SENIOR HIGH CORE COLLECTION

SEVENTEENTH EDITION

CORE COLLECTION SERIES

Formerly
STANDARD CATALOG SERIES

JOHN GREENFIELDT, GENERAL EDITOR

CHILDREN'S CORE COLLECTION
MIDDLE & JUNIOR HIGH CORE COLLECTION
SENIOR HIGH CORE COLLECTION
PUBLIC LIBRARY CORE COLLECTION: NONFICTION
PUBLIC LIBRARY CORE COLLECTION: FICTION

SENIOR HIGH
CORE COLLECTION

A SELECTION GUIDE

SEVENTEENTH EDITION

Former Title:
Senior High School Library Catalog

EDITED BY

RAYMOND W. BARBER

AND

PATRICE BARTELL

NEW YORK • DUBLIN

THE H. W. WILSON COMPANY

2007

Printed in the United States of America

ISBN 978-0-8242-1086-1

Abridged Dewey Decimal Classification and
Relative Index, Edition 14 is © 2004-2007
OCLC Online Computer Library Center,
Incorporated. Used with Permission. DDC,
Dewey, and Dewey Decimal Classification
are registered trademarks of OCLC.

Library of Congress Cataloging-in-Publication Data

Senior high core collection : a selection guide / edited by Raymond W. Barber
and Patrice Bartell. — 17th ed.
    p. cm.
    Includes index.
    Previous eds. published under title: Senior high school library catalog.

    ISBN 978-0-8242-1086-1 (alk. paper)

    1. High school libraries—United States—Book lists. I. Barber,
Raymond W. II. Bartell, Patrice.

Z1037.S435 2007
011.62—dc22

                                                           2007031812

CONTENTS

CONTENTS

PREFACE

With this edition the *Senior High School Library Catalog*, a standard collection development and maintenance tool for libraries, has changed its name to *Senior High Core Collection: A Selection Guide*. It is a selective list of fiction and nonfiction books for young adults, along with review sources and other professional aids for librarians and school media specialists. It includes analytical entries for parts of books, a list of recommended periodicals for high school libraries, and a list of recommended electronic resources. Annual Supplements to this volume will be published in 2008, 2009, and 2010.

In this Edition. This seventeenth edition of the *Senior High Core Collection* includes 6,268 book titles and 4,598 analytical entries. Of these more than half are new since the previous edition. Of special note in this edition are new books on sports, adult fiction of interest to young adults, and professional materials. In addition, a new separate section has been added for recommended periodicals. This section is in two parts, one of professional journals for teachers and librarians and one of periodicals for young adults. The section listing recommended Web-based resources, now entitled Recommended Electronic Resources, has been expanded. Another new feature is a selection of more than a hundred graphic novels. Fictional graphic novels and materials about graphic novels are listed at 741.5 in the Classified Collection, and nonfiction graphic novels are integrated throughout the rest of the classification. They are all listed together in the Index under Graphic novels.

For the first time in this edition a limited number of the most highly recommended titles are indicated with a rosette (*) at the end of the bibliographic data. This short list, as it were, can serve as a guide to the librarian with a limited budget or one who needs only one or two books in a given area.

History. The first edition of the Core Collection was published in 1926 as an author-title list, followed by a fuller version in 1928 that also included a subject index and analytical entries. Since the appearance of the second edition in 1932, the Collection has been published regularly every five years. From this edition forward it will be published every four years. Initially the work was called *Standard Catalog for High School Libraries*, but when *Junior High School Library Catalog* (now *Middle and Junior High Core Collection*) was introduced in 1965, its scope was changed. It became *Senior High School Library Catalog* in the ninth edition, published in 1967.

Preparation. In producing this edition the editors have worked closely with an advisory committee of distinguished librarians, who are listed below. Over the past five years they have participated in selecting the books that have entered the Collection. In preparation for this new edition they have reevaluated all the material in the previous edition of the Collection and its Supplements and proposed many new titles. Reviews in the professional literature have also been an important source of information in selecting the material for this Core Collection.

Scope and purpose. The Collection lists books for young people in grades nine through twelve. Separate sections list essential periodicals and electronic resources. Throughout the Collection special attention has been given to resources for the librarian or school media specialist, including works on the history and development of young adult literature, literary criticism, bibliographies, selection aids, guides to the operation of media centers, periodicals relating to library science and education, and other resources for the selection and evaluation of print and non-print materials and the use of the internet in instruction.

The three annual Supplements, which will expand the total coverage by approximately 2,400 additional titles, are intended for use with this volume. Libraries and media centers serving large systems and those with special curriculum needs or user groups will wish to supplement this list further. Schools that must accommodate students reading below their grade level may find it helpful to consult the latest edition of *Middle and Junior High Core Collection* and its Supplements. Materials for more advance and college-bound students can be found in the *Public Library Core Collection: Nonfiction* and its Supplements. To augment the fiction list with adult and genre titles the user is referred to *Public Library Core Collection: Fiction* and its Supplements.

All books listed are either published in the United States or published in Canada or the United Kingdom and distributed in the United States and are in print at the time this volume was printed. Original paperback editions are included, as well as paperback reprints of essential titles that have become unavailable in hardcover.

If a book was listed in a previous edition of the Collection and has been deleted in this edition, that deletion is not intended as a sign that the book is no longer valuable or that it should necessarily be weeded from the collection. A book can be deleted for a number of reasons, such as its no longer being in print, or simply to make room for newer titles in a volume of limited size.

Because of the lack of uniform national curriculum standards, this Collection does not aim to support any particular high school level curriculum but rather to cover a broad spectrum of topics. Material suitable for both college-bound and non-college-bound students is included, as well as material for independent study and recreational reading. In the nonfiction section special importance is given to curriculum support material in the social and physical sciences and to works devoted to current concerns of youth, such as interpersonal relationships, substance abuse, and health and fitness. New reference books are well represented. The fiction section contains a wide range of literary works that are of interest to young people and many that are frequently included on school reading lists—classics as well as contemporary and genre fiction. In recent years studies in literary criticism for young people have increasingly been published in series, with one volume devoted to each author. Because it is impossible to list, or even to evaluate, every volume in a voluminous series, a few representative samples have been listed from the most highly recommended series, with a note indicating the series and other titles available.

The periodicals and electronic resources sections are devoted primarily to reference works and other educational materials in support of the curriculum in many areas, especially science, social studies, geography, and mathematics. Neither section is intended to be comprehensive. The free Web resources are offered simply as added value, some favorite sites with substantial content that deserve attention.

The Collection excludes the following: non-print materials other than electronic resources; non-English-language materials, with the exception of dictionaries and similar items; textbooks; and books about specific vocations, individual computer programs, and other topics that quickly become outdated.

Organization. The Collection consists of four parts:

Part 1, the Classified Collection, is arranged according to the Dewey Decimal Classification for nonfiction, followed by sections for fiction and story collections. The information supplied for each book includes bibliographic description, suggested subject headings, a descriptive annotation, and frequently an evaluation from a quoted source.

Part 2, a List of Recommended Periodicals, is divided into professional journals for librarians and teachers and periodicals for young adults.

Part 3, a List of Recommended Electronic Resources, replaces the List of Recommended Web Resources found in the previous edition.

Part 4, the Author, Title, Subject, and Analytical Index, serves as a comprehensive key to the Classified Collection.

The section that follows, Directions for Use of the Collection, contains more detailed information about the uses and content of the Core Collection.

Acknowledgments. The H. W. Wilson Company is indebted to the publishers who supplied copies of their books and information about editions and prices. This Core Collection could not have been published without the efforts of the advisory committee, who gave so generously of their time and expertise.

Members of the Advisory Committee:

Betty Carter, Chair
Professor Emerita
School of Library and Information Studies
Texas Woman's University
Denton, Texas

Catherine Clancy
Branch Librarian
Dudley Branch Library
Boston Public Library
Boston, Massachusetts

Pamela Spencer Holley
Writer, Consultant on Young Adult Literature
Formerly Coordinator of School Libraries
Fairfax County, Virginia

Deborah Taylor
Coordinator of School and Student Services
Enoch Pratt Free Library
Baltimore, Maryland

Stephanie Zvirin
Books for Youth Editor
Booklist
American Library Association
Chicago, Illinois

Consultant on Electronic Resources:

Frances B. Bradburn
Director, Instructional Technologies
North Carolina Department of Public Instruction
Raleigh, North Carolina

Consultant on Graphic Novels:

Katharine L. Kan
Reviewer and consultant
Panama City, Florida

DIRECTIONS FOR USE OF THE COLLECTION

USES OF THE CORE COLLECTION

Senior High School Core Collection is designed to serve these purposes:

As an aid in purchasing. The Collection is designed to assist in the selection and acquisition of titles. Annotations are provided for each title along with information concerning publisher, ISBN, price, and availability. Since Part 1, the Classified Collection, is arranged according to the Dewey Decimal Classification, the Collection may be used to identify elements of the library collection that should be updated or strengthened. In evaluating the suitability of a work each library will want to consider the special character of the community and school it serves.

As an aid in reference. Reference work and readers' advisory service is furthered by the information about sequels and companion volumes and the descriptive and critical annotations in the Classified Collection, and by the subject access in the Index. The analytical entries in the Index augment the library's catalog by providing access to parts of composite works.

As an aid in verification of information. For this purpose full bibliographical data are provided in the Classified Collection. Entries also include recommended subject headings based upon *Sears List of Subject Headings* and a suggested classification derived from the fourteenth edition of the *Abridged Dewey Decimal Classification and Relative Index*. Notes describe editions available and publication history.

As an aid in curriculum support. The classified approach, subject indexing, and annotations are helpful in identifying materials appropriate for classroom use.

As an aid in collection maintenance. In addition to recently published works, the Core Collection includes titles listed in the previous edition and its Supplements that have retained their usefulness. This information affects decisions to rebind, replace, or discard older materials.

As an instructional aid. The Core Collection is essential in courses that deal with literature and book selection for young people.

DESCRIPTION OF THE COLLECTON

Part 1. Classified Collection

The Classified Collection is arranged with the nonfiction books first, classified by the Dewey Decimal Classification in numerical order from 000 to 999. Individual biographies are classed in 92 and follow the 920s (collective biography). Novels and short story collections, with the symbols "Fic" and "S C," follow the nonfiction.

An Outline of Classification, which serves as a table of contents to the Classified Collection, is reproduced on page xv. It should be remembered that many subjects are treated in more than one discipline and so are found in various parts of the classification. If a particular title is not found where it might be expected, the Index should be consulted to determine if the work is classified elsewhere.

Within classes, books are arranged alphabetically under main entry, usually the author. An exception is made for works of individual biography, classed in 92, which are arranged alphabetically under the name of the person written about. The following is an example of a typical entry and a description of its components:

Haynes, Charles C.
First freedoms; a documentary history of the First Amendment Rights in America; [by] Charles C. Haynes, Sam Chaltain, Susan M. Glisson. Oxford University Press 2005 255p il $40
Grades: 8 9 10 11 12 **342**
1. United States. Constitution. 1st-10th amendments 2. Constitutional history—United States
ISBN 978-0-19-515759-5; 0-19-515750-8
LC 2005-31880
This book features "information and primary documents concerning the origins and attacks on the First Amendment. The various documents go from the Charter of Rhode Island and Providence Plantations in 1663 through the Patriot Act of 2001." Lib Media Connect
This is "an excellent resource for all libraries, as well as enjoyable reading for history buffs." SLJ

The names of the authors, Charles C. Haynes, Sam Chaltain, and Susan M. Glisson, are given in conformity with *Anglo-American Cataloguing Rules*, 2nd edition, 1998 revision. They are inverted and printed in dark or bold face type. The title of the book is *First freedoms*, and the subtitle *A documentary history of the First Amendment Rights in America*. The book was published by Oxford University Press. The publication date is 2005. It has 255 pages and sells for $40. (Prices given were current when the Collection went to press.)

Following the last line of the body of the entry is the grade level indicator: "Grades 8 9 10 11 12," which lists every grade for which this title is recommended. At the end of that line is the figure 342 in bold face type. This is the classification number derived from the fourteenth edition of the *Abridged Dewey Decimal Classification*. The number 342 is the classification number for "Constitutional and administrative law."

The numbered term "1. United States. Constitution. 1st-10th amendments" is a uniform title used as a subject, the name given to the document the book is about. The numbered term "2. Constitutional history—United States" is the recommended

xii

topical subject heading for this book based on *Sears List of Subject Headings*. In some cases the subjects assigned to the entire book will not show that there are portions of the book dealing with more specific topics. In such cases subject analytic entries are made in the Index of the Collection for significant portions of the book.

The ISBN (International Standard Book Number) is included to facilitate ordering. The Library of Congress control number (also called the LC card number) is provided when available.

Following are two notes supplying additional information about the book. The first is a description of the book's content taken from a review in *Library Media Connection*. The second is a critical note from *School Library Journal*. Such annotations are useful in evaluating books for selection and in determining which of several books on the same subject is best suited for the individual reader. Further notes may describe special features of a book, such as a bibliography, sequels, companion volumes, other editions available, and publication history.

Part 2. List of Recommended Periodicals

The List of Recommended Periodicals is divided into two parts: Part I, Professional journals for librarians and teachers, and Part II, Periodicals for young adults. Within each part the journals are listed alphabetically by title. The information given for each periodical consists of title, publisher, price, ISSN (International Standard Serial Number), a note indicating frequency of publication, and a brief annotation.

Part 3. List of Recommended Electronic Resources

This section consists of two kinds of electronic resources—commercial subscription-based databases and free Web sites—all listed in a single alphabet. All of them have been chosen for their excellence of content and appropriate age level. The list includes professional resources.

Bibliographic information about Web resources includes the title, publisher's name and telephone number, an indication of the price range for subscription resources, and a URL. This is followed by a descriptive annotation and in some cases a quotation from a reviewing source.

Part 4. Author, Title, Subject, and Analytical Index

This section is an alphabetical index of all the works in the Classified Collection. Each of the books in the Classified Collection is entered under author; title, if distinctive; series; subject; and other added entry points as necessary. Following the name of the series all the titles in that series are listed. The classification number in bold face type is the key to the location of the main entry of the book in the Classified Collection. Works classed in 92, individual biography, will be found under the name of the person written about.

Subject, author, and title analytical entries for parts of composite works are also included in the index. Analytical entries provide indexing for parts of works and are an important feature of the Collection in that they maximize use of the library's holdings. Subject analytics afford access to parts of books not covered by the subject headings for the whole book, while author and title analytics provide an approach to anthologies and collections, especially of plays and short stories.

Cross-references are made in the index from variant forms of names, from terms not used as subject headings to the term that is used, and from terms used as subject headings to related or more specific headings.

The following are examples of Index entries for the book cited above:

Author	**Haynes, Charles C.**	**342**
Title	**First** freedoms. Haynes, Charles C.	**342**
Subject	**United States. Constitution. 1st-10th amendments**	
	Haynes, Charles C. First Freedoms	**342**
Joint Author		
	Chaltain, Sam	
	(jt. auth) Haynes, Charles C. First Freedoms	**342**

Examples of other types of entries:

Compiler

> **Allenbaugh, Kay**
> (comp) Chocolate for a teen's heart. See Chocolate
> for a teen's heart   **S C**

Subject Analytic

> **Burr, Aaron, 1756-1836**
> **About**
> *See/See also pages in the following book(s):*
> Ellis J.J. Founding brothers (11 12 Adult)
>   **920**

Author Analytic

> **Lowry, Lois**
> Holding
> *In* Am I blue? p175-87   **S C**

Title Analytic

> The **burning** man. Bradbury R.
> *In* Bradbury, R. Bradbury stories; 100 of his most
> celebrated tales   **S C**

Outline of Classification

Reproduced below is the Second Summary of the Dewey Decimal Classification. It will serve as a table of contents for the nonfiction section of the Classified Collection. (Fiction and Story Collections follow the nonfiction.) Note that the inclusion of this outline is not intended as a substitute for consulting the Dewey Decimal Classification itself. This outline is reproduced from Edition 14 of the Abridged Dewey Decimal Classification and Relative Index, published in 2004, by permission of OCLC Online Computer Library Center, Inc., owner of copyright.

000 Computer science, knowledge & systems
010   Bibliographies
020   Library & information sciences
030   Encyclopedias & books of facts
040   [Unassigned]
050   Magazines, journals & serials
060   Associations, organizations & museums
070   News media, journalism & publishing
080   Quotations
090   Manuscripts & rare books

100 Philosophy
110   Metaphysics
120   Epistemology
130   Parapsychology & occultism
140   Philosophical schools of thought
150   Psychology
160   Logic
170   Ethics
180   Ancient, medieval & eastern philosophy
190   Modern western philosophy

200 Religion
210   Philosophy & theory of religion
220   The Bible
230   Christianity & Christian theology
240   Christian practice & observance
250   Christian pastoral practice & religious orders
260   Christian organization, social work & worship
270   History of Christianity
280   Christian denominations
290   Other religions

300 Social sciences, sociology & anthropology
310   Statistics
320   Political science
330   Economics
340   Law
350   Public administration & military science
360   Social problems & social services
370   Education
380   Commerce, communications & transportation
390   Customs, etiquette & folklore

400 Language
410   Linguistics
420   English & Old English languages
430   German & related languages
440   French & related languages
450   Italian, Romanian & related languages
460   Spanish & Portuguese languages
470   Latin & Italic languages
480   Classical & modern Greek languages
490   Other languages

500 Science
510   Mathematics
520   Astronomy
530   Physics
540   Chemistry
550   Earth sciences & geology
560   Fossils & prehistoric life
570   Life sciences; biology
580   Plants (Botany)
590   Animals (Zoology)

600 Technology
610   Medicine & health
620   Engineering
630   Agriculture
640   Home & family management
650   Management & public relations
660   Chemical engineering
670   Manufacturing
680   Manufacture for specific uses
690   Building & construction

700 Arts
710   Landscaping & area planning
720   Architecture
730   Sculpture, ceramics & metalwork
740   Drawing & decorative arts
750   Painting
760   Graphic arts
770   Photography & computer art
780   Music
790   Sports, games & entertainment

800 Literature, rhetoric & criticism
810   American literature in English
820   English & Old English literatures
830   German & related literatures
840   French & related literatures
850   Italian, Romanian & related literatures
860   Spanish & Portuguese literatures
870   Latin & Italic literatures
880   Classical & modern Greek literatures
890   Other literatures

900 History
910   Geography & travel
920   Biography & genealogy
930   History of ancient world (to ca. 499)
940   History of Europe
950   History of Asia
960   History of Africa
970   History of North America
980   History of South America
990   History of other areas

SENIOR HIGH CORE COLLECTION
SEVENTEENTH EDITION
CLASSIFIED COLLECTION

000 COMPUTER SCIENCE, INFORMATION & GENERAL WORKS

001.4 Research; statistical methods

Feldman, Burton
The Nobel Prize; a history of genius, controversy, and prestige. Arcade Pub. 2000 489p il $29.95; pa $15.95 *
Grades: 11 12 Adult   **001.4**
1. Nobel Prizes
ISBN 1-55970-537-X; 1-55970-592-2 (pa)
                       LC 00-42002
The author provides a "history of the prizes awarded in the sciences, literature, social sciences, and humankind's . . . peace efforts. This is the first comprehensive critical history of the prizes to appear, and it's very good." Libr J
Includes bibliographical references

Tufte, Edward R., 1942-
The visual display of quantitative information. 2nd ed. Graphics Press 2001 197p il $40
Grades: 11 12 Adult   **001.4**
1. Statistics—Graphic methods
ISBN 0-9613921-4-2   LC 2001-271866
First published 1983
This book focuses "on statistical graphics, charts, tables. Theory and practice in the design of data graphics, 250 illustrations of the best (and a few of the worst) statistical graphics, with . . . analysis of how to display data for precise, effective, quick analysis." Publisher's note

Valenza, Joyce Kasman
Power research tools; learning activities & posters; illustrated by Emily Valenza. American Lib. Assn. 2003 113p il pa $55 *
Grades: Professional   **001.4**
1. Research 2. Internet resources 3. Internet searching 4. Report writing
ISBN 0-8389-0838-1   LC 2002-8972
Contents: Searching; Ethics; Evaluation; Organizing and communicating
A collection of "lessons, rubrics, graphic organizers, and curriculum designed to help students become successful users of information. Beginning with the first steps of research, the development of a thesis, the material progresses logically through the succeeding steps, covering Boolean operators; search tools and strategies; subject and keyword searching; ethics; plagiarism; documenting and citing resources; creating source and note cards; the process of writing the paper; and quoting, paraphrasing, and summarizing. . . . This is an invaluable resource for teaching information skills in any subject area, in middle school or high school." SLJ

Wilson, A. Paula
100 ready-to-use pathfinders for the Web; a guidebook and CD-ROM. Neal-Schuman Publishers 2005 xxiii, 247p il pa $75 *
Grades: Professional   **001.4**
1. Internet research 2. Reference services (Libraries)
ISBN 1-55570-490-5   LC 2004-40292
This "resource offers step-by-step instructions for creating pathfinders to post on your library's Web site. . . . The CD reproduces . . . specific examples in HTML and plain text as well as providing blank templates for immediate use. . . . The pathfinders are for all age ranges and skill levels and include books, online sources, government sources, magazines, and subject headings that could link to the library's catalog." Voice Youth Advocates
This "is an important addition to the literature of practical library guides." Ref & User Services Quarterly
Includes bibliographical references

001.9 Controversial knowledge

Alschuler, William R.
The science of UFOs; edited by Howard Zimmerman. St. Martin's Press 2001 211p il hardcover o.p. pa $13.95
Grades: 11 12 Adult   **001.9**
1. Unidentified flying objects
ISBN 0-312-26225-6; 0-312-30071-9 (pa)
                       LC 00-45760
An "examination of UFO accounts through the lens of science—its method, presently accepted theory, and possible future directions." SLJ
"Although Alschuler's analysis seems at times like an introductory physics text as it delves into the quantum mechanics and physics of propective alien technologies, readers will appreciate his objective, fact-based analysis of a range of purported extraterrestrial phenomena." Publ Wkly
Includes bibliographical references

Clark, Jerome
Unnatural phenomena; a guide to the bizarre wonders of North America; illustrations by John Clark. ABC-CLIO 2005 xxxiv, 369p il $85
Grades: 11 12 Adult   **001.9**
1. Curiosities and wonders
ISBN 1-57607-430-7   LC 2005-11206
"Organized geographically, . . . [this book] explores the history of bizarre natural phenomena in virtually every U.S. state." Publisher's note
Includes bibliographical references

Coleman, Loren
Cryptozoology A-Z; the encyclopedia of loch monsters, Sasquatch, Chupacabras, and other authentic mysteries of nature; {by} Loren Coleman and Jerome Clark. Simon & Schuster 1999 270p il pa $13 *
Grades: 11 12 Adult   **001.9**
1. Monsters—Encyclopedias
ISBN 0-684-85602-6   LC 99-31023
"A Fireside book"
Cryptozoology is defined as the study of hidden animals. This encyclopedia "contains nearly two hundred entries, including cryptids (the name given to these unusual beasts), new animal finds, and the explorers and scientists who search for them." Publisher's note
Includes bibliographical references

Eberhart, George M.
Mysterious creatures; a guide to cryptozoology. ABC-CLIO 2002 2v set $185
Grades: 11 12 Adult   **001.9**
1. Mythical animals 2. Monsters 3. Parapsychology 4. Occultism
ISBN 1-57607-283-5   LC 2002-13785
Also available online
This is a study of "cryptids as distribution anomalies, unknown variations of known species, survivors thought to be extinct, mythical animals, paranormal creatures with animal-like characteristics, and hoaxes. More than 1,085 unknown animals are covered in field-guide format, some with pictures or drawings. . . . Useful as a biological guide, a folklore reference, and a study of paranormal creatures." Booklist
Includes bibliographical references

Sagan, Carl, 1934-1996
The demon-haunted world; science as a candle in the dark. Random House 1996 457p hardcover o.p. pa $14.95
Grades: 11 12 Adult   **001.9**
1. Science
ISBN 0-394-53512-X; 0-345-40946-9 (pa)
     LC 95-34076
"Using basic tools of science—empiricism, rationalism, and experimentation—Sagan debunks . . . common fallacies of pseudoscience. In doing so, he speculates as to how such beliefs arise." Libr J
Sagan "links today's aliens with yesterday's demons in this lithe, well-supported, sometimes quite wry, and altogether refreshing performance." Booklist
Includes bibliographical references

Shermer, Michael
Why people believe weird things; pseudoscience, superstition, and other confusions of our time; foreword by Stephen Jay Gould. rev and expanded. Freeman, W.H. 2002 xxvi, 349p il pa $16 *
Grades: 11 12 Adult   **001.9**
1. Science 2. Belief and doubt 3. Parapsychology
ISBN 0-8050-7089-3   LC 2002-68784
"First Owl Books edition"
First published 1997
Contents: Science and skepticism; Pseudoscience and superstition; Evolution and creationism; History and pseudohistory; Hope springs eternal
The author "explores the very human reasons people find otherworldly phenomena, conspiracy theories, and cults so appealing. In . . . [the] chapter, 'Why Smart People Believe in Weird Things' he takes on science luminaries like physicist Frank Tippler and others, who hide their spiritual beliefs behind the trappings of science." Publisher's note
Includes bibliographical references

004   Data processing. Computer science

Barrett, Joanne R., 1960-
Teaching and learning about computers; a classroom guide for teachers, librarians, media specialists, and students. Scarecrow Press 2002 255p il $45 *
Grades: Professional   **004**
1. Computers 2. Data processing
ISBN 0-8108-4450-8   LC 2002-8350
"The 14 chapters in increasing complexity include information about word processing, spreadsheets, charts and graphics, databases, multimedia presentations, the Internet, the World Wide Web, creating Web pages, learning programming, and viruses and copyright law. . . . Every computer teacher should be in possession of this book, and it would make a terrific textbook for those who are teaching teachers." SLJ

Billings, Charlene W., 1941-
Supercomputers; charting the future of cybernetics; {by} Charlene W. Billings and Sean M. Grady. New ed. Facts on File 2004 228p $29.95
Grades: 7 8 9 10   **004**
1. Supercomputers
ISBN 0-8160-4730-8   LC 2003-3628
First published 1995
"Defining 'supercomputers' as 'usually . . . the fastest, and most expensive, computers available at any given time,' the authors present a thorough history of data storage and manipulation devices, from ancient Sumerian clay tablets through Charles Babbage's 'Difference Engine' to ENIAC, the sexy-looking creation of Seymour Cray, and the recent growth of multiple-unit cluster systems—not to mention the Internet. The development of office machines in general and the many uses

Billings, Charlene W., 1941-—*Continued*
to which computers have been put in business, science, military pursuits, and film animation are also examined." SLJ

Includes bibliographical references

Ceruzzi, Paul E.
A history of modern computing. 2nd ed. MIT Press 2003 445p il pa $22.95
Grades: 9 10 11 12 **004**
1. Computers 2. Data processing
ISBN 0-262-53203-4 LC 2002-40799
First published 1998
This history "concentrates on five key moments of transition: the transformation of the computer in the late 1940s from a specialized scientific instrument to a commercial product; the emergence of small systems in the late 1960s; the beginning of personal computing in the 1970s; the spread of networking after 1985; and . . . the period 1995-2001 [including] . . . the Microsoft antitrust suit, the rise and fall of the dot-coms, and the advent of open source software." Publisher's note
Includes bibliographical references

Cuddy, Colleen
Using PDAs in libraries; a how-to-do-it manual. Neal-Schuman Publishers 2005 145p il (How-to-do-it manuals for librarians) pa $65
Grades: Professional **004**
1. Libraries—Automation 2. Personal digital assistants
ISBN 1-55570-543-X
"After an opening chapter that defines PDAs (personal digital assistants) and provides an overview of their history and future, this practical manual's remaining six chapters discuss PDAs in terms of networking, storage devices, peripherals, software applications, content, library reference software, security, and vulnerability issues. . . . Information throughout the book is well researched, and readers will appreciate its deft organization and clear, accessible language." Booklist

Downing, Douglas
Dictionary of computer and Internet terms; [by] Douglas A. Downing, Michael A. Covington, Melody Mauldin Covington; with the assistance of Catherine Anne Covington. 9th ed. Barron's 2006 587p il (Barron's business guides) pa $12.99 *
Grades: 9 10 11 12 **004**
1. Computers—Dictionaries 2. Internet—Dictionaries
ISBN 0-7641-3417-5 LC 2005-52175
First published 1986 with title: Dictionary of computer terms
This work defines approximately 2,500 computer terms. Topics explained "include finding information with search tools on the Web, creating a home page with HTML, communicating via e-mail, tuning in to multimedia applications, and the technical details involved in connecting a computer with a modem to other computers and the Internet." Publisher's note

Encyclopedia of computer science. 4th ed, editors: Anthony Ralston, Edwin D. Reilly, David Hemmendinger. Grove's Dictionaries Inc. 2000 xxix, 2034p il $150
Grades: 11 12 Adult **004**
1. Computer science—Encyclopedias
ISBN 1-56159-248-X LC 2002-319006
First published 1976 by Van Nostrand Reinhold & Co.
Alphabetically arranged and classified into subject areas, the entries cover: hardware, systems, information and data, software, mathematics, theory of computation, methodologies, applications, and computing milieux.

The **Facts** on File dictionary of computer science; edited by John Daintith, Edmund Wright. Rev. ed. Facts on File 2006 273p il (Facts on File science library) $49.50
Grades: 11 12 Adult **004**
1. Computer science—Dictionaries
ISBN 0-8160-5999-3; 978-0-8160-5999-7
LC 2006-42004
First published 2001; based on the Minidictionary of computing, published 1986 by Oxford University Press
This dictionary provides over 2400 "entries that explain such fundamental concepts as hardware, software, and applications." Publisher's note
"The book will prove a handy reference for budding computer scientists." Voice Youth Advocates
Includes bibliographical references

Hafner, Katie
Where wizards stay up late; the origins of the Internet; [by] Katie Hafner and Matthew Lyon. Simon & Schuster 1996 304p il hardcover o.p. pa $15 *
Grades: 11 12 Adult **004**
1. Internet
ISBN 0-684-81201-0; 0-684-83267-8 (pa)
LC 96-19533
The authors tell the "story of some extraordinary computer scientists who, with the Department of Defense in the late 1960s, developed the Arpanet. It is based mostly on interviews with those scientists and engineers who designed and built a revolutionary computer network that spawned the global Internet." Libr J
This "book is excellent at enshrining little known but crucial scientist/administrators like Bob Taylor, Larry Roberts and Joseph Licklider, many of whom laid the groundwork for the computer science industry." Publ Wkly
Includes bibliographical references

Henderson, Harry, 1951-
Encyclopedia of computer science and technology. Facts on File 2003 450p il $82.50 *
Grades: 11 12 Adult **004**
1. Computer science—Encyclopedias
ISBN 0-8160-4373-6 LC 2002-6796
"In this A-to-Z resource, 400 mini essays . . . {offer} . . . an overview of the topic, a discussion of its significance, and a guide to further reading. An introduction ends with a list of subject groupings of related entries

Henderson, Harry, 1951-—*Continued*
such as 'Computer Languages,' 'Business Applications,' and 'AI and Robotics.' Biographies of historical figures . . . and modern visionaries . . . are often accompanied by captioned photographs. . . . An illustration of the inner workings of a mouse and a simple graphic of computer animation are useful . . . More complex flowcharts explain database structure, HTML, and network systems. . . . This solid resource succeeds in explaining technical aspects of these subjects to general readers." SLJ

High definition; an A to Z guide to personal technology. Houghton Mifflin 2006 361p il pa $14.95 *
Grades: 9 10 11 12 Adult   **004**
1. Electric household appliances—Dictionaries
ISBN 0-618-71489-8; 978-0-618-71489-6
LC 2006-19549
This dictionary "brings together more than 3000 terms used to describe the components, functions, and applications of devices found in today's homes and offices: cell phones, computers, MP3 players, gaming systems, CD and DVD players, and more. . . . This very affordable volume should be part of every reference collection, large and small." Libr J

Pfaffenberger, Bryan, 1949-
Webster's New World computer dictionary. Wiley 2003 422p pa $16.99
Grades: 9 10 11 12   **004**
1. Computer science—Dictionaries 2. Data processing—Dictionaries
ISBN 0-7645-2478-X   LC 2003-269226
First edition compiled by Laura Darcy and Louise Boston published 1983 by Simon & Schuster with title: Webster's New World dictionary of computer terms. Frequently revised
This dictionary defines more than 4,500 of the most frequently used computer terms and demonstrates how they relate to other terms

Reilly, Edwin D.
Milestones in computer science and information technology. Greenwood Press 2003 392p $70
Grades: 9 10 11 12   **004**
1. Computer science 2. Information technology
ISBN 1-573-56521-0   LC 2002-44843
"An Oryx book"
Over 600 alphabetically arranged entries describe the significant developments in computer science and advances in information technology
"The articles are clearly written and accessible, containing essential details without reliance on technical jargon. . . . Extremely useful tools include a listing of the 'Top Ten' milestones, and four separate indexes devoted to personal names, chronology, geography, and general topics." Libr Media Connect
Includes bibliographical references

004.6   Interfacing and communications. Networks

Johnson, Doug, 1952-
Learning right from wrong in the digital age; an ethics guide for parents, teachers, librarians, and others who care about computer-using young people. Linworth Pub. 2003 122p pa $44.55 *
Grades: Professional   **004.6**
1. Internet 2. Computers and children 3. Cheating (Education)
ISBN 1-586-83131-3   LC 2003-43320
"After an overview of the difference between the physical and virtual world in regard to ethical codes, several sections are devoted to scenarios of various behaviors that involve privacy, property, and appropriate use of information. Each scenario provides discussion topics as well as the relationship to National Learning Standards." Libr Media Connect
"Johnson's '3 P's of Technology Ethics,' Privacy, Property, and a(P)propriate use, are effectively and excitingly addressed through both discussion and instructional scenarios." SLJ
Includes bibliographical references

Magid, Lawrence J.
MySpace unraveled; a parent's guide to teen social networking from the directors of BlogSafety.com; [by] Larry Magid and Anne Collier. Peachpit Press 2007 184p il pa $14.99
Grades: 11 12 Adult   **004.6**
1. MySpace (Web site) 2. Internet and teenagers 3. Parenting
ISBN 0-321-48018-X; 978-0-321-48018-7
LC 2006-298800
This is a "look at what MySpace is, why teens use it, and what parents should know to help guarantee that their teen is safe when using MySpace or other social networking sites. . . . The book is easy to read, filled with colorful screenshots, and sure to help parents understand what their role is in their teen's involvement in social networking." Voice Youth Advocates

Simpson, Carol Mann, 1949-
Internet for schools; a practical guide; [by] Carol Simpson and Sharron L. McElmeel. 3rd ed. Linworth Pub. 2000 317p il (Professional growth series) pa $39.95
Grades: Professional   **004.6**
1. Internet
ISBN 0-938865-98-6   LC 99-86960
First published 1995 with title: Internet for library media specialists
A guide to using the Internet in curriculum-specific classroom situations. Topics discussed include web-based e-mail, bookmarking, filtering software, selecting search engines, virtual field trips, and authorized use policies.
Includes bibliographical references

Using the Internet, online services, and CD-ROMs for writing research and term papers; edited by Charles Harmon. 2nd ed. Neal-Schuman 2000 126p il (Neal-Schuman net-guide series) pa $35 *

Grades: 11 12 Adult   **004.6**
1. Report writing 2. Dissertations 3. Research 4. Internet
ISBN 1-55570-374-7   LC 00-39441
First published 1996
"This book explains prewriting, the thesis sentence, and methods of revising and proofreading, and offers tips concerning catalog searches. . . . Emphasis is placed on the necessity for evaluating Web pages. Web terminology and methods for searching the Internet are explained. The book also contains a valuable chapter on citing print and electronic sources in both MLA and APA Styles. For most students faced with a research paper assignment, this book would be of great assistance." Book Rep
Includes bibliographical references

005.7   Data in computer systems

Smith, Susan S.
Web-based instruction; a guide for libraries; [by] Susan Sharpless Smith. 2nd ed. American Library Association 2006 263p il pa $52 *
Grades: Professional   **005.7**
1. Bibliographic instruction 2. Computer-assisted instruction 3. Web sites 4. Library information networks
ISBN 0-8389-0908-6   LC 2005-15011
First published 2001
"Throughout the book's eight chapters, which are organized to offer a step-by-step approach for planning and implementing Web-based instruction, the author discusses the design and development of different types of Web projects and instruction, project development tools, user interfaces, multimedia, interactivity, evaluation, testing, and assessment. . . . [This is] an excellent resource notable for its practical content, thoroughness, and high readability." Booklist
Includes bibliographical references

006.3   Artificial intelligence

Henderson, Harry, 1951-
Artificial intelligence; mirrors for the mind. Chelsea House 2007 190p il (Milestones in discovery and invention) $35
Grades: 9 10 11 12   **006.3**
1. Artificial intelligence
ISBN 0-8160-5749-4; 978-0-8160-5749-8
                                       LC 2006-16639
This book includes "portraits of the men and women in the vanguard of this innovative field. Subjects include Alan Turing, who made the connection between mathematical reasoning and computer operations; Allen Newell and Herbert Simon, who created a program that could reason like a human being; Pattie Maes, who developed computerized agents to help people with research and shopping; and Ray Kurzweil, who, besides inventing the flatbed scanner and a reading machine for the blind, has explored relationships between people and computers that may exceed human intelligence." Publisher's note
Includes glossary and bibliographical references

006.6   Computer graphics

Bell, Ann, 1945-
Creating digital video in your school; how to shoot, edit, produce, distribute, and incorporate digital media into the curriculum. Linworth Pub. 2005 107p il pa $39.95 *
Grades: 9 10 11 12   **006.6**
1. Digital video recording 2. Instructional materials centers 3. Multimedia
ISBN 1-58683-186-0   LC 2004-30202
"This manual guides novices and supports hobby filmmakers through using and understanding video and audio recording, editing, and producing within an education setting. This author missed nothing: her guide is excellent." SLJ
Includes bibliographical references

Hansen, Brad
The dictionary of multimedia; terms & acronyms. 4th ed. Franklin, Beedle & Associates 2005 611p il $50
Grades: 9 10 11 12   **006.6**
1. Multimedia—Dictionaries
ISBN 1-88790-273-2
First published 1997
Contains over 5000 technical and multimedia terms from a multidisciplinary perspective including audio, graphics, video, networking, human factors, and general computing. Copyright issues and international standards are addressed. Includes a basic HTML tutorial and an appendix listing books, software, manuals and periodicals, as well as covering digital video, MIDI and Internet development.

006.7   Multimedia systems

Kline, David
Blog!: how the newest media revolution is changing politics, business, and culture; [by] David Kline and Dan Burnstein; contributing editors, Arne J. de Keijzer and Paul Berger. CDS Books 2005 xxvi, 402p $24.95
Grades: 9 10 11 12   **006.7**
1. Weblogs
ISBN 1-59315-141-1
The authors "examine the notion that weblogs, or 'blogs,' are redefining journalism and media consumption and conclude that, while blogging may not signal the death of big media, it has measurably impacted everything from political campaigns—as evidenced by Howard Dean's presidential bid—to the life of former child star Wil Wheaton, who found his 'second act' in a tell-all blog about the humiliations of show business." Publ Wkly

Kline, David—*Continued*

This book "focuses on the larger issues that make this such an exciting cultural moment while steering clear of details that will date quickly. Well worthwhile." Booklist

Stone, Biz

Who let the blogs out? a hyperconnected peek at the world of Weblogs; with a foreword by Wil Wheaton. St. Martin's Griffin 2004 244p pa $13.95 *

Grades: 11 12 Adult   **006.7**

1. Weblogs

ISBN 0-312-33000-6   LC 2004-50860

The author "presents a brief history of blogging in addition to covering the growth of the 'participatory web,' blogging in businesses, political blogging, and the 'blogosphere.' But he is at his best when providing advice to veteran and aspiring bloggers about blogrolling, blog culture dos and don'ts, easy HTML editing, and adding subtle advertising to blogs to create revenue. Stone's enthusiasm for his subject is infectious, and anyone who has toyed with the idea of starting a blog will be inspired to begin." Libr J

Includes bibliographical references

011 Bibliographies

American reference books annual 2007 edition; Shannon Graff Hysell, associate editor. Libraries Unlimited 2007 xxv, 704p $125

Grades: Professional   **011**

1. Reference books—Bibliography

ISSN 0065-9959

ISBN 978-1-59158-525-1; 1-59158-525-2

Cumulative indexes available 1990-1994; 1995-1999; 2000-2004

Annual. First published 1970

Editor: 1970-2001 Bohdan S. Wynar

"Each issue covers the reference book output (including reprints) of the previous year (i.e., the 1970 volume covers 1969 publications). Offers descriptive and evaluative notes (many of them signed by contributors), with references to selected reviews. Limited to titles in English. Classed arrangement; author-subject-title index." Guide to Ref Books. 11th edition

Magazines for libraries; for the general reader and school, junior college, college, university, and public libraries; edited by Cheryl LaGuardia; created by Bill Katz. 15th ed. Bowker 2006 xcii, 1101p $275

Grades: Professional   **011**

1. Periodicals—Bibliography

ISSN 0000-0914

ISBN 978-1-6003-0096-7; 1-6003-0096-0

First published 1969. Frequently revised

First-tenth edition edited by Bill Katz

"Annotated classified guide to recommended periodicals for the general reader and school, college, and public libraries. Provides comparative evaluations and grade- and age-level recommendations for all periodicals included." N Y Public Libr Book of How & Where to Look It Up

Recommended reference books for small and medium-sized libraries and media centers. Libraries Unlimited 2007 $70

Grades: Professional   **011**

1. Reference books—Bibliography 2. Reference books—Reviews

ISSN 0277-5948

ISBN 1-59158-526-0; 978-1-59158-526-8

Annual. First published 1981

On cover: 2007 edition. Editor, 2005-2007: Shannon Graff Hysell

Each annual volume includes reviews of about 550 titles chosen by the editor as the most valuable reference titles published during the previous year.

"Where budget restrictions are a consideration, this is an invaluable asset; for small libraries, a superior selection/acquisitions tool. Highly recommended." Voice Youth Advocates

Rosow, La Vergne

Accessing the classics; great reads for adults, teens, and English language learners. Libraries Unlimited 2006 301p pa $40

Grades: Professional   **011**

1. Best books 2. Reading—Remedial teaching

ISBN 1-56308-891-6; 978-1-56308-891-9

       LC 2005-30838

"This collection of annotated titles aims at providing resources for anyone who works with inexperienced or low-literacy teenagers or adults." Voice Youth Advocates

"The intended audience is wide-ranging and includes anyone who wishes to foster language and literacy skills. Essential reading." Booklist

Includes bibliographical references

011.6 General bibliographies of works for specific kinds of users and libraries

Books for you; an annotated booklist for senior high; Kylene Beers and Teri S. Lesesne, editors, and the Committee on the Senior High School Booklist of the National Council of Teachers of English; with a foreword by Michael Cart. 14th ed. National Council of Teachers of English 2001 xxviii, 411p il (NCTE bibliography series) $33.95

Grades: 9 10 11 12   **011.6**

1. Young adult literature—Bibliography 2. Best books

ISBN 0-8141-0372-3   LC 2001-276359

First published 1945

This bibliography of over 1,000 titles is arranged by subject into 35 thematic chapters. More than 150 titles of multicultural interest are included. Each entry provides bibliographic information, a summary of contents, and mention of any awards the book has won

Gillespie, John Thomas, 1928-
Best books for high school readers; grades 9-12; [by] John T. Gillespie, Catherine Barr. Libraries Unlimited 2004 1182p $75
Grades: Professional   **011.6**
1. Young adult literature—Bibliography 2. Best books
ISBN 1-59158-084-6   LC 2004-303598
Also available supplement published 2006 $40 (ISBN: 1-59158-410-8, ISBN-13: 978-1-59158-410-0)
First published 1991 by Bowker with title: Best books for senior high readers
"A total of 14,198 titles are listed. . . . Entries contain standard bibliographic information, as well as price for all in-print editions, the ISBN, a brief summary, a listing of publications where the book was reviewed, and the Dewey number where the item would be classified in a typical collection. . . . Librarians and teachers who work with high school students will find this guide a welcome addition to their readers' advisory resource shelf." Am Ref Books Annu, 2005

Classic teenplots; a booktalk guide to use with readers ages 12-18; [by] John T. Gillespie and Corinne J. Naden. Libraries Unlimited 2006 348p (Children's and young adult literature reference series) $55
Grades: Professional   **011.6**
1. Book talks 2. Young adult literature 3. Teenagers—Books and reading
ISBN 1-59158-312-8   LC 2006017624
"Prefaced by a brief guide to booktalking are one hundred entries for in-print classic titles for teens, taken from the out-of-print Juniorplots and Seniorplots series. Additional titles have been added to round out the eight theme/genre-based sections, which include topics such as Teenage Life and Concerns, Historical Fiction and Other Lands, and Important Nonfiction. . . . This excellent resource offers from sixteen to twenty titles per section. " Voice Youth Advocates
Includes bibliographical references

Jones, Patrick
A core collection for young adults; [by] Patrick Jones, Patricia Taylor, Kirsten Edwards. Neal-Schuman 2003 xxix, 405p (Teens @ the library series) pa $65
Grades: Professional   **011.6**
1. Young adult literature—Bibliography 2. Best books
ISBN 1-55570-458-1   LC 2002-45237
The authors "have selected and annotated over 1,000 titles, including adult and young adult fiction and nonfiction; biographies and personal narratives; graphic novels and illustrated works; underground classics; humor; science fiction/fantasy; Web sites; databases, and other electronic formats. Brief annotations . . . identify the primary audience for each book. Core collection entries include call numbers, full bibliographic information, and grade/audience level. . . . An accompanying title-checker disk allows librarians to . . . compare catalog holdings to the core collection." Publisher's note
"A useful book for both novice and experienced librarians who want to build a teen collection that actually circulates." SLJ
Includes bibliographical references

Latino periodicals; a selection guide; Salvador Güereña and Vivian M. Pisano, editors. McFarland & Co. 1998 147p pa $39.95
Grades: Professional   **011.6**
ISBN 0-7864-0540-6   LC 98-16582
An annotated list of 300 Spanish-and English-language publications. "It is organized by type of magazine (general interest, parenting, focus on teens, etc.), includes other types of periodicals ('fotonovelas', newspapers, etc.), and is indexed by topic and title. The book covers titles ranging from professional journals and fashion magazines to comic books and computer magazines." SLJ

Middle and junior high school library catalog; edited by Anne Price. 9th ed. H. W. Wilson Co. 2005 1237p $275
Grades: Professional   **011.6**
1. Classified catalogs 2. School libraries—Catalogs
ISBN 0-8242-1053-0
Also available on-line version
"Standard catalog series"
First published 1965 with title: Junior high school catalog
Kept up to date by annual supplements which are included in the price of the main volume
This collection of recommended materials includes entries for more than 6,000 books, plus over 2,000 analytic entries for stories, plays, and other items from anthologies and composite works, for grades five through nine. Entries contain full bibliographic information, Dewey Decimal Classification number, subject headings, descriptive, and when possible, critical annotations. Special sections include annotated lists of recommended periodicals for professionals and for children and young adults, and an annotated list of recommended electronic resources for student research

More outstanding books for the college bound; Young Adult Library Services Association, editor. American Library Association 2005 251p pa $35
Grades: Professional   **011.6**
1. College students 2. Best books
ISBN 0-8389-3553-2   LC 2005-13078
First published 1984 with title: Outstanding books for the college bound
In this book, "covering forty-five years of recommended titles—from 1959-2004—readers get to identify the most frequently cited titles and explore by genre." Publisher's note
Includes bibliographical references

New York Public Library
Books for the teen age, 2007. New York Public Lib. 2007 30p il pa $10
Grades: Professional   **011.6**
1. Young adult literature—Bibliography 2. Best books
ISBN 0-8710-4773-X; 978-0-8710-4773-1
Also available online
Annual. First published 1929
A list of approximately 1,000 books of interest to teenagers arranged in broad categories. Many of the titles address current concerns.

016.3054   Bibliographies of women

Bauermeister, Erica
500 great books by women; a reader's guide; [by] Erica Bauermeister, Jesse Larsen, and Holly Smith. Penguin Bks. 1994 425p pa $12.95
Grades: 11 12 Adult   **016.3054**
1. Women—Bibliography
ISBN 0-14-017590-3   LC 94-15989
"Representing diverse voices and cultures ranging from the thirteenth century to the contemporary period, the 500 works by women recommended in this guide are those that the compilers 'found to be thought-provoking, beautiful, and satisfying.' Among the selections are works by Aphra Behn, Jane Austen, Marguerite Duras, Barbara Tuchman, Gail Godwin, and Amy Tan. To be considered for inclusion, books had to be written in prose, available in English, and in print." Booklist

016.4   Bibliographies of language

McCaffery, Laura Hibbets
Building an ESL collection for young adults; a bibliography of recommended fiction and nonfiction for schools and public libraries. Greenwood Press 1998 182p $49.95
Grades: Professional   **016.4**
1. English as a second language—Bibliography
2. Young adult literature—Bibliography
ISBN 0-313-29937-4   LC 98-5271
"This annotated bibliography offers more than 500 titles for grades 5 through adult. The entries are organized by genre or topic and arranged alphabetically by author. They include complete bibliographic information, ISBN, price, Fry Reading Level, interest level, and possible uses in and out of the classroom. An introduction outlines the changing need for ESL materials in the United States and explains McCaffery's selection criteria." Libr J
"Teachers will find this an excellent source for titles to meet specific curriculum needs." Voice Youth Advocates
Includes bibliographical references

016.7   Bibliographies of the arts

Pawuk, Michael G.
Graphic novels; a genre guide to comic books, manga, and more; foreword by Brian K. Vaughn. Libraries Unlimited 2007 xxxv, 633p il (Genreflecting advisory series) $65 *
Grades: Professional   **016.7**
1. Graphic novels—Bibliography
ISBN 1-59158-132-X; 978-1-59158-132-1
                              LC 2006-34156
"This guide is intended to help you start, update, or maintain a graphic novel collection and advise readers about the genre. It covers more than 2,400 titles, including series titles, and organizes them according to genre, subgenre, and theme—from super-heroes and adventure to crime, humor, and nonfiction. Reading levels, awards/recognition, and core titles are identified; and tie-ins with gaming, film, anime, and television are noted." Publisher's note
Includes bibliographical references

Weiner, Stephen
The 101 best graphic novels. NBM 2005 60p il $15.95; pa $9.95 *
Grades: Professional   **016.7**
1. Graphic novels—Bibliography 2. Best books
ISBN   978-1-56163-443-9;   1-56163-443-3; 978-1-56163-444-6 (pa); 1-56163-444-1 (pa)
                              LC 2005-932866
"The young adult category has been subdivided into ages 12-15 and 16-19. . . . The greats you'd expect to find (Frank Miller, Alan Moore, Will Eisner, Neil Gaiman) are here along with many newer authors. . . . [This] is a useful tool for librarians and graphic-novel fans alike." SLJ
Includes bibliographical references

016.8   Bibliographies of literature

Anatomy of wonder; a critical guide to science fiction; {edited by} Neil Barron. 5th ed. Libraries Unlimited 2004 995p $80
Grades: 11 12 Adult   **016.8**
1. Science fiction—Bibliography 2. Science fiction—History and criticism
ISBN 1-59158-171-0
First published 1976 by Bowker
"Critical discussions of more than 1,400 science fiction novels, story collections, and anthologies, along with a . . . survey of the 'secondary' literature, chapters on teaching science fiction, titles appropriate for—or appealing to—teens, a directory of libraries containing significant collections of science fiction, and award-winning titles and titles of literary merit. Author, title, and theme indexes {are provided}." Publisher's note

Day, Frances Ann
Lesbian and gay voices; an annotated bibliography and guide to literature for children and young adults; foreword by Nancy Garden. Greenwood Press 2000 xxi, 268p $38.95
Grades: Professional   **016.8**
1. Children's literature—Bibliography 2. Young adult literature—Bibliography 3. Homosexuality in literature—Bibliography
ISBN 0-313-31162-5   LC 00-21047
This reference "lists over 275 recommended books that incorporate various aspects of homosexuality. . . . Each chapter looks at a particular literary genre. Listed alphabetically by author, each entry includes complete bibliographic information, a detailed annotation, topics, age level specifications, mention of any strong language or explicit sex, a summary of pertinent criticism, and a listing of literary awards." Book Rep
A "much-needed, thorough guide. . . . this is an extraordinary compilation that belongs in every collection." SLJ
Includes bibliographical references

Dickinson, A. T.

American historical fiction; an annotated guide to novels for adults and young adults. Oryx Press 1999 405p $65.95

Grades: Professional   **016.8**

1. Historical fiction—Bibliography 2. American fiction—Bibliography 3. United States—History—Fiction—Bibliography

ISBN 1-57356-067-7   LC 98-38044

Based on Dickinson's American historical fiction, 5th edition published 1986 by Scarecrow Press

Expanded and updated ed. of same title by A.T. Dickinson. 5th ed.

"Organized by time period, the entries include author, title, date of publication, number of pages, content notes, setting, main characters, and, where applicable, genres, awards, and series/sequel information. . . . This work should be a boon to reader's advisory and collection development librarians needing to build specific areas of the collection." Libr J

Fantasy and horror; a critical and historical guide to literature, illustration, film, TV, radio, and the Internet; edited by Neil Barron. Scarecrow Press 1999 816p $85

Grades: 11 12 Adult   **016.8**

1. Fantasy fiction—Bibliography

ISBN 0-8108-3596-7   LC 98-46564

"Extensive revision of two separate guides, Horror literature and Fantasy literature" Preface

This is a "guide to more than 2,300 works of fiction and poetry from 1762 to 1998. Barron states in his preface that Fantasy and Horror 'is an extensive revision of two separate guides, Horror Literature and Fantasy Literature, both published . . . in 1990 and now out of print.' . . . The first half of his new book lists titles in chronological chapters such as 'Early and Later Gothic Traditions, 1762-1896' or 'Contemporary Fantasy, 1957-1998.' . . . The second half of the book focuses more on secondary material." Booklist

Includes bibliographical references

Fichtelberg, Susan

Encountering enchantment; a guide to speculative fiction for teens. Libraries Unlimited 2007 328p (Genreflecting advisory series) $48

Grades: Professional   **016.8**

1. Fantasy fiction—Bibliography 2. Science fiction—Bibliography 3. Young adult literature—Bibliography

ISBN 1-59158-316-0; 978-1-59158-316-5

     LC 2006-33739

"This guide organizes by genre, subgenre, and theme some 1,400 titles of fantasy, science fiction and paranormal titles, most published within the last decade. Chapters cover such subgenres as epic fantasy, wizardry, romance, and mystery, which are further broken down by subgenres and themes. Annotations offer bibliographic information, brief plot summaries, reading levels, alternative media formats (including large print and Braille), and awards information." Publisher's note

"This useful guide should be in every YA collection." SLJ

Includes bibliographical references

Fonseca, Anthony J.

Hooked on horror; a guide to reading interests in horror fiction. 2nd ed. Libraries Unlimited 2003 xxiii, 464p il $55

Grades: 11 12 Adult   **016.8**

1. Horror fiction—Bibliography 2. Horror films

ISBN 1-56308-904-1

First edition published 1999

"Although we . . . refer to this guide as a second edition . . . it is, for all practical purposes, volume 2 of Hooked on horror. This is because space constraints make it impossible for us to list most of the titles that are found in the first edition. Therefore, readers' advisors . . . who own the first edition are advised to use this guide as a supplement rather than as a stand-alone product." pxxii

"Focusing on titles published in the last decade and older classics that are currently in print or commonly available in libraries, the authors cover 13 popular subgenres of horror fiction, including vampires and werewolves, techno horror, ghosts and haunted houses, and small town horror. . . . Special features of this book . . . [include] the inclusion of graphic novels; indications of audio, e-book, and large print formats." Publisher's note

Frolund, Tina

Genrefied classics; a guide to reading interests in classical literature. Libraries Unlimited 2007 xxiv, 365p (Genreflecting advisory series) $45 *

Grades: 11 12 Adult   **016.8**

1. Fiction—Bibliography

ISBN 1-59158-172-9; 978-1-59158-172-7

     LC 2006-33740

"By identifying the genre characteristics of more than 400 classic fiction works, and organizing titles according to these features, this guide helps readers find the type of books they enjoy." Publisher's note

Includes bibliographical references

Gannon, Michael B.

Blood, bedlam, bullets, and badguys; a reader's guide to adventure/suspense fiction. Libraries Unlimited 2004 385p (Genreflecting advisory series) $55

Grades: Professional   **016.8**

1. Adventure fiction—Bibliography 2. Suspense fiction—Bibliography

ISBN 1-563-08732-4   LC 2003-60527

"Fifteen chapters cover subgenres such as espionage, legal and medical thrillers, sea adventures, and novels with elements of the paranormal. Each chapter begins with a definition of the subgenre and brief discussions of its history and appeal. There is also a very useful list of things to keep in mind when advising a reader." Booklist

Includes bibliographical references

Herald, Diana Tixier

Genreflecting; a guide to popular reading interests; edited by Wayne A. Wiegand. 6th ed. Libraries Unlimited 2006 562p (Genreflecting advisory series) $60; pa $45 *

Grades: Professional　　　　　　**016.8**
　1. Fiction—Bibliography 2. Fiction—History and criticism 3. Books and reading
　ISBN 1-59158-224-5; 1-59158-286-5 (pa)
　　　　　　　　　　　LC 2005-30804
First published 1982 under the authorship of Betty Rosenberg

A listing of recommended titles in such genres as crime, adventure, romance, science fiction, Christian fiction, fantasy, horror, and their subgenres. Besides information on authors and titles, the volume provides information on anthologies, bibliographies, critical works, encyclopedias, organizations, and publishers.

Includes bibliographical references

Strictly science fiction; a guide to reading interests; [by] Diana Tixier Herald, Bonnie Kunzel. Libraries Unlimited 2002 xxii, 297p (Genreflecting advisory series) $55

Grades: Professional　　　　　　**016.8**
　1. Science fiction—Bibliography 2. Science fiction—History and criticism
　ISBN 1-56308-893-2　　　　LC 2002-3186

"The purpose of this volume is to serve as both a readers' advisory tool and as a guide for collection development. It lists approximately 900 mainly adult titles currently in print or likely to be found in library collections, and is organized by subgenres such as action/adventure, high tech, and short stories." SLJ

"Good indexing, by author, title, subject, and character name, along with chapters devoted to books written for children and young adults and genre-blended books (such as science fiction/ romance or science fiction/mystery), sets this reference apart." Libr J

Includes bibliographical references

Teen genreflecting; a guide to reading interests. 2nd ed. Libraries Unlimited 2003 275p lib bdg $40 *

Grades: Professional　　　　　　**016.8**
　1. Young adult literature—Bibliography 2. Teenagers—Books and reading
　ISBN 1-56308-996-3　　　　LC 2003-54610
First published 1997

"The first chapter offers an overview of teen readers' advisory services, and subsequent chapters focus on popular genres of young adult literature, including but not limited to suspense, adventure, fantasy, alternate formats (including graphic novels), and Christian fiction. Both recent and classic YA books are listed in their appropriate genres, and every entry contains the author, title, publication date, and age level of the book. . . . When appropriate, awards and any best lists on which a book might have appeared are cited. . . . In addition to its value as a readers' advisory guide, this book can serve as a key to building a core young adult fiction collection or as a guide to purchasing for a collection that is weak in some genres." Voice Youth Advocates

Includes bibliographical references

Jacob, Merle

To be continued; an annotated guide to sequels; by Merle Jacob and Hope Apple. 2nd ed. Oryx Press 2000 465p $67.95

Grades: 11 12 Adult　　　　　　**016.8**
　1. Fiction—Bibliography
　ISBN 1-57356-155-X　　　　LC 00-42782
First published 1995

"This book contains 1,762 entries, which span every possible genre and era. A list of genres is provided, and each genre is described. . . . Following the main entry is a title index, a genre index, a subject and literary forms index, and a time and place index." Book Rep

Includes bibliographical references

Johnson, Sarah L., 1969-

Historical fiction; a guide to the genre. Libraries Unlimited 2005 xxi, 813p (Genreflecting advisory series) $75

Grades: 11 12 Adult　　　　　　**016.8**
　1. Historical fiction—Bibliography
　ISBN 1-59158-129-X　　　　LC 2005-47483

"Each category, e.g., 'Traditional Historical Novels,' 'Historical Thrillers,' 'Time-Slip Novels,' is subdivided further by world region and historical era. . . . The annotations also indicate benchmarks of the genre, award winners, and titles recommended for young adults and reading groups. . . . This is an excellent resource." Choice

For a fuller review, see: Booklist, Sept. 15, 2005

Includes bibliographical references

Leeper, Angela

Poetry in literature for youth. Scarecrow Press 2006 303p (Literature for youth) pa $40

Grades: Professional　　　　　　**016.8**
　1. Poetry—Bibliography
　ISBN 0-8108-5465-1　　　　LC 2005030719

This "provides annotated listings of titles arranged by subjects. . . . More than 900 entries describe collections, anthologies, performance poetry, poet biographies, and more, for kindergarten through high school." Booklist

"This title is packed with innovative ways to integrate poetry into the K-12 curriculum." SLJ

Includes bibliographical references

Thomas, Rebecca L.

Popular series fiction for middle school and teen readers; a reading and selection guide; [by] Rebecca L. Thomas and Catherine Barr. Libraries Unlimited 2005 514p (Children's and young adult literature reference series) $50

Grades: Professional　　　　　　**016.8**
　1. Children's literature—Bibliography 2. Young adult literature—Bibliography
　ISBN 1-59158-202-4

"Covering some 800 series, this well-indexed, annotated guide to serial fiction will serve both as a reader's advisory and a collection-development tool. . . . This . . . is a must-buy for all librarians eager to keep up with the rapidly expanding teen market." SLJ

What do I read next? 2007; a reader's guide to current genre fiction, fantasy, western, romance, horror, mystery, science fiction; [by] Neil Barron [et al.] Gale Res. 2007 2v ea $185
Grades: 11 12 Adult **016.8**
1. Fiction—Bibliography
ISSN 1052-2212
ISBN 978-0-7876-9025-0 (v1); 0-7876-9025-2 (v1); 978-0-7876-9026-7 (v2); 0-7876-9026-0 (v2)
Also available online
Annual. First published 1991 for 1989-1990
A guide to locating new fiction titles in specific genres. Arranged by author within six genre sections, each entry provides publisher and publication date, series name, major characters, time period, geographic setting, review citations, and related books.

016.9   Bibliographies of geography and history

Adamson, Lynda G.
Literature connections to world history, 7-12; resources to enhance and entice. Libraries Unlimited 1998 511p pa $38.50
Grades: Professional **016.9**
1. History—Bibliography 2. Audiovisual materials—Catalogs
ISBN 1-56308-505-4   LC 97-35953
Also available Literature connections to world history, K-6
Covers books, CD-ROMs, and videotapes; Includes indexes
This resource is divided "into two main sections. The first section lists authors and book titles in the categories of historical fiction, biography, collective biography, history trade book, CD-ROM, and videotape within specific time periods according to grade levels. The second section contains annotated bibliographies of titles listed in the first part: books, CD-ROMs, and videotapes." Introduction

Barancik, Sue, 1944-
Guide to collective biographies for children and young adults. Scarecrow Press 2005 447p pa $44.95
Grades: Professional **016.9**
1. Biography—Bibliography
ISBN 0-8108-5033-8 (pa)   LC 2004-19560
"This text indexes 721 titles for children and young adults in order to provide access to 5,760 notable individuals from early to modern times. All of the referenced titles were published between 1988 and 2002." Booklist
"A current guide such as this one is essential. . . . A must-have for libraries serving grades 4 through 12." SLJ

Richards, Michael D., 1941-
Term paper resource guide to twentieth-century world history; [by] Michael D. Richards and Philip F. Riley. Greenwood Press 2000 335p $49.95
Grades: 9 10 11 12 **016.9**
1. Report writing 2. Modern history—Study and teaching
ISBN 0-313-30559-5   LC 99-88458
Companion volume to Term paper resource guide to twentieth-century United States history by Robert Muccigrosso
"The most significant 100 events in world history are arranged chronologically. . . . Each topic is followed by six suggestions for term papers, both traditional and nontraditional in approach, such as interviews, exploring connections between literature and history, group projects, mock trails, and film study." Book Rep
Includes bibliographical references

016.94053   Bibliographies of World War II, 1939-1945

Rosen, Philip, 1928-
Bearing witness; a resource guide to literature, poetry, art, music, and videos by Holocaust victims and survivors; [by] Philip Rosen and Nina Apfelbaum. Greenwood Press 2002 210p $52.95
Grades: Professional **016.94053**
1. Holocaust, 1933-1945—Bibliography
ISBN 0-313-31076-9   LC 00-69153
This is a resource guide to "over 800 first-person accounts, fiction, poetry, art interpretations, and music by Holocaust victims and survivors, as well as videos relating the testimony and experiences of Holocaust survivors." Publisher's note
"This volume will be valuable to all who are researching the Holocaust. Its strength lies in the inclusion of materials not often found elsewhere." Booklist
Includes bibliographical references

016.973   Bibliographies of United States history

Adamson, Lynda G.
Literature connections to American history, 7-12; resources to enhance and entice. Libraries Unlimited 1997 624p pa $41.50
Grades: Professional **016.973**
1. United States—History—Bibliography 2. Audiovisual materials—Catalogs 3. CD-ROMs—Reviews
ISBN 1-56308-503-8   LC 97-19560
Also available Literature connections to American history, K-6
"The first part of the book is divided into 13 time periods or topics, each of which is subdivided by grade level. . . . The books, identified only by author and title, are listed according to genre, including historical fiction, biography, collective biography, and history trade books. Multimedia listings include CD-ROMs and videos. The

Adamson, Lynda G.—*Continued*
bulk of the volume contains short annotated bibliographies of the nearly 3,000 books, CD-ROMs, and videos."
Book Rep

"This comprehensive title should be valuable as a reader's advisory tool, a purchasing guide, and a resource for curriculum enrichment." Bull Cent Child Books

Includes bibliographical references

Hardy, Lyda Mary
Women in U.S. history; a resource guide.
Libraries Unlimited 2000 344p pa $45
Grades: Professional   **016.973**
1. Women—United States—Bibliography 2. Women—United States—History
ISBN 1-56308-769-3   LC 00-55849
This overview of historical resources includes primary sources as well as biographies, autobiographies and compilations. Best books, Web sites, and videos are included. Subject and author/title indexes are appended.

Includes bibliographical references

Muccigrosso, Robert
Term paper resource guide to twentieth-century United States history; [by] Robert Muccigrosso, Ron Blazek, and Teri Maggio. Greenwood Press 1999 310p $49.95
Grades: 9 10 11 12   **016.973**
1. Report writing 2. United States—History—20th century—Chronology
ISBN 0-313-30096-8   LC 98-44592
Companion volume to Term paper resource guide to twentieth century world history by Michael Richards

This volume includes "500 term paper ideas and . . . print and nonprint sources on twentieth-century U.S. history. This guide presents entries on 100 of the most important events and developments in twentieth-century U.S. history organized in chronological order, from the Spanish-American War to the creation of NAFTA." Publisher's note

Includes bibliographical references

020   Library and information sciences

McCain, Mary Maude
Dictionary for school library media specialists; a practical and comprehensive guide; [by] Mary Maude McCain and Martha Merrill. Libraries Unlimited 2001 219p pa $42
Grades: Professional   **020**
ISBN 1-56308-696-4   LC 01-16506
"The book defines more than 375 terms. There are two types of definitions—shorter glossary descriptions (*capital outlay, reboot*) and longer, more detailed treatments (*poetry, proximity operators*). *See* references (especially from acronyms and abbreviations) and *see also* references facilitate use." Booklist

021.2   Relationships with the community

Gillespie, Kellie M., 1960-
Teen volunteer services in libraries. VOYA Books 2004 133p il (VOYA guides) pa $26.95
Grades: Professional   **021.2**
1. Volunteer work 2. Libraries
ISBN 0-8108-4837-6   LC 2003-17932
Contents: Why teens as volunteers?; Getting started; Marketing, recruiting, and placement; Orientation and training; Recognition and retention; Supervising volunteers; Volunteer program variations; How do they do it?: interviews with teen volunteer managers; Successful teen volunteer programs

This offers "advice about starting and maintaining effective teen volunteer programs in school and public libraries. . . . [The author discusses] recruitment, orientation and training, recognition and retention, and supervision." Publisher's note

"If you are even considering starting a teen volunteer program, you must read this book. If you already have one in your library, this volume still has much to offer." SLJ

Includes bibliographical references

021.7   Promotion of libraries, information centers

Wolfe, Lisa Ann
Library public relations, promotions, and communications; a how-to-do-it manual. 2nd ed. Neal-Schuman Publishers 2005 230p (How-to-do-it manuals for librarians) pa $65
Grades: Professional   **021.7**
1. Libraries—Public relations
ISBN 1-55570-471-9   LC 2004-25944
First published 1997
"The book is divided into two parts—'Planning and Evaluation' and 'Strategies and Methodologies'—with many examples of successful communicating and the impact and changes brought by technology. Ideas on putting together a communications plan, creating clear signage and print products, effectively using a library's Web site, and communicating during a crisis will be helpful for all types of libraries and positions." Booklist

Includes bibliographical references

023   Personnel management

Giesecke, Joan
Fundamentals of library supervision. American Library Association 2005 166p il (ALA fundamental series) pa $42
Grades: Professional   **023**
1. Libraries—Administration 2. Personnel management
ISBN 0-8389-0895-0   LC 2004-24654
This book teaches library "supervisors how to motivate staff, encourage a positive work ethic, and build

Giesecke, Joan—*Continued*
teams. The advice on interviewing, hiring, training, and working with new employees is highly relevant. . . . New managers needing an outline of the fundamental principles of supervision as well as old hands who can benefit from a refresher course will find all the practical advice they need to accomplish their jobs." Libr J
Includes bibliographical references

025.04 Automated information storage and retrieval systems

Berners-Lee, Tim, 1955-
Weaving the Web; the original design and ultimate destiny of the World Wide Web; by its inventor Tim Berners-Lee with Mark Fischetti. HarperSanFrancisco 1999 226p hardcover o.p. pa $15
Grades: 11 12 Adult   **025.04**
1. World Wide Web
ISBN 0-06-251586-1; 0-06-251587-X (pa)
    LC 99-27665
World Wide Web developer Berners-Lee "recounts the events leading up to his creation of the web, fusing hypertext and internetworking into the most dramatic development in communications since the printing press. In this important work, he also shares his personal vision of the web, what's right and wrong with it, and what its future may hold for us." Libr J

Braun, Linda W.
Hooking teens with the Net. Neal-Schuman 2003 133p (Teens @ the library series) pa $45 *
Grades: Professional   **025.04**
1. Internet resources 2. Internet searching—Study and teaching
ISBN 1-55570-457-3   LC 2002-45221
This is a "guide to integrating information-literacy skills into the curriculum via the Internet. Through the use of popular teen sites, the author suggests that students will make an easy transition to more traditional electronic tools. . . . Each chapter includes an overview and bulleted skills and technology requirements as well as skills taught and extension activities, and each one culminates with a resource list. . . . A detailed and useful teaching tool." SLJ
Includes bibliographical references

Diaz, Karen R.
IssueWeb: a guide and sourcebook for researching controversial issues on the Web; [by] Karen R. Diaz, Nancy O'Hanlon. Libraries Unlimited 2004 287p pa $30
Grades: Professional   **025.04**
1. Internet resources 2. Internet searching—Study and teaching
ISBN 1-591-58078-1   LC 2003-65946
The authors "open with an online research guide that concentrates on finding an appropriate topic, using the right terminology, and evaluating online research, consid-

ering bias, balance, and documentation. . . . Recommended Web sites follow, subdivided into reference, legal issues, news, data sources, and advocacy for and against." Choice
"A veritable gold mine of more than 40 well-organized, well-presented issues briefs follows three remarkably clear, concise chapters on finding, evaluating, and incorporating Internet resources." SLJ

Doggett, Sandra L.
Beyond the book; technology integration into the secondary school library media curriculum; edited by Paula K. Montgomery. Libraries Unlimited 2000 177p (Library and information problem-solving skills series) pa $29.50 *
Grades: Professional   **025.04**
1. High school libraries 2. Instructional materials centers 3. Computer-assisted instruction
ISBN 1-56308-584-4   LC 99-33151
"Chapters address everything from a history of technology in schools to the pros and cons of contemporary usage, tools and lesson plans, and debates over Internet filters. There's even a section on grant writing and securing additional funding to build up media center resources. Throughout, the author provides plenty of Web sites, and she includes an extensive bibliography." Booklist
Includes bibliographical references

Gordon, Rachel Singer
Best career and education Web sites; a quick guide to online job search; [by] Rachel Singer Gordon and Anne Wolfinger. 4th ed. Jist Works 2004 198p il pa $12.95 *
Grades: 9 10 11 12   **025.04**
1. Job hunting 2. Vocational guidance 3. Internet resources 4. Web sites
ISBN 1-563-70960-0   LC 2004-269117
First published 1998 under the authorship of Anne Wolfinger with title: The quick Internet guide to career and college information
This resource contains a directory of Web sites and "also offers guidance on e-mail etiquette when sending résumés and job inquiries, advice about avoiding online employment scams, and provides information about finding temporary and freelance work, telecommuting, and volunteering. The directory is organized into sections that enable a student or job seeker to focus on what they need without feeling intimidated by a large volume. The sections include career exploration, finding openings from job banks, researching a potential employer, and careers in the military." Voice Youth Advocates

Harris, Frances Jacobson
I found it on the Internet; coming of age online. American Library Association 2005 161p il pa $35
Grades: Professional   **025.04**
1. Young adults' libraries 2. Internet—Social aspects
ISBN 0-8389-0898-5 (pa)   LC 2004-30119
This is an "analysis of the fundamental differences in how teens (for whom the Internet is a primary language) and adults (who will always be second-language learners)

Harris, Frances Jacobson—*Continued*
view information and communication." SLJ

"Well-researched and easy to read, this roadmap through digital terrain and all of its potholes is proactive and practical." Ref & User Services Quarterly

Includes bibliographical references

Hernon, Peter, 1944-
U.S. government on the Web; getting the information you need; {by} Peter Hernon, Robert E. Dugan, John A. Shuler. 3rd ed. Libraries Unlimited 2003 xxvi, 465p il pa $50 *

Grades: 11 12 Adult   025.04

1. Government information—Directories 2. Internet 3. Web sites

ISBN 1-59158-086-2   LC 2003-51584

First published 1999

This guide to U.S. government information on the Web contains information from the current administration and includes material on the Patriot Act, the E-Government Act of 2002, and the Department of Homeland Security. The authors provide Web sites and suggest strategies for effectively accessing and using government information online

Includes bibliographical references

MacDonald, Randall M., 1961-
Successful keyword searching; initiating research on popular topics using electronic databases; by Randall M. MacDonald and Susan Priest MacDonald. Greenwood Press 2001 443p $44.95

Grades: Professional   025.04

1. Internet

ISBN 0-313-30676-1   LC 00-35323

"Beginning with a brief overview of seaching and the various types, the authors then address 144 topics most often researched by students. Each subject includes a list of keywords, a brief list of related organizations, notable people in the field, and three-to-eight . . . Web sites." SLJ

Includes bibliographical references

Peck, Robert S.
Libraries, the First Amendment, and cyberspace; what you need to know. American Lib. Assn. 2000 216p pa $32 *

Grades: Professional   025.04

1. Internet 2. Libraries—Censorship 3. Freedom of speech

ISBN 0-8389-0773-3   LC 99-39455

The author "discusses the First Amendment, its developing interpretation, and how it relates to state constitutional guarantees; the exceptions to free speech; and the concept of the public forum. Further chapters consider the religious connotations of free speech, free speech in the workplace, whether there is a right to offend, free speech and children, and other topics. Finally, he turns to the First Amendment in cyberspace and on the Internet." Booklist

Smith, J. Douglas, 1965-
World War II on the Web; a guide to the very best sites; [by] J. Douglas Smith and Richard Jensen. Scholarly Resources 2003 207p $65; pa $23.95

Grades: 11 12 Adult   025.04

1. World War, 1939-1945—Internet resources 2. Web sites

ISBN 0-8420-5020-5; 0-8420-5021-3 (pa)

LC 2002-29236

"Provides descriptions and ratings for 'the top 100+' sites, plus listings for an additional 140 'sites worth a visit.' Arrangement is topical, and separate ratings are given for content, aesthetics, and navigation. Each topical chapter includes a fairly extensive list of suggested readings, a nice addition that we don't often find in Web site guides. A CD-ROM, included with the guide, links to all the sites that are listed." Booklist

The United States government Internet manual 2007. Bernan 2007 pa $59 *

Grades: 11 12 Adult   025.04

1. Government information—Directories 2. Internet 3. Web sites

ISSN 1547-2892

ISBN 1-59888-073-X; 978-1-59888-073-1

Annual. First published 2004

Continues Government information on the Internet

This is a resource to "federal government data online, including laws, pamphlets, press releases, numerous statistics, grant and fellowship information, dictionaries, and much more. . . . Based on . . . Government Information on the Internet . . . and designed to complement . . . The United States Government Manual, the volume organizes sites by topic for easy browsing and, in addition to URLs, includes descriptions of numerous government agencies. It contains organizational charts for federal and congressional cabinet-level departments, which are great for student projects. Its user friendliness is further enhanced by three indexes, which list agencies, sites, or publications. . . . This reference is suitable for libraries offering Internet access, but it will also prove valuable to teachers, students, and even children (included are government sites containing online educational games, quizzes, and resources)." Libr J

Wolinsky, Art
Internet power research using the Big6 approach. rev ed. Enslow Publishers 2005 64p il (Internet library) lib bdg $22.60; pa $11.93

Grades: Professional   025.04

1. Information systems 2. Research

ISBN 0-7660-1563-7 (lib bdg); 0-7660-1564-5 (pa)

LC 2004-22185

First published 2002

Provides instructions for using the "Big6" research method and scenarios for applying the technique to research conducted on the Internet.

The information is presented in "a friendly, informal writing style. . . . This is a helpful resource for students who want to hone their research strategies." SLJ

Includes glossary and bibliographical references

025.1 Library administration

The **big** book of library grant money, 2006; profiles of private and corporate foundations and direct corporate givers receptive to library grant proposals. American Library Association 2006 1564p pa $275
Grades: Professional   025.1
1. Library finance 2. Endowments—Directories
ISSN 1086-0568
ISBN 0-8389-3558-3
Annual. First published 1994
This book "includes nearly 2,400 private and corporate foundations and givers that have either indicated an interest in giving money to libraries or have already done so. Potential donors in The Big Book are profiled with contact and portfolio information, past contributions summary and analysis, and application information." Publisher's note

Curzon, Susan Carol
Managing change; a how-to-do-it manual for librarians. rev. ed. Neal-Schuman Publishers 2005 129p (How-to-do-it manuals for librarians) pa $55
Grades: Professional   025.1
1. Libraries—Administration
ISBN 1-55570-553-7   LC 2005-22846
First published 1989
The author "outlines the step-by-step processes and . . . instructions necessary for conceptualizing the issues; planning; preparing; decision-making; controlling resistance; and implementing changes. Practical guidance for dealing with technology's impact on libraries, applying the latest research in change management, and developing new strategies for coping with change are included." Publisher's note
"The real-world approach makes the book a valuable addition to the professional collection." Booklist
Includes bibliographical references

Dresang, Eliza T.
Dynamic youth services through outcome-based planning and evaluation; foreword by Virginia Walter. American Library Association 2006 155p il pa $42
Grades: Professional   025.1
1. Libraries—Administration 2. School libraries—Activity projects
ISBN 0-8389-0918-3; 978-0-8389-0918-8
                            LC 2006-7487
In this "guide, three experts who have conducted extensive research and piloted . . . [an] outcome-based program for youth in the St. Louis Public Library, share their findings and proven strategies." Publisher's note
Includes bibliographical references

Gerding, Stephanie K.
Grants for libraries; a how-to-do-it manual. Neal-Schuman Publishers 2006 xxiii, 252p il (How-to-do-it manuals for librarians) $99.95 *
Grades: Professional   025.1
1. Grants-in-aid 2. Fund raising
ISBN 1-55570-535-9   LC 2005-27980

Includes CD-ROM
"The authors of this book take the reader through every phase of the grant-writing cycle, offering details, examples, and relevant tools. Dividing the process into 10 steps, each covered in a separate chapter, the book offers practical advice and easy-to-follow suggestions appropriate for every type of library. . . . This book should be at the side of every grant-writing librarian." Booklist
Includes bibliographical references

Hallam, Arlita
Managing budgets and finances; a how-to-do-it manual for librarians and information professionals. Neal-Schuman Publishers 2005 233p il (How-to-do-it manuals for librarians) pa $65 *
Grades: Professional   025.1
1. Library finance
ISBN 1-55570-519-7
"This budgeting manual . . . offers the new or seasoned library administrators, board members, department heads, or finance professionals a way to budget carefully and clearly by offering a variety of strategies, definitions, and suggestions. The manual is divided into three parts: basics for librarians, special topics in financial management for libraries, and alternative library funding." Booklist
Includes bibliographical references

Leadership and the school librarian; essays from leaders in the field; [compiled by] Mary D. Lankford. Linworth Pub. 2006 132p il pa $44.95
Grades: Professional   025.1
1. School libraries 2. Libraries—Administration
ISBN 1-58683-191-7   LC 2005-34166
"Written by seven Texas library media specialists, the essays examine primary areas of professional responsibility: advocacy, collection development, finances, collaboration, professional development, and information access, focusing on the leadership opportunities that these areas afford." Voice Youth Advocates
"This collection of essays is just what you need to develop your leadership skills." Libr Media Connect
Includes bibliographical references

MacDonell, Colleen
Essential documents for school libraries; I've-got-it! answers to I-need-it-now! questions. Linworth Pub. 2004 132p il $44.95 *
Grades: Professional   025.1
1. Libraries—Administration
ISBN 1-58683-174-7   LC 2004-19392
Contents: Planning documents; Official reports; Publicity; Teaching documents; Programming documents; Procedure sheets and guides; Library rules and regulations; Interactive forms
"Each chapter begins with why the documents are needed, followed by practical advice for writing the documents, and examples of how the documents make an effective change in the library media program." Libr Media Connect
"An excellent addition for school librarians who always want to be prepared." SLJ
Includes bibliographical references

Matthews, Joseph R.

Strategic planning and management for library managers. Libraries Unlimited 2005 150p il pa $40

Grades: Professional   **025.1**

1. Libraries—Administration

ISBN 1-59158-231-8   LC 2005-10099

"Part 1 defines a strategy, addresses the need for one, and presents 10 distinct schools of strategic thought. Part 2 differentiates between strategic planning and long-range planning, discusses the benefits of strategic planning, and identifies approaches to preparing and implementing such plans. Part 3 focuses on performance measures, ways to communicate the value of libraries to others, and the 'culture of assessment,' an environment where all library staff are routinely involved in the evaluation process. Information presented throughout the book is clear, practical, readily accessible, well documented, and amply supported by notes, tables, figures, diagrams, and quotes." Booklist

McGhee, Marla W.

The principal's guide to a powerful library media program; [by] Marla W. McGhee and Barbara A. Jansen. Linworth Pub. 2005 xxvi, 141p il pa $39.95

Grades: Professional   **025.1**

1. School libraries 2. Instructional materials centers 3. School superintendents and principals

ISBN 1-58683-193-3   LC 2004-30208

Five "chapters provide administrators with a knowledge base of library-related philosophy and research; best practices in collaboration and instructional issues; responsibilities that effective librarians assume; nuts and bolts of hiring, scheduling, budgeting, and facilities; and professional development." SLJ

This is "an excellent introduction to the school library media program, its impact on student learning, and the components necessary for a vital, effective program." Libr Media Connect

Includes bibliographical references

025.2 Acquisitions and collection development

Baumbach, Donna

Less is more; a practical guide to weeding school library collections. American Library Association 2006 194p il pa $32 *

Grades: Professional   **025.2**

1. Libraries—Collection development

ISBN 0-8389-0919-1; 978-0-8389-0919-5

LC 2006-7490

Contents: The role of weeding in collection development (why less is more); General weeding guidelines; Getting started and keeping on keeping on; Weeding criteria by topic and Dewey number; What automation hath wrought; What's next?

"This outstanding, easy-to-use guide makes weeding realistic and achievable. . . . This is an indispensable resource for every school library." Booklist

Includes bibliographical references

Doll, Carol Ann

Managing and analyzing your collection; a practical guide for small libraries and school media centers; [by] Carol A. Doll, Pamela Petrick Barron. American Lib. Assn. 2002 93p il pa $30 *

Grades: Professional   **025.2**

1. Libraries—Collection development

ISBN 0-8389-0821-7   LC 2001-53747

This guide to collection development is divided into chapters covering management objectives, gathering and analyzing collection data, and weeding

This is a "book that librarians will actually read from cover to cover. . . . [It] isn't overwhelming and technical. Instead, it is rather chatty with solid, useful information." Book Rep

Includes bibliographical references

Goldsmith, Francisca

Graphic novels now; building, managing, and marketing a dynamic collection. American Library Association 2005 113p il $35

Grades: Professional   **025.2**

1. Graphic novels 2. Libraries—Special collections

ISBN 0-8389-0904-3   LC 2005-12653

This book begins with a "theoretical discussion of graphic novels: an illustrative definition . . . ; a brief but informative history of the format; and a number of well-reasoned arguments for bringing the genre into library collections. The latter half of the book provides many concrete suggestions for creating, maintaining, promoting, and defending a graphic-novel collection." SLJ

Includes bibliographical references

Greiner, Tony

Analyzing library collection use with Excel; [by] Tony Greiner and Bob Cooper. American Library Association 2007 167p il pa $40 *

Grades: Professional   **025.2**

1. Library circulation 2. Libraries—Collection development 3. Excel (Computer program)

ISBN 0-8389-0933-7; 978-0-8389-0933-1

LC 2006-101539

The authors "show how to use Excel® to translate circulation and collection data into meaningful reports for making collection management decisions." Publisher's note

Includes bibliographical references

Hughes-Hassell, Sandra

Collection management for youth; responding to the needs of learners; [by] Sandra Hughes-Hassell, Jacqueline C. Mancall. ALA Editions 2005 103p il pa $35

Grades: Professional   **025.2**

1. Libraries—Collection development 2. Instructional materials centers

ISBN 0-8389-0894-2   LC 2004-26911

"The authors present 11 . . . tools for creating a learner-centered collection with suggestions on the best methods for easy implementation of these procedures.

Hughes-Hassell, Sandra—*Continued*

. . . Every library media specialist wanting a more practical approach to collection management would find this book an important addition to his or her professional development library." Libr Media Connect

Includes bibliographical references

Kravitz, Nancy E.

Censorship and the school library media center; [by] Nancy Kravitz. Libraries Unlimited 2002 223p il (Libraries Unlimited professional guides in school librarianship) pa $40

Grades: Professional   025.2

1. Libraries—Censorship 2. School libraries 3. Intellectual freedom

ISBN 0-313-31437-3   LC 2002-11603

Contents: Who and why; A historical perspective; Cases in law; Challenged material; Policies and procedures; Today's issues; In defense of intellectual freedom

"Kravitz begins with a discussion of the various types of challenges that arise from parents, political and religious groups, internal groups, and groups that oppose censorship. She then fills in the historical perspective. . . . She explains the case law on obscenity and school libraries and addresses challenged materials in terms of religion and literature, political suppression, sex, language and other taboos, and textbook censorship. . . . The six appendixes include important documents, the 100 most frequently challenged books, and a list of organizations for and against intellectual freedom. This is a solid addition to professional shelves . . . as well as for senior-high-school research and debates on censorship." Booklist

Includes bibliographical references

Lukenbill, W. Bernard

Community resources in the school library media center; concepts and methods; [by] W. Bernard Lukenbill. Libraries Unlimited 2004 195p il $40

Grades: Professional   025.2

1. School libraries 2. Libraries and community

ISBN 1-59158-110-9   LC 2004-48926

"This text outlines organizational strategies for managing community resources. . . . Lukenbill includes information such as agency directories, telementoring numbers, historical documents, museum exhibits, photos, and volunteer pools. Expanding the concept of the vertical file, the author presents ideas for developing, managing, marketing, and accessing electronic photo archives, Web site links, school documents, and bulletin boards. One chapter addresses sensitive community information, censorship, privacy, and terrorism concerns. . . . A definitive tool for developing community-resource collections." SLJ

Lyga, Allyson A. W.

Graphic novels in your media center; a definitive guide; by Allyson A. W. Lyga with Barry Lyga. Libraries Unlimited 2004 180p il pa $35

Grades: professional   025.2

1. Graphic novels—Administration 2. Book selection 3. Books and reading

ISBN 1-59158-142-7   LC 2004-46517

In the first section the authors "make cogent arguments for the inclusion of graphic novels. A second section introduces common terms and includes an extremely useful 'how to read' subsection, complete with sample pages. The remaining sections provide recommended titles for all ages, testimonials from teachers and comic book store proprietors, resource lists, and a set of 17 lesson plans." Booklist

"This indispensable, well-organized guide will provide school librarians with all of the necessary information for implementing and developing a graphic-novels collection." SLJ

Miller, Steve

Developing and promoting graphic novel collections. Neal-Schuman Publishers 2005 130p il (Teens @ the library series) pa $49.95 *

Grades: Professional   025.2

1. Graphic novels—Administration 2. Book selection 3. Books and reading

ISBN 1-55570-461-1   LC 2004-40159

This is an "overview of graphic novels and their use as reader development tools. Miller explores the evolution, categories, and genres of graphic novels; he then addresses the . . . details of collection development, acquisition, cataloging, and maintenance for this unique format. A special section shows how to promote graphic novels (include display ideas)." Publisher's note

"This volume is filled with practical information and savvy advice." SLJ

Includes bibliographical references

Reichman, Henry, 1947-

Censorship and selection; issues and answers for schools. 3rd ed. American Lib. Assn. 2001 223p pa $37 *

Grades: professional   025.2

1. Censorship 2. School libraries 3. Academic freedom

ISBN 0-8389-0798-9   LC 00-67657

First published 1988

The author "covers the different media (including books, school newspapers, and the Internet), the important court cases (including recent litigations involving Harry Potter, the Internet, and Huck Finn), the issues in dispute (including violence, religion, and profanity), and how the laws on the books can be incorporated into selection policies." Publisher's note

"Reichman's manual provides sound practical advice on how to handle this complex and emotionally charged subject." Voice Youth Advocates

Includes bibliographical references

Symons, Ann K.

Protecting the right to read; a how-to-do-it manual for school and public librarians; [by] Ann K. Symons, Charles Harmon; illustrations by Pat Race. Neal-Schuman 1995 211p il (How-to-do-it manuals for librarians) pa $55

Grades: Professional　　**025.2**

1. Libraries—Censorship 2. Intellectual freedom

ISBN 1-55570-216-3　　LC 95-42444

"The authors take readers from discussion of the policies and principles of intellectual freedom to considerations specific to school and public libraries to the protection of freedom on the Internet. . . . Appendixes consist of reprints of documents put out by the ALA and the Minnesota Coalition Against Censorship." Book Rep

"Intellectual freedom issues and guiding principles get a thorough and comprehensive treatment. . . . An essential book." Voice Youth Advocates

Includes bibliographical references

Walker, Barbara J.

The librarian's guide to developing Christian fiction collections for young adults. Neal-Schuman Publishers 2005 200p (The librarian's guides to developing Christian fiction collections) pa $55

Grades: Professional　　**025.2**

1. Libraries—Special collections 2. Christian fiction—Bibliography 3. Teenagers—Books and reading

ISBN 1-55570-545-6　　LC 2005-5112

The author discusses issues "such as censorship, the legalities in spending tax dollars on Christian novels, and marketing to an underserved clientele. 'Key Book Titles' offers an extensive, annotated bibliography, organized by topic (Apocalyptic, Bible, Contemporary, Fantasy, Historical, Mystery, Romance, Thrillers, Westerns). . . . A thorough, balanced approach." SLJ

Includes bibliographical references

025.3　Bibliographic analysis and control

Byrne, Deborah J.

MARC manual; understanding and using MARC records. 2nd ed. Libraries Unlimited 1998 xxiii, 263p pa $45

Grades: Professional　　**025.3**

1. MARC formats 2. Cataloging

ISBN 1-56308-176-8　　LC 97-35961

First published 1991

This handbook explains the 3 types of MARC records: bibliographic, author, and holdings. MARC database processing and online systems are discussed.

Includes bibliographical references

Fritz, Deborah A. (Deborah Angela), 1955-

Cataloging with AACR2 and MARC21; for books, electronic resources, sound recordings, videorecordings, and serials. 2nd ed. American Library Association 2004 various paging il loose leaf $68 *

Grades: professional　　**025.3**

1. American Library Association 2. Anglo-American cataloguing rules 3. Cataloging

ISBN 0-8389-0884-5　　LC 2004-6535

First published 1998 with title: Cataloging with AACR2R and USMARC

In this guide Fritz "provides the hands-on cross-references between AACR2 and MARC21 required for easy online cataloging. Designed to streamline the process and avoid errors, the book is organized in order of MARC tags." Publisher's note

"Although it does not present every rule or MARC tag, this fairly comprehensive and handy reference addresses all levels of cataloging expertise. Catalogers and instructors should add this to their collection." Libr J

Gorman, Michael, 1941-

The concise AACR2; prepared by Michael Gorman. 4th ed. American Library Association 2004 179p pa $40 *

Grades: Professional　　**025.3**

1. Anglo-American cataloguing rules 2. Cataloging

ISBN 0-8389-3548-6　　LC 2004-16088

On cover: Fourth edition

"This practical guidebook . . . has been fully revised and is now in concordance with AACR2, 2002 Revision 2004 Update. Michael Gorman . . . explains the more generally applicable AACR2 rules for cataloging library materials in simplified terms that make the rules more accessible and practical for practitioners and students who are in less complex library and bibliographic environments." Publisher's note

Intner, Sheila S., 1935-

Standard cataloging for school and public libraries; [by] Sheila S. Intner and Jean Weihs. 3rd ed. Libraries Unlimited 2001 346p il $47.50

Grades: professional　　**025.3**

1. Cataloging 2. Library classification

ISBN 1-56308-781-2　　LC 2001-18615

First published 1990

This explains the Anglo-American Cataloging Rules (AACR2), Sears and Library of Congress subject headings, Dewey decimal and Library of Congress classification systems, MARC format, large computer networks, policy manuals, and how to manage a cataloging department

Includes bibliographical references

025.4   Subject analysis and control

Dewey, Melvil, 1851-1931
  Abridged Dewey decimal classification and relative index; devised by Melvil Dewey. ed 14, edited by Joan S. Mitchell, Julianne Beall, Giles Martin, Winton E. Matthews, Jr., Gregory R. New. OCLC 2004 1050p $99 *
  Grades: professional   025.4
    1. Dewey Decimal Classification
    ISBN 0-910608-73-3   LC 2003-542823
  Also available online
  First abridged edition published 1894
  The 14th Abridged Edition is an abridgement of the four volume 22nd Edition. Adapted to the needs of small and growing libraries, the 14th Abridged Edition is designed primarily for school and public libraries with collections of up to 20,000 titles

Sears list of subject headings; Joseph Miller, editor; Barbara A. Bristow, associate editor. 19th ed. Wilson, H. W. 2007 li, 823p $145 *
  Grades: Professional   025.4
    1. Subject headings
    ISBN 978-0-8242-1076-2
  Also available Canadian companion. 6th edition published 2001
  First published 1923 with title: List of subject headings for small libraries, by Minnie Earl Sears
  This is "a standard authority list for subject cataloging in small and medium-sized libraries. It contains more than 8,000 established subject terms and . . . provisions for establishing further terms as needed. It also contains more than 500 authorized subdivisions with instructions in their application, scope notes, suggested cross-references, and suggestions for classification." Publisher's note

025.5   Services to users

Borne, Barbara Wood, 1945-
  100 research topic guides for students. Greenwood Press 1996 xx, 234p (Greenwood professional guides in school librarianship) $39.95
  Grades: 9 10 11 12   025.5
    1. Research 2. Report writing
    ISBN 0-313-29552-2   LC 95-42446
  The author "presents ideas for term papers and speeches. . . . The book is divided into four sections: Science and Technology, Social Issues, Social Studies, and Biography. . . . Appendixes give an overview of note-taking procedures; brief outline of MLA bibliographic citation form; and how best to search a database. Most resources have been published since 1990." Book Rep

Cooper, Gail, 1950-
  New virtual field trips; [by] Gail Cooper and Garry Cooper. Libraries Unlimited 2001 155p pa $27.50
  Grades: Professional   025.5
    1. Internet 2. World Wide Web 3. Field trips
    ISBN 1-56308-887-8   LC 00-45091
  First published 1997 with title: Virtual field trips
  This is an "annotated guide to 440 web sites . . . that were selected to tie in to National Science Standards and inquiry-based learning, and to encourage independent studies. Organized into 13 topics covered in most K-12 school curricula, the entries include museums, libraries, schools, scientific labs, and government and university sites. . . . An accessible, useful resource." SLJ
  Includes bibliographical references

Developing an information literacy program, K-12; a how-to-do-it manual and CD-ROM package; developed by the Iowa City Community School District; edited by Mary Jo Langhorne. 2nd ed. Neal-Schuman 2004 432p (How-to-do-it manuals for librarians) pa $89.95 *
  Grades: Professional   025.5
    1. Bibliographic instruction 2. School libraries 3. Library information networks
    ISBN 1-55570-509-X   LC 2004-46046
  First published 1998
  "Over twenty lessons . . . cover keyword research, library and library materials organization, using nonfiction books, using the library catalog, using online databases, using the Internet, note-taking, creating bibliographies, and more. You will also find planning and assessment forms, checklists, tables, and worksheets for developing, implementing, and instructing your information literacy programs—all reproduced in the book and accompanying CD-ROM." Publisher's note

Eisenberg, Michael
  Teaching information & technology skills; the Big6 in secondary schools; [by] Michael B. Eisenberg and Robert E. Berkowitz; with Robert Darrow and Kathleen L. Spitzer. Linworth Pub. 2000 203p il pa $39.95
  Grades: Professional   025.5
    1. Computer-assisted instruction 2. Research
    ISBN 1-58683-006-6   LC 00-60592
  The authors present an information literary model for secondary schools. Instructional tools and lesson/unit plans are discussed. Reproducible forms and evaluative matrices are included
  Includes bibliographical references

Farkas, Meredith, 1977-
  Social software in libraries; building collaboration, communication, and community online. Information Today, Inc. 2007 xxiv, 320p il pa $39.50
  Grades: Professional   025.5
    1. Libraries and community 2. Telecommunication 3. Information technology
    ISBN 978-1-57387-275-1   LC 2007-4515

Farkas, Meredith, 1977-—_Continued_
This "guide provides librarians with the information and skills necessary to implement the most popular and effective social software technologies: blogs, RSS, wikis, social networking software, screencasting, photo-sharing, podcasting, instant messaging, gaming, and more." Publisher's note
Includes bibliographical references

Farmer, Lesley S. Johnson, 1949-
Technology-infused instruction for the educational community; a guide for school library specialists; [by] Lesley S.J. Farmer. Scarecrow Press 2005 209p il pa $40
Grades: Professional   025.5
1. School libraries 2. Information technology
ISBN 0-8108-5118-0   LC 2004-18028
"Library media teachers who provide staff development would do well to read this concise manual, which provides a welcome shortcut for the training of teachers and parents in the use of technology. . . . Farmer keeps the information moving swiftly through an engaging text that sparks ideas that readers can transfer smoothly into practice. Useful checklists and worksheets that translate into visuals abound." SLJ
Includes glossary and bibliographical references

Lanning, Scott
Essential reference services for today's school media specialists; [by] Scott Lanning and John Bryner. Libraries Unlimited 2004 129p il pa $40
Grades: Professional   025.5
1. Reference services (Libraries) 2. School libraries
ISBN 1-59158-137-0   LC 2004-40833
This book "covers not only how to develop a quality reference section for school library media specialists, but also how to complete a reference interview and work with teachers to reach the most students. . . . All librarians will find something useful in this book." Libr Media Connect
Includes bibliographical references

Nonfiction reader's advisory; edited by Robert Burgin. Libraries Unlimited 2004 250p pa $39.95
Grades: Professional   025.5
1. Reference services (Libraries)
ISBN 1-591-58115-X   LC 2004-48642
This is a "collection of essays on the challenges of readers' advisory librarians who strive to meet the nonfiction reading needs of patrons." Booklist
Includes bibliographical references

Riedling, Ann Marlow, 1952-
Information literacy; what does it look like in the school library media center. Libraries Unlimited 2004 121p il pa $35 *
Grades: Professional   025.5
1. Bibliographic instruction 2. School libraries
3. Information networks
ISBN 1-59158-201-6   LC 2004-48773

This "instructional manual is designed to teach school library media specialists what information literacy 'looks like' in general, in the school, in the classroom, in your mind, in life, and in motion. . . . It discusses information literacy, research, independent learning, ethics and more. . . . Annotated resources are provided within each chapter, as are . . . related readings and Web sites." Publisher's note
This is "a worthwhile addition." SLJ
Includes bibliographical references

Reference skills for the school library media specialist; tips and tools. 2nd ed. Linworth Books 2005 141p pa $44.95 *
Grades: Professional   025.5
1. Reference services (Libraries) 2. School libraries
3. Instructional materials centers
ISBN 1-58683-190-9   LC 2004-25097
First published 2000
This book "is tailored specifically for the school library media specialist, focusing on reference processes, sources, services and skills. . . [It contains] terminology and techniques, research processes and models, selection, evaluation, maintenance of reference sources, and addresses the vast changes in technology." Publisher's note
"This is a helpful tool for those new to the profession. A good complement to the more general texts on librarianship that are often used." SLJ
Includes bibliographical references

Saricks, Joyce G.
The readers' advisory guide to genre fiction. American Lib. Assn. 2001 460p (ALA readers' advisory series) pa $38
Grades: Professional   025.5
1. Reference services (Libraries) 2. Fiction—Bibliography
ISBN 0-8389-0803-9   LC 2001-22750
The author explores popular fiction genres. "Each genre, from adventure to literary fiction, is given its own chapter in which the genre is defined, its characteristics and appeal to its fans are described, key authors and subgenres are discussed, the preparation needed to work with readers is detailed, and tips on the readers' advisory interview are offered." Voice Youth Advocates
Includes bibliographical references

Spratford, Becky Siegel
The horror readers' advisory; the librarian's guide to vampires, killer tomatoes, and haunted houses; [by] Becky Siegel Spratford [and] Tammy Hennigh Clausen. American Library Association 2004 161p il (ALA readers' advisory series) pa $36
Grades: Professional   025.5
1. Horror fiction—History and criticism 2. Reference services (Libraries)
ISBN 0-8389-0871-3   LC 2003-25530
This is a "guide to horror fiction, explaining its appeal and advising on how librarians unfamiliar with the genre can broaden their own knowledge and build a viable collection. The text briefly outlines the characteristics of the main categories, or subgenres, including the usual mon-

Spratford, Becky Siegel—*Continued*
sters and occult creatures; extreme suspense of all types; hauntings and possession; and a section on classic works of horror, along with tips for interviewing readers of each subgenre. . . . [This] small, helpful book will be a boon to readers' advisors needing fresh meat for horror fans." Libr J
Includes bibliographical references

Stebbins, Leslie F.
Student guide to research in the digital age; how to locate and evaluate information sources. Libraries Unlimited 2006 202p il pa $45
Grades: 9 10 11 12   025.5
1. Research 2. Information systems 3. Information resources
ISBN 1-59158-099-4   LC 2005-30844
"This research guide seeks to clarify and simplify the overload of research options that exist, and to provide a best practices approach to discovering, evaluating, and using the best information sources, Web or print, to obtain the most appropriate information for research needs." Choice
Includes bibliographical references

Volkman, John D.
Cruising through research; library skills for young adults. Libraries Unlimited 1998 207p il pa $29.50
Grades: Professional   025.5
1. Research 2. Bibliographic instruction
ISBN 1-56308-536-4   LC 97-40408
"The author uses the 'cruise' theme throughout the book calling each assignment an 'excursion.'. . . The first two excursions cover the use of reference materials that most students will need to use. . . . Other excursions guide students through the process of writing a term paper by identifying a topic, taking notes, outlining, and writing the paper and the bibliography." Voice Youth Advocates
This book "would be an asset to any professional collection and is an excellent personal choice for librarians looking for new ideas." Book Rep
Includes bibliographical references

025.7 Physical preparation for storage of library materials

Schechter, Abraham A.
Basic book repair methods; illustrated by the author. Libraries Unlimited 1999 102p il pa $37
Grades: Professional   025.7
1. Books—Conservation and restoration
ISBN 1-56308-700-6   LC 98-50950
Photographs accompany step-by-step instructions for common preservation techniques, from the cleaning of pages and their readhesion, to case reattachment and rebacking.
Includes bibliographical references

025.8 Maintenance and preservation of library collections

Halsted, Deborah D.
Disaster planning; a how-to-do-it manual for librarians with planning templates on CD-ROM. Neal-Schuman Publishers 2005 xx, 247p il (How-to-do-it manuals for librarians) pa $85
Grades: Professional   025.8
1. Disaster relief 2. Accidents—Prevention 3. Library resources—Conservation and restoration
ISBN 1-55570-486-7   LC 2003-65152
Includes CD-ROM
"Step-by-step instructions discuss creating a working disaster team, establishing a communications strategy, identifying relief and recovery agencies, developing response plans, and examining issues of cutting-edge library security. . . . This valuable resource is an important addition to most professional collections." Booklist
Includes bibliographical references

027 General libraries, information centers

The **whole** library handbook 4; current data, professional advice, and curiosa about libraries and library services; edited by George M. Eberhart. American Library Association 2006 585p il map pa $42
Grades: Professional   027
1. Library science 2. Libraries—United States 3. Library services
ISBN 0-8389-0915-9; 978-0-8389-0915-7
                                      LC 2005-33619
First published 1991
This is an "encyclopedic collection of factual data covering all aspects of the library world, together with readable excerpts from recent books and articles on 'librariana.'" Choice
Includes bibliographical references

027.6 Libraries for special groups and organizations

Byrd, Susannah Mississippi, 1971-
Bienvenidos! = Welcome! a handy resource guide for marketing your library to Latinos; foreword by Carol Brey-Casiano. American Library Association 2005 110p il pa $20 *
Grades: Professional   027.6
1. Libraries and Hispanic Americans
ISBN 0-8389-0902-7; 978-0-8389-0902-7
                                      LC 2005-6315
This "guide covers everything from survey analysis to access and outreach to collection development, and offers practical solutions and suggestions. . . . Byrd includes resources, services, government agencies, projects, professional organizations, etc., making this title a valuable addition to libraries and organizations that are initiating

Byrd, Susannah Mississippi, 1971——*Continued*
programs directed toward diverse Latino populations."
SLJ
Includes bibliographical references

Lerch, Maureen T.
Serving homeschooled teens and their parents.
Libraries Unlimited 2004 242p (Libraries
Unlimited professional guides for young adult
librarians) pa $39
Grades: Professional   **027.6**
1. Home schooling 2. Young adults' libraries
ISBN 0-313-32052-7   LC 2004-46518
"After introductory chapters that dispel many myths
about homeschooling and delve into adolescent psychology,
the two experts give sound advice and great examples
for service plan creation, collection development,
programming, and promotion of services." Libr Media
Connect
Includes bibliographical references

Library services to youth of Hispanic heritage;
Barbara Immroth and Kathleen de la Peña
McCook, editors; assisted by Catherine Jasper.
McFarland & Co. 2000 197p pa $42.50 *
Grades: Professional   **027.6**
1. Libraries and Hispanic Americans 2. Young adults'
libraries
ISBN 0-7864-0790-5   LC 00-37247
In this "collection of essays, more than 20 experts in
the field discuss library programs, collections, planning,
and evaluation of services for Hispanic youth." Booklist
Includes bibliographical references

027.62 Libraries for young people

Anderson, Sheila B.
Extreme teens; library services to nontraditional
young adults. Libraries Unlimited 2005 xxiii, 175p
(Libraries Unlimited professional guides for young
adult librarians) pa $36
Grades: Professional   **027.62**
1. Young adults' libraries 2. Teenagers—Books and
reading
ISBN 1-59158-170-2   LC 2005016076
"This accessible manual offers practical advice on
working with 'extreme teens,' young adults who, because
of their sexuality, educational circumstances, or living
situations, tend to be underserved by traditional public library services. Individual sections discuss definitions of
various populations, service specifications for subgroups,
collection development, and promotional programs. Additional features include statistics, scenarios, cited sources,
and lists of recommended print and electronic resources,
both fiction and nonfiction." Booklist
Includes bibliographical references

Braun, Linda W.
Technically involved; technology-based youth
participation activities for your library. American
Library Association 2003 138p il pa $34
Grades: Professional   **027.62**
1. Young adults' libraries
ISBN 0-8389-0861-6   LC 2003-12021
Contents: Youth participation - the what and the why;
Getting teens involved; On the road to greatness; Bringing generations together; Reading, writing, and youth
participation; Getting things done at the library; Overcoming obstacles
In this "title, Braun encourages librarians to involve
teens in technology-related activities and projects that
will benefit them and others. She responds to questions
regarding participation, benefits to patrons and libraries,
and training. The author provides numerous suggestions
for activities. . . . This excellent volume is a must for
libraries with teen groups, and a consideration for those
that don't have them." SLJ
Includes bibliographical references

Teens.library; developing internet services for
young adults. American Lib. Assn. 2002 82p pa
$30
Grades: Professional   **027.62**
1. Internet 2. Young adults' libraries
ISBN 0-8389-0824-1
This "resource for librarians in both the public and
school environment provides insight as to why teens
gravitate to the Internet and which sites are their favorites. . . . The book offers the clueless as well as the
knowledgeable librarian steps to take in developing library Web sites for teens and designing and maintaining
these sites. . . . Detailed descriptions of the cites Web
resources are included. A must-read for all librarians
who work with teenagers." Booklist
Includes bibliographical references

Edwards, Kirsten, 1965-
Teen library events; a month-by-month guide.
Greenwood Press 2002 166p (Greenwood
professional guides for young adult librarians)
$52.95 *
Grades: professional   **027.62**
1. Young adults' libraries 2. Public libraries
ISBN 0-313-31482-9   LC 00-52430
The author "presents step-by-step procedures covering
January through December, from developing booktalks
using the Printz Award titles to bookmaking (with de-
tailed diagrams) to designing a Teen Read Week con-
test." Booklist
"This is an excellent, no-nonsense guide that describes
programs that can be executed with a minimum amount
of effort." SLJ
Includes bibliographical references

Edwards, Margaret A., 1902-1988

The fair garden and the swarm of beasts; the library and the young adult; foreword by Betty Carter for the Young Adult Library Services Association. Centennial ed. American Lib. Assn. 2002 xxxiii, 206p il pa $20 *

Grades: Professional   **027.62**

1. Young adults' libraries 2. Books and reading

ISBN 0-8389-3533-8   LC 2002-33276

First published 1969 by Hawthorn Bks.

The author "describes methods of working with young adults, the training of young adult librarians and work in the public schools, and provides information on book selection, book talks and displays." Wis Libr Bull [review of 1969 edition]

"This great librarian's blazing devotion to teens and reading makes her book the classic in the field." Voice Youth Advocates

Includes bibliographical references

Evans, Earlene G.

3-D displays for libraries, schools and media centers; [by] Earlene Green Evans and Muriel Miller Branch. McFarland & Co. 2000 126p pa $38.50

Grades: Professional   **027.62**

1. Libraries—Exhibitions 2. School libraries 3. Instructional materials centers

ISBN 0-7864-0860-X   LC 00-64077

The authors present "the step-by-step process for constructing 19 thematic displays. . . . Each example includes a list of necessary supplies and materials, instructions for building the display, a black-and-white photograph of the completed work, and extended learning activities that include matching quizzes, research and writing assignments, and discussion questions. Each chapter shares different displays based on one of the following themes: apples, reading, flight, women, the Harlem Renaissance, and world cultures." Booklist

Excellence in library services to young adults; the nation's top programs; [by the] Young Adult Library Services Association; Renee Vaillancourt McGrath, editor. 4th ed. American Library Association 2004 75p il pa $28

Grades: Professional   **027.62**

1. Young adults' libraries

ISBN 0-8389-8280-8

First published 1994

Twenty-five library programs for young adults are presented here. . . . [They] "are organized into nine categories: After-School Programs, Career Preparation, Creative Expression, Life Skills, Literary Appreciation, Miscellany, Summer Reading, Teen Advisory Boards, and Young Adults with Disabilities. Basic information for each program is given, including program description, community demographics, how youth helped in the planning process, budget, evaluation, effect of the program on young adults, and contact information. . . . A must-read for anyone doing young adult programming." Voice Youth Advocates

Farmer, Lesley S. Johnson, 1949-

Digital inclusion, teens, and your library. Libraries Unlimited 2005 176p (Libraries Unlimited professional guides for young adult librarians) $39

Grades: Professional   **027.62**

1. Internet 2. Young adults' libraries

ISBN 1-59158-128-1   LC 2004-63833

"This guide helps librarians to identify 'tech-nots'—technologically disadvantaged teens—in a community or school and to reach out and build information literacy in underserved teen populations." Publisher's note

Includes bibliographical references

Honnold, RoseMary, 1954-

101+ teen programs that work. Neal-Schuman 2003 xxi, 195p il (Teens @ the library series) pa $49.95

Grades: Professional   **027.62**

1. Young adults' libraries 2. School libraries—Activity projects 3. Teenagers—Books and reading

ISBN 1-55570-453-0   LC 2002-29385

Program plans cover activities such as summer reading games, contests, crafts, coffeehouse style poetry and Mike nights.

"Those who work with teens will find plenty of year-round programming ideas in this useful volume. The author has incorporated tried-and-true activities complete with instructions on how to plan and present each one." SLJ

Includes bibliographical references

More teen programs that work. Neal-Schuman Publishers 2005 xxi, 245p il (Teens @ the library series) $49.95

Grades: Professional   **027.62**

1. Young adults' libraries 2. School libraries—Activity projects 3. Teenagers—Books and reading

ISBN 1-55570-529-4   LC 2004-19032

Follow-up to: 101+ teen programs that work

Contents: Measuring unmeasurable outcomes; Summer reading and teen read week; More independent programs; More craft programs; Book themed programs; Food programs; More parties, games, and lock-ins; Programs for girls; Programs for boys; Programs for tweens; More programs for teens and adults and teens and children; Writing programs; Teens in the spotlight; School and life skills; Teen volunteer and fund raising projects

"Full of practical and excellent information, this is a definite choice for any library that wants to expand its programming for teens." SLJ

Includes bibliographical references

Jones, Patrick

Connecting young adults and libraries; a how-to-do-it manual for librarians; [by] Patrick Jones, Michele Gorman, Tricia Suellentrop. 3rd ed. Neal-Schuman Publishers 2004 xxix, 438p il (How-to-do-it manuals for librarians) pa $75 *

Grades: Professional   **027.62**

1. Young adults' libraries 2. Young adult literature—Bibliography 3. Books and reading

ISBN 1-55570-508-1   LC 2004-46008

Jones, Patrick—*Continued*
First published 1992
"Not only are the building blocks of library services such as collection development, outreach, programs, booktalking, and teen space included, but the authors also discuss why they are important and why they work. Peppered throughout are examples of libraries successfully connecting with teens. . . . An upbeat, well-organized must-have for anyone working with this audience." SLJ

Do it right! best practices for serving young adults in school and public libraries; [by] Patrick Jones and Joel Shoemaker. Neal-Schuman 2001 182p il (Teens @ the library series) pa $45
Grades: Professional   **027.62**
1. Young adults' libraries 2. Public libraries
ISBN 1-55570-394-1   LC 2001-30718
"In the first half of the book, Shoemaker concentrates on turning the school library media center into 'library heaven,' while in the second half Jones addresses the challenges and rewards of working with young adults in the public library. . . . The book . . . provides plenty of training ideas, sample surveys, action plans, job descriptions, library policies, and interview questions." SLJ
Includes bibliographical references

Kan, Katharine
Sizzling summer reading programs for young adults; [by] Katharine L. Kan for the Young Adult Library Services Association. 2nd ed. American Library Association 2006 110p il pa $30
Grades: Professional   **027.62**
1. Young adults' libraries 2. Teenagers—Books and reading
ISBN 0-8389-3563-X
First published 1998
This "presents more than 50 summer reading programs that have been used successfully with preteens and teenagers. . . . Submissions represent a cross section of themes, incentives, activities and budgets. . . . Children and young adult services librarians will find a wealth of practical, hands-on information." Booklist

Koelling, Holly
Classic connections; turning teens on to great literature. Libraries Unlimited 2004 xxi, 405p (Libraries Unlimited professional guides for young adult librarians) pa $40
Grades: Professional   **027.62**
1. Teenagers—Books and reading
ISBN 1-59158-072-2   LC 2004-48644
"The book is divided into two sections: Laying the Groundwork and Making it Happen. The first section covers the essential elements that define a book as a classic, reviews adolescent development and reading habits, and discusses what types of classics have teen appeal. The second section contains a discussion of collection development, readers' advisory, programming, booktalking, and promotion of the classics. . . . It is a valuable book for anyone trying to connect teens to classic literature." Voice Youth Advocates
Includes bibliographical references

Kunzel, Bonnie Lendermon
The teen-centered book club; readers into leaders; [by] Bonnie Kunzel and Constance Hardesty. Libraries Unlimited 2006 xxi, 211p (Libraries Unlimited professional guides for young adult librarians) pa $40
Grades: Professional   **027.62**
1. Young adults' libraries 2. Teenagers—Books and reading
ISBN 1-59158-193-1
"Two experienced youth-services librarians introduce the idea of teen-centered book clubs. . . . In clear prose supported by research, the authors cover every aspect of the program, from assessing the needs of the library and teens to conducting successful meetings to evaluating activities. . . . . An excellent reference." SLJ
Includes bibliographical references

Learning and libraries in an information age; principles and practice; Barbara K. Stripling, editor. Libraries Unlimited 1999 375p (Principles and practice series) pa $39
Grades: Professional   **027.62**
1. School libraries 2. Bibliographic instruction 3. Instructional materials centers
ISBN 1-56308-666-2   LC 99-45329
"This collection of 13 essays from respected leaders in the field explores the structure and theory of the school library in the information age and looks ahead to its future changes. Some of the topics include learning theories and how they relate to library media practice, comparisons of several models for teaching information-literacy skills, collaborative teaching standards-based teaching, and assessment of student learning." SLJ
Includes bibliographical references

Mondowney, JoAnn G.
Hold them in your heart; successful strategies for library services to at-risk teens. Neal-Schuman 2001 139p (Teens @ the library series) pa $45
Grades: Professional   **027.62**
1. Young adults' libraries
ISBN 1-55570-393-3   LC 00-58413
"This book focuses on specific services for teens. . . . It includes sections on gaining support, needs assessment, funding, and planning and evaluation." SLJ
Includes bibliographical references

New directions for library service to young adults; Young Adult Library Services Association with Patrick Jones; edited by Linda Waddle. American Lib. Assn. 2002 146p pa $32 *
Grades: Professional   **027.62**
1. Young adults' libraries
ISBN 0-8389-0827-6   LC 2002-3377
This "covers guidelines on planning, implementing, and evaluating services with youth involved in each step of the process. Twelve goal statements for YA services and ten core values upon which these goals are built are presented. . . . Besides his usual clear writing, ubiquitous lists, and deft editorial organization, Jones writes a manifesto for how services for young adults should be conceptualized." Voice Youth Advocates
Includes bibliographical references

Ott, Valerie A.

Teen programs with punch; a month-by-month guide. Libraries Unlimited 2006 282p il tab (Libraries Unlimited professional guides for young adult librarians) pa $40

Grades: Professional   **027.62**

1. Young adults' libraries 2. Teenagers—Books and reading

ISBN 1-59158-293-8   LC 2006012775

"Ott has gathered together less-than-conventional program ideas arranged by month. She provides clear instructions, lists of supplemental materials, promotional ideas, reading lists, costs, and suggested grade levels for each one. For librarians with limited budgets, and who may be pressed for time, there are quick and easy ideas that cost little or no money. . . . Many of the programs are designed to draw underserved populations, such as goths, GLBTQ teens, and vegetarians, into the library. . . . This highly informative guide would make a great addition to any YA librarian's professional collection." SLJ

Includes bibliographical references

Reaching out to religious youth; a guide to services, programs, and collections; L. Kay Carman, editor; Carol S. Reich, assistant editor. Libraries Unlimited 2004 222p (Libraries Unlimited professional guides for young adult librarians) pa $38

Grades: Professional   **027.62**

1. Libraries—Special collections 2. Religion—Bibliography

ISBN 0-313-32041-1   LC 2003-69495

"Individual chapters describe the basic history and beliefs of Protestantism, Evangelical Christianity, Roman Catholicism, The Church of Jesus Christ of Latter-day Saints, Orthodox Christianity, Seventh-day Adventists, Judaism, Islam, Buddhism, and Hinduism. Discussion follows on programs that would appeal to teens practicing that religion or those interested in learning more about it." SLJ

"Librarians looking not only to build a well-balanced religious literature collection, but also to gain insight into their students, will find plenty of answers from this interesting and informative work." Libr Media Connect

Includes bibliographical references

Serving older teens; edited by Sheila B. Anderson. Libraries Unlimited 2004 xxiv, 240p il (Libraries Unlimited professional guides for young adult librarians) pa $38.50

Grades: Professional   **027.62**

1. Young adults' libraries 2. Teenagers—Books and reading

ISBN 0-313-31762-3   LC 2003-61053

"Just who the older teen is and what types of library services he or she needs are covered, backed up with statistics. Suggested books for teens are included, both fiction and nonfiction, divided by topics. Even the planning and designing of space for young adults in the library is covered. . . . This book will be an invaluable resource for young adult librarians in high schools or public libraries. . . . It's difficult to imagine anything that is not covered in this comprehensive volume." Libr Media Connect

Includes bibliographical references

Simpson, Martha Seif, 1954-

Reading programs for young adults; complete plans for 50 theme-related units for public, middle school and high school libraries. McFarland & Co. 1997 348p pa $45 *

Grades: Professional   **027.62**

1. Young adults' libraries 2. School libraries—Activity projects 3. Teenagers—Books and reading

ISBN 0-7864-0357-8   LC 97-1499

The author offers programs "that librarians can use or adapt to entice young people into reading for fun. Each unit is built around the same template, beginning with suggestions for book displays, related games, and book review ideas." SLJ

Includes bibliographical references

Stanley, Deborah B.

Practical steps to the research process for high school. Libraries Unlimited 1999 230p il (Information literacy series) pa $32 *

Grades: Professional   **027.62**

1. School libraries 2. Bibliographic instruction 3. Research

ISBN 1-56308-762-6   LC 99-50169

Stanley takes a "look at research techniques, teacher collaboration, and student learning. She supports her text with an abundance of figures and forms. . . . A repeated outline of the research method and sidebar icons encoding different learning skills and modifications for special student populations help bring the information together. Best of all, Stanley's personal anecdotes assure readers that her information is based on concrete experience." Booklist

Includes bibliographical references

Thinking outside the book; alternatives for today's teen library collections; edited by C. Allen Nichols. Libraries Unlimited 2004 xxvi, 189p il (Libraries Unlimited professional guides for young adult librarians) pa $34

Grades: Professional   **027.62**

1. Young adults' libraries 2. Audiovisual materials 3. Libraries and students

ISBN 1-59158-059-5   LC 2003-60592

The editor "believes that more 'alternative' materials need to be added to teen collections. These include magazines, graphic novels, comic books, audiobooks, music, videos, Web sites/on-line collections, and game- and CD-ROM-based reference sources. He provides helpful background information for each format as well as sources for reviews, criteria for selection, issues and obstacles to overcome, suggested titles, and purchasing advice. The [editor] also provides a complete chapter on 'shelving and display options' to entice teens into browsing new materials." Libr Media Connect

Includes bibliographical references

Tuccillo, Diane

Library teen advisory groups; [by] Diane P. Tuccillo. Scarecrow Press 2005 165p il (VOYA guides) pa $29.95 *

Grades: Professional   **027.62**

1. Young adults' libraries 2. Volunteer work

ISBN 0-8108-4982-8   LC 2004-13873

Tuccillo, Diane—*Continued*

Contents: Why teen advisory boards? -- Funding options for your teen library advisory program -- Ready, set— get started! -- Libraries are not boring: activities, events, and projects that make a difference with teens -- Teen representation on adult library boards and other community boards -- The perks of being a teen library advisory board member -- These groups work! -- Schools can have advisory groups, too!

"A comprehensive how-to guide that covers all the bases from theory to practice to nitty-gritty detail." SLJ

Includes bibliographical references

027.8   School libraries

American Association of School Librarians

Information power; building partnerships for learning; prepared by the American Association of School Librarians [and] Association for Educational Communications and Technology. American Lib. Assn. 1998 205p il pa $37 *

Grades: professional   **027.8**

1. School libraries 2. Instructional materials centers

ISBN 0-8389-3470-6   LC 98-23291

First published 1988

This resource "relates the library-media program to the entire educational infrastructure. The authors explicate their themes in terms of standards, indicators, levels of proficiency, goals, principles, and examples of student activities. The appendixes contain essential information on Library Power, AASL's ICON-nect project, the Library Bill of Rights, confidentiality, censorship, access equity, and ethics." SLJ

Includes bibliographical references

Bradburn, Frances Bryant

Output measures for school library media programs. Neal-Schuman 1999 95p pa $55

Grades: Professional   **027.8**

1. School libraries 2. Instructional materials centers

ISBN 1-55570-326-7   LC 98-45557

"Bradburn's handbook is intended to guide school library specialists in collecting data on budgets, staff, and services and in using the data to evaluate programs and argue for increased funding. Forms and work sheets as well as three case studies are included." Booklist

Includes bibliographical references

Church, Audrey P., 1957-

Leverage your library program to help raise test scores; a guide for library media specialists, principals, teachers, and parents. Linworth Pub 2003 123p il pa $39.95 *

Grades: professional   **027.8**

1. School libraries 2. Instructional materials centers

ISBN 1-586-83120-8   LC 2003-40080

"In chapter one, recent research on school libraries is provided and briefly explains the results in layman terms. This is followed by a chapter each for the administrators, teachers, and parents that describes what each needs to know about the library and librarian's roles. A chapter is included for the librarian on what they need to do. The final chapter pulls the book together with perspectives from principals and librarians . . . This book can serve as a means to start a dialog with the administration and at the same time as a reference book for the school librarian." Lib Media Connect

Includes bibliographical references

Craver, Kathleen W.

Creating cyber libraries; an instructional guide for school library media specialists. Libraries Unlimited 2002 xxvi, 222p (Greenwood professional guides in school librarianship) pa $40

Grades: Professional   **027.8**

1. Internet resources 2. School libraries

ISBN 0-313-32080-2   LC 2001-55619

"Nine chapters cover guidelines; policies to consider; Web-design issues; the use of portals; and strategies for maintaining, evaluating, and promoting a library Web site. Special-interest areas, such as providing a virtual reading room and online instruction, are also discussed. . . . This title is a one-stop-shopping bonanza of wonderful, useful ideas on how to create a cyber library that will meet the information needs of our patrons." Libr J

Includes bibliographical references

Curriculum connections through the library; edited by Barbara K. Stripling and Sandra Hughes-Hassell. Libraries Unlimited 2003 xxi, 229p (Principles and practice series) pa $37.50

Grades: Professional   **027.8**

1. School libraries

ISBN 1-56308-973-4   LC 2003-54628

The editors have chosen "essays that sample existing scholarship and direct professionals in ways to affect curriculum, collections, and collaboration across disciplines and to aid students who must perform under the scrutiny of the national standards movement. The book contains some suggestions for joint projects, but primarily promotes open-ended, inquiry-based learning. . . . The writing is clear and purposeful. . . . A stimulating choice for practicing librarians and students of library science." SLJ

Includes bibliographical references

Erikson, Rolf

Designing a school library media center for the future; [by] Rolf Erikson, Carolyn Markuson. American Lib. Assn. 2000 109p il pa $40

Grades: Professional   **027.8**

1. Instructional materials centers—Design and construction 2. School libraries—Design and construction

ISBN 0-8389-0790-3   LC 00-42025

"For the American Association of School Librarians"

"This book covers researching, planning, constructing, and moving into a new school media center. The chapters dealing with overseeing specification and bidding processes and meeting accessibility guidelines are particularly helpful." SLJ

Includes bibliographical references

Farmer, Lesley S. Johnson, 1949-

Student success and library media programs; a systems approach to research and best practice; [by] Lesley S. J. Farmer. Libraries Unlimited 2003 180p pa $45

Grades: Professional   **027.8**

1. School libraries 2. Academic achievement
ISBN 1-59158-058-7   LC 2003-53881

"Designed for school library media specialists, this book focuses on library media programs and examines the factors that influence student achievement." Publisher's note

This is a "comprehensive and thoroughly researched book. . . . An invaluable guide for media specialists." SLJ

Includes bibliographical references

Foundations for effective school library media programs; Ken Haycock, editor. Libraries Unlimited 1999 331p hardcover o.p. pa $52

Grades: Professional   **027.8**

1. School libraries 2. Instructional materials centers 3. Bibliographic instruction
ISBN 1-56308-720-0; 1-56308-368-X (pa)
    LC 98-40343

Explores the role of library media specialists in school improvement, curriculum design, collaboration with teachers, and building information literacy. Articles discuss learning theories, flexible scheduling, new technologies, and thematic units

Includes bibliographical references

Kearney, Carol A.

Curriculum partner; redefining the role of the library media specialist. Greenwood Press 2000 xxiv, 180p (Greenwood professional guides in school librarianship) $46.95

Grades: Professional   **027.8**

1. School libraries 2. Instructional materials centers
ISBN 0-313-31025-4   LC 99-462341

The author "includes chapters on leadership, change, vision, partnering, collaborative planning, staff development, and advocacy and provides examples from the experiences of practitioners to support her ideas." SLJ

Includes bibliographical references

Leslie, Roger

Igniting the spark; library programs that inspire high school patrons; [by] Roger Leslie and Patricia Potter Wilson. Libraries Unlimited 2001 172p il pa $35

Grades: Professional   **027.8**

1. High school libraries 2. School libraries—Activity projects
ISBN 1-56308-797-9   LC 01-38431

The authors provide "information for planning, executing, and assessing attention-getting school library media programs for grades 9-12. . . . Wilson's engaging first-person accounts of his experiences keep the focus on the 'how to' aspects." Book Rep

Includes bibliographical references

Loertscher, David V., 1940-

Taxonomies of the school library media program. 2d ed. Hi Willow Res. & Pub. 2000 250p pa $30 *

Grades: Professional   **027.8**

1. School libraries 2. Instructional materials centers
ISBN 0-931510-75-9

First published 1988 by Libraries Unlimited

A guide to creating and managing a library media center. Topics include: collaboration, reading, enhancing learning through technology, and information literacy. Discusses methods to evaluate the impact of the program on students and teachers.

Morris, Betty J.

Administering the school library media center. 4th ed, rev and expanded. Libraries Unlimited 2004 683p $70; pa $55 *

Grades: professional   **027.8**

1. School libraries 2. Instructional materials centers
ISBN 0-313-32261-9; 1-59158-183-4 (pa)
    LC 2004-41797

First published 1973 under the authorship of John T. Gillespie and Diana L. Spirt with title: Creating a school media program

"This volume covers library media center programming, facilities and technologies, student learning, policies and procedures, and library media specialist roles. . . . Highlights include budget planning and justification, library media job descriptions, and information on the bid process. The chapter on facilities contains infrequently found information on the psychology of color, URLs for Web sites with floor plans, and guidelines for space planning." Booklist

Schuckett, Sandy

Political advocacy for school librarians; you have the power! Linworth Pub 2004 128p pa $39.95

Grades: Professional   **027.8**

1. School libraries 2. Libraries and community 3. Lobbying
ISBN 1-58683-158-5   LC 2004-4869

"Schuckett motivates and explicitly details an exciting 'how-to' of political lobbying at all levels—from the school site and local board all the way to the national level. . . . School librarians need political clout, and Schuckett shows us how to get it." SLJ

Includes bibliographical references

Skaggs, Gayle, 1952-

Off the wall! school year bulletin boards and displays for the library. McFarland & Co. 1995 142p il pa $24.50

Grades: Professional   **027.8**

1. School libraries 2. Libraries—Exhibitions 3. Bulletin boards
ISBN 0-7864-0116-8   LC 95-5693

Arranged to correlate with the school year, this "guide contains more than 100 bulletin board and display ideas. . . . Skaggs has concentrated on ideas that can be inexpensively made and assembled fairly quickly." Booklist

"This is a handy aid for quick displays and to stimulate further creative ideas." Voice Youth Advocates

The **Technology** connection; building a successful library media program; Kathleen Schrock, editor. Linworth Pub. 2000 244p il (Professional growth series) pa $39.95

Grades: Professional   **027.8**
1. School libraries 2. Instructional materials centers
ISBN 1-58683-008-2   LC 00-44818

A collection of articles originally published in issues of The Technology Connection, The Book Report and Library Talk

"Topics include guidelines for evaluating Web pages, rubrics for scoring multimedia projects, using the Internet, building influence in the school library, technology integration, copyright issues, stress, scheduling, assisting students, volunteers, etc." SLJ

Includes bibliographical references

Valenza, Joyce Kasman
Power tools recharged; 125+ essential forms and presentations for your school library information program; illustrated by Emily Valenza. American Library Association 2004 various paging il pa $55
*

Grades: professional   **027.8**
1. School libraries 2. Libraries—Public relations
ISBN 0-8389-0880-2   LC 2004-5853
First published 1998 with title: Power tools

This offers a compilation of customizable, reproducible forms and handouts for school library administration and assessment, teaching information literacy, making presentations. Included are such items as templates for a gift book program, letters to parents and faculty members, a checklist of tasks, library equipment sign-out forms, and a reading interest survey.

Includes bibliographical references

Van Deusen, Jean Donham, 1946-
Enhancing teaching and learning; a leadership guide for school library media specialists. 2nd ed. Neal-Schuman Publishers 2005 337p il pa $59.95

Grades: Professional   **027.8**
1. School libraries 2. Instructional materials centers
ISBN 1-55570-516-2   LC 2004-53173
First published 1998

This attempts to show "how to develop and implement an effective library media program by integrating it into the total education environment. Part One covers all aspects of the school environment: students, curriculum and instruction, principals, school district administrators, and the community. Part Two shows you how to use interaction and collaboration to make the school library media program integral to all of these communities." Publisher's note

The **Whole** school library handbook; edited by Blanche Woolls and David V. Loertscher. American Library Association 2005 448p pa $45
*

Grades: professional   **027.8**
1. School libraries 2. Instructional materials centers
ISBN 0-8389-0883-7   LC 2004-20198

This reference resource to the school media center includes "facts, . . . articles, checklists, organization contact information, trivia, [and] advice from the field's experts. . . . [It also features] information on fundraising, grant writing, flexible scheduling, promoting the school library, and advocating its value in the school community." Publisher's note

Includes bibliographical references

Woolls, E. Blanche
The school library media manager. 3rd ed. Libraries Unlimited 2004 352p (Library and information science text series) $60; pa $45

Grades: Professional   **027.8**
1. School libraries 2. Instructional materials centers
ISBN 1-591-58144-3; 1-591-58182-6 (pa)
    LC 2004-48478
First published 1994

This provides an "overview of the profession and all aspects of school library management. . . . The new National Board for Professional Teaching Standards certification for school librarians is discussed as are budget, facilities, cataloging, copyright, selection of materials, staff evaluation, and all the other basic managerial functions. The book is current with discussions of the AASL national guidelines and standards, the USA Patriot Act, and the effect of Internet filtering on school libraries." Publisher's note

028   Reading and use of other information media

Fadiman, Clifton, 1904-1999
The new lifetime reading plan; [by] Clifton Fadiman and John S. Major. 4th ed. HarperCollins Pubs. 1997 xxi, 378p hardcover o.p. pa $14

Grades: 11 12 Adult   **028**
1. Best books 2. Books and reading
ISBN 0-06-270208-4; 0-06-272073-2 (pa)
    LC 97-4975
First published 1960 by Crowell

The author has selected a list of works ranging from the Koran and Confucius to Chinua Achebe and Gabriel Garcia Márquez. An appendix profiling books by 100 important 20th-century authors is included.

Includes bibliographical references

028.1   Reviews of books and other media

Bodart, Joni Richards
The world's best thin books; what to read when your book report is due tomorrow. new thinner ed. Scarecrow Press 2000 256p pa $18.95

Grades: 9 10 11 12   **028.1**
1. Young adult literature—Bibliography 2. Report writing 3. Best books
ISBN 1-57886-007-5   LC 99-38615
First published 1993 by Libraries Unlimited with title: 100 world-class thin books

Bodart, Joni Richards—*Continued*
"Bodart has compiled a list of high-quality, quick-to-read books. . . . Each entry provides just enough description to pique reader interest and includes bibliographic notation, information on readability and subjects covered, an annotated list of characters, and a cursory booktalk that emulates the author's tone and point of view. She concludes each entry with a list of major themes addressed in the book and possible book report or booktalk ideas." Booklist

028.5 Reading and use of other information media by young people

Aronson, Marc
Exploding the myths; the truth about teenagers and reading. Scarecrow Press 2000 146p (Scarecrow studies in young adult literature) $29.50
Grades: Professional 028.5
1. Teenagers—Books and reading
ISBN 0-8108-3904-0 LC 00-61948
Aronson discusses censorship, audience, authenticity, demographics, and YA publishing history. "Whether talking about the graphic novel, poetry, magic realism, or gritty contemporary fiction, he shows that teenagers today are often more open to challenge and diversity in narrative and format than their adult guardians are. What many librarians think is 'popular' is often condescending. Whether you agree with Aronson or not, you'll be caught up in issues that matter. A great starting place for YA literature classes." Booklist

Booth, Heather, 1978-
Serving teens through readers' advisory. American Library Association 2007 159p bibl (ALA readers' advisory series) pa $36 *
Grades: Professional 028.5
1. Teenagers—Books and reading 2. Young adult literature—Bibliography 3. Young adults' libraries
ISBN 0-8389-0930-2 (pa); 978-0-8389-0930-0 (pa)
LC 2006036134
"The first few chapters discuss teen reading habits and why readers' advisory for this group is different and also provide 'tips for the generalist' who may not be an expert in teen fiction. Other chapters cover elements of the readers' advisory interaction . . . and survey the appropriate books. Two unique chapters offer well-thought-out and practical advice on making reading-related homework assignments less painful for staff and students as well as suggestions for providing readers' advisory services to teens through their parents or other adults. . . . Filled with excellent tips and great ideas. . . . [This] is essential reading for all readers' advisors and any library staff who work with teens." Booklist
Includes bibliographical references

Bromann, Jennifer
Booktalking that works. Neal-Schuman 2001 155p (Teens @ the library series) pa $35 *
Grades: professional 028.5
1. Book talks 2. Young adults' libraries 3. Teenagers—Books and reading
ISBN 1-55570-403-4 LC 2001-18340
This presents "a variety of booktalking techniques, selection tips for booktalk titles, and how to write and prepare for booktalks. The book begins by addressing who today's teenagers are, what they want, and what they need. There are specific magazines, catalogs, and on-line Web sites mentioned for selection." Book Rep
"Practical, smart, hip, and irreverent. . . . A fun read that will encourage you to find your own personal style." Booklist
Includes bibliographical references

More booktalking that works. Neal-Schuman 2005 145p (Teens @ the library series) pa $49.95 *
Grades: Professional 028.5
1. Book talks 2. Young adults' libraries 3. Teenagers—Books and reading
ISBN 1-55570-525-1 LC 2005-2326
"Bromann has expanded on her previous booktalking title, *Booktalking That Works* (Neal-Schuman, 2001), with additional practical advice based on added years of experience. . . . The first part of this book is arranged in a question-and-answer format covering various aspects of booktalking, from creating and presenting booktalks to choosing books and developing hooks for reluctant readers. This section includes a list of the top-20 types of books to booktalk and 10 very brief quick talks. The second section offers 200 booktalks of varying length and covering several fiction and nonfiction genres that she encourages librarians to adapt for personal use. . . . School and public librarians will find many helpful hints, whether they are novice or veteran booktalkers." Booklist

Dear author; letters of hope; edited by Joan F. Kaywell; with an introduction by Catherine Ryan Hyde. Philomel Books 2007 222p $14.99 *
Grades: 8 9 10 11 12 028.5
1. Teenagers—Books and reading 2. Authors, American
ISBN 978-0-399-23705-8; 0-399-23705-4
LC 2006-21050
"Chris Lynch, Nancy Garden, and Christopher Paul Curtis and are just a few of the well-known authors who respond to real teens' letters in this powerful compilation. Not mere fan mail, the selections speak about teens' gravest concerns – bullying, derailed friendships, racism, date rape, incest, illness, divorce, and more – and they describe how the authors' books helped them face the heartaches. . . .For some readers, this dialogue between writers and readers will be inspiring; for those harboring their own wounding secrets, it may be lifesaving." Booklist
Includes bibliographical references

Donelson, Kenneth L.

Literature for today's young adults; [by] Kenneth L. Donelson, Alleen Pace Nilsen. 7th ed. Pearson/Allyn and Bacon 2004 c2005 478p il $93.33 *

Grades: professional   **028.5**
1. Young adult literature—History and criticism
2. Books and reading
ISBN 0-205-41035-9   LC 2004-44306
First published 1980
Authors' names appear in reverse order in 6th ed
This is an "introduction to young adult literature framed within . . . literary, historical, and social context. It also provides . . . criteria for evaluating books of all genres, from poetry and nonfiction to mysteries, science fiction, and horror. [It includes] coverage of . . . issues, such as pop culture and mass media." Publisher's note
Includes bibliographical references

Gillespie, John Thomas, 1928-

The Newbery/Printz companion; booktalk and related materials for award winners and honor books; [by] John T. Gillespie and Corinne J. Naden. 3rd ed. Libraries Unlimited 2006 503p $75 *

Grades: Professional   **028.5**
1. Newbery Medal 2. Michael L. Printz award
3. Children's literature—History and criticism
4. Authors
ISBN 1-59158-313-6   LC 2006-14955
First published 1996 with title: The Newbery companion
This guide to the "Newbery and Printz awards for children's and young adult literature provides information on each year's winners and honor books, as well as on the awards themselves and the librarians for whom they are named. For each award-winning book, there is a plot summary, list of characters and themes, background on the author, incidents for booktalking, related reads, and . . . ideas for introducing the book to young readers." Publisher's note
"This invaluable source should be in every school and public library." Booklist
Includes bibliographical references

Honnold, RoseMary, 1954-

The teen reader's advisor. Neal-Schuman Publishers 2006 491p (Teens @ the library series) pa $75 *

Grades: Professional   **028.5**
1. Teenagers—Books and reading 2. Young adults' libraries 3. Young adult literature—Bibliography
ISBN 1-55570-551-0   LC 2006-12640
"The first part deals with the challenges of working with teens, from developing a rapport and dealing with the more conservative adults in their lives, to marketing a YA collection to its audience. The author's descriptions of the major awards and lists relating to the literature as well as the list of print and online reader's advisory resources are sure to be helpful. Part two consists of subject and genre lists. Each one has at least 10 titles. The annotations are excellent." SLJ
Includes bibliographical references

Knowles, Elizabeth, 1946-

Boys and literacy; practical strategies for librarians, teachers, and parents; [by] Elizabeth Knowles and Martha Smith. Libraries Unlimited 2005 xxi, 164p il pa $35 *

Grades: Professional   **028.5**
1. Boys—Books and reading 2. Children's literature—Bibliography 3. Young adult literature—Bibliography
ISBN 1-59158-212-1
"Boys don't seem to like to read. . . . This book briefly explores the research about this situation, outlines strategies to reverse this trend, and lists books within genres that boys enjoy reading. . . . The best part of the book is the author section. . . . For each author covered, there is a complete list of books, contact information, . . . and Web sites. . . . This is a wonderful resource for teachers and parents to begin working on improving literacy with boys." Booklist

Moore, John Noell

Interpreting young adult literature; literary theory in the secondary classroom. Boynton/Cook Pubs. 1997 202p (Young adult literature series) $27.50

Grades: Professional   **028.5**
1. Young adult literature—History and criticism
2. Literature—Philosophy
ISBN 0-86709-414-1   LC 97-5045
Chapters address "formalism, archetypal criticism, structuralism/semiotics, deconstruction, reader-response, feminism, black aesthetics, and cultural studies. Each of these chapters cover key concepts and basic terms of the theory, introduces and interprets a young adult text from that perspective, and invites readers to join the conversation. The concluding section of each chapter discusses other young adult texts that can be approached from that theory and suggests additional critical studies appropriate for teaching these texts." Publisher's note
Includes bibliographical references

Reynolds, Tom K.

Teen reading connections. Neal-Schuman Publishers 2005 149p (Teens @ the library series) pa $49.95

Grades: Professional   **028.5**
1. Teenagers—Books and reading 2. Young adults' libraries
ISBN 1-55570-506-5 (pa)   LC 2004-47347
This "book offers strategies, programs, and tools to use to connect teen patrons, books, and reading. Chapters cover fiction; nonfiction; booktalks; promotional activities; design of Web sites, display, and facilities; public and school library cooperation; print and electronic resources; reader's advisory services; and library policies." Booklist
Includes bibliographical references

Schall, Lucy

Teen genre connections; from booktalking to booklearning. Libraries Unlimited 2005 318p $40

Grades: Professional   **028.5**
1. Young adult literature—Bibliography
2. Teenagers—Books and reading 3. Best books
ISBN 1-59158-229-6   LC 2005-14288

Schall, Lucy—*Continued*

"The author organizes over 100 popular titles into subject groupings with explanations as to why specific titles are included. . . . She provides themes, summaries, booktalk ideas, discussion starters, and related titles for each book included. . . . This volume will help librarians develop collections in specific areas of teen interest such as personal challenges, survival, paranormal suspense, and fantasy. A well-rounded effort." SLJ

Includes bibliographical references

Silvey, Anita

500 great books for teens. Houghton Mifflin Co. 2006 397p $26

Grades: Professional   **028.5**

1. Teenagers—Books and reading 2. Young adult literature—Bibliography

ISBN 978-0-618-61296-3; 0-618-61296-3

LC 2006003350

"A Frances Tenenbaum book"

"Silvey selects and annotates five hundred titles for young adults, arranging them loosely in twenty-one chapters by genre and/or area of interest, from 'Adventure and Survival' to 'War and Conflict.' Each book is coded for either younger (12-14) or older (14-18) teens and gets a couple hundred words or so. . . . The selections are both sturdy and wide-ranging." Horn Book

Includes bibliographical references

028.7 Use of books and other information media as sources of information

Smith, Jane Bandy

Teaching & testing information literacy skills; [by] Jane Bandy Smith; Lisa Churchill and Lucy Mason, contributors. Linworth Pub. 2005 xx, 138p il pa $44.95

Grades: Professional   **028.7**

1. Bibliographic instruction 2. School libraries 3. Library information networks

ISBN 1-58683-078-3   LC 2004-26004

The author "reviews the rise and acceptance of information literacy, traces a continuum from older ideas of isolated library skills to this more inclusive life skill, and presents a frame for curriculum development with five pages of excellent instructional objectives by category and grade level. . . . This powerful book will illuminate the inexperienced and reinvigorate veteran school librarians." SLJ

Includes bibliographical references

Student engagement and information literacy; edited by Craig Gibson. Association of College and Research Libraries 2006 197p pa $27

Grades: Professional   **028.7**

1. Information literacy 2. Libraries and students

ISBN 0-8389-8388-X; 978-0-8389-8388-1

LC 2006-16956

This book "addresses information literacy in a framework inspired by higher education scholarship and dialogue as it relates to student engagement. Articles are based on what librarians and faculty know about how students learn, how different learning environments affect engagement, and how different groups on campuses can collaborate on student engagement and learning." Publisher's note

Includes bibliographical references

Taylor, Joie

Information literacy and the school library media center. Libraries Unlimited 2006 148p il (Libraries Unlimited professional guides in school librarianship) pa $35

Grades: Professional   **028.7**

1. Information literacy 2. School libraries

ISBN 0-313-32020-9

"Beginning with a description of what it means to be information literate, the author goes on to highlight how the American Association of School Librarians (AASL) and Association for Educational Communications and Technology (AECT) standards can be integrated into the curriculum in ways that complement state and district standards, giving specific examples from several states. She discusses how the library media specialist through flexible scheduling and curriculum mapping can facilitate an environment where students can hone their information literacy skills. . . . Two things make this book exceptional. First the chapter on collaboration is a refreshingly frank discussion of the value of working with classroom teachers that delineates the roles of the teacher and the library media specialist, while being realistic in realizing that barriers do exist to real collaboration. Second the extensive bibliography is filled with books, journal articles, and Web resources that will guide readers to the best practices in information literacy at the current time." Voice Youth Advocates

030 General encyclopedic works

Schott, Ben, 1974-

Schott's almanac 2007. Bloomsbury 2006 367p il map $25.95

Grades: 9 10 11 12   **030**

1. Almanacs

ISBN 1-59691-171-9

This almanac is a "biography of the year: from Islam's outrage at cartoons of the Prophet to the winner of American Idol, from Google's expansion into China to the incidence of shark-bites worldwide, from the Nobel Prize for Literature to the Bad Sex in Fiction award." Publisher's note

031 General encyclopedic works in American English

The **Encyclopedia** Americana. Grolier 30v il maps set $699 *

Grades: 7 8 9 10 11 12 Adult   **031**

1. Encyclopedias and dictionaries

ISBN 0-7172-0139-2

Also available online

First published 1829. Frequently revised

The Encyclopedia Americana—*Continued*

"An encyclopedia suitable for junior and senior high school students as well as adults and college-level students. Cross-references are plentiful throughout the 45,000 articles. The index is comprehensive and analytical. *Americana* contains an exceptionally large number of U.S. place-names and biographies. The sciences, mathematics, American history, and the social sciences are particularly well developed. There are bibliographies at the end of major articles, nearly 400 of which have been updated for this edition." Ref Sources for Small & Medium-sized Libr. 6th edition

For a review of 2004 edition see: Booklist, Sept. 15, 2004

Hirsch, E. D. (Eric Donald), 1928-

The new dictionary of cultural literacy; [by] E.D. Hirsch, Joseph F. Kett, James Trefil. Completely rev and updated, 3rd ed. Houghton Mifflin 2002 647p il maps $29.95

Grades: 11 12 Adult   **031**
1. Civilization—Dictionaries 2. English language—Dictionaries
ISBN 0-618-22647-8   LC 2002-27609

First published 1988 with title: The dictionary of cultural literacy

"The text is divided into sections by subject—e.g., fine arts, world politics, life sciences—each with a brief introduction; access is also aided by a thorough index. The entries themselves are complete, concise, and clearly written as well as extensively and effectively cross-referenced." Libr J

Merriam-Webster's collegiate encyclopedia. Merriam-Webster 2000 1792p il maps $34.95 *

Grades: 11 12 Adult   **031**
1. Encyclopedias and dictionaries
ISBN 0-87779-017-5   LC 00-62189

"More than 25,000 brief articles range in length from 40 to 700 words. They are alphabetized letter by letter. Variant spellings or names are printed in bold type, and pronunciations are provided. Cross-references to other articles are indicated by bullets. More than 1,650 black-and-white photographs, maps, diagrams, and other illustrations enhance entries. . . . There is coverage of topics and people in art, business, geography, history, literature, medicine, music, religion, science, and more." Booklist

The New Encyclopaedia Britannica. Encyclopaedia Britannica 2007 32v il maps apply to publisher for price

Grades: 11 12 Adult   **031**
1. Encyclopedias and dictionaries
ISBN 1-59339-292-3

Also available CD-ROM version and online

First published 1768 in England; in the United States 1902. Now published with the editorial advice of the University of Chicago. First published with current title with the fifteenth edition in 1974. Frequently revised

"In three sections: Propaedia, or outline of knowledge; Macropaedia, with longer in-depth articles covering major topics; and Micropaedia, with shorter A-to-Z ready reference entries. *Britannica's* reputation as the basic encyclopedia for all libraries and reference collections is based on the writing and knowledge of thousands of expert contributors and consultants. Updated between major editions by the Britannica *Book of the Year.*" NY Public Libr Book of How & Where to Look It Up

Webster's new explorer desk encyclopedia. Federal Street Press 2003 1349p il map $19.98

Grades: 11 12 Adult   **031**
1. Encyclopedias and dictionaries
ISBN 1-892859-43-2   LC 2002-115261

"With more than 17,500 entries, this useful work provides very basic information on a wide variety of topics, from geography and biography to history, science, and literature. Additional features include photographs, diagrams, and maps, all in black and white." SLJ

The World Book encyclopedia. World Bk. 2006 22v il map set $1,079

Grades: 11 12 Adult   **031**
1. Encyclopedias and dictionaries
ISBN 0-7166-0106-0

Also available CD-ROM version, The World Book multimedia encyclopedia, and online

First published 1917-1918 by Field Enterprises. Frequently revised

Supplemented by: World Book's year in review; another available annual supplement is World Book's science year in review

"Curriculum-oriented, this superior encyclopedia is well-edited and produced to meet the reference and informational needs of students from grade four through high school. Long standing tradition of excellence for readability, accuracy, authoritativeness, objectivity, judicious and extensive use of outstanding graphics and timeliness." N Y Public Libr. Ref Books for Child Collect

For a review of 2004 edition see: Booklist, Sept. 15, 2004

031.02   American books of miscellaneous facts

Ash, Russell

The top 10 of everything 2008. Distributed in the U.S. and Canada by Sterling Publishing 2007 256p il $24.95 *

Grades: 9 10 11 12   **031.02**
1. Curiosities and wonders
ISSN 1541-7697
ISBN 0-600-61678-9; 978-0-600-61678-8

Annual. First published 1994 by Dorling Kindersley

Ash "has amassed thousands of statistics on topics of popular interest, listing the 10 most (or least) common, popular, expensive, or best in each category. . . . The wide range of categories reported spans from the natural sciences (the Earth, universe, and human body), to entertainment (music, stage, radio, sports, and travel). Bright, splashy, full-color photos enliven the columnar text, as do relevant 'Did you know' sidebars. . . . A browser's dream." SLJ

Brahms, William B.

Notable last facts; a compendium of endings, conclusions, terminations and final events throughout history; compiled by William B. Brahms. Reference Desk Press 2005 834p $145

Grades: 11 12 Adult **031.02**

1. Encyclopedias and dictionaries

ISBN 0-9765325-0-6 LC 2005-901194

"Notable last facts, as defined by the compiler, are 'any historically significant event, person, place or thing that marks the end of its kind or its era.' These facts [include] the last self-service Horn & Hardart Automat in Manhattan, the last theatrical performance of Sir John Gielgud, the last year hurricanes had no name, the last game played by Red Sox legend Ted Williams, and so forth." Booklist

"This extensive compilation is a groundbreaking core reference work for libraries of all kinds." Choice

Includes bibliographical references

Encyclopaedia Britannica almanac, 2006. Encyclopaedia Britannica 2005 pa $11.95

Grades: 11 12 Adult **031.02**

1. Almanacs 2. Statistics 3. United States—Statistics

ISSN 1540-8868

ISBN 1-4022-0604-6; 978-1-4022-0604-7

Annual. First published 2002

"Features include biographies of notable figures, from the past as well as the present; a lookup of thousands of facts covering various branches of knowledge (e.g., science, business, history, entertainment, sports, and the arts). . . . There are also entries for countries and their leaders, with maps, flags, and various statistics; for awards and award winners; for sporting events; and much more." Libr J

Famous first facts, international edition; a record of first happenings, discoveries, and inventions in world history; {edited by} Steven Anzovin & Janet Podell. Wilson, H.W. 2000 837p $140 *

Grades: 11 12 Adult **031.02**

1. Encyclopedias and dictionaries

ISBN 0-8242-0958-3 LC 99-86869

This work "contains more than 5000 firsts from hundreds of countries and ranging in time from 3.5 billion years ago (the age of the oldest continental land discovered) to 2001 (the scheduled date of completion of the first building over 1500 feet tall). . . . {It} groups related entries under broad subject categories (arranged alphabetically) and sub-categories. Within each category or sub-category, entries are arranged chronologically." Publisher's note

Feldman, David, 1950-

When do fish sleep? and other imponderables of everyday life; illustrated by Kassie Schwan. Harper & Row 1989 260p il hardcover o.p. pa $12.95

Grades: 11 12 Adult **031.02**

1. Questions and answers

ISBN 0-06-016161-2; 0-06-074093-0 (pa)

LC 89-45038

"Feldman offers answers to such 'imponderables' as Why are rented bowling shoes so ugly? and Why do doctors tap on our backs during physical exams? Delightful and informative browsing fare." Booklist

Why do clocks run clockwise? and other imponderables; mysteries of everyday life; explained by David Feldman; illustrated by Kas Schwan. Harper & Row 1987 251p il hardcover o.p. pa $12.95

Grades: 11 12 Adult **031.02**

1. Questions and answers

ISBN 0-06-015781-X; 0-06-074092-2 (pa)

LC 87-45045

The author "answers such recurring questions as 'What causes the ringing sound in your ears?' 'Why do nurses wear white?' and 'Why doesn't a "two-by-four" measure two inches by four inches?' Feldman answers them as authoritatively and truthfully as he can, relying on as trustworthy sources as he can find and sometimes, when the query submits to no single answer, fielding several different probable responses." Booklist

Kane, Joseph Nathan, 1899-2002

Famous first facts; a record of first happenings, discoveries, and inventions in American history; [by] Joseph Nathan Kane, Steven Anzovin, & Janet Podell. 6th ed. H.W. Wilson 2006 1307p il $185 *

Grades: 5 6 7 8 9 10 11 12 Adult

031.02

1. Encyclopedias and dictionaries 2. United States—History—Dictionaries

ISBN 978-0-8242-1065-6; 0-8242-1065-4

LC 2006-3096

Also available CD-ROM version and online

First published 1933

Over 7500 entries cover first occurences in American history, organized into 16 chapters each divided into sections. Sections are alphabetically organized, and individual entries are organized chronologically within each section. Includes five indexes: subject index, index by years, index by days, index to personal names, and geographical index.

"Besides serving as an essential ready-reference source, the book is also fun to read out loud to colleagues—when was bubble gum first manufactured in the U.S.? When was the spray can introduced?" Booklist

The **New** York Public Library desk reference. 4th ed. Hyperion 2002 999p il maps $34.95

Grades: 11 12 Adult **031.02**

1. Encyclopedias and dictionaries

ISBN 0-7868-6846-5 LC 2002-27480

"A Stonesong Press book"

First published 1989 by Webster's New World

Divided into chapters, this reference features charts, tables, lists, and illustrations providing information in such categories as signs and symbols, mathematics and science basics, the arts, grammar and punctuation, etiquette, personal finance, first aid, and household tips.

Includes bibliographical references

The **New** York Times almanac, 2007. Penguin Bks. 2006 il maps pa $10.95

Grades: 11 12 Adult **031.02**

The New York Times almanac, 2007—*Continued*
1. Almanacs 2. Statistics 3. United States—Statistics
ISSN 1523-7079
ISBN 0-14-303820-6; 978-0-14-303820-7
Annual. First published 1997
Edited by John W. Wright
This almanac contains a "chronology of the year; major news stories of the year; U.S. history; U.S. presidential biographies; world history; world geography; economic and climate data; major awards in the arts, sciences, and sports; and a wide variety of U.S. demographic information. . . . It is well organized, the table layout is easy to read, and the typeface does not invite eye strain." Am Ref Books Annu, 1998

The **New** York times guide to essential knowledge; a desk reference for the curious mind. St. Martin's Press 2004 1096p $35
Grades: 11 12 Adult   **031.02**
1. Encyclopedias and dictionaries
ISBN 0-3123-1367-5   LC 2004-304961
The main sections of this reference are: the arts, economics, business and finance and science and technology. "Each section is preceded by an essay providing a broad, global historical perspective that highlights major figures in the field. A glossary follows, and maps, sidebars, charts, tables, and one-page essays. . . . The volume's ready-reference component includes sections on writing and grammar, biographical sketches of prominent figures in every field, a guide to nutrition, a dictionary of food complemented by a section on wine, a guide to crossword puzzles, awards and prizes, nations and languages of the world, and US states and cities." Choice

The **Time** almanac 2007. Information Please 2007 il maps $31.95; pa $12.99 *
Grades: 11 12 Adult   **031.02**
1. Almanacs 2. Statistics 3. United States—Statistics
ISSN 1529-1154
ISBN   1-93340-522-8;   978-1-93340-522-3;
1-93340-549-X (pa); 978-1-93340-549-0 (pa)
Also available online
Annual. Time almanac began with 1998 edition; absorbed Information please in 1998
Also known as The Time almanac with Information please
Contains statistical and factual material with a general topical arrangement and subject index. Illustrated with news photos and maps.

The **World** almanac and book of facts, 2007. World Almanac Educ. 2007 1008p il maps $32.99; pa $12.99 *
Grades: 11 12 Adult   **031.02**
1. Almanacs 2. Statistics 3. United States—Statistics
ISSN 0084-1382
ISBN   0-88687-996-5;   978-0-88687-996-9;
0-88687-995-7 (pa); 978-0-88687-995-2 (pa)
Annual. First published 1868. Publisher varies
"This is the most comprehensive and well-known of almanacs. . . . Contains a chronology of the year's events, consumer information, historical anniversaries, annual climatological data, and forecasts. Color section has flags and maps. Includes detailed index." N Y Public Libr Book of How & Where to Look It Up

032.02   English books of miscellaneous facts

Guinness book of records 2008. Guinness Media 2008 il $28.95 *
Grades: 11 12 Adult   **032.02**
1. Curiosities and wonders
ISSN 1475-7419
ISBN 1-904994-19-9; 978-1-904994-19-0
Also available in paperback from Bantam Bks.
Annual. First published 1955 in the United Kingdom; in the United States 1962. Variant titles: Guinness book of world records; Guinness world records
Editors and publisher vary
"Ready reference for current record holders in all fields, some esoteric. Index provides access to information arranged in broad subject categories. Must be replaced annually." N Y Public Libr. Ref Books for Child Collect

060.4   General rules of order (Parliamentary procedure)

Robert, Henry Martyn, 1837-1923
Robert's Rules of order newly revised. Perseus Pub. 2000 various paging $37.50 *
Grades: 11 12 Adult   **060.4**
1. Parliamentary practice
ISBN 0-7382-0923-6   LC 2004-351757
First published 1876 as Pocket manual of rules of order for deliberate assemblies. Title and publisher vary
"A new and enlarged edition by Sarah Corbin Robert, Henry M. Robert III, William J. Evans, Daniel H. Honemann, Thomas J. Balch"
"Long the standard compendium of parliamentary law, explaining methods of organizing and conducting the business of societies, conventions, and other assemblies. Includes convenient charts and tables." Ref Sources for Small & Medium-sized Libr. 6th edition

Sturgis, Alice
The standard code of parliamentary procedure; original edition by Alice Sturgis. 4th ed, revised by the American Institute of Parliamentarians. McGraw-Hill 2001 xxiv, 285p pa $14.95
Grades: 11 12 Adult   **060.4**
1. Parliamentary practice
ISBN 0-07-136513-3   LC 2001-265929
First published 1950
This guide to the rules of parliamentary procedure includes explanations of their purpose and examples of their use. Also considers ways the Internet and other technologies have rewritten rules of meetings
Includes bibliographical references

Zimmerman, Doris P., 1931-
Robert's Rules in plain English. Collins 2005 171p pa $7.95
Grades: 9 10 11 12   **060.4**

Zimmerman, Doris P., 1931-—Continued
1. Parliamentary practice
ISBN 0-06-078779-1; 978-0-06-078779-0
First published 1997
Abbreviated essential parliamentary rules condensed from Robert's Rules of order newly revised
Covers methods of organizing and conducting business of societies, organizations, governing bodies, and other types of assemblies.

070.1 News media

Garner, Joe
We interrupt this broadcast; the events that stopped our lives—from the Hindenburg explosion to the attacks of September 11. Updated 3rd ed. Sourcebooks 2002 178p il + 2 sound discs $49.95
Grades: 11 12 Adult   **070.1**
1. Television broadcasting of news 2. Broadcast journalism 3. Disasters
ISBN 1-57071-974-8   LC 2003-265013
First published 1998
"This book and double-CD set documents, in text, audio and black-and-white photographs, the moments when history, for better or for worse (though usually for worse), was made in an instant. . . . In addition to the CDs' reports and sound bites dramatically introduced and explained . . . each event gets about four pages of coverage, with an efficient summary and at least half a dozen photos. . . . These are the kinds of moments that still shock and amaze. This moving book is 'a tribute of sorts' to the events that defined eras, the journalists who reported on them and the media television, radio that made us all witnesses." Publ Wkly

Henderson, Harry, 1951-
Power of the news media. Facts on File 2004 316p il (Library in a book) $45
Grades: 11 12 Adult   **070.1**
1. Broadcast journalism 2. Press
ISBN 0-8160-4768-5   LC 2003-18900
This book "covers the history of news traced through newspapers, television, radio, and the Internet; issues related to the media; and information on laws related to the media and how legislation affects our news coverage. Important cases are reviewed chronologically from 1735 to 2003." Libr Media Connect
The author's "format—breaking topics into quick-hit subsections—makes it an ideal source for students researching a particular aspect of news media. . . . Every American should have a working knowledge of the topic, and this book is a recommended resource." Voice Youth Advocates
Includes bibliographical references

Seib, Philip M., 1949-
Going live; getting the news right in a real-time, online world; [by] Philip Seib. Rowman & Littlefield 2001 197p $24.95
Grades: 9 10 11 12   **070.1**
1. Television broadcasting of news
ISBN 0-7425-0900-1   LC 00-42562

The author "looks at the challenges to news delivery, profits, and ethics borne of new technology that encourages speed over accuracy. Seib sees a convergence in news gathering styles of various media that is inspired by computer-based media. . . . Faced with competitive pressures, many traditional news outlets (with newspapers leading the way) have developed their own Web sites, including linkages to other sites and sources, blurring the line between professional news organizations and others. . . . This is a compelling look at how news gathering is changing, for better and worse." Booklist
Includes bibliographical references

070.4 Journalism

Colman, Penny
Where the action was; women war correspondents in World War II. Crown 2002 118p il maps $17.95; lib bdg $19.99
Grades: 9 10 11 12   **070.4**
1. Women journalists 2. World War, 1939-1945—Women 3. World War, 1939-1945—Journalists
ISBN 0-517-80075-6; 0-517-80076-4 (lib bdg)
LC 2001-28689
This describes the work of such journalists as Margaret Bourke-White, Martha Gellhorn, Dickey Chapelle, and Marguerite Higgins
"The text is briskly readable, and the 70 black-and-white photos are impressive and well chosen. . . . This well-handled book profoundly captures both the times and the struggle of women who had the talent to do the job male reporters did, but had to fight harder to do it." Booklist
Includes bibliographical references

Flash!: the Associated Press covers the world; introduction by Peter Arnett; edited by Vincent Alabiso, Kelly Smith Tunney, and Chuck Zoeller. Abrams 1998 200p il hardcover o.p. pa $24.95
Grades: 11 12 Adult   **070.4**
1. Associated Press 2. Journalism 3. Photojournalism
ISBN 0-8109-1974-5; 0-8109-2793-4 (pa)
LC 97-40307
"A collection of notable news photos 'from the AP wire' marks the 150th anniversary of the news cooperative begun in 1848, which was the first wire service to provide photographs. . . . The text here includes Peter Arnett's appreciation of the AP's ethos and achievements and a history of the service by Charles J. Hanley." Booklist
"The human side of history is especially evident in this book in the faces of refugees, movie stars, soldiers, athletes, and politicians. . . . This outstanding work will be eagerly pored over in all libraries." Voice Youth Advocates

Foerstel, Herbert N.
From Watergate to Monicagate; ten controversies in modern journalism and media. Greenwood Press 2001 279p il $60.95
Grades: 11 12 Adult   **070.4**
1. Journalism 2. Mass media
ISBN 0-313-31163-3   LC 00-61698

Foerstel, Herbert N.—*Continued*

Also available in paperback from Maissoneuve Press

The author discusses "problems facing the media, such as mergers that drastically reduce the number of independent media, government giveaway of the 'digital spectrum,' PR masquerading as news, the power of lobbyists, CIA agents in the media, government censorship, paparazzi, and journalistic plagiarism. . . . Chapters cover radio; TV; newspapers; the Internet; and unlicensed radio stations, which provide local news coverage that focus on minorities, community groups, and schools. An excellent book for journalism and government students and staff." Book Rep

Includes bibliographical references

Freedman, Samuel G.

Letters to a young journalist. Basic Books 2006 184p (Art of mentoring) $22.95

Grades: 11 12 Adult   **070.4**

1. Journalism 2. Vocational guidance

ISBN 0-465-02455-6; 978-0-465-02455-1

LC 2005-37974

The author takes a "look at the practice of American journalism. He recalls his own achievements and shortcomings over a long career as well as other great and not so great moments in American journalism. . . . Freedman speaks very directly and personally, offering encouragement with equal portions of reality about the state of modern journalism from corporate influences to the blurring of lines between truth and propaganda." Booklist

Includes bibliographical references

Real sports reporting; edited by Abraham Aamidor. Indiana Univ. Press 2003 260p $49.95; pa $19.95

Grades: 11 12 Adult   **070.4**

1. Reporters and reporting 2. Sports

ISBN 0-253-34273-2; 0-253-21616-8 (pa)

LC 2003-2448

This book "is divided into two sections. The first, 'Beat Coverage,' features articles on writing about various sports: football, hockey, soccer, golf, tennis, baseball; there's even a general article on how to write a sports column. . . . Part two, 'The Rest of the Story,' offers more general advice, with articles on covering highschool and college sports, doing freelance sports writing, and becoming a sports editor. It's a vastly informative book, a real treat for budding journalists and even a few sports fans with an interest in writing." Booklist

Reporting America at war; an oral history; compiled by Michelle Ferrari with commentary by James Tobin. Hyperion 2003 241p il $23.95

Grades: 11 12 Adult   **070.4**

1. War 2. Reporters and reporting

ISBN 1-401-30072-3   LC 2003-49966

"Beginning with Edward R. Morrow's live reports during the London blitz and ending with an epilogue on the second war in Iraq, this oral history contains transcripts of interviews with 11 top correspondents. Murrow is one of three deceased reporters included (the others are Martha Gellhorn and Homer Bigart), along with Walter Cronkite, Andy Rooney, Frank Gibney, Malcolm Browne, David Halberstam, Morley Safer, Ward Just, Gloria Emerson, Chris Hedges and Christiane Amanpour.

. . . Tobin's introductions and transitional and informational interpolations within the transcripts hold this informative volume together." Publ Wkly

Includes bibliographical references

070.5   Publishing

Todd, Mark

Whatcha mean, what's a zine? the art of making zines and mini comics; [by] Mark Todd + Esther Peal Watson; with contributions by more than 20 creators of Indie-comics and magazines. Houghton Mifflin 2006 110p il pa $12.99

Grades: 7 8 9 10   **070.5**

1. Zines 2. Desktop publishing 3. Comic books, strips, etc.

ISBN 978-0-618-56315-9; 0-618-56315-6

LC 2005-55026

"A zine is a mini-magazine or homemade comic about any topic of the creator's choice, designed for maximum creativity and expression. The authors present a history of self-publishing. . . . Other topics include ideas for zine subjects; copying, binding, and printing tips, including easy-to-understand silk-screening and gocco instruction. . . . Throughout, technical terms are deftly used and advice is dispensed in an accessible, rousing format that includes comics, drawings, and cut-and-paste zine techniques. This well-designed and entertaining resource is sure to find an audience among hip, artistic, and do-it-yourself enthusiasts." SLJ

071   Journalism and newspapers-- North America

Burns, Eric

Infamous scribblers; the founding fathers and the rowdy beginnings of American journalism. Public Affairs 2006 467p $27.50

Grades: 11 12 Adult   **071**

1. Journalism 2. Newspapers—United States

ISBN 978-1-58648-334-0; 1-58648-334-X

LC 2005-53542

The author "explores the role newspapers played in the founding of the country." Libr J

"From the sniping feuds among Boston's first papers to sex scandals involving Alexander Hamilton and Thomas Jefferson, the snappy patter gives clear indication of how much Burns . . . relishes telling his story." Publ Wkly

Includes bibliographical references

The New new journalism; conversations with America's best nonfiction writers on their craft; [edited and with an introduction by] Robert S. Boynton. Vintage Books 2005 xxxiv, 456p pa $13.95

Grades: 11 12 Adult   **071**

1. Journalism

ISBN 1-400-03356-X   LC 2004-57161

The New new journalism—*Continued*
The author "offers interviews with 19 writers who detail how and why they produce their work. . . . A fascinating book that makes the reader want to go out and get every book the writers have written as well as those mentioned as sources of inspiration." Booklist
Includes bibliographical references

Written into history; Pulitzer Prize reporting of the twentieth century from the New York times; edited and with an introduction by Anthony Lewis. Times Bks. 2001 xxv, 355p hardcover o.p. pa $17
Grades: 11 12 Adult   **071**
1. Journalism 2. Pulitzer Prizes
ISBN 0-8050-6849-X; 0-8050-7178-4 (pa)
                                            LC 2001-35555
The award-winning articles "are sorted into the following categories: investigative reporting; dangerous stories that put reporters at risk; international news; public advocacy; criticism of the arts; science reporting; and biographical and human-interest stories. Among the topics are Russian slave-labor camps during the 1950s, the Pentagon Papers, the Vietnam War, and exploitation of illegal aliens in the U.S." Booklist
"For anyone interested in recent history or journalism at its best, this book will prove worthwhile." Publ Wkly

080   General collections

Adler, Mortimer J., 1902-2001
How to think about the great ideas; from the great books of Western civilization; [by] Mortimer J. Adler; edited by Max Weismann. Open Court 2000 xxiv, 530p pa $24.95
Grades: 11 12 Adult   **080**
1. Great books of the Western world
ISBN 0-8126-9412-0   LC 99-45251
This volume contains the transcripts of 52 half-hour segments of Adler's 1953-1954 television program The great ideas
"The book showcases Adler's ideas about all the big categories—truth, beauty, freedom, love, sex, art, justice, rationality, humankind's nature, Darwinism, government." Publ Wkly

Great treasury of Western thought; a compendium of important statements on man and his institutions by the great thinkers in Western history; edited by Mortimer J. Adler & Charles Van Doren. Bowker 1977 xxv, 1771p $58
Grades: 11 12 Adult   **080**
1. Quotations
ISBN 0-8352-0833-8   LC 77-154
"Quotations are often long ones, the average lengths being about 100 words. . . . Arranged in twenty chapters (Man, Family, Love, Emotion, Mind, Knowledge, etc.) with introductory notes for each chapter and subsection. Overall subject and proper name index." Sheehy. Guide to Ref Books. 10th edition

098   Prohibited works, forgeries, hoaxes

Noble, William, 1932-
Bookbanning in America; who bans books?—and why? Eriksson 1990 349p hardcover o.p. pa $14.95
Grades: 9 10 11 12   **098**
1. Books—Censorship
ISBN 0-8397-1080-1; 0-8397-1081-X (pa)
                                            LC 90-3413
The author "quotes from transcripts of trials, school board meetings, and interviews with librarians, educators, and parents. Striving for balance, he presents both sides of the censorship issue." Booklist
"A useful entry point for individuals beginning elementary research on censorship. Recommended for most public and high school libraries." Choice
Includes bibliographical references

100   PHILOSOPHY & PSYCHOLOGY

Blackburn, Simon
Think: a compelling introduction to philosophy. Oxford Univ. Press 1999 312p $25
Grades: 11 12 Adult   **100**
1. Philosophy
ISBN 0-19-210024-6   LC 00-265266
The author explores such areas as knowledge, mind, free will, identity, God, goodness and justice. "His method is to introduce what other philosophers—primarily Plato, Descartes, Locke, Berkeley, Leibniz, Hume, and Kant—have had to say about these themes. . . . Readers new to the subject could very well be captivated." Libr J
Includes bibliographical references

Bloom, Harold, 1930-
Essayists and prophets. Chelsea House Publishers 2005 221p (Bloom's literary criticism 20th anniversary collection) $38.95; pa $19.95
Grades: 9 10 11 12   **100**
1. Philosophers
ISBN 0-7910-8523-6; 0-7910-8524-4 (pa)
                                            LC 2005-5523
"Bloom muses on some of the greatest philosophical and critical thinkers to have graced the page. Some of the writers covered included Friedrich Nietzsche, William Hazlitt, and Sigmund Freud." Publisher's note
Includes bibliographical references

Phillips, Christopher, 1959-
Socrates café; a fresh taste of philosophy. Norton 2001 232p hardcover o.p. pa $13.95
Grades: 11 12 Adult   **100**
1. Philosophy
ISBN 0-393-04956-6; 0-393-32298-X (pa)
                                            LC 00-62211

Phillips, Christopher, 1959-—_Continued_
"Former journalist Phillips travels around the country to elicit dialogs, questions, and philosophical investigations from nonacademic participants. Elementary schools, senior-citizen facilities, public coffeehouses, and other well-populated venues provide the backdrops for the discussions he reports in this account of what 'doing philosophy' can and does mean in contemporary culture." Libr J

Includes bibliographical references

Van Lente, Fred
Action philosophers! Evil Twin Comics 2006 92p il pa $6.95 *
Grades: 10 11 12　　　　　　　　　　　**100**
1. Graphic novels 2. Philosophy—Graphic novels 3. Humorous graphic novels
ISBN 0-9778329-0-2; 978-0-9778329-0-3
This book combines a summary of the basic tenets of philosophers Plato, Bodhidharma, Nietzsche, Thomas Jefferson, St. Augustine, Ayn Rand, Sigmund Freud, Carl Jung, and Joseph Campbell with irreverent artistic portrayals. Imagine Plato as a masked wrestler (shouting "Plato smash!"), or Bodhidharma as a kung fu master. The section on Freud frankly discusses and portrays some of his more controversial psychosexual ideas.

103　Dictionaries, encyclopedias, concordances of philosophy

The **Cambridge** dictionary of philosophy; edited by Robert Audi. 2nd ed. Cambridge Univ. Press 1999 xxxv, 1001p il hardcover o.p. pa $32.99
Grades: 11 12 Adult　　　　　　　　　**103**
1. Philosophy—Dictionaries
ISBN 0-521-63136-X; 0-521-63722-8 (pa)
　　　　　　　　　　　　　　LC 99-12920
First published 1995
This work contains some 4,400 entries including 50 on major contemporary philosophers. Wide coverage of Western philosophy as well as non-Western and non-European philosophers is included. The rapidly growing fields of philosophy of mind and applied ethics are also covered

The **Oxford** companion to philosophy; edited by Ted Honderich. 2nd ed., new ed. Oxford University Press 2005 1056p il $60 *
Grades: 11 12 Adult　　　　　　　　　**103**
1. Philosophy—Encyclopedias
ISBN 0-19-926479-1　　　　LC 2005-275452
First published 1995
"Including more than 2200 alphabetically arranged entries from nearly 300 contributors, . . . [this book] provides an encyclopedic view of philosophy's past and present, its ideas, disputes (the editor himself contributes an article on unlikely philosophical propositions), and key figures, living and dead. . . . This title makes an excellent companion for standard multivolume subject encyclopedias." SLJ
For a fuller review, see: Booklist, Nov. 15, 2005
Includes bibliographical references

109　Philosophy--History

Durant, William James, 1885-1981
The story of philosophy; the lives and opinions of the great philosophers; by Will Durant. {2nd ed}. Simon & Schuster 1933 412p hardcover o.p. pa $15
Grades: 11 12 Adult　　　　　　　　　**109**
1. Philosophy—History 2. Philosophers
ISBN 0-671-69500-2; 0-671-20159-X (pa)
First published 1926
A selective account of western thinkers from Socrates and Kant to Schopenhauer and Dewey
Includes bibliographical references

King, Peter J., 1935-
One hundred philosophers; the life and work of the world's greatest thinkers. Barron's Educ. Ser. 2004 192p il pa $19.95 *
Grades: 11 12 Adult　　　　　　　　　**109**
1. Philosophers
ISBN 0-7641-2791-8　　　　　LC 2003-110643
This is "an overview of 100 important philosophers, from the ancient Greek pre-Socratics to today's analytic philosophers. Each thinker is summarized in an illustrated page . . . with a biographical sketch and summary of major works and ideas." Publisher's note
The author "has done a masterful job in presenting the life and work of what he calls 'the world's greatest thinkers.' . . . The concise and clearly written description of the thinker's life and ideas are just what a student or a layperson needs to gather an overview of the thinker's life and intellectual contributions." Am Ref Books Annu, 2005
Includes bibliographical references

Russell, Bertrand, 1872-1970
A history of Western philosophy; and its connection with political and social circumstances from the earliest times to the present day. Simon & Schuster 1945 xxiii, 895p
Grades: 11 12 Adult　　　　　　　　　**109**
1. Philosophy—History 2. Philosophers
ISBN 0-671-31400-9; 0-671-20158-1 (pa)
Originally designed and partly delivered as lectures at the Barnes Foundation in Pennsylvania
Contents: Ancient philosophy; Catholic philosophy; Modern philosophy. A summary is given of the main contributions of each period
"My purpose is to exhibit philosophy as an integral part of social and political life; not as the isolated speculations of remarkable individuals." Preface

Solomon, Robert C., 1942-2007
A short history of philosophy; {by} Robert C. Solomon, Kathleen M. Higgins. Oxford Univ. Press 1996 329p hardcover o.p. pa $23.95
Grades: 11 12 Adult　　　　　　　　　**109**
1. Philosophy—History
ISBN 0-19-508647-3; 0-19-510196-0 (pa)
　　　　　　　　　　　　　　LC 95-12578

Solomon, Robert C., 1942-2007—*Continued*
"This general history of philosophy . . . focuses on Western philosophy, but also discusses non-Western philosophical traditions. The authors cover major philosophers and movements as well as minor but interesting figures. They treat serious religious thought as philosophical, and include information about the Jewish, Christian, and other religious traditions." Publisher's note
"This is a fine overview of the subject that any interested reader will find rewarding." Libr J
Includes bibliographical references

World philosophers and their works; editor, John K. Roth; managing editor, Christina J. Moose; project editor, Rowena Wildin. Salem Press 2000 3v il set $331
Grades: 11 12 Adult   **109**
1. Philosophers
ISBN 0-89356-878-3   LC 99-55143
The editor "presents substantial entries that for 226 philosophers give brief biographies, justify the inclusion of each thinker, list their most important works, analyze their lifework, and locate them within the context of philosophy." Choice
Includes bibliographical references

111 Ontology

Adler, Mortimer J., 1902-2001
Six great ideas; truth, goodness, beauty, liberty, equality, justice: ideas we judge by, ideas we act on. Simon & Schuster 1997 243p pa $12
Grades: 11 12 Adult   **111**
1. Truth 2. Good and evil 3. Aesthetics 4. Justice 5. Equality 6. Freedom
ISBN 0-684-82681-X
"A Touchstone book"
First published 1981 by Macmillan
"In the first half of this book, Adler discusses the question whether truth, goodness, and beauty are objective features of the world. . . . The second half of the book . . . distinguishes different ideals of equality, analyzes several senses of liberty, and argues for the priority of justice over equality and liberty." Libr J

113 Cosmology (Philosophy of nature)

Lynch, Thomas, 1948-
Bodies in motion and at rest; on metaphor and mortality. Norton 2000 275p hardcover o.p. pa $12.95 *
Grades: 11 12 Adult   **113**
1. Life 2. Death
ISBN 0-393-04927-2; 0-393-32164-9 (pa)
    LC 00-21355
This collection of essays shows how Americans live and how they die. It presents attitude toward death and offers counseling and comforting advice to the bereft
The author "engages the reader with a mixture of poetic and funerary elements . . . his voice is rich and generous." N Y Times

Marshall, Peter H., 1946-
Nature's web; rethinking our place on earth; [by] Peter Marshall. Paragon House 1994 513p $29.95
Grades: 11 12 Adult   **113**
1. Philosophy of nature
ISBN 1-55778-652-6   LC 93-17233
In this "search for a new environmental ethic, Marshall . . . traces the development of human attitudes about nature from ancient times to the present." Publ Wkly
"This is a wonderful history of 'green' ideas." Choice
Includes bibliographical references

The **Oxford** companion to the mind; edited by Richard L. Gregory. 2nd ed. Oxford University Press 2005 1004p il $75 *
Grades: 11 12 Adult   **128**
1. Psychology—Dictionaries
ISBN 0-19-866224-6   LC 2004-275127
First published 1987
This book "contains over 1000 alphabetically arranged entries on all aspects of the mind, including topics in neurophysiology, communication, psychology, and philosophy, as well as people relevant to the field." Libr J
This "is one of those texts one wishes for enough hours in the day to read from cover to cover. . . . For those interested in the mind, this is a wonderful reference and a resource for learning more about themselves." Sci Books Films

133.1 Apparitions

Classic American ghost stories; 200 years of ghost lore from the Great Plains, New England, the South, and the Pacific Northwest; edited by Deborah A. Downer. August House 1990 214p $19.95; pa $9.95
Grades: 11 12 Adult   **133.1**
1. Ghosts
ISBN 0-87483-115-6; 0-87483-118-0 (pa)
    LC 90-34782
"Editor Deborah Downer brings together stories from newspapers, journals, and magazines, none of which were written as fictitious. An index references story locations by city and state." Publisher's note

Guiley, Rosemary Ellen
The encyclopedia of ghosts and spirits. 2nd ed. Facts on File 2000 430p $65; pa $19.95 *
Grades: 11 12 Adult   **133.1**
1. Ghosts—Encyclopedias
ISBN 0-8160-4085-0; 0-8160-4086-9 (pa)
    LC 99-59617
First published 1992
This work examines famous hauntings, historical personages and happenings, and various legends and myths about ghosts and spirits throughout the world. Recent events, new findings about old myths and updated information on major figures in the field are covered.

133.3   Divinatory arts

Levitt, Susan
Teen feng shui; design your space, design your life. Bindu Books 2003 223p il pa $14.95 *
Grades: 9 10 11 12   133.3
1. Feng shui
ISBN 0-89281-916-2   LC 2003-745
"Feng shui, the Chinese art of placement . . . is explored here with a uniquely young adult perspective, focusing almost solely on a teen's bedroom. . . . Teens with an interest in feng shui, eastern philosophies, or self-improvement will find this book accessible and enjoyable." Voice Youth Advocates

Pickover, Clifford A.
Dreaming the future; the fantastic story of prediction. Prometheus Bks. 2001 452p $28 *
Grades: 9 10 11 12   133.3
1. Divination 2. Fortune telling 3. Prophecies
ISBN 1-573-92895-X   LC 00-51838
This work examines various methods of fortune-telling, such as tarot cards, the zodiac, astrology and human sacrifice. Major prophecies by famous soothsayers throughout the history of prediction are explored, including the insight of Nostradamus, Edgar Cayce, Jeanne Dixon and the children of Fatima
"True believers and skeptics alike cannot fail to be won over by Pickover's disarming affection for his subjects . . . this book should delight." Publ Wkly
Includes bibliographical references

133.4   Demonology and witchcraft

Alexander, Dominic
Spellbound: from ancient gods to modern Merlins; a time tour of myth and magic. Reader's Digest 2002 256p il $26.95 *
Grades: 9 10 11 12   133.4
1. Magic
ISBN 0-7621-0379-5   LC 2002-18979
This study "covers the origins of magic in the ancient Middle East and Egypt, classical approaches in Greece and Rome, the Christian encounter with magic, medieval concerns about the magical gifts of nonconformists, the famous 15th-century witch hunter's text Malleus Maleficarum (The Hammer of Witches), and the modern persistence of magical beliefs. Much of the book is dedicated to the development of popular notions about witchcraft." Libr J
"With a broad cultural perspective and insight into human psychology, the author presents a challenging exploration of the relationship between science and the supernatural. Lavish illustrtations, plus sidebars that demystify many occult subjects, make this a solid and fascinating title." SLJ
Includes bibliographical references

Aronson, Marc
Witch-hunt: mysteries of the Salem witch trials. Atheneum Bks. for Young Readers 2003 272p il $18.95 *
Grades: 9 10 11 12   133.4
1. Trials 2. Witchcraft 3. Salem (Mass.)—History
ISBN 0-689-84864-1   LC 2002-152768
Contents: Two Salem families, 1641-1692; Two mysteries; The mysteries end and the hearings begin; The accuser: Ann Putnam, Jr; The one and the many; From hearings to trials; The man in black; "Choosing death with a quiet conscience"; "That no more innocent blood be shed"; "A great delusion of Satan"
"An eye-opening exploration of what is known to have taken place in Salem in 1692, and of a variety of interpretations that have been perpetuated about the happenings. A dynamic narrative hooks readers into thinking about the mysteries of the past and their continued influence on modern life." SLJ
Includes bibliographical references

Burns, William E.
Witch hunts in Europe and America; an encyclopedia. Greenwood Press 2003 400p $75
Grades: 9 10 11 12   133.4
1. Witchcraft—Encyclopedias 2. Persecution 3. Trials
ISBN 0-313-32142-6   LC 2003-44074
"After an alphabetical list of entries, there's a chronology from 1307 to 1793, indicating the time span of coverage. Topics include witch hunts in various countries, major individual witch hunts and trials, aspects of the witch-hunting process, demonological writers who were both supporters and opponents of witch-hunting, and subsequent interpretations of the witch hunt by historians and others." Libr Media Connect

Carlson, Laurie M., 1952-
A fever in Salem; a new interpretation of the New England witch trials. Dee, I.R. 1999 197p hardcover o.p. pa $14.95 *
Grades: 11 12 Adult   133.4
1. Witchcraft 2. Salem (Mass.)—History
ISBN 1-56663-253-6; 1-56663-309-5 (pa)
                                 LC 99-27520
In this reading of the New England witch trials, Carlson argues that "the 'possessed' of Salem, and perhaps of many other places where witchcraft was suspected, were in thrall not to devilry but to a mysterious disease of the brain, encephalitis lethargica, popularly known as sleeping sickness." New Yorker
"Carlson's compelling narrative begs for assessment by medical experts. A valuable purchase for libraries seeking more than a basic summary of the witch trials." Libr J
Includes bibliographical references

Demos, John, 1937-
Entertaining Satan; witchcraft and the culture of early New England; [by] John Putnam Demos. Updated ed. Oxford University Press 2004 543p il map $74; pa $21.95 *

Grades: 9 10 11 12　　　　　**133.4**
1. Witchcraft 2. New England—History
ISBN 0-19-517484-4; 0-19-517483-6 (pa)
　　　　　　　　　　　LC 2004-54701
First published 1982
"This is not simply a monograph on witchcraft but a major attempt to understand the kind of society and the kind of culture in which witchcraft had a place. To that end Demos employs nearly every conceptual tool available to the historian, including those borrowed from psychology, anthropology, and sociology." N Y Rev Books
Includes bibliographical references

The **Greenhaven** encyclopedia of witchcraft; Patricia D. Netzley, {book editor}. Greenhaven Press 2002 288p il (Greenhaven encyclopedia of) lib bdg $74.95

Grades: 9 10 11 12　　　　　**133.4**
1. Witchcraft—Encyclopedias
ISBN 0-7377-0437-3　　　LC 2001-54533
This book brings together "traditions, rituals, concepts, and magical tools as well as important personages both historical and modern, deities, and historical events." Booklist
Includes bibliographical references

Guiley, Rosemary Ellen
The encyclopedia of vampires, werewolves, and other monsters; foreword by Jeanne Keyes Youngson. Facts on File 2004 352p il $75; pa $24.95

Grades: 9 10 11 12　　　　　**133.4**
1. Vampires—Encyclopedias 2. Werewolves—Encyclopedias 3. Monsters—Encyclopedias
ISBN 0-8160-4684-0; 0-8160-4685-9 (pa)
　　　　　　　　　　　LC 2003-26592
"From ancient customs to famous cases of beasts and vampires in popular culture, this . . . reference focuses on folklore, historical cases, cross-cultural mythology, and the presence of these creatures in the arts and entertainment fields. Covering Japanese, Mexican, Gypsy, and Bosnian variations, among others, the diversity of cultures represented is eye-opening, and similarities are amazing. General reference collections, especially those getting popular-culture questions, will want to add this volume." Booklist
Includes bibliographical references

The encyclopedia of witches and witchcraft. 2nd ed. Facts on File 2000 417p il hardcover o.p. pa $24.95

Grades: 11 12 Adult　　　　　**133.4**
1. Witchcraft—Encyclopedias
ISBN 0-8160-3848-1; 0-8160-3849-X (pa)
　　　　　　　　　　　LC 98-54386
First published 1989
With more than 500 articles, this work delves into the subject from antiquity to the present. The entries vary in length from a paragraph to several pages and examine rituals, traditions, and events as well as people and places

Kallen, Stuart A., 1955-
Witches. Lucent Bks. 2000 112p il (Mystery library) lib bdg $27.45

Grades: 9 10 11 12　　　　　**133.4**
1. Witchcraft
ISBN 1-56006-688-1　　　LC 00-8062
The first half of this book "covers the history of witchcraft in Europe and America until the mid-eighteenth century. The second half takes a look at modern witchcraft, mainly Wicca, explaining rituals and beliefs with an eye toward demystifying Wicca's practice as religion. The author acknowledges the controversy surrounding witchcraft that still exists today." Booklist
Includes bibliographical references

Salem witch trials; Laura Marvel, book editor. Greenhaven Press 2003 144p il map (At issue in history) $29.95

Grades: 7 8 9 10 11 12　　　　　**133.4**
1. Trials 2. Witchcraft 3. Salem (Mass.)—History
ISBN 0-7377-0823-9; 978-0-7377-0823-3
　　　　　　　　　　　LC 2001-8518
Presents some theories regarding factors leading to the seventeenth-century witch trials in Salem, Massachusetts, and possible explanations for the behavior and confessions of those accused.
Includes bibliographical references

Satanism; Tami Roleff, book editor. Greenhaven Press 2002 112p (At issue) lib bdg $27.45; pa $18.70

Grades: 9 10 11 12　　　　　**133.4**
1. Satanism
ISBN 0-7377-0807-7 (lib bdg); 0-7377-0806-9 (pa)
　　　　　　　　　　　LC 2001-40612
This collection of essays explores "Satanism's rituals, its influence on youth . . . its association with certain crimes, and the social and cultural forces that make its credos intriguing to some teens. . . . Throughout, the arguments are even-tempered, the information straightforward, and the details unsensationalized." Booklist
Includes bibliographical references

133.5　Astrology

Lewis, James R., 1949-
The astrology book; the encyclopedia of heavenly influences. 2nd ed. Visible Ink Press 2003 928p il pa $24.95

Grades: 11 12 Adult　　　　　**133.5**
1. Astrology—Encyclopedias
ISBN 1-57859-144-9
Also available in hardcover from Omnigraphics
First published 1994 by Gale Res. with title: The astrology encyclopedia
This "defines and explains more than 800 astrological terms and concepts from air signs to Zeus. . . . *The Astrology Book* includes a special section on casting a

Lewis, James R., 1949-—Continued
chart, plus a . . . chapter that explains and interprets every planet in every house and sign. The text also includes a table of astrological glyphs and abbreviations, and a list of organizations, books, periodicals, and Web sites." Publisher's note

"Although aimed at the believer, Lewis' work may be confidently consulted by the skeptic seeking basic information about astrology." Booklist

Woolfolk, Joanna Martine
The only astrology book you'll ever need. New ed. Madison Books, Distributed by National Book Network 2001 445p il pa $16.95 *
Grades: 9 10 11 12   **133.5**
1. Astrology
ISBN 1-56833-231-9   LC 2001-31798
Also available in paperback with CD-ROM from Taylor Trade Publishing
"First Madison Books edition"
First published 1982 by Stein and Day
This book covers "sun signs, moon signs, planets, and the significance of the 12 zodiacal houses, as well as the most recent discoveries in astronomy and 21st-century projections. The author gives an easy, logical way to integrate the interpretations of the sun signs, moon signs, planets, and houses in any given chart, something not easily done or often seen in general astrology books." Libr J
Includes bibliographical references

133.9 Spiritualism

Is there life after death? Rebecca K. O'Connor, book editor. Greenhaven Press 2005 106p (At issue) lib bdg $28.70; pa $19.95
Grades: 9 10 11 12   **133.9**
1. Future life
ISBN 0-7377-2406-4 (lib bdg); 0-7377-2407-2 (pa)
                                LC 2004-52399
"Authors in this anthology present both sides of the argument about the afterlife." Publisher's note
Includes bibliographical references

Roach, Mary
Spook; science tackles the afterlife. Norton 2005 311p il $24.95 *
Grades: 11 12 Adult   **133.9**
1. Future life 2. Religion and science
ISBN 0-393-05962-6   LC 2005-14450
The author investigates a range of theories and beliefs about the soul's migration after death.
"Roach perfectly balances her skepticism and her boundless curiosity with a sincere desire to know. . . . She is an original who can enliven any subject with wit, keen reporting and a sly intelligence." Publ Wkly
Includes bibliographical references

141 Idealism and related systems and doctrines

The **essential** transcendentalists; edited and introduced by Richard G. Geldard. J.P. Tarcher/Penguin 2005 265p pa $15.95 *
Grades: 11 12 Adult   **141**
1. Transcendentalism
ISBN 1-58542-434-X   LC 2005-44016
This study "is divided into three main sections. . . . The first is 'Primary Texts,' with selections from the writings of Sampson Reed, James Marsh, Amos Alcott (father of Louisa May), and Ralph Waldo Emerson. The second, 'Individual Voices,' introduces selections from Frederic Hedge, Margaret Fuller, and Henry David Thoreau. The last is 'The Transcendental Heritage,' which features the works of Walt Whitman, Emily Dickinson, Wallace Stevens, Loren Eiseley, and Annie Dillard. This is a highly informed, elegantly written, fascinating story told through commentary, historical overview, and selections from classic works. It belongs in all libraries." Libr J
Includes bibliographical references

150 Psychology

Reber, Arthur S.
The Penguin dictionary of psychology; {by} Arthur S. Reber and Emily S. Reber. 3rd ed. Penguin Bks. 2001 xxi, 831p il pa $16 *
Grades: 9 10 11 12   **150**
1. Psychology—Dictionaries
ISBN 0-14-051451-1   LC 2002-276265
First published 1985
Contains 17,000 entries on various aspects of psychology, including new developments in neuroscience and social psychology

150.19 Psychological systems, schools, viewpoints

De Laszlo, Violet S. (Violet Staub), 1900-1988
The basic writings of C. G. Jung; edited with an introduction by Violet Staub de Laszlo. Modern Lib. 1993 c1959 xxxiii, 691p $21.95
Grades: 11 12 Adult   **150.19**
1. Psychoanalysis
ISBN 0-679-60071-X   LC 93-17801
Also available in paperback from Princeton Univ. Press
This is a reissue of the 1959 edition
This volume contains excerpts from Symbols of transformation, On the nature of the psyche, Relations between the ego and the unconscious, Psychological types, Psychology of the transference, and Psychology and religion. It also includes Archetypes of the collective unconscious, Psychological aspects of the mother archetype, On the nature of dreams, On the psychogenesis of schizophrenia, Introduction to the religious and psychological problems of alchemy, and Marriage as a psychological relationship
Includes bibliographical references

Freud, Sigmund, 1856-1939
The basic writings of Sigmund Freud; translated and edited by A.A. Brill. Modern Lib. 1995 c1938 973p $24.95
Grades: 11 12 Adult   **150.19**
1. Psychoanalysis
ISBN 0-679-60166-X   LC 95-13411
A reissue of the 1938 edition
Contents: Psychopathology of everyday life; The interpretation of dreams; Three contributions to the theory of sex; Wit and its relations to the unconscious; Totem and taboo; The history of the psychoanalytic movement

Rogers, Carl R. (Carl Ransom), 1902-1987
A way of being. Houghton Mifflin 1980 395p pa $15 hardcover o.p.
Grades: 11 12 Adult   **150.19**
1. Psychology 2. Humanism
ISBN 0-395-75530-1 (pa)   LC 80-20275
The author offers a "collection of papers, talks, autobiographical sketches and vignettes of patients' experiences in workshops and therapy." Publ Wkly
"This is a book rich in theoretical insights and experiential sharing, and full of invigorating optimism." Libr J
Includes bibliographical references

Skinner, B. F. (Burrhus Frederic), 1904-1990
About behaviorism. Knopf 1974 256p pa $12 hardcover o.p.
Grades: 11 12 Adult   **150.19**
1. Behaviorism
ISBN 0-394-71618-3 (pa)
The author defines, analyzes and defends the science of behaviorism with chapters exploring the causes of behavior, operant behavior, verbal behavior, thinking, causes and reasons, knowledge, emotion and self
Includes bibliographical references

Thurschwell, Pamela, 1966-
Sigmund Freud. Routledge 2000 158p (Routledge critical thinkers) $75; pa $16.95 *
Grades: 11 12 Adult   **150.19**
1. Freud, Sigmund, 1856-1939 2. Psychoanalysis
ISBN 0-415-21520-X; 0-415-21521-8 (pa)
                                       LC 00-32823
"The book contains chapters on early theories, interpretation, sexuality, case histories, maps of the mind, society and religion, and psychoanalysis's aftermath, including feminist criticism and a remarkable summary of Jacques Lacan's role." Booklist
Includes bibliographical references

150.3 Psychology--Encyclopedias and dictionaries

Cordón, Luis A.
Popular psychology; an encyclopedia. Greenwood Press 2005 274p il $75 *
Grades: 11 12 Adult   **150.3**
1. Psychology—Encyclopedias
ISBN 0-313-32457-3   LC 2004-17426

This "encyclopedia explains the accuracies and fallacies of contemporary popular psychology when compared to the discipline practiced by professional psychologists. . . . Entries cover pop psychologists (Noam Chomsky, Deepak Chopra, Dr. Phil McGraw) and historical theoreticians (Erikson, Freud, Jung, Skinner). Other entries treat controversial topics and 'pseudoscience'—e.g., aromatherapy, dianetics/scientology, EMDR, facilitated communication, subliminal perception." Choice
This book "provides a concise guide for anyone seeking to understand the true scientific nature of psychology." Libr Media Connect
Includes bibliographical references

The **Gale** encyclopedia of psychology; Bonnie R. Strickland, executive editor. 2nd ed. Gale Group 2001 701p il $191.50
Grades: 11 12 Adult   **150.3**
1. Psychology—Encyclopedias
ISBN 0-7876-4786-1   LC 00-34736
First published 1996
Coverage includes noteworthy people, movements, theories, and important case studies and experiments. The articles, ranging from 25 to 1,500 words examine such diverse topics as abnormal psychology, bipolar disorder, Sigmund Freud and insomnia
Includes bibliographical references

Psychology basics; edited by Frank N. Magill. Salem Press 1998 2v il (Magill's choice) lib bdg set $118.75
Grades: 11 12 Adult   **150.3**
1. Psychology—Encyclopedias
ISBN 0-89356-963-1   LC 97-39249
Contents: v1 Abnormality defined—intelligence; 2v Intelligence tests—the visual system; Index
The encyclopedia includes "110 signed articles drawn from Salem's six-volume *Survey of Social Science: Psychology* (1993). Articles represent various areas of psychology, including cognition, developmental psychology, emotion, intelligence, learning, personality, psychopathology, and psychotherapy. . . . Each entry includes labels for type of psychology and field of study . . . a definition of the main entry term; a list of principal terms defined; the article itself divided into overview, applications, and context sections; an annotated bibliography; and a list of related topics in the set." Booklist

152.4 Emotions

Chocolate for a teen's heart; unforgettable stories for young women about love, hope, and happiness; [compiled by] Kay Allenbaugh. Simon & Schuster 2001 219p pa $12
Grades: 9 10 11 12   **152.4**
1. Teenagers 2. Girls
ISBN 0-7432-1380-7   LC 2001-20810
This work presents 55 stories about teen relationships written by teens and women reminiscing about their teen years. It relates the happiness of a first romance, conflicts with parents, and the joys and sorrows of peer relationships. In sum, the stories reveal the essence of being a teen
"This collection of positive stories should prove refreshing and will be popular with fans of inspirational tales." Booklist

Fromm, Erich, 1900-1980
The art of loving. Centennial ed. Continuum
2000 130p $18.95
Grades: 11 12 Adult　　　　　　　**152.4**
1. Love
ISBN 0-8264-1260-2　　　　　LC 00-21030
Also available in paperback from HarperCollins Pubs.
A reissue of the title first published 1956
"An astonishingly simple presentation of an abstract
subject." Booklist

Goleman, Daniel
Emotional intelligence. Bantam Bks. 1995 352p
$25.95; pa $16.95
Grades: 11 12 Adult　　　　　　　**152.4**
1. Emotions 2. Intellect
ISBN 0-553-09503-X; 0-553-37506-7 (pa)
　　　　　　　　　　　　　LC 95-16685
The author explains "how to develop our emotional
intelligence in ways that can improve our relationships,
our parenting, our classrooms, and our workplaces.
Goleman assures us that our temperaments may be deter-
mined by neurochemistry, but they can be altered."
Booklist
"Mr. Goleman, with an economy of style that serves
his reformer's convictions well, integrates a vast amount
of material on issues whose intricacy and problematic
character he reveals in an original and persuasive way."
N Y Times Book Rev
Includes bibliographical references

Lorenz, Konrad
On aggression; translated by Marjorie Kerr
Wilson. Harcourt Brace Jovanovich 1966 306p pa
$13 hardcover o.p.
Grades: 11 12 Adult　　　　　　　**152.4**
1. Aggressiveness (Psychology) 2. Comparative psy-
chology
ISBN 0-15-668741-0 (pa)
Also available in hardcover from Fine Communica-
tions
"A Helen and Kurt Wolff book"
Original German edition published 1963 in Austria
The author examines aggression in animals and hu-
mans, noting both the positive and destructive manifesta-
tions of such behavior
Includes bibliographical references

Provine, Robert R.
Laughter; a scientific investigation. Viking 2000
258p il $24.95; pa $14
Grades: 11 12 Adult　　　　　　　**152.4**
1. Laughter
ISBN 0-670-89375-7; 0-14-100225-5 (pa)
　　　　　　　　　　　　　LC 00-38227
The author "reviews recent scientific research, philo-
sophical and psychological literature, case studies of ab-
normal laughter and phenomena like laugh tracks." N Y
Times Book Rev
"As soon as Provine . . . introduces his
groundbreaking, fun-to-read anthropological study of
laughter, . . . the full scope of its strangeness and complexity begins to emerge." Booklist
Includes bibliographical references

153　Imagination, imagery, creativity

Rose, Steven Peter Russell, 1938-
The future of the brain; the promise and perils
of tomorrow's neuroscience; [by] Steven Rose.
Oxford University Press 2005 344p il $28; pa
$16.95
Grades: 11 12 Adult　　　　　　　**153**
1. Brain
ISBN　978-0-19-515420-7;　0-19-515420-7;
978-0-19-530893-8 (pa); 0-19-530893-X (pa)
　　　　　　　　　　　　　LC 2004-23578
The author "discusses the technologies for altering the
brain that are apt to appear in the next two decades . . .
The understanding of neuroscience he provides permits
his readers to consider the implications of imminent de-
velopments." Booklist
Includes bibliographical references

Sagan, Carl, 1934-1996
The dragons of Eden; speculations on the
evolution of human intelligence. Random House
1977 263p il pa $7.50 hardcover o.p.
Grades: 11 12 Adult　　　　　　　**153**
1. Intellect 2. Brain 3. Genetics
ISBN 0-345-34629-7 (pa)　　　LC 76-53472
In this study of human intellect "Sagan is principally
preoccupied with the neocortex, with its left hemisphere,
responsible for language and logic, a right hemisphere in
charge of intuition and spatial dimension, and a corpus
callosum that mediates and synthesizes the two." Atl
Mon
Includes bibliographical references

153.1　Memory and learning

Baddeley, Alan D., 1934-
Your memory; a user's guide; [by] Alan
Baddeley. New illustrated ed. Firefly Books 2005
288p il pa $24.95 *
Grades: 11 12 Adult　　　　　　　**153.1**
1. Memory
ISBN 1-55297-985-7　　　　LC 2005-357222
First published 1982 by Macmillan
"The 14 chapters alternate between discussions of
memory system function (short-term memory, working
memory, learning, organization, storage, retrieval, devel-
opmental issues, and forgetting) and practical application
(repression, amnesia, eyewitness testimony, Alzheimer's,
improving memory, and changes with age)." Sci Books
Films
Includes bibliographical references

Schacter, Daniel L.

The seven sins of memory; how the mind forgets and remembers. Houghton Mifflin 2001 272p il $25; pa $14

Grades: 11 12 Adult 153.1
1. Memory
ISBN 0-618-04019-6; 0-618-21919-6 (pa)
LC 00-53885

The author discusses "the curious processes of memory by classifying its malfunctions into seven categories: transience, absent-mindedness, blocking, misattribution, suggestibility, bias, and persistence. Schacter illustrates each of these 'sins' with examples of routine misfortunes common to all." Libr J

Includes bibliographical references

Turkington, Carol

The encyclopedia of memory and memory disorders; [by] Carol Turkington and Joseph R. Harris. 2nd ed. Facts on File 2001 296p (Facts on File library of health and living) $66 *

Grades: 11 12 Adult 153.1
1. Memory—Encyclopedias
ISBN 0-8160-4141-5 LC 00-52806
First published 1995

This volume includes over 70 entries describing: Alzheimer's disease; Football and memory loss; Huffing; Mad cow disease; Memory in infancy; Norepinephrine; "Punch drunk" syndrome; Social memory; Vitamins and memory.

Includes bibliographical references

153.4 Thought, thinking, reasoning

Gladwell, Malcolm

Blink: the power of thinking without thinking. Little, Brown and Co 2005 277p il $25.95

Grades: 11 12 Adult 153.4
1. Decision making 2. Intuition
ISBN 0-316-17232-4 LC 2004-13916
Also available large print edition $27.95 (ISBN 0-316-01178-9)

The author "decodes the science of rapid cognition, those snap judgments made with only the subtlest clues." Christ Sci Monit

Gladwell "has a dazzling ability to find commonality in disparate fields of study. . . . Each case study is satisfying, and Gladwell imparts his own evident pleasure in delving into a wide range of fields and seeking an underlying truth." Publ Wkly

Includes bibliographical references

153.6 Communication

Fast, Julius, 1918-

Body language. Evans & Co. 1970 192p pa $6.50 hardcover o.p.

Grades: 11 12 Adult 153.6

1. Nonverbal communication
ISBN 0-671-67325-4 (pa)

This book discusses the "science of kinesics, the use of non-verbal communication through the means of body movements which may support or contradict our verbal expressions." Best Sellers

Includes bibliographical references

153.8 Will (Volition)

Bachel, Beverly K., 1957-

What do you really want? how to set a goal and go for it! A guide for teens. Free Spirit 2000 134p il pa $12.95 *

Grades: 7 8 9 10 11 12 153.8
1. Success 2. Motivation (Psychology)
ISBN 1-57542-085-6 LC 00-57286

The book discusses various ways for teenagers to set goals, build support networks, keep themselves motivated in the process and reap the harvest of their successes

Bachel's "helpful advice is well supported by quotations from teens who have tried some of the techniques, and simple, appealing graphics keep things light. . . . Back matter includes goal-setting resources and some helpful organizations and Web sites." Booklist

153.9 Intelligence and aptitudes

Streznewski, Marylou Kelly, 1934-

Gifted grownups; the mixed blessings of extraordinary potential. Wiley 1999 292p $24.95

Grades: 11 12 Adult 153.9
1. Genius
ISBN 0-471-29580-9 LC 98-29536

Seeking to debunk "the myth that intellectually gifted people are either impractical social misfits or perfect specimens, . . . [the author presents a] study of 100 people aged 18 to 90. . . . [She] explores their experiences with schools, jobs, and in the social world." Libr J

"The book is interesting not only anecdotally, but because it provokes thought about the nature of intelligence and its interactive functioning in our changing society." Readings

Includes bibliographical references

154.6 Sleep phenomena

Hobson, J. Allan

Dreaming; an introduction to the science of sleep. Oxford Univ. Press 2002 170p il $22 *

Grades: 11 12 Adult 154.6
1. Dreams 2. Sleep
ISBN 0-19-280304-2 LC 2003-266389

The author "describes how the theory of dreaming has advanced dramatically over the past fifty years. . . . The book also discusses dream disorders (nightmares, night terrors, sleep walking), the possible link between dreaming and the regulation of body temperature, the effects of sleep deprivation, and much more." Publisher's note

Hobson, J. Allan—*Continued*

"As Hobson meticulously matches dream features to brain chemistry, he cajoles readers into replacing mystical interpretations with an understanding of the evidence indicating that our precious dreams are the results of the brain's routine processing of an overwhelming amount of memory." Booklist

Lewis, James R., 1949-

The dream encyclopedia. Gale Res. 1995 xxi, 416p il hardcover o.p. pa $19.95

Grades: 11 12 Adult   **154.6**

ISBN 0-7876-0155-1; 0-7876-0156-X (pa)

LC 95-10759

"This work presents brief articles on some 250 topics, from adaptive therapy and astral projections to Zulu and Zuni myths. . . . In addition to the main encyclopedia, a short introductory overview of dream and sleep research and a subject index are included. Also provided is a list of 'dream resources,' with the names and addresses of many of the organizations now focusing on the study of dreams and sleep research." Am Ref Books Annu, 1996

Parker, Julia, 1932-

Parkers' complete book of dreams. Dorling Kindersley 1995 208p il pa $15 hardcover o.p.

Grades: 11 12 Adult   **154.6**

1. Dreams

ISBN 0-7894-3295-1 (pa)   LC 94-27918

This guide covers the history as well as theories concerning the meaning of dreaming. Advice is given on how to record and improve the ability to recall specific dreams

154.7   Hypnotism

Rosen, Marvin

Meditation and hypnosis. Chelsea House Publishers 2005 121p il (Gray matter) $32.95

Grades: 9 10 11 12   **154.7**

1. Hypnotism 2. Meditation

ISBN 0-7910-8515-5   LC 2005-15848

This book "traces the history of and controversies about manipulating consciousness. Experimentation and medical and psychological applications are discussed in depth, including fascinating subtopics such as brainwashing, dissociation, multiple personalities, and multitasking." SLJ

Includes bibliographical references

155.2   Individual psychology

Burnham, Terry

Mean genes; from sex to money to food; taming our primal instincts; by Terry Burnham & Jay Phelan. Perseus Bks. 2000 263p $24

Grades: 11 12 Adult   **155.2**

1. Genetics 2. Psychology

ISBN 0-7382-0230-4

Also available in paperback from Penguin Bks.

The authors "explore the genetic evolution of behaviors that sabotage humans' willpower to resist temptation. Debt, fat, drugs, risk, greed, gender, beauty, infidelity, family, and friends and foes are presented as key issues that affect all people." Libr J

"A delightfully readable presentation of the evolutionary, as distinct from the moralized, appreciation of human nature." Booklist

Steinem, Gloria

Revolution from within; a book of self-esteem. Little, Brown 1992 377p pa $14.95 hardcover o.p.

Grades: 11 12 Adult   **155.2**

1. Self-esteem 2. Feminism

ISBN 0-316-81247-1 (pa)   LC 91-11356

The author discusses the importance of self-esteem and offers practical advice on ways of acquiring it

Steinem's "book unfolds like a flower: it offers literature, art, nature, meditation, and connectedness as ways of finding and exploring the self. . . . Her focus is women, but she is clear that what she has to say is for men, too, and she is neither strident nor dismissive." Libr J

Includes bibliographical references

155.5   Psychology of young people

Esherick, Joan

Balancing act; a teen's guide to managing stress. Mason Crest Publishers 2005 128p il (Science of health) $24.95 *

Grades: 9 10 11 12   **155.5**

1. Stress (Psychology)

ISBN 1-590-84853-5   LC 2004-10693

Contents: Stressed to the max: teens under pressure -- The causes of stress -- How stress affects your body, mind, and emotions -- How stress affects your relationships and responsibilities -- Handling stress, pt. 1: flight isn't always bad -- Handling stress, pt. 2: facing stress head-on

The author "describes the body's physical reaction to stress, using words and images that young people can easily understand." SLJ

Includes bibliographical references

Espeland, Pamela, 1951-

The gifted kids' survival guide; a teen handbook; [by] Judy Galbraith and Jim Delisle; edited by Pamela Espeland. revised, expanded and updated ed. Free Spirit 1996 295p il pa $15.95

Grades: 9 10 11 12   **155.5**

1. Gifted children

ISBN 1-57542-003-1   LC 96-29430

Also available in hardcover from Econo-Clad Bks.

First published 1983 by Wetherall Publishing Company

Examines issues that are of concern for young people who have been labeled "gifted," discussing what the label means, intelligence testing, educational options, and relationships with parents and friends. Includes first-person essays on being gifted

Includes bibliographical references

Palmer, Pat, 1928-
Teen esteem; a self-direction manual for young adults; {by} Pat Palmer with Melissa Alberti Froehner. 2nd ed. Impact Pubs. 2000 97p il pa $9.95 *
Grades: 9 10 11 12   **155.5**
1. Self-esteem 2. Conduct of life
ISBN 1-88623-014-5   LC 99-87865
"Little Imp books"
First published 1989
Provides guidance on developing self-esteem and the positive attitude necessary to cope with such adolescent challenges as peer pressure, substance abuse, and sexual expression
"Whether it's used for small group discussion or on an individual basis, this book is a thought-provoking guide that touches on many relevant issues affecting teens." Book Rep
Includes bibliographical references

155.7 Evolutional psychology

Ridley, Matt
Nature via nurture; genes, experience, and what makes us human. HarperCollins Pubs. 2003 326p $25.95 *
Grades: 11 12 Adult   **155.7**
1. Nature and nurture 2. Genetics
ISBN 0-06-000678-1   LC 2003-40687
"In February 2001 it was announced that the human genome contains not 100,000 genes, as originally postulated, but only 30,000. This . . . revision led some scientists to conclude that there are simply not enough human genes to account for all the different ways people behave: we must be made by nurture, not nature. . . . {Ridley argues that} nurture depends on genes, too, and genes need nurture. Genes not only predetermine the broad structure of the brain, they also absorb formative experiences, react to social cues, and even run memory. They are consequences as well as causes of the will." Publisher's note
Includes bibliographical references

155.9 Environmental psychology

Fitzgerald, Helen
The grieving teen; a guide for teenagers and their friends. Simon & Schuster 2000 222p pa $12
Grades: 11 12 Adult   **155.9**
1. Bereavement 2. Adolescent psychology
ISBN 0-684-86804-0   LC 00-38746
"A Fireside book"
"Chapters consist of typical questions that young adults may have about grief, followed by a 'What You Can Do' section. The topics covered include such contemporary issues as death from AIDS, post-traumatic stress disorder, and Internet support. Fitzgerald provides many real-life experiences and a true sensitivity to differing religious and cultural practices." Libr J
Includes bibliographical references

Gootman, Marilyn E., 1944-
When a friend dies; a book for teens about grieving & healing; edited by Pamela Espeland. Rev. and updated ed. Free Spirit Pub. 2005 118p pa $9.95 *
Grades: 7 8 9 10   **155.9**
1. Death 2. Bereavement
ISBN 1-57542-170-4   LC 2005-447
First published 1994
This offers "information on subjects including: How can I stand the pain? How should I be acting? What is 'normal'? What if I can't handle my grief on my own? and How can I find a counselor or a therapist? Interspersed throughout the book . . . are quotes by teenagers who have experienced grief. . . . Quotes from well-known writers and philosophers give insight into the grieving process and healing." SLJ

Hughes, Lynne Barribeau
You are not alone; teens talk about life after the loss of a parent; [by] Lynne B. Hughes. Scholastic Press 2005 192p $16.99; pa $8.99
Grades: 7 8 9 10   **155.9**
1. Bereavement 2. Death 3. Parent-child relationship
ISBN 0-439-58590-2; 0-439-58591-0 (pa)
LC 2005-2878
The author "begins with the author's own story (she lost both parents by the time she was 12) and integrates quotes from other teens who have experienced grief. Hughes addresses questions of added responsibilities, remarriage of a parent, and the wide range of emotions that can result from a parent's death. This is a thoughtful, conscientious approach to a challenging topic." Publ Wkly

Kübler-Ross, Elisabeth
On death and dying. Scribner Classics 1997 286p il $23; pa $13
Grades: 9 10 11 12 Adult   **155.9**
1. Death 2. Terminal care
ISBN 0-684-84223-8; 0-684-83938-5 (pa)
LC 97-177294
A reissue of the title first published 1969 by Macmillan
A look at the psychological, sociological and theological issues faced by the terminally ill and their caregivers
Includes bibliographical references

Myers, Edward, 1950-
When will I stop hurting? teens, loss, and grief; illustrations by Kelly Adams. Scarecrow Press 2004 159p il (It happened to me) $34.50
Grades: 7 8 9 10   **155.9**
1. Bereavement 2. Loss (Psychology)
ISBN 0-8108-4921-6   LC 2003-23698
"Outlining the phases of the grieving process, Myers incorporates . . . personal accounts and quotes from young adults who have experienced the death of a family member into the text. He discusses the range of emotions young people may have from anger and fear to relief and sadness and assures readers that these feelings are normal." SLJ

Myers, Edward, 1950-—*Continued*

This book "will be extremely helpful for teens struggling to understand their emotions following the loss of a loved one. Grieving is well explained and the individual nature of grief is stressed." Libr Media Connect

Includes bibliographical references

156 Comparative psychology

Waal, Frans de, 1948-

Our inner ape; a leading primatologist explains why we are who we are; photographs by the author. Riverhead Books 2005 274p il $24.95 *

Grades: 11 12 Adult   **156**

1. Human behavior 2. Primates—Behavior 3. Comparative psychology

ISBN 1-57322-312-3   LC 2005-42768

This book compares human "social behavior with that of two species of apes: chimpanzees and bonobos." N Y Times Book Rev

"Readers might be surprised at how much these apes and their stories resonate with their own lives, and may well be left with an urge to spend a few hours watching primates themselves at the local zoo." Publ Wkly

Includes bibliographical references

158 Applied psychology

Canfield, Jack, 1944-

Chicken soup for the teenage soul [I-III]; [by] Jack Canfield, Mark Victor Hansen, Kimberly Kirberger. Health Communications 1997-2000 3v il ea $24

Grades: 7 8 9 10 11 12   **158**

1. Interpersonal relations 2. Emotions

ISBN 1-55874-468-1 ([I]); 1-55874-615-3 ([II]); 1-55874-761-3 ([III])

Also available in paperback ea $12.95

These books cover "teenage subjects running the gamut from love, family ties, and self-esteem to developing values and life crises, such as a death in the family. . . . Teenagers not only helped select the poems, stories, and accounts that have been included but also have written some of them . . . with a few contributions by well-known people, including Sandra Cisneros, Helen Keller, and Robert Fulghum. . . . This isn't a religious book, but it is an inspirational and motivational one, sometimes funny, sometimes poignant." Booklist [review of 1997 volume]

Includes bibliographical references

Chicken soup for the teenage soul's the real deal; school: cliques, classes, clubs, and more; [compiled by] Jack Canfield, Mark Victor Hansen, Deborah Reber. Health Communications 2005 pa $12.95 *

Grades: 7 8 9 10   **158**

1. Interpersonal relations 2. Emotions

ISBN 0-7573-0255-6   LC 2005046051

"The stories included here were submitted by students and are based on their own experiences. Almost every page includes a fun fact, a statistic, or a quiz." SLJ

Evans, Patricia

Teen torment; overcoming verbal abuse at home and at school. Adams Media Corp. 2003 304p pa $12.95 *

Grades: 9 10 11 12   **158**

1. Teenagers 2. Invective 3. Aggressiveness (Psychology) 4. Self-esteem

ISBN 1-58062-845-1   LC 2002-14292

Contents: About verbal abuse? -- Where verbal abuse shows up -- What can we do about it?

In the first section the author "shows how teens are particularly affected: verbal abuse impairs the self-confidence and self-knowledge necessary to develop into healthy, functioning adults. And she discusses the role of verbal abuse in violent behavior. In the book's second half, Evans looks specifically at verbal abuse in the media, on the sports field, at home, and in school, and she closes with a section on stopping verbal abuse, with separate chapters for parents, teachers, teens, and 'boyfriends and girlfriends.' Evans' approach is more practical and anecdotal than scientific, using approachable language enhanced with plenty of checklists, charts, and an appended resources section. The result is an easily digested, empowering guide to identifying and curbing damaging behavior and to strengthening communication in general." Booklist

Includes bibliographical references

The **Friend** who got away; twenty women's true-life tales of friendships that blew up, burned out, or faded away; edited by Jenny Offill and Elissa Schappell; introd. by Francine Prose. Doubleday 2005 xxi, 294p $24.95

Grades: 11 12 Adult   **158**

1. Friendship 2. Loss (Psychology)

ISBN 0-385-51186-8   LC 2004-58259

Contributors to this anthology include "Francine Prose, Katie Roiphe, Dorothy Allison, Elizabeth Strout, Ann Hood, Diana Abu-Jaber, and Helen Schulman. . . . Each story is different, dealing with everything from relationships that gradually dissolved to those that broke up suddenly, but almost all address friendships from the authors' young adult years." Libr J

"Though often sad when read in succession, these pieces are deeply affecting." Publ Wkly

Goleman, Daniel

Social intelligence; the new science of human relationships. Bantam Books 2006 403p il $28

Grades: 9 10 11 12 Adult   **158**

1. Emotions 2. Intellect

ISBN 0-553-80352-2; 9780553803525

     LC 2006-45971

Also available large print edition $30 (ISBN: 0-7393-2679-1; ISBN-13: 978-0-7393-2679-4)

The author "argues for a new social model of intelligence drawn from the emerging field of social neuroscience. . . . Goleman illuminates new theories about attachment, bonding, and the making and remaking of memory as he examines how our brains are wired for altruism, compassion, concern and rapport." Publ Wkly

Includes bibliographical references

170 Ethics (Moral philosophy)

Encyclopedia of ethics; Susan Neiburg Terkel, consulting editor; R. Shannon Duval, editor. Facts on File 1999 302p $71.50 *
Grades: 11 12 Adult **170**
1. Ethics—Encyclopedias
ISBN 0-8160-3311-0   LC 98-39932
This encyclopedia covers such topics as moral development, character, justice, self-realization, existentialism, genetic engineering, the right to die, business, medical, and sexual ethics, and includes the ideas of such thinkers as Confucius, Hildegard von Bingen, and John Stuart Mill

Ethics: opposing viewpoints; Laurie diMauro and Tina Grant, book editors. Greenhaven Press 2007 260p il lib bdg $34.95; pa $23.70
Grades: 9 10 11 12   **170**
1. Ethics
ISBN 0-7377-3319-5 (lib bdg); 978-0-7377-3319-8 (lib bdg); 0-7377-3320-9 (pa); 978-0-7377-3320-4 (pa)
      LC 2006-41179
"Opposing viewpoints series"
"Issues tackled include the motivation, and reasons, for ethical behavior, the ethics of biomedical engineering, and the ethics of large corporations, from Enron to Wal-Mart. . . . This book will be of interest both for personal reading and research." SLJ
Includes bibliographical references

Harper, Hill, 1966-
Letters to a young brother. Gotham Books 2006 176p $20 *
Grades: 9 10 11 12   **170**
1. Boys 2. Conduct of life
ISBN 1-59240-200-3; 978-1-59240-200-7
      LC 2006-3699
The author "devotes separate chapters to school and work, sex, and life aspirations, tackling such issues as single parenthood, sexually transmitted diseases, the allure of materialism, and the power of words and faith. . . . Although aimed at young black men, this book, with its contemporary language and approach, should have appeal for youth of both sexes and all races." Booklist

174 Occupational ethics

Callahan, David, 1965-
The cheating culture; why more Americans are doing wrong to get ahead. Harcourt 2004 353p $26; pa $14 *
Grades: 11 12 Adult   **174**
1. Business ethics 2. Social ethics
ISBN 0-15-101018-8; 0-15-603005-5 (pa)
      LC 2003-15529
The author examines "government reports and statistics, studies by social scientists, public opinion polls, and journalistic investigations of scandals and cheating. Callahan also conducted interviews with people who deal

with the cheating culture: parents, students, teachers, coaches, athletes, experts in business ethics, stock analysts, lawyers, accountants, doctors, and law enforcement officials." Booklist
"If all business school students could be required to read one book, this should be it." Choice
Includes bibliographical references

Ethics; Brenda Stalcup, book editor. Greenhaven Press 2000 160p (Current controversies) $31.20; pa $19.95
Grades: 9 10 11 12   **174**
1. Ethics
ISBN 0-7377-0338-5; 0-7377-0337-7 (pa)
      LC 99-45248
Articles and essays explore philosophical and practical aspects of ethical behavior in business, medicine, and education.
This work "will assist not only debaters but also thoughtful students and adults looking at the issues behind some of today's headlines." Booklist
Includes bibliographical references

174.2 Medical ethics

Biomedical ethics: opposing viewpoints; Tamara L. Roleff, book editor. Greenhaven Press 1998 252p lib bdg $31.20; pa $19.95 *
Grades: 7 8 9 10   **174.2**
1. Medical ethics 2. Bioethics
ISBN 1-56510-793-4 (lib bdg); 1-56510-792-6 (pa)
      LC 97-51374
"Opposing viewpoints series"
Presents opposing viewpoints on biomedical ethics issues such as human cloning, genetic research and engineering, organ transplants and reproductive technologies.
Includes glossary and bibliographical references

Black, Laura
The stem cell debate; the ethics and science behind the research. Enslow Pubs. 2006 128p il (Issues in focus today) $31.93 *
Grades: 7 8 9 10 11 12   **174.2**
1. Stem cell research
ISBN 0-7660-2545-4; 978-0-7660-2545-5
      LC 2005-37880
The author "describes what stem cells are, how they work, and what scientists are trying to make them do. She explains the arguments on all sides of the stem cell controversy so that young readers can form their own opinions." Publisher's note
Includes bibliographical references

Caplan, Arthur L.
Smart mice, not-so-smart people; an interesting and amusing guide to bioethics. Rowman & Littlefield 2006 210p $21.95
Grades: 11 12 Adult   **174.2**
1. Medical ethics
ISBN 978-0-7425-4171-9; 0-7425-4171-1
      LC 2006-14275

Caplan, Arthur L.—*Continued*

The author discusses "issues at the center of the new genetics, cloning in the laboratory and in the media, stem cell research, experiments on human subjects, blood donation and organ transplantation, and healthcare delivery." Publisher's note

The **Ethics** of genetic engineering; Maurya Siedler, book editor. Greenhaven Press 2005 140p (At issue) lib bdg $27.45; pa $18.70
Grades: 9 10 11 12   **174.2**
1. Genetic engineering
ISBN 0-7377-2370-X (lib bdg); 0-7377-2371-8 (pa)
LC 2004-42517

A collection of articles presenting viewpoints on the ethical debates in genetic engineering with chapters on agricultural biotechnology, cloning humans and embryonic stem cell research.

Includes bibliographical references

Genetic engineering; Scott Barbour, book editor. Greenhaven Press 2006 126p il (Introducing issues with opposing viewpoints) lib bdg $32.45
Grades: 9 10 11 12   **174.2**
1. Genetic engineering
ISBN 0-7377-3223-7   LC 2005-50210

"This anthology explores issues raised by the promises of genetic science, genetically modified foods and human cloning." Publisher's note

Includes bibliographical references

Genetic engineering: opposing viewpoints; Louise I. Gerdes, book editor. Greenhaven Press 2005 221p il lib bdg $33.70; pa $22.45 *
Grades: 9 10 11 12   **174.2**
1. Genetic engineering
ISBN 0-7377-2236-3 (lib bdg); 0-7377-2237-1 (pa)
LC 2004-43660

"Opposing viewpoints series"

A collection of articles explore the social and ethical issues raised by genetic engineering. Governmental and agricultural implications are discussed.

Includes bibliographical references

Levy, Debbie

Medical ethics. Lucent Bks. 2001 128p il (Lucent overview series) lib bdg $27.45
Grades: 9 10 11 12   **174.2**
1. Medical ethics
ISBN 1-56006-547-8   LC 00-9708

Discusses the advances in medicine and science in fighting disease, promoting health and extending life together with the conflicting values and dilemmas that are raised when applying these new discoveries

The author "presents a balanced account of the principles involved and the dilemmas in prioritizing them. The text is clear and accessible . . . and case studies personalize what could easily be perceived as dry and technical." SLJ

Includes glossary and bibliographical references

Medical ethics; Laura K. Egendorf, book editor. Greenhaven Press 2005 190p (Current controversies) lib bdg $34.95; pa $23.70 *
Grades: 9 10 11 12   **174.2**
1. Medical ethics
ISBN 0-7377-2212-6 (lib bdg); 0-7377-2213-4 (pa)
LC 2004-60566

"Chapters in this volume include a debate on the fairness of the health care system and examinations of the ethics of organ transplants, reproductive technologies, and genetic technologies." Publisher's note

Includes bibliographical references

Uschan, Michael V., 1948-

Forty years of medical racism; the Tuskegee experiments. Gale/Lucent 2005 112p il (Lucent library of Black history) lib bdg $28.70
Grades: 9 10 11 12   **174.2**
1. Human experimentation in medicine 2. Syphilis 3. Tuskegee (Ala.)—Race relations
ISBN 1-59018-486-6   LC 2004-10678

Contents: Roots of the Tuskegee study -- The Tuskegee study begins -- The Tuskegee study continues for decades -- The Tuskegee study: questions and problems arise -- The Tuskegee study: a national scandal -- Epilogue: the Tuskegee study's twin legacies

This book's "inviting format and directness in addressing hard issues provide an accessibility that is vital to understanding the lessons to be learned from this era in American social history." SLJ

Includes bibliographical references

176   Ethics of sex and reproduction

Cloning; Lisa Yount, book editor. Greenhaven Press 2000 176p (Contemporary issues companion) lib bdg $31.20; pa $19.95
Grades: 9 10 11 12   **176**
1. Cloning
ISBN 0-7377-0330-X (lib bdg); 0-7377-0329-6 (pa)
LC 99-49733

This volume "presents more than two dozen articles on the science and ethics of cloning. . . . Included are chapters on media perceptions (and misconceptions) of cloning, as well as ethical discussions of the process as it affects both animals and humans. Most articles originally appeared in 1997 with a handful updating the issue to 1999. . . . High-school students preparing position papers will find much information here." Booklist

Includes bibliographical references

Cloning; Bruno Leone, book editor. Greenhaven Press 2003 93p (At issue) lib bdg $27.45; pa $18.70 *
Grades: 9 10 11 12   **176**
1. Cloning
ISBN 0-7377-1338-0 (lib bdg); 0-7377-1339-9 (pa)
LC 2002-74278

This presents various opinions about the ethics of cloning. "Each short article, essay, or excerpt has been taken from a recent publication. Writers include professors of social thought, religion, ethics, bioethics, biology,

Cloning—*Continued*
and Judeo-Christian ethics. Additional material is presented by representatives of anti-vivisection societies, embryologists, and freelance writers. . . . A comprehensive list of concerned organizations and a lenghthy bibliography are included. This is a valuable tool for developing critical-thinking skills and a fine source for research." SLJ
Includes bibliographical references

Cloning; Nancy Harris, book editor. Greenhaven Press 2005 192p (Exploring science and medical discoveries) lib bdg $34.95; pa $23.70
Grades: 9 10 11 12   **176**
1. Cloning
ISBN 0-7377-1965-6 (lib bdg); 0-7377-1966-4 (pa)
LC 2003-56829
"Current cloning controversies are discussed in eight essays, which consider everything from the overriding question of whether humans should be cloned, to the pros and cons of regulating cloning technologies, therapeutic and reproductive cloning, and whether animals should be used in research. Six essays delve into the future of cloning. Wide ranging and probing, this compilation . . . is a smart place to introduce the subject." Booklist
Includes bibliographical references

Cloning; Louise I. Gerdes, book editor. Greenhaven Press 2006 141p il (Introducing issues with opposing viewpoints) $32.45
Grades: 7 8 9 10 11 12   **176**
1. Cloning
ISBN 0-7377-3220-2   LC 2005-46292
"In this compilation, authors debate some of the controversies surrounding the cloning of people and animals." Publisher's note
Includes bibliographical references

Cloning; William Dudley, book editor. Greenhaven Press 2005 c2006 112p il (Writing the critical essay) $26.20 *
Grades: 7 8 9 10   **176**
1. Cloning
ISBN 0-7377-3196-6
"An Opposing viewpoints guide"
This presents essays representing various points of view on the ethics of cloning and includes questions designed to aid the reader in analyzing each essay.
Includes bibliographical references

Cloning: opposing viewpoints; Tamara L. Roleff, book editor. Greenhaven Press 2006 176p il lib bdg $34.95; pa $23.70 *
Grades: 9 10 11 12   **176**
1. Cloning
ISBN 0-7377-3311-X (lib bdg); 0-7377-3312-8 (pa)
LC 2005-46165
"Opposing viewpoints series"
"Scientists, politicians, and seriously ill patients examine the issue of cloning and the issues of whether cloning is ethical, whether cloning research can cure diseases, whether adult or embryonic stem cells should be used in research, and whether cloning should be banned." Publisher's note
Includes bibliographical references

The **ethics** of human cloning; John Woodward, book editor. Greenhaven Press 2005 111p (At issue) lib bdg $28.70; pa $19.95
Grades: 9 10 11 12   **176**
1. Cloning
ISBN 0-7377-2186-3 (lib bdg); 0-7377-2187-1 (pa)
LC 2004-48217
Starting with an overview of the problem, articles discuss the moral and religious aspects of the human cloning debate
Includes bibliographical references

Reproductive technology; Cindy Mur, book editor. Greenhaven Press 2004 90p (At issue) lib bdg $27.45; pa $18.70
Grades: 9 10 11 12   **176**
1. Reproductive technology
ISBN 0-7377-2412-9 (lib bdg); 0-7377-2413-7 (pa)
LC 2004-46079
This volume has chapters discussing In vitro fertilization, commercial surrogacy, posthumous conception, human cloning and sex selection

179   Other ethical norms

Animal experimentation: opposing viewpoints; Helen Cothran, book editor. Greenhaven Press 2002 202p il lib bdg $32.45; pa $21.20 *
Grades: 9 10 11 12   **179**
1. Animal experimentation
ISBN 0-7377-0903-0 (lib bdg); 0-7377-0902-2 (pa)
LC 2001-40790
"Opposing viewpoints series"
This is an exploration of scientific, religious, and ethical viewpoints on various issues of animal experimentation, including cloning, genetic engineering, and animal donors for human transplants
"A well-balanced anthology of opinions . . . with an excellent assortment of further resources to help students and others research the issues." Booklist
Includes bibliographical references

Animal rights; Shasta Gaughen, book editor. Greenhaven Press 2005 160p (Contemporary issues companion) lib bdg $33.70; pa $22.45 *
Grades: 9 10 11 12   **179**
1. Animal rights 2. Animal welfare 3. Animal experimentation
ISBN 0-7377-2653-9 (lib bdg); 0-7377-2654-7 (pa)
LC 2004-52352
This volume explores some of the salient issues in the animal rights debate "including whether or not animals should have the same rights as people, the debate over animal rights in the food industry, and the ethics of animal experimentation." Introduction

Animal rights; Nick Treanor, book editor. Greenhaven Press 2005 222p (History of issues) lib bdg $34.95; pa $23.70
Grades: 9 10 11 12   **179**
1. Animal rights
ISBN 0-7377-1905-2 (lib bdg); 0-7377-1906-0 (pa)
LC 2003-67680

Animal rights—*Continued*

"This anthology includes chapters on the historical roots of the issue, the philosophical debates about animal rights, the controversial tactics used by some animal rights activists, and on the relationship between animal rights and science." Publisher's note

Includes bibliographical references

McCain, John S., 1936-

Why courage matters; the way to a braver life; [by] John McCain with Mark Salter. Random House 2004 209p il $16.95

Grades: 11 12 Adult   **179**

1. Courage

ISBN 1-400-06030-3   LC 2003-58626

Also available large print edition $18.95 (ISBN 0-375-43234-5)

Senator McCain tells his favorite stories of courage. "In offering anecdotes of individuals whose actions embody the rarity of true courage, his well-drawn examples range from Navajo leaders to Colorado River explorers to Jewish freedom fighter Hannah Senesh and Burmese dissident and Nobel Peace Prize-recipient Aung San Suu Kyi. He reflects on the wellsprings of courage, defining it as conscious self-sacrifice 'for the sake of others or to uphold a virtue,' encompassing actions that may be spurred by honor, outrage, a sense of duty, one's conscience, or moral obligation." SLJ

Phillips, Christopher, 1959-

Six questions of Socrates; a modern-day journey of discovery through world philosophy. W. W. Norton 2004 320p $23.95; pa $14.95

Grades: 11 12 Adult   **179**

1. Philosophy

ISBN 0-393-05157-9; 0-393-32679-9 (pa)

LC 2003-18200

Contents: What is virtue? -- What is moderation? -- What is justice? -- What is good? -- What is courage? -- What is piety?

"As he travels the world, Phillips challenges ordinary people with the central questions of Socrates' philosophy." Booklist

The author's "smooth, natural style enables readers to feel that they are part of the discussion at hand, making the book engaging and accessible to those who may have been put off by the formality of traditional works." SLJ

Includes bibliographical references

Yount, Lisa

Animal rights. Facts on File 2004 298p (Library in a book) $45

Grades: 9 10 11 12   **179**

1. Animal rights

ISBN 0-8160-5027-9   LC 2003-17507

This volume examines "the debate regarding animal welfare in contemporary society. It covers the responsibilities of laboratories, farms, and businesses that use animals or animal products." Publisher's note

Includes glossary and bibliographical references

179.7   Respect and disrespect for human life

Assisted suicide; Karen F. Balkin, book editor. Greenhaven Press 2005 208p (Current controversies) lib bdg $33.70; pa $22.45

Grades: 9 10 11 12   **179.7**

1. Euthanasia

ISBN 0-7377-2198-7 (lib bdg); 0-7377-2199-5 (pa)

LC 2004-47375

"Individual chapters address both sides of legalization, ethics, constitutional rights, and the influence of assisted suicide on society as a whole. Each one includes at least four commentaries on each position. This well-balanced presentation provides points of consideration that require sophisticated readers." SLJ [review of 1998 edition]

Death and dying: opposing viewpoints; James Haley, book editor. Greenhaven Press 2003 224p il lib bdg $34.95

Grades: 7 8 9 10   **179.7**

1. Death

ISBN 0-7377-1224-4   LC 2002-72223

"Opposing viewpoints series"

"Doctors, scientists, and those who have lost loved ones discuss the difficult issues surrounding death and dying such as easing the dying process, coping with death, extending the human life span, and the possibility of life after death." Publisher's note

Includes bibliographical references

The **Ethics** of abortion; Christine Watkins, book editor. Greenhaven Press 2005 112p (At issue) lib bdg $28.70; pa $19.95 *

Grades: 9 10 11 12   **179.7**

1. Abortion

ISBN 0-7377-2709-8 (lib bdg); 0-7377-2710-1 (pa)

LC 2005-45119

"Members of the pro-choice and pro-life movements offer conflicting arguments about whether—and in what cases—abortion can be considered ethical." Publisher's note [review of 2000 edition]

Includes bibliographical references

Euthanasia; Lisa Yount, book editor. Greenhaven Press 2002 174p (Contemporary issues companion) lib bdg $32.45; pa $21.20

Grades: 9 10 11 12   **179.7**

1. Euthanasia

ISBN 0-7377-0829-8 (lib bdg); 0-7377-0828-X (pa)

LC 2001-33778

Areas covered include "new technology; medical ethics . . . the legal changes and implications, primarily in Oregon and the Netherlands; and religion and ethics, including the fine line between active and passive euthanasia." Booklist

Includes bibliographical references

Euthanasia; Loreta M. Medina, book editor. Greenhaven Press 2005 235p (History of issues) lib bdg $34.95; pa $23.70 *

Grades: 9 10 11 12   **179.7**

1. Euthanasia

ISBN 0-7377-2005-0 (lib bdg); 0-7377-2006-9 (pa)

LC 2004-40501

Euthanasia—*Continued*

The essays contained in this book discuss the history of and the legal battles and current ethical debate over euthanasia and assisted suicide. Contributors include Charles Francis Potter, William Rehnquist, and John Shelby Spong.

Includes bibliographical references

Euthanasia: opposing viewpoints; Carrie L. Snyder, book editor. Greenhaven Press 2006 269p il lib bdg $34.95; pa $23.70
Grades: 7 8 9 10   **179.7**
1. Euthanasia
ISBN 0-7377-2933-3 (lib bdg); 0-7377-2934-1 (pa)
    LC 2005-55110
"Opposing viewpoints series"
"The four chapters explore whether euthanasia is ethical, if it should be legalized, if legalization would lead to involuntary killing, and under what circumstances, if any, doctors should assist in suicide." Booklist [review of 2000 edition]
Includes bibliographical references

Physician-assisted suicide; Gail Hawkins, book editor. Greenhaven Press 2002 75p (At issue) lib bdg $24.95; pa $16.20
Grades: 9 10 11 12   **179.7**
1. Euthanasia 2. Medical ethics
ISBN 0-7377-1056-X (lib bdg); 0-7377-1055-1 (pa)
    LC 2001-54325
"The first two pieces question the morality and ethics of physician-assisted suicide. The remaining essays explore the possibility of legalizing it: Does society now favor it? Would legalization lead to new forms of patient abuse? Contributors include doctors, psychiatrists, and members of activist groups such as the Hemlock Society and Not Dead Yet." Booklist
Includes bibliographical references

The **right** to die; John Woodward, book editor. Greenhaven Press 2006 94p (At issue) lib bdg $28.70; pa $19.95
Grades: 9 10 11 12   **179.7**
1. Right to die 2. Euthanasia
ISBN 0-7377-3439-6 (lib bdg); 0-7377-3440-X (pa)
    LC 2005-50522
In this "anthology, the authors examine whether or not each person has a right to control the means and timing of his or her own death." Publisher's note
Includes bibliographical references

Yount, Lisa
Right to die and euthanasia. rev ed. Facts on File 2007 312p il (Library in a book) $45 *
Grades: 11 12 Adult   **179.7**
1. Right to die 2. Euthanasia
ISBN 978-0-8160-6275-1   LC 2006-33424
First published 2000 with title: Physician-assisted suicide and euthanasia
This reference source contains an overview of the subjects, a chronology of significant events (including the Terri Schiavo case), biographical information on important figures, a glossary of terms, and an annotated bibliography.
Includes glossary and bibliographical references

181   Eastern philosophy

Creel, Herrlee Glessner, 1905-1994
Chinese thought from Confucius to Mao Tsê-tung. University of Chicago Press 1953 292p pa $15 hardcover o.p. *
Grades: 9 10 11 12   **181**
1. Chinese philosophy
ISBN 0-226-12030-9 (pa)
This history of Chinese philosophy and thought features discussions of: Confucius, Mo Tzu, Menacius, Hsün Tzu, Taoism, Buddhism, and Neo-Confucianism
Includes bibliographical references

184   Platonic philosophy

Hare, R. M. (Richard Mervyn)
Plato. Oxford Univ. Press 1982 82p (Past masters series) pa $9.95 hardcover o.p. *
Grades: 11 12 Adult   **184**
1. Plato
ISBN 0-19-287585-X (pa)   LC 83-159441
The author examines the chief Platonic concepts in their political and intellectual contexts
Includes bibliographical references

Plato
The selected dialogues of Plato; the Benjamin Jowett translation; revised, and with an introduction by Hayden Pelliccia. Modern Lib. 2000 xxii, 323p $24.95; pa $12.95
Grades: 9 10 11 12   **184**
1. Philosophy
ISBN 0-679-60228-3; 0-375-75840-2 (pa)
    LC 00-30552
This compilation gathers together Plato's most important writings. The topics addressed include: poetic interpretation; cross-examination to arrive at the truth; the nature of rhetoric, psychology and love; and Socrates' art of persuasion in attempting to save his own life
"This {work} is a needed and welcome addition to the translations of the *Dialogues*. Recommended for all libraries with holdings of the major philosophical writers." Libr J
Includes bibliographical references

185   Aristotelian philosophy

Adler, Mortimer J., 1902-2001
Aristotle for everybody; difficult thought made easy. Macmillan 1978 206p pa $13 hardcover o.p.
Grades: 11 12 Adult   **185**
1. Aristotle, 384-322 B.C.
ISBN 0-684-83823-0 (pa)   LC 78-853
Adler traces "in the simplest language and with occasional modern analogues, the logic and growth of Aristotle's basic doctrines." Publ Wkly
Includes bibliographical references

190 Modern western and other non-eastern philosophy

Great thinkers of the Western world; edited by Ian P. McGreal. HarperCollins Pubs. 1992 572p $47
Grades: 11 12 Adult   190
1. Philosophy 2. Theology 3. Science
ISBN 0-06-270026-X   LC 91-38362
"The major ideas and classic works of more than 100 outstanding Western philosophers, physical and social scientists, psychologists, religious writers, and theologians." Title page
"This guide to 116 selected authors . . . spans the ancient Greeks to the first half of the twentieth century. . . . The guide is arranged chronologically by the birthdate of the writer. Each entry contains birth and death dates, a list of the author's major ideas, an essay of three to five pages, and a short annotated list of secondary sources. . . . Its readable essays . . . are accessible to the layperson." Booklist

Magee, Bryan
The story of philosophy. DK Pub. 1998 240p il $29.95; pa $20
Grades: 11 12 Adult   190
1. Philosophy
ISBN 0-7894-3511-X; 0-7894-7994-X (pa)
                                            LC 98-3780
This "illustrated volume converts two-and-a-half millennia of Western philosophy into a colorful parade of provocative figures—from Heraclitus to Heidegger—who have enlarged the boundaries of thought." Booklist
"Writing with a clear and lively style, Magee provides an excellent introduction to the topic." SLJ
Includes bibliographical references

Western philosophy; an illustrated guide; general editor, David Papineau. Oxford University Press 2004 224p il $35 *
Grades: 9 10 11 12   190
1. Philosophy
ISBN 0-19-522143-5   LC 2004-10215
Contents: World \ Tim Crane -- Mind and body \ Jesse Prinz -- Knowledge \ Adam Morton -- Faith \ John Cottingham -- Ethics and aesthetics \ Brenda Almond -- Society \ Jonathan Woolf
"The lucid writing, with multiple examples and illuminating analogies, will engage readers and provoke them into thought before they know it. . . . This most attractive volume makes its discipline irresistible." SLJ
Includes bibliographical references

191 North American philosophy

Rand, Ayn, 1905-1982
The Ayn Rand reader; edited by Gary Hull and Leonard Peikoff; introduction by Leonard Peikoff. Plume Bks. 1999 497p pa $16.95
Grades: 9 10 11 12   191
1. Capitalists and financiers
ISBN 0-452-28040-0   LC 98-26698

This compilation contains excerpts from all of Rand's novels and serves as an introduction to her basic philosophy expressed in all of her works, fiction as well as nonfiction

193 German and Austrian philosophy

Nietzsche, Friedrich Wilhelm, 1844-1900
The portable Nietzsche; selected and translated, with an introduction, prefaces, and notes, by Walter Kaufmann. Viking 1954 687p pa $17 hardcover o.p.
Grades: 11 12 Adult   193
ISBN 0-14-015062-5 (pa)
"The Viking portable library"
Includes the complete texts of Thus spake Zarathustra, Twilight of the idols, The antichrist, and Nietzsche contra Wagner. Selections from other works, notes and letters complete the volume

200 RELIGION

Armstrong, Karen
The battle for God; fundamentalism in Judaism, Christianity, and Islam. Knopf 2000 442p $29.95; pa $15.95 *
Grades: 11 12 Adult   200
1. Religious fundamentalism
ISBN 0-679-43597-2; 0-345-39169-1 (pa)
                                            LC 99-34022
This is a "study of fundamentalism among Jews (in Israel), Christians (American Protestants), and Muslims (Sunni Egyptians and Shiite Iranians). Armstrong argues that all strains of fundamentalism, despite their differences, are fearful defenses against modernity. . . . The author is sympathetic to the human need for spiritual meaning, but she points out that the intellectual flaws of fundamentalist beliefs are customarily accompanied by paranoia, anger, and aggression—which, in turn, frequently betray the message of the faith." New Yorker
Includes bibliographical references

Bowker, John, 1935-
World religions; contributing consultants: David Bowker [et al.] DK Pub. 1997 200p il maps $35; pa $16.95
Grades: 11 12 Adult   200
1. Religions 2. Religion
ISBN 0-7894-1439-2; 0-7566-1772-3 (pa)
                                            LC 96-38277
Each chapter begins with an "introduction and is followed by one-or-two page sections that explain the basic tenets of the faith, symbols, events, people, buildings, works of art, and the differences and similarities to other religions. Hinduism, Buddhism, Judaism, Christianity, and Islam are included as are Jainism, Sikhism, Chinese and Japanese religions, and Native religions." SLJ

Controversial new religions; edited by James R. Lewis and Jesper Aagaard Petersen. Oxford Univ. Press 2004 496p $74; pa $29.95

Grades: 11 12 Adult   **200**

1. Cults

ISBN 0-19-515682-X; 0-19-515683-8 (pa)

LC 2003-24374

"This volume collects papers on those specific New Religious Movements (NRMS) that have generated the most scholarly attention. With few exceptions, these organizations are also the controversial groups that have attracted the attention of the mass media, often because they have been involved in, or accused of, violent or anti-social activities. Among the movements . . . profiled are such groups as the Branch Davidians, Heaven's Gate, Aum Shinrikyo, Solar Temple, Scientology, and Falun Gong." Publisher's note

Includes bibliographical references

Encyclopedia of women and world religion; edited by Serinity Young. Macmillan Ref. USA 1999 2v il set $295

Grades: 11 12 Adult   **200**

1. Women—Religious life—Encyclopedias

ISBN 0-02-864608-8   LC 98-39292

This work contains "more than 600 articles and more than 300 photographs with information about women in relation to most of the world's religions past and present, with emphasis on the major religions. . . . The articles are concise and evenhanded, providing brief critiques of scholarship and concluding with well-chosen bibliographies. Accessible to the general reader and a useful initial reference." Libr J

The Founders on religion; a book of quotations; James H. Hutson, editor. Princeton University Press 2005 xxx, 244p $19.95

Grades: 11 12 Adult   **200**

1. Statesmen—United States 2. Quotations 3. United States—Religion

ISBN 978-0-691-12033-1; 0-691-12033-1

LC 2005-15974

The editor has "gleaned, introduced, and edited quotations from 17 founders of the US. . . . This scholarly compilation, organized under 79 categories, shows the variety and complexity of the founders' thought, and will challenge current political and religious opinions of the Left and Right." Choice

Includes bibliographical references

Gaskins, Pearl, 1957-

I believe in—; Christian, Jewish, and Muslim young people speak about their faith. Cricket Books 2004 205p il $18.95

Grades: 7 8 9 10 11   **200**

1. Faith 2. Teenagers—Religious life

ISBN 0-8126-2713-X   LC 2004-1146

This is a "collection of excerpts from interviews conducted with almost 100 Chicago-area teens—Jews, Christians, and Muslims. Individual chapters include such topics as religious symbols . . . ; following (and breaking) religious laws; women's issues; and the idea of 'many faiths, one world.'" Booklist

"From this well-structured, open-ended presentation of

viewpoints, stereotypes are challenged, moral and ethical conflicts are discussed, and varied perspectives emerge on current issues." SLJ

Includes bibliographical references

Guiley, Rosemary Ellen

The encyclopedia of angels; foreword by Lisa Schwebel. 2nd ed. Facts on File 2004 398p il $75; pa $24.95

Grades: 11 12 Adult   **200**

1. Angels—Dictionaries

ISBN 0-8160-5023-6; 0-8160-5024-4 (pa)

LC 2003-60147

First published 1996

"Guiley's encyclopedia provides researchers with a historical and phenomenological approach to studying angels by examining what folklore, myth, and religion have contributed to research in the field. . . . Brief bibliographies follow most of the alphabetically arranged entries, which cover topics such as encounters with angels and the roles of angels in religion, culture, and art." Choice

Includes bibliographical references

The Illustrated guide to world religions; general editor, Michael D. Coogan. Oxford Univ. Press 1998 288p il maps hardcover o.p. pa $19.95

Grades: 11 12 Adult   **200**

1. Religions

ISBN 0-19-521366-1; 0-19-521997-X (pa)

LC 98-6784

An introductory survey of seven major world religions: Judaism, Christianity, Islam, Hinduism, Buddhism, and Chinese and Japanese traditions.

The information presented "is accurate and presented in lively prose, and the color photographs and maps greatly enhance reading pleasure." Libr J

Includes bibliographical references

Introduction to the world's major religions; Lee W. Bailey, general editor. Greenwood Press 2006 6v set $325 *

Grades: 11 12 Adult   **200**

1. Religions

ISBN 0-313-33634-2   LC 2005-30883

Contents: v. 1. Judaism / Emily Taitz -- v. 2. Confucianism and Taoism / Randall L. Nadeau -- v. 3. Buddhism / John M. Thompson -- v. 4. Christianity / Lee W. Bailey -- v. 5. Islam / Zayn R. Kassam -- v. 6. Hinduism / Steven J. Rosen

"Each volume contains an introduction by the author, time line, and narrative chapters on the history, texts and tenets, branches, practice worldwide (including demographics), rituals and holidays, and major figures. The end matter consists of a glossary, bibliography, and index to the set. . . . The volumes are straightforward and well structured to help locate the answers to most questions asked about beliefs, practices, holidays, and definitions of the major religions people encounter." Booklist

Includes bibliographical references

Williams, Juan
 This far by faith; stories from the African-American religious experience; [by] Juan Williams and Quinton Dixie. Morrow 2003 326p il hardcover o.p. pa $15.95
Grades: 11 12 Adult   **200**
  1. African Americans—Religion 2. African Americans—History
  ISBN 0-06-018863-4; 0-06-093424-7 (pa)
                        LC 2002-71884
 This study of African American worship "interweaves stories of individual spiritual journeys and accounts of church leaders and religious movements. The authors . . . [aim to] link blacks' faith to their ongoing fight for equality." Christ Sci Monit
 "Brief topical articles and captioned illustrations supplement the main text, creating a balanced, readable, and nuanced introduction to the power of faith to sustain the African American community." Libr J

The **Wilson** chronology of the world's religions; edited by David Levinson with contributions from John Bowman {et al.}. Wilson, H.W. 2000 688p $110
Grades: 11 12 Adult   **200**
  1. Religion—History—Chronology
  ISBN 0-8242-0978-8   LC 99-52362
 "The entries cover religion in the prehistoric and ancient world; world religions, sects, and cults; religious tolerance and intolerance; state religions; and many other topics. The chronology is supplemented by 250 informational sidebars which provide coverage of religions and sects, religious leaders, texts, and major events." Publisher's note
 Includes bibliographical references

200.3   Religion--Encyclopedias and dictionaries

Encyclopedia of religious and spiritual development; editors, Elizabeth M. Dowling, W. George Scarlett. Sage Publications 2006 xxiv, 528p $150
Grades: 11 12 Adult   **200.3**
  1. Youth—Religious life—Encyclopedias
  ISBN 0-7619-2883-9   LC 2005-12704
 "A SAGE reference publication"
 "This work addresses the complexity of factors involved in religious and spiritual development. . . . The work includes over 250 entries written by 125 international scholars on religions and traditions, institutions, and important texts and practices that have had an impact throughout history." Libr J
 "This book deserves a place in every library because it is a rich source of insight and information on topics of growing relevance and interest." Choice
 Includes bibliographical references

The **encyclopedia** of world religions; Robert S. Ellwood, general editor; Gregory D. Alles, associate editor. Rev. ed. Facts on File 2006 514p il map (Facts on File library of religion and mythology) $50 *
Grades: 7 8 9 10 11 12   **200.3**
  1. Religions—Encyclopedias
  ISBN 0-8160-6141-6; 978-0-8160-6141-9
                        LC 2005-56750
 First published 1998
 This encyclopedia "covers all the major and minor religions of the world, including the religions of the ancient world; the major religions practiced around the world today; religions of contemporary indigenous peoples; definitions of religious symbols and ideas; key leaders and thinkers; and terms and definitions." Publisher's note
 Includes bibliographical references

The **HarperCollins** dictionary of religion; general editor, Jonathan Z. Smith; associate editor, William Scott Green; area editors, Jorunn Jacobsen Buckley {et al.}; with the American Academy of Religion. HarperSanFrancisco 1995 154p il maps $47.50
Grades: 11 12 Adult   **200.3**
  ISBN 0-06-067515-2   LC 95-37024
 Published "in association with the American Academy of Religion."
 "The 3200-plus articles are written by a team of 327 religion scholars, experts in their respective fields. . . . In addition to the standard alphabetically arranged articles on persons, holy days, rituals, deities, scriptures, etc., there are ten major articles dealing with ancient and modern religious traditions and one on the study of religion." Libr J

Wilkinson, Philip, 1955-
 Illustrated dictionary of religions. DK Pub. 1999 128p hardcover o.p. pa $12.95 *
Grades: 11 12 Adult   **200.3**
  ISBN 0-7894-4711-8; 0-7566-2018-X (pa)
                        LC 99-30403
 "Following an introductory section that discusses what religion is and what role it plays in society, content is divided into chapters covering the major religious traditions. There are also sections on ancient and primal religions and on new religions. Occultism, the New Age Movement, and the Moonies are mentioned here. . . . Throughout the text, a wealth of illustrations depicts religious practice and artifacts and representations of religion in art." Booklist

200.9 Religion--Historical and geographic treatment

Balmer, Randall Herbert
Religion in twentieth century America; {by} Randall Balmer. Oxford Univ. Press 2001 142p il (Religion in American life) $28
Grades: 7 8 9 10   **200.9**
1. United States—Religion
ISBN 0-19-511295-4   LC 00-60674
The author "traces the evolution of various movements, including the Pentecostal, Fundamentalist, Evangelical, and New Age movements, the emergence of the Religious Right, Promise Keepers, and televangelism." Booklist
"This title is accessible and reliable, brief and lively, and makes a fine addition to most libraries." SLJ
Includes bibliographical references

The **Cambridge** illustrated history of religions; edited by John Bowker. Cambridge Univ. Press 2002 336p il (Cambridge illustrated history) $40 *
Grades: 11 12 Adult   **200.9**
1. Religions
ISBN 0-521-81037-X   LC 2001-37866
"The major religions get thoroughgoing treatment, with short introductions also given to the Zoroastrianism; the religions of Greece, Rome, Egypt, and Mesopotamia; aboriginal religions; and new religious movements. . . . Christianity receives a separate chapter as well as substantial treatment in chapters on Chinese, Korean, and Japanese religions. . . . This volume presents a large amount of information in an engaging way, offering much scholarly insight for the lay reader." Libr J
Includes bibliographical references

Gaustad, Edwin Scott
New historical atlas of religion in America; by Edwin Scott Gaustad and Philip L. Barlow; with the special assistance of Richard W. Dishno. Oxford Univ. Press 2001 xxiii, 435p maps $160 *
Grades: 11 12 Adult   **200.9**
1. United States—Church history 2. United States—Religion
ISBN 0-19-509168-X   LC 00-30001
First published 1976 with title: Historical atlas of religion in America
"A completely reorganized, updated, and expanded edition of Gaustad's 1962 original work and the 1976 revision, this beautifully illustrated atlas presents a historical narrative of America's rich and diverse religious past. Lively text along with 260 colorful, detailed maps and 200 other graphics provide the histories, migration, developments, and growths of religious communities in the United States."—"Outstanding Reference Sources." Am Libr

Queen, Edward L.
The encyclopedia of American religious history; {by} Edward L. Queen II, Stephen R. Prothero, and Gardiner H. Shattuck, Jr.; foreword by Martin E. Marty, editorial advisor. rev ed. Facts on File 2001 2v il set $137.50 *
Grades: 11 12 Adult   **200.9**
1. United States—Religion—Encyclopedias
ISBN 0-8160-4335-3   LC 00-69512
First published 1995
This reference source presents over 500 articles, ranging from a few hundred words to approximately 9,000 examining different religions, religious leaders, events, and other topics that helped shape the history of religion in America. The coverage extends from Puritan America to the moral majority
This "is an excellent and readable resource for the study of the history of religion in the U.S." Booklist
Includes bibliographical references

Religion in America: opposing viewpoints; Mary E. Williams, book editor. Greenhaven Press 2006 224p il lib bdg $34.95; pa $23.70 *
Grades: 7 8 9 10   **200.9**
1. United States—Religion
ISBN 0-7377-2957-0 (lib bdg); 0-7377-2958-9 (pa)
                                          LC 2005-40386
"Opposing viewpoints series"
"Contributors provide . . . views on both the private religious attitudes of Americans and the social significance of religious belief in the following chapters: Is America a Religious Nation? What Effect Does Religion Have on American Society? What Should Be Done to Accommodate Religious Freedom in America? What Values Should Religious Americans Support?" Publisher's note
Includes bibliographical references

201 Religious mythology & social theology

Breuilly, Elizabeth
Religions of the world; the illustrated guide to origins, beliefs, traditions & festivals; [by] Elizabeth Breuilly, Joanne O'Brien, Martin Palmer; consultant editor, Martin E. Marty. rev ed. Facts on File 2005 160p il map $29.95 *
Grades: 7 8 9 10   **201**
1. Religions
ISBN 0-8160-6258-7   LC 2005051101
First published 1997
This "looks at the key issues of faith as it exists today. It includes features on beliefs, traditions, festivals and practices of the major faiths and also looks at and discusses the differences within as well as between the faiths." Publisher's note
This "is a valuable resource, covering the beliefs and practices of 10 major religions and lavishly illustrated with color photos, maps, diagrams, and charts." SLJ
Includes bibliographical references

Campbell, Joseph, 1904-1987

Creative mythology. Arkana 1991 c1968 730p
(The masks of God, v4) pa $18
Grades: 11 12 Adult　　　　　　　　　**201**
1. Mythology in literature
ISBN 978-0-14-019440-1; 0-14-019440-1
First published 1968 by Viking
"This volume explores the whole inner story of modern culture since the Dark Ages, treating modern man's unique position as the creator of his own mythology." Publisher's note
Includes bibliographical references

Occidental mythology. Arkana 1991 c1964 564p
(The masks of God, v3) pa $18
Grades: 11 12 Adult　　　　　　　　　**201**
1. Mythology
ISBN 978-0-14-019441-8; 0-14-019441-X
First published 1964 by Viking
"A systematic . . . comparison of the themes that underlie the art, worship, and literature of the Western world." Publisher's note
Includes bibliographical references

Oriental mythology. Arkana 1991 c1962 561p
(The masks of God, v2) pa $18
Grades: 11 12 Adult　　　　　　　　　**201**
1. Oriental mythology
ISBN 978-0-14-019442-5; 0-14-019442-8
First published 1962 by Viking
"An exploration of Eastern mythology as it developed into the distinctive religions of Egypt, India, China, and Japan." Publisher's note
Includes bibliographical references

The power of myth; [by] Joseph Campbell, with Bill Moyers; Betty Sue Flowers, editor. Doubleday 1988 231p il hardcover o.p. pa $29.95 *
Grades: 11 12 Adult　　　　　　　　　**201**
1. Mythology 2. Religious art 3. Spiritual life
ISBN 0-385-24773-7; 0-385-24774-5　　LC 88-4218
Also available in paperback from Anchor Bks. $14.95 (ISBN 0-385-41886-8)
This companion to a public television series records conversations between Campbell and Bill Moyers. Campbell reflects on themes and symbols from world religions and mythologies and explores their relevance for his own spiritual journey.
"Campbell is the hero on his own voyage of discovery. This well-bound book on lovely paper with helpful illustrations from art is highly recommended for all libraries." Choice

Primitive mythology. Arkana 1991 c1959 504p
(The masks of God, v1) pa $18
Grades: 11 12 Adult　　　　　　　　　**201**
1. Mythology
ISBN 978-0-14-019443-2; 0-14-019443-6
First published 1959 by Viking
The author "discusses the primitive roots of mythology, examining them in light of . . . discoveries in archaeology, anthropology, and psychology." Publisher's note
Includes bibliographical references

Davis, Kenneth C.

Don't know much about mythology; everything you need to know about the greatest stories in human history but never learned. HarperCollins Publishers 2005 545p $26.95; pa $14.95 *
Grades: 9 10 11 12 Adult　　　　　　　**201**
1. Mythology
ISBN　0-06-019460-X;　　978-0-06-019460-4;
0-06-093257-0 (pa); 978-0-06-093257-2 (pa)
　　　　　　　　　　　　　　　　LC 2005-43341
The author "examines the myths created by societies ranging from Egypt, Greece and Rome to Africa, India and the Americas, proceeding . . . by way of question and answer as he surveys each mythmaking culture. . . . His survey provides a superb starting point for entering the world of mythology." Publ Wkly
Includes bibliographical references

Eliot, Alexander

The universal myths; heros, gods, tricksters, and others; with contributions by Joseph Campbell and Mircea Eliade. New Am. Lib. 1990 310p pa $15
Grades: 9 10 11 12　　　　　　　　　**201**
1. Mythology
ISBN 0-452-01027-6　　　　　　LC 89-38161
"A Meridian book"
First published 1976 by McGraw Hill with title: Myths
This volume provides a "retelling of so-called universal myths, which Eliot and associates have drawn from various cultures worldwide and organized by commonality of theme. . . . It is Eliot's contention that the ubiquity of such myths argues strongly for the essential oneness of humankind. Essays by Joseph Campbell and Mircea Eliade bolster this view." Booklist
Includes bibliographical references

Frazer, Sir James George, 1854-1941

The new golden bough; a new abridgment of the classic work; edited and with notes and foreword by Theodor H. Gaster. Phillips 1959 xxx, 738p $51.95
Grades: 11 12 Adult　　　　　　　　　**201**
1. Mythology 2. Religions 3. Superstition
ISBN 0-87599-036-3
"A comparative study of world religions, magic, vegetation and fertility beliefs and rites, kingship, taboos, totemism and the like." New Century Handb of Engl Lit
Includes bibliographical references

Human rights and the world's major religions. Praeger 2005 5v set $399.95
Grades: 11 12 Adult　　　　　　　　　**201**
1. Human rights 2. Religions
ISBN 0-275-98425-7　　　　　　LC 2003-68987
"Using the 1948 UN Universal Declaration of Human Rights as a springboard, these five similarly structured volumes examine human rights within the context of Judaism, Christianity, Islam, Hinduism, and Buddhism. The first part of each volume considers the historical development and analysis of the religion; the second is a selection of excerpts from relevant texts followed by brief biographies of the major thinkers mentioned and an anno-

Human rights and the world's major religions—*Continued*
tated bibliography." Libr J

"This set will be indispensable to those researching human rights in religion, as it pulls together important elements of the topic previously unavailable in a single reference work." Choice

Includes bibliographical references

McIntosh, Kenneth, 1959-
When religion & politics mix; how matters of faith influence political policies; by Kenneth McIntosh, M.Div., and Marsha McIntosh. Mason Crest Publishers 2005 112p il (Religion and modern culture) $22.95 *

Grades: 7 8 9 10   **201**
1. Church and state—United States 2. Religion and politics
ISBN 1-59084-971-X; 978-1-59084-971-2
LC 2005-3057

This is an "overview of where U.S. voters stand on the relevance of religion in their personal and public lives. The book explores topics such as abortion, same-sex marriage, and stem cell research, and it compares religious views in the U.S. with Canada's more secular perspectives. . . . [The book provides] a lucid perspective on different beliefs within and beyond various religions." Booklist

Includes bibliographical references

World mythology; the illustrated guide; Roy Willis, general editor. Oxford University Press 2006 311p il map pa $22.50 *

Grades: 9 10 11 12   **201**
1. Mythology
ISBN 0-19-530752-6; 978-0-19-530752-8
LC 2005-30779

First published 1993 by Holt & Co.

This book describes "the myths of Egypt, the Middle East, India, China, Tibet, Mongolia, Japan, Greece, Rome, the Celtic lands, Northern and Eastern Europe, the Arctic, North and South America, Mesoamerica, Africa, Australia, Oceania, and Southeast Asia." Libr J [review of 1993 edition]

Includes bibliographical references

201.03 Religious mythology-- Encyclopedias and dictionaries

Leeming, David Adams, 1937-
A dictionary of creation myths; [by] David Adams Leeming with Margaret Adams Leeming. Oxford University Press 1995 330p il pa $23.95

Grades: 11 12 Adult   **201.03**
1. Creation—Encyclopedias
ISBN 0-19-510275-4   LC 95-39961

First published 1994 by ABC-CLIO with title: Encyclopedia of creation myths

This book "provides access to information on the beliefs (both exotic and ordinary) of ancient civilizations from Sumeria and Babylonia to Egypt, Greece, and an-

cient Rome, from India and China to Japan and Indonesia, as well as the rich mythological history of Native Americans, the indigenous peoples of Australia, and many other cultures." Publisher's note

Includes bibliographical references

Mercatante, Anthony S.
The Facts on File encyclopedia of world mythology and legend; revised by James R. Dow. 2nd ed. Facts on File 2003 2v il (Facts on File library of religion and mythology) set $125 *

Grades: 11 12 Adult   **201.03**
1. Mythology—Dictionaries
ISBN 0-8160-4708-1   LC 2003-40262
First published 1988

"The entries discuss the folktales of both ancient and modern Eastern and Western cultures and clarify the relationship of these tales to the scriptural traditions of Buddhism, Hinduism, Judaism, Christianity, and Islam. Various botanical, zoological, and other references with mythical implications are . . . identified, and brief portraits of gods, heroes, demons, saints, and universal mythic figures are provided. . . . This reliable resource will be used by both students and scholars in public and academic libraries." Libr J

Includes bibliographical references

Philip, Neil
Mythology of the world; [by] Neil A. Philip. Kingfisher 2004 159p il map $24.95 *

Grades: 9 10 11 12   **201.03**
1. Mythology
ISBN 0-7534-5779-2   LC 2003-26801

The author combines "analysis about mythology and culture, first in general and then about each region of each continent, with brief versions of particular myths, commentary on their origins, and their connections with history, geography, spirituality, and more. . . . Philip's lengthy discussion on myth and society is as fascinating as the particulars of each story." Booklist

203 Public worship and other practices

Encyclopedia of religious rites, rituals, and festivals; Frank A. Salamone, editor. Routledge 2004 487p il (Routledge encyclopedias of religion and society) $150

Grades: 11 12 Adult   **203**
1. Religions—Encyclopedias 2. Rites and ceremonies
ISBN 0-415-94180-6   LC 2003-20389

"A Berkshire Reference work"

"Articles describing types of practices common to many cultures treat such topics as death rituals, hunting rituals, puberty rites, and sport and ritual. Specific occasions that involve ceremonies include Divali, Easter, Ramadan, and Yom Kippur. Some practices like cannibalism, haircutting rituals, and snake handling are described in separate articles." SLJ

"The entries can be understood by readers unfamiliar with the topics covered, but the work is suitable for all levels of scholars." Choice

Includes bibliographical references

How to be a perfect stranger; the essential religious etiquette handbook; edited by Stuart M. Matlins & Arthur J. Magida. 4th ed. SkyLight Paths Pub. 2006 403p pa $19.99 *

Grades: 11 12 Adult   **203**

1. Etiquette 2. Rites and ceremonies

ISBN 1-59473-140-3; 978-1-59473-140-2

First published 1996-1997 in two volumes by Jewish Lights Pub.

This guide "provides brief overviews of many religions: services, life-cycle events, home celebrations. It explains rituals so that those unfamiliar with them will know what to expect, how to dress, whether to bring a gift, and so on. It also has a glossary, explains various religious calendars, and lists religious festivals." Booklist [review of 1996-1997 edition]

Includes bibliographical references

Religious holidays and calendars; edited by Karen Bellenir. 3rd ed. Omnigraphics 2004 424p $84 *

Grades: 11 12 Adult   **203**

1. Calendars 2. Religious holidays

ISBN 0-7808-0665-4   LC 2004-041500

First published 1993 under the editorship of Aidan A. Kelly, Peter Dresser, and Linda M. Ross

This "handbook provides an overview of the time-keeping and holiday traditions of the world's religions. Part 1 has four chapters that outline the history of calendars. Part 2 covers 24 religious groups in 17 chapters, each surveying the history of the religion, then listing it chronologically and describing the holidays it celebrates. The 28 contributors provide accurate information in readable, double-columned articles, ranging in length from 66 pages on types of Christianity to one on Scientology." Choice

204 Religious experience, life, practice

Chopra, Deepak

Fire in the heart; a spiritual guide for teens. Simon & Schuster Books for Young Readers 2004 199p $14.95 *

Grades: 9 10 11 12   **204**

1. Spiritual life 2. Teenagers

ISBN 0-689-86216-4   LC 2003-20174

Contents: Before you begin -- Day 1. Do I have a soul? ; Baba ; You won't believe your eyes ; Everything is connected ; Soul training ; The way of the heart ; The way of the mind ; The way of silence ; The way of action -- Day 2. How do wishes come true? ; Life is desire ; The wishing tree ; Follow the thread ; Trust your soul ; A tale of ups and downs ; "What Do I Need?" ; Your time is coming -- Day 3. What is the supreme force in the universe? ; Alchemy ; The boy who needed love ; The secret of attraction ; Shopping for people ; Looking in the mirror ; Good versus evil ; Loving yourself -- Day 4. How can I change the world? ; Chasing rainbows ; Out of my way! ; Pure gold ; The sweet life ; A soul alphabet -- The last word

By recounting his own experiences at age fifteen, Deepak Chopra, a noted Hindu author and physician provides a blueprint for teens who are seeking their own spiritual paths

209 Sects and reform movements

Barghusen, Joan D., 1935-

Cults. Lucent Bks. 1998 96p il (Lucent overview series) lib bdg $28.70

Grades: 7 8 9 10   **209**

1. Cults

ISBN 1-56006-199-5   LC 97-26652

Describes the nature and history of cults and the different aspects of living in a cult, including the difficulty of leaving it

"A balanced and informative look at the subject. . . . A smooth prose style and careful use of transitions contribute to the book's readability. . . . Detailed notes and a list of works consulted reflect the breadth of the author's research." SLJ

Includes bibliographical references

Cults; Jill Karson, book editor. Greenhaven Press 2000 144p (Contemporary issues companion) lib bdg $34.95; pa $23.70

Grades: 9 10 11 12   **209**

1. Cults

ISBN 0-7377-0163-3 (lib bdg); 0-7377-0162-5 (pa)   LC 99-20382

Personal accounts, case studies, commentaries and overviews on various alternative religions

Includes bibliographical references

Lewis, James R., 1949-

Cults: a reference handbook, second edition. 2nd ed. ABC-CLIO 2005 341p (Contemporary world issues) $50 *

Grades: 9 10 11 12   **209**

1. Cults 2. Sects 3. United States—Religion

ISBN 1-85109-618-3   LC 2005-4574

First published 1998 with title: Cults in America

This book "includes the Jonestown murder/suicides in 1978, the Solar Temple slayings in 1995, and the Falun Gong cultists in China. Among the topics covered are a chronology of groups and movements; court decisions, legislation and governmental actions; worldwide statistics and data on cults; biographical sketches of some of the core figures involved; and a list of academic organizations and web sites dedicated to cults and the corresponding issues." Libr J

Includes bibliographical references

220.3 Bible--Encyclopedias and topical dictionaries

Eerdmans dictionary of the Bible; David Noel Freedman, editor-in-chief; Allen C. Myers, associate editor; Astrid B. Beck, managing editor. Eerdmans 2000 xxxiii, 1425p il maps $45
Grades: 11 12 Adult   **220.3**
1. Bible—Dictionaries
ISBN 0-8028-2400-5   LC 00-56124
This "dictionary contains nearly 5,000 alphabetically ordered articles by 600 biblical scholars on the books, persons, places and significant terms found in the Bible." America
"Up-to-date, comprehensive, and well written, the *EDB* is highly recommended." Libr J

The **Oxford** companion to the Bible; edited by Bruce M. Metzger, Michael D. Coogan. Oxford Univ. Press 1993 xxi, 874p il map $70 *
Grades: 8 9 10 11 12 Adult   **220.3**
1. Bible—Dictionaries 2. Bible (as subject)—Dictionaries
ISBN 0-19-504645-5   LC 93-19315
This volume "contains more than 700 signed entries treating the formation, transmission, circulation, sociohistorical situation, interpretation, theology, uses, and influence of the Bible." Libr J
"The many contributors read as a veritable who's who among biblical scholars. Although this companion is not meant to be an exhaustive reference, it is a highly reliable guide." Booklist

Vine, W. E. (William Edwy), 1873-1949
Strong's concise concordance and Vine's concise expository dictionary of the Bible. Nelson, T. 1999 2v in 1 $29.99 *
Grades: 11 12 Adult   **220.3**
1. Bible—Concordance
ISBN 0-7852-4254-6   LC 99-29685
This omnibus volume includes Strong's concise concordance, a version of the original published in 1894
This reference provides definitions, explanations of text, and concordance entries in one reference source

220.5 Bible--Modern versions

Bible.
The Bible: Authorized King James Version; with an introduction and notes by Robert Carroll and Stephen Prickett. Oxford University Press 1998 lxxiv, 1039, 248, 445p il, maps (Oxford world's classics) pa $18.95 *
Grades: 5 6 7 8 9 10 11 12 Adult   **220.5**
ISBN 0-19-283525-4; 978-0-19-283525-3
                                         LC 96-28858
"Reissued as an Oxford world's classics paperback 1998" Verso of title page
The authorized or King James Version originally published 1611.
Includes bibliographical references

The Holy Bible; containing the Old and New Testaments with the Apocryphal/Deuterocanonical books: New Revised Standard Version. Oxford University Press 1989 xxi, 996, 298, 284p map $29.99 *
Grades: 5 6 7 8 9 10 11 12 Adult   **220.5**
ISBN 0-19-528330-9; 978-0-19-528330-3
                                         LC 90-222105
"Intended for public reading, congregational worship, private study, instruction, and meditation, it attempts to be as literal as possible while following standard American English usage, avoids colloquialism, and prefers simple, direct terms and phrases." Sheehy. Guide to Ref Books. 10th edition. suppl

The new Jerusalem Bible; [general editor: Henry Wansbrough] Doubleday 1985 2108p map $45; pa $29.95 *
Grades: 7 8 9 10 11 12 Adult   **220.5**
ISBN   0-385-14264-1;   978-0-385-14264-9;
0-385-24833-4 (pa); 978-0-385-24833-4 (pa)
                                         LC 85-16070
First published in this format 1966 with title: The Jerusalem Bible
"Derives from the French version edited at the Dominican Ecole Biblique de Jerusalem and known as 'La Bible de Jerusalem.' The introductions and notes are 'a direct translation from the French, though revised and brought up to date in some places' but translation of the Biblical text goes back to the original languages." Guide to Ref Books. 11th edition

Seek, find; the Bible for all people: Contemporary English Version. G.P. Putnam's Sons/American Bible Society 2006 1725p $24.95; pa $15.95 *
Grades: 11 12 Adult   **220.5**
ISBN   0-399-15385-3;   978-0-399-15385-3;
0-399-15397-7 (pa); 978-0-399-15397-6 (pa)
Also available large print edition $29.95 (ISBN: 0-399-15386-1; ISBN-13: 978-0-399-15386-0)
"The CEV was published by the American Bible Society in response to an urgent need for a translation that would reach those many millions who are not reading the Bible. The goal was a serious translation—not a paraphrase—combining historical and scholarly accuracy with contemporary language that everyone can understand." Publisher's note

220.9 Bible--Geography, history, biography, stories

Calvocoressi, Peter
Who's who in the Bible. New illustrated ed., rev. ed. Penguin Books 1999 xxiii, 200p il map (Penguin reference books) pa $19.95
Grades: 11 12 Adult   **220.9**
1. Bible—Biography
ISBN 0-14-051426-0   LC 00-266958
First published 1987
"This work provides profiles, ranging in length from a sentence to several pages, of some 450 biblical characters. It is unusual in discussing the literature, visual arts, and music associated with many of these characters." Libr J [review of 1987 edition]

The **Oxford** guide to people & places of the Bible; edited by Bruce M. Metzger, Michael D. Coogan. Oxford Univ. Press 2001 xxii, 374p maps $35 *
Grades: 11 12 Adult   220.9
1. Bible (as subject)
ISBN 0-19-514641-7   LC 00-66900
"This dictionary is a spinoff from *The Oxford Companion to the Bible* (1993) from which the compilers have extracted the articles about people and places. Many of the more than 300 articles in *People and Places* are exactly the same as those in the larger *Companion*, except that the frequent parenthetical references to biblical passages have been deleted. Some articles are extracts from longer articles in the *Companion*. Articles range in length from a short paragraph, such as the nine lines devoted to *Gethsemane*, to as many as nine pages (for *Jerusalem*) or thirteen pages (for *Jesus Christ*). Longer articles are divided into sections, each with a topical subheading. . . . The bibliography has been updated to include references as recent as 2000." Booklist
Includes bibliographical references

The **Oxford** history of the biblical world; edited by Michael D. Coogan. Oxford Univ. Press 1998 643p il maps $60; pa $19.95 *
Grades: 11 12 Adult   220.9
1. Bible—History of biblical events 2. Ancient civilization
ISBN 0-19-508707-0; 0-19-513937-2 (pa)
                                            LC 98-16042
"Organized chronologically, the essays explore the many cultures of ancient Canaan, Israel, Judea, and Palestine from 10,000 B.C.E. to the rise of Islam in the seventh century C.E. Illustrations, maps, charts, chronologies, and bibliographies enhance the uniformly well-written essays. But the strengths of the work are its currency and breadth of coverage and perspective." Libr J
Includes bibliographical references

Tischler, Nancy M., 1931-
Men and women of the Bible; a readers guide. Greenwood Press 2002 267p il $59.95
Grades: 11 12 Adult   220.9
1. Bible—Biography
ISBN 0-313-31714-3   LC 2002-75347
This resource provides "information on 100 biblical characters and their cultural significance in Western civilization. . . . Entries are arranged alphabetically from *Aaron* to *Zephaniah*, concisely written, and adhere to a uniform pattern. Subjects are listed by name with the addition of etymological information. A synopsis of the relevant biblical story follows, utilizing the King James version of the Bible. . . . The author also includes information on each person as a character in later works, including Western literature, legend, and painting." Booklist
Includes bibliographical references

Who's who in the Bible. Reader's Digest Assn. 1994 480p il maps $32
Grades: 11 12 Adult   220.9
1. Bible—Biography
ISBN 0-89577-618-9   LC 94-17591

"More than 500 people, Aaron to Job's friend Zophar, are profiled in the alphabetical entries. . . . At the head of each biography is the pronunciation, original language, and meaning (if known) of the name; following is a summary and interpretation of that person's story, complete with biblical citations and cross-references in 'bold' type to related entries." Publisher's note

221   Bible. Old Testament

Bible. O.T.
The Dead Sea scrolls Bible; the oldest known Bible; translated for the first time into English [by] Martin Abegg, Jr., Peter Flint, and Eugene Ulrich. HarperSan Francisco 1999 xxii, 649p $39.95; pa $21.95
Grades: 9 10 11 12   221
ISBN 0-06-060063-2; 0-06-060064-0 (pa)
                                            LC 99-26866
This book "presents all 220 of the Dead Sea biblical scrolls, arranged to be read in canonical order." Publisher's note
Includes bibliographical references

222   Historical books of Old Testament

Bible. O.T. Pentateuch.
The contemporary Torah; a gender-sensitive adaptation of the JPS translation; revising editor, David E.S. Stein; consulting editors, Adele Berlin, Ellen Frankel, and Carol L. Meyers. Jewish Publication Society 2006 xlii, 412p $28
Grades: 11 12 Adult   222
ISBN 0-8276-0796-2; 978-0-8276-0796-5
                                            LC 2006-40608
A modern adaptation of the Jewish Publication Society's translation of the Torah. "In places where the ancient audience probably would not have construed gender as pertinent to the text's plain sense, the editors changed words into gender-neutral terms; where gender was probably understood to be at stake, they left the text as originally translated, or even introduced gendered language where none existed before. They made these changes regardless of whether words referred to God, angels, or human beings." Publisher's note

The **Torah:** the five books of Moses; a new translation of the Holy Scriptures according to the Masoretic text; first section. Jewish Publ. Soc. 1963 393p $20; pa $15
Grades: 11 12 Adult   222
ISBN 0-8276-0015-1; 0-8276-0680-X (pa)
Also available large print edition $24 (ISBN: 0-8276-0683-4)
This "translation of Genesis, Exodus, Leviticus, Numbers, and Deuteronomy was prepared . . . to present a version of the Bible that takes into account modern insights and knowledge of ancient times. . . . Of chief value to persons of the Jewish religion but of interest to Bible scholars of any religion." Booklist

Chittister, Joan
The tent of Abraham; stories of hope and peace for Jews, Christians, and Muslims; [by] Joan Chittister, Saadi Shakur Chishti, Arthur Waskow; foreword by Karen Armstrong. Beacon Press 2006 218p $24.95 *
Grades: 9 10 11 12   **222**
1. Abraham (Biblical figure) 2. Christianity 3. Judaism 4. Islam
ISBN 0-8070-7728-3; 978-0-8070-7728-3
       LC 2006-1274
"The three coauthors, representing the three major Western faiths (Judaism, Christianity and Islam), explain each religion's basis for a monotheistic multifaith movement by delving into ancient stories." Publ Wkly
"Delicate in telling but bold in message, this book encourages every reader to take an inner pilgrimage to understand better others' viewpoints." Libr J

Kirsch, Jonathan
Moses; a life. Ballantine Bks. 1998 415p map hardcover o.p. pa $14.95
Grades: 11 12 Adult   **222**
1. Moses (Biblical figure)
ISBN 0-345-41269-9; 0-345-41270-2 (pa)
       LC 98-25299
The author "distills the vast secondary literature that has grown up around the sparse biblical material on Moses. He draws on the myths, legends, and midrashim of Moses to soften ragged edges left by competing images of him as warrior, magician, shepherd, God's favorite, sorcerer's apprentice, and reluctant prophet." Booklist
Includes bibliographical references

225.9   Bible. New Testament--Geography, history, biography, stories

Ehrman, Bart D.
Peter, Paul, and Mary Magdalene; the followers of Jesus in history and legend. Oxford University Press 2006 285p il $25
Grades: 11 12 Adult   **225.9**
1. Peter, the Apostle, Saint 2. Paul, the Apostle, Saint 3. Mary Magdalene, Saint
ISBN 0-19-530013-0; 978-0-19-530013-0
       LC 2005-58996
The author "examines discussions of Simon Peter, the apostle Paul, and Mary Magdalene in Scripture and other writings of the first few centuries." Libr J
Ehrman "presents three of the best known and most important of Jesus' followers and does so in a way that is uncompromising in its scholarship yet utterly engaging for general readers." Booklist
Includes bibliographical references

230   Christianity. Christian theology

The **Quotable** saint; [compiled by] Rosemary Ellen Guiley. Facts on File 2002 368p $45; pa $16.95
Grades: 9 10 11 12   **230**
1. Christian life—Quotations
ISBN 0-8160-4375-2; 0-8160-4376-0 (pa)
       LC 2002-23540
This is a "collection of excerpts from the lives, thoughts, writings, and sayings of the saints. More than 3,000 quotes cover [such topics as] . . . daily life, work, family, marriage, relationships, the afterlife, the soul, and more. The quotes are listed under more than 250 categories, such as God; Creation; Natural World; Humanity; Angels." Publisher's note
"This book will allow readers, especially neophytes to the topic, to brush elbows with much grand and glorious wisdom." SLJ
Includes bibliographical references

230.003   Christianity--Encyclopedias and dictionaries

Encyclopedia of Christianity; edited by John Bowden. Oxford University Press 2005 xli, 1364p il $125
Grades: 11 12 Adult   **230.003**
1. Christianity—Encyclopedias
ISBN 978-0-19-522393-4; 0-19-522393-4
       LC 2005-48801
"This single volume contains 33 gateway entries to pivotal subjects; 300 major articles . . . [166] boxed items on various themes; and a who's who of 400 (mainly male) historically influential Christians." Christ Century
"This is probably the most comprehensive single-volume encyclopedia of Christianity." Choice
Includes bibliographical references

242   Devotional literature

The **African** prayer book; selected and with an introduction by Desmond Tutu. Doubleday 1995 xx, 139p $21; pa $9.95 *
Grades: 11 12 Adult   **242**
1. Prayers
ISBN 0-385-47730-9; 0-385-51649-5 (pa)
       LC 94-43444
Tutu "draws on the breadth and depth of African spirituality to assemble this little treasury of prayer and devotion. He has arranged material from throughout the African continent and the African diaspora into a traditional pattern of adoration, contrition, thanksgiving, and supplication." Booklist

248 Christian experience, practice, life

Lewis, C. S. (Clive Staples), 1898-1963
The Screwtape letters; with, Screwtape proposes a toast. HarperSanFrancisco 2001 209p $22.95; pa $11.95
Grades: 11 12 Adult   **248**
1. Christian life 2. Satire
ISBN 0-06-065289-6; 0-06-065293-4 (pa)
                               LC 00-49860
First published 1943 by Macmillan with title: The Screwtape letters; this combined edition first published 1961 by Macmillan
"A popular work on Christian moral and theological problems. . . . It is in the form of a series of letters in which a devil, Screwtape, advises his nephew, Wormwood, on how to deal with his human 'patients.'" Reader's Ency. 4th edition

248.4 Christian life and practice

Campolo, Anthony
Letters to a young evangelical; the art of mentoring; [by] Tony Campolo. BasicBooks 2007 280p (Art of mentoring) $23 *
Grades: 9 10 11 12   **248.4**
1. Christian life
ISBN 0-465-00831-3; 978-0-465-00831-5
"In letters to two fictional young evangelicals, Campolo endeavors to challenge and encourage young Christians in much the same way Paul did in his epistles. . . . As Campolo covers such topics as the religious right, fundamentalism, dispensationalism, homosexuality, abortion and Christian-Muslim relations, he admirably steers clear of telling his readers what to think. Rather, he explains his position on the issue at hand, explains the positions of his detractors and leaves his readers to decide for themselves." Publ Wkly

252 Texts of sermons

American sermons; the pilgrims to Martin Luther King, Jr. Library of Am. 1999 939p $40
Grades: 11 12 Adult   **252**
1. Sermons
ISBN 1-88301-165-5   LC 98-34295
The contents of this "anthology appear chronologically according to publication or, because they were composed to be spoken, delivery dates. . . . [This is an] exceptionally rich collection." Booklist
Includes bibliographical references

John Paul II, we love you; World Youth Day reflections, 1984-2005; edited by Barbara A. Murray. Saint Mary's Press 2005 141p il pa $9.95
Grades: 9 10 11 12   **252**
1. John Paul II, Pope, 1920-2005 2. Youth—Religious life 3. Church work with youth
ISBN 0-88489-820-2   LC 2004-14396

This book features "excerpts from the pope's official addresses at World Youth Days past, reflections by youth from around the world, and an 8-page insert full of color photos." Publisher's note

King, Martin Luther, Jr., 1929-1968
Strength to love. Fortress 1981 c1963 155p pa $17
Grades: 11 12 Adult   **252**
1. Sermons
ISBN 0-8006-1441-0   LC 80-2374
First published 1963 by Harper & Row
A collection of sermons addressing social injustice and racism.
Includes bibliographical references

261.5 Christianity and secular disciplines

Grant, Edward, 1926-
Science and religion, 400 B.C. to A.D. 1550; from Aristotle to Copernicus. Greenwood Press 2004 xxvi, 307p il (Greenwood guides to science and religion) $67.95
Grades: 11 12 Adult   **261.5**
1. Religion and science
ISBN 0-313-32858-7   LC 2004-17429
Contents: Introduction — Aristotle and the beginnings of two thousand years of natural philosophy — Science and natural philosophy in the Roman empire — The first six centuries of Christianity: Christian attitudes toward Greek philosophy and science — The emergence of a New Europe after the Barbarian invasions — The medieval universities and the impact of Aristotle's natural philosophy — The interrelations between natural philosophy and theology in the fourteenth and fifteenth centuries — Relations between science and religion in the Byzantine empire, the world of Islam, and the Latin West
Includes bibliographical references

Olson, Richard, 1940-
Science and religion, 1450-1900; from Copernicus to Darwin; [by] Richard G. Olson. Greenwood Press 2004 292p il (Greenwood guides to science and religion) $65
Grades: 11 12 Adult   **261.5**
1. Religion and science
ISBN 0-313-32694-0   LC 2004-47501
This book "explores the many ways in which religion—its ideas, attitudes, practices, and institutions—interacted with science from the beginnings of the Scientific Revolution to the end of the 19th century." Publisher's note
The issues discussed "should be especially helpful to those who are interested in the historical background to current science-religion issues being debated in the United States." Sci Books Films
Includes bibliographical references

270 History of Christianity and Christian church

Chadwick, Owen
A history of Christianity. St. Martin's Press 1996 304p il pa $35 hardcover o.p.
Grades: 9 10 11 12 Adult   **270**
1. Church history
ISBN 0-312-18723-8 (pa)   LC 96-2631
"A Thomas Dunne book"
This overview of Christianity is "illustrated, with the text and pictures working well together to give the reader a clear meaning of basic Christian concepts. . . . The facts are correct, the time lines are accurate, the voice is that of a lover of Christian history rather than a purely academic scholar." Libr J

272 Persecutions in church history

The **Inquisition**; Brenda Stalcup, book editor.
Greenhaven Press 2001 267p (Turning points in world history) hardcover o.p. pa $19.95 *
Grades: 9 10 11 12   **272**
1. Inquisition 2. Church history
ISBN 0-7377-0486-1 (lib bdg); 0-7377-0485-3 (pa)
    LC 00-58690
This work is a collection of readings which cover the Inquisition in its 800-year history: its roots, the resulting trials and punishments, the Spanish Inquisition and its aftermath, and the gradual demise of the persecution. The impact on national governments, the Jews, and the native population of New Spain are also discussed.
Includes bibliographical references

Pérez, Joseph, 1931-
The Spanish Inquisition; a history; trans. by Janet Lloyd. Yale University Press 2005 248p $26; pa $17
Grades: 11 12 Adult   **272**
1. Inquisition 2. Spain—History
ISBN 0-300-10790-0; 0-300-11982-8 (pa)
    LC 2004-114614
The author "tells the history of the Spanish Inquisition from its medieval beginnings to its nineteenth-century ending. . . . He explores the inner workings of its councils, and shows how its officers, inquisitors, and leaders lived and worked." Univ Press Books for Public and Second Sch Libr, 2006
Includes bibliographical references

280 Christian denominations and sects

Mead, Frank Spencer, 1898-1982
Handbook of denominations in the United States; [by] Frank S. Mead, Samuel S. Hill, Craig D. Atwood. 12th ed. Abingdon Press 2005 430p il $20 *
Grades: 11 12 Adult   **280**
1. Sects 2. United States—Religion
ISSN 0072-9787
ISBN 0-687-05784-1; 978-0-687-05784-9
    LC 2005-11023
First published 1951. Periodically revised
"History and present structure of Christian religious bodies in the United States. Reports on doctrines of different churches. Includes bibliography and index." NY Public Libr Book of How & Where to Look It Up

282 Roman Catholic Church

Allen, John L., 1965-
The rise of Benedict XVI; the inside story of how the pope was elected and where he will take the Catholic Church; [by] John L. Allen, Jr. Doubleday 2005 249p il $19.95; pa $12.95
Grades: 9 10 11 12   **282**
1. Benedict XVI, Pope, 1927-
ISBN 0-385-51320-8; 0-385-51321-6 (pa)
This is an account of the death of Pope John Paul II and the election of his successor, Joseph Cardinal Ratzinger, elevated to the papacy under the name of Benedict XVI in 2005.
This is "a rich and thoughtful analysis of the present-day Catholic Church and its complex new spiritual leader." Publ Wkly

The **Catholic** Church: opposing viewpoints.
Greenhaven Press 2006 219p il lib bdg $34.95; pa $23.70
Grades: 9 10 11 12   **282**
1. Catholic Church
ISBN 0-7377-3229-6 (lib bdg); 0-7377-3230-X (pa)
    LC 2005-46115
"Opposing viewpoints series"
This "anthology examines several recent controversies involving the Catholic Church, including an exploration of factors contributing to the recent sex-abuse scandal, the church's influence on politics and culture, and whether the church needs reform." Publisher's note
Includes bibliographical references

Flinn, Frank K.
Encyclopedia of Catholicism. Facts on File 2006 xxxi, 670p (Encyclopedia of world religions) $75 *
Grades: 11 12 Adult   **282**
1. Catholic Church—Encyclopedias
ISBN 0-8160-5455-X; 978-0-8160-5455-8
    LC 2006-9645

Flinn, Frank K.—*Continued*

This encyclopedia "covers the key people, movements, institutions, practices, and doctrines of Roman Catholicism from its earliest origins." Publisher's note

Includes bibliographical references

New Catholic encyclopedia; prepared by an editorial staff at the Catholic University of America. 2nd ed. Gale Group 2003 15v il maps set $1,295

Grades: 11 12 Adult   **282**

1. Catholic Church—Encyclopedias

ISBN 0-7876-4004-2   LC 2002-924

First published 1967 as an update to the Catholic encyclopedia

Published "in association with the Catholic University of America."

This encyclopedia "covers the history of the eastern churches, the churches of the Protestant Reformation, and other ecclesial communities as well as the Christian roots based in ancient Israel and Judaism. No comprehensive resource on Catholicism can be complete without touching on other world religions as well, including Islam, Buddhism, and Hinduism. This resource provides entries not only on the doctrine, organization, and history of the church, but also on the people, institutions, and social changes that have affected the church over the years. Arranged alphabetically, the entries run in length from half a page to several pages in length. All entries provide the name of the contributor and a bibliography. Cross-references to related articles are located throughout the work. Adding to the usefulness of the set are more than 3,000 black-and-white photographs, maps, and charts that complement the scholarly articles." Am Ref Books Annu, 2003

New Catholic encyclopedia: jubilee volume, the Wojtyla years. Gale Group 2001 681p il $95 *

Grades: 11 12 Adult   **282**

1. Catholic Church

ISBN 0-7876-4787-X   LC 00-60991

Published in association with the Catholic University of America

"Arranged into two parts, . . . {this volume} closely chronicles the life, teachings, and activities of Karol Wojtyla. First, 12 thematic essays review and critique the contributions of Pope John Paul II and his influence on the 20th century." Libr J

Includes bibliographical references

289.3   Latter-Day Saints (Mormons)

Bushman, Claudia L.

Mormons in America; {by} Claudia Lauper Bushman and Richard Lyman Bushman. Oxford Univ. Press 1998 142p il (Religion in American life) $28

Grades: 7 8 9 10   **289.3**

1. Church of Jesus Christ of Latter-day Saints

ISBN 0-19-510677-6   LC 98-18605

Chronicles the history of the Church of Jesus Christ of Latter-Day Saints beginning in America in the early 1800s and continuing to the present day throughout the world

"A solid resource for libraries. Illustrated with historical material and black-and-white photos. Time line and bibliography appended." Booklist

Includes bibliographical references

289.7   Mennonite churches

Amish roots; a treasury of history, wisdom, and lore; [edited by] John A. Hostetler. Johns Hopkins Univ. Press 1989 319p il hardcover o.p. pa $21.95

Grades: 11 12 Adult   **289.7**

1. Amish

ISBN 0-8018-3769-3; 0-8018-4402-9 (pa)

                     LC 88-31688

This is a compilation of "writing by and about the Amish from journals and letters, family and farm records, newspaper stories, poems, songs and stories. Ranging from the observations of the first Anabaptist immigrants in the 1700s to the present, the over 150 entries—commenting on church, family life, work, school and the rich Amish agricultural heritage—form a remarkably complete portrait." Publ Wkly

Includes bibliographical references

Hostetler, John A., 1918-

Amish society. 4th ed. Johns Hopkins Univ. Press 1993 435p il maps hardcover o.p. pa $20 *

Grades: 11 12 Adult   **289.7**

1. Amish

ISBN 0-8018-4441-X; 0-8018-4442-8

                     LC 92-19304

First published 1963

This book discusses the sectarian origins of the Amish, immigration history, family and community life, population trends, farming practices, technological innovations, education, medicine and the effects of government regulation.

Includes bibliographical references

292   Classical religion (Greek and Roman religion)

Adkins, Lesley

Dictionary of Roman religion; [by] Lesley Adkins & Roy A. Adkins. Facts on File 1996 288p il $44

Grades: 11 12 Adult   **292**

1. Rome—Religion—Dictionaries

ISBN 0-8160-3005-7   LC 95-8355

Also available in paperback from Oxford Univ. Press

This dictionary "provides more than 1,400 brief definitions and descriptions of deities, myths, and persons; cult sites and practices, and terminology and technology drawn from the religions of the Roman Republic and Empire. . . . Although the entries decidedly emphasize archaeology and art history . . . they are clearly and concisely written and refreshingly free of the unexplicated jargon or terminology that can intimidate novices." Choice

Beauman, Sally

The genealogy of Greek mythology; an illustrated family tree of Greek myth from the first gods to the founders of Rome; {by} Vanessa James. Gotham Books 2003 107p il map $25

Grades: 9 10 11 12   **292**

1. Classical mythology
ISBN 1-592-40013-2   LC 2004-272120

This "book/chart begins with the earliest surviving account of the creation of the universe from Chaos and quickly covers the children of Gaia, the rise of the Titans, and the triumph of the Olympians. The origins of each of the Olympians, their symbols, and their characters are briefly described. . . . Lists of the gods' children are followed by an index of 3000-plus individuals. When the book is turned over, it opens to a large map of the Aegean Sea, showing the places associated with mythic heroes. This begins the genealogical chart of the mortals who participated in the Trojan War, starting with their immortal ancestors and concluding with their descendants. A map of the Mediterranean Sea shows the routes of the Argonauts, Aeneas, and Odysseus. Lists of Helen's suitors, the 12 labors of Hercules, and more conclude the volume. . . . The appeal here is in the beauty of the more than 125 color photographs of Greek and Roman artwork, the concise biographies, and the elegant ordering of a complex topic." SLJ

Daly, Kathleen N.

Greek and Roman mythology A to Z; a young readers companion; revised by Marian Rengel. rev ed. Facts on File 2003 132p il map $35 *

Grades: 9 10 11 12   **292**

1. Classical mythology—Dictionaries
ISBN 0-8160-5155-0   LC 2003-48535

First published 1992

Alphabetically listed entries identify and explain the characters, events, important places, and other aspects of Greek and Roman mythology

"The format is accessible, making the book useful for school assignments, as well as enjoyable for general reading. Each entry provides a clear definition, and retells the stories associated with the character or place. The broad coverage, ample cross-references, and extensive index enable readers to recognize the many connections and interrelationships between characters and myths." SLJ {review of 1992 edition}

Includes bibliographical references

Graves, Robert, 1895-1985

The Greek myths. Combined ed. Penguin Books 1992 782p pa $19.95

Grades: 11 12 Adult   **292**

1. Classical mythology
ISBN 0-14-017199-1

Also available in an illustrated paperback edition

First published 1955

On cover: Complete edition

A collection of the author's interpretations of Greek myths based on anthropological and archaeological findings

Hamilton, Edith, 1867-1963

Mythology; illustrated by Steele Savage. Little, Brown 1942 497p il $27.95; pa $13.95 *

Grades: 8 9 10 11 12 Adult   **292**

1. Classical mythology 2. Norse mythology
ISBN 0-316-34114-2; 0-316-34151-7 (pa)

Contents: The gods, the creation and the earliest heroes; Stories of love and adventure; Great heroes before the Trojan War; Heroes of the Trojan War; Great families of mythology; Less important myths; Mythology of the Norsemen; Genealogical tables

A retelling of Greek, Roman and Norse myths

The **Oxford** dictionary of classical myth and religion; edited by Simon Price and Emily Kearns. Oxford University Press 2003 599p maps $39.95; pa $17.95 *

Grades: 11 12 Adult   **292**

1. Classical mythology—Dictionaries
ISBN 0-19-280288-7; 0-19-280289-5 (pa)
                                 LC 2004-298013

Spine title: Classical myth & religion

"Instead of separating mythology and Judeo-Christian religion into separate references, this work covers all religious life in the ancient Greco-Roman world. The result is a generally accessible and academically current compendium of information on gods and holy beings, religious practices, festivals, sacred sites, myths, authors, and texts of the period. The reader will find not only Athena and Zeus but also Jesus Christ and St. Augustine, Mani and Zoroaster." Libr J

293 Germanic religion and religious mythology

Daly, Kathleen N.

Norse mythology A to Z; a young reader's companion; revised by Marian Rengel. rev ed. Facts on File 2003 116p il $35 *

Grades: 9 10 11 12   **293**

1. Norse mythology—Dictionaries
ISBN 0-8160-5156-9   LC 2003-45758

First published 1991

Alphabetically listed entries identify and explain the characters, events, and important places of Norse mythology.

"This exciting volume breathes fresh life into ancient Norse Mythology. . . . More than 100 pages of entries, most a paragraph in length, are clearly written and engaging. . . . This is a sturdy and attractive volume that is well bound. Its large format, combined with good typesetting and use of white space, makes it inviting and comfortable to use." Am Ref Books Annu, 2004

Includes bibliographical references

294 Religions of Indic origin

Mann, Gurinder Singh
Buddhists, Hindus, and Sikhs in America; [by] Gurinder Singh Mann, Paul David Numrich & Raymond B. Williams. Oxford Univ. Press 2001 158p il (Religion in American life) lib bdg $28 *
Grades: 7 8 9 10   **294**
1. Buddhism 2. Hinduism 3. Sikhism 4. Asian Americans—Religion
ISBN 0-19-512442-1   LC 2001-45151
Presents the basic tenets of these three Asian religions and discusses the religious history and experience of their practitioners after immigration to the United States
"Solid information, a large selection of historical and contemporary photographs, interesting readings from primary sources, and accounts from school-age Buddhists, Hindus, and Sikhs combine to make this is a valuable resource." Booklist
Includes bibliographical references

294.3 Buddhism

Dalai Lama XIV, 1935-
Ethics for the new millennium; [by] His Holiness The Dalai Lama. Riverhead Bks. 1999 237p hardcover o.p. pa $13
Grades: 11 12 Adult   **294.3**
1. Ethics 2. Buddhism
ISBN 1-57322-025-6; 1-57322-883-4 (pa)
                                                LC 99-15138
The Tibetan Buddhist spiritual leader presents advice on leading an ethical life. His book is divided into three sections: the foundation of ethics, ethics and the individual, and ethics and society
"An important book for thoughtful teens to muse over now, and return to in the future." SLJ

Smith, Huston
Buddhism: a concise introduction; [by] Hurston Smith and Philip Novak. HarperSanFrancisco 2003 242p hardcover o.p. pa $12.95 *
Grades: 11 12 Adult   **294.3**
1. Buddhism
ISBN 0-06-050696-2; 0-06-073067-6 (pa)
                                               LC 2003-544630
This "book grew out of Smith's *The World's Religions*. . . . The first 12 chapters present his outstanding survey of the life and fundamental teachings of the 'Perfectly Enlightened One,' basic Buddhist concepts, and the major divisions of Buddhism (e.g., Mahayana, Theravada, Zen, and Tibetan). . . . Novak . . . is the primary author of the final six chapters, all-new sections on the migration of Buddhism to the West. Impressively, this informative portion with its emphasis on Buddhism in America lives up to the standards of lucidity so evident in earlier chapters." Libr J
Includes bibliographical references

Wangu, Madhu Bazaz
Buddhism. 3rd ed. Facts on File 2006 128p il map (World religions) $30
Grades: 7 8 9 10 11 12   **294.3**
1. Buddhism
ISBN 0-8160-6609-4; 978-0-8160-6609-4
                                               LC 2006-44006
First published 1993
Presents the story of Buddhism's origins and growth through the centuries, discussing its basic philosophy and the evolution of the three major schools of Buddhist thought.
Includes bibliographical references

Winston, Diana
Wide awake: a Buddhist guide for teens. Perigee Bk. 2003 290p pa $13.95
Grades: 7 8 9 10 11 12   **294.3**
1. Buddhism
ISBN 0-399-52897-0   LC 2002-192666
"Switching between anecdotes of her own journey in Buddhism and advice on how teens can apply the Buddha's teachings to their lives, Winston offers a personal and thoughtful introduction to Buddhist thought and practice." Booklist

294.5 Hinduism

Ganeri, Anita, 1961-
The Ramayana and Hinduism. Smart Apple Media 2003 30p il (Sacred texts) $27.10
Grades: 5 6 7 8 9   **294.5**
1. Hinduism
ISBN 1-58340-242-X   LC 2003-42352
Contents: Origins; Texts and teaching; In daily life
Explains the history and practices of the religion of Hinduism, especially as revealed through its sacred book, the Ramayana

Jones, Constance, 1961-
Encyclopedia of Hinduism; [by] Constance A. Jones and James D. Ryan; J. Gordon Melton, series editor. Facts on File 2006 xxxvii, 552p il (Facts on File library of religion and mythology) $75 *
Grades: 9 10 11 12 Adult   **294.5**
1. Hinduism—Encyclopedias
ISBN 0-8160-5458-4; 978-0-8160-5458-9
                                               LC 2006-44419
This encyclopedia "focuses on the most significant groups within this religion, noteworthy teachers and their contributions, the religions and cultural movements that enriched its history, and the diaspora of Hindu thought and practice around the world. Two major religious traditions that sprang from Hindu influence, Jainism and Sikhism, also have many entries." Publisher's note
Includes bibliographical references

Wangu, Madhu Bazaz
Hinduism. 3rd ed. Facts on File 2006 128p il
(World religions) $30 *
Grades: 7 8 9 10 11 12   **294.5**
1. Hinduism
ISBN 0-8160-6611-6; 978-0-8160-6611-7
                              LC 2006-44573
First published 1991
Presents the history, customs, and beliefs of Hinduism,
describing the mysteries and the myths that sustained it
growth over the centuries. Also includes information on
the Hindu national movement, conflict in Kashmir, and
India's first nuclear bombs.
Includes bibliographical references

Yoga, mind & body; {by} Sivananda Yoga
Vedanta Center. DK Pub. 1996 168p il $24.95;
pa $15 *
Grades: 11 12 Adult   **294.5**
1. Yoga
ISBN 0-7894-0447-8; 0-7894-3301-X (pa)
                              LC 95-44387
"Five main principles of yoga based on the tenet of
'simple living and high thinking' are introduced. Each
one is explained and illustrated in a separate section of
the book. The chapter on proper exercise is the longest
section and goes through a complete workout session
with full-color photographs and drawings of each position. The mental and physical benefits of each position
are listed as well as possible problems, and variations for
different skill levels. The chapter on vegetarian diet has
20 pages of recipes." SLJ

296   Judaism

Morrison, M. A. (Martha A.), 1948-
Judaism; by Martha A. Morrison, Stephen F.
Brown. 3rd ed. Facts on File 2006 128p il (World
religions) $30 *
Grades: 7 8 9 10 11 12   **296**
1. Judaism
ISBN 0-8160-6613-2; 978-0-8160-6613-1
                              LC 2006-46245
First published 1991 under the authorship of Fay Car-
ol Gates
An account of the history and rituals of Judaism, ex-
amining such areas as sacred use of the Hebrew language
and the role of the faith in establishing the contemporary
nation of Israel.
Includes glossary and bibliographical references

Robinson, George
Essential Judaism; a complete guide to beliefs,
customs and rituals. Pocket Bks. 2000 xxi, 644p
hardcover o.p. pa $20
Grades: 11 12 Adult   **296**
1. Judaism
ISBN 0-671-03480-4; 0-671-03481-2 (pa)
                              LC 99-55288
This book "attempts to provide the essentials of Judaism for novices, outsiders and those who, like Robinson,
rediscovered their heritage as adults. It's an excellent in-

troductory resource, vast but accessibly organized." Publ
Wkly
Includes bibliographical references

296.03   Judaism--Encyclopedias and dictionaries

Karesh, Sara E.
Encyclopedia of Judaism; [by] Sara E. Karesh
and Mitchell M. Hurvitz. Facts on File 2006
xxxvi, 602p il (Facts on File library of religion
and mythology) $75 *
Grades: 11 12 Adult   **296.03**
1. Judaism—Encyclopedias
ISBN 0-8160-5457-6   LC 2004-26537
This encyclopedia "covers individuals, places, events,
theologies, ideologies, organizations, movements, and denominations that span Jewish history. . . . This is a very
good one-volume resource that is especially accessible to
young adults and non-Jews." Libr J
Includes bibliographical references

The **New** encyclopedia of Judaism; editor-in-chief,
Geoffrey Wigoder; coeditors, Fred Skolnik &
Shmuel Himelstein. New York Univ. Press 2002
856p il $79.95
Grades: 11 12 Adult   **296.03**
1. Judaism—Dictionaries
ISBN 0-8147-9388-6   LC 2002-16614
First published 1989 with title: The Encyclopedia of
Judaism
This reference "seeks to present a balanced picture,
offering current thinking among scholars in Reform,
Conservative, and Orthodox movements and a roster of
contributors hailing from Israel, England, and the United
States. While the scholarship is solid, the material is
readily accessible to a popular audience, and the work is
magnificently illustrated." Libr J
Includes bibliographical references

The **Oxford** dictionary of the Jewish religion;
editors in chief, R.J. Zwi Werblowsky, Geoffrey
Wigoder. Oxford Univ. Press 1997 764p $110
Grades: 8 9 10 11 12 Adult   **296.03**
1. Judaism—Dictionaries
ISBN 0-19-508605-8   LC 96-45517
"The 2400 entries in this dictionary include unsigned
but revised articles from the editors' Encyclopedia of the
Jewish Religion (1966), as well as . . . new signed arti-
cles covering {topics} . . . and biographies related to the
Jewish religion and interfaith relations." Libr J

The **student's** encyclopedia of Judaism;
editor-in-chief Geoffrey Wigoder; coeditors Fred
Skolnik and Shmuel Himelstein; educational
editor Barbara Sutnick. New York University
Press 2004 390p il map $39.95
Grades: 9 10 11 12   **296.03**
1. Judaism—Encyclopedias
ISBN 0-8147-4275-0   LC 2003-65125
Revised and condensed edition of The new encyclope-
dia of Judaism, published 2002

The student's encyclopedia of Judaism—*Continued*

Identifies and defines people, places, and terms important to the Jewish faith

"The approximately 1000 entries in this handsome and comprehensive volume describe virtually all aspects of Jewish life and culture, including significant and lesser-known people. The articles are clearly written and abundantly cross-referenced. . . . There have been a number of recent reference works about Jews and Judaism for this audience, but this encyclopedia stands out. It is a must for any collection supporting the study of religion." SLJ

296.4   Judaism--Traditions, rites, public services

Oppenheimer, Mark, 1974-

Thirteen and a day; the bar and bat mitzvah across America. Farrar, Straus and Giroux 2005 256p $24 *

Grades: 11 12 Adult   296.4
1. Bar mitzvah 2. Bat mitzvah
ISBN 0-374-10665-7   LC 2004-16793

This is an account of the bar and bat mistvah ceremony as it is observed in the United States. "The bar or bat mistvah is a religious ceremony that initiates a Jewish boy or girl into adulthood." N Y Times Book Rev

"Oppenheimer's revelations are well contextualized and thoughtful." Booklist

Includes bibliographical references

Rush, Barbara

The Jewish year; celebrating the holidays. Stewart, Tabori & Chang 2001 176p il $35 *

Grades: 9 10 11 12   296.4
1. Jewish holidays 2. Jews—Folklore
ISBN 1-58479-030-X   LC 00-29718

This is a guide to the traditional celebrations and observances of the Jewish people. Also included are the holidays that have been created in the 20th century

"This beautifully constructed guide through the Jewish year takes readers far beyond mere observance to a true appreciation of the significance of the holidays. . . . Combining history, tradition, literature, and art, Rush has created a multifaceted work that informs, entertains, and even challenges. . . . Exquisite, full-color reproductions augment the text." SLJ

297   Islam, Babism, Bahai Faith

Armstrong, Karen

Islam; a short history. Modern Lib. 2000 xxxiv, 222p maps $19.95; pa $11.95 *

Grades: 11 12 Adult   297
1. Islam
ISBN 0-679-64040-1; 0-8129-6618-X (pa)
                                     LC 00-25285

This history of the Islamic faith focuses on the religion's attitude toward politics

The author "does an admirable job of presenting Islamic history from an objective, unbiased point of view." Libr J

Includes bibliographical references

Aslan, Reza

No god but God; the origins, evolution, and future of Islam. Random House 2005 xxiv, 310p $25.95; pa $14.95

Grades: 11 12 Adult   297
1. Islam
ISBN 1-4000-6213-6; 0-8129-7189-2 (pa)
                                     LC 2004-54053

"Beginning with an exploration of the religious climate in the years before the Prophet's Revelation, Aslan traces the story of Islam from the Prophet's life and the so-called golden age of the first four caliphs all the way through European colonization and subsequent independence. . . . This is an excellent overview that doubles as an impassioned call to reform." Booklist

Includes bibliographical references

Ben Jelloun, Tahar, 1944-

Islam explained. New Press (NY) 2002 120p hardcover o.p. pa $13.95

Grades: 11 12 Adult   297
1. Islam
ISBN 1-56584-781-4; 1-56584-897-7 (pa)
                                     LC 2002-30500

Translated from the French by Franklin Philip

"Cast in the form of an extended conversation between Ben Jelloun and his young daughter. . . . Father and child discuss the history of Islam, what it means to be a Muslim today, the challenges facing the Islamic world, and terrorism. . . . Its openness and emotional honesty, particularly when discussing the tragedy of 9/11, make it a valuable addition to a growing public discourse. As an introduction to the religion, it is spotty, but as a liberal Muslim voice of reconciliation, heartbreak, and compassion, it is priceless." Booklist

Bloom, Jonathan

Islam: a thousand years of faith and power; [by] Jonathan Bloom and Sheila Blair. Yale University Press 2002 268p il map (Yale Nota bene) pa $13.95 *

Grades: 9 10 11 12   297
1. Islam—History
ISBN 0-300-09422-1   LC 2001-96195

First published 2000 by TV Bks.

This book narrates the rise of Islam from its origins and the prophet Muhammad, through its height during the Abbasid Empire, the Mongol invasions of the 13th century to the growth of the Ottoman, Persian, and Mughal empires.

Includes bibliographical references

Farah, Caesar E.

Islam: beliefs and observances. 7th ed. Barron's 2003 500p map pa $14.95 *

Grades: 9 10 11 12   297
1. Islam
ISBN 0-7641-2226-6   LC 2002-25354

Farah, Caesar E.—*Continued*
First published 1968
This book traces the historical development of Islam starting with its founder, the prophet Muhammad in the early seventh century A.D. Its rapid spread as a religious, cultural and political force is detailed along with an examination of the Koran and other Islamic beliefs and moral obligations
Includes bibliographical references

Gordon, Matthew
Islam; by Matthew S. Gordon. 3rd ed. Facts on File 2006 128p il map (World religions) $30
Grades: 7 8 9 10 11 12 297
1. Islam
ISBN 0-8160-6612-4 LC 2006-25391
First published 1991
Contents: Introduction: the modern Islamic world; Muhammad and the founding of Islam; The spread of Islam; Koran, hadith, and the law; The variety of religious life in Islam; Muslim ritual life; The patterns of Islamic life; Islam and the modern world
Includes bibliographical references

Islam; origins, practices, holy texts, sacred persons, sacred places; {by} Matthew S. Gordon. Oxford Univ. Press 2002 112p il $17.95 *
Grades: 11 12 Adult 297
1. Islam
ISBN 0-19-521885-X LC 2002-70371
Originally published: New York : Facts on File, 2001
The author "discusses the rise of Islam; the centrality of its sacred text, the Qur'an; the importance of the Prophet Muhammad; the major developments of both Sunni and Shi'i Islam . . . the ethical principles and 'Five Pillars' of the faith; the role of the mosque and of sacred sites such as Mecca; the concept of sacred time and the Islamic lunar calendar; Muslims' beliefs about death and the afterlife; and Islam in the modern world." Publ Wkly
Includes bibliographical references

Hartz, Paula
Baha'i Faith; by Paula R. Hartz. 2nd ed. Facts on File 2006 128p il (World religions) $30
Grades: 7 8 9 10 11 12 297
1. Bahai Faith
ISBN 0-8160-6608-6 LC 2006-25360
First published 2002
This describes the history, people, scriptures, and beliefs of the Baha'i faith.
Includes bibliographical references

Hasan, Asma Gull
American Muslims; the new generation. 2nd edition, with study guide. Continuum 2002 204p pa $19.95 *
Grades: 9 10 11 12 297
1. Islam 2. Muslims—United States
ISBN 0-8264-1416-8 LC 2003-270056
First published 2000

This book provides basic information about Islam in America: its major tenets, its various sects and its ethnic groups, including African Americans. In an effort to help Americans overcome anti-Muslim stereotypes the author focuses on Muslim American family values, religious freedom and adaptation of their faith to American culture
"From her perspective as a youthful American Muslim feminist, Hasan provides a fluent evaluation of the Islamic community in the US." Choice {review of 2000 edition}
Includes bibliographical references

Is Islam a religion of war or peace? Jann Einfeld, book editor. Greenhaven Press 2005 108p (At issue) lib bdg $28.70; pa $19.95
Grades: 7 8 9 10 297
1. Islam 2. Terrorism 3. War—Religious aspects
ISBN 0-7377-3099-4 (lib bdg); 0-7377-3100-1 (pa)
LC 2004-59678
"Eleven opinions are presented here. The book begins with Osama bin Laden's justification for his attacks on Americans. The portrayal of Islam as a predominantly peaceful religion by President George W. Bush is countered by evangelist Pat Robertson. Additional perspectives are offered by Islamic scholars, a former Muslim, a female Muslim reformer, and a rabbi who is an expert on Islam." SLJ
Includes bibliographical references

Islam: opposing viewpoints; William Dudley, book editor. Greenhaven Press 2005 203p il lib bdg $33.70; pa $22.45 *
Grades: 9 10 11 12 297
1. Islam
ISBN 0-7377-2238-X (lib bdg); 0-7377-2239-8 (pa)
LC 2003-67545
"Opposing viewpoints series"
"Islamic and non-Islamic scholars and contributors to this volume debate Islam's relationship to violence and the West, the status of Muslim women, and other . . . questions." Publisher's note
Includes bibliographical references

Living Islam out loud; American Muslim women speak; edited by Saleemah Abdul-Ghafur. Beacon Press 2005 209p pa $15
Grades: 9 10 11 12 297
1. Muslim women 2. Women in Islam 3. Muslims—United States
ISBN 0-8070-8383-6 LC 2004-28161
"Themes about negotiating culture, romantic relationships, and faith and spiritual journeys often intersect in the 18 short essays that comprise the book. The majority of writers come from families that immigrated to the United States from the Middle East and Asia, but the book also includes two essays by African-American Muslim women." Sojourners

The Oxford history of Islam; {edited by} John Esposito. Oxford Univ. Press 1999 749p il map $49.95 *
Grades: 11 12 Adult 297
1. Islam
ISBN 0-19-510799-3 LC 99-13219

The Oxford history of Islam—*Continued*

"Contributors treat, among other things, Muslim history, law, and society; art and architecture; and regional differences. Chapters on the 'Globalization of Islam' and 'Contemporary Islam' are particularly relevant to current events. . . . An ideal one-volume source." Libr J

Includes bibliographical references

Riddell, Peter G.

Islam in context; past, present, and future; {by} Peter G. Riddell and Peter Cotterell. Baker Academic 2003 231p il map pa $17.99

Grades: 11 12 Adult   **297**

1. Islam 2. Islamic civilization

ISBN 0-8010-2627-X   LC 2002-154564

"Written primarily for Christians, this overview of historical and contemporary conflicts of the Islamic world first briefly introduces Islam and Muhammad, and then portrays Islam as a movement containing coexisting strands of violence and pacifism from the very start of its existence as a political entity. . . . The viewpoint throughout is, of course, decidedly pro-Christian, but the information Riddell and Cotterell relay is accurate and well organized. Christians interested in the history of Islam and its relationship to Christianity would do well to start here." Booklist

Includes bibliographical references

Siddiqui, Haroon

Being Muslim. Groundwood Books 2006 160p il (Groundwork guides) $15.95

Grades: 8 9 10 11 12   **297**

1. Islam 2. Muslims

ISBN 978-0-88899-785-2; 0-88899-785-X

"House of Anansi Press"

"In the wake of 9/11, 'Islam-bashing' bears all the symptoms of racism. . . . That's the argument of award-winning Canadian journalist Siddiqui. . . . His clear, passionate discussion confronts international issues that are in the news now. . . . This timely volume . . . is sure to spark debate." Booklist

Includes bibliographical references

Women in Islam; Margaret Speaker Yuan, book editor. Greenhaven Press 2005 128p (At issue) lib bdg $28.70; pa $19.95 *

Grades: 9 10 11 12   **297**

1. Women in Islam

ISBN 0-7377-2759-4 (lib bdg); 0-7377-2760-8 (pa)

LC 2004-54104

"This book presents viewpoints that address many of the concerns for women in Islam, from dress to property rights to personal rights." Publisher's note

Includes bibliographical references

297.1   Sources of Islam

Koran.

The meaning of the glorious Koran; an explanatory translation by Marmaduke Pickthall; with an introduction by William Montgomery Watt. A.A. Knopf, Distributed by Random House 1992 xxiv, 693p il $22 *

Grades: 7 8 9 10 11 12 Adult   **297.1**

ISBN 0-679-41736-2; 978-0-679-41736-1

LC 92-52928

"Everyman's library"

This translation first published 1930

"The sacred scripture of Islam, regarded by Muslims as the Word of God, and except in sura I.—which is a prayer to God—and some few passages in which Muhammad or the angels speak in the first person, the speaker throughout is God." Ency Britannica

299   Religions not provided for elsewhere

The **Gnostic** Bible; edited by Willis Barnstone and Marvin Meyer. Shambhala 2003 860p $39.95; pa $24.95

Grades: 11 12 Adult   **299**

1. Gnosticism

ISBN 1-57062-242-6; 1-59030-199-4 (pa)

LC 2003-7148

"The book provides Gnostic texts from their Jewish origins, into early Christianities, on into the medieval world. Though it concentrates on the early Jewish-Christian matrix of early Gnosticism, the collection . . . manifests the breadth and depth of Gnostic variations in neo-Platonist, Manichean, Mandean, Islam, and Cathar movements." Choice

"This book may well be the most comprehensive collection of Gnostic materials ever gathered in one volume." Publ Wkly

Green, Miranda J. (Miranda Jane)

The world of the Druids. Thames & Hudson 1997 192p il maps pa $24.95

Grades: 9 10 11 12   **299**

1. Druids and Druidism 2. Celts

ISBN 0-500-05083-X; 0-500-28571-3 (pa)

LC 96-61291

Published in the United Kingdom with title: Exploring the world of the Druids

Green presents a study of the Druids. She "begins by analyzing the classical writings on Druids. She also discusses the role of historical and archaeological analysis. . . . The author examines the archaeological finds and the conclusions drawn from that. She discusses the Druid resurgence in the 19th century and the Druids' role in the 20th-century neopagan movement." Libr J

"The wide-ranging illustrations from ancient objects to modern ceremonies and modern Druids that are linked with an enthralling text make this a remarkable book." Hist Today

Includes bibliographical references

299.5 Religions of East and Southeast Asian origin

Berthrong, John H., 1946-
Confucianism; a short introduction; [by] John H. and Evelyn Nagai Berthrong. Oneworld Publs. 2000 209p il pa $23.95 *
Grades: 9 10 11 12   **299.5**
1. Confucianism
ISBN 1-85168-236-8
This book defines what Confucianism is, its underlying principles and its history, development and impact on Chinese life, from families to the imperial state
Includes bibliographical references

Birrell, Anne
Chinese myths. University of Tex. Press 2000 80p (Legendary past) pa $14.95
Grades: 9 10 11 12   **299.5**
1. Oriental mythology
ISBN 0-292-70879-3   LC 00-39296
Published in cooperation with British Museum Press
This book explores the tradition of Chinese myths in the context of world mythology. Topics include: origins and creation myths; myths of the flood; the divine cosmos; gender in myth; metamorphoses; mythic heroes and heroines; and fabled plants and animals

Brennan, J. H.
The magical I ching. Llewellyn Publs. 2000 247p pa $14.95
Grades: 9 10 11 12   **299.5**
1. I ching 2. Divination
ISBN 1-567-18087-6   LC 00-24132
This work presents the history of the I Ching and explains the magical spiritual technique behind this ancient oracle. It also shows how to develop the symbols used in I Ching by using several different methods and analyzes each of the possible sixty-four hexagrams that form the basis of the oracle
Includes bibliographical references

Hartz, Paula
Shinto; [by] Paula R. Hartz. updated edition. Facts on File 2004 128p il (World religions) $30 *
Grades: 9 10 11 12   **299.5**
1. Shinto 2. Japan—Religion
ISBN 0-8160-5725-7   LC 2004-40376
Discusses the history of the Shinto religion in Japan, describing its origins, basic beliefs, rituals, and festivals, and its place in Japanese society.
Includes bibliographical references

Taoism; by Paula R. Hartz. Updated ed. Facts on File 2004 128p il (World religions) $30 *
Grades: 7 8 9 10 11 12   **299.5**
1. Taoism
ISBN 0-8160-5724-9   LC 2004-43224
First published 1993

This book "traces the progress of Taoist thought, from the great *Tao Te Ching* or 'The Book of the Way and Its Power,' by Laozi to the contemporary *Tao of Physics* by Fritjof Capra. It also examines the restoration of Taoism under China's religious freedom clause, the slow rebirth of Taoist monasticism, renewed interest in Taoism in China and abroad, and the impact of tourism on the monastic tradition." Publisher's note
Includes bibliographical references

Hoobler, Thomas
Confucianism; by Thomas and Dorothy Hoobler. Updated ed. Facts on File 2004 128p il (World religions) $30 *
Grades: 9 10 11 12   **299.5**
1. Confucianism
ISBN 0-8160-5728-1   LC 2004-43250
First published 1993
Describes how the teachings of Confucius evolved from a social order to a religion, infusing all phases of Chinese life for 2000 years.

The **Wisdom** of the Tao; editor, Julian F. Pas. Oneworld Publs. 2000 223p il $15.95
Grades: 9 10 11 12   **299.5**
1. Taoism
ISBN 1-85168-232-5
Partial contents: The Scriptures of Taoism; The mystery of the Tao and its power; Cosmic reality, life and death; The sage-ruler; Mystical sparkles; Taoist moral principles; Language, dreams and utopias
Includes bibliographical references

299.6 Religions originating among Black Africans and people of Black African descent

Galembo, Phyllis
Vodou; visions and voices of Haiti. Ten Speed Press 2005 xxx, 113p il pa $24.95
Grades: 9 10 11 12   **299.6**
1. Voodooism 2. Haiti
ISBN 1-58008-676-4; 978-1-58008-676-9
First published 1998
The book delves into the symbols and spiritual tradition of Voodoo or Vodou. Both the divine and human faces of real Haitian Vodou are presented together with its current practice involving priestesses, zombies, snakes and swamps.
Includes bibliographical references

Lugira, Aloysius Muzzanganda
African religion; by Aloysius M. Lugira. rev ed. Facts on File 2004 128p il (World religions) $30 *
Grades: 9 10 11 12   **299.6**
1. Africa—Religion
ISBN 0-8160-5729-X   LC 2004-46906
First published 1999

Lugira, Aloysius Muzzanganda—*Continued*

Explores indigenous African religion and its basic beliefs, discussing oral tradition, ideas of the Supreme Being, rites and rituals, sacred spaces and places, and mystical forces.

"Students doing reports on religions should find this a useful source." Booklist

Includes bibliographical references

299.7 Religions of North American native origin

Hartz, Paula

Native American religions; by Paula R. Hartz. updated edition. Facts on File 2004 128p il (World religions) $30 *

Grades: 7 8 9 10 11 12   **299.7**

1. Native Americans—Religion 2. Native Americans—Rites and ceremonies

ISBN 0-8160-5727-3   LC 2004-46907

First published 1997

"Presents the common traits shared among the diverse Native American tribes, the ceremonies and rituals that are an intrinsic part of the lives of tribe members, the ethical and religious principles that guide believers to living a harmonious and balanced life, and the relationship between Native American religions and Christianity." Publisher's note

Includes bibliographical references

Hirschfelder, Arlene B.

The encyclopedia of Native American religions; [by] Arlene Hirschfelder, Paulette Molin; foreword by Walter R. Echo-Hawk. updated ed. Facts on File 2000 390p il $75

Grades: 11 12 Adult   **299.7**

1. Native Americans—Religion—Encyclopedias

ISBN 0-8160-2017-5   LC 99-21586

First published 1991

"The entries in this encyclopedia provide descriptions of religious ceremonies and terminology; biographies of native American religious leaders, missionaries, and others who have influenced the practice of these religions; summaries of major court cases affecting native religious practices; healing and other ceremonial practices that are spiritual rather than religious in nature; and some . . . mythology." Booklist [review of 1991 edition]

Includes bibliographical references

300 SOCIAL SCIENCES

300.3 Social sciences--Encyclopedias and dictionaries

Dictionary of the social sciences; edited by Craig Calhoun. Oxford Univ. Press 2002 563p $75

Grades: 11 12 Adult   **300.3**

1. Social sciences—Dictionaries

ISBN 0-19-512371-9   LC 00-68151

This dictionary provides "definitions of key terms, offering entries that also discuss the intellectual issues behind the terms' usage. The entries cover all the social sciences except for law, education, and public administration. . . . Some 275 biographies are included." Libr J

Includes bibliographical references

301 Sociology and anthropology

A **Doomsday** reader; prophets, predictors, and hucksters of salvation; edited by Ted Daniels. New York Univ. Press 1999 253p hardcover o.p. pa $18.95

Grades: 11 12 Adult   **301**

1. Survivalism 2. Millennium 3. Militia movements
4. White supremacy movements

ISBN 0-8147-1908-2; 0-8147-1909-0 (pa)

       LC 99-6337

This work is a collection of apocalyptic pronouncements, edicts, scriptures and other writings by such diverse groups as the Branch Davidians, the Order of the Solar Temple, Heaven's Gate, white supremacists as well as the soothsayers and portraits of doom.

"This crash course in doomsday literacy may provide as much as many libraries will ever need on some of its contents." Booklist

Includes bibliographical references

302.2 Communication

Biedermann, Hans, 1930-

Dictionary of symbolism; cultural icons and the meanings behind them; translated by James Hulbert. Meridan Book 1994 465p il pa $25 *

Grades: 11 12 Adult   **302.2**

1. Signs and symbols

ISBN 0-452-01118-3   LC 93-30616

Original German edition, 1989

This dictionary "incorporates symbols that originated in Asia, Africa, Europe and the 'New World'. There are almost 600 entries from mythology, fairy tale, psychology, religion, and sociology, plus historical and legendary figures. With 2000 black-and-white illustrations, the book is highly attractive. The symbols are accompanied by thorough interpretations based on various sources." SLJ

Includes bibliographical references

The **Complete** dictionary of symbols; Jack Tresidder, general editor. Chronicle Books 2005 544p il $22.95 *

Grades: 11 12 Adult   **302.2**

1. Signs and symbols

ISBN 0-8118-4767-5

First published 2004 in the United Kingdom

"The greater part of the dictionary consists of 2,000 alphabetical entries on figures (many biblical and classical), myths, animals, natural phenomena, ideograms, and artistic and cultural works. Entries include the Slavic Baba Iaga, the Japanese Susano, [and] the Indian Mahabharata. . . . The book is inexpensive and well-constructed." Choice

Liungman, Carl G., 1938-
Dictionary of symbols. W.W. Norton 1994 596p
il pa $21.95 *
Grades: 11 12 Adult   **302.2**
1. Signs and symbols 2. Picture writing
ISBN 0-393-31236-4; 978-0-393-31236-2
Original Swedish edition, 1974
This dictionary groups "icons according to their graphical style rather than their meaning. For example, all
symbols based upon the cross are included in one chapter, those based upon the triangle in another, and those
based upon the circle in yet another. Each symbol is succinctly defined and a source of origin (if known) is giv-
en. To enhance access, both name and form indexes are
provided. This work will certainly become one of the
key sources for tracing symbols and their meanings." Am
Libr
Includes bibliographical references

302.23 Media (Means of communication)

King, C. Richard
Media images and representations; foreword by
Walter Echo-Hawk; introduction by Paul Rosier.
Chelsea House Publishers 2006 117p il
(Contemporary Native American voices) lib bdg
$30
Grades: 9 10 11 12   **302.23**
1. Native Americans in mass media
ISBN 0-7910-7968-6   LC 2005-7546
This book "examines the wide spectrum of informa-
tion by and/or about American Indian cultures in film,
television, journalism, and on the Internet, as well as
high school, collegiate, and professional sports mascots."
SLJ
Includes bibliographical references

Mass media: opposing viewpoints; William
Dudley, book editor. Greenhaven Press 2005
218p il $33.70; pa $22.45 *
Grades: 8 9 10 11 12   **302.23**
1. Mass media
ISBN 0-7377-2242-8; 0-7377-2243-6 (pa)
LC 2004-42401
"Opposing viewpoints series"
Presents opposing viewpoints on various aspects of
mass media including television's affect on society,
whether or not advertising is harmful, the influence of
media on politics, whether or not pornography on the
Internet should be regulated, and the regulation of televi-
sion for children
Includes bibliographical references

McLuhan, Marshall, 1911-1980
Understanding media; the extensions of man;
introduction by Lewis H. Lapham. MIT Press
1994 xxiii, 365p pa $19.95 *
Grades: 11 12 Adult   **302.23**
1. Mass media 2. Communication 3. Technology and
civilization
ISBN 0-262-63159-8   LC 94-27722

A reissue of the title first published 1964 by McGraw-
Hill
The premise of the book is that the form of any medium, rather than its content determines what is being
communicated. The author examines the various media to
show how their forms effect "the patterning of human associations"
Includes bibliographical references

Media bias; Stuart A. Kallen, book editor.
Greenhaven Press 2005 96p (At issue) lib bdg
$28.70; pa $19.95
Grades: 9 10 11 12   **302.23**
1. Journalism 2. Mass media
ISBN 0-7377-2410-2 (lib bdg); 0-7377-2411-0 (pa)
LC 2004-40527
In this anthology opinions from across the political
spectrum debate the issue of whether the media is biased
towards conservative or corporate interests

Popular culture: opposing viewpoints; John
Donald Woodward, book editor. Greenhaven
Press 2005 202p il lib bdg $34.95; pa $23.70 *
Grades: 9 10 11 12   **302.23**
1. Popular culture—United States
ISBN 0-7377-3105-2 (lib bdg); 0-7377-3106-0 (pa)
LC 2005-40223
"Opposing viewpoints series"
"Various essays address the pros and cons of reality
TV, violent video games, rap music, professional wres-
tling, radio vulgarity, etc. . . . The writing is clear, the
information current, and the content ever present in the
social-issues curriculum." SLJ
Includes bibliographical references

Television: opposing viewpoints; Jamuna Carroll,
book editor. Greenhaven Press 2006 207p il lib
bdg $34.95; pa $23.70 *
Grades: 9 10 11 12   **302.23**
1. Television broadcasting
ISBN 0-7377-3337-3 (lib bdg); 0-7377-3338-1 (pa)
LC 2005-40152
"Opposing viewpoints series"
"This anthology explores the role television may play
in obesity, aggression, and stereotyping and its effects on
viewers' morals and self-esteem. Also covers how programming should be regulated." Publisher's note
Includes bibliographical references

303.3 Coordination and control

Best, Joel
Damned lies and statistics; untangling numbers
from the media, politicians, and activists.
University of Calif. Press 2001 190p $19.95 *
Grades: 9 10 11 12   **303.3**
1. Statistics
ISBN 0-520-21978-3   LC 00-64910
The author aims to "remind us that we need to treat
statistics skeptically. . . . Best explains {what he sees
as} the four basic sources of flawed statistics (bad guess-
es, deceptive definitions, confusing questions, biased

Best, Joel—*Continued*

samples). Then he examines mutant statistics and discusses the illogic of statistical comparisons that attempt to equate differing time periods, places, groups, or social problems." Christ Sci Monit

"Invaluable counsel for good citizenship." Booklist

Includes bibliographical references

More damned lies and statistics; how numbers confuse public issues. University of California Press 2004 200p il $19.95 *

Grades: 9 10 11 12   303.3

1. Statistics

ISBN 0-520-23830-3   LC 2003-28076

Companion volume to Damned lies and statistics

Contents: Missing numbers -- Confusing numbers -- Scary numbers -- Authoritative numbers -- Contentious numbers -- Toward statistical literacy?

In this volume, the author continues his "account of how statistics are produced, used, and misused by everyone from researchers to journalists. . . . {He} illustrates his points with contemporary statistics about such concerns as school shootings, fatal hospital errors, bullying, teen suicides, deaths at the World Trade Center, college ratings, risk of divorce, racial profiling, and fatalities caused by falling coconuts." Publisher's note

"The book is packed with helpful tips for understanding statistics, and it even manages to make a usually dull topic entertaining." Booklist

Includes bibliographical references

Cull, Nicholas John

Propaganda and mass persuasion; a historical encyclopedia, 1500 to the present; {by} Nicholas J. Cull, David Culbert, David Welch. ABC-CLIO 2003 xxi, 479p il $85

Grades: 11 12 Adult   303.3

1. Propaganda—Encyclopedias

ISBN 1-57607-820-5   LC 2003-9513

This is an "A-Z guide to five centuries of propaganda, in both wartime and peacetime, which covers key moments, techniques, concepts, and some of the most influential propagandists in history." Publisher's note

"This specialized encyclopedia does a good job of exploring the different uses of propaganda." Booklist

Includes bibliographical references

Huxley, Aldous, 1894-1963

Brave new world revisited. Harper & Row 1958 147p pa $11.95 hardcover o.p.

Grades: 11 12 Adult   303.3

1. Propaganda 2. Totalitarianism 3. Brainwashing 4. Culture

ISBN 0-06-089852-6 (pa)

Also available in hardcover from Amereon

In response to his 1932 novel Brave new world "Huxley reconsiders his prophecies and fears that some of these may be coming true much sooner than he thought." Oxford Companion to Engl Lit. 5th edition

303.4 Social change

Anderson, Terry H., 1946-

The movement and the sixties. Oxford Univ. Press 1995 500p il pa $19.95 hardcover o.p.

Grades: 11 12 Adult   303.4

1. Radicalism 2. Demonstrations 3. United States—Social conditions

ISBN 0-19-510457-9 (pa)   LC 94-16344

This "book is a national study of U.S. social activism from 1960 to 1973, focusing on how 'the Movement' was experienced by participants and exploring why this activism arose when it did, how it developed, and what it accomplished." Booklist

Anderson's "sweeping study is a valuable, refreshingly unbiased reassessment of the '60s legacy." Publ Wkly

Includes bibliographical references

Benjamin, Marina

Rocket dreams; how the space age shaped our vision of a world beyond. Free Press 2003 242p hardcover o.p. pa $14

Grades: 11 12 Adult   303.4

1. Astronautics

ISBN 0-7432-3343-3; 0-7432-5534-8 (pa)
                                     LC 2002-45590

The author "grew up watching NASA spaceflights on television. In six personal chapters, she describes how she and others have sought to find substitutes for space exploration by investigating aliens in Roswell, NM, shopping in enclosed malls that mimic space stations, colonizing cyberspace, and cooperatively searching for extraterrestrial intelligence." Libr J

This is "an elegantly written memoir, as the author tells about her youthful fascination with the space program and her travels to places like Arecibo and Roswell, as well as her virtual travels among various computer groups over the last 20 years. Space buffs will appreciate many aspects of her story." Publ Wkly

Includes bibliographical references

Diamond, Jared M.

Guns, germs, and steel; the fates of human societies; [by] Jared Diamond. Norton 2005 518p il map $24.95

Grades: 11 12 Adult   303.4

1. Technology and civilization 2. Social change 3. Environmental influence on humans

ISBN 0-393-06131-0; 978-0-393-06131-4
                                     LC 2005-284261

First published 1997

"This book poses a simple but profound question about the distribution of wealth and power in the modern world: 'Why weren't Native Americans, Africans, and Aboriginal Australians the ones who decimated, subjugated, or exterminated Europeans and Asians?'. . . To explore the discrepancies in technological and cultural development he looks not at peoples but at places, and at the natural resources available to different indigenous populations since 11,000 B.C. The scope and the explanatory power of this book are astounding." New Yorker [review of 1997 edition]

Includes bibliographical references

Dissent in America; voices that shaped a nation; [edited by] Ralph F.Young. Pearson Education 2006 792p $35 *

Grades: 11 12 Adult   **303.4**
1. United States—Politics and government—Sources
2. United States—Social conditions—Sources
ISBN 0-321-44297-0   LC 2006-15415

"Divided chronologically, the anthology collects essays, speeches, organizational statements, songs, posters, interviews, broadsides and texts in other media. . . . For readers with something on their minds, 400 years of precedent may be just what they need to stimulate some questions of their own." Publ Wkly

Encyclopedia of American social movements; edited by Immanuel Ness; foreword by Stephen Eric Bronner and Frances Fox Piven. Sharpe Reference 2004 4v il set $399 *

Grades: 11 12 Adult   **303.4**
1. Social movements—Encyclopedias
ISBN 0-7656-8045-9   LC 2002-42613

"The encyclopedia is organized according to 16 movements, among them the antislavery, civil rights, women's, labor, and environmental movements. After an introductory overview, each section contains from 5 to more than 30 articles that correspond to time periods . . . or subject. . . . The writing is lively, accurate, and balanced." Booklist

Includes bibliographical references

Globalization: opposing viewpoints; Louise I. Gerdes, book editor. Greenhaven Press 2006 224p lib bdg $34.95; pa $23.70 *

Grades: 9 10 11 12   **303.4**
1. Globalization
ISBN 0-7377-2937-6 (lib bdg); 0-7377-2938-4 (pa)   LC 2005-40431

"Opposing viewpoints series"

"Authors in this anthology debate controversies surrounding the impact of globalization on culture, on political processes and relations, and on developed and developing economies. The selections in this anthology also explore various globalization policies." Publisher's note

Includes bibliographical references

The **information** revolution; opposing viewpoints; Laura K. Egendorf, book editor. Greenhaven Press 2004 202p il $33.70; pa $22.45

Grades: 8 9 10 11 12   **303.4**
1. Information technology 2. Information society
ISBN 0-7377-1693-2; 0-7377-1694-0 (pa)   LC 2003-44813

"Opposing viewpoints series"

"This title looks at how the Internet and the Information Revolution have changed society, education, our individual rights, and the future . . . Students will find short, accurate articles here for their research, and they will be aided by the discussion questions, bibliographies, organizations to contact, and excellent index . . . The easily digested format is welcome as many resources on this topic are dense and scholarly. A solid addition for most libraries." SLJ

Includes bibliographical references

The **Internet:** opposing viewpoints; James D. Torr, book editor. Greenhaven Press 2005 204p il lib bdg $34.95; pa $23.70

Grades: 8 9 10 11 12   **303.4**
1. Internet
ISBN 0-7377-2941-4 (lib bdg); 0-7377-2942-2 (pa)   LC 2004-59699

"Opposing viewpoints series"

"The authors in this volume examine the diverse effects of the Internet revolution—and suggest ways in which the technology can be harnessed for the better." Publisher's note

Includes bibliographical references

The **Radical** reader; a documentary history of the American radical tradition; edited by Timothy Patrick McCarthy and John McMillian; foreword by Eric Foner. New Press 2003 688p $65; lib bdg $21.95 *

Grades: 11 12 Adult   **303.4**
1. Radicalism
ISBN 1-56584-827-6; 1-56584-682-6 (lib bdg)   LC 2002-41051

The editors present "more than 200 declarations, appeals, editorials, and essays by such radical thinkers (each introduced in a brief bio) as Frederick Douglass, Sarah Grimké, Henry David Thoreau, Upton Sinclair, Emma Goldman, Angela Davis, Betty Friedan, Mario Savio, César Chávez, Rachel Carson, Tony Kushner, and Ralph Nader." Booklist

"By bringing many hard-to-find documents under one cover, this anthology will excite readers in discussing why radicals from all walks of life have made progressive ideals meaningful to Americans. Recommended for college, high school, and public libraries." Libr J

Includes bibliographical references

Tenner, Edward

Our own devices; the past and future of body technology. Alfred A. Knopf 2003 336p hardcover o.p. pa $14.95

Grades: 11 12 Adult   **303.4**
1. Technology and civilization 2. Technological innovations
ISBN 0-375-40722-7; 0-375-70707-7 (pa)   LC 2002-40694

"Tenner examines the reciprocal relationship between technology (in the broad sense of useful created objects) and technique (the methods we use to employ them) as they have developed together culturally. . . . A handful of examples provide insight into the history, ergonomics, and symbolism of some of the tools that are figuratively and literally closest to us: shoes (thong sandals and athletic varieties), chairs, eyeglasses, and headgear. Tenner also explores technologies that have influenced medicine (bottle feeding), arts (musical keyboards), and commerce (typing keyboards)." Libr J

"For a work that covers such a broad topic, this book is a page-turner, largely due to its clear prose and the author's approach to the material. While not lavishly illustrated, there seems to be a picture every time one is needed to illustrate the technology being discussed." SLJ

Includes bibliographical references

303.6 Conflict

Bell, J. Bowyer, 1931-2003
Murders on the Nile; the World Trade Center and global terror. Encounter Bks. 2003 206p $26.95
Grades: 11 12 Adult   **303.6**
  1. Terrorism 2. Islamic fundamentalism 3. World Trade Center terrorist attack, 2001
  ISBN 1-89355-463-5   LC 2002-40885
The author describes "how Islamic terror arose along the banks of the Nile a century ago amidst the grievances of an Egypt held in bondage by foreign imperialists and local despots. . . . [He] shows how this movement which originated in Egypt spread to the rest of the Islamic world which also became converted to the notion of redemption through jihad . . . [and] how what began almost one hundred years ago along the Nile gradually became a global conspiracy found not only along the Nile but ultimately along the Hudson as well." Publisher's note
"Bell's relevantly detailed book should be one of the first to read for understanding of so-called Islamic terrorism, not least because Bell never blames the religion, Islam, for the excesses of Qutb and Rahman's movement, which he always calls Islamism." Booklist
Includes bibliographical references

Burns, Vincent
Terrorism; a documentary and reference guide; [by] Vincent Burns and Kate Dempsey Peterson; foreword by James K. Kallstrom. Greenwood Press 2005 xxxvii, 293p il $75 *
Grades: 11 12 Adult   **303.6**
  1. Terrorism
  ISBN 0-313-33213-4   LC 2005-3390
This is a "volume of 70 documents, some never before in print, pertaining to terrorism and the US. Readings include speeches, policy statements, letters, reports, and laws. . . . An easy-to-use resource that is full of pertinent information, this volume should be read all the way from the introduction . . . to the resources section." Choice
Includes bibliographical references

Combs, Cindy C.
Encyclopedia of terrorism; [by] Cindy C. Combs and Martin Slann. Rev ed. Facts on File 2007 478p il map (Facts on File library of world history) $95 *
Grades: 11 12 Adult   **303.6**
  1. Terrorism—Encyclopedias
  ISBN 0-8160-6277-3; 978-0-8160-6277-5
                                  LC 2006-15853
First published 2002
This encyclopedia provides articles on "the events, people, organizations, and places that have played a major role in international terrorism. the events, people, organizations, and places that have played a major role in international terrorism. Each entry is placed within its . . . historical context to help readers understand the wide-ranging motivations behind terrorist actions." Publisher's note
Includes bibliographical references

Encyclopedia of world terrorism; edited by Frank Shanty and Raymond Picquet; John Lalla, documents editor. Sharpe, M.E. 2003 2v il set $249
Grades: 11 12 Adult   **303.6**
  1. Terrorism
  ISBN 1-563-24807-7   LC 2002-75983
Contents: v1: 1996-2002 -- v2: Documents
"The text examines terrorist activity worldwide from the mid-1990's to the present while providing historical context and contemporary analysis. . . . The first volume is divided into three main sections: 'Twenty-First-Century Terrorism,' which offers an extensive analysis of the 9/11 attacks and their consequences; 'Global Terrorism, 1996-2002,' which covers terrorism worldwide during those years; and 'Future Trends.'" Libr J
Includes bibliographical references

Gottfried, Ted, 1928-
The fight for peace; a history of antiwar movements in America. 21st Century Bks. 2006 136p il (People's history) $26.60 *
Grades: 7 8 9 10   **303.6**
  1. Pacifism 2. Peace 3. War
  ISBN 0-7613-2932-3
"Gottfried starts out by explaining that a group in Connecticut rallied together in 2003 to peacefully protest the war against Iraq. . . . Then the author discusses the antiwar movement during the Civil War and proceeds through history, beginning with the ancient Greek play Lysistrata. . . . The pictures, political cartoons, and quotes are an excellent addition. . . . This is a book that can be read for general interest as well as for reports." SLJ
Includes bibliographical references

Gupta, Dipak K.
Who are the terrorists? Chelsea House 2006 116p il map (The roots of terrorism) lib bdg $35
Grades: 7 8 9 10   **303.6**
  1. Terrorism
  ISBN 0-7910-8306-3   LC 2005021627
This "volume discusses the world history as well as the groups and individuals behind today's headlines. . . . Gupta emphasizes that equating Islam with the barbaric acts of a few terrorists is like making the burning crosses of the Ku Klux Klan the essence of Christianity. He also points out the role of the American invasion of Iraq and the images from Abu Ghraib. . . . This is sure to spark vehement group discussion." Booklist
Includes bibliographical references

Henderson, Harry, 1951-
Global terrorism. Rev. ed. Facts on File 2004 316p il map (Library in a book) $45 *
Grades: 9 10 11 12   **303.6**
  1. Terrorism
  ISBN 0-8160-5337-5   LC 2003-63126
First published 2001 with title: Terrorism

Henderson, Harry, 1951——Continued

This book combines a "general perspective on terrorism (including a historical introduction and theoretical discussion) with recent events and publications. . . . This volume addresses issues such as the Israel-Palestine conflict as well as the U.S. military invasion of Iraq. The attitude toward terrorism in nations such as Pakistan, Saudi Arabia, and Egypt and the public involvement of U.S. armed forces as trainers and advisers in the Philippines and Columbia are covered. The book also sheds light on the actions of North Korea and U.S. responses." Publisher's note

Includes bibliographical references

Judson, Karen, 1941-

Resolving conflicts; how to get along when you don't get along. Enslow Pubs. 2005 112p il (Issues in focus today) $31.93 *

Grades: 7 8 9 10 11 12   **303.6**

1. Conflict management

ISBN 0-7660-2359-1   LC 2004-28119

The author "describes different kinds of conflicts and how they can be resolved, with a special focus on teens and building their conflict-resolution skills and understanding." Publisher's note

Includes bibliographical references

Kronenwetter, Michael

Terrorism: a guide to events and documents. Greenwood Press 2004 298p il $55 *

Grades: 11 12 Adult   **303.6**

1. Terrorism

ISBN 0-313-32578-2   LC 2004-6619

Contents: The philosophy of terror -- A short history of terrorism -- Turning to terror -- Varieties of terror -- Weapons of mass destruction -- Their name is legion: a selection of terrorist groups -- Four aspects of terror -- Chronology -- Documents

This "book examines the phenomenon of terrorism, discussing the methods, tactics, and weapons used by terrorists and exploring the attraction that terrorism holds for many individuals, groups, and movements." Publisher's note

"Kronenwetter's book is seminal to an understanding of terrorism. Honest, insightful, and easily understood, his book articulates the core ideals of terrorism and expertly presents its philosophical motivations within a historical context." Choice

For a fuller review, see: Booklist, Nov. 15, 2004

Includes bibliographical references

Media violence: opposing viewpoints; Louise I. Gerdes, book editor. Greenhaven Press 2004 191p il lib bdg $33.70

Grades: 7 8 9 10   **303.6**

1. Violence 2. Mass media

ISBN 0-7377-2011-5 (lib bdg)   LC 2003-44810

"Opposing viewpoints series"

"This volume opens with a history of the nationwide debate over violent content in television, video games, music, and film. . . . The following chapters address the impact of violent media, government intervention, and societal response. . . . The articles provide a truly di-

verse and divergent set of opinions. Short in length . . . and strong on substance, the essays will appeal to students preparing papers and debate topics." SLJ

Terrorism; Michelle E. Houle, book editor. Greenhaven Press 2005 170p il map (History of issues) lib bdg $34.95; pa $23.70

Grades: 9 10 11 12   **303.6**

1. Terrorism

ISBN 0-7377-1909-5 (lib bdg); 0-7377-1910-9 (pa)

LC 2004-49716

"The book is divided into five chapters, each one focusing on a different aspect of terrorism: religion-based terrorism, state-sponsored terrorism, terrorism committed in the pursuit of national liberation, terrorism and the U.S., and the difficulties of defining terrorism." Booklist

Includes bibliographical references

Terrorism; David M. Haugen and Matthew J. Box, book editors. Greenhaven Press 2006 110p il (Social issues firsthand) lib bdg $28.70 *

Grades: 9 10 11 12   **303.6**

1. Terrorism

ISBN 0-7377-2501-X   LC 2005-40218

This book designed to discuss the personal aspects of controversial issues "includes articles written by Osama bin Laden, Timothy McVeigh, Hizbullah, and a member of Aum Shinrikyo. All of these are in a chapter titled, 'What Motivates a Terrorist?' Later chapters include reports by survivors and family members of Sept. 11, 2001, the Oklahoma City bombing, Palestine, and other terrorist tragedies." Libr Media Connect

Includes bibliographical references

What motivates suicide bombers? Lauri S. Friedman, book editor. Greenhaven Press 2005 93p (At issue) lib bdg $28.70; pa $19.95

Grades: 9 10 11 12   **303.6**

1. Terrorism 2. Suicide bombers

ISBN 0-7377-2321-1 (lib bdg); 0-7377-2320-3 (pa)

LC 2004-52315

This anthology "explores the influence of religion, economics, politics, and technology on people who become willing to give their lives for terror." Publisher's note

Includes bibliographical references

Women on war; an international anthology of women's writings from antiquity to the present; edited and with an introduction by Daniela Gioseffi. 2nd ed. Feminist Press 2003 375p $55; pa $19.95 *

Grades: 11 12 Adult   **303.6**

1. Peace 2. War

ISBN 1-55861-408-7; 1-55861-409-5 (pa)

LC 2003-42407

First published 1988 by Simon & Schuster

This collection "gathers together writings by more than 150 women, including renowned poets, novelists, essayists, journalists, and activists, as well as ordinary women with first-hand experience of armed conflict as survivors, refugees, rape victims, nurses, and soldiers. . . . {Contributors include} Isabella Allende, Maya Angelou, Margaret Atwood, Simone de Beauvoir, Gwen-

Women on war—*Continued*
dolyn Brooks, Emily Dickinson, Marguerite Duras, Slavenka Drakulic, Barbara Ehrenreich, Cynthia Enloe, Martha Gelhorn {and} Nadine Gordimer." Publisher's note
This is a "powerful and important collection." Booklist
Includes bibliographical references

Woodward, John, 1958-
War; John Woodward, book editor. Greenhaven Press 2006 207p (Current controversies) lib bdg $34.95; pa $23.70
Grades: 9 10 11 12   **303.6**
1. War
ISBN 0-7377-3236-9 (lib bdg); 978-0-7377-3236-8 (lib bdg); 0-7377-3237-7 (pa)   LC 2005-46261
In this anthology the authors "examine the root causes of war and explore ways to prevent it." Publisher's note
Includes bibliographical references

304.2 Human ecology

The **Atlas** of US and Canadian environmental history; edited by Char Miller. Routledge 2003 248p il map $150 *
Grades: 11 12 Adult   **304.2**
1. Human ecology 2. Environmental policy
ISBN 0-415-93781-7   LC 2003-46799
"This resource offers essays written by history scholars on ecological issues for young people. Organized chronologically from 1492 to present times, chapters include two-page treatments of the era's hot topics . . . These controversial topics are explained in a simple, nonbiased way that will appeal to young adults. The statistics offered are frequently enlightening." Voice Youth Advocates
Includes bibliographical references

Diamond, Jared M.
Collapse: how societies choose to fail or succeed. Viking 2005 575p il $29.95; pa $17
Grades: 11 12 Adult   **304.2**
1. Social change 2. Environmental policy
ISBN 0-670-03337-5; 0-14-303655-6 (pa)
                                    LC 2004-57152
The author "examines storied examples of human economic and social collapse, and even extinction, including Easter Island, classical Mayan civilization and the Greenland Norse. He explores patterns of population growth, overfarming, overgrazing and overhunting, often abetted by drought, cold, rigid social mores and warfare, that lead inexorably to vicious circles of deforestation, erosion and starvation prompted by the disappearance of plant and animal food sources. . . . Readers will find his book an enthralling, and disturbing, reminder of the indissoluble links that bind humans to nature." Publ Wkly
Includes bibliographical references

Gunn, Angus M., 1920-
Unnatural disasters; case studies of human-induced environmental catastrophes. Greenwood Press 2003 143p il map $55
Grades: 9 10 11 12   **304.2**
1. Disasters 2. Human influence on nature
ISBN 0-313-31999-5   LC 2002-44848
This book focuses on human-induced "disasters including coalmine disasters, dam failures, industrial explosions, nuclear energy accidents, oil spills, terrorist acts, and industrial toxicity and government actions . . . Beginning in 1903 and continuing to September 11, 2001 each event is presented as a case study describing the situation, causes, consequences, and cleanup. The focus is on cases that significantly impacted the environment." Libr Media Connect
"The book is well written and well balanced, and the author . . . has a good grasp of the technical background behind each of the disasters he describes. He discusses not only the technical, but also the economic, political, and sociological backgrounds of each disaster. A good starting place for anyone wanting to research human-caused disasters." Choice
Includes bibliographical references

How geography affects the United States. Greenwood Press 2002 5v il map set $199.95
Grades: 9 10 11 12   **304.2**
1. Human geography 2. United States—Geography 3. United States—Local history
ISBN 0-313-32250-3   LC 2002-75304
Contents: v1 Northeast; v2 Southeast; v3 Midwest; v4 Northwest; v5 Southwest
Explores the ways in which geography has affected the lives of the people of the United States
"This helpful series blends physical characteristics, American history, pop culture, and modern travel information to offer a fresh take on geography, making a potentially dull subject interesting." Voice Youth Advocates
Includes bibliographical references

Leakey, Richard E., 1944-
The sixth extinction; patterns of life and the future of humankind; {by} Richard Leakey and Roger Lewin. Doubleday 1995 271p il pa $11.20 hardcover o.p.
Grades: 11 12 Adult   **304.2**
1. Evolution 2. Human influence on nature 3. Mass extinction of species
ISBN 0-385-46809-1 (pa)   LC 95-18286
The authors contend that "human beings, by destroying tropical rain forests and driving tens of thousands of species into extinction, are dangerously reducing biodiversity, damaging ecosystems and possibly precipitating the next major mass extinction." Publ Wkly
Leakey and Lewin "present a powerful message based on years of observation and fieldwork." Libr J
Includes bibliographical references

304.6 Population

The **American** people; Census 2000; Reynolds Farley and John Haaga, editors. Russell Sage 2005 456p il map pa $35 *
Grades: 11 12 Adult **304.6**
1. United States—Population 2. United States—Census
ISBN 0-8715-4273-0 LC 2005-50433
This book "is more than just a compilation of tables and charts of raw census data. It is an interpretative guide to understanding the demographic breakdown of American society. Chapters include: 'Gender Inequalities', 'Cohorts and Socioeconomic Progress' and 'The Lives and Times of the Baby Boomers'. Editors Farley and Haaga show trends in American culture that will not be found anywhere else." Univ Press Books for Public and Second Sch Libr, 2006
Includes bibliographical references

Encyclopedia of genocide and crimes against humanity; Dinah L. Shelton, editor in chief. Macmillan Reference 2004 3v il map set $415
Grades: 11 12 Adult **304.6**
1. Genocide—Encyclopedias 2. Atrocities
ISBN 0-02-865847-7 LC 2004-6587
The scope of this encyclopedia starts "with the Roman persecution of Christians and . . . [continues] to recent Sudanese Arab massacres of Sudanese Africans. Arranged alphabetically by topic, each entry contains a narrative, a bibliography including books, reports, and Web sites, and . . . cross-references." Choice
"The editorial team has cast its net wide to create an outstanding comprehensive sourcebook that will be the standard resource for many years." Booklist
Includes bibliographical references

Population: opposing viewpoints; Karen F. Balkin, book editor. Greenhaven Press 2005 186p il lib bdg $34.95; pa $23.70 *
Grades: 9 10 11 12 **304.6**
1. Population
ISBN 0-7377-2951-1 (lib bdg); 0-7377-2952-X (pa)
LC 2004-60862
"Opposing viewpoints series"
Considers opposing opinions on various issues concerning world population including problems of rapid growth, the effects of population on the environment, changes in age demographics within developed nations, and ways of decreasing human fertility.
Includes bibliographical references

Springer, Jane
Genocide. Groundwood Books 2006 144p (Groundwork guides) $15.95
Grades: 8 9 10 11 12 **304.6**
1. Genocide
ISBN 978-0-88899-681-7; 0-88899-681-0
"This disturbing history of mass ethnic killings across the world examines the why, when, where, and how genocide takes place. . . . In a lucid, informal text, Springer ably documents particular crimes against humanity, including the transatlantic slave trade, the slaughter of America's Native peoples, the Turkish massacre of the Armenians, the Nanking massacre, the Holocaust, and the Khmer Rouge slaughter in Cambodia." Booklist

304.8 Movement of people

Benson, Sonia
U.S. immigration and migration almanac; [by] Sonia G. Benson; Sarah Hermsen, project editor. UXL 2004 2v il (U. S. immigration and migration reference library) set $115
Grades: 9 10 11 12 **304.8**
1. United States—Immigration and emigration
ISBN 0-7876-7732-9 LC 2003-27833
This set "opens with an overview of immigration to and migration patterns within the U.S. and current theories about Pre-Columbian migrations to North America. Separate, well-written chronological chapters cover from the early arrival of the Spanish and English to the more recent immigration of Latino and Caribbean groups." SLJ
Includes bibliographical references

Immigration; Laura K. Egendorf, book editor. Greenhaven Press 2006 240p il map (History of issues) lib bdg $34.95 *
Grades: 9 10 11 12 **304.8**
1. United States—Immigration and emigration
ISBN 0-7377-2871-X LC 2005-46156
"Primary and secondary sources are used in this anthology to explore the efficacy of immigration policies and how immigrant populations have changed America for better and for worse." Publisher's note
Includes bibliographical references

Immigration in U.S. history; edited by Carl L. Bankston, III, Danielle Antoinette Hidalgo. Salem Press 2006 2v il (Magill's choice) set $114
Grades: 11 12 Adult **304.8**
1. United States—Immigration and emigration
ISBN 978-1-58765-266-0; 1-58765-266-8
LC 2005-33560
"The 193 entries cover issues related to U.S. immigration and are drawn from 13 different Salem publications. . . . Each of the alphabetically arranged articles begins with a brief definition of the article's topic. This is followed by a list of categories under which the topic falls (for example, 'Asian Immigrants,' 'Border Control,' 'Refugees') and a sentence on the significance of the topic as it relates to immigration. . . . The set is a good contribution to the study of immigration in the U.S." Booklist
Includes bibliographical references

Powell, John, 1954-
Encyclopedia of North American immigration. Facts on File 2005 464p il map (Facts on File library of American history) $75 *
Grades: 11 12 Adult **304.8**
1. United States—Immigration and emigration—Encyclopedias 2. Canada—Immigration and emigration—Encyclopedias
ISBN 0-8160-4658-1 LC 2004-7361
The author "presents an introduction to immigration to English and French-speaking regions over the past 500 years. . . . His intent is to offer 'a convenient one-

Powell, John, 1954——*Continued*

volume reference full of straightforward and concise information on people, groups, policies, and events that defined the world's greatest migration of peoples to a continent and shaped their reception in North America.'" Booklist

"This valuable reference work on a hot topic belongs in all types of libraries—not only in the US and Canada, which offered shelter to immigrants, but also in libraries worldwide." Choice

Includes bibliographical references

305 Social groups

Farmer, Paul, 1959-

Pathologies of power; health, human rights, and the new war on the poor; with a foreword by Amartya Sen. University of California Press 2003 402p (California series in public anthropology) $27.50; pa $16.95

Grades: 9 10 11 12   **305**

1. Poor—Medical care 2. Human rights

ISBN 0-520-23550-9; 0-520-24326-9 (pa)

LC 2002-13311

"The author's central argument is simple: Health care is a human right. Extreme poverty and the social and political conditions that give rise to it . . . deny people that right and produce 'unnecessary' deaths. 'Unnecessary,' because given present-day means of prevention and cure, those able to afford health care do not die in this manner . . . The argument is buttressed both by vivid accounts of the author's experience as a physician and of his patients' unbelievable hardships and courage, and by a thorough documentation of the larger issues." Antioch Rev

Includes bibliographical references

Muslims in America; Allen Verbrugge, book editor. Greenhaven Press 2005 159p (Contemporary issues companion) lib bdg $33.70; pa $22.45 *

Grades: 9 10 11 12   **305**

1. Muslims—United States

ISBN 0-7377-2315-7 (lib bdg); 0-7377-2316-5 (pa)

LC 2004-50096

This collection of articles is divided in the following chapters: A history of islam and Muslims in America; Muslim life in American society; Muslim American women; American Muslims after the September 11 attacks; Personal accounts of Muslims in America

"The selections present a good variety of viewpoints. . . . A very good annotated list of organizations to contact is included. This is a solid selection for reports as well as for students with a special interest in the subject." SLJ

Includes bibliographical references

305.23 Young people

The **Courage** to be yourself; true stories by teens about cliques, conflicts, and overcoming peer pressure; edited by Al Desetta with Educators for Social Responsibility. Free Spirit Pub. 2005 145p pa $13.95

Grades: 7 8 9 10 11 12   **305.23**

1. Teenagers 2. Conduct of life

ISBN 1-57542-185-2   LC 2005-5173

"In 26 first-person stories, real teens write about their lives." Publisher's note

"There is certainly some value in hearing teens of many ethnicities and orientations speaking plainly about being fat, or being from India in a school full of blond, blue-eyed folk, or being Arab after 9/11." Booklist

Includes bibliographical references

Feig, Paul

Kick me; adventures in adolescence. Three Rivers Press (NY) 2002 278p pa $12.95

Grades: 11 12 Adult   **305.23**

1. Adolescence 2. Boys

ISBN 0-609-80943-1   LC 2002-18121

"These interlocking essays—on everything from a sadistic gym teacher and geeky after-class pastimes to obsessive romantic tendencies and a prom that wasn't the best night of the author's life—are terrifically entertaining, although undoubtedly imaginatively amped up for maximum readability." Publ Wkly

The **Freedom** Writers diary; how a group of extraordinary teens used writing to change themselves and the world around them; the Freedom Writers with Erin Gruwell; foreword by Zlata Filipovic. Doubleday 1999 280p il pa $12.95 *

Grades: 9 10 11 12   **305.23**

1. Teenagers

ISBN 0-385-49422-X   LC 99-30342

"Main Street books"

"This collective journal brings together the work of a group of students, the Freedom Writers, from an English class taught by Gruwell at an 'at risk' public high school. Inspired by *The Diary of Anne Frank* and *Zlata's Diary*, the students recorded their responses to a world dominated by abuse, drugs, crime, homelessness, and racism. Taken together, the nearly 150 entries . . . tell a moving coming-of-age story in which the authors gradually become their own heroes." Booklist

GirlSource; a book by and for young women about relationships, rights, futures, bodies, minds, and souls; created by the GirlSource editorial team, Jessica Barnes . . . [et al.] Ten Speed Press 2003 96p il pa $12.95 *

Grades: 9 10 11 12   **305.23**

1. Young women 2. Conduct of life

ISBN 1-58008-555-5   LC 2003-60839

First published 2000 with title: It's about time!

"The topics covered include everything from stress, meditation, and depression to sex, STDs, and birth con-

GirlSource—*Continued*

trol; from rape and drugs to teens' rights with police; and from relationships and family issues to preparing for college. Every topic is dealt with in an open and honest fashion that will be refreshing for teens. . . . All public and school librarians should do their students the favor of having plenty of copies of this title on their shelves. Young women everywhere will thank you." Voice Youth Advocates

Includes bibliographical references

Jukes, Mavis

It's a girl thing; how to stay healthy, safe, and in charge; illustrations by Debbie Tilley. Knopf 1996 135p il hardcover o.p. pa $12

Grades: 5 6 7 8 9 10   **305.23**
1. Adolescence 2. Girls 3. Sex education
ISBN 0-679-94325-0; 0-679-87392-9 (pa)
LC 93-40296

"Jukes discusses a wide variety of subjects from buying a bra to sexual harassment and abuse. In a warm, conversational style, she covers body changes in both boys and girls, menstruation, general health, drinking and drugs, sexual feelings, pregnancy, contraceptives, and sexually transmitted diseases including AIDS. The text is sometimes humorous, but always conveys caring, respect, and concern." SLJ

Includes bibliographical references

Nazario, Sonia

Enrique's journey. Random House 2006 291p il $26.95; pa $14.95

Grades: 11 12 Adult   **305.23**
1. Illegal aliens 2. United States—Immigration and emigration
ISBN 1-4000-6205-5; 978-1-4000-6205-8; 0-8129-7178-7 (pa); 978-0-8129-7178-1 (pa)
LC 2005-44347

The author "retraces the travel of immigrants from Central America to El Norte and writes . . . about the trials and tribulations that besiege the journey. Specifically, she focuses on a Honduran boy, Enrique, left behind by his mother, Lourdes, who fled to the United States, like many Central American women before her, to make enough money to give her children a better life back home and ultimately return to them." Libr J

"Descriptions of rapes, beatings, and jailing of immigrant children and accounts of those who suffered loss of limbs falling from freight trains are graphic and disturbing. But no one can doubt the authenticity of this reporting." SLJ

Robbins, Alexandra, 1976-

The overachievers; the secret lives of driven kids. Hyperion 2006 439p $24.95 *

Grades: 11 12 Adult   **305.23**
1. Workaholism 2. High school students
ISBN 1-4013-0201-7; 978-1-4013-0201-6
LC 2006-41244

The author "follows the lives of students from a Bethesda, Md., high school as they navigate the SAT and college application process. These students are obsessed

with success, contending with illness, physical deterioration (senior Julie is losing hair over the pressure to get into Stanford), cheating (students sell a physics project to one another), obsessed parents (Frank's mother manages his time to the point of abuse) and emotional breakdowns." Publ Wkly

"The portraits of the teens are compelling and make for an easy read." Publ Wkly

Includes bibliographical references

Sherrow, Victoria

Encyclopedia of youth and war; young people as participants and victims. Oryx Press 2000 366p il $68.95

Grades: Professional   **305.23**
1. Children and war
ISBN 1-57356-287-4   LC 99-43452

"Beginning with the Thirty-Year War in the mid-1600s, this single volume containing over three hundred individual entries addresses the impact of war on young people from the perspectives of both victim and participant. . . . Students will find valuable and interesting information on broad subjects such as volunteers, land mines, disease, or resistance movements as they relate specifically to children aged eighteen or younger." Voice Youth Advocates

Includes bibliographical references

The **Struggle** to be strong; true stories by teens about overcoming tough times; edited by Al Desetta, Sybil Wolin. Free Spirit 2000 179p il pa $21.95

Grades: 9 10 11 12   **305.23**
1. Teenagers 2. Conduct of life
ISBN 1-57542-079-1   LC 99-56600

"The structure of the book is based on seven resiliencies: insight, independence, relationships, initiative, creativity, humor, and morality. Each chapter defines the resiliency and its importance, adding teen-authored essays to illustrate the topics and to highlight the importance of struggling to stay strong." Voice Youth Advocates

Sugar in the raw; voices of young black girls in America; {edited} by Rebecca Carroll; foreword by Ntozake Shange. Crown Trade Paperbacks 1997 144p pa $14 *

Grades: 11 12 Adult   **305.23**
1. African American youth 2. African American women 3. Teenagers
ISBN 0-517-88497-6   LC 96-37527

This compilation of profiles of 15 young black girls across the U.S. between the ages of 11 and 18, reveals both their inner and outer lives. Coming from vastly different social and economic backgrounds, they all share a sense of independence and pride as they speak of their lives, self-esteem, personal values, race and their dreams for the future

Teen life in Europe; edited by Shirley R. Steinberg; foreword by Richard M Lerner. Greenwood Press 2005 281p il (Teen life around the world) $55

Grades: 9 10 11 12   **305.23**
1. Youth—Europe
ISBN 0-313-32727-0   LC 2005-15183

Teen life in Europe—*Continued*

"Each chapter covers a country in the region, and is written by a native of that country. The 12 countries profiled include Denmark, England, France, Germany, Ireland, Italy, Malta, The Netherlands, Portugal, Spain, Sweden, and Turkey. Each chapter concludes with a resource guide providing print and electronic sources for additional research." Publisher's note

Includes bibliographical references

Teen life in Latin America and the Caribbean; edited by Cynthia Tompkins and Kristen Sternberg; foreword by Richard M. Lerner. Greenwood 2004 325p il (Teen life around the world) $57.95

Grades: 9 10 11 12   **305.23**

1. Youth—Latin America 2. Youth—Caribbean region

ISBN 0-313-31932-4   LC 2003-59644

This book describes "the unique challenges and opportunities of teens in 15 Latin American or Caribbean countries." Publisher's note

Includes bibliographical references

Williams, Terrie

Stay strong; simple life lessons for teens. Scholastic 2001 218p hardcover o.p. pa $4.99

Grades: 9 10 11 12   **305.23**

1. Teenagers 2. Conduct of life 3. Life skills

ISBN 0-439-12971-0; 0-439-12972-9 (pa)

"Drawing on her own success in public relations, the author gives straight-from-the-hip advice to teens on a range of topics. Most of her guidance deals with ethical situations, manners, and personal relationships. Anecdotes and success stories illustrate key ideas, while quotations from teenagers and instructive raps emphasize her point of view." Booklist

Yell-oh girls! emerging voices explore culture, identity, and growing up Asian American; {edited by} Vickie Nam. Quill 2001 xxxv, 297p il pa $13 *

Grades: 11 12 Adult   **305.23**

1. Asian Americans 2. Teenagers 3. Girls

ISBN 0-06-095944-4   LC 2001-18164

This is an "anthology of essays by young Asian American women. The contributors, from China, Hawaii, Laos, Vietnam, and even India, range in age from 13 to nearly 40. . . . Readers . . . who have felt the pain of being outsiders will be swept along by the authors' sincerity and their efforts to use writing to clarify who they are." Booklist

305.3   Men and women

Male/female roles: opposing viewpoints; Auriana Ojeda, book editor. Greenhaven Press 2005 219p il lib bdg $33.70; pa $22.45 *

Grades: 8 9 10 11 12   **305.3**

1. Sex role

ISBN 0-7377-2240-1 (lib bdg); 0-7377-2241-X (pa)
     LC 2004-40605

"Opposing viewpoints series"

"Authors in this anthology debate whether gender is biological or culturally determined, if male and female roles have changed for the better, and how best to improve relationships between men and women." Publisher's note

Includes bibliographical references

305.4   Women

Collins, Gail

America's women; four hundred years of dolls, drudges, helpmates, and heroines. Morrow 2003 556p il $27.95; pa $15.95

Grades: 11 12 Adult   **305.4**

1. Women—United States—History

ISBN 0-06-018510-4; 0-06-122722-6 (pa)
     LC 2003-51011

This is a history of American women from colonial times to the present

"Collins elegantly and eruditely celebrates the hard-won victories, overwhelming obstacles, and selfless contributions of a captivating array of influential women." Booklist

Includes bibliographical references

The **Columbia** documentary history of American women since 1941; edited by Harriet Sigerman. Columbia University Press 2003 690p $75 *

Grades: 11 12 Adult   **305.4**

1. Women—United States—History—Sources

ISBN 0-231-11698-5   LC 2002-41395

This collection of public and private primary sources includes such topics as employment opportunities, "the ideas and changes brought about by the women's movement, the challenges to and defense of reproductive rights, the backlash against feminism in the name of family values, and new visions for women's lives in the twenty-first century." Publisher's note

"This enormously valuable volume will provide documentary source materials for students from junior high school through college who are searching for voices of and about American women throughout the second half of the 20th century." Libr J

Includes bibliographical references

Coppens, Linda Miles, 1944-

What American women did, 1789-1920; a year-by-year reference. McFarland & Co. 2001 259p il $38.50

Grades: 7 8 9 10   **305.4**

1. Women—United States—History 2. Women—Social conditions

ISBN 0-7864-0899-5   LC 00-64010

"A chronological account of women's accomplishments in the areas of domesticity, work, education, religion, the arts, law and politics, and reform efforts. . . . This work will prove useful for students wishing to gain a better perspective of history, particularly social history, as it pertained to women." SLJ

Includes bibliographical references

Cullen-DuPont, Kathryn

Encyclopedia of women's history in America. 2nd ed. Facts on File 2000 418p il $71.50 *
Grades: 8 9 10 11 12 Adult   305.4
1. Women—United States—History 2. Feminism
ISBN 0-8160-4100-8   LC 99-87498
First published 1996

This work highlights the lives and contributions of women in American history ranging from Pocahontas to Hillary Clinton and Madeleine Albright. Entries cover individuals, movements, court cases and women's issues from Colonial times to the present

"Well-written and informative . . . . An excellent quick reference source . . . recommended . . . ." Choice
Includes bibliographical references

De Pauw, Linda Grant

Founding mothers; women in America in the Revolutionary era; wood engravings by Michael McCurdy. Houghton Mifflin 1975 228p il hardcover o.p. pa $7.95 *
Grades: 9 10 11 12 Adult   305.4
1. Women—United States—History 2. Women—Social conditions 3. United States—Social life and customs—1600-1775, Colonial period
ISBN 0-395-21896-9; 0-395-70109-0 (pa)
                             LC 75-17031
Also available in hardcover from Econo-Clad Bks.

"Viewing roles of women who lived during the Revolutionary era from a contemporary feminist perspective . . . {the author} examines Black, white and Native American women as well as women of all social classes, including slaves." SLJ
Includes bibliographical references

Du Bois, W. E. B. (William Edward Burghardt), 1868-1963

The souls of Black folk; edited with an introduction and notes by Brent Hayes Edwards. Oxford University Press 2007 xxxvi, 223p il (Oxford world's classics) pa $12.95
Grades: 11 12 Adult   305.4
1. African Americans
ISBN 978-0-19-280678-9; 0-19-280678-5
                             LC 2006-35193
First published 1903 by McClurg

"A collection of fifteen essays and sketches by W.E.B. Du Bois. In it he describes the lives of African American farmers, sketches the role of music in their churches, details the history of the Freedman's Bureau, discusses the career of Booker T. Washington, and advocates a commitment to higher education for the most talented African American youth." Benet's Reader's Ency of Am Lit
Includes bibliographical references

Encyclopedia of women in American history. Sharpe Ref. 2002 3v il set $299
Grades: 11 12 Adult   305.4
1. Women—United States—History—Encyclopedias
ISBN 0-7656-8038-6   LC 2001-42025
Contents: v1 Colonization, revolution, and the new nation, 1585-1820, general editor, Joyce Appleby; v2 Civil War, western expansion, and industrialization, 1820-

1900, general editor, Eileen K. Cheng; v3 Suffrage, world war, and modern times, 1900-present, general editor, Joanne Goodwin

The set "is divided into three chronologically arranged volumes. Each volume includes historical surveys and thematic essays on central issues and political changes affecting women's lives during the period. These are followed by A-Z entries on significant events and social movements, laws, court cases and more, as well as profiles of notable American women from all walks of life and all fields of endeavor. Primary sources and original documents are included throughout, and the set also features special highlights that appear next to the A-Z entries . . . and Charts and Graphs, which provide geographical and statistical data about women's history." Publisher's note
Includes bibliographical references

Esherick, Joan

Women in the Arab world. Mason Crest Publishers 2005 112p il map (Women's issues, global trends) $22.95
Grades: 7 8 9 10   305.4
1. Women—Arab countries
ISBN 1-59084-861-6   LC 2004-12709
Contents: The modern Arab world: extremes for women; Arab women in ages past; Religion and Arab women; Arab women and the public world; Family life; Changing their world: Arab women who are making a difference; Unfinished business: issues and controversies facing Arab women today

This examines the roles of women in Arab countries.
This is "physically attractive, browsable, and up-to-date. . . . It is detailed and thorough, includes many charts and facts, and takes great care to differentiate between what most Arabs do or believe and what may occur in specific countries or among specific groups." SLJ
Includes bibliographical references

The **Feminist** movement; Nick Treanor, book editor. Greenhaven Press 2002 238p il (American social movements) $33.70 *
Grades: 9 10 11 12   305.4
1. Feminism 2. Women—United States
ISBN 0-7377-1050-0   LC 2001-7289
An anthology of articles, speeches, interviews, and essays which discuss the development of the feminist movement, including world involvement and personal stories

"There's as much here for adults as there is for teens; in fact, the {book} would be excellent for family discussion." Booklist
Includes bibliographical references

Franck, Irene M.

The Wilson chronology of women's achievements; a record of women's achievements from ancient times to present; by Irene M. Franck and David M. Brownstone. Wilson, H.W. 1998 507p $105
Grades: 8 9 10 11 12 Adult   305.4
1. Women—History
ISBN 0-8242-0936-2   LC 97-34394
First published 1995 by HarperPerennial with title: Women's world

Franck, Irene M.—*Continued*

This chronicle of women's history ranges "from the Egyptian queen Nefertiti and the Greek poet Sappho to Susan B. Anthony, Marie Curie, Eleanor Roosevelt, and Janet Reno." Publisher's note

Includes bibliographical references

Goodwin, Jan

Price of honor; Muslim women lift the veil of silence on the Islamic world. rev ed. Plume Bks. 2003 351p il pa $16 *

Grades: 11 12 Adult   305.4

1. Muslim women 2. Islamic countries

ISBN 0-452-28377-9   LC 2002-28257

First published 1994 by Little, Brown

The author "examines the movement that is aggressively spreading a fundamentalist version of Islam throughout much of the world. Her interviews with Muslim women in ten countries both fascinate and disturb, for their candor reveals the movement's profound and often devastating effects on them. . . . A necessary purchase." Libr J {review of 1994 edition}

Lawler, Jennifer

Encyclopedia of women in the Middle Ages. McFarland & Co. 2001 279p $45

Grades: 9 10 11 12   305.4

1. Women—History—Encyclopedias 2. Middle Ages—Encyclopedias

ISBN 0-7864-1119-8   LC 2001-126809

"This encyclopedia contains several hundred entries on the culture, history and circumstances of women in the Middle Ages, from the years 500 to 1500 C.E. . . . There are entries on queens, empresses, and other women in positions of leadership as well as entries on topics such as work, marriage and family, households, employment, religion, and various other aspects of women's lives in the Middle Ages. Genealogies of queens and empresses accompany the text." Publisher's note

Includes bibliographical references

Levy, Ariel, 1974-

Female chauvinist pigs; women and the rise of raunch culture. Free Press 2005 224p $25; pa $14

Grades: 11 12 Adult   305.4

1. Feminism 2. Sexism

ISBN 0-7432-4989-5; 0-7432-8428-3 (pa)

LC 2005-48811

The author argues that "our popular culture . . . has embraced a model of female sexuality that comes straight from pornography and strip clubs, in which the woman's job is to excite and titillate—to perform for men." N Y Times Book Rev

"A piercing look at how women are sabotaging their own attempts to be seen as equals by going about the quest the wrong way, Levy's engrossing book should be required reading for young women." Booklist

Includes bibliographical references

Matthews, Glenna

American women's history; a student companion. Oxford Univ. Press 2000 368p il (Oxford student companions to American history) lib bdg $60 *

Grades: 9 10 11 12   305.4

1. Women—United States—History

ISBN 0-19-511317-9   LC 99-87245

Alphabetical articles on major events, documents, persons, social movements, and political and social concepts connected with the history of women in America

"Articles vary in length and are easy to read. Many articles are accompanied by a photograph. . . . This is a helpful reference tool that will be useful to students needing information about American women and their contributions to U.S. history." Booklist

Includes bibliographical references

Mays, Dorothy A.

Women in early America; struggle, survival, and freedom in a new world. ABC-CLIO 2004 xxi, 495p il $95

Grades: 9 10 11 12   305.4

1. Women—United States—History—Encyclopedias

ISBN 1-85109-429-6   LC 2004-19721

The author offers "overviews of the diversity, as well as the commonalities, of both immigrant and native women's experience between 1607 and the outbreak of the War of 1812. . . . This resource offers large doses of easily accessible, hard-to-find-elsewhere information. Collections of any size serving students of our country's past will find it a popular and worthwhile addition." SLJ

Includes bibliographical references

Peavy, Linda Sellers, 1943-

Pioneer women; the lives of women on the frontier; [by] Linda Peavy & Ursula Smith. Oklahoma paperbacks ed. University of Oklahoma Press 1998 144p il pa $21.95

Grades: 9 10 11 12 Adult   305.4

1. Frontier and pioneer life—West (U.S.) 2. Women—West (U.S.)

ISBN 0-8061-3054-7; 978-0-8061-3054-5

LC 97-40684

First published 1996 by Smithmark Pubs.

An illustrated exploration of women's lives on the Western frontier. Marriages between Anglo men and Indian and Hispanic women are examined as are the lives of women who found employment outside the homestead as teachers, physicians and journalists.

"YAs seeking primary source material for women's studies and on the westward movement will find this exceptional collection of journals, letters, oral histories, and rarely seen photographs an outstanding resource." Booklist

Includes bibliographical references

Peril, Lynn
College girls; bluestockings, sex kittens, and coeds, then and now. Norton 2006 408p il pa S16.95
Grades: 11 12 Adult   **305.4**
1. Women—Education 2. College students
ISBN 978-0-393-32715-1; 0-393-32715-9
                                   LC 2006-18896
This is a "history of the American college girl." N Y Times Book Rev
The author's "witty, irreverent style, her generous use of old advertisements and photos and her careful footnotes make this text unusually user-friendly." Publ Wkly
Includes bibliographical references

The **Reader's** companion to U.S. women's history; editors, Wilma Mankiller [et al.] Houghton Mifflin 1998 xxii, 696p il $45; pa $20
Grades: 11 12 Adult   **305.4**
1. Women—United States—History 2. Women—Social conditions 3. Feminism
ISBN 0-395-67173-6; 0-618-00182-4 (pa)
                                   LC 97-39923
"This handbook includes more than 400 articles that consider questions pertaining to women's day-to-day lives. The list of contributors, numbering more than 300 [includes] such notables as Bella Abzug, Rita Mae Brown, Letty Cottin Pogrebin, and Gloria Steinem." Booklist
"Easily a cornerstone of any women's history collection, this ready-reference book makes fascinating reading." SLJ

Rosen, Ruth
The world split open; how the modern women's movement changed America. Viking 2000 446p il hardcover o.p. pa $15
Grades: 11 12 Adult   **305.4**
1. Women's movement 2. Feminism
ISBN 0-670-81462-8; 0-14-009719-8 (pa)
                                   LC 99-54439
"Rosen details the rebirth of feminism, from the liberalism of NOW through women's liberation, which grew out of the civil rights movement. Her focus is on the 'hidden injuries of sex' and how what had been construed as 'personal' problems—abortion, compulsory heterosexuality, rape and sexual violence, prostitution and pornography—became political issues." Publ Wkly
Includes bibliographical references

Sexual harassment; confrontations and decisions; edited by Edmund Wall. rev ed. Prometheus Bks. 2000 294p (Contemporary issues) pa $20
*
Grades: 9 10 11 12   **305.4**
1. Sexual harassment
ISBN 1-57392-830-5   LC 99-45206
First published 1992
This collection of essays offers some of the major debates in the research on sexual harassment, including defination and description of the problem
Includes bibliographical references

Strom, Sharon Hartman
Women's rights. Greenwood Press 2003 xxii, 353p (Major issues in American history) $55
Grades: 9 10 11 12   **305.4**
1. Women's rights
ISBN 0-313-31135-8   LC 2002-75337
"In fifteen chapters, the author provides an overview of the women's rights movement from its inception until contemporary times. . . . Some of the topics discussed are the Seneca Falls convention, women's involvement in the fight for voting rights, and their participation in team sports. . . . Each chapter provides a brief summary of the topic or event followed by excerpts from actual historical documents." Voice Youth Advocates
"Students and teachers of women's history, as well as those just exploring the field, will find this a superb book to use. . . . The descriptive bibliographies are extremely useful." Choice
Includes bibliographical references

Voices of resistance; Muslim women on war, faith, & sexuality; edited by Sarah Husain. Seal Press 2006 284p il map pa $16.95 *
Grades: 9 10 11 12   **305.4**
1. Muslim women
ISBN 978-1-58005-181-1; 1-58005-181-2
                                   LC 2006-5459
This "collection of fiction, poetry, interviews, essays, letters, and artwork celebrates diversity across race, nation, sexuality, and gender. Most contributors live in the U.S., and the focus is on post-9/11 America, connecting multiple immigrant histories and memories of 'home' with the personal and political in contemporary daily life. . . . Sure to spark discussion in college classrooms and among feminist and peace activist groups." Booklist
Includes bibliographical references

Waking up American; coming of age biculturally; [edited by] Angela Jane Fountas. Seal Press 2005 232p pa $15.95
Grades: 11 12 Adult   **305.4**
1. Children of immigrants 2. Women—United States
ISBN 1-58005-136-7; 978-1-58005-136-1
                                   LC 2005-11765
"'Where are you from?' In one of the best of the recent anthologies by new immigrants, young women writers answer that question with immediacy and wit, displaying honesty about the pain, anger, and prejudice at home and outside." Booklist

Wolf, Naomi
The beauty myth; how images of beauty are used against women. Perennial 2002 348p pa $14.95
Grades: 11 12 Adult   **305.4**
1. Women 2. Sex role 3. Personal appearance
ISBN 0-06-051218-0   LC 2002-72516
First published 1991 by Morrow
A "book about the ways women enslave themselves—and their bank accounts—to an industry that promises physical perfection." N Y Times Book Rev
The author "presents a provocative and persuasive account of the pervasiveness of the beauty ideal in all facets of Western culture." Libr J
Includes bibliographical references

Women in the classical world; image and text; {by} Elaine Fantham {et al.}. Oxford Univ. Press 1994 430p il maps hardcover o.p. pa $38.95 *

Grades: 11 12 Adult   **305.4**

1. Women—History

ISBN 0-19-506727-4; 0-19-509862-5 (pa)

LC 92-47284

This volume chronicles "the lives of women both famous and anonymous, aristocratic and indentured, worshiped and abused. The result is a unique illustrated chronological survey of women's lives built upon a foundation of vivid cultural and social history and laced with poetry, anecdotes, and original interpretations." Booklist

Includes bibliographical references

Women in the Middle Ages; an encyclopedia; edited by Katharina M. Wilson and Nadia Margolis. Greenwood Press 2004 2v il set $199.95

Grades: 11 12 Adult   **305.4**

1. Middle Ages—Encyclopedias 2. Women—History—Encyclopedias

ISBN 0-313-33016-6   LC 2004-53042

"In addition to entries on renowned women, there is a . . . number of articles covering topics such as footbinding, clothing, medicine, law, literary motifs, and geography-specific information. Terminology is defined in context, making the work readily accessible to high school students and lay readers." Libr J

Includes bibliographical references

Women's letters; America from the Revolutionary War to the present; edited by Lisa Grunwald & Stephen J. Adler. Dial Press 2005 824p il $35

Grades: 11 12 Adult   **305.4**

1. Women—United States—History—Sources

ISBN 0-385-33553-9   LC 2005-41446

This "book, with over 400 letters, is arranged chronologically, covering 230 years of American history. Each of its sections is preceded by a . . . timeline of events, and each letter is introduced with an explanatory note." N Y Times Book Rev

"This is a delightful collection of belles letters in the most literal sense of the term." Publ Wkly

Includes bibliographical references

Women's lives in medieval Europe: a sourcebook; edited by Emilie Amt. Routledge 1993 347p il pa $32.95 hardcover o.p.

Grades: 11 12 Adult   **305.4**

1. Women—Europe 2. Europe—History—476-1492

ISBN 0-415-90628-8 (pa)   LC 92-12815

"Excerpts from primary sources provide information regarding the daily lives of European women from A.D. 500 to 1500. Following an overview of the times . . . the materials are arranged chronologically. They trace a heritage of ideas, describing living conditions of noblewomen, workers, religious sects, and outsiders. Full bibliographic information precedes each entry. Although religious texts, public law, and regulations constitute a large portion of the documents, materials written by women are included when possible. YAs interested in the subject . . . will have their knowledge expanded, and they'll be able to meet many primary-source research requirements." SLJ

Women's rights; Shasta Gaughen, book editor. Greenhaven Press 2003 160p (Contemporary issues companion) lib bdg $25.96; pa $16.96

Grades: 9 10 11 12   **305.4**

1. Women's rights

ISBN 0-7377-0849-2 (lib bdg); 0-7377-0848-4 (pa)

LC 2002-72226

"This book opens with 'Historic Perspectives on Women's Rights' . . . .The second section addresses 'Women and the Workplace'. . . . One of the most intelligent compositions is Frederica Mathewes-Green's 'Finding Common Ground on Abortion,' in which the author compassionately pleads for society to pave a new path to resolve this ongoing controversy. . . . A well-organized and thoughtful collection." SLJ

Includes bibliographical references

Woolf, Virginia, 1882-1941

A room of one's own. Harcourt Brace Jovanovich 1991 c1929 125p $17; pa $10

Grades: 11 12 Adult   **305.4**

1. Women—Social conditions 2. Women authors 3. Women—Great Britain

ISBN 0-15-178733-6; 0-15-678733-4 (pa)

LC 91-17953

"An HBJ modern classic"

A reissue of the title first published 1929

"Woolf begins by announcing her basic thesis: that 'a woman must have money and a room of her own if she is to write fiction.' . . . She then examines the educational, social, and financial disadvantages and prejudices which have thwarted women writers throughout (English) history." Camb Guide to Lit in Engl

305.5 Social classes

Ehrenreich, Barbara

Nickel and dimed; on (not) getting by in boom-time America. Metropolitan Bks. 2001 221p $23; pa $13

Grades: 11 12 Adult   **305.5**

1. Minimum wage 2. Labor—United States 3. Poverty

ISBN 0-8050-6388-9; 0-8050-6389-7 (pa)

LC 00-52514

This is an exposé "of such abstractions as 'living wage' and 'affordable housing.' Ehrenreich worked, for a month at a time, at 'unskilled' jobs—as a waitress and chambermaid in Florida, a housecleaner and nursing-home aide in Maine, a Wal-Mart clerk in Minnesota—to report on how people survive on wages of six or seven dollars an hour." New Yorker

"No real answers to the problem but a compelling sketch of its reality and pervasiveness." Libr J

305.8 Ethnic and national groups

The **African** American almanac. Gale Res. 2007 il $240 *

Grades: 8 9 10 11 12 Adult   **305.8**

The African American almanac—*Continued*
1. African Americans
ISSN 1071-8710
ISBN 0-7876-4021-2; 978-0-7876-4021-7
First edition under the editorship of Harry A. Ploski published 1967 by Bellwether with title: The Negro almanac. Periodically revised. Editors vary
"Reference covering the cultural and political history of Black Americans. Includes generous amount of statistical information and biographies of Black Americans, both historical and contemporary." N Y Public Libr. Book of How & Where to Look It Up

African American breakthroughs; 500 years of black firsts; Jay P. Pederson and Jessie Carney Smith, editors. U.X.L 1995 280p il (African American reference library) $58 *
Grades: 6 7 8 9   **305.8**
1. African Americans—History
ISBN 0-8103-9496-0   LC 95-122049
Also available adult version entitled Black firsts (1994) published by Visible Ink Press
"Organized by subject, events are then listed chronologically. Subjects include *Business and Labor*; *Justice, Law Enforcement, and Public Safety*; *Religion*; and *Science, Medicine, and Invention*. . . . Each of the 500 entries consists of three or four sentences on the person or event with the original source or sources cited." Booklist

Antisemitism; a historical encyclopedia of prejudice and persecution; Richard S. Levy, editor. ABC-CLIO 2005 2v il set $185 *
Grades: 11 12 Adult   **305.8**
1. Antisemitism—Encyclopedias
ISBN 1-85109-439-3   LC 2005-9480
This encyclopedia provides an "overview and examination of anti-Semitism, with 650 double-column entries by over 200 contributors from 21 countries. . . . The focus of this work is on modern times, particularly the 19th and 20th centuries, but there are also many entries on anti-Jewish expression and actions through the ages." Libr J
This is "a balanced, well-written, exceedingly useful, and often compelling tool. . . . Levy's encyclopedia is crucial for any library serving a thinking public." Choice
Includes bibliographical references

The Arabs; Jean Brodsky Schur, book editor. Greenhaven Press 2005 218p map (Coming to America) lib bdg $34.95 *
Grades: 9 10 11 12   **305.8**
1. Arab Americans
ISBN 0-7377-2148-0   LC 2004-52356
"After a short introduction about Arab immigration, subsequent chapters discuss the various reasons Arabs chose to leave their home countries, the ways in which Arab Christians and Muslims adapted to American culture, and the types of discrimination and anti-Arab stereotyping faced by this group. . . . The selections are clearly written and informative." SLJ
Includes bibliographical references

Asante, Molefi K., 1942-
Erasing racism; the survival of the American nation; [by] Molefi Kete Asante. Prometheus Bks. 2003 294p il $27
Grades: 11 12 Adult   **305.8**
1. Racism 2. African Americans—Civil rights 3. African Americans—Social conditions 4. United States—Race relations
ISBN 1-591-02069-7   LC 2003-43208
In this "analysis of the history of racism in America, Asante divides the nation into two camps: a white majority who perceives America as a land of promise, and a black minority that is relegated to exist in a wilderness on the margins of society. . . . The key to bridging the racial divide, he argues, lies in getting all Americans to understand and confront the history of slavery. . . . Anyone who has struggled to understand race relations in America or to engage others in open debate about it will glean something valuable from this book." Publ Wkly
Includes bibliographical references

Autobiography of a people; three centuries of African American history told by those who lived it; [compiled by] Herb Boyd. Doubleday 2000 549p hardcover o.p. pa $15 *
Grades: 11 12 Adult   **305.8**
1. African Americans—History—Sources 2. African Americans—Biography
ISBN 0-385-49278-2; 0-385-49279-0 (pa)
                                      LC 99-16576
This volume contains excerpts from slave narratives, diaries, poems, letters, autobiographies, memoirs and speeches.
"Boyd includes the writers one would expect, such as Phyllis Wheatley, Frederick Douglass, W. E. B. Dubois, Reverend King, Malcolm X, and Colin Powell. But his collection may be most valuable to twenty-first century readers for the less familiar voices he gathers: slaves, freedmen and women, and, later, intellectuals, workers, and activists, whose experiences are captured in a protest or letter or memoir." Booklist
Includes bibliographical references

Avakian, Monique
Atlas of Asian-American history. Facts on File 2002 214p il maps (Facts on File library of American history) $85 *
Grades: 11 12 Adult   **305.8**
1. Asian Americans—History
ISBN 0-8160-3699-3   LC 00-49509
This "overview of the political, social, and cultural history of Asian Americans opens with a discussion of the Asian heritage and ends with comments on Asian America today. Personal anecdotes throughout range from the Chinese miners in 19th-century California to modern day health-care workers from India. Sixty full-color maps, 100 historical photos, and 34 line drawings and graphs lead the reader through discussions of the people of China, Japan, Korea, India, the Philippines, and Southeast Asia." Libr J
Includes bibliographical references

The **Black** Americans; a history in their own words, 1619-1983; edited by Milton Meltzer. 1st Harper trophy ed. Harper & Row 1987 c1984 306p il pa $12.99 *

Grades: 5 6 7 8 9 10   **305.8**

1. African Americans—History—Sources

ISBN 0-06-446055-X

"A Harper trophy book"

This is a revised and updated edition of In their own words: a history of the American Negro, edited by Milton Meltzer and published in three volumes, 1964-1967

A history of Black people in the United States, as told through letters, speeches, articles, eyewitness accounts, and other documents.

Black firsts: 4,000 ground-breaking and pioneering historical events; [edited by] Jessie Carney Smith. 2nd ed rev and expanded. Visible Ink Press 2003 787p il $58; pa $24.95 *

Grades: 11 12 Adult   **305.8**

1. African Americans—History

ISBN 1-57859-153-8; 1-57859-142-2 (pa)

                   LC 2002-154346

First published 1994 by Gale Research with title: Black firsts; 2,000 years of extraordinary achievement

"The chapters survey broad fields such as 'Arts and Entertainment,' 'Government: Local,' and 'Science and Medicine' and are broken down into more specific subject headings. 'Arts and Entertainment,' for example, encompasses 'Architecture,' 'Dance,' 'Music,' and 'Television,' among others. Under each of these headings, firsts are arranged chronologically. Each is described in an entry ranging from a line or two to half a page, and sources are always cited. . . . Many of the sidebars highlight achievements by women. . . . *Black firsts* remains an important part of the reference collection." Booklist

Includes bibliographical references

Chang, Iris, 1968-2004

The Chinese in America; a narrative history. Viking 2003 496p il hardcover o.p. pa $16

Grades: 11 12 Adult   **305.8**

ISBN 0-670-03123-2; 0-14-200417-0 (pa)

                   LC 2002-44858

The author recounts "the immigration of Chinese people to the U.S. from the early nineteenth century to the end of the twentieth. . . . Chang threads personal stories of individuals she came across in her research into her book, making it a much more human account. . . . This is history at its most dramatic and relevant." Booklist

Includes bibliographical references

The **Chinese**; C.J. Shane, book editor. Greenhaven Press 2005 206p map (Coming to America) lib bdg $34.95 *

Grades: 9 10 11 12   **305.8**

1. Chinese Americans

ISBN 0-7377-2150-2   LC 2003-67533

This book focuses on the experiences of Chinese immigrants, including the prejudices they faced in America. Includes chronologies and profiles of prominent Chinese Americans.

Includes bibliographical references

Du Bois, W. E. B. (William Edward Burghardt), 1868-1963

The Oxford W. E. B. Du Bois reader; edited by Eric J. Sundquist. Oxford Univ. Press 1996 680p pa $34.95 *

Grades: 11 12 Adult   **305.8**

1. African Americans 2. United States—Race relations

ISBN 0-19-509178-7   LC 95-21307

This reader covers Du Bois's "writing career, from the 1890s through the early 1960s. The volume selects key essays and longer works that portray the range of Du Bois's thought on such subjects as African American culture, the politics and sociology of American race relations, art and music, black leadership, gender and women's rights, Pan-Africanism and anti-colonialism, and Communism in the U.S. and abroad." Publisher's note

Includes bibliographical references

Eisner, Will, 1917-2005

The plot; the secret story of the Protocols of the Elders of Zion; with an introduction by Umberto Eco. Norton 2005 148p il $19.95; pa $14.95 *

Grades: 9 10 11 12   **305.8**

1. Protocols of the wise men of Zion 2. Antisemitism

ISBN 0-393-06045-4; 0-393-32860-0 (pa)

                   LC 2005-40527

This is an account done in cartoons of the history of the anti-Semitic tract The Protocols of the Elders of Zion.

The author "provides a great service to the truth by detailing the history of an infamous hoax." Libr J

Encyclopedia Latina; history, culture, and society in the United States; Ilan Stavans, editor in chief, Harold Augenbraum, associate editor. Grolier Academic Reference 2005 4v il map set $499 *

Grades: 11 12 Adult   **305.8**

1. Hispanic Americans—Encyclopedias

ISBN 0-7172-5815-7   LC 2004-23603

Contents: v. 1. 1492-Cuban missile crisis -- v. 2. Cuban revolution-literature, gay and lesbian -- v. 3. Literature, Latina American-race -- v. 4 Radio-Zorro

"The 650 signed entries contain some 150 biographies of notable Latinos, plus hundreds of articles pertaining to history, sociology, politics, contemporary issues, law, arts and sciences, and other topics important to Latino culture. . . . [This set's] articles are thorough, informative, and objective." Libr J

Includes bibliographical references

Encyclopedia of African-American culture and history; the Black experience in the Americas; Colin A. Palmer, editor in chief. 2nd ed. Macmillan Reference USA 2006 6v il map set $695

Grades: 11 12 Adult   **305.8**

1. African Americans—Encyclopedias

ISBN 0-02-865816-7   LC 2005-13029

First published 1996 under the editorship of Jack Salzman, David L. Smith, and Cornel West

"Readers can find comparative analyses of social movements, languages, religions and family structures in

Encyclopedia of African-American culture and history—*Continued*
the context of an interdisciplinary framework." Publisher's note
For a fuller review, see: Booklist, March 15, 2006
Includes bibliographical references

Encyclopedia of African American history, 1619-1895; from the colonial period to the age of Frederick Douglass; editor in chief, Paul Finkelman. Oxford University Press 2006 3v il set $375
Grades: 11 12 Adult   **305.8**
1. African Americans—History—Encyclopedias
ISBN 0-19-516777-5; 978-0-19-516777-1
LC 2005-33701
This encyclopedia, the first of a projected two sets focusing on African-American history, documents "blacks' experiences from the first slave ships to Frederick Douglass's death. The set offers depth, reaching most important persons, events, and developments through 1895 but is written for easy access with multiple cross references, chronologies, topical outlines, and a comprehensive index." Libr J
Includes bibliographical references

Encyclopedia of African American society; Gerald D. Jaynes, general editor. Sage Publications 2005 2v il set $295
Grades: 11 12 Adult   **305.8**
1. African Americans—Social life and customs—Encyclopedias 2. African Americans—Social conditions—Encyclopedias
ISBN 0-7619-2764-6   LC 2004-25515
"A Sage reference publication"
"With particular focus on social issues, the more than 700 alphabetically arranged articles here seek to provide readers with background information on the history and place of African Americans in this country's cultural and economic matrix. . . . [The entries] encompass subjects as huge as the origins of slavery or the course of the Civil Rights movement down to discussions of the 'Cakewalk,' the 'Sambo stereotype,' and hip-hop's 'Zulu Nation.'" SLJ
"This reference source will prove useful to any African American studies collection, especially those serving high school students and undergraduates." Choice
Includes bibliographical references

Encyclopedia of racism in the United States. Greenwood Press 2005 3v il set $249.95 *
Grades: 11 12 Adult   **305.8**
1. Racism—Encyclopedias 2. United States—Race relations—Encyclopedias
ISBN 0-313-32688-6   LC 2005-8523
"The majority of the 450 entries run about a paragraph to a page in length, covering sociological terms, current and historical events, individuals, organizations, books, court cases, government programs, and legislation. Twenty-five of the entries deal with such broad concepts as affirmative action or the Civil Rights Movement." Libr J
"With nearly a hundred pages of primary documents, the Encyclopedia will be a valuable supplement to studies of racism and multiculturalism." Choice
Includes bibliographical references

Ethnic violence; Myra H. Immell, book editor. Greenhaven Press 2000 160p (Contemporary issues companion) lib bdg $31.20; pa $19.95
Grades: 9 10 11 12   **305.8**
1. Violence 2. Ethnic relations 3. Race relations
ISBN 0-7377-0164-1 (lib bdg); 0-7377-0165-X (pa)
LC 99-36834
Among the topics covered are the Armenian genocide, the Holocaust, Arab-Israeli conflicts, and U.S. racial violence during the 1960s. Recent ethnic conflicts in Bosnia, Croatia, Albania, Kosovo, Asia and Africa are discussed
"Pertinent original-source material for researchers interested in varied perspectives on the subject." SLJ
Includes bibliographical references

Feagin, Joe R.
White men on race; power, privilege, and the shaping of cultural consciousness; {by} Joe Feagin and Eileen O'Brien. Beacon Press 2003 275p hardcover o.p. pa $18 *
Grades: 11 12 Adult   **305.8**
1. United States—Race relations 2. United States—Social conditions
ISBN 0-8070-0980-6; 0-8070-0983-0 (pa)
LC 2003-11632
Contents: "Race" in America -- The white bubble: learning about whiteness and the racial others -- Perspectives on whiteness -- Perspectives on African Americans and other Americans of color -- Issues of interracial dating and marriage -- Situations of possible discrimination: action and inaction -- Views on public policy: affirmative action and "reverse discrimination" -- The multiracial future
"Racism in the U.S., the authors argue, is a far more subtle phenomenon than it used to be, but it exists nonetheless—and it still excludes minorities from opportunities afforded white males. Based on hundreds of interviews with . . . elite white men—business managers, corporate execs, and the like—the book covers a wide range of subjects from the respondent's first encounter with an African American to interracial dating, affirmative action, and (of course) crime. . . . This is not a balanced, multisided look at racism; the authors are presenting a thesis . . . not trying to cover every point of view. Still, they make their case powerfully and persuasively." Booklist
Includes bibliographical references

Finkelstein, Norman H., 1941-
Forged in freedom; shaping the Jewish-American experience. Jewish Publ. Soc. 2002 204p il $24.95
Grades: 9 10 11 12   **305.8**
1. Jews—United States
ISBN 0-8276-0748-2   LC 2002-453
A history in words and photographs of the growth of the Jewish community in the United States and its contributions to American culture, politics, and economics in the twentieth century
This offers "an easy, open style and spacious design with lots of black-and-white photos. . . . Everyone will find something to argue with here, but this close-up view presents diversity and controversy in many forms." Booklist
Includes bibliographical references

Franklin, John Hope, 1915-
From slavery to freedom; a history of African
Americans; [by] John Hope Franklin, Alfred A.
Moss, Jr. 8th ed. Alfred A. Knopf 2000 xxiv, 742p
il map $49.95 *
Grades: 11 12 Adult   **305.8**
1. African Americans—History 2. Slavery—United
States
ISBN 0-375-40671-9   LC 2005-299886
Also available edition with study guide CD-ROM and
in paperback from McGraw-Hill
First published 1947
A survey of African-Americans history from slavery
to the present.
Includes bibliographical references

Freedom on my mind; the Columbia documentary
history of the African American experience;
Manning Marable, general editor; Nishani
Frazier and John McMillian, assistant editors.
Columbia University Press 2003 734p $80 *
Grades: 11 12 Adult   **305.8**
1. African Americans—History—Sources
ISBN 0-231-10890-7   LC 2003-51605
This "anthology features the works of noteworthy figures of African American history and culture . . . and
provides a tapestry of personal correspondence, excerpts
from slave narratives and autobiographies, leaflets,
speeches, oral histories and interviews, political manifestos, song lyrics, and important statements of black institutions and organizations . . . A necessary text of readings for both introductory and advanced African American studies courses." Choice
Includes bibliographical references

Gale encyclopedia of multicultural America;
contributing editor, Robert von Dassanowsky;
author of introduction, Rudolph J. Vecoli; edited
by Jeffrey Lehman. 2nd ed. Gale Group 2000
3v il set $215 *
Grades: 11 12 Adult   **305.8**
1. Minorities—Encyclopedias
ISBN 0-7876-3986-9   LC 99-44226
First published 1995 in two volumes
Contents: v1 Acadians-Garifuna Americans; v2 Georgian Americans-Ojibwa; v3 Oneidas-Yupiat
Essays on approximately 150 culture groups of the
U.S., from Acadians to Yupiats, covering their history,
acculturation and assimilation, family and community dynamics, language and religion
Includes bibliographical references

Gonzalez, Juan
Harvest of empire; a history of Latinos in
America. Viking 2000 xx, 346p hardcover o.p. pa
$15 *
Grades: 11 12 Adult   **305.8**
1. Hispanic Americans
ISBN 0-670-86720-9; 0-14-025539-7 (pa)
     LC 99-33526
The author notes that with rising immigration "Latinos
will constitute the largest minority in the nation by 2010.
Gonzalez explores why Spanish and British colonization

experiences were so different, particularly the divergence
in attitudes on slavery and race. . . . This is an important book for understanding a major American ethnic
group." Booklist
Includes bibliographical references

The **Greenwood** encyclopedia of African
American civil rights; from emancipation to the
twenty-first century; Charles D. Lowery and
John F. Marszalek, editors; Thomas Adams
Upchurch, associate editor; foreword by David
J. Garrow. Greenwood Press 2003 2v il set $175
*
Grades: 11 12 Adult   **305.8**
1. African Americans—Civil rights—Encyclopedias
2. United States—Race relations—Encyclopedias
ISBN 0-313-32171-X   LC 2003-40837
First published 1992 with title: Encyclopedia of African-American civil rights
"Entries are alphabetically arranged and cross-
referenced, and each is followed by a selected bibliography. Many of the entries focus on seminal political issues of the 1950s and 1960s—*Black Power, March on
Washington, Voter Education Project*—but also cover
important developments both before and after this time.
Other entries are biographical, ranging from politicians to
writers, artists, actors, musicians, and athletes. Important
literary documents are covered, including not only novels, plays, and political treatises but also journals. . . .
This set is recommended for high-school, public, and academic libraries." Booklist

Griffin, John Howard, 1920-1980
Black like me; the definitive Griffin estate
edition, corrected from original manuscripts; with
a foreword by Studs Terkel ; historic photographs
by Don Rutledge; and an afterword by Robert
Bonazzi. 1st Wings Press ed. Wings Press 2004
239p il $24.95; lib bdg $29.95 *
Grades: 11 12 Adult   **305.8**
1. African Americans—Southern States 2. Prejudices
ISBN 0-930324-72-2; 0-930324-73-0 (lib bdg)
     LC 2004-1549
Also available in hardcover from Buccaneer Bks. and
in paperback from New Am. Lib.
First published 1961
The author, "who is white, a Catholic, and a Texan,
conceived and carried out the unusual notion of blackening his skin with a newly developed pigment drug and
traveling through the Deep South as a Negro. This book,
part of which appeared in the Negro magazine Sepia, is
a journal account of that experience." New Yorker
Includes bibliographical references

Growing up Jewish in America; an oral history;
[compiled by] Myrna Katz Frommer and Harvey
Frommer. University of Nebraska Press 1999
264p il pa $15.95 *
Grades: 9 10 11 12 Adult   **305.8**
1. Jews—United States
ISBN 0-8032-6900-5   LC 99-34630
First published 1995 by Harcourt Brace & Co.

Growing up Jewish in America—*Continued*

The compilers "mix the experiences of some 100 interviewees—a good fraction of them writers or Jewish community officials—into a rich mosaic portrait. . . . Interviewees discuss politicization, the impact of the Holocaust, the effects of Zionism and the ongoing tensions about assimilation and anti-Semitism. . . . An accessible introduction to the varieties of the American Jewish experience." Publ Wkly

Includes bibliographical references

Hall, Loretta

Arab American voices. U.X.L 2000 233p il $58
*

Grades: 9 10 11 12   **305.8**

1. Arab Americans
ISBN 0-7876-2956-1   LC 99-37500

Twenty primary source documents from speeches, memoirs, poems, novels, and autobiographies present the words of Americans with roots in Lebanon, Syria, Palestine, Iraq, Egypt, and other Arab nations

"The works selected, from Kahlil Gibran's 'Dead Are My People' to the text of the U.S. government's Antiterrorism and Effective Death Penalty Act of 1986, should provide many new openings for discussions with students." Booklist

Includes glossary and bibliographical references

Haney-López, Ian

Racism on trial; the Chicano fight for justice; [by] Ian F. Haney Lopez. Harvard Univ. Press 2003 324p il hardcover o.p. pa $17.95

Grades: 11 12 Adult   **305.8**

1. Mexican Americans 2. Los Angeles (Calif.)—Race relations
ISBN 0-674-01068-X; 0-674-01629-7 (pa)
    LC 2002-38267

"In 1968, ten thousand students marched in protest over the terrible conditions prevalent in the high schools of East Los Angeles, the largest Mexican community in the United States. . . . Ian Haney López tells the . . . story of the Chicano movement in Los Angeles by following two criminal trials, including one arising from the student walkouts. He demonstrates how racial prejudice led to police brutality and judicial discrimination that in turn spurred Chicano militancy." Publisher's note

"This is a penetrating look at racial politics and evolving race consciousness among Latinos." Booklist

Includes bibliographical references

The **Harvard** guide to African-American history; Evelyn Brooks Higginbotham, editor-in-chief; Leon F. Litwack and Darlene Clark Hine, general editors; Randall K. Burkett, associate editor; foreword by Henry Louis Gates, Jr. Harvard Univ. Press 2001 xxxvi, 923p (Harvard University Press reference library) $125 *

Grades: 11 12 Adult   **305.8**

1. African Americans—History
ISBN 0-674-00276-8   LC 00-53861

"The first section includes 12 essays on historical research aids divided by topics such as films, newspapers, Internet resources, primary sources on microform, government documents, manuscript collections, and oral history archives. The second section contains comprehensive bibliographies . . . further subdivided into specific themes such as race relations, religion, color and class, politics and voting, urban conditions, and science and technology. The third section provides sources related to special subject matters: autobiographies of African Americans, studies identified by geographic region, and studies of African American women." Libr J

Heaton, Tim B.

Statistical handbook on racial groups in the United States; by Tim B. Heaton, Bruce A. Chadwick, and Cardell K. Jacobson. Oryx Press 2000 355p $65 *

Grades: 9 10 11 12   **305.8**

1. Ethnic groups 2. United States—Population
ISBN 1-57356-266-1   LC 00-28477

This work provides statistical comparisons on many topics including: educational goals, attitudes about employment, leisure activities, marital happiness, attitudes about contraception, religious beliefs, arrest rates, and political party preference

"More than 400 charts and tables provide a broad range of data on non-Hispanic whites, Native Americans, and African, Hispanic, and Asian-Americans. Most of the data come from U.S. government sources." Booklist

Includes bibliographical references

The **Hispanic** American almanac; a reference work on Hispanics in the United States; edited by Sonia G. Benson. 3rd ed. Gale Group 2003 xxvii, 886p il maps $135 *

Grades: 11 12 Adult   **305.8**

1. Hispanic Americans
ISBN 0-7876-2518-3   LC 2002-10070

First published 1993 under the editorship of Nicolás Kanellos

This is a "resource covering people of the U.S. whose ancestors come from Mexico, Cuba, Puerto Rico, and Central America. The book contains 25 subject chapters (e.g., 'Spanish Explorers and Colonizers'; 'Law, Government, and Military'; 'Art'. . . . A chronology offers a year-by-year outline of the migration of Hispanics to this country. . . . The 'Historical Overview' chapter details the evolution of three major Hispanic groups: Mexicans, Puerto Ricans, and Cubans. The 'Significant Documents' chapter provides the researcher with documents such as the Treaty of Guadalupe Hidalgo (1948), the NAFTA agreement, and California's Proposition 227. . . . The final chapter contains more than 500 biographies highlighting Hispanics. . . . Well organized and written at a reading level that is easily understood, this volume is an excellent resource for high-school and public libraries." Booklist

Includes bibliographical references

Horst, Heather A.

Jamaican Americans; [by] Heather A. Horst and Andrew Garner; series editor, Robert D. Johnston. Chelsea House 2007 144p il map (The new immigrants) lib bdg $27.95

Grades: 7 8 9 10 11 12   **305.8**

1. West Indian Americans 2. Immigrants—United States

ISBN 0-7910-8790-5; 978-0-7910-8790-9

LC 2006-25904

"Drawing on personal stories and historical fact, this . . . book focuses on this dynamic people and assesses their lasting impact." Publisher's note

Includes bibliographical references

Interracial America: opposing viewpoints; Eleanor Stanford, book editor. Greenhaven Press 2006 205p il lib bdg $34.95; pa $23.70 *

Grades: 8 9 10 11 12   **305.8**

1. United States—Race relations 2. Ethnic relations

ISBN 0-7377-2943-0 (lib bdg); 0-7377-2944-9 (pa)

LC 2005-54893

"Opposing viewpoints series"

The question of racial and ethnic differences is addressed sociologically and politically. Attention is given to immigration, affirmative action, interracial marriage, biracial children, and transracial adoption.

"For social-studies classes wishing to delve into the matter of race, this volume should prove helpful when used in conjunction with other source materials. It will be a boon to debaters." SLJ

Includes bibliographical references

The Irish; Karen Price Hossell, book editor. Greenhaven Press 2005 207p il (Coming to America) lib bdg $34.95 *

Grades: 9 10 11 12   **305.8**

1. Irish Americans

ISBN 0-7377-2154-5   LC 2004-47582

"The contributors to this volume explore why the Irish left their homeland, the experiences of the immigrants and their descendants, and the achievements of notable Irish Americans." Publisher's note

Includes bibliographical references

The Italian American experience; an encyclopedia; editors, Salvatore J. LaGumina [et al.] Garland 2000 735p il (Garland reference library of the humanities) $130

Grades: 11 12 Adult   **305.8**

1. Italian Americans—Encyclopedias

ISBN 0-8153-0713-6   LC 99-38629

In addition to short biographies of prominent people, this "book contains essays on the ways in which Italian Americans changed American geography and history. There are entries describing the country's many Little Italys; on how Italian Americans changed pop music with singers such as Frank Sinatra and Madonna; and on Italians' formation of and influence on labor unions. . . . This is a thorough, accessible reference work." Libr J

The Italians; C.J. Shane, book editor. Greenhaven Press 2005 208p il (Coming to America) lib bdg $34.95 *

Grades: 9 10 11 12   **305.8**

1. Italian Americans

ISBN 0-7377-2765-9   LC 2004-54132

This book focuses on the experiences of Italian immigrants, including the ethnic stereotyping Italian Americans still face today. Includes chronologies and profiles of prominent Italian Americans.

Includes bibliographical references

Katz, William Loren

Black Indians; a hidden heritage. Atheneum Pubs. 1986 198p il $17.95; pa $10

Grades: 9 10 11 12   **305.8**

1. African Americans 2. Native Americans

ISBN 0-689-31196-6; 0-689-80901-8 (pa)

LC 85-28770

Traces the history of relations between blacks and American Indians, and the existence of black Indians, from the earliest foreign landings through pioneer days.

The author "has provided a valuable addition to titles on American Indians. Excellent for assignments, it contains important information many history instructors may be unaware of. His sections on black Indians and the Seminoles of Florida and their views about living together are particularly good." Child Book Rev Serv

Includes bibliographical references

Kennedy, Randall

Nigger; the strange career of a troublesome word. Pantheon Bks. 2002 226p hardcover o.p. pa $12

Grades: 11 12 Adult   **305.8**

1. African Americans 2. Racism 3. United States—Race relations

ISBN 0-375-42172-6; 0-375-71371-9 (pa)

LC 2001-36442

Kennedy examines the history of the use of the racial epithet in American society by both African Americans and whites and its implications for race relations

"An insightful and highly provocative book that raises vital questions about the relationship between language, politics, social norms and how society and culture confront racism." Publ Wkly

Includes bibliographical references

Langer, Elinor, 1939-

A hundred little Hitlers; the death of a black man, the trial of a white racist, and the rise of the neo-nazi movement in America. Metropolitan Bks. 2003 398p hardcover o.p. pa $15

Grades: 11 12 Adult   **305.8**

1. Seraw, Mulugeta 2. White supremacy movements 3. United States—Race relations

ISBN 0-8050-5098-1; 0-312-42363-2 (pa)

LC 2003-42167

"This book focuses on the 1988 murder of an Ethiopian man, Mulugeta Seraw, by three skinheads in Portland, Oregon. . . . Although the killers avoided trial, California hate-monger Tom Metzger and his son, John, did

Langer, Elinor, 1939-—*Continued*
stand trial in Portland for conspiracy, charged with inciting the murder through propaganda and an agent." Booklist

"Langer's valuable and chilling view into the modern American racist movement is recommended for all libraries." Libr J

Includes bibliographical references

Meagher, Timothy J.
The Columbia guide to Irish American history; [by] Timothy Meagher. Columbia University Press 2005 398p (Columbia guides to American history and cultures) $47.50 *

Grades: 11 12 Adult   **305.8**
1. Irish Americans
ISBN 0-231-12070-2   LC 2005-43233
The author "examines Irish American history from the first Irish settlements in the seventeenth century through the famine years in the nineteenth century to the unpredictability of 1960s America and beyond to the twentieth century. Teachers and students interested in the history of Irish America will welcome this book." Univ Press Books for Public and Second Sch Libr, 2006
Includes bibliographical references

The **Mexicans**; C.J. Shane, book editor. Greenhaven Press 2005 221p il map (Coming to America) lib bdg $34.95 *

Grades: 9 10 11 12   **305.8**
1. Mexican Americans
ISBN 0-7377-2156-1   LC 2004-46078
This book focuses on the experiences of Mexican immigrants, including those who became Americans by default after the Mexican-American War of 1848 and those who are immigrating today. Includes chronologies and profiles of prominent Mexican Americans
Includes bibliographical references

The **New** York Public Library African American desk reference. Wiley 1999 606p il $40 *

Grades: 11 12 Adult   **305.8**
1. African Americans—Encyclopedias
ISBN 0-471-23924-0
"A Stonesong Press book"
This reference is "arranged into 19 chapters covering topics such as slavery, education, health, law, science and technology, the arts, and sports. Chapters include numerous tables, lists, photographs, and sidebars and end with sources for additional information. Quotations are sprinkled throughout." Booklist
Includes bibliographical references

Race relations: opposing viewpoints; James D. Torr, book editor. Greenhaven Press 2005 208p il lib bdg $34.95; pa $23.70 *

Grades: 9 10 11 12   **305.8**
1. United States—Race relations
ISBN 0-7377-2955-4 (lib bdg); 0-7377-2956-2 (pa)
                                            LC 2004-59763
"Opposing viewpoints series"
This book explores race-related "topics in the following chapters: What Is the State of Race Relations in America? Is Racism a Serious Problem? What Should the Government Do to Improve Race Relations? How Can Society Improve Race Relations?" Publisher's note
Includes bibliographical references

Racism; Mary E. Williams, book editor. Greenhaven Press 2004 188p (Current controversies) $33.70; pa $22.45

Grades: 9 10 11 12   **305.8**
1. Racism 2. United States—Race relations
ISBN 0-7377-1629-0; 0-7377-1630-4 (pa)
                                            LC 2003-54020
"Some analysts believe that racism is no longer a serious problem, while others insist that discrimination continues to oppress minorities and impede their social and economic progress. Chapters in this anthology include: How Prevalent is Racism? How Can Racism Be Combated?" Publisher's note
Includes bibliographical references

Rangaswamy, Padma, 1945-
Indian Americans; series editor: Robert D. Johnston. Chelsea House 2007 158p il map (The new immigrants) lib bdg $27.95

Grades: 7 8 9 10 11 12   **305.8**
1. East Indians—United States 2. Immigrants—United States
ISBN 0-7910-8786-7   LC 2006-8384
The author traces the history of new immigrants from India "from the early days of the Punjabi pioneers in California to the triumphs of the 'dot-com generation.'" Publisher's note
Includes bibliographical references

Remembering Jim Crow; African Americans tell about life in the segregated South; edited by William H. Chafe {et al.}. New Press (NY) 2001 xxxv, 346p il $55; pa $16.95 *

Grades: 11 12 Adult   **305.8**
1. African Americans—Segregation 2. African Americans—Southern States 3. Southern States—Race relations
ISBN 1-56584-697-4; 1-56584-778-4 (pa)
                                            LC 2001-31224
Companion volume to Remembering slavery
Recollections taken from interviews compiled by the Behind the Veil Project at the Center for Documentary Studies at Duke University
This work offers "views into the thoughts, activities, and anxieties of black Americans. . . . Included are two one-hour CDs of the radio documentary produced by American Radio Works, a transcript of the audio program, 50 rare segregation-era photographs, biographical information, and suggestions for further reading. This {is a} superb primary source." Libr J
Includes bibliographical references

Sachar, Howard Morley, 1928-
A history of the Jews in America; by Howard M. Sachar. Knopf 1992 1051p pa $25 hardcover o.p. *

Grades: 11 12 Adult   **305.8**
1. Jews—United States
ISBN 0-679-74530-0 (pa)   LC 91-4261

Sachar, Howard Morley, 1928——*Continued*
The author examines "two different subjects. One is the rich, sometimes dark, ultimately triumphant story of Jews in the United States. The other is the relation between American Jews and Israel, a matter of the widest interest, for probably no other group in this country is so deeply committed to the success of a foreign state. That poses problems that Mr. Sachar confronts unflinchingly and in detail, making his narrative not only good history but a contribution to the current debate over American-Israeli relations." N Y Times Book Rev
Includes bibliographical references

Should America pay? slavery and the raging debate over reparations; {edited by} Raymond A. Winbush. Amistad 2003 396p hardcover o.p. pa $13.95
Grades: 11 12 Adult   **305.8**
1. African Americans 2. Slavery—United States
ISBN 0-06-008310-7; 0-06-008311-5 (pa)
                                    LC 2002-27927
The author addresses the issue "of paying reparations to black Americans for slavery. . . . He explores numerous voices within the reparations movement and commentary on the various stages and aspects of the movement. He also examines the significance of grassroots organizations in the development of the reparations movement, as well as legal perspectives and dissenting voices. This is a complete and balanced look at a controversial topic." Booklist
Includes bibliographical references

Takaki, Ronald T., 1939-
Strangers from a different shore; a history of Asian Americans; {by} Ronald Takaki. Updated and rev ed, 1st Back Bay ed. Little, Brown 1998 591p il pa $16.95 *
Grades: 11 12 Adult   **305.8**
1. Asian Americans—History
ISBN 0-316-83130-1   LC 98-218270
First published 1989
This work discusses the Chinese transcontinental railroad workers, the plantation workers in the Hawaii canefields, the Japanese Americans in the U.S. internment camps during World War II, the Hmong refugees in Wisconsin and the stereotypical image of Asian American youth as model students
Includes bibliographical references

U-X-L Asian American almanac; edited by Irene Natividad and Susan B. Gall. 2nd ed. U-X-L 2004 268p il map $58 *
Grades: 9 10 11 12   **305.8**
1. Asian Americans
ISBN 0-7876-7598-9   LC 2003-110047
First published 1995 with title: Asian American almanac
"Explores the culture and history of the diverse groups of Americans who descend from Asian and Pacific Island countries: Asian Indian, Cambodian, Chinese, Filipino, Native Hawaiian, Hmong, Indonesian, Korean, Japanese, Laotian, Pacific Island, Pakistani, Thai, and Vietnamese Americans. The Almanac is organized into 17 subject chapters on topics including family, health, religion, employment, civil rights and activism, education, law, demographics, literature and theater, and sports." Publisher's note
Includes glossary and bibliographical references

W.E.B. Du Bois; editor, Harold Bloom. Chelsea House 2001 (Modern critical views) $36.95
Grades: 9 10 11 12   **305.8**
1. Du Bois, W. E. B. (William Edward Burghardt), 1868-1963 2. African Americans—Intellectual life 3. African Americans—Political activity 4. United States—Race relations
ISBN 0-7910-5915-4   LC 00-50945
For complete list of series titles contact publisher
This collection of scholarly essays, articles and book excerpts focus on Du Bois's aesthetic and political views, his creative writing and his literary achievements. It also looks at his attempts to muster enthusiasm for the writing of a pan-African encyclopedia as well as Du Bois's early years as a young professor at the University of Pennsylvania in the 1890s.
Includes bibliographical references

What are you? voices of mixed-race young people; {edited by} Pearl Fuyo Gaskins. Holt & Co. 1999 273p il $18.95 *
Grades: 7 8 9 10   **305.8**
1. Racially mixed people 2. Teenagers 3. United States—Race relations
ISBN 0-8050-5968-7   LC 98-37381
Many young people of racially mixed backgrounds discuss their feelings about family relationships, prejudice, dating, personal identity, and other issues
"While underscoring the complexity of the mixed-race experience, these unadorned voices offer a genuine, poignant, enlightening and empowering message to all readers." SLJ
Includes bibliographical references

Williams, Lena
It's the little things; the everyday interactions that get under the skin of Blacks and whites. Harcourt 2000 268p $22; pa $14 *
Grades: 11 12 Adult   **305.8**
1. United States—Race relations 2. African Americans
ISBN 0-15-100407-2; 0-15-601348-7 (pa)
                                    LC 00-37027
The author discusses "a range of annoying to dangerous incidences that are caused by the lack of understanding between the races. Williams examines the arenas of the workplace, public places, school, home, social settings, and the media. She recounts incidents from the mundane to the infamous." Booklist

Wormser, Richard, 1933-
The rise and fall of Jim Crow; the African-American struggle against discrimination, 1865-1954. Watts 1999 144p il map lib bdg $23 *
Grades: 7 8 9 10   **305.8**
1. African Americans—Segregation 2. African Americans—Civil rights 3. United States—Race relations
ISBN 0-531-11443-0   LC 99-28254

Wormser, Richard, 1933—_Continued_

Discusses the laws and practices that supported discrimination against African Americans from Reconstruction to the Supreme Court decision that found segregation to be illegal

Wormser "writes quietly, without sensationalism, in an immediate present-tense narrative illustrated with occasional black-and-white photos." Booklist

Includes bibliographical references

The **Young** Oxford history of African Americans; Robin D. G. Kelley and Earl Lewis, general editors. Oxford Univ. Press 1994-1997 11v il maps set $264 *

Grades: 9 10 11 12   305.8

1. African Americans—History 2. United States—Race relations

ISBN 0-19-508502-7

Contents: v1 The first passage, by C. A. Palmer; v2 Strange new land, by P. H. Wood; v3 Revolutionary citizens, by D. C. Littlefield; v4 Let my people go, by D. G. White; v5 Break those chains at last, by N. Frankel; v6 Though justice sleeps, by B. Bair; v7 A chance to make good, by J. R. Grossman; v8 From a raw deal to a new deal? by J. W. Trotter; v9 We changed the world, by V. Harding; v10 Into the fire, by R. D. G. Kelley; v11 Biographical supplement and index, by D. M. Freund and M. McQuirter

This set "provides an in-depth examination of African-American involvement in every historical period from the Spanish explorers through the L. A. riots of 1992 and their aftermath. Each book has a detailed time-line, a thorough index and an extensive list for further reading." Child Book Rev Serv

Zia, Helen

Asian American dreams; the emergence of an American people. Farrar, Straus & Giroux 2000 356p il hardcover o.p. pa $14

Grades: 11 12 Adult   305.8

1. Asian Americans

ISBN 0-374-14774-4; 0-374-52736-9 (pa)

LC 99-26746

"Zia surveys the history of Asian Americans, the rapid development of their new political force, and the unique issues they face. This well-written book is an important addition to the growing field of Asian American studies." Libr J

Includes bibliographical references

305.9 Occupational and miscellaneous groups

Martínez, Rubén

The new Americans; photographs by Joseph Rodríguez. New Press 2004 251p il $25

Grades: 11 12 Adult   305.9

1. United States—Immigration and emigration

ISBN 1-565-84792-X   LC 2003-70621

"This book, a companion to a PBS miniseries, details the lives of seven families who have recently arrived in the United States from the West Bank, Nigeria, the Do-

minican Republic, Mexico, and India." Libr J

"Masterfully evoking such diverse settings as a Palestinian wedding in Chicago, a raucous ball game in Guatemala City and a torpid migrant trailer camp in California, Martínez's writing is clear-eyed and incisive—and sometimes heartbreaking and hilarious." Publ Wkly

Includes bibliographical references

Moorehead, Caroline

Human cargo; a journey among refugees. H. Holt 2005 330p maps $26; pa $16

Grades: 11 12 Adult   305.9

1. Refugees

ISBN 0-8050-7443-0; 0-312-42561-9 (pa)

LC 2004-54239

The author "tours a number of refugee milieus, visiting, among others, Liberian refugees in Cairo, Mexican migrants waiting to cross into the United States, Mideastern refugees detained in Australian internment camps and Palestinian refugees still nursing hopes of returning to a homeland they have never seen. . . . Moorehead draws sympathetic portraits of individual refugees, replete with horror stories of the travails they fled and their precarious but hopeful efforts to build new lives, but also pulls back to examine what she says are the sometimes counterproductive policies of aid organizations and the indifference and callousness of Western governments." Publ Wkly

Includes bibliographical references

306 Culture and institutions

American values: opposing viewpoints; Mary E. Williams, book editor. Greenhaven Press 2005 204p il $33.70; pa $22.45 *

Grades: 9 10 11 12   306

1. Social values 2. United States—Moral conditions

ISBN 0-7377-2220-7; 0-7377-2221-5 (pa)

LC 2004-40520

"Opposing viewpoints series"

In this "anthology, authors discuss the nature of such values as patriotism, consumerism, religion, and altruism. Chapters include: What Values Should America Uphold? Is America in Moral Decline? How Should Patriotism Be Defined? How Could American Values Be Improved?" Publisher's note

Includes bibliographical references

Current issues: Macmillan social science library. Macmillan Ref. USA 2003 4v set $375

Grades: 9 10 11 12   306

1. Social problems 2. United States—Social conditions 3. United States—Politics and government—1989-

ISBN 0-02-865744-6   LC 2002-8469

"Some 265 entries treat subjects ranging from _Abortion_ and _Academic freedom_ to _Women's rights_ and _Work_. . . . Information is clearly presented, usually providing an overview, historical background, constitutional or legal principles, ethical or social aspects, and several different points of view." Booklist

Includes glossary and bibliographical references

Fischer, Claude S., 1948-
Century of difference; how America changed in
the last one hundred years; [by] Claude S. Fischer
and Michael Hout. Russell Sage Foundation 2006
411p il map $45
Grades: 11 12 Adult　　　　　　　　**306**
1. American national characteristics 2. Social change
3. United States—History—20th century 4. United
States—Social conditions
ISBN 0-8715-4352-4; 978-0-8715-4352-3
　　　　　　　　　　　　　　LC 2006-21640
"Differences in American family life, work, and worship between the years of 1900 and 2000 are compared
and examined in concise details. While the included statistics and graphs are plentiful and easy to use, most value is provided in the extensive commentary that breaths
life into the data comparisons." Univ Press Books for
Public and Second Sch Libr, 2007
Includes bibliographical references

Johnson, Steven
Everything bad is good for you; how today's
pop culture is actually making us smarter.
Riverhead Books 2005 238p il $23.95; pa $14
Grades: 11 12 Adult　　　　　　　　**306**
1. Popular culture 2. Intellect
ISBN 1-57322-307-7; 1-59448-194-6 (pa)
　　　　　　　　　　　　　　LC 2005-42769
The author "makes the case that popular culture has
become more intellectually challenging in the past 30
years. . . . He suggests that increases in IQ scores in the
past century could be related to more challenging enter-
tainment." Christ Sci Monit
This "is a brisk, witty read, well versed in the history
of literature and bolstered with research." Time
Includes bibliographical references

Long, Douglas, 1967-
Fundamentalists and extremists. Facts on File
2002 266p (Library in a book) $45
Grades: 11 12 Adult　　　　　　　　**306**
1. Religious fundamentalism 2. Religion and politics
3. United States—Religion
ISBN 0-8160-4846-0　　　　　LC 2002-1291
"In his introduction, Long spells out the difference between fundamentalism and extremism. The author then
traces the history of both subjects, followed by a chronology of key events. An overview of key court cases
and paragraph-length entries on important figures are
also included. The next section provides hints on how
and where to look for more information. . . . Part three
excerpts from the transcripts of three court cases: the
Scopes trial, Brown v. Board of Education, and Roe v.
Wade." SLJ
"The subject overview is clear and concise. . . .
[This] is a must-have for research." Voice Youth Advocates
Includes glossary and bibliographical references

Underhill, Paco
The call of the mall; a walking tour through the
crossroads of our shopping culture. Simon &
Schuster 2004 227p $25.95; pa $14
Grades: 11 12 Adult　　　　　　　　**306**
1. Shopping centers and malls 2. Consumption (Economics) 3. Consumers
ISBN 0-7432-3591-6; 0-7432-3592-4 (pa)
　　　　　　　　　　　　　　LC 2003-64960
The author takes readers on a "tour of a typical Saturday at a large, regional mall. He examines the routes
there, the shopping center itself, the stores, food, entertainment, ambience. and the customers. He shows why
the mall is the way it is and how it could be improved.
He provides insight into how the stores are arranged,
how they display merchandise. and the different ways
that men and women respond to this environment." SLJ

306.4　Specific aspects of culture

Are athletes good role models? Geoff Griffin,
book editor. Greenhaven Press 2005 95p (At
issue) lib bdg $28.70; pa $19.95 *
Grades: 9 10 11 12　　　　　　　　**306.4**
1. Athletes 2. Conduct of life
ISBN 0-7377-2695-4 (lib bdg); 0-7377-2696-2 (pa)
　　　　　　　　　　　　　　LC 2004-54289
"In this anthology, the authors debate the positive and
negatives aspects of athletes as role models." Publisher's
note
Includes bibliographical references

306.7　Sexual relations

Encyclopedia of lesbian, gay, bisexual, and
transgender history in America; Marc Stein,
editor in chief. Thomson Learning 2003 3v set
$380
Grades: 11 12 Adult　　　　　　　　**306.7**
1. Homosexuality 2. Lesbianism
ISBN 0-684-31261-1　　　　　LC 2003-17434
This set "includes approximately 545 articles ranging
from short biographical entries to longer essays surveying topics such as the Stonewall riots, federal law and
policy, same-sex institutions and AIDS. . . . Features include a guide to archival sources, a chronology/timeline,
a historical overview essay and a comprehensive index."
Publisher's note
"Stein puts together an impressive set. . . . This information is available elsewhere, but this resource gathers
it in one easy-to-use source." Voice Youth Advocates
Includes bibliographical references

Sex: opposing viewpoints. Greenhaven Press 2006
208p il lib bdg $34.95; pa $23.70
Grades: 7 8 9 10　　　　　　　　**306.7**
1. Sexual behavior
ISBN 0-7377-2959-7 (lib bdg); 0-7377-2960-0 (pa)
　　　　　　　　　　　　　　LC 2005-52578
"Opposing viewpoints series"
"Authors debate several issues such as premarital sex,
gay marriage, and virginity pledges in this . . . antholo-
gy." Publisher's note
Includes bibliographical references

The **Sexual** revolution; Mary E. Williams, book editor. Greenhaven Press 2002 240p (American social movements) $33.70; pa $22.45 *

Grades: 9 10 11 12   **306.7**

1. Sexual behavior 2. Sexual ethics
ISBN 0-7377-1052-7; 0-7377-1051-9 (pa)
                              LC 2001-8358

An anthology of articles, speeches, interviews and essays which explore how changes in attitudes toward sexuality and developments such as readily available means of birth control transformed society throughout the twentieth century

"There's as much here for adults as there is for teens; in fact, the {book} would be excellent for family discussion." Booklist

Includes bibliographical references

Teen sex; Christine Watkins, book editor. Greenhaven Press 2005 124p (At issue) lib bdg $28.70; pa $19.95 *

Grades: 9 10 11 12   **306.7**

1. Youth—Sexual behavior
ISBN 0-7377-2426-9 (lib bdg); 0-7377-2427-7 (pa)
                              LC 2004-54288

This book "explores the issues of sex education, parental involvement, gay and lesbian clubs, television's influence, dangers of the Internet, and most importantly, how teenagers themselves feel about sex." Publisher's note

Includes bibliographical references

Turner, Jeffrey S.
Dating and sexuality in America; a reference handbook. ABC-CLIO 2003 300p (Contemporary world issues) $45 *

Grades: 9 10 11 12   **306.7**

1. Dating (Social customs) 2. Sexual behavior
ISBN 1-85109-584-5

Contents: Background and history -- Issues, controversies, and solutions -- Worldwide perspective -- Chronology -- Biographical sketches -- Facts and data -- Directory of organizations, associations, and Agencies -- Selected print and nonprint resources

This "preliminary overview of dating and sexuality in the United States includes a history, the standard issues (teenage pregnancy, birth control, sexually transmitted diseases) and contemporary concerns such as Internet dating and club drugs. Dating customs and attitudes toward sexuality in other countries are also explored. . . . Turner does a fine job of presenting the issues in an unbiased, concise, and readable style, avoiding the moralistic overtones found in some works on this topic for this age group." Libr Media Connect

Includes bibliographical references

306.76   Sexual orientation

The **Full** spectrum; a new generation of writing about gay, lesbian, bisexual, transgender, questioning, and other identities; edited by David Levithan & Billy Merrell. Knopf 2006 272p il pa $9.95 *

Grades: 8 9 10 11 12   **306.76**

1. Gay men 2. Lesbians 3. Sex role 4. Homosexuality
ISBN 0-375-93290-9   LC 2005-23435

"The 40 contributions to this invaluable collection about personal identity have two things in common: all are nonfiction and all are by writers under the age of 23. Beyond that, diversity is the order of the day, and the result is a vivid demonstration of how extraordinarily broad the spectrum of sexual identity is among today's gay, lesbian, bisexual, transgender, and questioning youth. . . . Insightful, extraordinarily well written, and emotionally mature, the selections offer compelling, dramatic evidence that what is important is not *what* we are but *who* we are." Booklist

Gay and lesbian rights in the United States; a documentary history; edited by Walter L. Williams and Yolanda Retter. Greenwood Press 2003 317p (Primary documents in American history and contemporary issues) $49.95 *

Grades: 9 10 11 12   **306.76**

1. Gay men—Civil rights 2. Gay liberation movement 3. Homosexuality
ISBN 0-313-30696-6   LC 2002-35218

"This collection of primary documents . . . [provides] varying viewpoints on the complex issue of gay and lesbian rights. Personal testimonies, laws, opinion pieces, court cases, and other documents, dating from colonial times to the present day [are examined]." Publisher's note

This volume "is fascinating to anyone interested in or researching GLBT history. The documents clearly show the evolution of thought on issues of homosexuality." Voice Youth Advocates

Includes bibliographical references

Gay rights; Kate Burns, book editor. Greenhaven Press 2006 237p (History of issues) lib bdg $34.95

Grades: 9 10 11 12   **306.76**

1. Gay men—Civil rights 2. Homosexuality
ISBN 0-7377-2867-1   LC 2005-46331

"This volume examines early gay rights efforts as well as the burgeoning gay liberation movement after Stonewall. Topics include gays in the military, lesbian-feminism, family issues, AIDS-related activism, hate crimes legislation and the battle over same-sex marriage." Publisher's note

Includes bibliographical references

The **Gay** rights movement; Jennifer Smith, book editor. Greenhaven Press 2003 222p (American social movements) $34.95; pa $23.70

Grades: 9 10 11 12   **306.76**

1. Gay liberation movement
ISBN 0-7377-1158-2; 0-7377-1157-4 (pa)
                              LC 2002-192516

The Gay rights movement—*Continued*

This is a "selection of pro-gay articles by a wide variety of authors in chapters like 'Origins of the Gay Rights Movement,' 'Coming Out and Coming Together,' and 'The Struggle for Survival.' The depth and scope of the information are noteworthy. . . . This clearly written, concise book has an excellent table of contents and index, as well as an outstanding list for further research consisting of books, periodicals, films, Internet sources, and Web sites." SLJ

Hear me out: true stories of Teens Educating and Confronting Homophobia; a project of Planned Parenthood of Toronto; [edited by Frances Rooney] Second Story Press 2004 197p il pa $9.95 *

Grades: 8 9 10 11 12   **306.76**
1. Homosexuality 2. Transsexualism 3. Bisexuality
ISBN 1-896764-87-8

"A project of Planned Parenthood of Toronto, this collection of personal accounts of sexual self-discovery by volunteers in the organization's peer-based T.E.A.C.H. program (Teens Educating and Confronting Homophobia) is remarkable for the diversity of social, economic, ethnic, and racial backgrounds represented. The 20 stories included demonstrate the wide spectrum of gay, lesbian, queer, transgender, transsexual, and questioning young-adult experiences. . . . An important and emotionally powerful collection that is sure to encourage thought and discussion." Booklist

Homosexuality: opposing viewpoints; Auriana Ojeda, editor. Greenhaven Press 2004 240p lib bdg $34.95 *

Grades: 7 8 9 10   **306.76**
1. Homosexuality
ISBN 0-7377-1687-8 (lib bdg)   LC 2003-44859

"Opposing viewpoints series"

This presents opposing viewpoints answering such questions as "Should Society Encourage Increased Acceptance of Homosexuality?" and "Is Homosexuality Immoral?"

"This well-researched, unbiased anthology includes a variety of provocative articles and essays that are sure to invite criticism, discussion, and debate." SLJ
Includes bibliographical references

Hudson, David L., 1969-

Gay rights; [by] David L. Hudson, Jr. Chelsea House 2004 114p (Point-counterpoint) $37.50
Grades: 7 8 9 10   **306.76**
1. Lesbians—Civil rights 2. Gay men—Civil rights
ISBN 0-7910-8094-3   LC 2004-13828

Contents: Point: same-sex couples have a fundamental right to marry; Counterpoint: marriage is between a man and a woman; Point: gays and lesbians should not face discrimination as parents; Counterpoint: states have the power to protect children by giving preference to heterosexual parents; Point: employers should not be able to discriminate against gays and lesbians; Counterpoint: gays and lesbians don't need special treatment in the workforce; Point: the military should end its discriminatory policy toward gays and lesbians; Counterpoint: the military can prohibit homosexual conduct in the military

"Gay marriage, adoption rights, workplace rights, and service in the armed forces are all argued pro and con in a clear, journalistic style. Both sides of an issue are reinforced with sidebars of pertinent U.S. court case decisions and provocative questions. Well-organized footnotes and an index provide easy access to more specific perspectives on each argument, and a section on 'Beginning Legal Research' is also included." SLJ
Includes bibliographical references

Huegel, Kelly

GLBTQ (Gay, Lesbian, Bisexual, Transgender, Questioning); the survival guide for queer & questioning teens. Free Spirit 2003 224p il pa $15.95 *

Grades: 7 8 9 10 11 12   **306.76**
1. Homosexuality 2. Transsexualism 3. Bisexuality
ISBN 1-57542-126-7   LC 2002-156692

Contents: GLBTQ basics; Homophobia; Coming out; Life at school; GLBTQ friends; Dating and relationships; Sex; Your health; Drugs, alcohol and tobacco; Religion and culture; Work, college & beyond; Transgender teens

Describes the challenges faced by gay, lesbian, bisexual, and transgendered teens, offers practical advice, real-life experiences, and accessible resources and support groups

"Huegel has written an indispensable guide for gay, lesbian, bisexual, transgender, and questioning teens, as well as for their straight peers and parents." Booklist
Includes bibliographical references

Kranz, Rachel

Gay rights; [by] Rachel Kranz, Tim Cusick. Rev ed. Facts on File 2005 362p (Library in a book) $45

Grades: 9 10 11 12   **306.76**
1. Gay men—Civil rights 2. Homosexuality
ISBN 0-8160-5810-5   LC 2005-9832

First published 2000

This is an "overview of gay rights in America. In three sections, the text presents a topical overview, further research, and appendixes." Libr J [review of 2000 edition]
Includes bibliographical references

Marcovitz, Hal

Teens & gay issues. Mason Crest Publishers 2005 112p il (Gallup Youth Survey) $22.95 *

Grades: 7 8 9 10   **306.76**
1. Homosexuality 2. Gay men—Civil rights 3. Lesbians—Civil rights
ISBN 1-59084-873-X   LC 2004-13755

"Marcovitz addresses the challenges affecting gay teens (like the decision to come out and homophobia in schools), as well as larger gay issues like the nature vs. nurture debate regarding whether sexual orientation is by choice or genetically assigned and recent controversies over gay marriage and adoption of children by gay and lesbian couples. . . . [This is] well documented." SLJ
Includes bibliographical references

306.8 Marriage and family

Daycare and diplomas; essays by teen mothers who stayed in school; by the students at South Vista Educational Center. Fairview Press 2000 89p il pa $9.95 *
Grades: 9 10 11 12   **306.8**
1. South Vista Education Center (Richfield, Minn.)
2. Teenage mothers
ISBN 1-57749-098-3   LC 00-37620
In this work 36 teen mothers share their experiences and views on pregnancy, parenting and staying in school

Gay and lesbian families; Kate Burns, book editor. Greenhaven Press 2005 110p (At issue) lib bdg $28.70; pa $19.95 *
Grades: 9 10 11 12   **306.8**
1. Same-sex marriage
ISBN 0-7377-2374-2 (lib bdg); 0-7377-2375-0 (pa)
    LC 2004-47471
"This anthology investigates key issues related to gay and lesbian families including gay parenting, marriage laws, gay children and teens, adoption policies, and religious viewpoints in the United States and Canada." Publisher's note
Includes bibliographical references

Gay marriage; Lauri S. Friedman, book editor. Greenhaven Press 2006 143p il (Introducing issues with opposing viewpoints) lib bdg $32.45 *
Grades: 9 10 11 12   **306.8**
1. Same-sex marriage
ISBN 0-7377-3222-9   LC 2005-45988
"The text is broken up with color photographs, fact boxes, political cartoons, and questions to engage readers. . . . The essays are grouped under the questions: Should Homosexuals Be Allowed to Marry? How Should Marriage Be Legislated? and Does Gay Marriage Threaten Society?" SLJ
Includes bibliographical references

Perez-Brown, Maria
Mamá: Latina daughters celebrate their mothers; photographs by Julie Bidwell. Rayo 2003 229p hardcover o.p. pa $14.95
Grades: 11 12 Adult   **306.8**
1. Hispanic American women 2. Mother-daughter relationship
ISBN 0-06-008386-7; 0-06-008387-5 (pa)
    LC 2002-37032
The author describes Hispanic American mother-daughter relationships based on her own experiences and on interviews
"Honest, funny, and deeply moving, these stories will resonate with all mothers and daughters, particularly first and second-generation Americans, while offering special insight into Latina American culture." Booklist

Schultz, Margaret A.
Teens with single parents; why me? Enslow Pubs. 1997 128p (Teen issues) lib bdg $26.60
Grades: 7 8 9 10   **306.8**
1. Single parent family 2. Children of divorced parents
ISBN 0-89490-913-4   LC 96-39439
Examines the effects of living in a single-parent family, discussing such topics as emotional aspects and economic factors.
"Interviews with teens, parents, and psychologists offer young people excellent coping strategies and a chance to see that their anger and frustration are hardly unique." Booklist
Includes bibliographical references

Snow, Judith E.
How it feels to have a gay or lesbian parent; a book by kids for kids of all ages. Harrington Park Press 2004 110p $19.95; pa $12.95
Grades: 5 6 7 8 9 10   **306.8**
1. Parent-child relationship 2. Homosexuality
ISBN 1-56023-419-9; 1-56023-420-2 (pa)
    LC 2003-18008
In their own words, children of different ages talk about how and when they learned of their gay or lesbian parent's sexual orientation and the effect it has had on them.
"This inspirational, eye-opening title gives readers who have gay and lesbian parents a much-deserved voice." SLJ

Teenage pregnancy and parenting; Lisa Frick, book editor. Greenhaven Press 2007 215p il (Current controversies) lib bdg $34.95; pa $23.70 *
Grades: 10 11 12   **306.8**
1. Teenage pregnancy 2. Teenage parents 3. Sex education
ISBN 0-7377-3295-4 (lib bdg); 978-0-7377-3295-5 (lib bdg); 0-7377-3296-2 (pa); 978-0-7377-3296-2 (pa)
    LC 2006-20089
"This book tackles, in familiar pro/con format, such dilemmas as whether teen pregnancy is really a serious problem, what factors contribute to it, the effectiveness of sex-education programs, adoption and abortion, and whether or not society should view teen parenting in a positive light. Researchers will find the differing views invaluable, allowing them to see both sides of an issue." SLJ
Includes bibliographical references

The **Truth** about family life; Mark J. Kittleson, general editor; William Kane, adviser; Richelle Rennegarbe, adviser; Renée Despres and Lynne Griffin, principal authors. Facts on File 2005 212p il (Truth about series) $35 *
Grades: 9 10 11 12   **306.8**
1. Family—United States
ISBN 0-8160-5305-7   LC 2005-1358
This book provides "information on family types, their history and role in society, and how to cope with the basic issues that confront families of all kinds." Publisher's note
Includes glossary and bibliographical references

306.89   Separation and divorce

The **truth** about divorce; Mark J. Kittleson, general editor; William Kane, advisor; Richelle Rennegarbe, advisor; Barry Youngerman, principal author. Facts on File 2005 180p il (Truth about series) $35 *
Grades: 9 10 11 12   **306.89**
1. Divorce 2. Marriage
ISBN 0-8160-5304-9   LC 2004-10236

Contents: Child support, spousal support; Children, psychological effects of divorce on; Communication and compromise in divorced families; Custody and visitation; Divorce, adjusting to the realities of; Divorce alternatives; Divorce in America; Divorce, the business side of; Divorce, the legal process of; Divorce, the psychological cost for spouses; Families, blended; Finances and divorce; Generational patterns and adult children of divorce; Help for troubled marriages; Love and marriage ; Marriage lifestyles, alternative; Media and divorce; Racially and culturally mixed marriages; Relationship after divorce, parents'; Relationship failure; Relationships, types of; Religion and divorce; Stress factors in marriage, external; Hotlines and helpsites

Includes glossary and bibliographical references

306.9   Institutions pertaining to death

Macmillan encyclopedia of death and dying; Robert Kastenbaum, editor in chief. Macmillan Ref. USA 2002 c2003 2v set $250
Grades: 11 12 Adult   **306.9**
1. Death—Encyclopedias
ISBN 0-02-865689-X   LC 2002-5809

"The 327 signed entries . . . range in length from a few paragraphs to several pages. . . . Types of entries include causes of death . . . practices surrounding death . . . individuals and events that have influenced the way we think about death . . . and entries on the nature or meaning of death from various multidisciplinary and multicultural perspectives. . . . An appendix profiles and gives contact information for 75 organizations active in death-related education, research, advocacy, or other areas." Booklist

310.5   General statistics--Serial publications

The **Statesman's** year-book 2007; the politics, cultures, and economies of the world. St. Martin's Press 2006 $235 *
Grades: 11 12 Adult   **310.5**
1. Statistics 2. Political science
ISSN 0081-4601
ISBN 1-4039-9276-2; 978-1-4039-9276-5
Also available online
Annual. First published 1864

"Descriptive and statistical information about international organizations and countries of the world—brief history, area, political status, economy, etc." N Y Public Libr. Ref Books for Child Collect. 2d edition

317.1   General statistics of Canada

Canadian almanac & directory 2007. Micromedia; distributed by Information Handling Services 2006 $315
Grades: 11 12 Adult   **317.1**
1. Canada—Directories 2. Almanacs
ISSN 0068-8193
ISBN 1-895021-49-9; 978-1-895021-49-3
Also available online
Annual. First published 1847. Publisher varies

"Contains reliable legal, commercial, governmental, statistical, astronomical, departmental, ecclesiastical, financial, educational, and general information." Guide to Ref Books. 11th edition

317.3   General statistics of the United States

CQ's state fact finder 2007; rankings across America. CQ Press 2007 $100; pa $60
Grades: 11 12 Adult   **317.3**
1. United States—Statistics
ISSN 1079-7149
ISBN   978-0-87289-495-2;   0-87289-495-9; 978-0-87289-496-9 (pa); 0-87289-496-7 (pa)
Annual. First published 1993 under the authorship of Victoria Van Son. Authors vary

"This guide provides data, state by state, under such headings as *Business and Economy, Education, Energy, Health, Population, Recreation, Social Services*, and *Transportation*. . . . A second section of the book rearranges the data by state, so that the user can go directly to a particular state and see where it ranks in each of 325 areas. . . . This is a must purchase for all academic, high-school, and public libraries, where information like this is sure to be in demand." Booklist

Includes bibliographical references

Historical statistics of the United States; earliest times to the present; [by] Susan B. Carter . . . [et al.] Millennial ed. Cambridge University Press 2006 5v il set $990 *
Grades: 11 12 Adult   **317.3**
1. United States—Statistics
ISBN 0-521-81791-9; 978-0-521-81791-2
                                  LC 2005-27089
Also available online
First published 1949 by U.S. Govt. Print. Off. with title: Historical statistics of the United States, 1789-1945

"Each of the 39 chapters begins with an essay on the 'quantitative history' of the topic and comments on the reliability of the data and possible limits to interpretation. Included are approximately 1900 tables and 170 maps, graphs, and time lines; the text is fully cross-referenced and indexed. . . . A bargain for all libraries supporting research." Libr J

Includes bibliographical references

United States. Bureau of the Census
Statistical abstract of the United States; 2007 The National Data Book. 12th ed. U.S. Govt. Ptg. Office 2007 999p il map $39; pa $35 *
Grades: 11 12 Adult   317.3
1. United States—Statistics 2. Statistics
ISBN   978-0-16-076302-1;   0-16-076302-9; 978-0-16-076301-4 (pa); 0-16-076301-0 (pa)
Also available online
"Issued October 2006"
Annual. First published for the year 1878
"Compendium of statistics on the social, political and economic organization of the U.S. presented in tables. Lists other sources of such information." N Y Public Libr. Ref Books for Child Collect. 2d edition

320   Political science

Living through the red scare; edited by Derek Maus. Greenhaven Press 2006 144p (Living through the Cold War) lib bdg $32.45
Grades: 9 10 11 12   320
1. Anticommunist movements 2. Internal security— United States
ISBN 0-7377-2915-5   LC 2005-46029
"This volume examines this contentious period from the perspectives of both accusers and accused, as well as chronicling some of its lingering effects on American culture." Publisher's note
Includes bibliographical references

Machiavelli, Niccolò, 1469-1527
The prince. Knopf 1992 xxxi, 190p (Everyman's library) $16 *
Grades: 11 12 Adult   320
1. Political science 2. Political ethics
ISBN 0-679-41044-9   LC 91-53225
Also available from the University of Chicago Press and in paperback from Penguin Bks.
Written in 1513
"A handbook of advice on the acquisition, use, and maintenance of political power, dedicated to Lorenzo de Medici." Haydn. Thesaurus of Book Dig

Paine, Thomas, 1737-1809
Collected writings. Library of Am. 1995 906p $35
Grades: 11 12 Adult   320
1. Political science
ISBN 1-883011-03-5   LC 94-25756
Contents: Common sense; The crisis and other pamphlets, articles and letters; Rights of man; The age of reason
Includes bibliographical references

320.03   Political science-- Encyclopedias and dictionaries

The **Oxford** guide to the United States Government; edited by John J. Patrick, Richard M. Pious, Donald A. Ritchie. Oxford Univ. Press 2001 802p $35
Grades: 11 12 Adult   320.03
1. United States—Politics and government—Encyclopedias
ISBN 0-19-514273-X   LC 00-51024
"In this alphabetical encyclopedia on topics relating to both the present activities and history of the U.S. government, entries include biographies of presidents and vice presidents, selected First Ladies and members of congress, and all Supreme Court justices who have ever served. Other types of biographical entries are those of unofficial groups of people who have played important roles in American government and history. . . . There are also articles on the various departments of the federal government; important historical events . . . issues and concepts . . . laws and decisions; and Supreme Court cases." Booklist
"This solid reference work is highly recommended for public, academic, and high school libraries." Libr J
Includes bibliographical references

320.1   The state

Social contract; essays by Locke, Hume, and Rousseau; with an introduction by Sir Ernest Barker. Oxford Univ. Press 1980 xliv, 307p pa $22.95
Grades: 11 12 Adult   320.1
1. Political science 2. State, The
ISBN 0-19-500309-8
Also available in hardcover from Greenwood Press
First published 1947 in the United Kingdom; 1948 in the United States
Contents: An essay concerning the true original, extent and end of civil government, by J. Locke; Of the original contract, by D. Hume; The social contract, by J. Rousseau
This book contains three major essays dealing with the social contract theory of government, first published 1690, 1748 and 1762 respectively. The introduction by Sir Ernest Barker discusses the history and transformations of the theory before focusing on the ideas of the three authors

320.3   Comparative government

Governments of the world; a global guide to citizens' rights and responsibilities; C. Neal Tate, editor-in-chief. Macmillan Reference USA 2006 4v il map set $395 *
Grades: 11 12 Adult   320.3
1. Comparative government—Encyclopedias
ISBN 0-02-865811-6   LC 2005-10436
"In these volumes, 310 alphabetically arranged articles range in length from 500 to 3,500 words and cover 198 regions ('including every independent nation and several

Governments of the world—*Continued*

territories') as well as international courts, supranational institutions, concepts central to understanding political organization and human rights, and key individuals who have had positive and negative impacts on the evolution of citizens' rights and responsibilities." Booklist

Includes bibliographical references

320.5   Political ideologies

Didion, Joan

Fixed ideas: America since 9.11; preface by Frank Rich. New York Review of Bks. 2003 44p pa $7.95

Grades: 11 12 Adult   **320.5**

1. Nationalism 2. September 11 terrorist attacks, 2001 3. United States—Politics and government—2001-

ISBN 1-590-17073-3   LC 2003-7251

The author contends that "after September 11, those who initiated discussions regarding the causes of the tragedy were instantly branded as traitors as the White House simultaneously launched the war on terrorism and a public relations campaign that blatantly oversimplified the complex realities involved. . . . First published in the *New York Review of Books*, this is an essential work of clarity in a time of obfuscation." Booklist

Laqueur, Walter, 1921-

Fascism; past, present, future. Oxford Univ. Press 1996 263p hardcover o.p. pa $17.95 *

Grades: 11 12 Adult   **320.5**

1. Fascism

ISBN 0-19-509245-7; 0-19-511793-X (pa)

     LC 95-17612

"Part 1 examines historical fascism's 'ideology, its specific features, the reasons that it received the support of many millions, and how it came to power;' part 2 sketches fascist, right-wing extremist, neofascist, and radical nationalist populist movements that have emerged since World War II, noting their similarities to and differences from Hitler's and Mussolini's regimes; and part 3 considers 'clerical fascism, that is, radical Islam and similar trends in other religions' and extremist groups in formerly communist states. Laqueur analyzes these subjects judiciously." Booklist

Includes bibliographical references

321.8   Democratic government

The **Concise** encyclopedia of democracy. CQ Press 2000 452p il $118.75 *

Grades: 11 12 Adult   **321.8**

ISBN 1-56802-426-6   LC 99-54450

Each of the nearly 300 articles "opens with a short definition of its topic, followed by background and general information about it. The entries include biographies of world leaders; information about international governments; analyses of important concepts; historical treatments of topics related to democracy; and coverage of primary sources, such as speeches, documents, and Supreme Court decisions." Book Rep

Includes bibliographical references

322   Relation of the state to organized groups and their members

Carter, Stephen L.

God's name in vain; how religion should and should not be involved in politics. Basic Bks. 2000 248p pa $15 hardcover o.p.

Grades: 11 12 Adult   **322**

1. Religion and politics 2. Church and state

ISBN 0-465-00887-9 (pa)   LC 00-33741

The author "argues that religion mustn't and can't be walled out of politics but that church and clergy involvement in political parties only sullies religion. One of the most important books about freedom of religion of this, or perhaps any, era." Booklist

Includes bibliographical references

Djupe, Paul A.

Encyclopedia of American religion and politics; [by] Paul A. Djupe and Laura R. Olson. Facts on File 2003 512p il (Facts on File library of American history) $85 *

Grades: 11 12 Adult   **322**

1. Religion and politics 2. United States—Religion—Encyclopedias

ISBN 0-8160-4582-8   LC 2002-33921

"An A-to-Z reference covering all facets of American politics and religion, from the early days of the American republic to the rise of the political power of the Christian Right. More than 600 entries cover key religious and political leaders, important historical events, descriptions of court cases, concepts, and religious denominations." Publisher's note

"The encyclopedia is timely and accessible. . . . Recommended for most reference collections in public libraries." Libr J

Includes bibliographical references

322.4   Political action groups

Chalmers, David Mark

Hooded Americanism: the history of the Ku Klux Klan. 3rd ed. Duke Univ. Press 1987 c1981 477p il pa $24.95 hardcover o.p. *

Grades: 11 12 Adult   **322.4**

1. Ku Klux Klan

ISBN 0-8223-0772-3 (pa)   LC 86-29133

First published 1965 by Doubleday; this is a reissue of the 1981 edition published by Watts

This book recounts the history of the Klan. It describes the sociological and psychological forces behind the Klan, and sets forth its dogmas

"The book is written in a breezy, journalistic style. . . . Especially instructive and sobering is Chalmers' account of the role of the Klan in politics." J Am Hist

Includes bibliographical references

Esposito, John L.

Unholy war; terror in the name of Islam. Oxford Univ. Press 2002 196p hardcover o.p. pa $15.95 *

Grades: 11 12 Adult 322.4

1. Terrorism 2. Islam and politics 3. United States—Foreign opinion

ISBN 0-19-515435-5; 0-19-516886-0 (pa)

LC 2001-58009

The author "explains the teachings of Islam—the Qur-an, the example of the Prophet, Islamic law—about jihad or holy war, the use of violence, and terrorism. He chronicles the rise of extremist groups and examines their frightening worldview and tactics." Publisher's note

"Engaging, evenhanded, and highly readable . . . this is essential reading for every concerned citizen and all those who wish to gain a deeper understanding of contemporary Islam and its internal struggles." Libr J

Includes bibliographical references

Extremist groups: opposing viewpoints; Karen F. Balkin, book editor. Greenhaven Press 2005 202p il map lib bdg $34.95; pa $23.70 *

Grades: 7 8 9 10 11 12 322.4

1. Radicalism 2. Right and left (Political science)

ISBN 0-7377-3594-5 (lib bdg); 978-0-7377-3594-9 (lib bdg); 0-7377-3595-3 (pa); 978-0-7377-3595-6 (pa)

"Opposing viewpoints series"

This "look at extremist groups focuses on the intense and often violent clashes that occur when these organizations push the limits of the law and societal tolerance. The anthology includes a . . . chapter on terrorist groups whose activities pose a threat worldwide." Publisher's note

Includes bibliographical references

Gandhi, Mahatma, 1869-1948

Gandhi on non-violence; selected texts from Mohandas K. Gandhi's Non-violence in peace and war; edited with an introduction by Thomas Merton. New Directions 1965 82p pa $7.95 *

Grades: 11 12 Adult 322.4

1. Passive resistance 2. India—Politics and government

ISBN 0-8112-0097-3

"A New Directions paperbook"

In an introductory essay Merton "considers Gandhi's ideas, not in relation to their Indian context, but in terms of their applicability to all men's lives. Brief quotations from Gandhi's writings make up most of the book." Asia: a Guide to Paperbacks

Gerges, Fawaz A.

Journey of the Jihadist; inside Muslim militancy. Harcourt 2006 312p $25

Grades: 11 12 Adult 322.4

1. Terrorism 2. Jihad 3. Islamic fundamentalism

ISBN 0-15-101213-X; 978-0-15-101213-8

LC 2005-37759

In this "account of the development of militant Islamist praxis and ideology in the contemporary Middle East, Gerges . . . explains what the jihadists are about and what they intend to accomplish. . . . The author's ability to explain complex issues in a jargon-free and easy-flowing narrative makes this book one of the best, most useful, and most timely volumes for nonspecialist readers." Libr J

Includes bibliographical references

Gitlin, Todd

Letters to a young activist. Basic Bks. 2003 174p (Art of mentoring) $22.50 *

Grades: 11 12 Adult 322.4

1. Political activists 2. Politics 3. Social movements

ISBN 0-465-02738-5 LC 2002-152385

The author "offers encouragement and cautionary notes to current-day activists. . . . Gitlin focuses on the character and discipline needed to sustain social movements, the need for compromise and tempering anger, and how to maintain patriotism and democratic ideals and continue to agitate for social justice. . . . This is a thoughtful and philosophical look at the personal delight and social efficacy of activism." Booklist

Includes bibliographical references

Hamilton, Neil A., 1949-

Rebels and renegades; a chronology of social and political dissent in the United States. Routledge 2002 361p il $100 *

Grades: 11 12 Adult 322.4

1. Radicalism 2. Right and left (Political science)

ISBN 0-415-93639-X LC 2002-8916

Contents: Colonization and settlement ; Revolution and nation-building; Expansion and reform ; Civil War and Reconstruction; Industrialization and the Progressive Era; World War I and the Roaring Twenties; The Great Depression and World War II; Postwar United States; Contemporary United States

The author "examines the historical role that radicals and reactionaries have played in shaping American society and culture. Arranged in nine chapters, the book features a chronological format that begins in 1620 with the Pilgrims and ends with the September 11, 2001 terrorist attacks. Each chapter opens with an overview of the time period, and individual entries consist of one- or two-page descriptions of radicals, their activities, and their impact." Libr J

Includes bibliographical references

The **White** separatist movement; Mary E. Williams, book editor. Greenhaven Press 2002 240p il (American social movements) $33.70; pa $22.45

Grades: 9 10 11 12 322.4

1. White supremacy movements

ISBN 0-7377-1054-3; 0-7377-1053-5 (pa)

LC 2001-8360

This anthology of essays, speeches, book excerpts, and personal observations explores the beliefs and activities of the Ku Klux Klan, the American Nazi Party, and such late twentieth-century white supremacist extremist groups as the Christian Identity movement

This "offers a solid starting point for research." Booklist

Includes bibliographical references

323   Civil and political rights

Civil liberties and war; edited by Andrea C. Nayaka. Greenhaven Press/Thomson Gale 2006 78p il (Examining issues through political cartoons) lib bdg $27.45
Grades: 7 8 9 10   **323**
1. Civil rights 2. War—Public opinion 3. Military policy—United States
ISBN 0-7377-2517-6

This "spotlights 16 cartoons related to the suspension of civil liberties and human rights during America's wars. The first chapter presents cartoons from the Civil War to the War in Vietnam, while chapter two considers 'America's War on Terrorism' and chapter three, the current war in Iraq. . . . Each political cartoon is accompanied by a paragraph or two of commentary and a brief note on the cartoonist. The book concludes with a bibliography and an excellent, varied list of 16 relevant organizations and government agencies, with descriptions and contact information." Booklist
Includes bibliographical references

Civil liberties: opposing viewpoints; Auriana Ojeda, book editor. Greenhaven Press 2004 204p il $33.70; pa $22.45 *
Grades: 7 8 9 10   **323**
1. Civil rights
ISBN 0-7377-1675-4; 0-7377-1676-2 (pa)
                         LC 2003-59647
"Opposing viewpoints series"
"This volume examines the pros and cons of such issues as regulation of hate speech, flag burning, banning of child pornography, posting of the Ten Commandments in public places, public surveillance cameras, the war on terrorism, and ethnic profiling. Twenty-two essays from contributors ranging from the ACLU to John Ashcroft and from such publications as the 'Humanist', the 'Seattle Times', and 'Midstream' offer arguments from a variety of perspectives. . . . This highly accessible book will prove useful for opinion and research papers." SLJ
Includes bibliographical references

Thompson, Cooper, 1950-
White men challenging racism; 35 personal stories; [by] Cooper Thompson, Emmett Schaefer, and Harry Brod; with a foreword by James W. Loewen. Duke Univ. Press 2003 xxxvi, 353p $64.95; pa $21.95
Grades: 9 10 11 12   **323**
1. Political activists 2. Racism
ISBN 0-8223-3084-9; 0-8223-3096-2 (pa)
                         LC 2002-14628
This book contains interviews with "35 white men with a range of ages and backgrounds and from across the U.S. . . . who have spent their lives combating racism and social injustice via community organizing, teaching, civil rights advocacy, and a variety of other efforts . . . . Among the subjects are Herbert Aptheker, radical historian; Stetson Kennedy, a Klan infiltrator in the 1940s; Richard Lapchick, advocate for racial and gender justice in sports. The contributors explore issues from immigrant rights to interracial relations to gay activism.

Readers interested in different perspectives on social justice will enjoy this collection." Booklist
Includes bibliographical references

323.1   Civil and political rights of nondominant groups

Allen, Zita
Black women leaders of the civil rights movement. Watts 1996 128p il (African-American experience) lib bdg $23 *
Grades: 7 8 9 10   **323.1**
1. African American women 2. African Americans—Civil rights
ISBN 0-531-11271-3   LC 96-26134
This volume includes stories of women who participated in the desegregation of schools, buses, lunch counters, and other public facilities
"The brief, but detailed text captures the spirit of the movement. . . . Libraries would do well to add this book to the many other titles available on the movement because of its central focus and perspectives." SLJ
Includes bibliographical references

American civil rights: primary sources; {compiled by} Phillis Engelbert; edited by Betz Des Chenes. U.X.L 1999 xl, 200p il $58 *
Grades: 9 10 11 12   **323.1**
1. Civil rights
ISBN 0-7876-3170-1   LC 99-27167
Presents fifteen documents, including speeches, autobiographical texts, and proclamations, related to the civil rights movement and arranged by category under economic rights, desegregation, and human rights
"The uniqueness of this set lies in the range of people covered. Students will find it an excellent resource for reports and interesting reading." Booklist
Includes bibliographical references

Boyd, Herb, 1938-
We shall overcome; a living history of the civil rights struggle told in words, pictures and the voices of the participants. Sourcebooks 2004 272p il $45 *
Grades: 11 12 Adult   **323.1**
1. African Americans—Civil rights
ISBN 1-402-20213-X   LC 2004-12509
Accompanied by 2 CDs
"Through text, images, and actual recordings (found on 2 CDs), Boyd . . . presents some of the major events in the Civil Rights Movement, including the murder of Emmett Till, the march on Washington, and the life and death of Martin Luther King Jr." Libr J
Includes bibliographical references

Civil rights; Jill Karson, book editor. Greenhaven Press 2003 238p il map (Great speeches in history series) lib bdg $33.70; pa $22.45 *
Grades: 7 8 9 10   **323.1**
1. African Americans—Civil rights 2. United States—Race relations 3. Speeches
ISBN 0-7377-1593-6 (lib bdg); 0-7377-1594-4 (pa)
                         LC 2002-32209

Civil rights—*Continued*

"A collection of the speeches of well-known individuals who participated in or supported the American Civil Rights Movement from early pioneers through the 1960s up until today. Selections from Frederick Douglass, Malcolm X, Fannie Lou Hamer, Jesse Jackson, and Nelson Mandela emphasize the power of oratory to inform, persuade, and make an impact." SLJ

Includes bibliographical references

Civil rights; Karen Balkin, book editor. Greenhaven Press 2004 187p (Current controversies) lib bdg $34.95; pa $23.70 *
Grades: 9 10 11 12   **323.1**
1. Civil rights
ISBN 0-7377-1178-7 (lib bdg); 0-7377-1177-9 (pa)
LC 2003-60822

The articles in this anthology explore civil rights issues ranging from censorship to segregation to gun control

Includes bibliographical references

Civil rights in the United States; Waldo E. Martin, Jr., Patricia Sullivan, editors. Macmillan Ref. USA 2000 2v set $260
Grades: 11 12 Adult   **323.1**
1. Civil rights 2. African Americans—Civil rights
ISBN 0-02-864765-3   LC 99-57548

"Covering the period from 1865 to the present, the set features more than 700 entries comprised of historical and state surveys, biographies, entries on civil rights and other organizations, political and social movements, legislation and government programs, court cases, overall concepts, cultural and educational institutions, as well as film, literature, music and art." Publisher's note

The **Eyes** on the prize civil rights reader; documents, speeches, and firsthand accounts from the black freedom struggle, 1954-1990; general editors, Clayborne Carson {et al.}. Penguin Bks. 1991 764p pa $18 *
Grades: 11 12 Adult   **323.1**
1. African Americans—Civil rights 2. United States—Race relations
ISBN 0-14-015403-5   LC 91-9507

First published 1987 with title: Eyes on the prize: America's civil rights years, a reader and guide

"An anthology of primary material important in the historiography of this country's civil rights movement. . . . Not simply for reference use, this compilation makes provocative cover-to-cover reading and is extremely worthy of consideration by every library." Booklist

Includes bibliographical references

Gold, Susan Dudley, 1949-
Korematsu v. United States; Japanese-American internment. Marshall Cavendish Benchmark 2005 c2006 159p il (Supreme Court milestones) lib bdg $39.93 *
Grades: 7 8 9 10   **323.1**
1. Korematsu, Fred, 1919-2005 2. Japanese Americans—Evacuation and relocation, 1942-1945 3. World War, 1939-1945—Reparations
ISBN 0-7614-1943-8   LC 2005-2534

Describes the historical context of the Korematsu versus United States Supreme Court Case in which a Japanese-American sought compensation for being sent to an internment camp during World War II.

Includes bibliographical references

Hampton, Henry
Voices of freedom; an oral history of the civil rights movement from the 1950s through the 1980s; {by} Henry Hampton and Steve Fayer with Sarah Flynn. Bantam Bks. 1990 692p hardcover o.p. pa $24
Grades: 11 12 Adult   **323.1**
1. African Americans—Civil rights 2. United States—Race relations
ISBN 0-553-05734-0; 0-553-35232-6 (pa)
LC 89-18297

This companion to the PBS series "'Eyes on the Prize,' composed of interviews done originally for the TV program, is a riveting document of the civil rights movement of the 1960s and 1970s. The text is arranged in a chronological sequence that reconstructs major events from the murder of Emmett Till in Mississippi in 1955 and the Little Rock integration crisis to the affirmative action cases of the 1970s." Booklist

Includes bibliographical references

King, Martin Luther, Jr., 1929-1968
A testament of hope; the essential writings of Martin Luther King, Jr.; edited by James Melvin Washington. Harper & Row 1986 xxvi, 676p hardcover o.p. pa $23.95 *
Grades: 11 12 Adult   **323.1**
1. African Americans—Civil rights 2. United States—Race relations
ISBN 0-06-250931-4; 0-06-064691-8 (pa)
LC 85-45370

"King's most important writings are gathered together in one source. The arrangement is topical: philosophy, sermons and public addresses, essays, interviews and excerpts of his books. The material within each of these categories is arranged chronologically. Included are Dr. King's writings on nonviolence, integration and politics." SLJ

Includes bibliographical references

Why we can't wait; {by} Martin Luther King, Jr. Harper & Row 1964 178p il hardcover o.p. pa $6.95 *
Grades: 11 12 Adult   **323.1**
1. African Americans—Civil rights 2. Birmingham (Ala.)—Race relations
ISBN 0-06-012395-8; 0-451-52753-4 (pa)

The author first reviews the background of the 1963 civil rights demands. He then describes the strategy of the Birmingham campaign and outlines future action

Nguyen, Tram

We are all suspects now; untold stories from immigrant communities after 9/11. Beacon Press 2005 187p pa $14 *

Grades: 11 12 Adult   **323.1**

1. Immigrants 2. United States—Ethnic relations 3. War on terrorism 4. September 11 terrorist attacks, 2001

ISBN 0-8070-0461-8 (pa)   LC 2005-11579

The author "reveals the human cost of the domestic war on terror and examines the impact of post-9/11 policies on people targeted because of immigration status, nationality, race, and religion." Publisher's note

"Mesmerizing personal accounts of poor treatment by the US government, as well as everyday trials and tribulations that immigrants face in the aftermath of September 11th, make this book impossible to put down." Univ Press Books for Public and Second Sch Libr, 2006

Includes bibliographical references

Olson, Lynne

Freedom's daughters; the unsung heroines of the civil rights movement from 1830 to 1970. Scribner 2001 460p il $30; pa $16

Grades: 11 12 Adult   **323.1**

1. African American women 2. African Americans—Civil rights

ISBN 0-684-85012-5; 0-684-85013-3 (pa)

LC 00-41306

Olson discusses the contribution of such women as Fannie Lou Hamer, Diane Nash, Rosa Parks and Ella Baker to the civil rights movement

This book "expertly mines oral history collections housed in Southern universities, biographies and testaments published in the last decade by Southern university presses and more general works by historians." N Y Times Book Rev

Includes bibliographical references

Reporting civil rights. Library of Am. 2003 2v ea $40 *

Grades: 11 12 Adult   **323.1**

1. African Americans—Civil rights 2. Journalism 3. United States—Race relations

ISBN 1-931082-28-6 (v1); 1-931082-29-4 (v2)

LC 2002-27459

Contents: pt1 American journalism, 1941-1963; pt2 American journalism, 1963-1973

These "volumes present newspaper and magazine articles from the popular and African American press. . . . The 151 writers whose works are collected here include Ralph Ellison, Langston Hughes, John Hersey, Robert Penn Warren, David Halberstam, Jimmy Breslin, James Baldwin, Marshall Frady, and Tom Wolfe. . . . Each volume also contains a chronology and biographical sketches of the contributors." Libr J

"An important anthology for readers interested in the history of the civil rights movement." Booklist

Williams, Juan

Eyes on the prize: America's civil rights years, 1954-1965; {by} Juan Williams with the Eyes on the prize production team; introduction by Julian Bond. Viking 1987 300p il hardcover o.p. pa $20 *

Grades: 7 8 9 10   **323.1**

1. African Americans—Civil rights 2. United States—Race relations

ISBN 0-670-81412-1; 0-14-009653-1 (pa)

LC 86-40271

"A Robert Lavelle book"

"This companion volume to the PBS TV series of the same name is an . . . account of black America's struggle for social and political equality, covering the civil rights battle from the landmark Brown v. Board of Education decision in 1954 to the Selma protest marches, and Voting Rights Act of 1965." Libr J

"Highly recommended both as a socio-historical document and as a heartfelt, poignant remembrance of a movement and its activists." Booklist

Includes bibliographical references

323.3 Civil and political rights of other social groups

Do children have rights? Jamuna Carroll, book editor. Greenhaven Press 2006 124p (At issue) lib bdg $28.70; pa $19.95 *

Grades: 9 10 11 12   **323.3**

1. Youth—Civil rights

ISBN 0-7377-2366-1 (lib bdg); 0-7377-2367-X (pa)

LC 2005-46327

This anthology offers "discussions on child labor laws, child pornography, abortion rights of minors, child privacy rights and the use of censorship to protect children." Publisher's note

Includes bibliographical references

323.44 Freedom of action (Liberty)

Fromm, Erich, 1900-1980

Escape from freedom 1941 305p pa $14 hardcover o.p. *

Grades: 9 10 11 12   **323.44**

1. Freedom 2. Social psychology 3. Totalitarianism

ISBN 0-8050-3149-9

"A searching inquiry into the meaning of freedom for modern man. . . . The author stresses the role of psychological factors in the social process, interpreting the historical development of freedom in terms of man's awareness of himself as a significant separate being." Libr J

Includes bibliographical references

Intellectual freedom manual; compiled by the Office for Intellectual Freedom of the American Library Association. 7th ed. American Library Association 2006 xx, 521p pa $52 *

Grades: Professional   **323.44**

1. Intellectual freedom 2. Libraries—Censorship

ISBN 0-8389-3561-3; 978-0-8389-3561-3

LC 2005-22409

Intellectual freedom manual—*Continued*
First published 1974

This guide to preserving intellectual freedom includes: ALA interpretations to the Library Bill of Rights; recommendations for special libraries and specific situations; information about legal decisions affecting school and public libraries; a section on the ALA's Intellectual Freedom Action Network.

"This manual details the professional standards to which librarians aspire and offers practical information about how to achieve those goals; it's a must for any librarian's professional library." Book Rep

Includes bibliographical references

323.6 Citizenship and related topics

Ellis, Richard
To the flag; the unlikely history of the Pledge of Allegiance; [by] Richard J. Ellis. University Press of Kansas 2005 297p il $29.95; pa $15.95 *
Grades: 11 12 Adult   **323.6**
1. Pledge of Allegiance
ISBN 0-7006-1372-2; 0-7006-1521-0 (pa)
                                    LC 2004-23110
The author provides an "account not only of the pledge's 19th century beginnings, but also of its recent use as a political tool. A must read for political junkies of any age!" Univ Press Books for Public and Second Sch Libr, 2006

Is it unpatriotic to criticize one's country? Mary E. Williams, book editor. Greenhaven Press 2005 77p (At issue) lib bdg $28.70; pa $19.95
Grades: 9 10 11 12   **323.6**
1. Patriotism 2. Dissent
ISBN 0-7377-2396-3 (lib bdg); 0-7377-2397-1 (pa)
                                    LC 2004-59694
The essays in this book discuss whether or not criticism of or protest against the actions of the U.S. government by its own citizens, especially during a time of war, undermines patriotism

Includes bibliographical references

324.025 The political process--Directories

Political handbook of the world 2007. CQ Press 2006 $225
Grades: 11 12 Adult   **324.025**
1. Political science—Handbooks, manuals, etc. 2. Political parties
ISSN 0913-175X
ISBN 978-0-87289-370-2; 0-87289-370-7
Annual. First published 1927 with title: A political handbook of Europe
Edited by Arthur S. Banks et al.

"Provides data for each country on chief officials, government and politics, political parties, and news media. Sections devoted to intergovernmental organizations and to issues concerned with particular regions; e.g., Middle East, Latin America. Index to geographical, organizational, and personal names." Ref Sources for Small & Medium-sized Libr. 6th edition

324.5 Nominating candidates

National party conventions, 1831-2004. CQ Press 2005 325p il pa $40
Grades: 11 12 Adult   **324.5**
1. Political conventions 2. Political parties
ISBN 1-56802-982-9
First published 1995 with title: National party conventions, 1831-1992

This volume offers information about Republican and Democratic Party national conventions including sites, delegates, chief officers and keynote speakers, party organization and rules, credential fights, platform fights, ballots, and candidates.

Includes bibliographical references

324.6 Election systems and procedures; suffrage

Frost-Knappman, Elizabeth
Women's suffrage in America; an eyewitness history; [by] Elizabeth Frost-Knappman and Kathryn Cullen-DuPont. Updated ed. Facts on File 2005 512p (Eyewitness history) $75 *
Grades: 9 10 11 12   **324.6**
1. Women—Suffrage 2. Women—United States—History
ISBN 0-8160-5693-5   LC 2004-43339
First published 1992

This volume provides "firsthand accounts of the women's movement—diary entries, letters, speeches, and newspaper accounts—that illustrate how historical events appeared to those who lived through them. Among the eyewitness testimonies included were those of Susan B. Anthony, Sojourner Truth, Lucretia Mott, Frederick Douglass, Helen Keller, and John Quincy Adams. . . . Critical documents such as the Declaration of Rights and Sentiments at Seneca Falls, the Emancipation Address of the Women's National League, the Constitution of the National Loyal Woman Suffrage Association, and the 19th Amendment are paired with capsule biographies of more than 80 key figures." Publisher's note

This is "a lively and important sourcebook for students of American political and cultural history." SLJ [review of 1992 edition]

Includes bibliographical references

Guide to U.S. elections. 5th ed. CQ 2005 2v il map set $335 *
Grades: 11 12 Adult   **324.6**
1. Elections—United States—Statistics
ISBN 1-56802-981-0
First published 1975 with title: Congressional Quarterly's guide to U.S. elections

This is a compilation of data drawn from different sources on gubernatorial, congressional, and presidential elections. "Data on elections is accompanied by historical background and essays on topics such as campaign finance and redistricting." Booklist

Includes bibliographical references

Henderson, Harry, 1951-
Campaign and election reform. Facts on File 2004 316p (Library in a book) $45
Grades: 11 12 Adult   **324.6**
1. Elections—United States 2. Campaign funds—United States
ISBN 0-8160-5136-4   LC 2003-6485
Contents: Introduction to campaign and election reform; The law of campaigns and elections; Chronology; Biographical listing; How to research campaign and election reform; Organizations and agencies
"Beginning with the Declaration of Independence and ending with the 2002 Bipartisan Campaign Reform Act, coverage includes the Electoral College and the complicated world of campaign-finance reform as well as the technology used to record individual voter records. Legislation and court cases that have determined the current electoral process in our country are reviewed and explanations of the legal battles waged during the 2000 presidential election between George Bush and Al Gore are included. . . . A solid one-stop resource." SLJ
Includes bibliographical references

Moore, John Leo, 1927-
Elections A to Z; [by] John L. Moore. 2nd ed. CQ Press 2003 614p il map (CQ's American government A to Z series) $125
Grades: 11 12 Adult   **324.6**
1. Elections—United States—Encyclopedias
ISBN 1-56802-801-6   LC 2003-11235
First published 1999
This "explains how campaigns and elections . . . are conducted in America and how voters, political parties and others participate in choosing their elected officials. . . . Entries range from short definitions of terms like 'front-runner' to in-depth essays exploring vital aspects of campaigns and elections such as the right to vote, turnout trends, and the history, evolution and current state of House, Senate, presidential, and some state-level elections." Publisher's note
Includes bibliographical references

Presidential elections, 1789-2004. CQ Press 2005 277p il map pa $43 *
Grades: 11 12 Adult   **324.6**
1. Presidents—United States—Election
ISBN 1-56802-983-7; 978-1-56802-983-2
     LC 2006-282339
First published 1995 with title: Presidential elections, 1789-1992
This offers information about the electoral college, electoral votes and popular votes in each presidential election, voter turnout, primary returns, and Democratic and Republican Party conventions.
Includes bibliographical references

Women's suffrage; Richard Haesly, book editor. Greenhaven Press 2003 223p il (History firsthand) $33.70; pa $22.45
Grades: 9 10 11 12   **324.6**
1. Women—Suffrage
ISBN 0-7377-1304-6; 0-7377-1305-4 (pa)
     LC 2002-23170

"Suffragists explain the long struggle to obtain voting rights for women. They reveal how a small group of organizers inspired a national movement that culminated in the passing of the Nineteenth Amendment." Publisher's note
"While excerpts from the writings of familiar participants like Elizabeth Cady Stanton, Frances D. Gage, Susan B. Anthony, Alice Stone Blackwell, and Sojourner Truth are included, it is the documents from the Supreme Court and the Congressional Record that round out the picture." SLJ
Includes bibliographical references

324.7   Conduct of election campaigns

Guide to political campaigns in America; Paul S. Herrnson, editor-in-chief; Colton Campbell, Marni Ezra, Stephen K. Medvic, associated editors. CQ Press 2005 457p il $125
Grades: 11 12 Adult   **324.7**
1. Politics 2. Elections—United States
ISBN 1-56802-876-8   LC 2005-18123
"Organized into seven sections, [this book] contains 27 chapters that discuss every aspect of the American political campaign process—including a historical overview, nomination politics, voter turnout, polling, debates, and campaign reform. The editors examine various political campaigns, e.g., presidential, congressional, gubernatorial, state, and local. They also look at judicial elections and initiatives and referenda. . . . This volume should be found in every reference collection." Choice
Includes bibliographical references

325.73   Immigration to the United States

Daniels, Roger
Coming to America; a history of immigration and ethnicity in American life. 2nd ed. Perennial 2002 515p il map pa $17.95 *
Grades: 11 12 Adult   **325.73**
1. Minorities 2. United States—Immigration and emigration
ISBN 0-06-050577-X   LC 2002-72436
First published 1990
"After discussing the topic of immigration in general and sociological theories of why people migrate between countries, Daniel discusses each racial or national group that came to the United States during the various eras of the nation's history." SLJ {review of 1990 edition}
Includes bibliographical references

Illegal immigration: opposing viewpoints; Margaret Haerens, book editor. Greenhaven Press 2007 212p il lib bdg $34.95; pa $23.70 *
Grades: 8 9 10 11 12   **325.73**
1. Illegal aliens 2. United States—Immigration and emigration
ISBN 0-7377-3356-X (lib bdg); 0-7377-3357-8 (pa)
     LC 2005-55049
"Opposing viewpoints series"

Illegal immigration: opposing viewpoints—*Continued*

"The writers present opposing perspectives on such topics as border-patrol efforts, immigration policy reform, racism, the development of a guest worker program, and the connection between illegal immigration and terrorism. . . . Even reluctant readers will find many compelling and inflammatory arguments to hold their interest." SLJ

Includes bibliographical references

Immigration; Louise I. Gerdes, book editor. Greenhaven Press 2005 224p (Current controversies) lib bdg $34.95; pa $23.70 *

Grades: 9 10 11 12   **325.73**

1. United States—Immigration and emigration

ISBN 0-7377-2779-9 (lib bdg); 0-7377-2780-2 (pa)
                                                           LC 2004-59788

"The authors in this anthology present differing views on the impact of immigration, the treatment of immigrants, and how legal and illegal immigration should be managed." Publisher's note

Includes bibliographical references

U.S. immigration and migration, Primary sources; [compiled by] James L. Outman; Lawrence W. Baker, editor. UXL 2004 xxxi, 232p il (U.S. immigration and migration reference library) $65 *

Grades: 9 10 11 12   **325.73**

1. United States—Immigration and emigration

ISBN 0-7876-7669-1   LC 2004-3553

"The 17 excerpts begin with Lord Baltimore's 1649 Declaration of Religious Tolerance and end with Pat Buchanan's views on immigration policies. The letters, articles, government documents, Supreme Court rulings, and the reflections of authors such as Willa Cather and Mark Twain offer a wide variety of viewpoints." SLJ

Includes bibliographical references

326 Slavery and emancipation

Altman, Linda Jacobs, 1943-

The politics of slavery; fiery national debates fueled by the slave economy; foreword by series advisor Henry Louis Gates. Enslow 2004 128p il map (Slavery in American history) lib bdg $26.60

Grades: 7 8 9 10   **326**

1. Slavery—United States 2. United States—Politics and government 3. United States—Race relations

ISBN 0-7660-2150-5   LC 2003-26532

Contents: The beginnings of American slavery; From servants to slaves; Slavery and the founding freedoms; Compromise and the Constitution; Slavery in a growing nation; Missouri and the westward expansion; Slavery and manifest destiny; North and South : a clash of cultures; The road to disunion

"Altman relates the beginning of 'the peculiar institution' and the constitutional, historical, and political issues and figures surrounding it from 1619 to the ratification of the Thirteenth Amendment in 1865. . . . [This book] will be useful in American-history collections." SLJ

Bailey, Anne C.

African voices of the Atlantic slave trade; beyond the silence and the shame. Beacon Press 2005 289p il map $26; pa $16 *

Grades: 11 12 Adult   **326**

1. Slave trade

ISBN 0-8070-5512-3; 0-8070-5513-1 (pa)
                                                           LC 2004-15082

The author "focuses on the slave trade from the African perspective. As there are few written African records, in contrast to those found in Europe and the Americas, on this topic, she centers her study on the oral tradition, what she refers to as 'African human libraries.' She primarily focuses on a region in Ghana around one particular oral remembrance told from various perspectives. . . . A fascinating perspective on slavery from the African continent." Booklist

Includes bibliographical references

Douglass, Frederick, 1817?-1895

Frederick Douglass: selected speeches and writings; edited by Philip S. Foner; abridged and adapted by Yuval Taylor. Hill Bks. 1999 789p pa $32.95 hardcover o.p. *

Grades: 11 12 Adult   **326**

ISBN 1-55652-352-1 (pa)   LC 99-23180

Based on Foner's five-volume The life and writings of Frederick Douglass (1950-1975), this volume "covers Douglass' speeches and writings over a 54-year period. The breadth and depth of his focus and concerns reflected in more than 2,000 speeches, editorials, articles, and letters provide a wellspring of knowledge about the man and his intellect." Booklist

Includes bibliographical references

Edwards, Judith

Abolitionists and slave resistance; breaking the chains of slavery; foreword by Henry Louis Gates. Enslow Publishers 2004 128p il map (Slavery in American history) lib bdg $26.60

Grades: 7 8 9 10   **326**

1. Abolitionists 2. Slavery—United States

ISBN 0-7660-2155-6   LC 2003-13457

Contents: Events leading to abolition; Slavery and the Revolution; The anti-slavery movement gathers force; Abolitionists organize; The Amistad and the new decade; The rebels and the runaways; Escape from slavery; John Brown's raid; On the antislavery side; From slave to soldier

"Edwards examines the growth of the abolition movement and provides examples of some of the ways slaves themselves protested, including theft, work slowdowns, and destruction of property. Rebellions, runaways, and the Underground Railroad are also covered. The sensitive and respectful approach leads to an understanding of the social issues that remain as a legacy of slavery in American society today." SLJ

Includes bibliographical references

Fradin, Dennis B.

Bound for the North Star; true stories of fugitive slaves; {by} Dennis Brindell Fradin. Clarion Bks. 2000 206p il $20 *

Grades: 7 8 9 10   326

1. Slavery—United States 2. Underground railroad 3. Abolitionists

ISBN 0-395-97017-2   LC 00-29052

"Fradin here draws on more than 16 slaves' personal experiences to show what slavery was like: the unrelenting racism; the physical brutality, including rape and flogging; the anguish of family separation. . . . The narrative is direct, with no rhetoric or cover-up. . . . This is painful reading about legal racist cruelty and those who resisted it." Booklist

Includes bibliographical references

Fradin, Judith Bloom

5,000 miles to freedom; Ellen and William Craft's flight from slavery; [by] Judith Bloom Fradin and Dennis Brindell Fradin. National Geographic 2006 96p il $19.95; lib bdg $29.90

Grades: 5 6 7 8 9 10   326

1. Craft, Ellen, 1826-1891 2. Craft, William, 19th cent. 3. Slavery—United States

ISBN 0-7922-7885-2; 0-7922-7886-0 (lib bdg)

"In 1848, light-skinned Ellen Craft, dressed in the clothing of a rich, white man, assumed the identity of Mr. William Johnson and, escorted by his black slave, William, traveled by railroad and boat to reach the North. With the passage of a more stringent Fugitive Slave Law in 1850, the couple . . . decided to travel to England. . . . In 1869, they returned to the United States, opening a school and operating a farm in Georgia. . . . This lively, well-written volume presents the events in their lives in an exciting, page-turner style that's sure to hold readers attention. Black-and-white photographs, illustrations, and reproductions enhance the text." SLJ

Includes bibliographical references

Growing up in slavery; stories of young slaves as told by themselves; edited by Yuval Taylor; illustrations by Kathleen Judge. Lawrence Hill Books 2005 xxv, 230p il $22.95; pa $9.95 *

Grades: 9 10 11 12   326

1. Slavery—United States

ISBN 1-55652-548-6; 1-55652-635-0 (pa)

"Ten African Americans—among them Frederick Douglass and Harriet Jacobs, as well as less well-known individuals—tell what it was like to be a child and teenager under slavery. . . . Invaluable for students in search of primary-source material, and many selections will make riveting read-alouds." Booklist

Includes bibliographical references

Hendrick, George

The Creole mutiny; a tale of revolt aboard a slave ship; {by} George Hendrick, Willene Hendrick. Dee, I.R. 2003 177p il $24.95; pa $14.95

Grades: 11 12 Adult   326

1. Washington, Madison 2. Creole (Brig) 3. Slavery—United States

ISBN 1-56663-493-8; 1-56663-550-0 (pa)

LC 2002-31589

"In the early 1840s, the slave ship *Creole* departed from the east coast of the American South en route to New Orleans with more than 130 slaves as cargo and some white common passengers. . . . The slaves rebelled, killed the captain, took control of the ship, and succeeded in finding freedom in the British-controlled Bahamas. Using court records and insurance documents, the Hendricks reconstructed this little-known tale of slave revolt at sea under the leadership of Madison Washington. . . . This compelling history is particularly fascinating as a look at international law and the differing social policies of the U.S. and Britain regarding slavery at the time." Booklist

Includes bibliographical references

Horton, James Oliver

Slavery and the making of America; [by] James Oliver Horton [and] Lois E. Horton. Oxford University Press 2004 254p il maps $35; pa $18.95 *

Grades: 11 12 Adult   326

1. Slavery—United States 2. African Americans—History

ISBN 0-19-517903-X; 0-19-530451-9 (pa)

LC 2004-13617

The authors "explore the economic, social, and cultural implications of the enslavement of Africans in America, from the selection of slaves from certain regions of Africa to harvest the newly introduced rice crops of the Carolinas to the incentive of freedom offered on both sides of the American Revolution and Civil War to induce the assistance of slaves." Booklist

"The oft-told tale is made fresh through up-to-date slavery scholarship, the extensive use of slave narratives and archival photos and, especially, a focus on individual experience." Publ Wkly

Jewett, Clayton E.

Slavery in the South; a state-by-state history; [by] Clayton E. Jewett and John O. Allen; foreword by Jon L. Wakelyn. Greenwood Press 2004 xxxiii, 305p il $59.95

Grades: 11 12 Adult   326

1. Slavery—United States

ISBN 0-313-32019-5   LC 2003-60004

The authors "profile 15 states and the District of Columbia. . . . All profiles contain a timeline, slave and free black census data, background on the origins of slavery for the state, and the state's Civil War experience. Many of the sketches include sections on subjects such as slave life, emancipation and reconstruction, slave codes, and economics of slavery." Choice

"Although the book is organized by state, the informa-

Jewett, Clayton E.—*Continued*
tion is valuable for students who are studying the institution of slavery as a whole." Libr Media Connect
Includes bibliographical references

King, Wilma, 1942-
Stolen childhood; slave youth in
nineteenth-century America. Indiana Univ. Press
1995 253p il hardcover o.p. pa $12.95 *
Grades: 11 12 Adult   326
1. Slavery—United States 2. African American children 3. African Americans—History 4. United
States—History—19th century
ISBN 0-253-32904-3; 0-253-21186-7 (pa)
                                    LC 94-49163
The author "traces how those born into slavery grew
old almost instantly, before their time, suffering atrocities
akin to those of war-ravaged populations. She examines
family, work, play, religion, punishment, and escape in
a pioneering survey to assess our understanding of slavery from the experiences and perspectives of those under
21 years of age." Libr J
"With moral authority and appreciation for the telling
anecdote, Wilma King takes up the neglected story of
black slave children in the American South." Christ Sci
Monit
Includes bibliographical references

Lester, Julius
To be a slave; paintings by Tom Feelings. 30th
anniversary ed. Dial Bks. 1998 160p il $20; pa
$6.99
Grades: 6 7 8 9   326
1. Slavery—United States
ISBN 0-8037-2347-4; 0-14-131001-4 (pa)
                                    LC 98-5213
A reissue of the title first published 1968
"Through the words of the slave, interwoven with
strongly sympathetic commentary, the reader learns what
it is to be another man's property; how the slave feels
about himself; and how he feels about others. Every aspect of slavery, regardless of how grim, has been painfully and unrelentingly described." Read Ladders for
Hum Relat. 6th edition
Includes bibliographical references

Passages to freedom; the Underground Railroad in
history and memory; edited by David W. Blight.
Smithsonian Books 2004 337p il map hardcover
o.p. pa $19.95 *
Grades: 11 12 Adult   326
1. Underground railroad 2. Abolitionists 3. Slavery—
United States
ISBN 1-58834-157-7; 0-06-085118-X (pa)
                                    LC 2003-44289
"Among the contributing scholars are Ira Berlin, Da-
vid Blight, Eddie S. Glaude, Jr., and Deborah Gray
White. This is a scholarly but thoroughly accessible re-
source." Booklist
Includes bibliographical references

Postma, Johannes
The Atlantic slave trade. Greenwood Press 2003
xxii, 177p map (Greenwood guides to historic
events, 1500-1900) $45
Grades: 11 12 Adult   326
1. Slave trade
ISBN 0-313-31862-X   LC 2002-35338
Also available in paperback from University Press of
Florida
The author "covers the entire Atlantic slave trade era,
from the 1400s to the final abolition of chattel slavery in
the New World in 1888. The focus is on Africa and the
entire New World. While he describes the many horrors
of the Middle Passage, he also examines how the slave
trade contributed to the development of the modern international economy. The last chapters discuss the efforts to
abolish the slave trade and its legacy." SLJ
Includes bibliographical references

Schneider, Dorothy
Slavery in America; [by] Dorothy Schneider and
Carl J. Schneider. Rev ed. Facts on File 2007
554p il map (American experience) $80; pa $21.95
*
Grades: 11 12 Adult   326
1. Slavery—United States
ISBN   0-8160-6241-2;   978-0-8160-6241-6;
0-8160-6839-9 (pa); 978-0-8160-6839-5 (pa)
                                    LC 2006-24798
First published 2000 as part of the Eyewitness history
series
This book recounts the history of slavery, "as well as
the Reconstruction period that followed, by examining,
chapter by chapter, many of its aspects: the slave catch-
ers and their coffles in Africa, the crowded slave ships,
slave auctions, life and labor on plantations, escape attempts and insurrections, and the Civil War and eventual
emancipation." Publisher's note
Includes bibliographical references

Segal, Ronald, 1932-
Islam's Black slaves; the other Black diaspora.
Farrar, Straus & Giroux 2001 273p maps
hardcover o.p. pa $14 *
Grades: 11 12 Adult   326
1. Slavery 2. Slave trade
ISBN 0-374-22774-8; 0-374-52797-0 (pa)
                                    LC 00-62256
This book presents "an overview of black slavery in
the Islamic world from its beginnings to modern Sudan
and Morocco. . . . {It} explores Islamic slavery in China, India, the Middle East, and Africa and focuses on the
differences between Islamic and Western slavery." Libr
J
"The strength of this account is the meticulous documentation of what is fact and what is surmise. The dramatic narrative is sure to spark discussion and further research." Booklist

Slave narratives. Library of Am. 2000 1,034p $40
*
Grades: 11 12 Adult   326
1. Slavery—United States 2. African Americans—Biography
ISBN 1-88301-176-0   LC 99-40360

Slave narratives—*Continued*

"Appearing in this collection are memoirs penned by well-known activists Nat Turner, Frederick Douglass, William Wells Brown, Henry Bibb, and Sojourner Truth. In addition, several powerful, evocative works by less celebrated writers are also featured. . . . Together these 10 narratives paint a vivid portrait of the cruelties of the institution of slavery. . . . A significant contribution to the literature of the African American experience." Booklist

Includes bibliographical references

Slavery; James D. Torr, book editor. Greenhaven Press 2004 240p map (Opposing viewpoints in world history series) $33.70; pa $22.45 *
Grades: 9 10 11 12   326
1. Slavery—United States
ISBN 0-7377-1705-X; 0-7377-1706-8 (pa)
LC 2003-44812

This book offers "perspectives on American slavery through a selection of primary sources. The excerpts, culled from speeches, pamphlets, and scholarly texts, are divided into four sections that cover moral issues, slave resistance, abolitionists, and events that led to the Civil War. . . . The entries that are included . . . will greatly enhance students' understanding of the issues. . . . An important, useful addition to the high-school history curriculum." Booklist

Includes bibliographical references

Slavery today; Auriana Ojeda, book editor. Greenhaven Press 2004 80p (At issue) lib bdg $28.70; pa $19.95 *
Grades: 9 10 11 12   326
1. Slavery 2. Slave trade
ISBN 0-7377-1613-4 (lib bdg); 0-7377-1614-2 (pa)
LC 2003-51617

"In this anthology, authors examine the modern slave trade. Issues discussed include child prostitution and kidnapping." Publisher's note

"This collection of articles . . . will raise awareness on many aspects of human trafficking and its repercussions in various areas around the world." SLJ

Includes bibliographical references

Thomas, Hugh, 1931-

The slave trade; the story of the Atlantic slave trade, 1440-1870. Simon & Schuster 1997 908p il maps hardcover o.p. pa $25
Grades: 11 12 Adult   326
1. Slave trade
ISBN 0-684-81063-8; 0-684-83565-7 (pa)
LC 97-17234

This "account begins with the 15th-century African trade, dominated by Portugal and Spain. The book then enters the 17th and 18th centuries. . . . The final sections focus on how the increased prohibition of the slave trade in the 19th century affected international relations and how, once slavery became illegal in some nations, conditions for the slaves became even worse." Publ Wkly

The author has "combined passion with first-rate scholarship . . . to produce a definitive survey of the origins, progression, and end of the slave trade." Booklist

Includes bibliographical references

Watkins, Richard Ross

Slavery: bondage throughout history; written and illustrated by Richard Watkins. Houghton Mifflin 2001 136p il $18
Grades: 7 8 9 10   326
1. Slavery—History
ISBN 0-395-92289-5   LC 00-40752

"The author discusses how people have been owned as property through history and across the world. . . . He takes a number of comprehensive subjects—capture, trading, law, escape, revolt, etc.—and talks about each one across cultures and civilizations." Booklist

"A brilliantly written treatment of an abhorrent topic." SLJ

Includes glossary and bibliographical references

White, Shane

The sounds of slavery; discovering African American history through songs, sermons, and speech; [by] Shane White and Graham White. Beacon Press 2005 xxii, 241p hardcover o.p. pa $17 *
Grades: 11 12 Adult   326
1. Slavery—United States 2. African Americans—History 3. Plantation life
ISBN 0-8070-5026-1; 0-8070-5027-X (pa)
LC 2004-21447

Includes audio CD

"Drawing on WPA interviews with former slaves, slave narratives, and other historical documents from the 1700s through the 1850s, the authors provide the context for the field calls, work songs, sermons, and other sounds and utterances of slaves on American plantations. The authors also focus on recollections of the wails of slaves being whipped, the barking of hounds hunting down runaways, and the keening of women losing their children to the slave block. The combination of the CD and the book brings vibrancy and texture to a complex history that has been long neglected." Booklist

Includes discography and bibliographical references

Worth, Richard, 1945-

Slave life on the plantation; prisons beneath the sun. Enslow Publishers 2004 128p il (Slavery in American history) lib bdg $26.60
Grades: 7 8 9 10   326
1. Slavery—United States 2. Plantation life
ISBN 0-7660-2152-1   LC 2003-24291

Contents: A slave's life; Slavery in the 1600s; Plantation life in 1700s; King Cotton; Relationships between owners and slaves; African-American culture on the plantation; Freedom

"Worth frames his account within the sweep of history, but his focus is on daily life—the work, the hardship (especially the breakup of family life), punishment, and resistance—and he discusses the relationship between owners and slaves, the importance of cotton, and African American culture. [This title includes] several stirring page-long slave narratives as well as black-and-white drawings and photos. The documentation is exemplary." Booklist

Includes glossary and bibliographical references

327.1 Foreign policy and international relations

Globalization; edited by Katrin Sjursen. Wilson, H.W. 2000 209p (Reference shelf) pa $45
Grades: 11 12 Adult   **327.1**
1. International relations
ISBN 0-8242-0986-9   LC 00-43887
Articles culled from various sources explore the economic, political and social ramifications of the rapidly changing landscape of international relations
Includes bibliographical references

Schram, Martin
Avoiding armageddon; our future, our choice: companion to the PBS series from Ted Turner Documentaries. Basic Bks. 2003 356p il $26
Grades: 11 12 Adult   **327.1**
1. Arms control 2. Terrorism
ISBN 0-465-07255-0   LC 2003-2721
This book "details the threats facing the U.S. today—from nuclear, chemical and biological attack and from terrorism—and outlines possible solutions." Publ Wkly
The author "offers fresh insights into such relevant subtopics as the Al-Qaeda operation and the mind-set of the typical suicide bomber. . . . The book . . . is shocking, discomfiting, and necessary." Booklist
Includes bibliographical references

327.12 Espionage and subversion

The **Central** Intelligence Agency; Helen Cothran, book editor. Greenhaven Press 2003 128p (At issue) lib bdg $26.60; pa $17.45
Grades: 9 10 11 12   **327.12**
1. United States. Central Intelligence Agency 2. Terrorism 3. Violence
ISBN 0-7377-1725-4 (lib bdg); 0-7377-1726-2 (pa)
                              LC 2002-29722
New edition in preparation
In this "volume, essayists argue about the CIA's role in the terrorist attacks that now threaten America. Some writers allege that the agency's mishandling of information led to the tragedy of 9/11; others argue for altering the CIA's powers based on our changing social climate. Still others deal with CIA assassinations, covert action, and accusations of CIA involvement in drug trafficking. . . . {This volume is} filled with interesting insights about the CIA's workings and responsibilities." Booklist
Includes bibliographical references

Espionage and intelligence gathering; [edited by] Louise I. Gerdes. Greenhaven Press 2004 192p (Current controversies) lib bdg $34.95; pa $23.70
Grades: 9 10 11 12   **327.12**
1. Intelligence service—United States 2. American espionage
ISBN 0-7377-1581-2 (lib bdg); 0-73771582-0 (pa)
                              LC 2003-49017
New edition in preparation

"This book attempts to look at both sides of such issues as the importance of U.S. intelligence gathering abroad, how much leeway the government has under the Patriot Act, and if better intelligence and operations could have prevented 9/11. . . . This is a useful book because of its hard-hitting, current essays." SLJ
Includes bibliographical references

Owen, David, 1939-
Spies: the undercover world of secrets, gadgets and lies; foreword by Antonio J. Mendez. Firefly Bks. 2004 128p il map $19.95; pa $9.95
Grades: 9 10 11 12   **327.12**
1. Spies 2. Espionage
ISBN 1-55297-795-1; 1-55297-794-3 (pa)
                              LC 2004-303819
This book covers "the history of espionage from its beginnings until the present day." Booklist
"This is a slick, colorful book. . . . Teens will find a great deal of intriguing information, along with wonderful photos. Social studies teachers will find a wealth of material to support their curriculums, as well." SLJ

Smith, W. Thomas
Encyclopedia of the Central Intelligence Agency; [by] W. Thomas Smith Jr. Facts on File 2003 282p il (Facts on File library of American history) $60; pa $19.95 *
Grades: 11 12 Adult   **327.12**
1. United States. Central Intelligence Agency
ISBN 0-8160-4666-2; 0-8160-4667-0 (pa)
This encyclopedia includes "more than 500 historical, biographical, and general entries about the intelligence-gathering, covert-action agency established in 1947. . . . Current through March 2003, the encyclopedia also covers predecessor organizations such as the World War II-era Office of Strategic Services (OSS). . . . The work covers terrorism extensively, not only in the entry *September 11, 2001, terrorist attacks on the United States,* which is one of the longest in the volume, but also in entries for Osama bin Laden and the Department of Homeland Security, among others." Booklist
Includes bibliographical references

327.47 Russia--Foreign relations

Rice, Earle
The Cold War; collapse of communism; by Earle Rice Jr. Lucent Bks. 2000 112p il maps (History's great defeats) lib bdg $27.45
Grades: 9 10 11 12   **327.47**
1. Cold war 2. World politics—1945-1991 3. Soviet Union—Foreign relations—United States 4. United States—Foreign relations—Soviet Union
ISBN 1-56006-634-2   LC 00-8311
"With concise writing, clearly structured arguments, and an array of supporting features, this . . . is a valuable resource. The thorough footnoting can serve as a model for student research. Appendixes also include a chronology, a glossary, a bibliography" Booklist
Includes bibliographical references

327.73 United States--Foreign relations

Hastedt, Glenn P., 1950-
Encyclopedia of American foreign policy; by Glenn Hastedt. Facts on File 2003 562p il map $85
Grades: 11 12 Adult   327.73
1. United States—Foreign relations—Encyclopedias
ISBN 0-8160-4642-5   LC 2003-49186
In this reference, Hastedt "addresses the four major foreign policy themes: selection of a grand strategy, the role of the public voice, the policymaking process, and the influence of the past. The more than 475 entries, all by Hastedt, are arranged alphabetically and include people, agencies, documents, and events rather than broader issues and ideological constructs of US foreign policy. Entries are quite readable and rarely run longer than a page; most are also cross-referenced and have bibliographies." Choice
Includes bibliographical references

Laxer, James
Empire. Groundwood Books 2006 144p il map (Groundwork Guides) $15.95
Grades: 8 9 10 11 12   327.73
1. Imperialism 2. United States—Foreign relations
ISBN 978-0-88899-706-7; 0-88899-706-X
LC 2006-497080
This book "compares the American Empire to those of the past, finding much can be learned from the fates of the British, Roman, Chinese, Incan, and Aztec empires." Publisher's note
Includes bibliographical references

U.S. policy toward rogue nations; James D. Torr, book editor. Greenhaven Press 2004 94p (At issue) lib bdg $28.70; pa $19.95
Grades: 9 10 11 12   327.73
1. United States—Foreign relations
ISBN 0-7377-2196-0 (lib bdg); 0-7377-2197-9 (pa)
LC 2003-62480
This book "considers the doctrine of preemptive war; whether the invasion of Iraq was justified; if the U.S. should support regime change in Syria and Iran; alternative approaches to dealing with North Korea; the value of peace efforts in Sudan; and whether the U.S. should lift sanctions in Libya." SLJ
Includes bibliographical references

328.73 The legislative process in the United States

Barone, Michael
The almanac of American politics, 2006; [by] Michael Barone and Grant Ujifusa. National Journal 2005 1907p il maps pa $69.95
Grades: 11 12 Adult   328.73

1. United States. Congress 2. United States—Politics and government 3. Almanacs
ISSN 0362-076X
ISBN 0-89234-112-2
First published 1972 by Gambit. Periodically revised Subtitle and publisher vary; "The senators, the representatives and the governors; their records and elections results, their states and districts." Subtitle
"Provides essential data for the assessment of each representative and senator in Congress. Specifics include political background on the state or congressional district, biographies, voting records, group ratings (by such groups as Americans for Democratic Action and Americans for Constitutional Action), and recent election results. Provides information on the governor of each state. Arranged by state. Congressional district maps." Ref Sources for Small & Medium-sized Libr. 6th edition

Congress A to Z; David R. Tarr, Ann O'Connor, editors. 4th ed. CQ Press 2003 605p il (CQ's American government A to Z series) $125 *
Grades: 11 12 Adult   328.73
1. United States. Congress
ISBN 1-56802-800-8   LC 2003-14802
First published 1988
This work provides information on the structure and work of Congress in some 250 alphabetical entries. "Entries range from short definitions to a series of core essays exploring the legislative process, the seniority system, the committee system, the budget process, and other broad areas." Publisher's note
"This volume is an excellent example of . . . readable, accessible, comprehensive, and unbiased coverage of American politics. . . . This is perhaps the best one-volume reference work on the U.S. Congress." Am Ref Books Annu, 2000
Includes bibliographical references

CQ's politics in America. CQ Press 2007 il maps $125; pa $85 *
Grades: 11 12 Adult   328.73
1. United States. Congress 2. Elections—United States
ISSN 1527-8913
ISBN   978-0-87289-545-4;   0-87289-545-9; 978-0-87289-547-8 (pa); 0-87289-547-5 (pa)
Biennial. First published 1981
Current editors: David J. Hawkings and Brian Nutting; Hardcover edition includes free access to online versions and updates
Profiles each current member of Congress, providing political background, statistical information, committee assignments, etc.

Dewhirst, Robert E.
Encyclopedia of the United States Congress; [by] Robert E. Dewhirst; John David Rausch, Jr., associate editor. Facts on File 2006 578p il (Facts on File library of American history) $95
Grades: 11 12 Adult   328.73
1. United States. Congress
ISBN 0-8160-5058-9   LC 2005-28124
This encyclopedia covers "the people, events, and terms involved in the legislative branch of government. It also provides explanations of the relationships between

Dewhirst, Robert E.—*Continued*
the legislative and other branches of government, court cases, elections, political opponents, congressional leaders, scandals, controversial issues, and the inner workings of Congress." Publisher's note
Includes bibliographical references

Greenberg, Ellen
The House and Senate explained; the people's guide to Congress. Norton 1996 173p il hardcover o.p. pa $12 *
Grades: 9 10 11 12 Adult   **328.73**
1. United States. Congress
ISBN 0-393-03984-6; 0-393-31496-0 (pa)
                                  LC 96-12291
Revised edition of the House & Senate explained published 1986
"Greenberg simplifies, explains, and presents the legislative branch in ways that bring clarity to confusion. She begins with the basics—how both the House and Senate are physically organized. . . . A typical congressional day is outlined and a pithy explanation of the steps from a bill to law is offered. An excellent reference source, the book includes a full index and sections on written and Internet accesses to the government." SLJ

Guide to Congress. 5th ed. CQ Press 2000 2v il set $345
Grades: 11 12 Adult   **328.73**
1. United States. Congress
ISBN 1-56802-477-0   LC 99-53914
First published 1971 with title: Congressional Quarterly's guide to the Congress of the United States
6th edition in preparation
"Covers history and workings of Congress, with biographical data on all members." N Y Public Libr Book of How & Where to Look It Up
Includes bibliographical references

How Congress works. 3rd ed. Congressional Quarterly 1998 184p il pa $35.50 *
Grades: 9 10 11 12   **328.73**
1. United States. Congress
ISBN 1-56802-391-X   LC 98-29616
First published 1983
This work explains the procedures, and rules that govern the Senate and the House as well as party leadership, the legislative process, the committee system and congressional staff
Includes bibliographical references

Remini, Robert Vincent, 1921-
The House: the history of the House of Representatives; [by] Robert V. Remini. HarperCollins Publishers 2006 614p il $34.95
Grades: 11 12 Adult   **328.73**
1. United States. Congress. House—History
ISBN 978-0-06-088434-5; 0-06-088434-7
                                  LC 2006-615801
"The Library of Congress"
The author "traces the development of this quintessential American institution from a struggling, nascent body

to the venerable powerhouse it has become since America's rise on the world stage." Publisher's note
"Published under the aegis of the House itself, Remini's work is nonpartisan, civic-minded, and deserving of every library's consideration." Booklist
Includes bibliographical references

Ritchie, Donald A.
The Congress of the United States; a student companion. 2nd ed. Oxford Univ. Press 2001 248p (Oxford student companions to American government) lib bdg $45 *
Grades: 9 10 11 12   **328.73**
1. United States. Congress 2. United States—Politics and government
ISBN 0-19-515007-4   LC 2001-36142
First published 1993 with title: The young Oxford companion to the Congress of the United States
An alphabetically arranged, illustrated guide to the United States Congress with short essays on such topics as congressional leadership, relations with the President, elections and succession, notable legislation, Capitol buildings, traditions, and more
This "provides an excellent starting point for junior high and high school students doing research and is up-to-date as of the start of the 107th Congress in January 2001." Booklist
Includes bibliographical references

United States. Congress
Official Congressional directory, 2005-2006. U.S. Govt. Ptg. Office 2005 $49; pa $39 *
Grades: 11 12 Adult   **328.73**
1. United States. Congress
ISBN 1-59804-022-7;   978-1-59804-022-7; 1-59804-023-5 (pa); 978-1-59804-023-4 (pa)
Biennial
"Covers biographical information, committee assignments of members of Congress, and officers of Congress." N Y Public Libr Book of How & Where to Look It Up

330.1   Economic systems, schools, theories

Heilbroner, Robert L., 1919-2005
The worldly philosophers; the lives, times, and ideas of the great economic thinkers. Rev. 7th ed. Simon & Schuster 1999 365p pa $16
Grades: 11 12 Adult   **330.1**
1. Economists 2. Economics 3. Imperialism 4. Utopias 5. Capitalism 6. Depressions
ISBN 0-684-86214-X   LC 99-14050
"A Touchstone book"
First published 1953
The author traces the story of economics and the great economists from Adam Smith, Malthus, Ricardo, the Utopians, Marx, Veblen and Keynes to those working with the problems of our contemporary world
Includes bibliographical references

330.9 Economic situation and conditions

Outman, James L., 1946-
Industrial Revolution: almanac; [by] James L. Outman, Elisabeth M. Outman. UXL 2003 242p il (Industrial revolution reference library) $55
Grades: 9 10 11 12 **330.9**
1. Industrial revolution
ISBN 0-7876-6513-4 LC 2002-155422
Contents: Origins of the Industrial Revolution; The revolution begins: steam engines, railroads, steamboats; New machines and the factory system; The social and political impact of the Industrial Revolution, part 1; The age of petroleum and electricity; The new business models; The social and political impact of the Industrial Revolution, part 2; Globalization
"This is an excellent adjunct to American and world history units and classes on economics and labor movements." Booklist
Includes bibliographical references

Industrial Revolution: primary sources; [by] James L. Outman, Elisabeth M. Outman. UXL 2003 212p il (Industrial revolution reference library) $55 *
Grades: 9 10 11 12 **330.9**
1. Industrial revolution
ISBN 0-7876-6515-0 LC 2002-155420
Contents: Economic theory; Adam Smith; The Wealth of Nations; Andrew Ure; The philosophy of manufacturers; Karl Marx; The Communist Manifesto; Andrew Carnegie; The gospel of wealth; Technological advances and criticisms; Thomas Savery; Uses of the fire engine; Leeds letters; Luddites; Samuel Morse; On the telegraph; J. Stillman; The last tie; The Industrial Revolution and working conditions; Sadler Report; Samuel Gompers; Germinal Zola and coal miners; Upton Sinclair; Excerpt from The Jungle; Triangle Shirtwaist fire; Jane Addams; Excerpt from Hull House; Carmen Teoli; Congressional testimony; Politics and law in the Industrial Revolution; United States Supreme Court; Northern Securities v. United States; Theodore Roosevelt; Progressive Party platform
"This is an excellent adjunct to American and world history units and classes on economics and labor movements." Booklist
Includes bibliographical references

330.973 United States--Economic conditions

Benson, Sonia
Development of the industrial U.S.: Almanac; [by] Sonia G. Benson; Jennifer York Stock, project editor. UXL 2006 lv, 216p il $63
Grades: 9 10 11 12 **330.973**
1. Industries—United States 2. Industrial revolution
ISBN 1-4144-0175-2 LC 2005-15915
This book "consists of 14 chapters, each thoroughly examining one aspect of industrialization, such as rail-

roads or early factories. User-friendly features (research and activity ideas, ample glossaries and word boxes, references to Web sites and print resources) further enhance this product's usefulness." Booklist
Includes bibliographical references

Development of the industrial U.S.: Primary sources; [by] Sonia G. Benson; Jennifer York Stock, project editor. UXL 2006 lii, 205p il $63 *
Grades: 9 10 11 12 **330.973**
1. Industries—United States 2. Industrial revolution
ISBN 1-4144-0179-5 LC 2005-16349
This book "provides excerpts and explications of seminal sources, including legislative acts, accounts of daily life from regular citizens, political cartoons and more." Publisher's note
Includes bibliographical references

The **Industrial** revolution: opposing viewpoints; William Dudley, editor. Greenhaven Press 1998 282p il (American history series) lib bdg hardcover o.p.; pa $22.45
Grades: 7 8 9 10 **330.973**
1. Industrial revolution 2. United States—Economic conditions
ISBN 1-56510-707-1 (lib bdg); 1-56510-706-3 (pa) LC 97-48274
"This anthology traces the evolution of the United States from a collection of small agricultural colonies to an industrial giant—a development that radically changed how Americans worked and lived. The views of industrialists, labor organizers, and social critics of industrialism are featured." Publisher's note
Includes bibliographical references

331 Labor economics

Murray, R. Emmett
The lexicon of labor; a glossary of more then 500 key terms, biographical sketches, and historical insights concerning labor in America. New Press (NY) 1998 208p il pa $14.95
Grades: 11 12 Adult **331**
ISBN 1-56584-456-4 LC 98-12783
This is an "encyclopedia of 500 entries for terms, concepts, people, legislation, places, and events in U.S. labor history." Booklist
Includes bibliographical references

U.S. labor in the twentieth century; studies in working-class struggles and insurgency; edited by John Hinshaw and Paul Le Blanc. Humanity Bks. 2000 397p (Revolutionary studies series) pa $25
Grades: 9 10 11 12 **331**
1. Working class 2. Labor—United States
ISBN 1-573-92865-8 LC 00-40723
Topics discussed "include the migration of African Americans to western Pennsylvania's industrial towns, the role of women and radicals in the first sit-down strikes, A. Philip Randolph's contributions to black American socialism, and the role of labor and radicals in the early civil rights movement." Booklist
Includes bibliographical references

331.1 Labor force and market

Affirmative action; Leora Maltz, book editor. Greenhaven Press 2005 77p (At issue) lib bdg $27.45; pa $18.70 *
Grades: 9 10 11 12   **331.1**
1. Discrimination in education 2. Affirmative action programs 3. Colleges and universities—United States
ISBN 0-7377-2002-6 (lib bdg); 0-7377-2001-8 (pa)
    LC 2004-42546
The articles in this volume focus on affirmative action in education with viewpoints "for and against affirmative action that have been made in the last few years. Some argue passionately for the merits of affirmative action while others insist it must be abolished." Introduction
Includes bibliographical references

Affirmative action; a documentary history; edited by Jo Ann Ooiman Robinson. Greenwood Press 2001 400p (Primary documents in American history and contemporary issues) $49.95 *
Grades: 11 12 Adult   **331.1**
1. Affirmative action programs
ISBN 0-313-30169-7   LC 00-49508
"Presents 400 documents, beginning in 1864 . . . and ending in mid-2000. In between are extracts from speeches, proceedings, legislation, court cases, articles, and more. Each document is accompanied by a brief explanation that puts it in context." Booklist
Includes bibliographical references

331.2 Conditions of employment

Paquette, Penny Hutchins
Apprenticeship; the ultimate teen guide. Scarecrow Press 2005 373p il (It happened to me) $42 *
Grades: 9 10 11 12   **331.2**
1. Apprentices 2. Occupational training 3. Vocational education
ISBN 0-8108-4945-3   LC 2005-8301
"After a brief discussion of the history of apprenticing, the text quickly shifts to apprenticeship today, explaining the organizational structure, various programs, and the nuts and bolts of applying for and entering into an apprenticeship position. Subsequent chapters discuss the various industries that accept apprentices and the benefits of these types of positions." Voice Youth Advocates
"An excellent starting point for teens." SLJ
Includes bibliographical references

331.4 Women workers

America's working women; a documentary history, 1600 to the present; edited by Rosalyn Baxandall and Linda Gordon, with Susan Reverby. rev and updated. Norton 1995 356p il pa $16.95 hardcover o.p. *
Grades: 11 12 Adult   **331.4**
ISBN 0-393-31262-3 (pa)   LC 94-32194

First published 1976 by Random House
"This chronologically arranged anthology presents an . . . overview of the changing roles and contributions of woman at home, in the fields, and in today's workplace." Booklist
Includes bibliographical references

Reber, Deborah
In their shoes; extraordinary women describe their amazing careers. Simon Pulse 2007 411p il pa $12.99
Grades: 8 9 10 11 12   **331.4**
1. Women—Employment 2. Occupations 3. Vocational guidance
ISBN 978-1-4169-2578-1; 1-4169-2578-3
    LC 2006-34801
"Each chapter contains an interview with its subject . . . as well as sidebars and lists on what to do now to prepare, what the person's day is like, and a time line of how her career took shape over the years. Concrete details about the women's current lives and about how they attained their goals are included. . . . A fine addition to any collection." SLJ

331.7 Labor by industry and occupation

Bolles, Richard Nelson
What color is your parachute? for teens; discovering yourself, defining your future; [by] Richard Nelson Bolles and Carol Christen, with Jean M. Blomquist. Ten Speed Press 2006 167p il (The Parachute library) pa $14.95 *
Grades: 9 10 11 12   **331.7**
1. Applications for positions 2. Vocational guidance 3. Job hunting
ISBN 1-58008-713-2; 978-1-58008-713-1
    LC 2006-5029
The authors "begin by prompting readers to consider their interests, the kinds of people they enjoy and their ideal work environment, and round out the text with quizzes, writing exercises and teen testimonials designed to get teens thinking. Then they offer concrete ideas on how to gain experience (internships, Web sites, etc.) and prepare for interviews." Publ Wkly
Includes bibliographical references

Encyclopedia of careers and vocational guidance. 13th ed. Ferguson 2005 5v il set $249.95
Grades: 8 9 10 11 12 Adult   **331.7**
1. Occupations 2. Vocational guidance
ISBN 0-8160-6055-X   LC 2004-22855
First published 1967
"Volume 1 starts with a . . . guidance section that provides . . . resources in career preparation, finding a job, applying for jobs, and information needed once hired. . . . The careers section, in volumes 1-5, gives . . . historical background for each field, followed by discussion of industry trends, resources, and outlook." Choice
Includes bibliographical references

Exploring tech careers. 4th ed. Ferguson Pub. Co.
2006 2v il set $125
Grades: 9 10 11 12   **331.7**
1. Technology—Vocational guidance 2. Occupations
ISBN 0-8160-6447-4; 978-0-8160-6447-2
            LC 2005-19101
First published 1995 under the editorship of Halli R.
Cosgrove
This "two-volume set covers more than 110 technician
careers and features interviews with professionals already
at work in the field." Publisher's note
Includes bibliographical references

Reeves, Diane Lindsey, 1959-
Career ideas for teens in education and training;
[by] Diane Lindsey Reeves with Gail Karlitz.
Ferguson 2005 183p il (Career ideas for teens)
$40; pa $16.95
Grades: 7 8 9 10   **331.7**
1. Teaching 2. Education 3. Vocational guidance
ISBN 0-8160-5295-6; 0-8160-6919-0 (pa)
            LC 2004024220
This book explorers 35 occupations in education and
training. "Information for each job includes education requirements, relevant Web sites, and median salaries. . . .
[It] also covers volunteer opportunities; lists entry-level
jobs within the field; provides interview tips and sample
questions. . . . [It offers a] lively style and variety of engaging activities." SLJ

Unger, Harlow G., 1931-
But what if I don't want to go to college? a
guide to success through alternative education. 3rd
ed. Ferguson 2006 246p $34.95; pa $16.95 *
Grades: 8 9 10 11 12   **331.7**
1. Occupational training 2. Vocational education
3. Vocational guidance
ISBN 0-8160-6557-8; 0-8160-6558-6 (pa)
            LC 2005-55521
First published 1992
This "volume examines careers in 16 industry categories and describes the skills and experiences required for
each. It also offers guidance for self-assessment and determining what essential employment skills readers already possess." Publisher's note

United States. Bureau of Labor Statistics
Occupational outlook handbook 2006-2007. U.S.
Govt. Ptg. Office 2006 709p il $24.95; pa $17.95
*
Grades: 11 12 Adult   **331.7**
1. Occupations 2. Vocational guidance
ISBN   1-59357-247-6;   978-1-59357-247-1;
1-59357-248-4 (pa); 978-1-59357-248-8 (pa)
Biennial. First published 1949. Supplemented by Oc-
cupational Outlook Quarterly, subscription $15
"Gives information on employment trends and outlook
in more than 800 occupations. Indicates nature of work,
qualifications, earnings and working conditions, how to
enter, where to go for more information, etc." Guide to
Ref Books. 11th edition

331.8   Labor unions and labor-management relations

Zinn, Howard, 1922-
Three strikes; miners, musicians, salesgirls, and
the fighting spirit of labor's last century; {by}
Howard Zinn, Dana Frank, Robin D.G. Kelley.
Beacon Press 2001 174p hardcover o.p. pa $16
Grades: 11 12 Adult   **331.8**
1. Strikes 2. Labor movement
ISBN 0-8070-5012-1; 0-8070-5013-X (pa)
            LC 2001-1135
"Zinn chronicles the 1913-14 Colorado coal strike,
which pitted immigrant miners against robber barons;
Frank describes a little-known Depression-era strike by
Woolworth's counter girls in Detroit; and Kelley studies
a New York musicians' strike against movie theaters.
. . . Provocative analysis of still relevant issues."
Booklist
Includes bibliographical references

332.024   Personal finance

Cash and credit information for teens: tips for a
successful financial life; edited by Kathryn R.
Deering. Omnigraphics 2005 407p (Teen finance
series) $58 *
Grades: 9 10 11 12   **332.024**
1. Personal finance
ISBN 0-7808-0780-4   LC 2005-16285
"Including facts about earning, spending, and borrow-
ing money, with topics such as budgeting, consumer
rights, banks, paychecks, taxes, loans, credit cards, and
more." Title page
"Covering everything from credit cards and consumer
fraud to keeping tax records, this will serve as a fine
core collection resource." Booklist
Includes bibliographical references

Gray, Farrah
Reallionaire; nine steps to becoming rich from
the inside out; [by] Farrah Gray, with Fran Harris.
Health Communications 2004 282p il pa $12.95
Grades: 11 12 Adult   **332.024**
1. Personal finance
ISBN 0-7573-0224-6   LC 2004-62555
The author "grew up in the projects in Chicago and
formed his first business organization at age 7, inspired
by his mother's will and determination. By age 15, he
had developed his own food company for kids, Farr-Out
Foods, which he sold for $1.5 million. . . . Although the
book is punctuated with what he calls 'Real Points' for
success and exercises for things like building a great
team and seizing opportunities, the real inspiration is his
personal story, which speaks strongly of the importance
of mentoring to young people and sends the message that
you should never underestimate anyone, especially yourself." Booklist

Kiyosaki, Robert T., 1947-
Rich dad, poor dad for teens; the secrets about money, that you don't learn in school! by Robert T. Kiyosaki with Sharon L. Lechter. Warner Books 2004 132p pa $14.99
Grades: 7 8 9 10   **332.024**
1. Personal finance
ISBN 0-446-69321-9   LC 2004-6069
Kiyosaki presents "his approach to how he thinks about accumulating wealth and about having money work for the earner. . . . Teens are encouraged to be creative in developing ways to earn cash and to limit spending. . . . Teens will be attracted by the notion of playing games to learn more about acquiring assets and managing money." SLJ

Savings and investment information for teens; edited by Kathryn R. Deering. Omnigraphics 2005 370p (Teen finance series) $65 *
Grades: 9 10 11 12   **332.024**
1. Saving and investment 2. Personal finance
ISBN 0-7808-0781-2   LC 2005-18743
"Tips for a successful financial life, including facts about making money grow, with information about the economy, bank accounts, stocks, bonds, mutual funds, online investing, and more." Title page
"A how-to book that will appeal to future business majors and budding entrepreneurs." SLJ
Includes bibliographical references

332.6 Investment

Bamford, Janet
Street wise; a guide for teen investors. Bloomberg Press 2000 223p pa $16.95
Grades: 11 12 Adult   **332.6**
1. Saving and investment 2. Personal finance
ISBN 1-57660-039-4   LC 00-24724
An investment guide for new investors, including stock market games and investment clubs, interviews with teens who have invested, investing advice, and additional resources

Blumenthal, Karen
Six days in October; the stock market crash of 1929. Atheneum Bks. for Young Readers 2002 156p il $17.95 *
Grades: 7 8 9 10   **332.6**
1. New York Stock Exchange, Inc. 2. Great Depression, 1929-1939 3. United States—Economic conditions—1919-1933
ISBN 0-689-84276-7   LC 2001-46360
"A Wall Street Journal book"
A comprehensive review of the events, personalities, and mistakes behind the Stock Market Crash of 1929, featuring photographs, newspaper articles, and cartoons of the day
"This fast-paced, gripping . . . account of the market crash of October 1929 puts a human face on the crisis." Publ Wkly
Includes bibliographical references

333.7 Land, recreational and wilderness areas, energy

How should America's wilderness be managed? Stuart A. Kallen, book editor. Greenhaven Press 2005 123p (At issue) lib bdg $28.70; pa $19.95
Grades: 9 10 11 12   **333.7**
1. Wilderness areas—Management 2. Human influence on nature 3. Natural resources—Management
ISBN 0-7377-2384-X (lib bdg); 0-7377-2385-8 (pa)
     LC 2004-42494
This collection of articles "explores land use issues from many points of view including those of loggers, environmentalists, oil geologists, backpackers, snowmobile riders, and others." Publisher's note
Includes bibliographical references

Magoc, Chris J., 1960-
Environmental issues in American history; a reference guide with primary documents. Greenwood Press 2006 xxxv, 328p il map (Major issues in American history) $85 *
Grades: 11 12 Adult   **333.7**
1. Environmental policy—United States 2. Human ecology 3. Nature conservation 4. Environmental protection
ISBN 0-313-32208-2   LC 2005-34852
In this "study, primary documents support different sides of various questions, such as the use of water as an energy source, deforestation, gold mining in California, and the emergence of wildlife conservation." Publisher's note
Includes bibliographical references

333.71 General topics of natural resources and energy

Global resources: opposing viewpoints; Helen Cothran, book editor. Greenhaven Press 2004 224p il lib bdg $34.95; pa $23.70 *
Grades: 9 10 11 12   **333.71**
1. Natural resources—Management 2. Conservation of natural resources
ISBN 0-7377-1681-9 (lib bdg); 0-7377-1682-7 (pa)
     LC 2002-41629
"Opposing viewpoints series"
New edition in preparation
"In this volume, scientists, activists, and policy makers debate what resources are being threatened and the best ways to protect them." Publisher's note

333.72 Conservation and protection

Conservation; Yael Calhoun, series editor; foreword by David Seideman. Chelsea House Publishers 2005 xxv, 162p il (Environmental issues) $26.95 *
Grades: 9 10 11 12   **333.72**
1. Conservation of natural resources 2. Nature conservation
ISBN 0-7910-8203-2   LC 2005-3661

Conservation—*Continued*

This volume examines major issues faced by environmentalists with sections on the oceans; rivers, lakes, and streams and federal lands

Includes bibliographical references

Hill, Julia

One makes the difference; inspiring actions to change our world; [by] Julia Butterfly Hill and Jessica Hurley. HarperSanFrancisco 2002 198p il pa $14.95

Grades: 11 12 Adult   **333.72**
1. Environmental protection
ISBN 0-06-251756-2   LC 2001-51542

The author "suggests steps that readers of all ages can take to reduce waste and pollution. Using nontoxic household products for cleaning, organizing recycling programs and buying locally grown produce are just a few of the measures Hill recommends . . . She also gives a crash course in nonviolent protesting and other forms of political action." Publ Wkly

"Salient facts that surprise and educate combine with extensive lists of organizations and resources to make this an invaluable guide for anyone who wants to make the world a better place but doesn't know what to do or how to begin." Booklist

McDaniel, Carl N., 1942-

Wisdom for a livable planet; the visionary work of Terri Swearingen, Dave Foreman, Wes Jackson, Helena Norberg-Hodge, Werner Fornos, Herman Daly, Stephen Schneider, and David Orr. Trinity University Press 2005 277p hardcover o.p. pa $17.95

Grades: 11 12 Adult   **333.72**
1. Environmental sciences
ISBN 1-595-34008-4; 1-595-34009-2 (pa)
                              LC 2004-19081

The author personalizes "critical environmental issues via profiles of eight 'visionaries' agitating for a more livable planet. . . . His subjects are prominent in the areas of hazardous waste incineration, biodiversity, sustainable agriculture, appropriate technology, population control, rational economic planning, climate concerns and environmental education. . . . The stories of these eight ecological warriors are profoundly appealing in that they show the diverse ways that people can commit to a common cause." Publ Wkly

Includes bibliographical references

Mongillo, John F.

Teen guides to environmental science; [by] John Mongillo; with assistance from Peter Mongillo. Greenwood Press 2004 5v il map set $249.95 *

Grades: 9 10 11 12   **333.72**
1. Environmental sciences 2. Human ecology
3. Human influence on nature
ISBN 0-313-32183-3   LC 2004-44869

Contents: v. 1. Earth systems and ecology -- v. 2. Resources and energy -- v. 3. People and their environments -- v. 4. Human impact on the environment -- v. 5. Creating a sustainable society

"This set would be useful for large public and school libraries with a curriculum that includes environmental studies." SLJ

Includes bibliographical references

333.79 Energy

Borowitz, Sidney, 1918-

Farewell fossil fuels; reviewing America's energy policy. Plenum 1999 220p il hardcover o.p. pa $19.95

Grades: 9 10 11 12   **333.79**
1. Renewable energy resources 2. Energy policy
ISBN 0-306-45780-6; 0-306-45781-4 (pa)
                              LC 98-5671

This volume discusses the major sources of energy currently in use throughout the world and explains how other sources of energy, such as nuclear, solar photovoltaics, biomass, wind, geothermal, fusion, hydrogen, and others can be developed and utilized

Energy alternatives: opposing viewpoints; Helen Cothran, book editor. Greenhaven Press 2002 220p il lib bdg $31.20; pa $19.95 *

Grades: 9 10 11 12   **333.79**
1. Energy resources 2. Renewable energy resources
ISBN 0-7377-0905-7 (lib bdg); 0-7377-0904-9 (pa)
                              LC 2001-40604

"Opposing viewpoints series"

"Section one includes articles that debate the abundance and danger of fossil fuels. Pieces in section two address alternate energy sources, including solar power, fuel cells, methane hydrates, geothermal energy, and wind farms. . . . Intriguing for readers who want the latest on how things may shape up in the future. Discussion questions and organizations to contact are appended." Booklist

Includes bibliographical references

Energy alternatives: opposing viewpoints; Barbara Passero, book editor. Greenhaven Press/Thomson Gale 2006 238p il lib bdg $34.95; pa $23.70 *

Grades: 9 10 11 12   **333.79**
1. Energy resources 2. Renewable energy resources
ISBN 0-7377-3350-0 (lib bdg); 978-0-7377-3350-1 (lib bdg); 0-7377-335-19 (pa); 978-0-7377-3351-8 (pa)
                              LC 2006-22293

"Each of the four chapters focuses on a question: 'Are Alternative Energy Sources Necessary?'; 'Is Nuclear Power a Viable Energy Alternative?'; 'What Renewable Energy Sources Should Be Developed?'; and 'Should Alternatives to Fossil Fuels Be Pursued?' . . . A timely addition." SLJ

Includes bibliographical references

Romm, Joseph J.
The hype about hydrogen; fact and fiction in the race to save the climate. Island; Eurospan 2004 238p il hardcover o.p. pa $16.95
Grades: 11 12 Adult   **333.79**
1. Hydrogen as fuel 2. Fuel cells 3. Greenhouse effect
ISBN 1-55963-703-X; 1-55963-704-8 (pa)
                             LC 2003-21418
The author "explains why hydrogen isn't the quick technological fix it's cracked up to be, and why cheering for fuel cells to sweep the market is not a viable strategy for combating climate change." Publisher's note
Romm "has produced a well-organized and thoroughly researched work that is also quite easy to read." Sci Books Films
Includes bibliographical references

What energy sources should be pursued? Stuart A. Kallen, book editor. Greenhaven Press 2005 112p (At issue) lib bdg $28.70; pa $18.70
Grades: 9 10 11 12   **333.79**
1. Energy resources
ISBN 0-7377-2757-8 (lib bdg); 0-7377-2758-6 (pa)
                             LC 2004-47479
"The advantages and disadvantages of solar energy and hydrogen fuel cells are among the issues debated in {this volume}. Throughout this anthology, energy industry experts, environmentalists, and others disagree as to the best path to follow, but most are convinced that the current energy system is not going to function in the next century the way it has in the past. All agree that renewable energy, more efficient oil production techniques, or technologies yet to be discovered must be developed in order to meet the energy needs of the future." Introduction

Yount, Lisa
Energy supply. Facts on File 2005 296p il (Library in a book) $45
Grades: 11 12 Adult   **333.79**
1. Energy resources 2. Energy consumption
ISBN 0-8160-5577-7   LC 2004-21607
"This title summarizes . . . the many aspects of important energy issues, furnishing a concise overview of major points needed for doing research on this topic. . . . A good source and guide for high school students and college freshmen." Choice
Includes bibliographical references

333.8 Subsurface resources

Foreign oil dependence; James Haley, book editor. Greenhaven Press 2004 93p (At issue) lib bdg $28.70 *
Grades: 9 10 11 12   **333.8**
1. Petroleum industry
ISBN 0-7377-2272-X (lib bdg)   LC 2003-66264
This anthology features "discussions on the pros and cons of fuel-economy standards, oil drilling in Alaska, and the feasibility of U.S. energy independence. Challenging articles from recent journals and newspapers tackle difficult questions." SLJ
Includes bibliographical references

333.9 Other natural resources

Space exploration; Daniel A. Leone, book editor. Greenhaven Press 2005 95p (At issue) lib bdg $28.70; pa $19.95
Grades: 9 10 11 12   **333.9**
1. Outer space—Exploration 2. Astronautics—United States
ISBN 0-7377-2747-0 (lib bdg); 0-7377-2748-9 (pa)
                             LC 2004-58028
The essays in this anthology explore NASA's space initiative involving manned missions to Mars and beyond, in addition to such issues as "weapons in space, privatizing space ventures, and protecting Earth from asteroids." Publisher's note
Includes bibliographical references

333.91 Water and lands adjoining bodies of water

Knapp, Bevil, 1949-
America's wetland; Louisiana's vanishing coast; photographs by Bevil Knapp; text by Mike Dunne. Louisiana State University Press 2005 129p il $39.95
Grades: 11 12 Adult   **333.91**
1. Wetlands 2. Coasts
ISBN 0-8071-3115-6; 978-0-8071-3115-2
                             LC 2005-9329
"In an eerie prophesy of the flooding to come in New Orleans, this book discusses the job of wetlands in keeping storm surges and waves out of the low-lying areas. Superb color photographs detail fishing, the oil industry, and marine life in the wetlands areas of Louisiana." Univ Press Books for Public and Second Sch Libr, 2006

333.95 Biological resources

Are the world's coral reefs threatened? Charlene Ferguson, book editor. Greenhaven Press 2005 110p (At issue) lib bdg $28.70; pa $19.95
Grades: 9 10 11 12   **333.95**
1. Coral reefs and islands 2. Marine ecology 3. Human influence on nature
ISBN 0-7377-2697-0 (lib bdg); 0-7377-2698-9 (pa)
                             LC 2004-53918
"This book examines the causes of [coral reef] destruction, the economic impact and the effect regulations will have on their future." Publisher's note
Includes bibliographical references

Endangered oceans: opposing viewpoints; Louise I. Gerdes, book editor. Greenhaven Press 2004 220p il lib bdg $34.95; pa $23.70 *
Grades: 7 8 9 10   **333.95**
1. Marine ecology 2. Environmental policy 3. Marine pollution
ISBN 0-7377-2274-6 (lib bdg); 0-7377-2275-4 (pa)
                             LC 2003-54015
"Opposing viewpoints series"

Endangered oceans: opposing viewpoints—*Continued*

"The collection includes views of scientists, policymakers, and other experts debating the future of the world's oceans." Publisher's note

Includes bibliographical references

Goodall, Jane, 1934-

The ten trusts; what we must do to care for the animals we love; {by} Jane Goodall and Marc Bekoff. HarperSanFrancisco 2002 xx, 200p hardcover o.p. pa $14.95

Grades: 11 12 Adult   333.95
1. Animal rights 2. Animal welfare 3. Wildlife conservation 4. Human influence on nature
ISBN 0-06-251757-0; 0-06-055611-0 (pa)
LC 2002-68717

The authors "offer a prescriptive conservation plan designed to protect animals as well as help educate people about the importance of saving both animals and the environment." Publ Wkly

"An accessible, compelling, and important exposé." Booklist

Includes bibliographical references

Life on earth; an encyclopedia of biodiversity, ecology, and evolution; edited by Niles Eldredge. ABC-CLIO 2002 2v set $185

Grades: 11 12 Adult   333.95
ISBN 1-57607-286-X   LC 2002-15852

"Four introductory essays outline the definition, importance, and preservation of biodiversity. Many of the 194 articles are about specific phyla or species . . . or important concepts. . . . Others address issues that will appeal to students and general readers. . . . Articles are clearly written, usually define specialized terms, and include bibliographies of books and popular and scholarly periodical articles." Booklist

Includes bibliographical references

Riley, Laura

Nature's strongholds; the world's great wildlife reserves; [by] Laura and William Riley. Princeton University Press 2005 672p il maps $49.50

Grades: 9 10 11 12   333.95
1. Wildlife refuges 2. National parks and reserves
ISBN 0-691-12219-9   LC 2004-97392

"The authors present summaries of the major reserves on each continent, discuss the backgrounds of those reserves and the flora and fauna found there, and give . . . guidelines for visiting the sites." Sci Books Films

Includes bibliographical references

Wildlife protection; Yael Calhoun, series editor; foreword by David Seideman. Chelsea House Publishers 2005 xxvii, 122p il (Environmental issues) $26.95 *

Grades: 9 10 11 12   333.95
1. Wildlife conservation
ISBN 0-7910-8204-0   LC 2004-29000

This discussion of wildlife protection issues and challenges includes sections on endangered species and reserves for wildlife protection

Includes bibliographical references

335.4 Marxian systems

Pipes, Richard

Communism: a history. Modern Lib. 2001 175p hardcover o.p. pa $10.95 *

Grades: 11 12 Adult   335.4
1. Communism
ISBN 0-679-64050-9; 0-8129-6864-6 (pa)
LC 2001-275458

"This is a short history on the essentials of communism—as an ideal, as a program outlined by Marx, and as a state established by Lenin to implement the program." Booklist

"As a brief, polemical diatribe . . . this short account of communism should provoke and instruct." Libr J

Includes bibliographical references

338.1 Agriculture

Pyle, George, 1956-

Raising less corn, more hell; the case for the independent farm and against industrial food. PublicAffairs 2005 xxv, 229p $25

Grades: 11 12 Adult   338.1
1. Family farms 2. Agricultural industry
ISBN 1-58548-115-0   LC 2005-41902

"Organizing his book into three neatly named sections—'Wealth,' 'Health,' and 'Security'—Pyle . . . addresses in turn the economic aspects of farming and feeding the United States and the much larger world beyond; health and environmental problems attributed to our present large-scale industrial food production methods; and issues of food safety and security, including genetically modified corn, soybeans, and other crops." Libr J

The author's "well-researched, lucid and passionate argument explains not only what is wrong with U.S. agricultural policy but why it matters." Publ Wkly

338.4 Secondary industries and services

Almond, Steve

Candyfreak: a journey through the chocolate underbelly of America. Algonquin Books of Chapel Hill 2004 266p $21.95

Grades: 11 12 Adult   338.4
1. Almond, Steve 2. Candy 3. Chocolate
ISBN 1-56512-421-9   LC 2003-70801

Also available in paperback from Harvest Bks.

The author tells how candy "shaped his childhood and continues to define his life in ways large and small. . . . Once hundreds of American confectioners delivered regional favorites to consumers, but now the big three of candy—Hershey, Mars, and Nestlé—control the market. To find out what happened to those candies of yesteryear, Almond talks to candy collectors and historians and visits a few of the remaining independent candy companies. . . . Flavored with the author's amusingly tart

Almond, Steve—*Continued*

sense of humor, *Candyfreak* is an intriguing chronicle of the passions that candy inspires and the pleasures it offers." Libr J

Includes bibliographical references

Chaplin, Heather, 1971-

Smartbomb; the quest for art, entertainment, and big bucks in the videogame revolution; [by] Heather Chaplin & Aaron Ruby. Algonquin Books of Chapel Hill 2005 287p $24.95; pa $13.95

Grades: 11 12 Adult 338.4

1. Video games

ISBN 1-56512-346-8; 978-1-56512-346-5; 1-56512-545-2 (pa) LC 2005-47845

"The story goes back in time to MIT in the late '50s and the development of the first video game. Moving onward to the present, readers meet developers at Nintendo, the creators of Doom, the developers of the Sims series, and players of Massively Multiplayer Online games. . . . This immensely readable book will have great appeal with gaming teens, but should also be required reading for librarians interested in learning more about gaming and its role in our culture and our teen-focused libraries." SLJ

Includes bibliographical references

338.5 General production economics

Galbraith, John Kenneth, 1908-2006

The Great Crash, 1929; with a new introduction by the author. Houghton Mifflin 1997 206p il pa $14 *

Grades: 11 12 Adult 338.5

1. Great Depression, 1929-1939 2. United States—Economic conditions—1919-1933

ISBN 0-395-85999-9 LC 97-22051

"A Mariner book"

First published 1955

Beginning with the bull market of Coolidge and Hoover and continuing through the stock market crash, the author analyzes its causes and speculates about the chances of another crash

Includes bibliographical references

338.7 Business enterprises

Corporate power in the United States; edited by Joseph Sora. Wilson, H.W. 1998 172p (Reference shelf) pa $45

Grades: 11 12 Adult 338.7

1. Corporations

ISBN 0-8242-0943-5 LC 98-8162

A collection of reprinted articles from various sources concerning the influence of corporations on American life

Includes bibliographical references

Katz, Jon

Geeks; how two lost boys rode the Internet out of Idaho. Villard Bks. 2000 xliii, 207p hardcover o.p. pa $13.95

Grades: 11 12 Adult 338.7

1. Data processing

ISBN 0-375-50298-X; 0-7679-0699-3 (pa)

LC 99-43150

This book focuses on "Jesse Dailey, a working-class 19-year-old trapped in rural Idaho, where he and his friend Eric Twilegar fixed computers for a living, and hacked and surfed the Web, convinced that they were losers and outcasts. Katz . . . traveled to Idaho to meet the pair, intending to chronicle their lives. He wound up encouraging and sometimes assisting Jesse and Eric as they tried to improve their lives by moving to Chicago, where they sought better jobs and even considered applying to college." Publ Wkly

"With Dailey and Twilegar. . . Katz has found the perfect hook to deliver his big theme: the ascension, via the Internet, of the once lowly nerd to a position of undeniable social primacy." N Y Times Book Rev

Zygmont, Jeffrey

Microchip: an idea, its genesis, and the revolution it created. Perseus Bks. 2003 xxii, 245p $25

Grades: 11 12 Adult 338.7

1. Computer industry 2. Microelectronics

ISBN 0-7382-0561-3 LC 2002-112395

"Comparing the invention of the integrated circuit to that of steel, Zygmont tracks the incredible story of the microchip from the visionaries who conceived of it to the rapid-fire advances that have made this complex technology integral to everyday life." Booklist

Includes bibliographical references

340 Law

Feinman, Jay M.

1001 legal words you need to know; [the ultimate guide to the language of law] Oxford University Press 2005 239p pa $10.95

Grades: 11 12 Adult 340

1. Law—United States—Dictionaries

ISBN 0-19-518133-6; 978-0-19-518133-3

First published 2003

Subtitle from cover

This "guide to the language of the American legal system . . . defines and explains every term with a sample sentence, and many entries have supplementary notes. In addition, the book includes a number of quick miniguides to legal troubleshooting that includes information on understanding wills, trusts, and inheritance, granting someone the power of attorney, understanding contracts, what to do if you're sued, how to choose a lawyer, exploring law school, and enjoying cop and lawyer dramas." Publisher's note

Includes bibliographical references

Feinman, Jay M.—*Continued*
Law 101; everything you need to know about the American legal system. 2nd ed. Oxford University Press 2006 363p $28 *
Grades: 11 12 Adult   **340**
1. Law—United States
ISBN 978-0-19-517957-6; 0-19-517957-9
LC 2005-55481
First published 2000
This is an "introduction to law, covering the main subjects found in the first year of law school, giving us a basic understanding of how it all works. Readers are introduced to every aspect of the legal system, from constitutional law and the litigation process to tort law, contract law, property law, and criminal law." Publisher's note

340.03   Law--Encyclopedias and dictionaries

Black's law dictionary; Bryan A. Garner, editor in chief. 8th ed. Thomson/West 2004 xxv, 1810p $66 *
Grades: 11 12 Adult   **340.03**
1. Law—Dictionaries
ISBN 0-314-15199-0   LC 2004-616324
Also available in an abridged paperback edition
First published 1891 with title: A dictionary of law, under the authorship of Henry Campbell Black. Periodically revised to bring terms up to date
"Definitions of the terms and phrases of American and English jurisprudence, ancient and modern." Subtitle
"This comprehensive work is the standard U.S. law dictionary. [It] includes more than 5,000 new or revised entries, as well as thousands of archaic or little-used legal terms. Many entries include references to cases or statutes. Appendixes include a table of abbreviations and the text of the U.S. Constitution." Guide to Ref Books. 11th edition [review of the 7th edition]

341.23   United Nations

Alger, Chadwick F., 1924-
The United Nations system; a reference handbook. ABC-CLIO 2005 375p (Contemporary world issues) $50 *
Grades: 9 10 11 12   **341.23**
1. United Nations
ISBN 1-85109-805-4   LC 2005-25406
"This book is divided into chapters that cover background and history, problems, controversies and solutions, ambivalent participation of the Untied [sic] States in the UN system, chronologically the emergence and development of the UN system, facts and data, alternative futures of the UN system, directors of organizations, associations and agencies, biographical sketches of present heads of the UN system, selective print and nonprint resources of the United Nations, and an index and information about the author. . . . This book should be in all libraries that need up-to-date information on globalization, the United Nations, and the interrelationship between countries." Am Ref Books Annu, 2006
Includes bibliographical references

Fasulo, Linda M.
An insider's guide to the UN. Yale University Press 2003 245p il hardcover o.p. pa $16
Grades: 11 12 Adult   **341.23**
1. United Nations
ISBN 0-300-10155-4; 0-300-10762-5 (pa)
LC 2003-10668
Contents: An overview -- UN founding documents -- The Secretary General and the Secretariat -- The American ambassadors -- The Security Council -- Peace operations -- The General Assembly -- Coordinating to fight international terrorism -- The UN village -- Rights versus sovereignty: the US and the International Criminal Court -- The call for reform -- UN finances -- A tour of UN headquarters -- The coup against Boutros-Ghali -- UN advocates, donors, and friends -- Keeping tabs on how nations vote -- Making a career at the UN -- ECOSOC -- Agencies, programs, and commissions -- Rule of law and human rights -- Social and economic development -- Protecting the biosphere and its inhabitants -- UN to the rescue -- Nuclear, biological, and chemical threats -- Guiding globalization: how the UN helps make things work -- International crime and drug trafficking
The author "describes how the U.N. actually works, surveys its humanitarian, crime-fighting, and peacekeeping programs, and argues that the organization continues to deserve American support." Univ Press Books for Public and Second Sch Libr
Includes bibliographical references

Gorman, Robert F.
Great debates at the United Nations; an encyclopedia of fifty key issues 1945-2000. Greenwood Press 2001 xli, 451p il $65
Grades: 11 12 Adult   **341.23**
1. United Nations
ISBN 0-313-31386-5   LC 00-57652
The introduction "provides some historical background on the United Nations and the nature of its debates since its inception. Next come discussions of specific issues . . . that have appeared on its agenda. Each entry contains four sections: the significance of the issue; its historical, social, and economic background; the history of the UN discussions . . . and the outcome of the debate. . . . Each discussion ends with a list of suggested readings." SLJ
Includes bibliographical references

Moore, John Allphin, 1940-
Encyclopedia of the United Nations; [by] John Allphin Moore, Jr., Jerry Pubantz. Facts on File 2002 xxvii, 484p il (Facts on File library of world history) $75
Grades: 11 12 Adult   **341.23**
1. United Nations 2. International relations
ISBN 0-8160-4417-1   LC 2002-72222
"Over 400 articles cover people associated with the UN, the countries and regions where it has been involved, its agencies and institutions, its affiliated organizations, specific project names, and other issues that the UN has addressed over the past 55 years. Appendixes provide a chronology of major UN events, a selected bibliography, and a very useful list of web addresses to navigate the complex UN web site." Libr J
Includes bibliographical references

341.242 European Union

The **European** Union; edited by Norris Smith; editorial advisor, Lynn M. Messina. H.W. Wilson 2005 177p il map (Reference shelf) $50 *

Grades: 11 12 Adult   **341.242**
  1. European Union
  ISBN 0-8242-1046-8   LC 2004-62511

This book "examines the EU from its formation, with a discussion of the economic, political, and social impact of the organization upon its own members and the rest of the international community." Publisher's note

Includes bibliographical references

341.6 Law of war

Barkan, Elazar
  The guilt of nations; restitution and negotiating historical injustices. Norton 2000 414p $29.95

Grades: 11 12 Adult   **341.6**
  1. Political ethics 2. Human rights 3. International relations 4. Minorities 5. History—Philosophy
  ISBN 0-393-04886-1   LC 99-88238

Also available in paperback from Johns Hopkins University Press

The author examines "historical injustices within and between nations over the past 50 years, urging that we move toward a theory of restitution that allows victims and perpetrators to negotiate their understandings of history and identity and to establish a basis for a common future. Most of Barkan's book is devoted to analysis of specifics: the Holocaust; U.S. internment of Japanese Americans; Nazi art in Russian museums and Nazi gold in Swiss banks; Japanese abuse of 'comfort wormen'; Eastern Europe after decades of Communism; {and} treatment of indigenous groups on the U.S. mainland." Booklist

Includes bibliographical references

War crimes; Henny H. Kim, book editor. Greenhaven Press 2000 176p (Contemporary issues companion) lib bdg $31.20; pa $19.95

Grades: 9 10 11 12   **341.6**
  1. War crimes
  ISBN 0-7377-0171-4 (lib bdg); 0-7377-0170-6 (pa)
    LC 99-16391

All of the articles in this collection "originated in the 1990s, except one on Vietnam that was written in 1966, and cover such topics as the Nuremberg trials, Bosnia, Rwanda, Cambodia, and the Japanese invasion of China. . . . A useful book for class discussions as well as for research papers." SLJ

Includes bibliographical references

342 Constitutional and administrative law

Amar, Akhil Reed
  America's constitution; a biography. Random House 2005 657p il $29.95; pa $16.95

Grades: 11 12 Adult   **342**
  1. Constitutional history—United States
  ISBN 1-400-06262-4; 0-8129-7272-4 (pa)
    LC 2004-61464

This is a "guide to the goals and meaning intended by those who drafted and ratified the original 1787 document and its 27 amendments." Economist

"Only rarely do you find a book that embodies scholarship at its most solid and invigorating; this is such a book." Publ Wkly

Includes bibliographical references

Are privacy rights being violated? Stuart A. Kallen, book editor. Greenhaven Press 2006 128p (At issue) lib bdg $28.70; pa $19.95

Grades: 9 10 11 12   **342**
  1. Right of privacy
  ISBN 0-7377-2360-2 (lib bdg); 0-7377-2361-0 (pa)
    LC 2005-45117

The topics discussed in this anthology include spyware, employee privacy rights, the use of video cameras in public places, and the Patriot Act. Contributors include Matthew Callan, Max Blumenthal, and Heather MacDonald.

Includes bibliographical references

The **Bill** of Rights; Gary Zacharias, book editor, Jared Zacharias, book editor. Greenhaven Press 2003 112p (At issue in history) lib bdg $28.70; pa $19.95 *

Grades: 9 10 11 12   **342**
  1. Civil rights 2. Constitutional law—United States 3. United States—Constitution—1-10th amendments
  ISBN 0-7377-1425-5 (lib bdg); 0-7377-1426-3 (pa)
    LC 2002-73857

"Articles and primary documents address the history of, and the issues and controversies surrounding the Bill of Rights. . . . The first section is devoted to the early debates over the need for the Bill of Rights. . . . The second section consists of articles that discuss, both positively and negatively, the amendments over the years." SLJ

Includes bibliographical references

Bowen, Catherine Drinker, 1897-1973
  Miracle at Philadelphia; the story of the Constitutional Convention, May to September, 1787; foreword by Warren E. Burger. Little, Brown 1986 c1966 346p pa $16.95 hardcover o.p. *

Grades: 11 12 Adult   **342**
  1. United States. Constitutional Convention (1787) 2. Constitutional history—United States
  ISBN 0-316-10398-5 (pa)   LC 86-205421

"An Atlantic Monthly Press book"

A reissue of the title first published 1966

Bowen, Catherine Drinker, 1897-1973—*Continued*

"Writing from sources—delegates' letters and diaries; contemporary reports; James Madison's faithful minutes—Catherine Drinker Bowen draws [a] . . . picture of the men, issues and background of the Constitutional Convention held at Philadelphia in the hot summer of 1787." Publ Wkly

Includes bibliographical references

Civil liberties; Andrea C. Nakaya, book editor. Greenhaven Press 2006 142p il (Introducing issues with opposing viewpoints) lib bdg $32.45 *

Grades: 7 8 9 10 11 12   342
1. Civil rights
ISBN 0-7377-3387-X   LC 2005-46144

The articles in this anthology "debate issues such as flag burning, Internet filters in public libraries, racial profiling, and the Patriot Act. Authors as disparate as NASCAR driver John Andretti and former U.S. Attorney General John Ashcroft trade arguments about civil liberties in essays that address issues such as media censorship and the treatment of immigrants during the war on terror. . . . A solid resource for research." SLJ

Includes bibliographical references

Civil liberties and the constitution; cases and commentaries; Lucius J. Barker . . . [et al.] 8th ed. Prentice Hall 1999 878p pa $119.20 *

Grades: 9 10 11 12   342
1. United States. Supreme Court 2. Civil rights 3. Constitutional law—United States
ISBN 0-13-082897-1   LC 98-54160

First published 1970

Topics covered include: Civil liberties in a political-social context; religious liberty; freedom of expression, assembly, and association; the rights of the accused; racial and sexual discrimination; political participation; and the right to privacy.

Includes bibliographical references

Civil liberties and war; Jamuna Carroll, book editor. Greenhaven Press 2006 173p il (Issues on trial) lib bdg $34.95 *

Grades: 9 10 11 12   342
1. Civil rights 2. War—Public opinion 3. Military policy—United States
ISBN 0-7377-2503-6; 978-0-7377-2503-2
                    LC 2005-52761

"This volume examines four significant Supreme Court cases: Charles T. Schenck v. United States (1919), involving suppressing speech that poses a clear and present danger; Toyosaburo Korematsu v. United States (1944), which deals with the evacuation of Japanese Americans; New York Times Co. v. United States (1971), which revolves around the publication of the Pentagon Papers and the issue of prior restraint; and Yaser Esam Hamdi et al. v. Donald H. Rumsfeld et al. (2004), which entails due-process rights and enemy combatants. . . . An important, timely addition for most collections." SLJ

Includes bibliographical references

The **Civil** Rights Act of 1964. Greenhaven Press 2004 128p il (At issue in history) lib bdg $29.95; pa $21.20

Grades: 9 10 11 12   342
1. Civil Rights Act of 1964 2. Civil rights
ISBN 0-7377-2304-1 (lib bdg); 0-7377-2305-X (pa)
                    LC 2003-47288

"This book reviews the history of the landmark legislation, the debate that surrounded it, and its legacy through essays and articles written at the time and more recent pieces that examine the progress made and outlook for the future. . . . A useful collection of primary and secondary sources for reports." SLJ

Includes bibliographical references

Encyclopedia of the American Constitution; edited by Leonard W. Levy and Kenneth L. Karst. 2nd ed, Adam Winkler, associate editor for the second ed. Macmillan Ref. USA 2000 6v set $595

Grades: 11 12 Adult   342
1. Constitutional law—United States
ISBN 0-02-864880-3   LC 00-29203

First published 1986 in 4 volumes

This "reference contains approximately 3000 contributions from academics, lawyers, and judges concerning key constitutional law cases and legislative developments relating to constitutional issues (e.g., abortion, welfare rights, and affirmative action)." Libr J

Feinberg, Barbara Silberdick, 1938-

The Articles of Confederation; the first constitution of the United States. 21st Cent. Bks. (Brookfield) 2002 110p il maps lib bdg $24.90

Grades: 7 8 9 10   342
1. United States. Articles of Confederation 2. Constitutional history—United States 3. United States—Politics and government—1775-1783, Revolution
ISBN 0-7613-2114-4   LC 2001-27441

"Feinberg introduces the history and text of 'The Articles of Confederation and Perpetual Union,' the constitution that guided the U.S. government from 1776 to 1787. . . . Attractively laid out, this solid choice includes many black-and-white illustrations, including portrait paintings, engravings, and maps." Booklist

Includes bibliographical references

Free speech; John Boaz, book editor. Greenhaven Press 2006 221p (Current controversies) lib bdg $34.95; pa $23.70

Grades: 7 8 9 10   342
1. Freedom of speech
ISBN 0-7377-2204-5 (lib bdg); 978-0-7377-2204-8 (lib bdg); 0-7377-2205-3 (pa)   LC 2005-46225

"This volume explores the challenges facing free speech post September 11, 2001, including the Patriot Act, commercial free speech, and consolidation of the media." Publisher's note

Includes bibliographical references

Freedom of religion; edited by Gary Zacharias. Greenhaven Press 2004 144p il (Bill of Rights) lib bdg $32.45

Grades: 9 10 11 12 **342**

1. Freedom of religion 2. Church and state

ISBN 0-7377-2647-4 (lib bdg)   LC 2004-46074

"This volume explains the history of church/state relations, the establishment and free expression clauses contained in the statement, and arguments that have arisen over it." Publisher's note

Includes bibliographical references

Freedom of speech; edited by William Dudley. Greenhaven Press 2005 128p (Bill of Rights) lib bdg $32.45

Grades: 9 10 11 12 **342**

1. Freedom of speech 2. Censorship

ISBN 0-7377-1929-X   LC 2004-54149

"This interesting anthology examines the historical origins of the free speech clause of the First Amendment, the evolving interpretations of the First Amendment by the Supreme Court, and the changing public attitudes toward free speech. Included are discussions of such issues as wartime dissent, censorship, hate speech, and flag burning." Publisher's note

Includes bibliographical references

Freedom of the press; Rob Edelman, book editor. Greenhaven Press 2007 181p (Issues on trial) lib bdg $34.95

Grades: 9 10 11 12 **342**

1. Freedom of the press

ISBN 0-7377-3449-3; 978-0-7377-3449-2

LC 2006-41173

"This anthology offers . . . [an] examination of four landmark court cases involving freedom of the press, each of which was heard by the U.S. Supreme Court." Publisher's note

Includes bibliographical references

Friedman, Ian C.

Freedom of speech and the press. Facts on File 2005 128p il map (American rights) $35

Grades: 7 8 9 10 **342**

1. Freedom of speech 2. Freedom of the press

ISBN 0-8160-5662-5   LC 2004-21003

Contents: Foundations of free speech and press; Defining free speech and press in a new nation; Influencing American society in the 19th century; Evolving roles in the early 20th century; Engaging patriotism, decency, and race; Vietnam and Watergate; Battles over hateful words; The present and future of free speech and press

Includes bibliographical references

Haynes, Charles C.

First freedoms; a documentary history of the First Amendment Rights in America; [by] Charles C. Haynes, Sam Chaltain, Susan M. Glisson. Oxford University Press 2005 255p il $40

Grades: 8 9 10 11 12 **342**

1. United States. Constitution. 1st-10th amendments 2. Constitutional history—United States

ISBN 978-0-19-515750-5; 0-19-515750-8

LC 2005-31880

This book features "information and primary documents concerning the origins and attacks on the First Amendment. The various documents go from the Charter of Rhode Island and Providence Plantations in 1663 through the Patriot Act of 2001." Libr Media Connect

This is "an excellent resource for all libraries, as well as enjoyable reading for history buffs." SLJ

Head, Tom

Freedom of religion. Facts on File 2005 146p il map (American rights) $35

Grades: 7 8 9 10 **342**

1. Freedom of religion 2. United States—Religion

ISBN 0-8160-5664-1   LC 2004-20547

Contents: Religious freedom in the American colonies; The freedom of conscience; A diverse religious nation; Religious expression and the law; Conscientious objectors and the draft; Religion in public schools; Freedom from religion?; Religious liberty around the world; The future of religious freedom in America

"This solid, readable volume walks readers through the part religion played in the formation of the colonies and looks at how faith informed the people's lives and the tensions among various religions." Booklist

Includes bibliographical references

Hinds, Maurene J.

You have the right to know your rights; what teens should know. Enslow Pubs. 2005 104p il (Issues in focus today) $31.93 *

Grades: 9 10 11 12 **342**

1. Youth—Civil rights

ISBN 0-7660-2358-3

The author "outlines for readers the ways in which the rights of young people have changed over time in the United States, and she brings them up-to-date on the topic of young people's rights today. Hinds covers such issues as privacy and self-expression and explains what teens can do if their rights are violated." Publisher's note

Includes bibliographical references

Icenoggle, Jodi, 1967-

Schenck v. United States and the freedom of speech debate. Enslow Pubs. 2005 128p il (Debating Supreme Court decisions) lib bdg $26.60

Grades: 7 8 9 10 **342**

1. Schenck, Charles 2. Freedom of speech

ISBN 0-7660-2392-3

In the "case of *Schenck v. United States,* the Supreme Court held that people who opposed World War I were not allowed to use their free speech rights to interfere with the draft. . . . [In this book the author] explains the different arguments that have been used for and against free speech." Publisher's note

Includes glossary and bibliographical references

Johnson, Terry, 1961-

Legal rights. Facts on File 2005 152p il map (American rights) $35

Grades: 7 8 9 10 **342**

1. Civil rights

ISBN 0-8160-5665-X   LC 2004-23350

Johnson, Terry, 1961-—*Continued*
Contents: Origins of American legal rights; The right
against unreasonable searches and seizures; The right to
fair treatment; The right to a fair trial; The right against
excessive or cruel and unusual punishments; Legal rights
and the war on terrorism; The USA Patriot Act and the
future of American legal rights
"The content is well organized, beginning with the origins and foundations of the rights, and proceeding with
a clear discussion of the challenges they face even today.
. . . Black-and-white maps, charts and graphs, photos,
reproductions, and political cartoons contribute useful information." SLJ
Includes bibliographical references

Keenan, Kevin M.
Invasion of privacy; a reference handbook.
ABC-CLIO 2005 259p (Contemporary world
issues) $50 *
Grades: 11 12 Adult   342
1. Right of privacy
ISBN 1-85109-630-2   LC 2005-18577
"This book provides a comprehensive overview of the
right to privacy through a series of essays. . . . Keenan
achieves balance by presenting the varying points of
view on the topic and manages to convey the essentials
of a complex and timely subject." Libr J
Includes bibliographical references

Lively, Donald E., 1947-
Landmark Supreme Court cases; a reference
guide. Greenwood Press 1999 374p $64.95 *
Grades: 11 12 Adult   342
1. United States. Supreme Court 2. Constitutional
law—United States
ISBN 0-313-30602-8   LC 98-44220
"This volume discusses 74 cases under four broad topics: the distribution of powers, the relationship between
the nation and its states, concepts of equality, and individual rights. These are divided further into more specific topics. . . . The thematic approach combined with
fairly detailed discussion of individual cases works well."
Booklist
Includes bibliographical references

Marzilli, Alan, 1970-
Fetal rights. Chelsea House Publishers 2006
150p il map (Point-counterpoint) $32.95 *
Grades: 9 10 11 12   342
1. Fetus
ISBN 0-7910-8643-7   LC 2005-6533
"This book examines whether the law should recognize an unborn child—or fetus—as a person. Other relevant topics include whether or not women should be
prosecuted for using drugs during pregnancy and whether
or not a pregnant woman should be forced to undergo
medical procedures for the benefit of a fetus." Publisher's note
Includes bibliographical references

Menez, Joseph Francis, 1917-
Summaries of leading cases on the Constitution;
[by] Joseph F. Menez and John R. Vile. 14th ed.
Rowman & Littlefield Publishers 2004 xxviii,
627p $80; pa $24.95
Grades: 9 10 11 12   342
1. United States. Supreme Court 2. Constitutional
law—United States
ISBN 0-7425-3276-3; 0-7425-3277-1 (pa)
                              LC 2003-13479

First published 1954
This volume presents summaries of major cases concerning constitutional law that have been decided by the
Supreme Court since its establishment. It is written for
students and laypersons.

The **Oxford** guide to United States Supreme Court
decisions; edited by Kermit L. Hall. Oxford
Univ. Press 1999 428p $39.95; pa $19.95 *
Grades: 11 12 Adult   342
1. United States. Supreme Court 2. Constitutional
law—United States
ISBN 0-19-511883-9; 0-19-513924-0 (pa)
                              LC 98-8747

This volume is a guide to approximately 400 Supreme
Court decisions. "Each case entry typically provides
background information on the case, explains the Court's
decision, {and} explores any disagreement among the
justices about the legal doctrines and societal values at
stake. . . . A glossary of terms, a copy of the U.S. Constitution, . . . appendixes charting the nominations and
succession of Supreme Court justices, a case index, and
a topical index complete the volume." Booklist
"An impressive accomplishment, this guide will be invaluable to all students of United States history and will
also appeal to sophisticated readers." Libr J

Patrick, John J.
The Bill of Rights; a history in documents.
Oxford Univ. Press 2003 205p il map (Pages from
history) lib bdg $32.95 *
Grades: 7 8 9 10   342
1. United States. Constitution. 1st-10th amendments
2. Civil rights
ISBN 0-19-510354-8   LC 2002-6294
Contents: The roots of American rights; Rights revolu-
tion and in America; The birth of the Bill of Rights; The
Bill of Rights marginalized; Rights renewed and denied;
A resurgence of rights; Nationalization of the Bill of
Rights; Political cartoons on the right to bear arms; Con-
sensus and controversy
Uses contemporary documents to explore the history
of the first ten amendments to the U.S. Constitution, the
British traditions on which they were based, and their
impact on American society
"This attractive and informative volume will be a
valuable resource for most collections." SLJ
Includes bibliographical references

Pendergast, Tom, 1964-
Constitutional amendments: from freedom of speech to flag burning; [by] Tom Pendergast, Sara Pendergast, and John Sousanis; Elizabeth Shaw Grunow, editor. U.X.L 2001 3v set $165
Grades: 7 8 9 10   **342**
1. United States. Constitution. 1st-10th amendments 2. Constitutional law—United States 3. Civil rights
ISBN 0-7876-4865-5   LC 00-67236
"Covering each of the 27 amendments, this 3-vol. resource provides the history and social context of the amendment process. Entries range in length from 10 to 15 pages and begin with the full text of the amendment followed by an essay on the social and political climate that gave rise to its proposal." Publisher's note
"Presentation is very clear. . . . This is definitely a set that belongs in school and public libraries." Booklist
Includes glossary and bibliographical references

Phillips, Tracy A.
Hazelwood v. Kuhlmeier and the school newspaper censorship debate; debating Supreme Court decisions. Enslow Publishers 2006 112p il (Debating Supreme Court decisions) lib bdg $26.60
Grades: 7 8 9 10   **342**
1. Hazelwood School District v. Kuhlmeier 2. Censorship 3. Freedom of the press 4. Students—Law and legislation
ISBN 0-7660-2394-X   LC 2005034655
This discusses the Supreme Court case involving the censorship of a high school newspaper in Hazelwood Missouri.
This is "objectively and clearly written and would be useful for reports." SLJ
Includes bibliographical references

Racial discrimination; Mitchell Young, book editor. Greenhaven Press 2006 183p il (Issues on trial) lib bdg $34.95
Grades: 9 10 11 12   **342**
1. Race discrimination
ISBN 0-7377-2787-X; 978-0-7377-2787-6
          LC 2005-55092
This anthology examines four major court cases involving racial discrimination: Plessy v. Ferguson (1896), Brown v. Board of Education (1954), Wisconsin v. Mitchell (1993), and Grutter v. Bollinger (2003).
Includes bibliographical references

Savage, David G., 1950-
The Supreme Court and individual rights. 4th ed. CQ Press 2004 399p il $39.95 *
Grades: 9 10 11 12   **342**
1. United States. Supreme Court 2. Civil rights 3. Constitutional law—United States
ISBN 1-568-02887-3   LC 2004-273178
First published 1980 under the editorship of Elder Witt
This volume "examines the impact of U.S. Supreme Court decisions on the rights and freedoms of the individual through the Court's 2002-2003 term. . . . [This

book] traces the Court's emergence as a defender of individual rights and liberties, even during the recent era of conservative judicial majorities." Publisher's note
Includes bibliographical references

The **Supreme** Court and the Constitution; readings in American constitutional history; edited by Stanley I. Kutler. 3rd ed. Norton 1984 765p pa $37.30 *
Grades: 9 10 11 12   **342**
1. United States. Supreme Court 2. Constitutional history—United States
ISBN 0-393-95437-4   LC 84-5969
First published 1969 by Houghton Mifflin. Periodically revised
This work includes extracts of judicial cases which have had significance for constitutional law. Arrangement is chronological, further subdivided by topical categories

Vile, John R.
The Constitutional Convention of 1787; a comprehensive encyclopedia of America's founding. ABC-CLIO 2005 2v il set $185
Grades: 11 12 Adult   **342**
1. Constitutional history—United States—Encyclopedias 2. Constitutional law—United States—Encyclopedias
ISBN 1-85109-669-8   LC 2005-24214
This "resource covers the people, events, committees, ideology, and documents related to the drafting of the Constitution." SLJ
For a fuller review, see: Booklist, Dec. 1, 2005
Includes bibliographical references

The United States Constitution; questions and answers. Greenwood Press 1998 316p il $39.95
Grades: 7 8 9 10   **342**
1. United States. Constitution 2. Constitutional law—United States
ISBN 0-313-30643-5   LC 97-32008
The author examines each section of the U.S. Constitution "and provides a question-and-answer format that allows for easy explanation of a complicated document. The amendments are addressed in detail. . . . The book is easy to read and well laid out." Book Rep
Includes bibliographical references

Weiner, Mark Stuart, 1967-
Black trials; citizenship from the beginnings of slavery to the end of caste; [by] Mark S. Weiner. Alfred A. Knopf 2004 421p $26.95; pa $16.95 *
Grades: 11 12 Adult   **342**
1. African Americans—Civil rights 2. Trials
ISBN 0-375-40981-5; 0-375-70884-7 (pa)
          LC 2004-40860
The author "examines how court proceedings involving black people—and whites trying to assist them—have served as windows onto race relations and the power of whites over blacks in the U.S. from its earliest days. . . . This book is the best of its kind—a serious, deeply felt reflection on the weight of history on contemporary affairs." Publ Wkly
Includes bibliographical references

Wernick, Allan

U.S. immigration & citizenship; your complete guide. 4th ed. Emmis Books 2004 347p pa $24.99 *

Grades: 9 10 11 12 **342**
1. United States—Immigration and emigration 2. Citizenship
ISBN 1-57860-169-X   LC 2004-56298
First published 1997
This guide to immigration law and procedures discusses the visa application process, how to get a green card and naturalization and citizenship requirements.

What rights should illegal immigrants have? Lori Newman, book editor. Greenhaven Press 2007 90p (At issue) lib bdg $28.70; pa $19.95
Grades: 9 10 11 12 **342**
1. Illegal aliens 2. United States—Immigration and emigration 3. Civil rights
ISBN 0-7377-3480-9 (lib bdg); 978-0-7377-3480-5 (lib bdg); 0-7377-3481-7 (pa); 978-0-7377-3481-2 (pa)
LC 2006-43415
This "book looks at such subjects as health care and college tuition for illegal immigrants, as well as the impact of the war on terrorism on their rights." SLJ
Includes bibliographical references

344 Labor, social service, education, cultural law

The **American** Bar Association guide to workplace law; [principle author, Barbara Fick] 2nd ed. Random House Reference 2006 301p pa $16.95
Grades: 11 12 Adult **344**
1. Labor—Law and legislation
ISBN 0-375-72140-1; 978-0-375-72140-3
LC 2006-45186
First published 1997
This guide covers laws affecting hiring, sexual harassment, leave time, health insurance, ending an employment relationship, retirement, unions, government employment and workplace rights.
Includes bibliographical references

Dudley, Mark E.

Engel v. Vitale (1962); religion in the schools. 21st Cent. Bks. (NY) 1995 96p il (Supreme Court decisions) $18.90
Grades: 7 8 9 10 **344**
1. Engel, Stephen 2. Vitale, William J. 3. Religion in the public schools 4. Church and state
ISBN 0-8050-3916-3   LC 95-19435
The author points out that although a 1962 Supreme Court case decided that official prayers in public schools are unconstitutional, the issue of separation of church and state remains.
This volume is "clearly written and well organized." SLJ
Includes bibliographical references

The **environment**; Andrea C. Nakaya, book editor. Greenhaven Press 2006 163p il (Issues on trial) lib bdg $34.95
Grades: 9 10 11 12 **344**
1. Environmental policy—United States
ISBN 0-7377-2797-7; 978-0-7377-2797-5
LC 2005-52713
"This anthology examines four court cases that offer insight into some of America's most important environmental conflicts. . . . There is a wealth of information in this title, which serves as a meaningful reference tool and a prelude to the study of law as a force for major social change." SLJ
Includes bibliographical references

Fridell, Ron, 1943-

Cruzan v. Missouri and the right to die debate; debating Supreme Court decisions. Enslow Publishers 2005 128p il (Debating Supreme Court decisions) lib bdg $26.60
Grades: 7 8 9 10 **344**
1. Cruzan, Nancy 2. Cruzan, Joe, d. 1996 3. Right to die—Law and legislation
ISBN 0-7660-2356-7   LC 2004-20028
Contents: Legal questions; The changing face of death; Through supporters' eyes; Through opponents' eyes; Right to die laws; Lower court cases; U.S. Supreme Court cases; The issues today; Debating the issues
This examines both sides of the debate concerning assisted suicide and related Supreme Court decisions.
Includes glossary and bibliographical references

Hull, N. E. H., 1949-

Roe v. Wade; the abortion rights controversy in American history; {by} N.E.H. Hull and Peter Charles Hoffer. University Press of Kan. 2001 315p (Landmark law cases & American society) hardcover o.p. pa $15.95
Grades: 11 12 Adult **344**
1. McCorvey, Norma 2. Wade, Henry, 1914-2001 3. Roe v. Wade 4. Abortion—Law and legislation
ISBN 0-7006-1142-8; 0-7006-1143-6 (pa)
LC 2001-1785
This "study begins with three chapters on U.S. abortion history: its nineteenth-century criminalization; the effect of improving birth-control methods in the twentieth century; and state-level legal changes in the 1960s. The authors then analyze the decision itself and trace the continuing battles of the next three decades." Booklist
This volume "is crammed with information but remains very readable and a good source for student papers." Libr J
Includes bibliographical references

Is gun ownership a right? Kelly Doyle, book editor. Greenhaven Press 2005 127p (At issue) lib bdg $28.70; pa $18.70
Grades: 9 10 11 12 **344**
1. Gun control
ISBN 0-7377-2394-7 (lib bdg); 0-7377-2395-5 (pa)
LC 2004-52283

Is gun ownership a right?—*Continued*

The authors "debate the meaning and purpose of the Second Amendment, the goals and actions of gun rights activists and gun control activists, and the issues related to gun rights and gun ownership in America." Introduction

Includes bibliographical references

Kowalski, Kathiann M., 1955-

The Earls case and the student drug testing debate; debating Supreme Court decisions. Enslow Publishers 2006 128p il (Debating Supreme Court decisions) lib bdg $26.60

Grades: 7 8 9 10 **344**

1. Earls, Lindsay 2. Students—Law and legislation 3. Drug testing

ISBN 0-7660-2478-4 LC 2005034654

This is an account of the Supreme Court case involving Lindsay Earls, a high school student in Oklahoma who was subjected to a random drug test.

This is "objectively and clearly written and would be useful for reports." SLJ

Includes glossary and bibliographical references

McPherson, Stephanie Sammartino

The Bakke case and the affirmative action debate. Enslow Pubs. 2005 128p il (Debating Supreme Court decisions) lib bdg $26.60

Grades: 7 8 9 10 **344**

1. Bakke, Allan Paul 2. Affirmative action programs

ISBN 0-7660-2526-8

"In 1973, [Allan] Bakke applied to medical school. . . . He was not admitted. When he found out that the medical school class reserved some positions for members of minority groups, he took the university to court, charging discrimination. His case went . . . to the Supreme Court. Is affirmative action an effort to 'level the playing field,' or is it unfair preferential treatment to minorities? . . . [This] explores both sides of the argument as well as related court cases and laws." Publisher's note

Reproductive rights; William Dudley, book editor.

Greenhaven Press 2006 178p il (Issues on trial) lib bdg $34.95 *

Grades: 9 10 11 12 **344**

1. Abortion—Law and legislation 2. Birth control—Law and legislation

ISBN 0-7377-2511-7; 978-0-7377-2511-7

LC 2005-54268

"This book examines various issues related to the topic via a series of writings about famous Supreme Court cases, ranging from Buck v. Bell in 1927 and Griswold v. Connecticut in 1965 to Roe v. Wade in 1973 and A.Z. v. B.Z. in 2000. The essays include court decisions and dissenting opinions as well as contemporary journalism pieces and retrospective commentary. . . . Students of modern science, biology, genetics, and the law will find this volume informative and interesting." SLJ

Includes bibliographical references

Students' rights; Laura K. Egendorf, book editor.

Greenhaven Press 2006 189p il (Issues on trial) lib bdg $34.95

Grades: 9 10 11 12 **344**

1. Students—Civil rights 2. Students—Law and legislation 3. Youth—Civil rights

ISBN 0-7377-2509-5; 978-0-7377-2509-4

LC 2005-52690

"In this anthology judges and commentators explore four key students' rights cases." Publisher's note

Includes bibliographical references

Students' rights: opposing viewpoints; Jamuna Carroll, book editor. Greenhaven Press 2005 207p lib bdg $34.95; pa $23.70 *

Grades: 9 10 11 12 **344**

1. Students—Civil rights

ISBN 0-7377-3088-9 (lib bdg); 0-7377-3089-7 (pa)

LC 2004-59761

"Opposing viewpoints series"

"Essays cover . . . topics such as No Child Left Behind, religion in schools, dress codes, The Patriot Act, access to family-planning information, random drug testing, and illegal immigrants' access to federal financial aide, while posing significant questions to help students develop critical-thinking skills." SLJ

Includes bibliographical references

Telgen, Diane

Brown v. Board of Education. Omnigraphics 2005 xxxiv, 246p il (Defining moments) lib bdg $38

Grades: 7 8 9 10 **344**

1. Brown, Oliver, 1919-1961 2. Topeka (Kan.). Board of Education 3. Segregation in education

ISBN 0-7808-0775-8

This "opens with an 'Important People, Places, and Terms' section and a detailed chronology that takes readers from an 1849 school-segregation case to the 2003 University of Michigan rulings on student diversity. The book includes a narrative overview, biographies of individuals involved, and primary sources. This latter, impressive section gives this treatment of Brown v. Board of Education depth and promotes a greater empathy from readers. . . . Telgen has done a fine job of making this topic accessible to and engaging for today's students." SLJ

Includes bibliographical references

Torrans, Lee Ann, 1952-

Law for K-12 libraries and librarians. Libraries Unlimited 2003 250p pa $25 *

Grades: professional **344**

1. Libraries—Law and legislation 2. School libraries

ISBN 1-59158-036-6 LC 2003-2592

Contents: Copyright; The scope of copyright; The fair use of material protected by copyright in education; Library archiving and section 108 of the DMCA; Tracing copyright; Library bibliographies criteria for selection and the legal implications and limitations of linking; Faculty created web sites: who owns them?; Patron privacy and filtering in the school library: guarding outgoing

Torrans, Lee Ann, 1952-—*Continued*
data, monitoring incoming data; Library bibliographies:
student web pages, metatags in websites and the law; Licensing in the library; Americans with disabilities and
the school library; Employment in the library; Policies
and procedures: a difference with significance
"Advice and regulations addressing what can be copied, taped, and used on school Web sites will be helpful
for both media specialists and teachers. Comprehensive
yet readable, this guide is logically organized and solidly
supported by examples and references. An indispensable
resource." SLJ
Includes bibliographical references

345   Criminal law

Berger, Leslie, 1928-1995
The grand jury; [by] Leslie Berger; Austin
Sarat, general editor. Chelsea House 2000 101p il
(Crime, justice, and punishment) $19.95
Grades: 9 10 11 12   345
1. Jury 2. Administration of criminal justice
ISBN 0-7910-4290-1   LC 99-40243
Explains how the American grand jury system operates and some of the abuses of this system, using classic
cases as illustrations
Includes bibliographical references

Cohen, Laura
The Gault case and young people's rights;
debating Supreme Court decisions. Enslow
Publishers, Inc. 2006 128p il (Debating Supreme
Court decisions) lib bdg $26.60
Grades: 7 8 9 10   345
1. Gault, Gerald 2. Juvenile courts 3. Children—Law
and legislation
ISBN 0-7660-2476-8   LC 2006001741
Examines the 1967 Supreme Court Case in which the
court ruled that juvenile courts cannot deprive children of
certain rights guaranteed by the Constitution.
This is "objectively and clearly written and would be
useful for reports." SLJ
Includes bibliographical references

The **death** penalty; Samuel Brenner, book editor.
Greenhaven Press 2006 190p il map (Issues on
trial) lib bdg $34.95 *
Grades: 9 10 11 12   345
1. Capital punishment—United States
ISBN 0-7377-2507-9; 978-0-7377-2507-0
LC 2005-58851
This book examines four major court cases involving
capital punishment.
Includes bibliographical references

Freedom from cruel and unusual punishment;
Kristin O'Donnell Tubb, book editor.
Greenhaven Press 2005 144p (Bill of Rights) lib
bdg $32.45
Grades: 9 10 11 12   345
1. Punishment 2. Capital punishment
ISBN 0-7377-1925-7 (lib bdg)   LC 2004-54223

"This anthology discusses the Eighth Amendment, including a history dating back to biblical times, its inseparable ties to the death penalty, and recent rulings and debates." Publisher's note
Includes bibliographical references

Gershman, Gary P.
Death penalty on trial; a handbook with cases,
laws, and documents. ABC-CLIO 2005 265p (On
trial) $55
Grades: 11 12 Adult   345
1. Capital punishment—United States
ISBN 1-85109-606-X; 978-1-85109-606-0
LC 2005-1438
"The first half of the book describes the history, court
cases, and decisions regarding the death penalty, and the
impact of the judicial determinations and how they affect
the current legal environment. The second half of the
volume consists of excerpts from important judicial decisions between 1892 and 2002; a short glossary related to
Key People, Laws, and Concepts; a chronology; a table
of cases; and an eight-page annotated bibliography." SLJ
This book "is an excellent choice for the library
shelf." Libr Media Connect
Includes bibliographical references

Hanson, Freya Ottem, 1949-
The Scopes monkey trial; a headline court case.
Enslow Pubs. 2000 128p il (Headline court cases)
$20.95
Grades: 9 10 11 12   345
1. Scopes, John Thomas 2. Evolution—Study and
teaching
ISBN 0-7660-1388-X   LC 99-50503
Discusses one of the most famous court cases in history, in which a Tennessee high school teacher was put on
trial for teaching evolution
Includes bibliographical references

Hoffer, Peter Charles
The Salem witchcraft trials; a legal history.
University Press of Kan. 1997 165p (Landmark
law cases & American society) hardcover o.p. pa
$12.95
Grades: 11 12 Adult   345
1. Trials 2. Salem (Mass.)—History
ISBN 0-7006-0858-3; 0-7006-0859-1 (pa)
LC 97-19986
"Hoffer discusses the legal nature of the charges of
witchcraft, the evidential and procedural characteristics of
the trials of the accused, and the roles and attitudes of
the ministers and magistrates who controlled the proceedings. . . . Hoffer offers little that is new in terms of interpretation, but he presents it well and in a manner easily grasped by the general reader." Choice
Includes bibliographical references

Individual rights and the police; Mark R. Nesbitt,
book editor. Greenhaven Press 2006 188p
(Issues on trial) lib bdg $34.95
Grades: 9 10 11 12   345
1. Criminal procedure 2. Civil rights
ISBN 0-7377-2505-2; 978-0-7377-2505-6
LC 2005-54542

Individual rights and the police—*Continued*

This anthology examines four court cases involving the rights of the accused: Mapp v. Ohio (1961), Miranda v. Arizona (1966), Katz v. United States (1967), and Terry v. Ohio (1968).

Includes bibliographical references

Jacobs, Thomas A.

They broke the law, you be the judge; true cases of teen crime; edited by Al Desetta. Free Spirit Pub 2003 213p il pa $15.95 *

Grades: 7 8 9 10   **345**
     1. Administration of justice 2. Juvenile courts
     ISBN 1-575-42134-8   LC 2003-4814
"This book details 21 cases ranging from truancy to auto theft. Following a description of events leading up to and including the crime itself, readers are given background about the individual, sentencing options, and questions to consider before sentencing, and then asked to make a decision about the case." SLJ
"An excellent introduction to how juvenile justice works, this will be a great resource for classroom and group discussions." Booklist

Includes bibliographical references

Kelly-Gangi, Carol

Miranda v. Arizona and the rights of the accused; debating Supreme Court decisions; [by] Carol Kelly-Gangi. Enslow Publishers 2006 128p il (Debating Supreme Court decisions) lib bdg $26.60

Grades: 7 8 9 10   **345**
     1. Miranda, Ernesto 2. Right to counsel
     ISBN 0-7660-2477-6   LC 2006011737
This discusses the Supreme Court case involving a suspect's rights while being questioned by police.

Includes bibliographical references

Khan, Lin Shi

Scottsboro, Alabama; a story in linoleum cuts; {by} Lin Shi Khan and Tony Perez; edited by Andrew H. Lee; foreword by Robin D.G. Kelley. New York Univ. Press 2002 147p il $55; pa $21

Grades: 11 12 Adult   **345**
     1. Scottsboro case
     ISBN 0-8147-5176-8; 0-8147-5177-6 (pa)
     LC 2001-59189
This "graphic book from 1935 reproduces 118 linocuts illustrating the history of African Americans up to and including the Scottsboro trials. . . . {This is} a highly charged political indictment and work of art. The reproductions are excellent, and Lee and Robin D.G. Kelley provide background essays on the trials and the provenance of the book." Libr J

Larson, Edward J.

The Scopes trial; a photographic history; introduction by Edward Caudill; photo captions by Edward Larson; afterword by Jesse Fox Mayshark. University of Tenn. Press 1999 88p il hardcover o.p. pa $18.95

Grades: 11 12 Adult   **345**
     1. Scopes, John Thomas 2. Evolution—Study and teaching
     ISBN 1-57233-080-5; 1-57233-081-3 (pa)
     LC 99-50735
The photographs are from the W.C. Robinson and Sue K. Hicks collections, Special Collections, University of Tennessee, Knoxville
"Sandwiching a clutch of generously annotated documentary photos, Caudill's introduction explains what led to the trial. . . . Mayshark's afterword presents the trial's larger historical and political context and its long-lived effects on Tennessee, textbook publishing, and plain speech about hot topics. The slim, handsome book is an ideal primer on its notorious subject." Booklist

Includes bibliographical references

Summer for the gods; the Scopes trial and America's continuing debate over science and religion. Basic Bks. 1997 318p il hardcover o.p. pa $15.95

Grades: 11 12 Adult   **345**
     1. Scopes, John Thomas 2. Trials 3. Evolution—Study and teaching
     ISBN 0-465-07509-6; 0-465-07510-X (pa)
     LC 97-9648
The author gives an account of the 1925 trial of John Scopes for violating a state law prohibiting the teaching of evolution.
"Careful and evenhanded analysis dispels the mythologies and caricatures in film and stage versions of the trial, leaving us with a far clearer picture of the cultural warfare that still periodically erupts in our classes and courts." Booklist

Includes bibliographical references

Lewis, Anthony, 1927-

Gideon's trumpet. Random House 1964 262p pa $12.95 hardcover o.p.

Grades: 11 12 Adult   **345**
     1. Gideon, Clarence Earl 2. United States. Supreme Court 3. Law—United States
     ISBN 0-679-72312-9 (pa)
An account of the case of a Florida man convicted of burglary which brought about a historic decision of the Supreme Court decreeing that in all states a defendant is entitled to counsel.

Includes bibliographical references

Monroe, Judy

The Sacco and Vanzetti controversial murder trial; a headline court case. Enslow Pubs. 2000 112p il (Headline court cases) $20.95

Grades: 9 10 11 12   **345**
     1. Sacco, Nicola, 1891-1927 2. Vanzetti, Bartolomeo, 1888-1927 3. Trials (Homicide)
     ISBN 0-7660-1387-1   LC 99-50540

Monroe, Judy—*Continued*

Discusses the trial of Nicola Sacco and Bartolomeo Vanzetti, two Italian immigrants who were tried and convicted for a murder that they did not appear to have committed

Includes bibliographical references

The **Patriot** Act: opposing viewpoints; Louise I. Gerdes, book editor. Greenhaven Press 2005 218p il lib bdg $34.95; pa $23.70 *
Grades: 9 10 11 12   **345**
1. USA Patriot Act of 2001
ISBN 0-7377-3097-8 (lib bdg); 0-7377-3098-6 (pa)
                                    LC 2004-60591
"Opposing viewpoints series"
"The authors in this anthology present differing views on whether the Patriot Act protects national security, violates civil liberties, and whether it should or should not be expanded." Publisher's note

Includes bibliographical references

The **right** to a trial by jury; edited by Robert Winters. Greenhaven Press 2005 142p (Bill of Rights) $32.45
Grades: 9 10 11 12   **345**
1. Jury
ISBN 0-7377-1937-0   LC 2004-52282
This book "examines medieval origins and the colonial implementation of English-style trial processes and includes Supreme Court decisions. It then presents the modern arguments for and against the jury system, with a time line of significant decisions." Voice Youth Advocates

Rights of the accused; Michelle Lewis, book editor. Greenhaven Press 2007 198p (Issues on trial) lib bdg $34.95 *
Grades: 9 10 11 12   **345**
1. Criminal procedure
ISBN 978-0-7377-2795-1; 0-7377-2795-0
                                    LC 2006-38192
This anthology examines in detail the following court cases: Coffin v. United States (1895), Gideon v. Wainwright (1963), Duncan v. Louisiana (1968), and Crawford v. Washington (2004).

Includes bibliographical references

Ruschmann, Paul

Legalizing marijuana. Chelsea House 2004 129p il (Point-counterpoint) $25.95
Grades: 7 8 9 10   **345**
1. Marijuana 2. Drugs—Law and legislation
ISBN 0-7910-7483-8   LC 2003-9497
Contents: Marijuana and prohibition; Marijuana use is harmless enough to be considered a personal choice; Laws are needed to protect uninformed people from the dangers of marijuana; Enforcement of marijuana laws is uneven, ineffective, and wasteful; Marijuana laws should be strictly enforced; Heavily regulated marijuana is a better alternative than the black market; Relaxing marijuana laws would lead to too many problems; The future of marijuana policy

This presents arguments for and against legalization of marijuana, including whether or not the drug is dangerous, how marijuana laws are enforced, and whether or not relaxing the laws would be good for society.

Includes bibliographical references

Miranda rights; series consulting editor, Alan Marzilli. Chelsea House Publications 2006 126p il (Point-counterpoint) lib bdg $32.95
Grades: 7 8 9 10   **345**
1. Miranda, Ernesto 2. Right to counsel
ISBN 0-7910-9229-1; 978-0-7910-9229-3
                                    LC 2006-23655
"This book examines both sides of Miranda-related questions: Is the Miranda decision a violation of separation of powers or the concept of federalism? Does making mandatory the reading of the rules free guilty criminals? Do the warnings affect the validity of confessions?" Publisher's note

Includes bibliographical references

Sherrow, Victoria

Gideon v. Wainwright; free legal counsel. Enslow Pubs. 1995 104p il (Landmark Supreme Court cases) lib bdg $18.95
Grades: 7 8 9 10   **345**
1. Gideon, Clarence Earl 2. Wainwright, Louie L. 3. Legal aid
ISBN 0-89490-507-4   LC 93-45981
This "volume details the genesis of the case that established the right to free legal counsel, the Supreme Court decision, and the arguments presented by the lawyers for each side. A fine addition to the thought-provoking series." Horn Book Guide

Includes bibliographical references

Should juveniles be tried as adults? Judy Layzell, book editor. Greenhaven Press 2005 107p (At issue) lib bdg $27.45; pa $18.70 *
Grades: 9 10 11 12   **345**
1. Juvenile delinquents 2. Criminal procedure 3. Administration of criminal justice
ISBN 0-7377-1977-X (lib bdg); 0-7377-1978-8 (pa)
                                    LC 2004-47463
This title provides articles discussing whether youthful offenders should be tried in adult courts. The papers point out that "the issue of trying juveniles as adults involves a range of legal, ethical, developmental, emotional, and pragmatic issues." Introduction

Includes bibliographical references

Sonneborn, Liz

Miranda v. Arizona. Rosen Pub. Group 2004 64p il (Supreme Court cases through primary sources) lib bdg $29.95
Grades: 9 10 11 12   **345**
1. Miranda, Ernesto 2. Right to counsel
ISBN 0-8239-4010-1   LC 2002-154575
Contents: A rape in Arizona; Confessing to the crime; The rights of the accused; Making a case; The Supreme Court decision; The legacy of Miranda

This discusses the case in which the Supreme Court ruled that suspects must be informed of their rights to re-

Sonneborn, Liz—*Continued*

main silent and the right to counsel when they they are being questioned by the police.

This "deserves a place in every library. . . .Copious and well-chosen primary source documents give extra value to this [book]. . . . Each document adds human drama to the already engaging text. " Libr Media Connect

Includes glossary and bibliographical references

Sorensen, Lita

The Scottsboro Boys Trial; a primary source account. Rosen Publishing Group 2004 64p il (Great trials of the 20th century) lib bdg $29.25

Grades: 9 10 11 12   **345**

1. Trials 2. African Americans—Civil rights

ISBN 0-8239-3975-8   LC 2002-153356

Contents: Background : a journey interrupted; The story of two white girls; A court in the Old South; The role of the NAACP and the ILD; Appeals, outcomes, and a landmark decision; A long road to justice; Impact of the Scottsboro Boys Trial in American history

An account of the 1931 trial in which African American youths were charged with rape.

This is "packed with information. . . . [An] attractive, intelligent offering." SLJ

Includes bibliographical references

346   Private law

Jacobs, Thomas A.

What are my rights? 95 questions and answers about teens and the law. Free Spirit 1997 199p il pa $14.95

Grades: 7 8 9 10   **346**

1. Youth—Law and legislation

ISBN 1-57542-028-7   LC 97-8599

Provides information to help the reader understand laws, recognize responsibilities, and appreciate rights especially in relation to parents, school, job, and personal matters.

"In clear, everyday language, with just a sprinkling of legal terms, Jacobs presents useful guidelines and background on a variety of topically organized concerns related to teens' rights." Booklist

Includes glossary and bibliographical references

Sherrow, Victoria

Cherokee Nation v. Georgia; Native American rights. Enslow Pubs. 1997 128p il (Landmark Supreme Court cases) lib bdg $26.60

Grades: 7 8 9 10   **346**

1. Native Americans—Government relations

ISBN 0-89490-856-1   LC 96-39651

Discusses the cases brought by the Cherokee Nation and its supporters against the state of Georgia beginning in the 1830s to protect the rights of the Cherokee living there.

This offers "cogently written prose." Horn Book Guide

Includes bibliographical references

346.04   Property law

Butler, Rebecca P.

Copyright for teachers and librarians. Neal-Schuman Publishers 2004 248p il pa $59.95

Grades: professional   **346.04**

1. Copyright 2. Fair use (Copyright)

ISBN 1-55570-500-6   LC 2004-46013

"The five chapters in Part I are . . . reviews of copyright law, the concept of fair use, determining what is in public domain, how to obtain permissions, and other general guidelines on such topics as licensing, loaning, penalties, plagiarism, and exemptions. The bulk of the book is in Part II, which deals with specific applications, such as Internet and public access, videos and DVDs, television, software, music, multimedia, distance learning and—oh, yes!—print! . . . An indispensable addition." SLJ

Includes bibliographical references

Complete copyright; an everyday guide for librarians; Carrie Russell, editor. American Library Association 2004 262p il spiral bdg $50

Grades: Professional   **346.04**

1. Copyright

ISBN 0-8389-3543-5   LC 2004-7681

Russell provides "guidance for both common copyright issues and latest trends, including the intricacies of copyright in the digital world. Through real-life examples, she also illustrates how librarians can be advocates for a fair and balanced copyright law." Publisher's note

Crews, Kenneth D.

Copyright law for librarians and educators; creative strategies and practical solutions; with contributions from Dwayne K. Buttler . . . [et al.] 2nd ed. American Library Association 2006 141p il pa $45 *

Grades: Professional   **346.04**

1. Copyright

ISBN 0-8389-0906-X   LC 2005-13804

First published 2000 with title: Copyright essentials for librarians and educators

The author "addresses 18 areas of copyright in 5 parts. He begins with the scope of protectable works as well as works without copyright protection. Next, he discusses the rights of ownership, including duration and exceptions. He then explains fair use and its related guidelines. Part 4 focuses on the TEACH Act, Section 108, and responsibilities and liabilities. Lastly, Crews examines special issues such as the Digital Millennium Copyright Act." Booklist

Includes bibliographical references

Gordon, Sherri Mabry

Downloading copyrighted stuff from the Internet; stealing or fair use? Enslow Publishers 2005 104p il (Issues in focus today) lib bdg $31.93

Grades: 7 8 9 10   **346.04**

1. Copyright 2. Internet

ISBN 0-7660-2164-5   LC 2004-9954

Gordon, Sherri Mabry—*Continued*

Contents: Downloading: a history; Tools of the underground Internet; The underground Internet today; Free speech? The argument for the underground Internet; Copyright infringement? the argument against the underground Internet;Underground Internet lawsuits and their outcomes; What's next? the future of the underground Internet

This presents "two sides of the ongoing controversy surrounding the use of the Internet to download copyrighted material. . . . The author presents specific legal action and instances to support each side of the debate. . . . Clearly written, this is an accessible treatment of a complex topic." SLJ

Includes glossary and bibliographical references

Hoffmann, Gretchen McCord

Copyright in cyberspace 2; questions and answers for librarians. Neal-Schuman Publishers 2005 271p pa $75 *

Grades: Professional   **346.04**

1. Copyright 2. Internet

ISBN 1-55570-517-0   LC 2004-18238

First published 2001 with title: Copyright in cyberspace

"The book is divided into four sections covering copyright fundamentals, applying them in cyberspace, specific library applications as they relate to the increasing types of material that can be copyrighted, and resources. . . . The intricacies of file-sharing, browsing and caching, hyperlinks and framing, licensing, and electronic reserves are covered separately, bolstered by court-case examples, notes, and bibliographies. . . . An indispensable reference for all types of libraries." SLJ

Includes bibliographical references

Internet piracy; James D. Torr, book editor. Greenhaven Press 2005 78p (At issue) lib bdg $28.70; pa $19.95

Grades: 9 10 11 12   **346.04**

1. Copyright—Music

ISBN 0-7377-2328-9 (lib bdg); 0-7377-2329-7 (pa)
     LC 2004-42524

This book discusses the effects of free online file sharing, particularly music sharing, on artists and the industry as well as how the government should get involved in the issue. Contributors include Janis Ian, Jack Valenti, and Orson Scott Card.

Includes bibliographical references

Simpson, Carol Mann, 1949-

Copyright catechism; practical answers to everyday school dilemmas; [by] Carol Simpson. Linworth Pub. 2005 192p pa $36.95

Grades: Professional   **346.04**

1. Fair use (Copyright) 2. Copyright

ISBN 1-58683-202-6; 979-1-58683-202-4
     LC 2005-18524

Companion volume to Copyright for schools: a practical guide

This "volume looks at practical applications for all types of schools, community organizations, daycare facilities, and colleges. . . . Educators will appreciate Simpson's clear and concise answers for almost every imaginable copyright dilemma." SLJ

Copyright for schools; a practical guide. 4th ed. Linworth Pub. 2005 223p il $44.95

Grades: Professional   **346.04**

1. Fair use (Copyright) 2. Copyright

ISBN 1-58683-192-5   LC 2005-5430

First published 1994 with title: Copyright for school libraries

This book "includes chapters on the law, public domain, fair use, print, audiovisual, music, multimedia, distance learning, and software. Simpson then discusses school library exemptions, permissions, managing copyright, administrators' roles, and policies." Libr Media Connect

Includes bibliographical references

347   Civil procedure and courts

Baum, Lawrence

The Supreme Court. 9th ed. CQ Press 2007 255p il pa $34.95 *

Grades: 9 10 11 12   **347**

1. United States. Supreme Court

ISBN 978-1-933116-85-3; 1-933116-85-4
     LC 2006-25340

First published 1981

This book provides an introduction to various aspects of the Supreme Court, including the selection of justices, types of cases chosen, and factors influencing the decisions rendered.

Includes glossary and bibliographical references

DeVillers, David

Marbury v. Madison; powers of the Supreme Court. Enslow Pubs. 1998 112p il (Landmark Supreme Court cases) lib bdg $19.95

Grades: 7 8 9 10   **347**

1. Marbury, William, 1761?-1835 2. Madison, James, 1751-1836 3. United States. Supreme Court

ISBN 0-89490-967-3   LC 97-24865

Discusses the case Marbury v. Madison in which the idea of judicial review became part of the federal government's system of checks and balances.

Includes glossary and bibliographical references

Finkelman, Paul, 1949-

Landmark decisions of the United States Supreme Court; {by} Paul Finkelman, Melvin I. Urofsky. CQ Press 2003 687p $225 *

Grades: 11 12 Adult   **347**

1. United States. Supreme Court 2. Constitutional law—United States

ISBN 1-568-02720-6   LC 2002-153035

New edition in preparation

"More than 1,000 of the Court's most important decisions are discussed in this title. The cases selected for inclusion fall into three categories: decisions recognized as the most important (Dred Scott v. Sandford, Roe v. Wade); cases that are significant but of lesser impact; and those that were narrow in influence. . . . Summaries are preceded by the type and date of the decision, the vote of each justice, and the authors of the majority and

Finkelman, Paul, 1949-—*Continued*
dissenting opinion. The summaries give the background, relevant legal points, and impact of each decision. Underlying principles are clearly explained." Booklist
Includes bibliographical references

Great world trials; Edward W. Knappman, editor. Gale Res. 1997 xxviii, 536p il $90
Grades: 11 12 Adult   347
1. Trials
ISBN 0-7876-0805-X   LC 96-38793
Also available in paperback from Visible Ink Press A New England Pub. Assocs. Bk.
This is a "narrative of 100 international trials of historical, political, or social significance." Libr J
"From the Alcibiades trial in 415 B.C. to the 1996 trial of Yigal Amir and covering crimes such as murder, treason, fraud, and negligence, this work paints a vivid portrait of international jurisprudence through the ages." Booklist
Includes bibliographical references

Hartman, Gary R.
Landmark Supreme Court cases; the most influential decisions of the Supreme Court of the United States; [by] Gary Hartman, Roy M. Mersky, [and] Cindy Tate Slavinski. Facts on File 2004 594p (Facts on File library of American history) $70
Grades: 11 12 Adult   347
1. United States. Supreme Court 2. Law—United States
ISBN 0-8160-2452-9   LC 2003-57776
"The authors describe some 350 influential US Supreme Court decisions. Arranged by subjects such as abortion and taxation, the . . . entries include an abstract of the decision, . . . the case's history, summary of the arguments, the salient issues involved, its significance, related cases, and recommended readings including law journal articles." Choice
This is "an excellent source for beginning researchers. . . . The discussion of the case's significance and its implications will be useful for students." SLJ
For a fuller review see: Booklist, Oct. 15, 2004
Includes bibliographical references

Jost, Kenneth
The Supreme Court A to Z. 4th ed. CQ Press 2007 622p il (CQ's American government A to Z series) $85 *
Grades: 8 9 10 11 12 Adult   347
1. United States. Supreme Court
ISBN 0-87289-335-9; 978-0-87289-335-1
                                     LC 2006-38701
First published 1993
This book "provides biographies of past and present justices, the history of important cases, and explanations of constitutional principles and legal concepts." Publisher's note
Includes bibliographical references

Mauro, Tony
Illustrated great decisions of the Supreme Court. 2nd ed. CQ Press 2006 415p il $81
Grades: 9 10 11 12 Adult   347
1. United States. Supreme Court 2. Constitutional law—United States
ISBN 1-56802-964-0; 978-1-56802-964-1
                                     LC 2005-30474
First published 2000
For each of the nearly 100 cases summarized the author provides background facts, highlights of the decision and assesses the impact on American society. Illustrated with photos, portraits, political cartoons, and drawings. Includes a bibliography and a case and subject index.
Includes bibliographical references

The **Oxford** companion to the Supreme Court of the United States; editor in chief, Kermit L. Hall; editors, James W. Ely, Jr., Joel B. Grossman. 2nd ed. Oxford University Press 2005 xxv, 1239p il $65
Grades: 11 12 Adult   347
1. United States. Supreme Court
ISBN 0-19-517661-8   LC 2004-29463
First published 1992
This encyclopedia includes over 1200 articles "on all aspects of the court's history, justices, operations, and cases. Over 300 experts contributed the entries, which vary in length; some have bibliographic references. The organization . . . [includes] alphabetical entries, portraits of the justices, cross-references, and indexes by both case name and topic." Choice
For a fuller review, see: Booklist, Oct. 15, 2005

Paddock, Lisa
Facts about the Supreme Court of the United States; historical overview by Paul Barrett. Wilson, H.W. 1996 xxx, 569p il $100
Grades: 11 12 Adult   347
1. United States. Supreme Court
ISBN 0-8242-0896-X   LC 95-53202
"A New England Pub. Assocs. book"
A look at the organization, function and history of the Supreme Court. The chronological arrangement places each Court, its justices, and individual cases in historical context. Includes a glossary of legal terms and concepts
Includes bibliographical references

Patrick, John J., 1935-
The Supreme Court of the United States; a student companion. 3rd ed. Oxford University Press 2006 415p il (Oxford student companions to American government) $60 *
Grades: 9 10 11 12   347
1. United States. Supreme Court
ISBN 978-0-19-530925-6; 0-19-530925-1
                                     LC 2006-8473
First published 1994 with title: The young Oxford companion to the Supreme Court of the United States
New edition in preparation
"Entries presented alphabetically include biographies of justices, decisions of the court, core concepts, ideas

Patrick, John J., 1935-—*Continued*
and issues, legal terms and phrases, and procedures,
practices, and personnel. . . . The inclusion of so many
illustrations makes this a welcome and necessary addition
to every high school library." Libr Media Connect
Includes bibliographical references

Savage, David G., 1950-
Guide to the U.S. Supreme Court. 4th ed. CQ
Press 2004 2v il map set $350 *
Grades: 9 10 11 12   **347**
1. United States. Supreme Court
ISBN 1-568-02743-5   LC 2004-1572
First published 1979 with title: Congressional Quarter-
ly's guide to the U.S. Supreme Court
This set "covers the Court's entire history; its opera-
tions; its power in relation to other branches of govern-
ment; major decisions affecting the other branches, the
states, individual rights and liberties; and biographies of
the justices." Publisher's note
"The insightful content is indispensable for courses in
U.S. history and government/political science, especially
advanced placement." Libr Media Connect
Includes bibliographical references

Schultz, David A., 1958-
The encyclopedia of the Supreme Court; [by]
David Schultz. Facts on File 2005 562p il (Facts
on File library of American history) $85 *
Grades: 11 12 Adult   **347**
1. United States. Supreme Court
ISBN 0-8160-5086-4   LC 2004-13174
"The purpose of this one-volume resource is to provide 'an overview of the major cases, concepts, and issues and of the personalities who have shaped' the Supreme Court, as well as to provide a sense of its history
and impact on American politics." Libr J
"The ease with which one can search this volume, as
well as the style of writing and depth of explanation
make this a truly valuable resource." Libr Media Connect
Includes bibliographical references

U.S. court cases; edited by the editors of Salem
Press. Salem Press 1999 2v (Magill's choice) set
$95 *
Grades: 11 12 Adult   **347**
1. Law—United States 2. Courts—United States
ISBN 0-89356-422-2   LC 99-19926
"The first part of the set has 13 chapters discussing
fundamentals of law, justice, and the court system. The
second part contains alphabetically arranged entries on
212 cases. Most of the cases were decided by the Supreme Court, but a few were decided by lower courts."
Booklist
"All of the articles have originally appeared in earlier
Salem Press publications. Appendixes include the complete text of the U.S. Constitution and a listing of Supreme Court justices annotated with career highlights.
Black-and-white photographs, primarily portraits, appear
intermittently. This is a resource that will be well
thumbed by students of American law." SLJ
Includes bibliographical references

348   Laws, regulations, cases

Major acts of Congress; Brian K. Landsberg,
editor in chief. Macmillan Reference USA 2004
3v il set $290
Grades: 11 12 Adult   **348**
1. Law—United States—Encyclopedias
ISBN 0-02-865749-7   LC 2003-18747
The editor "offers historical overviews of the importance and impact of 262 major congressional acts from
1789 to 2002. The signed, alphabetically arranged entries
range from one to five pages in length and conclude with
bibliographies and occasional Internet resources." SLJ
This "will be a top-tier reference work for students
and laypersons researching federal legislation." Booklist
Includes bibliographical references

U.S. laws, acts, and treaties; edited by Timothy L.
Hall. Salem Press 2003 3v (Magill's choice) set
$188
Grades: 11 12 Adult   **348**
1. Law—United States 2. United States—Foreign relations—Treaties
ISBN 1-58765-098-3   LC 2002-156063
Contents: v1 1776-1928; v2 1929-1970; v3 1970-2002
This "is a collection of 433 major U.S. acts of Congress and U.S. treaties covering the time period from
1776 through 2002, beginning with the Declaration of Independence and ending with the Homeland Security Act.
. . . The essays, chronically arranged and varying in
length from 500 to 2,000 words, cover the historical origins and main provisions of each law or treaty. . . . This
set presents a good coverage of landmark laws and treaties in a concise, easy-to-read, and easy-to-use work. It
is geared toward high-school and undergraduate students
but would also make a useful and functional reference
tool for public libraries." Booklist
Includes bibliographical references

349   Law of specific jurisdictions

Encyclopedia of American law; {edited by} David
Schultz. Facts on File 2002 542p il $75 *
Grades: 11 12 Adult   **349**
1. Law—United States—Encyclopedias
ISBN 0-8160-4329-9   LC 2001-40206
"This encyclopedia's entries average a page in length
and include contemporary topics such as affirmative ac-
tion and recent court cases as well as concepts such as
entrapment, equity, and insanity. . . . This resource
packs a lot of material and is easy to read and navigate."
Book Rep
Includes bibliographical references

West's encyclopedia of American law; Jeffrey
Lehman, editor, Shirelle Phelps, editor. 2nd ed.
Thomson/Gale 2004 13v set $1195
Grades: 9 10 11 12 Adult   **349**
1. Law—United States—Encyclopedias
ISBN 0-7876-6367-0   LC 2004-4918
First published 1983-1985 with title: The Guide to
American law
Over 5,000 alphabetically arranged entries explain le-
gal principles and concepts, landmark documents, laws,
famous trials, historical movements, and notable persons

352.13 State and provincial administration

The **Book** of the states, 2006. Council of State Govts. 2006 $125; pa $99
Grades: 11 12 Adult   **352.13**
1. State governments
ISSN 0068-0125
ISBN   0-87292-832-2;   978-0-87292-832-9;
0-87292-833-0 (pa); 978-0-87292-833-6 (pa)
Biennial, 1935-2001, Annual from 2002 Began publication 1935
"In addition to general articles on various aspects of state government, this source provides many statistical and directory data, the principal state officials, and such information as the nickname, motto, flower, bird, song, and tree of each state." Ref Sources for Small & Medium-sized Libr. 6th edition

352.2 Organization of administration

United States government manual 2007-2008; Office of the Federal Register, National Archives and Records Service, General Services Administration. Claitor's Law Bks. 2007 pa $27
*
Grades: 11 12 Adult   **352.2**
1. United States—Politics and government—Handbooks, manuals, etc.
ISBN 1-59804-377-3; 978-1-59804-377-8
Annual. First published 1935. Variant title: United States government organization manual
"Official handbook of the Federal government describing the purposes and programs of most Government agencies and listing the top personnel." N Y Public Libr. Ref Books for Child Collect. 2d edition

352.23 Chief executives

Guide to the presidency; Michael Nelson, editor. 3rd ed. CQ Press 2002 2v set $315
Grades: 11 12 Adult   **352.23**
1. Presidents—United States
ISBN 1-56802-714-1   LC 2002-151619
First published 1989 with title: Congressional Quarterly's guide to the presidency
New edition in preparation
Contents: v1 Origins and development of the presidency; Selection and removal of the president; Powers of the presidency; The president, the public, and the parties; v2 The White House and the executive branch; Chief executive and federal government; Biographies of the presidents and vice presidents
This "is an essential purchase for public and academic libraries." Booklist
Includes bibliographical references

My fellow Americans; the most important speeches of America's presidents, from George Washington to George W. Bush; {compiled} by Michael Waldman; CDs narrated by George Stephanopoulos. Sourcebooks 2003 337p il $45
*
Grades: 7 8 9 10   **352.23**
1. Presidents—United States 2. United States—Politics and government 3. American speeches
ISBN 1-402-20027-7   LC 2003-6879
This "resource contains 43 speeches from 17 presidents, nearly all unabridged, each with an introduction explaining its historical context and significance. Two companion CDs allow listeners to hear all 43 speeches, including the actual voices of presidents from Teddy Roosevelt to George W. Bush. . . . Waldman's stated purpose in putting together this volume is to show how the actions, the dreams, and the big ideas presented by these addresses furthered the American democratic spirit. Some early drafts are included, including several versions of the opening paragraph of JFK's Inaugural Address. The most recent entry is President Bush's Address on Iraq given on March 17, 2003, accompanied by the April news photo showing the fall of the Saddam Hussein statue in Baghdad. A fine addition." SLJ
Includes bibliographical references

Pious, Richard M., 1944-
The presidency of the United States; a student companion. 2nd ed. Oxford Univ. Press 2001 320p il (Oxford student companions to American government) lib bdg $45 *
Grades: 9 10 11 12   **352.23**
1. Presidents—United States 2. Vice-presidents—United States 3. United States—Politics and government
ISBN 0-19-515006-6   LC 2001-36136
First published 1994 with title: The young Oxford companion to the presidency of the United States
This volume covers "the political careers of all presidents up to and including Bill Clinton, there are articles on such diverse topics as campaign reform, third parties in American politics, the Electoral College, and the impeachment process. An extensive bibliography will be useful to students who wish to delve more deeply. . . . Black-and-white photographs and numerous appendixes detailing presidential election results, terms, historic sites, and libraries make this compendium an excellent starting point for report research." Booklist
Includes bibliographical references

The Presidency A to Z; Michael Nelson, advisory editor. 3rd ed. CQ Press 2003 603p (CQ's American government A to Z series) $125 *
Grades: 8 9 10 11 12 Adult   **352.23**
1. Presidents—United States—Encyclopedias
ISBN 1-56802-803-2   LC 2003-9464
First published 1992
New edition in preparation
"Approximately 300 entries describe the background of the presidents, their public experiences, daily and family life, powers and life in the White House, and deaths. Extensive essays explore concepts relating to the presidency such as Constitutional powers, the budget process,

The Presidency A to Z—*Continued*
diplomatic activity, the cabinet, and the relationship of
the presidency to Congress and the courts." Libr J {re-
view of 1992 edition}
Includes bibliographic references

State of the union; presidential rhetoric from
Woodrow Wilson to George W. Bush. CQ Press
2007 1185p il $140
Grades: 11 12 Adult   **352.23**
1.   Presidents—United   States—Messages
2. Presidents—United States—Inaugural addresses
3. American speeches 4. United States—Politics and
government—Sources
ISBN 978-0-87289-433-4; 0-87289-433-9
         LC 2006-35973
"This volume includes over 100 full-text addresses delivered by Presidents from 1913 to 2006 and comes complete with prefatory notes for context." Libr J
Includes bibliographic references

353.4   Administration of justice

Police corruption; Tamara L. Roleff, book editor.
Greenhaven Press 2003 94p (At issue) lib bdg
$20.96; pa $13.96
Grades: 9 10 11 12   **353.4**
1. Police corruption
ISBN 0-7377-1172-8 (lib bdg); 0-7377-1171-X (pa)
         LC 2002-21478
This volume examines "how the nature of the police
profession can breed corruption and deceit. . . . Without
directly implying that corruption abounds, the essayists
provide strong arguments about how new recruits are initiated into a profession that has its own version of the
law. . . . Disturbing stuff, bound to spark discussion."
Booklist
Includes bibliographic references

355   Military science

Axelrod, Alan, 1952-
The encyclopedia of the American armed forces.
Facts on File 2005 2v il (Facts on File library of
American history) set $175 *
Grades: 11 12 Adult   **355**
1. United States—Armed forces—Encyclopedias
ISBN 0-8160-4700-6   LC 2004-20549
"The four sections each document a major branch of
the United States military: Army, Navy, Marine Corps,
and Air Force. Each branch has an initial list of entries,
a list of branch-specific abbreviations and acronyms, and
a short bibliography." Choice
    For a fuller review, see: Booklist, Jan. 1 & 15, 2006
Includes bibliographic references

Black, Jeremy
The Cambridge illustrated atlas of warfare:
Renaissance to revolution, 1492-1792. Cambridge
Univ. Press 1996 192p il maps $44.95 *
Grades: 11 12 Adult   **355**
1. Military history 2. Military art and science
ISBN 0-521-47033-1   LC 95-36852
Color maps illustrate this "study of warfare during the
early modern period, ranging from the European Renais-
sance to the American Revolution. . . . Feature boxes
describe key events, important military confrontations, in-
dividual tacticians, battle strategies and weapons." Publisher's note
Includes bibliographic references

Buckley, Gail Lumet, 1937-
American patriots; the story of Blacks in the
military from the Revolution to Desert Storm; [by]
Gail Buckley. Random House 2001 xxiv, 534p il
hardcover o.p. pa $15.95
Grades: 11 12 Adult   **355**
1. African American soldiers 2. United States—Military history 3. United States—Race relations
ISBN 0-375-50279-3; 0-375-76009-1 (pa)
         LC 00-51825
This is an account "of blacks in the U.S. military,
both at home and abroad, from the 1770s to the 1990s.
. . . This readable, spirited story deserves a place in every U.S. history collection, as well as in the black or
military collections." Libr J
Includes bibliographic references

Encyclopedia of American military history;
Spencer C. Tucker, general editor; associate
editors David Coffey, John C. Fredriksen, Justin
D. Murphy. Facts on File 2003 3v il maps set
$225 *
Grades: 11 12 Adult   **355**
1. United States—Military history—Encyclopedias
ISBN 0-8160-4355-8   LC 2002-29658
"More than 1,200 entries cover military leaders, wars,
campaigns, battles, events, famous soldiers, military
branches, key technological developments, overviews of
weapons systems, and more. It covers the period from
the colonial wars to the present, and gives special attention to the minorities and women who have contributed
significantly to American military success." Publisher's
note
Includes bibliographic references

Facts about the American wars; edited by John S.
Bowman. Wilson, H.W. 1998 750p il maps
$110
Grades: 11 12 Adult   **355**
1. United States—Military history
ISBN 0-8242-0929-X   LC 97-40298
"A New England Publishing Associates book."
"An introduction explains the text's layout and ap-
proach to each war. The reader samples every conflict
from the Franco-Spanish War of the mid-1500s to the
Persian Gulf War of 1991. Most wars covered have
maps; illustrations, or photographs; each has a separate
bibliography. The details provided for each war are most
impressive." Book Rep
Includes bibliographic references

Lanning, Michael Lee

The battle 100; the stories behind history's most influential battles; maps by Bob Rosenburgh. Sourcebooks 2003 355p il map $24.95 *

Grades: 11 12 Adult   355

1. Battles 2. Military history 3. Naval history 4. Military art and science

ISBN 1-57071-799-0   LC 2002-153539

Partial contents: 1. Yorktown (1781) -- 2. Hastings (1066) 3. Stalingrad (1942 & 43) 4. Leipzig (1813) -- 5. Antietam (1862) -- 6. Cajamarca (1532) -- 7. Atomic bombing of Japan (1945) -- 8. Huai-Hai (1948) -- 9. Waterloo (1815) -- 10. Vienna (1529) -- 11. Zama (202 B.C.) -- 12. Tenochtitlan (1521) -- 13. Normandy (1944) -- 14. Salamis (480 B.C.) -- 15. Saratoga (1777) -- 16. Spanish Armada (1588) -- 17. Gettysburg (1863) -- 18. Arbela-Gaugamela (331 B.C.) -- 19. Mexico City (1847) -- 20. Actium (31 B.C.) -- 21. Mecca (630) -- 22. Moscow (1941) -- 23. San Jacinto (1836) -- 24. Tours (732) -- 25. Indus River (1221) -- 26. Alesia (52 B.C.) -- 27. Sedan (1870) -- 28. Marathon (490 B.C.) -- 29. Quebec (1759) -- 30. Milvian Bridge (312) -- 31. Manzikert (1071) -- 32. San Juan Hill (1898) -- 33. Crecy (1346) -- 34. Tsushima Strait (1905) -- 35. Granada (1491) -- 36. Trafalgar (1805) -- 37. Adrianople (378) -- 38. Marne (1914) -- 39. Chalons (451)

"This readable resource provides more information and analysis on individual battles than a general encyclopedia, and will be useful for students needing an overview on an engagement." SLJ

Includes bibliographical references

Living under the threat of nuclear war; Derek C. Maus, book editor. Greenhaven Press 2005 143p il map (Living through the Cold War) lib bdg $32.45

Grades: 9 10 11 12   355

1. Nuclear warfare

ISBN 0-7377-2130-8   LC 2003-67535

"The first part of the book offers excerpts from public statements and speeches by prominent officials such as Presidents Harry S. Truman, John F. Kennedy, and Ronald Reagan, and Soviet leader Mikhail Gorbachev. The following section discusses ways that the American public and the media dealt with the constant threat of nuclear war. Selections from antinuclear-proliferation activists, Albert Einstein, John Paul II, and Carl Sagan and Richard Turco's description of 'nuclear winter' follow." SLJ

Includes bibliographical references

Murray, Stuart, 1948-

Atlas of American military history. Facts on File 2004 248p il map $85; pa $29.95 *

Grades: 9 10 11 12   355

1. United States—Military history—Maps

ISBN 0-8160-5578-5; 0-8160-6221-8 (pa)

LC 2004-8994

This "resource traces American military history, beginning with a profile and a timeline, from wars of the colonial period up through the war in Iraq. Arranged chronologically, various aspects of each conflict and military campaign, both domestic and international, are explored. . . . This volume is a very complete treatment of American military history and would be a helpful addi-

tion to a library's collection, attracting both browsers and researchers." Libr Media Connect

Includes bibliographical references

Phillips, Charles, 1948-

Encyclopedia of wars; [by] Charles Phillips and Alan Axelrod. Facts on File 2005 3v map (Facts on File library of world history) set $300

Grades: 11 12 Adult   355

1. Military history—Encyclopedias

ISBN 0-8160-2851-6   LC 2003-28010

The authors "have compiled some 2,000 alphabetically arranged entries detailing wars, conflicts, and rebellions from ancient to modern times. Each entry comes in two parts. A leadoff summary section offers a simple statement on major causes of the conflict, lists major participants, where fighting took place, final outcome, names and dates of relevant treaties, number of combatants on each side, and casualties (if known). A narrative section then elucidates the overall conduct and context of the war and the major battles and events bearing upon the outcome." Choice

Phillips and Axelrod "have produced a very readable and . . . well-researched book that both scholars and history buffs will enjoy." Booklist

Includes bibliographical references

Rogue nations: opposing viewpoints; Louise Gerdes, book editor. Greenhaven Press 2007 209p il lib bdg $34.95; pa $23.70

Grades: 9 10 11 12   355

1. International security 2. United States—Foreign relations 3. Military policy—United States

ISBN 0-7377-3421-3 (lib bdg); 978-0-7377-3421-8 (lib bdg); 0-7377-3422-1 (pa); 978-0-7377-3422-5 (pa)

LC 2006-16737

"Opposing viewpoints series"

"This collection of essays examines what is meant by the term 'rogue,' to which nations it applies, what kinds of threats these countries pose, and how the world should deal with them. . . . Each viewpoint begins with a helpful summary and questions to help students focus on important points. Occasional insets with maps, political cartoons, and additional, brief viewpoints add to the text." SLJ

Includes bibliographical references

Sutherland, Jonathan, 1958-

African Americans at war; an encyclopedia; {by} Jonathan D. Sutherland. ABC-CLIO 2004 2v set $185 *

Grades: 11 12 Adult   355

1. African American soldiers 2. United States—Armed forces

ISBN 1-57607-746-2   LC 2003-21501

"There are more than 250 {alphabetically arranged} entries conveying biographical, thematic, and conceptual information. Well-known leaders (Colin Powell), groups (Buffalo Soldiers), specific units . . . and battles . . . have their own entries. . . . Most entries range from half a page to three pages, and the references range from one to six sources, including Web sites. . . . This is a superb resource for any high-school, public, or undergraduate library looking to enrich its history, military or African American studies collections." Booklist

Voices of war; stories of service from the home front and the front lines; edited by Tom Wiener. National Geographic Society 2004 336p il $30; pa $6.95 *

Grades: 11 12 Adult　　　　　　　　　**355**

1. Veterans 2. United States—Military history 3. United States—Armed forces—Military life

ISBN 0-7922-7838-0; 0-7922-4204-1 (pa)

　　　　　　　　　　　　　　LC 2004-49986

"Library of Congress Veterans History Project"

This book showcases "the oral histories collected by the Veteran's History Project, the Library of Congress's nationwide effort to collect and preserve the stories not only of war veterans, but also of those who served in support of the frontline troops. . . . The personal accounts cover the major conflicts of the 20th century, from World War I to the Persian Gulf War, and include letters, diaries, and journals. The chapters are nicely arranged to show the commonalities of military experience, e.g., basic training, daily life, combat, the home front, and returning home." Libr J

War: opposing viewpoints; Louise Gerdes, book editor. Greenhaven Press 2005 239p il lib bdg $34.95; pa $23.70 *

Grades: 9 10 11 12　　　　　　　　**355**

1. War

ISBN 0-7377-2591-5 (lib bdg); 0-7377-2592-3 (pa)

　　　　　　　　　　　　　　LC 2004-54283

"Opposing viewpoints series"

In this anthology the authors "debate controversies surrounding the causes and conduct of war, including under what circumstances war is justified, how prisoners and civilians should be treated, and what measures, if any, will prevent wars." Publisher's note

Includes bibliographical references

Warry, John, 1916-

Warfare in the classical world; an illustrated encyclopedia of weapons, warriors, and warfare in the ancient civilisations of Greece and Rome. University of Okla. Press 1995 224p il maps pa $29.95 *

Grades: 9 10 11 12　　　　　　　　**355**

1. Military art and science 2. Military history

ISBN 0-8061-2794-5　　　　　LC 95-18643

A reissue of the title first published 1980 by St. Martin's Press

"The many and various technologies of war developed and employed by the Greeks and Romans are shown along with the political and social arenas of the times. . . . Famous leaders—Alexander the Great, Julius Caesar, Bulla, Hannibal, and Pompey—are presented in mini-biographies with synopses of conditions that provoked war. . . . Useful for history and classical studies, and a terrific read." SLJ

What are the most serious threats to national security? Stuart A. Kallen, book editor. Greenhaven Press 2005 126p (At issue) lib bdg $28.70; pa $19.95

Grades: 9 10 11 12　　　　　　　　**355**

1. National security—United States 2. United States—Defenses

ISBN 0-7377-2753-5 (lib bdg); 0-7377-2754-3 (pa)

　　　　　　　　　　　　　　LC 2004-59679

"This title examines the many security pressures facing the United States today from bioterrorism to 'dirty' nuclear bombs and cyberterrorism." Publisher's note

Includes bibliographical references

Women in the military; James Haley, book editor. Greenhaven Press 2004 94p (At issue) $28.70; pa $19.95 *

Grades: 9 10 11 12　　　　　　　　**355**

1. Women in the armed forces

ISBN 0-7377-2298-3; 0-7377-2299-1 (pa)

　　　　　　　　　　　　　　LC 2003-64685

"Excerpted from books, journals, and magazines, the essays cover a wide range of topics, but center on women's physical suitability for combat and the impact of their presence in previously all-male units. Overall, the selections are well argued and represent the contrasting views of active and retired military personnel, professors, writers, conservatives, and liberals. . . . The book should prove useful for debates and position papers and should help readers form their own opinions on the subject." SLJ

Includes bibliographical references

355.8　Military equipment and supplies

Do nuclear weapons pose a serious threat? Helen Cochran, book editor. Greenhaven Press 2005 80p (At issue) lib bdg $28.70; pa $18.70

Grades: 9 10 11 12　　　　　　　　**355.8**

1. Nuclear weapons 2. World politics—1991- 3. Military policy—United States

ISBN 0-7377-2192-8 (lib bdg); 0-7377-2193-6 (pa)

　　　　　　　　　　　　　　LC 2004-42533

The authors of this anthology "discuss the extent of the nuclear danger facing the world today and debate the best methods for enchancing nuclear security." Introduction

Includes bibliographical references

Preston, Diana

Before the fallout; from Marie Curie to Hiroshima. Walker 2005 438p il $27 *

Grades: 11 12 Adult　　　　　　　**355.8**

1. Atomic bomb

ISBN 0-8027-1445-5　　　　　LC 2004-61953

Also available in paperback from Berkley Books

This history of the making of the atomic bomb covers "half a century, beginning with Marie and Pierre Curie's 1898 discovery of radium and continuing through other important scientific findings (e.g., Einstein's relativity theory and Heisenberg's quantum mechanics)." Libr J

Preston, Diana—*Continued*

"Avidly researched and gracefully constructed, Preston's revelatory history is rich in telling moments, powerful personalities, intense confrontations, and indelible images of the devastation delivered by nuclear weapons, our Damoclean sword." Booklist

Includes bibliographical references

356 Foot forces and warfare

Clancy, Tom, 1947-

Special forces; a guided tour of U.S. Army Special Forces; written with John Gresham. Berkley Bks. 2001 366p il pa $16 *

Grades: 11 12 Adult   356

1. United States. Special Operations Command

ISBN 0-425-17268-6   LC 00-65121

"The book covers recruitment and training of personnel . . . equipment, which includes an exotic mixture of high, low, and no tech components; and the variety of missions special forces execute." Booklist

Includes bibliographical references

Haney, Eric L.

Inside Delta Force; the story of America's elite counterterrorist unit. Delacorte Press 2002 324p il hardcover o.p. pa $14

Grades: 11 12 Adult   356

1. United States. Army. Delta Force

ISBN 0-385-33603-9; 0-385-33936-4 (pa)

LC 2001-58408

The author relates his "experiences during the formation and early operations of 1st Special Forces Operational Detachment-Delta. . . . He served three times in Beirut guarding the American ambassador, participated in the invasion of Grenada, served in several Central American countries and narrowly escaped death during the abortive rescue attempt of the American hostages in Iran. . . . Readers of other special forces memoirs will find this one distinctive for Haney's attention to interservice rivalries . . . that he believes compromised several missions, as well as for Haney's nuanced, often disgusted descriptions of the human cost of war." Publ Wkly

Inside Delta Force; the story of America's elite counterterrorist unit. Delacorte Press 2006 246p il $15.95; lib bdg $17.99 *

Grades: 8 9 10 11 12   356

1. United States. Army. Delta Force

ISBN 0-385-73251-1; 0-385-90273-5 (lib bdg)

LC 2004-30945

"In this adaptation of an adult book, Retired Command Sergeant Major Haney relates a . . . story of the 1977 founding of the ultrasecret counterterrorist unit of the U.S. Army known as Delta Force. . . . Better stock up on copies; you won't want to ration this one." Booklist

358 Air and other specialized forces and warfare

Biological and chemical weapons; Stuart A. Kallen, book editor. Greenhaven Press 2006 110p (At issue) lib bdg $28.70; pa $19.95 *

Grades: 9 10 11 12   358

1. Biological warfare 2. Chemical warfare

ISBN 0-7377-2699-7 (lib bdg); 0-7377-2700-4 (pa)

LC 2005-46186

Contributors to this anthology debating the potential threat of biological and chemical warfare include Jim A. Davis, Jonathan B. Tucker, and George W. Bush.

Includes bibliographical references

Gay, Kathlyn, 1930-

Silent death; the threat of chemical and biological terrorism. 21st Cent. Bks. (Brookfield) 2001 128p il lib bdg $24.90

Grades: 7 8 9 10   358

1. Chemical warfare 2. Biological warfare 3. Terrorism

ISBN 0-7613-1401-6   LC 00-41807

"Citing examples of military and civilian persons exposed to chemical-biological agents, primarily from World War I to the Persian Gulf War, Gay argues for the need to understand and curtail the use of agents that often cannot be detected until the damage is done. . . . Relevant, engrossing." Booklist

Includes bibliographical references

Weapons of mass destruction; an encyclopedia of worldwide policy, technology, and history; Eric A. Croddy and James J. Wirtz, editors. ABC-CLIO 2004 2v il set $185 *

Grades: 11 12 Adult   358

1. Nuclear weapons 2. Chemical warfare 3. Biological warfare

ISBN 1-85109-490-3   LC 2004-24651

This set covers "the history, context, current issues, and key concepts surrounding biological, chemical, and nuclear weapons." Publisher's note

"No other reference source covers such a wide array of topics related to WMD. It will dispel many myths but will also draw attention to the lethal consequences of WMD." Booklist

Includes bibliographical references

Weapons of mass destruction: opposing viewpoints; James D. Torr, book editor. Greenhaven Press 2005 207p il lib bdg $33.70; pa $22.45 *

Grades: 7 8 9 10   358

1. Weapons

ISBN 0-7377-2250-9 (lib bdg); 0-7377-2251-7 (pa)

LC 2004-47587

"Opposing viewpoints series"

"The viewpoints in the volume examine WMD threats from terrorist groups and 'axis of evil' nations in the following chapters: How Likely Is an Attack Involving Weapons of Mass Destruction? How Should the United States Deal with Countries that Threaten to Develop

Weapons of mass destruction: opposing viewpoints—*Continued*

Weapons of Mass Destruction? What Policies Should the United States Adopt Toward Nuclear Weapons? How Can the United States Defend Itself Against Weapons of Mass Destruction?" Publisher's note

Includes bibliographical references

358.4 Air forces and warfare

Boyne, Walter J., 1929-

The influence of air power upon history. Pelican 2003 447p $35

Grades: 11 12 Adult   **358.4**

1. Air power

ISBN 1-58980-034-6   LC 2002-155441

Contents: Fledgling wings; Air power in World War I; Fighters and bombers; Growth of air power theory; Air power between the wars; The search for air power 1939-41; The growth of air power 1941-43; True air superiority, then air supremacy; The cold war; The cold war 1963-73; Post World War II Middle Eastern wars

This is "a comprehensive, balanced overview of war in the air. . . . Boyne's clearly written book brings air power into the military-history mainstream." Booklist

Includes bibliographical references

361.2 Social action

Halpin, Mikki

It's your world—if you don't like it, change it; activism for teenagers. Simon Pulse 2004 305p pa $8.99 *

Grades: 7 8 9 10   **361.2**

1. Social action

ISBN 0-689-87448-0

"Animal rights, racism, war protest, AIDS, school violence and bullying, women's rights, and promoting tolerance are among the topics covered here. Halpin provides basic information about each one and then makes myriad suggestions for action at home, in the community, the 'five-minute activist,' etc. The ideas are easy to implement. . . . . This is an important book that will empower any young adult who would like to make a difference." SLJ

Includes bibliographical references

361.3 Social work

Gay, Kathlyn, 1930-

Volunteering; the ultimate teen guide. Scarecrow Press 2004 127p il (It happened to me) $32.50

Grades: 7 8 9 10   **361.3**

1. Volunteer work

ISBN 0-8108-4922-4   LC 2004-8174

Contents: Being a volunteer; Building and repairing; Closing the generation gap; Helping with health care; Helping the homeless, feeding the hungry; Protecting the environment and animals; Preserving the past; Counsel-

ing, teaching, and tutoring; Reducing bigotry, prejudice, and racism; Campaigning, communicating, and collecting; Getting started, reaping rewards

"This is a useful tool in that it provides a one-stop resource for teens interested in locating volunteer opportunities." SLJ

Includes bibliographical references

Marcovitz, Hal

Teens & volunteerism. Mason Crest 2005 112p il (Gallup Youth Survey) $22.95

Grades: 7 8 9 10   **361.3**

1. Volunteer work

ISBN 1-59084-877-2   LC 2004004827

This is "based on the findings of the Gallup Youth Survey (a 20-year ongoing survey of teens). . . . [It] covers the gamut of issues surrounding [volunteerism and youth], focusing on mandatory vs. optional community service in high school and college, military service, political community service, and activism. [The book is] well documented." SLJ

Includes bibliographical references

Volunteerism; edited by Frank McGuckin. Wilson, H.W. 1998 177p (Reference shelf) pa $45 *

Grades: 11 12 Adult   **361.3**

1. Volunteer work

ISBN 0-8242-0944-3   LC 98-35206

A collection of reprinted articles from various sources divided into four sections: Society's responsibility and commitment; Private volunteering and AmeriCorps; Volunteerism is not enough; and Rewards of volunteerism

Includes bibliographical references

361.6 Governmental action

Banerjee, Dillon

So you want to join the Peace Corps; what to know before you go. Ten Speed Press 2000 178p il pa $12.95 *

Grades: 11 12 Adult   **361.6**

1. Peace Corps (U.S.)

ISBN 1-58008-097-9   LC 99-53048

Banerjee discusses "preapplication jitters, training, packing, managing money, medical and safety concerns, adjusting to local food and customs, maintaining contact with home, rules and supervision, social concerns, traveling, and what to do after 'the toughest job you'll ever love.' The volume includes 11 appendixes, including general facts and a map, Peace Corps requirements and applications, and information on post-Peace Corps resources." Booklist

362.1 Physical illness

The **AIDS** crisis; a documentary history; edited by Douglas A. Feldman and Julia Wang Miller. Greenwood Press 1998 xxxix, 266p (Primary documents in American history and contemporary issues) $49.95 *

Grades: 11 12 Adult   362.1

1. AIDS (Disease)

ISBN 0-313-28715-5   LC 97-26891

This book "presents more than 200 documents on AIDS, from the first medical report in 1981. Most documents are full text, and each is accompanied by a short introduction providing context." Booklist

"An excellent glossary provides the reader with explanations of acronyms and medical terms. . . . This unusual volume is highly recommended." Voice Youth Advocates

Banish, Roslyn, 1942-

Focus on living; portraits of Americans with HIV and AIDS; photographs and interviews by Roslyn Banish ; introduction by Paul A. Volberding. University of Massachusetts Press 2003 xxiv, 263p il $50; pa $24.95 *

Grades: 9 10 11 12   362.1

1. AIDS (Disease)

ISBN 1-558-49394-8; 1-558-49395-6 (pa)

     LC 2002-14512

The author "has been interviewing and photographing Americans who are living with HIV or AIDS; this book collects 40 of her portraits along with transcriptions of her subjects' first-person testimony . . . Banish's unadorned portraits, often shot at her subjects' homes, are subtle and dignified, and the narratives have a lucid strength, even in despair . . . The disease crosses all lines of race, class, gender and sexual orientation, and Banish takes care to include people from all walks of life, fostering an expanded sense of community and further breaking the silence and statistics that surround people living with HIV and AIDS." Publ Wkly

Fleischman, John

Phineas Gage: a gruesome but true story about brain science. Houghton Mifflin 2002 86p il $16; pa $8.95 *

Grades: 5 6 7 8 9   362.1

1. Gage, Phineas P., d. 1861 2. Brain—Wounds and injuries

ISBN 0-618-05252-6; 0-618-49478-2 (pa)

     LC 2001-39253

"Phineas, a railroad construction foreman, was blasting rock near Cavendish, Vermont, in 1848 when a thirteen-pound iron rod was shot through his brain. Miraculously, he survived to live another eleven years and become a textbook case in brain science." Publisher's note

"The author deftly introduces readers to a diverse range of relevant scientific history as well as more specific beliefs that influenced the medical establishment's understanding of Gage, then goes on to examine subsequent neurological discoveries that have changed and enhanced our understanding of Gage's fate. The book's present-tense narrative is inviting and intimate, and the text is crisp and lucid." Bull Cent Child Books

Includes glossary and bibliographical references

Kaufman, Miriam

Easy for you to say; q & a's for teens living with chronic illness or disability. Rev. ed. Firefly Books 2005 285p pa $19.95 *

Grades: 9 10 11 12   362.1

1. Diseases 2. Physically handicapped

ISBN 1-55407-078-3

First published 1995

This work, "aimed exclusively at teens who are disabled or who have a chronic illness, focuses on individual needs. Written by a Canadian physician who works with adolescents, it is filled with very personal, even courageous questions from teens with varied medical conditions—from spina bifida to cystic fibrosis, to kidney disease. There are a few fairly general chapters—on family dynamics, friendship, and recreation. But the best sections concern medical issues and sexuality." Booklist [review of 1995 edition]

Includes bibliographical references

Shilts, Randy

And the band played on; politics, people, and the AIDS epidemic. St. Martin's Press 1987 xxiii, 630p pa $16.95 hardcover o.p. *

Grades: 11 12 Adult   362.1

1. AIDS (Disease)

ISBN 0-312-24135-6 (pa)   LC 87-16528

A "chronicle of the five-year political, scientific, and social battle to force government, the medical and blood-bank establishments, the news media, and gay men to take AIDS seriously." Booklist

"Shilts successfully weaves comprehensive investigative reporting and commercial page-turner pacing, political intrigue and personal tragedy into a landmark work." Publ Wkly

Includes bibliographical references

Terminal illness: opposing viewpoints; Andrea C. Nakaya, book editor. Greenhaven Press 2005 204p il lib bdg $34.95; pa $23.70

Grades: 7 8 9 10   362.1

1. Terminal care

ISBN 0-7377-2963-5 (lib bdg); 0-7377-2964-3 (pa)

     LC 2004-60595

"Opposing viewpoints series"

"The authors of this anthology present various opinions on the best way to care for the terminally ill and their friends and family, including a debate on the role of euthanasia." Publisher's note

Includes bibliographical references

Winick, Judd, 1970-

Pedro and me; friendship, loss, and what I learned. Holt & Co. 2000 187p il pa $16

Grades: 7 8 9 10   362.1

1. Zamora, Pedro, 1972-1994 2. Real world (Television program) 3. AIDS (Disease) 4. Friendship 5. Graphic novels

ISBN 0-8050-6403-6   LC 99-40729

Winick, Judd, 1970- —*Continued*

In this "volume—part graphic novel, part memoir—professional cartoonist Winick pays tribute to his *Real World* housemate and friend Pedro Zamora, an AIDS activist who died of the disease in 1994." Publ Wkly

"The author does a stellar job of marrying image to word to form a flowing narrative. . . . This is an important book for teens and the adults who care about them. Winick handles his topics with both sensitivity and a thoroughness that rarely coexist so seamlessly." SLJ

362.28   Suicide

Evans, Glen

The encyclopedia of suicide; {by} Glen Evans, Norman L. Farberow; foreword by Alan L. Berman. 2nd ed. Facts on File 2003 xxxiii, 329p $65

Grades: 11 12 Adult   **362.28**

ISBN 0-8160-4525-9   LC 2002-27166

First published 1988

Arranged in A-Z format, over 500 entries cover such aspects as causes, history and psychology of suicide. Also covered are philosophical and religious issues as well as sociological viewpoints and research and treatment concerns

Includes bibliographical references

Suicide information for teens; edited by Joyce Brennfleck Shannon. Omnigraphics, Inc 2005 368p (Teen health series) $65 *

Grades: 9 10 11 12   **362.28**

1. Suicide

ISBN 0-7808-0737-5   LC 2004-19972

"Health tips about suicide causes and prevention: including facts about depression, risk factors, getting help, survivor support, and more." Title page

"This book provides information about suicide warning signs, and it describes the behaviors of a person who may be contemplating suicide. . . . It offers information about treatments available through counseling, outpatient therapy, hospitalization, and residential facilities. Information about grief is provided for students whose lives have been touched by suicide." Publisher's note

Includes bibliographical references

Suicide: opposing viewpoints; Roman Espejo, book editor. Greenhaven Press 2003 207p il lib bdg $34.95; pa $23.70

Grades: 7 8 9 10 11 12   **362.28**

1. Suicide

ISBN 0-7377-1242-2 (lib bdg); 0-7377-1241-1 (pa)

           LC 2002-32214

"Opposing viewpoints series"

In this "anthology, authors debate the causes and possible solutions to this problem in the following chapters: Is Suicide Ever Acceptable? What are the Causes of Teen Suicide? Should Assisted Suicide Be Legalized? How Can Suicide Be Prevented?" Publisher's note

Includes bibliographical references

Teen suicide; John Woodward, book editor. Greenhaven Press 2005 90p (At issue) lib bdg $28.70; pa $19.95

Grades: 9 10 11 12   **362.28**

1. Suicide

ISBN 0-7377-2428-5 (lib bdg); 0-7377-2429-3 (pa)

           LC 2004-42427

A collection of articles discussing the problem of teen suicide and what parents, friends, teachers and society can do to prevent the tragedy

Includes bibliographical references

362.29   Substance abuse

Addiction: opposing viewpoints; Louise I. Gerdes, book editor. Greenhaven Press 2005 189p il $33.70; pa $22.45 *

Grades: 9 10 11 12   **362.29**

1. Drug abuse 2. Alcoholism 3. Tobacco habit

ISBN 0-7377-2216-9; 0-7377-2217-7 (pa)

           LC 2003-67520

"Opposing viewpoints series"

"Authors in this . . . anthology debate controversies surrounding the concept of addiction, including what behaviors should be considered addictive, what causes addiction, what treatments are most effective, and whether the government should intervene to reduce the costs associated with addiction." Publisher's note

Includes bibliographical references

Club drugs; Karen F. Balkin, book editor. Greenhaven Press 2005 96p (At issue) lib bdg $27.45; pa $18.70

Grades: 9 10 11 12   **362.29**

1. Ecstasy (Drug) 2. Designer drugs 3. Drug abuse

ISBN 0-7377-1607-X (lib bdg); 0-7377-1608-8 (pa)

           LC 2004-52289

Contents: Recreational use of club drugs is harmful, by D. M. McDowell; Recreational use of ecstasy may cause long-term brain damage, by B. P. Boot; The harmfulness of ecstasy has been exaggerated, by R. Doblin; Scientists disagree on the long-term effects of ecstasy use, by D. Concar; Club drugs facilitate rape, by N. Fitzgerald; Ecstasy helps heal the trauma of rape, by Lisa; The sexual effects of ecstasy are exaggerated, by J. Sullum; Ecstasy may help parkinson's disease sufferers, by J. Margolis; Anti-club drug laws help stop drug abuse, by B. Graham; Anti-club drug laws will prove to be ineffective, by Center for Cognitive Liberty and Ethics

Includes bibliographical references

Drug abuse: opposing viewpoints; Tamara L. Roleff, book editor. Greenhaven Press 2005 221p il lib bdg $33.70; pa $22.45 *

Grades: 7 8 9 10   **362.29**

1. Drug abuse

ISBN 0-7377-2226-6 (lib bdg); 0-7377-2227-4 (pa)

           LC 2004-42406

A collection of articles and speeches, book excerpts and quotations on various aspects of the drug abuse problem

Includes bibliographical references

Drugs, alcohol, and tobacco; learning about addictive behavior; Rosalyn Carson-DeWitt, editor in chief. Macmillan Ref. USA 2003 3v set $295 *

Grades: 7 8 9 10   **362.29**
ISBN 0-02-865756-X   LC 2002-9270

Based on the Encyclopedia of drugs, alcohol & addictive behavior, 2nd edition, published 2001

"The 190 alphabetically arranged articles range from one to six pages in length and yield a comprehensive look at the nature of, treatments for, and social issues surrounding addictive substances and behaviors. Topics include specific drugs, diagnoses, treatments, legal and social implications, drug trafficking, cultural pressures, and related compulsive behaviors." SLJ

Includes bibliographical references

Drugs and controlled substances; information for students; Stacey Blachford, Kristine Krapp, editors. Gale Group 2002 c2003 xxvi, 495p il $115 *

Grades: 11 12 Adult   **362.29**
1. Drugs 2. Drug abuse
ISBN 0-7876-6264-X   LC 2002-10925

Provides detailed information about the composition, history, effects, uses and abuses of common drugs, including illegal drugs and addictive substances, as well as commonly abused classes of prescription drugs.

"In addition to the well-written essays, sidebars discussing legal issues, misconceptions, history, and news stories add depth to each topic. . . . Currency, scope, and authority are the hallmarks of this highly recommended reference work." Booklist

Includes bibliographical references

Drugs and sports; edited by William Dudley. Greenhaven Press 2001 93p (At issue) lib bdg $28.70; pa $19.95

Grades: 7 8 9 10   **362.29**
1. Athletes—Drug use
ISBN 1-56510-697-0 (lib bdg); 1-56510-696-2 (pa)
     LC 00-59632

This collection of essays addresses "drug abuse among athletes and the ethical erosion of sports by unscrupulous athletes, trainers, doctors, and pharmacists who keep finding ways to outwit drug testers. . . . The information is eye-opening enough to give readers much to consider." Booklist

Encyclopedia of drugs, alcohol & addictive behavior; Rosalyn Carson-DeWitt, editor-in-chief. 2nd ed. Macmillan Ref. USA 2001 4v il set $425

Grades: 11 12 Adult   **362.29**
ISBN 0-02-865541-9   LC 00-46068

First published 1995 with title: Encyclopedia of drugs and alcohol

"In entries ranging from 'Addicted Babies' to 'Zero Tolerance' and covering topics such as ethnopharmacology, MDMA, and the history of alcohol in the US, this encyclopedia is an outstanding reference. . . . Social, legal, and historical aspects of substance abuse are well covered." Choice

Includes bibliographical references

Gottfried, Ted, 1928-
The facts about marijuana. Benchmark Books 2004 c2005 109p il (Drugs) lib bdg $37.07

Grades: 6 7 8 9   **362.29**
1. Marijuana
ISBN 0-7614-1806-7   LC 2004-5578

Contents: What is marijuana?; Highs and lows; Go directly to jail; Pot, pain and punishment; Tests that count!

The author describes the effects of marijuana use, varying opinions about legalization, marijuana laws, and drug testing in schools.

Includes glossary and bibliographical references

Hyde, Margaret Oldroyd, 1917-
Drugs 101; an overview for teens; {by} Margaret O. Hyde and John F. Setaro. 21st Cent. Bks. (Brookfield) 2003 159p il $25.95 *

Grades: 9 10 11 12   **362.29**
1. Drugs 2. Drug abuse
ISBN 0-7613-2608-1   LC 2002-8290

Contents: Drugs: the changing scene; Addiction and the brain; Marijuana, heroin, cocaine, and methamphetamine; Club drugs; Prescription drugs and inhalants; Drugs and the young brain; Drug abuses, you, and society; Starting and stopping: prevention and treatment; Reducing the supply; Should drugs be legalized?

This "overview of drugs and drug abuse offers . . . information about various illicit drugs often used by teens, and their emotional, physical, and psychological ramifications. . . . Black-and-white photographs, charts, and diagrams are scattered throughout this concise, well-researched overview." Booklist

Includes bibliographical references

LeVert, Suzanne
The facts about cocaine. Marshall Cavendish Benchmark 2005 c2006 96p il map (Drugs) lib bdg $37.07 *

Grades: 7 8 9 10   **362.29**
1. Cocaine 2. Drug abuse
ISBN 0-7614-1973-X   LC 2005-1313

Describes how cocaine affects the mind and body, the dangers of cocaine abuse, cocaine and the law, and how to deal with addiction.

Includes glossary and bibliographical references

The facts about ecstasy. Benchmark Books 2004 c2005 96p il (Drugs) lib bdg $37.07

Grades: 6 7 8 9   **362.29**
1. Ecstasy (Drug)
ISBN 0-7614-1807-5   LC 2004-9341

Contents: Ecstasy: number one club drug; Drugs by design; Risky business: the body and brain on X; Ecstasy and the law; Designing a drug-free life

The author describes the drug MDMA, commonly known as ecstasy, and how it is abused, its health risks, the laws against it, and how to recover from the habit

Inlcudes glossary and bibliographical references

LeVert, Suzanne—*Continued*
The facts about LSD and other hallucinogens;
[by] Suzanne LeVert. Marshall Cavendish
Benchmark 2005 c2006 96p il (Drugs) lib bdg
$37.07
Grades: 7 8 9 10   **362.29**
1. LSD (Drug) 2. Hallucinogens 3. Drug abuse
ISBN 0-7614-1974-8   LC 2005-3948
"Describes the history, characteristics, legal status, and
abuse of LSD." Publisher's note
This "useful [volumes is] attractively packaged and
will be of interest to report writers and general readers.
[Text] and photos do an excellent job of showing how
[this] group of drugs affects the body." SLJ
Includes glossary and bibliographical references

The facts about steroids. Benchmark Books
2004 c2005 96p il (Drugs) lib bdg $37.07
Grades: 6 7 8 9   **362.29**
1. Steroids 2. Athletes—Drug use
ISBN 0-7614-1808-3   LC 2004-11852
Contents: The game of steroids; Steroids and your
body; The health risks of taking steroids; Steroids and
the law; Treatment, prevention, and healthy fitness
The author "discusses the effects of steroids on the
body, health risks, the law, prevention, and treatment.
The medicinal use of steroids is very briefly mentioned.
. . . [This title has a] readable, well-organized [text], and
good use of color, graphics, photographs, tables, dia-
grams, and labels helps to spark readers' interest." SLJ
Includes glossary and bibliographical references

Marijuana: opposing viewpoints; Jamuna Carroll,
book editor. Greenhaven Press 2006 224p il lib
bdg $34.95; pa $23.70
Grades: 9 10 11 12   **362.29**
1. Marijuana
ISBN 0-7377-3323-3 (lib bdg); 0-7377-3324-1 (pa)
LC 2005-40421
"Opposing viewpoints series"
This book "examines the many controversies plaguing
marijuana: whether it harms the body, has potential for
addiction, and impairs driving abilities; whether current
marijuana legislation is fair and effective; whether the
drug should be legalized and under what circumstances;
and how its use should be discouraged." Publisher's note
Includes bibliographical references

Menhard, Francha Roffe
The facts about inhalants. Benchmark Books
2004 c2005 92p il (Drugs) lib bdg $37.07
Grades: 6 7 8 9   **362.29**
1. Solvent abuse
ISBN 0-7614-1809-1   LC 2004-11858
Contents: Introduction; What are inhalants?; A history
of inhalant abuse; The dangers of inhalant abuse; Help
for inhalant abusers; Inhalants and the law
The author "addresses the types of inhalants, the history, dangers, effects, available help for abuse of these
drugs, and the laws regulating them. . . . [This title has
a] readable, well-organized [text], and good use of color,
graphics, photographs, tables, diagrams, and labels helps
to spark readers' interest." SLJ
Includes glossary and bibliographical references

Smoking; Laurie S. Friedman, book editor.
Greenhaven Press 2006 126p il (Introducing
issues with opposing viewpoints) lib bdg $32.45
Grades: 8 9 10 11 12   **362.29**
1. Smoking 2. Tobacco habit
ISBN 0-7377-3342-X   LC 2005-46140
"The articles in this anthology expose multiple sides
of . . . [the smoking] debate." Publisher's note
Includes bibliographical references

Tobacco and smoking: opposing viewpoints;
Karen F. Balkin, book editor. Greenhaven Press
2005 188p il lib bdg $33.70; pa $22.45
Grades: 9 10 11 12   **362.29**
1. Tobacco habit 2. Smoking 3. Tobacco industry
ISBN 0-7377-2248-7 (lib bdg); 0-7377-2249-5 (pa)
LC 2003-67502
"Opposing viewpoints series"
"Many twenty-first century health and social issues
surrounding tobacco and smoking are examined. . . .
The anthology includes [an] international chapter that ex-
plores the worldwide health and economic impacts of to-
bacco use." Publisher's note
Includes bibliographical references

362.292 Alcoholism

Alcohol; Scott Barbour, book editor. Greenhaven
Press 2006 144p il (Introducing issues with
opposing viewpoints) lib bdg $32.45
Grades: 9 10 11 12   **362.292**
1. Alcoholism 2. Teenagers—Alcohol use 3. Drunk
driving
ISBN 0-7377-3219-9   LC 2005-40327
"Contributors to this volume debate the harms and
benefits of alcohol as well as measures to prevent underage drinking and drunk driving." Publisher's note

Alcohol: an opposing viewpoints guide; William
Dudley, book editor. Greenhaven Press 2006
96p il (Writing the critical essay) $26.20
Grades: 9 10 11 12   **362.292**
1. Alcoholism 2. Teenagers—Alcohol use 3. Essay
4. Authorship
ISBN 0-7377-3192-3   LC 2005-52557
"Selected articles examine how alcohol and alcoholism
affect people's lives. Writing exercises and model essays
examine some of the techniques used for powerful descriptive writing." Publisher's note
Includes bibliographical references

Gottfried, Ted, 1928-
The facts about alcohol. Benchmark Books 2004
c2005 111p il (Drugs) lib bdg $37.07
Grades: 6 7 8 9   **362.292**
1. Drinking of alcoholic beverages 2. Alcoholism
3. Youth—Alcohol use
ISBN 0-7614-1805-9   LC 2004-5388
Contents: What's in a drink?; The noble experiment;
Liquor: lobbies and laws; A problem in the family; Help,
hope, and healing

Gottfried, Ted, 1928-—*Continued*
The author "includes historical aspects of alcohol and society, including humans' first experimentations with fermentation, Prohibition, and the temperance movement; related laws and legislation; and definition, causes, treatment, and effects. . . . [This title has a] readable, well-organized [text], and good use of color, graphics, photographs, tables, diagrams, and labels helps to spark readers' interest." SLJ
Includes glossary and bibliographical references

Rosengren, John
Big book unplugged; a young person's guide to Alcoholics Anonymous. Hazelden 2003 121p pa $10.95
Grades: 9 10 11 12   **362.292**
1. Alcoholics Anonymous 2. Teenagers—Alcohol use 3. Alcoholism
ISBN 1-592-85038-3; 978-1-592-85038-9
LC 2003-50828
"Alcoholics Anonymous, more familiarly called The Big Book, was published in 1939. . . . The Big Book describes the basic AA 12-step program, including the personal story of Bill W., credited with founding AA. In this clearly written manual, John R. devotes an interpretive chapter that corresponds to each of the 11 chapters in The Big Book. . . . In addition to those in recovery, this guide will also be useful to their family, friends, counselors and teachers." Publ Wkly
Includes bibliographical references

The **Truth** about alcohol; Mark J. Kittleson, general editor; William Kane, adviser; Richelle Rennegarbe, adviser; Barry Youngerman, principal author. Facts on File 2004 196p (Truth about series) $35 *
Grades: 7 8 9 10   **362.292**
1. Teenagers—Alcohol use 2. Alcoholism
ISBN 0-8160-5298-0   LC 2004-509
This discusses such topics as binge drinking, underage drinking, the prevalence of drinking on college campuses, drunken driving, dealing with alcohol abuse in the family, alcohol advertising and counter-advertising, and seeking help for an alcohol problem.
This title does "an excellent job of providing accurate information for teens. For reports or for self-help, [it belongs] in any library serving young adults." SLJ
Includes glossary and bibliographical references

362.3   Mental retardation

Libal, Autumn
My name is not Slow; youth with mental retardation. Mason Crest Publishers Inc 2004 127p il (Youth with special needs) $24.95 *
Grades: 7 8 9 10   **362.3**
1. Mental retardation 2. Down syndrome
ISBN 1-590-84731-8   LC 2003-18435
Through the story of Penelope, a girl growing up with Down's syndrome, this book discusses "mental retardation, the special needs of individuals living with this form of disability, and the support systems available to

help people with mental retardation acquire independence and success." Publisher's note
Includes glossary and bibliographical references

362.4   Problems of and services to people with physical disabilities

Encyclopedia of disability; general editor, Gary L. Albrecht. Sage Publications 2006 5v il set $850
Grades: 11 12 Adult   **362.4**
1. Handicapped—Encyclopedias
ISBN 0-7619-2565-1   LC 2005-18301
"Almost 200 of the entries are biographical, treating individuals from Homer and Socrates to Helen Keller and Franklin Roosevelt. Others treat history . . . types of disability . . . [and] attitudes and conditions affecting daily life. . . . [This encyclopedia draws] in readers from a wide range of studies and interests and helping them to see disability in an entirely new way." Booklist
Includes bibliographical references

McHugh, Mary
Special siblings; growing up with someone with a disability. rev ed. Paul H. Brookes 2003 xxvii, 241p il pa $21.95 *
Grades: 9 10 11 12   **362.4**
1. Handicapped 2. Siblings
ISBN 1-557-66607-5   LC 2002-28179
First published 1999 by Hyperion
"A look at what it is like to be a sibling of someone with a physical, mental, or emotional disability. McHugh's brother has both cerebral palsy and mental retardation, a fact that has shaped every aspect of her life. In the course of writing this book, she spoke to siblings ranging in age from 6 to 76 years of age who expressed feelings that ran the gamut from compassion to resentment. She writes with painful honesty and includes information about research studies, interviews with experts, and the experiences and stories of many siblings." SLJ
Includes bibliographical references

362.5   Problems of and services to poor people

Encyclopedia of homelessness; David Levinson, editor. Sage Publications 2004 2v il $295
Grades: 11 12 Adult   **362.5**
1. Homelessness—Encyclopedias
ISBN 0-7619-2751-4   LC 2004-9279
"Entries cover homelessness in 8 major U.S. cities and 30 cities and nations around the world, as well as causes of homelessness; historical aspects; housing, policy, health and lifestyle issues; and service systems." Booklist
Includes bibliographical references

Encyclopedia of world poverty; general editor, Mehmet Odekon. SAGE Publications 2006 3v il map set $395
Grades: 11 12 Adult   **362.5**
1. Poverty—Encyclopedias 2. Poor—Encyclopedias
ISBN 1-4129-1807-3; 978-1-4129-1807-7
LC 2006-6495

Encyclopedia of world poverty—*Continued*

"A SAGE reference publication"

"This three-volume encyclopedia offers 800 signed entries that cover various definitions of poverty and techniques to measure it (in 78 articles); reviews of most countries, with their rank on the Human Development Index and Human Poverty Index and their condition (191 articles); and finally, potential causes and effects of poverty (more than 50 articles). Especially interesting are the articles discussing local organizations, intergovernmental organizations, and nongovernmental organizations, as well as theories on how gender, race, and age are intertwined with poverty." Choice

Includes bibliographical references

How can the poor be helped? Geoff Griffin, book
   editor. Greenhaven Press 2006 108p (At issue)
   lib bdg $28.70; pa $19.95
   Grades: 9 10 11 12   **362.5**
   1. Poverty
   ISBN 0-7377-2717-9 (lib bdg); 0-7377-2718-7 (pa)
                                    LC 2005-46234

The essays in this anthology address such questions as "Do living-wage laws help the poor or lead to unemployment? Do government programs help the poor or would market solutions work better? Does U.S. foreign aid help the third world or help corrupt governments to stay in power?" Publisher's note

Includes bibliographical references

Poverty; David M. Haugen and Matthew J. Box,
   book editors. Greenhaven Press 2006 108p il
   (Social issues firsthand) lib bdg $28.70 *
   Grades: 8 9 10 11 12   **362.5**
   1. Poverty 2. Poor—United States
   ISBN 0-7377-2899-X   LC 2005-45120

"Collecting intimate stories of individuals living in poverty and those helping them, this anthology includes personal narratives of poor people struggling to survive on little or no income, and also writings that convey the thoughts and deeds of people trying to alleviate the plight of the impoverished." Publisher's note

These "16 accounts from poverty's gritty trenches evaporate easy assumptions about the poor, and reveal the obstacles faced by stricken individuals and families hampered by catch-22 social policies, entrenched racial inequities, and logistics such as cleaning up for an interview." Booklist

Includes bibliographical references

Poverty and the homeless; Mary E. Williams,
   book editor. Greenhaven Press 2004 186p
   (Current controversies) lib bdg $34.95 *
   Grades: 9 10 11 12   **362.5**
   1. Homeless persons 2. Poverty
   ISBN 0-7377-2310-6 (lib bdg)   LC 2003-60012

"Contributors examine the root causes of poverty and what should be done to help the poor and the homeless." Publisher's note

Includes bibliographical references

362.6 Problems of and services to persons in late adulthood

Aging in America; edited by Olivia J. Smith.
   Wilson, H.W. 2000 224p (Reference shelf) pa
   $40 *
   Grades: 11 12 Adult   **362.6**
   1. Aging 2. Elderly—Care
   ISBN 0-8242-0984-2   LC 00-42629

A collection of articles exploring the social, economic, and political aspects of an aging population

Includes bibliographical references

362.7 Problems of and services to young people

Adoption; David M. Haugen and Matthew J. Box,
   book editors. Greenhaven Press 2005 108p
   (Social issues firsthand) lib bdg $28.70 *
   Grades: 8 9 10 11 12   **362.7**
   1. Adoption
   ISBN 0-7377-2881-7   LC 2005-46075

"The book explores such diverse issues as gay adoptive parents, open and transracial adoptions, the search for and reunion with birthparents, custody battles, and more. The editors have done an excellent job of selecting 16 lively, articulate, and poignant essays by birthparents, adoptive parents, and adoptees, all offering different perspectives on the process." SLJ

Includes bibliographical references

Adoption: opposing viewpoints; Mary E.
   Williams, book editor. Greenhaven Press 2006
   226p il lib bdg $34.95; pa $23.70
   Grades: 7 8 9 10   **362.7**
   1. Adoption
   ISBN 0-7377-3301-2 (lib bdg); 978-0-7377-3301-3 (lib
   bdg); 0-7377-3302-0 (pa); 978-0-7377-3302-0 (pa)
                                    LC 2006-43350

"Opposing viewpoints series"

This anthology addresses such topics as "whether adoption should be encouraged; conflicting views on transracial, international, and gay parent adoptions; whose rights are most in need of protection—adoptive or birth parents or those of adoptees; as well as what government policies should be implemented." SLJ

Includes bibliographical references

Feuereisen, Patti

   Invisible girls; the truth about sexual abuse; [by]
   Patti Feuereisen; with Caroline Pincus. Seal Press
   2005 233p pa $15.95
   Grades: 9 10 11 12   **362.7**
   1. Child sexual abuse
   ISBN 1-58005-135-9   LC 2004-30252

Subtitle on cover: Book for teen girls, young women, and everyone who cares about them

"This book sets personal narratives within a generalized discussion of sexual abuse of girls and young women. Feuereisen addresses myths about female sexuality and abuse, considers contributing family dynamics, and

Feuereisen, Patti—*Continued*
offers advice on preventing, reporting, and recovering from abuse. Individual chapters are given to father-daughter incest, other incest, abuse by teachers and clergy, and different types of rape. The writing is clear and frank, including sufficient details without becoming salacious." SLJ
Includes bibliographical references

Fodor, Margie Druss
Megan's law; protection or privacy. Enslow Pubs. 2001 128p il (Issues in focus) lib bdg $20.95
Grades: 9 10 11 12   362.7
1. Child sexual abuse 2. Sex crimes
ISBN 0-7660-1586-6   LC 00-12307
Contents: A child's murder shocks the nation and sparks change; The birth of Megan's law; History of laws protecting children against child molesters; Portrait of a child molester; The case for Megan's law: protection; The case against Megan's law: privacy violation; How Megan's law works in and out of the courtroom; Teaching children to watch out for themselves
This "presents the history of legislation regarding tracking convicted sex offenders and preventing crimes against children. . . . It includes balanced views on the drawbacks of Megan's Law, from problems with registration to crimes against men forced to register by their neighboring citizens." Voice Youth Advocates
Includes glossary and bibliographical references

Pledge, Deanna S., 1956-
When something feels wrong; a survival guide about abuse for young people. Free Spirit 2003 214p il pa $14.95 *
Grades: 7 8 9 10   362.7
1. Child abuse 2. Domestic violence
ISBN 1-575-42115-1   LC 2002-14060
Contents: What is abuse?; Taking action; Your healing journey
Provides checklists, journaling ideas, and other positive ways of dealing with being physically, sexually, and/or emotionally abused, emphasizing the importance of talking about what has happened and getting help
"This book will be a godsend for those struggling with any type of abuse. . . . The tone is light and encouraging, yet straightforward. The advice is seasoned and workable." SLJ
Includes bibliographical references

Strong at the heart; how it feels to heal from sexual abuse; [compiled] by Carolyn Lehman. Farrar, Straus & Giroux 2005 156p il $18 *
Grades: 8 9 10 11 12   362.7
1. Child sexual abuse 2. Incest 3. Rape
ISBN 0-374-37282-9   LC 2004-56280
"Melanie Kroupa Books"
This "gathers 11 personal stories by young men and women who experienced rape, molestation, or incest and found healing through speaking out about their abuse. . . . Clearly and candidly written, the narratives recounted here include sufficient details of abuse to be authentic, but never titillating. . . . An attractive, accessible format and black-and-white portraits throughout personalize the presentation." SLJ

Tucker, Neely
Love in the driest season; a family memoir. Crown Publishers 2004 242p il hardcover o.p. pa $14
Grades: 11 12 Adult   362.7
1. Adoption 2. Zimbabwe
ISBN 0-609-60976-9; 1-4000-8160-2 (pa)
LC 2002-154095
This is a "narrative of two Mississippians in Africa—a white reporter and his African-American wife—who struggle against Third World bureaucracy to adopt an abandoned Zimbabwean baby, as the continent is torn by crisis." SLJ
"This story about the adoption of a tiny, critically ill Zimbabwean orphan appeals to the head as much as the heart." Christ Sci Monit

362.82   Problems of and services to families

Battered women; Lane E. Volpe, book editor. Greenhaven Press 2004 138p (Contemporary issues companion) hardcover o.p. pa $22.45 *
Grades: 9 10 11 12   362.82
1. Domestic violence 2. Abused women
ISBN 0-7377-1617-7; 0-7377-1618-5 (pa)
LC 2003-56877
"Contributors to this . . . anthology investigate the nature of domestic violence and examine various measures that can protect battered women. Personal profiles of individuals whose lives have been touched by domestic violence round out this look at a disturbing but important issue." Publisher's note
Includes bibliographical references

Domestic violence: opposing viewpoints; David M. Haugen, book editor. Greenhaven Press 2005 186p il lib bdg $33.70; pa $22.45
Grades: 8 9 10 11 12   362.82
1. Domestic violence
ISBN 0-7377-2224-X (lib bdg); 0-7377-2225-8 (pa)
LC 2004-41168
"Opposing viewpoints series"
"This volume examines the prevalence of domestic violence in America, its causes, and its remedies." Publisher's note
Includes bibliographical references

362.83   Problems of and services to women

Violence against women; Karen Balkin, book editor. Greenhaven Press 2004 208p (Current controversies) lib bdg $33.70; pa $22.45 *
Grades: 9 10 11 12   362.83
1. Abused women 2. Violence
ISBN 0-7377-2041-7 (lib bdg); 0-7377-2042-5 (pa)
LC 2003-48328
Replaces the edition published 1999 under the editorship of James D. Torr
New edition in preparation

Violence against women—*Continued*

"Chapter headings include, 'Is Violence Against Women in the United States a Serious Problem?' 'What Causes Violence Against Women?' 'Are Current Approaches to Reducing Violence Against Women Effective?' and 'What is the Extent of Violence Against Women Worldwide?' Articles in each section present opposing viewpoints. . . . Contributors include men and women, feminists and antifeminists, activists, scholars, journalists, and social workers." SLJ

Includes bibliographical references

363.1   Public safety programs

Cummins, Ronnie

Genetically engineered food; a self-defense guide for consumers; [by] Ronnie Cummins and Ben Lilliston ; foreword by Frances Moore Lappé. [2nd, rev ed] Marlowe & Co 2004 237p pa $14.95

Grades: 11 12 Adult   363.1

1. Food—Biotechnology 2. Farm produce
ISBN 1-569-24469-3   LC 2004-45565
First published 2000

The authors "discuss genetically engineered or modified food focusing on the scientific, political, economic, and health issues. . . . [They] include information on what consumers can do, from smart shopping to grassroots lobbying, to reduce the threat of genetically engineered food." Booklist [review of 2000 edition]

Includes bibliographical references

Drunk driving; Louise I. Gerdes, book editor. Greenhaven Press 2004 138p (Contemporary issues companion) lib bdg $33.70; pa $22.45 *

Grades: 9 10 11 12   363.1

1. Drunk driving
ISBN 0-7377-3077-3 (lib bdg); 0-7377-3078-1 (pa)
                                   LC 2004-45562

This anthology discussing the problem of drunk driving is divided as follows: The problem of drunk driving; Solutions to the problem of drunk driving; Legal issues concerning drunk driving; Personal stories of tragedy and triumph

Includes bibliographical references

Fast food; Tracy Brown Collins, book editor. Greenhaven Press 2005 91p (At issue) lib bdg $27.45; pa $18.70 *

Grades: 9 10 11 12   363.1

1. Food industry 2. Convenience foods 3. Restaurants
ISBN 0-7377-2318-1 (lib bdg); 0-7377-2319-X (pa)
                                   LC 2004-47441

"Is Ronald McDonald a harmless advertising icon that represents a restaurant and good charities, or does he exploit children and seduce them into lifelong consumption of products that are bad for their health and the environment? More broadly, is the fast-food industry an unethical manipulator of people and exploiter of resources, or is it merely an example of capitalism at its best? Do corporations engineer people's habits and appetites, or is it up to individuals to make healthy choices for themselves? These and other issues are explored in *At Issue: Fast Food*." Introduction

Includes bibliographical references

Food safety; Stuart A. Kallen, book editor. Greenhaven Press 2005 125p (At issue) lib bdg $27.45; pa $18.70

Grades: 9 10 11 12   363.1

1. Food adulteration and inspection 2. Food contamination
ISBN 0-7377-2372-6 (lib bdg); 0-7377-2373-4 (pa)
                                   LC 2004-52361

Among the topics discussed in these 12 reprinted articles are agricultural terrorism, genetically engineered crops, mad cow disease, organic food and pesticides

Genetically engineered foods; Nancy Harris, book editor. Greenhaven Press 2004 112p (At issue) lib bdg $28.70; pa $19.95 *

Grades: 9 10 11 12   363.1

1. Food—Biotechnology
ISBN 0-7377-1786-6 (lib bdg); 0-7377-1787-4 (pa)
                                   LC 2002-35387

Controversial issues about genetically engineered foods discussed include "questions about their safety to human health and the environment, whether they should be labeled or not, and whether they will solve the problems of world hunger." Publisher's note

Includes bibliographical references

Pringle, Peter

Food, inc; Mendel to Monsanto—the promises and perils of the biotech harvest. Simon & Schuster 2003 239p hardcover o.p. pa $13

Grades: 11 12 Adult   363.1

1. Food—Biotechnology 2. Farm produce
ISBN 0-7432-2611-9; 0-7432-6763-X (pa)
                                   LC 2003-42823

The author "believes that there is nothing inherently unsafe about genetically modified (GM) foods and that technology has the potential to relieve hunger and pain for millions of people. However, in this discussion of the aspects of GM foods, he does not hesitate to point out the perils. . . . Especially troubling to the author is the degree to which plant biotechnology gives control to a few international conglomerates that own patents to the products and processes." Libr J

"This is a book to satisfy curiosity and engender concern, and any of its chapters would provide an excellent subject for discussion groups." SLJ

363.2   Police services

Ackerman, Thomas H.

FBI careers; the ultimate guide to landing a job as one of America's finest. 2nd ed. JIST Works 2006 340p pa $19.95

Grades: 9 10 11 12   363.2

1. United States. Federal Bureau of Investigation 2. Vocational guidance
ISBN 1-59357-237-9   LC 2005-21337
First published 2002

The author "outlines the history and organization of the FBI; the salary and benefits of a career with this agency; and opportunities and hiring processes, including ways to present an outstanding application. He also de-

Ackerman, Thomas H.—*Continued*

scribes the training for different positions. . . . This book is a must for career collections and for libraries with populations that are particularly interested in law enforcement, but it is not for those with only an idle interest in the FBI." SLJ

Ashabranner, Brent K., 1921-

Badge of valor; the National Law Enforcement Officers Memorial; by Brent Ashabranner; photographs by Jennifer Ashabranner. Millbrook Press 2000 64p lib bdg $24.90

Grades: 9 10 11 12   **363.2**
1. National Law Enforcement Officers Memorial (Washington, D.C.) 2. Police
ISBN 0-7613-1522-5   LC 00-20222
Describes the planning and creation of the National Law Enforcement Officers Memorial and profiles some of those police officers who gave their lives in the line of duty
Includes bibliographical references

Bell, Suzanne

Encyclopedia of forensic science; foreword by Barry A.J. Fisher; preface by Max M. Houck. Facts on File 2003 350p il $75 *

Grades: 11 12 Adult   **363.2**
1. Forensic sciences—Encyclopedias
ISBN 0-8160-4811-8   LC 2002-154971
"In addition to explaining the science of forensics, Bell . . . reviews various disciplines related to forensic science, among them entomology, odontology, and psychology. Other entries cover professional organizations, government agencies, famous names in the field of forensics, evidence, and legal issues. . . . With its clear language and brief entries [this] volume will provide readers with a nuts-and-bolts understanding of the real world of forensic science." Booklist
Includes bibliographical references

The Facts on File dictionary of forensic science. Facts on File 2004 278p il (Facts on File science library) $45; pa $17.95

Grades: 11 12 Adult   **363.2**
1. Forensic sciences—Dictionaries
ISBN 0-8160-5131-3; 0-8160-5153-4 (pa)
                                LC 2003-15735
"Definitions range from a few sentences to several paragraphs, provide fundamental knowledge of the key terms and concepts in forensics, and cover a . . . range of forensic knowledge, including blood, pharmacology, decomposition, and court and legal terms." Choice
The author "has created an exceptional forensic reference guide. . . . I recommend this text highly as a handy pocket reference guide for anyone interested in forensic science or working in a related scientific discipline. It will greatly benefit students, teachers, and high school, university, and public libraries." Sci Books Films

Friedlander, Mark P.

When objects talk; solving a crime with science; {by} Mark P. Friedlander, Jr., and Terry M. Phillips. Lerner Publs. 2001 120p il lib bdg $27.93

Grades: 9 10 11 12   **363.2**
1. Forensic sciences 2. Criminal investigation
ISBN 0-8225-0649-1   LC 00-10247
"This book explains the latest techniques and technology for DNA testing, ballistics, autopsies, bloodstain-pattern interpretation, and much more, but combines it with 'The Case,' a fictional account of how forensics is used to solve a hypothetical murder." Book Rep
"The readable, informative text gives students an understanding of the scientific methods and how they are used to help police, lawyers, judges, and juries bring criminals to justice." SLJ
Includes glossary and bibliographical references

Genge, Ngaire

The forensic casebook; the science of crime scene investigation; [by] N.E. Genge. Ballantine Bks. 2002 319p il pa $16.95

Grades: 9 10 11 12   **363.2**
1. Forensic sciences 2. Criminal investigation
ISBN 0-345-45203-8 (pa)   LC 2002-72063
This offers "examples of forensic crime fighting. It begins with the identification and protection of the area where a crime took place; the next three chapters focus on work at the scene, and the last one describes the roles of the dog handler and forensic photographer. . . . Experts provide an absorbing look at all aspects of the profession from imprint evidence to DNA fingerprinting and from document examination to forensic entomology." SLJ
Includes bibliographical references

Meeks, Kenneth, 1963-

Driving while black; highways, shopping malls, taxicabs, sidewalks : how to fight back if you are a victims of racial profiling. Broadway Bks. 2000 254p pa $12.95 *

Grades: 11 12 Adult   **363.2**
1. Race discrimination 2. African Americans—Civil rights
ISBN 0-7679-0549-0   LC 00-28932
"A practical guide for victims of racial profiling by police, security guards, and stores. . . . The book is divided into sections according to venue: driving while black, riding the train, shopping, and flying while black. Each chapter contains advice on how to respond to discrimination, including sample complaint letters, addresses of agencies to contact, and tips on information to cite." Libr J
Includes bibliographical references

Owen, David, 1939-

Hidden evidence; 40 true crimes and how forensic science helped solve them. Firefly Bks. (Buffalo) 2000 240p il $35; pa $24.95

Grades: 11 12 Adult   **363.2**

Owen, David, 1939-—*Continued*
1. Forensic sciences 2. Criminal investigation
ISBN 1-55209-492-8; 1-55209-483-9 (pa)

Owen "looks at how forensic science has developed and how techniques have evolved from methods of investigation used in ancient China to computerized DNA analysis. . . . This is fascinating reading for a range of readers from forensic scientists to professional and amateur sleuths, but the graphic illustrations are not for the squeamish." Booklist

Platt, Richard, 1953-
Crime scene; the ultimate guide to forensic science. DK Publishing 2003 144p il $25; pa $16.95 *
Grades: 9 10 11 12   **363.2**
1. Forensic sciences 2. Criminal investigation
ISBN 0-7894-8891-4; 0-7566-1896-7 (pa)
LC 2003-271170

"Techniques such as fingerprint analysis, shoe prints and tire tracks, tool marks and fabric prints, insect analysis, nuclear and mitochondrial DNA evidence, and other tools used by scene-of-the crime investigators are described; details of the collaborative roles of the medical examiner, law enforcement officers, and officers of the court are also included." Sci Books Films

"This is a solid, thorough, well-organized, and beautifully illustrated treatment of the subject of forensic science . . . This book would be invaluable for law classes and reports, as well as for mystery readers and writers." Libr Media Connect

Police brutality; Louise I. Gerdes, book editor. Greenhaven Press 2004 206p (Current controversies) lib bdg $34.95; pa $23.70 *
Grades: 9 10 11 12   **363.2**
1. Police brutality
ISBN 0-7377-1627-4 (lib bdg); 0-7377-1628-2 (pa)
LC 2003-60738

"Authors in this anthology examine the nature and scope of police brutality, possible causes, and potential reforms." Publisher's note

Includes bibliographical references

Racial profiling; Kris Hirschmann, book editor. Greenhaven Press 2007 115p (At issue) lib bdg $28.70; pa $19.95
Grades: 9 10 11 12   **363.2**
1. Racial profiling
ISBN 0-7377-1979-6 (lib bdg); 978-0-7377-1979-6 (lib bdg); 0-7377-1980-X (pa); 978-0-7377-1980-2 (pa)
LC 2006-43375

This anthology of selections by writers offering different opinions on the issue of racial profiling focuses on the profiling of Muslims and on airport security.

Includes bibliographical references

Wagner, E. J.
The science of Sherlock Holmes; from Baskerville Hall to the Valley of Fear, the real forensics behind the great detective's greatest cases. Wiley 2006 244p il $24.95
Grades: 11 12 Adult   **363.2**
1. Holmes, Sherlock (Fictitious character) 2. Forensic sciences 3. Criminal investigation
ISBN 0-471-64879-5; 978-0-471-64879-6
LC 2005-22236

The author discusses forensic science in Arthur Conan Doyle's stories of the 'consulting detective' Sherlock Holmes. She compares Holmes's investigative techniques to those used in actual cases such as the killing of Lizzie Borden's parents in 1892, the 1902 murder of Joseph Browne Elwell, and the disappearance of Dr. George Parkman in 1849.

This book "will intrigue readers with incredible stories and amazing tales from the early days of forensic science." Christ Sci Monit

Includes bibliographical references

Yount, Lisa
Forensic science; from fibers to fingerprints. Facts on File 2007 206p il (Milestones in discovery and invention) $35 *
Grades: 7 8 9 10 11 12   **363.2**
1. Forensic sciences 2. Criminal investigation
ISBN 0-8160-5751-6; 978-0-8160-5751-1
LC 2006-1748

This book "profiles key figures in this newsmaking field, both pioneers and today's top forensics experts." Publisher's note

Includes glossary and bibliographical references

363.3   Other aspects of public safety

Are efforts to reduce terrorism successful? Lauri S. Friedman, book editor. Greenhaven Press 2005 112p (At issue) lib bdg $28.70; pa $19.95
Grades: 9 10 11 12   **363.3**
1. Terrorism 2. War on terrorism
ISBN 0-7377-2334-3 (lib bdg); 0-7377-2335-1 (pa)
LC 2004-42421

The viewpoints presented in this title "explore the gamut of actions being taken in the war against terrorism and offer insight into the wide range of interpretations of their success." Introduction

Includes bibliographical references

363.31   Censorship

Censorship; Kate Burns, book editor. Greenhaven Press 2004 139p (Contemporary issues companion) lib bdg $34.95; pa $23.70
Grades: 9 10 11 12   **363.31**
1. Censorship 2. Mass media 3. Internet
ISBN 0-7377-1579-0 (lib bdg); 0-7377-1580-4 (pa)
LC 2003-55106

This anthology "examines several key censorship issues related to art and entertainment, the media, the Internet, and government regulation." Introduction

Includes bibliographical references

Censorship; Julia Bauder, book editor. Greenhaven Press 2007 275p (Current controversies) lib bdg $34.95; pa $23.70 *
Grades: 9 10 11 12 **363.31**
1. Censorship
ISBN 978-0-7377-3277-1 (lib bdg); 0-7377-3277-6 (lib bdg); 978-0-7377-3278-8 (pa); 0-7377-3278-4 (pa)
LC 2006-38688
Contents: Should offensive speech be censored? — Should high schools and universities censor? — Should pornographic and violent material be censored? — Should speech that endangers national security be censored?
Includes bibliographical references

Censorship: opposing viewpoints; Andrea C. Nakaya, book editor. Greenhaven Press 2005 192p il lib bdg $34.95; pa $23.70 *
Grades: 9 10 11 12 **363.31**
1. Censorship
ISBN 0-7377-2925-2 (lib bdg); 0-7377-2926-0 (pa)
LC 2004-54309
"Opposing viewpoints series"
The facets of the censorship debate explored in this anthology are "censorship on the Internet, censorship in relation to America's war on terrorism, whether free speech should be censored, and whether freedom in the United States is threatened by censorship." Publisher's note
Includes bibliographical references

Green, Jonathon
The encyclopedia of censorship; [by] Jonathon Green, Nicholas J. Karolides. rev ed. Facts on File 2005 xxii, 698p (Facts on File library of world history) $85
Grades: 11 12 Adult **363.31**
1. Censorship—Encyclopedias
ISBN 0-8160-4464-3 LC 2004-53211
First published 1990
"The crowded roster of those who have been affected by censorship, as well as the books, films, and other works attacked, are found in these . . . pages. Controversies that have arisen over the years are given historical context; highly valuable national wrap-ups treat the culture, law, and predominant trends of diverse lands." Libr J
Includes bibliographical references

363.32 Control of violence and terrorism

Gottfried, Ted, 1928-
Homeland security versus constitutional rights. 21st Century Books 2003 128p il lib bdg $24.90 *
Grades: 9 10 11 12 **363.32**
1. Terrorism 2. Civil rights 3. Civil defense 4. National security—United States
ISBN 0-76132-862-9 LC 2003-590

Contents: Response to terrorism; Dealing with terrorism; The detainees; Presidential power and the Constitution; Keeping the vigil; The POW controversy; Patriotic critics
Presents varying perspectives on the issue of whether the U.S. government is defending the country against terrorism at the expense of the rights of the individual citizen
"The book offers more in-depth information than most students receive from newspapers or television, giving opposing viewpoints in a logical, nonthreatening manner." SLJ
Includes bibliographical references

Henderson, Harry, 1951-
Terrorist challenge to America. Facts on File 2003 316p il (Library in a book) $45
Grades: 9 10 11 12 **363.32**
1. Terrorism
ISBN 0-8160-4975-0 LC 2002-14585
"This title focuses on the immediate and long-term challenges faced by America in the aftermath of the 9/11 attacks. Henderson examines the country's immediate response to these events and discusses 'the shifts in the understanding of the role' of the U.S. The author's . . . approach includes the differing points of view on the motivations of al-Qaeda, the 'Bush doctrine' with regard to weapons of mass destruction, and other topics. . . . Henderson's up-to-date volume should be considered by most libraries; it will be useful to students needing background information and/or suggestions for further research." SLJ
Includes bibliographical references

Homeland security; Andrea C. Nakaya, book editor. Greenhaven Press 2005 191p (Current controversies) lib bdg $34.95; pa $22.45 *
Grades: 9 10 11 12 **363.32**
1. United States. Dept. of Homeland Security 2. Terrorism 3. National security—United States 4. Civil rights
ISBN 0-7377-2777-2 (lib bdg); 0-7377-2778-0 (pa)
LC 2004-52292
The authors of the articles in this volume "offer various perspectives on the security of the United States. They debate how safe the United States is, whether the Department of Homeland Security is effective, what measures should be taken to ensure homeland security, and whether these measures threaten civil liberties." Introduction

Homeland security; edited by Norris Smith and Lynn M. Messina. H.W. Wilson Co 2004 197p il (Reference shelf) $50
Grades: 11 12 Adult **363.32**
1. National security—United States 2. Terrorism
ISBN 0-8242-1033-6 LC 2003-70366
"This book looks at the Office of Homeland Security, evaluating its effectiveness and its impact on civil liberties, law enforcement, and Americans' peace of mind." Publisher's note
Includes bibliographical references

Steven, Graeme C. S.

Counterterrorism: a reference handbook; [by] Graeme C. S. Steven and Rohan Gunaratna. ABC-CLIO 2004 xxiv, 293p (Contemporary world issues) $50

Grades: 9 10 11 12   **363.32**

1. Terrorism 2. War on terrorism

ISBN 1-85109-666-3   LC 2004-9632

Contents: Terrorism and counterterrorism in the global context -- Counterterrorism: perspectives, issues, and solutions -- Chronology -- Profiles of terrorist and counterterrorist leaders and organizations -- Framework for counterterrorism policy -- Directory of counterterrorism agencies and organizations -- Print and nonprint resources

"This handbook provides a useful and timely guide to all aspects of the terrorism issue." Am Ref Books Annu, 2005

Includes bibliographical references

Terrorism: opposing viewpoints; Laura K. Egendorf, book editor. Greenhaven Press 2004 204p il lib bdg $34.95; pa $23.70

Grades: 8 9 10 11 12   **363.32**

1. Terrorism

ISBN 0-7377-2246-0 (lib bdg); 0-7377-2247-9 (pa)
LC 2003-49497

"Opposing viewpoints series"

This anthology includes essays and writings on terrorism by John Ashcroft, Noam Chomsky, Michelle Malkin, and others. Chapters include: Is terrorism a serious threat?; What are the causes of terrorism?; How should America's domestic war on terrorism be conducted?; How should the international community respond to terrorism?

Includes bibliographical references

363.33   Control of explosives and firearms

Atkin, S. Beth

Gunstories; life-changing experiences with guns; interviews and photographs by S. Beth Atkin. HarperCollins Publishers 2006 245p il $16.99; lib bdg $17.89 *

Grades: 7 8 9 10 11 12   **363.33**

1. Firearms

ISBN 0-06-052659-9; 0-06-052660-2 (lib bdg)
LC 2005-2076

The author "gathers testimonials addressing how guns are an integral part of teens' lives. Situated between oral testimonials, and figuratively placing an exclamation mark on the topic, are summaries of thirty-four school shootings occurring between 1995 and 2005." Voice Youth Advocates

"This book should be useful for students involved in the debate about guns in our culture as well as for those with a general interest in the subject." SLJ

Crooker, Constance Emerson

Gun control and gun rights. Greenwood Press 2003 180p il (Historical guides to controversial issues in America) $49.95

Grades: 9 10 11 12   **363.33**

1. Gun control

ISBN 0-313-32174-4   LC 2002-35213

"This volume follows the evolution of the battle between gun control advocates and those who believe it is a constitutional right to bear arms. It looks at the historical perspectives and the increase of violence in the decisions that have been made to control gun ownership. The book looks at perspectives equally, covering both those who advocate gun control and those who believe it is their right to own guns." Libr Media Connect

Includes bibliographical references

Guns and violence; Laura K. Egendorf, book editor. Greenhaven Press 2005 202p (Current controversies) lib bdg $34.95; pa $23.70

Grades: 8 9 10 11 12   **363.33**

1. Gun control 2. Violence

ISBN 0-7377-2206-1 (lib bdg); 0-7377-2207-X (pa)
LC 2004-52287

Presents differing viewpoints on the seriousness of gun violence, whether or not gun control reduces crime and its constitutionality, the effectiveness of gun ownership as self defense, and what measures would reduce gun violence

Includes bibliographical references

Henderson, Harry, 1951-

Gun control. rev ed. Facts on File 2005 316p il (Library in a book) $45 *

Grades: 11 12 Adult   **363.33**

1. Gun control

ISBN 0-8160-5660-9   LC 2004-50651

First published 2000

This examination of the history and issues of gun control "includes an annotated bibliography, chronology, glossary, biographical listing, a chapter on how to research the topic, laws and court cases, and a list of applicable organizations and agencies." Publisher's note

363.34   Disasters

Allaby, Michael, 1933-

A chronology of weather; illustrations by Richard Garratt. Rev. ed. Facts on File 2004 196p il (Dangerous weather) $35

Grades: 9 10 11 12   **363.34**

1. Weather 2. Natural disasters

ISBN 0-8160-4792-8; 978-0-8160-4792-5
LC 2003-4000

First published 1998

The author answers "questions students and nonspecialists have about weather and provides a general overview of the . . . information that shapes the way weather is understood and studied. Features include discussion of how the climates of the world have changed over the centuries; a 5,000-year chronology of dangerous weather, from ca. 3200 BCE to the present; and a chro-

Allaby, Michael, 1933-—*Continued*
nology of discoveries listing important developments in the understanding of weather." Publisher's note
Includes bibliographical references

Hurricane Katrina; William Dudley, book editor. Greenhaven Press 2006 91p (At issue) lib bdg $28.70; pa $19.95
Grades: 7 8 9 10   363.34
1. Hurricane Katrina, 2005 2. Disaster relief
ISBN 0-7377-3551-1 (lib bdg); 978-0-7377-3551-2 (lib bdg); 0-7377-3552-X (pa); 978-0-7377-3552-9 (pa)
                                   LC 2005-55131
"This book is a collection of brief articles presenting contrasting views of the disaster. It includes discussions of the government's preparedness and response; the proper role for government; whether to rebuild New Orleans; the accuracy of news reporting; and racism and global warming as factors in the disaster. . . . An excellent introduction to the controversies surrounding the Katrina debacle." SLJ
Includes bibliographical references

Hurricane Katrina; the storm that changed America; by the editors of Time; [with an introduction by Wynton Marsalis] Time Books 2005 136p il map $21.95
Grades: 11 12 Adult   363.34
1. Hurricane Katrina, 2005 2. Disaster relief 3. Rescue work
ISBN 1-933405-13-9; 978-1-933405-13-1
                                   LC 2005-908814
This book on Hurricane Katrina features photographs from Time photographers and firsthand accounts from survivors and other witnesses of what happened during and after the storm.

Katrina: state of emergency; introduction by Ivor van Heerden. Andrews McMeel Pub. 2005 176p il pa $19.95
Grades: 11 12 Adult   363.34
1. Hurricane Katrina, 2005 2. Disaster relief
ISBN 0-7407-5844-6; 978-0-7407-5844-7
                                   LC 2005-935404
At head of title: CNN reports
This book "provides a chronological account of the hurricane through a selection of CNN transcripts and photos documenting all facets of the disaster starting from past studies predicting such a tragedy to the path of the hurricane to the consequences surrounding the flooding and delayed rescue efforts." Publisher's note

Kusky, Timothy M.
Geological hazards; a sourcebook. Greenwood Press 2003 297p il map (Sourcebooks on hazards and disasters) $65 *
Grades: 9 10 11 12   363.34
1. Geology 2. Natural disasters
ISBN 1-57356-469-9   LC 2002-192773
"An Oryx book"
"Beginning with an overview of geological processes and a definition of geologic hazards, Timothy Kusky then devotes a chapter to each type of hazard, including

earthquakes, volcanic eruptions, tsunami, mass wasting, streams and floods, coastal hazards, deserts, drought, and wind, glaciers, and subsidence hazards. Each chapter covers terminology, technology, and statistics and impacts of catastrophic events. Descriptions of specific events . . . are also included. . . . This is a useful resource for any earth science curriculum." Libr Media Connect
Includes bibliographical references

363.4   Controversies related to public morals and customs

Haugen, David, 1969-
Legalized gambling; [by] David M. Haugen. Facts on File 2006 298p (Library in a book) $45
Grades: 11 12 Adult   363.4
1. Gambling
ISBN 0-8160-6054-1   LC 2005-8916
Contents: Introduction to legalized gambling -- The law and legalized gambling -- Chronology -- Biographical listing -- Glossary -- How to research legalized gambling issues -- Annotated bibliography -- Organizations and agencies
This is "an excellent introduction and overview of legalized gambling in the United States." Choice
Includes bibliographical references

Hill, Jeff
Prohibition. Omnigraphics 2004 xxv, 201p il (Defining moments) $38 *
Grades: 7 8 9 10   363.4
1. Prohibition
ISBN 0-7808-0768-5   LC 2004-22643
This book provides an "historical analysis of the Prohibition era (1920-33), including the politics of the Eighteenth Amendment; the Mob wars; the roles played by important public figures, from mobster Al Capone to Prohibition activist Carry Nation to President Warren Harding; and much more. . . . With a detailed glossary, a chronology, and an annotated bibliography, this is an important curriculum resource on the social and political history of an era." Booklist
Includes bibliographical references

Pornography: opposing viewpoints; Helen Cothran, book editor. Greenhaven Press 2002 186p il lib bdg $34.95; pa $23.70
Grades: 7 8 9 10   363.4
1. Pornography
ISBN 0-7377-0761-5 (lib bdg); 0-7377-0760-7 (pa)
                                   LC 2001-16036
"Opposing viewpoints series"
This collection of essays "addresses both sides of the following questions: 'Is Pornography Harmful?' 'Should Pornography Be Censored?' 'How Should Internet Pornography Be Regulated?' 'What Should Be the Feminist Stance on Pornography?'" SLJ
Includes bibliographical references

The **war** on drugs: opposing viewpoints; Tamara L. Roleff, book editor. Greenhaven Press 2004 222p il lib bdg $34.95; pa $23.70
Grades: 7 8 9 10   363.4
1. Drug abuse
ISBN 0-7377-2284-3 (lib bdg); 0-7377-2285-1 (pa)
                                               LC 2003-63063

"Opposing viewpoints series"
"Chapters in this . . . anthology include Is the War on Drugs Succeeding? Is There a Link Between the War on Drugs and Terrorism? Which Policies Are Working in the War on Drugs? [and] Should Illegal Drugs Be Legalized?" Publisher's note
Includes bibliographical references

363.46   Abortion

Abortion: opposing viewpoints; James D. Torr, book editor. Greenhaven Press 2006 192p il lib bdg $34.95; pa $23.70 *
Grades: 7 8 9 10   363.46
1. Abortion
ISBN 0-7377-2921-X (lib bdg); 0-7377-2922-8 (pa)
                                               LC 2005-46396

"Opposing viewpoints series"
"The viewpoints in this anthology debate Roe v. Wade, the ethics of abortion, and related issues in the following chapters: Is Abortion Immoral? How Does Abortion Affect Women? Should Abortion Rights Be Restricted? How Are Controversies Over Embryo Testing and Research Related to the Abortion Debate?" Publisher's note
Includes bibliographical references

The **abortion** rights movement; Meghan Powers, book editor. Greenhaven Press/Thomson/Gale 2006 154p il (American social movements) $34.95
Grades: 9 10 11 12   363.46
1. Pro-choice movement 2. Abortion
ISBN 0-7377-1947-8   LC 2005-46108
"This anthology of 18 articles, interviews, speeches, and personal narratives makes a case for abortion as central to women's pursuit of social equality. . . . This book is an eloquent, in-depth introduction to a crucial contemporary issue." Booklist
Includes bibliographical references

Abortion wars; a half century of struggle, 1950-2000; edited by Rickie Solinger. University of Calif. Press 1998 413p pa $21.95 hardcover o.p.
Grades: 11 12 Adult   363.46
1. Abortion
ISBN 0-520-20952-4 (pa)   LC 97-12261
"A collection of 18 essays written by abortion providers, journalists, reproductive-rights activists, legal strategists, and philosophers. In the introduction the editor makes it clear that the book is 'unabashedly a pro-rights book.' . . . The time line alone is so valuable that it's practically worth the price of the book." SLJ

Herring, Mark Youngblood, 1952-
The pro-life/choice debate; [by] Mark Herring. Greenwood Press 2003 200p il (Historical guides to controversial issues in America) $49.95 *
Grades: 9 10 11 12   363.46
1. Abortion
ISBN 0-313-31710-0   LC 2002-32073
"Herring examines the [abortion] issue from the debate's origin to its current state and expected future. Narrative chapters include discussions of the pro and con arguments associated with abortion, featuring quotes from doctors, politicians, religious figures, and ordinary people." Publisher's note
The author's "discussion of the moral, medical, and legal developments leading up to the modern feminist movement is particularly informative in framing the historical context of current debate . . . Herring writes clearly and presents each side of the debate objectively." Libr J
Includes bibliographical references

363.6   Public utilities and related services

Farabee, Charles R., Jr.
National park ranger; an American icon; {by} Charles R. "Butch" Farabee Jr. Roberts Rinehart Publishers 2003 180p il pa $18.95
Grades: 11 12 Adult   363.6
1. United States. National Park Service 2. National parks and reserves—United States
ISBN 1-570-98392-5   LC 2003-1022
"In this study of the vocation of park ranger since Maryland's park caretakers in 1696 to the present day, former ranger Farabee not only explores a ranger's role but also touches on the establishment of the National Park Service, the introduction of women rangers, and early resource management. Readers will enjoy the abundance of archival photographs, ranger profiles, and numerous other features." Libr J
Includes bibliographical references

363.7   Environmental problems

Air quality; [edited by Yael Calhoun]; foreword by David Seidelman. Chelsea House Publishers 2005 126p il (Environmental issues) $26.95 *
Grades: 9 10 11 12   363.7
1. Air pollution
ISBN 0-7910-8201-6   LC 2004-29003
This volume discusses air quality concerns and challenges with sections on health issues: pollution from transportation and industry and global dust

Blatt, Harvey
America's environmental report card; are we making the grade? MIT Press 2004 277p il maps $27.95; pa $13.95
Grades: 11 12 Adult   363.7
1. Environmental policy—United States
ISBN 0-262-02572-8; 0-262-52467-8 (pa)
                                               LC 2004-40261

Blatt, Harvey—*Continued*
The author "breaks down environmental issues into their components, describing different aspects of the problem, offering solutions and suggesting a prognosis. . . . Frank but hopeful, serious but readable, this is an excellent environmental science primer." Publ Wkly
Includes bibliographical references

Carson, Rachel, 1907-1964
Silent spring; introduction by Linda Lear; afterword by Edward O. Wilson. 40th anniversary ed. Houghton Mifflin 2002 378p il $24; pa $14 *
Grades: 11 12 Adult   363.7
1. Pesticides—Environmental aspects 2. Pesticides and wildlife
ISBN 0-618-25305-X; 0-618-24906-0 (pa)
"A Mariner book"
First published 1962
In The silent spring, Carson "contended that the indiscriminate use of weed killers and insecticides constituted a hazard to wildlife and to human beings. Her provocative work inspired many subsequent environmental studies." Reader's Ency. 4th edition

Climate change; Yael Calhoun, series editor; foreword by David Seidman. Chelsea House Publishers 2005 128p il (Environmental issues) $26.95 *
Grades: 9 10 11 12   363.7
1. Climate—Environmental aspects
ISBN 0-7910-8206-7   LC 2004-28993
Issues and challenges discussed in this anthology include greenhouse gases and the ozone layer, climate change effects on wildlife and climate change effects on water
Includes bibliographical references

The **Environment:** opposing viewpoints; Laura K. Egendorf, book editor. Greenhaven Press 2005 202p il (Opposing viewpoints series) $33.70; pa $26.20 *
Grades: 9 10 11 12   363.7
1. Pollution 2. Human ecology 3. Environmental policy—United States
ISBN 0-7377-2230-4; 0-7377-2231-2 (pa)
                                        LC 2004-49292
"Opposing viewpoints series"
This collection of essays offers varying viewpoints on environmental pollution and protection
Includes bibliographical references

Environmental encyclopedia; edited by Marci Bortman [et al.] 3rd ed. Gale Res. 2002 2v set $275
Grades: 11 12 Adult   363.7
1. Environmental sciences—Encyclopedias 2. Ecology—Encyclopedias 3. Earth sciences—Encyclopedias
ISBN 0-7876-5486-8
First published 1994
"Entries range from 100 to more than 2,000 words. Some are complemented by black-and-white photographs and diagrams. Each entry is signed, and topical coverage

includes a broad range of environmental perspectives, including scientific, political, and social issues. . . . Additional sections include a brief (five page) 'Historical Chronology' of environmental events, a five-page chronology of 'Environmental Legislation in the United States,' organizations mentioned within the bibliographies accompanying encyclopedia entries, and an index to entries and terms." Booklist

Environmental policy; Yael Calhoun, series editor; foreword by David Seideman. Chelsea House Publishers 2005 143p il (Environmental issues) $26.95
Grades: 9 10 11 12   363.7
1. Environmental policy—United States
ISBN 0-791-08205-9   LC 2004-28998
Environmental policy concerns discussed in this anthology include federal land policy, air quality policy and climate change policy
Includes bibliographical references

Flannery, Tim F. (Tim Fridjof), 1956-
The weather makers; how man is changing the climate and what it means for life on Earth; [by] Tim Flannery. Atlantic Monthly Press 2006 357p il maps $24; pa $15
Grades: 11 12 Adult   363.7
1. Climate 2. Greenhouse effect
ISBN 0-8711-3935-9; 0-8021-4292-3 (pa)
                                        LC 2005-52350
This is a "look at the connection between climate change and global warming." Publ Wkly
"This work is distinctive in its marriage of science to an act-now attitude and should energize environmentally minded readers." Booklist
Includes bibliographical references

Gardner, Robert, 1929-
Science projects about the environment and ecology. Enslow Pubs. 1999 112p il (Science projects) lib bdg $20.95
Grades: 7 8 9 10   363.7
1. Environmental protection 2. Ecology 3. Science—Experiments 4. Science projects
ISBN 0-89490-951-7   LC 98-35049
Presents experiments and projects suitable for science fairs, dealing with such aspects of the environment and ecology as the atmosphere, soil, water, plants, animals, and climate
"Each project is clearly outlined with a list of generally available supplies. The text [is] concise and informative." SLJ
Includes bibliographical references

Global warming; Shasta Gaughen, book editor. Greenhaven Press 2005 144p (Contemporary issues companion) lib bdg $33.70; pa $22.45
Grades: 9 10 11 12   363.7
1. Greenhouse effect
ISBN 0-7377-2651-2 (lib bdg); 0-7377-2652-0 (pa)
                                        LC 2004-49294
Various perspective on the issue of global warming are presented "including discussions of the research and

Global warming—*Continued*
science of global warming, the possible consequences of unchecked global warming, and potential solutions." Introduction

Includes bibliographical references

Global warming: opposing viewpoints; Cynthia A. Bily, book editor. Greenhaven Press 2006 208p il lib bdg $34.95; pa $23.70 *
Grades: 8 9 10 11 12   363.7
1. Greenhouse effect
ISBN 0-7377-2935-X (lib bdg); 0-7377-2936-8 (pa)
                                    LC 2005-52779
"Opposing viewpoints series"
"The essays address and assess the magnitude of the threat of global warming, its causes and effects, and the measures to be taken to combat it. The discussions range from SUVs to power plants to the Kyoto Protocol and solar flares. The points of view are radically divergent and promote excellent classroom discussion." SLJ

Includes bibliographical references

Grossman, Elizabeth, 1957-
High tech trash; digital devices, hidden toxins, and human health. Island Press/Shearwater Books 2006 334p $25.95
Grades: 11 12 Adult   363.7
1. Refuse and refuse disposal 2. Electronic apparatus and appliances
ISBN 1-55963-554-1; 978-1-55963-554-7
                                    LC 2006-4549
The author "traces the toxic substances (lead, mercury, phosphorus, brominated flame retardants, and others) used in digital devices, along with their health hazards. Each of the book's nine chapters has notes and references; there is also an appendix on how to recycle computers. . . . [Grossman] has made a valiant effort to consolidate the information that general, nontechnical readers interested in the subject . . . would find very useful." Sci Books Films

Includes bibliographical references

Hillstrom, Kevin
North America; a continental overview of environmental issues; {by} Kevin Hillstrom, Laurie Collier Hillstrom. ABC-CLIO 2003 xxiv, 296p il $65 *
Grades: 9 10 11 12   363.7
1. Human ecology 2. Human influence on nature
ISBN 1-576-07684-9   LC 2002-156276
"The work consists of a collection of descriptive and interpretive essays in 10 broad categories: 'Population and Land Use'; 'Biodiversity'; 'Parks, Preserves, and Protected Areas'; 'Forests'; 'Agriculture'; 'Freshwater'; 'Oceans and Coastal Areas'; 'Energy and Transportation'; 'Air Quality and the Atmosphere'; and 'Environmental Activism'. The writing is clear and straightforward, and while the authors are clearly environmentalists, the book avoids polemics . . . This is a good overview that is not overly technical but intellectually sound." Am Ref Books Annu, 2004

Includes bibliographical references

Is air pollution a serious threat to health? Andrea C. Nakaya, book editor. Greenhaven Press 2005 94p (At issue) lib bdg $28.70; pa $18.70
Grades: 9 10 11 12   363.7
1. Air pollution
ISBN 0-7377-2392-0 (lib bdg); 0-7377-2393-9 (pa)
                                    LC 2004-40532
The authors "present various opinions on the effect of air pollution on health in the United States and around the world and debate ways to address pollution problems." Introduction

Includes bibliographical references

Kidd, J. S. (Jerry S.)
Air pollution; problems and solutions; [by] J.S. Kidd and Renee A. Kidd. Chelsea House 2005 196p il (Science and society) $35
Grades: 7 8 9 10   363.7
1. Air pollution
ISBN 0-8160-5605-6   LC 2005-52791
First published 1998 with title: Into thin air
This book "shows how scientists and engineers are working to help policy makers solve the problems of atmospheric pollution. It discusses society's delicate relationship with science and technology and covers the role citizens play in pushing for an atmospheric environment that is as clean as possible." Publisher's note

Includes bibliographical references

Kolbert, Elizabeth
Field notes from a catastrophe; man, nature, and climate change. Bloomsbury Pub. 2006 210p il map $22.95 *
Grades: 11 12 Adult   363.7
1. Greenhouse effect 2. Climate
ISBN 1-59691-125-5; 978-1-59691-125-3
                                    LC 2005-30972
This investigation of global warming is an outgrowth of a three-part series (The Climate of Man) that appeared in The New Yorker in 2005. "The book is organized around notes Ms. Kolbert took on 'field trips,' not only to places where climate change is affecting the natural world but also to ones—labs, offices, observatories—where humans are trying to understand the phenomenon of human-induced global warming." N Y Times (Late NY Ed))
"On the burgeoning shelf of cautionary but occasionally alarmist books warning about the consequences of dramatic climate change, Kolbert's calmly persuasive reporting stands out for its sobering clarity." Publ Wkly

Includes bibliographical references

Lynas, Mark, 1973-
High tide; the truth about our climate crisis. Picador 2004 xxxiii, 345p il map pa $14
Grades: 11 12 Adult   363.7
1. Greenhouse effect
ISBN 0-312-30365-3   LC 2004-44661
"In a series of . . . travel narratives, Lynas shows the human side of global warming, taking readers to Britain, North and South America, China, and the South Pacific. He introduces them to folks whose houses and roads are

Lynas, Mark, 1973—*Continued*

falling crazily through melting permafrost, who are going hungry because fishing lakes have disappeared, and who are becoming refugees because their grasslands have turned to desert. . . . The author clearly explains why these are not isolated incidents, but interrelated parts of a worldwide set of phenomena that soon will affect us all." SLJ

Includes bibliographical references

Mongillo, John F.

Encyclopedia of environmental science; by John Mongillo and Linda Zierdt-Warshaw. Oryx Press 2000 450p il $99.95 *

Grades: 11 12 Adult   **363.7**

1. Environmental sciences—Encyclopedias

ISBN 1-57356-147-9   LC 00-32657

This encyclopedia covers "the major topics of agriculture, atmosphere, biomes, ecology, endangered plant and wildlife species, energy, law and regulations, water, and wetlands. . . . The 1000 entries are arranged alphabetically and range from several paragraphs to two pages in a clear and straightforward style with plenty of cross references." Libr J

Includes bibliographical references

Pollution: opposing viewpoints; Louise I. Gerdes, book editor. Greenhaven Press 2006 221p il lib bdg $34.95; pa $23.70 *

Grades: 7 8 9 10   **363.7**

1. Pollution

ISBN 0-7377-2949-X (lib bdg); 0-7377-2950-3 (pa)
LC 2005-45983

"Opposing viewpoints series"

"The authors in this . . . anthology debate several controversial questions, including whether various forms of pollution continue to be a serious problem, whether pollution poses a public health threat, and what policies and programs will best reduce pollution." Publisher's note

Includes bibliographical references

Royte, Elizabeth

Garbage land; on the secret trail of trash. Little, Brown 2005 311p $24.95; pa $14.99 *

Grades: 11 12 Adult   **363.7**

1. Refuse and refuse disposal

ISBN 0-316-73826-3; 0-316-15401-X (pa)
LC 2004-24732

The author presents "a cultural tour guided and informed by the things she throws away. Structured around four separate journeys—those of Royte's household trash, compostable matter, recyclables, and sewage—[this] is a literary investigation of the . . . dirty side of consumption." Publisher's note

"There's little waste in Royte's winning words. . . . Seldom has garbage been handled with such care." Christ Sci Monit

Includes bibliographical references

Tanaka, Shelley

Climate change. Groundwood Books 2006 144p il (Groundwork guides) $15.95

Grades: 8 9 10 11 12   **363.7**

1. Climate—Environmental aspects 2. Greenhouse effect

ISBN 978-0-88899-783-8; 0-88899-783-3

"House of Anansi Press"

This "presents background on Earth's climate and about how, primarily through humankind's carelessness, global warming has escalated to a point of major concern. . . . The book also considers strategies people and nations might take to reverse the destructive trends. . . . Many students needing material for reports or debates will want this for the well-documented information and handy, backpack-friendly size." Booklist

Includes glossary and bibliographical references

Water pollution; Yael Calhoun, series editor; foreword by David Seideman. Chelsea House Publishers 2005 xxv, 164p il (Environmental issues) $26.95

Grades: 9 10 11 12   **363.7**

1. Water pollution

ISBN 0-7910-8202-4   LC 2004-28992

This compilation examines water pollution issues and challenges with sections on rivers, streams, and wetlands; groundwater and drinking water and oceans

Includes bibliographical references

Wyman, Bruce C.

The Facts on File dictionary of environmental science; [by] Bruce Wyman, L. Harold Stevenson. new ed. Facts on File 2001 458p (Facts on File science library) $44; pa $17.95

Grades: 11 12 Adult   **363.7**

1. Environmental sciences—Dictionaries

ISBN 0-8160-4233-0; 0-8160-4234-9 (pa)
LC 00-55554

First published 1991 with authors names in reverse order

New edition in preparation

This dictionary contains over 4,000 cross-referenced entries reflecting the diversity of subjects that are relevant to the environmental field.

"Entries contain clear and mostly concise definitions, but with no sources given. Significant place-names (Love Canal, Three Mile Island), a few environmentalists (Thoreau) and organizations, with Web sites included in the entry, are all useful additions." Choice

364 Criminology

Alternatives to prisons; Jennifer Skancke, book editor. Greenhaven Press 2005 123p (At issue) lib bdg $28.70; pa $19.95 *

Grades: 9 10 11 12   **364**

1. Prisons—United States 2. Corrections 3. Administration of criminal justice

ISBN 0-7377-2693-8 (lib bdg); 0-7377-2694-6 (pa)
LC 2004-53500

"The contributors to this anthology explore the reasons behind the exploding prison population, whether prisons are a successful deterrent to crime, and the various alternatives to imprisonment—drug courts, mental health courts, electronic monitoring, family-based therapies, and restorative justice—that are currently available." Publisher's note

Includes bibliographical references

Crime and criminals: opposing viewpoints; James D. Torr, book editor. Greenhaven Press 2005 208p il $33.70; pa $22.45 *
Grades: 9 10 11 12   **364**
1. Crime 2. Criminals
ISBN 0-7377-2222-3; 0-7377-2223-1 (pa)
                                                          LC 2004-42416
"Opposing viewpoints series"
"The authors in this volume examine the factors that influence crime—focusing on the economy, prison and sentencing policies, and gun control laws—in the following chapters: What Causes Crime? Does Controlling Guns Control Crime? How Should the Criminal Justice System Be Reformed? How Can Crime Be Reduced?" Publisher's note
"Students (and teachers and librarians) will find themselves reaching often for this book. . . . Students will {also} find the Web sites particularly helpful for further research. A useful resource." SLJ
Includes bibliographical references

Famous American crimes and trials; edited by Frankie Y. Bailey and Steven Chermak. Praeger 2004 5v il (Praeger perspectives) set $375
Grades: 11 12 Adult   **364**
1. Administration of criminal justice
ISBN 0-275-98333-1   LC 2004-50548
Contents: v. 1. 1607-1859 -- v. 2. 1860-1912 -- v. 3. 1913-1959 -- v. 4. 1960-1980 -- v. 5. 1981-2000
This set "examines 70 cases, beginning in 1607 with the trial of accused heretic Quaker Mary Dyer and ending with the 2001 execution of convicted Oklahoma City bomber Timothy McVeigh. . . . This work has definite multidisciplinary appeal." Choice
Includes bibliographical references

Hanes, Richard Clay, 1946-
Crime and punishment in America, Almanac; [by] Richard C. Hanes and Sharon M. Hanes; Sarah Hermsen, project editor. UXL 2005 2v il (Crime and punishment in America reference library) set $110
Grades: 9 10 11 12   **364**
1. Crime—United States 2. Administration of criminal justice
ISBN 0-7876-9163-1   LC 2004-17067
This book "covers topics such as the development of the American justice system; types of crime (violent, property, white collar, organized, environmental); the court system; juvenile and military justice; and the effects of race and ethnicity." Booklist
Includes bibliographical references

Hanes, Sharon M.
Crime and punishment in America, Primary sources; Sarah Hermsen, project editor. UXL 2005 232, lxip il (Crime and punishment in America reference library) $60 *
Grades: 9 10 11 12   **364**
1. Crime—United States 2. Administration of criminal justice
ISBN 0-7876-9168-2   LC 2004-17068

This book "has excerpts from 18 interviews and documents. . . . Examples include the Magna Carta, 'The Plea of Clarence Darrow,' the RICO Act, and 'The Al-Qaeda Training Manual.' In addition to the excerpts, entries are supplemented by helpful material such as definitions of words used." Booklist
Includes bibliographical references

364.03   Criminology--Encyclopedias and dictionaries

Encyclopedia of crime and punishment; edited by David Levinson. Sage Publs. 2002 4v set $600
Grades: 11 12 Adult   **364.03**
1. Crime—Encyclopedias 2. Administration of criminal justice
ISBN 0-7619-2258-X   LC 2002-1220
"The 439 signed entries cover 13 major themes: crimes and related behaviors, law and justice, policing, forensics, corrections, victimology, punishment, social and cultural context, international aspects, concepts and theories, research methods and information, organizations and institutions, and special populations. . . . [This is] easy to understand and useful for beginning research in the field of criminal justice." Booklist

364.1   Criminal offenses

Altschiller, Donald
Hate crimes; a reference handbook. 2nd ed. ABC-CLIO 2005 247p (Contemporary world issues) $50 *
Grades: 9 10 11 12   **364.1**
1. Hate crimes
ISBN 1-85109-624-8   LC 2005-7151
First published 1999
This book "covers the alarming increase in hate crimes in the United States and abroad, and the legal, political, and educational efforts to combat intolerance and violence against minority group members." Publisher's note
Includes bibliographical references

Bugliosi, Vincent
Helter skelter; the true story of the Manson murders; {by} Vincent Bugliosi with Curt Gentry. 25th anniversary ed. Norton 1994 528p il $25; pa $13.95
Grades: 11 12 Adult   **364.1**
1. Manson, Charles, 1934- 2. Homicide
ISBN 0-393-08700-X; 0-393-32223-8 (pa)
                                                          LC 94-20957
A reissue of the title published 1974
"This book by the prosecutor at the Tate-LaBianca murder trial tells the inside story of the Manson Family murders, the investigations, and the trial." Libr J

Capote, Truman, 1924-1984
In cold blood; a true account of a multiple murder and its consequences. Random House 2002 343p $22; pa $13
Grades: 11 12 Adult   **364.1**
1. Hickock, Richard, 1931-1965 2. Smith, Perry, 1928-1965 3. Homicide
ISBN 0-375-50790-6; 0-679-74558-0 (pa)
LC 2002-282920
Also available Modern Library edition $15.95 (0-679-60023-X)
A reissue of the title first published 1966
"This edition is set from the first American edition of 1966 and commemorates the seventy-fifth anniversary of Random House"—Jacket
"Truman Capote called his account of the 1959 murder of a Kansas farm family a nonfiction novel. Using information he collected through interviews with towns-people and the killers, Capote created a vivid portrait of the criminals and graphically described the crime, the criminals' escape to Mexico, capture, trial, appeals, and hanging." HarperCollins Reader's Ency of Am Lit. 2nd edition

Crowe, Chris
Getting away with murder: the true story of the Emmett Till case. Phyllis Fogelman Bks. 2003 128p il map $18.99
Grades: 7 8 9 10   **364.1**
1. Till, Emmett 2. Lynching 3. Racism 4. Trials (Homicide) 5. Mississippi—Race relations
ISBN 0-8037-2804-2   LC 2002-5736
Contents: The boy who triggered the civil rights movement; Kicking the hornets' nest; The boy from Chicago; The wolf whistle; Setting the stage; Getting away with murder; Aftershocks
This is the story of "the black 14-year-old from Chicago who was brutally murdered while visiting relatives in the Mississippi Delta in 1954. . . . The gruesome, racially motivated crime and the court's failure to convict the white murderers was a powerful national catalyst for the civil rights movement. . . . Crowe's powerful, terrifying account does justice to its subject in bold, direct telling, supported by numerous archival photos and quotes from those who remember." Booklist
Includes bibliographical references

Dolnick, Edward, 1952-
The rescue artist; a true story of art, thieves, and the hunt for a missing masterpiece. HarperCollins Publishers 2005 270p il $25.95; pa $14.95
Grades: 11 12 Adult   **364.1**
1. Munch, Edvard, 1863-1944 2. Art thefts
ISBN   0-06-053117-7;   978-0-06-053117-1; 0-06-053118-5 (pa); 978-0-06053118-8 (pa)
LC 2004-62060
This is an "account of the 1994 theft of one of the world's most famous paintings, The Scream. . . . This is a tightly woven, fast-paced story." SLJ
Includes bibliographical references

Encyclopedia of murder and violent crime; Eric Hickey, editor. Sage Publications 2003 xxxv, 603p il $125 *
Grades: 9 10 11 12   **364.1**
1. Homicide—Encyclopedias 2. Violence—Encyclopedias
ISBN 0-7619-2437-X   LC 2003-1505
"This volume contains more than 200 signed entries from more than 116 contributions on a variety of topics related to violent crime and murder. The majority of the alphabetically arranged entries can be divided into two categories: biographies of murderers or violent groups and overviews of theories of violence, legal processes, or types of violence." Booklist
"This work provides a wealth of information to create a background for student research and analysis. . . . The information presented is well written and accurate." Lib Media Connect
Includes bibliographical references

Gangs; Scott Barbour, book editor. Greenhaven Press 2006 128p il map (Introducing issues with opposing viewpoints) $32.45
Grades: 7 8 9 10   **364.1**
1. Gangs
ISBN 0-7377-3221-0   LC 2005-40395
"In such chapters as, How Can Gang Violence Be Reduced? the issue is presented viewpoint by viewpoint, with an introduction and the author's credentials provided for each essay. Thought-provoking queries are given. . . . Fast Facts are also included. The book is heavily illustrated with color photos, cartoons, and tables. This informative book encourages active reading and makes research accessible for less-able students who are learning critical reading and research skills. A top resource for every library." SLJ

Gangs: opposing viewpoints; William Dudley and Louise I. Gerdes, book editors. Greenhaven Press 2005 206p il lib bdg $33.70; pa $22.45 *
Grades: 9 10 11 12   **364.1**
1. Gangs
ISBN 0-7377-2234-7 (lib bdg); 0-7377-2235-5 (pa)
LC 2004-52288
"Opposing viewpoints series"
"The authors . . . debate the nature and scope of the {street gang} problem, its causes, and what society and the justice system can do to reduce the problems associated with gangs." Publisher's note
Includes bibliographical references

Hate groups: opposing viewpoints; Mary E. Williams, editor. Greenhaven Press 2004 192p il lib bdg $34.95; pa $23.70 *
Grades: 7 8 9 10 11 12   **364.1**
1. Hate crimes
ISBN 0-7377-2280-0 (lib bdg); 0-7377-2281-9 (pa)
LC 2003-54324
"Opposing viewpoints series"
"Contributors debate whether hate groups pose a serious threat and whether extra penalties should be applied to hate crimes." Publisher's note
Includes bibliographical references

Henderson, Harry, 1951-
Internet predators. Facts on File 2005 298p
(Library in a book) $45 *
Grades: 11 12 Adult   **364.1**
1. Computer crimes
ISBN 0-8160-5739-7   LC 2004-27537
"The book covers cybercrime, cyberfraud, scams, buy-
a-bride, and of course pornography and its attendant sex-
ual predators, mainly pedophiles. . . . This book goes a
long way to providing an opening discussion to . . .
[this] important topic." Am Ref Books Annu, 2006
Includes bibliographical references

Innes, Brian, 1928-
Fakes & forgeries; the true crime stories of
history's greatest deceptions: the criminals, the
scams, and the victims. Reader's Digest 2005 256p
il $26.95
Grades: 11 12 Adult   **364.1**
1. Forgery 2. Swindlers and swindling 3. Fraud
ISBN 0-7621-0625-5   LC 2005-46462
"Was a diary found in 1991 truly written by Jack the
Ripper? Was a young woman rescued from a Berlin canal actually Anastasia, daughter of Tsar Nicholas II? The
answers to these questions and others are explored. . . .
[The author] divides his research into seven categories
and provides details on how each case was solved. . . .
The book is lively and engaging and will satisfy anyone
who enjoys solving a good true-crime story." Libr J

The **Kennedy** assassination; Charles W. Carey, Jr.,
    book editor. Greenhaven Press 2005 208p il
    (Interpreting primary documents) lib bdg $34.95
Grades: 7 8 9 10   **364.1**
1. Kennedy, John F. (John Fitzgerald), 1917-1963—
Assassination
ISBN 0-7377-2112-X   LC 2004-40610
This book takes a "look at what happened on the day
President Kennedy was shot, summarizes the various
government investigations into his death, and considers a
number of the 'conspiracy' theories." Publisher's note
Includes bibliographical references

Naimark, Norman M.
Fires of hatred; ethnic cleansing in
twentieth-century Europe. Harvard Univ. Press
2001 248p hardcover o.p. pa $18.50 *
Grades: 11 12 Adult   **364.1**
1. Genocide 2. Atrocities 3. Ethnic relations
4. Europe—History—20th century
ISBN 0-674-00313-6; 0-674-00994-0 (pa)
                                    LC 00-57500
This "comparative work explores five examples of the
brutal separation or elimination of people from territory
in central Europe since WWI, illuminating common patterns of 'ethnic cleansing' as a modern phenomenon. In
these case studies—Armenians and Greeks in Turkey,
Nazis and Jews, Soviet deportations of Chechens/Ingush
and Crimean Tatars, expulsions of Germans from
Czechoslovakia and Poland, and contemporary Balkan
warfare." Choice
Includes bibliographical references

Newton, Michael, 1951-
The encyclopedia of high-tech crime and
crime-fighting. Facts on File 2004 377p il $75
Grades: 9 10 11 12   **364.1**
1. Computer crimes 2. Computer viruses 3. Criminal
investigation
ISBN 0-8160-4978-5   LC 2002-192847
"The alphabetical listing of more than 420 entries provides information about crimes, criminals, and crime-
fighting techniques, covering topics such as airport security, DNA evidence, Internet fraud, and weapons. It also
includes . . . computer virus attacks . . . blood-spatter
analysis, {and} explosive detection devices. . . . This is
a very interesting and addictive book, one that will appeal to its intended audience, browsers and report writers
alike. Because of its comprehensive scope, this title
stands alone in its coverage of the topic." Libr Media
Connect
Includes bibliographical references

The encyclopedia of unsolved crimes. Facts on
File 2004 340p il (Facts on File crime library)
$75; pa $21.95
Grades: 11 12 Adult   **364.1**
1. Crime—Encyclopedias
ISBN 0-8160-4980-7; 0-8160-4981-5 (pa)
                                    LC 2003-64286
"Entries range from the obvious (Jack the Ripper) to
the obscure (Jack the Stripper); from political assassinations (Martin Luther King) to countless acts of violence
against African Americans, especially those involved in
the civil rights struggle; and from killings along American highways to unsolved crimes in other countries (the
Butcher of Mons). Each entry is impressively researched
and accessible; the JonBenet Ramsey and West Memphis
Three entries, in particular, are models of economy and
clarity." Choice
Includes bibliographical references

President Kennedy has been shot; by the
    Newseum with Cathy Trost and Susan Bennett.
    Sourcebooks 2003 300p il $29.95; pa $19.95 *
Grades: 11 12 Adult   **364.1**
ISBN 1-4022-0158-3; 1-4022-0317-9 (pa)
                                    LC 2003-15512
Accompanied by Audio CD
This is a "multimedia reliving of Kennedy's assassination, beginning with Air Force One landing at Love Field
and ending with the president's internment at Arlington
National Cemetery. The commentaries from some of the
nation's foremost journalists, including Mike Wallace,
Dan Rather, and Walter Cronkite, have a clarity, drama,
and intensity that only newsmen of their stature can provide. . . . The book-CD combination is so well done that
many readers will feel as if they have experienced that
fateful day." SLJ
Includes bibliographical references

Sexual violence: opposing viewpoints; Helen
    Cothran, book editor. Greenhaven Press 2003
    218p il lib bdg $32.45; pa $21.20
Grades: 9 10 11 12   **364.1**
1. Sex crimes 2. Rape 3. Violence
ISBN 0-7377-1240-6 (lib bdg); 0-7377-1239-2 (pa)
                                    LC 2002-34728
"Opposing viewpoints series"

Sexual violence: opposing viewpoints—*Continued*
First published 1997
"Topics covered include rape, heterosexual pornography, pedophilia (especially by adults whose jobs include daily interaction with children), castration, battered woman syndrome, and rape-shield laws. . . . Except for one brief, compelling example of domestic violence in a lesbian relationship, same-sex situations are not addressed; and . . . abuse by priests is only glossed over here. But, overall, this book provides a varied, often enlightening, discussion of an often hidden problem." Booklist
Includes bibliographical references

364.36 Juvenile delinquents

Juvenile crime: opposing viewpoints; Andrea C. Nakaya, book editor. Greenhaven Press 2005 208p il map lib bdg $34.95; pa $23.70 *
Grades: 9 10 11 12 **364.36**
1. Juvenile delinquency
ISBN 0-7377-2945-7 (lib bdg); 0-7377-2946-5 (pa)
LC 2005-40320
"Opposing viewpoints series"
"This anthology investigates causes and possible solutions to the problem of juvenile crime." Publisher's note
Includes bibliographical references

364.6 Penology

Banks, Cyndi
Punishment in America; a reference handbook. ABC-CLIO 2005 319p il (Contemporary world issues) $50 *
Grades: 9 10 11 12 **364.6**
1. Punishment 2. Administration of criminal justice
ISBN 1-85109-676-0 LC 2005-659
"From the Salem witch trials to death row, this work is . . . [an] analysis of the evolution of punishment practices, policies, and problems in America." Publisher's note
Includes bibliographical references

364.66 Capital punishment

Capital punishment; Mary E. Williams, book editor. Greenhaven Press 2005 174p (Current controversies) lib bdg $33.70; pa $22.45 *
Grades: 9 10 11 12 **364.66**
1. Capital punishment
ISBN 0-7377-2200-2 (lib bdg); 0-7377-2201-0 (pa)
LC 2004-47486
Among the topics discussed are "arguments concerning the ethics, fairness, and deterrent effects of the death penalty in the United States." Introduction

The **Death** penalty; Jean Alicia Elster, book editor. Greenhaven Press 2005 237p (History of issues) lib bdg $34.95; pa $23.70 *
Grades: 9 10 11 12 **364.66**
1. Capital punishment—United States
ISBN 0-7377-1911-7 (lib bdg); 0-7377-1912-5 (pa)
LC 2004-43661

"This volume explores the history of capital punishment in America from the 17th century to the present while covering such . . . topics as cruel and unusual punishment, deterrence, race and gender discrimination, the morality of state-sanctioned killing, and protecting the innocent defendant." Publisher's note
Includes bibliographical references

The **Death** penalty; Lauri S. Friedman, book editor. Greenhaven Press 2006 144p il (Introducing issues with opposing viewpoints) lib bdg $32.45
Grades: 9 10 11 12 **364.66**
1. Capital punishment—United States
ISBN 0-7377-3341-1 LC 2005-40401
"This collection of articles helps students hone in on the main arguments that are used to support and to condemn the death penalty." Publisher's note
Includes bibliographical references

The **death** penalty: opposing viewpoints; Diane Andrews Henningfeld, book editor; Bonnie Szumski, publisher; Helen Cothran, managing editor. Greenhaven Press 2006 223p il $34.95; pa $23.70
Grades: 8 9 10 11 12 **364.66**
1. Capital punishment
ISBN 0-7377-2929-5; 0-7377-2930-9 (pa)
LC 2005052743
"Opposing viewpoints series"
"Powerful people and organizations contribute essays to the death-penalty debate. Supreme Court Justice Antonin Scala argues that the death penalty is just, and his former colleague, Sandra Day O'Connor, debates whether juveniles should be exempt from it. This nonbiased, comprehensive look at one of today's most difficult issues will be helpful for students writing persuasive essays and for debate groups." SLJ
Includes bibliographical references

Essig, Mark Regan, 1969-
Edison & the electric chair; a story of light and death; {by} Mark Essig. Walker & Co. 2003 358p il $26; pa $15
Grades: 11 12 Adult **364.66**
1. Edison, Thomas A. (Thomas Alva), 1847-1931
2. Capital punishment
ISBN 0-8027-1406-4; 0-8027-7710-4 (pa)
LC 2003-52507
This describes Thomas Edison's part in developing the electric chair for executions in 1889
"Essig relates Edison's furtive hand in the advent of the chair with flair, skill, and gallows humor." Booklist
Includes bibliographical references

The **Ethics** of capital punishment; Nick Fisanick, book editor. Greenhaven Press 2005 128p (At issue) lib bdg $27.45; pa $18.70 *
Grades: 9 10 11 12 **364.66**
1. Capital punishment
ISBN 0-7377-2338-6 (lib bdg); 0-7377-2339-4 (pa)
LC 2004-54352

The Ethics of capital punishment—*Continued*

This compilation of articles demonstrates "how the is-sue of capital punishment often presents people—even those with strong opinions on justice, the value of life, and the role of government—with ethical dilemmas." Introduction

Includes bibliographical references

Henderson, Harry, 1951-

Capital punishment. 3rd ed. Facts on File 2006 316p il (Library in a book) $45 *

Grades: 11 12 Adult   **364.66**

1. Capital punishment

ISBN 0-8160-5708-7   LC 2005-13671

First published 1991 under the authorship of Stephen A. Flanders

A look at both sides of this controversial issue from social, political, ethical, and religious perspectives. Includes a glossary, bibliographies, and Internet sources.

Includes bibliographical references

Kurtis, Bill

The death penalty on trial; crisis in American justice. Public Affairs 2004 218p $25; pa $13.95

Grades: 11 12 Adult   **364.66**

1. Capital punishment

ISBN 1-58648-169-X; 1-58648-446-X (pa)

     LC 2004-50564

The author "re-examines his lifelong support of the death penalty, arguing eloquently that the risk of executing the wrong person is too great to let capital punishment stand. His reflections are motivated by the 2003 actions of then governor George Ryan of Illinois . . . who commuted the sentences of the state's 164 death row inmates. Ryan's actions followed the exoneration through DNA evidence of 13 death row inmates. Kurtis frames his argument around two trials in which the wrong men were first convicted and then exonerated." Publ Wkly

Thompson, Bruce E. R., 1952-

The Greenhaven encyclopedia of capital punishment; Mary Jo Poole, consulting editor. Greenhaven Press/Thomson/Gale 2005 336p il (Greenhaven encyclopedia of) $76.20

Grades: 9 10 11 12   **364.66**

1. Capital punishment—Encyclopedias

ISBN 0-7377-2174-X   LC 2004-27429

This "resource offers historical, legal, and biographical entries related to the subject. Students will learn which Bible verses are most quoted in arguments for and against the death penalty; read about 'Monsieur New York,' one of history's most skilled hangmen; and find out about the role of DNA analysis in exoneration, among other topics." SLJ

Includes bibliographical references

365   Penal and related institutions

America's prisons: opposing viewpoints; Clare Hanrahan, book editor. Greenhaven Press 2006 203p il map lib bdg $34.95; pa $23.70 *

Grades: 8 9 10 11 12   **365**

1. Prisons—United States

ISBN 0-7377-3344-6 (lib bdg); 0-7377-3345-4 (pa)

     LC 2005-52659

"Opposing viewpoints series"

"This collection of opposing viewpoints provides students an opportunity to weigh the merits of arguments that support or oppose the operation of America's prisons." Publisher's note

Includes bibliographical references

Ferro, Jeffrey

Prisons. Facts on File 2006 314p il (Library in a book) $45 *

Grades: 11 12 Adult   **365**

1. Prisons—United States

ISBN 0-8160-6035-5   LC 2005-3370

The author "gives an overview of American penitentiaries, tracking the history of prisons and punishments and offering thumbnail biographies of notorious criminals and law enforcers. . . . The title's value is that everything is found in one concise unit." Libr J

Includes bibliographical references

How should prisons treat inmates? Kristen Bailey, book editor. Greenhaven Press 2005 95p (At issue) $28.70; pa $19.95

Grades: 9 10 11 12   **365**

1. Prisoners—Civil rights

ISBN 0-7377-2719-5; 0-7377-2720-9 (pa)

     LC 2004-54218

"The viewpoints in this volume explore issues such as inmates' right to vote, privatization of prisons, the necessity of super maximum security, and the general question of how prisoners should be treated on a day-to-day basis." Publisher's note

Includes bibliographical references

Hubner, John

Last chance in Texas; the redemption of criminal youth. Random House 2005 xxv, 277p $25.95

Grades: 11 12 Adult   **365**

1. Giddings State School (Tex.) 2. Juvenile delinquency

ISBN 0-375-50809-0   LC 2005-42892

This book is "about the Capital Offenders Group treatment program at Texas's Giddings State School. The institution houses nearly 400 of the most violent juvenile offenders in a program designed to alter the life trajectory of its residents." SLJ

"Readers of this eye-opening account will find themselves reflecting on their own attitudes about juvenile justice as it's administered today." Booklist

Prisons; James Haley, book editor. Greenhaven Press 2005 192p (Current controversies) lib bdg $34.95; pa $23.70
Grades: 9 10 11 12   365
1. Prisons—United States
ISBN 0-7377-2214-2 (lib bdg); 0-7377-2215-0 (pa)
LC 2004-47433
"Whether increased incarnation has reduced crime, how prisoners are being treated, and the rise of prison labor are among the issues under discussion in this anthology." Publisher's note

370   Education

Unger, Harlow G., 1931-
Encyclopedia of American education. 3rd ed. Facts on File 2007 3v il (Facts on File library of American history) set $250 *
Grades: 11 12 Adult   370
1. Education—United States—Encyclopedias
ISBN 0-8160-6887-9; 978-0-8160-6887-6
LC 2006-22174
First published 1996
This encyclopedia "contains more than 2,000 entries spanning the colonial period to the present. This . . . [reference provides information on different aspects] of education, from the evolution of school curriculum, education funding, and church-state controversies to . . . debates on multiculturalism, prayer in school, and sex education." Publisher's note
Includes bibliographical references

370.117   Multicultural education and bilingual education

Bilingual education; Loreta Medina, book editor. Greenhaven Press 2004 79p (At issue) lib bdg $27.45; pa $18.70 *
Grades: 9 10 11 12   370.117
1. Bilingual education
ISBN 0-7377-1605-3 (lib bdg); 0-7377-1606-1 (pa)
LC 2003-44863
"The anthology presents the arguments for and against bilingual education as an educational tool in helping school children that have limited proficiency in English, learn English early in school." Publisher's note
Includes bibliographical references

371   Schools & their activities; special education

Education: opposing viewpoints. Greenhaven Press 2005 191p il lib bdg $33.70; pa $22.45 *
Grades: 9 10 11 12   371
1. Public schools 2. School choice
ISBN 0-7377-2228-2 (lib bdg); 0-7377-2229-0 (pa)
LC 2004-42454
"Opposing viewpoints series"

"Standardized testing, No Child Left Behind, diversity, and character education are among the topics covered in this . . . anthology. Chapters include: What is the State of Education? Are Alternatives to Public Education Viable? What Role Should Religious and Moral Values Play in Public Education? How Could Public Education Be Improved?" Publisher's note
Includes bibliographical references

371.3   Methods of instruction and study

Directory of distance learning opportunities, K-12; compiled by Modoc Press, Inc. Greenwood Press 2003 302p $69.95
Grades: 11 12 Adult   371.3
1. Distance education—Directories 2. Correspondence schools and courses
ISBN 1-573-56515-6   LC 2002-35210
"An Oryx book"
"Designed for librarians, parents, and school counselors looking for information on specific K-12 distance learning courses of study, this work contains an overview of the current status of distance education in the U.S. and in-depth information on more than 6,000 courses offered by 154 U.S. institutions and consortia. . . . Both print-based (correspondence study) and electronic (via the Internet, satellite broadcast, or interactive television) programs are included. . . . This directory is sure to be a welcome addition in public and school libraries. Nothing else pulls so much information together in one print source." Booklist

371.7   Student welfare

Aronson, Elliot
Nobody left to hate; teaching compassion after Columbine. Freeman, W.H. 2000 194p pa $12.95 hardcover o.p.
Grades: 9 10 11 12   371.7
1. School violence 2. Interpersonal relations
ISBN 0-8050-7099-0 (pa)   LC 00-10462
The author "argues that the negative atmosphere in our schools—the exclusion, taunting, humiliation, and bullying—played a major role in triggering the pathological behavior of the shooters {at Columbine High School. This book offers} . . . strategies for creating a more supportive, stimulating, and compassionate environment in our schools." Publisher's note
Includes bibliographical references

Hester, Joseph P.
Public school safety; a handbook, with a resource guide. McFarland & Co. 2003 200p pa $35
Grades: professional   371.7
1. School violence 2. Education—Government policy
ISBN 0-7864-1483-9   LC 2003-2511
Contents: The state of youth violence and its roots; Public school safety, government initiatives; Strategies for building a school safety program; Measures to ensure

Hester, Joseph P.—*Continued*
school safety, model programs; Building a leadership culture; National resources for safe school programs; Resources for the Surgeon General's report
This "begins by discussing a number of important government reports that have identified the problems and causes of youth violence and some ideas for combating it. . . . The myriad strategies involving the community, parents, and teachers are discussed and both ineffective and effective programs are evaluated. . . . This is a solid and thorough guide." SLJ
Includes bibliographical references

How can school violence be prevented? Scott Barbour, book editor. Greenhaven Press 2005 80p (At issue) lib bdg $28.70; pa $19.95 *
Grades: 9 10 11 12   **371.7**
1. School violence
ISBN 0-7377-2382-3 (lib bdg); 0-7377-2383-1 (pa)
LC 2004-42514
In this anthology the authors examine the issue of school violence "and debate the best way to head off tragedies similar to those that have occurred in Columbine, Red Lion, Rocori, and other schools across the nation." Introduction

Hunnicutt, Susan
School shootings; Susan Hunnicutt, book editor. Greenhaven Press 2006 102p (At issue) lib bdg $28.70; pa $19.95
Grades: 9 10 11 12   **371.7**
1. School violence
ISBN 0-7377-2416-1 (lib bdg); 978-0-7377-2416-5 (lib bdg); 0-7377-2417-X (pa); 978-0-7377-2417-2 (pa)
LC 2005-54525
"This anthology explores various explanations for rampage school shootings, and examines ways communities have responded." Publisher's note
Includes bibliographical references

Orr, Tamra
Violence in our schools; halls of hope, halls of fear. Franklin Watts 2003 192p il $29.50
Grades: 7 8 9 10   **371.7**
1. School violence
ISBN 0-531-12268-9   LC 2003-104
Chronicles school violence and discusses its causes, perpetrators, and solutions, including "Questions to ponder" and specific advice for individual action
"This book takes an evenhanded, enlightening look at the problem of, and possible solutions for, school violence. . . . For students doing research, the book offers succinct summaries of incidents of school violence dating back to the 1920s, and it includes an overview of the Columbine tragedy. . . . For sociology research and for schools seeking proactive ideas for creating safe and inclusive campuses, this is an excellent resource." Booklist
Includes bibliographical references

School violence; Kate Burns, book editor. Greenhaven Press 2005 171p (Contemporary issues companion) lib bdg $33.70; pa $22.45 *
Grades: 9 10 11 12   **371.7**
1. School violence
ISBN 0-7377-3075-7 (lib bdg); 0-7377-3076-5 (pa)
LC 2004-47410
In addition to discussions about race and school violence, this title provides an "assortment of research and commentary that has come into circulation since the Columbine school massacre in 1999. {Included are} sections addressing the nature, causes, and prevention of school violence." Introduction
Includes bibliographical references

371.82   Specific kinds of students

Tooley, James
The miseducation of women. Continuum 2002 258p $44.95; pa $39.95
Grades: 9 10 11 12   **371.82**
1. Women—Education 2. Feminism
ISBN 0-8264-5094-6; 0-8264-5095-4 (pa)
Also available in paperback from Ivan R. Dee
The author "takes to task the U.S. and British educational systems for succumbing to feminists in the last 30 years and misdirecting young women into early careers instead of marriage and motherhood. . . . First published in England to scathing criticism, this book is sure to spark vociferous debate in the U.S. as well." Booklist
Includes bibliographical references

371.9   Special education

Cohen, Leah Hager
Train go sorry; inside a deaf world. Vintage Bks. 1995 296p pa $14.95
Grades: 11 12 Adult   **371.9**
1. Lexington School for the Deaf (New York, N.Y.)
2. Deaf—Means of communication
ISBN 0-679-76165-9   LC 94-23501
First published 1994 by Houghton Mifflin
"Cohen draws upon her experiences as the hearing grandchild of deaf immigrants to combine personal stories of hearing-impaired individuals with related aspects of deaf culture. Using her first home and her father's place of employment, the Lexington School for the Deaf in New York City, to connect characters and experiences, she shares tales of activities familiar to young adults." Libr J
"Well organized and beautifully written." Booklist

Conroy, Pat
The water is wide. Dial Press Trade Paperbacks 2006 294p pa $14
Grades: 11 12 Adult   **371.9**
1. Socially handicapped children 2. African Americans—Education 3. Public schools—South Carolina
ISBN 978-0-553-38157-3; 0-553-38157-1
LC 2005-285152
Also available in paperback from Bantam Bks.

Conroy, Pat—*Continued*
First published 1972 by Houghton Mifflin
"A young white teacher goes to an island off the coast of South Carolina to teach a group of functionally illiterate black children. Yamacraw Island is backward and primitive, a world for the most part left untouched by the 20th Century. . . . By ignoring the textbooks and concentrating on meaningful situations and dialogue . . . he begins to make headway. He also, unfortunately arouses the ire of the powers that be and, after fierce struggle, is fired." Libr J

A **Guide** to high school success for students with disabilities; edited by Cynthia Ann Bowman and Paul T. Jaeger; foreword by Chris Crutcher. Greenwood Press 2004 181p $45 *
Grades: 9 10 11 12   **371.9**
1. Handicapped students 2. Academic achievement
ISBN 0-313-32832-3   LC 2004-53041
"The book covers a wide array of issues including handling difficult teachers, advocating for self, setting high expectations for self and others, use of the library and media centers, extracurricular activities, dating and sexuality, and life after high school. . . . This is a good read for students, parents, and teachers alike." Choice
Includes bibliographical references

Paquette, Penny Hutchins
Learning disabilities; the ultimate teen guide; {by} Penny Hutchins Paquette, Cheryl Gerson Tuttle. Scarecrow Press 2003 301p il (It happened to me) lib bdg $32.50; pa $17.95 *
Grades: 7 8 9 10   **371.9**
1. Learning disabilities
ISBN 0-8108-4261-0 (lib bdg); 0-8108-5643-3 (pa)
                                  LC 2002-17588
This provides an "overview of the most common disabilities. . . . The book also teaches students how to advocate for themselves, informing them of their rights under law both during the school years and after high school graduation. . . . Assistive technology that can help students improve their learning abilities such as Optical Character Recognition (OCR) systems, screen reading software, books on tape, electronic notebooks, and other tools that aid student learning are covered." Publisher's note
"Far more detailed than similiar books from other publishers." Voice Youth Advocates
Includes bibliographical references

371.95 Gifted students

Karnes, Frances A.
Competitions for talented kids; win scholarships, big prize money, and recognition; [by] Frances A. Karnes & Tracy L. Riley. Prufrock Press 2005 245p pa $17.95 *
Grades: 7 8 9 10 11 12   **371.95**
1. Contests 2. Gifted children
ISBN 1-59363-156-1
"Featuring more than 140 competitions focused on a wide range of academic subjects, studio arts, performing arts, leadership, and service learning, this volume encourages students to seek scholarships, prize money, and recognition for their talents." Booklist
Includes bibliographical references

372.6 Language arts (Communication skills)

De Vos, Gail, 1949-
Storytelling for young adults; a guide to tales for teens. 2nd ed. Libraries Unlimited 2003 208p $35
Grades: Professional   **372.6**
1. Storytelling 2. School libraries—Activity projects 3. Books and reading
ISBN 1-563-08903-3   LC 2003-51648
First published 1991
This is a "collection of recommended stories for young adults . . . Brief synopses of the stories are arranged in themed chapters about the fantastic, laughter, folktales, tales of life, tales of the spirit, and tales of the arts and sciences. A few samples are given in their entirety. Author, theme, and title indexes are included as well as a list of the story collections in which the tales appear . . . The strength of this text is that the author has been storytelling with teens for fifteen years, so the recommended stories have the force of being 'tried and true' with this age group . . . It will be helpful for the beginning storyteller in choosing material, particularly in the school setting, and for educators who are trying to find popular stories for the teen audience." Voice Youth Advocates
Includes bibliographical references

373.1 Organization and activities in secondary education

Bluestein, Jane
High school's not forever; [by] Jane Bluestein and Eric Katz. HCI Teens 2005 302p il pa $12.95 *
Grades: 7 8 9 10 11 12   **373.1**
1. High school students
ISBN 0-7573-0256-4   LC 2005-50232
"Culled from the responses of some 2000 high and post-high school students, this title gives voice to young people who have lived through the experience and who offer both affirming and cautionary tales as they attempted to navigate the uncertain seas of friendship, depression, academic achievement, drugs, and sexuality. . . . There is no question that this book will enhance most YA collections." SLJ
Includes bibliographical references

Braun, Linda W.
Teens, technology, and literacy; or, Why bad grammar isn't always bad. Libraries Unlimited 2007 105p il pa $30
Grades: Professional **373.1**
1. Literacy 2. Teenagers—Books and reading 3. Bibliographic instruction 4. Computer-assisted instruction 5. Information technology
ISBN 1-59158-368-3; 978-1-59158-368-4
LC 2006-31714
"Braun shows teachers, administrators, and librarians how to incorporate today's technologies into the development of literacy skills. The author backs up the grammar used in IMs and text messaging by explaining how these technologies promote better literacy in the classroom. . . . This book is a must for most collections." SLJ
Includes bibliographical references

375 Curricula

Managing curriculum and assessment; a practitioner's guide; [by] Beverly Nichols . . . [et al.] Linworth Publishing 2006 170p pa $49.95
Grades: Professional **375**
1. Education—Curricula 2. Evaluation
ISBN 1-58683-216-6 LC 2006003202
"This is a guide by practitioners who give advice on how to respond to the laws and requirements of No Child Left Behind. It is an invaluable resource that provides new insights. . . . There are three sections to the guide with an accompanying CD that contains everything in the book and more. . . . This guide is loaded with examples and is a must have for your professional library." Libr Media Connect
Includes bibliographical references

378 Higher education

Balaban, Mariah, 1977-
Study away; the unauthorized guide to college abroad; {by} Mariah Balaban and Jennifer Shields. Anchor Bks. (NY) 2003 319p il pa $13.95
Grades: 11 12 Adult **378**
1. Foreign study—Directories
ISBN 1-4000-3189-3 LC 2003-52172
This guide provides facts about 70 "college programs, in 28 countries around the globe. . . . Entries for each school, organized alphabetically by country, include brief mention of campus location, academic and social life, admissions policies, and housing, with an 'At a Glance' box giving figures . . . for enrollment, tuition . . . and faculty-student ratio. . . . For curious students the book is a good place to start." Booklist

Berent, Polly
Getting ready for college. Random House 2003 209p il pa $12.95
Grades: 9 10 11 12 **378**
1. College students 2. Colleges and universities—United States
ISBN 0-8129-6896-4 LC 2003-41375

This "manual includes day planners, notes on how to take notes, tips on how to make a 'real life' file, and advice from scores of college students in the trenches as well as campus health-care professionals, college counselors, administrators, and financial-aid advisers." Publisher's note
This "will be useful to any young person getting ready to enter the college milieu. It's a quick, easy read, enriched by quotes from teens." Booklist

Cohen, Katherine
Rock hard apps; how to write a killer college application. Hyperion 2003 273p pa $16.95 *
Grades: 9 10 11 12 **378**
1. College applications
ISBN 0-7868-6862-7 LC 2003-44994
"Cohen deconstructs, then reconstructs the applications of three real Ivy-League-college-bound kids, working in enough about their backgrounds to give context to the advice she provides on recommendations, the 'brag' sheet, essays, etc." Booklist

The truth about getting in; a top college advisor tells you everything you need to know. Hyperion 2002 252p $21.95; pa $14.95 *
Grades: 9 10 11 12 **378**
1. College applications 2. Colleges and universities—Entrance requirements
ISBN 0-7868-8747-8; 0-7868-8849-0 (pa)
LC 2003-266705
"Chapters cover a wide variety of topics—from gathering information about colleges and preparing for admissions tests to writing an effective essay and securing financial aid. . . . Cohen's approach is pleasant and positive." Booklist

Coplin, William D.
10 things employers want you to learn in college; the know-how you need to succeed; {by} Bill Coplin. Ten Speed Press 2003 259p pa $14.95
Grades: 9 10 11 12 **378**
1. Vocational education 2. Vocational guidance
ISBN 1-580-08524-5 LC 2003-4083
Contents: The ten know-how groups (plus extra credit): Work ethic; Kick yourself in the butt; Be honest; Manage your time; Manage your money; Physical skills; Stay well; Look good; Type 35 wpm error free; Take legible notes; Verbal communications; Converse one-on-one; Present to groups; Use visual displays; Written communications; Write well; Proof and edit; Use word processing tools; Send information electronically; Working directly with people; Build good relationships; Work in teams; Teach; Influencing people; Manage; Sell; Politick; Lead; Gathering information; Use library holdings; Use commercial databases; Search the Web; Conduct interviews; Use surveys; Keep and use records; Quantitative tools; Use numbers; Use graphs and tables; Use spreadsheet programs; Asking and answering the right questions; Detect BS; Pay attention to detail; Apply knowledge; Evaluate actions and policies; Problem-solving; Identify problems; Create solutions; Launch
"This outstanding resource provides an overview of what the optimal college experience is about. All col-

Coplin, William D.—*Continued*
lege-bound students should be required to read this book." Voice Youth Advocates
Includes bibliographical references

Eye on apply; six true stories of college admissions; by the staff of The Princeton Review. Random House 2004 242p pa $15.95 *
Grades: 9 10 11 12   378
1. College applications
ISBN 0-375-76426-7   LC 2004-303198
At head of title: The Princeton Review
"During 2002, the Princeton Review posted journal entries online by six high school juniors. The postings continued throughout their senior year and gave birth to this work, designed to assist students through the college application process. . . . A useful and thought-provoking book." SLJ

Fiske, Edward B.
The Fiske guide to getting into the right college; {by} Edward B. Fiske & Bruce G. Hammond. Sourcebooks 2002 257p pa $14.95 *
Grades: 11 12 Adult   378
1. College choice 2. Colleges and universities—Entrance requirements 3. Colleges and universities—Finance
ISBN 1-57071-906-3   LC 2001-57590
First published 1997 by Times Bks.
New edition in preparation
"Information on everything from interviews to standardized tests, college essays, and financing is included, along with a handy 'road map' of institutions, organized into such categories as 'Small College Bargains,' 'Most Innovative Curriculums,' and 'Colleges for Students with Learning Disabilities.' In addition, there is a selective roundup of listings by subject specialty. . . . Further resources, including Web sites, appear in a separate chapter. In all, this is a first-rate introduction that will help students narrow the field while still allowing them to cover the territory." Booklist {review of 1997 edition}

Gottesman, Greg
College survival; [by] Greg Gottesman, Daniel Baer, and friends; [illustrations by Steve Ojemann] 7th ed. Thomson/Peterson's 2004 246p il pa $14.95 *
Grades: 9 10 11 12   378
1. College students 2. Colleges and universities—United States
ISBN 0-7689-1444-2   LC 2004-558549
"An Arco book"
First published 1991 by Macmillan. Periodically revised
Written by students for students and illustrated with cartoons, this guide presents ideas for coping with college life. Such subjects as clothing, choosing classes, time management, test-taking, dating, and roommates are addressed

Hernandez, Michele A.
Acing the college application; how to maximize your chances for admission to the college of your choice; {by} Michele Hernandez. Ballantine Bks. 2002 222p pa $13.95
Grades: 9 10 11 12   378
1. College applications
ISBN 0-345-45409-X   LC 2002-67570
New edition in preparation
The author "looks first at filling out the activities section, following with tips on writing the main and supplementary essays—including polishing the style ('eliminate almost every adjective and adverb'), selecting a subject, and injecting passion and enthusiasm into the work. Many sample essays illustrate her points. In addition, she includes a . . . section on the personal interview, which not only takes some of the fear out of the process but also explains how teens can use the opportunity to best advantage. A useful addition to the college shelf." Booklist

Jell, John R.
From school to a career; a student's guide to success in the real world; [by] John Jell. ScarecrowEducation 2005 77p il pa $10.95 *
Grades: 9 10 11 12   378
1. Vocational education 2. Vocational guidance
ISBN 1-57886-213-2   LC 2004-21308
The author "offers practical advice for how to develop good job skills while in college. He discusses . . . time management, the importance of both formal and informal learning, what makes for relevant work experience in a future career field, and networking. . . . The professional language is easy for teens to understand and sets a good example of how a job seeker or serious college student should speak and write." Voice Youth Advocates

Kaufman, Daniel, 1968-
Essays that will get you into college; by Daniel Kaufman, Chris Dowhan, Adrienne Dowhan. 2nd ed. Barron's 2003 166p il pa $11.95 *
Grades: 9 10 11 12   378
1. College applications
ISBN 0-7641-2034-4; 978-0-7641-2034-3
                                      LC 2003-48039
First published 1998 under the authorship of Amy Burnham, Daniel Kaufman and Chris Dowhan
"The authors discuss everything from assessing one's audience to revising and proofreading. The book also offers advice from admissions officers and college professionals. They explain exactly what they want to see in a college admissions essay. Many college-bound students will want to pick up this book because of the information provided in chapter four. Twenty-five admissions essays were graded, ranked, and commented on by a panel of judges. These essays are wonderful examples of what admissions officers expect and what will not make the grade." Voice Youth Advocates

The **Latino** student's guide to college success; edited by Leonard A. Valverde. Greenwood Press 2002 212p lib bdg $39.95; pa $29.95 *
Grades: 9 10 11 12 **378**
1. Hispanic Americans—Education 2. Colleges and universities—United States
ISBN 0-313-31113-7 (lib bdg); 0-313-31960-X (pa)
LC 00-64062
"After outlining the steps to take in finding and working toward success at a program of study, 10 Latinos and Latinas in various fields tell 'How I Did It,' and offer advice for today's students. A directory of top universities and community colleges in the United States for Latinos, an excellent index, and various checklists and examples of student aid forms are included." SLJ
Includes bibliographical references

Navigating your freshman year; how to make the leap to college life and land on your feet; [Natavi Guides, Inc.] Prentice Hall Press 2005 155p il (Students helping students) pa $12.95 *
Grades: 9 10 11 12 **378**
1. College students
ISBN 0-7352-0392-X LC 2004-56976
This student-authored guide covers topics such as what to bring with you to college, how to deal with roommates, social activites and dating, and study tips
"There's lots of good advice in the pages of this guide. . . . Leaving home, doing laundry, forming good study habits, finding friends, and seeking help are all dealt with efficiently." Booklist
Includes bibliographical references

Nist, Sherrie L. (Sherrie Lee), 1946-
College rules! how to study, survive, and succeed in college; [by] Sherrie Nist-Olejnik, and Jodi Patrick Holschuh. 2nd ed. Ten Speed Press 2007 304p pa $14.95
Grades: 9 10 11 12 **378**
1. College students 2. Study skills
ISBN 978-1-58008-838-1; 1-58008-838-4
LC 2006-101169
First published 2002
The authors offer "advice on every aspect of college life, from housekeeping skills to course selection to taking notes. . . . High school students will want to browse this book to get a realistic feel for college life. Current college students needing assistance with study skills will also find it useful." Voice Youth Advocates

Pierce, Valerie, 1957-
Countdown to college; 21 "to-do" lists for high school; [by] Valerie Pierce with Cheryl Rilly. Front Porch Press 2003 163p il pa $9.95
Grades: 9 10 11 12 **378**
1. Colleges and universities—Entrance requirements 2. College applications
ISBN 0-9656086-7-0
On cover: Step-by-step strategies for 9th, 10th, 11th, and 12th graders
The authors offer "academic and financial advice, such as connecting with couselors and teachers, planning an academic schedule, checking admission requirements at certified institutions, and launching a scholarship search. . . . The junior and senior year chapters include sources for getting through testing, campus visits, essays, Advanced Placement choices, application deadlines, 'senioritis,' and hidden costs as well as packing and planning for the big move." Voice Youth Advocates
"This book should be required for every high school freshman that hopes to attend college. . . . Every guidance office and library serving college prep students should have one." Libr Media Connect

Starkey, Lauren B., 1962-
Goof-proof college admissions essays; {by} Lauren Starkey. LearningExpress 2003 177p $12.95
Grades: 9 10 11 12 **378**
1. College applications
ISBN 1-576-85470-1 LC 2003-10397
The author "provides guidelines for essay writing, examples from successful essays and tips from admissions officers. The majority of the book is devoted to the basics of good writing (writing a draft, choosing and using words correctly and clearly, and how to revise, edit, and proofread). . . . A motivated student could use the book as a step-by-step manual for producing an admissions essay. A very useful appendix contains resource material, including online application Web sites and grammar, writing and spelling resources on the Internet." Libr Media Connect
Includes bibliographical references

Steinberg, Jacques
The gatekeepers; inside the admissions process of a premier college. Viking 2002 xxiii, 292p hardcover o.p. pa $15
Grades: 11 12 Adult **378**
1. Wesleyan University (Middletown, Conn.) 2. College applications
ISBN 0-670-03135-6; 0-14-200308-5 (pa)
LC 2002-16884
The author follows "the procedures at Wesleyan University for a year . . . [to] see how the admissions process really looks, to the admitters as well as the applicants." N Y Times Book Rev
"This insightful and readable book should be purchased by all academic and large public libraries." Libr J
Includes bibliographical references

Study abroad, 2007. Peterson's; distributed by UNIPUB 2006 pa $29 *
Grades: 11 12 Adult **378**
1. Foreign study—Directories 2. Scholarships
ISSN 0081-895X
ISBN 0-7689-2175-9; 978-0-7689-2175-5
First published 1948. Frequently revised
At head of title: Peterson's
"Lists, for 124 countries, financial aid and courses for foreign students, with information on scholarships, fellowships, and other assistance for study, teaching, research, training, and observation; university-level and short courses; continuing education and training programs; and student employment opportunities." Guide to Ref Books. 11th edition

378.1 Generalities of higher education

Bardin, Matt

Zen in the art of the SAT; how to think, focus, and achieve your highest score; [by] Matt Bardin and Susan Fine. Houghton Mifflin 2005 220p il pa $7.99 *

Grades: 9 10 11 12   **378.1**

1. Scholastic Assessment Test 2. Colleges and universities—Entrance requirements

ISBN 0-618-57488-3   LC 2005-4326

"Each chapter explores how students can use principles of Zen Buddhism to move beyond anxiety, build their confidence, and focus on solving the SAT's inscrutable, koanlike questions. . . . It's the advice about mindfulness and transforming nervous energy and negative thoughts, which readers can apply to every life experience, that really distinguishes this title." Booklist

Includes bibliographical references

Barron's ACT assessment; [by] George Ehrenhaft [et al.] Barron's Educ. Ser. 2006 il pa $18.99

Grades: 11 12 Adult   **378.1**

1. ACT assessment 2. Colleges and universities—Entrance requirements

ISBN 0-7641-3366-7; 978-0-7641-3366-4

    LC 2007-204127

Also available with CD-ROM for $34.99

First published 1972 with title: Barron's how to prepare for the American College Testing Program (ACT). Continues How to prepare for the ACT, American College Testing Assessment Program, and Barron's How to prepare for the ACT assessment. (14th edition 2007) Frequently revised. Editors vary

Title on cover: Barron's ACT

A guide to achieving higher scores on the ACT which includes subject reviews and practice exams with answers.

Includes bibliographical references

Cohen, Harlan, 1973-

The naked roommate; and 107 other issues you might run into in college. 2nd ed. Sourcebooks 2007 449p pa $14.95

Grades: 9 10 11 12   **378.1**

1. College students

ISBN 978-1-4022-0909-3; 1-4022-0909-6

    LC 2007-1793

First published 2004

On cover: Expert and student advice about: roommates, relationships, classes, friends, finances, dorm life, sex, no sex, alcohol, Greek life, laundry and everything that really matters in college. . .

This is "a hilarious and truthful book that gives high school students a look at college life. . . . The advice is sound; the tone is light." SLJ

Conley, David T., 1948-

College knowledge; what it really takes for students to succeed and what we can do to get them ready. Jossey-Bass 2005 xxii, 350p il (Jossey-Bass education series) $24.95 *

Grades: 11 12 Adult   **378.1**

1. College students 2. Academic achievement

ISBN 0-7879-7397-1   LC 2004-30569

The author "recounts the preparation or lack thereof during the high school years of three college-bound students and makes it clear that there is a difference between college-eligible and college-ready. He lays out chapter by chapter what is wrong and how it can be remedied. . . . This valuable book belongs in every high school library." SLJ

Includes bibliographical references

Cracking the PSAT/NMSQT, 2008 edition; by Jeff Rubenstein and Adam Robinson. Random House 2007 il pa $19

Grades: 9 10 11 12   **378.1**

1. Scholastic Assessment Test 2. Colleges and universities—Entrance requirements

ISSN 1549-6120

ISBN 0-375-76609-X; 978-0-375-76609-1

Annual. First published 2005 to partially replace Cracking the SAT & PSAT by Adam Robinson and John Katzman

At head of title: The Princeton Review

This guide on how to prepare for the PSAT exam includes practice tests, a listing of important vocabulary words, and the strategies and techniques needed to glean the correct answers to test questions.

Cracking the SAT, 2008 edition. Random House 2007 il pa $19.95

Grades: 9 10 11 12   **378.1**

1. Scholastic Assessment Test 2. Colleges and universities—Entrance requirements

ISSN 1934-239X

ISBN 0-375-76606-5; 978-0-375-76606-0

Also available with DVD for $33.95

Annual. First published 2005 with title Cracking the new SAT to partially replace Cracking the SAT & PSAT by Adam Robinson and John Katzman

At head of title: The Princeton Review

This guide offers practical advice on how to prepare for the SAT college entrance exam. Practice tests are provided with detailed explanations for each answer. Free access to extra tests, lessons, and drills online is also included.

Gruber, Gary R.

Gruber's complete SAT guide 2008. 11th ed. Sourcebooks 2007 pa $19.95

Grades: 9 10 11 12   **378.1**

1. Scholastic Assessment Test 2. Colleges and universities—Entrance requirements

ISBN 978-1-4022-1134-8   LC 2007-24991

First published 1985 with title: Gruber's complete preparation for the SAT by Critical Thinking Book Co.

The author explains the principles behind the test, reviews necessary skills and develops test-taking strategies. Sample tests with answers are provided.

Light, Richard J.
Making the most of college; students speak their minds. Harvard Univ. Press 2001 242p hardcover o.p. pa $14.95 *
Grades: 11 12 Adult　　　　　　　　**378.1**
1. College students
ISBN 0-674-00478-7; 0-674-01359-X (pa)
　　　　　　　　　　　　　　LC 00-59728
"Light addresses two major areas: the choices students make to get the most out of college and effective ways for faculty members to help students get the best experience. The book is based on research by more than 60 faculty members from 20 colleges and universities and interviews with undergraduates. . . . Parents and students either in college or headed there will find this book a valuable resource." Booklist
Includes bibliographical references

Master the SAT 2007. Thomson/Peterson's 2006 pa $17.99
Grades: 9 10 11 12　　　　　　　　**378.1**
1. Scholastic Assessment Test 2. Colleges and universities—Entrance requirements
ISBN 0-7689-2319-0
Also available with CD-ROM for $29.99
Annual. First published with title Master the new SAT
At head of title: Arco
This book prepares students for the SAT with content that will teach, review, and test students' essay writing abilities as well as their Algebra II and higher-level math skills. Also included are practice tests, a diagnostic test to help students identify problem areas, and a detailed review of fundamental subject principles.

Nemko, Marty, 1945-
The all-in-one college guide. 2nd ed. Barron's 2004 224p pa $10.95 *
Grades: 11 12 Adult　　　　　　　　**378.1**
1. College choice 2. College students
ISBN 0-7641-2298-3　　　　　LC 2003-63897
First published 1999 with title: You're gonna love this college guide
Subtitle on cover: More-results, less-stress plan for choosing, getting into, finding the money for, and making the most of college
This guide offers advice on how to choose, get into, find the money for, and make the most of college. Also included is information on how to choose a major and a career

Peterson, Brian, 1971-
The African American student's guide to excellence in college. Chance 22 2004 c2005 209p pa $14 *
Grades: 9 10 11 12　　　　　　　　**378.1**
1. African Americans—Education
ISBN 0-9664587-2-9
This book's "emphasis is on how to negotiate the college or university system to take advantage of all it has to offer in the way of academic and social resources. There are segments on taking exams; reading for comprehension; time management; and getting help from writing centers, study groups, and tutors. . . . It should prove helpful to many students, whether or not they are African American." SLJ
Includes bibliographical references

Rosen, Louis, Ph. D.
College is not for everyone; [by] Louis Rosen. ScarecrowEducation 2005 87p il pa $20.95 *
Grades: 9 10 11 12　　　　　　　　**378.1**
1. Vocational guidance 2. Higher education
ISBN 1-578-86245-0　　　　　LC 2004-29878
The author argues "that schools from secondary through community college are not doing enough to prepare students who are not university bound. . . . This book will find the most use in the counselors' offices of schools where there are the largest number of students moving straight into the work force after high school." Voice Youth Advocates
Includes bibliographical references

Rubenstein, Jeff
Crash course for the new SAT; the last-minute guide to scoring high. 3rd ed. Random House 2005 216p il pa $9.95
Grades: 9 10 11 12　　　　　　　　**378.1**
1. Scholastic Assessment Test 2. Colleges and universities—Entrance requirements
ISBN 0-375-76461-5　　　　　LC 2005-295513
First published 1999 with title: Crash course for the SAT
At head of title: The Princeton Review
This book provides strategies and practice questions for students who have little time left to study for the SAT.

378.3　Student aid and related topics

College Board guide to getting financial aid, 2007. College Board 2006 989p pa $19.95 *
Grades: 11 12 Adult　　　　　　　　**378.3**
1. College costs 2. Student loan funds
ISBN 0-8744-7766-2　　　　　LC 2006-903734
Annual. First published with title: The college cost book. Continues The college costs & financial aid handbook
This guide covers over 3000 two-and four-year institutions. Provides information on what each college really costs, describes aid packages and includes tips on application procedures

College Entrance Examination Board
The College Board scholarship handbook 2008. 11th ed. College Bd. 2007 pa $27.95
Grades: 9 10 11 12　　　　　　　　**378.3**
1. Scholarships
ISBN 0-87447-784-0; 978-0-87447-784-9
Annual. First published 1997 with title: Scholarship handbook

College Entrance Examination Board—*Continued*

Information on more than 2,100 undergraduate scholarships, internships, and loan programs. Entries are indexed by category, among them gender, minority status, field of study, and career interest. Includes a planning worksheet to help students organize applications.

College money handbook 2007. Peterson's 2006 pa $32 *

Grades: 11 12 Adult   **378.3**
1. College costs 2. Student loan funds 3. Scholarships
ISSN 1541-1591
ISBN 0-7689-2324-7; 978-0-7689-2324-7
Annual. First published 1983. Variant titles: Paying less for college; Peterson's college money handbook
At head of title: Peterson's
"Arranged alphabetically and covering more than $36 billion in institutional, state, and federal aid, this . . . book includes profiles of more than 1,600 colleges and universities and the need -and non-need-based scholarships they offer. It answers commonly asked questions about financial aid and provides a step-by-step explanation of the financial aid application process." Publisher's note

Schlachter, Gail A.

College student's guide to merit and other no-need funding 2007-2009; [by] Gail Ann Schlachter, R. David Weber. Reference Service Press 2007 $32.50

Grades: 11 12 Adult   **378.3**
1. Scholarships 2. Student aid
ISSN 1099-9086
ISBN 1-58841-166-4; 978-1-58841-166-2
First published 1998. Frequently revised
"Listed are nearly 1,600 sources for college financial aid. The types of sources in the volume include scholarships, forgivable loans, and research grants. . . . Entries are arranged alphabetically within general areas—humanities, sciences, and social sciences. Within each entry is a surprising amount of information for the user." Recomm Ref Books for Small & Medium-sized Libr & Media Cent, 2000

Directory of financial aids for women 2007-2009; {by} Gail Ann Schlachter. Reference Service Press 2007 $45 *

Grades: 11 12 Adult   **378.3**
1. Scholarships 2. Women—Education
ISSN 0732-5215
ISBN 1-58841-167-2; 978-1-58841-167-9
Biennial. First published 1978
Describes "scholarships, fellowships, loans, grants, awards, and internships designed primarily or exclusively for women. . . . Lists state sources of educational benefits and offers an annotated bibliography of directories that list general financial aid programs. Program title, sponsoring organization, geographic, subject, and filing date indexes." Ref Sources for Small & Medium-sized Libr. 5th edition

Financial aid for the disabled and their families, 2006-2008; [by] Gail Ann Schlacter [sic], R. David Weber. Reference Service Press 2006 504p $40 *

Grades: 11 12 Adult   **378.3**
1. Scholarships 2. Physically handicapped
ISBN 1-58841-148-6; 978-1-58841-148-8
Biennial. First published 1988
"Provides information on a wide range of funding needs in such areas as education, career development, research, and travel. Includes multiple indexes; cross-referenced." N Y Public Libr Book of How & Where to Look It Up

High school senior's guide to merit and other no-need funding; [by] Gail Ann Schlachter, R. David Weber. Reference Service Press 2007 $29.95

Grades: 11 12 Adult   **378.3**
1. Scholarships 2. Student aid
ISSN 1099-9132
ISBN 1-58841-165-6; 978-1-58841-165-5
Biennial. First published 1996
The authors focus on "middle-class students who don't qualify for need-based scholarships. They list scholarships based on academic record, artistic ability, religious or ethnic background, etc., that are granted by associations, labor unions, foundations, and other private groups. . . . Entries note eligibility, amount of award, duration, number of awards granted, and deadline." Booklist
"This well-designed survey takes some of the confusion out of the process and presents current information." SLJ

Wheeler, Dion

The sports scholarships insider's guide; getting money for college at any division. Sourcebooks 2005 342p pa $16.95 *

Grades: 9 10 11 12   **378.3**
1. Athletes 2. Scholarships 3. College sports
ISBN 1-4022-0376-4   LC 2005-3152
"Topics include the recruiting process, financial-aid opportunities, academic requirements, preparing credentials, school visits, and negotiating for financial assistance from NCAA division I, II, III and NAIA institutions. The second half of the book includes listings of sports for the various divisions, institution names, and Web addresses." SLJ

378.73   Institutions of higher education--United States

Asher, Donald

Cool colleges for the hyper-intelligent, self-directed, late blooming, and just plain different. 2nd ed. Ten Speed Press 2007 287p il pa $21.95

Grades: 9 10 11 12   **378.73**
1. College choice 2. Colleges and universities—United States—Directories
ISBN 978-1-58008-839-8; 1-58008-839-2
LC 2007-922323

Asher, Donald—*Continued*
First published 2000
Profiles more than 40 innovative and unusual schools of higher learning.

Barron's profiles of American colleges 2007; compiled and edited by the College Division of Barron's Educational Series. 27th ed. Barron's Educ. Ser. 2006 1656p map pa $28.99
Grades: 11 12 Adult   **378.73**
1. Colleges and universities—United States—Directories
ISSN 1065-5026
ISBN 0-7641-7903-9; 978-0-7641-7903-7
Annual. First published 1964
Includes CD-ROM
"More than 1,650 schools are profiled with details on admission requirements, academic programs, tuitions and other fees, sources of available financial aid, library facilities, computer facilities, descriptions of campus environments, athletic facilities, extracurricular activities, e-mail addresses, fax numbers, web sites, and more. Each school receives Barron's . . . academic rating system, which advises students on its degree of academic competitiveness." Publisher's note

College & university almanac 2007. Peterson's 2006 pa $15 *
Grades: 9 10 11 12   **378.73**
1. Colleges and universities—United States—Directories
ISSN 1523-9128
ISBN 0-7689-2163-5; 978-0-7689-2163-2
Annual. First published 1998
At head of title: Peterson's
A guide to selecting, getting in, and paying for a college. Lists over 2000 accredited colleges and universities in the United States.

College Entrance Examination Board
The College Board book of majors. 2nd ed. College Board 2006 1314p pa $24.95
Grades: 11 12 Adult   **378.73**
1. Colleges and universities—United States—Directories 2. Colleges and universities—Curricula
ISBN 0-8744-7765-4; 978-0-8744-7765-8
Annual. First published 1977 with title: The college handbook index of majors. Variant titles: The College Board index of majors and graduate degrees; Index of majors and graduate degrees
Features over nine hundred majors at thirty-six hundred accredited colleges and universities in the United States for degree levels from associate to Ph.D.

College Board college handbook 2008. 45th ed. College Bd. Publs. 2007 2151p pa $28.95
Grades: 11 12 Adult   **378.73**
1. Colleges and universities—United States—Directories
ISBN 0-8744-7783-2; 978-0-8744-7783-2
Accompanied by CD-ROM
Annual. First published 1941 by Ginn with title: Annual handbook. Formerly titled The college handbook

This work offers "detailed information for college-bound students on such subjects as freshman admissions requirements and procedures, enrollment, majors, expenses, financial aid, and many other areas of interest." N Y Public Libr. Book of How & Where to Look It Up

College exploration on the internet; a student and counselor's guide to more than 500 web sites. College & Career Press 2004 343p il pa $19.95 *
Grades: 9 10 11 12   **378.73**
1. College choice 2. Web sites
ISBN 0-9745251-0-3
This collection of college resource Web sites focuses on "categories such as financial aid, campus tours, scholarship scams, minority information, college planning, and studying abroad. Web sites are not offered by category, but alphabetically by Web site name. Each site is described with a general description, best points, and what you should know. Fee based sites are included." Libr Media Connect
"This book is invaluable and should be in every guidance counselor's office." Voice Youth Advocates

Colleges with programs for students with learning disabilities or attention deficit disorders. 8th ed. Peterson's 2007 pa $29.95 *
Grades: 9 10 11 12   **378.73**
1. Learning disabilities 2. Colleges and universities—United States—Directories
ISBN 0-7689-2506-1; 978-0-7689-2506-7
First published 1985 with title: Peterson's guide to colleges with programs for learning disabled students. Variant title: Peterson's colleges with programs for students with learning disabilities
Profiles two-year and four-year colleges offering special programs and services. Includes information on graduate-level options and financial aid.

Fiske, Edward B.
The Fiske guide to colleges 2008. 24th ed. Times Bks. 2007 xxxv, 756p pa $22.95 *
Grades: 11 12 Adult   **378.73**
1. Colleges and universities—United States—Directories 2. College choice
ISBN 1402208367; 9781402208362
Annual. First published 1982 with title: The New York Times selective guide to colleges
This guide to some 300 of the best colleges and universities nationwide includes information on admissions, costs, financial aid, housing, social life, and academic strengths and weaknesses.

Peterson's four-year colleges 2007. 37th ed. Peterson's 2006 2922p il pa $32 *
                                                       378.73
1. Colleges and universities—United States—Directories
ISSN 0894-9336
ISBN 0-7689-2153-8; 978-0-7689-2153-3
Accompanied by CD-ROM
Annual. First published 1966 as part of Peterson's annual guide to undergraduate study

Peterson's four-year colleges 2007—*Continued*

"In two major sections: (1) half-page entries for some 2,000 institutions, with details of enrollment, admission requirements, expenses, housing, student aid, and programs offered; (2) two-page in-depth descriptions of more than 800 institutions, prepared by their officials, which emphasize campus environment, student activities, and lifestyle. Indexes: major, entrance difficulty, cost, and name of institution." Guide to Ref Books. 11th edition

Peterson's two-year colleges 2007. 37th ed. Peterson's 2007 712p il pa $27 * pa $26.95

Grades: 11 12 Adult   **378.73**
1. Colleges and universities—United States—Directories
ISSN 0894-9328
ISBN 0-7689-2154-6; 978-0-7689-2154-0
Annual. First published 1966 as part of Peterson's annual guide to undergradute study

"Describes 1,400 accredited institutions in the U.S. and its territories awarding the associate degree as their most popular undergraduate offering, plus some non-degree-granting schools. . . . In addition to the usual information on admission and graduation requirements, programs, costs, etc., treats considerations peculiar to junior colleges, giving advice on profiting from two-year colleges and transferring to four-year schools, statistics on students transferring from individual colleges, and a list by major of colleges offering associate degree programs." Guide to Ref Books. 11th edition

The **Princeton** Review guide to college visits 2007; the staff of The Princeton Review. Random House 2007 pa $20

Grades: 9 10 11 12   **378.73**
1. College choice 2. Colleges and universities—United States
ISBN 978-0-375-76600-8; 0-375-76600-6
Annual. First published 1993 with title: The complete guide to college visits by Carol Pub. Group

On cover: Planning trips to popular campuses in the Northeast, Southeast, West and Midwest

This guide, which is divided by U.S. region, offers information such as maps and directions to campuses, lists of hotels and other accommodations, advice on the times of year to visit, campus tour dates and times, and information on meeting professors, coaches, and other important campus personnel.

They teach that in college!? a resource guide to more than 75 interesting college majors and programs; edited by Andrew Morkes. College and Career Press 2006 310p il pa $19.95

Grades: 9 10 11 12   **378.73**
1. Colleges and universities—United States—Directories 2. Colleges and universities—Curricula
ISBN 0-9745251-1-1; 978-0-9745251-1-2

"With 'ripped from the headlines' immediacy for students who are not interested in run-of-the-mill professions, this invaluable resource profiles careers that fill a job market deamnd and pay well; are offered as majors by no more than 25 percent of the nation's colleges; and are fun." Voice Youth Advocates

382 International commerce (Foreign trade)

Gifford, Clive
The arms trade. Chrysalis Education 2004 61p il (World issues) $29.95

Grades: 7 8 9 10   **382**
1. Firearms industry 2. Defense industry
ISBN 1-59389-154-7

"This book examines . . . questions surrounding the arms trade today. What is the arms trade? Is the arms trade legal? What are weapons of mass destruction? Are there benefits from the arms trade? Will the arms trade ever stop?" Publisher's note

"This book packs in copious information from a well-rounded perspective. . . . Very effective color photos . . . add a startling and engrossing element." Booklist

Includes glossary and bibliographical references

384 Communications. Telecommunication

Henderson, Harry, 1951-
Communications and broadcasting; from wired words to wireless Web. Rev. ed. Facts on File 2006 201p il (Milestones in discovery and invention) $35

Grades: 7 8 9 10 11 12   **384**
1. Telecommunication
ISBN 0-8160-5748-6; 978-0-8160-5748-1

LC 2006-5577

First published 1997

This is a "look at the development and interconnection of [the following] scientific ideas: electromagnetism, leading to the telegraph and telephone; Maxwell's wave theory, leading to radio and television; and communications and information theory, from Claude Shannon to the World Wide Web and beyond. In addition, there are . . . portraits of the inventors themselves." Publisher's note

Includes glossary and bibliographical references

387.2 Ships

Macaulay, David, 1946-
Ship. Houghton Mifflin 1993 96p il $19.95; pa $12.95 *

Grades: 4 5 6 7 8 9   **387.2**
1. Shipwrecks 2. Underwater exploration 3. Caribbean region—Antiquities
ISBN 0-395-52439-3; 0-395-74518-7 (pa)

LC 92-1346

This book "opens with an underwater find in the Caribbean and, in story and illustration, follows the work of marine archeologists in studying the wreck. As part of the background research in Spain, one of the team finds a diary recording the building of a caravel in 1504. The rest of the book contains a 'translation' of the diary with accompanying illustrations. Though a fictional account, the narrative gives a good feel for the maritime technology of the early 16th century." Sci Books Films

390   Customs, etiquette, folklore

The **Greenwood** encyclopedia of daily life; a tour through history from ancient times to the present; Joyce E. Salisbury, general editor. Greenwood Press 2004 6v il map set $599.95 *
Grades: 11 12 Adult   **390**
1. Manners and customs—Encyclopedias
2. Civilization—Encyclopedias
ISBN 0-313-32541-3   LC 2003-54724
Contents: v. 1. The ancient world / Gregory S. Aldrete, volume editor -- 2. The medieval world / Joyce E. Salisbury, volume editor -- 3. 15th and 16th centuries / Lawrence Morris, volume editor -- 4. 17th and 18th centuries / Peter Seelig, volume editor -- 5. 19th century / Andrew E. Kersten, volume editor -- 6. The modern world / Andrew E. Kersten, volume editor

This "work provides an overview of the material, domestic, recreational, religious, political, intellectual, and economic aspects of daily life in a selection of cultures from six broad historical periods. . . . Each of the six volumes gives a survey of the historical period in each culture covered, which is representative rather than exhaustive, then covers aspects of daily life from broad topics to narrower." Libr J
Includes bibliographical references

391   Costume and personal appearance

Cosgrave, Bronwyn
The complete history of costume and fashion; from ancient Egypt to the present day. Checkmark Bks. 2001 256p il $37.95 *
Grades: 11 12 Adult   **391**
1. Costume—History
ISBN 0-8160-4574-7   LC 00-64401
"This book explores the development of fashion from its simple and practical beginnings to the growth of the multibillion dollar global industry that it is today. . . . Trends in clothing style, fabric, accessories, and footwear {are examined}." Publisher's note
Includes bibliographical references

DeJean, Joan E.
The essence of style; how the French invented high fashion, fine food, chic cafés, style, sophistication, and glamour. Free Press 2005 303p il $25; pa $15
Grades: 11 12 Adult   **391**
1. Louis XIV, King of France, 1638-1715
2. Fashion—History 3. France—Social life and customs
ISBN 0-7432-6413-4; 0-7432-6414-2 (pa)
LC 2005-40019
A historian of seventeenth-century French culture argues that "the French under Louis XIV set the standards of sophistication, style, and glamour that still rule our lives today." Publisher's note
"An unusual and delightfully educational perspective on snob appeal." Booklist
Includes bibliographical references

Encyclopedia of clothing and fashion; Valerie Steele, editor in chief. Scribner 2005 3v (Scribner library of daily life) set $395
Grades: 11 12 Adult   **391**
1. Costume—Encyclopedias 2. Fashion—Encyclopedias
ISBN 0-684-31394-4   LC 2004-10098
Contents: v1 Academic dress to Futurist fashion, Italian -- v2 Gabardine to Quilting -- v3 Rabanne, Paco to Zoran

Alphabetically arranged entries range "from a half page for some particular items, clothing types, fibers, and techniques . . . to multiple pages for *Cross dressing; Dandyism; Hats, men's* and *Hats, women's; Kimono; Street style* and *Twentieth century fashion*, among others. Articles on designers or people who influenced fashion . . . are a significant part of the content, as are articles with a historical slant. . . . Many of the articles are entertaining as well as enlightening. . . . *Encyclopedia of Clothing and Fashion* is an exciting and unique resource that excels in depth and range of coverage." Booklist

Fashions of a decade [series] Chelsea House Publishers 2006 8v il set $280 *
Grades: 7 8 9 10 11 12   **391**
1. Costume
ISBN 0-8160-7059-8; 978-0-8160-7059-6
Volumes also available separately ea $35
First published 1991-1992
Contents: The 1920s by Jacqueline Herald; The 1930s by Maria Constantino; The 1940s by Patricia Baker; The 1950s by Patricia Baker; The 1960s by Yvonne Connikie; The 1970s by Jacqueline Herald; The 1980s by Vicky Carnegy; The 1990s by Anne McEvoy

This set describes clothing styles of the 20th century in the context of world events, social movements, and cultural movements of each decade.
"These titles provide colorful and fascinating information. . . . Attractive black-and-white illustrations, color photos, reproductions, sketches from magazines and newspapers, and fact boxes enhance and bring to life these lively and accessible texts." SLJ

Graydon, Shari
In your face; the culture of beauty and you. Annick 2004 176p il $24.94; pa $14.95 *
Grades: 7 8 9 10   **391**
1. Personal appearance
ISBN 1-55037-857-0; 1-55037-856-2 (pa)
The author "looks at fashion across time and cultures, and analyzes the underlying messages in today's focus . . . on thinness, long nails, and high heels. Along the way, she warns both young men and women of the very real dangers of eating disorders, plastic surgery, liposuction, and other body-image 'solutions.' . . . Graydon will make readers laugh as well as think about the issues." Booklist
Includes bibliographical references

Kelly, Clinton, 1969-

Dress your best; the complete guide to finding the style that's right for your body; [by] Clinton Kelly and Stacy London. Three Rivers Press 2005 255p il pa $18.95

Grades: 11 12 Adult   391

1. Clothing and dress 2. Fashion

ISBN 0-307-23671-4   LC 2005-13681

This fashion guide describes specific male and female body types, and the kinds of outfits that match well with them. "Each type's section opens with a photo of an average-looking model sporting a basic swimsuit, along with comments from the model and the authors. . . . Ladies and gentlemen, start your shopping engines—and don't leave home without this book!" Publ Wkly

Nunn, Joan

Fashion in costume, 1200-2000. 2nd ed. New Amsterdam Bks. 2000 280p pa $18.95 *

Grades: 11 12 Adult   391

1. Costume—History

ISBN 1-56663-279-X   LC 99-47516

First published 1984 by Schocken Bks. with title: Fashion in costume, 1200-1980

This history of American and European costume covers men's, women's, and children's dress, accessories and jewelry, fabrics, and color. Discusses how historical, social, economic, and artistic events influence fashion

Includes bibliographical references

Paterek, Josephine

Encyclopedia of American Indian costume. Norton 1996 516p il pa $24.95

Grades: 11 12 Adult   391

1. Native American costume

ISBN 0-393-31382-4

First published 1994 by ABC-CLIO

Paterek describes "the clothing used for everyday, war, rites, and ceremonies for men, women, and children in hundreds of tribes in diverse climates stretching over centuries. Well-organized text and 400 drawings and authentic photos plus the cultural essays prefacing the 10 regional groupings and each tribe put the costumes in historical, social, and geographic context. Appendixes cover terminology and the materials used in clothing. The excellent bibliographies in this classic work both document and encourage further reading." Am Libr

Includes bibliographical references

Scott, Georgia

Headwraps; a global journey. Public Affairs 2003 209p il $35

Grades: 11 12 Adult   391

1. Hats

ISBN 1-586-48109-6   LC 2003-60655

This "book examines headwraps from cultural, fashion and practical standpoints." Publ Wkly

"On any page, readers will find excellent color photos of Scott's many new friends in their headgear, or archival photos and artistic renderings. Illustrations and text mesh seamlessly to reveal an amazing variety of textiles and methods of tying." SLJ

Includes bibliographical references

393   Death customs

Colman, Penny

Corpses, coffins, and crypts; a history of burial. Holt & Co. 1997 212p il $17.95

Grades: 7 8 9 10   393

1. Funeral rites and ceremonies 2. Burial

ISBN 0-8050-5066-3   LC 97-7842

Documents the burial process throughout the centuries and in different cultures.

The author "is both candid and detailed in her handling of the gruesome nitty-gritty. . . . Many of the photographs in the liberally illustrated text are from her own explorations, and all are captioned, some in great detail. . . . She's filled her sensitive, solid book with answers to questions people often need and want to know but are too reluctant to ask." Booklist

Includes glossary and bibliographical references

Pringle, Heather Anne, 1952-

The mummy congress; science, obsession, and the everlasting dead; {by} Heather Pringle. Hyperion 2001 368p il hardcover o.p. pa $13.95

Grades: 11 12 Adult   393

1. Mummies 2. Forensic anthropology

ISBN 0-7868-6551-2; 0-7868-8463-0 (pa)

                                                LC 00-54487

"Besides outstanding members of the scientific association that gathers as the Mummy Congress, Pringle limns the many varieties of mummies, from the world's oldest, preserved by the high-altitude climate of the Andes, to modern Communist dictators, self-mummifying Buddhists, and the subjects of extreme cosmetic surgery. More astounding than all the fright flicks about shambling, gauze-wrapped menaces wound together." Booklist

Includes bibliographical references

394   General customs

Rydell, Robert W.

Fair America; world's fairs in the United States; {by} Robert W. Rydell, John E. Findling, and Kimberly D. Pelle. Smithsonian Institution Press 2000 166p il $29.95; pa $15.95

Grades: 11 12 Adult   394

1. Exhibitions 2. Fairs

ISBN 1-56098-968-8; 1-56098-384-1 (pa)

                                                LC 99-40957

This examines the world's fairs which were held in the United States from 1853 to 1984 and their effects, such as introducing Americans to new technologies and foreign cultures, and the ways in which they reflected and influenced American culture

Includes bibliographical references

394.1 Eating, drinking; using drugs

Tobacco in history and culture; an encyclopedia; Jordan Goodman, editor in chief. Thomson Gale 2005 2v il (Scribner turning points library) set $275

Grades: 11 12 Adult   **394.1**
1. Tobacco—Encyclopedias
ISBN 0-684-31405-3   LC 2004-7109
Contents: v. 1. Addiction--Music, popular -- v. 2. Native Americans--Zimbabwe

The author "focuses on the cultural aspects of tobacco as a drug, health hazard, social phenomena, and economic force." Ref & User Services Quarterly

"This makes an excellent starting point for readers looking for quick entrance to the vast body of knowledge of the history and diversity of tobacco uses, tobacco health, addiction, social control issues, advertising, production, and distribution, among other topics." Choice

Includes bibliographical references

394.26 Holidays

The **American** book of days; compiled and edited by Stephen G. Christianson. 4th ed. Wilson, H.W. 2000 xxvi, 945p $140 *

Grades: 8 9 10 11 12 Adult   **394.26**
1. Holidays 2. Festivals
ISBN 0-8242-0954-0   LC 99-86611
First edition, by George William Douglas, published 1937

This work "consists of essays that are a day-to-day recounting of selective American historic events, including those of festivals and celebrations. . . . The topics of these essays vary, with the editor highlighting notable activities from military, scientific, ethnic, political, and cultural occurrences. Not limited strictly to events, essays are also devoted to individuals who played a significant role in American history. . . . A comprehensive index and table of contents provide excellent means for finding specific topics." Am Ref Books Annu, 2001

Chase's calendar of events 2006. Contemporary Bks. 2006 pa $64.95 *

Grades: 11 12 Adult   **394.26**
1. Calendars 2. Holidays 3. Almanacs
ISSN 1083-0588
ISBN 0-07-146818-8; 978-0-07-146818-3

Annual. First published 1958 with title: Chase's calendar of annual events, under the editorship of William D. and Helen M. Chase. Variant title: Chase's annual events

Accompanied by CD-ROM

"Day-by-day listing of national and state holidays, religious observances, special events, festivals and fairs, and historical anniversaries and birthdays. Covers U.S. events primarily, but some international occasions and anniversaries are included." N Y Public Libr Book of How & Where to Look It Up

Christianson, Stephen G.
The international book of days; edited by Lynn M. Messina; contributors, Jennifer Peloso, Norris Smith, Laura Ware. H.W. Wilson 2004 xxxi, 889p il map $140

Grades: 11 12 Adult   **394.26**
1. Holidays 2. Festivals
ISBN 0-8242-0975-3   LC 2004-42285

This "book presents an international tour of holidays and major historical events. Organized by day of the year, the book covers some 1500 key events in world history." Libr J

Encyclopedia of holidays and celebrations; a country-by-country guide; Matthew Dennis, editor. Facts on File 2006 3v il map (Facts on File library of world history) set $275

Grades: 11 12 Adult   **394.26**
1. Holidays 2. Festivals
ISBN 0-8160-6235-8; 978-0-8160-6235-5
    LC 2005-27700

This is "a three-volume guide that explores holidays and festivals in 206 countries. Volumes I and II are organized alphabetically by country, and volume III contains overviews of major internationally observed holidays and religions. . . . This welcome addition to multicultural studies is attractively laid out, easy to use, great for browsing as well as fact finding, and is highly recommended for high school, public, and college libraries." Ref & User Services Quarterly

Includes bibliographical references

The **Folklore** of world holidays; Robert Griffin and Ann H. Shurgin, editors. 2nd ed. Gale Res. 1998 c1999 841p $150

Grades: 11 12 Adult   **394.26**
1. Holidays 2. Festivals 3. Folklore
ISBN 0-8103-8901-0   LC 98-37030
First published 1992 under the editorship of Margaret Read MacDonald

"Provides descriptive information on nearly 2,000 beliefs, stories, superstitions, proverbs, recipes, games, pageants, fairs, processions and other lore related to more than 350 special dates from 150 countries." Publisher's note

Includes bibliographical references

Gulevich, Tanya
Encyclopedia of Christmas and New Year's celebrations; illustrated by Mary Ann Stavros-Lanning. Omnigraphics 2003 xx, 977p il $68

Grades: 11 12 Adult   **394.26**
1. Christmas 2. New Year
ISBN 0-7808-0625-5   LC 2003-40580
First published 2000 with title: Encyclopedia of Christmas

"Over 240 alphabetically arranged entries covering Christmas, New Year's, and related days of observance, including folk and religious customs, history, legends, and symbols from around the world; supplemented by a bibliography and lists of Christmas Web sites and associations . . ." Title page

Gulevich, Tanya—*Continued*

The author "covers a variety of secular and sacred aspects of Christmas and New Year's celebrations. The volume discusses the history and meaning of the well known, such as Saint Nicholas, and the lesser well known, such as Knecht Ruprecht who was Saint Nicholas' companion visiting the not-so-good children. . . . This encyclopedic work is useful for those schools where folklore is covered, or for those interested in origins of the holidays." Lib Media Connect

Includes bibliographical references

Holidays and anniversaries of the world; Beth A. Baker, editor. 3rd ed. Gale Res. 1998 c1999 1184p $130

Grades: 11 12 Adult   **394.26**

1. Holidays 2. Festivals 3. Historical chronology

ISBN 0-8103-5477-2   LC 98-38866

First published 1985

New edition in preparation

"A comprehensive catalogue containing detailed information on every month and day of the year, with coverage of more than 26,000 holidays, anniversaries, fasts and feasts, holy days of the saints, the blesseds, and other days of religious significance, birthdays of the famous, important dates in history, and special events and their sponsors." Tilte page

Holidays, festivals, and celebrations of the world dictionary. 3rd ed. Omnigraphics 2005 xxxv, 906p $110 *

Grades: 11 12 Adult   **394.26**

1. Holidays 2. Festivals

ISBN 0-7808-0422-8   LC 2004-25017

First edition published 1994 compiled by Sue Ellen Thompson and Barbara W. Carlson

"Contains information about nearly 2,500 holidays, festivals, holy days, feasts and fasts, and other observances, including popular, secular, and religious celebrations for more than 100 countries and every state of the United States"—Title page

"From Labor Day in the United States to Kallemooi in the North Coast Islands of the Netherlands, the work covers a wide range of religious and political festivities." Libr J

Includes bibliographical references

Rajtar, Steve, 1951-

United States holidays and observances; by date, jurisdiction, and subject, fully indexed. McFarland & Co. 2003 165p $45 *

Grades: 11 12 Adult   **394.26**

1. Holidays 2. Festivals

ISBN 0-7864-1446-4   LC 2002-154293

Includes indexes

This "concentrates on observances and holidays established by statute in the U.S. and American Samoa, District of Columbia, Guam, the Northern Mariana Islands, Puerto Rico, and the U.S. Virgin Islands. In addition, UN-designated holidays are included. . . . The text is arranged by month, and chapters for each month are divided into 'Observances with Variable Dates' and 'Observances with Fixed Dates.' Each entry identifies the observance as federal or specific to a state and offers a de-

scription that ranges in length from three or four lines to a quarter page. . . . {This} would be a good addition to ready-reference desks in public libraries and information centers in schools." Booklist

Roy, Christian, 1963-

Traditional festivals; a multicultural encyclopedia. ABC-CLIO 2005 2v il set $185

Grades: 9 10 11 12   **394.26**

1. Festivals

ISBN 1-57607-089-1 (set)   LC 2005-10444

"The work attempts to cover festivals from all major religions. Moreover, the text also takes into account festival and feast days from ancient or extinct societies. . . . Articles trace the historical development of festivals as well as geographical variations of these holy and feast days in a comparative framework. . . . This will be a very helpful resource for researchers in the field of comparative religion and culture." Choice

Includes bibliographical references

Thompson, Sue Ellen, 1948-

Holiday symbols and customs. 3rd ed. Omnigraphics 2002 895p $68 *

Grades: 11 12 Adult   **394.26**

1. Holidays 2. Festivals

ISBN 0-7808-0501-1   LC 2002-193028

First published 1998 with title: Holiday symbols

"A guide to the legend and lore behind the traditions, rituals, foods, games, animals, and other symbols and activities associated with holidays and holy days, feasts and fasts, and other celebrations, covering calendar, ethnic, religious, historic, cultural, national, promotional, sporting, and ancient events, as observed in the United States and around the world." Title page

For a review see: Booklist, Jan. 1 and 15, 2004

Includes bibliographical references

395   Etiquette (Manners)

Baldrige, Letitia

Letitia Baldrige's new manners for new times; a complete guide to etiquette; illustrations by Denise Cavalieri Fike. Scribner 2003 xxvi, 709p il $35

Grades: 11 12 Adult   **395**

1. Etiquette

ISBN 0-7432-1062-X   LC 2003-65666

First published 1990 with title: Letitia Baldrige's complete guide to the new manners for the 90's

"Combining correctness, consideration, and common sense in equal measure, Baldrige advises readers on proper ways to approach intricate situations. She addresses same-sex unions, pregnant brides, blended and extended families, and sexual harassment with aplomb." Libr J

Martin, Judith, 1938-
Miss Manners' guide to excruciatingly correct behavior; illustrated by Gloria Kamen. freshly updated. Norton 2005 858p il $35
Grades: 11 12 Adult   395
1. Etiquette
ISBN 0-393-05874-3   LC 2005-00264
First published 1982 by Atheneum Pubs.
This book "covers such modern dilemmas as dealing with intrusive cell phones, handling guests who can't commit, and determining when e-mail is socially correct." Libr J
"Miss Manners is always as entertaining as she is civilized." Booklist

Packer, Alex J., 1951-
The how rude! handbook of family manners for teens; avoiding strife in family life; edited by Pamela Espeland. Free Spirit Pub. 2004 117p il pa $9.95
Grades: 9 10 11 12   395
1. Etiquette 2. Conduct of life
ISBN 1-57542-163-1   LC 2004-16142
"This book covers the basics of creating the civilized home—a place where people talk instead of yell, pick up after themselves, respect each other, and fight fair." Publisher's note

The how rude! handbook of school manners for teens; civility in the hallowed halls; edited by Pamela Espeland. Free Spirit Pub. 2004 117p il pa $9.95 *
Grades: 9 10 11 12   395
1. Etiquette 2. Conduct of life
ISBN 1-57542-164-X   LC 2004-18972
Contents: School manners 101: classroom decorum -- School manners 102: beyond the basics -- To cheat, or not to cheat? -- Responding to rudeness -- Getting along with teachers -- How to dress for school success -- Bullies, bigots, bashers, and harassers -- Civility at sporting events -- Applying to colleges -- Graduation -- Bonus chapter: A brief history of manners

Post, Elizabeth L.
Emily Post's teen etiquette; {by} Elizabeth L. Post and Joan M. Coles. HarperPerennial 1995 177p il pa $13 *
Grades: 7 8 9 10   395
1. Etiquette
ISBN 0-06-273337-0   LC 95-18503
Replaces Emily Post talks with teens about manners and etiquette (1986)
"Practical, commonsense advice on dealing with your family, communicating with others, mealtime manners, your appearance, social survival (friendship and dating), money, and getting a job. The basics of how to write a thank you note and which fork to use are covered as well as dealing with call waiting and beepers. The family section recognizes divorce and stepfamilies as well as situations involving abuse." Voice Youth Advocates

Post, Peggy, 1945-
Emily Post's Etiquette. 17th ed., [revised by] Peggy Post. HarperCollins Publishers 2004 876p $39.95 *
Grades: 7 8 9 10 11 12 Adult   395
1. Etiquette
ISBN 0-06-620957-9   LC 2004-40508
First published 1922 under the authorship of Emily Post. Periodically revised and updated. Title varies. 11th-15th editions revised by Elizabeth Post; 16th-17th editions revised by Peggy Post
"The classic reference for which fork to use has been expanded to include such modern situations as dating, living together, second marriages, and co-ed business traveling." N Y Public Libr Book of How & Where to Look It Up

398 Folklore

De Vos, Gail, 1949-
Tales, rumors, and gossip; exploring contemporary folk literature in grades 7-12. Libraries Unlimited 1996 xx, 405p $39
Grades: Professional   398
1. Folklore
ISBN 1-56308-190-3   LC 95-19553
"Aimed at the professional, the book is divided into three sections: an introduction to contemporary legends, the role of these legends in the world around us, and a discussion of individual legends. If you are looking for legends on cults, demonology or Satanism, you'll find them here. . . . Librarians and teachers will use this as a resource for contemporary literature classes." Book Rep
Includes bibliographical references

Nigg, Joe
Wonder beasts; tales and lore of the phoenix, the griffin, the unicorn, and the dragon. Libraries Unlimited 1995 160p il $27.50
Grades: 7 8 9 10   398
1. Animals—Folklore
ISBN 1-56308-242-X   LC 94-46797
The author "has compiled material ranging from Herodotus, Ovid, Pliny the Elder, to Chinese and Native American folk tales, and fantasies by Edith Nesbit. Each entry is carefully documented and a reference list at the end provides dozens of full citations for those who'd like to delve deeper. Wonder Beasts will be useful to students who are researching myth and folklore, and to librarians and scholars who are looking for a comprehensive source list on the topic." Voice Youth Advocates

398.03 Folklore--Encyclopedias and dictionaries

American folklore; an encyclopedia; edited by Jan Harold Brunvand. Garland 1996 794p il (Garland reference library of the humanities) pa $44.95 hardcover o.p. *
Grades: 11 12 Adult   398.03
1. Folklore—United States—Encyclopedias
ISBN 0-8153-3350-1 (pa)   LC 95-53734

American folklore—*Continued*

This volume contains "more than 500 articles covering American and Canadian folklore from holidays, festivals, and rituals to crafts, music, dance, and occupations. Well-chosen black-and-white photographs illustrate many aspects of our rich folklife tradition. Twenty-three ethnic groups receive lengthy articles describing their traditional and contemporary folklore—with the exception of Native Americans." Am Libr

Includes bibliographical references

398.2 Folk literature

Sagas, romances, legends, ballads, and fables in prose form, and fairy tales, folk tales, and tall tales are included here, instead of with the literature of the country of origin, to keep the traditional material together and to make it more readily accessible. Modern fairy tales are classified with Fiction, Story collections (SC)

African folktales; traditional stories of the black world; selected and retold by Roger D. Abrahams. Pantheon Bks. 1983 354p il (Pantheon fairy tale & folklore library) pa $18 hardcover o.p.
Grades: 9 10 11 12 **398.2**
1. Folklore—Africa
ISBN 0-394-72117-9 (pa) LC 83-2474
This collection contains almost one hundred tales gleaned from the storytelling traditions of Africa, south of the Sahara
Includes bibliographical references

Asian-Pacific folktales and legends; edited by Jeannette L. Faurot. Simon & Schuster 1995 252p pa $12
Grades: 11 12 Adult **398.2**
1. Folklore—Asia
ISBN 0-684-81197-9 LC 95-31549
"A Touchstone book"
"The 65 myths and folktales in this volume are gathered from the rich heritage of legends in eight East and Southeast Asian countries, with the largest number of stories coming from China (17). The editor herself translates or retells 14 of the Chinese stories for this collection, while the others are reprinted from existing anthologies. . . . The collection gives a quick, multinational overview of some favorite Asian legends." Libr J

Be afraid, be very afraid; the book of scary urban legends; [collected by] Jan Harold Brunvand. Norton 2004 256p pa $13.95 *
Grades: 9 10 11 12 **398.2**
1. Folklore 2. Legends
ISBN 0-393-32613-6 LC 2004-11798
In this collection of urban legends, the author "has compiled the scariest, grisliest ones—some that are unfamiliar but many that have been heard at sleepovers and depicted in horror movies over the past several years. . . . This is a good addition where such titles are popular." SLJ
Includes bibliographical references

Best-loved folktales of the world; selected and with an introduction by Joanna Cole; illustrated by Jill Karla Schwarz. Doubleday 1983 xxiv, 792p il pa $17
Grades: 9 10 11 12 **398.2**
1. Folklore 2. Fairy tales
ISBN 0-385-18949-4 LC 81-43288
"200 tales from widely ranging countries of the world make up this diversified collection. . . . Familiar classics and lesser known stories are arranged geographically by region, but access can also be obtained through an index of categories, which is appended. Here, users can find tales through motifs, such as trickster heroes, giants and ogres, fables with a moral, quests, and magical helpers." Booklist

Bulfinch, Thomas, 1796-1867
Bulfinch's mythology; foreword by Alberto Manguel. Modern Library pbk. ed. Modern Library 2004 862p pa $17.95
Grades: 11 12 Adult **398.2**
1. Mythology 2. Folklore—Europe 3. Chivalry
ISBN 0-375-75147-5 LC 2005-271850
First combined edition published 1913 by Crowell. Originally published in three separate volumes 1855, 1858 and 1862 respectively
Contents: The age of fable — The age of chivalry — Legends of Charlemagne
"The classic work on mythology, Bulfinch's gives brief summations of Greek, Roman, Norse, Arthurian, and other miscellaneous myths and includes notes on the 'Iliad,' the 'Odyssey,' and the 'Aeneid.'" N Y Public Libr Book of How & Where to Look It Up
Includes bibliographical references

Favorite folktales from around the world; edited by Jane Yolen. Pantheon Bks. 1986 498p pa $18 hardcover o.p. *
Grades: 11 12 Adult **398.2**
1. Folklore 2. Fairy tales
ISBN 0-394-75188-4 (pa) LC 86-42644
"Selections include tales from the American Indians, the brothers Grimm, Italo Calvino's Italian folk-tales, as well as stories from Iceland, Afghanistan, Scotland, and many other countries. Yolen provides each section with a relevant introduction, often including historical and literary factors, thus alerting readers as to what to look for." SLJ

Hearne, Betsy Gould, 1942-
Beauties and beasts; by Betsy Hearne; illustrated by Joanne Caroselli. Oryx Press 1993 179p il (Oryx multicultural folktale series) pa $33.95
Grades: 11 12 Adult **398.2**
1. Fairy tales 2. Folklore 3. Mythology
ISBN 0-89774-729-1 LC 93-16
"The theme of a lonely beast who is transformed by the magic of human love is threaded throughout worldwide variations of the 'Beauty and the Beast' folktale. Author Betsy G. Hearne presents 28 versions of the beloved fable with minimal adaptations from around the world." Publisher's note
"Professionals will be very grateful for this sensitively

Hearne, Betsy Gould, 1942-—*Continued*
written, thoughtful, and accessible interpretive collection." J Youth Serv Libr
Includes bibliographical references

Holt, David
Spiders in the hairdo; modern urban legends; collected and retold by David Holt & Bill Mooney. August House 1999 111p il pa $7.95
Grades: 11 12 Adult   **398.2**
1. Folklore—United States
ISBN 0-87483-525-9   LC 99-11973
This "collection of urban myths assembles 50 brief stories from modern oral tradition. Commonly attributed to FOAFs (friends of a friend), they are intriguing and often frightening tales passed along in casual conversation. These tales are the substance of modern folklore, an evolving treasury of evanescent narratives." Libr J
Includes bibliographical references

Latin American folktales; stories from Hispanic and Indian traditions; edited and with an introduction by John Bierhorst. Pantheon Bks. 2002 386p (Pantheon fairy tale & folklore library) hardcover o.p. pa $17
Grades: 11 12 Adult   **398.2**
1. Folklore—Latin America
ISBN 0-375-42066-5; 0-375-71439-1 (pa)
      LC 2001-34056
Bierhorst "has collected and translated more than 100 folktales from the Spanish oral tradition as practiced in the Americas, from New Mexico to Nicaragua to Chile. . . . {His} introduction provides the context not only for the evolution and telling . . . of the folktales but also for their recording, primarily by early-twentieth-century folklorists and anthropologists. He then sets his readers loose in a vivid world of tricksters, witches, amorous young men, sneaky wives {and} animals with magical powers. . . . A glossary and registry of motifs adds to this volume's value and enjoyment." Booklist
Includes bibliographical references

Lester, Julius
Black folktales; illustrated by Tom Feelings; with an introduction by the author. 1st Evergreen ed. Grove Press 1992 110p il pa $12
Grades: 9 10 11 12   **398.2**
1. Blacks—Folklore 2. Folklore—Africa
ISBN 0-8021-3242-1   LC 91-7619
"An Evergreen book"
First published 1969 by Baron, R.W.
"Lester gives 12 African and Afro-American folk tales such twentieth-century touches as the Lord's reading of the 'TV Guide' and the mention of Rap Brown and Aretha Franklin but his sprightly versions retain the spirit and shape of the original story. . . . These stories of creation, love, folk heroes, and everyday people have a direct simplicity and laconic humor that is both effective and appealing." Booklist

Lynch, Patricia Ann
Native American mythology A to Z. Facts on File 2004 130p il map (Mythology A-Z) $40 *
Grades: 11 12 Adult   **398.2**
1. Native Americans—Folklore
ISBN 0-8160-4891-6   LC 2004-47115
This book presents "coverage of the deities, legendary heroes and heroines, important animals, objects, and places that make up the mythic lore of the many peoples of North America from northern Mexico into the Arctic Circle." Publisher's note
Includes bibliographical references

Malory, Sir Thomas, 15th cent.
Le morte Darthur, or, The hoole book of Kyng Arthur and of his noble knyghtes of the Rounde Table; authoritative text, sources and backgrounds, criticism; [by] Sir Thomas Malory; edited by Stephen H.A. Shepherd. Norton 2004 lii, 954p (A Norton critical edition) pa $16.95
Grades: 11 12 Adult   **398.2**
1. Arthur, King
ISBN 0-393-97464-2   LC 2002-26534
Originally published 1485
"The work is a skillful selection and blending of materials taken from the mass of Arthurian legends. The central story consists of two main elements: the reign of King Arthur ending in catastrophe and the dissolution of the Round Table; and the quest of the Holy Grail." Oxford Companion to Engl Lit
Includes bibliographical references

Meeting the other crowd; the fairy stories of hidden Ireland; {collected and edited} by Eddie Lenihan with Carolyn Eve Green. Putnam 2003 332p hardcover o.p. pa $15.95
Grades: 11 12 Adult   **398.2**
1. Fairy tales 2. Folklore—Ireland
ISBN 1-58542-206-1; 1-58542-307-6 (pa)
      LC 2002-31985
This collection of short tales "feature the seanchai, the traditional teacher and tale spinner of Irish folklore, and can be divided into three major categories: fairy places and signs of their presence, who fairies are and what they want, and the gifts, punishments, and other outcomes of fairy encounters." Libr J
"A major contribution to its field, the book is also compulsively readable." Booklist

Orenstein, Catherine, 1968-
Little Red Riding Hood uncloaked; sex, morality, and the evolution of a fairy tale. Basic Bks. 2002 289p il hardcover o.p. pa $14.95
Grades: 11 12 Adult   **398.2**
1. Little Red Riding Hood
ISBN 0-465-04125-6; 0-465-04126-4 (pa)
      LC 2002-4240
"Once upon a time, Red Riding Hood was a good little girl. When she foolishly strayed from the path in the forest and spoke to strangers, she fell prey to the wicked wolf, but fortunately, the heroic woodcutter rescued her just in time. . . . With wit and insight, Orenstein makes

Orenstein, Catherine, 1968——*Continued*
us look again at the old childhood story, how it has
changed and what that says about us. From Perrault and
the Brothers Grimm to Bruno Bettelheim and Andrea
Dworkin, the lively informal narrative surveys the stories
and the scholarship in terms of folklore, psychology,
feminism, and pornography." Booklist
Includes bibliographical references

Pickering, David, 1958-
A dictionary of folklore. Facts on File 1999
324p $44 *
Grades: 11 12 Adult   **398.2**
1. Folklore—Dictionaries 2. Mythology—Dictionaries
ISBN 0-8160-4550-0
The author provides entries "on such subjects as herbal remedies, the superstitions connected with various
gemstones, the folklore associated with selected trees,
plants, birds, and animals. He also covers the ritual tradition of holidays and festivals and the origins of proverbs
and sayings. In addition, the dictionary mentions characters and heroes from selkies to Joe Magarac, fantasy beings such as sprites and pixies, and some urban myths."
Libr J

Pyle, Howard, 1853-1911
The story of King Arthur and his knights;
written and illustrated by Howard Pyle. Scribner
1984 312p il $22.95
Grades: 7 8 9 10   **398.2**
1. Arthur, King 2. Arthurian romances
ISBN 0-684-14814-5   LC 84-50167
Also available in paperback from Dover Publs. and
Signet Classics
A reissue of the title first published 1903
The first of a four-volume series retelling the Arthuri-
an legends
This is an account of the times "when Arthur, son of
Uther-Pendragon, was Overlord of Britain and Merlin
was a powerful enchanter, when the sword Excalibur was
forged and won, when the Round Table came into be-
ing." Publisher's note

The story of Sir Launcelot and his companions.
Dover Publications 1991 340p il pa $13.95
Grades: 9 10 11 12   **398.2**
1. Lancelot (Legendary character) 2. Arthurian ro-
mances
ISBN 0-486-26701-6   LC 90-22326
A reissue of the title first published 1907 by Scribner
This third book of the series follows "Sir Launcelot's
adventures as he rescues Queen Guinevere from the
clutches of Sir Mellegrans, does battle with the Worm of
Corbin, wanders as a madman in the forest and is finally
returned to health by the Lady Elaine." Best Sellers

The story of the champions of the Round Table;
written and illustrated by Howard Pyle. Dover
Publications 1968 328p il pa $11.95
Grades: 9 10 11 12   **398.2**
1. Arthurian romances
ISBN 0-486-21883-X
Available in hardcover from Amereon
A reissue of the title first published 1905 by Scribner

Contents: The story of Launcelot; The book of Sir
Tristram; The book of Sir Percival
"Pyle's second volume of Arthurian legends will be of
interest to motivated students of literature and history, as
well as useful in professional collections for comparisons
and source work. In spite of the archaic language . . .
the narrative depth and graphic force . . . will draw in
readers." Booklist

The story of the Grail and the passing of
Arthur. Dover Publications 1992 258p il pa $12.95
Grades: 7 8 9 10   **398.2**
1. Arthur, King 2. Arthurian romances 3. Grail—Fiction
ISBN 0-486-27361-X   LC 92-29058
A reissue of the title first published 1910 by Scribner
This fourth volume of the series follows the adventures of Sir Geraint, Galahad's quest for the holy Grail,
the battle between Launcelot and Gawaine, and the slaying of Mordred

Steig, Jeanne
A gift from Zeus; written by Jeanne Steig;
pictures by William Steig. HarperCollins Pubs.
2001 166p il $17.95
Grades: 9 10 11 12   **398.2**
1. Classical mythology
ISBN 0-06-028405-6   LC 00-31617
A retelling of sixteen myths including the tales of Prometheus and Pandora, Demeter and Persephone, Midas
and Orpheus and Eurydice
"All the brutality, rape, incest, bestiality, and abuse of
the original myths are here but presented in a voice
that's witty, playful, and filled with in-jokes and euphe-
misms. . . . High-schoolers studying the classics will
find relief in these lively, unpretentious, even blasphe-
mous interpretations of the ancient material that play up
the action and story over the archetypes." Booklist

Tingle, Tim
Walking the Choctaw road. Cinco Puntos Press
2003 142p il $16.95; pa $10.95
Grades: 7 8 9 10   **398.2**
1. Folklore—Southern States
ISBN 0-938317-74-1; 0-938317-73-3 (pa)
                                             LC 2003-1069
A collection of stories of the Choctaw people, including traditional lore arising from beliefs and myths, historical tales passed down through generations, and personal
stories of contemporary life
"Sophisticated narrative devices and some subtle character nuances give these stories a literary cast, but the
author's evocative language, expert pacing, and absorbing
subject matter will rivet readers and listeners both."
Booklist

Yiddish folktales; edited by Beatrice Silverman
Weinreich; translated by Leonard Wolf.
Pantheon Bks. 1988 xxxii, 413p il (Pantheon
fairy tale & folklore library) pa $18 hardcover
o.p.
Grades: 11 12 Adult   **398.2**
1. Jews—Folklore
ISBN 0-8052-1090-3 (pa)   LC 88-42594

Yiddish folktales—*Continued*

Published in cooperation with Yivo Institute for Jewish Research

A "collection of Yiddish folktales divided into various categories, including allegories, children's tales, humor, legends, and the supernatural. The more than 200 selections from the world of Eastern European Jewry are drawn from the archives of the YIVO Institute of Jewish Research. . . . {This work} brings the Yiddish culture of long ago vividly to life." Booklist

Zitkala-Sa, 1876-1938

American Indian stories, legends, and other writings; edited with an introduction and notes by Cathy N. Davidson and Ada Norris. Penguin Bks. 2003 xlvi, 268p il pa $13

Grades: 9 10 11 12   **398.2**

1. Native Americans—Folklore 2. Native Americans—Social conditions

ISBN 0-14-243709-3   LC 2002-32268

Also available in paperback from Bison books "Penguin classics"

This is a collection of stories and nonfiction writings by the Sioux writer and activist. "Her work, surprisingly, seems undated. . . . This first comprehensive collection . . . reveals Zitkala-Sa as a crusading, spiritually aware woman." Booklist

Includes bibliographical references

398.9 Proverbs

Cordry, Harold V., 1943-

The multicultural dictionary of proverbs; over 20,000 adages from more than 120 languages, nationalities and ethnic groups. McFarland & Co. 1997 406p pa $35

Grades: 11 12 Adult   **398.9**

1. Proverbs

ISBN 0-7864-0251-2; 0-7864-2262-9 (pa)

LC 96-33264

"The proverbs are arranged under 1300 headings (e.g., accidents, divided loyalty, marriage, and shame), and each includes the nationality, group or language in which it originated." Publisher's note

"This well-organized multicultural dictionary of proverbs not only illustrates the common insights that different cultures share but also provides a rich resource of wisdom that the casual reader can glean from perusing the proverbs in an entry." Am Ref Books Annu, 1998

A **Dictionary** of American proverbs; Wolfgang Mieder, editor in chief; Stewart A. Kingsbury and Kelsie B. Harder, editors. Oxford Univ. Press 1992 710p $65

Grades: 11 12 Adult   **398.9**

1. Proverbs

ISBN 0-19-505399-0   LC 91-15508

"This scholarly work includes 15,000 proverbs with variants currently used in the United States and parts of Canada. Entries are arranged alphabetically under key words and are often followed by variants and cross references. . . . This collection differs from most such compilations because the proverbs were collected by field workers rather than from written sources. The work sets new standards for understanding the oral tradition in America and is an essential purchase for ready-reference collections." Libr J

400 LANGUAGE

Crystal, David, 1941-

The Cambridge encyclopedia of language. 2nd ed. Cambridge Univ. Press 1997 480p il $85; pa $30

Grades: 11 12 Adult   **400**

1. Language and languages

ISBN 0-521-55050-5; 0-521-55967-7 (pa)

LC 96-3104

First published 1987

This encyclopedia "covers all the major themes of language study, including popular ideas about language, language and identity, the structure of language, speaking and listening, writing, reading, and signing, language acquisition, the neurological basis of language, and languages of the world. . . . [Also includes] advances in areas such as machine translation, speech interaction with machines, and language teaching." Univ Press Books for Public and Second Sch Libr, 1997

410 Linguistics

Crystal, David, 1941-

Language and the internet. 2nd ed. Cambridge University Press 2006 304p $29.99 *

Grades: 11 12 Adult   **410**

1. Language and languages 2. Internet

ISBN 978-0-521-86859-4; 0-521-86859-9

LC 2006-12916

First published 2001

"Covering a range of Internet genres, including e-mail, chat, and the Web, this is . . . [an] account of how the Internet is radically changing the way we use language." Publisher's note

Includes bibliographical references

Dalby, Andrew

Dictionary of languages; the definitive reference to more than 400 languages. Columbia Univ. Press 1999 734p il maps $73.50; pa $22.95 *

Grades: 11 12 Adult   **410**

1. Language and languages—Dictionaries

ISBN 0-231-11568-7; 0-231-11569-5 (pa)

LC 98-87178

This dictionary includes alphabetical entries that "cover all languages with official status as well as those with a written literature and 175 minor languages with significant historical and/or anthropological interest. A preface explains the author's pronunciation scheme. . . . The entries themselves are from two to four pages long. Each one discusses a specific language. . . . With coverage of languages from Abkhaz to Zulu, explanations of Egyp-

Dalby, Andrew—*Continued*
tian hieroglyphics and Sumerian script, and a discussion of Chinese dialects and characters, [this] . . . is a welcome addition to public and academic library collections." Booklist

412 Etymology

Hayakawa, S. I.
Language in thought and action; {by} S.I. Hayakawa and Alan R. Hayakawa. 5th ed. Harcourt Brace Jovanovich 1990 287p il $49.95; pa $16
Grades: 11 12 Adult   **412**
1. Semantics 2. Thought and thinking 3. English language
ISBN 0-15-550120-8; 0-15-648240-1 (pa)
                                                LC 89-84371
First published 1939 with title: Language in action
The author analyzes the nature of language, discusses the processes of thinking and writing, and gives advice on thinking and writing clearly
Includes bibliographical references

413 Dictionaries

Corbeil, Jean-Claude
The Firefly five language visual dictionary; [by] Jean-Claude Corbeil, [and] Ariane Archambault. Firefly Books 2004 1092p il map $49.95 *
Grades: 11 12 Adult   **413**
1. Polyglot dictionaries 2. Picture dictionaries
ISBN 1-55297-778-1   LC 2005-362868
This "is a compendium of more than 6000 full-color images and 35,000 terms in English, Spanish, French, German, and Italian, with entries arranged by subject and covering themes that range from astronomy to sports and everything in between. . . . The amount of detail jam-packed into each image is nothing short of remarkable. . . . Not only is this book useful in learning the details and nuances of a foreign language but it is a handy way to learn these terms in one's own language." Libr J

419 Verbal language not spoken and written

Costello, Elaine
Random House American sign language dictionary; illustrated by Lois Lenderman, Paul M. Setzer, Linda C. Tom. Random House 1994 xxxiv, 1067p il $55; pa $20
Grades: 11 12 Adult   **419**
1. Sign language
ISBN 0-394-58580-1; 0-679-78011-4 (pa)
Also available Random House Webster's concise American sign language dictionary pa $7.99 (ISBN 0-553-58474-X)

Costello "has compiled over 5000 signs in this massive dictionary. Each sign is illustrated with a full-torso picture showing hand configuration and movement, and both the common and alternate meanings are given where necessary. Arranged like a typical dictionary, this work is easy to use and very detailed." Libr J

Signing; how to speak with your hands; illustrated by Lois A. Lehman. rev ed. Bantam Bks. 1995 xx, 262p il pa $18.95
Grades: 11 12 Adult   **419**
1. Sign language
ISBN 0-553-37539-3   LC 94-46156
First published 1983
An illustrated introduction to American Sign Language (ASL) and its different uses by both the hearing and the deaf
Includes bibliographical references

The **Gallaudet** dictionary of American Sign Language; Clayton Valli, editor in chief; illustrated by Peggy Swartzel Lott, Daniel Renner, and Rob Hills. Gallaudet University Press 2005 xli, 558p il $49.95 *
Grades: 11 12 Adult   **419**
1. Sign language—Dictionaries
ISBN 1-56368-282-6; 978-1-56368-282-7
                                                LC 2005-51129
Includes DVD-ROM
This "reference work is composed of approximately 3000 illustrated entries, each showing the American Sign Language equivalent for an English word. The entries are arranged alphabetically and include synonyms where appropriate." Libr J
"This is a very valuable language resource for parents, students, and teachers learning ASL as a first language and as a second language." Choice
Includes bibliographical references

Grayson, Gabriel
Talking with your hands, listening with your eyes; a complete photographic guide to American Sign Language. Square One Pubs. 2002 373p il pa $26.95 *
Grades: 11 12 Adult   **419**
1. Sign language
ISBN 0-7570-0007-X   LC 2002-1125
"The book covers more than 900 signs that represent nearly 1,800 words and phrases, with signs grouped by topic. . . . Grayson provides instructions for each word, explaining the hand shape, the position in front of the body where the sign is made and the type of movement involved in expressing the word." Publ Wkly
"An outstanding, user-friendly resource for those interested in learning ASL." SLJ

Lewis, Karen B.
Sign language made simple; [by] Karen B. Lewis and Roxanne Henderson; illustrations by Michael Brown and Cassio Lynm; produced by The Philip Lief Group, Inc. Doubleday 1997 255p il pa $12.95
Grades: 11 12 Adult   **419**
1. Sign language
ISBN 0-385-48857-2   LC 97-9233
"A Made Simple book"
This book contains a brief history of signing and discusses its use of non-manual markers. The dictionary of American Sign Language signs is accompanied by approximately 1000 illustrations. Grammatical aspects such as word endings and tenses are addressed

Riekehof, Lottie L.
The joy of signing; the illustrated guide for mastering sign language and the manual alphabet. 2nd ed. Gospel Pub. House 1987 352p il $23.99
Grades: 11 12 Adult   **419**
1. Sign language
ISBN 0-88243-520-5   LC 86-80173
First published 1963 with title: Talk to the deaf
This manual presents over 1300 signs used for communicating with deaf adults, and provides basic vocabulary needed for entering interpreter training programs. Signs are arranged in 25 categories with an alphabetical index. For each sign there is a line drawing, description of how to make the sign, origin (concept) and notes on usage
Includes bibliographical references

Sternberg, Martin L. A.
American Sign Language; a comprehensive dictionary; illustrated by Herbert Rogoff. Unabridged. HarperCollins Pubs. 1998 xxi, 983p il $60; pa $24
Grades: 8 9 10 11 12 Adult   **419**
1. Sign language
ISBN 0-06-271608-5; 0-06-273634-5 (pa)
LC 98-26649
Also available American sign language concise dictionary pa $12 (ISBN 0-06-274010-5)
First published 1981
Arranged alphabetically, this dictionary features 7,000 sign entries, with cross-references and more than 12,000 illustrations
Includes bibliographical references

Essential ASL; the fun, fast, and simple way to learn American Sign Language; illustrations by Herbert Rogoff and Eduself. HarperPerennial 1996 322p il pa $7.95
Grades: 9 10 11 12   **419**
1. Sign language
ISBN 0-06-273428-8
This work is derived from the author's American sign language concise dictionary. It contains 700 of the more widely used signs illustrated with 2,000 pictures. 50 common phrases are also included

420 English and Old English

Crystal, David, 1941-
The Cambridge encyclopedia of the English language. 2nd ed. Cambridge Univ. Press 2003 499p il $75; pa $35 *
Grades: 11 12 Adult   **420**
1. English language
ISBN 0-521-82348-X; 0-521-53033-4 (pa)
LC 2003-272259
First published 1995
This "volume is divided into six broad topics that cover the English language's history, vocabulary, grammar, writing and speech systems, usage, and acquisition. Within these major topics, the book is divided into logical subtopics and finally into the basic unit of the text—the two-page spread. . . . The clear and spirited text is stunning, enhanced with over 500 illustrations, making this a particularly rich reference work and a browser's dream." Libr J {review of 1995 edition}

McCrum, Robert
The story of English; [by] Robert McCrum, Willam Cran [and] Robert MacNeil. 3rd rev ed. Penguin Bks. 2003 xxi, 468p pa $16
Grades: 11 12 Adult   **420**
1. English language—History
ISBN 0-14-200231-3   LC 2002-29818
First published 1986 by Viking
A "companion to the PBS television series of the same name. . . . The text covers the history of our language from its roots in Latin through its transplanting to other shores and its infusions from other cultures and languages. . . . Good for browsing, this book is a must for word and history buffs." SLJ [review of 1986 edition]
Includes bibliographical references

421 Written and spoken codes of standard English

Vos Savant, Marilyn Mach
The art of spelling; the madness and the method; by Marilyn vos Savant; illustrations by Joan Reilly. Norton 2000 204p il hardcover o.p. pa $12.95 *
Grades: 11 12 Adult   **421**
1. English language—Spelling
ISBN 0-393-04903-5; 0-393-32208-4 (pa)
LC 00-37228
The author "offers some suggestions for spelling improvement, supplying common roots like anim-, arch-, and spec- and a list of 500 commonly misspelled words. She also includes a few quizzes, with answers in the back of the book. This is not a how-to book, however, for more than half of it examines what spelling ability tells us about intelligence and personality. . . . The bibliography and web site list are nice additions as well." Libr J

421.03 Written and spoken codes of standard English--Dictionaries

The **Barnhart** abbreviations dictionary; edited by Robert K. Barnhart. Wiley 1995 xxi, 434p pa $39.95 *
Grades: 11 12 Adult   **421.03**
1. Abbreviations—Dictionaries 2. Signs and symbols 3. Acronyms
ISBN 0-471-57146-6   LC 96-115251
"This dictionary provides more than 60,000 entries for currently used abbreviations. . . . Two distinct parts form this work. The first is the list of abbreviation headwords with explanatory material. . . . The second part consists of a reverse list of words, phrases, and written symbols with current abbreviation forms. . . . [This work] belongs on ready reference shelves in academic and public libraries." Choice

422 Etymology of standard English

The **Oxford** dictionary of allusions; edited by Andrew Delahunty, Sheila Dignen, and Penny Stock. 2nd ed. Oxford University Press 2005 472p (Oxford paperback reference) pa $16.95 *
Grades: 11 12 Adult   **422**
1. Allusions
ISBN 0-19-860919-1; 978-0-19-860919-3
     LC 2005-44913
First published 2001
The text "categorizes entries under 190 general headings, ranging from fatness, destruction, and illusion to quest and outlaws. . . . Valuable to students are 22 special entries, nine from Greek mythology and an equal number from the Bible. . . . Selection of cited material is refreshingly unpedantic. Bram Stoker, Saki, V.S. Naipaul, Robertson Davies, Kurt Vonnegut, and Martin Amis are quoted alongside The Guardian, New Scientist, The Independent, and Observer and lines from classic English writers like Keats, Hardy, Thackeray, Pope, Wilde, and Richardson." Choice

422.03 Etymology of standard English--Dictionaries

Hendrickson, Robert, 1933-
The Facts on File encyclopedia of word and phrase origins. 3rd ed. Facts on File 2003 822p $82.50 *
Grades: 11 12 Adult   **422.03**
1. English language—Etymology—Dictionaries 2. English language—Terms and phrases
ISBN 0-8160-4813-4   LC 2003-44948
First published 1987
This work "contains definitions and origins of more than 12,500 words and expressions. . . . Anecdotes and information on the development of a wide range of words, including slang, proverbs, animal and plant names, place names, nicknames, historical expressions, foreign language expressions, and phrases from literature, are included. . . . The emphasis throughout is on words

and expressions whose origins are not adequately explained, or not addressed at all, in standard dictionaries." Publisher's note

The **Oxford** dictionary of English etymology; edited by C. T. Onions; with the assistance of G. W. S. Friedrichsen and R. W. Burchfield. Oxford Univ. Press 1966 1024p $65 *
Grades: 11 12 Adult   **422.03**
ISBN 0-19-861112-9
Also available in a concise edition pa $16.95 (ISBN 0-19-283098-8)
"Authoritative work tracing the history of common English words back to their Indo-European roots. The most complete and reliable etymological dictionary ever published, it serves as a complement to the OED." Ref Sources for Small & Medium-sized Libr. 6th edition

The **Oxford** dictionary of foreign words and phrases; edited by Jennifer Speake. Oxford Univ. Press 1997 512p pa $16.95 *
Grades: 11 12 Adult   **422.03**
ISBN 0-19-861051-3; 978-0-19-861051-9
     LC 96-49006
This dictionary features "a pronunciation guide for each word based on the International Phonetic Alphabet, and examples of usage. Some entries also feature notes on the historical or etymological background of the word or phrase. Approximately 8,000 words and phrases from more than 40 languages make up the main entries. . . . Included are words and phrases that have meaning in more than one sense or have come into general use in this century." Choice

423 Dictionaries of standard English

The **American** Heritage college dictionary. 4th ed. Houghton Mifflin 2007 xxviii, 1636p il map $26.95 *
Grades: 11 12 Adult   **423**
1. English language—Dictionaries
ISBN 978-0-618-83595-9; 0-618-83595-4
     LC 2007-276186
First published 1975 as an abridgment of The American Heritage dictionary of the English language
This dictionary is derived from the fourth edition of the American Heritage Dictionary of the English language. This edition includes over 2,000 photographs and drawings, usage advice, notes on synonyms, regionalisms, and word histories, biographical and geographical entries as well as a style manual.

The **American** heritage dictionary of phrasal verbs. Houghton Mifflin Co. 2005 466p $19.95
Grades: 11 12 Adult   **423**
1. English language—Terms and phrases
ISBN 0-618-59260-1; 978-0-618-59260-9
     LC 2005-12835
"This dictionary focuses on phrasal verbs, specifically those that have meaning beyond the literal definitions of the words involved." Libr J
"This unique resource belongs on the shelves of most

The American heritage dictionary of phrasal verbs—*Continued*

libraries as a complement to standard English-language dictionaries. It will be useful to native English speakers as well as to ESL students." Booklist

The American Heritage dictionary of the English language. 4th ed., New updated ed. Houghton Mifflin 2006 xxxvii, 2074p il $60 *

Grades: 11 12 Adult **423**

1. English language—Dictionaries
ISBN 0-618-70172-9; 978-0-617-70172-8

Also available CD-ROM version; print and CD-ROM edition $75 (ISBN: 0-618-70173-7; ISBN-13: 978-0-618-70173-5)

First published 1969

This dictionary provides over 210,000 main entries with over 4,000 full-color illustrations. Word histories, synonym paragraphs and regionalisms are also explored. The work also examines the influence of social factors such as age and ethnicity on how American English has been shaped by speakers from every social class.

This "eminently useful dictionary features fabulous full-color design that quickly and effectively guides users to the information they seek." Libr J

The American Heritage guide to contemporary usage and style. Houghton Mifflin 2005 512p $19.95 *

Grades: 11 12 Adult **423**

1. English language—Usage—Dictionaries
ISBN 978-0-618-60499-9; 0-618-60499-5

LC 2005-16513

"Drawing on the authoritative knowledge of its lexicographers and the considered collective judgment of a panel of noted writers, the book offers guidance on the simple (the pronunciations of bouquet); the perplexingly redundant (free gift); the often imprecisely used (impeach); the no longer distinct (healthful/healthy); the needless but persistent (irregardless); the easily confused (stationary/stationery); the unfortunately conflated (lay/lie); and many more pitfalls. Articles embodying the precision and lucidity of dictionary definitions explain the history of a word's or expression's usage issue, how and why the issue exists, and the preferred usage." Booklist

The American Heritage high school dictionary. 4th ed, updated ed. Houghton Mifflin 2007 xxvii, 1636p il map $26

Grades: 9 10 11 12 **423**

1. English language—Dictionaries
ISBN 978-0-618-71487-2; 0-618-71487-1

LC 2007-272676

Replaces the 4th ed. published 2002

A general dictionary of the English language adapted for high school students, including etymologies, biographical entries, geographical entries, usage notes, and synonyms.

Ammer, Christine

The Facts on File dictionary of clichés. 2nd ed. Facts on File 2006 534p (Facts on File library of language and literature) $50; pa $19.95

Grades: 9 10 11 12 **423**

1. English language—Terms and phrases 2. English language—Usage
ISBN 0-8160-6279-X; 0-8160-6280-3 (pa)

LC 2005-37999

First published 1992 with title: Have a nice day—no problem!: a dictionary of cliches

This dictionary "explains the meanings and origins of almost 4,000 clichés and common expressions. Each entry . . . includes the meaning of the cliché or expression, its origin and early uses, the historical development of the phrase, and its present-day usage." Publisher's note

"The book is inherently fascinating and an excellent place to look for old chestnuts galore." Libr J

Bartlett's Roget's thesaurus. Little, Brown 1996 xxxii, 1415p $21.95; pa $16.95 *

Grades: 8 9 10 11 12 Adult **423**

1. English language—Synonyms and antonyms
2. Americanisms
ISBN 0-316-10138-9; 0-316-73587-6 (pa)

LC 96-18343

This thesaurus "reflects the current state of American English, including terminology from the worlds of composers and television, with such sub-categories as 'Living Things,' 'The Arts,' 'Feelings.' But what really makes the book a joy to use is the tremendously useful lists—everything from phobias to styles and periods of furniture." Am Libr

Concise Oxford American thesaurus. Oxford University Press 2006 996p $19.95 *

Grades: 11 12 Adult **423**

1. English language—Synonyms and antonyms
ISBN 0-19-530485-3; 978-0-19-530485-5

LC 2005-35868

First published 1997 in the United Kingdom with title: The concise Oxford thesaurus; Original American edition published 1999 with title: The Oxford American thesaurus of current English

This "thesaurus contains over 15,000 entries with more than 350,000 synonyms and is . . . arranged with the typical synonyms listed first. . . . This simple arrangement makes this thesaurus particularly user-friendly." Libr J

Concise Oxford English dictionary; edited by Catherine Soanes, Angus Stevenson. 11th ed. Oxford University Press 2004 xx, 1708p $29.95 *

Grades: 11 12 Adult **423**

1. English language—Dictionaries
ISBN 0-19-860864-0; 978-0-19-860864-6

LC 2004-53134

First published 1911 under the editorship of H. W. Fowler and F. G. Fowler with title: The Concise dictionary of current English

This work contains over 240,000 entries, including derivatives, compounds and abbreviations. It includes explanatory notes on pronunciation, grammatical inflection and etymology.

Corbeil, Jean-Claude

Merriam-Webster's visual dictionary; [by] Jean-Claude Corbeil, Ariane Archambault; [illustrators, Jean-Yves Ahern . . . [et al.] Merriam-Webster 2006 952p il map $39.95 *

Grades: 11 12 Adult   423

1. English language—Dictionaries 2. Picture dictionaries

ISBN 978-0-8777-9051-8; 0-8777-9051-5

"Logically organized into 17 broad categories (e.g., astronomy, humans, animals, clothing, and society), with numerous subcategories to make finding the needed terms easy, this is the only visual dictionary that includes definitions with the terms. And its price is very reasonable for such a substantial book. Essential." Libr J

Davidson, Mark

Right, wrong, and risky; a dictionary of today's American English usage. Norton 2006 570p $29.95 *

Grades: 11 12 Adult   423

1. English language—Usage 2. English language—Dictionaries 3. Americanisms

ISBN 0-393-06119-1   LC 2005-17628

The author "offers a dictionary that 'views the real world of today's American English, identifying usage questions that are debatable, citing conflicting answers, and offering risk-free solutions for each conflict.' . . . Browsers will enjoy the colorful, interesting backstories on the origins of terms such as ground zero, on the sudden warming to the phrase girl talk, and on the widely misunderstood use of the word Neanderthal." Booklist

Includes bibliographical references

The **essential** high school dictionary. Random House 2006 xxvi, 630p il pa $12.95

Grades: 9 10 11 12   423

1. English language—Dictionaries

ISBN 0-375-76543-3; 978-0-375-76543-8

LC 2006-298226

First published 1993 with title: Random House Webster's school & office dictionary

At head of title: Princeton Review

This annotated dictionary includes synonyms, etymologies, cultural histories behind words, and lists of frequently misused words.

Garner, Bryan A.

Garner's modern American usage. 2nd ed. Oxford Univ. Press 2003 848p $39.95

Grades: 11 12 Adult   423

1. English language—Usage 2. Americanisms

ISBN 0-19-516191-2

First published 1998 with title: A dictionary of modern American usage

"Containing roughly 7000 main entries and many cross references, the dictionary offers intelligent, sensible, readable advice concerning usage demons involving problems of grammar, spelling, homonyms, variants, clichés, skunked words, redundancies, phrasal adjectives and verbs, and more." Libr J [review of 1998 edition]

Includes bibliographical references

Laird, Charlton, 1901-

Webster's New World Roget's A-Z thesaurus; [by] Charlton Laird and the editors of Webster's New World dictionaries; Michael Agnes, editor in chief. Macmillan USA 1999 xxxiii, 894p $21.99; pa $12.95 *

Grades: 11 12 Adult   423

1. English language—Synonyms and antonyms

ISBN 0-02-863122-6; 0-02-863123-4 (pa)

LC 99-13475

"A Webster's New World book"

First published 1948 by Holt with title: Laird's promptory; Variant title: Webster's New World thesaurus

This alphabetically arranged thesaurus contains more than 300,000 synonyms and derived terms of commonly used words and phrases. Includes information on usage and idioms. Brief definitions are included.

Merriam-Webster's collegiate dictionary. Eleventh ed. Merriam-Webster 2003 1623p il $23.95

Grades: 11 12 Adult   423

1. English language—Dictionaries

ISBN 0-87779-808-7   LC 2003-3674

Also available thumb-indexed print and CD-ROM edition $26.95 (ISBN 0-87779-809-5) and online

First published 1898

This edition includes over 165,000 entries, 10,000 new words and meanings, 38,000 etymologies, a handbook of style, an essay on the English language, a special section on signs and symbols, and a free one-year subscription to the Collegiate Web site.

Merriam-Webster's collegiate thesaurus. Merriam-Webster 1993 868p $17.95

Grades: 11 12 Adult   423

1. English language—Synonyms and antonyms

ISBN 0-87779-169-4   LC 93-3177

Also available on CD-ROM as part of Merriam-Webster's collegiate dictionary & thesaurus and online

First published 1976 with title: Webster's collegiate thesaurus

"Employs a conventional dictionary arrangement, and gives synonyms, related terms, idiomatic equivalents, antonyms, and contrasted words as applicable. Cross-references in small capitals." Guide to Ref Books. 11th edition

Merriam-Webster's dictionary of synonyms; a dictionary of discriminated synonyms with antonyms and analogous and contrasted words. Merriam-Webster 1984 909p $22.95

Grades: 9 10 11 12 Adult   423

1. English language—Synonyms and antonyms

ISBN 0-87779-341-7

Also available in paperback with title: The Merriam-Webster dictionary of synonyms and antonyms

First published 1942 with title: Webster's dictionary of synonyms

"This synonym dictionary is an outstanding work. . . . Synonyms and similar words, alphabetically arranged, are carefully defined, discriminated, and illustrated with thousands of quotations. The entries also include antonyms and analogous words." Nichols. Guide to Ref Books for Sch Media Cent. 4th edition

Metaphors dictionary; [edited by] Elyse Sommer, with Dorrie Weiss. Visible Ink Press 2001 xlvi, 612p $24.95 *

Grades: 11 12 Adult   423

1. English language—Terms and phrases
ISBN 1-57859-137-6

First published 1995 by Gale Res.

This is a "collection of 6,500 colorful classic and contemporary comparative phrases (with full annotations and a complete bibliography of sources) . . . organized under 500 timeless and timely themes, ranging from Aloneness to Love to Zeal." Publisher's note

"Any library serving patrons involved in creative writing, composition, public speaking, or literary criticism should add this volume." Am Ref Books Annu, 1996 [entry for 1995 edition]

The **New** Oxford American dictionary. 2nd ed. Oxford University Press 2005 xl, 2051p il map $60 *

Grades: 11 12 Adult   423

1. English language—Dictionaries 2. Americanisms
ISBN 0-19-517077-6

Also available Concise Oxford American dictionary $19.95 (ISBN-10: 0-19-530484-5; ISBN-13: 978-0-19-530484-8)

First published 1980 with title: The Oxford American dictionary

Includes CD-ROM

"The entries are organized around core meanings. . . . [Each entry] shows the major meaning or meanings of the word, plus any related senses. . . . Definitions are supplemented by illustrative, in-context examples of actual usage." Publisher's note

The **Oxford** American writer's thesaurus; compiled by Christine A. Lindberg. Oxford University Press 2004 xxiv, 1088p $40

Grades: 11 12 Adult   423

1. English language—Synonyms and antonyms
ISBN 0-1951-7076-8

"In addition to the more than 300,000 synonyms and 10,000 antonyms found in the thesaurus, each . . . editorial board member (including David Auburn, Michael Dirda, David Lehman, Stephin Merritt, Francine Prose, Zadie Smith, Jean Strouse, David Foster Wallace, and Simon Winchester) has contributed . . . mini-essays on words that they particularly love, hate, admire, or are just plain puzzled by." Publisher's note

"This work breaks away from the traditional format of simple lists of synonyms and antonyms by offering a number of ingenious and helpful features set within boxes in the text. . . . Although loaded with special features, this thesaurus doesn't undermine its more traditional duties." Libr J

Random House Webster's college dictionary. [Rev and updated ed] Random House Reference 2005 xxvi, 1597p il map $26.95 *

Grades: 11 12 Adult   423

1. English language—Dictionaries
ISBN 0-375-42600-0   LC 2005-280097

First published 1991 as a successor to The Random House college dictionary

Includes CD-ROM

"Each entry in the dictionary presents spelling, along with alternatives, syllabication, pronunciation used in conversational speech (with alternatives), and part of speech. Entries also include meanings and definitions, with the most common usage listed first; historical, technical, or other usages of the term; date of first usage, including place of origin; and other related words that use the same root or stem. . . . The dictionary includes over 207,000 definitions, many of them so new they are not yet found in competing products. . . . For libraries seeking a wide variety of dictionaries, this work will prove especially useful for its inclusion of recent terms and idioms." Am Ref Books Annu, 2001 [entry for 2001 edition]

Random House Webster's college thesaurus. Rev. and updated ed. Random House Reference 2000 820p $22.95 *

Grades: 11 12 Adult   423

1. English language—Synonyms and antonyms
ISBN 0-375-42596-9; 978-0-375-42596-7
                    LC 2005-279530

First published 1984 with title: Random House thesaurus

Based on Reader's digest family word finder; "Published as Random House Roget's college thesaurus in 2000, revised and updated by Enid Pearsons and Carol G. Braham" Verso of title page

An alphabetical listing of main-entry word lists which group together synonyms and antonyms by meaning. Also included are sample sentences for every main entry (and for each meaning).

Random House Webster's easy English dictionary. Random House 2001 620p il pa $12.95

Grades: 9 10 11 12   423

1. English language—Dictionaries
ISBN 0-375-70484-1   LC 2001-19985

This dictionary contains over 13,000 words and phrases and offers over 17,000 example sentences. It provides extensive usage, grammar, synonyms, has a basic word list for TOEFL (Test of English as a Foreign Language) and gives IPA (International Phonetic Alphabet) pronunciations

Random House Webster's intermediate English dictionary. Random House 2001 xx, 522p il pa $11.95

Grades: 9 10 11 12   423

1. English language—Dictionaries
ISBN 0-375-71964-4   LC 2001-19978

This dictionary includes over 45,000 words and phrases, provides definitions with additional grammatical assistance. Also included are international phonetic alphabet pronunciations and coverage of business and technical terms

Random House Webster's unabridged dictionary. 2nd ed. Random House 2005 xxvi, 2230p il map $59.95 *

Grades: 8 9 10 11 12 Adult   423

1. English language—Dictionaries
ISBN 0-375-42599-3

First published 1966 with title: The Random House dictionary of the English language

Random House Webster's unabridged dictionary—*Continued*

This dictionary contains over 315,000 entries. A new-words section and an essay on the growth of English are included. 2,400 spot maps and illustrations complement the text

Roget's 21st century thesaurus in dictionary form; the essential reference for home, school, or office; edited by the Princeton Language Institute; Barbara Ann Kipfer, head lexicographer. 3rd ed. Bantam Dell 2005 962p $15; pa $5.99 *

Grades: 11 12 Adult   **423**

1. English language—Synonyms and antonyms
ISBN 0-385-33895-3; 0-440-24269-X (pa)
"A Delta book"
First published 1992
"Produced by the Philip Lief Group, Inc."
This thesaurus, cross referencing each word with the same concept, provides 500,000 synonyms and antonyms in a dictionary format and includes recently coined and common slang terms and commonly used foreign terms.

Roget's II; the new thesaurus. Houghton Mifflin 2003 1200p $21

Grades: 11 12 Adult   **423**

1. English language—Synonyms and antonyms
ISBN 0-618-25414-5
Also available online
First published 1980
The work uses a dictionary format, with words and numbered definitions on the left column of a page, and corresponding numbered synonyms, near-synonyms, antonyms and near-antonyms on the right column.

Sheehan, Michael, 1939-
Word parts dictionary; standard and reverse listings of prefixes, suffixes, and combining forms. McFarland & Co. 2000 227p lib bdg $39.95 *

Grades: 11 12 Adult   **423**

1. English language—Dictionaries
ISBN 0-7864-0819-7   LC 00-37217
This dictionary "contains three sections: a standard dictionary that arranges the word parts in alphabetic order; a 'finder' dictionary that is really a reverse dictionary for words; and the categories, which is also a reverse dictionary but one that arranges the words in broad clusters of meanings. Although numbers are not given, the standard dictionary (the source for the word parts) contains more than 6,000 word definitions, ranging from the commonplace to the enjoyably obscure." Am Ref Books Annu, 2001

Visual dictionary. Rev. and updated. DK Pub. 2006 672p il map $40 *

Grades: 7 8 9 10 11 12 Adult   **423**

1. Picture dictionaries 2. English language—Dictionaries
ISBN 0-756-62606-4; 978-0-756-62606-8
First published 1994 with title: Dorling Kindersley ultimate visual dictionary. Variant titles: DK ultimate visual dictionary, Ultimate visual dictionary

This dictionary features over 33,000 terms and more than 6,000 color illustrations detailing everything from the prehistoric earth, the physical and biological science, to the visual arts, architecture, music, sports and common, ordinary everyday things.

Webster's II new college dictionary. 3rd ed. Houghton Mifflin 2004 c2005 1518p il $25.95

Grades: 9 10 11 12   **423**

1. English language—Dictionaries
ISBN 0-618-39601-2   LC 2003-57079
First published 1995
This dictionary includes over 150,000 definitions and hundreds of synonyms, usage notes and etymologies. Terminology from the fields of science and technology as well as computers is provided. Also includes a style guide with rules for capitalization and punctuation as well as biographical and geographical sections

Webster's third new international dictionary of the English language, unabridged; editor in chief, Philip Babcock Gove and the Merriam-Webster editorial staff. Merriam-Webster 2002 144a, 2662p il $129 *

Grades: 7 8 9 10 11 12 Adult   **423**

1. English language—Dictionaries
ISBN 0-87779-201-1   LC 2003-272164
Prices vary according to binding; Also available print and CD-ROM edition and online
Original edition by Noah Webster published 1828 with title: An American dictionary of the English language. Has also appeared under various other titles. First published with present title 1961
"Clear, accurate definitions are given in historical order. Outstanding for its numerous illustrative quotations, impeccable authority, and etymologies, Webster's third is regarded as the most reliable, comprehensive general unabridged dictionary." Ref Sources for Small & Medium-sized Libr. 6th edition

Young, Sue
The new comprehensive American rhyming dictionary. Morrow 1991 622p pa $14.95 hardcover o.p. *

Grades: 11 12 Adult   **423**

1. English language—Rhyme 2. Americanisms
ISBN 0-380-71392-6 (pa)   LC 90-19165
This book contains over 65,000 words and phrases categorized by sound, rather than spelling. It includes many colloquialisms and slang expressions.

427 English language variations

Ammer, Christine
The American Heritage dictionary of idioms. Houghton Mifflin 1997 729p $32; pa $14.95 *

Grades: 11 12 Adult   **427**

1. English language—Idioms 2. English language—Terms and phrases 3. Americanisms
ISBN 0-395-72774-X; 0-618-24953-2 (pa)
    LC 97-12390

Ammer, Christine—*Continued*

"In addition to idioms, the dictionary includes common figures of speech, formula phrases such as 'take care,' emphatic redundancies whose word order cannot be reversed such as 'cease and desist,' common proverbs, colloquialisms, and slang phrases. Each expression is defined briefly and then illustrated by a short, simple sentence showing how it is used in context." SLJ

Includes bibliographical references

The **Cassell** dictionary of English idioms; [editor, Rosalind Fergusson] Cassell 2000 392p hardcover o.p. pa $14.95

Grades: 11 12 Adult   **427**
1. English language—Idioms 2. English language—Terms and phrases
ISBN 0-304-35009-5; 0-304-36384-7 (pa)
                                        LC 00-340364

"Idiomatic expressions are arranged alphabetically by their 'core' or key terms. . . . Approximately 10,000 idioms have been selected from English as it is used today in North America, Australia, New Zealand, and the British Isles. Usage notes identify country of origin of expressions tied closely to one culture. Notes also label terms as colloquial or slang as appropriate." Booklist

Dickson, Paul

Slang! the topical dictionary of Americanisms. Walker & Co. 2006 418p $24.95 *

Grades: 11 12 Adult   **427**
1. English language—Slang—Dictionaries 2. Americanisms—Dictionaries
ISBN 0-8027-1531-1; 978-0-8027-1531-9
First published 1990 by Pocket Bks.

On cover: New and completely updated

This American slang dictionary "includes 30 topics, such as 'Bureaucratese' and 'Real Estate,' and more than 10,000 words." Libr J

"Informative, reliable, entertaining, and modern, this topical slang dictionary complements the more staid slang lexicons and more scholarly general dictionaries." Booklist

Includes bibliographical references

Green, Jonathon

Cassell's dictionary of slang. 2nd ed. Weidenfeld & Nicholson 2005 1565p $39.95 *

Grades: 11 12 Adult   **427**
1. English language—Slang—Dictionaries
ISBN 0-304-36636-6
First published 1998 by Cassell with title: The Cassell dictionary of slang

"Green includes words from the seventeenth century to the present with slang from all English-speaking areas: U.S., U.K., Canada, the Caribbean, New Zealand, Australia, and India. Each entry includes the part of speech, date of use, and definition. In a volume of this size it would be impossible to cite each source, so instead Green includes a bibliography of more than 200 books and numerous newspapers, comics, films, television scripts, and even Internet sites." Booklist [review of 1998 edition]

Hendrickson, Robert, 1933-

The Facts on File dictionary of American regionalisms. Facts on File 2000 786p $82.50

Grades: 11 12 Adult   **427**
1. English language—Dictionaries 2. Americanisms
ISBN 0-8160-4156-3   LC 00-28808

This "resource covers colorful and ordinary expressions spoken in several geographical regions, samples from the dialects spoken by Hawaiian and Pennsylvania Dutch people, and brief information about the dialects Bawlamerese, Bonac, Conch, Gullah, and Boont. A typical section includes a general discussion of the regional language or dialect (etymology, pronunciation, and grammatical variations) followed by alphabetized words and phrases briefly defined." Libr J

The **new** Partridge dictionary of slang and unconventional English; Tom Dalzell (senior editor) and Terry Victor (editor). Routledge 2006 2v set $220

Grades: 11 12 Adult   **427**
1. English language—Slang—Dictionaries
ISBN 0-415-21258-8; 978-0-415-21258-8
First published 1937

"New editorial matter and selection, Tom Dalzell and Terry Victor; material taken from The dictionary of slang and unconventional English, 8th edition (first published 1984), E. Partridge and P. Beale estates" Verso of title page

"Entries list the term, identify its part of speech, explain its meaning, identify the country of origin, and cite sources or provide quotations showing how the term is used. . . . This dictionary informs, but it also entertains." Booklist

Includes bibliographical references

Spears, Richard A.

McGraw-Hill's American idioms dictionary. 4th ed. McGraw-Hill 2007 xxiii, 743p il pa $16.95

Grades: 9 10 11 12   **427**
1. English language—Idioms 2. English language—Terms and phrases 3. Americanisms
ISBN 978-0-07-147893-9; 0-07-147893-0
                                        LC 2006-46933

First published 1987 with title: NTC's American idioms dictionary

This dictionary contains more than 14,000 idiomatic phrases in American parlance. Meaning, usage and appropriate contexts are given for each idiomatic phrase.

Includes bibliographical references

McGraw-Hill's dictionary of American slang and colloquial expressions. 4th ed. McGraw-Hill 2006 xxix, 546p pa $19.95 *

Grades: 11 12 Adult   **427**
1. English language—Slang—Dictionaries 2. Americanisms
ISBN 0-07-146107-8; 978-0-07-146107-8
                                        LC 2005-52220

First published 1989 with title: NTC's dictionary of American slang and colloquial expressions

This book offers "definitions of more than 12,000 slang and informal expressions from various sources, ranging from golden oldies such as . . . golden oldie, to

Spears, Richard A.—*Continued*
recent coinages like shizzle (gangsta), jonx (Wall Street), and ping (the Internet). Each entry is followed by examples illustrating how an expression is used in everyday conversation and, where necessary, International Phonetic Alphabet pronunciations are given, as well as cautionary notes for crude, inflammatory, or taboo expressions." Publisher's note

Includes bibliographical references

428   Standard English usage

Fowler, H. W., 1858-1933.
Fowler's modern English usage; first edition by H.W. Fowler. Rev. 3rd ed., by R.W. Burchfield. Oxford University Press 2004 xxi, 873p $35
Grades: 11 12 Adult   **428**
1. English language—Etymology 2. English language—Idioms 3. English language—Usage
ISBN 0-19-861021-1; 978-0-19-861021-2
                              LC 2005-271630
First published 1926 with title: A dictionary of modern English usage; 2000 edition published with title: The new Fowler's modern English usage
This alphabetically arranged guide gives "advice on grammar, syntax, style, and choice of words." Publisher's note

Merriam-Webster's dictionary of English usage.
Merriam-Webster 1994 978p $24.95 *
Grades: 9 10 11 12   **428**
1. English language—Usage
ISBN 0-87779-132-5   LC 93-19289
First published 1989 with title: Webster's dictionary of English usage
This guide looks at English usage from both historical and contemporary perspectives. Over 20,000 quotations illustrate the discussion of usage issues. Provides explanations of how accomplished writers have dealt with usage problems. Grammar, spelling and punctuation points are also covered

Includes bibliographical references

O'Conner, Patricia T.
Woe is I; the grammarphobe's guide to better English in plain English. Riverhead Bks. 2003 240p $19.95; pa $14
Grades: 11 12 Adult   **428**
1. English language—Grammar 2. English language—Usage
ISBN 1-57322-252-6; 1-59448-006-0 (pa)
                              LC 2003-41416
First published 1996
This guide to good English offers advice on punctuation, usage, style and grammar as well as e-mail.
"The author doesn't take herself or the subject matter too seriously, offering a delightful romp through the intricacies of our language. . . . She knows her subject, can convey her message with wit and ease, and does it all in a compact, easy-to-read format. In short, this is an entertaining and useful grammar reference." Libr J

Includes bibliographical references

Ostler, Rosemarie
Dewdroppers, waldos, and slackers; a decade-by-decade guide to the vanishing vocabulary of the twentieth century. Oxford University Press 2003 239p il $25
Grades: 9 10 11 12   **428**
1. English language—Slang
ISBN 0-19-516146-7   LC 2003-8302
"This reference work is not simply a slang dictionary. Along with definitions . . . Ostler includes in each decade's chapter both brief discussions of relevant cultural topics and a few photos. These short, often humorous essays are a way to provide examples for the terms defined. . . . Ostler's work is fun for browsing; it offers a unique presentation of recent cultural history." Libr J

Includes bibliographical references

Peters, Pam
The Cambridge guide to English usage.
Cambridge University Press 2004 608p il $35 *
Grades: 11 12 Adult   **428**
1. English language—Usage
ISBN 0-521-62181-X   LC 2004-301888
"Covering over 3000 points of word meaning, spelling, punctuation, grammar, and style, the alphabetically arranged entries often include references to resources where the information was found." Libr J
"Considering the abundance of peculiarities and challenges in English usage, *Cambridge* will strengthen even a library well stocked with other guides. It is a serious book for those serious about language." Booklist

Truss, Lynne
Eats, shoots & leaves; the zero tolerance approach to punctuation. Gotham Books 2004 xxvii, 209p $19.95
Grades: 11 12 Adult   **428**
1. Punctuation
ISBN 1-59240-087-6   LC 2004-40646
First published 2003 in the United Kingdom
The author "dissects common errors that grammar mavens have long deplored (often, as she readily points out, in isolation) and makes . . . arguments for increased attention to punctuation correctness. . . . Truss serves up delightful, unabashedly strict and sometimes snobby little book, with cheery Britishisms ('Lawks-a-mussy!') dotting pages that express a more international righteous indignation." Publ Wkly

Includes bibliographical references

433   German language--Dictionaries

Random House Webster's German-English, English-German dictionary. Rev. ed. Random House Reference 2006 c1998 547p $12.95 *
Grades: 11 12 Adult   **433**
1. German language—Dictionaries
ISBN 0-375-72194-0; 978-0-375-72194-6
Also available in paperback from Ballantine Bks.
First published 1997 with title: Random House German-English English-German dictionary

Random House Webster's German-English, English-German dictionary—*Continued*

In addition to more than 60,000 entries this dictionary also includes notes on pronunciation, lists of abbreviations, tables of irregular verbs and lists of geographical names.

440 Romance languages. French

Cracking the SAT: French subject test, 2007-2008 edition; [by] the Princeton Review. Random House 2007 il pa $18

Grades: 9 10 11 12 **440**

1. French language—Study and teaching 2. Scholastic Assessment Test 3. Colleges and universities—Entrance requirements

ISBN 0-375-76589-1; 978-0-375-76589-6

Annual. First published 2005. Continues Cracking the SAT II: French subject tests

At head of title: The Princeton Review

This guide provides test-taking strategies and sample tests on the subject of French.

443 French language--Dictionaries

Larousse concise dictionary: Spanish-English, English-Spanish; [project management/dirección, Sharon J. Hunter] Larousse 2006 various paging $22.95; pa $12.95

Grades: 9 10 11 12 **443**

1. Spanish language—Dictionaries

ISBN 2-03-542138-1; 978-2-03-542138-8; 2-03-542137-3 (pa); 978-2-03-542137-1 (pa)

First published 1999

"With more than 90,000 references and 120,000 translations, including English compounds, English phonetics, and a supplement on life and culture in Spain, Latin America, the United Kingdom, and the U.S., this concise bilingual dictionary provides essential, everyday vocabulary for language learners." Booklist [review of 1999 edition]

The **Oxford-Hachette** French dictionary; French-English, English-French; edited by Marie-Hélène Corréard, Valerie Grundy. 3rd ed, edited by Jean-Benoit Ormal-Grenon, Natalie Pomier. Oxford Univ. Press 2001 xxxviii, 1945p il $45 *

Grades: 11 12 Adult **443**

1. French language—Dictionaries

ISBN 0-19-860363-0

First published 1994

This work provides coverage of French and English vocabulary in general as well as scientific and technical areas with some 350,000 words and phrases and some 530,000 translations. Supplementary material includes information on French society and culture, including famous places, people and much practical information for those planning to reside in France

Le **petit** Larousse illustré; en couleurs. Larousse 2006 1855p il map $59.95

Grades: 9 10 11 12 **443**

1. French language—Dictionaries

ISBN 2-03-582491-5; 978-2-03-582491-2

First published 1906. Title varies

Earlier editions by Pierre Larousse, published with title: Nouveau petit Larousse illustré, and Petit Larousse. Frequently revised to keep up to date with new words and accepted expressions. Text in French.

Random House Webster's French-English, English-French dictionary. Random House Reference 2006 588p pa $12.95 *

Grades: 11 12 Adult **443**

1. French language—Dictionaries

ISBN 978-0-375-72193-9; 0-375-72193-2

LC 2006-297159

Also available in paperback from Ballantine Bks.

First published 1997 with title: Random House French-English, English-French dictionary

This dictionary of more than 60,000 entries includes thousands of idioms, phrases and common expressions. Tables of irregular verbs are included as is a single A-Z listing of countries and other geographical names. Informal usages are labeled.

460 Spanish and Portuguese languages

Cracking the SAT: Spanish subject test, 2007-2008 edition; [by] the Princeton Review. Random House 2007 il pa $18

Grades: 9 10 11 12 **460**

1. Spanish language—Study and teaching 2. Scholastic Assessment Test 3. Colleges and universities—Entrance requirements

ISSN 1558-3406

ISBN 0-375-76595-6; 978-0-375-76595-7

Annual. First published 2005. Continues Cracking the S A T II: Spanish subject test

At head of title: The Princeton Review

This guide provides test-taking strategies and sample tests on the subject of Spanish.

463 Dictionaries of standard Spanish

The **American** Heritage Spanish dictionary; Spanish/English, inglés/español. 2nd ed. Houghton Mifflin 2001 xxx, 1103p $26 *

Grades: 11 12 Adult **463**

1. Spanish language—Dictionaries

ISBN 0-618-12770-4 LC 2001-24524

Also available online; The Concise American Heritage Spanish dictionary, 2nd edition published 2001 is also available

"With an emphasis on American English and Latin American Spanish, . . . this bilingual dictionary includes new technological, scientific, and business terms. Speakers of all the Americas will appreciate the different meanings of more than 120,000 words, presented in an easy-to-understand design. Notes on grammar usage are a plus." Booklist

Cassell's Spanish-English, English-Spanish dictionary. Completely rev and reset ed, completely rev by Anthony Gooch, Angel Garcia de Paredes. Macmillan 1978 xxv, 1109p thumb-indexed $22.95 *

Grades: 8 9 10 11 12 Adult   **463**
1. Spanish language—Dictionaries
ISBN 0-02-522910-9   LC 77-18453
Also available in a concise edition for $13 (ISBN 0-02-522660-6)

First published 1959 in the United Kingdom. First American edition published 1960 by Funk & Wagnall's with title: Cassell's Spanish dictionary

This dictionary emphasizes the Spanish of Latin America, and includes both classical and literary Spanish as well as the language of the modern Spanish-speaking world

Corbeil, Jean-Claude
The Firefly Spanish/English junior visual dictionary; [by] Jean-Claude Corbeil; Ariane Archambault. Firefly Books 2006 368p il $19.95 *

Grades: 5 6 7 8 9 10 11 12   **463**
1. Spanish language—Dictionaries 2. Picture dictionaries
ISBN 978-1-55407-190-6; 1-55407-190-9
"Items are arranged under 22 broad topics such as 'Astronomy,' 'Music,' and 'Transportation.' . . . In the labels, the Spanish word appears under the English word. . . . There are 12,000 terms and 2,000 illustrations for everyday objects like suitcases, airplanes, and different kinds of gloves." Booklist

Larousse standard diccionario, español-inglés, inglés-español. 3. ed. Larousse 2004 575, 62, 664p $36

Grades: 11 12 Adult   **463**
1. Spanish language—Dictionaries
ISBN 2-03-542076-8   LC 2004-459150
Replaces the edition published 1996 with title: Larousse English-Spanish, Spanish-English dictionary

With over 174,000 references and 257,000 translations this dictionary covers general, professional and literary vocabulary. Abbreviations, acronyms and proper nouns are included. Contains special sections on language usage arranged alphabetically in main dictionary text.

Multicultural Spanish dictionary; how everyday Spanish differs from country to country. Schreiber Pub. 2006 281p pa $24.95 *

Grades: 9 10 11 12   **463**
1. Spanish language—Dictionaries
ISBN 978-0-884003-17-5; 0-884003-17-5
    LC 2006-13957
First published 1999 under the editorship of Agustín Martínez

"Divided into three parts (English-Spanish, Spanish-English and subject areas) this guide includes the most commonly used words throughout Latin America and Spain in the most common areas of everyday life. As stated in the introduction, it 'is not meant to replace the standard Spanish-English dictionary'; rather, it is a useful basic guide to a variety of common Spanish terms." Booklist [review of 1999 edition]

The **Oxford** Spanish dictionary; Spanish-English/English-Spanish; chief editors, Beatriz Galimberti Jarman, Roy Russell; edited by Carol Styles Carvajal, Jane Horwood. 3rd ed. Oxford Univ. Press 2003 xlviii, 1977p $49.95 *

Grades: 11 12 Adult   **463**
1. Spanish language—Dictionaries
ISBN 0-19-860475-0   LC 2003-272816
Also available CD-ROM version; print and CD-ROM edition $75 (ISBN: 0-19-860878-0; ISBN-13: 978-0-19-860878-3)

First published 1994
Title page in English and Spanish
This dictionary contains over 300,000 words and phrases, 500,000 translations and "covers over 24 varieties of Spanish as it is written and spoken throughout the Spanish-speaking world. . . . Special entries on life and culture explain the differences between institutions, administrative systems, educational systems, and general life in the Spanish and English-speaking worlds, offering vital background to the language." Publisher's note

473   Dictionaries of classical Latin

Cassell's Latin dictionary; Latin-English, English-Latin; by D. P. Simpson. Macmillan 1977 c1959 883p thumb-indexed $24.95

Grades: 11 12 Adult   **473**
1. Latin language—Dictionaries
ISBN 0-02-522580-4   LC 77-7670
Also available in a concise paperback edition for $7.99 (ISBN 0-02-013340-5; ISBN-13: 978-0-02-013340-7)

First published 1854. This edition first published 1959. Previous United States editions published by Funk & Wagnalls with title: Cassell's New Latin dictionary

"Cassell's incorporates current English idiom and Latin spelling into the traditional presentation of classical Latin. The 30,000 entries include generic terms, geographical and proper nouns. Etymological notes and illustrative quotations are provided within entries." Wynar. Guide to Ref Books for Sch Media Cent. 3d edition

491.7   East Slavic languages. Russian

Oxford Russian dictionary; Russian-English, edited by Marcus Wheeler and Boris Unbegaun; English-Russian, edited by Paul Falla; revised and updated by Della Thompson. 4th ed. Oxford University Press 2007 xxi, 1322p $65

Grades: 11 12 Adult   **491.7**
1. Russian language—Dictionaries
ISBN 978-0-19-861420-3; 0-19-861420-9
    LC 2007-9399
First published 1972 with title: The Oxford Russian-English dictionary

Oxford Russian dictionary—*Continued*

This dictionary features over 500,000 words, phrases, and translations and includes a correspondence section and cultural notes as well as special boxes to help with tricky words and terms.

492.4   Hebrew language

Zilkha, Avraham

Modern English-Hebrew dictionary. Yale Univ. Press 2002 457p (Yale language series) $55; pa $30

Grades: 11 12 Adult   492.4

1. Hebrew language—Dictionaries

ISBN 0-300-09004-8; 0-300-09005-6 (pa)

LC 2001-26830

This dictionary includes 30,000 entries, with listings for translating words with multiple meanings, newly coined and slang words, common idioms, vocalization of Hebrew words, acronyms, and gender identification and plural forms of irregular nouns

495.1   Chinese language

A **New** English-Chinese dictionary; edited by Zheng Yi Li [et al.] 2nd rev ed. Wiley 1985 1613p pa $64.95 hardcover o.p.

Grades: 11 12 Adult   495.1

1. Chinese language—Dictionaries

ISBN 0-471-80897-0 (pa)

Also available from French & European Publications

"Originally published in 1950 (Shanghai) with a first revision appearing in 1957 (Peking), this current volume presents more than 120,000 entries including abbreviations, compounds, and derivatives for a total of 6 million words in all." Choice

495.6   Japanese language

Basic Japanese-English dictionary. 2nd ed. Oxford University Press, Bonjinsha 2004 1000p pa $19.95

Grades: 7 8 9 10 11 12 Adult   495.6

1. Japanese language—Dictionaries

ISBN 0-19-860859-4   LC 2004-54786

First published 1986 in Japan; 1989 by Oxford University Press

This "dictionary contains over 3,000 entries which, along with providing basic meanings and grammatical information, also distinguish between senses, list compounds, and give sample sentences and idiomatic expressions. . . . It presents all the Japanese words and phrases in roman script with standard Japanese script alongside. . . . . Cross-references direct the user to words of contrasting or related meaning, and, where necessary, the dictionary provides notes on special usage. It also includes [an] appendix which gives an introduction to Japanese grammar." Publisher's note

Lammers, Wayne P., 1951-

Japanese the manga way; an illustrated guide to grammar & structure. Stone Bridge Press 2005 xxviii, 282p il pa $24.95

Grades: 9 10 11 12   495.6

1. Japanese language

ISBN 1-880656-90-6   LC 2005-296444

The author "intends to teach absolute beginners how to use manga to learn to speak and read conversational Japanese. . . . For someone who has the patience, drive, and desire to learn the language, the book will be an immense help." SLJ

Includes bibliographical references

495.7   Korean language

Shapiro, Norma

The Oxford picture dictionary, English-Korean; [by] Norma Shapiro and Jayme Adelson-Goldstein; translated by Techno-Graphics & Translations, Inc. Oxford Univ. Press 1998 228p pa $13.95

Grades: 11 12 Adult   495.7

1. Picture dictionaries 2. Korean language—Dictionaries

ISBN 0-19-435191-2   LC 98-10947

Over 3,700 words are defined in labeled illustrations grouped into 12 thematic areas. Exercises and a pronunciation guide are provided.

500   SCIENCE

Bryson, Bill

A short history of nearly everything. Broadway Bks. 2003 544p $27.50; pa $15.95 *

Grades: 9 10 11 12 Adult   500

1. Science

ISBN 0-7679-0817-1; 0-7679-0818-X (pa)

LC 2003-46006

Also available Random House large print edition

In presenting this history of science, Bryson's "interest is not simply to discover what we know but to find out how we know it. How do we know what is in the center of the earth, thousands of miles beneath the surface? How can we know the extent and the composition of the universe, or what a black hole is? How can we know where the continents were 600 million years ago?" Publisher's note

"Neither oversimplified nor overstuffed, this exceptionally skillful tour of the physical world covers the basic principles and still has room for profiles of some of the more engaging scientists." N Y Times Book Rev

Includes bibliographical references

Carlson, Dale Bick, 1935-

In and out of your mind; teen science: human bites; [by] Dale Carlson. Bick Pub. House 2002 xxvi, 218p il pa $14.95

Grades: 9 10 11 12   500

1. Science

ISBN 1-88415-827-7   LC 2001-25516

Carlson, Dale Bick, 1935-—*Continued*
This guide to modern science discusses the universe, atoms, physics as well as medical and science ethics
"Teens with an affinity for science and its workings will enjoy pondering the facts and ideas presented here." SLJ
Includes glossary and bibliographical references

Etzkowitz, Henry, 1940-
Athena unbound; the advancement of women in science and technology; {by} Henry Etzkowitz, Carol Kemelgor, Brian Uzzi, with Michael Neushatz {et al.}. Cambridge Univ. Press 2000 282p $55; pa $21 *
Grades: 11 12 Adult **500**
1. Women scientists
ISBN 0-521-56380-1; 0-521-78738-6 (pa)
LC 00-20997
This is an "inquiry into why there are so few women scientists. . . . The authors balance their extremely detailed analysis with a humanistic perspective as they compare and contrast the status of women scientists in different countries, characterize both exclusionary and supportive forms of networking, and, ultimately, offer some surprising and hopeful conclusions." Booklist
Includes bibliographical references

Feynman, Richard Phillips, 1918-1988
The meaning of it all; thoughts of a citizen scientist. Basic Books 2005 c1998 133p pa $13.95
Grades: 11 12 Adult **500**
1. Science 2. Religion
ISBN 0-465-02394-0
First published 1998 by Addison-Wesley
"Originally delivered as a three-part lecture series at the University of Washington in 1963, this collection touches on such far-ranging topics as the existence or nonexistence of God; the Constitution; and UFOs. . . . These memorable lectures confirm that Feynman's gift of insight extended from the subatomic world to the cosmic, and to the very human as well." Publ Wkly

The **Handy** science answer book; compiled by the Science and Technology Department of the Carnegie Library of Pittsburgh; edited by James E. Bobick and Naomi E. Balaban. Centennial ed. Visible Ink Press 2003 660p pa $21.95
Grades: 11 12 Adult **500**
1. Science 2. Technology
ISBN 1-57859-140-6
LC 2002-15562
First published 1994
"The text is divided into various subject areas including physics and chemistry, space, earth, climate and weather, minerals and other materials, energy, technology, and environment, gathering answers to reference questions. . . . A comprehensive index . . . makes the material accessible and easy to find. Pages are full of fascinating tidbits, complemented by illustrations, photos, charts, graphs, and maps. . . . A librarian will want a copy of this book behind the desk for ready reference, but students will want a copy for themselves to peruse time and again just for fun." Voice Youth Advocates

Johnson, Carolyn
Using Internet primary sources to teach critical thinking skills in the sciences. Libraries Unlimited 2003 339p (Libraries Unlimited professional guides in school librarianship) $39.95
Grades: Professional **500**
1. Science—Study and teaching 2. Internet in education
ISBN 0-313-31851-4
LC 2003-47722
"A navigation tool for steering students to excellent scientific resources available on the Internet. The sites included are principally primary documents and other sites that provide reliable data. . . . Each lesson begins with a URL and a site summary. A series of tasks follows that would serve as a starting point for science teachers to expand upon, and are designed to trigger discussion and analytical thinking and writing. . . . The 10 appendixes offer such helpful topics as subject guides to Web sites, career data, information available in journals and other periodicals, and Web guides to standards." SLJ
Includes bibliographical references

Oxford dictionary of scientific quotations; edited by W.F. Bynum and Roy Porter; assistant editors, Sharon Messenger, Caroline Overy. Oxford University Press 2005 712p $60; pa $18.95
Grades: 11 12 Adult **500**
1. Science 2. Quotations
ISBN 0-19-858409-1; 0-19-861443-8 (pa)
LC 2005-277260
"The quotations collected here are not only by scientists but by writers, politicians, and others with something to say about science. . . . Each entry includes the name of the person being quoted, his or her dates, a . . . biographical statement, and several quotes, with their sources." Booklist
"This hefty volume is a great reference but it is also a great read—open it up to any page and expand the mind with a sampling of scientific ideas and philosophy." Choice

Ray, C. Claiborne
The New York Times second book of science questions and answers; 225 new, intriguing, and just plain bizarre inquiries into everyday scientific mysteries; drawings by Victoria Roberts; edited by Henry Fountain. Anchor Bks. (NY) 2003 228p il pa $13 *
Grades: 11 12 Adult **500**
1. Science
ISBN 0-385-72258-3
LC 2002-26192
Also available The New York Times book of science questions and answers published 1997 pa $15 (ISBN 0-385-48660-X)
These selections from the author's weekly column in the science section of The New York Times answer such questions as "What would kill you if you fell into a black hole? Once people finally get to Mars, how will they get back? What makes the holes in Swiss cheese?" Publisher's note
"This eclectic volume of 228 questions with 200-word answers entices readers' interest in science. . . . There is no index and not much structure in this volume, but its

Ray, C. Claiborne—*Continued*
charm and interest make up for its informality." Sci
Books Films
Includes bibliographical references

Sagan, Carl, 1934-1996
Broca's brain; reflections on the romance of
science. Random House 1979 347p pa $7.99
hardcover o.p.
Grades: 11 12 Adult   **500**
1. Science 2. Philosophy
ISBN 0-345-33689-5 (pa)   LC 78-21810
In this volume Sagan considers the following: "the
quest for extraterrestrial life, popular science, and religious questions, as well as numerous concerns more immediate to his own specialty, astronomy." Libr J
The author "is a lucid, logical writer with a gift for
explaining science to the layman and infecting the reader
with his own boundless enthusiasm and curiosity." Natl
Rev
Includes bibliographical references

Scientific American's ask the experts; answers to
the most puzzling and mindblowing science
questions; by the editors of Scientific American.
HarperCollins Pubs. 2003 267p il pa $14.95
Grades: 11 12 Adult   **500**
1. Science
ISBN 0-06-052336-0   LC 2004-555579
This "is a book that answers questions big, little, and
in between. . . . The book uses the familiar question-
and-answer format, with a table of contents allowing the
reader to flip to a specific question. The questions are
answered by a variety of experts. . . . This is one of
those books you put on your reference shelf, and pull out
whenever the subject turns to matters of scientific interest. Great for trivia buffs, too." Booklist

Wiggins, Arthur W.
The five biggest unsolved problems in science;
{by} Arthur W. Wiggins {and} Charles M. Wynn;
with cartoon commentary by Sidney Harris. J.
Wiley & Sons 2003 234p il pa $14.95 *
Grades: 11 12 Adult   **500**
1. Science
ISBN 0-471-26808-9   LC 2003-284262
"The problems discussed in this volume are the duel-
ing concepts of mass and masslessness (physics), the
passage from chemicals to living matter (chemistry), the
complete structure of the proteome (biology), long-range
weather forecasting (geology), and the expansion of the
universe (astronomy)." Sci Books Films
Includes bibliographical references

500.2   Physical sciences

Encyclopedia of earth and physical sciences. 2nd
ed. Marshall Cavendish 2005 13v il map set
$657.07
Grades: 11 12 Adult   **500.2**
1. Earth sciences—Encyclopedias 2. Physical sciences—Encyclopedias
ISBN 0-7614-7583-4   LC 2004-58630

First published 1998
Contents: 1. Absolute zero-Barrier islands -- 2. Base
level-Clouds -- 3. Cloud seeding-Earth, structure of -- 4.
Earthquakes-Forests -- 5. Fossil record-Humidity -- 6.
Hurricanes-Magnetism -- 7. Maps and mapping-Musical
acoustics -- 8. Nanotechnology-Paleoclimatology -- 9. Pa-
leontology-Quasars -- 10. Quaternary period-Space -- 11.
Space exploration-Tin -- 12. Titanium-Zinc
Includes bibliographical references

500.5   Space sciences

Space sciences; Pat Dasch, editor in chief.
Macmillan Ref. USA 2002 4v il set $395
Grades: 11 12 Adult   **500.5**
1. Space sciences
ISBN 0-02-865546-X   LC 2002-1707
"The Macmillan science library." On cover
Contents: v1 Space business; v2 Planetary science and
astronomy; v3 Humans in space; v4 Our future in space
"The entries in each volume are in alphabetical order
and range from a single paragraph to several pages in
length, with most being one or two pages long. The front
and back matter are the same in each volume and include a few pages of reference tables such as conversion
charts, time lines of milestones in space history and human achievements in space, a list of contributors, a table
of contents for the set, and a glossary." Booklist
"A comprehensive and usable survey of space exploration, this marvelous encyclopedia works equally well as
a multivolume set and as four standalone volumes. . . .
The photographs are excellent." Libr J
Includes bibliographical references

501   Science--Philosophy and theory

The **next** fifty years; science in the first half of the
twenty-first century; edited by John Brockman.
Vintage Books 2002 301p pa $14.95
Grades: 11 12 Adult   **501**
1. Science 2. Forecasting
ISBN 0-375-71342-5   LC 2001-57368
"A Vintage original"
"This collection of essays provides some interesting
and provocative possibilities as to achievements in various areas of science over the next 50 years as projected
by current leaders (who are also articulate writers) in
their fields." Sci Books Films

502   Science--Miscellany

Ochoa, George
The Wilson chronology of science and
technology; {by} George Ochoa and Melinda
Corey. Wilson, H.W. 1997 440p $105 *
Grades: 11 12 Adult   **502**
1. Science—History 2. Technology—History
ISBN 0-8242-0933-8   LC 97-22060
This chronology begins in 2,500,000 B.C. and contin-
ues into 1997. "Within each year, entries are arranged al-
phabetically according to one of 13 categories: archaeol-

Ochoa, George—*Continued*

ogy; astronomy, space science, and space exploration; biology, biochemistry, agriculture, and ecology; chemistry; earth sciences (geology, oceanography, meteorology) and earth exploration; mathematics; medicine; miscellaneous; paleontology; physics; psychology, neuroscience, and artificial intelligence; social sciences (anthropology, sociology, economics, political science) and linguistics; and technology and engineering." Publisher's note

Includes bibliographical references

503 Science--Encyclopedias and dictionaries

The **American** Heritage science dictionary. Houghton Mifflin 2005 694p il maps $19.95 *
Grades: 8 9 10 11 12 Adult **503**
1. Science—Dictionaries
ISBN 0-618-45504-3 LC 2004-19696

This "science dictionary includes 8500 terms in anthropology, biology, chemistry, earth science, mathematics, medicine, physics, and technology. There are also 320 biographical entries of noted scientists as well as 30 biographical notes that explain how certain researchers found answers to major scientific problems. Written in clear, simple prose that general readers can understand, the entries are often more than simple definitions, offering in-depth discussions of scientific ideas." Libr J

The **American** Heritage student science dictionary. Houghton Mifflin 2002 376p il $18 *
Grades: 11 12 Adult **503**
1. Science—Dictionaries
ISBN 0-618-18919-X LC 2002-22726

Entries with definitions of basic scientific terms are accompanied by illustrations, "Did You Know" sidebars, and explanatory notes

Encyclopedia of science, technology, and ethics; edited by Carl Mitcham. Macmillan Reference USA 2005 4v il map set $450
Grades: 11 12 Adult **503**
1. Science—Ethical aspects
ISBN 0-02-865831-0 LC 2005-6968

This "set confronts the major ethical issues of our time in a series of 675 articles, 33 of which are overviews of topics like computer ethics, while the remainder deal with such 'hot-button' issues as abortion and animal rights." Libr J

This "multivolume work on ethics provides a superb introduction to the issues presented." Booklist

Includes bibliographical references

Gale encyclopedia of science; K. Lee Lerner & Brenda Wilmoth Lerner, editors. 3rd ed. Gale Group 2004 6v il maps set $575
Grades: 11 12 Adult **503**
1. Science—Encyclopedias
ISBN 0-7876-7554-7 LC 2003-15731

First published 1996

Including over 2000 alphabetically arranged entries, this "set covers all major areas of science, engineering, technology, as well as mathematics and the medical and health sciences. Entries typically describe scientific concepts, provide overviews of scientific areas and, in some cases, define terms. Longer entries conclude with a bibliography." Publisher's note

Includes bibliographical references

McGraw-Hill concise encyclopedia of science & technology. 5th ed. McGraw-Hill 2005 2651p il $185 *
Grades: 11 12 Adult **503**
1. Science—Encyclopedias 2. Technology—Encyclopedias
ISBN 0-07-142957-3; 978-0-07-142957-3 LC 2004-54909

First published 1984

A condensed version of the McGraw-Hill encyclopedia of science & technology

This encyclopedia features over 7300 articles on branches of technology and science ranging from acoustics to zoology.

Includes bibliographical references

McGraw-Hill encyclopedia of science & technology. 10th ed. McGraw-Hill 2007 20v il map set $2,995
Grades: 11 12 Adult **503**
1. Science—Encyclopedias 2. Technology—Encyclopedias
ISBN 978-0-07-144143-8; 0-07-144143-3 LC 2007-6137

"An international reference work in twenty volumes including an index"

First published 1960 in fifteen volumes

This encyclopedia "contains approximately 7,100 articles on major topics in all categories of science and technology, written for the non-specialist. Each entry begins with general information on the topic. Detailed information follows under headings so the reader can focus on specific areas of interest. All but general survey articles have a bibliography at the end. There is extensive cross-referencing between articles that leads to related topics. Scientists who have been major contributors to their field wrote many articles. The index volume contains a list of contributors, a guide to scientific notation, study guides, a topical index, and an analytical index." Sci Books Films [review of 2002 edition]

Includes bibliographical references

The **new** book of popular science. Grolier 2006 6v il set $279
Grades: 5 6 7 8 9 10 **503**
1. Science—Encyclopedias 2. Technology—Encyclopedias
ISBN 0-7172-1225-4 LC 2005-29898

First published 1924 with title: The Book of popular science. Frequently revised

Contents: v1 Astronomy, space science, mathematics, past and future; v2 Earth sciences, energy, environmental sciences; v3 Chemistry, physics, biology; v4 Plant life, animal life; v5 Mammals, human sciences; v6 Technology

The information in this set is classified under such broad categories as astronomy and space science, computers and mathematics, earth sciences, energy, environmental sciences, physical sciences, general biology, plant

The new book of popular science—*Continued*
life, animal life, mammals, human sciences and technology.

Includes bibliographical references

The **new** Penguin dictionary of science; editor, M.J. Clugston; author team, N.J. Lord . . . [et al.] 2nd ed. Penguin Books 2004 727p il (Penguin reference books) pa $20
Grades: 9 10 11 12   **503**
1. Science—Dictionaries
ISBN 0-14-101074-6; 978-0-14-101074-8
         LC 2004-273165
First published 1943 under the editorship of E.B. Uvarov and Alan Isaacs with title: The Penguin dictionary of science; replaces the edition with same title published 1998
This dictionary covers terms used in chemistry, physics, astronomy, human anatomy, mathematics, computing and other scientific fields. An appendix includes a periodic table, a list of chemical properties, diagrams of amino acids, and other information.

Swedin, Eric Gottfrid
Science in the contemporary world; an encyclopedia; [by] Eric G. Swedin. ABC-CLIO 2005 xxv, 382p il (ABC-CLIO's history of science series) $85
Grades: 9 10 11 12   **503**
1. Science—Encyclopedias
ISBN 1-85109-524-1   LC 2004-26950
This book "covers developments in the scientific disciplines from the end of World War II to the present day. . . . It makes a make good introductory text to the history of science in the late twentieth and early twenty-first centuries." Booklist
Includes bibliographical references

U.X.L encyclopedia of science. 2nd ed, Rob Nagel, editor. U.X.L 2002 10v il maps set $395
Grades: 9 10 11 12   **503**
1. Science—Encyclopedias
ISBN 0-7876-5432-9   LC 2001-35562
First published 1997
Includes 600 topics in the life, earth, and physical sciences as well as in engineering, technology, math, environmental science, and psychology
It's "difficult to find fault with this clearly written resource that uses simple, nontechnical terms to explain scientific concepts at a basic level." Booklist

Van Nostrand's scientific encyclopedia. 9th ed, Glenn D. Considine, editor; Peter H. Kulik, associate editor. Wiley-Interscience 2002 2v il maps set $350 *
Grades: 11 12 Adult   **503**
1. Science—Encyclopedias
ISBN 0-471-33230-5
First published 1938
"Animal life; biosciences; chemistry; earth and atmospheric sciences; energy sources and power technology; mathematics and engineering sciences; medicine, anatomy, and physiology; physics; plant science; space and planetary sciences." Title page

507.8 Science--Use of apparatus and equipment in study and teaching

Bochinski, Julianne Blair, 1966-
The complete handbook of science fair projects; illustrated by Judy DiBiase. Newly rev and updated. J. Wiley 2004 228p il hardcover o.p. pa $14.95 *
Grades: 9 10 11 12   **507.8**
1. Science projects
ISBN 0-471-45767-1; 0-471-46043-5 (pa)
         LC 2003-19494
First published 1991
Discusses various aspects of science fair projects including advice on choosing a topic, doing research, developing experiments, organizing data results, and presenting a project to the judges
"An excellent resource for students looking for ideas." Booklist

More award-winning science fair projects; illustrated by Judy J. Bochinski-DiBiase. J. Wiley 2004 228p il $29.95; pa $14.95 *
Grades: 7 8 9 10   **507.8**
1. Science projects 2. Science—Experiments
ISBN 0-471-27338-4; 0-471-27337-6 (pa)
         LC 2003-9477
Presents forty award-winning science fair projects, a section on how to do a science fair project, updates to science fair rules and science supply resources, as well as new material on useful web sites.

Brisk, Marion A.
1001 ideas for science projects. 3rd ed. Macmillan 1999 250p il pa $14.95
Grades: 9 10 11 12   **507.8**
1. Science projects 2. Science—Experiments
ISBN 0-02-862513-7   LC 97-81089
First published 1992
At head of title: ARCO
These science projects cover topics in archeology, astronomy, earth science, space science, and medicine, and are keyed to level of difficulty, availability of resources, and need for lab work
Includes bibliographical references

Downie, N. A., 1956-
Vacuum bazookas, electric rainbow jelly, and 27 other Saturday science projects; {by} Neil Downie. Princeton Univ. Press 2001 253p hardcover o.p. pa $18.95
Grades: 9 10 11 12   **507.8**
1. Science—Experiments 2. Science projects
ISBN 0-691-00985-6; 0-691-00986-4 (pa)
         LC 2001-36258
Most projects "illustrate the physics of waves or mechanics, and for the hard-core gadgeteer, Downie appends to each project an explanation of the mathematics describing what's going on with, say, a rotating, ribless

Downie, N. A., 1956——_Continued_
umbrella. . . . There is an upgrade of the classic cups-and-string telecom technology, which Downie calls the string radio. He illustrates the basic idea of modern smart-bomb warfare in the shape of a (perfectly safe) guided carpet missile, and throughout he sprinkles a number of amusingly useless labor-saving devices." Booklist
"This book is an excellent source of fun, light-hearted projects for young adults." Sci Books Films
Includes bibliographical references

Rosner, Marc Alan
Science fair success using the Internet. rev. and updated. Enslow Publishers 2006 112p il (Science fair success) lib bdg $26.60 *
Grades: 7 8 9 10   **507.8**
1. Science projects 2. Science—Experiments 3. Internet
ISBN 0-7660-2425-3 (lib bdg)   LC 2005-06749
First published 1999
Explains how to use Internet resources, including e-mailing experts and using search engines, to enhance science projects, with sample projects in biology, chemistry, physics, environment and earth science, and astronomy.
Includes bibliographical references

Vecchione, Glen
Blue ribbon science fair projects. Sterling Pub. Co. 2005 224p il $19.95
Grades: 9 10 11 12   **507.8**
1. Science projects 2. Science—Experiments
ISBN 978-1-4027-1073-5; 1-4027-1073-9
                                              LC 2005-13557
"After an introduction to the process of creating science-fair projects and a summary of tips from an experienced science-fair judge, Vecchione . . . [presents] project ideas within the following subject areas: animals, the human body, magnetism, botany, equipment, chemistry, astronomy, physics, and math. . . . Students planning science-fair projects will find this a solid resource." Booklist

508 Natural history

Daubert, Stephen
Threads from the web of life; stories in natural history; with illustrations by Chris Daubert. Vanderbilt University Press 2006 162p il $24.95
Grades: 11 12 Adult   **508**
1. Natural history
ISBN 0-8265-1509-6; 978-0-8265-1509-4
                                              LC 2005-23117
The author "illustrates 16 ecological processes with lively narratives in which he envisions how it might feel to be at the center of the action: for example, traveling with a green sea turtle from its feeding grounds in Brazil to its nesting beaches 2,000 kilometers away on Ascension Island in the eastern Atlantic; riding whirling air currents with migrating American white pelicans; or fleeing from a predator swordfish with a school of neon fly-

ing squid. . . . His natural history tales are instructive and entertaining, and each is followed by an annotation explaining the science behind it." Publ Wkly
Includes bibliographical references

DK nature encyclopedia. DK Pub. 1998 304p il map $29.99 *
Grades: 5 6 7 8 9 10   **508**
1. Natural history—Encyclopedias
ISBN 0-7894-3411-3   LC 98-16657
"The book is divided into six sections. 'The Natural World' describes the origins and evolution of life on earth. 'How Living Things Work' examines the basic characteristics shared by all living things—respiration, reproduction, life cycles, etc. 'Ecology' surveys the major types of habitats around the world and discusses topics such as food chains and endangered species. A short section explains 'How Living Things Are Classified,' while the final chapters look at specific groups of plants. . . . Well organized, clearly written, and with an amazing scope, this encyclopedia makes a valuable guide to nature." SLJ

Fothergill, Alastair
Planet Earth; as you've never seen it before; [by] Alastair Fothergill . . . [et al.]; foreword by David Attenborough. University of California Press 2006 309p il map $39.95 *
Grades: 11 12 Adult   **508**
1. Habitat (Ecology) 2. Earth
ISBN 978-0-520-25054-3; 0-520-25054-0
                                              LC 2006-50073
In this collection of over 400 photographs of natural landscapes and wildlife, the author "takes readers on a kaleidoscopic tour of the flora, fauna and natural history of the Earth's poles, forests, plains, deserts, mountains and oceans." Publ Wkly

Gould, Stephen Jay, 1941-2002
Dinosaur in a haystack; reflections in natural history. Harmony Bks. 1995 480p il pa $15.95 hardcover o.p. *
Grades: 11 12 Adult   **508**
1. Natural history
ISBN 0-517-88824-6 (pa)   LC 95-51333
In this collection the author "relates anecdotes from the history of science and demonstrates their relevance to contemporary scientific disputes and social trends." Libr J
"A discovery awaits in every essay—in every haystack—which solidifies Gould as one of the most eloquent science popularizers writing today." Booklist
Includes bibliographical references

The richness of life; the essential Stephen Jay Gould; edited by Paul McGarr and Steven Rose; with an introduction by Steven Rose and a foreword by Oliver Sacks. 1st American ed. Norton 2007 654p il $35
Grades: 11 12 Adult   **508**
1. Natural history 2. Evolution
ISBN 978-0-393-06498-8; 0-393-06498-0
                                              LC 2006-29208

Gould, Stephen Jay, 1941-2002—*Continued*

Frist published 2006 in the United Kingdom

"These 44 essays represent . . . [the author's] best-known pieces from his books and from essays for Natural History magazine, as well as never before published speeches." Publ Wkly

"For collections that have room for only one volume of his writing, this is the essential one." SLJ

Includes bibliographical references

Love, Rosaleen

Reefscape; reflections on the Great Barrier Reef. Joseph Henry Press 2001 264p map $24.95

Grades: 11 12 Adult   **508**

1. Great Barrier Reef (Australia)

ISBN 0-309-07260-3   LC 2001-24281

Love "presents information about the ecology of coral reefs and interweaves information about the history, anthropology, and archaeology of the area." Sci Books Films

Includes bibliographical references

Savage, Candace, 1949-

Prairie; a natural history; principal photography by James R. Page; illustrations by Joan A. Williams. Greystone Books 2004 308p il maps hardcover o.p. pa $28.95 *

Grades: 9 10 11 12   **508**

1. Prairies

ISBN 1-550-54985-5; 1-553-65190-1 (pa)

LC 2004-40623

Co-published by the David Suzuki Foundation

Savage examines the history and biology of the Great Plains of North America, which stretch "from northern Alberta down into Texas and from Montana to Missouri." Quill Quire

"This is not a research book, but rather a well-written, science-based overview of an underappreciated ecosystem. It will be a great addition to any library." Sci Books Films

Includes bibliographical references

509 Science--Historical and geographic treatment

Adler, Robert E., 1946-

Science firsts: from the creation of science to the science of creation; [by] Robert Adler. Wiley 2002 232p il $24.95 *

Grades: 11 12 Adult   **509**

1. Science—History 2. Scientists

ISBN 0-471-40174-9   LC 2002-727233

The author tells the engaging and inspiring stories of thirty-five landmark scientific discoveries from the first accurate prediction of an eclipse in 585 B.C. to the cloning of Dolly the sheep.

Includes bibliographical references

Bunch, Bryan H.

The history of science and technology; a browser's guide to the great discoveries, inventions, and the people who made them from the dawn of time to today; [by] Bryan Bunch with Alexander Hellemans. Houghton Mifflin 2004 776p il $40

Grades: 9 10 11 12   **509**

1. Science—History 2. Technology—History

ISBN 0-618-22123-9   LC 2004-40500

Based on the authors' The timetables of science (1988) and The timetables of technology (1993)

This "volume is divided into 10 periods, each beginning with an overview of major advances, many of which caused controversy in political, social, and religious arenas. The introductions are followed by yearly chronicles of specific accomplishments ranging from the time when hominoids used pebble tools through 2003." SLJ

This "book lives up to its marketing as a browser's guide to the history of science and technology. . . . This monograph is well organized for laypersons, students, and reference librarians." Choice

Includes bibliographical references

The **Chronology** of science; from Stonehenge to the human genome project; consulting editor, Lisa Rosner. ABC-CLIO 2002 566p $85 *

Grades: 11 12 Adult   **509**

1. Science—History 2. Scientists

ISBN 1-57607-954-6   LC 2001-7692

The chronologies are "divided into subject areas, including astronomy, biology, chemistry, ecology, mathematics, and physics; 16 feature essays on critical scientific discoveries . . . [are included as well as] biographies of key scientists." Publisher's note

Includes bibliographical references

Crease, Robert P.

The prism and the pendulum; the ten most beautiful experiments in science. Random House 2003 xxii, 244p il hardcover o.p. pa $14.95 *

Grades: 11 12 Adult   **509**

1. Science—History 2. Science—Experiments

ISBN 1-400-06131-8; 0-8129-7062-4 (pa)

LC 2003-54765

Each scientific experiment discussed here "is followed by an 'interlude,' or commentary, on how the experiment qualifies as most beautiful and how art and science both give meaning to the term 'beauty.'" Sci Books Films

Gribbin, John R.

The scientists; a history of science told through the lives of its greatest inventors; [by] John Gribbin. Random House 2003 xxii, 646p il hardcover o.p. pa $16.95 *

Grades: 11 12 Adult   **509**

1. Scientists 2. Science—History

ISBN 1-4000-6013-3; 0-8129-6788-7 (pa)

LC 2003-46607

First published 2002 in the United Kingdom with title: Science: a history, 1543-2001

Gribbin, John R.—*Continued*

"Starting with the Renaissance, Gribbin traces the development of science over the past 500 years through the lives of the people who made it. From Copernicus and Galileo to Albert Einstein and Linus Pauling, Gribbin carefully places the individual in the time in which he or she lived. . . . He also . . . shows the development of science to be the result of the interplay among three factors: the person, the historical time, and the available technology." Libr J

"Replete with scientific clarity, Gribbin's work is the epitome of what a general-interest history of science should be." Booklist

Includes bibliographical references

Hakim, Joy

The story of science: Aristotle leads the way. Smithsonian Books 2004 282p il map (Story of science) $21.95

Grades: 8 9 10 11 12   **509**
1. Science—History 2. Ancient civilization
ISBN 1-58834-160-7

"In the first book of her . . . Story of Science Joy Hakim invites readers . . . to meet the forebearers of modern science—Thales, Pythagoras, Archimedes, Aristotle, Arab and Chinese thinkers, Thomas Aquinas, Roger Bacon, and many others—and share in their . . . discoveries in astronomy, math, and physics." Publisher's note

"Hakim has interwoven creation myths, history, physics, and mathematics to present a seamless, multifaceted view of the foundation of modern science. . . . The entire volume is beautifully organized." SLJ

Includes bibliographical references

The story of science: Newton at the center. Smithsonian Books 2005 463p il maps (Story of science) $24.95

Grades: 8 9 10 11 12   **509**
1. Science—History
ISBN 1-58834-161-5   LC 2004-58465

This second volume of a projected six-book series is an account of the history of astronomy and physics from c.1500 to 1900

"Teachers will find anecdotal information to enliven their lessons; browsers will be fascinated by the sidebars and captioned illustrations that enhance the text or show related information." SLJ

Includes bibliographical references

History of modern science and mathematics; Brian S. Baigrie, editor. Scribner 2002 4v il set $395 *

Grades: 11 12 Adult   **509**
1. Science—History 2. Mathematics—History
ISBN 0-684-80636-3   LC 2002-4042

This "set attempts to synthesize the history of scientific developments in anthropology, astronomy, biology, chemistry, mathematics, physics, psychology, and the earth sciences. . . . This work ranges from the 17th century to the present without trying to include the most recent developments." Libr J

Includes bibliographical references

Horvitz, Leslie Alan

Eureka!: scientific breakthroughs that changed the world. Wiley 2002 246p il $24.95 *

Grades: 11 12 Adult   **509**
1. Science—History
ISBN 0-471-40276-1   LC 2001-46890

This examines twelve scientific discoveries and their discoverers, including Joseph Priestley and oxygen, Friedrich Kekulé and the structure of carbon compounds, Dmitri Mendeleev and the periodic table, Isaac Newton and gravity, Einstein and the theory of relativity, Philo Farnsworth and television, Alexander Fleming and penicillin, Charles Townes and the laser, Alfred Wegener and continental drift, Darwin and the origin of species, Watson and Crick and the double helix, and Benoit Mandelbrot and fractal geometry.

Includes bibliographical references

Krebs, Robert E., 1922-

Scientific laws, principles, and theories; a reference guide; illustrations by Rae Déjur. Greenwood Press 2001 402p il $65 *

Grades: 11 12 Adult   **509**
1. Science—History
ISBN 0-313-30957-4   LC 00-23297

The author discusses the history of such scientific concepts as quantum theory, the Doppler effect, Elton's theory of animal ecology, Newton's laws and principles, and Percival Lowell's theory of life

"By far the most comprehensive single-volume catalog of scientific principles and theories available, this book makes a convenient, easy-to-use tool for those studying science's present or past." SLJ

Includes bibliographical references

Lawson, Russell M., 1957-

Science in the ancient world; an encyclopedia. ABC-CLIO 2004 xxv, 291p il (ABC-CLIO's history of science series) $85 *

Grades: 11 12 Adult   **509**
1. Science—History—Encyclopedias
ISBN 1-85109-534-9   LC 2004-17715

This book "describes scientific concepts in ancient societies, including the Egyptian, Babylonian, Greek, and Roman worlds until the fall of the Roman Empire. Most of the entries are about people, concepts, and locales of the Greco-Roman world. Arrangement is alphabetical, supported by good cross-references and indexing." Booklist

Includes bibliographical references

Lightman, Alan P., 1948-

The discoveries; great breakthroughs in 20th century science; [by] Alan Lightman. Pantheon Books 2005 553p il $32.50; pa $16.95 *

Grades: 11 12 Adult   **509**
1. Science—History
ISBN 0-375-42168-8; 0-375-71345-X (pa)
                   LC 2005-40854

This book "chronicles 25 landmark findings in astronomy, physics, chemistry, and biology in the 20th century.

Lightman, Alan P., 1948-—*Continued*
Beginning with Max Planck's quantum theory and ending with Paul Berg's recombinant DNA, these breakthroughs are academically and playfully explored via the nature of the unknown, the circumstances and influences of discovery, and, most originally, the actual words of the scientists." Libr J
Includes bibliographical references

The **Oxford** companion to the history of modern science; editor in chief, J.L. Heilbron; editors, James Bartholomew {et al.}. Oxford Univ. Press 2003 xxviii, 941p il $110
Grades: 11 12 Adult   509
1. Science—History
ISBN 0-19-511229-6   LC 2002-153783
This reference on the history of science from the Renaissance through the 20th century includes some 600 articles covering "a broad spectrum of topics in all scientific disciplines (e.g., biotechnology, geology) as well as disciplines that influenced science, such as religion and politics. Also included are the biographies of 100 leading figures (e.g., Isaac Newton, Marie Curie) and coverage of scientific instruments (e.g., microscopes, Geiger counters). Organized alphabetically, the well-written articles include plenty of cross references. Over 100 black-and-white illustrations appear within their appropriate articles, but the eight pages of color illustrations in the middle of the volume are not associated with any article." Libr J
Includes bibliographical references

Science and its times; understanding the social significance of scientific discovery; Neil Schlager, editor; Josh Lauer, associate editor. Gale Group 2000-2001 8v set $625 *
Grades: 11 12 Adult   509
1. Science—History
ISBN 0-7876-3932-X   LC 00-37542
Contents: v1 2000 B.C.-700 A.D.; v2 700-1450; v3 1450-1699; v4 1700-1799; v5 19th century; v6 1900-1950; v7 1950-present; v8 Cumulative index
This set addresses "a wide variety of scientific developments with explanations of underlying factors and their effects on politics, economics, culture and daily life. [It includes] more than 20 topical essays, 25 full biographies and 85 sketches of notable people in each volume." Publisher's note

The **Scientific** revolution; Mitchell Young, book editor. Greenhaven Press 2006 240p il (Turning points in world history) lib bdg $34.95
Grades: 9 10 11 12   509
1. Science—History
ISBN 0-7377-2987-2   LC 2005-40268
"This volume offers many essays and articles discussing various aspects of a single subject—the scientific revolution. Each themed chapter includes about a half-dozen entries, introduced by the editor and written mainly by academics. . . . Though the book will be challenging for some students, others will find it a well-organized, informative resource." Booklist
Includes bibliographical references

Spangenburg, Ray, 1939-
The history of science; [by] Ray Spangenburg and Diane Kit Moser. Facts On File 2004 5v set $200
Grades: 7 8 9 10 11 12   509
1. Science—History
ISBN 0-8160-4850-9
First published 1993-1994 with title: On the shoulders of giants
Volumes also available separately ea $40
Contents: The birth of science: ancient times to 1699; The rise of reason: 1700-1799; The age of synthesis: 1800-1895; Modern science, 1896-1945; Science frontiers, 1946 to the present
This set discusses major scientists and the scientific issues and discoveries for which they are known.
Includes glossary and bibliographical references

Webster, Raymond B.
African American firsts in science and technology; foreword by Wesley L. Harris. Gale Group 1999 462p $80 *
Grades: 11 12 Adult   509
1. Scientists 2. African American inventors
ISBN 0-7876-3876-5   LC 99-27346
Presents capsule accounts of notable first achievements by African Americans, arranged in the categories "Agriculture and Everyday Life," "Dentistry and Nursing," "Life Science," "Math and Engineering," "Medicine," "Physical Science," and "Transportation."
Includes bibliographical references

Windelspecht, Michael, 1963-
Groundbreaking scientific experiments, inventions, and discoveries of the 19th century; illustrated by Sandra Windelspecht. Greenwood Press 2003 xxvii, 270p il (Groundbreaking scientific experiments, inventions, and discoveries through the ages) $65
Grades: 9 10 11 12   509
1. Science—History 2. Technology—History
ISBN 0-313-31969-3   LC 2002-75305
This volume presents material "alphabetically by topic with information about the specific experiments, inventions, and discoveries of both women and men. . . . Each entry provides a brief historical discussion that allows the reader to understand the climate of the time of discovery and builds a foundation for understanding the methodology by which the scientists and inventors approached their discoveries, experiments, and inventions and for realizing the implications of these on man's future." Lib Media Connect
Includes bibliographical references

510 Mathematics

Acheson, D. J.
1089 and all that; a journey into mathematics; [by] David Acheson. Oxford Univ. Press 2002 178p il $19.95
Grades: 11 12 Adult   510
1. Mathematics
ISBN 0-19-851623-1   LC 2002-71547

Acheson, D. J.—*Continued*

"This book aims to make mathematics accessible to non-experts and the lay reader. Providing an . . . overview of the subject, the text includes several . . . mathematical conundrums. . . . The book contains several cartoons, sketches and photos." Publisher's note

"Not a page passes without at least one intriguing insight. . . . Anyone who is baffled by mathematics should buy it." New Sci

Boyer, Carl B. (Carl Benjamin), 1906-

A history of mathematics; revised by Uta C. Merzbach. 2nd ed. Wiley 1989 762p il hardcover o.p. pa $39.95 *
Grades: 11 12 Adult   510
1. Mathematics
ISBN 0-471-09763-2; 0-471-54397-7 (pa)
                              LC 89-5325
First published 1969

"This good general history of mathematics is understandable to the student as well as authoritative for the mathematician." Malinowsky. Best Sci & Technol Ref Books for Young People
Includes bibliographical references

Cracking the SAT: math subject tests, 2007-2008 edition; [by] the Princeton Review. Random House 2007 il pa $19
Grades: 9 10 11 12   510
1. Mathematics—Study and teaching 2. Scholastic Assessment Test 3. Colleges and universities—Entrance requirements
ISBN 0-375-76593-X; 978-0-375-76593-3
First published 2005. Continues Cracking the SAT II: math subject tests

At head of title: The Princeton Review. Variant title: Cracking the SAT math 1 and 2 subject tests

This guide provides test-taking strategies and sample tests on the subject of mathematics.

Eastaway, Robert

Why do buses come in threes? the hidden mathematics of everyday life; [by] Rob Eastaway and Jeremy Wyndham; illustrations by Barbara Shore. Wiley 1998 156p il hardcover o.p. pa $15.95
Grades: 9 10 11 12   510
1. Mathematics
ISBN 0-471-34756-6; 0-471-37907-7 (pa)
                              LC 99-21915

This book "explains how math and the laws of probability are constantly at work in our lives, affecting everything we do, from getting a date to catching a bus to cooking dinner. . . . Rob Eastaway and Jeremy Wyndham present solutions to such conundrums as how fast one should run in the rain to stay dry and who was the greatest sportsman of all time." Publisher's note
Includes bibliographical references

Glazer, Evan, 1971-

Real-life math; everyday use of mathematical concepts; [by] Evan M. Glazer and John W. McConnell. Greenwood Press 2002 165p il $49.95
Grades: 11 12 Adult   510
1. Mathematics
ISBN 0-313-31998-7   LC 2001-58635

The authors "have written this book as a reply to students' complaints that they'll never use the mathematical concepts they're being taught. They look at dozens of mathematical concepts and . . . show how these math ideas relate to the world in which students live. . . . The book is thorough and accurate." Libr Media Connect
Includes bibliographical references

Using Internet primary sources to teach critical thinking skills in mathematics. Greenwood Press 2001 222p (Greenwood professional guides in school librarianship) pa $45 *
Grades: Professional   510
1. Mathematics—Study and teaching 2. Internet 3. Computer-assisted instruction
ISBN 0-313-31327-X   LC 00-52137

This offers activities and questions to promote critical thinking in mathematics including real-time data collection, information sharing, interactive learning environments, and collaboration with faraway students. Entries include web addresses and site summaries and cover pre-algebra, algebra, geometry, precalculus and calculus, probability, statistics, and math history.

"A highly valuable resource for mathematics teachers to enhance student learning." Choice

Henderson, Harry, 1951-

Mathematics: powerful patterns in nature and society. Facts on File 2007 170p il (Milestones in discovery and invention) $35
Grades: 7 8 9 10 11 12   510
1. Mathematics
ISBN 0-8160-5750-8; 978-0-8160-5750-4
                              LC 2006-24680

"Some mathematicians have discovered relatively simple yet exceedingly powerful patterns that yield insight into aspects of natural and human behavior. . . . [This book] presents 10 essays that profile the minds behind such patterns, many of which have surfaced in recent popular culture." Publisher's note
Includes glossary and bibliographical references

Jacobs, Harold R.

Mathematics, a human endeavor; a book for those who think they don't like the subject. 3rd ed. Freeman, W.H. 1994 678p il $79.40 *
Grades: 9 10 11 12   510
1. Mathematics
ISBN 0-7167-2426-X   LC 93-37458

Also available in a teachers edition with instruction manual, workbook, etc.

First published 1970

Contents: Mathematical ways of thinking; Number sequences; Functions and their graphs; Large numbers and logarithms; Symmetry and regular figures; Mathematical curves; Methods of counting; The mathematics of

Jacobs, Harold R.—*Continued*
chance; An introduction to statistics; Topics in topology
Includes bibliographical references

Stewart, Ian, 1945-
Letters to a young mathematician. Basic Books
2006 210p il (Art of mentoring) $22.95; pa $15 *
Grades: 11 12 Adult   **510**
1. Mathematics
ISBN   0-465-08231-9;   978-0-465-08231-5;
0-465-08232-7 (pa); 978-0-465-08232-2 (pa)
LC 2005-30384
This book "takes the form of letters from a fictitious
mathematician to his niece. The letters span a period of
20 years, from the time the niece is thinking about studying mathematics in high school through the early years
of her academic career. The format works wonderfully to
introduce readers to the basics of the discipline of mathematics while providing a sense of what mathematicians
actually do." Publ Wkly

Tabak, John
Mathematics and the laws of nature; developing
the language of science. Facts on File 2004 221p
il (History of mathematics) $40 *
Grades: 9 10 11 12   **510**
1. Mathematics 2. Science
ISBN 0-8160-4957-2   LC 2003-16961
"Examining the pioneering ideas, works, and applications that have made math the language of science, [this
book] looks at the many ways in which so-called 'pure'
math has been used in the applied sciences." Publisher's
note
Includes bibliographical references

510.3   Mathematics--Encyclopedias and dictionaries

Darling, David J.
The universal book of mathematics; from
Abracadabra to Zeno's paradoxes; [by] David
Darling. Wiley 2004 383p il $40
Grades: 11 12 Adult   **510.3**
1. Mathematics—Encyclopedias
ISBN 0-471-27047-4   LC 2003-24670
"The book's entries include numerous mathematical
terms, brief biographies of mathematicians from ancient
times to the present, and famous mathematical problems
(both solved and unsolved), as well as problems and puzzles of a more recreational nature. It is a spirit of whimsy, the fanciful, and the outrageous that makes this book
much more than a dry encyclopedia of mathematical
terms, however. Darling's writing style and choice of entries make this an easy book to pick up and page
through." Choice
Includes bibliographical references

The **Facts** on File dictionary of mathematics;
edited by John Daintith, Richard Rennie. 4th ed.
Facts on File 2005 262p il (Facts on File
science library) $45; pa $17.95 *
Grades: 9 10 11 12   **510.3**
1. Mathematics—Dictionaries
ISBN 0-8160-5651-X; 0-8160-5652-8 (pa)
LC 2005-48762
First published 1980
Among the topics covered are: fractals, sets, chaos
theory, computer graphics and hypertext.
Includes bibliographical references

Tanton, James S., 1966-
Encyclopedia of mathematics; [by] James
Tanton. Facts on File 2005 568p il (Facts on File
science library) $75 *
Grades: 11 12 Adult   **510.3**
1. Mathematics—Encyclopedias
ISBN 0-8160-5124-0   LC 2004-16785
This encyclopedia "offers more than 800 entries from
abacus and compound interest to Bertrand Russell and
vector along with essays on the history and evolution of
equations and algebra, calculus, functions, geometry,
probability and statistics, and trigonometry." SLJ
For a fuller review, see: Booklist, Dec. 1, 2005
Includes bibliographical references

511   General principles of mathematics

Kaplan, Robert
The nothing that is; a natural history of zero;
illustrations by Ellen Kaplan. Oxford Univ. Press
2000 225p $40; pa $11.95
Grades: 11 12 Adult   **511**
1. Zero (The number)
ISBN 0-19-512842-7; 0-19-514237-3 (pa)
LC 99-29000
"Kaplan presents cultural, philosophical, historical, and
mathematical developments that either encouraged or discouraged the recognition of the role of zero in counting
and computation." Sci Books Films

Seife, Charles
Zero; the biography of a dangerous idea. Viking
2000 248p il hardcover o.p. pa $15
Grades: 11 12 Adult   **511**
1. Zero (The number)
ISBN 0-670-88457-X; 0-14-029647-6 (pa)
LC 99-36693
"The zero emerges as a daunting intellectual riddle in
this . . . chronicle of a once controversial concept as
Seife deftly traces the gradual acceptance of the zero and
its role as catalyst for the evolution of everything from
business to physics to moral thought." Booklist
Includes bibliographical references

511.3 Mathematical logic (Symbolic logic)

Edwards, A. W. F. (Anthony William Fairbank), 1935-
Cogwheels of the mind; the story of Venn diagrams; foreword by Ian Stewart. Johns Hopkins University Press 2004 110p il $25
Grades: 11 12 Adult   **511.3**
1. Venn, John, 1834-1923 2. Symbolic logic
ISBN 0-8018-7434-3   LC 2003-10633
This book is about "who John Venn was, why he conceived of the diagram, and the properties that lie secreted beneath such a seemingly simple mathematical object." Booklist
"This title will appeal to readers studying mathematics and logic, to those who would like to know how scientific and mathematical research is carried out, and to those who are involved in graphic design and the study of the history of art as it relates to math." SLJ

512 Algebra

Miller, Robert, 1943-
Bob Miller's algebra for the clueless; algebra. 2nd ed. McGraw-Hill 2007 276p il (Bob Miller's clueless series) pa $12.95
Grades: 9 10 11 12   **512**
1. Algebra
ISBN 0-07-147366-1; 978-0-07-148846-4
LC 2006-8455
First published 1999
This guide to algebra explains such concepts as natural numbers, integers, equations, factoring, radicals and exponents and includes anxiety reducing features and tips for solving difficult problems.

Tabak, John
Algebra: sets, symbols, and the language of thought; John Tabak. Facts on File 2004 224p il (History of mathematics) $40
Grades: 9 10 11 12   **512**
1. Algebra
ISBN 0-8160-4954-8   LC 2003-17338
This volume examines "the question of why this type of math is so important that it arose in different cultures at different times. The book also discusses the relationship between algebra and geometry, shows the progress of thought throughout the centuries, and offers biographical data on the key figures." Publisher's note
Includes bibliographical references

Wingard-Nelson, Rebecca
Algebra I and algebra II. Enslow Publishers 2004 64p il (Math success) $22.60 *
Grades: 9 10 11 12   **512**
1. Algebra
ISBN 0-7660-2566-7   LC 2003-27620

Contents: The coordinate plane -- Lines and slope -- Linear equations -- More linear equations -- Direct variation -- Inequalities -- Graphs of inequalities -- Absolute value -- Systems and graphing -- Solving systems by substitution -- Solving systems by elimination -- Systems of inequalities -- Systems and problem solving -- Relations and functions -- Operations and functions -- Exponents -- Special exponents -- Exponential functions -- Polynomials -- Polynomial operations -- Binomial multiplication -- Factoring polynomials -- Special polynomials -- Quadratic functions -- Complete the square -- The quadratic formula -- Rationals -- Complex rationals
"The book follows a concise algebraic format and is clearly and simply presented." Sci Books Films
Includes bibliographical references

513 Arithmetic

Bunch, Bryan H.
The kingdom of infinite number; a field guide; [by] Bryan Bunch. Freeman, W.H. 2000 388p il hardcover o.p. pa $13.95
Grades: 11 12 Adult   **513**
1. Numbers 2. Number concept
ISBN 0-7167-3388-9; 0-7167-4447-3 (pa)
LC 99-53641
"Bunch limns the personalities, the species linkages, and the field marks of all kinds of numbers—from simple odds and evens to intricate logarithms and transcendentals." Booklist
"The reader will inevitably get caught up in the book's spellbinding mixture of history, language, mathematics, and science." Sci Books Films
Includes bibliographical references

Tabak, John
Numbers: computers, philosophers, and the search for meaning; John Tabak. Facts on File 2004 224p il (History of mathematics) $40
Grades: 9 10 11 12   **513**
1. Numbers 2. Counting
ISBN 0-8160-4955-6   LC 2003-16970
This book "deals with the development of numbers from fractions to algebraic numbers to transcendental numbers to complex numbers and their uses. The book also examines in detail the number *pi*, the evolution of the idea of infinity, and the representation of numbers in computers." Publisher's note
Includes bibliographical references

515 Analysis

Berlinski, David, 1942-
A tour of the calculus. Pantheon Bks. 1995 331p il pa $14.95 hardcover o.p.
Grades: 11 12 Adult   **515**
1. Calculus
ISBN 0-679-74788-5 (pa)   LC 95-4042
This is an introduction to "the foundations of calculus. It is in part an informal history of the subject; the author

Berlinski, David, 1942-—*Continued*
interweaves the historical fragments with expository sections that [seek to] explain the concepts from a modern viewpoint." Libr J

"Berlinski tangibly grounds the abstract notions, so that attentive readers can ease into and grasp the several full-blown proofs he sets forth." Booklist

Maor, Eli
The Facts on File calculus handbook. Facts on File 2003 164p il $35; pa $17.95 *
Grades: 9 10 11 12   **515**
1. Calculus
ISBN 0-8160-4581-X; 0-8160-6229-3 (pa)
         LC 2003-49027
This resource is "a supplement to calculus or trigonometry course work. The *Handbook*'s primary content is the glossary. Here, the author has compiled terms and expressions commonly used in calculus with . . . definitions and examples . . . The other sections include a historical overview of the development of calculus, a selection of brief biographies of mathematicians, a timeline of calculus, a collection of charts and tables, and a list of recommened readings and Websites . . . The conciseness of the definitions and examples, in addition to the historical data, make it a good 'study guide' or review resource for those high school students preparing for AP exams or similar college placement exams. For a quick look up of a definition that will be understandable to the non-math individual, this would be a practical ready-reference resource." Am Ref Books Annu, 2004
Includes bibliographical references

516 Geometry

Gorini, Catherine A.
The Facts on File geometry handbook. Facts on File 2003 280p il (Facts on File science library) $35; pa $17.95 *
Grades: 11 12 Adult   **516**
1. Geometry
ISBN 0-8160-4875-4; 0-8160-6230-7 (pa)
         LC 2002-12343
This includes a glossary of 3,000 entries with labeled diagrams, biographies of 300 scientists and mathematicians from ancient times to the present, a chronology of geometry history, charts, tables, recommended reading and websites.
Includes bibliographical references

Mlodinow, Leonard
Euclid's window; the story of geometry from parallel lines to hyperspace. Free Press 2001 306p il pa $15 hardcover o.p.
Grades: 11 12 Adult   **516**
1. Geometry
ISBN 0-684-86524-6 (pa)   LC 00-54351
Mlodinow's monograph "takes the form of five biographical stories, each about a key figure in the development of geometry: Euclid, Descartes, Gauss, Einstein and Witten." New Sci

"This engaging history does an excellent job of explaining the importance of the study of geometry without making the reader learn any geometry." Libr J
Includes bibliographical references

Tabak, John
Geometry: the language of space and form; John Tabak. Facts on File 2004 222p il (History of mathematics) $40
Grades: 9 10 11 12   **516**
1. Geometry
ISBN 0-8160-4953-X   LC 2003-17340
This book covers "the nature of ancient, projective (including non-Euclidian), and coordinate geometry. . . . [The author] analyzes the insights and accomplishments of many thinkers, ancient and modern, providing a generous array of illuminating demonstrations and examples while keeping extraneous biographical details . . . to a minimum, then closes with a time line, a specialized glossary, and annotated, multimedia reading lists." SLJ
Includes bibliographical references

516.2 Euclidean geometry. Trigonometry

Blatner, David
The joy of π. Walker & Co. 1997 129p il hardcover o.p. pa $12 *
Grades: 11 12 Adult   **516.2**
1. Pi
ISBN 0-8027-1332-7; 0-8027-7562-4 (pa)
         LC 97-23705
The author discusses the history of the number π, as well as the process of "calculating the ratio of a circle's circumference to its diameter, which has advanced from measuring lengths of string and the 'brute force' of measuring polygons to feeding supercomputers sophisticated algorithms. Sidebars . . . abound, containing a factoid, joke, or doggerel inspired by π." Booklist
Includes bibliographical references

Livio, Mario, 1945-
The golden ratio; the story of phi, the world's most astonishing number. Broadway Bks. 2002 294p hardcover o.p. pa $14.95
Grades: 11 12 Adult   **516.2**
1. Geometry
ISBN 0-7679-0815-5; 0-7679-0816-3 (pa)
         LC 2002-23084
The author examines the history and myths of phi, the "golden ratio" of 1.6180339887 that has been related to phenomena as diverse as the arrangements of petals on roses and the breeding patterns of rabbits.

"Overall, an enjoyable work, amply supported by index, extensive references, and ten appendixes presenting mathematical elaborations of text material." Choice
Includes bibliographical references

519.2   Probabilities

Orkin, Michael
What are the odds? chance in everyday life; {by} Mike Orkin. Freeman, W.H. 1999 154p pa $14.95
Grades: 11 12 Adult   **519.2**
1. Probabilities 2. Chance
ISBN 0-7167-3560-1   LC 99-51731
This "treatise covers the role of chance and probability, ranging from coin tosses to Heisenberg's uncertainty principle. . . . The author explains the role of chance and probability in terms that can, on the whole, be understood by those who have had neither course work nor any other type of exposure to probability and statistics." Sci Books Films
Includes bibliographical references

Rosenthal, Jeffrey, 1967-
Struck by lightning; the curious world of probabilities; [by] Jeffrey S. Rosenthal. HarperCollins Canada 2005 263p il pa $19.95
Grades: 11 12 Adult   **519.2**
1. Probabilities 2. Chance
ISBN 0-309-09734-7; 978-0-309-09734-5
LC 2005-37021
Rosenthal discusses ways in which probability theory affects such areas of everyday life as crime, travel, gambling, politics, and disease.
"The lighthearted presentation ensures that readers will not feel burdened by all the knowledge they are gaining and the concluding summary—disguised as a final exam—is sure to deliver an A to everyone, which is what Rosenthal deserves for this clever book." Publ Wkly

Tabak, John
Probability and statistics; the science of uncertainty. Facts on File 2004 226p il (History of mathematics) $40; pa $17.95 *
Grades: 9 10 11 12   **519.2**
1. Probabilities 2. Statistics
ISBN 0-8160-4956-4; 0-8160-6231-5 (pa)
LC 2003-16966
This book covers subjects ranging "from ancient games of chance played around the world and the theories of Fermat and Pascal to phrenology, the specious use of statistics, and statistical methods to stop epidemics." Publisher's note
Includes bibliographical references

519.5   Statistical mathematics

Cohen, I. Bernard, 1914-2003
The triumph of numbers; how counting shaped modern life. W. W. Norton 2005 209p il $24.95; pa $14.95
Grades: 11 12 Adult   **519.5**
1. Statistics
ISBN   0-393-05769-0;   978-0-393-05769-0; 0-393-32870-8 (pa); 978-0-393-32870-7 (pa)
LC 2004-27322

This is a "history of numbers and the birth of statistics." Publisher's note
"This book presents a persuasive narrative on how numbers have maintained a prominent role not only in science and government throughout time, but in the daily operations of life." Sci Books Films
Includes bibliographical references

Kault, David
Statistics with common sense. Greenwood Press 2003 257p il $49.95
Grades: 9 10 11 12   **519.5**
1. Statistics
ISBN 0-313-32209-0   LC 2002-75322
Aimed primarily at individuals who learned statistics at an earlier time but never fully grasped the concepts behind it, this resource emphasizes "a working knowledge of understanding the processes not merely memorizing the formulas. The book also illustrates common sense decision-making in the application process, and a . . . description of the full mathematical derivation of some statistical tests. . . . Having a clear understanding of when and how to use 'stats' is the driving force of this book. If your students and teachers need a great guide for statistics, add this volume to your library collection." Libr Media Connect
Includes bibliographical references

Paulos, John Allen
Once upon a number; the hidden mathematical logic of stories. Basic Bks. 1998 214p pa $13 hardcover o.p. *
Grades: 11 12 Adult   **519.5**
1. Statistics 2. Symbolic logic
ISBN 0-465-05159-6 (pa)   LC 98-39252
The author contends "that statistics cannot be disconnected from the stories—or narrative contexts—that attach them to the complexities of the world." Publ Wkly
"Paulos fills this book with so many intriguing nuggets of mathematically sound information about the stories we tell that it deserves rereading, which, because Paulos' voice is so enjoyable, seems no daunting task." Booklist
Includes bibliographical references

520   Astronomy and allied sciences

The **Amateur** astronomer; edited by Shawn Carlson. Wiley 2001 271p il pa $16.95 *
Grades: 11 12 Adult   **520**
1. Astronomy
ISBN 0-471-38282-5   LC 00-47773
At head of title: Scientific American
A collection of articles on the subject of astronomy published in Scientific American magazine from the 1950s to the 1990s
"Carlson provides fascinating assessments of both how much and how little was known 50 years ago, and he charts the evolution of theories and the rise and resolution of controversies, thus offering invaluable insights into the history of scientific thought and methodology. Technically precise yet always clear, these popular science columns remain vital and exciting." Booklist
Includes bibliographical references

Aveni, Anthony F.
Stairways to the stars; skywatching in three great ancient cultures; [by] Anthony Aveni. Wiley 1997 230p il hardcover o.p. pa $15.95 *
Grades: 11 12 Adult   **520**
1. Astronomy—History 2. Ancient civilization
ISBN 0-471-15942-5; 0-471-32976-2 (pa)
LC 96-36517
This book "examines the astronomy of three ancient societies: Great Britain and Stonehenge; the Mayas and the cult of Venus; and the Incas and the city of Cuzco, built as . . . [an] observatory. Also included is a chapter on 'naked eye' observing that allows readers to see the night sky as did our ancient ancestors." Libr J
"An insightful and interesting blend of ancient anthropology and ancient astronomy." Choice
Includes bibliographical references

Dickinson, Terence
The universe and beyond; foreword by Skylab Astronaut Edward G. Gibson. 4th ed. Firefly Books 2004 180p il $45; pa $29.95 *
Grades: 9 10 11 12   **520**
1. Astronomy
ISBN 1-55297-937-7; 1-55297-901-6 (pa)
LC 2005-357160
First published 1986
Illustrated with over 130 color illustrations and photographs, this describes the universe, comets, planets, black holes, galaxies, dark matter, quasars, and other topics.
"For its content and quality, the book is an excellent bargain as priced, and would be a fine addition to all school libraries. . . . Anyone interested in astronomy, planetary science, cosmology, stars, or the universe in general would benefit from having a copy for many years to come." Sci Books Films
Includes bibliographical references

Ferris, Timothy
Seeing in the dark; how backyard stargazers are probing deep space and guarding earth from interplanetary peril. Simon & Schuster 2002 379p il hardcover o.p. pa $14
Grades: 11 12 Adult   **520**
1. Astronomy 2. Astronomers
ISBN 0-684-86579-3; 0-684-86580-7 (pa)
LC 2002-20693
Ferris examines "the 20th-century in spectroscopic analysis of very distant light from celestial bodies through the personal experiences of . . . astronomers, mostly amateurs." Christ Sci Monit
"This book should turn many novices on to astronomy and captivate those already fascinated by the heavens." Publ Wkly

Kidger, Mark R., 1960-
Astronomical enigmas; life on Mars, the Star of Bethlehem, and other Milky Way mysteries. Johns Hopkins University Press 2005 297p il map $29.95
Grades: 9 10 11 12   **520**
1. Astronomy
ISBN 0-8018-8026-2   LC 2004-8937

The author "has organized Astronomical Enigmas around the answers to some questions laypersons frequently pose when meeting a professional astronomer." Choice
"This is a beautifully written book packed with narrative answers to major astronomical topics of current interest." Sci Books Films
Includes bibliographical references

NightWatch: a practical guide to viewing the universe; foreword by Timothy Ferris; illustrations by Adolf Schaller, Victor Costanzo, Roberta Cooke, Glenn LeDrew; principal photography by Terence Dickinson. 4th ed. Firefly Books 2006 192p il $35 *
Grades: 8 9 10 11 12   **520**
1. Astronomy
ISBN 978-1-55407-147-0; 1-55407-147-X
LC 2006-491527
First published 1983
This "handbook for amateur astronomers combines a text both meaty and hard to put down with a great array of charts, boxes, tables, and dazzling full-color photos of the sky." SLJ [review of 1998 edition]
Includes bibliographical references

Petersen, Carolyn Collins
Visions of the cosmos; {by} Carolyn Collins Petersen, John C. Brandt. Cambridge University Press 2003 218p il $40
Grades: 9 10 11 12   **520**
1. Astronomy
ISBN 0-521-81898-2   LC 2003-43043
This "book is a comprehensive exploration of astronomy through the eyes of the world's observatories and spacecraft missions." Publisher's note
"Almost every page holds stunningly detailed visual images. Full-page color digital photos such as the birth of a star or the Pillars of Creation captivate readers while the descriptive text explains how these visions were recorded and what they may mean. This book takes the scientific who, what, where, when, and why and puts them in terms a neophyte astronomer can comprehend." Libr Media Connect
Includes bibliographical references

Yount, Lisa
Modern astronomy; expanding the universe. Facts on File 2006 204p il (Milestones in discovery and invention) $35
Grades: 7 8 9 10 11 12   **520**
1. Astronomy
ISBN 0-8160-5746-X; 978-0-8160-5746-7
LC 2005-25113
This book profiles "12 men and women whose research and work in new technologies brought about a revolution in the understanding of time and space during the 20th century." Publisher's note
Includes glossary and bibliographical references

520.3 Astronomy--Encyclopedias and dictionaries

Angelo, Joseph A.
Encyclopedia of space and astronomy; [by] Joseph A. Angelo, Jr. Facts on File 2006 740p il (Facts on File science library) $75 *
Grades: 11 12 Adult   **520.3**
1. Astronomy—Encyclopedias 2. Space sciences—Encyclopedias
ISBN 0-8160-5330-8   LC 2004-30800
This encyclopedia presents "the main concepts, terms, facilities, and people in astronomy. . . . Coverage includes terms such as astrophysics, planetary science, and cosmology, as well as both American and international astronomy and space technology." Publisher's note
Includes bibliographical references

Astronomy encyclopedia; foreword by Leif J. Robinson; star maps created by Wil Tirion; general editor, Patrick Moore. fully rev and expanded ed. Oxford Univ. Press 2002 456p il maps $50 *
Grades: 11 12 Adult   **520.3**
1. Astronomy—Encyclopedias
ISBN 0-19-521833-7   LC 2003-535058
First published 1987 with title: International encyclopedia of astronomy
This encyclopedia ranges "from adaptive optics and cold dark matter, to Islamic astronomy and the lens defect known as vignetting. It includes . . . articles on the cornerstones of astronomical investigation, such as the Milky Way, the sun and the planets, optical and radio telescopes, stars, black holes, astrophysics, observatories, astronomical photography, space programs, the constellations, and famous astronomers. And there are concise entries on planetary features and satellites, asteroids, observational techniques, comets, satellite launchers, meteors, and subjects as diverse as life in the Universe and the structure of meteorites." Publisher's note
"This is a beautiful book, replacing many older encyclopedias that may be on the reference shelves. If a library has funds to purchase only one encyclopedia covering astronomy, this is the one to select." Booklist

Darling, David J.
The universal book of astronomy from the Andromeda Galaxy to the zone of avoidance; [by] David Darling. Wiley 2003 570p il $40
Grades: 11 12 Adult   **520.3**
1. Astronomy—Dictionaries
ISBN 0-471-26569-1   LC 2003-13941
This book features "over 3000 alphabetically arranged entries covering history, biography, celestial objects, cosmological phenomena, and more." Libr J
"Designed for nonspecialists, Darling's volume fills a niche in astronomy ready reference. . . . The volume is . . . highly readable and provides bonuses in 22 star charts outlining all 88 constellations in both north and south celestial hemispheres, instructional aids throughout the text, and charts that accompany entries for many stars, galaxies, and clusters and show size, position, etc." Choice
Includes bibliographical references

A **Dictionary** of astronomy; edited by Ian Ridpath. Rev ed. Oxford University Press 2003 518p il (Oxford paperback reference) pa $15.99 *
Grades: 11 12 Adult   **520.3**
1. Astronomy—Dictionaries
ISBN 0-19-860513-7
First published 1997
Cover title: Oxford dictionary of astronomy
This dictionary "contains over 4,000 entries, addressing topics such as objects in the solar system, astronomy and physics terms, and principle entries for stars and galaxies. This revised edition also provides up-to-date coverage of recent space exploration and discoveries. There are no photographs: over 40 illustrations highlight individual entries. Brief biographical sketches of major astronomers are also included. . . . This is an excellent, affordable dictionary for advanced high school users and academic researchers." Am Ref Books Annu, 2004

The **Facts** on File dictionary of astronomy; edited by John Daintith, William Gould. 5th ed. Facts on File 2006 550p il (Facts on File science library) $59.50 *
Grades: 7 8 9 10 11 12   **520.3**
1. Astronomy—Dictionaries
ISBN 0-8160-5998-5; 978-0-8160-5998-0
                    LC 2006-40860
First published 1979 under the editorship of Valerie Illingworth
This dictionary includes "more than 3,700 entries . . . that reflect all aspects of astronomy, together with associated terms in spectroscopy, photometry, and particle physics." Publisher's note
Includes bibliographical references

Firefly astronomy dictionary; [an illustrated A-Z guide to the universe] Firefly Books 2003 256p il pa $14.95
Grades: 11 12 Adult   **520.3**
1. Astronomy—Dictionaries
ISBN 1-55297-837-0   LC 2004-271068
First published 1995 in the United Kingdom under the editorship of Ian Ridpath and John Woodruff with title: Philip's astronomy dictionary
"As well as defining scientific terms and explaining theories, the dictionary provides brief biographies of over 100 famous astronomers including Ptolemy, Galileo, Johann Kepler, Copernicus and Edwin Hubble. An appendix provides tables of symbols and mathematical units and calculations used in astronomy." Publisher's note
"Attractively produced, . . . [this book] offers numerous small but sharp and attractive illustrations. Its more than 1,000 entries range from one to several paragraphs, with numerous cross-references in boldface. . . . Recommended." Choice

The **Firefly** encyclopedia of astronomy; edited by Paul Murdin & Margaret Penston. Firefly Books 2004 472p il $59.95 *
Grades: 11 12 Adult   **520.3**
1. Astronomy—Encyclopedias
ISBN 1-55297-797-8
"This book covers astronomical objects and phenomena, space missions, observatories, and astronomers and

The Firefly encyclopedia of astronomy—*Continued*

their organizations, among other topics." Libr J

This encyclopedia "provides an engaging trove of information for lay people. Articles on topics in astrophysics and cosmology convey several decades worth of findings in these fields without trying to explain the science to non-experts." Publ Wkly

522 Techniques, equipment, materials of astronomy

Angelo, Joseph A.

Spacecraft for astronomy; [by] Joseph A. Angelo, Jr. Facts on File, Inc. 2006 288p il (Frontiers in space) $39.50

Grades: 9 10 11 12   522

1. Space probes 2. Astronomical instruments 3. Astronomical observatories

ISBN 0-8160-5774-5; 978-0-8160-5774-0

LC 2006-4875

This "volume describes the historic events, scientific principles, and technical breakthroughs that allow complex orbiting astronomical observatories to increase our understanding of the universe, its origin, and its destiny." Publisher's note

Includes glossary and bibliographical references

Barnes-Svarney, Patricia

Through the telescope; a guide for the amateur astronomer; [by] Patricia L. Barnes-Svarney, Michael R. Porcellino. rev and updated. McGraw-Hill 2000 309p il pa $19.95

Grades: 9 10 11 12   522

1. Astronomy

ISBN 0-07-134804-2   LC 99-54054

First edition by Michael R. Porcellino published 1989 by TAB Bks.

This guide covers the use of the telescope and other tools of the astronomer, and provides instruction for observing the planets, the moon, stars, and other objects. Sky charts are also included

Includes bibliographical references

Harrington, Philip S.

Star ware; the amateur astronomer's guide to choosing, buying, and using telescopes and accessories. 4th ed. Wiley 2007 417p il pa $21.95

Grades: 11 12 Adult   522

1. Telescopes

ISBN 978-0-471-75063-5; 0-471-75063-8

LC 2006-25134

First published 1994

This guidebook on choosing and caring for telescopes and related equipment also features advice on practical issues such as keeping dew off a corrector plate, warding off mosquitoes, and staying warm outside.

Includes bibliographical references

Kerrod, Robin, 1938-

Hubble; the mirror on the universe. Firefly Books 2003 192p il $35 *

Grades: 11 12 Adult   522

1. Hubble Space Telescope 2. Outer space—Exploration

ISBN 1-55297-781-1   LC 2004-298072

This book is an "introduction to the objects found in our solar system and universe and to the techniques used to study them. In addition, there is a brief history of telescopes and the HST {Hubble Space Telescope}." Sci Books Films

"This resource can be considered two books in one. It is at once a photographic tour of the universe revealed by images from the Hubble Space Telescope (HST) and an astronomy textbook. Replete with full-page color photographs, the book matches up Hubble's well-labeled pictures to corresponding text nicely; however, it would be worth purchasing for the photos alone." Voice Youth Advocates

Stephenson, Bruce

The universe unveiled; instruments and images through history; [by] Bruce Stephenson, Marvin Bolt, Anna Felicity Friedman. Cambridge Univ. Press 2000 152p il $29.95

Grades: 9 10 11 12   522

1. Astronomical instruments 2. Astronomy

ISBN 0-521-79143-X   LC 00-59883

This book "depicts the shift from an Earth-centered understanding of the Universe to a Sun-centered view, the mapping of the stars, and the ever-expanding knowledge of the heavens using telescopes. It also examines the developing technologies of navigation and of the measuring and mapping of the Earth." Publisher's note

Includes bibliographical references

Taschek, Karen, 1956-

Death stars, weird galaxies, and a quasar-spangled universe; the discoveries of the Very Large Array telescope. University of New Mexico Press 2006 78p il $17.95

Grades: 9 10 11 12   522

1. Radio astronomy 2. Telescopes

ISBN 0-8263-3211-0; 978-0-8263-3211-0

LC 2005-22841

"The Very Large Array (VLA) radio telescope, located on the Plains of San Agustin, NM, is made up of 27 giant dish antennas. This book describes the array itself; the planets Mercury, Jupiter, and Uranus; the life and death of stars like the sun; death stars and black holes; different types of galaxies; and the future of radio astronomy. . . . The current, authoritative, and interesting text contains considerable astronomical data that would be useful in research and gives a good sense of how these telescopes are changing our view of the universe." SLJ

523 Specific celestial bodies and phenomena

Ekrutt, Joachim W.
Stars and planets; identifying them, learning about them, experiencing them; [by] Joachim Ekrutt; star maps and diagrams by Wil Tirion; maps of solar and lunar eclipses by Brian Sullivan; consulting editor, Clint Hatchett. 2nd ed. Barron's Educ. Ser. 2000 159p il pa $13.95
Grades: 9 10 11 12   523
1. Astronomy 2. Stars 3. Planets
ISBN 0-7641-1310-0   LC 99-35131
First English language edition published 1992
"With all important celestial events up to the year 2010 and with a lexicon of celestial bodies"
This book includes month-by-month sky maps for the northern and southern hemispheres, an astronomical calendar of the planets, a set of tables for phases of the moon, solar and lunar eclipses, and an illustrated dictionary of celestial objects and events

Firefly atlas of the universe; foreword by Arnold Wolfendale. 3rd ed. Firefly Books 2005 288p il $49.95 *
Grades: 11 12 Adult   523
1. Astronomy
ISBN 1-55407-071-6   LC 2006-275758
First published 1970 by Rand McNally; this edition first published 2003 in Canada. Variant title: Philip's atlas of the universe
This work begins with a "general historical overview, followed by individual sections on the solar system, the sun, the stars, the structure of the universe and our galaxy's place in it, and over 20 useful star maps, all incorporating the newest scientific data." Libr J [review of 2003 edition]

Moore, Patrick
Stargazing; astronomy without a telescope. 2nd ed. Cambridge Univ. Press 2001 209p il hardcover o.p. pa $19
Grades: 9 10 11 12   523
1. Astronomy
ISBN 0-521-79052-2; 0-521-79445-5 (pa)
                                       LC 00-37884
First published 1985
This is a guide to observing the night sky with the naked eye, showing how to find and identify the constellations, planets, comets, and meteors.

523.1 The universe, galaxies, quasars

Boslough, John
Stephen Hawking's universe. Morrow 1985 158p il pa $5.99 hardcover o.p. *
Grades: 9 10 11 12   523.1
1. Hawking, Stephen W., 1942- 2. Universe
ISBN 0-380-70763-2 (pa)   LC 84-4673

Published in the United Kingdom with title: Beyond the black hole
This book presents a profile of the English physicist along with a transcript of one of his lectures.
"Boslough captures the essence of Hawking's contributions to the fundamentals and the applications of physics to astronomy and cosmology. . . . Any reader at any level with an interest in the ideas of science will enjoy reading this man's views of the physical universe." Choice

Chaisson, Eric
Epic of evolution; seven ages of the cosmos; illustrated by Lola Judith Chaisson. Columbia University Press 2005 478p il $34.50; pa $22.95
Grades: 11 12 Adult   523.1
1. Cosmology 2. Life—Origin
ISBN   0-231-13560-2;   978-0-231-13560-3; 0-231-13561-0 (pa); 978-0-231-13561-0 (pa)
                                      LC 2005-45452
This is "a tour of the seven ages of the cosmos, from the formless era of radiation through the origins of human culture." Publisher's note
The author "has crafted a wonderful vehicle for exploring our universe." Sci Books Films
Includes bibliographical references

Hawking, Stephen W., 1942-
Black holes and baby universes and other essays; [by] Stephen Hawking. Bantam Bks. 1993 182p pa $18 hardcover o.p.
Grades: 11 12 Adult   523.1
1. Cosmology 2. Science—Philosophy
ISBN 0-553-37411-7 (pa)   LC 93-8269
A collection of essays and speeches ranging from autobiographical sketches to theoretical discussions of black holes, relativity and quantum mechanics.
The author "sprinkles his explanations with a wry sense of humor and a keen awareness that the sciences today delve not only into the far reaches of the cosmos, but into the inner philosophical world as well." N Y Times Book Rev

A briefer history of time; [by] Stephen Hawking and Leonard Mlodinow. Bantam Dell 2005 162p il $25 *
Grades: 11 12 Adult   523.1
1. Cosmology
ISBN 0-553-80436-7   LC 2005-42949
Also available Random House large print edition $27 (ISBN: 0-375-72833-3)
First published 1988 with title: A brief history of time
The authors describe concepts about space and time, black holes, the origin and nature of the universe, the uncertainty principle, and the unification of physics. It also discusses string theory, dark matter, and dark energy.
"Hawking and Mlodinow provide one of the most lucid discussions of this complex topic ever written for a general audience. Readers will come away with an excellent understanding of the apparent contradictions and conundrums at the forefront of contemporary physics." Publ Wkly
Includes bibliographical references

Hooper, Dan, 1976-
Dark cosmos; in search of our universe's missing mass and energy. HarperCollins Publishers 2006 240p il $24.95
Grades: 11 12 Adult   523.1
1. Cosmology 2. Astrophysics
ISBN 978-0-06-113032-8; 0-06-113032-X
LC 2006-44333
This book discusses "dark matter" and "dark energy," invisible substances which scientists speculate may make up over 95% of the universe.
"Hooper's clear presentation in very simple, jargon-free prose should appeal especially to young people just starting to get excited about the mysteries that still await them in science." Publ Wkly

Kaku, Michio
Parallel worlds; a journey through creation, higher dimensions, and the future of the cosmos. Doubleday 2005 428p il hardcover o.p. pa $15.95
Grades: 11 12 Adult   523.1
1. Cosmology 2. Big bang theory 3. String theory
ISBN 0-385-50986-3; 1-4000-3372-1 (pa)
LC 2004-56039
The author "begins by describing the extraordinary advances that have transformed cosmology over the last century, and particularly over the last decade, forcing scientists around the world to rethink our understanding of the birth of the universe, and its ultimate fate. . . . As astronomers wade through the avalanche of data from the WMAP satellite, a new cosmological picture is emerging. So far, the leading theory about the birth of the universe is the 'inflationary universe theory,' a major refinement on the big bang theory." Publisher's note
"This is a riveting popular treatment of the string revolution in physics written by a pioneering theorist in the field. Kaku expounds comprehensibly on why astrophysicists love strings and branes and the way they resolve various vexatious cosmological paradoxes." Booklist

Universe; written by Robert Dinwiddie . . . [et al.] DK 2005 512p il $50 *
Grades: 11 12 Adult   523.1
1. Cosmology
ISBN 0-7566-1364-7   LC 2005-4794
"The volume is divided into three sections. The first, called 'Introduction,' presents an overview of basic concepts, organized under the broad topics 'What Is the Universe?' 'The Beginning and End of the Universe,' 'The View from Earth,' and 'Exploring Space.' The next section, 'Guide to the Universe,' focuses on the features of the solar system, the Milky Way, and the regions beyond. Among the topics that are covered here are the planets; asteroids, comets, and meteors; the stars; and galaxy clusters. . . . Finally, the book has a section called 'The Night Sky,' with entries on each of the 88 constellations, including maps." Booklist
This is "a visually stunning reference that makes browsing irresistible. Every page of this oversized volume is full color, with an eye-pleasing balance of text and graphics." Libr J

523.2 Planetary systems

Encyclopedia of the solar system; editors, Lucy-Ann McFadden, Paul R. Weissman and Torrence V. Johnson. 2nd ed. Academic 2007 xx, 966p il map $99.95 *
Grades: 9 10 11 12   523.2
1. Solar system—Encyclopedias 2. Astronomy—Encyclopedias
ISBN 978-0-12-088589-3; 0-12-088589-1
LC 2006-937972
First published 1999
This encyclopedia covers "the origin and evolution of the solar system, historical discoveries, and details about planetary bodies and how they interact." Publisher's note
Includes bibliographical references

Sobel, Dava
The Planets. Viking 2005 270p il $24.95; pa $13 *
Grades: 11 12 Adult   523.2
1. Planets 2. Solar system
ISBN 0-670-03446-0; 0-14-200116-3 (pa)
Also available Random House large print edition
The author turns her attention to "the planets of our solar system. . . . Sobel explores the planets' origins and oddities through the lens of popular culture, from astrology, mythology, and science fiction to art, music, poetry, biography, and history." Publisher's note
"For newcomers to planetary astronomy, 'The Planets' offers a nimble summary of the latest findings on each planet's features and geology. For those who avidly followed the journeys of the Mariners, Voyagers and Vikings through interplanetary space, it lets us fall in love with the heavens all over again." N Y Times Book Rev
Includes bibliographical references

The solar system; edited by Giovanni Caprara; [translated by S.M. Harris] Firefly Books 2003 255p il (A Firefly guide) pa $24.95 *
Grades: 11 12 Adult   523.2
1. Solar system
ISBN 1-55297-679-3   LC 2004-272175
Original Italian edition, 2001
"Chapters on the sun, planets, and minor bodies discuss the physical characteristics of these objects as well as the history of their exploration." Libr J
"The book is a compact and easy-to-use resource providing factual information, tidbits from history, and descriptions of some critical space missions with related results. The tables (one for each planet) and the cutaway diagrams of planets and moons are especially well done." Choice
Includes bibliographical references

Upgren, Arthur R.
Many skies; alternative histories of the sun, moon, planets, and stars; [by] Arthur Upgren. Rutgers University Press 2005 198p il $24.95
Grades: 9 10 11 12   523.2
1. Astronomy 2. Solar system
ISBN 0-8135-3512-3   LC 2004-7533

Upgren, Arthur R.—*Continued*
The author "asks how the development of astronomy might be different if our solar system and the universe were different." Sci Books Films
"This book is not just for the science fiction aficionado, but for readers to ponder as they simultaneously learn astronomy." Choice
Includes bibliographical references

523.3 Moon

Legault, Thierry
New atlas of the moon; [by] Thierry Legault, Serge Brunier. Firefly Books 2006 127p il $55
Grades: 11 12 Adult   523.3
  1. Moon—Maps
  ISBN 978-1-55407-173-9; 1-55407-173-9
This lunar atlas features a day to day photographic record of the moon in its different phases with clear overlays over the lunar photos to identify major craters. It also features a section on lunar cartography that describes the location and details of different craters.
Includes bibliographical references

Mackenzie, Dana
The big splat; or, How our moon came to be. Wiley 2003 232p il $24.95
Grades: 11 12 Adult   523.3
  1. Moon
  ISBN 0-471-15057-6   LC 2003-535402
"Mackenzie's account of humanity's long relationship with Earth's only natural satellite, from a probable lunar calendar found in the Lascaux caves to the new 'giant impact' theory of the moon's origin, is magnetically readable, preternaturally clear, and amazingly concise."
Booklist
Includes bibliographical references

523.4 Planets

Bakich, Michael E.
The Cambridge planetary handbook. Cambridge Univ. Press 2000 336p il $30
Grades: 11 12 Adult   523.4
  1. Planets
  ISBN 0-521-63280-3   LC 99-10171
"The book is arranged in two parts. Part one presents planetary data, such as atmospheric pressure, composition, and future conjunctions and transits. Part two contains a summary on each planet, including its moons. . . . The handbook is well suited for amateur astronomers and students of astronomy." Booklist

Hartmann, William K.
A traveler's guide to Mars; the mysterious landscapes of the red planet. Workman Pub. 2003 468p map pa $18.95
Grades: 11 12 Adult   523.4
  1. Mars (Planet)
  ISBN 0-7611-2606-6   LC 2003-41149

"Following an opening chapter discussing what humans have believed and have come to verify about the red planet, the author discusses the three major eras of its 4.5 billion year history. He describes various regions, offering a geological tour of the craters, volcanoes, and the face of Mars. . . . Interspersed throughout are boxed inserts highlighting weather, hazards, financial considerations, geology, etc. Also appearing periodically are sections called 'My Martian Chronicles' in which the astronomer describes his own work and experiences in his quest to learn more about this unusual planet. His writing style will make teens want to keep reading. . . . If you can have only one title about Mars, this is the one to buy." SLJ
Includes bibliographical references

Weintraub, David A., 1958-
Is Pluto a planet? a historical journey through the solar system. Princeton University Press 2007 254p il $27.95
Grades: 11 12 Adult   523.4
  1. Planets 2. Solar system 3. Pluto (Planet)
  ISBN 0-691-12348-9; 978-0-691-12348-6
                                      LC 2006-929630
The author "places the Pluto controversy in context in his . . . account of the development of our solar system and the evolution of the meaning of the word planet, from Aristotle's theories to recent decrees by the International Astronomical Union." Publ Wkly
Weintraub "provides a very interesting and thought-provoking history concerning the whole idea of planets, and I recommend the book highly to anyone interested in the solar system." Sci Books Films
Includes bibliographical references

523.5 Meteoroids, solar wind, zodiacal light

Norton, O. Richard
The Cambridge encyclopedia of meteorites; fragments of other worlds. Cambridge Univ. Press 2002 xx, 354p il maps $50 *
Grades: 11 12 Adult   523.5
  1. Meteorites
  ISBN 0-521-62143-7   LC 2001-35621
This reference describes the classification, structure, history, and origins of meteorites
"Anyone wishing to know what meteorites are, where they come from, and what they reveal about the history of the universe need look no further. This thorough and accessible compilation covers all facets of the field." Libr J
Includes bibliographical references

Rocks from space; meteorites and meteorite hunters; illustrated by Dorothy S. Norton. 2nd ed. Mountain Press 1998 447p il maps $55; pa $32
Grades: 11 12 Adult   523.5
  1. Meteorites 2. Asteroids 3. Comets
  ISBN 0-87842-438-5; 0-87842-373-7 (pa)
                                      LC 97-51574
First published 1994

Norton, O. Richard—*Continued*

This illustrated introduction to meteorites and meteoritics includes "sections devoted to meteorite falls, finds, and craters in addition to descriptions of meteorites, how they are classified, their origins, and what they are. Also [included] . . . is a section on the history of meteoritics and the prominent personalities associated with the science." Choice [review of 1994 edition]

Includes bibliographical references

523.6   Comets

Burnham, Robert

Great comets; foreword by David H. Levy. Cambridge Univ. Press 2000 228p pa $22 *

Grades: 11 12 Adult   **523.6**

1. Comets

ISBN 0-521-64600-6   LC 98-50546

The author focuses on the comets Hyakutake in 1996 and Hale-Bopp in 1997, placing them in the context of their predecessors, including Halley's comet, profiles spaceprobes to the comets, and assesses the risks to humanity from comets

"The copious illustrations are . . . supported by a good deal of text. . . . The science is accurate and presented in a nontechnical way. . . . Overall, this is a very fine book." Sci Books Films

Includes bibliographical references and index

Levy, David H., 1948-

David H. Levy's guide to observing and discovering comets. Cambridge University Press 2003 177p il $70; pa $22.99 *

Grades: 11 12 Adult   **523.6**

1. Comets

ISBN 0-521-82656-X; 0-521-52051-7 (pa)

     LC 2002-31547

The author "describes the observing techniques that have been developed over the years—from visual observations and searching, to photography, through to electronic charge-coupled devices (CCDs). He combines the history of comet hunting with the latest techniques, showing how our understanding of comets has evolved over time." Publisher's note

Includes bibliographical references

523.7   Sun

Golub, Leon

Nearest star; the surprising science of our sun; {by} Leon Golub & Jay M. Pasachoff. Harvard Univ. Press 2001 267p il $29.95; pa $16.95

Grades: 11 12 Adult   **523.7**

1. Sun

ISBN 0-674-00467-1; 0-674-01006-X (pa)

     LC 00-63213

The authors "describe for a nonspecialist audience what is currently known of the structure of the sun, the source of its enormous energy, its history and future, its various effects on Earth and its atmosphere." Libr J

This is "a brilliant, richly illustrated survey." Booklist

Includes bibliographical references

Harrington, Philip S.

Eclipse! the what, where, when, why, and how guide to watching solar and lunar eclipses. Wiley 1997 280p il maps pa $16.95 *

Grades: 9 10 11 12   **523.7**

1. Solar eclipses 2. Lunar eclipses

ISBN 0-471-12795-7   LC 96-29777

This describes solar and lunar eclipses and offers advice on observing and photographing them

"This well-organized book . . . does a fine job of detailing the mechanics of solar and lunar eclipses. . . . Numerous black-and-white photographs and many line drawings and tables in the text are followed by seven helpful appendices and a good index." Sci Books Films

Includes bibliographical references

Lang, Kenneth R.

The Cambridge encyclopedia of the sun. Cambridge Univ. Press 2001 256p il $49.95 *

Grades: 11 12 Adult   **523.7**

1. Sun

ISBN 0-521-78093-4   LC 00-49365

"Each of the nine chapters addresses a different theme. These themes include physical properties, the magnetic solar atmosphere, solar winds and explosions, solar observations, and the Sun-Earth connection. The volume is well illustrated with figures and photographs in both color and black and white. A 35-page glossary provides definitions of terms and acronyms as well as information on telescopes, satellites, and instruments. A short annotated bibliography and an unannotated directory of Web sites are appended." Booklist

Includes bibliographical references and index

523.8   Stars

Calia, Charles Laird

The stargazing year; a backyard astronomer's journey through the seasons of the night sky. Jeremy P. Tarcher/Penguin 2005 273p il $24.95; pa $14.95

Grades: 11 12 Adult   **523.8**

1. Stars

ISBN 1-58542-391-2; 1-58542-470-6 (pa)

     LC 2004-63762

Also available Thorndike Press large print edition

"In a series of 12 essays, each dedicated to one month of the year, Calia describes his quest to build his own backyard observatory, providing . . . tidbits of astronomical history and mythological lore along the way. The book is part memoir, part travelogue through the constellations visible in the Northern Hemisphere. . . . The result is charming, witty, wistful and ultimately inspiring." Publ Wkly

Includes bibliographical references

Kaler, James B.

The hundred greatest stars. Copernicus 2002 xxvii, 213p il $32.50

Grades: 11 12 Adult   **523.8**

1. Stars

ISBN 0-387-95436-8   LC 2002-19774

Kaler, James B.—*Continued*

The author "picks a representative of the major star types, such as the red giant, and rounds out his group with a smattering of classical naked-eye stars. . . . Geared for popularity, the book's design presents one image of the star under discussion, either a field view of its position in a constellation or an exuberant HST closeup, faced by Kaler's one-page story about the star's characteristics and inferred history. For the astronomy buff, an alluring gallery of stars mysterious or simply odd awaits, from magnetars to pulsars to distended monsters on the verge of going supernova." Booklist

Includes bibliographical references

Kerrod, Robin, 1938-

The star guide; learn how to read the night sky star by star. 2nd ed. Wiley 2005 160p il $29.95 *

Grades: 11 12 Adult **523.8**

1. Stars—Atlases

ISBN 0-471-70617-5   LC 2004-22953

First published 1993

The presentation for this instructional guide to stargazing "is structured around monthly star maps (for midlatitude observers) in two-page spreads, with a follow-up feature on that month's outstanding constellation. . . . Photos featuring Hubble Space Telescope spectaculars, supplemented by tips for viewing the sun, moon, and planets, round out this attractive book on basic astronomy." Booklist

Miller, Ron, 1947-

Stars and galaxies. Twenty-First Century Books 2006 96p il (Worlds beyond) lib bdg $27.93

Grades: 7 8 9 10 **523.8**

1. Stars 2. Galaxies

ISBN 0-7613-3466-1   LC 2004-30813

"A cursory description of how the ancients observed and measured the stars leads into chapters about the sun, varieties of stars and the spaces between them, the Milky Way and surrounding galaxies, and theories about how the universe began and how it will end. Miller's text is thorough and substantial, yet his clear examples make the concepts accessible. . . . Miller's own original artwork mixes with stunning NASA photos." Booklist

Includes bibliographical references

526 Mathematical geography

Danson, Edwin, 1948-

Weighing the world; the quest to measure the Earth. Oxford University Press 2005 289p il $29.95

Grades: 11 12 Adult **526**

1. Science—History 2. Surveying 3. Earth

ISBN 978-0-19-518169-2; 0-19-518169-7

    LC 2004-66284

This is a "behind-the-scenes look at the scientific events leading to modern map making. . . . Danson presents the stories of the scientists and scholars that had to scale the Andes, cut through tropical forests and how they handled the hardships they faced in the attempt to revolutionize our understanding of the planet." Publisher's note

The author "enlivens data about geodetic surveying, transforming them into greatly interesting dramas of science." Booklist

Includes bibliographical references

The **Map** book; edited by Peter Barber. Levenger Press 2006 360p il map $45 *

Grades: 11 12 Adult **526**

1. Maps

ISBN 0-8027-1474-9

"More than 165 maps are chronologically arranged in this . . . volume, each with a descriptive and interpretative text by one of 68 international scholars. . . . This handsome collection of antique and modern cartography, brilliantly reproduced in full color, is highly recommended for all libraries, particularly those with cartographical or related collections." Libr J

Includes bibliographical references

Raymo, Chet

Walking zero; discovering cosmic space and time along the Prime Meridian. Walker & Co. 2006 194p il maps $22.95

Grades: 11 12 Adult **526**

1. Longitude 2. Great Britain—Description and travel

ISBN 0-8027-1494-3; 978-0-8027-1494-7

    LC 2006-282372

This is the author's "expression of his personal exploration of space, time, and scientific history, inspired partly by his walking the footpaths of southeast England in close proximity to the 0 degrees longitude line. . . . . This work is a thought-provoking, highly enlightening discussion of some of the most fascinating concepts in physics, astronomy, and geology, among other subjects." Sci Books Films

Includes bibliographical references

Sobel, Dava

Longitude; the true story of a lone genius who solved the greatest scientific problem of his time; with a new foreword by Neil Armstrong. Hardcover anniversary ed., [10th anniversary ed., 2005 anniversary ed.] Walker & Co. 2005 184p il $19 *

Grades: 11 12 Adult **526**

1. Harrison, John, 1693-1776 2. Longitude

ISBN 0-8027-1462-5; 978-0-8027-1462-6

Also available illustrated edition for $32.95; pa $22.95 (ISBN 0-8027-1344-0; pa 0-8027-7593-4)

First published 1995

"In 1714, Britain's Parliament offered the modern equivalent of $12 to anybody who could develop a means of determining longitude at sea. While the likes of Isaac Newton and Edmund Halley sought to calculate longitude by celestial measurement, John Harrison, an uneducated clockmaker, solved the problem with his invention of the chronometer. Science writer Sobel tells this story in a way that enables readers 'to see the globe anew.'" Libr J

Includes bibliographical references

528   Astronomical and nautical almanacs

Astronomical almanac for the year 2008; issued by the Nautical Almanac Office, United States Naval Observatory. . . . U.S. Govt. Ptg. Office 2007 il $40 *
Grades: 11 12 Adult   **528**
1. Nautical almanacs
ISSN 0737-6421
ISBN 0-16-077396-2; 978-0-16-077396-9
Also available online
Annual. Formed by the union in 1981 of The American ephemeris and nautical almanac and The Astronomical ephemeris published by Her Majesty's Nautical Almanac Office. Spine title: Astronomical almanac
"With basic information contributed by the ephemeris offices of a number of countries, this collection of tables is the authoritative source for annual astronomical data from the movement of heavenly bodies to the calculation of calendars." Ref Sources for Small & Medium-sized Libr. 6th edition

529   Chronology

Aveni, Anthony F.
Empires of time; calendars, clocks, and cultures; [by] Anthony Aveni. rev ed. University Press of Colo. 2002 332p il pa $22.95
Grades: 11 12 Adult   **529**
1. Time
ISBN 0-87081-672-1   LC 2002-7120
First published 1989 by Basic Bks.
The author "traces the modern calendar's roots back to Greek pastoral poetry and prehistoric African bone markings, then compares Western, Chinese, Maya, Inca and tribal time systems. He also fathoms our division of time into days, weeks, months, seasons and years for clues to our psychology and worldview." Publ Wkly
Includes bibliographical references

Gleick, James
Faster; the acceleration of just about everything. Pantheon Bks. 1999 324p il pa $14 hardcover o.p.
Grades: 11 12 Adult   **529**
1. Time
ISBN 0-679-77548-X (pa)   LC 99-21640
Gleick focuses on time and argues that the pace of life has grown faster. He discusses technologies such as "the watch, the typewriter, the phone, the TV, and [the computer, and] . . . the ways these 'time-saving' devices have influenced our world." Christ Sci Monit
The author's "shrewd dissection of the 'psychology of hurriedness' leads to many provocative observations." Booklist

Richards, E. G. (Edward Graham)
Mapping time; the calendar and its history. Oxford Univ. Press 1999 xxi, 438p il pa $43.50 hardcover o.p. *
Grades: 11 12 Adult   **529**
1. Calendars 2. Time
ISBN 0-19-286205-7 (pa)   LC 98-24957
"An overview of astronomy, time, clocks, writing, arithmetic, and other theoretical issues lays the groundwork for a description of calendar systems from prehistory to the present. Illustrations, charts, and diagrams, including algorithms for the conversion of calendar systems, are also provided." Libr J
Includes bibliographical references

530   Physics

Bloomfield, Louis
How things work; the physics of everyday life. 3rd ed. Wiley 2006 561p il pa $70.95 *
Grades: 11 12 Adult   **530**
1. Physics
ISBN 978-0-471-46886-8; 0-471-46886-X
       LC 2006-271695
First published 1997
This book is an "introduction to physics and science that starts with whole objects and looks inside them to see what makes them work. It's written for students who seek a connection between science and the world in which they live." Publisher's note

Cole, K. C.
First you build a cloud; and other reflections on physics as a way of life. Harcourt Brace & Co. 1999 231p il pa $14
Grades: 11 12 Adult   **530**
1. Physics
ISBN 0-15-600646-4   LC 98-47050
"A Harvest book"
Originally published 1985 by Morrow with title: Sympathetic vibrations
"Cole offers reflections on the place of physics in modern life. . . . Especially compelling are the essays on the aesthetic force behind scientific endeavors—the beauties of theory. For readers without scientific background, Cole gracefully introduces relativity, quantum theory, optics, astrophysics, and other significant disciplines, never getting bogged down in unnecessary explanation." Booklist
Includes bibliographical references

The hole in the universe; how scientists peered over the edge of emptiness and found everything. Harcourt 2001 274p il pa $14 hardcover o.p.
Grades: 11 12 Adult   **530**
1. Physics
ISBN 0-15-601317-7 (pa)   LC 00-44947
Cole discusses the history of nothing, "combining the history of zero (a mathematical nothing) with that of the vacuum (a physical nothing). . . . Until Einstein showed that light needed no tangible medium through which to travel, theorists filled the vacuum with 'ether'—the 'en-

Cole, K. C.—*Continued*
fant terrible' of substances, as Einstein put it. It was subsequently banished." Atl Mon
Includes bibliographical references

Cracking the SAT: physics subject test, 2007-2008 edition; [by] the Princeton Review. Random House 2007 il pa $19
Grades: 9 10 11 12   **530**
1. Physics—Study and teaching 2. Scholastic Assessment Test 3. Colleges and universities—Entrance requirements
ISSN 1558-0067
ISBN 0-375-76594-8; 978-0-375-76594-0
Annual. First published 2005. Continues Cracking the SAT II: Physics Subject Test
At head of title: The Princeton Review
This guide provides test-taking strategies and sample tests on the subject of physics.

The **Facts** on File dictionary of physics; edited by John Daintith, Richard Rennie. 4th ed. Facts on File 2005 278p il (Facts on File science library) $45; pa $17.95 *
Grades: 9 10 11 12   **530**
1. Physics—Dictionaries
ISBN 0-8160-5653-6; 0-8160-5654-4 (pa)
            LC 2005-40096
First published 1981
This dictionary contains over 2,500 entries. Among topics covered are: particle physics, cosmology, low-temperature physics, quantum theory, nanotechnology, and superconductivity. Tables list symbols for physical quantities and conversion factors.
Includes bibliographical references

The **Facts** on File physics handbook; the Diagram Group. rev ed. Facts on File 2006 272p il (Facts on File science library) $35 *
Grades: 8 9 10 11 12   **530**
1. Physics
ISBN 0-8160-5880-6   LC 2004-59265
First published 2000
Also covering mathematics and computer science, this reference "contains, in separate sections, a dictionary of around 1500 entries; 250-400 thumbnail biographies; a multipage chronology; and an array of field-specific charts, tables, and diagrams." SLJ [review of 2000 edition]
Includes bibliographical references

Feynman, Richard Phillips, 1918-1988
Six easy pieces; essentials of physics, explained by its most brilliant teacher; [by] Richard P. Feynman; originally prepared for publication by Robert B. Leighton and Matthew Sands; new introduction by Paul Davies. Helix Bks. (Reading) 1995 xxix, 145p il hardcover o.p. pa $15
Grades: 11 12 Adult   **530**
1. Physics
ISBN 0-201-40955-0; 0-201-40825-2 (pa)
            LC 94-30894
Also available in paperback with audio CD from Basic Bks.

This book reprints six chapters from Feynman's Lectures on Physics, which the "scientist delivered from 1961 to 1963 at the California Institute of Technology. . . . They discuss atoms, basic physics, the relation of physics to other sciences, the conservation of energy, gravitation, and quantum behavior." Libr J
"These 'easy pieces' cover key topics with a minimum of mathematics and a wealth of excellent analogies and vivid descriptions." Booklist

Jargodzki, Christopher, 1944-
Mad about physics; braintwisters, paradoxes, and curiosities; [by] Christopher Jargodzki and Franklin Potter. Wiley 2000 304p il pa $16.95
Grades: 11 12 Adult   **530**
1. Physics
ISBN 0-471-56961-5   LC 00-39914
The authors present 397 questions and answers in physics and astronomy such as why the full moon is nine times brighter than the half moon, why backspin is important in basketball, and why race car drivers accelerate when going around a curve
"This entertaining book is sure to appeal to anyone with an interest in what makes the world work the way it does. . . . The authors' explanations of even the most complicated phenomena are always clear and precise." Booklist

Kakalios, James
The physics of superheroes. Gotham 2005 365p il $26; pa $15
Grades: 11 12 Adult   **530**
1. Physics—Study and teaching 2. Comic books, strips, etc. 3. Heroes and heroines
ISBN 1-59240-146-5; 1-59240-242-9 (pa)
            LC 2005-46095
The author "looks at momentum, friction, special relativity, properties of matter, light, magnetism, atomic physics, quantum mechanics, and solid-state physics as demonstrated by his favorite comic book heroes—including Superman, Flash, and the Invisible Woman—and shows that much of the time, comic book physics is accurate (though he exposes the bloopers, too). The book's a treat for anyone interested in physical science and can be enjoyed readily by math phobes and those with little science education, since Kakalios explains it all with clear detail and a good measure of fun." Libr J
Includes bibliographical references

Lightman, Alan P., 1948-
Great ideas in physics; the conservation of energy, the second law of thermodynamics, the theory of relativity, and quantum mechanics; [by] Alan Lightman. 3rd ed. McGraw-Hill 2000 300p il pa $14.95
Grades: 9 10 11 12   **530**
1. Physics
ISBN 0-07-135738-6   LC 00-22999
First published 1992
The author explains the physics behind the conservation of energy, the second law of thermodynamics, the theory of relativity, and quantum mechanics, citing ex-

Lightman, Alan P., 1948-—*Continued*
cerpts from the writings of Newton, Kelvin, Einstein, and de Broglie and explaining the influences of these concepts

Includes bibliographical references

Rosen, Joe
Encyclopedia of physics. Facts on File 2004
386p il (Facts on File science library) $75 *
Grades: 11 12 Adult   **530**
1. Physics—Encyclopedias
ISBN 0-8160-4974-2   LC 2003-14963
The entries "cover physical concepts, prominent physicists (modern and historical), and physics laboratories, societies, and organizations. The alphabetically arranged entries are supplemented with 11 topical essays that aim to shed some light on physics in a philosophical or practical way. These essays cover such topics as beauty, the nature of the relationship between physics and philosophy, and the desire among some physicists to find the unifying laws governing all physical concepts. . . . The entries are well written, accurate, and include equations where appropriate." Booklist
Includes bibliographical references

530.1   Physics--Theories and mathematical physics

Al-Khalili, Jim, 1962-
Black holes, wormholes & time machines.
Institute of Physics 1999 xxii, 265p il pa $16.99
Grades: 9 10 11 12   **530.1**
1. Space and time
ISBN 0-7503-0560-6   LC 99-46327
This book seeks to explain the theories of relativity, the big bang, black holes, and time
The author "avoids mathematics, yet gives an admirably clear account of some of the concepts involved."
Economist
Includes bibliographical references

Bodanis, David
$E=mc^2$; a biography of the world's most famous equation. Walker & Co. 2000 337p il $25
Grades: 11 12 Adult   **530.1**
1. Einstein, Albert, 1879-1955 2. Force and energy 3. Space and time
ISBN 0-8027-1352-1   LC 00-40857
Also available in paperback from Berkley Pub. Group
The author relates the story of "Einstein's formulation of the equation in 1905 and its association ever after with relativity and nuclear energy. Parallel with the science, Bodanis populates his tale with dramatic lives."
Booklist

Clegg, Brian
The God effect; quantum entanglement, science's strangest phenomenon. St. Martin's Press 2006 269p il $24.95
Grades: 11 12 Adult   **530.1**
1. Quantum theory
ISBN 0-312-34341-8; 978-0-312-34341-5
                                            LC 2006-42503
This is a "survey of the history of entanglement, exploring ideas such as time travel, teleportation, and quantum computing itself. . . . There is plenty of historical detail and surprising bits of information that entertain, as well as some background personal information about several of the primary researchers in the field." Sci Books Films
Includes bibliographical references

Gott, J. Richard, 1947-
Time travel in Einstein's universe; the physical possibilities of travel through time; {by} J. Richard Gott, III. Houghton Mifflin 2001 291p il hardcover o.p. pa $14
Grades: 11 12 Adult   **530.1**
1. Space and time 2. Fourth dimension
ISBN 0-395-95563-7; 0-618-25735-7 (pa)
                                            LC 00-54243
"Gott tackles the complexities of attempting to turn the fantasy of time travel into a theoretical possibility in a lively and lucid discussion." Booklist
Includes bibliographical references

Guillen, Michael
Five equations that changed the world; the power and poetry of mathematics. Hyperion 1995 277p hardcover o.p. pa $14.95
Grades: 11 12 Adult   **530.1**
1. Physics 2. Mathematics
ISBN 0-7868-6103-7; 0-7868-8187-9 (pa)
                                            LC 95-15199
The author discusses "five significant equations in physics and the individuals who developed them. The individuals are Isaac Newton (Universal gravitation), Daniel Bernoulli (hydrodynamic pressure), Michael Faraday (thermodynamics), Rudolf Clausius (thermodynamics), and Albert Einstein (special relativity)." Libr J
"A seamless blend of dramatic biography and mathematical documentary that links the personal with the scientific." Publ Wkly

Hawking, Stephen W., 1942-
The nature of space and time; [by] Stephen Hawking and Roger Penrose. Princeton Univ. Press 1996 141p il (Isaac Newton Institute series of lectures) hardcover o.p. pa $18.95
Grades: 11 12 Adult   **530.1**
1. Space and time 2. Quantum theory 3. Astrophysics
ISBN 0-691-03791-4; 0-691-05084-8 (pa)
                                            LC 95-35582
This volume "takes the form of a debate between Hawking and Penrose at Cambridge in 1994. At the center of the discussion is a pair of powerful theories: the quantum theory of fields and the general theory of rela-

Hawking, Stephen W., 1942——*Continued*

tivity. The issue is how—if at all—one can merge the two into a quantum theory of gravity. . . . A substantial background in theoretical physics is needed for full comprehension." Libr J

Includes bibliographical references

The universe in a nutshell; [by] Stephen Hawking. Bantam Bks. 2001 216p il $35

Grades: 11 12 Adult   **530.1**

1. Quantum theory

ISBN 0-553-80202-X   LC 2001-35757

Companion volume to A brief history of time

Hawking "explains the basic laws of physics that govern the universe, beginning with a brief history of the concept of relativity, and then he is off and running to explore time, space, the future, and the possibility of time travel, among other fundamental rules of the universe's road. Admirers of Hawking's previous book will continue to appreciate his ability not only to air fresh, provocative ideas but also to say what he means clearly and without watering down his material or condescending to his audience—he even injects humor into his narrative. The profuse, beautifully rendered illustrations contribute greatly to the reader's understanding of his points." Booklist

Rigden, John S.

Einstein 1905; the standard of greatness. Harvard University Press 2005 173p il $21.95; pa $14.95 *

Grades: 11 12 Adult   **530.1**

1. Einstein, Albert, 1879-1955 2. Quantum theory

ISBN 0-674-01544-4; 0-674-02104-5 (pa)

LC 2004-54049

The author "chronicles the . . . theories that Einstein put forth beginning in March 1905: his particle theory of light, rejected for decades but now a staple of physics; his overlooked dissertation on molecular dimensions; his theory of Brownian motion; his theory of special relativity; and the work in which his famous equation, . . . [energy equals mass times the speed of light squared], first appeared." Publisher's note

"The book is a delight to read, with a lot of interesting, useful information." Choice

Includes bibliographical references

530.8   Measurement

The **Economist** desk companion; how to measure, convert, calculate, and define practically anything. Wiley 1998 272p il map $27.95 *

Grades: 11 12 Adult   **530.8**

1. Weights and measures

ISBN 0-471-24953-X   LC 98-17615

First published 1992 by Holt & Co.

"This reference manual provides essential information on measurements, formulas, and calculations on a wide variety of scientific, industrial, economic, and applied technological topics. The introductory section describes the three major world measurement systems, followed by sections containing conversion tables, local units of measurements around the world, and abbreviations and coun-

try codes. Subjects include agriculture, finance, health, and transport, among many other topics. . . . This ready-reference volume serves as a superb compilation of material scattered in numerous sources." Libr J

535.6   Color

Finlay, Victoria

Color: a natural history of the palette. Ballantine Bks. 2002 448p il maps hardcover o.p. pa $14.95

Grades: 11 12 Adult   **535.6**

1. Color

ISBN 0-345-44430-2; 0-8129-7142-6 (pa)

This "book is a blend of travelogue and historical exploration about the myriad ways color takes on meaning for us, whether as a matter of aesthetics, economics, war or culture. . . . Thanks to Finlay's impeccable reportorial skills and a remarkable degree of engagement, this is an utterly unique and fascinating read." Publ Wkly

Includes bibliographical references

536   Heat

Shachtman, Tom, 1942-

Absolute zero and the conquest of cold. Houghton Mifflin 1999 261p $25; pa $14 *

Grades: 11 12 Adult   **536**

1. Low temperatures—Research

ISBN 0-395-93888-0; 0-618-08239-5 (pa)

LC 99-33305

The author "analyzes the social impact of the chill factor, explains the science of cold and tells the curious tales behind inventions like the thermometer, the fridge and the thermos flask." N Y Times Book Rev

Includes bibliographical references

537   Electricity and electronics

Bodanis, David

Electric universe; the shocking true story of electricity. Crown Publishers 2004 308p $24 *

Grades: 11 12 Adult   **537**

1. Electricity 2. Force and energy

ISBN 1-400-04550-9   LC 2004-11275

The author "examines electricity's theoretical development and how 19th- and 20th-century entrepreneurs harnessed it to transform everyday existence. Going from 'Wires' to 'Waves' to computers and even the human body, Bodanis pairs electrical innovations with minibiographies of their developers, among them Thomas Edison, Alexander Graham Bell, Guglielmo Marconi, Heinrich Herz and Alan Turing." Publ Wkly

"As a storyteller, author David Bodanis is wonderful. . . . This book is directed at a general audience, but it should be required reading for all scientific professionals." Sci Books Films

Includes bibliographical references

538 Magnetism

Verschuur, Gerrit L., 1937-
Hidden attraction; the history and mystery of magnetism. Oxford Univ. Press 1993 256p il hardcover o.p. pa $14.95 *

Grades: 11 12 Adult **538**
1. Magnetism
ISBN 0-19-506488-7; 0-19-510655-5 (pa)
LC 92-37690

The author "uses the history of magnetism to illustrate the development of scientific theory and method, from natural phenomena rooted in superstition to the accurate simulations of modern science. An informative study, with details about such scientists as Michael Faraday and James Maxwell and their pioneering work." Booklist
Includes bibliographical references

539.7 Atomic and nuclear physics

Cathcart, Brian
The fly in the cathedral; how a small group of Cambridge scientists won the race to split the atom. Farrar, Straus & Giroux 2005 308p il hardcover o.p. pa $15 *

Grades: 11 12 Adult **539.7**
1. Cockcroft, Sir John, 1897-1967 2. Walton, Ernest T. S., 1903-1995 3. Nuclear physics
ISBN 0-374-15716-2; 0-374-53026-2 (pa)
LC 2004-56348

First published 2004 in the United Kingdom
This is an "account of the genesis of nuclear physics in the first third of the 20th century. Although the centerpiece of his story is the experiment performed on April 14, 1932, by John Cockcroft and Ernest Walton . . . Cathcart fully describes the experiment's scientific and social context. Through crisp prose, interesting analogies and ample insight, he makes the basics of nuclear physics accessible while demonstrating the passion scientists have for their work." Publ Wkly
Includes bibliographical references

The Facts on File dictionary of atomic and nuclear physics; edited by Richard Rennie. Facts on File 2002 250p il hardcover o.p. pa $19.95 *

Grades: 11 12 Adult **539.7**
ISBN 0-8160-4916-5; 0-8160-4917-3 (pa)
LC 2002-32545

This dictionary "covers areas such as atomic theory, the structure of matter, spectroscopy, quantum theory, nuclear physics, particle physics, and cosmology. Examples of specific entries are *Bohr model; Carbon dating; Grand unified theories* (GUTs); *Hadron; Hawking, Stephen William; Rydberg constant*; and *Self-organization.* Appendixes provide tables of fundamental constants, elementary particles, chemical elements, and a selected list of organizational Web pages." Booklist
Includes bibliographical references and index

Friedlander, Michael W.
A thin cosmic rain; particles from outer space. Harvard Univ. Press 2000 241p il hardcover o.p. pa $19.95

Grades: 11 12 Adult **539.7**
1. Cosmic rays
ISBN 0-674-00288-1; 0-674-00989-9 (pa)
LC 00-39594

First published 1989 with title: Cosmic rays
"This book tells the long-running detective story behind the discovery and study of cosmic rays, a story that stretches from the early days of subatomic particle physics in the 1890s to the frontiers of high-energy astrophysics today." Publisher's note
"A detailed, informative survey of the topic." Booklist
Includes bibliographical references

Henderson, Harry, 1951-
Nuclear physics. Facts on File 1998 132p il (Milestones in discovery and invention) $25

Grades: 7 8 9 10 **539.7**
1. Nuclear physics 2. Physicists
ISBN 0-8160-3567-9
LC 97-17380

This book profiles physicists Marie and Pierre Curie, Ernest Rutherford, Niels Bohr, Lise Meitner, Richard Feynman, and Murray Gell-Mann, explains their scientific discoveries, and outlines questions in current physics research.
Includes bibliographical references

540 Chemistry & allied sciences

Cobb, Cathy
The joy of chemistry; the amazing science of familiar things; [by] Cathy Cobb & Monty L. Fetterolf. Prometheus Books 2005 393p il $26

Grades: 11 12 Adult **540**
1. Chemistry
ISBN 1-591-02231-2
LC 2004-20144

The authors cover "the material of a general chemistry course along with organic, inorganic and analytical chemistry and biochemistry; there's even a chapter on forensic chemistry. . . . They explain everything from flatulence (the chemical composition of intestinal gas) to pizza cheese (why mozzarella rather than, say, parmesan?)." Publ Wkly
Includes bibliographical references

Cracking the SAT: chemistry subject test, 2007-2008 edition; [by] the Princeton Review. Random House 2007 il pa $18

Grades: 9 10 11 12 **540**
1. Chemistry—Study and teaching 2. Scholastic Assessment Test 3. Colleges and universities—Entrance requirements
ISSN 1556-844X
ISBN 0-375-76589-1; 978-0-375-76589-6

Annual. First published 2005. Continues Cracking the SAT II: chemistry subject test
At head of title: The Princeton Review
This guide provides test-taking strategies and sample tests on the subject of chemistry.

CRC handbook of chemistry and physics; a ready-reference book of chemical and physical data. 88th ed. CRC Press 2007 $139.95 *
Grades: 11 12 Adult   540
1. Chemistry—Tables 2. Physics—Tables
ISBN 0-8493-0488-1; 978-0-8493-0488-0
Also available CD-ROM version and online
First published 1913. Periodically revised
A "reference book containing much-used information on mathematics, chemistry, and physics, including tables, physical constants of chemical elements and compounds, definitions, formulae, etc." AAAS Sci Book List for Young Adults
Includes bibliographical references

The **Facts** on File chemistry handbook; the Diagram Group. Rev. ed. Facts on File 2006 272p il (Facts on File science library) $35 *
Grades: 8 9 10 11 12   540
1. Chemistry
ISBN 0-8160-5878-4   LC 2005-55496
First published 2000
In addition to a dictionary of around 1500 entries, this source also includes hundreds of thumbnail biographies and an extensive chronology. Charts, tables, and diagrams are included.
Includes bibliographical references

Lange's handbook of chemistry. 16th ed. McGraw-Hill 2005 various paging il $150 *
Grades: 11 12 Adult   540
1. Chemistry—Tables
ISBN 0-07-143220-5; 978-0-07-143220-7
First published 1934. Periodically revised
Originally compiled and edited by Norbert Adolph Lange. Editors vary
"A standard reference source for both students and professional chemists. Sections for: organic compounds; general information, conversion tables, and mathematics; inorganic chemistry; properties of atoms, radicals, and bonds; physical properties; thermodynamic properties; spectroscopy; electrolytes, electromotive force, and chemical equilibrium; physiochemical relationships; polymers, rubbers, fats, oils, and waxes; and practical laboratory information." Guide to Ref Books. 11th edition

Le Couteur, Penny, 1943-
Napoleon's buttons; how 17 molecules changed history; {by} Penny Le Couteur, Jay Burreson. Jeremy P. Tarcher/Penguin Books 2003 375p il hardcover o.p. pa $14.95 *
Grades: 11 12 Adult   540
1. Chemistry
ISBN 1-58542-220-7; 1-58542-331-9 (pa)
    LC 2002-032247
The authors "explore how chemical properties of compounds have altered history. The impacts run the gamut from medicine (e.g., penicillin, vitamin C) to social change (e.g., the contraceptive pill and slavery perpetuated by the farming of glucose, or sugar cane, and cellulose, or cotton) to more direct historical incidents such as the Opium Wars or the spice trade spurring New World exploration." Libr J

"Napoleon's Buttons is a fascinating attempt at recognizing the role of chemistry in the wider world. With its many structural diagrams, the book can resemble a course in organic chemistry, but the chemist-authors are good guides. . . . The best chapter is the one on dyes." Quill & Quire
Includes bibliographical references

Myers, Richard, 1951-
The basics of chemistry. Greenwood Press 2003 373p il (Basics of the hard sciences) $75
Grades: 11 12 Adult   540
1. Chemistry
ISBN 0-313-31664-3   LC 2002-28436
This work covers "atoms, molecules, elements, and compounds; states of matter, bonding, and solutions; kinetics and heat; acids/bases; electrochemistry; nuclear, environmental, organic, and biochemistry; and the chemical industry and careers. Reasonable and informative project ideas are included . . . with adequate instructions for completion." SLJ
"Recommended as a basic overview for public, school, or undergraduate libraries, but not for reference collections." Libr J
Includes bibliographical references

540.3   Chemistry--Encyclopedias and dictionaries

Chemistry: foundations and applications. Macmillan Ref. USA 2004 4v il set $395
Grades: 9 10 11 12   540.3
1. Chemistry—Encyclopedias
ISBN 0-02-865721-7   LC 2003-21038
The alphabetically arranged signed articles "range from concise definitions to multiple-page overviews. Broad areas covered include analytical chemistry applications, biochemistry, elements, energy, environmental chemistry, medicine, organic chemistry, physical chemistry, reactions, states of matter, and structure. . . . In addition to explaining scientific principles, this set relates chemistry to everyday life. . . . An 18-page glossary and 67-page subject index are included in each volume. Glossary definitions also appear in the margins next to the text. . . . Bibliographic references and related Internet resources are listed at the end of many articles." Booklist

The **Facts** on File dictionary of chemistry; edited by John Daintith. 4th ed. Checkmark Books 2005 310p il (Facts on File science library) $45; pa $17.95 *
Grades: 9 10 11 12   540.3
1. Chemistry—Dictionaries
ISBN 0-8160-5649-8; 0-8160-5650-1 (pa)
    LC 2005-43785
First published 1981
This reference work includes more than 3,000 cross-referenced entries that identify terms, reactions, techniques and applications in chemistry.
Includes bibliographical references

Rittner, Don
Encyclopedia of chemistry; [by] Don Rittner and Ronald A. Bailey. Facts on File 2005 342p il (Facts on File science library) $75 *
Grades: 11 12 Adult   **540.3**
1. Chemistry—Encyclopedias
ISBN 0-8160-4894-0   LC 2004-11242
This encyclopedia "offers more than 2000 articles on topics from ABO blood groups to zwitterionic compound." SLJ
For a fuller review, see: Booklist, Dec. 1, 2005
Includes bibliographical references

540.9   Chemistry--Historical and geographic treatment

Greenberg, Arthur
A chemical history tour; picturing chemistry from alchemy to modern molecular science. Wiley 2000 312p il $62.95 *
Grades: 9 10 11 12   **540.9**
1. Chemistry—History
ISBN 0-471-35408-2   LC 99-38865
"A Wiley-Interscience publication"
This is a history of chemistry from ancient times to the present illustrated by contemporary drawings, paintings, and charts.
Includes bibliographical references

541   Physical chemistry

Cobb, Cathy
Magick, mayhem, and mavericks; the spirited history of physical chemistry. Prometheus Books 2002 420p il $29
Grades: 11 12 Adult   **541**
1. Physical chemistry—History
ISBN 1-573-92976-X   LC 2002-70511
"The history moves from ancient astronomy, mathematics and natural philosophy through early modern developments in mathematics, physics, alchemy, medicinal remedies and chemistry, using the assumption that physical chemists could achieve their aims only after the foundations of mathematics, physics and chemistry were well laid. . . . Cobb's style is lively and swashbuckling." American Scientist
Includes bibliographical references

546   Inorganic chemistry

Knapp, Brian J.
Elements; [author, Brian Knapp; illustrations, David Woodroffe and David Hardy] New and rev ed. Grolier Educational 2002 18v il set $329
Grades: 5 6 7 8 9 10   **546**
1. Chemical elements
ISBN 0-7172-5674-X   LC 2001-280103
Vols. 1-15 first published 1996; vols. 16-18 first published 2002

Vols. 16-18 illustrated by David Woodroffe
Contents: 1. Hydrogen and the noble gases -- 2. Sodium and potassium -- 3. Calcium and magnesium -- 4. Iron, chromium, and manganese -- 5. Copper, silver, and gold -- 6. Zinc, cadmium, and mercury -- 7. Aluminum -- 8. Carbon -- 9. Silicon -- 10. Lead and tin -- 11. Nitrogen and phosphorus -- 12. Oxygen -- 13. Sulfur -- 14. Chlorine, fluorine, bromine, and iodine -- 15. Uranium and other radioactive elements -- 16. Actinium to fluorine -- 17. Francium to polonium -- 18. Potassium to zirconium
This set "discusses each element's discovery, forms, extraction, industrial uses, and unique character. In a one-topic-per-spread format, text blocks surround several large, clear, full-color photos or, more rarely, schematics. . . . This resource will strengthen both school labs and library collections." SLJ [review of 1996-2002 edition]

Krebs, Robert E., 1922-
The history and use of our earth's chemical elements; a reference guide; illustrations by Rae Déjur. 2nd ed. Greenwood Press 2006 422p il $75 *
Grades: 11 12 Adult   **546**
1. Chemical elements
ISBN 0-313-33438-2; 978-0-313-33438-2
     LC 2006-12032
First published 1998
"The elements are examined within their groups, enabling students to make connections between elements of similar structure. In addition, the discovery and history of each element—from those known from ancient times to those created in the modern laboratory—is explained." Publisher's note
Includes bibliographical references

Miller, Ron, 1947-
The elements. Twenty-First Century Books 2006 135p il lib bdg $28.90
Grades: 8 9 10 11 12   **546**
1. Chemical elements
ISBN 0-7613-2794-0   LC 2003-20874
Discusses the history of the periodic table of the elements, includes biographies of major figures in the field of chemistry, and provides information on each element. "A useful overview." SLJ
Includes bibliographical references

Newton, David E.
Chemical elements; from carbon to krypton; Lawrence W. Baker, editor. U.X.L 1999 3v set $165
Grades: 7 8 9 10   **546**
1. Chemical elements
ISBN 0-7876-2844-1   LC 98-31207
In this reference "the 112 elements of the periodic table are arranged alphabetically by chemical name. . . . {Each entry includes} 'basic information about the chemical element: its chemical symbol, atomic number, atomic mass, family and pronunciation.'. . . The entry then discusses the element's discovery and naming, physical and chemical properties, occurrence in nature, isotopes, methods of extraction, important compounds and uses, and health effects." Booklist

Stwertka, Albert
A guide to the elements. 2nd ed. Oxford Univ.
Press 2002 246p il $37.50; pa $18.95 *
Grades: 9 10 11 12   **546**
1. Chemical elements
ISBN 0-19-515026-0; 0-19-515027-9 (pa)
LC 2002-282309
First published 1996
At head of title: Oxford
Presents the basic concepts of chemistry and explains
complex theories before offering a separate article on
each of the building blocks that make up the universe
Includes bibliographical references

549 Mineralogy

Pellant, Chris
Rocks and minerals; Helen Pellant, editorial
consultant; photography by Harry Taylor. 2nd
American ed. Dorling Kindersley 2002 256p il
(Smithsonian handbooks) pa $20
Grades: 11 12 Adult   **549**
1. Rocks 2. Minerals
ISBN 0-7894-9106-0; 978-0-7894-9106-0
First published 1992 as part of the Eyewitness hand-
books series
This field guide to identification of rocks and minerals
includes techniques for collection and classification, and
facts about physical and chemical composition and formation.

Pough, Frederick H., 1906-2006
A field guide to rocks and minerals. 5th ed,
photographs by Jeff Scovil. Houghton Mifflin
1996 396p il hardcover o.p. pa $20 *
Grades: 9 10 11 12   **549**
1. Minerals 2. Rocks
ISBN 0-395-72778-2; 0-395-91096-X (pa)
LC 94-49005
"The Peterson field guide series"
First published 1953
"Sponsored by the National Audubon Society, the Na-
tional Wildlife Federation, and the Roger Tory Peterson
Institute"
This illustrated guide utilizes traditional identification
methods and includes discussions of crystallography,
mineralogy and home laboratory techniques.
Includes bibliographical references

550 Earth sciences

Earth; editor-in-chief, James F. Luhr. DK Pub.
2003 520p il map $50 *
Grades: 9 10 11 12 Adult   **550**
1. Earth
ISBN 0-7894-9643-7   LC 2003-51573
At head of title: Smithsonian Institution
This guide to Earth's physical dynamics is "divided
into five major sections—Planet Earth, Land, Ocean, Atmosphere and Tectonic Earth—the book explores the

planet's environment, weather systems and general physical makeup." Publ Wkly
"The writing is clear, animated, and engrossing. . . .
This superb and stunning volume should be kept handy
along with atlases and dictionaries." Booklist

Erickson, Jon, 1948-
Rock formations and unusual geologic
structures; exploring the earth's surface. rev ed.
Facts on File 2001 319p il maps (Facts on File
science library) $55
Grades: 9 10 11 12   **550**
1. Geology
ISBN 0-8160-4328-0   LC 00-49038
First published 1993
At head of title: The living earth
"The volume explores erosional effects and features,
dating methods for specific geologic structures, fossil for-
mation and fossil beds, plate tectonics, volcanic and geo-
logic activities, and more." Publisher's note
Includes bibliographical references

The Facts on File Earth science handbook; [by]
the Diagram Group. Rev. ed. Facts on File 2006
272p il (Facts on File science library) $35 *
Grades: 8 9 10 11 12   **550**
1. Earth sciences
ISBN 0-8160-5879-2   LC 2005-44692
First published 2000
This guide to earth sciences contains a dictionary with
around 1400 entries, a chronology, thumbnail biographies, an A to Z list of over 150 advances in earth science, and a list of Tyler Prize winners.
Includes bibliographical references

550.3 Earth sciences--Encyclopedias and dictionaries

The Facts on File dictionary of earth science. Rev.
ed., edited by Jacqueline Smith. Facts on File
2006 388p il map $55 *
Grades: 11 12 Adult   **550.3**
1. Earth sciences—Dictionaries
ISBN 0-8160-6000-2   LC 2006-42340
First published 1976 in the United Kingdom with title:
A dictionary of earth sciences
In this reference work more than 3700 "cross-
referenced entries . . . cover all aspects of Earth science:
geomorphology, stratigraphy, mineralogy, petrology, climatology, oceanography, paleontology, hydrology, geo-
physics, cartography, surveying, and soil science. Key
concepts in physics, chemistry, biology, and mathematics
are also defined." Publisher's note
Includes bibliographical references

Kusky, Timothy M.
Encyclopedia of earth science; [by] Timothy
Kusky. Facts on File 2005 510p il map (Facts on
File science library) $75 *
Grades: 11 12 Adult   **550.3**
1. Earth sciences—Encyclopedias
ISBN 0-8160-4973-4   LC 2004-4389

Kusky, Timothy M.—*Continued*

This encyclopedia covers "earth science subdisciplines (hydrology, oceanography, and so on) as well as concepts, theories and hypotheses, places, events, geological time periods, history, technology, and key individuals." Booklist

"Kusky's encyclopedia will appeal to a broad audience, from high school students to researchers." Choice

Includes bibliographical references

The **Oxford** companion to the earth; editors Paul L. Hancock and Brian J. Skinner; associate editor David L. Dineley: subject editor, Alistair G. Dawson. Oxford Univ. Press 2000 1174p il $75

Grades: 11 12 Adult   **550.3**
1. Earth sciences—Dictionaries
ISBN 0-19-854039-6   LC 2001-16311

This "resource offers concise explanations of earth phenomena and processes, with over 800 entries written by 200 experts. . . . Each entry is well written, with information suitable for undergraduates as well as researchers needing an overview." Libr J

551   Geology, hydrology, meteorology

Allaby, Michael, 1933-

Encyclopedia of weather and climate; [illustrations by Richard Garratt] Rev ed. Facts On File 2007 2v il (Facts on File science library) set $165 *

Grades: 11 12 Adult   **551**
1. Meteorology—Dictionaries
ISBN 0-8160-6350-8; 978-0-8160-6350-5
                                                  LC 2006-18295

First published 2002

"The main body of the encyclopedia consists of . . . entries describing processes such as cloud formation, atmospheric phenomena such as rainbows, and some of the techniques and instruments used to study the atmosphere, as well as the units of measurement that scientists use. The . . . coverage also includes the classification systems that are used for climate types, winds, and clouds. Ten appendixes contain . . . supplementary material—such as biographical notes on scientists and lists of the most severe tropical cyclones and tropical storms, weather disasters, and milestones in atmospheric research." Publisher's note

Includes bibliographical references

Kovach, Robert L. (Robert Louis)

Firefly guide to global hazards; {by} Robert Kovach and Bill McGuire. Firefly Books 2004 256p il pa $14.95 *

Grades: 11 12 Adult   **551**
1. Natural disasters
ISBN 1-55297-815-X   LC 2004-300692

An illustrated guide to the many large-scale natural disasters that affect life on Earth, both globally and locally

This title "includes hazards not always easily found in

resources: droughts, landslides, avalanches, extinctions, and diseases, to name a few. Various aspects of pollution are included so that students may see what humans are doing to the environment." SLJ

Lambert, David, 1932-

The field guide to geology; [by] David Lambert and the Diagram Group. New ed. Checkmark Books 2006 304p il map $39.95; pa $16.95 *

Grades: 11 12 Adult   **551**
1. Geology
ISBN   0-8160-6509-8;   978-0-8160-6509-7;
0-8160-6510-1 (pa); 978-0-8160-6510-3 (pa)
                                                  LC 2006-48533

First published 1988

This is an "overview of the processes that forged the planet and the technologies that have revolutionized the way that scientists investigate Earth's systems." Publisher's note

Includes bibliographical references

Newton, David E.

Encyclopedia of air. Greenwood Press 2003 252p il $79.95 *

Grades: 11 12 Adult   **551**
1. Air 2. Meteorology
ISBN 1-573-56564-4   LC 2003-44076

"An Oryx book"

"Entries discuss the science of air (biology, chemistry, meteorology, physics), its technology (air bag, airbrush, air conditioner), and even its social, mythological, and cultural aspects. Newton also includes biographical entries and descriptions of related organizations and associations." Choice

Includes bibliographical references

551.1   Gross structure and properties of the earth

Erickson, Jon, 1948-

Plate tectonics: unraveling the mysteries of the earth; foreword by Ernest H. Muller. rev ed. Facts on File 2001 289p il maps (Facts on File science library) $55 *

Grades: 9 10 11 12   **551.1**
1. Plate tectonics
ISBN 0-8160-4327-2   LC 00-49039

First published 1992

At head of title: The living earth

"Beginning with a historical overview of plate tectonic theory in this century, the book describes . . . how plate tectonics work, how it has affected evolution and extinction, and what the future holds." Publisher's note

Includes bibliographical references

551.2 Volcanoes, earthquakes, thermal waters and gases

Bolt, Bruce A., 1930-2005
Earthquakes; [by] Bruce Bolt. 5th ed. W.H. Freeman and Co. 2005 390p il map pa $45.95 *
Grades: 9 10 11 12   **551.2**
1. Earthquakes
ISBN 0-7167-7548-4; 978-0-7167-7548-5
LC 2005-925607
Also available online
First published 1978
On cover: 2006 centennial update: the big one
The author "provides a brief overview of the history of earthquakes and seismology, including topics such as geologic faults, intensity patterns, side effects of earthquakes (such as tsunamis), and protection of people and property." Publisher's note
Includes bibliographical references

Clarkson, Peter
Volcanoes. Voyageur Press 2000 39p il (World life library) pa $16.95 *
Grades: 9 10 11 12   **551.2**
1. Volcanoes
ISBN 0-89658-502-6   LC 00-36465
This describes the physical nature of volcanoes and explores many of the world's famous volcanoes and eruptions, illustrated with color photos and diagrams
Includes bibliographical references

Gates, Alexander E.
Encyclopedia of earthquakes and volcanoes; [by] Alexander E. Gates, PH.D and David Ritchie. 3rd ed. Facts on File 2007 346p il map (Facts on File science library) $75 *
Grades: 11 12 Adult   **551.2**
1. Earthquakes—Encyclopedias 2. Volcanoes—Encyclopedias
ISBN 0-8160-6302-8   LC 2005-46619
First published 1994
"The book's entries cover information on key environmental issues, economic dilemmas, ethical concerns, advances in research and technology, organizations, and individuals who have left their mark on the fields of volcanology and seismology." Publisher's note
Includes bibliographical references

Levy, Matthys
Why the earth quakes; [by] Matthys Levy and Mario Salvadori; illustrations by Michael Lilly. Norton 1995 215p il maps pa $13 hardcover o.p.
Grades: 11 12 Adult   **551.2**
1. Volcanoes 2. Earthquakes
ISBN 0-393-31527-4 (pa)   LC 95-1021
Levy and Salvadori "use examples from history to explore how human-made structures fare in the wake of earthquakes and volcanic eruptions. The authors briefly explain the nature of the earth, then discuss modern engineering solutions for keeping buildings upright during

earthquakes." Libr J
This is a "popularly written, illustrated account, suitable for science students and other interested readers." Booklist
Includes glossary and bibliographical references

Page, Jake
The big one; the earthquake that rocked early America and helped create a science; [by] Jake Page and Charles Officer. Houghton Mifflin 2004 239p il $24
Grades: 11 12 Adult   **551.2**
1. Earthquakes
ISBN 0-618-34150-1   LC 2004-40536
Page and Officer "delve into the geological history of the [New Madrid seismic zone] area, which begins . . . with the famous set of earthquakes that occurred in 1811-12. . . . The authors turn in a solid presentation; strong regional interest combined with the natural audience for earthquake stories will boost demand for this title." Booklist

551.3 Surface and exogenous processes and their agents

Erickson, Jon, 1948-
Asteroids, comets, and meteorites; cosmic invaders of the earth; foreword by Timothy Kusky. Facts on File 2003 256p il maps (Living earth) $55 *
Grades: 9 10 11 12   **551.3**
1. Asteroids 2. Comets 3. Meteorites
ISBN 0-8160-4873-8   LC 2002-2434
"Facts on File science library"
Partial contents: Origin of the solar system: formation of the sun and planets; The formation of earth: planetary origins; Cratering events: historic meteorite impacts; Planetary impacts: exploring meteorite craters; Impact effects: The global changes; Death star: impact extinction of species
This volume explores cosmic invaders from the days of the dinosaurs to the present environment
Includes bibliographical references

Frankel, Charles
The end of the dinosaurs; Chicxulub crater and mass extinctions. Cambridge Univ. Press 1999 223p il $27.95 *
Grades: 11 12 Adult   **551.3**
1. Catastrophes (Geology) 2. Mass extinction of species
ISBN 0-521-47447-7   LC 98-49427
Translated from the French
The author "recounts the birth of the cosmic hypothesis, which holds that the crash of a meteor on the Earth's surface killed two-thirds of life and all the dinosaurs. He first provides . . . {an} account of the impact and its aftermath. Frankel then goes on to detail the controversy that preceded the acceptance of the cosmic hypothesis, the search for the crater, its discovery and ongoing exploration, and the effect of the giant impact on the biosphere." Publisher's note
Includes bibliographical references

Fredston, Jill A.

Snowstruck; in the grip of avalanches; [by] Jill Fredston. Harcourt 2005 342p il $24; pa $14 *

Grades: 11 12 Adult   **551.3**

1. Avalanches 2. Survival skills

ISBN   978-0-15-101249-7;   0-15-101249-0; 978-0-15-603254-4 (pa); 0-15-603254-6 (pa)

LC 2005-20454

"As avalanche experts, . . . [the author and her husband] are often called upon to forecast, trigger, and teach about avalanches as well as rescue survivors—or, sadly, more often to recover remains. Fredston's decades of experience distilled into this instructive and personal narrative will leave readers with a newfound appreciation for the force, the fury, and the cold sorrow of avalanches." Libr J

Gordon, J. E. (James Edward), 1913-

Glaciers; text by John Gordon. Voyageur Press 2001 70p il (World life library) pa $16.95

Grades: 9 10 11 12   **551.3**

1. Glaciers

ISBN 0-89658-559-X   LC 2001-26862

Introduces the formation, flow, changing nature, and effects of glaciers

Includes bibliographical references

551.4 Geomorphology and hydrosphere

Yount, Lisa

Modern marine science; exploring the deep. Chelsea House 2006 204p il map (Milestones in discovery and invention) $35

Grades: 9 10 11 12   **551.4**

1. Marine sciences

ISBN 0-8160-5747-8   LC 2005-30562

This book "profiles 12 men and women who led the way into the oceans' deepest waters through research and new technologies. From Charles Darwin to Henry Stommel to Robert Ballard, this volume explores the lives and accomplishments of these scientific revolutionaries." Publisher's note

Includes glossary and bibliographical references

551.46 Hydrosphere and submarine geology. Oceanography

Ellis, Richard, 1938-

Encyclopedia of the sea; written and illustrated by Richard Ellis. Knopf 2000 380p il $35

Grades: 11 12 Adult   **551.46**

1. Oceanography—Encyclopedias

ISBN 0-375-40374-4   LC 99-42401

"The alphabetically arranged text consists of short paragraphs on topics in marine biology, oceanography, fisheries, geography, and maritime and naval history. . . . Eight pages of Ellis's color paintings . . . and hundreds of his own illustrations enhance the text. . . . The handy format makes the book useful as a ready-reference source for public and college libraries." Libr J

Erickson, Jon, 1948-

Marine geology; exploring the new frontiers of the ocean; foreword by Timothy Kusky. rev ed. Facts on File 2003 317p il (Living earth) $55 *

Grades: 7 8 9 10   **551.46**

1. Submarine geology 2. Marine biology

ISBN 0-8160-4874-6   LC 2002-1295

"Facts on File science library"

First published 1996

This "examines the interrelationship between water and its life forms and geologic structures. It looks at several ideas for the origins of the Earth, continents and oceans, and how these processes fit into the origin of the universe." Publisher's note

Includes glossary and bibliographical references

Hutchinson, S., 1959-

Oceans: a visual guide; [by] Stephen Hutchinson [and] Lawrence E. Hawkins. Firefly Books 2005 303p il map $29.95 *

Grades: 11 12 Adult   **551.46**

1. Oceanography 2. Marine biology

ISBN 1-55407-069-4

"Beginning with the birth of the oceans, the 'cradle of life,' the authors explain tides, salinity, currents, waves, and the diverse and complex ecosystems of the polar, equatorial, and temperate oceans with diagrams, photographs, and concise and clear commentary." Booklist

Rice, Tony

Deep ocean. Smithsonian Institution Press 2000 96p il (Natural world series) pa $14.95

Grades: 9 10 11 12   **551.46**

1. Ocean 2. Oceanography

ISBN 1-56098-867-3   LC 00-28537

This "book tells how oceanography developed as a science and summarizes what is known about the organisms that live in the deep ocean." Publisher's note

Includes glossary and bibliographical references

Stow, Dorrik A. V.

Oceans: an illustrated reference; [by] Dorrik Stow. University of Chicago Press 2006 c2005 256p il map $55 *

Grades: 11 12 Adult   **551.46**

1. Oceanography 2. Ocean 3. Marine biology

ISBN 0-226-77664-6   LC 2004-55333

"An Andromeda book"

This "reference work presents a thorough overview of the physical, geological, chemical, and biological properties of the world's oceans. . . . [The author's] up-to-date and well-organized volume would make a valuable introduction to a huge field of knowledge." Libr J

Includes bibliographical references

551.5 Meteorology

Buckley, Bruce

Weather: a visual guide; [by] Bruce Buckley, Edward J. Hopkins [and] Richard Whitaker. Firefly Books 2004 303p il maps $29.95

Grades: 11 12 Adult   551.5

1. Weather 2. Meteorology

ISBN 1-55297-957-1   LC 2004-303909

The authors "set the local and seasonal conditions that every person experiences within the context of the global forces that generate weather. Each force, such as giant atmospheric convection cells, is illustrated with a combination of a diagram, satellite photographs, ground-level photographs (often depicting the destruction wrought by violent storms), and . . . captions." Booklist

This is "a comprehensive academic resource with information and glorious color photographs on virtually every aspect of weather." SLJ

Burt, Christopher C.

Extreme weather; a guide & record book; with cartography by Mark Stroud. W.W. Norton 2004 304p il maps pa $24.95 *

Grades: 11 12 Adult   551.5

1. United States—Climate 2. Weather

ISBN 0-393-32658-6 (pa)   LC 2004-12199

The author "explores extreme weather phenomena in . . . mini-essays complemented by sidebars on such oddities as colored snow and luminous tornadoes. The whole is supplemented by maps, lists of destructive storms, and photos of towering thunderheads, raging floodwaters and the devastated remains of human settlement." Publ Wkly

"This book has enough information packed within its pages to keep the most ardent weather watchers busy." Booklist

Includes bibliographical references

The **Facts** on File dictionary of weather and climate; edited by Jacqueline Smith. Rev. ed. Facts on File 2006 262p il map (Facts on File science library) $49.50 *

Grades: 9 10 11 12 Adult   551.5

1. Meteorology—Dictionaries

ISBN 0-8160-6296-X; 978-0-8160-6296-6

LC 2006-42865

First published 2001

This volume includes "definitions for more than 2000 terms and concepts drawn from meteorology, climatology, and related geoscience disciplines. Entries are conveniently cross-referenced and include common acronyms. More than 60 line drawings complement definitions. The book features useful appendices providing a chronology of important events in the atmospheric sciences and unit conversion tables." Sci Books Films [review of 2001 edition]

Includes bibliographical references

Reynolds, Ross

Cambridge guide to the weather. Cambridge Univ. Press 2000 192p il pa $17 *

Grades: 11 12 Adult   551.5

1. Weather 2. Meteorology 3. Weather forecasting

ISBN 0-521-77489-6   LC 00-266555

This offers "country-by-country climate data and statistics, along with in-depth explanations of global weather patterns. . . . In addition, Ross Reynolds gives . . . {an} account of the implications of environmental issues currently in the headlines, such as global warming and the depletion of the ozone layer, as well as the effects of El Niño and other phenomena on world weather patterns." Publisher's note

This book's "rather complete coverage of all major topics is enhanced by excellent illustrations, including clear photographs, drawn figures, and maps." Sci Books Films

Includes bibliographical references

551.51 Composition, regions, dynamics of atmosphere

Amato, Joseph Anthony

Dust; a history of the small and the invisible; {by} Joseph A. Amato. University of Calif. Press 2000 288p il hardcover o.p. pa $15.95 *

Grades: 11 12 Adult   551.51

1. Dust 2. Science—Philosophy

ISBN 0-520-21875-2; 0-520-23195-3 (pa)

LC 99-27115

The author "writes only incidentally about dust; rather, he reviews how humanity's view of the unseen world changed throughout the ages as the ability to see it, through magnification, increased. . . . Amato touches on such diverse topics as the role of light in art, germ theory and medical advances, particle physics, and the effect of artificially made dusts on the environment. He concludes with a philosophical view of the future of humanity as medical and scientific advances takes it into uncharted waters." Choice

Includes bibliographical references

Bowen, Mark

Thin ice; unlocking the secrets of climate in the world's highest mountains. Henry Holt 2005 463p il $30; pa $17 *

Grades: 11 12 Adult   551.51

1. Upper atmosphere 2. Climate—Research

ISBN 0-8050-6443-5; 0-8050-8135-6 (pa)

LC 2005-40426

"A John Macrae book"

The author "documents the specialized techniques that Thompson used to extract and preserve ice cores from the highest mountains around the world's equator while also examining Thompson's research, which is based on the provocative premise that equatorial mountain glaciers, rather than polar ice, provide the clues to understanding global warming." Libr J

"This book will appeal to mountaineering and climatology buffs, but should be read by everyone concerned about the future of our planet." Publ Wkly

Holmes, Hannah, 1963-
The secret life of dust; from the cosmos to the kitchen counter, the big consequences of little things. Wiley 2001 240p hardcover o.p. pa $14.95
Grades: 11 12 Adult   **551.51**
   1. Dust 2. Science—Philosophy
   ISBN 0-471-37743-0; 0-471-42635-0 (pa)
                    LC 2001-22368
"Holmes explores how dust has been crucial in the birth of planets, how it affects the earth's environment and weather, and how humans create it as well. Out to communicate straight facts and science, she considers technical points in language that is clear and comprehensible even for those lacking a science background. In addition to the bibliography, Holmes provides a listing of web sites for each chapter so that readers may easily obtain current information and graphics." Libr J
Includes bibliographical references

551.55   Atmospheric disturbances and formations

Emanuel, Kerry A., 1955-
Divine wind; the history and science of hurricanes; [by] Kerry Emanuel. Oxford Univ. Press 2005 285p il $45 *
Grades: 11 12 Adult   **551.55**
   1. Hurricanes
   ISBN 0-19-514941-6   LC 2004-13078
This is a study of hurricanes.
"A gripping popular treatment of peril, that will have great resonance in light of recent disasters." Booklist
Includes bibliographical references

Norcross, Bryan
Hurricane almanac 2007; the essential guide to storms past, present, and future. Rev. and updated ed. St. Martin Griffin 2007 335p il (All about hurricanes) pa $12.99
Grades: 9 10 11 12 Adult   **551.55**
   1. Hurricanes
   ISSN 1935-8571
   ISBN 0-312-37152-7; 978-0-312-37152-4
   Annual. First published 2006
This almanac features "stories of the powerful hurricanes of the past that would be catastrophes if they happened today and explores how explosive coastal development during a time of relatively few hurricanes has set the stage for mega-disasters." Publisher's note

551.57   Hydrometeorology

Allaby, Michael, 1933-
Droughts; illustrations by Richard Garratt. rev ed. Facts on File 2003 212p il map (Dangerous weather) $35 *
Grades: 7 8 9 10   **551.57**
   1. Droughts
   ISBN 0-8160-4793-6   LC 2002-13035
   First published 1997

This examination of droughts and their impact includes "coverage of topics such as the geography of deserts; climate cycles and oscillations. . . . [Sidebars explain concepts] from atmospheric science, such as adiabatic cooling and warming, potential temperature, lapse rates, and the intertropical convergence and equatorial trough, as well as biological processes." Publisher's note

551.6   Climatology and weather

Dow, Kirstin, 1963-
The atlas of climate change; mapping the world's greatest challenge; [by] Kirstin Dow and Thomas E. Downing. University of California Press 2006 112p il map pa $19.95 *
Grades: 11 12 Adult   **551.6**
   1. Climate—Environmental aspects—Maps
   ISBN 978-0-52025-023-9; 0-52025-023-0
                    LC 2006-50098
This atlas "examines the signs of climate change—glacial and polar melting, rising sea levels, erratic weather patterns—and explains how global warming is being driven by the emission of greenhouse gases. It looks at the serious implications of these changes for food and water supplies, human health, sensitive ecologies, vulnerable cities, and cultural treasures—especially in those countries lacking the resources to adapt." Publisher's note
Includes bibliographical references

Fagan, Brian M., 1936-
The Little Ice Age; how climate made history 1300-1850; [by] Brian Fagan. Basic Bks. 2000 xxi, 246p il maps hardcover o.p. pa $16.95
Grades: 11 12 Adult   **551.6**
   1. Climate 2. Europe—History
   ISBN 0-465-02271-5; 0-465-02272-3 (pa)
                    LC 00-48627
"During the Little Ice Age—approximately the 14th to the mid-19th centuries—the climate of northern Europe turned volatile and markedly cooler. . . . [The author explains how] it catalyzed significant social, political, and economic changes throughout the region." Libr J
Includes bibliographical references

The long summer: how climate changed civilization. Basic Books 2003 284p il hardcover o.p. pa $16
Grades: 11 12 Adult   **551.6**
   1. Climate 2. Civilization—History
   ISBN 0-465-02281-2; 0-465-02282-0 (pa)
                    LC 2003-13917
Fagan discusses global climate change and its relation to human society. He "argues that as humans have organized themselves in increasingly complex ways, their susceptibility to large-scale devastation wrought by climate change has also risen. Ice Age hunter-gatherers were vulnerable to the vagaries of their harsh world, but they had a 'flexibility, mobility, and opportunism' that allowed them to move on if their immediate environment became too difficult. As people formed villages, cities, and empires, they became rooted to environments that in-

Fagan, Brian M., 1936-—*Continued*
evitably changed." Archaeology
"This book is highly recommended for general audiences considering the implications and the challenges posed by human-induced global climate change." Sci Books Films
Includes bibliographical references

Philander, S. George, 1942-
Our affair with El Niño; how we transformed an enchanting Peruvian current into a global climate hazard. Princeton University Press 2004 275p il maps hardcover o.p. pa $17.95 *
Grades: 11 12 Adult   **551.6**
1. El Niño Current 2. Climate
ISBN 0-691-11335-1; 0-691-12622-4 (pa)
LC 2003-44235
"The book begins by outlining the history of El Niño, an innocuous current that appears off the coast of Peru around Christmastime—its name refers to the Child Jesus—and originally was welcomed as a blessing. It goes on to explore how our perceptions of El Niño were transformed." Publisher's note
"This is an exceptional book, enjoyable to read and educational at several levels. El Niño is the springboard for a book that thoroughly explains the phenomenon and even goes far beyond it." Sci Books Films
Includes bibliographical references

551.7 Historical geology

Alvarez, Walter, 1940-
T. rex and the Crater of Doom. Princeton Univ. Press 1997 185p il $35
Grades: 11 12 Adult   **551.7**
1. Catastrophes (Geology) 2. Dinosaurs
ISBN 0-691-01630-5   LC 96-49208
Also available in paperback from Vintage Bks.
The author relates the story of how he "along with four other Berkeley scientists, found the geologic evidence that implicated a cosmic collision in the extinction of the dinosaurs. . . . [Their research involved] the evaluation of a thin iridium-rich layer of clay found in Italy and the search for an impact crater." Booklist
This book "gets the facts across in a lighthearted, almost playful manner. But it's also solid science, a clear and efficient exposition." N Y Times Book Rev
Includes bibliographical references

Erickson, Jon, 1948-
Historical geology; understanding our planet's past; foreword by Peter D. Moore. Facts on File 2002 307p il (Living earth) $55 *
Grades: 9 10 11 12   **551.7**
1. Stratigraphic geology
ISBN 0-8160-4726-X   LC 2001-51107
"Facts on File science library"
"An introductory chapter details basic geologic concepts, followed by chapters—organized according to different geologic time periods—that chronicle the emergence of each successive group of plants and animals." Publisher's note
Includes glossary and bibliographical references

Fortey, Richard A.
Earth; an intimate history; by Richard Fortey. Knopf 2004 429p il hardcover o.p. pa $19
Grades: 11 12 Adult   **551.7**
1. Stratigraphic geology
ISBN 0-375-40626-3; 0-375-70620-8 (pa)
LC 2004-46470
The author "relates his walks in places that visually reveal the deep earth (Vesuvius, Hawaii, the Grand Canyon) as well as sites, which, if not so spectacular, contain puzzling elements that provoked great interpretive controversies. . . . The Alps, the Scottish Highlands, Newfoundland, the Deccan Traps of India—these are among Fortey's destinations as he explains the theory of plate tectonics, showing how the theory came to be, as well as the continents and oceans whose skein of connections it explains. This is a marvelously inviting presentation." Booklist
Includes bibliographical references

552 Petrology

Bishop, A. C. (Arthur Clive)
Guide to minerals, rocks & fossils. Firefly Books 2005 336p il pa $19.95 *
Grades: 9 10 11 12   **552**
1. Minerals 2. Rocks 3. Fossils
ISBN 1-55407-054-6   LC 2005-280972
First published 1974 in the United Kingdom with title: The Hamlyn guide to minerals, rocks, and fossils; 1999 edition published by Cambridge Univ. Press with title: Cambridge guide to minerals, rocks, and fossils
"Minerals, rocks, and fossils are described, illustrated, explained, and related to their natural environment in this splendid compact volume. . . . As a most useful field guide for explorers or as a straightforward, beautifully illustrated and written general reference, this book is unparalleled." Choice
Includes bibliographical references

Coenraads, Robert Raymond, 1956-
Rocks and fossils; a visual guide; [by] Robert R. Coenraads. Firefly Books 2005 304p il $29.95
Grades: 11 12 Adult   **552**
1. Rocks 2. Fossils 3. Minerals
ISBN 1-55407-068-6
In this "introduction to geology and paleontology . . . [the author presents the] facts of how fossils are formed, how rocks are formed, and how plate tectonics work. . . . A science work perfectly suited for general use." Booklist

553.2 Carbonaceous materials

Freese, Barbara
Coal: a human history. Perseus Bks. 2003 308p il $37.95
Grades: 11 12 Adult   **553.2**
1. Coal
ISBN 0-7382-0400-5   LC 2002-114066
Also available in paperback from Penguin Bks.

Freese, Barbara—*Continued*

This is "an engrossing account of the comparatively cheap, usually dirty fuel that supported the Industrial Revolution, inspired the building of canals and railroads to move it, and once made London and Pittsburgh famous for their air." N Y Times Book Rev

The author's "balancing of ecological concerns with realistic analyses of resource use is impressive. Although the ecological implications of coal use are great, Freese effectively demonstrates the dependence on coal of countries around the world for sustaining economic growth. Most important, she offers clearheaded opinions on what we need to do to make our use of coal as clean as possible and what we must eventually do to replace it. Highly recommended for all libraries." Libr J

Includes bibliographical references

553.6   Other economic materials

Kurlansky, Mark

Salt: a world history. Penguin Books 2003 484p il map pa $16 *

Grades: 11 12 Adult   **553.6**

1. Salt

ISBN 0-14-200161-9   LC 2004-270006

First published 2002 by Walker & Co.

The author shows how salt "has influenced and affected wars, cultures, governments, religions, societies, economies, cooking (there are a few recipes), and foods. In addition, he provides information on the chemistry, geology, mining, refining, and production of salt." Libr J

"Throughout his engaging, well-researched history, Kurlansky sprinkles witty asides and amusing anecdotes. A piquant blend of the historic, political, commercial, scientific and culinary, the book is sure to entertain as well as educate." Publ Wkly

Includes bibliographical references

553.7   Water

Kandel, Robert S.

Water from heaven; the story of water from the big bang to the rise of civilization, and beyond; [by] Robert Kandel. Columbia Univ. Press 2003 311p il maps $29.95; pa $24

Grades: 11 12 Adult   **553.7**

1. Water

ISBN 0-231-12244-6; 0-231-12245-4 (pa)

LC 2002-31229

Original French edition, 1998

The author "explains the earth's elaborate and essential-to-life water cycle . . . beginning cosmologically with the birth of the solar system and an analysis of various theories as to where the earth's water . . . originated." Booklist

"While dense with facts and figures, Kandel's aquatic history is riveting, an exhaustive and complex examination of our most precious chemical compound." Publ Wkly

Includes bibliographical references

Newton, David E.

Encyclopedia of water. Greenwood Press 2002 401p il $75

Grades: 11 12 Adult   **553.7**

1. Water—Encyclopedias

ISBN 1-57356-304-8   LC 2002-70031

"The 236 entries in this book comprise an A-Z overview of water's manifold roles in human society and the natural world throughout history." Publisher's note

Includes bibliographical references

UXL encyclopedia of water science; K. Lee Lerner and Brenda Wilmoth Lerner, editors; Lawrence W. Baker, project editor. UXL 2005 3v il set $172

Grades: 9 10 11 12   **553.7**

1. Water—Encyclopedias

ISBN 0-7876-7617-9   LC 2004-21651

Contents: v. 1. Water science -- v. 2. Humans and water: economics, technology, and culture -- v. 3. Humans and water: environmental, legal, and political issues

"This set makes a good addition to libraries in which science or social studies students need current useful information for research projects." Libr Media Connect

Includes bibliographical references

Water: science and issues; E. Julius Dasch, editor in chief. Macmillan Ref. USA 2003 4v il maps set $395 *

Grades: 11 12 Adult   **553.7**

1. Water—Encyclopedias

ISBN 0-02-865611-3

Contents: v1 Acid-Drought; v2 Earle-Lakes; v3 Land-Pricing; v4 Prior-Women

"This reference contains more than 300 topical entries . . . about a wide array of topics surrounding the nature, sources, use, desecration, and protection of this most valuable resource. *Acid rain, Bottled water, Careers in oceanography, Hoover Dam, Leonardo da Vinci, Plankton, Salmon decline and recovery* and *Wetlands* are examples of entries and help illustrate the set's range. . . . At the beginning of each volume are several tables: metric conversions; symbols, abbreviations, and acronyms; and geologic eras, periods and epochs. Entries range in length from 500 to 2,500 words and include short bibliographies of print and electronic sources. Pages have wide margins, which contain picture captions, definitions of key terms, and boxes of important facts and explanations . . . Photographs, illustrations, and tables are attractive and add meaning to the text. Each volume concludes with the 36-page, detailed cumulative index and the 60-page glossary. . . . The scientific and social aspects of water are well introduced in this set, which is recommended for high-school, public, and undergraduate libraries." Booklist

Includes bibliographical references

553.8   Gems

Oldershaw, Cally

Firefly guide to gems. Firefly Bks. 2004 224p il map $14.95 *

Grades: 11 12 Adult   **553.8**

Oldershaw, Cally—*Continued*
1. Precious stones 2. Gems
ISBN 1-55297-814-1
This book "opens with extensive introductory material including history, various properties, and lore. Then, each gem is presented with text and charts of specific chemical properties. While most gems are discussed on a single page, some that are well known have longer articles." SLJ

Schumann, Walter
Gemstones of the world; [translated by Annette Englander and Daniel Shea] Newly rev. & expanded 3rd ed. Sterling Publishing Co. 2006 311p il $24.95
Grades: 9 10 11 12   **553.8**
1. Precious stones
ISBN 1-4027-4016-6; 978-1-4027-4016-9
First English language edition published 1977
"All the gemstones are treated in their many variations: more than 1,500 full-color photos showcase each precious and semiprecious stone in both its rough, natural, and its polished and cut renditions. Each entry offers . . . information on the gemstone's formation, structure, physical properties, and characteristics, along with the best methods of working, cutting, and polishing it." Publisher's note

Zoellner, Tom
The heartless stone; a journey through the world of diamonds, deceit, and desire. St. Martins Press 2006 293p map $24.95 *
Grades: 11 12 Adult   **553.8**
1. Diamonds
ISBN 0-312-33969-0; 978-0-312-33969-2
LC 2005-33037
The author "probes how 'blood diamonds' are used to fund vicious civil wars in Africa; how De Beers, seeing new markets to exploit, linked diamonds to the ancient yuino ceremony in Japan and played on caste obsession in India; and how India is pushing Belgium and Israel out of the gem trade. . . . This is a superior piece of reportage." Publ Wkly
Includes bibliographical references

560 Paleontology. Paleozoology

Encyclopedia of paleontology; editor, Ronald Singer. Fitzroy Dearborn Pubs. 1999 2v il set $295
Grades: 11 12 Adult   **560**
1. Fossils—Encyclopedias
ISBN 1-88496-496-6   LC 00-271769
This work has "328 articles that cover all areas of paleontology, including 79 biographies for individuals such as Jean Agassiz, Charles Darwin, and Louis Leakey. The articles are extremely well written, with line drawings, photographs, charts, and other illustrative matter, plus a list of works cited and a further reading list." Booklist

Erickson, Jon, 1948-
An introduction to fossils and minerals; seeking clues to the earth's past; foreword by Donald R. Coates. rev ed. Facts on File 2000 272p il maps (Facts on File science library) $55
Grades: 11 12 Adult   **560**
1. Fossils 2. Minerals 3. Geology
ISBN 0-8160-4236-5   LC 00-37203
First published 1992
At head of title: Living Earth
"The focus of this book is primarily the geological occurrence of fossils and minerals. . . . The kinds of enclosing rock formations and the geologic processes that produced them are explained. Types of fossils, mostly of animals, but some of plants, and their geographic distributions are . . . described. The occurrence of minerals, gems, and natural metal in the earth are explained." Sci Bks
Includes bibliographical references

Haines, Tim
The complete guide to prehistoric life; [by] Tim Haines and Paul Chambers. Firefly Books 2006 216p il $35; pa $24.95 *
Grades: 9 10 11 12   **560**
1. Fossils 2. Dinosaurs
ISBN 1-55407-125-9; 978-1-55407-125-8; 1-55407-181-X (pa); 978-1-55407-181-4 (pa)
LC 2005-9042575
This book covers "112 of the earliest beasts dating from the Cambrian Period to the Pleistocene Period, with . . . profiles on physical characteristics, lifestyle, habitat and behavior." Publisher's note

Marven, Nigel
Chased by sea monsters; prehistoric predators of the deep; [by] Nigel Marven, Jasper James. DK Pub 2004 167p il $25
Grades: 9 10 11 12   **560**
1. Extinct animals 2. Sea monsters 3. Marine animals
ISBN 0-7566-0375-7; 978-0-7566-0375-5
LC 2004-297988
"This book is published to accompany the television series entitled 'Chased by sea monsters' which was produced by Impossible Pictures and first broadcast on Discovery in 2004" Verso of title page
The authors "survey the last half-billion years of marine life to rank the 'seven most deadly seas' (i. e., geological epochs) in order of the scariness of their sea creatures. . . . The book's combination of sensationalism, lurid graphics and solid scientific exposition is well judged to stimulate budding paleontologists." Publ Wkly

Ottaviani, Jim

Bone sharps, cowboys, and thunder lizards; a tale of Edwin Drinker Cope, Othniel Charles Marsh, and the gilded age of paleontology; by Jim Ottaviani & Big Time Attic. G.T. Labs 2005 165p il pa $22.95 *

Grades: 9 10 11 12 **560**
1. Cope, E. D. (Edward Drinker), 1840-1897 2. Marsh, Othniel Charles, 1831-1899 3. Fossils—Graphic novels 4. Graphic novels
ISBN 0-9660106-6-3; 978-0-9660106-6-4
LC 2005-920326

Cover title

"Ottaviani portrays the heyday of American dinosaur hunting with a ripsnorting Western feel. Rival scientist/dinosaur hunters Marsh and Cope play out their real-life drama in a mostly accurate historical telling. Copious notes at the back of the book point out where Ottaviani departs from the facts; science and history become fun in his hands." Voice Youth Advocates

Includes bibliographical references

Thompson, Ida

The Audubon Society field guide to North American fossils; with photographs by Townsend P. Dickinson; visual key by Carol Nehring. Knopf 1982 846p il maps flexible bdg $19.95 *

Grades: 11 12 Adult **560**
1. Fossils
ISBN 0-394-52412-8 LC 81-84772

"A Chanticleer Press edition. The Audubon Society field guide series"

"This softbound field guide to fossils is divided into a section of color photographs followed by a section of detailed descriptions. It covers 420 fossils of marine and freshwater invertebrates, insects, plants, and vertebrates that are likely to be found by the amateur." Malinowsky. Best Sci & Technol Ref Books for Young People

567.9 Fossil reptiles. Dinosaurs

Lambert, David, 1932-

Dinosaur encyclopedia; from dinosaurs to the dawn of man; [by David Lambert, Darren Naish, Elizabeth Wyse] Dorling Kindersley 2001 376p il maps $29.95 *

Grades: 11 12 Adult **567.9**
1. Dinosaurs—Encyclopedias
ISBN 0-7894-7935-4 LC 2001-28433

In association with the American Museum of Natural History

"After a brief discussion of how paleontologists reconstruct the details of prehistory, this comprehensive volume breaks the animal kingdom into four major sections, 'Fish and Invertebrates,' 'Amphibians and Reptiles,' 'Dinosaurs and Birds' and 'Mammals and Their Ancestors.'" Publ Wkly

"This book is an excellent volume for both the uninitiated and the person who wishes to expand his or her knowledge from the basics. The book is logically laid out by groups of animals, and evolutionary connections between the animals are explained clearly. . . . As an encyclopedia, this one accomplishes its mission of providing a good basic foundation for each animal group it presents." Sci Books Films

Parker, Steve

Dinosaurus; the complete guide to dinosaurs. Firefly Books 2004 448p il $49.95 *

Grades: 9 10 11 12 **567.9**
1. Dinosaurs
ISBN 1-55297-772-2 LC 2004-299417

"Arrangement is by group, and 500 dinosaurs are described. Each entry includes an illustration and brief information about the dinosaur's discovery and characteristics. Each entry also includes a 'Dino Factfile' containing data on scientific name with pronunciation and meaning, location, size, diet, and time period." Booklist

This is "is a must-have source for libraries where dinosaur study is an annual research unit." Voice Youth Advocates

Includes bibliographical references

570 Life sciences. Biology

Biology; Richard Robinson, editor in chief. Macmillan Ref. USA 2002 4v set $395 *

Grades: 11 12 Adult **570**
1. Biology
ISBN 0-02-865551-6 LC 2001-40211

This set "provides 432 signed entries on a broad range of topics pertaining to biology, including basic concepts . . . history of the science . . . related fields . . . and issues . . . as well as topics of interest to young adults, such as smoking, birth control, alcohol, and STDs. . . . The eye-pleasing layout features many colorful photographs and diagrams that will appeal to casual browsers and the articles contain more than enough information to meet the needs of students. This informative set is highly recommended." Booklist

Includes bibliographical references

Cracking the SAT: biology E/M subject test, 2007-2008 edition; [by] the Princeton Review. Random House 2007 il pa $19

Grades: 9 10 11 12 **570**
1. Biology—Study and teaching 2. Scholastic Assessment Test 3. Colleges and universities—Entrance requirements
ISSN 1556-8431
ISBN 0-375-76588-3; 978-0-375-76588-9

Annual. First published 2005. Continues Cracking the SAT II: biology subject test

At head of title: The Princeton Review

This guide provides test-taking strategies and sample tests for the subject of biology.

The Facts on File biology handbook; [by] The Diagram Group. rev ed. Facts on File 2006 272p il (Facts on File science library) $35 *

Grades: 8 9 10 11 12 **570**
1. Biology
ISBN 0-8160-5877-6 LC 2004-59270

First published 2000

The Facts on File biology handbook—*Continued*

Topics covered include: amniocentesis, synthesis, hormones, glands, embryo, ventricle, and zygote. Francis Bacon, Edwin Hubble, and Linus Pauling are among the 400 scientists profiled. Includes a chronology of significant developments and discoveries from ancient Greece to the present day. Illustrated with tables, charts, and diagrams.

Includes bibliographical references

Stone, Carol Leth

The basics of biology; Carol Leth Stone. Greenwood Press 2004 280p il (Basics of the hard sciences) $75

Grades: 9 10 11 12   **570**

1. Biology

ISBN 0-313-31786-0   LC 2004-8510

This book "offers an overview of the discipline, including its history and key concepts and principles. Chapter coverage includes ecology, evolution, genetics, body systems, and the classes of living organisms. A handful of experiments accompanies each chapter. The final section is devoted to additional open-ended experiments for assignments or personal study. . . . This overview is well suited to novice students." SLJ

Includes bibliographical references

570.3 Life sciences--Encyclopedias and dictionaries

The **Facts** on File dictionary of biology; edited by Robert Hine. 4th ed. Facts on File 2005 406p il (Facts on File science library) $45; pa $17.95 *

Grades: 9 10 11 12   **570.3**

1. Biology—Dictionaries

ISBN 0-8160-5647-1; 0-8160-5648-X (pa)

LC 2005-40698

First published 1981

Over 3,000 entries cover basic terms as well as names of organs, biological processes, genera and species. Global warming, DNA fingerprinting, and the Human Genome Project are among the topics covered

"The volume is worthwhile for consideration by libraries in need of an up-to-date, relatively inexpensive dictionary that covers basic biological terminology." Booklist

Includes bibliographical references

McGraw-Hill dictionary of bioscience. 2nd ed. McGraw-Hill 2002 662p pa $19.95 *

Grades: 11 12 Adult   **570.3**

1. Biology—Dictionaries

ISBN 0-07-141043-0   LC 2002-33193

First published 1997

"All text in the dictionary was published previously in the McGraw-Hill dictionary of scientific and technical terms, sixth edition" Verso of title page

This dictionary includes 18,000 entries in more than 20 areas of life science and includes synonyms, acronyms, abbreviations, pronunciations, and an appendix of data tables.

"Given its reasonable price, the dictionary . . . would

be useful for offices, laboratories, or classrooms. The source of the definitions is a guarantee of quality." Am Ref Books Annu, 1998

Rittner, Don

Encyclopedia of biology; [by] Don Rittner and Timothy L. McCabe. Facts on File 2004 400p il $75 *

Grades: 9 10 11 12   **570.3**

1. Biology—Encyclopedias

ISBN 0-8160-4859-2   LC 2003-21279

Contains approximately 800 alphabetical entries, prose essays on important topics, line illustrations, and black-and-white photographs

Includes bibliographical references

571.6 Cell biology

The **Facts** on File dictionary of cell and molecular biology; edited by Robert Hine. Facts on File 2002 248p il $49.50 *

Grades: 11 12 Adult   **571.6**

ISBN 0-8160-4912-2   LC 2002-32540

"There are 2,000 entries for terms in all major areas of biochemistry, molecular biology, molecular genetics, and cell biology. . . . Brief biographies of significant scientists are included. The appendixes include a chronology of the major discoveries in biochemistry and molecular biology. Also provided are molecular diagrams of 20 amino acids, a chart of the genetic code, a brief list of Web pages, and a bibliography. . . . Each entry is well written and clear. The illustrations are good, and there appear to be all the major terms needed for the purpose of this dictionary." Am Ref Books Annu, 2003

Includes bibliographical references

Harold, Franklin M.

The way of the cell; molecules, organisms, and the order of life. Oxford Univ. Press 2001 305p il $37.50; pa $17.95

Grades: 11 12 Adult   **571.6**

1. Cells 2. Life (Biology)

ISBN 0-19-513512-1; 0-19-516338-9 (pa)

LC 00-56670

"Harold tackles the largest of questions (What is life?) within the smallest of settings (the cell) in order to consider where and why a strictly genetic approach to life leads us astray." Booklist

Includes bibliographical references

Panno, Joseph

The cell; evolution of the first organism. Facts on File 2004 186p il (New biology) $35 *

Grades: 11 12 Adult   **571.6**

1. Cells

ISBN 0-8160-4946-7   LC 2003-25841

Contents: The origin of life -- Procaryotes: laying the foundations -- Eucaryotes: dawn of a new era -- The cell cycle -- Genes -- From cells to bodies -- Neurons: pushing back the night -- Resource center

Panno, Joseph—*Continued*

"From the origins of the first cell to the diseases that attack different types of cells, this . . . volume tells the full story of this organism." Publisher's note

Includes bibliographical references

571.7   Biological control and secretions

Foster, Russell G.

Rhythms of life; the biological clocks that control the daily lives of every living thing. Yale University Press 2004 276p il $30; pa $18

Grades: 11 12 Adult   571.7

1. Biological rhythms

ISBN   0-300-10574-6;   978-0-300-10574-2; 0-300-10969-5 (pa); 978-0-300-10969-6 (pa)

LC 2004-105609

The authors "survey the biological clocks that dictate circadian rhythms, the daily cycles that affect creatures from cockroaches to humans. . . . Biology buffs will marvel at the fascinating material." Publ Wkly

Includes bibliographical references

572.8   Biochemical genetics

Carroll, Sean B.

The making of the fittest; DNA and the ultimate forensic record of evolution; with illustrations by Jamie W. Carroll and Leanne M. Olds. W.W. Norton & Co. 2006 301p il map $25.95 *

Grades: 11 12 Adult   572.8

1. DNA 2. Evolution

ISBN 978-0-393-06163-5; 0-393-06163-9

LC 2006-17197

The author presents "discoveries gathered from DNA evidence that confirm Charles Darwin's theory of evolution 'beyond any reasonable doubt.' . . . Readers will gain insight into the evolutionary process and expand their knowledge of how the 'fittest' species were made, from fish that live in subfreezing water to birds that communicate via ultraviolet colors." Libr J

Includes bibliographical references

Watson, James D., 1928-

The double helix; a personal account of the discovery of the structure of DNA. Scribner 1998 226p il $25; pa $14

Grades: 11 12 Adult   572.8

1. DNA 2. Biochemistry—Research

ISBN 0-684-85279-9; 0-7432-1630-X (pa)

LC 98-136787

Also available in paperback from Norton

A reissue of the title first published 1968 by Atheneum Pubs.

Portions of this book were first published in The Atlantic Monthly

This book is a "personal, day-by-day account of how Watson, [Francis] Crick and their collaborators in the years between 1951 and 1963 hit upon the famous 'double helix' model of the 'DNA' [deoxyribonucleic acid] molecule, the fundamental genetical material." America

576.5   Genetics

Encyclopedia of genetics; editor, revised edition, Bryan D. Ness; editor, first edition, Jeffrey A. Knight. rev ed. Salem Press 2004 2v il set $210 *

Grades: 11 12 Adult   576.5

1. Genetics—Encyclopedias

ISBN 1-587-65149-1   LC 2003-26056

First published 1999

"Each volume starts with an alphabetical list of contents. The essays all follow a similar format. Each begins with top matter that lists 'Field of Study' offering one or more subdisciplines under which the topic falls. This is followed by 'Significance', which provides a definition of the topic and a summary of its importance. Next are definitions of 'Key Terms'. Headings break the main body of each essay into clearly defined subtopics. . . . About half of the essays include 'Web Sites of Interest' directing users to Web sites of government agencies, professional or academic societies, support organizations, and a few relevant personal URLs." Booklist

Includes bibliographical references

Genetics; Richard Robinson [editor in chief] Macmillan Ref. USA 2003 4v set $395

Grades: 11 12 Adult   576.5

1. Genetics—Encyclopedias

ISBN 0-02-865606-7   LC 2002-3560

This set contains "approximately 250 signed entries from *Accelerated aging: Progeria* to *Zebrafish*. Articles range from a few paragraphs to a few pages in length and focus on a variety of topics, including inheritance, genes and chromosomes, genetic diseases, biotechnology, history, careers, and the ethical, legal, and social issues associated with genetically modified foods and cloning. The entries appear in alphabetical order and include cross-references to related entries. Most have a list of suggested readings and Internet resources. . . . The clear and well-written articles are informative and should meet the needs of most students." Booklist

Includes bibliographical references

Watson, James D., 1928-

DNA: the secret of life; [by] James D. Watson, with Andrew Berry. Knopf 2003 446p il hardcover o.p. pa $25.95

Grades: 11 12 Adult   576.5

1. Genetics 2. DNA

ISBN 0-375-41546-7; 0-375-71007-8 (pa)

LC 2002-190725

"Watson begins by describing the history of molecular genetics, pausing at times to introduce the scientific players and to describe the . . . experiments showing how DNA is replicated, how its code is translated into the proteins that compose our bodies and how genes are turned on and off as needed. The remaining two-thirds of the book treats the implications of the new genetics: biotechnology, genetically modified food, the forensic use of DNA, the sequencing of the human genome, the development of genetically based medicine and the search for genes affecting human behavior. . . . [There is] a chapter on DNA-based approaches to understanding the human past." N Y Times Book Rev

Watson, James D., 1928-—*Continued*

"Watson sensitively and sensibly treats the controversies aroused by genetically modified foods and organisms, patenting genes, and playing with the 'stuff of life.' Written for the educated and biologically aware reader, this is recommended for most public and academic libraries." Libr J

Includes bibliographical references

Yount, Lisa

Modern genetics; engineering life. Rev. ed. Facts on File 2006 204p il map (Milestones in discovery and invention) $35

Grades: 7 8 9 10 11 12   **576.5**
1. Genetics 2. Genetic engineering
ISBN 0-8160-5744-3; 978-0-8160-5744-3
LC 2005-18152
First published 1997 with title: Genetics and genetic engineering

This book "profiles 14 men and women who were among the leaders in making important genetic discoveries in research and new technologies. Profiles include James Watson, Francis Crick, Herbert Boyer, Stanley N. Cohen, Michael Bishop, and Harold Varmus." Publisher's note

Includes glossary and bibliographical references

576.8   Evolution

Creationism versus evolution; Eric Braun, book editor. Greenhaven Press 2005 91p (At issue) lib bdg $28.70; pa $19.95

Grades: 9 10 11 12   **576.8**
1. Creationism 2. Evolution 3. Religion and science
ISBN 0-7377-2703-9 (lib bdg); 0-7377-2704-7 (pa)
LC 2004-60631

This anthology debates common misconceptions of both evolution and the theory of creationism, including a discussion of Intelligent Design theory.

Includes bibliographical references

Darwin, Charles, 1809-1882

The Darwin reader; edited by Mark Ridley. 2nd ed. Norton 1996 315p il pa $21.30 *

Grades: 11 12 Adult   **576.8**
1. Evolution 2. Natural selection
ISBN 0-393-96967-3   LC 95-50297
First published in the United Kingdom with title: The essential Darwin; first Norton edition published 1987

This collection presents excerpts from Darwin's most important works including Origin of the species, The descent of man and Coral reef. Illustrations are taken from the original editions

Includes bibliographical references

The portable Darwin; edited, with an introduction, notes, and epilogue by Duncan M. Porter and Peter W. Graham. Penguin Bks. 1993 xxii, 561p il pa $16

Grades: 11 12 Adult   **576.8**
1. Evolution 2. Natural selection
ISBN 0-14-015109-5   LC 93-17106
"The Viking portable library"

This collection of Darwin's writings includes five chapters from The origin of species; excerpts from The voyage of the Beagle, The descent of man, and The variation of animals and plants under domestication; scientific papers, travel writings, and letters.

Includes bibliographical references

Dixon, Dougal, 1947-

The future is wild; {by} Dougal Dixon, John Adams. Firefly Bks. 2003 160p il maps hardcover o.p. pa $24.95 *

Grades: 9 10 11 12   **576.8**
1. Evolution 2. Forecasting
ISBN 1-55297-724-2; 1-55297-723-4 (pa)
"A natural history of the future." Cover; Companion book to the Discovery Channel television series

"This work speculates on the evolution of the Earth and its beings, minus human life, over the next 5, 100, and 200 million years." SLJ

"The computer-generated illustrations of the hypothetical species are gorgeous and detailed. . . . The clever, creative forces behind this work have a real chance of opening some young adults' eyes to the possibilities of science." Voice Youth Advocates

Encyclopedia of evolution; Mark Pagel, editor in chief. Oxford Univ. Press 2002 2v il set $325

Grades: 11 12 Adult   **576.8**
1. Evolution—Encyclopedias
ISBN 0-19-512200-3   LC 2001-21588

This reference covers topics in evolutionary theory "including developmental biology, social behavior, consciousness, evolution of disease, systematics, population biology, complexity theory, and even art in prehistory. Some biographical articles are also included. . . . [Contributors include] Stephen Jay Gould, Jane Goodall, Sarah Blaffer Hrdy, and John Maynard Smith." Libr J

Evolution; Clay Farris Naff, book editor. Greenhaven Press 2005 222p (Exploring science and medical discoveries) lib bdg $34.95 *

Grades: 8 9 10 11 12   **576.8**
1. Evolution
ISBN 0-7377-2823-X   LC 2004-60590

In this anthology, "nineteen selections are arranged in roughly chronological order, beginning with ancient Greek philosophers whose ideas about nature hinted at evolutionary theories to come. . . . This solid survey provides a good overview with manageable amounts of primary-source materials that would be dauntingly difficult to comprehend in their entirety." SLJ

Includes bibliographical references

Evolution; Don Nardo, book editor. Greenhaven Press 2005 240p il (History of issues) lib bdg $34.95; pa $23.70

Grades: 9 10 11 12   **576.8**
1. Evolution
ISBN 0-7377-2098-0 (lib bdg); 0-7377-2099-9 (pa)
LC 2004-47481

"In this volume, scientists, religious leaders, and others square off in pairs of pro and con essays. Topics include: the nineteenth-century controversy over evolution, modern advances in evolutionary theory, and the debate

Evolution—*Continued*
over teaching evolution in schools." Publisher's note
Includes bibliographical references

Extraterrestrial life; Tamara L. Roleff, book editor. Greenhaven Press 2001 144p (Contemporary issues companion) lib bdg $31.20; pa $19.95
Grades: 9 10 11 12　　　　　576.8
1. Life on other planets
ISBN 0-7377-0462-4 (lib bdg); 0-7377-0461-6 (pa)
LC 00-64045

A collection of articles discussing various aspects of extraterrestrial life including UFO sightings, alien abductions, and scientific evidence for life on other planets from NASA's explorations
Includes bibliographical references

Jones, Steve, 1944-
Darwin's ghost; the origin of species updated. Random House 2000 xxix, 377p il pa $15.95 hardcover o.p. *
Grades: 11 12 Adult　　　　　576.8
1. Natural selection 2. Evolution
ISBN 0-345-42277-5 (pa)　　　　LC 99-53246
First published 1999 in the United Kingdom with title: Almost like a whale
Jones "has updated Charles Darwin's *On the origin of species* (1859) so that the fact of organic evolution is both understandable and relevant to today's general reader. . . . Very informative and cogently argued, this book is an important addition to the natural history literature." Libr J
Includes bibliographical references

Koerner, David
Here be dragons; the scientific quest for extraterrestrial life; [by] David Koerner, Simon LeVay. Oxford Univ. Press 2000 264p il pa $24.95 hardcover o.p.
Grades: 11 12 Adult　　　　　576.8
1. Life on other planets 2. Life—Origin
ISBN 0-19-514600-X (pa)　　　　LC 99-38170
In this book the authors explore "the origin of life and its occurrence outside Earth. . . . They offer a broad overview of up-to-date research and thought on topics ranging from the chemistry of life's origins to the search for extra-solar planets, the process of evolution, and the nature of life and the cosmos." Booklist
Includes bibliographical references

Larson, Edward J.
Evolution: the remarkable history of a scientific theory. Modern Library 2004 337p il (Modern Library chronicles) $21.95; pa $14.95 *
Grades: 11 12 Adult　　　　　576.8
1. Evolution
ISBN 0-679-64288-9; 0-8129-6849-2 (pa)
LC 2003-64888
This is an "overview of evolutionary thought from ancient speculations to the emergence of a neo-Darwinian

synthesis. It focuses on those essential facts, events, and ideas that have contributed to the successes of scientific evolutionism. . . . Larson is to be commended for stressing the value of both scientific inquiry and the evolutionary framework. This outstanding book is highly recommended for all academic and public libraries." Libr J
Includes bibliographical references

Parker, Andrew, 1967-
In the blink of an eye. Perseus Pub 2003 316p il hardcover o.p. pa $15
Grades: 11 12 Adult　　　　　576.8
1. Evolution 2. Fossils
ISBN 0-7382-0607-5; 0-465-05438-2 (pa)
LC 2003-282077
The author "provides a relatively simple explanation for the sudden explosion of life forms that defines the boundary between the pre-Cambrian and Cambrian eras approximately 543 million years ago: 'The Cambrian explosion was triggered by the sudden evolution of vision' in simple organisms. . . . In readable prose, Parker provides detailed information on the fossil record as well as a wealth of interesting material on the role light plays in environments and how vision operates across a host of species. Although at times his tangents are a bit distracting, Parker's book will bring his controversial ideas to the general public." Publ Wkly

Pennock, Robert T.
Tower of Babel; the evidence against the new creationism. MIT Press 1999 429p $55; pa $21.95
Grades: 11 12 Adult　　　　　576.8
1. Evolution 2. Creationism 3. Religion and science
ISBN 0-262-16180-X; 0-262-66165-9 (pa)
LC 98-27286
"A Bradford book"
The author "catalogues the wide range of creationist beliefs, dissects their main arguments and highlights what he sees as their internal inconsistencies." Publ Wkly
By "disentangling the scientific issues from the religious and philosophic ones, Pennock has made a valuable contribution to a too-often-overheated debate." Booklist
Includes bibliographical references

Powell, James Lawrence, 1936-
Night comes to the Cretaceous; dinosaur extinction and the transformation of modern geology; [by] James L. Powell. Freeman, W.H. 1998 250p il map $22.95
Grades: 11 12 Adult　　　　　576.8
1. Catastrophes (Geology) 2. Mass extinction of species 3. Dinosaurs
ISBN 0-7167-3117-7　　　　LC 98-13192
Also available in paperback from Harcourt
The author "summarizes arguments for and against the controversial 'impact theory' of the extinction of the dinosaurs first proposed by Nobel physicist Luis Alvarez and his geologist son Walter and others in 1980. . . . Powell's book is written for a broad audience. It is slow reading in places, but explanations added in parentheses clarify technical materials." Sci Books Films
Includes bibliographical references

Rice, Stanley Arthur, 1957-
Encyclopedia of evolution; [by] Stanley A. Rice; foreword by Massimo Pigliucci. Facts on File 2007 468p il (Facts on File science library) $75 *
Grades: 11 12 Adult 576.8
1. Evolution—Encyclopedias
ISBN 0-8160-5515-7; 978-0-8160-5515-9
LC 2005-31646
This encyclopedia "contains more than 200 entries that span modern evolutionary science and the history of its development. . . . Five essays that explore . . . questions resulting from studies in evolutionary science are included as well. The appendix consists of a summary of Charles Darwin's Origin of Species." Publisher's note
Includes bibliographical references

Scott, Eugenie Carol, 1945-
Evolution vs. creationism; an introduction; [by] Eugenie C. Scott; foreword by Niles Eldredge. Greenwood Press 2004 272p il $51.95 *
Grades: 9 10 11 12 576.8
1. Evolution 2. Creationism
ISBN 0-313-32122-1 LC 2004-44214
Also available in paperback from Univ. of California Press
"Prior to addressing differing sides of the question, the author provides the reader with an introduction to the concepts of science, evolution, religion, and creationism. A history of the controversy and the varying theories and opinions about it follows. The third section contains approximately 100 pages of excerpts from major works dealing with the scientific, legal, educational, and religious arguments. . . . This informative work provides the reader with a clear, insightful summary of the complicated issues and viewpoints surrounding the evolution/creationism debate." Libr Media Connect
Includes bibliographical references

Whitfield, Philip J.
Evolution; [by] Philip Whitfield. Gale Group 2000 220p il (Living universe series) $95
Grades: 9 10 11 12 576.8
1. Evolution
ISBN 0-02-865593-1
First published 1993 in the United Kingdom with title: The natural history of evolution
Contents: Life and change; The rules of change; Life fits the world; New perspectives
This book discusses the history of evolutionary theory from Darwin's theory of natural selection to DNA and genetic research, and considers such questions as "How can evolution be observed and measured? How can we interpret the fossil record? What are the ethical implications of gene manipulation?" Publisher's note
Includes glossary and bibliographical references

Young, Christian C., 1968-
Evolution and creationism; a documentary and reference guide; [by] Christian C. Young and Mark A. Largent. Greenwood Press 2007 298p il $85 *
Grades: 11 12 Adult 576.8
1. Evolution 2. Creationism
ISBN 978-0-313-33953-0 LC 2007-10682

"This reference work provides over 40 of the most important documents to help readers understand the [evolution versus creationism] debate in the eyes of the people of the time. Each document is from a major participant in the debates from the predecessors of Darwin to the judges of the influential court cases of the present day." Publisher's note
Includes bibliographical references

Zimmer, Carl
Evolution; the triumph of an idea; introduction by Stephen Jay Gould; foreword by Richard Hutton. HarperCollins Pubs. 2001 xx, 364p il maps hardcover o.p. pa $15.95
Grades: 11 12 Adult 576.8
1. Evolution
ISBN 0-06-019906-7; 0-06-113840-1 (pa)
LC 2001-24077
This companion to the PBS documentary series provides an overview of topics related to evolution such as Darwin's life, patterns of human evolution and its relation to language, genetics, modern implications in agriculture and medicine, and the fallacies of creationism
"Zimmer's synthesis of evolution is a valuable introduction to the subject." Booklist

577 Ecology

Agosta, William C.
Thieves, deceivers, and killers; tales of chemistry in nature; [by] William Agosta. Princeton Univ. Press 2001 241p $26.95; pa $16.95
Grades: 11 12 Adult 577
1. Ecology 2. Animal communication
ISBN 0-691-00488-9; 0-691-09273-7 (pa)
LC 00-32627
The author "discusses chemical substances used for protection or communications in plants and animals and how these substances have found use as bactericides, repellents, and medicinals. This small book contains many detailed and fascinating descriptions of interspecies interactions and how nature uses chemical substances for communications, defense, and offense in the world of microbes, insects, and mammals." Choice
Includes glossary and bibliographical references

Baskin, Yvonne
A plague of rats and rubbervines; the growing threat of species invasions. Island Press (Washington, D.C.) 2002 377p il hardcover o.p. pa $16
Grades: 11 12 Adult 577
1. Biological invasions 2. Nature conservation
ISBN 1-55963-876-1; 1-55963-051-5 (pa)
LC 2002-4029
"A SCOPE-GISP project"
The author "describes her visits to several environments where alien species have run amok, such as Hawaii, the Galapagos Islands, South Africa, and New Zealand, skillfully revealing her zoological and botanical

Baskin, Yvonne—*Continued*

knowledge. . . . Her survey—with historical perspective on biological interchange since the time of Columbus—of an extinction threat second only to habitat destruction will appeal to ecologically minded readers." Booklist

Includes bibliographical references

Burdick, Alan

Out of Eden; an odyssey of ecological invasion. Farrar, Straus & Giroux 2005 324p il $25; pa $14

Grades: 11 12 Adult **577**

1. Biological invasions 2. Ecology

ISBN 0-374-21973-7; 0-374-53043-2 (pa)

LC 2005-922517

This book argues that "exotic animals and plants are crossing the globe, borne on the . . . tide of human traffic to places where nature never intended them to be. . . . [These species] increasingly crowd native and endangered species out of existence." Publisher's note

"A sober report, Burdick's work still sounds an alarm for readers concerned with the way humans alter nature." Booklist

Slobodkin, Lawrence B.

A citizen's guide to ecology. Oxford University Press 2003 245p $40; pa $14.95

Grades: 11 12 Adult **577**

1. Ecology 2. Human influence on nature

ISBN 0-19-516286-2; 0-19-516287-0 (pa)

LC 2002-72826

This book attempts to explain "the ecological world, and how individual citizens can participate in practical decisions on ecological issues. It tackles such issues as global warming, ecology and health, organic farming, species extinction and adaptation, and endangered species." Publisher's note

"Slobodkin's sober examination of {the issues} . . . offers the empowerment that arises from genuine knowledge about problems." Booklist

Includes bibliographical references

577.2 Specific factors affecting ecology

Russell, Edmund, 1957-

War and nature; fighting humans and insects with chemicals from World War I to Silent Spring. Cambridge Univ. Press 2001 315p (Studies in environment and history) $55; pa $20

Grades: 9 10 11 12 **577.2**

1. Chemical warfare 2. Pest control 3. Insect pests

ISBN 0-521-79003-4; 0-521-79937-6 (pa)

LC 00-40323

The author "traces military and agricultural use of poison gases, incendiaries, smokes, insecticides and pesticides, while exploring the toll on human life, culture and the environment." Publ Wkly

This is an "innovative and illuminating study." Booklist

Includes bibliographical references

577.3 Forest ecology

Martin, Patricia A. Fink, 1955-

Woods and forests; illustrations by Bob Italiano and Steve Savage. Watts 2000 143p il (Exploring ecosystems) lib bdg $24

Grades: 7 8 9 10 **577.3**

1. Forest ecology 2. Science—Experiments

ISBN 0-531-11697-2 (lib bdg) LC 99-33044

"In six chapters with 20 projects and 13 investigations, Martin starts students on a journey of understanding and appreciating our woods and forests. Topics in this book include tree identification, forest wildlife, and life cycles in the forest. . . . Appended are a glossary, an index, and a listing of books, videos, organizations, Web sites, and equipment suppliers." Book Rep

Includes bibliographical references

577.5 Ecology of miscellaneous environments

Gritzner, Charles F.

Deserts. Chelsea House 2006 127p il map (Geography of extreme environments) lib bdg $24.95

Grades: 9 10 11 12 **577.5**

1. Deserts

ISBN 0-7910-9234-8; 978-0-7910-9234-7

LC 2006-25584

This book on deserts discusses desert weather and climate, geography, the ecosystem, the native cultres that live there, and future prospects for the people that live there.

Includes bibliographical references

Polar regions. Chelsea House 2006 126p il map (Geography of extreme environments) lib bdg $24.95

Grades: 9 10 11 12 **577.5**

1. Polar regions

ISBN 0-7910-9235-6; 978-0-7910-9235-4

LC 2006-19636

"This volume introduces readers to the climatic 'ends of the Earth,' one of the planet's most unique and perhaps most challenging ecosystems. Polar Regions reveals how these stark locations, once believed to be inhospitable, have in fact been home to a number of culture groups." Publisher's note

Includes glossary and bibliographical references

577.7 Marine ecology

Carson, Rachel, 1907-1964

The edge of the sea; with illustrations by Bob Hines. Houghton Mifflin 1955 276p il pa $14 hardcover o.p.

Grades: 7 8 9 10 **577.7**

1. Marine biology 2. Seashore

ISBN 0-395-92496-0 (pa)

Also available in hardcover from P. Smith

Carson, Rachel, 1907-1964—_Continued_

"The seashores of the world may be divided into three basic types: the rugged shores of rock, the sand beaches, and the coral reefs and all their associated features. Each has its typical community of plants and animals. The Atlantic coast of the United States [provides] clear examples of each of these types. I have chosen it as the setting for my pictures of shore life." Preface

Ellis, Richard, 1938-

The empty ocean; plundering the world's marine life; written and illustrated by Richard Ellis. Island Press 2003 367p il hardcover o.p. pa $25 *

Grades: 11 12 Adult   **577.7**

1. Marine ecology 2. Endangered species

ISBN 1-55963-974-1; 1-55963-637-8 (pa)

The author "explains the economic, political, historical, and biological reasons for declining fisheries, the plight of sea turtles, disappearance of marine birds, slaughter of marine mammals, and destruction of coral reefs." Libr J

"Rather than writing the 'Silent Spring' of the oceans, {Ellis} has produced a book that is likely to provide the inspiration and source materials for such a badly needed work . . . It is also a splendid example of history illuminating ecology, with well-chosen facts that enable us to picture a largely invisible catastrophe." N Y Times Book Rev

Includes bibliographical references

Sheppard, Charles, 1962-2005

Coral reefs. Voyageur Press 2002 72p il (World life library) pa $16.95

Grades: 9 10 11 12   **577.7**

1. Coral reefs and islands 2. Marine ecology

ISBN 0-8965-8220-5   LC 2002-3005

Describes the nature, growth, location, and ecology of coral reefs.

Includes bibliographical references

Walker, Pamela, 1958-

The coral reef; [by] Pam Walker and Elaine Wood. Facts on File 2005 140p (Life in the sea) $35 *

Grades: 6 7 8 9   **577.7**

1. Coral reefs and islands

ISBN 0-8160-5703-6

"An opening chapter gives detailed coverage of how reefs are formed. Later chapters examine the reefs' inhabitants, from essential microbes to the larger, showier fish, reptiles, and other animals. The final chapter . . . mentions environmental hazards and conservation efforts. . . . The range and depth of information . . . make this a fine addition for science collections." Booklist

577.8 Synecology and population biology

Whitfield, Philip J.

Biomes and habitats; {by} Philip Whitfield, Peter D. Moore, Barry Cox. Macmillan Ref. USA 2002 220p il maps (Macmillan living universe series) $95 *

Grades: 11 12 Adult   **577.8**

1. Ecology

ISBN 0-02-865633-4

This volume deals with "global patterns, habitat patterns, niche patterns, changing patterns, and the human impact. The first section examines the history of our planet, plate tectonics, and evolution from earliest life forms to the complex biological world we live in. In the following section, seventeen specific habitats are described in some detail, including some less often considered, such as chaparral lands and savanna. Narrowing the focus, the authors next look at the way species evolve to particular niches, in response to environment and predation." Voice Youth Advocates

578 Natural history of organisms and related subjects

Gould, Stephen Jay, 1941-2002

I have landed; the end of a beginning in natural history. Harmony Bks. 2002 418p il hardcover o.p. pa $16 *

Grades: 11 12 Adult   **578**

1. Natural history 2. Evolution

ISBN 0-609-60143-1; 1-4000-4804-4 (pa)

LC 2002-24145

In this anthology of "essays from Natural History magazine . . . Gould writes on Darwinism, evolutionary theory, the history of science, and the joys of doing scientific research." Libr J

"Gould is at the peak of his abilities in this latest menagerie of wonders." Publ Wkly

Weidensaul, Scott

Return to wild America; a yearlong journey in search of the continent's natural soul. North Point Press 2005 xx, 394p il map $26; pa $15 *

Grades: 11 12 Adult   **578**

1. Peterson, Roger Tory, 1908-1996 2. Fisher, James Maxwell McConnell, 1912-1970 3. Natural history—North America

ISBN 0-8654-7688-8; 0-8654-7731-0 (pa)

LC 2005-47720

Fifty years after the publishing of Roger Tory Peterson's and James Fisher's _Wild America_, the author retraces Peterson and Fisher's steps "from Newfoundland's craggy coastline, down the East Coast, into Mexico and up the West Coast to Alaska. . . . This engrossing state-of-nature memoir, making a vibrant case for preserving America's wild past for future Americans, promises to become a classic in its own right." Publ Wkly

Includes bibliographical references

Wolfe, David W.

Tales from the underground; a natural history of subterranean life. Perseus Bks. 2001 221p il pa $18 hardcover o.p.

Grades: 11 12 Adult 578

1. Soil microbiology

ISBN 0-7382-0679-2 (pa)

The author discusses the ecology of life in the soil and the earth's rocky crust, including Darwin's experiments with earthworms, Lewis and Clark's first encounter with prairie dogs, the use of genetic tools, and the possible role of primitive underground microbes in evolution.

Wolfe "explains in a straightforward, readable style that there is probably as much biodiversity and even as much biomass below ground as above." New Sci

Includes bibliographical references

578.4 Adaptation

Gross, Michael, 1963-

Life on the edge; amazing creatures thriving in extreme environments. Plenum Trade 1998 200p il pa $15 hardcover o.p.

Grades: 11 12 Adult 578.4

1. Adaptation (Biology) 2. Stress (Physiology) 3. Life—Origin

ISBN 0-7382-0445-5 (pa) LC 98-4622

Translated from the German

Gross introduces a variety of extremophiles, or "organisms that survive in the most hostile habitats—extremes of temperature, salinity, acidity, alkalinity—as well as deep below the earth's surface." Choice

"The book constitutes an accessible introduction to an exciting outpost on the scientific frontier." Booklist

Includes glossary and bibliographical references

578.6 Miscellaneous nontaxonomic kinds of organisms

Fleisher, Paul

Parasites; latching on to a free lunch. Twenty-First Century Books 2006 112p il (Discovery!) lib bdg $29.27

Grades: 7 8 9 10 578.6

1. Parasites

ISBN 978-0-8225-3415-0; 0-8225-3415-0

LC 2005-10521

This book describes "all sorts of unpleasant creatures that can feed on your body—head lice, fleas, ticks, tapeworms, and fungi—as well as the huge variety of parasites that feed on animals and plants all around you." Publisher's note

This is "well organized and quite up to date. The photos . . . are plentiful, colorful, and excellent. . . . Clear, concise, and interesting." Voice Youth Advocates

Includes bibliographical references

Foster, Steven, 1957-

A field guide to venomous animals and poisonous plants; North America, North of Mexico; [by] Steven Foster and Roger A. Caras. Houghton Mifflin 1994 244p il pa $21 hardcover o.p. *

Grades: 11 12 Adult 578.6

1. Poisonous animals 2. Poisonous plants

ISBN 0-395-93608-X (pa) LC 94-1641

"The Peterson field guide series"

Sponsored by National Audubon Society, National Wildlife Federation, and Roger Tory Peterson Institute

This guide includes "90 animals from the mildly irritating to the deadly venomous: stinging and biting insects, scorpions and spiders, mammals, and reptiles, with an emphasis on snakes. More than 250 plants are described: wildflowers, weeds and exotic aliens, shrubs, trees, ferns, and mushrooms. The list includes plants that often cause allergies or dermatitis, such as Poison Ivy, as well as those that are toxic to eat." Publisher's note

Includes glossary and bibliographical references

578.68 Rare and endangered species

Endangered species: opposing viewpoints; Helen Cothran, book editor. Greenhaven Press 2000 156p il lib bdg $34.95; pa $23.70 *

Grades: 7 8 9 10 578.68

1. Endangered species

ISBN 0-7377-0506-X (lib bdg); 0-7377-0505-1 (pa)

LC 99-85752

"Opposing viewpoints series"

This collection of articles offers varying viewpoints on extinction, preservation, property rights, and international cooperation.

Includes bibliographical references

578.7 Organisms characteristic of specific kinds of environments

Guide to wetlands; Patrick Dugan, general editor. Firefly Books 2005 304p il maps pa $19.95 *

Grades: 9 10 11 12 578.7

1. Wetlands

ISBN 1-55407-111-9 LC 2006-276145

At head of title on cover: Firefly

This handbook provides "information on the major wetlands of the world, with an emphasis on their ecological roles, human impact, and conservation. The diversity of habitats includes estuaries, tidal flats, floodplains, freshwater marshes, and swamps." Choice

"This book would be a great resource for addressing the ecological role, diversity, and human use of wetlands." Sci Books Films

Marent, Thomas, 1966-
Rainforest; [by] Thomas Marent with Ben Morgan. DK Pub. 2006 360p il map $40 *
Grades: 11 12 Adult   **578.7**
   1. Rain forests—Pictorial works
   ISBN 0-7566-1940-8; 978-0-7566-1940-4
                     LC 2006-6774
   Includes audio CD
This "book is the product of Swiss photographer Marent's passion for exploring rainforests on five continents and over 16 years. His spectacularly beautiful photographs show about the nature of rainforests and their curious inhabitants, and the accompanying text explains what you are seeing and what it can tell you about these ecosystems. . . . An accompanying CD provides rainforest sounds from various locations. This book . . . is not only beautiful but an excellent source of information. It also shows the amazing diversity of species that makes rainforests unique and valuable." Libr J

Oldfield, Sara
Rainforest; photography by Bruce Coleman Collection; foreword by Mark Rose. MIT Press 2003 160p il map $29.95
Grades: 11 12 Adult   **578.7**
   1. Rain forests
   ISBN 0-262-15106-5
                    LC 2002-29559
"Each chapter covers a major rainforest region: Africa, Madagascar, India and Southeast Asia, Indonesia and the Philippines, Central America, the Caribbean, the Amazon . . . and Brazil, as well as the temperate rainforests in areas such as Tasmania and North America. The book details habitat, plants and animals, and threats to the precarious balance between humans and rainforests. The introduction provides an overview of the world's rainforests and a summary of current conservation issues." Publisher's note
The author "presents a wonderful overview of both tropical and temperate rainforests. . . . An excellent primer on this imperiled ecosystem." Booklist

579 Microorganisms, fungi, algae

Farrell, Jeanette
Invisible allies; microbes that shape our lives. Farrar, Straus & Giroux 2005 165p il lib bdg $17 *
Grades: 9 10 11 12   **579**
   1. Microorganisms
   ISBN 0-374-33608-3 (lib bdg)   LC 2004-53750
This describes the roles of microbes in the making of cheese, bread, and chocolate, in digestion and killing harmful microbes, and in decomposition for waste treatment.
This is "a fascinating, broad-ranging and imminently readable book. . . . Illustrations include photos as well as interesting archival material." Booklist
Includes glossary and bibliographical references

Rainis, Kenneth G.
A guide to microlife; [by] Kenneth G. Rainis and Bruce J. Russell. Watts 1996 287p il lib bdg $40
Grades: 9 10 11 12   **579**
   1. Microorganisms 2. Microbiology
   ISBN 0-531-11266-7   LC 95-44973
Serves as a guide to be used for the identification of microorganisms and provides information about microlife forms and how they affect other life forms, including human
"A good resource for classrooms, this colorful volume is packed with information." SLJ
Includes bibliographical references

Sankaran, Neeraja
Microbes and people: an A-Z of microorganisms in our lives. Oryx Press 2000 297p il $62.95
Grades: 11 12 Adult   **579**
   ISBN 1-57356-217-3   LC 00-10117
"Entries cover environmental, industrial, and food microbiology, in addition to the microbiology of health and disease. Scientific techniques used for studying microorganisms are discussed, and biographies of key individuals are provided. A chronology of infections and disease epidemics from 430 BC to the present is included as an appendix." Publisher's note
"Because it provides very readable coverage of topics so much in the news lately, this dictionary will be much used in high school, undergraduate, and public libraries." Booklist
Includes bibliographical references

579.6 Mushrooms

Læssøe, Thomas
Mushrooms; editorial consultant, Gary Lincoff; photography by Neil Fletcher. 2nd American ed. DK Pub. 2002 304p il (Smithsonian handbooks) $20
Grades: 9 10 11 12   **579.6**
   1. Mushrooms
   ISBN 0-7894-8986-4
   First published 1998 as part of the Eyewitness handbooks series
This is a "guide to more than 500 species of mushroom and other macrofungi found in northern temperate zones worldwide. . . . For each species, there are one to four sharp, detailed color photos with clues about their identity. There is also a small color painting of habitat suitable for the growth of the species. . . . This book should prove invaluable at any level, from casual nature observer to professional mycologist." Sci Books Films [review of 1998 edition]

Lincoff, Gary
The Audubon Society field guide to North American mushrooms; [by] Gary H. Lincoff; visual key by Carol Nehring. Knopf 1981 926p il flexible bdg $19.95 *
Grades: 7 8 9 10 11 12 Adult   **579.6**
   1. Mushrooms
   ISBN 0-394-51992-2   LC 81-80827

Lincoff, Gary—*Continued*

"A Chanticleer Press edition. The Audubon Society field guide series"

This guide to 703 species of common mushrooms provides 762 color photographs and descriptions as keys to identifying these plants.

"The author is an expert on mushroom toxins and instills responsible cautions. The photos are uncommonly beautiful." SLJ

McKnight, Kent H.

A field guide to mushrooms, North America; [by] Kent H. McKnight and Vera B. McKnight; illustrations by Vera B. McKnight. Houghton Mifflin 1987 429p il pa $21 hardcover o.p. *

Grades: 11 12 Adult 579.6

1. Mushrooms

ISBN 0-395-91090-0 (pa) LC 86-27799

"The Peterson field guide series"

"Sponsored by the National Audubon Society and the National Wildlife Federation"

"More than 500 species [of mushrooms] are described and depicted. . . . Edibility of each species is noted and signified by marginal pictograms both in the text and on the colorplates. . . . Appended: a genial chapter of recipes by Anne Dow, glossary, selected references, and index." Booklist

580 Plants

The **Facts** on File dictionary of botany; edited by Jill Bailey. Facts on File 2002 250p il $49.50 *

Grades: 11 12 Adult 580

ISBN 0-8160-4910-6 LC 2002-35202

"Facts on File science library"

This dictionary covers "pure and applied plant science, including the taxonomy and classification of plants, with entries for the higher-ranking taxa. Techniques of nucleic acid technology are included, with references made to applications in horticulture and agriculture." Publisher's note

Includes bibliographical references

Huxley, Anthony Julian, 1920-

Green inheritance; the WWF book of plants; [by] Anthony Huxley; foreword by Sir David Attenborough. Rev., by Martin Walters. University of California Press 2005 192p il map pa $29.95

Grades: 9 10 11 12 580

1. Plant conservation

ISBN 0-520-24359-5 LC 2005-52876

"A completely revised and expanded edition of the WWF book of plants"

First published 1985

This book "draws attention to the problems facing the planet at large as well as the ways each individual can conserve natural resources. Overall, the educational and wide-ranging text promotes an appreciation for the wondrous properties of plant life, from basic sustenance and curative powers to the ecology of insects and flowers." Booklist

Includes bibliographical references

Magill's encyclopedia of science; plant life; editor, Bryan D. Ness. Salem Press 2002 4v il map set $457

Grades: 11 12 Adult 580

1. Botany—Encyclopedias

ISBN 1-58765-084-3 LC 2002-13319

This encyclopedia provides "information for any study related to plants, archaea, bacteria, algae, or fungi, from molecular-level processes to planet-wide economic or environmental issues. The 379 signed articles, about half of which are published with revisions and updated bibliographies from several of the publisher's earlier reference books, are arranged into a single alphabet." SLJ

Includes bibliographical references

Plant; editor-in-chief, Janet Marinelli. DK 2005 512p il map $50 *

Grades: 11 12 Adult 580

1. Botany 2. Plants

ISBN 0-7566-0589-X; 978-0-7566-0589-6

LC 2004-22207

"The goal of this book is to provide novice gardeners to professional horticulturalists with a resource that relates each plant to its original biome and assist them with making informed decisions about buying, propagating, and nurturing threatened plants. Divided into encyclopedic sections based on plant type, each section provides a general introduction to the plant type, followed by detailed entries for each plant within that group." Am Ref Books Annu, 2006

This is a "massive, colorful, and delightful guide to the plant kingdom." Libr J

Plant sciences; Richard Robinson, editor in chief. Macmillan Ref. USA 2001 4v il set $415

Grades: 7 8 9 10 580

1. Botany 2. Plants

ISBN 0-02-865434-X LC 00-46064

This set covers "plant-related topics from acid rain to wood products. While this set includes complex information . . . it also offers basic facts on biomes, leaves, cells, individual scientists, related careers, and other subjects. The writing is clear and well organized, and depending on the topic, it's concise or very detailed." SLJ

580.7 Plants--Education, research, related topics

Gardner, Robert, 1929-

Science projects about plants. Enslow Pubs. 1999 112p il (Science projects) lib bdg $26.60

Grades: 7 8 9 10 580.7

1. Plants 2. Science projects 3. Science—Experiments

ISBN 0-89490-952-5 LC 98-6821

Provides instructions for over thirty experiments appropriate for science fairs, involving plant physiology, reproduction, and growth

"The book offers solid ideas for projects." Booklist

Includes bibliographical references

582.13 Plants noted for their flowers

Burger, William C., 1932-
Flowers: how they changed the world. Prometheus Books 2006 337p il $23
Grades: 11 12 Adult   **582.13**
1. Flowers
ISBN 1-59102-407-2; 978-1-59102-407-1
LC 2006-2739
This book "begins with basic facts about the morphology and physiology of plant growth and concludes by explaining how plants have played a major role in creating the modern world." Sci Books Films
This is "an engaging and beautifully written look at how flowering plants, over more than 100 million years, have 'transformed terrestrial ecosystems, supported the origin of primates, and helped us humans become the masters of our planet.'" Publ Wkly
Includes bibliographical references

Spellenberg, Richard
Familiar flowers of North America: eastern region; Ann H. Whitman, editor. Knopf 1986 192p il pa $9
Grades: 11 12 Adult   **582.13**
1. Wild flowers
ISBN 0-394-74843-3   LC 86-045587
"Chanticleer Press editions. The Audubon Society pocket guides"
This guide to 80 eastern wildflowers is arranged by color and shape of the flower and includes color photos, drawings, and descriptions of the plants habitat and range, folklore and history

Familiar flowers of North America: western region; Ann H. Whitman, editor. Knopf 1986 192p il pa $4.95
Grades: 11 12 Adult   **582.13**
1. Wild flowers
ISBN 0-394-74844-1   LC 86-045586
"Chanticleer Press editions. The Audubon Society pocket guides"
Eighty "color plates, arranged by the color and shape of the flower, fill the main section of this truly pocket-size field guide. Each entry also includes a line drawing, a description of the plant's habitat and range, and a paragraph explaining its place among other flowers and its folklore or history. . . . Appendices include a brief glossary and an alphabetic and a family index." BAYA Book Rev

National Audubon Society field guide to North American wildflowers, western region. 2nd ed rev. Knopf 2001 862p il map $19.95 *
Grades: 7 8 9 10 11 12 Adult   **582.13**
1. Wild flowers
ISBN 0-375-40233-0   LC 2001-269242
"A Chanticleer Press edition"
First published 1979
"More than 940 . . . full-color images show the wildflowers of western North America close-up and in

their natural habitats. . . . Images are grouped by flower color and shape and keyed to . . . descriptions that reflect current taxonomy." Publisher's note

Thieret, John W., 1926-2005
National Audubon Society field guide to North American wildflowers: eastern region; revising author, John W. Thieret; original authors, William A. Niering and Nancy C. Olmstead. Knopf 2001 879p il map (National Audubon Society field guide series) $19.95 *
Grades: 7 8 9 10 11 12 Adult   **582.13**
1. Wild flowers
ISBN 0-375-40232-2   LC 2001-269241
"A Chanticleer Press edition"
First published 1979 under the authorship of William A. Niering and Nancy C. Olmstead
Spine title: Field guide to wildflowers, eastern region
"Covers the area east of the Rockies and east of the Big Bend area of Texas to the Atlantic. Color photographs together with family and species descriptions make this a most useful field guide." Sci News {review of 1979 edition}

582.16 Trees

Benvie, Sam
The encyclopedia of North American trees. Firefly Bks. (Buffalo) 2000 304p il maps pa $24.95 hardcover o.p. *
Grades: 11 12 Adult   **582.16**
1. Trees—North America
ISBN 1-55297-641-6 (pa)   LC 2001-521107
In this tree encyclopedia the species "are listed alphabetically by Latin name with the common name given in dark print at the top of the entry as well as on the top of the right-hand page. Each species is described in a page or less. . . . For the most common trees, a box lists key features. . . . Additional larger boxes provide a detailed history of the species and line drawings of the leaves, buds, and flowers." Booklist
Includes bibliographical references

Familiar trees of North America: eastern region; Ann H. Whitman, editor; Jerry F. Franklin, John Farrand, Jr., consultants. Knopf 1986 192p il pa $9
Grades: 11 12 Adult   **582.16**
1. Trees—North America
ISBN 0-394-74851-4   LC 86-045585
"Chanticleer Press editions. The Audubon Society pocket guides"
This pocket field guide covers eighty trees commonly found in the eastern United States. Includes color photos and descriptions of characteristics, habitat, range, history, and uses

Familiar trees of North America: western region;
Ann H. Whitman, editor; Jerry F. Franklin, John
Farrand, Jr., consultants. Knopf 1986 192p il pa
$9

Grades: 11 12 Adult   **582.16**
1. Trees—North America
ISBN 0-394-74852-2   LC 86-045584
"Chanticleer Press editions. The Audubon Society
pocket guides"

This pocket field guide covers eighty trees commonly
found in the western United States. "Each color plate is
accompanied by a black silhouette of the tree and a
small photo of its bark as well as a written description
of its characteristics, its habitat and range, and its history
and uses. . . . Introductory essays and illustrations provide a key to tree identification. Appendices include descriptions of tree families and an index to common and
botanical names." BAYA Book Rev

Firefly Encyclopedia of trees; edited by Stephen
Cafferty. Firefly Books 2005 288p il map
$49.95 *

Grades: 11 12 Adult   **582.16**
1. Trees
ISBN 1-55407-051-1
"Delineating the principle genera of trees, from primeval cycads to ancient conifers, deciduous broadleaves to
tropical tree ferns, the compendium augments its . . .
background on the horticultural, ornamental, and economic significance of each species with . . . sidebars
and distribution maps, as well as . . . [color photographs
and] illustrations." Booklist

Includes bibliographical references

Plotnik, Arthur, 1937-
The urban tree book; an uncommon field guide
for city and town; {by} Arthur Plotnik; in
consultation with the Morton Arboretum;
illustrated by Mary H. Phelan. Three Rivers Press
(NY) 2000 432p il pa $18.95 *

Grades: 11 12 Adult   **582.16**
1. Trees—United States
ISBN 0-8129-3103-3   LC 99-42452
An inquiry into the characteristics and survival strategies of nearly 200 species of trees

The author "expresses his sense of wonder about urban trees found all over the U.S. with warmth and wit
as he recounts their history and lore and medicinal and
spiritual legacies. . . . Plotnik also celebrates landmark
trees, assesses the new urban forestry movement, and
provides a wealth of useful resources." Booklist

Includes bibliographical references

Reader's Digest North American wildlife, trees
and nonflowering plants. Reader's Digest Assn.
1998 269p il $17.95

Grades: 9 10 11 12   **582.16**
1. Trees—North America
ISBN 0-7621-0037-0   LC 97-32725
Contains material originally published in 1982 in the
Readers Digest book, North American wildlife

This explains how to identify trees by examining their
leaves, bark, flowers, fruits and shapes and includes a
survey of such non-flowering plants as ferns, mosses, liv-
erworts, and lichen

590   Animals

Dinerstein, Eric, 1952-
Tigerland and other unintended destinations.
Island Press 2005 279p $25.95; pa $16.95 *
Grades: 9 10 11 12   **590**
1. Ecology 2. Nature conservation
ISBN 1-55963-578-9; 1-59726-152-1 (pa)
    LC 2005-13822
This book "takes readers on Dinerstein's unlikely jour-
ney to conservation's frontiers, from early research in
Nepal to recent expeditions as head of Conservation Sci-
ence at the World Wildlife Fund." Publisher's note

The author's "compelling tour of wild places and his
vivid portraits of intrepid wildlife defenders offer convincing arguments for providing the treasures of nature
with the same reverence and protection we accord cherished works of art." Booklist

Noyes, Deborah, 1965-
One kingdom; our lives with animals—the
human-animal bond in myth, history, science, and
story. Houghton Mifflin Company 2006 128p il
$18

Grades: 7 8 9 10   **590**
1. Animals
ISBN 0-618-49914-8   LC 2005-25446
In this "photo-essay, Noyes examines the ways that
human lives have overlapped with animals and how our
beliefs, culture, and science have been impacted throught
history by the essential but frequently paradoxical human-animal connection. . . . Readers will find the provocative questions Noyes raises compelling and challenging, and the lyrical, urgent prose, along with beautiful
black-and- white photos of the animals up close, will
draw serious students and browsers alike." Booklist

Includes bibliographical references

590.3   Animals--Encyclopedias and dictionaries

Animal sciences; Allan B. Cobb, editor in chief.
Macmillan Ref. USA 2002 4v il (Macmillan
science library) set $395 *

Grades: 11 12 Adult   **590.3**
1. Animals—Encyclopedias
ISBN 0-02-865556-7   LC 2001-26627
This "work contains approximately 300 signed entries
on a variety of topics relating to animal science, including animal development, functions, behavior, ecology,
and evolution. The connection between animals and humans is also explored. . . . Also included are biographies of noted scientists who have made 'significant contributions' to the field. . . . Articles appear in alphabetical order and range in length from several paragraphs to
several pages. . . . Articles are clear and well written,
and the appealing layout includes many colorful photographs, diagrams, and sidebars. . . . This set contains
sufficient information to serve the needs of a variety of
student users and will appeal to the casual browser as
well." Booklist

The **encyclopedia** of animals; a complete visual guide; [text, Jenni Bruce . . . et al.] University of California Press 2004 608p il map $39.95 *
Grades: 9 10 11 12   **590.3**
1. Animals—Encyclopedias
ISBN 0-520-24406-0   LC 2004-303646
"The book starts with an introduction to animal evolution, biology, behavior, classification, habitats, and current conservation issues. This is followed by a survey of animals, divided into the standard taxonomic classifications of mammals, birds, reptiles, amphibians, fishes, and invertebrates. . . . Icons and symbols indicate habitat, size, weight, and social and reproductive habits of the various species." Libr J
"This lavishly illustrated chronicle of Earth's biodiversity is a visual delight." Booklist

Grzimek's animal life encyclopedia. 2nd ed. Gale Group 2003 17v il maps set $1,750
Grades: 11 12 Adult   **590.3**
1. Zoology—Encyclopedias
ISBN 0-7876-5362-4   LC 2002-3351
Original German edition, 1968; first English language edition published 1972-1975 by Van Nostrand Reinhold
Contents: v1 Lower metazoans and lesser deuterosomes; v2 Protostomes; v3 Insects; v4-5 Fishes I-II; v6 Amphibians; v7 Reptiles; v8-11 Birds I-IV; v12-16 Mammals I-V; v17 Cumulative index
"Even after 30 years, the original *Grzimek's* is still considered a core title for reference collections. Biologists and nonbiologists alike will appreciate the excellent organization, well-written text, and beautiful illustrations. . . . Highly recommended for all types of libraries." Libr J
Includes bibliographical references

Magill's encyclopedia of science: animal life; editor, Carl W. Hoagstrom. Salem Press 2002 4v il set $435
Grades: 11 12 Adult   **590.3**
1. Zoology—Encyclopedias
ISBN 1-58765-019-3   LC 2001-49799
This "is a major revision and update of the six-volume *Magill's Survey of Science: Life Science*, published in 1991. . . . There are 385 signed main entries, ranging in length from 1000 to 3000 words each. . . . The entries cover a wide variety of topics related to animal life and include articles on subjects such as biodiversity and defense mechanisms as well as those on specific species or individual animals. Each entry begins with ready-reference information and a list of principal terms with definitions." Libr J
Includes bibliographical references

590.7   Animals--Education, research, related topics

Dashefsky, H. Steven
Zoology: high school science fair experiments. TAB Bks. 1995 145p il pa $12.95 hardcover o.p.
Grades: 9 10 11 12   **590.7**
1. Zoology 2. Science projects 3. Science—Experiments
ISBN 0-07-015687-5 (pa)   LC 94-29631

"Dashefsky offers 20 experiments about human and nonhuman form of life. . . . Helpful chapters on the scientific method, zoology basics, and research tips set the stage nicely for the experiments, which fall into four categories: people-related, biocides, animal lives, and animals and the environment." Booklist
Includes glossary and bibliographical references

590.73   Collections and exhibits of living animals

Hancocks, David
A different nature; the paradoxical world of zoos and their uncertain future. University of Calif. Press 2001 xxii, 279p il hardcover o.p. pa $21.95 *
Grades: 11 12 Adult   **590.73**
1. Zoos
ISBN 0-520-21879-5; 0-520-23676-9 (pa)
                                          LC 00-53209
The author discusses the history of zoos and their current status. He "questions the ongoing role of zoos as places for recreation, research, conservation, and education. He believes they can become much more if designed well and turned into conservation centers." Christ Sci Monit
Includes bibliographical references

Robinson, Phillip T.
Life at the zoo: behind the scenes with the animal doctors. Columbia University Press 2004 293p il $27.95; pa $17.95 *
Grades: 11 12 Adult   **590.73**
1. Zoos
ISBN 0-231-13248-4; 0-231-13249-2 (pa)
                                          LC 2004-43893
A "look at how animal exhibits are designed, how the animals are cared for, and how illness is detected in animals that want to hide any weakness." Booklist
"It would be difficult to cover even one aspect, such as animal health, that might affect the overall management of a zoo, but Dr. Philip Robinson manages to provide an excellent coverage of just about everything that might be involved in the operation of a zoo." Sci Books Films
Includes bibliographical references

591.3   Genetics, evolution, young of animals

Arthur, Wallace
Creatures of accident; the rise of the animal kingdom. Hill & Wang 2006 255p $25
Grades: 11 12 Adult   **591.3**
1. Natural selection 2. Evolution
ISBN 0-8090-4321-1; 978-0-8090-4321-7
                                          LC 2005-33540
The author "advances the argument that the process [of the evolution of life] tends toward greater complexity

Arthur, Wallace—*Continued*

over time. . . . Arthur sketches out the main structural attributes of complexity in animals, from the cell to organs to embryology to body forms, and when they appeared. . . . Championing naturalistic clarity, Arthur's precision about the processes of evolution will benefit serious students of the topic." Booklist

Includes bibliographical references

O'Brien, Stephen J.

Tears of the cheetah; and other tales from the genetic frontier; foreword by Ernst Mayr. St. Martin's Press 2003 287p il $25.95; pa $14.95

Grades: 11 12 Adult   **591.3**

1. Genetics 2. Endangered species

ISBN 0-312-27286-3; 0-312-33900-3 (pa)

LC 2003-53164

The author discusses the genetic "histories of exotic species such as Indonesian orangutans, humpback whales, and the imperiled cheetah. . . . Among these genetic detective stories we also discover how the Serengeti lions have lived with FIV (the feline version of HIV), where giant pandas really come from, how bold genetic action pulled the Florida panther from the edge of extinction, how the survivors of the medieval Black Death passed on a genetic gift to their descendents, and how mapping the genome of the domestic cat solved a murder case in Canada." Publisher's note

"O'Brien's exploration of the genetic landscape of a particular species is marvelously revelatory of its history . . . . Molecular biology *can* be difficult to absorb, but not when a clear expositor such as O'Brien has such good stories to tell." Booklist

Includes bibliographical references

591.5   Behavior

Crump, Martha L.

Headless males make great lovers; & other unusual natural histories; [by] Marty Crump; with illustrations by Alan Crump. University of Chicago Press 2005 199p il $25; pa $14 *

Grades: 11 12 Adult   **591.5**

1. Animal behavior

ISBN 0-226-12199-2; 0-226-12202-6 (pa)

LC 2005-7592

"The author draws upon her own observations of nature, and on the scientific literature, to reveal how animals mate, parent, feed, defend, and communicate among themselves in unusual ways." Choice

"Illustrated throughout with line drawings, and bolstered with a chapter-by-chapter list of references, this marvelous introduction to the whys and wherefores of animal behavior will find an audience in all libraries." Booklist

Includes bibliographical references

Encyclopedia of animal behavior; edited by Marc Bekoff; foreword by Jane Goodall. Greenwood Press 2004 3v il set $349.95

Grades: 11 12 Adult   **591.5**

1. Animal behavior

ISBN 0-313-32745-9   LC 2004-56073

This encyclopedia describes "what makes animals tick using techniques that range from molecular approaches to analysis of species. The 300 entries, some stretching to 7000 words, discuss topics as diverse as concept learning in pigeons and stress in dolphins." Libr J

Includes bibliographical references

Grandin, Temple

Animals in translation; using the mysteries of autism to decode animal behavior; [by] Temple Grandin and Catherine Johnson. Scribner 2005 356p $25; pa $15 *

Grades: 11 12 Adult   **591.5**

1. Animal behavior 2. Autism

ISBN 0-7432-4769-8; 0-15-603144-2 (pa)

LC 2004-58498

Also available in paperback from Harvest Books

The author contends "that her autistic sensory perceptions (in particular, her intense focus on visual details) enable her to take in the world as animals do. In fact, she argues that autistic people and animals are essentially alike—they see, feel and think in remarkably similar ways." N Y Times Book Rev

"This fascinating book will teach readers to see as animals see, to be a little more visual and a little less verbal, and, as a unique analysis of animal behavior, it belongs in all libraries." Booklist

Includes bibliographical references

Grice, Gordon, 1944-

The red hourglass; lives of the predators. Delacorte Press 1998 259p pa $19 hardcover o.p.

Grades: 11 12 Adult   **591.5**

1. Predatory animals 2. Poisonous animals

ISBN 0-385-31890-1 (pa)   LC 97-41544

"This collection of seven essays examines several smaller predators, including black widows ('the red hourglass'), tarantulas, mantids, brown recluse spiders, and rattlesnakes. . . . Two essays about larger predators, the pig and the 'canid,' are [also included]." Libr J

"This book will delight those interested in either animals or literature." Booklist

McCarthy, Susan

Becoming a tiger; how baby animals learn to live in the wild. HarperCollins 2004 418p hardcover o.p. pa $13.95

Grades: 11 12 Adult   **591.5**

1. Animal intelligence

ISBN 0-06-620924-2; 0-06-093484-0 (pa)

LC 2003-67553

The author examines "the ways that animals figure out how to function in their worlds. . . . One of the basic things a baby animal must learn is how to get from one place to another in a manner appropriate to its species. Other basics involve learning to recognize your own species, to communicate, to find food, and *not* to become some other species' food. McCarthy discusses species as various as horses, bonobos, zebra finches, and fruit-fly maggots to illustrate the learning process." Booklist

"McCarthy writes clearly and her penchant for humor . . . makes the book an easy read, both for students of

McCarthy, Susan—*Continued*
learning and those who can't get enough of television's *Animal Planet*." Publ Wkly
Includes bibliographical references

McDougall, Len
The complete tracker; tracks, signs, and habits of North American wildlife. Lyons & Burford 1997 273p il maps pa $14.95 *
Grades: 11 12 Adult   **591.5**
1. Animal tracks 2. Animal behavior
ISBN 1-55821-458-5   LC 96-37815
This book "provides detailed information on: habitat and range, foods, mating habits, seasonal habits, tracks, scat, signs, and vocalizations. A brief section provides basic advice on how to equip yourself, track, stalk, read sign, and, once found, observe the animals. . . . This field guide is very useful and engagingly written." Libr J

591.59   Animal communication

Friend, Tim
Animal talk; breaking the codes of animal language. Free Press 2004 274p il $25; pa $15 *
Grades: 11 12 Adult   **591.59**
1. Animal communication
ISBN 0-7432-0157-4; 0-7432-0158-2 (pa)
                                        LC 2003-63107
"The author describes the methods of, and reasons behind, animal communication and demonstrates that human and animal communication are not so widely disparate as once believed. Friend also gives background details on the basics of communication theory, genetics, evolution, and the progression of scientific thought regarding animal communication. . . . His humorous and engaging prose style makes this a captivating read." Libr J
Includes bibliographical references

591.6   Miscellaneous nontaxonomic kinds of animals

Bachleda, F. Lynne, 1951-
Dangerous wildlife in California & Nevada; a guide to safe encounters at home and in the wild. Menasha Ridge Press 2002 306p il map pa $22.95
Grades: 9 10 11 12   **591.6**
1. Dangerous animals 2. Poisonous plants
ISBN 0-89732-536-2   LC 2002-24431
Third volume of a projected nine volume set on dangerous animals begun with Dangerous wildlife in the Southeast
This "reference describes which creatures and plants can cause you harm—and when, why, and how to avoid them—in California and Nevada." Publisher's note
Includes bibliographical references

Dangerous wildlife in the mid-Atlantic; a guide to safe encounters at home and in the wild. Menasha Ridge Press 2001 305p il map pa $22.95
Grades: 9 10 11 12   **591.6**
1. Dangerous animals 2. Poisonous plants
ISBN 0-89732-406-4   LC 2001-54360
Second volume in a projected nine volume set on dangerous wildlife begun with Dangerous wildlife in the Southeast
This "reference describes which creatures and plants can cause you harm and when, why, and how to avoid them—in Delaware, Maryland, New Jersey, New York, Pennsylvania, Virginia, and West Virginia." Publisher's note
Includes bibliographical references

Dangerous wildlife in the Southeast; a guide to safe encounters at home and in the wild. Menasha Ridge Press 2001 321p il map pa $22.95
Grades: 9 10 11 12   **591.6**
1. Dangerous animals 2. Poisonous plants
ISBN 0-89732-335-1   LC 2001-30874
First volume of a projected nine volume set on dangerous wildlife
Each section of "this volume on the dangerous reptiles and amphibians, insects and arachnids, mammals, plants, and seashore creatures of the Southeast . . . includes general natural history information on the particular type of wildlife; an in-depth explanation of how the animal or plant is dangerous; tips on identification, first aid, and avoidance; and a description of each of the dangerous species of that type of wildlife found in the region. . . . The writing is suffused with humor, anecdotes abound, and the illustrations and photos are excellent." Libr J
Includes bibliographical references

591.7   Animal ecology, animals characteristic of specific environments

Couturier, Lisa, 1962-
The hopes of snakes; and other tales from the urban landscape. Beacon Press 2005 159p $23; pa $14
Grades: 9 10 11 12   **591.7**
1. Urban ecology 2. Wildlife
ISBN 0-8070-8564-2; 0-8070-8565-0 (pa)
                                        LC 2004-15081
The essays in this collection, "ranging in time from . . . [the author's] childhood to that of her young daughter's, are based on a multitude of experiences with wildlife, chiefly in the New York City metropolitan area and in Washington, D.C. and its suburbs. Teens will be encouraged by these stand-alone essays to study the world around them." SLJ

Hoyt, Erich, 1950-
Creatures of the deep; in search of the sea's "monsters" and the world they live in. Firefly Bks. 2001 160p il map $40
Grades: 9 10 11 12   **591.7**
1. Marine animals
ISBN 1-55209-340-9   LC 2003-389055

Hoyt, Erich, 1950-—*Continued*
"The book is divided into three parts. The first discusses ocean layers from surface to the deepest level and the unusual animals that inhabit them. Part two examines the food chain, with emphasis on the giant predators, although the phytoplankton and copepods that feed myriad creatures from giant whales and sharks to smaller animals are included. Part three looks at the great ridges and trenches that make the oceans as diverse geologically as the land." Voice Youth Advocates

"Startling facts abound, and Hoyt's enthusiasm for his subject shows on every page." Publ Wkly

Includes bibliographical references

Naskrecki, Piotr
The smaller majority; the hidden world of the animals that dominate the tropics. Belknap Press of Harvard University Press 2005 278p il $35
Grades: 11 12 Adult   **591.7**
1. Invertebrates 2. Animals—Pictorial works
3. Tropics
ISBN 0-674-01915-6; 978-0-674-01915-7
                                   LC 2005-46060
In this book the author "includes over 400 . . . full-color photographs of animals that are generally smaller than the human finger. The author . . . [has] collected images of animals from Costa Rica, Guinea, the Dominical Republic, the Solomon Islands, Australia, South Africa, Botswana, and Namibia." Choice

"Naskrecki's exuberant, expert knowledge of this microscopic world has been distilled down to the most arresting details. Crisp, enjoyable prose, clearly explains complex biological processes." Publ Wkly

Includes bibliographical references

591.9 Treatment of animals by continents, countries, localities

The **new** encyclopedia of aquatic life. Facts on File 2005 2v il map (Facts on File natural science library) set $150 *
Grades: 9 10 11 12   **591.9**
1. Marine animals 2. Freshwater animals
ISBN 0-8160-5119-4
First published 1985 under the editorship of Keith Banister and Andrew Campbell with title: The encyclopedia of aquatic life

This book "examines the behavior, ecology, and evolution of all fish and invertebrate groups living in Earth's waters." Publisher's note

Includes bibliographical references

592 Invertebrates

Attenborough, David, 1926-
Life in the undergrowth. Princeton University Press 2006 288p il $29.95
Grades: 11 12 Adult   **592**
1. Invertebrates
ISBN 0-691-12703-4   LC 2005-934727

The author "explores the lives of the planet's land-based invertebrates. Concentrating mainly on insects and spiders, the author investigates all aspects of the animals' life cycles." Booklist

"This wonderful exploration of invertebrates exceeds the requirements for a great nature book through the strength of its photographs and the quality of its prose." Publ Wkly

Barrow, Lloyd H.
Science fair projects investigating earthworms. Enslow Pubs. 2000 104p (Science fair success) lib bdg $20.95
Grades: 9 10 11 12   **592**
1. Worms 2. Science projects 3. Science—Experiments
ISBN 0-7660-1291-3   LC 99-36381
Presents experiments, suitable for science fairs, that explore the structure, function, movement, preferences, and reactions of earthworms
Includes bibliographical references

Petersen, Christine
Invertebrates. Watts 2002 128p il $24
Grades: 9 10 11 12   **592**
1. Invertebrates
ISBN 0-531-12021-X   LC 2001-3031
A close look at past and present invertebrates, including sponges, jellies, worms, mollusks, and arthropods
The text is "concisely written, logically organized, and relatively free of scientific jargon." Booklist
Includes glossary and bibliographical references

Stewart, Amy, 1969-
The earth moved; on the remarkable achievements of earthworms. Algonquin Bks. 2004 223p $23.95; pa $12.95
Grades: 11 12 Adult   **592**
1. Worms
ISBN 1-565-12337-9; 1-565-12468-5 (pa)
                                   LC 2003-52379
The author explores "the impact worms have on humans and on our planet. . . . {She} educates on the vital roles these creatures play in growing crops, how they can neutralize the effects of nuclear waste on soil, and their ability to regenerate new body parts. . . . A book that's as enlightening as it is entertaining." SLJ
Includes bibliographical references

595.7 Insects

Arnett, Ross H., Jr.
Simon and Schuster's guide to insects; by Ross H. Arnett, Jr., and Richard L. Jacques, Jr. Simon & Schuster 1981 511p il pa $17 hardcover o.p. *
Grades: 11 12 Adult   **595.7**
1. Insects
ISBN 0-671-25014-0 (pa)   LC 80-29485
"A Fireside book"
This field guide identifies 350 insect species found in North America. Entries include information about the

Arnett, Ross H., Jr.—*Continued*
habits and biology of each species, as well as the scientific and common names of the species and its impact on the environment. Also included is a history of the study of insects, and instructions for collecting insects.
Includes glossary

Brock, James P.
Kaufman field guide to butterflies of North America; [by] Jim P. Brock and Kenn Kaufman; with the collaboration of Rick and Nora Bowers and Lynn Hassler. Houghton Mifflin 2006 c2003 391p il map pa $19.95 *
Grades: 11 12 Adult   595.7
1. Butterflies
ISBN 0-618-76826-2; 978-0-618-76826-4
LC 2006-287515
First published 2003 with title: Butterflies of North America
"Each species is listed by common name and scientific name and receives a several-sentence description, including flight time and larval food plants. All except very local or accidental species also are shown on range maps. The illustrations are opposite the written description, with most species pictured in multiple images. . . . The illustrations are created by digital enhancement of photographs. . . . An essential purchase for all libraries." Booklist [review of 2003 edition]

Capinera, John L.
Field guide to grasshoppers, crickets, and katydids of the United States; [by] John L. Capinera, Ralph D. Scott, and Thomas J. Walker. Cornell University Press 2004 249p il maps hardcover o.p. pa $29.95 *
Grades: 11 12 Adult   595.7
1. Grasshoppers 2. Crickets
ISBN 0-8014-4260-5; 0-8014-8948-2 (pa)
LC 2004-10727
This "field guide to U.S. and Canadian orthoptera introduces 206 of the most common species. . . . It explains classification, morphology (illustrated), biology, sound production, and collection and preservation, and presents pictorial keys to families and subfamilies." Libr J
"The highlight is certainly the 50 pages of Scott's color illustrations. . . . For those who want to know what's plaguing them when locusts descend, this is the book." Publ Wkly
Includes bibliographical references

Eisner, Thomas
For love of insects. Belknap Press of Harvard University Press 2003 448p il $35; pa $19.95
Grades: 11 12 Adult   595.7
1. Insects
ISBN 0-674-01181-3; 0-674-01827-3 (pa)
LC 2003-44399
"Ranging from a caterpillar who feeds on flowers while disguising as one by affixing petals to his back, to a beetle who can resist a pull 200 times his own weight, the book is full of little known information about how

insects feed, fight, and reproduce." Univ Press Books for Public and Second Sch Libr, 2006
Includes bibliographical references

Secret weapons; defenses of insects, spiders, scorpions, and other many-legged creatures; [by] Thomas Eisner, Maria Eisner, Melody V.S. Siegler. Belknap Press of Harvard University Press 2005 372p il $29.95; pa $18.95
Grades: 11 12 Adult   595.7
1. Animal defenses 2. Insects 3. Spiders
ISBN 0-674-01882-6; 0-674-02403-6 (pa)
LC 2005-41042
"This volume presents 69 case studies of organisms from 4 orders of spiders, 2 of centipedes, 5 of millipedes, and 10 of insects. Most of the studies address defensive chemistry and identify the chemical(s) involved, how each is acquired, stored, and deployed." Sci Books Films
"This very readable and well-illustrated book will appeal to all those interested in disciplines like biology, entomology, and ecology." Choice
Includes bibliographical references

Ellis, Hattie, 1967-
Sweetness & light; the mysterious history of the honeybee. Harmony Books 2004 243p il hardcover o.p. pa $13.95
Grades: 11 12 Adult   595.7
1. Bees 2. Beekeeping
ISBN 1-400-05405-2; 1-400-05406-0 (pa)
LC 2004-4116
The author tells the story of the bee in human history, "from Stone Age honey hunters to modern-day hives on the rooftops of New York City." Publisher's note
"What a delightful volume on the honeybee this is: Not only is the reader treated to a wealth of information on the biology, ecology, and economic importance of that insect, but the interrelationship of the honeybee and humanity throughout history is very nicely presented." Sci Books Films
Includes bibliographical references

The **Firefly** encyclopedia of insects and spiders; edited by Christopher O'Toole. Firefly Bks. 2002 240p il $40 *
Grades: 11 12 Adult   595.7
1. Insects 2. Spiders
ISBN 1-55297-612-2
First published 1986 by Facts on File with title: The Encyclopedia of insects
This work "treats all the major taxonomic groups of arthropods except for the marine groups. The 28 orders of insects are all given separate treatment, as well as millipedes, centipedes, and arachnids. The work focuses in fascinating detail on behavior, morphology, ecology, life cycles, and economic or medical importance. Strikingly beautiful photographs of arthropods around the world supplement drawings that illustrate specific features. Separate essays discuss topics such as flight, pheromones and mating, mimicry, and social life. . . . There is no rival encyclopedia." Choice

Halpern, Sue M.

Four wings and a prayer; caught in the mystery of the monarch butterflies; [by] Sue Halpern. Pantheon Bks. 2001 212p il maps pa $13 hardcover o.p.

Grades: 11 12 Adult 595.7

1. Monarch butterflies

ISBN 0-375-70194-X (pa) LC 00-51055

Halpern discusses her experiences studying the migration of monarch butterflies. "She spends much of her time assisting Bill Calvert, a . . . field biologist, as they drive through rural Mexico tagging, weighing, and counting butterflies." Christ Sci Monit

Marshall, Stephen A.

Insects: their natural history and diversity; with a photographic guide to insects of eastern North America. Firefly Books 2006 718p il $95 *

Grades: 11 12 Adult 595.7

1. Insects

ISBN 978-1-55297-900-6; 1-55297-900-8
LC 2006-389462

This "offers more than 4000 excellent color photographs and concise, accurate information about every major insect family worldwide. . . . This book is simply bigger, prettier, and more comprehensive than any previous publication on insects and will be useful to amateur and professional alike." Libr J

Includes bibliographical references

Pyle, Robert Michael

The Audubon Society field guide to North American butterflies; visual key by Carol Nehring and Jane Opper. Knopf 1981 916p il $19.95

Grades: 7 8 9 10 11 12 Adult 595.7

1. Butterflies

ISBN 0-394-51914-0 LC 80-84240

"A Chanticleer Press edition. The Audubon Society field guide series"

This guide "introduces more than 600 species of North American butterfly, including those native to the Hawaiian Islands. A section of brilliant color plates (more than 1,000 of them) featuring butterflies in their natural habitats, follows a general introduction and notes on text organization and use." Booklist

Sbordoni, Valerio

Butterflies of the world; {by} Valerio Sbordoni, and Saverio Forestiero. Firefly Bks. (Buffalo) 1998 c1985 312p il maps $45 *

Grades: 11 12 Adult 595.7

1. Butterflies

ISBN 1-55209-210-0

This is a reissue of the edition published 1985 by Times Books

This is an illustrated reference on "butterflies (and some moths) and their evolution, anatomy, physiology, and ecology. . . . The information has been synthesized and presented in logical groupings with beautifully rendered illustrations. . . . The narrative combines good science with good science writing." Booklist

Includes bibliographical references

Schappert, Phil, 1956-

The last Monarch butterfly; conserving the Monarch butterfly in a brave new world. Firefly Books 2004 113p il pa $19.95

Grades: 11 12 Adult 595.7

1. Monarch butterflies 2. Wildlife conservation

ISBN 1-55297-969-5 (pa) LC 2005-357220

"Firefly Books"

Overview of both eastern and western monarch butterflies, including their life cycle and migratory patterns. The impact of natural disasters and increasing residential and industrial development on monarch butterfly populations is also discussed.

"The narrative is enhanced by beautiful photographs and backed up by some 180 references to the scientific literature. . . . Let's hear it for the monarch, an amazing insect; if the reader has any doubts about that, this book will put them to rest." Sci Books Films

Waldbauer, Gilbert

Millions of monarchs, bunches of beetles; how bugs find strength in numbers. Harvard Univ. Press 2000 264p il $27.50; pa $16.95

Grades: 11 12 Adult 595.7

1. Insects

ISBN 0-674-00090-0; 0-674-00686-0 (pa)
LC 99-42453

The author "examines many of the reasons that insects form groups. . . . Insects come together for a host of reasons, Waldbauer explains: to find mates, to avoid predators, to enhance their food-gathering abilities, to manipulate their environment and to subdue prey. In each case, Waldbauer provides evocative descriptions of particular species' behaviors while discussing the underlying evolutionary reasons for that behavior." Publ Wkly

Includes bibliographical references

A walk around the pond; insects in and over the water. Harvard University Press 2006 286p il $22.95

Grades: 11 12 Adult 595.7

1. Insects 2. Freshwater animals

ISBN 0-674-02211-4 LC 2005-44737

The author "introduces us to the aquatic insects that have colonized ponds, lakes, streams, and rivers, especially those in North America." Publisher's note

"Readers will be inspired to take a closer look at their favorite pond or stream." Booklist

Includes bibliographical references

What good are bugs? insects in the web of life. Harvard University Press 2003 384p il $29.95; pa $17.50

Grades: 11 12 Adult 595.7

1. Insects

ISBN 0-674-01027-2; 0-674-01632-7 (pa)
LC 2002-27335

The author "instructs readers on the major roles insects play. He provides . . . examples for every aspect of insect ecology he discusses, sprinkling reports from the scientific literature with personal anecdotes from his many years of research." Booklist

This "is an excellent work about the beneficial insects, that vast majority of insect species of which we are gen-

Waldbauer, Gilbert—*Continued*
erally unaware. . . . The author is an excellent writer and provides many interesting examples." Choice
Includes bibliographical references

596 Chordates

Petersen, Christine
Vertebrates. Watts 2002 128p il $24
Grades: 9 10 11 12   **596**
1. Vertebrates
ISBN 0-531-12020-1   LC 2001-3032
A close look at past and present vertebrates, including fish, birds, amphibians, reptiles, and mammals
The text is "concisely written, logically organized, and relatively free of scientific jargon." Booklist
Includes glossary and bibliographical references

597 Cold-blooded vertebrates. Fishes

Allen, Thomas B., 1929-
The shark almanac. Lyons Press 1999 274p il pa $19.95 hardcover o.p.
Grades: 11 12 Adult   **597**
1. Sharks
ISBN 1-584-74808-0 (pa)   LC 98-38524
The author "discusses the evolution, anatomy, and physiology of more than 100 shark species. A description and illustration of each family is presented, giving its common name, size, distribution, and degree of danger to humans. The same information is given for the related skates and rays. Detailed historical information on shark attacks, a list of shark avoidance rules, and an extensive bibliography are included." Libr J
Includes bibliographcial references

Benchley, Peter, 1940-2006
Shark trouble; true stories about sharks and the sea. Random House 2002 186p il hardcover o.p. pa $12.95
Grades: 11 12 Adult   **597**
1. Sharks 2. Marine animals
ISBN 0-375-50824-4; 0-8129-6633-3 (pa)
LC 2002-283533
"Benchley describes the many types of sharks (including the ones that pose a genuine threat to man), what is and isn't known about shark behavior, the odds against an attack and how to reduce them even further—all reinforced with the lessons he has learned, the mistakes he has made, and the personal perils he has encountered." Publisher's note
"Handy with statistics and quick to crack a joke with himself as the target, Benchley offers riveting accounts of his ups close and personal encounters with sharks, a gigantic manta ray, a friendly killer whale, barracuda, and sundry other wild creatures." Booklist

Capuzzo, Mike
Close to shore; a true story of terror in an age of innocence. Broadway Bks. 2001 317p map pa $14.95 hardcover o.p.
Grades: 11 12 Adult   **597**
1. Sharks 2. Animal attacks
ISBN 0-7679-0414-1 (pa)   LC 2001-25750
This describes a series of shark attacks in 1916 off the coast of New Jersey.
"A book full of adventure, mounting tension, some gore and excitement, and lots of history." SLJ
Includes bibliographical references

Compagno, Leonard J. V.
Sharks of the world; [by] Leonard Compagno, Marc Dando, Sarah Fowler. Princeton University Press 2005 368p il map (Princeton field guides) hardcover o.p. pa $29.95
Grades: 11 12 Adult   **597**
1. Sharks
ISBN 0-691-12071-4; 0-691-12072-2 (pa)
LC 2004-111901
First published in the United Kingdom with title: Field guide to the sharks of the world
The authors cover "over 450 species, including many as-yet-unnamed species and some that are only known from a single specimen. Each is illustrated with both a line drawing and a beautifully rendered color painting; in most cases a ventral view of the head and illustrations of the teeth are included. . . . Packed with information, this is an invaluable guide for anyone interested in this fascinating group." Choice
Includes bibliographical references

Ferrari, Andrea
Sharks; {by} Andrea and Antonella Ferrari; foreword by Doug Perrine. Firefly Bks. 2002 256p il pa $24.95 *
Grades: 11 12 Adult   **597**
1. Sharks
ISBN 1-55209-629-7   LC 2002-511486
Also available in paperback from Voyageur Press
Original Italian edition, 2000
Translated from the original Italian 2000 ed., Tutto squali, by Anna Bennett
"A guide to the appearance and behavior of 120 species of sharks and rays. . . . Illustrated with photographs of sharks and rays in their natural environment. Essays on history, biology, and ecology accompany the text." Publisher's note
"Perrine offers a spellbinding shark gallery." Booklist
Includes bibliographical references

Gilbert, Carter Rowell, 1930-
National Audubon Society field guide to fishes, North America; [by] Carter R. Gilbert, James D. Williams. rev ed, 2nd ed, fully rev. Alfred A. Knopf 2002 607p il maps pa $19.95 *
Grades: 6 7 8 9 10 11 12 Adult   **597**
1. Fishes—North America
ISBN 0-375-41224-7   LC 2002-20773
"A Chanticleer Press edition"

Gilbert, Carter Rowell, 1930-—_Continued_
First published 1983 with title: The Audubon Society field guide to North American fishes, whales, and dolphins

This guide covers over 600 freshwater and saltwater species in detail, with notes on 771 more species.

Page, Lawrence M.
A field guide to freshwater fishes: North America north of Mexico; {by} Lawrence M. Page, Brooks M. Burr; illustrations by Eugene C. Beckham III, John Parker Sherrod, Craig W. Ronto. Houghton Mifflin 1991 432p il maps pa $19 hardcover o.p. *
Grades: 7 8 9 10 11 12 Adult   597
1. Fishes—North America
ISBN 0-395-91091-9 (pa)   LC 90-42049
"The Peterson field guide series"
"Sponsored by the National Audubon Society, the National Wildlife Federation, and the Roger Tory Peterson Institute"
This guide "covers all 790 species known in North America north of Mexico. Over 700 illustrations, most in color, show identifying marks. Also includes 377 distribution maps and additional line drawings of key details." Publisher's note
Includes bibliographical references

Parker, Steve
The encyclopedia of sharks; [by] Steve and Jane Parker. Rev. ed. Firefly Books 2002 192p il pa $24.95
Grades: 9 10 11 12   597
1. Sharks—Encyclopedias
ISBN 1-55297-638-6   LC 2002-726873
First published 1999
The authors "discuss the evolution of sharks, their senses, internal organs, behavior, foods and feeding, and reproduction. Well illustrated with photographs, color drawings, maps, and diagrams, the text is basic yet informative in discussing sharks as a group." Booklist [review of 1999 edition]

Perrine, Doug
Sharks and rays of the world. Voyageur Press 1999 132p il hardcover o.p. pa $21.95
Grades: 9 10 11 12   597
1. Sharks 2. Rays (Fishes)
ISBN 0-89658-448-8; 0-89658-011-3 (pa)
LC 99-25791
Examines the natural history and evolution of various species of sharks and rays. Describes their physical characteristics, feeding, reproduction, and encounters with humans.
Includes bibliographical references

Schweid, Richard
Consider the eel. University of North Carolina Press 2002 181p il map $24.95
Grades: 11 12 Adult   597
1. Eels
ISBN 0-8078-2693-6   LC 2001-48067

Also available De Capo paperback edition
The author "tries to fill in the gaps in the eel's astonishing natural history and tie that to sketches of fishery traditions, folklore, literary excerpts and reportage. . . . Anyone with a curiosity about the sea will find Schweid's taste of the eel strangely appealing." Publ Wkly
Includes bibliographical references

Shark: stories of life and death from the world's most dangerous waters; edited by Nathaniel May. Thunder's Mouth Press 2002 298p il $17.95
Grades: 11 12 Adult   597
1. Sharks
ISBN 1-56025-397-5   LC 2002-18002
"An Adrenaline book"
This "is an anthology of excerpts from previously published books and articles, including Peter Benchley's Jaws, Eugenie Clark's Lady with a Spear, Ernest Hemingway's The Old Man and the Sea, and Jean-Michel Cousteau's Cousteau's Great White Shark. . . . The selections feature people being attacked by sharks or sharks being attacked by people." Libr J
"We emerge from this exciting anthology with a deeper appreciation not only of sharks but also of the men and women who devote their lives to them." Booklist
Includes bibliographical references

597.8   Amphibians

Beltz, Ellin
Frogs: inside their remarkable world. Firefly Books 2005 175p il $34.95
Grades: 11 12 Adult   597.8
1. Frogs 2. Toads
ISBN 1-55297-869-9   LC 2006-365517
The author "picture of the history of the frog, its anatomical makeup, its place in the natural world and the threats that are seriously reducing its numbers around the world." Publisher's note
"Beltz presents an entertaining and comprehensive introduction to the order Anura (frogs and toads)." Booklist
Includes bibliographical references

597.9   Reptiles

Badger, David
Lizards; a natural history of some uncommon creatures, extraordinary chameleons, iguanas, geckos, and more; text by David Badger; photography by John Netherton. Voyageur Press 2003 160p il $35; pa $21.95
Grades: 11 12 Adult   597.9
1. Lizards
ISBN 0-89658-520-4; 0-7603-2579-0 (pa)
LC 2002-12138
This describes the behavior and characteristics of more than 25 species of lizards including chameleons, geckos, skinks, anoles, iguanas, monitors, and Komodos, and in-

Badger, David—*Continued*
cludes folklore and quotes
"In a conversational tone, Badger lets the reader into the lizards' world. Their traits are amply illustrated by photographer Netherton's remarkable close-up pictures." Booklist
Includes bibliographical references

Conant, Roger, 1909-
A field guide to reptiles & amphibians; eastern and central North America; {by} Roger Conant and Joseph T. Collins; illustrated by Isabelle Hunt Conant and Tom R. Johnson. 3rd ed, expanded. Houghton Mifflin 1998 616p il maps (Peterson field guide series) $21
Grades: 11 12 Adult   597.9
1. Reptiles 2. Amphibians
ISBN 0-395-90452-8   LC 98-13622
First published 1958 with title: A field guide to reptiles and amphibians of the United States and Canada east of the 100th meridian
"Sponsored by the National Audubon Society, the National Wildlife Federation, and the Roger Tory Peterson Institute"
This guide describes 595 species and subspecies, featuring color photos, black and white drawings, and color distribution maps of reptiles and amphibians of the region. Also includes information on transporting live reptiles and amphibians
Includes bibliographical references

Peterson first guide to reptiles and amphibians; [by] Roger Conant, Robert C. Stebbins, Joseph T. Collins. Houghton Mifflin 1999 c1992 128p il pa $5.95 *
Grades: 9 10 11 12   597.9
1. Reptiles 2. Amphibians
ISBN 0-395-97195-0
First published 1992
On cover: A simplified field guide to the snakes, turtles, frogs, lizards, and other reptiles, and amphibians of North America
This is a guide to identification of reptile and amphibian species.
This is "easy to use. The information is accurate and easy to understand. . . . Useful for browsing as well as for identification in the field." Voice Youth Advocates

Discovery Channel reptiles & amphibians; an explore your world handbook. Discovery Bks. (NY) 2000 192p il maps pa $14.95
Grades: 9 10 11 12   597.9
1. Reptiles 2. Amphibians
ISBN 1-56331-839-3   LC 99-59155
This work examines defense mechanisms, camouflage, mimicry, and symbiosis. Suggestions for acquiring and caring for reptiles and amphibians are provided
Illustrations of common specimens are organized by biome, with a particularly good map of biomes of the world." Voice Youth Advocates

Firefly encyclopedia of reptiles and amphibians; edited by Tim Halliday and Kraig Adler. Firefly Bks. 2002 240p il maps $40 *
Grades: 11 12 Adult   597.9

1. Reptiles 2. Amphibians
ISBN 1-55297-613-0
First published 1986 by Facts on File with title: The Encyclopedia of reptiles and amphibians
This volume "presents information about evolution, form, function, distribution, diet, reproduction, development, locomotion, social behavior, and conservation of the various families of amphibians and reptiles. Special feature articles cover other important aspects of their lives, from vocal communication to play. . . . The book includes a glossary, a bibliography with Web sites, and an extensive index." Choice

597.92   Turtles

Davidson, Osha Gray
Fire in the turtle house; the green sea turtle and the fate of the ocean. PublicAffairs 2001 258p il hardcover o.p. pa $15
Grades: 11 12 Adult   597.92
1. Sea turtles 2. Ocean 3. Human influence on nature
ISBN 1-58648-000-6; 1-58648-199-1 (pa)
LC 2001-31868
"A horrible disease of unknown origin is ravaging the already diminished ranks of green sea turtles, causing nonmalignant tumors. . . . Davidson tracks the course of the disease as he dives with turtle researchers in Hawaii, observes surgeries to remove tumors in a rehabilitation hospital in Florida, and visits laboratory researchers questing for the cause. . . . Following the strands of evidence, the author reminds us of the interrelatedness of life and the environment." Booklist
Includes bibliographical references

Ferri, Vincenzo
Tortoises and turtles. Firefly Bks. 2002 c1999 255p il pa $24.95 *
Grades: 11 12 Adult   597.92
1. Turtles
ISBN 1-55209-631-9
Original Italian edition, 1999
Cover title: Turtles & tortoises
An "illustrated guide to 190 land, marine and freshwater turtles and tortoises . . . describing the physical and biological characteristics of the majority of species." Publisher's note
"Turtle enthusiasts and students writing papers will find this guide and the additional resources it cites invaluable." Voice Youth Advocates
Includes bibliographical references

Ripple, Jeff, 1963-
Sea turtles. Voyageur Press 1996 85p il (World life library) pa $16.95
Grades: 7 8 9 10   597.92
1. Sea turtles
ISBN 0-89658-315-5   LC 95-22059
This book covers sea turtle distribution, biology, behavior, historical background and conservation techniques. The text is "lavishly illustrated with more than 50 full-color photographs that bring these animals to vibrant life." SLJ
Includes bibliographical references

Safina, Carl, 1955-
Voyage of the turtle; in pursuit of the Earth's last dinosaur. Holt 2006 383p il map $27.50; pa $17 *

Grades: 11 12 Adult   **597.92**
1. Turtles
ISBN   978-0-8050-7891-6;   0-8050-7891-6;
978-0-8050-8318-7 (pa); 0-8050-8318-9 (pa)
LC 2005-55023
"A John Macrae book"
The author's "main subject is the leatherback, Dermochelys coriacea, largest of all living turtles, which grows to 800 pounds as an average adult." N Y Times Book Rev
"This is a well-written natural history/conservation narrative. General readers will enjoy the book and hopefully will become excited to learn more about critical environmental issues." Sci Books Films
Includes bibliographical references

Spotila, James R., 1944-
Sea turtles; a complete guide to their biology, behavior, and conservation. Johns Hopkins University Press 2004 227p il $24.95 *

Grades: 11 12 Adult   **597.92**
1. Sea turtles
ISBN 0-8018-8007-6   LC 2004-8935
"The volume covers various aspects of sea turtle biology, such as their life history, diving physiology, sense organs, and magnetic orientation. Following the general chapters, individual chapters are devoted to each of the seven species of extant sea turtles." Sci Books Films
"The author is eloquent in his appeal for the conservation of sea turtles. The best single book on the subject." Booklist
Includes bibliographical references

597.96 Snakes

Ernst, Carl H.
Snakes of the United States and Canada; [by] Carl H. Ernst, Evelyn M. Ernst. Smithsonian Books 2003 668p il map $70 *

Grades: 11 12 Adult   **597.96**
1. Snakes
ISBN 1-58834-019-8   LC 2002-26924
This "reference begins with an introduction to snake biology and evolution, which is followed by an identification guide and key to the North American species. The heart of the book is the species accounts which . . . [provide] information on identifying features, geographic variation, known fossils, current distribution, habitat type, behavior, reproduction, growth, diet, and predators. Completing the book is a glossary of terms and a . . . reference section." Publisher's note
"This current and comprehensive volume contains all the information currently available on the 131 species of snakes living in North America." Libr J
Includes bibliographical references

O'Shea, Mark
Venomous snakes of the world. Princeton University Press 2005 160p il map $29.95 *

Grades: 11 12 Adult   **597.96**
1. Snakes 2. Poisonous animals
ISBN 0-691-12436-1   LC 2005-920576
The author "has produced a compendium of more than 170 venomous snakes, along with their markings, geographical distribution, maximum length, venom, prey, and similar species. But instead of opting for the traditional taxonomic arrangement, he lists these snakes geographically by continent (a final chapter on sea snakes is also included)." Libr J
"Fascinating photographs and descriptions will make this title a favorite." Univ Press Books for Public and Second Sch Libr, 2006
Includes bibliographical references

Ricciuti, Edward R.
The snake almanac; a fully illustrated natural history of snakes worldwide. Lyons Press 2001 192p il $29.95

Grades: 11 12 Adult   **597.96**
1. Snakes
ISBN 1-58574-178-7   LC 2001-29116
This "describes the general physical and behavioral characteristics of all snakes, their evolution, types of habitats, images in mythology and folklore, human encounters with dangerous species, international conservation efforts, and more. The longest chapter, entitled 'Snake Sketches,' is a mini-field guide to 95 representative world species. . . . The text is well organized and clearly written in a lively style." SLJ
Includes bibliographical references

Stafford, Peter J.
Snakes; [by] Peter Stafford. Smithsonian Institution Press 2000 112p il pa $14.95

Grades: 9 10 11 12   **597.96**
1. Snakes
ISBN 1-560-98997-1   LC 00-29145
"From garter snakes and vipers to boas and pythons, snakes are described in terms of evolution, anatomy, locomotion, senses, prey, feeding, growth, and reproduction. Stafford also details the habitats, conservation status, markings, and unusual behaviors of individual species." Publisher's note
Includes bibliographical references

597.98 Crocodilians

Behler, John L.
Alligators & crocodiles; [by] John L. Behler & Deborah A. Behler. Voyageur Press 1998 72p il (World life library) pa $16.95

Grades: 9 10 11 12   **597.98**
1. Alligators 2. Crocodiles
ISBN 0-89658-370-8   LC 97-28583
This book "examines the natural history of the crocodilians—alligators, crocodiles, caiman, and gharials—collectively and individually. Its 'Crocodilian Gallery' in-

Behler, John L.—*Continued*
cludes information on all 23 existing crocodilians. . . .
Information about the range, diet, appearance, behavior,
and mating practices of these creatures [is provided]."
Publisher's note
Includes bibliographical references

598 Birds

Attenborough, David, 1926-
The life of birds. Princeton Univ. Press 1998
320p il $29.95 *
Grades: 11 12 Adult   **598**
1. Birds
ISBN 0-691-01633-X   LC 98-30705
This survey of bird behavior describes "eating habits,
flight, communication, mating, parenthood and environ-
mental adaptability." Publ Wkly
"Well illustrated with color photographs,
Attenborough's latest goes a long way to converting all
readers into bird lovers." Booklist
Includes bibliographical references

The **Bedside** book of birds; an avian miscellany.
Nan A. Talese 2005 369p il $29.95
Grades: 9 10 11 12 Adult   **598**
1. Birds
ISBN 0-385-51483-2   LC 2005-47068
The compiler "employs poems, folk tales, parables,
legends, and extracts from the works of naturalists and
others to explore humans' relationship with birds through
the centuries." Publ Wkly
"This is a book to dip into during those spare minutes,
and the reader will be well rewarded by these glimpses
into avian-human relations." Booklist
Includes bibliographical references

Berger, Cynthia
Owls; illustrations by Amelia Hansen. Stackpole
Books 2005 131p il (Wild guide) pa $19.95
Grades: 11 12 Adult   **598**
1. Owls
ISBN 0-8117-3213-4   LC 2005-2317
The author "explores the lives of [owls] . . . including their fearsome hunting abilities, their surprisingly tender courtship rituals, and, of course, their haunting vocalizations. Also included is an identification guide covering
the full range of North American species." Publisher's
note
Berger "has produced a wonderfully complete yet
compact introduction to owls." Booklist
Includes bibliographical references

Bird, David M., 1949-
The bird almanac; a guide to essential facts and
figures of the world's birds. Completely rev and
updated. Firefly Books 2004 xx, 460p il pa $22.95
Grades: 9 10 11 12   **598**
1. Birds
ISBN 1-552-97925-3   LC 2004-273747
First published 2004

This is a guide to aspects of avarian biology, including anatomy, reproduction and mortality of bird species
worldwide.
Includes bibliographical references

Blaugrund, Annette
The essential John James Audubon. Harry N.
Abrams 1999 112p il (Essential series) $12.95
Grades: 9 10 11 12   **598**
1. Audubon, John James, 1785-1851
ISBN 0-8109-5807-4; 978-0-8109-5807-4
                                        LC 99-73513
This book examines the art of ornithologist John
James Audubon.

Burger, Joanna
Birds: a visual guide. Firefly Books 2006 304p
il map $29.95 *
Grades: 11 12 Adult   **598**
1. Birds
ISBN 978-1-55407-177-7; 1-55407-177-1
"Divided into six sections, the text considers all aspects of birds' lives. Basic anatomy, evolution, physiology, and intelligence are all touched on in the first section, while bird behavior . . . is covered in the second.
A large section examines the taxonomy of birds . . . accompanied by a world map showing its distribution.
Habitat, migration, and how birds fill their space are discussed in the fourth section, followed by a look at avian
adaptations and lifestyles. The final section, on birds and
humans, covers such disparate topics as birds in legend,
bird-watching, captive birds, and habitat loss. Beautifully
illustrated." Booklist

Choiniere, Joseph
What's that bird? getting to know the birds
around you, coast-to-coast; [by] Joseph Choiniere
& Claire Mowbray Goldin; photography by Tom
Vezo ; ill. by James Robins. Storey Pub. 2005
117p il map $24.95; pa $14.95
Grades: 9 10 11 12   **598**
1. Birds 2. Bird watching
ISBN 1-58017-555-4; 1-58017-554-6 (pa)
                                        LC 2004-17307
This book features "facts about bird nesting sites, hab-
itat, song, diet, lifestyle, and migration patterns." Publish-
er's note
Includes bibliographical references

Chu, Miyoko
Songbird journeys; four seasons in the lives of
migratory birds. Walker & Co. 2006 312p il map
$23
Grades: 11 12 Adult   **598**
1. Birds—Migration
ISBN 0-8027-1468-4; 978-0-8027-1468-8
                                        LC 2006-278075
The author describes the "seasonal migrations of
American songbirds. . . . In addition to descriptions of
the birds' migrations, habits, and life histories for each
season, there are details on hotspots for observing the

Chu, Miyoko—*Continued*

birds, including web sites, addresses, when to go, and special activities. . . . An excellent overview of a compelling subject; highly recommended." Libr J

Includes bibliographical references

City birding; true tales of birds and birdwatching in unexpected places; [by] Kenn Kaufman [et al.] Stackpole Bks. 2003 179p $18.95

Grades: 11 12 Adult   **598**

1. Bird watching 2. Birds

ISBN 0-8117-0027-5   LC 2002-9268

This is a collection of essays about "finding birds in seemingly blighted cities. . . . Many well-known birding authors are represented here: Marie Winn writes of a rare shorebird found in a Brooklyn marina, Kenn Kaufman reveals the wonders of parking lots, Clay Sutton observes a river of migrating raptors from a hotel roof, and Paul Johnsgard waxes lyrical about the town dump of Lincoln, Nebraska." Booklist

Dunne, Pete

Pete Dunne on bird watching; the how-to, where-to, and when-to of birding. Houghton Mifflin 2003 334p il pa $12

Grades: 11 12 Adult   **598**

1. Bird watching

ISBN 0-395-90686-5   LC 2002-27558

The author "describes how to attract more birds to the yard by feeding, landscaping, and providing water, then he moves on to the tools needed to see and identify the new additions to the yard, discussing binoculars and field guides and how to choose the best ones. The next chapters cover the fundamentals of birding. Birding ethics and the responsibilities of birders are covered in the final chapter." Booklist

This "book is a superlative introduction to bird watching." Libr J

Includes bibliographical references

Ehrlich, Paul R.

The birder's handbook; a field guide to the natural history of North American birds: including all species that regularly breed north of Mexico; [by] Paul R. Ehrlich, David S. Dobkin, Daryl Wheye. Simon & Schuster 1988 xxx, 785p il pa $21.95 hardcover o.p.

Grades: 11 12 Adult   **598**

1. Birds—North America

ISBN 0-671-65989-8 (pa)   LC 87-32404

This volume contains "basic information on each of the 646 species of birds in North America, enriched by 250 short essays on all aspects of avian behavior and biology. This book is a companion volume to any illustrated field guide." Am Libr

Includes bibliographical references

Firefly encyclopedia of birds; edited by Christopher Perrins. Firefly Bks. 2003 655p il maps $59.95

Grades: 11 12 Adult   **598**

1. Birds

ISBN 1-55297-777-3

"An Andromeda book"

First published 1985 by Facts on File with title: The encyclopedia of birds

"Organized in phylogenetic order, the volume covers almost 10,000 bird species; for each bird family (owls, woodpeckers, thrushes, et al.) there is a map, a general text, and sidebars with paragraphs on nesting, voice, size, diet, plumage, habitat, etc. There are also random essays on appropriate related subjects, such as conservation, courtship, and many family-specific topics of interest as well as a helpful glossary. The volume is highly illustrated in color, both by quality paintings and the approximately 1000 lively, engaging photographs. This excellent reference title in an attractive format is highly recommended for most public and academic libraries." Libr J

Gallagher, Tim

The grail bird; hot on the trail of the Ivory-billed woodpecker. Houghton Mifflin 2005 272p il map $25; pa $14.95

Grades: 11 12 Adult   **598**

1. Woodpeckers

ISBN 0-618-45693-7; 0-618-70941-X (pa)

                                   LC 2005-42792

The author "was one of the first to rediscover the ivory-billed woodpecker, a fabled bird long believed extinct." Booklist

"An engaging story of the triumph of conservation, this book is highly recommended for most collections." Libr J

Includes bibliographical references

Hoose, Phillip M., 1947-

The race to save the Lord God Bird; [by] Phillip Hoose. Farrar, Straus and Giroux 2004 196p il map $20

Grades: 7 8 9 10   **598**

1. Woodpeckers 2. Endangered species

ISBN 0-374-36173-8

Tells the story of the ivory-billed woodpecker's extinction in the United States, describing the encounters between this species and humans, and discussing what these encounters have taught us about preserving endangered creatures

"Sharp, clear, black-and-white archival photos and reproductions appear throughout. The author's passion for his subject and high standards for excellence result in readable, compelling nonfiction." SLJ

Includes glossary and bibliographical references

Jacquet, Luc

March of the penguins; from the film by Luc Jacquet; narration written by Jordan Roberts; photographs by Jérôme Maison. National Geographic 2006 unp il $30

Grades: 9 10 11 12   **598**

1. Penguins

ISBN 0-7922-6182-8; 978-0-7922-6182-7

                                   LC 2006-295371

"The book delves further than the hit movie into the lives of these remarkable penguins and their story of survival, and it also covers the conditions endured by the film crew to get the footage." Publisher's note

Jacquet, Luc—*Continued*
"This fine book works as a stand-alone volume, thanks to its charming photographs and revealing text." Publ Wkly

Kaufman, Kenn
Kaufman field guide to birds of North America; with the collaboration of Rick and Nora Bowers and Lynn Hassler Kaufman. Houghton Mifflin 2005 c2000 392p il map pa $18.95
Grades: 11 12 Adult   598
1. Birds—North America
ISBN 0-618-57423-9; 978-0-618-57423-0
First published 2000 with title: Birds of North America
For this identification guide "Kaufman selected over 2000 digitally edited photographs, enhanced to improve contrast, color, and the like. The excellent result will appeal to beginning birders perhaps intimidated by illustrations. . . . Kaufman's text is simple and uncluttered, a plus for novices." Libr J

Leahy, Christopher W.
The birdwatcher's companion to North American birdlife; illustrations by Gordon Morrison. Princeton University Press 2004 1039p il hardcover o.p. pa $19.95
Grades: 11 12 Adult   598
1. Birds—North America
ISBN 0-691-09297-4; 0-691-11388-2 (pa)
LC 2003-66383
First published 1982 by Hill & Wang
"This alphabetical compendium of ornithology offers entries ranging from single-line definitions of avian terminology ('Erne') to 12-page essay-style articles ('Systemics') that concentrate primarily on the US and Canada. Entries include a substantial number of biographies and black-and-white drawings. . . . Comprehensive entries on conservation, evolution of birdlife, optical equipment, and human threats to birdlife provide welcome up-to-date information. . . . Leahy's style is by turns serious and scholarly or personal and whimsical, appropriate to a comprehensive reference for both novice and expert birders. There is no recent comparable work." Choice
Includes bibliographical references

Matthiessen, Peter
The birds of heaven; travels with cranes; paintings and drawings by Robert Bateman. North Point Press 2001 349p il $27.50; pa $16
Grades: 11 12 Adult   598
1. Cranes (Birds) 2. Endangered species
ISBN 0-374-19944-2; 0-86547-657-8 (pa)
LC 2001-32986
The author writes "of his journeys in search of all the crane species and of his conversations with the scientists working to understand and preserve them." Booklist
"Eloquent and graceful, this lovely, moving narrative will inspire and delight readers with or without ornithological background or interests." Publ Wkly

National Geographic complete birds of North America; edited by Jonathan Alderfer. National Geographic 2006 664p il map $35 *
Grades: 11 12 Adult   598
1. Birds—North America
ISBN 0-7922-4175-4   LC 2005-54495
Companion volume to Field guide to the birds of North America
This guide includes "chapters for the more than 80 avian families, with an overview of plumage, behavior, distribution, taxonomy, and conservation. This is followed by descriptions of all 962 species (covering identification, similar species, voice, status, and distribution) and sidebars that address such topics as difficult identifications." Libr J
"The book pulls together a remarkable amount of information into what can only be described as one of the finest one-volume reference works ever published on North American birds." Booklist
Includes bibliographical references

National Geographic field guide to the birds of North America; edited by Jon L. Dunn and Jonathan Alderfer. 5th ed. National Geographic 2006 503p il map pa $24 *
Grades: 11 12 Adult   598
1. Birds—North America
ISBN 0-7922-5314-0 (pa); 978-0-7922-5314-3 (pa)
LC 2006-49420
First published 1983 with title: Field guide to the birds of North America
An identification guide to more than 800 species of North American birds. Arranged in family groups, the information for each species includes a full-color illustration, a range map, common and scientific names, measurement, and a description of plumage, distinctive songs and calls, behavior, abundance, and habitat.
Includes bibliographical references

Nielsen, John T.
Condor; to the brink and back—the life and times of one giant bird; [by] John Nielsen. HarperCollins Publishers 2006 257p il map $25.95
Grades: 11 12 Adult   598
1. Condors
ISBN 0-06-008862-1; 978-0-06-008862-0
LC 2004-54336
The author "focuses on the process and players in the $20-million California Condor Recovery program, describing the infighting in the scientific and environmental communities, at war about whether a 'hands on' or a 'hands off' approach will work best." Publ Wkly
"This is popular science writing at its peak." Booklist
Includes bibliographical references

Peterson, Roger Tory, 1908-1996
A field guide to the birds of eastern and central North America; by Roger Tory Peterson and Virginia Marie Peterson. 5th ed. Houghton Mifflin 2002 xxii, 427p il maps $30; pa $19 *
Grades: 6 7 8 9 10 11 12 Adult   598
1. Birds—North America
ISBN 0-395-74047-9; 0-395-74046-0 (pa)
LC 2001-51879

Peterson, Roger Tory, 1908-1996—*Continued*

Also available large print edition $24 (ISBN 0-395-96371-0)

"The Peterson field guide series"

First published 1934 with title: A field guide to the birds

"Sponsored by the National Audubon Society, the National Wildlife Federation, and the Roger Tory Peterson Institute"

This guide to birds found east of the Rocky Mountains contains colored illustrations painted by the author, with a description of each species on the facing page. Views of young birds and seasonal variations in plumage are included. Birds are arranged in eight major groups of body shape

A field guide to western birds; text and illustrations by Roger Tory Peterson; maps by Virginia Marie Peterson. 3rd ed, completely rev and enl. Houghton Mifflin 1998 432p il maps $27 *

Grades: 6 7 8 9 10 11 12 Adult   598
1. Birds—West (U.S.)
ISBN 0-395-91174-5   LC 89-31517
Also available vinyl-bound edition (ISBN 0-618-13218-X) $20

"The Peterson field guide series"

First published 1941

"Sponsored by the National Audubon Society, the National Wildlife Federation, and the Roger Tory Peterson Institute"

"A completely new guide to field marks of all species found in North America west of the 100th meridian and north of Mexico." Title page

This guide illustrates over 1,000 birds (700 species) on 165 color plates. In addition, over 400 distribution maps are included

Sibley, David

The Sibley field guide to birds of eastern North America; written and illustrated by David Allen Sibley. Knopf 2003 431p il pa $19.95 *

Grades: 11 12 Adult   598
1. Birds—North America
ISBN 0-679-45120-X   LC 2002-114931
Companion volume to The Sibley field guide to birds of western North America

This portable "guide features 650 bird species, plus regional populations found east of the Rocky Mountains. Accounts include . . . illustrations . . . with descriptive caption text pointing out the most important field marks. Each entry contains . . . text concerning frequency, nesting, behavior, food and feeding, voice description, and key identification features." Publisher's note

"All the qualities to be expected in a field guide are here. . . . Image reproduction is crisp, colors are distinct, shading shows well, and despite the very small size, range map colors are clear. . . . Sibley has accomplished the difficult task of condensing . . . {The Sibley guide to birds} to practical field size." Libr J

The Sibley field guide to birds of western North America; written and illustrated by David Allen Sibley. Knopf 2003 473p il pa $19.95 *

Grades: 11 12 Adult   598
1. Birds—North America
ISBN 0-679-45121-8   LC 2002-114930
Companion volume to The Sibley field guide to birds of eastern North America

This portable "guide features 703 bird species, plus regional populations found west of the Rocky Mountains. Accounts include . . . illustrations . . . with descriptive caption text pointing out the most important field marks. Each entry contains . . . text concerning frequency, nesting, behavior, food and feeding, voice decription, and key identification features." Publisher's note

"All the qualities to be expected in a field guide are here. . . . Image reproduction is crisp, colors are distinct, shading shows well, and despite the very small size, range map colors are clear. . . . Sibley has accomplished the difficult task of condensing . . . [The Sibley guide to birds] to practical field size." Libr J

The Sibley guide to bird life & behavior; illustrated by David Allen Sibley; edited by Chris Elphick, John B. Dunning, Jr., David Allen Sibley. Knopf 2001 588p il maps $45 *

Grades: 11 12 Adult   598
1. Birds—North America
ISBN 0-679-45123-4   LC 2001-33903
At head of title: National Audubon Society

This companion volume to The Sibley guide to birds provides "information about birds' lives and behavior. . . . Part 1 ('The World of Birds') discusses basic avian biology, including form, distribution, population, and conservation, in about 100 pages. Part 2 ('Bird Families of North America'), to which over 40 ornithologists contributed, uses a standard format to describe taxonomy, foraging, breeding, range, nests, eggs, longevity, conservation, and more." Libr J

The Sibley guide to birds; written and illustrated by David Sibley. Knopf 2000 544p il maps pa $35 *

Grades: 11 12 Adult   598
1. Birds—North America
ISBN 0-679-45122-6   LC 00-41239
"A Chanticleer Press edition"

At head of title: National Audubon Society

"The treatments of each of the 810 species have detailed paintings to show the natural variations in plumage (e.g., juveniles, male/female adults, seasonal and geographic changes). In all, there are more than 6,600 full-color illustrations. . . . The text for each species has a short summary of identification key points, description of vocalizations, and an up-to-date range map." Choice

"This stunning volume stands out as a must have for even casual birders." SLJ

Tennant, Alan, 1943-
On the wing; to the edge of the earth with the peregrine falcon. Alfred A. Knopf 2004 304p il $26.95; pa $14.95
Grades: 11 12 Adult   **598**
1. Falcons
ISBN 0-375-41551-3; 1-4000-3182-6 (pa)
LC 2003-69496
The author "describes his efforts to trail peregrine falcons on their epic migratory flights from the Caribbean to the Arctic. . . . After radio-tagging a young peregrine off the coast of Texas, Tennant teams up with George Vose, a former WWII combat flight instructor, to follow the bird on its spring migration north." Publ Wkly
"An exhilarating and illuminating storyteller, Tennant offers exquisitely poetic descriptions of peregrine falcons—magnificently aerodynamic, keen-sighted, and fearless birds of prey—a galvanizing history of falconry, and a sobering accounting of the consequences of rampant chemical pollution and environmental destruction." Booklist

The **world** atlas of birds; [consultant editor, Sir Peter Scott; foreword by Roger Tory Peterson] 2006 ed. Gramercy Books 2006 272p il map $19.99 *
Grades: 9 10 11 12   **598**
1. Birds
ISBN 0-517-22732-0; 978-0-517-22732-9
LC 2006-295814
First published 1974 in the United Kingdom with title: The Mitchell Beazley world atlas of birds
This "reference guide to the birds of the world includes . . . full-color illustrations of 500 species of birds, as well as more than 200 line drawings." Publisher's note
Includes bibliographical references

599 Mammals

Attenborough, David, 1926-
The life of mammals. Princeton University Press 2002 320p il $35
Grades: 11 12 Adult   **599**
1. Mammals
ISBN 0-691-11324-6   LC 2002-106846
The author "treks across every continent and kind of terrain to introduce us to such unusual and evolutionarily successful creatures as the Patagonian opossum, the Canadian pygmy shrew, the Alpine marmot, and the Malaysian sun bear." Publisher's note
"Heavily illustrated with beautiful photographs and enlivened by Attenborough's friendly, informative writing style, this is a terrific introduction to the wonders of our hairy, milk-producing relatives." Booklist

Elbroch, Mark
Mammal tracks & sign; a guide to North American species. Stackpole Bks. 2003 779p il maps $44.95 *
Grades: 11 12 Adult   **599**
1. Animal tracks
ISBN 0-8117-2626-6   LC 2002-10549

This guide provides "track and trail illustrations, range maps, and full-color photographs showing feeding signs, scat, tunnels, burrows, bedding areas, remains, and more. . . . {It explains} how to find, identify, measure, and interpret the clues mammals leave behind. . . . Includes essays that contextualize tracking as a developing science." Publisher's note
The author "brings an ideal combination of practical experience and careful research to this work. . . . A definitive treatment, Elbroch's book will set the standard for years to come and is essential to anyone interested in tracking this continent's mammals." Libr J
Includes bibliographical references

The **encyclopedia** of mammals; edited by David W. Macdonald. 2nd ed. Facts on File 2006 3v il map (Facts on File natural science library) set $325
Grades: 9 10 11 12   **599**
1. Mammals—Encyclopedias
ISBN 0-8160-6494-6; 978-0-8160-6494-6
LC 2006-48409
First published 1984 in one volume edition; published in a three volume edition 2001
Contents: v. 1. Marsupials, insect eaters, elephants, and rodents -- v. 2. Primates, shrews, bats, weasels, bears, and seals -- v. 3. Dogs, cats, hoofed mammals, and whales
"Any collection supporting a science curriculum would find this set invaluable. It's also very attractive for browsing." Book Rep [review of 2001 edition]
Includes bibliographical references

Forsyth, Adrian
Mammals of North America. Firefly Bks. (Buffalo) 1999 352p il maps $40; pa $29.95
Grades: 11 12 Adult   **599**
1. Mammals
ISBN 1-55209-409-X; 1-55407-233-6 (pa)
"The author has limited his work to approximately 150 species that inhabit some of the same territory as humans. . . . Each chapter follows the same format: the common name of the species followed by the Latin name; a color photograph; a sidebar consisting of a map with the habitat shaded, a description, and vital statistics, including life span, diet, habitat, predators, and dental formula; and an article of a few paragraphs to several pages describing the mammal's life in the wild. . . . This resource can be used by students for reports because the text is clear and easy to comprehend." Booklist

Mammals; editorial consultants, Juliet Clutton-Brock, Don E. Wilson. DK 2002 400p il map (Smithsonian handbooks) hardcover o.p. pa $20
Grades: 9 10 11 12   **599**
1. Mammals
ISBN 0-7513-3374-3; 0-7894-8404-8 (pa)
LC 2001-47823
This book features over 500 profiles of mammals including descriptions, color photos, and facts about the animals.

Whitaker, John O., Jr.
National Audubon Society field guide to North
American mammals. rev ed. Knopf 1996 937p il
maps pa $19.95 *
Grades: 6 7 8 9 10 11 12 Adult   **599**
1. Mammals
ISBN 0-679-44631-1   LC 95-81456
First published 1980
This field guide describes 390 species of mammals of
North America and includes keys for identification, range
maps, information on tracks and anatomy, and 375 color
photos

599.2 Marsupials and monotremes

Moyal, Ann
Platypus; the extraordinary story of how a
curious creature baffled the world. Smithsonian
Institution Press 2001 226p il maps $21.95
Grades: 11 12 Adult   **599.2**
1. Platypus
ISBN 1-56098-977-7   LC 2001-20892
Also available in paperback from Johns Hopkins Univ.
Press
The author offers an "account of this odd Australian
mammal as she follows the story of its discovery, the
scientific infighting over its place in taxonomy, and modern efforts to understand its biology and keep and breed
it in captivity. The author captures the state of nineteenth-century scientific inquiry beautifully. Well illustrated with period engravings of both the animal and the
scientists who fought over it, as well as photographs of
the living animal." Booklist
Includes glossary and bibliographical references

599.3 Miscellaneous orders of placental mammals

Sullivan, Robert
Rats: observations on the history and habitat of
the city's most unwanted inhabitants. Bloomsbury
2003 242p $23.95; pa $14.95
Grades: 11 12 Adult   **599.3**
1. Rats
ISBN 1-582-34385-3; 1-582-34477-9 (pa)
LC 2003-16293
This book contains observations on and a history of
"rats in New York City, from bar fights in the 1840s to
the World Trade Center catastrophe." SLJ
The author "has an excellent sense of narrative, blending interesting anecdotes and snippets of history in such
an engaging way that it really is hard to put down the
book. The result is a fascinating account that is much
bigger than the title implies." Voice Youth Advocates

599.5 Cetaceans and sea cows

Baird, Robin W.
Killer whales of the world; natural history and
conservation. Voyageur Press 2002 132p il map (A
WorldLife discovery guide) $29.95; pa $19.95
Grades: 11 12 Adult   **599.5**
1. Whales
ISBN 0-89658-512-3; 0-7603-2654-1 (pa)
LC 2002-2982
"Using examples from populations around the world,
. . . [this book] explores the history of killer whales and
outlines what can be done to conserve one of the legends
of the deep." Publisher's note
"This in-depth introduction is an excellent primer to
these sea mammals." Booklist
Includes bibliographical references

Bonner, W. Nigel (William Nigel)
Whales of the world; [by] Nigel Bonner. Facts
on File 2002 191p il $35
Grades: 9 10 11 12   **599.5**
1. Whales 2. Dolphins
ISBN 0-8160-5216-6   LC 2002-34738
First published 1989
"Ten chapters treat all aspects of the species' biology
and natural history, exploring such topics as evolution,
social structure, feeding, breeding, migration patterns,
and environmental influences." Publisher's note
Includes bibliographical references

Clapham, Phil
Whales of the world. Voyageur Press 1997 132p
il hardcover o.p. pa $19.95
Grades: 11 12 Adult   **599.5**
1. Whales 2. Whaling
ISBN 0-89658-359-7; 0-89658-537-9 (pa)
LC 97-1860
The author "examines all the species, from humpback
to blue whales to right whales and sperm whales, and reveals the often complex ways in which whales interact,
communicate and breed. He also recounts the history of
whaling from its earliest days among aboriginal peoples
to the large-scale commercial operations which left several populations on the brink of extinction. The book
concludes by surveying the many images of whales
found in legend and myth." Publisher's note
"The wonderful photos illustrate many aspects of
whale life, showing some behaviors never before pictured." Booklist
Includes bibliographical references

Powell, James
Manatees: natural history & conservation.
Voyageur Press 2002 72p il (World life library) pa
$16.95
Grades: 11 12 Adult   **599.5**
1. Manatees
ISBN 0-89658-583-2   LC 2002-7540
Contents: Origins; Form and function; A year in the
life of a Florida manatee; Sirenian conservation; Recom-
mended reading and organizations

Powell, James—*Continued*
Discusses the evolution, movement, habitat, and physical description of manatees and dugongs, as well as what can be done to protect them
This is "distinguished by full-page color photos, well-written [text] and objective views about the future." SLJ

Reep, Roger L.
The Florida manatee; biology and conservation; [by] Roger L. Reep and Robert K. Bonde. University Press of Florida 2006 189p il map $34.95
Grades: 11 12 Adult   599.5
1. Manatees
ISBN 978-0-8130-2949-8; 0-8130-2949-X
                                    LC 2005-58578
"The authors explore Sirenian history . . . and detail the manatee lifestyle. They explain, with expertise, the neuroanatomy, senses, perception, and behavior, revealing (in a comparative framework) how the aquatic environment demanded solutions very different from those found in terrestrial animals. No other source fulfills more admirably the goal of inspiring and recruiting young talent into the fold of Sirenian conservation around the world." Choice
Includes bibliographical references

599.63   Even-toed ungulates

Watson, Lyall
The whole hog; exploring the extraordinary potential of pigs; Lyall Watson. Smithsonian Books 2004 208p il $24.95
Grades: 11 12 Adult   599.63
1. Pigs
ISBN 1-588-34216-6   LC 2004-52248
The author "investigates several distinct pig types, including bushpigs, wild boars, forest hogs and peccaries . . . and offers anecdotes about his childhood pet warthog. . . . Anthropology, biology, geography, psychology are all here in a clearly written, amiable text peppered with trivia tidbits . . . and lots of photos. Even those who read but a handful of these pages will find their opinion of pigs much rosier." Publ Wkly
Includes bibliographical references

599.67   Elephants

Poole, Joyce, 1956-
Elephants. Voyageur Press 1997 72p il (World life library) pa $14.95
Grades: 9 10 11 12   599.67
1. Elephants
ISBN 0-89658-357-0   LC 97-15272
This describes elephants' "society and strong sense of family, their complex infrasonic communication, their feeding and mating habits, and their chances for survival in a rapidly changing world." Publisher's note
Includes bibliographical references

599.75   Cat family

Alderton, David, 1956-
Wild cats of the world; photographs by Bruce Tanner. Facts On File 2002 192p il map $35 *
Grades: 7 8 9 10   599.75
1. Wild cats
ISBN 0-8160-5217-4   LC 2002-34736
First published 1993
This "volume explores the development and behavior of wild cats, with chapters covering form and function, evolution, and distribution. It also examines each species in detail, providing information on distinctive features such as sight, hearing, hunting techniques, and locomotion." Publisher's note
Includes bibliographical references

Caputo, Philip
Ghosts of Tsavo; stalking the mystery lions of East Africa. National Geographic Soc. 2002 275p il $27; pa $15
Grades: 11 12 Adult   599.75
1. Lions 2. Tsavo National Park (Kenya)
ISBN 0-7922-6362-6; 0-7922-4100-2 (pa)
                                    LC 2002-22642
This is a study of the Tsavo lions of Kenya. Philip Caputo discusses "why they are bigger than their counterparts of the Serengeti plains, why the males do not normally grow manes, and why Tsavo lions are more prone than Serengeti lions to make humans a part of their diet. The observable differences between Tsavo lions and Serengeti lions have led some behavioral scientists whom Mr. Caputo interviews to believe that the Tsavo lions are actually a different species." N Y Times (Late N Y Ed)

Gamble, Cyndi
Leopards; natural history & conservation; text by Cyndi Gamble; photography by Rodney Griffiths. Voyageur Press 2004 48p il map (World life library) pa $12.95
Grades: 7 8 9 10   599.75
1. Leopards
ISBN 0-89658-656-1   LC 2004-14316
"The text offers a comprehensive look at these endangered animals and raises awareness of various efforts to preserve their habitats and to save them from extinction. Excellent-quality photographs appear throughout. . . . An attractive and informative addition." SLJ
Inlcudes bibliographical references

599.77   Dog family

Grambo, Rebecca L., 1963-
Wolf; legend, enemy, icon; photographs by Daniel J. Cox. Firefly Books 2006 176p il $34.95
Grades: 11 12 Adult   599.77

Grambo, Rebecca L., 1963——*Continued*
1. Wolves
ISBN 1-55407-044-9
Shifting "between science and myth, with sociological, anthropological, and ethological stops along the way, Grambo explores all sides of the wolf, from both lupine and human perspectives. The many illustrations, which include Daniel Cox's images of wolves in the wild, reinforce the premise of the text." Booklist
Includes bibliographical references

Smith, Douglas W.
Decade of the wolf; returning the wild to Yellowstone; [by] Douglas W. Smith & Gary Ferguson. Lyons Press 2005 212p il maps $23.95; pa $16.95
Grades: 11 12 Adult   **599.77**
1. Wolves 2. Endangered species 3. Yellowstone National Park
ISBN 1-59228-700-X; 1-59228-886-3 (pa)
LC 2005-40767
This is an "inside look at the Yellowstone Wolf Recovery Project, covering the 10 years that have passed since the U.S. Fish and Wildlife Service made the controversial decision to reintroduce wolves into the national park." Publ Wkly
"Well illustrated with black-and-white and color photographs, this intimate history of the return of the top predator to Yellowstone will find an eager audience." Booklist
Includes bibliographical references

Steinhart, Peter
The company of wolves. Knopf 1995 374p il maps hardcover o.p. pa $14.95
Grades: 11 12 Adult   **599.77**
1. Wolves
ISBN 0-679-41881-4; 0-679-74387-1 (pa)
LC 94-26913
This is "an examination of the relationship between humans and wolves in the wolves' last refuges in the Arctic and in places where the two species live together again as wolves move into new areas, either through their own natural movements or through attempts at reintroduction. Steinhart . . . speaks with wolf biologists, wildlife managers, trappers, ranchers, Native Americans, and others. Though it is clear where Steinhart's sympathies lie, the book is balanced between the wolves' advocates and their opponents." Libr J
Includes bibliographical references

599.78   Bears

Angel, Heather, 1941-
Pandas. Voyageur Press 1998 72p il maps (World life library) pa $16.95
Grades: 9 10 11 12   **599.78**
1. Giant panda
ISBN 0-89658-364-3   LC 97-42001
This book "relates details of the panda's eating habits, habitat, and behaviors, as well as conservation issues re-

lating to its survival and endangered species status." Publisher's note
"The author, a trained zoologist and professional wildlife photographer, has traveled extensively in China and writes eloquently of the land and plants of the mountainous regions that are the giant panda's home. . . . The high quality of the photographs and the popularity of the subject recommend this book for all libraries." Booklist
Includes bibliographical references

Breiter, Matthias
Bears: [a year in the life] Firefly Books 2005 176p il $34.95
Grades: 11 12 Adult   **599.78**
1. Bears
ISBN 1-55407-077-5   LC 2006-295648
The author offers a "look at three species of bears by following their lives through each month of the year. . . . Breiter works a tremendous amount of natural history into this calendar approach, and his photo illustrations are both apt and beautiful." Booklist
Includes bibliographical references

Busch, Robert
The grizzly almanac; {by} Robert H. Busch. Lyons Press 2000 229p il maps hardcover o.p. pa $19.95
Grades: 11 12 Adult   **599.78**
1. Grizzly bear
ISBN 1-58574-143-4; 1-59228-320-9 (pa)
LC 00-58587
The author "traces the evolution of the 'big bear' from its earliest days, describes its habitat and behavior, and recounts grizzly folklore and tales of grizzly attacks. Maintaining that the grizzly's reputation as a vicious killer is undeserved, he makes recommendations for a more peaceful coexistence with humans." Libr J
Includes bibliographical references

Croke, Vicki
The lady and the panda; the true adventures of the first American explorer to bring back China's most exotic animal; [by] Vicki Constantine Croke. Random House 2005 372p il $25.95; pa $14.95
Grades: 11 12 Adult   **599.78**
1. Harkness, Ruth 2. Giant panda
ISBN 0-375-50783-3; 0-375-75970-0 (pa)
LC 2004-51356
Also available Thorndike Press large print edition
The author tells the "story of Ruth Harkness, the Manhattan bohemian socialite who, against all but impossible odds, trekked to Tibet in 1936 to capture the most mysterious animal of the day: a bear that had for countless centuries lived in secret in the labyrinth of lonely cold mountains." Publisher's note
"This well-written, exhaustively researched and documented book should be on every library's shelves." Libr J
Includes bibliographical references

Rosing, Norbert
The world of the polar bear. Firefly Books 2006 203p il $45
Grades: 11 12 Adult   **599.78**
1. Polar bear
ISBN 978-1-55407-155-5; 1-55407-155-0
This book contains "a season-by-season account of the life of the polar bear, including feeding, mating, rearing of cubs and journeying from the ice; an intimate look at the animals that share the polar bear's environment, including seals, arctic foxes, walruses and muskoxen; a section on such northern sky phenomena as sun dogs and the northern lights; [and] many anecdotes and insights about the polar bear." Publisher's note
Includes bibliographical references

Turbak, Gary
Grizzly bears. Voyageur Press 1997 71p il maps (World life library) pa $14.95
Grades: 9 10 11 12   **599.78**
1. Grizzly bear
ISBN 0-89658-334-1   LC 96-42373
This describes grizzly bear habits and habitats, hibernation, and what threatens the bear's existence
Includes bibliographical references

599.79   Marine carnivores

Miller, David, 1959-
Seals & sea lions. Voyageur Press 1998 72p il (World life library) pa $16.95
Grades: 9 10 11 12   **599.79**
1. Seals (Animals)
ISBN 0-89658-371-6   LC 97-44771
This describes the habits and habitats of seals and sea lions and threats to their existence
Includes bibliographical references

599.8   Primates

Goodall, Jane, 1934-
In the shadow of man; photographs by Hugo van Lawick. rev ed. Houghton Mifflin 1988 297p il map pa $15 *
Grades: 11 12 Adult   **599.8**
1. Chimpanzees
ISBN 0-618-05679-9   LC 87-36965
Also available in hardcover from P. Smith
First published 1971
The author describes the chimpanzee group she studied during ten years of field observation in the Gombe Stream Chimpanzee Reserve in Tanzania
Includes bibliographical references

Through a window; my thirty years with the chimpanzees of Gombe. Houghton Mifflin 1990 268p il map pa $16 hardcover o.p. *
Grades: 11 12 Adult   **599.8**
1. Chimpanzees
ISBN 0-618-05677-7 (pa)   LC 90-36974

This continuation of In the shadow of man "tells two stories: first of how the chimps of Gombe in Tanzania have grown, changed and died, and second, how Goodall and her dedicated group of Tanzanian observers have survived the rigours of the past thirty years. It is beautifully written, and evokes both sympathy and understanding of these animals." Times Lit Suppl

Preston-Mafham, Rod
Primates of the world; [by] Rod and Ken Preston-Mafham. Facts On File 2002 191p il $35
Grades: 9 10 11 12   **599.8**
1. Primates
ISBN 0-8160-5211-5   LC 2002-34733
First published 1992
"The authors discuss the various species of lemurs, monkeys, and apes; their habitats, social systems, breeding habits and rearing of youth, methods of communication, and feeding preferences; and their ambivalent relationship with the human race." Publisher's note

Russon, Anne E.
Orangutans: wizards of the rainforest. Rev. ed. Firefly Books 2004 240p il map pa $24.95
Grades: 9 10 11 12   **599.8**
1. Orangutan
ISBN 1-55297-998-9   LC 2005-357221
First published 1999 in the United Kingdom
A firsthand account of the lives of orangutans including a scientific history of orangutans, a description of orangutans and their natural habitat, their behavior patterns, rehabilitation operations, the politics of orangutan rescue work, and a look at orangutans released back into the forest.
Includes bibliographical references

Swindler, Daris Ray
Introduction to the primates; [by] Daris R. Swindler; illustrated by Linda E. Curtis. University of Wash. Press 1998 284p il pa $22
Grades: 9 10 11 12   **599.8**
1. Primates
ISBN 0-295-97704-3   LC 97-47149
"Swindler begins with a history of primate research and then covers systematics and an overview of the living primates. He covers such systems as genetics, skull, teeth (with diet and guts), brain, skeleton and locomotion, growth and development (one of his specialities), and social behavior. The fossil history of primates is briefly reviewed, and the book closes with prospects for conservation." Choice
Includes bibliographical references

World atlas of great apes and their conservation; edited by Julian Caldecott and Lera Miles; foreword by Kofi A. Annan. University of California Press, in association with UNEP-WCMC 2005 456p il map $45 *
Grades: 11 12 Adult   **599.8**
1. Apes 2. Biogeography 3. Atlases 4. Wildlife conservation
ISBN 0-520-24633-0; 978-0-520-24633-1
                               LC 2006-272653

World atlas of great apes and their conservation—*Continued*

Images, maps and 130-page bibliography available electronically via the World Wide Web

"Each great ape specie is given a separate chapter that contains information on behavior and ecology, communication and tool use, threats and conservation, and exceptionally detailed distribution maps. What sets this book apart is the section that details each country in which apes are found and exactly what conservation efforts are underway." Univ Press Books for Public and Second Sch Libr, 2006

Includes bibliographical references

599.93   Genetics, sex and age characteristics, evolution

Ackerman, Jennifer

Chance in the house of fate; a natural history of heredity. Houghton Mifflin 2001 252p $25; pa $14
Grades: 11 12 Adult   **599.93**
1. Heredity 2. Genetics
ISBN 0-618-08287-5; 0-618-21909-9 (pa)
                LC 00-54122

"Ackerman's subject {is} the genetic links between humans and the rest of the natural world. . . . Along with stories about generational change, Ackerman examines the scientific history of heredity, including the work of scientists like Darwin and Anton van Leeuwenhoek." NY Times Book Rev

"Ackerman proves to be an exciting and eloquent tour guide through the complex realm of heredity. . . . Adept at selecting vivid analogies sure to please nonscientific readers." Booklist

Includes bibliographical references

Encyclopedia of human evolution and prehistory; editors, Eric Delson {et al.}. 2nd ed. Garland 2000 xlv, 753p il (Garland reference library of the humanities) lib bdg $175 *
Grades: 9 10 11 12   **599.93**
ISBN 0-815-31696-8

First published 1988 under the editorships of Ian Tattersall, Eric Delson, and John Van Couvering

This reference "contains nearly 800 articles written by 54 international, but largely U.S., contributors. The articles are divided between shorter specific articles and longer integrative articles, including articles on concepts and methods, localities and sites, fossils, primate taxa, tool types, archaeological industries, and eminent deceased and living anthropologists. There are also long, integrative articles on major regions such as Western Asia." Am Ref Books Annu, 2001

"This is a very readable, thorough reference source covering every aspect of human evolution and prehistory. The scientific facts, theories, and philosophies pertaining to evolution are presented skillfully and understandably." Booklist

Gibbons, Ann

The first human; the race to discover our earliest ancestors. Doubleday 2006 306p il map $26 *
Grades: 11 12 Adult   **599.93**
1. Fossil hominids 2. Evolution
ISBN 0-385-51226-0; 978-0-385-51226-8
             LC 2005-53780

The author "explains what paleoanthropologists have been doing over the past 15 years: competing, feuding, and making dramatic discoveries. Anchoring her narrative to the anatomy that is the foundation of physical anthropology, Gibbons intentionally emphasizes the personalities involved." Booklist

This "is a near insider's account that still has the critical distance a nonpartisan can offer." Libr J

Includes bibliographical references

Johanson, Donald C.

From Lucy to language; [by] Donald Johanson & Blake Edgar; principal photography, David L. Brill. Rev., updated, and expanded. Simon and Schuster 2006 288p il map $65
Grades: 11 12 Adult   **599.93**
1. Human origins 2. Fossil hominids
ISBN 0-7432-8064-4; 978-0-7432-8064-8
            LC 2007-270098

"A Peter N. Nèvraumont book"

First published 1996

This is a "photographic showcase of the essential physical evidence of human origins. . . . Permitting a face-to-face encounter with human ancestors, this work furnishes essential information, [and] an incomparable visual experience." Booklist

Includes bibliographical references

Lucy: the beginnings of humankind; [by] Donald C. Johanson and Maitland A. Edey. Simon & Schuster 1981 409p il pa $16 hardcover o.p.
Grades: 11 12 Adult   **599.93**
1. Human origins 2. Fossil mammals
ISBN 0-671-72499-1 (pa)   LC 80-21759

In November 1974 at a place called Hadar in Ethiopia Donald Johanson "discovered the partial skeleton of an extremely primitive female, erect-walking primate or hominid. . . . The skeleton received the name 'Lucy.' Much later, Lucy received the scientific name, Australopithecus afarensis, and it was determined she was some 3.5 million years old. . . . This book is Johanson's own story of the events leading up to and subsequent to Lucy's discovery." Best Sellers

Includes bibliographical references

Jolly, Alison

Lucy's legacy; sex and intelligence in human evolution. Harvard Univ. Press 1999 518p il hardcover o.p. pa $18.95
Grades: 11 12 Adult   **599.93**
1. Evolution 2. Intellect
ISBN 0-674-00069-2; 0-674-00540-6 (pa)
            LC 99-32252

"Lucy is the name given to the fossil skeleton of an Australopithecine, a human ancestor, discovered in Ethio-

Jolly, Alison—*Continued*

pia. The name may be a misnomer, since there's no way yet of telling whether Lucy was female. No matter. Primatologist Jolly's interest is not so much in Lucy as in the crucial role that females in general have played in human evolution. . . . In clear and clever prose, Jolly shows us how we got so smart, what sex had to do with it, and how our brains have become the central force in evolution." Booklist

Includes bibliographical references

Jordan, Paul

Neanderthal: Neanderthal Man and the story of human origins. Sutton Pub. 1999 239p il pa $19.95 hardcover o.p.

Grades: 11 12 Adult   **599.93**
1. Fossil hominids 2. Human origins
ISBN 0-7509-2676-7 (pa)

This discusses the discovery of Neanderthal fossils, the technology and way of life of these hominids and their relationship to homo sapiens.

Leakey, Richard E., 1944-

The origin of humankind; [by] Richard Leakey. Basic Bks. 1994 171p il maps (Science masters series) pa $14.95 hardcover o.p.

Grades: 11 12 Adult   **599.93**
1. Human origins
ISBN 0-465-05313-0 (pa)   LC 94-3617

"Leakey summarizes the evolution of theories, from Darwin's to his own, in the process demonstrating the scientific method in action. . . . Covering the taxonomy of skeletons and craniums, shapes of tools, and the first sprouts of art and culture, Leakey knowledgeably points the enthralled neophyte to the wide avenues of future discoveries." Booklist

This "is a worthwhile addition to many kinds of libraries—public, general, science, biological, and psychological." Sci Books Films

Includes bibliographical references

Origins reconsidered; in search of what makes us human; [by] Richard Leakey and Roger Lewin. Doubleday 1992 375p il pa $16.95 hardcover o.p.

Grades: 11 12 Adult   **599.93**
1. Human origins
ISBN 0-385-46792-3 (pa)   LC 92-6661

"Leakey and Lewin discuss how conceptions of human anatomical and behavioral development have been radically altered within the last 12 years by new discoveries and research in other fields. They review the developments and assert Leakey's own hypotheses based on these discoveries. . . . This is an engrossing book written for the layperson, fully explaining anthropological terms and theories when necessary. It's a solid introduction to current theory concerning human development." SLJ

Reilly, Philip, 1947-

Is it in your genes? the influence of genes on common disorders and diseases that affect you and your family; [by] Philip R. Reilly. Cold Spring Harbor Laboratory Press 2004 288p hardcover o.p. pa $19.95 *

Grades: 9 10 11 12   **599.93**
1. Medical genetics
ISBN 0-87969-719-9; 0-87969-721-0 (pa)
LC 2004-2458

"Drawing on the many questions he has been asked (for example, 'My sister has multiple sclerosis. Am I at an increased risk?'), Reilly discusses over 90 common conditions, diseases, and disorders, arranged from conception to old age." Publisher's note

Includes bibliographical references

Ridley, Matt

Genome; the autobiography of a species in 23 chapters. HarperCollins Pubs. 2000 344p pa $14 hardcover o.p.

Grades: 11 12 Adult   **599.93**
1. Genomes 2. Genetics
ISBN 0-06-093290-2 (pa)   LC 99-40933

Ridley presents a "summation of our ever increasing understanding of the roles that genes play in disease, behavior, sexual differences, and even intelligence. More important, though, he addresses not only the ethical quandaries faced by contemporary scientists but the reductionist danger in equating inheritability with inevitability." New Yorker

Includes bibliographical references

Sloan, Christopher

The human story; our evolution from prehistoric ancestors to today; foreword by Meave Leakey and Louise Leakey; photographs by Kenneth L. Garrett; art by Kennis and Kennis. National Geographic Society 2004 80p il $21.95 *

Grades: 7 8 9 10   **599.93**
1. Evolution 2. Human origins
ISBN 0-7922-6325-1   LC 2003-13978

Contents: Of bones and genes; Our next of kin; Out of Africa; Becoming modern; Being human today

Explores the origins of humans, including how such developments as Linnaeus' classification system and recent understanding of the human genome have improved scientists' comprehension of evolution

"What many . . . readers will find most exciting is how today's cutting-edge technology helps us learn about the prehistoric connections all humans share. Great for classroom discussion." Booklist

Includes glossary and bibliographical references

Tattersall, Ian

Extinct humans; by Ian Tattersall and Jeffrey H. Schwartz. Westview Press 2000 256p il pa $35 hardcover o.p.

Grades: 11 12 Adult   **599.93**
1. Human origins 2. Fossil hominids 3. Evolution
ISBN 0-8133-3918-9 (pa)   LC 00-22088

Tattersall, Ian—*Continued*

The authors explain "why the idea of the one-track, lineal descent of human beings is obsolete and the notion of a 'bushy' evolutionary history, like that of other genera, fits the fossil evidence better." Booklist

Includes bibliographical references

Tudge, Colin

The time before history; 5 million years of human impact. Scribner 1996 366p il maps pa $17.95 hardcover o.p.

Grades: 11 12 Adult   **599.93**

1. Human origins 2. Evolution 3. Mammals

ISBN 0-684-83052-3 (pa)   LC 95-42026

Tudge "begins by putting time into perspective so that we can understand how vast is our past; he helps us see that all evolution is part of a bigger whole—an unfolding process affected by shifting continents, climactic changes, and our own impact on the planet and its ecosystems. . . . He defines our origins in a biological, as well as historical context and applies the lessons that we should learn from our mistakes as well as our achievements to provide a blueprint for the future." Libr J

"With majestic sweep and subtle wit, . . . Tudge brings an astonishing perspective to the story of humanity." Publ Wkly

Includes bibliographical references

Wade, Nicholas

Before the dawn; recovering the lost history of our ancestors. Penguin Press 2006 312p il map $24.95

Grades: 11 12 Adult   **599.93**

1. Evolution 2. Social change

ISBN 1-59420-079-3; 978-1-59420-079-3

                   LC 2005-55293

This is a "survey of human evolution for lay readers which considers the emergence of man in his entirety: physical, psychological, and social. . . . Wade's book concentrates on the recent evolutionary past: our last 50,000 years. . . . [It] emphasizes genetic over paleontological evidence." N Y Rev Books

"This is highly recommended for readers interested in how DNA analysis is rewriting the history of mankind." Publ Wkly

Includes bibliographical references

Wells, Spencer, 1969-

The journey of man; a genetic odyssey; photographs by Mark Read. Princeton University Press 2003 224p il map $29.95

Grades: 11 12 Adult   **599.93**

1. Evolution 2. Genetics 3. Human origins

ISBN 0-691-11532-X

Also available in paperback from Random House

The author "chronicles the history of genetic population studies, starting with Darwin's puzzlement over the diversity of humanity he saw first-hand from the deck of the Beagle, and ending with the various attempts to classify human variation on the basis of different political and social agendas." Nature

"Fortunately for the lay reader, Wells has a knack for

clear descriptions and clever analogies to help explain the intricacies of the science involved." Libr J

Includes bibliographical references

600 TECHNOLOGY

Cool stuff and how it works; written by Chris Woodford [et al.] Dorling Kindersley Pub. 2005 256p il $24.99 *

Grades: 9 10 11 12 Adult   **600**

1. Inventions

ISBN 0-7566-1465-1   LC 2005-13587

This book "uses advanced imaging technology such as X rays, scanning electron micrographs, and infrared thermograms, along with traditional graphics, to reveal the workings of . . . [high-tech gadgets and appliances] from the Internet and computers to advanced textiles, space-age materials, and medical marvels. . . . This will rate high on the 'cool' factor, whether at home, school, or library." Booklist

Forbes, Peter, 1947-

The gecko's foot; bio-inspiration: engineering new materials from nature. Norton 2006 272p il $24.95

Grades: 11 12 Adult   **600**

1. Technological innovations 2. Nature

ISBN 0-393-06223-6; 978-0-393-06223-6

                   LC 2006-06731

First published 2005 in the United Kingdom

This is an introduction to the "field of bio-inspiration and its use of life's microscopic features to engineer novel technologies. The volume overviews the history and current status of this field's major research areas and includes material on new adhesives based on the little lizard of the title, on self-cleaning paints modeled on the lotus leaf, and on photonic cells fashioned after butterfly wings." Sci Books Films

"Readers interested in how invention imitates nature, and vice versa, will find much to savor." Publ Wkly

Includes bibliographical references

Langone, John, 1929-

The new how things work; everyday technology explained; art by Pete Samek, Andy Christie, and Bryan Christie. National Geographic Society 2004 272p il $35 *

Grades: 9 10 11 12 Adult   **600**

1. Technology 2. Inventions

ISBN 0-7922-6956-X   LC 2004-50438

First published 1999 with title: National Geographic's how things work

"With eleven chapters, including 'At Home,' 'Building and Buildings,' 'Transportation,' 'At Play,' and 'Tools of Medicine,' the book covers . . . familiar items such as refrigerators and washing machines, planes and trains, elevators and escalators, as well as the not-so-familiar, such as laser surgery and DNA manipulation. . . . {Coverage of recent innovations range} from DVDs and MP3s to plasma screen TVs and wireless Internet technology." Publisher's note

Macaulay, David, 1946-

The new way things work; [by] David Macaulay with Neil Ardley. Houghton Mifflin 1998 400p il $35

Grades: 4 5 6 7 8 9 10 11 12 Adult   **600**
1. Technology 2. Machinery 3. Inventions
ISBN 0-395-93847-3   LC 98-14224

First published 1988 with title: The way things work

Arranged in five sections this volume provides information on "the workings of hundreds of machines and devices—holograms, helicopters, airplanes, mobile phones, compact disks, hard disks, bits and bytes, cash machines. . . . Explanations [are also given] of the scientific principles behind each machine—how gears make work easier, why jumbo jets are able to fly, how computers actually compute." Publisher's note

Parker, Barry R.

Death rays, jet packs, stunts, & supercars; the fantastic physics of film's most celebrated secret agent; [by] Barry Parker. Johns Hopkins University Press 2005 231p il $25

Grades: 11 12 Adult   **600**
1. Bond, James (Fictitious character) 2. Physics
ISBN 0-8018-8248-6   LC 2005-7782

"A longtime James Bond fan, Parker takes a look at the science behind the movies and explains what works and what doesn't, and the basic physics involved. . . . A book that's sure to appeal to teens with an interest in gadgets, cars, stunts, trick cinematography, and sports (skiing, bungee jumping)." SLJ

Includes bibliographical references

608   Inventions and patents

Katoh, Tadashi

Project X Challengers: Cup Noodle; the miracle of 8.2 billion served: the magic noodle, Nissin Cup Noodle; [translated by Sachiko Sato] Digital Manga Publishing 2006 208p il pa $12.95

Grades: 7 8 9 10 11 12 Adult   **608**
1. Graphic novels 2. Manga 3. Food industry—Japan—Graphic novels 4. Inventions—Graphic novels
ISBN 1-56970-959-9

This book chronicles the hard work, innovation, and imagination of a small team of men who invented the instant cup noodle that just about every college student knows today. Just designing the container took a long time, then the noodles, and choosing the flavors. Many companies now make versions of the cup noodle, but not many people understand how revolutionary it was back in 1971. The book includes a photo line-up of Nissin Cup Noodle from 1971 to 2000, photos of the people who worked on the project, and a timeline from 1948 to 1999. This series is based on a series of business documentaries aired on Japan's national television network, NHK. Akira Imai was the series' chief producer.

609   Technology--Historical and geographic treatment

Brown, David E.

Inventing modern America; from the microwave to the mouse; text by David E. Brown; foreword by Lester C. Thurow; introductions by James Burke. MIT Press 2001 c2002 209p il hardcover o.p. pa $19.95

Grades: 11 12 Adult   **609**
1. Inventions 2. Inventors
ISBN 0-262-02508-6; 0-262-52349-3 (pa)
    LC 2001-44768

"A publication of the Lemelson-MIT program for invention and innovation"

This "profiles thirty-five inventors . . . {including} such well-known figures as George Washington Carver, Henry Ford, and Steve Wozniak, as well as . . . Stephanie Kwolek, inventor of Kevlar, and Wilson Greatbatch, inventor of the first implantable cardiac pacemaker." Publisher's note

"Brown simplifies technical data and uses an enthusiastic, almost proselytizing tone. . . . Full color photographs, diagrams and intriguing tidbits . . . make this a good book for most to browse." Publ Wkly

Includes bibliographical references

Carlisle, Rodney P.

Scientific American inventions and discoveries; all the milestones in ingenuity—from the discovery of fire to the invention of the microwave oven. Wiley 2004 502p il $40 *

Grades: 9 10 11 12   **609**
1. Inventions—History 2. Technology—History 3. Technological innovations
ISBN 0-471-24410-4   LC 2003-23258

The author presents a "guide to some 418 inventions and discoveries. He organizes his presentation in a chronological manner, using six major periods from ancient times to the present." Sci Books Films

"This fact-filled compendium will delight students with a passion for science and technology, no matter what their age." Publ Wkly

Harrison, Ian, 1965-

The book of inventions; how'd they come up with that. National Geographic Society 2004 288p il $30 *

Grades: 9 10 11 12 Adult   **609**
1. Inventions—History
ISBN 0-7922-8296-5   LC 2004-49922

"This volume provides the dates, details, and . . . stories of how some of our most interesting and useful objects have been invented. . . . Entries include objects . . . [such] as the disposable diaper, the zipper, the hair dryer, the photocopier, the artificial heart, and the traffic light." Publisher's note

"With sliced bread and the lava lamp among his selected inventions, Harrison aims to please more than teach. . . . Fun and colorful, Harrison's volume will attract would-be Edisons." Booklist

Includes bibliographical references

Inventions and inventors; edited by Roger Smith. Salem Press 2001 2v il (Magill's choice) set $99

Grades: 9 10 11 12   **609**

1. Inventions 2. Inventors

ISBN 1-58765-016-9   LC 2001-49412

This reference "examines 160 of the most significant inventions of the 20th century, and the people behind the inventions. . . . Essays cover such diverse subject areas as High-Tech, including computers, compact discs and cellular phones, to common Household Devices such as polyester, Tupperware and Velcro, and Medical Advances including heart-lung machines, artificial kidneys, and mammography." Publisher's note

"This set is a well-organized and diverse compilation." Choice

Includes bibliographical references

James, Peter

Ancient inventions; {by} Peter James & Nick Thorpe. Ballantine Bks. 1994 xxiii, 672p il hardcover o.p. pa $21

Grades: 11 12 Adult   **609**

1. Inventions—History

ISBN 0-345-36476-7; 0-345-40102-6 (pa)

LC 94-7738

The authors "define the ancient period as the time before A.D. 1492, analyzing the evolution of inventions from brain surgery to playing cards, and putting into perspective the accomplishments of many diverse cultures while laying to rest some 'distorted Western views of history.'" Booklist

This "is thoroughly researched and profusely illustrated; it is doubtful that anyone could examine it without coming away enlightened in one of its broadly ranging areas." Libr J

Includes bibliographical references

Macdonald, Anne L., 1920-

Feminine ingenuity; women and invention in America; {by} Anne Macdonald. Ballantine Bks. 1992 xxiv, 514p il pa $25 hardcover o.p. *

Grades: 9 10 11 12 Adult   **609**

1. Women inventors 2. Inventions

ISBN 0-345-38314-1 (pa)   LC 91-55502

This is a "study of American women's contribution to science, engineering, and technology as represented in the issuance of U.S. patents. From the first patent issued to a woman in 1809, Macdonald traces the uphill struggle women have faced in their efforts to obtain equal rights—in the area of patent awards as well as in the broader educational, economic, and social arenas." Libr J

Includes bibliographical references

The **Seventy** great inventions of the ancient world; edited by Brian M. Fagan. Thames & Hudson 2004 304p il $40 *

Grades: 9 10 11 12 Adult   **609**

1. Inventions—History 2. Technology—History

ISBN 0-500-05130-5   LC 2004-100250

"Fagan organizes into six categories the 70 things his three dozen scholarly contributors present. The first cate-gory describes the basic natural materials—stone, clay, and wood—with which humanity began to alter the environment. Ensuing categories catalog their uses, such as in hunting, farming, or artwork. . . . Stuffed with hundreds of color photographs, Fagan's work is an estimable spruce-up option for any library." Booklist

Includes bibliographical references

Sluby, Patricia Carter

The inventive spirit of African Americans; patented ingenuity. Praeger 2004 xxxviii, 313p il $39.95 *

Grades: 9 10 11 12   **609**

1. African American inventors

ISBN 0-275-96674-7   LC 2003-64767

This "portrait of many black inventors and scientists is derived from a comprehensive review of all the patents that have been issued to African Americans from the days of slavery to the present high-tech era. Sluby also includes a brief biography of many little-known male and female African Americans whose ingenuity contributed to American industry. . . . An important addition to the literature on contributions of African Americans to US history." Choice

Includes bibliographical references

Van Dulken, Stephen, 1952-

Inventing the 20th century; 100 inventions that shaped the world: from the airplane to the zipper; {by} Stephen Van Dulken; with an introduction by Andrew Phillips. New York Univ. Press 2000 246p il hardcover o.p. pa $17.95

Grades: 11 12 Adult   **609**

1. Inventions

ISBN 0-8147-8808-4; 0-8147-8812-2 (pa)

LC 00-41141

This briefly describes inventions of the 20th century, arranged by decade, with text and diagrams from the patent applications

"A fascinating compendium for trivia seekers." Publ Wkly

Includes bibliographical references

610 Medicine & health

Bortolotti, Dan

Hope in hell; inside the world of Doctors Without Borders. Firefly Bks. 2004 303p il $29.95; pa $19.95

Grades: 11 12 Adult   **610**

1. Médecins Sans Frontières (Organization)

ISBN 1-55297-865-6; 1-55407-142-9 (pa)

LC 2005-357206

This "portrait of Doctors Without Borders/*Médecins Sans Frontières* (aka MSF), the nonprofit that won the Nobel Peace Prize in 1999, emphasizes the inner workings of the organization and is animated by interviews with mid-level staffers and by site visits to MSF projects in Angola, Afghanistan and Pakistan. In between, . . . Bortolotti traces the history of the world's largest independent medical humanitarian organization, whose gene-

Bortolotti, Dan—*Continued*

sis was the Biafran horrors of the late '60s." Publ Wkly

"Much of what Bortolotti reports is noticeably absent from the daily headlines, so this eye-opening account is all the more chilling, and MSF's efforts achingly more compelling." Booklist

Includes bibliographical references

The **Harvard** Medical School family health guide; edited by Anthony L. Komaroff. Simon & Schuster 1999 1288p il hardcover o.p. pa $25 *
Grades: 11 12 Adult   **610**
1. Medicine 2. Health
ISBN 0-684-84703-5; 0-684-86373-1 (pa)
                                                  LC 99-27223

"Divided into ten parts, the text begins with a discussion on how to navigate current healthcare systems; the major areas then covered include health maintenance, how diseases are diagnosed, symptom management illustrated by numerous decision trees, and diseases and disorders." Libr J

Hyde, Margaret Oldroyd, 1917-

Medicine's brave new world; bioengineering and the new genetics; {by} Margaret O. Hyde and John F. Setaro. 21st Cent. Bks. (Brookfield) 2001 143p il lib bdg $29.90
Grades: 7 8 9 10   **610**
1. Medical technology 2. Medical ethics
ISBN 0-7613-1706-6   LC 00-69083
"The authors present a host of medical breakthroughs and ponder the future of many versions of genetic manipulation to support medical science. Topics include fertility advances, xenotransplants (the transfer of animal organs or cells to humans), stem cell research, cloning, the Human Genome Project, and genetic testing." Booklist

"What makes this work stand out is the way that incredibly complex cellular processes are lucidly explained." SLJ

Includes glossary and bibliographical references

610.3   Medical sciences-- Encyclopedias and dictionaries

American Medical Association complete medical encyclopedia; medical editors, Jerrold B. Leikin, Martin S. Lipsky. Crown 2003 1408p il $45 *
Grades: 9 10 11 12 Adult   **610.3**
1. Medicine—Encyclopedias
ISBN 0-8129-9100-1   LC 2002-67340
This "medical compendium contains over 5000 alphabetically arranged entries (with 2000 on illnesses) and 1750 illustrations (mostly line drawings, as well as photographs). . . . Definitions include parts of the body (e.g., the spinal cord, with a line drawing of the 'Communication Highway,' as the book calls it), procedures (e.g., in vitro fertilization, with four detailed line drawings of the steps involved), disorders (e.g., ectropion, with a line drawing of a sagging lower eyelid), and specialties (e.g., oncologist). . . . Owing to its relatively modest price, reliability of source, and coverage of popular areas in medicine, it is recommended not only for public libraries and consumer health collections but also for high school libraries." Libr J

Black's medical dictionary; edited by Harvey Marcovitch. 41st ed. Scarecrow Press 2006 814p il $55
Grades: 9 10 11 12   **610.3**
1. Medicine—Dictionaries
ISBN 0-8108-5713-8
First published 1906. Frequently revised
Editors vary
"This dictionary, illustrated with line drawings and graphs, has longer entries than most. Many are several paragraphs long, with extensive information on diseases and parts of the body. The language is accessible to educated lay readers." Ref Sources for Small & Medium-sized Libr. 6th edition

Dorland's illustrated medical dictionary. 31st ed. Saunders Elsevier 2007 xxvii, 2175p il $49.95 *
Grades: 11 12 Adult   **610.3**
1. Medicine—Dictionaries
ISBN 978-1-4160-2364-7; 1-4160-2364-X
Also available deluxe edition with CD-ROM $99.95 and online
First published 1900. Periodically revised
This standard reference includes terms used in medicine, surgery, dentistry, pharmacy, chemistry, nursing, veterinary science, biology, and medical biology. Pronunciation, derivation, and definitions are given.
"This is considered one of the most comprehensive medical dictionaries in print." N Y Public Libr Book of How & Where to Look It Up

The **Gale** encyclopedia of medicine; Jacqueline L. Longe, project editor. 3rd ed. Thomson Gale 2005 5v il set $625
Grades: 11 12 Adult   **610.3**
1. Medicine—Encyclopedias
ISBN 1-4144-0368-2   LC 2005-11418
First published 1999
This encyclopedia "covers more than 1750 disorders, medications, tests, and treatments. . . . Articles incorporate a definition and related key terms and detail causes and symptoms of the disorder, how diagnoses are made, possible treatments (including alternative treatment methods), and the general prognosis. Articles addressing medical tests discuss preparations, aftercare, risks, and normal/abnormal results." Libr J

Includes bibliographical references

Magill's medical guide; medical consultants, Anne Chang . . . [et al.] 3rd rev ed. Salem Press 2005 4v il set $341 *
Grades: 9 10 11 12   **610.3**
1. Medicine—Encyclopedias
ISBN 1-58765-159-9   LC 2004-11759
First published 1995
"Coverage includes conditions, procedures, agencies, and broad themes or topics (e.g., death and dying). Each entry begins by indicating what body system or part of the anatomy is affected, designating related fields and specialties, and defining the headword and any other key terms. . . . The last volume has a glossary . . . a general index, and lists of diseases and other medical conditions, types of health care providers, professional journals, and relevant organizations and Web sites." Choice

The **Merck** manual of diagnosis and therapy; [edited by] Mark H. Beers . . . [et al.] 18th ed. Merck Research Laboratories 2006 xxxii, 2991p il $65 *

Grades: 11 12 Adult   **610.3**

1. Medicine—Handbooks, manuals, etc.

ISSN 0076-6526

ISBN 0-911910-18-2; 978-0-911910-18-6

Also available online

First published 1899

"A one-volume reference that attempts to cover all but the most obscure diseases. Sections are organized by type of disease or medical specialty." N Y Public Libr Book of How & Where to Look It Up

Stedman, Thomas Lathrop, 1853-1938
Stedman's medical dictionary. Lippincott Williams & Wilkins 2006 various paging $49.95

Grades: 11 12 Adult   **610.3**

1. Medicine—Dictionaries

ISBN 0-7817-3390-1   LC 2005-21544

First published 1911. Periodically revised

Accompanied by CD-ROM

Provides definitions, pronunciation and derivations for terms used in general medicine, veterinary medicine, biochemistry and other related fields

Webster's new explorer medical dictionary; created in cooperation with the editors of Merriam-Webster. Federal Street Press 2006 23a, 937p $10.98 *

Grades: 9 10 11 12   **610.3**

1. Medicine—Dictionaries

ISBN 978-1-59695-020-7; 1-59695-020-X

First published 1999

This dictionary features entries for "frequently used words in human and veterinary medicine. Features include end-of-line divisions, variant spellings, pronunciation, functional labels, and inflected forms. Many entries contain abbreviations and symbols, proprietary and generic names of medicines, and both scientific and common names of plants and animals. Eponymous entries contain brief biographical information." Choice [review of 1999 edition]

610.69 Medical personnel and relationships

Reeves, Diane Lindsey, 1959-
Career ideas for teens in health science; [by] Diane Lindsey Reeves with Gail Karlitz and Anna Prokos. Ferguson 2005 184p il (Career ideas for teens) $40; pa $16.95

Grades: 7 8 9 10   **610.69**

1. Vocational guidance 2. Medicine

ISBN 0-8160-5290-5; 0-8160-6920-4 (pa)

     LC 2004-15040

The careers covered in this book include home health aide, chiropractor, dietician, biochemist, and pharmacist.

610.9 Medical sciences--Historical and geographic treatment

Adler, Robert E., 1946-
Medical firsts; from Hippocrates to the human genome. Wiley 2004 232p il $24.95

Grades: 11 12 Adult   **610.9**

1. Medicine—History

ISBN 0-471-40175-7   LC 2003-14212

"The contributors to the annals of medical knowledge [the author] cites include the most famous names—Hippocrates, Pasteur, Freud, Alexander Fleming—and some not so commonly known, such as pioneering gynecologist Soranus (first century C.E.); Ibn al-Nafis (ca. 1210-88), credited as the first to understand and describe pulmonary circulation; and John Snow, an important figure in the war on cholera. . . . Adler discusses each figure's personal, social, and political history as it affected his or her contribution." Booklist

"Adler ably combines good storytelling, clear and cogent scientific explanations [and] a respect for science over superstition." Publ Wkly

Includes bibliographical references

The **Cambridge** illustrated history of medicine; edited by Roy Porter. Cambridge Univ. Press 1996 400p il maps hardcover o.p. pa $35 *

Grades: 9 10 11 12 Adult   **610.9**

1. Medicine—History

ISBN 0-521-44211-7; 0-521-00252-4 (pa)

     LC 95-38000

This is a history of medicine from antiquity to the present. In ten "chapters, Roy Porter and his collaborators examine the changing form of medicine and . . . [the] technical successes that it has achieved." Sci Am

Includes bibliographical references

Dawson, Ian
Greek and Roman medicine. Enchanted Lion 2005 64p il map (History of medicine) $19.95

Grades: 9 10 11 12   **610.9**

1. Medicine—History 2. Classical civilization

ISBN 1-59270-036-5   LC 2004-56272

This book covers the methods used by Greek and Roman doctors to heal the sick, the influence of the Greek and Roman gods in medicine of the period, and the importance of the physicians Galen and Hippocrates.

Includes bibliographical references

Medicine in the Middle Ages. Enchanted Lion 2005 64p il map (History of medicine) $19.95

Grades: 9 10 11 12   **610.9**

1. Medicine—History 2. Middle Ages

ISBN 1-59270-037-3   LC 2004-61996

This book "focuses on how travel, which brought the Black Death and competing eastern viewpoints, forced practitioners to reevaluate bleeding, pus generation, battlefield surgery, and the importance of cleanliness." Voice Youth Advocates

Includes bibliographical references

Friedman, Meyer, 1910-2001

Medicine's 10 greatest discoveries; {by} Meyer Friedman, Gerald W. Friedland. Yale Univ. Press 1998 363p il hardcover o.p. pa $14.95

Grades: 11 12 Adult   **610.9**

1. Vesalius, Andreas, 1514-1564 2. Harvey, William, 1578-1657 3. Leeuwenhoek, Antoni van, 1632-1723 4. Long, Crawford W., 1815-1878 5. Röntgen, Wilhelm Conrad, 1845-1923 6. Harrison, Ross G., 1870-1959 7. Anichkov, N. N. (Nikolai Nikolaevich), 1885-1964 8. Fleming, Alexander, 1881-1955 9. Florey, Howard, Baron Florey, 1898-1968 10. Watson, James D., 1928- 11. Crick, Francis, 1916-2004 12. Jenner, Edward, 1749-1823 13. Wilkins, Maurice Hugh Frederick, 1916-2004 14. Medicine—History 15. Scientists

ISBN 0-300-07598-7; 0-300-08278-9 (pa)

LC 98-19921

This describes such medical discoveries as the circulation of blood by William Harvey, the X-ray by Roentgen, Penicillin by Alexander Fleming, and DNA by Watson, Crick and Maurice Hugh Frederick Wilkins

Includes bibliographical references

Great medical discoveries; C.J. Shane, book editor. Greenhaven Press 2004 251p il (Turning points in world history) lib bdg $33.70

Grades: 9 10 11 12   **610.9**

1. Medicine—History 2. Medicine—Research

ISBN 0-7377-1437-9 (lib bdg)   LC 2003-54005

"This collection of essays explores everything from the ancient study of human anatomy to genetic research. The chapters look at discoveries with regard to the structure and function of the human body, disease and disease prevention, medical procedures, and pharmaceuticals. The concluding chapter addresses the social impact of great medical discoveries. Articles are gathered from diverse sources. . . . Young adults will find this book useful for science or history assignments or if they are researching inventions or the history of disease." SLJ

Includes bibliographical references

Harding, Anne

Milestones in health and medicine; by Anne S. Harding. Oryx Press 2000 267p il $59.95

Grades: 11 12 Adult   **610.9**

1. Medicine—History

ISBN 1-57356-140-1   LC 00-32660

"Alphabetically arranged entries emphasize discoveries and contributions related to medical advancements, although synopsized information is provided on symptoms and treatments where appropriate. The entries are clear and concise and assume a reading level commensurate with the subject matter." SLJ

Includes bibliographical references

Hellman, Hal, 1927-

Great feuds in medicine; ten of the liveliest disputes ever. Wiley 2001 237p $24.95; pa $15.95

Grades: 11 12 Adult   **610.9**

1. Medicine—History 2. Scientists

ISBN 0-471-34757-4; 0-471-20833-7 (pa)

LC 00-63349

This considers disputes involving such medical scientists as William Harvey, Galvani, Volta, Pasteur, Freud, Sabin, Salk, and Montagnier

"Hellman eschews comprehensiveness for pith and entertainment, neglecting no unusual 'twist,' 'strange coincidence,' 'cloud of suspicion' or 'lucky break' to heighten the drama of these medical milestones." Publ Wkly

Includes bibliographical references

611   Human anatomy, cytology, histology

Abrahams, Peter H.

McMinn's color atlas of human anatomy. 5th ed, [by] Peter H. Abrahams, Sandy C. Marks Jr., Ralph Hutchings; new dissections prepared by Lynette Nearn Hardwick; radiological adviser, J. Spratt. Mosby 2003 378p il pa $74.95

Grades: 9 10 11 12   **611**

1. Human anatomy

ISBN 0-7234-3212-0   LC 2002-29923

Also available CD-ROM version with title: McMinn's interactive clinical anatomy

First published 1977 under the authorship of R. M. H. McMinn with title: Color atlas of human anatomy

Includes CD-ROM

This anatomy atlas presents "photographs of dissections of all areas of the human body. A . . . number overlay labeling system helps students . . . identify key structures. . . . Brief explanatory text describes important anatomical features." Publisher's note

Gray's anatomy; the anatomical basis of clinical practice; editor-in-chief, Susan Standring; lead editors, Harold Ellis . . . [et al.]; editors, Barry K.B. Berkovitz . . . [et al.] 39th ed. Elsevier Churchill Livingstone 2005 xx, 1627p il $190 *

Grades: 11 12 Adult   **611**

1. Human anatomy

ISBN 0-44307-168-3; 978-0-44307-168-3

LC 2004-63458

First published 1858. Periodically revised. Publisher varies

Variant title: Gray's anatomy of the human body

A comprehensive standard reference work with illustrations, descriptions and definitions.

"Holds its place as a major and authoritative text on systematic anatomy. Recommended." Annals of Internal Medicine

Includes bibliographical references

Leonardo, da Vinci, 1452-1519

Leonardo on the human body; [by] Leonardo da Vinci. Dover Publs. 1983 506p il pa $26.95

Grades: 9 10 11 12   **611**

1. Human anatomy

ISBN 0-486-24483-0   LC 82-18285

First published 1952 by H. Schuman with title: Leonardo Da Vinci on the human body

This volume includes 215 black-and-white plates containing some 1200 illustrations. Each plate is accompanied by explanatory notes

Light, Douglas B.
Cells, tissues, and skin; by Douglas Light; introduction by Denton A. Cooley. Chelsea House 2003 154p il (Your body, how it works) lib bdg $25.95
Grades: 9 10 11 12   **611**
1. Cells 2. Tissues 3. Skin
ISBN 0-7910-7708-X   LC 2003-13667
Contents: Cells; Cell membranes; Movement through cell membranes; Cytoplasm; The nucleus; Tissues; Skin; Skin derivatives; Common skin disorders
"This book explores the properties of cells and the various different types, and how they work together to sustain life." Publisher's note
Includes bibliographical references

Photographic atlas of the body; pictures supplied by the Science Photo Library; foreword by Baroness Susan Greenfield. Firefly Books 2004 288p il $49.95 *
Grades: 9 10 11 12   **611**
1. Human anatomy—Atlases
ISBN 1-55297-973-3; 978-1-55297-973-0
LC 2005-357208
"Close-up photography of human anatomy is combined with . . . text to explain the human body's functions and inner workings." Publisher's note
"Anyone, old or young, fascinated with the inner workings of the body will be delighted by these strangely compelling images, which look more like strange landscapes and life forms than the interior of our own physical selves." Publ Wkly

Roach, Mary
Stiff; the curious lives of human cadavers. Norton 2003 303p il $23.95; pa $13.95
Grades: 11 12 Adult   **611**
1. Human experimentation in medicine 2. Dead 3. Dissection
ISBN 0-393-05093-9; 0-393-32482-6 (pa)
LC 2002-152908
The author "explains how surgeons and doctors use cadavers donated for research purposes to help the living, and also examines potential new variations on how we bury the dead." Libr J
"For those who are interested in the fields of medicine or forensics and are aware of some of the procedures, this book makes excellent reading." SLJ
Includes bibliographical references

The **Structure** of the body. World Almanac Libr. 2002 64p il (21st century science) lib bdg $21.95
Grades: 9 10 11 12   **611**
1. Human anatomy 2. Physiology
ISBN 0-8368-5008-4   LC 2002-22704
Produced by Gareth Stevens Publishing
This "discusses 'The Body's Building Blocks,' including cells, tissues, and the role of DNA; 'The Architecture of the Body,' including skin, bones, muscles, and joints; and 'Blood Circulation.'" SLJ
This offers "succinct text and crisp, computer-generated images." Booklist
Includes bibliographical references

612   Human physiology

Mai, Larry L.
The Cambridge Dictionary of human biology and evolution; [by] Larry L. Mai, Marcus Young Owl, M. Patricia Kersting. Cambridge University Press 2005 648p il pa $60 *
Grades: 9 10 11 12 Adult   **612**
1. Biology—Dictionaries 2. Evolution—Dictionaries
ISBN 0-521-66486-1; 978-0-521-66486-8
LC 2004-43553
"This dictionary covers many aspects of human biology: anatomy, growth, physiology, genetics, paleontology, physical anthropology, primatology, and zoology." Am Ref Books Annu, 2006
"This is one of those dictionaries that will keep even casual browsers intrigued." Choice

Major systems of the body. World Almanac Libr. 2002 63p il (21st century science) lib bdg $21.95
Grades: 9 10 11 12   **612**
1. Human anatomy 2. Physiology
ISBN 0-8368-5007-6   LC 2002-21193
This "discusses 'Respiration and Nutrition,' including the teeth and stomach; 'The Five Senses'; 'The Nervous System'; and 'Reproduction.'" SLJ
This offers "succinct text and crisp, computer-generated images." Booklist

Margulies, Sheldon
The fascinating body; how it works. ScarecrowEducation 2004 412p il pa $34.95
Grades: 9 10 11 12   **612**
1. Human body
ISBN 1-57886-076-8   LC 2003-18883
Contents: Organ systems -- Skin -- Immunologic system -- Eyes -- Ears -- Respiratory system -- Cardiac system -- Gastrointestinal system -- Endocrine system -- Vascular system -- Urologic system -- Genital system -- Hematologic system -- Bones and joints -- Neurologic system -- How doctors make a diagnosis -- Final thoughts for teenagers
"This title should be made available to every biology classroom or library media center, not only for the wealth of information, but for its concise and useful explanations of the way our bodies function. . . . This resource is an invaluable tool for the high school science curriculum." Libr Media Connect

McMillan, Beverly
Human body; a visual guide. Firefly Books 2006 304p il $29.95 *
Grades: 9 10 11 12 Adult   **612**
1. Physiology 2. Human anatomy
ISBN 978-1-55407-188-3; 1-55407-188-7
This book provides "scientific information on the human body, using microphotography, advanced medical imaging and annotated illustrations. The book reveals all the intricacy and beauty of the human body and shows the structure and functions of all the systems that make up a human being." Publisher's note
Includes bibliographical references

Walker, Richard, 1951-
Encyclopedia of the human body. DK Pub 2002
304p il $29.99 *
Grades: 7 8 9 10   **612**
1. Human anatomy 2. Physiology
ISBN 0-7894-8672-5   LC 2002-73489
This "volume contains 116 entries divided into 5 categories: 'Working Parts,' 'Moving Framework,' 'Control
and Sensation,' 'Supply and Maintenance,' and 'New
Generations.' Within these sections each spread takes a
closer look at an aspect of the topic ('Cells,' 'Cell Structure,' 'Cell Chemistry,' etc.). Almost 900 . . . illustrations, photographs, models, diagrams, and electron micrographs are incorporated into this work." SLJ
"This encyclopedia is attractive and a good beginning
reference source for basic information or quick answers.
Browsers will appreciate the appealing layout, especially
the closeup images of various body structures." Booklist
Includes bibliographical references

World of anatomy and physiology; K. Lee Lerner
and Brenda Wilmoth Lerner, editors. Gale
Group 2002 2v set $160
Grades: 11 12 Adult   **612**
1. Physiology—Encyclopedias 2. Anatomy—Encyclopedias
ISBN 0-7876-5684-4   LC 2002-5517
"This reference provides basic information on human
anatomy and physiology. The 650 alphabetically arranged
entries, ranging in length from several paragraphs to several pages, are written at a level accessible to high
school students and the general reader. Topics covered
range from classical human anatomy and physiology to
developmental and reproductive biology. . . . Lengthy
biographies of about 200 famous as well as lesser-known
scientists, among them Francis Crick, Herophilus, Rita
Levi-Montalcini, Susumu Tonegawa, and Otto Heinrich
Warburg, are also included. . . . Although primarily
aimed at high-school students and general readers, this
reference source could also be of use to undergraduate
students in introductory courses." Booklist
Includes bibliographical references

612.1   Blood and circulation

Brynie, Faith Hickman, 1946-
101 questions about blood and circulation, with
answers straight from the heart. 21st Cent. Bks.
(Brookfield) 2001 176p il lib bdg $27.90 *
Grades: 7 8 9 10   **612.1**
1. Cardiovascular system 2. Blood 3. Heart
ISBN 0-7613-1455-5   LC 00-32570
"The book is divided into five chapters in a question-
and-answer format: 'That Should Come First' (on the
structure and function of the circulatory system), 'The
Heart,' 'Blood', 'When Things Go Wrong'. . . and
'Your Healthy Heart'. . . . Comprehensive, informative,
and highly instructional. . . . The reader will appreciate
the many graphs, diagrams, tables, and photomicro-
graphs." Sci Books Films
Includes bibliographical references

612.2   Respiration

Petechuk, David
The respiratory system. Greenwood Press 2004
202p il (Human body systems) $65 *
Grades: 9 10 11 12 Adult   **612.2**
1. Respiratory system
ISBN 0-313-32434-4   LC 2004-40445
This book "discusses the functions of each organ and
how they work together to allow us to breathe. Respiration is discussed both externally (breathing) and internally at the cellular level. The cardiovascular, nervous, and
muscular systems are discussed in relation to the respiratory system." Publisher's note
Includes bibliographical references

612.3   Digestion

Windelspecht, Michael, 1963-
The digestive system. Greenwood Press 2004
xx, 191p il (Human body systems) $65 *
Grades: 9 10 11 12 Adult   **612.3**
1. Digestion
ISBN 0-313-32680-0   LC 2004-40446
This book covers "the upper and lower gastrointestinal
tract and accessory organs, such as the gall bladder and
liver. . . . The endocrine, circulatory, and lymphatic system are discussed in relation to the digestive system. The
history of the research on the digestive system is presented and the future of research in this field is considered." Publisher's note
Includes bibliographical references

612.4   Hematopoietic, lymphatic, glandular, urinary systems

McDowell, Julie
The lymphatic system; [by] Julie McDowell and
Michael Windelspecht. Greenwood Press 2004
172p il (Human body systems) $65 *
Grades: 9 10 11 12 Adult   **612.4**
1. Lymphatic system
ISBN 0-313-32494-8   LC 2004-44218
In this book "the lymph system, including lymph
nodes and lymphatic circulation are explored and lymphatic functions of the spleen, appendix, and tonsils are
discussed. The history of the research on the lymphatic
system is presented and the future of research in this
field is considered." Publisher's note
Includes bibliographical references

Watson, Stephanie, 1969-
The endocrine system; [by] Stephanie Watson,
and Kelli Miller. Greenwood Press 2004 210p il
(Human body systems) $65 *
Grades: 9 10 11 12 Adult   **612.4**
1. Endocrine glands
ISBN 0-313-32699-1   LC 2004-40447

Watson, Stephanie, 1969-—*Continued*
This book "discusses the anatomy and function of
each organ in the endocrine system. . . . Discussions on
insulin, metabolism and menopause are included. . . .
The history of the research on the endocrine system is
presented and the future of research in this field is considered. Current controversies and dilemmas of scientists
performing this research are explored." Publisher's note
Includes bibliographical references

612.6 Reproduction, development, maturation

Brynie, Faith Hickman, 1946-
101 questions about reproduction; or how 1 + 1
= 3 or 4 or more. Twenty-First Century Books
2006 176p il lib bdg $27.90
Grades: 7 8 9 10   612.6
1. Pregnancy 2. Childbirth 3. Sex education
ISBN 0-7613-2311-2   LC 2003-16350
Uses a question-and-answer format to present information about physical, medical, and social issues surrounding human reproduction, including birth control, pregnancy, and childbirth.
"This is a splendid companion to Brynie's 101 Questions about Sex and Sexuality (21st Century Bks, 2003);
together the books present informative, complementary
coverage for browsers and researchers." SLJ
Includes bibliographical references

Nilsson, Lennart, 1922-
A child is born; [photography], Lennart Nilsson;
text, Lars Hamberger; translated from the Swedish
by Linda Schenck. 4th ed, completely rev and
updated. Delacorte Press 2003 239p il $35; pa $21
Grades: 11 12 Adult   612.6
1. Pregnancy 2. Embryology 3. Childbirth
ISBN 0-385-33754-X; 0-385-33755-8 (pa)
                                  LC 2003-43854
"A Merloyd Lawrence book"
Original Swedish edition, 1965; first United States
edition, 1966
An illustrated look at male and female reproductive
anatomy and physiology, the processes of ovulation and
fertilization, fetal development, and labor and delivery.

Panno, Joseph
Aging; theories and potential therapies. Facts on
File 2005 c2004 157p il (New biology) $35; pa
$18.95 *
Grades: 9 10 11 12 Adult   612.6
1. Aging 2. Longevity
ISBN 0-8160-4951-3; 0-8160-6930-1 (pa)
                                  LC 2003-25469
Published in paperback with title: The science of
aging
This book discusses the subject of aging, "from natu-
ral processes to technological developments, and de-
scribes past and present research on extending the human
life span." Publisher's note
Includes bibliographical references

612.7 Musculoskeletal system, integument

Adams, Amy
The muscular system. Greenwood Press 2004
209p il (Human body systems) $65 *
Grades: 9 10 11 12 Adult   612.7
1. Muscles
ISBN 0-313-32403-4   LC 2004-47595
This book "discusses the parts of the muscular system
and how they work together to help us move from place
to place and to maintain many internal processes, such as
a heart beat. Muscle contraction, development, and response during exercise are covered. . . . Muscular system diseases and disorders, symptoms and treatments are
[also] explored." Publisher's note
Includes bibliographical references

Kelly, Evelyn B.
The skeletal system; [by] Evelyn Kelly.
Greenwood Press 2004 231p il (Human body
systems) $65 *
Grades: 9 10 11 12 Adult   612.7
1. Skeleton 2. Bones
ISBN 0-313-32521-9   LC 2003-67643
In this book, "both the axial bones of the skeleton and
the appendicular bones of the limbs are explored. Joints,
ligaments, tendons and cartilage are discussed in relation
to the bones of the skeletal system. . . . Skeletal system
disorders, symptoms and treatments are [also] explored,
including sprains, fractures, arthritis, lyme disease, and
carpal tunnel syndrome." Publisher's note
Includes bibliographical references

612.8 Nervous functions. Sensory functions

Brynie, Faith Hickman, 1946-
101 questions about sleep and dreams that kept
you awake nights . . . until now. Twenty-First
Century Books 2006 176p il lib bdg $27.93 *
Grades: 8 9 10 11 12   612.8
1. Sleep 2. Dreams
ISBN 978-0-7613-2312-9; 0-7613-2312-0
                                  LC 2005-17276
This book describes the physical and psychological aspects of sleep and dreams.
The author "presents sometimes rather complicated
scientific material in a way that is not only easily understood, but also thoroughly enjoyable." Sci Books Films
Includes bibliographical references

Hudmon, Andrew
Learning and memory. Chelsea House
Publishers 2005 136p il (Gray matter) $32.95
Grades: 8 9 10 11 12   612.8
1. Psychology of learning 2. Memory 3. Brain
ISBN 0-7910-8638-0   LC 2005-11699

Hudmon, Andrew—*Continued*

This "volume provides fascinating insights into various processes involved in how we learn different things in different ways. Particularly enlightening is the section differentiating explicit memory (learning facts) and implicit memory (learning processes) . . . The [book features] colorful historical photos and illustrations, process models, and shaded insets." SLJ

Includes bibliographical references

McDowell, Julie

The nervous system and sense organs. Greenwood Press 2004 201p il (Human body systems) $65 *

Grades: 9 10 11 12 Adult   **612.8**

1. Nervous system 2. Senses and sensation

ISBN 0-313-32456-5   LC 2003-67638

In this book, "major areas of the brain and the autonomic and peripheral nervous systems are covered. The five senses are discussed in relation to the nervous system. The history of the research on the nervous system is presented and the future of research in this field is considered." Publisher's note

Includes bibliographical references

Morgan, Michael, 1960-

The midbrain. Chelsea House 2006 114p il (Gray matter) $32.95

Grades: 8 9 10 11 12   **612.8**

1. Brain

ISBN 0-7910-8637-2   LC 2005-11988

This "stars the least flashy, less-well-researched part of the brain responsible for various movements (including Parkinson's problems), vision, hearing, sensuality, defense, and complex eye movements. . . . [This book proceeds] from a physiological model of the brain and address structure and behavior in various species while focusing on humans." SLJ

Includes bibliographical references

Rapport, Richard

Nerve endings; the discovery of the synapse. Norton 2005 240p il $23.95

Grades: 11 12 Adult   **612.8**

1. Ramón y Cajal, Santiago, 1852-1934 2. Golgi, Camillo, 1843-1926 3. Nervous system

ISBN 0-393-06019-5   LC 2005-942

This book discusses "Santiago Ramon y Cajal and Camillo Golgi, joint recipients of the 1906 Nobel Prize in Medicine and Physiology. . . . Even when Golgi's own groundbreaking advances in histology allowed him to see a gap between nerve cells, he insisted that cells were connected. At the same time, Cajal used Golgi's own histology methods to propose that neurons communicate over a gap—later called the synapse." Sci Books Films

"Teens studying biology and medicine will find that the book provides an accessible introduction to understanding the structure and function of the nervous system." SLJ

Includes bibliographical references

Turkington, Carol

The encyclopedia of the brain and brain disorders; foreword by Joseph R. Harris. 2nd ed. Facts on File 2002 369p $65

Grades: 11 12 Adult   **612.8**

1. Brain—Encyclopedias

ISBN 0-8160-4774-X   LC 2002-66512

"Library of health and living series"

First published 1996 with title: The brain encyclopedia

This volume "includes more than 600 clear, concise entries about the brain and treatments for neurological disorders. Articles, alphabetically arranged, are followed by directories of self-help organizations and of professional and government organizations in the fields of neurology, chronic pain, and mental illness. The list of references is extensive, the subject index is well organized." Choice

613   Personal health and safety

The **Black** women's health book; speaking for ourselves; edited by Evelyn C. White. new expanded ed. Seal Press 1994 375p pa $16.95

Grades: 11 12 Adult   **613**

1. African American women—Health and hygiene

ISBN 1-878067-40-0   LC 93-28901

First published 1990

Contributors to this collection include Zora Neale Hurston, Lucille Clifton, Marian Wright Edelman, bell hooks, and Toni Morrison. Topics covered include: suicide, midwives, the politics of black women's health, sexual abuse, domestic violence, skin color, HIV infection, menopause, etc.

Includes bibliographical references

Goldstein, Mark A., 1947-

Boys to men; staying healthy through the teen years; by Mark A. Goldstein and Myrna Chandler Goldstein. Greenwood Press 2000 197p il $45

Grades: 9 10 11 12   **613**

1. Boys—Health and hygiene 2. Teenagers—Health and hygiene

ISBN 0-313-30966-3   LC 00-21045

"Dividing adolescence into three time frames—twelve to fourteen, fifteen to eighteen, and nineteen to twenty-one years old—the Goldsteins present information on various areas of physical and emotional growth and development." Voice Youth Advocates

Includes bibliographical references

Libal, Autumn

Can I change the way I look? a teen's guide to the health implications of cosmetic surgery, makeovers, and beyond. Mason Crest Publishers 2005 128p il (Science of health) $24.95

Grades: 7 8 9 10   **613**

1. Teenagers—Health and hygiene 2. Personal grooming

ISBN 1-59084-843-8   LC 2004-1883

"Framing her discussion within an examination of the media influence on our culture's definition of beauty,

Libal, Autumn—*Continued*
Libal does an excellent job of discussing the risks and benefits of cosmetics, piercing and tattooing, diet, exercise, and cosmetic surgery. . . . The author also considers, in some detail, the dangers of anorexia nervosa, bulimia, and steroid use." SLJ
Includes bibliographical references

Our bodies, ourselves; a new edition for a new era; [by] The Boston Women's Health Book Collective. 35th anniversary ed. Simon & Schuster 2005 832p il pa $24.95 *
Grades: 11 12 Adult   **613**
1. Women—Health and hygiene 2. Women—Psychology
ISBN 0-7432-5611-5 (pa)   LC 2004-65374
Also available in hardcover from P. Smith
"A Touchstone book"
First published 1971
This encyclopedia of women's health covers such topics as body image, food, alcohol and drugs, holistic healing, psychotherapy, occupational health, violence, relationships and sexuality, sexual health and controlling fertility, childbearing, aging and politics of women and health.
This book "is exceedingly readable, strikingly comprehensive, and thoroughly documented." Libr J
Includes bibliographical references

613.2   Dietetics

Diet information for teens; edited by Karen Bellenir. 2nd ed. Omnigraphics 2006 432p (Teen health series) $58 *
Grades: 8 9 10 11 12   **613.2**
1. Nutrition 2. Teenagers—Health and hygiene
ISBN 0-7808-0820-7   LC 2006-4413
First published 2000
"Health tips about diet and nutrition including facts about dietary guidelines, food groups, nutrients, healthy meals, snacks, weight control, medical concerns related to diet, and more." Title page
This "is a compilation of articles on all facets of nutrition, drawn mainly from FDA documents. The information is presented in a straightforward, plainspoken manner." SLJ [review of 2000 edition]
Includes bibliographical references

The **Encyclopedia** of vitamins, minerals, and supplements; {compiled by} Tova Navarra; foreword by Wendy Shankin-Cohen. 2nd ed. Facts on File 2004 xxiii, 353p (Facts on File library of health and living) $65
Grades: 11 12 Adult   **613.2**
1. Vitamins 2. Nutrition 3. Dietary supplements—Encyclopedias
ISBN 0-8160-4998-X   LC 2003-61662
First published 1996
Over 900 entries in A-Z format focus on how to use vitamins, minerals, and food supplements "safely, their effects on nutrition, their uses as treatment for assorted health concerns, and common misconceptions about them. Articles on individual vitamins and minerals are

detailed." Booklist
Includes bibliographical references

Gillespie, Gregg R., 1934-
501 recipes for a low-carb life; [by] Gregg R. Gillespie and Mary B. Johnson. Sterling 2003 416p pa $9.95
Grades: 9 10 11 12   **613.2**
1. Cooking 2. Low-carbohydrate diet
ISBN 1-4027-0814-9   LC 2003-269543
The authors "emphasize the importance of distinguishing 'good' versus 'bad' carbohydrates in achieving both sound nutrition and weight loss. The book's recipes arise from an all-American cuisine that borrows freely from many ethnic traditions." Booklist

Ingram, Scott, 1948-
Want fries with that? obesity and the supersizing of America. Franklin Watts 2006 128p il $26 *
Grades: 7 8 9 10   **613.2**
1. Obesity 2. Convenience foods 3. Eating customs
ISBN 0-531-16756-9   LC 2005-5619
This is an "exploration of the physical phenomenon of obesity and its emotional and social ramifications. The text is packed with information on specific dangers such as increased risks of diabetes, cancer, and other health problems. The author casts a critical eye on the effect of advertising and the availability of fast food, both in and out of school, and covers recent state legislation seeking to inform parents of diagnoses of obesity in their children." SLJ
Includes glossary and bibliographical references

Mayo Clinic on healthy weight; Donald D. Hensrud, editor in chief. Mason Crest 2002 208p il $29.95 *
Grades: 9 10 11 12 Adult   **613.2**
1. Weight loss 2. Nutrition
ISBN 1-59084-225-1
Also available in paperback from Kensington Bks. and in a Spanish language edition
"Answers to help you achieve and maintain the weight that's right for you." On cover
This guide "begins with Getting Motivated. This portion defines obesity, covers the causes and health risks, and assists in setting goals and analyzing the fundamentals of healthy eating. How To Lose Weight . . . investigates physical activity, helps with changing attitudes and actions, and provides support for when the going gets tough. A chapter also covers the better-known eating plans, such as the Atkins Diet, the Zone, Blood-Type diet, Jenny Craig, and Weight Watchers. The third section, When You Need More Help, explains medications and surgery for weight loss." Voice Youth Advocates

Nichter, Mimi
Fat talk; what girls and their parents say about dieting. Harvard Univ. Press 2000 263p $25; pa $16.95
Grades: 11 12 Adult **613.2**
1. Obesity 2. Weight loss 3. Girls—Health and hygiene
ISBN 0-674-00229-6; 0-674-00681-X (pa)
LC 99-59521
The author "spent three years studying and interviewing teenage girls about their attitudes toward appearance, eating habits, and dieting. . . . Over two hundred girls were followed over a three-year period so that changing attitudes could be measured. The reader gains a better understanding of teenage girls through the readable narrative that describes the results of the study." Voice Youth Advocates
Includes bibliographical references

Nutrition and well-being A to Z; Delores C.S. James, editor in chief. Macmillan Reference USA 2004 2v il set $175 *
Grades: 9 10 11 12 Adult **613.2**
1. Nutrition—Encyclopedias
ISBN 0-02-865707-1 LC 2004-6088
Topics covered "include dietary habits, eating diseases and disorders, health risks and food safety, the eating habits of various ethnic groups, weight loss issues as well as professional matters, and health programs and organizations." Libr J
This is "a no-nonsense, comprehensive encyclopedia that will be of use to students researching health and food-science topics." SLJ
For a fuller review see: Booklist, Dec. 1, 2004
Includes bibliographical references

Obesity: opposing viewpoints; Andrea C. Nakaya, book editor. Greenhaven Press 2006 203p il lib bdg $34.95; pa $23.70 *
Grades: 9 10 11 12 **613.2**
1. Obesity
ISBN 0-7377-3233-4 (lib bdg); 0-7377-3234-2 (pa)
LC 2005-40333
"Opposing viewpoints series"
"Each of the four chapters discusses a different aspect of obesity (the severity of the problem, what's causing it, how to reduce it, and who is responsible), and each chapter includes six to eight articles that represent different views. Each one includes a few thought-provoking questions to consider while reading. An excellent starting point for reports." SLJ
Includes bibliographical references

Shanley, Ellen L.
Fueling the teen machine; [by] Ellen L. Shanley, Colleen A. Thompson. Bull 2001 288p il pa $12.95
Grades: 9 10 11 12 **613.2**
1. Nutrition 2. Teenagers—Health and hygiene
ISBN 0-923521-57-7 LC 2001-18432
This volume covers such topics as vitamins and minerals, weight management, eating disorders, vegetarianism, sports nutrition, fast food, meal planning and cooking
Includes bibliographical references

Smolin, Lori A.
Basic nutrition; [by] Lori A. Smolin, Mary B. Grosvenor; preface, Lori A. Smolin and Mary B. Grosvenor; introduction by Richard J. Deckelbaum. Chelsea House 2005 190p il (Eating right) $35
Grades: 9 10 11 12 **613.2**
1. Nutrition
ISBN 0-7910-7850-7 LC 2004-2745
Contents: What is nutrition? -- Carbohydrates -- Dietary fiber -- Lipids -- Protein -- Water -- Vitamins -- Minerals -- Choosing a healthy diet
Includes bibliographical references

Nutrition and weight management; [by] Lori A. Smolin, Mary B. Grosvenor. Chelsea House 2005 175p il (Eating right) $35
Grades: 9 10 11 12 **613.2**
1. Nutrition 2. Weight loss
ISBN 0-7910-7852-3 LC 2004-11615
Contents: The obesity crisis -- What is a healthy body weight? -- Body weight and health -- Food, nutrition, and body weight -- Balancing intake and expenditure: how many calories do you need? -- Biological factors that affect what you weigh -- Achieving and maintaining a healthy weight -- Diets and other weight loss fixes -- Weight management in children and adolescents
Includes bibliographical references

Nutrition for sports and exercise; [by] Lori A. Smolin [and] Mary B. Grosvenor; introduction, Richard J. Deckelbaum. Chelsea House 2005 158p il (Eating right) $35 *
Grades: 9 10 11 12 **613.2**
1. Nutrition 2. Athletes—Nutrition
ISBN 0-7910-7853-1 LC 2004-9563
Contents: What is nutrition? -- Energy for exercise -- How your body changes when you exercise -- What should athletes eat? -- Keeping cool: water and electrolyte balance during exercise -- Ergogenic aids for athletes: are they safe? -- Nutritional problems common among athletes -- Diet and exercise for a healthy life
Includes bibliographical references

Vegetarian sourcebook; basic consumer health information about vegetarian diets, lifestyle, and philosophy . . .; edited by Chad T. Kimball. Omnigraphics 2002 360p il (Health reference series) $78 *
Grades: 9 10 11 12 Adult **613.2**
1. Vegetarianism
ISBN 0-7808-0439-2 LC 2002-70236
"This work answers questions that people might have about the healthfulness of a vegetarian diet as well as how to incorporate it into one's everyday life. . . . The articles in this volume are easy to read and come from authoritative sources." Am Ref Books Annu, 2003
Includes bibliographical references

613.6 Personal safety and special topics of health

Bocij, Paul
Cyberstalking; harassment in the Internet age and how to protect your family. Praeger Publishers 2004 268p $39.95 *
Grades: 9 10 11 12 Adult   613.6
1. Computer crimes
ISBN 0-275-98118-5; 978-0-275-98118-1
LC 2003-68988
This book is devoted "to an examination of cyberstalking, providing an overview of the problem, its causes and consequences, and practical advice for protecting yourself and your loved ones." Publisher's note
"This is an extremely alarming book that focuses on the dark side of the Internet and makes it clear that we are all potential victims of cyberstalkers. . . . It's certain to be popular in libraries." Booklist
Includes bibliographical references

Greenbank, Anthony Hunt, 1933-
The book of survival; the original guide to staying alive in the city, the suburbs, and the wild lands beyond; by Anthony Greenbank. 3rd rev ed. Hatherleigh Press 2004 315p il pa $15.95
Grades: 11 12 Adult   613.6
1. Survival skills
ISBN 1-57826-149-X   LC 2003-26656
First published 1967 in the United Kingdom; first published in the United States 1968 by Harper & Row
This survival manual covers topics such as how to prevent frostbite, survive electrical blackouts, escape from quicksand and prepare for possible terrorist attacks.

Piven, Joshua
The worst-case scenario survival handbook; by Joshua Piven and David Borgenicht. Chronicle Bks. 1999 176p il pa $14.95
Grades: 9 10 11 12   613.6
1. Safety education 2. Survival after airplane accidents, shipwrecks, etc. 3. Wilderness survival
ISBN 0-8118-2555-8   LC 2001-268229
This offers advice on safety and survival in emergencies from such dangers as quicksand, erupting volcanoes, terrorist attacks, sharks, plane crashes, and bombs.

Wiseman, John, 1940-
SAS survival handbook; how to survive in the wild, in any climate, on land or at sea; [by] John "Lofty" Wiseman. New ed. HarperResource 2004 576p il pa $19.95
Grades: 11 12 Adult   613.6
1. Wilderness survival 2. Survival after airplane accidents, shipwrecks, etc.
ISBN 0-06-057879-3   LC 2004-302194
First published 1986 in the United Kingdom
This book "is the Special Air Service's complete course in being prepared for any type of emergency. John 'Lofty' Wiseman presents real strategies for surviv-
ing in any type of situation, from accidents and escape procedures, including chemical and nuclear to successfully adapting to various climates (polar, tropical, desert), to identifying edible plants and creating fire." Publisher's note

613.7 Physical fitness

Barough, Nina
Walking for fitness; the low-impact workout that tones and shapes. DK Pub. 2003 160p il pa $15
Grades: 9 10 11 12   613.7
1. Walking 2. Physical fitness
ISBN 0-7894-9693-3; 978-0-7894-9693-5
LC 2004-298141
This book provides information and advice about different aspects of fitness walking including techniques, what clothes to wear, nutrition, and training programs.
Includes bibliographical references

Burke, Ed, 1949-
The complete book of long-distance cycling; build the strength, skills, and confidence to ride as far as you want; by Edmund R. Burke and Ed Pavelka. Rodale 2000 292p il pa $19.95
Grades: 11 12 Adult   613.7
1. Cycling
ISBN 1-57954-199-2   LC 00-9615
This overview covers bike gear, proper nutrition, and what type of bike to buy
"The authors give the lowdown on the latest equipment and explain bike technology without oversimplifying." Booklist

Fahey, Thomas D., 1947-
Basic weight training for men and women. 6th ed. McGraw-Hill 2007 248p il pa $30.63
Grades: 11 12 Adult   613.7
1. Weight lifting
ISBN 0-07-304688-4; 978-0-07-304688-4
LC 2005-53132
First published 1989 by Mayfield Pub. Co. with title: Basic weight training
This is a "guide to developing a personalized weight-training program with both free weights and machines. Weight training concepts and specific exercises are grouped by body region, and many photographs, illustrations, diagrams, and figures demonstrate proper technique and form." Publisher's note
Includes bibliographical references

Hesson, James L.
Weight training for life. 8th ed. Thomson Wadsworth 2006 165p il pa $30.95
Grades: 11 12 Adult   613.7
1. Weight lifting
ISBN 0-495-01275-0; 978-0-495-01275-7
LC 2005-937607
First published 1985 by Morton

Hesson, James L.—*Continued*

This weight training guide features "photos demonstrating exercises and proper techniques, forms for writing goals, for planning a personal weight-training program, and for recording circumference measurements, strength measurements, and muscle endurance measurements." Publisher's note

Includes bibliographical references

McFarlane, Stewart

The complete book of t'ai chi. DK Pub. 1997 120p il pa $15 hardcover o.p. *

Grades: 9 10 11 12 Adult   **613.7**

1. Tai chi

ISBN 0-7894-4259-0 (pa)   LC 96-33596

This is an illustrated guide to the Chinese art of t'ai chi, which is aimed at promoting physical and mental well-being.

"The gentle movements are diagrammed in detail with full-color step-by-step photographs and precise explanations. A good how-to book for beginners." BAYA Book Rev

Pagano, Joan

Strength training for women; tone up, burn calories, stay strong. Dorling Kindersley 2005 160p il pa $15 *

Grades: 9 10 11 12 Adult   **613.7**

1. Weight lifting 2. Physical fitness 3. Women— Health and hygiene

ISBN 0-7566-0595-4; 978-0-7566-0595-7

LC 2005-295208

The author "begins with a three-part fitness test and questionnaire to assess whether the reader should consult a doctor before beginning her program. For true beginners, she provides an anatomy chart that depicts the major muscle groups and the exercises that are best suited to them. She dispels fitness myths like 'lifting weights will bulk you up' and 'you can spot reduce,' and talks about the risk factors, exercise guidelines and restrictions of osteoporosis. . . . This book may be one of the best substitutes for pricey gym memberships and personal trainers." Publ Wkly

Schwartz, Ellen, 1949-

I love yoga; a guide for kids and teens; illustrated by Ben Hodson. Tundra Books 2003 122p il pa $9.95 *

Grades: 9 10 11 12   **613.7**

1. Yoga

ISBN 0-88776-598-X   LC 2002-117468

The author "presents the history of yoga, different styles, yoga benefits, concerns, cautions, misconceptions, equipment, and basic postures." Publisher's note

"This is less a how-to book than an upbeat introduction to yoga, well designed to spark the interest of kids and teens." Quill & Quire

Includes bibliographical references

613.9 Birth control, reproductive technology, sex hygiene

Bell, Ruth

Changing bodies, changing lives; a book for teens on sex and relationships; {by} Ruth Bell and other co-authors of Our bodies, ourselves and Ourselves and our children, together with members of the Teen Book Project. expanded 3rd ed. Times Bks. 1998 411p il pa $24 *

Grades: 7 8 9 10   **613.9**

1. Sex education

ISBN 0-8129-2990-X   LC 97-29249

First published 1980

This is a "book on sex, physical and emotional health, and personal relationships. . . . Readers . . . will find emotional support as well as specific answers to most of their questions in this nonjudgmental resource." Booklist

Brynie, Faith Hickman, 1946-

101 questions about sex and sexuality—; with answers for the curious, cautious, and confused. Twenty-First Century Books 2003 176p il lib bdg $27.90

Grades: 7 8 9 10   **613.9**

1. Sex education

ISBN 0-7613-2310-4   LC 2002-11209

Uses a question-and-answer format to present information about the physical, emotional, and social topics surrounding sex and sexuality

"Brynie emphasizes abstinence as the only sure way of avoiding STDs and pregnancies, but also gives detailed information on contraception. . . . The matter-of-fact style is never condescending or alarmist in tone. . . . Explicit black-and-white illustrations lend an almost clinical touch. . . . The glossary; resource list of books, articles, and Web sites; and extensive citations make Brynie's title good for reports, while the directness of the presentation will appeal to general readers." SLJ

Hyde, Margaret Oldroyd, 1917-

Safe sex 101; an overview for teens; by Margaret O. Hyde and Elizabeth H. Forsyth. Twenty-First Century Books 2006 128p il (Teen overviews) lib bdg $26.60

Grades: 9 10 11 12   **613.9**

1. Youth—Sexual behavior 2. Safe sex in AIDS prevention 3. Birth control 4. Sexually transmitted diseases

ISBN 0-8225-3439-8 (lib bdg); 978-0-8225-3439-6 (lib bdg)   LC 2005-18806

Contents: How do you decide if you are ready for sex? -- Do you choose abstinence? -- Why learn about safe sex? -- Secret lives of teens -- Where you can learn about safe sex -- How your sex organs work -- What you should know about contraception -- Working to prevent teen pregnancy and sexually transmitted diseases

"This thoughtfully written, well-organized introduction to safe-sex issues will make an excellent addition to any public or school library collection." Booklist

Includes bibliographical references

Pardes, Bronwen
Doing it right. Simon & Schuster 2007 143p il
pa $14.99
Grades: 7 8 9 10 11 12	**613.9**
1. Sex education
ISBN 978-1-4169-1823-X; 1-4169-1823-X
LC 2006-928450
On cover: making smart, safe, and satisfying choices
about sex
The author "tackles the tough questions about sexual
orientation, size, abuse, orgasm, pregnancy, STDs, and
masturbation among others." Voice Youth Advocates
Pardes "strives to give teens the information they
need, without judgment, to make their own decisions.
She freely discusses sex without love, reproductive anatomy, transitioning as a transsexual, and sexually transmitted diseases. . . . The openness of this book will be
a boon to teens looking for frank discussions of sexuality
and making choices." SLJ
Includes bibliographical references

Sex education; Kristen Bailey, book editor.
Greenhaven Press 2005 110p (At issue) lib bdg
$27.45; pa $18.70
Grades: 9 10 11 12	**613.9**
1. Sex education
ISBN 0-7377-2418-8 (lib bdg); 0-7377-2419-6 (pa)
LC 2004-49293
The articles in this anthology offer a variety of viewpoints on how sexuality should be taught to America's
youth with chapters on abstinence and one addressing the
needs of gay teens
Includes bibliographical references

Sexual health information for teens; edited by
Deborah A. Stanley. Omnigraphics 2003 391p
(Teen health series) $58 *
Grades: 9 10 11 12	**613.9**
1. Sex education
ISBN 0-7808-0445-7	LC 2003-53636
"Health tips about sexual development, human reproduction, and sexually transmitted diseases: including facts
about puberty." Title page
"This straightforward sex education text offers clinical
accuracy, but limited coverage of puberty, reproductive
health, sexuality, pregnancy, and sexually transmitted diseases. The layout and tone enhance the treatment of sensitive issues for youth. Contributing to the text are two
anatomical charts, sidebars, and glosses. Extensive lists
of Internet and family service sources enable young readers to locate data from a number of sources." Libr Media
Connect

Teenage sexuality: opposing viewpoints; Ken R.
Wells, book editor. Greenhaven Press 2006 224p
il lib bdg $34.95; pa $23.70 *
Grades: 9 10 11 12	**613.9**
1. Youth—Sexual behavior 2. Sex education
ISBN 0-7377-3362-4 (lib bdg); 0-7377-3363-2 (pa)
LC 2005-52664
"Opposing viewpoints series"
Issues covered include teenagers' attitudes about sex,
teen pregnancy, sex education, and teenage homosexuali-
ty.
Includes bibliographical references

# 614	Forensic medicine, incidence & prevention of disease

Bass, William M., 1928-
Death's acre; inside the legendary forensic lab
the Body Farm where the dead do tell tales; [by]
Bill Bass and Jon Jefferson; foreword by Patricia
Cornwell. Putnam 2003 304p il $24.95; pa $15 *
Grades: 9 10 11 12 Adult	**614**
1. Forensic anthropology
ISBN 0-399-15134-6; 0-425-19832-4 (pa)
LC 2003-46908
"The author explains the process of decomposition and
how bones give clues to identify: approximate age, sex,
height, and race, all of which are needed to bring the forensic scientist one step closer to putting a name to a
corpse. He describes some of the cases he has been involved with and laughs at himself when he shares stories
of mistakes and assumptions. Young adults will gain insight into the forensic process and appreciate Bass's dedication to the truth and his work." SLJ

Evans, Colin
The casebook of forensic detection; how science
solved 100 of history's most baffling crimes.
Wiley 1996 310p il pa $17.95 hardcover o.p.
Grades: 11 12 Adult	**614**
1. Forensic sciences 2. Medical jurisprudence
3. Criminal investigation
ISBN 0-471-28369-X (pa)	LC 95-26002
Also available in paperback from Berkley Trade
"Covers cases from 1751 to 1991, arranged according
to the methodology by which they were solved. Fifteen
areas are listed alphabetically, ranging from ballistics
through DNA typing, fingerprinting, odontology, serolo-
gy and toxicology to the still-disputed voiceprint analysis." Publ Wkly
"Written in a popular style as clear as it is brief, this
book is suitable for general true-crime collections." Libr
J

Fridell, Ron, 1943-
DNA fingerprinting; the ultimate identity. Watts
2001 112p il lib bdg $25
Grades: 7 8 9 10	**614**
1. DNA fingerprinting 2. Forensic sciences
ISBN 0-531-11858-4	LC 00-26925
Discusses the discovery of DNA fingerprinting, the
processes involved, its initial use, and its past and present role in forensic identification, conservation biology,
and human genetics
"Fridell consistently gets right to the heart of his subject, melding scientific, forensic, and historic information
in an easy-to-grasp, often eye-opening fashion." Booklist
Includes bibliographical references

Hoff, Brent H.

Mapping epidemics; a historical atlas of disease; [by] Brent H. Hoff and Carter Smith III; Charles H. Calisher, consulting editor. Watts 2000 112p il map hardcover o.p. pa $19.95 *

Grades: 7 8 9 10   **614**

1. Epidemiology 2. Diseases

ISBN 0-531-11713-8; 0-531-16487-X (pa)

LC 99-16502

"More than 30 potentially deadly human illnesses are profiled in this volume. . . . Each two-to-six page article includes a boxed compilation of basic facts and a map showing global distribution. Most present the causative agent, transmission systems, treatment, prevention, and control measures. The bulk of each article links the history of human experience with the illness, major outbreaks, and its *modus operandi*." SLJ

This work offers a "wealth of information expressed clearly enough for younger students and deeply enough for students doing higher-level research." Booklist

Includes glossary and bibliographical references

Lee, Henry C.

Blood evidence; how DNA is revolutionizing the way we solve crimes; [by] Henry C. Lee, Frank Tirnady. Perseus Bks. 2003 xxx, 418p $26

Grades: 11 12 Adult   **614**

1. DNA fingerprinting 2. Forensic sciences

ISBN 0-7382-0602-4   LC 2002-105970

This book "explains the principles and science behind DNA testing and shows how it has both helped solve some of the most puzzling criminal cases in recent history and been used to discredit eyewitness accounts and physical evidence found at the crime scene." Publisher's note

"This volume is an excellent introduction to the science and use of DNA analysis." Publ Wkly

Includes bibliographical references

Tocci, Salvatore

High-tech IDs; from finger scans to voice patterns. Watts 2000 127p il lib bdg $20 *

Grades: 7 8 9 10   **614**

1. Biometry 2. Fingerprints 3. DNA fingerprinting

ISBN 0-531-11752-9 (lib bdg)   LC 99-37380

Describes a variety of devices and systems used for identifying individuals, including finger and hand scans, iris and retinal scans, fingerprinting, DNA fingerprinting, and voice pattern recognition, and gives examples of how they are used

"This title fills a need for topical and timely information on current technology. It is easy to read, and the information is presented in a clear and logical style." SLJ

Includes bibliographical references

Wecht, Cyril H., 1931-

Tales from the morgue; forensic answers to nine famous cases including the Scott Peterson & Chandra Levy cases; [by] Cyril Wecht and Mark Curriden with Angela Powell. Prometheus Books 2005 314p il $26

Grades: 11 12 Adult   **614**

1. Forensic sciences 2. Criminal investigation

ISBN 1-59102-353-X   LC 2005-17805

Pathologist Wecht "sorts out the evidence, or lack thereof, in the scandalous circumstances of Scott Peterson and Chandra Levy, explains why he thinks the JFK assassination was a conspiracy and agrees with the original Marilyn Monroe autopsy that found no signs of foul play. . . . What makes Wecht's arguments so persuasive is that he lets scientific facts—or at least his expert interpretation of them—do the talking." Publ Wkly

Includes bibliographical references

Zedeck, Beth E.

Forensic pharmacology; [by] Beth E. Zedeck and Morris S. Zedeck; series editor, Lawrence Kobilinsky. Chelsea House Publishers 2006 138p il (Inside forensic science) $30

Grades: 9 10 11 12   **614**

1. Forensic sciences 2. Pharmacology

ISBN 0-7910-8920-7; 978-0-7910-8920-0

LC 2006-20624

"This book describes one aspect of forensic science: forensic pharmacology and toxicology of drugs and abuse. The reader is introduced to the daily work of the scientists, the principles of pharmacology and toxicology, the technical anaylsis of drugs, and the characteristics of eight major categories of drugs of abuse." Publisher's note

Includes glossary and bibliographical references

Zugibe, Frederick T.

Dissecting death; secrets of a medical examiner; [by] Frederick Zugibe and David L. Carroll. Broadway Books 2005 240p il $24.95; pa $14

Grades: 11 12 Adult   **614**

1. Forensic sciences 2. Medical jurisprudence 3. Criminal investigation

ISBN 0-7679-1879-7; 0-7679-1880-0 (pa)

LC 2004-62889

Zugibe "presents 10 challenging cases he encountered, as well as his insights as a self-described Monday-morning quarterback on two of the most notorious crimes of the 1990s: the brutal slaying of JonBenét Ramsey and the murders of Nicole Brown Simpson and Ronald Goldman." Publ Wkly

The authors' "straightforward style makes for clear and fascinating reading, and the cases chosen are intriguing." Booklist

614.4   Incidence of and public measures to prevent disease

Do infectious diseases pose a serious threat? Viqi Wagner, book editor. Greenhaven Press 2005 126p (At issue) lib bdg $28.70; pa $19.95
Grades: 9 10 11 12   **614.4**
1. Communicable diseases 2. Public health
ISBN 0-7377-2330-0 (lib bdg); 0-7377-2331-9 (pa)
                                    LC 2004-40582
"Public- and private- sector experts debate the reasons for, scope of, and best responses to infectious disease threats including SARS, bioterrorism agents, and AIDS." Publisher's note
Includes bibliographical references

Encyclopedia of plague and pestilence; from ancient times to the present; George Childs Kohn, editor. rev ed. Facts on File 2001 454p (Facts on File library of world history) $77 *
Grades: 9 10 11 12 Adult   **614.4**
ISBN 0-8160-4263-2   LC 2001-18946
First published 1995
New edition in preparation
"This volume provides concise descriptions of more than 700 epidemics, listed alphabetically by location of the outbreak. Each . . . entry includes when and where a particular epidemic began, how and why it happened, who it affected, how it spread and ran its course, and its outcome and significance." Publisher's note
The author "does an excellent job of including 'noteworthy epidemics and outbreaks.' . . . This title would be useful for a variety of subject areas." Book Rep
Includes bibliographical references

Epidemics: opposing viewpoints; Mary E. Williams, book editor. Greenhaven Press 2005 208p il lib bdg $34.95; pa $23.70
Grades: 9 10 11 12   **614.4**
1. Epidemics
ISBN 0-7377-2282-7 (lib bdg); 0-7377-2283-5 (pa)
                                    LC 2004-61657
"Opposing viewpoints series"
In this "anthology, authors examine the resurgent problem of infectious disease around the world and discuss how governments and individuals should respond to the threats posed by epidemics." Publisher's note
Includes bibliographical references

Farrell, Jeanette
Invisible enemies; stories of infectious diseases. 2nd ed. Farrar, Straus & Giroux 2005 272p il $18 *
Grades: 7 8 9 10   **614.4**
1. Communicable diseases
ISBN 0-374-33607-5   LC 2004-57668
First published 1998
The author "focuses on seven dreaded human diseases: smallpox, leprosy, plague, tuberculosis, malaria, cholera, and AIDS. Each chapter provides a description of the physical and psychological effects of the disease on its victims, early theories about its causes, and efforts made

to avoid or cure it. Then the methods of research that revealed its cause and developed the means to control its spread are explained in fascinating detail. . . . If every science book for nonspecialists were written with such flair and attention to detail, science would soon become every student's favorite subject." SLJ
Includes glossary and bibliographical references

Giblin, James, 1933-
When plague strikes; the Black Death, smallpox, AIDS; by James Cross Giblin; woodcuts by David Frampton. HarperCollins Pubs. 1995 212p pa $8.99 hardcover o.p. *
Grades: 9 10 11 12   **614.4**
1. Plague 2. Smallpox 3. AIDS (Disease) 4. Epidemics
ISBN 0-06-446195-5 (pa)   LC 94-39881
"Giblin takes a look back to ancient Egypt, to the Dark Ages, and to the age of the smallpox epidemics and finds intriguing historic parallels. Then he traces what is known about the *AIDS* epidemic from its earliest suspected case to the present. Giblin closes his study with the report of a new plague, a mutation of the hantavirus, which seems to be ready to continue to wreck havoc on populations worldwide." Book Rep
The author "writes with simplicity and drama about three terrible plagues and about the suffering, bigotry, and humanity of people, then and now." Booklist
Includes bibliographical references

Goldsmith, Connie, 1945-
Invisible invaders; new and dangerous infectious diseases. Twenty-First Century Books 2006 111p il (Discovery!) lib bdg $29.27
Grades: 7 8 9 10   **614.4**
1. Communicable diseases
ISBN 978-0-8225-3416-7; 0-8225-3416-9
                                    LC 2005-17271
This book covers "topics associated with current infectious diseases." Sci Books Films
"This title is a thorough, understandable, and accessible source of current information and medical definitions, and a trail to further research." SLJ
Includes bibliographical references

Grady, Denise
Deadly invaders; virus outbreaks around the world, from Marburg fever to avian flu. Kingfisher 2006 128p il map $16.95
Grades: 7 8 9 10   **614.4**
1. Communicable diseases
ISBN 978-0-7534-5995-9; 0-7534-5995-7
                                    LC 2006004441
"A New York Times book"
"In the first half of the book . . . Grady discusses the Marburg virus, the incurable disease it causes, and its effects on individuals and communities, as seen through the lens of her personal experiences in Angola. . . . Next she offers a short . . . chapter on each of seven deadly diseases: Marburg fever, avian flu, HIV/AIDS, Hantavirus pulmonary syndrome, West Nile disease, SARS, and monkeypox." Booklist

Grady, Denise—*Continued*

The "writing is informative and compelling. . . . The layout is appealing and includes good-quality, full-color, relevant photographs on almost every spread. . . . A fast-paced, timely, and important book." SLJ

Includes bibliographical references

McKenna, Maryn

Beating back the devil; on the front lines with the disease detectives of the Epidemic Intelligence Service. Free Press 2004 303p $26

Grades: 11 12 Adult   614.4

1. Centers for Disease Control and Prevention (U.S.).
Epidemic Intelligence Service Program
ISBN 0-7432-5132-6   LC 2004-53214

"This book celebrates a group of unsung heroes, the Epidemic Intelligence Service (EIS) of the U.S. Centers for Disease Control. Since its inception in 1951, the EIS has sent officers around the world to investigate outbreaks of diseases from polio, smallpox, tuberculosis, SARS, and West Nile Virus to the bioterrorist anthrax attacks." Libr J

"This book should serve as an effective antidote for anyone suffering from the misconception that epidemologists must lead boring lives." Sci Books Films

Includes bibliographical references

Walters, Mark Jerome

Six modern plagues and how we are causing them. Island Press 2003 206p $22; pa $14

Grades: 11 12 Adult   614.4

1. Epidemiology 2. Communicable diseases
3. Environmental health 4. Human ecology
ISBN   1-55963-992-X;   978-1-55963-992-7;
1-55963-714-5 (pa); 978-1-55963-714-5 (pa)
                                              LC 2003-15137

The author "examines six modern diseases: mad cow disease, HIV/AIDS, salmonella DT104, Lyme disease, hantavirus, and West Nile virus. Highlighting the main features of the history and impact of each of these diseases, he presents them as 'parables of the unintended consequences of the careless human disruption of the natural systems that are our home.'" Choice

"A quick read and a great introduction to the topic." Libr J

Includes bibliographical references

Ward, Brian R.

Epidemic; by Brian Ward. Dorling Kindersley 2000 64p il (DK eyewitness books) $15.99; lib bdg $19.99

Grades: 9 10 11 12   614.4

1. Epidemics
ISBN 0-7894-6296-6; 0-7894-6989-8 (lib bdg)
                                              LC 00-27948

Discusses what an epidemic is, how it evolves, various causes and carriers, and efforts to prevent epidemics

614.5 Incidence & prevention of specific diseases

AIDS; Andrea C. Nakaya, book editor. Greenhaven Press 2006 144p il (Introducing issues with opposing viewpoints) lib bdg $32.45 *

Grades: 9 10 11 12   614.5

1. AIDS (Disease)
ISBN 0-7377-3218-0   LC 2005-47417

"This anthology combines . . . articles with . . . visual elements like cartoons, charts, maps and pictures to help students gain an understanding of the causes of, and possible solutions to, this devastating pandemic." Publisher's note

Includes bibliographical references

Byrne, Joseph Patrick

The black death; [by] Joseph P. Byrne. Greenwood Press 2004 xxx, 231p il map (Greenwood guides to historic events of the medieval world) $45

Grades: 9 10 11 12   614.5

1. Plague
ISBN 0-313-32492-1   LC 2004-43640

This book "describes the bubonic plague that destroyed large European populations in the 14th century. . . . [The author] has compiled an outstanding reference discussing many theories about the possible causes, transmission, societal implications, economic consequences, and impact on modern medicine." SLJ

Includes bibliographical references

Cantor, Norman F., 1929-2004

In the wake of the plague; the Black death and the world it made. 1st Perennial ed. Perennial/HarperCollins 2002 245p il map pa $13.95

Grades: 11 12 Adult   614.5

1. Plague
ISBN 0-06-001434-2   LC 2001-51819

First published 2001 by Free Press

The author "looks at the effects of the Black Death on 14th-century Europe." Libr J

"By animating history and demonstrating our times' connections to even as remote an event as the Black Death, Cantor's erudite excursion proves most engrossing." Booklist

Includes bibliographical references

Crosby, Molly Caldwell

The American plague; the untold story of yellow fever, the epidemic that shaped our history. Berkley Books 2006 308p il $24.95

Grades: 11 12 Adult   614.5

1. Yellow fever
ISBN 0-425-21202-5; 978-0-425-21202-8
                                              LC 2006-50497

This book tells the "story of yellow fever, recounting Memphis Tennessee's near-destruction and resurrection

Crosby, Molly Caldwell—*Continued*
from the epidemic—and the four men who changed medical history with their battle against an invisible foe that remains a threat to this very day." Publisher's note

The author "offers a forceful narrative of a disease's ravages and the quest to find its cause and cure." Publ Wkly

Includes bibliographical references

Emmeluth, Donald

Botulism; [by] Don Emmeluth. Chelsea House 2005 136p il (Deadly diseases and epidemics) $31.95

Grades: 7 8 9 10   **614.5**

1. Botulism

ISBN 0-7910-8674-7   LC 2005-16673

Contents: Historical perspective; Causes of botulism; Transmission of botulism; Diagnosis of botulism; Botulism and the nervous system; Treating botulism; Preventing botulism; Concerns for the future; Hopes for the future

Includes glossary and bibliographical references

Goldsmith, Connie, 1945-

Influenza: the next pandemic? Twenty-First Century Books 2007 112p il (Twenty-first century medical library) lib bdg $27.93

Grades: 6 7 8 9 10   **614.5**

1. Influenza

ISBN 978-0-7613-9457-0; 0-7613-9457-5 (lib bdg)

LC 2005-23588

The author "traces the history of the flu, giving attention to past outbreaks and epidemics. She also describes flu viruses of today, explains treatments, and details health officials' concerns about bird flu. . . . Good for reports, and a worthy source to update collections." SLJ

Includes bibliographical references

Grady, Sean M., 1965-

Biohazards; humanity's battle with infectious disease; [by] Sean M. Grady and John Tabak. Facts on File 2006 194p il map (Science & technology in focus) $35 *

Grades: 7 8 9 10   **614.5**

1. Communicable diseases

ISBN 0-8160-4687-5   LC 2005-5610

This "work . . . examines the bacteria and viruses that make up a significant part of our world. The threat of bioterrorism; the risks of international travel; the spread, control, and treatment of such newly important diseases as anthrax, hantavirus, and HIV/AIDS, as well as historical ones like the Black Plague and smallpox, are clearly discussed." SLJ

Includes bibliographical references

Greenfeld, Karl Taro, 1964-

China syndrome; the true story of the 21st century's first great epidemic. HarperCollins 2006 442p map $25.95

Grades: 11 12 Adult   **614.5**

1. SARS (Disease)

ISBN 0-06-058722-9; 978-0-06-058722-2

LC 2005-52684

In this book about the 2002 SARS outbreak in China, the author "traces the origins and spread of the disease in a chronological drumbeat that sometimes follows the events by day." Libr J

"The story unfolds like a whodunnit, with a large cast of rogues, victims and heroes. . . . This book is a parable for our times." New Statesman

Includes bibliographical references

Johnson, Steven, 1968-

The ghost map; the story of London's most terrifying epidemic—and how it changed science, cities, and the modern world. Riverhead 2006 299p il map $26.95

Grades: 11 12 Adult   **614.5**

1. Snow, John, 1813-1858 2. Cholera

ISBN 1-59448-925-4; 978-1-59448-925-9

LC 2006-23114

This book "takes place in the summer of 1854. A devastating cholera outbreak seizes London just as it is emerging as a modern city. . . . Dr. John Snow—whose ideas about contagion had been dismissed by the scientific community—is spurred to intense action when the people in his neighborhood begin dying. . . . Johnson chronicles Snow's day-by-day efforts, as he risks his own life to prove how the epidemic is being spread." Publisher's note

"From Snow's discovery of patient zero to Johnson's compelling argument for and celebration of cities, this makes for an illuminating and satisfying read." Publ Wkly

Includes bibliographical references

Kelly, John, 1945-

The great mortality; an intimate history of the Black Death, the most devastating plague of all time. HarperCollins Publishers 2005 364p $25.95; pa $14.95

Grades: 11 12 Adult   **614.5**

1. Plague

ISBN 0-06-000692-7; 0-06-000693-5 (pa)

LC 2004-54213

"Western Europe is the primary focus of Kelly's compact history, which is 'intimate' in that it highlights many particular persons' passages through the crucible years, 1348-49. . . . Kelly proceeds chronologically, beginning with the plague's prehistory in north central Asia and its spread through China before empire-building Mongols brought it west. . . . This sweeping, viscerally exciting book contributes to a literature of perpetual fascination: the chronicles of pestilence." Booklist

Includes bibliographical references

Marlink, Richard G., 1954-

Global AIDS crisis; a reference handbook; [by] Richard G. Marlink and Alison G Kotin. ABC-CLIO 2004 283p il map (Contemporary world issues) $50 *

Grades: 9 10 11 12   **614.5**

1. AIDS (Disease)

ISBN 1-85109-655-8   LC 2004-21402

Marlink, Richard G., 1954- —*Continued*

"Focusing on the worldwide scope of the crisis, this handbook examines a variety of aspects of AIDS in historical, contemporary, and future contexts. . . . A useful resource for students doing research on the worldwide impact of AIDS." SLJ

Includes bibliographical references

Oshinsky, David M., 1944-

Polio; an American story. Oxford University Press 2005 342p il $30; pa $16.95

Grades: 11 12 Adult   **614.5**

1. Poliomyelitis vaccine

ISBN 0-19-515294-8; 0-19-530714-3 (pa)

LC 2004-25249

This is an account of the "effort to find a cure [for polio], from the March of Dimes to the discovery of the Salk and Sabin vaccines." Publisher's note

This book "is a rich and illuminating analysis that convincingly grounds the ways and means of modern American research in the response to polio." N Y Times Book Rev

Includes bibliographical references

Pierce, John R.

Yellow jack; how yellow fever ravaged America and Walter Reed discovered its deadly secrets; [by] John R. Pierce, Jim Writer. J. Wiley 2005 278p il $24.95

Grades: 11 12 Adult   **614.5**

1. Reed, Walter, 1851-1902 2. Yellow fever

ISBN 0-471-47261-1   LC 2004-13845

The authors "describe the probable African origins of the disease, its 350-year history in the Caribbean, and the deadly epidemics that terrorized the colonies and early United States." Sci Books Films

"This chronicle of the rise and eventual fall of yellow fever traces a substantial medical history." Booklist

Includes bibliographical references

Preston, Richard

The hot zone. Random House 1994 300p pa $14 hardcover o.p.

Grades: 11 12 Adult   **614.5**

1. Ebola virus 2. Animal experimentation

ISBN 0-385-49522-6 (pa)   LC 94-13415

"Ebola, a lethal virus that slumbers in an unknown host somewhere in the rain forest, sneaked into the United States in 1989 in a shipment of primates that ended up in a monkey house in Reston, Virginia. This virus jumps between species easily, and takes only weeks to kill its victim, with gory hemorrhaging from various orifices. Preston tells the suspenseful tale of its detection, and gives vivid life to the members of the SWAT team that, for eighteen bio-hazardous days, combatted the strain now known as Ebola Reston." New Yorker

Sehgal, Alfica

Leprosy; foreword by David Heymann. Chelsea House 2006 88p il (Deadly diseases and epidemics) $31.95

Grades: 9 10 11 12   **614.5**

1. Leprosy

ISBN 0-7910-8502-3   LC 2005-10391

Contents: An introduction to leprosy -- The spread, signs, and types of leprosy -- Leprosy around the world -- What causes leprosy? -- Host-pathogen interactions -- Bringing leprosy under control -- Bacteria do not like test tubes -- Ongoing reforms and the future

Includes glossary and bibliographical references

Siegel, Marc, 1956-

Bird flu; everything you need to know about the next pandemic. Wiley 2006 202p pa $12.95

Grades: 11 12 Adult   **614.5**

1. Avian influenza

ISBN 978-0-470-03864-2; 0-470-03864-0

LC 2005-36110

The author "cites evidence that the death rate from avian flu could be much lower than the reported estimate of 50% and it will probably not mutate to be readily transmissible between humans. . . . Revisiting the West Nile virus, anthrax, SARS and bioterrorism panics, Siegel sees bird flu as the latest 'bug du jour' hyped by government and media alarmism. . . . Siegel's exemplary bedside manner makes this dose of common sense go down easy." Publ Wkly

Includes bibliographical references

Spurlock, Morgan, 1970-

Don't eat this book; fast food and the supersizing of America. G. P. Putnam's Sons 2005 308p $21.95; pa $14 *

Grades: 9 10 11 12 Adult   **614.5**

1. Convenience foods 2. Food industry 3. Restaurants

ISBN 0-399-15260-1; 0-425-21023-5 (pa)

LC 2005-43196

The author "describes America's obesity epidemic, its relation to the fast food industry, the industry's cozy relations to U.S. government agencies and how the problem is spreading worldwide. . . . His book is a powerful tool in his rip-roaring campaign to turn around America's love-hate relationship with fast food." Publ Wkly

Includes bibliographical references

615 Pharmacology and therapeutics

Amphetamines; edited by Nancy Harris. Greenhaven Press 2005 174p (History of drugs) $34.95

Grades: 9 10 11 12   **615**

1. Amphetamines 2. Methamphetamine

ISBN 0-7377-1949-4   LC 2004-40577

This anthology discusses the history of amphetamine use and the different varieties used over the years, including Ecstacy and methamphetamines. It also discusses how some amphetamines have been used as medicine.

Includes bibliographical references

Antidepressants; edited by William Dudley.
Greenhaven Press 2005 188p (History of drugs)
$34.95
Grades: 9 10 11 12   **615**
1. Antidepressants
ISBN 0-7377-1951-6   LC 2004-52357
This "anthology traces the history of the invention and
selling of antidepressants and their impact on American
society. It also examines controversies about their safety
and effectiveness." Publisher's note
Includes bibliographical references

Antidepressants; Katherine Dunbar, book editor.
Greenhaven Press 2006 91p (At issue) lib bdg
$28.70; pa $19.95
Grades: 9 10 11 12   **615**
1. Antidepressants
ISBN 0-7377-3115-X (lib bdg); 0-7377-3116-8 (pa)
                                      LC 2005-40330
"The authors in this anthology debate the safety and
efficacy of antidepressants in both children and adults,
exploring issues such as overprescription, the placebo effect and suicide." Publisher's note
Includes bibliographical references

Chevallier, Andrew
Encyclopedia of herbal medicine. 2nd ed. DK
Pub. 2000 336p il $40
Grades: 11 12 Adult   **615**
1. Materia medica 2. Medical botany
ISBN 0-7894-6783-6   LC 2001-268250
First published 1996 with title: The encyclopedia of
medicinal plants
This provides information about the current uses, cul-
tivation, habitat, and folklore of over 550 herbs
This "volume remains a top choice for a library refer-
ence on the medicinal use of herbs for the public." Libr
J

Facklam, Margery, 1927-
Modern medicines; the discovery and
development of healing drugs; Margery Facklam,
Howard Facklam, and Sean M. Grady. Rev. ed.
Facts on File 2004 226p il (Science & technology
in focus) $29.95 *
Grades: 7 8 9 10   **615**
1. Pharmacology 2. Drugs
ISBN 0-8160-4706-5   LC 2003-11489
First published 1992 with title: Healing drugs: the history of pharmacology
Contents: Ancient remedies; A garden of simples; Patent cures and medicine shows; Formalizing pharmacology; A world of wonder drugs; Preemptive strikes; Biological systems management; Miracles in the medicine
cabinet; From the laboratory to the pharmacy; Producing
modern pills and potions; New uses for old drugs; When
drugs go wrong; Back to the Garden?; Herbalists and scientists; Warning signs; Drug-resistant germs; The perils
of medicine; Distribution woes; Future trends in pharmacology
"Straightforward, sensibly organized, and well researched, this volume . . . is an excellent introduction."
Booklist

Hager, Thomas
The demon under the microscope; from
battlefield hospitals to Nazi labs, one doctor's
heroic search for the world's first miracle drug.
Harmony Books 2006 340p $24.95
Grades: 11 12 Adult   **615**
1. Domagk, Gerhard, 1895-1964 2. Sulfonamides
ISBN 1-4000-8213-7; 978-1-4000-8213-1
                                      LC 2006-4510
The author "narrates the story of the race [by doctors
such as Gerhard Domagk] to find the 'magic bullet' to
eliminate diseases such as pneumonia, childbed fever,
and gonorrhea. . . . Hager connects early innovations in
medicine to the fortuitous and intuitive leaps that allowed
early 20th-century researchers to create sulfa, the first antibiotic. . . . One is left with a sense of gratitude for the
relative safety of modern medical practices." Libr J
Includes bibliographical references

Hallucinogens; edited by Mary E. Williams.
Greenhaven Press 2005 203p (History of drugs)
$34.95
Grades: 9 10 11 12   **615**
1. Hallucinogens
ISBN 0-7377-1959-1   LC 2004-52394
"Authors discuss the development of such drugs as
LSD, mescaline, and psilocybin, defining their dangers,
describing their influence on the 1960s counterculture,
and debating their potential therapeutic uses." Publisher's
note
Includes bibliographical references

Kidd, J. S. (Jerry S.)
Potent natural medicines; Mother Nature's
pharmacy; [by] J.S. Kidd and Renee A. Kidd. rev
ed. Chelsea House 2006 212p il (Science and
society) $35 *
Grades: 7 8 9 10   **615**
1. Pharmacology 2. Medical botany
ISBN 0-8160-5607-2   LC 2005041741
First published 1998 with title: Mother Nature's pharmacy
This introduces "plants' medicinal properties, pioneers
who hunted for sources of and applications for botanical
treatments, and the ways phytochemical nutrients prevent
disease. . . . [Also included] are chapters about recent
research, including investigation into animal sources for
medicine; the impact of field research on native peoples;
and the federal regulation of herb and plant supplements.
. . . This [is] a good choice to support research and debate projects." Booklist
Includes bibliographical references

Lax, Eric
The mold in Dr. Florey's coat; the story of the
penicillin miracle. Henry Holt and Co. 2004 307p
il $25; pa $15 *
Grades: 9 10 11 12 Adult   **615**
1. Penicillin
ISBN 0-8050-6790-6; 0-8050-7778-2 (pa)
                                      LC 2003-56685
"A John Macrae book"

Lax, Eric—*Continued*

Penicillin was discovered in 1928. "But it took a team of Oxford scientists headed by Howard Florey and Ernest Chain four more years to develop it as the first antibiotic. . . . Lax tells the story behind the discovery and why it took so long to develop the drug." Publisher's note

"In this fluent, entertaining report on the history of the arguably most significant medical discovery of the twentieth century, Lax delves into the lives of the colorful scientists who played significant roles in developing the antibiotic." Booklist

Includes bibliographical references

Marijuana; edited by Jordan McMullin. Greenhaven Press 2005 188p (History of drugs) $34.95 *
Grades: 9 10 11 12   615
1. Marijuana
ISBN 0-7377-1957-5   LC 2004-47474

"This book chronicles the history of marijuana in various cultures, specifically focusing on its role in Western society and the heated debates that have surrounded its use and abuse." Publisher's note

This anthology's "atypical approach, healthy quantities of additional documentation at the end, and an international point of view earn it a place in deeper subject collections." Booklist

Includes bibliographical references

Mehling, Randi

Hallucinogens. Chelsea House 2003 125p (Drugs: the straight facts) lib bdg $22.95
Grades: 9 10 11 12   615
1. Hallucinogens
ISBN 0-7910-7261-4   LC 2002-153504

Contents: The history of hallucinogens; The psychodelic effects of hallucinogens; The properties of hallucinogens; The health effects of hallucinogens; Teenage trends and attitudes; Hallucinogen dependency; Hallucinogens and the law

"The book covers the history and physical properties of hallucinogens, and provides the reader with information on the health effects, trends and attitudes, and legal ramifications associated with the use of the drugs." Publisher's note

The **Merck** index; an encyclopedia of chemicals, drugs, and biologicals; Maryadele J. O'Neil, editor; Patricia E. Heckelman, senior associate editor; Cherie B. Koch, associate editor; Kristin J. Roman, assistant editor; Catherine M. Kenny, editorial assistant; Maryann R. D'Arecca, administrative assistant. 14th ed. Merck 2006 various paging il $125 *
Grades: 11 12 Adult   615
1. Materia medica 2. Drugs
ISBN 0-911910-00-X; 978-0-911910-00-1
Also available CD-ROM version and online
First published 1889. Periodically revised
Includes CD-ROM

"Technical descriptions of the preparation, properties, uses, commercial names, and toxicity of drugs and medicines." N Y Public Libr Book of How & Where to Look It Up

Miller, Richard Lawrence

The encyclopedia of addictive drugs. Greenwood Press 2002 491p $75 *
Grades: 9 10 11 12 Adult   615
ISBN 0-313-31807-7   LC 2002-75332

"The more than 130 substances included are both natural and pharmaceutical products, all associated with misuse and addiction. Listed by common name, the initial citation includes pronunciation, Chemical Abstracts Service Registry Number, formal and informal names, drug type, U.S. availability, and more. The accompanying article discusses uses, drawbacks, abuse factors, drug interactions, cancer risks, and effects on pregnancy, and concludes with a bibliography." SLJ

615.5 Therapeutics

Billitteri, Thomas J.

Alternative medicine. 21st Cent. Bks. (Brookfield) 2001 112p il (Twenty-first century medical library) lib bdg $26.90
Grades: 7 8 9 10   615.5
1. Alternative medicine
ISBN 0-7613-0965-9   LC 00-57707

"Among the topics covered are homeopathic medicine, hypnosis, chiropractic touch therapy, and acupuncture. . . . This book is a solid choice for general information and for reports." SLJ

Includes bibliographical references

Navarra, Tova

The encyclopedia of complementary and alternative medicine; foreword by Adam Perelman. Facts on File 2004 xxiii, 276p $75; pa $18.95
Grades: 11 12 Adult   615.5
1. Alternative medicine—Encyclopedias
ISBN 0-8160-4997-1; 0-8160-6226-9 (pa)
                                            LC 2003-43415

"The topics in this book . . . range from yoga, chiropractic, and homeopathy to herbal remedies, imagery and visualization, massage, medication, and naturopathy. . . . Besides the entries, this important resource offers appendixes that list professional and lay organizations and herbs used in varieties of medical disciplines, and a time line of the various therapies." Choice

For a fuller review, see: Booklist, May 15, 2004
Includes bibliographical references

The **New** York Times guide to alternative health; a consumer reference; by Jane E. Brody, Denise Grady, and the reporters of the New York Times. Times Bks. 2001 394p il pa $16 *
Grades: 9 10 11 12 Adult   615.5
1. Alternative medicine 2. Consumer education
ISBN 0-8050-6743-4   LC 2001-17160

This guide "offers facts, theories, and anecdotal evidence related to several of the most popular alternative therapies, including acupuncture, massage therapy, herbal medicine, and chiropractic. . . . This is a useful resource for libraries that receive frequent questions about alternative therapies. It will also be a good resource for students who are writing papers on alternative therapies, as it includes both historical and current information about the therapies." Libr J

615.8 Specific therapies and kinds of therapies

Gene therapy; Roman Espejo, book editor. Greenhaven Press 2005 74p (At issue) lib bdg $28.70; pa $19.95

Grades: 9 10 11 12 **615.8**
1. Gene therapy
ISBN 0-7377-2256-8 (lib bdg); 0-7377-2257-6 (pa)
LC 2004-40587

In this collection of articles "the authors explore the benefits and risks involved in this young field of research as well as the significant implications gene therapy will have on human health if it becomes an acceptable form of treatment." Introduction

Includes bibliographical references

Gene therapy; Clay Farris Naff, book editor. Greenhaven Press 2005 224p il (Exploring science and medical discoveries) lib bdg $34.95; pa $23.70 *

Grades: 9 10 11 12 **615.8**
1. Gene therapy
ISBN 0-7377-1967-2 (lib bdg); 0-7377-1968-0 (pa)
LC 2003-62482

"This anthology charts the discoveries and the blind alleys, the bold experiments and the misguided fiascos, and the hype and hysteria along the path to gene-therapy cures." Publisher's note

Panno, Joseph
Gene therapy; treating disease by repairing genes. Facts on File 2004 172p il (New biology) $35 *

Grades: 9 10 11 12 Adult **615.8**
1. Gene therapy
ISBN 0-8160-4948-3 LC 2003-25851

"This book provides an account of the research leading to the first successful gene therapy trial and discusses the worldwide attention and subsequent controversy caused by the tragic death of a patient receiving gene therapy, as well as the future prospects and general ethics of gene therapy." Publisher's note

Includes bibliographical references

615.9 Toxicology

Brands, Danielle A.
Salmonella. Chelsea House 2005 102p il (Deadly diseases and epidemics) $31.95

Grades: 7 8 9 10 **615.9**
1. Salmonellosis
ISBN 0-7910-8500-7 LC 2005-5348

Contents: Salmonella strikes at the senior prom; Salmonella and food-borne illness; Hosts, sources, and carriers; Salmonella in the body; Treating salmonellosis; Salmonella outbreaks and current research; Other bacteria that cause food poisoning; Preventing salmonellosis

Includes glossary and bibliographical references

Callahan, Joan R.
Biological hazards; an Oryx sourcebook. Oryx Press 2002 385p il (Oryx sourcebooks on hazards and disasters) $64.95

Grades: 11 12 Adult **615.9**
1. Communicable diseases 2. Poisons and poisoning 3. Environmental health
ISBN 1-57356-385-4 LC 2001-55184

This sourcebook provides "introductory information on a wide range of biological hazards. . . . Chapters divide hazards into categories: human pathogens in water, food, and air; those transmitted by contact; plant and animal pathogens and pests; venoms, toxins, and allergens; and animals that are a threat for predatory or other behavior. Another chapter provides information on controversial topics such as immunization and biological warfare. . . . The chapters that deal with different kinds of hazards offer extensive references and recommended readings. Lists of additional resources, including statistics and documents, print resources, nonprint resources, and organizations, comprise the final chapters." Booklist

Includes bibliographical references

Food-borne illnesses; Karen F. Balkin, book editor. Greenhaven Press 2004 80p (At issue) lib bdg $28.70; pa $19.95

Grades: 9 10 11 12 **615.9**
1. Food adulteration and inspection 2. Food poisoning
ISBN 0-7377-1334-8 (lib bdg); 0-7377-1335-6 (pa)
LC 2003-66265

This book features "information on Mad Cow Disease, genetically modified foods, food irradiation, [and] bioterrorism. . . . There are also three pieces devoted to the meat-packing industry and market inspection. . . . A good starting point for discussion or for term papers." SLJ

Includes bibliographical references

616 Diseases

Bakalar, Nick
Where the germs are; a scientific safari; {by} Nicholas Bakalar. Wiley 2003 262p il $24.95 *

Grades: 9 10 11 12 Adult **616**
1. Microbiology 2. Germ theory of disease 3. Bacteria
ISBN 0-471-15589-6 LC 2003-271569

This book is "about our everyday interactions with microbes. . . . It reveals some of the extraordinary things scientists now know about these most ordinary companions." Publisher's note

The author's "excellent chapter on childhood diseases and vaccines should be required reading for parents, and teenagers should be plunked down in a chair with the chapter on sexually transmitted diseases. . . . His writing is witty, and he gives all the details of germs and illnesses without medical school jargon." Publ Wkly

Crawford, Dorothy H.
The invisible enemy; a natural history of viruses. Oxford Univ. Press 2000 275p il hardcover o.p. pa $14.95 *
Grades: 9 10 11 12 Adult   616
1. Viruses
ISBN 0-19-850332-6; 0-19-856481-3 (pa)
LC 00-36756
The author begins by explaining how viruses "subvert the internal machinery of living cells to reproduce and spread. . . . Ms. Crawford examines the threats posed by the Lassa and Hanta viruses—as well as Ebola, . . . and assesses the prospects for a flu pandemic like that of 1918, which infected half the world's population." Economist
"Crawford offers new knowledge and insights for any reader, regardless of the depth of their science education." New Sci
Includes bibliographical references

Diseases; Bryan Bunch and Jenny Tesar, editors. 3rd rev. ed. Scholastic Library Pub. 2006 8v il set $349
Grades: 6 7 8 9 10   616
1. Diseases—Encyclopedias
ISBN 0-7172-6205-7   LC 2006-7986
First published 1997
Alphabetically arranged articles presenting medical information on more than 500 diseases, discussing causes, symptoms, stages of the disease, its likelihood of striking, treatments, prevention, and long-term effects.
"Students will find a goldmine of basic reference information in these attractive . . . volumes." SLJ
Includes bibliographical references

The **Gale** encyclopedia of genetic disorders; Brigham Narins, editor. 2nd ed. Thomson Gale 2005 2v il set $340
Grades: 9 10 11 12   616
1. Medical genetics—Encyclopedias
ISBN 1-4144-0365-8   LC 2005-7599
First published 2001 under the editorship of Stacey L. Blachford
This encyclopedia offers "coverage of more than 400 conditions with genetic origins or connections, among them the well known (e.g., Down syndrome, sickle cell disease) and the lesser known (e.g., neuraminidase deficiency, cadasil)." Libr J
For a fuller review, see: Booklist, Feb. 1, 2006
Includes bibliographical references

Hains, Bryan C.
Pain; series editor, Eric H. Chudler. Chelsea House Publishers 2006 121p il (Gray matter) lib bdg $32.95
Grades: 8 9 10 11 12   616
1. Pain 2. Brain
ISBN 0-7910-8951-7; 978-0-7910-8951-4 (lib bdg)
LC 2006-15133
This book "explores the workings of the somatosensory and pain systems, how disorders can affect how we process information with these systems, and how pain can be treated." Publisher's note
Includes glossary and bibliographical references

Human diseases and conditions; Neil Izenberg, editor in chief. Scribner 2000 3v il set $325 *
Grades: 9 10 11 12 Adult   616
1. Medicine
ISBN 0-684-80543-X   LC 99-51442
Also available: Supplement II, Infectious diseases and the immune system $100 (ISBN 0-684-31260-3)
Published in association with the Center for Children's Health Media, the Nemours Foundation
"Almost 300 diseases and conditions are included (with an equal number of color photographs, charts, and illustrations), covering such topics as cleft palate, kuru, obsessive-compulsive disorder, slipped disk, and typhoid fever. . . . Each entry, ranging in length from one to eight pages, contains information on natural history, causes, cures, and prevention, when appropriate. . . . Children and teenagers are obviously the intended audience, though any adult would find this book valuable."
Includes bibliographical references

Newton, David E.
Stem cell research. Facts on File 2007 284p il (Library in a book) $45 *
Grades: 9 10 11 12 Adult   616
1. Stem cell research
ISBN 978-0-8160-6576-9; 0-8160-6576-4
LC 2005-32803
"Covering court cases, legislation, and relevant policies, this volume also includes a chronology; a glossary; a guide to further research; an annotated bibliography . . . ; appendixes; as well as an index." Publisher's note
Includes bibliographical references

Panno, Joseph
Stem cell research; medical applications and ethical controversy. Facts on File 2005 178p il (New biology) $35; pa $18.95
Grades: 11 12 Adult   616
1. Stem cell research
ISBN 0-8160-4949-1; 0-8160-6931-X (pa)
LC 2003-25975
The author "explains how stem cells can be used to treat, and possibly cure, a wide variety of diseases, and he predicts that the use of adult stem cells will soon be routine. . . . In addition, there is a chapter summarizing cell biology and recombinant DNA technology. A carefully done, in-depth . . . [book] that will work well for researchers and debaters, adults as well as teens." Booklist
Includes bibliographical references

Shnayerson, Michael
The killers within; the deadly rise of drug-resistant bacteria; {by} Michael Shnayerson, Mark Plotkin. Little, Brown 2002 328p hardcover o.p. pa $14.95
Grades: 11 12 Adult   616
1. Bacteria 2. Antibiotics
ISBN 0-316-71331-7; 0-316-73566-3 (pa)
LC 2002-24177

Shnayerson, Michael—*Continued*

The authors provide a "look at the overuse of antibiotics, the methods bacteria use to develop resistance, the role of antibiotics as animal growth promoters, and the outlook for antibiotics. . . . Shnayerson and Plotkin have managed to demonstrate their concern over the future of antibiotics while keeping the scientific background manageable for lay readers." Libr J

Includes bibliographical references

Stark, Peter

Last breath; cautionary tales from the limits of human endurance. Ballantine Bks. 2001 300p hardcover o.p. pa $14.95

Grades: 11 12 Adult   **616**

1. Outdoor life—Accidents 2. Adventure and adventurers 3. Death

ISBN 0-345-44150-8; 0-345-44151-6 (pa)

LC 2001-37553

A "look at how individuals can face death in the course of adventure and daring. . . . Scenarios include hypothermia, drowning while kayaking on a treacherous Chinese river, suffocation by avalanche, and heatstroke in a competitive bike race. Other dangers include altitude sickness, scurvy, falling, jellyfish stings, the bends, malaria, and dehydration. . . . Each story is compelling and the mystery of the outcome holds readers' attention." SLJ

Includes bibliographical references

Tierno, Philip M., Jr.

The secret life of germs; observations and lessons of a microbe hunter; [by] Philip M. Tierno, Jr. Pocket Bks. 2002 c2001 290p hardcover o.p. pa $14

Grades: 11 12 Adult   **616**

1. Microorganisms

ISBN 0-7434-2187-6; 0-7434-2188-4 (pa)

LC 2001-36937

This is "the story of bacteria, viruses, and prions and their myriad effects on human beings. From toxic shock syndrome to Lyme disease to diarrheal infections of the Third World, Tierno offers a broad overview of the impact of these microbes on the world today. . . . An interesting book for popular science readers as well as for students doing reports on disease." Libr J

Includes bibliographical references

Wynbrandt, James

The encyclopedia of genetic disorders and birth defects; by James Wynbrandt and Mark D. Ludman. 2nd ed. Facts on File 2000 xx, 474p $71.50 *

Grades: 9 10 11 12 Adult   **616**

1. Phobias 2. Fear

ISBN 0-8160-3989-5   LC 98-53568

First published 1991

New edition in preparation

This volume covers "clinical and research information on hereditary conditions and birth defects. The text includes a general essay on the basics of genetic science and its medical applications. More than 600 entries are

. . . cross-referenced and explore genetic anomalies, diagnostic procedures, causes of mutations, and high risk groups." Publisher's note

"The clearly written text . . . makes a complex and difficult subject comprehensible." Am Ref Books Annu, 2001

Includes bibliographical references

616.02   Domestic medicine and medical emergencies

American Medical Association family medical guide. 4th ed., completely rev. and updated. John Wiley & Sons 2004 1184p il $45 *

Grades: 9 10 11 12 Adult   **616.02**

1. Medicine 2. Health self-care

ISBN 0-471-26911-5   LC 2004-5764

First published 1982

Contents: What you should know: information to keep you healthy -- Staying healthy -- Diet and health -- Exercise, fitness, and health -- A healthy weight -- Reducing stress -- Staying safe -- Preventing violence -- Preventive health care -- Complementary and alternative medicine -- First aid and caregiving -- First aid -- Home caregiving -- What are your symptoms? -- Symptoms charts -- Health issues throughout life -- Children's health -- Adolescent health -- Sexuality -- Infertility -- Pregnancy and childbirth -- Dying and death -- Diseases, disorders, and other problems -- Disorders of the heart and circulation -- Blood disorders -- Disorders of the respiratory system -- Disorders of the brain and nervous system -- Behavioral, emotional, and mental disorders -- Disorders of the digestive system -- Disorders of the urinary tract -- Disorders of the male reproductive system -- Disorders of the female reproductive system and urinary tract -- Hormonal disorders -- Disorders of the immune system -- Infections and infestations -- Genetic disorders -- Disorders of the bones, muscles, and joints -- Disorders of the ear -- Eye disorders -- Disorders of the skin, hair, and nails -- Cosmetic surgery -- Teeth and gums

"This is a well-organized volume, considering the amount of information it covers." Publ Wkly

The **American** Red Cross first aid and safety handbook; [prepared by] American Red Cross and Kathleen A. Handal; foreword by Elizabeth Dole. Little, Brown 1992 321p il hardcover o.p. pa $18.95 *

Grades: 9 10 11 12 Adult   **616.02**

1. First aid

ISBN 0-316-73645-7; 0-316-73646-5 (pa)

LC 91-24847

This first aid guidebook is based on course materials used by the Red Cross and covers how to handle such emergencies as allergic reactions, bleeding, choking, and heart attacks.

The **Merck** manual of medical information; Mark H. Beers, editor-in-chief; Andrew J. Fletcher, Thomas V. Jones, and Robert Porter, senior assistant editors; Michael Berkwitz, and Justin L. Kaplan, assistant editors. 2nd home ed. Merck Res. Labs. 2003 xxxviii, 1907p il $37.50; pa $19.95 *

Grades: 11 12 Adult   **616.02**

1. Medicine

ISBN 0-9119-1035-2; 0-7434-7733-2 (pa)

LC 2002-115250

Also available online

First published 1997

"A detailed table of contents lists 25 sections divided into chapters. The first, 'Fundamentals,' explains basic anatomy and physiology, the aging process, fitness, communicating with health professionals, and legal and ethical issues. The others cover specific organs, systems, diseases and disorders, drugs, and first aid. The sections dealing with organs and systems begin with the biology of the system and then explain the symptoms, diagnosis, prognosis, and treatment of diseases that may affect it. There are color diagrams of relevant anatomy as well as an eight-page insert of anatomical charts." Booklist

"Written for the layperson, articles are clear, comprehensive and detailed. There are excellent charts and illustrations to further make the material more understandable. Almost every conceivable medical condition is covered." Publ Wkly

616.07   Pathology

Brynie, Faith Hickman, 1946-

101 questions about your immune system you felt defenseless to answer . . . until now 2000 176p il lib bdg $25.90

Grades: 9 10 11 12   **616.07**

1. Immune system 2. Allergy 3. Vaccination

ISBN 0-7613-1569-1   LC 99-33368

"In addition to the physiology of the immune system, there are detailed sections about allergies and vaccines. The best chapter, however, is the up-to-date discussion about AIDS. The design is clear and open, with illustrations that include tables, photos, charts, and diagrams, and a detailed glossary and a long bibliography round out this volume." Booklist

Includes bibliographical references

Segen, J. C.

The patient's guide to medical tests; everything you need to know about the tests your doctor orders; [by] Joseph C. Segen and Josie Wade. 2nd ed. Facts on File 2002 418p (Facts on File library of health and living) $44 *

Grades: 9 10 11 12 Adult   **616.07**

1. Diagnosis

ISBN 0-8160-4651-4   LC 2002-18824

First published 1997 with Joseph Stauffer as joint author

This "guide presents information on more than 1,000 commonly prescribed tests and procedures. Each entry

includes a description of the test, patient preparation required, a description of the procedure itself, the reference range, what abnormal values may signify, and the approximate cost of each test." Publisher's note

616.1   Diseases of the cardiovascular system

Mertz, Leslie A.

The circulatory system; [by] Leslie Mertz. Greenwood Press 2004 xx, 217p il (Human body systems) $65 *

Grades: 11 12 Adult   **616.1**

1. Cardiovascular system

ISBN 0-313-32401-8   LC 2004-42449

In addition to the parts and functions of the circulatory system, "blood pressure, blood type and fetal circulation are covered. The history of research on the circulatory system is presented and the future of research in this field is considered. Current controversies and dilemmas, such as stem cell research, are explored." Publisher's note

Includes bibliographical references

616.2   Diseases of the respiratory system

Apel, Melanie Ann

Cystic fibrosis; the ultimate teen guide. Scarecrow Press 2006 259p il (It happened to me) $42

Grades: 9 10 11 12   **616.2**

1. Cystic fibrosis

ISBN 0-8108-4821-X   LC 2005-22073

"The first four chapters focus on the definition, source, diagnosis, and grueling treatments of cystic fibrosis before moving on to discuss patient and family reactions to the information and challenges. . . . Gripping personal accounts will pull in readers, teenage and adult, who are not familiar with the disease." Voice Youth Advocates

Includes bibliographical references

Asthma information for teens; edited by Karen Bellenir. Omnigraphics 2005 386p il (Teen health series) $65

Grades: 7 8 9 10   **616.2**

1. Asthma

ISBN 0-7808-0770-7

"Health tips about managing asthma and related concerns including facts about asthma causes, triggers, symptoms, diagnosis, and treatment." Title page

"Although this volume is nearly 400 pages long, it is so clearly written and well organized that even hesitant readers will be able to find the facts they need, whether for reports or for personal information. . . . A succinct but complete resource." SLJ

Emmeluth, Donald

Influenza; consulting editor I. Edward Alcamo; foreword by David Heymann. Chelsea House 2003 129p il (Deadly diseases and epidemics) lib bdg $25.95

Grades: 9 10 11 12   **616.2**

1. Influenza

ISBN 0-7910-7305-X   LC 2002-155110

Contents: Deadly world traveler; What is a virus?; Viral replication; "I've got the flu. What can I do?"; Diagnosis; Influenza—nature's frequent flyer: prevention; Dealing with complications; What may the future bring? the past and future concerns; The future: hopes and dreams

"This book discusses the history of influenza—some of the earliest recorded appearances of the disease to the largest epidemics in recent history. Emmeluth also provides information about the structure of the virus and the mechanism by which it causes disease." Publisher's note

Includes glossary and bibliographical references

Fanta, Christopher H.

The Harvard Medical School guide to taking control of asthma; a comprehensive prevention and treatment plan for you and your family; [by] Christopher H. Fanta, Lynda M. Cristiano, Kenan E. Haver, with Nancy Waring. Free Press 2003 331p il pa $14 *

Grades: 11 12 Adult   **616.2**

1. Asthma

ISBN 0-7432-2478-7   LC 2003-63145

"The authors explain how asthma is diagnosed and how the various symptoms, such as shortness of breath, wheezing and tightness in the chest, manifest themselves in different individuals. A large portion of the book is devoted to a lengthy and highly useful discussion of the current therapies available, as well as the pros and cons of specific medications." Publ Wkly

Includes bibliographical references

Finer, Kim R., 1956-

Tuberculosis; consulting editor I. Edward Alcamo; foreword by David Heymann. Chelsea House 2003 112p il (Deadly diseases and epidemics) lib bdg $25.95

Grades: 9 10 11 12   **616.2**

1. Tuberculosis

ISBN 0-7910-7309-2   LC 2002-155988

Contents: Tuberculosis throughout time; Robert Koch, Selman Waksman, and the near defeat of tuberculosis; The tuberculosis bacterium; Consumption: what happens once you become infected; Transmission from organism to organism; The immune response to tuberculosis infection; Screening for and diagnosis of tuberculosis; The BCG vaccine; Treatment of tuberculosis I: sanatoriums and early drug treatments; Treatment of tuberculosis II: modern drug therapy; The human immunodeficiency virus and tuberculosis

This book examines techniques for identifying, treating, and preventing tuberculosis as well as the social impact of the disease.

Includes glossary and bibliographical references

Lung disorders sourcebook; edited by Dawn D. Matthews. Omnigraphics 2002 678p il (Health reference series) $78 *

Grades: 11 12 Adult   **616.2**

1. Lungs—Diseases

ISBN 0-7808-0339-6   LC 2002-16976

"Basic consumer health information about emphysema, pneumonia, tuberculosis, asthma, cystic fibrosis, and other lung disorders. Including facts about diagnostic procedures, treatment strategies, disease prevention efforts, and such risk factors as smoking, air pollution, and exposure to asbestos, radon, and other agents: along with a glossary and resources for additional help and information." Title page

"This title is a great addition for public and school libraries because it provides concise health information on the lungs. Readers can start with this reference source and get satisfactory answers before proceeding to other medical reference tools for more in-depth information." Am Ref Books Annu, 2003

Paquette, Penny Hutchins

Asthma; the ultimate teen guide. Scarecrow Press 2003 171p il (It happened to me) $32.50; pa $14.95 *

Grades: 9 10 11 12   **616.2**

1. Asthma

ISBN 0-8108-4633-0; 0-8108-5759-6 (pa)

LC 2002-153542

Contents: How long has this been going on? A history of asthma; What is it? Asthma defined; Diagnosing asthma; Asthma triggers and how to avoid them; What to do about it? Asthma treatments; Dealing With asthma at school; When asthma becomes deadly; Coping with asthma; On your own

"The text explains exactly what is happening to the body as a result of an asthma attack, introduces ways to monitor symptoms or situations that may trigger an asthma attack, and provides an overview of medications that can help teens cope. Young readers will find the numerous sidebars and factoids quite interesting and informative." Lib Media Connect

Includes bibliographical references

Serradell, Joaquima

SARS; consulting editor, the late I. Edward Alcamo; foreword by David Heymann. Chelsea House 2005 112p il (Deadly diseases and epidemics) $31.95

Grades: 9 10 11 12   **616.2**

1. SARS (Disease)

ISBN 0-7910-8184-2   LC 2004-29797

Contents: A SARS tale: introduction -- SARS: a global epidemic -- SARS and other viral infections -- Spread and symptoms -- Diagnosis and management of SARS -- Treatment of SARS -- Prevention and public health measures -- Impact and significance of SARS: economics, society, and public health

Includes glossary and bibliographical references

Yancey, Diane
Tuberculosis. 21st Cent. Bks. (Brookfield) 2001 128p il (Twenty-first century medical library) $26.90
Grades: 7 8 9 10   **616.2**
1. Tuberculosis
ISBN 0-7613-1624-8
The author begins this book with a history of tuberculosis, "tracing evidence of it back to the Neolithic Age and then explores the variety of treatments used to combat it. . . . The three personal cases related are from three different socioeconomic situations. Good-quality, black-and-white photos appear throughout." SLJ
Includes bibliographical references

616.3   Diseases of the digestive system

Chow, James H., 1948-
The encyclopedia of hepatitis and other liver diseases; [by] James H. Chow, Cheryl Chow. Facts on File 2005 372p (Facts on File library of health and living) $75
Grades: 11 12 Adult   **616.3**
1. Liver—Diseases—Encyclopedias
ISBN 0-8160-5710-9; 978-0-8160-5710-8
                  LC 2005-18489
"With more than 150 entries, coverage ranges from symptoms, treatments, and research to tests, social issues, and much more. Appendixes list . . . relevant organizations, transplantation and Internet resources, and support groups for those with liver-related issues." Publisher's note
For a fuller review, see: Booklist, Dec. 1, 2006
Includes bibliographical references

Minocha, Anil, 1957-
The encyclopedia of the digestive system and digestive disorders; {by} Anil Minocha, Christine Adamec. Facts on File 2004 xxviii, 350p il (Facts on File library of health and living) $65 *
Grades: 11 12 Adult   **616.3**
1. Gastrointestinal system—Encyclopedias
2. Digestive organs—Encyclopedias
ISBN 0-8160-4993-9   LC 2003-21432
This reference addresses "the gastrointestinal system, normal digestive functions, diseases, and preventive measures in more than 300 alphabetically arranged entries. . . . Entries on specific disorders (e.g., acid reflux, gallstones, and ulcers) include definitions, risk factors, symptoms, diagnosis, and treatment, when applicable. Extensive appendixes identify U.S. and Canadian organizations, associations, support groups, and poison control; they also list helpful web sites and suggested readings." Libr J

Palmer, Melissa
Dr. Melissa Palmer's guide to hepatitis & liver disease. Avery 2004 470p il pa $16.95
Grades: 11 12 Adult   **616.3**
1. Liver—Diseases
ISBN 1-58333-188-3   LC 2003-63905

First published 1999
The author "discusses all facets of liver disease, from symptoms and tests to treatment options and lifestyle changes." Publisher's note

616.4   Diseases of endocrine system

American Diabetes Association complete guide to diabetes. 4th ed. American Diabetes Association 2005 554p il pa $29.95 *
Grades: 11 12 Adult   **616.4**
1. Diabetes
ISBN 1-58040-237-2   LC 2005-2996
First published 1996
Includes CD-ROM
This book describes types of insulin and the best ways to use them, insulin pumps and injection-free insulin techniques in research, new oral diabetes medications and therapies, the use of carbohydrate counting techniques as a meal planning tool as well as information on diabetes in the workplace, school, and day care.
Includes bibliographical references

Betschart, Jean, 1948-
Type 2 diabetes in teens; secrets for success; [by] Jean Betschart-Roemer. Wiley 2002 223p il pa $14.95
Grades: 9 10 11 12   **616.4**
1. Diabetes
ISBN 0-471-15056-8   LC 2002-2967
This book offers teens advice on "how to keep blood sugar in control; what to do when you get cravings; how to manage your diabetes in school; what to say to your friends and your dates; how to balance exercise and food when you take insulin; where to find help when you need it; ways to eat healthier; [and] how to be patient with yourself and enjoy life." Publisher's note
Includes bibliographical references

Diabetes information for teens; edited by Sandra Augustyn Lawton. Omnigraphics 2006 410p il (Teen health series) $65
Grades: 8 9 10 11 12   **616.4**
1. Diabetes
ISBN 0-7808-0811-8   LC 2005036597
"Health tips about managing diabetes and preventing related complications including information about insulin, glucose control, healthy eating, physical activity, and learning to live with diabetes" Title page
"Students dealing with their own diabetes or that of a friend or family member or those writing reports on the topic will find this a valuable resource." SLJ
Includes bibliographical references

Mayo Clinic on managing diabetes; Maria Collazo-Clavell, medical editor-in-chief. 2nd ed. Mayo Clinic 2006 229p il pa $19.95 *
Grades: 11 12 Adult   **616.4**
1. Diabetes
ISBN 1-893005-38-0; 978-1-893005-38-9
                  LC 2005-925743
First published 2002

Mayo Clinic on managing diabetes—Continued
This guidebook is divided into five areas: The Facts, which provides details about the disease; Taking Control, which discusses blood testing, weight management, and dieting; Medical Treatments, which discusses insulin and drug treatments, dialysis, and transplantation; Successful Management, which discusses self-care and medical tests; and Special Issues, which discusses sexual issues and children with diabetes.

Moran, Katherine J., 1959-
Diabetes; the ultimate teen guide; illustrations by Lisa P. Merriman. Scarecrow Press 2004 181p il (It happened to me) $34.50; pa $14.95 *
Grades: 11 12 Adult   616.4
1. Diabetes
ISBN 0-8108-4806-6; 0-8108-5642-5 (pa)
                              LC 2003-18500
Provides practical information on living with diabetes, discussing what the disease is, how to manage it, treatment options, and related issues
"This tightly focused title looks at specific problems or issues that teens with diabetes may face. . . . Interesting facts are included about the history of the disease." SLJ
Includes bibliographical references

Warshaw, Hope S., 1954-
The diabetes food & nutrition bible; a complete guide to planning, shopping, cooking, and eating; with foreword by Graham Kerr. American Diabetes Association 2001 324p il pa $18.95 *
Grades: 11 12 Adult   616.4
1. Diabetes—Diet therapy
ISBN 1-58040-037-X   LC 2001-22343
This book features information on counting carbohydrates, planning meals, vitamins, minerals, and methods of meal preparation. It includes more than 100 recipes.

616.5   Diseases of integument

Turkington, Carol
The encyclopedia of skin and skin disorders; [by] Carol Turkington, Jeffrey S. Dover; medical illustrations, Birck Cox. 3rd ed. Facts on File 2007 459p (Facts on File library of health and living) $75; pa $17.95 *
Grades: 11 12 Adult   616.5
1. Skin—Encyclopedias
ISBN   0-8160-6403-2;   978-0-8160-6403-8;
0-8160-6404-0 (pa); 978-0-8160-6404-5 (pa)
                              LC 2005-57402
First published 1996 with title: Skin deep
Paperback published with title: Skin deep
"More than 1,100 entries cover everything from the sun, skin, and acne to skin cancer, cosmetics, and skin lotions." Publisher's note
Includes bibliographical references

616.6   Diseases of the urogenital system. Diseases of the urinary system

Watson, Stephanie, 1969-
The urinary system. Greenwood Press 2004 207p il (Human body systems) $65 *
Grades: 11 12 Adult   616.6
1. Urinary organs
ISBN 0-313-32402-6   LC 2003-67648
The author "discusses the role and function of each part of the urinary system. . . . Watson also explores how the urinary system maintains chemical balance and hydration in the body. The history of research related to the urinary system is presented and the future of research in this field is considered." Publisher's note
Includes bibliographical references

616.7   Diseases of the musculoskeletal system

Sayler, Mary Harwell
The encyclopedia of the muscle and skeletal systems and disorders; foreword by Lori Siegel. Facts on File 2005 xx, 389p (Facts on File library of health and living) $75 *
Grades: 11 12 Adult   616.7
1. Musculoskeletal system—Encyclopedias
ISBN 0-8160-5447-9   LC 2003-26606
"The encyclopedia explores and explains why, by midlife, the body visibly complains of overuse and abuse through its aches, pains, stiffness, muscle weakness, and other symptoms of aging. Approximately 500 entries relating to muscle and skeletal disorders, arranged alphabetically, are presented." Booklist
The author "writes each entry with wit and skill—amazing among health science encyclopedias. It will be useful to health care consumers and students for years to come." Choice
Includes bibliographical references

616.8   Diseases of the nervous system and mental disorders

B., David, 1959-
Epileptic. Pantheon Books 2005 361p il $25; pa $17.95
Grades: 11 12 Adult   616.8
1. Epilepsy—Graphic novels 2. Graphic novels
ISBN 0-375-42318-4; 0-375-71408-5 (pa)
                              LC 2004-53419
Original French edition, 2002
"Growing up in the 1960s and 1970s in France's Loire Valley, Jean-Christophe developed grand mal epilepsy around the age of 11. Pierre-Francois, nine, observes his brother's battle with the physical and social implications of the disease; their parents' efforts to find management of it through medical, macrobiotic, and even

B., David, 1959-—_Continued_

psychic interventions; and the author's own development in this milieu as a boy obsessed with history and warfare and as a dedicated artist." SLJ

The author's "artwork is magnificent—gorgeously bold, impressionistic representations of the world not as it is but as he's taught himself to perceive it. . . . B.'s illustrations constantly underscore his writing's wrenching psychological depth; readers can literally see how the chaos of his childhood shaped his vision and mind." Publ Wkly

Bloom, Ona

Encephalitis; [by] Ona Bloom and Jennifer Morgan; foreword by David Heymann. Chelsea House 2006 125p il (Deadly diseases and epidemics) $31.95

Grades: 9 10 11 12 **616.8**
1. Encephalitis
ISBN 0-7910-8503-1 LC 2005-5518

Contents: An introduction to viral encephalitis -- An introduction to viruses: the molecular basis for encephalitis -- The immune system and viral infections -- The nervous system and viral infections: etiology of encephalitis -- Diagnosis and treatment of encephalitis -- Viral and nonviral causes of encephalitis -- Treatment and prevention of encephalitis -- Scientific research and the future of encephalitis

Includes glossary and bibliographical references

Brill, Marlene Targ, 1945-

Tourette syndrome. 21st Cent. Bks. (Brookfield) 2002 112p il (Twenty-first century medical library) lib bdg $26.90

Grades: 7 8 9 10 **616.8**
1. Tourette syndrome
ISBN 0-7613-2101-2 LC 2001-41747

Examines the tic disorder known as Tourette syndrome, its symptoms and manifestations, how it can be controlled and treated, and, through case studies, what it is like to live with Tourette's

The author covers "most of the information report writers would be seeking and a section about home and school is especially helpful to anyone trying to understand the problems faced by a person with this disorder." Book Rep

Includes glossary and bibliographical references

Goodfellow, Gregory

Epilepsy. Lucent Bks. 2001 95p il (Diseases and disorders series) lib bdg $27.45 *

Grades: 9 10 11 12 **616.8**
1. Epilepsy
ISBN 1-56006-701-2 LC 00-8657

Discusses the causes, diagnosis, and treatment of epilepsy, the types of seizures, and the challenges of living with the disease

Includes bibliographical references

Hecht, Alan

Polio; consulting editor I. Edward Alcamo; foreword by David Heymann. Chelsea House 2003 101p il (Deadly diseases and epidemics) lib bdg $25.95

Grades: 9 10 11 12 **616.8**
1. Poliomyelitis
ISBN 0-7910-7462-5 LC 2003-826

Contents: The history of polio; The transmission of polio and how it affects the body; Vaccines and how they work; The life of Jonas Salk; The life of Albert Sabin; Nobody is exempt; Just when we thought it was safe: post-polio syndrome; What lies ahead? the future of polio

The author "explains how the poliovirus infects the human body, multiplies and spreads, and, in particular, how the virus invades nerve cells and the spinal cord to cause paralysis. Considerable attention is also paid to the triumphant search for a cure for the disease, most notably the work of Jonas Salk and Albert Sabin." Publisher's note

Includes glossary and bibliographical references

Landau, Elaine

Alzheimer's disease; a forgotten life. Franklin Watts 2005 112p il (Health and human disease) $26

Grades: 7 8 9 10 **616.8**
1. Alzheimer's disease
ISBN 0-531-16755-0 LC 2005-01736

"Landau offers a well-researched, clearly written presentation on Alzheimer's and its effects. Topics discussed include diagnostic tools, possible causes, symptoms, stages, medications, research, and the problems faced by caregivers." Booklist

Includes glossary and bibliographical references

McPhee, Andrew T.

Sleep and dreams. Watts 2001 111p il lib bdg $24

Grades: 9 10 11 12 **616.8**
1. Sleep 2. Dreams
ISBN 0-531-11735-9 LC 00-28971

Discusses the nature of sleep and dreams, the causes of and treatments for sleep disorders, and the possible meaning of common dreams

"The information is best suited for supporting reports on sleep biology. . . . Teens will have fun with the dream dictionary at book's end." Booklist

Includes glossary and bibliographical references

Schwartz, Maxime, 1940-

How the cows turned mad; translated by Edward Schneider. University of Calif. Press 2003 238p $24.95; pa $15.95

Grades: 11 12 Adult **616.8**
1. Prion diseases
ISBN 0-520-23531-2; 0-520-24337-4 (pa)
LC 2002-75514

The author discusses the spread of "mad-cow disease and its human counterpart, variant Creutzfeldt-Jakob disease (vCJD). . . . His book maps out . . . the scientific

Schwartz, Maxime, 1940-—*Continued*

investigation into how scrapie—a disease that has long been known to afflict sheep—came to cross the species barrier to cows, and then from cows to humans." Economist

"Writing with immense concentration and clarity, French molecular biologist Schwartz makes the long hunt for the unexpected culprit gene utterly engrossing." Booklist

Includes bibliographical references

Silverstein, Alvin

Parkinson's disease; [by] Alvin and Virginia Silverstein and Laura Silverstein Nunn. Enslow Pubs. 2001 128p il (Diseases and people) lib bdg $26.60

Grades: 7 8 9 10   **616.8**
1. Parkinson's disease
ISBN 0-7660-1593-9   LC 00-12073
This describes the history of Parkinson's disease, its causes, symptoms, diagnosis and treatment, the disease and society, and research

Includes glossary and bibliographical references

Polio; {by} Alvin and Virginia Silverstein and Laura Silverstein Nunn. Enslow Pubs. 2001 128p il (Diseases and people) lib bdg $26.60

Grades: 7 8 9 10   **616.8**
1. Poliomyelitis
ISBN 0-7660-1592-0   LC 00-10993
The authors "describe the symptoms, causes, and treatments of this crippling disease. They trace its history from evidence of polio in ancient times to the epidemics of the first half of the twentieth century. The authors include the stories of well-known patients, such as Franklin D. Roosevelt, and important researchers, such as Salk, Sabin, and Sister Kenny." Publisher's note

Includes glossary and bibliographical references

616.85 Neuroses; speech and language disorders; disorders of personality, intellect, impulse control

Anorexia; Karen F. Balkin, book editor. Greenhaven Press 2005 110p (At issue) lib bdg $28.70; pa $19.95 *

Grades: 9 10 11 12   **616.85**
1. Anorexia nervosa
ISBN 0-7377-2178-2 (lib bdg); 0-7377-2179-0 (pa)
      LC 2004-61693
This book "considers the physical, social, and psychological aspects of this puzzling disorder and includes . . . viewpoints exploring anorexia in men, older women, and women throughout the world." Publisher's note

Includes bibliographical references

Cassell, Dana K.

Encyclopedia of obesity and eating disorders; [by] Dana Cassell, David H. Gleaves. 3rd ed. Facts on File 2006 xx, 362p (Facts on File library of health and living) $75 *

Grades: 9 10 11 12   **616.85**
1. Obesity—Encyclopedias 2. Eating disorders—Encyclopedias
ISBN 0-8160-6197-1; 978-0-8160-6197-6
      LC 2005-51375

First published 1994

This encyclopedia "includes more than 450 entries . . . [and features] a history of obesity and eating disorders; chronology of key events, research, and breakthroughs; tables listing key facts and statistics; and a directory of resources and Web sites." Publisher's note

For a fuller review, see: Booklist, Dec. 1, 2006

Includes bibliographical references

Clark, Arda Darakjian, 1956-

Dyslexia. Thomson Gale 2005 112p il (Diseases and disorders series) $28.70 *

Grades: 9 10 11 12   **616.85**
1. Dyslexia
ISBN 1-59018-040-2   LC 2004-14704
This book "explores theories of causation, symptoms, assessments, and remediation. The psychosocial impact of dyslexia on dyslexics and their families is discussed, along with strategies for coping and living with dyslexia." Publisher's note

Includes bibliographical references

Cobain, Bev, 1940-

When nothing matters anymore; a survival guide for depressed teens; edited by Elizabeth Verdick. Free Spirit 1998 165p il pa $13.95 *

Grades: 7 8 9 10   **616.85**
1. Depression (Psychology)
ISBN 1-57542-036-8   LC 98-24911
A guide to understanding and coping with depression, discussing the different types, how and why the condition begins, how it may be linked to substance abuse or suicide, and how to get help.

"Cobain has written a book that ought to be on every teacher's desk and in every place teens gather." Book Rep

Includes bibliographical references

Corman, Catherine A.

Positively ADD; real success stories to inspire your dreams; [by] Catherine A. Corman and Edward M. Hallowell. Walker 2006 172p il $16.95; lib bdg $17.85 *

Grades: 8 9 10 11 12   **616.85**
1. Attention deficit disorder
ISBN   978-0-8027-8988-4;   0-8027-8988-9; 978-0-8027-8071-3 (lib bdg); 0-8027-8071-7 (lib bdg)
      LC 2005037184
This "profiles 17 adults who began dealing with attention deficit disorder in childhood. Along with political strategist [James] Carville, subjects include a Pulitzer

Corman, Catherine A.—*Continued*
Prizewinning photographer, a major league pitcher, and a young Rhodes scholar. . . . [This is] an encouraging, helpful book for teens with ADD as well as for their parents, teachers, and friends." Booklist
Includes bibliographical references

Eating disorders: opposing viewpoints; Jennifer A. Hurley, book editor. Greenhaven Press 2001 173p lib bdg $34.95; pa $23.70
Grades: 7 8 9 10   **616.85**
1. Eating disorders
ISBN 0-7377-0652-X (lib bdg); 0-7377-0651-1 (pa)
LC 00-69183
"Opposing viewpoints series"
This collection of essays offers various points of view about eating disorders
Includes bibliographical references

Gilbert, Paul, 1951-
Overcoming depression; a step-by-step approach to gaining control over depression. 2nd ed. Oxford Univ. Press 2001 xxiii, 382p pa $15.95
Grades: 9 10 11 12   **616.85**
1. Depression (Psychology)
ISBN 0-19-514311-6   LC 00-57471
First published 1997 in the United Kingdom; first United States edition 1999
The author offers a program for overcoming depression using cognitive behavioral therapy and explains how problems such as perfectionism, shame, anger, and aggression can be exacerbated by depression
Includes bibliographical references

Hyde, Margaret Oldroyd, 1917-
Depression; what you need to know; [by] Margaret O. Hyde and Elizabeth H. Forsyth. Watts 2002 112p il lib bdg $24
Grades: 9 10 11 12   **616.85**
1. Depression (Psychology)
ISBN 0-531-11892-4   LC 2002-2488
Discusses the causes and symptoms of depression, who suffers from this condition, and how it can be treated
"The compelling information will keep teens reading. . . . Many examples of teens who have recovered from depression personalize the text, and there are useful help checklists." Booklist
Includes glossary and bibliographical references

Hyman, Bruce M.
Obsessive-compulsive disorder; by Bruce M. Hyman and Cherry Pedrick. Twenty-First Century Books 2003 96p (The Twenty-first century medical library) $26.90
Grades: 7 8 9 10   **616.85**
1. Obsessive-compulsive disorder
ISBN 0-7613-2758-4   LC 2002-14252
Contents: What is OCD?; The symptoms of OCD; Treatment of OCD; The impact on family and friends; Living with OCD

Examines the anxiety disorder known as OCD, its symptoms and manifestations, how it can be controlled and treated, and, through case studies, what it is like to live with obsessive-compulsive disorder
"With little else written specifically for young adults on this topic—which has risen to prominence recently in the popular media—this will be useful to report writers as well as to those concerned about their own anxieties." Booklist
Includes glossary and bibliographical references

Moragne, Wendy
Depression. 21st Cent. Bks. (Brookfield) 2001 112p il (Twenty-first century medical library) lib bdg $26.90
Grades: 7 8 9 10   **616.85**
1. Depression (Psychology)
ISBN 0-7613-1774-0   LC 00-36424
"Moragne presents the stories of seven teens diagnosed with different forms of depression, following the kids from the onset of their condition to successful treatment. Her profiles are respectful as well as thorough, including a surprising amount of information about symptoms, kinds of depression, causative factors, treatment . . . and the impact on one's self-esteem and personal relationships. . . . Difficult medical information . . . is presented clearly and without condescension." Booklist
Includes glossary and bibliographical references

Stewart, Gail, 1949-
Phobias; by Gail B. Stewart. Lucent Bks. 2001 96p il (Diseases and disorders series) lib bdg $27.45
Grades: 9 10 11 12   **616.85**
1. Phobias
ISBN 1-56006-726-8   LC 00-10223
The author discusses the history, symptoms, and treatment of phobias
"A solid addition to mental-health sections." SLJ
Includes bibliographical references

Teens with eating disorders; by Gail B. Stewart. Lucent Bks. 2001 112p il lib bdg $27.45
Grades: 9 10 11 12   **616.85**
1. Eating disorders
ISBN 1-56006-764-0   LC 00-8754
Profiles four teenagers with eating disorders, discussing their problems, therapy, and ways in which they have dealt with their food obsession with varying degrees of success
Includes bibliographical references

Strada, Jennifer L., 1970-
Eating disorders. Lucent Bks. 2001 96p il (Lucent overview series) lib bdg $27.45
Grades: 9 10 11 12   **616.85**
1. Eating disorders
ISBN 1-56006-659-8   LC 00-10392
"Strada gives teens an overview of anorexia, bulimia, and binge eating. . . . She describes food obsessions, then explains their causes and risks. Subsequent chapters address effects, treatment, and prevention." Booklist
Includes bibliographical references

The **Truth** about eating disorders; Mark J. Kittleson, general editor; William Kane, adviser; Richelle Rennegarbe, adviser; Gerri Freid Kramer, principal author. Facts on File 2004 166p il (Truth about series) $35 *

Grades: 7 8 9 10   **616.85**
1. Eating disorders
ISBN 0-8160-5300-6   LC 2004-6389

This discusses anorexia, bulimia, fad diets, and laxative abuse, the causes of eating disorders, how to recognize the disorders, the portrayal of eating disorders in the media, and obesity and weight control.

This title does "an excellent job of providing accurate information for teens. For reports or for self-help, [it belongs] in any library serving young adults." SLJ

Includes glossary and bibliographical references

The **Truth** about fear and depression; Mark J. Kittleson, general editor; William Kane, adviser; Richelle Rennegarbe, adviser; Heather Denkmire, principal author. Facts on File 2004 164p il (Truth about series) $35 *

Grades: 7 8 9 10   **616.85**
1. Depression (Psychology) 2. Anxiety
ISBN 0-8160-5301-4   LC 2004-7364

This "title includes discussions of anxiety disorders and their treatment, causes of depression, and defense mechanisms. . . . [This title does] an excellent job of providing accurate information for teens. For reports or for self-help, [it belongs] in any library serving young adults." SLJ

Includes glossary and bibliographical references

Turkington, Carol
The encyclopedia of autism spectrum disorders; [by] Carol Turkington, Ruth Anan. Facts On File 2007 324p $75 *

Grades: 11 12 Adult   **616.85**
1. Autism—Encyclopedias
ISBN 0-8160-6002-9; 978-0-8160-6002-3
                                       LC 2005-27227

"More than 300 entries address the different types of autism, causes and treatments, institutions, associations, leading scientists, research, social impact, and much more." Publisher's note

Includes bibliographical references

Veague, Heather Barnett
Personality disorders; consulting editor, Christine Collins; foreword by Pat Levitt. Chelsea House Publishers 2007 116p il (Psychological disorders) lib bdg $37.50

Grades: 9 10 11 12   **616.85**
1. Personality disorders
ISBN 0-7910-9002-7; 978-0-7910-9002-2
                                       LC 2006-24072

This book "defines and explains the spectrum of personality disorders, the social and medical issues related to them, and how they can be recognized and treated." Publisher's note

Includes glossary and bibliographical references

Williams, Julie
Pyromania, kleptomania, and other impulse control disorders. Enslow Pubs. 2002 128p il (Diseases and people) lib bdg $20.95

Grades: 9 10 11 12   **616.85**
1. Impulse control disorders
ISBN 0-7660-1899-7   LC 2001-5945

Contents: What are impulse control disorders?; History and legal consequences of impulse control disorders; Causes and treatment of impulse control disorders; Pyromania; Kleptomania; Pathological gambling; Intermittent explosive disorder

Describes the characteristics of impulsive control disorders, their possible genetic, developmental, and chemical causes, related disorders, and treatments

Includes glossary and bibliographical references

616.86   Substance abuse (Drug abuse)

Booley, Theresa Anne
Alcohol and your liver; the incredibly disgusting story. Rosen Pub. Group 2000 48p il (Incredibly disgusting drugs) lib bdg $25.25

Grades: 9 10 11 12   **616.86**
1. Alcoholism 2. Liver—Diseases
ISBN 0-8239-3254-0   LC 00-10039

This discusses the effects of alcohol on the body with emphasis on liver damage

Includes glossary and bibliographical references

Hyde, Margaret Oldroyd, 1917-
Smoking 101; an overview for teens; [by] Margaret O. Hyde, John F. Setaro. Twenty-First Century Books 2006 128p il lib bdg $26.60

Grades: 7 8 9 10   **616.86**
1. Smoking 2. Tobacco
ISBN 0-7613-2835-1   LC 2004-22757

Contents: The first cigarette won't kill me; Nicotine: the addiction culprit; I'll get my tobacco elsewhere; My smoking and my body: the physiology of smoking; My smoking and your body: second hand smoke; Ads: a reality check; The global view: what's happening with tobacco in the rest of the world?; The corporate view: what tobacco companies do; Now that I'm informed . . . some ideas for quitting

"The message is clear, the facts are well-presented, and the tone is insightful. These authors understand the teen audience and how to reach it." SLJ

Includes bibliographical references

616.89 Mental disorders

Hicks, James Whitney, 1964-
Fifty signs of mental illness; a guide to understanding mental health. Yale University Press 2005 389p (Yale University Press health & wellness) hardcover o.p. pa $17 *
Grades: 11 12 Adult   **616.89**
1. Mental illness 2. Abnormal psychology
ISBN 0-300-10657-2; 0-300-11694-2 (pa)
                                   LC 2004-21535
Contents: Anger -- Antisocial behavior -- Anxiety -- Appetite disturbances -- Avoidance -- Body image problems -- Compulsions -- Confusion -- Cravings -- Deceitfulness -- Delusions -- Denial -- Depression -- Dissociation -- Euphoria -- Fatigue -- Fears -- Flashbacks -- Grandiosity -- Grief -- Hallucinations -- Histrionics -- Hyperactivity -- Identity confusion -- Impulsiveness -- Intoxication -- Jealousy -- Learning difficulties -- Mania -- Memory loss -- Mood swings -- Movement problems -- Nonsense -- Obsessions -- Oddness -- Panic -- Paranoia -- Physical complaints and pain -- Psychosis -- Religious preoccupations -- Self-esteem problems -- Self-mutilation -- Sexual performance problems -- Sexual preoccupations -- Sleep problems -- Sloppiness -- Speech difficulties -- Stress -- Suicidal thoughts -- Trauma
"A reservoir of useful knowledge, this belongs in almost every library serving real people." Libr J

Noll, Richard, 1959-
The encyclopedia of schizophrenia and other psychotic disorders; foreword by Leonard George. 3rd ed. Facts on File 2007 xx, 409p (Facts on File library of health and living) $75 *
Grades: 11 12 Adult   **616.89**
1. Schizophrenia—Encyclopedias
ISBN 0-8160-6405-9; 978-0-8160-6405-2
                                   LC 2005-56749
First published 1992
"Biologically related schizophrenic disorders, genetics, antipsychotic drug treatments, and pathophysiology are a few of the topics explored in the more than 600 entries. . . . The language is clear, making this volume equally suitable for use by patients, scholars, and general readers. A solid addition for health collections." Booklist
Includes bibliographical references

616.9 Other diseases

Coleman, William H., 1937-
Cholera; consulting editors I. Edward Alcamo; foreword by David Heymann. Chelsea House 2003 114p il (Deadly diseases and epidemics) lib bdg $25.95
Grades: 9 10 11 12   **616.9**
1. Cholera
ISBN 0-7910-7303-3   LC 2002-155048
Contents: Discovering cholera; Properties of Vibrio cholerae; Dr. Snow and cholera; Transmission and epidemiology of cholera; Signs and symptoms of cholera; The virulence of Vibrio cholerae; The genome of Vibrio cholerae; Treatments for cholera; Prevention and vaccines; Cholera in the future
"This book describes the history of this infectious disease and discusses characteristics that enable this microorganism to cause serious health problems. The book also discusses the basic bacteriology, immunology, treatment, and epidemiology of the disease. Research that seeks both to cure and to understand the cholera bacillus is also highlighted." Publisher's note
Includes glossary and bibliographical references

Decker, Janet M.
Anthrax; [by] Janet Decker; consulting editor I. Edward Alcamo; foreword by David Heymann. Chelsea House 2003 122p il (Deadly diseases and epidemics) lib bdg $25.95
Grades: 9 10 11 12   **616.9**
1. Anthrax
ISBN 0-7910-7302-5   LC 2002-155987
Contents: A cloud of death; The fifth plague; Human anthrax; How anthrax causes disease; Deadly letters (outbreak 2001); Diagnosing and treating anthrax; Anthrax vaccine; Anthrax and bioterrorism
"This book describes the symptoms, diagnosis, and treatment of anthrax, as well as disinfection of contaminated buildings (even a whole island). It also examines the use of anthrax as a biowarfare agent, from ancient times through the terrorist attacks of 2001." Publisher's note
Includes glossary and bibliographical references

Mononucleosis; [by] Janet Decker; consulting editor I. Edward Alcamo; foreword by David Heymann. Chelsea House 2004 112p il (Deadly diseases and epidemics) lib bdg $25.95
Grades: 9 10 11 12   **616.9**
1. Mononucleosis 2. Epstein-Barr virus
ISBN 0-7910-7700-4   LC 2003-20143
Contents: Infectious mononucleosis and the Epstein-Barr virus (ebv); The discovery of Epstein-Barr virus; The life of Epstein-Barr virus; Immune system response to Epstein-Barr virus; Signs and symptoms; Ebv transmission and latent infection; Diagnosis of infectious mononucleosis; Treatments for infectious mononucleosis; Ebv and cancer; Ebv and other diseases
"Mononucleosis is caused by the Epstein Barr virus. This book explores the microbiology of the virus as well as treatment and prevention options." Publisher's note
Includes glossary and bibliographical references

Edlow, Jonathan A., 1952-
Bull's-eye: unraveling the medical mystery of Lyme disease. Yale University Press 2003 285p il $35; pa $17
Grades: 11 12 Adult   **616.9**
1. Lyme disease
ISBN 0-300-09867-7; 0-300-10370-0 (pa)
                                   LC 2002-154119
This account of the discovery of Lyme disease relates how connections were "established between symptoms and tick bites, leading to the discovery of the stages of the disease, its specific microbial cause, and its treat-

Edlow, Jonathan A., 1952——*Continued*
ment." Publisher's note

"This well-documented book is . . . as important for the light it sheds on the nature of scientific inquiry within the contemporary social and political context as it is for its information about Lyme disease." Booklist

Includes bibliographical references

Freeman-Cook, Lisa

Staphylococcus aureus infections; [by] Lisa and Kevin Freeman-Cook. Chelsea House 2006 182p il (Deadly diseases and epidemics) $31.95

Grades: 9 10 11 12   **616.9**

1. Bacterial infections

ISBN 0-7910-8508-2   LC 2005-4958

Contents: The dangers of staphylococcus aureus infection -- Introduction to bacteria -- Staphylococcus aureus -- The immune system and bacterial virulence factors -- Fighting S. aureus infections -- Mechanisms of resistance -- Methicillin- and vancomycin-resistant S. aureus: a modern epidemic -- Prevention of antibiotic resistance -- The future of staphylococcus aureus treatment

Includes bibliographical references

Glynn, Ian, 1928-

The life and death of smallpox; [by] Ian and Jenifer Glynn. Cambridge Univ. Press 2004 278p il $25

Grades: 11 12 Adult   **616.9**

1. Smallpox

ISBN 0-521-84542-4; 978-0-521-84542-7

LC 2005-297126

The authors "describe the history of the disease from the time of the ancient Egyptian pharaohs to the last natural case, which occurred in Somalia in 1977. . . . This book is thoroughly researched and eminently readable. Although several books have been written on the history of smallpox, this is the definitive work on the subject." Choice

Includes bibliographical references

Guilfoile, Patrick

Antibiotic-resistant bacteria; [by] Patrick G. Guilfoile; founding editor, I. Edward Alcamo; foreword by David Heymann. Chelsea House Publishers 2006 128p il (Deadly diseases and epidemics) $31.95

Grades: 9 10 11 12   **616.9**

1. Microorganisms 2. Drugs

ISBN 0-7910-9188-0; 978-0-7910-9188-3

LC 2006-17589

This book "describes pathogens that have become particularly adept at evading a wide range of antibiotics, and highlights how scientists continue to strive to develop new treatments and countermeasures to fight this onslaught." Publisher's note

Includes glossary and bibliographical references

Kienzle, Thomas E.

Rabies; founding editor, the late I. Edward Alcamo; foreword by David Heymann. Chelsea House Publishers 2006 143p il map (Deadly diseases and epidemics) $31.95

Grades: 7 8 9 10 11 12   **616.9**

1. Rabies

ISBN 0-7910-9261-5; 978-0-7910-9261-3

LC 2006-10420

This book provides an "analysis of this dangerous disease, from prevention and treatment to recent research and developments." Publisher's note

Includes glossary and bibliographical references

Kowalski, Kathiann M., 1955-

Attack of the superbugs; the crisis of drug-resistant diseases. Enslow Pubs. 2005 128p il (Issues in focus today) $31.93 *

Grades: 7 8 9 10   **616.9**

1. Diseases 2. Microorganisms 3. Drugs

ISBN 0-7660-2400-8; 978-0-7660-2400-7

The author "supplies evidence that many existing infections and diseases are becoming resistant to current treatments and provides examples of new, lethal outbreaks and epidemics emerging in this era of modern medicine. . . . This title is a good choice for young adults because it explains what they can do to prevent or minimize infection." SLJ

Includes bibliographical references

Preston, Richard

The demon in the freezer; a true story. Random House 2002 240p hardcover o.p. pa $7.99 *

Grades: 11 12 Adult   **616.9**

1. Smallpox 2. Biological warfare

ISBN 0-375-50856-2; 0-345-46663-2 (pa)

Also available large print edition $26.95 (ISBN 0-375-43186-1) and in paperback from Fawcett Bks.

Contents: Something in the air; The dreaming demon; To Bhola Island; The other side of the moon; A woman with a peaceful life; The demon's eyes; The anthrax skulls; Superpox

The author explains "the chemical properties of the smallpox virus; how a single infected person . . . can set off an epidemic; and what this horrendous disease can be like. . . . We learn how the disease was eliminated by an international vaccination campaign in the 1970's; why there are reasons to believe that the Soviet Union grew staggering quantities of the virus, allegedly in part to arm intercontinental missiles; and how the virus might now be used by others as a 'strategic weapon.'" N Y Times Book Rev

Rocco, Fiammetta

The miraculous fever tree; malaria and the quest for a cure that changed the world. HarperCollins Pubs. 2003 348p il maps $24.95; pa $13.95

Grades: 11 12 Adult   **616.9**

1. Malaria 2. Quinine

ISBN 0-06-019951-2; 0-06-095900-2 (pa)

LC 2003-51128

Rocco, Fiammetta—*Continued*

Rocco presents a history of malaria and the drug that eventually cured it, quinine. The tree of the title is the cinchona, whose bark is the source of the drug.

The author's "clear prose and personal investment—having grown up in Africa, she knows malaria and quinine all too personally—ensure that every episode of her narrative enthralls." Booklist

Includes bibliographical references

Saffer, Barbara

Anthrax. Lucent Books 2004 112p il (Diseases and disorders series) $27.45

Grades: 9 10 11 12   **616.9**

1. Anthrax

ISBN 1-59018-405-X   LC 2003-20277

Contents: Anthrax in animals -- A human scourge -- Preventing and treating anthrax -- Anthrax biological weapons -- Detecting and responding to anthrax bioweapons

Examines the history, diagnosis, symptoms, and treatment options of anthrax, as well as ongoing research for a way to defend the people of the United States from anthrax biological weapons

This book presents "important material in a clear, readable format." SLJ

Includes bibliographical references

Smith, Tara C., 1976-

Ebola. Chelsea House 2005 104p il (Deadly diseases and epidemics) $31.95

Grades: 7 8 9 10   **616.9**

1. Ebola virus

ISBN 0-7910-8505-8   LC 2005-6515

Contents: A modern plague; Ebola in Africa; Ebola hits close to home; General characteristics of the virus; Ecology of the virus; Immunological methods of detection; Developing a vaccine; Other hemorrhagic fevers

Includes glossary and bibliographical references

Turkington, Carol

The encyclopedia of infectious diseases; [by] Carol Turkington, Bonnie Lee Ashby. 3rd ed. Facts On File 2007 412p (Facts on File library of health and living) $75 *

Grades: 11 12 Adult   **616.9**

1. Communicable diseases—Encyclopedias

ISBN 0-8160-6397-4; 978-0-8160-6397-0

LC 2006-13795

First published 1998

"The alphabetically arranged volume covers diseases, treatment options, and relevant organizations. . . . Information is provided for each disease and includes its cause, symptoms, treatment, and prevention. Major diseases that have had an impact on the world's population (tuberculosis, AIDS) are covered . . . and include a history. This feature makes the volume useful to researchers and students." Booklist [review of 2003 edition]

Includes bibliographical references

Willett, Edward, 1959-

Ebola virus. Enslow Pubs. 2003 112p il map (Diseases and people) $26.60

Grades: 9 10 11 12   **616.9**

1. Ebola virus

ISBN 0-7660-1595-5   LC 2002-10149

Contents: Profile; A terrifying killer; The history of ebola; What is ebola hemorrhagic fever?; Diagnosing ebola hemorrhagic fever; Treatment of ebola hemorrhagic fever; Social implications of ebola hemorrhagic fever; Preventing ebola hemorrhagic fever; Research and future prospects; Q&A; Ebola hemorrhagic fever timeline

The author "explores the history and symptoms of the Ebola virus, from how it was first discovered to treatment options available for those who may contract this extremely rare—but deadly—disease. He also addresses the media attention and social factors that may add to the fear and stigma related to this virus." Publisher's note

Includes bibliographical references

616.95   Sexually transmitted diseases

Moore, Elaine A., 1948-

Encyclopedia of sexually transmitted diseases; [by] Elaine A. Moore with Lisa Marie Moore; illustrations by Marvin G. Miller. McFarland 2005 280p il $65 *

Grades: 11 12 Adult   **616.95**

1. Sexually transmitted diseases—Encyclopedias

ISBN 0-7864-1794-3   LC 2004-18309

"This encyclopedia offers entries on such topics as diseases, treatments, statistics, care centers and departments, risk factors, prevention issues, legal issues, associations and organizations, procedures, and relevant historical and political information. Entries on sexually transmitted diseases include history, causes and origins, risk factors, precautions, incidence, symptoms, special problems relating to gender, race, or poverty level, diagnosis, descriptions of diagnostic tests, defining illnesses and related disorders, treatment (drug regimens, therapies, side effects, and alternative medicine), and considerations in pregnancy." Publisher's note

For a fuller review, see: Booklist, May 15, 2005

Includes bibliographical references

Sexually transmitted diseases; Bryan J. Grapes, book editor. Greenhaven Press 2001 158p (Current controversies) lib bdg $31.20; pa $19.95

Grades: 9 10 11 12   **616.95**

1. Sexually transmitted diseases

ISBN 0-7377-0687-2 (lib bdg); 0-7377-0686-4 (pa)

LC 2001-18751

This collection of essays debates such questions as "Are sexually transmitted diseases a serious problem? Should public health measures be used to prevent the spread of HIV? How can sexually transmitted diseases be prevented?" Publisher's note

Includes bibliographical references

Sexually transmitted diseases: opposing viewpoints; Margaret Haerens, book editor. Greenhaven Press 2007 213p lib bdg $34.95; pa $23.70 *

Grades: 10 11 12   **616.95**

1. Sexually transmitted diseases

ISBN 0-7377-3333-0 (lib bdg); 978-0-7377-3333-4 (lib bdg); 0-7377-3334-9 (pa); 978-0-7377-3334-1 (pa)

LC 2006-17067

Topics discussed in this anthology include "whether sexually transmitted diseases are serious problems, how the government should educate youth about STDs, what individuals should do to reduce their spread, and how the global AIDS crisis should be addressed." SLJ

Includes bibliographical references

Shmaefsky, Brian

Syphilis; consulting editor I. Edward Alcamo; foreword by David Heymann. Chelsea House 2003 140p il (Deadly diseases and epidemics) lib bdg $25.95

Grades: 9 10 11 12   **616.95**

1. Syphilis

ISBN 0-7910-7308-4   LC 2002-155109

Contents: History and lore of syphilis; Syphilis as an STD; Syphilis: the organism; Syphilis: the disease; Syphilis: cures, prevention, and treatment; Syphilis: epidemiology; Syphilis in modern society; A case study in syphilis research

The author "explores the origin, cause, and treatment of the disease from scientific and historical perspectives." Publisher's note

Includes glossary and bibliographical references

Spencer, Juliet V.

Herpes. Chelsea House 2005 119p il (Deadly diseases and epidemics) $31.95

Grades: 9 10 11 12   **616.95**

1. Herpesvirus diseases

ISBN 0-7910-8196-6   LC 2004-29798

Contents: A painful discovery -- Epidemiology of sexually transmitted diseases -- Nature's design: virus structure -- Virus replication -- Lying in wait: virus latency -- Clinical syndromes -- Diagnosis and treatment -- Prevention and control -- The future of herpes

Includes glossary and bibliographical references

Yancey, Diane

STDs; what you don't know can hurt you. 21st Cent. Bks. (Brookfield) 2002 128p (Twenty-first century medical library) lib bdg $24.90 *

Grades: 9 10 11 12   **616.95**

1. Sexually transmitted diseases

ISBN 0-7613-1957-3   LC 2001-27793

Explains different types of sexually transmitted diseases, how they are contracted, their symptoms, and treatment

"Without being didactic or overly graphic, Yancey shares valuable information about STDs in a tone that honors readers' intelligence while warning them about the sometimes-fatal consequences of sexual activity." Booklist

Includes glossary and bibliographical references

616.97   Diseases of the immune system

Gordon, Sherri Mabry

Peanut butter, milk, and other deadly threats; what you should know about food allergies. Enslow Publishers 2006 112p il (Issues in focus today) $31.93 *

Grades: 7 8 9 10   **616.97**

1. Food allergy

ISBN 0-7660-2529-2   LC 2005-29219

Discusses what it is like to live with food allergies, how teens and their families cope with them, the causes of food allergies, and the research being done to prevent and control them.

"The format is open, with plenty of white space, making the book accessible to reluctant readers. Full-color photos, helpful case studies, and a list of reputable organizations to contact for further information are included." SLJ

Includes glossary and bibliographical references

Watstein, Sarah B.

The encyclopedia of HIV and AIDS; {by} Sarah Barbara Watstein, Stephen E. Stratton; foreword by Evelyn J. Fisher. 2nd ed. Facts on File 2003 660p $71.50 *

Grades: 11 12 Adult   **616.97**

1. AIDS (Disease)—Dictionaries

ISBN 0-8160-4808-8   LC 2002-35220

"Facts on File library of health and living"

First published 1998 with title: The AIDS dictionary

This volume includes "entries covering the basic biological, medical, financial, legal, political, and social issues and terms associated with HIV and AIDS. Entries explain symptoms and treatments, opportunistic infections, prevention strategies, and much more. Appendixes include HIV/AIDS associations, education centers, clinical trials, hotlines, publications, and additional material." Publisher's note

"The coverage is . . . broad and the language is pitched for the intended audience of nonspecialists . . . vastly expanded and brought up to date . . . Recommended." Choice

Includes bibliographical references

616.99   Tumors and cancers

Cramer, Scott D.

Prostate cancer; founding editor, the late I. Edward Alcamo; foreword by David Heymann. Chelsea House 2006 136p il map (Deadly diseases and epidemics) $31.95

Grades: 7 8 9 10 11 12   **616.99**

1. Prostate gland—Cancer

ISBN 0-7910-8935-5; 978-0-7910-8935-4

LC 2006-24074

"This book provides a . . . look at this dangerous disease with insights on prevention, recognition, and treatment." Publisher's note

Includes glossary and bibliographical references

Ferreiro, Carmen, 1958-
Lung cancer; founding editor, the late, I. Edward Alcamo; foreword by David Heymann. Chelsea House 2006 144p il (Deadly diseases and epidemics) $31.95
Grades: 7 8 9 10 11 12   **616.99**
1. Lung cancer
ISBN 0-7910-8937-1; 978-0-7910-8937-8
LC 2006-10422
This book offers "details on new methods for early detection, improvements in conventional treatment (surgery, chemotherapy, and radiotherapy), and the development of new therapies that specifically target cancer cells." Publisher's note
Includes glossary and bibliographical references

Fies, Brian
Mom's cancer. Abrams Image 2006 117p il $12.95
Grades: 9 10 11 12 Adult   **616.99**
1. Graphic novels 2. Biographical graphic novels 3. Cancer—Graphic novels
ISBN 0-8109-5840-6   LC 2005-21824
2005 Eisner Award for Best Digital Comic
When writer/cartoonist Fies learned his mother had cancer and that it had already spread from her lungs, he used webcomics to depict what was happening to his mother and the rest of the family as Mom fought the cancer. All the pain, the heartache, the little battles won, the effects on Fies' relationships with his sisters, the ultimate hope are all on the page. In the end, Mom beat the cancer. In an afterword, Fies tells the reader that some of the medications just wore down his mother's body, and she died shortly before the book was published.

Informed decisions; the complete book of cancer diagnosis, treatment, and recovery; [edited by] Harmon Eyre, Dianne Partie Lange; Lois B. Morris, consulting editor. 2nd ed. American Cancer Soc. 2001 768p il pa $29.95 *
Grades: 11 12 Adult   **616.99**
1. Cancer
ISBN 0-944235-27-1   LC 2001-1880
First published 1997 by Viking
"Covering all types of cancer in general terms, this tome from the American Cancer Society discusses detection, diagnosis, and treatment in five parts, subdivided into 31 chapters. Throughout, the information is presented logically, clearly, and in a visually accessible manner, with copious subheads, sidebars (case histories, checklists, dos and don'ts, etc.), headnotes (Tips and Advice, Cancer Basics), and questions to ask the doctor." Libr J

Majure, Janet, 1954-
Breast cancer. Enslow Pubs. 2000 128p il (Diseases and people) lib bdg $20.95 *
Grades: 9 10 11 12   **616.99**
1. Breast cancer
ISBN 0-7660-1312-X   LC 99-32153
Discusses the history, diagnosis, prevention, and treatments of breast cancer and explores its effects on society
Includes bibliographical references

Panno, Joseph
Cancer: the role of genes, lifestyle, and environment. Facts on File 2004 162p il (New biology) $35 *
Grades: 11 12 Adult   **616.99**
1. Cancer
ISBN 0-8160-4950-5   LC 2003-25840
This book "begins with a . . . summary of cell biology and continues with an overview of the way cancer cells work and how researchers have discovered the nature of these cells. The book looks . . . at the successes and failures of treatments using high doses of chemo- or radiation therapy; the plight of cancer survivors; recent advances in the use of light-activated compounds, monoclonal antibodies, gene therapy, and stem cells . . . as well as the extensive research that has been done to determine the causes of different types of cancer." Publisher's note
Includes bibliographical references

Silverstein, Alvin
Cancer; [by] Alvin & Virginia Silverstein & Laura Silverstein Nunn. Twenty-First Century Books 2006 121p il (Twenty-first century medical library) lib bdg $26.90
Grades: 9 10 11 12   **616.99**
1. Cancer
ISBN 0-7613-2833-5; 978-0-7613-2833-9
LC 2003-12638
Explains different types of cancer, their causes, symptoms and treatment, and, through case studies, what it is like to live with cancer.
This book "will interest readers who want to learn everything they can about the current medical state of cancer research, diagnosis, and treatment." SLJ
Includes bibliographical references

Spencer, Juliet V.
Cervical cancer; founding editor, the late I. Edward Alcamo; foreword by David Heymann. Chelsea House 2006 128p il map (Deadly diseases and epidemics) $31.95
Grades: 7 8 9 10 11 12   **616.99**
1. Cervix—Cancer
ISBN 0-7910-8941-X; 978-0-7910-8941-5
LC 2006-12586
This "volume explains the causes, symptoms, progress, and treatment of cervical cancer." Publisher's note
Includes glossary and bibliographical references

617.1 Injuries and wounds. Sports medicine

Oakes, Elizabeth H., 1951-
The encyclopedia of sports medicine; [by] Elizabeth Oakes; foreword by Connie Lebrun. Facts on File 2005 322p il (Facts on File library of health and living) $75 *
Grades: 11 12 Adult   **617.1**
1. Sports medicine—Encyclopedias
ISBN 0-8160-5334-0   LC 2003-24720

Oakes, Elizabeth H., 1951-—*Continued*

"More than 150 entries . . . describe causes, diagnosis, prevention, and treatment of sports injuries for amateur and professional athletes." Booklist

"This is an excellent resource for weekend, varsity high school and college, and professional athletes, and for trainers." Choice

Includes bibliographical references

Sports injuries information for teens; health tips about sports injuries and injury prevention; edited by Joyce Brennfleck Shannon. Omnigraphics 2004 405p il (Teen health series) $58 *

Grades: 7 8 9 10   **617.1**

1. Sports medicine 2. Wounds and injuries

ISBN 0-7808-0447-3

"Including facts about specific injuries, emergency treatment, rehabilitation, sports, safety, competition stress, fitness, sports nutrition, steroid risks, and more." Title page

"Along with physiological information about injuries and treatments, the special needs of teen athletes are considered in this comprehensive overview. . . . The information presented is copious and concise." SLJ

Includes bibliographical references

617.7   Ophthalmology

Kornmehl, Ernest W., 1959-

LASIK: a guide to laser vision correction; [by] Ernest W. Kornmehl, Robert K. Maloney, Jonathan M. Davidorf. 2nd ed. Addicus Books 2006 121p il pa $14.95 *

Grades: 11 12 Adult   **617.7**

1. Eye—Surgery

ISBN 1-886039-79-8; 978-1-886039-79-7

LC 2005-35027

First published 2001

"Among the topics the authors cover: how laser surgery works, who is a good candidate for surgery, finding a qualified surgeon, what to expect from the procedure, and post-procedure care." Publisher's note

"The color illustrations are clear and instructive, and the risks and complications associated with the procedure are well delineated." Libr J

617.8   Otology and audiology

Mayo Clinic on hearing; Wayne Olsen, editor in chief. Library ed. Mason Crest 2004 194p il $34.95 *

Grades: 7 8 9 10 11 12   **617.8**

1. Hearing 2. Deafness

ISBN 1-59084-805-5   LC 2003-107354

First published 2003 by Mayo Clinic

On cover: Strategies for managing hearing loss, dizziness and other ear problems

Contents: Understanding common hearing problems — How you hear — Getting a hearing exam — Common problems of the outer ear and middle ear — Common

problems of the inner ear — Tinnitus — The management of hearing loss — Living with hearing impairment — Hearing aids — Cochlear implants — Other communication aids — Dizziness and problems with balance

617.9   Transplantation of tissue and organs

Cheney, Annie

Body brokers; inside America's underground trade in human remains. Broadway Books 2006 205p $23.95; pa $14 *

Grades: 11 12 Adult   **617.9**

1. Procurement of organs, tissues, etc.

ISBN   0-7679-1733-2;   978-0-7679-1733-9; 0-7679-1734-0 (pa); 978-0-7679-1734-6 (pa)

LC 2005-54278

This is an exposé of "the lucrative business of procuring, buying, and selling human cadavers and body parts." Publisher's note

This book "speeds along like a circular saw through a thigh joint. It's a zippy, entertaining read, and more formal, scholarly works on the topic are not." N Y Times Book Rev

Includes bibliographical references

McClellan, Marilyn

Organ and tissue transplants; medical miracles and challenges. Enslow Pubs. 2003 128p il (Issues in focus) lib bdg $20.95

Grades: 7 8 9 10   **617.9**

1. Transplantation of organs, tissues, etc. 2. Artificial organs

ISBN 0-7660-1943-8   LC 2002-8401

Explores the history of organ transplantation, as well as its medical, ethical, financial, and personal aspects, providing insights into the latter through stories of organ donors and recipients

"With its useful black-and-white photos, anatomical diagram, pie chart, and statistics, this book is equally approachable for curious readers and report writers." SLJ

Includes glossary and bibliographical references

Schwartz, Tina P., 1969-

Organ transplants; a survival guide for the entire family: the ultimate teen guide. Scarecrow Press 2005 243p il (It happened to me) $36.50 *

Grades: 7 8 9 10   **617.9**

1. Transplantation of organs, tissues, etc.

ISBN 0-8108-4924-0   LC 2004-21563

"The 13 chapters, written in a question-and-answer format, detail the steps involved from diagnosis and being placed on a waiting list to pre and post-surgery. . . .The well-written text is complemented by a comprehensive section of suggestions for additional information. . . . Texts with this breadth of coverage are rare." SLJ

Includes bibliographical references

618 Gynecology and obstetrics

Hollen, Kathryn H.
The reproductive system. Greenwood Press 2004
xx, 193p il (Human body systems) $65 *
Grades: 11 12 Adult   **618**
1. Reproductive system
ISBN 0-313-32449-2   LC 2004-43638
This book "discusses the reproductive organs, hormones, conception through childbirth and development after birth including puberty. The history of research on the reproductive system is presented and the future of research in this field is considered. Current controversies and dilemmas are also explored." Publisher's note
Includes bibliographical references

Zach, Kim K., 1958-
Reproductive technology. Lucent Books 2005
112p il (Great medical discoveries) $27.45 *
Grades: 9 10 11 12   **618**
1. Reproductive technology
ISBN 1-59018-344-4   LC 2003-15403
Contents: Reproductive technology: new hope for infertile couples -- Treating male infertility: artificial and donor insemination -- Fertility enhancement: drug therapy and microsurgery -- The keystone of assisted reproduction: in vitro fertilization -- Surrogacy, egg donation, and embryo adoption -- Preventing inherited disease: preimplantation genetic diagnosis -- Drawing the line: ethical, moral, and social questions
"For students studying ethics or science, this book will provide concise, clear information for reports. . . . Teens will find understandable, complete explanations for their assignments or clarification if there are fertility issues within their families" SLJ
Includes bibliographical references

618.1 Gynecology

Minkin, Mary Jane
The Yale guide to women's reproductive health; {by} Mary Jane Minkin, Carol V. Wright. Yale Univ. Press 2003 448p il $29.95 *
Grades: 11 12 Adult   **618.1**
1. Women—Health and hygiene
ISBN 0-300-09820-0   LC 2002-35738
"Aiming to provide readers with information needed to make choices that may be presented in a gynecologist's office, the text covers menstruation, contraceptives, infections and sexually transmitted diseases, breast and genital tract cancer, pregnancy and infertility, and abortion and miscarriage." Libr J
Includes bibliographical references

618.3 Diseases and complications of pregnancy

Tsiaras, Alexander
From conception to birth; a life unfolds; {by} Alexander Tsiaras; text by Barry Werth. Doubleday 2002 283p il $35 *
Grades: 9 10 11 12   **618.3**
1. Prenatal diagnosis 2. Pregnancy
ISBN 0-385-50318-0   LC 2002-24707
Using images created with newly developed medical imaging technology, "the book tracks the development of a baby from the moment of conception, through the explosively complex early stages of development and the amazing stages of growth as the baby is nurtured by the mother, ending with the joy of birth." Publisher's note

618.92 Pediatrics

Attention deficit/hyperactivity disorder; William Dudley, book editor. Greenhaven Press 2005 77p (At issue) lib bdg $28.70; pa $19.95 *
Grades: 9 10 11 12   **618.92**
1. Attention deficit disorder
ISBN 0-7377-2258-4 (lib bdg); 0-7377-2259-2 (pa)
LC 2004-54303
"This anthology features . . . opinions on the extent of ADHD, its causes, and what kinds of treatment are best." Publisher's note
Includes bibliographical references

Esherick, Joan
The journey toward recovery; youth with brain injury. Mason Crest Publishers 2004 127p il (Youth with special needs) $24.95 *
Grades: 7 8 9 10   **618.92**
1. Brain damaged children
ISBN 1-59084-734-2   LC 2003-18640
Through the story of Jerome, a teenager who suffers a traumatic brain injury from a bike accident, this book discusses different "forms of brain injury; how these injuries affect people's lives; and how schools, doctors, and lawmakers are helping youth with this form of special need." Publisher's note
Includes glossary and bibliographical references

620 Engineering and allied operations

Berlow, Lawrence H., 1945-
The reference guide to famous engineering landmarks of the world; bridges, tunnels, dams, roads, and other structures. Oryx Press 1997 c1998 250p il $73.95 *
Grades: 11 12 Adult   **620**
ISBN 0-89774-966-9   LC 97-36051
"The main section is an alphabetically arranged, double-column compendium of facts and histories of 600

Berlow, Lawrence H., 1945——*Continued*
structures. The format of each entry begins with the structure's location and date of construction. Size is often given, including metric, and the basic facts of the construction are provided. . . . A biography section provides background on 52 significant engineers or designers. A chronology section begins with the oldest surviving dam in the world (in Egypt) and continues to 2010, when a monster skyscraper, Millennium Tower, will be completed in Tokyo." Booklist

Hall, J. Storrs
Nanofuture; what's next for nanotechnology; foreword by K. Eric Drexler. Prometheus Books 2005 333p il $29 *
Grades: 11 12 Adult   **620**
1. Nanotechnology
ISBN 1-59102-287-8   LC 2005-1789
The author covers "the physical principles of engineering at the atomic scale, possible applications of nanomachines, and their potential alteration of human society." Booklist
"This book fills a niche as a brief, inspirational introduction to nanotechnology for budding nanoscientists as well as the general public." Choice

Molotch, Harvey Luskin
Where stuff comes from; how toasters, toilets, cars, computers, and many other things come to be as they are; [by] Harvey Molotch. Routledge 2003 324p il $24.95; pa $24.95
Grades: 11 12 Adult   **620**
1. Engineering
ISBN 0-415-94400-7; 0-415-95042-2 (pa)
                                      LC 2003-1191
The author examines "the complicated, dynamic relationships between inventor, society, corporation, regulator, shopkeeper, community, family and customer. . . . Myriad links, he argues, ultimately produce and constantly change what we want, buy, keep and throw away; thus, neither consumers nor producers are to be blamed for our numerous possessions. . . . Molotch's description of systemic person-product complexes could work to end blame-the-consumer guilt-mongering in the popular discourse." Publ Wkly
Includes bibliographical references

Petroski, Henry
Success through failure; the paradox of design. Princeton University Press 2006 235p il $22.95
Grades: 11 12 Adult   **620**
1. Engineering 2. Design
ISBN 978-0-691-12225-0; 0-691-12225-3
                                      LC 2005-34126
The author explores the "relationship between success and failure in engineering design. Ingenuity is explored as a pendulum that swings between success and failure, driven by design philosophy and practices in a given place and time. Case studies and examples include bridges, spacecrafts, airports, buildings with architectural celebrity, New Coke, U-Locks, and notable structures that have suffered from performance issues." Libr J

An "engaging and readable book. . . . Petroski uses countless interesting case histories to show how failure motivates technological advancement." IEEE Spectrum
Includes bibliographical references

Tobin, James, 1956-
Great projects; the epic story of the building of America: from the taming of the Mississippi to the invention of the Internet. Free Press 2001 322p il maps $40
Grades: 11 12 Adult   **620**
ISBN 0-7432-1064-6   LC 2001-33016
This describes eight construction projects and innovations including "the flood-control works of the lower Mississippi, Hoover Dam, Edison's lighting system, the spread of electricity across the nation, the great Croton Aqueduct, the bridges of New York City, Boston's revamped street system, known as the Big Dig, and the [Internet]." Publisher's note
"The clearly written, nontechnical narratives are lively and comprehensive." Libr J
Includes bibliographical references

621.3   Electrical, magnetic, optical, communications, computer engineering; electronics, lighting

Jonnes, Jill, 1952-
Empires of light; Edison, Tesla, Westinghouse, and the race to electrify the world. Random House 2003 416p il hardcover o.p. pa $15.95
Grades: 9 10 11 12   **621.3**
1. Edison, Thomas A. (Thomas Alva), 1847-1931
2. Tesla, Nikola, 1856-1943 3. Westinghouse, George, 1846-1914 4. Electric power
ISBN 0-375-50739-6; 0-375-75884-4 (pa)
                                      LC 2002-31866
The author "details the rise and fall of the three visionaries who harnessed electricity, while also offering a critique of corporate greed. Her tale emphasizes the 'War of the Electric Currents,' in which Thomas Edison sought to defend the primacy of his direct current electrical system against George Westinghouse's higher-voltage and more broadly applicable alternating current system. Nikola Tesla, the somewhat kooky Serbian genius (and former Edison man), joined the fray on Westinghouse's side with his AC induction motor. Jonnes serves up plenty of color in an engaging and relaxed style." Publ Wkly
Includes bibliographical references

621.31   Generation, modification, storage, transmission of electric power

Ford, R. A.
Homemade lightning; creative experiments in electricity. 3rd ed. McGraw-Hill 2001 257p il $24.95
Grades: 9 10 11 12   **621.31**
1. Electric generators 2. Science—Experiments
ISBN 0-07-137323-3   LC 2001-41014

Ford, R. A.—*Continued*
First published 1991
This offers information about electrostatic generators and instruction for building various types, including experiments with electrohorticulture, gravitation and electricity, cold light, and electric tornadoes

621.381 Electronics

Reid, T. R.
The chip; how two Americans invented the microchip and launched a revolution. rev ed. Random House 2001 309p pa $13.95
Grades: 11 12 Adult   621.381
1. Kilby, Jack, 1923-2005 2. Noyce, Robert, 1927-1990 3. Microelectronics
ISBN 0-375-75828-3   LC 2001-19694
First published 1984
"Reid explains the technology, traces the history of electronics, and tells the stories of the two young engineers who created the silicon microchip and launched the global information industry." Booklist
"Reid has successfully combined a work in the history of technology with important insights concerning today's world of high technology." Choice
Includes bibliographical references

Schultz, Mitchel E.
Grob's basic electronics. McGraw-Hill 2006 c2007 various paging il $130 *
Grades: 11 12 Adult   621.381
ISBN 0-07-322276-3
First published 1959 under the authorship of Bernard Grob. Periodically revised
Accompanied by computer laser optical disc
An introductory text on the fundamentals of electricity and electronics for technicians in radio, television, and industrial electronics
Includes bibliographical references

621.3841 Amateur radio

The **ARRL** handbook for radio communications 2007. American Radio Relay League 2006 il $59.95; pa $44.95
Grades: 11 12 Adult   621.3841
1. Radio—Handbooks, manuals, etc.
ISSN 0890-3565
ISBN   0-87259-977-9;   978-0-87259-977-2; 0-87259-976-0 (pa); 978-0-87259-976-5 (pa)
Also available CD-ROM version
Annual. Began publication 1926. Editions 1 through 61 published with title: The Radio amateur's handbook. Editions 62 through 79 published with title: The ARRL handbook for radio amateurs
Includes CD-ROM
"Chapters cover fundamentals and changing technology in the field and include many tables, circuit diagrams, photographs, and occasional references." Guide to Ref Books. 11th edition

621.48 Nuclear engineering

Lüsted, Marcia Amidon, 1962-
A nuclear power plant; by Marcia and Greg Lüsted. Lucent Books 2005 112p il map (Building history series) lib bdg $28.70 *
Grades: 9 10 11 12   621.48
1. Nuclear power plants 2. Nuclear engineering
ISBN 1-59018-392-4   LC 2004-10681
The authors "recount the discovery of nuclear power, its positive aspects, and its uses beyond atomic bombs. They then describe the types of plants, outline the geographic requirements for building them, and discuss safety issues. The last chapter looks at the future of nuclear power." SLJ
Includes bibliographical references

621.8 Machine engineering

Gurstelle, William
Adventures from the technology underground; catapults, pulsejets, rail guns, flamethrowers, tesla coils, air cannons, and the garage warriors who love them. Clarkson Potter 2006 224p $25; pa $13.95
Grades: 11 12 Adult   621.8
1. Machine design
ISBN 1-4000-5082-0; 0-307-35125-4 (pa)
     LC 2005-20412
The author takes "readers into the hidden communities of people involved in developing hurling machines (catapults and trebuchets), pulse jet engines, flamethrowers, tesla coil-powered electric current theater, air cannons, robots, high-powered rockets, and magnetic linear accelerator guns. . . . Gurstelle balances scientific explanations of the technologies with profiles of the people who built them and descriptions of the events at which they were showcased." Libr J
Includes bibliographical references

622 Mining and related operations

Reece, Erik
Lost mountain; a year in the vanishing wilderness: radical strip mining, and the devastation of Appalachia; foreword by Wendell Berry; photographs by John J. Cox. Riverhead Books 2006 250p il $24.95; pa $14 *
Grades: 11 12 Adult   622
1. Coal mines and mining 2. Human influence on nature 3. Appalachian region
ISBN 1-59448-908-4; 1-59448-236-5 (pa)
     LC 2005-52921
The author explores the effects of strip mining on the landscape of Eastern Kentucky.
Reece "has written an impassioned account of a business rife with industrial greed, devious corporate ownership and unenforced environmental laws. It's also a heartrending account of the rural residents whose lives

Reece, Erik—*Continued*
are being ruined by strip-mining's relentless, almost unfettered, encroachment." Publ Wkly
Includes bibliographical references

623.4 Ordnance

Conant, Jennet
109 East Palace; Robert Oppenheimer and the secret city of Los Alamos. Simon & Schuster 2005 425p map hardcover o.p. pa $14
Grades: 11 12 Adult   **623.4**
1. McKibbin, Dorothy Scarritt, 1897-1985 2. Oppenheimer, J. Robert, 1904-1967 3. Los Alamos Scientific Laboratory 4. Manhattan Project 5. Atomic bomb
ISBN 0-7432-5007-9; 0-7432-5008-7 (pa)
LC 2005-42497
In this history of the creation of the atomic bomb, the author focuses "on daily life in Los Alamos. She tells the story largely through the eyes of Dorothy McKibben, who was in charge of the project's Santa Fe office, at 109 East Palace Street. This unassuming storefront was the portal to Los Alamos for all the physicists and military personnel who arrived in New Mexico." Booklist
"Anyone interested in the history of atomic weapons will find this book totally engrossing." Sci Books Films
Includes bibliographical references

Gonzales, Doreen
The Manhattan Project and the atomic bomb in American history. Enslow Pubs. 2000 128p il (In American history) lib bdg $20.95 *
Grades: 9 10 11 12   **623.4**
1. Manhattan Project 2. Atomic bomb
ISBN 0-89490-879-0   LC 99-16690
Describes the events and people surrounding the creation of the atomic bomb, and examines the effects of its use during World War II
This "account is well-documented and includes a time line and reading and organization lists." Booklist
Includes bibliographical references

Weapons; an international encyclopedia from 5000 B.C. to 2000 A.D; {by} the Diagram Group. St. Martin's Press 1990 336p il hardcover o.p. pa $22.95 *
Grades: 11 12 Adult   **623.4**
1. Weapons—History
ISBN 0-312-03951-4 (pa); 0-312-03950-6 (pa)
LC 90-28498
First published 1980
This "is a visual display of combat weapons of every century and culture. It is not, however, arranged alphabetically or chronologically. Instead, chapters are ordered by function. . . . The historical and regional indexes will be useful to readers who want to focus on weapons of a particular time or place. . . . The quality of illustrations is what distinguishes Diagram Group publications, and these are up to the usual standards. More than 2,500 black-and-white drawings are included." Booklist
Includes bibliographical references

623.88 Seamanship

Pawson, Des
The handbook of knots. Expanded ed. DK 2004 176p il pa $17
Grades: 11 12 Adult   **623.88**
1. Knots and splices
ISBN 0-7566-0374-9; 978-0-7566-0374-8
LC 2004-274491
First published 1998
"This is a step-by-step guide to tying and using more than 100 knots. . . . There's a chapter on rope construction, rope materials, and properties of ropes and their main uses. It's very informative and put together concisely." BAYA Book Rev [review of 1998 edition]

624 Civil engineering

Macaulay, David, 1946-
Underground. Houghton Mifflin 1976 109p il $19; pa $9.95
Grades: 5 6 7 8 9   **624**
1. Civil engineering
ISBN 0-395-24739-X; 0-395-34065-9 (pa)
In this "examination of the intricate support systems that lie beneath the street levels of our cities, Macaulay explains the ways in which foundations for buildings are laid or reinforced, and how the various utilities or transportation services are constructed." Bull Cent Child Books
"Introduced by a visual index—a bird's eye view of a busy, hypothetical intersection with colored indicators marking the specific locations analyzed in subsequent pages—detailed illustrations are combined with a clear, precise narrative to make the subject comprehenssible and fascinating." Horn Book
Includes glossary

Reeves, Diane Lindsey, 1959-
Career ideas for teens in architecture and construction; [by] Diane Lindsey Reeves with Gail Karlitz and Don Rauf. Ferguson 2005 170p il (Career ideas for teens) $40
Grades: 7 8 9 10   **624**
1. Vocational guidance 2. Architecture 3. Building 4. Engineering
ISBN 0-8160-5289-1   LC 2004-20030
The careers described in this book include architect, carpenter, electrician, interior designer, and urban planner.

624.2 Bridges

Brown, David J., 1946-
Bridges: three thousand years of defying nature. Firefly Books 2005 208p il pa $29.95 *
Grades: 11 12 Adult   **624.2**

Brown, David J., 1946-—*Continued*
1. Bridges
ISBN 1-55407-099-6 (pa)
The author "offers a history of more than 100 of the world's greatest bridges, organized chronologically. He explains their origins and structure principle, beginning with the ancient world (Rome and China) and the medieval period (France, Italy, and the Czech Republic). . . . There are more than 300 color and black-and-white illustrations in this very informative account." Booklist

628.9   Fire-fighting technology

Fire fighters; stories of survival from the front lines of firefighting; edited by Clint Willis. Thunder's Mouth Press 2002 351p il pa $17.95 *

Grades: 11 12 Adult   **628.9**
1. Fire fighting
ISBN 1-56025-402-5   LC 2002-18147
This is a collection of 21 accounts of fighting fires in urban, rural, and forest environments, previously published in books and magazines between 1963 and 2001, by such authors as Edward Abbey, Norman Maclean, Stephen Pyne, and Studs Terkel
"Mere display guarantees this collection's circulation." Booklist
Includes bibliographical references

629.1   Aerospace engineering

Abrams, Michael
Birdmen, batmen, and skyflyers; wingsuits and the pioneers who flew in them, fell in them and perfected them. Harmony Books 2006 304p il $23.95; pa $13.95 *
Grades: 11 12 Adult   **629.1**
1. Aeronautics—History
ISBN   1-4000-5491-5;   978-1-4000-5491-6;
1-4000-5492-3 (pa); 1-978-1-4000-5492-3 (pa)
LC 2005-32409
"From ancient myths through China 'sometime in the sixth century A.D.' to present-day skydivers, Abrams chronicles the men and their various models of wings that have taken to the air in hope of flying like a bird. The tales of flight range from the silly and mysterious to the inspiring and unbelievable." Publ Wkly
Includes bibliographical references

629.13   Aeronautics

Dick, Ron, 1931-
The golden age; [by] Ron Dick and Dan Patterson. Boston Mills Press 2004 287p il (Aviation century) $39.95
Grades: 11 12 Adult   **629.13**
1. Aeronautics—History
ISBN 1-55046-409-4; 978-1-55046-409-2
LC 2005-298220

This book "chronicles the history of aviation from 1919 to 1939. . . . Any readers interested in the history of flying will treasure this profusely illustrated book." Booklist
Includes bibliographical references

War & peace in the air; [by] Ron Dick and Dan Patterson. Boston Mills Press 2006 352p il (Aviation century) $49.95
Grades: 11 12 Adult   **629.13**
1. Aeronautics—History
ISBN 978-1-55046-430-6; 1-55046-430-2
This book "explores the influence of aviation in the major wars and minor conflicts since World War II. The authors also examine the dangers of flight, including airborne disasters, accident investigations and threats from terrorism, and speculate on the myriad ways in which aviation will change in the near and far future." Publisher's note
Includes bibliographical references

Grant, R. G. (Reg G.)
Flight: 100 years of aviation. DK Pub. 2002 440p il $50; pa $24.95 *
Grades: 11 12 Adult   **629.13**
1. Aeronautics—History
ISBN 0-7894-8910-4; 0-7566-1902-5 (pa)
LC 2002-73935
Grant "divides this book into sections that include a prehistory of flight and the Wright brothers; accounts of air combat in World War I, and a focus on the 'golden age' that recounts the flights of Charles Lindbergh, Amelia Earhart, Jimmy Doolittle, and the great airships and flying boats. He also presents a history of aircraft's role in World War II (the Battle of Britain, the air war at sea, and the Allied bombing raids on Axis cities); the cold war and Vietnam; space travel; and jet passenger travel." Booklist
"The impressive illustrations include over 300 gorgeous, full-color profiles of the world's major military and civilian aircraft and space vehicles." Libr J

Haynsworth, Leslie
Amelia Earhart's daughters; the wild and glorious story of American women aviators from World War II to the dawn of the space age; {by} Leslie Haynsworth and David Toomey. Morrow 1998 322p il pa $14 hardcover o.p. *
Grades: 11 12 Adult   **629.13**
1. Women air pilots 2. Women astronauts
ISBN 0-380-72984-9 (pa)   LC 98-8727
This "study of American women aviators concentrates almost exclusively on the WASPs of World War II and the would-be female astronauts of the early 1960s." Booklist
Includes bibliographical references

Marshall, David
Wild about flying! dreamers, doers, and daredevils; [by] David Marshall & Bruce Harris. Firefly Books 2003 232p il $35 *
Grades: 9 10 11 12   **629.13**
1. Aeronautics—History
ISBN 1-55297-849-4   LC 2004-297806

Marshall, David—*Continued*

This is a "history of aviation told through brief biographies of the most central people in the saga of flight. . . . With its unique focus and accurate, understandable technical data, this volume is a great addition to YA collections." SLJ

Tobin, James, 1956-

To conquer the air; the Wright Brothers and the great race for flight. Free Press 2003 433p il hardcover o.p. pa $16

Grades: 11 12 Adult   **629.13**

1. Wright, Orville, 1871-1948 2. Wright, Wilbur, 1867-1912 3. Aeronautics—History

ISBN 0-684-85688-3; 0-7432-5536-4 (pa)

LC 2002-44778

"In this centenary of the airplane, Tobin recreates the course, in its technological and biographical dimensions, of the Wright brothers' claim to its invention." Booklist

"This book represents the most forceful argument to date for the brothers' monumental legacy to the history of flight. . . . This lucidly written and exhaustively researched study is recommended for all aviation collections and all libraries." Libr J

Includes bibliographical references

629.22   Types of vehicles

Kettlewell, Caroline

Electric dreams; one unlikely team of kids and the race to build the car of their dreams. Carroll & Graf 2004 290p $24; pa $14.95 *

Grades: 9 10 11 12   **629.22**

1. Electric automobiles

ISBN 0-7867-1271-6; 0-7867-1485-9 (pa)

This "story tells how a twice-totaled 1985 two-door Ford Escort was transformed by students from the poorest county in North Carolina to win the first Mid-Atlantic High School Electric Vehicle Challenge." SLJ

"The word 'inspirational' is applied to too many books, but it comfortably fits this one, with its genuinely likable cast of unlikely achievers. This is essential reading for any serious environmentalist, as it makes the case that EVs might play even in the conservative South." Publ Wkly

629.222   Passenger automobiles

Edmonston, Louis-Philippe

Car smarts; hot tips for the car crazy; [by] Phil Edmonston and Maureen Sawa; illustrated by Gordon Suavé. Tundra 2004 76p il pa $15.95

Grades: 7 8 9 10   **629.222**

1. Automobiles

ISBN 0-88776-646-3

This offers a "look at the history and design of automobiles. . . . [It] discusses how cars work. . . . A chapter on ownership talks about financial issues, negotiating, and maintenance. The closing section covers the automotive future, with information on ecological issues, alter-

native fuels, hybrids, and fuel cells." SLJ

"Written in a lively style, the book provides solid information. . . . The many illustrations include colorful paintings, drawings, and photos as well as excellent diagrams of a car's working parts." Booklist

629.227   Cycles

Davidson, Jean, 1937-

Jean Davidson's Harley-Davidson family album; 100 years of the world's greatest motorcycle in rare photos; foreword by Sarah Harley and Arthur Harley. Voyageur Press 2003 128p il $19.95

Grades: 9 10 11 12   **629.227**

1. Davidson family 2. Harley family 3. Harley-Davidson, Inc. 4. Motorcycles

ISBN 0-89658-629-4   LC 2002-151809

The granddaughter of one of the founders of the Harley-Davidson company "shares the history, legends, and many personal photos of the marque that simply defines *motorcycle* for most people. . . . As fun as the book is for motorcycle enthusiasts, it also is important in terms of filling a niche in the overall history of the American vehicle business." Booklist

Sidwells, Chris, 1956-

Complete bike book. DK Pub. 2003 240p il hardcover o.p. pa $17.95 *

Grades: 8 9 10 11 12 adult   **629.227**

1. Cycling 2. Bicycles—Maintenance and repair

ISBN 0-7894-9337-3; 0-7566-1427-9 (pa)

LC 2003-40985

"The author begins with a short history of the bicycle, charting its evolution from a simple two-wheeled machine propelled by foot power . . . to today's ultramodern, high-tech vehicle. Individual chapters discuss such matters as proper cycling attire, how to teach a child to ride, how to tailor your diet to maximize its effectiveness, and how to maintain and repair your bike. . . . The book is perfect for newbies, for someone who cycles to work, and for the off-roader, the racer, and the person who sees cycling as a healthy workout." Booklist

Includes bibliographical references

Wilson, Hugo

The ultimate Harley-Davidson book. Dorling Kindersley 2000 192p il $24.95

Grades: 9 10 11 12   **629.227**

1. Harley-Davidson motorcycle

ISBN 0-7894-5165-4   LC 99-53958

This is an illustrated history of Harley-Davidson motorcycles and the company that built them from 1911 to 1999

Includes glossary

629.28 Motor land vehicles and cycles--Tests, driving, maintenance, repairs

Bicycling magazine's basic maintenance and repair; simple techniques to make your bike ride better and last longer; edited by Ed Pavelka. Rodale Press 1999 135p il pa $9.99
Grades: 11 12 Adult **629.28**
1. Bicycles—Maintenance and repair
ISBN 1-57954-170-4 LC 99-35338
An illustrated guide to do-it-yourself repairs and maintenance procedures designed to prevent on-road breakdowns

Chilton's auto repair manual. Chilton il *
Grades: 11 12 Adult **629.28**
1. Automobiles—Maintenance and repair
ISSN 0069-3634
For information on availability and price contact publisher
First published 1953 with title: Chilton's automobile repair manual
"Covers all mass-produced American cars of the past six or seven years plus the current year. Illustrated; includes charts to help diagnose problems. Useful for both novices and experts." N Y Public Libr Book of How & Where to Look It Up

Christensen, Lisa
Clueless about cars; an easy guide to car maintenance and repair. Firefly Bks. 2004 160p il pa $14.95
Grades: 11 12 Adult **629.28**
1. Automobiles—Maintenance and repair
ISBN 1-55297-975-X LC 2004-303528
New edition in preparation
The author "discusses a car's systems, maintenance both by the owner and the mechanic, and emergencies. She explains how and why actions must be taken to insure the safety and reliability of the vehicle. Environmental concerns are also considered. The clear, chatty voice is perfect for novice drivers, and the author makes no assumptions about prior knowledge. . . . A resource that is sure to be popular." SLJ

Cuthbertson, Tom
Anybody's bike book; illustrated by Rick Morrall. Totally rev new ed. Ten Speed Press 1998 228p il pa $14.95
Grades: 9 10 11 12 Adult **629.28**
1. Bicycles—Maintenance and repair
ISBN 0-89815-996-2 LC 98-168280
First published 1971
On cover: A comprehensive manual of bike repairs
This book covers such topics as how to fix different parts of a bicycle, what to look for when buying one, and how to handle emergencies when riding.

Downs, Todd
The bicycling guide to complete bicycle maintenance & repair; for road & mountain bikes. Rodale 2005 378p il pa $19.95 *
Grades: 11 12 Adult **629.28**
1. Bicycles—Maintenance and repair
ISBN 1-57954-883-0 LC 2004-24331
First published 1986 with title: Bicycling magazine's Complete guide to bicycle maintenance and repair
This illustrated guide includes step-by-step instructions for major and minor repairs and maintenance for many types of bicycles.

Florence, Mike
The everything car care book; how to maintain your car and keep it running smoothly; [by] Mike Florence and Rob Blumer. Adams Media Corporation 2002 289p il (Everything series) pa $14.95 *
Grades: 9 10 11 12 **629.28**
1. Automobiles—Maintenance and repair
ISBN 1-58062-732-3 LC 2002-10017
This book "provides step-by-step instruction on: Changing oil; Avoiding ripoffs; maintaining the car to prevent problems; monitoring brake, power steering, and transmission fluids; replacing and adjusting headlights; troubleshooting major problems; [and] understanding basic body repair and touch-ups." Publisher's note

Gravelle, Karen
The driving book; everything new drivers need to know but don't know to ask; illustrated by Helen Flook. Walker & Co. 2005 170p il $16.95; pa $9.95 *
Grades: 9 10 11 12 **629.28**
1. Automobile drivers
ISBN 0-8027-8933-1; 0-8027-7706-6 (pa)
LC 2004-58485
This guide covers such topics as "automobile maintenance, getting gasoline, the differences between city and country driving, bad weather, the usefulness of cell phones in emergencies, and road rage. The book is clearly written and well organized, but it is also humorous and appealing, with lighthearted illustrations throughout." SLJ

Vose, Kenneth E.
Inside Monster garage; written by Ken Vose. Meredith Books 2003 175p il pa $19.95
Grades: 9 10 11 12 **629.28**
1. Monster garage (Television program) 2. Automobiles—Design and construction
ISBN 0-696-21890-9 LC 2003-104195
This book features interviews, photos and stories with the mechanics, welders, and designers on the Discovery Channel show Monster Garage.

629.4 Astronautics

Angelo, Joseph A.
The Facts on File dictionary of space technology; [by] Joseph A. Angelo, Jr. rev ed. Facts on File 2004 474p $49.95; pa $19.95 *
Grades: 11 12 Adult   629.4
1. Astronautics—Dictionaries
ISBN 0-8160-5222-0; 0-8160-5223-9 (pa)
LC 2003-49148
"Facts on File science library"
First published 1982 with title: The dictionary of space technology
This dictionary contains approximately 1,500 cross-referenced entries that present the basic concepts and phrases in the science of space, spaceflight, and space technology. Among the topics covered are: abort modes; ballistic missile defense; launch vehicles; Milstar; ocean remote sensing; robotics and space stations

Space technology. Greenwood Press 2003 394p il (Sourcebooks in modern technology) $65
Grades: 9 10 11 12   629.4
1. Astronautics 2. Space sciences 3. Outer space—Exploration
ISBN 1-57356-335-8   LC 2002-75310
This book examines "the history, technology, impact, and goals of space flight. Angelo organizes his material into 10 topical chapters, beginning with a historical overview, followed by a chronology encompassing both Ptolemy and the February 2003 loss of the space shuttle Columbia, then discussions of space-related physics and technology, military and civilian applications, current issues, and future plans." SLJ
"This book is a good source of general information, easily read and understood by most high school students, and will provide plenty of good information for reports and papers." Lib Media Connect
Includes bibliographical references

Burrows, William E.
This new ocean; the story of the first space age. Random House 1998 723p il pa $18.95 hardcover o.p.
Grades: 11 12 Adult   629.4
1. Astronautics 2. Outer space—Exploration
ISBN 0-375-75485-7 (pa)   LC 98-3252
This is a "history of space exploration, from its ancient roots in mythology and literature to the theoreticians and pioneering engineers who made it a reality in this century." Libr J
"'This New Ocean' is most distinguished by the successful integration of three different story lines: manned space flight, the militarization of space and space science." N Y Times Book Rev
Includes bibliographical references

Chaikin, Andrew, 1956-
Space; a history of space exploration in photographs; [by] Andrew Chaikin; foreword by James A. Lovell. Firefly Books 2004 c2002 249p il pa $24.95 *
Grades: 6 7 8 9   629.4

1. Outer space—Exploration
ISBN 1-55297-987-3
First published 2002 in the United Kingdom
This is a "collection of more than 300 images that pay tribute to and trace the history of space exploration." Publisher's note
"This book is proof that scientific photos not only can educate but also can be admired for their beauty. Text explains the intriguing photos and helps introduce each chapter." Voice Youth Advocates

National Geographic encyclopedia of space; [compiled by] Linda K. Glover; with Andrew Chaikin . . . [et al.]; foreword by Buzz Aldrin. National Geographic Society 2004 400p il map $40 *
Grades: 11 12 Adult   629.4
1. Astronautics 2. Astronomy—Encyclopedias 3. Outer space—Exploration
ISBN 0-7922-7319-2   LC 2004-55229
The essays in this encyclopedia "discuss deep space, our solar system and space travel. There are also sections on using space to study Earth and on the military and intelligence uses of space. The essays in general are readable and show the implications of astronomy for life on Earth, such as the impact of solar flares on the weather. . . . This volume will suit astronomy enthusiasts better than total novices. Everyone, however, can enjoy the gorgeous photos." Publ Wkly

Walsh, Patrick J.
Echoes among the stars; a short history of the U.S. space program. Sharpe, M.E. 2000 204p $35.95; pa $29.95
Grades: 11 12 Adult   629.4
1. Astronautics—United States
ISBN 0-7656-0537-6; 0-7656-0538-4 (pa)
LC 99-38899
Walsh "recounts the early successes of the Mercury and Gemini missions that paved the way for the Apollo moon landings as well as the Skylab and Apollo-Soyuz mission that marked the end of the first era of U.S. manned space flight." Libr J
Includes bibliographical references

Zimmerman, Robert
The chronological encyclopedia of discoveries in space. Oryx Press 2000 410p il maps $95 *
Grades: 11 12 Adult   629.4
1. Outer space—Exploration 2. Astronautics
ISBN 1-57356-196-7
"Over 1,000 entries record the date of launch, name of the spacecraft(s), summary of the mission, names of the crew members, experiments, problems, and discoveries in a clear and concise fashion. Seemingly every single space mission is included, encompassing spaceflight with and without human crews, military and civilian ventures, public and commercial ventures, planetary probes, and communications satellites. . . . An excellent, cross-referencing system within the text, as well as extensive subject indices by satellite, mission, and nation or consortia, helps the reader follow particular interests in detail. . . . There is no comparable source to this volume

Zimmerman, Robert—*Continued*
for its comprehensiveness and conciseness." Sci Books Films
Includes bibliographical references

629.45   Manned space flight

Ackmann, Martha
The Mercury 13: the untold story of thirteen American women and the dream of space flight. Random House 2003 239p il hardcover o.p. pa $13.95 *
Grades: 11 12 Adult   629.45
1. Project Mercury 2. Women astronauts
ISBN 0-375-50744-2; 0-375-75893-3 (pa)
                             LC 2002-37118
Also available Thorndike Press large print edition
Ackmann discusses the 1961 testing of women pilots who were being considered for the Mercury space program, and why the initiative was eventually dropped. "The trials narrowed the field of women to 13—hence Ackmann's title—and . . . the women performed at the same level as the men. {Ackmann also addresses} what happened to them afterward." Time
"Mercury 13 is both an outstanding work of research and an exceptionally readable and well-told story. Readers will gain new perspectives on space, medicine, women, and American culture, and will appreciate the magnitude of what was lost when the women were grounded." SLJ
Includes bibliographical references

Kevles, Bettyann
Almost heaven; the story of women in space; [by] Bettyann Holtzmann Kevles. Basic Books 2003 274p il $25.95
Grades: 11 12 Adult   629.45
1. Women astronauts
ISBN 0-7382-0209-6   LC 2003-13801
Also available in paperback from MIT Press
This is a "history of the U.S. space program, with special emphasis on, and stories about, the women who have had the courage to venture into space. Each one is special, the book reveals; yet they all share a spirit of adventure and a willingness to put up with hardship in order to fulfill their dream." Sci Books Films
Includes bibliographical references

Kranz, Eugene F., 1933-
Failure is not an option; mission control from Mercury to Apollo 13 and beyond; {by} Gene Kranz. Simon & Schuster 2000 415p il $26
Grades: 11 12 Adult   629.45
1. United States. National Aeronautics and Space Administration 2. Space flight 3. Astronautics—United States
ISBN 0-7432-0079-9   LC 00-27720
Also available in paperback from Berkley Pub. Group
This memoir by the NASA flight director "follows his and NASA's careers from the start of the space race through 'the last lunar strike,' Apollo 17 (1972-1973)."

Publ Wkly
"A welcome contribution to the history of space flight. More than any previous book, it gives the view of that history as lived by the brotherhood of Mission Control. The writing, like Kranz himself, is brisk, unadorned and informative, but warmed from time to time by characteristic expressions of irony and humor." N Y Times Book Rev

Launius, Roger D.
Frontiers of space exploration. 2nd ed. Greenwood Press 2004 245p il $45 *
Grades: 11 12 Adult   629.45
1. Astronautics—International cooperation 2. Outer space—Exploration
ISBN 0-313-32524-3   LC 2003-60402
First published 1998
"The text includes a chronology, a general historical overview of space flight, 3 lengthy essays on space exploration, and 21 biographical essays. In addition, 26 primary documents trace U.S. space flight history, and there is an up-to-date listing of all U.S. space flights up to and including the Columbia disaster of January 2003. A fine annotated bibliography rounds out the volume." Booklist

Pyle, Rod
Destination moon; the Apollo missions in the astronauts' own words. HarperCollins Publishers 2005 192p il $24.95; pa $14.95 *
Grades: 11 12 Adult   629.45
1. Project Apollo 2. Space flight to the moon
ISBN 0-06-087349-3; 0-06-087350-7 (pa)
                             LC 2005-51350
This "survey of the Apollo moon program includes a brief summary of each flight and attempted flight of the great effort, from the fatal fire on Pad 34 in 1967 to the landing of a scientist on the moon in Apollo 17 in 1972. . . . Space collections of all sizes should welcome Pyle's book, and smaller ones will find it invaluable." Booklist

Wolfe, Tom
The right stuff. Farrar, Straus & Giroux 1983 463p $30
Grades: 9 10 11 12   629.45
1. Astronauts 2. Astronautics—United States
ISBN 0-374-25033-2   LC 84-162805
Also available in paperback from Bantam Bks.
A reissue of the title first published 1979
This is a "history of the early years of the space program. Starting with an account of the lives of military pilots [the book progresses] through the selection of the first seven astronauts, their training, and the Mercury flights." Libr J

The right stuff; illustrated. Black Dog & Leventhal 2004 265p il $35
Grades: 11 12 Adult   629.45
1. Astronauts 2. Astronautics—United States
ISBN 1-57912-458-5
Also available in paperback from Bantam Bks.
First published 1979 by Farrar, Straus & Giroux

Wolfe, Tom—*Continued*

This is a "history of the early years of the space program. Starting with an account of the lives of military pilots [the book progresses] through the selection of the first seven astronauts, their training, and the Mercury flights." Libr J

629.47　Astronautical engineering

Reynolds, David West

Kennedy Space Center; gateway to space. Firefly Books 2006 248p il $40

Grades: 11 12 Adult　　629.47

1. John F. Kennedy Space Center 2. Astronautics—United States

ISBN 1-55407-039-2; 978-1-55407-039-8

Containing an "overview of the space program from the view of the facilities that launched the missions and the people who made it happen, Reynolds's work is full of elegant descriptions and compelling details that highlight the vast technology and the indomitable human spirit." Voice Youth Advocates

Includes bibliographical references

629.8　Automatic control engineering

Brooks, Rodney Allen

Flesh and machines; how robots will change us. Pantheon Bks. 2002 260p il $26; pa $14

Grades: 11 12 Adult　　629.8

1. Robots 2. Artificial intelligence

ISBN 0-375-42079-7; 0-375-72527-X (pa)

　　　　　　　　　　LC 2001-36636

"A scientist at MIT's famous artificial intelligence lab, Brooks here splits his book in two: the first part describes various robots he and his group have built; the second part philosophizes on the nature of artificial intelligence." Booklist

A "stimulating book written by one of the major players in the field . . . about the state of robotics and its short-term future. It also offers surprisingly deep glimpses into what it is to be human. Brooks appears to have gained a boundless appreciation for human beings by attempting to copy them." N Y Times Book Rev

Henderson, Harry, 1951-

Modern robotics; building versatile machines. Chelsea House 2006 xx, 188p il (Milestones in discovery and invention) $35

Grades: 9 10 11 12　　629.8

1. Robots

ISBN 0-8160-5745-1　　　LC 2005-31805

This book presents "biographies of the men and women who were and are the leaders in bringing about this change through research and new technologies." Publisher's note

Includes glossary and bibliographical references

Jones, David

Mighty robots; mechanical marvels that fascinate and frighten. Annick Press 2006 126p il $24.95; pa $14.95

Grades: 5 6 7 8 9 10　　629.8

1. Robots

ISBN 1-55037-929-1; 1-55037-928-3 (pa)

"From the development of robotic technology to the history of robots in books and films, this informative offering surveys the field broadly but zeroes in with detailed accounts of many topics. . . . Many clear color photos and detailed sidebars expand the text. . . . Jones presents a great deal of information in a well-organized, accessible manner." Booklist

Malone, Robert

Ultimate robot. DK Publishing 2004 192p il $30 *

Grades: 9 10 11 12　　629.8

1. Robots

ISBN 0-7566-0270-X　　　LC 2004-303591

"This volume examines the uses of robots in popular culture. . . . From the tinplate productions of the 1940s to today's computer-driven toys, the robots on display in Malone's fun tour will amuse rather than alarm readers." Booklist

Sobey, Ed

How to build your own prize-winning robot. Enslow Pubs. 2002 128p il (Science fair success) lib bdg $20.95

Grades: 9 10 11 12　　629.8

1. Robots 2. Science—Experiments 3. Science projects

ISBN 0-7660-1627-7　　　LC 2001-4875

The author covers the fundamentals of robotics, from motors to wheel alignment, and provides instructions for the construction of a personal robot. Includes clubs, organizations, and robotic component suppliers

Includes bibliographical references

632　Plant injuries, diseases, pests

Waldbauer, Gilbert

Insights from insects; what bad bugs can teach us. Prometheus Books 2005 311p il $18

Grades: 11 12 Adult　　632

1. Insect pests

ISBN 1-59102-277-0　　　LC 2004-26928

The author "profiles a rogue's gallery of unhealthful, unprofitable and unsavory creatures from the mosquito and house fly to an array of agricultural scourges. From their ingenious strategies for wreaking havoc and evading retribution from predators, toxic plant chemicals, insecticides and eradication programs, he gleans lessons about the Darwinian struggle for survival and the complex, easily upset balance of ecosystems. Waldbauer's lucid, engaging style, informed by accessible discussions of his and other scientists' research, maintains a lab-coated tone of interested objectivity." Publ Wkly

Includes bibliographical references

634.9 Forestry

Brown, Daniel, 1951-
Under a flaming sky; the great Hinckley firestorm of 1894; [by] Daniel James Brown. Lyons Press 2006 256p il map $22.95
Grades: 11 12 Adult   **634.9**
1. Forest fires 2. Minnesota
ISBN 1-59228-863-4; 978-1-59228-863-2
"On September 1, 1894, a firestorm consumed timber-boomtown Hinckley, Minnesota, and three nearby hamlets. Brown, grandson of an 11-year-old survivor, makes riveting, affecting, white-knuckle reading of that horrifying, internationally reported day's lethal passage." Booklist
Includes bibliographical references

635 Garden crops (Horticulture)

Smith, Miranda, 1944-
Your backyard herb garden; a gardener's guide to growing over 50 herbs plus how to use them in cooking, crafts, companion planting, and more. Rodale Press 1997 160p map hardcover o.p. pa $16.95
Grades: 9 10 11 12   **635**
1. Herb gardening 2. Herbs
ISBN 0-87596-767-1; 0-87596-994-1 (pa)
                                   LC 96-23153
This guide offers information about planning and preparing an herb garden, growing and caring for herbs, using them for cooking, health, and beauty, and includes an illustrated directory of more than 70 herbs
Includes bibliographical references

Step-by-step yard & garden basics. Better Homes & Gardens Bks. 2000 323p il pa $24.95
Grades: 11 12 Adult   **635**
1. Gardening 2. Lawns 3. Landscape architecture
ISBN 0-6962-1288-9; 978-0-6962-1288-8
                                   LC 0013-4297
At head of title: Better Homes and Gardens; "Writer, Liz Ball." Verso of title page
This guidebook covers "starting a lawn and growing roses . . . pruning trees and creating a front yard garden. It provides 200 . . . weather-related tips for lawns and lawn alternatives—flowers, vines, edibles, trees, shrubs and ornaments. [It features] more than 750 photos . . . plus a . . . list of tools and supplies needed for each project. Each chapter closes with a seasonal checklist of related chores for yards and gardens in both northern and southern climates." Publisher's note

635.9 Flowers and ornamental plants

The **American** Horticultural Society A-Z encyclopedia of garden plants; Christopher Brickell, H. Marc Cathey, editors-in-chief. Rev. US ed. DK Pub. 2004 1099p il map $80 *
Grades: 11 12 Adult   **635.9**
1. Ornamental plants—Encyclopedias
ISBN 0-7566-0616-0   LC 2004-559196
First published 1997
This volume "covers over 2000 genera with more than 15,000 individual entries of annuals, perennials, trees, shrubs, climbers, rock plants, biennials, bulbs, orchids, and much more. . . . Arranged by genus, each entry includes family name, a description of the genus, native habitat, garden uses, cultivation, propagation, and pests and diseases. The entries contain a description, height, width, USDA hardiness zones, heat zones, and cultivars." Libr J
"Equal parts gem and tool, this book is like a diamond. Clear, concise, and thoroughly useful, it fits the needs of all gardeners." Am Ref Books Annu, 2005

American Horticultural Society encyclopedia of plants and flowers; editors in chief, Christopher Brickell & Trevor Cole. Rev and updated ed. DK Pub. 2002 720p il $60 *
Grades: 11 12 Adult   **635.9**
1. Ornamental plants
ISBN 0-7894-8993-7   LC 2002-73553
First published 1989 in the United Kingdom with title: The Royal Horticultural Society gardeners' encyclopedia of plants and flowers
This "volume features design information, an illustrated catalog of plants arranged by color as well as kind, and a plant dictionary. With over 8000 trees, shrubs, water plants, cacti, succulents, and more profiled here, there is something for nearly every kind of garden." Libr J

Bawden-Davis, Julie
Flower gardening; a practical guide to creating colorful gardens in every yard; photographs by John M. Rickard. Reader's Digest 2004 288p il $32.95
Grades: 9 10 11 12   **635.9**
1. Flower gardening
ISBN 0-7621-0502-X   LC 2003-58756
This guide features "plans containing new flower species and trends in flower gardening. Includes an A-to-Z section of 477 easy-to-grow plants, ideas for plants, and combinations that will thrive based on where you live and soil type, moneysaving tips, and seasonal advice." Publisher's note
"The most valuable chapters focus on dirt-under-the-nails how-to's. These sections are clear and complete enough for beginners or novices, but also offer tips, tricks and clever ideas seasoned veterans will appreciate." Publ Wkly

Care-free plants; a guide to growing the 200 hardiest, low-maintenance, long-living beauties. Reader's Digest 2002 352p il map $35

Grades: 9 10 11 12   635.9

1. Landscape gardening 2. Ornamental plants

ISBN 0-7621-0358-2   LC 2001-48924

"The book features encyclopedia-style entries on no-fuss annuals, perennials, vines, bulbs, shrubs and trees. Each entry includes photographs, growing tips and vital statistics like preferred soil type and 'critter resistance' level." Publ Wkly

This is a "straightforward, nicely illustrated guide for the gardener." Libr J

Hewitt, Terry

The complete book of cacti & succulents. Dorling Kindersley 1993 176p il hardcover o.p. pa $20

Grades: 11 12 Adult   635.9

1. Cactus 2. Succulent plants

ISBN 1-56458-337-6; 0-7894-1657-3 (pa)

LC 93-22107

An illustrated look at the history and cultivation of more than 300 plants. Ideas for containers and display are included.

Taylor's encyclopedia of garden plants; edited by Frances Tenenbaum. Houghton Mifflin 2003 464p il map (Taylor's guides to gardening) $45

Grades: 11 12 Adult   635.9

1. Ornamental plants—Encyclopedias

ISBN 0-618-22644-3   LC 2002-27630

"A Frances Tenenbaum book"

"The text includes over 1000 species (with myriad cultivars) of trees, shrubs, roses, perennials, annuals, bulbs, and ground covers. The book is arranged by scientific name, with each entry including genus name, pronunciation, plant family, where the plant is native, number of species, a general description, cultivation, uses in the landscape, where the plant grows best (from area of the country to garden site), and any pests or diseases." Libr J

"This beautifully illustrated encyclopedia offers North American gardeners a definitive resource for all their questions, from flowers to trees to shrubs." Publ Wkly

636   Animal husbandry

Hayhurst, Chris

Cool careers without college for animal lovers. Rosen Pub. Group 2002 144p il (Cool careers without college) lib bdg $33.25

Grades: 9 10 11 12   636

1. Animal specialists 2. Vocational guidance

ISBN 0-8239-3500-0   LC 2001-3170

Profiles the characteristics of and qualifications needed for twelve jobs that involve working with animals.

Includes bibliographical references

636.089   Veterinary sciences. Veterinary medicine

Nakaya, Shannon Fujimoto

Kindred spirit, kindred care; making health decisions on behalf of our animal companions. New World Library 2005 155p pa $13.95 *

Grades: 9 10 11 12   636.089

1. Pets—Health and hygiene

ISBN 1-57731-507-3   LC 2005-880

"Devoting entire chapters to choosing a veterinarian, understanding diagnostic and treatment options, managing care, and coping with death and its aftermath, and providing sidebars filled with pertinent questions to ask at various stages of treatment management, Nakaya arms conscientious caregivers with the information they will need to make the best choices for their animal companions. A necessary and noble guide to easing those stressful situations every animal lover must face." Booklist

Includes bibliographical references

636.1   Equines. Horses

Edwards, Elwyn Hartley

The new encyclopedia of the horse; photography by Bob Langrish, Kit Houghton; foreword by Sharon Ralls Lemon. [rev ed] DK Pub. 2000 464p il maps $40 *

Grades: 11 12 Adult   636.1

1. Horses—Encyclopedias

ISBN 0-7894-7181-7   LC 2001-271665

"A Dorling Kindersley book"

First published 1994 with title: The encyclopedia of the horse

The author "traces the evolution of the horse, covering every major breed of horse and pony as well as the contribution the horse has made to civilization—in the wild, at work, at war, and in sport and recreation. . . . The origin, history, and uses of each breed are explained. . . . Specimens of familiar as well as obscure breeds are featured, including Dutch Warmbloods and Camargues, Icelandic and Timor Ponies, Morgans and Shetlands, Andalucian and Lusitano, and the Cutting Horse. . . . Sections on horse management, training, and equipment explain the basics of the proper care of the horse. Information is also included on farriers, feeding, grooming, horse behavior, training techniques, and which equipment to use, including saddles, bridles, and bits." Publisher's note

"A beautiful reference work for the true horse enthusiast." Libr J

Faurie, Bernadette

The horse riding & care handbook. Lyons Press 2000 160p il hardcover o.p. pa $19.95

Grades: 11 12 Adult   636.1

1. Horses 2. Horsemanship

ISBN 1-58574-058-6; 1-58574-517-0 (pa)

"Each section contains pictures or diagrams to clarify the explanations, from horse evolution and history with

Faurie, Bernadette—*Continued*

humans to markings, colors, and breeds. Topics such as tack, how to mount, a first riding lesson, and techniques of western riding are all simply described with wonderful graphics." Libr J

Price, Steven D., 1940-

The horseman's illustrated dictionary. Lyons Press 2000 214p il hardcover o.p. pa $16.95

Grades: 11 12 Adult   **636.1**

1. Horses 2. Horsemanship

ISBN 1-58574-146-9; 1-59228-098-6 (pa)

LC 00-62147

This dictionary includes definitions and derivations of words about horses and horsemanship

636.4 Swine

Montgomery, Sy

The good good pig; the extraordinary life of Christopher Hogwood. Ballantine Books 2006 228p il $21.95; pa $13.95

Grades: 11 12 Adult   **636.4**

1. Pigs

ISBN   0-345-48137-2;   978-0-345-48137-5;
0-345-49609-4 (pa); 978-0-345-49609-6 (pa)

LC 2005-57094

Also available Thorndike Press large print edition

This is a "description of the 14-year life of a 750-pound pet pig who was named after the conductor [Christopher Hogwood]. Anyone who has ever loved a pet can enjoy reading about the relationship between Montgomery and her Christopher." Sci Books Films

636.7 Dogs

American Kennel Club

The complete dog book; American Kennel Club. 20th ed. Ballantine Books 2006 xxi, 858p il $35 *

Grades: 7 8 9 10 11 12 Adult   **636.7**

1. Dogs

ISBN 0-345-47626-3; 978-0-345-47626-5

LC 2005-48263

"Official publication of the American Kennel Club" First published 1935. Periodically revised

"The official guide to 124 AKC registered breeds and their history, appearance, selection, training, care and feeding, and first aid. Some color plates." N Y Public Libr. Ref Books for Child Collect. 2d edition

Budiansky, Stephen

The truth about dogs; an inquiry into the ancestry, social conventions, mental habits, and moral fiber of Canis familiaris. Viking 2000 263p il pa $13 hardcover o.p.

Grades: 11 12 Adult   **636.7**

1. Dogs

ISBN 0-14-100228-X (pa)   LC 00-34966

The author "uses scientific and genetic research to explain why dogs do what they do and are the way they are. In a conversational and entertaining way, the author shows how dog behavior is much more complex and interesting than we have previously thought, and how that behavior is firmly grounded in the breed's successful evolution." Booklist

Includes bibliographical references

Coppinger, Raymond

Dogs; a startling new understanding of canine origin, behavior, and evolution; [by] Raymond Coppinger and Lorna Coppinger. Scribner 2001 352p il $26

Grades: 11 12 Adult   **636.7**

1. Dogs

ISBN 0-684-85530-5   LC 00-54137

"Taking a biological approach to the study of canine behavior and intelligence, the authors promulgate a theory of how the dog evolved. They explain in depth how the interplay of nature and nurture and critical periods of development produced an animal that has more shapes and sizes and uses than any other. . . . They define what constitutes a breed and criticize today's purebred breeding programs." Libr J

"This important book belongs in all libraries." Booklist

Includes bibliographical references

Davis, Caroline, 1971-

Essential dog; the ultimate guide to owning a happy and healthy pet. Reader's Digest Association 2006 192p il $26.95 *

Grades: 9 10 11 12   **636.7**

1. Dogs

ISBN 0-7621-0669-7; 978-0-7621-0669-1

LC 2005-54747

This is a "primer for those wanting a dog book to read both before and after acquiring a canine. The first section on choosing a dog sets up the structure of the rest of the book. Each chapter begins with a checklist of what is covered in the text." Booklist

Dibra, Bashkim

Dogspeak; how to learn it, speak it, and use it to have a happy, healthy, well-behaved dog; {by} Bash Dibra; with Mary Ann Crenshaw; illustrations by José Dennis. Simon & Schuster 1999 270p il pa $13 hardcover o.p.

Grades: 11 12 Adult   **636.7**

1. Dogs

ISBN 0-684-86548-3 (pa)   LC 99-30194

"Discusses the social, or pack, nature of dogs and explains eight factors important to pack dynamics: the dominance hierarchy aggression, territorial behavior, food guarding, flight behavior, chase behavior, socialization, and vocalization. Throughout, Dibra provides examples of how these factors come into play when training the family dog." Libr J

Fogle, Bruce

New complete dog training manual; {by} Bruce Fogle and Patricia Holden White. Dorling Kindersley 2002 176p il $25 *

Grades: 11 12 Adult   **636.7**

1. Dogs—Training

ISBN 0-7894-8398-X   LC 2001-47931

First published 1994 with title: ASPCA complete dog training manual

This book "shows you how to establish routines, implement commands, break bad habits, and learn how to train various breeds." Publisher's note

The new encyclopedia of the dog; photography by Tracy Morgan. 2nd American ed. Dorling Kindersley 2000 416p il $40

Grades: 11 12 Adult   **636.7**

1. Dogs—Encyclopedias

ISBN 0-7894-6130-7   LC 00-22642

First published 1995 with title: The encyclopedia of the dog

This describes over 420 breeds and varieties of dogs, including their histories, temperments, and physical features

Geeson, Eileen

Ultimate dog grooming; additional material by Barbara Vetter & Lia Whitmore. Firefly Books 2004 288p il $29.95; pa $27.95

Grades: 11 12 Adult   **636.7**

1. Dogs

ISBN 1-55297-873-7; 1-55407-328-6 (pa)

The author "offers a three-part introduction to grooming for both owners and professionals. In Part 1, she briefly addresses what an owner needs to know about grooming as well as how to choose the right groomer. Part 2 is geared toward those who want to become professional groomers. . . . The bulk of the book offers well-done profiles of 170 dog breeds—arranged by coat type—that include worthwhile tips and hints. Supplementing the text are more than 500 color illustrations, ranging from detailed drawings to photographs." Libr J

Katz, Jon

A dog year; twelve months, four dogs, and me. Villard Bks. 2002 xxi, 200p hardcover o.p. pa $12.95

Grades: 11 12 Adult   **636.7**

1. Dogs

ISBN 0-375-50297-1; 0-8129-6690-2 (pa)

LC 2001-45506

The author describes his adoption of "a homeless Border collie, Devon. . . . Katz details the long and torturous months spent helping Devon adapt to his new life and to helping the dog overcome his deep-seated fears and insecurities. Katz tells an honest story, carefully detailing how difficult it can be to take responsibility for a dog, particularly a maladjusted one." Booklist

A good dog; the story of Orson, who changed my life. Villard Books 2006 224p il $21.95; pa $13.95

Grades: 11 12 Adult   **636.7**

1. Dogs

ISBN   978-1-4000-6189-1;   1-4000-6189-X; 978-0-8129-7149-1 (pa); 0-8129-7149-3 (pa)

LC 2006-42163

"Orson was Katz's 'lifetime dog,' the one he felt a powerful, life-changing connection with—but Orson was a difficult dog. In a lyrical series of vignettes, the author writes of his working border collie, Rose (the personality opposite of Orson); the rooster, Winston; sheep; donkeys; and the impossible Orson, whom Katz thought was destined to work sheep but whose work became the author. This is a lovely memoir." Booklist

The **Original** dog bible; the definitive new source for all things dog; edited by Kristin Mehus-Roe. Bowtie Press 2005 750p il pa $24.95

Grades: 11 12 Adult   **636.7**

1. Dogs

ISBN 1-931993-34-3   LC 2004-9985

This "volume covers every aspect of responsible dog ownership and includes additional details on evolution, genetics, history, folklore, competitive events, careers, and rescue groups. Appendixes include explanations of performance titles, lists of record holders, a glossary, and a 54-page listing of resources." Libr J

Thomas, Elizabeth Marshall, 1931-

The hidden life of dogs; [illustrations by Jared T. Williams] Pocket Books [1996] xxiii, 148p il pa $12.95

Grades: 9 10 11 12 Adult   **636.7**

1. Dogs—Psychology

ISBN 0-671-51700-7

First published 1993 by Houghton Mifflin

In this book about animal behavior the author's "intention is to find out, by observing her own animals, what it is that dogs 'want'. The dogs were free to make their own decisions; Thomas fed them, sheltered them, and provided medical care, but otherwise didn't train them or direct their activities." Libr J

The author's "writing is so good not only because of her sense of language but also because of the quality of her observations. . . . A splendid book." Natl Rev

Includes bibliographical references

636.8 Cats

Christensen, Wendy

The Humane Society of the United States complete guide to cat care; [by] Wendy Christensen and the staff of the Humane Society of the United States. St. Martin's Press 2002 322p il hardcover o.p. pa $16.95 *

Grades: 11 12 Adult   **636.8**

1. Cats

ISBN 0-312-26929-3; 0-312-32608-4 (pa)

LC 2001-57892

Christensen, Wendy—*Continued*
This "guide includes sections on choosing a healthy cat, feeding and nutrition, training, grooming, disease, vet visits, caring for an aging cat, feline first-aid kits and emergency care." Publisher's note

Davis, Caroline, 1971-
Essential cat; the ultimate guide to caring for your cat. Reader's Digest Assn. 2005 192p il $26.95
Grades: 7 8 9 10   **636.8**
  1. Cats
  ISBN 0-7621-0496-1   LC 2003-60556
This book covers topics such as "feline behavior, healthcare, reproduction, first aid, illness, and aging. Numerous checklists, sidebars, and tips and remedies supply the reader with a wealth of quick information. Hundreds of delightful full-color instructional photographs provide clear steps for tasks such as feeding, grooming, giving medications, bathing, and even brushing a cat's teeth." Libr J

Edney, A. T. B.
ASPCA complete cat care manual; [by] Andrew Edney; foreword by Roger Caras. Dorling Kindersley 1992 192p il hardcover o.p. pa $14.95 *
Grades: 11 12 Adult   **636.8**
  1. Cats
  ISBN 1-56458-064-4; 0-7566-1742-1 (pa)
                     LC 92-52783
Subtitle on cover: The ultimate illustrated guide to caring for your cat
"Cat care is made easy through step-by-step photographs that illustrate grooming, handling, detecting illness, first aid, and other concerns. Difficult-to-explain procedures, such as how to administer medication or transport an injured cat, are clearly understandable." Libr J
Includes bibliographical references

Fogle, Bruce
The new encyclopedia of the cat. DK Pub. 2001 288p il maps $35
Grades: 11 12 Adult   **636.8**
  1. Cats—Encyclopedias
  ISBN 0-7894-8021-2   LC 2001-275714
First published 1997 with title: The encyclopedia of the cat
"Opening sections cover the cat family, cats and people, and feline design and behavior. Entries on more than 60 longhair and shorthair breeds include discussions on the ancestry of each breed, shape and form, colors and patterns, and standards and temperament. Over 1300 beautiful color illustrations make this an essential purchase for both circulating and reference collections." Libr J [review of 1997 edition]
Includes bibliographical references

Herriot, James
James Herriot's cat stories; with illustrations by Lesley Holmes. St. Martin's Press 1994 161p $17.95
Grades: 11 12 Adult   **636.8**
  1. Cats
  ISBN 0-312-11342-0   LC 94-20131
A "collection of favorite cat tales from Herriot's veterinary practice. Retired after over 50 years in practice, Herriot continues to entertain young and old alike with his storytelling ability. His current collection includes 'Alfred, the Sweet-Shop Cat,' 'Boris and Mrs. Bond's Cat Establishment,' 'Moses Found Among the Rushes,' and others." Libr J

Wilbourn, Carole, 1940-
The total cat; understanding your cat's physical and emotional behavior from kitten to old age. HarperCollins Pubs. 2000 xxxvii, 233p il pa $14
Grades: 11 12 Adult   **636.8**
  1. Cats
  ISBN 0-380-79051-3   LC 00-40846
Wilbourn presents "general information about the care, feeding, and medical needs of cats. . . . From the selection of a cat by its age and personality type, along with suggestions for finding a good match for the character and lifestyle of the potential owner, to fitting a cat into a household that may include other pets to causes and cures of less desirable feline behavioral traits, the author covers all aspects of cat behavior." Booklist

639.2   Commercial fishing, whaling, sealing

Murphy, Jim, 1947-
Gone a-whaling; the lure of the sea and the hunt for the great whale. Clarion Bks. 1998 208p il $18; pa $8.95
Grades: 7 8 9 10   **639.2**
  1. Whaling—History
  ISBN 0-395-69847-2; 0-618-43243-4 (pa)
                     LC 97-13051
Diary entries form the backbone of this "look at whale hunting in America, from the nineteenth century to today." Booklist
"Murphy makes history fascinating and immediate with a lively, engrossing narrative that both informs and entertains." Voice Youth Advocates
Includes glossary and bibliographical references

639.34   Aquariums

Alderton, David
Encyclopedia of aquarium & pond fish. Dorling Kindersley 2005 400p il $35 *
Grades: 11 12 Adult   **639.34**
  1. Fishes—Encyclopedias
  ISBN 0-7566-0941-0
This reference provides care and identification information on over 800 freshwater, saltwater, coldwater and

Alderton, David—*Continued*

tropical fish, showing "what each fish looks like, what food they eat, which species they can cohabit with and how big they grow." Publisher's note

The author "has created the definitive work on the subject, with photos to match." Libr J

Dawes, John

Complete encyclopedia of the freshwater aquarium. Firefly Books 2001 304p il $40

Grades: 9 10 11 12   **639.34**

1. Aquariums—Encyclopedias 2. Fishes—Encyclopedias

ISBN 1-55297-544-4   LC 2003-535209

"A brief section is devoted to aquaria, their maintenance, and suitable plants, but the major part of the book consists of photographs and descriptions of almost all freshwater fishes suitable for aquaria. . . . For students interested in learning about freshwater fishes and their care, this book would be a good place to start." Choice

Includes bibliographical references

Maître-Allain, Thierry

Aquariums; the complete guide to freshwater and saltwater aquariums; [by] Thierry Maitre-Allain and Christian Piednoir; [English translation by Matthew Clarke] Firefly Books 2006 281p il $39.95 *

Grades: 11 12 Adult   **639.34**

1. Aquariums 2. Marine aquariums

ISBN 1-55407-085-6

The authors "walk the novice through all aspects of setting up and maintaining an underwater habitat. . . . Beautiful photos clearly illustrate this good all-in-one handbook that will fill the needs of beginning aquarists." Booklist

Includes bibliographical references

Rogers, Geoff

Focus on freshwater aquarium fish; [by] Geoff Rogers, Nick Fletcher. Firefly Bks. 2004 208p il $29.95

Grades: 11 12 Adult   **639.34**

1. Fishes

ISBN 1-55297-936-9   LC 2004-303841

"The book presents the fish based on their families or fishkeeping groups. . . . Each section opens with an overview that introduces the range of fish within that group and explores their adaptations. The images and text provide details of the mature size and main characteristics of each fish, its behavior in the aquarium and a brief look at how it breeds." Publisher's note

"This beautiful book is supplemental to aquarium how-to books." Booklist

639.9   Conservation of biological resources

Owens, Delia

The eye of the elephant; an epic adventure in the African wilderness; [by] Delia and Mark Owens. Houghton Mifflin 1992 305p il hardcover o.p. pa $16

Grades: 11 12 Adult   **639.9**

1. Elephants 2. Wildlife conservation

ISBN 0-395-42381-3; 0-395-68090-5 (pa)

LC 92-17691

This is an account of the authors' efforts to save elephants in the Luangwa Valley of Zambia from poachers by involving and educating the local people.

This "is a provocative, disturbing, and eminently readable work." Nat Hist

Includes bibliographic references

Followed by Secrets of the savanna

Owens, Mark

Secrets of the savanna; twenty-three years in the African wilderness unraveling the mysteries of elephants and people; [by] Mark and Delia Owens. Houghton Mifflin 2006 230p il map $26; pa $14.95

Grades: 11 12 Adult   **639.9**

1. Elephants 2. Wildlife conservation

ISBN 978-0-395-89310-4; 0-395-89310-0; 978-0-618-87250-3 (pa); 0-618-87250-7 (pa)

LC 2005-23842

Sequel to The eye of the elephant

The authors "describe traveling to the 'remote and ruggedly beautiful' Luangwa Valley, in northeastern Zambia, to help save the North Luangwa National Park, where the elephant population had been decimated by poachers." Publ Wkly

"This book, full of adventure and a few hair-raising moments, deserves a wide readership." Libr J

Includes bibliographical references

640   Home and family management

The **experts'** guide to 100 things everyone should know how to do; created by Samantha Ettus. Clarkson Potter Publishers 2004 326p $19.95 *

Grades: 9 10 11 12   **640**

1. Home economics 2. Life skills

ISBN 1-4000-5256-4; 978-1-4000-5256-1

LC 2004-2546

"These experts and 94 more show you how to read a newspaper (New York Times publisher [Arthur] Sulzberger), tell a joke (comedian [Howie] Mandel), save money (financial guru [Suze] Orman), and, well, pretty much anything else you can think of. . . . The authors call the book 'Cliff Notes to life,' and that about sums it up. It's more fun than Cliff Notes, though." Booklist

641 Food and drink

641.3 Food

Allen, Stewart Lee

In the devil's garden; a sinful history of forbidden food. Ballantine Bks. 2002 315p hardcover o.p. pa $13.95

Grades: 11 12 Adult **641**

1. Food 2. Eating customs 3. Cooking 4. Menus

ISBN 0-345-44015-3; 0-345-44016-1 (pa)

LC 2001-43882

"Different cultures and religions have defined certain foods as taboo over the centuries. Allen examines these taboos and looks for possible explanations for forbidding some otherwise edible foodstuffs from human consumption." Booklist

"The historical and cultural links between food, sex and religion make for fascinating reading." Publ Wkly

Includes bibliographical references

641.03 Food and drink--Encyclopedias and dictionaries

Davidson, Alan, 1924-2003

The Oxford companion to food; edited by Tom Jaine; illustrations by Soun Vannithone. 2nd ed. Oxford University Press 2006 907p il map $65 *

Grades: 11 12 Adult **641.03**

1. Food—Encyclopedias

ISBN 0-19-280681-5; 978-0-19-280681-9

LC 2006-48602

First published 1999

"Covering everything from individual ingredients and cooking techniques to food celebrities and national cuisines, the authoritative and engaging The Oxford Companion to Food is one of the best basic culinary reference books available." Libr J

Includes bibliographical references

Rolland, Jacques L., 1945-

The food encyclopedia; over 8,000 ingredients, tools, techniques and people; [by] Jacques L. Rolland and Carol Sherman with other contributors. Robert Rose 2006 701p il $49.95

Grades: 11 12 Adult **641.03**

1. Food—Encyclopedias 2. Cooking

ISBN 978-0-7788-0150-4; 0-7788-0150-0

This encyclopedia "has 8,000 entries, with cross-reference on foods, wines, beverages, cooking methods and techniques, and biographies of prominent people." Publisher's note

Includes bibliographical references

Albala, Ken, 1964-

Food in early modern Europe. Greenwood Press 2003 360p il (Food through history) $49.95

Grades: 9 10 11 12 **641.3**

1. Food—History 2. Eating customs 3. Europe—Social life and customs

ISBN 0-313-31962-6 LC 2002-28431

The author "explores the complex and interrelated changes that took place in the production and consumption of food in Europe roughly between 1504 and 1800, from first contact with the New World to the beginning of the Industrial Revolution." Choice

"This very scholarly book provides interesting information for both the researcher and browser alike." Libr Media Connect

Includes bibliographical references

The **Cambridge** world history of food; editors, Kenneth F. Kiple, Kriemhild Coneè Ornelas. Cambridge Univ. Press 2000 2v set $190 *

Grades: 11 12 Adult **641.3**

1. Food—History

ISBN 0-521-40216-6 LC 00-57181

In slipcase

"The two volumes are arranged in eight parts covering the diet of early man, staple foods, dietary liquids, nutrients and food-related disorders, food and drink around the world, nutrition and health, current food-related issues and concluding with a dictionary of plant foods. . . . The Cambridge World History of Food is a thorough study of a topic that is eternally popular. It should become a standard source in reference collections." Booklist

Includes bibliographical references

Dunn-Georgiou, Elisha

Everything you need to know about organic foods. Rosen Pub. Group 2002 64p il (Need to know library) lib bdg $23.95 *

Grades: 7 8 9 10 **641.3**

1. Natural foods 2. Organic gardening

ISBN 0-8239-3551-5 LC 2001-3789

Discusses the organic food movement and recent information about the United States Department of Agriculture's criteria for what defines an organic food.

Includes bibliographical references

Goldstein, Myrna Chandler, 1948-

Controversies in food and nutrition; {by} Myrna Chandler Goldstein and Mark A. Goldstein. Greenwood Press 2002 260p il (Contemporary controversies) $45

Grades: 11 12 Adult **641.3**

1. Food 2. Nutrition

ISBN 0-313-31787-9 LC 2002-69605

This book explains varying opinions and underlying issues that surround such topics as popular diets, vegetarianism, food irradiation, organic and imported food, vitamin supplementation, food allergies, and genetic modifi-

Goldstein, Myrna Chandler, 1948——*Continued*
cations

"For anyone confused about the barrage of messages we get every day about nutrition, this is an excellent book. . . . Thoroughly enjoyable to read, the book is designed as a high school or college reference text, but it would also interest the general public." Choice

Includes bibliographical references

Kaufman, Cathy K.

Cooking in ancient civilizations. Greenwood Press 2006 liv, 224p il map (Greenwood Press "Daily life through history" series) $45 *

Grades: 11 12 Adult   **641.3**

1. Food—History 2. Cooking 3. Ancient civilization
ISBN 0-313-33204-5; 978-0-313-33204-3

                           LC 2006-15692

This cookbook focuses "on the main ancient peoples studied today—the Romans, Mesopotamians, Egyptians, and Greeks. . . . Each group is covered in a chapter that begins with a narrative overview of the environment and resources, cuisine and social class, and a note on sources." Publisher's note

Includes bibliographical references

Menzel, Peter

Hungry planet; what the world eats; photographed by Peter Menzel; written by Faith D'Aluisio. Ten Speed Press 2005 287p il map $40; pa $24.95

Grades: 11 12 Adult   **641.3**

1. Food—Pictorial works
ISBN 978-1-58008-681-3; 978-1-58008-869-5 (pa)

                           LC 2005-13455

This is "a photographic study of families from around the world, revealing what people eat during the course of one week." Publisher's note

"This is a beautiful, quietly provocative volume." Publ Wkly

Includes bibliographical references

The **Oxford** encyclopedia of food and drink in America; Andrew F. Smith, editor in chief. Oxford University Press 2004 2v il set $250 *

Grades: 11 12 Adult   **641.3**

1. Food—Encyclopedias 2. Beverages
ISSN 978-0-19-515437-5
ISBN 0-19-515437-1   LC 2003-24873

This reference covers "the regions, people, ingredients, foods, drinks, publications, advertising, companies, historical periods, and political and economic aspects pertinent to American cuisine." Publisher's note

"Whether readers make a living studying culinary traditions or just enjoy eating, they'll find this book a marvel. . . . For food lovers of all stripes, this work inspires, enlightens and entertains." Publ Wkly

For a fuller review see: Booklist, Dec. 1, 2004

Rosenblum, Mort

Chocolate: a bittersweet saga of dark and light. North Point Press 2005 290p il $24; pa $14

Grades: 11 12 Adult   **641.3**

1. Chocolate
ISBN 0-86547-635-7; 0-86547-730-2 (pa)

                           LC 2004-54734

Also available Thorndike Press large print edition

The author "unveils chocolate's history and its various incarnations, including in his fresh and insightful discussions the origins of mole; the differences between, say, Hershey's kisses and Valrhona's products; the invention of Nutella; and the small boutique chocolate artisans found nearly everywhere. . . . A compelling and tasty read." Booklist

Shulman, Martha Rose

Foodlover's atlas of the world. Firefly Bks. 2002 288p il $35 *

Grades: 11 12 Adult   **641.3**

ISBN 1-55297-571-1   LC 2003-535048

"This overview of food around the world is divided into 'Europe,' 'Africa and the Middle East,' 'Asia and Australia' and 'the Americas,' and is subdivided by country and region. In each section Shulman discusses the staple foods, culinary history, specialties and mealtime customs of each area. Sidebars spotlight signature dishes and special ingredients, beverages and . . . concoctions. . . . The book concludes with a sampling of 80-plus recipes from every continent." Publ Wkly

"An excellent resource for geography, foreign language, and home-economics students." SLJ

Includes bibliographical references

Tannahill, Reay

Food in history. new, fully rev and updated ed. Crown 1989 c1988 424p il pa $16 hardcover o.p.

Grades: 9 10 11 12   **641.3**

1. Food—History 2. Dining
ISBN 0-517-88404-6   LC 89-671

First published 1973 by Stein & Day; this edition first published 1988 in the United Kingdom

"A world history of food from prehistoric times . . . this book also traces the way in which food has influenced the entire course of human development." Publisher's note

Includes bibliographical references

641.5 Cooking

Albyn, Carole Lisa, 1955-

The multicultural cookbook for students; by Carole Lisa Albyn and Lois Sinaiko Webb. Oryx Press 1993 xxii, 287p maps pa $29.50

Grades: 9 10 11 12   **641.5**

1. Cooking
ISBN 0-89774-735-6   LC 92-41634

Presents a collection of recipes from over 120 countries and briefly discusses the culture and culinary habits of each country

Bayless, Rick
Rick & Lanie's excellent kitchen adventures; chef-dad, teenage daughter, recipes and stories; [by] Rick Bayless & Lanie Bayless, with Deann Groen Bayless; photographs by Christopher Hirsheimer. Stewart, Tabori & Chang 2004 231p il $29.95 *
Grades: 7 8 9 10   **641.5**
1. Cooking
ISBN 1-58479-331-7   LC 2004-12627
"The volume is organized by region, with almost every continent covered. Each section begins with a few personal stories from the authors. . . . The recipes range from ultrasimple, such as 'The Simplest Fried Beans' to elaborate, such as 'Chinese Celebration Hot Pot,' which involves several exotic ingredients and numerous steps. . . . This is a volume filled with delicious recipes that are not necessarily all easy—but are always described in a way that is easy to follow." SLJ

Better homes and gardens new cook book. 14th ed. Meredith Books 2006 656p il $29.95; pa $19.95 *
Grades: 11 12 Adult   **641.5**
1. Cooking
ISBN   0-696-22403-8;   978-0-696-22403-4; 0-696-22565-4 (pa); 978-0-696-22565-9 (pa)
LC 2006-921302
First published 1930 with title: My Better Homes and Gardens cook book. Periodically revised
"A standard cookbook . . . with staple recipes and types of cooking." N Y Public Libr. Book of How & Where to Look It Up

Betty Crocker cookbook; everything you need to know to cook today. 10th ed. Wiley 2005 575p il $29.95; pa $17.95 *
Grades: 11 12 Adult   **641.5**
1. Cooking
ISBN   0-7645-6877-9;   978-0-7645-6877-0; 0-7645-8374-3 (pa); 978-0-7645-8374-2 (pa)
LC 2006-281166
First published with this title 1969 by Golden Press. Periodically revised. Publisher varies. Variant title: Betty Crocker's new cookbook
"This book gives easily readable and understandable recipes. Also has a glossary of cooking terms in back, as well as nutritional guidelines and 'special helps.'" N Y Public Libr. Book of How & Where to Look It Up

Butts, Lauren
Okay, so now you're a vegetarian; advice and 100 recipes from one vegetarian to another. Broadway Books 2000 244p il pa $12.95
Grades: 9 10 11 12   **641.5**
1. Vegetarian cooking
ISBN 0-7679-0527-X; 978-0-7679-0527-5
LC 99-86652
In addition to offering 100 recipes ranging "from a Breakfast Burrito and Thai Tofu-Veggie Wrap to the Fake-Steak Burger and Death-by-Chocolate Brownies, . . . [the author] also deciphers vegetarian jargon and gives nutritional advice on maintaining a healthy diet." Publisher's note
Includes bibliographical references

Carle, Megan
Teens cook; how to make what you want to eat; [by] Megan and Jill Carle with Judi Carle. Ten Speed Press 2004 146p il pa $19.95
Grades: 9 10 11 12   **641.5**
1. Cooking
ISBN 1-58008-584-9
This cookbook features "recipes for a variety of dishes including chocolate chip scones, potato skins, broccoli cheese soup, steak fajitas, baked macaroni and cheese, and toffee bars. Because Megan is a vegetarian, there are several vegetarian recipes or vegetarian substitutes. . . . Attractive, engaging, and told from a teen perspective, this cookbook will make an excellent addition to any nonfiction collection." Voice Youth Advocates

Cunningham, Marion
The Fannie Farmer cookbook; illustrated by Lauren Jarrett. 13th ed. Knopf 1996 874p il $30 *
Grades: 11 12 Adult   **641.5**
1. Cooking
ISBN 0-679-45081-5   LC 97-162330
First published 1896 under the authorship of Fannie Merritt Farmer. Periodically revised
This standard cookbook focuses on the selection, preparation, and serving of a wide variety of foods

Dragonwagon, Crescent
Passionate vegetarian; by Crescent Dragonwagon; illustrated by Robin Gourley. Workman 2002 1110p il hardcover o.p. pa $24.95 *
Grades: 9 10 11 12   **641.5**
1. Vegetarian cooking
ISBN 1-56305-711-5; 0-7611-2825-5 (pa)
LC 2002-72584
This book features "more than 1000 recipes, from 'Welcoming Hors d'Oeuvres' to 'Just Desserts.' . . . In addition to the recipes, . . . [the author] includes hundreds of boxes and sidebars on ingredients and myriad other subjects; the vegetable chapter, for example, features an A-Z guide to her favorites." Libr J
Includes bibliographical references

Grant, Mark
Roman cookery; ancient recipes for modern kitchens; decorations by Jane Smith. Serif 1999 191p il pa $14.95
Grades: 9 10 11 12 Adult   **641.5**
1. Roman cooking
ISBN 1-89795-939-7
The author's "theme is everyday Roman food: bread and olive oil form the basic of the simple cuisine that he tells us even emperors ate when not attending extravagant banquets. . . . [He] brings together recipes from the whole span of Roman cookery: . . . sources range from about 400 B.C. to A.D. 500, and from Egypt to northern France." Classical Rev
Includes bibliographical references

Greene, Gloria Kaufer, 1950-

The new Jewish holiday cookbook; an international collection of recipes and customs. Completely rev and updated with more than 80 new recipes! Times Bks. 1999 539p $29.95

Grades: 11 12 Adult   **641.5**

1. Jewish cooking 2. Jewish holidays

ISBN 0-8129-2977-2   LC 98-55721

First published 1985 with title: The Jewish holiday cookbook

"Starting with the chief and weekly holiday, Sabbath, Greene offers tasty recipes that occasionally draw on ingredients outside traditional ones. . . . Greene labels each recipe as 'meat,' 'dairy,' or 'pareve' so that readers may determine instantly how the recipe correlates with dietary laws." Booklist

Jacob, Jeanne

The world cookbook for students; [by] Jeanne Jacob, Michael Ashkenazi. Greenwood Press 2007 5v il map set $225 *

Grades: 7 8 9 10 11 12   **641.5**

1. Cooking 2. Eating customs

ISBN 0-313-33454-4; 978-0-313-33454-2

     LC 2006-26184

"The volumes are organized alphabetically by country or group name. Each entry includes a brief introduction to the land and people and their cuisine and then an overview of the foodstuffs, typical dishes, and styles of eating in simple bulleted lists. Approximately 5 recipes are provided per country/ethnic group of typical dishes and holiday fare, for a total of 1,198." Publisher's note

Includes bibliographical references

Lieberman, Dave, 1980-

Young and hungry; photography by George Whiteside. Hyperion 2005 262p il $22.95

Grades: 11 12 Adult   **641.5**

1. Cooking

ISBN 1-4013-0128-2   LC 2004-59926

The author "offers a variety of appealing, easy, budget-conscious dishes for various occasions, including casual and romantic dinners, brunches, barbecues, tailgate parties and buffets." Publ Wkly

Madison, Deborah

Vegetarian cooking for everyone. Broadway Bks. 1997 742p il $40

Grades: 11 12 Adult   **641.5**

1. Vegetarian cooking

ISBN 0-7679-0014-6   LC 97-11138

Following information on ingredients and techniques, the recipes focus "mainly on vegetables and grains, aiming at flavor and variety, both often arrived at via assorted ethnic approaches." Publ Wkly

McFeely, Mary Drake

Can she bake a cherry pie? American women and the kitchen in the twentieth century. University of Mass. Press 2000 194p hardcover o.p. pa $16.95

Grades: 9 10 11 12   **641.5**

1. Cooking 2. Women—United States

ISBN 1-55849-250-X; 1-55849-333-6 (pa)

     LC 00-23452

"This book shows how cooking developed and evolved during the twentieth century. From Fannie Farmer to Julia Child, new challenges arose to replace the old. Women found themselves still tied to the kitchen, but for different reasons and with the need to acquire new skills." Publisher's note

"This book would be an excellent beginning for in-depth research or for a pleasant introduction to the field. It will have a wide appeal to those interested in women's roles in the 20th century and in home cooking." Choice

Includes bibliographical references

The **new** American Heart Association cookbook. 7th ed. Clarkson Potter 2004 xx, 700p il $30; pa $19.95 *

Grades: 11 12 Adult   **641.5**

1. Cooking 2. Low-cholesterol diet

ISBN 1-4000-4826-5; 0-307-35205-6 (pa)

     LC 2004-11239

Also available in paperback 25th anniversary edition

First published 1973 with title: American Heart Association cookbook

"Each recipe comes with a breakdown of calories, protein content, carbohydrates, cholesterol, fats (broken down by saturated, polyunsaturated and monounsaturated) and sodium content, along with a table of dietary exchange. . . . This book remains a basic in many heart-conscious kitchens." Publ Wkly

The **new** American plate cookbook; recipes for a healthy weight and a healthy life; American Institute for Cancer Research. University of California Press 2005 306p il $24.95

Grades: 11 12 Adult   **641.5**

1. Cooking

ISBN 0-520-24234-3   LC 2004-17993

The recipes in this book are "built around vegetables and whole grains, with an emphasis on brown rice, wheat pasta, and other healthful foods, rather than protein. . . . Recipes are appealing and easy to make and cover every course of a meal. Well-known dishes are reworked, e.g., New England Clam Chowder, to help with the transition to healthier eating." Libr J

Robertson, Robin

Vegan planet; 400 irresistible recipes with fantastic flavors from home and around the world. Harvard Common Press 2003 576p hardcover o.p. pa $21.95

Grades: 11 12 Adult   **641.5**

1. Vegetarian cooking

ISBN 1-55832-210-8; 1-55832-211-6 (pa)

     LC 2002-7435

Robertson, Robin—*Continued*

The author "offers dozens of imaginative vegan recipes inspired by a wide range of cuisines, from Five-Spiced Portobello Satays and Lebanese Fattoush (bread salad) to Cajun-Style Collards and Moroccan Fava Bean Stew." Libr J

Rombauer, Irma von Starkloff, 1877-1962

Joy of cooking; [by] Irma S. Rombauer, Marion Rombauer Becker, Ethan Becker; illustrated by John Norton. 75th anniversary ed. Scribner 2006 1132p il $30 *

Grades: 11 12 Adult   **641.5**
  1. Cooking
  ISBN 978-0-7432-4626-2; 0-7432-4626-8
                                        LC 2006-51231
First published 1931

"All-purpose cookbook for informal and formal use with American and foreign recipes. Includes menu planning suggestions, nutrition, basic information on foods, basic cooking terminology, and methods of preparation." N Y Public Libr Book of How & Where to Look It Up

This is the "backbone for any library's cookery reference collection, its nearly 4,000 recipes defining essential American home cooking." Booklist

Segan, Francine

Shakespeare's kitchen; Renaissance recipes for the contemporary cook; photographs by Tim Turner. Random House 2003 270p il $35

Grades: 9 10 11 12   **641.5**
  1. British cooking
  ISBN 0-375-50917-8   LC 2002-36839

"Updating dozens of classic Elizabethan recipes, Segan leads a culinary foray into Shakespeare's time. Each recipe is supplemented with a historical note that places the dish in context. . . . Its playful tone, fascinating side-notes, and apt citations from the Bard's plays make this book as fun to read as it is to cook from." Publ Wkly

Includes bibliographical references

Shimbo, Hiroko

The Japanese kitchen; 250 recipes in a traditional spirit; illustrations by Rodica Prato. Harvard Common Press; distributed by National Bk. Network 2000 512p il hardcover o.p. pa $21.95

Grades: 11 12 Adult   **641.5**
  1. Japanese cooking
  ISBN 1-55832-176-4; 1-55832-177-2 (pa)
                                        LC 00-33505

The author provides a "guide to equipment, techniques, and ingredients, followed by a wide-ranging selection of recipes of all sorts. There are both the homestyle dishes she grew up on and more elaborate ones for special occasions, as well as the traditional Japanese classics, with her own touches, of course, and innovative new recipes. . . . An essential purchase." Libr J

Stern, Sam, 1990-

Cooking up a storm; [by] Sam Stern, with Susan Stern. Candlewick Press 2006 128p il pa $16.99 *

Grades: 6 7 8 9   **641.5**
  1. Cooking
  ISBN 978-0-7636-2988-5; 0-7636-2988-X (pa)
                                        LC 2006-42571

"English teen Sam Stern, with his mother's help, offers this slender, photo-packed cookbook, unusual not only because of its author but also because it focuses on guys. . . . That said, the recipes, presented in a casual but clear voice, will draw both genders. . . . The bright, energetic text and color photos of Sam and his photogenic friends and family will easily pull in aspiring foodies." Booklist

Webb, Lois Sinaiko, 1922-

Holidays of the world cookbook for students. Oryx Press 1995 xxxiv, 297p il maps pa $36.95

Grades: 5 6 7 8 9 10   **641.5**
  1. Cooking 2. Holidays
  ISBN 0-89774-884-0   LC 95-26019

In this cookbook "more than 136 countries are represented, with 388 recipes. The U.S. is divided into six sections with 10 recipes for regional celebrations. History behind the holiday is included where possible, as is pertinent background information on the culture represented. . . . A discussion of different calendars used around the world is an interesting inclusion. The recipes' directions are clear and include equipment lists." SLJ

Includes glossary and bibliographical references

Zanger, Mark H.

The American history cookbook. Greenwood Press 2003 xxiii, 459p il (Cookbooks for students) pa $29.95

Grades: 11 12 Adult   **641.5**
  1. Cooking
  ISBN 1-57356-376-5   LC 2002-69608

"An Oryx book"

"This book uses historical commentary and recipes to trace the history of American cooking from the first European contact with Native Americans to the 1970s. Each of 50 chronologically arranged topical chapters contain 500-1,000 words of general commentary followed by descriptions and . . . step-by-step instructions for 3-4 recipes. The recipes are drawn from a wide variety of historical cookbooks and other historical sources." Publisher's note

Includes bibliographical references

643 Housing and household equipment

Complete do-it-yourself manual; with the editors of Family handyman. rev and updated. Reader's Digest 2005 528p il $35 *

Grades: 11 12 Adult   **643**
  1. Houses—Maintenance and repair
  ISBN 0-7621-0579-8   LC 2004-50945

First published 1973 with title: Reader's Digest complete do-it-yourself manual

Complete do-it-yourself manual—*Continued*
At head of title: Reader's Digest
This manual for homeowners covers topics such as power tools, plumbing, landscaping, and storage projects with photos, diagrams and illustrations
"Intriguing sidebars on wood refinishers (the fastest drying versus the safest), the financial benefits of renting specialty tools for a large drywall project and other subjects round out this must-have guide." Publ Wkly

646.2 Sewing and related operations

The **complete** book of sewing. Rev ed. DK Pub. 2003 320p il $40 *
Grades: 11 12 Adult   **646.2**
1. Sewing 2. Dressmaking
ISBN 0-7894-9658-5   LC 2002-41761
First published 1996
Subtitle on cover: A practical step-by-step guide to every technique
This "sewing guide provides a detailed reference for both novices and experts. . . . Chapters explain how to pick and use patterns; select fabrics and notions; sew basic stitches and seams; attach interfacings and interlinings; form darts, tucks, pleats, and gathers; sew necklines, collars, waistlines, sleeves, and cuffs; hem; and add edges, fastenings, and pockets." SLJ [review of 1996 edition]

The **complete** photo guide to sewing; [created by by the editors of Creative Publishing International] Creative Pub. International 2005 320p il pa $19.95
Grades: 9 10 11 12   **646.2**
1. Sewing
ISBN 1-58923-226-7   LC 2005-6049
First published 1999
"Sections include choosing the right tools and notions, using conventional machines and sergers, fashion sewing, tailoring, special-occasion sewing, and home décor projects. Included are step-by-step instructions for basic projects like pillows, tablecloths, and window treatments." Publisher's note

646.4 Clothing and accessories construction

Holkeboer, Katherine Strand
Patterns for theatrical costumes; garments, trims, and accessories from ancient Egypt to 1915; [by] Katherine Strand Holkeboer. Drama Book Publishers 1992 342p il pa $35
Grades: 9 10 11 12   **646.4**
1. Costume 2. Sewing
ISBN 0-89676-125-8   LC 92-34985
First published 1984 by Prentice-Hall
Each design "includes black-and-white drawings of the completed garment, pattern pieces for enlarging embellishments to be copied, and, when necessary, illustrations of how to wear the particular costume. A few special

costumes—clergy, animals, oriental—are featured as are notes on constructing important accessories." Booklist
Includes bibliographical references

Rogers, Barb, 1947-
Costumes, accessories, props, and stage illusions made easy. Meriwether Pub. 2005 205p il pa $19.95 *
Grades: 9 10 11 12   **646.4**
1. Costume
ISBN 1-56608-103-3; 978-1-56608-103-0
                                                LC 2005-4359
This book details ways to make theater "costumes with simple tools such as scissors, glue guns, and paint. In addition, there are chapters on how to make hats, gloves, armor, and animal heads, as well as other props and accessories from rummage-sale finds and a little imagination. . . . This is a useful volume for schools and community theaters with little or no budgets for costumes and props." SLJ
Includes bibliographical references

646.7 Management of personal and family life

Beker, Jeanne
The big night out; Nathalie Dion, illustrator. Tundra Books 2005 80p il pa $15.95 *
Grades: 7 8 9 10   **646.7**
1. Rites and ceremonies 2. Parties 3. Etiquette 4. Personal grooming
ISBN 0-88776-719-2
"This book is for young women who are seeking to develop and display their own sense of style as they prepare for a special event. . . . [The author] provides realistic advice on budgeting, planning ahead, and attending to all the details, from accessorizing to practicing hairstyles and makeup application in advance. . . . This book will hold an obvious appeal. Its straightforward style and playful, whimsical illustrations make it easily accessible." Voice Youth Advocates

Brown, Bobbi
Bobbi Brown teenage beauty; everything you need to look pretty, natural, sexy & awesome; [by] Bobbi Brown & Annemarie Iverson. Cliff St. Bks. 2000 200p il $25; pa $18.95
Grades: 9 10 11 12   **646.7**
1. Personal grooming 2. Skin—Care
ISBN 0-06-019636-X; 0-06-095724-7 (pa)
                                                LC 00-711795
"Brown and Iverson give teens basic beauty tips and a large boost to their self-esteem. . . . The authors stress the importance of diet and exercise." SLJ

Dating; Jennifer A. Hurley, book editor. Greenhaven Press 2002 154p (Teen decisions) hardcover o.p. pa $19.95 *
Grades: 9 10 11 12   **646.7**
1. Dating (Social customs)
ISBN 0-7377-0921-9; 0-7377-0920-0 (pa)
                                                LC 2001-40611

Dating—*Continued*

"In this anthology, teens relate their experiences with dating, breakups, and sex." Publisher's note

Includes bibliographical references

Espeland, Pamela, 1951-

Life lists for teens; tips, steps, hints, and how-tos for growing up, getting along, learning, and having fun. Free Spirit 2003 264p pa $11.95

Grades: 9 10 11 12   **646.7**

1. Conduct of life 2. Life skills

ISBN 1-57542-125-9   LC 2002-152116

Hundreds of lists provide guidance in areas of young adult life as diverse as selecting a book or a hair color to selecting a mentor

"Espeland's well-organized book has lots of useful information and teen appeal." SLJ

Fornay, Alfred

Born beautiful; the African American teenager's complete beauty guide. John Wiley & Sons 2002 166p il pa $14.95 *

Grades: 9 10 11 12   **646.7**

1. Teenagers—Health and hygiene 2. African American women—Health and hygiene 3. Personal appearance 4. Personal grooming

ISBN 0-471-40275-3   LC 2002-18131

"An Amber book"

This book on beauty and grooming for African American teenage girls includes information on makeup, hairstyles, nail and skin care, diet, and clothing.

Morgenstern, Julie

Organizing from the inside out for teens; the foolproof system for organizing your room, your time, and your life; {by} Julie Morgenstern and Jessi Morgenstern-Colón; illustrations by Janet Pedersen. Holt & Co. 2002 238p il pa $15 *

Grades: 7 8 9 10   **646.7**

1. Life skills 2. Time management

ISBN 0-8050-6470-2   LC 2002-68552

The authors "offer practical advice to teenagers who want to get organized. After considering what might be holding them back and the three steps to success (analyze, strategize, attack), the discussion shifts to the two major areas of concern: managing space and managing time. . . . Useful advice in an accessible paperback format." Booklist

Nakone, Lanna

Organizing for your brain type; finding your own solution to managing time, paper, and stuff. St. Martin's Griffin 2005 xlvii, 222p pa $13.95 *

Grades: 11 12 Adult   **646.7**

1. Home economics 2. Time management

ISBN 0-312-33977-1   LC 2004-60159

"A quiz at the beginning assigns readers to the maintaining, harmonizing, innovating, or prioritizing style. Nakone then describes the strengths and weaknesses of each type and matches a prescription for how that type

can best manage time. . . . This book should do well in most libraries." Libr J

Includes bibliographical references

The **New** York Times practical guide to practically everything; the essential companion for everyday life; edited by Amy D. Bernstein and Peter W. Bernstein. St. Martin's Press 2006 834p il map $29.95

Grades: 11 12 Adult   **646.7**

1. Life skills

ISBN 0-312-35388-X; 978-0-312-35388-9

LC 2006-45081

This "guide covers a wide range of topics—from 'Getting and Staying Trim' to 'The Braille System'—broken up into broad subject categories such as 'Health,' 'Food & Drink,' 'Money,' 'Careers,' 'House & Garden,' 'Sports & Games,' 'Arts & Entertainment' and 'Everyday Science.' . . . This is a browse-worthy collection of general knowledge that should come in handy next time you're traveling to the Galapagos, building an igloo, or in any of more than 800 other 'everyday' situations." Publ Wkly

Odes, Rebecca

The looks book; a whole new approach to beauty, body image, and style; [by] Rebecca Odes, Esther Drill, Heather McDonald; illustrated by Rebecca Odes. Penguin Bks. 2002 151p il pa $18

Grades: 9 10 11 12   **646.7**

1. Personal appearance 2. Personal grooming 3. Fashion

ISBN 0-14-200211-9   LC 2002-28997

This offers a brief history of fashion and information and advice about body types and body image, personal grooming and style

"While frothy fashion and beauty factoids abound, the basic message of empowerment—that girls should be happy with their inner and outer selves—is presented here with intelligence and humor." Publ Wkly

Includes bibliographical references

Taylor, Sally, 1963-

On my own; the ultimate how-to guide for young adults: a manual for excelling in your independent life. Silly Goose Productions 2002 xxix, 609p il pa $34.95 *

Grades: 9 10 11 12   **646.7**

1. Life skills

ISBN 0-9711500-0-1   LC 2003-267891

"Advice and detailed information are offered about such important life skills as finding a job, living on a budget, living with a roommate, caring for a pet, and the responsibilities of car ownership. Several chapters deal with health-related topics. . . . It's sound, straightforward advice and information in a sensibly organized, accessible format; an interactive CD-ROM is included, supplementing the text with audio and visual content." Booklist

Willdorf, Nina
City chic; an urban girl's guide to livin' large on less. Sourcebooks 2003 247p il pa $12.95
Grades: 9 10 11 12 **646.7**
1. Young women 2. Life skills 3. Personal finance
ISBN 1-4022-0054-4 LC 2002-153629
This is a guide for "women dealing with life on a budget in a big city. . . . There are chapters on home decorating (complete with tips on seasonal curbside shopping); body care (suggesting exercises you can do anywhere); food and drink (listing cash-saving dinner options); and clothes." Publ Wkly
Includes bibliographical references

649 Child rearing & home care of persons

Dayee, Frances S.
Babysitting. rev ed. Watts 2000 159p il $25 *
Grades: 9 10 11 12 **649**
1. Babysitting
ISBN 0-531-11745-6 LC 99-87945
First published 1990
A guide to earning money as a babysitter, with advice on getting customers, safety, and handling emergencies
Includes bibliographical references

Lanchon, Anne
All about adoption; how to deal with the questions of your past; illustrated by Monike Czarnecki; edited by Tucker Shaw. Abrams/Amulet 2006 104p il (Sunscreen) pa $9.95 *
Grades: 7 8 9 10 **649**
1. Adoption
ISBN 0-8109-9227-2
"This guide covers an adopted child's traditional worries and concerns, such as establishing identity and living with overprotective parents. It also addresses such squirm-worthy issues as the fear of abandonment, racist comments, and discussing birth parents with adoptive parents. . . . Originally published in France, this handsomely designed self-help title . . . provides practical advice and reassurance for adopted teens and their families." Booklist
Includes bibliographical references

Lindsay, Jeanne Warren
Teen dads; rights, responsibilities, and joys. rev ed. Morning Glory Press 2001 223p il $18.95; pa $12.95
Grades: 9 10 11 12 **649**
1. Teenage fathers 2. Child rearing 3. Parenting
ISBN 1-88535-667-6; 1-88535-668-4 (pa)
LC 00-135006
First published 1993
This "guide integrates comments from teen fathers highlighting their various emotions as they confront their new family responsibilities into a text that discusses a variety of moral, legal, sexual, and social issues that teen

dads face. This healthy dose of reality mixed with commonsense advice is illustrated with black-and-white photos." Horn Book Guide
Includes bibliographical references

Stoppard, Miriam
Complete baby & child care. Rev. ed. Dorling Kindersley 2006 352p il $27.50 *
Grades: 11 12 Adult **649**
1. Child care 2. Infants—Care 3. Child development 4. Child rearing
ISBN 0-7566-1707-3 LC 2006-274086
First published 1995 in the United Kingdom
The author offers advice on behavior, clothing, choosing nursery equipment and supplies, and traveling with children.

650.14 Success in obtaining jobs and promotions

Enelow, Wendy S.
Best resumes for people without a four-year degree. Impact Publications 2004 185p pa $19.95
Grades: 9 10 11 12 **650.14**
1. Résumés (Employment)
ISBN 1-57023-204-0 LC 2003-100522
This collection of professionally-written résumés "includes four . . . résumé-writing exercises as well as contact information for the professional résumé writers who contributed to this book." Publisher's note
Includes bibliographical references

Fry, Ronald W.
Your first resume; for students and anyone preparing to enter today's job market; by Ron Fry. 5th ed. Career Press 2001 188p pa $11.99 *
Grades: 9 10 11 12 Adult **650.14**
1. Résumés (Employment)
ISBN 1-56414-583-2 LC 2001-35875
First published 1988
A step-by-step guide for preparing a successful résumé. Numerous examples accompany the text.

Hinds, Maurene J.
The Ferguson guide to resumes and job hunting skills; a step-by-step guide to preparing for your job search. Ferguson 2005 248p il $45; pa $16.95 *
Grades: 9 10 11 12 **650.14**
1. Résumés (Employment) 2. Job hunting
ISBN 0-8160-5792-3; 0-8160-5796-6 (pa)
LC 2004-24445
"Included are an annotated roundup of assessment tests, from Myers-Briggs to the Strong Interest Inventory; a litany of common job-hunters' mistakes (for instance, not looking an interviewer directly in the eyes); and, of course, a variety of resumes and cover letters." Booklist

Potter, Ray

Résumés that get jobs. 10th ed. Thomson/ARCO 2002 179p il pa $14.95 *

Grades: 9 10 11 12   **650.14**

1. Résumés (Employment) 2. Applications for positions

ISBN 0-7689-0869-8   LC 2002-512345

First published 1963 under the editorship of Edward C. Gruber. Periodically revised

This guide for job-seekers covers job-hunting, interview conduct and focuses on resume writing skills with sample resumes included for a wide variety of positions in various fields.

Schwager, Tina, 1964-

Cool women, hot jobs . . . and how you can go for it, too! {by} Tina Schwager & Michele Schuerger. Free Spirit 2002 278p il pa $15.95

Grades: 7 8 9 10   **650.14**

1. Vocational guidance 2. Women—Employment 3. Occupations

ISBN 1-57542-109-7   LC 2001-40908

Profiles twenty-two women and the jobs they do, from choreographer to FBI agent, describing their education, duties, personality traits, and other factors in their career success, and gives specific ways to determine one's own future work

This "is a valuable contribution to a young adult collection. The pages burst with the inspiration and motivation." Voice Youth Advocates

Troutman, Kathryn K.

Creating your high school resume; a step-by-step guide to preparing an effective resume for jobs, college, and training programs; Kathryn Kraemer Troutman. 2nd ed. Jist Works 2003 154p il pa $8.95

Grades: 9 10 11 12   **650.14**

1. Résumés (Employment)

ISBN 1-56370-902-3   LC 2004-270050

First published 1998

This book "explains why high school students need to work on a resume and keep updating it. In addition to job searching, students will be able to use a resume when applying for college, asking people for recommendations, and applying for scholarships. There are examples from teenagers that demonstrate how to present oneself in the best possible light." Lib Media Connect

651 Office services

The **New** York Public Library business desk reference. Wiley 1998 494p il map hardcover o.p. pa $24.95 *

Grades: 11 12 Adult   **651**

1. Office practice—Handbooks, manuals, etc.

ISBN 0-471-14442-8; 0-471-32835-9 (pa)

LC 97-7408

"A Stonesong Press book"

This work "has sections focusing on information delivery, communications, the office environment, equipment, supplies and systems, human resources, finances, law, public relations, marketing, travel, and information resources. The lists of further information that end each section include organizations, service providers, books, and online resources." Booklist

651.7 Business communication. Creation and transmission of records

Geffner, Andrea B.

How to write better business letters. 4th ed. Barron's 2007 173p il pa $14.99 *

Grades: 9 10 11 12   **651.7**

1. Business letters

ISBN 0-7641-3539-2; 978-0-7641-3539-2

LC 2006-42953

First published 1982

"This book instructs on how to write effective examples of every kind of business letter. It presents about 75 model letters in categories that include credit applications, letters of inquiry, orders of goods and services, formal business announcements, letters of recommendation, and sales promotional letters of the type used by direct marketers. This book also features examples of different letter formatting styles." Publisher's note

Thomason-Carroll, Kristi L.

Young adult's guide to business communications. Business Books 2004 117p il $14.95 *

Grades: 9 10 11 12   **651.7**

1. Business communication 2. Résumés (Employment) 3. Interviewing

ISBN 0-9723714-4-3   LC 2002-115501

This "guide covers writing a résumé, filling out job applications, interviewing skills, and work etiquette (e.g., the proper form for memos, e-mails, and reports, and interactions with others). Throughout the lively text, the author stresses the importance of making a good impression through careful preparation and presentation." SLJ

Includes bibliographical references

652 Processes of written communication

Butler, William S.

Secret messages; concealment, codes, and other types of ingenious communication; [by] William S. Butler and L. Douglas Keeney. Simon & Schuster 2001 192p il $23

Grades: 11 12 Adult   **652**

1. Cryptography 2. Ciphers

ISBN 0-684-86998-5   LC 00-46368

"Through a series of short stories and anecdotes, this book gives . . . [a] quick tour of codes used by common folk as well as spies. . . . Much of the book is devoted to codes used to convey messages in everyday life. Those used by hospitals, police officers, restaurant staff,

Butler, William S.—*Continued*
and bridge players are addressed. . . . An engaging book
that may entice readers to pursue a more in-depth exploration of the topic." SLJ
Includes bibliographical references

Singh, Simon
The code book; the evolution of secrecy from
Mary, Queen of Scots, to quantum cryptography.
Doubleday 1999 402p il map hardcover o.p. pa
$15
Grades: 11 12 Adult   **652**
1. Cryptography
ISBN 0-385-49531-5; 0-385-49532-3 (pa)
LC 99-35261
This survey explores the evolution of cryptography.
"Along the way, we encounter Charles Babbage, the
nineteenth-century British polymath who conceived of a
steam-powered computer; archeologists who used crypto-
graphic methods to translate Egyptian hieroglyphics; and
Navajo code-talkers employed by the U.S. military in the
Second World War." New Yorker
Includes bibliographical references

658.4   Executive management

Encyclopedia of leadership; editors, George R.
Goethals, Georgia J. Sorenson, James
MacGregor Burns. Sage Publications 2004 4v il
map set $595
Grades: 11 12 Adult   **658.4**
1. Leadership—Encyclopedias
ISBN 0-7619-2597-X   LC 2004-1252
"What is leadership? What is a great leader? What is
a great follower? What are the types of leadership? And
how does someone become a leader? This set was designed with the needs of several user communities in
mind, including students, scholars, and professionals who
want to explore such questions." Booklist
Includes bibliographical references

658.8   Management of marketing

Ikuta, Tadashi
Project X Challengers: Seven Eleven; the
miraculous story of Japan's 7-Eleven stores;
[translated by Sachiko Sato] Digital Manga
Publishing 2006 191p il pa $12.95
Grades: 8 9 10 11 12 Adult   **658.8**
1. Graphic novels 2. Manga 3. Retail trade—Japan—
Graphic novels
ISBN 1-56970-958-0
In 1971, two young business executives, Toshifumi
Suzuki and Hideo Shimizu, discovered the 7-11 convenience stores in the U. S., and they decided this could
become just the thing to help their company succeed in
the Japanese retail industry. The whole concept of a
small convenience store went totally against reigning retail philosophy in Japan at that time. This book tells how
Suzuki and Shimizu, with a small team of retail novices,
started Seven Eleven in Japan. This business manga is

based on an NHK (Japan's national television network)
documentary series produced in 2000. It includes a section of photographs and a timeline from 1957 to 2000.

Underhill, Paco
Why we buy; the science of shopping. Simon &
Schuster 1999 255p hardcover o.p. pa $15
Grades: 11 12 Adult   **658.8**
1. Marketing 2. Consumers
ISBN 0-684-84913-5; 0-684-84914-3 (pa)
LC 99-12125
"Each chapter delves into a particular aspect of a store
environment and its interface with customers: the importance of signage and why less is more, how men shop,
. . . the need to cater to boomers, and clues about waiting time. Throughout, insights are peppered with one or
several examples." Booklist

659.1   Advertising

Advertising: opposing viewpoints; edited by Laura
K. Egendorf. Greenhaven Press 2006 205p il lib
bdg $34.95; pa $23.70 *
Grades: 9 10 11 12   **659.1**
1. Advertising
ISBN 0-7377-3226-1 (lib bdg); 0-7377-3228-8 (pa)
LC 2005-40262
"Opposing viewpoints series"
"In this anthology the authors consider the impact of
advertising in the following chapters: Is Advertising
Harmful? Does Advertising Exploit Children? Should Po-
litical Advertising Be Reformed? What Is the Future of
Advertising?" Publisher's note
Includes bibliographical references

660.6   Biotechnology

Panno, Joseph
Animal cloning; the science of nuclear transfer.
Facts on File 2005 c2004 164p il (New biology)
$35
Grades: 11 12 Adult   **660.6**
1. Cloning
ISBN 0-8160-4947-5   LC 2003-25471
The "entries discuss natural cloning and early cloning
experiments beginning in the 1950s; the research that led
to the creation of Dolly, the first animal cloned from an
adult cell; as well as the recent sheep-human, goat-
human, and pig-human hybrids scientists have experi-
mented with using cloning technology." Publisher's note
Includes bibliographical references

Seiple, Samantha
Mutants, clones, and killer corn; unlocking the
secrets of biotechnology; [by] Samantha Seiple and
Todd Seiple. Lerner 2005 112p il (Discovery!)
$27.93
Grades: 7 8 9 10   **660.6**

Seiple, Samantha—*Continued*
1. Biotechnology
ISBN 0-8225-4860-7
"The Seiples present an overview of biotechnology from its origins in selective breeding to its possible future implications. The writing is clear and a brief outline of genetics is offered. . . . The appealing layout features color photographs, charts, and graphs, as well as informative sidebars. . . . A solid, up-to-date addition for reports and general-interest reading." SLJ

Shannon, Thomas A. (Thomas Anthony), 1940-
Genetic engineering; a documentary history; edited by Thomas A. Shannon. Greenwood Press 1999 xxxi, 282p (Primary documents in American history and contemporary issues) $49.95 *
Grades: 9 10 11 12   660.6
1. Genetic engineering
ISBN 0-313-30457-2   LC 98-46808
This volume "includes documents on such topics as cloning, diagnostic applications, ethics, genetically altered food, and the Human Genome Project." Booklist
Includes bibliographical references

Yount, Lisa
Biotechnology and genetic engineering. rev ed. Facts on File 2004 316p $45
Grades: 8 9 10 11 12   660.6
1. Biotechnology 2. Genetic engineering
ISBN 0-8160-5059-7   LC 2003-64223
First published 2000
This provides "medical, political, and ethical viewpoints behind headline stories about DNA research and fingerprinting, the Human Genome Project, cloning, and the patenting of living organisms. The author also includes a chronology, a glossary of technical terms, and short biographical sketches of the scientists and others involved in the history and current issues surrounding the new science. . . . She completes the volume with addresses and Web sites of biotechnical agencies and organizations as well as abstracts of landmark Court cases." Voice Youth Advocates {review of 2000 edition}
"In one comprehensive volume, Yount provides the ultimate resource for students, teachers, and library media specialists." Booklist {review of 2000 edition}
Includes bibliographical references

664   Food technology

Hayhurst, Chris
Everything you need to know about food additives. Rosen Pub. Group 2002 64p il (Need to know library) lib bdg $27.95
Grades: 9 10 11 12   664
1. Food additives
ISBN 0-8239-3548-5   LC 2001-1980
This book "introduces common additives and explains reasons for their use, including consumers' finicky preferences; discusses health risks associated with many additives; and offers exciting alternatives to processed foods, such as produce from community-supported agriculture programs." Booklist
Includes bibliographical references

Winter, Ruth, 1930-
A consumer's dictionary of food additives; descriptions in plain English of more than 12,000 ingredients both harmful and desirable found in foods. Completely rev. and updated 6th ed. Three Rivers Press 2004 579p pa $16.95 *
Grades: 11 12 Adult   664
1. Food additives—Dictionaries
ISBN 1-4000-5232-7   LC 2004-5062
First published 1972. Periodically revised
This book provides "facts about the relative safety and side effects of more than 12,000 ingredients that end up in your food as a result of processing and curing, such as preservatives, food-tainting pesticides, and animal drugs." Publisher's note

667   Cleaning, color, coating, related technologies

Garfield, Simon
Mauve; how one man invented a color that changed the world. Norton 2001 222p il pa $13.95 hardcover o.p.
Grades: 11 12 Adult   667
1. Perkin, William Henry, 1838-1907 2. Dyes and dyeing
ISBN 0-393-32313-7 (pa)   LC 00-69533
This volume discusses how a British student, William Henry Perkin, while trying to synthesize quinine from coal tar, developed mauve, "the first mass-produced artificial dye. . . . By the turn of the 20th century, because of Perkin's novel idea, dye makers had 2,000 synthesized colors at their disposal." N Y Times Book Rev
"The text is understandable by the average layman and is enjoyable reading for the scientist and non-scientist alike." Sci Books Films
Includes bibliographical references

674   Lumber processing, wood products, cork

The **Encyclopedia** of wood; a tree-by-tree guide to the world's most versatile resource; general editor, Aidan Walker. Facts on File 2005 192p il map $35 *
Grades: 11 12 Adult   674
1. Wood
ISBN 0-8160-6181-5   LC 2004-60849
First published 1989
This book "provides an A-to-Z directory featuring more than 150 of the world's most popular woods, with information on growth rate, distribution, key characteristics, working properties, and commercial uses." Publisher's note
"A nice addition to libraries with strong interior design or DIY collections." Libr J
Includes bibliographical references

676 Pulp and paper technology

Asunción, Josep
The complete book of papermaking. Lark Books 2003 160p il $24.95
Grades: 11 12 Adult **676**
1. Papermaking
ISBN 1-57990-456-4 LC 2002-155637
The author "covers the history and present-day techniques of the craft in a well-illustrated book that includes paper samples. . . . This excellent guide is highly recommended for all arts and crafts collections." Libr J
Includes bibliographical references

684 Furnishings and home workshops

Horwood, Roger
The woodworker's handbook. Lyons Press 2003 160p il pa $19.95 *
Grades: 11 12 Adult **684**
1. Woodwork
ISBN 1-58574-839-0
First published 1999 in the United Kingdom
This book "features sections on: the most popular natural and manmade woods; use, care and maintenance of tools and equipment; techniques and basic woodworking skills; a . . . range of step-by-step projects; repairs and restoration of old wood." Publisher's note

Taunton's complete illustrated guide to woodworking; [by] Lonnie Bird . . . [et al.] Taunton Press 2005 311p il $29.95
Grades: 11 12 Adult **684**
1. Woodwork
ISBN 1-56158-769-9 LC 2004-28678
This "guide covers a wide array of woodworking topics. . . . The arrangement is consistent and well thought out, with illustrated referencing at the beginning of each chapter." Libr J

687 Clothing and accessories

Sullivan, James, 1965-
Jeans: a cultural history of an American icon. Gotham Books 2006 303p il $26 *
Grades: 11 12 Adult **687**
1. Jeans (Clothing)
ISBN 1-59240-214-3; 978-1-59240-214-4
LC 2005-35698
This book "traces the itinerary of denim pants from their 19th-century origins as a workingman's wardrobe staple to their present status as 'the best-selling garment of all time.'" N Y Times Book Rev
The author "keeps the writing brisk and the major players . . . distinct while ranging across continents and decades, giving devotees the definitive account of the development of the denim that decorates their derrieres." Publ Wkly
Includes bibliographical references

690 Buildings

Macaulay, David, 1946-
Mill. Houghton Mifflin 1983 128p il $18; pa $9.95
Grades: 4 5 6 7 8 9 10 **690**
1. Mills 2. Textile industry—History
ISBN 0-395-34830-7; 0-395-52019-3 (pa)
LC 83-10652
This is an "account of the development of four fictional 19th-Century Rhode Island cotton mills. In explaining the construction and operation of a simple water-wheel powered wooden mill, as well as the more complex stone, turbine and steam mills to follow, the author also describes the rise and decline of New England's textile industry." SLJ

Unbuilding. Houghton Mifflin 1980 78p il $18; pa $9.95
Grades: 4 5 6 7 8 9 **690**
1. Empire State Building (New York, N.Y.) 2. Building 3. Skyscrapers
ISBN 0-395-29457-6; 0-395-45425-5 (pa)
LC 80-15491
This fictional account of the dismantling and removal of the Empire State Building describes the structure of a skyscraper and explains how such an edifice would be demolished
"Save for the fact that one particularly stunning double-page spread is marred by tight binding, the book is a joy: accurate, informative, handsome, and eminently readable." Bull Cent Child Books

698 Detail finishing

Lord, Gary, 1952-
It's faux easy by Gary Lord. North Light Books 2005 144p il pa $24.99
Grades: 11 12 Adult **698**
1. House painting
ISBN 1-58180-554-3 LC 2004-49282
On cover: Paint 30 fabulous finishes for your home
The author's "20 projects, graduated in difficulty from simple texturizing to complicated stencil work, take handy home owners from gathering supplies and wall prep to application techniques. . . . A first-rate addition to the do-it-yourself shelf." Booklist

700 ARTS & RECREATION

Aronson, Marc
Art attack; a short cultural history of the avant-garde. Clarion Bks. 1998 192p il $24
Grades: 7 8 9 10 **700**
1. Modern art 2. Art appreciation 3. Art and society
ISBN 0-395-79729-2 LC 97-22372
"*Art Attack* would make an excellent resource for the secondary level student who might be interested in exploring some creative outlets or as a catalyst for discus-

Aronson, Marc—_Continued_

sions about aesthetics, expression, or contemporary lifestyles." ALAN

Includes bibliographical references

Arts and humanities through the eras. Gale 2004 5v il set $450

Grades: 11 12 Adult **700**

1. Arts—History 2. Civilization—History

ISBN 0-7876-5695-X LC 2004-10243

Also available as separate volumes ea $105

Contents: v1 Ancient Egypt (2675 B.C.E.-332 B.C.E.) -- v2 Ancient Greece and Rome (1200 B.C.E.-476 C.E.) -- v3 Medieval Europe (814-1450) -- v4 Renaissance Europe (1300-1600) -- v5 The age of Baroque and Enlightenment (1600-1800)

"Each volume consists of nine chapters covering the major branches of the humanities: architecture and design, dance, fashion, literature, music, philosophy, religion, theater, and visual arts. . . . This outstanding series offers a wealth of information; the chapters on architecture, dance, and theater alone are worth the price of each volume." Libr J

Includes bibliographical references

Delacampagne, Ariane, 1959-

Here be dragons; a fantastic bestiary; [by] Ariane Delacampagne and Christian Delacampagne. Princeton University Press 2003 199p il $45

Grades: 9 10 11 12 **700**

1. Mythical animals 2. Animals in art

ISBN 0-691-11689-X LC 2003-51741

After an "assessment of animals in art as dream imagery and religious symbols, the Delacampagnes' five subsequent chapters consider, respectively, the evolution of the bestiary of nonexistent creatures, portrayals of unicorns and partially human beasts, images of four-footed flying things and dragons, the issue of influence versus coincidence in accounting for the similarity of fantastic animals in disparate cultures, and fantastic animals in contemporary art . . . The pictures of everything from the two-horned unicorn . . . on the walls of the Lascaux caves to a yeti from the pages of _Tintin au Tibet_ (1960) are invariably gorgeous." Booklist

Includes bibliographical references

Dictionary of the arts. Facts on File 1994 564p $29.95 *

Grades: 11 12 Adult **700**

1. Artists—Dictionaries

ISBN 0-8160-3205-X LC 94-16276

A "one-volume reference that includes 6,000 alphabetically arranged entries on architecture, cinema, literature, craft and design, dance, fashion, music, mythology, painting, photography, sculpture, and theater. . . . Students will find quick, cross-referenced, and user-friendly info on such topics as detective fiction, leprechauns, Priam, Abba, Calvin Klein, Snow White, synthesizers, and Dickens, plus 1,000 quotations. A basic reference tool." SLJ

Encyclopedia of the Harlem Renaissance; Cary D. Wintz, Paul Finkelman, editors. Routledge 2004 2v il map set $325 *

Grades: 11 12 Adult **700**

1. African American arts 2. Harlem Renaissance—Encyclopedias

ISBN 1-57958-389-X LC 2004-16353

This encyclopedia features "essays on the life and works of major writers, artists, and musicians of the period as well as broader articles on the impact of contemporary political, social, economic, and legal issues on the movement. . . . This thorough and well-organized reference work should appeal to a wide range of users from high school to graduate school students and is recommended for all libraries." Libr J

Includes bibliographical references

Encyclopedia of the romantic era, 1760-1850; Christopher John Murray, general editor. Fitzroy Dearborn 2003 2v il set $325

Grades: 11 12 Adult **700**

1. Romanticism

ISBN 1-57958-361-X LC 2003-42406

"This two-volume cultural encyclopedia contains 770 entries on the arts and sciences of the Romantic Era, including, but not limited to, the Romantic movement. The strengths of this encyclopedia are many, including its geographical coverage (Britain, continental Europe, and the Americas); entries on individuals; discussions of specific works of literature, art, and music; and thematic entries that focus on a broad-range of subjects (e.g. the Dandy, Orientalism, and the Sublime)." Libr Media Connect

Includes bibliographical references

Eyerdam, Pamela J.

Using Internet primary sources to teach critical thinking skills in visual arts. Libraries Unlimited 2003 329p (Libraries Unlimited professional guides in school librarianship) pa $45

Grades: Professional **700**

1. Art—Internet resources 2. Art—Study and teaching 3. Internet in education

ISBN 0-313-31555-8 LC 2002-7891

"Introductory chapters explore the history of art education and critical-thinking skills along with practical suggestions for utilizing the Internet in art research. The majority of the book, however, provides exhaustive lists of Web sites that feature works of art, biographies of artists, background information, critical reviews, scholarly treatment of art topics, and museums . . . This substantial resource will undoubtedly set the standard for using the Internet in art education." SLJ

Includes bibliographical references

Makosz, Rory

Latino arts and their influence on the United States; songs, dreams, and dances. Mason Crest Publishers 2005 112p il (Hispanic heritage) $22.95 *

Grades: 7 8 9 10 **700**

1. Latin American art 2. Arts—United States

ISBN 1-59084-938-8 LC 2004022968

Makosz, Rory—*Continued*

This "book begins with a general discussion of the ways in which cultures express themselves through their arts. It goes on to discuss the arts of Latin American cultures and their growing prominence in the United States, with emphasis on dance and music. Writing, painting, theater arts, and holidays are also included. . . . [This is] an excellent resource both for students researching Latino arts for reports and for general readers." SLJ

Includes bibligraphical references

Ochoa, George

The Wilson chronology of the arts; [by] George Ochoa and Melinda Corey. Wilson, H.W. 1998 476p $110 *

Grades: 11 12 Adult   **700**

1. Arts—History

ISBN 0-8242-0934-6   LC 97-23541

First published 1995 by Ballantine Books with title: The timeline book of the arts

"The authors provide a timeline detailing human creativity that progresses from ca. 43,000 B.C.E. to 1997, with 4,000 entries spread over 13 categories of artistic endeavor. . . . The chronology is global in scope and comprehensive in coverage, emphasizing well-established art forms without neglecting the oral traditions and decorative art forms of nonliterate societies and currently emerging art forms. . . . The straightforward organization of this work makes it suitable for many different uses." Recomm Ref Books for Small & Medium-sized Libr & Media Cent, 1999

Rovin, Jeff

Adventure heroes; legendary characters from Odysseus to James Bond. Facts on File 1994 314p il $38.50

Grades: 11 12 Adult   **700**

1. Characters and characteristics in literature—Dictionaries

ISBN 0-8160-2881-8   LC 93-46603

"Charlie Chan, Modesty Blaise, Jonny Quest, and Beowulf are just some of the more than 500 characters listed here along with the works in which they appeared. Rovin . . . has drawn entries from the realms of comic books, comic strips, folklore, literature, mythology, motion pictures, opera, radio, television, video, and computer games. For each character or show he offers date and place of first appearance, a biography, and comments that are chock full of interesting information. . . . A good ready reference for popular culture collections." Libr J

Smith, Anna Deavere

Letters to a young artist. Anchor Books 2006 227p il pa $13

Grades: 11 12 Adult   **700**

1. Artists 2. Creation (Literary, artistic, etc.) 3. Conduct of life

ISBN 1-4000-3238-5; 978-1-4000-3238-9

LC 2005-48318

The author "casts her reflections on the creative process, the artist's life and the acting profession as a series

of brief letters addressed to a fictitious teenager. . . . With a pithiness that wards away the preachy, Smith succeeds in conveying the pain, the joy and the effort that characterize a life on the stage and in the world." Publ Wkly

Includes bibliographical references

701 Art--Philosophy and theory

Yenawine, Philip

Key art terms for beginners. Abrams 1995 160p $24.95 *

Grades: 7 8 9 10   **701**

1. Art appreciation

ISBN 0-8109-1225-2   LC 94-26911

In this illustrated introduction to art appreciation, the author "divides the discussion into three main parts. The longest chapter covers the periods and schools of art history from 'Aboriginal' to 'Western.' A shorter section on mediums and materials ranges from 'Acrylics' to 'Welding.' A third section introduces the vocabulary of analysis and criticism. . . . The volume is filled with wonderful black-and-white and full-color photographs and reproductions." SLJ

Includes bibliographical references

702.8 Art--Technique, procedures, apparatus, equipment, materials

Smith, Ray, 1949-

The artist's handbook. Rev ed. DK Pub. 2003 384p il $30; pa $21.95 *

Grades: 11 12 Adult   **702.8**

1. Art—Technique 2. Artists' materials

ISBN 0-7894-9336-5; 0-7566-2621-8 (pa)

LC 2002-41583

First published 1987 by Knopf

Cover title: New artist's handbook; equipment, materials, procedures, techniques

The author presents "information on established materials that he organizes first by function—pigments, resins, solvents, and the like—then by media categorized according to discipline. . . . This excellent overall guide to the visual arts boasts multiple appendixes on color, perspective, health, and safety. With glossary and index, this far-ranging overview is hard to beat." Booklist

703 Art--Encyclopedias and dictionaries

Facts on File encyclopedia of art; Sir Lawrence Gowing, general editor. Facts on File 2005 5v il map set $325 *

Grades: 11 12 Adult   **703**

1. Art—Encyclopedias

ISBN 0-8160-5797-4   LC 2005-40505

First published 1983 by Prentice-Hall as volume one of Encyclopedia of visual art

Facts on File encyclopedia of art—*Continued*
"The chapters cover not only aesthetics but social and cultural context as well and not only Western arts (which do seem to dominate) but arts from other parts of the world. The most striking feature is the vivid, full-color photography on nearly every page, with three-dimensional objects ranging from Aegean armor to a Japanese Zen temple particularly well treated." Libr J
For a fuller review, see: Booklist, Jan. 1 & 15, 2006
Includes bibliographical references

Landi, Ann
Schirmer encyclopedia of art. Schirmer Reference 2001 4v il set $345
Grades: 11 12 Adult   **703**
1. Art—Encyclopedias
ISBN 0-02-865414-5   LC 2001-40067
This encyclopedia provides a "survey of world art, from prehistory to the present. More than 400 A-to-Z entries . . . cover painting, sculpture, photography, architecture, movements and genres around the world—from Europe and Asia to South America and the Middle East." Publisher's note
"Color reproductions of artworks are good. The especially strong bibliography of suggested resources, including Web sites, is subdivided by subject. The set reflects new thinking about art, for example, the amplification of art formerly termed 'primitive' and the inclusion of artists and schools outside the Western mainstream. . . . This attractive set is recommended for high-school and public libraries." Booklist
Includes bibliographical references

Langmuir, Erika
Yale dictionary of art and artists; [by] Erika Langmuir and Norbert Lynton. Yale Univ. Press 2000 753p $30; pa $12.95
Grades: 11 12 Adult   **703**
1. Art—Dictionaries 2. Artists—Dictionaries
ISBN 0-300-08702-0; 0-300-06458-6 (pa)
                          LC 00-25800
"Varying in length from a few lines to several pages for artists such as Leonardo da Vinci, Pablo Picasso, or John Constable, the 3000 entries cover Western art from 1300 until the present. The work covers painters, sculptors, graphic artists, patrons, technical processes, movements, and terminology." Libr J

The **Oxford** companion to western art; edited by Hugh Brigstocke. Oxford Univ. Press 2001 820p il $75
Grades: 11 12 Adult   **703**
1. Art—Dictionaries
ISBN 0-19-866203-3
"A partial successor to the 1970 *Oxford Companion to Art*, this title limits itself to European-language cultures, dropping architecture and non-Western subjects. The 2600 signed entries generally range in length from 100 to 1000-plus words . . . and they include artist, historian, theorist, and patron biographies as well as entries on institutions, cities and museums, styles, movements, and art historical theory and methodology." Libr J
Includes bibliographical references

The **Oxford** dictionary of art; edited by Ian Chilvers. 3rd ed. Oxford University Press 2004 xlvi, 816p $45 *
Grades: 11 12 Adult   **703**
1. Art—Dictionaries
ISBN 0-19-860476-9   LC 2004-41540
First published 1988
This "reference contains 3000 entries that discuss Western and Western-inspired art from antiquity on. It considers paintings, graphics, sculpture, and architecture in terms of artistic figures, periods, schools, techniques, critical terms, and museums; lesser artists are treated more concisely than major ones." Libr J

704   Art--Special topics

The **Arts** of the North American Indian; native traditions in evolution; edited by Edwin L. Wade; Carol Haralson, coordinating editor. Hudson Hills Press 1986 324p il hardcover o.p. pa $35
Grades: 9 10 11 12   **704**
1. Native American art
ISBN 0-933920-55-5; 0-933920-56-3 (pa)
                          LC 85-21932
Published in association with the Philbrook Art Center, Tulsa
"Detailed explanatory captions accompany each illustration and serve as a significant 'subtext' for exhibition materials, which represent a span of time from the prehistoric to today's avant-garde. . . . A competent glossary as well as bibliography and index enhance the overall excellence of this volume. Some prior knowledge of the general topic is advised; this is not a selection for beginners." Choice
Includes bibliographical references

Bolden, Tonya
Wake up our souls; a celebration of Black American artists; Published in association with Smithsonian American Art Museum. Harry N. Abrams 2004 128p il $24.95 *
Grades: 6 7 8 9   **704**
1. African American art
ISBN 0-8109-4527-4
Published in association with Smithsonian American Art Museum.
Presents a history of African American visual arts and artists from the days of slavery to the present
"Bolden's writing is rich and lyrical. She smoothly incorporates the historical context, explaining pivotal events and relevant artistic movements clearly and succinctly." SLJ

Cockcroft, James D.
Latino visions; contemporary Chicano, Puerto Rican, and Cuban American artists; by James D. Cockcroft, Jr; assisted by Jane Canning. Watts 2000 143p il (Book report biography) hardcover o.p. pa $12.95 *

Grades: 7 8 9 10   **704**
1. Hispanic American art 2. Modern art
ISBN 0-531-11312-4; 0-531-16523-X (pa)
                                          LC 99-89464
Describes the evolution of Latino art in America through discussion of various artistic movements and important Latino artists

The author "makes you value 'people's art,' to be viewed not in imposing museums but as part of public life. At the same time, he does talk about individual Latino artists . . . with stirring detail." Booklist
Includes bibliographical references

Farrington, Lisa E.
Creating their own image; the history of African-American women artists. Oxford University Press 2005 354p il $55 *

Grades: 11 12 Adult   **704**
1. African American women 2. African American artists 3. Women artists
ISBN 0-19-516721-X   LC 2003-66171
This is a "study of women of color and their works, starting with slavery, moving through the Harlem Renaissance, and continuing to the new millennium." Libr J

"A richly detailed yet fluent work of trailblazing research, fresh interpretations, and cogent argument, Farrington's treatise discusses vital aesthetic as well as social and cultural issues and creates a vibrant context for such seminal artists as Augusta Savage, Faith Ringgold, Barbara Chase-Riboud, Kara Walker, and many more." Booklist

704.9 Iconography

Carr-Gomm, Sarah
Dictionary of symbols in Western art. Facts on File 1995 240p il $30

Grades: 11 12 Adult   **704.9**
1. Art—Dictionaries 2. Symbolism—Dictionaries
ISBN 0-8160-3301-3   LC 95-17577
This dictionary focuses on "the meaning of symbols in Western art. Visual themes, religious and mythological, that occur in figurative paintings and sculpture from the late Middle Ages to the nineteenth century are covered alphabetically. . . . Interspersed alphabetically are feature panels on the treatment in art of major themes (the ages of man, the nude, virtues). See also references and footnotes are printed in the margins." Booklist

Hall, James, 1918-
Dictionary of subject and symbols in art; introduction by Kenneth Clark. rev ed. Harper & Row 1979 c1974 xxix, 349p il pa $32 hardcover o.p. *

Grades: 11 12 Adult   **704.9**
1. Art—Dictionaries
ISBN 0-06-430100-1 (pa)   LC 79-116436
"Icon editions"
First published 1974
This book seeks "to help the museum-goer and student identify and understand the subject matter of Western art, using subjects from the Old and New Testaments, the Christian saints and symbols, and classical mythology and literature . . . {as well as} historical episodes, figures and devices of moral allegory, themes of romantic epic poetry, and popular genre representations of Northern European art." Choice
Includes bibliographical references

Patel, Sanjay
The little book of Hindu deities; from the Goddess of Wealth to the Sacred Cow. Plume 2006 141p il pa $14

Grades: 9 10 11 12   **704.9**
1. Gods and goddesses 2. Hinduism
ISBN 0-452-28775-8; 978-0-452-28775-4
                                          LC 2006-12110
The author describes "the exploits of various deities while drawing us in—literally—with his joyous and unexpected full-color illustrations. . . . Both funny and informative, this is a fresh and breezy introduction to the Hindu gods." Publ Wkly

708 Art--Galleries, museums private collections

The **Israel** Museum, Jerusalem. Vendome Press 1995 240p il $65

Grades: 11 12 Adult   **708**
1. Israel Museum
ISBN 0-86565-960-5   LC 95-15860
Editor/project coordinator, Irene Lewitt
This volume "contains introductory essays on the Museum's history, which precede a chronologically and culturally organized sampling of archaeological objects. Modern painting, sculpture, graphics, and decorative arts (most donated by emigrés) follow." Choice

National Gallery of Art; [foreword by Earl A. Powell III] 2nd ed. Thames and Hudson 2006 332p il (World of art) pa $18.95

Grades: 11 12 Adult   **708**
1. National Gallery of Art (U.S.)
ISBN 0-500-20390-3; 978-0-500-20390-3
                                          LC 2005-904459
First published 2004 by National Gallery of Art; Based on John Walker's National Gallery of Art, published 1984

"The collection of the National Gallery of Art in Washington includes works by the greatest masters of Western art from the twelfth century to the present. . . .

National Gallery of Art—*Continued*

[In this] look at the National Gallery's masterpieces . . . the works are illustrated in full color, and the curators have written the texts." Publisher's note

Treasures from the Art Institute of Chicago; selected by James N. Wood, with commentaries by Debra N. Mancoff; {edited by Laura J. Kozitka and Catherine A. Steinmann}. Art Inst. of Chicago 2000 344p il $34.95

Grades: 11 12 Adult   **708**
1. Art Institute of Chicago
ISBN 0-300-11622-5   LC 99-69501

"This compendium is not only a catalog of pieces owned by the museum, but it is virtually an introduction to the history of art throughout the world. . . . Superb examples from Asian, African; classical Greek and Roman; and other regional art, crafts, ceramics, and media add a wonderfully broad scope." SLJ

709   Art--Historical and geographic treatment

Atlas of world art; edited by John Onians. Oxford University Press 2004 352p il maps $150 *

Grades: 11 12 Adult   **709**
1. Art—History—Maps
ISBN 0-19-521583-4   LC 2003-55029

This atlas offers a "framework for coverage of art activity around the world from prehistoric times to 2000. . . . Each of the book's seven parts (each covers a period in art history) includes a brief illustrated introduction followed by a standardized sequence of sections on World, American, European, African, Asian and Pacific Art." Choice

"Groundbreaking and handsomely produced, this is a welcome addition to any reference collection." Libr J

For a fuller review see: Booklist, Nov. 1, 2004

Includes bibliographical references

Cole, Bruce, 1938-

Art of the Western world; from ancient Greece to post-modernism; by Bruce Cole and Adelheid Gealt; with an introduction by Michael Wood. Summit Bks. 1989 xx, 345p il pa $22 hardcover o.p.

Grades: 11 12 Adult   **709**
1. Art—History
ISBN 0-671-74728-2 (pa)   LC 89-4311

"A companion volume to the PBS television series of the same title, this compact survey of Western art history is a . . . recapitulation of the conventional high art canon. Written on a level suitable for high school students and general readers, the volume includes good reproductions of one or two of the best known works by famous masters of painting, sculpture, and architecture." Libr J

Gardner, Helen, d. 1946

Gardner's art through the ages; [revised by] Fred S. Kleiner, Christin J. Mamiya. 12th ed. Thomson/Wadsworth 2005 2v il map set $133.95 *

Grades: 11 12 Adult   **709**
1. Art—History
ISBN 0-15-505090-7; 978-0-15-505090-7
    LC 2003-111627

First published 1926 by Harcourt Brace & Co.

This book surveys world art from prehistoric times to the present day. Painting, sculpture, architecture and some decorative arts are considered. Although the focus is on European art, there are also chapters on ancient Near Eastern, Asian, pre-Columbian, American Indian, African and Oceanic art.

Includes bibliographical references

Gombrich, E. H. (Ernst Hans), 1909-2001

The story of art. 16th ed rev and expanded. Phaidon Press 1995 688p il $49.95; pa $29.95

Grades: 11 12 Adult   **709**
1. Art—History
ISBN 0-7148-3355-X; 0-7148-3247-2 (pa)
    LC 96-140698

First published 1950

This survey of art examines artistic achievements in historical context to consider how prevailing social, political, and economic factors may have influenced the succession and popularity of certain artistic styles.

Includes bibliographical references

Hartt, Frederick, 1914-1991

Art: a history of painting, sculpture, architecture. Prentice Hall 2003 c1993 2v il pa $157

Grades: 9 10 11 12   **709**
1. Art—History
ISBN 0-13-151749-X

Each volume is also available separately

A reprint of the volumes first published 1976 by Abrams. Periodically revised

An illustrated chronological history of art from prehistory to the contemporary period. Timelines link the political history, religions, literature, science and technology, with the painting, sculpture and architecture of each era

Hollingsworth, Mary

Art in world history. M.E. Sharpe 2004 2v set $199

Grades: 11 12 Adult   **709**
1. Art—History
ISBN 0-7656-8069-6   LC 2003-15510

"Consisting of 52 short chapters covering the history of art from early civilizations through the late 20th century, this extensively illustrated reference by Hollingsworth offers short snippets of facts and descriptions of artists, artworks, media, and movements. In addition to the main narrative body of each chapter, sidebar articles focus on specific highlights of the area covered by the chapter. . . . An excellent purchase for public libraries or other collections that need a good, heavily illustrated survey of art history." Libr J

For a fuller review see: Booklist, July 2004

Janson, H. W. (Horst Woldemar), 1913-1982

Janson's history of art; the western tradition; Penelope J.E. Davies . . . [et al.] 7th ed. Pearson Prentice-Hall 2007 various paging il map $120.20 *

Grades: 11 12 Adult   **709**
1. Art—History
ISBN 0-13-193455-4; 978-0-13-193455-9
                                          LC 2005-54647
Also available in a two-volume paperback edition ea $101.20
First published 1962 by Abrams with title: History of art

A history of art from prehistoric cave paintings to video art. While the focus is primarily on Western art, brief discussions of Oriental, Near Eastern, Islamic, African and Latin American arts are included.

Includes bibliographical references

Kampen O'Riley, Michael

Art beyond the west; the arts of Africa, India and Southeast Asia, China, Japan and Korea, the Pacific, and the Americas; afterword by Anne D'Alleva. Abrams 2002 c2001 344p il maps $75 *

Grades: 11 12 Adult   **709**
1. Art
ISBN 0-8109-1433-6   LC 2001-27923
Also available from Prentice-Hall
First published 2001 in the United Kingdom

The author "has attempted to encapsulate the entirety of non-Western art in one volume. . . . {Chapters} range over Africa, India, Southeast Asia, China, Japan and Korea, the Americas, and the Pacific and consider such issues as post- and intercolonialism and postmodernism." Libr J

The author "succeeds in defining the essence of each distinct artistic tradition. Add to that impressive feat a clear, relaxed, and engaging prose style and superb illustrations, and the sum is a prime introductory guide to much of the world's art." Booklist

Includes bibliographical references

Kasfir, Sidney Littlefield

Contemporary African art. Thames & Hudson 2000 224p il map (World of art) pa $14.95 *
Grades: 11 12 Adult   **709**
1. African art 2. Art—20th century
ISBN 0-500-20328-8   LC 99-70939

This survey of contemporary African art "emphasizes the changes in the art of this continent in the last half of the 20th century. . . . The illustrations are fully captioned and they alone could justify purchase." SLJ

Includes bibliographical references

Little, Stephen, 1954-

. . . isms: understanding art. Universe 2004 159p il pa $16.95
Grades: 11 12 Adult   **709**
1. Art—History
ISBN 0-7893-1209-3   LC 2004-94996

The author "identifies four types of isms: trends specific to the visual arts (perspectivism), broad cultural trends (romanticism), artist-defined movements (cubism), and retrospectively named movements (mannerism). He then moves forward chronologically, deftly defining more than 50 isms, naming key artists, and showcasing splendid examples." Booklist

Walden, Sarah

Whistler and his mother: an unexpected relationship; secrets of an American masterpiece. University of Neb. Press 2003 242p il $35
Grades: 9 10 11 12   **709**
1. Whistler, James McNeill, 1834-1903
ISBN 0-8032-4811-3   LC 2003-104221

"Walden, a restorer, was hired by the Louvre to bring the Portrait of the Artist's Mother: Arrangement in Grey and Black back from decrepitude. She came to admire Whistler's formal achievement even as she discovered the shoddy methods that led to its deterioration. The book is entrancing. Walden's is a view we seldom get: the detail of individual brush strokes and choices of paint and varnish." London Rev Books

Includes bibliographical references

709.01   Arts of nonliterate peoples, and earliest times to 499

Bahn, Paul G.

The Cambridge illustrated history of prehistoric art. Cambridge Univ. Press 1998 xxxii, 302p il $45 *
Grades: 11 12 Adult   **709.01**
1. Prehistoric art
ISBN 0-521-45473-5   LC 96-51099

The author "discovers the initial 'discoveries' of this art form, then weaves an excellent accounting of research, from the earliest to the recent. This discourse encompasses mobiliary art, art on rocks and walls, the application of scientific scrutiny, literal and symbolic interpretations, and the press of time. Bahn also describes current threats and future prospects. The writing is lucid and descriptive, satisfying to the advanced anthropologist or artist while quite comprehensible to uninitiated readers." Choice

709.02   Art--6th-15th centuries, 500-1499

Cole, Alison

Renaissance. Dorling Kindersley 2000 64p il (DK eyewitness books) lib bdg $19.99 *
Grades: 9 10 11 12   **709.02**
1. Art—15th and 16th centuries
ISBN 0-7894-6624-4   LC 00-503613
First published 1994 in the Eyewitness art series

A guide to the art of Northern Europe and Italy from the 14th to the 16th century. Color photographs of paintings, sculpture and architecture representative of the peri-

Cole, Alison—*Continued*
od include the works of Giotto, Leonardo, Dürer, Titian, Raphael and Michelangelo. Features include detailed close-ups, diagrams and charts
Includes glossary

Graham-Dixon, Andrew
Renaissance. University of Calif. Press 1999 336p il $29.95 *
Grades: 11 12 Adult   **709.02**
1. Art—15th and 16th centuries 2. Renaissance
ISBN 0-520-22375-6   LC 00-698469
This companion to a BBC television series is an "introduction to Renaissance art and the cultural milieu that spawned it. . . . The bulk of the text is given over to canonic figures ranging from Giotto to Michelangelo. . . . In addition, the author discusses religion, humanistic thought, the changing social status of the artist, and the larger historic ebb and flow." Libr J

Snyder, James
Art of the Middle Ages; [by] James Snyder, Henry Luttikhuizen, Dorothy Verkerk. 2nd ed. Prentice Hall 2006 530p il map $90 *
Grades: 11 12 Adult   **709.02**
1. Medieval art 2. Christian art 3. Medieval architecture
ISBN 0-13-193825-8   LC 2004-60135
First published 1989 with title Medieval art
"Church architecture and decoration receive the bulk of Snyder's attention, with manuscript illumination and sumptuary and secular arts presented rather briefly. The volume is well illustrated, though chiefly in black-and-white photographs." Libr J [review of 1989 edition]
Includes bibliographical references

709.04   Art--20th century, 1900-1999

Arwas, Victor
Art deco. rev ed. Abradale Press 2000 316p il $34.98
Grades: 9 10 11 12   **709.04**
1. Art deco
ISBN 0-8109-8199-8
First published 1980. This is a reprint of the 1992 Abrams edition
The author "traces Art Deco's flowering in furniture, metal, silver, jewelry, enamel, lacquer, figurines, bronzes, sculpture, painting, posters, graphics, book illustrations, bookbinding, glass and ceramics. The extraordinary objects shown in 437 plates (340 in color) are among the finest Art Deco creations ever made." Publ Wkly

Livingstone, Marco
Pop art: a continuing history. Abrams 1990 271p il $49.50
Grades: 11 12 Adult   **709.04**
1. Pop art
ISBN 0-8109-3707-7   LC 90-99

With 300 color plates this volume chronicles the work of 130 artists of the Pop Art movement, including Jasper Johns, Robert Rauschenberg, Andy Warhol, and Roy Lichtenstein
"Recommended as the best single historical survey on Pop Art." Libr J
Includes bibliographical references

Moszynska, Anna
Abstract art. Thames & Hudson 1990 240p il (World of art) pa $14.95
Grades: 9 10 11 12   **709.04**
1. Abstract art
ISBN 0-500-20237-0   LC 88-51347
"The author explains both the general philosophy of abstractionism and the approaches of many individual artists to the form. Paintings and sculptures are featured, as are examples of graphic design and architecture." Booklist

709.1   Art--Treatment by areas, regions, places in general

Khalili, Nasser D., 1945-
Islamic art and culture; a visual history. Overlook Press 2006 186p il $60 *
Grades: 11 12 Adult   **709.1**
1. Islamic art 2. Islamic civilization
ISBN 1-58567-839-2; 978-1-58567-839-6
This "visual history of Islamic art introduces readers to the diverse peoples, cultures, and styles making up Islam today. Spanning 12 centuries and covering everything from miniature painting to architecture, it shows, e.g., various Qur'ans, coins, armor, and scientific instruments. . . . This is an excellent introduction to the subject that combines aptly chosen and beautifully reproduced photographs with a concise and informative text." Libr J
Includes bibliographical references

709.32   Ancient Egyptian art

Egyptian treasures from the Egyptian Museum in Cairo; edited by Francesco Tiradritti; photographs by Araldo De Luca. Abrams 1999 416p il $75
Grades: 11 12 Adult   **709.32**
1. Egyptian Museum 2. Egyptian art 3. Egypt—Antiquities
ISBN 0-8109-3276-8   LC 99-72419
Also published in the United Kingdom with title: The Cairo Museum
This is a "descriptive guide to the ancient history exhibit at the Egyptian Museum in Cairo. . . . Following the introduction are educational essays by Egyptologists from around the world, on topics ranging from the early dynastic eras through to the later periods of invasion by the Greeks. Throughout the book, there are vivid photographs of artifacts with a narration explaining the historical and artistic significance of each piece." Booklist
Includes bibliographical references

709.45   Italian art

Hirst, Michael
Michelangelo and his drawings. Yale Univ.
Press 1988 132p il pa $25 hardcover o.p.
Grades: 11 12 Adult   **709.45**
1. Michelangelo Buonarroti, 1475-1564
    ISBN 0-300-04796-7 (pa)   LC 88-50431
The text of this book "is organized by type of drawing: initial sketches, life studies, compositional drawings, architectural designs, and finished drawings used as gifts. It is followed by a thematically arranged index of drawings and a section of . . . plates." Libr J
"An informative, insightful, and eminently readable book. . . . This is an important contribution to Michelangelo scholarship." Choice

709.51   Chinese art

Tregear, Mary
Chinese art. rev ed. Thames & Hudson 1997
216p il maps (World of art) pa $14.95 *
Grades: 11 12 Adult   **709.51**
1. Chinese art
    ISBN 0-500-20299-0
First published 1980 by Oxford Univ. Press
An introduction to major decorative, ceremonial, figurative and narrative aspects of Chinese art. Coverage ranges from works of Neolithic groups and the bronzes of the Shang dynasty to Buddhist sculpture, ceramics, garden design and architecture. Emphasis is also placed on the interaction of poetry, painting and calligraphy.
Includes bibliographical references

709.73   American art

The **American** art book. Phaidon Press 1999 512p
il hardcover o.p. pa $9.95 *
Grades: 11 12 Adult   **709.73**
1. American art
    ISBN 0-7148-3845-4; 0-7148-4119-6 (pa)
                     LC 99-231734
A "survey of American art from colonial days to the present. By presenting one well-chosen example of the work of each of 500 painters, photographers, sculptors, and folk artists in alphabetical order, the editors liberate their creations from chronology, regionalism, and the categorization of schools and movements, an approach that creates some wonderfully unexpected and revealing juxtapositions." Booklist

Bearden, Romare, 1914-1988
A history of African-American artists; from 1792 to the present; {by} Romare Bearden & Harry Henderson. Pantheon Bks. 1992 541p il $75 *
Grades: 11 12 Adult   **709.73**
1. African American artists 2. American art
    ISBN 0-394-57016-2   LC 89-42782

"Opening in the 18th century with Joshua Johnston, the authors go on to examine the work of Robert S. Duncanson, Henry O. Tanner, Aaron Douglas, Edmonia Lewis, Jacob Lawrence, Auguste Savage, Ellis Wilson, Archibald Motley, Alma Thomas, and others born before 1925. Their lives and careers, which often involved overcoming racial barriers, are portrayed against the backdrop of artistic, social, and political events; black Renaissance and Depression artists receive the most attention." Libr J
"Richly illustrated and written with resounding empathy and pride, this is a major contribution to the literature on African American history and to the annals of American art." Booklist

Creation's journey; Native American identity and belief; edited by Tom Hill and Richard W. Hill, Sr. Smithsonian Institution Press 1994 255p il $45 *
Grades: 11 12 Adult   **709.73**
1. National Museum of the American Indian (U.S.)
2. Native American art
    ISBN 1-56098-453-8   LC 94-4757
Published in conjunction with an exhibition held at the National Museum of the American Indian, New York City, October 1994-February 1997
This "volume links stories, anecdotes, descriptions of rituals, and spiritual beliefs to specific art objects, including an Osage cradleboard and a Winnebago bandolier bag. In each essay, the connection between spirituality and the making of art is articulated; each pattern, image, and symbol is shown to be an expression of dreams, visions, and beliefs." Booklist
Includes bibliographical references

Harlem Renaissance; art of Black America; introduction by Mary Schmidt Campbell; essays by David Driskell, David Levering Lewis, and Deborah Willis Ryan. Studio Museum in Harlem; Abradale Press 1994 200p il $17.98
Grades: 11 12 Adult   **709.73**
1. Harlem Renaissance 2. African American artists
3. American art
    ISBN 0-8109-8128-9   LC 93-20814
A reissue of the title first published 1987
This book "features four black artists: the sculptor Meta Warrick Fuller and the painters Aaron Douglas, Palmer Hayden and William H. Johnson. Also included are photographs . . . by James Van Der Zee." N Y Times Book Rev [review of 1987 edition]
"An eye-catching and eye-opening introduction to the black intelligensia who created the Harlem Renaissance of 1919-1930. . . . Black-and-white figures and color plates are plentiful and of fine quality." Choice [review of 1987 edition]
Includes bibliographical references

Roark, Elisabeth Louise
Artists of colonial America; [by] Elisabeth L. Roark. Greenwood Press 2003 207p il (Artists of an era) $59.95
Grades: 9 10 11 12   **709.73**
1. American art 2. United States—History—1600-1775, Colonial period
    ISBN 0-313-32023-3   LC 2003-47240

Roark, Elisabeth Louise—*Continued*
"This book presents . . . information and . . . pictures regarding the history and symbolism of colonial art. . . . Important colonial painters such as John Singleton Copely are included. . . . Based on its depth of information, eye-appeal, and value for research, this is a must-buy for every high school art or history collection." Libr Media Connect
Includes bibliographical references

709.8   Latin American art

Scott, John F., 1936-
Latin American art; ancient to modern. University Press of Fla. 1999 xxiv, 240p il $49.95; pa $29.95 *
Grades: 11 12 Adult   **709.8**
   1. Latin American art
   ISBN 0-8130-1645-2; 0-8130-1826-9 (pa)
                                        LC 98-46535
A study "of Latin American art from pre-Columbian times to the present, encompassing media ranging from sculpture, pottery, and painting to architecture. Scott . . . addresses the major styles and artists that define each period." Libr J
Includes bibliographical references

711   Area planning

Macaulay, David, 1946-
City: a story of Roman planning and construction. Houghton Mifflin 1974 112p il $18; pa $7.95 *
Grades: 4 5 6 7 8 9   **711**
   1. City planning—Rome 2. Civil engineering 3. Roman architecture
   ISBN 0-395-19492-X; 0-395-34922-2 (pa)
                                        LC 74-4280
"By following the inception, construction, and development of an imaginary Roman city, the account traces the evolution of Verbonia from the selection of its site under religious auspices in 26 B.C. to its completion in 100 A.D." Horn Book
Includes glossary

720   Architecture

Macaulay, David, 1946-
Building big. Houghton Mifflin 2000 192p il $30; pa $12.95 *
Grades: 5 6 7 8 9 10   **720**
   1. Architecture 2. Engineering
   ISBN 0-395-96331-1; 0-618-46527-8 (pa)
                                        LC 00-28116
"Walter Lorraine books"
This companion to the PBS series examines the architecture and engineering of "bridges, tunnels, dams, domes, and skyscrapers. Each section offers an implicitly chronological analysis as it focuses on several significant

examples of that particular kind of structure." Bull Cent Child Books
"Macaulay combines his detailed yet vaguely whimsical illustrations with simple, straightforward prose that breaks down complex architectural and engineering accomplishments into easily digestible tidbits that don't insult the intelligence of the reader of any age." N Y Times Book Rev
Includes glossary

720.3   Architecture--Encyclopedias and dictionaries

Burden, Ernest E., 1934-
Illustrated dictionary of architecture; [by] Ernest Burden. 2nd ed. McGraw-Hill 2001 389p il pa $39.95
Grades: 11 12 Adult   **720.3**
   1. Architecture—Dictionaries
   ISBN 0-07-137529-5   LC 2001-34558
First published 1998
This volume "is a compilation of more than 5,000 photographs and drawings in nearly 1,500 entries that define the technical and stylistic elements of both current and historical architecture. . . . It is an excellent resource for interested laypeople as well as professionals in the field and is recommended as a ready-reference tool for public, academic, and high-school libraries." Booklist

Ching, Frank, 1943-
A visual dictionary of architecture; {by} Francis D. K. Ching. Van Nostrand Reinhold 1995 319p il $44.95; pa $39.95 *
Grades: 11 12 Adult   **720.3**
   1. Architecture—Dictionaries
   ISBN 0-471-28451-3; 0-471-28821-7 (pa)
                                        LC 95-1476
This volume arranges some "5,000 entries thematically under 68 concepts covering architectural design, history, and technology. The topics, which are treated alphabetically, include building types (church, house, theater), sections (door, roof, stair), features (arch, column, vault), and materials (brick, paint, wood). Terms are logically clustered on oversize pages and defined with both line drawings and text, usually 20 to 100 words." Booklist

Dictionary of architecture & construction; edited by Cyril M. Harris. 4th ed. McGraw-Hill 2005 1089p il $74.95 *
Grades: 11 12 Adult   **720.3**
   1. Architecture—Dictionaries 2. Building—Dictionaries
   ISBN 0-07-145237-0   LC 2005-42340
First published 1975
This dictionary features "definitions of more than 27,000 important architecture and construction terms . . . [including] terms in legal areas, technologies, techniques, materials, organizations, historic architectural styles, and architectural trends." Publisher's note
"The handy one-volume format, the reasonable cost, the clarity and accuracy of entries, the legible type and drawings, and the inclusive approach to current develop-

Dictionary of architecture & construction—*Continued*

ments in the design, building, and scholarly professions related to architecture make this publication a crucial tool." Choice

The **Penguin** dictionary of architecture and landscape architecture; edited by John Fleming, Hugh Honour and Nikolaus Pevsner. 5th ed. Penguin Bks. 1998 643p il pa $16.95 hardcover o.p.

Grades: 11 12 Adult　　　　　　　　　**720.3**
1. Architecture—Dictionaries
ISBN 0-14-051323-X (pa)

First published 1966 with title: The Penguin dictionary of architecture

This reference covers "architecture from ancient times to the present. Major entries on key individuals, styles, movements, materials, and terms range up to several pages in length and include cross references and bibliographies for further reading." Publisher's note

"A magnificent panorama of world architecture, scholarly conciseness at its best." Art Review

720.9　Architecture--Historical and geographic treatment

Glancey, Jonathan
Architecture. DK Pub. 2006 512p il (Eyewitness companions) pa $30 *
Grades: 11 12 Adult　　　　　　　　　**720.9**
1. Architecture—History
ISBN 0-7566-1732-4　　　　　　LC 2005-36013

First published 2000 with title: The story of architecture

The author "examines 5000 years of architecture throughout the world. In well-executed and consistent writing, he briefly introduces each era and region, then touches on significant buildings and complexes (e.g., the Parthenon, the Sydney Opera House)." Libr J

The **Seventy** wonders of the modern world; 1500 years of extraordinary feats of engineering and construction; edited by Neil Parkyn. Thames & Hudson 2002 304p il $40
Grades: 11 12 Adult　　　　　　　　　**720.9**
1. Architecture 2. Curiosities and wonders
ISBN 0-500-51047-4　　　　　　LC 2002-100549

Published in the United Kingdom with title: The seventy architectural wonders of our world

"Most of the featured 'wonders' date from the second half of the 20th century. The selections are divided into seven categories: churches, palaces, public buildings, towers and skyscrapers, bridges and railways, canals and dams, and statues. Each entry includes basic information on history, structural and engineering details, innovations, aesthetics, and a sidebar 'fact-file.'" Libr J

Watkin, David, 1941-
A history of Western architecture. 3rd ed. Watson-Guptill 2000 704p il $50; pa $40
Grades: 9 10 11 12　　　　　　　　　**720.9**
1. Architecture—History
ISBN 0-8230-2273-0; 0-8230-2274-9 (pa)
　　　　　　　　　　　　　　LC 00-42870

First published 1986
This study focuses on the development of architecture in Europe and the United States and includes chapters on Mesopotamian and Egyptian architecture
Includes bibliographical references

720.973　Architecture--United States

Chollet, Laurence B.
The essential Frank O. Gehry. Harry N. Abrams 2001 112p il (Essential series) $12.95
Grades: 9 10 11 12　　　　　　　　　**720.973**
1. Gehry, Frank
ISBN 0-8109-5829-5; 978-0-8109-5829-6

"This portrait of one of the hottest cultural icons of our day examines Gehry's life and work—and his continuing search for new forms and new means of architectural expression." Publisher's note

726　Buildings for religious and related purposes

King, Ross, 1962-
Brunelleschi's dome; how a Renaissance genius reinvented architecture. Penguin Books 2001 194p il pa $14
Grades: 11 12 Adult　　　　　　　　　**726**
1. Brunelleschi, Filippo, 1377-1446 2. Santa Maria del Fiore (Cathedral: Florence, Italy) 3. Church buildings
ISBN 0-14-200015-9　　　　　　LC 2001-280068

First published 2000 by Walker & Co.
"King illuminates the mysterious sources of inspiration and the secretive methods of architectural genius Filippo Brunelleschi in a fascinating chronicle of the building of his masterwork, the dome of Santa Maria del Fiore in Florence. A remarkable saga of how one incandescent mind performed the one matchless feat that would forever transform architecture from a mechanical craft into a creative art." Booklist
Includes bibliographical references

Macaulay, David, 1946-
Mosque. Houghton Mifflin 2003 96p il $18 *
Grades: 4 5 6 7 8 9 10　　　　　　　**726**
1. Mosques—Design and construction
ISBN 0-618-24034-9　　　　　　LC 2003-177

"Walter Lorraine books"
Using "a fictional framework to hold his nonfictional material, the author introduces readers to Admiral Suha Mehmet Pasa, a wealthy aristocrat living in Istanbul, who decides in his declining years to fund the building of a mosque and its associated buildings—religious school, soup kitchen, public baths, public fountain, and tomb.

Macaulay, David, 1946-—_Continued_
Detailing the activities of the architect and workers, Macaulay creates a from-the-ground-up look not only at the actual construction, but also at the uses of the various buildings." SLJ

"Once again Macaulay uses clear words and exemplary drawings to explore a majestic structure's design and construction. . . . In his respectful, straightforward explanation of the mosque's design, Macaulay offers an unusual, inspiring perspective into Islamic society." Booklist
Includes glossary

Pyramid. Houghton Mifflin 1975 80p il $18; pa $9.95 *
Grades: 4 5 6 7 8 9   **726**
1. Pyramids 2. Egypt—Civilization
ISBN 0-395-21407-6; 0-395-32121-2 (pa)
LC 75-9964
The construction of a pyramid in 25th century B.C. Egypt is described. "Information about selection of the site, drawing of the plans, calculating compass directions, clearing and leveling the ground, and quarrying and hauling the tremendous blocks of granite and limestone is conveyed as much by pictures as by text." Horn Book
Includes glossary

728.8   Large and elaborate private dwellings

Macaulay, David, 1946-
Castle. Houghton Mifflin 1977 74p il $18; pa $9.95 *
Grades: 4 5 6 7 8 9   **728.8**
1. Castles 2. Fortification
ISBN 0-395-25784-0; 0-395-32920-5 (pa)
LC 77-7159
Macaulay depicts "the history of an imaginary thirteenth-century castle—built to subdue the Welsh hordes—from the age of construction to the age of neglect, when the town of Aberwyfern no longer needs a fortified stronghold." Economist
Includes glossary

730   Plastic arts. Sculpture

Celebrating Inuit art, 1948-1970; edited by Maria von Finckenstein; foreword by Adrienne Clarkson; essays by James Houston and Ann Meekitjuk Hanson. Key Porter Bks. 2000 c1999 192p il hardcover o.p. pa $26.95
Grades: 11 12 Adult   **730**
1. Inuit—Art
ISBN 1-55263-104-4; 1-55263-803-0 (pa)
LC 00-304267
This volume was published to accompany an exhibition of Inuit sculpture at the Canadian Museum of Civilization. "The text comprises CMC curator von Finckenstein's . . . introduction to the economic and social context; journalist Ann Meekitjuk Hanson's account of one artist's transition; and Houston's recollections of discovering the native talent and developing it in the

1940s and 1950s." Libr J
"If you can have only one book on Inuit sculpture in your library, let it be this one. Not only do the fabulous photographs . . . recommend it. So do the absorbing accompanying essays." Booklist
Includes bibliographical references

731.4   Sculpture--Techniques and procedures

Bütz, Richard
How to carve wood; a book of projects and techniques. Taunton Press 1984 215p il pa $19.95
Grades: 11 12 Adult   **731.4**
1. Wood carving
ISBN 0-918804-20-5   LC 83-50680
"A Fine Woodworking Bk."
The author introduces "the most common types of carving, whittling, chip carving, relief carving, lettering, and architectural carving. The information on tools and their care is very helpful. This is the best book available on the subject." Libr J
Includes bibliographical references

737.4   Coins

A **Guide** book of United States coins, 2008; by R. S. Yeoman; edited by Kenneth Bressett. Western 2007 il $16.95 *
Grades: 11 12 Adult   **737.4**
1. Coins
ISSN 0072-8829
ISBN 0-7948-2267-3; 978-0-7948-2267-5
Also available in spiral-binding format
Annual. First published 1946 by Whitman
At head of title: The official red book
This guide "known as the 'Red Book' is an outstanding reference on U.S. coins designed for use in identifying and grading coins. All issues from 1616 to the present are covered. The guide provides historical data, statistics, values, and detailed photographs for each coin. Additional sections deal with specialties such as Civil War and Hard Times tokens, misstruck coins, and uncirculated and proof sets." Nichols. Guide to Ref Books for Sch Media Cent. 4th edition

Krause, Chester L.
Standard catalog of world coins; by Chester L. Krause and Clifford Mishler. Krause Publs. il pa $55 *
Grades: 11 12 Adult   **737.4**
1. Coins
ISSN 1556-2263
ISBN 0-8968-9365-0; 978-0-8968-9365-8
Also available volumes covering the 17th, 19th and 21st centuries
First published 1972. Periodically revised
This illustrated volume currently covers coins from throughout the world minted 1901-2000. Prices are provided for each coin in up to four grades of preservation. Includes commemorative issues.

738.1   Ceramic arts--Techniques, equipment, materials

Nelson, Glenn C.

Ceramics: a potter's handbook; [by] Glenn C. Nelson, Richard Burkett. 6th ed. Wadsworth/Thomson Learning 2002 439p il pa $90.95 *

Grades: 11 12 Adult   **738.1**

1. Ceramics 2. Pottery

ISBN 0-03-028937-8   LC 2001-96329

First published 1960. Periodically revised

This manual for beginner to advanced potters presents forming and decorating techniques, body and glaze recipes, and sources for raw materials and equipment.

Includes bibliographical references

739.27   Jewelry

Codina, Carles

The complete book of jewelry making. Lark Bks. 2000 160p il hardcover o.p. pa $19.95

Grades: 11 12 Adult   **739.27**

1. Jewelry

ISBN 1-57990-188-3; 1-57990-304-5 (pa)

     LC 00-42809

This book covers "the basics, from the ABCs of metallurgy to such complicated techniques as enameling and lacquering. . . . Most of the examples are contemporary, taken from European designers, and all blessed with great color photographs." Booklist

741.2   Drawing--Techniques, equipment, materials

Complete guide to drawing & painting. Reader's Digest Assn. 1997 288p il $29.95 *

Grades: 11 12 Adult   **741.2**

1. Drawing 2. Painting—Technique

ISBN 0-89577-956-0   LC 96-52461

A guide to drawing in pencil, charcoal, ink, and pastels. Oil, watercolor, and acrylic painting techniques are covered. Composition, color, and working from photographs are discussed

Includes glossary

Kutch, Kristy Ann

Drawing and painting with colored pencil; basic techniques for mastering traditional and watersoluble colored pencils. Watson-Guptill Publications 2005 144p il pa $24.95

Grades: 9 10 11 12   **741.2**

1. Colored pencil drawing—Technique 2. Watercolor painting—Technique

ISBN 0-8230-1568-8; 978-0-8230-1568-9

     LC 2005-10466

This book "covers traditional colored pencil techniques as well as tips on mastering the new water-soluble

colored pencils." Publisher's note

"This excellent book will inspire artists and wannabe artists alike." Voice Youth Advocates

Includes bibliographical references

Micklewright, Keith, 1933-

Drawing: mastering the language of visual expression. Harry N. Abrams 2005 168p il (Abrams studio) pa $29.95

Grades: 11 12 Adult   **741.2**

1. Drawing—Technique

ISBN 0-8109-9238-8   LC 2005-5862

"Using examples of master artists such as Ingres and Michelangelo as well as more contemporary work of Cezanne, Hockney, and others, different aspects of drawing are examined. Each chapter ends with 'Ideas to Explore,' in which the reader is given suggestions for practice. . . . This book is valuable for those learning the theory behind the elements of drawing and for those looking for practical instruction." Voice Youth Advocates

Includes bibliographical references

Scott, Damion

How to draw hip-hop; [by] Damion Scott and Kris Ex. Watson-Guptill 2006 144p il pa $19.95

Grades: 7 8 9 10   **741.2**

1. Drawing 2. Hip-hop

ISBN 0-8230-1446-0   LC 2005-29156

"This book combines the bold and energetic lines of graffiti art with the bright colors of cel-shaded video games and an obvious Japanese manga influence. . . . [It discusses] genre-specific concepts like wild style lettering [and] hip-hop clothing. The teaching . . . is unique and totally accessible. . . . There is no other book of this kind on the market, making it a necessary and relevant purchase." SLJ

741.5   Cartoons, caricatures, comics

Abouet, Marguerite, 1971-

Aya; [by] Marguerite Abouet & Clément Oubrerie; [translation by Helge Dascher] Drawn & Quarterly 2007 96p il $19.95

Grades: 10 11 12 Adult   **741.5**

1. Graphic novels 2. Friendship—Graphic novels 3. Ivory Coast—Graphic novels

ISBN 1-894937-90-2; 978-1-894937-90-0

2006 award for Best First Album at the Angouleme International Comics Festival

In Ivory Coast of 1978, nineteen-year-old Aya and her friends Adjoua and Bintou live in an oasis of peace and prosperity. Studious Aya wants to become a doctor, but her friends just want to have a good time and enjoy nights with handsome lovers. Soon enough, Adjoua finds out she's pregnant, and she says the father is Moussa, Bintou's boyfriend and the young man Aya's parents were hoping to get for her husband. Moussa's rich parents agree to a wedding, but they show their prejudice against poor townspeople in their arrangements.

An **Anthology** of graphic fiction, cartoons, and true stories; edited by Ivan Brunetti. Yale University Press 2006 400p il $28
Grades: 11 12 Adult   **741.5**
1. Comic books, strips, etc. 2. American wit and humor
ISBN 978-0-300-11170-5; 0-300-11170-3
LC 2006-14095
Brunetti presents "an overview of the art-comics movement, complete with a handful of the classic newspaper strips that informed today's creators. He finds room for such established veterans as R. Crumb, Lynda Barry, Gilbert and Jaime Hernandez, Daniel Clowes, Gary Panter, and Chester Brown as well as many less-familiar creators. . . . Brunetti admits that his selection criteria are highly personal, but as a cartoonist himself, whose work combines a socially transgressive spirit and impressive formal capability, his idiosyncratic approach is based in professional expertise. If his choices are sometimes arguable, his iconoclasm makes the book livelier and less predictable than such anthologies are wont to be." Booklist

Asamiya, Kia, 1963-
Batman: child of dreams; English adaptation by Max Allan Collins. DC Comics 2003 332p il pa $19.95 hardcover o.p.
Grades: 9 10 11 12   **741.5**
1. Batman (Comic strip) 2. Graphic novels 3. Superhero graphic novels
ISBN 1-56389-907-8   LC 2004-266983
"The intrepid Dark Knight is thrown into battle with a Japanese impostor who pushes a drug that seems to promise the realization of one's dreams. Asamiya's *manga*, in grainy black and grays, sets the mood superbly." Booklist

Azuma, Kiyohiko, 1968-
Azumanga Daioh, Vol. 1; [creator, Kiyohiko Azuma]; translators, Kay Bertrand . . . [et al.]; graphic design, Tawna Franze & Windi Martin; graphic artist, Windi Martin. ADV Manga 2003 160p il pa $9.99 *
Grades: 8 9 10 11 12   **741.5**
1. Graphic novels 2. Manga 3. Humorous graphic novels 4. High school students—Graphic novels
ISBN 1-4139-0000-3; 978-1-4139-0000-2
First published 2001 in Japan
This is a four-volume manga series.
"This episodic . . . manga . . . hilariously depicts the hijinks and misadventures of a high school class with the ditziest teacher in the world." Voice Youth Advocates
Readers will also get a good idea of Japanese suburban high school culture amidst the laughter. The adult teachers go drinking occasionally, and there's one male teacher who ogles the girls in their P.E. uniforms.

Barry, Lynda
One hundred demons. Sasquatch Bks. 2002 216p il $24.95
Grades: 9 10 11 12   **741.5**
1. Graphic novels
ISBN 1-57061-337-0   LC 2002-21657

"Whether she's talking about head lice, old boy-friends, or hippies who 'forgot' to pay her wages, Barry playfully explores, in 'autobifictionalographical' text and art, those demons common to teens—and to us all." Booklist

Batman in the eighties; Batman created by Bob Kane; [introduction by John Wells] DC Comics 2004 191p il pa $19.95
Grades: 9 10 11 12   **741.5**
1. Batman (Comic strip) 2. Graphic novels 3. Comic books, strips, etc. 4. Superhero graphic novels
ISBN 1-4012-0241-1
The events featured in this collection "include Dick Grayson's transformation into Nightwing, Barbara Gordon's final days as Batgirl and the introduction of not one, but two new versions of Robin. The stories in this volume may not include the greatest highlights of the decade, but do serve to round out many of the events that affected the Batman mythos during the 1980's." Libr Media Connect

Batman in the forties; Batman created by Bob Kane; {introduction by Bill Schelly}. DC Comics 2004 192p il pa $19.95
Grades: 9 10 11 12   **741.5**
1. Batman (Comic strip) 2. Graphic novels 3. Comic books, strips, etc. 4. Superhero graphic novels
ISBN 1-4012-0206-3
Originally published (1939-1949) in single magazine form as Batman 7, 15, 20, 31, 37, 47, 48, 49, Detective Comics 27, 33, 38, 49, 80, Real Fact Comics 5, Star-Spangled Comics 70, World's Finest Comics 30
"The 17 selections include such milestones as Batman's first appearance in May 1939, the two-page story of his origins from November 1939, and the 1940 introduction of his young partner, Robin. . . . Other stories feature early appearances by some of Batman's most renowned arch-enemies: the Joker, Catwoman, and Two-Face. . . . Most compelling are the earliest stories; crude as they are, their naive verve and raw directness remain effective." Booklist

Beatty, Scott
Batgirl: year one; Scott Beatty, Chuck Dixon, writers; Marcos Martin, penciller; Alvaro Lopez, inker; Javier Rodriguez, colorist; Willie Schubert, letterer; Marcos Martin, Alvaro Lopez, original covers. DC Comics 2003 212p il pa $17.95
Grades: 9 10 11 12   **741.5**
1. Graphic novels 2. Comic books, strips, etc. 3. Superhero graphic novels
ISBN 1-4012-0080-X
"Her police captain father doesn't want her on the force. The FBI says she's too short to be a field agent. But Barbara Gordon is determined to find a place among crime fighters and transcend her existence as an 'Underpaid Librarian and Potential Defaulter of Student Loans.' . . . Batgirl is a joy from start to finish, with smart, barbed dialogue; a dense (but not migraine-inducing) plot; exuberantly drawn action; and impressive characterization." SLJ

Beatty, Scott—*Continued*

Catwoman: the visual guide to the feline fatale; written by Scott Beatty. DK Pub. 2004 63p il $19.99

Grades: 9 10 11 12   **741.5**
1. Batman (Comic strip) 2. Comic books, strips, etc.
ISBN 0-7566-0383-8   LC 2003-26750
This illustrated history of the Batman villain seeks to answer such questions as, "What kind of equipment does Catwoman carry? . . . [and] How did Catwoman become who she is? . . . In *Catwoman* the art is lush and varied, covering nearly 65 years of history." Booklist

Superman; the ultimate guide to the Man of Steel; written by Scott Beatty. Rev. ed. DK 2006 144p il $24.99

Grades: 7 8 9 10   **741.5**
1. Superman (Comic strip) 2. Comic books, strips, etc.
ISBN 978-0-7566-2067-7; 0-7566-2067-8
       LC 2005035040
First published 2002
Surveys the nature and history of the hero Superman, discussing his birth, career, secrets, equipment, and enemies

Busiek, Kurt

Superman: secret identity; Kurt Busiek, writer; Stuart Immonen, artist, colorist, original covers; Todd Klein, letterer; Superman created by Jerry Seigel and Joe Schuster. DC Comics 2004 206p il pa $19.95

Grades: 9 10 11 12   **741.5**
1. Superman (Comic strip) 2. Graphic novels 3. Comic books, strips, etc. 4. Superhero graphic novels
ISBN 1-4012-0451-1   LC 2005-299025
First published in single magazine form in Superman: secret identity 1-4
"The teenage Clark Kent of this book is a Kansas farm boy, but in his world, Superman is just a comic book character, and Clark gets teased for having his name. But one day, Clark discovers that he actually has all of Superman's powers. As he starts to use them, he draws government attention—but this book isn't as much about superheroics and men in black as it is about Clark the man. . . . Strongly recommended for teen and adult superhero fans and for anyone who feels that the genre lacks 'human interest.'" Libr J

Castellucci, Cecil, 1969-

The Plain Janes. DC Comics/Minx 2007 unp il pa $9.99

Grades: 7 8 9 10 11 12   **741.5**
1. Graphic novels 2. Friendship—Graphic novels 3. Art—Graphic novels 4. High school students—Graphic novels
ISBN 978-1-4012-1115-8
This is the first book in a new line of comics being written for and marketed to teen girls.
After a bomb attack in Metro City, Jane's parents move to suburban Kent Waters, where Jane feels lost. Then she meets three other Janes at the "reject" table in the high school lunch room, and she convinces them to

help her form their own secret club: P.L.A.I.N.—People Loving Art in Neighborhoods. However, their "art attacks" cause the authorities to think that P.L.A.I.N. is a terrorist group.

Chiarello, Mark

The DC Comics guide to coloring and lettering comics; [by] Mark Chiarello and Todd Klein; introduction by Jim Steranko. Watson-Guptill Publications 2004 144p il pa $19.95

Grades: 9 10 11 12   **741.5**
1. Comic books, strips, etc. 2. Cartoons and caricatures 3. Drawing
ISBN 0-8230-1030-9   LC 2004-9753
Contents: Lettering -- The lettering profession -- Hand lettering -- Tools and materials -- Getting started with lettering -- Lettering text and balloons -- Display lettering and sound effects -- Elements on the page -- Advanced techniques -- Logo design -- Computer lettering -- Hardware and software -- Fonts and type -- Using Illustrator -- Working with Art and Scans -- Working with color -- The final product
"This is a great resource for YAs seriously interested in graphic storytelling; it will also find an appreciative audience among adults." Booklist

Chinn, Mike, 1954-

Writing and illustrating the graphic novel; everything you need to know to create great graphic works. Barron's Educ. Ser. 2004 128p il pa $21.95 *

Grades: 11 12 Adult   **741.5**
1. Graphic novels—Drawing 2. Comic books, strips, etc.—Authorship
ISBN 0-7641-2788-8   LC 2003-110234
"A Quarto book"
The author "helps intermediate writers and illustrators marry narrative to visuals and create lively characters in dynamic locations. He also offers advice on establishing one's own style, building a portfolio, and making a professional presentation. Whether for creating new varieties of superheroes or adapting the classics, this will be the standard resource for most collections." Libr J
Includes bibliographical references

Couch, N. C. Christopher

The Will Eisner companion; the pioneering spirit of the father of the graphic novel; [by] N.C. Christopher Couch and Stephen Weiner; introduction by Dennis O'Neil; afterword by Denis Kitchen. DC Comics 2004 174p il $19.95

Grades: 11 12 Adult   **741.5**
1. Eisner, Will, 1917-2005 2. Comic books, strips, etc.
ISBN 1-4012-0422-8
"This book is part mini-biography and part summary of the major works of the man who invented and reinvented the art of the graphic novel." SLJ
"Wherever Eisner's books—either the Spirit collections that DC Comics is lavishly republishing, or the graphic novels—have proven popular, their fans will value this authoritative supplement to them." Booklist
Includes bibliographical references

Crawford, Philip Charles

Graphic novels 101; selecting and using graphic novels to promote literacy for children and young adults: a resource guide for school librarians and educators. Hi Willow Research & Pub. 2003 76p il $30 *

Grades: Professional   **741.5**
1. Graphic novels—Administration 2. Libraries—Collection development
ISBN 0-931510-91-0; 978-0-931510-91-5

In this resource on the graphic novel genre, Crawford discusses "why it should be included in the collection, what's available, what to avoid (there really are 'graphic' graphic novels), and how to purchase and handle them."
Publisher's note
Includes bibliographical references

Daly, Paul

Athena Voltaire; the collected webcomics. APE Entertainment 2006 unp il pa $13.95

Grades: 9 10 11 12 Adult   **741.5**
1. Graphic novels 2. Adventure graphic novels 3. Fantasy graphic novels
ISBN 978-0-9741398-9-0

The stories originally appeared as webcomics, and the series was nominated for the first Eisner Award for Best Digital Comic in 2005

In "The Terror in Tibet," adventurous pilot (and widow) Athena Voltaire agrees to guide a group of British gentlemen on an expedition into the Himalayas. The time is the 1930s, and Nazis are on the rise in Germany. Athena soon finds out that the British are up to no good, nor are the Germans pursuing them. They're all after something in a remote monastery halfway up Mount Everest, and she decides to prevent anyone from succeeding. In "The Wrath from the Tomb," Dracula's daughter seeks revenge against the men who killed her father; she makes a mistake when she sends men to attack Athena's Arizona ranch. Teens who love the Indiana Jones and Mummy movies will enjoy Athena's adventures. The violence level is about the same as those movies, although the scene in which the vampire is run through with a spear might bother more sensitive readers.

Daniels, Les, 1943-

Marvel; five fabulous decades of the world's greatest comics; introduction by Stan Lee. Abrams 1991 287p il pa $26.95 hardcover o.p.

Grades: 11 12 Adult   **741.5**
1. Marvel comics (New York, N.Y.) 2. Comic books, strips, etc.
ISBN 0-8109-2566-4   LC 91-8783

"Daniels' behind-the-scenes look at the development of Marvel, his profiles of the line's foremost heroes and villains, and biographies of leading writers and artists will entice . . . young fans. . . . But the book's strongest appeal lies in the generous samplings of artwork spread throughout." Booklist

The **DC** Comics encyclopedia; the definitive guide to the characters of the DC universe; written by Phil Jimenez . . . [et al.] DK Publishing 2004 351p il $40

Grades: 11 12 Adult   **741.5**
1. DC Comics Group 2. Comic books, strips, etc.
ISBN 0-7566-0592-X   LC 2004-3379

This is a "one-volume encyclopedia of more than 1,000 characters created by DC Comics . . . featuring some of DC's most creative artists and heroes and villains from the world famous to lesser known one-offs."
Publisher's note
"The colorful design makes this book a pleasure to browse." Libr J

Dead High yearbook; [edited by Mark McVeigh and Ivan Velez; art by Shawn Martinbrough . . . [et al.] Dutton 2007 70p il pa $18.99

Grades: 9 10 11 12   **741.5**
1. Graphic novels 2. Horror graphic novels 3. High school students—Graphic novels
ISBN 978-0-525-47783-9

An undead staff of students work on their high school yearbook in the framing story that binds this anthology of stories depicting the many bad ends students meet. In "What's Got Into Grandma?" Louis does one selfish deed that may bind him to Grandma forever. Pretty Rowena adopts a demonic chihuahua. Studious Clara insists on taking her final exam even after losing her head (literally) in "Head of the Class." The stories are gruesome and gory, and some show a dark humor.

"McVeigh and Velez expertly assemble a collection of messed-up Aesopian fables blended together with a bunch of bad zombie movies and John Hughes films." Voice Youth Advocates

DeMatteis, J. M.

Brooklyn dreams; written by J. M. DeMatteis; art by Glenn Barr; lettering by Bob Lappan. Paradox Press 1994 unp il pa $12.95

Grades: 9 10 11 12   **741.5**
1. Graphic novels 2. High school students—Graphic novels
ISBN 1-4012-0051-6

"Originally published in single volume form as Brooklyn dreams, Vols. 14."—Verso of title page

In this "graphic novel, fortyish Vincent Carl Santini recalls his senior year (1970–71) in high school. But first he retreats to August, before school opened, when he adopted a scruffy dog his parents quickly made him give up, before advancing a little into senior year and the time he got arrested while carrying drugs . . . As graphically distinguished and creatively novelistic a graphic novel as has ever been, this is a classic of the form." Booklist

Drooker, Eric, 1958-

Blood song; a silent ballad; introduction by Joe Sacco. Harcourt 2002 unp il pa $20

Grades: 9 10 11 12   **741.5**
1. Graphic novels 2. Stories without words
ISBN 0-15-600884-X   LC 2002-24263
"A Harvest original"

Drooker, Eric, 1958----*Continued*

"Driven by war from their rural home in Southeast Asia, a young woman and her dog ride the ocean currents to a city in the West. A deeply moving graphic novel, masterfully done." SLJ

Eisner, Will, 1917-2005

Comics & sequential art. Poorhouse Press 1985 154p il pa $22.99 hardcover o.p. *

Grades: 9 10 11 12   **741.5**

1. Comic books, strips, etc.

ISBN 0-9614728-1-2   LC 85-61669

This offers the author's ideas, theories, and advice about graphic storytelling and the uses to which the comic book art form can be applied

"Eisner has written an important, possibly definitive guide book to the creative process." Publ Wkly

Eldred, Tim

Grease monkey; written and drawn by Tim Eldred; [edited by Teresa Nielsen Hayden] Tor 2006 352p il $27.95

Grades: 9 10 11 12 Adult   **741.5**

1. Graphic novels 2. Science fiction graphic novels

ISBN 0-7653-1325-1

When hostile aliens attacked Earth and left it after killing most of the humans, another group of aliens came and offered to "uplift" one of the animal species to human intelligence so that Earth could rebuild. The dolphins turned them down, but the gorillas went for it. Some generations later, new mechanic Robin Plotnik comes to the space station called Fist of Earth, where he's assigned to work with Chief Mac Gimbensky. Mac is a no-nonsense gorilla who works on the ships of the all-woman Barbarian Squadron. He and Robin work together well, but they each have their romantic problems. This is science fiction from a viewpoint not always seen in most stories.

Flight v2; [editor/art director, Kazu Kibuishi] Image Comics 2005 432p il pa $24.95

Grades: 9 10 11 12   **741.5**

1. Graphic novels 2. Short stories—Graphic novels 3. Fantasy graphic novels

ISBN 1-58240-477-1

Stories are by various authors; At head of title: Image comics presents; v1 published 2004

In this themed story collection, "more than 30 accomplished young artists take off on the theme, sometimes loosely construed, of flight. . . . At more than 400 pages, there is something in this elegantly produced collection for everyone, including readers who usually snub comics." Booklist

Flight v3; [editor/art director, Kazu Kibuishi] Ballantine Books 2006 351p il pa $24.95

Grades: 9 10 11 12 Adult   **741.5**

1. Graphic novels 2. Fantasy graphic novels

ISBN 978-0-345-49039-1; 0-345-49039-8

LC 2006-45883

Sequel to Flight v2 (2005)

v1 published 2004

This third volume of Flight includes 26 short stories by mostly young writers, many of whom have webcomics. Some, such as Michael Gagne and Becky Cloonan, have published a number of books. The stories range from whimsical interludes to ironic fables to mini-epics of derring-do; ironically, most of the stories have only a tangential connection to the theme of flight.

Friedman, Aimee, 1979-

Breaking up; a Fashion High graphic novel; art by Christine Norrie. Graphix 2007 192p il pa $9.99 *

Grades: 8 9 10 11 12   **741.5**

1. Graphic novels 2. Friendship—Graphic novels 3. High school students—Graphic novels

ISBN 978-0-439-74867-4; 0-439-74867-4

LC 2007-270601

It's junior year at Georgia O'Keeffe School for the Arts (aka Fashion High) for Chloe and her best friends Erika, Isabel, and MacKenzie. But now, changes might break them up: MacKenzie seems to prefer hanging out with uber-popular Nicola while trying to get Nicola's boyfriend, Gabe, for herself; and she lost her virginity during summer vacation. Erika's boyfriend is demanding she go the next physical step with him. But Chloe's developing friendship with Adam, the biggest nerd in school, may be the one thing that breaks up the circle of friends.

"Friedman moves from giggly gossip, instant messages and lattes, to a thoughtful exploration of the difficult time the girls have reconciling their friendships, and learning to accept each other for who they are. For teens going through similar dilemmas, this book will likely be a great source of comfort." Publ Wkly

Fujii, Mihona, 1974-

Gals! Vol. 1. DC Comics/CMX 2005 unp il pa $9.95

Grades: 9 10 11 12   **741.5**

1. Graphic novels 2. Manga 3. Shojo manga 4. Conduct of life—Graphic novels

ISBN 1-4012-0550-X

Ran Kotobuki and her friends hang out in trendy Shibuya, where they love to shop and con free meals out of guys. They are kogals, the trendsetters of teen fashion and harbingers of cool. Ran also comes from a family of policemen, so she knows how to deal with street thugs, kogal rivals, and others. But when she discovers that Hoshino, one of her classmates, has been dating older men for money and may be getting into trouble, she decides she has to help.

Gaiman, Neil, 1960-

Marvel 1602; [Neil Gaiman, writer; Andy Kubert, illustrator; Richard Isanove, digital painting; Todd Klein, lettering] Marvel Comics 2005 unp il $24.99; pa $19.99

Grades: 9 10 11 12   **741.5**

1. Graphic novels 2. Comic books, strips, etc. 3. Superhero graphic novels

ISBN 0-7851-1073-9; 0-7851-1073-9 (pa)

First published in magazine form as Marvel 1602 #1-8

Gaiman, Neil, 1960-—Continued

This book "takes the Marvel superheroes and villains of the 1960s—the original X-Men, Daredevil, Dr. Doom, and many others—and places them in the early 17th century." Libr J

"The improbable combination works remarkably well, as the superheroes' strange abilities adapt to Elizabethan culture. This glorious adventure is peppered with Scott McKowen's gorgeous, moody cover-art woodcuts." Publ Wkly

Gallagher, Fred

Megatokyo v2; story & art, Fred Gallagher; co-creator, Rodney Caston; "shirt guy dom" comics by Dominic Nguyen. Dark Horse Bks. 2004 182p il pa $9.95

Grades: 9 10 11 12   741.5
1. Graphic novels 2. Japan—Graphic novels
ISBN 1-59307-118-3

Second volume of an ongoing series; v1 published 2002 by I.C. Entertainment

This book "follows the misadventures of two young geeks: Piro, an artist obsessed with all things anime and *manga*, and Largo, a hard-core video gamer. After things go wrong at a gaming expo, the pair set off on a last-minute pilgrimage to Japan. Unfortunately, they discover they have no funds to return. . . . Although most of the characters here are in their mid-twenties, their inexperience and shyness will appeal to young adults." Booklist

Gorman, Michele

Getting graphic! using graphic novels to promote literacy with preteens and teens; with a foreword by Jeff Smith. Linworth Pub. 2003 100p il pa $36.95 *

Grades: Professional   741.5
1. Graphic novels—Administration
ISBN 1-58683-089-9   LC 2003-13199

"This title serves as an introduction to the world of fiction and nonfiction comics. Collection-development policies are addressed as well as cataloging, shelving, and maintaining these . . . books. Gorman provides ideas for the genre's integration into classroom curriculum and suggests promotional activities for school and public libraries." SLJ

"A must-have first resource for school and public libraries that are considering adding graphic novels to their collections but are unsure how to proceed." Booklist

Includes bibliographical references

Graphic Classics Volume Eleven: O. Henry; edited by Tom Pomplun. Eureka Productions 2005 144p il pa $11.95

Grades: 7 8 9 10 11 12   741.5
1. Henry, O., 1862-1910—Adaptations 2. Graphic novels 3. Short stories—Graphic novels
ISBN 978-0-9746648-2-0

This volume of Graphics Classics adapts some of the short stories by O. Henry, the master of the surprise ending. Stories include 'The Ransom of Red Chief,' illustrated by Johnny Ryan, 'The Gift of the Magi,' illustrated by Lisa Weber, 'The Caballero's Way' (the original story of the Cisco Kid), illustrated by Mark A. Nelson, and more.

Gravett, Paul

Graphic novels; everything you need to know. Collins Design 2005 192p il pa $24.95 *

Grades: Professional   741.5
1. Graphic novels—History and criticism
ISBN 0-06-082425-5; 978-0-06-082425-9

"Selecting 30 highly recommended works from many countries . . . [the author] groups them in separate chapters by theme (childhood, fantasy, crime, sex, superheroes) and devotes a two-page spread to each work, presenting sample pages and discussing them in annotations. . . . This is a genuinely substantial contribution to the growing literature on graphic novels." Libr J

Includes bibliographical references

Hage, Anika

Gothic sports, Vol. 1. Tokyopop 2007 176p il pa $9.99

Grades: 8 9 10 11 12   741.5
1. Manga 2. Soccer—Graphic novels 3. High school students—Graphic novels
ISBN 978-1-59816-992-8

When Anya starts at Lucrece High, she wants to join one of the sports teams for which the school is famed. Since she's never played on a school's team before, she gets rejected. But this time, she's determined to succeed, so she joins with some of the other school misfits and they form their own soccer team. And with the help of a Goth-Lolita classmate, they have fantastically fashionable Goth-Lolita uniforms (even for the boys!). This is the first volume of a series translated from German, making it a global manga title.

Hale, Tricia Riley

Grand Theft Galaxy, Vol. 1. Tokyopop 2007 unp il pa $9.99

Grades: 8 9 10 11 12   741.5
1. Graphic novels 2. Humorous graphic novels 3. Science fiction graphic novels
ISBN 978-1-59816-713-9

College freshman Samantha Beagley has her life all figured out. She's a pre-law student, and she lives by her charts and planners. On her eighteenth birthday, Sam loses control of her life. She receives a very strange present from her parents, and learns to her horror that they are alien thieves. Some years ago they stole a certain object, the Evo Cube, and they hid it away so well they can't remember where it is. And now the Galactic Order Directorate has found Sam's parents, and they will destroy the Earth in three days if the Evo Cube isn't returned. When her parents grab her and go off-planet to save themselves, Sam decides to find the Evo Cube herself; and that leads her to find the master thief Jackal. He turns out to be her former pet cat, Mr. Fluffy. This is the first of a global manga series.

Hart, Christopher

Cartooning for the beginner. Watson-Guptill 2000 144p il pa $19.95

Grades: 11 12 Adult   741.5
1. Cartoons and caricatures
ISBN 0-8230-0586-0   LC 00-101905

Hart, Christopher—*Continued*

This guide to cartooning techniques "covers the world of cartoon animals, animation, and 'edgy 'toons.'" Libr J

Drawing cutting edge anatomy; the ultimate reference guide for comic book artists. Watson-Guptill Publications 2004 144p il pa $19.95

Grades: 9 10 11 12   741.5
1. Artistic anatomy 2. Figure drawing 3. Cartoons and caricatures 4. Comic books, strips, etc.

ISBN 0-8230-2398-2   LC 2004-12864

"This drawing tutorial shows artists how to draw the exaggerated musculature of super-sized figures in action poses." Publisher's note

"This book covers the basics in good detail. . . . Attractively presented and educational, this title will be popular with comic-book fans who like to draw." SLJ

How to draw animation. Watson-Guptill 1997 144p il pa $18.95 *

Grades: 11 12 Adult   741.5
1. Animated films 2. Drawing

ISBN 0-8230-2365-6   LC 97-13064

Illustrated step-by-step instructions to character design, animation techniques, and layout. Human and animal anatomy and movement are analyzed. Costume design is discussed

Harvey, Robert C.

The art of the comic book; an aesthetic history. University Press of Miss. 1996 288p il (Studies in popular culture) pa $22 hardcover o.p. *

Grades: 11 12 Adult   741.5
1. Comic books, strips, etc. 2. Popular culture—United States

ISBN 0-87805-758-7   LC 95-377

Harvey "attempts to situate the comic book in terms of its evolution from the comic strip to the world of publishing as a whole. . . . {He describes the} change brought upon comics by the institution of the Comics Code in 1954, which put horror and detective stories out of business and ushered in the primacy of superheroes. He also {examines} . . . the art itself, focusing on the development of the vocabulary of panel, layout, story, and style, and the relationship between writer and artist during various stages of comic book history. In addition, he . . . {discusses Will Eisner}, Gil Kane, Frank Miller, and Robert Crumb." Libr J

Includes bibliographical references

Hatfield, Charles, 1965-

Alternative comics; an emerging literature. University Press of Mississippi 2005 182p il hardcover o.p. pa $20

Grades: 11 12 Adult   741.5
1. Comic books, strips, etc.

ISBN 1-57806-718-9; 1-57806-719-7 (pa)
LC 2004-25709

The author "establishes a historical and theoretical framework in which graphic novels can be considered 'literature.' . . . It's hard to imagine anyone coming

away from this book without new insights, a deeper respect for comics as a challenging artistic form and sharper reading skills to use when enjoying new comics." Publ Wkly

Includes bibliographical references

Hickman, Troy

Common Grounds: Baker's dozen. Image Comics/Top Cow Productions 2004 2004p il pa $14.99

Grades: 9 10 11 12 Adult   741.5
1. Graphic novels 2. Superhero graphic novels

ISBN 1-58240-436-4

Superheroes and supervillains need a place where they can relax, unwind, and not worry about the next battle. Common Grounds is just such a place a chain of coffee shops with bakery counters, totally neutral ground. Here, hero and villain can relax and take a break in the restroom ("Head Games"), a teenage superhero who doubts herself and an older superpowered religious Jew can encourage each other ("Sanctuary"), a group of overweight heroes can meet ("Fat Chance"), or formerly evil monsters can get custom takeout and shoot the breeze ("Where Monsters Dine"). The book includes a baker's dozen (thirteen) stories.

Hinds, Gareth, 1971-

Beowulf; adapted and illustrated by Gareth Hinds. Candlewick Press 2007 unp il $21.99; pa $9.99 *

Grades: 9 10 11 12   741.5
1. Beowulf 2. Graphic novels

ISBN   978-0-7636-3022-5;   0-7636-3022-5;
978-0-7636-3023-2 (pa); 0-7636-3023-3 (pa)
LC 2006-49023

Graphic novel adaptation of the Old English epic poem, Beowulf.

"For fantasy fans both young and old, this makes an ideal introduction to a story without which the entire fantasy genre would look very different; many scenes may be too intense for very young readers." Publ Wkly

Hornschemeier, Paul

Mother, come home; with an introduction by Thomas Tennant. Dark Horse 2004 unp il pa $14.95

Grades: 9 10 11 12   741.5
1. Graphic novels 2. Mental illness—Graphic novels

ISBN 1-59307-037-3

In this "story, a young child struggles with the death of his mother and his father's collapse. Clean-lined artwork leaves plenty of room for strong emotional content linked to themes of euthanasia, suicide, and depression." Booklist

Inada, Shiho

Ghost hunt, Vol. 1; manga by Shiho Inada; story by Fuyumi Ono; translated by Akira Tsubasa; adapted by David Walsh; lettered by Foltz Design. Del Rey Manga 2005 216p il pa $10.95

Grades: 8 9 10 11 12 Adult   741.5

Inada, Shiho—*Continued*
1. Graphic novels 2. Manga 3. Shojo manga 4. Horror graphic novels
ISBN 0-345-48624-2

A decrepit old building stands on the campus of Mai's high school; every time the school tries to demolish it, unexplained accidents occur. Finally, the school hires a psychic researcher, and when Mai accidentally injures his assistant and damages an expensive camera, Shibuya (the researcher) insists she work off her debt by helping him. A miko (Shinto priestess), a Buddhist monk, and a Roman Catholic exorcist also come—but none of their methods work to stop the strange occurrences. Despite herself, Mai gets drawn into the investigation. This is the first of an ongoing manga series that provides some ghostly thrills without graphic violence, bad language, or sexual innuendo.

Jolley, Dan
JSA: the liberty files. DC Comics 2004 258p il pa $19.95
Grades: 9 10 11 12   **741.5**
1. Batman (Comic strip) 2. Graphic novels 3. World War, 1939-1945—Graphic novels 4. Superhero graphic novels 5. Comic books, strips, etc.
ISBN 1-4012-0203-9   LC 2003-267212

"Originally published in single magazine form in JSA: the liberty file #1-2, JSA: the unholy three #1-2"—Verso of title page

Set during World War II, Batman teams up with the Clock and the Owl in Egypt to locate Jack the Grin, who may have information regarding a Nazi superweapon called the Super-man.

"The action stays hot and heavy, through WWII and into cold war H-bomb espionage. . . . This Batman is a domineering, rather paranoid good guy in a dangerous world that Harris' active compositions and sharp lines, colored in dark shades lit by explosions, make more exciting than, to date, Batman movies have been." Booklist

Jones, Gerard
Men of tomorrow; geeks, gangsters and the birth of the comic book. Basic Books 2004 320p il $26; pa $15 *
Grades: 11 12 Adult   **741.5**
1. Comic books, strips, etc. 2. Cartoonists
ISBN 0-465-03656-2; 0-465-03657-0 (pa)
LC 2004-9031

This book tells "the surprising story of the young Jewish misfits, hustlers and nerds who invented the superhero and the comic book industry. . . . Springing unheralded out of working-class Jewish immigrant neighborhoods in the depths of the Depression, these young men transformed an odd mix of geekdom, science fiction, and outsider yearnings into blue-eyed chisel-nosed crime-fighters and adventurers who quickly captured the mainstream imagination. . . . He chronicles how the comics sparked a frightened counterattack that nearly destroyed the industry in the 1950's and how later they surged back at an underground level, to inspire a new generation to transmute those long-ago fantasies into art, literature, blockbuster movies and graphic novels." Publisher's note

Kelso, Megan, 1968-
The squirrel mother; stories. Fantagraphics 2006 147p il pa $16.95
Grades: 10 11 12   **741.5**
1. Graphic novels
ISBN 1-56097-746-9; 978-1-56097-746-9

This is a "collection of graphic short stories, all of which originally appeared in various magazines and anthologies between 2000 and 2005. Kelso's work is characterized by subject matter that fits roughly into two disparate camps: personal and semi-autobiographical stories that draw heavily on the details of her childhood and adolescence and stories about the idea of America and American history, such as a trilogy of short pieces about Alexander Hamilton." Publisher's note

"Beautifully packaged, this is a gem of a collection." Publ Wkly

Kibuishi, Kazu
Daisy Kutter; the last train. Viper Comics 2005 190p il pa $10.95 *
Grades: 9 10 11 12   **741.5**
1. Graphic novels 2. Adventure graphic novels 3. Science fiction graphic novels
ISBN 0-9754193-2-3; 978-0-9754193-2-8

Daisy Kutter lives in a world where high tech weapons, machines, and sentient robots coexist with humans in communities that resemble towns in the American Old West. Daisy was a war hero, then an outlaw (a good one), and now she runs a general store and plays Texas Hold 'Em poker. The owner of a train asks her to rob it to test his new security, and Daisy is forced to take the job when she loses her store in a poker game. Only when she's in the middle of her job does she realize the owner has set an elaborate trap to kill her. The action and violence never exceeds what one can see on network television.

Kirkman, Robert
Invincible: ultimate collection, Vol. 1. Image Comics 2005 400p il $34.95
Grades: 9 10 11 12   **741.5**
1. Graphic novels 2. Superhero graphic novels
ISBN 1-58240-500-X

Originally published as Invincible, issues #1-13

High school senior Mark Grayson develops super powers, but it's only logical because his father is superhero Omni-Man. Soon enough Mark gets a costume, a mask, and a name—Invincible. He also joins a team of teenage superheroes as they track down the person who is turning fellow students into walking bombs. Then Mark learns that evil sometimes wears the face of someone familiar, someone respected, and loved. And he'll need all the power he can muster to save himself—and Earth. This edition includes extra features, including a sketchbook section.

"The story is compelling, presenting teenage melodrama without a trace of condescension, and even the inevitable superhero-crush-on-a-girl-he-can-never-have subplot receives a fresh spin." Voice Youth Advocates

Kishimoto, Masashi, 1974-
Naruto. vol. 1, The tests of the Ninja; story and art by Masashi Kishimoto; [English adaptation by Jo Duffy] Viz 2003 186p il (Shonen jump graphic novel) pa $7.95
Grades: 9 10 11 12   **741.5**
1. Graphic novels 2. Manga 3. Shonen manga
ISBN 1-56931-900-6; 978-1-56931-900-0
First published 1999 in Japan
Volume one of an ongoing series; "This graphic novel contains material that was originally published in English in Shonen jump #6-10" Verso of title page
"Teen orphan Naruto wants to become the greatest ninja of all, despite the fact that most people in his village have despised him from birth because of a terrible demon has been imprisoned in his body. . . . Teens love this series." Voice Youth Advocates

Klein, Grady
The Lost Colony Book 1; the Snodgrass conspiracy. First Second Books 2006 119p il pa $14.95
Grades: 8 9 10 11 12 Adult   **741.5**
1. Graphic novels 2. United States—History—1783-1865—Graphic novels 3. Humorous graphic novels
ISBN 1-59643-097-4
Life is good on the Island, off the maps and isolated from the rest of the country. Then Mr. Stoop stumbles upon the place and puts up posters advertising a slave auction in a nearby port. Little Birdy Snodgrass, fed up with doing all the chores because of her new little brother, decides to go buy a slave and sneaks off the island. In the meantime, wealthy eccentric Rex Carter is trying to invent a machine that will replace slaves. Chaos ensues when his invention gets into the wrong hands. Klein uses racial epithets on one page to show how banal and stupid they are. He populates the Island with a mixed group of ethnicities and uses his story to confront stereotypes.
"At first glance, this novel appears to be a cartoony rendition of America in the nineteenth century, but it quickly proves to be chock full of insight into the controversies of the past." Voice Youth Advocates

Kotegawa, Yua, 1975-
Line; editor, Javier Lopez; translator, Kaoru Bertrand. ADV Manga 2006 168p il pa $9.99
Grades: 10 11 12   **741.5**
1. Graphic novels 2. Manga 3. Suicide—Graphic novels
ISBN 1-4139-0249-9
Chiko is just another Tokyo high school student, but then one morning she finds a cell phone on the subway. When the phone rings and she answers it, the caller says she has only minutes to stop a suicide. It's got to be a crank call, right? But within minutes a fellow student has jumped from the subway station roof. The caller calls again and gives Chiko fifteen minutes to get to the Shibuya station; but someone dies before she can get there. After the third death, which Chiko and her classmate Bando witness from the next building over, the caller tells her that she's the last hope to stop people from committing suicide; and for that night, Chiko and Bando run all over Tokyo to stop the deaths if they can. This is a one-volume manga full of intense action and some harsh language.

Kubo, Tite, 1977-
Bleach, Vol. 1; [story and art by Tite Kubo; English adaptation, Lance Caselman; translation, Joe Yamazaki] Viz Shonen Jump 2004 190p il pa $7.95
Grades: 9 10 11 12   **741.5**
1. Graphic novels 2. Manga 3. Shonen manga 4. Supernatural graphic novels 5. Adventure graphic novels
ISBN 1-59116-441-9
Teenage Ichigo Kurasaki has always been able to see ghosts, but that never really affected his life, until the night a Hollow, an evil spirit that preys on humans, attacks him. Soul Reaper Rukia Kuchiki tries to help Ichigo save himself and his family, but somehow he manages to absorb all her powers. Now he's a Soul Reaper, and he must work to protect the innocent from the Hollows. This is the first volume of an ongoing manga series that is full of fighting action and irreverent humor.

Kuper, Peter, 1958-
The jungle; [based on the story by] Upton Sinclair; adapted by Peter Kuper; co-writer, Emily Russell. ComicsLit 2004 46p il $15.95; pa $10.95
Grades: 9 10 11 12   **741.5**
1. Graphic novels
ISBN 1-56163-404-2; 1-56163-411-5 (pa)
           LC 2004-53095
First published 1991 by First Publishing
"Jurgis and his family have immigrated to America from Lithuania, settled in Chicago, and found jobs in the meatpacking plant. The family seems to be living the American dream: having their own home, and a means of support, even if the work is hard and disgusting. Peter Kuper's dark, colored, cartoon-style illustrations, framed in black, bring to life Sinclair's original work and highlight the atrocities perpetuated upon the Rudkus family." Libr Media Connect

The metamorphosis; {based on the story by} Franz Kafka; adapted by Peter Kuper. Crown 2003 77p il hardcover o.p. pa $10.95
Grades: 9 10 11 12   **741.5**
1. Graphic novels
ISBN 1-4000-4795-1; 1-4000-5298-8 (pa)
           LC 2003-273589
"Gregor Samsa wakes up and discovers he has been changed into a giant cockroach. Thus begins 'The Metamorphosis,' and Kuper translates this story masterfully with his scratchboard illustrations. The text is more spare, but the visuals are so strongly rendered that little of the original is changed or omitted." SLJ

Sticks and stones; an epic in pictures. Three Rivers Press 2004 unp il pa $13.95
Grades: 9 10 11 12   **741.5**
1. Graphic novels 2. Stories without words
ISBN 1-4000-5257-2   LC 2004-45969

Kuper, Peter, 1958-—_Continued_
"A stone giant is born from a volcano and demands the fealty of the people around him. He makes them build him a stone castle; then he discovers a nearby peaceful village made entirely of wood and sets about conquering it and plundering its resources. Meanwhile, a small resistance front develops, led by a woman from the stone tribe and a boy from the wood tribe, and eventually the stone empire and its despot meet a grim fate. Kuper's narrative is beautifully constructed, from its grand sweep to its minute details." Publ Wkly

Larson, Gary
The far side. Andrews & McMeel 1982 unp il pa $8.95
Grades: 9 10 11 12   741.5
1. Comic books, strips, etc.
ISBN 0-8362-1200-2   LC 82-72418
A collection of Larson's Far side cartoons

The prehistory of the Far side; a 10th anniversary exhibit. Andrews & McMeel 1989 288p il pa $14.95 hardcover o.p.
Grades: 9 10 11 12   741.5
1. Comic books, strips, etc.
ISBN 0-8362-1851-5   LC 89-84813
Retrospective of Larson's work that includes childhood drawings, and stories that evolved into Far side cartoons

Lash, Batton
Tales of supernatural law. Exhibit A Press 2005 184p il pa $16.95
Grades: 9 10 11 12 Adult   741.5
1. Graphic novels 2. Humorous graphic novels 3. Supernatural graphic novels 4. Lawyers—Graphic novels
ISBN 0-9633954-9-1
This volume reprints the first eight issues of the ongoing comics series that used to be called Wolff & Byrd, Counselors of the Macabre and is now called Supernatural Law. Alanna Wolff and Jeff Byrd provide legal services for monsters, vampires, zombies, ghosts, and other things that go bump in the night. In these stories, they help a couple who foolishly used a monkey's paw to make wishes, another couple whose house becomes haunted every full moon, a supermodel seeking redress for a curse, a horror television host accused of exposing children to violence, a swamp monster who would like his fifteen minutes of fame, and the interdimensional being Th'Lulu.

Lat
Kampung boy. First Second 2006 141p il pa $16.95 *
Grades: 8 9 10 11 12   741.5
1. Malaysia—Graphic novels 2. Family life—Graphic novels 3. Muslims—Graphic novels 4. Graphic novels
ISBN 1-59643-121-0   LC 2005-34135
First published 1979 in Malaysia with title: Lat, the kampung boy

"Malaysian cartoonist Lat uses the graphic novel format to share the story of his childhood in a small village, or kampung. From his birth and adventures as a toddler to the enlargement of his world as he attends classes in the village, makes friends, and, finally, departs for a prestigious city boarding school, this autobiography is warm, authentic, and wholly engaging." Booklist

Lehman, Timothy
Manga: masters of the art. Collins Design 2005 255p il pa $24.95
Grades: 11 12 Adult   741.5
1. Cartoonists 2. Comic books, strips, etc.—Authorship
ISBN 978-0-06-083331-2; 0-06-083331-2
This is a collection of the author's interviews with 12 different manga artists, including Kia Asamiya and the four-woman collective CLAMP, in which the artists "discuss how they became interested in manga, their first published work, where they get their ideas, the creative process, tips and techniques, artistic influences, the genre itself, and much more." Publisher's note
Fans "will be fascinated by the behind-the-scenes details and the generous samples from stories that prompt seeking out more." Booklist

Lewis, A. David, 1977-
The lone and level sands; artists, Marvin Perry Mann and Jennifer Rodgers. 2nd ed. Archaia Studio 152 147p il pa $17.95
Grades: 9 10 11 12 Adult   741.5
1. Bible. O.T. Exodus—Graphic novels 2. Graphic novels 3. Egypt—History—Graphic novels
ISBN 1-932386-12-2
First published 2005 in black and white by Caption Box
Told mostly from the viewpoint of the Pharaoh, this book recounts the well-known story of the Exodus. Moses is portrayed as an old desert rascal, and Ramses II finds himself buffeted on all sides as he contends with a God who speaks through his family and friends and manipulates him to bring about the freedom of the Hebrews.
"The plot moves with inexorable tragedy toward its conclusion, but the book never reads like a catalogue of vignettes about the miseries the Egyptians and Hebrews inflicted on each other. Instead, it is a powerful, moving reconsideration of an otherwise familiar tale. It is guaranteed to provoke." Voice Youth Advocates

Little, Jason
Shutterbug follies. Doubleday Graphic Novels 2002 153p il $24.95
Grades: 9 10 11 12   741.5
1. Graphic novels 2. Mystery graphic novels
ISBN 0-385-50346-6   LC 2002-727189
This novel was "originally serialized as both a weekly newspaper comic strip and a web comics serial. . . . Scrappy 18-year-old Bee is working in a New York photo lab when a picture of a naked female corpse that's not quite what it appears to be piques her interest. Her amateur investigation of its photographer leads her to an ever-deepening mystery, a friendly cab driver, a cute but

Little, Jason—*Continued*

nervous photo assistant, some scary doings with the Russian mob and finally, into deadly danger." Publ Wkly

"With nearly implausible coincidences, a dash of slapstick humor, and a few red herrings, this is a detective romp, and the ending panel leaves readers breathlessly awaiting a sequel." SLJ

Masters of American comics; essay by John Carlin; with contributions by Stanley Crouch . . . [et al.]; edited by John Carlin, Paul Karasik, and Brian Walker. Yale University Press 2005 316p il $45

Grades: 11 12 Adult　　　　　　　**741.5**

1. Comic books, strips, etc. 2. Cartoonists

ISBN 0-300-11317-X　　　　　LC 2005-19449

"This catalogue was published in conjunction with Masters of American Comics, an exhibition jointly organized by The Hammer Museum and The Museum of Contemporary Art, Los Angeles"—Verso of title page

This book focuses "on the 15 'Masters' of American comics, including George Herriman, Jack Kirby and R. Crumb. . . . Jules Feiffer, Pete Hamill and Matt Groening, among others, contribute essays on each of the artists." Publ Wkly

"Hundreds of color reproductions allow the ingenuity of the artists' work to speak for itself." New Yorker

Includes bibliographical references

McCloud, Scott

Making comics; storytelling secrets of comics, manga, and graphic novels. HarperCollins 2006 264p il pa $22.95 *

Grades: 11 12 Adult　　　　　　　**741.5**

1. Comic books, strips, etc.—Authorship 2. Graphic novels—Drawing

ISBN 0-06-078094-0; 978-0-06-078094-4

The author "explores practical matters, including comics devices such as panels, word balloons, and sound effects; facial expressions and body language; the creation of convincing and evocative settings; and the different tools artists can use for the job, from pencils to computers. He also delves into the framing of images in panels, the flow of panels on a page, and the relationships between words and pictures in comics. . . . This is thoughtful, fascinating, stimulating, potentially controversial, and inspiring." Libr J

Includes bibliographical references

Reinventing comics; how imagination and technology are revolutionizing an art form. Paradox Press 2000 237p il pa $22.95 *

Grades: 11 12 Adult　　　　　　　**741.5**

1. Comic books, strips, etc. 2. Cartoons and caricatures

ISBN 0-06-095350-0　　　　　　LC 00-710457

The author maps out "'12 revolutions', which, he believes, need to take place for comics to survive and finally be recognized as a legitimate art form. The topics progress from the oldest of comic-related arguments (seeking respect) to the use of computer technology to renew and expand its audience. These brilliantly presented discussions concern comics as literature, comics as art, creators' rights, industry innovation, and public perception, among other topics." Libr J

Understanding comics; the invisible art. HarperPerennial 1994 c1993 215p il pa $22.95 *

Grades: 9 10 11 12　　　　　　　**741.5**

1. Comic books, strips, etc.

ISBN 0-06-097625-X

First published 1993 by Kitchen Sink Press

The author "traces the 3,000-year history (from Egyptian paintings on) of telling stories through pictures; describes the language of comics—its 'grammar' and 'vocabulary'; explains the use of different types of images ranging from ironic to realistic; depicts how artists convey movement and the passage of time and use various symbols as shorthand; and [seeks to demonstrate] the expressive emotional qualities of different drawing styles." Booklist [review of 1993 edition]

Includes bibliographical references

Medley, Linda

Castle waiting. Fantagraphics 2006 456p il $29.95 *

Grades: 5 6 7 8 9 10　　　　　　**741.5**

1. Graphic novels 2. Fairy tales

ISBN 1-56097-747-7

All of Medley's previously self-published comics are collected here in one volume for the first time. The titular castle was the home of Sleeping Beauty, whose story is retold from the viewpoint of the flibbertigibbet ladies in waiting. After the flighty princess awakens with the kiss of a handsome but not too bright prince, the castle becomes a sanctuary for various misfits. Readers will find references to many fairy tales, folk tales, and nursery rhymes in Medley's book, and her clean, clear black-and-white art reflects the works of classic illustrators such as Arthur Rackham.

Miller, Frank

Batman: the Dark Knight strikes again; {by} Frank Miller, Lynn Varley, Todd Klein, Batman created by Bob Kane. DC Comics 2002 247p il $29.95; pa $19.99

Grades: 9 10 11 12　　　　　　　**741.5**

1. Batman (Comic strip) 2. Graphic novels 3. Comic books, strips, etc. 4. Superhero graphic novels

ISBN 1-56389-844-6; 1-56389-929-9 (pa)

　　　　　　　　　　　　　　LC 2003-544916

Sequel to Batman: the Dark Knight returns (1986)

"Originally published in single magazine form as Batman: the Dark Knight strikes again 1-3." p {8}

Based on Batman comic strip

"Batman leads the opposition in a dystopian near-future when security concerns have spurred a repressive crackdown. Other costumed heroes side with either the government or Batman. . . . The book's authoritarian society resonates with the post-9/11 environment, though Miller's cheekiness dispels notions that this is serious commentary." Booklist

Miller, Steve

Scared!: how to draw fantastic horror comic characters; [by] Steve Miller and Bryan Baugh. Watson-Guptill Publications 2004 144p il pa $19.95

Grades: 9 10 11 12   **741.5**

    1. Monsters in art 2. Cartoons and caricatures 3. Drawing 4. Comic books, strips, etc.

    ISBN 0-8230-1664-1   LC 2004-112245

This book "begins with a brief history of horror comics (mostly in the U.S.), profiles of some popular illustrators, useful tips on drawing for the genre (creating 'creepy characters,' for example), and advice on references and resources. The bulk of the book is dedicated to straightforward how-to, with illustrations for a gallery of ghouls showing each character broken down into basic shapes. The approach is especially suited to YA artists just developing an interest in how comics are drawn." Booklist

Miyuki, Takahashi

Musashi #9, Vol. 1; [translation and adaptation by Tony Ogasawara] CMX Manga 2005 206p il pa $9.95

Grades: 9 10 11 12 Adult   **741.5**

    1. Graphic novels 2. Manga 3. Adventure graphic novels 4. Spies—Graphic novels

    ISBN 1-4012-0540-2

Musashi #9 is the code name for one of the top operatives of ultimate Blue, a secret organization operating independently of any government, whose goal is to maintain world peace. A teenager who displays incredible martial arts skills, wields weapons with aplomb, moves with stealth, and uses disguises, Musashi #9 protects tough teen girl Yayoi when assassins come after her, helps an ex-FBI agent save his kidnapped sister, protects a Russian scientist and his son from spies, and helps two teen boys who stumble upon terrorists targeting the Russian president. The reader discovers, along with Yayoi, that Musashi #9 is actually a girl who usually disguises herself as a boy. This is the first volume of an ongoing manga series. There's lots of action, but minimal graphic depictions of violence and little in the way of harsh language or adult content.

Moore, Alan

America's best comics. America's Best Comics 2004 185p il pa $17.95

Grades: 9 10 11 12   **741.5**

    1. Comic books, strips, etc. 2. Graphic novels 3. Superhero graphic novels

    ISBN 1-4012-0147-4   LC 2004-541180

Comics by Alan Moore and 32 collaborators

"Moore reinvigorates the superhero genre in a collection featuring a variety of quirky, satiric, occasionally sexy characters." Booklist

Watchmen; Alan Moore, writer; Dave Gibbons, illustrator/letterer; John Higgins, colorist. DC Comics 2005 various paging il $75

Grades: 9 10 11 12   **741.5**

    1. Graphic novels 2. Comic books, strips, etc. 3. Superhero graphic novels

    ISBN 1-4012-0713-8

"Originally published in single magazine form as Watchmen 1-12"—verso of title page

Issued in slipcase

This graphic novel "begins with the paranoid delusions of a half-insane hero called Rorschach. But is Rorschach really insane or has he in fact uncovered a plot to murder super-heroes and, even worse, millions of innocent civilians? On the run from the law, Rorschach reunites with his former teammates in a desperate attempt to save the world and their lives." Publisher's note

"Nearly 20 years after the original publication, 'Watchmen' shows an eerie prescience: the symmetry between current events and the conclusion of its story, concerning a villain who believes he can stave off real war by distracting the populace with a trumped-up one, and an act of mass murder perpetrated in the heart of New York City, is almost too fearful to bear." N Y Times Book Rev

Morse, Scott

The barefoot serpent. Top Shelf Productions 2003 128p il pa $14.95

Grades: 9 10 11 12   **741.5**

    1. Graphic novels 2. Hawaii—Graphic novels

    ISBN 1-891830-37-6

"A little girl journeys to Hawaii with her parents after her older brother's death. There she meets a little-boy wheeler-dealer and tags along as he hustles a mask he has carved and plays in sand and surf. Rejoining her father, she infects him with her restored spirits; the family flies home refreshed. Sandwiching that story is a child's-picture-book-like sketch of Japanese filmmaker Akira Kurosawa." Booklist

Nagatomo, Haruno

Draw your own Manga; beyond the basics; translated by Françoise White. Kodansha International 2005 111p il pa $19.95 *

Grades: 7 8 9 10   **741.5**

    1. Graphic novels—Drawing 2. Drawing

    ISBN 4-7700-2304-9; 978-4-7700-2304-9

Also available: Draw your own Manga; all the basics (2003)

"This advanced manual looks at how to enhance manga with a range of special effects as well as how to use various types of color ink, markers, and airbrushes to reach more creative levels. Supplemented by an interview with the immensely popular Japanese sports manga artist Shinji Mizushima, this book is recommended for any cartoon or animation library." Libr J

Nibot, Root

Banana Sunday; written by Root Nibot; illustrated by Colleen Coover; book design by Keith Wood; edited by James Lucas Jones. Oni Press 2006 105p il pa $11.95

Grades: 6 7 8 9 10 11 12   **741.5**

    1. Graphic novels 2. Humorous graphic novels 3. Monkeys—Graphic novels 4. High school students—Graphic novels

    ISBN 1-932664-37-8   LC 2006-280742

Nibot, Root—*Continued*

Originally published as a four-part miniseries.

Kirby Steinberg is the new student at Forest Edge High School, but that's the least of her problems. She's also the guardian of three talking monkeys, who are ostensibly subjects of her scientist father's research. Caring for pompous Chuck, flirty Knobby, and Go Go (who likes to sleep and eat) makes life hard for Kirby, but her new friend Nickels (school newspaper reporter) has also decided there's more to these monkeys and she's determined to find their secret.

Nonaka, Eiji

Cromartie High School, Vol. 1; [translated by Brendan Frayne] ADV Manga 2005 158p il pa $10.95

Grades: 10 11 12 Adult   **741.5**

1. Graphic novels 2. Manga 3. Humorous graphic novels 4. High school students—Graphic novels
ISBN 1-4139-0257-X

Takashi Kamiyama enrolled at Cromartie High School, the worst high school in Tokyo, to help a friend, who then flunked the entrance exam. Now he's stuck in a school filled with juvenile delinquents, street toughs, and some very strange characters. They include a shirtless guy who looks like Freddy Mercury and never says anything, a gorilla who is smarter than everyone else, and Mechazawa, who looks like a canister-shaped robot. American readers may not be aware that, in Japan, students must pass entrance exams to get into the high school of their choice. It doesn't matter how rich your family is if you can't pass an entrance exam with a high enough score to get into a top school. This is the first volume of an ongoing manga full of wacky and sometimes deadpan humor.

Nowak, Naomi, 1984-

Unholy kinship. NBM 2006 unp il pa $9.95

Grades: 10 11 12 Adult   **741.5**

1. Graphic novels 2. Sisters—Graphic novels 3. Mental illness—Graphic novels 4. Dreams—Graphic novels
ISBN 1-56163-482-4

Young college student Luca has taken care of her mentally unstable older sister Gae ever since their single mother became a permanent resident of St. Mark's Asylum for the Demented. As the fall term starts, Luca starts having strange dreams as Gae begins to deteriorate emotionally. The doctors and nurses from St. Mark's Asylum claim they want to help Gae, but their drugs make things worse. And the dreams become stranger, until Luca can't be sure what is real. The cool tones of the artwork underscore the building sense of doom as the story progresses.

O, Se-Yong, 1955-

Buja's diary. NBM 2005 280p il pa $19.95

Grades: 11 12 Adult   **741.5**

1. Graphic novels 2. Korea (South)—Graphic novels
ISBN 1-56163-448-4; 978-1-56163-448-4

LC 2005-50519

The thirteen "stories by this Korean 'manwha' (comic book) author relate poignant tales of distressed humanity

struggling with family, history, and culture. . . . Although O's eye is not unsympathetic, the world he depicts is unforgiving, sometimes graphically so. . . . Originally published in 1995, this book is a thoughtful examination of the human condition in the Korea of the recent past as well as universally." Voice Youth Advocates

O'Neil, Dennis, 1939-

The DC comics guide to writing comics; introduction by Stan Lee. Watson-Guptill 2001 128p il $19.95 *

Grades: 11 12 Adult   **741.5**

1. Comic books, strips, etc.—Authorship
ISBN 0-8230-1027-9   LC 2001-26101

The author "discusses story structure, characterization, script preparation, and other general writing topics. He also covers those more specific to comics writing such as miniseries, maxiseries, and continuity. O'Neil addresses the visual component of the art, the importance of page layout, and the relationship between the writer and the artist." SLJ

"O'Neil addresses the universals of writing in a way that makes the book useful to all aspiring scripters, regardless of their knowledge of comics." Booklist

Pilcher, Tim

The essential guide to world comics; [by] Tim Pilcher, Brad Brooks. Collins & Brown, Distributed in the U.S. by Sterling 2005 319p il pa $19.95 *

Grades: 11 12 Adult   **741.5**

1. Comic books, strips, etc.
ISBN 1-84340-300-5

The authors "examine the cultural impact of comics in over 20 countries, from Japan—where popular titles sell 6.5 million copies per week—to France, where comics are considered an art from on par with music and poetry." Publisher's note

"A stunning eye-opener to the comics medium's variety." Booklist

Rodionoff, Hans

Lovecraft; from a screenplay written by Hans Rodionoff; adapted by Keith Giffen; illustrated by Enrique Breccia; lettered by Todd Klein. DC Comics 2003 ca.140p il hardcover o.p. pa $17.95

Grades: 9 10 11 12   **741.5**

1. Lovecraft, H. P. (Howard Phillips), 1890-1937 2. Graphic novels 3. Horror graphic novels
ISBN 1-4012-0110-5; 1-4012-0143-1 (pa)

LC 2004-271756

"When young Howard Phillips Lovecraft becomes the reluctant guardian of the Necronomicon, an accursed book that is the doorway to the beyond, his life veers into strange territory. From an odd upbringing through his later success as a weaver of 'weird' tales, Lovecraft maintains a tenuous balance between reality and the bizarre nightmares of his 'fictional' horror." Publisher's note

"Cthulhu Mythos fans who aren't pedantic nitpickers will enjoy the way the book blends bits of biographical detail with Lovecraft's frightening fictional concepts to create a grotesque and disturbing visual experience." Publ Wkly

Roman, Dave

Agnes Quill; an anthology of mystery; all transcripts written by Dave Roman; illustrated by Jason Ho, Raina Telgemeier, Jeff Zornow and Dave Roman. SLG Publishing 2006 130p il pa $10.95

Grades: 7 8 9 10 11 12   **741.5**
   1. Graphic novels 2. Mystery graphic novels 3. Horror graphic novels
   ISBN 978-1-59362-052-3

Orphaned teen Agnes Quill lives in the city of Legerdemain and carries on a family tradition; she can see and communicate with ghosts, and she works as a detective to help them. Her cases range from recovering the mummified head of a ghost's old body in order to save the valuable necklace hidden there, to helping a little girl ghost find her doll, to helping a man find his legs, and more. Roman works with artists including Raina Telgemeier, and their styles range from childlike cartoons to gloomy, atmospheric art fulll of shadows.

"The variety of drawing styles and Agnes' story of being a teenage detective who can see the dead among the living combine in an interesting read that will likely keep readers' attention." Voice Youth Advocates

Sable, Mark

Grounded, Vol. 1: Powerless; writer/creator, Mark Sable; artist, Paul Azaceta. Image Comics 2006 160p il pa $14.99

Grades: 10 11 12 Adult   **741.5**
   1. Graphic novels 2. Superhero graphic novels 3. High school students—Graphic novels
   ISBN 978-1-58240-641-1

Originally published as a comics miniseries

Ever since he was a little boy, Jonathan just knew that superheroes are real, and that he would eventually come into his power. Now he's in high school, and he has just discovered that he was right all along superheroes are real. In fact, his parents are two of the most famous heroes in the world. Disillusionment sets in when he catches his father in bed with another woman. He also has to face the fact that he has no powers at all, which doesn't help when his parents put him into a school for the children of heroes; he's the only one who doesn't have any. Even as he deals with bullying and nasty pranks, he learns that there's a dark side to the powers.

Sacks, Adam

Salmon doubts. Alternative Comics 2004 128p il pa $14.95

Grades: 10 11 12 Adult   **741.5**
   1. Graphic novels 2. Salmon—Graphic novels
   ISBN 1-89186-771-7

Geoff, an introverted salmon, struggles all his life from hatching to the homecoming upriver to spawn; he experiences all the things any teenager does during puberty—questioning authority, wondering about his purpose in life, worrying about body image, wondering if that pretty salmon likes him or not . . .

"Using only cool underwater tones of blue and purple, Sacks somehow manages to convey the vividness and vibrancy of submerged life just by the reaction of his main character." Voice Youth Advocates

Sakai, Stan

Usagi Yojimbo, book one. Fantagraphics Books 1999 144p il pa $15.95

Grades: 9 10 11 12   **741.5**
   1. Graphic novels 2. Adventure graphic novels
   ISBN 0-930193-35-0; 978-0-930193-35-5
                        LC 93-239124

First published 1987

Vol. 1 of a 20-book series; Vols. 1-7 published by Fantagraphics; Vols. 8-20 published by Dark Horse Comics

This series contains the adventures of Miyamoto Usagi, a ronin samurai rabbit in 17th-century Japan.

Sfar, Joann

The professor's daughter; [story by] Joann Sfar & [illustrated by] Emmanuel Guibert; translated by Alexis Siegel. First Second Books 2007 63p il pa $16.95

Grades: 7 8 9 10 11 12 Adult   **741.5**
   1. Graphic novels 2. Humorous graphic novels 3. Romance graphic novels 4. Mummies—Graphic novels
   ISBN 978-1-59643-130-0 (pa); 1-59643-130-X (pa)
                        LC 2006-22177

In Victorian London, Lillian, the daughter of a famed archeologist, has fallen in love with the mummy of Imhotep IV; he thinks that Lillian bears a strong resemblance to this long-dead wife. Their love faces many obstacles, from Lillian's father, the police, a pirate who is actually Imhotep III (yes, the father and another mummy), even Queen Victoria herself. Dainty Victorian manners mix with broad farce and black comedy in a beautifully illustrated book with muted colors and sepia tones.

The rabbi's cat. Pantheon Books 2005 142p il $21.95; pa $16.95

Grades: 9 10 11 12   **741.5**
   1. Graphic novels 2. Cats—Graphic novels 3. Judaism—Graphic novels
   ISBN 0-375-42281-1; 0-375-71464-2 (pa)
                        LC 2004-61406

"A slinky gray cat lives with a rabbi and his beautiful young daughter. One day, the feline eats their parrot, only to find that he has gained the bird's ability to talk. Witty and highly intelligent, the cat immediately decides that he wants to learn more about Judaism, from the Kabbalah to the Torah. . . . There is plenty for teens to like—humor, romance, and theological questioning combined with a folkloric quality to bring to life a multifaceted work." SLJ

Vampire loves; color by Audré Jardel; translation by Alexis Siegel. First Second Books 2006 187p il pa $16.95

Grades: 9 10 11 12 Adult   **741.5**
   1. Graphic novels 2. Vampires—Graphic novels 3. Romance graphic novels
   ISBN 978-1-59643-093-8; 1-59643-093-1
                        LC 2005-21498

First published in four volumes in France with title: Grand vampire

When the vampire Ferdinand breaks up with Lani, his cheating girlfriend, he starts looking for love and ro-

Sfar, Joann—*Continued*

mance. In the process he meets the vampire sisters Ritaline and Aspirine, tries his hand at detective work, goes on a cruise and meets the ghost, Sigh, and gets mixed up in a fight between mummy pirates and Professor Joseph Bell.

"Edgy and creepy but at the same time universal and normal, Vampire Loves is a unique study in contrasts that will be a pleasurable discovery for graphic novel enthusiasts." Voice Youth Advocates

Sizer, Paul

Moped army, Vol. 1. Cafe Digital Comics 2005 136p il pa $12.95

Grades: 11 12 Adult   741.5

1. Graphic novels 2. Science fiction graphic novels
ISBN 0-9768565-4-9; 978-0-9768565-4-2

This graphic novel is set in the same universe as Little White Mouse (2005). "Feeling unsatisfied with her circumscribed life and rich, cruel boyfriend, a privileged teenaged girl runs away to the lower city where the poor dwell, finding a home and a new 'family' among the young rebels who call themselves the Moped Army. Even readers who don't like science fiction will enjoy this story that depends on strong characterization." Voice Youth Advocates

Stassen, Jean-Philippe

Deogratias; a tale of Rwanda; [by] Stassen; translated by Alex Siegel. Roaring Brook 2006 79p il pa $17.95

Grades: 11 12 Adult   741.5

1. Rwanda—Graphic novels 2. Graphic novels
ISBN 1-59643-103-2; 978-1-59643-103-4

LC 2005-17576

In this "fictionalized account of the Rwandan genocide, readers meet Deogratias, a teenaged Hutu. His friends Benina and Apollinaria are Tutsi—a race that is being ethnically cleansed by Hutu extremists. As the conflict escalates, Deogratias witnesses murders and is forced to become involved in brutal acts of violence. He suffers a mental breakdown. The story is told through a series of flashbacks while he skates the line between rational and insane. Stassen spares his readers none of the brutality and visceral cruelties of this atrocity. Scenes of rape, harsh language, and some sexual content solidly designate this book for a mature audience. . . . A masterful work with vibrant, confident art, this book will stay with and haunt its readers." SLJ

Sturm, James, 1965-

James Sturm's America; God, gold, and golems. Drawn & Quarterly 2007 192p il $24.95

Grades: 10 11 12 Adult   741.5

1. Graphic novels 2. United States—History—Graphic novels 3. Gold mines and mining—Graphic novels 4. Baseball—Graphic novels 5. Revivals—Graphic novels
ISBN 978-1-897299-05-0

This book compiles three of Sturm's stories that are set in quieter periods of American history, during relatively peaceful non-war and pre-Depression times. "The Revival," set around 1801, portrays frontier life and early religious revival movements as a couple makes their way from Ohio westward and stop off at a camp where people push themselves into religious frenzies. "Hundreds of Feet Below Daylight" examines the people who continue gold mining after the euphoria has died down and life becomes tough. Some readers may be shocked by the brutality exhibited by some of the miners who so desperately hunt for money. "The Golem's Mighty Swing" features a Jewish professional baseball team traveling the country just trying to get by in the 1920s. Facing racial and religious taunts and sometimes violence, they try a gimmick—disguising their African American player as a golem—in order to generate ticket sales.

"Social issues, including racial prejudice and intolerance, poverty, and family dynamics, are broached via both plot and character. . . . This [is] an easy crossover graphic novel for readers who enjoy American history made into well-told stories." Booklist

Suenobu, Keiko

Life, Vol. 1; created by Keiko Suenobu; [translation Michelle Kobayashi; English adaptation, Darcy Lockman] Tokyopop 2006 unp il pa $9.99

Grades: 10 11 12 Adult   741.5

1. Graphic novels 2. Manga 3. Shojo manga 4. Self-mutilation—Graphic novels 5. High school students—Graphic novels
ISBN 1-59532-931-5   LC 2006-285451

Ayumu and her best friend Shii-chan (Shinozuka) study for their high school entrance exam; Ayumu needs help to study because she wants to get a high score to join Shii-chan. While cramming, Ayumu jabs herself with her compass point, using the pain to help her focus. While she succeeds, Shii-chan doesn't do as well on the exam; she blames Ayumu and breaks off with her. Now in a school full of strangers and struggling to keep up, Ayumu eases her loneliness by cutting herself. The book includes an epilogue by licensed clinical psychologist Susan M. Axtell, who provides advice and helpful web links.

"The visuals of Ayumu cutting herself are fairly graphic and make this book more suitable for older teen readers. The pain felt by the characters is palpable and affecting." Voice Youth Advocates

The **Superhero** book; the ultimate encyclopedia of comic-book icons and Hollywood heroes; edited by Gina Misiroglu with David A. Roach. Visible Ink Press 2004 xxi, 725p il $29.95

Grades: 7 8 9 10   741.5

1. Cartoons and comics 2. Superheroes (Fictional characters) 3. Motion pictures
ISBN 0-7808-0772-3   LC 2004-19059

This is an "encyclopedic reference work that profiles superheroes from all companies and in all media. . . . Its 300 full entries provide information on more than 1,000 mythic overachievers, covering . . . comic book, movie, television, and novel superheroes." Publisher's note

This "is a must-buy for comic readers interested in knowing the early roots and conceptions of comic-book heroes." SLJ

Talbot, Bryan, 1952-
The tale of one bad rat. Dark Horse 1995 unp il pa $14.95
Grades: 11 12 Adult 741.5
1. Child sexual abuse—Graphic novels 2. Runaway teenagers—Graphic novels 3. Graphic novels
ISBN 1-56971-127-5; 978-1-56971-077-7
"This book collects issues one through four of the Dark Horse comic-book series, The tale of one bad rat" Verso of title page
This book's "heroine is teenager Helen Potter, who has run away from an abusive father and whose path to recovery takes her from a squat in London to refuge at an inn in the British countryside. Along the way, she meets characters and situations that Talbot derives from the work of Helen's namesake, Beatrix Potter, whose life he symbolically links to Helen's. Talbot's vivid, realistic full-color illustration brilliantly evokes the story's settings, yet even more effective are his compassionate characterizations." Booklist

Tanabe, Yellow
Kekkaishi, Vol. 1. Viz Action 2005 192p il pa $9.99
Grades: 9 10 11 12 Adult 741.5
1. Graphic novels 2. Manga 3. Shonen manga 4. Supernatural graphic novels
ISBN 1-59116-968-2
Junior high student Yoshimori Sumimura is a kekkaishi, a demon hunter; it's the family business. The Yukimuras next door are also kekkaishi, rivals of the Sumimuras. Their daughter Tokine is also a demon hunter. Yoshimori would much rather become a pastry chef, but he can't let Tokine always get the demons. This is the first of an ongoing manga series that has lots of demon hunting action but not too much violence, and considerable humor.

TenNapel, Douglas R.
Iron West. Image Comics 2006 160p il pa $14.99
Grades: 8 9 10 11 12 Adult 741.5
1. Graphic novels 2. Science fiction graphic novels 3. Western stories—Graphic novels
ISBN 978-1-58240-630-5
Preston Struck has worked as a con artist and crooked gambler, but when he encounters a horde of technological killers while escaping bounty hunters, he discovers an unfortunate streak of responsibility. Awakened by greedy miners, an alien artifact has begun manufacturing humanoid form robots to kill every human, starting with the town of Twain Harte. Aided by a wizened shaman, a Sasquatch, and the not-too-trusting sheriff, Struck reluctantly sets out to stop the killer robots.
TenNapel uses well-worn cliches of American Westerns and turns them on their heads, including Native American stereotypes, the saloon gal with a heart of gold. The level of violence is similar to that seen in any classic Western movie (think John Wayne films). "This finely balanced piece of work is polished with style." Voice Youth Advocates

Trudeau, G. B. (Garry B.), 1948-
The long road home. Andrews McMeel Pub. 2005 93p il (A Doonesbury book) pa $9.95
Grades: 11 12 Adult 741.5
1. Doonesbury (Comic strip) 2. Comic books, strips, etc.
ISBN 0-7407-5385-1; 978-0-7407-5385-5
LC 2004-116364
A collection of the Doonesbury strips from a seven month period that chronicle the wounding of B.D. in Iraq and his experiences along the road to rehabilitation.
"Trudeau is a great comic writer whose devotion to politics and capacity for moral outrage are apparently undiminished . . . but he is a great comic writer first, with the intellectual honesty that implies." N Y Times Book Rev

Watsuki, Nobuhiro, 1970-
Buso Renkin, Vol. 1; story & art by Nobuhiro Watsuki; [translation and English adaptation, Mayumi Kobayashi; touch-up art & lettering, James Gaubatz] Viz Shonen Jump Advanced 2006 188p il pa $7.99
Grades: 10 11 12 Adult 741.5
1. Graphic novels 2. Manga 3. Shonen manga 4. Fantasy graphic novels
ISBN 978-1-4215-0615-9
High school student Kazuki Muto thought he was saving a girl from a monster, but actually Tokiko saved Kazuki's life. They had been attacked by a homunculus, a malevolent creature who was disguised as a teacher. Homunculi attach themselves to people's brains, and the only thing that can kill them is a weapon called a buso renkin. Tokiko had to implant a kakugane into Kazuki's heart to save him; the alchemical device can become a buso renkin—but Kazuki has no idea how to wield it. Now he and Tokiko team up to hunt the homunculi overrunning his school. The series features a lot of monsters and monster fighting action.

Rurouni Kenshin; Meiji swordsman romantic story. vol. 1; [English adaptation, Gerard Jones; translation, Kenichiro Yagi] Viz Comics 2003 196p il (Shonen Jump graphic novel) pa $7.95
Grades: 10 11 12 741.5
1. Graphic novels 2. Manga 3. Shonen manga
ISBN 1-59116-220-3
Volume one of an ongoing series
"The story of a young wandering samurai—who bears a reverse blade sword and strives not to kill after seeing and committing much bloodshed in the battles to bring the Emperor back to power in 1868—becomes much more than mere historical saga. Kenshin's relationships with new and old friends and enemies makes compelling storytelling." Voice Youth Advocates

Weinstein, Lauren
Girl stories; by Lauren R. Weinstein. Henry Holt 2006 237p il pa $16.95
Grades: 7 8 9 10 741.5
1. Graphic novels
ISBN 978-0-8050-7863-3; 0-8050-7863-0
LC 2005-46205

Weinstein, Lauren—*Continued*

"Smart, creative Lauren sheds her geeky rep in high school in Weinstein's collection of comic strips, which have to intimacy of a teen's diary. The color-washed sketches have an edgy quality." Booklist

Weissman, Steven

White flower day. Fantagraphics 2002 112p il pa $14.95

Grades: 9 10 11 12   741.5

1. Graphic novels 2. Humorous graphic novels

ISBN 1-56097-514-8

"Another 'Yikes' book."

Contents: I saw you; White flower day; Look out for big Della

"Scratch panels highlighted in ocher cast {a} jaundiced pall over three . . . twisted tales of rascaldom. They feature the Frankenstein-like Pullapart Boy, devilish L'il Bloody, and several equally weird young characters who venture forth to create mayhem, from innocent to morbid." Booklist

Wight, Eric, 1974-

My dead girlfriend, Vol. 1. Tokyopop 2007 unp il pa $9.99

Grades: 8 9 10 11 12 Adult   741.5

1. Graphic novels 2. Romance graphic novels 3. High school students—Graphic novels

ISBN 978-1-59816-996-6

As a perfectly normal boy, Finney Bleak stands out among the monsters and ghosts of his town and in school, Mephisto Prep. He's the youngest in a family known for the many weird and wacky ways everyone has died. In school, Finney must deal with bullies such as Karl the Frankenstein-type monster, teen vampire Drake, and others. He had one memorable night at the carnival with the perfect girl, Jenny, months ago, but she never made it to the meeting they had arranged for the next day. Now, as he's chased in the woods by Karl and company, somebody comes to his aid—it's Jenny, who's now a ghost. So, nobody's ever perfect, right? This is another global manga title, the first of a projected series.

Yang, Gene

American born Chinese; color by Lark Pien. First Second 2006 233p il pa $16.95 *

Grades: 9 10 11 12   741.5

1. Graphic novels

ISBN 978-1-59643-152-2; 1-59643-152-0 (pa)

LC 2005-58105

2006 nominee, National Book Awards Young People's Literature; 2007 Michael L. Printz Award for excellence in young adult literature

In three interconnected stories, the reader meets the Monkey King, who wants to be more than he is, Jin Wang, a Chinese American middle school student who desperately wants to fit in at his new school, and Caucasian-looking Danny, who unaccountably has an extremely stereotypically Chinese cousin, Chin-Kee, whose visit causes great embarrassment.

"True to its origin as a Web comic, this story's clear, concise lines and expert coloring are deceptively simple yet expressive. Even when Yang slips in an occasional Chinese ideogram or myth, the sentiments he's depicting need no translation. Yang accomplishes the remarkable feat of practicing what he preaches with this book: accept who you are and you'll already have reached out to others." Publ Wkly

Gordon Yamamoto and the king of the geeks. AmazeInk/SLG Publishing 2004 100p il pa $9.95

Grades: 7 8 9 10 11 12 Adult   741.5

1. Graphic novels 2. Bullies—Graphic novels 3. Humorous graphic novels

ISBN 0-943151-95-3

First published as a three-issue miniseries by Humble Comics

Gordon Yamamoto is a Japanese American teenager, but unlike the stereotypical Japanese American teen, he's not very bright, he's quite large, and he's a bully. He's been a bully most of his life, and he started a tradition; this year he "crowns" Miles the King of the Geeks with a ripe pair of undies. This year, however, something weird happens, and alien technology leaves him with Miles' memories and knowledge. When his attempt to clear his mind goes wrong and Miles' hate takes physical form, the bully and the geek need to team up to save themselves. This is one of Yang's earlier works before American Born Chinese.

Loyola Chin and the San Peligran Order. AmazeInk/SLG Publishing 2004 100p il pa $9.95

Grades: 8 9 10 11 12   741.5

1. Graphic novels 2. Science fiction graphic novels 3. Dreams—Graphic novels

ISBN 1-59362-005-5

High school sophomore Loyola Chin discovers that the food she eats before going to bed can determine where her dreams take her. Tamales with hoisin sauce put her onto a giant chessboard, while kimchee and a glass of horchata take her under the sea with angel fish. It is plain old, ordinary cornbread, however, that causes her to meet Saint Danger. He tells her he's had a vision of the future and that he has a plan to save the Earth. She learns that his solution may cause more trouble for people, and in her dream visions she begins to reconcile with her dead mother's fate. In her waking hours, she has to deal with big, goofy Gordon Yamamoto, who has a crush on her. Loyola just happens to be Chinese American. This early work by Yang follows Gordon Yamamoto and the King of the Geeks.

741.6 Graphic design, illustration and commercial art

Bancroft, Tom

Creating characters with personality; introduction by Glen Keane. Watson-Guptill 2006 160p il pa $19.95

Grades: 9 10 11 12   741.6

1. Cartoons and caricatures 2. Graphic arts

ISBN 0-8230-2349-4; 978-0-8230-2349-3

LC 2005-28462

This book "shows artists how to create a distinctive character, then place that character in context within a script, establish hierarchy, and maximize the impact of pose and expression." Publisher's note

Barnicoat, John, 1924-
Posters: a concise history. Thames and Hudson
1985 288p il (World of art) pa $11.95
Grades: 9 10 11 12   **741.6**
1. Posters—History
ISBN 0-500-20118-8   LC 88-50151
First published 1972 by Abrams with title: A concise
history of posters
"A survey of the poster art of the past century. . . .
Both text and illustration cover the subject on an international scale, with expanded coverage of works from major periods such as Art Nouveau and Surrealism, as well
as political and war posters." Libr J
Includes bibliographical references

Jude, Dick
More fantasy art masters; the best fantasy and
science fiction artists show how they work.
Watson-Guptill Publications 2003 144p il pa
$24.95
Grades: 9 10 11 12   **741.6**
1. Fantasy in art 2. Science fiction—Illustrations
ISBN 0-8230-3127-6   LC 2002-154358
Also available Fantasy art masters pa $24.95 (ISBN 0-
8230-1636-6)
First published 2002 in the United Kingdom
This "collects the work of 10 different artists in the
fantasy and science-fiction fields. . . . Some of the artists, such as Keith Parkinson, work primarily in oils,
while others choose pastel, watercolor, or digitally altered photography. . . . There is something here for almost everyone. Especially valuable is the text that accompanies the breathtaking graphics. Each artist discusses the method used to execute the images, and some of
them offer insights into what made a painting successful,
or unsuccessful for that matter." SLJ
Includes bibliographical references

742 Perspective in drawing

DuBosque, Doug
Draw 3-D; a step-by-step guide to perspective
drawing. Peel Productions 1999 63p il pa $8.99
Grades: 6 7 8 9 10   **742**
1. Perspective 2. Drawing
ISBN 0-939217-14-7   LC 98-42174
"Using easy-to-follow, step-by-step sketches,
DuBosque introduces readers to the techniques of three-
dimensional drawing. Beginning with such elementary
concepts as depth, he progresses logically through shading, reflections, and multiple vanishing points. The supportive tone encourages novices to keep trying and not
become discouraged." SLJ

743 Drawing and drawings by subject

Graves, Douglas R.
Drawing portraits. Watson-Guptill 1974 159p il
pa $16.95 hardcover o.p. *
Grades: 9 10 11 12   **743**

1. Drawing 2. Artistic anatomy
ISBN 0-8230-1431-2
The author discusses "the art and craft of portraiture
from beginning to end—seeing and drawing the anatomy
of the head and hands, posing and lighting the sitter,
conveying the weight, texture, and drape of the sitter's
clothing, composing the portrait (individual as well as
group), and dealing with such auxiliary problems as the
relationship between the artist and his sitter." Introduction
Includes bibliographical references

Hart, Christopher
Human anatomy made amazingly easy.
Watson-Guptill 2000 114p il pa $19.95 *
Grades: 11 12 Adult   **743**
1. Artistic anatomy 2. Figure drawing
ISBN 0-8230-2497-0   LC 00-43514
In this work for the beginning artist "Hart simplifies
the process in an accessible manual that concentrates on
line and forgoes the complexity of color." Libr J

745.5 Handicrafts

Arendt, Madeline
Altered art for the first time. Sterling Pub. 2005
112p il $19.95
Grades: 11 12 Adult   **745.5**
1. Handicraft
ISBN 1-4027-1655-9   LC 2005-10344
"A Sterling/Chapelle Book"
"This guide concentrates on altering books. Beginning
with complete coverage of needed and suggested materials and supplies, and taking the reader/crafter step-by-
step through a series of specific projects, Arendt shows
how to take a book and make, among other things, an attractive journal, a display for souvenirs of a special occasion, or, using a book's covers, a box for holding commemorative items. Her encouraging tone will inspire
even new crafters to venture into this rewarding activity." Booklist
Includes bibliographical references

Taylor, Terry
Altered art; techniques for creating altered
books, boxes, cards & more. Lark Books 2004
144p il $19.95 *
Grades: 11 12 Adult   **745.5**
1. Handicraft
ISBN 1-57990-550-1   LC 2004-5313
Taylor "begins with a brief history of altered art (Joseph Cornell was an early practitioner), discusses copyright issues with regard to borrowed images, then moves
straight into techniques, tools, and a . . . gallery of a variety of artists' works. The author includes a few projects
with step-by-step instructions. . . . [This book] is without a doubt one of the finest craft books available." SLJ

745.54 Paper handicrafts

Foose, Sandra Lounsbury
Simply super paper; over 50 projects to cut, curl, twist and tease from paper. Contemporary Bks. 2000 132p il pa $16.95
Grades: 11 12 Adult   **745.54**
1. Paper crafts
ISBN 0-8092-2864-5   LC 98-46895
"The book opens with information about the types of paper available and where to find them, and suggests useful tools. The crafts themselves are followed by patterns for each project. The instructions are highly detailed and sometimes complex, but most of the activities contain how-to drawings that show important details. Nicely laid-out photographs of the completed work provide a clear illustration of what crafters are working toward." SLJ

Maurer-Mathison, Diane V., 1944-
Paper art; the complete guide to papercraft techniques; [by] Diane Maurer-Mathison with Jennifer Philippoff. Watson-Guptill 1997 160p il (Watson-Guptill crafts) flexible bdg $27.50
Grades: 9 10 11 12   **745.54**
1. Paper crafts
ISBN 0-8230-3840-8   LC 97-28466
This includes a history of papermaking and describes materials and techniques for such paper arts as stamping, embossing, stenciling, spattering, marbling, ink blowing, decoupage, quilling, paper weaving, and pop-ups
Includes bibliographical references

The **Michaels** book of paper crafts; edited by Dawn Cusick & Megan Kirby; [photography, Steve Mann, Evan Bracken; contributing writers, Kelly Banner . . . et al.] Lark Books 2005 319p il $24.95 *
Grades: 11 12 Adult   **745.54**
1. Paper crafts
ISBN 1-57990-638-9   LC 2004-25211
The authors discuss "the basics of nine different paper-based crafts—from decoupage to scrapbooking to quilling . . . Once it's discovered, this won't sit on the craft shelf for long." Booklist

Sowell, Sharyn
Paper cutting techniques for scrapbooks & cards. Sterling Pub. 2005 128p il $19.95 *
Grades: 11 12 Adult   **745.54**
1. Paper crafts 2. Scrapbooks 3. Greeting cards
ISBN 1-4027-1921-3   LC 2005-15043
"A Sterling/Chapelle book"
The author shows how to "fashion delicate borders, alphabets, flowery frames, and 3D embellishments. How to use vintage papers, cut with patterns or freehand, and understand positive and negative space, are also here." Publisher's note
"Both experienced and novice paper users will learn something from this beautifully illustrated book, which is pretty enough to be an art book in and of itself." Booklist

745.58 Handicrafts from beads, found and other objects

Discover beading; compiled by Lesley Weiss. Kalmbach Books 2006 96p il pa $19.95
Grades: 9 10 11 12 Adult   **745.58**
1. Beadwork 2. Beads 3. Jewelry
ISBN 0-8711-6239-3   LC 2007-273183
All projects have appeared previously in BeadStyle magazine, except for Classic Knotted Pearls and Easy Macramé Necklace
"Focuses on using basic, beginner-friendly beading techniques to create . . . bracelets, necklaces, earrings, and more." Publisher's note
"This visually pleasing beading book for crafters is a smart purchase. . . . This book will appeal to crafting teens and adults and would be a nice addition to any size public library." Voice Youth Advocates

Taylor, Carol, 1943-
Creative bead jewelry; weaving, looming, stringing, wiring, making beads. Sterling 1995 144p il pa $18.95
Grades: 9 10 11 12   **745.58**
1. Beadwork 2. Jewelry
ISBN 0-8069-1306-1   LC 95-4595
The author provides information and gives guidance on many projects introducing different methods and designs. Color photographs and black-and-white illustrations are included

745.6 Calligraphy, illumination, heraldic design

Harris, David, 1929-
The art of calligraphy. Dorling Kindersley 1995 128p il hardcover o.p. pa $17.95 *
Grades: 11 12 Adult   **745.6**
1. Calligraphy
ISBN 1-56458-849-1; 0-75661-304-3 (pa)
                               LC 94-26722
An "introduction to a wide variety of written scripts used from Roman times to modern days. The detailed, practical instructions for 26 styles focus on step-by-step, clear visuals, as well as on the proper equipment--brushes, pens, pencils, paper, and ink. A brief history with examples from calligraphic masters introduces each style." SLJ

Marsh, Don, 1957-
Calligraphy. North Light Bks. 1996 128p (First steps series) $18.99
Grades: 11 12 Adult   **745.6**
1. Calligraphy
ISBN 0-89134-666-X   LC 96-4014
This guide to calligraphy is aimed at the beginner and includes various projects such as greeting cards and invitations
"Excellent for secondary school age and above." Libr J
Includes bibliographical references

746.43 Knitting, crocheting, tatting

Eckman, Edie, 1960-
The crochet answer book. Storey Pub. 2005 320p il pa $12.95
Grades: 11 12 Adult   **746.43**
　　1. Crocheting
　　ISBN 1-58017-598-8   LC 2005-16484
This book features "chapters on topics ranging from equipment needs to resources for more information. . . . Appended are standard crochet abbreviations, common crochet terms and phrases, standard body measurements and sizing, suggested sizes for accessories and household items, and yarn care symbols." Booklist
Includes bibliographical references

Okey, Shannon
Knitgrrl; learn to knit with 15 fun and funky projects; photography by Shannon Fagan, Christine Okey, and Tamas Jakab; illustrations by Kathleen Jacques. Watson-Guptill 2005 96p il pa $9.95 *
Grades: 7 8 9 10   **746.43**
　　1. Knitting
　　ISBN 0-8230-2618-3
This offers instructions for basic knitting techniques and for such projects as scarves, hats, leg warmers, mittens, and bags.
"A lively, teen-friendly book with all the basics, plenty of additional information, and appealing color photos and illustrations." SLJ

Knitgrrl 2; learn to knit with 16 all-new patterns; photography by Shannon Fagan, Christine Okey, and Tamas Jakab; Illustrations by Kathleen Jacques. Watson-Guptill 2006 96p il pa $9.95 *
Grades: 7 8 9 10   **746.43**
　　1. Knitting
　　ISBN 0-8230-2619-1
This offers instructions for basic knitting techniques and for projects including flipflops, book covers, a jacket collar, a headband/choker, a pencil purse, a water-bottle holder, a beauty-to-go bag, a belt, a kerchief, a cardigan, a scarf, a necklace, wrist/ankle bracelets, a poncho, a tank top, and a beach bag.
"Varied typeface and print color as well as a mix of excellent color photography and illustrations make this book fun to read and explore. Clear, step-by-step directions are extremely helpful for learning the basics." SLJ

Radcliffe, Margaret
The knitting answer book. Storey Pub. 2005 400p il pa $14.95
Grades: 11 12 Adult   **746.43**
　　1. Knitting
　　ISBN 1-58017-599-6   LC 2005-16466
Framed as a series of questions that might be asked by knitters, this manual covers knitting "materials, techniques, and resources. . . . Radcliffe answers such specific queries as 'What is the best cast-on when you're planning to add fringe to a piece?' and 'Is there a more durable cast-on I can use for children's clothes?'" Libr J

Taylor, Kathleen
Knit one, felt too; discover the magic of knitted felt with 25 easy patterns. Storey Books 2003 176p il pa $18.95
Grades: 11 12 Adult   **746.43**
　　1. Knitting
　　ISBN 1-58017-497-3   LC 2003-50558
"If you knit a loose, oversize garment and then shrink it on purpose, you have turned a wool object into felt . . . Taylor offers 25 projects, first showing how to knit the item, then how to get the desired look. The projects are quite inventive, from toddler slippers shaped like bunnies to wine bags decorated with grapes. Taylor's enthusiasm combined with the straightforward and eye-catching color photos will entice knitters." Booklist

746.46 Patchwork and quilting

Beyer, Jinny
Quiltmaking by hand; simple stitches, exquisite quilts. Breckling Press 2003 262p il pa $29.95
Grades: 11 12 Adult   **746.46**
　　1. Quilting
　　ISBN 0-9721218-2-X   LC 2003-15827
In this guide to the "traditional methods of quilt assembly—all by hand, the author begins with threading the needle and progresses to perfecting hand quilting stitches." Libr J
Includes bibliographical references

751 Techniques, procedures, apparatus, equipment, materials, forms

Clément, Serge
The joy of art; a creative guide for beginning painters; {by} Serge Clément and Marina Kamena; translated from the French by Anthony Roberts. Abrams 2000 unp il $35 *
Grades: 11 12 Adult   **751**
　　1. Painting—Technique
　　ISBN 0-8109-4225-9   LC 00-38972
Translated from an undetermined language
This "book describes the fundamentals of art, including types of painting and drawing materials, incorporating texture, organizing space, and understanding perspective. . . . Instructions are accompanied by illustrations by the creators and by reproductions of celebrated works of art to articulate specific styles and processes." Book Rep
Includes bibliographical references

Ganz, Nicholas
Graffiti world; street art from five continents; edited by Tristan Manco. H.N. Abrams 2004 376p il $35 *
Grades: 11 12 Adult   **751**
　　1. Street art 2. Graffiti
　　ISBN 0-8109-4979-2   LC 2004-4248

Ganz, Nicholas—*Continued*

Contents: History of graffiti -- Styles of graffiti -- Definition of terms -- The Americas -- Europe -- The rest of the world

Ganz's survey of graffiti art includes "upward of 2,000 full-color photographs. . . . An ephemeral, often despised, yet irrefutably powerful mode of expression, graffiti has always been political, and although many of the street artists Ganz succinctly profiles have moved away from illegal spray painting, they have not compromised the inherent subversiveness of their work. . . . Ganz's global array captures the power and synergy of this vibrant alternative art world in which artists form crews and collectiveness to ensure that their art is seen." Booklist

Includes bibliographical references

751.4 Painting--Techniques and procedures

All about techniques in acrylics; {an indispensable manual for artists}; {author, Parramón's Editorial Team}. Barron's 2004 143p il (All about techniques) $26.95

Grades: 11 12 Adult   **751.4**
1. Acrylic painting—Technique
ISBN 0-7641-5710-8   LC 2003-68843
Originally published in Spain

"A brief history of the use of acrylics by people such as Jackson Pollack is followed by sections on the varieties of acrylics available, tools for their use, and techniques for skies, vegetation, landscapes, still lifes, interiors, animals, and the nude. The demonstrations of color mixing, sgraffito, texturing, transparent impastos, and layering with glazes are especially well done." Libr J

"The book is a delight for anyone interested in acrylics and definitely a worthy acquisition for teen collections and art departments anywhere." Voice Youth Advocates

751.42 Watercolor painting

Clarke, Michael, 1952-
Watercolor. Dorling Kindersley 2000 64p il (DK eyewitness books) lib bdg $19.99 hardcover o.p. *
Grades: 9 10 11 12   **751.42**
1. Watercolor painting
ISBN 0-7894-6817-4   LC 00-503616
First published 1993 in the Eyewitness art series

"Providing a quick overview of the medium, this book . . . is adorned with photographic reproductions of some of the world's finest paintings. Short paragraphs and blurbs provide quick points of reference for browsers. Because of its broad appeal, this volume will be quite useful to teachers, and should be included in basic art collections." SLJ

Harrison, Hazel
The encyclopedia of watercolor techniques. rev ed. Running Press 1999 192p il $24.95
Grades: 9 10 11 12   **751.42**

1. Watercolor painting—Technique
ISBN 0-7624-0465-5
First published 1990

"Harrison gives instructions for using water-based media. . . . In some 35 lessons, she covers the laying down of washes, working wet-in-wet, spattering, scumbling, and creating texture with salt." Libr J

752 Color in painting

Pyle, David
What every artist needs to know about paints & colors. Krause Publs. 2000 144p il $29.95
Grades: 11 12 Adult   **752**
ISBN 0-87341-831-X   LC 99-69484
"Covers the history of how color is used, how paints and colors are made, pigment characteristics, and how to choose and use modern artists' colors." Libr J

Includes bibliographical references

753 Symbolism, allegory, mythology, legend

How to read a painting; lessons from the old masters; [edited by] Patrick de Rynck. H.N. Abrams 2004 383p il $35 *
Grades: 11 12 Adult   **753**
1. Symbolism in art 2. Art appreciation
ISBN 0-8109-5576-8   LC 2004-9511
The editor "presents 150 paintings and frescoes that have attained the status of masterpieces. Each work is displayed on a full-color two-page spread that includes detailed closeups and a meticulous decoding of the painting's subject, symbols, and intent. This is a truly felicitous approach, and the selections are supreme." Booklist

Includes bibliographical references

759 Painting--Historical and geographic treatment

Beckett, Wendy
Sister Wendy's 1000 masterpieces; [by] Sister Wendy Beckett; contributing consultant, Patricia Wright. DK Pub. 1999 512p il $40
Grades: 11 12 Adult   **759**
1. Painting 2. Art appreciation
ISBN 0-7894-4603-0   LC 99-20355
This work reproduces 1000 works of art from over 500 artists. Arranged alphabetically, each artist is represented by two paintings. Use of symbolism, technique and artistic inspiration are discussed. Includes a directory of museums and galleries where the original works are displayed

759.05   Painting--1800-1899

Welton, Jude, 1955-
Impressionism. Dorling Kindersley 2000 64p il maps (DK eyewitness books) $15.99; lib bdg $19.99
Grades: 9 10 11 12   **759.05**
  1. Impressionism (Art) 2. French painting
  ISBN 0-7894-5583-8; 0-7894-6812-3 (lib bdg)
                                           LC 00-503615
First published 1993 in the Eyewitness art series
This visual introduction to the impressionist movement features full-color artworks, details of paintings, and photographs of artists' materials, equipment, and studios
This book is "eye-catching, informative, and priced nicely for high school collections." Booklist

759.1   North American painting

Spring, Justin, 1962-
The essential Jackson Pollock. Harry N. Abrams 1998 112p il (Essential series) $12.95
Grades: 9 10 11 12   **759.1**
  1. Pollock, Jackson, 1912-1956
  ISBN 0-8109-5809-0; 978-0-8109-5809-8
                                           LC 98-71936
This book examines the life and art of abstract expressionist painter Jackson Pollock.

759.13   American painting

Eldredge, Charles C.
Georgia O'Keeffe. Abrams 1991 160p il (Library of American art) $45
Grades: 11 12 Adult   **759.13**
  1. O'Keeffe, Georgia, 1887-1986
  ISBN 0-8109-3657-7   LC 90-48459
Numerous reproductions, many in color, "chart the course of O'Keeffe's lengthy career, while Eldredge's accessible text discusses her artistic themes and stylistic subtleties. A beautiful retrospective." Booklist
Includes bibliographical references

Feelings, Tom, 1933-2003
The middle passage; white ships/black cargo; introduction by John Henrik Clarke. Dial Bks. 1995 unp il map $45
Grades: 7 8 9 10   **759.13**
  1. Blacks in art 2. Slavery—Pictorial works
  ISBN 0-8037-1804-7   LC 95-13866
"Consisting entirely of Feeling's uncaptioned black-and white illustrations, this . . . picture book chronicles the inhumane conditions endured by enslaved Africans during 'four centuries of the slave trade.'" Booklist
"A book for careful study and discussion, both at home and in the classroom." N Y Times Book Rev
Includes bibliographical references

Gouveia, Georgette
The essential Mary Cassatt; by Georgette G. Gouveia. Harry N. Abrams 2001 112p il (Essential series) $12.95
Grades: 9 10 11 12   **759.13**
  1. Cassatt, Mary, 1844-1926
  ISBN 0-8109-5814-7; 978-0-8109-5814-2
                                           LC 99-73512
First published 2000 in the United Kingdom
"This book explores Cassatt's unique position as a woman artist among the Impressionists, her enduring popularity as a celebrated painter of motherhood, and this Victorian suffragist's continuing influence as a feminist role model today." Publisher's note

Hennessey, Maureen Hart
Norman Rockwell; pictures for the American people; [by] Maureen Hart Hennessey and Ann Knutson. Abrams 1999 199p il $35
Grades: 11 12 Adult   **759.13**
  1. Rockwell, Norman, 1894-1978
  ISBN 0-8109-6392-2   LC 99-73071
A catalogue of a traveling exhibition of Rockwell's work. "Colorplates reproduce Rockwell's paintings in . . . detail, and the essays set them in fresh contexts, discussing such themes as Rockwell's urban scenes; the reaction by both black and white Southerners to Rockwell's historic civil rights painting *The Problem We All Live With*; and Rockwell's role in the development of American illustration." Publisher's note
Includes bibliographical references

Spring, Justin, 1962-
The essential Edward Hopper. Harry N. Abrams 1998 112p il (Essential series) $12.95
Grades: 9 10 11 12   **759.13**
  1. Hopper, Edward, 1882-1967
  ISBN 0-8109-5805-8; 978-0-8109-5805-0
                                           LC 98-71937
This book examines the art of realist Edward Hopper, who painted such works as A Woman In The Sun and Nighthawks.

759.4   French painting

Jaffe, Hans Ludwig C., 1915-1985
Pablo Picasso; text by Hans L.C. Jaffé. Abradale Press 1996 160p il (Library of great painters) $19.98
Grades: 9 10 11 12   **759.4**
  1. Picasso, Pablo, 1881-1973
  ISBN 0-8109-8142-4   LC 95-20642
Concise edition of the author's Pablo Picasso, originally published 1964 by Abrams
Translated by Norbert Guterman
"This work gathers together 133 illustrations (48 full-color plates) along with background text on each work." Libr J

Lucie-Smith, Edward, 1933-
Toulouse-Lautrec. rev and enl ed. Phaidon Press 1983 31p il pa $9.95 hardcover o.p.
Grades: 9 10 11 12   **759.4**
1. Toulouse-Lautrec, Henri de, 1864-1901
ISBN 1-7148-2761-4
First published 1977
"The introductory overview of the artist's life is followed by 48 chronologically arranged color plates and concise, paragraph-length analyses of individual works. . . . An intelligently written and well-illustrated survey." Choice

Morris, Catherine
The essential Claude Monet. Harry N. Abrams 1999 112p il (Essential series) $12.95
Grades: 9 10 11 12   **759.4**
1. Monet, Claude, 1840-1926
ISBN 0-8109-5802-3; 978-0-8109-5802-9
This book examines the work of Impressionist painter Claude Monet.

Schaffner, Ingrid
The essential Henri Matisse. Henry N. Abrams 1999 112p il (Essential series) $12.95
Grades: 9 10 11 12   **759.4**
1. Matisse, Henri
ISBN 0-8109-5816-3; 978-0-8109-5816-6
                                          LC 98-74611
This book examines the art of the French painter Henri Matisse.

759.5   Italian painting

Hartt, Frederick, 1914-1991
Michelangelo. Abrams 1984 128p il $24.95 *
Grades: 11 12 Adult   **759.5**
1. Michelangelo Buonarroti, 1475-1564
ISBN 0-8109-1335-6
Concise edition of the author's Michelangelo, originally published 1964
At head of title: Michelangelo Buonarroti
The forty colorplates in this book include broad views and close details of Michelangelo's frescoes in the Sistine Chapel and of his other paintings

Marani, Pietro C.
Leonardo da Vinci—the complete paintings; appendices edited by Pietro C. Marani and Edoardo Villata. Abrams 2000 384p il $85 *
Grades: 11 12 Adult   **759.5**
1. Leonardo, da Vinci, 1452-1519
ISBN 0-8109-3581-3   LC 00-27556
Original Italian edition, 1999
This guide covers Leonardo's 31 paintings "intensively, recording possible precedents for design and technique in the work of other artists, calling attention to significant details, offering preparatory drawings and cartoons for comparison with the finished, which is not to say completed, works, and presenting X rays to elucidate

the gestation of the *Mona Lisa* and other paintings Leonardo spent years striving to perfect. Such scrupulous attention to Leonardo's total creative process boosts the number of illustrations, mostly colorplates, to 295." Booklist
Includes bibliographical references

Ottmann, Klaus, 1954-
The essential Michelangelo. Harry N. Abrams 2000 112p il (Essential series) $12.95
Grades: 9 10 11 12   **759.5**
1. Michelangelo Buonarroti, 1475-1564
ISBN 0-8109-5817-1; 978-0-8109-5817-3
This book examines the works of Italian sculptor and painter Michelangelo Buonarroti, including the Pieta and the ceiling of the Sistene Chapel.

Wasserman, Jack, 1921-
Leonardo; text by Jack Wasserman. Abrams 1984 128p il $24.95
Grades: 11 12 Adult   **759.5**
1. Leonardo, da Vinci, 1452-1519
ISBN 0-8109-1285-6
Concise edition of the author's Leonardo, originally published 1975
At head of title: Leonardo da Vinci
"Included here . . . are such masterpieces as the 'Mona Lisa' and the 'Last Supper,' and all the paintings known to be fully or in part by Leonardo's hand. A special section features his incomparably original drawings, including material from his famous notebooks." Publisher's note

759.6   Spanish painting

Goff, Robert
The essential Salvador Dali. Wonderland Press, Harry N. Abrams 1998 112p il (Essential series) $12.95
Grades: 9 10 11 12   **759.6**
1. Dalí, Salvador, 1904-1989
ISBN 0-8109-5800-7   LC 98-71952
This book examines the paintings of surrealist Salvador Dali, in which one finds melting clocks and mixtures of sexual and religious images.

759.9492   Dutch painting

Bernard, Bruce, 1928-2000
Van Gogh. Dorling Kindersley 2000 63p il (DK eyewitness books) $15.99
Grades: 9 10 11 12   **759.9492**
1. Gogh, Vincent van, 1853-1890
ISBN 0-7894-4878-5
First published 1992 as part of the Eyewitness art series
This "volume combines concise biographical material with brilliant color illustrations identified by detailed captions to convey [Van Gogh's lifestyle], influences, creative output, and unique accomplishments. . . . A brief chronology, the locations of the works presented, and a glossary conclude [the] volume." Libr J

Campbell, W. John, 1951-
The essential Hieronymus Bosch. H. N. Abrams 2000 112p il map (Essential series) $12.95
Grades: 9 10 11 12   **759.9492**
   1. Bosch, Hieronymus, d. 1516
   ISBN 0-8109-5810-4; 978-0-8109-5810-4
   This book examines Hieronymus Bosch's paintings, in which one finds demons, demi-humans, and other fantastic creatures and images.

Schaffner, Ingrid
The essential Vincent van Gogh. Harry N. Abrams 1998 112p il (Essential series) $12.95 *
Grades: 9 10 11 12   **759.9492**
   1. Gogh, Vincent van, 1853-1890
   ISBN 0-8109-5813-9; 978-0-8109-5813-5
                   LC 98-71931
   This book examines the art of disturbed Dutch painter Vincent Van Gogh.

Sweet, Christopher
The essential Johannes Vermeer. Harry N. Abrams 1999 112p il (Essential series) $12.95
Grades: 9 10 11 12   **759.9492**
   1. Vermeer, Johannes, 1632-1675
   ISBN 0-8109-5801-5; 978-0-8109-5801-2
   This book examines the art of great Dutch painter Jan Vermeer.

769.5   Forms of prints

Friedberg, Robert, 1912-
Paper money of the United States; a complete illustrated guide with valuations. 18th ed. Coin & Currency Inst. 2006 il $42.50
Grades: 9 10 11 12   **769.5**
   1. Paper money
   ISSN 1099-9981
   ISBN 0-87184-518-0; 978-0-87184-518-4
   First published 1953. Periodically revised
   A guide to paper money of the United States from 1861 to the present. Contains descriptions, valuations, and illustrations of notes, fractional currency, and certificates.

770   Photography, photographs, computer art

Goldberg, Vicki
The power of photography; how photographs changed our lives. Abbeville Press 1991 279p pa $35 hardcover o.p.
Grades: 11 12 Adult   **770**
   1. Photography
   ISBN 1-55859-467-1   LC 91-3116
   This study of photography "traces the medium from its beginnings with the French daguerreotype of the 1840s to the powerful social tool and all-pervasive 'eye' {the author considers} it has become." SLJ
   Includes bibliographical references

Willis, Deborah, 1952-
Reflections in Black; a history of Black photographers, 1840-1999. Norton 2000 348p il $50; pa $35
Grades: 11 12 Adult   **770**
   ISBN 0-393-04880-2; 0-393-32280-7 (pa)
                   LC 99-55185
   Companion volume to A Smithsonian traveling exhibition
   "Willis sketches important figures and traces both developments in photographic techniques and the practice of photography by African Americans. . . . A beautiful and informative album." Booklist
   Includes bibliographical references

770.9   Photography--Historical and geographic treatment

Newhall, Beaumont, 1908-1993
The history of photography; from 1839 to the present day. completely rev and enl ed. Museum of Modern Art 1982 319p il pa $38 hardcover o.p. *
Grades: 11 12 Adult   **770.9**
   1. Photography—History
   ISBN 0-87070-381-1   LC 82-81430
   First published 1949
   An illustrated history of photography focusing on important innovators and master photographers
   Includes bibliographical references

Sandler, Martin W.
Photography: an illustrated history. Oxford Univ. Press 2002 156p il (Oxford illustrated histories) $29.95
Grades: 11 12 Adult   **770.9**
   1. Photography—History
   ISBN 0-19-512608-4   LC 2001-36602
   Presents the history of photography from the daguerreotypes of the mid-1800s to its acceptance as an art form and more
   "Most exciting are the images . . . which range from famous examples of photojournalism . . . to fine art. . . . [A] well-done, clearly written overview." Booklist
   Includes bibliographical references

775   Digital photography

Ang, Tom
KISS guide to digital photography. DK Pub 2004 288p il (Keep it simple series) pa $20
Grades: 11 12 Adult   **775**
   1. Photography—Digital techniques
   ISBN 0-7894-9696-8   LC 2003-55522
   This guide aims to help readers "find the right camera and accessories, master digital tricks, lighting and composition, while demystifying buzzwords, from pixels and jpegs to cropping and cloning." Publisher's note

Freeman, Michael, 1945-
The complete guide to digital photography. 2nd ed fully rev and updated. Lark Bks. 2003 224p il pa $29.95 *
Grades: 11 12 Adult   775
1. Digital cameras
ISBN 1-57990-534-X   LC 2003-47653
First published 2001
The author "arranges the text in four sections: hardware, software (including tools and filters), techniques, and creative imagery. . . . The strengths of this guide are the clear, easily understood text and the comprehensive manner in which he addresses this broad subject. A very helpful introduction to this exciting field for both amateur and professional photographers." Libr J
Includes bibliographical references

Seamon, Mary Ploski, 1943-
Digital cameras in the classroom; [by] Mary Ploski Seamon and Eric J. Levitt. Linworth Pub 2003 66p il pa $29.95 *
Grades: Professional   775
1. Digital cameras 2. Digital photography
3. Photography in education
ISBN 1-58683-095-3   LC 2003-43337
This offers advice on such topics as "selecting the right camera, how digital imagery works, storing and downloading pictures, and incorporating images into PowerPoints, Web sites, and other projects. A chapter on classroom activities shows . . . how to use digital cameras as an idea generator and . . . teaching tool." Publisher's note
"The author's emphasis on the active learning involved in using digital cameras will encourage the most reluctant teachers and media specialists to see the value of this medium while concise chapters make learning to use a digital camera a reality." SLJ
Includes bibliographical references

778.5 Cinematography, video production, related activities

Netzley, Patricia D.
The encyclopedia of movie special effects. Oryx Press 2000 291p il $73.95 *
Grades: 11 12 Adult   778.5
1. Cinematography
ISBN 1-57356-167-3   LC 99-47733
"This volume provides 366 entries on visual, mechanical, and makeup effects and techniques used in film and includes discussions of every movie to win an Oscar for special effects." Libr J
Includes bibliographical references

Shaner, Peter A.
Digital filmmaking for teens; [by] Pete Shaner and Gerald Everett Jones. Thomson Course Technology Professional Trade Reference 2005 237p il $24.99 *
Grades: 7 8 9 10   778.5
1. Cinematography 2. Video recording
ISBN 1-59200-603-5   LC 2004-114416

"The highlight of this guide is the DVD included in the package with which one can watch some films made by teens in a workshop in New York. . . . Only 2 of the 10 chapters are specifically about shooting the film. The other sections describe equipment, storyboarding, lighting, planning, editing, adding music, and releasing the film. . . . The instructions and suggestions are meticulously documented and easy to follow. This book . . . could serve as a superb guide for filmmaking at home or as a text for a class." SLJ
Includes bibliographical references

778.9 Photography of specific subjects

Caputo, Robert
National Geographic photography field guide; people & portraits: secrets to making great pictures. National Geographic Soc. 2001 159p il $21.95 *
Grades: 11 12 Adult   778.9
1. Photography
ISBN 0-7922-6499-1   LC 2001-44918
Also available companion volumes: National Geographic photography field guide landscapes (2002); National Geographic photography field guide: secrets to making great pictures (1999)
This guide explains "the best angles, lighting, and lenses to capture candid photos and portraits of family, friends, and everyone else. How to evoke a subject's true character on film {and} how to compose a formal family portrait." Publisher's note
Includes bibliographical references

779 Photographs

In focus; National Geographic greatest portraits. National Geographic Society 2004 504p il $30
Grades: 11 12 Adult   779
1. Portrait photography
ISBN 0-7922-7363-X   LC 2004-44953
"Comprising 280 portraits by 150 of National Geographic's celebrated photographers . . . the book spans over 100 years and covers the entire globe. Organized chronologically as well as thematically and enriched with essays on the development of photographic styles through decades, it is a tasteful celebration of the medium but even more so of human diversity." Libr J

Mitchell, John G.
National Geographic, the wildlife photographs. National Geographic Soc. 2001 304p il maps $50
Grades: 11 12 Adult   779
1. National Geographic Society (U.S.) 2. Animals—Pictorial works
ISBN 0-7922-6356-1   LC 2001-37021
This is a collection of over 170 wildlife images from National Geographic organized by habitat. "A sidebar portfolio in each section features the work of one photographer well known for his or her images of animals from the featured habitat. Mitchell's text gives informa-

Mitchell, John G.—*Continued*
tion on each region, discussing the environment, the politics of conservation, and a profile of the featured photographer. This beautiful book will be welcome in large photography collections." Booklist

Myers, Walter Dean, 1937-
One more river to cross; an African American photograph album. Harcourt Brace & Co. 1995 166p il hardcover o.p. pa $18
Grades: 7 8 9 10   **779**
1. African Americans—Pictorial works
ISBN 0-15-100191-X; 0-15-202021-7 (pa)
     LC 95-3839
"This collection of period photography documents the African-American struggle from captivity to freedom." Book Rep
"This oversized, superbly produced album is dramatic, with spare, almost poetic narration by Myers. . . . Although there are some photos of well-known individuals, the strength of this book is the pictures of ordinary people, engaged in the everyday tasks and enjoyments of life." Voice Youth Advocates

O'Donnell, Joe, 1922-2007
Japan 1945; a U.S. Marine's photographs from Ground Zero. Vanderbilt University Press 2005 87p il $39.95
Grades: 11 12 Adult   **779**
1. War photography 2. World War, 1939-1945—Pictorial works
ISBN 0-8265-1467-7   LC 2004-17367
This is a "visual document of the atomic bombings of Japanese cities in 1945. . . . Except for a few photographs ('Burn Victim'), the only images of devastation are panoramic views of the rubble that the bombed cities had become." Choice
"This stunning work . . . is essential for all World War II collections." Libr J

Photos that changed the world; the 20th century; edited by Peter Stepan; with contributions by Claus Biegerd {et al.}. Prestel-Verlag 2000 183p il $35 *
Grades: 11 12 Adult   **779**
1. Photojournalism
ISBN 3-7913-2395-4
Translated from the German
Stepan provides "105 images that had the lasting visual power to capture a moment that could be the image of an era held in the instant of a shutter's click for distribution to a generation. . . . The photos are well reproduced and gain from the explanations of time, place, and context included in the excellent short essays that accompany each." Libr J

Pletka, Bob
My so-called digital life; 2,000 teenagers, 300 cameras, and 30 days to document their world; created by Bob Pletka. Santa Monica Press 2005 168p il pa $24.95
Grades: 11 12 Adult   **779**
1. Teenagers—Pictorial works
ISBN 1-59580-005-0   LC 2005-9678

The author "gave 2,000 middle and high school students from across California digital cameras and thirty days to document their lives. The results are compiled in this beautifully produced book of big, bold collages of photographs accompanied by short quotes and a few longer passages, written and formatted by the participants." Voice Youth Advocates

Spirit capture; photographs from the National Museum of the American Indian; edited by Tim Johnson. Smithsonian Institution Press 1998 205p il $60; pa $34.95 *
Grades: 11 12 Adult   **779**
1. National Museum of the American Indian (U.S.)
2. Native Americans—Pictorial works
ISBN 1-56098-924-6; 1-56098-765-0 (pa)
     LC 98-4173
The more than 200 reproductions included in this volume range from daguerrotypes to color slides. Essays by Native American authors explore how Indians of the Western hemisphere were documented and depicted
Includes bibliographical references

Through the lens; National Geographic greatest photographs. National Geographic Soc. 2003 504p il $30
Grades: 11 12 Adult   **779**
1. Documentary photography
ISBN 0-7922-6164-X   LC 2003-52757
This is a "collection of 250 photos, mostly in color and drawn from the National Geographic Society's archive. . . . The society's signature blend of dramatic, rigorously composed natural shots and 'family of nations'-style culture peeps are backed by broad captions and text. . . . The six sections ('Europe'; 'Asia'; 'Africa & the Middle East'; 'The Americas'; 'Oceans and Isles'; 'The Universe') include the first color underwater photographs, as well as collaborative work with NASA, and prominently credit the 84 photographers whose work is featured." Publ Wkly

780   Music

Marsalis, Wynton
Marsalis on music. Norton 1995 171p il music $29.95
Grades: 9 10 11 12 Adult   **780**
1. Music
ISBN 0-393-03881-5   LC 95-4470
This book "is designed to show how basic elements of music are shared by different musical styles. Chapters are divided into rhythm, form, wind bands and jazz bands, and practice. Musical examples are provided on an accompanying audio CD. . . . Also included are biographical sketches of composers featured in the book." Libr J
"An outstanding companion to a PBS series. . . . A superb resource for students and for other readers." Booklist
Includes glossary

780.3 Music--Encyclopedias and dictionaries

Ammer, Christine
The Facts on File dictionary of music. 4th ed.
Facts on File, Inc 2004 495p il $50; pa $19.95 *
Grades: 9 10 11 12   **780.3**
1. Music—Dictionaries
ISBN 0-8160-5266-2; 0-8160-5267-0 (pa)
                   LC 2003-61284
First published 1972 by Harper & Row with title:
Harper's dictionary of music
"This book's emphasis is on classical music. The
more than 3000 entries include definitions of terminology, explanations of styles, biographies of composers, and
descriptions of musical instruments. Phonetic pronunciations are given for all non-English terms. Many clear, detailed line drawings of instruments and musical notation
are included. . . . This is a good basic reference tool for
collections in need of classical music resources." SLJ

Baker, Richard, 1925-
Richard Baker's companion to music; a personal
A-Z guide to classical music. Parkwest Publs.
1994 208p $27.95
Grades: 11 12 Adult   **780.3**
1. Music—Dictionaries
ISBN 0-563-36414-9
"Intended for the layperson interested in classical music, the . . . entries, which cover from Palestrina to the
1990's, include composers, soloists, orchestras, concert
halls, famous compositions, musical forms, and instruments. Most entries are 6-10 lines in length, although
broad subjects (*Choral Music, Jazz,* the *Proms*) receive
a two-page spread." Booklist

Baker's student encyclopedia of music; edited by
Laura Kuhn. Schirmer Bks. 1999 3v set $368.75
*
Grades: 11 12 Adult   **780.3**
1. Music—Dictionaries
ISBN 0-02-865315-7   LC 99-31758
"More than 5,500 entries cover musical terms; musicians, composers, conductors, and performers; instruments; genres; and individual works. Text is enhanced by
a number of student-friendly features: time lines for major composers, icons indicating entries for people or instruments, snippets of text moved into small sidebars;
and black-and-white photographs and illustrations."
Booklist

The **Harvard** concise dictionary of music and
musicians; edited by Don Michael Randel.
Belknap Press 1999 757p il $35; pa $18.95 *
Grades: 11 12 Adult   **780.3**
1. Music—Dictionaries 2. Music—Bio-bibliography
ISBN 0-674-00084-6; 0-674-00978-9 (pa)
                   LC 99-40644
"Entries are arranged alphabetically and encompass
terms, musical forms and styles, individual works, and
instruments, as well as composers, performers, and theorists." Booklist

The **Oxford** companion to music; edited by Alison
Latham. Oxford Univ. Press 2002 1434p il $65
*
Grades: 11 12 Adult   **780.3**
1. Music—Dictionaries 2. Musicians—Dictionaries
ISBN 0-19-866212-2   LC 2002-537302
"New edition of two quite different earlier companions
. . . Oxford companion to music . . . The new Oxford
companion to music." Preface
"Among the 8000 entries are articles on composers,
theorists, and some performers; instruments, forms, and
terms; subjects like electronic music, individual countries, and politics and music; and some pieces (and even
some famous arias). Each entry is presented in a dictionary format, with a select index of names appended and
sometimes with bibliographic references. . . . The bias is
still English, but the book provides cross references to
American terms and includes plenty of American composers and musical subjects. A solid reference with a
grand pedigree, usefully improved for home and general
library use, this is highly recommended for all public libraries." Libr J
Includes bibliographical references

780.89 Music of racial, ethnic, national groups

Floyd, Samuel A.
The power of black music; interpreting its
history from Africa to the United States; {by}
Samuel A. Floyd, Jr. Oxford Univ. Press 1995
316p il pa $18.95 hardcover o.p.
Grades: 11 12 Adult   **780.89**
1. African American music
ISBN 978-0-19-510975-7   LC 94-21
The range of genres the author discusses includes
"slaves' ring shouts, turn-of-the-century cotillion dances,
jazz, R & B, etc. . . . Complementing the discourse are
plenty of musical examples. Academics, critics, scholars,
and fans alike stand to gain much from carefully reading
this impressive work." Booklist
Includes discography, filmography, and bibliographical
references

Southern, Eileen
The music of black Americans; a history. 3rd
ed. Norton 1997 xxii, 678p il music hardcover o.p.
pa $53.65 *
Grades: 11 12 Adult   **780.89**
1. African American musicians
ISBN   0-393-03843-2;   978-0-393-97141-5;
0-393-97141-4 (pa)   LC 96-28811
First published 1971
A chronological survey of African American music in
the United States tracing black music from its origin in
Africa through colonial America and up to the present
Includes discography and bibliographical references

780.9 Music--Historical and geographical treatment

Grout, Donald Jay, 1902-1987
A history of western music; [by] J. Peter Burkholder, Donald Jay Grout, Claude V. Palisca. 7th ed. W.W. Norton 2006 xxviii, 965, 128p il map $71.25 *
Grades: 11 12 Adult   **780.9**
1. Music—History and criticism
ISBN 0-393-97991-1; 978-0-393-97991-6
LC 2005-48797
First published 1960
The authors survey the course of Western music from the ancient world to modern atonalism and dodecaphony. They cover vocal and instrumental forms, notation, performance, music-printing, the development of instruments, and biographical information on composers.
Includes bibliographical references

Hart, Mickey
Songcatchers; in search of the world's music; [by] Mickey Hart with K.M. Kostyal. National Geographic Society 2003 172p il $30
Grades: 11 12 Adult   **780.9**
1. Folk music 2. Music—History and criticism
ISBN 0-7922-4107-X   LC 2003-45901
"For some time now, Grateful Dead drummer Hart has been a songcatcher, a collector of the originally noncommercial music popularly called traditional music. Many anthropologists, musicians, political and labor organizers, composers, social workers, and others were songcatchers before him, and it is their collective story that he and professional writer Kostyal tell in this engaging book. . . . A book for every popular library." Booklist
Includes bibliographical references

Perlis, Vivian
Composer's voices from Ives to Ellington; an oral history of American music; [by] Vivian Perlis and Libby Van Cleve. Yale University Press 2005 477p il $50
Grades: 11 12 Adult   **780.9**
1. Composers—United States 2. Jazz musicians
ISBN 0-300-10673-4; 9780300106732
LC 2005-361
"In the first of four planned volumes, the authors cover the early 20th century, tapping reminiscences from the OH archives by and about such luminaries as Charles Ives, Edgard Varèse, Carl Ruggles, Charles Seeger, Henry Cowell, George Gershwin, Duke Ellington, and three of Nadia Boulanger's most illustrious students: Aaron Copland, Roy Harris, and Virgil Thompson." Libr J
"This volume offers the reader a unique perspective on the composers who created ragtime, 'new' music, and early jazz. A very enjoyable read supplemented by 2 compact discs that contain excerpts of interviews." Univ Press Books for Public and Second Sch Libr, 2006
Includes bibliographical references

Slonimsky, Nicolas, 1894-1995
The great composers and their works; edited by Electra Yourke. Schirmer Bks. 2000 2v il set $200 *
Grades: 11 12 Adult   **780.9**
1. Music—History and criticism 2. Music appreciation 3. Composers
ISBN 0-02-864955-9   LC 99-42808
"This alphabetically arranged work made up of . . . writings by the late Nicolas Slonimsky . . . is edited by his daughter, Electra Yourke, and treats 19 composers, from Bach to Shostakovich. Arrangement is chronological." Booklist
"These volumes will attract individuals with a serious interest in classical music, and supplement standard resources." SLJ

Terkel, Studs, 1912-
And they all sang; adventures of an eclectic disc jockey. New Press 2005 xxii, 301p $25.95; pa $16.95
Grades: 11 12 Adult   **780.9**
1. Musicians
ISBN 1-59558-003-4; 978-1-59558-118-1; 1-59558-118-9 (pa)   LC 2005-43866
In this "collection of 40 interviews, . . . Terkel recalls his venerable radio program, The Wax Museum, which premiered shortly after the end of WWII in 1945, profiling composers, entertainers and impresarios of nearly every type of music. . . . Insightful and daring, Terkel always asks the right questions, whether culturally or musically." Publ Wkly

781.4 Techniques of music

Evans, Roger
How to read music; for singing, guitar, piano, organ, and most instruments. Crown 1979 c1978 112p music pa $10 hardcover o.p. *
Grades: 9 10 11 12   **781.4**
1. Music—Study and teaching 2. Musical notation
ISBN 0-517-88438-0 (pa)   LC 79-20844
First published 1978 in the United Kingdom
An introduction to "music notation and score reading for an individual interested in learning and mature enough to follow directions. Some ability to play an instrument is useful but not mandatory. Examples are given showing both a piano keyboard and a guitar tablature." Voice Youth Advocates
"Fundamental musical concepts are presented here in a well-planned, logical order. . . . Evans has done a good job overall and has included a very useful directory of musical signs, note directory, and a brief musical dictionary." SLJ

781.6   Traditions of music. Classical music

Swafford, Jan

The Vintage guide to classical music. Vintage Bks. 1992 xxi, 597p il pa $17 *

Grades: 11 12 Adult   **781.6**

1. Music appreciation 2. Music—History and criticism

ISBN 0-679-72805-8   LC 91-50217

This guide contains "chronologically arranged essays on nearly 100 composers, from Guillaume de Machaut (ca. 1300-1377) to Aaron Copland (1900-1990), that combine biography with detailed analyses of the major works while assessing their role in the social, cultural, and political climate of their times." Publisher's note

Includes glossary and bibliographical references

781.64   Western popular music

Chang, Jeff

Can't stop, won't stop; a history of the hip-hop generation; introduction by D.J. Kool Herc. St. Martin's Press 2005 546p il hardcover o.p. pa $16 *

Grades: 11 12 Adult   **781.64**

1. Rap music

ISBN 0-312-30143-X; 0-312-42579-1 (pa)

LC 2004-56656

This is "a history of hip-hop and the cultural movement the music inspired." N Y Times Book Rev

"A fascinating, far-reaching must for pop-music and pop-culture collections." Booklist

Includes bibliographical references, discography, and filmography

Morales, Ed

The Latin beat; the rhythms and roots of Latin music from bossa nova to salsa and beyond. Da Capo Press 2003 xxviii, 372p pa $18.95 *

Grades: 9 10 11 12   **781.64**

1. Music—Latin America

ISBN 0-306-81018-2   LC 2003-16423

This book "outlines the musical styles of each country, then traces each form as it migrates north. Morales travels from the Latin ballad to bossa nova to Latin jazz, chronicles the development of the samba in Brazil and salsa in New York, explores the connection between the mambo craze of the 1950's with the Cuban craze of today, and uncovers the hidden history of Latinos in rock and hip hop." Publisher's note

"Displaying an incredible depth of historical and musical knowledge and insight, this book will be a joy to read both for those already steeped in the Latin musical tradition as well as for those recently introduced to the music of, for instance, Tito Puente." Publ Wkly

Includes bibliographical references

781.643   Blues music

Santelli, Robert

The big book of blues; a biographical encyclopedia. Penguin Bks. 2001 559p pa $20 *

Grades: 9 10 11 12   **781.643**

1. Musicians—Dictionaries 2. Blues music

ISBN 0-14-100145-3   LC 00-49212

First published 1993

This biographical dictionary contains some 600 entries profiling blues artists "from Bessie Smith to Koko Taylor, Charlie Patton to Robert Cray, Blind Willie McTell to Stevie Ray Vaughn. Each biographical sketch {includes} . . . biographical data and discographies . . . a discussion of the artist's style, musical contribution, and 'essential listening.'" Publisher's note

Includes bibliographical references and discographies

781.65   Jazz music

Gioia, Ted

The history of jazz. Oxford Univ. Press 1997 471p il $37.50; pa $16.95

Grades: 11 12 Adult   **781.65**

ISBN 0-19-509081-0; 0-19-512653-X (pa)

LC 97-102

The author relates the story of African American music from its roots in Africa to the international respect it enjoys today. . . . This well-researched, extensively annotated volume covers the major trends and personalities that have shaped jazz. The excellent bibliography and list of recommended listening make this a valuable purchase for libraries building a jazz collection. Libr J

The author traces jazz's origins to the slave dances of early 19th-century New Orleans. . . . Gioia documents the genre's evolution from the 19th century to today's hip downtown New York scene. Chapters detail each of the genre's major stylistic shifts, profiling unsung innovators as well as celebrities of each era. Publ Wkly

Includes bibliographical references

Marsalis, Wynton

Jazz A-B-Z; [by] Wynton Marsalis and Paul Rogers; with biographical sketches by Phil Schaap. Candlewick Press 2005 unp il $24.99

Grades: 5 6 7 8 9 10   **781.65**

1. Jazz music 2. Jazz musicians

ISBN 0-7636-2135-8   LC 2005-48448

This is an illustrated alphabetically arranged introduction to jazz musicians.

This is a "witty, stunningly designed alphabet catalog. . . . The biographical sketches and notes on poetic forms by Phil Schaap are concise and genuinely informative. . . . Rogers's pastiche full-page portraits, his use of expressive typography and the smaller vignettes he sprinkles throughout are bound to heighten any reader's appreciation of both the musicians and the music. . . . [Marsalis offers] clever . . . poems, wordplays, odes and limericks." N Y Times Book Rev

The **New** Grove dictionary of jazz; edited by Barry Kernfeld. 2nd ed. Grove's Dictionaries Inc. 2002 3v set $250

Grades: 11 12 Adult   **781.65**
1. Jazz music
ISBN 1-56159-284-6   LC 2001-40794
First published 1988 in two volumes

This reference to jazz and jazz musicians includes "more than 7750 entries. . . . [It covers] jazz styles, instruments, record labels, nicknames, guilds and associations, jazz language, libraries and archives, false fingering techniques for horns, festivals, titles of films containing jazz scenes, a list of contrafacts . . . and even biographies of a few jazz writers and critics." Libr J

Includes bibliographical references and discographies

Ratliff, Ben
Jazz: a critic's guide to the 100 most important recordings. Times Bks. 2002 xx, 250p il (New York Times essential library) pa $16

Grades: 11 12 Adult   **781.65**
1. Jazz music—Discography
ISBN 0-8050-7068-0   LC 2002-69551

The author "presents essays on what he considers the 100 most important jazz recordings. In each, he discusses a recording's merits and shortcomings and includes a list of its performers. . . . As a guide for the uninitiated it is essential for academic music libraries and public libraries large and small. It would also be most useful for collection development librarians building a well-rounded jazz CD collection." Libr J

Szwed, John F., 1936-
Jazz 101; a complete guide to learning and loving jazz; {by} John Szwed. Hyperion 2000 354p pa $14.95 *

Grades: 11 12 Adult   **781.65**
1. Jazz music
ISBN 0-7868-8496-7   LC 00-35055

Szwed "proceeds chronologically through jazz history, managing to explore the different trends in jazz that often overlapped and the key players who often reinvented themselves over decades. There even are accounts of the famous nightclubs where jazz history was made. Strong, descriptive reviews of key albums are included as sidebars to give the reader good places to start listening. Very worthwhile." Booklist

Includes bibliographical references

Ward, Geoffrey C.
Jazz; a history of America's music; based on a documentary film by Ken Burns written by Geoffrey C. Ward; with a preface by Ken Burns. Knopf 2000 489p il $65; pa $29.95 *

Grades: 11 12 Adult   **781.65**
1. Jazz music
ISBN 0-679-44551-X; 0-679-76539-5 (pa)
LC 00-22604

Companion volume to PBS series of the same title

The authors "have assembled a comprehensive history with a focus on the musicians and the sociology of jazz.

. . . The short articles by Wynton Marsalis, Dan Morgenstern, Gerald Early, Stanley Crouch, and Gary Giddins, which are woven into the text, provide a . . . specific focus on a number of jazz's aspects." Libr J

"The illustrations are copious, including about 500 pieces and running from cover to cover; the text, picture captions, and sidebars reflect the research that went into the six-year project. A very competent and lovingly rendered history." Booklist

Includes bibliographical references

781.66   Rock (Rock 'n' roll)

The **Beatles** anthology. Chronicle Bks. 2000 367p il $60; pa $35

Grades: 11 12 Adult   **781.66**
1. Beatles
ISBN 0-8118-2684-8; 0-8118-3636-3 (pa)
LC 00-23685

The story of the Beatles as "told through quotes from John, Paul, George, and Ringo, as well as the group's closest aides: George Martin, Neil Aspinall, and Derek Taylor. . . . The density of the text is daunting, but the book's browsability makes it as appealing to casual readers as it is indispensable to Beatlemaniacs." Libr J

Includes bibliographical references

Beaujon, Andrew
Body piercing saved my life; inside the phenomenon of Christian rock. Da Capo Press 2006 291p il $16.95

Grades: 11 12 Adult   **781.66**
1. Christian rock music
ISBN 0-306-81457-9; 978-0-306-81457-0
LC 2006-6254

The author "chronicles the Christian rock subculture, beginning with the 'Jesus People' of the early 1970s to its substantial popularity today. . . . This important, well-written study of the Christian rock phenomenon brings the personalities to life." Libr J

Includes bibliographical references

Crampton, Luke
Rock & roll year by year; {by} Luke Crampton & Dafydd Rees. DK Publishing 2003 599p il hardcover o.p. pa $30

Grades: 11 12 Adult   **781.66**
1. Rock music
ISBN 0-7894-9649-6; 0-7566-1334-5 (pa)
LC 2003-51655

Contents: 1950s: the birth of rock 'n' roll; 1960s: from Mersey beat to flower power; 1970s: a blend of glam rock, glitter, and punk; 1980s: the decade of MTV and Live Aid; 1990s: from Seattle grunge to girl power; 2000s: the new breed

"Beginning with January 1950 . . . rock history is chronicled month by month through December 2002 . . . In addition to the facts, figures, and personalities highlighted within each month, lively essays summarize significant developments of each decade, charts compare No. 1 hits in the U.S. and U.K. during identical periods, and entertaining sidebars provide expanded commentary

Crampton, Luke—*Continued*

and quotations. Every page includes fascinating historical photographs and color images of artifacts from the {Rock and Roll Hall of Fame Museum}." SLJ

Mulholland, Garry

This is uncool: the 500 greatest singles since punk and disco. Cassell Illustrated; distributed by Sterling 2002 456p il $29.95

Grades: 11 12 Adult **781.66**

ISBN 0-304-36186-0 LC 2003-427773

The author's "pick singles of 1976-99 appear chronologically. . . . Mulholland spaces pithy commentaries with sleeve and label art. . . . List books are great for warm memories and heated debates. With its in-your-face attitude and strong opinions, this is a good one." Booklist

Rock and roll is here to stay; an anthology; edited by William McKeen; introduction by Peter Guralnick. Norton 2000 672p il $35

Grades: 11 12 Adult **781.66**

1. Rock music

ISBN 0-393-04700-8 LC 99-31759

McKeen "presents 94 excerpts from novels, rock criticism, lyrics, interviews, speeches, personal recollections, and other sources to weave together the history of rock'n'roll." Libr J

The **Rolling** Stone illustrated history of rock & roll; the definitive history of the most important artists and their music; edited by Anthony DeCurtis and James Henke with Holly George-Warren; original editor: Jim Miller. {new ed}. Random House 1992 710p il pa $36.95 *

Grades: 7 8 9 10 **781.66**

1. Rock music

ISBN 0-679-73728-6 LC 92-6339

First published 1976

This history of four decades of rock music includes essays and photographs covering individual artists, groups, trends and styles

Talevski, Nick, 1962-

The unofficial encyclopedia of the Rock and Roll Hall of Fame. Greenwood Press 1998 402p il $60

Grades: 11 12 Adult **781.66**

1. Rock & Roll Hall of Fame and Museum 2. Rock musicians 3. Rock music

ISBN 0-313-30032-1 LC 97-41928

"This book covers the first 150 inductees into the Rock and Roll Hall of Fame. . . . Individuals and groups who have been inducted into the Rock and Roll Hall of Fame are listed alphabetically, with the entries providing both personal and professional information. Each description includes not only dry factual annotations about the individual's achievements, records, etc., but also interesting personal information, anecdotes, comments, and insights. At the end of each entry is a bibliography for further reading." Voice Youth Advocates

782 Vocal music

Tommasini, Anthony, 1948-

Opera: a critic's guide to the 100 most important recordings. Times Books 2004 316p il (The New York times essential library) pa $17

Grades: 11 12 Adult **782**

1. Opera

ISBN 0-8050-7459-7 LC 2004-49846

"Tommasini presents the pillars of the repertory—including stories about their composers, details of their plots and comments on their performance history—in a style that will appeal to informed readers without scaring off those whose knowledge of the music is limited. In addition, for readers who wish to explore further, Tommasini recommends CDs of each opera." Publ Wkly

Includes bibliographical references

782.25 Sacred songs

We'll understand it better by and by; pioneering African American gospel composers; edited by Bernice Johnson Reagon. Smithsonian Institution Press 1992 384p il music pa $27.95 hardcover o.p.

Grades: 11 12 Adult **782.25**

1. Gospel music 2. African American musicians 3. Composers

ISBN 1-56098-167-9 LC 91-37954

"Reagon and her contributors explore every aspect of gospel's history, spiritual significance, and influence on secular music, but the primary focus is on individuals. The lives and achievements of six pioneering gospel music composers are examined in detail. . . . A splendidly comprehensive and invaluable history." Booklist

Includes discography and bibliographical references

782.42 Songs

Bynoe, Yvonne

Encyclopedia of rap and hip-hop culture. Greenwood Press 2006 449p il $69.95 *

Grades: 11 12 Adult **782.42**

1. Rap music—Encyclopedias 2. Hip-hop—Encyclopedias

ISBN 0-313-33058-1 LC 2005-19215

This encyclopedia describes "the separate elements embraced by rap and hip-hop: the verbal (MCing), and the musical (DJing), break dancing, and aerosol painting. The alphabetical entries cover all these elements and include most of the well-known rap artists and groups, along with some less-familiar names. The articles also acknowledge some of rap's detractors. . . . This title will be of interest to browsers and report writers." SLJ

Includes bibliographical references

Furia, Philip, 1943-
The poets of Tin Pan Alley; a history of America's great lyricists. Oxford Univ. Press 1990 322p pa $14.95 hardcover o.p.
Grades: 11 12 Adult   **782.42**
1. Lyricists 2. Popular music 3. American songs
ISBN 0-19-507473-4   LC 90-35937
This work examines "lyrics from stage and movie musicals and the work of ten lyricists: Irving Berlin, Lorenz Hart, Ira Gershwin, Cole Porter, Oscar Hammerstein, Howard Dietz, Yip Harburg, Dorothy Fields, Leo Robin, and Johnny Mercer. . . . Although primarily a record of one aspect of show business, the book is a good history of American popular culture." Choice
Includes bibliographical references

Lommel, Cookie
The history of rap music. Chelsea House 2001 120p il (African-American achievers) $21.95
Grades: 9 10 11 12   **782.42**
1. Rap music
ISBN 0-7910-5820-4   LC 00-22274
Traces the development of rap music from origins in the hip hop of the 1970s through various controversies to its widespread popularity in the 1990s
Includes bibliographical references

National anthems of the world. 11th ed.
Weidenfeld & Nicolson 2006 629p $90 *
Grades: 5 6 7 8 9 10 11 12 Adult
                                            782.42
1. National songs
ISBN 0-304-36826-1
First published 1943 in the United Kingdom with title: National anthems of the United Nations and France
This volume contains national anthems of about 198 nations, including melody and accompaniment. Words are presented in the native language with transliteration provided where necessary. English translations follow. Brief historical notes on the adoption of each anthem are included.
"An essential reference resource for all libraries." Libr J

Songwriter's market 2007. Writer's Digest Bks. 2006 pa $26.99
Grades: 11 12 Adult   **782.42**
1. Popular music—Writing and publishing
ISSN 0161-5971
ISBN 1-58297-431-4; 978-1-58297-431-6
Annual. First published 1978
The main section of this guide consists of listings of music publishers, record companies, producers, managers, booking agents, and firms interested in original music. Also included are articles which present an overview of the songwriting field, and listings of resources such as organizations, workshops, and contests.

The **Vibe** history of hip hop; edited by Alan Light. Three Rivers Press (NY) 1999 418p il pa $27.50 *
Grades: 11 12 Adult   **782.42**
1. Rap music
ISBN 0-609-80503-7   LC 99-36003

This history of rap music answers "questions about hip-hop culture, such as how rap got started, who the earliest performers were, etc. Even larger issues such as the role of women as rap artists, regional rivalries, money, power, and the merge of rock and roll are examined in great detail. . . . This gargantuan masterpiece is profusely illustrated." SLJ
Includes discographies

784.19   Musical instruments

Baines, Anthony
The Oxford companion to musical instruments; written and edited by Anthony Baines. Oxford Univ. Press 1992 404p il $55
Grades: 7 8 9 10   **784.19**
1. Musical instruments—Dictionaries
ISBN 0-19-311334-1   LC 92-8635
Based on The New Oxford companion to music (1983)
This volume presents alphabetically arranged entries for musical instruments. "The individual entries cover specific instruments and families thereof (e.g., Wind Instruments) as well as their representation in different countries (e.g., Africa) and time periods (e.g., Baroque). . . . Playing techniques, a brief history, and a list of the major repertory are [discussed]." Booklist

784.2   Full orchestra (Symphony orchestra)

Steinberg, Michael
The symphony; a listener's guide. Oxford Univ. Press 1995 678p music $42.50; pa $25 *
Grades: 11 12 Adult   **784.2**
1. Symphony 2. Music appreciation 3. Composers
ISBN 0-19-506177-2; 0-19-512665-3 (pa)
                                       LC 95-5568
"Steinberg describes 36 composers and, movement by movement, 118 symphonies, including all the standard repertory . . . as well as a few by less well known composers such as Gorecki, Harbison, Martinu, and Sessions. The writing varies from formal and factual to chatty, with candid asides and stories relevant to the composer, the composition, or an important performance." Libr J
Includes bibliographical references

784.8   Wind band

Bailey, Wayne, 1955-
The complete marching band resource manual; techniques and materials for teaching, drill design, and music arranging; [by] Wayne Bailey; percussion chapter by Thomas Caneva. 2nd ed. University of Pennsylvania Press 2003 290p il spiral bdg $34.95
Grades: 9 10 11 12   **784.8**
1. Bands (Music)
ISBN 0-8122-1856-6   LC 2003-50768

Bailey, Wayne, 1955-—*Continued*
First published 1994
This guidebook for band directors features drill charts and instrumental arrangements.

787.8   Plectral lute family

Ellis, Rex M., 1951-
With a banjo on my knee; a musical journey from slavery to freedom. Watts 2001 160p il lib bdg $27
Grades: 7 8 9 10   **787.8**
1. Banjos 2. African American music
ISBN 0-531-11747-2   LC 00-33035
"Ellis explains the banjo's place in African American history. . . . He includes banjo talents such as James A. Bland, who wrote @Carry Me Back to Old Virginny,' and Johnny St. Cyr, who played with Louis Armstrong." Voice Youth Advocates
This is a "well-written, attractive work, which unveils a segment of social history both powerful and far reaching." Booklist
Includes glossary, discography and bibliographical references

787.87   Guitars

Bacon, Tony
The ultimate guitar book; {by} Tony Bacon & Paul Day. Knopf 1991 192p il pa $27.50 hardcover o.p.
Grades: 11 12 Adult   **787.87**
1. Guitars
ISBN 0-375-70090-0   LC 91-52714
This is a "chronological history of the guitar, beginning with an example from 1552 and continuing through current times. Covering acoustic, electrical, and bass guitars, including all the big-name manufacturers such as Fender, Gibson, Martin, and Stratocaster, this informative and beautifully illustrated work will have wide appeal." SLJ

Denyer, Ralph
The guitar handbook. {rev ed}. Knopf 1992 256p il pa $25 *
Grades: 11 12 Adult   **787.87**
1. Guitars
ISBN 0-679-74275-1   LC 92-53164
"A Dorling Kindersley book"
First published 1982
Contains a learning program covering the range of guitar techniques from simple chords to improvised lead solos, profiles of famous and influential guitarists, an illustrated chord dictionary, chapters on guitar customizing and recording techniques, and sections on a variety of acoustic and electric guitars, amplification, special effects and stage sound systems

790   Recreational and performing arts

Encyclopedia of recreation and leisure in America; Gary S. Cross, editor in chief. Charles Scribner's Sons 2004 2v il (Scribner American civilization series) set $270 *
Grades: 11 12 Adult   **790**
1. Recreation—Encyclopedias
ISBN 0-684-31265-4   LC 2004-4617
"This work provides information on all aspects of leisure in America, including historical influences, cultural changes, economic effects, and more. . . . This is a fascinating look at data useful for research papers, sociological studies, and historical evaluations or simply to satisfy curiosity." Libr J
Includes bibliographical references

790.1   General kinds of recreational activities

Owens, Tom, 1960-
Collecting baseball memorabilia; [by] Thomas S. Owens. Millbrook Press 1996 96p il lib bdg $26.90
Grades: 9 10 11 12   **790.1**
1. Collectors and collecting 2. Baseball
ISBN 1-56294-579-3   LC 95-19827
"This introduction delves into a wide array of baseball collectibles including tickets stubs, team schedules, autographs, and other items that can be obtained at little or no cost. . . . This book has a crisp layout with full-color photos or reproductions on nearly every page. While not a price guide, this title will be of interest to young baseball enthusiasts." SLJ
Includes glossary

Unique games and sports around the world; a reference guide; edited by Doris Corbett, John Cheffers, and Eileen Crowley Sullivan. Greenwood Press 2001 407p $59.95 *
Grades: 11 12 Adult   **790.1**
1. Games 2. Sports
ISBN 0-313-29778-9   LC 00-33125
A guide to more than 300 games. "Some involve physical action, like France's *Clubs royale;* others, like *Authors,* played in the U.S., are more intellectual. But most combine cognitive and physical activity. Organized by continents and then individual countries, entries for games note the typical players . . . the object of the game; number of players; equipment and apparel; type and amount of space needed; length of time; origin, purpose, or symbolic meaning; and the rules of play and scoring." Booklist
Includes bibliographical references

791.43 Motion pictures

The **Actor's** book of movie monologues; edited by Marisa Smith and Amy Schewel. Penguin Bks. 1986 xxx, 240p pa $14 *
Grades: 11 12 Adult   **791.43**
1. Motion pictures 2. Monologues
ISBN 0-14-009475-X   LC 86-8093
"Although designed as a sourcebook for aspiring thespians who need material for auditions, this collection of famous movie monologues makes great browsing for all film buffs. . . . Featuring memorable speeches from more than 80 films, the text is arranged chronologically." Booklist

Cavelos, Jeanne
The science of Star Wars. St. Martin's Press 1999 255p hardcover o.p. pa $14.95
Grades: 11 12 Adult   **791.43**
1. Space sciences 2. Star Wars films
ISBN 0-312-20958-4; 0-312-26387-2 (pa)
                                    LC 99-22007
An examination of space travel, aliens, planets, and robots as portrayed in the Star Wars films and books
"If you are willing to address this material seriously, you will find the book stimulating and fun. At points, it does get a bit deeper than, for example, a high school student will be ready to go, but a stretch is not a bad thing." Sci Books Films
Includes bibliographical references

Henderson, C. J.
The encyclopedia of science fiction movies; foreword by William Shatner. Facts on File 2001 516p il $75
Grades: 11 12 Adult   **791.43**
1. Science fiction films—Encyclopedias
ISBN 0-8160-4043-5   LC 00-61001
The main part of this work "consists of alphabetically arranged entries for more than 1,300 theatrical-release science fiction movies. Some basic credits are included, as well as the availability of the title on video, DVD, or laser disc. Then follows a synopsis and the author's opinions of the movie's watchability, validity as science fiction, and overall contribution to the genre. . . . The entries are followed by four appendixes, one a useful list of literature adapted to the screen and another of science fiction at the Oscars." Booklist

Lenburg, Jeff
The encyclopedia of animated cartoons; foreword by June Foray. 2nd ed. Facts on File 1999 576p il $75; pa $24.95
Grades: 9 10 11 12   **791.43**
1. Animated films
ISBN 0-8160-3831-7; 0-8160-3832-5 (pa)
                                    LC 98-46100
First published 1981 by Arlington House with title: The encyclopedia of animated cartoon series
"More than 2,200 cartoon entries encompass . . . creators, directors, production studios, voice talents, episode titles, and dates of release. . . . [Includes] more than 150 illustrations, and a nutshell history of American animation." Publisher's note
Includes bibliographical references

Maltin, Leonard
Leonard Maltin's movie guide 2007. Signet Bks. 2006 pa $20
Grades: 11 12 Adult   **791.43**
1. Motion pictures 2. Videotapes
ISSN 1555-7235
ISBN 0-452-28756-1; 978-0-452-28756-3
Annual. First published 1969 with title: TV movies. Title varies
This contains summaries and capsule reviews of thousands of films, videos, DVDs, and laserdisc releases, a list of recommended family films, filmographies of famous actors, and a list of specialty video mail-order companies.

Muir, John Kenneth, 1969-
The encyclopedia of superheroes on film and television. McFarland & Co 2004 621p il $59.95
Grades: 11 12 Adult   **791.43**
1. Heroes and heroines 2. Motion pictures 3. Television programs
ISBN 0-7864-1723-4   LC 2003-25048
"Each entry gives the comic-book origins, its super powers, technological gadgets, and arch-villains. Readers get critical reviews of the cinematic experience, cast and crew lists, a synopsis of the film or of each episode in a series, and a listing of spin-offs. . . . Hard-core superhero enthusiasts will treasure it." Libr Media Connect
Includes bibliographical references

Patmore, Chris
Movie making course; principles, practice, and techniques: the ultimate guide for the aspiring filmmaker. Barron's Educational Series, Inc. 2005 144p il pa $19.99 *
Grades: 11 12 Adult   **791.43**
1. Motion pictures—Production and direction
ISBN 0-7641-3191-5; 978-0-7641-3191-2
                                    LC 2004-111722
"All aspects of the moviemaking process are covered in five sections, including preproduction considerations (types of cameras and film, script writing, and storyboarding), the logistics of the actual shoot, postproduction activities (editing, special effects), suggested projects, and how to market the final product via film festivals and the Internet. . . . This volume will give students the tools necessary to produce a first film with little more than an idea, a video camera, and basic word-processing software." SLJ
Includes bibliographical references

Sanello, Frank
Reel v. real; how Hollywood turns fact into fiction. Taylor Pub. Co. 2003 303p il pa $19.95
Grades: 11 12 Adult   **791.43**
1. Motion pictures
ISBN 0-87833-268-5   LC 2001-27525

Sanello, Frank—*Continued*

This is "Sanello's comparison of the screen to the record for 70 'historical' flicks . . . [including] such Oscar winners as *Braveheart, Dances with Wolves, Shakespeare in Love, Titanic,* and *A Beautiful Mind.*" Booklist

Includes bibliographical references

Sansweet, Stephen J., 1945-

Star Wars encyclopedia; with an introduction by Timothy Zahn. Ballantine Bks. 1998 xxii, 354p il $49.95

Grades: 11 12 Adult   **791.43**

1. Star Wars films

ISBN 0-345-40227-8   LC 97-15066

"A Del Rey book"

This volume presents information on Star Wars "characters, planets, weapons, technology, events, and just about anything else that appears in any of the various comics, movies, books, toys, and collectibles currently available. . . . Serious fans will find this a major source of helpful facts presented in a useful format." SLJ

Includes bibliographical references

Sklar, Robert

A world history of film. rev & expanded ed. Abrams 2002 600p il $75 *

Grades: 11 12 Adult   **791.43**

1. Motion pictures

ISBN 0-8109-0606-6   LC 2001-22853

First published 1993 with title: Film: an international history of the medium

"Beginning with such precursors of cinema as the magic lantern and such pioneer filmmakers as the Lumières and Griffith, Sklar thereafter chronicles the rise of Hollywood, the development of genres, the advent of sound, and modern developments, right up to Pixar and the Farrelly brothers. . . . Well-selected photos profusely enhance the incisive text." Booklist

Includes filmography and bibliographical references

Welsch, Janice R.

Multicultural films; a reference guide; [by] Janice R. Welsch and J. Q. Adams. Greenwood Press 2005 231p il $49.95

Grades: Professional   **791.43**

1. Minorities in motion pictures

ISBN 0-313-31975-8   LC 2004-22529

This book "is a collection of synopses and brief analyses of selected American films. . . . It is divided into six sections, each of which covers a particular racial or ethnic group. The groups covered are African Americans, Arab and Middle Eastern Americans, Asian Americans, European Americans, Latino/a Americans, and Native Americans. . . . Each entry examines the way race or ethnicity functions in the film." Ref & User Services Quarterly

Includes bibliographical references

791.45   Television

Lackmann, Ronald W.

The encyclopedia of American television, broadcast programming Post World War II to 2000; {by} Ron Lackmann. Facts on File 2002 466p il $75

Grades: 11 12 Adult   **791.45**

1. Television broadcasting—Encyclopedias

ISBN 0-8160-4554-2   LC 2001-56856

Also available Lackmann's The encyclopedia of America radio: an A-Z guide to radio from Jack Benny to Howard Stern pa $18.95 (ISBN 0-8160-4077-X)

"The majority of entries are for programs and actors. Each program entry includes a description of the show, times the show aired, complete cast listings and notable guest stars, and the occasional interesting fact. Biographical entries include dates of birth and death, along with the actor's television credits. Any significant acting work done outside of television is also mentioned. All entries are enhanced with excellent cross-references to related shows and actors. Coverage of special television events and programs is also included." Am Ref Books Annu, 2003

Includes bibliographical references

Morris, Holly, 1965-

Adventure divas; searching the globe for a new kind of heroine. Villard 2005 xx, 283p il $23.95; pa $14.95

Grades: 11 12 Adult   **791.45**

1. Adventure divas (Television program)

ISBN 0-375-50827-9; 0-375-76063-6 (pa)

      LC 2005-45171

The author describes the "people and places she's encountered on the road while filming her PBS series Adventure Divas and other programs." Publisher's note

This "is a delightful triangulation of adventure travel, telecommuting and self-reinvention that proves it does not, in fact, take a rocket scientist to achieve personal flight." N Y Times Book Rev

Includes bibliographical references

Stashower, Daniel

The boy genius and the mogul; the untold story of television. Broadway Bks. 2002 xx, 277p il $24.95

Grades: 11 12 Adult   **791.45**

1. Farnsworth, Philo T., 1906-1971 2. Sarnoff, David, 1891-1971 3. Television—History

ISBN 0-7679-0759-0   LC 2002-283169

Stashower chronicles the life of the "farm boy who came up with the revolutionary idea that would ultimately make television possible as we know it today. Yet young Philo Farnsworth, with limited funding and a handful of friends to help build the apparatus, could not compete with the powerful David Sarnoff, president of RCA, who was determined to become the leader in the television effort. This book intermingles biographies of both men with the broader story of television's early years. . . . The amount of technical detail [Stashower] provides . . . is enough to give the reader an idea of

Stashower, Daniel—*Continued*
what the inventors had to work with, yet simplified
enough to be accessible to a general audience." Booklist
Includes bibliographical references

791.5 Puppetry and toy theaters

Blumenthal, Eileen, 1948-
Puppetry; a world history. Abrams 2005 272p il
$65 *
Grades: 11 12 Adult   791.5
  1. Puppets and puppet plays
  ISBN 0-8109-5587-3   LC 2004-29349
This is a "history of the puppet world, from prehistor-
ic times to Tony-winning Broadway hit Avenue Q. . . .
This would be a welcome addition to the libraries of per-
forming arts buffs who want to learn more about a lesser
known form." Publ Wkly
Includes bibliographical references

792 Stage presentations

Brustein, Robert, 1927-
Letters to a young actor; a universal guide to
performance. Basic Books 2005 234p (Art of
mentoring) $22.50; pa $15
Grades: 11 12 Adult   792
  1. Acting 2. Vocational guidance
  ISBN 0-465-00806-2; 0-465-00814-3 (pa)
                                        LC 2004-23438
The author "covers all aspects of an emerging actor's
life, from the 'actor's calling' to getting a strong liberal
education . . . to strategies for finding work and staying
employed." Booklist
"This is a sharp, accessible but far from simplistic
Cliffs Notes on being an actor." Publ Wkly

Corson, Richard
Stage makeup; [by] Richard Corson, James
Glavan. 9th ed. Allyn and Bacon 2001 xix, 428p
il $130 *
Grades: 11 12 Adult   792
  1. Theatrical makeup
  ISBN 0-13-606153-2   LC 00-46879
First published 1942 by Appleton. Periodically revised
The authors discuss the art and technique of theatrical
makeup, covering such topics as facial anatomy, various
methods for applying greasepaint and other makeup, and
the use of beards, wigs, and prosthetic pieces

Ellis, Roger, 1943-
The complete audition book for young actors; a
comprehensive guide to winning by enhancing
acting skills. Meriwether Pub 2003 295p il pa
$17.95
Grades: 9 10 11 12   792
  1. Acting
  ISBN 1-566-08088-6   LC 2003-21120
First published 1986 by Nelson-Hall with title: An audition handbook for student actors

A step-by-step guide for training young actors to audition well by developing acting skills.
This guide features "chapters on training, background
skills, how to select and prepare material for an audition,
cold readings, musical theater, and supporting materials
such as résumé and head shots . . . The writing is so engaging that it is a pleasure to read straight through. Ellis
speaks to his readers as a trusted advisor or coach . . .
Acting teachers looking for a text and students looking
for a useful and inspiring guidebook will welcome this
title." SLJ
Includes bibliographical references

Gillette, J. Michael
Theatrical design and production; an
introduction to scene design and construction,
lighting, sound, costume, and makeup. 4th ed.
Mayfield 1999 587p il $69.60 *
Grades: 11 12 Adult   792
  1. Theaters—Stage setting and scenery
  ISBN 0-7674-1191-9   LC 99-28595
First published 1987
This is a "survey of the technical and design aspects
of play production, including scene design and construction, lighting, sound, costume, and makeup. Health and
safety precautions for the backstage crew appear throughout in boxes labeled 'Safety Tips,' and 'Design Inspiration' boxes show how professional designers create the
desired look." Publisher's note
Includes bibliographical references

Jay, Annie
Stars in your eyes—feet on the ground; a
practical guide for teenage actors and their parents
too! [by] Annie Jay with LuAnne Feik; illustrated
by Ron Crawford. Theatre Directories 1999 150p
il pa $16.95
Grades: 9 10 11 12   792
  1. Acting
  ISBN 0-933919-42-5
The author "offers a practical guide for others like
herself with a serious yearning for a stage or screen career. . . . In chapters devoted to come-on scams, other
entertainment venues besides film and theater, unions,
and education, there is a positive, informative, down-to-
earth tone that sweeps the reader along. A final chapter,
written by Jay's mother, is devoted to a parent's role."
Booklist

Kuritz, Paul
Fundamental acting; a practical guide. Applause
Theatre Bk. Pubs. 1998 157p $24.95 *
Grades: 11 12 Adult   792
  1. Acting
  ISBN 1-55783-304-4   LC 97-27053
"Aimed at the beginning acting student, this book
takes a commonsense approach to the craft, building on
basic techniques in the first part and then going on to
cover two distinct types of theater: comedy and Shakespearean verse. . . . Warm-up exercises, comic dialect
guidelines, and a general stage terminology contribute to
the usefulness of the book." Libr J

Lee, Robert L., 1945-
Everything about theatre! the guidebook of theatre fundamentals. Meriwether 1996 216p il pa $17.95
Grades: 11 12 Adult   **792**
1. Theater—Production and direction 2. Acting
ISBN 1-56608-019-3   LC 96-6742
The author "covers topics such as costumes, stage directions, set design, and basic acting. Several chapters begin with brief historical accounts, such as the one containing the chronological development of stage types. . . . Lee presents a well-organized concise approach to the world of stage and drama that's appropriate for both aspiring actors and the adults who work with them." SLJ

Levy, Gavin
112 acting games; a comprehensive workbook of theatre games for developing acting skills. Meriwether Pub. 2005 237p il pa $17.95
Grades: 9 10 11 12   **792**
1. Acting 2. Games
ISBN 1-56608-106-8; 978-1-56608-106-1
     LC 2005-1784
"The games in this workbook for acting students are divided into twenty different categories, including Relaxtion, Memorization, and Improvision. The author explains the instructions for each game in a clear manner, including tips on student placement, the appropriate number of participants, and modifications for varying ages. . . . This book is a definite asset to any drama teacher." Voice Youth Advocates
Includes bibliographical references

Varley, Joy
Places, please! a manual for high-school theater directors. Smith & Kraus 2001 196p (Young actor series) pa $16.95 *
Grades: 9 10 11 12   **792**
1. Theater—Production and direction
ISBN 1-57525-282-1   LC 01-20316
This guide offers guidance on choosing a script, casting, costuming, working with faculty, rehearsing, directing young actors, stage design and lighting

792.03   Theater--Encyclopedias and dictionaries

Bordman, Gerald Martin
The Oxford companion to American theatre; {by} Gerald Bordman, Thomas S. Hischak. 3rd ed. Oxford University Press 2004 681p $75 *
Grades: 11 12 Adult   **792.03**
1. Theater—United States—Dictionaries 2. American drama—Dictionaries
ISBN 0-19-516986-7   LC 2003-21367
First published 1984
"The volume includes playwrights, plays, actors, directors, producers, songwriters, famous playhouses, {and} dramatic movements. . . . The book covers not only classic works (such as *Death of a Salesman*) but also many commercially successful plays (such as *Getting Gertie's Garter*), plus entries on foreign figures that have influenced our dramatic development (from Shakespeare to Beckett and Pinter)." Publisher's note
"Individual entries are packed with detail. . . . Hischak provides ample material for researchers, and should be a mainstay of any performing arts reference collection." Choice

Cambridge guide to American theatre; edited by Don B. Wilmeth and Tice L. Miller. Cambridge Univ. Press 1993 547p il $64.95; pa $24.95
Grades: 11 12 Adult   **792.03**
1. Theater—United States—Dictionaries 2. American drama—Dictionaries
ISBN 0-521-40134-8; 0-521-56444-1 (pa)
     LC 92-35030
Based on The Cambridge guide to world theatre
This guide "offers brief, alphabetically arranged essays on American theatrical figures—actors, playwrights, producers, directors, designers—plays, and major theatres from the art form's origins in native American rituals to the present. . . . Wonderfully compact, well written and generously illustrated, this is recommended for most libraries." Libr J

792.09   Theater--Historical and geographic treatment

Brockett, Oscar Gross, 1923-
History of the theatre; [by] Oscar G. Brockett, Franklin J. Hildy. 9th ed. Allyn and Bacon 2003 692p il map $116 *
Grades: 11 12 Adult   **792.09**
1. Theater—History 2. Drama—History and criticism
ISBN 0-205-35878-0   LC 2002-25352
First published 1968
This work traces the development of the theater from primitive times to the present, with an emphasis on European theater.
Includes bibliographical references

Kermode, Frank, 1919-
The age of Shakespeare. Modern Library 2004 214p il $21.95
Grades: 11 12 Adult   **792.09**
1. Shakespeare, William, 1564-1616—Stage history
ISBN 0-679-64244-7   LC 2003-044287
"Modern Library chronicles"
"The book moves . . . through the latest critical debates about the Bard's origins, and . . . summarizes the historical background of the Elizabethan and Jacobean periods in which he lived and worked. The great political and religious issues of the times are explicated . . . and linked to the development of live theater as a mainstay of English popular culture. . . . This is an excellent choice for students curious (or struggling) to understand what all the fuss is about the Bard of Avon." SLJ
Includes bibliographical references

The **Oxford** illustrated history of theatre; edited by John Russell Brown. Oxford Univ. Press 1995 582p il pa $27.50 hardcover o.p. *
Grades: 11 12 Adult   **792.09**
1. Theater—History
ISBN 0-19-285442-9   LC 95-231683
Covering theatre history from the ancient Greeks to the 1990s, this "resource provides a wide variety of information from basic theatre chronology to detailed analyses of several well-known and important plays and playwrights. . . . The emphasis is on European and Western theatre, but a chapter provides a concise summary on Southern and Eastern Asian theatre." SLJ
Includes bibliographical references

Sova, Dawn B.
Banned plays; censorship histories of 125 stage dramas. Facts on File 2003 400p (Facts on File library of world literature) $55; pa $16.95
Grades: 11 12 Adult   **792.09**
1. Drama—History and criticism 2. Censorship
ISBN 0-8160-4018-4; 0-8160-5070-8 (pa)
                                             LC 2003-63113
This book "details the censorship of plays throughout 2,500 years of theater history. Each entry begins with a . . . list of the play's author or authors, date and place of original production, characters, and filmed versions. A . . . plot summary is followed by . . . [an] account of the play's censorship history." Choice
The author "has chosen a fine, representative selection of suppressed plays throughout the centuries. . . . This meticulously researched title offers valuable information for both scholars and casual readers." SLJ
Includes bibliographical references

792.6 Musical plays

Boland, Robert, 1925-
Musicals! directing school and community theatre; {by} Robert Boland and Paul Argentini. Scarecrow Press 1997 xxv, 202p il pa $35
Grades: 11 12 Adult   **792.6**
1. Musicals—Production and direction
ISBN 0-8108-3323-9   LC 97-11996
This is "a handbook for novice directors of the musical. This illustrated nuts-and-bolts compendium includes 22 chapters divided among three major sections addressing preparation, production, and performance. Through accessible prose and a you-can-do-it tone, the authors provide an overview of preproduction planning, auditioning and casting, blocking, stage composition, rehearsals, and choreography, as well as the more technical layers of set design, costumes, and lights." Libr J
Includes bibliographical references

Bordman, Gerald Martin
American musical theatre; a chronicle; {by} Gerald Bordman. 3rd ed. Oxford Univ. Press 2001 917p $75
Grades: 11 12 Adult   **792.6**
1. Musicals
ISBN 0-19-513074-X   LC 00-59812

First published 1978
This book offers "show-by-show, season-by-season descriptions—from the first musical to the 1999/2000 Broadway season. . . . {It} encompasses all musical entertainment from plays, revues, opera bouffe and operettas to one-man and one-woman shows. {It} includes mini-biographies and . . . song, show and people indexes." Publisher's note

Kantor, Michael, 1961-
Broadway: the American musical; [by] Michael Kantor; Laurence Maslon. Bulfinch Press 2004 480p il $60 *
Grades: 11 12 Adult   **792.6**
1. Musicals
ISBN 0-8212-2905-2   LC 2003-69715
Contents: A real live nephew of my Uncle Sam (1893-1919) -- Syncopated city (1920-1929) -- I got plenty o' nuttin' (1930-1941) -- Oh, what a beautiful mornin' (1942-1960) -- Tradition (1960-1980) -- Lullaby of Broadway (1980-present)
This companion volume to a PBS documentary includes interviews and photographs of Broadway musicals from 1893 to 2004
"With its beguiling blend of entertainment and history, this splendid work is a must-have." Publ Wkly
Includes bibliographical references

Lamb, Andrew
150 years of popular musical theatre. Yale Univ. Press 2000 380p il $39.95
Grades: 11 12 Adult   **792.6**
1. Musicals
ISBN 0-300-07538-3   LC 00-25281
This volume covers "popular music theater from mid-nineteenth-century French operettas to British and American musical comedies to late-twentieth-century rock operas." Booklist

792.7 Variety shows and theatrical dancing

Nevraumont, Edward J., 1975-
The ultimate improv book; a complete guide to comedy improvisation; [by] Edward J. Nevraumont and Nicholas P. Hanson, with additional material from Kurt Smeaton. Meriwether 2001 272p pa $16.95
Grades: 9 10 11 12   **792.7**
1. Comedy 2. Acting
ISBN 1-56608-075-4   LC 2001-51396
"Suggestions for assembling a capable, compatible team of players, setting up performances guidelines, and keeping the action flowing and on target for the audience preface setups for 60 games. The game-exercises . . . are specifically designed to assist players in using language, literature, song, and movement in their skits." Booklist
Includes bibliographical references

792.8 Ballet and modern dance

Craine, Debra
The Oxford dictionary of dance; by Debra Craine, Judith Mackrell. Oxford Univ. Press 2000 527p $49.95; pa $16.95 *
Grades: 11 12 Adult   **792.8**
1. Dance—Dictionaries
ISBN 0-19-860106-9; 0-19-860400-9 (pa)
    LC 2001-274422
Based on The concise Oxford dictionary of ballet by Horst Kroegler
"The styles covered range from the Brazilian martial art form of *capoeria* to American hip-hop. . . . Most entries are brief, except for those on major individuals, institutions, and works. Some themes are treated (shoes, film, dance notation). Work lists are provided, as well as an extensive bibliography." Choice
Includes bibliographical references

Fishman, Katharine Davis
Attitude!: eight young dancers come of age at the Ailey School. J.P. Tarcher\Penguin 2004 285p il $23.95
Grades: 11 12 Adult   **792.8**
1. Ailey School (New York, N.Y.) 2. Modern dance 3. Dancers
ISBN 1-585-42355-6   LC 2004-49847
"Fishman spent a year at one of the nation's top dance academies to observe eight gifted students and try to ascertain why some, and not others, go on to pursue dance careers." Publ Wkly
The author "opens a fascinating window onto the world of these exceptional yet normal teenagers." Booklist
Includes bibliographical references

Reynolds, Nancy, 1938-
No fixed points; dance in the twentieth century; {by} Nancy Reynolds and Malcolm McCormick. Yale Univ. Press 2003 907p il $50
Grades: 11 12 Adult   **792.8**
1. Dance 2. Ballet 3. Modern dance
ISBN 0-300-09366-7   LC 2003-10754
This is a "narrative of the development of ballet, modern dance, and postmodern choreography. Synthesizing a century's worth of observation and opinion, Reynolds and McCormick chart the pendulum swing of styles and isolate individual contributions. . . . They highlight the significance of factors as large as government funding and as small as the depth of Baryshnikov's demi-plié." New Yorker
"Although everyone will be using the book for reference, Reynolds and McCormick have produced a work that is completely unlike a standard reference book; you don't just look things up in it—you read it. Here is a coherent, reasoned and entertaining chronicle of dance performance in the West over the hundred years that are unquestionably the fullest and most complicated in the long history of this fragmented and elusive art." N Y Times
Includes bibliographical references

Warren, Gretchen
Classical ballet technique; [by] Gretchen Ward Warren; photographs by Susan Cook. University of S. Fla. Press 1989 395p il $85; pa $39.95
Grades: 11 12 Adult   **792.8**
1. Ballet
ISBN 0-8130-0895-6; 0-8130-0945-6 (pa)
    LC 89-31141
Text and numerous photographs explain the correct execution of ballet steps
"General material on basic concepts, body structure and proportion, and ballet class proceed this extraordinary manual and guide." Booklist
Includes glossary and bibliographical references

793.73 Puzzles and puzzle games

Pulliam, Tom
The New York times crossword puzzle dictionary; by Tom Pulliam and Clare Grundman. 3rd ed. Times Bks. 1995 656p $27.50; pa $18.95 *
Grades: 11 12 Adult   **793.73**
1. Crossword puzzles—Dictionaries
ISBN 0-8129-2373-1; 0-8129-2823-7 (pa)
    LC 95-11416
"A Hudson Group book"
First published 1977
This dictionary of synonyms for crossword puzzles includes more than 50,000 entries.
"One of the more useful works of its kind." Ref Sources for Small & Medium-sized Libr. 6th edition

793.74 Mathematical games and recreations

Banks, Robert B.
Slicing pizzas, racing turtles, and further adventures in applied mathematics. Princeton Univ. Press 1999 286p il $39.95; pa $17.95
Grades: 9 10 11 12   **793.74**
1. Mathematical recreations
ISBN 0-691-05947-0; 0-691-10284-8 (pa)
    LC 98-53513
This "is a collection of mathematical investigations. . . . Topics range from prime numbers, sequences, and famous numbers (e.g., pi and e) to questions like what rivers run uphill, what would happen if all ice on the planet were to melt, and how many people have ever lived." Choice
"Banks's style is entertaining but never condescending. Some of the math is pretty tough; it helps if you did well in trigonometry as well as introductory calculus and analytic geometry." Christ Sci Monit
Includes bibliographical references

793.8 Magic and related activities

Gardner, Martin, 1914-
The colossal book of short puzzles and problems; combinatorics, probability, algebra, geometry, topology, chess, logic, cryptarithms, wordplay, physics and other topics of recreational mathematics; edited by Dana Richards. Norton 2006 494p il $35
Grades: 11 12 Adult   **793.8**
1. Mathematical recreations 2. Scientific recreations
ISBN 0-393-06114-0; 978-0-393-06114-7
LC 2005-24080
This is a compilation of puzzles from Martin Gardner's "column, 'Mathematical Games,' which appeared for over 25 years in Scientific American. . . . [The topics] include combinatorics, probability, algebra, plane and solid geometry, topology, games, chess, logic, wordplay, and physics, among others. . . . Anyone interested in recreational mathematics should like this book. The puzzles are fascinating and the book is easily browsed. It can also serve as a good reference for (high school and college) teachers seeking interesting problems to complement routine ones in mathematics texts." Sci Books Films

794.1 Chess

King, Daniel, 1963-
Chess; from first moves to checkmate. Kingfisher (NY) 2000 64p il $16.95 *
Grades: 5 6 7 8 9 10 11 12   **794.1**
1. Chess
ISBN 0-7534-5387-8   LC 00-26353
Introduces the rules and strategies of chess, as well as its history and some of the great players and matches
The author "offers training exercises, strategy quizzes, and trivia, all of which add depth and texture to his explanations. The computer-generated graphics are staggering. The colorful, multi-image illustrations are not only aesthetically appealing but also crystal clear and very effectively placed to enhance the text." Booklist

United States Chess Federation
U.S. Chess Federation's official rules of chess; compiled and sanctioned by the U.S. Chess Federation; Tim Just, chief editor; Daniel B. Burg, editor. 5th ed. Random House Puzzles & Games 2003 xxxvii, 370p il (McKay chess library) pa $18.95
Grades: 11 12 Adult   **794.1**
1. Chess
ISBN 0-8129-3559-4   LC 2003-278349
"This book supersedes the Official rules of chess, first edition, 1974, second edition, 1978, third edition, 1987, and fourth edition, 1993"
This "edition features the latest rules, including guidelines for the popular game of speed chess, an updated quick rating system, and the latest conventions of governing tournaments. It also contains explanations of every

legal move, a guide to calculating lifetime rankings, guidelines for sponsoring and running a tournament, and a lesson on how to read and write chess notation." Publisher's note

794.6 Bowling

Anthony, Earl, 1938-2001
Winning bowling; [by] Earl Anthony with Dawson Taylor. Contemporary Bks. 1994 198p il pa $12.95
Grades: 11 12 Adult   **794.6**
1. Bowling
ISBN 0-8092-3526-9   LC 94-21344
First published 1977
This is a guide to bowling techniques for beginners.

795.4 Card games

Hugard, Jean, 1872-1959
Encyclopedia of card tricks; revised and edited by Jean Hugard, associate editor, John J. Crimmins, Jr.; illustrations by Nelson Hahne. Dover Publs. 1974 402p il pa $9.95
Grades: 9 10 11 12   **795.4**
1. Card tricks
ISBN 0-486-21252-1
Revised edition of the Encyclopedia of self working card tricks by G. G. Gravatt
Explains how to perform over 600 card tricks

796 Athletic and outdoor sports and games

American women in sport, 1887-1987; a 100-year chronology; compiled by Ruth M. Sparhawk {et al.}. Scarecrow Press 1989 149p il $30 *
Grades: 11 12 Adult   **796**
1. Women athletes
ISBN 0-8108-2205-9   LC 89-6150
The main section of this "chronology is a year-by-year listing of accomplishments made by women in amateur and professional sports. This chronology can be accessed by a subject index to over 70 sports or by an extensive name index. There is also an unannotated bibliography." Voice Youth Advocates

Becoming an ironman; first encounters with the ultimate endurance event; edited by Kara Douglass. Breakaway Bks. 2001 286p il hardcover o.p. pa $14
Grades: 11 12 Adult   **796**
1. Triathlon
ISBN 1-891369-24-5; 1-891369-31-8 (pa)
This book surveys the history of the Ironman triathlon, a competition consisting "of a 2.4-mile swim, a 112-mile bike race, and a full marathon (26.2-mile run), all done in one day." Libr J

The **Best** American sports writing of the century; edited by David Halberstam. Houghton Mifflin 1999 776p $30; pa $18 *

Grades: 11 12 Adult **796**

1. Sports

ISBN 0-395-94513-5; 0-395-94514-3 (pa)

"Although there are pieces about mountain climbing, tennis and chess, fully half of the selections are about two sports: baseball and boxing. The book begins with a Best of the Best section led by Gay Talese's 1966 profile of Joe DiMaggio, 'The Silent Season of a Hero.'. . . The final section is a special six-piece tribute to a man who himself claimed to be the best of the best—Muhammad Ali." Publ Wkly

Craig, Steve, 1961-

Sports and games of the ancients. Greenwood Press 2002 271p il (Sports and games through history) $49.95 *

Grades: 11 12 Adult **796**

1. Ancient history

ISBN 0-313-31600-7 LC 2001-50101

This "book, arranged by geographic regions, focuses on the development of sports and games and the effect they had on the lives of people from the first Olympiad to the fall of Rome. . . . The author provides descriptions of each sport, explains essential equipment (including how to make it), and the rules of play. . . . Mancala, stick fighting, sumo wrestling (for both men and women), go, the log run, tejo, boomerangs, buzkashi, kabaddi, and Chinese football are among the topics covered. The material provided is not readily available in other single resources." SLJ

Includes bibliographical references

ESPN sports almanac 2006. Pearson Education 2006 il pa $12.99 *

Grades: 9 10 11 12 **796**

1. Sports

ISSN 1555-8304

ISBN 1-93306-016-6; 978-1-93306-016-3

Annual. First published 2004 as a continuation of ESPN information please sports almanac

"The almanac examines in detail baseball, college football, professional football, college basketball, professional basketball, other college sports, and hockey. The editors touch upon many other less conventional sports, such as archery, dog sledding, gymnastics, auto racing, boxing, and so on. Each section looks at statistics of the game and offers an essay highlighting an important event of the past year. Related topics cover ballparks and arenas, halls of fame and awards, who's who, and business." Recomm Ref Books in Paperback. 3d edition

Franck, Irene M.

Famous first facts about sports; {by} Irene M. Franck & David M. Brownstone. Wilson, H.W. 2001 903p $160 *

Grades: 7 8 9 10 **796**

1. Sports

ISBN 0-8242-0973-7 LC 00-43883

"Franck and Brownstone have compiled 5,415 'firsts' covering more than 110 sports. . . . Arranged alphabetically by sport, the concisely described events are listed in chronological order, with headers for time periods. Entries are given consecutive four-digit numbers, which are cited in the five indexes (subjects, years, days, personal names, and geographical locations). . . . The indexes provide essential access and are easy to use. . . . The depth of coverage is impressive." Choice

Includes bibliographical references

Game face; what does a woman athlete look like? {created and developed by} Jane Gottesman; edited by Geoffrey Biddle; foreword by Penny Marshall. Random House 2001 223p il hardcover o.p. pa $19.95

Grades: 9 10 11 12 **796**

1. Women athletes 2. Sports

ISBN 0-375-50602-0; 0-812-96868-9 (pa)

      LC 00-45976

Book will coincide with a 3-month exhibition at the Smithsonian Institution in Washington, D.C. and will continue as a traveling exhbit over the next five years

"This collection of black-and-white photographs features female athletes-amateurs and professional; team and individual standouts; stars of the past and present; portraits and snapshots; and young and old—engaged in various physical endeavors. The theme is variety and progress in women's sports. Each photo is accompanied by an identification of the sport, occasionally with a quote from the player depicted. . . . A welcome and timely addition for sports' collections." SLJ

Hastings, Penny

Sports for her; a reference guide for teenage girls. Greenwood Press 1999 254p il $45 *

Grades: 11 12 Adult **796**

1. Sports for women

ISBN 0-313-30551-X LC 99-21279

Discusses issues related to girls' participation in sports and provides information on the rules, equipment, training, and more for eight sports which high school girls are most likely to play

Includes bibliographical references

Hickok, Ralph

The encyclopedia of North American sports history. 2nd ed. Facts on File 2002 594p il $75 *

Grades: 11 12 Adult **796**

1. Sports—Encyclopedias

ISBN 0-8160-4660-3 LC 2001-55646

First published 1992

"Entries fall into eight categories: sports; general history; biography; sporting events; major awards; cities; stadiums, fields, and arenas; and sports organizations, such as leagues, college conferences, and halls of fame. . . . The importance of this volume is in its coverage of a variety of minor sports, such as women's synchronized swimming, steamboat racing, skin diving, and sled dog racing, for which finding information may be difficult." Booklist

Men in sports; great sports stories of all time from the Greek Olympic games to the American World Series; edited and with an introduction by Brandt Aymar. Crown 1994 499p pa $25 hardcover o.p.

Grades: 11 12 Adult   **796**

1. Sports

ISBN 0-517-88395-3   LC 93-19818

A "collection of nearly fifty sporting entries. Arranged alphabetically, the anthology includes fiction, nonfiction, sports reporting, and excerpts from longer works." Voice Youth Advocates

Musiker, Liz Hartman

The smart girl's guide to sports; a hip handbook for women who don't know a slam dunk from a grand slam. Hudson Street Press 2005 301p il $19.95

Grades: 9 10 11 12   **796**

1. Sports

ISBN 1-59463-011-9   LC 2005-18858

This book "covers all the major professional sports: football, basketball, baseball, hockey, golf, soccer, boxing, and even car racing. Each chapter includes a 'Here's How It Works' section that explains the basics of the game; [and] profiles of each sport's timeless greats and 'contemporary cool' players." Publisher's note

"Armed with both facts and humor, Musiker has written what could become an invaluable resource for football, baseball, hockey, basketball, golf, boxing, or NASCAR widows. . . . This guidebook will be a welcome helper for millions of sports-shy women (and men)." Booklist

Includes bibliographical references

Nike is a goddess; the history of women in sports; edited by Lissa Smith; introduction by Mariah Burton Nelson. Atlantic Monthly Press 1998 331p il pa $14 hardcover o.p.

Grades: 11 12 Adult   **796**

1. Sports 2. Women athletes

ISBN 0-87113-761-5   LC 98-27049

This "anthology documents the athletic achievements of female athletes during the late-nineteenth and twentieth centuries. Separate chapters written by noted sports journalists (Grace Lichtenstein, Michelle Kaufman, Karen Karbo) cover such disciplines as basketball, soccer, baseball, swimming, horseback riding, tennis, golf, and hockey, among others." Booklist

"The quality of writing in the different sections varies but each writer is well connected with her field and all give a good background history as well as an assessment of current developments in the sport. Controversial issues are not ignored, and lesbianism is addressed." SLJ

Professional sports; James D. Torr, editor. Greenhaven Press 2004 192p (Examining pop culture) lib bdg $26.96; pa $17.96 *

Grades: 9 10 11 12   **796**

1. Professional sports 2. Popular culture—United States

ISBN 0-7377-1587-1 (lib bdg); 0-7377-1588-X (pa)   LC 2002-192519

"Articles written by journalists, college professors, authors, and researchers {discuss} topics such as, 'The Super Bowl and U.S. Chauvinism' and 'Femininity and Feminism in the WNBA.' A wide variety of subjects is covered, including the rise of extreme sports, the market power of professional athletes, the history of professional sports, and fanatic fans. Each in-depth article covers a topic from many angles. This is a useful tool for students doing research or simply looking for expert opinions on some of today's hottest sports topics." SLJ

Includes bibliographical references

Sports and athletes: opposing viewpoints; James D. Torr, book editor. Greenhaven Press 2005 188p il lib bdg $33.70; pa $22.45 *

Grades: 9 10 11 12   **796**

1. Sports

ISBN 0-7377-2244-4 (lib bdg); 0-7377-2245-2 (pa)   LC 2004-53924

"Opposing viewpoints series"

"Authors in this volume examine a variety of sports controversies in chapters such as Is Drug Use a Problem in Sports? and Do Sports Benefit Children?" Publisher's note

Includes bibliographical references

Sports Illustrated . . . almanac 2007; by the editors of Sports Illustrated. Little, Brown 2006 il pa $12.99 *

Grades: 7 8 9 10 11 12 Adult   **796**

1. Sports

ISBN 1-933405-46-5; 978-1-933405-46-9

Annual. First published 1991 with title: Sports illustrated . . . sports almanac

"Provides team and individual records and highlights for all major sports. . . . A brief essay opens the section on each sport, followed by page upon page of records, both current and retrospective. Interspersed throughout . . . are black-and-white and color photographs and notable quotations by sports figures." Am Ref Books Annu, 1993

Sports: the complete visual reference; François Fortin {general editor}. Firefly Bks. 2000 372p il $39.95; pa $24.95 *

Grades: 11 12 Adult   **796**

1. Sports

ISBN 1-55209-540-1; 1-55297-807-9 (pa)

This is a "reference source on 120 contemporary sports . . . pulling together the history, physical environment for competitions, roles of the players and officials, specific terms and expressions, and dynamics of each. All of this is done with an emphasis on visual presentation, and each entry includes copious illustrations." Booklist

"A sure winner for any sports reference collection." Am Libr

796.03 Sports--Encyclopedias and dictionaries

Berkshire encyclopedia of world sport; David Levinson and Karen Christensen, editors. Berkshire Pub. Group 2005 4v il set $475 *
Grades: 11 12 Adult   **796.03**
1. Sports—Encyclopedias
ISBN 0-9743091-1-7   LC 2005-13050
"This encyclopedia covers a range of topics from professional and amateur sports and sporting events to national sports and issues and influences affecting athletics. . . . A broad, well-written resource." SLJ
For a fuller review, see: Booklist, Sept. 1, 2005
Includes bibliographical references

Encyclopedia of women and sport in America; edited by Carole A. Oglesby; with [contributions by] Doreen L. Greenberg [et al.] Oryx Press 1998 xxiii, 360p il $77.95 *
Grades: 8 9 10 11 12 Adult   **796.03**
1. Women athletes—Encyclopedias 2. Sports—Encyclopedias
ISBN 0-89774-993-6   LC 97-52787
"This encyclopedia provides short biographical entries with time and place of birth and then spells out the women's athletic accomplishments. It also includes historical articles, such as 'Badminton and Women' and sociological/psychological entries, such as 'Goal Setting and Women'." Voice Youth Advocates
"This clearly written book offers more information about American female athletes than any other single source." SLJ
Includes bibliographical references

International encyclopedia of women and sports; edited by Karen Christensen, Allen Guttmann, Gertrud Pfister. Macmillan Ref. USA 2000 3v set $375
Grades: 11 12 Adult   **796.03**
1. Women athletes—Encyclopedias
ISBN 0-02-864954-0   LC 00-62518
This "set provides articles on all aspects of the history and the current state of women's sports. Included are more than 230 biographies, 170 individual and group sports, and 75 country profiles, plus examinations of cultural, societal, health, and ethical issues." Am Libr
"A monumental undertaking. . . . This encyclopedia's strengths lie in its unique, cross-cultural treatment of all subjects. . . . A scholarly resource for public libraries and schools at all levels, middle school through college." Libr J
Includes bibliographical references

Rules of the game; the complete illustrated encyclopedia of all the sports of the world. [rev ed] St. Martin's Press 1990 320p il pa $21.95 hardcover o.p. *
Grades: 11 12 Adult   **796.03**
1. Sports—Encyclopedias
ISBN 0-312-11940-2   LC 90-37196
First published 1974 with title: The rule book

This volume covers 150 sports "grouped under 13 headings such as water, court, team, wheels, and air. Each article contains a detailed discussion of major objectives, playing area and equipment, rules, timing and scoring, and participants and officials." Booklist

796.21 Roller skating

Dugard, Martin
In-line skating made easy; a manual for beginners with tips for the experienced. Globe Pequot Press 1996 149p il pa $16.95
Grades: 9 10 11 12   **796.21**
1. In-line skating
ISBN 1-56440-903-1   LC 96-19861
"An East Woods book"
"Dugard discusses the various protective devices and how to wear them effectively. Basic foot positions for novices and more advanced skills for experienced skaters are explained. Excellent diagrams clearly show the dynamics of in-line skating. . . . All phases of the sport from preparation to cross training are demonstrated by action photos." SLJ

Werner, Doug, 1950-
In-line skater's start-up; a beginner's guide to in-line skating and roller hockey. Tracks Pub. 1995 159p il (Start-up sports) pa $9.95
Grades: 9 10 11 12   **796.21**
1. In-line skating
ISBN 1-884654-04-5   LC 95-60153
This work discusses the various techniques and equipment required for both skating and hockey. This illustrated guide also provides safety tips

796.22 Skateboarding

Jay, Jackson
Skateboarding basics. Capstone Press 1996 48p il (New action sports) $17.95
Grades: 7 8 9 10   **796.22**
1. Skateboarding
ISBN 1-56065-374-4; 978-1-56065-374-5
                              LC 95-44719
Describes the history, equipment, and techniques involved in the sport of skateboarding.
Includes bibliographical references

796.323 Basketball

Coffey, Wayne R.
Winning sounds like this; a season with the women's basketball team at Gallaudet, the world's only university for the deaf; {by} Wayne Coffey. Crown 2002 239p il hardcover o.p. pa $13 *
Grades: 11 12 Adult   **796.323**

Coffey, Wayne R.—*Continued*
1. Basketball 2. Women athletes 3. Deaf
ISBN 0-609-60765-0; 1-4000-4678-5 (pa)

"Coffey's account of the 1999-2000 women's basketball season at Gallaudet University not only follows the team from game to game but also examines the school's close-knit deaf community. . . . What comes through most clearly is the independence and identity that Gallaudet and basketball foster in these determined young women." Booklist

Colton, Larry, 1942-
Counting coup; a true story of basketball and honor on the Little Big Horn. Warner Bks. 2000 420p hardcover o.p. pa $14.95 *
Grades: 11 12 Adult **796.323**
1. Hardin High School (Hardin, Mont.)—Basketball 2. Basketball 3. Women athletes 4. Native Americans—Social conditions
ISBN 0-446-52683-5; 0-446-67755-8 (pa)
LC 00-24987

The author discusses the basketball team of Hardin High School on the Crow Indian Reservation in Montana.

"Readers, male and female, interested in a snapshot of modern Native culture, the normal stresses of high school, or the travails and triumphs of an underdog sports team will love this fascinating, beautifully written book." Voice Youth Advocates

D'Orso, Michael
Eagle blue; a team, a tribe, and a high school basketball season in Arctic Alaska. Bloomsbury Pub. 2006 323p il map $23.95 *
Grades: 11 12 Adult **796.323**
1. Basketball 2. School sports 3. Fort Yukon (Alaska)
ISBN 978-1-58234-623-6; 1-58234-623-2
LC 2005-25430

The author "follows the Fort Yukon Eagles through their 2005 season to the state championship, shifting between a mesmerizing narrative and the thoughts of the players, their coach and their fans. What emerges is more than a sports story; it's a striking portrait of a community consisting of a traditional culture bombarded with modernity, where alcoholism, domestic violence and school dropout rates run wild." Publ Wkly

Einhorn, Eddie, 1936-
How march became madness; how the NCAA tournament became the greatest sporting event in America; [by] Eddie Einhorn with Ron Rapoport. Triumph Books 2005 266p il $27.95
Grades: 9 10 11 12 **796.323**
1. Basketball
ISBN 978-1-57243-809-5; 1-57243-809-6
LC 2005-54903

Includes DVD

This is an "account of how the telecast between Houston and UCLA laid the foundation for what became one of the greatest sporting events in America." Publisher's note

"Drawing on interviews with nearly 50 college basketball greats—both players and coaches—Einhorn and Rapoport . . . provide a big-picture history of the tournament." Booklist

Feinstein, John
A march to madness; the view from the floor in the Atlantic Coast Conference. Little, Brown 1997 464p il hardcover o.p. pa $14
Grades: 11 12 Adult **796.323**
1. Atlantic Coast Conference 2. Basketball
ISBN 0-316-27740-1; 0-316-27712-6 (pa)
LC 97-31060

Feinstein "covers one year with all of the teams in the perennially powerful Atlantic Coast Conference. After introducing each of the schools, their teams, their coaches, and their expectations for the 1996/97 basketball season, the book describes their progress week by week, culminating with Dean Smith's run to the NCAA Final Four. Such a detailed accounting of a sports season could seem interminable to readers, but Feinstein has again produced a narrative that is not only interesting but often exciting." Libr J

Joravsky, Ben
Hoop dreams; a true story of hardship and triumph; introduction by Charles Barkley. Turner Pub. (Atlanta) 1995 301p il pa $13.50 hardcover o.p.
Grades: 9 10 11 12 **796.323**
1. Basketball 2. Chicago (Ill.)—Social conditions
ISBN 0-06-097689-6 (pa) LC 94-46398

"Based on the documentary film of the same name, this book . . . looks at the dream of ghetto youths to play in the NBA." Publ Wkly

Lannin, Joanne
A history of basketball for girls and women; from bloomers to big leagues. Lerner Publs. 2000 144p il lib bdg $26.60; pa $9.95
Grades: 9 10 11 12 **796.323**
1. Basketball 2. Women athletes
ISBN 0-8225-3331-6 (lib bdg); 0-8225-9863-9 (pa)
LC 99-50643

Traces the development of women's basketball, from its beginnings at Smith College to today's Women's National Basketball Association

"This well-researched, inspiring account will appeal to fans of both genders who follow the game, as well as to those interested in feminist studies and equal rights." Booklist

Includes bibliographical references

Lieberman, Nancy, 1958-
Basketball for women; becoming a complete player; [by] Nancy Lieberman-Cline [and] Robin Roberts with Kevin Warneke. Human Kinetics 1996 283p il pa $16.95 *
Grades: 11 12 Adult **796.323**
1. Basketball 2. Women athletes
ISBN 0-87322-610-0 LC 95-17945

Lieberman, Nancy, 1958-—*Continued*

The author "begins with a history of the game dating back to the first official women's basketball game at Smith College in 1893. From there she discusses not only the dedication it takes to be a true player, but also basketball's position in her, and hopefully the reader's priorities. . . . Next she suggests the building of the plan, mentally and physically, to begin the ascent to the next level of playing. The following seven chapters are devoted to . . . drill techniques." Voice Youth Advocates

Includes bibliographical references

796.325 Volleyball

Dearing, Joel

Volleyball fundamentals. Human Kinetics 2003 135p il (Sports fundamentals series) pa $14.95

Grades: 9 10 11 12   **796.325**

1. Volleyball

ISBN 0-7360-4508-2   LC 2002-15234

Contents: The W formation -- Creating topspin -- Serving -- Receiving serve -- Setting -- Attacking -- Blocking -- Digging -- Team defense -- Team offense -- Transition -- Modified games -- Scoring systems -- Off to the endline

796.332 American football

Bissinger, H. G.

Friday night lights; a town, a team, and a dream. Da Capo Press 2000 367p il pa $15.95

Grades: 11 12 Adult   **796.332**

1. Permian High School (Odessa, Tex.) 2. Football

ISBN 0-306-80990-7   LC 00-40510

First published 1990 by Addison-Wesley

In 1988, the author, a "Philadelphia Inquirer editor, left his job to spend a year with a high school sports team. The sport he picked was football, the location, the . . . West Texas oil town of Odessa. . . . Here 20,000 fans turn out regularly to watch their Permian Panthers win." Libr J

"It is a tricky balancing act, but Mr. Bissinger carries it off: 'Friday Night Lights' offers a biting indictment of the sports craziness that grips not only Odessa but most of American society, while at the same time providing a moving evocation of its powerful allure." N Y Times Book Rev

Complete guide to special teams; American Football Coaches Association; edited by Bill Mallory and Don Nehlen. Human Kinetics 2005 254p il pa $21.95 *

Grades: 11 12 Adult   **796.332**

1. Football

ISBN 0-7360-5291-7   LC 2004-20518

Contents: Punts \ Robin Ross -- Kickoffs \ Greg McMahon -- Punt returns \ John Harbaugh -- Kickoff returns \ Dave Ungerer -- Extra points and field goals \ Lester Erb and Ronald Aiken -- Two-point conversions \ Urban Meyer -- Punt and field goal blocks \ Bud Foster

-- Developing special teams units \ Mike Sabock -- Punting \ Jeff Hays -- Kicking off \ Joe Robinson -- Kicking extra points and field goals \ Brian Polian -- Long snapping \ Bill Legg -- Holding for kicks \ Steve Kidd -- Returning punts and kickoffs \ Bill Lynch -- Developing special teams players \ Joe DeForest

MacCambridge, Michael, 1963-

America's game; the epic story of how pro football captured a nation. Random House 2004 552p il hardcover o.p. pa $15

Grades: 11 12 Adult   **796.332**

1. National Football League 2. Football

ISBN 0-375-50454-0; 0-375-72506-7 (pa)

LC 2004-52003

The author traces pro football's history "with particular attention paid to six key franchises—the Rams, Browns, Colts, Cowboys, Chiefs, and Raiders—and how their fortunes reflected the larger growth of the game itself." Publisher's note

"This magisterial history is a fitting acknowledgment of the sport's legacy." Publ Wkly

Includes bibliographical references

796.334 Soccer

Buxton, Ted

Soccer skills for young players; {by} Ted Buxton, with Alex Leith and Jim Drewitt; foreword by Gordon Jago. Firefly Bks. (Buffalo) 2000 128p il pa $14.95 *

Grades: 9 10 11 12   **796.334**

1. Soccer

ISBN 1-55209-329-8

"Buxton presents more than 70 drills for beginner to advanced players. The book opens with a few warm-up and stretching exercises. Specific types of drills are illustrated by at least one colorful action photograph; many are also accompanied by a diagram of the play on the field and additional tips outlined in a skill box." SLJ

Longman, Jere

The girls of summer; the U.S. women's soccer team and how it changed the world. HarperCollins Pubs. 2000 318p il hardcover o.p. pa $14 *

Grades: 11 12 Adult   **796.334**

1. Soccer 2. Women athletes

ISBN 0-06-019657-2; 0-06-093468-9 (pa)

This "retelling of the 1999 Women's World Cup championship match between the U.S. and China weaves together gender issues, the influence of Title IX, and biographies and interviews with key players." Booklist

Includes bibliographical references

Luongo, Albert M., 1939-

Soccer drills; skill-builders for field control. McFarland & Co. 2000 182p pa $24.50

Grades: 9 10 11 12   **796.334**

1. Soccer

ISBN 0-7864-0682-8   LC 99-47698

Luongo, Albert M., 1939—*Continued*

The author "suggests a systematic plan for skill development, from beginning to advanced drills, based on selected techniques of top competitive world-class players and managers. . . . Thirty-eight illustrations—with clear and concise legends—provide an easy-to-follow visual guide for various playing techniques. Diagrams show proper body positions and stages of progression for drills." Voice Youth Advocates

Luxbacher, Joe

Soccer: steps to success; [by] Joseph A. Luxbacher. 3rd ed. Human Kinetics 2005 198p il (Steps to success activity series) pa $17.95

Grades: 9 10 11 12 Adult   **796.334**

1. Soccer

ISBN 0-736-05435-9   LC 2004-18570

First published 1991

This book describes the skills and concepts used in soccer in twelve steps.

796.34   Racket games

Boga, Steve, 1947-

Badminton; {by} Steven Boga. Stackpole Bks. 1996 100p il pa $10 *

Grades: 9 10 11 12   **796.34**

1. Badminton (Game)

ISBN 0-8117-2487-5   LC 95-22434

This volume begins with "a brief history of the sport as well as the rules and the court dimensions. Also attended to are equipment selection and such basics as racket grip, positioning, footwork, and shotmaking. Singles, doubles, and mixed-doubles are presented in terms of both rules and strategy. . . . A glossary and national list of badminton clubs and organizations are appended. If you need a badminton how-to, this is the one to buy." Booklist

Hinkson, Jim

Lacrosse for dummies; [by] Jim Hinkson, John Jiloty, and Robert Carpenter; foreword by Brian Shanahan. Wiley 2002 xxii, 374p il pa $24.99

Grades: 9 10 11 12 Adult   **796.34**

1. Lacrosse

ISBN 1-89441-349-0

This guide "opens with the basics of the game, and familiarizes you with such things as the ball and the stick, the position of the players on the field, the equipment used, and the way the game is played. The other parts of the book illustrate how you should watch the game for maximum enjoyment, how you can become a better player, and how you can become a better coach." Publisher's note

Hodges, Larry, 1960-

Table tennis; steps to success. Human Kinetics 1993 151p il (Steps to success activity series) pa $17.95

Grades: 9 10 11 12 Adult   **796.34**

1. Table tennis

ISBN 0-87322-403-5   LC 92-37606

"In cooperation with United States Table Tennis Association"

This book describes the skills and concepts used in table tennis in fifteen steps.

Swissler, Becky

Winning lacrosse for girls; foreword by Anna Maria Vesco. Facts on File 2004 192p il $35; pa $16.95 *

Grades: 7 8 9 10   **796.34**

1. Lacrosse

ISBN 0-8160-5183-6; 0-8160-5184-4 (pa)

     LC 2003-51446

This "teaches the game's basic skills, strategies, and drills and how to master them. Chapters cover the history of the game, the basics of stick handling, the rules of play, passing and receiving, offense and defense, key strategies, skills and tactics, conditioning, and much more." Publisher's note

This is "well organized, clear, and concise. . . . Accurate . . . pictures accompany the instruction in a logical and clear fashion." SLJ

Includes bibliographical references

Urick, Dave

Sports illustrated lacrosse; fundamentals for winning; photography by Heinz Kluetmeier. {rev ed}. Sports Illustrated 1991 255p il pa $12.95 *

Grades: 9 10 11 12   **796.34**

1. Lacrosse

ISBN 1-56800-071-5

"Sports illustrated winner's circle books"

First published 1988

An introduction to the game of lacrosse providing information about equipment, rules, skills, strategy, and training

796.342   Tennis

Douglas, Paul

Tennis. Dorling Kindersley 1995 72p il pa $5

Grades: 7 8 9 10   **796.342**

1. Tennis

ISBN 0-7566-0225-4

At head of title: 101 essential tips

Aspects covered include strokes, positions, playing surfaces, dress and equipment

"This is a good text for those just picking up the sport, as well as for those seasoned players who want to brush up on their game or improve their strategy." Voice Youth Advocates

International book of tennis drills; over 100 skill-specific drills adopted by tennis professionals worldwide; by the United States Professional Tennis Registry. Triumph Bks. (Chicago) 1998 289p il pa $14.95

Grades: 9 10 11 12   **796.342**

1. Tennis

ISBN 1-57243-283-7

First published 1993

International book of tennis drills—*Continued*

This guide for enhancing tennis skills covers such topics as serving, groundstrokes, midcourt shots, volleys, lobs, singles and doubles play tactics, as well as speed and agility

796.352   Golf

Campbell, Malcolm, 1944-

The new encyclopedia of golf. 3rd American ed. DK Pub. 2000 384p il $40

Grades: 11 12 Adult   **796.352**

1. Golf—Encyclopedias

ISBN 0-7894-8036-0   LC 2001-28349

First published 1991 by Random House with title: The Random House international encyclopedia of golf

The author "traces the history and lore of the game in this volume, which includes hundreds of full-color photographs and . . . [an] introduction on the modern game and its players." Libr J

Includes bibliographical references

Ultimate golf techniques; contributor, Steve Newell; special photography, Dave Cannon. DK Pub. 1996 216p il hardcover o.p. pa $14.95

Grades: 11 12 Adult   **796.352**

1. Golf

ISBN 0-7894-0442-7; 0-7894-3302-8 (pa)

LC 95-44327

Text and numerous illustrations present the basic techniques of the golf swing

"The effective mix of jump-off-the-page graphics and straightforward captions takes golf instruction into the realm of visual learning, where it naturally belongs." Booklist

796.355   Field hockey

Swissler, Becky

Winning field hockey for girls; foreword by Tracey Belbin. Facts on File 2003 201p il hardcover o.p. pa $16.95

Grades: 9 10 11 12   **796.355**

1. Field hockey

ISBN 0-8160-4724-3; 0-8160-4725-1 (pa)

LC 2002-5990

"A Mountain Lion book"

Contents: History, rules, and equipment — Understanding the basics — Dribbling — Passing and receiving — Shooting — Tackling — Goal keeping — Offensive strategy — Defensive strategy — Conditioning

Includes bibliographical references

796.357   Baseball

Adair, Robert Kemp

The physics of baseball. 3rd ed, rev, updated, and expanded. Perennial 2002 169p il pa $12.95

Grades: 11 12 Adult   **796.357**

1. Physics 2. Baseball 3. Force and energy

ISBN 0-06-008436-7   LC 2001-39886

First published 1990

A look at how some physical principles are applied to the game of baseball. Pitching, batting and the properties of bats are discussed

Includes bibliographical references

Angell, Roger

Game time: a baseball companion; edited by Steve Kettmann. Harcourt 2003 398p $25; pa $15

Grades: 11 12 Adult   **796.357**

1. Baseball

ISBN 0-15-100824-8; 0-15-601387-8 (pa)

LC 2002-152611

"A Harvest original"

Contents: Spring; The old folks behind home; Sunny side of the street; Easy lessons; Takes: waltz of the geezers; Put me in, coach; Takes: digging up Willie; For openers; Takes: pride; Let go, Mets; Summer; Early innings; The companions of the game; Scout; Distance; The web of the game; Takes: penmen; Takes: payback; Wings of fire; The bard in the booth; Style; Takes: three Petes; Fall; Takes: Jacksonian; Blue collar; Takes: the confines; Ninety feet; One for the good guys; Legends of the fens; Can you believe it?; Takes: the purist; Kiss kiss, bang bang

"Half of the essays in this compilation of highlights from Angell's 40 years of covering baseball for the *New Yorker* have not previously appeared in book form, and even those that have are well worth revisiting. Angell . . . remains the dean of baseball writers." Booklist

Asinof, Eliot, 1919-

Eight men out; the Black Sox and the 1919 World Series. Holt & Co. 1963 302p il pa $15 hardcover o.p.

Grades: 11 12 Adult   **796.357**

1. Baseball

ISBN 0-8050-6537-7 (pa)

"An Owl book"

The author has reconstructed the story of the Chicago White Sox baseball scandal, and describes the 1921 trial of the eight players who had arranged with gamblers to throw the 1919 World Series to Cincinnati

Baseball, the perfect game; an all-star anthology celebrating the game's greatest players, teams, and moments; Josh Leventhal, editor. Voyageur Press 2005 223p il $29.95

Grades: 11 12 Adult   **796.357**

1. Baseball

ISBN 0-89658-668-5   LC 2004-23541

Partial contents: The national game -- The origins of baseball -- Opening day \ by Jim Brosnan -- The collector: J.R. Burdick and the world of baseball cards \ by Mark Lamster -- Dynasties, more than just those damn Yankees \ by Gary Gillette and Pete Palmer -- The Red Stockings, baseball's first professional team -- The Black Sox scandal \ by Eliot Asinof -- 1941, an unmatchable summer \ by Ray Robinson -- Next year arrives, the 1955 Brooklyn Dodgers \ by Doris Kearns Goodwin -- The 1975 World Series, an October classic \ by Bill Lee -- The greatest World Series \ by Josh Leventhal -- 1998: the year that baseball came back . . . \ by Alan Schwarz

Baseball, the perfect game—*Continued*

"Hardcore fans of 'America's Game' have a gem in this book. . . . The selections, all beautifully written, clearly are intended for older teens comfortable with documentary-style descriptions." Voice Youth Advocates

Baseball's best shots. DK Pub. 2000 159p il $30
Grades: 9 10 11 12   **796.357**
1. Baseball—Pictorial works
ISBN 0-7894-66119-6   LC 00-30691
This pictorial history of baseball includes over 100 photographs of such players as Ty Cobb, Babe Ruth, Ted Williams, Joe DiMaggio, Ken Griffey, Jr., Mark McGuire, Sammy Sosa, and Derek Jeter

Biographical dictionary of American sports, Baseball; edited by David L. Porter. rev and expanded ed. Greenwood Press 2000 3v set $295 *
Grades: 11 12 Adult   **796.357**
1. Baseball
ISBN 0-313-29884-X   LC 99-14840
First published 1987
This set "contains 1,450 signed entries. Individuals were chosen because of their 'impressive statistical records' or because they 'made a major impact on professional baseball' and include major league players; prominent minor league, Negro League, and Girls League players; and various executives, coaches, managers, and umpires. . . . Any library that wants to have a serious baseball reference section will need {this work}." Booklist
Includes bibliographical references

Encyclopedia of women and baseball; edited by Leslie A. Heaphy and Mel Anthony May; foreword by Laura Wulf. McFarland & Co. 2006 438p il $49.95 *
Grades: 11 12 Adult   **796.357**
1. All-American Girls Professional Baseball League 2. Women athletes 3. Baseball
ISBN 0-7864-2100-2; 978-0-7864-2100-8
                                       LC 2006-8719
"This encyclopedia provides information on women players, managers, teams, leagues, and issues since the mid-19th century. Players are listed by maiden name with married name, when known, in parentheses. Information provided includes birth date, death date, team, dates of play, career statistics and brief biographical notes when available." Publisher's note
The editors "have produced a valuable resource on a seldom studied area of baseball." Choice
Includes bibliographical references

Enders, Eric
100 years of the World Series. Sterling 2003 320p il $19.95
Grades: 11 12 Adult   **796.357**
1. Baseball 2. World series (Baseball)
ISBN 1-586-63597-2   LC 2002-29850
"This compilation begins with the 1903 Boston Pilgrims and concludes with . . . the 2002 Anaheim Angels. The series are ordered chronologically and grouped

by major periods . . . with a concise, well-written introduction preceding each period. This handsome, oversized book includes box scores, composite statistics, and reproductions of programs, as well as hundreds of spectacular photographs, many of which won't be found in other baseball histories." Libr J
Includes bibliographical references

Halberstam, David, 1934-2007
Summer of '49. Morrow 1989 304p il pa $13.95 hardcover o.p.
Grades: 11 12 Adult   **796.357**
1. New York Yankees (Baseball team) 2. Boston Red Sox (Baseball team)
ISBN 0-06-000781-8   LC 89-2886
"This book is ostensibly about the pennant race between the Yankees and Red Sox {in 1949} and the 'rivalry' between Joe DiMaggio and Ted Williams. . . . It is a study of all the elements and personalities that influenced baseball that year and beyond. Halberstam brings them together in such an enjoyable, interesting, and informative manner that a reader needn't be a baseball fan to appreciate the book." Libr J

Hogan, Lawrence D., 1944-
Shades of glory; the Negro Leagues and the story of African-American baseball; with a foreword by Jules Tygiel. National Geographic 2006 422p il $26 *
Grades: 11 12 Adult   **796.357**
1. Negro leagues 2. Baseball 3. African American athletes
ISBN 0-7922-5306-X; 978-0-7922-5306-8
                                       LC 2006-273216
Published in association with the National Baseball Hall of Fame and Museum
This book "traces the history of black baseball from the 19th century to the first great teams, such as the Cuban Giants, and on to the era of the vibrant barnstorming teams from the East Coast, Chicago, and Cuba." Publisher's note
"This is an important, informative, and entertaining contribution to sports history." Booklist

Kahn, Roger, 1927-
Beyond the boys of summer; the very best of Roger Kahn; edited by Rob Miraldi. McGraw-Hill 2005 xxxvi, 364p $24.95
Grades: 11 12 Adult   **796.357**
1. Baseball
ISBN 0-07-144727-X   LC 2004-24851
This book "presents a showcase of 50 years worth of Kahn's . . . work." Publisher's note
"Kahn is a giant among sports journalists, and this is a fine sampling of his most memorable work." Booklist
Includes bibliographical references

Kelley, Brent P.

Voices from the Negro leagues; conversations with 52 baseball standouts of the period 1924-1960. McFarland & Co. 1998 334p il $45 *

Grades: 11 12 Adult   **796.357**

1. Baseball 2. African American athletes

ISBN 0-7864-2279-3   LC 97-37332

This "book is divided into two sections: the first comprises those who played prior to Jackie Robinson's breaking the color barrier; the second section features those who continued to play in the Negro leagues after Robinson's debut. . . . Kelley also provides biographies of each subject for context and whatever statistics are available. A wonderful book that should be exceedingly popular among fans with an interest in the game's history." Booklist

Includes bibliographical references

Light, Jonathan Fraser, 1957-

The cultural encyclopedia of baseball. 2nd ed. McFarland & Co. 2005 1105p il $75 *

Grades: 11 12 Adult   **796.357**

1. Baseball—Encyclopedias

ISBN 0-7864-2087-1   LC 2005-1718

First published 1997

This encyclopedia "profiles every Hall of Fame player, as well as every National and American League club (and predecessors). . . . Statistics play a large role in this resource, which includes facts and figures on just about every conceivable event in the game. Cultural references to baseball are noted throughout in numerous quotations. Some of the more fascinating sections include 'Nicknames,' 'Presidents,' and 'Salaries.' Other entries that make for offbeat perusal include 'Freak Accidents,' 'Sex,' and 'Injuries and Illnesses.'" Choice

Includes bibliographical references

McGuire, Mark, 1963-

The 100 greatest baseball players of the 20th century ranked; by Mark McGuire and Michael Sean Gormley. McFarland & Co. 2000 207p $30

Grades: 11 12 Adult   **796.357**

1. Baseball

ISBN 0-7864-0914-2   LC 00-20230

"The authors of this work looked at statistics, the different eras, the 'five tools,' and even oral legend in compiling this list. . . . They've ranked the Negro League players and superstars from around the globe alongside the Major League legends." Publisher's note

Monteleone, John J.

The Louisville Slugger complete book of women's fast-pitch softball; by John Monteleone and Deborah Crisfield; photography by Michael Plunkett. H. Holt 1999 219p il pa $22

Grades: 9 10 11 12   **796.357**

1. Softball

ISBN 0-8050-5809-5   LC 98-55221

"An Owl book"

"A Mountain Lion book"

In addition to covering topics such as "hitting, fielding, offensive strategy, and defensive tactics, the book features interviews with top-level collegiate, Olympic, and professional players and coaches." Publisher's note

Neft, David S.

The sports encyclopedia: baseball 2007; [by] David S. Neft, Richard M. Cohen. St. Martin's Press 2007 pa $23.95 *

Grades: 9 10 11 12 Adult   **796.357**

1. Baseball—Statistics

ISSN 1043-688X

ISBN 0-312-36359-1; 978-0-312-36359-8

Annual. First published 1974 by Grosset & Dunlap

Covers baseball from 1876 to the present and contains team statistics, alphabetical registers of batters and pitchers, and summaries of each season.

Ripken, Cal, Jr.

Play baseball the Ripken way; the complete illustrated guide to the fundamentals; [by] Cal Ripken, Jr. and Bill Ripken with Larry Burke. Random House 2004 236p il $24.95; pa $15.95

Grades: 11 12 Adult   **796.357**

1. Baseball

ISBN 1-4000-6122-9; 0-8129-7050-0 (pa)

     LC 2003-66725

"Chapters written by Cal cover batting, base running, infield play, and catching; Bill's chapters outline pitching and outfield play. The text is interspersed with . . . photographs as well as sidebars on special tips, and each chapter closes with a review checklist." Libr J

"This book is the next best thing to a personal lesson with the man who broke Lou Gehrig's record of playing in 2,632 consecutive games; it's a comprehensive look at all aspects of how to play baseball that will benefit young players and adult weekend warriors." Publ Wkly

Sokolove, Michael Y.

The ticket out: Darryl Strawberry and the boys of Crenshaw; [by] Michael Sokolove. Simon & Schuster 2004 291p hardcover o.p. pa $14

Grades: 11 12 Adult   **796.357**

1. Strawberry, Darryl 2. Crenshaw High School (Los Angeles, Calif.) 3. Baseball

ISBN 0-7432-2673-9; 0-7432-7885-2 (pa)

     LC 2004-41745

"The individual stories of a vastly talented 1979 L.A. high-school baseball team come to life in this heartbreaking account of the players' last season and the difficulties they faced in the years that followed." Booklist

Includes bibliographical references

Total baseball; the ultimate baseball encyclopedia; [edited by] John Thorn, Phil Birnbaum, Bill Deane. 8th ed. SPORT Classic Bks. 2004 2676p $59.95 *

Grades: 9 10 11 12   **796.357**

1. Baseball

ISBN 1-894963-27-X

"Sport Classic Books"

First published 1989

This reference volume includes yearly results, awards, detailed postseason and all-star accounts, and the complete career statistics of every major-league player.

Vecsey, George
Baseball: a history of America's favorite game. Modern Library 2006 252p il (Modern Library chronicles) $21.95 *
Grades: 11 12 Adult   **796.357**
1. Baseball
ISBN 0-679-64338-9; 978-0-679-64338-8
                                    LC 2006-45033
This history of baseball "unfolds much like a highlights tape, with a breezy background narrative of the game from its pre-Civil War roots to its current drug scandals, structured around set pieces spotlighting the outsized deeds of luminaries like Babe Ruth, Jackie Robinson, Branch Rickey and George Steinbrenner. . . . Vivid, affectionate and clear-eyed, Vecsey's account makes for an engaging sports history." Publ Wkly
Includes bibliographical references

Wendel, Tim
The new face of baseball; the one-hundred year rise and triumph of Latinos in America's favorite sport; foreword by Bob Costas; color photographs by Victor Baldizon. Rayo 2003 266p il hardcover o.p. pa $13.95
Grades: 11 12 Adult   **796.357**
1. Baseball 2. Hispanic Americans
ISBN 0-06-053631-4; 0-06-053632-2 (pa)
                                    LC 2004-300834
"Going as far back as the mid-nineteenth century, to the early days of Cuban baseball, Wendel traces the spread of American baseball fever in the Caribbean and Mexico." Publisher's note
"Fans will recognize names like Minoso, Clemente, Cepeda, or Sosa, but it is enlightening to see them presented as part of a single accomplished group . . . This is an excellent overview." Libr J
Includes bibliographical references

Wilson, Nick
Voices from the pastime; oral histories of surviving major leaguers, Negro leaguers, Cuban leaguers, and writers, 1920-1934. McFarland & Co. 2000 208p il pa $29.95 *
Grades: 11 12 Adult   **796.357**
1. Baseball
ISBN 0-7864-0824-3   LC 00-26695
The players and sportswriters not only recount their own careers, they talk of some of the greatest players in the history of the game, including Babe Ruth, Josh Gibson, Satchel Paige, Walter Johnson and Martin Dihigo
Includes bibliographical references

796.42 Track and field

Carr, Gerald A., 1936-
Fundamentals of track and field; [by] Gerry Carr. 2nd ed. Human Kinetics 1999 285p il pa $24.95
Grades: 9 10 11 12   **796.42**
1. Track athletics
ISBN 0-7360-0008-9   LC 98-52218

First published 1991 by Leisure Press
This book provides "information for teaching and coaching every track and field event, including such frequently excluded events as the 400-meter hurdles, steeplechase, triple jump, hammer throw, and race walking." Publisher's note
Includes bibliographical references

Complete book of running; everything you need to know to run for fun, fitness and competition; edited by Amby Burfoot. Rodale 2004 312p il pa $17.95
Grades: 11 12 Adult   **796.42**
ISBN 1-57954-929-2
First published 1997 with title: Runner's world complete book of running
Among this volume's contributors are Liz Applegate, Hal Higdon, Joe Henderson and Joan Benoit Samuelson. Topics covered include: nutrition, injury prevention and treatment, shoe selection, mental readiness, and marathon preparation.

Housewright, Ed
Winning track and field for girls; foreword by Buzz Andrews. Facts on File 2004 188p il $35 *
Grades: 7 8 9 10   **796.42**
1. Track athletics
ISBN 0-8160-5231-X   LC 2003-49241
"Housewright starts with a . . . history of women's track. The chapters are then divided into topics such as sprints, hurdles, middle and long distances, relays, jumping events, throwing events, the heptathlon, cross-country, and the triathlon. Each of these chapters then goes into detail about the individual event and concludes with a section about record holders. Helpful drills and sample workouts are also provided." SLJ
Includes bibliographical references

Scott, Dagny
Runner's world complete book of women's running; the best advice to get started, stay motivated, lose weight, run injury-free, be safe, and train for any distance. Rodale 2000 308p hardcover o.p. pa $16.95 *
Grades: 11 12 Adult   **796.42**
1. Running
ISBN 1-57954-118-6; 1-57954-466-5 (pa)
                                    LC 99-59609
Topics covered include racing, nutrition, running during pregnancy, stretching techniques, exercise drills and proper clothing.

796.44 Sports gymnastics

Ryan, Joan
Little girls in pretty boxes; the making and breaking of elite gymnasts and figure skaters. Warner Bks. 2000 268p il pa $13.95
Grades: 9 10 11 12   **796.44**
1. Gymnastics 2. Ice skating 3. Women athletes
ISBN 0-446-67682-9   LC 00-31981

Ryan, Joan—*Continued*

First published 1995 by Doubleday

"In an attempt to focus attention on the high price paid through pain, pressure, and humiliation to become an Olympic champion, Ryan has researched the stories behind some of the young female superstar gymnasts and figure skaters. The extraordinary cost to these young women in body, mind, and spirit is dramatized through the intense subculture dominated by gyms, trainers, parents, and sports officials who press for excellence and success without regard to the health and well-being of those involved. . . . A book to be pondered by coaches, parents, and young people." SLJ [review of 1995 edition]

796.48   Olympic games

Guttmann, Allen

The Olympics, a history of the modern games. 2nd ed. University of Ill. Press 2002 214p il (Illinois history of sports) $39.95; pa $16.95

Grades: 11 12 Adult   **796.48**

1. Olympic games

ISBN 0-252-02725-6; 0-252-07046-1 (pa)

LC 2001-41383

First published 1992

"The author's premise is that politics have been at the foundation of modern Olympics from its inception in Athens (1896) to Seoul (1988). Gold, silver, and bronze medals have shared the victory stand with nationalism, and have even been tarnished by arrogance, protests, terrorists, and boycotts. Although the text emphasizes the political and socioeconomic climate of the Olympics, it also contains memorable accounts of athletic competition." Libr J {review of 1992 edition}

"Guttmann discusses the intended and actual meaning of the modern Olympic Games, from 1896 to 2000. Recounting the memorable and significant athletic events of the Olympics in terms of their social and political impact, Guttmann . . . {attempts to demonstrate} that the modern games were revived to propagate a political message and continue to serve political purposes." Publisher's note

Includes bibliographical references

Mallon, Bill

Historical dictionary of the Olympic movement; [by] Bill Mallon, with Ian Buchanan. 3rd ed. Scarecrow Press 2006 cxvi, 411p il (Historical dictionaries of religions, philosophies, and movements) $90 *

Grades: 9 10 11 12   **796.48**

1. Olympic games

ISBN 0-8108-5574-7   LC 2005-16706

First published 1995

"The volume covers a wide range of persons, places, and events over a long historical period, stretching back more than a millennium. Entries are in dictionary format and include significant events, Olympic bodies, pioneers of the games, organizations, athletes, and the many participating countries, which now number 202." Booklist

Includes bibliographical references

796.5   Outdoor life

Paulsen, Gary

Woodsong. Bradbury Press 1990 132p map $17.95; pa $5.99

Grades: 7 8 9 10   **796.5**

1. Sled dog racing 2. Outdoor life 3. Minnesota

ISBN 0-02-770221-9; 0-689-85250-9 (pa)

LC 89-70835

Also available in paperback from Puffin Bks.

For the author and his family, life in northern Minnesota is a wild experience involving wolves, deer, and the sled dogs that make their way of life possible. Includes an account of Paulsen's first Iditarod, a dogsled race across Alaska

"The book is packed with vignettes that range among various shades of terror and lyrical beauty." Voice Youth Advocates

Stilwell, Alexander

Encyclopedia of survival techniques; {illustrations, Tony Randall and Anne Cakebread}. Lyons Press 2000 192p il maps pa $19.95 *

Grades: 11 12 Adult   **796.5**

1. Wilderness survival

ISBN 1-58574-062-4   LC 2001-271839

This guide covers preparation, basic skills, equipment, various terrains, natural disasters, and first aid

"Campers, scouts, hikers, or anyone interested in outdoor-survival techniques will find easy to use information here." SLJ

796.51   Walking

Berger, Karen, 1959-

Advanced backpacking; illustrations by Ron Hildebrand. Norton 1998 224p il maps (Trailside series guide) flexible bdg $18.95

Grades: 11 12 Adult   **796.51**

1. Backpacking

ISBN 0-393-31769-2   LC 97-43849

This book "is comprised of three sections: Part 1 covers the basics of expedition planning, including route selection, food and water supply, and the treatment of physical ailments that can occur on the trail; Part 2 considers the special gear and skills necessary for different weather and terrain and for trekking in foreign countries; and Part 3 offers a sampling of the most spectacular trails in the United States along with contact information." Publisher's note

Includes bibliographical references

Hart, John, 1948-

Walking softly in the wilderness; the Sierra Club guide to backpacking. 4th ed, complete rev and updated. Sierra Club Books 2005 508p il map (Sierra Club outdoor adventure guide) pa $16.95 *

Grades: 11 12 Adult   **796.51**

1. Backpacking 2. Wilderness areas

ISBN 1-578-05123-1   LC 2004-56554

Hart, John, 1948-—*Continued*
First published 1977
This guide for both the novice and experienced hiker reflects the environmental concerns of the Sierra Club. Among topics covered are: clothing and equipment; making and breaking camp; problem animals and plants; hiking and camping with kids. Listings of conservation and wilderness travel organizations, map and equipment sources, land management agencies, and Internet contacts are appended.
Includes bibliographical references

796.52   Walking and exploring by kind of terrain

Taylor, Michael Ray, 1959-
Caves; exploring hidden realms. National Geographic Soc. 2001 216p il maps $35 *
Grades: 11 12 Adult   **796.52**
1. Caves
ISBN 0-7922-7904-2   LC 00-52710
This book was produced in conjunction with an IMAX project filming two caver's explorations in the Yucatan, Greenland, and the South-Central United States
"The photographs and the story of the explorations would be sufficient to recommend this work, but it also includes fascinating background material on the history of the caves, their biological diversity, {and} the tools used by spelunkers." Booklist
Includes bibliographical references

796.522   Mountaineering

Climb: stories of survival from rock, snow, and ice; edited by Clint Willis. Thunder's Mouth Press 2000 259p il pa $16.95
Grades: 11 12 Adult   **796.522**
1. Mountaineering
ISBN 1-56025-250-2   LC 99-26747
"An Adrenaline book"
This anthology brings together "writings by some of the world's best climbers, such as American Jim Wickwire, Scotsman Hamish MacInnes, and literary icons Evelyn Waugh and H. G. Wells. This collection will surely appeal to die-hard veterans of the sport and newcomers intrigued by risk taking. . . . For all readers, lessons abound—although the writers may have survived their ordeals presented here, some did not survive others." Booklist

Coburn, Broughton
Everest: mountain without mercy; introduction by Tim Cahill, afterword by David Breashears. National Geographic Soc. 1997 256p il maps $35; pa $24
Grades: 11 12 Adult   **796.522**
1. Mount   Everest   Expedition   (1996)
2. Mountaineering
ISBN 0-7922-7014-2; 0-7922-6984-5 (pa)
LC 97-10765

"Bringing an understated yet powerful Buddhist/Sherpa ethical perspective to the tragedy on Everest chronicled in Jon Krakauer's Into Thin Air, Coburn reports on the IMAX film crew who participated in the rescue effort when the May 1996 expeditions led by guides Rob Hall and Scott Fischer ended in death and crippling injury." Publ Wkly

Krakauer, Jon
Into thin air; a personal account of the Mount Everest disaster. Villard Bks. 1997 xx, 293p il $25.95; pa $14.95 *
Grades: 11 12 Adult   **796.522**
1. Mount   Everest   Expedition   (1996)
2. Mountaineering
ISBN 0-679-45752-6; 0-385-49478-5 (pa)
LC 96-30031
This is an account of the author's May 1996 Mount Everest climbing expedition in which twelve fellow climbers died during a snow storm
"This tense, harrowing story is as mesmerizing and hard to put down as any well-written adventure novel." SLJ
Includes bibliographical references

796.6   Cycling and related activities

Bicycling magazine's 900 all-time best tips; top riders share their secrets to maximize fun, safety, and performance; edited by Ed Pavelka. Rodale 2000 138p il pa $9.95 *
Grades: 11 12 Adult   **796.6**
1. Cycling
ISBN 1-57954-227-1   LC 99-56768
Replaces Bicyling magazine's 600 tips for better bicycling
A collection of information on such topics as bicycle models, accessories, riding styles, and repair techniques

Carmichael, Chris
The ultimate ride; get fit, get fast, and start winning with the world's top cycling coach; [by] Chris Carmichael with Jim Rutberg. G.P. Putnam's Sons 2003 325p il hardcover o.p. pa $15 *
Grades: 11 12 Adult   **796.6**
1. Cycling 2. Physical fitness
ISBN 0-399-15071-4; 0-425-19601-1 (pa)
LC 2003-43214
The author offers advice to "serious cyclists wanting to improve their abilities, compete more successfully and train without incurring injuries." Publ Wkly
"This is an excellent guide to obtaining peak performance in cycling competition, but the wealth of training tips and intelligent discussion of nutrition will be almost as valuable to noncompetitive cyclists and even to other athletes serious about conditioning." Booklist

Crowther, Nicky

The ultimate mountain bike book; the definitive illustrated guide to bikes, components, techniques, thrills and trails; maintenance section by Melanie Allwood. rev 3rd ed. Firefly Bks. 2002 191p il pa $24.95 *

Grades: 9 10 11 12 Adult   **796.6**
1. Mountain bikes
ISBN 1-55297-653-X
First published 1996 by Motorbooks International
"Some of the topics covered are as basic as how to choose a bike, required accessories, and nitty-gritty instructions on how to maintain and care for your equipment. Crowther also includes information about racing, downhill, cross-country, and stunt riding. Although certain topics are written with advanced and competitive riders in mind . . . the book is jam-packed with everything beginner and experienced bikers need to know." SLJ

796.63   Mountain biking

Bicycling magazine's mountain biking skills; skills and techniques to master any terrain. Rodale 2005 122p pa $9.95

Grades: 9 10 11 12 Adult   **796.63**
1. Mountain biking
ISBN 978-1-59486-299-1; 1-59486-299-0
                                        LC 2005-23045
First published 1990
This guide to mountain biking covers basic and intermediate skills and techniques including "ways to handle tough terrain, steer clear of hazardous obstacles, and even crash properly to avoid injury." Publisher's note

796.72   Automobile racing

Menzer, Joe

The wildest ride; a history of NASCAR (or, How a bunch of good ol' boys built a billion-dollar industry out of wrecking cars). Simon & Schuster 2001 311p il hardcover o.p. pa $14 *

Grades: 11 12 Adult   **796.72**
1. National Association for Stock Car Auto Racing
2. Automobile racing
ISBN 0-7432-0507-3; 0-7432-2625-9 (pa)
                                        LC 2001-031088
Also available G.K. Hall large print edition
This history focuses on the "legacy of the founding France family, the evolution of the cars from modified stock cars to purpose-built racers, and the fan-base expansion of the 1980s and 1990s. . . . Highly entertaining and full of facts." Libr J
Includes bibliographical references

O'Malley, J. J.

Daytona 24 Hours; the definitive history of America's great endurance race; [by] J.J. O'Malley; foreword by Hurley Haywood; design by Tom Morgan; photos edited by Buz McKim; results and index by Janos Wimpffen. David Bull Pub. 2003 400p il $89.95 *

Grades: 9 10 11 12   **796.72**
1. Automobile racing
ISBN 1-893618-24-2   LC 2003-103993
The author delivers a "chronicle of the race, year by year (1974 was the only year it wasn't run), and the clear, mostly full-color photos, one on nearly every page, show the crew, the cars, the drivers, the track, and the pulsing action." Booklist

Thunder and glory; the 25 most memorable races in NASCAR Winston Cup history; [from the editors of NASCAR scene] Triumph Books 2004 160p il $34.95; pa $19.95

Grades: 9 10 11 12   **796.72**
1. National Association for Stock Car Auto Racing
2. Automobile racing
ISBN 1-57243-677-8; 1-57243-830-4 (pa)
                                        LC 2006-297046
Includes DVD
"The focus is on 25 of the editors' most memorable Winston Cup races, which are analyzed and recounted with utter reverence. . . . Even nonracing fans will find the drama compelling." Booklist

796.8   Combat sports

Beekman, Scott

Ringside; a history of professional wrestling in America; [by] Scott M. Beekman. Praeger 2006 188p il $39.95 *

Grades: 11 12 Adult   **796.8**
1. Wrestling
ISBN 0-275-98401-X; 978-0-275-98401-4
                                        LC 2006-8230
"This chronological work begins with a brief account of wrestling's global history, and then proceeds to investigate the sport's growth as a specifically American institution." Publisher's note
"An eye-opening reappraisal of a much-maligned sport, and (for wrestling fans) perhaps a much-needed vindication." Booklist
Includes bibliographical references

Greenberg, Keith Elliot, 1959-

Pro wrestling; from carnivals to cable TV. Lerner Publs. 2000 128p il (Sports legacy series) lib bdg $26.60; pa $9.95

Grades: 9 10 11 12   **796.8**
1. Wrestling
ISBN 0-8225-3332-4 (lib bdg); 0-8225-9864-7 (pa)
                                        LC 99-50554
A history of professional wrestling from its roots in legitimate sport to its days as a carnival attraction followed by the growth of regional rivalries and culminating as television-centered entertainment
Includes bibliographical references

Kreidler, Mark

Four days to glory; wrestling with the soul of the American heartland. HarperCollins Publishers 2007 262p il $24.95 *

Grades: 11 12 Adult   **796.8**

1. Wrestling 2. School sports

ISBN 978-0-06-082318-4; 0-06-082318-6

LC 2007-272997

Jay Borschel and Dan LeClere aspire to be four-time high school wrestling champions in Iowa.

The author's "deftness in 'Four Days' is in turning a niche sport into one as accessible as baseball or basketball." N Y Times Book Rev

Park, Yeon Hwan

Black belt tae kwon do; the ultimate reference guide to the world's most popular martial art; by Y.H. Park & Jon Gerrard. Facts on File 2000 272p il hardcover o.p. pa $16.95 *

Grades: 11 12 Adult   **796.8**

1. Tae kwon do

ISBN 0-8160-4240-3; 0-8160-4241-1 (pa)

LC 99-57876

Coverage includes practice, warm-up, and advanced techniques and forms, sparring strategies, self-defense, and breaking. Over 700 photographs accompany the text. Appendixes cover official competition rules, weight classes, governing bodies, and international organizations and associations. Includes two glossaries, English to Korean and Korean to English

Pedro, Jimmy, 1970-

Judo techniques & tactics; [by] Jimmy Pedro with William Durbin. Human Kinetics 2001 183p il (Martial arts series) pa $16.95

Grades: 9 10 11 12 Adult   **796.8**

1. Judo

ISBN 0-7360-0343-6   LC 00-54236

This instructional guide describes the fundamentals of judo, including its history, definitions of terms used, and guides on competition and conditioning.

Includes bibliographical references

Scott, Danna

Boxing: the complete guide to training and fitness. Berkley Pub. Group 2000 127p il pa $14.95

Grades: 9 10 11 12 Adult   **796.8**

1. Boxing

ISBN 0-399-52601-3   LC 99-59079

"A Perigee book"

This guide to boxing includes "tips on: equipment; punches and combinations; defensive skills and movement; ring strategy; boxing styles; proper training techniques; tricks of the trade; and much more." Publisher's note

796.9   Ice and snow sports

Stark, Peter

Winter adventure; a complete guide to winter sports; by Peter Stark and Steven M. Krauzer. Norton 1995 224p il (Trailside series guide) flexible bdg $17.95 *

Grades: 11 12 Adult   **796.9**

1. Winter sports

ISBN 0-393-31400-6   LC 95-34646

This guide to winter sports covers sledding, snowshoeing, dogsledding and skijoring, snowboarding, games such as cross-country tag and hare and hounds, the nature of snow and ice, ice skating, iceboating, ice climbing, curling and barrel jumping, winter camping, walking on snow and ice, dressing for winter, and winter safety. It lists organizations, mail-order sources, and information sources

796.93   Skiing and snowboarding

Cazeneuve, Brian

Cross-country skiing; a complete guide; illustrations by Ron Hildebrand. Norton 1995 192p il (Trailside series guide) flexible bdg $17.95 *

Grades: 11 12 Adult   **796.93**

1. Skiing

ISBN 0-393-31335-2   LC 95-5529

This illustrated guide to cross-country skiing covers equipment, techniques, backcountry skiing, clothing, safety, and fitness, and lists organizations, mail-order sources, and information sources

Kleh, Cindy

Snowboarding skills; the back-to-basics essentials for all levels; [photographer, Jed Jacobson] Firefly Books 2007 c2002 128p il pa $16.95

Grades: 7 8 9 10 11 12 Adult   **796.93**

1. Snowboarding

ISBN 1-55297-626-2   LC 2003-467271

This book features "information on taking lessons, proper nutrition before hitting the slopes, safety, clothing, stretching and preseason exercises, maintaining the equipment, basic moves, proper etiquette, and riding in a variety of snow conditions." SLJ

"Kleh's combination of dead-on practical advice, insider lingo, and near-religious enthusiasm makes this guide to snowboarding an invaluable resource for anyone wanting to try the sport or to advance his or her skills." Booklist

Masoff, Joy, 1951-

Snowboard! your guide to freeriding, pipe & park, jibbing, backcountry, alpine, boardercross, and more; illustrations by Jack Dickason. National Geographic Soc. 2002 64p il (Extreme sports) pa $8.95 *

Grades: 4 5 6 7 8 9   **796.93**

1. Snowboarding

ISBN 0-7922-6740-0   LC 2001-44392

Masoff, Joy, 1951-—*Continued*

Describes different kinds of snowboarding—freeriding, in the pipe, jibbing, backcountry—and the techniques, equipment, and terminology involved

"Sharp, action-packed photos and punchy, magazine-style prose add to the appeal. . . . Relaxed, readable, and filled with helpful information." Booklist

796.962   Ice hockey

A **basic** guide to ice hockey; the U.S. Olympic Committee. Griffin Pub, Distributed by G. Stevens Pub 2002 152p il (Olympic guides) lib bdg $23.93; pa $9.95

Grades: 9 10 11 12 Adult   **796.962**

1. Hockey

ISBN 0-8368-3103-9 (lib bdg); 1-58000-085-1 (pa)
                                         LC 2001-55096

Provides information on such aspects of ice hockey as the history of Olympic competition, game rules and strategies, relevant nutrition, safety and first aid, and more. Describes Olympic and ice hockey organizations.

McKinley, Michael, 1961-

Hockey: a people's history. McClelland & Stewart 2006 346p il $45

Grades: 11 12 Adult   **796.962**

1. Hockey

ISBN 0-7710-5769-5; 978-0-7710-5769-4

This history "chronicles hockey from its genesis as a winter substitute for lacrosse. A companion to a similarly titled CBC TV series, the lavishly illustrated book combines punchy boxed features celebrating individuals and hockey oddments and a detailed tracing of the game's development. . . . Essential for general sports as well as hockey-intensive collections." Booklist

Includes bibliographical references

796.98   Winter Olympic games

Wallechinsky, David, 1948-

The complete book of the Winter Olympics. 2002 ed. Overlook Press 2001 xxxviii, 353p il $25.95; pa $15.95

Grades: 11 12 Adult   **796.98**

1. Olympic games

ISBN 1-58567-195-9; 1-58567-185-1 (pa)
                                         LC 2001-36018

First published 1984

This compendium of Olympic history provides "backgrounds, stories, and statistics from every Winter Olympics since the Chamonix games of 1924." Publisher's note

797.1   Boating

Grant, Gordon

Canoeing; illustrations by Ron Hildebrand. Norton 1997 192p il (Trailside series guide) flexible bdg $18.95

Grades: 11 12 Adult   **797.1**

1. Canoes and canoeing

ISBN 0-393-31489-8   LC 96-2151

This guide to canoeing covers equipment, safety, paddling techniques, camping, moving water and white water canoeing. Grant provides lists of organizations, schools, tour organizers and guides, information sources, mail-order sources of equipment, and canoe manufacturers

Harrison, David, 1938-

Canoeing; the complete guide to equipment and technique; [by] Dave Harrison. Stackpole Bks. 1996 190p il map pa $15.95

Grades: 9 10 11 12   **797.1**

1. Canoes and canoeing

ISBN 0-8117-2426-3   LC 95-44934

First published 1981 by Harper & Row with title: Sports illustrated canoeing

This introduction to canoeing covers equipment, paddling technique, competitions, and more

Krauzer, Steven M.

Kayaking; whitewater and touring basics; introduction by John Viehman; illustrations by Ron Hildebrand. Norton 1995 192p il (Trailside series guide) flexible bdg $18.95 *

Grades: 11 12 Adult   **797.1**

1. Canoes and canoeing

ISBN 0-393-31336-0   LC 95-5527

This illustrated guide to kayaking covers equipment, techniques, and safety. Includes lists of organizations, mail-order sources, and information sources

Sleight, Steve

New complete sailing manual. Rev ed., 1st American ed. DK 2005 448p il map $35

Grades: 9 10 11 12 Adult   **797.1**

1. Sailing

ISBN 0-7566-0944-5; 978-0-7566-0944-3
                                         LC 2005-277514

First published 1999 with title: DK complete sailing manual

This sailing manual covers such topics as navigation, ropes and knots, boating safety, boat maintenance, and handling emergencies.

Stuhaug, Dennis O.

Kayaking made easy; a manual for beginners with tips for the experienced. 3rd ed. Globe Pequot Press 2006 264p il (Made easy series) pa $17.95

Grades: 9 10 11 12   **797.1**

1. Canoes and canoeing

ISBN 0-7627-3859-6   LC 2006-43437

Stuhaug, Dennis O.—*Continued*
First published 1995
This guide offers a step-by-step approach, first famil-
iarizing you with the gear, then proceeding through the
various strokes, and finally covering the complexities of
long-distance navigation. Publisher's note

Swenson, Allan A.
The L.L. Bean canoeing handbook. Lyons Press
1999 136p il pa $18.95 *
Grades: 11 12 Adult   **797.1**
1. Canoes and canoeing
ISBN 1-55821-977-3   LC 99-41186
Includes instruction on selecting equipment, handling
varying water conditions, and solo and tandem canoeing
techniques. Also offers advice on supplies, transporting
equipment, environmental stewardship, and trip planning

797.3 Other aquatic sports

The **Perfect** day; 40 years of Surfer magazine;
edited by Sam George. Chronicle Bks. 2001
167p il $35
Grades: 9 10 11 12   **797.3**
1. Surfing
ISBN 0-8118-3117-5   LC 00-57098
An illustrated anthology of articles spanning the history of Surfer magazine. Coverage is international in
scope.

798.4 Horse racing

Hillenbrand, Laura
Seabiscuit; an American legend. Random House
2001 399p il $25.95; pa $15.95
Grades: 11 12 Adult   **798.4**
1. Horse racing 2. Seabiscuit (Race horse)
ISBN 0-375-50291-2; 0-449-00561-5 (pa)
                                    LC 2001-267852
Also available Thorndike Press large print edition
Hillenbrand tells the story of the race horse who de-
feated "Triple Crown Winner War Admiral in what [has
been] called the greatest horse race of all time [Pimlico,
Nov. 1, 1938]." Newsweek
"This is a remarkable tale well told by a writer who
deftly blends history and sport." Economist
Includes bibliographical references

Ours, Dorothy
Man o' War; a legend like lightning. St Martin's
Press 2006 342p il $24.95
Grades: 11 12 Adult   **798.4**
1. Man o' War (Race horse) 2. Horse racing
ISBN 0-312-34099-0; 978-0-312-34099-5
                                    LC 2006-41631
This is an account of the thoroughbred racehorse Man
o' War, also known as Big Red.
This book "is clearly a labor of love, and it certifies
Big Red's claim to immortality." N Y Times Book Rev
Includes bibliographical references

798.8 Dog racing

Paulsen, Gary
Winterdance; the fine madness of running the
Iditarod. Harcourt Brace & Co. 1994 256p il $26;
pa $15
Grades: 6 7 8 9   **798.8**
1. Iditarod Trail Sled Dog Race, Alaska 2. Sled dog
racing
ISBN 0-15-126227-6; 0-15-600145-4 (pa)
                                    LC 93-42096
"This book is primarily an account of Paulsen's first
Iditarod and its frequent life-threatening disasters. . . .
However, the book is more than a tabulation of tribula-
tions; it is a meditation on the extraordinary attraction
this race holds for some men and women." Libr J

799 Fishing, hunting, shooting

Paulsen, Gary
Father water, Mother woods; essays on fishing
and hunting in the North Woods; with illustrations
by Ruth Wright Paulsen. Delacorte Press 1994
159p il pa $4.99 hardcover o.p.
Grades: 9 10 11 12   **799**
1. Hunting 2. Fishing
ISBN 0-440-21984-1   LC 94-2737
"This collection of autobiographical essays, identifies
{Paulsen's} youthful experiences in the woods and rivers
of northern Minnesota. . . . Throughout it all, descriptions of light and water, of fish and wildlife, kindle in
the reader a measure of the author's own complex respect for nature." Publ Wkly

799.1 Fishing

Mason, Bill, 1929-
Sports illustrated fly fishing; learn from a
master. [rev ed] Sports Illustrated 1994 255p il pa
$14.95 *
Grades: 9 10 11 12   **799.1**
1. Fishing 2. Fly casting
ISBN 1-56800-033-2
"Sports illustrated winner's circle books"
First published 1988
An illustrated introduction to the sport of fly fishing.
Emphasis is placed on equipment and technique.

Merwin, John
Fly fishing; a Trailside guide; illustrations by
Ron Hildebrand. Norton 1996 192p il (Trailside
series guide) flexible bdg $19.95 *
Grades: 11 12 Adult   **799.1**
1. Fishing 2. Fly casting
ISBN 0-393-31476-6   LC 96-2141
This illustrated guide to fly fishing covers equipment,
tying knots, types of flies, fly casting techniques for dif-
ferent types of fish, and lists organizations, schools,
mail-order sources, and information sources.
Include bibliographical references

799.3   Shooting other than game

Engh, Douglas
Archery fundamentals. Human Kinetics 2005
125p il (Sports fundamentals series) pa $15.95
Grades: 9 10 11 12 Adult   **799.3**
1. Archery
ISBN 0-7360-5501-0; 978-0-7360-5501-7
LC 2004-11221
Contents: Bows — Arrows — Shooting recurve —
Shooting compound — Grips, anchors, and releases —
Taking aim — Tight groups — Scoring performance —
Accessories — Tuning and repair — Competition
This book provides instruction in the basic skills of
archery, including shooting techniques, improving aim,
and how to keep score as well as information on care
and repair of bows, arrows and other equipment.

800   LITERATURE

Baker, Nancy L., 1950-
A research guide for undergraduate students;
English and American literature; [by] Nancy L.
Baker and Nancy Huling. 6th ed. Modern
Language Association of America 2006 96p il pa
$12
Grades: 11 12 Adult   **800**
1. Literature—Research 2. English literature—Bibliog-
raphy 3. American literature—Bibliography
ISBN 978-0-8735-2924-2; 0-8735-2924-3
LC 2006-7360
First published 1982
This book "provides dozens of research samples from
the library's online catalog to new databases. Includes a
. . . chapter with bibliographic citation managers." Univ
Press Books for Public and Second Sch Libr, 2007
Includes bibliographical references

Cracking the SAT: literature subject test,
2007-2008 edition; [by] the Princeton Review.
Random House 2005 il pa $18
Grades: 9 10 11 12   **800**
1. Literature—Study and teaching 2. Scholastic As-
sessment Test 3. Colleges and universities—Entrance
requirements
ISBN 0-375-76589-1; 978-0-375-76589-6
Annual. First published 2005. Continues Cracking the
SAT II: Writing and literature subject tests
At head of title: The Princeton Review
This guide provides test-taking strategies and sample
tests on the subject of literature.

Kent-Drury, Roxanne M.
Using Internet primary sources to teach critical
thinking skills in world literature. Libraries
Unlimited 2005 194p (Libraries Unlimited
professional guides in school librarianship) pa $42
Grades: Professional   **800**
1. Literature—Study and teaching 2. Internet in educa-
tion
ISBN 0-313-32009-8; 978-0-313-32009-5
LC 2004-63834

"This book provides creative and interesting thinking
activities to enhance student understanding of literature
and culture and to promote critical thinking." Publisher's
note
Includes bibliographical references

803   Literature--Encyclopedias and dictionaries

Abrams, M. H. (Meyer Howard), 1912-
A glossary of literary terms; with contributions
by Geoffrey Galt Harpham. 8th ed. Thomson,
Wadsworth 2005 370p pa $34.95 *
Grades: 11 12 Adult   **803**
1. Literature—Dictionaries
ISBN 1-4130-0218-8; 978-1-4130-0218-8
LC 2004-111345
First published 1957
In a series of essays, the author discusses literary
terms and definitions ranging from the traditional to the
avant-garde. Subsidiary terms are included under major
or generic terms.

Baldick, Chris
The concise Oxford dictionary of literary terms.
2nd ed. Oxford University Press 2004 280p
(Oxford paperback reference) pa $16.95 *
Grades: 11 12 Adult   **803**
1. Literature—Dictionaries 2. English language—
Terms and phrases
ISBN 0-19-860883-7   LC 2003-70163
Also available online
First published 1990
"Reissued with new covers" Verso of title page
This work defines more than 1,000 literary terms.
Also provides coverage of traditional drama, rhetoric, lit-
erary history, and textual criticism. Includes pronuncia-
tion guides on over 200 terms.

Benét's reader's encyclopedia; edited by Bruce
Murphy. 4th ed. HarperCollins Pubs. 1996
1144p $50 *
Grades: 11 12 Adult   **803**
1. Literature—Dictionaries
ISBN 0-06-270110-X   LC 96-217151
First published 1948 under the editorship of William
Rose Benet
This encyclopedia contains over 10,000 entries and
covers world literature from early times to the present.
Includes entries on authors, literary movements, principal
characters, plot synopses, terms, awards, myths and leg-
ends, etc.

Brewer's dictionary of modern phrase & fable;
edited by John Ayto & Ian Crofton. 2nd ed.
Weidenfeld & Nicolson 2006 853p $34.95 *
Grades: 9 10 11 12 Adult   **803**
1. Literature—Dictionaries 2. Allusions
ISBN 0-304-36809-1; 978-0-304-36809-9
First published 2000 by Cassell

Brewer's dictionary of modern phrase & fable—*Continued*

This modern version of Brewer's dictionary of phrase and fable "focuses on material from the 20th and 21st centuries. More than 800 entries, arranged alphabetically with cross-references and accompanying quotations, contain insightful and informative descriptions and etymologies. . . . The contemporary phrases contain slang usage as well as technical terms." Choice [review of 2001 edition]

Brewer's dictionary of phrase & fable. 17th ed., revised by John Ayto. Collins 2005 xxvii, 1523p il $55 *

    Grades: 5 6 7 8 9 10 11 12 Adult   **803**
    1. Literature—Dictionaries 2. Allusions
    ISBN 0-06-112120-7; 978-0-06-112120-3

First published 1870 under the editorship of Ebenezer Cobham Brewer

"Over 15,000 brief entries give the meanings and origins of a broad range of terms, expressions, and names of real, fictitious and mythical characters from world history, science, the arts and literature." N Y Public Libr. Ref Books for Child Collect. 2d edition

"This classic for the ages is immensely browseable; one can get lost in it for hours." Libr J

Carey, Gary

A multicultural dictionary of literary terms; [by] Gary Carey and Mary Ellen Snodgrass. McFarland & Co. 1999 184p hardcover o.p. pa $29.95
    Grades: 11 12 Adult   **803**
    1. Literature—Dictionaries
    ISBN 0-7864-0552-X; 0-7864-2950-X (pa)
                      LC 98-35221

"Using the full spectrum of literature, including drama, poetry, and novels, the authors . . . draw from a cross section of works by people of many races and traditions for both literary terms and the examples used to define them." Libr J

Includes bibliographical references

Harmon, William, 1938-

A handbook to literature. 10th ed. Pearson/Prentice Hall 2006 675p pa $16.95 *
    Grades: 11 12 Adult   **803**
    1. Literature—Dictionaries
    ISBN 0-13-134442-0   LC 2005-49285

First published 1936 by Doubleday under the authorship of William Flint Thrall and Addison Hibbard; later editions by William Harmon and C. Hugh Holman

This work provides "explanations of terms, concepts, schools, and movements in literature. Alphabetical arrangement with numerous cross-references as well as bibliographic references for some entries." Guide to Ref Books. 11th edition

Oxford dictionary of phrase and fable; edited by Elizabeth Knowles. 2nd ed. Oxford University Press 2005 805p $40; pa $18.95 *
    Grades: 11 12 Adult   **803**
    1. Literature—Dictionaries 2. Allusions
    ISBN 978-0-19-860981-0; 978-0-19-920246-1 (pa)
First published 2000

This work seeks to define words and phrases of British cultural history.

This "is a highly useful tool to help understand what phrases mean and where they come from and should definitely be added to all reference collections." Booklist

Quinn, Edward, 1932-

A dictionary of literary and thematic terms. 2nd ed. Facts on File 2006 474p (Facts on File library of language and literature) $55; pa $19.95 *
    Grades: 11 12 Adult   **803**
    1. Literature—Dictionaries
    ISBN 0-8160-6243-9; 978-0-8160-6243-0;
    0-8160-6244-7 (pa); 978-0-8160-6244-7 (pa)
                      LC 2005-29826

First published 1999

In addition to basic definitions of terms "this general literary dictionary . . . covers common themes in literature such as love, death, alienation, and time. Literary schools are treated with just enough depth to offer a basic understanding of the major tenets." Libr J [review of 1999 edition]

Includes bibliographical references

Webber, Elizabeth, 1946-

Merriam-Webster's dictionary of allusions; {by} Elizabeth Webber & Mike Feinsilber. Merriam-Webster 1999 592p pa $14.95 *
    Grades: 11 12 Adult   **803**
    1. Allusions
    ISBN 0-87779-628-9   LC 99-33125

"More than 900 entries are listed alphabetically. Each includes a short definition and a longer history of the word or phrase; some also include pronunciation. Length varies from five to six sentences to a page or more, and all include one or more examples of the term in use, complete with date, author (when available), and print or media sources. . . . Almost all of the usage examples are from the late 1980s and 1990s." Booklist

Includes bibliographical references

808 Rhetoric

Agress, Lynne, 1941-

Working with words in business and legal writing. Perseus Bks. 2002 123p il pa $13.50
    Grades: 11 12 Adult   **808**
    1. Authorship—Handbooks, manuals, etc.
    ISBN 0-7382-0562-1

The author "provides a framework for good writing in business and law. . . . She addresses common failings such as poor grammar, the use of jargon, awkward sentences, excess verbiage, pretentious writing, and poor punctuation, clearly presenting each problem and offering possible solutions." Libr J

Bly, Carol
Beyond the writers' workshop; new ways to write creative nonfiction. Anchor Bks. (NY) 2001 xxiv, 376p il pa $12
Grades: 11 12 Adult   **808**
1. Creative writing 2. Rhetoric 3. Authorship
ISBN 0-385-49919-1   LC 00-50233
In this study the author provides "advice on how to write meaningful nonfiction by incorporating techniques from psychotherapy and neuroscience. . . . She ends the book with 15 writing exercises, usage sheets, and sample writing class agendas." Libr J
Includes bibliographical references

The **Chicago** manual of style. 15th ed. University of Chicago Press 2003 956p il $55
Grades: 11 12 Adult   **808**
1. Authorship—Handbooks, manuals, etc. 2. Publishers and publishing—Handbooks, manuals, etc. 3. English language—Usage
ISBN 0-226-10403-6   LC 2003-1860
First published 1906 with title: A manual of style
Updated to reflect current style, technology, and professional practice, this style manual includes journals and electronic publications, descriptive headings on all numbered paragraphs, and reorganized chapters on grammar, usage, and documentation, including guidance on citing electronic sources
Includes bibliographical references

Dunn, Jessica, 1980-
A teen's guide to getting published; publishing for profit, recognition, and academic success; [by] Jessica Dunn & Danielle Dunn. 2nd ed. Prufrock Press 2006 249p pa $14.95 *
Grades: 7 8 9 10 11 12   **808**
1. Authorship 2. Publishers and publishing
ISBN 1-59363-182-0   LC 2006005109
First published 1997
Danielle Dunn's name appears first on the earlier edition
"Adding new Internet opportunities such as online journals, writer-support blogs, and e-mail editing, this volume covers the full gamut of possibilities and pitfalls for aspiring writers. . . . In addition to standard advice on publishers and agents, the authors give practical suggestions for finding a writing environment that is accessible to teens, such as school publication staffs and local newspaper internships. . . . Annotated appendixes list Web sites, books, journals, and contests. Also provided is information on mentors, writing camps, and courses catering to young authors, and a valuable list of mainstream publishers who have expressed openness to submissions from teens. This compact, sensible book discusses all kinds of writing." SLJ

Fleming, Robert
The African American writer's handbook; how to get in print and stay in print. One World (NY) 2000 339p pa $12
Grades: 11 12 Adult   **808**
1. Authorship—Handbooks, manuals, etc. 2. African American authors
ISBN 0-345-42327-5   LC 00-102059

The author "discusses the basics of manuscript submissions, tools of writing, and the publishing world. He speaks of issues that many African-American writers must deal with in producing and marketing their books. He also reveals the importance of self-promotion. In subsequent chapters, Fleming entertains book lovers of any race with a tour of the African-American literary world." Libr J
Includes bibliographical references

Francis, Barbara, 1948-
Other people's words; what plagiarism is and how to avoid it. Enslow Pubs. 2005 112p il (Issues in focus today) $31.93 *
Grades: 6 7 8 9   **808**
1. Plagiarism
ISBN 0-7660-2525-X
"This title offers students a clear explanation of plagiarism and its consequences as well as specific ways to avoid it. . . . Chapters address cheating, Internet downloading, fabrication, and how teachers curb plagiarism. . . . A must-have for middle and high school libraries." SLJ
Includes glossary and bibliographical references

Gibaldi, Joseph, 1942-
MLA handbook for writers of research papers. 6th ed. Modern Lang. Assn. of Am. 363p il pa $14.75 *
Grades: 9 10 11 12   **808**
1. Report writing
ISBN 0-87352-975-8
First published 1977 with title: MLA handbook for writers of research papers, theses, and dissertations.
This manual discusses research strategies, formatting, documenting sources, writing basics and utilizing electronic sources
Includes bibliographical references

Harper, Elizabeth, 1934-
Your name in print; a teen's guide to publishing for fun, profit, and academic success. St. Martin's Griffin 2005 186p pa $13.95
Grades: 7 8 9 10   **808**
1. Authorship—Handbooks, manuals, etc.
ISBN 0-312-33759-0   LC 2004-24675
The authors "offer chapters and features on a variety of subjects: writing outlets (such as local papers and blogs); article topics; workspaces; book publishing and agents; tips from pros; sample columns; [and] 'glances' at current teen writers. . . . This book will be a useful addition for most libraries." Voice Youth Advocates
Includes bibliographical references

Johnson, Sarah Anne
The art of the author interview; and interviewing creative people. University Press of New England 2005 158p pa $19.95
Grades: 11 12 Adult   **808**
1. Interviewing 2. Reporters and reporting
ISBN 1-58465-397-3   LC 2004-23688

Johnson, Sarah Anne—*Continued*

This book "shows readers how to initiate, research, conduct, and publish interviews with authors and other creative people." Publisher's note

Lasch, Christopher

Plain style; a guide to written English; edited and with an introduction by Stewart Weaver. University of Pa. Press 2002 121p hardcover o.p. pa $14.95

Grades: 11 12 Adult   808

1. Rhetoric 2. English language—Grammar
ISBN 0-8122-3673-4; 0-8122-1814-0 (pa)
LC 2002-19163

"The guide is divided into six parts, covering the principles of literary construction; conventions governing punctuation, capitalization, typography, and footnotes; characteristics of bad writing; words often misued; words often mispronounced; and a table of proofreaders' marks." Booklist

Includes bibliographical references

Plotnik, Arthur, 1937-

Spunk & bite; a writer's guide to punchier, more engaging language & style. Random House 2005 263p $16.95; pa $12.95

Grades: 11 12 Adult   808

1. Rhetoric
ISBN 0-375-72115-0; 0-375-72227-0 (pa)
LC 2005-44934

The author "demonstrates how . . . unexpected humor, loquaciousness, and apt description can jolt a writer into engaged authorship. This primer is dotted with illustrative examples that range from Shakespeare and J.K. Rowling to Dave Barry and Maeve Binchy. . . . This is an entertaining and engaging choice for writers." Libr J

Prose, Francine, 1947-

Reading like a writer; a guide for people who love books and for those who want to write them. HarperCollins Publishers 2006 273p $23.95; pa $13.95

Grades: 11 12 Adult   808

1. Rhetoric 2. Creative writing 3. Books and reading
ISBN   978-0-06-077704-3;   0-06-077704-4;
978-0-06-077705-0; 0-06-077705-2 (pa)
LC 2005-58457

The author "devotes a chapter each to eight elements of writing: words, sentences, paragraphs, narration, character, dialog, details, and gesture. These chapters are framed by an opening piece that urges close reading as most productive for writers; a chapter devoted to Chekhov, particularly his short stories, as translated by Constance Garnett; and a closing chapter, 'Reading for Courage.'" Libr J

This book "should be greatly appreciated in and out of the classroom. Like the great works of fiction, it's a wise and voluble companion." N Y Times Book Rev

Salzman, Mark

True notebooks. Alfred A. Knopf 2003 330p hardcover o.p. pa $13.95

Grades: 11 12 Adult   808

1. Creative writing 2. Juvenile delinquency
ISBN 0-375-41308-1; 0-375-72761-2 (pa)
LC 2002-43435

"While teaching writing to 17-year-olds detained in Los Angeles Central Juvenile Hall, Salzman found himself surprised by the boys' talent. The teens' heartwarming, funny voices are included in his irresistible, provocative memoir." Booklist

Schiwy, Marlene A.

A voice of her own; women and the journal writing journey. Simon & Schuster 1996 380p pa $15

Grades: 11 12 Adult   808

1. Diaries
ISBN 0-684-80342-9   LC 96-5325

"A Fireside book"

The author considers various aspects "of journal keeping, from how and why keeping a journal can make life more meaningful to various types of journals and writing styles. She offers advice about choosing blank books, keeping a journal private, and deciding when to reread old journals. Schiwy also delves into the history of women diarists and discusses the many reasons women keep diaries at different stages of life." Booklist

Includes bibliographical references

Shields, Nancy E., 1928-

Where credit is due; a guide to proper citing of sources, print and nonprint; [by] Nancy E. Shields, with the assistance of Mary E. Uhle. 2nd ed. Scarecrow Press 1997 189p $41.50 *

Grades: 7 8 9 10   808

1. Bibliographical citations 2. Research
ISBN 0-8108-3211-9   LC 96-6523

First published 1985

"This book is a style guide for students to properly document the vast array of sources for the research paper. It includes every possible source that could be used as a reference with examples of footnotes and bibliography entries. . . . This book is exactly what the librarian needs to provide students with up-to-date styles for documentation in their writing." Book Rep

Strunk, William, 1869-1946

The elements of style; with revisions, an introduction, and a chapter on writing by E.B. White. 4th ed. Allyn & Bacon 1999 105p $14.95; pa $7.95 *

Grades: 11 12 Adult   808

1. Rhetoric
ISBN 0-205-31342-6; 0-205-30902-X (pa)
LC 99-16419

First privately printed in 1918

This work provides guidelines for proper usage and composition. Misused expressions and commonly misspelled words are discussed. Includes examples

Strunk, William, 1869-1946—*Continued*

This work is "prescriptive, conservative, and humorous; in sum, it is the best book available on how to write English prose." Nichols. Guide to Ref Books for Sch Media Cent. 4th edition

Turabian, Kate L., 1893-1987

A manual for writers of research papers, theses, and dissertations; Chicago style for students and researchers; revised by Wayne C. Booth, Gregory G. Colomb, Joseph M. Williams, and University of Chicago Press editorial staff. 7th ed. University of Chicago Press 2007 466p il (Chicago guides to writing, editing, and publishing) $35; pa $17 *

Grades: 11 12 Adult **808**

1. Report writing 2. Dissertations
ISBN   978-0-226-82336-2;   0-226-82336-9;
978-0-226-82337-9 (pa); 0-226-82337-7 (pa)
LC 2006-25443

First published 1937 with title: A manual for writers of dissertations

Designed to serve as a guide to suitable style in the presentation of formal papers—term papers, reports, articles, theses, dissertations—both in scientific and in nonscientific fields.

Walker, Janice R.

The Columbia guide to online style; [by] Janice R. Walker and Todd Taylor. 2nd ed. Columbia University Press 2006 xxi, 288p il $45; pa $19.50 *

Grades: 11 12 Adult **808**

1. Authorship—Data processing—Handbooks, manuals, etc. 2. Bibliographical citations
ISBN   0-231-13210-7;   978-0-231-13210-7;
0-231-13211-5 (pa); 978-0-231-13211-4 (pa)
LC 2006-24383

First published 1998

This is a "resource for citing electronic and electronically accessed sources. It is also a . . . style guide for creating documents electronically for submission for print or electronic publication." Publisher's note

Includes bibliographical references

Winkler, Anthony C.

Writing the research paper; a handbook with both the MLA and APA documentation styles; {by} Anthony C. Winkler, Jo Ray McCuen. 5th ed. Harcourt Brace College Pubs. 1999 358p il pa $37 *

Grades: 9 10 11 12 **808**

1. Report writing 2. Research
ISBN 0-15-508440-2   LC 98-88048

First published 1979

New edition in preparation

Among the topics covered are: choosing a topic; libraries and background sources; outlining; rough drafts; documentation; punctuation, mechanics, and spelling. A sample student paper is included

Includes bibliographical references

The **Writer's** handbook 2007. Writer 2006 pa $24.95 *

Grades: 11 12 Adult **808**

1. Authorship—Handbooks,   manuals,   etc.
2. Publishers and publishing
ISSN 0084-2710
ISBN 1-4050-4937-5; 978-1-4050-4937-5

Annual. First published 1936

Current editor Barry Turner

"A collection of articles, most of which appeared originally in *The writer*, on various phases of professional writing, including fiction, nonfiction, and specialties. Some articles are carried over from earlier editions, some are new, none are dated. The specialties section is a market guide, mainly to the periodical field, giving for each title: address, editor, and type of material accepted with indication of rate of payment. Also has sections for greeting card and drama markets, including regional and university theaters, television, and for book publishers." Guide to Ref Books. 11th edition

The **Writer's** market, 2007. Writer's Digest Bks. 2007 pa $29.99

Grades: 11 12 Adult **808**

1. Authorship—Handbooks,   manuals,   etc.
2. Publishers and publishing
ISSN 0084-2729
ISBN 1-58297-427-6; 978-1-58297-427-9

Also available deluxe edition with access to Writer's Market online database $49.99

Annual. First published 1922

"A guide for freelance writers, covering the practical side of writing for publication, including information about book publishers; consumer magazines; trade, technical and a few professional journals; scriptwriting; syndicates; greeting card and gift markets. Provides extensive lists of contests and awards and of relevant organizations and publications. Subject index of book publishers." Guide to Ref Books. 11th edition

808.06   Writing children's literature

Peck, Richard, 1934-

Invitations to the world; teaching and writing for the young. Dial Bks. 2002 204p $16.99 *

Grades: 9 10 11 12 **808.06**

1. Authorship 2. Books and reading 3. Young adult literature—Technique
ISBN 0-8037-2734-8   LC 2001-53691

First published 1994 by Delacorte Press with title: Love and death at the mall

"Peck puts down his thoughts on writing for young people and reminisces about the inspiration behind his books and his motivation to become an author. . . . The earlier version of this book addressed two questions: 'How did you get your start?' and 'Where do you get your ideas?' Here Peck adds a chapter to answer the question, 'How much longer are you going to write?'. . . Also new to this edition is a section at the end of the book called For Sharing that includes advice to encourage reading and discussion questions for novels." Voice Youth Advocates

Includes bibliographical references

808.1 Rhetoric of poetry

Bugeja, Michael J.
The art and craft of poetry. Writer's Digest Bks. 1994 339p hardcover o.p. pa $16.99 *
Grades: 11 12 Adult **808.1**
1. Poetics
ISBN 0-89879-633-4; 1-58297-101-3 (pa)
LC 93-38192
The author begins this handbook for aspiring poets by describing "how keeping a journal helps poets focus their observations, contemplations, and discoveries. Bugeja goes on to describe various genres of poetry, the elements of poems, styles such as narrative and lyric poetry, and forms such as the sonnet, villanelle, and sestina. His explanations are lucid, his examples illuminating, and his suggested exercises useful and geared to different levels of proficiency." Booklist

Deutsch, Babette, 1895-1982
Poetry handbook: a dictionary of terms. 4th ed. HarperResource 2002 203p pa $14 *
Grades: 11 12 Adult **808.1**
1. Poetics—Dictionaries 2. Poetry—Terminology
ISBN 0-06-463548-1
First published 1957 by Funk & Wagnalls
"The craft of verse described in dictionary form. Terms and techniques are defined and illustrated." N Y Public Libr. Ref Books for Child Collect. 2d edition

Drury, John, 1950-
The poetry dictionary; foreward by Dana Gioia. 2nd ed. Writer's Digest Books 2006 374p pa $14.99 *
Grades: 11 12 Adult **808.1**
1. Poetry—Dictionaries 2. Poetics
ISBN 1-58297-329-6; 978-1-58297-329-6
LC 2005-15113
First published 1995 by Story Press (Cincinnati)
"Spanning the centuries from ode to rap, The Poetry Dictionary contains 284 entries that define movements and schools of poetry, forms of verse, rhyme and stress patterns, and poetic devices. Entries range in length from a paragraph for canto to more than seven pages for sonnet." Booklist [review of 1995 edition]

Fooling with words; a celebration of poets and their craft; edited by Bill Moyers. Morrow 1999 230p hardcover o.p. pa $12
Grades: 11 12 Adult **808.1**
1. Poetics
ISBN 0-688-17346-2; 0-688-17792-1 (pa)
LC 99-34965
"Moyers here interviews 11 American poets (e.g., Robert Pinsky, Mark Doty, Shirley Geok-lin Lim, and Paul Muldoon) whose voices echo the diversity of the United States—a wonderful jumble of genders, ethnic groups, and religions. This book is not a how-to; interviews (accompanied by the interviewee's poetry) focus on the poet as an individual, the creative process, and enjoying poetry and reveling in its sound." Libr J

Higginson, William J., 1938-
The haiku handbook; how to write, share, and teach haiku; [by] William J. Higginson with Penny Harter. Kodansha International 1989 c1985 331p pa $14 *
Grades: 11 12 Adult **808.1**
1. Haiku
ISBN 4-770-01430-9
First published 1985 by McGraw-Hill
The author "surveys the original and related forms (renga, haibun, senryu), inventors and developers (Basho, Buson, Issa, Shiki), and the numerous variations that later authors, especially in other languages, have wrought on haiku's simple principles. He discusses the many uses—artistic, personal, psychological—that the mode can serve, encouraging the reader all along the way to use the form, to experiment, and thus to express thoughts and feelings. . . . An extensive reference section gives word lists, a glossary, and good bibliographies." Booklist

Hirsch, Edward
How to read a poem; and fall in love with poetry. Harcourt Brace & Co. 1999 352p $23; pa $15
Grades: 11 12 Adult **808.1**
1. Poetics 2. Poetry—History and criticism
ISBN 0-15-100419-6; 0-15-600566-2 (pa)
LC 98-50065
"A DoubleTake book."; "Published by the Center for Documentary Studies in association with---."
The author "has gathered an eclectic group of poems from many times and places, with selections as varied as postwar Polish poetry, works by Keats and Christopher Smart, and lyrics from African American work songs. A prolific, award-winning poet in his own right, Hirsch suggests helpful strategies for understanding and appreciating each poem. The book is scholarly but very readable and incorporates interesting anecdotes from the lives of the poets." Libr J
Includes bibliographical references

Jerome, Judson
The poet's handbook. Writer's Digest Bks. 1980 224p pa $15.99 hardcover o.p.
Grades: 9 10 11 12 **808.1**
1. Poetics
ISBN 1-58297-136-6 LC 80-17270
"This is not the usual alphabetized handbook. It gives a brief but scholarly background of the poet's place in early times and later history and moves on to discuss in individual chapters the craft of poetry: syllable-counting, meter, rhyme, free verse, the rhythms of the English language, and so on. It is more personal than one usually finds such a book to be, and it presents almost everything a beginning poet, as well as one who has mastered the craft, should know." Choice

Kooser, Ted

The poetry home repair manual; practical advice for beginning poets. University of Nebraska Press 2005 163p $19.95; pa $13.95 *

Grades: 11 12 Adult   **808.1**

1. Poetics

ISBN 0-8032-2769-8; 0-8032-5978-6 (pa)

LC 2004-24700

The author's advice "includes both broad and specific ideas on revising, and . . . discussion of matters ranging from the often-underestimated power of simile to employing narrative effectively." Booklist

"Among the many books offering advice on writing poetry, . . . [this book] stands out for its usefulness and, at the same time, for its inspiring view of the purposes of poetry." Midwest Quarterly

Includes bibliographical references

Myers, Jack Elliott, 1941-

Dictionary of poetic terms; [by] Jack Myers, Don Charles Wukasch. University of N. Tex. Press 2003 434p pa $22.95 *

Grades: 11 12 Adult   **808.1**

1. Poetics—Dictionaries

ISBN 1-57441-166-7   LC 2003-11482

First published 1985 by Longman Press with title: Longman dictionary and handbook of poetry

This volume "contains over 1,600 entries on the devices, techniques, history, theory, and terminology of poetry from the Classical period to the present." Publisher's note

"Particularly useful is the plethora of samples from the works of such greats as James Joyce, Edna St. Vincent Millay, Ezra Pound, and Ogden Nash. Although some of the vocabulary is lofty, the definitions, fascinating history, and brief essays combine to form a useful handbook." Libr J

Includes bibliographical references

Oliver, Mary, 1935-

A poetry handbook. Harcourt Brace & Co. 1994 130p pa $13

Grades: 11 12 Adult   **808.1**

1. Poetics

ISBN 0-15-672400-6   LC 93-49676

"A Harvest original"

A "handbook for young poets on the formal aspects and structure of poetry. Oliver excels at explaining the sound and sense of poetry—from scansion to imagery, diction to voice. She stresses the importance of reading poetry, since, in order to write well, 'it is entirely necessary to read widely and deeply.' Sage advice is given in an entire chapter dedicated to revision, wherein Oliver urges poets to consider their first draft 'an unfinished piece of work' that can be polished and improved later. Written in a pleasant and lucid style, this book is a wonderful resource." Libr J

Packard, William

The poet's dictionary; a handbook of prosody and poetic devices. Harper & Row 1989 212p pa $15 hardcover o.p.

Grades: 11 12 Adult   **808.1**

1. Poetics 2. Versification

ISBN 0-06-272045-7   LC 88-45899

This "dictionary gives succinct definitions enhanced by some historical and other explanatory notes, always followed by examples from familiar sources. . . . Reliability and authenticity are hallmarks of this dictionary." Choice

Includes bibliographical references

Poetry from A to Z; a guide for young writers; compiled by Paul B. Janeczko; illustrated by Cathy Bobak. Bradbury Press 1994 131p il $16.95 *

Grades: 5 6 7 8 9 10   **808.1**

1. Poetics 2. American poetry—Collections

ISBN 0-02-747672-3   LC 94-10528

"In his guide, Janeczko gives many examples and ideas to get young writers started writing poetry. The book is organized alphabetically with seventy-two poems on almost any topic you could imagine. In addition, fourteen exercises labeled 'Try This' explain how to write different types of poems and help a young writer get started." Voice Youth Advocates

Includes bibliographical references

Seeing the blue between; advice and inspiration for young poets; compiled by Paul B. Janeczko. Candlewick Press 2002 132p $18.99; pa $7.99

Grades: 7 8 9 10   **808.1**

1. Poetics 2. American poetry—Collections

ISBN 0-7636-0881-5; 0-7636-2909-X (pa)

LC 2001-25882

"Here, thirty-two established poets share their writing secrets in short letters addressed directly to the readers. Although each poet has a distinct voice . . . a familiar mantra quickly develops: read, observe, love words, write, rewrite. . . . Accompanying poems may connect directly to a letter's content, give a representative sample of an individual's body of work, or impart advice." Horn Book Guide

"The letters are personal, friendly, and supportive. . . . A valuable addition to public and school libraries, with the potential for much classroom and personal use." SLJ

808.2   Rhetoric of drama

Straczynski, J. Michael, 1954-

The complete book of scriptwriting. rev and expanded [ed] Writer's Digest Bks. 1996 424p il pa $19.99 hardcover o.p.

Grades: 11 12 Adult   **808.2**

1. Drama—Technique 2. Television authorship 3. Motion picture plays—Technique 4. Radio authorship

ISBN 1-58297-158-7 (pa)   LC 96-30630

First published 1982

Straczynski, J. Michael, 1954—*Continued*
This "encyclopedic exploration of writing scripts for TV, motion pictures, animation, radio, and the stage includes examples of actual scripts formatted for each medium." Libr J

808.3 Rhetoric of fiction

Gardner, John, 1933-1982
The art of fiction; notes on craft for young writers. Knopf 1984 224p pa $12.95 hardcover o.p. *
Grades: 11 12 Adult   808.3
1. Fiction—Technique
ISBN 0-679-73403-1   LC 83-47850
"This essay distills the late Gardner's ripest thoughts about what fiction is and how to go about learning to write it. The initial section deals with 'literary-aesthetic theory,' the second with 'the fictional process.' . . . The book concludes with two sets of exercises, one for class use and one for individual use. Recommended for any young writer or writing class, and for all readers who care about the craft of fiction." Booklist

Henry, Laurie
The fiction dictionary. Story Press (Cincinnati) 1995 324p hardcover o.p. pa $20.99 *
Grades: 11 12 Adult   808.3
1. Fiction—Technique
ISBN 1-884910-05-X; 1-884910-54-8 (pa)
    LC 95-4269
Henry provides "definitions of 345 terms relating to fiction, including genres, narrative devices, elements of fictional works, and critical theories. In addition to citing examples of works that illustrate a term, she frequently supplements her explanations with brief excerpts from novels and short stories." Booklist

Lukeman, Noah
The plot thickens; 8 ways to bring fiction to life. St. Martin's Press 2002 221p $19.95; pa $12.95
Grades: 11 12 Adult   808.3
1. Fiction—Technique
ISBN 0-312-28467-5; 0-312-30928-7 (pa)
    LC 2001-58564
"Lukeman focuses on the mechanics of storytelling. He introduces budding writers to the techniques of characterization (ask yourself questions about the people you've created), the various ways of generating suspense (danger, a ticking clock), and the importance of conflict." Booklist

Piercy, Marge
So you want to write; how to master the craft of writing fiction and memoir; [by] Marge Piercy and Ira Wood. 2nd ed. Leapfrog Press 2005 324p pa $16.95
Grades: 11 12 Adult   808.3
1. Fiction—Technique 2. Biography as a literary form
ISBN 0-9728984-5-X
First published 2001

This book "uses talks, exercises, anecdotes and examples proven in the classroom, to address: How to begin a piece by seducing your reader, How to create characters that embody the infinite contradictions of human behavior, How to master the elements of plotting fiction, How to create a strategy for telling the story of your life, How to learn to read critically, like a professional writer, How to write about painful personal material without coming off as a victim, [and] How to proceed if your work is continually rejected by publishers." Publisher's note
Includes bibliographical references

808.4 Rhetoric of essays

Orr, Tamra
Extraordinary essays. Franklin Watts 2005 128p il (F. W. Prep) $30.50; pa $9.95 *
Grades: 7 8 9 10   808.4
1. Essay 2. Authorship
ISBN 0-531-16761-5; 0-531-17576-6 (pa)
"This concise, appealingly designed writing guide offers practical advice to students on how to successfully complete essay assignments. Topics covered include choosing a topic, brainstorming, researching, crafting and defending a thesis statement, and revising." Booklist
Includes bibliographical references

808.5 Rhetoric of speech

Latrobe, Kathy Howard
Readers theatre for young adults; scripts and script development; {by} Kathy Howard Latrobe, Mildred Knight Laughlin. Teacher Ideas Press 1989 130p pa $22
Grades: Professional   808.5
1. Drama—Collections 2. Drama in education
ISBN 0-87287-743-4   LC 89-4552
Presents plays adapted from sixteen literary classics and includes scenes from novels with suggestions for adapting them into scripts
Includes bibliographical references

Pinsky, Robert
The sounds of poetry; a brief guide. Farrar, Straus & Giroux 1998 129p pa $13 hardcover o.p. *
Grades: 11 12 Adult   808.5
1. Poetry
ISBN 0-374-52617-6   LC 98-18873
Pinsky presents "a manual of proposals on how to read poems—or, more accurately, how to 'hear more of what is going on in poems.' That distinction, in Pinsky's view is vital." Atl Mon
"By bringing his passion for the sound of language—so evident in his own poems—to his expert interpretations of the work of others, Pinsky cracks open the glass case that seems to separate poetry from everyday language, allowing the song of each poem to ring bright and clear." Booklist
Includes bibliographical references

Ryan, Margaret, 1950-
Extraordinary oral presentations. Franklin Watts 2005 128p il (F. W. Prep) $30.50; pa $9.95 *
Grades: 7 8 9 10   **808.5**
1. Public speaking
ISBN 0-531-16758-5; 0-531-17577-4 (pa)
This offers advice on preparing oral presentations. This book provides "good, practical ideas for students." SLJ
Includes bibliographical references

808.53 Debating

The **debatabase** book; a must-have guide for successful debate; [by] the editors of IDEA; introduction by Robert Trapp. 3rd ed. International Debate Education Association 2007 240p il pa $25.95 *
Grades: 9 10 11 12   **808.53**
1. Debates and debating
ISBN 978-1-932716-27-6; 1-932716-27-0
LC 2006-39746
First published 2003
Presents background, arguments, and resources on approximately 150 debate topics in diverse areas. Includes the resolution, context, pro and con, sample motions, and web links and print resources.
Includes bibliographical references

Discovering the world through debate; a practical guide to educational debate for debaters, coaches and judges; [by] Robert Trapp . . . [et al.]; with the assistance of Judith K. Bowker. 3rd ed. International Debate Education Association 2005 258p il pa $29.95 *
Grades: 9 10 11 12   **808.53**
1. Debates and debating
ISBN 1-932716-06-8   LC 2005-10911
First published 2000 under the authorship of William Driscoll
This book discusses how to prepare, structure, and carry out a debate. Includes chapters on judging and the appendix presents 50 debate exercises.

Merali, Alim, 1984-
Talk the talk; speech and debate made easy. Gravitas Pub. 2006 269p $25.95
Grades: 7 8 9 10 11 12   **808.53**
1. Debates and debating 2. Public speaking
ISBN 0-9738682-0-1
"This outstanding guide to all aspects of debate is a practical and easy-to-read source for students. Beginning with helpful physical preparations and mental exercises, the book goes on to discuss kinds of speeches, ingredients of style, steps to winning an argument, and special types of speech, such as cross-examination and parliamentary exchanges." Voice Youth Advocates
Includes glossary and bibliographical references

Miller, Joe, 1968-
Cross-X; a turbulent, triumphant season with an inner-city debate squad. Farrar, Straus & Giroux 2006 480p $26
Grades: 11 12 Adult   **808.53**
1. Debates and debating
ISBN 978-0-374-13194-4; 0-374-13194-5
LC 2005-29829
This "book considers in depth the lives and competitions of Kansas City Central High's debate team." Libr J
"The reporting is both lively and engrossing, and even at nearly 500 pages, the book encourages most readers to learn more about these remarkable teens." Publ Wkly

808.8 Literature--Collections

The **Green** Man: tales from the mythic forest; edited by Ellen Datlow & Terri Windling; introduction by Terri Windling; decorations by Charles Vess. Viking 2002 384p $18.99; pa $8.99
Grades: 7 8 9 10   **808.8**
1. Literature—Collections 2. Fantasy fiction
ISBN 0-670-03526-2; 0-14-240029-7 (pa)
LC 2001-46976
"The stories are thematically connected yet tonally varied, and each strongly plotted tale conjures a credible fantasy world. A brief biography of and remarks by the writer are included with each story. . . . This title will be eagerly devoured." Bull Cent Child Books

Growing up gay; an anthology for young people; edited by Bennett L. Singer. New Press (NY) 1993 317p pa $14.95 hardcover o.p.
Grades: 11 12 Adult   **808.8**
1. Literature—Collections 2. Homosexuality
ISBN 1-56584-103-4
Paperback edition has title: Growing up gay/growing up lesbian
"Culled from the writings of 56 authors, this book offers a message to gay and lesbian youth that they are not alone. The material here ranges from fiction by James Baldwin, Rita Mae Brown, and David Leavitt to autobiographical essays by Audre Lord, Quentin Crisp, and Martina Navratilova. The book is arranged into categories that encompass self-discovery, relationships, family, and 'facing the world.' . . . Essential for all high school/college libraries and highly recommended for all public libraries." Libr J

Journalistas; 100 years of the best writing and reporting by women journalists; edited by Eleanor Mills with Kira Cochrane. Carroll & Graf 2005 xx, 364p pa $14.95
Grades: 11 12 Adult   **808.8**
1. Women journalists 2. Literature—Collections
ISBN 0-7867-1667-3
Published in the United Kingdom with title: Cupcakes and kalashnikovs
This anthology contains work by such authors as "Martha Gellhorn, Rebecca West, Susan Sontag and Mary McCarthy. . . . The book is divided into subject

Journalistas—*Continued*
areas." N Y Times Book Rev

"From Djuna Barnes' 1914 account of being force-fed to end her hunger strike, to Eleanor Roosevelt's 1938 'My Day' column, to Rose George's 2004 article about gang rapes in France, this collection provides a broad and deep look at reporting by women in the past century." Booklist

Leaving home: stories; selected by Hazel Rochman and Darlene Z. McCampbell. HarperCollins Pubs. 1997 231p pa $11.99 hardcover o.p.
Grades: 6 7 8 9   **808.8**
1. Youth—Fiction 2. Short stories
ISBN 0-06-440706-3   LC 96-28979
An international anthology that reflects the thoughts and feelings of young people as they make their way into the world. Authors represented include Amy Tan, Sandra Cisneros, Tim Wynne-Jones, and Toni Morrison

"The editors have varied the tones, the music, the voices, and the meanings of the pieces, which provide both humorous and heartbreaking stories of the meaning of adolescence." ALAN

Night is gone, day is still coming; stories and poems by American Indian teens and young adults; edited by Annette Pina Ochoa, Betsy Franco, and Traci L. Gourdine; with an introduction by Simon J. Ortiz. Candlewick Press 2003 145p $16.99 *
Grades: 7 8 9 10   **808.8**
ISBN 0-7636-1518-8   LC 2002-74086
"In poems and short stories, young Indian writers, ages 11 to 22, tell about their lives on the reservations, in small towns, and in large cities." Booklist

"These are honest voices in a well-organized anthology that gives an excellent look into an important American culture." SLJ

Nothing makes you free; writings by descendants of Jewish Holocaust survivors; edited by Melvin Jules Bukiet. Norton 2002 394p $27.95; pa $15.95
Grades: 11 12 Adult   **808.8**
1. Holocaust survivors 2. Holocaust, 1933-1945, in literature 3. Literature—Collections
ISBN 0-393-05046-7; 0-393-32425-7 (pa)
                                      LC 2001-55863
"Excerpts from the works of 30 writers whose parents survived the Holocaust make up this anthology of fiction and memoirs. . . . In these remarkable pieces issues such as guilt, anger, faith, and accountability are explored. They capture not only the experience of the concentration camps but also its powerful legacy, passed down to a new generation through the bond of love that ties parent and child." Booklist

Read all about it! great read-aloud stories, poems, and newspaper pieces for preteens and teens; edited by Jim Trelease. Penguin Bks. 1993 489p il pa $13.95
Grades: 9 10 11 12   **808.8**
1. Young adult literature 2. Literature—Collections 3. Authors
ISBN 0-14-014655-5   LC 93-21781

This is a collection of 52 selections of fiction, poetry, and nonfiction from newspapers, magazines, and books by such authors as Cynthia Rylant, Jerry Spinelli, Howard Pyle, Rudyard Kipling, Robert W. Service, Maya Angelou, Moss Hart, Pete Hamill, and Leon Garfield. Includes biographical information about the authors

808.81   Poetry--Collections

Ain't I a woman! classic poetry by women from around the world; edited by Illona Linthwaite. Contemporary Books 2000 xxiii, 264p pa $14.95 *
Grades: 11 12 Adult   **808.81**
1. Poetry—Women authors—Collections
ISBN 0-8092-2534-4   LC 99-43286
First published 1988 by Bedrick Bks.

"The poems range from ancient Greek lyrics to contemporary Jamaican 'Dub,' with emphasis on Commonwealth writers. . . . The editor's arrangement of the poems to tell the story of a woman's life from childhood through death provides a compelling framework." Booklist

Americans' favorite poems; the Favorite Poem Project anthology; edited by Robert Pinsky and Maggie Dietz. Norton 1999 327p $27.50 *
Grades: 11 12 Adult   **808.81**
1. Poetry—Collections
ISBN 0-393-04820-9   LC 99-31979
"People across America, including many teens, share the poetry they love, and talk about what it means in their lives. Their choices—from John Keats to Lucille Clifton—defy stereotypes, and their comments are heartfelt." Booklist

Animal poems; selected and edited by John Hollander. Knopf 1994 256p (Everyman's library pocket poets) $12.50
Grades: 9 10 11 12   **808.81**
1. Animals—Poetry 2. Poetry—Collections
ISBN 0-679-43631-6
This anthology focuses on the poetic treatment of animals from various traditions

The **Body** eclectic; an anthology of poems; edited by Patrice Vecchione. Holt & Co. 2002 192p $16.95
Grades: 7 8 9 10   **808.81**
1. Poetry—Collections
ISBN 0-8050-6935-6   LC 2001-51900
This collection of poetry focuses on the human body and its parts, including works by poets such as Gary Soto, Shel Silverstein, Paul Laurence Dunbar, Pablo Neruda, Walt Whitman and Shakespeare

"Excellent notes at the back introduce each writer and suggest more books to read. A great collection to show teens that literature is about their intimate selves and their connections with people everywhere." Booklist

Includes bibliographical references

A **Book** of love poetry; edited and with an introduction by Jon Stallworthy. Oxford Univ. Press 1974 c1973 393p pa $18.95 hardcover o.p.
Grades: 11 12 Adult   **808.81**

A Book of love poetry—*Continued*
1. Love poetry
ISBN 0-19-504232-8
First published 1973 in the United Kingdom with title:
The Penguin book of love poetry
A collection of poems written during the past 2000
years arranged thematically from young love to the "long
look back" of the aged
Includes indexes of poets, translators, titles and first
lines

**A Book of lumininous things; an international
anthology of poetry; edited and with an
introduction by Czeslaw Milosz. Harcourt Brace
& Co. 1996 xx, 320p pa $15 hardcover o.p.**
Grades: 11 12 Adult   **808.81**
1. Poetry—Collections
ISBN 0-15-600574-3   LC 95-38060
"Nobel laureate Milosz states in his introduction that
the purpose of this personal and eclectic collection is to
present poetry that is 'short, clear, readable, and . . . realistic, that is, loyal toward reality and attempting to describe it as concisely as possible.' . . . Most of the selections are from classical Chinese and 20th-century
American and European (primarily Eastern European,
Scandinavian, and French) poets." Libr J

**A Book of women poets from antiquity to now;
edited by Aliki Barnstone & Willis Barnstone.
rev ed. Schocken Bks. 1992 xxiv, 822p pa $22
***
Grades: 9 10 11 12   **808.81**
ISBN 0-8052-0997-2   LC 91-52701
First published 1980
An anthology of representative work by women poets
of various literary traditions

**City lights pocket poets anthology; edited by
Lawrence Ferlinghetti. City Lights Bks. 1995
259p $18.95**
Grades: 11 12 Adult   **808.81**
1. Poetry—Collections
ISBN 0-87286-311-5   LC 95-31608
"Drawing from the 52 volumes published in the Pocket Poets series since 1956, this selection provides a
handy sampler of many of the prominent avant-garde and
leftist poets of the post-WW II era. . . . The series' extensive international scope is highlighted in poems culled
from German, Russian, Italian, Dutch, Nicaraguan and
Spanish poets." Publ Wkly

**Faith & doubt; an anthology of poems; edited by
Patrice Vecchione. Henry Holt and Co. 2006
138p $16.95**
Grades: 9 10 11 12   **808.81**
1. Poetry—Collections
ISBN 978-0-8050-8213-5; 0-8050-8213-1
                                            LC 2006-18228
A collection of poems from around the world that ex-
plores the many facets of faith and doubt.
"This book will be read, considered, and discussed.
Some who have been lost will find themselves; others
will realize that there is direction even on the misguided
path. Lucky are those who stumble upon this unassuming
but powerful read." Voice Youth Advocates
Includes bibliographical references

**Holocaust poetry; compiled and introduced by
Hilda Schiff. St. Martin's Press 1995 xxiv, 234p
$22; pa $14.95 ***
Grades: 11 12 Adult   **808.81**
1. Poetry—Collections
ISBN 0-312-13086-4; 0-312-14357-5 (pa)
                                            LC 95-2708
"In English and in translation from many languages,
more than 80 poets—including Wiesel, Fink, Brecht,
Yevtushenko, Auden, and Sachs—give voice to what
seems unspeakable. Schiff points out that compelling historical accounts document the facts and numbers, but a
poem, like a story, makes us imagine how it felt for one
person. These poems are stark and deceptively simple."
Booklist
Includes bibliographical references

**I feel a little jumpy around you; a book of her
poems & his poems collected in pairs; {by}
Naomi Shihab Nye and Paul B. Janeczko.
Simon & Schuster Bks. for Young Readers 1996
256p pa $10 hardcover o.p. ***
Grades: 7 8 9 10   **808.81**
1. Poetry—Collections
ISBN 0-689-81341-4   LC 95-44904
A collection of poems, by male and female authors,
presented in pairings that offer insight into how men and
women look at the world, both separately and together
"Though the gender counterpoint really plays little
part in the juxtaposition, the pairings are piquant and
provide a manageable way to start talking about a very
large collection of poetry. An engaging marginal dialogue, taken from Nye's and Janeczko's collaborative fax
correspondence, appears alongside the appendix and permits a revealing peek behind the scences. Highly readable notes from contributors are included, as is an index
of poems and a gender-segregated index of poets." Bull
Cent Child Books

**I just hope it's lethal; poems of sadness, madness,
and joy; collected by Liz Rosenberg and Deena
November. Houghton Mifflin 2005 190p pa
$7.99**
Grades: 9 10 11 12   **808.81**
1. Poetry—Collections
ISBN 0-618-56452-7   LC 2005-4257
The editors "have brought together poems that, as Ro-
senberg writes, address 'various aspects of sanity and
madness.' . . . There are works by famous writers, such
as Shakespeare, Sylvia Plath, Emily Dickinson, and
Rumi, as well as contemporary poets, such as Naomi
Shihab Nye." SLJ
"This interesting and rich collection of poetry will
have special significance for teen readers." Voice Youth
Advocates

**Light-gathering poems; edited by Liz Rosenberg.
Holt & Co. 2000 146p $15.95**
Grades: 7 8 9 10   **808.81**
1. Poetry—Collections
ISBN 0-8050-6223-8   LC 99-49231
Companion volume to Earth-shattering poems (1997)
"Poems were chosen for their ability to 'gather light,'
some representing beauty, some joy, some fascinating

Light-gathering poems—*Continued*
imagery, and some the illusive light at the end of a dark tunnel. . . . Notable writers such as Robert Frost, Walt Whitman, Langston Hughes, Edna St. Vincent Millay, Emily Dickinson, and Allen Ginsberg share the spotlight with contemporaries such as Gary Soto, Kate Schmitt, Mary Oliver, Steven Dauer, and Henry M. Seiden." Voice Youth Advocates

Includes bibliographical references

Love poems. Knopf 1993 256p (Everyman's library pocket poets) $12.50
Grades: 11 12 Adult   **808.81**
1. Love poetry 2. Poetry—Collections
ISBN 0-679-42906-9   LC 93-11427
Among the poets included are Robert Graves, W. B. Yeats, Pablo Neruda, Boris Pasternak, William Carlos Williams, Anna Akhmatova, Robert Browning and Christina Rossetti. An index of first lines is appended

Music of a distant drum; classical Arabic, Persian, Turkish, and Hebrew poems; translated and introduced by Bernard Lewis. Princeton Univ. Press 2001 222p il $22.95
Grades: 11 12 Adult   **808.81**
1. Arabic poetry—Collections 2. Hebrew poetry—Collections 3. Persian poetry—Collections 4. Turkish poetry—Collections
ISBN 0-691-08928-0   LC 2001-19858
"Lewis, one of the foremost scholars of the Middle East, has devoted much of his career to the history of Islam; this volume collects his translations of poems—nearly all appearing in English for the first time—that span eleven centuries and four major Middle Eastern traditions. Many of the most striking works address, in spare, stirring lines, the twin demands of serving the self and serving God." New Yorker

Includes bibliographical references

The **Oxford** book of war poetry; chosen and edited by John Stallworthy. Oxford Univ. Press 1984 xxxi, 358p $31.95; pa $16.95
Grades: 11 12 Adult   **808.81**
1. War poetry 2. Poetry—Collections
ISBN 0-19-214125-2; 0-19-280454-5 (pa)
    LC 83-19303
"This comprehensive anthology focuses on poetic treatment of warfare ranging from the battlefields of ancient history to the conflicts in Vietnam, Northern Ireland, and El Salvador." Univ Press Books for Second Sch Libr

This collection "reminds one of the large numbers and great variety of war poems from many centuries that are very good poems. Mr. Stallworthy's selections include most of the best, at least the best in English." N Y Times Book Rev

Includes bibliographical references

Poems to read; a new favorite poem project anthology; edited by Robert Pinsky and Maggie Dietz. Norton 2002 xxv, 352p $27.95 *
Grades: 11 12 Adult   **808.81**
1. Poetry—Collections
ISBN 0-393-01074-0   LC 2002-321

This anthology "features works by a wide selection of well-known, mostly American and European writers from throughout the ages: Henry King, Rabindranath Tagore, Gwendolyn Brooks, J.W. von Goethe, Issa, Jorie Graham, Robert Herrick, Dionisio Martinez and Frank O'Hara are just a few of them." Publ Wkly
"A graceful, sometimes jubilant, sometimes lyrical, sometimes brooding, but always welcoming and stirring collection." Booklist

Includes bibliographical references

Poetry in motion; 100 poems from the subways and buses; edited by Molly Peacock, Elise Paschen, Neil Neches. Norton 1996 157p pa $13.95 hardcover o.p.
Grades: 11 12 Adult   **808.81**
1. Poetry—Collections
ISBN 0-393-31458-8   LC 95-47922
This anthology contains the first hundred poems displayed on placards in the subways and buses of New York City as part of a program to promote poetry to the general public. Poems included range from Sappho and Sophocles to Sylvia Plath and Robert Creeley

Includes bibliographical references

The **Poetry** of our world; an international anthology of contemporary poetry; edited by Jeffrey Paine. HarperCollins Pubs. 2000 xxviii, 511p hardcover o.p. pa $18.95 *
Grades: 11 12 Adult   **808.81**
1. Poetry—Collections
ISBN 0-06-055369-3; 0-06-095193-1 (pa)
    LC 99-34921
In this global anthology "each section is preceded by a thoughtful introduction of several pages by the selector in that area. . . . A stunning and highly readable anthology." Libr J

Poetry speaks; hear great poets read their work from Tennyson to Plath; editors, Elise Paschen and Rebekah Presson Mosby; narrator, Charles Osgood. Sourcebooks 2001 336p il $49.95 *
Grades: 11 12 Adult   **808.81**
1. American poetry—Collections 2. English poetry—Collections
ISBN 1-57071-720-6   LC 2001-31317
This anthology "comes with three CD's. . . . Each audio selection is prefaced by . . . {an} introduction by Charles Osgood, and the book has an essay on each poet written by a contemporary poet." N Y Times Book Rev
"A cornucopia of pleasurable reading and listening. . . . A must for poetry lovers." SLJ

Revenge and forgiveness; an anthology of poems; edited by Patrice Vecchione. Henry Holt 2004 148p $16.95
Grades: 7 8 9 10   **808.81**
1. Poetry—Collections
ISBN 0-8050-7376-0   LC 2003-56631
A collection of nearly sixty poems dealing with revenge and forgiveness, plus suggested readings about each contributing poet
"For students who are of a philosophical bent and for teachers of poetry, this book of poems about love, hate, and war will be a useful resource." Libr Media Connect

Includes bibliographical references

Risking everything; 110 poems of love and revelation; edited by Roger Housden. Harmony Bks. 2003 173p $20

Grades: 11 12 Adult   **808.81**

1. Poetry—Collections

ISBN 1-400-04799-4   LC 2002-14410

The editor "has placed strong emphasis on contemporary voices such as the American poet laureate Billy Collins and the Nobel Prize–winners Czeslaw Milosz and Seamus Heaney, but the collection also includes some . . . echoes of the past in the form of work by masters such as Goethe, Wordsworth, and Emily Dickinson." Publisher's note

This is "an inspirational anthology sans inspirational chestnuts." Booklist

The **Space** between our footsteps; poems and paintings from the Middle East; selected by Naomi Shihab Nye. Simon & Schuster Bks. for Young Readers 1998 144p il maps $19.95 *

Grades: 7 8 9 10   **808.81**

1. Poetry—Collections 2. Middle East—Poetry

ISBN 0-689-81233-7   LC 97-18622

"Lyrical verse about family, friendship, nature, and daily life makes up this collection of poems from 19 countries in the Middle East, with gloriously colored paintings in a wide range of styles." Booklist

This same sky; a collection of poems from around the world; selected by Naomi Shihab Nye. Four Winds Press 1992 212p il hardcover o.p. pa $9.99 *

Grades: 9 10 11 12   **808.81**

1. Poetry—Collections

ISBN 0-02-768440-7; 0-689-80630-2 (pa)

     LC 92-11617

A poetry anthology in which 129 poets from sixty-eight different countries celebrate the natural world and its human and animal inhabitants

"Notes on the contributors, a map, suggestions for further reading, an index to countries, and an index to poets are appended, adding additional luster to a book which should prove invaluable for intercultural education as well as for pure pleasure." Horn Book

Voices: poetry and art from around the world; selected by Barbara Brenner. National Geographic Soc. 2000 96p il $18.95 *

Grades: 5 6 7 8 9 10   **808.81**

1. Poetry—Collections

ISBN 0-7922-7071-1   LC 00-20232

In this anthology "the arrangement is by continent. The large-size pages include poetry, much of it in translation, and beautifully reproduced full-color art from each region. . . . Many of the selections are compelling, beautiful in their particulars and universal in their reach. . . . With each selection there are brief facts about the artist, poet, or translator, as well as the culture and history of the place. The open design will attract browsers, and the geographical focus will make this an excellent tool for teachers across the curriculum." Booklist

War and the pity of war; edited by Neil Philip; illustrated by Michael McCurdy. Clarion Bks. 1998 96p il $20 *

Grades: 5 6 7 8 9 10   **808.81**

1. War poetry 2. Poetry—Collections

ISBN 0-395-84982-9   LC 97-32897

"The selections, covering conflicts from ancient Persia to modern-day Bosnia, are by a wide variety of poets, from the well known (Tennyson, Whitman, Sandburg, Auden), to the obscure (Anakreon from ancient Greece and 11th-century Chinese poet Bunno). . . . The stark and simple scratchboard drawings are reminiscent of the Ernie Pyle illustrations from World War II and are as memorable as the best propaganda." SLJ

World poetry; an anthology of verse from antiquity to our time; Katharine Washburn and John S. Major, editors; Clifton Fadiman, general editor. Norton 1998 xxii, 1338p $45 *

Grades: 11 12 Adult   **808.81**

1. Poetry—Collections

ISBN 0-393-04130-1   LC 97-10879

This volume presents poetry "arranged chronologically in eight sections, from the Bronze and Iron Ages to the 20th century, with each time period subdivided by region and language." Christ Sci Monit

The anthology's "stated aim—'to surprise and delight the common reader'—may seem rather quaint; yet it is a worthy one, and is, on the whole, impressively fulfilled." Times Lit Suppl

Includes bibliographical references

808.82   Drama--Collections

24 favorite one-act plays; edited by Bennett Cerf and Van H. Cartmell. Doubleday 1958 455p pa $14.95 *

Grades: 11 12 Adult   **808.82**

1. Drama—Collections 2. One act plays

ISBN 0-385-06617-1

A wide assortment of one-act plays includes comedies, tragedies, new and old, Irish, American, Russian, English, and Austrian. Includes the work of such playwrights as Eugene O'Neill, Noel Coward, George S. Kaufman, William Inge, and Dorothy Parker

"A good collection showing the variety of form and subject used by modern masters of the short play." Good Read

100 great monologues from the neo-classical theatre; edited by Jocelyn A. Beard. Smith & Kraus 1994 157p (Monologue audition series) pa $9.95

Grades: 9 10 11 12   **808.82**

1. Monologues 2. Acting

ISBN 1-88039-960-1   LC 94-33114

"Among the neoclassical soliloquies chosen for inclusion are excerpts from the works of Congreve, Dryden, and Comielle. Molière is perhaps the most prominently featured of all the assembled playwrights. Dramatic plays such as Racine's *Phedre* are drawn upon to provide some very potent material, while more comic passages are contained in Sheridan's splendid *The Rivals*." Booklist

The **Actor's** book of scenes from new plays; edited by Eric Lane and Nina Shengold. Penguin Bks. 1988 424p pa $14

Grades: 9 10 11 12   **808.82**
1. Drama—Collections 2. Acting
ISBN 0-14-010487-9   LC 87-33389
"A Smith and Kraus Inc. book"

A collection of two-character scenes by contemporary dramatists for classroom and audition use

The **Best** men's stage monologues of 2006; edited by Jocelyn A. Beard. Smith & Kraus 2007 pa $11.95 *

Grades: 11 12 Adult   **808.82**
1. Monologues 2. Acting
ISSN 1067-134X
ISBN 1-57525-554-5; 978-1-57525-554-5
Annual. First published 1991 for the 1990 theater season

This title and The Best women's stage monologues provide monologues "from contemporary dramatic luminaries, including Charles L. Mee and Daisy Foote. Both volumes offer scenic descriptions and brief leads into the speechs and indicate the tone (dramatic, comic, or seriocomic). In the volume for women, there are no strictly comedic pieces." Libr J [review of 2000 edition]

The **Best** women's stage monologues of 2006; edited by Jocelyn A. Beard. Smith & Kraus 2006 pa $11.95 *

Grades: 11 12 Adult   **808.82**
1. Monologues 2. Acting
ISSN 1067-134X
ISBN 1-575-25555-3; 978-1-575-25555-2
Annual. First published 1991 for the 1990 theater season

This title and The Best men's stage monologues, provide monologues "from contemporary dramatic luminaries, including Charles L. Mee and Daisy Foote. Both volumes offer scenic descriptions and brief leads into the speechs and indicate the tone (dramatic, comic, or seriocomic). In the volume for women, there are no strictly comedic pieces." Libr J [review of 2000 edition]

The **Book** of monologues for aspiring actors; {edited by} Marsh Cassady. NTC Pub. Group 1995 212p il pa $23.96 *

Grades: 7 8 9 10   **808.82**
1. Monologues 2. Acting
ISBN 0-8442-5771-0   LC 94-66239
"The selections range from the classical Greeks to Sam Shepard and Oscar Wilde; they give YA's the opportunity to develop characters of like ages in many different settings. Several questions to probe the actors' imaginations appear at the end of each monologue." SLJ

Caruso, Sandra
The young actor's book of improvisation; dramatic situations from Shakespeare to Spielberg: ages 12-16; {by} Sandra Caruso with Susan Kosoff. Heinemann (Portsmouth) 1998 xx, 259p $22.95 *

Grades: 9 10 11 12   **808.82**
1. Acting
ISBN 0-325-00049-2   LC 97-46817
A sourcebook of techniques designed to develop improvisional skills in young actors

Scenes "are divided thematically—confrontation, fantasy, solo moment, relationships, etc.—and according to the number and gender of the actors. Each brief entry includes the source, characters, place, and time period if relevant, an explanation of the situation, and comments, including tips, notes, and supplemental information to 'enhance the actors' understanding of story and character.'" Booklist
Includes bibliographical references

Cassady, Marsh, 1936-
The book of scenes for aspiring actors. NTC Pub. Group 1995 202p il pa $16.95

Grades: 9 10 11 12   **808.82**
1. Acting 2. Drama—Collections
ISBN 0-8442-5769-9   LC 94-66240
"A collection of scripts for characters between the ages of 12-21. An introductory chapter analyzes the scene and the characters and gives information for both directors and actors on diagraming the set and blocking the action. . . . The selections come from Shakespeare, Jean Anouilh, and Maxwell Anderson and range in diversity from William Gillette's *Secret Service* to Brandon Thomas's *Charley's Aunt* and Arthur Laurents's *West Side Story*." Libr J

International plays for young audiences; contemporary works from leading playwrights; edited by Roger Ellis. Meriwether 2000 419p pa $16.95 *

Grades: 9 10 11 12   **808.82**
1. Drama—Collections
ISBN 1-56608-065-7   LC 00-55921
"The 12 short plays feature young characters in a variety of settings and situations. While some of the selections are straightforward in style (such as Gustavo Ott's *Minor Leagues)*, others require a creative stretch in order to be able to read and produce them (such as Neil Duffield's racial fable *Skin and Bones*). . . . All, however, have characters that would be intriguing to young people and all deal with themes of cultural conflict and understanding." SLJ
Includes bibliographical references

Multicultural scenes for young actors; Craig Slaight and Jack Sharrar, editors. Smith & Kraus 1995 237p (Young actor series) pa $11.95 *

Grades: 9 10 11 12   **808.82**
1. Drama—Collections 2. Acting
ISBN 1-880399-48-2   LC 94-44187

Multicultural scenes for young actors—*Continued*

This collection "is organized according to cast requirements, and each of the cuttings from over 40 plays is preceded by source notes and a brief plot summary. Information regarding performance rights is appended. Although a few of the plays have been included in standard compilations, the multicultural theme makes this collection unique." SLJ

Play index. Wilson, H.W. 1953-2003 10v v10 $255 *

    Grades: 11 12 Adult   **808.82**

    1. Drama—Indexes

    ISSN 0554-3037

    ISBN 999083-4164 (v10); 978-999083-4161 (v10)

    Also available on-line version

First published 1953 covering the years 1949-1952, and edited by Dorothy Herbert West and Dorothy Margaret Peake $80. Additional volumes: 1953-1960 $80 edited by Estelle A. Fidell and Dorothy Margaret Peake; 1961-1967 $70 edited by Estelle A. Fidell; 1968-1972 $80 edited by Estelle A. Fidell; 1973-1977 $80 edited by Estelle A. Fidell; 1978-1982 $80 edited by Juliette Yaakov; 1983-1987 $240 edited by Juliette Yaakov and John Greenfieldt; 1988-1992 $240 edited by Juliette Yaakov and John Greenfieldt; 1993-1997 edited by Juliette Yaakov and John Greenfieldt $240; 1998-2002 edited by John Greenfieldt $240

Play index indexes plays in collections and single plays; one-act and full-length plays; radio, television, and Broadway plays; plays for amateur production; plays for children, young adults, and adults. It is divided into four parts. Part I is an author, title, and subject index; the author or main entry includes the title of the play, brief synopsis of the plot, number of acts and scenes, size of cast, number of sets, and bibliographic information. Part II is a list of collections indexed, and Part III, a cast analysis, lists plays by the type of cast and number of players required.

"This index is an excellent source for locating published plays." Safford. Guide to Ref Materials for Sch Media Cent. 5th edition

The Scenebook for actors; great monologs & dialogs from contemporary & classical theatre; edited by Norman A. Bert. Meriwether 1990 246p pa $15.95

    Grades: 9 10 11 12   **808.82**

    1. Drama—Collections 2. Acting

    ISBN 0-916260-65-8   LC 90-52983

A collection of scenes, monologues and dialogues from scripts produced after 1975. Selections are for characters aged 18 to 30 and several are written for Afro-American and Hispanic actors

    Includes bibliographical references

Scenes from classic plays, 468 B.C. to 1970 A.D.; Jocelyn A. Beard, editor. Smith & Kraus 1993 310p pa $11.95 *

    Grades: 9 10 11 12   **808.82**

    1. Drama—Collections 2. Acting

    ISBN 1-880399-36-9   LC 93-33010

"Arranged chronologically, the selected scenes average three pages in length and involve two to three characters.

A one-line description of the setting and of each character is given, as well as a one- to two-sentence synopsis of what is occurring at the opening of the scene. This book must be commended for such a well-balanced representation of time-honored classics." Booklist

Stevens, Chambers, 1968-

Sensational scenes for teens; the scene studyguide for teen actors. Sandcastle Pub. 2001 104p il (Hollywood 101) $14.95

    Grades: 9 10 11 12   **808.82**

    1. Drama—Collections 2. Acting

    ISBN 1-883995-10-8   LC 99-76948

"Stevens presents more than 30 short comedy and drama scenes, all written for two actors with an even mix of boy-boy, girl-girl, and boy-girl casts. The contemporary urban and suburban settings coupled with culturally neutral names allow for racial and ethnic diversity." SLJ

    Includes bibliographical references

The Ultimate audition book; 222 monologues, 2 minutes & under; edited by Jocelyn A. Beard. Smith & Kraus 1997-2002 2v + v4 (Monologue audition series) ea pa $19.95 *

    Grades: 11 12 Adult   **808.82**

    1. Monologues 2. Acting

    ISBN 1-57525-066-7 (v1); 1-57525-270-8 (v2); 1-57525-420-4 (v4)   LC 97-10471

Volume 2 edited by John Capecci, Laurie Walker, and Irene Ziegler; Variant title: 222 monologues, 2 minutes & under from literature. Volume 4 edited by Irene Ziegleraston and John Capecci; variant title for v4: 222 comedy monologues, 2 minutes & under

This collection draws "upon lesser-known works from significant writers and those of contemporary favorites and reflects a wide range of tone, age, time period, and voice. Divided among female, male, and unisex categories, all meet the obligatory two minutes or less time limit imposed by most directors and auditions." Libr J [review of volume 2]

    Includes bibliographical references

808.85   Speeches--Collections

Lend me your ears; great speeches in history; selected and introduced by William Safire. rev and expanded ed. Norton 1997 1,055p $39.95 *

    Grades: 11 12 Adult   **808.85**

    1. Speeches

    ISBN 0-393-05931-6   LC 96-43423

    First published 1992

Pope Urban II, Bob Dole, Cicero, Jesus, Boris Yeltsin, Richard Nixon and Colin Powell are among the orators represented in this anthology of over 200 speeches grouped chronologically into thematic categories

The Penguin book of twentieth-century speeches; edited by Brian MacArthur. 2nd rev ed. Penguin Books 1999 xxix, 525p pa $15.95 *

    Grades: 9 10 11 12   **808.85**

    1. Speeches

    ISBN 0-14-028500-8   LC 00-267955

    First published 1992 in the United Kingdom

The Penguin book of twentieth-century speeches—*Continued*

"Nelson Mandela, Winston Churchill, Emmeline Pankhurst, Martin Luther King, Jr., and Adolf Hitler are among the more than 140 famous speakers whose words are collected in this anthology that teens will use for reference and for browsing." Booklist [review of 1992 edition]

808.88 Collections of miscellaneous writings

African American quotations; [compiled by] Richard Newman; foreword by Julian Bond. Checkmark Books 2000 504p pa $18 *

Grades: 11 12 Adult   **808.88**
1. African Americans—Quotations
ISBN 0-8160-4439-2
First published 1998 by Oryx Press

"This collection of more than 2500 memorable quotations from African Americans covers a wide range of historical, contemporary, mainstream, and controversial figures from the 18th century to the present. Activists, actors, artists, athletes, clergy, educators, and writers are well represented." Libr J

American Indian quotations; compiled and edited by Howard J. Langer. Greenwood Press 1996 260p il $65.95 *

Grades: 11 12 Adult   **808.88**
ISBN 0-313-29121-7   LC 95-33151

"This volume offers 800 quotations covering more than four centuries of American life. Arranged chronologically, the quotations include the words of warriors, poets, politicians, doctors, lawyers, athletes, and others. . . . The book provides brief biographical information about those quoted, including both historical and contemporary figures, and cross-references the material through subject, author, and tribal indexes." Publisher's note

Andrews, Robert, 1957-
The Columbia dictionary of quotations. Columbia Univ. Press 1993 1092p $50.95

Grades: 11 12 Adult   **808.88**
1. Quotations
ISBN 0-231-07194-9   LC 93-27305

This work "offers 18,000 quotes arranged alphabetically by speaker under 1500 well-selected topics. Brief citations to original sources are noted, and *See references* guide one to related quotes under other topics. For those who feel most comfortable quoting contemporaries, this sourcebook supplies an ample serving. . . . This should prove a popular general quotation sourcebook for academic, public, and school libraries." Libr J

Famous lines; a Columbia dictionary of familiar quotations. Columbia Univ. Press 1997 xxiii, 625p $38.95

Grades: 11 12 Adult   **808.88**
1. Quotations
ISBN 0-231-10218-6   LC 96-43879

This work "contains more than 6,000 witticisms, enduring observations, and incendiary statements from all kinds of people from antiquity to yesterday. Besides identifying the source, Andrews . . . provides details of the first publication, specific chapter and scene, and even the character speaking. Besides quotes from Shakespeare and Oscar Wilde, readers will find fascinating quotes from Monty Python, Gloria Steinem, and maybe your favorite author, for example, Agatha Christie. The more than 500 subject headings include homelessness, AIDS, sexual harassment, murder, and war." Booklist
Includes bibliographical references

Bartlett, John, 1820-1905
Bartlett's familiar quotations; a collection of passages, phrases, and proverbs traced to their sources in ancient and modern literature. Little, Brown 2002 1431p $50 *

Grades: 11 12 Adult   **808.88**
1. Quotations
ISBN 0-316-08460-3   LC 2003-269668
First published 1855. Periodically revised. Editors vary

"Arranged chronologically by author, with exact references. Includes many interesting footnotes, tracing history or usage of analogous thoughts, the circumstances under which a particular remark was made, etc. Author and keyword indexes. One of the best books of quotations with a long history." Guide to Ref Books. 11th edition
Includes bibliographical references

Cassell's humorous quotations; [compiled by] Nigel Rees. Cassell 2001 543p hardcover o.p. pa $12.95 *

Grades: 11 12 Adult   **808.88**
1. Quotations 2. Wit and humor
ISBN 0-304-35720-0; 0-304-36588-2 (pa)
     LC 2002-392062
First published 1998 with title: Cassell dictionary of humorous quotations

Contains "more than 5,000 entries arranged under 1,200 themes ranging from 'Advertising' and 'Advice' to 'Comedy, Nonsense' and 'Writers and Writing.' Many of the quotations are annotated, and most provide references to books, interviews, plays, and more in addition to the speaker's name, years of birth and death, and brief identifying phrase." Booklist

"A comprehensive index makes it easy for researchers to locate 'half-remembered lines.' A welcome addition to literature and ready-reference collections." Choice

Chambers dictionary of quotations; editor, Alison Jones; with the assistance of Stephanie Pickering [and] Megan Thomson. Chambers; distributed by Larousse Kingfisher Chambers 1997 1515p $39.95

Grades: 11 12 Adult   **808.88**
1. Quotations
ISBN 0-550-21019-9

"There are more than 20,000 quotations from more than 4,000 sources. Quotations are arranged alphabetically by author, from *Abbott, Diane Julie*, the first black woman member of Parliament; to *Zwerlin, Mike*, U.S. writer and jazz musician. Just these two examples are an indication of the diversity the editors have sought in the people who are represented by quotes." Booklist

Collins quotation finder. rev ed. HarperCollins
Pubs. 1999 829p hardcover o.p. pa $16.95
Grades: 11 12 Adult   **808.88**
1. Quotations
ISBN 0-00-472384-8; 0-00-712184-9 (pa)
This "compilation contains quotes by a wide variety of
persons, from standards like Virgil and Churchill to
newer expressions from Woody Allen and Camille
Paglia. Arrangement is alphabetical by broad subjects,
. . . subarranged by names of authors or speakers and
citing titles of works. Context is provided where
neccessary." Choice

The **Columbia** Granger's dictionary of poetry
quotations; edited by Edith P. Hazen. Columbia
Univ. Press 1992 1132p $131
Grades: 11 12 Adult   **808.88**
1. Quotations
ISBN 0-231-07546-4   LC 91-42240
This work contains the "most memorable lines written
by the greatest poets of English. Quotations are organized alphabetically by poet, and coded so one can find
full text in hundreds of current anthologies. With
keyword and subject indexing." Univ Press Books for
Public and Second Sch Libr

Concise Oxford dictionary of quotations; edited by
Susan Ratcliffe. 5th ed. Oxford University Press
2006 580p (Oxford paperback reference) pa
$17.95 *
Grades: 11 12 Adult   **808.88**
1. Quotations
ISBN 0-19-861417-9; 978-0-19-861417-3
                                       LC 2006-48714
First published 1964
Collected here are quotations by over 2,000 authors
from around the world ranging in time from the 8th century BC to the present. Arrangement is alphabetical by
the names of authors with sections such as Anonymous,
Ballads, The Bible, the Mass in Latin, etc. included in
the alphabetical order. Foreign quotations are given in
the original language followed by the English translation.
Indexed by key words.

Contemporary quotations in black; compiled and
edited by Anita King. Greenwood Press 1997
298p il $45
Grades: 11 12 Adult   **808.88**
1. Quotations
ISBN 0-313-29122-5   LC 96-47431
"This collection features the words of contemporary
African Americans and black Africans. . . . Many of the
over 1000 quotations are drawn from magazines and
newspaper articles published from 1990 to 1996, and
most have never before appeared in anthologies. Those
quoted range from journalists and musicians to athletes
and physicians. . . . Entries are presented alphabetically
by author, quotes are numbered sequentially, and indexing is by author and subject/keyword." Libr J

The **Girls'** book of wisdom; empowering,
inspirational quotes from 500 fabulous females;
selected and edited by Catherine Dee. Little,
Brown 1999 192p pa $8.95
Grades: 9 10 11 12   **808.88**
1. Quotations 2. Women—Quotations
ISBN 0-316-17956-6   LC 99-24741
A collection of quotations from 500 famous women,
including suffragists, pioneers, politicians, moms, musicians, athletes, and actors, grouped in such categories as
"Friendship," "Confidence," and "Creativity."
"While the included quotes are not revolutionary and
are occasionally clichèd, attractive fonts, funky small
graphics, and the mix of historical and modern powerful
women will make this choice popular among teen girls."
Voice Youth Advocates

Heart full of grace; a thousand years of black
wisdom; edited by Venice Johnson. Simon &
Schuster 1995 unp pa $19.95 hardcover o.p.
Grades: 11 12 Adult   **808.88**
1. African Americans—Quotations
ISBN 0-684-82542-2   LC 95-38106
"This is a diverse anthology of quotations, from the
sayings of Martin Luther King and Langston Hughes to
political speeches and African proverbs." Libr J

Oxford dictionary of humorous quotations; edited
by Ned Sherrin. 3rd ed. Oxford University Press
2005 xxxii, 525p $40
Grades: 11 12 Adult   **808.88**
1. Quotations 2. Wit and humor
ISBN 0-19-861004-1; 978-0-19-861004-5
                                       LC 2005-541489
First published 1995 with title: The Oxford book of
humorous quotations
A compilation of nearly 6,000 quotations arranged in
themes. Shakespeare, Austen, Groucho Marx, Monty Python and Roseanne are among humorists and pundits represented. Includes author and key word indexes.
"Readers will benefit from this reference work cover
to cover, soaking in the insights while smiling and
chuckling to themselves along the way." Am Ref Books
Annu, 2006

The **Oxford** dictionary of modern quotations;
edited by Elizabeth Knowles. 2nd ed. Oxford
Univ. Press 2002 483p hardcover o.p. pa $16.95
*
Grades: 9 10 11 12   **808.88**
1. Quotations
ISBN 0-19-866275-0; 0-19-860951-5 (pa)
                                       LC 2002-74256
First published 1991
New edition in preparation
This compendium "provides, besides the usual lines
from speeches, publications, and public commentary, lists
of song titles, lines from films, and famous last words."
Choice

Oxford dictionary of phrase, saying, and
quotation; edited by Susan Ratcliffe. 3rd ed.
Oxford University Press 2006 xxi, 689p $39.95
*
Grades: 9 10 11 12   **808.88**

Oxford dictionary of phrase, saying, and quotation—*Continued*

1. Quotations 2. Proverbs 3. English language—Terms and phrases
ISBN 978-0-19-280650-5; 0-19-280650-5
First published 1997

This book "brings together a profusion of proverbs, phrases, and quotations, arranged by subject or themes from Ability to Youth. The design and layout are clear and well organized. More than 12,000 bon mots from around the globe are included, and the origins and links of these treasured sayings in our language are traced through numerous cross-references." Booklist

The **Oxford** dictionary of quotations; edited by Elizabeth Knowles. 6th ed. Oxford University Press 2004 1140p $50 *
Grades: 11 12 Adult   **808.88**
1. Quotations
ISBN 0-19-860720-2   LC 2004-558811
First published 1941

This edition "has over 17,000 quotations. . . . The quotations are arranged alphabetically by author of the quotation. . . . An individual quotation entry includes, besides the quotation itself: the author; dates of birth and death; brief descriptions of the author; cross-references to other quotations about the author in the book and to references to him or her; the context (if necessary); and published source." Am Ref Books Annu, 2005

The **Quotable** woman; the first 5,000 years; compiled and edited by Elaine T. Partnow. Facts on File 2001 974p $75 *
Grades: 11 12 Adult   **808.88**
1. Quotations 2. Women—Quotations
ISBN 0-8160-4012-5   LC 00-37660
Replaces The New quotable woman, published 1992

This is a "collection of notable quotations by women, from Eve to Madeleine Albright. It includes more than 18,000 quotations from more than 3,600 women throughout history, on subjects from friendship and love to politics, religion, art, and women's role in society." Publisher's note
Includes bibliographical references

Quotations for all occasions; compiled by Catherine Frank. Columbia Univ. Press 2000 260p $55; pa $18.95 *
Grades: 11 12 Adult   **808.88**
1. Quotations
ISBN 0-231-11290-4; 0-231-11291-2 (pa)
LC 00-24048

This title "organizes its 1500-plus quotes into three sections that cover 150 different occasions. 'Every Year' contains quotes for such annual events as holidays, birthdays, days of the week, and seasons, while 'Occasionally' encompasses quotes for less frequent events, like going back to school, breaking up, quitting smoking, and school reunions. The final section is for 'Once in a Lifetime' experiences, such as turning 16, getting a first car, menopause, and retirement." Libr J
Includes bibliographical references

Random House Webster's quotationary. Random House 1999 1039p hardcover o.p. pa $27.95
Grades: 11 12 Adult   **808.88**
1. Quotations
ISBN 0-679-44850-0; 0-375-71968-7 (pa)
LC 98-30433

"The 20,000 quotations in this volume are arranged by subject, from *ability* to *Zen,* and then alphabetically by author. . . . The quotations include factual statements, song lyrics, slogans, titles, and phrases." Booklist
Includes bibliographical references

Science fiction quotations; from the inner mind to the outer limits; edited by Gary Westfahl; with a foreword by Arthur C. Clarke. Yale University Press 2005 xxi, 461p pa $25
Grades: 11 12 Adult   **808.88**
1. Science fiction 2. Quotations
ISBN 0-300-10800-1   LC 2005-3195

The author "defines a science fiction quotation as coming from novels, short stories, films, and TV programs (with some attention given to plays, radio dramas, and comic books) and being about works of science fiction or from science fiction writers. Organized under topical headings, more than 2,900 quotations offer the wisdom and wit of well-known authors like Arthur C. Clarke and Isaac Asimov as well as lesser-known personalities like J. O. Bailey and Stirling Silliphant and from titles as varied as The Strawberry Window, Cat's Cradle, and The Thing (from another World)." Booklist

The **Yale** book of quotations; edited by Fred R. Shapiro; foreword by Joseph Epstein. Yale University Press 2006 1104p $50 *
Grades: 11 12 Adult   **808.88**
1. Quotations
ISBN 978-0-300-10798-2; 0-300-10798-6
LC 2006-12317

The more than 12,000 "range over literature, history, popular culture, sports, computers, science, politics, law, and the social sciences, and although American quotations are emphasized, the book's scope is global. The authors represented are as diverse as William Shakespeare, John Lennon, Jack Dempsey, both Presidents Bush, J.K. Rowling, Rita Mae Brown, Confucius, Warren Buffet, and Deng Xiaoping. The entries are arranged by author, then chronologically and alphabetically by source title within the same year. A significant effort was made to trace the first published occurrence of a quotation, and whenever possible the wording is taken from the original source. . . . Electronic products such as the Times Digital Archive, JSTOR, Proquest Historical Newspapers and American Periodical Series, LexisNexis, Newspaperarchive.com, Questia, Eighteenth Century Collections Online, and Literature Online were all used." Libr J

809 Literary history and criticism

African literature and its times; {edited by} Joyce Moss & Lorraine Valestuk. Gale Group 2000 xlv, 544p il (World literature and its times) lib bdg $145.25 *
Grades: 11 12 Adult   **809**
ISBN 0-7876-3727-0   LC 00-24488

African literature and its times—*Continued*

Contributors discuss "50 literary works in relation to their social and historical contexts. Each article begins with comments on the genre, setting, and the historical period in which the work takes place, along with information about the author. . . . The work of key writers such as Athol Fugard, Camara Laye, Doris Lessing and Wole Soyinka is discussed as is the writing of others who have more recently emerged on the scene." SLJ

Includes bibliographical references

Bloom, Harold, 1930-

The epic. Chelsea House Publishers 2005 265p (Bloom's literary criticism 20th anniversary collection) $38.95; pa $19.95

Grades: 9 10 11 12   **809**

1. Epic literature—History and criticism

ISBN 0-7910-8229-6; 0-7910-8368-3 (pa)

                LC 2005-5379

"In this volume, Bloom writes on the ancient works of Homer through more modern epics such as Hart Crane's 'The Bridge'." Publisher's note

Brown, Jean E., 1945-

Teaching young adult literature; sharing the connection; {by} Jean E. Brown, Elaine C. Stephens. Wadsworth Pub. Co. 1995 320p il $41.95

Grades: Professional   **809**

1. Young adult literature—Study and teaching
2. Youth—Books and reading

ISBN 0-534-19938-0   LC 94-35183

This work combines "theory and practical ideas for enhancing the study of an important genre for adolescents. . . . The authors challenge teachers to expand their own reading repertoires, combining traditional and non-traditional works. Particularly helpful are sections detailing developmental tasks for YAs and applying those tasks to specific characters in YA literature. Also useful are in-depth interviews with YA authors, suggestions for 'bridging' potential connections between a YA work and other literature, and numerous effective pedagogical strategies for the classroom." Voice Youth Advocates

Includes bibliographical references

Burt, Daniel S.

The literary 100; a ranking of the most influential novelists, playwrights, and poets of all time. Facts on File 2001 400p il $45; pa $19.95

Grades: 11 12 Adult   **809**

1. Authors 2. Literature—History and criticism

ISBN 0-8160-4382-5; 0-8160-4383-3 (pa)

              LC 00-34093

Burt profiles not only familiar authors such as Tolstoy, Shakespeare, Dickens, and Jane Austen, but non-western writers such as Murasaki Shikibu, Tu Fu, and Cao Xueqin

This "makes for a fascinating dip through history and across cultures in a reference work that manages to be both concise and filled with enticing personal tidbits of information." Voice Youth Advocates

Includes bibliographical references

Cook, James Wyatt, 1932-

Encyclopedia of Renaissance literature. Facts on File 2006 xxvi, 598p (Facts on File library of world literature) $70

Grades: 9 10 11 12   **809**

1. Renaissance literature

ISBN 0-8160-5624-2   LC 2004-29417

This encyclopedia "spans the years between 1500 and 1700 and covers works in many European and Asian languages as well as a few African languages. Individuals featured include Giovanni Boccaccio, John Bunyan, John Calvin, Nicolaus Copernicus, John Dryden, and Edmund Spenser." SLJ

"Students and general readers . . . will find the concise summaries of unfamiliar non-European works and genres especially handy." Am Ref Books Annu, 2006

Includes bibliographical references

The Facts on File dictionary of classical and biblical allusions; [edited by] Martin H. Manser; associate editor, David H. Pickering. Facts on File 2003 448p (Facts on File writer's library) $45

Grades: 11 12 Adult   **809**

1. Allusions 2. Literature—Dictionaries

ISBN 0-8160-4868-1   LC 2002-192752

"This companion volume to The Facts On File Dictionary of Cultural and Historical Allusions (2000) focuses on literary references from Greek, Roman, Norse, Egyptian, and Celtic mythology, as well as the Bible. The book contains approximately 2000 alphabetically arranged entries with pronunciations, definitions examples, origins, and quotes. . . .This is a valuable book for students and for casual readers to find word or phrase origins." SLJ

Includes bibliographical references

Foster, Brett

Rome; [by] Brett Foster and Hal Marcovitz; introduction by Harold Bloom. Chelsea House 2005 197p il map (Bloom's literary places) $40

Grades: 9 10 11 12   **809**

1. Rome (Italy) 2. Literary landmarks

ISBN 0-7910-7839-6; 978-0-7910-7839-6

             LC 2005-13294

This guide to the city of Rome focuses on the places within it that have had an impact on literature. "Rome, the eternal city, boasts a long and rich literary history with strong connections to the English Romantic poets Keats and Shelley, as well as Stendhal, Goethe, and Henry James." Publisher's note

Includes bibliographical references

Harris, Laurie Lanzen

Characters in 20th-century literature. Gale Res. 1990 480p $75

Grades: 11 12 Adult   **809**

1. Literature—History and criticism 2. Characters and characteristics in literature

ISBN 0-8103-1847-4   LC 89-25709

"Descriptions of over 2,000 characters, drawn from 250 of the twentieth century's major novelists, dramatists, and short story writers, are included. . . . The book

Harris, Laurie Lanzen—*Continued*
is arranged alphabetically by author. . . . The essay on each work contains a brief plot synopsis as well as commentary on thematic and stylistic aspects of the work and the way in which the characters illustrate the central themes and aesthetics of the author." Preface

Herz, Sarah K.
From Hinton to Hamlet; building bridges between young adult literature and the classics; [by] Sarah K. Herz and Donald R. Gallo. 2nd ed., rev. and expanded. Greenwood Press 2005 256p $39.95
Grades: Professional   809
1. Young adult literature—Study and teaching 2. Youth—Books and reading
ISBN 0-313-32452-2   LC 2005-12728
First published 1996
"Aimed at teachers and librarians, the text offers personal experiences, testimonials, data, and theory for incorporating young adult literature into classrooms. . . . This resource is a must-have for all school libraries." Voice Youth Advocates
Includes bibliographical references

Highet, Gilbert, 1906-1978
The classical tradition; Greek and Roman influences on Western literature. Oxford Univ. Press 1949 xxxviii, 764p pa $29.95 hardcover o.p.
Grades: 11 12 Adult   809
1. Literature—History and criticism 2. Comparative literature 3. Classical literature
ISBN 0-19-500206-7
"The twenty-four chapters fall into four main sections. The first takes in the Dark and Middle Ages—Anglo-Saxon poetry and prose, French epic and romance, Dante, Petrarch, Boccaccio, Chaucer. The second section comprises eight chapters on the Renaissance—drama, epic, pastoral and romance, lyric, the literature of translation, Rabelais, Montaigne. . . . {The} third section {is} 'The Baroque Age.' . . . After baroque, we come to our fourth and last section, the romantic, or . . . the revolutionary period 'and afterwards.'" Spectator
Includes bibliographical references

Holocaust literature; an encyclopedia of writers and their work; S. Lillian Kremer, editor. Routledge 2002 2v set $250
Grades: 11 12 Adult   809
1. Holocaust, 1933-1945, in literature
ISBN 0-415-92985-7   LC 2002-23694
"This encyclopedia synthesizes a wide range of literary voices and provides a compelling look at more than 300 novelists, poets, memoirists, dramatists, and other writers who experienced the Holocaust or otherwise integrated the subject into their works." Publisher's note
Includes bibliographical references

Howes, Kelly King
Characters in 19th-century literature. Gale Res. 1993 597p $75
Grades: 11 12 Adult   809
1. Literature—History and criticism 2. Characters and characteristics in literature
ISBN 0-8103-8398-5   LC 92-75005
This reference work "provides brief plot summations and detailed character analyses for approximately 200 novels, plays, and short stories by 100 nineteenth-century writers who are currently studied in U.S. classrooms. . . . The book is arranged alphabetically by author and provides the individual's dates, nationality, and principal genres. Then the various works are considered in individual essays that analyze how the characters develop the author's themes." Booklist
"This volume will be of much use to students and teachers and just might entice some readers into books they might otherwise ignore." Voice Youth Advocates

Kurian, George Thomas
Timetables of world literature. Facts on File 2003 457p $65 *
Grades: 11 12 Adult   809
ISBN 0-8160-4197-0   LC 2002-3891
Chronicles world literature from the Classical Age through the twentieth century, discussing literary developments and the relationship between literature and the political and social climate of each historical period
"This comprehensive reference . . . helps academic researchers place major works of literature from 58 countries in historical and cultural context." Libr J
Includes bibliographical references

Literary movements for students; presenting analysis, context, and criticism on literary movements; David Galens, project editor. Gale Group 2002 2v il set $185
Grades: 11 12 Adult   809
1. Literature—History and criticism
ISBN 0-7876-6517-7   LC 2002-10928
Entries provide "historical background information on each movement as well as modern critical interpretation of each movement's characteristic styles and themes. Approximately 25 movements are covered, including absurdism, Greek drama, modernism, science fiction/fantasy, surrealism and many others." Publisher's note
Includes bibliographical references

Literature and its times; profiles of 300 notable literary works and the historical events that influenced them. Gale Res. 1997 5v set $570 *
Grades: 11 12 Adult   809
1. Literature—History and criticism
ISBN 0-7876-0606-5   LC 97-34339
Also available supplement $199 (ISBN 0-7876-6550-9)
Edited by Joyce Moss and George Wilson
"The editors chose the selections (fiction, poetry, short stories, plays, biographies, and speeches) with the input of public libraries and secondary-school teachers. . . . Each volume covers a time range subdivided by dates and a general description . . . and begins with a brief

Literature and its times—*Continued*
overview of the historical events of the era, with a time-line providing a synopsis of each period." Libr J

Literature of developing nations for students; Michael L. LaBlanc, Elizabeth Bellalouna, and Ira Mark Milne, editors. Gale Group 2000 2v set $160

Grades: 11 12 Adult   **809**
1. Fiction—History and criticism 2. Developing countries in literature
ISBN 0-7876-4928-7   LC 00-56023

"Each entry begins with an introduction of a few paragraphs to the author and specific novel and then . . . provides plot summary and analysis. Excerpts from essays and articles about the novel are provided . . . and short summaries of major characters, an overview of important themes, historical context, a critical overview, and a bibliography are also included." Libr J

Includes bibliographical references

Literature of the Holocaust; edited and with an introduction by Harold Bloom. Chelsea House 2003 325p (Bloom's period studies) lib bdg $37.95

Grades: 9 10 11 12   **809**
1. Holocaust, 1933-1945, in literature
ISBN 0-7910-7677-6   LC 2003-16888

Contents: The Holocaust in the stories of Elie Wiesel, by T. A. Idinopulos; The problematics of Holocaust literature, by A. H. Rosenfeld; Tragedy and the Holocaust, by R. Skloot; Holocaust documentary fiction: novelist as eyewitness, by J. E. Young; Holocaust and autobiography: Wiesel, Friedländer, Pisar, by J. Sungolowsky; The Holocaust, by D. E. Lipstadt; Primo Levi and the language of witness, by M. Tager; The Utopian space of a nightmare: the diary of Anne Frank, by B. Chiarello; The literature of Auschwitz, by L. L. Langer; Comedic distance in Holocaust literature, by M. Cory; Public memory and its discontents, by G. H. Hartman; Two Holocaust voices: Cynthia Ozick and Art Spiegelman, by L. L. Langer; The Holocaust and literary studies, by J. M. Peck; Rafael Seligmann's Rubinsteins Versteigerung: the German-Jewish family novel before and after the Holocaust, by R. Robertson; Memorizing memory, by A. Hungerford

Includes bibliographical references

Masterpieces of world literature; edited by Frank N. Magill. Harper & Row 1989 957p $55 *

Grades: 11 12 Adult   **809**
1. Literature—History and criticism
ISBN 0-06-270050-2   LC 89-45052

"The work, arranged alphabetically by title, contains plot summaries, character portrayals, and critical evaluations of 270 classics of world literature (novels, plays, stories, poems, and essays), all reprints from other Magill guides." Nichols. Guide to Ref Books for Sch Media Cent. 4th edition

Ruud, Jay
Encyclopedia of medieval literature. Facts on File 2005 734p (Facts on File library of world literature) $75

Grades: 11 12 Adult   **809**
1. Medieval literature—Encyclopedias
ISBN 0-8160-5497-5   LC 2004-31066

"Each article focuses on key authors, characters, titles, and aspects of works that exemplify the importance of the Middle Ages. The selections are from Europe and Asia and represent various cultural backgrounds. . . . Individuals interested in a source of basic information from which to begin a study of the Middle Ages will find this volume to be especially useful." Am Ref Books Annu, 2006

Includes bibliographical references

Snodgrass, Mary Ellen
Encyclopedia of Gothic literature. Facts on File 2005 480p (Facts on File library of world literature) $65

Grades: 11 12 Adult   **809**
1. Gothic revival literature
ISBN 0-8160-5528-9   LC 2004-46986

"This encyclopedia examines the literature in alphabetical entries that describe people, places, works, literary and psychological terms, characters, subgenres, and concepts." SLJ

This is a "solid, very readable and essential contribution to the field of literary genre reference materials." Am Ref Books Annu, 2005

Includes bibliographical references

Stripling, Mahala Yates
Bioethics and medical issues in literature. Greenwood Press 2005 xxviii, 224p (Exploring social issues through literature) $49.95

Grades: 9 10 11 12   **809**
1. Fiction—History and criticism 2. Medicine in literature 3. Ethics in literature
ISBN 0-313-32040-3   LC 2005-1493

"Chapters look at such . . . topics as technology's creature, illness and culture, and end of life issues, with each chapter offering a close examination of two major literary works." Publisher's note

Includes bibliographical references

Twentieth-century literary movements dictionary; Helene Henderson and Jay P. Pederson, editors. Omnigraphics 1999 xxix, 1037p $80

Grades: 11 12 Adult   **809**
1. Literature—History and criticism
ISBN 1-55888-426-2   LC 99-41091

"A compendium to more than 500 literary, critical, and theatrical movements, schools, and groups from more than 80 nations, covering the novelists, poets, short-story writers, dramatists, essayists, theorists, and works, genres, techniques, and terms associated with each movement." Title page

Includes bibliographical references

Whitson, Kathy J.
Encyclopedia of feminist literature. Greenwood Press 2004 300p $65 *
Grades: 11 12 Adult **809**
1. Feminism in literature 2. American literature—Women authors—Bio-bibliography 3. English literature—Women authors—Bio-bibliography
ISBN 0-313-32731-9 LC 2004-42478
"The women authors included in this volume range from the very familiar—Toni Morrison and Virginia Woolf—to the less well-known—Judith Ortiz Cofer and Shirley Geok-Lin Lim. Nearly 70 writers are represented with an additional 22 'topic' entries on subjects ranging from abolition to the 'woman question.' Author entries include biographical information, major works, and an analysis of at least one work." Libr J
For a fuller review, see: Booklist, Apr. 1, 2005
Includes bibliographical references

Women in literature; reading through the lens of gender; edited by Jerilyn Fisher and Ellen S. Silber; foreword by David Sadker. Greenwood Press 2003 xxxix, 358p $65
Grades: 9 10 11 12 **809**
1. Women in literature 2. Literature—History and criticism
ISBN 0-313-31346-6 LC 2002-35212
This is a "collection of two- to three-page signed essays looking at 96 works of fiction (both canonical works and newer/less familiar titles) . . . The literary works run the gamut from Homer and William Shakespeare to Alice Walker and Amy Tan. . . . Teachers looking for ways to shake up their traditional reading lists and students looking for a different approach to some classics will find this book of interest." SLJ
Includes bibliographical references

809.1 Poetry--History and criticism

Bloom, Harold, 1930-
Poets and poems. Chelsea House Publishers 2005 487p (Bloom's literary criticism 20th anniversary collection) $38.95
Grades: 9 10 11 12 **809.1**
1. Poetry—History and criticism
ISBN 0-7910-8225-3 LC 2005-8636
"In this volume, Bloom considers poets Emily Dickinson, Walt Whitman, Hart Crane, William Shakespeare, Samuel Taylor Coleridge, William Butler Yeats, and many others." Publisher's note

Classic writings on poetry; edited by William Harmon. Columbia University Press 2003 538p $79; pa $27.50 *
Grades: 11 12 Adult **809.1**
1. Poetry—History and criticism
ISBN 0-231-12370-1; 0-231-12371-X (pa)
LC 2003-40917
This anthology contains "writing on poetry by such philosophical royalty as Plato, Aristotle, Milton, Sir Philip Sidney, Wordsworth, and Emily Dickinson. Readers are given a peek through the hole of history's fence into the lives and worlds of our poetic geniuses and reminded of the poem's matchless role in conveying reverence, remembering wars, recording history, entertaining, expressing deep emotion, and above all, allowing the finite mind, for one moment, to contain infinity." Libr J
Includes bibliographical references

Planet on the table; poets on the reading life; editors, Sharon Bryan & William Olsen. Sarabande Bks. 2003 361p il (Writer's studio) pa $16.95
Grades: 11 12 Adult **809.1**
1. Poetry—History and criticism 2. Books and reading
ISBN 1-88933-091-4 LC 2002-7234
In this collection of essays, such writers as Maxine Kumin, Jacqueline Osherow, Edward Hirsch, and Campbell McGrath discuss their personal reading habits as well as their thoughts on various works of literary criticism
This is a "vital and illuminating collection. . . . In all, 25 poets share their love for and insights into the fine art of reading in this glowing sphere of an anthology." Booklist
Includes bibliographical references

Schwedt, Rachel E., 1944-
Young adult poetry; a survey and theme guide; [by] Rachel Schwedt and Janice DeLong; foreword by Mel Glenn. Greenwood Press 2002 192p $49.95
Grades: 9 10 11 12 **809.1**
1. Poetry—History and criticism 2. Teenagers—Books and reading
ISBN 0-313-31336-9 LC 2001-33719
This resource features an annotated bibliography of 198 poetry volumes and a thematic guide to over 6000 individual poems. Works span the reading levels from sixth to twelfth grade and range in style
"This book will certainly help with decisions about adding specific poetry anthologies to classrooms and library shelves, and, most importantly, knowing the grade levels for which they are intended." SLJ
Includes bibliographical references

809.2 Drama--History and criticism

Bloom, Harold, 1930-
Dramatists and dramas. Chelsea House Publishers 2005 306p (Bloom's literary criticism 20th anniversary collection) $38.95
Grades: 9 10 11 12 **809.2**
1. Drama—History and criticism
ISBN 0-7910-8226-1 LC 2005-3094
"Bloom's coverage ranges from the Ancient Greeks to modern day and includes writers like Aristophanes, Shakespeare, Moliere, Anton Chekhov, Tennessee Williams, and Arthur Miller." Publisher's note

Critical survey of drama; edited by Carl Rollyson. 2nd rev ed. Salem Press 2003 8v set $499
Grades: 11 12 Adult **809.2**
1. Drama—Dictionaries 2. English drama—Dictionaries 3. American drama—Dictionaries
ISBN 1-58765-102-5 LC 2003-2190

Critical survey of drama—*Continued*

"Combines, updates, and expands two earlier Salem Press reference sets: Critical survey of drama, revised edition, English language series, published in 1994, and Critical survey of drama, foreign language series, published in 1986." Preface

This set contains "about 630 essays, of which 570 discuss individual dramatists and 60 cover overview topics. . . . Each essay on a dramatist provides . . . material as birth and death dates, lists of the author's major dramatic works (with dates of first production and publication). Each essay opens with a brief survey of the author's publications in literary forms other than drama, a summary of the writer's professional achievements and awards, an extended biographical sketch that centers on the writer's development as a dramatist, and an extensive critical analysis of the writer's major dramatic works. Following this discussion is a list of major publications in fields other than drama and an annotated bibliography of critical works about the author." Publisher's note

Includes bibliographical references

Griffiths, Trevor R., 1949-

The Ivan R. Dee guide to plays and playwrights. Ivan R. Dee 2003 424p il pa $28.95

Grades: 11 12 Adult   **809.2**
1. Theater—Dictionaries 2. Drama—Dictionaries
ISBN 1-566-63566-7   LC 2003-70127

First published 2003 in the United Kingdom with title: The theatre guide

This guide "contains biographical sketches and critical commentary about more than 550 playwrights and their plays. Griffiths emphasizes the writers rather than their works and includes only those likely to be produced nowadays." Choice

This book "provides something that similar guides often omit: scribes, however obscure, who are being published and produced today. . . . Readers will find big names like George Abbott, Aeschylus, and Edward Albee as well as newcomers like Welsh dramatist Gary Owen and Briton Amanda Whittington." Libr J

Partnow, Elaine, 1941-

The female dramatist; profiles of women playwrights from the Middle Ages to contemporary times; by Elaine T. Partnow with Leslie Anne Hyatt. Facts on File 1998 xxix, 271p il $49.50

Grades: 11 12 Adult   **809.2**
1. Drama—Women authors 2. Drama—Bio-bibliography
ISBN 0-8160-3015-4   LC 97-26501

"While most playwrights covered are twentieth-century Americans, there is representation from all continents and from 1000 A.D. onward. . . . Entries are alphabetically arranged and vary from a quarter page to three pages. Approximately a quarter of the entries have portraits. Information includes personal history, contributions to the field, a selected list of plays and other works, and selected secondary materials. Some entries open with excerpts from plays. The writing is accessible—clear and concise, not pedantic." Booklist

Includes bibliographical references

Patterson, Michael

The Oxford dictionary of plays. Oxford University Press 2005 xxxv, 523p $50 *

Grades: 11 12 Adult   **809.2**
1. Drama—Dictionaries
ISBN 0-19-860417-3   LC 2004-23698

This is a "digest of 1000 works that span the history of theater from Aristophanes to Michael Frayn's Democracy (2003). The entries, which run between 200 and 400 words, include the date and place of first performance, genre (descriptions of which are included in the preface), setting, cast required, and a synopsis of the action with a one-paragraph assessment of the play." Libr J

For a fuller review, see: Booklist, Dec. 15, 2005
Includes bibliographical references

809.3   Fiction--History and criticism

Beacham's encyclopedia of popular fiction; edited by Kirk H. Beetz. Beacham Pub. 1996-2002 19v

Grades: 11 12 Adult   **809.3**
1. Fiction—Bio-bibliography
ISSN 1530-1028
ISBN 0-93383-338-5   LC 96-20771

This reference work consists of a three volume set of Biography series and sixteen volumes of Analyses series. Available separately or in sets. Apply to publisher for price

Bloom, Harold, 1930-

Novelists and novels. Chelsea House Publishers 2005 588p (Bloom's literary criticism 20th anniversary collection) $38.95

Grades: 9 10 11 12   **809.3**
1. Fiction—History and criticism
ISBN 0-7910-8227-X   LC 2005-3269

The author discusses "the world's great novelists including Miguel de Cervantes, Charles Dickens, Jane Austen, Franz Kafka, Ernest Hemingway, William Faulkner, and more." Publisher's note

Includes bibliographical references

Short story writers and short stories. Chelsea House Publishers 2005 188p (Bloom's literary criticism 20th anniversary collection) $38.95

Grades: 9 10 11 12   **809.3**
1. Short stories—History and criticism
ISBN 0-7910-8228-8   LC 2005-6399

This book contains the author's "considerations on those writers who shaped the art of the short story; [including] Guy de Maupassant, Edgar Allan Poe, and Sherwood Anderson." Publisher's note

Critical survey of short fiction; editor, Charles E. May. 2nd rev ed. Salem Press 2001 7v il set $473

Grades: 11 12 Adult   **809.3**
1. Short stories—History and criticism 2. Short stories—Bio-bibliography
ISBN 0-89356-006-5   LC 00-46384

First published 1981 under the editorship of Frank Magill

Critical survey of short fiction—*Continued*
"The first six volumes contain 515 author entries arranged alphabetically. . . . They vary in length but have the same items included, beginning with birth and death dates, and a portrait if available, followed by a list of principle works of short fiction. . . . Volume 7 consists of 29 survey essays on history, theory, and genre as well as world cultures. These vary in length from 3,000 to 10,000 words. A new feature, 'Research Tools,' provides lists of award winners as well as a chronology, glossary, and bibliography." Booklist

Encyclopedia of the novel; editor, Paul Schellinger; assistant editors, Christopher Hudson, Marijke Rijsberman. Fitzroy Dearborn Pubs. 1998 2v set $295
Grades: 11 12 Adult   **809.3**
1. Fiction—Encyclopedias
ISBN 1-57958-015-7   LC 99-165908
This work's "650 essays are arranged alphabetically and focus on classic novels, great novel writers, types of novels, novels identified with particular countries or regions, technical and formal aspects of novels, theory, influence, and novel criticism. All of the entries are signed and have been contributed by specialists, and conclude with brief biographies, lists of works, and further readings. There are two indexes: a title index and a detailed, general index." Am Libr

Hooper, Brad
The short story readers' advisory; a guide for librarians. American Lib. Assn. 2000 135p pa $32
Grades: 11 12 Adult   **809.3**
1. Short stories—History and criticism
ISBN 0-8389-0782-2   LC 99-85751
This work contains over 200 critical essays covering short story authors past and present. A step-by-step guide on how to interview readers in order to match their tastes with appropriate stories is included.
Includes bibliographical references

Murphy, Bruce, 1962-
The encyclopedia of murder and mystery; [by] Bruce F. Murphy. St. Martin's Minotaur 1999 543p hardcover o.p. pa $24.95
Grades: 11 12 Adult   **809.3**
1. Mystery fiction—Encyclopedias
ISBN 0-312-21554-1; 0-312-29414-X (pa)
                                                            LC 99-25316
"Alongside summaries of significant novels, Murphy offers descriptions of various subgenera, common plot devices and movie adaptations, as well as biographical entries on classic authors such as Raymond Chandler and Agatha Christie, and on newer luminaries like James Ellroy." Publ Wkly
Includes bibliographical references

Mystery and suspense writers; the literature of crime, detection, and espionage; Robin W. Winks, editor in chief; Maureen Corrigan, associate editor. Scribner 1998 2v set $250
Grades: 11 12 Adult   **809.3**
1. Mystery fiction—Dictionaries 2. Spies in literature
ISBN 0-684-80521-9   LC 98-36812

"Articles on 68 mystery writers ranging from Edgar Allen Poe to Sarah Paretsky run from ten to 20 pages and include information on the life and works as well as solid bibliographies for each author." Libr J

Short story writers; edited by Frank N. Magill; consulting editor, Charles E. May. Salem Press 1997 3v il (Magill's choice) set $188 *
Grades: 11 12 Adult   **809.3**
1. Short stories—History and criticism
ISBN 0-89356-950-X   LC 97-23079
Vol. 1, Alice Adams - Hamlin Garland; Vol. 2, Nikolai Gogol - Edna O'Brien; Vol. 3, Flannery O'Connor - Richard Wright
"The three volumes consist of essays on 102 writers who are arguably the most popular and most acclaimed of the genre. Extracted from among the 363 essays in the 1993 edition of *Critical Survey* [of short fiction], the essays were updated for this edition." Libr J

St. James guide to fantasy writers; editor, David Pringle. St. James Press 1996 711p (St. James guide to writers series) $185
Grades: 11 12 Adult   **809.3**
1. Fantasy fiction—Bio-bibliography
ISBN 1-55862-205-5   LC 95-48783
This volume "offers an A-to-Z compendium of major fantasy writers. Each entry consists of a brief biography, a complete list of published works, a signed critical essay, and comments from some living authors on their work." Libr J

810   American literature

Modern American literature. 5th ed. St. James Press 1999 3v set $495 *
Grades: 11 12 Adult   **810**
1. American literature—History and criticism
ISBN 1-55862-379-5   LC 98-38952
First published 1960 by Ungar and edited by Dorothy Nyren. The 5th edition incorporates the 3 volumes of the 4th edition and its 3 supplements and adds 70 new entries. Features expanded coverage of black, Hispanic, Native American and women writers
Includes bibliographical references

810.3   American literature-- Encyclopedias and dictionaries

The **Companion** to southern literature; themes, genres, places, people, movements, and motifs; edited by Joseph M. Flora and Lucinda H. MacKethan; associate editor, Todd Taylor. Louisiana State Univ. Press 2001 xxvi, 1054p $69.95
Grades: 11 12 Adult   **810.3**
1. Southern States—Intellectual life
ISBN 0-8071-2692-6   LC 2001-29959
This sourcebook "explores the multifaceted aspects of the 'southern experience as it is depicted in literature.' Focusing on common threads that run through southern writing and set it apart from the literature of other re-

The Companion to southern literature—*Continued*

gions, the more than 500 alphabetical entries cover a wide range of topics." Booklist

"This unique compilation {is} . . . an excellent addition to libraries that support studies of Southern literature." Libr J

Includes bibliographical references

Encyclopedia of American literature. Facts on File 2002 3v set $225 *

Grades: 11 12 Adult   **810.3**
1. American literature—Encyclopedias
ISBN 0-8160-4121-0   LC 2001-40900
New edition in preparation

Contents: v1 The colonial and revolutionary era {by} Carol Ruth Berkin; v2 The age of romanticism and realism {by} Lisa Paddock; v3 The modern and post-modern period {by} Carl Rollyson

"All three volumes feature an introductory essay followed by alphabetically arranged entries and a chronology. The entries, which range from literary figures, genres, and literary characters to specific works, topical entries such as 'Lost Generation,' and musicals, provide not just facts but interpretation of the topic's importance as well." Libr J

Includes bibliographical references

HarperCollins Reader's encyclopedia of American literature. HarperResource 2002 1126p $49.95 *

Grades: 11 12 Adult   **810.3**
1. American literature—Encyclopedias
ISBN 0-06-019815-X

"Portions of this book appeared in a somewhat modified form in The Reader's Encyclopedia of American Literature published by T.Y. Crowell in 1962 and in Benet's Reader's Encyclopedia, third edition, published by Harper & Row in 1987." Verso of title page

"The bulk of the book consists of entries on authors, titles, characters, literary genres, periodicals, groups and movements, and historical persons and events directly related to literature. The social, political, religious, and philosophical backgrounds of American literature are treated in entries on presidents, political figures, and military personnel who have figured prominently in literature or themselves contributed to it. Many American military actions are given separate entries, as are documents such as the Mayflower Compact, the Declaration of Independence, the Federalist papers, and the Constitution. American Indian tribes receive coverage along with individual entries on Native American writers." Preface

Hart, James David, 1911-1990

The Oxford companion to American literature; [by] James D. Hart; with revisions and additions by Phillip W. Leininger. 6th ed. Oxford Univ. Press 1995 779p $49.95 *

Grades: 11 12 Adult   **810.3**
1. American literature—Dictionaries
ISBN 0-19-506548-4   LC 94-45727
First published 1941

In addition to over 2000 entries for individual authors and more than 1,100 for important works this reference includes entries for literary movements, awards, maga-

zines, printers, book collectors and newspapers. A chronological index of literary and social history is appended.

The Oxford encyclopedia of American literature; Jay Parini, editor-in-chief. Oxford University Press 2004 4v il set $495 *

Grades: 11 12 Adult   **810.3**
1. American literature—Encyclopedias
ISBN 0-19-515653-6   LC 2002-156325

Contents: v. 1. Academic novels-The essay in America -- v. 2. William Faulkner -Mina Loy -- v. 3. Norman Mailer-Sentimental literature -- v. 4. Anne Sexton-Writing as a woman in the twentieth century

This set "provides a wealth of reliable information on standard bearers of American literature in an easy-on-the eyes format for students and general readers." SLJ

Snodgrass, Mary Ellen

Encyclopedia of frontier literature. Oxford Univ. Press 1999 540p il pa $19.95

Grades: 9 10 11 12   **810.3**
1. American literature—Encyclopedias 2. Frontier and pioneer life in literature
ISBN 0-19-513318-8   LC 99-11766
First published 1997 by ABC-CLIO

This "reference explores over 400 years worth of the extensive body of literature about the exploration and settlement of North America, presenting dominant themes, literary history, genres, writers, individuals, peoples, and themes." Book Rep

810.8   American literature-- Collections

911: the book of help; edited by Michael Cart; with Marianne Carus and Marc Aronson. Cricket Bks. 2002 178p $17.95; pa $9.95

Grades: 9 10 11 12   **810.8**
1. September 11 terrorist attacks, 2001 2. Terrorism 3. American literature—Collections
ISBN 0-8126-2659-1; 0-8126-2676-1 (pa)
         LC 2002-4707

"A Marcato book"

A collection of essays, poems, and short fiction, created in response to the terrorist attacks of September 11, 2001. Contributors include Katherine Paterson, Joan Bauer, Walter Dean Myers, Nikki Giovanni, Arnold Adoff, and Russell Freedman

This "stands out for its rich prose, its unusual reporting, its search for context, its reminder of wonders." NY Times Book Rev

American dragons: twenty-five Asian American voices; edited by Laurence Yep. HarperCollins Pubs. 1993 237p pa $6.99 hardcover o.p. *

Grades: 7 8 9 10   **810.8**
1. American literature—Asian American authors—Collections
ISBN 0-06-440603-2   LC 92-28489

These "short stories, poems, and other selections are written by a cross section of Asian Americans, with roots in China, Vietnam, Japan, Korea, Tibet, and Thailand.

American dragons: twenty-five Asian American voices—*Continued*
The book is organized by theme, covering such issues of interest to adolescents as identity, family relationships, generational and cultural conflicts, and love." Horn Book
"A kaleidoscopic, occasionally brilliant, illumination of the Asian-American experience." SLJ
Includes bibliographical references

Baseball: a literary anthology; edited by Nicholas Dawidoff. Library of Am. 2002 721p $35
Grades: 11 12 Adult   810.8
1. Baseball 2. American literature—Collections
ISBN 1-931082-09-X   LC 2001-38654
"Beginning with Thayer's *Casey at the Bat* and ending with Buster Olney, there are more than 700 pages of prose and poetry, fiction and sportswriting, writers and players. Scanning the table of contents, it almost seems like *everybody* wrote about baseball: Damon Runyon, Ring Lardner, James Weldon Johnson, William Carlos Williams, James Thurber. But so did Paul Gallico, Nelson Algren, Tallulah Bankhead, and Jacques Barzun. . . . Ineffable, indispensable, inimitable—just like baseball." Booklist

The Best American nonrequired reading 2006; edited by Dave Eggers; introduction by Matt Groening. Houghton Mifflin 2006 377p il $28; pa $14
Grades: 9 10 11 12   810.8
1. American literature—Collections
ISBN   0-618-57050-0;   978-0-618-57050-8; 0-618-57051-9 (pa); 978-0-618-57051-5 (pa)
LC 2002-213163
Annual. First published 2002
An anthology of fiction and nonfiction selections intended for readers aged 15 to 25. Includes pieces ranging from popular culture and music to investigative reporting on politics and international affairs.

Crossing into America; the new literature of immigration; edited by Louis Mendoza and S. Shankar. New Press (NY) 2003 xxvi, 365p hardcover o.p. pa $18.95 *
Grades: 11 12 Adult   810.8
1. American literature—Collections 2. Immigrants
ISBN 1-56584-720-2; 1-56584-895-0 (pa)
LC 2002-41055
"This anthology includes a few poems and some fictional works, but most of the selections are memoirs. The political oppression and economic desperation that prompted immigration to the United States as well as the prejudice and discrimination that people often face once they arrive here are addressed in many of the pieces." SLJ
"A beautiful piece by Cuban American Achy Obejas captures the intergenerational conflict without heroics, and there are electrifying selections from Sandra Cisneros, Jamaica Kincaid, and other famous writers as well as some exciting new voices." Booklist
Includes bibliographical references

Crossing the danger water; three hundred years of African-American writing; edited and with an introduction by Deirdre Mullane. Anchor Bks. (NY) 1993 xxii, 769p pa $20 *
Grades: 11 12 Adult   810.8
ISBN 0-385-42243-1   LC 93-17194
This anthology "includes fiction, autobiography, poetry, songs, and letters by such writers as Frederick Douglass, Sojourner Truth, W.E.B. Du Bois, Zora Neale Hurston, and Richard Wright. Many topics are covered, from slavery, education, the Civil War, Reconstruction, and political issues to spirituals, songs of the Civil Rights movement, and rap music." Libr J
Includes bibliographical references

Grand mothers: poems, reminiscences, and short stories about the keepers of our traditions; edited by Nikki Giovanni. Holt & Co. 1994 xxi, 168p hardcover o.p. pa $7.95
Grades: 9 10 11 12   810.8
1. Grandmothers
ISBN 0-8050-2766-1; 0-8050-4903-7 (pa)
LC 94-6144
"This anthology brings together writings about grandmothers. . . . Though the topic of grandmothers might be expected to bring out a certain sentimentality, the writers cut through the clichés to the basic human needs that grandmothers fill and the fundamental questions their lives and their memories raise in those who know them, remember them, or pass down their stories. Varied in quality, but still a unique collection of writings." Booklist

Growing up Latino; memoirs and stories; edited with an introduction by Harold Augenbraum and Ilan Stavans; foreword by Ilan Stavans. Houghton Mifflin 1993 xxix, 344p pa $15 hardcover o.p. *
Grades: 6 7 8 9   810.8
1. American literature—Hispanic American authors—Collections
ISBN 0-395-66124-2   LC 92-32624
"A Marc Jaffe book"
A collection of short stories and excerpts from novels and memoirs written by twenty-five Latino authors. Among the contributors are Julia Alvarez, Oscar Hijuelos, Denise Chávez, Rolando Hinojosa, and Sandra Cisneros.
Includes bibliographical references

Guys write for Guys Read; edited by Jon Scieszka. Viking 2005 272p il $16.99; pa $10.99
Grades: 6 7 8 9   810.8
1. American literature—Collections
ISBN 0-670-06007-0; 0-670-06027-5 (pa)
LC 2004-28984
This is a collection of short stories, essays, columns, cartoons, anecdotes, and artwork by such writers and illustrators as Brian Jacques, Jerry Spinelli, Chris Crutcher, Mo Willems, Chris Van Allsburg, Matt Groening, and Neil Gaiman, selected by voters at the Guys Read web site.
This is "a diverse and fast-paced anthology . . . that

Guys write for Guys Read—*Continued*
deserves a permanent place in any collection . . . .
There's something undeniably grand about this collective
celebration of the intellectual life of the common boy."
SLJ

I thought my father was God and other true tales
from the National Story Project; edited and
introduced by Paul Auster; Nelly Reifler,
assistant editor. Holt & Co. 2001 xxi, 383p il
$25; pa $15
Grades: 11 12 Adult   **810.8**
1. American literature—Collections
ISBN 0-8050-6714-0; 0-312-42100-1 (pa)
                                    LC 00-54397
Also available in paperback from Picador USA
"In 1999, novelist Paul Auster . . . and the hosts of
National Public Radio's All Things Considered asked listeners to send in true stories to be read on-air as part of
the National Story Project. Auster received more than
4,000 submissions; the 180 best are published here."
Publ Wkly
"These are stop-you-in-your-tracks stories about hair-
raising coincidences, miracles, tragedies, redemption, and
moments of pure hilarity." Booklist

Infinite divisions: an anthology of Chicana
literature; {edited by} Tey Diana Rebolledo,
Eliana S. Rivero. University of Ariz. Press 1993
xxii, 393p il pa $24.95 hardcover o.p. *
Grades: 11 12 Adult   **810.8**
ISBN 0-8165-1384-8   LC 92-45101
"This collection, which includes 178 texts by 56 wom-
en, is organized historically and thematically. The first
chapter includes early narratives from both oral and written traditions. Later chapters focus on personal identity,
relationships within the community, and archetypes and
myths. Authors include Gloria Anzaldúa, Denise Chavez,
Sandra Cisneros, Margarita Cota Cárdenas, Pat Mora,
and Antonia Quantana Pigno. Introductory essays set the
tone for each new chapter, and extensive footnotes are
included. Texts originally in Spanish are presented in
both Spanish and English." Libr J
Includes bibliographical references

Jewish American literature; a Norton anthology;
[compiled and edited by] Jules Chametzky [et
al.] Norton 2000 xxiv, 1221p il $39.95
Grades: 11 12 Adult   **810.8**
1. American literature—Jewish authors 2. American
literature—Collections
ISBN 0-393-04809-8   LC 00-55393
The editors have attempted "to encompass Jewish literature from 1654 to the present in this collection of poems, cartoons, sermons, diaries, letters, stories, speeches,
plays, prayers, novel excerpts, and critical writings either
translated from Hebrew or Yiddish or written in English.
Major sections group the literature chronologically to
help identify large movements. . . . This great anthology
is essential for Jewish studies and American literature
collections." Libr J
Includes bibliographical references

Latina: women's voices from the borderlands;
edited by Lillian Castillo-Speed. Simon &
Schuster 1995 284p pa $14 hardcover o.p. *
Grades: 11 12 Adult   **810.8**
1. American literature—Hispanic American authors—
Collections
ISBN 0-684-80240-6   LC 95-10397
"A Touchstone book"
This anthology contains short stories, novel excerpts,
personal essays, memoirs and political writings by thirty-
one Latina writers. Sandra Cisneros, Julia Alvarez, Judith
Ortiz Cofer and Christina Garcia are among the contribu-
tors

The **Norton** anthology of African American
literature; Henry Louis Gates, Jr., general editor,
Nellie Y. McKay, general editor. 2nd ed. Norton
2003 2800p 2 computer laser optical discs pa
$70.30 *
Grades: 11 12 Adult   **810.8**
1. American literature—African American authors—
Collections
ISBN 0-393-97778-1   LC 2003-66176
First published 1996
"The anthology is divided into seven sections, each
with a separate introduction giving the sociopolitical factors that impacted on the material included therein. Featured are 120 writers, 52 of whom are women, richly
representing African American vernacular literature, poetry, drama, short stories, novels, slave narratives, and autobiographies." Libr J [review of 1996 edition]
Includes bibliographical references

The **Oxford** book of women's writing in the
United States; edited by Linda Wagner-Martin,
Cathy N. Davidson. Oxford Univ. Press 1995
596p pa $27.50 hardcover o.p. *
Grades: 11 12 Adult   **810.8**
ISBN 0-19-513245-9   LC 95-1499
This anthology provides "samples of the public and
private work of 99 women of diverse racial and ethnic
backgrounds who write in English and were born in or
have lived in the United States over the past four centuries. They include short fiction (almost half of the book),
poems, essays, plays, and speeches but have also gone
beyond traditional genre categories to include performance pieces, erotica, diaries, letters, and recipes." Libr
J

A **Patriot's** handbook; songs, poems, stories, and
speeches celebrating the land we love; selected
and introduced by Caroline Kennedy. Hyperion
2003 xxiii, 663p il $27.95; pa $16.95
Grades: 11 12 Adult   **810.8**
1. Patriotism 2. American literature—Collections
ISBN 0-7868-6918-6; 1-4013-0707-1 (pa)
                                   LC 2003-49983
In this compilation of prose and poetry, "Kennedy arranges her material into chapters based on general
themes, including the flag, portraits of Americans, freedom, and equality. The first selection is the lyrics to the
national anthem, and the last one is an excerpt from the
fiction of highly esteemed contemporary writer Annie
Proulx; selections in between include George Washing-

A Patriot's handbook—*Continued*

ton's 'Farewell Address,' Sojourner Truth's speech 'Ain't I a Woman,' the text of *Brown v. the Board of Education*, and the words to the Grateful Dead's song 'U.S. Blues.' Kennedy provides a general introduction to the book and introduces each chapter. For personal enjoyment and education, but the reference value is obvious, too." Booklist

The **Portable** Harlem Renaissance reader; edited and with an introduction by David Levering Lewis. Viking 1994 xlvii, 766p pa $18 hardcover o.p. *

Grades: 11 12 Adult   **810.8**
1. American literature—African American authors—Collections 2. Harlem Renaissance
ISBN 0-14-017036-7   LC 93-30233

"General categories include essay, memoir, fiction, poetry, and drama; specific writers include such expected names as Langston Hughes, Zora Neale Hurston, and Claude McKay, but lesser-known names are also represented. There is anger in these pages and also frustration, pride, pain, and elation, but above all there is incredible talent. Reading the collection straight through would be a wonderful education, but most readers will dip in here and there, and that is edifying, too." Booklist

The **Portable** sixties reader; edited by Ann Charters. Penguin Bks. 2003 xli, 628p il pa $16 *

Grades: 11 12 Adult   **810.8**
1. United States—History—1961-1974 2. American literature—Collections
ISBN 0-14-200194-5   LC 2002-32266

This reader includes "essays, poetry, and fiction under thematic subjects, such as civil rights; women's rights; the sexual revolution; environmental issues; the antiwar, free-speech, and black-arts movements; and the use of drugs in pursuit of enlightenment. . . . [Includes works by] James Baldwin, Thomas Merton, Susan Sontag, Gary Snyder, Allen Ginsburg, Rachel Carson, Kate Millett, Nikki Giovanni, and many more." Booklist
Includes bibliographical references

The **Portable** Western reader; edited and with an introduction by William Kittredge. Penguin Bks. 1997 xxi, 600p pa $14.95

Grades: 11 12 Adult   **810.8**
1. American literature—West (U.S.)—Collections
ISBN 0-14-023026-2   LC 96-47243

"Viking portable library"
"Part 1, 'Ancient Stories,' shows the evolution of Native American storytelling from the early legends to contemporary stories and includes writings by Catherine McClellan, John Graves, and Louise Erdrich. Parts 2 and 3 contrast the mythology of the 19th-century 'Western' with the actual experience of living in the West. Most of these authors, from Walt Whitman to Larry McMurtry, will be familiar to readers. Part 4, 'Brilliant Possibilities,' showcases the new generation of Western writers, including Gretel Ehrlich, Jimmy Santiago Baca, and Sherman Alexie." Libr J

Rising voices; writings of young Native Americans; selected by Arlene B. Hirschfelder and Beverly R. Singer. Random House 1993 c1992 131p pa $6.99 *

Grades: 5 6 7 8 9 10   **810.8**
1. American literature—Native American authors—Collections 2. Native Americans 3. Children's writings
ISBN 0-8041-1167-7

First published 1992 by Scribner
A collection of poems and essays in which young Native Americans speak of their identity, their families and communities, rituals, and the harsh realities of their lives.

Shooting the rat; stories and poems by outstanding high school writers; edited by Mark Pawlak and Dick Lourie. Hanging Loose Press 2003 280p hardcover o.p. pa $16 *

Grades: 9 10 11 12   **810.8**
ISBN 1-931236-24-0; 1-931236-23-2 (pa)
                    LC 2003-40748

"The 170 pieces are divided into 5 sections with themes ranging from the writer as observer to poems and stories about family, the transition between childhood and adulthood, and awakening sexuality. Images and language will speak directly to teens, and range from coarse to eloquent. This is a book that may be used in classrooms to introduce poetry or in libraries to celebrate the writing of today's youth." SLJ

Sidman, Joyce, 1956-
The world according to dog; poems and teen voices; with photographs by Doug Mindell. Houghton Mifflin 2003 71p il $15

Grades: 9 10 11 12   **810.8**
1. Dogs 2. Teenagers' writings
ISBN 0-618-17497-4   LC 2002-476

A collection of poems about dogs is accompanied by essays by young people about the dogs in their lives
"The teen essays are heartfelt and honest. . . . Sidman's poetic form is succinct, evoking images, memories, and even smells. . . . Readers of all ages who appreciate their canine companions will thoroughly enjoy this slim book." Voice Youth Advocates

Sister to sister; women write about the unbreakable bond; edited by Patricia Foster. Doubleday 1995 354p hardcover o.p. pa $12.95

Grades: 11 12 Adult   **810.8**
ISBN 0-385-47128-9; 0-385-47129-7 (pa)
                    LC 95-10486

"Contributors to this volume include bell hooks, Robin Behn, Letty Cottin Pogrebin, and Joy Williams. The essays, while all centering on the themes of sisterly relationships, run the literary gamut. Fanciful fiction pieces are included, as are straightforward autobiographical anecdotes and a couple of critical essays. Any library with a demand for contemporary women's literature should have this collection." Libr J

Things I have to tell you; poems and writing by teenage girls; edited by Betsy Franco; photographs by Nina Nickles. Candlewick Press 2001 63p il $15.99; pa $8.99

Grades: 7 8 9 10 **810.8**

1. Teenagers' writings 2. Girls

ISBN 0-7636-0905-6; 0-7636-1035-6 (pa)

LC 99-46884

A collection of poems, stories, and essays written by girls twelve to eighteen years of age and revealing the secrets which enabled them to overcome the challenges they faced

Where we are, what we see; the best young artists and writers in America: a Push anthology; edited by David Levithan. PUSH/Scholastic 2005 220p il pa $7.99

Grades: 7 8 9 10 **810.8**

1. Teenagers' writings

ISBN 0-439-73646-3 LC 2005-296492

The "young writers and artists in this anthology have been selected from the winners of the Scholastic Art & Writing Awards program. The offerings range from an intense recollection, 'What Cancer Meant,' to a whimsical dictionary of words that don't exist but should. . . . This collection is a real boon for budding writers and artists, who will feel the encouragement and see the possibility of publication." Booklist

You hear me? poems and writing by teenage boys; edited by Betsy Franco. Candlewick Press 2000 107p hardcover o.p. pa $6.99

Grades: 7 8 9 10 **810.8**

1. Teenagers' writings 2. Boys

ISBN 0-7636-1158-1; 0-7636-1159-X (pa)

LC 99-57129

This is an "anthology of poems, essays, and stories written by young men aged twelve through twenty." Harv Educ Rev

"The voices range from painfully honest to playfully ironic, but all are controlled and powerful as they speak to subjects that teen readers will be familiar with." Voice Youth Advocates

810.9 American literature--History and criticism

Aberjhani

Encyclopedia of the Harlem Renaissance; {by} Aberjhani and Sandra L. West; foreword by Clement Alexander Price. Facts on File 2003 xxi, 424p il maps $65 *

Grades: 11 12 Adult **810.9**

1. Harlem Renaissance—Encyclopedias 2. American literature—African American authors—Encyclopedias

ISBN 0-8160-4539-9 LC 2002-152067

This work includes essays about personalities, places, literary themes, political and sociological movements, newspapers, and discussions that highlighted the Harlem Renaissance

"An appendix of museums and centers that feature works from the Harlem Renaissance round out this indis-

pensable encyclopedia's 350 entries. An excellent and inspiring work of scholarship." Choice

Includes bibliographical references

African American literary criticism, 1773 to 2000; edited by Hazel Arnett Ervin. Twayne Pubs. 1999 xxix, 543p $50 *

Grades: 11 12 Adult **810.9**

1. American literature—African American authors—History and criticism

ISBN 0-8057-1683-1 LC 99-29491

This resource assembles more than 150 critical statements about African American literature "including public addresses, literary manifestoes, letters, journal entries, reviews, and analytical studies by such authors as W.E.B. Du Bois, Charles Chesnutt, Langston Hughes, Ann Petry, Toni Morrison, Henry Louis Gates, Jr. and many others. Each entry includes a list of sources for further reading." Publisher's note

Includes bibliographical references

African-American voices in young adult literature; tradition, transition, transformation; edited by Karen Patricia Smith. Scarecrow Press 1994 xxxv, 405p pa $50.50 hardcover o.p.

Grades: Professional **810.9**

1. Young adult literature 2. African Americans in literature

ISBN 0-8108-4272-6 LC 94-13800

"Citing a need for professional reading about African-American young adult narratives, the editor of this collection of fourteen original essays has gathered writings which make audible diverse voices within a dynamic literature. . . . The book, anxious to hear from both established and new voices, includes examinations of frequently recognized African-American authors—Virginia Hamilton, Mildred Taylor, and Walter Dean Myers, for instance—as well as writers with growing reputations, such as Angela Johnson." Voice Youth Advocates

Includes bibliographical references

The **American** renaissance; edited and with an introduction by Harold Bloom. Chelsea House 2003 370p (Bloom's period studies) $37.95

Grades: 9 10 11 12 **810.9**

1. American literature—History and criticism 2. United States—Intellectual life

ISBN 0-7910-7676-8 LC 2003-19991

"Ralph Waldo Emerson's transcendental writings influenced Henry David Thoreau and Walt Whitman, whose works are considered cornerstones of the American literary movement. This volume examines the impact of the American Renaissance on the Western canon of literature." Publisher's note

Includes bibliographical references

American women writers, 1900-1945; a bio-bibliographical critical sourcebook; edited by Laurie Champion; Emanuel S. Nelson, advisory editor. Greenwood Press 2000 407p $95

Grades: 11 12 Adult **810.9**

1. American literature—Women authors—Bio-bibliography

ISBN 0-313-30943-4 LC 00-22336

American women writers, 1900-1945—*Continued*
"This reference book profiles 58 American women writers who published their significant works between 1900 and 1945. . . . The information is arranged in four sections: 'Biography,' 'Major Works and Themes,' 'Critical Reception,' and 'Bibliography.' . . . The biographical information is brief and includes the most basic details, while the overview of the major works and themes is quite substantive and will be very useful for research. 'Critical Reception,' considers reactions both at the time of publication and today. . . . This book will be a valuable tool for research because it balances coverage of the prominent and the lesser known." Booklist

Beat culture; lifestyles, icons, and impact; edited by William T. Lawlor. ABC-CLIO 2005 liv, 390p il $85
Grades: 9 10 11 12   **810.9**
1. Beat generation—Encyclopedias
ISBN 1-85109-400-8   LC 2005-2772
"This volume covers the Beat Generation: the musicians, writers, and artists as well as the culture and history." Booklist
This "single-volume work is possibly the best overview of the topic for high school students." SLJ
Includes bibliographical references

The **Beat** generation; a Gale critical companion; Lynn M. Zott, project editor. Gale 2003 3v (Gale critical companion collection) set $350
Grades: 11 12 Adult   **810.9**
1. American literature—History and criticism 2. Beat generation
ISBN 0-7876-7569-5   LC 2002-155786
"Volume 1 gathers a variety of sources that place the movement in cultural context. . . . Volumes 2-3 supply entries for 28 Beat authors. . . . Author entries include a brief biography, notes on major works and critical reception, a list of principal works, a selection of primary sources and secondary criticism, and further readings. . . . The selections include contributions by major Beat Generation scholars and provide a well-balanced, representative view of the Beats." Choice
Includes bibliographical references

Brown, Lois, 1966-
The encyclopedia of the Harlem literary renaissance. Facts on File 2006 612p il map $65; pa $21.95
Grades: 11 12 Adult   **810.9**
1. Harlem Renaissance—Encyclopedias 2. American literature—African American authors—Encyclopedias
ISBN 0-8160-4967-X; 0-8160-6925-5 (pa)
                                              LC 2004-22097
This book features "800 alphabetically arranged articles on writers, their works, periodicals, editors, publishers, critics, and related topics. . . . For a one-volume work on a prescient period of literary history, complete with a map of the Harlem Literary Renaissance, this is the book this reviewer would carry around to see the sights." Choice
Includes bibliographical references

The **Butterfly's** way; voices from the Haitian dyaspora [sic] in the United States; edited by Edwidge Danticat. Soho Press 2001 251p pa $15
Grades: 11 12 Adult   **810.9**
1. American literature—Haitian American authors—Collections
ISBN 1-56947-218-1   LC 00-64085
These "essays and poems talk about the pain and pride of young people who don't belong, both in Haiti and in their places of refuge. A landmark anthology." Booklist

The **Cambridge** history of American literature; general editor, Sacvan Bercovitch; associate editor, Cyrus R.K. Patell. Cambridge Univ. Press 1994-2003 8v set $900
Grades: 11 12 Adult   **810.9**
1. American literature—History and criticism
ISBN 0-521-85760-0   LC 92-42479
Contents: v1 1590-1820 $100, pa $33 (ISBN 0-521-30105-X; 0-521-58571-6); v2 Prose writing 1820-1865 $100 (ISBN 0-521-30106-8); v3 Prose writing, 1860-1920 $140 (ISBN 0-521-30107-6); v4 Nineteenth-century poetry, 1800-1910 $125 (ISBN 0-521-30108-4); v5 Poetry and criticism, 1900-1950 $95 (ISBN 0-521-30109-2); v6 Prose writing, 1910-1950 $95 (ISBN 0-521-49731-0); v7 Prose writing, 1940-1990 $90 (ISBN 0-521-49732-9); v8 Poetry and criticism, 1940-1995 $100 (ISBN 0-521-49733-7)
Scholars contribute essays assessing major authors, movements and trends in the development of American literature

Censored books [I]-II; critical viewpoints; edited by Nicholas J. Karolides, Lee Burress, John M. Kean. Scarecrow Press 1993-2001 2v v1 pa $39.50; v2 $45
Grades: 9 10 11 12   **810.9**
1. American literature—History and criticism 2. Censorship
ISBN 0-8108-4038-3 (v1); 0-8108-4147-9 (v2)
Volume two covering 1985-2000 edited by Nicholas J. Karolides
Authors, librarians, and teachers contribute essays in support of books that are frequently challenged. They examine each work as literature and assess its content relative to societal values

The **Chronology** of American literature; America's literary achievements from the colonial era to modern times; edited by Daniel S. Burt. Houghton Mifflin 2004 805p il $40 *
Grades: 11 12 Adult   **810.9**
1. American literature—Collections
ISBN 0-618-16821-4   LC 2003-51142
"This chronology includes more than 8,400 literary works by more than 5,000 writers. Sections for each year are grouped in five chapters by period, from 1582 to 1999. Within each year, entries are grouped by genre, such as diaries and other personal writings, fiction, essays, literary criticism and scholarship, nonfiction, poetry, and drama. Within each genre, authors are listed alphabetically, generally with birth and death dates and short

The Chronology of American literature—*Continued*

descriptions of named works for the year. . . . *The Chronology of American Literature* is easy to browse and, for book lovers, difficult to put down." Booklist

Includes bibliographical references

Davis, Cynthia J., 1964-
Women writers in the United States; a timeline of literary, cultural, and social history; {by} Cynthia Davis and Kathryn West. Oxford Univ. Press 1996 488p $60 *

Grades: 11 12 Adult   **810.9**
1. American literature—Women authors 2. Women—United States
ISBN 0-19-509053-5   LC 95-31815

In a timeline format, the authors "present information on the full spectrum of women's writing—including fiction, poetry, biography, political manifestos, essays, advice columns, and cookbooks, alongside a chronology of developments in social and cultural history that are especially pertinent to women's lives." Publisher's note

Drew, Bernard A. (Bernard Alger), 1950-
100 more popular young adult authors; biographical sketches and bibliographies. Libraries Unlimited 2002 379p il (Popular authors series) $65

Grades: 7 8 9 10 11 12   **810.9**
1. Young adult literature—Bio-bibliography
ISBN 1-56308-920-3   LC 2002-12170

Sequel to The 100 most popular young adult authors

A ready reference for teenagers who seek information about well-known writers, either for school work, out of curiosity, to find more books by a favorite author, or to learn about the writing process.

The 100 most popular young adult authors;
biographical sketches and bibliographies. rev. Libraries Unlimited 1997 xxviii, 531p $58

Grades: 7 8 9 10 11 12   **810.9**
1. Young adult literature—Bio-bibliography
ISBN 1-56308-615-8   LC 97-25882

First published 1996

A "tool for brief biographical information about authors writing books from upper elementary to adult levels which are of interest to young adults. Coverage is of mostly contemporary American authors, but other nationalities and classic writers are included as well. Arranged alphabetically, each entry gives biographical data, the types of books written and some critical analysis. Lists for further reading are appended." Safford. Guide to Ref Materials for Sch Libr Media Cent. 5th edition

Includes bibliographical references

Followed by 100 more popular young adult authors

Encyclopedia of American war literature; edited by Philip K. Jason and Mark A. Graves. Greenwood Press 2001 424p $95

Grades: 11 12 Adult   **810.9**
1. American literature—Encyclopedias 2. War in literature
ISBN 0-313-30648-6   LC 00-42225

The "284 entries provide brief biographical and literary information about writers. . . . The editors focus on fiction rather than historical or nonfictional works. Besides biographical entries, arranged in alphabetical order, the editors include topical entries that provide overviews of particular wars and literary genres. Entries include all wars in which Americans have participated." Choice

The Greenwood encyclopedia of African American literature; edited by Hans Ostrom and J. David Macey, Jr. Greenwood Press 2005 5v il set $499.95 *

Grades: 11 12 Adult   **810.9**
1. American literature—African American authors—Encyclopedias
ISBN 0-313-32972-9   LC 2005-13679

This "set provides coverage of the foundations, development, and proliferation of African American literature, from Colonial times to the present. . . . The depth and breadth of the 1,029 entries make this an invaluable resource." Choice

Includes bibliographical references

The Greenwood encyclopedia of multiethnic American literature. Greenwood Press 2005 5v il set $499.95 *

Grades: 11 12 Adult   **810.9**
1. American literature—Encyclopedias 2. Minorities—Encyclopedias
ISBN 0-313-33059-X   LC 2005-18960

This encyclopedia contains "more than 1100 entries, approximately 1000 of them devoted to individual authors. The remaining entries describe relevant literary topics (e.g., The Blues, Tricksters), key literary works (e.g., The Bluest Eye, Tracks), and other relevant topics (e.g., Holocaust narratives)." Libr J

"A comprehensive set unique in its scope, this encyclopedia is an excellent foundational resource that adds much to the growing field of ethnic American literature." Choice

Includes bibliographical references

The Harlem Renaissance; edited and with an introduction by Harold Bloom. Chelsea House 2003 336p (Bloom's period studies) $37.95

Grades: 9 10 11 12   **810.9**
1. American literature—African American authors—History and criticism 2. Harlem Renaissance
ISBN 0-7910-7679-2   LC 2003-16873

"This volume examines the defining themes and style of African-American literature during . . . [the Harlem Renaissance] which laid the groundwork for contemporary African-American writers." Publisher's note

Includes bibliographical references

The Harlem Renaissance: a Gale critical companion; foreword by Trudier Harris-Lopez; Janet Witalec, project editor. Gale Res. 2003 3v il (Gale critical companion collection) set $325

Grades: 11 12 Adult   **810.9**
1. Harlem Renaissance
ISBN 0-7876-6618-1   LC 2002-10076

Contents: v1 Topics; v2 Authors A-H; v3 Authors I-Z

The Harlem Renaissance: a Gale critical companion—*Continued*

"Volume 1 focuses on five topic areas, starting with an overview and background information, then moving on to chapters on social, economic, and political factors; publishing and periodicals; performing arts; and the visual arts. . . . Volumes 2 and 3 are devoted to writers. Eleven female and twenty-two male authors are discussed, among them Arna Bontemps, Marcus Garvey, Angelina Weld Grimké, James Weldon Johnson, and Dorothy West. . . . Most author entries include biographical profiles, lists of principal works, some primary source material, critical essays, and further reading lists. . . . The breadth and depth of *Harlem Renaissance* make it a valuable and unique reference source for academic, public, and high-school libraries." Booklist

Hill, Laban Carrick

Harlem stomp! a cultural history of the Harlem Renaissance. Little, Brown 2004 151p il $18.95 *

Grades: 7 8 9 10   **810.9**

1. Harlem Renaissance 2. African Americans—Intellectual life

ISBN 0-316-81411-3   LC 2002-73067

"This is an account of cultural and intellectual life in Harlem during the first half of the 20th century." Bull Cent Child Books

"The vibrancy, energy, and color of the Harlem Renaissance come to life in this gem of a book packed with poetry, prose, song lyrics, art, and photography created by some of the period's most influential figures. . . . Informative and highly entertaining, it deserves to be shelved in any library." Voice Youth Advocates

Includes bibliographical references

Johnson, Claudia D.

Labor and workplace issues in literature; [by] Claudia Durst Johnson. Greenwood Press 2006 183p (Exploring social issues through literature) $49.95

Grades: 9 10 11 12   **810.9**

1. Fiction—History and criticism 2. Work in literature

ISBN 0-313-33286-X   LC 2005-25974

"Each chapter examines the historical background and plot of the work, and discusses the labor and workplace issues raised by the author. It then overviews the history of these issues since the publication of the work and relates the literary text to modern concerns. The volume discusses such issues as low wages, long hours, workplace dangers, unemployment, sexual harassment, lack of job security or medical care, and the struggle of immigrants." Publisher's note

Includes bibliographical references

Magill's survey of American literature; edited by Steven G. Kellman. Rev. ed. Salem Press 2007 6v il set $499

Grades: 11 12 Adult   **810.9**

1. Literature—History and criticism 2. Literature—Bio-bibliography

ISBN 978-1-58765-285-1; 1-58765-285-4

LC 2006-16503

First published 1992 with two volume supplement published 1996 under the editorship of Frank Northen Magill

"Examining selected works of 339 U.S. and Canadian writers, from Anne Bradstreet and Benjamin Franklin to Edward Bloor and Octavia E. Butler, this clearly written resource provides sturdy support for assignments, and will also be popular with discussion groups and with general readers of literature." SLJ

Includes bibliographical references

Modern American women writers; edited by Elaine Showalter, Lea Baechler, and A. Walton Litz. Collier Bks. 1993 416p pa $15

Grades: 11 12 Adult   **810.9**

1. American literature—History and criticism 2. Women authors

ISBN 0-02-082025-9   LC 93-22193

First published 1991 by Scribner

"This work focuses on 41 representative American women who have published since 1870. Among those included are Anne Tyler, Alice Walker, and Emily Dickinson. The essays, ranging from 8 to 22 pages, emphasize the social and historical environment in which each wrote." Nichols. Guide to Ref Books for Sch Media Cent. 4th edition

Molin, Paulette Fairbanks

American Indian themes in young adult literature; [by] Paulette F. Molin. Scarecrow Press 2005 183p (Scarecrow studies in young adult literature) $40

Grades: Professional   **810.9**

1. Native Americans in literature 2. Young adult literature—History and criticism

ISBN 0-8108-5081-8   LC 2004-26420

"Eight essays survey literature, mostly published in the past 10 years, with American Indian themes, and written for an audience that includes a wide range of Young Adults—approximately 11 to 18-year-olds." SLJ

This "is a useful reference work, especially for the readers she targets—teachers, librarians, and even publishers and editors of young adult literature—and it provides the most complete bibliography of the genre in print." Amer Indian Culture and Research Journal

Includes bibliographical references

New immigrant literatures in the United States; a sourcebook to our multicultural literary heritage; edited by Alpana Sharma Knippling; Emmanuel S. Nelson, advisory editor. Greenwood Press 1996 386p $90

Grades: 11 12 Adult   **810.9**

1. American literature—History and criticism 2. Minorities in literature 3. Immigrants in literature

ISBN 0-313-28968-9   LC 95-45211

"Knippling offers a critical overview of post-WW II literature written by new immigrants to the U.S. The author excludes Native Americans and African Americans, but marginalized literatures of Asian, Caribbean, and Mexican origins have been included. A blend of reference and critical interpretation, the sourcebook's chapters focus on writing in English. Twenty-two contributors of diverse background and expertise describe skillfully the origin, nature, and literary traditions of the new immigrants covered in the text." Choice

Nineteenth-century American women writers; a bio-bibliographical critical sourcebook; edited by Denise D. Knight; Emmanuel S. Nelson, advisory editor. Greenwood Press 1997 534p $110

Grades: 11 12 Adult **810.9**

1. American literature—Women authors—Bio-bibliography

ISBN 0-313-29713-4   LC 96-35351

This volume "contains entries for 77 writers whose inclusion was determined by the fact that their best-known works were published during the nineteenth century. . . . Designed as a primary reference guide for researchers, the book includes fiction writers, poets, autobiographers, essayists, and abolitionists." Booklist

Phillips, Jerry

Romanticism and transcendentalism: 1800-1860; Jerry Phillips, Andrew Ladd, principal authors; Jerry Phillips, general editor; Michael Anesko, adviser and contributor. Facts on File 2005 96p il (Backgrounds to American literature) $30

Grades: 9 10 11 12   **810.9**

1. American literature—History and criticism 2. Romanticism 3. Transcendentalism

ISBN 0-8160-5668-4   LC 2005-21490

"This book focuses on American Romantic literature and transcendentalism. In addition to discussions of those two movements, the book also addresses the historical and philosophical foundations of Romantic thought; the impact of social reform movements, such as the abolitionists, on literature; and the emergence of uniquely American poets, specifically Emily Dickinson and Walt Whitman." Booklist

Includes bibliographical references

Slave narratives; James Tackach, book editor. Greenhaven Press 2001 190p il (Greenhaven Press companion to literary movements and genres) lib bdg $32.45; pa $19.95

Grades: 9 10 11 12   **810.9**

1. American prose literature—African American authors 2. Slavery—United States

ISBN 0-7377-0550-7 (lib bdg); 0-7377-0549-3 (pa)
          LC 00-37577

Critical essays explore works by Frederick Douglass, Harriet Jacobs, Nat Turner, and others

Includes bibliographical references

U.S. Latino literature; a critical guide for students and teachers; edited by Harold Augenbraum and Margarite Fernández Olmos under the auspices of the Mercantile Library of New York. Greenwood Press 2000 215p $49.95

Grades: 9 10 11 12   **810.9**

1. American literature—Hispanic American authors—History and criticism 2. Hispanic Americans in literature

ISBN 0-313-31137-4   LC 99-462065

Among the works discussed in these eighteen essays are Rudolfo A. Anaya's Bless me, Ultima, Richard Rodriguez's Hunger of memory, Sandra Cisneros' The house on Mango Street, and Julia Alvarez's How the Garcia girls lost their accents

"The critical essays begin with a brief biography of the author and then center on an analysis of the work's themes and forms. The essays also include ideas for teaching the work and suggestions for further reading. . . . An excellent addition to the professional shelf as well as literary criticism collections." Book Rep

Wilson, Charles E., 1961-

Race and racism in literature; [by] Charles E. Wilson, Jr. Greenwood Press 2005 154p (Exploring social issues through literature) $49.95 *

Grades: 9 10 11 12   **810.9**

1. American literature—History and criticism 2. Race in literature

ISBN 0-313-32820-X; 978-0-313-32820-6
          LC 2005-1494

"The novels discussed here were chosen to represent various racial and ethnic identities (e.g., black, Asian, Hispanic, Jewish, Italian, Native American). Each novel . . . is summarized, discussed in terms of its historical and social significance, and then discussed again as a work of literature. . . . [The author] is to be commended for drawing together a dozen novels that focus on race, and treating these works in a thoughtful and focused way." Am Ref Books Annu, 2006

Includes bibliographical references

811 American poetry

Alvarez, Julia, 1950-

The woman I kept to myself; poems. Algonquin Books of Chapel Hill 2004 155p $17.95

Grades: 11 12 Adult   **811**

ISBN 1-56512-406-5   LC 2003-70807

This "collection of 75 poems is divided into three sections, and each poem has three stanzas, exactly . . . The poet, who is from the Dominican Republic, writes about being raised with her sisters in New York. The subjects are personal—love, marriage, rejection, divorce, death, religion—but also universal. . . . Teens approaching adulthood will appreciate the poet who turned to 'paper solitude' and through many drafts discovered 'the woman I kept to myself.'" SLJ

Angelou, Maya

The complete collected poems of Maya Angelou. Random House 1994 273p $24.95 *

Grades: 11 12 Adult   **811**

ISBN 0-679-42895-X   LC 94-14501

This volume contains all of Angelou's published poems including her inaugural poem On the pulse of morning

Appelt, Kathi, 1954-

Poems from homeroom; a writer's place to start. Holt & Co. 2002 114p $16.95

Grades: 7 8 9 10   **811**

1. Poetics

ISBN 0-8050-6978-X   LC 2002-67886

Appelt, Kathi, 1954-—Continued

A collection of poems about the experiences of young people and a section with information about how each poem was written to enable readers to create their own original poems.

Appelt's "poems are at times sensual, dramatic, or violent, and always rhythmic. They are fascinating, smooth, and 'with it.' " SLJ

Includes bibliographical references

Benét, Stephen Vincent, 1898-1943

John Brown's body; [by] Stephen Vincent Benét. I.R. Dee 1990 c1928 336p pa $11.95

Grades: 11 12 Adult   **811**

1. Brown, John, 1800-1859—Poetry 2. United States—History—1861-1865, Civil War—Poetry 3. United States—History—Poetry

ISBN 0-929587-26-X   LC 89-25707

Awarded the Pulitzer Prize, 1929

First published 1928 by Doubleday, Doran

"First Elephant paperback edition" Verso of title page

"A narrative of the Civil War, it opens with a prelude on the introduction of slavery, which is followed by a description of John Brown and his raid on Harpers Ferry. The poem, which considers both sides of the conflict with sympathy, includes sketches of famous participants, battles, the hardships of those on the home front, etc." Reader's Ency. 4th edition

Bishop, Elizabeth, 1911-1979

The complete poems, 1927-1979. Farrar, Straus & Giroux 1983 287p pa $15 hardcover o.p.

Grades: 11 12 Adult   **811**

ISBN 0-374-51817-3   LC 82-21119

Supersedes the author's Complete poems, published 1969

This volume contains poems from four collections: North & South (1946); A cold spring (1955, winner of Pulitzer prize); Questions of travel (1965); and Geography III (1977). Also included are translations, uncollected poems, and sections entitled "Poems written in youth" and "Occasional poems"

Bishop's "reputation is founded on perhaps 25 poems. . . . Altogether that looks like a modest achievement until one considers that most of the larger poetic reputations of the past century have been founded on similar evidence. The difference is that Bishop's masterpieces stand in a higher ratio to her work as a whole." N Y Times Book Rev

Brooks, Gwendolyn

In Montgomery, and other poems. Third World Press 2003 146p $22.95

Grades: 11 12 Adult   **811**

ISBN 0-88378-232-4   LC 2003-50749

This is a "posthumous collection consisting primarily of dramatic monologues in a stunning variety of voices, from those of urban children to Winnie Mandela's. Reading the title sequence resembles randomly tuning a radio dial to listen to the diverse voices of Montgomery, Alabama, a city of 'leaning and lostness, glazed paralysis.' . . . Especially moving are the children's monologues. . . . Brooks captures the fierce purity of these children's needs and desires. Her loving witness never sounded more clearly than in these late poems." Booklist

Selected poems. Harper & Row 1963 127p pa $12.95 hardcover o.p. *

Grades: 11 12 Adult   **811**

ISBN 0-06-088296-4   LC 63-16503

"The subject of this poetry is the lives of African American residents of Northern urban ghettos, particularly women, and Brooks has been praised for her depiction of that experience in forms ranging from terza rima to blues meter." Benet's Reader's Ency of Am Lit

Cummings, E. E. (Edward Estlin), 1894-1962

Complete poems, 1904-1962; containing all the published poetry; edited by George J. Firmage. rev corr & expanded ed. Norton 1994 xxxii, 1102p $50 *

Grades: 9 10 11 12   **811**

ISBN 0-87140-152-5   LC 91-29158

Expanded version of Complete poems, 1913-1962 (1972)

"This volume has been prepared directly from the poet's original manuscripts, preserving the original typography and format. It includes all the previously published works, from *Tulips* (1922) to *Etcetera* (1983), as well as 36 uncollected poems that originally appeared in little magazines or anthologies." Libr J

Love; selected poems; art by Christopher Myers. Hyperion Books for Children 2005 unp il $16.99

Grades: 9 10 11 12   **811**

ISBN 0-7868-0796-2; 978-0-7868-0796-3

"Jump at the sun"

"In this astonishing picture book about sensual love, Myers . . . combines evocative photographs of people and paintings to create collages that match the startling imagery in cummings's poems." Publ Wkly

Dickey, James

The whole motion; collected poems, 1949-1992. Wesleyan Univ. Press 1992 477p (Wesleyan poetry) pa $27.95 hardcover o.p.

Grades: 11 12 Adult   **811**

ISBN 0-8195-1218-4   LC 91-50811

"A definitive retrospective of an American poet known for his experimental and probing approach. . . . This robust collection embraces more than 200 poems from over a dozen books, including his first, *Into the Stone,* to *Buckdancer's Choice,* winner of the 1966 National Book Award, his latest monograph, *The Eagle's Mile* (Wesleyan Univ., 1990), as well as a set of previously uncollected or unpublished works." Booklist

Dickinson, Emily, 1830-1886

The complete poems of Emily Dickinson; edited by Thomas H. Johnson. Little, Brown 1960 770p $35; pa $19.95 *

Grades: 11 12 Adult   **811**

ISBN 0-316-18414-4; 0-316-18413-6 (pa)

A chronological arrangement of all known Dickinson poems and fragments

Dickinson, Emily, 1830-1886—*Continued*

Final harvest; Emily Dickinson's poems; selection and introduction by Thomas H. Johnson. Little, Brown 1961 331p pa $14.99 hardcover o.p.

Grades: 11 12 Adult **811**

ISBN 0-316-18415-2

A selection of 575 poems from: The complete poems of Emily Dickinson. The editor's aim has been to allow the reader to realize the full scope and diversity of the poet's work

New poems of Emily Dickinson; edited by William H. Shurr with Anna Dunlap & Emily Grey Shurr. University of N.C. Press 1993 125p hardcover o.p. pa $13.95

Grades: 11 12 Adult **811**

ISBN 0-8078-2115-2; 0-8078-4416-0 (pa)

LC 93-20353

This volume increases Dickinson's "body of work by 498 selections. Shurr has accomplished this by combining three volumes of the poet's letters and identifying epigrams, riddles, and various longer lyrical pieces within the prose. These will both challenge and delight serious readers, for wit, unusual rhythms, and musical rhymes predominate." SLJ

Includes bibliographical references

The selected poems of Emily Dickinson. Modern Lib. 1996 295p hardcover o.p. pa $9.95 *

Grades: 11 12 Adult **811**

ISBN 0-679-60201-1; 0-679-78335-0 (pa)

This "edition presents the more than four hundred poems that were published between Dickinson's death and 1900. They express her concepts of life and death, of love and nature, and of what Henry James called 'the landscape of the soul.'" Publisher's note

Dillard, Annie

Mornings like this; found poems. HarperCollins Pubs. 1995 75p pa $12.95 hardcover o.p.

Grades: 11 12 Adult **811**

ISBN 0-06-092725-9 LC 95-8675

"What Dillard has done is construct poems out of 'bits of broken text'; that is, she's lifted sentences and used them to create original poems on her own themes. So these are language collages, meticulous and surprisingly effective. Dillard found gems embedded in such unlikely and obscure sources as a boys' project manual, nineteenth-century scientific texts, and memoirs, and she has turned them into poems of wonderful resonance, some very moving, others quite funny." Booklist

Dove, Rita

American smooth; poems. W.W. Norton 2004 143p $22.95; pa $13.95

Grades: 11 12 Adult **811**

ISBN 0-393-05987-1; 0-393-32744-2 (pa)

LC 2004-11793

"In these free-verse poems, Dove speaks from her own perspective—as well as from that of biblical characters, black soldiers from World War I, a ten-year-old girl from Harlem, several musicians, and a pair of dancers.

The selections work by lists, line breaks where ideas collide, and a juxtaposition of voices. Then using razor-sharp metaphors, Dove goes for the jugular and usually finds it. Although the book's sense of audience seems inconsistent, with some poems suitable for *A Child's Garden of Verses* and others for *The Kama Sutra*, the poems are evocative." Libr J

Mother love; poems. Norton 1995 77p $17.95; pa $11

Grades: 11 12 Adult **811**

ISBN 0-393-03808-4; 0-393-31444-8 (pa)

LC 95-5394

"Most poems included here are autobiographical. Dove writes of childhood bullies, rock songs crooned in the driveway, and, in the long poem, 'Persephone in Hell,' a stay in Paris over 20 years ago. Her language is simple and clear." Libr J

On the bus with Rosa Parks; poems. Norton 1999 95p pa $12.95 hardcover o.p.

Grades: 11 12 Adult **811**

ISBN 0-393-32026-X LC 98-45057

Dove's "poems effortlessly suggest grand narratives and American myths, yet ground themselves tersely in localities, characters, practicalities and particulars. This seventh collection leads off with a Dove specialty, the historical sequence: her 'Cameos' lend broad, social relevance to an intermittently abandoned Depression-era wife and her family." Publ Wkly

Selected poems. Vintage Bks. 1993 xxvi, 210p pa $13 *

Grades: 11 12 Adult **811**

ISBN 0-679-75080-0 LC 93-26112

"This volume places three previous collections under one cover. . . . The selection begins with *The Yellow House on the Corner*, Dove's first book, most notable for its poems derived from slave narratives. *Museum*, her second book, offers a potpourri of work that ranges over several continents and many millenia; Dove's tirelessly exact language illuminates the lives of saints, contemporary lifestyles, and Greek myths." Booklist

Eliot, T. S. (Thomas Stearns), 1888-1965

Collected poems, 1909-1962. Harcourt Brace Jovanovich 1963 221p $23 *

Grades: 11 12 Adult **811**

ISBN 0-15-118978-1

This volume contains the complete text of 'Collected poems, 1909-1935,' the 'Four quartets,' and several other poems accompanied by brief prefatory notes

The waste land, and other poems. Harcourt Brace Jovanovich 1955 c1934 88p pa $8 *

Grades: 9 10 11 12 **811**

ISBN 0-15-694877-X

Also available in paperback from Penguin Bks.

"A Harvest book"

In addition to Eliot's long poem of despair this volume contains a representative selection of his best known shorter works

Emerson, Ralph Waldo, 1803-1882

Collected poems & translations. Library of Am.
1994 637p $35 *

Grades: 11 12 Adult **811**
1. Dante Alighieri, 1265-1321. The new life
ISBN 0-940450-28-3 LC 93-40245

Contains Emerson's published poetry, plus selections of his unpublished poetry from journals and notebooks, and some of his translations of poetry from other languages, notably Dante's La vita nuova

Fairchild, B. H. (Bertram H.), 1942-

Early occult memory systems of the Lower Midwest. Norton 2002 125p $22.95; pa $14.95

Grades: 11 12 Adult **811**
ISBN 0-393-05096-3; 0-393-32566-0 (pa)
LC 2002-71886

This poetry "collection journeys through the intersections of imagination and history across the plains of the Midwest." Publisher's note

This is a "strong, compelling collection. . . . If strong emotion courses through Fairchild's work, it never makes it lachrymose, thanks to concrete vocabulary and images, direct syntax, and propulsive rhythms." Booklist

Ferlinghetti, Lawrence

How to paint sunlight; lyric poems & others (1997-2000). New Directions 2001 94p $19.95; pa $13.95

Grades: 11 12 Adult **811**
ISBN 0-8112-1463-X; 0-8112-1463-X (pa)
LC 00-67860

"A late-career miscellany divided into four sections, this . . . collection draws some of life's great polarities—light and dark, tragedy and comedy, ecstasy and despair—into the quotidian whorl of this beloved West Coast-transplant poet." Publ Wkly

These are my rivers; new & selected poems, 1955-1993. New Directions 1993 308p il pa $13.95 hardcover o.p. *

Grades: 11 12 Adult **811**
ISBN 0-8112-1273-4 LC 93-10383

"Reading this hefty selection from 12 previous volumes, plus 50 pages of new poems, we realize how accurately the poet described himself in 1979: a man who 'thinks he's Dylan Thomas and Bob Dylan rolled together with Charlie Chaplin thrown in.' . . . His style is recognizable throughout—phlegmatic poems running several pages, often lacking stanza breaks, with short lines at the left margin or moving across the page as hand follows eye." Libr J

Frost, Robert, 1874-1963

The poetry of Robert Frost; edited by Edward Connery Lathem. Holt & Co. 1969 607p hardcover o.p. pa $18 *

Grades: 11 12 Adult **811**
ISBN 0-8050-0502-1; 0-8050-6986-0 (pa)

"A one-volume edition of Frost's eleven volumes of poetry and two short blank-verse plays. The collection

ranges in time from A Boy's Will (1913) to In the Clearing (1962). . . . {There is} an appendix of bibliographical and textual notes for each of the poems." Nation

Gibran, Kahlil, 1883-1931

The Prophet. Knopf 1923 107p il $15 *

Grades: 11 12 Adult **811**
ISBN 0-394-40428-9

Also available pocket library editions

A collection of poems by the mystical writer/artist, who was born in Lebanon and died in the United States, in which the prophet Almustafa deals with fundamental aspects of human life such as love, friendship, good and evil, self-knowledge, passion and reason, joy and sorrow, freedom, work, marriage and children, prayer and death

Ginsberg, Allen, 1926-1997

Collected poems, 1947-1997. HarperCollins Publishers 2006 xx, 1189p il $39.95

Grades: 11 12 Adult **811**
ISBN 978-0-06-113974-1; 0-06-113974-2
LC 2006-41191

First published 1984 with title: Collected poems, 1947-1980

This books "reprints the complete text of 1984's Collected Poems 1947-1980, along with the collections that followed: White Shroud, Cosmopolitan Greetings, and Death and Fame, including the original book attributes of each collection. A poet of extremes at times too trusting of his instincts, Ginsberg could be playful, angry, strident, obscene, graceful, and hilarious in the space of a page, and by now his readers know they are likely to encounter as many embarrassing poems as enlightening ones. Still, this compendium provides the most complete edition of Ginsberg available." Libr J

Cosmopolitan greetings: poems, 1986-1992. HarperCollins Pubs. 1994 118p pa $15 hardcover o.p.

Grades: 11 12 Adult **811**
ISBN 0-06-092623-6 (pa) LC 93-43627

This collection is "suffused with a range of emotional colors that gives Ginsberg's work an added depth, a restless energy and ultimately an elegiac tone. Writing from China, Warsaw, Nicaragua and New York City, the poet makes strong statements on two of his favorite subjects, politics . . . and sexuality." Publ Wkly

Giovanni, Nikki

Blues; for all the changes: new poems. Morrow 1999 100p $15

Grades: 11 12 Adult **811**
ISBN 0-688-15698-3 LC 98-50996

"Giovanni never loses sight of the people in her work. In poems built with broken lines and paragraphs of prose, she spars with the ills that confront us, but every struggle has a human face." Libr J

Quilting the black-eyed pea; poems and not quite poems. William Morrow 2002 110p $16.95

Grades: 11 12 Adult **811**
ISBN 0-06-009952-6 LC 2002-66025

Giovanni, Nikki—*Continued*

"Arranged in six untitled sections whose themes are not self-evident, the poems take an artifact from life and examine its cultural impact." VOYA

Giovanni "entwines the political and the personal and celebrates womanhood and black society and culture. Hers is an embracing, uplifting, and sustaining voice, one given to both anger and humor." Booklist

The selected poems of Nikki Giovanni (1968-1995). Morrow 1996 224p $22 *

Grades: 11 12 Adult   811
    ISBN 0-688-14047-5   LC 95-31646

"Writing as an African American and as a woman, Giovanni speaks with powerful music about politics, love, feminism, and family." Booklist

Haas, Jessie

Hoofprints: horse poems. Greenwillow Books 2004 208p $15.99; lib bdg $16.89

Grades: 9 10 11 12   811
    1. Horses—Poetry
    ISBN 0-06-053406-0; 0-06-053407-9 (lib bdg)
    LC 2003-49066

A collection of more than one hundred poems celebrating horses, from ancient times to the present

"Haas's poetic talent is apparent in her deft use of rhymes and rhythms, descriptive narrative verse, occasional touches of humor, and subtle inferences. Her poems display cleverness and, often, spare, vividly descriptive, well-turned phrases." SLJ

Includes glossary and bibliographical references

Harjo, Joy, 1951-

The woman who fell from the sky; poems. Norton 1994 69p pa $12.95 hardcover o.p.

Grades: 11 12 Adult   811
    ISBN 0-393-31362-X (pa)   LC 96-23014

"Harjo sets 25 prayer-like prose poems in a spooky land of myth . . . depicting an ongoing moral 'war' between forces of creation (northern lights, wolves) vs. destruction (alcoholism, Vietnam). Like contemporary Jobs, the people in these pieces search for an intelligible response to 'the wreck of culture,' their efforts symbolizing the impact of alienation on the psyche." Libr J

Hemphill, Stephanie

Your own, Sylvia; a verse portrait of Sylvia Plath. Alfred A. Knopf 2007 261p $15.99; lib bdg $18.99

Grades: 8 9 10 11 12   811
    1. Plath, Sylvia—Poetry
    ISBN 978-0-375-83799-9; 978-0-375-93799-6 (lib bdg)   LC 2006-07253

The author interprets the people, events, influences and art that made up the brief life of Sylvia Plath.

"Hemphill's verse, like Plath's, is completely compelling: every word, every line, worth reading." Horn Book

Includes bibliographical references

Hughes, Langston, 1902-1967

The collected poems of Langston Hughes; Arnold Rampersad, editor; David Roessel, associate editor. Knopf 1994 708p $39.95; pa $18 *

Grades: 11 12 Adult   811
    ISBN 0-679-42631-0; 0-679-76408-9 (pa)
    LC 94-14509

"The editors have attempted to collect every poem (860 in all) published by the writer in his lifetime, and have also provided a brief but informative introduction, a detailed chronology and extensive textual notes that include the original date and place of publication for each poem. . . . Although Hughes is best known for his poems celebrating African American life, he was also a passionately political poet." Publ Wkly

Poems; selected and edited by David Roessel. Knopf 1999 252p $12.50

Grades: 11 12 Adult   811
    1. African Americans—Poetry
    ISBN 0-375-40551-8   LC 98-55136

The editor presents a representative selection of poetry by the prominent African American writer

Jarrell, Randall, 1914-1965

The complete poems. Farrar, Straus & Giroux 1969 507p pa $22 hardcover o.p. *

Grades: 11 12 Adult   811
    ISBN 0-374-51305-8 (pa)

Collected here are the entire contents of three published volumes Selected poems (1955), The woman at the Washington Zoo (1960), and The Lost World (1965) plus poems published from 1934 to 1964 but never collected and some never before published

Johnson, James Weldon, 1871-1938

Complete poems; edited with an introduction by Sondra Kathryn Wilson. Penguin Bks. 2000 xxxiii, 202p pa $14 *

Grades: 11 12 Adult   811
    1. African Americans—Poetry
    ISBN 0-14-118545-7   LC 00-39969

This volume contains Fifty years and other poems (1917), God's trombones (1927), Saint Peter relates an incident of the resurrection day (1935), and a number of previously unpublished poems. The editor's introduction considers Johnson's achievements and influence

Includes bibliographical references

Kerouac, Jack, 1922-1969

Pomes all sizes; introduction by Allen Ginsberg. City Lights Bks. 1992 175p pa $13.95 *

Grades: 11 12 Adult   811
    ISBN 0-87286-269-0   LC 92-1204

"This book, which Kerouac prepared for publication before his death in 1969, collects poems written between 1954 and 1965. Most are playful—comments about friends, variations on the sounds of words. Yet a few extremely sensitive longer pieces appear, including 'Caritas,' in which the poet runs after a barefoot beggar

Kerouac, Jack, 1922-1969—*Continued*
boy to give him money for shoes and then begins to
doubt the boy's veracity. Other intriguing poems reflect
the poet's religious concerns of the moment, running the
gamut of Eastern and Western religions." Libr J

Kunitz, Stanley, 1905-2006
The collected poems. Norton 2000 285p $27.95;
pa $15.95
Grades: 11 12 Adult   **811**
  ISBN 0-393-05030-0; 0-393-32294-7 (pa)
                                    LC 00-41130
In this volume "Kunitz brings together his entire oeu-
vre, including many unavailable early works and poems
from the recent *Passing Through*." Libr J
"What makes this collection of a lifetime's work so
valuable is the way it allows us to perceive the
interconnectedness of all Kunitz has written. Each poem
stands alone, but each also enriches the others." N Y
Times Book Rev
Includes bibliographical references

Le Guin, Ursula K., 1929-
Sixty odd; new poems. Shambhala Publs. 1999
98p pa $14
Grades: 11 12 Adult   **811**
  ISBN 1-57062-388-0   LC 98-37084
"A veritable collage of verse, capturing short literary
snapshots of real and imagined people, places, animals,
and events. . . . Writing with passion, wit, and vision,
Le Guin gives readers sharp, vivid imagery stimulating
all the senses." SLJ

Levertov, Denise, 1923-1997
Sands of the well. New Directions 1996 136p pa
$9.95 hardcover o.p.
Grades: 11 12 Adult   **811**
  ISBN 0-8112-1361-7 (pa)   LC 96-4324
"The outstanding sections in Levertov's eighteenth
collection are 'Sojourns in the Parallel World' and 'Close
to a Lake,' which contain, respectively, poems about nature and religious poems. . . . In other sections are poems about music, spring, memory, and political protest;
all are technically marvelous, for Levertov remains the
best free verse poet writing in English" Booklist

This great unknowing; last poems; with a note
on the text by Paul A. Lacey. New Directions
1999 68p pa $9.95 hardcover o.p.
Grades: 11 12 Adult   **811**
  ISBN 0-8112-1458-3 (pa)   LC 98-51469
"At once as intimate as Creeley and as visionary as
Duncan—two Black Mountain poets with whom she is
often associated—Levertov has always written a poetry
that ranges from the specifically personal to the search-
ingly mystical. Yet Levertov, from the mid-'60s until her
death in 1997, has been one of the few writers of her
generation to show that one need not mimic the oracular
qualities of the Beats to make a sociopolitical poetry."
Publ Wkly

Lewis, J. Patrick
Black cat bone; [by] J. Patrick Lewis;
illustrations by Gary Kelley. Creative Editions
2006 48p il $19.95 *
Grades: 6 7 8 9 10   **811**
  1. Johnson, Robert, 1911-1938—Poetry 2. African
American musicians—Poetry 3. Blues music—Poetry
4. Mississippi—Poetry
  ISBN 978-1-56846-194-6   LC 2005052298
"Robert Johnson, the celebrated blues musician, is said
to have sold his soul to the devil for his skills on the
guitar. . . . Lewis's verse echoes Johnson's music. . . .
A single line of text parades ghostlike across the bottom
of each page, explaining the aspect of the man's life that
the poem sings of, and becoming a cumulative mini-bio
in itself. A couple of Johnson's own lyrics appear with
the sequence of Lewis's poems where they add to the
narrative tension. Kelley's mixed-media illustrations in
blues and browns add to the mood and enliven the layout." SLJ

Longfellow, Henry Wadsworth, 1807-1882
Poems and other writings. Library of Am. 2000
854p $35 *
Grades: 11 12 Adult   **811**
  ISBN 1-88301-185-X   LC 00-26678
  Edited by J. D. McClatchy
This volume includes "*Hiawatha, Evangeline, The
Courtship of Miles Standish* and 'The Midnight Ride of
Paul Revere.' Here, too, are some surprisingly powerful
lyric and meditative poems—well made, deeply felt, and
not much like the schoolhouse favorites." Publ Wkly
Includes bibliographical references

Lowell, Robert, 1917-1977
Selected poems. Expanded ed., 1st expanded ed.
Farrar, Straus and Giroux 2006 420p pa $18 *
Grades: 11 12 Adult   **811**
  ISBN 0-374-53006-8; 978-0-374-53006-8
                                    LC 2005-54313
  First published 1976
A selection of over 200 poems tracing the develop-
ment of one of the premier confessional poets of his gen-
eration.
Includes bibliographical references

MacLeish, Archibald, 1892-1982
Collected poems, 1917-1982; with a prefatory
note to the newly collected poems by Richard B.
McAdoo. Houghton Mifflin 1985 524p pa $19
hardcover o.p.
Grades: 11 12 Adult   **811**
  ISBN 0-395-39569-0 (pa)   LC 85-14392
Collects all the known poetry of the author/public ser-
vant. As an expatriate in Paris his early work was heavi-
ly influenced by Pound and Eliot. After returning to the
States his verse concerned itself more with America's
political, social, and cultural heritage

Masters, Edgar Lee, 1868-1950
Spoon River anthology; edited and with an introduction and annotations by John E. Hallwas. University of Ill. Press 1992 436p il map hardcover o.p. pa $19 *
Grades: 9 10 11 12   **811**
  ISBN 0-252-01561-4; 0-252-06363-5 (pa)
                                    LC 91-16968
First published 1915 by Macmillan
"The men and women of Spoon River narrate their own biographies from the cemetery where they lie buried. Realistic and sometimes cynical, these free-verse monologues often contradict the pious and optimistic epitaphs written on the gravestones." Reader's Ency. 4th edition

Merrell, Billy, 1982-
Talking in the dark; a poetry memoir. PUSH 2003 136p pa $6.99
Grades: 9 10 11 12   **811**
  ISBN 0-439-49036-7
This "memoir told in verse . . . is about sons and brothers, friends and lovers. The individual poems enhance one another yet stand alone." SLJ
Merrell has "packed away a lot of wisdom about life, death, self-acceptance, and the vararies of love and lust. Likewise, he has honed his writing craft, and his free-verse memoir is rich with metaphor, words carefully chosen to say enough but not to much." Booklist

Merrill, James
The collected poems of James Merrill; edited by J.D. McClatchy and Stephen Yenser. Knopf 2001 xx, 885p $40; pa $27.50
Grades: 11 12 Adult   **811**
  ISBN 0-375-41139-9; 0-375-70941-X (pa)
                                    LC 00-40542
"Excluded are some juvenilia and light verse, as well as Merrill's book-length poem *The Changing Light at Sandover,* in print as a separate volume. Merrill's sonnets, sapphics, longer sequences and sinuous sentences encompass lyric pathos, ebullient comedy, rapt romance and acrid satire. Their formal sophistication can belie their depth of feeling, which is exactly what some readers love best about Merrill's work." Publ Wkly

Millay, Edna St. Vincent, 1892-1950
Collected poems; edited by Norma Millay. Harper & Row 1956 xxi, 738p pa $22.95 hardcover o.p. *
Grades: 11 12 Adult   **811**
  ISBN 0-06-090889-0 (pa)
Also available in hardcover from Buccaneer Books
The poems in this collection "are divided into two separate sections of lyrics and sonnets, arranged chronologically and printed in groups under the titles of the original volumes, ranging from 'Renascence' of 1917 to 'Mine the harvest,' published in 1954, four years after the poet's death." Booklist

Moore, Marianne, 1887-1972
The complete poems of Marianne Moore. Macmillan 1981 305p pa $16 hardcover o.p. *
Grades: 11 12 Adult   **811**
  ISBN 0-14-018851-7 (pa)   LC 80-13586
This "definitive edition of 'The Complete Poems' was prepared by Clive Driver and presents all of Moore's final emendations and cuts, punctuation, hyphens, line arrangements, and revised notes (all critical components of her poetry). It also includes five poems Moore wrote between the publication of the 1967 edition and the time of her death." Libr J

The poems of Marianne Moore; edited by Grace Schulman. Viking 2003 449p pa $18 hardcover o.p.
Grades: 11 12 Adult   **811**
  ISBN 0-14-303908-3 (pa)   LC 2003-50159
This collection "contains all of Moore's poems, including 120 previously uncollected and unpublished ones. Organized chronologically to allow readers to follow Moore's development as a poet, the volume includes an introduction, all of Moore's original notes to the poems, along with Schulman's notes, attributions, and some variants." Publisher's note
"The great modernist poet finally gets her due with this outstanding compliation." Libr J
Includes bibliographical references

Mora, Pat
My own true name; new and selected poems for young adults, 1984-1999; [by] Pat Mora with line drawings by Anthony Accardo. Piñata Bks. 2000 81p il $11.95
Grades: 9 10 11 12   **811**
  1. Mexican Americans—Poetry
  ISBN 1-55885-292-1   LC 00-23969
"Interlaced with Mexican phrases and cultural symbols, these powerful selections, representing more than 15 years of work, address bicultural life and the meaning of family. Mora speaks very much from an adult perspective, but her poems are about universal experiences." Booklist

Myers, Walter Dean, 1937-
Harlem; a poem; pictures by Christopher Myers. Scholastic 1997 unp il $16.95
Grades: 5 6 7 8 9 10   **811**
  1. African Americans—Poetry 2. Harlem (New York, N.Y.)—Poetry
  ISBN 0-590-54340-7   LC 96-8108
A Caldecott Medal honor book, 1998
A poem celebrating the people, sights, and sounds of Harlem
"Myers's paean to Harlem sings, dances, and swaggers across the pages, conveying the myriad sounds on the streets. . . . Christopher Myers's collages add an edge to his father's words, vividly bringing to life the sights and scenes of Lenox Avenue." Horn Book Guide

Myers, Walter Dean, 1937——*Continued*
Here in Harlem; poems in many voices; written by Walter Dean Myers. Holiday House 2004 88p il $16.95
Grades: 7 8 9 10 **811**
1. African Americans—Poetry 2. Harlem (New York, N.Y.)—Poetry
ISBN 0-8234-1853-7   LC 2003-67605
"In each poem here, a resident of Harlem speaks in a distinctive voice, offering a story, a thought, a reflection, or a memory. The poetic forms are varied and well chosen. . . . Expressive period photos from Myers' collection accompany the text of this handsome book." Booklist

Nelson, Marilyn, 1946-
Carver, a life in poems. Front St. 2001 103p il $16.95
Grades: 7 8 9 10 **811**
1. Carver, George Washington, 1864?-1943
ISBN 1-88691-053-7   LC 00-63624
A Newbery Medal honor book, 2002
"A series of fifty-nine poems portrays George Washington Carver as a private, scholarly man of great personal faith and social purpose. Nelson fills in the trajectory of Carver's life with details of the cultural and political contexts that shaped him even as he shaped history. As individual works, each poem stands as a finely wrought whole of . . . high caliber." Horn Book Guide

Fortune's bones; the manumission requiem. Front Street 2004 32p il $16.95
Grades: 7 8 9 10 **811**
1. Slavery—Poetry 2. African Americans—Poetry
ISBN 1-932425-12-8   LC 2004-46917
"This requiem honors a slave who died in Connecticut in 1798. His owner, a doctor, dissected his body, boiling down his bones to preserve them for anatomy studies. The skeleton . . . hung in a local museum until 1970. . . . The museum . . . uncovered the skeleton's provenance, created a new exhibit, and led to the commissioning of these six poems. The selections. . . arc from grief to triumph. . . . The facts inform the verse and open up a full appreciation of its rich imagery and rhythmic, lyrical language." SLJ
Includes bibliographical references

A wreath for Emmett Till; illustrated by Philippe Lardy. Houghton Mifflin 2005 unp il $17 *
Grades: 8 9 10 11 12 **811**
1. Till, Emmett—Poetry 2. Lynching—Poetry 3. Mississippi—Poetry 4. African Americans—Poetry
ISBN 0-618-39752-3   LC 2004-9205
This is a "poetry collection about Till's brutal, racially motivated murder. The poems form a heroic crown of sonnets—a sequence in which the last line of one poem becomes the first line of the next. . . . The rigid form distills the words' overwhelming emotion into potent, heart-stopping lines that speak from changing perspectives. . . . When matched with Lardy's gripping, spare, symbolic paintings of tree trunks, blood-red roots, and wreaths of thorns, these poems are a powerful achievement that teens and adults will want to discuss together." Booklist

Nye, Naomi Shihab, 1952-
19 varieties of gazelle; poems of the Middle East. Greenwillow Bks. 2002 142p $16.95; lib bdg $16.89; pa $6.99 *
Grades: 7 8 9 10 **811**
1. Middle East—Poetry
ISBN 0-06-009765-5; 0-06-009766-3 (lib bdg); 0-06-050404-8 (pa)   LC 2002-771
In this "volume, Nye collects her poems about growing up as an Arab American (her ancestry is Palestinian), including previously published poems and newly written pieces. This rich and varied volume offers insights into the experience of childhood in two very different worlds. . . . This volume will fill a need for classroom use, for young people seeking a more personal understanding of the Middle East, and for readers seeking a connection with their own Middle Eastern background." Bull Cent Child Books

You & yours: poems. BOA Editions 2005 87p (American poets continuum series) hardcover o.p. pa $15.50
Grades: 11 12 Adult **811**
ISBN 1-929918-68-2; 1-929918-69-0 (pa)   LC 2005-11360
"Part one covers Nye's personal experience, at home with her child in San Antonio or as a 'Frequent Frequent Flyer' enjoying the sights of Scotland. . . . Part two covers the Middle East." Publ Wkly
"Tender yet forceful, funny and commonsensical, reflective and empathic, Nye writes radiant poems of nature and piercing poems of war, always touching base with homey details and radiant portraits of family and neighbors." Booklist

Off the cuffs; poetry by and about the police; edited by Jackie Sheeler; foreword by Bob Holman. Soft Skull Press 2003 281p pa $15
Grades: 11 12 Adult **811**
ISBN 1-887128-81-6
This "anthology is both about police brutality *and* a tribute to the police. The poems in it appear in sections according to perspective. . . . Unjust, but not entirely baseless, rants sit next to expressions of deep love. The formal poems 'An Operation' by master poet Thom Gunn and 'Street Justice,' a Kiplingesque ballad by the LAPD's Nat Read, stand out amid all the free verse, but nearly every piece here is a stunner." Booklist

Oliver, Mary, 1935-
New and selected poems. Beacon Press 2005 c1992 2v v1 $28.50; pa $16; v2 $24.95; pa $16
Grades: 11 12 Adult **811**
ISBN 0-8070-6878-0 (v1); 0-8070-6877-2 (v1 pa); 0-8070-6886-1 (v2); 0-8070-6887-X (v2 pa)
Vol. 1 first published 1992; redesigned ed. to accompany the publication of vol. 2
Volume one contains poems written from 1965 to 1992. Volume two contains poems written from 1994 to 2005.

Plath, Sylvia
The collected poems; edited by Ted Hughes.
Harper & Row 1981 351p pa $17.95 hardcover
o.p. *
Grades: 11 12 Adult 811
ISBN 0-06-090900-5 (pa)
Also available in hardcover from Buccaneer Bks.
The collection contains "all the poems Plath wrote,
published and unpublished, from 1956 to 1963, as well
as a sample of her early work." Publ Wkly
"Although her best poems deal with suffering and
death, others are exhilarating and affectionate, and her
tone is frequently witty as well as disturbing." Concise
Oxford Companion to Engl Lit

Crossing the water; transitional poems. Harper
& Row 1971 56p pa $10 hardcover o.p.
Grades: 11 12 Adult 811
ISBN 0-06-090789-4 (pa)
This posthumous collection of poems written in 1960
and 1961 evidences "Plath's preoccupation with death
{which} is conveyed in obsessive use of the word black
to connote despair and in other metaphors. . . . Desperate funnels of words, structured in strength and discipline, allude to nature, people, time and painful experiences of living." Booklist

Poe, Edgar Allan, 1809-1849
Complete poems; edited by Thomas Ollive
Mabbott. University of Ill. Press 2000 xxx, 627p
il pa $25 *
Grades: 11 12 Adult 811
ISBN 0-252-06921-8 LC 00-38639
First published 1969 as volume 1 of: Collected works
of Edgar Allan Poe by Belknap Press of Harvard University Press
This book contains 101 poems and their variants. In
addition to classic poems such as The raven, The bells,
and Annabel Lee, this volume contains previously uncollected poems, fragments, verses published in reviews,
and poems attributed to Poe
Includes bibliographical references

Poems and poetics; Richard Wilbur, editor.
Library of Am. 2003 xxv, 179p (American poets
project) $20
Grades: 11 12 Adult 811
ISBN 1-931082-51-0 LC 2003-46637
"Wilbur wants Poe to be appreciated as a transcendental cosmic theorist and 'the most difficult of the symbolist writers of his century,' and he appends selections
from Poe's writings about poetics to help understanding
of his cosmology and discusses some of Poe's most intense stories to exemplify his symbolism. The poems,
presented chronologically, show again what a young
prodigy Poe was, formulating his poetic thought while
still in his teens, and what a sonorous Romantic musician
he became." Booklist
Includes bibliographical references

Pound, Ezra, 1885-1972
Selected poems. new ed. New Directions 1957
184p pa $8.95 *
Grades: 11 12 Adult 811

ISBN 0-8112-0162-7
First published 1949
This "provides a good sampling of the Pound who
wrote 'A Virginal,' the latter-day Renaissance poet, as
well as the reincarnate Li Po and the other 'personae'
that Ezra wore during the years he spent absorbing the
styles (and not the political thinking) of other centuries."
Saturday Rev

Roethke, Theodore, 1908-1963
The collected poems of Theodore Roethke.
Doubleday 1966 279p pa $14.95 hardcover o.p. *
Grades: 11 12 Adult 811
ISBN 0-385-08601-6 (pa)
Roethke's "refreshingly original rhythms are keenly
articulated and often hypnotic. Although his work is uneven and he sometimes gives way to self-indulgence or
to surprising naiveté, many of his best poems recreate
disconcertingly intense psychic or mystical experience.
He also had a flair for the seductively lyrical and the
brashly irreverent. He ranks as one of the best poets of
the first postmodern generation." Benet's Reader's Ency
of Am Lit

Rylant, Cynthia
Something permanent; photographs by Walker
Evans; poetry by Cynthia Rylant. Harcourt Brace
& Co. 1994 61p il $18
Grades: 7 8 9 10 811
ISBN 0-15-277090-9 LC 93-3861
"Nearly 60 years ago, Walker Evans and James Agee
documented the lives of poor Southern sharecroppers.
Their efforts resulted in a devastating, legendary account
of the Depression, Let Us Now Praise Famous Men.
Here, Rylant pairs Evans's photographs with 29 short,
lyrical poems." SLJ
"For students in junior high and high school, the jux-
taposition of Evans' photos and Rylant's poems will
demonstrate how emotions can be rooted in objects and
how, to dig them out, you need to use strong, sturdy
words." Booklist

Sandburg, Carl, 1878-1967
The complete poems of Carl Sandburg. rev and
expanded ed. Harcourt Brace Jovanovich 1970
xxxi, 797p $40
Grades: 11 12 Adult 811
ISBN 0-15-100996-1
First published 1950
Introduction by Archibald MacLeish
A collection of seven of the author's books: Chicago
poems, 1916; Cornhuskers, 1918; Smoke and steel, 1920;
Slabs of the sunburnt West, 1922; Good morning, America, 1925; The people, yes, 1936; Honey and salt, 1963
"Known for his free verse, written under the influence
of Walt Whitman and celebrating industrial and agricultural America, American geography and landscape, figures in American history, and the American common
people, {Sandburg} frequently makes use of contemporary American slang and colloquialisms." Herzberg.
Reader's Ency of Am Lit

Sandburg, Carl, 1878-1967—*Continued*

Poems for the people; edited with an introduction by George and Willene Hendrick. Dee, I.R. 1999 184p $22.50; pa $14.95

Grades: 11 12 Adult   **811**
    ISBN 1-56663-236-6; 1-56663-403-2 (pa)
                        LC 98-44501

A collection of 73 previously uncollected poems. Sandburg "began writing poetry in the 1910s, when he was a radical socialist, a stance he modified in the wake of the second Wilson administration's severe persecution of the Left. Since most of these poems date from that time, and since several were withheld from earlier publication because of their fervor, they give us Sandburg-as-radical straight." Booklist

Includes bibliographical references

Selected poems; edited by George Hendrick and Willene Hendrick. Harcourt Brace & Co. 1996 xxix, 285p pa $16 *

Grades: 11 12 Adult   **811**
    ISBN 0-15-600396-1   LC 95-50686
    "A Harvest original"
    "With a preface that puts the poet and his work in perspective, this 'one-volume edition of Sandburg's best and most characteristic poetry' is ideal for student and poetry enthusiast alike." Booklist
    Includes bibliographical references

Sexton, Anne

The complete poems; with a foreword by Maxine Kumin. Houghton Mifflin 1981 xxiv, 622p pa $19 hardcover o.p. *

Grades: 11 12 Adult   **811**
    ISBN 0-395-95776-1 (pa)   LC 81-2482
    "This collection contains all the poems in the eight volumes published in Sexton's lifetime, the two published after her death, and seven poems never before in print." Libr J
    "Even before her death in 1974, Sexton's work was the subject of critical controversy, often dismissed as mere confessionalism. But, as Maxine Kumin observes in an insightful introductory essay, Sexton 'delineated the problematic position of women—the neurotic reality of the time' and in so doing 'earned her place in the canon.'" Choice

Silverstein, Shel

Where the sidewalk ends; the poems & drawings of Shel Silverstein. 30th anniversary special ed. HarperCollins 2004 183p il $17.99; lib bdg $18.89 *

Grades: 3 4 5 6 7 8 9 10   **811**
    1. Humorous poetry 2. Nonsense verses
    ISBN 0-06-057234-5; 0-06-058653-2 (lib bdg)
                    LC 2004-269335
    First published 1974
    This edition contains 12 new poems
    "There are skillful, sometimes grotesque line drawings with each of the 127 poems, which run in length from a few lines to a couple of pages. The poems are tender, funny, sentimental, philosophical, and ridiculous in turn, and they're for all ages." Sat Rev

Soto, Gary

Junior college; poems. Chronicle Bks. 1997 83p pa $12.95

Grades: 11 12 Adult   **811**
    ISBN 0-8118-1543-9   LC 96-36049
    "The poems trace a trajectory of deepening ethnicity, documenting the Mexican American heritage and emphasize higher education's role in expanding options. Sometimes labeled 'America's foremost Chicano poet,' Soto would more accurately be called one of America's foremost contemporary poets." Libr J

New and selected poems. Chronicle Bks. 1995 177p hardcover o.p. pa $14.95

Grades: 11 12 Adult   **811**
    ISBN 0-8118-0761-4; 0-8118-0758-4 (pa)
                    LC 94-27081
    "In one of his more striking poems, Soto stares longingly at the unkempt lot in the California slum where his family's house used to be. Elsewhere, a Mexican American simply jogs and laughs after he has been ushered out the back door when immigration officials show up at his workplace. With rare lyricism, gentleness, and a touch of humor, Soto covers the ground that leads many highly touted poets to erupt in pulsating anger. Soto has it all— the learned craft, the intrinsic abilities with language, a fascinating autobiography, and the storyteller's ability to manipulate memories into folklore." Libr J

Stevens, Wallace, 1879-1955

The collected poems of Wallace Stevens. Knopf 1954 534p $40; pa $16 *

Grades: 11 12 Adult   **811**
    ISBN 0-394-40330-4; 0-679-72669-1 (pa)
    Steven's "poems range from descriptive and dramatic lyrics to meditative and discursive discourse, but all show a deep engagement in experience and in art. His musical verse, rich in tropic imagery but precise and intense in statement, is marked by concern with means of knowledge, with the contrast between reality and appearance, and the emphasis upon imagination as giving an aesthetic insight and order to life." Oxford Companion to Am Lit. 6th edition

Strand, Mark, 1934-

Chicken, shadow, moon and more. Turtle Point Press 2000 91p il $21.95

Grades: 11 12 Adult   **811**
    ISBN 1-885586-45-X
    This volume "is a book of lists that at times sounds like a collection of one-line poems and at other times like a collection of epigrams. Each list is constructed by a repeated use of a single word." N Y Rev Books
    "Startling visions, unexpected truths, an aura of wistfulness, and trills of playful humor waft from every page, and always the language is exact, musical, and transcendent." Booklist

Swenson, May, 1919-1989

Nature; poems old and new. Houghton Mifflin 1994 xxiii, 240p pa $15 hardcover o.p.

Grades: 11 12 Adult   **811**
    ISBN 0-618-06408-7 (pa)   LC 93-45642

Swenson, May, 1919-1989—*Continued*

This collection of Swenson's poetry "brings together poems from several earlier books, as well as poems published only in magazines, and introduces us to nine splendid poems published here for the first time. This collection . . . is brought together with special attention to poems describing the environment; poems of tides and the sea, of birds and gardens, of moods and seasons, of self and others. . . . This is a collection to be treasured; it belongs in all libraries with even a modest selection of poetry." Libr J

Updike, John

Americana and other poems. Knopf 2001 95p $23 *

Grades: 11 12 Adult   811
ISBN 0-375-41254-9   LC 2001-88571

This volume "ranges from a number of brilliant, expositional epics that converse as they describe, to shorter works with their quicksilver epiphanies." Christ Sci Monit

Walcott, Derek

Collected poems, 1948-1984. Farrar, Straus & Giroux 1986 515p pa $20 hardcover o.p. *

Grades: 11 12 Adult   811
ISBN 0-374-52025-9 (pa)   LC 85-20688

"It is difficult to think of a poet in our century who—without ever betraying his native sources—has so organically assimilated the evolution of English literature from the Renaissance to the present, who has absorbed the Classical and Judeo-Christian past, and who has mined the history of Western painting as Walcott has. Throughout his entire body of work he has managed to hold in balance his passionate moral concerns with the ideal of art." Poetry

Includes bibliographical references

Omeros. Farrar, Straus & Giroux 1990 325p pa $16 hardcover o.p.

Grades: 11 12 Adult   811
ISBN 0-374-52350-9 (pa)   LC 90-33592

This epic poem "follows the wanderings of a present-day Odysseus and the inconsolable sufferings of those who are displaced and traveling with trepidation toward their homes. Written in seven circling books and . . . tercets, the poem illuminates the classical past and its motifs through an extraordinary cast of contemporary characters from the island of Santa Lucia." Publ Wkly

"No poet rivals Mr. Walcott in humor, emotional depth, lavish inventiveness in language or in the ability to express the thoughts of his characters and compel the reader to follow the swift mutations of ideas and images in their minds. This wonderful story moves in a spiral, replicating human thought." N Y Times Book Rev

Walker, Alice, 1944-

Her blue body everything we know; earthling poems, 1965-1990, complete. Harcourt Brace Jovanovich 1991 463p pa $15 hardcover o.p.

Grades: 11 12 Adult   811
ISBN 0-15-602861-1 (pa)   LC 90-5160

In this volume of Walker's "complete earlier work, joined to new, previously uncollected poems, we see a quarter century of impressive artistic development." Booklist

Warren, Robert Penn, 1905-1989

The collected poems of Robert Penn Warren; edited by John Burt; with a foreword by Harold Bloom. Louisiana State Univ. Press 1998 xxvi, 830p $44.95

Grades: 11 12 Adult   811
ISBN 0-8071-2333-1   LC 98-26104

"This immense volume gathers 15 books of poetry—as well as uncollected verse from the beginning and end of his writing life—from a formidable American man of letters and our first poet laureate. . . . Scholars will especially cherish the careful, copious textual and explanatory notes provided by Warren's literary executor Burt . . . and fans of American poetry and literary history alike should welcome this opportunity to explore the prodigious oeuvre of one of the New Criticism's most forceful, convincing proponents." Publ Wkly

Whitman, Walt, 1819-1892

Leaves of grass; edited and with a new afterword by David S. Reynolds. 150th anniversary ed. Oxford University Press 2005 167p $23 *

Grades: 11 12 Adult   811
ISBN 0-19-518342-8   LC 2004-26509

Also available in paperback from Penguin Classics and Bantam Books

First published 1855

"The book, radical in form and content, takes its title from the themes of fertility, universality, and cyclical life. . . . As he revised and added to the original edition, Whitman arranged the poems in a significant autobiographical order." Reader's Ency. 4th edition

Williams, Norman, 1952-

One unblinking eye; poems. Swallow Press; Ohio University Press 2003 48p $24.95; pa $14.95

Grades: 9 10 11 12   811
ISBN 0-8040-1057-9; 0-8040-1058-7 (pa)
     LC 2003-42381

This collection contains "poems about tragedy in America's heartland, aging fathers, departed lovers, and surviving children who died in infancy . . . In Williams' work, precise imagery unites with humanity of feeling to become poetry of everlasting refreshment." Booklist

Williams, William Carlos, 1883-1963

The collected poems of William Carlos Williams. New Directions 1986-1988 2v v1 $40; pa $23.95; v2 $38; pa $22.95 *

Grades: 11 12 Adult   811
ISBN 0-8112-0999-7 (v1); 0-8112-1187-8 (v1 pa); 0-8112-1063-4 (v2); 0-8112-1188-6 (v2 pa)

Contents: v1 1909-1939; edited by A. Walton Litz and Christopher MacGowan; v2 1939-1962; edited by Christopher MacGowan

Williams, William Carlos, 1883-1963—*Continued*

"Williams's poetry is firmly rooted in the commonplace detail of everyday American life. He conceived of the poem as an object: a record of direct experience that deals with the local and the particular. He abandoned conventional rhyme and meter in an effort to reduce the barrier between the reader and his consciousness of his immediate surroundings. . . . Williams's original approach to poetry, his insistence on the importance of the ordinary, and his successful attempts at making his verse as 'tactile' as the spoken word had a far-reaching effect on American poetry." Reader's Ency. 4th edition

Wright, Richard, 1908-1960

Haiku; this other world; edited and with notes and afterword by Yoshinobu Hakutani and Robert L. Tener; introduction by Julia Wright. Arcade Pub. 1998 304p $23.50

Grades: 11 12 Adult   **811**
ISBN 1-55970-445-4   LC 98-23049

Also available in paperback from Doubleday

"During the last 18 months of his life, the great African American novelist wrote some 4,000 poems in the 3-line, 17-syllable Japanese form called haiku. He selected 817 of them to be published as a collection." Booklist

"If not quite a major literary event, these poems nonetheless testify to the fruitful East-West confluences of the period, and to the respite they offered one of our all-time great writers." Publ Wkly

Includes bibliographical references

811.008 American poetry-- Collections

180 more; extraordinary poems for every day; selected and with an introduction by Billy Collins. Random House 2005 xxiii, 373p pa $14.95

Grades: 11 12 Adult   **811.008**
1. American poetry—Collections
ISBN 0-8129-7296-1   LC 2005-42798

Sequel to: Poetry 180

This is a second collection of 180 poems for each day of the school year, designed to expose high school students to poetry.

American poetry: the nineteenth century; edited by John Hollander. Library of Am. 1993 2v ea $35 *

Grades: 11 12 Adult   **811.008**
1. American poetry—Collections
ISBN 0-940450-60-7 (v1); 0-940450-78-X (v2)
                                       LC 93-10702

Volume 1 also available in paperback $14.95 (ISBN 1-88301-136-1)

Vol. 1, Philip Freneau to Walt Whitman; Vol. 2, Herman Melville to Trumbull Stickney, American Indian poetry, folk songs and spirituals

Contents: v1 Freneau to Whitman; v2 Melville to Stickney; American Indian poetry; Folk songs and spirituals

An anthology of more than 1,000 poems by nearly 150 poets. Arrangement is chronological by poet's date of birth. Biographical sketches of the poets, a chronology of significant events from 1800 to 1900, and an essay on textual selection are included

Hollander has compiled "a selection of nineteenth-century American verse so wonderfully catholic that it not just augments but supersedes every other similar collection." Booklist

American poetry, The twentieth century. Library of Am. 2000 2v ea $35 *

Grades: 11 12 Adult   **811.008**
1. American poetry—Collections
ISBN 1-88301-177-9 (v1); 1-88301-178-7 (v2)
                                       LC 99-43721

The first two volumes of a projected four volume set

Contents: v1 Henry Adams to Dorothy Parker; v2 E.E. Cummings to May Swenson

"Over 200 poets are represented, all born before 1914, and presented in birth-date order." Publ Wkly

These volumes represent a "remarkable feat of assemblage, with excellent capsule biographies and explanatory notes at the end of each volume—the biographies, especially, are well worth reading." N Y Times Book Rev

Includes bibliographical references

American religious poems; an anthology by Harold Bloom; Harold Bloom and Jesse Zuba, editors. Library of America 2006 685p $40

Grades: 11 12 Adult   **811.008**
1. American poetry—Collections 2. Religious poetry
ISBN 1-931082-74-X   LC 2006-41031

An anthology of "verse on Christian, Jewish, Islamic, Buddhist, Native American spiritual, Transcendentalist and even agnostic themes, from 17th-century European colonists (one poet is Roger Williams, who founded Rhode Island) to up-and-comers in contemporary verse. Pious readers will have no trouble finding high-quality poetry that confirms their beliefs—from the monk Thomas Merton, the Anglican T.S. Eliot, the Jewish liturgical poet Esther Schor and the Louisiana-based Christian poet Martha Serpas. Yet from the 19th century to the present, from the decidedly heterodox Emily Dickinson forwards, the anthology often highlights the ways in which American spirituality has challenged all doctrines about who God is and what God does. . . . More than half of the book is taken up by 20th-century poets, who offer varied takes on what religion has come to mean in America." Publ Wkly

American war poetry; an anthology; edited by Lorrie Goldensohn. Columbia University Press 2006 413p $27.95 *

Grades: 11 12 Adult   **811.008**
1. War poetry 2. American poetry—Collections
ISBN 0-231-13310-3   LC 2005-54762

"Arranged by war, the book begins with the Colonial period and proceeds through Whitman admiring Civil War soldiers crossing a river to end with Brian Turner, who published his first book in 2005, beckoning a bullet in contemporary Iraq. Many voices, by turns elegiac, outraged, rhetorical and ecstatic are represented." Publ Wkly

Includes bibliographical references

Angst! teen verses from the edge! edited by Karen
Tom and Kiki; illustrations by Matt Frost.
Workman 2001 133p il pa $8.95
Grades: 9 10 11 12   **811.008**
1. American poetry—Collections 2. Youths' writings
ISBN 0-7611-2383-0   LC 2001-23803
"This collection of poetry derives from the Web site
PlanetKiki.com. . . . With the look of a fanzine and the
uncensored flavor of an Internet chat room (there's some
strong language here), the selections, written by teen
girls, will no doubt find an audience due to the quick
pacing, fresh look, and offbeat attitude. This is poetry on
the verge with trash-talking verse about crushes, rumors,
multiracial issues, smoking, and individuality." SLJ

Black poets; [a new anthology] Bantam Books
1985 c1971 xxvi, 353p pa $7.99
Grades: 11 12 Adult   **811.008**
1. American poetry—African American authors—Collections
ISBN 0-553-27563-1; 978-0-553-27563-6
This anthology covers African American poetry from
slave songs to the works of Gwendolyn Brooks and
Nikki Giovanni.

Catch the fire!!! a cross-generational anthology of
contemporary African-American poetry; edited
by Derrick I.M. Gilbert (a.k.a. D-Knowledge)
with the special editorial assistance of Tony
Medina. Riverhead Bks. 1998 xxiii, 288p pa $13
Grades: 11 12 Adult   **811.008**
1. American poetry—African American authors—Collections 2. American poetry—Collections
ISBN 1-57322-654-8   LC 97-30173
An anthology of poems by over 100 new and "established African American men and women poets. . . .
[The volume] includes work by performers, writers,
filmmakers, poets, songwriters, and a 'rainbow of others,' including basketball star center Shaquille O'Neal
and actor Malcolm-Jamal Warner." Libr J
This is "no ordinary poetry anthology, but the record
of a rite of passage: the handing down, from one generation to the next, of the torch of poetry and the story of
African American experience." Booklist

The **Columbia** anthology of American poetry;
edited by Jay Parini. Columbia Univ. Press 1995
757p $40.95 *
Grades: 11 12 Adult   **811.008**
1. American poetry—Collections
ISBN 0-231-08122-7   LC 94-32423
"Ranging from Anne Bradstreet to Louise Glück, editor Parini aims to represent 'the main schools of poetry
that have co-existed in the United States . . . in proportion to their influence,' including more poetry by women
and minorities 'than one generally finds' in older anthologies." Libr J

The **Columbia** book of Civil War poetry; Richard
Marius, editor; Keith W. Frome, associate
editor. Columbia Univ. Press 1994 xxxvi, 543p
il $37.95
Grades: 11 12 Adult   **811.008**
1. American poetry—Collections 2. United States—
History—1861-1865, Civil War—Poetry
ISBN 0-231-10002-7   LC 94-6481

"Bret Harte, Walt Whitman, and Robert Frost are but
three of the many writers whose poems about the Civil
War fill this noteworthy collection." Booklist

Cool salsa; bilingual poems on growing up Latino
in the United States; edited by Lori M. Carlson;
introduction by Oscar Hijuelos. Holt & Co.
1994 xx, 123p il $16.95 *
Grades: 5 6 7 8 9 10   **811.008**
1. American poetry—Hispanic American authors—
Collections 2. Bilingual books—English-Spanish
ISBN 0-8050-3135-9   LC 93-45798
Also available in paperback from Fawcett Bks.
"This collection presents poems by 29 Mexican-
American, Cuban-American, Puerto Rican, and other
Central and South American poets, including Sandra Cis-
neros, Luis J. Rodriguez, Pat Mora, Gary Soto, Ana
Castillo, Oscar Hijuelos, Ed J. Vega, Judith Ortiz-Cofer,
and other Latino writers both contemporary and histori-
cal. Brief biographical notes on the authors are provided.
All the poems deal with experiences of teenagers." Book
Rep

Eight American poets; an anthology: Theodore
Roethke, Elizabeth Bishop, Robert Lowell, John
Berryman, Anne Sexton, Sylvia Plath, Allen
Ginsberg, James Merrill; edited by Joel
Conarroe. Random House 1994 xxiv, 306p il pa
$14.95 hardcover o.p.
Grades: 11 12 Adult   **811.008**
1. American poetry—Collections
ISBN 0-679-77643-5 (pa)   LC 94-10186
This anthology contains representative work by eight
20th century American confessional poets

Every shut eye ain't asleep; an anthology of
poetry by African Americans since 1945; edited
by Michael Harper and Anthony Walton. Little,
Brown 1994 327p pa $19 hardcover o.p.
Grades: 11 12 Adult   **811.008**
1. American poetry—African American authors—Collections
ISBN 0-316-34710-8 (pa)   LC 93-10788
"Using Robert Hayden and Gwendolyn Brooks's poetry as 'emblematic' successes, this anthology selects 35
African American poets (spanning three generations) who
were born between 1913 and 1962 and came of age after
1945. Besides the well-known Imamu Baraka, Lucille
Clifton, Rita Dove, and Etheridge Knight, the editors feature little-known or younger poets like Elizabeth Alexander, Gerald Barrax, Jayne Cortex, and Dolores
Kendrick." Libr J

From both sides now; the poetry of the Vietnam
War and its aftermath; edited by Phillip
Mahony. Scribner 1998 314p hardcover o.p. pa
$16
Grades: 11 12 Adult   **811.008**
1. American poetry—Collections
ISBN 0-684-84946-1; 0-684-84947-X (pa)
     LC 98-16628
The editor "arranges poems by 135 poets in chrono-
logical order 'to simulate the progression of the Vietnam
War.' Poems of the North and South Vietnamese, 'boat

From both sides now—*Continued*

people,' and postwar Vietnamese American second-generation poets appear beside well-known names (e.g., Ehrhart, Komunyakaa, and Weihl)." Libr J

From totems to hip-hop; edited by Ishmael Reed. Thunder's Mouth Press 2003 xxx, 523p $34.95; pa $17.95

Grades: 11 12 Adult   **811.008**

1. American poetry—Collections

ISBN 1-56025-500-5; 1-56025-458-0 (pa)

LC 2002-75691

"Reed's selections range from classic poems like Carl Sandburg's 'Chicago' to contemporary texts like Tupac Shakur's 'Why Must U Be Unfaithful (4 women).' Along the way, readers will encounter familiar names like Marianne Moore, Claude McKay, Robert Frost, and T.S. Eliot but will also find less anthologized writers like Agha Shadid Ali, Bessie Smith, Speckled Red, Lorna Dee Cervantes, Haki Madhubuti, and the rock'n'roll composers Jerry Leiber and Mike Stoller." Libr J

This is "a dynamic and original anthology, an unprecedented amalgam of poets representing many facets of American culture and society." Booklist

Good poems; selected and introduced by Garrison Keillor. Viking 2002 xxvi, 476p $25.95; pa $15

Grades: 11 12 Adult   **811.008**

1. American poetry—Collections 2. English poetry—Collections

ISBN 0-670-03126-7; 0-14-200344-1 (pa)

LC 2002-16881

Keillor "has put together a collection of close to 300 poems he has read during . . . [the] PBS broadcast, The Writer's Almanac. . . . Poems are arranged by 19 general themes, such as 'Snow,' 'Failure,' and 'A Good Life.' Authors range from well-known oldies like Emily Dickinson and Robert Frost to unknowns like C.K. Williams. . . . An outstanding feature of this collection is that the selections are all so accessible—even folks who say they don't like poetry can find something here to enjoy." SLJ

Harper's anthology of 20th century Native American poetry; edited by Duane Niatum. Harper & Row 1988 xxxii, 396p pa $24.95 hardcover o.p. *

Grades: 11 12 Adult   **811.008**

1. American poetry—Native American authors

ISBN 0-06-250666-8 (pa)   LC 86-45023

This collection "contains the work of 36 native American poets, with hearty selections from each. Among the 36 are poets near the mainstream (Scott Momaday, James Welch, Louise Erdrich); those in academe (Gerald Vizenor, Linda Hogan, Jim Barnes); those writing in the tribal oral tradition (Barney Bush, Peter Blue Cloud, Wendy Rose); and those working in a modernist voice (Gladys Cardiff, Paula Gunn Allen). This book belongs in every collection that claims to represent the multiple voices of American literature today." Booklist

Includes bibliographical references

Heart to heart; new poems inspired by twentieth-century American art; edited by Jan Greenberg. Abrams 2001 80p il map $19.95 *

Grades: 5 6 7 8 9 10   **811.008**

1. American poetry—Collections 2. American art 3. Art—20th century

ISBN 0-8109-4386-7   LC 99-462335

A compilation of poems by Americans writing about American art in the twentieth century, including such writers as Nancy Willard, Jane Yolen, and X. J. Kennedy.

"From a tight diamante and pantoum to lyrical free verse, the range of poetic styles will speak to a wide age group. . . . Concluding with biographical notes on each poet and artist, this rich resource is an obvious choice for teachers, and the exciting interplay between art and the written word will encourage many readers to return again and again to the book." Booklist

I am the darker brother; an anthology of modern poems by African Americans; edited and with an afterword by Arnold Adoff; drawings by Benny Andrews; introduction by Rudine Sims Bishop; foreword by Nikki Giovanni. rev ed. Simon & Schuster Bks. for Young Readers 1997 208p il hardcover o.p. pa $5.99 *

Grades: 6 7 8 9   **811.008**

1. American poetry—African American authors—Collections

ISBN 0-689-81241-8; 0-689-80869-0 (pa)

LC 97-144181

First published 1968

This anthology presents "the African-American experience through poetry that speaks for itself. . . . Because of the historical context of many of the poems, the book will be much in demand during Black History Month, but it should be used and treasured as part of the larger canon of literature to be enjoyed by all Americans at all times of the year. An indispensable addition to library collections." SLJ

Is this forever, or what? poems and paintings from Texas; selected by Naomi Shihab Nye. Greenwillow Books 2004 164p il $19.99

Grades: 7 8 9 10   **811.008**

1. Texas—Poetry 2. Texas in art 3. American poetry—Collections

ISBN 0-06-051178-8   LC 2003-4441

"The poems include moving family tributes, furious self-revelations, and quiet, atmospheric vignettes that find grace and beauty in sunbaked neighborhoods, basic work, and everyday faces. . . . The accompanying artworks are arresting without overpowering the words, and they echo the poems' wide range of styles." Booklist

Letters to America; contemporary American poetry on race; edited by Jim Daniels. Wayne State Univ. Press 1995 230p pa $21.95

Grades: 9 10 11 12   **811.008**

1. American poetry—Collections 2. United States—Race relations—Poetry

ISBN 0-8143-2542-4   LC 95-19996

This volume collects "the probings of several dozen American poets on their nation's nightmare. . . . If a

Letters to America—*Continued*

large proportion of the poets selected are black, Indian, Chicano, or Asian, that is unsurprising, for they are the ones upon whom the subject thrusts itself most insistently." Booklist

The **Oxford** anthology of African-American poetry; edited by Arnold Rampersad; associate editor, Hilary Herbold. Oxford University Press 2006 432p $32.50 *

Grades: 11 12 Adult   **811.008**

1. American poetry—African American authors—Collections

ISBN 0195125630; 978-0-19-512563-4

LC 2005-15242

"Predicated on the fact that there is a vast body of poetry written by gifted black poets, this . . . anthology tells the story of African American culture and explicates its crucial role within the larger literary tradition. . . . There is much to admire about the artistry of the poems, and even more to discover about the African American experience." Booklist

The **Oxford** book of American poetry; chosen and edited by David Lehman; associate editor, John Brehm. Oxford University Press 2006 lvii, 1132p $35 *

Grades: 8 9 10 11 12 Adult   **811.008**

1. American poetry—Collections

ISBN 0-19-516251-X; 978-0-19-516251-6

LC 2005-36590

First published 1950 with title: The Oxford book of American verse

This is an anthology of "American poetry from its origins in the 17th century right up to the present." Publisher's note

"The book is not only a sound historical survey, but also gives the reader a powerful taste of poetry's impact upon the wider world." Economist

Includes bibliographical references

Paint me like I am; teen poems from WritersCorps. HarperTempest 2003 128p hardcover o.p. pa $6.99

Grades: 7 8 9 10   **811.008**

1. American poetry—Collections 2. Teenagers' writings

ISBN 0-06-029288-1; 0-06-447264-7 (pa)

LC 2002-5942

"The teen voices in these poems, collected from the WritersCorps youth program, are LOUD—raging, defiant, giddy, lusty, and hopeful. Grouped into arbitrary categories, the poems explore identity, creative expressions, family, neighborhood, drugs, and relationships. . . . A foreword from Nikki Giovanni rounds out this moving collection, which also includes a few thoughtful writing exercises." Booklist

Paper dance; 55 Latino poets; edited by Victor Hernández Cruz, Leroy V. Quintana, and Virgil Suarez. Persea Bks. 1995 242p $14 *

Grades: 11 12 Adult   **811.008**

1. American poetry—Hispanic American authors—Collections

ISBN 0-89255-201-8   LC 94-15586

"This collection of poetry attests to the richness of culture in the Hispanic diaspora in the U.S., and includes well-known writers such as Julia Alvarez, Luis J. Rodriguez, and Lucha Corpi, to name a few. . . . The poets' themes are as varied as they are intriguing. Ranging in scope from contemplations on race and ethnicity to love and death, they demand that readers pay attention to vital threads in the fabric of the American literary tapestry." SLJ

Poetry 180; a turning back to poetry; selected and with an introduction by Billy Collins. Random House Trade Paperbacks 2003 xxiv, 323p pa $13.95

Grades: 11 12 Adult   **811.008**

1. American poetry—Collections

ISBN 0-8129-6887-5   LC 2002-36949

Also available online

The editor "has collected 180 accessible modern poems: one for each day of the school year and together signifying a 180° turning back to poetry. These are poems, he says, you can 'get' the first time around, and he hopes that high schools will expose students to a poem a day via public address system or assemblies. A fine gathering of contemporary poets." Libr J

Includes bibliographical references

The **Poetry** anthology, 1912-2002; ninety years of America's most distinguished verse magazine; edited by Joseph Parisi & Stephen Young; with an introduction by Joseph Parisi. Ivan R. Dee 2002 lv, 509p $29.95; pa $16.95

Grades: 11 12 Adult   **811.008**

1. American poetry—Collections

ISBN 1-56663-468-7; 1-56663-604-3 (pa)

LC 2002-31178

A collection of 600 poems previously published in Poetry magazine, written by such poets as W.H. Auden, Elizabeth Bishop, Sylvia Plath, James Merrill, and Susan Hahn

This is a "comprehensive and thrilling anthology, a veritable history of twentieth-century poetry in English." Booklist

The **Poetry** of black America; anthology of the 20th century; introduction by Gwendolyn Brooks. Harper & Row 1973 xxxi, 552p $25.95

Grades: 11 12 Adult   **811.008**

1. American poetry—African American authors—Collections

ISBN 0-06-020089-8   LC 72-76518

A collection of over 600 poems by 145 authors. James Weldon Johnson, Paul Laurence Dunbar, Langston Hughes, Gwendolyn Brooks, Sonia Sanchez, Don Lee and Nikki Giovanni are among the poets represented. Biographical sketches are provided

A **Poke** in the I; [selected by] Paul Janeczko; illustrated by Chris Raschka. Candlewick Press 2001 35p il $16.99; pa $7.99 *

Grades: 4 5 6 7 8 9   **811.008**

1. American poetry—Collections

ISBN 0-7636-0661-8; 0-7636-2376-8 (pa)

LC 00-33675

A Poke in the I—*Continued*

"Thirty concrete poems of all shapes and sizes are carefully laid on large white spreads, extended by Raschka's quirky watercolor and paper-collage illustrations. . . . Beautiful and playful, this title should find use in storytimes, in the classroom, and just for pleasure anywhere." SLJ

Postmodern American poetry; a Norton anthology; edited by Paul Hoover. Norton 1994 xxxix, 701p pa $26.95

Grades: 11 12 Adult **811.008**

1. American poetry—Collections

ISBN 0-393-31090-6 LC 93-22753

Hoover "brings together more than 100 writers from the 1950s and since—Olson, Duncan, O'Hara, Ginsberg, Corso, Dorn, Major, Ashbery, Guest—whose adventures with the language renew it for far more than a readymade membership." Publ Wkly

Red hot salsa; bilingual poems on being young and Latino in the United States; edited by Lori Marie Carlson; introduction by Oscar Hijuelos. Henry Holt 2005 140p $14.95 *

Grades: 7 8 9 10 **811.008**

1. American poetry—Hispanic American authors—Collections 2. Hispanic Americans—Poetry 3. Bilingual books—English-Spanish

ISBN 0-8050-7616-6 LC 2004-54005

This is a "bilingual collection of poems that appear in both Spanish and English. Included are many well-known writers, such as Gary Soto and Luis J. Rodriguez . . . as well as emerging poets. . . . The poems often speak about the complex challenges of being bicultural. . . . Most poems are translated by the poets themselves, and many are written in an inventive blend of languages, which English speakers will easily follow with help from the appended glossary. Powerful and immediate." Booklist

Reflections on a gift of watermelon pickle—and other modern verse; [compiled by] Stephen Dunning, Edward Lueders, Hugh Smith. Lothrop, Lee & Shepard Bks. 1967 c1966 139p il $19.99

Grades: 6 7 8 9 **811.008**

1. American poetry—Collections

ISBN 0-688-41231-9

First published 1966 by Scott, Foresman in a text edition

"Although some of the {114} selections are by recognized modern writers, many are by minor or unknown poets, and few will be familiar to the reader. Nearly all are fresh in approach and contemporary in expression. . . . Striking photographs complementing or illuminating many of the poems enhance the attractiveness of the volume." Booklist

Shimmy shimmy shimmy like my sister Kate; looking at the Harlem Renaissance through poems; {edited by} Nikki Giovanni. Holt & Co. 1995 186p $17.95 *

Grades: 8 9 10 11 12 **811.008**

1. American poetry—African American authors—Collections 2. Harlem Renaissance

ISBN 0-8050-3494-3 LC 95-38617

This anthology includes poems by such authors as Paul Laurence Dunbar, Langston Hughes, Countee Cullen, Gwendolyn Brooks, and Amiri Baraka. Commentary and a discussion of the development of African American arts known as the Harlem Renaissance is provided by editor Giovanni

Includes bibliographical references

Six American poets; an anthology; edited by Joel Connaroe. Random House 1991 xxxiv, 281p il pa $14.95 hardcover o.p.

Grades: 11 12 Adult **811.008**

1. American poetry—Collections

ISBN 0-679-74525-4 (pa) LC 91-15375

This anthology contains 247 representative poems by Walt Whitman, Emily Dickinson, Wallace Stevens, William Carlos Williams, Robert Frost and Langston Hughes

Songs from this Earth on turtle's back; contemporary American Indian poetry; edited by Joseph Bruchac. Greenfield Review Press 1983 294p il pa $14.95 *

Grades: 11 12 Adult **811.008**

1. American poetry—Native American authors

ISBN 0-912678-58-5 LC 82-82420

"A biographical statement accompanies each sampling from 50 poets representing more than 35 different Native American nations." Libr J

"The collection provides a balance to the volumes of compiled chants and translated (or mistranslated) songs already in most libraries. . . . Writing in English, they display a variety of styles and themes and draw from urban, rural, and reservation backgrounds, yet they share a reverence for the earth and the natural world and a keen understanding of the power of language to create and shape that world." Choice

The **Spoken** word revolution; slam, hip-hop, & the poetry of a new generation; edited by Marc Eleveld; advised by Marc Smith; introduction by Billy Collins. Sourcebooks 2003 241p il $24.95; pa $19.95 *

Grades: 11 12 Adult **811.008**

1. American poetry—Collections 2. American poetry—History and criticism

ISBN 1-4022-0037-4; 1-4022-0246-6 (pa)

LC 2003-841

Includes audio CD

The editors "trace the evolution of spoken-word poetry from the Beats to rap, hip-hop, and performance art. The result is a dynamic and clarifying volume chock-full of fresh and informative commentary by the likes of Billy Collins, Marvin Bell, and Jerry Quickley and an exciting array of knock-out poems by Patricia Smith, Tara Betts, Jeff McDaniel, Roger Bonair-Agard . . . and many more. Eleveld and his contributors not only celebrate the verve, artistry, and significance of performance poetry but also anchor it firmly within the splendid, age-old, and life-sustaining universe of poetry. . . . An accompanying CD presents poets performing their work." Booklist

Sweet nothings; an anthology of rock and roll in American poetry; edited, with an introduction, by Jim Elledge. Indiana Univ. Press 1994 283p pa $16.95 hardcover o.p. *

Grades: 11 12 Adult   **811.008**

1. American poetry—Collections

ISBN 0-253-20864-5 (pa)   LC 93-11795

In this anthology the editor "explores the influence that rock 'n' roll has had on American poets who came of age to the sexy and defiant beat of Otis Redding, Buddy Holly, Aretha Franklin, Bob Dylan, and the Rolling Stones. Elledge's introduction provides a peppy . . . overview of the rise of rock 'n' roll and a sensitive assessment of how rock has shaped poetry both overtly and subtly. His theories are well supported by the poems themselves." Booklist

Includes bibliographical references

Three centuries of American poetry, 1623-1923; edited by Allen Mandelbaum and Robert D. Richardson, Jr. Bantam Bks. 1999 733p hardcover o.p. pa $24 *

Grades: 11 12 Adult   **811.008**

1. American poetry—Collections

ISBN 0-553-10250-8; 0-553-37518-0 (pa)

    LC 98-31408

This anthology contains works by well-known poets (Bradstreet, Whitman, Dickinson, Stevens) as well as obscure names such as Ellen Sturgis Hooper and Lucretia Davidson. Spirituals, popular song lyrics and Native American poems are included

Twentieth-century American poetry; edited by Dana Gioia, David Mason, Meg Schoerke. McGraw Hill 2004 xlvi, 1143p il pa $79.69 *

Grades: 11 12 Adult   **811.008**

1. American poetry—Collections

ISBN 0-07-240019-6   LC 2003-61449

"The text is divided into sections like 'Realism and Naturalism' and 'The Harlem Renaissance,' with each section prefaced by a penetrating overview and each poet introduced by a biographical essay. Included are poets as diverse as Sherman Alexie, Ezra Pound, and Lucille Clifton, along with Nuyorican poets, New Formalists, Beats, imagists, and surrealists. Make room for this affordable, remarkable volume." Libr J

Includes bibliographical references

Unsettling America; an anthology of contemporary multicultural poetry; edited by Maria Mazziotti Gillan and Jennifer Gillan. Penguin Bks. 1994 xxv, 406p pa $18 hardcover o.p.

Grades: 11 12 Adult   **811.008**

1. American poetry—Collections

ISBN 0-14-023778-X (pa)   LC 94-722

This "anthology provides exposure to poets, emerging and established—Louis Simpson, Rita Dove, Luis Rodriguez—who write directly from the immigrant, ethnic and/or religious experience. . . . This collection is a must for anyone seeking an inclusive, unwincing catalogue of the American experience." Publ Wkly

The **Vintage** book of African American poetry; edited and with an introduction by Michael S. Harper and Anthony Walton. Vintage Bks. 2000 xxxiii, 403p pa $14.95 *

Grades: 11 12 Adult   **811.008**

1. American poetry—African American authors—Collections

ISBN 0-375-70300-4   LC 99-39428

"A Vintage original"

"Included in chronological order here are over two centuries of poets, from Jupitor Hammon (1720-1800) to Reginald Shepherd (b.1963). . . . The editors' eloquent, outspoken vision provides a springboard for further examination of what constitutes the mainstream of American poetry." Libr J

Includes bibliographical references

The **Vintage** book of contemporary American poetry; edited and with an introduction by J.D. McClatchy. 2nd ed., newly rev. and expanded ed. Vintage Books 2003 xxxiv, 617p pa $17.95 *

Grades: 11 12 Adult   **811.008**

1. American poetry—Collections

ISBN 1-400-03093-5   LC 2003-269652

"A Vintage original"

First published 1990

"With selections from 65 poets writing over the last 40 years, and with brief notes on their lives and work, this anthology will introduce YAs to much of the best modern poetry." Booklist [review of 1990 edition]

Includes bibliographical references

Visions of war, dreams of peace; writings of women in the Vietnam War; edited by Lynda Van Devanter and Joan A. Furey. Warner Bks. 1991 214p pa $9.95

Grades: 11 12 Adult   **811.008**

1. Vietnam War, 1961-1975—Poetry—Collections

ISBN 0-446-39251-0   LC 90-23284

This anthology collects poetry about the Vietnam War as experienced by women who served and those who remained stateside while their husbands, brothers and fathers fought

Walk on the wild side; urban American poetry since 1975; edited by Nicholas Christopher. Collier Bks. 1993 230p pa $15.75 hardcover o.p.

Grades: 11 12 Adult   **811.008**

1. American poetry—Collections

ISBN 0-02-042725-5 (pa)   LC 93-29443

The editor has "selected 120 evocative poems by such radiant poets as Diane Ackerman, Amy Clampitt, Jessica Hagedorn, Edward Hirsch, Garrett Hongo, Mark Jarman, Joseph Lawrence, Philip Levine, and Carol Muske to demonstrate the 'infinite range of subject matter' generated by an urban perspective and urban settings. . . . This is an incandescent and powerful volume." Booklist

Wherever home begins; 100 contemporary poems; selected by Paul B. Janeczko. Orchard Bks. 1995 114p $15.95

Grades: 7 8 9 10 **811.008**

1. American poetry—Collections

ISBN 0-531-09481-2 LC 94-48740

"A Richard Jackson book"

"This collection of thoughtful unrhymed poems reflects the myriad places people call home from the sleepy, rural towns to the noisy, city streets. . . . The volume contains poems by familiar writers including Gary Soto, George Ella Lyon, Ronald Koertge, X.J. Kennedy, and Naomi Shihab Nye." Voice Youth Advocates

Word of mouth; poems featured on NPR's All things considered; edited and introduced by Catherine Bowman. Random House 2003 xx, 182p pa $12

Grades: 11 12 Adult **811.008**

1. American poetry—Collections

ISBN 0-375-71315-8 LC 2002-28077

This collection includes works by 33 poets, such as Lucille Clifton, Kevin Young, C.D. Wright, Naomi Shihab Nye, Lucia Perillo, and Marilyn Chin

"These inspired selections . . . make for a fresh and enjoyable poetry anthology." Booklist

811.009 American poetry--History and criticism

African-American poets: Phillis Wheatley through Melvin B. Tolson; edited and with an introduction by Harold Bloom. Chelsea House 2002 c2003 335p (Modern critical views) lib bdg $37.95 *

Grades: 9 10 11 12 **811.009**

1. American poetry—African American authors—History and criticism 2. African Americans in literature

ISBN 0-7910-6332-1 LC 2002-6352

A collection of critical essays about African American poets from the colonial era through the Harlem Renaissance.

"A wonderful text for honors or AP English literature classes." SLJ

Includes bibliographical references

African-American poets: Robert Hayden through Rita Dove; edited and with an introduction by Harold Bloom. Chelsea House Publishers 2003 318p (Modern critical views) lib bdg $45 *

Grades: 9 10 11 12 **811.009**

1. American poetry—African American authors—History and criticism 2. African Americans in literature

ISBN 0-7910-7396-3 LC 2003-2038

"This text examines contemporary African-American poets from Robert Hayden to Rita Dove." Publisher's note

Includes bibliographical references

Borus, Audrey

A student's guide to Emily Dickinson. Enslow Publishers 2005 152p il (Understanding literature) $27.93

Grades: 7 8 9 10 **811.009**

1. Dickinson, Emily, 1830-1886

ISBN 0-7660-2285-4 LC 2004-18098

"A short discussion of Dickinson's life and times is followed by a chapter on how to read and analyze her poems, which would be particularly useful for students reading her work for the first time. Subsequent chapters focus on particular themes in the poems such as death and eternity, truth, faith and reality, the natural world, and the influence of the Civil War." SLJ

Includes bibliographical references

Burns, Allan

Thematic guide to American poetry. Greenwood Press 2002 309p $54.95 *

Grades: 9 10 11 12 **811.009**

1. American poetry—History and criticism

ISBN 0-313-31462-4 LC 2001-58646

This "features 21 narrative essays on such broad themes in American poetry as 'Art and Beauty,' 'Family Relations,' 'Loss,' and 'War.' The essays are arranged alphabetically, and each begins with a theme-related quotation followed by a chronologically arranged discussion of how the theme is treated differently across individual poems. . . . The narratives for each poem are pithy and clear, discussing only generally how the poem portrays the theme under discussion." Booklist

Includes bibliographical references

Encyclopedia of American poetry, the twentieth century; edited by Eric L. Haralson. Fitzroy Dearborn Pubs. 2001 846p $125 *

Grades: 11 12 Adult **811.009**

1. American poetry—Bio-bibliography 2. Poets, American—Dictionaries

ISBN 1-57958-240-0

"The volume features more than 400 entries written by academic contributors on individual poets, landmark poems, and major topics. The poet entries are usually 1,000 to 2,000 words long and offer critical treatment of the poet's career and major achievements along with a capsule biography. . . . Approximately one-third of the poet entries include subentries for one or more landmark poems. The 'major topics' entries are longer (around 3,000 words) and include periods or movements (*Black Arts movement, Dada*), verse traditions (often ethnic, such as *Asian American poetry*), and styles and themes (*Confessional poetry, War and antiwar poetry*)." Booklist

The **Facts** on File companion to 20th-century poetry; [edited by] Burt Kimmelman. Facts on File 2004 572p (Facts on File library of American literature) $65; pa $19.95 *

Grades: 11 12 Adult **811.009**

1. American poetry—History and criticism

ISBN 0-8160-4698-0; 0-8160-6224-2 (pa)

LC 2004-50661

The entries in this book reference "poems, poets, poetry institutions, and poetic movements. . . . Biographical information about poets is often coupled with a critical

The Facts on File companion to 20th-century poetry—*Continued*

evaluation of their works. References to specific poems offer an analysis of the writer's style, influences or consistent themes, and the period in which the work was composed. . . . The articles are academic, cross-referencing and comparing works, authors, and time periods." SLJ

Includes bibliographical references

Fagan, Deirdre

Critical companion to Robert Frost; a literary reference to his life and work. Facts on File 2007 454p il $75

Grades: 9 10 11 12 Adult   **811.009**

1. Frost, Robert, 1874-1963

ISBN 0-8160-6182-3; 978-0-8160-6182-2

LC 2006-13269

"This encyclopedic guide offers critical entries on each of Frost's published poems, including such classics as 'The Road Not Taken,' 'Stopping By Woods on a Snowy Evening,' and 'The Death of the Hired Man.'" Publisher's note

Includes bibliographical references

The Greenwood encyclopedia of American poets and poetry; Jeffrey Gray, editor; James McCorkle and Mary McAleer Balkun, associate editors. Greenwood Press 2006 5v set $599.95

Grades: 11 12 Adult   **811.009**

1. American poetry—Encyclopedias 2. Poets, American—Encyclopedias

ISBN 0-3133-2381-X   LC 2005-25445

"Of the more than 900 alphabetically arranged articles found here, approximately one third deal with writers and movements prior to the 20th century. The rest cover 20th- and 21st-century poets and poetry movements." SLJ

This encyclopedia "provides an excellent overview for students learning about American poetry." Ref & User Services Quarterly

Includes bibliographical references

Gwendolyn Brooks; edited and with an introduction by Harold Bloom. Chelsea House 2000 216p (Modern critical views) $36.95

Grades: 9 10 11 12   **811.009**

1. Brooks, Gwendolyn

ISBN 0-7910-5656-2   LC 99-51327

Some other available titles in this series are: Sylvia Plath; Emily Dickinson; Walt Whitman; Robert Frost. For complete list of titles contact publisher

Analytical essays explore the work of the first African American woman named Poetry Consultant to the Library of Congress.

Includes bibliographical references

A Historical guide to Walt Whitman; edited by David S. Reynolds. Oxford Univ. Press 2000 280p il (Historical guides to American authors) $39.95; pa $19.95 *

Grades: 9 10 11 12   **811.009**

1. Whitman, Walt, 1819-1892

ISBN 0-19-512081-7; 0-19-512082-5 (pa)

LC 99-12608

Following a brief biography contributors discuss Whitman's poetics, themes and influence. An illustrated chronology and a bibliographical essay are included

Includes bibliographical references

Kennedy, Richard S., 1920-

E.E. Cummings revisited. Twayne Pubs. 1993 155p il (Twayne's United States authors series) $33 *

Grades: 11 12 Adult   **811.009**

1. Cummings, E. E. (Edward Estlin), 1894-1962

ISBN 0-8057-3995-5   LC 93-4853

Some other available series titles in this class are: Sylvia Plath, Charles Bukowski, Emily Dickinson, Shel Silverstein, Nikki Giovanni. For complete list of titles contact publisher

"In nine chapters tracing Cummings' development as a writer, Kennedy defines his subject's primary styles and their sources in naturalism, cubism, expressionism, surrealism, and other manifestations in the visual arts." Publisher's note

Includes bibliographical references

Kirk, Connie Ann, 1951-

A student's guide to Robert Frost. Enslow Pubs. 2006 160p il (Understanding literature) $27.93 *

Grades: 7 8 9 10   **811.009**

1. Frost, Robert, 1874-1963

ISBN 0-7660-2434-2   LC 2005-13392

In this book, "the career of this literary giant is examined. . . . Poems are put into historical and biographical context, with special emphasis placed on curriculum-related works, including 'Stopping by Woods on a Snowy Evening,' 'The Road Not Taken,' 'The Gift Outright,' and 'Fire and Ice.'" Publisher's note

Leiter, Sharon

Critical companion to Emily Dickinson; a literary reference to her life and work. Facts on File 2006 448p il $75

Grades: 11 12 Adult   **811.009**

1. Dickinson, Emily, 1830-1886

ISBN 0-8160-5448-7; 978-0-8160-5448-0

LC 2005-28123

This book "opens with a foreword by poet and Dickinson scholar Gregory Orr and includes an introduction; an approximately 20-page biography of Dickinson; explications of 150 of her best-known poems (e.g., 'Because I Could Not Stop for Death'); an A-to-Z dictionary of relevant persons, places, and ideas illustrated with black-and-white photos; a chronology; bibliographies; and a comprehensive index." Libr J

Includes bibliographical references

Oliver, Charles M.

Critical companion to Walt Whitman; a literary reference to his life and work. Facts on File 2005 408p il (Facts on File library of American literature) $65

Grades: 11 12 Adult   **811.009**

1. Whitman, Walt, 1819-1892

ISBN 0-8160-5768-0   LC 2005-4172

Oliver, Charles M.—*Continued*

The author "begins this work with a biographical essay that includes several illustrations. A large portion of this book addresses Whitman's works, with entries for the individual poems and for the complete volumes. Each entry describes when and where the book was published and includes a brief account of the poem and its context. The third section of the volume covers people, places, publications, and topics related to Whitman's life and work." Choice

Includes bibliographical references

Sylvia Plath; edited by Harold Bloom. Chelsea House 2000 96p (Bloom's major poets) lib bdg $21.95

Grades: 9 10 11 12   **811.009**
1. Plath, Sylvia
ISBN 0-7910-5935-9   LC 00-55590

Other available series titles in this class include: Gwendolyn Brooks; Emily Dickinson; Hilda Doolittle. For complete list of titles contact publisher

Literary scholars analyze The colossus, The arrival of the bee box, Daddy, Ariel, and Lady Lazarus

Includes bibliographical references

812   American drama

Albee, Edward, 1928-
Who's afraid of Virginia Woolf? Scribner Classics 2003 243p $24 *

Grades: 11 12 Adult   **812**
ISBN 0-7432-5525-9   LC 2003-54206

Also available in paperback from Dramatists Play Service and Signet Bks.

A reissue of the title first published 1962 by Atheneum Pubs.

Characters: 2 men, 2 women. 3 acts. First produced at the Billy Rose Theatre, New York City, October 13, 1962

"The play is a virulent unveiling of the relationship between George, a history professor, and his wife, Martha, the college president's daughter. Another couple, Nick and Honey, get caught in the crossfire of George and Martha's verbal and emotional lacerations, and it becomes clear that each character is engaged in an isolated struggle through a personal hell." Reader's Ency. 4th edition

Dabrowski, Kristen
Twenty 10-minute plays for teens. Smith & Kraus 2004 129p (Young actor series) pa $14.95

Grades: 9 10 11 12   **812**
1. Acting 2. One act plays
ISBN 1-57525-405-0

Also available vols. 2 and 3; new volumes released annually

On cover: 20 10-minute plays for teens

"These brief plays deal with typical adolescent concerns, including dating, parties, sports, and school life, as well as some more controversial topics like being gay, drinking, and suicide. There are roles for up to 14 females and 11 males, but the number of characters can easily be reduced or increased. . . . The content and language make the plays teen-friendly but more appropriate for older high school students, who will recognize the lingo and situations and will enjoy performing them." SLJ

Darion, Joe, 1917-2001
Man of La Mancha; a musical play; lyrics by Joe Darion; music by Mitch Leigh. Random House 1966 82p il hardcover o.p. pa $9.95

Grades: 11 12 Adult   **812**
ISBN 0-394-40621-4; 0-394-40619-2 (pa)

Winner of the New York Drama Critics Circle award "Best Musical 1966"

Characters: 14 men, 5 women, extras. First produced at the ANTA Washington Square Theatre, New York City, November 22, 1965

Fairbanks, Stephanie S., 1950-
Spotlight; solo scenes for student actors. Meriwether 1996 115p pa $14.95

Grades: 9 10 11 12   **812**
1. Acting 2. Monologues
ISBN 1-56608-020-7   LC 96-6169

"Fifty five monologues that feature typical teenage concerns. They run an average of 55 lines each; require minimal props and costumes; and have numbered lines for easy directing and practicing." SLJ

Fleischman, Paul
Zap. Candlewick Press 2005 83p $16.99; pa $5.99

Grades: 9 10 11 12   **812**
ISBN 0-7636-2774-7; 0-7636-3234-1 (pa)
                                            LC 2005-50790

Characters: 2 men, 8 women. 1 act. First produced at Pacific Grove High School, Pacific Grove, California, November 1, 2002.

"Framed as a performance for an imaginary audience armed with remote-control 'zappers,' this is actually seven plays mashed into one: a turgid rendition of Shakespeare's Richard III alternating at audience's whim among six spoofs of other dramaturgical biggies, among them, 'The Russian Play,' 'The English Mystery,' and 'The Southern Play.' Playgoers and actors alike . . . will relish the irreverent chaos as the boundaries between the plays gradually erode." Booklist

Garner, Joan
Stagings; short scripts for middle and high school students; written and illustrated by Joan Garner. Teacher Ideas Press 1995 233p il pa $27

Grades: 9 10 11 12   **812**
1. Acting 2. One act plays
ISBN 1-56308-343-4   LC 95-19013

"This book presents nine science fiction and fantasy one-act plays for young people to perform. . . . Each script begins with a thorough description of characters and costumes, followed by a scene design, set description and a props list. Other notes describe how a teacher could use the play in the classroom and specifically discuss the best staging possibilities for the script." Book Rep

Gibson, William, 1914-
The miracle worker. Pocket Books 2002 120p
pa $5.99 *
Grades: 11 12 Adult   **812**
1. Keller, Helen, 1880-1968—Drama 2. Sullivan,
Anne, 1866-1936—Drama
ISBN 0-7434-5758-7; 978-0-7434-5758-3
First published 1957
Dramatic portrayal of relationship between Helen Keller and her teacher Anne Sullivan.
"The present text is meant for reading, and differs
from the telecast version in that I have restored some
passages that read better than they play and others omitted in performance for simple lack of time." Author's
note

Goodrich, Frances, 1891-1984
The diary of Anne Frank; by Frances Goodrich
and Albert Hackett; newly adapted by Wendy
Kesselman. Dramatists Play Service 2000 70p il pa
$7.50
Grades: 9 10 11 12 Adult   **812**
1. Netherlands—History—1940-1945, German occupa-
tion—Drama 2. World War, 1939-1945—Jews—Dra-
ma 3. Jews—Netherlands—Drama
ISBN 0-8222-1718-X   LC 2006-455205
Awarded the Pulitzer Prize and the New York Drama
Critics Circle Award for 1956
First published 1956 by Random House
Characters: 5 men, 5 women. 2 acts. First produced at
the Cort Theatre, New York City, October 5, 1955.
Dramatization of Anne Frank: diary of a young girl.
Portrays ultimately unsuccessful attempt of Jewish family
to remain hidden during the German occupation of Hol-
land.

Hansberry, Lorraine, 1930-1965
A raisin in the sun. Modern Lib. 1995 xxvi,
135p $14.95; pa $6.50 *
Grades: 11 12 Adult   **812**
1. African Americans—Drama
ISBN 0-679-60172-4; 0-679-75533-0 (pa)
                                  LC 95-16074
Also available in paperback from Plume Bks.
Awarded the New York Drama Critics Circle Award
for the 1958-1959 season
First published 1959
Characters: 8 men, 3 women. 6 scenes in 3 acts. First
produced at the Ethel Barrymore Theatre, New York
City, March 11, 1959
"Hansberry's drama focuses on the Youngers, a 1950s
African-American working-class family in Chicago striv-
ing to realize their individual dreams of prosperity and
education, and their collective dream of a better life. It
was the first play by an African-American woman to be
produced on Broadway." Reader's Ency. 4th edition

Hughes, Langston, 1902-1967
Five plays; edited with an introduction by
Webster Smalley. Indiana Univ. Press 1963 258p
hardcover o.p. pa $14.95
Grades: 11 12 Adult   **812**

ISBN 0-253-32230-8; 0-253-20121-7 (pa)
Contents: Mulatto; Soul gone home; Little Ham; Simply heavenly; Tambourines to glory

Inge, William, 1913-1973
4 plays. Grove Press 1979 c1958 304p $13.50
Grades: 11 12 Adult   **812**
ISBN 0-8021-3209-X   LC 78-73032
The author was awarded the Pulitzer Prize, 1953, for
Picnic
"A Black cat book"
First published 1958 by Random House
Contents: Come back, Little Sheba; Picnic; Bus stop;
The dark at the top of the stairs

Krell-Oishi, Mary, 1953-
Perspectives; relevant scenes for teens.
Meriwether 1997 241p pa $14.95
Grades: 9 10 11 12   **812**
1. Acting 2. Teenagers—Drama
ISBN 1-56608-030-4   LC 97-5405
Consists of 23 original scenes in a variety of styles for
high school and college acting students
The scripts "vary in length and tone but have an equal
number of male and female parts. Several scenes deal
with sensitive subjects (premarital sex, abortion, homo-
sexuality), but they are thoughtfully presented, and the
occasional use of strong language is never gratuitous."
Booklist

Kushner, Tony
Angels in America; a gay fantasia on national
themes. 1st combined pbk. ed. Theatre
Communications Group 2003 289p pa $15.95
Grades: 11 12 Adult   **812**
1. Cohn, Roy, 1927-1986—Drama 2. Gay men—Dra-
ma
ISBN 1-55936-231-6   LC 2003-17904
Part one awarded the Pulitzer Prize, 1993
Contents: pt. 1. Millennium approaches — pt. 2.
Perestroika
Millennium approaches first presented at the Eureka
Theatre Company, San Francisco, May 1991. Perestroika
first presented at the Mark Taper Forum, Los Angeles,
November 1992.
A look at the political, sexual and religious aspects of
contemporary American life set against the AIDS epi-
demic and the life of Roy Cohn.

McCullers, Carson, 1917-1967
The member of the wedding; a play; an
introduction by Dorothy Allison. New Directions
2006 118p pa $11.95 *
Grades: 11 12 Adult   **812**
ISBN 0-8112-1655-1; 978-0-8112-1655-5
                                  LC 2005-36493
Awarded the New York Drama Critics Circle Award
for 1950
First published 1951
Characters: 6 men, 7 women. 3 acts with 3 scenes in
the last act. First produced at the Empire Theatre, New

McCullers, Carson, 1917-1967—*Continued*
York City, January 3, 1950

Based on the author's book of the same title, this is "a study of the loneliness of an overimaginative young Georgian girl." Saturday Rev

McNally, Terrence, 1939-
15 short plays. Smith & Kraus 1994 373p (Contemporary playwrights series) pa $16.95 *
Grades: 11 12 Adult   812
    ISBN 1-880399-34-2   LC 94-10070
    Contemporary playwrights series; Plays for actors series

"By providing a sampling of McNally's plays from the late 1960s to the early 1990s, the entire span of his career, this volume allows a great deal of insight into the range and depth of his development as he courses his way through some of the social, political, and sexual forces that have shaped the American temperament. . . . This is a splendid collection and these plays cut to the emotional bone." Voice Youth Advocates

Medoff, Mark Howard
Children of a lesser god; by Mark Medoff. Dramatists Play Service 1998 c1980 87p pa $7.50
Grades: 11 12 Adult   812
    1. Deaf—Drama
    ISBN 0-8222-0203-4   LC 81-132181
    Characters: 3 men, 4 women. 2 acts. First produced at the Longacre Theatre, New York City, March 30, 1980

"The sensitive drama of the love and growth of James Leeds, a speech teacher at a state school for the deaf, and Sarah Norman, one of his students, may lack some impact in reading since the effect of Sarah's isolation and skilled signing is lost, but Medoff's story remains a powerful, valuable one." Booklist
    Includes bibliographical references

Miller, Arthur, 1915-2005
The crucible; a play in four acts. Viking 1953 145p pa $12 hardcover o.p.
Grades: 11 12 Adult   812
    1. Witchcraft—Drama 2. Salem (Mass.)—Drama
    ISBN 0-14-048138-9 (pa)
    Also available in paperback from Dramatists Play Service
    Characters: 11 men, 10 women. First produced at the Martin Beck Theatre in New York City, January 22, 1953

A play based on the Salem witchcraft trials of 1692. It deals particularly with the hounding to death of the nonconformist John Proctor.

Death of a salesman; certain private conversations in two acts and a requiem; with an introduction by Christopher Bigsby. Penguin 1998 xxvii, 113p (Penguin twentieth-century classics) pa $12 *
Grades: 11 12 Adult   812
    ISBN 0-14-118097-8   LC 97-37223
    Winner of the New York Drama Critics Circle Award and the Pulitzer Prize, 1949
    First published 1949

Characters: 8 men, 5 women. First produced at the Morosco Theatre, New York City, February 10, 1949.

"The tragedy of a typical Americana salesman who at the age of sixty-three is faced with what he cannot face: defeat and disillusionment. It is a bitter and moving experience of groping for values and for material success." Wis Libr Bull
    Includes bibliographical references

The portable Arthur Miller; original introduction by Harold Clurman; revised edition edited with an introduction by Christopher Bigsby. Penguin Books 2003 xli, 575p (Penguin classics) pa $17 *
Grades: 11 12 Adult   812
    ISBN 0-14-243755-7   LC 2003-276344
    First published 1955

This volume contains the complete texts of Death of a salesman, The crucible, After the fall, The American clock, The last Yankee, and Broken glass. An excerpt from a radio play thought lost for years and two very brief selections from the memoir Timebends are also included.
    Includes bibliographical references

O'Neill, Eugene, 1888-1953
The iceman cometh; a play. Vintage Bks. 1946 260p pa $12
Grades: 11 12 Adult   812
    ISBN 0-375-70917-7
    Characters: 16 men, 3 women. First produced at the Martin Beck Theatre, New York City, October 9, 1946

Long day's journey into night; a play; with a foreword by Harold Bloom. 2nd ed. Yale Univ. Press 2002 c1989 179p $22.95; pa $12.95
Grades: 11 12 Adult   812
    ISBN 0-300-09410-8; 0-300-09305-5 (pa)
                                         LC 2001-97735
    Also available in paperback from Dramatists Play Service
    Awarded the Pulitzer Prize, 1957
    First published 1956
    Characters: 3 men, 2 women. 4 acts, 5 scenes. First produced in Stockholm, Sweden, February, 1956

"Among the papers Eugene O'Neill left when he died in 1953 was the manuscript of an autobiography. Not an autobiography in the usual sense, however. For 'Long Day's Journey Into Night' is in the form of a play—a true O'Neill tragedy, set in 1912 in the summer home of a theatrical family that is isolated from the community by a kind of ingrown misery and a sense of doom." N Y Times Book Rev

Rose, Reginald, 1920-2002
Twelve angry men; introduction by David Mamet. Penguin Books 2006 73p (Penguin classics) pa $11
Grades: 9 10 11 12   812
    ISBN 0-14-310440-3; 978-0-14-310440-7
                                         LC 2006-46006
    First published 1955 by Dramatic Pub.

Rose, Reginald, 1920-2002—*Continued*
Characters: 12 men. 3 acts. Original television broadcast on CBS program Studio One, September 20, 1954.
Television play in which one man in a jury tries to convince the other eleven jurors that the defendant in a murder trial is not guilty.

Shange, Ntozake
For colored girls who have considered suicide, when the rainbow is enuf; a choreopoem. 1st Scribner poetry ed. Scribner Poetry 1997 64p pa $9.95 *
Grades: 11 12 Adult   812
   1. African American women—Drama
ISBN 0-684-84326-9   LC 98-164958
First published 1977 by Macmillan
Choreopoem performed by seven women exploring the joys and sorrows of being a black woman.

Simon, Neil
Brighton Beach memoirs. Plume 1995 130p pa $12 *
Grades: 11 12 Adult   812
   1. Jews—New York (N.Y.)—Drama
ISBN 0-452-27528-8   LC 95-21788
Awarded the New York Drama Critics Circle Award for best play, 1983
First published 1984 by Random House
"Sex and baseball are the primary preoccupations of 15-year-old Eugene Jerome, narrator of a seriocomic slice of lower-middle-class Jewish family life in Depression-era New York City. The several adolescent characters in the extended family add to the teenage appeal of Simon's . . . play." Booklist

The collected plays of Neil Simon; with an introduction by Neil Simon. New Am. Lib. 1986-1998 4v v1-2 pa ea $19.95 *
Grades: 9 10 11 12   812
   ISBN 0-452-25870-7 (v1); 0-452-26358-1 (v2)
                   LC 86-12639
v4 available from Touchstone Bks. $15
"A Plume book"
Volume 1 originally published 1971 by Random House with title: The comedy of Neil Simon
Contents v1: Come blow your horn; Barefoot in the park; The odd couple; The star-spangled girl; Promises, promises; Plaza suite; Last of the red hot lovers; v2: Little me; The gingerbread lady; The prisoner of Second Avenue; The Sunshine Boys; The good doctor; God's favorite; California suite; Chapter two; v3: Sweet Charity; They're playing our song; I ought to be in pictures; Fools; The odd couple (female version); Brighton Beach memoirs; Biloxi blues; Broadway bound; v4: Rumors; Lost in Yonkers; Jake's women; Laughter on the 23rd floor; London suite

Lost in Yonkers. Plume 1993 120p (Plume drama) pa $12
Grades: 11 12 Adult   812
ISBN 0-452-26883-4   LC 92-29111
Awarded the Pulitzer Prize, 1991
First published 1991 by Random House

Characters: 4 men, 3 women. 2 acts. First presented at the Stevens Center for the Performing Arts, Winston-Salem, December 31, 1990.
This play, "set in 1940s New York, is a sad-funny portrait of a dysfunctional family, headed by a woman who provided for her children but never showed them love." Booklist

Soto, Gary
Novio boy; a play. Harcourt Brace & Co. 1997 78p pa $8 *
Grades: 7 8 9 10   812
   1. Dating (Social customs)—Drama 2. Mexican Americans—Drama
ISBN 0-15-201531-0   LC 96-32605
Rudy anxiously prepares for and then goes out on a first date with an attractive girl who is older than he is
"A hip, funny play. . . . Since the Mexican-American cast spouts frequent Spanish words, several lines of dialogue could be lost on an audience unfamiliar with the language. The visual clues of a live performance might serve to clarify some unfamiliar words. . . . Young actors should be able to perform this entertaining play with or without adult assistance." SLJ

Surface, Mary Hall, 1958-
Most valuable player and four other all-star plays for middle and high school audiences. Smith & Kraus 1999 176p il (Young actor series) pa $16.95
Grades: 9 10 11 12   812
   1. Children's plays, American
ISBN 1-57525-178-7   LC 99-30018
"The title play is a compelling piece about Jackie Robinson's early days in the major leagues. The other selections deal with Mozart's childhood and issues such as high school drug dealing, racial conflict, learning disability, and the need for artistic expression. They all move along at a fast clip, the characters speak simply and directly, and the language is realistic and occasionally rough. In most cases, the staging is fairly simple." SLJ

Ullom, Shirley, 1938-
Tough acts to follow; seventy-five monologs for teens. Meriwether 2000 155p pa $14.95
Grades: 9 10 11 12   812
   1. Monologues 2. Acting
ISBN 1-56608-057-6   LC 00-24678
This collection of original short character sketches "is overflowing with one-of-a kind monologues of equal length for both guys and girls, each with a clever title that provides quick insight into the subject matter." Voice Youth Advocates

Wasserstein, Wendy, 1950-2006
The Heidi chronicles and other plays. Vintage Bks. 1991 249p pa $13.95
Grades: 11 12 Adult   812
ISBN 0-679-73499-6   LC 90-55681
First published 1990 by Harcourt Brace Jovanovich
Contents: Uncommon women and others; Isn't it romantic; The Heidi chronicles

Wasserstein, Wendy, 1950-2006—*Continued*

This collection traces "three decades of changing styles, mores, life objectives, and intellectual challenges. Wasserstein examines her characters and their times with great good humor, complexity, depth of feeling, and a firm refusal to accept trite and easy images." Libr J

Wilder, Thornton, 1897-1975

Our town; a play in three acts; foreword by Donald Margulies. HarperCollins Pubs. 2003 xx, 181p $19.95; pa $9.95

Grades: 11 12 Adult   **812**
   ISBN 0-06-053525-3; 0-06-051263-6 (pa)
A reissue with a new foreword of the title first published 1938 by Coward-McCann
Large mixed cast. First produced at McCarter's Theatre, Princeton, N.J., January 22, 1938
"Presented without scenery of any kind, utilizing a narrator and loose episodic form, adventurous and imaginative in style, this unique play . . . is one of the most distinguished in the modern repertoire. It deals with the simplest and most touching aspects of life in a small town." HarperCollins Reader's Ency of Am Lit

Three plays: Our town, The skin of our teeth, The matchmaker; with a preface. Harper & Row 1957 401p pa $15.95 hardcover o.p. *

Grades: 11 12 Adult   **812**
   ISBN 0-06-051264-4 (pa)
Wilder was awarded the Pulitzer Prize, 1938 for Our town, and 1943 for The skin of our teeth
A collection of three titles first copyrighted 1938, 1942, and 1955 respectively. An earlier version of: The matchmaker, was first copyrighted 1939 with title: The merchant of Yonkers
Our town is a portrait of family life in small town America. The skin of our teeth is an allegorical fantasy about man's struggle to survive. The matchmaker is a romantic farce set in the 1880's

Williams, Tennessee, 1911-1983

The glass menagerie; introduction by Robert Bray. New Directions 1999 xxii, 105p pa $7.95

Grades: 9 10 11 12   **812**
   ISBN 0-8112-1404-4   LC 98-54624
Also available in paperback from Dramatists Play Service
Awarded the New York Drama Critics Circle Award for 1945
First published 1945 by Random House; this reissue of New Directions 1949 edition contains Williams' essay The catastrophe of success and production notes. A new critical introduction has been added
Characters: 2 men, 2 women. 2 parts. One set of scenery. First produced at the Civic Theatre, Chicago, December 26, 1944
"A poignant and painful family drama set in St. Louis, in which a frigid and frustrated mother's dreams of her glamorous past as a Southern belle conflict with the grimness of her reduced circumstances, as she persuades her rebellious son Tom to provide a 'gentleman caller' for her crippled daughter, Laura." Oxford Companion to Engl Lit. 6th edition

Wilson, August

Fences; a play; introduction by Lloyd Richards. New Am. Lib. 1986 101p pa $11 *

Grades: 11 12 Adult   **812**
   ISBN 0-452-26401-4   LC 86-5264
Awarded the Pulitzer Prize, 1987
"A Plume book"
Characters: 5 men, 1 woman, 1 girl. 2 acts, 9 scenes. First produced at the Yale Repertory Theatre, New Haven, Connecticut, April 30, 1985

Jitney. Overlook Press 2001 96p hardcover o.p. pa $14.95

Grades: 11 12 Adult   **812**
   1. African Americans—Drama
   ISBN 1-58567-186-X; 1-58567-370-6 (pa)
                  LC 2001-33962
Winner of the New York Drama Critics Circle Award, 2000
Characters: 8 men, 1 woman. 2 acts, 8 scenes. This is a revised version of a play written 1979

Joe Turner's come and gone; a play in two acts. New Am. Lib. 1988 94p pa $11

Grades: 11 12 Adult   **812**
   1. African Americans—Drama
   ISBN 0-452-26009-4   LC 88-1660
"A Plume book"
Characters: 6 men, 5 women. 2 acts, 10 scenes. 1 setting. First produced at the Yale Repertory Theatre, New Haven, Connecticut, April 29, 1986

Ma Rainey's black bottom; a play in two acts. New Am. Lib. 1985 111p pa $11

Grades: 11 12 Adult   **812**
   ISBN 0-452-26113-9   LC 84-27156
"A Plume book"
Characters: 8 men, 2 women. 2 acts. First produced at the Yale Repertory Theatre, New Haven, Connecticut, April 6, 1984
Recording session by Black blues great Ma Rainey for white-owned studio, is setting for exploration of racial relations and conflicts.

The piano lesson. New Am. Lib. 1990 108p hardcover o.p. pa $11 *

Grades: 11 12 Adult   **812**
   ISBN 0-525-24926-5; 0-452-26534-7 (pa)
                  LC 90-38734
Awarded the Pulitzer Prize and the New York Drama Critics Circle Award, 1990
Characters: 5 men, 3 women. 2 acts, 7 scenes. First presented at the Yale Repertory Theatre, New Haven, November 26, 1987

With their eyes; September 11th: the view from a high school at ground zero; edited by Annie Thoms; created by Taresh Batra {et al.}; photos by Ethan Moses. HarperTempest 2002 228p il hardcover o.p. pa $6.99

Grades: 7 8 9 10   **812**
   1. Stuyvesant High School (New York, N.Y.)
   ISBN 0-06-051806-5; 0-06-051718-2 (pa)
                  LC 2002-4552

With their eyes—*Continued*

"The students of Stuyvesant High School watched through their classroom windows as the World Trade Center was attacked on September 11. This book contains the play that they created based on what students, teachers, janitors, and others within their school community experienced." Voice Youth Advocates

"The speakers reveal their emotions with painful honesty. . . . The book is an obvious choice for reader's theater and for use across the curriculum; its deeply affecting contents will also make compelling personal-interest reading." Booklist

Zindel, Paul

The effect of gamma rays on man-in-the-moon marigolds; a drama in two acts; drawings by Dong Kingman. Harper & Row 1971 108p il pa $6.99 hardcover o.p. *

Grades: 11 12 Adult   **812**

ISBN 0-06-075738-8 (pa)

Also available in paperback from Dramatists Play Service

Awarded the Pulitzer Prize, 1971, and the 1969-70 New York Drama Critics Circle Award

Characters: 5 women. First produced at the Mercer-O'Casey Theatre, New York City, April 7, 1970

"The play, in the naturalistic tradition, deals with a widow and her two daughters, the imagination of one of whom has been captured by the atom and the possibilities it offers of producing mutations." McGraw-Hill Ency of World Drama

812.008   American drama--Collections

Audition monologs for student actors [I]-[II]; selections from contemporary plays; edited by Roger Ellis. Meriwether 1999-2001 2v pa ea $15.95

Grades: 9 10 11 12   **812.008**

1. Monologues 2. Acting

ISBN 1-56608-055-X (v1); 1-56608-073-8 (v2)

            LC 99-37962

"An introduction discusses choosing and performing the monologues, including specific sections on characterization and staging. The selections are evenly divided between those for males and females, and many are for minority actors. Each selection is prefaced by thoughtful character insights and performance suggestions. An excellent, up-to-the-minute resource for serious teen actors." Booklist [review of volume 1]

Black theatre USA; plays by African Americans, 1847 to today; edited by James V. Hatch, Ted Shine. rev and expanded ed. Free Press 1996 pa in 2v 916p hardcover o.p. v1 pa $26; v2 pa $25 *

Grades: 11 12 Adult   **812.008**

1. American drama—African American authors—Collections

ISBN 0-684-82306-3; 0-684-82308-X (v1 pa); 0-684-82307-1 (v2 pa)   LC 95-40329

First published 1974

Contents: v1 The early period, 1847-1938; v2 The recent period, 1935-today

Among the plays are: Star of Ethiopia, by W. E. B. Du Bois; A soldier's play, by C. Fuller; Sally's rape, by R. McCauley; Contribution, by T. Shine; Fires in the mirror, by A. D. Smith.

Includes bibliographical references

Great monologues for young actors; Craig Slaight, Jack Sharrar, editors. Smith & Kraus 1992-1999 3v v1 pa $11.95; v2-v3 pa ea $14.95

Grades: 9 10 11 12   **812.008**

1. Monologues 2. Acting

ISBN 1-880399-03-2 (v1); 0-57525-106-X (v2); 1-57525-408-1 (v3)

"The Young Actors series."

These volumes provide an introduction and acting notes for monologues for men and women drawn from contemporary and classic works

Great scenes from minority playwrights; seventy-four scenes of cultural diversity; edited by Marsh Cassady. Meriwether 1997 341p pa $16.95 *

Grades: 9 10 11 12   **812.008**

1. American drama—Collections 2. Minorities in literature 3. Acting

ISBN 1-56608-029-0   LC 97-298

A collection of scenes from Hispanic as well as Native-American, African-American, Jewish-American, and Asian-American theater

"Cassady introduces the plays and precedes each scene with questions intended to clarify characters' motivations or the playwright's intentions. Most plays concern the tragic aspects of prejudice, but two playwrights have chosen a satirical approach. A useful collection for drama classes and theater groups." Booklist

Millennium monologs; 95 contemporary characterizations for young actors; edited by Gerald Lee Ratliff. Meriwether 2002 261p pa $15.95

Grades: 9 10 11 12   **812.008**

1. Monologues 2. Acting

ISBN 1-56608-082-7   LC 2002-13009

An anthology of monologues by contemporary writers, divided into four categories: "Hope and Longing," "Spirit and Soul," "Fun and Fantasy," and "Doubt and Despair." Includes audition techniques

"This fine collection of American monologues is notable for its diversity as well as for the high quality of the material." Booklist

Monologues for young actors; [edited by] Lorraine Cohen. Avon Bks. 1994 198p pa $5.99

Grades: 9 10 11 12   **812.008**

1. Monologues 2. Acting

ISBN 0-380-76187-4   LC 94-94067

This "collection of monologues, compiled specifically for young actors, contains an audition piece for even the hard to please performer. Whether students are looking for comedy, tragedy, or something in between, this has what they need. It even includes monologues written specifically for young African American actors. All audition pieces in this excellent source are from celebrated contemporary or classical plays." Voice Youth Advocates

Under 30; plays for a new generation; edited by Eric Lane and Nina Shengold. Vintage 2004 639p pa $17

Grades: 9 10 11 12   **812.008**

1. American drama—Collections

ISBN 1-4000-7616-1   LC 2004043041

Contents: As bees in honey drown; Be aggressive; None of the above; Refuge; This is our youth; Cowtown; Fishing; Harriet Tubman visits a therapist; Icarus's mother; On the edge; Photographs from S-21; Shari says; Small world; Sweet hunk O' trash; Time flies; War at home

The editors "have assembled five full-length plays, 11 shorter plays, and excerpts from four plays, all written for actors under 30." Libr J

"This collection offers thespians plenty of characters to portray in situations that crackle with teen appeal." SLJ

812.009 American drama--History and criticism

Abbotson, Susan C. W., 1961-

Critical companion to Arthur Miller; a literary reference to his life and work. Facts on File 2006 518p il (Facts on File library of American literature) $75

Grades: 9 10 11 12 Adult   **812.009**

1. Miller, Arthur, 1915-2005

ISBN 0-8160-6194-7; 978-0-8160-6194-5

     LC 2006-22902

This book "covers Miller's entire canon, including plays, screenplays, fiction, short stories, and poetry, as well as many of his important essays and critical pieces. Also included are . . . entries on literary, theatrical, and personal figures important to Miller; key terms and topics connected to his work; and various theatrical companies and places with which he has been associated." Publisher's note

Includes bibliographical references

Student companion to Arthur Miller. Greenwood Press 2000 169p (Student companions to classic writers) lib bdg $35 *

Grades: 9 10 11 12   **812.009**

1. Miller, Arthur, 1915-2005

ISBN 0-313-30949-3   LC 99-89069

Another available series title in this class is: Student companion to Tennessee Williams. For complete list of titles contact publisher

A biographical section is followed by "discussion of eight of Miller's major plays that incorporates the impact of other literature and historical events on his work and links themes, language, and characters to events and periods in the writer's life. Chapters on each play address the development of setting and plot, characters, and point of view; provide a historical context; and touch on other relevant literary devices. A bibliography of Miller's play and other works, as well as extensive listings of critical studies, reviews, and criticisms complete the text." SLJ

Includes bibliographical references

Arthur Miller's Death of a salesman; edited and with an introduction by Harold Bloom. Updated ed. Chelsea House Publishers 2006 169p (Modern critical interpretations) $45

Grades: 9 10 11 12 Adult   **812.009**

1. Miller, Arthur, 1915-2005

ISBN 0-7910-9302-6; 978-0-7910-9302-3

     LC 2006-15137

Other available series titles in this class include: Arthur Miller's the crucible; Tennessee Williams' The glass menagerie. For complete list of titles contact publisher

First published 1988

A collection of ten critical essays on Miller's play "Death of A Salesman" arranged in chronological order of publication.

Includes bibliographical references

August Wilson; edited and with an introduction by Harold Bloom. Chelsea House 2002 85p (Bloom's major dramatists) lib bdg $21.95

Grades: 9 10 11 12   **812.009**

1. Wilson, August

ISBN 0-7910-6362-3   LC 2001-42336

Some other available series titles in this class are: Arthur Miller; Eugene O'Neill; Tennessee Williams. For complete list of titles contact publisher

Following a biography of Wilson this volume provides plot summaries, and critical interpretations of the plays and their characters.

Includes bibliographical references

Dunkleberger, Amy

A student's guide to Arthur Miller. Enslow Publs. 2005 160p il (Understanding literature) lib bdg $27.93 *

Grades: 7 8 9 10   **812.009**

1. Miller, Arthur, 1915-2005

ISBN 0-7660-2432-6

This discusses the life of Arthur Miller and his works *All My Sons, Death of a Salesman, The Crucible, A View From the Bridge, After the Fall, Incident at Vichy,* and *The Price*

"Engaging and informative. . . . The very accessible format and the solid information make [this book] useful to students, and the engaging style should interest casual readers." SLJ

Includes glossary and bibliographical references

Eugene O'Neill; edited and with an introduction by Harold Bloom. Updated ed. Chelsea House Publishers 2007 240p (Modern critical views) $31.95

Grades: 9 10 11 12 Adult   **812.009**

1. O'Neill, Eugene, 1888-1953

ISBN 0-7910-9366-2; 978-0-7910-9366-5

     LC 2006-36859

For a complete list of series titles contact publisher

First published 1987

This is an "exploration into the life and works of a playwright whose searing dramas continue to be a powerful presence on the American stage." Publisher's note

Includes bibliographical references

Heintzelman, Greta

Critical companion to Tennessee Williams; [by] Greta Heintzelman, Alycia Smith Howard. Facts on File 2005 436p il (Facts on File library of American literature) $65; pa $19.95

Grades: 11 12 Adult   **812.009**

1. Williams, Tennessee, 1911-1983
ISBN 0-8160-4888-6; 0-8160-6429-6 (pa)

LC 2004-7362

"The first comprises a 14-page biography with recommendations for further reading. The second and largest section includes entries for each of Williams's plays, stories, and miscellaneous publications. . . . The third section consists of brief entries on subjects relating to Williams and his work, covering, for example, awards, the Dramatists Guild, Truman Capote, and Washington University. The final section includes a chronology of Williams's life, a bibliography of his work, and a bibliography of secondary sources." Libr J

The authors "offer an excellent resource for those studying Williams's life and extensive body of work." Choice

Includes bibliographical references

Hermann, Spring

A student's guide to Tennessee Williams. Enslow Publishers 2007 160p il (Understanding literature) lib bdg $27.93

Grades: 7 8 9 10   **812.009**

1. Williams, Tennessee, 1911-1983
ISBN 978-0-7660-2706-0; 0-7660-2706-6

LC 2006-36458

"The life and work of Williams are examined. . . . Each work is placed in historical and biographical context, with special emphasis placed on curriculum-related works The Glass Menagerie, A Streetcar Named Desire, and Cat On a Hot Tin Roof, in addition to many other lesser-known works." Publisher's note

Includes glossary and bibliographical references

The **Tennessee** Williams encyclopedia; edited by Philip C. Kolin. Greenwood Press 2004 xxx, 350p $89.95

Grades: 11 12 Adult   **812.009**

1. Williams, Tennessee, 1911-1983
ISBN 0-313-32101-9   LC 2003-59583

The contributors "provide approximately 160 entries on individuals, places, works, and concepts of special significance in Williams's life and career. Entries are alphabetical. . . . This reviewer cannot imagine a more engaging or more useful reference resource for students and scholars of Williams." Choice

Includes bibliographical references

813.009   American fiction--History and criticism

Alice Walker; edited and with an introduction by Harold Bloom. Chelsea House 2000 83p (Bloom's major novelists) $21.95 *

Grades: 9 10 11 12   **813.009**

1. Walker, Alice, 1944-
ISBN 0-7910-5250-8   LC 99-14577

Some other available series titles in this class are: Willa Cather; Stephen Crane; Ernest Hemingway; Toni Morrison. For complete list of titles contact publisher

"This title includes detailed plot summaries . . . lists of characters, and excerpts from 25 critical essays on two of Walker's novels—*Meridian* and *The Color Purple*—along with a brief biography of the writer and a thematic index." SLJ

Includes bibliographical references

Bernard, Catherine

Understanding To kill a mockingbird. Lucent Books 2003 112p il map (Understanding great literature) $27.45 *

Grades: 7 8 9 10   **813.009**

1. Lee, Harper, 1926-—About
ISBN 1-560-06860-4   LC 2002-156251

An introduction to Harper Lee's famous novel, "To Kill a Mockingbird," discussing the author's life, the historical context of the novel, its plot, themes, characters, literary criticism, and pertinence for today's audiences.

Includes bibliographical references

Bloom, Susan P.

Presenting Avi; [by] Susan P. Bloom, Cathryn M. Mercier. Twayne Pubs. 1997 206p il (Twayne's young adult authors series) $30

Grades: 7 8 9 10   **813.009**

1. Avi, 1937-
ISBN 0-8057-4569-6   LC 96-53878

A critical introduction to the life and work of the prolific writer of young adult and children's books.

"The text shows painstakingly careful reading of Avi's work." SLJ

Includes bibliographical references

Buckwalter, Stephanie

A student's guide to Jack London. Enslow Publishers 2007 160p il (Understanding literature) lib bdg $27.93

Grades: 7 8 9 10   **813.009**

1. London, Jack, 1876-1916
ISBN 978-0-7660-2707-7; 0-7660-2707-4

LC 2006-32815

"The career of this literary giant is examined. . . . Each of his works is placed in historical and biographical context, with special emphasis placed on curriculum-related works. These include The Call of the Wild, White Fang, and several other autobiographical works and short stories." Publisher's note

Includes glossary and bibliographical references

Burkhead, Cynthia

Student companion to John Steinbeck. Greenwood Press 2002 180p (Student companions to classic writers) lib bdg $35.95 *

Grades: 9 10 11 12   **813.009**

1. Steinbeck, John, 1902-1968
ISBN 0-313-31457-8   LC 2002-17134

Another available series title in this class is: Student companion to Ernest Hemingway. For complete list of titles contact publisher

Burkhead, Cynthia—*Continued*

"Examines the life, career, and works of John Steinbeck. . . . Each criticism explores plot and character development, major themes, symbolism, and literary devices. An alternative critical theme is also included. . . . Because Steinbeck is required reading in many high school curriculums, this would be a valuable resource for students." Libr Media Connect

Includes bibliographical references

Campbell, Patricia J., 1930-

Robert Cormier; daring to disturb the universe. Delacorte Press 2006 287p pa $41.95; lib bdg $17.99

Grades: 9 10 11 12   **813.009**

1. Cormier, Robert

ISBN 0-385-73046-2 (pa); 978-0-385-73046-4 (pa); 0-385-90074-0 (lib bdg); 978-0-385-90074-4 (lib bdg)

LC 2005-23595

The author "writes both a tribute to Robert Cormier and . . . [a] literary analysis that examines the common themes in his work. She emphasizes Cormier's place in the history of young adult literature, the contrast between the man and his work, and the quality of the works he provided the world." Voice Youth Advocates

"Campbell treats . . . [Cormier's] fans to rare glimpses of his process, and, with her wide perspective on YA literature, puts Cormier's work—including such landmark novels as The Chocolate War and I Am the Cheese—and its wide-reaching reverberations in a context for today's readers and writers." Publ Wkly

Includes bibliographical references

Carson McCullers; edited and with an introduction by Harold Bloom. Chelsea House 1986 159p (Modern critical views) $36.95 *

Grades: 9 10 11 12   **813.009**

1. McCullers, Carson, 1917-1967

ISBN 0-87754-630-4   LC 86-9718

Some other available series titles in this class are: John Irving; John Steinbeck; Eudora Welty; Tom Wolfe. For complete list of titles contact publisher

Scholars evaluate the author of The ballad of the sad cafe, The heart is a lonely hunter, Reflections in a golden eye and The member of the wedding.

Includes bibliographical references

Cart, Michael

The heart has its reasons; young adult literature with gay/lesbian/queer content, 1969-2004; [by] Michael Cart [and] Christine A. Jenkins. Scarecrow Press 2006 207p (Scarecrow studies in young adult literature, no 18) $42

Grades: Professional   **813.009**

1. Homosexuality in literature 2. Young adult literature—History and criticism 3. Teenagers—Books and reading

ISBN 0-8108-5071-0   LC 2005-31320

"Both a comprehensive overview and a lively, detailed discussion of individual landmark books, this highly readable title . . . discusses 35 years of YA books with gay, lesbian, bisexual, transgender, and queer/questioning (GLBTQ) content. . . . With fully annotated bibliographies, including a chronological list, this is a valuable YA and adult resource, sure to be in great demand for personal reference and group discussion." Booklist

Includes bibliographical references

The **Columbia** companion to the twentieth-century American short story; Blanche H. Gelfant, editor. Columbia Univ. Press 2000 660p $83.50; pa $24.50 *

Grades: 11 12 Adult   **813.009**

1. Short stories—History and criticism 2. American fiction—Bio-bibliography

ISBN 0-231-11098-7; 0-231-11099-5 (pa)

LC 00-31610

"The first 100 pages are devoted to thematic essays that focus on the form of the short story, the development of the genre, several distinct subject types (e.g., short stories of the Holocaust or of the working class), and four different ethnic groups (African American, Asian American, Chicano Latino American, and Native American). . . . The remainder of the book is devoted to over 100 individual author essays that focus on reading for pleasure and understanding rather than critical interpretation. Entries discuss the development of each author and the content and meaning of his or her major short stories." Libr J

Includes bibliographical references

Crayton, Lisa A.

A student's guide to Toni Morrison. Enslow Publs. 2006 160p il (Understanding literature) lib bdg $27.93 *

Grades: 7 8 9 10   **813.009**

1. Morrison, Toni, 1931-

ISBN 0-7660-2436-9   LC 2005-19069

"Each work is placed in historical and biographical context, with special emphasis placed on curriculum-related material, including The Bluest Eye, Song of Solomon, and Beloved, along with several other noteworthy works." Publisher's note

Includes glossary and bibliographical references

Devlin, James E., 1938-

Elmore Leonard. Twayne Pubs. 1999 164p (Twayne's United States authors series) $32 *

Grades: 11 12 Adult   **813.009**

1. Leonard, Elmore, 1925-

ISBN 0-8057-1694-7   LC 99-42756

Some other available series titles in this class are: Beverly Cleary; F. Scott Fitzgerald; James Salter; Russell Banks. For complete list of titles contact publisher

Following a brief biography the author offers critical interpretation and explication of Leonard's major works. A chronology and annotated bibliography are included.

Includes bibliographical references

Diorio, Mary Ann L.

A student's guide to Herman Melville. Enslow Publs. 2006 160p il (Understanding literature) lib bdg $27.93 *

Grades: 7 8 9 10   **813.009**

1. Melville, Herman, 1819-1891

ISBN 0-7660-2435-0   LC 2005-10159

Diorio, Mary Ann L.—*Continued*

"Each work is placed in historical and biographical context, with special emphasis placed on curriculum-related works, including his masterpiece, Moby Dick, along with Billy Budd, several of his short stories, including 'Bartleby the Scrivener,' and several of his poetic works." Publisher's note

Includes glossary and bibliographical references

Ernest Hemingway; edited and with an introduction by Harold Bloom. Chelsea House Publishers 2005 243p (Modern critical views) $37.95 *

Grades: 9 10 11 12　　　　　**813.009**

1. Hemingway, Ernest, 1899-1961
ISBN 0-7910-8135-4

Other series titles in this class include: Stephen King; Carson McCullers. For complete list of titles contact publisher

Scholars evaluate Hemingway's novels and short stories.

Includes bibliographical references

Eudora Welty; edited and with an introduction by Harold Bloom. Chelsea House 1999 69p (Bloom's major short story writers) $21.95 *

Grades: 9 10 11 12　　　　　**813.009**

1. Welty, Eudora, 1909-2001
ISBN 0-7910-5126-9　　　　　LC 98-49499

Some other available series titles in this class are: Sherwood Anderson; Raymond Carver; John Cheever, O. Henry; Katherine Anne Porter. For complete list of titles contact publisher

"An examination of four of Welty's short stories: 'Death of a Traveling Salesman,' 'Why I Live at the P.O.,' 'The Wide Net,' and 'No Place for You, My Love.' For each, a summary is followed by an annotated list of characters and extracts from five or six authoritative critical sources analyzing different aspects of the story or the author's themes. The book begins with a two-page biography of Welty and concludes with lists of works by and about her as well as a helpful 'Index of Themes and Ideas.'" SLJ

The **Facts** on File companion to the American novel; edited by Abby H.P. Werlock; assistant editor, James P. Werlock. Facts on File 2005 3v (Facts on File library of American literature) set $195 *

Grades: 11 12 Adult　　　　　**813.009**

1. American fiction—Encyclopedias 2. American fiction—Bio-bibliography
ISBN 0-8160-4528-3; 978-0-8160-4528-0
LC 2005-12437

"This A-to-Z reference contains 450 biographical overviews of American and foreign-born authors living in the United States and 500 signed analytical essays on their novels. . . . Libraries will value this compact set for including classics as well as hard-to-find contemporary authors." SLJ

Includes bibliographical references

Fargnoli, A. Nicholas

William Faulkner A to Z; the essential reference to his life and work; {by} A. Nicholas Fargnoli and Michael Golay. Facts on File 2001 340p il $65; pa $17.95 *

Grades: 11 12 Adult　　　　　**813.009**

1. Faulkner, William, 1897-1962
ISBN 0-8160-3860-0; 0-8160-4159-8 (pa)
LC 2001-23821

New edition in preparation

The authors "provide detailed entries on Faulkner, his works, family, friends, contemporaries, and prominent places in his life. The volume also contains entries on publishers, magazines, and other social, historical, and cultural influences on Faulkner's work, including the response from not only critics but also the public. The appendixes are rich in resources, including family trees for Faulkner's family as well as for several families in his books." Voice Youth Advocates

Includes bibliographical references

Gale, Robert L.

An F. Scott Fitzgerald encyclopedia. Greenwood Press 1998 526p $90 *

Grades: 11 12 Adult　　　　　**813.009**

1. Fitzgerald, F. Scott (Francis Scott), 1896-1940
ISBN 0-313-30139-5　　　　　LC 98-13976

"In entries from Abbot, Hamilton ('Ham') (a character in The Love Boat) to 'Zone of Accident' (a story published in 1935), Gale covers all Fitzgerald's works and named fictional characters; and biographical sketches of his family, friends, and associates are included. Entries range in length from a single sentence to nearly three pages for Fitzgerald, Zelda and The Great Gatsby. Longer entries include bibliographies." Booklist

Includes bibliographical references

Gloria Naylor: critical perspectives past and present; edited by Henry L. Gates, Jr., and K.A. Appiah. Amistad Press 1993 322p (Amistad literary series) pa $14.95 hardcover o.p.

Grades: 11 12 Adult　　　　　**813.009**

1. Naylor, Gloria
ISBN 1-56743-030-9 (pa)　　　　　LC 92-45758

This volume collects critical responses to Mama Day, The women of Brewster Place, Linden Hills and Bailey's Cafe

Includes bibliographical references

The **Greenwood** encyclopedia of science fiction and fantasy; themes, works, and wonders; edited by Gary Westfahl; foreword by Neil Gaiman. Greenwood Press 2005 3v set $349.95

Grades: 11 12 Adult　　　　　**813.009**

1. Science fiction—Encyclopedias 2. Fantasy fiction—Encyclopedias
ISBN 0-313-32950-8　　　　　LC 2005-13677

This "encyclopedia consists of two parts. The first part (volumes 1 and 2) takes 400 of the most popular themes found in both science fiction and fantasy literature, and puts them into historical and cultural context. The second (volume 3) contains entries for a selected list of classic novels, films, and television series; these include entries

The Greenwood encyclopedia of science fiction and fantasy—*Continued*

for all the different Star Trek series, Dr. Who, Farscape, Buffy the Vampire Slayer, The Twilight Zone, and The X-Files." Choice

"This is an authoritative and extensive survey of themes and classic works of science fiction and fantasy stories, books, and themes." Libr Media Connect

Includes bibliographical references

Harper Lee's To kill a mockingbird; edited & with an introduction by Harold Bloom. Chelsea House Publishers 2003 98p (Bloom's guides) $30 *

Grades: 9 10 11 12   **813.009**
1. Lee, Harper, 1926-—About
ISBN 0-7910-7561-3   LC 2003-14153

Other available series titles include: Sandra Cisneros's The house on Mango Street; Aldous Huxley's Brave new world; William Shakespeare's Macbeth. For complete list of titles contact publisher

Examines different aspects of Harper Lee's novel about race relations in 1930s Alabama, with a biographical sketch of the author and critical essays on this work.

Includes bibliographical references

A Historical guide to Ernest Hemingway; edited by Linda Wagner-Martin. Oxford Univ. Press 1999 248p il (Historical guides to American authors) $45; pa $16.95 *

Grades: 11 12 Adult   **813.009**
1. Hemingway, Ernest, 1899-1961
ISBN 0-19-512151-1; 0-19-512152-X (pa)
     LC 99-10910

Following a brief biography contributors discuss nature, machismo, gender, war and wilderness as themes in Hemingway's fiction. An illustrated chronology and a bibliographical essay are included

Includes bibliographical references

A Historical guide to Nathaniel Hawthorne; edited by Larry J. Reynolds. Oxford Univ. Press 2001 223p il (Historical guides to American authors) $34.95; pa $15.95 *

Grades: 9 10 11 12   **813.009**
1. Hawthorne, Nathaniel, 1804-1864
ISBN 0-19-512413-8; 0-19-512414-6 (pa)
     LC 00-58917

Contents: Marble and mud: a biographical sketch, by Brenda Wineapple; Mysteries of mesmerism: Hawthorne's haunted house, by Samuel Coale; Hawthorne and children in the nineteenth century: daughters, flowers, stories, by Gillian Brown; Hawthorne and the visual arts, by Rita K. Colin; Nathaniel Hawthorne and the slavery question, by Jean Fagan Yellin; Illustrated chronology; Hawthorne and history: a bibliographical essay, by Leland S. Person

Includes bibliographical references

Hogan, Walter
Humor in young adult literature; a time to laugh. Scarecrow Press 2005 223p (Scarecrow studies in young adult literature) $40

Grades: Professional   **813.009**
1. Wit and humor—History and criticism
2. Teenagers—Books and reading
ISBN 0-8108-5072-9   LC 2004-18903

The author's "study is organized into eight chapters that generally reflect the stages of YA development, looking at books on family, friends, bullies, and authorities; then books dealing with self-image, love, and ironic perception; and, finally, books that are 'coming-of-age' novels." Booklist

"As a reader's advisory tool, this book is invaluable, paving the way for many laughter-filled hours to come." Voice Youth Advocates

Includes bibliographical references

J.D. Salinger's The catcher in the rye; edited & with an introduction by Harold Bloom. Chelsea House Publications 2007 127p (Bloom's guides) $30 *

Grades: 9 10 11 12   **813.009**
1. Salinger, J. D. (Jerome David), 1919-
ISBN 0-7910-9296-8; 978-0-7910-9296-5
     LC 2006-31070

Other available series titles in this class include: Kurt Vonnegut's Slaughterhouse-five; Ray Bradbury's Fahrenheit 451; Chaim Potok's The Chosen; Harper Lee's To kill a mockingbird. For complete list of titles contact publisher

This book's "critical extracts cover distinct elements of Salinger's novel, offering a variety of viewpoints and interpretations. Additional features answer questions about the author, characters, and the story's main points, and direct readers to further reading, with comments on the significance of each source." Publisher's note

Includes bibliographical references

MacRae, Cathi Dunn
Presenting young adult fantasy fiction. Twayne Pubs. 1998 xxx, 464p (Twayne's young adult authors series) $30

Grades: 7 8 9 10   **813.009**
1. Fantasy fiction—History and criticism
ISBN 0-8057-8220-6   LC 98-12896

MacRae "examines alternate worlds, magic realism, myth, legend, magic bestiary, and time fantasy. She includes in-depth critical analysis and interviews with four authors: Terry Brooks, Barbara Hambly, Jane Yolen, and Meredith Anne Pierce." Booklist

The author "is obviously enamored of her subject and its writers; her enthusiasm is contagious, and her research outstandingly useful." Bull Cent Child Books

Includes bibliographical references

Mark Twain's The adventures of Huckleberry Finn; edited and with an introduction by Harold Bloom. Updated ed. Chelsea House 2007 248p (Modern critical interpretations) $45 *

Grades: 9 10 11 12 Adult   **813.009**
1. Twain, Mark, 1835-1910
ISBN 0-7910-9426-X; 978-0-7910-9426-6
     LC 2006-36858

Mark Twain's The adventures of Huckleberry Finn—*Continued*

Other available series titles in this class include: Harper Lee's To kill a mockingbird; F. Scott Fitzgerald's The great Gatsby; The tales of Poe; Ernest Hemingway's The old man and the sea. For a complete list of titles contact publisher

First published 1986

A collection of twelve critical essays on Mark Twain's classic novel.

Includes bibliographical references

Newman, Gerald, 1939-

A student's guide to John Steinbeck; [by] Gerald Newman, Eleanor Newman Layfield. Enslow Publs. 2004 176p il (Understanding literature) $27.93 *

Grades: 9 10 11 12   **813.009**

1. Steinbeck, John, 1902-1968

ISBN 0-7660-2259-5   LC 2004-2304

"The authors discuss . . . [Steinbeck's] books in terms of characters, themes, plots, and symbolism. They devote separate chapters to Of Mice and Men, The Grapes of Wrath, and East of Eden but include other writings as well. . . . A good choice for reports and for a general understanding of this much-studied writer's works." SLJ

Includes glossary and bibliographical references

Oliver, Charles M.

Critical companion to Ernest Hemingway; a literary reference to his life and work. Facts on File 2006 630p il (Facts on File library of American literature) $75

Grades: 9 10 11 12 Adult   **813.009**

1. Hemingway, Ernest, 1899-1961

ISBN 0-8160-6418-0; 978-0-8160-6418-2

LC 2006-7970

First published 1999 with title: Ernest Hemingway A to Z

"This volume features entries on all of Hemingway's major and minor works, places and events related to his works, major figures in his life, and more. Appendixes include a complete list of Hemingway's works; a chronology; a genealogy; a . . . map for readers of Islands in the Stream; a list of film, stage, and radio adaptations; and a bibliography of secondary sources." Publisher's note

Includes filmography and bibliographical references

Pingelton, Timothy J.

A student's guide to Ernest Hemingway. Enslow Publs. 2005 160p il map (Understanding literature) lib bdg $27.93 *

Grades: 7 8 9 10   **813.009**

1. Hemingway, Ernest, 1899-1961

ISBN 0-7660-2431-8

This discusses Hemingway's life and his novels *In Our Time, The Sun Also Rises, A Farewell to Arms*, and *The Old Man and the Sea*

"Engaging and informative. . . . The very accessible format and the solid information make [this book] useful to students, and the engaging style should interest casual readers." SLJ

Includes glossary and bibliographical references

Reed, Arthea J. S.

Norma Fox Mazer; a writer's world. Scarecrow Press 2000 140p (Scarecrow studies in young adult literature) $36

Grades: 7 8 9 10   **813.009**

1. Mazer, Norma Fox, 1931-

ISBN 0-8108-3814-1   LC 00-38759

Other available series titles in this class are: What's so scary about R. L. Stine; Caroline Cooney; Ann Rinaldi. For a complete list of titles contact publisher

"Quoting heavily from the author herself and published reviews of her work, the author provides a chronology of major events in Mazer's life and then goes into deeper detail about her subject's childhood and adolescence and how her upbringing played a vital role in her novels and partnership with her husband, Harry Mazer. Several works are comprehensively analyzed." SLJ

Includes bibliographical references

Rehak, Melanie

Girl sleuth; Nancy Drew and the women who created her. Harcourt 2005 364p il $25; pa $14

Grades: 11 12 Adult   **813.009**

1. Wirt, Mildred A. (Mildred Augustine), 1905- 2. Keene, Carolyn 3. Stratemeyer, Edward, 1862-1930 4. Drew, Nancy (Fictitious character)

ISBN 0-15-101041-2; 0-15-603056-X (pa)

LC 2005-9129

Also available Thorndike Press large print edition

This is an account of "the writers and editors who constituted Carolyn Keene, the pseudonymous author of the [Nancy Drew] series." N Y Times Book Rev

"Packed with revealing anecdotes, Rehak's meticulously researched account of the publishing phenomenon that survived the Depression and WWII . . . will delight fans of the beloved gumshoe whose gumption guaranteed that every reprobate got his due." Booklist

Includes bibliographical references

Reid, Suzanne Elizabeth

Presenting young adult science fiction. Twayne Pubs. 1998 230p (Twayne's young adult authors series) $31

Grades: 9 10 11 12   **813.009**

1. Science fiction—History and criticism

ISBN 0-8057-1653-X   LC 98-35178

A critical introduction to science fiction authors Orson Scott Card, Douglas Hill, H. M. Hoover, Pamela Sargent, Octavia Butler, Pamela Service, Piers Anthony, and Douglas Adams, with chapters discussing the classical masters of science fiction, cyberpunk, Star trek, and new themes and trends.

Includes filmography and bibliographical references

Richard Wright; critical perspectives past and present; edited by Henry Louis Gates, Jr., and K.A. Appiah. Amistad Press 1993 476p (Amistad literary series) pa $14.95 hardcover o.p. *

Grades: 11 12 Adult   **813.009**
1. Wright, Richard, 1908-1960
ISBN 1-56743-027-7 (pa)   LC 92-45757
A collection of critical writings which examine Wright's fiction, nonfiction, and autobiographical works. The volume begins with a selection of reviews, written by such authors as Zora Neale Hurston, Clifton Fadiman, Ralph Ellison, Sinclair Lewis and Irving Howe. The second part consists of twenty-two present-day essays. Also included are a chronology and a bibliography.

Rollyson, Carl
Critical companion to Herman Melville; a literary reference to his life and work; [by] Carl Rollyson, Lisa Paddock, and April Gentry. Facts on File 2006 394p il (Facts on File library of world literature) $75

Grades: 9 10 11 12 Adult   **813.009**
1. Melville, Herman, 1819-1891
ISBN 0-8160-6461-X; 978-0-8160-6461-8
                                            LC 2005-36733
First published 2000 with title: Herman Melville A to Z

Entries in this "volume examine the characters and settings of Melville's novels and short stories, the critics and scholars who commented on his work, and his friends and associates, including such prominent literary figures as Oliver Wendell Holmes and Nathaniel Hawthorne." Publisher's note
Includes bibliographical references

Russell, Sharon A.
Revisiting Stephen King; a critical companion. Greenwood Press 2002 171p (Critical companions to popular contemporary writers) $34.95 *

Grades: 9 10 11 12   **813.009**
1. King, Stephen, 1947-
ISBN 0-313-31788-7   LC 2001-58641
This volume discusses the plot review, character development, and theme of eight of King's books from Desperation (1996) through Dreamcatcher (2001)
"Easy to read and understand, this title would be a good choice for secondary researchers. It's also interesting enough for King fans to enjoy." Libr Media Connect
Includes bibliographical references

Stephen King: a critical companion. Greenwood Press 1996 171p (Critical companions to popular contemporary writers) $35 *

Grades: 9 10 11 12   **813.009**
1. King, Stephen, 1947-
ISBN 0-313-29417-8   LC 95-50460
Some other available series titles in this class are: Kurt Vonnegut; Ray Bradbury; Gloria Naylor; Larry McMurtry; Louise Erdrich. For complete list of titles contact publisher

"Biographical information about King and background information on the horror genre in which he writes are contained in the first two chapters. The chapters that follow cover in detail the author's most important, most popular, and most recent works in chronological order, examining plot and character development and theme." Voice Youth Advocates
Includes bibliographical references

Schultz, Jeffrey D., 1966-
Critical companion to John Steinbeck; a literary reference to his life and work; [by] Jeffrey Schultz, Luchen Li. Facts on File 2005 406p il (Facts on File library of American literature) $65; pa $19.99 *

Grades: 11 12 Adult   **813.009**
1. Steinbeck, John, 1902-1968
ISBN 0-8160-4300-0; 0-8160-4301-9 (pa)
                                            LC 2004-26100
This "resource is divided into three parts: Biography, Works A-Z, and Related People, Places, and Topics. The first and shortest section provides a summary of Steinbeck's birth, early childhood, education, and career. The bulk of the book offers descriptions of all of his works— published and unpublished." SLJ
"Useful, succinct, and reasonably priced, it packs an abundance of information into one compact resource." Libr J
Includes bibliographical references

Skaggs, Peggy
Kate Chopin. Twayne Pubs. 1985 130p (Twayne's United States authors series) $34

Grades: 11 12 Adult   **813.009**
1. Chopin, Kate, 1851-1904
ISBN 0-8057-7439-4   LC 84-27977
The author "provides careful analyses of Chopin's two volumes of published short stories ('Bayou Folks' and 'A Night in Arcadie'), the stories of her unpublished volume, 'A Vocation and a Voice,' her uncollected short stories, poems, and essays, as well as her two novels, 'At Fault' and 'The Awakening.' A thorough critical study of interest to both general readers and scholars." Booklist
Includes bibliographical references

Sorrentino, Paul
Student companion to Stephen Crane; [by] Paul M. Sorrentino. Greenwood Press 2006 171p (Student companions to classic writers) $39.95 *

Grades: 9 10 11 12   **813.009**
1. Crane, Stephen, 1871-1900
ISBN 0-313-33104-9   LC 2005-26301
The author "includes facts about Crane's family, background on the Civil War, critical commentaries, as well as discussions about his writings, his literary heritage, and his revered place in American literature. . . . This volume includes a wealth of useful material that will help students better understand and interpret the writings of this great 19th-century author." SLJ
Includes bibliographical references

Tate, Mary Jo

Critical companion to F. Scott Fitzgerald; a literary reference to his life and work; foreword by Matthew J. Bruccoli. Facts on File 2006 464p il (Facts on File library of American literature) $75 *

Grades: 9 10 11 12 Adult   **813.009**
   1. Fitzgerald, F. Scott (Francis Scott), 1896-1940
   ISBN 0-8160-6433-4; 978-0-8160-6433-5
                                   LC 2006-11393
First published 1998 with title: F. Scott Fitzgerald A to Z

This book "studies the legacy of this writer, highlighting significant themes and historical references of his various works." Publisher's note

Includes bibliographical references

The **Toni** Morrison encyclopedia; edited by Elizabeth Ann Beaulieu. Greenwood Press 2003 428p $89.95 *

Grades: 11 12 Adult   **813.009**
   1. Morrison, Toni, 1931-
   ISBN 0-313-31699-6   LC 2002-21617

"This encyclopedia covers Morrison's works, characters, locations, themes (e.g., *Children*), and general topics (e.g., *Oprah's Book Club*). . . . Also included is a 14-page selected bibliography citing Morrison's novels, essays, stories, and interviews, as well as criticism on Morrison's works selected from books and articles. Typically, articles on themes, general topics, and works span several pages, while entries on characters and locations range from one sentence to one paragraph. A list of references concludes many, but not all, entries." Booklist

Includes bibliographical references

Tyson, Edith S.

Orson Scott Card; writer of the terrible choice. Scarecrow Press 2003 xxv, 187p (Scarecrow studies in young adult literature) $40 *

Grades: 9 10 11 12   **813.009**
   1. Card, Orson Scott
   ISBN 0-8108-4790-6   LC 2003-5730

"Tyson begins her book with a . . . preface gleaned from Card's own explanation of the purpose of his writing, followed by a light biographical skimming of his life and development as a writer. The best features of the book are Tyson's excellent analyses of Card's books. Each book is summarized . . . and then enriched with different perspectives on the meaning, or some relevant background information, or something that Card himself wrote about that particular book. The sequence and interrelatedness of his books are also well documented. This book is a must-have for both professional and circulating collections." Voice Youth Advocates

Includes bibliographical references

Wright, Sarah Bird

Critical companion to Nathaniel Hawthorne; a literary reference to his life and work. Facts on File 2006 392p il (Facts on File library of American literature) $75

Grades: 11 12 Adult   **813.009**
   1. Hawthorne, Nathaniel, 1804-1864
   ISBN 0-8160-5583-1; 978-0-8160-5583-8
                                   LC 2005-34648

This book "offers critical entries on Hawthorne's novels, short stories, travel writing, criticism, and other works, as well as portraits of characters, including Hester Prynne and Roger Chillingworth. This . . . reference also provides entries on Hawthorne's family, friends—ranging from Herman Melville to President Franklin Pierce—publishers, and critics, as well as periodicals that published his work and important places and events in his life." Publisher's note

Includes bibliographical references

814   American essays

Angelou, Maya

Wouldn't take nothing for my journey now. Random House 1993 141p hardcover o.p. pa $12

Grades: 11 12 Adult   **814**
   ISBN 0-679-42743-0; 0-553-38017-6 (pa)
                                   LC 93-5904
Also available in paperback from Bantam Bks.

The author "shares her thoughts about humankind: how to respect others of different cultures, opinions, and values as taught by universal philosophies. . . . Angelou's prose is brisk, fluid, and entrancing. This work will provide a taste of wisdom to all who read it." Libr J

Baldwin, James, 1924-1987

Collected essays. Library of Am. 1998 869p $35

Grades: 11 12 Adult   **814**
   ISBN 1-88301-152-3   LC 97-23496

The essays in this volume were selected by Toni Morrison. "Morrison has reprinted all of the material contained in Baldwin's previous collected essays, The Price of the Ticket (1985). She has added eleven pieces, the earliest of which dates from 1947—Baldwin's first published review, of a biography of Frederick Douglass, in the Nation—and the latest from 1984." Times Lit Suppl

The **beholder's** eye; a collection of America's finest personal journalism; edited and with an introduction by Walt Harrington. Grove Press 2005 xxii, 256p pa $14

Grades: 11 12 Adult   **814**
   ISBN 0-8021-4224-5 (pa)   LC 2005-46242

"Each writer takes a unique approach to the subject, drawing the reader into the experience of pit-bull fighting or hunting with the Inuit. Among the collection: Harrington, who is married to a black woman, explores his evolving attitudes on race through the lens of his relationship with his in-laws, Pete Earley returns to his hometown in search of the meaning of a sister's death in their youth, Ron Rosenbaum explores his own outlook

The beholder's eye—*Continued*

on life in a philosophical discourse with then-New York governor Mario Cuomo, Davis Miller is unabashedly starstruck in a comfortable and closeup look at Muhammad Ali at the home of Ali's mother, and Stephen S. Hall is personally probing in his exploration, via MRI, of his own brain and its functioning. These stories are amusing, insightful, and touching in a way that only something personal can be." Booklist

The **Best** American essays of the century; Joyce Carol Oates, editor; Robert Atwan, coeditor; with an introduction by Joyce Carol Oates. Houghton Mifflin 2000 596p hardcover o.p. pa $18 *

Grades: 11 12 Adult **814**

ISBN 0-618-04370-5; 0-618-15587-2 (pa)

This anthology includes essays "that contemplate diverse worlds, from nature to courtrooms, war and family memories. Race is a pervasive theme, explored with candor and insight by many, including James Baldwin, Zora Neale Hurston, and, in a jolting 1912 condemnation of a Coatesville, Pennsylvania, lynching, John Jay Chapman." Booklist

"Oates has assembled a provocative collection of masterpieces reflecting both the fragmentation and surprising cohesiveness of various American identities." Publ Wkly

Includes bibliographical references

Bradbury, Ray, 1920-

Bradbury speaks; too soon from the cave, too far from the stars. William Morrow 2005 243p hardcover o.p. pa $14.95

Grades: 11 12 Adult **814**

ISBN 0-06-058568-4; 0-06-058569-2 (pa)

LC 2005-41489

In this collection of essays, the author "weighs in on a medley of topics, including the allure of Paris, his enthusiasm for trains, the genesis of his most popular novels, and his reasons for remaining a diehard optimist. . . . By turns whimsical, insightful, and unabashedly metaphoric, his prose is immediately accessible as well as thought-provoking. Fans and nonfans alike should enjoy." Booklist

Everything I needed to know about being a girl I learned from Judy Blume. Pocket Books 2007 275p $23

Grades: 11 12 Adult **814**

1. Blume, Judy

ISBN 978-1-4165-3104-3; 1-4165-3104-1

"This collection of 24 essays . . . pays tribute to the influence of Judy Blume and her work about coming-of-age as a girl in America. In each piece, the writer reveals what O'Connell calls her 'Judy Blume moment,' telling a heartfelt and revealing story that reflects the same social awkwardness and true-to-life experiences Blume conveys in her novels, from menstruation to childhood bullying to masturbation. . . . Readers who similarly found solace and support in Blume's work should relate easily to these writers through the Blumian characters and themes they evoke." Publ Wkly

Hamill, Pete

Piecework; writings on men and women, fools and heroes, lost cities, vanished friends, small pleasures, large calamities, and how the weather was; foreword by Jimmy Breslin. Little, Brown 1996 432p $32; pa $16

Grades: 11 12 Adult **814**

ISBN 0-316-34104-5; 0-316-34098-7 (pa)

LC 95-4738

This is a collection of previously-published essays by the New York newspaper reporter and columnist

"These essays are opinionated, hard-hitting, passionate, and sometimes disturbing. Writing for magazines ranging from Esquire to Art & Antiques, Hamill's writings show readers the decay of New York and other cities, the violence and heartbreak of Lebanon and Nicaragua, and the unraveling of civil life in many parts of our society." Libr J

A **Historical** guide to Ralph Waldo Emerson; edited by Joel Myerson. Oxford Univ. Press 2000 322p il (Historical guides to American authors) $45; pa $17.95

Grades: 11 12 Adult **814**

1. Emerson, Ralph Waldo, 1803-1882

ISBN 0-19-512093-0; 0-19-512094-9 (pa)

LC 99-13122

Contributors discuss the prominent transcendentalist's views on religion, slavery, women's rights, natural science and individualism. Includes a biographical essay and a chronology

Includes bibliographical references

In fact; the best of Creative nonfiction; edited by Lee Gutkind; introduction by Annie Dillard. Norton 2005 xxxvi, 440p pa $15.95

Grades: 9 10 11 12 **814**

ISBN 0-393-32665-9 LC 2004-16506

This anthology of 25 essays from the literary journal Creative Nonfiction "covers the creative nonfiction universe from the personal essay to nature writing, literary journalism, and science writing. . . . This stellar volume will stand as an exciting and defining creative nonfiction primer." Booklist

Kingsolver, Barbara

Small wonder; essays; illustrations by Paul Mirocha. HarperCollins Pubs. 2002 267p $23.95; pa $12.95

Grades: 11 12 Adult **814**

ISBN 0-06-050407-2; 0-06-050408-0 (pa)

LC 2002-276255

"This set of 19 penetrating autobiographical musings on humankind and how we treat each other and the rest of nature coalesced in the stunned aftermath of September 11. . . . Food, motherhood, gardening, literature, television, homelessness, globalization, scientific illiteracy, selfishness, and forgiveness all come under sharp and revelatory scrutiny." Booklist

815.008 American speeches-- Collections

American Heritage book of great American speeches for young people; edited by Suzanne McIntire. Wiley 2001 292p il pa $14.95 *

Grades: 7 8 9 10 **815.008**
1. American speeches
ISBN 0-471-38942-0   LC 00-43749

This is a "compendium of more than 100 speeches that span nearly 400 years of American history, from Powhatan (1609) to Senator Charles Robb (2000). Prominent orators include Patrick Henry, Thomas Jefferson, John Kennedy, Richard Nixon, Martin Luther King, Jr., and Malcolm X. . . . The speeches inform readers and provide examples of how the spoken word has affected Americans throughout our past." SLJ

American speeches. Library of America 2006 2v ea $35

Grades: 9 10 11 12 Adult **815.008**
1. American speeches
ISBN 1-93108-297-9 (v1); 1-93108-298-7 (v2)
                              LC 2006-40928

Contents: pt. 1. Political oratory from the Revolution to the Civil War — pt. 2. Political oratory from Abraham Lincoln to Bill Clinton

This is a collection of over 120 historical speeches delivered between 1761 and 1997.

Includes bibliographical references

Historic speeches of African Americans; introduced and selected by Warren J. Halliburton. Watts 1993 192p il (African-American experience) lib bdg $23 *

Grades: 7 8 9 10 11 12 **815.008**
1. African Americans—History 2. American speeches
ISBN 0-531-11034-6 (lib bdg)   LC 92-39318

Presents speeches by various African American religious and political leaders from the days of slavery to the present, along with biographical information and historical background.

"Kids will dip into this for personal reading, and for curriculum research; they'll also find stirring pieces to read aloud and think about. The detailed sources at the end of the book make it easy to find out more about the individuals and their ideas." Booklist

In our own words; extraordinary speeches of the American century; edited by Robert G. Torricelli and Andrew Carroll. Kodansha Int. 1999 xxx, 450p $28 *

Grades: 11 12 Adult **815.008**
1. American speeches
ISBN 1-56836-291-9   LC 99-29995

Also available in paperback from Washington Sq. Press

"Arranged by decade from the Progressive Era to the '90s Technological Revolution, this book includes eulogies, sermons, fireside chats, public tributes, commencement addresses, and more. . . . Entries are attributed to Jane Addams, Clarence Darrow, Al 'Scarface' Capone, General George S. Patton, Jack Kerouac, Vince Lombardi, Jane Fonda, Ronald Reagan, and others." SLJ

Includes bibliographical references

UXL Asian American voices; edited by Deborah Gillan Straub. 2nd ed. UXL, Thomson\Gale 2004 xxv, 315p il $58 *

Grades: 7 8 9 10 11 12 **815.008**
1. Asian Americans 2. Speeches
ISBN 0-7876-7600-4   LC 2003-110048

First published 1997 with title: Asian American voices

This "reference presents full or excerpted speeches, sermons, orations, poems, testimony and other notable spoken words of Asian Americans. Each entry is accompanied by an introduction and boxes explaining terms and events to which the speech refers. The volume is illustrated with photographs and drawings." Publisher's note

816 American letters

Letters of the century; America, 1900-1999; edited by Lisa Grunwald and Stephen J. Adler. Dial Press (NY) 1999 741p il $35 *

Grades: 11 12 Adult **816**
1. American letters 2. United States—Civilization
ISBN 0-385-31590-2   LC 99-16808

This anthology "contains four hundred and twelve letters arranged chronologically to demonstrate the effects of war, the Depression, demographic change, scientific innovation, medical discovery, and artistic experimentation on American life." New Yorker

Among the letter writers gathered are "Carl Van Doren, Huey Long, Franklin D. Roosevelt, Lillian Hellman and a Vietnam soldier named Dusty. This is one of the most original literary tributes to the closing century." Publ Wkly

Includes bibliographical references (p. {677}-709) and index

817 American humor and satire

Macaulay, David, 1946-
Motel of the mysteries. Houghton Mifflin 1979 95p il pa $13 hardcover o.p.

Grades: 9 10 11 12 **817**
ISBN 0-395-28425-2 (pa)   LC 79-14860

In this satire the author pictures an amateur archeologist, who in the year 4022 stumbles upon an American motel which has been buried in 1985 in "a cataclysmic coincidence of previously unknown proportion {which} extinguished virtually all forms of life on the North American continent." The excavation of the motel and the ensuing explanations and interpretations of its human remains and artifacts provide a humorous satire of archeological finds and civilization, circa 1980

817.008 American humor and satire--Collections

Honey, hush! an anthology of African American women's humor; edited by Daryl Cumber Dance; foreword by Nikki Giovanni. Norton 1997 xxxix, 673p il pa $17.95 hardcover o.p.
Grades: 11 12 Adult **817.008**
1. American wit and humor 2. African American women
ISBN 0-393-31818-4 (pa)　　LC 97-6772
The editor "has collected folktales, proverbs, slave narratives, and cartoons reflecting the humor of African American women. Among those included are authors Audre Lorde and Toni Morrison and comedian Whoopi Goldberg." Libr J
Includes bibliographical references

Russell Baker's book of American humor. Norton 1993 598p $30 *
Grades: 11 12 Adult **817.008**
1. American wit and humor
ISBN 0-393-03592-1　　LC 93-22733
"Two hundred years of American humor have gone into the making of this anthology. . . . In the lineup are many of the old pros—Mark Twain, Fred Allen, James Thurber—and several relative newcomers—Fran Lebowitz, Nora Ephron, P.J. O'Rourke, and Dave Barry. The selections are nicely assorted in substance and are arranged by theme rather than chronology." Libr J
Includes bibliographical references

817.009 American humor and satire--History and criticism

American humor; Michael Nolan, book editor. Greenhaven Press 2001 160p il (Greenhaven Press companion to literary movements and genres) hardcover o.p. pa $14.96 *
Grades: 9 10 11 12 **817.009**
ISBN 0-7377-0415-2; 0-7377-0414-4 (pa)
　　LC 00-45472
A "study in which 15 five-to-ten-page essays are divided among three chapters: 'Sources of American Humor,' 'From Regional to National Types,' and 'The Twentieth-Century Transformation.' Specific works that are covered in depth include *The Adventures of Huckleberry Finn, Invisible Man, Catch-22, Catcher in the Rye, One Flew over the Cuckoo's Nest,* and *Slaughterhouse Five.* The articles are relatively easy to read. . . . A solid work." SLJ
Includes bibliographical references

818 American miscellany

The **Best** of the West; an anthology of classic writing from the American West; edited by Tony Hillerman. HarperCollins Pubs. 1991 528p pa $18 hardcover o.p.
Grades: 11 12 Adult **818**
1. West (U.S.) in literature
ISBN 0-06-092352-0 (pa)　　LC 90-55930

This anthology's "nonfiction sources run from 500 B.C. to the late nineteenth century; fictional selections by Harte, Crane, Scarborough, Davis, Stegner, and Norris are included. . . . Hillerman's subject groupings (e.g., explorers, settlers, Navajos, Hispanics, cowboys, miners, women, travel, and the military) make sense, and his juxtapositions encourage a thoughtful response." Booklist

Capote, Truman, 1924-1984
A Christmas memory, One Christmas, & The Thanksgiving visitor. Modern Lib. 1996 107p $13.95
Grades: 9 10 11 12 **818**
ISBN 0-679-60237-2　　LC 96-26022
In addition to two autobiographical stories A Christmas memory (1966) and The Thanksgiving visitor (1968), this volume includes the memoir One Christmas (1983)
One Christmas describes the Christmas Capote spent with his father in New Orleans when he was six years old. A Christmas memory and The Thanksgiving visitor "center on the author's early years with a family of distant relatives in rural Alabama. Both pay loving tribute to an eccentric old-maid cousin, Miss Sook Faulk, who became his best friend." Publisher's note

Cather, Willa, 1873-1947
Stories, poems, and other writings. Library of Am. 1992 1039p $35 *
Grades: 11 12 Adult **818**
ISBN 0-940450-71-2　　LC 91-62294
This volume contains the novels Alexander's bridge (1912) and My mortal enemy (1926); the poetry collection April twilights, and other poems (1923); the essay collection Not under forty (1936); and the following short story collections: Youth and the bright Medusa (1920); Obscure destinies (1932); The old beauty, and others (1948); and uncollected stories from 1892-1929

Crane, Stephen, 1871-1900
Prose and poetry. Library of Am. 1984 1379p $40; pa $15.95 *
Grades: 11 12 Adult **818**
1. Short stories
ISBN 0-940450-17-8; 1-883011-39-6 (pa)
　　LC 83-19908
Contents: Maggie: a girl of the streets; The red badge of courage; George's mother; The third violet; The monster; Stories, sketches, and journalism, by place and time; Poems
"This collection also includes both Crane's collections of epigrammatic free verses—'The Black Riders' and 'War is kind'—and selections from his uncollected poems." Publisher's note

Dillard, Annie
The Annie Dillard reader. HarperCollins Pubs. 1994 455p pa $15.95 hardcover o.p.
Grades: 11 12 Adult **818**
ISBN 0-06-092660-0 (pa)　　LC 94-19482

Dillard, Annie—_Continued_

This reader includes Holy the firm; excerpts from Pilgrim at Tinker Creek, An American childhood, and Teaching a stone to talk; and a reworked version of her 1978 short story The living

"This selection of writings, chosen by Dillard herself, provides a perfect sampling of her incisive, versatile, and impeccable achievements." Booklist

Pilgrim at Tinker Creek. Harper & Row 1974 271p hardcover o.p. pa $14.95

Grades: 9 10 11 12   **818**
  1. Natural history—Virginia
  ISBN 0-06-123332-3; 978-0-06-123332-6 (pa)
Also available in hardcover from Buccaneer Bks.

Starting with January, Dillard "records the seasons as they come and go at Tinker Creek in Virginia." Time

This work is "in an honored tradition of literature, not quite environmentalism and not the philosophy of science, it is rather the refraction of natural philosophy through the prismatic conscience of art. Highly recommended for the general reader—any general reader, anywhere—who wishes to deepen his awareness of his yard of world and to reflect upon it more profoundly." Choice

Du Bois, W. E. B. (William Edward Burghardt), 1868-1963

Writings. Library of Am. 1986 1334p $40; pa $15.95 *

Grades: 11 12 Adult   **818**
  ISBN 0-940450-33-X; 1-883011-31-0 (pa)
                                        LC 86-10565
Edited by Nathan Huggins
Contents: The suppression of the African slave-trade; The souls of black folk; Dusk of dawn; Essays; Articles from The crisis
Includes bibliographical references

Eliot, T. S. (Thomas Stearns), 1888-1965

The complete poems and plays, 1909-1950. Harcourt Brace & Co. 1952 392p $35 *

Grades: 11 12 Adult   **818**
  ISBN 0-15-121185-X
This book is made up of six individual titles formerly published separately: Collected poems (1909-1935); Four quartets; Old Possum's book of practical cats; Murder in the cathedral; Family reunion; Cocktail party

Eliot; poems and prose. Knopf 1998 221p (Everyman's library pocket poets) $12.50

Grades: 11 12 Adult   **818**
  ISBN 0-375-40185-7
A representative selection of work by the influential modernist poet and critic

Emerson, Ralph Waldo, 1803-1882

The portable Emerson. [rev ed], edited by Carl Bode in collaboration with Malcolm Cowley. Penguin Bks. 1981 xxxix, 670p pa $16.95 *

Grades: 11 12 Adult   **818**
  1. Plato 2. Thoreau, Henry David, 1817-1862 3. Napoleon I, Emperor of the French, 1769-1821
  ISBN 0-14-015094-3   LC 81-4047

"The Viking portable library"
First published 1946 by Viking
The editors have provided the following selections: essays, including History, Self-reliance, The over-soul, Circles and The poet; The complete texts of Nature and English traits; biographical essays on Plato, Napoleon, Henry David Thoreau, Thomas Carlyle, and others as well as twenty-two poems.
Includes bibliographical references

Franklin, Benjamin, 1706-1790

Autobiography, Poor Richard, and later writings; letters from London, 1757-1775, Paris, 1776-1785, Philadelphia, 1785-1790, Poor Richard's almanack, 1733-1758, The autobiography. Library of America 1997 816p $30 *

Grades: 11 12 Adult   **818**
  ISBN 1-88301-153-1   LC 97-21611
"J.A. Leo Lemay wrote the notes and selected the texts for this volume" Prelim. paging

"This collection of Franklin's works begins with letters sent from London (1757-1775) describing the events and diplomacy preceding the Revolutionary War. The volume also contains political satires, bagatelles, pamphlets, and letters written in Paris (1776-1785), where he represented the revolutionary United States at the court of Louis XVI, as well as his speeches given in the Constitutional Convention and other works written in Philadelphia (1785-1790), including his last published article, a . . . satire against slavery. Also included are the . . . prefaces to Poor Richard's Almanack (1733-1758). . . . [The] Autobiography, Franklin's last word on his greatest literary creation—his own invented personality—is presented here in a new edition." Publisher's note
Includes bibliographical references

Frost, Robert, 1874-1963

Collected poems, prose, & plays. Library of Am. 1995 1036p $35 *

Grades: 11 12 Adult   **818**
  ISBN 1-883011-06-X   LC 94-43693
This volume contains "all of the plays, a generous selection of prose, all collected poems, and 94 uncollected poems, as well as 17 poems that were previously unpublished." Libr J

Hawthorne, Nathaniel, 1804-1864

The portable Hawthorne; edited with an introduction by William C. Spengemann. Penguin Books 2005 439p (Penguin classics) pa $18

Grades: 11 12 Adult   **818**
  ISBN 0-14-303928-8; 978-0-14-303928-0
                                        LC 2004-65791
This collection "includes writings from each major stage in the career of Nathaniel Hawthorne: a number of his . . . early tales, all of The Scarlet Letter, excerpts from his three subsequently published romances—The House of Seven Gables, The Blithedale Romance, and The Marble Faun—as well as passages from his European journals and a sampling of his last, unfinished works." Publisher's note
Includes bibliographical references

A **Historical** guide to Edgar Allan Poe; edited by
J. Gerald Kennedy. Oxford Univ. Press 2001
247p il (Historical guides to American authors)
$39.95; pa $15.95 *
Grades: 11 12 Adult   **818**
1. Poe, Edgar Allan, 1809-1849
ISBN 0-19-512149-X; 0-19-512150-3 (pa)
                                        LC 00-20192
Following an introduction this volume presents a "capsule biography situating Poe in his historical context. The
subsequent essays in this book cover such topics as Poe
and the American publishing industry, Poe's sensationalism, his relationships to gender constructions, and Poe
and American privacy. The volume also includes a bibliographic essay, a chronology of Poe's life, a bibliography, illustrations, and an index." Publisher's note
Includes bibliographical references

A **Historical** guide to Henry David Thoreau;
edited by William E. Cain. Oxford Univ. Press
2000 285p il maps (Historical guides to
American authors) $39.95; pa $16.95 *
Grades: 9 10 11 12   **818**
1. Thoreau, Henry David, 1817-1862
ISBN 0-19-513862-7; 0-19-513863-5 (pa)
                                        LC 99-55276
Scholars assess the essays, social criticism, and natural
history writing of the influential Transcendentalist. Includes a biographical essay and chronology
Includes bibliographical references

Hughes, Langston, 1902-1967
The return of Simple; edited by Akiba Sullivan
Harper; introduction by Arnold Rampersad. Hill &
Wang 1994 xxii, 218p pa $11 hardcover o.p.
Grades: 11 12 Adult   **818**
ISBN 0-8090-1582-X (pa)   LC 93-45373
This collection brings together the "narrations of the
fictional Jesse B. Semple, or 'Simple,' which first ap-
peared in 1943 in {Hughes'} column in the *Chicago De-
fender* and, later, in the *New York Post*. Here, edited by
a teacher at Spelman College, is an enlightening collection of these social commentaries." Publ Wkly

Hurston, Zora Neale, 1891-1960
Folklore, memoirs, and other writings. Library
of Am. 1995 1001p il $35 *
Grades: 11 12 Adult   **818**
ISBN 0-940450-84-4   LC 94-21384
Companion volume to Novels and stories (1995)
"This is the first time the unexpurgated version of
Hurston's 1942 autobiography, *Dust Tracks on the Road*,
is being published; sections deemed too provocative
(dealing with politics, race, and sex) have been restored.
Mules and Men (1935) is a collection of African Ameri-
can folklore she gleaned on travels in the South, while
Tell My Horse (1938) tenders her personal findings on
African-based religion in Jamaica and Haiti. Additionally,
22 magazine and book articles with anthropological
themes . . . that have never been gathered into book
form are corralled here." Booklist

Jefferson, Thomas, 1743-1826
Writings. Library of Am. 1984 1600p $35 *
Grades: 11 12 Adult   **818**
ISBN 0-940450-16-X   LC 83-19917
Edited by Merrill D. Peterson
"Autobiography—A summary view of the rights of
British America—Notes on the State of Virginia—Public
papers—Addresses, messages, and replies—Miscellany—
Letters." Title page
This is "the largest and most skillfully edited single-
volume Jefferson ever published." N Y Times Book Rev
Includes bibliographical references

Kerouac, Jack, 1922-1969
The portable Jack Kerouac; edited by Ann
Charters. Viking 1995 xxv, 625p pa $17 hardcover
o.p. *
Grades: 11 12 Adult   **818**
ISBN 0-14-017819-8 (pa)   LC 94-20120
New edition in preparation
"Charters has chosen selections from each of
Kerouac's 14 novels, which comprise a complex and
evocative autobiographical series Kerouac called the Leg-
end of Duluoz. . . . Charters has also included poetry
from *San Francisco Blues* and *Book of Haikus,* as well
as a group of essays that cover Kerouac's main passions
and interests: writing, traveling, jazz, and Buddhism."
Booklist
Includes bibliographical references

Langston Hughes; edited and with an introduction
by Harold Bloom. Chelsea House 2002 143p
(Bloom's biocritiques) lib bdg $25.95 *
Grades: 9 10 11 12   **818**
1. Hughes, Langston, 1902-1967
ISBN 0-7910-6186-8   LC 2001-55281
Other available series titles include: Edgar Allan Poe;
Dante Alighieri; Walt Whitman; Tennessee Williams. For
complete list of titles contact publisher
A biocritical exploration of the African American
poet, activist, and essayist
Includes bibliographical references

Langston Hughes; critical perspectives past and
present; edited by Henry Louis Gates, Jr., and
K.A. Appiah. Amistad Press 1993 255p
(Amistad literary series) pa $14.95 hardcover
o.p. *
Grades: 11 12 Adult   **818**
1. Hughes, Langston, 1902-1967
ISBN 1-56743-029-5 (pa)   LC 92-45756
A collection of critical writings about Hughes's poet-
ry, novels, short stories and other works. The first part
contains reviews by Countee Cullen, Richard Wright,
James Baldwin, and others. The second part of the book
consists of ten critical essays.
Includes bibliographical references

London, Jack, 1876-1916
The portable Jack London; edited by Earle
Labor. Penguin Bks. 1994 xxxvii, 563p pa $15.95
*
Grades: 11 12 Adult   **818**
ISBN 0-14-017969-0   LC 93-38740

London, Jack, 1876-1916—*Continued*

This volume contains selected short stories, the complete text of The call of the wild, personal letters, and a sampling of journalistic pieces.

Includes bibliographical references

Magistrale, Tony

Student companion to Edgar Allan Poe. Greenwood Press 2001 139p (Student companions to classic writers) $35 *

Grades: 9 10 11 12   **818**

1. Poe, Edgar Allan, 1809-1849

ISBN 0-313-30992-2   LC 00-49071

Another available series title in this class is: Student companion to Mark Twain. For complete list of titles contact publisher

An introduction to the life, times and major works. Includes contemporary interpretations of The raven and The purloined letter

Includes bibliographical references

The **Mark** Twain encyclopedia; editors, J.R. LeMaster, James D. Wilson; editorial and research assistant, Christie Graves Hamric. Garland 1993 xxx, 848p (Garland reference library of the humanities) $155

Grades: 11 12 Adult   **818**

1. Twain, Mark, 1835-1910

ISBN 0-8240-7212-X   LC 92-45662

This "reference guide consists of approximately 740 signed articles by noted authorities. The articles cover all aspects of Twain's life. . . . Each article includes a bibliography. There are a detailed chronology of Twain's life and a lengthy Clemens genealogy." Am Libr

Maya Angelou; edited and with an introduction by Harold Bloom. Chelsea House 1998 240p (Modern critical views) $36.95 *

Grades: 9 10 11 12   **818**

1. Angelou, Maya

ISBN 0-7910-4782-2   LC 97-50357

Some other available series titles in this class are: Tom Wolfe; Edgar Allan Poe; Zora Neale Hurston; Ralph Waldo Emerson. For a complete list of titles contact publisher

Scholars explore social, political and religious themes in Angelou's prose and poetry

Includes bibliographical references

Maya Angelou's I know why the caged bird sings; edited and with an introduction by Harold Bloom. Chelsea House Publishers 1998 197p $29.95

Grades: 11 12 Adult   **818**

1. Angelou, Maya

ISBN 0-7910-4773-3   LC 97-53105

Critical essays analyze Angelou's classic autobiography. Contributors include Sidonie Ann Smith, Christine Froula, Opal Moore, and James Bertolino.

Includes bibliographical references

Poe, Edgar Allan, 1809-1849

The collected tales and poems of Edgar Allan Poe. Modern Lib. 1992 1026p $20 *

Grades: 11 12 Adult   **818**

ISBN 0-679-60007-8   LC 92-50231

A reissue of The complete tales and poems of Edgar Allan Poe published 1938

This volume contains short stories, poems, and a sampling of Poe's essays, criticism and journalistic writings

Rasmussen, R. Kent

Critical companion to Mark Twain; a literary reference to his life and work; with critical commentary by John H. Davis and Alex Feerst. Rev. ed. Facts on File 2007 2v il map (Facts on File library of American literature) set $125

Grades: 11 12 Adult   **818**

1. Twain, Mark, 1835-1910

ISBN 0-8160-5398-7; 978-0-8160-5398-8

                                        LC 2004-46910

First published 1995 in one volume with title: Mark Twain A to Z

Contents: v1. Part I: Biography; Part II: Works A-Z v2. Part III: Related people, places, and topics; Part IV: Appendices

This companion to the life and works of Mark Twain includes a biography, synopses and critical commentaries on each of his works, discussions about major characters and places in his works, and entries on important people, places, and other aspects of his life.

Includes glossary, filmography and bibliographical references

Sova, Dawn B.

Edgar Allan Poe, A-Z; the essential reference to his life and work. Facts on File 2001 310p il $65; pa $17.95 *

Grades: 11 12 Adult   **818**

1. Poe, Edgar Allan, 1809-1849

ISBN 0-8160-3850-3; 0-8160-4161-X (pa)

                                        LC 00-61039

New edition in preparation

This "reference work, consisting of some 3400 entries and illustrated with 50 black-and-white illustrations, treats all of the author's work—some 350 stories, poems, essays, and articles. Together with the entries covering Poe's literary works . . . are factual treatments of the people, places, and events associated with him. . . . The encyclopedia contains chronologies of the author's life and work, a directory of 'Poe Research Collections,' and a selective bibliography." Libr J

Includes bibliographical references

Stein, Gertrude, 1874-1946

Selected writings; edited with an introduction and notes by Carl Van Vechten and with an essay on Gertrude Stein by F. W. Dupee. Modern Lib. 1962 706p pa $18 hardcover o.p.

Grades: 11 12 Adult   **818**

ISBN 0-679-72464-8 (pa)

In addition to the autobiography of Alice B. Toklas and the libretto Four saints in three acts, this volume

Stein, Gertrude, 1874-1946—*Continued*
contains representative selections of Stein's poetry, prose, drama, and criticism.

Writings, 1932-1946. Library of Am. 1998 844p $40

Grades: 11 12 Adult   **818**
  ISBN 1-88301-141-8   LC 97-28916
  Contents: Stanzas in meditation; Lectures in America; The geographical history of America; Ida; Brewsie and Willie; Other works
  In addition to theater pieces, fiction, and poetry "memoir, philosophical speculation, literary criticism and theory, all sorts of briefer forms that are hard to account for but easy to marvel at and even to delight in, pack these volumes, and constitute, as the editors surely intended us to discover, the most consistently achieved representation of new ways of responding to life and new possibilities of getting experience into words that American literature has to show." N Y Times Book Rev

Stein, Karen F.
Margaret Atwood revisited. Twayne Pubs. 1999 xx, 176p (Twayne's world authors series) $33
Grades: 11 12 Adult   **818**
  1. Atwood, Margaret, 1939-
  ISBN 0-8057-1614-9   LC 99-33696
  For complete list of series titles contact publisher
  The author provides critical readings of Atwood's novels, short stories, poetry, nonfiction and children's books
  Includes bibliographical references

Steinbeck, John, 1902-1968
The grapes of wrath and other writings, 1936-1941. Library of Am. 1996 1067p $35 *
Grades: 9 10 11 12   **818**
  ISBN 1-883011-15-9   LC 96-3725
  This volume contains the short story collection The long valley (1938) and the novel The grapes of wrath. Also included is The log from the Sea of Cortez (1941) Steinbeck's narrative about marine research in the Gulf of California and The harvest gypsies,a series of newspaper articles on migrant labor that was published with title Their blood is strong (1938)

Stowe, Harriet Beecher, 1811-1896
The Oxford Harriet Beecher Stowe reader; edited with an introduction by Joan D. Hedrick. Oxford Univ. Press 1999 560p pa $34.95 *
Grades: 11 12 Adult   **818**
  ISBN 0-19-509117-5   LC 97-32020
  The editor provides an "introduction that assesses Stowe's vital impact on nineteenth-century American literature, politics, and culture. The readings are divided into three sections: Early Sketches, Antislavery Writings, and Domestic Culture and Politics. Early Sketches presents the finest writing of Stowe's literary apprenticeship. Antislavery Writings includes *Uncle Tom's Cabin* in its entirety. . . . Domestic Culture and Politics shows the scope of Stowe's thinking on the Victorian home, for which she was a major propagandist." Publisher's note
  Includes bibliographical references

Thoreau, Henry David, 1817-1862
Collected essays and poems. Library of Am. 2001 703p $35 *
Grades: 11 12 Adult   **818**
  ISBN 1-88301-195-7   LC 00-46234
  Edited by Elizabeth Hall Witherell
  Among the 27 essays included are Civil disobedience, Walking, Martyrdom of John Brown, A Yankee in Canada, and Life without principle. Many of the poems were taken from Thoreau's journals and manuscripts
  Includes bibliographical references

Walden, or, Life in the woods; with an introduction by Verlyn Klinkenborg. Knopf : Distributed by Random House 1992 xxxi, 295p $19 *
Grades: 11 12 Adult   **818**
  ISBN 0-679-41896-2   LC 92-54444
  Hardcover and paperback editions also available from various publishers
  "Everyman's library"
  First published 1854
  "Philosophy of life and observations of nature drawn from the author's solitary sojourn of two years in a cabin on Walden Pond near Concord, Massachusetts." Pratt Alcove
  Includes bibliographical references

Thurber, James, 1894-1961
Writings and drawings. Library of Am. 1996 1004p il $35
Grades: 11 12 Adult   **818**
  1. American wit and humor
  ISBN 1-883011-22-1   LC 96-5853
  Edited by Garrison Keillor
  Includes the complete texts of The seal in the bedroom (1932), the autobiography My life and hard times (1933); the anti-war parable The last flower (1939) and the children's tale The 13 clocks (1950)
  "These stories, parodies, reminiscences, cartoons, and drawings present Thurber's unique and masterful take on work, psychotherapy, fantasizing, domesticity, and the battle between the sexes." Booklist

Twain, Mark, 1835-1910
The innocents abroad [and] Roughing it. Library of Am. 1984 1027p il $35
Grades: 9 10 11 12   **818**
  1. Voyages and travels
  ISBN 0-940450-25-9   LC 84-11296
  Edited by Guy Cardwell
  The innocents abroad (1869) is Twain's humorous account of his adventures in the Holy Land, Italy, and Paris. Roughing it (1872) recounts a trip across the plains to California and then Hawaii in the early 1860s

Life on the Mississippi; with an introduction by James M. Cox. Penguin Books 1984 450p (Penguin Classics) pa $9.95 *
Grades: 9 10 11 12   **818**
  1. Mississippi River valley
  ISBN 0-14-039050-2   LC 84-1194
  A reissue of the title first published 1874

Twain, Mark, 1835-1910—*Continued*

"Its historical sketches, its frequent passages of vivid description, and its humorous episodes combine to make [this] a masterpiece of the literature of the Middle West." Eng and Pope's What to Read

Roughing it; edited with an introduction by Hamlin Hill. Penguin 1981 590p il (The Penguin American library) pa $14

Grades: 11 12 Adult   **818**

1. Hawaii—Description and travel

ISBN 0-14-039010-3   LC 81-10593

Hardcover and paperback editions also available from other publishers

First published 1872

A humorous account of a trip across the plains to California and then to Hawaii in the early 1860s.

Includes bibliographical references

Walker, Alice, 1944-

Anything we love can be saved; a writer's activism: essays, speeches, statements & letters. Random House 1997 xxv, 225p pa $15.95 hardcover o.p.

Grades: 11 12 Adult   **818**

ISBN 0-345-40796-2 (pa)   LC 96-41159

Walker has assembled a "wide-ranging collection of personal essays, remarks, letters, speeches and statements, many previously published. . . . Constantly testing and stretching her readers' imaginations and boundaries, Walker expresses her warmth, her anger, her optimism in this provocative, lively collection." Publ Wkly

Wharton, Edith, 1862-1937

Novellas and other writings. Library of Am. 1990 1137p il $45 *

Grades: 11 12 Adult   **818**

ISBN 0-940450-53-4   LC 89-62930

Contents: Madame de Treymes; Ethan Frome; Summer; Old New York; The mother's recompense; A backward glance

This volume contains the following novelettes: Madame de Troyes (1907); Ethan Frome (1911); Summer (1917); The mother's recompense (1925). Old New York (1924) is a collection of four novelettes: False dawn; The old maid; The spark; New Year's day. Also included is the autobiographical A backward glance (1934)

Includes bibliographical references

Whitman, Walt, 1819-1892

Complete poetry and collected prose. Library of Am. 1982 1380p $35; pa $17.95 *

Grades: 11 12 Adult   **818**

ISBN 0-940450-02-X; 1-883011-35-3 (pa)

LC 81-20768

Edited by Justin Kaplan

Contents: Leaves of grass (1855); Leaves of grass (1891-92); Complete prose works (1892); Supplementary prose

Wright, Richard, 1908-1960

Works. Library of Am. 1991 2v ea $35 *

Grades: 11 12 Adult   **818**

1. African Americans—Fiction 2. African Americans

ISBN 0-940450-66-6 (v1); 0-940450-67-4 (v2)

LC 91-60540

Contents: v1 Early works; v2 Later works

This set contains the complete novels Native son; The outsider (1953); and Lawd today! (1963); the story collection Uncle Tom's children; and the memoir Black boy

820.3   English literature-- Encyclopedias and dictionaries

The **Continuum** encyclopedia of British literature; Steven R. Serafin and Valerie Grosvenor Myer, editors. Continuum 2003 1184p $175

Grades: 11 12 Adult   **820.3**

1. English literature—Encyclopedias

ISBN 0-8264-1456-7   LC 2002-9231

"Most of the encyclopedia's 1,700 entries are devoted to writers. . . . The 69 topical articles provide . . . historical overviews of specific genres, themes, literary periods, and geographical areas. Among these are *Caribbean literature in English*, *Feminism*, *Old English*, and *War and literature*. With the exception of brief author entries of approximately 300 words or less, articles are signed and include bibliographical references." Booklist

"This reference work provides a fascinating current take on the canon. . . . The historical/literary time line and the lists of prize titles alone will keep researchers happy." SLJ

Includes bibliographical references

The **Oxford** companion to English literature; edited by Margaret Drabble. 6th ed., rev. Oxford University 2006 1172p $60 *

Grades: 11 12 Adult   **820.3**

1. English literature—Dictionaries 2. English literature—Bio-bibliography 3. American literature—Dictionaries

ISBN 0-19-861453-5; 978-0-19-861453-1

LC 2006-49353

First published 1932 under the editorship of Sir Paul Harvey

Entries "cover authors, literary movements and terms, critical theories, genres, publishers, plot summaries, and characters. . . . [This] is the best available one-volume reference on English literature." Libr J

The **Oxford** encyclopedia of British literature; David Scott Kastan, editor in chief. Oxford University Press 2006 5v il set $595 *

Grades: 11 12 Adult   **820.3**

1. English literature—Encyclopedias

ISBN 978-0-19-516921-8; 0-19-516921-2

LC 2005-25187

This "work contains more than 500 alphabetically arranged, signed articles covering 1400 years of British literature. While many entries examine fiction and nonfiction writers from the seventh century to the present, related articles describe themes, institutions, movements, literary terms, genres, and an occasional literary work or

The Oxford encyclopedia of British literature—
Continued

poem (Beowulf, Piers Plowman, etc.). . . . A vast and valuable resource." SLJ

For a fuller review, see: Booklist, Sept. 15, 2006

Includes bibliographical references

820.8   English literature--Collections

The **Norton** anthology of literature by women; the traditions in English; {compiled by} Sandra M. Gilbert, Susan Gubar. 2nd ed. Norton 1996 xxxviii, 2452p pa $61.25 *

Grades: 11 12 Adult   **820.8**
ISBN 0-393-96825-1   LC 96-5751
First published 1985

The editors provide representative selections of prose and poetry by women. Period introductions, biographical headnotes and bibliographies are provided

The **Oxford** anthology of English literature; general editors: Frank Kermode and John Hollander. Oxford Univ. Press 1973 6v in 2 il maps v1 2v pa set $65.95; v2 2v pa set $65.95

Grades: 11 12 Adult   **820.8**
1. English literature—Collections
ISBN 0-19-501657-2 (v1 2v pa); 0-19-501658-0 (v2 2v pa)

Each of the six parts collected here were published separately. Apply to publisher for prices and availability

Contents: v1 The Middle Ages through the eighteenth century: Medieval English literature, edited by J. B. Trapp; The literature of Renaissance England, edited by John Hollander and Frank Kermode; The Restoration and the eighteenth century, edited by Martin Price; v2 1800 to the present: Romantic poetry and prose, edited by Harold Bloom and Lionel Trilling; Victorian prose and poetry, edited by Lionel Trilling and Harold Bloom; Modern British literature, edited by Frank Kermode and John Hollander

820.9   English literature--History and criticism

Backgrounds to English literature. Facts on File 2002 5v set $150

Grades: 11 12 Adult   **820.9**
1. English literature—History and criticism 2. Great Britain—Civilization
ISBN 0-8160-5125-9   LC 2002-71284
Also available separately ea $27

Contents: v1 The Renaissance, by P. Lee-Browne; v2 The romantics, by N. King; v3 The Victorians, by A. Cruttenden; v4 The modernist period, 1900-1945, by P. Lee-Browne; v5 Post-war literature 1945 to the present, by C. Merz and P. Lee-Browne

This set provides "the historical, cultural, and social background of each major period. Each volume is a basic introduction to the period: its history, leaders, important laws, social and religious movements, scientific developments, and details of daily life in different regions and classes within Great Britain. The set summarizes the lit-

erary genres of each period and discusses representative writers and works." Publisher's note

"Will be useful for students studying the social, historical, and cultural influences on authors of the post-war period." SLJ

Includes bibliographical references

Burrow, J. A. (John Anthony)

Medieval writers and their work; Middle English literature and its background, 1100-1500. Oxford Univ. Press 1982 148p pa $20.95 hardcover o.p.

Grades: 9 10 11 12   **820.9**
1. English literature—History and criticism
ISBN 0-19-289122-7 (pa)   LC 81-16967

This book concentrates on "some of the chief differences which confront a reader of modern literature when he first approaches {Middle English writings:} differences in the notion of literature itself (Chapter 1), in the circumstances under which writings were produced and received (Chapter 2), in the types of writing produced (Chapter 3), and in the kinds of meaning to be found in them (Chapter 4). Chapters 1 and 5 also attempt to characterize the Middle English period in relation to earlier and later periods of English literature." Preface

Includes bibliographical references

The **Cambridge** guide to literature in English; edited by Dominic Head. 3rd ed. Cambridge University Press 2006 xxiii, 1241p il $50

Grades: 11 12 Adult   **820.9**
1. English literature—Dictionaries 2. English literature—Bio-bibliography 3. American literature—Dictionaries
ISBN 978-0-521-83179-6; 0-521-83179-2
                                                LC 2006-271458
First published 1988 under the editorship of Ian Ousby

"The scope of material covered . . . extends to the literature of the United Kingdom and well beyond: Africa, Asia, Australia, Canada, the Caribbean, India, New Zealand, and the U.S. are all well represented. . . . Literary terms are explained, literary movements are summarized, and literary magazines are sketched in unsigned entries ranging in length from a few lines to a few paragraphs or more. . . . With its broad coverage, clearly written and accessible text, and relatively modest price, this is a must purchase for most reference collections." Booklist

Dailey, Donna

London; [by] Donna Dailey and John Tomedi; introduction by Harold Bloom. Chelsea House 2005 231p il map (Bloom's literary places) $40

Grades: 9 10 11 12   **820.9**
1. London (England) in literature 2. Literary landmarks
ISBN 0-7910-7841-8   LC 2004-18928

Contents: London today -- After the conquest -- Elizabethan London -- London and the restoration -- Georgian and Regency London -- Victorian times -- London at the turn of the twentieth century -- London between the wars -- The London of Gravity's rainbow -- The millennial city

This guide to the city of London focuses on the places within it that have had an impact on literature.

Includes bibliographical references

Encyclopedia of British writers, 16th-18th centuries; [written and developed by Book Builders LLC] Facts on File 2005 2v set $150
Grades: 11 12 Adult   **820.9**
1. Authors, English—Dictionaries 2. English literature—Bio-bibliography 3. English literature—History and criticism
ISBN 0-8160-5132-1   LC 2004-47070
Also included in a four-volume set along with Encyclopedia of British writers, 19th and 20th centuries
"Writers 'from Christopher Marlowe to John Donne' and of numerous genres are covered: dramatists, novelists, nonfiction authors, poets, historians, publishers, translators, literary critics, and editors. The alphabetical entries are brief. . . . Those on individuals contain biographical information, works, and a short bibliography. . . . Where patrons do extensive research on these periods, these encyclopedias will prove useful." SLJ

The **Oxford** companion to Irish literature; edited by Robert Welch, assistant editor, Bruce Stewart. Oxford Univ. Press 1996 xxv, 614p maps $55 *
Grades: 11 12 Adult   **820.9**
1. Irish literature—Dictionaries
ISBN 0-19-866158-4   LC 95-44943
Encompassing "Ireland's literary heritage from the bardic poets and Celtic sagas to twentieth-century authors like Brian Friel, Edna O'Brien, and Nuala Ni Dhomhnaill, the more than 2,000 unsigned entries cover writers, titles of major works, literary genres and motifs, folklore, mythology, periodicals, associations, and historical figures and events." Booklist

Pool, Daniel
What Jane Austen ate and Charles Dickens knew; from fox hunting to whist: the facts of daily life in nineteenth-century England. Simon & Schuster 1993 416p il maps pa $14 hardcover o.p.
Grades: 11 12 Adult   **820.9**
1. English literature—History and criticism 2. Great Britain—Social life and customs
ISBN 0-671-88236-8 (pa)   LC 93-16240
"Modern American readers of 19th-century English novels are often brought up short by bizarre references and puzzling words that did not need explaining when the books were written. Now they do, and Daniel Pool does a charming job of clearing things up in a witty, informal survey of daily life in the Hanoverian-Victorian era." N Y Times Book Rev
Includes bibliographical references

Tomedi, John, 1978-
Dublin; introduction by Harold Bloom. Chelsea House 2005 191p il map (Bloom's literary places) $40
Grades: 9 10 11 12   **820.9**
1. Dublin (Ireland) 2. Literary landmarks
ISBN 0-7910-7836-1   LC 2005-13971
This guide to the city of Dublin focuses on the places within it that have had an impact on literature. "Most notably known as the home of James Joyce and the setting for his masterwork, Ulysses, Dublin is also the birthplace of George Bernard Shaw and was the childhood home of Oscar Wilde." Publisher's note
Includes bibliographical references

The **Victorian** novel; edited and with an introduction by Harold Bloom. Chelsea House 2004 412p (Bloom's period studies) $37.95
Grades: 9 10 11 12   **820.9**
1. English literature—History and criticism
ISBN 0-7910-7678-4
This study of the Victorian novel examines the work of major influential authors including "Charles Dickens, The Brontës, Anthony Trollope, George Eliot, Mrs. Elizabeth Gaskell, William Makepeace Thackeray, and Thomas Hardy." Publisher's note
Includes bibliographical references

World writers in English; Jay Parini, editor. Scribner 2003 2v set $250 *
Grades: 9 10 11 12   **820.9**
1. Literature—History and criticism 2. Literature—Bio-bibliography
ISBN 0-684-31289-1   LC 2003-14873
"A collection of 40 critical and biographical essays on writers from around the postcolonial world, including India and Asia, Australia and New Zealand, Africa, the Caribbean, and Canada, who write primarily in English. Most write fiction, though poets (Derek Walcott) and playwrights (Wole Soyinka) are also represented. Each 18- to 22-page signed essay includes excerpts from major works along with explication, with 'special attention paid to the cultural matrix that figures in the evolution of {the} writer.'" SLJ
"An essential addition to any general or academic reference collection." Booklist
Includes bibliographical references

821   English poetry

Agard, John, 1949-
Half-caste and other poems. Hodder & Stoughton 2004 80p il $16.99
Grades: 7 8 9 10 11 12   **821**
ISBN 0-340-89382-6
"This collection of poems . . . deftly covers race, identity, and other topics. . . . Agard uses rhyme, repetition, and refrains to make his work sing. His skillful use of humor to get his serious points across is in evidence here, and several concrete poems display both visual and verbal wit." Horn Book Guide
Includes bibliographical references

Auden, W. H. (Wystan Hugh), 1907-1973
Auden; poems; selected by Edward Mendelson. Knopf 1995 256p (Everyman's library pocket poets) $12.50
Grades: 11 12 Adult   **821**
ISBN 0-679-44367-3
A representative selection of lyrics that span the influential poet's career

Auden, W. H. (Wystan Hugh), 1907-1973—Continued

Collected poems; edited by Edward Mendelson. 2007 Modern Library ed. Modern Library 2007 xxxi, 928p $40

Grades: 11 12 Adult   **821**
    ISBN 978-0-679-64350-0; 0-679-64350-8
                                    LC 2006-47163
Also available in paperback from Vintage Bks.

Originally published in different form by Random House in 1976

A compilation of all the poems Auden wished to preserve, in his final revisions. Previous collected editions and later shorter poems are included. There is also an absurdist play written 1928: Paid on both sides.

Blake, William, 1757-1827

The essential Blake; selected and with an introduction by Stanley Kunitz. Ecco Press 1987 92p (Essential poets) hardcover o.p. pa $9.95 *

Grades: 11 12 Adult   **821**
    ISBN 0-88001-138-6; 0-06-088793-1 (pa)
                                    LC 86-24087
The editor has selected the poems he feels provide the best introduction to Blake's craft.

Poems. Knopf 1994 283p (Everyman's library pocket poets) $12.50 *

Grades: 11 12 Adult   **821**
    ISBN 0-679-43633-2
A collection of representative and epic poems by the visionary Romantic poet, painter and engraver

Brontë, Emily, 1818-1848

Brontë: poems. Knopf 1996 255p (Everyman's library pocket poets) $12.50

Grades: 11 12 Adult   **821**
    ISBN 0-679-44725-3
A representative selection of Brontë's poetical output including many of her mythical works

Browning, Elizabeth Barrett, 1806-1861

Sonnets from the Portuguese; a celebration of love. 1st U.S. ed. St. Martin's Press 1986 [63]p il $9.95 *

Grades: 11 12 Adult   **821**
    ISBN 0-312-74501-X   LC 86-13755
Hardcover and paperback editions also available from other publishers

A series of sonnets which "were written during a period of seven years and are considered by some scholars to have been inspired by her love for her husband poet Robert Browning." New Century Handb of Engl Lit

Browning, Robert, 1812-1889

Robert Browning's poetry; authoritative texts, criticism; selected and edited by James F. Loucks and Andrew M. Stauffer. 2nd ed. W. W. Norton & Co. 2007 689p (A Norton critical edition) pa $14.50 *

Grades: 11 12 Adult   **821**
    ISBN 978-0-393-92600-2; 0-393-92600-1
                                    LC 2006-47308
First published 1980

This collection of Browning's poetry, which includes Pauline, "reprints the texts of the seventeen-volume 'Fourth and complete edition' (Smith, Elder), of which all but the final volume were approved by Browning before his death. The poems are ordered chronologically according to their first appearance in book form." Publisher's note

Byron, George Gordon Byron, 6th Baron, 1788-1824

Byron; poems; [this selection by Peter Washington] Knopf 1994 288p (Everyman's library pocket poets) $12.50 *

Grades: 11 12 Adult   **821**
    ISBN 0-679-43630-8
A selection of lyric and dramatic poetry by the English Romantic poet and satirist.

Chaucer, Geoffrey, d. 1400

The Canterbury tales; translated into modern English by Nevill Coghill. Penguin Books 2003 504p (Penguin Classics) pa $10 *

Grades: 11 12 Adult   **821**
    ISBN 0-14-042438-5   LC 2003-265749
"A collection of twenty-four stories, all but two of which are in verse, written by Geoffrey Chaucer mainly between 1386 and his death in 1400. The stories are supposed to be related by members of a company of thirty-one pilgrims (including the poet himself) who are on their way to the shrine of St. Thomas at Canterbury. The prologue which tells of their assembly at the Tabard Inn in Southwark and their arrangement that each shall tell two stories on the way to Canterbury and two on the return journey, is a remarkable picture of English social life in the fourteenth century, inasmuch as every class is represented from the gentlefolks to the peasantry." Keller. Reader's Dig of Books

The portable Chaucer; selected, translated and edited by Theodore Morrison. rev ed. Viking 1975 611p pa $15.95 hardcover o.p. *

Grades: 11 12 Adult   **821**
    ISBN 0-14-015081-1 (pa)
"The Viking portable library"

First published 1949

Contains Troilus and Cressida, The Canterbury tales, selections from The book of the duchess and The bird's parliament, and some short verse.

Includes bibliographical references

Gawain and the Grene Knight (Middle English poem).

Sir Gawain and the Green Knight; a new verse translation by W. S. Merwin. Knopf 2002 hardcover o.p. pa $14 *

Grades: 9 10 11 12   821
  1. Arthurian romances
  ISBN 0-375-41476-2; 0-375-70992-4 (pa)
                                              LC 2002-20815
"Merwin's *Sir Gawain* replicates the propulsive alliteration and the rhymed-quatrain stanza endings of the original, and the translation appears face-to-face with the Middle English original. A major translation of a major English, and a major horror, classic." Booklist

Hardy, Thomas, 1840-1928

Poems. Knopf 1995 254p (Everyman's library pocket poets) $10.95

Grades: 11 12 Adult   821
  ISBN 0-679-44368-1
A representative selection of the English author's verse. An index of first lines is included

Heaney, Seamus

Electric light. Farrar, Straus & Giroux 2001 98p $20; pa $13

Grades: 11 12 Adult   821
  ISBN 0-374-14683-7; 0-374-52841-1 (pa)
                                                LC 00-67278
Heaney's "book of poems is a compendium of poetic genres set in an array of forms and tuned to many kinds of experience, the work of a mature poet and world citizen, aware of his cultural authority as a public man and of the rights and responsibilities that go with it." N Y Times Book Rev

Opened ground; selected poems, 1966-1996. Farrar, Straus & Giroux 1998 443p pa $16 hardcover o.p.

Grades: 11 12 Adult   821
  ISBN 0-374-52678-8 (pa)   LC 98-4331
"The best of nobel laureate Heaney's poems, gathered from 12 previous collections, create a substantial volume that charts the course of one man's thoroughly examined personal life and reflects a volatile era in the life of his troubled country, Northern Ireland, though the particulars Heaney renders so vibrantly become archetypal and unbounded in their tragedy and bliss." Booklist

Housman, A. E. (Alfred Edward), 1859-1936

The collected poems of A. E. Housman. Holt & Co. 1965 254p pa $16

Grades: 11 12 Adult   821
  ISBN 0-8050-0547-1
Also available in hardcover from Buccaneer Bks.
This anthology "constitutes the authorized canon of A. E. Housman's verse as established in 1939." Note on the text

Hughes, Ted, 1930-1998

Selected poems, 1957-1994. Farrar, Straus & Giroux 2002 333p hardcover o.p. pa $15

Grades: 11 12 Adult   821
  ISBN 0-374-25875-9; 0-374-52864-0 (pa)
                                              LC 2002-21603
"With poems that are characteristically alert to the processes of creation as well as self-destruction, this selection displays Hughes's mighty, even terrifying, talent." N Y Times Book Rev

Keats, John, 1795-1821

The major works; edited with an introduction and notes by Elizabeth Cook. Oxford Univ. Press 2001 xxxvi, 667p pa $16.95

Grades: 9 10 11 12   821
  ISBN 0-19-284063-0   LC 2001-272404
First published 1990
This volume contains all the poetry published during Keats' lifetime, including Endymion in its entirety, the Odes, Lamia, and both versions of Hyperion. A number of posthumously published poems are presented along with a selection of Keats' letters. Includes a bibliography, chronology, and a glossary of classical names

Poems. Knopf 1994 253p (Everyman's library pocket poets) $12.50 *

Grades: 11 12 Adult   821
  ISBN 0-679-43319-8   LC 94-2495
A representative collection by the influential English romantic.

Includes bibliographical references

Kipling, Rudyard, 1865-1936

Complete verse; definitive edition. Doubleday 1989 c1940 850p pa $20 hardcover o.p. *

Grades: 11 12 Adult   821
  ISBN 0-385-26089-X (pa)   LC 88-7364
Replaces Rudyard Kipling's verse: definitive edition, published 1940
This edition includes all of Kipling's published poetry and, in addition, more than 20 poems which have not previously appeared in the inclusive edition of his verse

Rossetti, Christina Georgina, 1830-1894

Poems. Knopf 1993 256p (Everyman's library pocket poets) $12.50

Grades: 11 12 Adult   821
  ISBN 0-679-42908-5   LC 93-14362
The poems in this collection are grouped under the following headings: Lyric poems, Dramatic and narrative poems, Rhymes and riddles, Sonnet sequences, Prayers and meditations. An index of first lines is included

Shakespeare, William, 1564-1616

Poems. Knopf 1994 252p (Everyman's library pocket poets) $12.50 *

Grades: 11 12 Adult   821
  ISBN 0-679-43320-1   LC 94-2494
Also available CD-ROM version
A representative selection of Shakespeare's verse.

Shakespeare, William, 1564-1616—*Continued*

The sonnets; edited by Rex Gibson. Cambridge Univ. Press 1997 204p il pa $12.50 *
Grades: 9 10 11 12   **821**
ISBN 0-521-55947-2   LC 97-149257
"Each of Shakespeare's 154 sonnets is given at least one page, which includes the text of the sonnet, its theme and meaning, one possible interpretation, an explanation of difficult phrases and imagery, and a glossary of the unfamiliar words. The information is not thrust on the reader as the final and only 'correct' interpretation." Book Rep

The sonnets; edited by Stephen Orgel; with an introduction by John Hollander. Penguin Books 2001 xliv, 164p (The Pelican Shakespeare) pa $4.95 *
Grades: 11 12 Adult   **821**
ISBN 0-14-071453-7   LC 2001-33200
"A series of 154 sonnets by Shakespeare. Probably composed between 1593 and 1601, they are written in the form of three quatrains and a couplet that has come to be known as Shakespearean. Influenced by, and often reacting against, the popular sonnet cycles of the time, notably Sir Philip Sidney's 'Astrophel and Stella', Shakespeare's sonnets are among the finest examples of their kind." Reader's Ency. 4th edition

Tennyson, Alfred Tennyson, Baron, 1809-1892

Tennyson; a selected edition, incorporating the Trinity College manuscripts; edited by Christopher Ricks. University of Calif. Press 1989 xxxi, 1032p hardcover o.p. pa $27.50 *
Grades: 11 12 Adult   **821**
ISBN 0-520-06588-3; 0-520-06666-9 (pa)
                                LC 88-40556
Included in this annotated selection of the Victorian poet's work are the complete texts of The princess, In memoriam, Maud, and Idylls of the King.

Thomas, Dylan, 1914-1953

The poems of Dylan Thomas; edited with an introduction and notes by Daniel Jones; with a preface by Dylan Thomas. rev ed. New Directions 2003 xxix, 320p il $34.95 *
Grades: 11 12 Adult   **821**
ISBN 0-8112-1541-5   LC 2002-155790
Includes CD of the poet reading his work
First published 1971
"To the 90 poems Thomas published in Collected Poems, 1934-1952 Jones has added 102 and placed the total, as far as he could determine, in the chronological order of their composition. Some of the poems were still in manuscript form when Thomas died; others had been published in periodicals and anthologies. In an appendix, Jones offers Thomas' early poems—including one written when the poet was 12." Libr J {review of 1971 edition}
Includes bibliographical references

Selected poems, 1934-1952. rev ed. New Directions 2003 214p pa $14.95
Grades: 11 12 Adult   **821**
ISBN 0-8112-1542-3   LC 2002-155792

First published 1953 with title: The collected poems of Dylan Thomas
"The prologue in verse, written for this collected edition of my poems, is intended as an address to my readers, the strangers. This book contains most of the poems I have written, and all, up to the present year, that I wish to preserve. Some of them I have revised a little." Preface {of 1953 edition}

William Wordsworth; edited and with an introduction by Harold Bloom. Chelsea House 1999 75p (Bloom's major poets) lib bdg $21.95
Grades: 9 10 11 12   **821**
1. Wordsworth, William, 1770-1850
ISBN 0-7910-5114-5   LC 98-37752
Other available series titles in this class include: Robert Browning; John Donne; John Milton; Alfred, Lord Tennyson. For complete list of titles contact publisher
Following a biography of the poet this volume contains thematic analysis of several poems. Includes extracts from critical essays.
Includes bibliographical references

Wordsworth, William, 1770-1850

Poems. Knopf 1995 256p (Everyman's library pocket poets) $12.50 *
Grades: 11 12 Adult   **821**
ISBN 0-679-44369-X
A selection of work representative of the prominent Romantic's poetic legacy

Yeats, W. B. (William Butler), 1865-1939

The poems; edited by Richard J. Finneran. 2nd ed. Scribner 1997 xxix, 752p il $40; pa $20 *
Grades: 11 12 Adult   **821**
ISBN 0-684-83935-0; 0-684-80731-9 (pa)
                                LC 97-23065
First published 1983 by Macmillan
This edition of the Nobel Laureate's verse contains complete texts of all the poems Yeats is known to have written. Yeats' original rhetorical punctuation has been restored. The editor provides textual histories

821.008   English poetry--Collections

100 essential modern poems; selected and introduced by Joseph Parisi. Ivan R. Dee 2005 305p $24.95 *
Grades: 11 12 Adult   **821.008**
1. English poetry—Collections 2. American poetry—Collections
ISBN 1-56663-612-4   LC 2005-9897
"Each of the 70 individuals whose work is represented receives a short, readable introduction that includes pertinent biographical information, a description of the poet's place in modern literary history, and an analysis of the writer's style. One to three representative poems follow each entry." SLJ
"Preceded by wonderfully conversational and expertly appreciative biocritical essays about each poet, his choices are superb as he lingers over Yeats and Stevens and includes often-overlooked witty and satirical poets, among them Dorothy Parker, Ogden Nash, Kay Ryan, Frank O'Hara, and Billy Collins." Booklist

100 great poems of the twentieth century; [edited by] Mark Strand. Norton 2005 320p $24.95

Grades: 11 12 Adult   **821.008**

1. English poetry—Collections 2. American poetry—Collections

ISBN 0-393-05894-8   LC 2005-2150

The editor "has selected works by poets of Europe and North and South America, and because there are so many gifted American poets, he restricted himself to those born before 1927. The result is a marvelously graceful, shimmering cosmos of poems by the likes of Anna Akhmatova, A. R. Ammons, Amy Clampit, Robert Desnos, Robert Frost, Nazim Hikmet, Kenneth Koch, Edna St. Vincent Millay, Gabriela Mistral, Eugenio Montale, Octavio Paz, and Derek Walcott." Booklist

The **Best** poems of the English language; from Chaucer through Robert Frost; selected and with commentary by Harold Bloom. HarperCollins Publishers 2004 xxviii, 972p $34.95; pa $19.95 *

Grades: 11 12 Adult   **821.008**

1. English poetry—Collections 2. American poetry—Collections

ISBN 0-06-054041-9; 0-06-054042-7 (pa)

     LC 2003-51104

"Arranged chronologically by author, the poems are preceded by commentaries that extol their specific virtues and place them in historical context. Taken together, they provide an overview of Bloom's own theories of writing, such as his notion that the greatest poems manifest an 'inevitability' of phrasing . . . Bloom rarely bores, and at his best he achieves a cogency . . . worthy of the poets he so deeply admires." Libr J

Includes bibliographical references

Blushing: expressions of love in poems & letters; collected by Paul B. Janeczko. Orchard Bks. 2004 98p il lib bdg $15.95

Grades: 7 8 9 10   **821.008**

1. Love poetry 2. Poetry—Collections

ISBN 0-439-53056-3   LC 2003-48697

A collection of love poetry and letters by such authors as Lord Byron, William Shakespeare, Sir Walter Scott, Nikki Giovanni, Maya Angelou, Emily Dickinson, Elizabeth Barrett Browning, and Edna St. Vincent Millay

"Janeczko chooses a subject that will certainly draw interest, and the combination of letters and poetry offers a fine glimpse of what poets do: make beautiful, disciplined work from their deepest, undisciplined feelings." Booklist

Chapters into verse; poetry in English inspired by the Bible; assembled and edited by Robert Atwan & Laurance Wieder. Oxford Univ. Press 1993 2v hardcover o.p. set pa $24.95

Grades: 11 12 Adult   **821.008**

ISBN 0-19-508493-4; 0-19-513676-4 (pa)

     LC 92-37206

Volumes 1 and 2 also available separately in hardcover v1 $45; v2 $42

Contents: v1 Genesis to Malachi; v2 Gospels to Revelation

"An anthology of poems from all eras, styles, and degree of reverence, which take as their major inspiration lines, verses, or chapters from the Bible. Arranged in Biblical order in two volumes . . . the poems are preceded by the appropriate chapters and verses (the King James version has been used throughout). Poets as wide-ranging as Emily Dickinson, Sylvia Plath, and Delmore Schwartz are interspersed with D.H. Lawrence and writers from the Harlem Renaissance." Libr J

The **Columbia** anthology of British poetry; edited by Carl Woodring and James Shapiro. Columbia Univ. Press 1995 xxxi, 891p $41 *

Grades: 11 12 Adult   **821.008**

1. English poetry—Collections

ISBN 0-231-10180-5   LC 94-46333

This anthology "contains major British poetry from Beowulf to the present day. Poets receive a short biographical introduction along with their poetry. . . . It includes more female poets than most comparable anthologies, and is conducive to browsing. Major poems such as Coleridge's 'Rime of the Ancient Mariner,' Britain's best-loved poems, and newly rediscovered poems are part of this collection." SLJ

The **New** Oxford book of Irish verse; edited, with translations, by Thomas Kinsella. Oxford Univ. Press 2001 xxx, 423p pa $16.95 *

Grades: 11 12 Adult   **821.008**

1. Irish poetry—Collections

ISBN 0-19-280192-9   LC 2001-278442

Replaces The Oxford Book of Irish verse, XVIIth century-XXth century, chosen by Donagh MacDonagh and Lennox Robinson (1958); this is a reissue of the 1986 edition

"This selection is divided into three parts. Book I opens with the earliest pre-Christian poetry in Old Irish and ends in the fourteenth century with the first Irish poetry in the English language. Book II covers the fourteenth to the eighteenth centuries and Book III the nineteenth and twentieth centuries." Publisher's note

The **New** Oxford book of Victorian verse. Oxford Univ. Press 1987 xxxiv, 654p pa $19.95 hardcover o.p. *

Grades: 11 12 Adult   **821.008**

1. English poetry—Collections

ISBN 0-19-284084-3 (pa)   LC 86-23701

Replaces The Oxford book of Victorian verse, edited by Sir Arthur Quiller-Couch (1912)

An anthology of 19th century English poetry. Among the poets prominently featured are: Clough, Morris, Arnold, the Decadents, Emily Brontë, Clare, Barnes, and Christina Rossetti

"While general collections should all add Ricks, those retaining {the Quiller-Couch edition} should dust him off and keep him available in order to represent fully Victorian verse and changing attitudes toward it." Libr J

The **Norton** anthology of modern and contemporary poetry; edited by Jahan Ramazani, Richard Ellmann, Robert O'Clair. 3rd ed. Norton 2003 2v pa set $75 *

Grades: 11 12 Adult   **821.008**
1. English poetry—Collections 2. American poetry—Collections
ISBN 0-393-32429-X   LC 2002-37990

Volumes 1 and 2 also available separately in paperback each $55

First published 1973 with title: The Norton anthology of modern poetry

Contents: v1 Modern poetry; v2 Contemporary poetry

This volume includes "1596 poems by 195 poets. . . . The anthology includes the works of such masters as Walt Whitman, Ezra Pound, Dylan Thomas, Langston Hughes, Gertrude Stein, Lucille Clifton, Louise Erdrich, and Allen Ginsberg. . . . Extensive, and beautifully composed introductions provide insight, observations, and historical context for the selections. . . . This ambitious, highly successful work is a veritable tribute to the enduring power of literature and language." SLJ

Includes bibliographical references

The **Norton** book of light verse; edited by Russell Baker; with the assistance of Kathleen Leland Baker. Norton 1986 447p $29.95

Grades: 11 12 Adult   **821.008**
1. English poetry—Collections 2. American poetry—Collections 3. Humorous poetry
ISBN 0-393-02366-4   LC 86-18172

Arranged by subject, this anthology presents some four hundred British and American light verse selections. The poems date from the sixteenth-century to the present

The **Oxford** book of English verse; edited by Christopher Ricks. Oxford Univ. Press 1999 xxxii, 690p $39.95 *

Grades: 11 12 Adult   **821.008**
1. English poetry—Collections
ISBN 0-19-214182-1   LC 99-20831

First published 1900 under the editorship of Sir Arthur Quiller-Couch with title: The Oxford book of English verse, 1250-1900. Present edition replaces The New Oxford book of English verse, 1250-1950, edited by Helen Gardner published 1972

This collection "starts with anonymous 13th-century lyric and ends with Seamus Heaney; in between are seven centuries' worth of poems in English from Britain and Ireland. . . . Ricks brings in plenty of dialect verse, excerpts from long poems and verse plays, and a few translations into English. . . . Long after reviewers stop debating how Ricks chose each item, readers will keep returning to these pages to find yet another good poem they've not before seen." Publ Wkly

The **Oxford** book of twentieth-century English verse. Oxford Univ. Press c1973 xlii, 654p $35 *

Grades: 11 12 Adult   **821.008**
1. English poetry—Collections
ISBN 0-19-812137-7

This anthology of more than 600 poems by more than 200 twentieth-century British writers includes works by John Masefield, T. S. Eliot, W. B. Yeats, W. H. Auden, Dylan Thomas and Alan Sillitoe

"A strong vein of neo-Georgianism runs throughout the book, resulting in a clear partiality for work that is explicitly, even documentarily, English in locale, for poems that are narrative or anecdotal, for neat, well-populated fables and for moralistic ruminations." New Statesman

Poetry out loud; edited by Robert Alden Rubin; with an introduction by James Earl Jones. Algonquin Bks. 1993 215p il pa $9.95 hardcover o.p.

Grades: 9 10 11 12   **821.008**
1. English poetry—Collections 2. American poetry—Collections
ISBN 1-56512-122-8 (pa)   LC 93-3946

An anthology of over 100 poems specifically chosen for reading aloud

Includes bibliographical references

The **Top** 500 poems; edited by William Harmon. Columbia Univ. Press 1992 xxx, 1132p $36.95

Grades: 11 12 Adult   **821.008**
1. English poetry—Collections 2. American poetry—Collections
ISBN 0-231-08028-X   LC 91-42239

"Harmon devises an interesting method (collecting the 500 most anthologized shorter English and American poems as indexed in the *Columbia Granger's Index to Poetry,* 8th and 9th eds.) to bring together poetry of the last 750 years that he calls the 'greatest successes'. . . . Each of the 500 poems, arranged in chronological order, has a biographical headnote and editorial comments by the editor." Libr J

Understanding poetry; [edited by] Cleanth Brooks, Robert Penn Warren. 4th ed. Holt, Rinehart & Winston; distributed by Harcourt Brace College Pubs. 1976 xxii, 602p pa $55.50

Grades: 9 10 11 12   **821.008**
1. English poetry—Collections 2. American poetry—Collections 3. Poetry—History and criticism
ISBN 0-03-076980-9

First published 1938

This volume explores the meaning and structure of poetry with discussions of the nuances of theme, dramatic structure and metrics. Approximately 350 English and American poems ranging from the 16th century to the present are included in this collection

821.009   English poetry--History and criticism

Elizabeth Barrett Browning; edited and with an introduction by Harold Bloom. Chelsea House 2002 311p (Modern critical views) $36.95

Grades: 9 10 11 12   **821.009**
1. Browning, Elizabeth Barrett, 1806-1861
ISBN 0-7910-6450-6   LC 2001-47214

Other available series titles in this class are: Geoffrey Chaucer; John Keats; William Wordsworth; William Butler Yeats. For complete list of titles contact publisher

Elizabeth Barrett Browning—*Continued*
A collection of contemporary critical views on the author of Sonnets from the Portuguese
Includes bibliographical references

Glancy, Ruth F., 1948-
Thematic guide to British poetry; [by] Ruth Glancy. Greenwood Press 2002 303p $64.95
Grades: 9 10 11 12   **821.009**
1. English poetry—History and criticism
ISBN 0-313-31379-2   LC 2002-23252
"This thematic guide offers interpretations of 415 poems, representing the work of over 110 poets spanning seven centuries of B poetry." Publisher's note
This is a "well-organized, easy-to-navigate, authoritative volume." SLJ
Includes bibliographical references

Graham, Peter W., 1951-
Lord Byron. Twayne Pubs. 1998 189p il (Twayne's English authors series) $33
Grades: 11 12 Adult   **821.009**
1. Byron, George Gordon Byron, 6th Baron, 1788-1824
ISBN 0-8057-7065-8   LC 98-13079
For a complete list of titles in series contact publisher
The author considers Byron's major poems, lyrics, satires and dramas. The poet's letters and journals serve as source material.
Includes bibliographical references

Hallissy, Margaret
A companion to Chaucer's Canterbury tales. Greenwood Press 1995 333p il $52.50 *
Grades: 11 12 Adult   **821.009**
1. Chaucer, Geoffrey, d. 1400. Canterbury tales
ISBN 0-313-29189-6   LC 95-16017
This work is "designed specifically for first-time readers. . . . It provides students with simple interpretations and amplifications and makes their journey through this great unfinished work enjoyable and rewarding. Particularly helpful are the opening sections on Chaucer's world and language. There are essays of explanation as well on each of the major tales." SLJ
Includes bibliographical references

Poets of World War I: Rupert Brooke & Siegfried Sassoon; edited and with an introduction by Harold Bloom. Chelsea House 2003 83p (Bloom's major poets) lib bdg $22.95
Grades: 9 10 11 12   **821.009**
1. Brooke, Rupert, 1887-1915 2. Sassoon, Siegfried, 1886-1967
ISBN 0-7910-7388-2   LC 2003-6927
This volume includes biographies of the two poets and critical analysis of their poems
Includes bibliographical references

Poets of World War I: Wilfred Owen & Isaac Rosenberg; Harold Bloom, editor. Chelsea House 2002 111p (Bloom's major poets) lib bdg $22.95
Grades: 9 10 11 12   **821.009**
1. Owen, Wilfred 2. Rosenberg, Isaac, 1890-1918
ISBN 0-7910-5932-4   LC 2001-28515
"This volume contains a short biography of each poet and the analysis of eight poems (four from each poet) from thematic and structural foundations. These criticisms are supported by primary source material, such as letters, diaries, and notes." Book Rep

Rossignol, Rosalyn
Critical companion to Chaucer; a literary reference to his life and work. Facts on File 2006 648p il $85
Grades: 11 12 Adult   **821.009**
1. Chaucer, Geoffrey, d. 1400
ISBN 0-8160-6193-9; 978-0-8160-6193-8
                                LC 2006-99
First published 1999 with title: Chaucer A to Z
This book on the works of Chaucer includes a biography of Chaucer, synopses and critical commentary on his works (including the Canterbury Tales), and lists of related people, places and topics.
Includes bibliographical references

822   English drama

Bolt, Robert
A man for all seasons; a play in two acts. Random House 1962 xxv, 163p il pa $9.50 hardcover o.p.
Grades: 11 12 Adult   **822**
1. More, Sir Thomas, Saint, 1478-1535—Drama
2. Great Britain—History—1485-1603, Tudors—Drama
ISBN 0-679-72822-8 (pa)
Characters: 11 men, 2 women. First produced in the United States at the ANTA Theatre, New York City, November 22, 1961
A play set in sixteenth century England about Sir Thomas More, a devout Catholic, and his conflict with Henry VIII.

Christie, Agatha, 1890-1976
The mousetrap and other plays. New American Library 2000 742p hardcover o.p. pa $7.99
Grades: 7 8 9 10 11 12 Adult   **822**
ISBN 0-451-20118-3; 0-451-20114-0 (pa)
                                LC 00-64727
First published 1978 by Dodd, Mead
Contents: Ten little Indians — Appointment with death — The hollow — The mousetrap — Witness for the prosecution — Towards zero — Verdict — Go back for murder
"The noted mystery writer composed adaptations of seven novels and stories into arresting plays as well as creating one original theater piece ('Verdict'). . . . All are as delightful to read for pleasure as Christie's mystery novels, especially since some that earlier appeared in the latter form have been intriguingly altered." Booklist

Fugard, Athol

"Master Harold"— and the boys. Penguin Books 1984 60p pa $11

Grades: 11 12 Adult **822**

    1. South Africa—Race relations—Drama

    ISBN 0-14-048187-7   LC 84-1008

First published 1982 by Random House

Characters: 3 men. 1 act. First produced at the Yale Repertory theatre, New Haven, Connecticut, 1982.

Drama with racial overtones set in Port Elizabeth tea room focuses on precocious white South African teenager's relationship with two black men who work for his family, both old enough to be his father.

Pinter, Harold, 1930-

The birthday party, and The room; two plays. Grove Press 1961 120p il pa $10

Grades: 9 10 11 12 **822**

    ISBN 0-8021-5114-0

"An Evergreen original"

The birthday party, first performed in 1958 and published in 1959, portrays the mental destruction of a young pianist living obscurely in an English seaside town. In The room, first produced in 1957, an elderly couple seems about to be evicted from their boarding house

Pomerance, Bernard

The Elephant Man; a play. Grove Press 1979 71p pa $11 hardcover o.p.

Grades: 11 12 Adult **822**

    1. Merrick, Joseph Carey, 1862 or 3-1890—Drama

    2. Physically handicapped—Drama

    ISBN 0-8021-3041-0 (pa)   LC 79-7792

Characters: 5 men, 2 women. 21 scenes. First produced at the Hampstead Theatre, London, 1977

Play based on the life of John [i.e., Joseph Carey] Merrick who from birth was so grotesquely deformed that he became known as the Elephant Man. Merrick was exhibited as a freak until a London surgeon found him permanent residence in a hospital where he became a favorite of aristocracy and literati.

Shaffer, Peter

Peter Shaffer's Amadeus; with an introduction by the director Sir Peter Hall and a wholly new preface by the author. Perennial Bks. 2001 xxxiv, 124p pa $15

Grades: 11 12 Adult **822**

    1. Mozart, Wolfgang Amadeus, 1756-1791—Drama

    2. Salieri, Antonio, 1750-1825—Drama

    ISBN 0-06-093549-9   LC 2001-278382

First published 1980 in the United Kingdom

Characters: 9 men, 1 woman, extras. 2 acts. First produced at the National Theater of Great Britain, November 1979

Explores relationship between Autrian court composer Antonio Salieri and the divinely gifted young Wolfgang Amadeus Mozart.

Shaw, Bernard, 1856-1950

Pygmalion . . . and My fair lady; [Pygmalion] by George Bernard Shaw; and My fair lady/ based on Shaw's Pygmalion; adaptation and lyrics by Alan Jay Lerner; music by Frederick Loewe. 50th anniversary ed. Signet Classic [2006] 219p pa $5.95

Grades: 11 12 Adult **822**

    ISBN 0-451-53009-8

My fair lady was awarded the New York Drama Critics Circle Award for 1956

"This is an authorized original paperback edition published by New American Library" Verso of title page

This volume includes the complete texts of Shaw's Pygmalion and Lerner's musical adaptation My fair lady.

Sheridan, Richard Brinsley, 1751-1816

The rivals; [by] Sheridan; edited with introduction and notes by C. J. L. Price. Oxford Univ. Press 1968 140p pa $19.95

Grades: 9 10 11 12 **822**

    ISBN 0-19-831908-8

In this satirical comedy, first presented in 1775, two gentlemen woo Lydia Languish, a young woman with highly romantic ideas concerning love whose fortune will be forfeited if she marries without the consent of her aunt. The aunt, Mrs. Malaprop, has become famous for her eccentric use of the English language

Stoppard, Tom

Rosencrantz and Guildenstern are dead. Grove Press 1967 126p pa $12 hardcover o.p.

Grades: 11 12 Adult **822**

    1. Shakespeare, William, 1564-1616—Parodies, imitations, etc.

    ISBN 0-8021-3275-8 (pa)

Characters: 13 men, 2 women, extras. First produced in this form April 11, 1967 in London

This play "took the theatre world on both sides of the Atlantic by storm. The originality of the idea which put Hamlet's two insignificant friends centerstage was matched by the brilliance of the dialogue between these bewildered nonentities." Reader's Ency. 4th edition

Thomas, Dylan, 1914-1953

Under milk wood; a play for voices. New Directions 1954 107p music pa $8.95

Grades: 11 12 Adult **822**

    ISBN 0-8112-0209-7

"A radio play for voices. Written in poetic, inventive prose, this play is full of humor, a joyful sense of the goodness of life and love, and a strong Welsh flavor. It is an impression of a spring day in the lives of the people of Llareggub, a Welsh village situated under Milk Wood. It has no plot, but a wealth of characters who dream aloud, converse with one another, and speak in choruses of alternating voices." Reader's Ency. 4th edition

Wilde, Oscar, 1854-1900

The importance of being earnest and other plays; introduction by Terrence McNally; notes by Michael F. Davis. Modern Library paperback ed. Modern Library 2003 257p pa $9.95

Grades: 11 12 Adult   **822**

ISBN 0-8129-6714-3   LC 2003-44566

Contents: Lady Windermere's fan -- An ideal husband -- The importance of being earnest

The title play, written in 1895, is a drawing room comedy exposing quirks and foibles of Victorian society with plot revolving around amorous pursuits of two men who face social obstacles when they woo young ladies of quality. The book also features Lady Windermere's fan (1893), a four act comedy about a woman who has an affair when she suspects her husband of adultery, and An ideal husband (1895), a comedy about a blackmail scheme involving a lord's investment in the Suez Canal days before the British government's purchase of it, and his wife's reaction to her husband's past misdeeds.

822.008   English drama--Collections

100 great monologues from the Renaissance theatre; edited by Jocelyn A. Beard. Smith & Kraus 1994 186p pa $9.95

Grades: 9 10 11 12   **822.008**

1. Monologues 2. Acting

ISBN 1-880399-59-8   LC 94-19393

A collection of monologues for men and women selected to represent the range of English Renaissance stage roles

822.009   English drama--History and criticism

Ben Jonson; edited and with an introduction by Harold Bloom. Chelsea House 2001 104p (Bloom's major dramatists) $21.95

Grades: 9 10 11 12   **822.009**

1. Jonson, Ben, 1573?-1637

ISBN 0-7910-6359-3   LC 2001-53677

Another available series title in this class is: Christopher Marlowe. For a complete list of titles contact publisher

Includes a biographical essay, plot summaries, and critical interpretations of the plays and their characters.

Includes bibliographical references

822.3   William Shakespeare

Aliki

William Shakespeare & the Globe; written & illustrated by Aliki. HarperCollins Pubs. 1999 48p il hardcover o.p. lib bdg $15.89; pa $6.99 *

Grades: 4 5 6 7 8 9   **822.3**

1. Shakespeare, William, 1564-1616 2. Globe Theatre (London, England) 3. Shakespeare's Globe (London, England)

ISBN 0-06-027820-X; 0-06-027821-8 (lib bdg); 0-06-443722-1 (pa)   LC 98-7903

The "text describes Shakespeare's life, the Elizabethan world and entertainments, and the ups and downs of the theatrical industry . . . including tidbits such as the Burbage brothers' piece-by-piece theft of the original Globe Theatre. A fast-forward to the twentieth century then treats Sam Wanamaker's dream of making the Globe rise again." Bull Cent Child Books

"A logically organized and engaging text, plenty of detailed illustrations with informative captions, and a clean design provide a fine introduction to both bard and theater." Horn Book Guide

Appignanesi, Richard

Manga Shakespeare: Romeo and Juliet; by William Shakespeare; adapted by Richard Appignanesi; illustrated by Sonia Leong. Amulet Books 2007 195p il pa $9.95

Grades: 9 10 11 12   **822.3**

1. Shakespeare, William, 1564-1616—Adaptations 2. Graphic novels

ISBN 978-0-8109-9325-9; 0-8109-9325-2
                                  LC 2006-100362

First published in the United Kingdom

Shakespeare's classic play of star-crossed young lovers gets the manga treatment. Set in modern Tokyo with rival yakuza gangs, and using somewhat abridged text from the play for the dialogue, the story becomes an accessible, action-packed read most teens will like.

"Although the richness of the language may be lost, the script keeps the spirit of the story intact, hitting all the major speeches." Booklist

Bieman, Elizabeth

William Shakespeare: the romances. Twayne Pubs. 1990 151p (Twayne's English authors series) $23.95

Grades: 11 12 Adult   **822.3**

1. Shakespeare, William, 1564-1616—Criticism

ISBN 0-8057-6995-1   LC 89-26857

Other available titles about Shakespeare in this series are: William Shakespeare: his life and times; William Shakespeare: sonnets and poems; William Shakespeare: the comedies; William Shakespeare: the tragedies

An examination of the themes and techniques used in Pericles, Cymbeline, The winter's tale and The tempest

Includes bibliographical references

Bloom, Harold, 1930-

Hamlet: poem unlimited. Riverhead Bks. 2003 154p hardcover o.p. pa $13

Grades: 11 12 Adult   **822.3**

1. Shakespeare, William, 1564-1616. Hamlet

ISBN 1-573-22233-X; 1-573-22377-8 (pa)
                                  LC 2002-31691

This "is Bloom's attempt to uncover the mystery of both Prince Hamlet and the play itself. . . . Bloom takes us through the major soliloquies, scenes, characters, and action of the play, to explore the enigma at the heart of the drama." Publisher's note

"Far superior to existing theories of performance and worth yards of criticism for each well-wrought page." Libr J

Bloom, Harold, 1930- —*Continued*

Shakespeare: the invention of the human. Riverhead Bks. 1998 xx, 745p pa $18 hardcover o.p.

Grades: 11 12 Adult   **822.3**

1. Shakespeare, William, 1564-1616—Criticism

ISBN 1-57322-751-X (pa)   LC 98-21325

In this critical study, Bloom argues "that the plays and poems of Shakespeare are not just 'the center of the Western canon'; they are nothing less than 'secular scripture.'. . . Bloom's book proceeds through genre groupings in rough chronological order." Commentary

"The passion and obsessiveness of Bloom's approach are its greatest recommendation." N Y Rev Books

Boyce, Charles

Critical companion to William Shakespeare; a literary reference to his life and work. Rev. ed. Facts on File 2005 2v il (Facts on File library of world literature) set $104.50 *

Grades: 11 12 Adult   **822.3**

1. Shakespeare, William, 1564-1616

ISBN 0-8160-5373-1   LC 2004-25769

First published 1990 with title: Shakespeare A to Z

"The first two-thirds [of this set] covers the plays. Arranged alphabetically by title, the 3000 entries generally consist of a scene-by-scene summary, a commentary, sources, theatrical history, and character sketches. The last one-third features entries for actors, composers, musicians, places that figured in the plays, and miscellaneous items." Libr J

For a fuller review, see: Booklist, Sept. 1, 2005

Includes bibliographical references

Butler, Colin

The practical Shakespeare; the plays in practice and on the page. Ohio University Press 2005 205p $39.95; pa $19.95 *

Grades: 11 12 Adult   **822.3**

1. Shakespeare, William, 1564-1616—Dramatic production

ISBN 0-8214-1621-9; 0-8214-1622-7 (pa)
          LC 2004-30580

"Notes on staging, acting behaviors, scenes not shown, entrances, exits, characterizations, prologues, choruses, and staging are each featured in the text. References to specific scenes in the plays are used to illustrate and support the material. Any group preparing a production of one of the plays should find this a useful reference." Univ Press Books for Public and Second Sch Libr, 2006

Includes bibliographical references

Cahn, Victor L.

The plays of Shakespeare; a thematic guide. Greenwood Press 2001 361p $49.95

Grades: 9 10 11 12   **822.3**

1. Shakespeare, William, 1564-1616

ISBN 0-313-30981-7   LC 00-22337

The author approaches Shakespeare "through an analysis of his major themes across several plays. The book contains 19 separate thematic essays devoted to such topics as Fate, Honor, Justice, Love, Money, and Power. Each analysis is abundantly supported with quotations from well-known and often-studied plays." Book Rep

Includes bibliographical references

Coursen, Herbert R.

Macbeth; a guide to the play. Greenwood Press 1997 212p il (Greenwood guides to Shakespeare) $60

Grades: 9 10 11 12   **822.3**

1. Shakespeare, William, 1564-1616. Macbeth
2. Tragedy

ISBN 0-313-30047-X   LC 96-49733

For complete list of series titles contact publisher

"In its examination of fate and ambition, the guide shows how the play relates to modern times though set in the 17th century. Discussion of these themes is directed to the student level. . . . The final section of the book is an analysis of *Macbeth* productions on stage, film, and television. Coursen offers insightful interpretation of the various productions and the challenge of providing a bridge from the text to the performance." Book Rep

Includes bibliographical references

Cover, Arthur Byron

Macbeth; [by] William Shakespeare; Arthur Byron Cover, adapter; Tony Leonard Tamai, illustrator. Puffin Graphics 2005 176p il pa $9.99 *

Grades: 9 10 11 12   **822.3**

1. Shakespeare, William, 1564-1616—Adaptations
2. Graphic novels

ISBN 0-14-240409-8

Ambitious lord Macbeth murders his king to take the throne because of the predictions of some witches, but his position is never secure, and he takes ever more violent measures to stay in power. Shakespeare's classic play is reinvented here with Japanese manga style art and a futuristic setting on a vast ringworld around a sun.

Coye, Dale F.

Pronouncing Shakespeare's words; a guide from A to zounds. Greenwood Press 1998 724p $125.95

Grades: 11 12 Adult   **822.3**

1. Shakespeare, William, 1564-1616—Dictionaries

ISBN 0-313-30655-9   LC 97-44868

Also available in paperback from Routledge

This work provides the correct pronunciation of over 300 words from Shakespeare's plays and poems. An "introduction precedes a phonetic pronunciation guide that includes definitions. Organized by play or poem, words are given in the order in which they appear in a linear reading. Lists at the beginning of each work contain pronunciation guides for place and proper names, the most common 'hard' words, and the most common reduced forms." Libr J

Includes bibliographical references

Dunton-Downer, Leslie

Essential Shakespeare handbook; [by] Leslie Dunton-Downer, Alan Riding. DK Pub 2004 480p il pa $25 *

Grades: 11 12 Adult   **822.3**
     1. Shakespeare, William, 1564-1616
     ISBN 0-7894-9333-0   LC 2004-274586

This is an "illustrated guide to every play in the Shakespeare canon, as well as a portrait of the Bard's life and the world of Elizabethan and Jacobean theater." Publisher's note

"This is an excellent basic tool for gaining insight into the Bard's poetic genius. . . . It is an informative, visually enticing introduction to the world's most famous dramatist." SLJ

Fallon, Robert Thomas

A theatergoer's guide to Shakespeare. Dee, I.R. 2001 479p $29.95; pa $18.95 *

Grades: 11 12 Adult   **822.3**
     1. Shakespeare, William, 1564-1616
     ISBN 1-56663-342-7; 1-56663-508-X (pa)
                         LC 00-57018

Fallon "begins each summary with a brief scholarly introduction that places the particular play in the Shakespearean canon and in some cases provides helpful historical information. Thereafter Fallon maps out, with faultless accuracy, the twists and turns of every play from *King Lear* to *The Two Noble Kinsmen.*" Booklist

Includes bibliographical references

Garber, Marjorie

Shakespeare after all. Pantheon Books 2004 989p hardcover o.p. pa $20

Grades: 11 12 Adult   **822.3**
     1. Shakespeare, William, 1564-1616—Criticism
     ISBN 0-375-42190-4; 0-385-72214-1 (pa)
                         LC 2004-40063

The author "provides a handbook on Shakespeare's plays. After an introduction supplying standard overviews of the Renaissance theater and Shakespeare's life, she offers a critical essay on each play, complete with bibliographies and filmographies. The strength of this work is that Garber shows how the plays are interrelated by recurring language, characters, and themes, how each era has interpreted Shakespeare for itself, and how Shakespeare continues to shape today's culture." Libr J

Includes bibliographical references

Garfield, Leon, 1921-1996

Shakespeare stories {I}-II; illustrated by Michael Foreman. Houghton Mifflin 1991-1995 c1985-c1994 2v il v1 $26; pa $17; v2 $26

Grades: 9 10 11 12   **822.3**
     1. Shakespeare, William, 1564-1616—Adaptations
     ISBN 0-395-56397-6 (v1); 0-395-86140-3 (v1 pa);
     0-395-70893-1 (v2)

Original volume first published 1985 by Schocken Bks.

In these volumes Garfield has rewritten twenty-one of Shakespeare's plays in narrative form, retaining much of the original language

The **Greenwood** companion to Shakespeare; a comprehensive guide to students; edited by Joseph Rosenblum. Greenwood Press 2005 4v set $299.95 *

Grades: 11 12 Adult   **822.3**
     1. Shakespeare, William, 1564-1616
     ISBN 0-313-32779-3   LC 2004-28690

"Each of the set's four volumes relates to a specific genre—Overviews and the History Plays (Vol. 1), The Comedies (Vol. 2), The Tragedies (Vol. 3), and The Romances and Poetry (Vol. 4)—and is organized in 'Cliff Notes' fashion, devoting each entry to a single play, long poem, sonnet, or sonnet pair. . . . A great introduction to the Bard." Libr J

Includes bibliographical references

Nostbakken, Faith, 1964-

Understanding Macbeth; a student casebook to issues, sources, and historical documents. Greenwood Press 1997 235p (Greenwood Press literature in context series) $39.95

Grades: 9 10 11 12   **822.3**
     1. Shakespeare, William, 1564-1616. Macbeth
     ISBN 0-313-29630-8   LC 96-35013

For complete list of series titles contact publisher

This work "cites primary 17th-century documents showing the political events that may have influenced Shakespeare's decision to write a tragedy based on royal treason and the evils of witchcraft. The casebook also includes a dramatic analysis of *Macbeth*, showing the elements—character and theme—that shape the play and guiding the reader to a critical understanding of the work." Book Rep

Includes bibliographical references

Olsen, Kirstin

All things Shakespeare; an encyclopedia of Shakespeare's world. Greenwood Press 2002 2v il maps set $150 *

Grades: 11 12 Adult   **822.3**
     1. Shakespeare, William, 1564-1616
     ISBN 0-313-31503-5   LC 2002-69732

This "encyclopedia describes Shakespeare's physical environment, including common objects, daily activities, and popular beliefs and attitudes. Information is grouped into general topic clusters such as 'Behavior,' 'Clothing and Dress,' 'Furniture,' 'Fire,' and 'War and Peace.' . . . Within the 200-plus entries, references are made to the play, act, and scene in which Shakespeare mentions the item or activity being discussed." Libr J

The **Oxford** companion to Shakespeare; general editor, Michael Dobson; associate general editor, Stanley Wells. Oxford Univ. Press 2001 xxix, 541p il maps $60 *

Grades: 11 12 Adult   **822.3**
     1. Shakespeare, William, 1564-1616
     ISBN 0-19-811735-3   LC 2001-277478

This volume "illuminates not only Shakespeare's life and works but also the many forms that interpretation of Shakespeare has taken in the centuries since his death." Booklist

Includes bibliographical references

Riley, Dick

The bedside, bathtub & armchair companion to Shakespeare; {by} Dick Riley & Pam McAllister. Continuum 2001 288p il hardcover o.p. pa $19.95
Grades: 11 12 Adult   **822.3**
  1. Shakespeare, William, 1564-1616
  ISBN 0-8264-1249-1; 0-8264-1250-5 (pa)
                              LC 2001-17332
"Provides synopses of plays, information about the period in which each play is set, possible plot sources, and notable features and productions of 36 of Shakespeare's plays (Pericles and The Two Noble Kinsmen are not included). Interspersed with chapters on each play are short discussions about topics such as Shakespeare's sonnets, authorship problems, women's roles in 15th- and 16th-century society, and Shakespeare's language." Libr J

Includes bibliographical references

Saccio, Peter

Shakespeare's English kings; history, chronicle, and drama. 2nd ed. Oxford Univ. Press 2000 284p il map hardcover o.p. pa $14.95
Grades: 9 10 11 12   **822.3**
  1. Shakespeare, William, 1564-1616—Histories
  2. Great Britain—History 3. Great Britain—Kings and rulers
  ISBN 0-19-512318-2; 0-19-512319-0 (pa)
                              LC 99-43297
First published 1977
This book explores the medieval histories and Tudor chronicles that served as source material for Shakespeare's ten history plays. In addition to explicating the plots, the author also discusses where Shakespeare deviated from his sources. Includes genealogical charts and an appendix of names and titles

Includes bibliographical references

Scheeder, Louis, 1946-

All the words on stage; a complete pronunciation dictionary for the plays of William Shakespeare; {by} Louis Scheeder and Shane Ann Younts. Smith & Kraus 2002 292p (Career development series) pa $24.95 *
Grades: 11 12 Adult   **822.3**
  1. Shakespeare, William, 1564-1616—Language
  ISBN 1-57525-214-7   LC 2001-20182
"This reference work is first a pronunciation dictionary, but also can aid in understanding the rhythm and variants of the iambic pentameter and the interweaving of word ahd rhythm produced by Shakespeare's blank verse. . . . Schools that read or perform Shakespeare in their curriculum will want to have this fine dictionary in the reference collection." Book Rep

Includes glossary and bibliographical references

Shakespeare, William, 1564-1616

The Columbia dictionary of quotations from Shakespeare; {selected by} Mary and Reginald Foakes. Columbia Univ. Press 1998 516p $63
Grades: 11 12 Adult   **822.3**
  1. Shakespeare, William, 1564-1616—Quotations
  2. Quotations
  ISBN 0-231-10434-0   LC 97-44894

"The book is organized by topics ('Age,' 'Duplicity,' 'Fish'), followed by passages of about five or six lines. After each selection, the citation, the character, and usually the context of the lines are given. If a reference is obscure, the explanation is more elaborate. Indexes provide access by play and poem, by character, and by keyword." SLJ

The complete works; general editors, Stanley Wells and Gary Taylor; editors, Stanley Wells . . . [et al.]; with introductions by Stanley Wells. 2nd ed. Clarendon Press; Oxford University Press 2005 lxxv, 1344p il $40 *
Grades: 11 12 Adult   **822.3**
  ISBN 0-19-926717-0   LC 2005-47272
First published 1986
On cover: The Oxford Shakespeare
This anthology "features a brief introduction to each work as well as [a] General Introduction. . . . [The volume includes] essay on language, a list of contemporary allusions to Shakespeare, an index of Shakespearean characters, a glossary, a consolidated bibliography, and an index of first lines of the Sonnets." Publisher's note

The essential Shakespeare; selected and with an introduction by Ted Hughes. Ecco Press 1991 230p (Essential poets) pa $8 hardcover o.p.
Grades: 11 12 Adult   **822.3**
  ISBN 0-06-088795-8 (pa)   LC 91-17522
Ted Hughes has selected a "combination of sonnets, songs, speeches, and poetry that best illustrate the incredible breadth of Shakespeare's genius. In his introduction, Hughes explores the origins of Shakespeare's language." Publisher's note

The first part of King Henry the Fourth; edited by Claire McEachern. Penguin Books 2000 xlii, 117p il (The Pelican Shakespeare) pa $5 *
Grades: 9 10 11 12   **822.3**
  ISBN 0-14-071456-1   LC 00-269943
Drama concerning problems arising from the deposition and murder of Richard II, of which Henry of Bolingbroke has had a part. Now king and faced with rebellion in Scotland and Wales, Henry and his sons Prince Hal (the Prince of Wales) and Prince John defeat the Percys and wage war against the armies of Northumberland and the Archbishop of York

Includes bibliographical references

King Lear; edited by Stephen Orgel. New ed. Penguin Books 1999 142p il (The Pelican Shakespeare) pa $5 *
Grades: 9 10 11 12   **822.3**
  ISBN 0-14-071476-6   LC 00-503596
The King of Britain divides his kingdom between his two scheming elder daughters and estranges himself from his favorite daughter when she speaks out against him

Macbeth; edited by Stephen Orgel. Penguin Books 2000 xlvi, 98p il (The Pelican Shakespeare) pa $5 *
Grades: 9 10 11 12   **822.3**
  ISBN 0-14-071478-2   LC 00-266703

Shakespeare, William, 1564-1616—*Continued*

Tragedy concerning a general who murders his king after hearing the prophecies of three witches. Spurred on by his wife, Lady Macbeth, they instigate a series of murders, as well as a war, in his quest (and her ambitions) for the throne of Scotland, ultimately leading to their demise

Includes bibliographical references

The merchant of Venice; edited by A. R. Braunmuller. Penguin Books 2000 lii, 103p (The Pelican Shakespeare) pa $5 *

Grades: 9 10 11 12   **822.3**

ISBN 0-14-071462-6   LC 00-702935

In this dark comedy, a young man, Bassiano, squanders his fortune and, in order to woo the wealthy lady he loves, must borrow money from his friend, Antonio, a Venetian merchant. Antonio, whose own money is invested in merchant ships, must borrow the sum from Shylock, the Jewish moneylender, who later demands a pound of Antonio's flesh when the merchant falls into his debt

A midsummer night's dream; edited by Russ McDonald. Penguin Books 2000 liii, 88p (The Pelican Shakespeare) pa $5 *

Grades: 9 10 11 12   **822.3**

ISBN 0-14-071455-3   LC 00-33635

Comedy about the strange events that take place in a forest inhabited by fairies who magically transform the romantic fate of two young couples

Includes bibliographical references

Much ado about nothing; edited by Peter Holland. [New ed.] Penguin Books 1999 xliv, 98p (The Pelican Shakespeare) pa $5 *

Grades: 9 10 11 12   **822.3**

ISBN 0-14-071480-4   LC 99-462498

Romantic comedy about two couples, Hero and Claudio, and Beatrice and Benedick, who, despite personal and familial obstacles, finally unite through the forces of local constables Dogberry and Verges

Includes bibliographical references

The Norton Shakespeare; based on the Oxford edition; Stephen Greenblatt, general editor {et al.}; with an essay on the Shakespearean stage by Andrew Gurr. Norton 1997 3420p il $62.50 *

Grades: 11 12 Adult   **822.3**

ISBN 0-393-97087-6   LC 97-7083

The editors' "mission is to make Shakespeare accessible to modern readers. With lengthy introductions providing insight into Shakespeare's life and times as well as textual notes, marginal glosses, footnotes, and bibliographies, they more than achieve their aim . . . {Includes} an illustrated chronology of Shakespeare's life, and over 150 illustrations. The result is a work of immense scope, scholarship, and richness." Libr J

Othello; [by] William Shakespeare; advisory editors, David Bevington, Barbara Gaines, and Peter Holland. Sourcebooks MediaFusion 2005 402p il (Sourcebooks Shakespeare) pa $14.95

Grades: 9 10 11 12   **822.3**

ISBN 1-4022-0102-8   LC 2005-23285

Includes CD-ROM

This book features the full text of Othello with performance annotations and glossary. The audio CD included features a 1944 performance of the play by Paul Robeson.

Romeo and Juliet; edited by Peter Holland. Penguin Books 2000 xlvi, 128p il (The Pelican Shakespeare) pa $5 *

Grades: 9 10 11 12   **822.3**

ISBN 0-14-071484-7   LC 00-269942

Young couple defies long-standing feud that divides their families—the Capulets and the Montagues—as their desperate need to be together, secret meetings, and secret marriage propel them toward tragedy

Includes bibliographical references

Romeo and Juliet; [by] William Shakespeare; advisory editors, David Bevington, Barbara Gaines, and Peter Holland. Sourcebooks MediaFusion 2005 360p il (Sourcebooks Shakespeare) pa $14.95

Grades: 9 10 11 12   **822.3**

ISBN 1-4022-0101-X   LC 2005-23286

Includes CD-ROM

This book features the full text of the play Romeo and Juliet with performance annotations and a glossary. The audio CD included features recordings of both Ellen Terry and Kate Beckinsale in the roles of Juliet.

The tempest; edited by Peter Holland. [New ed.] Penguin Books 1999 xliv, 84p (The Pelican Shakespeare) pa $5 *

Grades: 9 10 11 12   **822.3**

ISBN 0-14-071485-5   LC 99-462496

Prospero, the exiled Duke of Milan, living on an island with his daughter Miranda, raises a tempest that brings his shipwrecked enemies ashore. Now, faced with advancing age, he has the opportunity to punish and forgive his enemies as well as relinquish his magic powers

Includes bibliographical references

The tragedy of Julius Caesar; edited by William Montgomery; with an introduction by Douglas Trevor. Penguin Books 2000 xlvi, 114p (The Pelican Shakespeare) pa $5 *

Grades: 9 10 11 12   **822.3**

ISBN 0-14-071468-5   LC 2001-266965

Brutus, best friend of the Roman ruler Caesar, reluctantly joins a successful plot to murder Caesar and subsequently destroys himself

The tragedy of Othello, the Moor of Venice; edited by Russ McDonald. Penguin Books 2001 xxix, 145p il (The Pelican Shakespeare) pa $5 *

Grades: 9 10 11 12   **822.3**

ISBN 0-14-071463-4   LC 2001-33135

A general serving the Venetian state, Othello is duped by a jealous ensign into thinking that his wife, Desdemona, has been unfaithful. Succumbing to jealousy, he murders her and then, upon learning the truth, commits suicide

Shakespeare, William, 1564-1616—*Continued*
The tragical history of Hamlet prince of Denmark. Penguin Books 2001 lviii, 148p (The Pelican Shakespeare) pa $5 *

Grades: 9 10 11 12   **822.3**
ISBN 0-14-071454-5   LC 2001-31340

Story about the Prince of Wales who, upon learning of the death of his father at the hands of his uncle, Claudius, seeks revenge

Includes bibliographical references

Shakespeare; editor, Joseph Rosenblum; managing editor, Christina J. Moose. Salem Press 1998 xx, 482p il (Magill's choice) $68

Grades: 11 12 Adult   **822.3**
1. Shakespeare, William, 1564-1616
ISBN 0-89356-966-6   LC 97-43460

This work "divides the plays into histories, comedies, tragedies, and romances. The plays are indexed alphabetically and a time line also is included. *Shakespeare* begins with background of the man, the dramatist, and the poet. Each play is examined, including a summary, critical analysis, and bibliography. The poetry section explains each poem, analyzes it, and offers theories on theme." Book Rep

Includes bibliographical references

Shakespeare's histories; edited and with an introduction by Harold Bloom. Chelsea House 2000 117p (Bloom's major dramatists) $19.95

Grades: 9 10 11 12   **822.3**
1. Shakespeare, William, 1564-1616—Criticism
ISBN 0-7910-5241-9   LC 99-36774

Other available titles about Shakespeare in this series are: Shakespeare's comedies; Shakespeare's tragedies

This "title contains criticism on Richard III, Henry IV, Parts 1 and 2, and Henry V. Discussion of the individual plays is prefaced by an introduction and a three-page biography of Shakespeare. The entry on each play gives a succinct plot summary, brief descriptions of major characters, and six to eight critical excerpts. A list of the bard's works, further reading, and indexes of themes and ideas complete this comprehensive volume." SLJ

Includes bibliographical references

Shakespeare's world and work; an encyclopedia for students; John F. Andrews, editor in chief. Scribner 2001 3v il set $340

Grades: 7 8 9 10   **822.3**
1. Shakespeare, William, 1564-1616
ISBN 0-684-80629-0   LC 00-68743

This set "complements its examination of Shakespeare as literature with glimpses of the customs, beliefs, politics, and historical personages that had an impact on his writing. An attractive design and many student-friendly features help make a challenging topic palatable and even appealing." Booklist

Includes bibliographical references

Spurgeon, Caroline F. E., 1869-1942
Shakespeare's imagery and what it tells us; with charts and illustrations. Cambridge Univ. Press 1935 408p il pa $29.95 hardcover o.p.

Grades: 9 10 11 12   **822.3**

1. Shakespeare, William, 1564-1616—Technique
ISBN 0-521-09258-2 (pa)

"A scholarly study of Shakespeare's use of images and of his personality and thought as they may be deduced from his imagery." Booklist

"A distinctive contribution to Shakespeare's criticism, bold and original in idea, scrupulous and exhaustive in method, and of all things, readable as a detective story." N Y Times Book Rev

William Shakespeare; edited and with an introduction by Harold Bloom. Chelsea House 2002 142p (Bloom's biocritiques) lib bdg $25.95 *

Grades: 9 10 11 12   **822.3**
1. Shakespeare, William, 1564-1616
ISBN 0-7910-6171-X   LC 2002-5480

Other available series titles include: Gabriel Garcia Marquez; Herman Melville; Miguel de Cervantes; Gwendolyn Brooks. For complete list of titles contact publisher

Cleanth Brooks, Ralph Waldo Emerson, Yoojin Grace Kim, and Samuel Johnson provide critical readings of the Shakespearean canon. A biographical profile and a chronology are included

Includes bibliographical references

823.009   English fiction--History and criticism

Critical essays on Jane Austen; edited by Laura Mooneyham White. Hall, G.K. & Co. 1998 247p (Critical essays on British literature) $50 *

Grades: 11 12 Adult   **823.009**
1. Austen, Jane, 1775-1817
ISBN 0-7838-0093-2   LC 98-22545

Some other available series titles in this class are: Critical essays on Salman Rushdie; Critical essays on Angela Carter. For complete list of titles contact publisher

Scholars assess Austen's plots, characters, and themes. Particular emphasis is placed on Emma, Mansfield Park, and Sanditon.

Includes bibliographical references

Davis, Paul B. (Paul Benjamin), 1934-
Critical companion to Charles Dickens; a literary reference to his life and work. Rev ed. Facts on File 2007 676p il (Facts on File library of world literature) $75 *

Grades: 9 10 11 12 Adult   **823.009**
1. Dickens, Charles, 1812-1870
ISBN 0-8160-6407-5; 978-0-8160-6407-6
LC 2006-3026

First published 1998 with title: Charles Dickens A-Z

This "reference contains entries on this writer's works, including the characters in each work, . . . historical and thematic information, and critical discussion. It also includes entries on related people, places, themes, topics, and influences. Additional features include 116 illustrations, a chronology, a bibliography of primary and secondary sources, and much more." Publisher's note

Includes bibliographical references

The **Facts** on File companion to the British novel. Facts on File 2005 2v (Facts on File library of world literature) set $140 *

Grades: 9 10 11 12 Adult   **823.009**

1. English fiction—History and criticism

ISBN 0-8160-6377-X; 978-0-8160-6377-2

    LC 2004-20914

Contents: v. 1. Beginnings through the 19th century / Virginia Brackett -- v. 2. 20th century / Victoria Gaydosik

"This two-volume companion to the British novel contains more than 1000 A-to-Z entries (each averaging several pages in length) on English-writing authors hailing from either the British Isles or the Commonwealth as well as on novels, pertinent literary terms, themes, concepts, influential periodicals, and subgenres." Libr J

"With more than one thousand entries, each with a selected bibliography and a set of very usable appendixes, this work accomplishes much in a compact set." Ref & User Services Quarterly

Includes bibliographical references

Fargnoli, A. Nicholas

Critical companion to James Joyce; a literary companion to his life and work; [by] A. Nicholas Fargnoli, Michael Patrick Gillespie. Rev. ed. Facts On File 2006 450p il (Facts on File library of world literature) $65; pa $19.95

Grades: 11 12 Adult   **823.009**

1. Joyce, James, 1882-1941

ISBN   0-8160-6232-3;   978-0-8160-6232-4; 0-8160-6689-2 (pa); 978-0-8160-6689-6 (pa)

    LC 2005-15721

First published 1995 with title: James Joyce A to Z

The authors "divide this reference to the writer's life and work into four parts. Part 1 is a brief biography. Part 2 focuses on individual works (e.g., Dubliners), including its publication date, a brief history, a synopsis, early critical reception, contemporary perspectives, and one or two recommended titles for further reading. The entries in Part 3 cover people (including friends and relatives), places, and ideas related to Joyce. Part 4 contains an appendix, a bibliography of the writer's work, a bibliography of secondary sources, chronologies, family trees, and more. . . . [This is] a great primer for those needing a detailed introduction into Joyce's world." Libr J

Includes bibliographical references

Fonstad, Karen Wynn

The atlas of Middle-earth. rev ed. Houghton Mifflin 2001 c1991 1v il maps pa $24

Grades: 9 10 11 12   **823.009**

1. Tolkien, J. R. R. (John Ronald Reuel), 1892-1973

ISBN 0-618-12699-6

"A Mariner book"

First published 1981

A guide to the journeys, lands, peoples, and history of Tolkien's imaginary kingdom

Includes bibliographical references

Horror: another 100 best books; edited by Stephen Jones and Kim Newman; with a foreword by Peter Straub. Carroll & Graf Publishers 2005 456p pa $16.95

Grades: 11 12 Adult   **823.009**

1. Horror fiction—History and criticism 2. Best books

ISBN 0-7867-1577-4

First published 1988

This book "features one hundred of the top names in the horror field discussing one hundred of the most spine-chilling novels ever written. Each entry includes a synopsis of the work as well as publication history, biographical information about the author of each title, and recommended reading and biographical notes on the contributor." Publisher's note

"Horror fans seeking what to read next will not only find out here; they'll also have their taste and appreciative capacity refined by the intelligent, passionate commentary of the 100 writers who selected these 100 books." Booklist

Jane Austen; Harold Bloom, editor. Chelsea House 2002 127p (Bloom's biocritiques) lib bdg $25.95 *

Grades: 9 10 11 12   **823.009**

1. Austen, Jane, 1775-1817

ISBN 0-7910-6184-1   LC 2002-5626

Other available series titles include: James Joyce; Mark Twain; Emily Dickinson; T. S. Eliot. For complete list of titles contact publisher

Includes a biography and a chronology of Austen's life. Provides critical analysis of her work as well as critical views by significant literary critics

Includes bibliographical references

Jane Austen; edited and with an introduction by Harold Bloom. Chelsea House 2004 300p (Modern critical views) $37.95

Grades: 9 10 11 12   **823.009**

1. Austen, Jane, 1775-1817

ISBN 0-7910-7656-3   LC 2003-14156

Other available series titles in this class are: Charles Dickens; Doris Lessing; George Eliot; J.R.R. Tolkien. For complete list of titles contact publisher

These critical essays "examine aspects of *Pride and Prejudice*, *Mansfield Park*, *Emma*, *Persuasion*, and *Sense and Sensibility*. Themes explored include manners and morals, comic aggression, knowledge and opinion, gender roles, and the relationship of Austen's novels to William Shakespeare's plays. Essays discuss specifics of the novels and place them within the context of Austen's other woks. Characters are examined in depth, as are situations, feelings, and social context." SLJ

Includes bibliographical references

Lord of the Flies; edited and with an introduction by Harold Bloom. Chelsea House 1999 263p (Modern critical interpretations) $45

Grades: 9 10 11 12   **823.009**

1. Golding, William, 1911-1993

ISBN 0-7910-4777-6   LC 98-23884

Other available series titles in this class include: George Orwell's 1984; Emily Bronte's Wuthering Heights; Jane Austen's Pride and prejudice; Chinua Achebe's Things fall apart. For complete list of titles contact publisher

Lord of the Flies—*Continued*

"Sixteen critical selections from both journals and books are arranged in chronological order by date of publication from 1961 to 1993. The examined topics, length and completeness of entries, and depth of analysis present a wide range of material. Articles selected by Bloom have not previously appeared in works easily accessible to most readers." SLJ

Includes bibliographical references

Mary Shelley's Frankenstein; edited & with an introduction by Harold Bloom. Bloom's Literary Criticism 2007 150p (Bloom's guides) $30
Grades: 9 10 11 12   **823.009**
1. Shelley, Mary Wollstonecraft, 1797-1851
ISBN 978-0-7910-9358-0; 0-7910-9358-1
LC 2007-10199
Other series titles in this class include: Charles Dickens's A tale of two cities; George Orwell's Animal Farm; Charles Dickens's Great expectations; William Golding's Lord of the flies. For a complete list of titles contact publisher
This study guide on Mary Shelley's classic novel includes a brief biographical sketch of Shelley, a list of characters, a summary and analysis, and selections from critical essays by different scholars about the work.

Includes bibliographical references

Maunder, Andrew
The Facts on File companion to the British short story. Facts on File 2006 528p (Facts on File library of world literature) $75 *
Grades: 11 12 Adult   **823.009**
1. Short stories—History and criticism
ISBN 0-8160-5990-X; 978-0-8160-5990-4
LC 2006-6897
More than 450 alphabetically arranged entries cover authors, characters, and major short stories. Literary terms, themes, and motifs are covered. Winners of prizes and awards are noted.

Includes glossary and bibliographical references

Mellor, Anne Kostelanetz
Mary Shelley, her life, her fiction, her monsters. Methuen 1988 xx, 275p il pa $26.95 hardcover o.p. *
Grades: 11 12 Adult   **823.009**
1. Shelley, Mary Wollstonecraft, 1797-1851
ISBN 0-415-90147-2 (pa)   LC 87-31249
The author "blends biography and informed criticism here to give a feminist reevaluation of Mary Shelley and her fiction, especially *Frankenstein*. . . . Mellor's book is clearly written and forcefully argued." Choice

Includes bibliographical references

Nardo, Don, 1947-
Understanding Frankenstein. Lucent Bks. 2003 128p il (Understanding great literature) lib bdg $27.45 *
Grades: 7 8 9 10   **823.009**
1. Shelley, Mary Wollstonecraft, 1797-1851
ISBN 1-59018-147-6   LC 2002-12560

Discusses Mary Shelley's sources of ideas for the compelling plot, well-developed characters, and universal themes of "Frankenstein" which have led to its enduring popularity.

"The text is easy to understand. A solid introduction for middle school students." SLJ

Includes bibliographical references

Olsen, Kirstin
All things Austen; an encyclopedia of Austen's world. Greenwood Press 2005 2v il maps set $149.95 *
Grades: 11 12 Adult   **823.009**
1. Austen, Jane, 1775-1817
ISBN 0-313-33032-8   LC 2004-28664
This Jane Austen encyclopedia contains "more than 150 well-designed and well-written A-to-Z articles on such topics as clothing, education, politics, religion, science, business, society, and the military of 18th- and 19th-century England." Libr J

"This well-written and meticulously researched work provides a convenient means for general readers, students, and scholars to gain a better understanding of the social, cultural, and political climate of Austen's time." Booklist

Poplawski, Paul
A Jane Austen encyclopedia. Greenwood Press 1998 411p il $95 *
Grades: 11 12 Adult   **823.009**
1. Austen, Jane, 1775-1817
ISBN 0-313-30017-8   LC 97-44880
This volume "examines the life, works, characters, and minutiae of Austeniana. The alphabetically arranged entries include extensive plot summaries that end with lists of major and minor characters, brief character descriptions, and short articles on the author's family and friends." SLJ

Includes bibliographical references

Regis, Pamela
A natural history of the romance novel. University of Pennsylvania Press 2003 224p $24.95; pa $19.95
Grades: 9 10 11 12   **823.009**
1. Love stories—History and criticism
ISBN 0-8122-3303-4; 0-8122-1522-2 (pa)
LC 2002-45412
The author "traces the genre's history from Samuel Richardson's Pamela to the present. Her excellent study adds much-needed research to the slowly but steadily growing body of scholarship on the popular romance novel." Libr J

Includes bibliographical references

Thomas Hardy; edited and with an introduction by Harold Bloom. Chelsea House 2003 160p (Bloom's major novelists) lib bdg $22.95 *
Grades: 9 10 11 12   **823.009**
1. Hardy, Thomas, 1840-1928
ISBN 0-7910-6348-8   LC 2002-151007
Other available series titles in this class include: George Eliot; Charles Dickens. For complete list of titles contact publisher

Thomas Hardy—*Continued*

This title includes a biographical essay, plot summaries, and critical interpretations of the novels and their characters.

Includes bibliographical references

828   English miscellany

Blake, William, 1757-1827

The complete poetry and prose of William Blake; edited by David V. Erdman; commentary by Harold Bloom. newly rev ed. University of Calif. Press 1982 xxvi, 990p $65

Grades: 11 12 Adult   **828**

ISBN 0-520-04473-8   LC 81-40323

First published 1965 with title: Poetry and prose of William Blake

This collection contains the complete poetry and prose of Blake, including his letters, as well as critical commentary.

The portable Blake; selected and arranged with an introduction by Alfred Kazin. Viking 1946 713p il pa $15.95 hardcover o.p. *

Grades: 11 12 Adult   **828**

ISBN 0-14-015026-9 (pa)

"The Viking portable library"

A "generous selection of verse, prose, letters, and essays. Blake is shown as an artist and poet against all institutions but ever seeking unity (though his was the mystic's quest) while hunting for realism and naturalism." Cincinnati Public Libr

Includes bibliographical references

Brunsdale, Mitzi

Student companion to George Orwell; [by] Mitzi M. Brunsdale. Greenwood Press 2000 173p (Student companions to classic writers) $35 *

Grades: 9 10 11 12   **828**

1. Orwell, George, 1903-1950

ISBN 0-313-30637-0   LC 99-49690

For complete list of series titles contact publisher

The author explores the works of the noted novelist and social critic. Particular emphasis is placed on Animal farm and Nineteen eighty-four.

Includes bibliographical references

Conrad, Joseph, 1857-1924

The portable Conrad; edited and with an introduction and notes by Morton Dauwen Zabel. rev ed, [edited] by Frederick R. Karl. Viking 1969 762p pa $18 hardcover o.p. *

Grades: 11 12 Adult   **828**

ISBN 0-14-015033-1 (pa)

"The Viking portable library"

First published 1947

Contains two novels: The Nigger of the Narcissus and Typhoon; three long stories; six shorter stories; and a selection from Conrad's prefaces, letters and autobiographical writings.

Includes bibliographical references

DeGategno, Paul J.

Critical companion to Jonathan Swift; a literary reference to his life and works; [by] Paul J. DeGategno, R. Jay Stubblefield. Facts on File 2006 474p il (Facts on File library of world literature) $75

Grades: 11 12 Adult   **828**

1. Swift, Jonathan, 1667-1745

ISBN 0-8160-5093-7; 978-0-8160-5093-2

LC 2005-25470

This "work is divided into five parts. These parts consist of a ten-page biography of satirist Jonathan Swift (1667-1745); a 'Works A-Z' section that includes synopses and commentaries that generally run to several hundred words on virtually all of Swift's poems, essays, and books; a 'Related Entries' section with similar brief articles on persons, topics, and places relevant to Swift studies; appendixes that include a chronology of Swift's life; a . . . bibliography of primary and secondary works; and an index." Libr J

For a fuller review, see: Booklist, Feb. 1, 2007

Includes bibliographical references

Donne, John, 1572-1631

The complete poetry and selected prose of John Donne; edited by Charles M. Coffin; introduction by Denis Donoghue; notes by W. T. Chmielewski. Modern Library pa. ed. Modern Lib. 2001 xxxii, 697p pa $14.95

Grades: 11 12 Adult   **828**

ISBN 0-375-75734-1   LC 2001-30077

A reissue of the Modern Library edition published 1994

This volume contains Donne's love poetry, satires, epigrams, verse letters and holy sonnets. Also includes selected prose and a sampling of private letters.

Hopkins, Gerard Manley, 1844-1889

Poems and prose of Gerard Manley Hopkins; selected with an introduction and notes by W.H. Gardner. Penguin 1984 c1953 xxxvi, 260p (Penguin classics) pa $16

Grades: 11 12 Adult   **828**

ISBN 0-14-042015-0

"On entering the Society of Jesus at the age of twenty-four, . . . [the author] burnt all his poetry and 'resolved to write no more, as not belonging to my profession, unless by the wishes of my superiors'. The poems, letters and journal entries selected for this edition were written in the following twenty years of his life, and published posthumously in 1918." Publisher's note

Includes bibliographical references

Hussey, Mark, 1956-

Virginia Woolf A-Z; a comprehensive reference for students, teachers, and common readers to her life, work, and critical reception. Facts on File 1995 452p il $55 *

Grades: 11 12 Adult   **828**

1. Woolf, Virginia, 1882-1941

ISBN 0-8160-3020-0   LC 94-36500

Hussey, Mark, 1956-—_Continued_

This work provides: synopses and publishing histories of works; discussions of intellectual and literary influences on Woolf; biographical entries on important people in her life, including family and friends; and an overview of the critical reception to her work

Includes bibliographical references

Huxley, Aldous, 1894-1963

Brave new world: and, Brave new world revisited; foreword by Christopher Hitchens. HarperCollins 2004 xxi, 340p $23.95 *

Grades: 11 12 Adult   **828**

ISBN 0-06-053526-1   LC 2004-40611

First published 1960; a combined edition of the two titles published 1932 and 1958 respectively

Brave new world is a satirical novel "set in the year 632 AF (After Ford), it is a grim picture of the world which Huxley thinks our scientific and social developments have already begun to create." Reader's Ency. 4th edition

Kipling, Rudyard, 1865-1936

The portable Kipling; edited and with an introduction by Irving Howe. Viking 1982 xlii, 687p pa $18 hardcover o.p.

Grades: 9 10 11 12   **828**

ISBN 0-14-015097-8 (pa)   LC 81-52466

"The Viking portable library"

This volume collects short stories and verse. Included are about 50 poems. "The twenty-eight stories included give about equal weight to 'Stories of India' and 'Soldiers' Tales' and analyses of the effects of world war on disappointed idealists and activists." Christ Sci Monit

Means, A. L.

A student's guide to George Orwell. Enslow Pubs. 2005 176p il (Understanding literature) lib bdg $27.93 *

Grades: 7 8 9 10   **828**

1. Orwell, George, 1903-1950

ISBN 0-7660-2433-4

An introduction to the life and work of the author of _1984, Animal Farm_ and other works

Includes glossary and bibliographical references

Milton, John, 1608-1674

The portable Milton; edited and with an introduction by Douglas Bush. Viking 1949 693p pa $15.95 hardcover o.p. *

Grades: 11 12 Adult   **828**

ISBN 0-14-015044-7 (pa)

"The Viking portable library"

A selection of the early poems and sonnets; "Areopagitica" complete; lengthy selections from the other chief prose works; and the three major poems, "Paradise lost," "Paradise regained," and "Samson Agonistes," complete

Includes glossary and bibliographical references

The **New** Oxford book of literary anecdotes. Oxford University Press 2006 385p il $29.95

Grades: 11 12 Adult   **828**

1. English literature—Anecdotes 2. Authors, English—Anecdotes 3. Authors, American—Anecdotes

ISBN 0-19-280468-5; 978-0-19-280468-6

LC 2005-33698

First published 1975 under the editorship of James Sutherland with title: The Oxford book of literary anecdotes

The editor "has compiled more than 700 anecdotes about English-language writers, from Geoffrey Chaucer to J.K. Rowling. The brief, chronologically-arranged (by subject's birth date) entries offer a glimpse into the personalities and times of these authors." Libr J

Includes bibliographical references

Shippey, T. A. (Tom A.)

J.R.R. Tolkien; author of the century. Houghton Mifflin 2001 xxxv, 347p $26; pa $13 *

Grades: 11 12 Adult   **828**

1. Tolkien, J. R. R. (John Ronald Reuel), 1892-1973
2. Fantasy fiction—History and criticism

ISBN 0-618-12764-X; 0-618-25759-4 (pa)

LC 2001-16973

Originally published: London : HarperCollins, 2000

"Shippey examines Tolkien's published and many unfinished works (such as _The Silmarillion_), as well as the shorter poems and stories. He convincingly argues that Tolkien deserves to be ranked as a major literary figure." Libr J

Includes bibliographical references

Thomas, Dylan, 1914-1953

A child's Christmas in Wales; illustrated by Chris Raschka. Candlewick Press 2004 unp il $17.99 *

Grades: 2 3 4 5 6 7 8 9   **828**

1. Christmas—Wales

ISBN 0-7636-2161-7   LC 2003-65274

The Welsh poet Dylan Thomas recalls the celebration of Christmas with his family and the feelings it evoked in him as a child.

"Applied to torn paper, the ink and watercolors spread through the fibers, freely forming soft outlines and shadows. The result is an intrguing contemporary take on a story that is by now part of the rather staid canon of Christmas classics." N Y Times Book Rev

Wilde, Oscar, 1854-1900

The portable Oscar Wilde; selected and edited by Richard Aldington and Stanley Weintraub. rev ed. Viking 1981 741p pa $15.95 hardcover o.p. *

Grades: 11 12 Adult   **828**

ISBN 0-14-015093-5 (pa)   LC 80-39827

"The Viking portable library"

First published 1946

This volume contains The critic as artist, The picture of Dorian Gray, Salomé, The importance of being Earnest, De profundis, and selected poems, reviews, letters and phrases from other works.

Woolf, Virginia, 1882-1941
The Virginia Woolf reader; edited by Mitchell
A. Leaska. Harcourt Brace Jovanovich 1984 371p
pa $16 hardcover o.p. *
Grades: 11 12 Adult   **828**
    ISBN 0-15-693590-2 (pa)   LC 84-4478
"A Harvest book"
Excerpts from Woolf's "novels form less than 20 percent of a reader whose selections of short stories, essays,
letters, and diary entries are excellent. This collection
will be useful to those already familiar with Woolf's
novels and seeking an introductory selection of her other
writings." Libr J

Yeats, W. B. (William Butler), 1865-1939
The Yeats reader; a portable compendium of
poetry, drama, and prose; edited by Richard J.
Finneran. Rev. ed. Scribner Poetry 2002 xxii, 566p
il $35; pa $18 *
Grades: 11 12 Adult   **828**
    ISBN 0-7432-3315-8; 0-7432-2798-0
                  LC 2002-70670
First published 1997
This book "presents more than one hundred and fifty
of his best-known poems . . . plus eight plays, a sampling of his prose tales, and excerpts from his published
autobiographical and critical writings. In addition, an appendix offers six early texts of poems that Yeats later revised. Also included are selections from the memoirs left
unpublished at his death and complete introductions written for a projected collection that never came to fru-
ition." Publisher's note
Includes bibliographical references

829   Old English (Anglo-Saxon) literature

Beowulf.
Beowulf; [translated by] Seamus Heaney. Farrar,
Straus & Giroux 1999 220p $25 *
Grades: 11 12 Adult   **829**
    ISBN 0-374-11119-7   LC 99-23209
This edition also available in paperback from Norton;
other verse and prose translations available from various
publishers
"Much that seemed off-putting about Beowulf to modern readers becomes, in Heaney's retelling, eerily intriguing instead. . . . Beowulf may, by modern standards,
seem bloodthirsty and deluded, but Heaney's poetry
makes eloquently persuasive the hero's tragic stature."
Time

830.3   German literature-- Encyclopedias and dictionaries

Garland, Henry B. (Henry Burnand)
The Oxford companion to German literature; by
Henry and Mary Garland. 3rd ed, by Mary
Garland. Oxford Univ. Press 1997 951p maps $95
*
Grades: 11 12 Adult   **830.3**
    1. German literature—Bio-bibliography
    ISBN 0-19-815896-3   LC 96-53309
    First published 1976
Entries include biographies, synopses of important
works, literary terms and movements, historical events
and figures, and material relevant to the social and intel-
lectual background of German literature from the earliest
records to the present

830.9   German literature--History and criticism

The **Cambridge** history of German literature;
edited by Helen Watanabe-O'Kelly. Cambridge
Univ. Press 1997 613p $90; pa $32 *
Grades: 11 12 Adult   **830.9**
    1. German literature—History and criticism
    ISBN 0-521-43417-3; 0-521-78573-1 (pa)
                  LC 95-52412
This work provides a history of German literature "up
to the Unification of Germany in 1990. It is a history for
our times: well-known authors and movements are set in
a wider literary, cultural and political context, standard
judgments are reexamined where appropriate, and a new
prominence is given to writing by women. . . . Titles
and quotations are translated, and there is an extensive
bibliography." Publisher's note
A "briskly written survey of German literature that
grounds literary practice in the social and historical context of each period and yet does not shortchange the aesthetic qualities of the representative works discussed."
Choice

831   German poetry

Rilke, Rainer Maria, 1875-1926
Selected poems of Rainer Maria Rilke; a
translation from the German and commentary by
Robert Bly. Harper & Row 1981 224p pa $15
hardcover o.p. *
Grades: 9 10 11 12   **831**
    ISBN 0-06-090727-4 (pa)   LC 78-2114
A bilingual edition of the German poet's verse select-
ed from A Book for the Hours of Prayer, The Book of
Pictures, New Poems, The Uncollected and Occasional
Poems, and Sonnets to Orpheus. The translator also in-
cludes five introductory essays
"Bly's comments make us see Rilke's work in relation
to events of the poet's life and to creative inner tensions
within certain periods. They also afford an awareness of
Rilke's specific inwardness, a sensibility and disposition
of soul very different from that of any American poet."
Libr J

832 German drama

Brecht, Bertolt, 1898-1956
Galileo; English version by Charles Laughton; edited and with an introduction by Eric Bentley. Grove Weidenfeld 1991 155p pa $6.95
Grades: 9 10 11 12   **832**
1. Galilei, Galileo, 1564-1642—Drama
ISBN 0-8021-3059-3   LC 91-22966
"An Evergreen book"
Written 1938-39, first performed 1943
"The play concerns Galileo Galilei's conflict with the church over the application of the Copernican system, which the church viewed as anathema. Brecht deliberately portrays Galileo as a self-serving and decidedly unheroic character, willing to compromise his principles in the face of pressure." Reader's Ency. 4th edition

833.009 German fiction--History and criticism

Franz Kafka's The metamorphosis; edited & with an introduction by Harold Bloom. Chelsea House Publishers 2007 87p (Bloom's guides) $30 *
Grades: 9 10 11 12   **833.009**
1. Kafka, Franz, 1883-1924
ISBN 0-7910-9298-4; 978-0-7910-9298-9
          LC 2006-25342
Other available series titles include: Charlotte Bronte's Jane Eyre; William Shakespeare's Romeo and Juliet; Maya Angelou's I know why the caged bird sings. For complete list of titles contact publisher
This book's "critical extracts cover distinct elements of Kafka's novella, offering a variety of viewpoints. Additional features answer questions about the author, characters, and the story's main points, and direct readers to further reading, with comments on the significance of each source." Publisher's note
Includes bibliographical references

838 German miscellany

Hermann Hesse; edited and with an introduction by Harold Bloom. Chelsea House 2002 246p (Modern critical views) $37.95 *
Grades: 9 10 11 12   **838**
1. Hesse, Hermann, 1877-1962
ISBN 0-7910-7398-X   LC 2002-152671
For complete list of series titles contact publisher
"Essays here include discussions of Hesse's personal life, writing style, themes, characters, philosophy, and influences. His novels *Siddhartha, Narcissus and Goldmund, The Glass Bead Game, Steppenwolf,* and *Demian* are analyzed as is some of his poetry. Similarities of Hesse's writings with those of André Gide, Marcel Proust, and James Joyce are discussed in several essays. Excerpts of his poems are included in both German and English." SLJ
Includes bibliographical references

839.3 Dutch, Flemish, Afrikaans literatures

Frank, Anne, 1929-1945
Anne Frank's Tales from the secret annex; with translations by Ralph Manheim and Michel Mok. Doubleday 1984 c1983 136p pa $4.95 hardcover o.p. *
Grades: 11 12 Adult   **839.3**
ISBN 0-553-58638-6 (pa)   LC 82-45871
Original Dutch edition copyrighted 1949. First English translation published 1960 in the United Kingdom with title: Tales from the house behind
This volume presents all of Anne Frank's existing stories, sketches and drafts as well as her personal reminiscences and essays
"The themes and plots of her brief fables are not extraordinary. But their very ordinariness reminds readers that the writer who kept one of the world's most widely read diaries was an ordinary child." Horn Book

839.8 Danish and Norwegian literatures

Ibsen, Henrik, 1828-1906
Ibsen: four major plays; translated by Rick Davis and Brian Johnston. Smith & Kraus 1995 286p (Great translations for actors) pa $19.95 *
Grades: 11 12 Adult   **839.8**
ISBN 1-880399-67-9   LC 95-13632
Designated v1 on cover
Contents: A doll house; Ghosts; An enemy of the people; Hedda Gabler
"All four of these versions have been 'production-tested,' which shows in their graceful and believable dialogue and their sheer theatricality. Davis and Johnston have unlocked the power in Ibsen's works and made it clear why Ibsen was once *the* playwright for firebrands, Fabians, and other progressives throughout the world." Booklist

840.3 French literature-- Encyclopedias and dictionaries

The **New** Oxford companion to literature in French; edited by Peter France. Oxford Univ. Press 1995 li, 865p maps $80 *
Grades: 11 12 Adult   **840.3**
ISBN 0-19-866125-8
First published 1959 with title: The Oxford companion to French literature
"This work views literature from the perspective of its greater cultural context. Accordingly, topics discussed go beyond the poets, novelists, and dramatists of the traditional French canon, and include philosophy, science, art, history, linguistics, and cinema. Even strip cartoons and pamphlets are treated. . . . The more than 3,000 entries are written by approximately 130 international experts. In addition to brief entries, there are long articles on general

The New Oxford companion to literature in French—*Continued*

topics, such as Québec, feminism, Occitan literature, and the history of the French language." Am Ref Books Annu, 1996

841 French poetry

Baudelaire, Charles, 1821-1867
Poems. Knopf 1993 256p (Everyman's library pocket poets) $12.50
Grades: 11 12 Adult **841**
ISBN 0-679-42910-7 LC 93-14363
A representative selection of poetry by the French symbolist.

Chanson de Roland.
The song of Roland; translated, with an introduction, by W.S. Merwin. Modern Library 2001 137p pa $11.95 *
Grades: 11 12 Adult **841**
1. Roland (Legendary character)
ISBN 0-375-75711-2 LC 00-48989
Also available in paperback from Penguin Classics
"This heroic poem celebrates the mighty feats of Roland, the great French hero in the time of Charlemagne. The medieval legend has replaced and transformed the actual facts of history to a great extent but the epic poem has continued in popularity." Bookman's Manual
Includes bibliographical references

Rimbaud, Arthur, 1854-1891
Poems. Knopf 1994 288p (Everyman's library pocket poets) $12.50
Grades: 11 12 Adult **841**
ISBN 0-679-43321-X LC 94-2496
A collection of work by the French Symbolist known for his daring images and pioneering prose poems

842 French drama

Anouilh, Jean, 1910-1987
Antigone; a play; translated by Jeremy Sams. French 2002 48p pa $6.50
Grades: 11 12 Adult **842**
ISBN 0-573-62819-X
Characters: 7 men, 3 women. 1 act.
This version of Sophocles' tragedy was composed and originally produced in German-occupied Paris in 1942. Antigone's death represents resistance against a totalitarian regime.

Beckett, Samuel, 1906-1989
Waiting for Godot; tragicomedy in 2 acts. Grove Press 1954 60p il pa $13 hardcover o.p.
Grades: 11 12 Adult **842**
ISBN 0-8021-3034-8 (pa)
Translated from the French by the author

Originally written in French. The play was first produced in Paris during the winter of 1952
"There are strong biblical references throughout, but Beckett's powerful and symbolic portrayal of the human condition as one of ignorance, delusion, paralysis, and intermittent flashes of human sympathy, hope, and wit has been subjected to many varying interpretations. The theatrical vitality and versatility of the play have been demonstrated by performances throughout the world." Oxford Companion to Engl Lit. 5th edition

Ionesco, Eugène
Four plays; translated by Donald M. Allen. Grove Press 1958 160p pa $13
Grades: 9 10 11 12 **842**
ISBN 0-8021-3079-8
Original French edition, 1954
Contents: The bald soprano; The lesson; Jack; or, The submission; The chairs
The bald soprano is a comedy satirizing English middle class life, while Jack, concerns a sulky young man who disappoints his family by refusing to marry the girl of their choice. An avant-garde drama, The chairs focuses on an old couple who receives many imaginary guests. The murder of a young student by his elderly teacher ends a bizarre lesson in The lesson

Rhinoceros, and other plays; translated by Derek Prouse. Grove Press 1960 141p pa $10
Grades: 11 12 Adult **842**
ISBN 0-8021-3098-4
Also available in hardcover from P. Smith
"An Evergreen book"
Contents: Rhinoceros; The future is in eggs; The leader
Three satirical comedies by a leading dramatist of the "theater of the absurd." In Rhinoceros, one man resists the pressure to conform as everyone about him accepts their transformation into rhinoceroses and he finds himself socially isolated. In The future is in eggs, a couple must produce eggs destined to become intellectuals. The leader is a satire on the mass adulation of political figures in which the leader turns out to be a headless figure

Molière, 1622-1673
The misanthrope and other plays; translated, and with an introduction by Donald M. Frame; and a new afterword by Lewis C. Seifert. Signet Classics 2005 524p pa $7.95
Grades: 11 12 Adult **842**
ISBN 0-451-52987-1; 978-0-451-52987-9
LC 2006-276841
Contents: The misanthrope — The doctor in spite of himself — The miser — The would-be gentleman — The mischievous machinations of Scapin — The learned women — The imaginary invalid

Molière; edited and with an introduction by Harold Bloom. Chelsea House 2003 122p (Bloom's major dramatists) lib bdg $22.95 *
Grades: 9 10 11 12 **842**
1. Molière, 1622-1673
ISBN 0-7910-7034-4 LC 2002-155108
For a complete list of series titles contact publisher

Molière—*Continued*

Includes a biographical essay, plot summaries, and critical interpretations of the plays and their characters.

Includes bibliographical references

Sartre, Jean Paul, 1905-1980

No exit, and three other plays. Vintage Bks. 1989 275p pa $12 *

Grades: 11 12 Adult   842

ISBN 0-679-72516-4   LC 89-40097

Contents: No exit; The flies; Dirty hands; The respectful prostitute

No exit is a modern morality play; The flies is a reworking of the Orestes-Electra story. The third play concerns a young Communist intellectual's attempt to maintain his integrity as party line changes and personal relationships alter perceptions of his murder of a party boss who had fallen out of favor, but whose memory is later rehabilitated. The last play concerns a prostitute's involvement in false charges of rape against a murdered black man and his companion in a town in the American South

844   French essays

Camus, Albert, 1913-1960

The myth of Sisyphus, and other essays; translated from the French by Justin O'Brien. Knopf 1955 212p pa $12.95 hardcover o.p. *

Grades: 11 12 Adult   844

ISBN 0-679-73373-6 (pa)

Personal reflections on the meaning of life and the philosophical questions surrounding suicide

848   French miscellany

Conroy, Peter V.

Jean-Jacques Rousseau. Twayne Pubs. 1998 171p (Twayne's world authors series) $33

Grades: 11 12 Adult   848

1. Rousseau, Jean-Jacques, 1712-1778

ISBN 0-8057-1616-5   LC 98-23266

For complete list of series titles contact publisher

An overview of the themes and issues that run through the writings of the 18th century French philosopher, author and political theorist. Works discussed include: the Discourses; Julie; The social contract; Emile; The confessions, and The reveries

Includes bibliographical references

Jean-Paul Sartre; editor, Harold Bloom. Chelsea House 2001 220p (Modern critical views) $36.95 *

Grades: 9 10 11 12   848

1. Sartre, Jean Paul, 1905-1980

ISBN 0-7910-5917-0   LC 00-64440

Another available series title in this class is Albert Camus. For complete list of titles contact publisher

Analytical essays explore the work and influence of the existentialist dramatist, novelist and philosopher

Includes bibliographical references

Voltaire, 1694-1778

The portable Voltaire; edited, and with an introduction by Ben Ray Redmen. Viking 1949 569p pa $17 hardcover o.p. *

Grades: 11 12 Adult   848

ISBN 0-14-015041-2 (pa)

"The Viking portable library"

The selections from Voltaire's works include: Candide, part one; Three stories: Zadig, Micromegas, and Story of a good Brahmin; Letters, and selections from the Philosophical Dictionary and other works. The editor's introduction gives a biographical sketch of Voltaire.

850.9   Italian literature--History and criticism

The **Cambridge** history of Italian literature; edited by Peter Brand and Lino Pertile. Cambridge Univ. Press 1996 xxi, 701p map hardcover o.p. pa $36.99

Grades: 11 12 Adult   850.9

ISBN 0-521-43492-0; 0-521-66622-8 (pa)

LC 95-50622

"Leading scholars describe and assess the work of a wide range of writers who have contributed to the Italian literary tradition from its earliest origins to the present day. . . . Translations are provided, along with maps, chronological charts, and . . . bibliographies." Publisher's note

"Contemporary readers will no doubt be delighted to learn more about such topics as the evolution of opera, compositions by Italian women writers, and the development of feminism." Choice

851   Italian poetry

Dante Alighieri, 1265-1321

The portable Dante; translated, edited, and with an introduction and notes by Mark Musa. Penguin Bks. 1995 xliii, 654p pa $17 *

Grades: 11 12 Adult   851

ISBN 0-14-243754-9   LC 94-15988

First published 1947

This book "contains complete verse translations of Dante's two masterworks, The Divine Comedy and La Vita Nuova, as well as a bibliography, notes, and an introduction by . . . Mark Musa." Publisher's note

Contains complete verse translations of The Divine comedy and La vita nuova

Includes bibliographical references

Purgatorio; a new verse translation by W.S. Merwin. Knopf 2000 xxix, 359p hardcover o.p. pa $19.95

Grades: 11 12 Adult   851

ISBN 0-375-40921-1; 0-375-70839-1 (pa)

LC 99-40708

A translation of the central section of The divine comedy. "The 'Purgatorio' is the only section to take place on Earth, and it is also the most human and hopeful. In his introduction, Merwin confides that he has been read-

Dante Alighieri, 1265-1321—*Continued*
ing Dante since his adolescence, and his reverence for the poet, his erudition, and the incredible elasticity and naturalness of his translation render this masterpiece (presented in its original Italian on facing pages) fresh and radiant." Booklist

860.3 Spanish literature-- Encyclopedias and dictionaries

Concise encyclopedia of Latin American literature; editor, Verity Smith. Fitzroy Dearborn Pubs. 2000 xxi, 678p $75 *

Grades: 11 12 Adult   **860.3**
1. Latin American literature—Encyclopedias 2. Latin American literature—Bio-bibliography
ISBN 1-57958-252-4

Based on the Encyclopedia of Latin American literature (1997)

Contains entries on 50 leading writers and 50 important works of Latin American and Caribbean literature. Also includes survey articles on the literature of individual countries and topical essays. Bibliographies of primary and secondary sources are listed

Includes bibliographical references

Dictionary of Mexican literature; edited by Eladio Cortés. Greenwood Press 1992 xliii, 768p $115

Grades: 11 12 Adult   **860.3**
ISBN 0-313-26271-3   LC 91-10529

This volume contains "500 entries covering the most important writers, literary schools, and cultural movements in Mexican literary history. The 41 contributors include American, Mexican, and Hispanic scholars with assistance from some of the authors themselves." Libr J

860.8 Spanish literature--Collections

The Tree is older than you are; a bilingual gathering of poems & stories from Mexico with paintings by Mexican artists; selected by Naomi Shihab Nye. Simon & Schuster Bks. for Young Readers 1995 111p il pa $13.95 hardcover o.p. *

Grades: 7 8 9 10   **860.8**
1. Mexican literature—Collections 2. Bilingual books—English-Spanish
ISBN 0-689-82087-9   LC 95-1565

"This bilingual anthology of poems, stories, and paintings by Mexican writers and artists brims over with a sense of wonder and playful exuberance, its themes as varied and inventive as a child's imagination." Voice Youth Advocates

860.9 Spanish literature--History and criticism

Moss, Joyce, 1951-
Latin American literature and its times; [by] Joyce Moss, Lorraine Valestuk. Gale Group 1999 xxxix, 562p il (World literature and its times) $125

Grades: 11 12 Adult   **860.9**
1. Latin American literature—History and criticism
ISBN 0-7876-3726-2   LC 99-29292

"Highlights Latin American literature and Latino works 'produced in the United States.' Arrangement is alphabetical by title. Lengthy, informative essays discuss individual poems and fiction and nonfiction titles with a focus on the political, economical, social contexts in which the pieces were written. . . . Each essay concludes with a list 'For More Information.' Black-and-white photographs, movie stills, and reproductions are sprinkled throughout." SLJ

Includes bibliographical references

861 Spanish poetry

Borges, Jorge Luis, 1899-1986
Selected poems; edited by Alexander Coleman. Viking 1999 477p pa $20 hardcover o.p.

Grades: 11 12 Adult   **861**
ISBN 0-14-058721-7 (pa)   LC 99-10318

"Poetry is the heart of Borges' metaphysical, mythical, and cosmopolitan oeuvre. . . . Editor Coleman commissioned a wealth of new translations for this unprecedented and invaluable collection, and the roster of translators includes such luminaries as Robert S. Fitzgerald, W.S. Merwin, Mark Strand, and John Updike." Booklist

Cid, ca. 1043-1099
The poem of the Cid; translated by Rita Hamilton and Janet Perry; with an introduction and notes by Ian Michael. Penguin 1984 c1975 242p map pa $14 *

Grades: 11 12 Adult   **861**
ISBN 0-14-044446-7

Paperback editions also available from other publishers

Parallel Spanish text and English translation, with English introduction and notes

"The poem is based on the exploits of Rodrigo or Ruy Diaz de Bivar (c.1043-1099), who was known as 'el Cid.' . . . Similar in form to the 'Chanson de Roland,' the poem is notable for its simplicity and directness and for its exact, picturesque detail. Despite the inclusion of much legendary material, the figure of the Cid who is depicted as the model Castilian warrior, is not idealized to an extravagant degree." Reader's Ency. 4th edition

Neruda, Pablo, 1904-1973

The poetry of Pablo Neruda; edited and with an introduction by Ilan Stavans. Farrar, Straus and Giroux 2003 996p hardcover o.p. pa $20

Grades: 11 12 Adult   **861**

ISBN 0-374-29995-1; 0-374-52960-4 (pa)

LC 2002-32548

This volume contains translations of nearly 600 poems. "Arranged chronologically and often newly translated, the poems are sometimes accompanied by the Spanish original." Libr J

"Stavans has assembled the most complete anthology of Neruda yet available in English, drawing evenhandedly from the various stages of the poet's long and complex career. Neruda was, it seems, at least half a dozen poets, many of them in competition with the others. Needless to say, there are wonders in these pages that will delight readers unfamiliar with the tumultuously varied planet known as Neruda." Nation

Includes bibliographical references

Selected odes of Pablo Neruda; translated, with an introduction by Margaret Sayers Peden. University of Calif. Press 1990 375p (Latin American literature and culture) pa $18.95 hardcover o.p.

Grades: 11 12 Adult   **861**

ISBN 0-520-22708-5 (pa)   LC 90-10707

"With the Spanish text and the English translation on facing pages, the beautiful odes of the great Chilean poet pay tribute to simple things in simple words, from bicycles and birds to his suit." Booklist

Twenty love poems and a song of despair; translated by W. S. Merwin; introduction by Cristina García; illustrations by Pablo Picasso. Penguin Books 2004 94p il pa $13 *

Grades: 9 10 11 12   **861**

ISBN 0-14-243770-0   LC 2003-67611

Original Spanish edition 1924; this translation first published 1971 by Grossman Pubs.

This bilingual collection presents a series of poems that contains "sea and nature imagery that associates woman with the productive forces of Mother Earth." Choice

Includes bibliographical references

Paz, Octavio, 1914-1998

Selected poems; edited by Eliot Weinberger; translated from the Spanish by G. Aroul [et al.] New Directions 1984 147p pa $11.95 hardcover o.p.

Grades: 11 12 Adult   **861**

ISBN 0-8112-0899-0 (pa)   LC 84-9856

"The 67 well-chosen selections show Paz in his several phases and guises—in lyrics and prose poems, in long, free-form pieces and short, impressionistic works—a range of styles representing the best modes of East and West as practiced South over the last half-century. Many of the translations are by his peers (Elizabeth Bishop, Mark Strand, W. C. Williams)." Booklist

863.009   Spanish fiction--History and criticism

Williams, Raymond L.

The modern Latin American novel; [by] Raymond Leslie Williams. Twayne Pubs. 1998 177p (Twayne's critical history of the novel) $33

Grades: 11 12 Adult   **863.009**

1. Latin American fiction—History and criticism

ISBN 0-8057-1655-6   LC 98-25148

Among the authors discussed in this critical survey of Latin American fiction are Alejo Carpentier, Juan Carlos Onetti, Julio Cortázar, Carlos Fuentes, and Mario Vargas Llosa

Includes bibliographical references

870.8   Latin literature--Collections

Atchity, Kenneth John

The classical Roman reader; new encounters with Ancient Rome; edited by Kenneth J. Atchity; associate editor, Rosemary McKenna. Oxford University Press 1998 xxxvi, 438p il pa $24.95 *

Grades: 11 12 Adult   **870.8**

1. Latin literature—Collections

ISBN 0-19-512740-4   LC 98-29785

Also available The Classical Greek reader (1996)

First published 1996 by Holt & Co.

"Excerpts by well-known authors are here—Virgil, Horace, Ovid, Juvenal—but so too are nonartistic authors who exemplify Rome's characteristic emphasis on the practical over the abstract. . . . For those uninitiated to Rome's written legacy but eager to meet it, this varied set of readings makes a memorable match." Booklist

Includes bibliographical references

The **Portable** Roman reader; edited, and with an introduction by Basil Davenport. Viking 1951 656p pa $18 hardcover o.p. *

Grades: 11 12 Adult   **870.8**

1. Latin literature—Collections

ISBN 0-14-015056-0 (pa)

"The Viking portable library"

This anthology includes selections from Plautus, Terence, Caesar, Virgil, Seneca, Juvenal as well as complete plays by Plautus and Terence and the anonymous poem Vigil of Venus

870.9   Latin literature--History and criticism

Hamilton, Edith, 1867-1963

The Roman way. Norton 1932 281p pa $12.95 hardcover o.p. *

Grades: 11 12 Adult   **870.9**

1. Latin literature—History and criticism 2. Rome—Civilization

ISBN 0-393-31078-7 (pa)

Companion volume to The Greek way

Hamilton, Edith, 1867-1963—*Continued*

An interpretation of Roman life from the descriptions in the works of great writers from Plautus and Terence to Virgil and Juvenal.

871.008   Latin poetry--Collections

The **Roman** poets; selected and edited by Peter Washington. Knopf 1997 253p il (Everyman's library pocket poets) $12.50 *

Grades: 11 12 Adult   **871.008**

1. Latin poetry

ISBN 0-375-40071-0   LC 98-124022

A representative selection of classical Latin verse.

873   Latin epic poetry and fiction

Ovid, 43 B.C.-17 or 18

Tales from Ovid; [translated by] Ted Hughes. Farrar, Straus & Giroux 1997 257p pa $14 hardcover o.p. *

Grades: 11 12 Adult   **873**

ISBN 0-374-52587-0   LC 97-36061

Hughes retells 24 Greco-Roman myths from Ovid's Latin epic *Metamorphoses*.

This is "an inspired act of translation that stands as vigorous poetry in its own right." N Y Times Book Rev

Includes bibliographical references

Virgil

The Aeneid; translated by Robert Fagles; introduction by Bernard Knox. Viking 2006 486p map $40 *

Grades: 11 12 Adult   **873**

ISBN 0-670-03803-2   LC 2006-47220

Also available in paperback from Vintage and Cambridge Univ. Press

"The Aeneid is in twelve books: the first six in imitation of the Odyssey; the last six, of the Iliad. The Trojan hero is led to Italy, where he is to be the father of a race and of an empire supreme among nations. On his way thither he tarries at Carthage, whose queen, Dido, loves him as with the first love of a virgin. To her he tells the story of Troy. For love of him she slays herself when the gods lead him from her shores. Arrived in Italy he seeks the underworld, under the protection of the Sibyl of Cumae. He emerges thence to overcome his enemies." Keller. Reader's Dig of Books

878   Latin miscellany

Caesar, Julius, 100-44 B.C.

The Gallic War; with an English translation by H. J. Edwards. Harvard Univ. Press 1958 xxii, 616p il maps $21.50 *

Grades: 11 12 Adult   **878**

1. Rome—History

ISBN 0-674-99080-3

"The Loeb classical library"

Caesar's account of his campaign (58-50 B.C.) to bring the province of Gaul (France) under his control.

880   Hellenic literatures. Classical Greek

Thorburn, John E., Jr.

The Facts on File companion to classical drama. Facts on File 2005 680p map (Facts on File library of world literature) $71.50

Grades: 11 12 Adult   **880**

1. Classical drama

ISBN 0-8160-5202-6   LC 2004-16803

This "compendium covers ancient Greek and Roman drama from the 500s B.C.E. through 100 C.E. Approximately 400 alphabetical entries, ranging in length from one sentence to several pages, delve into plays, authors, characters, settings, genres, themes, theatrical terms, historical events, etc." SLJ

"It is difficult to think of any other resource quite this thorough that combines all of Greek and Roman drama into a convenient single-volume publication." Libr J

Includes bibliographical references

880.3   Classical Greek literature--Encyclopedias and dictionaries

The **Oxford** companion to classical literature; edited by M. C. Howatson. 2nd ed. Oxford Univ. Press 1989 615p il maps $65; pa $29.95 *

Grades: 11 12 Adult   **880.3**

ISBN 0-19-866121-5; 0-19-860081-X (pa)

                        LC 88-27330

First published 1937 under the editorship of Sir Paul Harvey

This work "covers classical literature from the appearance of the Greeks, around 2200 B.C., to the close of the Athenian philosophy schools in A.D. 529. It includes articles on authors, major works, historical notables, mythological figures, and topics of literary significance. Short summaries of major works, chronologies, charts, and maps are special features." Nichols. Guide to Ref Books for Sch Media Cent. 4th edition

880.8   Classical Greek literature--Collections

The **Norton** book of classical literature; edited by Bernard Knox. Norton 1993 866p $29.95 *

Grades: 11 12 Adult   **880.8**

ISBN 0-393-03426-7   LC 92-10378

"A comprehensive volume of more than 300 pieces of classical literature, primarily Greek but also some Roman." Booklist

The **Portable** Greek reader; edited, and with an introduction by W. H. Auden. Viking 1948 726p pa $18 hardcover o.p. *

Grades: 11 12 Adult   **880.8**

The Portable Greek reader—*Continued*
ISBN 0-14-015039-0 (pa)
"Selections from representative Greek writers, from Homer to Galen, aimed at providing the reader with an introduction to all facets of Greek culture, rather than to its literature alone. Mr. Auden's preface deals chiefly with the various Greek concepts of the hero, in comparison with our own, and points up the immense differences between the two civilizations." New Yorker

880.9   Classical Greek literature-- History and criticism

Ancient Greek literature; K.J. Dover, editor [et al.] 2nd ed. Oxford Univ. Press 1997 187p maps pa $21.95
Grades: 9 10 11 12   **880.9**
ISBN 0-19-289294-0   LC 98-120951
First published 1980
A historical survey of Greek poetry, tragedy, comedy, history, science, philosophy, and oratory from 700 BC to 550 AD. Passages from the works of principal authors are provided in translation
Includes bibliographical references

Hamilton, Edith, 1867-1963
The Greek way. Norton 1943 347p pa $12.95 hardcover o.p. *
Grades: 11 12 Adult   **880.9**
1. Greece—Civilization
ISBN 0-393-31077-9 (pa)
Companion volume to The Roman way
First published 1930. Variant title: The great age of Greek literature
An account of writers and literary forms of the Periclean Age including discussions of Pindar, Aristophanes, Aeschylus, tragedy, Greek religion and philosophy

881.008   Classical Greek poetry-- Collections

The **Oxford** book of classical verse in translation; edited by Adrian Poole and Jeremy Maule. Oxford University Press 1995 xlix, 606p $45 *
Grades: 11 12 Adult   **881.008**
1. Classical poetry—Collections
ISBN 0-19-214209-7
A "collection of classical verse from Homer to Boethius. Translations, modern and older, are brought together in a rich blending of Greek and Latin writings. Some of the greatest poets in the English language—Dryden, Pope, Tennyson, Poe, Byron, Yeats, Browning, Houseman, Wilde, Shelley, and Pound are among the translators. They emphasize the debt English poetry owes to the classics." SLJ

882   Classical Greek dramatic poetry and drama

Aeschylus; comprehensive research and study guide; edited and with an introduction by Harold Bloom. Chelsea House 2002 97p (Bloom's major dramatists) $21.95
Grades: 9 10 11 12   **882**
1. Aeschylus
ISBN 0-7910-6355-0   LC 2001-47591
Other available series titles in this class are: Aristophanes; Euripides; Sophocles. For complete list of titles contact publisher
This volume covers several plays and provides a plot summary of each work. Extracts from critical essays examine important aspects of each play. A biography of the playwright is included
Includes bibliographical references

Aristophanes
Lysistrata; translated, with notes and topical commentaries by Sarah Ruden. Hackett Pub. Co 2003 126p $24.95; pa $5.95
Grades: 11 12 Adult   **882**
ISBN 0-87220-604-1; 0-87220-603-3 (pa)
                                    LC 2002-38750
This is a translation of Aristophanes' comedy with notes and commentary. "The 'topical commentaries' are essays on 'Athenian Democracy', 'Ancient Greek Warfare', 'Athenian Women', and 'Greek Comedy'. . . . The volume is topped off with a selected bibliography and an index to the commentaries." Classical Rev

Sophocles
Antigone; translated by Richard Emil Braun. Oxford University Press 1989 101p (Greek tragedy in new translations) pa $11.95 *
Grades: 11 12 Adult   **882**
ISBN 0-19-506167-5   LC 89-22867
"One of the earliest extant tragedies of Sophocles. After the defeat of the expedition of The Seven Against Thebes, Creon, now king, decrees that the body of Polynices shall be unburied, in defiance of the rites due the dead. Antigone, Oedipus' daughter, gives her brother a token burial and, though she is affianced to his son Haemon, Creon condemns her to be buried alive. Warned by Tiersias, he regrets his act too late; Antigone and Haemon kill themselves, and Creon's wife, Eurydice does the same on hearing the news." Reader's Ency. 4th edition

Oedipus the King; translated by Stephen Berg and Diskin Clay. Oxford 1978 114p (Greek tragedy in new translations) hardcover o.p. pa $9.95 *
Grades: 11 12 Adult   **882**
ISBN 0-19-502325-0; 0-19-505493-8 (pa)
                                    LC 77-10964
This classical tragedy deals with the fulfillment of a prophecy as it is revealed that Oedipus has unwittingly killed his father, married his mother and brought the

Sophocles—*Continued*
plague to Thebes. He blinds himself in horror and becomes an outcast.
Includes bibliographical references

Sophocles' Oedipus rex; edited and with an introduction by Harold Bloom. Updated ed. Chelsea House Publishers 2006 245p (Modern critical interpretations) $45 *
Grades: 11 12 Adult　　　　　　　　　**882**
1. Sophocles
ISBN 0-7910-9309-3; 978-0-7910-9309-2
　　　　　　　　　　　　　　　LC 2006-25276
Other available series titles include: Beowulf; Herman Melville's Moby-Dick; Upton Sinclair's The jungle. For complete list of titles contact publisher
First published 1988
"This collection of essays draws upon a . . . history of criticism and commentary to examine the questions of fate, free will, heroism, and humanity that this powerful tragedy continues to provoke." Publisher's note
Includes bibliographical references

882.008　Classical Greek dramatic poetry and drama--Collections

Four Greek plays; edited by Dudley Fitts. Harcourt Brace Jovanovich 2002 310p pa $14 *
Grades: 9 10 11 12　　　　　　　　**882.008**
1. Greek drama—Collections
ISBN 0-15-602795-X
"A Harvest/HBJ book"
First published 1960
Contents: The Agamemnon of Aeschylus; The Oedipus Rex of Sophocles; The Alcestis of Euripides; The birds of Aristophanes

Seven famous Greek plays; edited, with introductions by Whitney J. Oates and Eugene O'Neill, Jr. Modern Lib. 1950 xxv, 446p pa $10 hardcover o.p. *
Grades: 9 10 11 12　　　　　　　　**882.008**
ISBN 0-394-70125-9 (pa)
Contents: Prometheus bound and Agamemnon by Aeschylus; Oedipus the king and Antigone by Sophocles; Alcestis and Medea by Euripides; The frogs by Aristophanes
Includes bibliographical references

883　Classical Greek epic poetry and fiction

Homer
The Iliad; translated by Robert Fagles; introduction and notes by Bernard Knox. Viking 1990 683p $35; pa $15.95 *
Grades: 11 12 Adult　　　　　　　　　**883**
1. Trojan War
ISBN 0-670-83510-2; 0-14-027536-3 (pa)
　　　　　　　　　　　　　　　LC 89-70695

Homer's epic of the Trojan War.
This "translation is lively . . . fun, [and] . . . a worthy companion to the best. Notes, introduction, bibliography, glossary of names." Booklist

The Odyssey; translated by Robert Fitzgerald; with an introduction by Seamus Heaney. Distributed by Random House 1992 xxvii, 509p $21
Grades: 9 10 11 12　　　　　　　　　**883**
ISBN 0-679-41047-3　　　　　　LC 92-52903
This translation also available in paperback from Farrar, Straus, and Giroux; Hardcover and paperback editions of The Odyssey also available from other publishers
"An epic poem in Greek hexameters. . . . The 'Odyssey' is a sequel to the 'Iliad' and narrates the ten years' adventures of Ulysses during his return journey from Troy to his own kingdom, the island of Ithaca." Keller. Reader's Dig of Books
Includes bibliographical references

The Odyssey; translated by Robert Fagles; introduction and notes by Bernard Knox. Viking 1996 541p $35; pa $14.95 *
Grades: 11 12 Adult　　　　　　　　　**883**
ISBN 0-670-82162-4; 0-14-026886-3 (pa)
　　　　　　　　　　　　　　　LC 96-17280
This is a verse translation of Homer's epic poem.
"Fagles' *Odyssey* is the one to put into the hands of younger, first-time readers, not least because of its paucity of notes, which, though sometimes frustrating, is a sign that translation has been used to do the work of explanation. Altogether, an outstanding piece of work." Booklist
Includes bibliographical references

Homer; edited and with an introduction by Harold Bloom. Updated ed. Chelsea House 2006 221p $45
Grades: 9 10 11 12　　　　　　　　　**883**
1. Homer
ISBN 0-7910-9313-1; 978-0-7910-9313-9
　　　　　　　　　　　　　　　LC 2006-25325
First published 1986
This book "explores Homer's transformative effect on epic and bardic poetry, as well as his narrative technique and use of language and meter." Publisher's note
Includes bibliographical references

McCarty, Nick
The Iliad; retold by Nick McCarty; illustrated by Victor Ambrus. Kingfisher (NY) 2000 95p il hardcover o.p. pa $15.95
Grades: 5 6 7 8 9 10　　　　　　　　**883**
1. Trojan War
ISBN 0-7534-5330-4; 0-7534-5321-5 (pa)
　　　　　　　　　　　　　　　LC 00-30442
A retelling of Homer's story of the Trojan War.
"An exciting text in large print and action-packed illustrations create an accessible version of a classic tale." SLJ

Willcock, Malcolm M.
A companion to the Iliad; based on the translation by Richmond Lattimore. University of Chicago Press 1976 293p il maps pa $14 hardcover o.p.
Grades: 9 10 11 12 **883**
1. Homer—Iliad—Concordances
ISBN 0-226-89855-5 (pa)
"The notes here are directed mostly toward the explanation of words, expressions, and allusions in the text; but they also include summaries of books and sections, and assistance toward the appreciation of Homer's broader composition, by drawing attention to the implications of the narrative and the very effective characterization of the major heroes." Preface
Includes bibliographical references

888 Classical Greek miscellany

Aristotle, 384-322 B.C.
The basic works of Aristotle; edited, and with an introduction by Richard McKeon. Random House 1941 xxxix, 1487p $49.95; pa $19.95
Grades: 11 12 Adult **888**
ISBN 0-394-41610-4; 0-375-75799-6 (pa)
Follows the Oxford translation of 1931
Contains entire texts of the following: Physica; De generatione et corruptione; De anima; Parva naturalia; Metaphysica; Ethica Nicomachea; Politica; De poetica
Includes bibliographical references

Plato
The republic; edited by G.R.F. Ferrari; translated by Tom Griffith. Cambridge Univ. Press 2000 xlviii, 382p (Cambridge texts in the history of political thought) $38; pa $11 *
Grades: 11 12 Adult **888**
1. Utopias 2. Political science
ISBN 0-521-48173-2; 0-521-48443-X (pa)
LC 00-24471
Translation from the Ancient Greek
Griffith's "aim was to translate the Greek text as if it were a conversation, and he has succeeded admirably. The text does indeed flow like a conversation, with the entire back-and-forth interaction that such exchanges involve. . . . [He] has also written a very useful introduction that places the work in a historical context and provides a glossary that will help readers identify individuals and places mentioned in the work." Libr J
Includes bibliographical references

890 Literatures of other languages

The **Literature** of ancient Egypt; an anthology of stories, instructions, and poetry; edited and with an introduction by William Kelly Simpson; with translations by Robert K. Ritner . . . {et al.}. 3rd. ed., rev. and expanded. Yale Univ. Press 2003 544p il pa $20
Grades: 9 10 11 12 **890**

1. Egyptian literature
ISBN 0-300-09920-7
First published 1973
This is a collection of ancient Egyptian literature, including writings from the late Demotic period
Includes bibliographical references

891 East-Indo European literatures

Mahabharata.
The Mahābhārata; an English version based on selected verses; [translated by] Chakravarthi V. Narasimhan. rev ed, with a new preface. Columbia University Press 1998 xxix, 254p (Translations from the Asian classics) hardcover o.p. pa $25.50 *
Grades: 11 12 Adult **891**
ISBN 0-231-02624-2; 0-231-11055-3 (pa)
Also available in an illustrated paperback edition from the University of California Press
"One of the two great epic poems of ancient India (the other being the 'Ramayana'), about eight times as long as the 'Iliad' and 'Odyssey' together. It is a great compendium, added to as late as AD 600, although it had very nearly acquired its present form by the 4th century. Covering an enormous range of topics, the Mahabharata, with its famous interpolation, the 'Bhagavadgita', has as its central theme the great war between the sons of two royal brothers, in a struggle for succession." Reader's Ency. 4th edition

Mahabharata. Bhagavadgita.
Bhagavad Gita; a new translation; [translated by] Stephen Mitchell. Harmony Bks. 2000 223p hardcover o.p. pa $13.95 *
Grades: 11 12 Adult **891**
ISBN 0-609-60550-X; 0-609-81034-0 (pa)
LC 00-28286
Hardcover and paperback editions also available from other publishers
"An eighteen-part discussion between the god Krishna, an avatar of Vishnu appearing as a charioteer, and Arjuna, a warrior about to enter battle, on the nature and meaning of life. Sometimes called the New Testament of Hinduism, it is an interpolation in the great Hindu epic the Mahabharata." Reader's Ency. 4th edition

Narayan, R. K., 1906-2001
The Ramayana; a shortened modern prose version of the Indian epic (suggested by the Tamil version of Kamban); introduction by Pankaj Mishra. Penguin Books 2006 157p (Penguin classics) pa $13 *
Grades: 11 12 Adult **891**
ISBN 0-14-303967-9
LC 2006-45201
First published 1972
A retelling of Prince Rama's courtship of the fourteen-year-old Sita, their exile, Sita's abduction, the search, and the great battle with her abductor Ravana, involving a pantheon of gods, heroes, and evil spirits.

Omar Khayyam

Rubáiyát of Omar Khayyám; rendered into English verse by Edward FitzGerald; with illustrations by Edmund J. Sullivan. St. Martin's Press 1983 75p il $9.95

Grades: 11 12 Adult   **891**

ISBN 0-312-69527-6   LC 83-9767

Hardcover and paperback editions also available from other publishers

"The Rubaiyat' (Quatrains) of Omar the Tentmaker, of Persia, is composed of a series of stanzas forming 'a medley of love and tavern songs, tinged with Sufi mysticism, and with the melancholy of Eastern fatalism.'" Dickinson. Best Books Ser

891.7   East Slavic literatures. Russian

Chekhov, Anton Pavlovich, 1860-1904

The plays of Anton Chekhov; a new translation by Paul Schmidt. HarperCollins Pubs. 1997 387p pa $15.95 hardcover o.p. *

Grades: 11 12 Adult   **891.7**

ISBN 0-06-092875-1 (pa)   LC 96-42456

Available in hardcover from P. Smith

Contents: Swan song; The bear; The proposal; Ivanov; The seagull; A reluctant tragic hero; The wedding reception; The festivities; Uncle Vanya; Three sisters; The dangers of tobacco; The cherry orchard

Handbook of Russian literature; edited by Victor Terras. Yale Univ. Press 1985 558p pa $42 hardcover o.p.

Grades: 11 12 Adult   **891.7**

ISBN 0-300-04868-8 (pa)   LC 84-11871

"The volume includes entries on authors, genres, literary movements, and period studies, together with reviews of notable journals. The lengthiest entries run to more than 6,000 words, and the shortest have been kept to a single paragraph." Booklist

"A valuable resource for students, scholars, and general readers." Libr J

Includes bibliographical references

Leo Tolstoy: comprehensive research and study guide; edited and with an introduction by Harold Bloom. Chelsea House 2002 96p (Bloom's major novelists) $21.95

Grades: 9 10 11 12   **891.7**

1. Tolstoy, Leo, graf, 1828-1910

ISBN 0-7910-6347-X   LC 2001-53678

Another available series title in this class is: Fyodor Dostoevsky. For complete list of titles contact publisher

This volume includes a biography of the great Russian novelist, plot summaries for several of his novels, and extracts from critical essays

Includes bibliographical references

Malcolm, Janet

Reading Chekhov; a critical journey. Random House 2001 209p hardcover o.p. pa $13.95

Grades: 11 12 Adult   **891.7**

1. Chekhov, Anton Pavlovich, 1860-1904

ISBN 0-375-50668-3; 0-375-76106-3 (pa)

LC 2001-19585

"The author's pilgrimage to Chekhov's Russia—Moscow, St. Petersburg, the gardens of his villa in Yalta—is a reunion with this most reticent of literary fathers. Malcolm analyzes the transformations that Chekhov grants his redeemable roués and guileless heroines, and illuminates the hidden surreality and waywardness of his realism." New Yorker

Includes bibliographical references

The **Portable** nineteenth-century Russian reader; edited by George Gibian. Penguin Bks. 1993 xxii, 641p pa $15.95 *

Grades: 11 12 Adult   **891.7**

ISBN 0-14-015103-6   LC 92-39863

This collection includes Pushkin's poem 'The Bronze Horseman'; Gogol's 'The Overcoat'; Turgenev's 'First Love'; Chekhov's 'Uncle Vanya'; Tolstoy's 'The Death of Ivan Ilych'; and 'The Grand Inquisitor' episode from Dostoyevsky's 'The Brothers Karamazov'; plus poetry, plays, short stories, novel excerpts, and essays by such writers as Griboyedov, Pavlova, Herzen, Goncharov, Saltykov-Shchedrin, and Maksim Gorky

The **portable** twentieth-century Russian reader; edited with an introduction and notes by Clarence Brown. Rev. and updated ed. Penguin Books 1993 615p (Penguin classics) pa $18 *

Grades: 9 10 11 12   **891.7**

1. Russian literature—Collections

ISBN 0-14-243757-3   LC 2003-283124

First published 1985

This collection "includes stories by Chekhov, Gorky, Bunin, Zamyatin, Babel, Nabokov, Solzhenitsyn, and Voinovich; excerpts from Andrei Bely's Petersburg, Mikhail Bulgakov's The Master and Margarita, Boris Pasternak's Dr. Zhivago, and Sasha Solokov's A School for Fools; the complete text of Yuri Olesha's 1927 masterpiece Envy; and poetry by Alexander Blok, Anna Akhmatova, and Osip Mandelstam." Publisher's note

892   Afro-Asiatic literatures. Semitic literatures

Ancient Egyptian literature; an anthology; translated by John L. Foster. University of Tex. Press 2001 272p hardcover o.p. pa $19.95 *

Grades: 11 12 Adult   **892**

ISBN 0-292-72526-4; 0-292-72527-2 (pa)

LC 00-61607

An anthology of ancient Egyptian poetry, stories, hymns, prayers, and wisdom texts. Includes a discussion of translation, as well as brief information about authorship and date of each selection

Includes bibliographical references

Gilgamesh.

Gilgamesh; a new English version [by] Stephen Mitchell. Free Press 2004 290p $25; pa $14 *

Grades: 11 12 Adult **892**

ISBN 0-7432-6164-X; 0-7432-6169-0 (pa)

LC 2004-50072

"Relying on existing translations (and in places where there are gaps, on his own imagination), Mitchell seeks language that is as swift and strong as the story itself. . . . This wonderful new version of the story of Gilgamesh shows how the story came to achieve literary immortality—not because it is a rare ancient artifact, but because reading it can make people in the here and now feel more completely alive." Publ Wkly

Includes bibliographical references

892.7 Arabic literature

Anthology of modern Palestinian literature; edited and introduced by Salma Khadra Jayyusi. Columbia Univ. Press 1992 xxxiii, 744p hardcover o.p. pa $30.50 *

Grades: 11 12 Adult **892.7**

1. Arabic literature—Collections

ISBN 0-231-07508-1; 0-231-07509-X (pa)

LC 92-5189

"Presented here are translations of poems, stories, and excerpts from novels, as well as works by Palestinian poets who write in English. Also included are personal narratives by Palestinian writers depicting the varied aspects of Palestinian life from the turn of the century to the present. . . . Biographical sketches introduce the authors, and a chronology of modern Palestinian history provides background for some of the events and places referred to in the selections. The introduction by the editor provides a concise but comprehensive political history of Palestinian literature during the twentieth century." Publisher's note

Includes bibliographical references

Night and horses and the desert; an anthology of classical Arabic literature; edited by Robert Irwin. 1st Anchor Books ed. Anchor Books 2001 462p pa $16 *

Grades: 11 12 Adult **892.7**

1. Arabic literature—Collections 2. Arabic literature—History and criticism

ISBN 0-385-72155-2 LC 2001-53721

First published 2000 by Overlook Press

This "anthology presents a wide range of classical Arabic poetry and prose, covering the fifth to the 16th centuries from Afghanistan to Andalusia, Spain." Libr J

"The chapter on the Qur'an is perhaps the most essential as it examines just how vital the dogma of Islam has been for the Arabic understanding of culture and art. . . . This persuasive work will surely fill in the gap in the study of Arabic literature in this country." Publ Wkly

Includes bibliographical references

895.1 Chinese literature

Anthology of modern Chinese poetry; edited and translated by Michelle Yeh. Yale Univ. Press 1993 245p pa $21 hardcover o.p. *

Grades: 11 12 Adult **895.1**

ISBN 0-300-05947-7 (pa) LC 92-16322

Published with assistance from Mary Cady Tew Memorial Fund

"Arranged chronologically, this selection of twentieth-century poetry from China and Taiwan offers a few poems by each of 67 poets born between 1891 and 1963. Its scope is enormous, its range impressive. Editor Yeh's translations are accessible and fluid; her introduction and notes are helpful without being overbearingly scholarly." Booklist

Includes bibliographical references

Liu Siyu, 1964-

A thousand peaks; poems from China; [by] Siyu Liu and Orel Protopopescu; illustrated by Siyu Liu. Pacific View Press 2002 52p il $19.95 *

Grades: 5 6 7 8 9 **895.1**

1. Chinese poetry 2. Bilingual books—English-Chinese

ISBN 1-88189-624-2 LC 2001-34008

A collection of thirty-five poems spanning nineteen centuries, representing both famous and lesser-known poets, including both the Chinese text and a literal translation.

This "is an anthology of considerable fascination and broad utility. . . . The layout is neat, tidily fitting each poem's material on a single page and adding a line drawing featuring a relevant Chinese character. The wealth of material here provides a more stimulating entree to Chinese history than any dry textbook." Bull Cent Child Books

Includes bibliographical references

One hundred poems from the Chinese; {edited and translated} by Kenneth Rexroth. New Directions 1956 159p pa $11.95 hardcover o.p. *

Grades: 11 12 Adult **895.1**

ISBN 0-8112-0180-5 (pa)

Also available: One hundred more poems from the Chinese pa $10.95 (ISBN 0-8112-0179-1)

"Nine poets, who lived centuries ago, speak with the poignancy of understatement of unchanging things; the brevity of life, the richness of friendship, the beauties of nature, the inevitability of old age and death." Booklist

Includes bibliographical references

The Shorter Columbia anthology of traditional Chinese literature; Victor H. Mair, editor. Columbia Univ. Press 2000 xxx, 741p map (Translations from the Asian classics) $65; pa $26

Grades: 11 12 Adult **895.1**

1. Chinese literature—Collections

ISBN 0-231-11998-4; 0-231-11999-2 (pa)

LC 00-35878

Abridged version of Columbia anthology of traditional Chinese literature, published 1994

The Shorter Columbia anthology of traditional Chinese literature—*Continued*

This "abridged volume, which, like the original includes selections of Chinese literature from the beginnings to 1919 . . . retains the characteristics of the original in that it is arranged according to genre rather than chronology and interprets 'literature' very broadly to include not just literary fiction, poetry, and drama, but folk and popular literature, lyrics and arias, elegies and rhapsodies, biographies, autobiographies and memoirs, letters, criticism and theory, and travelogues and jokes. It also contains fresh translations by newer voices in the field." Publisher's note

Includes bibliographical references

895.6   Japanese literature

Anthology of Japanese literature from the earliest era to the mid-nineteenth century; edited by Donald Keene. Grove Press 1955 442p il pa $14.50

Grades: 9 10 11 12   **895.6**
1. Japanese literature—Collections
ISBN 0-8021-5058-6

"UNESCO Collection of representative works: Japanese series"

"Covers the period from 712 A.D., when 'Record of Ancient Matters,' the earliest surviving Japanese book, was completed to about 1850. . . . The selections here include self-contained episodes from plays and novels (among them the classic 'The Tale of Genji'), fairy tales, short stories, and personal reminiscences, and numerous . . . poems." New Yorker

The Classic Noh theatre of Japan; [edited and translated] by Ezra Pound and Ernest Fenollosa. New Directions 1959 163p pa $10.95

Grades: 9 10 11 12   **895.6**
1. Nō plays
ISBN 0-8112-0152-X

A collection of classical Japanese No verse dramas, dealing with various aspects of social life and incorporating folklore

From the country of eight islands; an anthology of Japanese poetry; edited and translated [from the Japanese] by Hiroaki Sato and Burton Watson; with an introduction by Thomas Rimer; associate editor: Robert Fagan. Columbia Univ. Press 1987 xliv, 652p pa $29.50

Grades: 11 12 Adult   **895.6**
1. Japanese poetry—Collections
ISBN 0-231-06395-4   LC 86-7881

First published 1981 by University of Wash. Press

This anthology ranges "from the Kojiki (Record of Ancient Matters) . . . to a nineteenth-century transcript of a cycle of rice-planting songs, and from Kakinomoto no Hitimaro, [a] writer of elegies, who lived in the sixth century, to such recent poets as Tomioka Taeko. . . . Also included are Fujiwara no Teika's anthology of one hundred three 'tanka,' a no play, six sequences of 'renga' or linked verse, the 'frog matches' in which Basho participated, and some longer modern poems rendered in full." Publisher's note [1981 edition]

Includes bibliographical references

One hundred poems from the Japanese; {edited and translated} by Kenneth Rexroth. New Directions 1956 143p pa $11.95 hardcover o.p. *

Grades: 11 12 Adult   **895.6**
1. Japanese poetry—Collections
ISBN 0-8112-0181-3 (pa)

Also available: One hundred more poems from the Japanese pa $8.95 (ISBN 0-8112-0619-X)

A bilingual collection of poems drawn chiefly from the traditional Manyōshu, Kokinshū, and Hyakunin Isshu collections and also containing examples of haiku and other later forms. The translator's introduction provides background information on the history and nature of Japanese poetry

Includes bibliographical references

One man's moon; 50 haiku; by Bashō {et al.}; versions by Cid Corman. Gnomon Press 1984 50p pa $10 *

Grades: 9 10 11 12   **895.6**
1. Haiku
ISBN 0-917788-26-5

Poet/translator Corman offers his versions of haiku by some of its most adept practitioners

896   African literatures

The Penguin book of modern African poetry; edited by Gerald Moore and Ulli Beier. 4th ed. Penguin Bks. 1999 xxvi, 448p pa $15.95 *

Grades: 11 12 Adult   **896**
1. African poetry—Collections
ISBN 0-14-118100-1

First published 1963 in the United Kingdom with title: Modern poetry from Africa

New edition in preparation

This anthology includes over 200 poems by 67 poets from 23 countries

Includes bibliographical references

Women writing Africa: the eastern region; edited by Amandina Lihamba . . . [et al.] 1st ed. The Feminist Press at the City University of New York 2007 xxv, 478p (Women writing Africa project) $75; pa $29.95

Grades: 11 12 Adult   **896**
1. African literature—Collections 2. Literature—Women authors 3. East Africa
ISBN   978-1-55861-535-9;   1-55861-535-0;
978-1-55861-534-2 (pa); 1-55861-534-2 (pa)
         LC 2006-36534

This collection offers a "portrait of women's lives in Kenya, Malawi, Tanzania, Uganda and Zambia. These pieces span the centuries from 1711 to 2003, address topics ranging from religion to HIV and represent prose and poetry, fiction and nonfiction, lullabies and protest songs. . . . General readers who want to be entertained, educated and chastened about women's struggles and triumphs in east Africa will delight in this literary feast." Publ Wkly

Includes bibliographical references

Women writing Africa: the southern region; edited by M.J. Daymond {et al.}. Feminist Press 2002 xxx, 554p (Women writing Africa project) $75; pa $29.95

Grades: 11 12 Adult   **896**

1. African literature—Collections 2. Literature—Women authors 3. Southern Africa

ISBN 1-55861-406-0; 1-55861-407-9 (pa)

         LC 2002-29483

This "resource brings together more than 120 selections by women in six countries of southern Africa, in English and in translation from more than 20 different languages, ranging from wedding songs and work songs to letters, prison diaries, poetry, memoirs, and recent testimony before South Africa's Truth and Reconciliation Commission. . . . The first in a projected series of four regional African collections, this is a must for women's studies and African history and literature collections." Booklist

Includes bibliographical references

Women writing Africa: West Africa and the Sahel; edited by Esi Sutherland-Addy and Aminata Diaw. Feminist Press 2005 477p (Women writing Africa project) $75; pa $29.95

Grades: 9 10 11 12   **896**

1. African literature—Collections 2. Literature—Women authors 3. West Africa 4. Sahel

ISBN 1-55861-501-6; 1-55861-500-8 (pa)

         LC 2005-50708

"This second of four volumes representing the literary expression of African women focuses on 12 West African nations, documenting the history of this expression since upward of six centuries before colonialism and 20th-century independence. . . . [The 132 texts compiled] showcase not just the written word—in the form of letters, diaries, historical documents—but the spoken word as well, in lullabies, songs, and other oral traditions. . . . This anthology provides an epic tale of African history while highlighting African women's valuable contributions to their culture and bringing their voices to life for readers everywhere." Libr J

Includes bibliographical references

897   North American native literatures

Coltelli, Laura, 1941-

Winged words: American Indian writers speak; {reported by} Laura Coltelli. University of Neb. Press 1990 211p il (American Indian lives) pa $9.95 hardcover o.p. *

Grades: 11 12 Adult   **897**

1. Allen, Paula Gunn 2. Erdrich, Louise 3. Dorris, Michael 4. Harjo, Joy, 1951- 5. Momaday, N. Scott 6. Ortiz, Simon J., 1941- 7. Hogan, Linda 8. Rose, Wendy 9. Silko, Leslie, 1948- 10. Vizenor, Gerald Robert, 1934- 11. Welch, James, 1940-2003 12. American literature—Native American authors

ISBN 0-8032-6351-1 (pa)   LC 89-39323

A compilation of interviews with Louise Erdrich, N. Scott Momaday, James Welch and eight other Native American writers

"Coltelli's questions probe the writers' sources of inspiration, methods of composition, and perceptions of their own and their works' relationship to tribal culture, among other broad areas. But it's the questions Coltelli has tailored to each individual that hit pay dirt and result in some illuminating moments." Booklist

Includes bibliographical references

Coming to light; contemporary translations of the native literatures of North America; edited and with an introduction by Brian Swann. Random House 1994 801p pa $22 hardcover o.p.

Grades: 11 12 Adult   **897**

1. Native American literature 2. American literature—Native American authors—Collections

ISBN 0-679-74358-8 (pa)   LC 94-13457

"Swann has gathered intact texts from storytellers, singers, and orators. Arranged by region and tribe, each set of translations is prefaced by a lengthy introduction by the translator that sets the stories in context. The focus varies, depending on whether the translator is a linguist, anthropologist, or educator and whether he or she is a Native speaker, of which a fair number are. This wide-ranging collection goes far toward achieving Swann's goal of presenting a collection of reliable translations placed in their cultural and historical environments." Libr J

Includes bibliographical references

Dictionary of Native American literature; Andrew Wiget, editor. Garland 1994 598p (Garland reference library of the humanities) $140

Grades: 11 12 Adult   **897**

1. American literature—Native American authors 2. Native American literature

ISBN 0-8153-1560-0   LC 94-3811

Wiget "offers 73 essays, written by experts and arranged by subject and by period in three parts. The first, 'Native American Oral Literatures,' has an overview by Wiget and nine chapters on the oral literature of different geographic areas of Native America, followed by chapters on themes such as oratory, the trickster, dreams and songs, and revitalization movements. The second section, 'The Historical Emergence of Native American Writing,' with an introduction by Ruoff, is followed by chapters on topics such as federal Indian policy, autobiography, women's autobiography, and humor, as a backdrop to descriptions of the major native writers of the period. The third section, 'A Native American Renaissance: 1967 to the Present,' presents an overview by Joseph Bruchac followed by chapters on critical responses to Native American literature, teaching American Indian literature, the literature of Canada, fiction, theater, and Indians in Anglo-American literature." Choice

Includes bibliographical references

Returning the gift; poetry and prose from the first North American Native Writers Festival; Joseph Bruchac, editor, with the support of the Association for the Study of American Indian Literatures. University of Ariz. Press 1994 xxix, 369p (Sun tracks) hardcover o.p. paperback available $19.95

Grades: 11 12 Adult   **897**
1. Native American literature

               LC 94-4845

An "anthology of poetry and prose from the recent North American Native Writers' Festival, this provides a rich introduction to the diversity of contemporary Native writing in Canada and the U.S." Booklist

900 HISTORY & GEOGRAPHY

Cracking the SAT: U.S. and world history subject tests; [by] the Princeton Review. Random House 2007 il pa $19

Grades: 9 10 11 12   **900**
1. History—Study and teaching 2. Scholastic Assessment Test 3. Colleges and universities—Entrance requirements

ISSN 1558-3120

ISBN 0-375-76591-3; 978-0-375-76591-9

Annual. First published 2005. Continues Cracking the S A T II: U.S. and world history subject tests

At head of title: The Princeton Review

This guide provides test-taking strategies and sample tests on the subjects of both American and world history.

Shiveley, James M.
Using Internet primary sources to teach critical thinking skills in government, economics, and contemporary world issues; [by] James M. Shiveley and Phillip J. VanFossen. Greenwood Press 2001 xxv, 244p (Libraries Unlimited professional guides in school librarianship) $50

Grades: Professional   **900**
1. Social sciences—Study and teaching 2. Internet in education

ISBN 0-313-31283-4   LC 00-52147

"Part 1 offers an explanation of what critical thinking is and how it relates to social studies. Part 2 discusses what a primary source is and how one can differentiate it from a secondary and other sources. Part 3 describes 118 Web sites which contain primary source documents, giving for each site the URL, a brief abstract of the content, and questions and activities utilizing critical thinking skills. . . . This is an excellent professional resource for any public or school library that caters to the middle or high-school student." Booklist

Includes bibliographical references

902   History--Miscellany. Chronologies

Grun, Bernard, 1901-1972
The timetables of history; a historical linkage of people and events. 4th ed. Simon & Schuster 2005 835p $25

Grades: 11 12 Adult   **902**
1. Historical chronology

ISBN 0-7432-7003-7; 978-0-7432-7003-8

               LC 2005-49766

"A Touchstone book"

Original German edition, 1946; first published in the United States 1975

"Based on Werner Stein's Kulturfahrplan"

This chronology "includes material from 4500 BCE to 2004. . . . The information is listed by year in seven columns labeled 'History, Politics', 'Literature, Theater', 'Religion, Philosophy, Learning', 'Visual Arts', 'Music', 'Science, Technology, Growth', and 'Daily Life.' . . . This work is an excellent chronological tool, and should be found in all libraries." Choice

National Geographic concise history of the world; an illustrated timeline; edited by Neil Kagan. National Geographic Society 2005 416p il map $40 *

Grades: 11 12 Adult   **902**
1. Historical chronology

ISBN 0-792-28364-3   LC 2005-52248

This history is organized in time line format and broken up into eight historical eras. Includes maps, sidebars, and illustrations.

Includes bibliographical references

National Geographic visual history of the world; [authors, Klaus Berndl . . . et al.] National Geographic Society 2005 656p il $35 *

Grades: 11 12 Adult   **902**
1. World history

ISBN 0-7922-3695-5   LC 2005-541553

"Over 4,000 illustrations and photographs cover individuals and events from prehistory (the beginning to ca. 4000 BCE) to the contemporary world (1945 to the present). . . . This educational and entertaining volume of social, cultural, and military history will appeal to a wide readership." Choice

Stewart, Robert
Mysteries of history; [by] Robert Stewart, with Clint Twist and Edward Horton. National Geographic Society 2003 191p il $29.95

Grades: 11 12 Adult   **902**
1. History—Miscellanea

ISBN 0-7922-6232-8   LC 2003-11268

"A Marshall ed"

Contents: Why did the pharaohs build the pyramids? -- What was the purpose of Stonehenge? -- Was there a Trojan Horse? -- Why did Rome fall? -- Was there a real King Arthur? -- What happened to the Knights Templars and their gold? -- Did Marco Polo reach China? -- Why was the great Zimbabwe built? -- Did Columbus discover

Stewart, Robert—*Continued*
America? -- Was there a real El Dorado? -- What happened to America's "lost colony"? -- How did Japan remain in total isolation from the outside world for more than 250 years? -- Was King George III really mad? -- Was Napoleon poisoned? -- What is the truth behind the myth of the Underground Railroad? -- Why did Custer choose to fight the Battle of the Little Bighorn? -- Why did the Hindenburg crash? -- Did FDR know about Pearl Harbor in advance? -- Who killed John F. Kennedy?

"Attractive enough for browsing, this volume is a good starting place for exploring any of the questions raised, and the extensive bibliography suggests books for further reading on each topic." Booklist

Teeple, John B., 1928-
Timelines of world history. DK Pub. 2002 666p il map hardcover o.p. pa $30 *
Grades: 11 12 Adult   **902**
1. Historical chronology
ISBN 0-7894-8926-0; 0-7566-1703-0 (pa)
        LC 2002-73896
"This volume uses time lines to provide 'a visual chronicle of human history and development' from 10,000 B.C.E. to the present. Time lines appear in four columns—one each for Asia, Africa, Europe, and the Americas and Australasia—and are accompanied by gorgeous illustrations and maps. The outer column of each page has sidebars containing summaries of key events, condensed biographies, or descriptions of places." Booklist
"This superb reference tool will be especially appreciated in smaller libraries." Voice Youth Advocates

The **timetables** of American history; Laurence Urdang, editor; with an introduction by Henry Steele Commager and a new foreword by Arthur Schlesinger, Jr. Simon & Schuster [2001] c1996 534p il pa $24 *
Grades: 11 12 Adult   **902**
1. Historical chronology
ISBN 0-7432-0261-9
"A Touchstone book"
First published 1982
"A Laurence Urdang reference book" Verso of title page
Presents information chronologically in tabular form. Each double-page spread has columns for history and politics, the arts, science and technology, and miscellaneous.

Williams, Hywel
Cassell's chronology of world history; dates, events and ideas that made history. Weidenfeld & Nicolson 2005 752p $39.95 *
Grades: 11 12 Adult   **902**
1. Historical chronology
ISBN 0-304-35730-8
"Starting with the earliest human fossils, discovered in Ethiopia, the book settles into a sequential listing of the leading events of world history through the early 21st century. The text is arranged into four major sections—'The Ancient and Medieval Worlds, 135,000 B.P.–1449,'

'The Early Modern World, 1450-1799,' 'The Nineteenth Century World, 1800-1899,' and 'The Modern World, 1900-2004'—each of which is subdivided by continent and such categories as 'Economy and Society,' 'Science and Technology,' and 'Arts and Humanities.'" Libr J

The **Wilson** calendar of world history; edited by John Paxton and Edward W. Knappman; contributors: Rodney Carlisle [et al.] Wilson, H.W. 1999 460p il $100
Grades: 11 12 Adult   **902**
1. Historical chronology 2. Calendars
ISBN 0-8242-0937-0   LC 98-50998
"A New England Publishing Associates book"
"Based on S.H. Steinberg's Historical table." Title page
This successor to Steinberg's chronology reports on 25,000 historical events and includes expanded coverage of the arts and sciences as well as events in Latin America, Asia, and Africa. Includes index for people, places, events, concepts, inventions, discoveries, and titles of works.
Includes bibliographical references

903   History--Encyclopedias and dictionaries

Berkshire encyclopedia of world history; William H. McNeill, senior editor; Jerry H. Bentley [et al.] editorial board. Berkshire Pub. Group 2004 5v set $525
Grades: 11 12 Adult   **903**
1. World history—Encyclopedias
ISBN 0-97430-910-9
This encyclopedia traces "the development of human history—with a focus on area studies, global history, anthropology, geography, science, arts, literature, economics, women's studies, African-American studies, and cultural studies related to all regions of the world." Publisher's note
For a review see: Booklist, Jan. 1 & 15, 2005

Encyclopedia of world history. Facts on File 2000 524p il maps $93.50 *
Grades: 11 12 Adult   **903**
1. World history—Encyclopedias 2. History—Outlines, syllabi, etc.
ISBN 0-8160-4249-7   LC 00-34721
Editorial Board: Patrick K. O'Brien
"The 6,500 entries are alphabetical with cross-references and include colored maps, paintings, photographs, charts, and tables. Difficult-to-find topics, such as regions of Russia and the Balkans, Africa, and Oceania, are covered through the year 2000. The article on former President Bill Clinton discusses his full term. Interesting quotes from famous people accompany the articles, usually with illustrations." Voice Youth Advocates

Kohn, George C.
Dictionary of historic documents; George Childs Kohn, editor; foreword by Leonard Latkovski. rev ed. Facts on File 2003 646p $75 *
Grades: 9 10 11 12   **903**
ISBN 0-8160-4772-3   LC 2002-73856

Kohn, George C.—*Continued*

First published 1990

This dictionary provides "information about more than 2,400 significant historic documents in world history. Included are key acts, constitutions, proclamations, treaties, bills, laws, agreements, and speeches, among others, from ancient codes, such as Hammurabi's Code, to modern agreements and speeches, such as the Kyoto Protocol or President George W. Bush's 'Freedom and Fear Are at War' speech. . . . Each entry includes a concise summary describing the principal details of the document, its significance and historical context, as well as primary or secondary sources for further reference." Publisher's note

New dictionary of the history of ideas; edited by Maryanne Cline Horowitz. Charles Scribner's Sons 2005 6v il map set $695 *

Grades: 11 12 Adult   **903**

1. Civilization—History—Dictionaries

ISBN 0-684-31377-4   LC 2004-14731

First published 1973 in five volumes under the editorship of Philip P. Wiener with title: Dictionary of the history of ideas

The 700 articles include "entries on feminism and antifeminism, queer theory, and nongender topics like diversity, social capital, and third cinema [as well as] standard subjects, like beauty and love. . . . Each entry explores origin, cultural interpretations, and historical themes. . . . This delightful foray into humankind's ideas, from abolitionism to Zionism, is a bargain highly recommended." Libr J

Includes bibliographical references

World monarchies and dynasties; John Middleton, editor. Sharpe Reference 2005 3v il map set $325

Grades: 11 12 Adult   **903**

1. Kings and rulers—Dictionaries

ISBN 0-7656-8050-5   LC 2003-23236

"This three-volume work provides introductions to almost 400 individual monarchs, 450 dynasties, and 140 topics related to monarchies, covering all regions of the world and all historical periods." Libr J

"This is an impressive and evenhanded approach to an interesting topic, and one that definitely fills a niche." Ref & User Services Quarterly

Includes bibliographical references

904   Collected accounts of events

Beyer, Rick

The greatest stories never told; 100 tales from history to astonish, bewilder, & stupefy. HarperResource 2003 214p il $17.95

Grades: 7 8 9 10   **904**

1. History—Miscellanea

ISBN 0-06-001401-6   LC 2004-296419

Based on the television program: Timelab 2000

"Beginning with the year 46 B.C. and ending in 1990, Beyer presents a chronological account of one hundred unknown, partially known, and familar tales about an array of people and events that have shaped the world. . . . They range from the mundane to the fantastic. . . .

Extensive research went into the production of this charming work. Primary documents in the form of letters, laws, illustrations, and photographs bring to life these unique and incredible anecdotes." Voice Youth Advocates

Includes bibliographical references

Davis, Lee Allyn

Man-made catastrophes; [by] Lee Davis. rev ed. Facts on File 2002 402p il $60

Grades: 11 12 Adult   **904**

1. Disasters

ISBN 0-8160-4418-X   LC 2001-54324

"Facts on File science library"

First published 1993

This describes man-made disasters "from the burning of Babylon in 538B.C. to the 2001 terrorist attack on the World Trade Center in New York City. . . . [The entries] are organized by disaster type: air crashes, civil unrest and terrorism, explosions, maritime disasters, nuclear and industrial accidents, railway disasters, and space disasters." Publisher's note

Includes bibliographical references

Davis, Paul K., 1952-

100 decisive battles; from ancient times to the present. Oxford University Press 2001 462p il map pa $19.95 *

Grades: 11 12 Adult   **904**

1. Battles 2. Military history

ISBN 0-19-514366-3   LC 00-49183

First published 1999 by ABC-CLIO

Surveys the one hundred most decisive battles in world history from the Battle of Megiddo in 1469 B.C. to Desert Storm, 1991. "Entries are approximately two thousand words long, limiting background details and confining the descriptions to the combatants, the historical setting, the battle itself, and the results. Each entry ends with a list of references used by the author in his research." Voice Youth Advocates

Includes bibliographical references

909   World history. Civilization

The **1100s**; Helen Cothran, book editor. Greenhaven Press 2001 304p il maps (Headlines in history) hardcover o.p. pa $27.45

Grades: 9 10 11 12   **909**

1. World history—12th century 2. Medieval civilization

ISBN 0-7377-0530-2; 0-7377-0529-9 (pa)

     LC 00-64035

"This anthology chronicles the major events occurring in the twelfth century including the Crusades, the rise of knights and samurai warriors, the development of the first universities, the coming of Genghis Khan, and the fall of the Toltec civilization. Chapters include essays on these topics and many other twelfth-century events occurring in Europe, Asia, and the Americas." Publisher's note

Includes bibliographical references

The **1200s**; Thomas Siebold, book editor.
Greenhaven Press 2001 240p il maps (Headlines
in history) lib bdg $43.70; pa $27.45
Grades: 9 10 11 12 **909**
1. World history—13th century 2. Medieval civilization
ISBN 0-7377-0532-9 (lib bdg); 0-7377-0531-0 (pa)
LC 2001-16035
The readings in this volume "are organized by geography, and they cover such crucial themes as the conflict
between nomadic and sedentary peoples, the move to
secularization, and the growth of trade. . . . There's an
appendix of primary documents. The combination of big-
picture, detailed focus, and authoritative voices makes
this a strong . . . [book] for discussion and research in
advanced history classes." Booklist
Includes bibliographical references

The **1300s**; Stephen Currie, book editor.
Greenhaven Press 2001 272p il (Headlines in
history) lib bdg $43.70
Grades: 9 10 11 12 **909**
1. World history—14th century 2. Medieval civilization
ISBN 0-7377-0534-5 (lib bdg) LC 00-69509
This collection of primary and secondary source articles examines such topics as famine and plague in Europe, political infighting in Japan, Aztec civilization, "the
rise of the Ottomans, the Mali Empire, the Great Schism,
and Geoffrey Chaucer's poetry." Publisher's note
Includes bibliographical references

Africana: the encyclopedia of the African and
African American experience; editors, Kwame
Anthony Appiah, Henry Louis Gates, Jr. 2nd ed.
Oxford University Press 2005 5v set $425
Grades: 11 12 Adult **909**
1. Blacks—Encyclopedias 2. African diaspora—Ency-
clopedias 3. African Americans—Encyclopedias
4. Africa—Encyclopedias
ISBN 0-19-517055-5 LC 2004-20222
First published 1999 by Basic Civitas Bks.
This encyclopedia covers "prominent individuals,
events, trends, places, political movements, art forms,
business and trade, religions, ethnic groups, organiza-
tions, and countries on both sides of the ocean. . . .
There are articles on contemporary nations of sub-
Saharan Africa, ethnic groups from various regions of
Africa, African American Academy award winners, Ca-
ribbean musical styles, African religions in Brazil, and
European colonial powers." Booklist [review of 1999
edition]
Includes bibliographical references

Boorstin, Daniel J., 1914-2004
The creators. Random House 1992 811p il
hardcover o.p. pa $18.95
Grades: 11 12 Adult **909**
1. Civilization 2. Arts 3. Creation (Literary, artistic,
etc.)
ISBN 0-394-54395-5; 0-679-74375-8 (pa)
LC 91-39948
In this volume "Boorstin undertakes an interpretive
history of creativity in Western civilization. Packed with

shrewd, entertaining profiles of Dante, Goethe, Benjamin
Franklin and dozens of others, this stimulating synthesis
sets the achievements of individual geniuses into a coher-
ent narrative of humanity's advance from ignorance."
Publ Wkly
Includes bibliographical references

The discoverers. Random House 1983 745p
hardcover o.p. pa $18.95
Grades: 11 12 Adult **909**
1. Civilization 2. Exploration 3. Science—History
ISBN 0-394-40229-4; 0-394-72625-1 (pa)
LC 83-42766
The author "leads his reader through . . . anecdotal
information of the discoveries of timekeeping,
mapmaking, observations of nature, both large and small,
and of insights into human social organizations, past and
present, in this popularized, general history of 'mankind's need to know.'" Choice
Includes bibliographical references

The seekers; the story of man's continuing quest
to understand his world. Random House 1998
298p hardcover o.p. pa $15.95
Grades: 11 12 Adult **909**
1. Civilization—History
ISBN 0-679-43445-3; 0-375-70475-2 (pa)
LC 98-15430
Concluding volume of author's trilogy begun with The
discoverers and The creators
"This is an account, generally chronological, of how
the Western world's heritage of ideas of meaning and
purpose was shaped by the thinking of the great philosophers and religious leaders from ancient times to the
present. Until the rise of scientific thinking in the 17th
century, Boorstin observes, answers were sought from
history and human events, but in modern times, ideologies and dogmas overcame that way of thinking." Libr J
Includes bibliographical references

Cahill, Thomas, 1940-
The gifts of the Jews; how a tribe of desert
nomads changed the way everyone thinks and
feels. Talese 1998 291p (Hinges of history)
$23.50; pa $14
Grades: 11 12 Adult **909**
1. Bible. O.T. —History of Biblical events
2. Judaism—History 3. Jews—History
ISBN 0-385-48248-5; 0-385-48249-3 (pa)
LC 97-45139
In this colloquial look at the influence of the Hebrew
Bible on civilization, the author gives "the Jews credit
for revolutionizing the concepts of democracy, universal
law, monotheism, linear time, personal vocation, destiny,
self-improvement and the belief in the equality of all humans. He stumbles on the odd aside and occasionally is
surprisingly insensitive. . . Still, his passion and breadth
of knowledge are admirable." N Y Times Book Rev
Includes bibliographical references

Cahill, Thomas, 1940-—*Continued*

Sailing the wine-dark sea; why the Greeks matter. Talese 2003 304p (Hinges of history) $27.50; pa $14.95

Grades: 11 12 Adult   **909**

1. Greece—Civilization

ISBN 0-385-49553-6; 0-385-49554-4 (pa)

LC 2003-50725

This author "begins with a discussion of Homer's *Iliad* and *Odyssey* and how these two epic poems relate to the history of Greece. He then focuses on such themes as the Greek alphabet, literature, and political system, and its playwrights, philosophers, and artists. A final chapter examines the effects that Greco-Roman and Judeo-Christian traditions had on each other." Booklist

Includes bibliographical references

The **Cambridge** illustrated history of the Islamic world; edited by Francis Robinson. Cambridge Univ. Press 1996 xxiii, 328p il maps hardcover o.p. pa $36.99

Grades: 11 12 Adult   **909**

1. Islamic countries—History

ISBN 0-521-43510-2; 0-521-66993-6 (pa)

LC 95-37562

"Facts about Islam's history and practice are presented, along with its economic, societal, and intellectual structures. Excellent graphics support the text. Maps are extensive and exact." SLJ

Includes bibliographical references

Cocker, Mark

Rivers of blood, rivers of gold; Europe's conquest of indigenous peoples. Grove Press 2000 416p il hardcover o.p. pa $16

Grades: 11 12 Adult   **909**

1. Imperialism 2. Genocide 3. Colonies

ISBN 0-8021-1666-3; 0-8021-3801-2 (pa)

LC 99-87927

The author "looks in detail at the Spanish conquest of Mexico, the British near-extermination of the Tasmanian Aborigines, the white settlers' dispossession of the Apaches, and the German subjugation of the Herero and Nama of South-West Africa. Cocker shows that European imperialism involved the deaths of millions and the complete extinction of numerous distinct peoples." Booklist

Includes bibliographical references

Encyclopedia of the developing world; Thomas M. Leonard, editor. Routledge 2005 3v set $625

Grades: 11 12 Adult   **909**

1. Developing countries—Encyclopedias

ISBN 1-57958-388-1   LC 2005-49976

The entries "detail developments from 1945 forward. In addition to basic statistical and geographical information, country-focused entries detail history, economy, and political situation. Thematic entries cover people (e.g., Jomo Kenyatta), historical topics (e.g., colonialism), economic and government models (e.g., communism), the environment (e.g., water) and organizations (e.g., WTO)." Libr J

Includes bibliographical references

Encyclopedia of the Palestinians; edited by Philip Mattar. Rev. ed. Facts on File 2005 684p il map (Facts on File library of world history) $90 *

Grades: 9 10 11 12   **909**

1. Palestinian Arabs—Encyclopedias

ISBN 0-8160-5764-8   LC 2004-57673

First published 2000

This book focuses on "Palestinian history, politics, and society from the late Ottoman period to the present. . . . [This is] the most objective reference compendium to treat Palestinian history as a subject in its own right." Choice

Includes bibliographical references

Evans, Colin, 1948-

Great feuds in history; ten of the liveliest disputes ever. Wiley 2001 242p $24.95; pa $15.95

Grades: 11 12 Adult   **909**

1. History—Miscellanea

ISBN 0-471-38038-5; 0-471-22588-6 (pa)

LC 00-43919

This discusses the following feuds: Elizabeth I vs. Mary, Parliament vs. Charles I, Burr vs. Hamilton, Hatfields vs. McCoys, Stalin vs. Trotsky, Amundsen vs. Scott, Duchess of Windsor vs. Queen Mother, Montgomery vs. Patton, Johnson vs. Kennedy, Hoover vs. King.

This places "emphasis on the global issues often at stake and how, for better or worse, the feuds changed history. Evans . . . captures all the drama and controversy in these streamlined accounts brimming with invigorated, well-paced prose." Publ Wkly

Includes bibliographical references

Events that changed the world in the seventeenth century; edited by Frank W. Thackeray & John E. Findling. Greenwood Press 1999 213p il (Greenwood Press "Events that changed the world" series) $39.95

Grades: 9 10 11 12   **909**

1. World history—17th century

ISBN 0-313-29078-4   LC 99-25506

This title covers "the Manchu conquest of China, the Thirty Years' War, the Scientific Revolution, and other events." Booklist

Includes bibliographical references

Events that changed the world through the sixteenth century; edited by Frank W. Thackeray and John E. Findling. Greenwood Press 2001 223p il (Greenwood Press "Events that changed the world" series) $39.50

Grades: 9 10 11 12   **909**

1. World history—15th century 2. World history—16th century

ISBN 0-313-29079-2   LC 00-52132

This volume focuses "on the fifteenth and sixteenth centuries, with 10 events ranging from the *Reconquista* (circa 711-1492) to the defeat of the Spanish Armada in 1588." Booklist

Includes bibliographical references

Fargues, Philippe
The atlas of the Arab world; [by] Philippe Fargues & Rafic Boustani. Facts on File 1991 144p il maps $55
Grades: 11 12 Adult **909**
1. Arab countries
ISBN 0-8160-2346-8 LC 89-675447
"Translation by Darla Rudy," "Copyright 1990 by Bordas S.A., Paris; translation copyright 1991 by Facts on File" Verso of title page
"A wealth of information presented in colorful maps, graphs, diagrams, and charts. Arranged by broad cultural topics such as ethnic groups and religions, society, cities, oil and industry, facts not readily available in standard resources are presented and compared." SLJ
Includes bibliographical references

Global history; cultural encounters from antiquity to the present. M.E. Sharpe 2004 4v set $325
Grades: 11 12 Adult **909**
1. Civilization—History
ISBN 0-7656-8043-2 LC 2004-41560
This reference set "covers significant cultural encounters from 5,000 B.C.E. to the present. Each volume encompasses a specific time period with articles chronologically arranged. In total, the set contains 80 articles representing important instances of cross-cultural contacts. . . . Many of the articles focus on historical events or particular civilizations, but some treat recent social and technological developments, such as AIDS and satellite broadcasting. . . . The articles are clearly written and engaging enough to hold the attention of most readers from high school up. *Global History's* cross-cultural approach differentiates it from standard world history reference sources, and it is recommended for high-school, public, and college libraries." Booklist

Great events from history, The 17th century, 1601-1700; editor, Larissa Juliet Taylor. Salem Press 2005 2v il map set $160
Grades: 11 12 Adult **909**
1. World history—17th century
ISBN 1-58765-225-0; 978-1-58765-225-7
LC 2005-17362
Companion volume to Great lives from history, The 17th century, 1601-1700
Some of the essays in this work were originally published in Chronology of European history, 15,000 B.C. to 1997 (1997) and Great events from history: North American series. Rev. ed. (1997)
This set "offers two to three-page essays that detail the major milestones of the century as well as social developments that were reflective of daily life during the period. The perspective here is international and spans a variety of categories, including religion and theology, cultural and intellectual history, expansion and land acquisition, and natural disasters. A list of key figures involved in each event is provided." SLJ
Includes bibliographical references

Great events from history, The Renaissance & early modern era, 1454-1600; editor, Christina J. Moose. Salem Press 2005 2v il map set $160
Grades: 11 12 Adult **909**
1. Renaissance 2. World history—15th century 3. World history—16th century
ISBN 1-58765-214-5; 978-1-58765-214-1
LC 2004-28878
Companion volume to Great lives from history, The Renaissance & early modern era, 1454-1600
Some of the essays were previously published in various works
This collection of essays covers events in the scientific, intellectual, literary, sociological, political and military disciplines that happened worldwide during the Renaissance.
Includes bibliographical references

A **Historical** atlas of the Jewish people; from the time of the patriarchs to the present; general editor, Eli Barnavi; English edition editor, Miriam Eliav-Feldon; cartography, Michel Opatowski; new edition revised by Denis Charbit. new ed. Schocken Bks. 2002 321p il maps $45
Grades: 11 12 Adult **909**
1. Jews—History—Maps
ISBN 0-8052-4226-0 LC 2003-279553
First published 1992 by Knopf
"Covering three millennia of Jewish history and culture through a combination of concise text, accurate and well-drawn maps, and a sumptuous array of photographs, diagrams, and reproductions of paintings, this atlas succeeds in covering all the main themes of the Jewish experience. The material is arranged chronologically and systematically. . . . The result is a reference that will profit both scholars and lay readers." Libr J [review of 1992 edition]

The **Islamic** world; past and present; John L. Esposito, editor in chief . . . {et al.}. Oxford University Press 2004 3v il map set $325 *
Grades: 9 10 11 12 **909**
1. Islam—Encyclopedias
ISBN 0-19-516520-9 LC 2003-19665
This book "contains more than 300 entries, ranging in length from a few paragraphs to several pages; many black-and-white photos; color inserts; numerous sidebars, including definitions of unfamiliar terms; an extensive bibliography; and (in each volume) a chronology, glossary, and list of 'People and Places.' The material is accessible, browsable, and current; topics treated include religion and history ('Prayer,' 'Prophets,' 'Crusades'), culture and customs, and political and social issues ('Architecture,' 'Clothing,' 'Intifadah,' 'Taliban,' 'Sexuality')." SLJ
For a fuller review, see: Booklist, Nov. 15, 2004

James, Lawrence
The rise and fall of the British Empire. St. Martin's Press 1995 704p il hardcover o.p. pa $21.95

Grades: 11 12 Adult   **909**
1. Great Britain—Colonies 2. Commonwealth countries—History
ISBN 0-312-14039-8; 0-312-16985-X (pa)
LC 95-38774
First published 1994 in the United Kingdom
The author "*surveys* the major periods and events in Britain's rise and decline as a global power without attempting to be the definitive study of any one of those periods or events. . . . James' focus rests primarily on individuals—those who built the British Empire, those who maintained it, and those who, when it came time, eased it out of existence." Booklist

Ochoa, George
The Wilson chronology of ideas; {by} George Ochoa and Melinda Corey. Wilson, H.W. 1998 431p $105 *

Grades: 11 12 Adult   **909**
1. Civilization—History 2. Philosophy
ISBN 0-8242-0935-4   LC 97-17591
A chronological presentation of influential philosophical, political, theological and social thought from ancient times to the late 20th century. Sidebars feature profiles of celebrated thinkers
Includes bibliographical references

Pagden, Anthony
Peoples and empires; a short history of European migration, exploration, and conquest from Greece to the present. Modern library ed. Modern Lib. 2001 xxv, 206p hardcover o.p. pa $10.95

Grades: 11 12 Adult   **909**
1. World history 2. Colonies 3. Immigration and emigration
ISBN 0-679-64096-7; 0-8129-6761-5 (pa)
LC 00-66204
"A Modern chronicles book"
This "overview of European empire building and colonization commences with the diffusion of Greek civilization and traces the subsequent evolution of the ensuing Roman, Spanish, French, and British empires. More interesting than how those empires physically expanded is the insightful discussion on what motivated individual men and entire nations to migrate and conquer." Booklist
Includes bibliographical references

Reformation, exploration, and empire. Grolier 2005 10v il map set $389

Grades: 6 7 8 9   **909**
1. World history—16th century 2. World history—17th century 3. Renaissance 4. Modern civilization
ISBN 0-7172-6071-2
"This set describes a key period of Western history from appoximately 1500 to 1700. The more than 240 entries provide a sense of the development of international trade, great cultural achievements, and the spirit of learning. . . . The layout is bright and colorful and features hundreds of illustraions, including maps, charts, tables, and more. Sidebars are plentiful and are used to highlight suplemental stories, information, and primary source materials." Booklist

Smith, Bonnie
Imperialism; a history in documents. Oxford Univ. Press 2000 175p il map (Pages from history) $32.95

Grades: 9 10 11 12   **909**
1. Imperialism 2. World history
ISBN 0-19-510801-9   LC 00-28552
The author "examines the 'high tide' of colonial imperialism, an era characterized by the expansion of European empires in Africa and Asia for financial gain and national power. She opens with background about the racial and economic rationales for imperialism, and then provides chapters about the rapid growth of empires, the role of technology and profits in imperialism, and its impact on the environment." SLJ
Includes bibliographical references

Smith, Tom, 1953-
Discovery of the Americas, 1492-1800. Facts on File 2005 206p il map (Discovery and exploration) $40 *

Grades: 9 10 11 12   **909**
1. Explorers 2. America—Exploration
ISBN 0-8160-5262-X   LC 2004-16155
This book on the initial exploration and discovery of the Americas covers such topics as the role of California missions, the legend of El Dorado, and the impact of the introduction of the horse to North America.
Includes bibliographical references

Somerset Fry, Plantagenet, 1931-
The Dorling Kindersley history of the world. Rev. ed., Rev. American ed. DK Pub. 2005 400p il map $39.95 *

Grades: 9 10 11 12   **909**
1. World history
ISBN 0-7566-1244-6   LC 2005-280605
First published 1994
"Coverage begins in the Cambrian era, 570 million years ago, and is current through 2004. The volume divides history into 20 chronological chapters, beginning with 'Early People' and moving through such sections as 'Traders and Warriors,' 'Monks and Invaders,' 'Commerce and Colonies,' 'The World Goes to War,' and, finally, 'One World.' . . . This visually enticing compilation will prove irresistible to browsers and offers a wealth of support material to student researchers." Booklist

Technology in world history; W. Bernard Carlson, editor. Oxford University Press 2005 7v il maps set $299

Grades: 7 8 9 10   **909**
1. Technology and civilization
ISBN 0-19-821820-5; 978-0-19-521820-6
LC 2003-55300

Technology in world history—*Continued*
"Seeking to explore how people have used technology to shape societies, Carlson and 10 other scholars examine the distinctive development and effects of technology in 18 cultures—defined either geographically (Pacific Peoples, Sub-Saharan Africa) or by historical period (Stone Age, The World Since 1970)." SLJ
For a fuller review, see: Booklist, Dec. 1, 2005
Includes bibliographical references

The **Third** World: opposing viewpoints; David M. Haugen, book editor. Greenhaven Press 2006 230p il lib bdg $34.95; pa $23.70
Grades: 11 12   **909**
1. Developing countries
ISBN 0-7377-2965-1 (lib bdg); 978-0-7377-2965-8 (lib bdg); 0-7377-2966-X (pa); 978-0-7377-2966-5 (pa)
LC 2005-54544
"Opposing viewpoints series"
This book is a collection of essays on the problems facing Third World countries.
"This volume would be an excellent resource for more advanced students researching the subject or looking for debate topics." SLJ
Includes bibliographical references

Western civilization; original and secondary source readings; Benjamin C. Sax, book editor. Greenhaven Press 2001 2v (Perspectives on history) hardcover o.p. v1-v2 pa ea $28.70 *
Grades: 11 12 Adult   **909**
1. Western civilization—History
ISBN 1-56510-989-9 (v1); 1-56510-988-0 (v1 pa); 1-56510-991-0 (v2); 1-56510-990-2 (v2 pa)
LC 00-50339
Contents: v1 From the origins of civilization to the age of absolutism; v2 From the scientific revolution to the present
"Kings, philosophers, saints, dictators, scholars, common folk—all of these voices emerge in the sweep of these very useful offerings." Booklist
Includes bibliographical references

909.07   World history -- ca. 500-1450/1500

Andrea, Alfred J., 1941-
Encyclopedia of the crusades. Greenwood Press 2003 xxiii, 356p il, maps $75 *
Grades: 11 12 Adult   **909.07**
1. Crusades—Encyclopedias 2. Europe—Church history—Encyclopedias
ISBN 0-313-31659-7   LC 2003-48544
This encyclopedia includes "more than 200 entries, each one between approximately 10 lines and four pages in length. . . . The introduction gives the entries some historical context and defines the term *crusade* for the reader. The entries are in alphabetical order and include cross-references in bold type to other entries in the book. Many entries also include suggested readings, both primary sources and historical studies. At the end of the work, the author has included a chronology of important

dates and events, a 'Basic Crusade Library' of further readings in bibliographic essay style, and a general index. . . . This encyclopedia is recommended for high-school, undergraduate, and public libraries." Booklist
Includes bibliographical references

The **Crusades**; an encyclopedia; Alan V. Murray, editor. ABC-CLIO 2006 4v il map set $385 *
Grades: 11 12 Adult   **909.07**
1. Crusades—Encyclopedias
ISBN 1-57607-862-0; 978-1-57607-862-4
LC 2006-19410
This encyclopedia "surveys all aspects of the crusading movement from its origins in the 11th century to its decline in the 16th century." Publisher's note
For a fuller review, see: Booklist, Dec. 1, 2006
Includes bibliographical references

The **Early** Middle Ages; Jeff Hay, book editor. Greenhaven Press 2001 234p il (Turning points in world history) lib bdg $34.95; pa $23.70
Grades: 7 8 9 10   **909.07**
1. Medieval civilization 2. Europe—History—476-1492
ISBN 0-7377-0482-9 (lib bdg); 0-7377-0481-0 (pa)
LC 00-34110
This is a collection of essays concerning the period marked by "the beginning of feudalism; the invention of new, more efficient farming techniques; and the shifting of European civilization away from the Mediterranean Sea." Publisher's note
Includes bibliographical references

Great events from history, The Middle Ages, 477-1453; editor, Brian A. Pavlac; consulting editors, Byron Cannon, . . . [et al.] Salem Press 2005 2v il map set $160
Grades: 11 12 Adult   **909.07**
1. Middle Ages 2. Medieval civilization
ISBN 1-58765-167-X; 978-1-58765-167-0
LC 2004-16640
Companion volume to Great lives from history, The Middle Ages, 477-1453
Some essays were previously published in Great events from history (1972-1980), Chronology of European history: 15,000 B.C. to 1997 (1997), Great events from history: North American series, revised edition (1997), Great events from history: ancient and medieval series (1972), and Great events from history: modern European series (1973)
This set "offers 322 essays, beginning with Confucianism arrives in Japan (fifth or sixth century) and ending with Fall of Constantinople (May 29, 1453)." Booklist
Includes bibliographical references

Jones, J. Sydney
The Crusades, Primary sources; written by J. Sydney Jones; edited by Marcia Merryman Means and Neil Schlager. UXL 2005 c2004 xxvii, 179p il (The Crusades reference library) $63 *
Grades: 11 12 Adult   **909.07**
1. Crusades
ISBN 0-7876-9178-X   LC 2004-18001

Jones, J. Sydney—*Continued*

This book "consists of 24 full or excerpted documents, first-person accounts, treaties, and speeches; the complete Magna Carta; and a section from the epic poem The Song of Roland. . . . All excerpts from the primary sources are followed by text that illuminates the history of the document and poses discussion questions." Booklist

Includes bibliographical references

Knight, Judson

Middle ages: almanac; edited by Judy Galens. U.X.L 2001 lxv, 226p il map $60

Grades: 9 10 11 12   **909.07**

1. Middle Ages 2. World history 3. Medieval civilization

ISBN 0-7876-4856-6   LC 00-59442

This reference's 19 chapters review world history from the fall of the Roman Empire in 500 A.D. to the beginning of the Renaissance in 1500 A.D.

"The volume's strength is its broad coverage; it includes material on India, Southeast Asia, China, Japan, the Americas, and Africa as well as Europe and the Middle East, making it unique among other books for this age group." SLJ

Includes bibliographical references

Medieval world. Grolier Educ. 2001 10v il maps set $345

Grades: 7 8 9 10   **909.07**

1. Middle Ages 2. Medieval civilization

ISBN 0-7172-5520-4   LC 00-46649

Contents: v1 Abelard-Burgundy; v2 The Byzantine Empire-Constantinople; v3 Copts-Feudalism; v4 Florence-Hospitals; v5 House and home-Joan of Arc; v6 Justinian-The Mediterranean; v7 Mehmet II-Painting and sculpture; v8 The papacy-Roman Empire; v9 Rome-Thomas Aquinas; v10 Tools and technology-Writing

"The 226 alphabetical entries in this set cover all aspects of the time period between 476 A.D. and 1453 A.D. . . . The set focuses on Europe, but it also shows how other civilizations were developing during this time period." Book Rep

This "is an attractive and helpful reference source that will provide information on a variety of subjects related to this complex historical period." Booklist

Includes bibliographical references

Middle ages: primary sources; {compiled by} Judson Knight; Judy Galens, editor. U.X.L 2000 xxxiv, 161p il $60 *

Grades: 9 10 11 12   **909.07**

1. Middle Ages

ISBN 0-7876-4860-4   LC 00-59441

This volume contains "19 full or excerpted documents written during this period, including the work of celebrated writers such as St. Augustine, Marco Polo, and Dante as well as less familiar individuals such as Anna Comnena and Lo Kuan-chung. Each selection is placed in its historical context and followed by a section entitled 'What happened next'. . . . Unfamiliar words or terms are defined in sidebars. Each entry has a box profiling the author of the documents and at least two illustrations." Booklist

Includes bibliographical references

O'Neal, Michael, 1949-

The Crusades, Almanac; written by Michael J. O'Neal; edited by Marcia Merryman Means and Neil Schlager. UXL 2005 c2004 xxv, 207p il (The Crusades reference library) $63

Grades: 11 12 Adult   **909.07**

1. Crusades

ISBN 0-7876-9176-3   LC 2004-18003

This book "discusses such topics as the conquering of Jerusalem by the caliph Umar, pilgrimages to the Holy Land, the traditions of chivalry, and territorial expansion and colonization as motivations for the Crusades. Its explanation of the difference and divisions between Sunni and Shiite Islam alone is useful reading for a wider audience." Booklist

Includes bibliographical references

The **Oxford** illustrated history of the Crusades; edited by Jonathan Riley-Smith. Oxford Univ. Press 1995 436p il maps hardcover o.p. pa $26.50 *

Grades: 11 12 Adult   **909.07**

1. Crusades

ISBN 0-19-820435-3; 0-19-285428-3 (pa)

       LC 94-24229

Scholars explore the complex religious, economic, and military aspects of the Crusades.

Includes bibliographical references

909.08   Modern history, 1450/1500-

Gonick, Larry

The cartoon history of the modern world; Part 1: from Columbus to the U.S. Constitution. Collins 2007 259p il pa $17.95

Grades: 9 10 11 12   **909.08**

1. Graphic novels 2. Modern history—Graphic novels

ISBN 978-0-06-076004-5; 0-06-076004-4

       LC 2006-49146

The book begins with a "15-page distillation of pre-Columbian America; and while Europe and North America receive most of the attention, Gonick does include at least some highlights from other parts of the world. Covering such topics as the Protestant Reformation, the British defeat of the Spanish Armada, the Copernican model of the universe, and the American Revolution, he writes and draws with considerable wit and authority, and is obviously well versed in his subject." SLJ

Tuchman, Barbara Wertheim

The march of folly; from Troy to Vietnam; [by] Barbara W. Tuchman. Knopf 1984 447p il hardcover o.p. pa $16.95

Grades: 11 12 Adult   **909.08**

1. Modern history

ISBN 0-394-52777-1; 0-345-30823-9 (pa)

       LC 83-22206

The author analyzes examples of governmental bumbling including the Trojan horse, the U.S. involvement in Vietnam, and the British loss of the American colonies.

Includes bibliographical references

909.7 World history--18th century, 1700-1799

The **Age** of Revolution; Stuart A. Kallen, book editor. Greenhaven Press 2002 219p il maps (World history by era) lib bdg $43.70; pa $27.45
Grades: 9 10 11 12   **909.7**
1. World history—18th century 2. World history—19th century 3. United States—History—1783-1865
ISBN 0-7377-0704-6 (lib bdg); 0-7377-0703-8 (pa)
LC 2001-23579
This book examines the era between 1774 and 1848, "with articles exploring . . . changes in world governments, transportation, industrial manufacturing, music, art, and poetry." Publisher's note
Includes bibliographical references

Events that changed the world in the eighteenth century; edited by Frank W. Thackeray & John E. Findling. Greenwood Press 1998 215p il (Greenwood Press "Events that changed the world" series) $39.95
Grades: 9 10 11 12   **909.7**
1. World history—18th century
ISBN 0-313-29077-6   LC 97-21968
This "book covers Peter the Great's Reforms of Russia, the War of Spanish Succession, the First British Empire, the War of Austrian Succession and Seven Years' War, the Enlightenment, the Agricultural Revolution, the American Revolution, the Industrial Revolution, the Atlantic Slave Trade, and the French Revolution. For each event, an introductory essay provides concise, background information. An interpretative essay follows, then both the long- and short-term implications of the event."
Book Rep
Includes bibliographical references

Great events from history, The 18th century, 1701-1800; editor John Powell. Salem Press 2006 2v il map set $160
Grades: 11 12 Adult   **909.7**
1. World history—18th century
ISBN 978-1-58765-279-0; 1-58765-279-X
LC 2006-5406
Companion volume to Great lives from history, The 18th century, 1701-1800
Some essays previously published in Great events from history: North American series (1997) and Chronology of European history (1997)
"Topics include geopolitical events, social and intellectual issues, scientific developments, philosophy, and the arts. The global coverage emphasizes turning points that redirected and shaped history and helped create the modern world. Essays have an average length of 1600 words. Each one begins with a short summary of the topic and includes dates, locales, categories, key figures, text, significance, further reading, see-also references, and cross-referencing to other essays in this set and in the rest of the series. . . . An informative resource." SLJ
Includes bibliographical references

909.81 World history--19th century, 1800-1899

1800-1820: the nineteenth century; Jodie L. Zdrok, book editor. Greenhaven Press 2005 173p map (Events that changed the world) lib bdg $34.95
Grades: 7 8 9 10 11 12   **909.81**
1. World history—19th century
ISBN 0-7377-2029-8   LC 2004-52322
Events covered in this book include "the end of the Holy Roman Empire, the Louisiana Purchase, the War of 1812, and the Battle of Waterloo." Publisher's note
Includes bibliographical references

1820-1840: the nineteenth century; Jennifer Bussey, book editor. Greenhaven Press 2005 143p il map (Events that changed the world) lib bdg $34.95
Grades: 7 8 9 10 11 12   **909.81**
1. World history—19th century
ISBN 0-7377-2031-X   LC 2004-52393
"This anthology highlights the most influential events between 1820 and 1840, with special attention to the far-reaching effects those events had in world history." Publisher's note
Includes bibliographical references

1840-1860: the nineteenth century; Jodie L. Zdrok, book editor. Greenhaven Press 2005 175p il map (Events that changed the world) lib bdg $34.95
Grades: 7 8 9 10 11 12   **909.81**
1. World history—19th century
ISBN 0-7377-2033-6   LC 2004-42513
"This title encompasses the political actions, military conflicts, social movements, and scientific and cultural innovations of this period." Publisher's note
Includes bibliographical references

1860-1880: the nineteenth century; Kelly Doyle, book editor. Greenhaven Press 2005 224p il (Events that changed the world) lib bdg $34.95
Grades: 7 8 9 10 11 12   **909.81**
1. World history—19th century
ISBN 0-7377-2035-2   LC 2004-42443
Events described in this book include the abolition of slavery, the birth of new secular governments in Europe, and the beginnings of the labor movement.
Includes bibliographical references

1880-1900: the nineteenth century; Jodie L. Zdrok, book editor. Greenhaven 2004 187p il (Events that changed the world) lib bdg $34.95
Grades: 7 8 9 10 11 12   **909.81**
1. World history—19th century
ISBN 0-7377-2037-9   LC 2003-67762
Events described in this book include the birth of Adolf Hitler, the Boxer rebellion, and the discovery of radium. Both primary and secondary sources are used.
Includes bibliographical references

Events that changed the world in the nineteenth century; edited by Frank W. Thackeray & John E. Findling. Greenwood Press 1996 217p il (Greenwood Press "Events that changed the world" series) $39.95

Grades: 9 10 11 12   **909.81**

1. World history—19th century

ISBN 0-313-29076-8   LC 95-53133

This volume "covers 10 important occurrences, such as the Meiji Restoration in Japan, the freeing of the serfs in Russia, and the revolutions of 1848. . . . For each, there is an unsigned five-page history of the event, followed by a 10-page interpretative essay by a historian of the period." Booklist

Includes bibliographical references

Great events from history, The 19th century, 1801-1900; editor, John Powell. Salem Press 2006 4v il map set $360

Grades: 11 12 Adult   **909.81**

1. World history—19th century

ISBN 978-1-58765-297-4; 1-58765-297-8
       LC 2006-19789

Companion volume to Great lives from history, The 19th century, 1801-1900

Some of the essays in this work appeared in various other Salem Press sets

"These volumes cover the world's most important events and developments from 1801 through 1900. . . . Essays address important social and cultural developments in daily life: major literary movements, significant developments in art and music, trends in immigration, and progressive social legislation." Publisher's note

Includes bibliographical references

909.82   World history--20th century, 1900-1999

1900-1920: the twentieth century; Gary Zacharias, book editor. Greenhaven Press 2004 224p il map (Events that changed the world) lib bdg $34.95

Grades: 9 10 11 12   **909.82**

1. World history—20th century

ISBN 0-7377-1752-1   LC 2003-48332

"The period from 1900-1920 marked not only the beginning of a new century but also the seed of many trends and movements that would bear fruit throughout the rest of the 20th century. This book covers major events of this time period, including wars, theories, inventions, disasters, and revolutions." Publisher's note

"There's plenty to intrigue history students, who will relish seeing disparate pieces of history slide smoothly together." Booklist

Includes bibliographical references

1920-1940: the twentieth century; Sharon M. Himsl, book editor. Greenhaven Press 2004 204p il (Events that changed the world) lib bdg $34.95

Grades: 7 8 9 10   **909.82**

1. World history—20th century

ISBN 0-7377-1754-8   LC 2003-44864

"Ratification of Nineteenth Amendment, first assembly of League of Nations, . . . Mussolini's March on Rome, Lindbergh's transatlantic flight, Jazz Singer debut, Gandhi's 'Salt March', Hitler's rise, stock market crash, and 'Operation Dynamo' (rescue at Dunkirk) are among the events discussed, describing a . . . period that begins with the aftermath of World War I and ends with the outbreak of World War II." Publisher's note

Includes bibliographical references

1940-1960: the twentieth century; Jennifer Bussey, book editor. Greenhaven Press 2004 188p il (Events that changed the world) lib bdg $34.95

Grades: 7 8 9 10   **909.82**

1. World history—20th century

ISBN 0-7377-1756-4   LC 2002-192798

"The world in 1960 was a very different place than it had been in 1940. . . . How did so much change unfold in twenty years' time? This anthology retraces those fateful footsteps, presenting articles about events spanning from the attack on Pearl Harbor to the launch of Sputnik." Publisher's note

"Several articles (e.g., an excerpt describing the killing of unarmed German guards by concentration camp liberators) are vivid enough to disturb some readers. . . . There's plenty to intrigue history students, who will relish seeing disparate pieces of history slide smoothly together." Booklist

Includes bibliographical references

1960-1980: the twentieth century; Jennifer A. Bussey, book editor. Greenhaven Press 2004 176p il (Events that changed the world) $34.95

Grades: 7 8 9 10   **909.82**

1. World history—20th century

ISBN 0-7377-1758-0   LC 2003-53929

"This anthology covers the major events that shaped the world during the pivotal decades of the 1960s and 1970s. Topics covered include the Bay of Pigs invasion, the building of the Berlin Wall, U.S. president Kennedy's assassination, the first moon landing, the U.S. legalization of abortion, the Vietnam War, and the Ayatollah Khomeini's deposition of the shah of Iran." Publisher's note

Includes bibliographical references

1980-2000: the twentieth century; Bryan Grapes, book editor. Greenhaven Press 2004 187p il map (Events that changed the world) lib bdg $34.95

Grades: 7 8 9 10   **909.82**

1. World history—20th century

ISBN 0-7377-1760-2   LC 2003-53928

"This anthology follows the 1980s and 1990s as the world moved through the rise of the AIDS epidemic, the fall of the Berlin Wall and the demise of communism in Eastern Europe, the death of the Soviet Union, and the rise of the computer age. Also covered in this volume: The birth of MTV, the nuclear disaster at Chernobyl, the Chinese government's bloody crackdown in Tiananmen Square, the death of apartheid, the dissolution of Yugoslavia, and the cloning of Dolly." Publisher's note

Includes bibliographical references

Bjornlund, Britta

The Cold War ends: 1980 to the present. Lucent Bks. 2003 112p il maps (American war library, Cold War) $27.45

Grades: 7 8 9 10 **909.82**

1. Cold war 2. World politics—1991-

ISBN 1-59018-209-X   LC 2002-8590

This book examines "the evolving relationship between the United States and the Soviet Union, the roles of Ronald Reagan, Mikhail Gorbachev, and others, the democratic revolutions in Eastern Europe, and the breakup of the U.S.S.R." Publisher's note

Includes bibliographical references

The **Columbia** history of the 20th century; {edited by} Richard W. Bulliet. Columbia Univ. Press 1998 651p $62; pa $29

Grades: 11 12 Adult **909.82**

1. World history—20th century

ISBN 0-231-07628-2; 0-231-07629-0 (pa)

LC 97-39426

Scholars contribute chapters on topics ranging "from 'Ethnicity and Racism,' to 'Nationalism,' 'Communications,' 'Industry and Business,' and others. The idea is for readers to peruse those chapters that appeal to them. Articles average under 25 pages, so content is quite broad. While the level of scholarship varies a bit, overall quality is good." Libr J

Includes bibliographical references

Cook, Chris, 1945-

The Facts on File world political almanac; from 1945 to the present. 4th ed, revised by Whitney Walker. Facts on File 2000 576p hardcover o.p. pa $21.95

Grades: 9 10 11 12 **909.82**

1. World politics—1945-

ISBN 0-8160-4295-0; 0-8160-4296-9 (pa)

LC 00-44222

First published 1989

Facts and figures about post World War II national and international politics. Topics covered include: heads of state; legislatures and constitutions; treaties and alliances; population and urbanization trends; the nuclear era; terrorism.

Events that changed the world in the twentieth century; edited by Frank W. Thackeray & John E. Findling. Greenwood Press 1995 233p il (Greenwood Press "Events that changed the world" series) $39.95

Grades: 9 10 11 12 **909.82**

1. World history—20th century

ISBN 0-313-29075-X   LC 94-38488

This title offers descriptions and "analysis of the twentieth century's most important events: World War I, the Russian Revolution, the rise of Fascism, the Great Depression, World War II, the Cold War, the Chinese Revolution, the end of Colonialism and the rise of the Third World, European unification, and the collapse of the Soviet Union." Publisher's note

Includes bibliographical references

Gaddis, John Lewis

The Cold War; a new history. Penguin Press 2005 333p il $27.95

Grades: 11 12 Adult **909.82**

1. Cold war 2. World politics—1945-1991

ISBN 1-594-20062-9   LC 2005-53406

The authors "account of Soviet-U.S. relations from WWII to the collapse of the U.S.S.R." Publ Wkly

"Energetically written and lucid, . . . [this book] makes an ideal introduction to the subject." N Y Times (Late N Y Ed)

Includes bibliographical references

Great events; 1900-2001; from the editors of Salem Press. rev ed. Salem Press 2002 8v il set $475 *

Grades: 9 10 11 12 **909.82**

1. World history—20th century

ISBN 1-587-65053-3   LC 2002-2008

First published 1992

Contents: v1 1900-1920; v2 1920-1939; v3 1939-1957; v4 1957-1971; v5 1971-1984; v6 1984-1993; v7 1993-1998; v8 1998-2001

"This set revises the publisher's *The Twentieth Century: Great Events* (1992) and supplement (1996) and *The Twentieth Century: Great Scientific Achievements* (1994) and its supplement (1997). . . . Arrangement is chronological. Each volume has a complete list of contents as well as a 'Category Index' that lists entry headings alphabetically under more than 60 topics. . . . Each one-thousand-word article begins with a headline-style title that announces the event . . . followed by a sentence or two summarizing the event and its significance." Booklist

Hillstrom, Kevin

The Cold War; foreward by Christian Ostermann. Omnigraphics 2006 xx, 536p il (Primary sourcebook series) $65

Grades: 11 12 Adult **909.82**

1. Cold war 2. World politics—1945-1991

ISBN 0-7808-0934-3; 978-0-7808-0934-5

LC 2006-15330

"Examines the Cold War and its impact on America, the Soviet Union, and the world. Features include narrative overviews of key events and trends, 100+ primary source documents, chronology, glossary, bibliography, and subject index." Publisher's note

"The wide-ranging scope of documents compiled in this volume will provide AP history and social studies classes with a wealth of information for research and analysis." Libr Media Connect

Includes glossary and bibliographical references

Kallen, Stuart A., 1955-

Primary sources. Lucent Bks. 2003 112p il map (American war library, Cold War) $27.45 *

Grades: 9 10 11 12 **909.82**

1. Cold war 2. United States—Foreign relations—Soviet Union 3. Soviet Union—Foreign relations—United States

ISBN 1-59018-243-X   LC 2002-7896

This "contains documents and essays relating to the Cold War written by some of its key players including

Kallen, Stuart A., 1955- —*Continued*
diplomats, ambassadors, presidents, and premiers." Publisher's note
Includes bibliographical references

National Geographic eyewitness to the 20th century. National Geographic Soc. 1998 400p il hardcover o.p. pa $22.95 *
Grades: 11 12 Adult   **909.82**
1. World history—20th century
ISBN 0-7922-7049-5; 0-7922-8063-6 (pa)
                                        LC 98-22756
"Chapters are arranged thematically by decade and open with a six-page essay discussing each era. . . . Most useful of all are the double-page spreads for each year presenting events, people, and themes in short paragraph entries. Brief trends and trivia are listed vertically. A time line appears along the bottom of the pages. Photographs bring the discussions to life and sidebars present interesting developments and people." SLJ

Tuchman, Barbara Wertheim
The proud tower; a portrait of the world before the war, 1890-1914; [by] Barbara W. Tuchman. 1st Ballantine Books ed. Ballantine Books 1996 528p il pa $15.95
Grades: 11 12 Adult   **909.82**
1. World history—20th century 2. World history—19th century 3. Europe—Social conditions 4. United States—Social conditions
ISBN 0-345-40501-3   LC 96-96511
First published 1966 by Macmillan
The author describes prewar social conditions in the U.S., France, England and Germany.
Includes bibliographical references

Winkler, Allan M., 1945-
The Cold War; a history in documents. Oxford Univ. Press 2000 159p il maps (Pages from history) $36.95; pa $19.95 *
Grades: 9 10 11 12   **909.82**
1. Cold war 2. United States—Foreign relations—Soviet Union 3. Soviet Union—Foreign relations—United States
ISBN 0-19-512356-5; 0-19-516637-X (pa)
                                        LC 00-27270
Uses contemporary documents to explore the Cold War struggle of the 1950s and 1960s and the lasting effects on American social and cultural patterns.
Includes bibliographical references

910   Geography and travel

De Porti, Andrea, 1968-
Explorers; the most exciting voyages of discovery, from the African expeditions to the lunar landing; [English translation, Paul Holberton] Firefly Books 2005 56p il $49.95 *
Grades: 11 12 Adult   **910**

1. Explorers 2. Exploration
ISBN 1-55407-101-1
This book "details 58 expeditions from the past 150 years—from Robert Peary and Matthew Henson's trek to the North Pole in 1909 to Edmund Hillary's 1953 climb up Everest (called by Tibetans 'the mother goddess of the world') to Neil Armstrong's 'one small step' onto the moon in 1969. . . . The creative way these journeys are presented will impress armchair adventurers." Publ Wkly
Includes bibliographical references

The **DK** geography of the world. DK 2003 304p il map $29.99; pa $19.99 *
Grades: 5 6 7 8 9 10   **910**
1. Geography
ISBN 0-7894-8594-X; 0-7566-1952-1 (pa)
                                        LC 2003-269290
First published 1996
Maps and text describe countries around the world and the ways of life of the inhabitants.
"This surprisingly comprehensive and affordable reference source is a joy to browse." Voice Youth Advocates

Fleming, Fergus, 1959-
Off the map; tales of endurance and exploration; as told by Fergus Fleming. Atlantic Monthly Press 2005 518p il maps $24.95; pa $16
Grades: 11 12 Adult   **910**
1. Explorers 2. Exploration
ISBN 0-8711-3899-9; 0-8021-4272-9 (pa)
                                        LC 2005-47849
First published 2004 in the United Kingdom
This book "consists of 45 biographical essays divided into three parts. 'The Age of Reconnaissance' begins in the 13th century with Marco Polo's wanderings in the Mongol Empire. 'The Age of Inquiry' takes the reader through the 18th century and halfway into the 19th, concluding with the . . . search for Sir John Franklin in the high Arctic. 'The Age of Endeavour' proceeds from the crossing of the Australian continent by Robert Burke and William Wills in 1861 to Umberto Nobile's . . . 1928 flight to the North Pole." N Y Times Book Rev
"Almost comprehensive enough to serve as a reference, this densely packed tome supplies a bewildering wealth of information about some of humanity's most compelling adventures." Publ Wkly
Includes bibliographical references

Moore, Robert
A time to die; the untold story of the Kursk tragedy. Crown 2003 c2002 271p il maps hardcover o.p. pa $13.95
Grades: 11 12 Adult   **910**
1. Kursk (Submarine) 2. Disasters 3. Nuclear submarines
ISBN 0-609-61000-7; 1-4000-5124-X (pa)
                                        LC 2002-15802
First published 2002 in the United Kingdom
The author "recounts the story of the botched attempt to rescue the 118 men stranded at the bottom of the Barents Sea when their nuclear-powered attack submarine went down on August 12, 2000. Based on two years of interviews with the crew's families, Norwegian and

Moore, Robert—*Continued*
British rescue workers, and even some Northern Fleet officers (despite a Russian navy prohibition), Moore uncovers details that few know, and which have never been reported in the Russian press." The Bulletin of the Atomic Scientists

Neufeld, Josh
A few perfect hours and other stories from Southeast Asia and Central Europe. Alternative Comics 2004 128p il pa $12.95
Grades: 10 11 12 Adult   **910**
1. Graphic novels 2. Travel—Graphic novels 3. Southeast Asia—Graphic novels 4. Central Europe—Graphic novels 5. Autobiographical graphic novels
ISBN 1-891867-79-2
Neufeld and his girlfriend (now wife) Sari Wilson traveled through such places as Thailand and Serbia, which Neufeld recounts in this book. Chapters recounting such adventures as serving as extras in Chinese-language television and meeting monks are interspersed with informative "Travel Tips," including one Wilson wrote frankly on dealing with feminine disorders in a foreign country.
"Besides providing entertainment purely as storytelling, this graphic-format memoir gives an intimacy of people and places often missing from travel tales. . . . The lesson on the use of squat toilets alone is worth the price of admission for many would-be travelers." Voice Youth Advocates

Poole, Robert M.
Explorers house; [by] Robert Poole. Penguin Press 2004 342p pa $16
Grades: 11 12 Adult   **910**
1. National Geographic Society (U.S.)
ISBN 1-59420-032-7; 0-14-303593-2 (pa)
                                            LC 2004-50536
This is an account of the National Geographic Society founded by Alexander Graham Bell and Gardner Hubbard. In 1888 "its journal first appeared, shedding light on subjects like volcanism and botany and establishing itself as an authority in scientific and technical arcana. The organization grew, but the magazine stalled until Gilbert H. Grosvenor, a young schoolteacher, signed on as editor, and the stories of the Grosvenor family and the magazine have been linked ever since." Publ Wkly

Worldmark chronology of the nations; Timothy L. Gall, Susan Bevan Gall, editors. Gale Group 2000 4v il maps set $275
Grades: 11 12 Adult   **910**
1. Geography 2. Historical chronology
ISBN 0-7876-0521-2   LC 99-44217
"This alphabetically arranged chronology contains articles on 192 countries. Each of the volumes, 'Africa,' 'Americas,' 'Asia,' and 'Europe,' begins with a general time line of world history from prehistory to the present, providing a context for entries on individual nations. . . . Profiles begin with an overview providing general information on the country, its people, and its history, followed by a time line that consists of dated entries cover-

ing an era, a decade, or a specific year or date. These entries briefly describe key people and events that shaped the nation. Each profile ends with a bibliography." Booklist

910.3   Geography--Dictionaries, encyclopedias, gazetteers

Facts about the world's nations; edited by Michael O'Mara. Wilson, H.W. 1999 1065p maps $100
Grades: 11 12 Adult   **910.3**
ISBN 0-8242-0955-9   LC 98-51148
Original edition published 1990 in the United Kingdom with title: ITN factbook; first published 1992 in Australia with title: The SBS world guide
A sourcebook on the nations of the world and their territories. Each alphabetical entry covers: geography; history; constitution and government; international relations; economy; communications; education and welfare. A Web site section at the end of each entry provides Internet addresses for official government, embassy, and United Nations permanent mission home pages. Chapters on the Vatican and such supranational entities as the Commonwealth of Independent States and the European Union are included
Includes bibliographical references

Firefly geography dictionary. Firefly Books 2003 256p il map pa $14.95
Grades: 11 12 Adult   **910.3**
1. Geography—Dictionaries
ISBN 1-55297-838-9   LC 2003-273971
First published 1995 in the United Kingdom with title: Philip's geography dictionary
This dictionary "provides more than 1,500 entries and 130 illustrations for words and concepts in physical, human, and environmental geography. . . . Entries, arranged alphabetically, are defined in complete sentences. . . . Despite its small size, this dictionary lives up to its claim to be comprehensive. It would be valuable for readers of elementary to advanced textbooks and journal articles." Choice

Merriam-Webster's geographical dictionary. 3rd ed. Merriam-Webster 1997 26a, 1361p maps $32.95 *
Grades: 11 12 Adult   **910.3**
1. Geography—Dictionaries
ISBN 0-87779-546-0   LC 96-52365
First published 1949 with title: Webster's geographical dictionary
This guide contains data about countries, cities, and physical features. More than 48,000 entries and over 250 maps provide population, size, economic data and historical notes. Pronunciations are included and a table of foreign terms used in English is provided

Waldman, Carl
Encyclopedia of exploration; [by] Carl Waldman and Alan Wexler. Facts on File 2004 2v il map (Facts on File library of world history) set $225
Grades: 11 12 Adult   **910.3**
1. Exploration 2. Explorers 3. Voyages and travels
ISBN 0-8160-4678-6   LC 2004-10625

Waldman, Carl—*Continued*

Vol. 2 by Carl Waldman and Jon Cunningham

Contents: v. 1. The explorers -- v. 2. Places, technologies, and culture trends

"The first volume is all biographical entries with accompanying appendixes that list explorers by occupation, area(s) explored, chronology, and the respective explorers' nationality. The second volume has topical entries about all things related to exploration, such as specific areas, technologies, and routes." Am Ref Books Annu, 2005

"This set is well organized and very readable." Booklist

Includes bibliographical references

The **World** factbook 2007; [produced by] Central Intelligence Agency. US Central Intelligence Agency 2007 $60 *

Grades: 9 10 11 12   **910.3**

ISSN 0277-1527

ISBN 1-59797-109-X; 978-1-59797-109-6

Annual. First published 1981

"For each country of the world (in alphabetical order), provides brief data on geography, people, government, economy, membership in international intergovernmental organizations, communications, and defense forces. Small maps of each country; regional maps in color. Includes introductory notes, definitions, and abbreviations." Guide to Ref Books. 11th edition

Worldmark encyclopedia of the nations; [Timothy L. Gall and M. Hobby, editors] 12th ed. Thomson Gale 2007 c2006 5v il map $535

Grades: 11 12 Adult   **910.3**

1. United Nations 2. Geography—Encyclopedias 3. World history—Encyclopedias 4. World politics—Encyclopedias

ISBN 1-414410-89-1

First published 1960

"Factual and statistical information on the countries of the world, exhibited in uniform format under such rubrics as topography, population, public finance, language, and ethnic composition. Country articles appear in volumes 2 through 5, arranged geographically by continent. Volume 1 is devoted to the United Nations and its affiliated agencies. Illustrations, maps." Ref Sources for Small & Medium-sized Libr. 6th edition

910.4   Accounts of travel and facilities for travelers

Ballard, Robert D., 1942-

Return to Titanic; a new look at the world's most famous lost ship; [by] Robert D. Ballard with Michael Sweeney. National Geographic Society 2004 192p il map $30

Grades: 11 12 Adult   **910.4**

1. Titanic (Steamship) 2. Shipwrecks 3. Underwater exploration

ISBN 0-7922-7288-9   LC 2004-55930

The author reviews *Titanic's* "history and the catastrophic events that led to her demise. He describes his dream of turning the ship into a museum on the ocean floor, easily explored from above by computer. . . . It's Ballard's passion and expertise that make this book tick." Publ Wkly

Includes bibliographical references

Butler, Daniel Allen

Unsinkable: the full story of the RMS Titanic. Stackpole Bks. 1998 292p il $19.95

Grades: 11 12 Adult   **910.4**

1. Titanic (Steamship) 2. Shipwrecks

ISBN 0-8117-1814-X   LC 98-9294

Also available in paperback from Da Capo Press

This is a history "of the disaster and aftermath, drawing on first-person accounts and solid secondary sources." Libr J

Includes bibliographical references

Delaney, Frank, 1942-

Simple courage; a true story of peril on the sea. Random House 2006 300p il $24.95

Grades: 11 12 Adult   **910.4**

1. Carlsen, Henrik Kurt, 1915-1989 2. Flying Enterprise (Ship) 3. Shipwrecks

ISBN 1-4000-6524-0; 978-1-4000-6524-0

LC 2006-41766

Also available large print edition $26.95 (ISBN: 0-7393-2662-7; ISBN-13: 978-0-7393-2662-6)

This book tells the story "of Captain Kurt Carlsen and the Flying Enterprise. On Christmas Day 1951, the World War II Liberty ship Flying Enterprise began splitting apart in a North Atlantic gale, and her cargo of pig iron shifted. Captain Carlsen saw to the safe abandonment of passengers and crew, then remained aboard to help with salvage efforts. He remained aboard, accompanied only by a young radioman who leaped aboard from a rescue ship, until the Flying Enterprise was about to sink under him." Booklist

Includes bibliographical references

Heyerdahl, Thor

Kon-Tiki; across the Pacific by raft; translated by F.H. Lyon. Washington Square Press 1984 240, 48p map (Enriched classics series) pa $5.99

Grades: 11 12 Adult   **910.4**

1. Kon-Tiki Expedition (1947) 2. Pacific Ocean 3. Ethnology—Polynesia

ISBN 0-671-72652-8   LC 84-42785

Original Norwegian edition, 1948

The "story of the six men who crossed the Pacific from Peru to the Polynesians on a primitive balsa-log raft such as Peruvian natives of the fifth century used, to prove that it was possible that the legendary race that came to Easter Island and the Polynesians could have come from Peru." Wis Libr Bull

Jacobson, Mark, 1948-
12,000 miles in the nick of time; a family tale; with additional commentary by Rae Jacobson. Atlantic Monthly Press 2003 271p hardcover o.p. pa $13
Grades: 11 12 Adult   **910.4**
1. Voyages around the world
ISBN 0-87113-852-2; 0-8021-4138-2 (pa)
LC 2003-41821
"A few years ago, the Jacobsons . . . spent the summer touring Asia, the Middle East, and part of Europe on the cheap. It wasn't easy to take three middle-class American kids, ages 9 to 16, to Cambodia's Killing Fields, India's Burning Gat, or the sex-shop strewn thoroughfares of Thailand. The book recounts the many trials, tribulations, and ironies of the trip as well as its more usual wonders." SLJ
"The book is very funny—the trip doesn't go exactly as the parents plan—but it is also hugely educational, history presented as a grand adventure. The kids learned a lot, and so do we." Booklist

Junger, Sebastian
The perfect storm; a true story of men against the sea. Norton 1997 226p il map $23.95
Grades: 11 12 Adult   **910.4**
1. Storms 2. Shipwrecks
ISBN 0-393-04016-X   LC 96-42412
Also available in paperback from HarperCollins Pubs.
"With waves as high as a hundred feet and winds so strong that anemometers were torn from their moorings, the storm of the title struck unsuspecting mariners off the coast of Nova Scotia in October, 1991. Junger traces the last voyage of the Andrea Gail—a commercial swordfishing boat that was lost, with all six hands, in the storm—and his account is relentlessly suspenseful." New Yorker

Kinder, Gary
Ship of gold in the deep blue sea. Vintage Books 1999 536p il pa $15.95
Grades: 11 12 Adult   **910.4**
1. Central America (Steamship) 2. Shipwrecks
ISBN 0-375-70337-3; 978-0-375-70337-9
LC 98-52933
First published 1998 by Atlantic Monthly Press
"On September 12, 1857, the steamship Central America sank in a great storm off the coast of South Carolina and settled a mile and a half beneath the waves. Most of the 423 souls on board perished. Lost, too, was $2,189,000 (now worth $1 billion) in California gold. . . . In 1989, a group of investors and treasure salvagers equipped with the latest underwater equipment was able to bring back much of the cargo, including the largest treasure ever recorded. The discovery of this vessel and its riches led to protracted litigation between various claimants, and the case is still in the courts. Kinder has followed the story from its beginning." Libr J

Lord, Walter, 1917-2002
A night to remember. Holt & Co. 1955 209p il hardcover o.p. pa $14 *
Grades: 11 12 Adult   **910.4**

1. Titanic (Steamship) 2. Shipwrecks
ISBN 0-03-027615-2; 0-8050-7764-2 (pa)
A detailed account of "the tragic drama of that terrible night—April 4, 1912—when the 'Titanic,' the unsinkable ship, struck an iceberg and went down in the icy waters of the Atlantic." Libr J

Martin, Jesse
Lionheart; a journey of the human spirit; [by] Jesse Martin with Ed Gannon. Allen & Unwin 2002 c2000 253p il maps pa $14.95
Grades: 7 8 9 10   **910.4**
1. Voyages around the world
ISBN 1-86508-347-X
First published 2000 in Australia
"In 1999, Martin sailed around the world solo and unassisted. In a 34-foot yacht named Lionheart, the 17-year-old Australian used no fossil fuels, received no supplies or visitors, and never stepped off the boat for the entire 10-month trip. His narrative is conversational in tone and unsparingly honest, revealing his insecurities as well as a quick wit. . . . The narrative form is simple, and the book hits all the marks for scope, teen appeal, and emotion." SLJ

Middleton, Nick
Extremes: surviving the world's harshest environments. Thomas Dunne Books/St. Martin's Press 2005 260p $24.95
Grades: 11 12 Adult   **910.4**
1. Wilderness survival 2. Voyages and travels
ISBN 0-312-34266-7   LC 2005-40750
The author writes of his travels among "the Inuit of Greenland, the Biaka of Congo, the Tubu of Niger and the Kombai of Papua New Guinea." N Y Times Book Rev
"Unlike many books of its kind, the account doesn't bemoan environmental damage or displaced natives. Rather, it's a lighthearted and entertaining look at places most will never see." Publ Wkly

National Geographic expeditions atlas; foreword by Peter H. Raven. National Geographic Soc. 2000 310p il maps $40
Grades: 11 12 Adult   **910.4**
1. Voyages and travels
ISBN 0-7922-7616-7   LC 99-86883
"Organized into seven topical sections, this book . . . includes time lines, more than 220 vibrant photographs and illustrations, 60 maps recounting National Geographic's 112-year history of exploration, and first-hand accounts that introduce the reader to some of the bravest adventurers of our time, such as Jacques Cousteau, Richard Byrd, Amelia Earhart, Jane Goodall, and many more." Libr J
Includes bibliographical references

Netzley, Patricia D.
Encyclopedia of women's travel and exploration.
Oryx Press 2000 259p il $88.95
Grades: 11 12 Adult   **910.4**
1. Voyages and travels—Encyclopedias 2. Women—
Travel—Encyclopedias
ISBN 1-573-56238-6; 978-1-57356-238-6
                                        LC 00-10720
"The 315 entries, arranged alphabetically, focus on a
wide variety of women explorers, adventurers, and trav-
elers throughout history and across continents. Most en-
tries are biographical, but some examine related topics
such as accommodations, solo travel, guide books, and
mountaineering, occasionally offering perceptive insights
into women's travel experiences and motivations."
Choice
Includes bibliographical references

Open your eyes; extraordinary experiences in
faraway places; edited by Jill Davis. Viking
2003 201p il $16.99
Grades: 7 8 9 10   **910.4**
1. Voyages and travels 2. Authors, American
ISBN 0-670-03616-1
A collection of memories and stories about a variety
of travel experiences that changed the lives of such well-
known writers as Lois Lowry, Suzie Morgenstern, and
Harry Mazer
"This unusual anthology spotlights 10 people whose
lives were changed by living or traveling abroad during
their youth. . . . Though not every piece is excellent, the
voices, vivid and distinctive." Booklist

Paine, Lincoln P.
Ships of discovery and exploration. Houghton
Mifflin 2000 188p il maps pa $17
Grades: 11 12 Adult   **910.4**
1. Exploration 2. Ships
ISBN 0-395-98415-7   LC 00-40802
"A Mariner original"
A look at 125 vessels that have played significant
roles in voyages of geographical exploration and scientific discovery. The physical characteristics, construction,
and history of each ship is described. Chronologies cover
underwater archaeology sites, maritime technology, exploration, and disasters at sea. Illustrated with drawings
paintings, photographs, and maps
Includes bibliographical references

Philbrick, Nathaniel
In the heart of the sea; the tragedy of the
whaleship Essex. Viking 2000 302p il $24.95; pa
$15
Grades: 11 12 Adult   **910.4**
1. Essex (Whale-ship) 2. Shipwrecks
ISBN 0-670-89157-6; 0-14-100182-8 (pa)
                                        LC 99-53740
"On November 20, 1820, the Nantucket whaleship
Essex was rammed by a large sperm whale and sank in
the Pacific, 'just about as far from land as it was possible to be anywhere on earth.' The episode inspired Melville, but this climactic moment proves less interesting
than the story of the survivors' voyage in the ship's

whaleboats, a months-long ordeal that included madness
and cannibalism. Philbrick nicely links the experiences
aboard ship with the values of Nantucket society." New
Yorker

Read, Piers Paul, 1941-
Alive; sixteen men, seventy-two days, and
insurmountable odds—the classic adventure of
survival in the Andes. Harper Perennial 2005 398p
il pa $13.95
Grades: 11 12 Adult   **910.4**
1. Survival after airplane accidents, shipwrecks, etc.
2. Andes
ISBN 0-06-077866-0
First published 1974 by Lippincott
The author describes the extraordinary hardships endured by the survivors of a horrific plane crash in the
Andes.

Rogozinski, Jan
Pirates! brigands, buccaneers, and privateers in
fact, fiction, and legend. Facts on File 1995 398p
il $55
Grades: 11 12 Adult   **910.4**
1. Pirates
ISBN 0-8160-2761-7   LC 94-12717
Entries in this work cover "actual and fictional pirates
since the fourth century B.C., movies, operas, and fiction
about pirates, nautical slang, and terminology. There is
an emphasis throughout on differentiating pirate myth
from fact. Narratives range from a few lines to detailed
profiles of several pages. . . . Rogozinski's treatment
should have [broad] appeal given its worldwide coverage
and inclusion of films and novels from which much of
our familiarity with pirate history and lore is derived."
Libr J
Includes bibliographical references

White, Pamela
Exploration in the world of the Middle Ages,
500-1500. Facts on File 2005 176p il map
(Discovery and exploration) $40
Grades: 7 8 9 10   **910.4**
1. Exploration 2. Middle Ages
ISBN 0-8160-5264-6   LC 2004-14564
This "looks at exploration and discovery in the medieval world. Well-known adventurers like Marco Polo are
discussed as well as lesser-known stories such as a fifteenth-century Chinese emperor's exploration of Africa,
Muslim travelers, Vikings, the exploratory contributions
of pilgrims and missionaries, and the prevalence and
long-ranging impact of untrustworthy travel accounts of
the day. This . . . is an intriguing and informative resource." Voice Youth Advocates
Includes bibliographical references

911 Historical geography

Atlas of classical history; edited by Richard J.A.
Talbert. Routledge 1988 217p maps pa $37.95
Grades: 9 10 11 12   **911**
1. Historical atlases
ISBN 0-415-03463-9   LC 89-162237

Atlas of classical history—*Continued*
First published 1985 by Macmillan
"Covers Greek and Roman history from Troy and Knossos to the Roman Empire in 314 CE. The black-and-white maps, though small, are very clear. Many city maps. The text is brief, in many cases good mainly for identification, a skeletal history, or verification of a few key dates." Guide to Ref Books. 11th edition

Atlas of world history; Patrick O'Brien, general editor. Oxford Univ. Press 1999 367p il maps $85 *
Grades: 11 12 Adult   **911**
1. Historical atlases
ISBN 0-19-521567-2
Also available concise edition $45 (ISBN 0-19-521921-X)
Published in the United Kingdom with title: Philip's atlas of world history
"The volume is divided into five main chronological sections, from 'The Ancient World' to 'The Twentieth Century.' Each of these sections contains numerous two-page spreads featuring maps and accompanying essays. Following the maps are a 24-page 'Timechart,' a 32-page section called 'Events, People and Places' that features brief entries on major subjects within the maps, a 24-page index, and a 4-page bibliography." Booklist

Beck, Warren A.
Historical atlas of the American West; by Warren A. Beck and Ynez D. Haase. University of Okla. Press 1989 xlii, 78p maps hardcover o.p. pa $24.95
Grades: 11 12 Adult   **911**
1. West (U.S.)—Historical geography 2. Historical atlases
ISBN 0-8061-2193-9; 0-8061-2456-3 (pa)
                                    LC 88-40540
"Defining the West as that part of the United States lying west of the 100th meridian, Beck and Haase provide a cartographic survey of the history of the region. In addition to maps illustrating such standard themes as natural resources, exploration and travel routes, the growth of the transportation network, and Indian tribal lands, the authors have included detailed maps on such topics as the Spanish-Mexican land grants and the Mt. St. Helens's eruption. . . . This atlas is an essential purchase for most libraries." Libr J

Farrington, Karen
Historical atlas of expeditions. Checkmark Bks. 2000 189p il maps $35 *
Grades: 9 10 11 12   **911**
1. Explorers 2. Exploration 3. Voyages and travels
ISBN 0-8160-4432-5
"An overview of explorers and adventurers from 3200 B.C.E. to the late 20th century. . . . Farrington covers travels before 1600 in two chapters and divides the remainder of the book by geographic area (Asia, Africa, the Americas, the Arctic and Antarctic, and Australasia). Each section includes full-color and black-and-white photos, reproductions, maps, and time lines." SLJ
"Few titles provide such expansive and well-organized coverage of human exploration." Book Rep

Fisher, Ronald M., 1938-
National Geographic historical atlas of the United States; text adapted by Ron Fisher. National Geographic 2004 240p il map $40 *
Grades: 11 12 Adult   **911**
1. United States—Historical geography—Maps
ISBN 0-7922-6131-3   LC 2004-50421
"Beginning in 1450 and leading up to the capture of Saddam Hussein by U.S. Forces, the atlas highlights the landmark events of our nation's history in chronological order." Publisher's note

Goetzmann, William H.
The atlas of North American exploration; from the Norse voyages to the race to the Pole; [by] William H. Goetzmann, Glyndwr Williams; [cartographic director, Malcolm Swanston; maps created by Isabelle Lewis and Jacqueline Land] University of Okla. Press 1998 222p il map pa $29.95
Grades: 9 10 11 12   **911**
1. America—Exploration 2. Explorers 3. Historical atlases
ISBN 0-8061-3058-X   LC 97-45731
First published 1992
"This survey atlas, emphasizing exploration from the late 1400s to the late 1800s, is firmly directed toward a general audience. It features excellent color maps and illustrations with two-page 'spreads,' each devoted to the analysis of a particular explorer and each with extracts from the explorer's journals (translated to English if necessary). The atlas takes Columbus and his predecessors as a starting point, and covers all of North America. . . . The writers have endeavored to maintain an objective tone, and in the bibliography give full citations for works mentioned in the text." Libr J
Includes bibliographical references

Hammond atlas of United States history. Rev 2001 ed. Hammond World Atlas Corp. 2001 c1997 il map $16.95; pa $11.95 *
Grades: 9 10 11 12   **911**
1. United States—Historical geography—Maps
ISBN 0-8437-1449-2; 0-8437-1761-0 (pa)
                                    LC 2005-632483
First published 1968. Periodically revised. Title varies.
Variant title: Atlas of United States history
Includes more than sixty maps, graphs, and diagrams depicting the economic, social, political, demographic, and ecological factors that have molded American history

Magocsi, Paul R.
Historical atlas of Central Europe; [by] Paul Robert Magocsi. rev and expanded ed. University of Wash. Press 2002 274p maps (History of East Central Europe) hardcover o.p. pa $45
Grades: 11 12 Adult   **911**
1. Central Europe—Historical geography—Maps
ISBN 0-295-98193-8; 0-295-98146-6 (pa)
                                    LC 2001-27907
First published 1993 with title: Historical atlas of East Central Europe

Magocsi, Paul R.—*Continued*
"The volume is arranged chronologically, with coverage beginning about A.D. 400 (roughly the time of the demise of the Roman Empire) and continuing through the end of the 20th century. The maps and tables provide information on military affairs; population and population movements; economy; ethnolinguistic distributions; and religious, cultural, and educational institutions. All are extremely well done." SLJ

McKitterick, Rosamond
Atlas of the medieval world. Oxford University Press 2004 304p il map $45
Grades: 11 12 Adult   **911**
1. Historical atlases 2. Middle Ages
ISBN 0-19-522158-3   LC 2004-56816
First published 2003 in the United Kingdom with title: The Times medieval world
This atlas explores "through maps and narrative the millennium from the end of the Roman Empire to the colonization of the Americas. . . . The work features more than 90 digitally produced color political and thematic maps as well as hundreds of sumptuous photographs of art and architecture." Libr J
Includes bibliographical references

Nash, Gary B.
Atlas of American history; [by] Gary B. Nash and Carter Smith. Facts on File 2006 346p il map (Facts on File library of American history) $95 *
Grades: 9 10 11 12   **911**
1. United States—Historical geography—Maps
ISBN 0-8160-5952-7; 978-0-8160-5952-2
                              LC 2006-15915
This book "uses more than 200 full-color maps to help bring into focus both the dramatic events and enduring developments that have shaped our national heritage." Publisher's note
Includes bibliographical references

World history atlas; general editor, Jeremy Black. 2nd ed. Dorling Kindersley Pub. 2005 352p il map $50 *
Grades: 9 10 11 12   **911**
1. Historical atlases
ISBN 0-7566-0967-4
First published 2000 with title: Atlas of world history
"The atlas traces the entire 20,000-year history of humankind in two parts: the first focuses on major historical eras (e.g., the Crusades and European expansion), while the second covers regional history (e.g., the Ottoman Empire, the Pacific theater of World War II)." Libr J
Includes bibliographical references

912   Atlases. Maps

Aczel, Amir D.
The riddle of the compass; the invention that changed the world. Harcourt 2001 178p il maps hardcover o.p. pa $13
Grades: 11 12 Adult   **912**
1. Compass
ISBN 0-15-100506-0; 0-15-600753-3 (pa)
                              LC 00-47153
This book tracks "down the roots of the compass and tells the story of navigation through the ages." Publisher's note
Includes bibliographical references

Atlas of North America; H.J. de Blij, editor; [cartography by Philip's] Oxford University Press 2004 320p il map $125 *
Grades: 5 6 7 8 9 10   **912**
1. Atlases
ISBN 0-19-516993-X   LC 2004-45005
This "atlas of the three largest countries of North America . . . [features a] thematic section covering physical, historic, economic, urban, social, and cultural topics ranging from environmental change to religious practice and from indigenous peoples to migration patterns." Publisher's note
"This exhaustive, authoritative resource presents a dynamic view of Canada, the U.S., and Mexico." SLJ

Atlas of the world; [prepared by National Geographic Maps for the Book Division] 8th ed. National Geographic Society 2005 various paging il map $165 *
Grades: 5 6 7 8 9 10   **912**
1. Atlases
ISBN 0-7922-7543-8   LC 2004-45002
First published 1963
At head of title: National Geographic
This edition features 60 political maps, 17 thematic maps, and 10 panoramic satellite views of the world. Also includes views of all five ocean floors and both polar regions, the latest imagery from the Hubble Space Telescope, and new information from Mars. A world-thematic section addressing such global concerns as biodiversity, the world economy, and terrorism is also provided. The Web site that accompanies the atlas includes interactive maps
For a review see: Booklist, Feb. 15, 2005

The Canadian atlas; our nation, environment and people; edited by Andrew R. Byers [et al.] Reader's Digest 2005 192p il map $37.95
Grades: 9 10 11 12   **912**
1. Atlases 2. Canada—Maps
ISBN 0-88850-770-4
This atlas "introduces the geography of Canada in a series of over 30 thematic maps and explores the country's geology, climate, ecology, historical development, population demographics, and infrastructure." Libr J
"This colorful and educational look at Canada from a geographic perspective would be of use in any school library where Canada is part of the curriculum." Booklist

Firefly atlas of North America; United States, Canada & Mexico. Firefly Books 2006 272p il map $55

Grades: 11 12 Adult   **912**
1. Atlases
ISBN 978-1-55407-207-1; 1-55407-207-7

This atlas is "divided into three sections covering the United States (including Puerto Rico and the U.S. Pacific Territories), Canada and Mexico. . . . Each country section opens with a map and a color-coded legend to the regional maps that follow. All 50 U.S. states (plus Washington, D.C.), the 13 Canadian provinces and territories (including Nunavut) and Mexico's 32 states are illustrated." Publisher's note

Goode, J. Paul, 1862-1932
Goode's world atlas; Howard Veregin, editor. 21st ed. Rand McNally 2005 371p il map $49.95 *

Grades: 4 5 6 7 8 9 10 11 12 Adult   **912**
1. Atlases
ISBN 0-528-85339-2

First published 1922 with title: Goode's school atlas
At head of title: Rand McNally

"Contains thematic maps and tables showing distribution of population, minerals, manufacturing, and other subjects. Also included are metropolitan-area maps, physical-political maps of regions, geographic tables, and ocean-floor maps showing earth movement. Pronouncing index included." N Y Public Libr Book of How & Where to Look It Up
Includes bibliographical references

Hammond world atlas. 4th ed. Hammond 2002 287p il maps $75 *

Grades: 11 12 Adult   **912**
1. Atlases
ISBN 0-8437-1836-6   LC 2002-68882

First published 1992 with title: Hammond atlas of the world

Contents: Thematic section; Satellite section; Map section: Europe; Asia; Africa; Australia, New Zealand, and Central Pacific; North and Middle America; South American and polar regions; Statistical tables and index

"The fourth edition of the *Hammond World Atlas* is recommended as a first purchase among medium-sized atlases for academic, public, and high school libraries. It is a complete revision with new material, and, most importantly, the maps are fantastic." Booklist

The **road** atlas '07: U.S., Canada, Mexico; by Rand McNally and Company. Rand McNally 2007 138p il map pa $13.95 *

Grades: 11 12 Adult   **912**
1. United States—Maps 2. Road maps
ISBN 0-528-95826-7

Also available in spiral-binding with travel guide $24.95

"More than 350 detailed city maps"
First published 1924

"Road maps of each state in the United States, Canada, and Mexico. Distances shown on the maps. Index of place names and mileage charts included." Ref Sources for Small & Medium-sized Libr. 6th edition

915 Geography of and travel in Asia

Polo, Marco, 1254-1323?
The travels of Marco Polo; edited and revised from William Marsden's translation, by Manuel Komroff; introduction by Jason Goodwin. Modern Library pbk. ed. Modern Library 2001 322p map pa $13.95

Grades: 11 12 Adult   **915**
1. Asia—Description and travel 2. Voyages and travels
ISBN 0-375-75818-6   LC 2001-45030

Also available in paperback from Penguin Bks.

An autobiographical account of Marco Polo's thirteenth century travels in Asia.

915.1 Geography of travel in China and adjacent areas

Salzman, Mark
Iron & silk. Random House 1987 c1986 211p hardcover o.p. pa $12.95

Grades: 11 12 Adult   **915.1**
1. China—Description and travel 2. Martial arts
ISBN 0-394-55156-7; 0-394-75511-1 (pa)
                                          LC 86-11846

The author tells of his two years teaching English to medical students in China's Hunan Province following his graduation from Yale University in 1982.

This book is "not so much a treatise on modern Chinese mores as a series of telling vignettes. . . . [The author] describes his encounter with Pan Qingfu, the country's foremost master of wushu, the traditional Chinese martial art." Time

916 Geography of and travel in Africa

Bangs, Richard
Mystery of the Nile; the epic story of the first descent of the world's deadliest river; [by] Richard Bangs and Pasquale Scaturro. G.P. Putnam's Sons 2005 294p il map $25.95; pa $16

Grades: 11 12 Adult   **916**
1. Nile River
ISBN   0-399-15262-8;   978-0-399-15262-7; 0-451-21755-1 (pa); 978-0-451-21755-4 (pa)
                                          LC 2004-60164

"Scaturro and his partner, Gordon Brown, led an expedition that on April 28, 2004, completed the first descent of the Blue Nile River; it took 114 days. . . . Bangs relied on Scaturro's journals in writing this book. He describes the journey's perils—dangerous rapids, armed guerrillas, man-eating crocodiles, polluted water, temperatures as high as 125 degrees, sandstorms, windstorms, and exhaustion. . . . This is a moving account of an incredible journey." Booklist

916.6 West Africa and offshore islands

Benanav, Michael
Men of salt; across the Sahara with the caravan of white gold. Lyons Press 2006 220p il map $23.95
Grades: 11 12 Adult   **916.6**
1. Sahara Desert—Description and travel 2. Salt
ISBN 1-59228-772-7; 978-1-59228-772-7
     LC 2005-23205
The author describes his experiences after he "joined what is known as the Caravan of White Gold—so-called because the salt was once literally worth its weight in gold—on its mission into the deadly heart of the Sahara to haul back gleaming slabs of solid salt for sale at market." Publisher's note
"Even if readers don't find the idea of spending 40 harrowing days with a caravan crossing some of the world's most unforgiving desert as enticing as Benanav does, that doesn't mean they won't quickly devour his thrilling account of that otherworldly journey." Publ Wkly
Includes bibliographical references

917 Geography of and travel in North America

The **Columbia** gazetteer of North America; edited by Saul B. Cohen. Columbia Univ. Press 2000 1157, 24p il $156
Grades: 11 12 Adult   **917**
1. North America—Gazetteers
ISBN 0-231-11990-9   LC 00-27512
"This work includes more than 50,000 entries covering every incorporated place and country in the United States, along with many unincorporated places and physical features throughout North America. Arranged alphabetically, each entry includes a pronunciation guide, location information, and longitude and latitude where appropriate. If the listing is a municipality, brief population figures are provided as well. . . . Color maps of the physical regions of North America, along with political maps of the region, are included as reference points."
Am Ref Books Annu, 2001

Cox, Caroline, 1954-
Opening up North America, 1497-1800; [by] Caroline Cox, Ken Albala. Facts on File 2005 196p il map (Discovery and exploration) $40 *
Grades: 9 10 11 12   **917**
1. Explorers 2. America—Exploration
ISBN 0-8160-5261-1   LC 2004-10500
Contents: Triumph and disappointment: 1789-1793 -- The race for spices and the land of codfish: 1497-1509 -- France and Spain along the Mid-Atlantic coast: 1504-1536 -- Jacques Cartier's voyages: 1534-1543 -- Spanish, French, and English failures: mid-16th century -- Europeans colonize and contest northeastern America: early 17th century -- The French lead the way: 1607-1635 -- Furs, friars, and French expansion: 1635-1673 -- La Salle's adventures and wartime misery: 1673-1715 -- Gaining knowledge—coming to blows: 1715-1756 -- Wartime and exploration: 1754-1783 -- In the footsteps of MacKenzie: 1783-1800 -- North America in 1800
Includes bibliographical references

Isserman, Maurice
Exploring North America, 1800-1900. Facts on File 2005 198p il map (Discovery and exploration) $40 *
Grades: 9 10 11 12   **917**
1. Explorers 2. West (U.S.)—Exploration
ISBN 0-8160-5263-8   LC 2004-11587
This book "offers insight into various events and themes that occurred in the exploration of North America from 1800 to 1900. Powell at the Grand Canyon, Thomas Jefferson's 'other explorers' (a separate volume discusses Lewis and Clark), the explorations of Alaska and California, the role of the U.S. Army Corps of Engineers, and the contributions of fur traders to exploration are discussed." Voice Youth Advocates
Includes bibliographical references

917.3 Geography of and travel in the United States

The **Cambridge** gazetteer of the United States and Canada; a dictionary of places; edited by Archie Hobson. Cambridge Univ. Press 1995 743p maps $80 *
Grades: 11 12 Adult   **917.3**
1. United States—Gazetteers 2. Canada—Gazetteers
ISBN 0-521-41579-9   LC 95-8898
The over 12,000 listings for places in the U.S. and Canada include entries for municipalities, states, countries, geographical features, notable neighborhoods, regional names, and a few legendary places. Includes definitions of about 170 geographical terms
"The inclusion of such a wide variety of places, from streets and ballparks to battlefields and forests, makes this a valuable work that will be welcome in all reference departments." Booklist

Curtis, Nancy C.
Black heritage sites; an African American odyssey and finder's guide. American Lib. Assn. 1996 677p il $75
Grades: 11 12 Adult   **917.3**
1. Historic sites 2. African Americans—History
ISBN 0-8389-0643-5   LC 95-5788
Also available in a two volume paperback edition from New Press
This "guide locates significant places in African-American history and supplies . . . recent addresses, phone numbers, and visitors' information. . . . Organized by region, a historical essay introduces each section, presenting the culture and history in that area." Publisher's note

Ferris, Gary W.
Presidential places; a guide to the historic sites of U.S. presidents; [by] Gary Ferris. Blair 1999 284p il pa $15.95
Grades: 11 12 Adult **917.3**
1. Presidents—United States—Homes 2. Historic sites 3. United States—Description and travel
ISBN 0-89587-176-9 LC 98-50395
This is a "guide to historic places of interest relating to all the American presidents. Included are, among other things, presidential birthplaces, where they lived, where they went to school, the churches they attended, where they are buried, and the monuments, museums, and libraries dedicated to their lives and administrations." Libr J

Includes bibliographical references

National Geographic guide to the national parks of the United States. 5th ed. National Geographic Society 2006 480p il pa $25 *
Grades: 11 12 Adult **917.3**
1. National parks and reserves—United States
ISBN 0-7922-5322-1
First published 1989
This guide provides information on each of the fifty national parks, including things to do, campgrounds and accommodations, and facilities for the disabled.

National Geographic guide to the state parks of the United States; prepared by the Book Division, National Geographic Society. 2nd ed. National Geographic Soc. 2004 384p il maps pa $24
Grades: 11 12 Adult **917.3**
1. Parks—United States
ISBN 0-7922-6628-5 LC 2003-61515
First published 1997
A guide to more than 200 parks in all 50 states. Each entry provides information on: outstanding scenery and nature; historic and cultural sites; recreational activities; wildlife watching; camping and lodging. 32 maps and 250 color photographs accompany the text.

917.9 Geography of and travel in Great Basin and Pacific Coast states

Brower, Kenneth, 1944-
Yosemite; an American treasure; prepared by the Special Publications Division. National Geographic Soc. 1990 199p il map $15
Grades: 11 12 Adult **917.9**
1. Yosemite National Park (Calif.)
ISBN 0-87044-789-0 LC 90-5655
Text and photographs "chronicle how rivers of ice shaped the valley and relate the saga of Yosemite—from the time it was the secret refuge of the Ahwahneechee Indians through its first one hundred years as a national park. . . . Brower details the captivating variety of Yosemite's plants and animals. He portrays, too, the people." Publisher's note
Includes bibliographical references

919 Geography of and travel in Pacific Ocean Islands

Vail, Martha
Exploring the Pacific. Facts on File 2005 162p il map (Discovery and exploration) $40
Grades: 9 10 11 12 **919**
1. Explorers 2. Exploration 3. Pacific Ocean
ISBN 0-8160-5258-1 LC 2004-6807
This book "features the travels of Europeans such as Ferdinand Magellan and James Cook, but also looks at early Polynesian voyages and more recent explorers." SLJ
Includes bibliographical references

920 Biography

Books of biography are arranged as follows: 1. Biographical collections (920) 2. Biographies of individuals alphabetically by name of biographee (92)

Aaseng, Nathan, 1953-
Athletes. Facts on File 1995 xxv, 118p il (American Indian lives) $25 *
Grades: 9 10 11 12 **920**
1. Athletes 2. Native Americans—Biography
ISBN 0-8160-3019-7 LC 94-12469
The author profiles a number of Native American athletes, including Jim Thorpe, Olympic track star Billy Mills, and baseball stars Harley Bender, John Meyers and Allie Reynolds
This book is "written in crisp sports journalistic style. . . . A welcome addition to Native American, biography, and sports collections." Booklist
Includes bibliographical references

Black inventors. Facts on File 1997 128p il (American profiles) $25 *
Grades: 7 8 9 10 **920**
1. African American inventors 2. Inventions
ISBN 0-8160-3407-9 LC 96-40486
"Aaseng tells of 10 black inventors, the problems they overcame, and the often slow, frustrating road to ingenious achievement. A bibliography, a chronology, and photographs supplement each chapter as do patent drawings where appropriate." Booklist

Abdul-Jabbar, Kareem, 1947-
Black profiles in courage; a legacy of African American achievement; [by] Kareem Abdul-Jabbar and Alan Steinberg; foreword by Henry Louis Gates, Jr. Morrow 1996 xxiv, 232p il hardcover o.p. pa $13
Grades: 11 12 Adult **920**
1. African Americans—Biography
ISBN 0-688-13097-6; 0-380-81341-6 (pa)
LC 96-26245
This book "profiles the historical achievements of 11 historical black figures from Estevanico de Dorantes to Rosa Parks." Libr J

Abdul-Jabbar, Kareem, 1947-—*Continued*
The authors have provided "interesting and nuanced accounts of heroic African Americans whose accomplishments changed U.S. history. . . . Although Abdul-Jabbar is highly critical of past and present racism in the U.S., he gives credit to the abolitionist movement and leaders such as William Lloyd Garrison for their efforts toward ending slavery." Publ Wkly
Includes bibliographical references

Aikman, David, 1944-
Great souls; six who changed the century. Lexington Books 2003 388p pa $17
Grades: 11 12 Adult   **920**
ISBN 0-7391-0438-1
First published 1998 by Word Pub.
The author interviews six people, "Billy Graham, Nelson Mandela, Aleksandr Solzhenitsyn, Mother Teresa, Pope John Paul II, and Elie Wiesel. He explains how each of these luminaries personify specific virtues that are sorely needed today: salvation, forgiveness, truth, compassion, human dignity, and remembrance." Publisher's note
Includes bibliographical references

American first ladies; editor, Robert P. Watson. 2nd ed. Salem Press 2006 446p il $142
Grades: 9 10 11 12   **920**
1. Presidents' spouses—United States
ISBN 978-1-58765-271-4; 1-58765-271-4
        LC 2006-54
First published 2002
"The main text contains 44 biographical entries arranged chronologically. Coverage includes presidents' wives, spouses who died before their husbands became president, and female relatives who performed First Lady duties for unmarried or widowed presidents. . . . [This book] is enlightening and highly readable." Booklist
Includes bibliographical references

Angelo, Bonnie
First families; the impact of the White House on their lives. Morrow 2005 336p il $25.95; pa $15.95
Grades: 11 12 Adult   **920**
1. White House (Washington, D.C.) 2. Presidents—United States—Family
ISBN 0-06-056356-7; 0-06-056358-3 (pa)
        LC 2005-41474
Also available Thorndike Press large print edition
The author "takes readers inside the lives of the presidential families." Libr J
"Relying heavily on the recollections and memoirs of presidential family members, White House staff, and D.C. journalists, this chatty slice of Americana is chock-full of fun First Family facts." Booklist
Includes bibliographical references

Benson, Sonia
Development of the industrial U.S.: Biographies; [by] Sonia G. Benson; Carol Brennan, contributing writer; Jennifer York Stock, project editor. UXL 2006 lvi, 252p il $63
Grades: 9 10 11 12   **920**
1. Industries—United States 2. Industrial revolution
ISBN 1-4144-0176-0   LC 2005-16350
"Subjects range from social workers to society divas and from industrialists to labor organizers and political activists. Articles average about 10 pages and include portraits, illustrations, and sidebars." Booklist
Includes bibliographical references

Black leaders of the nineteenth century; edited by Leon Litwack and August Meier. University of Ill. Press 1988 344p il (Blacks in the new world) pa $22 hardcover o.p. *
Grades: 9 10 11 12   **920**
1. African Americans—Biography
ISBN 0-252-06213-2 (pa)   LC 87-19439
"Including individual essays on the famous, such as Frederick Douglass and Harriet Tubman, as well as a general discussion of black Reconstructionist leaders at the grass roots, this scholarly collection provides in-depth information." Booklist
Includes bibliographical references

Bradley, Michael J., 1956-
The age of genius; 1300 to 1800. Facts On File 2006 162p il (Pioneers in mathematics) $29.95
Grades: 7 8 9 10   **920**
1. Mathematics—History 2. Mathematicians
ISBN 0-8160-5424-X   LC 2005-32354
This volume presents profiles of mathematicians such as "Viete, Napier, Fermat, Pascal, Newton, Leibniz, Euler, and Agnesi. . . . The last chapter profiles Benjamin Banneker, an African-American from the colonial period in America." Sci Books Films
Includes glossary and bibliographical references

The birth of mathematics; ancient times to 1300. Facts on File 2006 148p il (Pioneers in mathematics) $29.95
Grades: 7 8 9 10   **920**
1. Mathematics—History 2. Mathematicians
ISBN 0-8160-5423-1   LC 2005-30563
The author "explores in exact detail the mathematical advances and other discoveries of 10 early mathematicians, from Thales of Miletus to Leonardo Fibonnaci. Illustrated with many mathematical figures and equations." Booklist
Includes glossary and bibliographical references

The foundations of mathematics; 1800 to 1900. Facts On File 2006 162p il (Pioneers in mathematics) $29.95
Grades: 7 8 9 10   **920**
1. Mathematics—History 2. Mathematicians
ISBN 0-8160-5425-8   LC 2005-33736
This volume presents information on mathematicians such as Augusta Ada Lovelace, Marie-Sophie Germain, Mary Fairfax Somerville, Evariste Galois, Georg Cantor, and Henri Poincare.
Includes glossary and bibliographical references

Bradley, Michael J., 1956-—*Continued*

Mathematics frontiers; 1950 to the present. Facts on File 2006 148p il (Pioneers in mathematics) $29.95
Grades: 7 8 9 10 **920**
  1. Mathematics—History 2. Mathematicians
  ISBN 0-8160-5427-4   LC 2005-36154
This volume presents profiles of mathematicians such as John Nash, Stephen Hawking, Julia Robinson, Ernest Wilkins, Jr., John Conway, Fan Chung, Andrew Wiles, and Sarah Flannery.
Includes glossary and bibliographical references

Modern mathematics; 1900 to 1950. Facts on File 2006 164p il (Pioneers in mathematics) $29.95
Grades: 7 8 9 10 **920**
  1. Mathematics—History 2. Mathematicians
  ISBN 0-8160-5426-6   LC 2005-36152
This volume presents profiles of mathematicians such as Alan Turing, David Hilbert, Norbert Wiener, Grace Chisholm Young, Amalie Emmy Noether, and Grace Murray Hopper.
Includes glossary and bibliographical references

Bruno, Leonard C.

Math and mathematicians; the history of math discoveries around the world; Lawrence W. Baker, editor. U.X.L 1999-2002 4v il set $235 *
Grades: 7 8 9 10 **920**
  1. Mathematicians 2. Mathematics
  ISBN 1-4144-0494-8   LC 99-32424
v1 and v2 available as a 2 volume set $120; v3 and v4 also available separately pa $67
Compilation of biographies, 50 to 60 per volume, of mathematicians from throughout history and articles describing math concepts and principles.
"This effective resource is marked by its attention to detail and variety of information. Readers can readily cross-reference concepts, people, and discoveries. Easy to use, this wonderful reference will be appropriate for middle, high school, and public libraries." Voice Youth Advocates [review of vols 1 & 2]
Includes glossary and bibliographical references

Bussing-Burks, Marie, 1958-

Influential economists. Oliver Press 2003 160p il (Profiles) $19.95
Grades: 7 8 9 10 **920**
  1. Economists
  ISBN 1-881508-72-2   LC 2001-59310
Presents information on the lives and work of the economists Thomas Gresham, Adam Smith, Thomas Robert Malthus, Karl Marx, John Maynard Keynes, Milton Friedman, and Alan Greenspan
"The author discusses sometimes complex theories in a straightforward, jargon-free text accessible to most sophisticated teen readers. . . . Informative, well-written, and fairly interesting." Booklist
Includes glossary and bibliographical references

Butts, Edward, 1951-

She dared; true stories of heroines, scoundrels, and renegades; [by] Ed Butts; illustrated by Heather Collins. Tundra Bks. 2005 121p il pa $8.95
Grades: 6 7 8 9 **920**
  1. Women—Biography 2. Canada—Biography
  ISBN 0-88776-718-4
This "details the lives of some of Canada's most famous and infamous women. The stories showcase explorers, spies, criminals, and pioneers in a variety of career fields. Organized chronologically from the 16th to the mid-20th century, this 12-chapter offering is historically sound and well researched." SLJ

Carey, Charles W.

American inventors, entrepreneurs, and business visionaries; {by} Charles W. Carey, Jr. Facts on File 2002 xx, 410p il (American biographies) $65
*
Grades: 11 12 Adult **920**
  1. Inventors 2. Businesspeople 3. United States—Biography
  ISBN 0-8160-4559-3   LC 2001-53252
"More than 280 individuals from the seventeenth through twentieth centuries who helped change the American economy are profiled here. . . . Each entry provides birth date (and death date where applicable), followed by a page or two on the person's life and innovations, and concludes with a brief further reading list. . . . This volume is worthy of inclusion in reference collections of public, academic, and high-school libraries. Its content is wide-ranging and its entries provide interesting reading." Booklist
Includes bibliographical references

Cropper, William H.

Great physicists; the life and times of leading physicists from Galileo to Hawking. Oxford Univ. Press 2001 500p il hardcover o.p. pa $19.95 *
Grades: 11 12 Adult **920**
  1. Physicists
  ISBN 0-19-513748-5; 0-19-517324-6 (pa)
            LC 2001-21611
"Among the scientists presented are Galileo, Newton, Bohr, Einstein, Gibbs, Faraday, Marie Curie, Rutherford, Chandrasekhar, and Hawking." Sci Books Films
The author "incorporates nothing beyond the ken of high-school calculus students. . . . His reworking of the abundant extant biographical material enhances the appeal of his book for reflective science students." Booklist
Includes bibliographical references

Cullen, Katherine E.

Science, technology, and society; the people behind the science; [by] Katherine Cullen. Chelsea House 2006 xx, 172p il (Pioneers in science) $29.95
Grades: 9 10 11 12 **920**
  1. Scientists
  ISBN 0-8160-5468-1; 978-0-8160-5468-8
            LC 2004-30605

Cullen, Katherine E.—*Continued*

This book "looks at 10 pioneers who have changed the way society views science and technology forever. Each chapter contains . . . information on the scientist's childhood, research, discoveries, and lasting contributions to the field and concludes with a chronology and a list of print and Internet references specific to that individual." Publisher's note

"Readers with substantially different levels of scientific knowledge will find the book comprehensible and interesting." Sci Books Films

Includes bibliographical references

Davis, Sampson

The pact: three young men make a promise and fulfill a dream; by Samson Davis, George Jenkins, and Remeck Hunt; with Lisa Frazier Page. Riverhead Bks. 2002 248p hardcover o.p. pa $14

Grades: 11 12 Adult   **920**

1. African Americans—Biography 2. Physicians

ISBN 1-57322-216-X; 1-57322-989-X (pa)

LC 2001-59647

"Three young black men in the medical professions (a dentist, an emergency-room physician, and an internist) recall an informal pact they made as youths that guided them out of their inner-city Newark neighborhoods and into successful careers. . . . In their own voices, these three young men tell a compelling story that will inspire other young people to form and value supportive, long-term friendships." Booklist

Denlinger, Elizabeth Campbell

Before Victoria; extraordinary women of the British Romantic era; by Elizabeth Campbell Denlinger; foreword by Lyndall Gordon. Columbia University Press 2005 188p il $41.50 *

Grades: 11 12 Adult   **920**

1. Women—Great Britain 2. Great Britain—History—19th century

ISBN 0-231-13630-7   LC 2004-59267

"Published on the occasion of the exhibition, Before Victoria: extraordinary women of the British Romantic era, presented at the New York Public Library, Humanities and Social Sciences Library, D. Samuel and Jeane H. Gottesman Exhibition Hall, April 8-July 30, 2005" Verso of title page

This book "offers portraits of a group of women who were scientists, artists, writers, poets, philanthropists and reformers during the Romantic Era and details how their accomplishments changed the social and economic landscape for women." Univ Press Books for Public and Second Sch Libr, 2006

Includes bibliographical references

Distinguished African American scientists of the 20th century; {by} James H. Kessler {et al.}; with Sigrid Berge, portrait artist, and Alyce Neukirk, computer graphics artist. Oryx Press 1996 382p il $73.95 *

Grades: 7 8 9 10   **920**

1. Scientists 2. African Americans—Biography

ISBN 0-89774-955-3   LC 95-43880

"One hundred famous and not-so-famous African American scientists (both living and dead) are covered in this biographical reference. . . . Men and women accomplished in anthropology, biology, chemistry, engineering, geology, mathematics, medicine, and physics are included. Those profiled include lesser-known scientists such as Christine Darden (an engineer with NASA) as well as the better known, e.g., George Washington Carver." Libr J

Includes bibliographical references

Dunn, Brad, 1973-

When they were 22; 100 famous people at the turning point in their lives. Andrews McMeel Pub. 2006 179p $12.95

Grades: 9 10 11 12   **920**

1. Celebrities

ISBN 978-0-7407-5810-2; 0-7407-5810-1

LC 2005-57170

This book "tells the stories of famous people and the fateful events and choices they faced at the all-important age of 22. . . . [The personalities profiled range from] writers, actors, and musicians to politicians, hip-hop moguls, criminals, and porn stars." Publisher's note

Includes bibliographical references

Earls, Irene

Young musicians in world history. Greenwood Press 2002 139p il $44.95

Grades: 9 10 11 12   **920**

1. Musicians

ISBN 0-313-31442-X   LC 2001-40559

Contents: Louis Armstrong; Johann Sebastian Bach; Ludwig van Beethoven; Pablo Casals; Sarah Chang; Ray Charles; Charlotte Church; Bob Dylan; John Lennon; Midori; Wolfgang Mozart; Niccolo Paganini; Isaac Stern

Profiles thirteen musicians who achieved high honors and fame before the age of twenty-five, representing many different time periods and musical styles

"A useful introduction to some of the musical giants of the last four centuries." SLJ

Includes glossary and bibliographical references

Ellsberg, Robert, 1955-

Blessed among all women; women saints, prophets, and witnesses for our time. Crossroad Pub. 2005 316p $19.95; pa $16.95

Grades: 9 10 11 12   **920**

1. Christian saints 2. Religious biography 3. Women—Biography

ISBN 0-8245-2251-6; 0-8245-2439-X (pa)

LC 2005-11363

Companion volume to All saints (1997)

The author presents short biographies of 136 women he considers holy. The "entries are grouped according to the virtues of the Beatitudes, an arrangement that reflects Ellsberg's definition of saints as 'people who made the Gospel concrete'. . . . Although Ellsberg is yet another man narrating tales of women saints, his accounts are far from one-dimensional. The women he depicts are fully human, which makes them useful spiritual guides." America

Includes bibliographical references

Evans, Harold
They made America; [by] Harold Evans, with Gail Buckland and David Lefer. Little, Brown 2004 496p $40; pa $18.95 *
Grades: 11 12 Adult   **920**
1. Inventors 2. Inventions
ISBN 0-316-27766-5; 0-316-01385-4 (pa)
LC 2003-65954
The author "profiles 70 of America's leading inventors, entrepreneurs and innovators, some better known than others. Along with such obvious choices as Henry Ford, Thomas Edison and the Wright brothers, Evans profiles Lewis Tappan (an abolitionist who dreamed up the idea of credit ratings), Gen. Georges Doriot (pioneer of venture capital) and Joan Ganz Cooney, of the Children's Television Workshop." Publ Wkly

First daughters: letters between U.S. presidents and their daughters; {compiled by} Gerard W. Gawalt and Ann G. Gawalt. Black Dog & Leventhal Publishers 2004 320p il $17.95
Grades: 9 10 11 12   **920**
1. Presidents—United States—Children 2. Presidents—United States 3. Letters
ISBN 1-57912-370-8   LC 2004-13803
"The Gawalts offer a look at the lives of first daughters through letters between them and their fathers. The selections range from chatty notes to insights into the political ambitions of the country's leaders. The text includes supplementary information about each correspondent, and puts each letter into a historical context. . . . An excellent primary resource for American history students." SLJ

Ford, Carin T.
Legends of American dance and choreography; [by] Carin Ford. Enslow Pubs. 2000 112p (Collective biographies) lib bdg $20.95
Grades: 9 10 11 12   **920**
1. Dancers 2. Choreographers
ISBN 0-7660-1378-2   LC 99-38818
Profiles ten influential and dedicated dancers and choreographers who worked in America, including Martha Graham, Fred Astaire, and Mikhail Baryshnikov
"A rich portrait of the vitality and the diversity of dance in America throughout the 20th century. . . . This collective biography may whet the appetite of young readers and encourage them to seek longer accounts of these luminaries of the dance world." SLJ
Includes bibliographical references

Freedman, Russell
Indian chiefs. Holiday House 1987 151p il lib bdg $22.95; pa $12.95
Grades: 6 7 8 9   **920**
1. Native Americans—Biography
ISBN 0-8234-0625-3 (lib bdg); 0-8234-0971-6 (pa)
LC 86-46198
This "book chronicles the lives of six renowned Indian chiefs, each of whom served as a leader during a critical period in his tribe's history. . . . The text relates information about the lives of each chief and aspects of Indian/white relationships that illuminate his actions. Interest-

ing vignettes and quotations are well integrated into the narrative as are dramatic accounts of battles. While the tone of the text is nonjudgmental, an underlying sympathy for the Indians' situation is apparent." Horn Book
Includes bibliographical references

Garrison, Mary, 1952-
Slaves who dared; the stories of ten African-American heroes. White Mane Kids 2002 142p il $19.95 *
Grades: 9 10 11 12   **920**
1. Slavery—United States 2. African Americans—History
ISBN 1-57249-272-4   LC 2002-22666
"Garrison does a great job of weaving into each narrative many actual quotes, illustrations . . . and the drama of how and where the stories were recorded." Booklist
Includes bibliographical references

Gates, Henry Louis
The African-American century; how Black Americans have shaped our country; {by} Henry Louis Gates, Jr. and Cornel West. Free Press 2000 414p il hardcover o.p. pa $16 *
Grades: 11 12 Adult   **920**
1. African Americans—Biography 2. African Americans—Intellectual life
ISBN 0-684-86414-2; 0-684-86415-0 (pa)
LC 00-63596
"Gates and West have listed and written biographies of their choices of the 100 most important and influential [African Americans] of the . . . twentieth century. In their opinion the subjects that they have selected have made significant impacts and contributions to American society. . . . The entries are arranged by decade and by the person's period of prominence in society, 1900-1909 through 1990-1999. Profiles include Madame C.J. Walker, Langston Hughes, Carter G. Woodson, Paul Robeson, Thurgood Marshall, and Colin Powell." MultiCult Rev
Includes bibliographical references

Goldman, Elizabeth, 1949-
Believers; spiritual leaders of the world. Oxford Univ. Press 1995 190p il (Oxford profiles) lib bdg $40
Grades: 9 10 11 12   **920**
1. Religious biography
ISBN 0-19-508240-0   LC 94-41673
This volume contains "biographical profiles of 43 religious and spiritual leaders. . . . The two-to-five page essays are arranged chronologically and span from the time of Moses to living leaders such as Tenzin Gyatso (the Dalai Lama) and Desmond Tutu. Black-and-white photographs, drawings, and reproductions appear throughout." SLJ
"Unlike many books about religion, this is very accessible and fact oriented, yet thought provoking." Booklist
Includes bibliographical references

Hanes, Richard Clay, 1946-

Crime and punishment in America, Biographies; [by] Richard C. Hanes and Kelly Rudd; Sarah Hermsen, project editor. UXL 2005 191, lixp il (Crime and punishment in America reference library) $60

Grades: 9 10 11 12   **920**

1. Criminals 2. Administration of criminal justice
ISBN 0-7876-9167-4   LC 2004-17066

This book "includes entries on important figures, such as Jane Addams, Allan Pinkerton, Clarence Darrow, Senator Estes Kefauver and others." Publisher's note

Includes bibliographical references

Hatch, Robert

The hero project; 2 teens, 1 notebook, 13 extraordinary interviews; by Robert Hatch and William Hatch. McGraw-Hill 2006 204p pa $14.95 *

Grades: 6 7 8 9   **920**

ISBN 0-07-144904-3   LC 2005017518

Contents: Introduction; Sample letter; Pete Seeger; Madeleine L'Engle; Florence Griffith-Joyner; Jimmy Carter; Orson Scott Card; Yo Yo Ma; Elouise Cobell; Carroll Spinney; Desmond Tutu; Lance Armstrong and Linda Kelly Armstrong; Steven Wozniak; Dolores Huerta; Jackie Chan

This is a collection of interviews by two teenaged brothers with some of their heroes.

"The selections are candid and thoughtful, with the boys asking questions about political and spiritual beliefs as well as queries about childhood heroes and family pets." SLJ

Hillstrom, Kevin

American Civil War: biographies; {by} Kevin Hillstrom and Laurie Collier Hillstrom; Lawrence W. Baker, editor. U.X.L 2000 2v il set $110

Grades: 9 10 11 12   **920**

1. United States—History—1861-1865, Civil War—Biography
ISBN 0-7876-3820-X   LC 99-46920

This set "chronicles the lives of 60 famous and lesser-known men and women, including abolitionists, spies, commanders, and writers." SLJ

Vietnam War: biographies; {by} Kevin Hillstrom and Laurie Collier Hillstrom; Diane Sawinski, editor. U.X.L 2001 2v il set $110 *

Grades: 7 8 9 10   **920**

1. Vietnam War, 1961-1975—Biography 2. United States—Biography
ISBN 0-7876-4884-1   LC 00-56378

This "focuses on 60 important figures, including military and political leaders (Spiro Agnew, Ngo Dinh Diem, Pol Pot), activists (Daniel Berrigan, Jane Fonda), writers (Le Ly Hayslip, Tim O'Brien), and prominent veterans (Ron Kovic, John McCain) on both sides of the conflict. . . . A picture of each personality accompanies the informative text." Booklist

Includes bibliographical references

Howes, Kelly King

World War II: biographies; {by} Kelly K. Howes; edited by Christine Slovey. U.X.L 1999 xxxiii, 288p il $60

Grades: 9 10 11 12   **920**

1. World War, 1939-1945—Biography
ISBN 0-7876-3895-1   LC 99-27166

"In addition to political and military leaders, the 31 alphabetical entries in *Biographies* include conscientious objector Franz Jaggerstatter, journalists Dorothy Thompson and Ernie Pyle, physicist J. Robert Oppenheimer, and Holocaust victim Edith Stein. The profiles range in length from 6 to 13 pages and most contain at least one black-and-white photo. Sidebars cover myriad topics such as Shintoism and examples of the Navajo code." SLJ

Includes bibliographical references

Invisible giants; fifty Americans that shaped the nation but missed the history books; edited by Mark C. Carnes. Oxford Univ. Press 2002 316p il hardcover o.p. pa $19.95

Grades: 11 12 Adult   **920**

1. United States—Biography
ISBN 0-19-515417-7; 0-19-516883-6 (pa)
                                        LC 2001-58785

"All American National Biography entries copyright 2000 by the American Council of Learned Societies." Verso of title page

The publisher of American National Biography recruited "50 well-known contemporary authors to pick from it a once-significant, now-obscure person, and reprint the ANB article prefaced by the selector's one-page justification. . . . As varied as the individal subjects, some selectors, such as Jacques Barzun (on critic John Jay Chapman) or Arthur Schlesinger Jr. (on historian George Bancroft), concisely point to changing tastes. . . . Each of these ANB subjects left a mark perceptible in modern America, filling this volume with surprises for even the most widely read." Booklist

Includes bibliographical references

Kane, Joseph Nathan, 1899-2002

Facts about the presidents; Janet Podell & Steven Anzovin {editors}. 7th ed. Wilson, H.W. 2001 721p il $120 *

Grades: 11 12 Adult   **920**

1. Presidents—United States
ISBN 0-8242-1007-7   LC 2001-26261

First published 1959

The main part of this work provides an individual chapter on each President, from Washington through George W. Bush, presenting such information as family, education, election, Vice President, main events and accomplishments of his administration, and First Lady. Part two contains tables and lists presenting comparative data on all the Presidents

Includes bibliographical references

Katz, William Loren
Black pioneers; an untold story. Atheneum Bks. for Young Readers 1999 193p il maps $19.95
Grades: 9 10 11 12 **920**
1. African Americans—History 2. Frontier and pioneer life 3. Abolitionists 4. Underground railroad
ISBN 0-689-81410-0 LC 98-19104
The author "describes the settlement of the Ohio and Mississippi Valleys (covering Ohio, Indiana, Illinois, Michigan, Wisconsin, Minnesota, Iowa, Kansas, and Missouri) by African Americans seeking freedom, including biographical sketches of men and women who formed churches, started schools, or were politically active in their region." SLJ
"The narration is clear, fluid, and enlivened with quotes from the pioneers themselves." Horn Book Guide
Includes bibliographical references

Kennedy, John F. (John Fitzgerald), 1917-1963
Profiles in courage. HarperCollins Pubs. 2003 xxii, 245p $19.95; pa $13.95 *
Grades: 7 8 9 10 11 12 Adult **920**
1. Politicians—United States 2. Courage
ISBN 0-06-053062-6; 0-06-085493-6 (pa)
LC 2003-40676
A reissue of the title first published 1956
This series of profiles of Americans who took courageous stands at crucial moments in public life includes John Quincy Adams, Daniel Webster, Thomas Hart Benton, Sam Houston, Edmund G. Ross, Lucius Q. C. Lamar, George Norris, Robert A. Taft and others.
Includes bibliographical references

Kennedy Cuomo, Kerry
Speak truth to power; human rights defenders who are changing our world; photographs by Eddie Adams; edited by Nan Richardson. Crown 2000 256p il $50
Grades: 7 8 9 10 **920**
1. Human rights
ISBN 0-8129-3062-2 LC 00-34557
"An Umbrage editions book"
This book "is composed of fifty three-page interviews with people who have made strides in the global fight to ensure basic human rights for everyone. . . . The Dalai Lama, Desmond Tutu, and Elie Wiesel are included, but most subjects are everyday people who have survived imprisonment, death threats, and torture to bring about change. . . . Their reports are sad but inspiring. . . . The haunting photographs and stories are gripping." Voice Youth Advocates

Knight, Judson
Middle ages: biographies; edited by Judy Galens. U.X.L 2000 2v set $110
Grades: 9 10 11 12 **920**
1. Middle ages—Biography 2. Medieval civilization
ISBN 0-7876-4857-4 LC 00-64864
Among the 50 people profiled are Eleanor of Aquitaine, Henry the Navigator, Kublai Khan, Montezuma I, and St. Patrick
Each "entry contains illustrations, date spans and pronunciations of names for individuals, sidebars, and a bibliography of books, periodicals, and Web sites." Booklist

Koopmans, Andy
Filmmakers. Lucent Books 2005 112p il (History makers) $28.70
Grades: 7 8 9 10 **920**
1. Motion picture producers and directors
ISBN 1-59018-598-6 LC 2004-12774
Contents: Alfred Hitchcock; Stanley Kubrick; Francis Ford Coppola; Spike Lee; Peter Jackson
"This collective biography . . . focuses on the struggles, successes, and setbacks of five film directors: Alfred Hitchcock, Stanley Kubrick, Francis Ford Coppola, Spike Lee, and Peter Jackson. The subjects are well chosen. . . . These biographies inform about cinema history and have the potential to inspire readers interested in pursuing a career in film." Booklist
Includes bibliographical references

Lanier, Shannon
Jefferson's children; the story of one American family; by Shannon Lanier and Jane Feldman; with photographs by Jane Feldman; and an introduction by Lucian K. Truscott IV. Random House 2000 144p il hardcover o.p. pa $16.95
Grades: 7 8 9 10 **920**
1. African Americans—Biography 2. Racially mixed people 3. United States—Race relations
ISBN 0-375-80597-4; 0-375-82168-6 (pa)
LC 00-44551
This is an "anthology of personal meditations by a variety of Jefferson's living descendants. Edited by Shannon Lanier, a descendant through Sally's son Madison Hemings's line, the portraits that emerge are as generous and jumbled as America itself. The statements range from hostile to conciliatory to indifferent to eloquent." NY Times Book Rev
Includes bibliographical references

Lifetimes: the Great War to the stock market crash: American history through biography and primary documents; edited by Neil A. Hamilton; writers, Mark LaFlaur, James M. Manheim, Renée Miller. Greenwood Press 2002 328p il $74.95 *
Grades: 11 12 Adult **920**
1. United States—History—20th century 2. United States—Biography
ISBN 0-313-31799-2 LC 2001-54700
"Each entry includes a one- to two-page biographical essay, complete with a black-and-white photo. Primary sources include autobiographical sketches, reviews of the subjects' works, commentary from contemporaneous journals, political cartoons, and other materials. The essays are accurate, readable, and objective." Libr J
Includes bibliographical references

Light, Alan
The skills to pay the bills; the story of the Beastie Boys. Three Rivers Press 2005 206p il pa $14
Grades: 11 12 Adult **920**
1. Beastie Boys (Musical group) 2. Rap music
ISBN 0-609-60478-3; 978-0-609-60478-6
LC 2005-24001

Light, Alan—*Continued*

This book "chronicles the Beasties' unique journey from the hardcore New York underground to the top of the Billboard charts." Publisher's note

"Light's notably well written presentation of their story explores the Beasties phenomenon with wit and purpose far too rarely manifested in the rock-bio genre." Booklist

Includes discography

Malone, John Williams

It doesn't take a rocket scientist; great amateurs of science; {by} John Malone. Wiley 2002 232p $24.95

Grades: 11 12 Adult   920

1. Scientists

ISBN 0-471-41431-X   LC 2003-269159

This examines the lives and work of ten amateur scientists, including Gregor Mendel, David H. Levy, Henrietta Swan Leavitt, Joseph Priestley, Michael Faraday, Grote Reber, Arthur C. Clarke, Thomas Jefferson, Susan Hendrickson, and Felix d'Herelle

Includes bibliographical references

Martin, James

My life with the saints. Loyola Press 2006 411p $22.95

Grades: 11 12 Adult   920

1. Christian saints

ISBN 0-8294-2001-0   LC 2005-28466

The author "relates how he discovered various 'saints' and how each has affected his life. . . . Despite a theme built on a particular facet of Catholic belief, Martin's animated style and wide-ranging experiences make this a book readers of diverse backgrounds will enjoy." Publ Wkly

Includes bibliographical references

Matuz, Roger

Reconstruction era: biographies; Lawrence W. Baker, project editor. UXL 2004 xxiv, 246p il (Reconstruction Era reference library) $60 *

Grades: 11 12 Adult   920

1. Reconstruction (1865-1876)

ISBN 0-7876-9218-2   LC 2004-17300

This "volume covers political and military leaders as well as activists, artists, writers, and more. Among them are Louisa May Alcott, Frederick Douglass, Ulysses S. Grant, and Zebulon Vance. Within each biographical entry are cross-references to other individuals covered in this volume." Booklist

Includes bibliographical references

Mendoza, Patrick M.

Extraordinary people in extraordinary times; heroes, sheroes, and villains. Libraries Unlimited 1999 142p il pa $21

Grades: 7 8 9 10   920

1. United States—Biography

ISBN 1-56308-611-5   LC 99-14238

Stories of little-known historical characters from American history. Subjects range from that of the first woman to receive the Congressional Medal of Honor to the first woman to be hanged in the United States. Jeanette Rankin, Jose Marti and two survivors of the Sand Creek Massacre are among those profiled

Includes bibliographical references

Morell, Virginia

Ancestral passions; the Leakey family and the quest for humankind's beginnings. Simon & Schuster 1995 638p il hardcover o.p. paperback available $28.95

Grades: 11 12 Adult   920

1. Leakey, Louis Seymour Bazett, 1903-1972 2. Leakey, Mary D., 1913-1996 3. Leakey, Richard E., 1944- 4. Anthropologists 5. Human origins

LC 95-14306

"The Leakey family, now in its third generation of hunting hominid fossils in East Africa, is the subject of this exquisitely written biography about the search for the beginnings of humankind. . . . With access to volumes of personal and professional papers and extensive interviews with Mary, Richard, and Meave Leakey, as well as many others who played a role in the story of human origins, Virginia Morell has allowed the reader to gain unparalleled insight into the oftentimes complex lives of the world's 'first family of human evolution.'" Sci Books Films

Includes bibliographical references

My folks don't want me to talk about slavery; twenty-one oral histories of former North Carolina slaves; edited by Belinda Hurmence. Blair 1984 103p hardcover o.p. pa $6.95 *

Grades: 9 10 11 12   920

1. Slavery—United States 2. African Americans—Biography

ISBN 0-89587-038-X; 0-89587-039-8 (pa)

LC 84-16891

The narratives presented here were part of a Federal Writers' project during which some 2,000 former slaves were interviewed during the 1930s

A "unique glimpse of slavery viewed from the less well-recorded side, the side of the subjugated." Sci Books Films

Includes bibliographical references

New York Times Company

Sultans of swat; the four great sluggers of the New York Yankees; as originally reported by The New York Times; with an introduction by Yogi Berra. St. Martin's Press 2006 345p il $29.95

Grades: 11 12 Adult   920

1. Ruth, Babe, 1895-1948 2. Mantle, Mickey, 1931-1995 3. Gehrig, Lou, 1903-1941 4. DiMaggio, Joe 5. New York Yankees (Baseball team) 6. Baseball—Biography

ISBN 0-312-34014-1; 978-0-312-34014-8

LC 2005-52039

"Babe Ruth, Lou Gehrig, Joe DiMaggio, and Mickey Mantle were four of the greatest hitters in the history of baseball. . . . This volume uses sports reporting—game

New York Times Company—*Continued*
accounts, features, sidebars, photographs, and box scores—to recreate the four sluggers' careers. . . . To peruse these pages is to hop aboard a baseball time machine and experience the highlights of four great careers much as fans did at the time." Booklist

Open the unusual door; true life stories of challenge, adventure, and success by black Americans; edited and with an introduction by Barbara Summers. Graphia 2005 206p pa $7.99
Grades: 7 8 9 10   **920**
1. African Americans—Biography
ISBN 0-618-58531-1
"A wonderful cross section of excerpts from published autobiographies. The 16 stories tell of challenges met and opportunities recognized and realized. Colin Powell's recollection of his introduction to the military life at City College in New York City stands alongside Russell Simmons's retelling of the turning point in his life when, at 16 years of age, he shot at and missed a fellow drug dealer. . . . This little gem of a book should be a first purchase for public and school libraries." SLJ

Opfell, Olga S.
Women prime ministers and presidents. McFarland & Co. 1993 237p il lib bdg $38.50 *
Grades: 11 12 Adult   **920**
1. Heads of state 2. Women—Biography
ISBN 0-89950-790-5   LC 92-56675
This book contains "profiles of all women heads of government to the date of publication. The entries are in chronological order. Each gives biographical information and the history and politics of the woman's country during her lifetime. . . . This is an essential purchase for women's studies collections." Voice Youth Advocates
Includes bibliographical references

Ottaviani, Jim
Dignifying science: stories about women scientists. G. T. Labs 2003 144p il pa $16.95 *
Grades: 6 7 8 9   **920**
1. Graphic novels 2. Women scientists—Graphic novels 3. Biographical graphic novels
ISBN 0-9660106-4-7
Ottaviani provides biographical sketches of women scientists such as Lise Meitner, Rosalind Franklin, Barbara McClintock, and Hedy Lamarr (yes, the actress was also an inventor); all the stories are illustrated by women comics artists, including Lea Hernandez, Linda Medley, Anne Timmons, and others.

Outman, James L., 1946-
Industrial Revolution: biographies; {by} James L. Outman, Elisabeth M. Outman. UXL 2003 218p il (Industrial revolution reference library) $55 *
Grades: 9 10 11 12   **920**
1. Industrial revolution
ISBN 0-7876-6514-2   LC 2002-155421
Contents: Henry Bessemer; Andrew Carnegie; Henry Ford; Robert Fulton; Samuel Gompers; Jay Gould; James J. Hill; Mother Jones; Karl Marx; Rockefeller; Theodore Roosevelt; Adam Smith; George Stephenson; Ida Tarbell; James Watt; George Westinghouse; Eli Whitney

"The 25 essays in {this volume} provide biographical information with an emphasis on each person's contribution or impact on the Industrial Revolution. . . . More than 50 black-and-white photographs complement the text. . . . This is an excellent adjunct to American and world history units and classes on economics and labor movements." Booklist
Includes bibliographical references

U.S. immigration and migration. Biographies; James L. Outman, Roger Matuz, Rebecca Valentine; Lawrence W. Baker, editor. UXL 2004 2v il (U.S. immigration and migration reference library) set $115 *
Grades: 9 10 11 12   **920**
1. United States—Immigration and emigration
ISBN 0-7876-7733-7   LC 2004-3552
This set "profiles 50 men and women who either immigrated to this country or influenced the debate on the treatment of immigrants." SLJ
Includes bibliographical references

Pendergast, Tom, 1964-
The sixties in America. Biographies; [by] Tom Pendergast and Sara Pendergast; Kathleen J. Edgar, project editor. UXL 2005 lvi, 204p il (U-X-L the sixties in America reference library) $63 *
Grades: 9 10 11 12   **920**
1. United States—History—1961-1974
ISBN 0-7876-9247-6   LC 2004-16600
"Biographical entries cover counterculture icons (Bob Dylan, Abbie Hoffman), politicians and newsmakers (John F. Kennedy, Ralph Nader), mainstream celebrities (Vince Lombardi, Walter Cronkite), and individuals associated with specific events." Booklist
Includes bibliographical references

Westward expansion: biographies. U.X.L 2001 xxv, 251p il maps $60 *
Grades: 7 8 9 10   **920**
1. Frontier and pioneer life 2. West (U.S.)—Biography
ISBN 0-7876-4863-9   LC 00-109475
This collective biography profiles a number of legendary figures of the Wild West, including Buffalo Bill, George Custer, Wyatt Earp, Kit Carson, Annie Oakley, Andrew Jackson, Sarah Winnemucca, and Belle Starr

Pioneers of human rights; Cheryl Fisher Phibbs, book editor. Greenhaven Press 2005 240p il (Profiles in history) lib bdg $34.95
Grades: 7 8 9 10   **920**
1. Political activists 2. Human rights
ISBN 0-7377-2146-4   LC 2003-68585
"This collective biography focuses on human rights activists, with lengthy sections on Mohandas Gandhi and Nelson Mandela and chapters on Iqbal Masih, Eleanor Roosevelt, Frederick Douglass, Natasia Kandic (fighter against abuse in Serbia and Kosovo), and others. . . . The personal stories about courageous resistance that changed the world will draw activist teens as well as students researching the history." Booklist
Includes bibliographical references

Profiles in courage for our time; edited and introduced by Caroline Kennedy. Hyperion 2002 354p $23.95; pa $14.95

Grades: 11 12 Adult   **920**

1. Politicians—United States 2. Courage

ISBN 0-7868-6793-0; 0-7868-8678-1 (pa)

LC 2001-51894

This book "compiles 14 essays lauding political courage. Contributors include Michael Beschloss, E. J. Dionne, Bob Woodward, Anna Quindlen, and Pete Hamill, among others. Each of the 14 essay subjects was a recipient of the Profiles in Courage Award, created by the Kennedy family a decade ago." Booklist

"Unabashedly liberal and pro-government, this collection is a stirring look at people who rarely thought about what they could do for themselves, but always about what they could do for their country." Publ Wkly

Renaissance & Reformation: biographies; Peggy Saari & Aaron Saari, editors. U.X.L 2002 2v il set $105

Grades: 7 8 9 10   **920**

1. Renaissance

ISBN 0-7876-5470-1   LC 2001-8609

Profiles fifty people who played a significant role during the Renaissance and Reformation periods in Europe, including John Calvin, Peter Paul Rubens, Catherine de Medici, and Johannes Kepler.

Includes bibliographical references

Roberts, Cokie

Founding mothers; the women who raised our nation. William Morrow 2004 xx, 359p il $24.95; pa $14.95 *

Grades: 11 12 Adult   **920**

1. Women—United States—History

ISBN 0-06-009025-1; 0-06-009026-X (pa)

LC 2004-042873

"Focusing mainly on the wives, daughters, sisters, and mothers of the Founding Fathers, this . . . title chronicles the adventures and contributions of numerous women of the era between 1740 and 1797." SLJ

"In addition to telling wonderful stories, Roberts also presents a very readable, serviceable account of politics—male and female—in early America. If only our standard history textbooks were written with such flair!" Publ Wkly

Scandiffio, Laura

Evil masters; the frightening world of tyrants. Annick Press 2005 230p il map $24.95; pa $12.95

Grades: 7 8 9 10   **920**

1. Dictators

ISBN 1-55037-895-3; 1-55037-894-5 (pa)

This "title examines the lives and reigns of seven rulers. The profiles range from the frightening ancient world of the first emperor of China and Nero, emperor of Rome during the first century, to Ivan the Terrible and Robespierre. More recent rulers include Hitler, Stalin, and Saddam Hussein. . . . Maps, photos, reproductions, and half-page fact boxes make the events easier to understand. . . . This is an excellent and thought-provoking resource." SLJ

Includes bibliographical references

Schiff, Karenna Gore

Lighting the way; nine women who changed modern America. Miramax Books/Hyperion 2006 528p il $25.95; pa $17.95

Grades: 11 12 Adult   **920**

1. Women—United States—Biography

ISBN 1-4013-5218-9; 1-4013-6015-7 (pa)

LC 2005-56247

The author "profiles nine women who helped change the course of history by overcoming injustice in their own lives." Libr J

"This is an inspirational collection of biographies of women of various social, ethnic, and racial backgrounds fighting for social justice." Booklist

Includes bibliographical references

See, Lisa

On Gold Mountain; the one-hundred-year odyssey of my Chinese-American family. 1st Vintage Books ed. Vintage Books 1996 xxi, 394p il, maps pa $15.95

Grades: 11 12 Adult   **920**

1. Seay family 2. Chinese Americans

ISBN 0-679-76852-1   LC 96-11821

First published 1995 by St. Martin's Press

"See's chronicle melds together the life stories of her Chinese and American ancestors, beginning with a great-great-grandfather's journey from China to San Francisco. . . . Her tale is most specific in its descriptions of the hardships and discrimination endured for decades by large numbers of Chinese immigrants." Booklist

"Facing the nimble shell game her family plays with its history, Ms. See has done a gallant and fair-minded job of fashioning anecdote, fable and fact into an engaging account." N Y Times Book Rev

Includes bibliographical references

Sifters: Native American women's lives; edited by Theda Perdue. Oxford Univ. Press 2001 260p (Viewpoints on American culture) $55; pa $19.95 *

Grades: 11 12 Adult   **920**

1. Native American women

ISBN 0-19-513080-4; 0-19-513081-2 (pa)

LC 00-39950

"From Pocahontas, a Powhatan woman of the seventeenth century, to Ada Deer, the Menominee woman who headed the Bureau of Indian Affairs in the 1990s, the essays span four centuries. Each one recounts the experiences of women from vastly different cultural traditions. . . . Contributors focus on the ways in which different women have fashioned lives that remain firmly rooted in their identity as Native women." Publisher's note

Includes bibliographical references

Stark, Steven D.

Meet the Beatles; a cultural history of the band that shook youth, gender, and the world. HarperEntertainment 2005 344p il $26.95; pa $14.95

Grades: 11 12 Adult   **920**

1. Beatles 2. Rock musicians

ISBN 0-06-000892-X; 0-06-000893-8 (pa)

LC 2004-59794

Stark, Steven D.—*Continued*

In this biography of the Beatles, the author focuses "as much on the cultural trends that produced the Beatles—and the trends they created—as on the Fab Four themselves. . . . Throughout, Stark is sharp and insightful, even when he wades into the psychoanalytic waters of the John/Yoko and Paul/Linda relationships." Publ Wkly

Starkey, David

Six wives: the queens of Henry VIII. HarperCollins Pubs. 2003 xxvii, 852p il hardcover o.p. pa $16.95 *

Grades: 11 12 Adult   920

1. Great Britain—History—1485-1603, Tudors 2. Queens

ISBN 0-694-01043-X; 0-06-000550-5 (pa)

The author covers each of Henry's six wives, "their personalities, their place in the family networks and religious currents at court and the overall patterns of the king's infatuations and disillusionments." Publ Wkly

"Solidly researched and delightfully told, this is highly recommended." Libr J

Includes bibliographical references

Stefoff, Rebecca, 1951-

Women pioneers. Facts on File 1995 126p il (American profiles) $25

Grades: 9 10 11 12   920

1. Frontier and pioneer life—West (U.S.) 2. Women—West (U.S.)

ISBN 0-8160-3134-7   LC 95-13552

The author presents "nine stories of pioneer women and their courage, ingenuity, and triumph. Based on primary sources, the accounts are delivered in a narrative style that enhances readability without sacrificing detail or accuracy. A variety of figures are represented, from Rebecca Burlend, raised in England; to Clara Brown, born a slave in Virginia; to Polly Bemis, born in China." SLJ

Includes bibliographical references

Stolen voices; young people's war diaries from World War I to Iraq; edited with commentaries by Zlata Filipovic and Melanie Challenger; foreword by Olara A. Otunnu. Penguin 2007 xxiii, 293p il pa $14 *

Grades: 11 12 Adult   920

1. Children and war

ISBN 978-0-14-303871-9; 0-14-303871-0

"A Penguin original"

The editors have "compiled 14 diaries that were kept by children during wartime, from World War I to Iraq. Their poignant voices will break your heart." Libr J

Terkel, Studs, 1912-

Hope dies last; keeping the faith in difficult times. New Press 2003 xxix, 326p hardcover o.p. pa $16.95

Grades: 11 12 Adult   920

1. Hope 2. United States—Social conditions

ISBN 1-56584-837-3; 1-56584-937-X (pa)

LC 2003-50989

"Terkel talks with objectors, dissenters, observers, protestors, and do-gooders to find out what makes these committed and generous souls tick. He speaks with Ohio congressman and Democratic presidential candidate Dennis Kucinich, a doctor who treats the homeless, teachers, labor activists, recent immigrants, Pete Seeger, and John Kenneth Galbraith. . . . As a collector of true stories and a guardian of free speech, Terkel ensures that grass-root alternatives to the 'official word' are heard from sea to shining sea." Booklist

To the best of my ability; the American presidents; James McPherson, editor. DK Pub. 2000 480p il map hardcover o.p. pa $20 *

Grades: 11 12 Adult   920

1. Presidents—United States

ISBN 0-7894-5073-9; 0-7566-0777-9 (pa)

LC 00-21569

The first half of this book summarizes the "lives and administrations of the 42 men who have held the presidency. Each has a chapter generally running between six to eight pages . . . written by one of 32 contributing historians or biographers. . . . The second half of the book contains chapters on each election campaign, including very short essays describing issues, tables of results, and the full text of each president's inaugural address." Libr J

Vare, Ethlie Ann

Patently female; from AZT to TV dinners: stories of women inventors and their breakthrough ideas; [by] Ethlie Ann Vare, Greg Ptacek. Wiley 2002 220p il $27.95 *

Grades: 11 12 Adult   920

1. Women inventors

ISBN 0-471-02334-5   LC 2001-26950

Sequel to: Mothers of invention (1988)

The authors "detail how women's ideas like the cotton gin, automatic sewing machine and even the Brooklyn Bridge have often been attributed to men and how history books and museums like the Smithsonian and the National Inventors Hall of Fame have ignored women's achievements. The book's lighthearted, colloquial style makes it ideal for classrooms." Publ Wkly

Includes bibliographical references

Vowell, Sarah, 1969-

Assassination vacation. Simon & Schuster 2005 258p il hardcover o.p. pa $14

Grades: 11 12 Adult   920

1. Presidents—United States—Assassination 2. United States—Description and travel 3. United States—Local history

ISBN 0-7432-6003-1; 0-7432-6004-X (pa)

LC 2004-59134

Also available Thorndike Press large print edition

The author "takes readers on a pilgrimage of sorts to the sites and monuments that pay homage to Lincoln, Garfield and McKinley, visiting everything from grave sites and simple plaques (like the one in Buffalo that marks the place where McKinley was shot) to places like the National Museum of Health and Medicine, where fragments of Lincoln's skull are on display." Publ Wkly

Vowell, Sarah, 1969-—*Continued*
"[Vowell] has done her homework, providing lucid descriptions of the murders and agile summations of the scholarly assessments of each era." America

Watson, Robert P., 1962-
First ladies of the United States; a biographical dictionary. Lynne Rienner Pubs. 2001 327p $49.95 *

Grades: 9 10 11 12   920
1. Presidents' spouses—United States
ISBN 1-55587-907-1   LC 00-28068
"This work presents in chronological order . . . thorough sketches of every first lady from Martha Dandridge Custis Washington through Laura Welch Bush. Each entry begins with a picture, birth and death dates, presidential husband and his term of office, marriages, and children. Family background and early years are discussed, followed by courtship and marriage. The greater part of each entry covers the first lady's experiences during her husband's presidency." Voice Youth Advocates
Includes bibliographical references

Zach, Kim K., 1958-
Hidden from history; the lives of eight American women scientists. Avisson Press 2002 152p il (Avisson young adult series) pa $19.95 *
Grades: 9 10 11 12   920
1. Women scientists
ISBN 1-88810-554-2   LC 2002-28151
Short biographies of eight women who excelled in various scientific fields: Ellen Swallow Richards, Nettie Maria Stevens, Annie Jump Cannon, Alice Hamilton, Florence Sabin, Alice Catherine Evans, Grace Murray Hopper, and Gertrude Belle Elion
"With smooth, effortless delivery, these brief profiles of eight history-making scientists from the mid-1800s to the present will captivate readers." Booklist
Includes bibliographical references

920.003 Biographical reference works

Aaseng, Nathan, 1953-
African-American athletes. Facts on File 2003 262p il (A to Z of African Americans) $44 *
Grades: 11 12 Adult   920.003
1. African American athletes—Dictionaries
ISBN 0-8160-4805-3   LC 2002-5989
"Facts on File library of American history"
"Profiles cover more than 155 athletes, with information on their lives and their athletic accomplishments. Individuals were selected for inclusion based on a variety of factors—statistics, championships, recognition by peers, or pioneering efforts. Among them are Hank Aaron (baseball's career home-run leader), John Davis (two-time Olympic weightlifter), Emmitt Smith (professional football player), and Debi Thomas (Olympic figure skater). All but a handful are from the twentieth century. Failures and missteps of the athletes are not ignored, nor are they sensationalized." Booklist
Includes bibliographical references

Abridged encyclopedia of world biography. Gale Group 1999 6v il set $525 *
Grades: 11 12 Adult   920.003
1. Biography—Dictionaries
ISBN 0-7876-3904-4   LC 99-29293
Contents: v1 American history; v2 World history; v3 Literature; v4 Science and mathematics; v5 Arts and entertainment; v6 Social science
"This set is an abridgement of Gale's *Encyclopedia of World Biography*. . . . It provides complete biographical sketches for more than 2,000 well-known individuals and brief sketches on approximately 5,000 others. Each sketch includes key biographical data, such as date and place of birth, date of death (if deceased), nationality, and occupation. The 'complete' or lengthier sketches are accompanied by portraits and suggests for further reading." Recomm Ref Books for Small & Medium-sized Libr & Media Cent, 2000
"This is a solid resource for students in need of basic information." SLJ
Includes bibliographical references

Adamson, Lynda G.
Notable women in world history; a guide to recommended biographies and autobiographies. Greenwood Press 1998 401p $52.95 *
Grades: 11 12 Adult   920.003
1. Women—Biography—Dictionaries
ISBN 0-313-29818-1   LC 97-33136
"The entries are arranged alphabetically by last name with appropriate cross-references for alternative designations. Each contains the woman's name, key dates, occupation or avocation, and birthplace. A short biographical sketch about parents, education, general achievement, and recognition or awards follows. Women of all time periods are included. . . . Because it includes only those born outside the U.S., it complements sources on American women. *Notable Women in World History* is a useful addition to academic, public, and high-school libraries. It would be especially useful for women's studies collections." Booklist

African American lives; edited by Henry Louis Gates, Jr. and Evelyn Brooks Higginbotham. Oxford University Press 2004 xxvi, 1025p $55 *
Grades: 11 12 Adult   920.003
1. African Americans—Biography
ISBN 0-19-516024-X   LC 2003-23640
This compilation offers "biographies of 611 African-Americans over more than four centuries, beginning with Esteban, the first African known to have set foot in North America, up through writers, academics, artists, activists and more of today. A few of these profiles have been written by notable names—Gerald Early on Muhammad Ali, Clayborne Carson on Martin Luther King Jr. and Malcolm X, John Szwed on Miles Davis—though most are by lesser-known contributors." Publ Wkly
"This work opens multiple fresh vistas on proper African American history . . . Essential for any serious African American collection." Libr J
For a fuller review see: Booklist, July 2004
Includes bibliographical references

Allaby, Michael, 1933-
Makers of science; {by} Michael Allaby & Derek Gjertsen. Oxford Univ. Press 2002 5v il maps set $185 *
Grades: 11 12 Adult   **920.003**
1. Scientists 2. Science—History
ISBN 0-19-521680-6   LC 2001-48396
"This set incorporates the political and social setting as well as the scientific achievements of each scientist. Volumes are arranged chronologically, beginning with Aristotle and ending with Stephen Hawking. In between are biographies of more than 40 European and U.S. scientists 'whose discoveries were crucial to the development of science,' ranging in length from 8 to 16 pages. . . . Scientific principles are clearly explained, often with diagrams. Intriguing personal stories are also woven in." Booklist
Includes bibliographical references

American authors, 1600-1900; a biographical dictionary of American literature; edited by Stanley J. Kunitz and Howard Haycraft. Wilson, H.W. 1938 846p il (Authors series) $120 *
Grades: 11 12 Adult   **920.003**
1. Authors, American—Dictionaries 2. American literature—Bio-bibliography
ISBN 0-8242-0001-2
"Complete in one volume with 1300 biographies and 400 portraits." Title page
"This volume contains biographies of 1,300 authors who contributed to the development of American literature, from the founding of Jamestown (1607) to the end of the nineteenth century. Each essay describes the author's life, discusses past and present significance, and evaluates principal works." Safford. Guide to Ref Materials for Sch Media Cent. 5th edition

American Indian biographies; edited by Carole Barrett, Harvey Markowitz, project editor, R. Kent Rasmussen. Rev. ed. Salem Press 2005 623p il map (Magill's choice) $62
Grades: 8 9 10 11 12 Adult   **920.003**
1. Native Americans—Biography
ISBN 1-58765-233-1; 978-1-58765-233-2
     LC 2004-28872
First published 1999; some essays originally appeared in Dictionary of world biography, Great lives from history: the Renaissance & early modern era, 1454-1600 (2005), and American ethnic writers (2000)
"The book contains essays on religious, social, and political leaders; warriors; and reformers from the past as well as modern activists, writers, artists, entertainers, scientists, and athletes. . . . A great bargain and an asset in any library that supports an American history curriculum." Booklist
Includes bibliographical references

American national biography; general editors, John A. Garraty, Mark C. Carnes. Oxford Univ. Press 1999 24v set $795 *
Grades: 11 12 Adult   **920.003**
1. United States—Biography—Dictionaries
ISBN 0-19-520635-5   LC 98-20826

Also available online; Also available Supplement 1 published 2002 $150 (ISBN 0-19-515063-5) and Supplement II published 2005 $150 (0-19-522202-4), the first two in an ongoing series of Supplements
Conceived as the successor to the Dictionary of American biography, first published between 1926 and 1937; Published under the auspices of the American Council of Learned Societies
"ANB defines 'American' broadly as a person whose significance, achievement, fame, or influence occurred during residence within what is now the US, or whose life or career directly influenced the course of US history. Subjects must have died before 1996. . . . Subjects are arranged alphabetically. The typical entry, 750 to 7,500 words in length, proceeds chronologically, following the major personal and professional events of the subject's life, birth to death. The concluding paragraph attempts to assess the subject's contributions from today's perspective. A brief bibliography after each entry, not meant to be comprehensive, lists major sources, including locations of archives and collections of personal papers." Choice
Includes bibliographical references

American writers; a collection of literary biographies; Leonard Unger, editor in chief. Scribner 1974-1998 4v + supplement I-IV (in 8v) + retrospective supplement 1 set $1845
Grades: 11 12 Adult   **920.003**
1. Authors, American—Dictionaries 2. American literature—History and criticism
ISBN 0-684-80586-3
Continued by ongoing series of supplementary volumes each $145
"Signed essays on the life and works of selected American authors; selective bibliographies by and about each author. The basic set (1974. 4 v.) contains 97 essays originally published in the University of Minnesota pamphlets on American writers series; some have been revised and updated. Each of the 2-v. supplements covers 29 writers not included in the parent series; the supplements give greater attention to women and minorities." Guide to Ref Books. 11th edition
American writers: selected authors; a three volume set containing sixty-four essays from the parent publication is available $325 (ISBN 0-684-80604-5)

American writers: selected authors; Leonard Unger, A. Walton Litz, editors in chief. Scribner 1998 3v set $325
Grades: 9 10 11 12   **920.003**
1. Authors, American—Dictionaries 2. American literature—History and criticism
ISBN 0-684-80604-5   LC 98-36810
This set contains 64 articles from the four-volume American writers series and its various supplements
"Written by contemporary scholars, these essays provide fresh looks at some of the most-studied authors." SLJ

Bader, Philip
    African-American writers. Facts on File 2004
294p (A to Z of African Americans) $44 *
    Grades: 11 12 Adult   **920.003**
    1. American literature—African American authors—
Bio-bibliography 2. African American authors—Dictionaries
    ISBN 0-8160-4860-6   LC 2003-8699
    "This volume features biographical entries on 145 African American authors. Emphasizing writers whose works are still in print and are regularly part of high school and college curricula, it covers novelists, poets, journalists, children's and young adult authors, nonfiction writers, and critics. Among them are well-known figures like Ralph Ellison and Countee Cullen and contemporary voices like Suzan-Lori Parks and Edwidge Danticat. . . . All of the entries are clear and focused and manage to be comprehensive. . . . This volume's longer entries, illustrations, and indexes make it a worthwhile addition to high school, public, and academic libraries." Libr J
    Includes bibliographical references

Baker's biographical dictionary of musicians;
    Nicolas Slonimsky, editor emeritus; Laura Kuhn,
    Baker's series advisory editor. Centennial ed.
    Schirmer Bks. 2001 6v set $800 *
    Grades: 11 12 Adult   **920.003**
    1. Music—Bio-bibliography 2. Musicians—Dictionaries
    ISBN 0-02-865525-7   LC 00-46375
    First published 1900 in one volume under the authorship of Theodore Baker
    "Brief articles about composers, performers, critics, conductors, and teachers arranged alphabetically under surname with pronunciation, list of musical works, and a bibliography of print sources. Includes classical, jazz, rock, country, blues, and other popular musicians." Ref Sources for Small & Medium-sized Libr. 6th edition
    "This monumental work collocates information from classical, popular, and jazz music on a scale greater than any other source. Essential for all libraries." Choice
    Includes bibliographical references and discographies

Baker's biographical dictionary of popular
    musicians since 1990; introduction by David
    Freeland. Schirmer Ref. 2003 2v il set $195 *
    Grades: 11 12 Adult   **920.003**
    1. Popular music—Dictionaries
    ISBN 0-02-865799-3   LC 2003-13956
    This dictionary includes more than 500 artists and groups active from 1990-2000. Rock, rhythm and blues, rap, country, classical, and jazz are among the popular styles covered. Select discographies, bibliographies, and a glossary of musical terms are provided
    "An excellent companion to the 2001 expansion of *Baker's Biographical Dictionary of Musicians*. . . . Given the broad spectrum of musical styles covered here, this would make an excellent reference for public and academic libraries." Libr J
    Includes bibliographical references and discographies

Barthelmas, Della Gray, 1920-
    The signers of the Declaration of Independence;
a biographical and genealogical reference; with a
foreword by Frank Borman. McFarland & Co.
1997 334p il hardcover o.p. pa $35
    Grades: 11 12 Adult   **920.003**
    1. United States. Declaration of Independence
    ISBN 0-7864-0318-7; 0-7864-1704-8 (pa)
                               LC 97-11663
    Entries begin "with a full-page portrait of the signer and a facsimile of his signature as it appears on the document. The biographies range from one to 10 pages, followed by family information on the person (wives and children), then by genealogies of his and his spouse's ancestors for as many generations as possible." Book Rep

The **Biographical** dictionary of scientists. 3rd ed,
    consultant editors, Roy Porter, Marilyn Ogilvie.
    Oxford Univ. Press 2000 2v il set $125 *
    Grades: 11 12 Adult   **920.003**
    1. Scientists—Dictionaries
    ISBN 0-19-521663-6   LC 00-36752
    First published 1983-1985 in the United Kingdom; first United States edition edited by David Abbott published 1984-1986 by Bedrick Books
    This reference offers over 1,280 entries for men and women in all fields of science ranging in length from 500 to 1,200 words, with 150 illustrations, chronologies, quotations, tables of scientific discoveries and Nobel Prize Winners
    Includes bibliographical references

The **Biographical** dictionary of women in science;
    pioneering lives from ancient times to the
    mid-20th century; Marilyn Ogilvie and Joy
    Harvey, editors. Routledge 2000 2v set $250
    Grades: 11 12 Adult   **920.003**
    1. Women scientists—Dictionaries
    ISBN 0-415-92038-8   LC 99-17668
    "This title includes approximately 2,500 women scientists. . . . Science is defined broadly to include related fields like anthroplogy and sociology. . . . Entries begin with a brief biographical description, with birth and death dates, educational background, and area of professional work. The essays, typically 250 to 750 words long, give only brief early life history before focusing on the subjects' principal scientific contributions. . . . Ogilvie and Harvey's work is a must-have reference tool." Am Ref Books Annu, 2001
    Includes bibliographical references

Biographical encyclopedia of artists; Sir Lawrence
    Gowing, general editor. Facts on File 2005 4v
    il set $260 *
    Grades: 11 12 Adult   **920.003**
    1. Artists—Biography—Encyclopedias
    ISBN 0-8160-5803-2   LC 2005-40500
    First published 1983 by Prentice-Hall as volume two of Encyclopedia of visual art
    At head of title: Facts on File
    "The artists covered include Laurie Anderson, Frank Gehry, Anselm Kiefer, Jan Vermeer, and Andy Warhol. . . . A visual chronology of artists by country and era functions as an index to artists, and an alphabetical art-

Biographical encyclopedia of artists—*Continued*
ist/subject index concludes the work." Libr J
For a fuller review, see: Booklist, Jan. 1 & 15, 2006
Includes bibliographical references

Black women in America; Darlene Clark Hine,
editor in chief. 2nd ed. Oxford University Press
2005 3v il set $325
Grades: 11 12 Adult   **920.003**
1. African American women—Dictionaries
ISBN 0-19-515677-3   LC 2005-1532
First published 1993 by Carlson Pub.
This set features over 300 "profiles of women from
the 1800s to the present, including writers, activists, entrepreneurs, educators, ambassadors, and many others, interspersed with the roles they played in Islam, the Left,
librarianship, journalism, the labor movement, and more."
Libr J
"The essays offer fascinating glimpses into black
women's economic, social, and political contributions,
even at the grassroots level, and explore issues such as
spirituality, domestic servitude, and mixed-race identity
in terms of how they have shaped history." SLJ
Includes bibliographical references

Blanchard, Mary Loving, 1952-
Poets for young adults; their lives and works;
[by] Mary Loving Blanchard and Cara Falcetti.
Greenwood Press 2006 287p il $59.95 *
Grades: 9 10 11 12   **920.003**
1. American poetry—Bio-bibliography 2. Poets, American—Dictionaries
ISBN 0-313-32884-6; 978-0-313-32884-8
                               LC 2006-29475
This book "examines the lives and works of seventy-
five poets that are read and loved by teens. . . . [The
poets covered range] from the modern songwriters such
as Bob Dylan and Tupac Shakur, to the nineteen sixties
icons Jack Kerouac and Sylvia Plath, to such traditional
poets as Edgar Allan Poe and William Blake." Publisher's note
Includes bibliographical references

British authors before 1800; a biographical
dictionary; edited by Stanley J. Kunitz and
Howard Haycraft; complete in one volume with
650 biographies and 220 portraits. Wilson, H.W.
1952 584p il (Authors series) $95 *
Grades: 11 12 Adult   **920.003**
1. Authors, English—Dictionaries 2. English literature—Bio-bibliography
ISBN 0-8242-0006-3
"Short biographical essays on principal and marginal
figures in British literature. Bibliographies appended to
essays." N Y Public Libr. Book of How & Where to
Look It Up

British authors of the nineteenth century; edited
by Stanley J. Kunitz; associate editor: Howard
Haycraft; complete in one volume with 1000
biographies and 350 portraits. Wilson, H.W.
1936 677p il (Authors series) $105 *
Grades: 11 12 Adult   **920.003**

1. Authors, English—Dictionaries 2. English literature—Bio-bibliography
ISBN 0-8242-0007-1
"More than a thousand authors of the British Empire
(including Canada, Australia, South Africa, and New
Zealand) are represented by sketches varying in length
from approximately 100 to 2500 words, roughly propor-
tionate to the importance of the subjects." Preface

British writers; edited under the auspices of the
British Council; Ian Scott-Kilvert, general editor.
Scribner 1979-1992 7v + supplement I-IV set
$1835
Grades: 11 12 Adult   **920.003**
1. Authors, English—Dictionaries 2. English literature—Bio-bibliography 3. English literature—History
and criticism
ISBN 0-684-80587-1
Also available Retrospective supplement I published
2002 $168 and Retrospective supplement II published
2002 $168; Continued by ongoing supplementary vol-
umes each $168; Volumes 1-7 also available separately
ea $168
For subscription options apply to publisher
"This work presents articles by distinguished contributors on major British writers from the fourteenth century
to the present. . . . The biographical sketch that opens
each entry is followed by a survey of the author's principal works, a critical evaluation, and an updated bibliography." Ref Sources for Small & Medium-sized Libr. 6th
edition

Business leader profiles for students; Sheila M.
Dow, editor. Gale Group 1999-2002 2v il $130
Grades: 9 10 11 12   **920.003**
1. Businesspeople
ISBN 0-7876-2935-9 (v1 op); 0-7876-4889-2 (v2)
"This resource provides information on past and present giants of business and industry. Each alphabetical entry includes an overview of the person's life and career,
a discussion of his or her social and economic impact, a
brief chronology, and a bibliography. For some, a black-
and-white photograph and contact information are also
included. Among the approximately 250 entrepreneurs
profiled are: L. L. Bean, Andrew Carnegie, Berry Gordy,
Jr., Steve Jobs, Ralph Lauren, Joseph Pulitzer, Donald
Trump, Lillian Vernon, and Oprah Winfrey. . . . This
reference tool will be appreciated by business and economics students and others seeking information on these
sometimes elusive subjects." SLJ

Butler, Alban, 1711-1773
Butler's Lives of the saints. Christian Classics
1956 4v set $149.95; pa $109.95 *
Grades: 11 12 Adult   **920.003**
1. Christian saints—Dictionaries
ISBN 0-87061-045-7; 0-87061-137-2 (pa)
Also available in concise editions in paperback from
HarperSanFrancisco (edited by Michael Walsh) and in
hardcover from Liturgical Press (edited by Paul Burns)
A reprint of the four volume set published 1956 by
Kenedy; New edition of a work first published 1756-
1759. The calendar arrangement is retained, but the number of entries has almost doubled and many of the en-
tries have been rewritten in whole or part

Butler, Alban, 1711-1773—*Continued*
"The biographies of the saints and beati are arranged by their feast days with each of the four volumes containing three months. . . . Each volume has a table of contents arranged by the days of the month with a list of the feasts for each day." Booklist

Concise dictionary of scientific biography. 2nd ed. Scribner 2000 1097p il $135
Grades: 9 10 11 12   **920.003**
1. Scientists—Dictionaries
ISBN 0-684-80631-2   LC 00-61231
First published 1981
This volume "integrates the 5,100 biographies from the base set with the 400 biographies found in the *Supplement* and includes photos and portraits of the most-studied scientists." Publisher's note
"This book would be useful as a quick introduction and as a starting point for further study." Am Ref Books Annu, 2001

Contemporary African American novelists; a bio-bibliographical critical sourcebook; edited by Emmanuel S. Nelson. Greenwood Press 1999 xx, 530p $100 *
Grades: 11 12 Adult   **920.003**
1. African American authors—Dictionaries
2. American fiction—Bio-bibliography
ISBN 0-313-30501-3   LC 98-26438
"The 79 profiled writers include major novelists, such as Toni Morrison and John Edgar Wideman, as well as such lesser-known writers as Steven Corbin and Dawn Turner Trice. . . . Each author's profile begins with a short biography. A discussion of the writer's major works and themes follows, with an overview of the critical reception in both popular and scholarly journals. Each entry concludes with a bibliography that lists the works of the profiled author and secondary sources for further investigation." Booklist

Contemporary novelists; editors, Neil Schlager and Josh Lauer. 7th ed. St. James Press 2001 xxiv, 1166p (Contemporary writers series) $230
Grades: 9 10 11 12   **920.003**
1. Novelists, English—Dictionaries 2. American fiction—Bio-bibliography
ISBN 1-55862-408-2
First published 1972 by St. Martin's Press
Contains bio-critical information on English-language novelists from around the world. Each entry lists essential biographical data; publications according to genre; a brief bibliography of secondary sources; the location of the author's manuscript collection; and a short critical essay on the novels
Includes bibliographical references

Contemporary poets; editor, Thomas Riggs; with a preface by Diane Wakoski. 7th ed. St. James Press 2001 xxiii, 1443p (Contemporary writers series) $230
Grades: 11 12 Adult   **920.003**
1. Poets, English—Dictionaries 2. Poets, American—Dictionaries 3. American poetry—Bio-bibliography
ISBN 1-55862-349-3   LC 00-45882
First published 1970 with title: Contemporary poets of the English language

"A biographical handbook of contemporary poets, arranged alphabetically. Entries consist of a short biography, full bibliography, comments by many of the poets, and a signed critical essay." Ref Sources for Small & Medium-sized Libr. 6th edition
Includes bibliographical references

Current biography yearbook 2006. Wilson, H.W. 2006 il $160 *
Grades: 11 12 Adult   **920.003**
1. Biography—Periodicals
ISSN 0084-9499
ISBN 0-8242-1074-3; 978-0-8242-1074-8
Also available online; Current biography: cumulated index, 1940-2005 available $85 (ISBN 0-8242-1054-9)
Annual. First published 1940 with title: Current biography
Also issued monthly except December at a subscription price of $160 per year (ISSN 0011-3344). Yearbooks 1940-2003 available ea $150; yearbooks 2004-2005 available ea $160
"Biographies of prominent people written in lively, popular prose. Emphasis is on entertainers, star athletes, politicians, and other celebrities. Series is cumulative, with biographies revised and updated occasionally. Each volume has seven-year index." N Y Public Libr Book of How & Where to Look It Up

Dictionary of Hispanic biography; Joseph C. Tardiff & L. Mpho Mabunda, editors; foreword by Rudolfo Anaya. Gale Res. 1996 xxv, 1011p il $150 *
Grades: 11 12 Adult   **920.003**
1. Hispanic Americans—Dictionaries
ISBN 0-8103-8302-0   LC 95-38261
"Ranging from the 'period of discovery' to the present (70 percent of the entries are from the contemporary period), this work covers some 471 notable Hispanics of Spain, Spanish America, and the United States. Virtually all vocations are represented." Libr J

Dictionary of scientific biography; Charles Coulston Gillispie, editor in chief. Scribner 1981 c1980-c1990 18v in 10 set $1800
Grades: 11 12 Adult   **920.003**
ISBN 0-684-16962-2
This is a reprint of the title published 1970-1980 in 16 volumes. Volumes 15-18 are Supplements
Published under the auspices of the American Council of Learned Societies; New edition in preparation
This "biographical dictionary covers over forty-five hundred people ranging from Einstein, Newton, and Pasteur to Marx, Columbus, and Abailard. Its focus is on the biographee's place in the history of science, rather than on his or her life story. The signed entries run from part of a page to many pages and include excellent bibliographies." RQ

Distinguished Asian Americans; a biographical dictionary; edited by Hyung-chan Kim; contributing editors, Dorothy Cordova {et al.}. Greenwood Press 1999 430p il $65 *
Grades: 11 12 Adult   **920.003**
ISBN 0-313-28902-6   LC 98-41423

Distinguished Asian Americans—*Continued*

"This volume features 166 entries, most ranging from two to three pages, arranged alphabetically by person. The Asian Americans included may be native or foreign-born. . . . All were 'chosen for their outstanding accomplishments in professions that range from labor leaders to political leaders, tennis players to football players, scientists to distinguished inventors, Hollywood actors to Wall Street investors, schoolteachers to scholars, and comedians to community activists.' Among those profiled are Michael Chang, Connie Chung, S.I. Hayakawa, Lance Ito, Bruce Lee, Yo-Yo Ma, I.M. Pei, and Kristi Yamaguchi. . . . {There is} a selected bibliography for each entry." Booklist

Durham, Jennifer L.

World cultural leaders of the twentieth century. ABC-CLIO 2000 2v il set $175

Grades: 11 12 Adult **920.003**

1. Biography—Dictionaries 2. Arts

ISBN 1-57607-038-7 LC 00-9209

"This book presents over 400 of the most famous men and women of the twentieth century in the areas of literature, art, film, dance, music, and theater. The contributions of each person are discussed in the context of the time in which they lived, and their works and achievements are detailed. The articles are concise and readable." Book Rep

Encyclopedia of women's autobiography; edited by Victoria Boynton and Jo Malin; Emmanuel S. Nelson, advisory editor. Greenwood Press 2005 2v set $249.95 *

Grades: 11 12 Adult **920.003**

1. Autobiography 2. Women—Biography—Encyclopedias

ISBN 0-313-32737-8 LC 2005-8526

The contents "range from autobiographies of individuals (e.g., Adrienne Rich, Sojourner Truth, Isak Dinesen) to those of specific ethnicities or nationalities (e.g., African American Women's Autobiography) to important genres and terms (e.g., Captivity/Prison Narrative, Diary, Feminism, and Voice)." Choice

This set's "encyclopedic and culturally diverse nature should appeal to a wide audience and provide a valuable starting point for further research." Libr J

Includes bibliographical references

Encyclopedia of world biography. 2nd ed. Gale Res. 1998 17v il set $1255

Grades: 11 12 Adult **920.003**

1. Biography—Dictionaries

ISBN 0-7876-2221-4 LC 97-42327

Kept up-to-date by yearly supplements. Volumes available 1998-2007 designated volumes 18-27 at $150 ea

First published 1973 with title: McGraw-Hill encyclopedia of world biography

Presents brief biographical sketches which provide vital statistics as well as information on the importance of the person listed. Volumes 1-16 are arranged alphabetically; volume 17 is the index

Encyclopedia of world writers; Thierry Boucquey, general editor; Gary Johnson, advisor; Nina Chordas advisor; [written and developed by Book Builders LLC] Facts on File 2005 3v (Facts on File library of world literature) set $225 *

Grades: 9 10 11 12 **920.003**

1. Authors—Dictionaries

ISBN 0-8160-6143-2 LC 2004-20551

Vol. 3 first published 2003 with title: Encyclopedia of world writers: 19th and 20th centuries

General editor for Vol. 3: Marie Josephine Diamond; advisors, Maria DiBattista and Julian Wolfreys

This set is "an introduction to the world's writers, not only literary authors but also philosophers, religious thinkers, and essayists. The first two volumes (beginnings through the 18th century) also treat anonymous works and oral traditions." Choice

"This reference will stand out for its scope, particularly the accessible entries on the earliest literary activity." SLJ

Includes bibliographical references

European authors, 1000-1900; a biographical dictionary of European literature; edited by Stanley J. Kunitz and Vineta Colby; complete in one volume with 967 biographies and 309 portraits. Wilson, H.W. 1967 1016p il (Authors series) $115 *

Grades: 11 12 Adult **920.003**

1. Literature—Bio-bibliography

ISBN 0-8242-0013-6

Includes continental European writers born after the year 1000 and dead before 1925. Nearly a thousand major and minor contributors to thirty-one different literatures are discussed.

"These biographies provide quick, satisfactory introductions to a staggering variety of authors and literatures." Choice

Extraordinary women of the Medieval and Renaissance world; a biographical dictionary; [by] Carole Levin [et al.] Greenwood Press 2000 327p il $65

Grades: 11 12 Adult **920.003**

1. Women—History 2. Women—Biography 3. Renaissance 4. Middle Ages

ISBN 0-313-30659-1 LC 99-55218

This volume presents seventy women who "lived between the tenth and seventeenth centuries. . . . The entries are arranged in alphabetical order, with a brief subheading noting country and occupation. As much information as is known about the person is summarized, including education, family, and achievements. Each article ends with a bibliography of additional sources of information. A number of the articles include portraits." Booklist

Flores, Angel, 1900-1992
Spanish American authors; the twentieth century. Wilson, H.W. 1992 915p $150
Grades: 11 12 Adult   **920.003**
1. Authors, Latin American—Dictionaries 2. Latin American literature—Bio-bibliography
ISBN 0-8242-0806-4   LC 92-7591
"A monumental and distinguished work covering more than 330 novelists and poets from Central and South America, Puerto Rico, and the Caribbean, some appearing for the first time in a reference source. Essential in any library supporting study of Latin America. . . . For each writer, provides biographical information, critical analysis and summaries of criticism, and a bibliography of primary and secondary works, excluding dissertations." Guide to Ref Books. 11th edition

Gates, Alexander E.
A to Z of earth scientists. Facts on File 2002 336p il (Notable scientists) $45
Grades: 11 12 Adult   **920.003**
1. Earth sciences 2. Scientists—Dictionaries
ISBN 0-8160-4580-1   LC 2002-14616
This "profiles the lives of 192 people who devoted their careers to the disciplines and subdisciplines of the earth sciences during the 18th century to the present. . . . Entries appear in alphabetic order under the name by which the scientist is most commonly known. Also included are birth date, date of death (if applicable), nationality, and earth science specialty. An essay containing more personal data, including an emphasis on the scientist's main work and contributions to the field follows this information." Am Ref Books Annu, 2003
Includes bibliographical references

Grant, Michael, 1914-2004
Greek and Latin authors, 800 B.C.-A.D. 1000; a biographical dictionary. Wilson, H.W. 1980 490p il (Authors series) $105
Grades: 11 12 Adult   **920.003**
ISBN 0-8242-0640-1   LC 79-27446
Covers more than 370 classical authors. Each entry includes "the pronunciation of the author's name, biographical background, an overview of major works with critical commentary on the nature and quality of those works, and, where relevant, a brief discussion of the influence of the author's works on later literature." Ref Sources for Small & Medium-sized Libr. 5th edition

Great lives from history, The 17th century, 1601-1700; editor, Larissa Juliet Taylor. Salem Press 2005 2v il set $160
Grades: 11 12 Adult   **920.003**
1. Biography—Dictionaries 2. World history—17th century
ISBN 1-58765-222-6; 978-1-58765-222-6
     LC 2005-17804
Companion volume to Great events from history, The 17th century, 1601-1700
First published as part of the Great lives from history series, published 1987-1995 under the editorship of Frank N. Magill; previously published as half of volume 4 of Dictionary of world biography, published 1998-1999

This "is a collection of biographical essays, ranging from three to five pages in length and documenting the lives of those individuals who helped to shape the history of the 17th century. The coverage is also global and includes both well-known and lesser-known figures." SLJ
Includes bibliographical references

Great lives from history, The 18th century, 1701-1800; editor, John Powell; editor, first edition, Frank N. Magill. Salem Press 2006 2v il map set $160
Grades: 11 12 Adult   **920.003**
1. Biography—Dictionaries 2. World history—18th century
ISBN 978-1-58765-276-9; 1-58765-276-5
     LC 2006-5336
Companion volume to Great events from history, The 18th century, 1701-1800
First published as part of the Great lives from history series, published 1987-1995 under the editorship of Frank N. Magill; previously published as half of volume 4 of Dictionary of world biography, published 1998-1999
"The alphabetically listed subjects encompass 36 areas of expertise and include John Newbery, Pontiac, Qianlong, Hannah More, Pius IV, Paul Revere, and Shah Wali Allah, among others. Each article is approximately three pages long and lists the subject's major accomplishments, important dates, and areas of achievement. . . . A well-written, useful set." SLJ
Includes bibliographical references

Great lives from history, The 19th century, 1801-1900; editor, John Powell. Salem Press 2006 4v il map set $360
Grades: 11 12 Adult   **920.003**
1. Biography—Dictionaries 2. World history—19th century
ISBN 978-1-58765-292-9; 1-58765-292-7
     LC 2006-20187
Companion volume to Great events from history, The 19th century, 1801-1900
First published as part of the Great lives from history series, published 1987-1995 under the editorship of Frank N. Magill; previously published as volumes 5 and 6 of Dictionary of world biography, published 1998-1999
"A total of 737 essays covering 757 major figures including 123 on women make up the set. . . . Major world leaders appear here, as well as the giants of religious faith who dominated the century: monarchs, presidents, popes, philosophers, writers, social reformers, educators, and military leaders who left their imprint on political as well as spiritual institutions." Publisher's note
Includes bibliographical references

Great lives from history, The ancient world, prehistory-476 C.E; editor, Christina A. Salowey. Salem Press 2004 2v il, maps set $160
Grades: 11 12 Adult   **920.003**
1. Biography—Dictionaries 2. Ancient history
ISBN 1-587-65152-1; 978-1-58765-164-9
     LC 2004-705
Companion volume to Great events from history, The ancient world, prehistory-476 C.E
First published as part of the Great lives from history series, published 1987-1995 under the editorship of Frank

Great lives from history, The ancient world, prehistory-476 C.E—*Continued*
N. Magill; previously published as volume 1 of Dictionary of world biography, published 1998-1999

This "set provides three-to-six-page biographies on major personages from the ancient world. Arranged alphabetically, each article gives basic information such as when and where the individual was born and also where and when he or she died, a description of his or her early life and life's work, the significance of the individual, an annotated bibliography, and related entries in both this set and in the . . . [Great events from history] set." Ref & User Services Quarterly

Includes bibliographical references

Great lives from history, the Middle Ages, 477-1453; editor, Shelley Wolbrink. Salem Press 2005 2v il map set $160
Grades: 11 12 Adult   **920.003**
1. Biography—Dictionaries 2. Middle ages—Biography
ISBN 1-58765-164-5; 978-1-58765-164-9
LC 2004-16696
Companion volume to Great events from history, the Middle Ages, 477-1453

First published as part of the Great lives from history series, published 1987-1995 under the editorship of Frank N. Magill; previously published as volume 2 of Dictionary of world biography, published 1998-1999

These "volumes focus on the people throughout the world from after the Fall of Rome, in 476 C.E., to 1453. Coverage is worldwide. . . . Each entry begins with ready-reference information, followed by a summary of the person's life, a paragraph or two on 'Significance,' a list of further readings, and cross-references to entries both within the set and within the [Great events in history] companion set." Booklist

Includes bibliographical references

Great lives from history, the Renaissance & early modern era, 1454-1600; editor, Christina J. Moose. Salem Press 2005 2v il map set $160
Grades: 11 12 Adult   **920.003**
1. Biography—Dictionaries 2. Renaissance
ISBN 1-58765-211-0; 978-1-58765-211-0
LC 2004-28875
Companion volume to Great events from history, the Renaissance & early modern era, 1454-1600

First published as part of the Great lives from history series, published 1987-1995 under the editorship of Frank N. Magill; previously published as volume 3 of Dictionary of world biography, published 1998-1999

"This two-volume work offers biographies of 338 historical figures in entries that range from two to five pages in length. A publisher's note in volume 1 explains the set's format and use. All the biographies include name, nationality or ethnicity, historical role, dates, and area(s) of achievement; description of early life, work, and significance; an annotated bibliography; and cross-references." Choice

Includes bibliographical references

Grossman, Mark
World military leaders; a biographical dictionary. Facts on File 2007 414p il (Facts on File library of world history) $75
Grades: 9 10 11 12 Adult   **920.003**
1. Military history—Dictionaries 2. Biography—Dictionaries
ISBN 0-8160-4732-4; 978-0-8160-4732-1
LC 2005-8908
"Spanning the centuries from 3500 BCE to the present, this . . . A-to-Z dictionary presents the stories of the military leaders whose actions precipitated enormous change in the world around them." Publisher's note

Includes bibliographical references

Hamilton, Neil A., 1949-
Presidents: a biographical dictionary. 2nd ed. Facts on File 2005 480p il (Facts on File library of American history) $70; pa $19.95 *
Grades: 11 12 Adult   **920.003**
1. Presidents—United States—Dictionaries
ISBN 0-8160-5733-8; 978-0-8160-5733-7; 0-8160-6424-5 (pa); 978-0-8160-6424-3 (pa)
LC 2005-6683
First published 2001

"The entries, arranged chronologically and including black-and-white portraits, chronologies, and references, are focused on policy but also reveal the characters of the men as well as their accomplishments and shortcomings in the political arena. An appendix provides tables that show each man's election results, administration, family data, and 'Unusual Facts.' . . . The readability of this title makes it appealing as well as informative." Booklist

Includes bibliographical references

Holy people of the world; a cross-cultural encyclopedia; Phyllis G. Jestice, editor. ABC-CLIO 2004 3v il set $285
Grades: 11 12 Adult   **920.003**
1. Religious biography
ISBN 1-576-07355-6   LC 2004-22606
"More than 1,000 of the 1,183 entries are biographical sketches of men and women from a variety of religious traditions, including African religions, Amerindian religions, Bahaism, Buddhism, Christianity, Hinduism, Islam, Judaism, Shinto, and Sikhism. There are also survey articles that address aspects of holy people across religious traditions." Booklist

"This edition deserves to become well-worn by the time a second appears." Libr J

Includes bibliographical references

Index to the Wilson authors series. rev 1997 {ed}. Wilson, H.W. 1997 135p $45 *
Grades: 9 10 11 12   **920.003**
ISBN 0-8242-0900-1   LC 96-48600
"Biographical dictionaries in the Wilson authors series; Greek and Latin authors, 800 B.C.-A.D. 1000; European authors, 1000-1900; British authors before 1800; British authors of the nineteenth century; American authors, 1600-1900; Twentieth century authors; Twentieth century authors: first supplement; World authors, 1900-1950; World authors, 1950-1970; World authors, 1970-

Index to the Wilson authors series—*Continued*
1975; World authors, 1975-1980; World authors, 1980-1985; World authors, 1985-1990; Spanish American authors: the twentieth century; The junior book of authors; More junior authors; Third book of junior authors; Fourth book of junior authors and illustrators; Fifth book of junior authors and illustrators; Sixth book of junior authors and illustrators; Seventh book of junior authors and illustrators." Title page

Jones, J. Sydney
The Crusades, Biographies; written by J. Sydney Jones; edited by Marcia Merryman Means and Neil Schlager. UXL 2005 c2004 xxii, 230p il (The Crusades reference library) $63
Grades: 11 12 Adult   **920.003**
1. Crusades
ISBN 0-7876-9177-1   LC 2004-18000
This book "includes entries on 25 key figures. Both well-known figures, such as the Muslim leader Saladin and Eleanor of Aquitaine, and those who are maybe less familiar, such as Anna Comnena, the twelfth-century author and Byzantine princess, are covered. Each entry has a boxed quotation by its subject, and most include portraits. The entries are readable and well organized." Booklist
Includes bibliographical references

Kuhlman, Erika A., 1961-
A to Z of women in world history; [by] Erika Kuhlman. Facts on File 2002 452p il (Facts on File library of world history) $49.50 *
Grades: 11 12 Adult   **920.003**
1. Women—Biography—Dictionaries
ISBN 0-8160-4334-5   LC 2001-54327
"The 260 women who are profiled here have not only made a mark on their own cultures but have also 'influenced other women from diverse cultures and different historical periods pursuing the same goals.'. . . Entries are organized first under 14 areas of accomplishment, from 'Adventurers and Athletes' to 'Writers.'. . . Entries are generally around two pages in length, and each offers suggestions for further reading. . . . *A to Z of Women in World History* is a good place to start for researchers who are taking a sphere-of-activity approach to women's history. This highly readable volume is recommended for high-school, public, and academic libraries." Booklist
Includes bibliographical references

Life sciences before the twentieth century; biographical portraits; Everett Mendelsohn, editor. Scribner 2002 211p il (Scribner science reference series) $80
Grades: 9 10 11 12   **920.003**
1. Scientists—Dictionaries 2. Life sciences
ISBN 0-684-80661-4   LC 2001-32045
A collection of about 90 biographical profiles of famous anatomists, biologists, bacteriologists, biochemists, and others involved in the life sciences from ancient times through the nineteenth century

Life sciences in the twentieth century; biographical portraits; Everett Mendelsohn, editor; Brian S. Baigrie, consulting editor. Scribner 2001 207p il (Scribner science reference series) $80
Grades: 11 12 Adult   **920.003**
1. Scientists—Dictionaries 2. Life sciences
ISBN 0-684-80647-9   LC 00-63789
A collection of about 90 biographical profiles of 20th century scientists in such fields as "anthropology, paleontology, bacteriology, immunology, organic chemistry, crystallography [and] biochemistry." Publisher's note

The **Lincoln** library of sports champions. 8th ed. Lincoln Library 2007 14v il set $523 *
Grades: 9 10 11 12   **920.003**
1. Athletes
ISBN 0-912168-25-0; 978-0-912168-25-8
                                       LC 2006-907320
First published 1975
Presents brief, alphabetically arranged biographies of nearly 300 great sports personalities, past and present, from around the world. Features a table of contents arranged by sport and a supplementary reading list.
Includes bibliographical references

MacNee, Marie J.
Outlaws, mobsters & crooks; from the Old West to the Internet; edited by Jane Hoehner. U.X.L 1998-2002 5v il 3v set $165; ea $60
Grades: 9 10 11 12   **920.003**
1. Criminals—Dictionaries
ISBN 0-7876-2803-4 (v1-3); 0-7876-6482-0 (v4); 0-7876-6483-9 (v5)   LC 98-14861
Contents: v1 Mobsters, racketeers & gamblers, robbers; v2 Computer criminals, spies, swindlers, terrorists; v3 Bandits & gunslingers, bootleggers, pirates; v4 From the Old West to the Internet [1] ; v5 From the Old West to the Internet [2]
Presents the lives of seventy-five North American criminals including the nature of their crimes, their motivations, and information relating to the law officers who challenged them
"Browsers and researchers alike will make good use of this enjoyable reference set due to its fact-filled content and peek into the lives of such a wide variety of outlaws." Voice Youth Advocates

McBrien, Richard P.
Lives of the saints; from Mary and Francis of Assisi to John XXIII and Mother Teresa. HarperSanFrancisco 2001 xxiii, 646p il pa $19.95 hardcover o.p.
Grades: 11 12 Adult   **920.003**
1. Christian saints—Dictionaries
ISBN 0-06-123283-1 (pa)   LC 00-53933
"This work goes beyond the Roman Catholic Church's list of saints to include those of the Orthodox, Anglican, and Lutheran churches. Concise and well-researched biographical sketches are arranged by feast days, with access provided by indexes for saints, personal names, and subjects. Complementing the biographies are thoughtful essays on the history of saints, their place in religious

McBrien, Richard P.—*Continued*
history, and canonization; a series of seven tables on feast days, patron saints, iconography, and papal canonization." Libr J
Includes bibliographical references

McElroy, Tucker
A to Z of mathematicians. Facts on File 2005 308p il (Notable scientists) $45 *
Grades: 11 12 Adult **920.003**
1. Mathematicians—Dictionaries
ISBN 0-8160-5338-3   LC 2004-5460
"This volume profiles 150 mathematicians from around the globe. . . . Each entry has basic biographical information when known and a description of the subject's accomplishments. . . . Students whose course of study focuses on mathematics would be most likely to benefit from this work." SLJ

Musicians since 1900; performers in concert and opera; compiled and edited by David Ewen. Wilson, H.W. 1978 974p il $120
Grades: 11 12 Adult   **920.003**
1. Musicians—Dictionaries
ISBN 0-8242-0565-0   LC 78-12727
"Replaces 'Living musicians' and its supplement (1940-57). Gives 'detailed biographical, critical and personal information about 432 of the most distinguished performing musicians in concert and opera since 1900.'—*Introd.*' . . . A few bibliographical references are given at the end of each biography; a classified list of musicians concludes the volume." Sheehy. Guide to Ref Books. 10th edition

Notable American women; a biographical dictionary completing the twentieth century; Susan Ware, editor; Stacy Braukman, assistant editor. Belknap Press 2004 xxx, 729p $45
Grades: 11 12 Adult   **920.003**
1. Women—United States—Biography 2. United States—Biography—Dictionaries
ISBN 0-674-01488-X   LC 2004-48859
This volume includes "stars of the golden ages of radio, film, dance, and television; scientists and scholars; politicians and entrepreneurs; authors and aviators; civil rights activists and religious leaders; Native American craftspeople and world-renowned artists. Women from a broad spectrum of ethnic, class, political, religious, and sexual identities are all acknowledged." Publisher's note
Includes bibliographical references

Notable American women, 1607-1950; a biographical dictionary; Edward T. James, editor; Janet Wilson James, associate editor; Paul S. Boyer, assistant editor. Harvard Univ. Press 1971 3v hardcover o.p. pa set $52
Grades: 11 12 Adult   **920.003**
1. Women—United States—Biography 2. United States—Biography—Dictionaries
ISBN 0-674-62731-8; 0-674-62734-2 (pa)
1,359 American "women—art patrons, astronomers, Indian captives, circus performers, entrepreneurs, inventors, philosophers—are treated in well written articles which range from 400 to 7,000 words. . . . Each article is followed by bibliographical references." Choice

Notable Asian Americans; Helen Zia and Susan B. Gall, editors; foreword by George Takei. Gale Res. 1995 xxxviii, 468p il $95 *
Grades: 11 12 Adult   **920.003**
ISBN 0-8103-9623-8   LC 94-33638
This volume "features 250 role models, most of whom are contemporary. Coverage includes Asian Indians, those from Southeast Asia and the Far East, Pacific Islanders, and Hawaiians. The largest number of biographees are of Chinese or Japanese descent. Typical entrants include Judge Ito, author Deepak Chopra, cellist Yo Yo Ma, actor Bruce Lee, comedian Margaret Cho, and sculptor Isamu Noguchi. . . . Accessible to high-schoolers and up, *Notable Asian Americans* is an interesting place to start reading about these personalities." Booklist

Notable Latino writers; from the editors of Salem Press. Salem Press 2005 3v il (Magill's choice) set $207
Grades: 11 12 Adult   **920.003**
1. American literature—Hispanic American authors—History and criticism
ISBN 1-58765-243-9; 978-1-58765-243-1
          LC 2005-17567
These volumes feature "122 essays about Latino novelists, short-story writers, poets, and playwrights of the Western Hemisphere who write in English, Spanish, or Portuguese. . . . This set may prove to be a useful research tool for students, teachers, and librarians." Libr J
Includes bibliographical references

Notable poets; {edited by Frank N. Magill and the editors of Salem Press}. Salem Press 1998 3v il (Magill's choice) set $175 *
Grades: 11 12 Adult   **920.003**
ISBN 0-89356-967-4   LC 98-26164
"This set largely comprises essays on individual poets reprinted from Frank Magill's much larger Critical Survey of Poetry sets, the English Language Series, and the Foreign Language Series. Coverage 'is designed to survey the essential poets' studied most often in US curricula. The poems range from Homer to Seamus Heany, from Anna Akhmatova to Anne Sexton." Choice

Notable women in mathematics; a biographical dictionary; edited by Charlene Morrow and Teri Perl. Greenwood Press 1998 302p il $52.95 *
Grades: 11 12 Adult   **920.003**
1. Women mathematicians—Dictionaries
ISBN 0-313-29131-4   LC 97-18598
"This book features five-to-six page profiles of 59 mathematicians and scientific computing researchers from around the world. Each profile describes the woman's major life events and educational and career milestones, includes a discussion of her areas of mathematical research in nontechnical terms, and lists works by and about that person. All entries have an accompanying black-and-white photograph. The majority of essays are based on interviews by the authors." SLJ

Notable women in the life sciences; a biographical dictionary; edited by Benjamin F. Shearer and Barbara S. Shearer. Greenwood Press 1996 440p il $52.50 *

Grades: 11 12 Adult   **920.003**
1. Women scientists—Dictionaries
ISBN 0-313-29302-3   LC 95-25603

"Biographical entries of 97 women who have made significant contributions to the life sciences from antiquity to the present. Essays vary in length from two pages to seven and include a biographical essay, notes, bibliography, and a photograph if available." SLJ

Oakes, Elizabeth H., 1951-
Encyclopedia of world scientists. Rev. ed. Facts on File 2007 2v il (Facts on File science library) set $170 *

Grades: 9 10 11 12 Adult   **920.003**
1. Scientists—Encyclopedias
ISBN 978-0-8160-6158-7; 0-8160-6158-0
      LC 2007-6076
First published 2001

This work contains "stories of nearly 1,000 scientists—almost half of whom are female—who have contributed significantly to their fields. All scientific disciplines are represented, as well as all periods of history as far back as 600 BCE." Publisher's note
Includes bibliographical references

Pendergast, Tom, 1964-
U-X-L graphic novelists; [by] Tom Pendergast and Sara Pendergast; Sarah Hermsen, project editor. U-X-L/Thomson Gale 2007 3v il set $181 *

Grades: 9 10 11 12 Adult   **920.003**
1. Graphic novels—Dictionaries 2. Cartoonists—Dictionaries
ISBN 1-4144-0440-9; 978-1-4144-0440-0
      LC 2006-13711

The three volumes include 75 alphabetically-arranged articles that profile authors, illustrators, and author-illustrators, and include European, American, and Japanese creators. The introduction provides some history of graphic novels, and there is a separate essay on manga.

"This accessible and readable survey of a timely topic should generate considerable attention in school library media center and public library collections. Well researched and documented, with subject and language appropriate for its intended audience, this set is highly recommended." Booklist
Includes bibliographical references

Popular contemporary writers; editor, Michael D. Sharp. Marshall Cavendish Reference 2005 11v il set $657.07

Grades: 8 9 10 11 12 Adult   **920.003**
1. Authors—Dictionaries 2. Literature—Bio-bibliography
ISBN 0-7614-7601-6   LC 2005-42005

"This alphabetically arranged encyclopedia offers information on 96 contemporary writers, primarily British and North American, whose works tend to mine populist as well as artistic veins—usually with bestselling results. Each extensive, readable entry opens with stage-setting biographical and critical comments, then goes on in successive sections to describe the writers life and career to date, examine his or her dominant themes in a critical light, summarize and evaluate major works, and close with leads to Web-based resources of interest." SLJ
Includes bibliographical references

Reef, Catherine
African Americans in the military. Facts on File 2004 256p il (A to Z of African Americans) $45
Grades: 11 12 Adult   **920.003**
1. African American soldiers—Dictionaries
ISBN 0-8160-4901-7   LC 2003-7491

With "profiles organized alphabetically, this volume gives readers . . . biographical essentials—year and place of birth, rank, family information—and then delves into the challenges and major accomplishments of each individual." Publisher's note

This "will find an important role in most general reference collections." Am Ref Books Annu, 2005
Includes bibliographical references

The **Renaissance** and the scientific revolution; biographical portraits; Brian S. Baigrie, editor. Scribner 2001 210p il (Scribner science reference series) $80
Grades: 11 12 Adult   **920.003**
1. Scientists—Dictionaries
ISBN 0-684-80646-0   LC 00-63565

A collection of about 90 biographical profiles of scientists from 1500 to 1800

Schneider, Dorothy
First ladies; a biographical dictionary; [by] Dorothy Schneider, Carl J. Schneider. 2nd ed. Facts on File 2005 420p il (Facts on File library of American history) $70 *
Grades: 11 12 Adult   **920.003**
1. Presidents' spouses—United States
ISBN 0-8160-5752-4   LC 2005-6682
First published 2001

"The entries, arranged chronologically and including black-and-white portraits, chronologies, and lists of further reading, show how . . . [the first ladies'] backgrounds and personal strengths and abilities influenced the women's approach to their times 'in office' and how the public's expectations changed through the years. . . . The readability of this volume makes it appealing as well as informative." Booklist
Includes bibliographical references

Science fiction, fantasy, and horror writers; [edited by] Marie J. MacNee. U.X.L 1995 2v il set $65
Grades: 7 8 9 10   **920.003**
1. Science fiction—Bio-bibliography 2. Authors—Dictionaries
ISBN 0-8103-9865-6   LC 94-32459

"In this two-volume set, classic authors such as Jules Verne and Mary Shelley rub elbows with newcomers such as Christopher Pike and R.L. Stine. The 80 biographical entries run three to six pages each. . . . The

Science fiction, fantasy, and horror writers—
Continued
entries include discussions of the author's major or critically acclaimed works. B&W photos of the authors and stills from motion pictures enhance the text. Best Bets, a chronological listing of some of an author's best works, and Real Life, a list of movie adaptations, are extra bonuses." Book Rep

Includes bibliographical references

Scientists, mathematicians, and inventors; lives and legacies: an encyclopedia of people who changed the world; edited by Doris Simonis; writers, Caroline Hertzenberg [et al.] Oryx Press 1999 244p il (Lives and legacies) $69.95
Grades: 11 12 Adult   **920.003**
1. Scientists—Dictionaries 2. Mathematicians—Dictionaries 3. Inventors—Dictionaries
ISBN 1-57356-151-7   LC 98-48484
Profiles people "who influenced their discipline or society at large or who overcame some societal barrier in conducting their careers. Each full-page biography has the person's name; dates; a short title or tag line describing the individual's accomplishments . . . a brief biography; a description of the person's work and its importance, ramifications, and intellectual legacy; a time line that puts personal and professional events in context of world political events; and suggestions for further reading." Sci Books Films

Scientists: their lives and works; Peggy Saari and Stephen Allison, editors. U.X.L 1996-2002 7v il v1-7 set $350; v1-3 set $165; v4, 5, 6, & 7 ea $60
Grades: 9 10 11 12   **920.003**
1. Scientists—Dictionaries
ISBN 1-4144-0487-5 (v1-7); 0-7876-0959-5 (v1-3); 0-7876-1874-8   (v4);   0-7876-2797-6   (v5); 0-7876-3682-7 (v6); 0-7876-6383-2 (v7)
                              LC 96-25579

Volume 4-6 edited by Marie C. Ellavich; volume 7 edited by Tanya Lee Stone; original 3 volume set has subtitle: the lives and works of 150 scientists
"The alphabetically arranged volumes profile figures . . . ranging from the Industrial Revolution to the present. Each entry lists birth and death dates and birthplace, followed by an accessible, fact-filled text that accurately chronicles the subject's early life, educational background, career milestones, discoveries, and awards." SLJ [review of original 3 volume set]

The **Scribner** encyclopedia of American lives; Kenneth T. Jackson, editor in chief; Karen Markoe, general editor; Arnold Markoe, executive editor. Scribner 1998-2003 6v il set $540
Grades: 11 12 Adult   **920.003**
1. United States—Biography—Dictionaries
ISBN 0-684-31292-1   LC 98-33793
Individual volumes also available ea $140
Contents: v1 1981-1985; v2 1986-1990; v3 1991-1993; v4 1994-1996; v5 1997-1999; v6 2000-2002; v7 2003-2005

"Scribner envisions SEAL as the continuation of the *Dictionary of American Biography* (DAB). . . . Selection criteria are that the biographees made significant contributions to American life and culture. . . . An appreciable number of women and people of color are recognized. All biographies are signed contributions by 332 scholars." Libr J {review of first two volumes}

Snodgrass, Mary Ellen
Who's who in the Middle Ages; illustrations research by Linda Campbell Franklin. McFarland & Co. 2001 312p il $75
Grades: 11 12 Adult   **920.003**
1. Middle Ages—Biography 2. Medieval civilization
ISBN 0-7864-0774-3   LC 00-56243
"Entries are alphabetical; the scope is from the fifth century to the fifteenth. Each entry, giving an array of names and alternate names for the person, includes both personal and historical details. References are included with each entry, and a bibliography accompanies the whole. Appendices cover the colleges and universities that educated many of the people, and the period's noteworthy events, major monasteries, abbeys and convents and their founders and dates, individuals listed by occupation or contribution, and popes, emperors and monarchs." Publisher's note

UXL encyclopedia of world biography; Laura B. Tyle, editor. U.X.L 2003 10v il set $475 *
Grades: 8 9 10 11 12   **920.003**
1. Biography—Dictionaries
ISBN 0-7876-6465-0   LC 2002-4316
A collection of 750 biographies and portraits of notable historic and current figures in American and world history, literature, science and math, arts and entertainment, and the social sciences
"The biographies are well written and, although brief, provide information that will be interesting to young adults." Am Ref Books Annu, 2003

Vice presidents; a biographical dictionary; edited by L. Edward Purcell. 3rd ed. Facts on File 2005 504p il $70
Grades: 9 10 11 12   **920.003**
1. Vice-presidents—United States
ISBN 0-8160-5740-0   LC 2005-40013
First published 1998
"The articles explain how these men came to office, demonstrate their range of experiences and skills, and document what they did with the power they had. The 50-page 'Chronology of Events' appended to the entries is useful background material for anyone needing to put a specific vice president's era in political perspective." Booklist
Includes bibliographical references

Who was who in America; with world notables. Marquis Who's Who 1942-2006 18v & Index set $999.95 * v1-13 ea $90; v14-16 ea $95; v17 $98; v17 & Index $155.95
Grades: 11 12 Adult   **920.003**
1. United States—Biography—Dictionaries
ISBN 0-8379-0254-1
Also available online; Also available historical volume 1607-1896 $90 (ISBN 0-8379-0236-3)

Who was who in America—*Continued*

Contents: v1 1897-1942 (ISBN 0-8379-0201-0); v2 1943-1950 (ISBN 0-8379-0206-1); v3 1951-1960 (ISBN 0-8379-0203-7); v4 1961-1968 (ISBN 0-8379-0204-5); v5 1969-1973 (ISBN 0-8379-0205-3); v6 1974-1976 (ISBN 0-8379-0207-X); v7 1977-1981 (ISBN 0-8379-0210-X); v8 1982-1985 (ISBN 0-8379-0214-2); v9 1985-1989 (ISBN 0-8379-0217-7); v10 1989-1993 (ISBN 0-8379-0220-7); v11 1993-1996 (ISBN 0-8379-0225-8); v12 1996-1998; v13 1998-2000; v14 2000-2002 (ISBN 0-8379-0245-2); v15 2002-2004 (ISBN 0-8379-0247-9);v16 2004-2005 (0-8379-0251-7); v17 2005-2006 0-8379-0255-X)

"Includes sketches removed from 'Who's who in America' because of death of the biographee; date of death and, often, interment location is added. With the 'Historical volume' these volumes form a series entitled 'Who's who in American history.'" Guide to Ref Books. 11th edition

World artists, 1950-1980; an H.W. Wilson biographical dictionary; {edited} by Claude Marks. Wilson, H.W. 1984 912p il $130 *

Grades: 11 12 Adult   **920.003**
1. Artists—Dictionaries
ISBN 0-8242-0707-6   LC 84-13152

"The 312 painters, sculptors, and graphic artists in this biographical dictionary were selected from the outstanding artistic figures in the US, Europe, and Latin America. . . . The biographical information includes family, working background, and aesthetic beliefs. There are many quotations from the artist and from critics. Also included is a list of significant collections and a bibliography." Choice

World artists, 1980-1990; an H.W. Wilson biographical dictionary; edited by Claude Marks. Wilson, H.W. 1991 413p il $95 *

Grades: 11 12 Adult   **920.003**
1. Artists—Dictionaries
ISBN 0-8242-0827-7   LC 91-13183

This volume contains brief biographies of 118 artists from around the world who have been influential in the 1980's

World authors, 1950-1970; a companion volume to Twentieth century authors; edited by John Wakeman; editorial consultant: Stanley J. Kunitz. Wilson, H.W. 1975 1594p il (Authors series) $160 *

Grades: 11 12 Adult   **920.003**
1. Authors—Dictionaries   2. Literature—Bio-bibliography
ISBN 0-8242-0419-0

This volume includes 959 "authors who came into prominence between 1950 and 1970. . . . Authors were chosen for literary importance or outstanding popularity." Wilson Libr Bull

World authors, 1970-1975; editor, John Wakeman; editorial consultant, Stanley J. Kunitz. Wilson, H.W. 1980 894p il (Authors series) $140 *

Grades: 11 12 Adult   **920.003**
1. Authors—Dictionaries   2. Literature—Bio-bibliography
ISBN 0-8242-0641-X   LC 79-21874

This volume provides biographical or autobiographical sketches for 348 of the most influential and popular men and women of letters who have come into prominence between 1970 and 1975

World authors, 1975-1980; editor, Vineta Colby. Wilson, H.W. 1985 829p il (Authors series) $140 *

Grades: 11 12 Adult   **920.003**
1. Authors—Dictionaries   2. Literature—Bio-bibliography
ISBN 0-8242-0715-7   LC 85-10045

This work profiles the lives and works of 379 writers

World authors, 1980-1985; editor, Vineta Colby. Wilson, H.W. 1990 938p il (Authors series) $140 *

Grades: 11 12 Adult   **920.003**
1. Authors—Dictionaries   2. Literature—Bio-bibliography
ISBN 0-8242-0797-1   LC 90-49782

This volume covers 320 contemporary writers

World authors, 1985-1990; a volume in the Wilson authors series; editor, Vineta Colby. Wilson, H.W. 1995 970p il (Authors series) $140 *

Grades: 11 12 Adult   **920.003**
1. Authors—Dictionaries   2. Literature—Bio-bibliography
ISBN 0-8242-0875-7   LC 95-41656

This volume covers 345 novelists, playwrights, poets, and other authors who have risen to prominence in the late 1980s

World authors, 1990-1995; editor, Clifford Thompson. Wilson, H.W. 1999 863p il (Authors series) $155 *

Grades: 11 12 Adult   **920.003**
1. Authors—Dictionaries   2. Literature—Bio-bibliography
ISBN 0-8242-0956-7   LC 99-48161

The 317 authors treated in this volume include novelists, playwrights, and poets who have published significant work in the early 1990s. Also covers essayists, historians, biographers, critics, philosophers, and social scientists who have made exceptional contributions to the literature of our time.

Includes bibliographical references

World authors, 1995-2000; editors, Clifford Thompson, Mari Rich [et al.] Wilson, H.W. 2003 872p il (Authors series) $160 *

Grades: 8 9 10 11 12 Adult   **920.003**
1. Authors—Dictionaries   2. Literature—Bio-bibliography
ISBN 0-8242-1032-8   LC 2003-45062

This reference includes 320 novelists, poets, dramatists, essayists, social scientists, and biographers who have published significant works from 1995 through 2000. Each profile details the author's life and career, the circumstances under which their works were produced, and their literary significance.

Includes bibliographical references

World authors, 2000-2005; editors, Jennifer Curry, David Ramm, Mari Rich, Albert Rolls. Wilson, H. W. 2007 800p il (Authors series) $170 *

Grades: 11 12 Adult 920.003

1. Authors—Dictionaries 2. Literature—Bio-bibliography

ISBN 978-0-8242-1077-9

This book "covers some 300 novelists, poets, dramatists, essayists, scientists, biographers, and other authors whose books [were] published 2000 through 2005." Publisher's note

World musicians; edited by Clifford Thompson; staff contributors: Denise Bonilla {et al.}; consultants: Justin Dello Joio, Lewis Porter. Wilson, H.W. 1999 1181p il $115 *

Grades: 11 12 Adult 920.003

1. Musicians—Dictionaries

ISBN 0-8242-0940-0 LC 98-29205

International in coverage, this volume profiles "contemporary musicians whose specialties range from classical to pop, opera to rap, bluegrass to rock. . . . Written in a lively style and ranging in length from 500 to 3,500 words, the articles cover each musician's personal and professional life and are frequently spiced with quotations from published interviews with the subject and excerpts from critical commentary. Many entries include a black-and-white photo of the musician, and all conclude with a selected bibliography of additional publications and recordings." Booklist

World poets; Ron Padgett, editor in chief. Scribner 2000 3v il set $295 *

Grades: 11 12 Adult 920.003

ISBN 0-684-80591-X LC 00-24801

"This resource examines the lives and works of 110 poets often studied in high school. The individuals included represent writers from all over the world, from prehistory to the present time. . . . Following the entries on the individual poets are 15 thematic essays covering such topics as the troubadours, the poetry of the Harlem Renaissance, and Asian-American poetry. Appendixes include information on poetic meter and lists of major prizewinners. This useful set concludes with a comprehensive index." SLJ

Writers of the American Renaissance; an A-to-Z guide; edited by Denise D. Knight. Greenwood Press 2003 458p $99.95

Grades: 9 10 11 12 920.003

1. Authors, American 2. Literature—Bio-bibliography

ISBN 0-313-32140-X LC 2003-52846

This "book is intended as a primary reference guide to 74 authors who wrote during the 19th century. Arranged alphabetically by author last name, each entry in the book includes a biography of the author; a discussion of the author's major works and themes; an overview of the critical reception of the author's works; works cited; and a two-part bibliography that includes works by the author and studies about the author. . . . This volume provides a comprehensive reference tool for students doing author studies and will add greatly to any high school library collection." Libr Media Connect

Includes bibliographical references

Yount, Lisa

A to Z of biologists. Facts on File 2003 390p il (Notable scientists) $45

Grades: 11 12 Adult 920.003

ISBN 0-8160-4541-0 LC 2002-13816

"Facts on File science library"

"Each profile focuses on a particular biologist's research and contributions to the field and his or her effect on scientists whose work followed. Their lives and personalities are also discussed through incidents, quotations, and photographs. The profiles are culturally inclusive and span a range of biologists from ancient times to the present day." Publisher's note

Includes bibliographical references

A to Z of women in science and math. Facts on File 1999 254p il (Encyclopedia of women) $45 *

Grades: 9 10 11 12 920.003

1. Women scientists—Dictionaries 2. Women mathematicians—Dictionaries

ISBN 0-8160-3797-3 LC 98-46093

New edition in preparation

Profiles over 150 women "who have made contributions in a wide range of fields—medicine, genetics, ecology, archaeology, astronomy, botany, mathematics, physics, computer science, zoology, chemistry, and related scientific fields. The selections cover women from antiquity to the present. . . . Essays on each woman are generally 300 to 1000 words, recounting essential biographical information: education, career, contributions to the field, and, perhaps most interestingly, obstacles they faced in male-dominated careers." Libr J

Includes bibliographical references

92 Individual biography

Lives of individuals are arranged alphabetically under the name of the person written about. Some subject headings have been added to aid in curriculum work.

Aaron, Hank, 1934-

Stanton, Tom. Hank Aaron and the home run that changed America. William Morrow 2004 249p il hardcover o.p. pa $13.95 *

Grades: 7 8 9 10 92

1. Baseball—Biography 2. African American athletes 3. United States—Race relations

ISBN 0-06-057976-5; 0-06-072290-8 (pa) LC 2004-46092

The author "covers the time from the funeral of Jackie Robinson in 1972 to the spring of 1974, when Hank Aaron hit his 715th home run and passed Babe Ruth's record." Booklist

"Stanton deftly balances the story of Aaron's professional career, his personal life, and the changes in baseball between the years of Jackie Robinson and today's megastars, such as Ken Griffey, Jr. and Barry Bonds. . . . This book is a must for young adult collections." Voice Youth Advocates

Includes bibliographical references

Abbott, Berenice, 1898-1991

Sullivan, George. Berenice Abbott, photographer; an independent vision. Clarion Books 2006 170p il $20

Grades: 7 8 9 10   92

    1. Women photographers

    ISBN 978-0-618-44026-9; 0-618-44026-7

                     LC 2005-30736

A biography of Berenice Abbott, who was a pioneer in the field of professional photography and is particularly acclaimed for her photographs of the streets and buildings of New York City before they were replaced by skyscrapers during a building boom in the 1920s and early 1930s.

"Sullivan brings together an enormous amount of information about Abbott and presents it in a clear, thoughtful manner. . . . Large, clear reproductions of Abbott's photos appear throughout the book." Booklist

Includes bibliographical references

Abeel, Samantha, 1977-

Abeel, Samantha. My thirteenth winter; a memoir. Orchard Bks. 2003 203p $15.95; pa $15.95

Grades: 9 10 11 12   92

    1. Learning disabilities

    ISBN 0-439-33904-9; 0-439-33905-6 (pa)

                     LC 2003-40465

"Abeel recounts her life, from kindergarten through college, with a learning disability that compromises her ability to learn skills based on sequential processing—especially math, spelling, and grammar. . . . Her narrative is interjected with first-person remembrances of painful incidents that left a vivid imprint on her self-worth." Booklist

"This introspective book provides a valuable resource for teachers or counselors working with youth with learning disabilities." VOYA

Adams, Ansel, 1902-1984

Gherman, Beverly. Ansel Adams; America's photographer; a biography for young people. Little, Brown and Company 2002 110p il $19.95

Grades: 7 8 9 10   92

    1. Photographers

    ISBN 0-316-82445-3; 978-0-316-82445-3

                     LC 2002-103229

Notable Children's Trade Books in the Field of Social Sciences (2003)

This is a "look into Adams' life, beginning with his childhood in San Francisco, following him as he becomes enamored with both photography and the piano, and detailing the long-range effects that growing up amid natural beauty had on him. . . . Readers being introduced to Adams' work for the first time will be awed by the photographs, and Adams' fans will appreciate both the numerous offerings and the book's handsome design." Booklist

Includes bibliographical references

Adams, Samuel, 1722-1803

Irvin, Benjamin. Samuel Adams; son of liberty, father of revolution; {by} Benjamin H. Irvin. Oxford Univ. Press 2002 176p il (Oxford portraits) $28 *

Grades: 7 8 9 10   92

    1. United States—History—1775-1783, Revolution

    ISBN 0-19-513225-4   LC 2002-4283

Contents: The elusive Samuel Adams; Samuel Adams's Boston; Raised for rebellion; Tis not in mortals to command success; Sam the publican and the Stamp Act Riots; Mobs and massacre; To save the country; The Coercive Acts and the Continental Congress; Is not America already independent; The storm is now over

Examines the life of Samuel Adams, a hero of the American Revolution who is credited by some with having fired the first shot at Lexington Green, the "shot heard 'round the world"

"Irvin's account of events is exciting and written in a compelling narrative style. He presents an unbiased assessment of Adams's actions and character." SLJ

Includes bibliographical references

Addams, Jane, 1860-1935

Fradin, Judith Bloom. Jane Addams; champion of democracy; by Judith Bloom Fradin and Dennis Brindell Fradin. Clarion Books 2006 216p il $21 *

Grades: 7 8 9 10   92

    1. Hull House (Chicago, Ill.) 2. Chicago (Ill.)—Social conditions

    ISBN 0-618-50436-1

A biography of the social activist, pacifist, author, founder of Hull House in Chicago, and winner of the Nobel Peace Prize.

"A fascinating and rich life is related in strong, unfussy prose." Booklist

Includes bibliographical references

Alcott, Louisa May, 1832-1888

Alcott, Louisa May. The selected letters of Louisa May Alcott; edited by Joel Myerson and Daniel Shealy; with an introduction by Madeleine B. Stern, associate editor. University of Ga. Press 1995 352p il pa $24.95

Grades: 11 12 Adult   92

    1. Authors, American 2. Women authors

    ISBN 0-8203-1740-3   LC 95-8400

First published 1987 by Little, Brown

This volume contains "a wealth of colorful, determined, cranky, humorous, affectionate correspondence, salted with Yankee colloquialisms. The recipients range from eminent people like Lucy Stone, Ralph Waldo Emerson and publisher Thomas Niles to friends of the Alcott and May families. A large part of the correspondence is about her books. . . . The voice of the writer and woman is palpable throughout, insistent and appealing." Publ Wkly

Includes bibliographical references

Alexander, the Great, 356-323 B.C.

Arrian. Alexander the Great; selections from Arrian; [translated by] J. G. Lloyd. Cambridge Univ. Press 1981 104p il maps (Translations from Greek and Roman authors) pa $17.95

Grades: 9 10 11 12   **92**

1. Greece—History 2. Kings and rulers

ISBN 0-521-28195-4   LC 81-9453

Born over four hundred years after the death of Alexander the Great, Arrian served in the Roman army and devoted his life's work to the study of Alexander's empire, a section of which he governed under the auspices of Rome. Here are selections from his history which focus primarily on Alexander's military campaigns

"This book may seem to be a military account, but first and foremost it is the story of a man." Introduction

Includes bibliographical references

Foreman, Laura. Alexander the Conqueror; the epic story of the warrior king. Da Capo Press 2004 211p il map $35 *

Grades: 11 12 Adult   **92**

1. Greece—History 2. Kings and rulers

ISBN 0-306-81293-2   LC 2003-62573

"A Tehabi book"

This illustrated biography of the Macedonian ruler "follows the progression of his conquests through the Near East and Central Asia to the Indus Valley, and introduces Alexander's family, the personalities of his generals, and the cultures of the lands he conquered. Foreman examines the complex character of Alexander as student, friend, lover, military genius, and emperor." Publisher's note

This is "a lively, engrossing account of the life of one of the world's greatest military commanders." SLJ

Includes bibliographical references

Alhazen, 965-1039

Steffens, Bradley. Ibn al-Haytham; first scientist. Morgan Reynolds Pub. 2007 128p il (Profiles in science) lib bdg $27.95

Grades: 7 8 9 10   **92**

1. Scientists 2. Mathematicians

ISBN 978-1-59935-024-0 (lib bdg); 1-59935-024-6 (lib bdg)   LC 2006-23970

The author "has organized what is known of his subject's life and work into a coherent narrative. . . . Like the history of mathematics, the history of science is incomplete without an acknowledgment of early scholars in the Middle East. This clearly written introduction to al-Haytham, his society, and his contributions does that." Booklist

Includes bibliographical references

Ali, Muhammad, 1942-

Remnick, David. King of the world: Muhammad Ali and the rise of an American hero. Random House 1998 326p il hardcover o.p. pa $14

Grades: 11 12 Adult   **92**

1. African American athletes

ISBN 0-375-50065-0; 0-375-70229-6 (pa)   LC 98-24539

This book focuses on Ali's career "in the early sixties—roughly, late 1962 to late 1965. . . . Five heavyweight title fights are dealt with in depth: the first Patterson-Liston fight on September 25, 1962, and their rematch on July 22, 1963: the first Liston-Ali fight on February 25, 1964, and their rematch on May 25, 1965: and the first Ali-Patterson fight on November 22, 1965." Nation

"This is the best book ever on Muhammad Ali and one of the best on America in the 1960s." Booklist

Includes bibliographical references

Allende, Isabel

Allende, Isabel. Paula; translated from the Spanish by Margaret Sayers Peden. HarperCollins Pubs. 1995 330p hardcover o.p. pa $13.95

Grades: 11 12 Adult   **92**

1. Allende family

ISBN 0-06-017252-5; 0-06-092721-6 (pa)   LC 95-2452

Allende "interweaves the story of her own life with the slow dying of her 28-year-old daughter, Paula." Publ Wkly

This "is a deeply affecting tale, written in the rich, luminous prose typical of Allende's novels, that investigates the sources of her writing as it paints a vivid portrait of Chile." Libr J

Anderson, Marian, 1897-1993

Keiler, Allan. Marian Anderson; a singer's journey. University of Illinois Press 2002 447p hardcover o.p. pa $21.95

Grades: 11 12 Adult   **92**

1. African American singers 2. African American women

ISBN 0-684-80711-4; 0-252-07067-4 (pa)   LC 99-43319

"A Lisa Drew book"

"Keiler offers an assessment of the great contralto, the first African American soloist at the Metropolitan Opera." Libr J

The author's "clear, succinct prose, initially lacking narrative coherence, gains strength and momentum as his subject matures from a young and struggling artist into one of the enduring voices of our century." Publ Wkly

Includes discography and bibliographical references

Angelou, Maya

Angelou, Maya. I know why the caged bird sings. Random House 2002 281p $21.95 *

Grades: 11 12 Adult   **92**

1. African American authors 2. Women authors

ISBN 0-375-50789-2   LC 2001-41914

Also available in paperback from Bantam Bks.

First published 1969

The first volume in the author's autobiographical series covers her childhood and adolescence in rural Arkansas, St. Louis, and San Francisco.

"Angelou is a skillful writer; her language ranges from beautifully lyrical prose to earthy metaphor, and her descriptions have power and sensitivity." Libr J

Angelou, Maya—_Continued_

Followed by Gather together in my name (1974); Singin' and swingin' and gettin' merry like Christmas (1976); The heart of a woman (1981); All God's children need traveling shoes (1986); A song flung up to heaven (2002)

Anthony, Susan B., 1820-1906

Ward, Geoffrey C. Not for ourselves alone: the story of Elizabeth Cady Stanton and Susan B. Anthony. See entry under Stanton, Elizabeth Cady, 1815-1902

Archimedes, ca. 287-212 B.C.

Hasan, Heather. Archimedes: the father of mathematics. Rosen Pub. Group 2006 112p il (The library of Greek philosophers) lib bdg $33.25
Grades: 9 10 11 12   92
1. Mathematicians
ISBN 1-4042-0774-0   LC 2005-9992
"This biography charts the life of Archimedes while . . . explaining his mathematical postulates." Publisher's note
Includes bibliographical references

Armstrong, Karen

Armstrong, Karen. The spiral staircase; my climb out of darkness. Knopf 2004 xxii, 305p $24; pa $14
Grades: 11 12 Adult   92
ISBN 0-375-41318-9; 0-385-72127-7 (pa)
LC 2003-47550
This "is the story of Armstrong's personal spiritual quest, which led her at age 17 to join a convent. However, she found that her own skeptical nature and the physical constraints of convent life crippled her intellectually and spiritually. . . . After seven years, Armstrong left the convent." SLJ

Armstrong, Lance

Armstrong, Lance. It's not about the bike; my journey back to life; [by] Lance Armstrong with Sally Jenkins. Putnam 2000 275p il $24.95; pa $14
Grades: 11 12 Adult   92
1. Athletes
ISBN 0-399-14611-3; 0-425-17961-3 (pa)
LC 00-35612
Armstrong describes his early years growing up in Plano, Texas, his rise through the sports world as a champion American cyclist, his diagnosis and recovery from testicular cancer and his triumph in the 1999 Tour de France.
"Readers will respond to the inspirational recovery story, and they will appreciate the behind-the-scenes cycling information." Booklist

Arthur, King

Ashe, Geoffrey. The discovery of King Arthur; Geoffrey Ashe in association with Debrett's Peerage. H. Holt 1987 224p il map pa $15
Grades: 11 12 Adult   92
1. Great Britain—Kings and rulers 2. Great Britain—History—0-1066
ISBN 0-8050-0115-8   LC 86-9784
First published 1985 by Anchor Press/Doubleday
The author explores archeological findings that support the theory that Arthur was a real leader in the 5th century. Arthurian themes in literature and art are also examined.
Includes bibliographical references

Asayesh, Gelareh

Asayesh, Gelareh. Saffron sky; a life between Iran and America. Beacon Press 1999 222p hardcover o.p. pa $15
Grades: 11 12 Adult   92
1. Women journalists 2. Iranian Americans
ISBN 0-8070-7210-9; 0-8070-7211-7 (pa)
LC 99-27889
The author "chronicles her life as a series of trips to and from Iran—as a child who spoke no English, on the eve of the 1992 Gulf War as a green card-holding adult, and as the parent of a young biracial American citizen—and in doing so, tells the story of both her family's and Iran's tumultuous recent history. This beautifully written narrative provides a rare, humanizing glimpse into the politics, culture, and geography of {Iran}." Libr J

Aseel, Maryam Qudrat, 1974-

Aseel, Maryam Qudrat. Torn between two cultures; an Afghan-American woman speaks out; {by} Maryam Qudrat. Capital Bks. 2003 191p $22.95; pa $14.95 *
Grades: 11 12 Adult   92
1. Afghan Americans 2. Muslims—United States 3. Muslim women 4. Afghanistan
ISBN 1-931868-36-0; 1-931868-70-0 (pa)
LC 2002-41108
"Capital currents book"
"Aseel, a first-generation Afghan American woman, is an activist in the Muslim community in general and the Afghani community in particular. Woven around her commentary on current events is the fascinating story of her life, including a childhood that balanced both modernity and tradition. Throughout the . . . engaging narrative, Aseel manages to clear up numerous misconceptions about her culture and religion." Booklist
Includes bibliographical references

Ashe, Arthur, 1943-1993

Ashe, Arthur. Days of grace; a memoir; by Arthur Ashe and Arnold Rampersad. Knopf 1993 317p il hardcover o.p. pa $6.99
Grades: 11 12 Adult   92
1. Tennis—Biography 2. African American athletes
ISBN 0-679-42396-6; 0-345-38681-7 (pa)
LC 92-54919

Ashe, Arthur, 1943-1993—*Continued*

Ashe discusses "the issues of greatest import to him: family, education, religion, athletics, health, politics, and social injustice. . . . The bulk of the work centers on his life after retirement from tennis . . . and his championing of various causes, including the fight against AIDS. In anticipation of his passing, he closes with an open letter to his daughter, Camera." Libr J

"This is a truly gripping book. It's gripping, it's moving, it's admirable; and what makes it so is Ashe's capacity for evaluating himself and the world with intelligence and honor." N Y Times Book Rev

Asimov, Isaac, 1920-1992

Asimov, Isaac. It's been a good life; edited by Janet Jeppson Asimov. Prometheus Books 2002 309p il $27

Grades: 9 10 11 12 Adult   92
1. Authors, American 2. Scientists
ISBN 1-573-92968-9   LC 2002-20570

The author's widow has "condensed his three-volume autobiography into one handy book covering his life from birth in Russia and immigration with his parents and through careers as a scientist, an sf writer, and a science popularizer, and touching on matters of his humanist faith and his numerous works on the way to his final illness. . . . This is a good introduction to one of the most prolific and distinguished careers in twentieth-century American letters, especially for those unready to immerse themselves in the complete Asimov self-life." Booklist

Includes bibliographical references

Audubon, John James, 1785-1851

Rhodes, Richard. John James Audubon; the making of an American. Knopf 2004 528p il $30; pa $16

Grades: 11 12 Adult   92
1. Artists—United States 2. Naturalists
ISBN 0-375-41412-6; 0-375-71393-X (pa)
                                  LC 2003-69489

The author "chronicles Audubon's ineluctable sense of mission, phenomenal skills, and triumph over adversity. . . . Rhodes sets Audubon's engrossing tale within the context of the War of 1812, the Louisiana Purchase, the wars against Native Americans (whom Audubon profoundly admired), and the rapid decimation of the American wilderness. . . . Full of passion and discovery, hardship and transcendence, Audubon's story is at once intimate and mythic, and Rhodes' fresh, comprehensive biography will capture the imagination of readers everywhere." Booklist

Includes bibliographical references

Austen, Jane, 1775-1817

Shields, Carol. Jane Austen. Viking 2001 185p (Penguin lives series) hardcover o.p. pa $13

Grades: 11 12 Adult   92
1. Authors, English 2. Women authors
ISBN 0-670-89488-5; 0-14-303516-9 (pa)
                                  LC 00-43807

"Penguin lives series"

"In chronicling her subject's life and personality, Shields emphasizes Austen's keen ability to listen, observe, and capture clearly the social mores of her time and explore human nature in her writing. Shields contends that historical references are behind many of the scenes and characters in Austen's novels, and as a way of more clearly personalizing Austen's experiences or feelings, she interjects commentary regarding writing and publishing that is presumably based on personal experience." Libr J

Baek, Hongyong, 1912-2002

Lee, Helie. Still life with rice; a young American woman discovers the life and legacy of her Korean grandmother. Scribner 1996 320p pa $13 hardcover o.p.

Grades: 11 12 Adult   92
1. Korean Americans
ISBN 0-684-82711-5 (pa)   LC 95-41921

"Lee traveled from California to Korea to recapture the life of her grandmother. Hongyong Baek (b. 1912) grew up in northern Korea, the daughter of wealthy parents, and at 22 entered into an arranged marriage. . . . Drawing on interviews with her grandmother and writing in her voice, Lee . . . describes the aftermath of the Japanese occupation of Korea, which forced Baek, her husband (with whom she ultimately fell in love) and their children to flee to China in 1939, where they supported themselves by selling opium. After they returned to Korea, the 1950s' civil war caused them extreme hardship. . . . Baek emigrated to the U.S. in 1972." Publ Wkly

"Written with great narrative power and attention to detail, a testament to the will to survive." Booklist

Baker, Russell, 1925-

Baker, Russell. Growing up. New American Library 1983 c1982 278p pa $15

Grades: 11 12 Adult   92
1. Journalists
ISBN 0-452-25550-3
Also available in paperback from Signet Bks.
"A Plume book"
First published 1982 by Congdon & Weed

This book "recounts the first 24 years of [Baker's] life as the son of an independent and deep-rooted Virginian family." Natl Rev

Balanchine, George, 1904-1983

Gottlieb, Robert Adams. George Balanchine: the ballet maker. HarperCollins\Atlas Books 2004 224p (Eminent lives) $19.95

Grades: 11 12 Adult   92
1. Choreographers 2. Ballet
ISBN 0-06-075070-7   LC 2004-48856

This biography tells Balanchine's life story "from his near-accidental enrollment, at the age of nine, in St. Petersburg's Imperial School of Ballet, through the deprivation and hunger of Bolshevik Russia, to Diaghilev's Ballets Russes, and finally, in 1933, to the United States and eventually to the New York City Ballet, to which his reputation is forever tied." Publisher's note

"This loving tribute captures Balanchine's legacy: his

Balanchine, George, 1904-1983—*Continued*
energy, confidence, lack of pretension and, most important, his joy in creation." Publ Wkly
Includes bibliographical references

Baldwin, James, 1924-1987
Baldwin, James. Conversations with James Baldwin; edited by Fred L. Standley and Louis H. Pratt. University Press of Miss. 1989 297p (Literary conversations series) hardcover o.p. pa $17 *
Grades: 11 12 Adult   **92**
     1. Authors, American 2. African American authors
     ISBN 0-87805-388-3; 0-87805-389-1 (pa)
           LC 88-36560
"During the sixties, seventies, and eighties, Baldwin participated in more than fifty situations having the format of interview, conversation, discussion or dialogue. . . . The twenty-seven pieces selected for this collection range from 1961 after his fourth book, 'Nobody Knows My Name,' to just prior to his death in a last formal conversation with poet Quincy Troupe." Introduction

Banneker, Benjamin, 1731-1806
Litwin, Laura Baskes. Benjamin Banneker; astronomer and mathematician. Enslow Pubs. 1999 112p il (African-American biographies) lib bdg $26.60 *
Grades: 9 10 11 12   **92**
     1. Astronomers 2. African Americans—Biography
     ISBN 0-7660-1208-5   LC 98-34913
A biography of the eighteenth-century African-American who taught himself mathematics and astronomy and helped survey what would become Washington, D.C
Includes bibliographical references

Barakat, Ibtisam
Barakat, Ibtisam. Tasting the sky; a Palestinian childhood. Farrar, Straus and Giroux 2007 176p $16
Grades: 6 7 8 9 10   **92**
     1. Israel-Arab conflicts 2. Palestinian Arabs
     ISBN 0-374-35733-1   LC 2006041265
"In 1981 the author, then in high school, boarded a bus bound for Ramallah. The bus was detained by Israeli soldiers at a checkpoint on the West Bank, and she was taken to a detention center before being released. The episode triggers sometimes heart-wrenching memories of herself as a young child, at the start of the 1967 Six Days' War, as Israeli soldiers conducted raids, their planes bombed her home, and she fled with her family across the border to Jordan. . . . What makes the memoir so compelling is the immediacy of the child's viewpoint, which depicts both conflict and daily life without exploitation or sentimentality." Booklist

Barton, Clara, 1821-1912
Oates, Stephen B. A woman of valor: Clara Barton and the Civil War. Free Press 1994 527p il map hardcover o.p. pa $16.95
Grades: 11 12 Adult   **92**
     1. United States—History—1861-1865, Civil War
     ISBN 0-02-923405-0; 0-02-874012-2 (pa)
           LC 93-38830
The author "uses both primary and secondary sources in addressing the Civil War career of Clara Barton. . . . An 'angel of the battlefield' who succored the wounded while under fire, Barton also raised funds and supplies through a network of women's support groups, while challenging the conventional belief that nursing was inappropriate for respectable women." Publ Wkly
"This is a carefully written and researched work that brings to life both the Civil War and a period of Barton's life that was to affect her forever." Libr J
Includes bibliographical references

Basie, Count, 1904-1984
Basie, Count. Good morning blues: the autobiography of Count Basie; as told to Albert Murray. Da Capo Press 1995 399p il pa $17.95
Grades: 11 12 Adult   **92**
     1. Jazz musicians 2. African American musicians
     ISBN 0-306-81107-3   LC 94-44697
First published 1985 by Random House
"Basie pays tribute to his colleagues and managers (and to John Hammond for 'discovering' him), but does not hesitate to discuss their weaknesses and shortcomings; his language is direct and earthy. Although some of the book reads more like a catalogue or itinerary than an autobiography, it will have strong appeal for jazz buffs and fans of the late bandleader." Publ Wkly

Bates, Daisy
Fradin, Judith Bloom. The power of one; Daisy Bates and the Little Rock Nine; by Judith Bloom Fradin & Dennis Brindell Fradin. Clarion Books 2004 178p il $19
Grades: 7 8 9 10   **92**
     1. Central High School (Little Rock, Ark.) 2. School integration 3. Arkansas—Race relations
     ISBN 0-618-31556-X   LC 2004-4618
This is a biography of Daisy Bates. Born in a small town in rural Arkansas, Bates was a journalist and activist. In 1957 she mentored the nine black students who were integrated into Central High School in Little Rock, Arkansas
"This compelling biography clearly demonstrates that one person can indeed make a difference." SLJ
Includes bibliographical references

Beah, Ishmael
Beah, Ishmael. A long way gone; memoirs of a boy soldier. Farrar, Straus & Giroux 2007 229p map $22 *
Grades: 11 12 Adult   **92**
     1. Sierra Leone—History—Civil War, 1991-
     ISBN 978-0-374-10523-5; 0-374-95191-8
           LC 2006-17101
"Sarah Crichton Books"

Beah, Ishmael—*Continued*

"In 1993, when the author was twelve, rebel forces attacked his home town, in Sierra Leone, and he was separated from his parents. For months, he straggled through the war-torn countryside, starving and terrified, until he was taken under the wing of a Shakespeare-spouting lieutenant in the government army. Soon, he was being fed amphetamines and trained to shoot an AK-47. . . . Beah's memoir documents his transformation from a child into a hardened, brutally efficient soldier who high-fived his fellow-recruits after they slaughtered their enemies—often boys their own age—and who 'felt no pity for anyone.'" New Yorker

Beethoven, Ludwig van, 1770-1827

Morris, Edmund. Beethoven: the universal composer. HarperCollins Publishers 2005 243p (Eminent lives) $21.95 *

Grades: 11 12 Adult   **92**

1. Composers

ISBN 0-06-075974-7; 978-0-06-075974-2

LC 2006-274925

This is a biography of the German composer.

The author "clearly admires his subject not only for the work but also for his constant fight against the odds, and he has written an ideal biography for the general reader." Publ Wkly

Includes bibliographical references

Bernstein, Leonard, 1918-1990

Blashfield, Jean F. Leonard Bernstein; conductor and composer. Ferguson, J.G. 2000 127p il (Ferguson's career biographies) lib bdg $21.95

Grades: 7 8 9 10   **92**

1. Conductors (Music) 2. Composers

ISBN 0-89434-337-8   LC 00-37580

This illustrated biography looks at the life, career, and influence of the prominent composer/conductor

"A comprehensive time line of Bernstein's life and information about becoming a conductor or a composer are appended. There are three lists of further reading that give books, Web sites, and related places to contact or visit." SLJ

Birkeland, Kristian, 1867-1917

Jago, Lucy. The northern lights. Knopf 2001 297p hardcover o.p. pa $14

Grades: 11 12 Adult   **92**

1. Scientists

ISBN 0-375-40980-7; 0-375-70882-0 (pa)

LC 2001-29895

"The true story of the man who unlocked the secrets of the aurora borealis." Jacket

This is a "biography of Kristian Birkeland, a Norwegian scientist who discovered the origins of the aurora borealis." Economist

"Instead of a stiff, scholarly biography, British journalist Jago has written a poignantly human story filled with minute, extensively researched details." Libr J

Includes bibliographical references

Black Elk, 1863-1950

Black Elk. Black Elk speaks; being the life story of a holy man of the Oglala Sioux; [as told through] John G. Neihardt; foreword by Vine Deloria, Jr.; with illustrations by Standing Bear; essays by Alexis N. Petri and Lori Utecht. University of Nebraska Press 2004 xxix, 270p il map pa $14.95

Grades: 11 12 Adult   **92**

1. Oglala Indians

ISBN 0-8032-8385-7   LC 2004-12692

A reprint of the title first published 1932 by Morrow

The Indian whose life story this is, was born in 1863. He was a famous warrior and hunter in his youth, and became a practicing medicine man among his people. Of him Neihardt says, "As an indubitable seer, he seemed to represent the consciousness of the Plains Indian more fully than any other I had ever known."

This "is about as near as you can get to seeing life and death, war and religion, through an Indian's eyes." Outlook

Blackwell, Unita, 1933-

Blackwell, Unita. Barefootin'; life lessons from the road to freedom; with JoAnne Prichard Morris. Crown Publishers 2006 258p $23

Grades: 11 12 Adult   **92**

1. African American women 2. African Americans—Civil rights

ISBN 0-609-61060-0; 978-0-609-61060-2

LC 2005-34953

"This memoir by activist, organizer, politician and sage Unita Blackwell is valuable chronicle of one woman's heroism in the face of the brutality that was Jim Crow-era Mississippi." Ms.

Includes bibliographical references

Bohr, Niels Henrik David, 1885-1962

Ottaviani, Jim. Suspended in language; Niels Bohr's life, discoveries, and the century he shaped; illustrated and lettered by Leland Purvis. G. T. Labs 2004 318p il pa $24.95 *

Grades: 9 10 11 12   **92**

1. Graphic novels 2. Physicists—Graphic novels 3. Biographical graphic novels

ISBN 0-9660106-5-5   LC 2003-91535

"Quantum physics gets an accessible yet substantive introduction through art that mixes fantasy and realism. Great for teens who like science." Booklist

Includes bibliographical references

Bourgeois, Louise

Greenberg, Jan. Runaway girl: the artist Louise Bourgeois; {by} Jan Greenberg and Sandra Jordan. Abrams 2003 80p il $19.95

Grades: 7 8 9 10   **92**

1. Artists—United States

ISBN 0-8109-4237-2   LC 2002-11922

Contents: Family tapestry; Family secrets; A young artist in Paris ; Runaway girl; The New York art scene; The great decade; Spider, spider burning bright

Bourgeois, Louise—*Continued*

Introduces the life of renowned modern artist Louise Bourgeois, who is known primarily for her sculptures

"In clear, elegant prose, bolstered with numerous quotes from the artist, the authors seamlessly juxtapose stories of Bourgeois' life with relevant artworks. . . . Beautifully reproduced photographs, printed on well-designed pages, offer an excellent mix of the artist's personal life and her art." Booklist

Includes bibliographical references

Bourke-White, Margaret, 1904-1971

Rubin, Susan Goldman. Margaret Bourke-White; her pictures were her life; photographs by Margaret Bourke-White. Abrams 1999 96p il $19.95 *

Grades: 9 10 11 12   92

1. Women photographers

ISBN 0-8109-4381-6   LC 98-53967

"Rubin traces the celebrated photographer's life." SLJ

"Filled with Bourke-White's marvelous photographs, this stellar biography seamlessly blends the personal and the professional." Booklist

Includes bibliographical references

Bragg, Rick

Bragg, Rick. All over but the shoutin'. Pantheon Bks. 1997 xxii, 329p hardcover o.p. pa $14

Grades: 11 12 Adult   92

1. Journalists

ISBN 0-679-44258-8; 0-679-77402-5 (pa)

LC 97-9918

"Honest, unsentimental, and so elegantly spare it nearly hurts to read, this memoir by Pulitzer Prize-winning journalist Bragg recounts a dirt-poor childhood in Alabama and the debt he owes his mother." Libr J

Brave Bird, Mary

Brave Bird, Mary. Lakota woman; by Mary Crow Dog and Richard Erdoes. 1st HarperPerennial ed. HarperPerennial 1991 263p il pa $13.95   92

1. American Indian Movement 2. Political activists 3. Dakota Indians

ISBN 0-06-097389-7   LC 90-55980

First published 1990 by Grove Weidenfeld

"Born in 1955 and raised in poverty on the Rosebud Reservation, Mary Crow Dog escaped an oppressive Catholic boarding school but fell into a marginal life of urban shoplifting and barhopping. A 1971 encounter with AIM (the American Indian Movement), participation in the 1972 Trail of Broken Treaties march on Washington, and giving birth to her first child while under fire at the 1973 siege of Wounded Knee radicalized her." Libr J

"The story of Mary Crow Dog's coming of age in the Indian civil rights movement is simply told—and, at times, simply horrifying." N Y Times Book Rev

Breazeal, Cynthia

Brown, Jordan. Robo world; the story of robot designer Cynthia Breazeal; by Jordan D. Brown. Franklin Watts 2005 108p il (Women's adventures in science) $31

Grades: 7 8 9 10   92

1. Robots 2. Women scientists

ISBN 0-531-16782-8   LC 2005000826

Also available in paperback from Joseph Henry Press

A biography of Cynthia Breazeal who designs, builds, and experiments with robots at the MIT Media Lab.

Includes bibliographical references

Brokaw, Tom, 1940-

Brokaw, Tom. A long way from home; growing up in the American heartland. Random House 2002 272p $24.95; pa $12.95

Grades: 11 12 Adult   92

1. Journalists

ISBN 0-375-50763-9; 0-375-75935-2 (pa)

LC 2002-31865

News anchor Brokaw "shares the events, tone, and tenor of his midwestern upbringing." Booklist

"Peppered with photographs . . . this tribute to an idyllic childhood should please Brokaw's loyal fans." Publ Wkly

Brooks, Gwendolyn

Hill, Christine M. Gwendolyn Brooks; "poetry is life distilled". Enslow Publishers 2005 128p il (African-American biography library) lib bdg $31.93

Grades: 7 8 9 10   92

1. African American authors 2. Women authors 3. Women poets

ISBN 0-7660-2292-7   LC 2004-16801

"The first African American to win the Pulitzer Prize, in 1950, Brooks wrote poetry about the people she knew in her segregated South Side Chicago neighborhood. Later, feminists would credit her for being one of the first writers to treat the lives of everyday women in serious poetry. . . . This lively, readable title . . . provides plenty about Brooks' personal life and her politics." Booklist

Includes bibliographical references

Rhynes, Martha E. Gwendolyn Brooks; poet from Chicago. Morgan Reynolds 2003 112p il (World writers) lib bdg $21.95 *

Grades: 7 8 9 10   92

1. Poets, American 2. African American authors 3. Women poets

ISBN 1-931798-05-2   LC 2002-151122

Presents a biography of the African American poet who has received the National Book Award and the Pulitzer Prize

"The writing is clear, lively, and detailed." SLJ

Includes bibliographical references

Brown, Bradford B., 1929-
Brown, Bradford B. While you're here, Doc; farmyard adventures of a Maine veterinarian. Tilbury House 2006 174p il pa $15
Grades: 9 10 11 12   **92**
1. Veterinary medicine
ISBN 978-0-8844-8279-6; 0-8844-8279-0
LC 2005-32418
This veterinary memoir features "tales of animal doctoring in a small coastal town in 1950s Maine. . . . Full of laconic farmers, hysterical owners, and more feisty animal patients than one can imagine, these stories of backwoods veterinary care are sure to be popular among James Herriot lovers." Booklist

Brown, Claude, 1937-2002
Brown, Claude. Manchild in the promised land. Touchstone 1999 415p pa $14.95 *
Grades: 11 12 Adult   **92**
1. African Americans—Biography 2. African Americans—Harlem (New York, N.Y.)
ISBN 0-684-86418-5
First published 1965 by Macmillan
This is "the autobiography of a young black man raised in Harlem. It is a realistic description of life in the ghetto. . . . The core of the book concerns the 'plague' of heroin addiction that swept through Harlem in the 1950s taking the lives of many of Brown's contemporaries." Publ Wkly

Bruchac, Joseph, 1942-
Bruchac, Joseph. Bowman's store; a journey to myself. 1st Lee & Low ed. Lee & Low Books 2001 315p il pa $9.95
Grades: 7 8 9 10   **92**
1. Abnaki Indians 2. Authors, American
ISBN 1-584-30027-2   LC 2001-16435
A reissue of the title first published 1997 by Dial Books
"Combining Native American stories with personal memories and dreams, Bruchac crafts a memoir of his childhood growing up with his grandparents in upstate New York." Horn Book Guide
"Each episode is constructed with a true storyteller's attention to language and plot development. Students of modern Native American cultures will find plenty of food for thought." Booklist

Bunche, Ralph J. (Ralph Johnson), 1904-1971
Urquhart, Brian E. Ralph Bunche; an American life; [by] Brian Urquhart. Norton 1993 496p il maps hardcover o.p. pa $15.95
Grades: 11 12 Adult   **92**
1. African Americans—Biography 2. United States—Race relations
ISBN 0-393-03527-1; 0-393-31859-1 (pa)
LC 92-46564
The author "describes Bunche's itinerant childhood, academic background, teaching and research, OSS service in World War II, significant contributions at the Dumbarton Oaks Conference of Allied leaders, and troubleshooting and mediation on behalf of the UN

throughout the Middle East, Africa, and Asia. . . . Urquhart has made a fascinating narrative of the accomplishments of an American-born international diplomat." Booklist
Includes bibliographical references

Bush, George W.
Bruni, Frank. Ambling into history: the unlikely odyssey of George W. Bush. HarperCollins Pubs. 2002 278p pa $12.95 hardcover o.p.
Grades: 11 12 Adult   **92**
1. Presidents—United States
ISBN 0-06093782-3 (pa)
The author, who covered Bush's 2000 presidential campaign for the New York Times, focuses on Bush's personality and mannerisms as well as his basic interactions with family, friends, and the public.
"Given [Bruni's] familiarity with Bush, one would expect his book to contain revealing insights, and this superb, incisive, and surprising account does not disappoint." Booklist
Includes bibliographical references

Carson, Rachel, 1907-1964
Levine, Ellen. Rachel Carson; a twentieth-century life. Viking 2007 224p il (Up close) $15.99 *
Grades: 6 7 8 9 10   **92**
1. Women scientists
ISBN 0-670-06220-1
A biography of the environmental scientist.
"Direct, eloquent, and precise. . . . A balanced, thoroughly researched introduction to an original scientist whose work remains of urgent importance today." Booklist
Includes bibliographical references

Carter, Jimmy, 1924-
Carter, Jimmy. An hour before daylight; memories of my rural boyhood. Simon & Schuster 2001 284p il hardcover o.p. pa $15
Grades: 11 12 Adult   **92**
1. Carter family
ISBN 0-7432-1193-6; 0-7432-1199-5 (pa)
LC 00-48248
Also available large print edition $26 (ISBN 0-7432-1220-7)
In this memoir, the thirty-ninth president of the United States remembers his childhood in rural Georgia
This "is social and agricultural history as plain and honest as one of the tables the author makes in his workshop—an American classic." New Yorker

Carter, Robert, 1728-1804
Levy, Andrew. The first emancipator; the forgotten story of Robert Carter, the founding father who freed his slaves. Random House 2005 310p $25.95
Grades: 11 12 Adult   **92**
ISBN 0-375-50865-1   LC 2004-54054

Carter, Robert, 1728-1804—*Continued*

The author "examines the unique life of Robert Carter III, one of the wealthiest men in 18th-century America, and his monumental 'Deed of Gift.' This legal document, recorded in 1791, allowed for the largest single emancipation of slaves until the Emancipation Proclamation." Libr J

"This well-written and thoroughly engaging book will certainly appeal to readers interested in the history of 18th- and 19th-century Virginia, but also to those interested in the history of slavery and racism in America and in historical biography." Publ Wkly

Includes bibliographical references

Cary, Lorene

Cary, Lorene. Black ice. Knopf 1991 237p hardcover o.p. pa $10

Grades: 11 12 Adult   92

1. St. Paul's School (Concord, N.H.) 2. African American women

ISBN 0-394-57465-6; 0-679-73745-6 (pa)

LC 90-52988

"In the early 1970's, an Eastern prep school recruiting minority students opened its doors to Cary, then a 15-year-old Philadelphia high school girl. These affecting recollections explore her experiences—interactions with teachers, an affair with another student, friendships, and problems with prejudice—as well as her struggle to determine her own black identity." Booklist

Cash, Johnny

Neimark, Anne E. Johnny Cash; a twentieth-century life. Viking Childrens Books 2007 207p il (Up close) $15.99

Grades: 8 9 10 11 12   92

1. Country musicians

ISBN 978-0-670-06215-7   LC 2006010198

"The life of the deeply troubled and powerfully influential music legend is brought vividly to life in this richly detailed biography. . . . Cash's genius as a songwriter and musician as well as his incalculable influence upon music are skillfully explored, and Neimark frequently uses excerpts from Cash's own songs to enrich his compelling life story." Booklist

Includes bibliographical references

Castro, Fidel, 1926-

Coltman, Sir Leycester. The real Fidel Castro; with a foreword by Julia E. Sweig. Yale Univ. Press 2003 335p il map $30; pa $20 *

Grades: 11 12 Adult   92

1. Cuba—Politics and government

ISBN 0-300-10188-0; 0-300-10760-9 (pa)

LC 2003-12942

This biography "offers a fresh assessment of the revolutionary leader. . . . It chronicles the events of Castro's extraordinary life and explores the contradiction between the private character and the public reputation." Univ Press Books for Public and Second Sch Libr, 2004

Includes bibliographical references

Catherine II, the Great, Empress of Russia, 1729-1796

Whitelaw, Nancy. Catherine the Great and the Enlightenment in Russia. Morgan Reynolds Pub. 2005 160p il map (European queens) lib bdg $24.95 *

Grades: 9 10 11 12   92

1. Russia—Kings and rulers

ISBN 1-931798-27-3; 978-1-931798-27-3

LC 2004-14711

The author "follows Catherine from her youth as a struggling German princess to Russia, where at 16 she wed the profoundly unimpressive Grand Duke Peter, whom she embraced as a means to the throne. . . . In language both straightforward and compelling, Whitelaw describes the formidable czarina's reign, her love affairs, her vast cultural influence, and the political treachery that surrounded her court." Booklist

Includes bibliographical references

Cézanne, Paul, 1839-1906

Rewald, John. Cézanne; a biography. Abrams 1986 288p il $75 *

Grades: 11 12 Adult   92

1. Artists, French

ISBN 0-8109-0775-5   LC 86-1017

This biography of the French painter is a revised and expanded version of the author's 1936 Sorbonne doctoral dissertation. An English translation was published in 1948 by Simon & Schuster under the title: Paul Cézanne: a biography

"The artist's character is revealed in his own words and in those of his friends . . . making Cézanne accessible in a way simple narrative cannot. Adding greatly to our understanding of Cézanne's development as a painter are the 270 illustrations." Libr J

Includes bibliographical references

Chagall, Marc, 1887-1985

Kagan, Andrew. Marc Chagall. Abbeville Press 1989 128p il (Modern masters series) hardcover o.p. pa $14.95 *

Grades: 11 12 Adult   92

1. Artists

ISBN 0-89659-932-9; 0-89659-935-3 (pa)

LC 89-6693

This illustrated biography of the Russian Jewish artist explores his paintings, graphics, mosaics, tapestries, and stained glass works. A biochronology and a selected exhibitions list are appended

Includes bibliographical references

Charbonneau, Jean-Baptiste, 1805-1866

Nelson, W. Dale. Interpreters with Lewis and Clark: the story of Sacagawea and Toussaint Charbonneau. See entry under Sacagawea, b. 1786

Charbonneau, Toussaint, ca. 1758-ca. 1839

Nelson, W. Dale. Interpreters with Lewis and Clark: the story of Sacagawea and Toussaint Charbonneau. See entry under Sacagawea, b. 1786

Charlemagne, Emperor, 742-814

Wilson, Derek A. Charlemagne. Doubleday 2006 226p il map $26; pa $14.95 *

Grades: 11 12 Adult   92

1. Kings and rulers

ISBN 0-385-51670-3; 0-307-27480-2 (pa)

LC 2005-48483

This biography of the Frankish emperor "demonstrates how the empire he built led to the development of the European identity." SLJ

The author "writes with clarity and passion, and his thesis is food for thought for both general readers and students." Libr J

Includes bibliographical references

Charles, Ray

Duggleby, John. Uh huh!: the story of Ray Charles. Morgan Reynolds Pub. 2005 160p il $26.95 *

Grades: 7 8 9 10   92

1. African American singers

ISBN 1-93179-865-6   LC 2005-1287

The author "traces Charles' long career and displays a sensitivity to the events surrounding his life (including his bitter battles with heroin and alcohol addiction), as well as a genuine understanding of his music and the breadth of his musical influence. Sidebars on 'race' music, Braille, the Grammys, soul, and rock and roll enrich the narrative." Booklist

Includes bibliographical references

Chavez, Cesar, 1927-1993

Cruz, Bárbara. César Chávez; a voice for farmworkers; [by] Bárbara C. Cruz. Enslow Publishers, Inc. 2005 128p il (Latino biography library) lib bdg $31.93

Grades: 7 8 9 10   92

1. Mexican Americans 2. Migrant labor

ISBN 0-7660-2489-X   LC 2004-27538

"Cruz takes readers from Chavez's first job as a migrant worker in California at age 10 through his decision to help his fellow workers: his fasts, his activism, the founding and continued involvement in the United Farm Workers Union until his death in 1993. Black-and-white and full-color photos appear throughout." SLJ

Griswold del Castillo, Richard. César Chávez; a triumph of spirit; by Richard Griswold del Castillo and Richard A. Garcia. University of Okla. Press 1995 206p il (Oklahoma western biographies) pa $14.95 hardcover o.p.

Grades: 11 12 Adult   92

1. Migrant labor 2. Mexican Americans

ISBN 0-8061-2957-3 (pa)   LC 95-15230

"In this biography of the embattled farm labor organizer, del Castillo . . . focuses on Chávez's formation, growth, and development as a leader in the movement to unionize farm workers in the Southwest. . . . Del Castillo's account is balanced, highly readable, and engaging." Libr J

Includes bibliographical references

Chávez Frías, Hugo

Levin, Judith. Hugo Chávez. Chelsea House Publishers 2007 128p il (Modern world leaders) $30 *

Grades: 7 8 9 10   92

1. Venezuela 2. Presidents—Venezuela

ISBN 0-7910-9258-5; 978-0-7910-9258-3

LC 2006-10611

This is a biography of the Venezuelan president.

Includes bibliographical references

Churchill, Sir Winston, 1874-1965

Rubin, Gretchen Craft. Forty ways to look at Winston Churchill; a brief account of a long life; {by} Gretchen Rubin. Ballantine Books 2003 307p il hardcover o.p. pa $14.95 *

Grades: 9 10 11 12   92

1. Prime ministers—Great Britain 2. Great Britain—Politics and government—20th century

ISBN 0-345-45047-7; 0-8129-7144-2 (pa)

LC 2003-271389

This biography is in the form of "40 brief chapters looking at the British prime minister from multiple angles: Churchill as son, father, husband, orator, painter, historian, enemy of Hitler and many other roles." Publ Wkly

"Rubin has much to offer teens, especially those with only vague notions of the great man." SLJ

Includes bibliographical references

Clemente, Roberto, 1934-1972

Maraniss, David. Clemente; the passion and grace of baseball's last hero. Simon & Schuster 2006 401p il maps $26; pa $15 *

Grades: 11 12 Adult   92

1. Baseball—Biography

ISBN   0-7432-1781-0;   978-0-7432-1781-1; 0-7432-9999-X; 978-0-7432-9999-2 (pa)

LC 2006-42235

Also available Thorndike Press large print edition

This is a "biography of the first Latin American player named to the Baseball Hall of Fame." Libr J

The author "has produced a baseball-savvy book sensitive to the social context that made Clemente, a black Puerto Rican, a leading indicator of baseball's future." N Y Times Book Rev

Includes bibliographical references

Cleopatra, Queen of Egypt, d. 30 B.C.

Burstein, Stanley M. The reign of Cleopatra. Greenwood Press 2004 xxiii, 179p il map (Greenwood guides to historic events of the ancient world) $45 *

Grades: 9 10 11 12   92

1. Queens 2. Egypt—History

ISBN 0-313-32527-8   LC 2004-14672

Contents: Historical background -- Cleopatra's life -- Ptolemaic Egypt: how did it work? -- Cleopatra's Egypt: a multicultural story -- Alexandria: city of culture and conflict -- Conclusion: queen and symbol

Includes bibliographical references

Cleopatra, Queen of Egypt, d. 30 B.C.—*Continued*

Nardo, Don. Cleopatra. Lucent Books 2005 112p il map (Lucent library of historical eras, Ancient Egypt) $28.70
Grades: 7 8 9 10   92
1. Queens 2. Egypt—History
ISBN 1-59018-660-5; 978-1-59018-660-2
LC 2004-22071
Subtitle on cover: Egypt's last pharaoh
This biography of the Egyptian queen "features quotations from ancient authors, along with Nardo's discussion of how many of these authors were biased, for or against one of the most powerful women in history. He includes her romantic liaisons with Julius Caesar and Marc Antony. . . . A final chapter looks at how Cleopatra has been rendered in literature." SLJ
Includes bibliographical references

Cochise, Apache Chief, d. 1874

Sweeney, Edwin R. (Edwin Russell). Cochise, Chiricahua Apache chief. University of Okla. Press 1991 xxiii, 501p il maps (Civilization of the American Indian series) pa $24.95 hardcover o.p.
Grades: 11 12 Adult   92
1. Apache Indians
ISBN 0-8061-2606-X (pa)   LC 90-50699
The author traces Cochise's "rise to leadership of his Apache band, his . . . skirmishes with the military and others in both the United States and Mexico, and his successful negotiations for a reservation in the homeland of his peoples." Libr J
"An insightful, and exciting work that ranks with the best efforts of ethnohistory. . . . This book is the definitive life story of history's most important Apache chief and restores him to his proper preeminent role in the region's history." Choice
Includes bibliographical references

Conroy, Pat

Conroy, Pat. My losing season. Talese 2002 402p $27.95; pa $14.95
Grades: 11 12 Adult   92
1. Authors, American
ISBN 0-385-48912-9; 0-553-38190-3 (pa)
LC 2002-66212
"Novelist Conroy ruminates on the profound effect of his final year as a point guard for the Citadel's basketball team, interweaving stories about the years leading up to college, his abusive father, his love-hate relationship with his school, and his growing fondness for books and writing." Booklist
"A wonderfully rich, informative, and well-researched reminiscence." Libr J

Cornwell, John, 1940-

Cornwell, John. Seminary boy. Doubleday 2006 321p il $24.95
Grades: 11 12 Adult   92
ISBN 978-0-385-54186-6; 0-385-51486-7
LC 2005-56026

The author "tells the story of his life at an all-male school in the 1950s. Son of a struggling working-class family in London, John was sent to Cotton College to become a Catholic priest. Here, during his teen years, he experienced the best and worst of pre-Vatican II seminary life. Some of his teachers were pious and dedicated men; others were sexual predators. . . . Part spiritual odyssey, part boarding school story, Cornwell's well-crafted memoir is filled with vivid descriptions of people and places and a young boy's struggle to find himself." Libr J

Cox, Lynne

Cox, Lynne. Swimming to Antarctica; tales of a long-distance swimmer. Knopf 2004 323p $24.95
Grades: 11 12 Adult   92
1. Women athletes
ISBN 0-375-41507-6   LC 2003-47577
Also available in paperback from Harvest Bks.
The author "has swum the Mediterranean, the three-mile Strait of Messina, under the ancient bridges of Kunning Lake, [and] below the old summer palace of the emperor of China in Beijing. . . . She writes about the ways in which these swims . . . became vehicles for personal goals." Publisher's note
"Cox is a pleasure. . . . Many passages are grip-the-page exciting, whether she's dodging Antarctic icebergs or Nile River sewage." Booklist

Crane, Kathleen, 1951-

Crane, Kathleen. Sea legs; tales of a woman oceanographer. Westview Press 2003 318p il map hardcover o.p. pa $16
Grades: 11 12 Adult   92
1. Oceanography 2. Women scientists
ISBN 0-8133-4004-7; 0-8133-4285-6 (pa)
LC 2003-1690
"Crane chronicles the relentless adversity she faced in becoming a world-class oceanographer with a modest matter-of-factness that almost camouflages the high caliber of her achievements. . . . She was the first to postulate the existence of the now famous deep-sea hot springs. . . . Crane's experiences are diverse, dramatic, and important; her understanding of international affairs and environmental realities laudable and moving; and her triumphs over personal sorrows and illness impressive and inspiring." Booklist
Includes bibliographical references

Crazy Horse, Sioux Chief, ca. 1842-1877

Freedman, Russell. The life and death of Crazy Horse; drawings by Amos Bad Heart Bull. Holiday House 1996 166p il maps $22.95 *
Grades: 5 6 7 8 9 10   92
1. Oglala Indians
ISBN 0-8234-1219-9   LC 95-33303
A biography of the Oglala Indian leader who relentlessly resisted the white man's attempt to take over Indian lands
This is "a compelling biography that is based on primary source documents and illustrated with pictographs by a Sioux band historian." Voice Youth Advocates
Includes bibliographical references

Crazy Horse, Sioux Chief, ca. 1842-1877—*Continued*

McMurtry, Larry. Crazy Horse. Viking 1999 148p (Penguin lives series) $19.95; pa $13
Grades: 11 12 Adult   92
1. Dakota Indians
ISBN 0-670-88234-8; 0-14-303480-4 (pa)
LC 98-26644
"Though essentially a loner and devoid of political ambition, Crazy Horse was a respected military tactician, equally feared and admired for the strength and the intensity of his convictions. Rather than merely attempting to sort out fact from fiction, McMurtry incorporates conjecture and legend into this philosophical portrait of both the man and the myth." Booklist

Crick, Francis, 1916-2004
Edelson, Edward. Francis Crick and James Watson and the building blocks of life. See entry under Watson, James D., 1928-

Ridley, Matt. Francis Crick; discoverer of the genetic code. Atlas Books 2006 213p (Eminent lives) $19.95 *
Grades: 11 12 Adult   92
1. Scientists 2. Genetics
ISBN 0-06-082333-X; 978-0-06-082333-7
LC 2005-55878
This "biography examines the paired strands of Crick's life and work." N Y Times Book Rev
"A briskly written essential for the DNA shelf." Booklist
Includes bibliographical references

Cromwell, Oliver, 1599-1658
Aronson, Marc. John Winthrop, Oliver Cromwell, and the Land of Promise. See entry under Winthrop, John, 1588-1649

Crutcher, Chris, 1946-
Crutcher, Chris. King of the mild frontier: an ill-advised autobiography. Greenwillow Bks. 2003 260p il $16.99; pa $6.99 *
Grades: 8 9 10 11 12   92
1. Authors, American
ISBN 0-06-050249-5; 0-06-050251-7 (pa)
LC 2002-11224
Chris Crutcher, author of young adult novels such as "Ironman" and "Whale Talk," as well as short stories, tells of growing up in Cascade, Idaho, and becoming a writer
"Like his novels, Crutcher's autobiography is full of heartbreak, poignancy, and hilarity. . . . This honest, insightful, revealing autobiography is a joy to read." Booklist

Cummings, E. E. (Edward Estlin), 1894-1962
Reef, Catherine. E. E. Cummings. Clarion Books 2006 149p il $21 *
Grades: 7 8 9 10 11 12   92
1. Poets, American
ISBN 978-0-618-56849-9; 0-618-56849-2
LC 2006-10453
Subtitle on cover: A poet's life
This is a biography of Edward Estlin Cummings, the author of Fifty Poems (1941), 1 x 1(1944), Xaipe (1950), Poems, 1923-1954 (1954), 95 Poems (1958), 73 Poems (1963), Complete Poems, 1913-1962 (1972), and Tulips & Chimneys (1976).
This "is an engaging look behind the typography at one of the twentieth century's most familiar poets." Bull Cent Child Books
Includes bibliographical references

Curie, Marie, 1867-1934
McClafferty, Carla Killough. Something out of nothing; Marie Curie and radium. Farrar, Straus & Giroux 2006 134p il $18 *
Grades: 5 6 7 8 9 10   92
1. Chemists 2. Women scientists
ISBN 0-374-38036-8   LC 2004-56414
This "biography examines Curie's life and work as a groundbreaking scientist and as an independent woman. . . . The groundbreaking science is as thrilling as the personal story. . . . The spacious design makes the text easy to read, and occasional photos . . . bring the story closer." Booklist

Yannuzzi, Della A. New elements; the story of Marie Curie; [by] Della Yannuzzi. Morgan Reynolds Pub. 2006 144p il (Profiles in science) lib bdg $27.95
Grades: 7 8 9 10   92
1. Chemists 2. Women scientists
ISBN 978-1-59935-023-3; 1-59935-023-8
LC 2006-18887
This is a biography "of the first woman to win a Nobel Prize in science. . . . Readers will come away with a strong portrait of the heralded scientist's life and times (the historical context is nicely integrated), and serious researchers will turn to the bibliography's sturdy selection of titles." Booklist
Includes bibliographical references

Dahl, Roald
Gelletly, LeeAnne. Gift of imagination; the story of Roald Dahl. Morgan Reynolds 2007 160p il (World writers) lib bdg $27.95 *
Grades: 7 8 9 10   92
1. Authors, English
ISBN 978-1-59935-026-4; 1-59935-026-2 (lib bdg)
LC 2006-17078
This biography "draws connections between the events in Dahl's life and the stories he created." SLJ
"A succinct, informative, and quite readable resource." Booklist
Includes bibliographical references

Dalai Lama II, 1476-1542
Mullin, Glenn H. The second Dalai Lama; his life and teachings; translated, edited, introduced, and annotated by Glenn H. Mullin. Snow Lion Publications 2005 270p pa $16.95
Grades: 9 10 11 12   **92**
  ISBN 1-55939-233-9   LC 2005-281580
The author "has divided his book into three parts: a general introduction to Tibetan religious history and the lineage of the Dalai Lamas, a biography of the Second Dalai Lama (1475-1541), particularly noted for his poetry, and a selection in 25 chapters of his mystical poems, translated and commented on by Mullin." Libr J

Dalai Lama XIV, 1935-
Dalai Lama XIV. Freedom in exile; the autobiography of the Dalai Lama. HarperCollins Pubs. 1990 288p il maps pa $15 hardcover o.p. *
Grades: 11 12 Adult   **92**
  ISBN 0-06-098701-4   LC 89-46523
"A Cornelia & Michael Bessie book"
"The Dalai Lama's story is, in part, a chapter in the 2,500-year history of Buddhism as well as a testament to the 'mendacity and barbarity' of Communist China. He shares the details of his amazing life, a glimpse at some of the mysteries of Tibetan Buddhism, and his unshakable belief in the basic good of humanity." Booklist

Dalí, Salvador, 1904-1989
Ross, Michael Elsohn. Salvador Dali and the surrealists; their lives and ideas: 21 activities. Chicago Review Press 2003 132p il pa $17.95 *
Grades: 9 10 11 12   **92**
  1. Artists, Spanish 2. Surrealism
  ISBN 1-556-52479-X   LC 2002-155628
Examines the lives and creative work of the surrealist artist Salvador Dalí and other artists and friends who shared his new ways of exploring art. Features art activities that engage the subconscious thoughts and spontaneity of the reader
"This visually stunning work enhances the body of material on the artist and his contemporaries. Eminently readable, the crisply written text is detailed and thorough, including pronunciations of many place and personal names. Dalí's life is presented familiarly, drawing in many details of life as an artist during that period in Europe and the relationships among the surrealists. . . . The attractive layout includes numerous excellent-quality reproductions of the work of Dali and many of the other artists mentioned in the text, and period photographs. . . . A valuable addition to any collection." SLJ
Includes bibliographical references

Darwin, Charles, 1809-1882
Eldredge, Niles. Darwin: discovering the tree of life. Norton 2005 256p il map $35
Grades: 11 12 Adult   **92**
  1. Naturalists
  ISBN 0-393-05966-9   LC 2005-18636
This is the companion volume to an exhibition on Darwin presented by the American Museum of Natural History in 2005.

"By closely analyzing Darwin's numerous notebooks, letters, and edited manuscripts, Eldredge draws a multidimensional portrait of the man as a humanist, naturalist, and reluctant evolutionist." Choice
Includes bibliographical references

Quammen, David. The reluctant Mr. Darwin; an intimate portrait of Charles Darwin and the making of his theory of evolution. Atlas Books/Norton 2006 304p (Great discoveries) $22.95; pa $14.95 *
Grades: 11 12 Adult   **92**
  1. Naturalists
  ISBN   0-393-05981-2;   978-0-393-05981-6;
  0-393-32995-X (pa); 978-0-393-32995-7 (pa)
                                             LC 2006-9864
The author "concentrates on how Darwin privately developed his theory of evolution and reluctantly made his ideas public when [Alfred] Wallace began to publish similar theories." Libr J
"This often slyly witty book stands out among the flood of books being published for Darwin's bicentenary." Publ Wkly
Includes bibliographical references

Delany, Bessie
Delany, Sadie. Having our say. See entry under Delany, Sadie

Delany, Sadie
Delany, Sadie. Having our say; the Delany sisters' first 100 years; [by] Sarah and A. Elizabeth Delany; with Amy Hill Hearth. Kodansha Int. 1993 210p il $20
Grades: 11 12 Adult   **92**
  1. Delany, Bessie 2. Delany family
  ISBN 1-56836-010-X   LC 93-23890
Also available in paperback from Dell
"The Delany sisters' story is a collective meditation on American life since Sadie's birth in 1889 and Bessie's in 1891 in Raleigh, North Carolina. . . . The sisters migrated to New York City's Harlem in the 1910s and in the 1950s to the suburb of Mt. Vernon, New York. The assertive Bessie battled racism and sexism as the only black female member of her Columbia University Dental School class in the 1920s. The more reticent Sadie became the first black domestic science teacher in the New York City high schools." Libr J
"The combination of the two voices, beautifully blended by Ms. Hearth, evokes an epic history, often cruel and brutal, but always deeply humane in their spirited telling of it." N Y Times Book Rev

Delman, Carmit
Delman, Carmit. Burnt bread & chutney; growing up between cultures; a memoir of an Indian Jewish girl. One World/Ballantine Bks. 2002 xxiv, 261p hardcover o.p. pa $13.95
Grades: 9 10 11 12   **92**
  1. Jews 2. Culture conflict
  ISBN 0-345-44593-7; 0-345-44594-5 (pa)
                                             LC 2002-22855

Delman, Carmit—*Continued*
The author's "mother is a direct descendant of the Bene Israel, a tiny, ancient community of Jews . . . of Western India. Her father is American, a Jewish man of Eastern European descent. They met while working the land of a nascent Israeli state. . . . They hardly took notice of the interracial aspect of their union. But their daughter, Carmit, growing up in America, was well aware of her uncommon heritage." Publisher's note

"Delman's troubled, but ultimately inspiring passage leads her to some universal truths." SLJ

Dickens, Charles, 1812-1870
Caravantes, Peggy. Best of times: the story of Charles Dickens. Morgan Reynolds Pub. 2005 160p il (World writers) $26.95
Grades: 7 8 9 10   92
1. Authors, English
ISBN 1-93179-868-0   LC 2005-8405
"Beginning with Dickens' childhood trauma (his father was put in debtors' prison, and Charles, 12, had to work in a blacking factory), this highly readable [book] . . . relates the extraordinary writer's stories to his life and times. . . . [It includes] many interesting quotes, color prints, and photos." Booklist
Includes bibliographical references

Smiley, Jane. Charles Dickens. Viking 2002 212p (Penguin lives series) $19.95 *
Grades: 11 12 Adult   92
1. Authors, English
ISBN 0-670-03077-5   LC 2001-45607
"A Penguin life; A Lipper\Viking book"
This "biography examines Dickens' life through his work, starting not with his birth but rather the beginnings of his literary career. After writing short essays for a monthly magazine, Dickens began the serialization of his first novel, *The Pickwick Papers*. Dickens quickly became both a best-selling novelist and a famous man, who had to contend with both the envy of other authors and, much later on, the very public dissolution of his marriage. . . . Smiley's superb and thoughtful analysis should appeal to anyone familiar with the great author's work." Booklist

Dickinson, Emily, 1830-1886
Longsworth, Polly. The world of Emily Dickinson. Norton 1990 136p il maps pa $19.95 hardcover o.p.
Grades: 11 12 Adult   92
1. Poets, American 2. Women poets
ISBN 0-393-31656-4 (pa)   LC 90-31672
Drawings, maps, and photographs illustrate the home, friends, landscape and influence of the nineteenth-century American poet.

Meltzer, Milton. Emily Dickinson; a biography. Twenty-first Century Books 2006 128p il (American literary greats) lib bdg $31.93 *
Grades: 7 8 9 10   92
1. Poets, American 2. Women poets
ISBN 0-7613-2949-8; 978-0-7613-2949-7
                               LC 2003-22978

Examines the life of the reclusive nineteenth-century Massachusetts poet whose posthumously published poetry brought her the public attention she had carefully avoided during her lifetime.

"This introduction to an important American literary figure is notable for its clear and succinct writing. . . . Excerpts from her letters and poems appear throughout. A worthwhile book for students who might have difficulty with more scholarly works." SLJ
Includes bibliographical references

Dinesen, Isak, 1885-1962
Leslie, Roger. Isak Dinesen; Gothic storyteller. M. Reynolds 2004 128p il (World writers) lib bdg $21.95
Grades: 11 12 Adult   92
1. Authors, Danish 2. Women authors
ISBN 1-931798-17-6   LC 2003-22484
Contents: A restless childhood; A romantic youth; A new life in a new land; Difficulty and illness; Life in Africa; Making a home; Leaving Africa; Another new life; Swan song
"Danish author Dinesen, born 1885, was a strong-willed spirit who sought independence and adventure. With her long battle with syphilis figuring prominently in this accounting, this traces the path the writer followed, which led her away from her bourgeois upbringing in Denmark to the unfettered life she enjoyed on her coffee farm at the foot of the Ngong Hills of Nairobi." Booklist
Includes bibliographical references

Dornstein, David Scott, 1963-1988
Dornstein, Ken. The boy who fell out of the sky; a true story. Random House 2006 304p il $23.95; pa $13.95
Grades: 11 12 Adult   92
1. Pan Am Flight 103 Bombing Incident, 1988
ISBN 0-375-50359-5; 0-375-70769-7 (pa)
                               LC 2005-42683
"On December 21, 1988, Dornstein's older brother, David, went down with Pan Am Flight 103 over Lockerbie, Scotland. Shattered, Dornstein returned to college and tried to move on. But eight years later, he started reading the papers left behind by his brother, who was an unpublished but prolific writer. . . . This memoir cobbles together the author's memories, past news accounts and David's . . . journal entries and letters." Publ Wkly
"Dornstein's account of his relationship with his brother and of his own self-examination is a startlingly honest, completely absorbing look at loss and brotherly love." Booklist
Includes bibliographical references

Douglass, Frederick, 1817?-1895
Douglass, Frederick. Autobiographies. Library of Am. 1994 1126p $35; pa $13.95
Grades: 11 12 Adult   92
1. Abolitionists 2. African Americans—Biography
ISBN 0-940450-79-8; 1-883011-30-2 (pa)
                               LC 93-24168

Douglass, Frederick, 1817?-1895—*Continued*
Contents: Narrative of the life of Frederick Douglass, an American slave; My Bondage and my freedom; Life and times of Frederick Douglass
"This one volume containing Douglass's seminal works is highly recommended for black history collections." Libr J
Includes bibliographical references

Frederick Douglass; John R. McKivigan, book editor. Greenhaven Press 2004 202p (People who made history) lib bdg $33.70; pa $22.45
Grades: 9 10 11 12   92
1. Abolitionists 2. African Americans—Biography
ISBN 0-7377-1522-7 (lib bdg); 0-7377-1523-5 (pa)
LC 2002-45488
This volume is composed of essays describing "the seminal moments of Douglass' life, from slave roots, learning to read, association with free blacks in Baltimore, discovery of the Columbian Oratory, publication of his narrative, to editing and publishing his own newspaper, and more. . . . A chronology of his life follows the essays, along with a detailed bibliography and selections from primary source documents taken from his autobiographies, letters. speeches, and editorials." Libr Media Connect
"Though the articles are abridged and accompanied by helpful summaries, the dense prose will still prove too challenging for many high-schoolers. However, advanced history students and teachers should find this a convenient all-in-one resource, especially for supplementing units on Douglass' autobiographies." Booklist
Includes bibliographical references

Du Bois, W. E. B. (William Edward Burghardt), 1868-1963
Hinman, Bonnie. A stranger in my own house; the story of W.E.B. Du Bois. Morgan Reynolds Pub. 2005 176p il map $26.95 *
Grades: 7 8 9 10   92
1. African Americans—Biography 2. African Americans—Civil rights
ISBN 1-93179-845-1   LC 2004-26460
"The long, complex life of this scholar and controversial civil rights leader is examined in this . . . biography. Hinman offers insights into the background, beliefs, and conflicts that shaped and defined Du Bois. . . . The engaging, informative, balanced text is enhanced with documentary photographs and illustrations." SLJ
Includes bibliographical references

Dumas, Firoozeh
Dumas, Firoozeh. Funny in Farsi; a memoir of growing up Iranian in America. Villard Bks. 2003 187p il hardcover o.p. pa $12.95
Grades: 9 10 11 12   92
1. Iranian Americans
ISBN 1-4000-6040-0; 0-8129-6837-9 (pa)
LC 2002-34921
"In 1972, when she was seven, Firoozeh Dumas and her family moved from Iran to Southern California, arriving with no firsthand knowledge of this country beyond her father's glowing memories of his graduate school years here. . . . Funny in Farsi chronicles the American journey of Dumas's . . . family: her engineer father . . . who first sought riches on Bowling for Dollars and in Las Vegas, and later lost his job during the Iranian revolution; her elegant mother, who never fully mastered English (nor cared to); her uncle, who combated the effects of American fast food with an army of miraculous American weight-loss gadgets; and Firoozeh herself, who as a girl changed her name to Julie, and who met a second wave of culture shock when she met and married a Frenchman." Publisher's note
"Dumas has a unique perspective on American culture, and she effortlessly balances the comedy of her family's misadventures with the more serious prejudices they face." Booklist

Dylan, Bob, 1941-
Roberts, Jeremy. Bob Dylan: voice of a generation. Lerner Publications Co. 2005 128p il (Lerner biography) $27.93 *
Grades: 9 10 11 12   92
1. Rock musicians
ISBN 0-8225-1368-4   LC 2004-2460
This is a biography of the folk-rock singer and songwriter.
"The overall spirit of rebellion and uncompromising emotional honesty . . . will appeal as urgently to today's YAs as it did to an earlier generation." Booklist
Includes bibliographical references

Earhart, Amelia, 1898-1937
Van Pelt, Lori. Amelia Earhart; the sky's no limit. Forge 2005 239p il (American heroes series) $19.95; pa $12.95 *
Grades: 11 12 Adult   92
1. Air pilots
ISBN 0-7653-1061-9; 0-7653-1062-7 (pa)
LC 2004-56316
"A Tom Doherty Associates book"
This is an "introduction to the best-known of pioneering female airplane pilots. . . . Everybody ought to have basic knowledge of Earhart; this is a good place to acquire it." Booklist
Includes bibliographical references

Edison, Thomas A. (Thomas Alva), 1847-1931
Tagliaferro, Linda. Thomas Edison; inventor of the age of electricity. Lerner Publs. 2003 128p il (Lerner biography) lib bdg $25.26 *
Grades: 7 8 9 10   92
1. Inventors
ISBN 0-8225-4689-2   LC 2002-7603
A biography of Thomas Alva Edison, the inventor of the electric lighting system and the phonograph.
"The life of this remarkable inventor and scientific genius is explored in lively and accessible detail. . . . In this clearly written and thoroughly researched volume, the information flows smoothly and logically." SLJ
Includes bibliographical references

Einstein, Albert, 1879-1955

Bernstein, Jeremy. Albert Einstein and the frontiers of physics. Oxford Univ. Press 1996 189p il (Oxford portraits in science) lib bdg $24; pa $12.95

Grades: 7 8 9 10   92

1. Physicists

ISBN 0-19-509275-9 (lib bdg); 0-19-512029-9 (pa)

LC 95-37500

At head of title: Oxford portraits in science

"Bernstein devotes considerable space in this . . . biography to explanations of relativity, quantum mechanics, gravitation, and the relevant mathematical formulas, and to the various scientists whose theories influenced Einstein in some way." SLJ

"Einstein's personal life, his political and religious beliefs, and his work for control of nuclear arms are well covered. . . . Recommended for those who want to know as much about Einstein's science as about his life." Voice Youth Advocates

Includes bibliographical references

Strathern, Paul. Einstein and relativity. Anchor Bks. (NY) 1999 102p pa $9.95

Grades: 11 12 Adult   92

1. Physicists 2. Relativity (Physics)

ISBN 0-385-49244-8   LC 98-44059

First published 1997 in the United Kingdom

"Strathern examines Albert Einstein, whose theory of relativity changed thinking on space and time and launched the nuclear age. . . . Einstein saw others go on to develop quantum physics, based on his theory; he used his fame to fight against anti-Semitism and nuclear weapons." Booklist

Includes bibliographical references

Eisner, Will, 1917-2005

Eisner, Will. Eisner/Miller: a one-on-one interview; conducted by Charles Brownstein. Dark Horse Books 2005 347p il pa $19.95

Grades: 9 10 11 12   92

1. Miller, Frank, 1957- 2. Comic books, strips, etc.

ISBN 1-56971-755-9

"In 2002, cartoonist Frank Miller visited with Will Eisner for a free-ranging discussion across several days. Brownstein provided shape to their encounters, giving the two artists a medium in which they could use words to explore the history of American graphic-novel expression, the business concerns of comics publishing, the relationship between art forms such as comics and film, and the meanings of success to each individual. . . . Students will find it valuable both for curriculum support and casual reading." SLJ

Includes bibliographical references

Eleanor, of Aquitaine, Queen, consort of Henry II, King of England, 1122?-1204

Kelly, Amy Ruth. Eleanor of Aquitaine and the four kings; [by] Amy Kelly. Harvard Univ. Press 1950 431p il pa $20.50 hardcover o.p.

Grades: 11 12 Adult   92

1. Queens 2. France—History—0-1328 3. Great Britain—History—1154-1399, Plantagenets

ISBN 0-674-24254-8 (pa)   LC 50-6545

This life story of Eleanor of Aquitaine, wife of two kings and mother of two others, is also a study of the twelfth century in which she lived.

Includes bibliographical references

Sapet, Kerrily. Eleanor of Aquitaine; medieval queen. Morgan Reynolds Pub. 2006 192p il map (European queens) lib bdg $27.95 *

Grades: 7 8 9 10 11 12   92

1. Queens 2. France—History—0-1328 3. Great Britain—History—1154-1399, Plantagenets

ISBN 978-1-931798-90-7; 1-931798-90-7

LC 2006-4865

This "biography provides . . . [an] account of Eleanor's eventful life as well as sets her story within the broader context of her times. . . . An attractive resource for library collections, this biography is rich in both narrative and visual details." Booklist

Includes bibliographical references

Elizabeth I, Queen of England, 1533-1603

Elizabeth I, Queen of England. Elizabeth I; her life in letters; {compiled by} Felix Pryor. University of Calif. Press 2003 144p il $34.95 *

Grades: 9 10 11 12   92

1. Queens 2. Great Britain—Kings and rulers 3. Great Britain—History—1485-1603, Tudors

ISBN 0-520-24106-1   LC 2003-59636

This "volume has been published to commemorate the 400th anniversary of Elizabeth I's death in 1603. It illustrates in color and, where possible, in actual size, sixty manuscripts—either by Elizabeth or to her. Each one is accompanied by a running commentary, explaining the document and placing it in its historical context, and selected transcriptions or, where necessary, translations from the originals." Publisher's note

Includes bibliographical references

Erlbaum, Janice, 1969-

Erlbaum, Janice. Girlbomb; a halfway homeless memoir. Villard 2006 252p $21.95; pa $13.95

Grades: 11 12 Adult   92

1. Runaway teenagers

ISBN 1-4000-6422-8; 978-1-4000-6422-9; 0-8129-7456-5 (pa); 978-0-8129-7456-0 (pa)

LC 2005-48643

"At 14, Erlbaum . . . became fed up with her mother's latest abusive husband and left their Brooklyn apartment. This memoir chronicles Erlbaum's teenage years, rife with typical issues that were intensified and complicated by her ongoing search for a place to call home. . . . Erlbaum perfectly captures the gritty landscape of the shelters, streets, and social scene of 1980s Manhattan and the gritty thoughts and feelings of a teenager immersing herself in flaky friends, lewd boys, violence, and drugs." Libr J

Euclid

Hayhurst, Chris. Euclid: the great geometer. Rosen Pub. Group 2006 112p il (The library of Greek philosophers) lib bdg $33.25 *

Grades: 9 10 11 12   92

1. Mathematicians

ISBN 1-4042-0497-0   LC 2005-6692

Euclid—*Continued*
"This book takes readers into Euclid's life, and to the ancient Greece in which he was raised." Publisher's note
Includes bibliographical references

Faraday, Michael, 1791-1867
Russell, Colin Archibald. Michael Faraday; physics and faith; [by] Colin A. Russell. Oxford Univ. Press 2000 124p il (Oxford portraits in science) lib bdg $24.95
Grades: 9 10 11 12   **92**
1. Physicists
ISBN 0-19-511763-8   LC 00-27008
A biography of the nineteenth-century English scientist whose religious beliefs guided his exploration of electricity and magnetism
"Give this to good readers who need a fresh biography subject, especially those who want to know about the history of science and technology." Booklist
Includes bibliographical references

Farmer, Paul, 1959-
Kidder, Tracy. Mountains beyond mountains. Random House 2003 336p $25.95; pa $14.95
Grades: 11 12 Adult   **92**
1. Physicians
ISBN 0-375-50616-0; 0-8129-7301-1 (pa)
      LC 2003-41253
This is a "portrait of Paul Farmer (MacArthur 'genius' grant, 1993), a driven, dedicated, rigidly idealistic doctor who commutes between Harvard and Haiti, where he works . . . to relieve the suffering of some of the poorest people on earth." N Y Times Book Rev
"This story is remarkable, and Kidder's skill in sequencing both dramatic and understated elements into a reflective commentary is unsurpassed." SLJ
Includes bibliographical references

Fermi, Enrico, 1901-1954
Cooper, Dan. Enrico Fermi and the revolutions in modern physics. Oxford Univ. Press 1999 117p il (Oxford portraits in science) lib bdg $28 *
Grades: 7 8 9 10   **92**
1. Physicists
ISBN 0-19-511762-X   LC 98-34471
A biography of the Nobel Prize-winning physicist whose work led to the discovery of nuclear fission, the basis of nuclear power and the atom bomb
"This book will be useful for reports. . . . The extensive list for further reading includes biographies of Fermi, books on both scientific and political aspects of the atomic-bomb project, and information on tours of laboratories involved in nuclear research today." SLJ

Firlik, Katrina
Firlik, Katrina. Another day in the frontal lobe; a neurosurgeon exposes life on the inside. Random House 2006 271p $24.95
Grades: 11 12 Adult   **92**
1. Physicians
ISBN 1-4000-6320-5   LC 2005-55260

The author "recounts how her background as a surgeon's daughter with a strong stomach and a keen interest in the brain led her to this rarefied specialty, and she describes her . . . trek from medical student to fully qualified surgeon." Publisher's note
"This witty and lucid . . . book demythologizes a complex medical specialty for those of us who aren't brain surgeons." Publ Wkly
Includes bibliographical references

Fitzgerald, F. Scott (Francis Scott), 1896-1940
Boon, Kevin A. F. Scott Fitzgerald; [by] Kevin Alexander Boon. Marshall Cavendish Benchmark 2005 c2006 142p (Writers and their works) lib bdg $25.95 *
Grades: 7 8 9 10   **92**
1. Authors, American
ISBN 0-7614-1947-0
"A biography of writer F. Scott Fitzgerald, that describes his era, his major works, his life, and the legacy of his writing." Publisher's note
This "attractive, well-organized [book fills] a gap in literary criticism for intermediate readers. Heavily illustrated with color and black-and-white photographs, [it] will appeal to students who might be intimidated by longer or more scholarly titles." SLJ
Includes bibliographical references

Fitzgerald, F. Scott (Francis Scott). A life in letters; edited by Matthew J. Bruccoli; with the assistance of Judith S. Baughman. Scribner 1994 xxiii, 503p $30; pa $18
Grades: 11 12 Adult   **92**
1. Authors, American
ISBN 0-684-19570-4; 0-684-80153-1 (pa)
      LC 93-31011
"Early letters to his editor, Maxwell Perkins, and friends, Edmund Wilson and Ernest Hemingway, document Fitzgerald's devotion to craft, exemplified by *The Great Gatsby* (1925), as well as the novelist's ever-present financial problems. . . . Letters to his wife, Zelda—when she was hospitalized for mental illness—detail the destruction of their marriage." Publ Wkly
"Essential reading for a full understanding of Fitzgerald as an artist and a man." Libr J

Fossey, Dian
De la Bédoyère, Camilla. No one loved gorillas more; Dian Fossey, letters from the mist; with photographs by Bob Campbell. National Geographic Society 2005 191p il $30 *
Grades: 11 12 Adult   **92**
1. Women scientists 2. Gorillas
ISBN 0-7922-9344-4   LC 2004-57944
This biography featuring an assemblage of Dian Fossey's letters to family and friends "reveals both the intense joy and immense suffering Fossey experienced during her 18-year sojourn among Rwanda's mountain gorillas." Booklist
Includes bibliographical references

France, Diane L.

Hopping, Lorraine Jean. Bone detective; the story of forensic anthropologist Diane France. Franklin Watts 2005 118p il (Women's adventures in science) lib bdg $31

Grades: 7 8 9 10   **92**

1. Forensic anthropology 2. Women scientists

ISBN 0-531-16776-3   LC 2005-0784

Also available in paperback from Joseph Henry Press

This "introduces the life and work of a contemporary forensic anthropologist, from her rural childhood to her work identifying the victims of the 9/11 tragedies. . . . The extensive detail gives readers a vivid sense of the daily work of a 'bone detective,' and clear explanations of the science will intrigue and inspire readers." Booklist

Includes glossary and bibliographical references

Francis, of Assisi, Saint, 1182-1226

Green, Julien. God's fool: the life and times of Francis of Assisi; translated by Peter Heinegg. Harper & Row 1985 273p pa $14 hardcover o.p. *

Grades: 11 12 Adult   **92**

1. Christian saints

ISBN 0-06-063464-2   LC 84-48771

Original French edition, 1983

An "account of the life of Francesco Bernardone, the riotous, reveling son of a silk merchant, who underwent a dramatic, God-inspired personal transformation, eventually becoming known to the world as the beloved saint of Assisi. Green has woven a thick fabric of history into his tale. . . . A remarkable and absorbing profile." Booklist

Frank, Anne, 1929-1945

Frank, Anne. The diary of a young girl: the definitive edition; edited by Otto H. Frank and Mirjam Pressler; translated by Susan Massotty. Doubleday 1995 340p $27.50; pa $6.99 *

Grades: 6 7 8 9   **92**

1. World War, 1939-1945—Jews 2. Netherlands—History—1940-1945, German occupation 3. Jews—Netherlands 4. Holocaust, 1933-1945

ISBN 0-385-47378-8; 0-553-57712-3 (pa)

LC 94-41379

"This new translation of Frank's famous diary includes material about her emerging sexuality and her relationship with her mother that was originally excised by Frank's father, the only family member to survive the Holocaust." Libr J

Frank, Anne. The diary of Anne Frank: the critical edition. rev Critical ed. Doubleday 2003 851p il $75

Grades: 11 12 Adult   **92**

1. World War, 1939-1945—Jews 2. Netherlands—History—1940-1945, German occupation 3. Jews—Netherlands 4. Holocaust, 1933-1945

ISBN 0-385-50847-6   LC 2003-269527

First published 1989

"Prepared by the Netherlands State Institute for War Documentation; introduced by Harry Paape, Gerrold van der Stroom, and David Barnouw; with a summary of the report by the Netherlands Forensic Institute; compiled by H.J.J. Hardy; edited by David Barnouw and Gerrold van der Stroom; translated by Arnold J. Pomerans, B.M. Mooyaart-Doubleday and Susan Massotty." Title page

This volume brings together "the three known versions of Frank's diary—the original, a self-edited version . . . {and} another edited by her father. It also contains . . . handwriting and paper analyses, new documentation regarding the Frank family's arrest, and . . . information about the diary's troubled publication history." Libr J {review of 1989 edition}

Includes bibliographical references

Pressler, Mirjam. Anne Frank: a hidden life; foreword by Rabbi Hugo Gryn; translated by Anthea Bell; with a note from Eva Schloss. Dutton Children's Bks. 2000 176p il hardcover o.p. pa $7.99

Grades: 9 10 11 12   **92**

1. World War, 1939-1945—Jews 2. Netherlands—History—1940-1945, German occupation 3. Jews—Netherlands 4. Holocaust, 1933-1945

ISBN 0-525-46330-5; 0-14-131226-2 (pa)

LC 99-89604

Also available in paperback from Puffin Bks.

Original German edition, 1992

"Rather than highlighting Anne's idealism, the author examines the tensions in her diary, performing a critical reading of Anne's description of herself and others, and analyzing how Anne reworked her diary in hopes of postwar publication. Pressler's work could serve as a model for how to read a subjective narrative." Publ Wkly

Includes bibliographical references

Franklin, Benjamin, 1706-1790

Franklin, Benjamin. Not your usual founding father; selected readings from Benjamin Franklin; edited by Edmund S. Morgan. Yale University Press 2006 303p il map $26 *

Grades: 11 12 Adult   **92**

ISBN 0-300-11394-3; 978-0-300-11394-5

LC 2006-45706

The editor "explains that this anthology differs from the typical selections of writings by founders, which showcase themes of revolution, war, and political philosophy. Here Morgan pursues the man himself, particularly Franklin's fascination with the curiosities of human behavior. . . . Franklin's humane solicitude and observational acuity surface in varied places (on ship, in Parisian salons) and in varied formats (personal letters, published satires) in such a way that readers encounter directly Franklin's seeming simplicity, which actually masked a deep complexity and which continually makes him the most interesting founder." Booklist

Gaustad, Edwin Scott. Benjamin Franklin; [by] Edwin S. Gaustad. Oxford University Press 2005 143p il (Lives and legacies) $17.95

Grades: 11 12 Adult   **92**

ISBN 0-19-530535-3   LC 2005-22906

This is a biography of the American statesman and scientist.

"Only diehard detractors of Franklin's Enlightenment

Franklin, Benjamin, 1706-1790—*Continued*
rationalism may deny that Gaustad has written an excellent introduction to this foremost founding father."
Booklist
Includes bibliographical references

Wood, Gordon S. The Americanization of Benjamin Franklin. Penguin Press 2004 299p il hardcover o.p. pa $16
Grades: 11 12 Adult   92
ISBN 1-59420-019-X; 0-14-303528-2 (pa)
LC 2003-63254
The author argues that "Franklin's conversion to American patriot was an evolutionary process; for most of his public life, he was a staunch supporter of the British empire. Once he committed to the patriot cause, though, he did so with considerable personal pain and loss. This superbly written work provides a fresh perspective on a justly admired but enigmatic figure."
Booklist
Includes bibliographical references

Franklin, Rosalind, 1920-1958
Polcovar, Jane. Rosalind Franklin and the structure of life. Morgan Reynolds 2006 144p il lib bdg $26.95 *
Grades: 7 8 9 10   92
1. Women scientists 2. DNA
ISBN 978-1-59935-022-6; 1-59935-022-X (lib bdg)
LC 2006-16864
A biography of the scientist whose unpublished research led to the discovery of the structure of DNA.
"Polcovar writes a rattling good story on two fronts: a woman becoming a scientist in an age when that was still unusual and the complex dynamics of personalities in a field sometimes thought of as impersonal." Booklist
Includes bibliographical references

Freud, Sigmund, 1856-1939
Reef, Catherine. Sigmund Freud: pioneer of the mind. Clarion Bks. 2001 152p il $19 *
Grades: 7 8 9 10   92
1. Psychiatrists
ISBN 0-618-01762-3   LC 00-43008
"Reef weaves the developing theories of the first psychoanalyst into a chronological report of his eventful life, setting both in the political and social currents of his era." Horn Book
"Effective use of personal details that reveal Freud's intellect, emotions, and personality, plus photos of his family, friends, and professional life, make this book rich and visually appealing." Voice Youth Advocates
Includes bibliographical references

Frey, James, 1969-
Frey, James. A million little pieces. Talese 2003 381p hardcover o.p. pa $14.95
Grades: 11 12 Adult   92
1. Drug addicts—Rehabilitation
ISBN 0-385-50775-5; 0-307-27690-2 (pa)
LC 2002-44393

"Frey's high school and college years are a blur of alcohol and drugs, culminating in a full-fledged crack addiction at age 23. As the book begins, his fed-up friends have convinced an airline to let him on the plane and shipped him off to his parents, who promptly put him in Hazelden, the rehabilitation clinic with the greatest success rate, 20 percent. Frey doesn't shy away from the gory details of addiction and recovery; all of the bodily fluids make major appearances here. What really separates this title from other rehab memoirs, apart from the author's young age, is his literary prowess. He doesn't rely on traditional indentation, punctuation, or capitalization, which adds to the nearly poetic, impressionistic detail of parts of the story. . . . This book is highly recommended for teens interested in the darker side of human existence." SLJ
Followed by My friend Leonard (2005)

Friedan, Betty, 1921-2006
Bohannon, Lisa Frederiksen. Woman's work; the story of Betty Friedan. Morgan Reynolds Pub 2004 144p il lib bdg $21.95 *
Grades: 9 10 11 12   92
1. Feminism
ISBN 1-931798-41-9   LC 2004-8444
"From her early years as a journalist through the publication of *The Feminine Mystique* to her role in the founding of the National Organization for Women, and her more recent support for seniors' rights, this title describes Friedan's considerable influence and significance." SLJ
"The chapters that follow Friedan chronologically through life nicely incorporate relevant cultural and historical background. . . . Throughout, Bohannon balances frankly portrayed unflattering subject matter with Friedan's extraordinary achievements." Booklist
Includes bibliographical references

Frost, Robert, 1874-1963
Caravantes, Peggy. Deep woods; the story of Robert Frost. Morgan Reynolds 2006 176p il (World writers) $27.95 *
Grades: 7 8 9 10   92
1. Poets, American
ISBN 978-1-931798-92-1; 1-931798-92-3
LC 2005037514
This "introduces poet Robert Frost. . . . Though focused on the man, Caravantes' presentation includes a few short selections from Frost's verse and, in sidebars, a bit of information about poetic forms. . . . Well organized and clearly written, the book offers a very readable account of Frost's often troubled life as an individual, a family man, a poet, and a public figure." Booklist
Includes bibliographical references

Fugard, Athol
Fugard, Athol. Cousins; a memoir. Theatre Communications Group 1997 152p $19.95
Grades: 11 12 Adult   92
1. Dramatists
ISBN 1-55936-132-8   LC 97-6241

Fugard, Athol—*Continued*

In this "memoir, South Africa's best-known contemporary playwright pays homage to two men who strongly influenced him when he was an impressionable young artist—his cousins Johnnie and Garth. . . . In passing, Fugard also tells a little about his family and boyhood in Port Elizabeth and environs, and he reveals, in tantalizing, brief snatches, which moments in his plays are taken from his life." Booklist

Fung, Inez, 1949-

Skelton, Renee. Forecast Earth; the story of climate scientist Inez Fung. Franklin Watts 2005 116p il (Women's adventures in science) $31
Grades: 7 8 9 10   92
  1. Climate 2. Women scientists
  ISBN 0-531-16777-1   LC 2005-05618
Also available in paperback from Joseph Henry Press
This is a biography of Inez Fung, "a climate scientist, someone who studies the causes of weather patterns and how they change over time." Publisher's note
This "volume is filled with full-color photographs of the subject and her work. Students will be comfortable with the style [of this book] and the easy reading level makes [it] accessible for even nonscience-oriented students." SLJ
Includes bibliographical references

Gaines, Ernest J., 1933-

Gaines, Ernest J. Conversations with Ernest Gaines; edited by John Lowe. University Press of Miss. 1995 335p il (Literary conversations series) hardcover o.p. pa $15.95 *
Grades: 11 12 Adult   92
  1. Authors, American 2. African American authors
  ISBN 0-87805-782-X; 0-87805-783-8 (pa)
       LC 95-13838
This is a collection of interviews given by the African American author between 1969 and 1994.

Gandhi, Mahatma, 1869-1948

Martin, Christopher. Mohandas Gandhi. Lerner Pubs. 2000 112p il map (Biography) lib bdg $25.26 *
Grades: 9 10 11 12   92
  1. India—Politics and government 2. Passive resistance
  ISBN 0-8225-4984-0   LC 99-28431
"This largely chronological overview provides some insight into the roots of Gandhi's beliefs in nonviolence and nonpossession, and his customary strategies such as fasting, civil disobedience, and turning the other cheek. . . . Back matter includes a brief epilogue pointing out the influence of Gandhi's teaching. While written in rather pedestrian prose, this title is . . . useful." SLJ
Includes bibliographical references

Gantos, Jack

Gantos, Jack. Hole in my life. Farrar, Straus & Giroux 2002 199p il $16; pa $8 *
Grades: 7 8 9 10   92
  1. Authors, American
  ISBN 0-374-39988-3; 0-374-43089-6 (pa)
       LC 2001-40957
The author relates how, as a young adult, he became a drug user and smuggler, was arrested, did time in prison, and eventually got out and went to college, all the while hoping to become a writer
"Gantos' spare narrative style and straightforward revelation of the truth have, together, a cumulative power that will capture not only a reader's attention but also empathy and imagination." Booklist

Gardner, Rulon, 1971-

Gardner, Rulon. Never stop pushing; [my life from a Wyoming farm to the Olympic medals stand]; [by] Rulon Gardner with Bob Schaller. Carroll & Graf 2005 341p il pa $15.95
Grades: 9 10 11 12   92
  1. Athletes
  ISBN 0-7867-1593-6   LC 2006-272981
Also available Thorndike Press large print edition
Subtitle from cover
This "is a motivational autobiography by Olympic Greco-Roman champion wrestler Rulon Gardner (Gold Medal, 2000; Bronze Medal, 2004)." Publisher's note
The authors "minimize the 'look-at-me' factor with a self-deprecating tone and a stern admonition that it's the work that is admirable and the triumphs only a byproduct. Nice reading for those who prefer athletes with tolerable egos." Booklist

Gautama Buddha

Armstrong, Karen. Buddha. Viking 2001 xxix, 205p map (Penguin lives series) hardcover o.p. pa $13 *
Grades: 11 12 Adult   92
  ISBN 0-670-89193-2; 0-14-303436-7 (pa)
       LC 00-43808
"A Penguin life"
"Armstrong interprets the mythologized story of the Buddha's abandonment of his life of comfort and privilege; commitment to practicing advanced forms of yoga and nearly fatal asceticism; enlightenment beneath a bodhi tree; and 45 years of wandering and teaching until his death in 483. And as she does so, she lucidly explains her revelations and influence." Booklist
Includes bibliographical references

Herbert, Patricia. The life of the Buddha; [by] Patricia M. Herbert. Pomegranate; In association with British Library 2005 96p il $19.95
Grades: 9 10 11 12   92
  ISBN 0-7649-3155-5   LC 2004-58721
First published 1993 in the United Kingdom
"Drawing on manuscript sources from Burma, Patricia Herbert recounts the story of the Buddha's life as it evolved over the centuries, incorporating legends, miracles, and local variations. The episodes are illustrated in full page color reproductions taken from two Burmese

Gautama Buddha—*Continued*
manuscripts that are among the British Library's most prized items." Publisher's note

Genghis Khan, 1162-1227
Rice, Earle. Empire in the east: the story of Genghis Khan. Morgan Reynolds Pub. 2005 160p il $26.95 *
Grades: 9 10 11 12   **92**
1. Mongolia—Kings and rulers
ISBN 1-931798-62-1   LC 2004-30743
"The biography offers background information about social customs of the times as well as details on the personal history of the man originally called Temujin. . . . A good introduction to the leader's life and brutal times." Booklist
Includes bibliographical references

Gilbreth, Frank Bunker, 1868-1924
Gilbreth, Frank B. Cheaper by the dozen; [by] Frank B. Gilbreth, Jr., Ernestine Gilbreth Carey. HarperCollins 2005 207p $19.95
Grades: 9 10 11 12 Adult   **92**
1. Gilbreth family
ISBN 0-06-076313-2; 978-0-06-076313-8
    LC 2005-296378
Also available Perennial Classics paperback edition
First published 1948 by Crowell
This biographical portrait of family life highlights the reminiscences of the twelve Gilbreth children and their adventures with their father, whose time and efficiency studies were applied to domestic life.
Followed by Belles on their toes (1950)

Gogh, Vincent van, 1853-1890
Greenberg, Jan. Vincent Van Gogh; portrait of an artist; {by} Jan Greenberg and Sandra Jordan. Delacorte Press 2001 132p il hardcover o.p. pa $6.99 *
Grades: 9 10 11 12   **92**
1. Artists, Dutch
ISBN 0-385-32803-6; 0-440-41917-4 (pa)
    LC 00-31850
This "book begins with van Gogh's boyhood and traces the various career paths (art dealer, missionary) he pursued before dedicating himself to painting. The authors draw on the artist's voluminous correspondence with his brother Theo to elicit his thoughts and feelings. . . . This outstanding, well-researched biography is fascinating reading." SLJ
Includes glossary and bibliographical references

González, Rigoberto, 1970-
González, Rigoberto. Butterfly boy; memories of a Chicano mariposa. University of Wisconsin Press 2006 207p (Writing in Latinidad) $24.95
Grades: 11 12 Adult   **92**
1. Gay men 2. Mexican Americans
ISBN 0-299-21900-3; 978-0-299-21900-0
    LC 2006-6990

"The son and grandson of farmworkers, constantly moving between Mexico and the U.S., then and now, Gonzalez weaves together three narrative threads: his angry present journey across the border with his estranged father; childhood memories of growing up as a fat, bookish 'sissy-boy'; and his urgent longing now for his sexy, abusive older lover." Booklist
"This moving memoir of a young Chicano boy's maturing into a self-accepting gay adult is a beautifully executed portrait of the experience of being gay, Chicano and poor in the United States." Publ Wkly

Goodall, Jane, 1934-
Greene, Meg. Jane Goodall; a biography. Greenwood Press 2005 146p il (Greenwood biographies) $29.95 *
Grades: 9 10 11 12   **92**
1. Women scientists
ISBN 0-313-33139-1; 978-0-313-33139-8
    LC 2005-16818
"Goodall's life is revealed from her earlier days growing up in England and the influence of her mother, to her experiences living and observing chimpanzees in Africa, and her undying efforts to promote conservation of wildlife." Publisher's note
Includes bibliographical references

Gottlieb, Lori
Gottlieb, Lori. Stick figure; a diary of my former self. Simon & Schuster 2000 222p il $22
Grades: 11 12 Adult   **92**
1. Anorexia nervosa
ISBN 0-684-86358-8   LC 99-52226
Also available in paperback from Berkley Bks.
This memoir in diary format is an account of the author's experience with anorexia. "At age 11, Gottlieb decided that she needed to lose weight. . . . Buying every diet book available, she became obsessed with calories. When she reached 60 pounds, she was hospitalized." SLJ
Gottlieb's "compelling narrative is undoubtedly based on her diaries, but her saucy wit, shrewd caricatures of hypocritical and shockingly unloving adults, lack of emotion, and confident pacing and structure all evince a more mature mind at work." Booklist

Graham, Martha
Freedman, Russell. Martha Graham, a dancer's life. Clarion Bks. 1998 175p il $18 *
Grades: 7 8 9 10   **92**
1. Dancers 2. Choreographers 3. Modern dance
ISBN 0-395-74655-8   LC 97-15832
A photo-biography of the American dancer, teacher, and choreographer who was born in Pittsburgh in 1895 and who became a leading figure in the world of modern dance
"A showstopping biography that captures its dynamic subject's personality, vision, and artistry." SLJ
Includes bibliographical references

Grant, Ulysses S. (Ulysses Simpson), 1822-1885
Rice, Earle. Ulysses S. Grant: defender of the Union; [by] Earle Rice, Jr. Morgan Reynolds 2005 176p il map lib bdg $24.95 *
Grades: 9 10 11 12   92
1. Presidents—United States
ISBN 1-931798-48-6   LC 2004-22345
The author "presents Ulysses S. Grant, touching upon his Ohio boyhood, education at West Point, service in the Mexican War, military leadership during the Civil War, and two terms as president. Rice portrays Grant in an evenhanded manner, making good use of source materials for apt quotations." Booklist
Includes bibliographical references

Grealy, Lucy, 1963-2002
Patchett, Ann. Truth & beauty; a friendship. HarperCollins Publishers 2004 257p $23.95; pa $13.95
Grades: 11 12 Adult   92
1. Women authors
ISBN 0-06-057214-0; 0-06-057215-9 (pa)
                                             LC 2003-67586
"As young writers. Patchett and Lucy Grealy began an intense friendship that lasted until Grealy's tragic death. With intimacy, gracy, and humor, Patchett's memoir captures Lucy's exuberance and her roller-coaster struggles with disfigurement and depression." Booklist

Gregory, Julie
Gregory, Julie. Sickened; the memoir of a Munchausen by proxy childhood; foreword by Marc D. Feldman. Bantam Books 2003 244p il hardcover o.p. pa $13
Grades: 9 10 11 12   92
1. Child abuse
ISBN 0-553-80307-7; 0-553-38197-0 (pa)
                                             LC 2003-52405
"Gregory's childhood was marred by a particularly insidious form of child abuse. Her mother used a combination of malnutrition, overwork, and prescription drugs to keep the girl in a perpetual state of ill health. . . . She relays her story not as a victim but as a strong survivor. . . . As well as being a fascinating read, this book could give others in similar situations a lifeline back to health." SLJ

Guevara, Ernesto, 1928-1967
Miller, Calvin Craig. Che Guevara; in search of revolution. Morgan Reynolds Pub. 2006 192p il map (World leaders) lib bdg $27.95 *
Grades: 7 8 9 10   92
ISBN 978-1-931798-93-8; 1-931798-93-1
                                             LC 2006-5975
This biography of the guerilla leader is "woven into . . . [an] account of the global politics of his day, including his role in the Cuban revolution and the showdown with the U.S. The design is appealing, with clear type, occasional photos, and maps, and teens will be drawn to the account of the young leader who made a difference in spite of an inglorious defeat." Booklist
Includes bibliographical references

Gunther, John, 1929-1947
Gunther, John. Death be not proud; a memoir. Harper & Row 1949 261p il pa $13.95 hardcover o.p.
Grades: 7 8 9 10   92
ISBN 0-06-123097-9 (pa)
Also available in hardcover from Buccaneer Bks.
A memoir of John Gunther's seventeen-year-old son, who died after a series of operations for a brain tumor. Not only a tribute to a remarkable boy but an account of a brave fight against disease

Guthrie, Woody, 1912-1967
Partridge, Elizabeth. This land was made for you and me: the life and songs of Woody Guthrie. Viking 2002 217p il $21.99 *
Grades: 7 8 9 10   92
1. Singers
ISBN 0-670-03535-1   LC 2001-46770
A biography of Woody Guthrie, a singer who wrote over 3,000 folk songs and ballads as he traveled around the United States, including "This Land is Your Land" and "So Long It's Been Good to Know Yuh"
This "presents an unflinchingly accurate portrait of a rambling and unpredictable man. . . . In addition to a panoply of archival photographs, which add realism to this engrossing story of a life, the book includes carefully selected quotes from songs, acquaintances, and documents to punctuate the story with authenticating detail without detracting from the momentum of the narrative." Bull Cent Child Books
Includes bibliographical references

Hahn, David
Silverstein, Ken. The radioactive boy scout; the true story of a boy and his backyard nuclear reactor. Random House 2004 209p hardcover o.p. pa $13.95 *
Grades: 9 10 11 12   92
ISBN 0-375-50351-X; 0-8129-6660-0 (pa)
                                             LC 2003-54811
"In the summer of 1995, a teenager in a Detroit suburb . . . managed to build a rudimentary nuclear breeder reactor in a shed behind his mother's house, using radioactive elements obtained from items as ordinary as smoke detectors. He got so far along in his efforts that when the Feds finally caught up with him, the EPA used Superfund money (usually spent on the worst hazardous waste sites) to clean up the shed. . . . [The author] fleshes out David Hahn's atomic escapades." Publ Wkly
"Silverstein tells his shocking story in lively detail that personalizes Hahn's world without sensationalizing." Booklist

Hakakian, Roya
Hakakian, Roya. Journey from the land of no; a girlhood caught in revolutionary Iran. Crown Publishers 2004 245p map $23; pa $13
Grades: 9 10 11 12   92
1. Iran—History—1979-
ISBN 1-4000-4611-4; 0-609-81030-8 (pa)
                                             LC 2003-21662

Hakakian, Roya—*Continued*

The author "recounts her past as a girl growing up in the second largest Jewish community in the Middle East—Tehran—during the takeover of the Ayatollah Khomeini." SLJ

"Political upheavals like the fall of the Shah of Iran and the rise of Islamic fundamentalism may be analyzed endlessly by scholars, but eyewitness accounts like Hakakian's help us understand what it was like to experience such a revolution firsthand. . . . Hakakian's story—so reminiscent of the experiences of Jews in Nazi Germany—is haunting." Publ Wkly

Hammel, Heidi B.

Bortz, Alfred B. Beyond Jupiter; the story of planetary astronomer Heidi Hammel; [by] Fred Bortz. Franklin Watts 2005 110p il (Women's adventures in science) $31

Grades: 7 8 9 10   92

1. Women astronomers
ISBN 0-531-16775-5   LC 2005-0778

Also available in paperback from Joseph Henry Press

This is a biography of the American astronomer Heidi Hammel.

The author "has captured some of the engaging qualities of Heidi Hammel's personality through extensive work with her and with the cooperation of her friends and family." Sci Books Films

Includes glossary and bibliographical references

Hansberry, Lorraine, 1930-1965

Hansberry, Lorraine. To be young, gifted, and Black; Lorraine Hansberry in her own words; adapted by Robert Nemiroff; with drawings and art by Lorraine Hansberry; introduction by James Baldwin; and a new preface by Jewell Handy Gresham Nemiroff. 1st Vintage Books ed. Vintage Books 1995 xxx, 261p il pa $13.95 *

Grades: 11 12 Adult   92

1. African American women 2. Dramatists
ISBN 0-679-76415-1   LC 96-119999

First published 1969 by Prentice-Hall

Work on this book and on the script for the play of the same title, which was presented at New York's Cherry Lane Theatre in 1969, "proceeded concurrently, each drawing upon the experiences and creative discoveries of the other, but ultimately diverging quite drastically." Postscript

Harmon, Adam

Harmon, Adam. Lonely soldier; the memoir of an American in the Israeli Army. Ballantine Books 2006 256p il $25.95

Grades: 11 12 Adult   92

1. Soldiers—Israel
ISBN 0-89141-874-1; 978-0-89141-874-0
                                                    LC 2005-58656

This is an "account of a sincere New Englander's move to Israel in 1990, where he enlists as a paratrooper just before the beginning of the Gulf War. . . . An illuminating account of a much-covered conflict, this is a memoir for anyone who wants a look behind the daily headlines." Publ Wkly

Harrison, Benjamin, 1833-1901

Calhoun, Charles W. (Charles William). Benjamin Harrison. Times Books 2005 206p il (American presidents series) $20

Grades: 11 12 Adult   92

1. Presidents—United States
ISBN 0-8050-6952-6; 978-0-8050-6952-5
                                                    LC 2004-63778

The author "dusts off an almost thoroughly forgotten chief executive, known primarily for serving between Cleveland's two terms, to disclose a harbinger of the modern, activist president. . . . One of the most revelatory entries in the American Presidents series." Booklist

Includes bibliographical references

Hart, Elva Trevino

Hart, Elva Trevino. Barefoot heart; stories of a migrant child. Bilingual Press/Editorial Bilingüe 1999 236p pa $17

Grades: 9 10 11 12   92

1. Migrant labor 2. Mexican Americans
ISBN 0-927534-81-9   LC 99-11731

The author recounts her life growing up in a family of migrant farm workers and "reveals the harsh toll that poverty and discrimination took on her family." Publ Wkly

This is "a powerful collection of vignettes." Libr J

Hawk, Tony, 1968-

Hawk, Tony. Hawk; occupation, skateboarder; {by} Tony Hawk with Sean Mortimer. ReganBooks 2000 289p il hardcover o.p. pa $15 *

Grades: 9 10 11 12   92

ISBN 0-06-019860-5; 0-06-095831-6 (pa)
                                                    LC 00-40279

In this memoir, the author recalls how he diverted the rebellious nature of his childhood into his love for and determination to excel in skateboarding. He also discusses his experiences with such skateboarding figures as Stacy Peralta, Mark Gonzalez, and Bob Burnquist

Hayslip, Le Ly

Hayslip, Le Ly. When heaven and earth changed places; a Vietnamese woman's journey from war to peace; [by] Le Ly Hayslip with Jay Wurts. Plume 1990 368p pa $16 *

Grades: 11 12 Adult   92

1. Vietnam War, 1961-1975—Personal narratives
ISBN 0-452-27168-1   LC 89-13711

First published 1989 by Doubleday

"Hayslip was born a Vietnamese peasant in 1949; little more than 20 years later she left for the United States with an American husband. Her early years were spent as a Viet Cong courier and lookout; a black marketeer; an unwed mother; a bar girl; a hospital aide. . . . She was tortured by the South Vietnamese army, raped by Viet Cong, and harassed by Americans. This story is juxtaposed with the tale of her . . . return to Vietnam in 1986." Libr J

"The book is a searing and human account of Viet-

Hayslip, Le Ly—*Continued*

nam's destruction and self-destruction. Lucidly, sometimes even lyrically, Ms. Hayslip paints an intensely intimate portrait." N Y Times Book Rev

Hemingway, Ernest, 1899-1961

Strathern, Paul. Hemingway in 90 minutes. Ivan R. Dee 2005 117p (Great writers in 90 minutes) $16.95; pa $8.95 *

Grades: 9 10 11 12   92

1. Authors, American

ISBN 1-56663-659-0; 1-56663-658-2 (pa)

LC 2005-7511

In this book, the author offers an "account of Hemingway's life and ideas, and explains their influence on literature and on man's struggle to understand his place in the world." Publisher's note

Includes bibliographical references

Henry, O., 1862-1910

Caravantes, Peggy. Writing is my business; the story of O. Henry. Morgan Reynolds Pub. 2006 160p il map (World writers) lib bdg $27.95 *

Grades: 7 8 9 10   92

1. Authors, American

ISBN 978-1-59935-031-8; 1-59935-031-9

LC 2006-16126

This is a biography of the short story writer.

"This title grabs readers' attention and never lets go." SLJ

Includes bibliographical references

Herriot, James

Herriot, James. All creatures great and small. 20th anniversary ed. St. Martin's Press 1992 442p $21.95; pa $13.95

Grades: 11 12 Adult   92

1. Veterinary medicine

ISBN 0-312-08498-6; 0-312-33085-5 (pa)

LC 92-18975

First published 1972

The first volume of Herriot's autobiographical account of the practice of veterinary medicine in Yorkshire, England in the 1930s

Followed by All things bright and beautiful (1974), All things wise and wonderful (1977), and The Lord God made them all (1981)

Hickam, Homer H., 1943-

Hickam, Homer H. Rocket boys; a memoir; {by} Homer H. Hickam, Jr. Delacorte Press 1998 368p $25.95; pa $14 *

Grades: 7 8 9 10   92

ISBN 0-385-33320-X; 0-385-33321-8 (pa)

LC 98-19304

"Raised in Appalachian coal country, Homer H. Hickam, Jr., might well have followed his father and grandfather into the mine. But when he was 14, his life was changed by a space launch on the other side of the world. Hickam's story of how a teenage boy's handmade

rockets lifted the hopes of a hardscrabble town is told in his {memoir}." Smithsonian

"Even if Hickam stretched the strict truth to metamorphose his memories into Stand By Me-like material for Hollywood . . . the embellishing only converts what is a good story into an absorbing, rapidly readable one that is unsentimental but artful about adolescence, high school, and family life." Booklist

Hitler, Adolf, 1889-1945

Adolf Hitler; Brenda Stalcup, book editor. Greenhaven Press 2000 202p (People who made history) lib bdg $31.20

Grades: 9 10 11 12   92

1. Dictators 2. National socialism 3. Germany—Politics and government—1933-1945

ISBN 0-7377-0223-0 (lib bdg)   LC 99-36361

An introduction "is followed by 16 essays, most of which have been excerpted from adult books. The selections are organized into sections devoted to exploring Hitler's early life and influences, his rise in power and its effects on the German people, World War II and the Holocaust, and his historical impact. Appendixes include discussion questions for each chapter, excerpts from speeches and original documents, a lengthy chronology, and an extensive list of materials for further research." SLJ

Includes bibliographical references

Hitler and his henchmen; Marylou Morano Kjelle, book editor. Greenhaven Press 2005 238p il (Profiles in history) lib bdg $34.95

Grades: 9 10 11 12   92

1. Dictators 2. National socialism 3. Germany—Politics and government—1933-1945

ISBN 0-7377-1713-0   LC 2004-54142

This book "explores the lives of the Führer and several key players in the Nazi reign, a regime Hitler had planned to last one thousand years." Publisher's note

Includes bibliographical references

Rice, Earle. Adolf Hitler and Nazi Germany. Morgan Reynolds 2005 176p il map $26.95 *

Grades: 7 8 9 10   92

1. Dictators 2. National socialism 3. Germany—Politics and government—1933-1945

ISBN 1-931798-78-8   LC 2005-17825

"Rice begins with details about Hitler's childhood, his early years as an artist, and his time as a soldier in World War I. He then focuses on Hitler's rise to power as dictator and leader of the Nazi Party, the causes and course of World War II, and the Fuhrer's obsessive determination to exterminate the Jews and other 'undesirables.'" Booklist

"Clear, concise writing coupled with impressive illustrations that include black-and-white and color photos of cityscapes and individuals make this book a useful resource." SLJ

Hockenberry, John

Hockenberry, John. Moving violations; war zones, wheelchairs, and declarations of independence. Hyperion 1995 367p pa $15.95 hardcover o.p.

Grades: 11 12 Adult   92
1. Journalists 2. Physically handicapped
ISBN 0-7868-8162-3 (pa)   LC 94-37190

"Correspondent Hockenberry covered the war in the Middle East in a wheelchair, but that's only one of the many triumphs in a life steeped in adversity. Hockenberry describes his struggles to live a full life in spite of his paraplegia in this frank and searing memoir." Booklist

Holiday, Billie, 1915-1959

Holiday, Billie. Lady sings the blues; [Billie Holiday with William Dufty] 50th anniversary ed., 1st Harlem Moon trade pbk. ed. Harlem Moon 2006 231p il pa $15.95 *

Grades: 11 12 Adult   92
1. African American singers
ISBN 978-0-7679-2386-6; 0-7679-2386-3
     LC 2007-271682

First published 1956 by Doubleday
Includes audio CD

"A hard, bitter and unsentimental book, written with brutal honesty and having much to say not only about Billie Holiday, the person, but about what it means to be poor and black in America." N Y Her Trib Books
Includes discography

Holman, James, 1786-1857

Roberts, Jason. A sense of the world; how a blind man became history's greatest traveler. HarperCollins Publishers 2006 382p il $26.95; pa $14.95

Grades: 11 12 Adult   92
1. Blind
ISBN   0-00-716106-9;   978-0-00-716106-5;
0-00-716126-3 (pa); 978-0-00-716126-3 (pa)
     LC 2005-58166

The author "narrates the life of a 19th-century British naval officer who was mysteriously blinded at 25, but nevertheless became the greatest traveler of his time. . . . Roberts does Holman justice, evoking with grace and wit the tale of this man once lionized as 'The Blind Traveler.'" Publ Wkly
Includes bibliographical references

House, Callie, 1861-1928

Berry, Mary Frances. My face is black is true; Callie House and the struggle for ex-slave reparations. Knopf 2005 314p il $26.95; pa $14.95

Grades: 11 12 Adult   92
1. African American women 2. African Americans—Reparations
ISBN 1-4000-4003-5; 0-307-27705-4 (pa)
     LC 2004-51330

The author "unearths the intriguing story of Callie House (1861–1928), a Tennessee washerwoman and seamstress become activist, and the organization she led, the National Ex-Slave Mutual Relief, Bounty and Pension Association. . . . Students and scholars of African-American history, as well as those engaged in the current reparations debates, will be deeply informed by the rise and fall of the Ex-Slave Association." Publ Wkly
Includes bibliographical references

Houze, David, 1965-

Houze, David. Twilight people; one man's journey to find his roots. University of California Press 2006 329p il $24.95

Grades: 11 12 Adult   92
1. African Americans—Civil rights 2. Apartheid
ISBN 0-520-24398-6; 978-0-520-24398-9
     LC 2005-35322

"The George Gund Foundation imprint in African American studies"

"The 1960s U.S. civil rights movement, South Africa's antiapartheid struggle, and the ramifications of mixed-race identity resonate personally with South African-born, Mississippi-raised Houze." Booklist
This "graceful memoir is a sensitive look into racial history in Africa and America, as well as a riveting personal narrative." Publ Wkly
Includes bibliographical references

Hughes, Langston, 1902-1967

Leach, Laurie F. Langston Hughes; a biography. Greenwood Press 2004 xx, 176p (Greenwood biographies) $29.95 *

Grades: 9 10 11 12   92
1. Poets, American
ISBN 0-313-32497-2   LC 2003-60131

This book covers the poet's life "from his tumultuous relationship with his father, various patrons, and romantic associations to his desire for recognition as an accomplished African-American literary artist. . . . This book would be a welcome addition to a high school library with a collection of in-depth biographies on literary artists." Libr Media Connect
Includes bibliographical references

Hurston, Zora Neale, 1891-1960

Hurston, Zora Neale. Dust tracks on a road; an autobiography; with a foreword by Maya Angelou. 1st Harper Perennial Modern Classic ed. Harper Perennial Modern Classics 2006 308p il pa $13.95 *

Grades: 11 12 Adult   92
1. African American authors 2. African American women
ISBN 0-06-085408-1; 978-0-06-085408-9
     LC 2005-52616

"The restored text established by The Library of America"

First published 1942 by Lippincott
On cover: P.S. insights, interviews & more
The author describes her wanderings in and out of schools and jobs as a young girl, finishing her course work at Barnard, and beginning her life's work.
Includes bibliographical references

Hurston, Zora Neale, 1891-1960—Continued

Lyons, Mary E. Sorrow's kitchen; the life and folklore of Zora Neale Hurston. 1st Collier Books ed. Collier Books, Maxwell Macmillan Canada, Maxwell Macmillan International 1993 144p il (Great achievers) pa $7.99 *

Grades: 7 8 9 10   **92**
  1. African American authors 2. African American women
  ISBN 0-02-044445-1   LC 92-30600
  First published 1990 by Scribner

This biography details "Hurston's migration from Florida to Baltimore, Washington, D.C., and finally Harlem as well as her travels through the West Indies to collect folklore. The text contains eleven excerpts from Hurston's books. . . . Lyons has created a prime example of biography—fascinating, enlightening, stimulating, and satisfying." Horn Book

Includes bibliographical references

Hynes, Samuel Lynn

Hynes, Samuel Lynn. The growing seasons; an American boyhood before the war. Viking 2003 291p il hardcover o.p. pa $14

Grades: 11 12 Adult   **92**
  ISBN 0-670-03193-3; 0-14-200396-4 (pa)
                                              LC 2003-283017

This is "a memoir of {the author's} Midwestern boyhood and youth during the 1930's. . . . 'The Growing Seasons' ends where 'Flights of Passage' began, at the Rock Island Depot in Minneapolis, with the 18-year-old Hynes saying farewell to his father and waiting for the train that will carry him off to war." N Y Times Book Rev

Hynes' "crisp writing evokes nostalgic memories of a time long past while succesfully avoiding sentimentality." Booklist

Jackson, Andrew, 1767-1845

Marrin, Albert. Old Hickory; Andrew Jackson and the American people. Dutton Children's Books 2004 262p il $30 *

Grades: 7 8 9 10   **92**
  1. Presidents—United States
  ISBN 0-525-47293-2   LC 2003-28299

"More than a biography, this fine study of our seventh president is also a history and analysis of the times in which he lived. . . . Marrin discusses the changes to society brought about by the Industrial Revolution, the railroads, and the rise of the market economy. Written in an engaging style and with a wealth of detail, the book is enhanced by numerous black-and-white illustrations." SLJ

Includes bibliographical references

Wilentz, Sean. Andrew Jackson. Times Books 2005 195p (American presidents series) $20

Grades: 11 12 Adult   **92**
  1. Presidents—United States
  ISBN 0-8050-6925-9   LC 2005-52857

The author "shows that our complicated seventh president was a central figure in the development of Ameri-

can democracy. . . . It is rare that historians manage both Wilentz's deep interpretation and lively narrative." Publ Wkly

Includes bibliographical references

Jackson, Jon

Jackson, Jon. On edge; backroom dealing, cocktail scheming, triple axels, and how top skaters get screwed; [by] Jon Jackson with James Pereira. Thunder's Mouth Press 2006 298p il $25; pa $14.95

Grades: 9 10 11 12   **92**
  1. Ice skating
  ISBN 1-56025-804-7; 978-1-56025-804-9; 1-56025-953-1; 978-1-56025-953-4 (pa)
                                              LC 2006-297463

In this memoir, the author describes figure skating's "double-dealing and corruption while simultaneously telling the . . . story of a young man who tried to make his way through this cutthroat world without losing his way. With co-author Pereira, Jackson writes about encountering bribery, manipulation, cowardice, substance abuse, sexual predation, and other sordid goings-on. . . . The book offers a much-needed look behind the scenes." Booklist

Jackson, Shirley Ann, 1946-

O'Connell, Diane. Strong force; the story of physicist Shirley Ann Jackson. Franklin Watts 2005 110p il (Women's adventures in science) lib bdg $31

Grades: 7 8 9 10   **92**
  1. Physicists 2. Women scientists 3. African American women
  ISBN 0-5311-6784-4   LC 2005-827

A biography of African American physicist Shirley Ann Jackson.

This is "interesting, substantive, and eminently readable." SLJ

Includes bibliographical references

Jackson, Stonewall, 1824-1863

Robertson, James I., Jr. Standing like a stone wall: the life of General Thomas J. Jackson; by James I. Robertson, Jr. Atheneum Bks. for Young Readers 2001 185p il maps $22

Grades: 7 8 9 10   **92**
  1. Generals 2. United States—History—1861-1865, Civil War
  ISBN 0-689-82419-X   LC 00-36253

"Robertson finds a good balance between Jackson's life before [the Civil War] and his experiences in the campaigns that made him famous. . . . The many illustrations include reproductions of period photographs and prints as well as several maps and photos of artifacts. Robertson's extensive source notes and a bibliography are appended. A good choice for biography collections." Booklist

Includes bibliographical references

Jennings, Kevin, 1963-

Jennings, Kevin. Mama's boy, preacher's son; a memoir. Beacon Press 2006 267p $24.95; pa $15 *

Grades: 11 12 Adult   92

1. Gay men 2. Political activists

ISBN   0-8070-7146-3;   978-0-8070-7146-5;
0-8070-7147-1 (pa); 978-0-8070-7147-2 (pa)

LC 2006-1275

The author, the "founder of a national advocacy group that supports safety and equality for students and teachers in public education, grew up in an impoverished Southern home, the son of an itinerant Baptist preacher and an outspoken firebrand of a mother. Self-described trailer trash, he fought against a sickly childhood, the early death of his father and the resulting feelings of guilt, and his own nascent homosexuality. He overcame these challenges and more to win an undergraduate scholarship to Harvard." Libr J

"Jennings writes of his journey with graciousness and candor." Voice Youth Advocates

Jeter, Derek, 1974-

Jeter, Derek. The life you imagine; ten steps to ultimate achievement. Crown 2000 xxii, 279p il $21.95; pa $12

Grades: 11 12 Adult   92

1. Baseball—Biography

ISBN 0-609-60786-3; 0-609-980718-8 (pa)

LC 00-34533

In this autobiography, Jeter outlines the "ten practical steps, . . . [he] used to fulfill his dream of playing baseball in the major leagues. The ten principles, which reflect the author's journey as an athlete, are based on input from family members, whom he credits for his success." Libr J

Joan, of Arc, Saint, 1412-1431

Pernoud, Régine. Joan of Arc: her story; Régine Pernoud, Marie-Véronique Clin; translated and revised by Jeremy duQuesnay Adams; edited by Bonnie Wheeler. St. Martin's Griffin 1999 xxii, 304p il map hardcover o.p. pa $16.95 *

Grades: 11 12 Adult   92

1. Christian saints 2. France—History—1328-1589, House of Valois

ISBN 0-312-21442-1; 0-312-22730-2 (pa)

LC 98-45059

Original French edition, 1986

This work "traces the appearance of Joan as a documented historical character rather than adhering to a standard chronological sequence. Informing the narrative is a novel interpretation of Joan as a political prisoner. Moving beyond the narrative, the American translator . . . has added a series of appendixes containing valuable contextual material. . . . These materials discuss key historical events, provide biographical information on Joan's contemporaries, and discuss Joan's afterlife in history, literature, folklore, art, and iconography." Libr J

Includes bibliographical references

John Paul II, Pope, 1920-2005

Flynn, Raymond. John Paul II; a personal portrait of the pope and the man. St. Martin's Press 2001 204p il pa $14.95 hardcover o.p.

Grades: 11 12 Adult   92

ISBN 0-312-28328-8 (pa)   LC 00-45965

Flynn, the "former mayor of Boston and ex-ambassador to the Vatican, tells us . . . what his book is not: It is not a biography, or an analysis. . . . Flynn views it, rather, as a profile based on his own experiences with Pope John Paul II, dating back to a 1969 visit to Boston of then-Cardinal Karol Wojtyla." Natl Rev

Mainardi, Alessandro. The life of Pope John Paul . . . in comics! illustrated by Werner Maresta. Papercutz 2006 96p il $16.95; pa $9.95

Grades: 7 8 9 10   92

1. Graphic novels 2. Biographical graphic novels

ISBN   1-59707-039-4;   978-1-59707-039-3;
1-59707-057-2 (pa); 978-1-59707-057-7 (pa)

"Translation by Kathleen Koeneman and Stafano Gaudiano" Verso of title page

This biography in graphic novel format focuses on "the very human side of this revered holy man. Maresta animates key episodes from Karol Wojtyla's childhood and John Paul II's papacy, including the assassination attempt he endured." Publ Wkly

"Handsome and in full color, the carefully considered pictures bring freshness to a familiar story." Booklist

Renehan, Edward J. Pope John Paul II; [by] Edward J. Renehan, Jr. Chelsea House 2007 109p il (Modern world leaders) $30 *

Grades: 7 8 9 10 11 12   92

ISBN 0-7910-9227-5; 978-0-7910-9227-9

LC 2006-10612

This "biography follows the arch of the pontiff's life in the context of world politics." Publisher's note

Includes bibliographical references

Johnson, Robert, 1911-1938

Wald, Elijah. Escaping the delta; Robert Johnson and the invention of the blues. Amistad 2004 342p $24.95; pa $14.95

Grades: 11 12 Adult   92

1. Blues music 2. African American musicians

ISBN 0-06-052423-5; 0-06-052427-8 (pa)

LC 2003-52287

"In this combination history of blues music and biography of Robert Johnson, Wald . . . explores Johnson's rise from a little known guitarist who died in 1938 to one of the most influential artists in rock and roll. From the blues' meager beginning in the early 1900s to its '30s heyday and its 1960s revival, Wald gives a revisionist history of the music, which he feels, in many instances, has been mislabeled and misjudged." Publ Wkly

The author "writes better than anyone else ever has about the blues. If you read only one book about blues—maybe ever—read this one." Booklist

Includes bibliographical references

Jones, John Paul, 1747-1792

Brager, Bruce L. John Paul Jones; America's sailor. Morgan Reynolds Pub. 2006 160p il map lib bdg $26.95

Grades: 7 8 9 10   **92**

1. Admirals

ISBN 978-1-931798-84-6; 1-931798-84-2

LC 2005-30443

The author "begins with Jones's Scottish childhood, where he developed a bitter resentment of the British class system. He then traces the man's career as a commercial seaman, privateer, naval commander, and soldier of fortune. . . . This often-unflattering portrait of Jones will require readers who can place his good and bad traits in perspective and judge his place in history, making it a good choice for mature students." SLJ

Includes bibliographical references

Jordan, Barbara, 1936-1996

Mendelsohn, James. Barbara Jordan; getting things done. 21st Cent. Bks. (Brookfield) 2000 192p il $23.90

Grades: 9 10 11 12   **92**

1. Women politicians 2. African American women

ISBN 0-7613-1467-9   LC 00-57776

"An introductory chapter addresses the climate of segregation into which Jordan was born. Illustrated with selected photos of Jordan and period political events, the following chapters trace her rise through elected office to become the first black woman from the South ever elected to the U.S. Congress, followed by her abrupt retirement from public office." Booklist

Includes bibliographical references

Jordan, Michael, 1963-

Halberstam, David. Playing for keeps: Michael Jordan and the world he made. Random House 1999 426p pa $16.95 hardcover o.p.

Grades: 11 12 Adult   **92**

1. Chicago Bulls (Basketball team) 2. African American athletes 3. Basketball—Biography

ISBN 0-7679-0444-3 (pa)   LC 98-49964

Halberstam presents a biography of basketball player Michael Jordan.

"What's particularly effective about Halberstam's storytelling is that he follows Jordan's athletic trajectory, not in chronological order but through juxtaposed images of a hot-blooded college player with an as-yet unpolished game and an even-tempered 30-year-old at the height of his career. Jordan was not born a flawless pro, but developed his gifts by working tirelessly and intensely." Natl Rev

Joseph, Nez Percé Chief, 1840-1904

Moulton, Candy Vyvey. Chief Joseph; guardian of the people; [by] Candy Moulton. Forge Books 2005 239p map (American heroes series) $19.95; pa $12.95 *

Grades: 11 12 Adult   **92**

1. Nez Percé Indians

ISBN 0-7653-1063-5; 0-7653-1064-3 (pa)

LC 2004-56318

"A Tom Doherty Associates book"

The author "focuses on Chief Joseph of the Nez Perce tribe, who, after trying for years to accommodate encroaching white men on his tribal lands, gave up and attempted, in the fall of 1877, to lead his people to safety in Canada. . . . Moving and well documented, this is a superb addition to the American Heroes series." Booklist

Includes bibliographical references

Scott, Robert Alan. Chief Joseph and the Nez Percés; {by} Robert A. Scott. Facts on File 1993 134p il maps (Makers of America) lib bdg $25

Grades: 9 10 11 12   **92**

1. Nez Percé Indians

ISBN 0-8160-2475-8   LC 92-15885

A biography of the nineteenth-century Nez Percé chief, concentrating on his unending struggle to win peace and equality for his people

Includes bibliographical references

Karr, Mary

Karr, Mary. The Liars' Club; a memoir; [with a new introduction by the author] 10th anniversary ed. Penguin Books 2005 320p pa $15

Grades: 11 12 Adult   **92**

ISBN 0-14-303574-6; 978-0-14-303574-9

LC 2005-276148

First published 2005

Poet "Karr and her older sister grew up in an east Texas oil town where they learned to cope with their mother's psychotic episodes, the ostracism by neighbors and their father's frequent absences. Karr's happiest times were the afternoons she spent at the 'Liars Club,' where her father and a group of men drank and traded boastful stories." Publ Wkly

"This barbed memoir of a close and calamitous family from a Texas oil town moves with the same quickness as its doubledged title. . . . The revelations continue to the final page, with a misleading carelessness as seductive as any world-class liar's." New Yorker

Katin, Miriam

Katin, Miriam. We are on our own; a memoir. Drawn & Quarterly 2006 122p il $19.95

Grades: 9 10 11 12 Adult   **92**

1. World War, 1939-1945—Graphic novels 2. Holocaust, 1933-1945—Graphic novels 3. Autobiographical graphic novels

ISBN 1-896597-20-3   LC 2005-9063602

In this WWII memoir, the author recounts "how she and her mother faked their deaths and fled Budapest after the Nazis occupied the city. With forged papers obtained from a black marketer, they escaped to the countryside in the guise of a servant girl and her illegitimate child. Katin relates their harrowing lives there and her mother's desperate search for her missing husband after the war. . . . This impressive book belongs in all serious graphic novel collections and is also a natural for Jewish studies." Booklist

Keckley, Elizabeth, ca. 1818-1907

Fleischner, Jennifer. Mrs. Lincoln and Mrs. Keckley. See entry under Lincoln, Mary Todd, 1818-1882

Keller, Helen, 1880-1968

Keller, Helen. Helen Keller: selected writings; edited by Kim E. Nielsen; consulting editor, Harvey J. Kaye. New York University Press 2005 317p il (History of disability series) $35
Grades: 11 12 Adult   92
1. Blind 2. Deaf
ISBN 0-8147-5829-0   LC 2004-28974
"Published in conjunction with the American Foundation for the Blind"
This is a collection "of Keller's personal letters, political writings, speeches, and excerpts of her published materials from 1887 to 1968." Univ Press Books for Public and Second Sch Libr, 2006
Includes bibliographical references

Keller, Helen. The story of my life; edited and with a preface by James Berger. The restored ed. Modern Library 2003 xlvi, 343p il hardcover o.p. pa $9.95 *
Grades: 8 9 10 11 12 Adult   92
1. Blind 2. Deaf
ISBN 0-679-64287-0; 0-8129-6886-7 (pa)
                                      LC 2002-40971
First published 1903
This biography of the inspirational Keller contains accounts of her home life and her relationship with her devoted teacher Anne Sullivan.
Includes bibliographical references

Kennedy, John F. (John Fitzgerald), 1917-1963

Burner, David. John F. Kennedy and a new generation. 2nd ed. Pearson\Longman 2005 210p il (Library of American biography) pa $20.67
Grades: 11 12 Adult   92
1. Presidents—United States 2. United States—Politics and government—1961-1974
ISBN 0-321-10143-X; 978-0-321-10143-3
                                      LC 2004-46520
First published 1988 by Little, Brown
"Though the author offers significant insight into how Kennedy's domineering father and privileged background strongly influenced the pragmatic nature of his politics, he does not entirely discount Kennedy's tremendous impact upon the ideals and expectations of a new generation of voters. This meditative analysis provides a welcome balance between increasingly extremist interpretations of Kennedy's career." Booklist
Includes bibliographical references

Cooper, Ilene. Jack: the early years of John F. Kennedy. Dutton Children's Bks. 2003 168p il $22.99
Grades: 9 10 11 12   92
1. Presidents—United States
ISBN 0-525-46923-0   LC 2002-75912
A description of the childhood and youth of John Fitzgerald Kennedy, the thirty-fifth president of the United States.
"Intelligent design and numerous fabulous, well-placed, and well-captioned black-and-white photographs enrich Cooper's clear prose. . . . This sensitive, well-researched biography will enhance any collection." Voice Youth Advocates
Includes bibliographical references

Dallek, Robert. Let every nation know; John F. Kennedy in his own words; [by] Robert Dallek and Terry Golway. Sourcebooks MediaFusion 2006 289p il $29.95; pa $19.95
Grades: 11 12 Adult   92
1. Presidents—United States 2. United States—Politics and government—1961-1974
ISBN   1-4022-0647-X;   978-1-4022-0647-4;
1-4022-0922-3 (pa); 978-1-4022-0922-2 (pa)
                                      LC 2005-37973
This book gives "brief analyses of 31 of JFK's speeches and debates, presented in audio selections on the accompanying CD-ROM. The results reveal Kennedy's eloquence, humor, and grace under pressure. . . . This work illuminates the importance of public address to the success and reputation of presidents and shows that Kennedy mastered this art." Libr J
Includes bibliographical references

Kenney, Charles. John F. Kennedy; the presidential portfolio: history as told through the collection of the John F. Kennedy Library and Museum; introduction by Michael Beschloss. PublicAffairs 2000 241p il $35 *
Grades: 11 12 Adult   92
1. Presidents—United States 2. United States—Politics and government—1961-1974
ISBN 1-891620-36-3   LC 00-57581
Includes computer optical disc
This volume features approximately 250 photos and documents and highlights "the many remarkable events of Kennedy's life and his presidency." Publisher's note
"The text is less detailed (and less focused on controversy) than a full-scale biography, but it emphasizes what most would consider the key elements of JFK's presidency . . . while also devoting chapters to Jacqueline and Robert F. Kennedy. Likely to appeal to Kennedy fans and to others seeking a sense of the period." Booklist

Kepler, Johannes, 1571-1630

Voelkel, James R. Johannes Kepler and the new astronomy. Oxford Univ. Press 1999 141p il (Oxford portraits in science) lib bdg $28 *
Grades: 7 8 9 10   92
1. Astronomers
ISBN 0-19-511680-1 (lib bdg)   LC 99-23844
A biography of the German astronomer who discovered three laws of planetary motion
"This book is enhanced with fascinating and informative reproductions, including facsimiles of Kepler's writings. Overall, an enjoyable introduction to a complex scientific life." SLJ
Includes bibliographical references

Khomeini, Ruhollah

Moin, Baqer. Khomeini; life of the Ayatollah. Thomas Dunne Bks. 2000 355p $27.95
Grades: 11 12 Adult   92
1. Iran—Politics and government
ISBN 0-312-26490-9   LC 2001-269491
First published 1999 in the United Kingdom

Khomeini, Ruhollah—*Continued*

The author "describes the harsh side of the cleric who forever changed the course of Iran's history. . . . The most interesting parts of the book deal with the human side of a man who was little known before his ascent to power and widely misunderstood both before and after." N Y Times Book Rev

Includes bibliographical references

Kincaid, Jamaica

Kincaid, Jamaica. My brother. Farrar, Straus & Giroux 1997 197p hardcover o.p. pa $10

Grades: 11 12 Adult   92

1. Women authors

ISBN 0-374-21681-9; 0-374-52562-5 (pa)

LC 97-16190

This is "Jamaica Kincaid's account of the life and death of her brother Devon Drew in their homeland of Antigua." N Y Times Book Rev

"Honest, unapologetic, and pure, this is an eloquent and searching elegy for the dead and a prayer of thankfulness for the living." Booklist

King, B. B.

King, B. B. Blues all around me; the autobiography of B.B. King; [by] B.B. King with David Ritz. Avon Bks. 1996 336p il hardcover o.p. pa $14

Grades: 11 12 Adult   92

1. Blues music 2. African American musicians

ISBN 0-380-97318-9; 0-380-80760-2 (pa)

LC 96-27773

King recounts his humble beginnings and his career as a prominent blues guitarist.

"This is one of the best recent pop-music bios. King speaks straight from the soul, it seems, just like he plays the guitar." Booklist

King, Martin Luther, Jr., 1929-1968

Anderson, Ho Che. King: a comic book biography; [Ho Che Anderson; introduction by Stanley Crouch; edited by Gary Groth] Fantagraphics 2005 228p il pa $22.95 *

Grades: 9 10 11 12   92

1. Graphic novels 2. Biographical graphic novels 3. African Americans—Biography—Graphic novels 4. African Americans—Civil rights—Graphic novels

ISBN 1-56097-622-5

"This collection brings together Anderson's . . . three-issue series covering the life of Dr. Martin Luther King, Jr., from his early days in college through the Civil Rights movement to his assassination." SLJ

"Anderson's biographical graphic novel has the weight and depth of a lifetime of research. . . . Through a varied graphic arsenal and subtle prose, Anderson's King comes alive." Publ Wkly

Johnson, Charles Richard. King: the photobiography of Martin Luther King, Jr.; Charles Johnson & Bob Adelman; foreword by Julian Bond; editor Mary Beth Brewer; designed by Will Hopkins & Mary K. Baumann. Harry N. Abrams 2004 288p il pa $19.95

Grades: 11 12 Adult   92

1. African Americans—Biography 2. African Americans—Civil rights

ISBN 0-8109-9182-9   LC 2004-8562

"A Bob Adelman book"

First published 2000 by Viking Studio

This photobiography uses "archival sources to narrate the life of the leader of the civil rights struggle. . . . The novelist Charles Johnson contributes a masterly elegiac text that does not paper over the philosophical differences between King's sustained vision of peaceful interracial cooperation and the vocal advocates of black power who claimed national attention in his last years." N Y Times Book Rev [review of 2000 edition]

Includes bibliographical references

King, Stephen, 1947-

King, Stephen. On writing; a memoir of the craft. Scribner 2000 288p $25; pa $14.95

Grades: 11 12 Adult   92

1. Authors, American 2. Authorship

ISBN 0-684-85352-3; 0-671-02425-6 (pa)

LC 00-30105

The author recounts "his life from early childhood through the aftermath of the 1999 accident that nearly killed him. Along the way, King touts the writing philosophies of William Strunk and Ernest Hemingway, advocates a healthy appetite for reading, expounds upon the subject of grammar, critiques a number of popular writers, and offers the reader a chance to try out his theories. . . . Recommended for anyone who wants to write and everyone who loves to read." Libr J

Whitelaw, Nancy. Dark dreams; the story of Stephen King. Morgan Reynolds 2005 128p il map (World writers) $26.95 *

Grades: 7 8 9 10   92

1. Authors, American 2. Horror fiction

ISBN 1-931798-77-X   LC 2005-20112

"This well-documented look at King's life introduces the man who has become a legend for reinventing and legitimizing horror. Whitelaw has put together a seamless synthesis of interviews, biographies, and King's own writing, pared down for younger readers and illustrated with plenty of full-color photographs." Booklist

Kingsley, Anna, d. 1870

Schafer, Daniel L. Anna Madgigine Jai Kingsley; African princess, Florida slave, plantation slaveowner. University Press of Fla. 2003 177p il maps $24.95

Grades: 11 12 Adult   92

1. Slavery—United States 2. African American women 3. Plantation life

ISBN 0-8130-2616-4   LC 2002-33372

Kingsley, Anna, d. 1870—*Continued*

"Schafer traces the history of Anna Madgigine Jai from her homeland of Senegal, where she was captured at about 13 years of age in 1806 and sold to Zephaniah Kingsley, a maritime merchant, slave trader, and later an abolitionist. Kingsley eventually married Anna, made her manager of his plantation, and fathered four children with her. . . . This is a fascinating look at an extraordinary woman and the complexities of slavery beyond the common image of slavery in the South." Booklist

Includes bibliographical references

Koehl, Mimi, 1948-

Parks, Deborah. Nature's machines; the story of biomechanist Mimi Koehl; by Deborah Amel Parks. Joseph Henry Press 2005 118p il (Women's adventures in science) lib bdg $31; pa $9.95

Grades: 7 8 9 10   92

1. Biologists 2. Human engineering 3. Women scientists

ISBN 0-531-16780-1 (lib bdg); 0-309-09559-X (pa)

LC 2005-10201

Mimi Koehl "wanted to know more about sea anemones, particularly how they survive the turbulent surf on rocky beaches. Her inquiries and experiments led to discoveries in a new field, biomechanics, in which scientists examine how form determines movement and function in the animal kingdom. . . . This [book] should spark the curiosity of any reader." Voice Youth Advocates

Includes bibliographical references

Kraus, Caroline

Kraus, Caroline. Borderlines; a memoir. Broadway Bks. 2004 360p hardcover o.p. pa $12.95

Grades: 9 10 11 12   92

ISBN 0-7679-1403-1; 0-7679-1428-7 (pa)

LC 2003-69592

"Caroline, an intelligent but somewhat naive college graduate, finds herself in a severely dysfunctional and dangerous friendship with troubled and manipulative Jane. Her downward spiral and recovery make for a compelling and suspenseful read." SLJ

Kuffel, Frances

Kuffel, Frances. Passing for thin; losing half my weight and finding myself. Broadway Books 2004 260p $24; pa $14

Grades: 9 10 11 12   92

1. Obesity

ISBN 0-7679-1291-8; 0-7679-1292-6 (pa)

LC 2003-52455

"Kuffel acknowledges that she began overeating because she loves food and because eating can be a mind-blowing sensual experience. (Here food descriptions are divine, but even better is her confession that she loved the 'Little House' books primarily for Laura Ingalls Wilder's great food writing.) At the same time, she doesn't let anyone off the hook for how she was treated after she became fat." SLJ

Lange, Dorothea, 1895-1965

Dorothea Lange—a visual life; edited by Elizabeth Partridge. Smithsonian Institution Press 1994 168p il hardcover o.p. pa $34.95

Grades: 11 12 Adult   92

1. Women photographers

ISBN 1-56098-350-7; 1-56098-455-4 (pa)

LC 94-25869

This is a "collection of photos and insightful essays about the photographer whose work captured more than four decades of American history. . . . Interwoven with Lange's personal story are the photographic records of the '30s, '40s, and '50s so dramatically captured by her insightful choices." SLJ

Includes bibliographical references

Partridge, Elizabeth. Restless spirit: the life and work of Dorothea Lange. Viking 1998 122p il $19.99; pa $10.99 *

Grades: 6 7 8 9   92

1. Women photographers

ISBN 0-670-87888-X; 0-14-230024-1 (pa)

LC 98-9807

A biography of Dorothea Lange, whose photographs of migrant workers, Japanese American internees, and rural poverty helped bring about important social reforms

"Generously placed throughout this accessibly written biography are the photographic images that make Lange a pre-eminent artist of the century. The book is elegantly designed and the photographic reproductions are excellent." Bull Cent Child Books

Includes bibliographical references

Lavender, Bee

Lavender, Bee. Lessons in taxidermy. Punk Planet Books 2005 160p pa $12.95

Grades: 9 10 11 12   92

ISBN 978-1-888451-79-5; 1-888451-79-3

LC 2004-115618

The author "recounts her life spent in and out of hospitals and her subsequent dissociation from her own body and emotions. She struggles with health problems from birth, which are compounded by her surroundings, including frequent encounters with street fights, domestic violence and poverty. . . . Witnessing her strength and sheer determination to live makes this striking book completely engrossing." Publ Wkly

Lee, Bruce, 1940-1973

Lee, Bruce. Bruce Lee; artist of life; compiled and edited by John Little. Tuttle 1999 269p il $24.95; pa $16.95

Grades: 11 12 Adult   92

1. Martial arts 2. Actors

ISBN 0-8048-3131-9; 0-8048-3263-3 (pa)

LC 99-33401

This is a "collection of Lee's private letters and writing, offering insight into the many facets of his life—including his poetry, life philosophies, and his thoughts on martial arts, love, fatherhood, friendship." Publisher's note

"Lee's writings are inspired and inspirational, of interest to his fans and to the multitudes seeking the meaning of life." Booklist

Includes bibliographical references

Lee, Bruce, 1940-1973—*Continued*

Miller, Davis. The Tao of Bruce Lee; a martial arts memoir. Harmony Bks. 2000 193p hardcover o.p. pa $15 *
Grades: 11 12 Adult   **92**
   1. Martial arts 2. Actors
   ISBN 0-609-60477-5; 0-609-80538-X (pa)
               LC 99-87697
Miller chronicles the life of film star and martial arts legend Bruce Lee and the impact Lee had on his life
This book "is equally a study of the nature and role of the hero in popular culture, a poignant and unusual coming-of-age story, and an informative biography." Booklist

Lee, Robert E. (Robert Edward), 1807-1870
Blount, Roy. Robert E. Lee; a Penguin life; [by] Roy Blount, Jr. Lipper/Viking Bk. 2003 210p (Penguin lives series) $19.95; pa $13 *
Grades: 11 12 Adult   **92**
   1. Generals 2. United States—History—1861-1865, Civil War
   ISBN 0-670-03220-4; 0-14-303866-4 (pa)
               LC 2002-32423
This is a biography of "the famous Southern general admired for his military leadership but also scorned for defending the Confederacy. Blount's concise writing keeps his biography trim and succinct, and his admiration for the subject allows for enjoyable reading." Booklist
Includes bibliographical references

Robertson, James I., Jr. Robert E. Lee; Virginian soldier, American citizen; [by] James I. Robertson, Jr. Atheneum Books for Young Readers 2005 159p il maps $21.95
Grades: 7 8 9 10   **92**
   1. Generals 2. United States—History—1861-1865, Civil War
   ISBN 0-689-85731-4   LC 2003-22108
Contents: The making of a soldier; Nation vs. country; Rocky path to army command; Brilliance in the field; The bloodiest day; Loss of an arm; Gettysburg; Forced on the defensive; From siege to defeat; National symbol
This portrait of the Confederate general "puts particular emphasis on his life during the Civil War years but provides plenty of information on his youth, his early military career, and his postwar years. . . . Useful for reports and interesting in its own right, this well-researched biography will be a solid addition to library collections." Booklist
Includes bibliographical references

Lennon, John, 1940-1980
Partridge, Elizabeth. John Lennon; all I want is the truth; a photographic biography by Elizabeth Partridge. Viking 2005 232p il $24.99 *
Grades: 8 9 10 11 12   **92**
   1. Beatles 2. Rock musicians
   ISBN 0-670-05954-4   LC 2005-11850

The author presents a "portrait of a legendary musician, tracing Lennon's life from his birth in 1940 during a German air raid on Liverpool to his murder in Manhattan 40 years later." Publ Wkly
"This handsome book will be eagerly received by both Beatles fans, who are legion, and their elders, who will enjoy reliving the glory days of the Fab Four and exploring the inner workings of a creative talent." SLJ
Includes bibliographical references

Lerner, Gerda, 1920-
Lerner, Gerda. Fireweed; a political autobiography. Temple Univ. Press 2002 377p (Critical perspectives on the past) $34.50; pa $22.95
Grades: 11 12 Adult   **92**
   1. Historians 2. Feminism
   ISBN 1-56639-889-4; 1-59213-236-7 (pa)
               LC 2001-54248
This is an autobiography by the feminist historian. Lerner "has been a privileged child, a resister, a prisoner, a refugee, a governess, an immigrant, an 'enemy alien,' a lover and wife, an X-ray technician, a mother, a grandmother, a novelist, a musical librettist, an organizer, a student and, ultimately, a historian. . . . 'Beginnings,' the first of four parts covers her early life in Vienna. . . . The remaining three parts of the book deal with Lerner's experiences as an immigrant to, then a proud, though critical, citizen of the United States." Women's Rev Books
"A fascinating memoir." Booklist
Includes bibliographical references

Lewis, John, 1940-
Lewis, John. Walking with the wind; a memoir of the movement; [by] John Lewis with Michael D'Orso. Harcourt 1999 526p il pa $16
Grades: 11 12 Adult   **92**
   1. United States. Congress. House 2. Student Nonviolent Coordinating Committee 3. African Americans—Biography 4. African Americans—Civil rights
   ISBN 0-15-600708-8   LC 99-28356
First published 1998 by Simon & Schuster
"The memoirs of Lewis, an African American congressman from Georgia, emphasize his participation in the . . . Civil Rights Movement of the 1960s, when the author served as national chair of the Student Nonviolent Coordinating Committee (SNCC) and held leadership positions in other Civil Rights organizations." Libr J
"The strength of Lewis's powerful new book is not only the witness he bears but also the simplicity of his voice." Newsweek

Lincoln, Abraham, 1809-1865
Freedman, Russell. Lincoln: a photobiography. Clarion Bks. 1987 149p il $18; pa $7.95 *
Grades: 5 6 7 8 9 10   **92**
   1. Presidents—United States 2. United States—History—1861-1865, Civil War
   ISBN 0-89919-380-3; 0-395-51848-2 (pa)
               LC 86-33379
Awarded the Newbery Medal, 1988

Lincoln, Abraham, 1809-1865—*Continued*
The author "begins by contrasting the Lincoln of legend to the Lincoln of fact. His childhood, self-education, early business ventures, and entry into politics comprise the first half of the book, with the rest of the text covering his presidency and assassination." SLJ
This is "a balanced work, elegantly designed and enhanced by dozens of period photographs and drawings, some familiar, some refreshingly unfamiliar." Publ Wkly
Includes bibliographical references

Keneally, Thomas. Abraham Lincoln. Viking 2003 183p (Penguin lives series) $19.95
Grades: 11 12 Adult   92
1. Presidents—United States 2. United States—History—1861-1865, Civil War
ISBN 0-670-03175-5   LC 2003-268078
"Keneally's Lincoln is a self-actuated farm boy made good by self-discipline, savvy instincts, wit, the wisdom acquired from courtrooms, friendships, and political huckstering—and luck . . . [The author] recounts Lincoln's early missteps in romance, business, and politics and his self-doubts and depression as his star dimmed several times, and he concedes Lincoln's erratic course toward emancipation and a successful strategy for Union victory during the Civil War . . . This is an epic compressed into a tightly written biography that all Americans might read with profit. Keneally's occasional tendency to let folklore stand as fact notwithstanding, there is no better brief introduction to Lincoln and his American dream." Libr J

Lincoln, Abraham. Abraham Lincoln the writer; a treasury of his greatest speeches and letters; compiled and edited by Harold Holzer. Boyds Mills Press 2000 106p il lib bdg $15.95 *
Grades: 7 8 9 10   92
1. Presidents—United States 2. United States—History—1861-1865, Civil War
ISBN 1-56397-772-9   LC 99-66551
"Lincoln's writings include personal letters, notes on the law, excerpts from speeches, debates, and inaugural addresses, letters to parents of fallen soldiers, and telegrams to his family. Reproductions of period photos, portraits, and documents illustrate the text effectively. . . . Highly interesting and a fine resource for students seeking quotations or for those wanting to meet Lincoln through his own words." Booklist

Lincoln in The times; the life of Abraham Lincoln, as originally reported in the New York times; edited by David Herbert Donald and Harold Holzer. St. Martin's Press 2005 413p il $29.95
Grades: 11 12 Adult   92
1. Presidents—United States 2. United States—History—1861-1865, Civil War—Sources
ISBN 0-312-34919-X   LC 2005-44293
The New York Times "covered the political career and presidency of Abraham Lincoln. . . . [This book] includes coverage of the major events in Lincoln's political life, such as his campaign, his . . . election, and his inaugurals; the State of the Union addresses, the Gettysburg Address, and the Emancipation Proclamation; the assassination and funeral." Publisher's note
"The editors' annotations, interspersed throughout,

help interpret the primary sources. Lincoln buffs will enjoy going back in time with this delightfully antiquarian anthology." Publ Wkly

Sullivan, George. Picturing Lincoln; famous photographs that popularized the president. Clarion Bks. 2000 88p il $16
Grades: 9 10 11 12   92
1. Presidents—United States 2. United States—History—1861-1865, Civil War
ISBN 0-395-91682-8   LC 00-27576
Examines some of the famous photographs taken of President Abraham Lincoln, discussing the circumstances under which they were taken and how these images were used
"This unique and sharply focused volume offers an introductory exploration of photographic processes and photographers while tracing the political fortunes of our 16th president." SLJ
Includes bibliographical references

Lincoln, Mary Todd, 1818-1882
Fleischner, Jennifer. Mrs. Lincoln and Mrs. Keckley; the remarkable story of the friendship between a first lady and a former slave. Broadway Bks. 2003 372p il map hardcover o.p. pa $15.95
Grades: 11 12 Adult   92
1. Keckley, Elizabeth, ca. 1818-1907 2. Presidents' spouses—United States
ISBN 0-7679-0258-0; 0-7679-0259-9 (pa)
                                        LC 2002-34493
"A dual biography of two women—one white, free, and privileged in all but happiness and the other black, initially enslaved, and adept in human relationships, sewing, and money matters—whose lives came together in Washington, DC, during the Civil War and remained stitched together thereafter." Libr J
"The book gives an in-depth look at a time, a friendship, and two very different women. The author's almost conversational writing style will keep readers engrossed." SLJ
Includes bibliographical references

Lindbergh, Charles, 1902-1974
Giblin, James. Charles A. Lindbergh; a human hero; {by} James Cross Giblin. Clarion Bks. 1997 212p il $22 *
Grades: 6 7 8 9   92
1. Air pilots
ISBN 0-395-63389-3   LC 96-9501
A biography of the pilot whose life was full of controversy and tragedy, but also fulfilling achievements
"This sympathetic and informed account (beautifully illustrated with contemporary photographs) is an excellent introduction to Lindbergh and also to the early years of the celebrity society in which we live now." N Y Times Book Rev
Includes bibliographical references

Hardesty, Von. Lindbergh: flight's enigmatic hero; foreword by Erik Lindbergh. Harcourt 2002 229p il map $40
Grades: 11 12 Adult   92
1. Air pilots
ISBN 0-15-100973-2   LC 2002-27305

Lindbergh, Charles, 1902-1974—*Continued*

The author "examines both the hero flyer's failures and his successes. Grandson Erik Lindbergh provides an introduction, and the book is lavishly illustrated with over 400 photographs and illustrations (including time lines and flight maps)." Libr J

"Attractively laid out, the hundreds of photographs do not overwhelm Hardesty's narrative, and ensure certain popularity." Booklist

Includes bibliographical references

Lobel, Anita, 1934-

Lobel, Anita. No pretty pictures; a child of war. Greenwillow Bks. 1998 193p il $16

Grades: 7 8 9 10   92

1. Jews—Poland 2. Holocaust, 1933-1945—Personal narratives 3. Holocaust survivors

ISBN 0-688-15935-4   LC 97-48392

Also available in paperback from Avon Camelot Bks.

The author, known as an illustrator of children's books, describes her experiences as a Polish Jew during World War II and for years in Sweden afterwards

"Lobel brings to these dramatic experiences an artist's sensibility for the telling detail, a seemingly unvarnished memory and heartstopping candor." Publ Wkly

London, Jack, 1876-1916

Stefoff, Rebecca. Jack London; an American original. Oxford Univ. Press 2002 127p il maps (Oxford portraits) lib bdg $28

Grades: 7 8 9 10   92

1. Authors, American

ISBN 0-19-512223-2   LC 2001-53087

"This volume does an excellent job of illuminating London's extraordinary life and career. The narrative is exciting and accessible. . . . The text is supplemented by interesting and informative illustrations, and includes excerpts from primary-source material." SLJ

Includes bibliographical references

Lowman, Margaret

Lowman, Margaret. Life in the treetops; adventures of a woman in field biology; [by] Margaret D. Lowman. Yale Univ. Press 1999 219p il maps $37.50; pa $13.95

Grades: 11 12 Adult   92

1. Botanists 2. Women scientists

ISBN   0-300-07818-8;   978-0-300-07818-3; 0-300-08464-1 (pa); 978-0-300-08464-1 (pa)

LC 98-48691

The author is a botanist who studies canopies, the uppermost layers of forests. "Interwoven with her narrative of field work is the story of how she balanced the needs of marriage, housewifery, children, and eventual single parenthood with college teaching and research trips to locales such as Panama, Australia, and Cameroon." Booklist

Lowman "gives a funny, unassuming and deeply idiosyncratic chronicle of her trials and triumphs as a field biologist of tree canopies and other ecosystems in Australia, New England, Belize, Panama and elsewhere." N Y Times Book Rev

Includes bibliographical references

Followed by It's a jungle up there! (2006)

Lyons, Maritcha Rémond, 1848-1929

Bolden, Tonya. Maritcha; a nineteenth-century American girl. Abrams 2005 47p il $17.95

Grades: 4 5 6 7 8 9 10   92

1. African American women 2. New York (N.Y.)—Race relations 3. African Americans—New York (N.Y.)

ISBN 0-8109-5045-6   LC 2004-05849

This is a "life history of Maritcha Rémond Lyons, born a free black in 1848 in lower Manhattan. The author draws her biographical sketch primarily from Lyons's unpublished memoir, dated one year before her death in 1929. . . . One of the . . . sections of the book documents the Draft Riots . . . of July 1868, and the impact of them on Maritcha and other citizens." Publ Wkly

"The high quality of writing and the excellent documentation make this a first choice for all collections." SLJ

Madison, James, 1751-1836

Wills, Garry. James Madison. Times Bks. 2002 xx, 184p (American presidents series) $20 *

Grades: 11 12 Adult   92

1. Presidents—United States

ISBN 0-8050-6905-4   LC 2002-19692

The author "maintains that Madison possessed qualities that served him well early in his career but proved to be a handicap during his Presidency. . . . Written with flair, this clear and balanced account is based on a sure handling of the material." Libr J

Includes bibliographical references

Malcolm X, 1925-1965

Helfer, Andrew. Malcolm X; a graphic biography; written by Andrew Helfer; art by Randy DuBurke. Hill and Wang 2006 102p il $15.95 *

Grades: 11 12 Adult   92

1. African Americans—Biography—Graphic novels 2. Black Muslims—Graphic novels 3. Graphic novels 4. Biographical graphic novels

ISBN 978-0-8090-9504-9; 0-8090-9504-1

LC 2006-13743

The authors "tell the story of Malcolm X's short life—his meeting with Dr. Martin Luther King Jr., the two leaders describing the opposite ideological ends of the fight for civil rights; and his eventual assassination by other members of the Nation of Islam (NOI)—in narration and detailed b&white drawings, sharp as photographs in a newspaper. . . . Helfer and DuBurke have created an evocative and studied look at not only Malcolm X but the racial conflict that defined and shaped him." Publ Wkly

Malcolm X, 1925-1965—*Continued*

Malcolm X. The autobiography of Malcolm X; with the assistance of Alex Haley; introduction by M. S. Handler; epilogue by Alex Haley; afterword by Ossie Davis. Ballantine Bks. 1992 500p $25; pa $15 *

Grades: 11 12 Adult   **92**
  1. African Americans—Biography 2. Black Muslims
  ISBN 0-345-37975-6; 0-345-37671-4 (pa)
                          LC 92-52659

Also available in hardcover from Amereon

First published 1965 by Grove Press

Based on tape-recorded conversations with Alex Haley, this account of the life of the Black Muslim leader was completed shortly before his murder

Alex Haley "did his job with sensitivity and with devotion. . . . {The book} will have a permanent place in the literature of the Afro-American struggle." N Y Rev Books

The Malcolm X encyclopedia; edited by Robert L. Jenkins, co-edited by Mfanya Donald Tryman. Greenwood Press 2002 643p il $74.95

Grades: 11 12 Adult   **92**
  ISBN 0-313-29264-7   LC 2001-23318

"The major section of the volume consists of 500 essays that create a cross-disciplinary, textured description of the man, his life, his times, and events. . . . Topics include *African nationalism, Civil rights movement, Police brutality, Socialism,* and *White liberals,* among others. Also included are a detailed chronology as well as several thematic essays that provide a framework for the entries that follow. . . . All encyclopedia entries have a short bibliography, but there is an extensive bibliography of books, articles, newspapers, electronic resources, and oral interviews included as a separate section in the volume. . . . The encyclopedia would add a first-stop resource for library users seeking information on this important figure of contemporary American history." Booklist

Mandela, Nelson

Gaines, Ann. Nelson Mandela and apartheid in world history; {by} Ann Graham Gaines. Enslow Pubs. 2001 128p il maps (In world history) $20.95 *

Grades: 9 10 11 12   **92**
  1. South Africa—Race relations 2. South Africa—Politics and government
  ISBN 0-7660-1463-0   LC 00-10369

This biography of the Nobel Peace Prize laureate "does a fine job of integrating Mandela's personal story with an overview of early South African history and the rise and fall of apartheid." Booklist

Includes bibliographical references

Mandela, Nelson. Mandela; an illustrated autobiography. Little, Brown 1996 208p il map $29.95 *

Grades: 11 12 Adult   **92**
  1. South Africa—Race relations 2. South Africa—Politics and government
  ISBN 0-316-55038-8   LC 96-77497

"This is an illustrated and abridged edition of Long walk to freedom: the autobiography of Nelson Mandela." Verso of title page

"The photos, from a variety of archives and journalistic sources, ably illustrate Mandela and, even more so, the South Africa around him." Libr J

Manet, Édouard, 1832-1883

Wright, Patricia. Manet. Dorling Kindersley in association with National Gallery Publications 1999 64p il (Eyewitness art) pa $15.99 *

Grades: 9 10 11 12   **92**
  1. Artists, French
  ISBN 0-7894-4879-3

First published 1993

This visual introduction to the life and works of the French painter includes many reproductions of his paintings, photographs of his studio and tools, and closeup details to show his technique.

Includes glossary

Manzano, Juan Francisco, 1797-1854

Engle, Margarita. The poet slave of Cuba; a biography of Juan Francisco Manzano; art by Sean Qualls. Henry Holt 2006 183p il $16.95 *

Grades: 7 8 9 10   **92**
  1. Poets
  ISBN 0-8050-7706-5; 978-0-8050-7706-3
                          LC 2005-46200

In "free verse, Engle dramatizes the boyhood of the nineteenth-century Cuban slave Juan Francisco Manzano, who secretly learned to read and wrote poetry about beauty and courage in his world of unspeakable brutality." Booklist

"This is a book that should be read by young and old, black and white, Anglo and Latino." SLJ

Marie Antoinette, Queen, consort of Louis XVI, King of France, 1755-1793

Lever, Evelyne. Marie Antoinette; the last queen of France; translated from the French by Catherine Temerson. Farrar, Straus & Giroux 2000 357p il pa $16.95 hardcover o.p.

Grades: 11 12 Adult   **92**
  1. Queens 2. France—History—1589-1789, Bourbons
  ISBN 0-312-08333-4 (pa)   LC 00-28763

The author examines "the opulent Versailles subculture and the queen whose royal excesses served as a major catalyst for the revolutionary upheaval of 1789. Through the skillful use of memoirs and other primary documents, Lever creates an empathic picture of Louis XVI's headstrong wife." Libr J

Includes bibliographical references

Marley, Bob

Talamon, Bruce. Bob Marley; spirit dancer; {by} Bruce W. Talamon; text by Roger Steffens; foreword by Timothy White. Norton 1994 128p il pa $13 hardcover o.p. *

Grades: 11 12 Adult   **92**
  1. Singers 2. Black musicians
  ISBN 0-393-32173-8 (pa)   LC 94-18321

Marley, Bob—*Continued*

This book consists mainly of Talamon's photographs of the Jamaican reggae musician, with brief text by Steffens

"Tasteful and well done, Talamon's photographic essay stands in stark contrast to some of the raw, slapdash products intended primarily to cash in on Marley's fame. . . . A moving portrait of a great musician." Booklist

Marshall, Thurgood, 1908-1993

Marshall, Thurgood. Thurgood Marshall; his speeches, writings, arguments, opinions, and reminiscences; edited by Mark Tushnet; foreword by Randall Kennedy. Hill Bks. 2001 xxvi, 548p (Library of Black America) $40; pa $24.95

Grades: 11 12 Adult   92
  1. United States. Supreme Court 2. African Americans—Biography 3. African Americans—Civil rights
  ISBN 1-55652-385-8; 1-55652-386-6 (pa)
                                        LC 2001-16793

"In a career ranging from his trial and appellate work for the NAACP to his tenure as an associate justice of the Court, Marshall wrought revolutionary changes in U.S. law and politics, and this collection of his legal briefs, writings, speeches, and judicial opinions, plus a never-before-published oral interview, gives us a superior analysis of the advocate, the democrat, the dissenter, and the unflagging fighter for equality." Libr J

Includes bibliographical references

Williams, Juan. Thurgood Marshall; American revolutionary. Times Bks. 1998 459p il pa $16 hardcover o.p.

Grades: 11 12 Adult   92
  1. United States. Supreme Court 2. African Americans—Biography 3. African Americans—Civil rights
  ISBN 0-8129-3299-4 (pa)   LC 98-9735

"Williams presents Marshall as a revolutionary 'of grand vision,' but this well-rounded portrait of the man also addresses his vanities and warts, from his ascension to his deflation and subsequent redemption. This is a must read for all Americans concerned with the struggle for civil and individual rights." Booklist

Includes bibliographical references

Martí, José, 1853-1895

Sterngass, Jon. José Martí. Chelsea House Publishers 2007 123p il (Great Hispanic heritage) lib bdg $30 *

Grades: 9 10 11 12   92
  1. Cuba—History
  ISBN 0-7910-8841-3; 978-0-7910-8841-8
                                        LC 2006-19601

This book "follows the life of the dynamic Cuban poet, journalist, and patriot." Publisher's note

Includes bibliographical references

Mathis, Greg, 1960-

Mathis, Greg. Inner city miracle; {by} Greg Mathis; with Blair S. Walker. Ballantine Bks. 2002 197p $23.95

Grades: 11 12 Adult   92
  1. African Americans—Biography
  ISBN 0-345-44642-9   LC 2002-26149

"Mathis, a former Detroit district court judge, shares stories of his upbringing in a strict household with a mother who worked several jobs to support her four sons. He also reveals that he lived on both sides of the law, eventually escaping to become Michigan's youngest judge ever." Libr J

The authors "poetically render the rhythms of street language, at least to those who don't speak it, and fairly present Mathis's sometimes testosterone-driven male attitude, making this an honest feel-good story. Mathis's parable from the projects explores a world that will be crucially familiar to many and offers a way to reach poor teens who rightly feel misunderstood and underrepresented in the mainstream." Publ Wkly

McCall, Nathan

McCall, Nathan. Makes me wanna holler; a young black man in America. Random House 1994 404p pa $14.95 hardcover o.p.

Grades: 11 12 Adult   92
  1. African Americans—Biography
  ISBN 0-679-74070-8 (pa)   LC 93-30654

The author relates the "story of his rise from poverty to success as a journalist at the *Washington Post*. He uses graphic language, blunt descriptions, honest expression, introspection, and careful observation to describe his early years in Portsmouth, Virginia, as a young black male, the recipient of a 12-year prison sentence for armed robbery, whose life was dangerously out of control. Insensitivity, alienation, racial hatred, drugs (especially crack), guns, rape, robbery, the black American as an endangered species—McCall covers it all in a depressing yet spellbinding documentary." Libr J

McCandless, Christopher, 1968-1992

Krakauer, Jon. Into the wild. Villard Bks. 1996 207p maps hardcover o.p. pa $12.95 *

Grades: 11 12 Adult   92
  1. Alaska—Description and travel
  ISBN 0-679-42850-X; 0-385-48680-4 (pa)
                                        LC 95-20008

"Christopher McCandless was a disaffected, idealistic young man who trekked into the Alaskan wilderness in search of transcendence and perished there. This narrative, which ponders his journey and inner life with sympathy and imagination, has YA appeal on many levels." Booklist

McCourt, Frank

McCourt, Frank. Angela's ashes; a memoir. Scribner 1996 364p il $25; pa $14

Grades: 11 12 Adult   92
  1. Irish Americans
  ISBN 0-684-87435-0; 0-684-84267-X (pa)
                                        LC 96-5335

"Frank McCourt, a teacher, grandfather and occasional actor, was born in New York City, but grew up in the Irish town of Limerick during the grim 1930's and 40's before he came back here as a teen-ager. His recollections of childhood are mournful and humorous, angry and forgiving." N Y Times Book Rev

McGee, Charles E., 1919-
Smith, Charlene E. McGee. Tuskegee airman; the biography of Charles E. McGee, Air Force fighter combat record holder. Branden 1999 204p il $24.95 *
Grades: 11 12 Adult   **92**
1. African Americans—Biography 2. Air pilots
ISBN 0-8283-2046-2   LC 99-18279
A biography of a middle-class African American who became one of the Tuskegee Airmen during World War II and flew combat missions in Korea and Vietnam. McGee retired from the Air Force with the rank of colonel
Includes bibliographical references

McGough, Matthew
McGough, Matthew. Bat boy; my true life adventures coming of age with the New York Yankees. Doubleday 2005 273p il $22.95; pa $12.95
Grades: 11 12 Adult   **92**
1. New York Yankees (Baseball team)
ISBN 0-385-51020-9; 0-307-27864-6 (pa)
                             LC 2004-61756
The author "tells the tale of his two years as batboy for the New York Yankees, in 1992-93." Booklist
This "memoir is much more than an all-access pass to Yankee Stadium and baseball—it is an exquisitely written and observed book about growing up and the beauty of the game." SLJ

McNeill, Robert
Pekar, Harvey. Harvey Pekar's American splendor; unsung hero; artist, David Collier. Dark Horse Comics 2003 79p il pa $11.95
Grades: 9 10 11 12   **92**
1. Vietnam War, 1961-1975—Graphic novels 2. African Americans—Biography—Graphic novels 3. Graphic novels 4. Biographical graphic novels
ISBN 1-59307-040-3
"The story of Robert McNeill"
"Writing in McNeill's voice, Pekar relates the story of his African American friend's experiences as a 17-year-old marine enlistee. The sturdy, black-and-white art stunningly visualizes the racial tensions, the daily struggle, and the horror." Booklist

Mead, Margaret, 1901-1978
Mark, Joan T. Margaret Mead; coming of age in America; {by} Joan Mark. Oxford Univ. Press 1998 110p il (Oxford portraits in science) $28 *
Grades: 7 8 9 10   **92**
1. Anthropologists
ISBN 0-19-511679-8   LC 98-18604
An "account of the life and works of the influential, pioneering anthropologist. . . . Mark does a fine job of abstracting Mead's research and published works and showing why they were both critically acclaimed and criticized. The reader-friendly prose is peppered with fascinating anecdotes and photos. Mead herself is presented as a complex, intriguing figure, with fascinating, often contradictory, public and private lives." Booklist
Includes bibliographical references

Meltzer, Milton, 1915-
Meltzer, Milton. Milton Meltzer; writing matters. Franklin Watts 2004 160p il lib bdg $29
Grades: 7 8 9 10   **92**
1. Authors, American
ISBN 0-531-12257-3   LC 2004-2947
Meltzer "writes about his own life through the prism of his craft. He tells about his growing up in Worcester, Massachusetts, the child of immigrants from the Austro-Hungarian empire, and his coming-of-age during the Depression." Booklist
"The author includes clear, interesting explanations about the American historical and economic events that influenced his life. While this book is a pleasure to read for general interest, it would also supplement units on American history." SLJ
Includes bibliographical references

Menchú, Rigoberta
Menchú, Rigoberta. I, Rigoberta Menchú; an Indian woman in Guatemala; edited and introduced by Elisabeth Burgos-Debray; translated by Ann Wright. Verso Eds. 1984 xxi, 251p hardcover o.p. pa $8.95
Grades: 9 10 11 12   **92**
1. Political activists 2. Native Americans—Guatemala
ISBN 0-86091-083-0; 0-86091-788-6 (pa)
                             LC 84-157775
This is the story of a twenty-three year old Guatemalan Indian woman. "It was recorded in the course of a single week in Paris, during January 1982, by a Venezuelan friend and admirer, Elizabeth Burgos-Debray. She then edited it as Rigoberta's autobiography, excluding her original questions and inserting linking passages." Times Lit Suppl
Includes bibliographical references

Michelangelo Buonarroti, 1475-1564
Hibbard, Howard. Michelangelo. Harper & Row 1974 347p il hardcover o.p. pa $39 *
Grades: 9 10 11 12   **92**
1. Artists, Italian
ISBN 0-06-433323-X; 0-06-430148-6 (pa)
"Icon editions"
The author provides an introduction to Michelangelo's life and his achievements as sculptor, painter, and architect
"Every work is illustrated where it is discussed. . . . The reader is painlessly made to understand such complicated matters as the iconographical scheme of the Sistine ceiling." Natl Rev
Includes bibliographical references

Somervill, Barbara A. Michelangelo; sculptor and painter. Compass Point Books 2005 112p il map (Signature lives) $30.60; pa $9.95
Grades: 6 7 8 9 10   **92**
1. Artists, Italian
ISBN   0-7565-0814-2;   978-0-7565-0814-2;
0-7565-1060-0 (pa); 978-0-7565-1060-2 (pa)
                             LC 2004-17116
This is a biography of the Renaissance painter and sculptor.

Michelangelo Buonarroti, 1475-1564—*Continued*
The author "presents a candid introduction to her famous Renaissance subject. Her text has a casual tone, and her direct, sometimes colloquial language will capture some reluctant readers." Booklist
Includes bibliographical references

Miller, Arthur, 1915-2005
Andersen, Richard. Arthur Miller. Marshall Cavendish Benchmark 2005 c2006 144p il (Writers and their works) lib bdg $25.95 *
Grades: 7 8 9 10   **92**
    1. Authors, American
    ISBN 0-7614-1946-2
"A biography of writer Arthur Miller that describes his era, his major works, his life, and the legacy of his writing." Publisher's note
This "attractive, well-organized [book fills] a gap in literary criticism for intermediate readers. Heavily illustrated with color and black-and-white photographs, [it] will appeal to students who might be intimidated by longer or more scholarly titles." SLJ

Miller, Frank, 1957-
Eisner, Will. Eisner/Miller: a one-on-one interview. See entry under Eisner, Will, 1917-2005

Miró, Asha, 1967-
Miró, Asha. Daughter of the Ganges; a memoir; translated by Jamal Mahjoub. Atria Books 2006 274p il $24
Grades: 11 12 Adult   **92**
    1. Adoptees
    ISBN 0-7432-8672-3; 978-0-7432-8672-5
                                              LC 2006-40791
"English-language compilation of two books, La hija del Ganges and Las dos caras de la luna, originally published as separate editions" Verso of title page
"This memoir is an assemblage of two books chronicling Miró's first trips back to her native land of India since being adopted in Barcelona at the age of six in 1974." Publ Wkly
"A unique memoir with wide appeal." SLJ

Moaveni, Azadeh, 1976-
Moaveni, Azadeh. Lipstick jihad; a memoir of growing up Iranian in America and American in Iran. Public Affairs 2005 249p $25; pa $13
Grades: 11 12 Adult   **92**
    1. Iran
    ISBN 1-58648-193-2; 1-58648-378-1 (pa)
                                              LC 2004-43184
"Moaveni, an Iranian-American who grew up in California, decided to embark on a journey in spring 2000 to rediscover her Iranian heritage. In this account, she . . . conveys the tensions she observed between the fundamentalist mullahs and younger Iranians, who are pushing for a more Westernized, modern Iran. . . . A charming and informative memoir." Libr J

Monet, Claude, 1840-1926
Waldron, Ann. Claude Monet. Abrams 1991 92p il (First impressions) $19.95 *
Grades: 9 10 11 12   **92**
    1. Artists, French 2. Impressionism (Art)
    ISBN 0-8109-3620-8   LC 91-8602
Examines the life and work of Monet, describing his struggle for artistic recognition and providing examples of his paintings
"Lavishly illustrated with photographs and color reproductions, {this} readable introduction will interest art students and browsers." Booklist

Monroe, James, 1758-1831
Hart, Gary. James Monroe. Times Books 2005 170p il (American presidents series) $20
Grades: 11 12 Adult   **92**
    1. Presidents—United States
    ISBN 978-0-8050-6960-0; 0-8050-6960-7
                                              LC 2005-41928
The author "studies James Monroe, the last of the Virginia dynasty, who, although president at an important time in U.S. history (1817-25), is often overlooked. Hart argues that in the years after the disastrous War of 1812, Monroe was 'the first "national security president."' . . . [This] is a satisfying and informative read." Libr J
Includes bibliographical references

Morris, Jim
Morris, Jim. The oldest rookie; big-league dreams from a small-town guy; {by} Jim Morris with Joel Engel. Little, Brown 2001 276p $22.95; pa $13.95
Grades: 11 12 Adult   **92**
    1. Baseball—Biography
    ISBN 0-316-59156-4; 0-446-67837-6 (pa)
                                              LC 00-64269
Paperback published with title: The rookie
"Morris, a high-school baseball coach and former minor-league pitcher, makes a deal with the kids on his team: if they make the play-offs, he'll try for the majors one last time. They do, and he does. It's a fabulous baseball story, full of wonderful humor, but it isn't all about dreams coming true; it also shows how much dreams cost, to the dreamers and to their loved ones." Booklist

Morrison, Toni, 1931-
Andersen, Richard. Toni Morrison. Marshall Cavendish Benchmark 2005 c2006 144p il (Writers and their works) lib bdg $25.95 *
Grades: 7 8 9 10   **92**
    1. Authors, American 2. African American authors
    3. Women authors
    ISBN 0-7614-1945-4
A biography of writer Toni Morrison that describes her era, her major works, her life, and the legacy of her writing.
This "attractive, well-organized [book fills] a gap in literary criticism for intermediate readers. Heavily illustrated with color and black-and-white photographs, [it] will appeal to students who might be intimidated by longer or more scholarly titles." SLJ
Includes bibliographical references

Morrison, Toni, 1931-—_Continued_

Haskins, James. Toni Morrison: telling a tale untold. 21st Cent. Bks. (Brookfield) 2002 144p il lib bdg $26.90

Grades: 9 10 11 12   **92**
1. Authors, American 2. Women authors 3. African American authors
ISBN 0-7613-1852-6   LC 2001-8036

Contents: Superior people; What it's like to be a grown-up; Developing a canon of Black work; Telling a tale untold; America's storyteller; Being there before the light arrives; To write the book I'd like to read

"Morrison's life, and Haskins' interpretation of her work, will make an interesting read for mature high school students who want to know more about the African-American experience and about one of the most gifted authors in the United States." ALAN

Includes bibliographical references

Morrison, Toni. Conversations with Toni Morrison; edited by Danille Taylor-Guthrie. University Press of Miss. 1994 293p (Literary conversations series) pa $20 hardcover o.p.

Grades: 11 12 Adult   **92**
1. Authors, American 2. Women authors 3. African American authors
ISBN 0-87805-692-0 (pa)   LC 93-44738

This is a collection of interviews with and essays about the Nobel prize winning African American novelist from a variety of sources from 1974 to 1992.

Muhammad, d. 632
Armstrong, Karen. Muhammad; a prophet for our time. Atlas Books/HarperCollins Publishers 2006 249p map (Eminent lives) $21.95; pa $14.95
*

Grades: 11 12 Adult   **92**
ISBN   0-06-059897-2;   978-0-06-059897-6; 0-06-115577-2 (pa); 978-0-06-115577-2 (pa)
LC 2006-45864

First published 1991 in the United Kingdom with subtitle: A Western attempt to understand Islam; Original American edition published 1992 with subtitle: A biography of the prophet

This is a biography of the founder of Islam.

"Readers of these pages cannot escape the genius of Muhammad and his aim for peace and compassion among nations and among Muslims themselves. . . . Recommended for all libraries." Libr J

Includes bibliographical references

Muir, John, 1838-1914
Ehrlich, Gretel. John Muir; nature's visionary. National Geographic Soc. 2000 240p il map $35
*

Grades: 11 12 Adult   **92**
1. Naturalists
ISBN 0-7922-7954-9   LC 00-60944

The author chronicles Muir's "life—from his self-education as a boy in Scotland and Wisconsin to his solitary cross-country treks, fruitful mountain hermitage, and cofounding of the Sierra Club. . . . Ehrlich beautifully captures Muir's essence and clearly defines the ongoing significance of his accomplishments. Lynn Johnson's gorgeous landscape photography and a wealth of wonderful archival images provide the perfect accompaniment." Booklist

Wilkins, Thurman. John Muir; apostle of nature. University of Okla. Press 1995 xxvii, 302p il maps (Oklahoma western biographies) pa $21.95 hardcover o.p.

Grades: 11 12 Adult   **92**
1. Naturalists
ISBN 0-8061-2797-X (pa)   LC 95-11426

"Wilkins follows Muir from his Scottish boyhood, clouded by a harsh, fundamentalist father, to an adolescence of arduous farmwork in Wisconsin to a lifelong career of exploration and study of wildernesses, particularly those of the western U.S., and vividly relates some of Muir's more perilous adventures on cliffside and snowfield. . . . An affectionate, uncluttered tale of an American folk hero." Booklist

Includes bibliographical references

Muller, Salomé, b. ca. 1809
Bailey, John. The lost German slave girl; the extraordinary true story of the slave Sally Miller and her fight for freedom. Atlantic Monthly Press 2004 268p hardcover o.p. pa $14

Grades: 11 12 Adult   **92**
ISBN 0-87113-921-9; 0-8021-4229-X (pa)
LC 2004-50264

"A series of highly contentious trials was held in the mid-1800s to determine whether Sally Miller, a New Orleans woman, was born a multiracial slave or was in fact a German immigrant trapped in bondage from childhood. The stuff of television miniseries, this sensational and emotional cause celebre of its time is revived into a fresh drama from the vantage point of the present." Libr J

Includes bibliographical references

Murrow, Edward R.
Edwards, Bob. Edward R. Murrow and the birth of broadcast journalism; [by] Robert A. Edwards. Wiley 2004 174p (Turning points) $19.95

Grades: 11 12 Adult   **92**
1. Journalists
ISBN 0-471-47753-2   LC 2003-21223

"The author chronicles Murrow's innovations in radio and television broadcasting, including live radio reports of the war in progress in Europe in 1940; exposure of the despotism of Senator Joseph McCarthy on CBS in 1953; the powerful television documentary _Harvest of Shame_ on the deplorable conditions of migrant workers in the U.S.; and the first in-depth television news program, _See It Now_. . . . Edwards brings to life the early days of radio and television and the innovations that Murrow sparked. . . . Readers interested in journalism will enjoy this slim book." Booklist

Includes bibliographical references

Myers, Walter Dean, 1937-

Myers, Walter Dean. Bad boy; a memoir. HarperCollins Pubs. 2001 214p $15.95; lib bdg $16.89; pa $6.99 *

Grades: 7 8 9 10   92

1. Authors, American 2. African American authors

ISBN 0-06-029523-6; 0-06-029524-4 (lib bdg); 0-06-447288-4 (pa)   LC 00-52978

Also available Thorndike Press large print edition

In this memoir "young adult author Walter Dean Myers recalls the life path that lead him to a career in writing. . . . His personal account allows the reader to get a glimpse of Myers, the man, touching on the issues of racism, adoption, self-identity, alcoholism, gang violence, and a speech impediment that almost altered Myers's path to the written word." Voice Youth Advocates

This "is a story full of funny anecdotes, lofty ideals, and tender moments." SLJ

Myrick, Leland

Myrick, Leland. Missouri Boy; color by Hilary Sycamore. Roaring Brook 2006 110p il pa $16.95

Grades: 10 11 12   92

1. Graphic novels 2. Autobiographical graphic novels

ISBN 1-59643-110-5; 978-1-59643-110-2

LC 2006-286622

"This memoir offers glimpses into the author's childhood and the onset of adulthood. . . . Each chapter paints a picture of Myrick's life, from birth with a twin brother and the death of the grandmother he never met in chapter one to the final chapter of his departure from Missouri to California to be with a girl from college. His childhood friendships with neighbors and his twin are portrayed in both good and bad situations. The good includes an old swimming hole where the boys would go during hot, muggy days or building a paper airplane with his brother, and the bad is being buried in fallen leaves only to emerge and discover friends urinating on him." Voice Youth Advocates

"A fine example of the graphic novel." Booklist

Nader, Ralph

Bowen, Nancy. Ralph Nader; man with a mission. 21st Cent. Bks. (Brookfield) 2002 144p $24.99

Grades: 9 10 11 12   92

1. Consumer protection

ISBN 0-7613-2365-1   LC 2001-41464

A biography of the consumer advocate who has devoted his life to crusading for citizens' rights, and who ran as the Green Party's presidential candidate in 2000

"Young people researching third-party movements, activism, consumer rights, or the role of Lebanese Americans will find this clearly written, well-documented biography an informative resource." Booklist

Includes bibliographical references

Napoleon I, Emperor of the French, 1769-1821

Johnson, Paul. Napoleon. Viking 2002 190p (Penguin lives series) hardcover o.p. pa $13 *

Grades: 11 12 Adult   92

1. France—Kings and rulers

ISBN 0-670-03078-3; 0-14-303745-5 (pa)

LC 2001-45605

"A Lipper\Viking book"

Johnson "presents a concise appraisal of Napoleon's career and a precise understanding of his enigmatic character. The author views Napoleon, not as an 'idea man' whose ideology was the ladder by which he propelled himself to heights of power, but as an opportunist who took advantage of a series of events and situations he could manipulate into achieving supreme control." Booklist

Includes bibliographical references

Nelson, Horatio Nelson, Viscount, 1758-1805

Czisnik, Marianne. Horatio Nelson; a controversial hero. Hodder Arnold 2005 192p il pa $35 *

Grades: 11 12 Adult   92

1. Great Britain. Royal Navy 2. Admirals

ISBN 0-340-90021-0 (pa); 978-0-340-90021-5 (pa)

LC 2006-298161

This work on the British admiral "is a collection of essays, offering reflections on aspects of his career, and on his contemporary and posthumous reputation." Engl Hist Rev

Includes bibliographical references

Newton, Sir Isaac, 1642-1727

Boerst, William J. Isaac Newton; organizing the universe. Morgan Reynolds Pub. 2004 144p il (Renaissance scientists) lib bdg $23.95

Grades: 7 8 9 10   92

1. Scientists

ISBN 1-931798-01-X   LC 2003-14571

"Boerst describes Newton's life from his premature birth through an isolated adulthood dominated by study and experimentation to his death at the age of 84. The author deftly explores his subject's accomplishments in relation to the scientific community and notable historical events of the time and includes information concerning his religious views. . . . This well-written book makes an excellent choice for teens exploring scientists or just looking for a good biography." SLJ

Includes bibliographical references

Christianson, Gale E. Isaac Newton. Oxford University Press 2005 144p il (Lives and legacies) $18.95

Grades: 11 12 Adult   92

1. Scientists

ISBN 978-0-19-530070-3; 0-19-530070-X

LC 2005-9600

This is a biography of the English mathematician and physicist.

"This enjoyable book gives a more in-depth view of Newton than one can get from any of the brief presentations one finds in science texts. . . . There are minor misstatements of both physics and chemistry in the book, but they should not detract from the excellent job author Gale Christianson does of bringing to light the many facets of the man and his great contributions to all of science." Sci Books Films

Includes bibliographical references

Newton, Sir Isaac, 1642-1727—*Continued*

Christianson, Gale E. Isaac Newton and the scientific revolution. Oxford Univ. Press 1996 155p il (Oxford portraits in science) lib bdg $28 *

Grades: 7 8 9 10   92
1. Scientists
ISBN 0-19-509224-4   LC 96-13179
Explores the life and scientific contributions of the famed English mathematician and natural philosopher

This book "reads easily and with a pleasant and comfortable flow. Structured around pivotal moments in Newton's life, the book is an excellent reference for biographical data on the great English scientist; in addition, it affords a fine historical perspective of the scientific revolution." Sci Books Films

Includes bibliographical references

Nostradamus, 1503-1566

Randi, James. The mask of Nostradamus. Scribner 1990 256p il pa $26

Grades: 11 12 Adult   92
1. Prophecies
ISBN 0-87975-830-9   LC 89-70189
A biographical study of "Michel de Notredame, better known as Nostradamus, the famous 16th-century French physician, astrologer and seer. Commentators claim that Nostradamus's cryptic verses accurately prophesied such events and personalities as Napoleon, Hitler, the French Revolution, the Great Fire of London and the invention of the Montgolfier balloon. Nonsense, argues Randi, and his meticulous readings of key quatrains make a potent case for his contention." Publ Wkly

Includes bibliographical references

Ochoa, Ellen, 1958-

Hasday, Judy L. Ellen Ochoa. Chelsea House Publishers 2007 106p il (Great Hispanic heritage) lib bdg $30

Grades: 9 10 11 12   92
1. Women astronauts
ISBN 0-7910-8842-1; 978-0-7910-8842-5
                                          LC 2006-19632
This book "follows the life of the first Hispanic female astronaut who traveled in space." Publisher's note

Includes bibliographical references

O'Neal, Shaquille, 1972-

O'Neal, Shaquille. Shaq talks back; [by] Shaquille O'Neal with Mike Wise. St. Martin's Press 2001 259p il hardcover o.p. pa $7.99

Grades: 11 12 Adult   92
1. African American athletes 2. Basketball—Biography
ISBN 0-312-27845-4; 0-312-98259-3 (pa)
                                          LC 2001-19021
O'Neal "recounts his life story, from his childhood in Newark through winning the 2000 NBA Championship. . . . He speaks frankly about his current and former teammates and coaches, as well as the state of the NBA and of the world in general. . . . Though Shaq devotes a lot of the book to his life off the court (his movies, rap albums, celebrity life), there's enough basketball here to satisfy hardcore hoops junkies." Publ Wkly

Oufkir, Malika

Oufkir, Malika. Freedom: the story of my second life; translated by Linda Coverdale. Hyperion 2006 241p $23.95

Grades: 9 10 11 12   92
ISBN 1-4013-5206-5; 978-1-4013-5206-6
"Miramax books"
The author, "whose first book, Stolen Lives, recounted her family's 20 years in Moroccan prisons, now continues her story up to the present, revealing what it was like to be thrust into the free world after years of confinement. . . . Ever charming and gracious, Oufkir is a delight to spend time with." Libr J

Oufkir, Malika. Stolen lives; twenty years in a desert jail; {by} Malika Oufkir and Michele Fitoussi; translated by Ros Schwartz. Miramax Bks. 2001 293p il map hardcover o.p. pa $14

Grades: 11 12 Adult   92
ISBN 0-7868-6732-9; 0-7868-8630-7 (pa)
                                          LC 00-53220
Original French edition, 1999
This memoir recounts the experiences of Oufkir and her family after she was adopted by King Muhammad V of Morocco as a companion for his daughter. She and her family were imprisoned by Muhammad's son King Hassan II for almost 20 years after her father, General Muhammad Oufkir, was executed for leading an unsuccessful plot to assassinate the king in 1972

This book "will fascinate readers with its singular tale of two kindly fathers, political struggles in a strict monarchy and a family's survival of cruel, prolonged deprivation." Publ Wkly

Paine, Thomas, 1737-1809

Collins, Paul. The trouble with Tom: the strange afterlife and times of Thomas Paine. Bloomsbury 2005 278p map $24.95 *

Grades: 11 12 Adult   92
ISBN 1-58234-502-3   LC 2005-45240
The author "traces the bizarre story of Thomas Paine's remains through nearly two centuries of American and English history. . . . Part travelogue, part memoir and part historical mystery, this book reads like a wry, witty novel and offers a delicious twist at the end." Publ Wkly

Includes bibliographical references

Palden Gyatso

Palden Gyatso. The autobiography of a Tibetan monk; [by] Palden Gyatso, with Tsering Shakya; foreword by the Dalai Lama; translated from the Tibetan by Tsering Shakya. Grove Press 1997 232p il maps $24; pa $13

Grades: 9 10 11 12   92
1. Tibet (China)
ISBN 0-8021-1621-3; 0-8021-3574-9 (pa)
                                          LC 97-39679
Published in the United Kingdom with title: Fire under the snow

Palden Gyatso offers an "account of his life in Tibet—first as a Buddhist monk, then as a prisoner of the Chinese for more than 30 years." Booklist

This is a "wrenching memoir of extraordinary suffering, resistance and endurance." N Y Times Book Rev

Pantoja, Antonia, 1922-2002

Pantoja, Antonia. Memoir of a visionary: Antonia Pantoja. Arte Público Press 2002 199p il hardcover o.p. pa $14.95

Grades: 11 12 Adult **92**

1. Puerto Ricans—United States 2. Political activists
ISBN 1-55885-365-0; 155885-385-5 (pa)

LC 2001-56695

"Puerto Rican activist Pantoja was awarded the prestigious Medal of Freedom in 1996 in recognition of her work in organizing Puerto Ricans to challenge the barriers of poverty, increase political involvement, and promote economic development. In her memoir, Pantoja recalls a youth of poverty and a family that sparked her passion and commitment to improving conditions for her neighbors and other Puerto Ricans. . . . This is an inspiring look at a community-spirited individual and the development of a grassroots organization." Booklist

Includes bibliographical references

Parker, Quanah, Comanche Chief, 1845?-1911

Neeley, Bill. The last Comanche chief: the life and times of Quanah Parker. Wiley 1995 276p il maps hardcover o.p. pa $16.95

Grades: 11 12 Adult **92**

1. Comanche Indians
ISBN 0-471-11722-6; 0-471-16076-8 (pa)

LC 94-38101

The author traces Parker's "life from youth to warrior chief to respected cattleman. He describes the last wars between the Comanches and settlers, the peyote ritual and pressures on Native Americans to conform to white society. . . . This is a fine portrait of the legendary chief and an illuminating glimpse into the history of the American West." Publ Wkly

Includes bibliographical references

Parks, Rosa, 1913-2005

Brinkley, Douglas. Rosa Parks. Viking 2000 246p (Penguin lives series) $19.95; pa $13 *

Grades: 11 12 Adult **92**

1. African American women 2. African Americans—Civil rights
ISBN 0-670-89160-6; 0-14-303600-9 (pa)

LC 00-35916

"A Lipper/Viking book"

"Rosa Parks' story takes readers from rural Alabama to the Montgomery Industrial School for Girls, marriage to barber Raymond Parks, quiet activism in the '30s and '40s, a first experience of integration at the Highlander Folk School, arrest in 1955 and the bus boycott, a move to Detroit, and more than 20 years on the staff of Rep. John Conyers (D-Mich.)." Booklist

Includes bibliographical references

Parks, Rosa. Quiet strength; the faith, the hope, and the heart of a woman who changed a nation; reflections by Rosa Parks with Gregory J. Reed. Zondervan 1994 93p il pa $9.99 hardcover o.p.

Grades: 11 12 Adult **92**

1. African American women 2. African Americans—Civil rights
ISBN 0-310-23587-1 (pa)

LC 94-46141

"Parks, one of the U.S.' authentic living legends, is the black lady who on December 1, 1955, refused to surrender her bus seat to a white man, was arrested under the Jim Crow law that required blacks to make way for whites, and thereby launched the yearlong bus boycott by blacks in Birmingham, Alabama, which led to the national overturning of that city's and similar segregation laws across the nation. In this tiny collection of what seem like outtakes from oral-history tapes, she rehearses her great day." Booklist

Includes bibliographical references

Pasteur, Louis, 1822-1895

Ackerman, Jane. Louis Pasteur and the founding of microbiology. Morgan Reynolds Pub. 2003 144p il (Renaissance scientists) lib bdg $23.95 *

Grades: 7 8 9 10 **92**

1. Scientists
ISBN 1-931798-13-3   LC 2003-17655

Follows the life and career of the French scientist who proved the existence of germs and their connection with diseases

"Students interested in science, biography, or medicine will find this an interesting account." SLJ

Includes bibliographical references

Pauling, Linus C., 1901-1994

Pasachoff, Naomi E. Linus Pauling; advancing science, advocating peace; [by] Naomi Pasachoff. Enslow Publishers 2004 128p il (Nobel Prize-winning scientists) $26.60

Grades: 9 10 11 12 **92**

1. Chemists
ISBN 0-7660-2130-0   LC 2003-6475

Profiles the Nobel Prize-winning chemist who described the nature of chemical bonds, made important discoveries in the fields of quantum mechanics, immunology, and evolution, and used his scientific fame to help advance political causes

Includes glossary and bibliographical references

Paulsen, Gary

Paulsen, Gary. The beet fields; memories of a sixteenth summer. Delacorte Press 2000 160p hardcover o.p. pa $5.99

Grades: 11 12 Adult **92**

1. Authors, American
ISBN 0-385-32647-5; 0-440-41557-8 (pa)

LC 00-23184

The author recalls his experiences as a migrant laborer and carnival worker after he ran away from home at age sixteen.

"Paulsen's coming-of-age memoir is nearly Steinbeckian in its unadorned but effective prose, and the events of the author's young life have a universality that will draw in readers heading for their own rites of passage." Bull Cent Child Books

Paulsen, Gary—*Continued*

Paulsen, Gary. Eastern sun, winter moon; an autobiographical odyssey. Harcourt Brace Jovanovich 1993 244p il hardcover o.p. pa $16 *

Grades: 11 12 Adult   **92**

1. Authors, American

ISBN 0-15-127260-3; 0-15-600203-5 (pa)

LC 91-47127

This is an account of the writer's childhood. Paulsen describes his journey to the Philippines at the end of World War II. He and his mother traveled there to join his father, a soldier whom Paulsen had never met.

This "memoir is wonderfully readable. The book is also an interesting portrait of adults as viewed by a child from whom little of the adult world is hidden." Libr J

Picasso, Pablo, 1881-1973

McNeese, Tim. Pablo Picasso. Chelsea House Publishers 2006 122p il (Great Hispanic heritage) lib bdg $30 *

Grades: 7 8 9 10   **92**

1. Artists, French

ISBN 0-7910-8843-X   LC 2005025999

A biography of the 20th century artist.

"McNeese does a wonderful job of describing [this man's life] and, more importantly, the times in which [he] lived. . . .[The book] includes representative pictures from each phase of the artist's career." SLJ

Includes bibliographical references

Pirsig, Robert M., 1928-

Pirsig, Robert M. Zen and the art of motorcycle maintenance; an inquiry into values. Morrow 1974 412p $26; pa $13.95

Grades: 11 12 Adult   **92**

ISBN 0-688-00230-7; 0-06-083987-2 (pa)

A collection of the author's philosophical musings inspired by a motorcycle trip with his son

Pocahontas, d. 1617

Woodward, Grace Steele. Pocahontas. University of Okla. Press 1969 227p il (Civilization of the American Indian series) pa $17.95 hardcover o.p.

Grades: 9 10 11 12   **92**

1. Powhatan Indians 2. United States—History—1600-1775, Colonial period

ISBN 0-8061-1642-0 (pa)

This is the "story of the appealing daughter of Chief Powhatan and her friendship with the colonists of the Jamestown settlement. . . . Her marriage and brief life in England are vividly re-created." Booklist

Includes bibliographical references

Poe, Edgar Allan, 1809-1849

Meltzer, Milton. Edgar Allan Poe; a biography. Twenty-First Century Books 2003 144p $31.90 *

Grades: 7 8 9 10   **92**

1. Authors, American

ISBN 0-7613-2910-2   LC 2002-155802

Contents: Theater in the blood; A quick and clever boy; The teenager; Soldier and poet; In West Point, and out; Satire and science fiction; Editor, novelist, husband; Hoaxes and horrors; The first ever detective story; A popular lecturer; New York : the rich and the poor; "The raven" and fame; Death of the beloved; The last years; Chronology of Poe's life

"More than most other biographers for young people, Meltzer places his subject within the framework of his society. Readers will come away not only with greater knowledge of Poe's life and accomplishments but also a clearer picture of American life in the first half of the nineteenth century." Booklist

Includes bibliographical references

Strathern, Paul. Poe in 90 minutes. Ivan R. Dee 2006 111p (Great writers in 90 minutes) $16.95; pa $8.95

Grades: 9 10 11 12   **92**

1. Authors, American

ISBN 978-1-56663-691-9; 1-56663-691-4; 978-1-56663-690-2 (pa); 1-56663-690-6 (pa)

LC 2006-19763

This biographical study of Edgar Allan Poe examines his life and appraises his works, discussing their overall influence on literature. It includes a chronology of his life.

Includes bibliographical references

Polk, James K. (James Knox), 1795-1849

Seigenthaler, John. James K. Polk. Times Books 2004 188p (American presidents series) $20

Grades: 11 12 Adult   **92**

1. Presidents—United States

ISBN 0-8050-6942-9   LC 2003-56368

This biography of the often forgotten eleventh president focuses on his accomplishments while in office.

Includes bibliographical references

Presley, Elvis, 1935-1977

Mason, Bobbie Ann. Elvis Presley. Viking 2002 178p (Penguin lives series) $19.95; pa $13 *

Grades: 11 12 Adult   **92**

1. Rock musicians

ISBN 0-670-03174-7; 0-14-303889-3 (pa)

LC 2002-28873

"A Lipper/Viking book"

The author "chronicles Elvis' sad story: humble origins, 1954 breakthrough, adoption by 'the Colonel' (manager Tom Parker), early TV appearances, army hitch, the death of his mother, marriage to Priscilla, Hollywood, 1968 'comeback', Las Vegas headliner, prescription drug abuse, meeting with Nixon, and death at 42 in 1977." Booklist

Includes discography, filmography and bibliographical references

Pullman, Philip, 1946-

Speaker-Yuan, Margaret. Philip Pullman. Chelsea House 2006 118p il (Who wrote that?) lib bdg $30

Grades: 6 7 8 9   **92**

1. Authors, English

ISBN 0-7910-8658-5   LC 2005-8184

Pullman, Philip, 1946-—*Continued*
This "draws upon an impressive array of sources—particularly Pullman's own writings—to present the groundbreaking author's life and work. . . . What may thrill readers most . . . are the insights into the writing process." Booklist
Includes bibliographical references

Pythagoras
Karamanides, Dimitra. Pythagoras: pioneering mathematician and musical theorist of Ancient Greece. Rosen Pub. Group 2006 112p il map (The library of Greek philosophers) lib bdg $33.25 *
Grades: 9 10 11 12   92
1. Mathematicians
ISBN 1-4042-00500-4   LC 2005-11968
Contents: The early years -- The traveling student -- Egypt and Babylon -- A return to Greece -- The Pythagorean school -- Pythagorean thought -- Pythagoras' legacy
This is a biography of Greek mathematician and philosopher.
Includes bibliographical references

Ragusa, Kym
Ragusa, Kym. The skin between us; a memoir of race, beauty, and belonging. W.W. Norton 2006 238p $23.95
Grades: 11 12 Adult   92
1. Racially mixed people
ISBN 978-0-393-05890-1; 0-393-05890-5
                                LC 2005-33673
The author "discusses her 'complex heritage'—her mother is African-American, Native American, Chinese and German; her father is Italian-American." Publ Wkly
"The particulars of Ragusa's story reveal the universal anxiety about belonging and about finding a home in America." Booklist

Raleigh, Sir Walter, 1552?-1618
Aronson, Marc. Sir Walter Ralegh and the quest for El Dorado. Clarion Bks. 2000 222p il map $20
Grades: 7 8 9 10   92
1. Explorers
ISBN 0-395-84827-X   LC 99-43096
In this biographical portrait "Ralegh—warrior, champion of North American colonialism, court favorite of Queen Elizabeth I, adventurer and writer—is placed in the center of a broad canvas depicting life in sixteenth-century England and beyond." Horn Book
"Incorporating critical examinations of period art and poetry as well as standard historical documentary evidence and pausing frequently to review and explicitly support its thesis, this title is at once lively, accessible, and challenging. Period illustrations, an index, and fastidiously annotated endnotes and bibliography are included." Bull Cent Child Books
Includes bibliographical references

Randolph, Asa Philip, 1889-1979
Miller, Calvin Craig. A. Philip Randolph and the African American labor movement. Morgan Reynolds 2005 160p il (Portraits of Black Americans) $24.95
Grades: 9 10 11 12   92
1. African Americans—Biography 2. African Americans—Civil rights 3. Labor unions
ISBN 1-931798-50-8   LC 2004-23706
A biography of the African American leader.
"Miller lucidly traces Randolph's spectacular career while presenting a case study in the effective use of hard-nosed rhetoric and nonviolent tactics to achieve breakthroughs in the fight against segregation. Profusely illustrated with photographs, sometimes in color, and capped by resource lists." Booklist
Includes bibliographical references

Reiss, Johanna
Reiss, Johanna. The upstairs room. Crowell 1972 273p $16.99; pa $5.99
Grades: 5 6 7 8 9 10   92
1. World War, 1939-1945—Jews 2. Netherlands—History—1940-1945, German occupation 3. Jews—Netherlands 4. Holocaust, 1933-1945—Personal narratives
ISBN 0-690-85127-8; 0-06-440370-X (pa)
Also available Spanish language edition
A Newbery Medal honor book, 1973
"In a vital, moving account the author recalls her experiences as a Jewish child hiding from the Germans occupying her native Holland during World War II. . . . Ten-year-old Annie and her twenty-year-old sister Sini, . . . are taken in by a Dutch farmer, his wife, and mother who hide the girls in an upstairs room of the farm house. Written from the perspective of a child the story affords a child's-eye-view of the war." Booklist
Followed by The journey back

Rice, Condoleezza, 1954-
Felix, Antonia. Condi; the Condoleezza Rice story. New updated ed. Newmarket Press 2005 288p il $19.95
Grades: 11 12 Adult   92
1. United States. National Security Council 2. Presidents—United States—Staff 3. African American women
ISBN 1-55704-675-1   LC 2005-284121
Also available in hardcover from Zondervan and in paperback from Pocket Bks.
First published 2002
"In this portrait of President Bush's national security advisor, Felix . . . presents Rice as perhaps the most influential woman in the history of the U.S. government." Libr J [review of 2002 edition]
Includes bibliographical references

Riis, Jacob A. (Jacob August), 1849-1914
Pascal, Janet B. Jacob Riis. Oxford University Press 2006 175p il $28
Grades: 9 10 11 12   92
1. Reformers
ISBN 978-0-19-514527-4; 0-19-514527-5
                                LC 2005-7757

Riis, Jacob A. (Jacob August), 1849-1914—*Continued*

Subtitle on cover: Reporter and reformer

"This biography traces Riis's life and evolution into a progressive social reformer. . . . [This is] an insightful work that is sure to hold readers' interest." SLJ

Includes bibliographical references

Ripken, Cal, Jr.

Ripken, Cal, Jr. The only way I know; [by] Cal Ripken, Jr., and Mike Bryan. Viking; distributed by Penguin Putnam 1997 326p il hardcover o.p. pa $12.95

Grades: 11 12 Adult   92
1. Baseball—Biography
ISBN 0-670-87193-1; 0-14-026626-7 (pa)
LC 97-9159

"Cal Junior chronicles his moves through the minor leagues and into the majors in great detail, always pointing out what he learned at each step of the journey and who taught it to him. There are some great baseball anecdotes—especially involving fiery Oriole skipper Earl Weaver—and plenty of the behind-the-scenes detail." Booklist

Robinson, Jackie, 1919-1972

Fussman, Cal. After Jackie; pride, prejudice, and baseball's forgotten heroes: an oral history. ESPN Books 2007 243p il $24.95

Grades: 11 12 Adult   92
1. Baseball—Biography 2. African American athletes
ISBN 1-93306-018-2; 978-1-93306-018-7

The author "traces Robinson's enormous legacy in sports, politics, and the civil rights movement through the men and women who came after him." Publisher's note

Robinson, Jackie. I never had it made; an autobiography; by Jackie Robinson as told to Alfred Duckett; foreword by Cornel West; introduction by Hank Aaron. Ecco Press 1995 xxii, 275p il pa $13.95 hardcover o.p. *

Grades: 11 12 Adult   92
1. Baseball—Biography 2. African American athletes
ISBN 0-06-055597-1   LC 94-45279

A reissue of the title first published 1972 by Putnam

This book "focuses on Robinson's political involvements after his career ended in 1956 and his friendships with such diverse characters as Martin Luther King, Malcolm X, William Buckley and Nelson Rockefeller." Publ Wkly

"Included are introductions by Hank Aaron and Cornel West that provide fresh perspectives on the significance of the legendary star's breaking of major league baseball's color barrier. With each retelling, it is clear that Robinson's story has become less a baseball story than a major cultural milestone in the nation's history." Libr J

Rodriguez, Richard, 1944-

Rodriguez, Richard. Hunger of memory; the education of Richard Rodriguez: an autobiography. Bantam trade pbk. ed. Bantam Books 2004 212p pa $15

Grades: 11 12 Adult   92
1. Mexican Americans
ISBN 0-553-38251-9   LC 2004-269979
First published 1982 by Godine

An account "of the coming of age of a person of Mexican descent and culture in American society and the inevitable transition in the private life of his family. Rodriguez focuses on his educational experiences, from his parochial elementary school . . . to his university years and subsequent experience as an educator." Libr J

Rogers, Will, 1879-1935

Yagoda, Ben. Will Rogers; a biography. Knopf 1993 409p il pa $24.95

Grades: 11 12 Adult   92
1. Entertainers
ISBN 0-8061-3238-8   LC 92-40177

This is a biography of "the rope-twirling vaudeville monologist, salty political commentator, silent film actor and *New York Times* columnist. . . . [This is] a resonant portrait imbued with Rogers's irreverent spirit, yet attuned to both the strengths and limitations of his commonsense, crackerbarrel world view." Publ Wkly

Includes bibliographical references

Roosevelt, Eleanor, 1884-1962

The Eleanor Roosevelt encyclopedia; edited by Maurine H. Beasley, Holly C. Shulman, and Henry R. Beasley; foreword by Blanche Wiesen Cook; introduction by James McGregor Burns. Greenwood Press 2000 xxvi, 628p il $73.95

Grades: 11 12 Adult   92
1. United States—Politics and government—1933-1945
ISBN 0-313-30181-6   LC 00-23530

This reference work "examines the many roles of our foremost First Lady. Given Roosevelt's significance and appeal, this volume is an exception to the rule that encyclopedic treatments of single individuals belong only in larger collections." Booklist

Includes bibliographical references

Freedman, Russell. Eleanor Roosevelt; a life of discovery. Clarion Bks. 1993 198p il $17.95; pa $10.95 *

Grades: 5 6 7 8 9 10   92
1. Presidents' spouses—United States
ISBN 0-89919-862-7; 0-395-84520-3 (pa)
LC 92-25024

"Readers are made privy to the telling details of a full life through numerous quotes from Roosevelt and her wide inner circle in this frank, well-documented portrait of the 'First Lady of the World.' A superlative biography." SLJ

Includes bibliographical references

Roosevelt, Franklin D. (Franklin Delano), 1882-1945

Freedman, Russell. Franklin Delano Roosevelt. Clarion Bks. 1990 200p il $20; pa $9.95 *

Grades: 5 6 7 8 9 10 **92**

1. Presidents—United States 2. United States—Politics and government—1933-1945

ISBN 0-89919-379-X; 0-395-62978-0 (pa)

LC 89-34986

The author "traces the personal and public events in a life that led to the formation of one of the most influential and magnetic leaders of the twentieth century." Horn Book

"The carefully researched, highly readable text and extremely effective coordination of black-and-white photographs chronicle Roosevelt's priviledged youth, his early influences, and his maturation. . . . Even students with little or no background in American history will find this an intriguing and inspirational human portrait." SLJ

Includes bibliographical references

Jenkins, Roy, Baron. Franklin Delano Roosevelt; completed with the assistance of Richard Neustadt. Times Books 2003 186p (American presidents series) $20

Grades: 11 12 Adult **92**

1. Presidents—United States 2. United States—Politics and government—1933-1945

ISBN 0-8050-6959-3

LC 2003-51136

The author "develops FDR's marked propensity to dissemble, which in domestic politics enabled him to best rivals such as presidential also-ran Al Smith, but which in other areas, such as foreign affairs, left his reputation vulnerable to trenchant criticism from historians . . . reminding readers that FDR was initially regarded as a political lightweight, in whom no seer could predict the confidence-inspiring leader of the Depression and World War II." Booklist

"Breezy and brief, 'Franklin Delano Roosevelt' is a small-scale biography of an outsize personality, and succeeds brilliantly. The joy that Jenkins takes in Roosevelt, and the reformers and rogues that surround him, is manifest, and difficult not to share." N Y Times Book Rev

Includes bibliographical references

Roosevelt, Theodore, 1858-1919

Renehan, Edward J. The lion's pride: Theodore Roosevelt and his family in peace and war; [by] Edward J. Renehan, Jr. Oxford Univ. Press 1998 289p il $30; pa $27.95 *

Grades: 11 12 Adult **92**

1. Roosevelt family 2. Presidents—United States

ISBN 0-19-512719-6; 0-19-513424-9 (pa)

LC 98-23998

Although this work explores Roosevelt's influential role as a former president, it primarily explores his relationship with his four sons and daughter.

"Renehan's portraits of the children further enrich a superb, real-life family saga." Booklist

Includes bibliographical references

Rosenberg, Ethel, 1915-1953

Philipson, Ilene J. Ethel Rosenberg; beyond the myths; by Ilene Philipson. Watts 1988 390p

Grades: 11 12 Adult **92**

1. Trials (Espionage)

LC 87-31634

"Without attempting a definitive judgment on whether Ethel Rosenberg was a Communist spy or a martyr to political paranoia, Philipson aims for a deeper understanding of her subject's personality, beliefs, and actions. The book covers the many complex conflicts that made up Rosenberg's life and career." Booklist

This is "a fine psycho-historical study of a complex figure." BAYA Book Rev

Includes bibliographical references

Rowling, J. K.

Kirk, Connie Ann. J.K. Rowling: a biography. Greenwood Press 2003 141p il (Greenwood biographies) $29.95

Grades: 9 10 11 12 **92**

1. Authors, English

ISBN 0-313-32205-8

LC 2002-75330

"Rowling's biography opens with a brief chapter defining her current status in the celebrity world. Subsequent chapters cover her early life and family, her school years, and her early career as a teacher. A long chapter is devoted to Harry Potter, and the volume concludes with controversies and criticisms surrounding the author's life and work." Voice Youth Advocates

"Although there is information about the author herself, the majority of the content is devoted to analyzing her writing. . . . The scholarly writing style and evaluative content make this volume useful to high school students studying Rowling and her work." SLJ

Includes bibliographical references

Runyon, Brent

Runyon, Brent. The burn journals. Alfred A. Knopf 2004 373p $17.95; lib bdg $18.99; pa $13.95 *

Grades: 7 8 9 10 **92**

1. Burns and scalds 2. Suicide

ISBN 0-375-82621-1; 0-375-92621-6 (lib bdg); 1-4000-9642-1 (pa)

LC 2004-5643

"One February day in 1991, Runyon came home from eighth grade . . . and set himself on fire. . . . The dialogue between Runyon and his nurses, parents, and especially his hapless psychotherapists is natural and believable, and his inner dialogue is flip, often funny, and sometimes raw. . . . The authentically adolescent voice of the journals will engage even those reluctant to read such a dark story." SLJ

Russell, Charles M. (Charles Marion), 1864-1926

Hassrick, Peter H. Charles M. Russell. University of Okla. Press 1999 155p il pa $34.95

Grades: 11 12 Adult **92**

1. Artists—United States

ISBN 0-8061-3142-X

LC 98-44419

First published 1989 by Abrams as part of the Library of American art series

Russell, Charles M. (Charles Marion), 1864-1926—*Continued*

A biographical and critical "study of the quintessential cowboy artist. . . . Hassrick describes Russell's career ably and verifies his reputation as a most appealing workingman artist via 52 resplendent colorplates and nearly as many black-and-white figures." Booklist

Includes bibliographical references

Rustin, Bayard, 1910-1987

Miller, Calvin Craig. No easy answers; Bayard Rustin and the civil rights movement. Morgan Reynolds Pub 2005 160p il lib bdg $24.95

Grades: 7 8 9 10   **92**

1. African Americans—Civil rights

ISBN 1-931798-43-5   LC 2004-18518

"Miller combines the life story of a great social activist with the history of the struggle for civil rights in the U.S. The politics are exciting, with details of the radical campaigns in the 1940s and 1950s, Rustin's impassioned call for nonviolent protest, and his role in organizing both the Montgomery Bus Boycott and the 1963 March on Washington." Booklist

Includes bibliographical references

Sacagawea, b. 1786

Nelson, W. Dale. Interpreters with Lewis and Clark: the story of Sacagawea and Toussaint Charbonneau. University of North Texas Press 2003 174p il, maps $24.95; pa $14.95 *

Grades: 9 10 11 12   **92**

1. Charbonneau, Toussaint, ca. 1758-ca. 1839 2. Charbonneau, Jean-Baptiste, 1805-1866 3. Lewis and Clark Expedition (1804-1806)

ISBN 1-57441-165-9; 1-57441-181-0 (pa)

LC 2003-4343

This is a biography of the husband and wife team of interpreters that were a part of the Lewis and Clark Expedition, as well as their son, Jean Baptiste

Includes bibliographical references

Sacks, Oliver W.

Sacks, Oliver W. Uncle Tungsten; memories of a chemical boyhood; [by] Oliver Sacks. Knopf 2001 337p il hardcover o.p. pa $14

Grades: 11 12 Adult   **92**

1. Physicians

ISBN 0-375-40448-1; 0-375-70404-3 (pa)

LC 2001-33738

"Sacks' first scientific love was chemistry, and he presents an avid history of the field within a memoir that pays tribute to his uncle, who welcomed Sacks into his lab, thus encouraging his passion for chemistry and learning." Booklist

Salbi, Zainab

Salbi, Zainab. Between two worlds; escape from tyranny: growing up in the shadow of Saddam; [by] Zainab Salbi and Laurie Becklund. Gotham Books 2005 295p $26; pa $14

Grades: 11 12 Adult   **92**

1. Hussein, Şaddām 2. Women—Iraq

ISBN   1-59240-156-2;   978-1-59240-156-7; 1-59240-244-5 (pa); 978-1-59240-244-1 (pa)

LC 2006-276819

The author discusses her childhood in Iraq, how life was changed by the accession to power of Saddam Hussein, her arranged marriage in America to an abusive husband, and her founding of an organization called Women for Women International.

"Through a journey colored with loss and hope, readers encounter a story of self-awakening and of realizing the will to live and survive." Libr J

Salk, Jonas, 1914-1995

Kluger, Jeffrey. Splendid solution: Jonas Salk and the conquest of polio. G.P. Putnam's Sons 2004 373p il hardcover o.p. pa $15 *

Grades: 11 12 Adult   **92**

1. Poliomyelitis

ISBN 0-399-15216-4; 0-425-20570-3 (pa)

LC 2004-50527

The author "tells how polio was beaten 50 years ago in one of the triumphs of modern medicine. The narrative naturally centers on Jonas Salk, whose lab developed the first polio vaccine." Publ Wkly

"Can't-put-it-down medical-science history." Booklist

Includes bibliographical references

Sanger, Margaret, 1879-1966

Reed, Miriam. Margaret Sanger: her life in her words; foreword by Margaret Sanger Lampe. Barricade Bks. 2003 288p il $29.95; pa $16.95 *

Grades: 11 12 Adult   **92**

1. Birth control 2. Women's rights

ISBN 1-56980-255-6; 1-56980-246-7 (pa)

LC 2003-40416

Reed "seeks to revitalize our appreciation for Sanger in this invaluable collection of her seminal, intelligent, and compassionate writings, which are accompanied by Reed's vibrant and illuminating commentary and a charming introduction by Sanger's granddaughter, Margaret Sanger Lampe." Booklist

Includes bibliographical references

Santiago, Esmeralda

Santiago, Esmeralda. When I was Puerto Rican; [a memoir] Da Capo Press 2006 c1993 278p pa $13.95

Grades: 11 12 Adult   **92**

1. Puerto Ricans—United States

ISBN 0-306-81452-8; 978-0-306-81452-5

First published 1993 by Addison-Wesley

The author "tells of her childhood in Puerto Rico in the 1950s and of her family's move to New York when she was 13." Libr J

Santiago, Esmeralda—*Continued*

"At once heart-wrenching and remarkably inspirational, this lyrical account depicts rural life in Puerto Rico amid the hardships and tensions of everyday life and Santiago's awakening as a young woman, who, although startled by culture shock, valiantly confronted New York head-on. When in the epilogue Santiago refers to her studies at Harvard, it is both a stirring and poignant reminder of the capacities of the human spirit." Booklist

Other autobiographical titles by the author are:

Almost a woman (1998)

The Turkish lover (2004)

Satrapi, Marjane, 1969-

Satrapi, Marjane. Persepolis. Pantheon Bks. 2003 153p il $17.95; pa $11.95 *

Grades: 11 12 Adult   **92**

1. Iran—Graphic novels 2. Graphic novels 3. Autobiographical graphic novels

ISBN 0-375-42230-7; 0-375-71457-X (pa)

LC 2002-190806

This is an "autobiography in . . . comic book form by a woman born to the leftish secular bourgeoisie of 1960's Iran; she was 10 when the shah fell and his tyranny was replaced by the ayatollah version. The book ends when she is 14 and her parents put her on a plane for some safer place (she now lives in France)." N Y Times Book Rev

"Satrapi's cursive, geometrical drawing style . . . eloquently conveys her ingenuousness and fervor as a child." Booklist

Satrapi, Marjane. Persepolis 2; [the story of a return] Pantheon Books 2004 187p il $17.95; pa $12.95 *

Grades: 11 12 Adult   **92**

1. Graphic novels 2. Autobiographical graphic novels

ISBN 0-375-42288-9; 0-375-71466-9 (pa)

LC 2003-70699

Sequel to: Persepolis

This continuation of Satrapi's memoir-in-comics begins "in the areligious West. There Satrapi endured initiations into sex, drugs, and partying, and travails over peer and love relationships that mirrored those of her Western fellow students. . . . After breaking up with her first love . . . she became homeless for three months and, after hospitalization for exposure, returned to Tehran, where the second half of this book transpires. . . . Satrapi's high-contrast, bold-lined, stencil-ish artwork remains very much at the service of one of the most compelling youth memoirs of recent years." Booklist

Scheeres, Julia, 1967-

Scheeres, Julia. Jesus land; a memoir. Counterpoint 2005 356p $23; pa $14

Grades: 11 12 Adult   **92**

ISBN 1-58243-338-0; 1-58243-354-2 (pa)

LC 2005-14816

The author writes about her "bond with the boy her fundamentalist family adopted and abused." N Y Times Book Rev

"Tinged with sadness yet pervaded by a sense of triumph, Scheeres's book is a crisply written and earnest examination of the meaning of family and Christian values." Publ Wkly

Schutz, Samantha, 1978-

Schutz, Samantha. I don't want to be crazy; a memoir of anxiety disorder. PUSH Books 2006 280p $16.99

Grades: 8 9 10 11 12   **92**

1. Anxiety 2. Panic disorders

ISBN 0-439-80518-X   LC 2005028964

"In this moving memoir, Schutz details her struggle with anxiety disorder. . . . Written in verse, this memoir successfully conveys what it is like to suffer from panic attacks." Voice Youth Advocates

Shakur, Tupac

Dyson, Michael Eric. Holler if you hear me: searching for Tupac Shakur. Basic Bks. 2001 292p il hardcover o.p. pa $15

Grades: 11 12 Adult   **92**

1. African American musicians 2. Rap music

ISBN 0-465-01755-X; 0-465-01728-2 (pa)

LC 2001-36564

In this biography of the late rapper, Dyson "examines Tupac both culturally and spiritually through a loosely organized series of meditations that begin in Tupac's childhood . . . and move through his manhood." New Yorker

"Dyson's discussion goes beyond slogans and poses to the actualities of 'thug life' and the consequences of Shakur's passions and allegiances. Piquant and analytical." Booklist

Includes bibliographical references

White, Armond. Rebel for the hell of it; the life of Tupac Shakur; [new foreword by S.H. Fernando] New ed. Thunder's Mouth Press 2002 xxii, 230p il pa $14.95

Grades: 11 12 Adult   **92**

1. African American musicians 2. Rap music

ISBN 1-56025-461-0

First published 1997

In this biography of the rap musician and actor, "White outlines his stint as a dancer with the Digital Underground, his breakthrough second album, his three subsequent multiplatinum efforts, and his various roles in such movies as Juice and Poetic Justice. He also details the rapper's trouble with the law, his incarceration at Riker's Island prison, and his untimely death. . . . This will appeal mostly to fans of standard rock biography." Libr J

Includes discography and filmography

Shen, Fan, 1955-

Shen, Fan. Gang of one; memoirs of a Red Guard. University of Nebraska Press 2004 279p (American lives) $24.95; pa $15.95

Grades: 9 10 11 12   **92**

1. China—History—1949-1976—Personal narratives

ISBN 0-8032-4308-1; 0-8032-9336-4 (pa)

LC 2003-17901

"Shen, age 12 at the start of the Cultural Revolution in 1966, recounts being complicit in arduous Red Guard activities that directly or indirectly led to several gruesome deaths of political 'enemies'—and later falling in love with and marrying the daughter of a man brutally

Shen, Fan, 1955-—*Continued*

tortured and killed by one of his fellow Red Guards."
Publ Wkly

"Teens will strongly identify with Shen's maneuverings around repressive regulations." Booklist

Siana, Jolene

Siana, Jolene. Go ask Ogre; letters from a deathrock cutter. Process 2005 188p il pa $18.95

Grades: 11 12 Adult　　　　　　　92

1. Self-mutilation

ISBN 0-9760822-1-7; 978-0-9760822-1-7

"When she was 17, Siana wrote a series of letters to punk rocker Ogre, the front man of the '80s band Skinny Puppy. The letters speak of depression and cutting, drug abuse and sex, music and poetry. At one concert, Ogre told her that he saved all her letters and one day would return them. True to his word, two boxes arrived at her door nine years later; inside were illustrated letters and journals filled with her most intimate thoughts and fears. . . . Almost every page of the book is filled with heartbreaking artwork and photos, which brilliantly link the journal entries and letters together, allowing readers to get a look inside the mind of a very creative but disturbed young woman." SLJ

Simon, Beth

Simon, Rachel. Riding the bus with my sister. See entry under Simon, Rachel, 1959-

Simon, Lizzie

Simon, Lizzie. Detour; my bipolar road trip in 4-D. Pocket Books 2001 211p hardcover o.p. pa $13

Grades: 11 12 Adult　　　　　　　92

1. Mental illness

ISBN 0-7434-4659-3; 0-7434-4660-7 (pa)

LC 2001-60261

"In fall 1999, twentysomething Simon, who had suffered one full-blown manic episode in her late teens and who controlled her symptoms with lithium, decided to put aside her career as a theatrical producer to seek out other highly successful young manic-depressives. Instead, she encounters a differing array of bipolars, from a multimillionaire who can't control his drug and alcohol use to people who have been institutionalized. . . . This book will resonate with younger readers." Libr J

Simon, Rachel, 1959-

Simon, Rachel. Riding the bus with my sister; a true life journey. Houghton Mifflin 2002 296p $23

Grades: 11 12 Adult　　　　　　　92

1. Simon, Beth 2. Mentally handicapped

ISBN 0-618-04599-6　　　　　　LC 2002-33930

Also available in paperback from Plume Bks.

"Simon's memoir . . . tells the story of her relationship with her sister, Beth, who is mentally retarded. . . . [Rachel] is perplexed by how Beth spends all of her time: riding buses. . . . Rachel's story begins when a newspaper editor suggests that she write a column about

riding the bus with her sister. Beth is so pleased to spend time with her that she asks her to continue riding with her for a year. Reluctantly, Rachel agrees." Women's Rev Books

"Clear writing and repeated conversations allow readers to hear the voices of both sisters. There is much to mull over, to enjoy, and to savor in this book." SLJ

Simpson, Colton

Simpson, Colton. Inside the Crips; life inside L.A.'s most notorious gang; [by] Colton Simpson with Ann Pearlman. St. Martin's Press 2005 xxiii, 323p $24.95; pa $14.95

Grades: 11 12 Adult　　　　　　　92

1. Crips (Gang)

ISBN 0-312-32929-6; 0-312-30930-X (pa)

LC 2005-42704

The author "provides an insider's perspective on day-to-day life in the Crips, the gang's history (including quite a bit about its rival, the Bloods), and the plight of growing up in the 'hood while wanting a better life. . . . This unvarnished portrayal of gang life is enlightening and even inspiring about a subject badly in need of illumination." Booklist

Smith, Alison, 1968-

Smith, Alison. Name all the animals; a memoir. Scribner 2004 319p $24; pa $13

Grades: 9 10 11 12　　　　　　　92

ISBN 0-7432-5522-4; 0-7432-5523-2 (pa)

LC 2003-60432

"When Smith was 15, her beloved older brother died suddenly. In a poignant, ultimately hopeful memoir that reads like fiction, Smith describes her own and her parents' journeys through grief and the thrill of a first love that was taboo in her religious community." Booklist

Smith, Joseph, 1805-1844

Remini, Robert Vincent. Joseph Smith. Viking 2002 190p (Penguin lives series) $19.95 *

Grades: 11 12 Adult　　　　　　　92

1. Mormons

ISBN 0-670-03083-X　　　　　　LC 2001-56762

In this biography of the founder of the Mormon Church, the author "places Smith in the context of his time in terms of the broader social, political, and economic events that influenced him and his church." Libr J

"A masterful evenhanded précis that will engross history and religion readers alike." Booklist

Includes bibliographical references

Stalin, Joseph, 1879-1953

Cunningham, Kevin. Joseph Stalin and the Soviet Union. M. Reynolds 2006 208p il map (World leaders) lib bdg $27.95 *

Grades: 9 10 11 12　　　　　　　92

1. Dictators 2. Soviet Union—History

ISBN 978-1-93179-894-5; 1-93179-894-X

LC 2005-32540

Stalin, Joseph, 1879-1953—*Continued*
"This biography reviews the life of Soviet leader Joseph Stalin and the changes within the country during his long tenure. Although not ignoring his youth and his personal life, the discussion centers on his political leadership and its far-reaching effects. . . . This attractive volume offers a solid biography of Stalin." Booklist
Includes bibliographical references

Stanton, Elizabeth Cady, 1815-1902
Banner, Lois W. Elizabeth Cady Stanton; a radical for woman's rights. Addison Wesley Longman 1997 c1980 189p (Library of American biography) pa $20
Grades: 9 10 11 12   **92**
1. Feminism
ISBN 0-673-39319-4
This biography of the nineteenth-century American feminist describes her upbringing, marriage, motherhood, and development as a leader.
Includes bibliographical references

Ward, Geoffrey C. Not for ourselves alone: the story of Elizabeth Cady Stanton and Susan B. Anthony; an illustrated history; based on a documentary film by Ken Burns, written by Geoffrey C. Ward; with a preface by Ken Burns; introduction by Paul Barnes; and contributions by Martha Saxton, Ann D. Gordon, Ellen Carol DuBois. Knopf 1999 240p $35; pa $19.95 *
Grades: 11 12 Adult   **92**
1. Anthony, Susan B., 1820-1906 2. Feminism
ISBN 0-375-40560-7; 0-375-70969-X (pa)
LC 99-31056
This biographical study of Cady and Anthony, leaders of the women's rights movement in the United States, was published to accompany a television film by Ken Burns.
"Ward writes beautifully, and he knows how to weigh evidence and how to assess the salience of events. He quotes shrewdly from the words of his protagonists. Although the interpretation is far from exciting or original, he freshens his material by including new essays by scholars." New Repub
Includes bibliographical references

Steinbeck, John, 1902-1968
Reef, Catherine. John Steinbeck. Clarion Bks. 1996 163p il $17.95; pa $8.95
Grades: 7 8 9 10   **92**
1. Authors, American
ISBN 0-395-71278-5; 0-618-43244-2 (pa)
LC 95-11500
"The book traces Steinbeck's life from his childhood in California, to his burgeoning writing career and his passion for social justice, to his worldwide recognition. Reef does an excellent job of synthesizing Steinbeck's work, his private life, and his politics and philosophy." Bull Cent Child Books
Includes bibliographical references

Steinbeck, John. Conversations with John Steinbeck; edited by Thomas Fensch. University Press of Miss. 1988 xxi, 116p (Literary conversations series) pa $18 hardcover o.p.
Grades: 11 12 Adult   **92**
1. Authors, American
ISBN 0-87805-360-3 (pa)   LC 88-17538
"This collection of Steinbeck's interviews allows him to speak on his own behalf in an illuminating expression of his intentions, goals, and achievements. From the beginning of his career through his last years the interviews reveal a fascinating, controversial, and captivating personality." Univ Press Books for Second Sch Libr
Includes bibliographical references

Steiner, Matt
Warren, Andrea. Escape from Saigon; how a Vietnam War orphan became an American boy. Farrar, Straus and Giroux 2004 110p il map $17
Grades: 9 10 11 12   **92**
1. Vietnamese Americans 2. Vietnam War, 1961-1975 3. Interracial adoption
ISBN 0-374-32224-4   LC 2003-60672
"Melanie Kroupa books"
Chronicles the experiences of an orphaned Amerasian boy from his birth and early childhood in Saigon through his departure from Vietnam in the 1975 Operation Babylift and his subsequent life as the adopted son of an American family in Ohio.
"The child-at-war story and the facts about the Operation Babylift rescue are tense and exciting. Just as gripping is the boy's personal conflict." Booklist

Stringer, Caverly
Stringer, Caverly. Sleepaway school; stories from a boy's life; [by] Lee Stringer. A Seven Stories Press 1st ed. Seven Stories Press 2004 227p $21.95; pa $13.95
Grades: 11 12 Adult   **92**
1. African Americans—Biography
ISBN 1-58322-478-5; 1-58322-701-6 (pa)
LC 2004-3610
"In more than 30 connected true stories, Stringer portrays his boyhood as a poor, black foster child coincidentally growing up in a wealthy white neighborhood after he was sent to a school for troubled boys—mostly white, middle-class boys." Booklist
The author "deftly tells a believable, candid and vivid tale of a person scarred by his past." Publ Wkly

Swift, Jonathan, 1667-1745
Aykroyd, Clarissa. Savage satire; the story of Jonathan Swift. Morgan Reynolds Pub. 2006 160p il (World writers) lib bdg $27.95 *
Grades: 7 8 9 10   **92**
1. Authors, Irish
ISBN 1-59935-027-0; 978-1-59935-027-1
LC 2006-18142
A biography of the Anglo-Irish writer who enjoyed shocking his readers.
"High-school students will find this a useful, informa-

Swift, Jonathan, 1667-1745—*Continued*
tive introduction to the man's life, politics, and writings."
Booklist
Includes bibliographical references

Telfair, Sebastian, 1985-
O'Connor, Ian. The jump; Sebastian Telfair and the high stakes business of high school ball. Rodale 2005 307p il $23.95; pa $13.95
Grades: 11 12 Adult   92
    1. Basketball—Biography
    ISBN 1-59486-107-2; 1-59486-447-0 (pa)
                     LC 2004-26366
In this biography of the up-and-coming basketball player, the author "chronicles Telfair's senior year at Brooklyn's Lincoln High. . . . This will be the most discussed book of the NBA season." Booklist

Teresa, Mother, 1910-1997
Spink, Kathryn. Mother Teresa; a complete authorized biography. HarperSanFrancisco 1997 306p il pa $15.95 hardcover o.p.
Grades: 11 12 Adult   92
    1. Missionaries of Charity 2. Missions—India
    ISBN 0-06-251553-5 (pa)   LC 97-41349
"Spink's biography benefits from her own 18-year involvement with the work of the Missionaries of Charity Order as well as from the intimate relationship she developed over the years with Mother Teresa. . . . A final chapter in the book provides glimpses of Mother Teresa's affection for Princess Diana, a brief description of Mother Teresa's funeral and a short account of the election of Sister Nirmal as her successor." Publ Wkly

Tesla, Nikola, 1856-1943
Aldrich, Lisa J. Nikola Tesla and the taming of electricity. Morgan Reynolds Pub. 2005 160p il $26.95 *
Grades: 9 10 11 12   92
    1. Inventors
    ISBN 1-931798-46-X   LC 2004-18786
The author writes "of Tesla's life, while using sidebars to carry information on related topics such as alternating and direct current, the patent system, and Tesla's dream of wireless power." Booklist
Includes bibliographical references

Thomas, Aquinas, Saint, 1225?-1274
Strathern, Paul. Thomas Aquinas in 90 minutes. Ivan R. Dee 1998 90p (Philosophers in 90 Minutes) $14.95; pa $7.95
Grades: 9 10 11 12   92
    1. Philosophers
    ISBN 1-56663-193-9; 1-56663-194-7 (pa)
                     LC 98-13264
The author offers an "account of Aquinas' life and ideas, and explains their influence on man's struggle to understand his existence in the world. The book also includes selections from Aquinas' writings; a brief list of suggested reading for those who wish to push further;

and chronologies that place Aquinas within his own age and in the broader scheme of philosophy." Publisher's note
Includes bibliographical references

Thompson, Craig, 1975-
Thompson, Craig. Blankets; an illustrated novel. Top Shelf 2003 582p il pa $29.95
Grades: 9 10 11 12   92
    1. Graphic novels 2. Family life—Graphic novels 3. Autobiographical graphic novels
    ISBN 1-891830-43-0   LC 2004-297892
This "memoir recreates the confusion, emotional pain and isolation of the author's rigidly fundamentalist Christian upbringing, along with the trepidation of growing into maturity. Skinny, naive and spiritually vulnerable, Thompson and his younger brother manage to survive their parents' overbearing discipline (the brothers are sometimes forced to sleep in 'the cubbyhole,' a forbidding and claustrophobic storage chamber) through flights of childhood fancy and a mutual love of drawing . . . Thompson manages to explore adolescent social yearnings, the power of young love and the complexities of sexual attraction with a rare combination of sincerity, pictorial lyricism and taste. His exceptional b&w drawings balance representational precision with a bold and wonderfully expressive line for pages of ingenious, inventively composed and poignant imagery." Publ Wkly

Thorpe, Jim, 1888-1953
Crawford, Bill. All American; the rise and fall of Jim Thorpe. John Wiley & Sons, Inc 2004 284p il $24.95
Grades: 11 12 Adult   92
    1. Athletes
    ISBN 0-471-55732-3   LC 2004-14376
This "terse, punchy biography of sports legend Thorpe (1888–1953) illuminates the current debate over the exploitation of unpaid college athletes by moneymaking, headline-grabbing educational institutions." Publ Wkly
Includes bibliographical references

Tienda, Marta
O'Connell, Diane. People person; the story of sociologist Marta Tienda. Franklin Watts 2005 108p il map (Women's adventures in science) lib bdg $31
Grades: 7 8 9 10   92
    1. Sociology 2. Mexican Americans—Biography
    ISBN 0-531-16781-X   LC 2005000825
Also available in paperback from Joseph Henry Press
A biography of Mexican American sociologist Marta Tienda.
This is "interesting, substantive, and eminently readable." SLJ
Includes bibliographical references

Tillage, Leon, 1936-
Tillage, Leon. Leon's story; [by] Leon Walter Tillage; collage art by Susan L. Roth. Farrar, Straus & Giroux 1997 107p il $15; pa $4.95
Grades: 4 5 6 7 8 9 10   **92**
1. African Americans—Biography 2. North Carolina—Race relations
ISBN 0-374-34379-9; 0-374-44330-0 (pa)
LC 96-43544
The son of a North Carolina sharecropper recalls the hard times faced by his family and other African Americans in the first half of the twentieth century and the changes that the civil rights movement helped bring about
The author's "voice is direct, the words are simple. There is no rhetoric, no commentary, no bitterness. . . . This quiet drama will move readers of all ages . . . and may encourage them to record their own family stories." Booklist

Traig, Jennifer
Traig, Jennifer. Devil in the details; scenes from an obsessive girlhood. Little, Brown 2004 246p il hardcover o.p. pa $14.99
Grades: 9 10 11 12   **92**
1. Obsessive-compulsive disorder
ISBN 0-316-15877-1; 0-316-01074-X (pa)
LC 2004-1417
"When she was an adolescent, Traig's loose collection of neuroses coalesced into a hyperreligious form of obsessive-compulsive disorder known as scrupulosity. The condition finds the once spiritually indifferent teenager purifying her school binders, using separate bathrooms for milk and meat, and perplexing and vexing her mixed-faith family." Booklist
The author's "efforts to adhere, in a vacuum, to Jewish law, are particularly amusing. She also writes affectionately about her long-suffering family members, who are funny enough to stage their own sitcom. In the end, she succeeds in overcoming her illness, providing a provocative yet entertaining memoir in the process." Libr J

Transue, Emily R.
Transue, Emily R. On call; a doctor's days and nights in residency. St. Martin's Press 2004 242p $23.95; pa $13.95
Grades: 9 10 11 12   **92**
1. Physicians
ISBN 0-312-32483-9; 0-312-32484-7 (pa)
LC 2004-46893
"During her three years as a resident in internal medicine at the University of Washington in Seattle, Transue wrote about her patients as a way to guard against burnout and share her experiences with friends and family. This [is a] moving collection of her stories. . . . Her descriptions of medical procedures can be graphic, but she presents an intriguing picture of a side of medicine many people never see." Publ Wkly

Truth, Sojourner, d. 1883
Painter, Nell Irvin. Sojourner Truth; a life, a symbol. Norton 1996 370p il hardcover o.p. pa $15.95 *
Grades: 11 12 Adult   **92**
1. Abolitionists 2. Feminism
ISBN 0-393-02739-2; 0-393-31708-0 (pa)
LC 95-47595
"Sojourner Truth's remarkable career as a powerful, impassioned speaker and advocate of abolitionism and women's rights spanned more than 30 years. Painter . . . traces Truth's life and legacy using a variety of sources, including her many photographs." Libr J
"Painter persuasively offers us the real woman behind the myth." Publ Wkly
Includes bibliographical references

Tubman, Harriet, 1820?-1913
Clinton, Catherine. Harriet Tubman; the road to freedom. Little, Brown 2004 272p hardcover o.p. pa $14.95 *
Grades: 11 12 Adult   **92**
1. Abolitionists
ISBN 0-316-14492-4; 0-316-15594-2 (pa)
LC 2003-56185
The author "places Tubman's life within its times, describing, among other things, the history of the abolitionist movement and the impact of the Fugitive Slave Law of 1850." N Y Times Book Rev
"Clinton turns sobriquets into meaningful descriptors of a unique person. In her hands, a familiar legend acquires human dimension with no diminution of its majesty and power." Publ Wkly
Includes bibliographical references

Turner, Nat, 1800?-1831
Baker, Kyle. Nat Turner Encore Edition Vol. 1. Kyle Baker Publishing 2006 95p il pa $10
Grades: 10 11 12 Adult   **92**
1. Graphic novels 2. Biographical graphic novels 3. Slavery—Graphic novels
ISBN 978-0-9747214-2-2
Originally published as Nat Turner issues #1 and 2
Baker starts his story by depicting a slavers' raid upon an African village and then the horrible voyage to America. In nearly wordless panels, striking black-and-white art effectively conveys the emotions. When Nat Turner is born, Baker uses excerpts from The Confessions of Nat Turner to reveal his thoughts as a boy, as a young man, and then the vision which gave him the purpose to "fight against the Serpent." Some images may be disturbing to sensitive teens, such as when a desperate mother throws her baby to the sharks, or slaves are bound and whipped by cruel masters.
Followed by Nat Turner Vol. 2: Revolution (2006)

Twain, Mark, 1835-1910
Powers, Ron. Dangerous water: a biography of the boy who became Mark Twain. Basic Bks. 1999 328p $24; pa $17.50
Grades: 11 12 Adult   **92**
1. Authors, American
ISBN 0-465-07670-X; 0-306-81086-7 (pa)
LC 99-228994

Twain, Mark, 1835-1910—*Continued*

"Powers regularly draws convincing links between Twain's early life and events and characters in his fiction." Publ Wkly

Includes bibliographical references

Ward, Geoffrey C. Mark Twain; by Geoffrey C. Ward and Dayton Duncan; based on a documentary film directed by Ken Burns; written by Dayton Duncan and Geoffrey C. Ward; with a preface by Ken Burns; picture research by Susanna Steisel and Pam Tubridy Baucom, and contributions by Russell Banks [et al.] Knopf 2001 269p il map $40

Grades: 11 12 Adult   92

1. Authors, American

ISBN 0-375-40561-5   LC 2001-33820

Companion volume to the PBS television series

"This fascinating biography of Twain contains a treasure trove of photographs and pictures." Booklist

Includes bibliographical references

Typhoid Mary, d. 1938

Bourdain, Anthony. Typhoid Mary; an urban historical. Bloomsbury Pub. 2001 148p $19.95 *

Grades: 11 12 Adult   92

ISBN 1-58234-133-8   LC 2001-18444

The subject of Bourdain's book is the cook "Mary Mallon, who became known as Typhoid Mary after infecting 33 people with typhoid fever . . . in turn-of-the-century New York." N Y Times Book Rev

"Investing a tragic tale with a new twist, Bourdain plays historical detective, providing an entertaining and suspenseful evocation of turn-of-the-century New York." Booklist

Includes bibliographical references

Ung, Loung, 1970-

Ung, Loung. Lucky child; a daughter of Cambodia reunites with the sister she left behind. HarperCollins Publishers 2005 268p il $24.95; pa $13.95

Grades: 11 12 Adult   92

1. Ung, Chou 2. Cambodian Americans 3. Cambodia—History—1975-

ISBN 0-06-073394-2; 0-06-073395-0 (pa)

                              LC 2004-54346

Sequel to First they killed my father

In this "memoir, Ung picks up where her first . . . left off, with the author escaping a devastated Cambodia in 1980 at age 10 and flying to her new home in Vermont. . . . She and her eldest brother, with whom she escaped, left behind their three other siblings. This book is alternately heart-wrenching and heartwarming, as it follows the parallel lives of Loung Ung and her closest sister, Chou, during the 15 years it took for them to reunite." Publ Wkly

Includes bibliographical references

Unger, Zac

Unger, Zac. Working fire; the making of an accidental fireman. Penguin Press 2004 262p hardcover o.p. pa $15

Grades: 11 12 Adult   92

1. Fire fighters—Biography

ISBN 1-59420-001-7; 0-14-303495-2 (pa)

                              LC 2003-50676

"A young rookie provides a look behind the firehouse doors, bringing close the danger, excitement, and challenge of fighting fire in a big city." Booklist

Van Buren, Martin, 1782-1862

Widmer, Edward L. Martin Van Buren; [by] Ted Widmer. Times Bks. 2005 189p (American presidents series) $20

Grades: 11 12 Adult   92

1. Presidents—United States

ISBN 0-8050-6922-4   LC 2004-53652

This is a "portrait of our eighth president, who, Widmer says, created the modern political party system." Publ Wkly

The author "keenly evokes the environment that enabled Van Buren to thrive. . . . Widmer also lends a certain dignity to Van Buren's post-presidential attempts to resolve the sectional crisis." N Y Times Book Rev

Includes bibliographical references

Vasishta, Madan, 1941-

Vasishta, Madan. Deaf in Delhi; a memoir. Gallaudet University Press 2006 220p il (Deaf lives) pa $29.95

Grades: 11 12 Adult   92

1. Deaf 2. Delhi (India)

ISBN 1-56368-284-2; 978-1-56368-284-1

                              LC 2005-55214

"A bout with mumps and typhoid left 11-year-old Vasishta deaf. In an India where the word for deaf in at least three languages means someone less than human, there was not much hope for his future. . . . The author weaves stories, set in the India of the 1950s and early '60s, of the holy men to whom his family turned for a cure for him, of his arranged marriage, and of the class system. . . . This book is a must for collections accessed by deaf teens, and it will appeal to young adults interested in Indian culture, multicultural studies, or disabilities." SLJ

Includes bibliographical references

Vlad III, Prince of Wallachia, 1430 or 31-1476 or 7

Florescu, Radu R. N. Dracula; prince of many faces, his life and his times; [by] Radu R. Florescu, Raymond T. McNally. Little, Brown 1989 xxii, 261p il maps pa $16.99 hardcover o.p.

Grades: 11 12 Adult   92

1. Kings and rulers

ISBN 0-316-28656-7 (pa)   LC 89-8164

This is a biography of the "fifteenth-century Romanian prince. The authors present him as a . . . national hero still revered for defending Romania from the Turks, yet also a psychopath who used his power indiscriminately

Vlad III, Prince of Wallachia, 1430 or 31-1476 or 7—*Continued*

to torture and murder thousands of his enemies and subjects." Libr J

This book "will probably be reckoned the last word on the real man behind the fictional vampire for many years to come." Booklist

Includes bibliographical references

Von Braun, Wernher, 1912-1977

Spangenburg, Ray. Wernher von Braun; space visionary and rocket engineer; {by} Ray Spangenburg and Diane K. Moser. Facts on File 1995 134p il (Makers of modern science) $25 *

Grades: 9 10 11 12   92

1. Rocketry 2. Scientists

ISBN 0-8160-2924-5   LC 94-22520

"The story of rocket development is . . . integrated with the story of von Braun's life. . . . Varied sources of information, including oral histories and archival materials are interwoven with diagrams and photographs that aptly explain the accompanying text. Lucid explanations are provided for scientific concepts such as jet rocket propulsion. They are simple but not simplistic." Appraisal

Includes glossary and bibliographical references

Vonnegut, Kurt, 1922-2007

Vonnegut, Kurt. Conversations with Kurt Vonnegut; edited by William Rodney Allen. University Press of Miss. 1988 305p (Literary conversations series) pa $15.95 hardcover o.p.

Grades: 11 12 Adult   92

1. Authors, American

ISBN 0-87805-358-1 (pa)   LC 88-13968

"In the twenty years of interviews collected here . . . the reader can hear Vonnegut working through his various personae of science fiction writer, black humorist, pop culture guru, and elder statesman toward a truer definition of himself and his art." Univ Press Books for Second Sch Libr

Walker, Rebecca, 1969-

Walker, Rebecca. Black, white and Jewish; autobiography of a shifting self. Riverhead Bks. 2001 320p hardcover o.p. pa $14

Grades: 11 12 Adult   92

1. Racially mixed people

ISBN 1-57322-169-4; 1-57322-907-5 (pa)

LC 00-35292

This is an autobiography by "the daughter of the black writer Alice Walker and a white Jewish lawyer, Mel Leventhal. Rebecca Walker writes that her confusion about being biracial began when her parents divorced when she was 8 years old. From then on, every two years, Walker alternated coast-to-coast between them." NY Times Book Rev

This is an "involving, honest, poignant memoir." Booklist

Wallenberg, Raoul

Linnea, Sharon. Raoul Wallenberg: the man who stopped death. Jewish Publ. Soc. 1993 151p il hardcover o.p. pa $9.95

Grades: 9 10 11 12   92

1. Jews—Hungary

ISBN 0-8276-0440-8; 0-8276-0448-3 (pa)

LC 93-12140

Traces the life of the Swedish diplomat who saved Hungarian Jews during World War II and then mysteriously disappeared after the Russians occupied Budapest

"Linnéa has a sound sense of her young audience. Her writing is lucid and vivid." Voice Youth Advocates

Walls, Jeannette

Walls, Jeannette. The glass castle; a memoir. Scribner 2005 288p $25; pa $14 *

Grades: 11 12 Adult   92

ISBN 0-7432-4753-1; 0-7432-4754-X (pa)

LC 2004-58907

The author "describes a childhood spent careering across the country, from California to West Virginia, in a succession of ever more rattletrap cars, in pursuit of increasingly implausible get-rich-quick schemes." Time

"Shocking, sad, and occasionally bitter, this gracefully written account speaks candidly, yet with surprising affection, about parents and about the strength of family ties—for both good and ill." Booklist

Warhol, Andy, 1928?-1987

Greenberg, Jan. Andy Warhol; prince of pop; [by] Jan Greenberg & Sandra Jordan. Delacorte Press 2004 193p il $16.95 *

Grades: 7 8 9 10   92

1. Artists—United States 2. Pop art

ISBN 0-385-73056-X   LC 2003-24102

A biography of the 20th century American artist famous for his Pop art images of Campbell's soup cans and Marilyn Monroe.

"Greenberg and Jordan offer a riveting biography that humanizes their controversial subject without making judgments or sensationalizing." Booklist

Includes glossary and bibliographical references

Washington, Booker T., 1856-1915

Washington, Booker T. Up from slavery; with a new introduction by Ishmael Reed. New American Library 2000 xxii, 228p (Edwards Black Heritage Collection) pa $4.95 *

Grades: 7 8 9 10 11 12 Adult   92

1. Tuskegee Institute 2. African Americans—Biography

ISBN 0-451-52754-2   LC 99-34954

First published 1901

"The classic autobiography of the man who, though born in slavery, educated himself and went on to found Tuskegee Institute." N Y Public Libr

Includes bibliographical references

Washington, George, 1732-1799

Ellis, Joseph J. His Excellency; George Washington. Knopf 2004 320p il $26.95; pa $15 *

Grades: 11 12 Adult 92
1. Presidents—United States
ISBN 1-4000-4031-0; 1-4000-3253-89 (pa)
LC 2004-46576
Also available large print edition $28.95 (ISBN 0-375-43190-X)

This is a "look at America's premier Founding Father, revealing a man with incredible energy, stamina, integrity, and vision as well as one who could be quite insecure, controlling, and shortsighted. Ellis examines the evolution of Washington's personality and challenges conventional scholarship. . . . He also determines that Washington's decisions on slavery were driven more by economics and posterity than purely by morality." Libr J

The author "offers a magisterial account of the life and times of George Washington, celebrating the heroic image of the president whom peers like Jefferson and Madison recognized as 'their unquestioned superior' while acknowledging his all-too-human qualities." Publ Wkly
Includes bibliographical references

Johnson, Paul. George Washington: the Founding Father. HarperCollins Publishers 2005 126p (Eminent lives) $19.95

Grades: 11 12 Adult 92
1. Presidents—United States
ISBN 0-06-075365-X LC 2004-52907

This is a biography of the first president of the United States.

The author "submits a beautifully cogent, enthrallingly perceptive, and . . . startlingly fresh take on the ultimate American icon." Booklist
Includes bibliographical references

Marrin, Albert. George Washington and the founding of a nation. Dutton Children's Bks. 2000 276p il $30 *

Grades: 9 10 11 12 92
1. Presidents—United States
ISBN 0-525-46481-6 LC 00-34088

This work documents the "life of a man who wanted only to be at home caring for his land and family but ended up spending years away from home, fighting one battle after another. . . . Much of the book is filled with descriptions of the battles Washington had to fight and of the people fighting at his side and against him. Some material is taken from diaries and letters." Voice Youth Advocates

"Copious notes and an extensive bibliography, as well as an index and a broad sampling of period artwork, will certainly benefit report writers, but real history buffs will just settle in for a satisfying cover to cover read." Bull Cent Child Books

Washington, Martha, 1731-1802

Brady, Patricia. Martha Washington; an American life. Viking 2005 276p il $24.95; pa $15

Grades: 11 12 Adult 92
1. Presidents' spouses—United States
ISBN 0-670-03430-4; 0-14-303713-7 (pa)
LC 2004-61242

In this book, the original first lady "is depicted as a very human but true heroine who remained steadfast through personal adversity and the uncertainties of war and revolution." Libr J

"Brady's splendid biography offers a compelling new portrait of this passionate, committed founding mother who has unjustly been obscured by others, such as Abigail Adams." Publ Wkly
Includes bibliographical references

Watson, James D., 1928-

Edelson, Edward. Francis Crick and James Watson and the building blocks of life. Oxford Univ. Press 1998 110p il (Oxford portraits in science) pa $28

Grades: 7 8 9 10 92
1. Crick, Francis, 1916-2004 2. Scientists 3. Genetics 4. Molecular biology
ISBN 0-19-511451-5 LC 97-42791

Describes the collaboration of Watson and Crick in the effort to discover DNA.

This dual biography is "also a history of the development of modern molecular biology. . . . The science is well presented and quite current." Sci Books Films
Includes bibliographical references

Wells, David

Wells, David. Perfect I'm not; Boomer on beer, brawls, backaches, and baseball; {by} David Wells with Chris Kreski. Morrow 2003 414p il hardcover o.p. pa $13.95

Grades: 11 12 Adult 92
1. Baseball—Biography
ISBN 0-06-050824-8; 0-06-074811-7 (pa)
LC 2002-35757

"In these pages Wells uses his colorful language to give the reader a locker-room view of baseball, from the minor leagues and winter ball to the World Series. . . . He also chronicles the dedication, physical grit and camaraderie that help sustain players in their short careers." N Y Times (Late N Y Ed)

Welty, Eudora, 1909-2001

Welty, Eudora. One writer's beginnings. Harvard Univ. Press 1984 104p il (William E. Massey, Sr. lectures in the history of American civilization) $20.95; pa $12 *

Grades: 11 12 Adult 92
1. Authors, American
ISBN 0-674-63925-1; 0-674-63927-8 (pa)
LC 83-18638

A series of lectures in which the author reflects on her Southern heritage and her early artistic influences.

Wexler, Nancy S.

Glimm, Adele. Gene hunter; the story of neuropsychologist Nancy Wexler. Franklin Watts 2005 118p il (Women's adventures in science) $31

Grades: 7 8 9 10   **92**

1. Huntington's chorea 2. Women scientists

ISBN 0-531-16778-X   LC 2005-06645

Also available in paperback from Joseph Henry Press

Contents: The dancing disease; Family secrets; Taking on the world; We won't give up; Risk and death; We are all one family; Testing the future; We found it!; In quest of cure

This is a biography of neuropsychologist Nancy Wexler who is seaching for the gene responsible for a fatal, inherited sickness called Huntington's disease.

This "volume is filled with full-color photographs of the subject and her work. Students will be comfortable with the style of [this book], and the easy reading level makes [it] accessible for even nonscience-oriented students." SLJ

Includes bibliographical references

White, Ryan

White, Ryan. Ryan White: my own story; by Ryan White and Ann Marie Cunningham. Dial Bks. 1991 277p il hardcover o.p. pa $7.99

Grades: 11 12 Adult   **92**

1. AIDS (Disease)—Personal narratives

ISBN 0-8037-0977-3; 0-451-17322-8 (pa)

    LC 90-21038

Ryan White describes how he got AIDS, engaged in a legal battle to return to school, and became a celebrity and spokesman for issues concerning the deadly disease

The book contains "surprising snatches of humor and insight that lend dimension to the vulnerable young man whose positive outlook shines through so clearly. Not saccharine, not angry, not bitter, this unusual book, delivered without an ounce of self-pity, seems as honest as it is inspiring. It will touch both adults and teens." Booklist

Whitman, Walt, 1819-1892

Meltzer, Milton. Walt Whitman; a biography. 21st Cent. Bks. (Brookfield) 2002 160p il lib bdg $31.90

Grades: 7 8 9 10   **92**

1. Poets, American

ISBN 0-7613-2272-8   LC 2001-27798

"The book honestly explores Whitman's character and actions, including his racial prejudice and his tendency to write anonymous (and effective) praises of his own writing. Ultimately, this has a definite edge and relevance that gives it more resonance than blander overviews of the poet. . . . Photographs of Whitman and his family, images of his work, and reproductions of period illustrations . . . liven up the formatting." Bull Cent Child Books

Includes bibliographical references

Reef, Catherine. Walt Whitman. Clarion Bks. 1995 148p il $16.95; pa $7.95 *

Grades: 7 8 9 10   **92**

1. Poets, American

ISBN 0-395-68705-5; 0-618-24616-9 (pa)

    LC 94-7405

"Here is a biography of Whitman that presents the life of the subject, the world in which he lived, and representative passages from his writings." Voice Youth Advocates

"This is not a biography for pleasure reading, but it could be a source for those interested in historical events of 19th century America. It also would be a good resource for students doing a critique of Whitman's work for an American literature course." Book Rep

Includes bibliographical references

Wiesel, Elie, 1928-

Wiesel, Elie. Night; translated from the French by Marion Wiesel; [with a new preface by the author; foreword by FranSoise Mauriac] Hill and Wang 2006 xxi, 120p $19.95; pa $9 *

Grades: 9 10 11 12   **92**

1. Holocaust, 1933-1945—Personal narratives 2. Holocaust survivors

ISBN 0-374-39997-2; 978-0-374-39997-9; 0-374-50001-0 (pa); 978-0-374-50001-6 (pa)

    LC 2005-936797

Original French edition, 1958

This is "the autobiographical account of an adolescent boy and his father in Auschwitz. Wiesel writes of their battle for survival, and of his battle with God for a way to understand the wanton cruelty he witnesses each day." Publisher's note

Williams, Roger, 1604?-1683

Gaustad, Edwin Scott. Roger Williams; prophet of liberty; {by} Edwin S. Gaustad. Oxford Univ. Press 2000 139p il maps (Oxford portraits) $28

Grades: 7 8 9 10   **92**

1. Puritans 2. United States—History—1600-1775, Colonial period

ISBN 0-19-513000-6   LC 00-56675

"Gaustad recounts Williams's life and identifies his contribution to the concept of religious liberty. His lively prose never transgresses scholarly limits, but makes the most of the few biographical details available. . . . The author makes excellent use of primary-source excerpts." SLJ

Includes bibliographical references

Wilson, Woodrow, 1856-1924

Lukes, Bonnie L. Woodrow Wilson and the Progressive Era. Morgan Reynolds 2005 192p il lib bdg $26.95

Grades: 7 8 9 10   **92**

1. Presidents—United States 2. United States—Politics and government—1898-1919

ISBN 978-1-93179-879-2; 1-93179-879-6

    LC 2005-15999

"This well-documented, chronological account begins with Wilson's birth in 1856, describes his varied careers, and continues through his death in 1924. . . . The author describes the intense political conflicts of the time, mostly concerning Americas involvement in World War I and then in the League of Nations. Lukes's approach is balanced. . . . Good-quality, full-color and black-and-white photos and reproductions appear throughout." SLJ

Includes bibliographical references

Winthrop, John, 1588-1649

Aronson, Marc. John Winthrop, Oliver Cromwell, and the Land of Promise. Clarion Books 2004 205p il map $20

Grades: 7 8 9 10   92

1. Cromwell, Oliver, 1599-1658 2. Puritans 3. Massachusetts—History—1600-1775, Colonial period 4. Great Britain—History—1603-1714, Stuarts

ISBN 0-618-18177-6   LC 2003-16418

"The accessible text is accompanied by excerpts from primary source documents and vivid illustrations. The author's passion for the period comes across in his writing. Aronson provides an excellent source for historical and biographical data." Voice Youth Advocates

Includes bibliographical references

Wolff, Tobias, 1945-

Wolff, Tobias. This boy's life: a memoir. Atlantic Monthly Press 1989 288p hardcover o.p. pa $14 *

Grades: 11 12 Adult   92

1. Authors, American

ISBN 0-871-13248-6; 0-8021-3668-0 (pa)

LC 88-17600

The novelist and short story writer "offers an engrossing and candid look into his childhood and adolescence in his first book of nonfiction. In unaffected prose he recreates scenes from his life that sparkle with the immediacy of narrative fiction. The result is an intriguingly guileless book, distinct from the usual reflective commentary of autobiography." Libr J

Woolf, Virginia, 1882-1941

Brackett, Virginia. Restless genius; the story of Virginia Woolf. Morgan Reynolds Pub 2004 144p il (World writers) lib bdg $24.95 *

Grades: 9 10 11 12   92

1. Authors, English

ISBN 1-931798-37-0   LC 2003-25043

This biography "begins with the people, events, and dynamics of Woolf's childhood, then quickly progresses to her adult life. Throughout, Brackett discusses in some detail the writer's relationships with her father, sister, husband, and, to a lesser extent, other relatives and members of the Bloomsbury group while focusing increasingly on her writings and her mental health." Booklist

Includes bibliographical references

Mills, Cliff. Virginia Woolf; introduction by Betty McCollum. Chelsea House Publishers 2004 130p il (Women in the arts) $22.95; pa $13.25

Grades: 9 10 11 12   92

1. Authors, English

ISBN 0-7910-7459-5; 0-7910-7953-8 (pa)

LC 2003-9505

Discusses the life and work of the twentieth-century English author, Virginia Woolf.

Woolf's "history is presented in an interesting manner as are the controversies that swirled around her. There are many color illustrations and pictures including insets giving more insight." Libr Media Connect

Includes bibliographical references

Wright, Orville, 1871-1948

Crouch, Tom D. The Wright brothers and the invention of the aerial age. See entry under Wright, Wilbur, 1867-1912

Freedman, Russell. The Wright brothers: how they invented the airplane; with original photographs by Wilbur and Orville Wright. Holiday House 1991 129p il hardcover o.p. pa $14.94 *

Grades: 5 6 7 8 9 10   92

1. Wright, Wilbur, 1867-1912 2. Aeronautics—History

ISBN 0-8234-0875-2; 0-8234-1082-X (pa)

LC 90-48440

A Newbery Medal honor book, 1992

In this "combination of photography and text, Freedman reveals the frustrating, exciting, and ultimately successful journey of these two brothers from their bicycle shop in Dayton, Ohio, to their Kitty Hawk flights and beyond. . . . An essential purchase for younger YAs." Voice Youth Advocates

Includes bibliographical references

Wright, Orville. How we invented the airplane; an illustrated history; edited with an introduction and commentary by Fred C. Kelly; additional text by Alan Weissman. Dover Publs. 1988 c1953 87p il pa $9.95 *

Grades: 11 12 Adult   92

1. Wright, Wilbur, 1867-1912 2. Aeronautics—History

ISBN 0-486-25662-6   LC 87-33037

First published 1953 by D. McKay

This "account by the two inventors . . . covers experiments, discovery of aeronautical principles, construction of planes and motors, first flights, and much more. Also included is a later account written by both brothers." Publisher's note

Includes bibliographical references

Wright, Richard, 1908-1960

Wright, Richard. Black boy; (American hunger): a record of childhood and youth; foreword by Edward P. Jones. 60th anniversary ed., 1st ed. HarperCollinsPublishers 2005 419p $24.95; pa $14.95

Grades: 11 12 Adult   92

1. African American authors 2. African Americans—Social conditions

ISBN   0-06-083400-5;   978-0-06-083400-5; 0-06-113024-9 (pa); 978-0-06-113024-3 (pa)

LC 2005-52698

First published 1945 by World Publishing Company

"The restored text established by the Library of America"

This autobiographical work concludes with Wright "newly arrived in Chicago in 1927 as a fugitive from the white South that never knew him. [It] relates his nomadic life in Tennessee, Arkansas, and Mississippi, abandoned by his father and with his mother working at menial jobs or incapacitated by illness." Benet's Reader's Ency of Am Lit

Includes bibliographical references

Wright, Wilbur, 1867-1912

Crouch, Tom D. The Wright brothers and the invention of the aerial age; {by} Tom D. Crouch and Peter L. Jakab. National Geographic Soc. 2003 240p il $35

Grades: 11 12 Adult **92**

1. Wright, Orville, 1871-1948 2. Aeronautics—History

ISBN 0-7922-6985-3   LC 2002-44924

Crouch and Jakab "trace the brothers' lives from their early years in Dayton, Ohio, and the events leading up to the invention of the airplane. . . . With 100 archival photographs, this work offers the most comprehensive portrait of these ingenious brothers yet written." Booklist

Includes bibliographical references

Freedman, Russell. The Wright brothers: how they invented the airplane. See entry under Wright, Orville, 1871-1948

Wright, Orville. How we invented the airplane. See entry under Wright, Orville, 1871-1948

Wyeth, Andrew, 1917-

Wyeth, Andrew. Andrew Wyeth, autobiography; introduction by Thomas Hoving; with commentaries by Andrew Wyeth. Little, Brown 1995 168p il hardcover o.p. pa $29.95

Grades: 11 12 Adult **92**

1. Artists—United States

ISBN 0-8212-2159-0; 0-8212-2569-3 (pa)

LC 94-48305

"A Bulfinch Press book"

Published "in association with the Nelson-Atkins Museum of Art."

Published in conjunction with a retrospective exhibit, this book reproduces 137 paintings. "Each painting is accompanied by commentary from the artist that lends insight into his life and character. Several nude studies are included." Booklist

Includes bibliographical references

Yamazaki, James N., 1916-

Yamazaki, James N. Children of the atomic bomb; an American physician's memoir of Nagasaki, Hiroshima, and the Marshall Islands; {by} James N. Yamazaki with Louis B. Fleming. Duke Univ. Press 1995 182p il maps (Asia-Pacific) $21.95 *

Grades: 11 12 Adult **92**

1. Physicians 2. Atomic bomb victims 3. Japanese Americans

ISBN 0-8223-1658-7   LC 95-6683

"An army surgeon who was captured at the Battle of the Bulge, Yamazaki practiced pediatrics after the war. In this . . . memoir, he recalls his enlistment in the official commission investigating the casualities inflicted by the Nagasaki explosion." Booklist

The author "describes the incredible destruction of lives and buildings, cooperation from Japanese officials and health care personnel (doctors, nurses, midwives), firsthand reports from survivors, and the medical studies of pregnancies and short- and long-term effects on children. . . . This autobiography is unique in the history of this genre." Choice

Includes bibliographical references

Yeager, Chuck, 1923-

Yeager, Chuck. Yeager; an autobiography; {by} Chuck Yeager & Leo Janos. Bantam Bks. 1985 342p il hardcover o.p. pa $7.99

Grades: 11 12 Adult **92**

1. Air pilots

ISBN 0-553-05093-1; 0-553-25674-2 (pa)

LC 85-3959

Yeager "describes his early life in the hills of West Virginia; his years as fighter pilot in World War II, where he was shot down in occupied France and escaped with the help of the French Resistance. . . . He tells his story vividly and pulls no punches in describing the events and the people who made history with him." SLJ

Zaharias, Babe Didrikson, 1911-1956

Cayleff, Susan E. Babe: the life and legend of Babe Didrikson Zaharias. University of Ill. Press 1995 327p il (Women in American history) $29.95; pa $15.95

Grades: 11 12 Adult **92**

1. Women athletes

ISBN 0-252-01793-5; 0-252-06593-X (pa)

LC 94-35584

The author "presents a feminist analysis of the life, sports career, and legacy of Mildred Ella 'Babe' Didrikson Zaharias. . . . Cayleff examines Babe's amateur athletic career from high school through the 1932 Olympics, as well as her professional and amateur golf accomplishments. . . . Although it will undoubtedly be controversial, *Babe* is a very important book about a unique and significant figure in US sports." Choice

Includes bibliographical references

Freedman, Russell. Babe Didrikson Zaharias; the making of a champion. Clarion Bks. 1999 192p il $18

Grades: 5 6 7 8 9 10 **92**

1. Women athletes

ISBN 0-395-63367-2   LC 98-50208

A biography of Babe Didrikson, who broke records in golf, track and field, and other sports, at a time when there were few opportunities for female athletes

"Freedman's measured yet lively style captures the spirit of the great athlete. . . . Plenty of black-and-white photos capture Babe's spirit and dashing good looks; the documentation . . . is impeccable." Horn Book

Includes bibliographical references

Zenatti, Valérie, 1970-

Zenatti, Valérie. When I was a soldier; a memoir; translated by Adriana Hunter. Bloomsbury Children's Books 2005 235p $16.95

Grades: 7 8 9 10 **92**

1. Women soldiers 2. Israel

ISBN 1-58234-978-9

In this "memoir, Zenatti, first among her group of friends to be called for compulsory military service, chronicles two years of growing up in the Israeli army between 1988 and 1990." SLJ

A "fast, wry, present-tense memoir. . . . Readers on all sides of the war-peace continuum, here and there, will find much to talk about." Booklist

929   Genealogy, names, insignia

Shepherdson, Nancy

Ancestor hunt; finding your family online. Franklin Watts 2003 144p il, maps $29.50 *

Grades: 9 10 11 12   **929**

1. Genealogy

ISBN 0-531-15454-8   LC 2002-11646

Contents: The ancestry mystery : are you related to someone famous?; Collecting clues : what does your family say?; Get a net : is great-grandma hiding online?; Tell the world : you've got mail!; Tracking ancestors : where did they come from?; The value of off-line searching : digging for proof; Were your ancestors soldiers, farmers, rich? finding the threads of their lives; Share it! your family history home page; Happy trails! having fun with your ancestors

This "volume shows you how to search your family history by using the Internet. Although you usually start by interviewing your older relatives, Shepherdson shows you how to take these clues and use them in various Internet sites and links. She also gives you things to avoid and tips for doing the interviews. . . . This book is so chock full of information that you will be returning to it constantly as you search for your family ancestry." Libr Media Connect

Includes bibliographical references

Smith, Franklin Carter, 1954-

A genealogist's guide to discovering your African-American ancestors; how to find and record your unique heritage; {by} Franklin Carter Smith and Emily Anne Croom. Betterway Bks. 2003 250p il pa $21.99 *

Grades: 11 12 Adult   **929**

1. Genealogy 2. African Americans

ISBN 1-55870-605-4   LC 2002-152014

"The book provides a three-part approach to researching family history. Part 1 covers the post-Civil War era to the present, showing readers how to search census records and oral histories. Part 2 focuses on pre-Civil War research, and part 3 offers case studies of how three African American families traced their ancestry. . . . This book, which includes outlines, maps and other materials to assist in research, will be greatly appreciated by black readers searching for their family roots." Booklist

Includes bibliographical references

929.4   Personal names

Dictionary of American family names; Patrick Hanks, editor. Oxford Univ. Press 2003 3v set $295 *

Grades: 11 12 Adult   **929.4**

1. Personal names—United States

ISBN 0-19-508137-4   LC 2003-3844

This is a "guide to 70,000 of the most frequently found surnames in the United States. Based on an 88.7 million-name sample culled from a commercial telephone database, the entries indicate the frequency of the name within the sample, plus an explanation of the name."

Libr J

"This set will be useful for genealogists, historians, and others curious about their family roots." SLJ

Includes bibliographical references

Hanks, Patrick

A concise dictionary of first names; {by} Patrick Hanks and Flavia Hodges. 3rd ed. Oxford Univ. Press 2001 314p pa $12.95 *

Grades: 9 10 11 12   **929.4**

1. Personal names

ISBN 0-19-866259-9

First published 1992 in the United Kingdom

This volume includes "answers to . . . the meanings and histories of names, how they have risen or fallen in popularity, and who the famous bearers of the names are from history, fiction, and the screen. Detailed appendix material includes European, Arabic, and Indian names." Publisher's note

Room, Adrian

Dictionary of first names. New ed. Cassell 2002 368p pa $14.95

Grades: 11 12 Adult   **929.4**

1. Personal names—Dictionaries

ISBN 0-304-36226-3

First published 1995

Cover title: Cassell's dictionary of first names

This offers information about more than 2000 personal names, including definitions, origin, history, and development, people real and fictional who shared particular names and lists the top five personal names given to children each year over the past 50 years

929.9   Flags

Druckman, Nancy

American flags; designs for a young nation; with commentaries by Jeffrey Kenneth Kohn. Abrams 2003 79p il $16.95

Grades: 9 10 11 12   **929.9**

1. Flags—United States

ISBN 0-8109-4506-1   LC 2002-152403

"The more than 60 flags that fill these pages include many variations and interpretations of the Stars and Stripes. Standardization did not occur until 1912." SLJ

"Here's a handsome, well-designed guide to American flag history, illustrated with many excellent photos of flags from different periods. . . . The book is accessible and useful to history students; flag collectors and illustrators will also find it quite informative." Booklist

Leepson, Marc, 1945-

Flag: an American biography. Thomas Dunne Books/St. Martin's Press 2005 334p il $24.95; pa $14.95

Grades: 11 12 Adult   **929.9**

1. Flags—United States

ISBN 978-0-312-32308-0; 0-312-32308-5; 978-0-312-32309-7 (pa); 0-312-32309-3 (pa)

     LC 2004-65920

Leepson, Marc, 1945-—*Continued*

"Chronicling the two-centuries-plus history of the U.S. flag, Leepson considers the abundant stories that purport to be the truth about Old Glory." Booklist

"From reverence to kitsch, Americans' attitudes to their flag and its mythology have changed over the years, and Leepson does a creditable job of recounting those changes." Publ Wkly
Includes bibliographical references

Schneider, Richard H.

Stars & stripes forever; the history, stories, and memories of our American flag. Morrow 2003 192p il $14.95 *

Grades: 11 12 Adult   **929.9**
1. Flags—United States
ISBN 0-06-052537-1   LC 2002-43213

"Beginning with a brief history of banners and flags in general, the author traces the historical roots of the American flag and its subsequent evolution into one of the most potent and inspiring symbols of freedom and democracy in the modern world. In addition to analyzing myths, legends, and facts associated with the Stars and Stripes, he includes a host of flag-related trivia and a number of touching personal anecdotes written by celebrities, soldiers, and ordinary American citizens." Booklist

Shearer, Benjamin F.

State names, seals, flags, and symbols; a historical guide. 3rd ed, rev and expanded. Greenwood Press 2001 495p il $73.95

Grades: 11 12 Adult   **929.9**
1. Geographic names—United States 2. Seals (Numismatics) 3. Flags—United States
ISBN 0-313-31534-5   LC 2001-23525
First published 1987

"Chapters on mottoes, flowers, trees, birds, songs, holidays, and license plates are just a sampling of what is covered, and the format is such that the concisely written material can be found as expeditiously as possible. Even though the book is touted predominantly as a reference tool, the information provided makes fascinating and enlightening reading." Libr J {review of 1994 edition}
Includes bibliographical references

930   History of ancient world to ca.499

Encyclopedia of the ancient world; editor, Thomas J. Sienkewicz. Salem Press 2002 3v il maps set $341

Grades: 11 12 Adult   **930**
1. Ancient civilization—Encyclopedias
ISBN 0-89356-038-3   LC 2001-49896
Contents: v1 Overviews, 'Abd al-Malik-Corinthian War; v2 Coriolanus, Gnaeus Marcius-Pharsalus, Battle of; v3 Phidias-Zurvanism indexes

This reference work encompasses "not only Greece and Rome but also 'the civilizations, cultures, traditions, monuments and artifacts, significant wars and battles, and important personages of the rest of the world: Europe (outside Greece and Rome), Africa, the Americas,

Asia, and Oceania.' The time span is from prehistory to approximately 700 C.E." Booklist
Includes bibliographical references

Great events from history, The ancient world, prehistory-476 C.E.; editor, Mark W. Chavalas; consulting editors, Mark S. Aldenderfer . . . [et al.] Salem Press 2004 2v il map set $160

Grades: 11 12 Adult   **930**
1. Ancient history
ISBN 1-58765-155-6; 978-1-58765-155-7
                                LC 2004-1360
Companion volume to Great lives from history, The ancient world, prehistory-476 C.E.

Some essays previously published in Great events from history (1972-1980), Chronology of European history, 15,000 B.C. to 1997 (1997), and Great events from history, North American series (1997)

"Articles are arranged chronologically, beginning around 25,000 B.C.E. with the San Peoples, who created the first discernible art in Africa, and ends on September 4, 476 C.E. with the fall of Rome, when the last Roman emperor, Romulus Augustulus, was deposed. Articles cover the entire world, with special attention paid to non-European areas. . . . All articles maintain the same structure and give the locale of the event, its category, a summary of the event, its significance, an annotated list of further readings, and cross references to related events." Ref & User Services Quarterly
Includes bibliographical references

Obregón, Mauricio

Beyond the edge of the sea; sailing with Jason and the Argonauts, Ulysses, the Vikings, and other explorers of the Ancient World. Random House 2001 132p il maps hardcover o.p. pa $11.95

Grades: 11 12 Adult   **930**
1. Explorers 2. Ancient geography
ISBN 0-679-46326-7; 0-679-78344-X (pa)
                                LC 00-27173
Obregón "writes of Jason, Ulysses, Far Eastern peoples, and the Vikings. He gives . . . maps of sites possibly visited by these travelers and discusses the difficulties and challenges facing the explorers. . . . He writes about the way such sailors must have navigated and describes the ships they sailed in." Sci Books Films

"Sweeping in scope . . . this book offers several surprisingly provocative and plausible conclusions. . . . The fascinating history of the sea, its mythic and historical figures, and the boats that changed the world are brought into a fresh and interesting perspective." Booklist
Includes bibliographical references

Skelton, Debra

Empire of Alexander the Great; [by] Debra Skelton and Pamela Dell. Facts on File 2005 128p il map (Great empires of the past) $35

Grades: 9 10 11 12   **930**
1. Alexander, the Great, 356-323 B.C. 2. Greece—History
ISBN 0-8160-5564-5   LC 2004-56430
This book "looks at what made Alexander a brilliant military tactician and a charismatic leader. It also ex-

Skelton, Debra—*Continued*

plores what the Eastern world learned through contact with Alexander, and what Alexander brought the West from the Persian Empire." Publisher's note

Includes bibliographical references

Starr, Chester G., 1914-

A history of the ancient world. 4th ed. Oxford Univ. Press 1991 742p il maps $49.95 *

Grades: 11 12 Adult 930

1. Ancient history

ISBN 0-19-506629-4 LC 90-34970

First published 1965

Incorporating recent archaeological and anthropological discoveries, the author surveys the changing economic and social structures of societies, from prehistory to the fifth century A.D. Egyptian, Assyrian, Chinese and Greek are among the civilizations discussed

Includes bibliographical references

930.1 Archaeology

Ceram, C. W., 1915-1972

Gods, graves, and scholars; the story of archaeology; translated from the German by E. B. Garside and Sophie Wilkins. 2nd rev and substantially enl ed. Knopf 1967 441p il maps pa $11.16 hardcover o.p.

Grades: 11 12 Adult 930.1

1. Archeology

ISBN 0-394-74319-9 (pa)

Original German edition, 1949; first English language edition, 1951

"The story of Champollion and the reading of the Rosetta Stone, the decipherment of the inscriptions on the monument of Darius the Great, Leonard Woolley's famous excavations at Ur, and John Lloyd Stephens' discovery of the ruins of a great Mayan city are . . . told in this book." Doors to More Mature Read

Includes bibliographical references

Encyclopedia of underwater and maritime archaeology; edited by James P. Delgado. Yale Univ. Press 1998 493p il $75

Grades: 11 12 Adult 930.1

1. Underwater exploration—Encyclopedias

ISBN 0-300-07427-1 LC 97-61536

First published 1997 in the United Kingdom with title: British Museum encyclopaedia of underwater and maritime archaeology

"The volume's 450 alphabetically arranged entries cover sites from prehistory to the modern era (including *Titanic*), legislation and legal issues, organizations, nations and regions, research themes, and technology and techniques. . . . More than 100 illustrations in color are complemented by more than 200 black-and-white drawings and photos." Booklist

Includes bibliographical references

The **Oxford** companion to archaeology; editor in chief, Brian M. Fagan; editors, Charlotte Beck {et al.}. Oxford Univ. Press 1996 xx, 844p il maps $75 *

Grades: 11 12 Adult 930.1

ISBN 0-19-507618-4 LC 96-30792

"In addition to broad discussions of specific civilizations such as Islamic, Olmec, and African, there are entries on theories (post processual), ethics, processes (lithics), dating techniques, pop culture (archaeology in film and television), specific sites and site management, plantation archaeology, and human evolution." Booklist

931 China to 420 A.D.

Hardy, Grant

The establishment of the Han empire and imperial China; [by] Grant Hardy and Anne Behnke Kinney. Greenwood Press 2005 xxx, 170p il (Greenwood guides to historic events of the ancient world) $45

Grades: 9 10 11 12 931

1. China—History

ISBN 0-313-32588-X LC 2004-22475

Contents: The establishment of the Han empire: an overview -- The center and the periphery -- Technological innovation and empire -- Social change in Han times -- Imperial China in world history -- Biographies -- Primary documents

This "is a promising eastward expansion of this series on the ancient world." SLJ

Includes bibliographical references

Kleeman, Terry F., 1955-

The ancient Chinese world; [by] Terry Kleeman & Tracy Barrett. Oxford University Press 2005 174p il map (World in ancient times) $32.95

Grades: 7 8 9 10 931

1. China—History

ISBN 0-19-517102-0 LC 2004-14408

This book "uses primary sources to describe the history of ancient China and how it still influences the lives of billions of people today." Publisher's note

"Readers seriously interested in history, in archaeology—or in China—will be well served by this engrossing book." SLJ

Includes bibliographical references

932 Egypt to 640 A.D.

Ancient Egypt; general editor, David P. Silverman. Oxford Univ. Press 1997 256p il maps hardcover o.p. pa $21.50

Grades: 11 12 Adult 932

1. Egypt—Civilization

ISBN 0-19-521270-3; 0-19-521952-X (pa)

LC 96-37171

"Twelve contributing scholars have joined Silverman in writing this . . . book that contains 200 color photographs, maps, and charts. Their essays cover such . . .

Ancient Egypt—*Continued*

subjects as history, geography, legends, archaeology, religion, economy, art, architecture, and language. There are pieces on international trade and travel, farming, hunting, fishing, mining, capital cities, palaces, fortresses, gender and society, mathematics, medicine, magic, the pharaohs, the cosmos, the cult of the dead, ritual games, the pyramids, tombs, temples, the solar cycle, and hieroglyphs." Booklist

Includes glossary and bibliographical references

Baker, Rosalie F.

Ancient Egyptians; people of the pyramids; {by} Rosalie F. and Charles F. Baker. Oxford Univ. Press 2001 189p il maps (Oxford profiles) $50

Grades: 7 8 9 10   932
   1. Egypt—Civilization 2. Egypt—Biography
   ISBN 0-19-512221-6   LC 2001-21209
   "Divided into five periods from the Old Kingdom, about 2686 B.C., to the declining New Kingdom, about 245 B.C., this book profiles some 30 Egyptian leaders, devoting a three- to seven-page chapter to each one. . . . The entries are well written and researched. . . . A useful addition for report writers and subject enthusiasts." SLJ

Includes glossary and bibliographical references

Brier, Bob

The murder of Tutankhamen; a true story. Berkley Books 2005 xx, 264p il pa $14

Grades: 11 12 Adult   932
   1. Tutankhamen, King of Egypt 2. Egypt—History
   ISBN 0-425-20690-4; 978-0-425-20690-4
                                   LC 2005-41085
   First published 1998 by Putnam
   By "combining known historical events with evidence gathered by advanced technologies, Brier has recreated the suspenseful story of religious upheaval and political intrigue that likely resulted in the murder of the teenage King Tutankhamen." Booklist
   "Brier obviously knows his subject and is impassioned by it. Readers who enjoy history or true-crime stories will be intrigued by this work." SLJ

Includes bibliographical references

Bunson, Margaret R.

Encyclopedia of ancient Egypt. rev ed. Facts on File 2002 462p il maps $70 *

Grades: 11 12 Adult   932
   1. Egypt—Civilization—Encyclopedias
   ISBN 0-8160-4563-1   LC 2002-3550
   First published 1991
   This work consists of "alphabetically arranged entries covering Egypt from around 3200 B.C. to the fall of the New Kingdom in 1070 B.C. There are several broad entries such as *Egypt, Agriculture, and Religion*. The bulk of the book, however, consists of specific entries for kings and queens, gods and goddesses, cities, important documents, etc." Booklist [review of 1991 edition]

Casson, Lionel, 1914-

Everyday life in ancient Egypt. rev and expanded ed. Johns Hopkins Univ. Press 2001 163p il hardcover o.p. pa $15.95

Grades: 9 10 11 12   932
   1. Egypt—Civilization
   ISBN 0-8018-6600-6; 0-8018-6601-4 (pa)
                                   LC 00-59091
   First published 1975 by American Heritage Pub. with title: The Horizon book of daily life in ancient Egypt
   The author describes the structure of ancient Egyptian society including social classes, family, the role of women, farm life, leisure, the professions and craftsmen, religion, and travel.

Includes bibliographical references

David, A. Rosalie (Ann Rosalie)

Handbook to life in ancient Egypt; [by] Rosalie David. rev ed. Facts on File 2003 417p il maps (Facts on File library of world history) $50 *

Grades: 11 12 Adult   932
   1. Egypt—Civilization
   ISBN 0-8160-5034-1   LC 2002-35229
   First published 1998
   This covers such topics as the geography of Ancient Egypt, society and government, religion, funerary beliefs and customs, architecture, trade and transport, the army and navy, economy and industry, and everyday life.

Includes bibliographical references

Hawass, Zahi A.

Tutankhamun and the golden age of the pharaohs; [by] Zahi Hawass; photographs by Kenneth Garrett. National Geographic Books 2005 285p il map $35

Grades: 11 12 Adult   932
   1. Tutankhamen, King of Egypt 2. Egypt—Antiquities
   ISBN 0-7922-3873-7   LC 2005-41678
   This companion to an exhibition displaying about 130 items found in the tombs of Tutankhamun and other kings from the same dynasty "describes the physical and symbolic attributes of each object and explains its purpose in the afterlife. . . . An arrestingly visual album destined for high demand." Booklist

Includes bibliographical references

Nardo, Don, 1947-

Arts, leisure, and sport in ancient Egypt. Lucent Books 2005 112p il map (Lucent library of historical eras, Ancient Egypt) $28.70

Grades: 7 8 9 10   932
   1. Egypt—Civilization 2. Egyptian art
   ISBN 1-59018-706-7   LC 2004030542
   Contents: Artistry in stone; Production of pottery and glass; Clothmaking and leatherworking; Working with metal and wood; Jewelry-making and painting; Writing and literature; Leisure games and sports; Hunting and fishing; Music, singing, and dancing
   "Quoting extensively from 19th- and 20th-century Egyptologists, as well as from available ancient sources, Nardo presents a great deal of information in a smooth narrative, accompanied by archival photographs and re-

Nardo, Don, 1947-—*Continued*
productions of artifacts, illustrations from the past century or so, and even scenes taken from films and documentaries." SLJ
Includes bibliographical references

Netzley, Patricia D.
The Greenhaven encyclopedia of ancient Egypt.
Greenhaven Press 2003 336p (Greenhaven encyclopedia of) $74.95
Grades: 8 9 10 11 12   **932**
1. Egypt—Antiquities—Encyclopedias
ISBN 0-7377-1150-7   LC 2002-6965
"Alphabetical entries range from prehistory to the time of Greco-Roman domination and are generally between a paragraph and a page in length. Coverage includes individual pharaohs, places, practices, trades, beliefs, artwork, and aspects of daily and family life with entries such as 'furniture,' 'children,' and 'entertaining guests.' Important individuals such as archaeologist Howard Carter are also included." SLJ
Includes bibliographical references

The **Oxford** encyclopedia of ancient Egypt;
Donald B. Redford, editor in chief. Oxford Univ. Press 2001 3v set $450 *
Grades: 11 12 Adult   **932**
1. Egypt—Civilization—Encyclopedias 2. Egypt—Antiquities—Encyclopedias
ISBN 0-19-510234-7   LC 99-54801
This reference work covers "archaeology, biography, history, language, social history, and more. . . . [It features] essays from more than 250 contributors from various countries and scholarly pursuits, all with solid academic credentials. . . . One is not likely to encounter another work of this magnitude on a subject of such universal interest for some time." Booklist
Includes bibliographical references

Taylor, John H.
Unwrapping a mummy; the life, death and embalming of Horemkenesi. University of Tex. Press 1996 111p il (Egyptian bookshelf) pa $18.95
Grades: 9 10 11 12   **932**
1. Horemkenesi 2. Mummies 3. Egypt—Civilization
ISBN 0-292-78141-5   LC 95-61446
An exploration of ancient Egyptian civilization based on the study of the mummy of Horemkenesi. Customs surrounding death and the process of mummification are discussed in detail
Includes bibliographical references

935 Mesopotamia and Iranian Plateau to 637 A.D.

Roaf, Michael
Cultural atlas of Mesopotamia and the ancient Near East. Facts on File 1990 238p il maps $45 *
Grades: 11 12 Adult   **935**
1. Iraq—Civilization 2. Middle East
ISBN 0-8160-2218-6   LC 90-3429

"An Equinox book"
This is a "study of the geography, history, archaeology, and anthropology of Mesopotamia and the Near East. . . . Special topics and archaeological sites are featured, described, and illustrated. Some of the topics include the origin of writing, ivory carving, and Mesopotamian warfare. . . . Excellent full-page maps and a wealth of full-color illustrations add to the reference value." SLJ
Includes glossary and bibliographical references

936 Europe north and west of Italian peninsula to ca. 499 A.D.

Cunliffe, Barry, 1939-
The ancient Celts. Penguin Books 1999 324p il map pa $21.95
Grades: 11 12 Adult   **936**
1. Celts
ISBN 0-14-025422-6
First published 1997 by Oxford Univ. Press
This is a "survey of the origins of the Celts and their expansion during the Iron Age through their largely successful subjection by the Romans. . . . [Cunliffe] has written a readable and informative book with many attractive illustrations." Libr J
Includes bibliographical references

936.1 Scotland to 410 A.D.

Burl, Aubrey
The stone circles of Britain, Ireland and Brittany. Yale Univ. Press 2000 462p il $60; pa $30
Grades: 9 10 11 12   **936.1**
1. Great Britain—Antiquities 2. Ireland—Antiquities
ISBN 0-300-08347-5; 0-300-11406-0 (pa)
LC 99-87909
First published 1976 with title: The stone circles of the British Isles
This describes the prehistoric stone circles built some 6000 years ago, such as Stonehenge in England, Callanish in Scotland and the cromlechs in Brittany, how and why they were constructed, and how they have been excavated and studied.
"Burl's authoritative book is indispensable for anyone pursuing this tantalizing enigma." Publ Wkly
Includes bibliographical references

937 Roman Empire

Adkins, Lesley
Handbook to life in ancient Rome; [by] Lesley Adkins and Roy A. Adkins. Updated ed. Facts on File 2004 450p il, maps (Facts on File library of world history) $85 *
Grades: 9 10 11 12   **937**
1. Rome—Civilization 2. Rome—Social life and customs
ISBN 0-8160-5026-0   LC 2003-49255
First published 1994

Adkins, Lesley—*Continued*

This work covers politics, military affairs, literature, religion, architecture, geography, and social life in ancient Rome from the 8th century B.C. to the 5th century A.D. Illustrated with site-specific photographs and line drawings.

Includes bibliographical references

Allan, Tony, 1946-

Life, myth, and art in Ancient Rome. J. Paul Getty Museum 2005 144p il pa $19.95 *

Grades: 11 12 Adult   **937**

1. Roman art 2. Roman mythology 3. Rome—Civilization 4. Rome—Antiquities

ISBN 0-89236-821-7   LC 2004-114326

This is an "illustrated guide to the cultural and political heritage of ancient Rome, including the enduring legacy of its art and architecture, the engineering innovations of its vast system of roads and aqueducts, the . . . myths of its gods and goddesses, and the power of its emperors and legions." Publisher's note

Includes bibliographical references

Baker, Rosalie F.

Ancient Romans; expanding the classical tradition; [by] Rosalie F. and Charles F. Baker III. Oxford Univ. Press 1998 267p il (Oxford profiles) $40

Grades: 9 10 11 12   **937**

1. Rome—History 2. Rome—Biography

ISBN 0-19-510884-1   LC 97-21531

"Drawing on the work of Plutarch, Livy, Tacitus, and Suetonius, the authors recount the history of Rome's rise to power through brief biographies of 39 notable Romans. The five periods covered span the years 400 B.C.E. to A.D. 350." SLJ

"Challenging reading, the book will best serve college-bound students with a basic knowledge of ancient Roman culture and history." Booklist

Includes glossary and bibliographical references

Bunson, Matthew

Encyclopedia of the Roman Empire. rev ed. Facts on File 2002 636p il maps $75 *

Grades: 11 12 Adult   **937**

ISBN 0-8160-4562-3   LC 2001-53253

First published 1994

This reference work provides information on the key places, people, events, and culture of Roman history, from the reign of Julius Caesar to the fall of the last Roman emperor in 476 A.D.

"An excellent ready-reference source." Booklist {review of 1994 edition}

Includes bibliographical references

Cambridge illustrated history of the Roman world; edited by Greg Woolf. Cambridge University Press 2003 384p il map (Cambridge illustrated history) $45

Grades: 11 12 Adult   **937**

1. Rome—History

ISBN 0-521-82775-2   LC 2004-298480

Contents: Discovering ancient Rome—Greg Woolf; The republic— Christopher S. Mackay; The emperors — David Potter; An imperial people— Greg Woolf; Rome and Greece— Greg Woolf; Domination—Emma Dench; An imperial metropolis—Jon Coulston & Hazel Dodge; The empire of letters—Simon Swain; An empire of cities—Penelope M. Allison; Knowledge and empire—Rebecca Flemming; The gods of empire—Richard Lim; The profits of empire—Neville Morley; War and peace—Ian Haynes

This book explores such topics as "religion, Rome's relationship with Greece, warfare and Empire, and science and culture." Publisher's note

Includes bibliographical references

Connolly, Peter, 1935-

The ancient city; life in classical Athens & Rome; [by] Peter Connolly, Hazel Dodge. Oxford Univ. Press 1998 256p il maps $35; pa $21.95 *

Grades: 11 12 Adult   **937**

1. Classical civilization 2. Rome—Civilization 3. Athens (Greece) 4. Greece—Civilization

ISBN 0-19-917242-0; 0-19-521582-6 (pa)

LC 98-201131

The authors "focus specifically on city life in two 'golden ages' of ancient times: Athens in fifth-century B.C. and Rome in second-century A.D. [They] place each city in its historical and geographical perspective, and then highlight how people really lived in those times and places. Detailed color drawings, cutaways, photographs, and maps make this an extremely useful as well as an outstandingly attractive book." Voice Youth Advocates

Includes bibliographical references

Davis, William Stearns, 1877-1930

A day in old Rome; a picture of Roman life. Biblo & Tannen 1959 xxiv, 482p il maps hardcover o.p. pa $25

Grades: 9 10 11 12   **937**

1. Rome—Social life and customs 2. Rome—Civilization

ISBN 0-8196-1206-5; 0-8196-0106-3 (pa)

A reprint of the title first published 1925 by Allyn

Depicts the daily life and customs of Roman civilization, including government, religion, games, courts and orators, country life, and occupations.

The **End** of ancient Rome; Don Nardo, book editor. Greenhaven Press 2000 208p il maps (Turning points in world history) lib bdg $31.20

Grades: 9 10 11 12   **937**

1. Rome—History

ISBN 0-7377-0372-5 (lib bdg)   LC 00-25740

"The book is divided into three broad chapters, each with four to six articles excerpted from books. The first group discusses Rome's ability to recover temporarily from its 'near demise' in the third century and its rule under Emperors Diocletian and Constantine I; the second, the disintegration of the empire in the West and the threats and attacks from the Huns and Vandals. The final section examines the many other factors that contributed to Rome's decline including a failing economy, poor

The End of ancient Rome—*Continued*

leadership, internal and external military threats, and the rise of Christianity." SLJ

Includes bibliographical references

Ermatinger, James William, 1959-

The decline and fall of the Roman Empire; [by] James W. Ermatinger. Greenwood Press 2004 xxxi, 187p il map (Greenwood guides to historic events of the ancient world) $45

Grades: 9 10 11 12   **937**

1. Rome—History

ISBN 0-313-32692-4   LC 2004-14674

"An overview of the period is presented in the introduction, and is followed by chapters on late Roman culture, society, and economics in late antiquity; religious conflicts in Christian Rome; enemies of Rome; and why and when Rome fell. The narrative chapters conclude with a section placing Rome's fall in modern perspective." Publisher's note

Includes bibliographical references

938   Greece to 323 A.D.

Adkins, Lesley

Handbook to life in ancient Greece; [by] Lesley Adkins and Roy A. Adkins. Updated ed. Facts on File 2005 514p il map (Facts on File library of world history) $70 *

Grades: 11 12 Adult   **938**

1. Greece—Civilization

ISBN 0-8160-5659-5   LC 2004-47105

First published 1997

This book covers "all aspects of ancient Greek life—from the beginnings of the Minoan civilization in Crete to the final defeat by the Roman world in 30 BCE." Publisher's note

Includes bibliographical references

Baker, Rosalie F.

Ancient Greeks; creating the classical tradition; {by} Rosalie F. Baker and Charles F. Baker. Oxford Univ. Press 1997 254p il maps (Oxford profiles) $50

Grades: 7 8 9 10   **938**

1. Greece—Biography 2. Greece—Civilization

ISBN 0-19-509940-0   LC 95-26637

"The influence of ancient Greek civilization is chronicled in concise biographies of over 37 Greek statesmen, playwrights, artists, mathematicians, philosophers, and military leaders." Book Rep

"Students looking for biographical or historical information on ancient Greece will find it valuable, as will teachers seeking to integrate the classics into other disciplines." Booklist

Includes glossary and bibliographical references

Classical Greece and Rome; Don Nardo, book editor. Greenhaven Press 2002 287p il maps (World history by era) hardcover o.p. pa $27.45

Grades: 9 10 11 12   **938**

1. Classical civilization 2. Ancient civilization

ISBN 0-7377-0578-7; 0-7377-0577-9 (pa)

LC 2001-16157

This study of the classical world that lasted from about 500 B.C. to A.D. 500 details "how the Greeks and Romans gained control of the Mediterranean world." Publisher's note

Includes bibliographical references

Classical Greek civilization, 800-323 B.C.E; edited by John T. Kirby. Gale Group 2001 xxxi, 395p il maps (World eras) $99

Grades: 11 12 Adult   **938**

1. Greece—Civilization

ISBN 0-7876-1707-5   LC 00-47648

"A Manly, Inc. book"

"The volume is divided into 10 topical chapters, among them 'The Arts,' 'Social Class System and the Economy,' 'The Family and Social Trends,' and 'Religion and Philosophy.' . . . Except for chapter one, 'World Events,' which provides context with a list of events outside Greece, each chapter follows the same general plan. A chronology and an overview precede a series of articles on various topics. . . . These articles generally range in length from two to four pages and are followed by biographical profiles." Booklist

This book's "comprehensive coverage of the entire classical Greek period makes it a valuable addition for your library's ancient history collection." Book Rep

Includes glossary and bibliographical references

Tritle, Lawrence A., 1946-

The Peloponnesian War; [by] Lawrence Tritle. Greenwood Press 2005 xxiv, 206p il map (Greenwood guides to historic events of the ancient world) $45

Grades: 9 10 11 12   **938**

1. Greece—History—431-404 B.C., Peloponnesian War

ISBN 0-313-32499-9   LC 2004-47506

This book features "biographical sketches, and annotated primary documents. An overview of the war is presented, followed by a presentation of Thucydides' account of the war's causes. A look at the intertwined . . . relation of democracy and empire is offered, as are chapters on how the war was represented in plays, statuary, and pottery." Publisher's note

Includes bibliographical references

Williams, Jean Kinney

Empire of ancient Greece; [by] Jean Williams. Facts on File 2005 128p il map (Great empires of the past) $35

Grades: 9 10 11 12   **938**

1. Greece—History—0-323 2. Greece—Civilization

ISBN 0-8160-5561-0   LC 2004-24952

This book "chronicles the remarkable legacy of the Greeks, as well as the diversity of their societies—from

Williams, Jean Kinney—*Continued*
the thriving democracy of Athens to the militarism of Sparta to the oligarchy of Thrace. . . . The book also looks at everyday life in ancient Greece, from the wealthy citizens who grappled in the Olympic arena to the farmers who found 50 different ways to use olive oil." Publisher's note
Includes bibliographical references

Wood, Michael, 1948-
In the footsteps of Alexander the Great; a journey from Greece to Asia. University of Calif. Press 1997 256p il maps hardcover o.p. pa $18.95 *
Grades: 11 12 Adult   **938**
1. Alexander, the Great, 356-323 B.C. 2. Historic sites 3. Asia—Description and travel
ISBN 0-520-21307-6; 0-520-23192-9 (pa)
LC 97-19188
Based on the PBS series, this "book recreates Alexander's 22,000 mile, ten-year expedition from Greece to India, following as much as possible the actual route of his journey." Publisher's note
This book is "illustrated with a mixture of Alexandrine art from a variety of cultures, landscapes that capture the wide range of geographies through which Alexander and his imperial armies passed, and portraits of cultures . . . in which the influence of that long-ago juggernaut is still visible." Booklist
Includes bibliographical references

938.003   Classical dictionaries

Ancient Greece; edited by Thomas J. Sienkewicz. Salem Press 2007 3v il map (Magill's choice) set $207
Grades: 11 12 Adult   **938.003**
1. Greece—History—Encyclopedias
ISBN 1-58765-281-1; 978-1-58765-281-3
LC 2006-16525
Some of the essays in this work appeared in various other Salem Press sets
This is a "comprehensive examination of Greek civilization and its impact on Western history, 'from its earliest archaeological remains until the Battle of Actium in 31 B.C.E.' . . . [The essays included] cover art, daily life and customs, government, literature, medicine and science, war, the role of women, and mythology. Biographical entries profile statesmen, artists, writers, scientists, and philosophers, and relevant entries probe battles, philosophical movements, and types of literature." SLJ
Includes bibliographical references

The **Cambridge** dictionary of classical civilization; edited by Graham Shipley . . . [et al.] Cambridge University Press 2006 xliv, 966p il map $180 *
Grades: 11 12 Adult   **938.003**
1. Classical civilization—Dictionaries
ISBN 0-521-48313-1; 978-0-521-48313-1
LC 2006-299203
The "entries and more than 500 illustrations focus on social, economic, and cultural aspects of these civiliza-

tions from the mid-eighth century BCE to the end of the fifth century." Booklist
Includes bibliographical references

The **Oxford** classical dictionary; edited by Simon Hornblower and Antony Spawforth. 3rd rev ed. Oxford Univ. Press 2003 lv, 1640p $110 *
Grades: 11 12 Adult   **938.003**
1. Classical dictionaries
ISBN 0-19-860641-9
First published 1949 under the editorship of M. Cary and others
This reference includes over 6,000 entries about the ancient Greco-Roman world, covering such topics as politics, government and economy, religion and mythology, law and philosophy, science and geography, languages, literature, art and architecture, archeology, historical writing, military history, social history, sex, and gender
"This is a work that makes a fascinating world of learning accessible to a broad audience." Booklist
Includes bibliographical references

Sacks, David
Encyclopedia of the ancient Greek world; editorial consultant, Oswyn Murray; revised by Lisa R. Brody. Rev ed. Facts on File 2005 xx, 412p il map (Facts on File library of world history) $75
Grades: 11 12 Adult   **938.003**
1. Greece—History—Encyclopedias
ISBN 0-8160-5722-2   LC 2004-56429
First published 1995
This encyclopedia covers "ancient Greece, from the dawning of Minoan civilization to the conquest of Rome—2000 years of a remarkable civilization that left an indelible imprint on human history. . . . This is a first-rate purchase for libraries on a topic of endless inquiry and fascination." SLJ
Includes bibliographical references

939   Other parts of ancient world to ca. 640

Civilizations of the Ancient Near East; Jack M. Sasson, editor in chief; John Baines, Gary Beckman, Karen S. Rubinson, associate editors. Hendrickson Publishers 2000 4v in 2 il map set $169.95 *
Grades: 11 12 Adult   **939**
1. Middle East—Civilization
ISBN 1-56563-607-4   LC 00-63144
First published 1995 by Scribner
This "work concentrates on the Near East, broadly defined to include a region from Northeast Africa to India, Pakistan, and Burma, with principal focus on the core areas of Egypt, Syro-Palestine, Mesopotamia, and Anatolia. The time span ranges from the third millennium B.C.E., when writing was invented, to 330 B.C.E., when Alexander triumphed over the Persian Empire. The 189 contributors from five continents and 16 countries include some of the world's finest scholars." Libr J [review of 1995 edition]
Includes bibliographical references

Dictionary of the ancient Near East; edited by Piotr Bienkowski and Alan Millard. University of Pa. Press 2000 342p il maps $49.95

   Grades: 11 12 Adult   **939**
   1. Middle East—Antiquities—Dictionaries
   ISBN 0-8122-3557-6   LC 00-21715

"The time period covered is from the Lower Paleolithic (around 1.5 million years ago) to the fall of Babylon to Cyrus the Great in 539 B.C. The geographic scope encompasses Mesopotamia, Iran, Anatolia, the Caucasus, the Levant, and Arabia. There are some entries on major archaeologists and explorers from modern times as well as on ancient cultures, historic and legendary figures, concepts, aspects of daily life, and individual archaeological sites. The 500 articles range from brief paragraphs to a few columns on double-columned pages." Booklist

"The volume's easy-to-follow format, very readable content and affordable price assure its use by general readers, students and scholars." Choice

Shanower, Eric

   A thousand ships. Image Comics 2001 223p il (Age of bronze) hardcover o.p. pa $19.95

   Grades: 10 11 12   **939**
   1. Trojan War—Graphic novels 2. Graphic novels
   ISBN 1-58240-212-4; 1-58240-200-0 (pa)

This is "the first part of a seven-volume graphic novel about the Trojan War. . . . The book begins with the story of Paris, the milk-white bull and the kidnapping of Helen, and goes up to the start of the war." Publ Wkly

Includes bibliographical references

Followed by Sacrifice (2004)

Thomas, Carol G., 1938-

   The Trojan War; [by] Carol G. Thomas and Craig Conant. Greenwood Press 2005 209p il map (Greenwood guides to historic events of the ancient world) $45 *

   Grades: 9 10 11 12   **939**
   1. Trojan War
   ISBN 0-313-32526-X   LC 2004-17660

"An overview of Troy and the world of the late Bronze Age is presented in the first chapter, followed by sections on: finding Troy and the Trojan War, Homer and the epic tradition, the force of legend, and Troy in the 21st century." Publisher's note

Includes bibliographical references

940   History of Europe

Davies, Norman

   Europe: a history. HarperCollins Publishers 1998 1365p il map pa $25.95

   Grades: 9 10 11 12   **940**
   1. Europe—History
   ISBN 0-06-097468-0   LC 97-32889

First published 1996 by Oxford Univ. Press

This book covers "the rise and fall of Rome, the sweeping invasions of Alaric and Atilla, the Norman Conquests, the Papal struggles for power, the Renaissance and the Reformation, the French Revolution and the Napoleonic Wars, Europe's rise to become the powerhouse of the world, and its eclipse in our own century, following two devastating World Wars." Publisher's note

Includes bibliographical references

The History of Europe; general editor, John Stevenson. Facts on File 2002 512p il maps $75 *

   Grades: 9 10 11 12   **940**
   1. Europe—History 2. Europe—Civilization
   ISBN 0-8160-5152-6   LC 2002-27125

This work documents the history of Europe from the beginnings of Ancient Greece in 2500 BC to the conflicts in the Balkans of the late 1990s. "Topics introduced along the way include science and technology, intellectual and political thought, literature, art, music and popular culture of the times." Publisher's note

940.1   Europe--Early history to 1453

The 1000s; Brenda Stalcup, book editor. Greenhaven Press 2001 314p il maps (Headlines in history) lib bdg $42.45; pa $27.45

   Grades: 9 10 11 12   **940.1**
   1. Medieval civilization 2. Middle ages—History
   ISBN 0-7377-0528-0 (lib bdg); 0-7377-0527-2 (pa)
     LC 00-52831

A collection of articles on such topics as "feudalism, the Norman Conquest, Vikings, Crusades, Islam, the culture of Asia, and the rise of civilizations in the New World." SLJ

Includes bibliographical references

Baker, Alan

   The knight. Wiley 2003 217p $22.95 *

   Grades: 11 12 Adult   **940.1**
   1. Knights and knighthood 2. Middle Ages
   ISBN 0-471-25135-6   LC 2002-9956

Contents: Introduction -- The mounted warrior -- From blood to laughter -- The knight's equipment -- Love and war -- Castles and siegecraft -- The fall of Jerusalem -- Warriors of Christ -- Mercenaries -- Conclusion : from lance to firearm

This "book takes a closer look at the knight and the environment in which he served. Each chapter covers a different topic, such as castle sieges, jousting tournaments, the weapons used by medieval warriors, and the Crusades. . . . Baker offers a good starting point for students or those with a casual interest in the knights of yore." Booklist

Includes bibliographical references

Bishop, Morris, 1893-1973

   The Middle Ages. 1st Mariner Books ed. Houghton Mifflin Co. 2001 350p il pa $17 *

   Grades: 9 10 11 12   **940.1**
   1. Middle Ages 2. Medieval civilization
   ISBN 0-618-05703-X   LC 2001-271448

"A Mariner book"

First published 1968 by American Heritage with title: The Horizon book of the Middle Ages

This volume covers the period from the conversion of Constantine in 312 A.D. through the conclusion of the Hundred Years War in 1461.

English, Edward D.
Encyclopedia of the medieval world. Facts on File 2004 2v il map (Facts on File library of world history) set $150 *
Grades: 11 12 Adult 940.1
1. Middle Ages—Encyclopedias
ISBN 0-8160-4690-5 LC 2003-27825
This encyclopedia "covers the time period from the late antique world to about 1500 C.E and includes events, people, institutions, and culture in western and eastern Europe, Scandinavia, North Africa, Byzantium, and the Near East. The 2,000 entries discuss significant people, art, politics, literature, religion, economics, law, science, and warfare in an A-Z format." Booklist
Includes bibliographical references

Gies, Frances
The knight in history. Harper & Row 1984 255p il maps hardcover o.p. pa $14.95
Grades: 11 12 Adult 940.1
1. Knights and knighthood 2. Middle Ages
ISBN 0-06-015399-3; 0-06-091413-0 (pa)
LC 84-47571
This book describes the rise and fall of the institution of knighthood and the influence of the medieval knight throughout history.
Includes bibliographical references

Life in a medieval village; [by] Frances and Joseph Gies. Harper & Row 1990 257p il maps hardcover o.p. pa $14.95
Grades: 11 12 Adult 940.1
1. Medieval civilization 2. Middle Ages
ISBN 0-06-016215-5; 0-06-092046-7 (pa)
LC 89-33759
"Elton, England, is the focal point of the authors' efforts to portray the everyday life and social structure of the High Middle Ages. After giving a brief summary of Elton's origins and development in the Roman and Anglo-Saxon periods, the book examines just how the residents lived and worked within the feudal structure at the beginning of the fourteenth century." Booklist
Includes bibliographical references

The **Oxford** history of medieval Europe; edited by George Holmes. Oxford Univ. Press 2001 395p il maps pa $16.95 *
Grades: 11 12 Adult 940.1
1. Europe—History—476-1492
ISBN 0-19-280133-3 LC 2002-281715
This is an abridged edition of The Oxford illustrated history of medieval Europe, published 1988
This compact edition covers such subjects as the chivalric code of knights, popular festivals, new art forms, the Black Death, the fall of Rome, and the emergence of the Reformation
Includes bibliographical references

Singman, Jeffrey L.
Daily life in medieval Europe. Greenwood Press 1999 268p il $49.95 *
Grades: 9 10 11 12 940.1
1. Europe—Social life and customs 2. Europe—History—476-1492 3. Medieval civilization
ISBN 0-313-30273-1 LC 98-46816
Also available online
The author "focuses on details that help readers picture rural and urban medieval life among peasants, monks, and the aristocracy—medieval heating and lighting, bedchambers in cottages and castles, clothing, money and prices, even sanitation. Singman narrows his focus to the years 1100-1300, portraying life in Northern France, England, the Low Countries, and some of Germany." Voice Youth Advocates
Includes bibliographical references

940.2 Europe--1453-

Encyclopedia of the Enlightenment; Alan Charles Kors, editor in chief. Oxford Univ. Press 2003 4v il set $495
Grades: 11 12 Adult 940.2
1. Enlightenment—Encyclopedias 2. Philosophy—Encyclopedias
ISBN 0-19-510430-7 LC 2002-3766
Contents: v1 Abbadie-Enlightenment studies; v2 Enthusiasm-Lyceums and museums; v3 Mably-Ruysch; v4 Sade-Zoology
This reference includes over 700 articles about "philosophic and social changes engendered by the Enlightenment. It {covers} . . . not only France, England, Scotland, the Low Countries, Italy, English-speaking North America, the German states, and Hapsburg Austria but also Iberian, Ibero-American, Jewish, Russian, and Eastern European cultures." Publisher's note
Includes bibliographical references

Europe 1450 to 1789; encyclopedia of the early modern world; Jonathan Dewald, editor in chief. Charles Scribner's Sons 2004 6v il map set $695
Grades: 11 12 Adult 940.2
1. Europe—History—Encyclopedias 2. Europe—Civilization—Encyclopedias
ISBN 0-684-31200-X LC 2003-15680
Contents: v1 Absolutism to Coligny; v2 Cologne to fur trade; v3 Gabrieli to Lyon; v4 Macau to Pope; v5 Popular culture to Switzerland; v6 Tasso to Zwingli
This reference set focuses "on Europe within the context of world history, including meaningful developments in the arts, religion, politics, exploration, and warfare. Alphabetical entries range from broad and expected topics like the Enlightenment and the Renaissance to the more narrowly defined. . . . Cross references are numerous, and each signed entry is followed by a bibliography." Booklist
Includes bibliographical references

The **European** Renaissance and Reformation, 1350-1600; edited by Norman J. Wilson. Gale Group 2001 xxix, 522p il maps (World eras, v1) $130.75 *

Grades: 11 12 Adult   **940.2**
1. Renaissance 2. Reformation
ISBN 0-7876-1706-7   LC 00-52802

This resource "is comprised of 10 chapters. The first two, focusing on world events and geography, respectively, provide users a global perspective and context for the culture and time period in question. Remaining chapters treat other cultural elements. . . . Each chapter is subdivided into five types of material: chronological, overview, topical, biographical, and documentary. . . . This volume, in addition to its fine organization, structure, and arrangement, is equally impressive for its inclusive, well-written content." Booklist

Includes bibliographical references

Gies, Joseph
Life in a medieval castle; [by] Joseph and Frances Gies. Harper & Row 1979 c1974 272p il pa $14.95

Grades: 11 12 Adult   **940.2**
1. Castles 2. Middle Ages
ISBN 0-06-090674-X   LC 79-103901
First published 1974 by Crowell

Using Chepstow Castle on the Welsh border as a model, the authors provide "descriptions of the medieval world where the castle was household, feudal center, and military target, and by concentrating on Anglo-Norman examples illustrate what existence was like as the dark ages began to brighten." Booklist

Includes glossary and bibliographical references

The **Oxford** illustrated history of modern Europe; edited by T. C. W. Blanning. Oxford Univ. Press 1996 362p il maps hardcover o.p. pa $24.95 *

Grades: 11 12 Adult   **940.2**
1. Europe—History—1789-1900 2. Europe—History—20th century
ISBN 0-19-820374-8; 0-19-285426-7 (pa)

This volume covers "politics, economics, warfare, class structure, art, and culture from the time of the revolution through 1995. Central themes include the idea that revolution against established order was possible, successful, and, once underway, perhaps unstoppable." Libr J

Includes bibliographical references

The **panorama** of the Renaissance; edited by Margaret Aston. H.N. Abrams 2000 c1996 367p il map $24.98

Grades: 9 10 11 12   **940.2**
1. Renaissance
ISBN 0-8109-8188-2
First published 1996

Eight sections are "devoted to such subjects as 'God and Man'; 'Rulers of the World'; 'Living and Dying'; and 'Science, Invention, and Discovery.' Once the stage is set in the introduction and openings of each chapter, readers are given an illustrated tour through myriad pathways that include houses, medicine, women, interior design, preaching and the Reformation, as well as mythology, charity, grotesqueries, and finance." SLJ

"Whatever the viewers' particular tastes—for pictures of everyday life, biblical imagery, or contemporary rulers—Aston's layout almost compels them to linger over the gamut of other topics as well." Booklist

Includes bibliographical references

The **Renaissance**; Raymond Obstfeld and Loretta Obstfeld, book editors. Greenhaven Press 2002 220p il (History firsthand) lib bdg $32.45; pa $21.20 *

Grades: 9 10 11 12   **940.2**
1. Renaissance
ISBN 0-7377-1080-2 (lib bdg); 0-7377-1079-9 (pa)
LC 2001-51296

This anthology gathers primary accounts from religious, artistic, scientific and secular leaders dealing with social and political topics of the day

Includes bibliographical references

The **Renaissance**; Jeff Hay, book editor. Greenhaven Press 2002 255p il maps (World history by era) lib bdg $44.95; pa $28.70

Grades: 9 10 11 12   **940.2**
1. Renaissance
ISBN 0-7377-0765-8 (lib bdg); 0-7377-0764-X (pa)
LC 2001-23842

This collection of primary and secondary source articles examines the Renaissance in Europe, Africa and the Americas, the Ottoman Turkish Empire and the Mughal Empire in India

Includes bibliographical references

The **Renaissance**; an encyclopedia for students; {edited by} Paul F. Grendler. Charles Scribner's Sons 2003 4v set $395 *

Grades: 11 12 Adult   **940.2**
1. Renaissance—Encyclopedias
ISBN 0-684-31281-6   LC 2003-15672

Adaptation of Encyclopedia of the Renaissance, published 1999

Contents: Vol. 1. Africa ; Americas ; Asia and the Indian Ocean -- Vol. 2. City of Florence ; France ; Habsburg lands ; Holy Roman Empire ; Italy, 1500 -- Vol. 3. London ; The Netherlands ; The Ottoman Empire ; The Papal States in Italy -- Vol. 4. Rome ; Russia ; The Scandinavian kingdoms ; Spain ; Universities ; Venetian territories in the Eastern Mediterranean

This encyclopedia includes articles on various aspects of social, cultural, and political history such as literature, government, warfare, and technology, plus maps, charts, definitions, and chronology

"Researchers should find their needs more than satisfied by this appealing and student-friendly resource." SLJ

Renaissance & Reformation: almanac; Peggy Saari & Aaron Saari, editors; Julie Carnagie, project editor. U.X.L 2002 2v il set $105 *

Grades: 7 8 9 10   **940.2**
1. Renaissance 2. Reformation
ISBN 0-7876-5467-1   LC 2002-6152

Renaissance & Reformation: almanac—Continued

This "is organized into topical chapters that include sidebars with additional information and more than 100 black-and-white illustrations. Volume 1 begins with a time line of important events. Following the time line are a 17-page vocabulary list and a research and activity guide. Chapters . . . deal with topics such as the rise of European monarchies, the Protestant and Catholic Reformations, the scientific revolution, the status of women, and daily life. A concluding bibliography lists books, Web sites, and video recordings and DVDs." Booklist

Includes bibliographical references

Renaissance & Reformation: primary sources; Peggy Saari & Aaron Saari, editors; Julie Carnagie, project editor. U.X.L 2002 201p il $58 *

Grades: 7 8 9 10   **940.2**
1. Renaissance 2. Reformation
ISBN 0-7876-5473-6   LC 2002-3928
Contents: On the equal or unequal sin of Eve and Adam, by I. Nogarola; The Prince, by N. Machiavelli; The Muqaddimah, by I. Khaldûn; Notebooks, by L. da Vinci; The Starry messenger, "A grand revolution" (box) by G. Galilie; Merchant of Venice, William Shakespeare (box) by W. Shakespeare; Heptaméron, by Margaret of Navarre; Don Quixote, by M. Cervantes; "Of cannibals", by M. de Montaigne; The description of the new world called the blazing world, by M. Cavendish; "The ninety-five theses or disputation on the power and efficacy of indulgences", by M. Luther; "The sixty-seven articles of Ulrich Zwingli", by H. Zwingli; Ecclesiastical ordinances, Institutes of the Christian religion, by J. Calvin; "Elizabeth, a dutch anabaptist martyr: a letter", by Elizabeth; Spiritual exercises, by Ignatius of Loyola; Centuries, by Nostradamus; The life of Teresa of Jesus, by Teresa de Avila; "Profession of the Tridentine faith", by The Roman Catholic Church; Malleus maleficarum, by H. Kramer and J. Sprenger

This "provides selected specific writings of the time. Introductory information about the original author begins each section, and sidebars list definitions of obscure or antiquated words. Following each document piece is a discussion of the historical effects of the piece along with additional readings." Booklist

Includes bibliographical references

Renaissance and Reformation; editor, James A. Patrick. Marshall Cavendish 2007 6v il set $671.36

Grades: 9 10 11 12 Adult   **940.2**
1. Renaissance—Encyclopedias 2. Reformation—Encyclopedias
ISBN 978-0-7614-7650-4; 0-7614-7650-4
                            LC 2006-42600

This encyclopedia provides a "background on the historical period that bridged the medieval and modern worlds, roughly 1300-1700, with emphasis on 1350-1650. . . . This is an extremely impressive publication, lavishly presented, informative, and remarkably enjoyable to read. . . . A must-have for all high-school collections and for public libraries patronized by young adults. Adults will find it appealing as well." Booklist

Includes bibliographical references

Sider, Sandra

Handbook to life in Renaissance Europe. Facts on File 2005 382p il map (Facts on File library of world history) $70

Grades: 11 12 Adult   **940.2**
1. Renaissance 2. Europe—Civilization
ISBN 0-8160-5618-8   LC 2004-20088

This "volume concentrates on Italy's impact on the Renaissance in both northern and southern Europe 1400-c.1600, covering the major movements in government, religion, art and architecture, literature, music, science, education, warfare, commerce, exploration, and daily life." SLJ

This book "furnishes a good, general introduction to the Renaissance, and does so succinctly and with some of the breadth usually found in longer works." Choice

Includes bibliographical references

Streissguth, Thomas

The Napoleonic wars; defeat of the Grand Army. Lucent Books 2003 112p il map (History's great defeats) $27.45

Grades: 9 10 11 12   **940.2**
1. Napoleon I, Emperor of the French, 1769-1821
2. France. Armeé. Grande Armeé 3. France—History—1799-1815
ISBN 1-590-18065-8   LC 2002-151712
Contents: The rise and fall of the First Empire; The failed Egyptian Campaign; Failed economics; The Peninsular War; Underestimating the enemy; Choosing the sword; A failure of deception

Provides a look at how Napoleon Bonaparte's egotism, unrealistic dreams, and tendency to underestimate enemies led to the downfall of his Grand Armée during the Napoleonic Wars.

Includes bibliographical references

Thomson, Melissa

Women of the Renaissance; [by] Melissa Thomson and Ruth Dean. Lucent Books 2004 128p il map (Women in history) $28.70

Grades: 9 10 11 12   **940.2**
1. Renaissance 2. Women—History
ISBN 1-59018-473-4   LC 2004-10849
Contents: Introduction: worlds of the Renaissance; Wives, mothers, and caregivers; Women at work; Women in religious life; Women who filled the role of queen; Political leaders, rebels, and pirates; Women scholars and scientists; Women writers; Women artists

This discusses the roles of women in the Renaissance, as wives, mothers, workers, religious figures, queens, politicians, pirates, scholars and scientists, writers, and artists

"A concise, accessible account of life during this period and the issues specific to women. . . . The index is comprehensive, the endnotes are extensive, and the full-color reproductions and a few maps are well placed. This attractive title will serve report writers and general readers." SLJ

Includes bibliographical references

Wilson, Ellen Judy

Encyclopedia of the Enlightenment; Peter Hanns Reill, consulting editor; Ellen Judy Wilson, principal author. rev ed. Facts on File 2004 670p $75 *

Grades: 11 12 Adult   **940.2**

1. Enlightenment—Encyclopedias 2. Philosophy—Encyclopedias 3. Europe—Intellectual life

ISBN 0-8160-5335-9   LC 2003-22973

First published 1996

This reference provides a "review of the important ideas, people, and events that shaped the world during the Enlightenment. [It] covers the major changes in science, education, philosophy, art and architecture, and politics which took place during the 17th and 18th centuries and led to the birth of the modern era. . . . The biographical entries cover such notables as Robespierre, Schiller, Fielding, Kant, and Voltaire. . . . Larger public, school, and academic libraries looking for a comprehensive overview of the subject for the student or interested reader will find this a valuable and accessible resource." Libr J

Includes bibliographical references

940.3   World War I, 1914-1918

Allan, Tony, 1946-

The causes of World War I. Heinemann Lib. 2003 48p il (20th-century perspectives) lib bdg $25.64

Grades: 9 10 11 12   **940.3**

1. World War, 1914-1918—Causes

ISBN 1-403-40148-9   LC 2002-4362

Explores key topics involving World War I and shows the causes that led up to the outbreak of war, including France's defeat in the Franco-Prussian War, the assassination of Franz Ferdinand, the heir to the Austro-Hungarian throne, and Germany's attack on France

"Useful for reports." Booklist

Includes glossary and bibliographical references

Bosco, Peter I.

World War I; revised by Antoinette Bosco. updated ed. Facts on File 2003 162p il map (America at war) $35

Grades: 7 8 9 10   **940.3**

1. World War, 1914-1918—United States

ISBN 0-8160-4940-8   LC 2002-5106

First published 1991

In words and pictures this "illustrates the military strategies and tactics of combatants involved as well as the national mindsets of the nations and soldiers who fought in World War I. . . . [It is] a must-read volume for both adults and younger readers. . . . Highly recommended for both public and school libraries." Am Ref Books Annu, 2004

Includes bibliographical references

Burg, David F.

Almanac of World War I; [by] David F. Burg and L. Edward Purcell; introduction by William Manchester. University Press of Ky. 1998 320p il maps hardcover o.p. pa $22

Grades: 11 12 Adult   **940.3**

1. World War, 1914-1918

ISBN 0-8131-2072-1; 0-8131-9087-8 (pa)

     LC 98-26625

"The bulk of the text is arranged chronologically by year and date, listing almost daily occurrences from 1914 through 1918. . . . The work is international in scope, covering political and military happenings from around the world. . . . There is really nothing comparable to this volume." Booklist

Includes bibliographical references

Carlisle, Rodney P.

World War I. Facts on File 2006 454p il map (Eyewitness history) $75

Grades: 8 9 10 11 12   **940.3**

1. World War, 1914-1918—Personal narratives

ISBN 0-8160-6061-4; 978-0-8160-6061-0

     LC 2005-27236

First published 1992 under the authorship of Joe H. Kirchberger with title: The First World War

This book "provides hundreds of firsthand accounts—from diary entries, letters, speeches, and newspaper accounts—that focus on different warfare issues and on the social and cultural impacts of the war on Europe and the United States. . . . This volume also includes critical documents related to this topic, as well as capsule biographies of key figures, narrative sections, eyewitness testimonies, 102 black-and-white photographs, maps and graphs, a bibliography, notes, a glossary, chronologies, appendixes, and an index." Publisher's note

Includes bibliographical references

Coetzee, Frans, 1955-

World War I: a history in documents; [by] Frans Coetzee and Marilyn Shevin-Coetzee. Oxford Univ. Press 2002 174p il maps (Pages from history) lib bdg $36.95 *

Grades: 7 8 9 10   **940.3**

1. World War, 1914-1918—Sources

ISBN 0-19-513746-9   LC 2001-36605

"Introductory essays define 'document' and then point out strategies for analyzing and evaluating one so that it can be of value to students. Personal letters, posters, song lyrics, and poems are among the documents included. The book has extensive citations and sidebar quotes with dates, speaker, position held, and the context." SLJ

Includes bibliographical references

Gilbert, Martin, 1936-

The First World War; a complete history. Holt & Co. 1994 xxiv, 615p il maps hardcover o.p. pa $22.50

Grades: 11 12 Adult   **940.3**

1. World War, 1914-1918

ISBN 0-8050-1540-X; 0-8050-4734-4 (pa)

     LC 94-27268

Gilbert, Martin, 1936-—_Continued_

This work "covers WW I on all major fronts—domestic, diplomatic, military—as well as such bloody preludes as the Armenian massacre of 1915." Publ Wkly

"What Mr. Gilbert seeks to do, and frequently succeeds in doing, is to humanize, indeed to personalize, World War I. His effort and accomplishment make this a rewarding and significant book." N Y Times Book Rev

Includes bibliographical references

Heyman, Neil M.

World War I. Greenwood Press 1997 xxiii, 257p il maps (Greenwood Press guides to historic events of the twentieth century) $45

Grades: 11 12 Adult   940.3
1. World War, 1914-1918
ISBN 0-313-29880-7   LC 97-1686

This work is "divided into three sections. The first gives an overview of the causes, issues, and ultimately the consequences of a world at war. . . . The second section of the book is a series of biographies of the major political and military participants in the war. . . . The third section of the book is devoted to primary documents from the period." Book Rep

Includes bibliographical references

Keegan, John, 1934-

An illustrated history of the First World War. Knopf 2001 429p il $50

Grades: 11 12 Adult   940.3
1. World War, 1914-1918
ISBN 0-375-41259-X   LC 2001-41410

The text is an abridgment of the author's The First World War. For this illustrated volume the text is complemented by "almost 500 photographs, posters, drawings and maps, a cross-section of material produced by all the major combatants and clarified by Keegan's extensive captions." Publ Wkly

Includes bibliographical references

Pendergast, Tom, 1964-

World War I almanac; [by] Tom Pendergast, Sara Pendergast; edited by Christine Slovey. U.X.L 2001 xl, 210p $60

Grades: 7 8 9 10   940.3
1. World War, 1914-1918
ISBN 0-7876-5476-0   LC 2001-53012

This "contains 12 chapters covering major topics related to the period, including the roots of the war; causes of U.S. involvement; the Espionage Act and Sedition Act; weapons of mass destruction; and more. Other features include maps, a detailed chronology of events, sidebars featuring related information, a glossary of 'Words to Know,' research and activity ideas, and a list of further reading sources." Publisher's note

Includes bibliographical references

Stokesbury, James L.

A short history of World War I. Morrow 1981 348p maps hardcover o.p. pa $14.95

Grades: 11 12 Adult   940.3
1. World War, 1914-1918
ISBN 0-688-00128-9; 0-688-00129-7 (pa)
     LC 80-22206

This chronologically arranged history of World War I presents both the political and military perspectives.

Includes bibliographical references

Strachan, Hew

The First World War. Viking 2004 364p il maps hardcover o.p. pa $16

Grades: 11 12 Adult   940.3
1. World War, 1914-1918
ISBN 0-670-03295-6; 0-14-303518-5 (pa)
     LC 2003-62191

The author details the "factors behind World War I, covers the major ground and naval campaigns and battles, and assesses the roles of leading officers and statesmen while simultaneously highlighting the home fronts and the non-European aspects of this cataclysmic event." Libr J

"Readers already familiar with the sequence of events in strict order will benefit most. But all readers will eventually be gripped, and even the most seasoned ones will praise the insights and the original choice of illustrations." Publ Wkly

Includes bibliographical references

The **Treaty** of Versailles; Jeff Hay, book editor. Greenhaven Press 2002 124p il (At issue in history) hardcover o.p. pa $18.70 *

Grades: 9 10 11 12   940.3
1. Treaty of Versailles (1919) 2. World War, 1914-1918—Peace
ISBN 0-7377-0827-1 (lib bdg); 0-7377-0826-3 (pa)
     LC 2001-40609

This collection of articles examines "the expectations of those who negotiated the treaty, the responses to the treaty by those who were close observers or participants in the negotiations, and more recent assessments of the treaty." Publisher's note

Includes bibliographical references

Tuchman, Barbara Wertheim

The guns of August; [by] Barbara W. Tuchman; [with a new foreword by Robert K. Massie] 1st Ballantine Books ed. Ballantine 1994 xxiv, 511p il, maps pa $14

Grades: 11 12 Adult   940.3
1. World War, 1914-1918
ISBN 0-345-38623-X   LC 93-90461

First published 1962 by Macmillan

A history of the negotiations that preceded World War I and the course of the war's first month.

Includes bibliographical references

The Zimmermann telegram. Ballantine Books [1985] c1966 244p il pa $14

Grades: 11 12 Adult   940.3
1. World War, 1914-1918—Causes
ISBN 0-345-32425-0   LC 84-91737

Tuchman, Barbara Wertheim—*Continued*
First published 1958 by Macmillan
The author discusses the German plan to induce Mexico to attack the U.S. during World War I.
Includes bibliographical references

The **United** States in the First World War; an encyclopedia; editor, Anne Cipriano Venzon; consulting editor, Paul L. Miles. Garland 1995 xx, 830p maps (Garland reference library of the humanities) $155; pa $45 *
Grades: 11 12 Adult   **940.3**
1. World War, 1914-1918
ISBN 0-8240-7055-0; 0-8153-3353-6 (pa)
LC 95-1782
"Biography, economics, civil rights, women's issues, foreign relations, battles, armaments, and conferences are among the topics included. Arrangement is alphabetical, and most articles are brief—between one column and a page. . . . Most articles include brief bibliographies. There are six maps, but no other illustrations." Libr J

World War I: a student encyclopedia; Spencer C. Tucker, editor; Priscilla Mary Roberts, editor, documents volume. ABC-CLIO 2005 5v il map set $485
Grades: 9 10 11 12   **940.3**
1. World War, 1914-1918—Encyclopedias
ISBN 1-85109-879-8   LC 2005-25638
"More than 900 A-to-Z entries that range in length from one to 20 pages cover major campaigns, individual battles, countries, biographies, weapons, diplomatic efforts, and the social and cultural impacts of the war. . . . This well-written and accessible resource is highly recommended for school and public libraries." Libr J
Includes bibliographical references

940.4   World War I, 1914-1918 (Military conduct of the war)

Eisenhower, John S. D., 1922-
Yanks: the epic story of the American Army in World War I; {by} John S. D. Eisenhower with Joanne Thompson Eisenhower. Free Press 2001 353p il maps hardcover o.p. pa $16
Grades: 11 12 Adult   **940.4**
1. United States. Army 2. World War, 1914-1918—Campaigns
ISBN 0-684-86304-9; 0-7432-2385-3 (pa)
LC 2001-23124
"This history focuses entirely on the challenges, victories, sacrifices . . . and long-term consequences of the American Expeditionary Force (AEF) in Europe during World War I." Libr J
"This is an important work that should help alter the historical picture of the American role in the conflict." Booklist
Includes bibliographical references

Farwell, Byron
Over there; the United States in the Great War, 1917-1918. Norton 1999 336p $27.95; pa $15.95 *
Grades: 11 12 Adult   **940.4**
1. World War, 1914-1918—United States
ISBN 0-393-04698-2; 0-393-32028-6 (pa)
LC 98-35705
This history of American intervention in World War I focuses primarily on the military aspects of the war but also discusses its social and economic impact
"This title does provide good coverage on the intervention in Russia and the role of women in the war, notably the 'Hello Girls.' " Libr J
Includes bibliographical references

Mosier, John, 1944-
The myth of the Great War; a new military history of World War I. HarperCollins Pubs. 2001 381p il hardcover o.p. pa $14.95
Grades: 11 12 Adult   **940.4**
1. World War, 1914-1918—Campaigns
ISBN 0-06-019676-9; 0-06-008433-2 (pa)
LC 00-46103
"After dissecting the major campaigns on the western front, Mosier concludes that Germany's ultimate defeat was the direct result of the influx of American soldiers into France in 1917 and 1918. . . . This is revisionist history that convincingly smashes the myths that Allied governments, leaders, and propagandists worked so hard to promulgate. Mosier's masterful account is a welcome addition." Booklist
Includes bibliographical references

940.53   World War II, 1939-1945

Adler, David A., 1947-
We remember the Holocaust. Holt & Co. 1989 147p il pa $16.95 hardcover o.p. *
Grades: 9 10 11 12   **940.53**
1. Holocaust, 1933-1945—Personal narratives
2. World War, 1939-1945—Jews
ISBN 0-8050-3715-2 (pa)   LC 87-21139
"Survivors of the Holocaust share their unique stories in an informative, moving account that serves to remind readers of the terrible effects of hatred." Soc Educ
Includes glossary and bibliographical references

And justice for all; an oral history of the Japanese American detention camps; [compiled by] John Tateishi; foreword by Roger Daniels. University of Washington Press 1999 xxvii, 262p il, map pa $19.95 *
Grades: 9 10 11 12   **940.53**
1. Japanese Americans—Evacuation and relocation, 1942-1945 2. World War, 1939-1945—United States
ISBN 0-295-97785-X   LC 98-49105
First published 1984 by Random House
"Recollections from 30 Japanese Americans who were placed in government detention camps following Japan's attack on Pearl Harbor lend valuable insight into this tragic event in U.S. history." Booklist

Art from the ashes; a Holocaust anthology; edited by Lawrence L. Langer. Oxford Univ. Press 1995 689p il hardcover o.p. pa $47.95 *
Grades: 11 12 Adult   **940.53**
1. Holocaust, 1933-1945—Personal narratives 2. Holocaust, 1933-1945, in literature
ISBN 0-19-507559-5; 0-19-507732-6 (pa)
LC 94-11446
This collection "includes both fiction and nonfiction, as well as drama and poetry. Among the nonfiction pieces are excerpts from the ghetto diaries of Abraham Lewin (Warsaw) and Avraham Tory (Kovno), an essay from Primo Levi's *The Drowned and the Saved,* and an essay from Elie Wiesel's *Legends of Our Time.*" Booklist
A "remarkable volume, perfectly suited for anyone studying the Holocaust. . . . Compared with [the] first-hand accounts, fiction could be, one would think, only a pallid version of reality. Yet the fiction Mr. Langer collects . . . highlights the reality of the Holocaust with stunning intensity." N Y Times Book Rev

Ayer, Eleanor H.
In the ghettos; teens who survived the ghettos of the Holocaust. Rosen Pub. Group 1998 64p il map (Teen witnesses to the Holocaust) $26.50 *
Grades: 7 8 9 10   **940.53**
1. Holocaust, 1933-1945—Personal narratives
ISBN 0-8239-2845-4   LC 98-43859
Chronicles the deportation of Jews into ghettos during Hitler's Third Reich and presents the narratives of three individuals who, as teenagers, lived in the ghettos of Lodz, Theresienstadt, and Warsaw and survived physical deprivations, abuse, and deportation to the death camps
Includes bibliographical references

Parallel journeys; [by] Eleanor H. Ayer with Helen Waterford and Alfons Heck. Atheneum Bks. for Young Readers 1995 244p il hardcover o.p. pa $5.99
Grades: 7 8 9 10   **940.53**
1. Holocaust, 1933-1945 2. Germany—History—1933-1945 3. Jews—Germany
ISBN 0-689-31830-8; 0-689-83236-2 (pa)
LC 94-23277
"Alternating chapters contrast the wartime experiences of two young Germans—Waterford, who was interned in a Nazi concentration camp, and Heck, a member of the Hitler Youth. The volume is composed mainly of excerpts from their published autobiographies, connected by Ayer's overall account of the era. A powerful and painful picture emerges, vividly describing life before, during, and, most impressively, after the Holocaust." Horn Book Guide
Includes bibliographical references

Berenbaum, Michael, 1945-
The world must know; the history of the Holocaust as told in the United States Holocaust Memorial Museum; Arnold Kramer, editor of photographs. 2nd ed. United States Holocaust Memorial Museum; Distributed by the Johns Hopkins University Press 2006 xxi, 250p il pa $29.95 *
Grades: 11 12 Adult   **940.53**

1. United States Holocaust Memorial Museum
2. Holocaust, 1933-1945
ISBN 0-8018-8358-X
First published 1993 by Little, Brown
This book documents the "stories of the Holocaust as told in the renowned permanent exhibition of the United States Holocaust Memorial Museum in Washington, D.C." Publisher's note
"Visually evocative and unsettling, the book, supplemented with a useful bibliography, is an excellent choice for those with little acquaintance of the subject or those needing a concise synopsis." Libr J [review of 1993 edition]
Includes bibliographical references

Bitton-Jackson, Livia
I have lived a thousand years; growing up in the Holocaust; by Livia E. Bitton-Jackson. Simon & Schuster Bks. for Young Readers 1997 224p pa $4.99
Grades: 7 8 9 10   **940.53**
1. Holocaust, 1933-1945—Personal narratives 2. Jews—Hungary
ISBN 0-689-81022-9; 0-689-82395-9 (pa)
LC 96-19971
Based on the author's book for adults, Elli: coming of age in the Holocaust (1980)
"This memoir covers the last fourteen months of World War II, during which thirteen-year-old Elli Friedmann (as the author was then named) and members of her family are deported from their home . . . to two ghettos and several camps, including Auschwitz." Bull Cent Child Books
"This is a memorable addition to the searing accounts of Holocaust survivors." Horn Book
Includes glossary

Chesnoff, Richard Z., 1937-
Pack of thieves; how Hitler and Europe plundered the Jews and committed the greatest theft in history. Doubleday 1999 325p il hardcover o.p. pa $14
Grades: 11 12 Adult   **940.53**
1. Holocaust, 1933-1945 2. Jews—Persecutions
ISBN 0-385-48763-0; 0-385-72064-5 (pa)
LC 99-33257
The author outlines the "Nazi plot to segregate Jews from the economic mainstream by expropriating their businesses, savings accounts, jewelry, art collections, and other personal belongings. What is startling, though, is not the fact that many Germans supported and profited from this plan, but that large numbers of government officials and private citizens in conquered and neutral European nations enthusiastically jumped on the bandwagon." Booklist

Children in the Holocaust and World War II; their secret diaries; [compiled by] Laurel Holliday. Pocket Bks. 1995 xxi, 409p il map hardcover o.p. pa $15 *
Grades: 11 12 Adult   **940.53**
1. Holocaust, 1933-1945—Personal narratives 2. World War, 1939-1945—Children
ISBN 0-671-52054-7; 0-671-52055-5 (pa)
LC 95-3211

Children in the Holocaust and World War II—
Continued

"Diary entries written by young people in ghettos, concentration camps, cities, and a Copenhagen prison camp offer . . . glimpses of life during World War II. Each selection is introduced by a brief biography that includes the author's name, country, age, family circumstances before and during the war, and concludes with circumstances of death or postwar life. Nine girls and 14 boys, Jews and gentiles, aged 10 to 18, are featured." SLJ

"This anthology is a haunting reminder of the impact of war on children. The powerful images will long be remembered." Voice Youth Advocates

Includes bibliographical references

Croci, Pascal
Auschwitz. Harry N. Abrams 2004 87p il $16.95
Grades: 11 12 Adult   **940.53**
1. Graphic novels 2. Auschwitz (Poland: Concentration camp)—Graphic novels 3. Holocaust, 1933-1945—Graphic novels
ISBN 0-8109-4831-1   LC 2003-13337
Original French edition, 2000
This graphic novel "focuses on the story of a Polish couple, Kazik and Cessnia, who lost their daughter at the infamous concentration camp. . . . Using a series of alternating flashbacks, the author shows the family's internment, enslavement, and torture, and the eventual death of their child. . . . The frighteningly realistic black-and-white illustrations make this book memorable." SLJ
Includes bibliographical references

Daniels, Roger
Prisoners without trial; Japanese Americans in World War II. Rev. ed. Hill and Wang 2004 162p il (Critical issue series) pa $12
Grades: 11 12 Adult   **940.53**
1. Japanese Americans—Evacuation and relocation, 1942-1945 2. World War, 1939-1945—United States
ISBN 0-8090-7896-1   LC 2004-47328
First published 1993
An account of "the relocation of Japanese Americans during World War II, an injustice prompted not by military necessity but by political and racial motivations. The purpose of this volume is to tell the story in light of the redress legislation enacted in 1988." Libr J [review of 1993 edition]
Includes bibliographical references

Dawidowicz, Lucy S.
The war against the Jews, 1933-1945. 10th anniversary ed. Bantam Books 1986 xxxx, 466p il pa $19
Grades: 11 12 Adult   **940.53**
1. Holocaust, 1933-1945 2. Jews—Europe
ISBN 0-553-34302-5   LC 85-48051
A reissue with new introduction and supplementary bibliography of the title first published 1975 by Holt, Rinehart & Winston

"One of the best histories of the mass murder of Jews in World War II. Argues for the centrality of anti-Semitism in Hitler's program." Reader's Adviser
Includes bibliographical references

Drez, Ronald J.
Twenty-five yards of war; the extraordinary courage of ordinary men in World War II. Hyperion 2001 xxii, 296p il hardcover o.p. pa $16
Grades: 11 12 Adult   **940.53**
1. World War, 1939-1945 2. United States—Armed forces
ISBN 0-7868-6783-3; 0-7868-8668-4 (pa)
                                  LC 2001-39077
Based on interviews with World War II veterans, Drez describes the experiences of ten soldiers in such battles as Midway, Tarawa, and Iwo Jima.
"To be sure, some of these veterans' stories have been previously published . . . but Drez manages to present them with freshness and adequate context." Booklist
Includes bibliographical references

Drucker, Olga Levy, 1927-
Kindertransport. Holt & Co. 1992 146p hardcover o.p. pa $9.95 *
Grades: 9 10 11 12   **940.53**
1. Holocaust, 1933-1945—Personal narratives 2. Jewish refugees
ISBN 0-8050-1711-9; 0-8050-4251-2 (pa)
                                  LC 92-14121
The author describes the circumstances in Germany after Hitler came to power that led to the evacuation of many Jewish children to England and her experiences as a young girl in England during World War II.
This is a "quiet, candid account. . . . Drucker writes with spare truth about how a refugee adjusts and what's both lost and gained." Booklist

Encyclopedia of the Holocaust; Schmuel Spector, Robert Rozett, editors. Facts on File 2000 528p il $93.50 *
Grades: 11 12 Adult   **940.53**
1. Holocaust, 1933-1945—Encyclopedias
ISBN 0-8160-4333-7   LC 00-30917
Following several introductory essays are "alphabetical entries on people, places, events, organizations, laws, and concepts. The language is clear, but more important is the authenticity of the information and the refusal to surrender to a simplification of issues. There are ample good-quality, black-and-white photographs, some unfamiliar, and also maps and tables. A detailed chronology and a thematic bibliography conclude the volume." SLJ
Includes bibliographical references

Epstein, Eric Joseph, 1959-
Dictionary of the Holocaust; biography, geography, and terminology; [by] Eric Joseph Epstein and Philip Rosen; foreword by Henry R. Huttenbach. Greenwood Press 1997 416p $67.95
Grades: 11 12 Adult   **940.53**
1. Holocaust, 1933-1945—Dictionaries
ISBN 0-313-30355-X   LC 97-8779

Epstein, Eric Joseph, 1959-—*Continued*

The nearly 2,000 alphabetically arranged entries cover people, places and events related to the Holocaust. "Among the personalities profiled here are Dietrich Bonhoeffer, Anne Frank, Primo Levi, Oskar Schindler, Harry S. Truman, and Elie Wiesel. Place entries include references to well-known locations, the number of prewar Jewish inhabitants, the date of liberation, and the number of Jews left after liberation. Entries dealing with concentration camps are generally the longest and identify camps by location, type, when opened and liberated, nationalities incarcerated, numbers murdered, other victimization, and camp commandants. Among the terms that are defined are many foreign expressions." Booklist

Epstein, Helen, 1947-

Children of the Holocaust; conversations with sons and daughters of survivors. Penguin Books 1988 c1979 355p pa $16

Grades: 9 10 11 12   **940.53**
  1. Holocaust, 1933-1945
  ISBN 0-14-011284-7   LC 88-9606
  First published 1979 by Putnam
  A series of interviews with the children of Holocaust survivors living in the U.S., Canada, South America, and Israel.
  Includes bibliographical references

Feldman, George

Understanding the Holocaust. U.X.L 1998 2v il maps set $110 *

Grades: 9 10 11 12   **940.53**
  1. Holocaust, 1933-1945 2. Germany—Politics and government—1933-1945 3. Germany—History—1933-1945
  ISBN 0-7876-1740-7   LC 97-26864
  "This overview describes the Holocaust, the events that led up to it, and how the Nazis attempted to eradicate an entire people while fighting a war on two fronts. Sidebars provide information on related individuals, events, and policies. Black-and-white photographs help clarify the text." SLJ
  Includes bibliographical references

Friedman, Ina R.

The other victims; first-person stories of non-Jews persecuted by the Nazis. Houghton Mifflin 1990 214p pa $6.95 hardcover o.p. *

Grades: 6 7 8 9   **940.53**
  1. Holocaust, 1933-1945—Personal narratives 2. Holocaust survivors
  ISBN 0-395-74515-2 (pa)   LC 89-27036
  Personal narratives of Christians, Gypsies, deaf people, homosexuals, and blacks who suffered at the hands of the Nazis before and during World War II.
  "Well organized and edited, the tales are harrowing, though they all end happily, often with escape or immigration to America and highly successful careers. Friedman points out that these were the lucky ones, and her book serves as a much-needed reminder that the Nazi nightmare extended far beyond Europe's Jewish population." Bull Cent Child Books
  Includes bibliographical references

Gies, Miep, 1909-

Anne Frank remembered; the story of the woman who helped to hide the Frank family; [by] Miep Gies with Alison Leslie Gold. Simon & Schuster 1987 252p il maps hardcover o.p. pa $14 *

Grades: 11 12 Adult   **940.53**
  1. Frank family 2. Netherlands—History—1940-1945, German occupation 3. Holocaust, 1933-1945
  ISBN 0-671-54771-2; 0-671-66234-1 (pa)
                                        LC 86-25991
  "A memoir by the courageous Dutch woman who helped hide the Frank family, this book augments the Anne Frank story. Perceptive characterizations, with insight into life in Amsterdam during the Nazi occupation." SLJ

Gilbert, Martin, 1936-

The Holocaust; a history of the Jews of Europe during the Second World War. Holt & Co. 1986 c1985 959p il maps hardcover o.p. pa $17.95

Grades: 11 12 Adult   **940.53**
  1. Holocaust, 1933-1945
  ISBN 0-03-062416-9; 0-8050-0348-7 (pa)
                                        LC 85-5523
  "Proceeding chronologically from Hitler's rise to power in 1933 to Germany's surrender and the liberation of the concentration camps, [the author] documents the countless horrors of this 'unprecedented explosion of evil over good,' drawing extensively on records and testimonies of those who survived (as well as some who eventually perished)." Booklist
  Includes bibliographical references

The Routledge atlas of the Holocaust. 3rd ed. Routledge 2002 282p il maps $75; pa $19.95 *

Grades: 11 12 Adult   **940.53**
  1. Holocaust, 1933-1945
  ISBN 0-415-28145-8; 0-415-28146-6 (pa)
  First published 1982 in the United Kingdom with title: The Dent atlas of the Holocaust
  The author "uses 317 maps, text, and photographs to document Hitler's attempt to destroy Europe's Jews. . . . Commentary offers statistical information, historical background, and something about the people of the area. Archival photographs bring the events to life. . . . This small but effective work demonstrates the magnitude of the Nazi terror by bringing it down to a personal level." Am Ref Books Annu, 2003
  Includes bibliographical references

Goldhagen, Daniel

Hitler's willing executioners; ordinary Germans and the Holocaust; {by} Daniel Jonah Goldhagen. Knopf 1996 622p il maps $35; pa $16 *

Grades: 11 12 Adult   **940.53**
  1. Holocaust, 1933-1945 2. Germany—History—1933-1945 3. Antisemitism 4. National socialism
  ISBN 0-679-44695-8; 0-679-77268-5 (pa)
                                        LC 95-38591
  The author "endeavors to show that the common apologia for the Germans—that Hitler 'brainwashed' them—

Goldhagen, Daniel—_Continued_

is nonsense and that most Germans gave their active assent to genocide. An ordinary German commander, for example, might feel himself bound by a strict code of conduct yet not be at all averse to murdering Jews. The book ends with a detailed notes section and an appendix that explains the correct methodology for studying the Nazi period." Libr J

Gottfried, Ted, 1928-

Children of the slaughter; young people of the Holocaust; illustrations by Stephen Alcorn. 21st Cent. Bks. (Brookfield) 2001 112p il (Holocaust) lib bdg $29.90

Grades: 7 8 9 10   **940.53**

1. Hitler-Jugend 2. Holocaust, 1933-1945 3. World War, 1939-1945—Children

ISBN 0-7613-1716-3   LC 00-30222

This discusses "the effect of the Holocaust not only on the Jewish children but also on the German youngsters who were forced to join the Hitler youth and on the offspring of Holocaust survivors." Voice Youth Advocates

"With clear, direct prose and a very spacious, readable design {this volume presents} the history without rhetoric or exploitation. There is much here for classroom discussion. . . . Stephen Alcorn's illustrations at the start of each chapter are jagged and dramatic; even more moving are the occasional black-and-white archival photos." Booklist

Includes glossary and bibliographical references

Deniers of the Holocaust; who they are, what they do, why they do it; illustrations by Stephen Alcorn. 21st Cent. Bks. (Brookfield) 2001 112p il (Holocaust) lib bdg $29.90 *

Grades: 7 8 9 10   **940.53**

1. Holocaust, 1933-1945

ISBN 0-7613-1950-6   LC 00-51221

This takes a "look at the people and organizations that claim the Holocaust never happened. This book looks at the rise of Nazi-affiliated groups, explores the techniques of moral relativism, and examines the current use of the Internet by the ring of deniers." Voice Youth Advocates

The book is "rich with topics for discussion, and the documentation is meticulous. . . . The spacious design, with lots of subheads, photos, and dramatic woodcuts at the start of each chapter, makes the {book} very readable." Booklist

Includes glossary and bibliographical references

Displaced persons; the liberation and abuse of Holocaust survivors. 21st Cent. Bks. (Brookfield) 2001 127p il maps (Holocaust) lib bdg $29.90

Grades: 7 8 9 10   **940.53**

1. Jewish refugees 2. Holocaust survivors

ISBN 0-7613-1924-7   LC 00-51225

This book "looks at the suffering of survivors immediately following {World War II} when many people returned 'home' to face racism, displacement, even massacre, and when countries, including the U.S., denied shelter to most refugees. . . . {This volume is} rich with topics for discussion, and the documentation is meticulous." Booklist

Includes glossary and bibliographical references

Heroes of the Holocaust; illustrations by Stephen Alcorn. 21st Cent. Bks. (Brookfield) 2001 112p il (Holocaust) lib bdg $29.90

Grades: 7 8 9 10   **940.53**

1. Holocaust, 1933-1945 2. World War, 1939-1945—Jews—Rescue 3. World War, 1939-1945—Underground movements

ISBN 0-7613-1717-1   LC 00-32571

This book "focuses on the Jews and Gentiles who risked their lives to save others." Horn Book Guide

This offers "clear, direct prose and a very spacious, readable design. . . . There is much here for classroom discussion." Booklist

Includes bibliographical references

History of World War II. Marshall Cavendish Corp 2004 3v il map set $357.07

Grades: 11 12 Adult   **940.53**

1. World War, 1939-1945

ISBN 0-7614-7482-X   LC 2002-34896

Contents: v. 1. Origins and outbreak -- v. 2. Global war -- v. 3. Victory and aftermath

"These three volumes cover not only the key political and military events during World War II but also the causes and aftermath of the war. Focus includes all aspects of the war and ranges from the historical and political backdrop of the period, to military tactics and strategies, to new technologies. Topics also encompass social and economic change caused by the global conflict, the persecution of various peoples, and the home fronts of the warring nations." Publisher's note

This is an "exceptionally well-researched and documented set. The depth and amount of material covered is remarkable." Libr Media Connect

Includes bibliographical references

The **Holocaust** encyclopedia; Walter Laqueur, editor; Judith Tydor Baumel, associate editor. Yale Univ. Press 2001 xxxix, 765p il maps $60

Grades: 11 12 Adult   **940.53**

1. Holocaust, 1933-1945—Encyclopedias

ISBN 0-300-08432-3   LC 00-106567

This "encyclopedia provides fresh and lengthy articles on such topics as antisemitism, historiography, Jewish women, memorials, and resistance, just to brush the surface." Choice

Includes bibliographical references

Houston, Jeanne Wakatsuki, 1933-

Farewell to Manzanar; a true story of Japanese American experience during and after the World War II internment; [by] Jeanne Wakatsuki Houston and James D. Houston. Houghton Mifflin 2002 c1973 188p $15

Grades: 7 8 9 10   **940.53**

1. Manzanar War Relocation Center 2. Japanese Americans—Evacuation and relocation, 1942-1945 3. World War, 1939-1945—United States

ISBN 0-618-21620-0   LC 2002-727748

Also available in paperback from Bantam Bks.

A reissue with a new afterword of the title first published 1973

Houston, Jeanne Wakatsuki, 1933——*Continued*
"The author tells of the three years she and her family spent at Manzanar, a Japanese internment camp. . . . The last part of the book deals with her postwar adolescence and reentry into American life." Libr J
"A spare, powerful memoir." Rochman. Against borders

Kopf, Hedda Rosner, 1946-
Understanding Anne Frank's The diary of a young girl; a student casebook to issues, sources, and historical documents. Greenwood Press 1997 272p il maps (Greenwood Press literature in context series) $39.95 *
Grades: 9 10 11 12 **940.53**
1. Frank, Anne, 1929-1945 2. Holocaust, 1933-1945
ISBN 0-313-29607-3 LC 96-50294
This work explores "the diary as literature, the history of the Frank family, Anne's childhood, the plight of Holland's Jewish population, rescuers of Holocaust children, and anti-Semitism in modern Germany. Primary texts, such as diaries and letters of other Holocaust children; excerpts from the Nuremberg Laws; minutes of the Wannsee Conference; and articles from the *New York Times*, are used extensively throughout the book. The author writes compassionately yet objectively." SLJ
Includes glossary and bibliographical references

Lewy, Guenter, 1923-
The Nazi persecution of the gypsies. Oxford Univ. Press 2000 306p il hardcover o.p. pa $24.95
Grades: 11 12 Adult **940.53**
1. Gypsies 2. World War, 1939-1945—Atrocities 3. National socialism
ISBN 0-19-512556-8; 0-19-514240-3 (pa)
LC 98-52545
The author "begins with a brief history of the maltreatment of Gypsies all over Europe, from the fifteenth century onward; then, by dint of exhaustive research, Lewy documents the horrors of their expulsions, detentions, deportations, and deaths during the systematic madness of the Holocaust." Booklist
Includes bibliographical references

Life: World War 2; history's greatest conflict in pictures; edited by Richard B. Stolley. Little, Brown 2001 351p il hardcover o.p. pa $29.95 *
Grades: 11 12 Adult **940.53**
1. World War, 1939-1945—Pictorial works 2. World history—20th century—Pictorial works
ISBN 0-8212-2771-8; 0-8212-5713-7 (pa)
LC 2001-93633
"A Bulfinch Press book"
This "album of 665 photographs taken from the archives of *Life* magazine and other collections begins with the years 1919 to 1939, the two decades leading up to World War II. Editor Stolley then proceeds to chronicle the war, year by year through 1945, and ends with what he calls 'the war's aftermath,' 1946 to 2001. . . . For World War II buffs, the book is a natural treasure." Booklist

Meltzer, Milton, 1915-
Never to forget: the Jews of the Holocaust. Harper & Row 1976 217p maps pa $9.99 hardcover o.p. *
Grades: 6 7 8 9 **940.53**
1. Holocaust, 1933-1945
ISBN 0-06-446118-1 (pa)
"The mass murder of six million Jews by the Nazis during World War II is the subject of this compelling history. Interweaving background information, chilling statistics, individual accounts and newspaper reports, it provides an excellent introduction to its subject." Interracial Books Child Bull
Includes bibliographical references

Mothers, sisters, resisters; oral histories of women who survived the Holocaust; edited by Brana Gurewitsch. University of Ala. Press 1998 xxi, 396p (Judaic studies series) $49.95; pa $22.95 *
Grades: 9 10 11 12 **940.53**
1. Holocaust, 1933-1945—Personal narratives 2. Holocaust survivors 3. World War, 1939-1945—Underground movements 4. Jewish women
ISBN 0-8173-0931-4; 0-8173-0952-7 (pa)
LC 98-19753
This is a collection of 25 personal narratives of Jewish women survivors of the Holocaust and their attempts to save themselves, their families and others
Includes bibliographical references

Ng, Wendy L.
Japanese American internment during World War II; a history and reference guide; [by] Wendy Ng. Greenwood Press 2002 xxvi, 204p $45
Grades: 11 12 Adult **940.53**
1. Japanese Americans—Evacuation and relocation, 1942-1945
ISBN 0-313-31375-X LC 00-69128
Contents: Chronology of events in Japanese American history: the Japanese in America before World War II; Evacuation; Life within barbed wire; The question of loyalty: Japanese Americans in the military and draft resisters; Legal challenges to the evacuation and internment; After the war: resettlement and redress; Photographic essay
"The combination of historical facts as presented in the essays and the ideas and sentiments expressed in the primary documents gives readers a vivid sense of this period in history. This readable book would be a solid addition to high school, public, and academic libraries." Voice Youth Advocates
Includes bibliographical references

Nicholas, Lynn H.
Cruel world; the children of Europe in the Nazi web. A.A. Knopf 2005 632p il maps $35; pa $17.95
Grades: 11 12 Adult **940.53**
1. World War, 1939-1945—Children 2. Children and war 3. Holocaust, 1933-1945
ISBN 0-679-45464-0; 0-679-77663-X (pa)
LC 2004-57745

Nicholas, Lynn H.—*Continued*
This is an account of the lives of children in Europe
during the Holocaust and World War II.
The author "has put together a well-written, compel-
ling history that makes us look at the war era anew."
Publ Wkly
Includes bibliographical references

O'Neill, William L.
World War II: a student companion. Oxford
Univ. Press 1999 384p il (Oxford student
companions to American history) lib bdg $60
Grades: 7 8 9 10   **940.53**
1. World War, 1939-1945
ISBN 0-19-510800-0   LC 98-54918
This volume includes "entries on individuals, battles,
military organizations, theaters, origins, weapon systems,
and countries. . . . Articles vary in length from two or
three paragraphs to several pages. . . . *Literature* and
motion pictures have brief lists of classic World War II
novels and films, respectively. A chronology, a list of
museums and historic sites, and a general bibliography
that includes Web sites give students additional tools to
expand their original search." Booklist
"A readable, concise, and informative book." SLJ

Only what we could carry; the Japanese American
internment experience; edited with introduction
by Lawson Fusao Inada; preface by Patricia
Wakida; afterword by William Hohri. Heyday
Bks. 2000 xxiii, 439p il maps pa $18.95 *
Grades: 11 12 Adult   **940.53**
1. Japanese Americans—Evacuation and relocation,
1942-1945
ISBN 1-89077-130-9   LC 00-9182
This anthology includes "poetry, prose, biography,
news accounts, formal government declarations, letters,
and autobiography along with photographs, sketches, and
cartoons. . . . Readers will come away from this book
with a deep understanding of the times, the sense of betrayal, and the conflicting feelings among the three major
groups of Japanese who went through the ordeal." SLJ
Includes bibliographical references

Oppenheim, Joanne
Dear Miss Breed; true stories of the Japanese
American incarceration during World War II and
a librarian who made a difference; foreword by
Elizabeth Kikuchi Yamada; afterword by Snowden
Becker. Scholastic 2006 287p il $22.99 *
Grades: 7 8 9 10   **940.53**
1. Breed, Clara E., 1906-1994 2. Japanese Americans—Evacuation and relocation, 1942-1945
3. World War, 1939-1945—United States
4. Librarians
ISBN 0-439-56992-3; 978-0-439-56992-7
      LC 2004-59009
This "account focuses on Clara Breed, a children's librarian at the San Diego Public Library, and the Japanese-American children she served prior to World War II
and whom she continued to serve after their families
were sent to an Arizona internment camp. . . . Illustrated
with numerous photographs . . . and incorporating copi-

ous letters and documents, the book is . . . compelling."
Horn Book
Includes bibliographical references

The **Oxford** companion to World War II; general
editor, I.C.B. Dear; consultant editor, M.R.D.
Foot. New ed. Oxford University Press 2005
1072p il map $75
Grades: 11 12 Adult   **940.53**
1. World War, 1939-1945—Encyclopedias
ISBN 0-19-280670-X; 978-0-19-280670-3
First published 1995
Entries in this companion include "surveys of the
countries involved in the conflict; politics and strategy;
domestic and economic issues; resistance and intelligence; campaigns and battles; warfare and weapons; wartime leaders and influential people; [and] slogans and
slang." Publisher's note
Includes bibliographical references

Reporting World War II. Library of Am. 1995 2v
ea $35 *
Grades: 11 12 Adult   **940.53**
1. World War, 1939-1945 2. Reporters and reporting
ISBN 1-883011-04-3 (v1); 1-883011-05-1 (v2)
      LC 94-45463
Contents: v1 American journalism, 1938-1944; v2
American journalism, 1944-1946
This "collection of some 200 entries by nearly 90
writers, drawn from newspapers, magazine articles,
broadcast transcripts and book excerpts, recalls WW II
campaigns and battles in all theaters but pays attention
to the home front as well. It begins with an excerpt from
William L. Shirer's *Berlin Diary* and ends with one from
John Hersey's *Hiroshima*. . . . This is a treasure trove
of war reporting, featuring writing of the highest order."
Publ Wkly

Robinson, Greg, 1966-
By order of the president; FDR and the
internment of Japanese Americans. Harvard Univ.
Press 2001 322p $27.95; pa $19.95 *
Grades: 11 12 Adult   **940.53**
1. Roosevelt, Franklin D. (Franklin Delano), 1882-
1945 2. Japanese Americans—Evacuation and
relocation, 1942-1945 3. World War, 1939-1945—
United States
ISBN 0-674-00639-9; 0-674-01118-X (pa)
      LC 2001-24609
"Using memos, reports, diary entries, letters, and other
documents written by FDR and his staff, this book offers
[a] look at the role of Roosevelt and his advisers in making the decision to intern." Libr J
This is a "lucid, comprehensive and balanced examination." Publ Wkly
Includes bibliographical references

Rogasky, Barbara, 1933-
Smoke and ashes; the story of the Holocaust.
rev and expanded ed. Holiday House 2002 256p il
maps $27.50; pa $14.95 *
Grades: 6 7 8 9   **940.53**
   1. Holocaust, 1933-1945
   ISBN 0-8234-1612-7; 0-8234-1677-1 (pa)
                                    LC 2001-16797
   First published 1988
   The author "details the dark horror of Nazism—from
the beginning pogroms the Nazis organized against German Jews to the setting up of concentration camps and
death factories. . . . In clear and simple prose, she relates how the Jews lived and died in the camps . . . and
how a small number of non-Jews helped them in their
struggle. She concludes with an account of the
Nuremburg Trials and the many instances of contemporary anti-Semitism that have outlived Hitler." SLJ {re-
view of 1988 edition}
   Includes bibliographical references

Samuel, Wolfgang W. E.
The war of our childhood; memories of World
War II; {reported by} Wolfgang W.E. Samuel.
University Press of Miss. 2002 356p il $30
Grades: 11 12 Adult   **940.53**
   1. World War, 1939-1945—Children 2. World War,
   1939-1945—Personal narratives
   ISBN 1-57806-482-1   LC 2002-6172
   These "memories by 27 German survivors of World
War II relate how as children—ages 3 to 12—they en-
dured air raids, hunger, terror, invading armies, and de-
privation. Samuel tells of their resilience under the most
trying circumstances and the critical role their mothers
played in their lives." Booklist

Schneider, Carl J.
World War II; [by] Carl J. Schneider and
Dorothy Schneider. Facts on File 2003 472p il
map (Eyewitness history) $75; pa $21.95
Grades: 9 10 11 12   **940.53**
   1. World War, 1939-1945—United States 2. United
   States—History—1933-1945
   ISBN 0-8160-4484-8; 0-8160-4485-6 (pa)
                                    LC 2002-15268
   This volume includes letters, speeches and newspaper
articles as well as excerpts from documents and from
capsule biographies of key figures.
   "This useful volume offers a good blend of historical
fact and primary-source material." SLJ
   Includes bibliographical references

Shermer, Michael
Denying history; who says the Holocaust never
happened and why do they say it? [by] Michael
Shermer, Alex Grobman; foreword by Arthur
Hertzberg. University of Calif. Press 2000 312p
hardcover o.p. pa $17.95 *
Grades: 11 12 Adult   **940.53**
   1. Holocaust, 1933-1945
   ISBN 0-520-21612-1; 0-520-23469-3 (pa)
                                    LC 00-28690

   The authors "respond to specific attacks that have
been made over the years against the veracity of the accepted 'facts' of the Holocaust;. . .[they also] discuss
historical truth, how we know it, and what motivates
some people to become deniers." New Leader
   "Using the deniers' own words to tear down their arguments, Shermer and Grobman provide a clear method
for determining the reality of past events and supply a
powerful weapon for anyone who cares about learning
from the credible historical record." Publ Wkly
   Includes bibliographical references

Spiegelman, Art
Maus; a survivor's tale. Pantheon Bks. 1996 2v
in 1 il $35 *
Grades: 7 8 9 10   **940.53**
   1. Spiegelman, Vladek 2. Holocaust, 1933-1945—
   Graphic novels 3. Graphic novels
   ISBN 0-679-40641-7   LC 96-32796
   Also available The complete Maus; available paper-
back boxed set edition $28 (ISBN 0-679-74840-7)
   A combined edition of Maus (1986) and Maus II
(1991)
   Contents: My father bleeds history; And here my trou-
bles began
   In this work "Spiegelman takes the comic book to a
new level of seriousness, portraying Jews as mice and
Nazis as cats. Depicting himself being told about the
Holocaust by his Polish survivor father, Spiegelman not
only explores the concentration-camp experience, but
also the guilt, love, and anger between father and son."
Rochman. Against borders

Stargardt, Nicholas
Witnesses of war; children's lives under the
Nazis. Distributed by Random House 2006 493p il
map $30; pa $16.95
Grades: 11 12 Adult   **940.53**
   1. World War, 1939-1945—Children
   ISBN   1-4000-4088-4;   978-1-4000-4088-9;
   1-4000-3379-9 (pa); 978-1-4000-3379-9 (pa)
                                    LC 2005-50409
   First published 2005 in the United Kingdom
   The author "divides this work into chapters following
the rise, escalation, and defeat of Nazism, concentrating
on how children (Jews, patients at mental hospitals, inmates in juvenile homes, 'regular' Germans, and con-
quered nationalities) coped with this existence." Libr J
   This is "a sharp and taut account of misery." Publ
Wkly
   Includes bibliographical references

Takaki, Ronald T., 1939-
Double victory; a multicultural history of
America in World War II; [by] Ronald Takaki.
Little, Brown 2000 282p il $28; pa $19.99 *
Grades: 11 12 Adult   **940.53**
   1. World War, 1939-1945—United States 2. United
   States—Race relations
   ISBN 0-316-83155-7; 0-316-83156-5 (pa)
                                    LC 99-40374

Takaki, Ronald T., 1939-—*Continued*

"Takaki discusses the experiences of African Americans, Indians, Chicanos, Asian Americans from several nations, German and Italian Americans, and Jewish Americans. . . . Despite Jim Crow, internment camps, neglected slums, barrios, reservations, and rejection of Jewish refugees, the nation's not-quite-Americans fought bravely in World War II." Booklist

Includes bibliographical references

Voices of the Holocaust; Lorie Jenkins McElroy, editor. U.X.L 1997 2v set $120
Grades: 9 10 11 12   **940.53**
1. Holocaust, 1933-1945 2. World War, 1939-1945—Jews
ISBN 0-7876-1746-6   LC 97-33195
Contents: v1 Antisemitism, escalation, victims; v2 Resistors, liberation, understanding

"A collection of 34 excerpted or full-text poems, memoirs, articles, essays, speeches, and newspaper accounts written by people who were either victims of the Holocaust or commentators on it at the time. . . . Each document is introduced and followed by information about its impact, what happened to its author, and a list for further reading." SLJ

Includes bibliographical references

Weglyn, Michi, 1926-1999

Years of infamy; the untold story of America's concentration camps; [by] Michi Nishiura Weglyn; with an introduction by James A. Michener. Updated ed. University of Wash. Press 1996 351p il map pa $25
Grades: 9 10 11 12   **940.53**
1. Japanese Americans—Evacuation and relocation, 1942-1945 2. World War, 1939-1945—United States
ISBN 0-295-97484-2   LC 95-45374
First published 1976 by Morrow

A first-person account of the injustices experienced during the evacuation and relocation of Japanese Americans during World War II.

Includes bibliographical references

Witness; voices from the Holocaust; edited by Joshua M. Greene and Shiva Kumar in consultation with Joanne Weiner Rudof; foreword by Lawrence L. Langer; in association with the Fortunoff Video Archive for Holocaust Testimonies, Yale University. Free Press 2000 xxx, 270p il $26; pa $15 *
Grades: 11 12 Adult   **940.53**
1. Holocaust, 1933-1945—Personal narratives
ISBN 0-684-86525-4; 0-684-86526-2 (pa)
                                      LC 99-58401

In this companion to the PBS series the editors "have woven together the testimonies of 27 individuals into an unforgettable narrative of the Holocaust: starting with pre-WWII Jewish life, they go on to describe the war's out-break, ghettos, resistance and hiding, death camps, death marches, liberation and life after the Holocaust." Publ Wkly

Includes bibliographical references

Women in the Holocaust; [edited by] Dalia Ofer and Lenore J. Weitzman. Yale Univ. Press 1998 402p hardcover o.p. pa $16.95
Grades: 11 12 Adult   **940.53**
1. Holocaust, 1933-1945 2. Jewish women
ISBN 0-300-07354-2; 0-300-08080-8 (pa)
                                      LC 97-46011

This is a collection of 21 articles by historians, sociologists, writers, literary scholars and survivors. "The book is divided into four parts: before the war, life in the ghettos, resistance and rescue, and labor camps and concentration camps." Booklist

Includes bibliographical references

World War II; Myra Immell, book editor. Greenhaven Press 2001 283p il maps (Turning points in world history) lib bdg $34.95; pa $23.70
Grades: 7 8 9 10   **940.53**
1. World War, 1939-1945
ISBN 0-7377-0699-6 (lib bdg); 0-7377-0698-8 (pa)
                                      LC 2001-16033

This is a collection of essays about World War II, with an introduction placing the essays in context and summaries of each one

Includes bibliographical references

World War II: a student encyclopedia; Spencer C. Tucker, editor; Priscilla Mary Roberts, editor, Documents volume; Jack Greene . . . [et al.], assistant editors. ABC-CLIO 2005 5v il map set $485
Grades: 9 10 11 12   **940.53**
1. World War, 1939-1945—Encyclopedias
ISBN 1-85109-857-7; 978-1-85109-857-6
                                      LC 2004-29951

This "encyclopedia covers the entire scope of the Second World War, from its earliest roots to its continuing impact on global politics and human society." Publisher's note

Includes bibliographical references

WWII: the people's story; Nigel Fountain, general editor. Reader's Digest 2003 315p il map $39.95
Grades: 9 10 11 12   **940.53**
1. World War, 1939-1945
ISBN 0-7621-0376-0   LC 2003-43172
Accompanied by computer disc

"Through letters, speeches, diaries, and interviews, this title provides insight into the thoughts and feelings of presidents and prime ministers during this period as well as soldiers, journalists, and children. Between excerpted comments, the text fills in the background information. . . . Pages are peppered with black-and-white and color photographs and reproductions depicting numerous aspects of the war. . . . An accompanying CD will allow students to hear the firsthand accounts included in the book." SLJ

Includes bibliographical references

Yancey, Diane
The internment of the Japanese. Lucent Bks. 2001 112p il (World history series) lib bdg $27.45
Grades: 7 8 9 10 **940.53**
1. Japanese Americans—Evacuation and relocation, 1942-1945 2. World War, 1939-1945—United States
ISBN 1-59018-013-5 LC 2001-6270
This is a history of the internment of Japanese Americans during World War II.
"Well designed for research and reports, this account includes primary- and secondary-source quotations. . . . The numerous black-and-white photos set the tone and enhance the information. . . . This informative, approachable text will be useful in most collections." SLJ
Includes bibliographical references

Yellin, Emily, 1961-
Our mothers' war; American women at home and at the Front during World War II. Free Press 2004 447p il hardcover o.p. pa $14 *
Grades: 11 12 Adult **940.53**
1. World War, 1939-1945—Women
ISBN 0-7432-4514-8; 0-7432-4516-4 (pa)
LC 2004-40496
Also available Thorndike Press large print edition
"Yellin reveals all of the responsibilities held by women, including helping to manufacture aircraft, ships, and other munitions; and, in the process, outproducing all of America's allies and enemies, by far. Readers see war brides who worked hard to maintain the morale of their husbands while surviving long separation, fear, and shortages of virtually everything necessary to support a family. . . . [This book] is an important book because the role played by women in World War II has been regularly ignored." SLJ
Includes bibliographical references

940.54 World War II, 1939-1945 (Military conduct of the war)

Aaseng, Nathan, 1953-
Navajo code talkers. Walker & Co. 1992 114p il map hardcover o.p. pa $8.95
Grades: 6 7 8 9 **940.54**
1. World War, 1939-1945 2. Navajo Indians 3. Cryptography
ISBN 0-8027-8182-9; 0-8027-7589-6 (pa)
LC 92-11408
Describes how the American military in World War II used a group of Navajo Indians to create an indecipherable code based on their native language.
"A good choice for an offbeat 'war book,' this would also make an unusual complement for both history and language arts classes. Historical photos of the code-talkers in action are included." Bull Cent Child Books
Includes bibliographical references

The **Attack** on Pearl Harbor; Thomas Streissguth, book editor. Greenhaven Press 2002 128p map (At issue in history) lib bdg $27.45 *
Grades: 9 10 11 12 **940.54**
1. Pearl Harbor (Oahu, Hawaii), Attack on, 1941
ISBN 0-7377-0752-6 (lib bdg) LC 2001-42922

"This book details the day of the attack and debates the role of the Roosevelt administration and senior army and naval officers in one of America's worst military defeats." Publisher's note
This is "a well-balanced treatise on who knew what, and when, and who was responsible for the lack of preparedness before the attack. . . . The text draws no conclusions, but permits readers to reach their own. . . . Nonetheless, this title deals with a debate that is seldom addressed." SLJ
Includes bibliographical references

Ballard, Robert D., 1942-
Graveyards of the Pacific; from Pearl Harbor to Bikini Atoll; [by] Robert D. Ballard with Michael Hamilton Morgan. National Geographic Soc. 2001 255p il maps $45
Grades: 11 12 Adult **940.54**
1. World War, 1939-1945—Naval operations 2. Shipwrecks
ISBN 0-7922-6366-9
This "overview of the Pacific war begins with [an] . . . account of Ballard's search for an elusive midget sub sunk just prior to the attack on Pearl Harbor, and ends with the American nuclear tests on Bikini Island, where captured German and Japanese craft were scuttled." Publisher's note
Includes bibliographical references

Bradley, James
Flags of our fathers; [by] James Bradley with Ron Powers. Bantam Bks. 2000 376p $24.95; pa $14 *
Grades: 11 12 Adult **940.54**
1. Rosenthal, Joe, 1911-2006 2. United States. Marine Corps 3. Iwo Jima, Battle of, 1945
ISBN 0-553-11133-7; 0-553-38415-5 (pa)
LC 00-25803
Also available large print edition $16.95 (ISBN: 0-7393-2659-7)
This is the "story of the most famous photograph to come out of World War II, the flag-raising on Mount Suribachi during the Battle of Iwo Jima in February 1945. Bradley is the son of one of the six men immortalized in that remarkable photo, and his gripping narrative, vivid descriptions, and heartfelt style make this a powerful story of courage, humility, and tragedy." Libr J
Includes bibliographical references

Brokaw, Tom, 1940-
An album of memories; personal histories from the greatest generation. Random House 2001 314p il maps $29.95; pa $14.95 *
Grades: 11 12 Adult **940.54**
1. World War, 1939-1945—Personal narratives
ISBN 0-375-50581-4; 0-375-76041-5 (pa)
LC 2001-273436
Also available large print edition $29.95 (ISBN 0-375-43134-9)
This volume "gathers letters written to Brokaw by Americans who lived through the Depression and World War II and, in some cases, letters written by their chil-

Brokaw, Tom, 1940-—*Continued*
dren. Brokaw provides a brief introduction and a time
line for each chapter; these cover the Depression, the war
in Europe and in the Pacific, and the wartime 'home
front,' closing with 'Reflections.' The book is lavishly illustrated with reproductions of photographs, drawings,
documents, and other memorabilia of the era." Booklist

Dunnigan, James F.
The Pacific War encyclopedia; {by} James F.
Dunnigan and Albert A. Nofi. Facts on File 1998
2v il maps set $137.50 *
Grades: 11 12 Adult   **940.54**
1. World War, 1939-1945—Encyclopedias
ISBN 0-8160-3439-7   LC 97-15634
"Entries are arranged alphabetically and include . . .
(military personnel and politicos from all sides, as well
as persons such as Charles Lindbergh and Ernie Pyle),
places (Manchukuo, Melbourne, Nagasaki, Timor, etc.)
and events (Battle of Iwo Jima, Port Chicago mutiny)."
Booklist
This work "is lively as well as informative, and . . .
will be attractive to military buffs while still useful to
more serious researchers." Libr J

Frank, Richard B.
Downfall; the end of the Imperial Japanese
Empire. Penguin 2001 484p il map pa $18
Grades: 11 12 Adult   **940.54**
1. World War, 1939-1945—Japan 2. World War,
1939-1945—Aerial operations 3. Japan—History—
1868-1945
ISBN 0-14-100146-1
First published 1999 by Random House
"Weaving together the strands of military and diplo-
matic events, Frank contends that absent the bombings of
Hiroshima and Nagasaki the war would have continued
for at least several more months, at a cost in Japanese
and Allied civilian and combatant lives far in excess of
the admittedly awful toll that the atomic bombs exacted.
A powerful work of history." Libr J
Includes bibliographical references

Fussell, Paul, 1924-
The boys' crusade; the American infantry in
Northwestern Europe, 1944-1945. Modern Lib.
2003 184p hardcover o.p. pa $12.95
Grades: 11 12 Adult   **940.54**
1. World War, 1939-1945—Campaigns 2. World War,
1939-1945—Europe
ISBN 0-679-64088-6; 0-8129-7488-3 (pa)
                                   LC 2003-44556
"A Modern Library chronicles book"
This memoir of World War II includes "a series of essays dealing with strategy, tactics, and leadership from
the landings at Normandy to the fall of Berlin. . . .
Fussell describes the typical GI as 18 to 20 years old,
from all types of social and educational backgrounds,
taken from minimal training and thrown into ground
combat of the fiercest kind. . . . This work is aimed at
correcting the sanitized works of 'sentimental' history the
war has inspired. Highly recommended." Libr J
Includes bibliographical references

Goldstein, Donald M.
The way it was; Pearl Harbor, the original
photographs; [by] Donald M. Goldstein, Katherine
V. Dillon and J. Michael Wenger.
Pergamon-Brassey's 1991 181p il maps hardcover
o.p. pa $19.95
Grades: 11 12 Adult   **940.54**
1. Pearl Harbor (Oahu, Hawaii), Attack on, 1941—
Pictorial works
ISBN 0-08-040573-8; 1-57488-359-3 (pa)
                                   LC 90-49572
This is a collection of photographs of the Japanese at-
tack on Pearl Harbor in 1941.
"The 430 prints in this . . . collection were gathered
from various Japanese and U.S. sources, and most have
never been seen by the general public. The majority were
taken during the height of the air raid itself, many from
Japanese cockpits. . . . The overall effect is to give the
reader an uncanny sense of being present at the battle."
Libr J

The **good** war; an oral history of World War Two;
[edited by] Studs Terkel. New Press 1997 589p
pa $16.95 *
Grades: 11 12 Adult   **940.54**
1. World War, 1939-1945—Personal narratives
ISBN 1-56584-343-6   LC 2003-389322
First published 1984 by Pantheon Bks.
In a series of interviews Terkel depicts how WWII affected the lives of average Americans.

Hastings, Max
Overlord: D-Day and the battle for Normandy.
Simon & Schuster 1984 368p il maps hardcover
o.p. pa $22.95
Grades: 11 12 Adult   **940.54**
1. Operation Overlord 2. Normandy (France), Attack
on, 1944
ISBN 0-671-46029-3; 0-671-55435-2 (pa)
                                   LC 83-20439
Also available in paperback from Vintage Books
Hastings presents an "analysis of the Normandy cam-
paign. He . . . [considers] the limits of the Allied ar-
mies' fighting power compared to the Wehrmacht." Libr
J
"Hastings' reportage of the battle is not unworthy to
stand with that of the best journalists and writers who
witnessed it. . . . He has managed to recreate what it
was like for almost everyone who was there." N Y
Times Book Rev
Includes bibliographical references

Hersey, John, 1914-1993
Hiroshima; a new edition with a final chapter
written forty years after the explosion. Knopf 1985
196p il $26; pa $6.50 *
Grades: 11 12 Adult   **940.54**
1. Hiroshima (Japan)—Bombardment, 1945
2. Atomic bomb 3. World War, 1939-1945—Japan
ISBN 0-394-54844-2; 0-679-72103-7 (pa)
                                   LC 85-40346
First published 1946
An account of the aftermath of the first atomic bomb
as reflected in the lives of six survivors

Kurson, Robert, 1963-
Shadow divers; the true adventure of two Americans who risked everything to solve one of the last mysteries of World War II. Random House 2004 375p il $26.95; pa $14.95
Grades: 9 10 11 12   940.54
1. U-869 (Submarine) 2. Excavations (Archeology) 3. Shipwrecks 4. Underwater exploration
ISBN 0-375-50858-9; 0-375-76098-9 (pa)
                                LC 2003-60362
Also available large print edition $28.95 (ISBN 0-375-43387-2)
"A journalist recounts the adventures of two deep-sea divers who discover a World War II German U-boat off the coast of New Jersey." Booklist
This book "features undersea thrills, a gripping mystery, incredible discoveries, true-blue friendship, life-or-death crises and history unfolding before the reader's eyes." N Y Times (Late N Y Ed)
Includes bibliographical references

Leckie, Robert
Okinawa; the last battle of World War II. Viking 1995 220p il hardcover o.p. pa $13.95
Grades: 11 12 Adult   940.54
1. World War, 1939-1945—Campaigns—Okinawa Island
ISBN 0-670-84716-X; 0-14-017389-7 (pa)
                                LC 94-39145
In this history of the Battle of Okinawa "Leckie supplies an accessible historical overview of a perplexing war tactic, the kamikaze attack." Booklist

Lord, Walter, 1917-2002
Day of infamy. [60th anniversary ed] Holt & Co. 2001 241p il hardcover o.p. pa $14 *
Grades: 9 10 11 12   940.54
1. Pearl Harbor (Oahu, Hawaii), Attack on, 1941
ISBN 0-8050-6809-0; 0-8050-6803-1 (pa)
                                LC 00-54247
A reissue of the title first published 1957
Based on over 500 eyewitness reports, this book provides a minute-by-minute account of the Japanese attack on Pearl Harbor.

Megellas, James
All the way to Berlin; a paratrooper at war in Europe. Presidio Press 2003 xxi, 309p il maps $25.95
Grades: 11 12 Adult   940.54
1. World War, 1939-1945—Personal narratives 2. World War, 1939-1945—Campaigns 3. World War, 1939-1945—Europe
ISBN 0-89141-784-2   LC 2002-192563
This is the author's account of "the September 1944 assault across the Waal River. . . . The attrition Megellas witnessed over months on the front line, at Anzio and in the Battle of the Bulge, shapes his narrative, but his observations about the craft of killing lend it a distinctive tone. . . . Strongly put and unsentimental, this memoir is a must for the World War II collection." Booklist

Nelson, Pete
Left for dead; a young man's search for justice for the USS Indianapolis; [by] Peter Nelson; with a preface by Hunter Scott. Delacorte Press 2002 xx, 201p il hardcover o.p. pa $8.95 *
Grades: 7 8 9 10   940.54
1. McVay, Charles Butler, III 2. Scott, Hunter 3. Indianapolis (Cruiser) 4. World War, 1939-1945—Naval operations
ISBN 0-385-72959-6; 0-385-73091-8 (pa)
                                LC 2001-53774
Recalls the sinking of the U.S.S. Indianapolis at the end of World War II, the navy cover-up and unfair court martial of the ship's captain, and how a young boy helped the survivors set the record straight fifty-five years later.
"Written in simple chronological order, it tells a powerful story." Book Rep
Includes bibliographical references

Overy, R. J. (Richard James), 1947-
The Battle of Britain; the myth and the reality; by Richard Overy. Norton 2001 177p maps hardcover o.p. pa $13.95 *
Grades: 11 12 Adult   940.54
1. Britain, Battle of, 1940
ISBN 0-393-02008-8; 0-393-32297-1 (pa)
                                LC 00-69249
First published 2000 in the United Kingdom with title: The Battle
This is an "account of the battle, its effects on the civilian population and its current place in history." N Y Times Book Rev
Includes bibliographical references

The **Pacific** war companion; from Pearl Harbor to Hiroshima; editor, Daniel Marston. Osprey 2005 272p il map $29.95; pa $12.95
Grades: 11 12 Adult   940.54
1. World War, 1939-1945—Campaigns—Pacific Ocean
ISBN   1-84176-882-0;   978-1-84176-882-3; 1-84603-212-1 (pa); 978-1-84603-212-7 (pa)
"These essays on the Pacific theater of WW II, written by a group of international scholars representing Australia, Great Britain, Japan, and the US, cover the wellknown events at Pearl Harbor, the Coral Sea, and Midway; MacArthur's push to the Philippines; Nimitz's island campaign in the central Pacific; Okinawa; and the dropping of the atomic bomb on Hiroshima and Nagasaki. . . . A chronology, detailed maps, and photographs greatly enhance this excellent volume on the Pacific phase of WW II." Choice
Includes bibliographical references

Stanton, Doug

In harm's way; the sinking of the USS Indianapolis and the extraordinary story of its survivors. Holt & Co. 2001 333p il hardcover o.p. pa $14

Grades: 11 12 Adult   **940.54**
  1. Indianapolis (Cruiser) 2. World War, 1939-1945—Naval operations 3. Shipwrecks
  ISBN 0-8050-6632-2; 0-8050-7366-3 (pa)
                                     LC 00-68254
Stanton discusses the loss of the USS Indianapolis, which was given the "job of carrying components of the Hiroshima bomb from San Francisco to Tinian. . . . The Indianapolis (then) headed for Leyte in the Philippines. . . . On July 30, 1945, the Indianapolis was cruising, unescorted, west of Guam when two torpedoes struck it, sinking the ship in a few minutes. An estimated 300 men were killed by the blast or entombed below. About 900 went into the Pacific. . . . Only 321 survived; of these, some died later in the hospital." Natl Rev

"Illuminating and emotional without being maudlin, Stanton's book helps explain what many have long considered an inexplicable catastrophe." Publ Wkly

Takaki, Ronald T., 1939-

Hiroshima; why America dropped the atomic bomb; [by] Ronald Takaki. Little, Brown 1995 193p il $28; pa $14.95 *

Grades: 11 12 Adult   **940.54**
  1. World War, 1939-1945—United States 2. Atomic bomb 3. Hiroshima (Japan)—Bombardment, 1945
  ISBN 0-316-83122-0; 0-316-83124-7 (pa)
                                     LC 95-13546
This study of the bombings of Hiroshima and Nagasaki focuses on the psychological motivations of the American decision-makers, especially Harry Truman.

"Right or wrong, the study is a provocative addition to the unresolved debate over the dropping of the atomic bombs." Publ Wkly

Includes bibliographical references

Tomblin, Barbara

G.I. nightingales; the Army Nurse Corps in World War II; [by] Barbara Brooks Tomblin. University Press of Ky. 1996 254p il hardcover o.p. pa $22 *

Grades: 11 12 Adult   **940.54**
  1. United States. Army Nurse Corps
  ISBN 0-8131-1951-0; 0-8131-9079-7 (pa)
                                     LC 96-1018
This is "an account of the 80,000 army nurses who served during World War II. These nurses participated in every theater of the war; some died while on duty, and many were decorated for their bravery. Along with their deserving stories, the reader learns the history of women nurses in the military." Libr J

Includes bibliographical references

World War II; Don Nardo, book editor. Greenhaven Press 2005 203p il (Opposing viewpoints in world history) lib bdg $34.95; pa $23.70 *

Grades: 9 10 11 12   **940.54**
  1. World War, 1939-1945
  ISBN 0-7377-2587-7 (lib bdg); 0-7377-2588-5 (pa)
                                     LC 2004-52277
"Four chapters discuss the assessment of blame for the attack on Pearl Harbor, the justification for the internment of Japanese Americans, the necessity and morality of using the atomic bomb, and whether the war deserves its nostalgic 'good war' image." SLJ

Includes bibliographical references

940.55   Europe--1945-

Living through the end of the Cold War; edited by Jeff Hay. Greenhaven Press 2005 141p il (Living through the Cold War) lib bdg $32.45

Grades: 9 10 11 12   **940.55**
  1. Cold war 2. World politics—1945-1991
  ISBN 0-7377-2132-4   LC 2004-42437
This book "captures the drama and historical significance of declining hostilities between the United States and Russia. The text offers speeches by Reagan, Gorbachev, Yelstin, and Havel, plus commentary on change in Russian lives and the collapse of the Iron Curtain." Libr Media Connect

Includes bibliographical references

Speakman, Jay

The Cold War. Greenhaven Press 2001 128p il (Opposing viewpoints digests) hardcover o.p. pa $19.95 *

Grades: 7 8 9 10   **940.55**
  1. Cold war 2. World politics—1945-1991 3. United States—Foreign relations—Soviet Union 4. Soviet Union—Foreign relations—United States
  ISBN 0-7377-0421-7; 0-7377-0420-9 (pa)
                                     LC 00-11681
This explores the causes and consequences of the Cold War and whether the cost was justified, using primary and secondary sources to place each viewpoint in the context of its supporters and detractors.

Includes bibliographical references

941   British Isles

The **British** inheritance; a treasury of historic documents; edited by Elizabeth Hallam and Andrew Prescott. University of Calif. Press 1999 150p il maps $39.95 *

Grades: 9 10 11 12   **941**
  1. Manuscripts 2. Great Britain—History
  ISBN 0-520-22470-1   LC 00-712550
"This volume displays, in chronological order, key documents which illuminate defining moments in British history. The documents are accompanied by . . . commentaries by experts and curators, placing the material in context and explaining its significance. Alongside such

The British inheritance—*Continued*
{documents} . . . as the Domesday Book and Magna Carta are many less-well-known . . . items such as Oscar Wilde's calling card and the last letter of Mary, Queen of Scots." Publisher's note

Includes bibliographical references

Events that changed Great Britain, from 1066 to 1714; edited by Frank W. Thackeray and John E. Findling. Greenwood Press 2003 201p il $46.95
Grades: 9 10 11 12   **941**
1. Great Britain—History
ISBN 0-313-31666-X   LC 2003-45527
This "resource describes and evaluates ten of the most important events in British history between the Norman Conquest of 1066 and the Glorious Revolution of 1689 and its aftermath." Publisher's note

Includes bibliographical references

Events that changed Great Britain since 1689; edited by Frank W. Thackeray & John E. Findling. Greenwood Press 2002 217p il $44.95
Grades: 9 10 11 12   **941**
1. Great Britain—History
ISBN 0-313-31686-4   LC 2002-16103
Contents: The Industrial Revolution, c.1750-c.1850, by D. Mitch; The Seven Years' War, 1756-1763, by F. M. Stowell; The Napoleonic Wars, 1789-1815, by S. J. Stearns; Pax Britannica, 1815-1914, by L. J. Satre; The Reform Act of 1832, by T. C. Mackey; The Great Exhibition of 1851, by D. J. Reynolds; Sinn Fein and the Suffragettes, by K. L. Campbell; World War I, 1914-1919, by L. P. Thornton; World War II, 1939-1945, by G. P. Blum; The Thatcher era, 1979-1990, by R. A. Leiby
"Each chapter deals with a different event and contains an overview, an interpretive essay by an expert on the topic, an illustration or photograph, and a selected annotated bibliography. . . . With its concentrated view on British historic events, this book will be a valuable resource for high school history collections." Libr Media Connect

The Lives of the kings & queens of England; edited by Antonia Fraser. rev and updated. University of Calif. Press 1998 384p il maps hardcover o.p. pa $27.50 *
Grades: 9 10 11 12   **941**
1. Great Britain—Kings and rulers
ISBN 0-520-21938-4; 0-520-22460-4 (pa)
                               LC 99-169506
First published 1975 in the United Kingdom; first United States edition 1995
"A collection of biographical sketches that encompasses the period from the establishment of monarchical power by the early Norman kings through the reign of Elizabeth II. . . . Accompanying the text are 175 contemporary illustrations and drawings of the royal coats of arms." Publisher's note

The **Oxford** illustrated history of Britain; edited by Kenneth O. Morgan. Oxford Univ. Press 1984 640p il maps hardcover o.p. pa $19.95
Grades: 11 12 Adult   **941**
1. Great Britain—History
ISBN 0-19-822684-5; 0-19-280135-X (pa)
                               LC 83-21990
"2,000 years of British history as told by ten leading historians. Details how the past has shaped British character, patriotism, and ethnocentrism. Includes over 250 illustrations, chronologies, genealogies of monarchs, and a table of Prime Ministers." N Y Public Libr Book of How & Where To Look It Up

Tompson, Richard S.
Great Britain: a reference guide from the Renaissance to the present. Facts on File 2003 552p il (European nations series) $85 *
Grades: 11 12 Adult   **941**
1. Great Britain—History
ISBN 0-8160-4474-0   LC 200219
This guide contains "an introductory overview of British history, Renaissance to the present; a narrative history; a historical dictionary, topical and biographical; a chronology; appendixes (maps, genealogies of English royal houses, lists of English sovereigns from 899, and prime ministers from 1721). The work concludes with an unannotated bibliography, arranged in sections for bibliogaphies, dictionaries and encyclopedias, general works, surveys, and topics." Choice

941.081 British Isles--Reign of Victoria, 1837-1901

Mitchell, Sally, 1937-
Daily life in Victorian England. Greenwood Press 1996 311p il (Greenwood Press daily life through history series) $49.95 *
Grades: 11 12 Adult   **941.081**
1. Great Britain—History—19th century 2. Great Britain—Civilization
ISBN 0-313-29467-4   LC 96-2539
Also available online
This overview of rural and urban life in Victorian England describes the "physical, social, economic, and legal aspects of life in the three basic classes of English society—working class, middle class, and aristocracy—and the rules and traditions that governed each. Each chapter deals with a different subject: work, technology and science, home life, education, health and medicine. The chapters make interesting reading for general background or can be used as a reference." Book Rep

Includes glossary and bibliographical references

Victorian England; Clarice Swisher, book editor. Greenhaven Press 2000 263p (Turning points in world history) lib bdg $31.20; pa $19.95
Grades: 9 10 11 12   **941.081**
1. Great Britain—History—19th century
ISBN 0-7377-0221-4 (lib bdg); 0-7377-0220-6 (pa)
                               LC 99-12771

Victorian England—*Continued*
This collection "includes essays on Queen Victoria's reign, the Great Exhibition of 1851, health and medicine, child labor in cotton mills, prison life, reactions to Darwin's theory of evolution, and changing attitudes toward the education of women and the working class." Booklist
Includes bibliographical references

941.5 Ireland

Bartoletti, Susan Campbell, 1958-
Black potatoes; the story of the great Irish famine, 1845-1850. Houghton Mifflin 2001 184p il $18; pa $9.95 *
Grades: 7 8 9 10   **941.5**
1. Famines 2. Ireland—History
ISBN 0-618-00271-5; 0-618-54883-1 (pa)
                        LC 2001-24156
The author "examines the causes of the famine, considering the roles of both the potato blight and of social conditions in mid-nineteenth century Ireland." Voice Youth Advocates
"The bibliography (also narrative) provides some of the most fascinating historical reading in the book. Overall, a useful addition to collections, for both personal and research uses." SLJ
Includes bibliographical references

The **Encyclopedia** of Ireland; edited by Brian Lalor; foreword by Frank McCourt. Yale University Press 2003 xxxvii, 1218p il map $65 *
Grades: 11 12 Adult   **941.5**
1. Ireland—Encyclopedias
ISBN 0-300-09442-6   LC 2003-103834
This encyclopedia contains alphabetically arranged entries from Abbey Theatre to Zozimus, a nineteenth-century balladeer. Coverage includes art, cinema, current events, fashion, food, history, Irish language, literature, music, politics, religion, sports, and biographies of a wide range of famous people of Irish descent, including St. Brigid, Éamon de Valera, John F. Kennedy, Bono, Eugene O'Neill, Mary Robinson, and William Butler Yeats
"This wonderful reference work will delight researchers and lovers of Ireland and the Irish." Choice

941.6 Ulster. Northern Ireland

Cottrell, Robert C., 1950-
Northern Ireland and England; the troubles; foreword by George J. Mitchell; introduction by James I. Matray. Chelsea House 2005 c2004 139p il map (Arbitrary borders) $31.50
Grades: 9 10 11 12   **941.6**
1. Northern Ireland
ISBN 0-7910-8020-X   LC 2004-14440
This book deals with the conflicts involved in the establishment of Northern Ireland and the Peace Line.
Includes bibliographical references

942.01 England--Early history to 1066

Lacey, Robert
The year 1000; what life was like at the turn of the first millennium: an Englishman's world; {by} Robert Lacey, Danny Danziger. Little, Brown 1999 230p hardcover o.p. pa $13.99
Grades: 11 12 Adult   **942.01**
1. Great Britain—History—0-1066
ISBN 0-316-55840-0; 0-316-51157-9 (pa)
                        LC 98-31254
Lacey and Danziger "have set out to capture what life was like in Anglo-Saxon England at the end of the first millennium. The framework for their story was provided by a priceless written work from that period, 'The Julius Work Calendar.'" Libr J
"This is a superb time capsule, and the authors distill a wealth of historical information into brightly entertaining reading." Publ Wkly
Includes bibliographical references

942.02 England--Norman period, 1066-1154

Howarth, David Armine, 1912-
1066: the year of the conquest; [by] David Howarth; illustrations to chapter headings by Gareth Floyd. Viking 1978 c1977 207p il hardcover o.p. pa $14 *
Grades: 11 12 Adult   **942.02**
1. Great Britain—History—1066-1154, Norman period
2. Hastings (East Sussex, England), Battle of, 1066
ISBN 0-670-69601-3; 0-14-005850-8 (pa)
                        LC 77-21694
First published 1977 in the United Kingdom
A history of the invasion of England by the Normans and William the Conqueror's victory at the Battle of Hastings.
Includes bibliographical references

942.03 England--Period of House of Plantagenet, 1154-1399

Singman, Jeffrey L.
Daily life in Chaucer's England; [by] Jeffrey L. Singman and Will McLean. Greenwood Press 1995 252p il (Greenwood Press daily life through history series) $49.95 *
Grades: 11 12 Adult   **942.03**
1. Chaucer, Geoffrey, d. 1400 2. Great Britain—History—1154-1399, Plantagenets
ISBN 0-313-29375-9   LC 95-7568
Also available online
"Included are descriptions of the feudal system in the 1300s, the medieval calendar, homes (including manors, but not castles), clothing, armor, food and entertainment, with enough detail to actually recreate certain aspects of

Singman, Jeffrey L.—*Continued*
daily life. For instance, patterns are provided for selected clothing, sample recipes come with modern equivalents, and medieval songs include notations." Book Rep
Includes bibliographical references

942.04 England--Period of Houses of Lancaster and York, 1399-1485

Weir, Alison
The Wars of the Roses. Ballantine Bks. 1995 462p il hardcover o.p. pa $15.95
Grades: 11 12 Adult   **942.04**
1. Great Britain—History—1455-1485, War of the Roses
ISBN 0-345-39117-9; 0-345-40433-5 (pa)
This is an account "of the first phase of the War of the Roses. Accepting the Tudor view that the conflict originated with Richard II's deposition, [the author] devotes half of the book to relations between Lancaster and York from 1399 to 1455. The second half deals with the period from the first Battle of St. Albans (1455) to the Battle of Tewkesbury (1471)." Libr J
"No history collection should do without this perfectly focused and beautifully unfolded account." Booklist

942.05 England--Tudor period, 1485-1603

Singman, Jeffrey L.
Daily life in Elizabethan England. Greenwood Press 1995 227p il (Greenwood Press daily life through history series) $49.95 *
Grades: 11 12 Adult   **942.05**
1. Great Britain—History—1485-1603, Tudors
ISBN 0-313-29335-X   LC 95-3807
Also available online
"Following a brief history of the era, an overview chapter discusses the social structure, governmental organization, religious establishment, and economy of the period. Subsequent chapters outline the cycle of life, from birth to death, and the cycles of time, moving through the day, week, and year as experienced by the people of the era. . . . Appendixes give instructions for organizing a living-history event and list useful suppliers and contacts for such an event. Bibliographies include audiovisual material." Booklist

943 Central Europe. Germany

Fulbrook, Mary, 1951-
A concise history of Germany. 2nd ed. Cambridge University Press 2004 277p il, maps (Cambridge concise histories) $65; pa $22
Grades: 11 12 Adult   **943**
1. Germany—History
ISBN 0-521-83320-5; 0-521-54071-2 (pa)
                    LC 2004-271599
First published 1990 in the United Kingdom

Contents: Introduction: The German lands and people — Mediaeval Germany — The age of confessionalism, 1500-1648 — The age of absolutism, 1648-1815 — The age of industrialisation, 1815-1918 — Democracy and dictatorship, 1918-45 — The two Germanies, 1945-90 — The Federal Republic of Germany since 1990 —Patterns and problems of German history
This history of Germany "spans the early Middle Ages to the present day. . . . Mary Fulbrook explores the interrelationships between social, political and cultural factors in the light of the latest scholarly controversies." Publ Wkly
Includes bibliographical references

Kort, Michael
The handbook of the new Eastern Europe; [by] Michael G. Kort. 21st Cent. Bks. (Brookfield) 2001 256p il maps lib bdg $39.90
Grades: 7 8 9 10   **943**
1. Eastern Europe 2. Central Europe
ISBN 0-7613-1362-1   LC 00-57708
This handbook begins with a "overview of the region. Economic and historical profiles are given for seven nations plus those in the former Yugoslavia, with an emphasis on post-1989 events after the fall of Communism. . . . Other reference material includes flags of each nation, a chronology of events since 1989, and an encyclopedia. The latter emphasizes names and places, with a few general topics such as environmental pollution." Voice Youth Advocates
"The book will be useful for serious students needing research materials." Horn Book Guide
Includes bibliographical references

Schmemann, Serge
When the wall came down; the Berlin Wall and the fall of Soviet Communism. Kingfisher 2006 127p il map $15.95
Grades: 7 8 9 10   **943**
1. Berlin Wall (1961-1989) 2. Germany (East)—Politics and government 3. Germany—History—1945-1990 4. Cold war
ISBN 0-7534-5994-9; 978-0-7534-5994-2
                    LC 2005-23892
"A New York Times book"
The author "describes the rise and defeat of the Nazis and the events that made Berlin and Germany a focal point for the Cold War. He then describes life in divided Germany and the events that led to the fall of the Berlin Wall and the reunification of Germany. A writer with a unique perspective, Schmemann creates an informative and quite readable account. The volume is well illustrated with black-and-white photos." Voice Youth Advocates
Includes bibliographical references

943.086   Germany--Period of Third Reich, 1933-1945

Bartoletti, Susan Campbell, 1958-
Hitler Youth; growing up in Hitler's shadow.
Scholastic Nonfiction 2005 176p il map $19.95 *
Grades: 7 8 9 10   **943.086**
  1. National socialism 2. Germany—History—1933-
1945 3. Holocaust, 1933-1945
  ISBN 0-439-35379-3   LC 2004-51040
  A Newbery Medal honor book, 2006
  The author "explores how Hitler gained the loyalty,
trust, and passion of so many of Germany's young peo-
ple." Publisher's note
  "Bartoletti draws on oral histories, diaries, letters, and
her own extensive interviews with Holocaust survivors,
Hitler Youth, resisters, and bystanders to tell the history
from the viewpoints of people who were there. . . . The
stirring photos tell more of the story. . . . The extensive
back matter is a part of the gripping narrative." Booklist
  Includes bibliographical references

Dvorson, Alexa
The Hitler Youth; marching toward madness.
Rosen Pub. Group 1999 64p il (Teen witnesses to
the Holocaust) $19.95
Grades: 9 10 11 12   **943.086**
  1. Hitler-Jugend 2. National socialism 3. Germany—
Politics and government—1933-1945 4. Holocaust,
1933-1945—Personal narratives 5. World War, 1939-
1945—Underground movements
  ISBN 0-8239-2783-0   LC 98-29025
  This book "begins with a discussion of the roots of
Nazism and then focuses on Edgar Gielsdorf, who tells
how he became an enthusiastic member of the Nazi
youth movement, later even a group leader—to his everlasting shame. He describes how he was seduced and
manipulated, how in school learning to hate Jews was as
much a part of the lesson plan as math and grammar."
Booklist
  Covers the armed and unarmed teenaged resistance to
the Nazis in the ghettos, concentration camps, and forests
of World War II Europe
  Includes bibliographical references

Hay, Jeff
A history of the Third Reich; by Jeff T. Hay;
Christopher R. Browning, consulting editor.
Greenhaven Press 2003 4v il maps set $299.80
Grades: 11 12 Adult   **943.086**
  1. National socialism 2. Germany—History—1933-
1945
  ISBN 0-7377-1283-X   LC 2002-33900
  Contents: v1 A-L; v2 M-Z; v3 Personalities; v4 Primary sources/index
  "Combines A-Z articles, biographical profiles, and primary source material to help high-school students understand the social and political forces that shaped, or were
shaped by, the Third Reich. An accessible, reliable
source." Booklist

Keeley, Jennifer, 1974-
Life in the Hitler Youth. Lucent Bks. 2000 112p
il (Way people live) lib bdg $27.45
Grades: 9 10 11 12   **943.086**
  1. Hitler-Jugend 2. National socialism 3. Germany—
Politics and government—1933-1945
  ISBN 1-56006-613-X   LC 99-37017
  Discusses life among the Hitler Youth, including their
ideology and activities, school and home life, and involvement in World War II
  "The text is compelling, thoroughly documented, and
enriched with eyewitness accounts, including news reports and testimonies from former Hitler Youth members.
The book certainly belongs in collections supporting the
study of World War II, and it also has a place in a curriculum that addresses broader issues, such as propaganda, genocide, and eugenics." Booklist
  Includes bibliographical references

943.087   Germany--1945-1990

Bernstein, Eckhard
Culture and customs of Germany. Greenwood
2004 xvi 217p il map (Culture and customs of
Europe) $45
Grades: 9 10 11 12   **943.087**
  1. Germany—Civilization
  ISBN 0-313-32203-1   LC 2003-55491
  "The author introduces readers and researchers to post
Cold War and post Berlin Wall Germany. . . . Holidays,
leisure activities, the German work ethic, eating and
drinking, the arts and performing arts, and other aspects
of the life of the Germans are portrayed. In light of the
many changes in Europe in the past century, this title offers a new, modern update of Germany and its people,
culture, and customs. Social studies classes and students
in German studies classes will find uses for this title."
Libr Media Connect
  Includes bibliographical references

944   France and Monaco

Haine, W. Scott
Culture and customs of France. Greenwood
Press 2006 315p il map (Culture and customs of
Europe) $49.95
Grades: 9 10 11 12   **944**
  1. France—Civilization
  ISBN 0-313-32892-7; 978-0-313-32892-3
                         LC 2006-17935
  Contents: The land, people, and history -- Religion
and thought -- Gender, marriage, family and education --
Social customs: leisure, holidays, sports, and festivals --
Cuisine and fashion -- Literature -- Media -- Cinema --
Performing arts -- Art, architecture, and housing
  Includes bibliographical references

944.04 France--Revolutionary period, 1789-1804

Anderson, James Maxwell, 1933-
Daily life during the French Revolution; [by] James M. Anderson. Greenwood Press 2007 268p il map (Greenwood Press "Daily life through history" series) $49.95
Grades: 9 10 11 12 **944.04**
1. France—History—1789-1799, Revolution
ISBN 0-313-33683-0; 978-0-313-33683-6
LC 2006-34084
"Chapters include the physical makeup of France; the social and political background of the revolution; the First Republic; religion, church and state; urban life; rural life; family life; the fringe society; clothes and fashion; food and drink; the role of women; military life; education; health and medicine; and writers, artists, musicians and entertainment." Publisher's note
Includes bibliographical references

Doyle, William, 1942-
The Oxford history of the French Revolution. 2nd ed. Oxford University Press 2003 481p maps pa $19.95
Grades: 9 10 11 12 **944.04**
1. France—History—1789-1799, Revolution
2. Europe—History—1789-1900
ISBN 0-19-925298-X LC 2002-29004
First published 1989
"Beginning with the accession of Louis XVI in 1774, . . . William Doyle traces the history of France through revolution, terror, and counterterror, to the triumph of Napoleon in 1802, along the way analyzing the impact of these events in France upon the rest of Europe." Publisher's note
Includes bibliographical references

The **encyclopedia** of the French revolutionary and Napoleonic Wars; a political, social, and military history; Gregory Fremont-Barnes, editor. ABC-CLIO 2006 3v il map set $285
Grades: 11 12 Adult **944.04**
1. France—History—1789-1799, Revolution—Encyclopedias 2. France—History—1799-1815—Encyclopedias
ISBN 1-85109-646-9; 978-1-85109-646-6
LC 2006-19409
This encyclopedia "provides information on a variety of issues from military topics to cultural, social, and political aspects of this period. Entries include significant battles, weaponry, and important individuals who made a mark, e.g., generals, politicians, writers, composers, and members of the clergy. . . . The last volume has full-text primary source documents, including firsthand accounts of battles, texts of treaties, speeches, and dispatches." Choice
"This is a fantastic resource for anyone researching the period. It is straightforward and user-friendly enough to be helpful to the beginner, but the detail and extensive references will appeal to the more advanced and experienced researcher as well." Booklist
Includes bibliographical references

945 Italian Peninsula and adjacent islands. Italy

Cohen, Elizabeth Storr, 1946-
Daily life in Renaissance Italy; [by] Elizabeth S. Cohen and Thomas V. Cohen. Greenwood Press 2001 316p il maps (Greenwood Press "Daily life through history" series) $49.95 *
Grades: 7 8 9 10 **945**
1. Renaissance 2. Italy—Civilization
ISBN 0-313-30426-2 LC 00-69150
Also available online
"A brief historical background precedes chapters covering society, families, morality, schooling, marriage, disease, and death, as well as many aspects of rural and city life. . . . The documented information is ideal for student reports and reference questions." Voice Youth Advocates
Includes bibliographical references

Lace, William W.
The Vatican; by William W. Lace. Lucent Books 2004 128p il (Building history series) $28.70
Grades: 9 10 11 12 **945**
1. Vatican City
ISBN 1-560-06843-4 LC 2003-11218
History of the buildings, occupants, and uses of the Vatican in Rome.
This is written "in accessible, straightforward language. . . . Quotes from Michelangelo and others, fascinating details, and intriguing mysteries . . . will draw readers easily into the text. . . . . Black-and-white reproductions of maps, etchings, and portraits mix with a central section of glossy color photographs that showcase some of the Vatican's artistic treasures." Booklist
Includes bibliographical references

The **Oxford** history of Italy; edited by George Holmes. Oxford Univ. Press 1997 386p il maps hardcover o.p. pa $29.95
Grades: 11 12 Adult **945**
1. Italy—History
ISBN 0-19-820527-9; 0-19-285444-5 (pa)
LC 98-100006
Paperback published with title: The Oxford illustrated history of Italy
Twelve scholars survey Italian social, political and cultural history from the time of the Roman Empire to the present.
"An excellent choice for readers wanting either a refresher course on Italian history or those who have no background whatsoever in the subject but have a desire to learn the basics." Booklist

946   Iberian Peninsula and adjacent islands. Spain

Fuentes, Carlos, 1928-
The buried mirror; reflections on Spain and the New World. Houghton Mifflin 1992 399p il hardcover o.p. pa $29.95
Grades: 11 12 Adult   **946**
1. Spain—Civilization 2. Latin America—Civilization
ISBN 0-395-47978-9; 0-395-92499-5 (pa)
                 LC 91-34312
Also available in hardcover from P. Smith
The author "believes that a common cultural heritage can help the countries of Latin America transcend disunity and fragmentation. . . . He . . . explores Spanish America's love-hate relationship with Spain and its search for an identity in its multicultural roots." Publ Wkly
"Every page in this lapidary essay offers profound insight into the Spanish American psyche." Libr J
Includes bibliographical references

Kern, Robert W., 1934-
The regions of Spain; a reference guide to history and culture; photographs by Chuck Smith. Greenwood Press 1995 411p il maps $57.75 *
Grades: 9 10 11 12   **946**
1. Spain—Civilization
ISBN 0-313-29224-8   LC 95-6481
"Each chapter deals with one of Spain's eighteen regions, begins with a brief description of regional characteristics, and then describes the provinces that fall into that region. The description of each province is much more detailed than the description of the region as a whole and is broken up into categories that offer information about topics such as history, economy, social life and customs, and fine arts." Voice Youth Advocates
Includes bibliographical references

Mann, Kenny, 1946-
Isabel, Ferdinand and fifteenth-century Spain. Benchmark Bks. 2002 80p il maps (Rulers and their times) lib bdg $29.93
Grades: 6 7 8 9   **946**
1. Ferdinand V, King of Spain, 1452-1516 2. Isabella I, Queen of Spain, 1451-1504 3. Spain—History
ISBN 0-7614-1030-9   LC 00-41450
This covers the lives of King Ferdinand and Queen Isabella of Spain "as well as everyday life and the literature of the times. Interesting facts about society, clothing, housing, food, cosmetics, sports, and other daily activities are brought to life. . . . Illustrated with plentiful archival art." Horn Book Guide
Includes glossary and bibliographical references

Millar, Heather, 1963-
Spain in the age of exploration. Benchmark Bks. (Tarrytown) 1999 80p il map (Cultures of the past) $28.70
Grades: 6 7 8 9   **946**
1. Spain—History
ISBN 0-7614-0303-5   LC 97-2090

Surveys the important events in the history of Spain between the voyages of Columbus and the defeat of the Spanish Armada and examines the role of the arts and religion during these two centuries.
Includes bibliographical references

Vincent, Mary
Cultural atlas of Spain and Portugal; {by} Mary Vincent and R.A. Stradling. Facts on File 1994 240p il maps $45 *
Grades: 11 12 Adult   **946**
1. Spain 2. Portugal
ISBN 0-8160-3014-6   LC 94-31211
This volume explores the cultural history of the Iberian peninsula. "The text and maps are complemented by 240 beautiful color photographs that highlight many important historical and cultural events. These encompass features on art, palaces, buildings, artists, posters, food, and even Expo'92 in Seville. A chronology, dynastic chart, glossary, short bibliography, and gazetteer complete the volume." Am Ref Books Annu, 1996

947   Eastern Europe. Russia

Borrero, Mauricio, 1959-
Russia: a reference guide from the Renaissance to the present. Facts on File 2004 497p il map (European nations series) $85 *
Grades: 11 12 Adult   **947**
1. Russia—History—Dictionaries
ISBN 0-8160-4454-6   LC 2003-60547
Alphabetically arranged entries cover "influential individuals, significant places, important policies . . . {and} various moments that have profoundly impacted the historical development of the country and its people." Publisher's note
"Readers will find an authoritative reference work distinguished by readability throughout and by wise decision making regarding what information to include and how it might best be presented. . . . It is a splendid resource, which is designed to serve the needs of students . . . as well as academic specialists and general readers." Booklist
Includes bibliographical references

Dornberg, John
Central and Eastern Europe. Oryx Press 1995 238p il maps (International government & politics series) pa $47.95
Grades: 11 12 Adult   **947**
1. Eastern Europe—History—1989- 2. Central Europe—History
ISBN 0-89774-942-1   LC 95-16582
"This book addresses the developments, changes, and issues that have occurred in Central and Eastern Europe since 1990 when the Cold War ended. . . . The first part of the book examines the area's geography, diverse mixture of peoples and ethnic groups, and history. Also covered are the region's current political, economic, social, and cultural developments, problems, and prospects. Maps and photographs add interest and clarification of

Dornberg, John—*Continued*

borders. Part II treats each country separately, providing a statistical profile and map for each one." SLJ

Includes bibliographical references

Eastern Europe; an introduction to the people, lands, and culture; edited by Richard Frucht. ABC-CLIO 2004 3v set $285

Grades: 11 12 Adult   **947**

1. Eastern Europe 2. Central Europe 3. Balkan Peninsula

ISBN 1-57607-800-0   LC 2004-22300

Contents: v. 1. The northern tier: Poland \ Piotr Wrobel. Estonia \ Mel Huang. Latvia \ Aldis Purs. Lithuania \ Terry D. Clark -- v. 2. Central Europe: Czech Republic \ Daniel E. Miller. Slovakia \ June Alexander. Hungary \ Andras Boros-Kazai. Croatia \ Mark Biondich. Slovenia \ Brigit Farley -- v. 3. Southeastern Europe: Serbia and Montenegro \ Nicholas T. Miller. Macedonia \ Aleksandar Panev. Bosnia-Hercegovina \ Katherine Mc-Carthy. Albania \ Robert Austin. Romania \ James P. Niessen. Bulgaria \ Richard Frucht. Greece \ Alexandros K. Kyrou

For a review see: Booklist, March 15, 2005

Includes bibliographical references

Gottfried, Ted, 1928-

The road to Communism; illustrated by Melanie Reim. 21st Cent. Bks. (Brookfield) 2002 144p il lib bdg $28.90

Grades: 9 10 11 12   **947**

1. Soviet Union—History—1917-1921, Revolution

ISBN 0-7613-2557-3   LC 2001-52252

Chronicles the Czarist Russian Empire in the 1800s, the birth of Bolshevism, events leading to the Russian Revolution of 1917, and the development of new political structures in its aftermath

"Gottfried writes with clarity and distance even as he narrates the dramatic details of the political conflict and the emotion of the 'dream that failed.'" Booklist

Includes glossary and bibliographical references

Kort, Michael

Russia. 3rd ed. Facts on File 2004 228p il map (Nations in transition) $40 *

Grades: 7 8 9 10   **947**

1. Russia (Federation)

ISBN 0-8160-5075-9

First published 1995

Examines the people, religion, environmental problems, politics, culture, history, and geography of Russia, emphasizing its transition, since 1991, from a communist to a free nation

Includes bibliographical references

Riasanovsky, Nicholas Valentine, 1923-

A history of Russia; [by] Nicholas V. Riasanovsky, Mark D. Steinberg. 7th ed. Oxford University Press 2005 2v il map set $56

Grades: 11 12 Adult   **947**

1. Russia—History 2. Soviet Union—History

ISBN 0-19-515394-4; 978-0-19-515394-1

LC 2004-49594

First published 1963

This narrative history includes discussions of economics, social organization, religion, and culture.

Includes bibliographical references

Schultze, Sydney

Culture and customs of Russia. Greenwood Press 2000 169p il maps $45 *

Grades: 11 12 Adult   **947**

1. Russia—Civilization

ISBN 0-313-31101-3   LC 00-34135

The author offers a "description of Russia's geography, history, religion, society, education, food, and the arts, making this an excellent, introductory reference work." Libr J

Includes bibliographical references

Stokes, Gale

The walls came tumbling down; the collapse of communism in Eastern Europe. Oxford Univ. Press 1993 319p hardcover o.p. pa $31.95

Grades: 11 12 Adult   **947**

1. Communism 2. Eastern Europe—Politics and government

ISBN 0-19-506644-8; 0-19-506645-6 (pa)

LC 92-44862

The author "deals with all the formerly Communist countries in Eastern Europe except Albania, and he traces the history of the collapse of the Soviet-type regimes rather than concentrating . . . on their evolution since the collapse." N Y Times Book Rev

This book "can be recommended as a coherent, well-written history that defines its time frame well, provides sound coverage, makes prudent judgments, and wears its analysis lightly. . . . Stokes's overview traces the ebb and flow of personalities and events in a manner that is both accessible to lay readers and informative to scholars." Libr J

947.08   Russia since 1855

Kurth, Peter

Tsar: the lost world of Nicholas and Alexandra; photographs by Peter Christopher. Little, Brown 1995 229p il hardcover o.p. pa $29.95

Grades: 11 12 Adult   **947.08**

1. Nicholas II, Emperor of Russia, 1868-1918 2. Alexandra, Empress, consort of Nicholas II, Emperor of Russia, 1872-1918 3. Russia—History

ISBN 0-316-50787-3; 0-316-55788-9 (pa)

LC 95-12820

In text and photographs, this volume examines the lives of Tsar Nicholas II, the Empress Alexandra, and the Russian Imperial family.

"A large format and a profusion of illustrations ostensibly mark it a picture book; instead it is a remarkably comprehensive overview of the reign of the last czar and his consort. . . . Kurth sensitively documents the imperial family's suffering as prisoners of the Bolsheviks and their eventual execution." Booklist

Includes bibliographical references

Massie, Robert K., 1929-
The Romanovs; the final chapter. Random House 1995 308p il hardcover o.p. pa $14.95
Grades: 11 12 Adult   **947.08**
1. Nicholas II, Emperor of Russia, 1868-1918 2. House of Romanov 3. Russia—Kings and rulers
ISBN 0-394-58048-6; 0-345-40640-0 (pa)
     LC 95-4718
This book "is divided into three major parts. The first segment—by far the most fascinating and original—focuses on the complex scientific process used in identifying the Romanovs' remains. . . . The second part concerns the various impostors who have claimed to be members of the Russian imperial family. . . . [The] third segment [is] a report on those Romanov émigrés—close relatives of the Czar's—who survived the Bolsheviks' persecution." N Y Times Book Rev
Includes bibliographical references

947.084   Russia (Soviet Union)-- 1917-1991

Eaton, Katherine Bliss
Daily life in the Soviet Union; [by] Katherine B. Eaton. Greenwood Press 2004 320p il map (Greenwood Press "Daily life through history" series) $49.95
Grades: 9 10 11 12   **947.084**
1. Soviet Union—History
ISBN 0-313-31628-7   LC 2004-12486
Contents: Ethnic groups and nationalities -- Government and law -- The military -- Economy, class structure, food, clothing, and shopping -- Rural life -- Housing -- Health care and health problems -- Education -- The arts -- Mass media, leisure, and popular culture -- Religion
"This would be an ideal addition to libraries in high schools offering a course on Russian and Soviet history." SLJ

The **Rise** and fall of the Soviet Union; Laurie Stoff, book editor. Greenhaven Press 2006 192p il (Opposing viewpoints in world history) lib bdg $34.95 *
Grades: 9 10 11 12   **947.084**
1. Soviet Union—History
ISBN 0-7377-2027-1   LC 2005-45991
"A 12-page introduction to the history of the Soviet Union is followed by four chapters on topics relating to different chronological periods. Each one includes from four to six viewpoints preceded by a summary of background information and a specific introduction to each piece. . . . The book will be a useful source for teachers who like the format of the series and can expand on the historical context." SLJ
Includes bibliographical references

Wade, Rex A.
The Bolshevik revolution and Russian Civil War. Greenwood Press 2001 xxiii, 220p il maps (Greenwood Press guides to historic events of the twentieth century) $45 *
Grades: 11 12 Adult   **947.084**
1. Soviet Union—History—1917-1921, Revolution
ISBN 0-313-29974-9   LC 00-35322
"A narrative history of the political, economic, and social background; causes and events of the revolution and civil war. . . . This book is a product of solid scholarship and an excellent choice for libraries." SLJ
Includes glossary and bibliographical references

947.085   Russia (Soviet Union)-- 1953-1991

Langley, Andrew
The collapse of the Soviet Union; the end of an empire. Compass Point Books 2006 96p il map (Snapshots in history) $31.93
Grades: 7 8 9 10   **947.085**
1. Soviet Union—History
ISBN 978-0-7565-2009-0; 0-7565-2009-6
     LC 2006003003
This "describes leaders, their plans, and their ultimate downfalls, from the removal of Tsar Nicholas II to the problems of present-day Russia. [This book is] great for research . . . brief but comprehensive." SLJ
Includes glossary and bibliographical references

947.7   Ukraine

Otfinoski, Steven, 1949-
Ukraine. Second ed. Facts on File 2004 139p il map (Nations in transition) $40
Grades: 7 8 9 10   **947.7**
1. Ukraine
ISBN 0-8160-5115-1   LC 2004-43241
First published 1999
Gives a historical and cultural overview of the country of Ukraine with particular emphasis on changes that have occurred since the collapse of the Soviet Union
Includes bibliographical references

948   Scandinavia

The **Oxford** illustrated history of the Vikings; edited by Peter Sawyer. Oxford Univ. Press 1997 298p il maps hardcover o.p. pa $27.50 *
Grades: 11 12 Adult   **948**
1. Vikings
ISBN 0-19-820526-0; 0-19-285434-8 (pa)
     LC 97-16649
This illustrated collection of articles includes discussion of the Vikings' impact on England, Iceland, Greenland, Russia, and the Frankish and Danish Empires; Viking ships and ship-building; Viking religion; and the ways in which Vikings have been portrayed throughout history. Significant archaeological finds are featured.
Includes bibliographical references

949.6 Balkan Peninsula

Judah, Tim, 1962-
The Serbs; history, myth, and the destruction of Yugoslavia. Yale Univ. Press 1997 350p il maps $40
Grades: 11 12 Adult   **949.6**
1. Serbs 2. Yugoslavia—History
ISBN 0-300-07113-2   LC 96-52212
Also available revised paperback edition
Judah explores the role of the Serbs in the Yugoslav conflict. "The early part is devoted to a summary of Serbian history since the Middle Ages, and the remaining two-thirds to recent events." London Rev Books
A "balanced well-written account. . . . This is a first-rate profile of the Serb nation from which general readers can derive a great deal." Choice
Includes bibliographical references

Mazower, Mark
The Balkans: a short history. Modern Lib. 2000 xliii, 188p maps (Modern Library chronicles) hardcover o.p. pa $11.95
Grades: 11 12 Adult   **949.6**
1. Balkan Peninsula—History
ISBN 0-679-64087-8; 0-8129-6621-X (pa)
                                  LC 00-56244
Mazower "has written a concise history of Europe's troubled southeastern corner that is both sympathetic to the region's never-ending struggle for identity and freedom from invaders and critical of its inhabitants' recurring failure to reconcile the religious and cultural differences imposed on them by the powers of the West and the East." Publ Wkly
This "is an excellent primer on the region's history, especially the growth of the nation-state in the 19th century." Economist
Includes bibliographical references

949.7 Serbia and Montenegro, Croatia, Slovenia, Bosnia and Hercegovina, Macedonia

Black, Eric
Bosnia; fractured region. Lerner Publs. 1999 96p il maps (World in conflict) lib bdg $25.26
Grades: 7 8 9 10   **949.7**
1. Yugoslav War, 1991-1995 2. Bosnia and Hercegovina
ISBN 0-8225-3553-X   LC 96-24951
Describes the history of the ethnic conflict in Bosnia, including current issues
"A book that attempts to explain the history of the Balkans in a way that is clear, concise, fair, and thorough is taking on a huge burden. This title succeeds and then some, for it is also interestingly written and engaging." Booklist
Includes bibliographical references

Daalder, Ivo H.
Winning ugly; NATO's war to save Kosovo; [by] Ivo H. Daalder, Michael E. O'Hanlon. Brookings Institution Press 2000 343p il maps $26.95; pa $19.95
Grades: 9 10 11 12   **949.7**
1. North Atlantic Treaty Organization 2. Kosovo (Serbia)
ISBN 0-8157-1696-6; 0-8157-1697-4 (pa)
                                  LC 00-9198
Also available online
This is an "examination of Western, and especially American, policy [in the Kosovo conflict]." N Y Rev Books
Includes bibliographical references

950 Asia. Orient. Far East

Columbia chronologies of Asian history and culture; edited by John S. Bowman. Columbia University Press 2000 751p map $93 *
Grades: 9 10 11 12   **950**
1. Asia—History
ISBN 0-231-11004-9   LC 99-47017
"This volume offers chronologies for the countries of Asia from the Paleolithic era through 1998. . . . The Middle East and Asiatic Russia are excluded. Chapters for each of the 26 individual countries are treated range from four or five pages . . . to more than 100 pages. Chronologies for most countries are subdivided by time periods representing major developments in their history." Booklist
"This reference work breaks new ground in the scope of its coverage." Libr J

Higham, Charles
Encyclopedia of ancient Asian civilizations; [by] Charles F.W. Higham. Facts on File 2004 xxi, 440p il map (Facts on File library of world history) $85 *
Grades: 11 12 Adult   **950**
1. Asia—Civilization—Encyclopedias
ISBN 0-8160-4640-9   LC 2003-48513
This "volume 'concentrates on civilizations that arose east of the Caspian Sea,' from modern Afghanistan and the Aral Sea south to India and Sri Lanka and east to Japan, Korea, and the islands of Southeast Asia. The years covered range from 3000 B.C.E. through the 15th century." SLJ
"This is a good beginning point for research, especially in regard to archaeological excavations." Booklist
Includes bibliographical references

Lane, George, 1952-
Genghis Khan and Mongol rule. Greenwood Press 2004 xlv, 224p il map (Greenwood guides to historic events of the medieval world) $45 *
Grades: 9 10 11 12   **950**
1. Genghis Khan, 1162-1227 2. Mongols
ISBN 0-313-32528-6   LC 2004-43639

Lane, George, 1952-—*Continued*

The author argues "that the Mongols were not necessarily the destructive barbarians of popular history, but rather an empire that encouraged cultural achievement, international trade, and even religious tolerance." SLJ

"The book tells a grand story in the brief compass of seven chapters." Hist Teach

Includes bibliographical references

The **Wilson** chronology of Asia and the Pacific; edited by David M. Brownstone and Irene M. Franck. Wilson, H.W. 1999 442p $105 *

Grades: 11 12 Adult   **950**

1. Asia—History 2. Pacific region—History

ISBN 0-8242-0950-8   LC 99-29402

"This volume features events in politics, government, and law; war; religion; education; economic life; arts and entertainment; science and technology; and medicine. A subject index is included." Publisher's note

Includes bibliographical references

Wood, Frances

The Silk Road; two thousand years in the heart of Asia. University of Calif. Press 2002 270p il maps $29.95; pa $19.95

Grades: 9 10 11 12   **950**

1. Central Asia—History

ISBN 0-520-23786-2; 0-520-24340-4 (pa)

LC 2003-273631

"Covering more than 5,000 years, this book . . . illustrated with photographs, manuscripts, and paintings from the collections of the British Library and other museums worldwide, presents an overall picture of the history and cultures of the Silk Road. It also contains many previously unpublished photographs by the great explorers Stein, Hedin, and Mannerheim. " Publisher's note

"This historical journey through the byways of the old Silk Road is a beautifully rendered tribute to the thousands of years in which these routes served as the center of trade." Publ Wkly

Includes bibliographical references

951 China and adjacent areas

Burgan, Michael

Empire of the Mongols. Facts on File 2004 128p il (Great empires of the past) $35

Grades: 9 10 11 12   **951**

1. Mongols

ISBN 0-8160-5563-7   LC 2004-28479

This book "details how the Mongols were able to sweep so swiftly and effectively across the plains and establish a great empire, and why it was ultimately an empire they could not control. Providing a . . . look into the daily life of the Mongols, this guide explains what they ate, how they dressed, how they raised their children, and what they believed." Publisher's note

Includes bibliographical references

China: opposing viewpoints; David M. Haugen, book editor. Greenhaven Press 2006 255p il lib bdg $34.95; pa $23.70 *

Grades: 9 10 11 12   **951**

1. China

ISBN 0-7377-3389-6 (lib bdg); 0-7377-3390-X (pa)

LC 2005-52815

"Opposing viewpoints series"

"In 28 (mostly brief) articles or excerpts, writers make arguments for and against China's progress toward democracy, military threat (especially to Taiwan), developing economy, and major crises (environmental, health, governance). . . . A great resource for critical reading, debate, papers, and discussion." SLJ

Includes bibliographical references

Facts about China; edited by Xiao-bin Ji; contributors, Eric Dalle. Wilson, H.W. 2003 751p map $105 *

Grades: 11 12 Adult   **951**

1. China

ISBN 0-8242-0961-3   LC 2001-45510

This "reference source covers all major topics regarding the People's Republic of China. Part 1 includes chapters on its geography and climate, peoples and language, systems of thought and belief, health and medicine, arts, entertainment and sports, literature, science and technology, economy and trade, and institutions (government and other) of Chinese society. Part 2 provides a chronology of important events in Chinese history; part 3, an alphabetical list of common Chinese concepts, important figures and events; and part 4, information and advice for future travelers." Choice

Includes bibliographical references

Fairbank, John King, 1907-1991

The great Chinese revolution: 1800-1985. Harper & Row 1986 396p maps hardcover o.p. pa $16 *

Grades: 11 12 Adult   **951**

1. China—History

ISBN 0-06-039057-3; 0-06-039076-X (pa)

LC 86-665

"A Cornelia & Michael Bessie book"

Contents: Late imperial China: growth and change, 1800-1895; The transformation of the late imperial order, 1895-1911; The era of the first Chinese Republic, 1912-1949; The Chinese People's Republic, 1949-1985

"The book is never pedantic, but gathers together a lifetime of scholarship plus a true gift for presentation of complex issues and a fine eye for telling illustration." Libr J

Includes bibliographical references

Slavicek, Louise Chipley, 1956-

The Great Wall of China; foreword by George J. Mitchell; intro. by James I. Matray. Chelsea House 2004 118p il map (Arbitrary borders) $31.50 *

Grades: 9 10 11 12   **951**

1. Great Wall of China 2. China—History

ISBN 0-7910-8019-6   LC 2004-10127

Slavicek, Louise Chipley, 1956--—*Continued*
Contents: China's legendary wall -- Before the great walls -- China's first Great Wall: the wall of Qin Shi Huang Di -- The Great Wall of the Han dynasty -- From the period of disunity through the Mongol conquest: the great wall in war and peace -- The Ming wall -- The Great Wall in Western and Chinese eyes
Includes bibliographical references

951.05   China--Period of People's Republic, 1949-

Jiang, Ji-li
Red scarf girl; a memoir of the Cultural Revolution; foreword by David Henry Hwang. HarperCollins Pubs. 1997 285p $16.99; pa $6.99
Grades: 6 7 8 9   **951.05**
1. China—History—1949-1976—Personal narratives
ISBN 0-06-027585-5; 0-06-446208-0 (pa)
                                          LC 97-5089
"This is an autobiographical account of growing up during Mao's Cultural Revolution in China in 1966. . . . Jiang describes in terrifying detail the ordeals of her family and those like them, including unauthorized search and seizure, persecution, arrest and torture, hunger, and public humiliation. . . . Her voice is that of an intelligent, confused adolescent, and her focus on the effects of the revolution on herself, her family, and her friends provides an emotional focal point for the book, and will allow even those with limited knowledge of Chinese history to access the text." Bull Cent Child Books

Schoppa, R. Keith, 1943-
The Columbia guide to modern Chinese history. Columbia Univ. Press 2000 356p il map (Columbia guides to Asian history) $49
Grades: 11 12 Adult   **951.05**
1. China—History
ISBN 0-231-11276-9   LC 99-53420
This narrative overview of Chinese history focuses on five areas: domestic politics, society, the economy, culture, and relations with the outside world. Contains approximately 500 annotated entries for further research in English as well as electronic resources and films. A chronology, excerpts from primary documents, and numerous graphs and tables are appended

Twentieth century China; a history in documents. Oxford University Press 2004 222p il map (Pages from history) $36.95 *
Grades: 9 10 11 12   **951.05**
1. China—History
ISBN 0-19-514745-6   LC 2004-2804
The author presents a "narrative of the last century using . . . excerpts from key primary sources: speeches, treaties, journalism, poems, letters, laws, etc. . . . Captions, selected quotations in sidebars, marginal glosses, text and picture credits, and a pronunciation guide all add to this well-organized book's utility and educational value." SLJ
Includes bibliographical references

The **Tiananmen** Square massacre; Kelly Barth, book editor. Greenhaven Press 2003 124p map (At issue in history) $28.70
Grades: 7 8 9 10   **951.05**
1. Tiananmen Square Incident, Beijing (China), 1989
ISBN 0-7377-1176-0   LC 2001-8517
A collection of articles using primary and secondary sources analyzes the Tiananmen Square incident and "discusses communism, the divided leadership of the Chinese, the citizens' protest in the square, how the protests were handled, the imposition of martial law, the crackdown, and the aftermath of the crackdown." Libr Media Connect
Includes bibliographical references

951.9   Korea

Edwards, Paul M., 1933-
Korean War almanac. Facts on File 2006 592p il map (Almanacs of American wars) $85
Grades: 11 12 Adult   **951.9**
1. Korean War, 1950-1953
ISBN 0-8160-6037-1   LC 2005-9374
First published 1990 under the authorship of Harry G. Summers
This book "contains a day-by-day chronology of the events and the people involved in this important war." Publisher's note
Includes bibliographical references

Encyclopedia of the Korean War; a political, social, and military history; Spencer C. Tucker, editor; Jinwung Kim . . . [et al.], assistant editors; [foreword by John S. D. Eisenhower] Checkmark Books 2002 xlii, 851p il map pa $29.95
Grades: 11 12 Adult   **951.9**
1. Korean War, 1950-1953—Encyclopedias
ISBN 0-8160-4682-4   LC 2001-37155
First published 2000 as volumes 1 and 2 in a 3-volume set by ABC-CLIO
This reference work covers "personalities, events, technical and military information, political and social background, and battles and campaigns." Libr J [review of 2000 edition]
Includes bibliographical references

Granfield, Linda
I remember Korea; veterans tell their stories of the Korean War, 1950-53. Clarion Books 2003 136p il $16
Grades: 9 10 11 12   **951.9**
1. Korean War, 1950-1953—Personal narratives
ISBN 0-618-17740-X   LC 2003-5397
Personal accounts of more than thirty men and women who served with the American and Canadian forces in Korea during the years 1950-1953
This title "has much to recommend it. . . . The text is timely, given both the renewed U.S.-North Korean tension and the increasing age of the veterans of the conflict. . . . The stories range from short anecdotes to more

Granfield, Linda—Continued

developed reminiscences; none are more than a few pages. Many are moving, some are surprisingly funny, and all offer insight into life at war from an insider's perspective." Quill & Quire

Includes bibliographical references

Hastings, Max

The Korean War. Simon & Schuster 1987 391p il maps hardcover o.p. pa $16

Grades: 11 12 Adult   **951.9**
1. Korean War, 1950-1953
ISBN 0-671-52823-8; 0-671-66834-X (pa)
                                        LC 87-16547

The author covers the political and military background of the Korean War, and also discusses how it served as a prelude to the American involvement in the Vietnam War, 15 years later.

This is a "readable, informative and sensible study." Booklist

Includes bibliographical references

Isserman, Maurice

Korean war. updated ed. Facts on File 2003 146p il map (America at war) lib bdg $35 *

Grades: 7 8 9 10   **951.9**
1. Korean War, 1950-1953
ISBN 0-8160-4939-4   LC 2002-7916
First published 1992

Contents: Task force Smith; Background to war; Defeat and retreat; Pusan and Inchon; Disaster in the north; Ridgway takes command; Long road to peace; Lessons from a forgotten war

Examines the political climate and military situation that led to the Korean War and discusses the key people and events involved in the conflict itself.

This volume provides "a great deal of information." Libr J

Includes bibliographical references

The **Korean** War; Dennis Nishi, book editor. Greenhaven Press 2003 240p (Interpreting primary documents) lib bdg $34.95; pa $23.70

Grades: 7 8 9 10   **951.9**
1. Korean War, 1950-1953
ISBN 0-7377-1202-3 (lib bdg); 0-7377-1201-5 (pa)
                                        LC 2002-40890

"This anthology contains documents by influential Washington policy makers as well as popular editorialists of the day." Publisher's note

Includes bibliographical references

Stokesbury, James L.

A short history of the Korean War. Morrow 1988 276p maps hardcover o.p. pa $13.95

Grades: 11 12 Adult   **951.9**
1. Korean War, 1950-1953
ISBN 0-688-06377-2; 0-688-09513-5 (pa)
                                        LC 88-5229

Stokesbury seeks to "trace the background of the Korean situation during the . . . years prior to July and August 1950. . . . [There is a discussion] of the first year

of maneuvers and battles before and after the Chinese Communists intervened, and also of the . . . fighting from time to time during the two years of peace negotiations." Publisher's note

"Stokesbury's combination of scholarship, clear writing, balanced judgments, and wit has reached a new high. It would be hard to imagine better personality portraits or better coverage of the prisoner-of-war issue." Booklist

Includes bibliographical references

951.93 North Korea (People's Democratic Republic of Korea)

Delisle, Guy, 1966-

Pyongyang: a journey in North Korea; translated by Helge Dascher. Drawn & Quarterly 2005 176p il map $19.95; pa $14.95 *

Grades: 11 12 Adult   **951.93**
1. Korea (North)—Graphic novels 2. Graphic novels
ISBN 1-896597-89-0; 1-897299-21-4 (pa)

This book "documents the two months French animator Delisle spent overseeing cartoon production in North Korea. . . . He records everything from the omnipresent statues and portraits of dictators Kim Il-Sung and Kim Jong-Il to the brainwashed obedience of the citizens." Booklist

"Pyongyang will appeal to multiple audiences: current events buffs, Persepolis fans and those who just love a good yarn." Publ Wkly

North Korea; Debra A. Miller, book editor. Greenhaven Press 2004 127p il map (World's hot spots) $28.70 *

Grades: 9 10 11 12   **951.93**
1. Korea (North)
ISBN 0-7377-2294-0   LC 2003-59903

"A collection of essays and periodical excerpts that discusses the situation within the country and its relationships within the world community. The book expounds on the reasons that North Korea is so often in the news. The introduction outlines the nation's history and its relationships with South Korea, the United States, and the Soviet Union. . . . The majority of the selections lean toward a United States bias and a post-9/11 mentality, but perspectives that are critical of the United States are still evident, which results in a well-rounded, interesting collection of views. . . . A useful tool for debate and discussion." SLJ

Includes bibliographical references

952 Japan

The **Cambridge** encyclopedia of Japan; editors, Richard Bowring, Peter Kornicki. Cambridge Univ. Press 1993 400p il maps $70 *

Grades: 11 12 Adult   **952**
1. Japan
ISBN 0-521-40352-9   LC 92-8167

This volume is divided "into eight categories: geography, history, language, thought and religion, arts and crafts, society, politics, and the economy. Each of these

The Cambridge encyclopedia of Japan—*Continued*

categories is further divided into 7-11 subjects that deal with numerous topics, such as the physical structure of the country, climate, education, family, judicial system, cinema, products, foreign policy, and important historical figures." Am Ref Books Annu, 1994

Dunn, Charles James
Everyday life in traditional Japan. C.E. Tuttle Co. 1972 c1969 197p il map (TUT books) pa $14.95
Grades: 9 10 11 12   952
1. Japan—Civilization 2. Japan—Social life and customs
ISBN 0-8048-1384-1   LC 72-186748
First published 1969 by Putnam
"A description of Japanese life during the stable . . . reign of the Tokugawa shoguns [1600-1850]." Cincinnati Public Libr
Includes bibliographical references

Kamachi, Noriko
Culture and customs of Japan. Greenwood Press 1999 187p (Culture and customs of Asia) $45 *
Grades: 9 10 11 12   952
1. Japan—Civilization
ISBN 0-313-30197-2   LC 99-13707
An "overview of Japanese culture including its language, mythology, history, religion, philosophy, fine arts, cuisine, clothing, holidays, and social customs. A section on the fine arts includes ikebana, bonsai, and the tea ceremony. Leisure activities include pachinko, karaoke, sumo, manga and anime, and other forms of entertainment. . . . The scholarly but accessible text is succinct and clear." SLJ
Includes bibliographical references

Roberson, John R., 1930-
Japan meets the world; the birth of a super power. Millbrook Press 1998 208p il maps $24.90
Grades: 7 8 9 10   952
1. Japan—History
ISBN 0-7613-0407-X   LC 98-6071
First published 1985 with title: Japan from Shogun to Sony, 1543-1984
Examines the history of Japan through various stages of progress and isolationism, including its rise to world power, up to the present day and the current Asian economic crisis
"This is an accessible, must-have resource for students needing detailed information about the history and current status of Japan. Glossary; bibliography; well-chosen but average-quality black-and white-photos." Booklist

Schomp, Virginia, 1953-
Japan in the days of the samurai. Benchmark Bks. 2002 80p il maps (Cultures of the past) lib bdg $19.95
Grades: 9 10 11 12   952
1. Japan—Civilization
ISBN 0-7614-0304-3   LC 98-12228

Describes the Japanese way of life during the samurai eras through information about the politics, military, culture, and the belief system; also indicates the legacy of the period.
"Offering balanced, thoughtfully interpreted material, this book effectively introduces Japan's early culture." Horn Book Guide
Includes glossary and bibliographical references

952.03   Japan--1868-1945

Buruma, Ian
Inventing Japan, 1853-1964. Modern Lib. 2003 194p hardcover o.p. pa $12.95
Grades: 11 12 Adult   952.03
1. Japan—History
ISBN 0-679-64085-1; 0-8129-7286-4 (pa)
                                             LC 2002-26346
"A Modern Library chronicles book"
"Buruma traces the remarkable metamorphosis that transformed an isolated island shogunate into an expansive military empire and then into a pacified and prosperous democracy. . . . An excellent introductory study." Booklist
Includes bibliographical references

954   South Asia. India

McLeod, John, 1963-
The history of India. Greenwood Press 2002 xx, 223p (Greenwood histories of the modern nations) $39.95 *
Grades: 11 12 Adult   954
1. Mogul Empire 2. India—History—1526-1765
ISBN 0-313-31459-4   LC 2002-276829
The author presents "in broad outlines some of the major events and episodes that make up India's history. . . . This is a useful compilation of important facts relating to Indian history. Its strength lies primarily in the last six chapters in which brief narratives of the struggle for independence and post-independence India down to the close of the twentieth century are nicely presented. All in all, this is a book that all libraries should have." Recomm Ref Books for Small & Medium-sized Libr & Media Cent, 2003
Includes bibliographical references

Singh, Patwant, 1925-
The Sikhs. Knopf 2000 276p il $27.50; pa $14 *
Grades: 11 12 Adult   954
1. Sikhs
ISBN 0-375-40728-6; 0-385-50206-0 (pa)
                                             LC 99-31807
The author "traces Sikh history from its origins in the 15th century through Indira Gandhi's 1984 storming of the Golden Temple. . . . Sikhs, he argues, have for centuries been an embattled people because their culture and religion defy the predominant religions in the region, as well as the Indian caste system with its ruling elite." Publ Wkly
Includes bibliographical references

954.91   Pakistan

Sinkler, Adrian
Pakistan. Greenhaven Press 2005 127p il map
(Nations in transition) lib bdg $28.70
Grades: 9 10 11 12   **954.91**
1. Pakistan
ISBN 0-7377-1208-2   LC 2004-47598
"This volume opens with the area's history from 15th-
century Mogul times up to Pakistan's creation in 1947.
It then focuses on three major issues: disputed Kashmir
and the costs of the resultant military competition and
conflict with India; the role of Islam in the country's
politics, especially as played out under the leadership of
the various regimes; and demands for ethnic separatism.
. . . This title is a solid offering for report writers." SLJ
Includes bibliographical references

955   Iran

Iran; Mikko Canini, book editor. Greenhaven
Press 2005 127p map (World's hot spots) lib
bdg $29.95 *
Grades: 9 10 11 12   **955**
1. Iran—History—1979-
ISBN 0-7377-1723-8 (lib bdg)   LC 2004-42500
"This title opens with a discussion of Iranian history
from the 1979 Revolution through the Iran-Iraq War up
to the present day. This overview is followed by a selection of essays by Western experts on the Middle East
and Iranian political figures, including Ayatollah
Khomeini, Iranian President Mohammad Khatami, and
Reza Pahlavi, son of the last shah. The book is nicely
balanced between Western and Middle Eastern points of
view, and is also quite up to date with essays on Iran as
a nuclear threat and Iran-Iraq relations after the defeat of
Saddam Hussein." SLJ
Includes bibliographical references

Iran: opposing viewpoints; Laura K. Egendorf,
book editor. Greenhaven Press 2007 208p il lib
bdg $34.95; pa $23.70 *
Grades: 9 10 11 12   **955**
1. Iran
ISBN 978-0-7377-3417-1 (lib bdg); 0-7377-3417-5 (lib
bdg); 978-0-7377-3418-8 (pa); 0-7377-3418-3 (pa)
     LC 2006-16934
"Opposing viewpoints series"
"These 23 essays represent differing points of view on
whether Iran is a threat to global security, the state of
human rights there, how the United States should respond to the country and its future. . . . This would be
a valuable source of current information for students researching argumentative essays or preparing for debates."
SLJ
Includes bibliographical references

Ramen, Fred
A historical atlas of Iran. Rosen Pub. Group
2003 64p il map (Historical atlases of South Asia,
Central Asia, and the Middle East) lib bdg $30.60
*
Grades: 9 10 11 12   **955**
1. Iran
ISBN 0-8239-3864-6   LC 2002-31031
This focuses on the political history of Iran "as determined by geography and religion. . . . Brief descriptions
of the art and architecture of [the] country testify to the
richness of [this culture]. . . . [This] well-organized and
ambitious [book provides] needed information." SLJ

Wright, Robin
The last great revolution; turmoil and
transformation in Iran. Knopf 2000 xxiv, 339p il
hardcover o.p. pa $14
Grades: 11 12 Adult   **955**
1. Iran—Politics and government
ISBN 0-375-40639-5; 0-375-70630-5 (pa)
     LC 99-27798
The author "talks to journalists, educators, politicians,
entertainers, and others to present a picture of the cultural and political changes in Iran: the softening of cultural
restrictions, the empowerment of women, and the mod-
ernization of industry and the economy." Booklist
Includes bibliographical references

956   Middle East

The **Continuum** political encyclopedia of the
Middle East; Avraham Sela, editor. rev and
updated ed. Continuum 2002 944p maps $175
Grades: 11 12 Adult   **956**
1. Middle East—Politics and government 2. Middle
East—History
ISBN 0-8264-1413-3   LC 2001-8542
First published 1999 with title: The political encyclo-
pedia of the Middle East
This "contains entries on countries ranging from Afghanistan to Yemen; political movements and leaders;
major foreign nations that impact this area, such as the
United States and Russia; religions and religious movements; and regional topics of concern including 'Oil,'
'Terrorism,' 'Water Politics,' and 'Women, Gender and
Politics.'. . . Alphabetical entries range from a few paragraphs to lengthy commentaries. . . . Large libraries
serving older students will find this a useful . . . source
of objective information on the history and issues affecting the contemporary Middle East." SLJ
Includes bibliographical references

Encyclopedia of the modern Middle East & North
Africa; Philip Mattar, editor in chief. 2nd ed.
Macmillan Reference USA 2004 4v il map set
$475
Grades: 11 12 Adult   **956**
1. Middle East—Encyclopedias 2. North Africa—En-
cyclopedias
ISBN 0-02-865769-1   LC 2004-5650
First published 1996

Encyclopedia of the modern Middle East & North Africa—*Continued*

"The set covers the modern history of the Middle East and North Africa, with major sections on Colonialism and Imperialism, the World Wars, the Israeli-Palestinian conflict and the United Nations involvement in the region. Each country in the region is reviewed, detailing its population, economy and government." Publisher's note

"For current, accurate, and non-partisan information on the Middle East and North Africa, this excellent reference set . . . will answer basic questions and serve as a starting point for research on the region." Libr Media Connect

Includes bibliographical references

Halliday, Fred

100 myths about the Middle East. University of California Press 2005 269p $39.95; pa $12.95
Grades: 11 12 Adult   956
1. Middle East—Politics and government
ISBN   0-520-24720-5;   978-0-520-24720-8;
0-520-24721-3 (pa); 978-0-520-24721-5 (pa)
LC 2005-53824
The author "debunks one hundred of the most commonly misconstrued 'facts' concerning the Middle East—in the political, cultural, social, and historical spheres." Publisher's note

"The book is a valuable addition to post-9/11 political literature (it also contains a fascinating glossary of terms that have entered the language since the September 2001 terrorist attacks)." Booklist

Kort, Michael

The handbook of the Middle East; {by} Michael G. Kort. 21st Cent. Bks. (Brookfield) 2002 303p il maps $39.90
Grades: 7 8 9 10   956
1. Middle East
ISBN 0-7613-1611-6   LC 2001-37330
Examines the past, present, and future of all the countries in the Middle East, discussing their history and culture

"The writing is clear, concise, lively, and full of fascinating details that will motivate readers to do more than just browse for facts. . . . This outstanding and timely resource should be purchased for all middle and high school libraries." Voice Youth Advocates

Includes glossary and bibliographical references

Lewis, Bernard

The Middle East; a brief history of the last 2,000 years. Scribner 1995 433p il $30; pa $16
Grades: 11 12 Adult   956
1. Middle East—History
ISBN 0-684-80712-2; 0-684-83280-1 (pa)
LC 96-4384
"Lewis has chosen to accentuate the social, economic, and cultural changes that have occurred over 20 centuries. He ranges from seemingly trivial concerns (changes in dress and manners in an Arab coffeehouse) to earth-shaking events (the Mongol conquest of Mesopotamia) in painting a rich, varied, and fascinating portrait of a region that is steeped in traditionalism while often forced by geography and politics to accept change." Booklist
Includes bibliographical references

The **Middle** East. Greenwood Press 2004 5v il map (Discovering world cultures) set $200 *
Grades: 9 10 11 12   956
1. Middle East
ISBN 0-313-32922-2
"A Creative Media Applications, Inc. production"
Contents: v1 Bahrain, Cyprus, Egypt; v2 Iran, Iraq, Israel; v3 Jordan, Kuwait, Lebanon, Oman; v4 Qatar, Saudi-Arabia, Syria; v5 Turkey, United Arab Emirates, Yemen

This "set profiles the 16 countries that lie in the geographic region between the Mediterranean Sea and India. . . . Each country . . . is covered in a multipage chapter providing detailed information on ethnic groups, land and resources, history, economy, religion, everyday life, holidays, and the arts. . . . Readers in need of a source of solid, unbiased information will be well served by this resource." Booklist

The **Middle** East: opposing viewpoints; William Dudley, book editor. Greenhaven Press 2004 203p il lib bdg $34.95; pa $23.70
Grades: 7 8 9 10 11 12   956
1. Middle East—Politics and government 2. Religion and politics
ISBN 0-7377-1805-6 (lib bdg); 0-7377-1806-4 (pa)
LC 2003-49020
"Opposing viewpoints series"
"This anthology features voices within and outside the region debating the Israeli/Palestinian conflict, the role of religion, and American foreign policy in the region, and other key issues." Publisher's note
Includes bibliographical references

Pouwels, Randall L.

The African and Middle Eastern world, 600-1500. Oxford University Press 2006 175p il map (Medieval and early modern world) $32.95 *
Grades: 9 10 11 12   956
1. Islamic civilization 2. Middle East—History
3. Africa—History
ISBN 0-19-517673-1; 978-0-19-517673-5
LC 2004-21476
"The author places readers in the midst of the action, allowing them to witness what it might have been like to live as a young caravan guide in A.D. 600. Thereafter, chapters are enlivened by the lives and exploits of Muhammad and his various successors, an in-depth discussion of the appeal of Islam, and a review of the leadership of men such as Mansa Musa and Sundiata. . . . This accessible and attractive volume is a wonderful introduction to the medieval Islamic world." SLJ
Includes bibliographical references

956.04   Middle East--1945-1980

The **Arab-Israeli** conflict; Mark Rackers, book editor. Greenhaven Press 2004 234p (Great speeches in history series) $34.95 *
Grades: 7 8 9 10   956.04

The Arab-Israeli conflict—*Continued*
1. Israel-Arab conflicts 2. Speeches
ISBN 0-7377-1649-5
"This book offers 20 speeches by major players in the history of this turmoil, beginning with David Ben-Gurion's 1946 address to the Anglo-American Committee that would decide the fate of the future state of Israel and ending with Ariel Sharon's 2002 plea for peace. An excellent introductory essay sets the stage for the modern conflict. . . . This volume is a core resource for Middle East collections." SLJ

The **Palestinians** and the disputed territories; Neil Alger, book editor. Greenhaven Press 2004 144p il map (World's hot spots) lib bdg $28.70 *
Grades: 7 8 9 10   **956.04**
1. Israel-Arab conflicts
ISBN 0-7377-1489-1   LC 2003-48327
This "collection of essays, articles, and analyses traces the history of strife in the region and looks at the current situation from a variety of perspectives. The writers discuss the complex issues with attention toward readers who may be unfamiliar with the circumstances of the Middle Eastern conflict. The selections expound on the importance of Jerusalem and the groups, both the religious and political, that wish to control the city. International influences and involvement by the U.S., Britain, and Russia are also addressed." SLJ
Includes bibliographical references

956.7 Iraq

Al-Windawi, Thura
Thura's diary; my life in wartime Iraq; translated by Robin Bray. Viking 2004 131p il map $15.99 *
Grades: 7 8 9 10   **956.7**
1. Iraq War, 2003
ISBN 0-670-05886-6   LC 2004-44031
"The author, now a scholarship student at an American university, writes of her daily life in war-besieged Baghdad. She describes the events just prior to the U.S. and Britain's 'shock & awe' attack on Iraq. . . . Political sentiments occasionally poke through, but the focus is on explicitly and calmly exposing the ravages of war on the vulnerable members of society." SLJ

Atkinson, Rick
In the company of soldiers; a chronicle of combat. H. Holt 2004 319p il maps $25; pa $14 *
Grades: 11 12 Adult   **956.7**
1. United States. Army. Airborne Division, 101st
2. Iraq War, 2003
ISBN 0-8050-7561-5; 0-8050-7773-1 (pa)
                                       LC 2003-67607
This is an eyewitness account of the war in Iraq. "In the spring of 2003, the author accompanied combat units to Iraq. He spent two months embedded with the 101st Airborne Division's headquarters staff, sharing their daily experiences from initial deployment out of Fort Campbell, KY, to overseas staging areas in Kuwait, and ulti-

mately bearing witness to the unit's march on Baghdad. His view of the war was from a vantage point that permitted scrutiny of strategy, planning, and decision making at the senior command level." SLJ

Bogdanos, Matthew
Thieves of Baghdad; one marine's passion for ancient civilizations and the journey to recover the world's greatest stolen treasures; [by] Matthew Bogdanos with William Patrick. Bloomsbury 2005 302p il map $25.95; pa $15.95 *
Grades: 11 12 Adult   **956.7**
1. Iraq War, 2003—Destruction and pillage 2. Iraq—Antiquities
ISBN 1-58234-645-3; 1-59691-146-8 (pa)
                                       LC 2005-27652
The author describes the events that took place after he "and several colleagues volunteered to investigate the theft of treasures from Baghdad's Iraq Museum in 2003." Booklist
Bogdanos "cuts through politics and hyperbole to tell an engrossing story abundant with history, colored by stories of brave Iraqis and Americans, and shaded with hope for the future." Publ Wkly
Includes bibliographical references

Carlisle, Rodney P.
Iraq war; [by] Rodney P. Carlisle; John S. Bowman, general editor. Updated ed. Facts on File 2007 198p il map (America at war) $35 *
Grades: 11 12 Adult   **956.7**
1. Iraq War, 2003 2. Iraq—History
ISBN 978-0-8160-7129-6   LC 2006-35763
First published 2004
This book "explains how coalition forces destroyed the Iraqi army and defeated the regime of Saddam Hussein. The . . . narrative describes such later events as the capture of Saddam Hussein by U.S. forces while also addressing the aftermath of the military campaign and the continuing unrest in the country." Publisher's note
Includes bibliographical references

Feuer, Alan
Over there; from the Bronx to Baghdad. Counterpoint 2005 283p $24
Grades: 11 12 Adult   **956.7**
1. Iraq War, 2003—Personal narratives
ISBN 1-58243-327-5; 978-1-58243-327-1
                                       LC 2004-27149
The author describes the events that occured after he "was bustled off to the Middle East to cover the invasion of Iraq. . . . This is one war memoir that demands to be read." Booklist

How should the United States withdraw from Iraq? Neal Pozner, book editor. Greenhaven Press 2005 80p (At issue) lib bdg $28.70; pa $19.95 *
Grades: 9 10 11 12   **956.7**
1. Iraq War, 2003 2. United States—Foreign relations—Iraq 3. Iraq—Foreign relations—United States
ISBN 0-7377-2322-X (lib bdg); 0-7377-2323-8 (pa)
                                       LC 2004-45563

How should the United States withdraw from Iraq?—*Continued*

This volume "presents speeches and articles by dignitaries such as George W. Bush, John Kerry, and Paul Bremer as well as journalists and representatives of various think tanks. The 10 selections fairly reflect different points of view and are argued with varying degrees of intensity and persuasiveness." Booklist

Includes bibliographical references

Iraq; David Schaffer, book editor. Greenhaven Press 2004 240p map (History of nations) lib bdg $33.70
Grades: 11 12 Adult   **956.7**
1. Iraq—History
ISBN 0-7377-1660-6   LC 2003-49019

"This book endeavors to show readers how the ancient roots and long history of Iraq continue to affect what is going on there today. From the early culture of Mesopotamia to the rise of Islam to the Ottoman Empire to the emergence of modern Iraq, the groundwork is laid for the reign of Saddam Hussein. The last section of entries includes George W. Bush's October 2002 speech in which he provides a rationale for taking military action against the regime, an essay in opposition to military intervention, a February 2003 interview with Hussein himself, and an essay on achieving lasting stability in Iraq. . . . For students doing in-depth research on current events, it will be invaluable." SLJ

Iraq; Andrea C. Nakaya, book editor. Greenhaven Press 2005 202p (Current controversies) lib bdg $34.95; pa $23.70
Grades: 9 10 11 12   **956.7**
1. Iraq War, 2003
ISBN 0-7377-2210-X (lib bdg); 0-7377-2211-8 (pa)
     LC 2004-42522

"This anthology examines justifications for the 2003 war, whether the United States should remain actively involved in Iraq, what the quality of life is like for Iraqis, and how reconstruction efforts should proceed." Introduction

Iraq: opposing viewpoints; William Dudley, book editor. Greenhaven Press 2004 202p il $33.70; pa $22.45 *
Grades: 9 10 11 12   **956.7**
1. Iraq War, 2003
ISBN 0-7377-2286-X; 0-7377-2287-8 (pa)
     LC 2003-49374

"Opposing viewpoints series"

The editor "presents different opinions about the current controversy concerning Iraq and the United States intervention, from the justifications given to go to war to what the future might hold for Iraq. The issues are examined via a compilation of speeches and articles written and given by individuals of varied backgrounds, from Middle East analysts and heads of not-for-profit organizations to the President of the United States. . . . The information is well organized and the pro/con viewpoints are placed back to back. . . . A valuable and far-reaching resource." SLJ

Includes bibliographical references

Koopman, John

McCoy's marines; Darkside to Baghdad. Zenith Press 2004 304p il map $25.95
Grades: 11 12 Adult   **956.7**
1. United States. Marine Corps 2. Iraq War, 2003—Personal narratives
ISBN 0-760-32088-8; 978-0-760-32088-4
     LC 2005-274038

The author "was embedded in the Third Battalion, Fourth Marines, during the most recent war in Iraq. He enjoyed a close working relationship with the CO, the battalion sergeant major, and several other members of the battalion. . . . . [He offers] a rare perspective on the gritty (literally, when a sandstorm blew up) details of ground combat in Iraq and how the modern American marine relates to his buddies, his enemies, and his family back home." Booklist

La Guardia, Anton

War without end; Israelis, Palestinians, and the struggle for a promised land. St. Martin's Griffin 2003 xxii, 436p il map pa $16.95
Grades: 11 12 Adult   **956.7**
1. Israel-Arab conflicts 2. Israeli national characteristics 3. Palestinian Arabs 4. Zionism
ISBN 0-312-31633-X   LC 2003-41288

First published 2001 in the United Kingdom with title: Holy Land, unholy war: Israelis and Palestinians

"This is fundamentally an examination of two wounded peoples, neither of whom seems capable of surmounting national myths and past hatreds to forge a new future. La Guardia is evenhanded in his criticism of both Israeli and Palestinian leaders, but he does not spare ordinary people. . . . This is an absorbing but heartbreaking examination of a seemingly endless tragedy that continues to unfold before our eyes." Booklist [review of 2002 edition]

Includes bibliographical references

Munier, Gilles

Iraq; an illustrated history. Interlink Books 2003 230p il $18 *
Grades: 11 12 Adult   **956.7**
1. Iraq—History
ISBN 1-566-56513-8   LC 2003-13372

Contents: Ten thousand years of civilization -- A brief history of modern Iraq -- Baghdad : madinat al-salam, or city of peace -- The last disciples of St. John the Baptist -- Near Baghdad -- From Baghdad to Najaf -- Karbala and environs -- Abraham : Prophet and Iraqi -- From Baghdad to Basra, via Kut -- Basra : Venice of the Orient -- From Najaf to Basra -- From Baghdad to Mosul -- Hatra : city of the sun-god -- Mosul and environs -- From Baghdad to Kanaqin (valley of the Diyala) -- From Baghdad to al-Haditha (upper Euphrates valley) -- From Baghdad to Erbil, via Kirkuk -- The Kurdistan autonomous Region

This work "betrays the French view of recent events on the Middle East. Its usefulness, however, lies in its offering an excellent introduction to Iraq's 4000-year history and culture. . . . Features like a glossary, sidebars with statistics, schematic maps, a list of relevant web sites, and the book's compact size make this a timely, useful choice for anyone interested in learning more

Munier, Gilles—*Continued*
about Iraq." SLJ
Includes bibliographical references

Schwartz, Richard Alan, 1951-
Encyclopedia of the Persian Gulf War.
McFarland & Co. 1998 216p il maps $45
Grades: 11 12 Adult   **956.7**
1. Persian Gulf War, 1991
ISBN 0-7864-0451-5   LC 97-51886
"Beginning with a seven-page overview, this encyclopedia presents alphabetically arranged entries that describe the conflict, including key figures, places, battles, diplomacy, and more." SLJ
Includes bibliographical references

Sinkler, Adrian
Iraq. Gale/Greenhaven 2006 128p il map
(Nations in transition) lib bdg $28.70
Grades: 9 10 11 12   **956.7**
1. Iraq—History
ISBN 0-7377-3085-4   LC 2004-60646
"This political history emphasizes events from 1932, when Britain formally granted Iraq independence, to the January 2005 elections and March 2005 convening of the Iraqi National Assembly. . . . [This book] contains detailed and accurate background information on the current situation in Iraq that would be useful for reports or debates." SLJ
Includes bibliographical references

Skiba, Katherine M.
Sister in the Band of Brothers; embedded with the 101st Airborne in Iraq. University Press of Kansas 2005 257p il (Modern war studies) $29.95
Grades: 11 12 Adult   **956.7**
1. United States. Army. Airborne Division, 101st
2. Iraq War, 2003—Personal narratives
ISBN 0-7006-1382-X   LC 2004-26475
The author "was the only woman embedded with the 101st Airborne when the United States invaded Iraq in 2003. She has written a fascinating memoir of her time within the training with other reporters, waiting to invade Iraq and spending the first few months of the war with soldiers in Iraq." Univ Press Books for Public and Second Sch Libr, 2006

Stout, Jay A., 1959-
Hammer from above; marine air combat over Iraq. Presidio Press 2006 xxi, 392p il map $25.95; pa $15.95
Grades: 11 12 Adult   **956.7**
1. Iraq War, 2003—Aerial operations
ISBN   0-89141-865-2;   978-0-89141-865-8;
0-89141-871-7 (pa); 978-0-89141-871-9 (pa)
LC 2005-49175
This is an "account of the role that Marine aircraft played in the launching of Operation Iraqi Freedom in 2003. Stout relies primarily on first-person testimony from dozens of Marines whom he interviewed shortly after they returned from the war." Publ Wkly

"This solid study of marine aviation in the current Iraq war will interest a wide range of aviation buffs and students of the Marine Corps." Booklist
Includes bibliographical references

Swofford, Anthony
Jarhead: a Marine's chronicle of the Gulf War and other battles. Scribner 2003 260p $25; pa $15
*
Grades: 11 12 Adult   **956.7**
1. United States. Marine Corps
ISBN 0-7432-3535-5; 0-7432-4491-5 (pa)
LC 2002-30866
The author, "who served in a United States Marine Corps Surveillance and Target Acquisition/Scout-Sniper platoon during the [1991 Gulf War] operation known as Desert Storm [presents an account of his experiences]." N Y Times (Late NY Ed)
This book offers "an unflinching portrayal of the loneliness and brutality of modern warfare and sophisticated analyses of—and visceral reactions to—its politics." Publ Wkly

What was asked of us; an oral history of the Iraq War by the soldiers who fought it; [compiled by] Trish Wood. Little, Brown and Co. 2006 xxii, 309p il map $25.99 *
Grades: 11 12 Adult   **956.7**
1. Iraq War, 2003—Personal narratives
ISBN 0-316-01670-5; 978-0-316-01670-4
LC 2006-930963
This is "a collection of 41 interviews conducted by Canadian investigative journalist Wood with veterans of the current war in Iraq." Libr J
"Colloquial, coarse and compelling, these narratives flash with humor, horror, nihilism and poesy." Publ Wkly

Yetiv, Steve
The Persian Gulf crisis; [by] Steve A. Yetiv. Greenwood Press 1997 xxi, 197p il maps (Greenwood Press guides to historic events of the twentieth century) $45
Grades: 11 12 Adult   **956.7**
1. Persian Gulf War, 1991
ISBN 0-313-29943-9   LC 96-6554
This work "opens with a chronology, followed by an overview of the crisis, a history of diplomatic initiatives leading to the war, and an account of operations Desert Shield and Desert Storm and their impact on the combatants." Choice
"The author incorporates only that which is pertinent in a style that is interesting and, at times, exciting to read. The inclusion of primary documents from the war, such as UN resolutions and speeches . . . make this title unique." SLJ
Includes bibliographical references

Zeinert, Karen, 1942-2002

The brave women of the Gulf Wars; Operation Desert Storm and Operation Iraqi Freedom; [by] Karen Zeinert & Mary Miller. 21st Century Bks. 2006 112p il $30.60 *

Grades: 7 8 9 10   **956.7**

    1. Women in the armed forces 2. Iraq War, 2003 3. Persian Gulf War, 1991—Women

    ISBN 0-7613-2705-3

"Zeinert and Miller reinforce the argument that women do, indeed, belong in the U.S. military by highlighting their contributions in Operations Desert Storm (Kuwait) and Iraqi Freedom. . . . The narrative paints a picture of consistent courage under fire and, one terse mention of the abuses at Abu Ghraib Prison aside, of professional conduct. The authors extend their purview with a chapter on women journalists in the campaigns, and while thoroughly villainizing Saddam Hussein, they also indicate that the official justifications for the war in Iraq turned out to be weak at best. A utilitarian but cogent assessment of the topic, well supported by notes and sources." Booklist

Includes bibliographical references

956.94   Palestine. Israel

Armstrong, Karen

Jerusalem; one city, three faiths. Knopf 1996 xxi, 471p il maps hardcover o.p. pa $17.95 *

Grades: 11 12 Adult   **956.94**

    ISBN 0-679-43596-4; 0-345-39168-3 (pa)

    LC 96-75888

Armstrong's "overarching theme, that Jerusalem has been central to the experience and 'sacred geography' of Jews, Muslims and Christians and thus has led to deadly struggles for dominance, is a familiar one, yet she brings to her sweeping, profusely illustrated narrative a grasp of sociopolitical conditions seldom found in other books." Publ Wkly

Blumberg, Arnold, 1925-

The history of Israel. Greenwood Press 1998 218p (Greenwood histories of the modern nations) $45 *

Grades: 7 8 9 10   **956.94**

    1. Israel—History 2. Zionism

    ISBN 0-313-30224-3   LC 97-45659

"Starting with a description of life in modern Israel, Blumberg . . . quickly covers Israel's early history, from 3,500 years ago to World War I. . . . The battles leading to independence, the isolation of Israel, conflicts within Israel, the Suez Crisis and subsequent wars, the Intifada, the development of the PLO, and the Peace Process are described in a manner that enables readers to have a much better understanding of the events happening in Israel now." Voice Youth Advocates

Includes bibliographical references

Children of Israel, children of Palestine; our own true stories; [edited by] Laurel Holliday. Pocket Bks. 1998 xxi, 358p il map hardcover o.p. pa $21.95 *

Grades: 9 10 11 12   **956.94**

    1. Israel-Arab conflicts 2. Israelis 3. Palestinian Arabs

    ISBN 0-671-00802-1; 0-671-00804-8 (pa)

    LC 97-42545

Also available in paperback from Washington Square Press

This is "a collection of autobiographical tales of growing up in Israel written by both Jews and Palestinians." Libr J

"Holliday says in her eloquent introduction that there is no sweet upbeat solution of easy neutrality, . . . but there is hope in their agreeing to tell their stories in a book together. They are listening to each other, and they make us hear all sides." Booklist

Includes bibliographical references

Frank, Mitch

Understanding the Holy Land; answering questions about the Israeli-Palestinian Conflict. Viking 2005 152p il map $17.99; pa $8.99 *

Grades: 6 7 8 9 10   **956.94**

    1. Israel-Arab conflicts

    ISBN 0-670-06032-1; 0-670-06043-7 (pa)

    LC 2004-14973

The author "tackles the complex subject of the Israeli-Palestinian conflict, making it comprehensible, if not any less horrific. . . . He uses a simple yet wonderfully effective technique to present the information: questions and answers. . . . Evenhanded and honest." Booklist

Includes bibliographical references

Greenfeld, Howard

A promise fulfilled; Theodor Herzl, Chaim Weizmann, and David Ben-Gurion, and the creation of the state of Israel. Greenwillow Books 2005 143p il $18.99 *

Grades: 7 8 9 10   **956.94**

    1. Herzl, Theodor, 1860-1904 2. Weizmann, Chaim, 1874-1952 3. Ben-Gurion, David, 1886-1973 4. Israel—History 5. Zionism

    ISBN 0-06-051504-X   LC 2004-54029

"A short history of events that, over the course of 66 years, led to the creation of the state of Israel, focusing on the lives and political involvement of the three men most responsible. . . . Captioned black-and-white photos add realism to the text." SLJ

Includes bibliographical references

Grossman, David

Death as way of life; Israel ten years after Oslo; translated from the Hebrew by Haim Watzman; edited by Efrat Lev. Farrar, Straus & Giroux 2003 188p $22

Grades: 11 12 Adult   **956.94**

    1. Israel-Arab conflicts 2. Israel—Politics and government

    ISBN 0-374-10211-2   LC 2002-44766

Grossman, David—*Continued*

This is "a collection of commentaries written between 1993 in the . . . time of the Oslo accords and late [2002]." N Y Times (Late N Y Ed)

This is "required reading for anyone hoping to get a basic knowledge of what the Israeli-Palestinian conflict is about and what it's like to live in a nation under fire." Booklist

Israel: opposing viewpoints; John Woodward, book editor. Greenhaven Press 2005 203p il lib bdg $34.95; pa $23.70 *

Grades: 8 9 10 11 12   **956.94**

1. Israel 2. Zionism 3. Palestinian Arabs

ISBN 0-7377-2589-3 (lib bdg); 0-7377-2590-7 (pa)
     LC 2004-60586

"Opposing viewpoints series"

"The authors in this book explore the founding of Israel, potential solutions to the Arab-Israeli dispute, America's relationship with the Jewish state, and the question of its right to exist." Publisher's note

Includes bibliographical references

Miller, Jennifer, 1980-

Inheriting the Holy Land; an American's search for hope in the Middle East. Ballantine Books 2005 xxxiii, 261p map $24.95; pa $14.95 *

Grades: 11 12 Adult   **956.94**

1. Israel-Arab conflicts

ISBN   0-345-46924-0;   978-0-345-46924-3; 0-345-46925-9 (pa); 978-0-345-46925-0 (pa)
     LC 2004-66349

The author "is the daughter of one of the chief American negotiators in the Israeli-Palestinian conflict and a longtime participant in the Seeds of Peace program, bringing together Israeli and Palestinian children. Using the many contacts that she has made, from the highest leaders to the children on the street, Miller explores . . . the many different viewpoints and preconceptions of the people involved in the conflict, not excluding her own. . . . This is a superb book on a crucial issue of our time." SLJ

Includes bibliographical references

Reich, Bernard

A brief history of Israel. Facts on File 2005 350p il map $45; pa $19.95 *

Grades: 9 10 11 12   **956.94**

1. Israel—History 2. Israel-Arab conflicts

ISBN 0-8160-5118-6; 0-8160-5793-1 (pa)
     LC 2004-2313

The author's "purpose is to seek to encompass a complex and continuing history by focusing on the main themes of establishing the state of Israel and ensuring its continued existence. He begins by tracing its history from biblical times to the Ottoman period and continues with the prehistory of the country from 1880 to 1948. In the remaining chapters, Reich chronicles the nation's development." Booklist

Includes bibliographical references

Rosaler, Maxine

Hamas: Palestinian terrorists. Rosen Pub. Group 2003 64p il map (Inside the world's most infamous terrorist organizations) lib bdg $26.50

Grades: 9 10 11 12   **956.94**

1. Hamas 2. Terrorism 3. Israel-Arab conflicts 4. Palestinian Arabs

ISBN 0-8239-3820-4   LC 2002-7769

Contents: A land divided; Inside Hamas; The suicide bombers; The cycle of violence

Discusses the origins, philosophy, and most notorious attacks of the Hamas terrorist group, including their present activities, possible plans, and counter-terrorism efforts directed against them.

"With color photos that aren't too shocking and long reading lists updated by links gathered on a dedicated Web site [this] will be useful for school reports." Booklist

Includes bibliographical references

958   Central Asia

Hanks, Reuel R.

Central Asia; a global studies handbook. ABC-CLIO 2005 xvii, 467p il map (Global studies) $55 *

Grades: 11 12 Adult   **958**

1. Central Asia

ISBN 1-85109-656-6   LC 2005-14716

This book covers Uzbekistan, Kazakhstan, and Kyrgyzstan. "Each part of the book is divided into a narrative and a reference section. The narrative portion covers the geography and history of each country, along with essays on current economic, social, and cultural trends. The reference section contains a historical chronology; encyclopedic entries on significant people, places, and events in each country; an overview of typical food and drink consumption; basic etiquette; a directory of country-related organizations; and a short, annotated bibliography." Choice

"The superb text makes accessible, whether for reports or general reading, former Silk Road lands that may play increasingly important roles—think of oil-rich Kazakhstan—in the world's economy." SLJ

Includes bibliographical references

Rall, Ted, 1963-

Silk road to ruin; is Central Asia the new Middle East? NBM 2006 303p il map $22.95

Grades: 11 12 Adult   **958**

1. Graphic novels 2. Central Asia—Graphic novels

ISBN 1-56163-454-9; 978-1-56163-454-5
     LC 2006-42041

"Moving between narrative and graphic novella interludes, . . . [the author] recounts several trips that he has made in the past decade to the five 'Stans,' those Central Asian nations that were so recently part of the USSR. . . . Rall takes readers on scary bus trips where armed guards threaten Westerners. . . . Diarrhea is a constant and bloody companion. Sports include a deadly horseback event in which opponents whip one another in the eyes." Voice Youth Advocates

Rall, Ted, 1963-—*Continued*

Rall's "awestruck descriptions of the region's natural beauty, crowded bazaars, and chaotic sporting tournaments will make adventurous readers want to see it all firsthand." SLJ

Includes bibliographical references

958.1 Afghanistan

Afghanistan; Jann Einfeld, book editor. Greenhaven Press 2005 188p (Current controversies) lib bdg $34.95; pa $23.70 *

Grades: 9 10 11 12   958.1

1. Afghanistan

ISBN 0-7377-2470-6 (lib bdg); 0-7377-2471-4 (pa)

LC 2004-54298

"In this anthology, scholars, officials, politicians, and warlords debate the progress and prospects of the war-weary Afghan people as they strive to rebuild their country and reshape their destiny." Publisher's note

Includes bibliographical references

Akbar, Said Hyder

Come back to Afghanistan; a California teenager's story; [by] Said Hyder Akbar and Susan Burton. Distributed to the trade by Holtzbrinck Publishers 2005 339p map $24.95; pa $14.95

Grades: 11 12 Adult   958.1

1. Afghanistan

ISBN 1-58234-520-1; 1-59691-068-2 (pa)

LC 2005-9249

The author "provides a firsthand account of his trips back home balancing his observations and experiences of Afghanistan's sources of instability, such as tribalism and narcotics, with personal notations on American failures, such as a tortured detainee, unfulfilled promises, and a security detail that leaves President Karzai a 'virtual prisoner.'" Libr J

"This is required reading for anyone seeking a better understanding of Afghanistan and of what it feels like to be a bicultural young person pulled between continents." Booklist

Ansary, Mir Tamim

West of Kabul, East of New York; an Afghan American story. Farrar, Straus & Giroux 2002 292p hardcover o.p. pa $13

Grades: 11 12 Adult   958.1

1. Afghanistan—Social conditions 2. Islamic civilization

ISBN 0-374-28757-0; 0-312-42151-6 (pa)

The author, an Afghan American, reflects on his dual heritage. In light of the events of September 11, he focuses particular attention on the relationship between Islam and the West.

"While Ansary's political insights can be detached or perhaps purposefully aloof his descriptions of having lived in and identified alternately with the West and the Islamic world are utterly compelling." Publ Wkly

Bergen, Peter L.

Holy war, Inc.; inside the secret world of Osama bin Laden. Free Press 2001 242p hardcover o.p. pa $14 *

Grades: 11 12 Adult   958.1

1. Terrorism

ISBN 0-7432-0502-2; 0-7432-3495-2 (pa)

LC 2001-54732

The author was a member of the CNN team that interviewed Saudi terrorist Osama bin Laden in 1997. Here he discusses "the history of Al Qaeda as a terrorist organization, profiles its leaders and more prominent members and examines its evolution as a global network." NY Times

"Although it may be impossible to fully understand bin Laden, Bergen does an admirable job of portraying him as a person, not just the face of terrorism. Readers will come away from this book understanding why bin Laden has been successful and how difficult it will be to dismantle his organization of terror." Booklist

Includes bibliographical references

Emadi, Hafizullah

Culture and customs of Afghanistan. Greenwood Press 2005 252p il map (Culture and customs of Asia) $49.95 *

Grades: 9 10 11 12   958.1

1. Afghanistan

ISBN 0-313-33089-1   LC 2005-3526

"This title looks at Afghanistan from ancient times to the present U.S. military involvement and provides useful background information for motivated readers." SLJ

Includes bibliographical references

MacPherson, Malcolm C., 1943-

Roberts ridge; a story of courage and sacrifice on Takur Ghar Mountain, Afghanistan; [by] Malcolm MacPherson. Delacorte Press 2005 338p il map $25

Grades: 11 12 Adult   958.1

1. Afghan War, 2001-

ISBN 0-553-80363-8; 978-0-553-80363-1

LC 2005-45494

"In March 2002 a team of U.S. Navy SEALs attempted the capture of Takur Ghar, a 10,000-foot-high mountain whose seizure would give the American forces in Afghanistan a key observation post. But the mountain was defended, and when the special forces helicopter reached the peak, it was shredded by enemy fire, and Petty Officer First Class Neil Roberts was thrown from the aircraft. His fellow SEALs were determined to bring him out. This is the story of that attempt. Well told and frightening as well as true, this is a book that bridges the breach between the increasingly professional American military and a civilian culture possessing little knowledge or experience of the military." Booklist

Includes bibliographical references

Marsden, Peter, 1945-

The Taliban; war and religion in Afghanistan. new expanded ed. Zed Bks. 2002 162p maps hardcover o.p. pa $21.95

Grades: 9 10 11 12   **958.1**

1. Taliban (Afghanistan) 2. Afghanistan—Politics and government 3. Islamic fundamentalism

ISBN 1-8427-7166-3; 1-85649-522-1 (pa)

LC 2001-58139

First published 1998

In this introduction to the radical Islamic movement in Afghanistan the author explains the sources of the Taliban, including early support from the U.S., and explores political, social and religious life under Taliban rule. Includes a chapter on the influence of Osama bin Laden.

Includes bibliographical references

Otfinoski, Steven, 1949-

Afghanistan. Facts on File 2004 130p il map (Nations in transition) $35

Grades: 9 10 11 12   **958.1**

1. Afghanistan

ISBN 0-8160-5056-2   LC 2003-49030

This volume provides an "examination of Afghanistan's long history and the traditions, religions, and cultural heritage of its many ethnic groups. It examines the different factions vying for power in Afghanistan today, as well as the difficulties Afghan people encounter in their daily life, and it outlines the staggering problems that the country faces in the future." Publisher's note

This is "informative, thought-provoking, and well-organized . . . well-researched . . . include{s} interesting and pertinent sidebars . . . the in-depth presentations provide solid and balanced overviews." SLJ

Includes bibliographical references

Rashid, Ahmed

Taliban: militant Islam, oil, and fundamentalism in Central Asia. Yale Univ. Press 2000 274p maps $40; pa $14.95

Grades: 11 12 Adult   **958.1**

1. Taliban (Afghanistan) 2. Afghanistan—Politics and government 3. Islamic fundamentalism

ISBN 0-300-08340-8; 0-300-08902-3 (pa)

LC 99-68718

The author "covers the origin and rise of the Taliban, its concepts of Islam on questions of gender roles and drugs, and the importance of the country to the development of energy resources in the region. . . . A lucid and thoroughly researched account." Libr J

The **rise** and fall of the Taliban; Kelly Barth, book editor. Greenhaven Press 2005 126p map (At issue in history) lib bdg $29.95 *

Grades: 9 10 11 12   **958.1**

1. Taliban (Afghanistan) 2. Afghanistan—Politics and government

ISBN 0-7377-1987-7   LC 2003-67515

This selection of source material and interpretations is divided as follows: Why the Taliban rose to power; Life under Taliban rule; The U.S. war and the fall of the Taliban.

Includes bibliographical references

Romano, Amy, 1978-

A historical atlas of Afghanistan. Rosen Pub. Group 2003 64p il map (Historical atlases of South Asia, Central Asia, and the Middle East) lib bdg $30.60

Grades: 9 10 11 12   **958.1**

1. Afghanistan

ISBN 0-8239-3863-8   LC 2002-31034

Maps and text chronicle the history of Afghanistan, from the Aryan invasion in 1500 B.C. to the rise of the Taliban.

This "well-organized and ambitious [book provides] needed information." SLJ

Includes glossary and bibliographical references

Stewart, Gail, 1949-

Life under the Taliban; by Gail B. Stewart. Lucent Books 2005 112p il map (Way people live) lib bdg $27.45 *

Grades: 9 10 11 12   **958.1**

1. Afghanistan

ISBN 1-590-18291-X   LC 2004-10378

Contents: The land of The Great Game; The coming of the Taliban; Life under the Sharia; Women under the Taliban; A life of grinding poverty; A training ground for terrorism; Resistance to the Taliban

Discusses the history of Afghanistan, the rise and fall of the Taliban, and daily life under the regime.

"Quotes from residents, journalists, aid workers, and U.N. officials enliven the clearly presented, accurate material. . . . An excellent resource for reports." SLJ

Includes bibliographical references

The **U.S.** attack on Afghanistan; John Boaz, book editor. Greenhaven Press 2005 142p il (At issue in history) lib bdg $29.95

Grades: 10 11 12   **958.1**

1. Afghan War, 2001-

ISBN 0-7377-1983-4; 978-0-7377-1983-3

LC 2004-61689

"Point-and-counterpoint essays and speeches, contributed by major political leaders such as Bush and Rumsfeld and by noted authors and historians, give balanced arguments for and against the attack prompted by 9/11. . . . Although politically pointed, strong arguments from both views are well supported." Booklist

Includes bibliographical references

959 Southeast Asia

Phillips, Douglas A.

Southeast Asia; series consulting editor Charles F. Gritzner. Chelsea House Publishers 2006 129p (Modern world cultures) lib bdg $30

Grades: 7 8 9 10   **959**

1. Southeast Asia

ISBN 0-7910-8149-4

This describes the geography, history, people and cultures, politics, economics, and possible future of Southeast Asia.

This "accessible [title is] generously illustrated with colorful photos, maps, and clear charts, graphs, and other

Phillips, Douglas A.—*Continued*
statistical data. . . . Phillips does an excellent job of organizing each topic by providing clear and outlined information. The research is well done, and information and statistics are up to date." SLJ

Southeast Asia; a historical encyclopedia from Angkor Wat to East Timor; edited by Ooi Keat Gin. ABC-CLIO 2004 3v il map set $285
Grades: 11 12 Adult   **959**
1. Southeast Asia
ISBN 1-576-07770-5   LC 2004-4813
The countries covered in this book include "Myanmar (Burma), Thailand (Siam), Laos, Cambodia, Vietnam, Malaysia, Singapore, Brunei, the Philippines, Indonesia, and East Timor. This A-Z aims to help students and researchers grasp the fragmented region through 800 detailed articles on archaeology, politics, culture, economic transformation, and more." Libr J
Includes bibliographical references

959.6   Cambodia

Ung, Loung, 1970-
First they killed my father; a daughter of Cambodia remembers. HarperCollins Pubs. 2000 240p il hardcover o.p. pa $13.95
Grades: 11 12 Adult   **959.6**
1. Cambodia—History—1975-
ISBN 0-06-019332-8; 0-06-085626-2 (pa)
LC 99-34707
The author's father was a "high-ranking government official in Phnom Penh. She was only five when the Khmer Rouge stormed the city and her family was forced to flee. They sought refuge in various camps, hiding their wealth and education, always on the move and ever fearful of being betrayed. After 20 months, Ung's father was taken away, never to be seen again. Her story of starvation, forced labor, beatings, attempted rape, separations, and the deaths of her family members is one of horror and brutality." SLJ

959.704   Vietnam--1949-

America in Vietnam; a documentary history; edited with commentaries by William Appleman Williams [et al.] Anchor Press/Doubleday 1985 345p map hardcover o.p. pa $19 *
Grades: 11 12 Adult   **959.704**
1. Vietnam War, 1961-1975
ISBN 0-385-19752-7; 0-385-19201-0 (pa)
LC 84-9321
Also available in paperback from Norton
In this collection of original essays and documentary sources, historians try to explain the U.S.-Vietnamese War of 1963-75 within the greater context of two centuries of American involvement in Asia.
Includes bibliographical references

Bloods: an oral history of the Vietnam War by black veterans; [edited by] Wallace Terry. Random House 1984 311p il hardcover o.p. pa $6.99 *
Grades: 11 12 Adult   **959.704**
1. Vietnam War, 1961-1975—Personal narratives
2. African American soldiers
ISBN 0-394-53028-4; 0-345-31197-3 (pa)
LC 83-42775
Black Vietnam War veterans discuss their experiences in battle and stateside.
This is "an intimate overview that often makes the reader stop, sit back, and think about this war that tore at America. . . . The accounts are moving, powerful and offer several views." Voice Youth Advocates
Includes bibliographical references

Caputo, Philip
A rumor of war; with a twentieth anniversary postscript by the author. Henry Holt and Co. 1996 xxi, 356p pa $15
Grades: .11 12 Adult   **959.704**
1. Vietnam War, 1961-1975—Personal narratives
ISBN 0-8050-4965-X   LC 96-19314
"An Owl book"
First published 1977 by Holt, Rinehart & Winston
These are "the combat recollections of a very young Marine officer in Vietnam in 1965-1966. Caputo later became a newspaperman. . . . He remembers himself as a patriotic youngster, eager to prove his manhood, and then . . . he takes us through his step-by-step discovery that war and manhood and their interrelation are more complicated than he had dreamed." New Yorker

Dear America: letters home from Vietnam; edited by Bernard Edelman for the New York Vietnam Veterans Memorial Commission. Norton 1985 316p il maps hardcover o.p. pa $13.95 *
Grades: 9 10 11 12   **959.704**
1. Vietnam War, 1961-1975—Personal narratives
ISBN 0-393-01998-5; 0-393-32304-8 (pa)
LC 85-273
"The letters have been intelligently organized to follow a typical tour of duty in Vietnam. . . . Readers will be struck by the variations in attitudes reflected in these letters of the combatants. . . . This is a wonderful book of raw data for the reader to sift through and interpret." Readings

Encyclopedia of the Vietnam War; by Jeffrey T. Hay, book editor. Greenhaven Press 2004 336p il (Greenhaven encyclopedia of) $74.95 *
Grades: 9 10 11 12   **959.704**
1. Vietnam War, 1961-1975—Encyclopedias
ISBN 0-7377-1149-3   LC 2003-5547
"Alphabetical entries provide easy access to information on numerous topics including major battles and missions; significant persons such as generals, antiwar activists, leaders, and ambassadors; policies and initiatives; weapons; incidents; and more. Most articles range from a paragraph to a page but a number of topics are examined in longer entries. . . . Cross-references guide readers to related topics, helping to place the war within its

Encyclopedia of the Vietnam War—*Continued*
larger historical and global context. . . . A four-page annotated list for further reading includes both print and
Web resources. Finally, there is a comprehensive index
to further ease access to information." SLJ

Includes bibliographical references

Everything we had; an oral history of the
Vietnam War; by thirty-three American soldiers
who fought it; [edited by] Al Santoli. Random
House 1981 265p il hardcover o.p. pa $6.99
Grades: 9 10 11 12   **959.704**
1. Vietnam War, 1961-1975—Personal narratives
2. Veterans
ISBN 0-394-51269-3; 0-345-32279-7 (pa)
                                        LC 80-5309
Interviews with 33 veterans assess the impact the
Vietnam War has had on their lives.

Includes glossary

FitzGerald, Frances, 1940-
Fire in the lake; the Vietnamese and the
Americans in Vietnam. Little, Brown 1972 491p
maps pa $16.95 hardcover o.p. *
Grades: 11 12 Adult   **959.704**
1. Vietnam War, 1961-1975 2. Vietnam—Politics and
government
ISBN 0-316-15919-0 (pa)
"An Atlantic Monthly Press book"
This book looks at the effects American intervention
had on the Vietnamese social and intellectual landscape.

Includes bibliographical references

Hillstrom, Kevin
Vietnam War: almanac; {by} Kevin Hillstrom
and Laurie Collier Hillstrom; Diane Sawinski,
editor. U.X.L 2001 293p il $60
Grades: 7 8 9 10   **959.704**
1. Vietnam War, 1961-1975
ISBN 0-7876-4883-3   LC 00-56379
This "combines early history from the colonial period,
U.S. involvement, and the war years and continues
through the reestablishment of diplomacy and trade in recent years. Arranged chronologically, each of the 17
chapters includes 'Words to Know' and 'People to
Know.' . . . Highly recommended for the junior- and senior-high-school libraries and public libraries." Booklist
Includes bibliographical references

Vietnam War: primary sources; {by} Kevin
Hillstrom and Laurie Collier Hillstrom; Diane
Sawinski, editor. U.X.L 2001 various paging $60
*
Grades: 7 8 9 10   **959.704**
1. Vietnam War, 1961-1975
ISBN 0-7876-4887-6   LC 00-56377
This "presents 13 full or excerpted speeches and writings 'that reflect the painfully diversified points of view
on the war.' . . . Each excerpt includes background material to provide context. Unfamiliar terms and their definitions fill sidebars, along with other relevant information
and photographs. The numerous sidebars, photographs,
and maps enhance the text." Booklist
Includes bibliographical references

Isserman, Maurice
Vietnam War; [by] Maurice Isserman; John S.
Bowman, general editor. Updated ed. Facts on File
2003 180p il map (America at war) $35
Grades: 9 10 11 12   **959.704**
1. Vietnam War, 1961-1975
ISBN 0-8160-4937-8   LC 2002-8762
First published 1992
This history includes a "discussion of the roots of
U.S. involvement in Indochina in the days just after
World War II and goes on to explore the varied and
complex motives behind America's effort to halt the
spread of communism in Asia." Publisher's note
Includes bibliographical references

Karnow, Stanley
Vietnam; a history. 2nd rev & updated ed.
Penguin Bks. 1997 768p il maps pa $17.95 *
Grades: 11 12 Adult   **959.704**
1. Vietnam War, 1961-1975 2. Vietnam—History
ISBN 0-14-026547-3
First published 1983
A summation "of over two centuries of conflict in In-
dochina. Chronicling a tragic history, Karnow presents a
balanced and sympathetic view of Vietnamese aspirations
and the mishaps that led to American involvement in a
'war nobody won.'" Voice Youth Advocates [review of
1983 edition]
Includes bibliographical references

Kovic, Ron
Born on the Fourth of July. Akashic Books
2005 216p pa $14.95
Grades: 9 10 11 12   **959.704**
1. Vietnam War, 1961-1975—Personal narratives
ISBN 978-1-88845-178-8; 1-88845-178-5
                                        LC 2004-115734
First published 1976 by McGraw-Hill
The autobiography of a young marine who was physi-
cally and emotionally scarred by his experience in Viet-
nam.

Living through the Vietnam War; edited by
Samuel Brenner. Greenhaven Press 2005 142p
map (Living through the Cold War) lib bdg
$32.45
Grades: 9 10 11 12   **959.704**
1. Vietnam War, 1961-1975 2. United States—History—1961-1974
ISBN 0-7377-2308-4   LC 2003-62477
"This volume discusses how American life was
changed and shaped by the longest war in American history. In separate chapters the volume presents the words
of the U.S. government, the views of those against the
war, the experiences of soldiers and veterans, and the
ways in which Vietnam was portrayed in media and popular culture." Publisher's note
Includes bibliographical references

Maraniss, David
They marched into sunlight; war and peace in Vietnam and America, October 1967. Simon & Schuster 2003 592p il map $29.95; pa $16
Grades: 11 12 Adult   959.704
  1. Vietnam War, 1961-1975
  ISBN 0-7432-1780-2; 0-7432-6104-6 (pa)
                                        LC 2003-52885
This is a "narrative by a reporter who juxtaposes a ghastly little battle in Vietnam with an antiwar and anti-Dow demonstration at the University of Wisconsin, Madison, on the same day; it captures moral ambiguity everywhere, without stereotyping or condescension." N Y Times Book Rev
Includes bibliographical references

Murray, Stuart, 1948-
Vietnam War; written by Stuart Murray. DK Pub. 2005 71p il (DK eyewitness books) $15.99; lib bdg $19.99
Grades: 7 8 9 10   959.704
  1. Vietnam War, 1961-1975
  ISBN   0-7566-1166-0;   978-0-7566-1166-8;
  0-7566-1165-2 (lib bdg); 978-0-7566-1165-1 (lib bdg)
                                        LC 2004-24516
"Besides identifying major political and military figures from both sides of the conflict, photos and text also document supporters and protesters, as well as the medical workers and civilians caught in the crossfire. Pictures and descriptions of weaponry and machinery will please military buffs, while troubling descriptions of Napalm and Agent Orange expose the grim realities of warfare." Booklist

Palmer, Laura, 1950-
Shrapnel in the heart; letters and remembrances from the Vietnam Veterans Memorial. Random House 1987 xx, 243p il hardcover o.p. pa $13 *
Grades: 9 10 11 12   959.704
  1. Vietnam Veterans Memorial (Washington, D.C.)
  2. Vietnam War, 1961-1975—Personal narratives
  ISBN 0-394-56027-2; 0-394-75988-5 (pa)
                                        LC 87-42652
"A collection of letters and poems that have been left at the Vietnam Veterans Memorial, with background information on the deceased and the bereaved writers." Booklist

Reporting Vietnam. Library of Am. 1998 2v il maps v1-v2 ea $35; pa $17.95 *
Grades: 11 12 Adult   959.704
  1. Vietnam War, 1961-1975 2. Reporters and reporting
  ISBN 1-88301-158-2 (v1); 1-88301-159-0 (v2);
  1-88301-190-6 (pa)   LC 98-12267
  Contents: Pt.1 American journalism, 1959-1969; pt.2 American journalism, 1969-1975
This collection includes "newspaper, magazine, book excerpts, and one TV commentary, Walter Cronkite's post-Tet report concluding that the United States should quickly negotiate its way out." Commonweal
"This book will help readers understand better what it was like to live through that tumultuous period of American history." Publ Wkly
Includes bibliographical references

Sherwood, John Darrell, 1966-
Fast movers; America's jet pilots and the Vietnam experience. St. Martin's Paperbacks 2001 il map pa $6.99
Grades: 11 12 Adult   959.704
  1. Vietnam War, 1961-1975—Aerial operations
  ISBN 0-312-97962-2
  First published 2000 by Free Press
The author discusses aerial operations during the Vietnam War and profiles about a dozen fliers. He describes "the specs of their jets, their ordnance, and the dogfighting dangers encountered on specific missions. These war stories propel the text." Booklist
Includes bibliographical references

Vadas, Robert E., 1952-
Cultures in conflict—the Viet Nam War. Greenwood Press 2002 xxi, 244p il map (Greenwood Press cultures in conflict series) $44.95
Grades: 9 10 11 12   959.704
  1. Vietnam War, 1961-1975 2. Culture conflict
  ISBN 0-313-31616-3   LC 2001-54716
A "picture of the Vietnam war, as experienced by Americans and Vietnamese. . . . [The author] presents the combined factors of competing communist, nationalist, and capitalist ideology; political arrogance; and deception that led to the great military conflagration in South East Asia. Cultural information describes ancient Vietnamese nationalism in contrast with American Cold War fears of the 'domino theory.'" Voice Youth Advocates
"This volume is an excellent resource for any person interested in knowing more about this war and how it affected Vietnam and the United States." Libr Media Connect
Includes glossary and bibliographical references

The **Vietnam** War; Nick Treanor, book editor. Greenhaven Press 2004 234p il map (Interpreting primary documents) hardcover o.p. pa $23.70
Grades: 7 8 9 10   959.704
  1. Vietnam War, 1961-1975
  ISBN 0-7377-2262-2 (lib bdg); 0-7377-2263-0 (pa)
                                        LC 2003-49058
"This anthology presents primary documents tracing the development of American intervention in Southeast Asia from Ho Chi Mingh's 1945 declaration of Vietnamese independence through to the fall of Saigon." Publisher's note
Includes bibliographical references

Yancey, Diane
Life of an American soldier. Lucent Bks. 2001 128p il (American war library, Vietnam War) lib bdg $27.45
Grades: 9 10 11 12   959.704
  1. Vietnam War, 1961-1975
  ISBN 1-56006-676-8   LC 00-8386
Describes the men and women who fought in the Vietnam War, the kind of war they fought, and the distress and difficulty they suffered on their return to the

Yancey, Diane—*Continued*

United States.

This is "liberally illustrated with good-quality, black-and-white captioned photos. Vocabulary is appropriate while at the same time describing the situation without softening the impact or tempering the language in the soldiers' statements." SLJ

Includes glossary and bibliographical references

Young, Marilyn Blatt

The Vietnam War: a history in documents; [by] Marilyn B. Young, John J. Fitzgerald, A. Tom Grunfeld. Oxford Univ. Press 2002 175p il maps (Pages from history) lib bdg $32.95; pa $19.95 *

Grades: 7 8 9 10   **959.704**

1. Vietnam War, 1961-1975

ISBN 0-19-512278-X (lib bdg); 0-19-516635-3 (pa)
LC 2001-52338

This is a "collection of original documents and photographs that detail the war in Vietnam. The text includes speeches, cartoons, news articles, and parallel events occurring in the United States and in Asia." Soc Educ

"The documents are skillfully tied together by brief text that gives good background information. . . . The book is well balanced in showing both sides. . . . Good-quality, black-and-white photos and illustrations are plentiful and informative." SLJ

Includes glossary and bibliographical references

960 Africa

Africa: an encyclopedia for students; John Middleton, editor. Scribner 2002 4v il maps set $395

Grades: 7 8 9 10   **960**

1. Africa—Encyclopedias

ISBN 0-684-80650-9   LC 2001-49348

A comprehensive look at the continent of Africa and the countries that comprise it, including peoples and cultures, the land and its history, art and architecture, and daily life

Africa: opposing viewpoints; Laura K. Egendorf, book editor. Greenhaven Press 2005 208p il $34.95; pa $23.70 *

Grades: 9 10 11 12   **960**

1. Africa

ISBN 0-7377-2218-5; 0-7377-2219-3 (pa)
LC 2004-42432

"Opposing viewpoints series"

"The authors in this book debate the issues facing modern Africa in the following chapters: What Problems Does Africa Face? How Can the Spread of AIDS in Africa Be Reduced? What Policies Will Best Help Africa? How Can Africa's Wild Lands Be Preserved?" Publisher's note

Includes bibliographical references

Cultural atlas of Africa; edited by Jocelyn Murray. rev ed. Checkmark Bks. 1998 240p il maps $50 *

Grades: 11 12 Adult   **960**

1. Africa—Civilization

ISBN 0-8160-3813-9

"An Andromeda book"

First published 1981

This survey of African civilization is divided into three parts. Part One: The physical background, describes the geography of the continent. Part Two: The Cultural background, includes such topics as languages, religions, early man, history, the arts, and education. Part Three: The Nations of Africa, offers information about individual countries divided by region

This "is an important contribution to our understanding of the African continent." Booklist {review of 1981 edition}

Includes bibliographical references

Encyclopedia of African history; Kevin Shillington, editor. Fitzroy Dearborn 2004 3v il map set $395

Grades: 11 12 Adult   **960**

1. Africa—Encyclopedias

ISBN 1-579-58245-1   LC 2004-16779

"The scope of the coverage encompasses the entire continent, including North Africa, and features all historical periods, with special attention to recent events. Most entries are given 1000 words, though major topics, such as regional surveys, stretch to 3000-4000 words. Topics range from art to anthropology to economics, but emphasis is placed on biographies and country studies, both pre- and postcolonial. . . . Simply put, this is an essential reference resource for students of African history." Libr J

Includes bibliographical references

Encyclopedia of African history and culture; Willie F. Page, editor. rev ed, by R. Hunt Davis, Jr. Facts on File 2005 5v il map set $425 *

Grades: 9 10 11 12 Adult   **960**

1. Africa—Encyclopedias

ISBN 0-8160-5199-2   LC 2004-22929

"A Learning Source Book"

First published 2001

This encyclopedia's "arrangement is chronological, with each of the five volumes representing a major era of African history: 'Ancient Africa,' 'African Kingdoms,' 'From Conquest to Colonization,' 'The Colonial Era,' and 'Independent Africa.'" Choice

This set "fulfills its information and education goals and is highly recommended for high-school, public, and academic libraries." Booklist

Includes bibliographical references

Falola, Toyin, 1953-

Key events in African history; a reference guide. Greenwood Press 2002 xxiii, 347p il maps $64.95

Grades: 11 12 Adult   **960**

1. Africa—History

ISBN 0-313-31323-7   LC 2001-58644

"An Oryx book"

"Falola surveys the . . . history of the African continent by focusing on 36 pivotal events that either caused or led to significant changes and developments in African social, political, and cultural life from around 40,000 B.C.E. to the collapse of apartheid in the 1990s. . . .

Falola, Toyin, 1953-—*Continued*
Following a detailed time line of historical events, each topic is highlighted in an individual chapter including cross-references, historical and political maps, illustrations, a notes section, and a suggested list for further reading." Booklist

Includes bibliographical references

Gates, Henry Louis
Wonders of the African world; [by] Henry Louis Gates, Jr. Knopf 1999 275p il map hardcover o.p. pa $24.95

Grades: 11 12 Adult   **960**
1. Africa—Civilization
ISBN 0-375-40235-7; 0-375-70948-7 (pa)
                   LC 99-18496

"In conjunction with the PBS television series of the same title, Gates offers a 12-nation reprise of the magnificence of ancient African civilizations . . . [moving] in clusters—from the black gods and kings of Nubia, to Ethiopia's links to the Holy Land and the Lost Ark of the Covenant, to Timbuktu's commercial and intellectual center, to the slave kingdoms, and to the Lost Cities of Great Zimbabwe." Libr J

"Gates writes with concentration and clarity, and anticipates the questions that arise in the wary reader's mind, delivering the answers at just the right time." N Y Times Book Rev

Includes bibliographical references

Lefkowitz, Mary R., 1935-
Not out of Africa; how Afrocentrism became an excuse to teach myth as history; [by] Mary Lefkowitz. Basic Bks. 1996 222p il map hardcover o.p. pa $19

Grades: 11 12 Adult   **960**
1. Africa—Historiography 2. History—Study and teaching
ISBN 0-465-09837-1; 0-465-09838-X (pa)
                   LC 95-49109

"A New Republic book"

"Those classicists who believe there are Egyptian antecedents for Greek philosophy are known as Afrocentrists. . . . Lefkowitz claims that the Afrocentrists are perpetuating myths and that they protect their claims by labeling those who question those claims as narrow-minded or racist." Libr J

"The book is a case study in historical methods, the value and limits of scholarship, and the preciousness of hard-bitten reason and objectivity. The book is also lucid and accessible." Christ Sci Monit

Includes bibliographical references

Reader, John, 1937-
Africa: a biography of the continent. Knopf 1998 801p il maps hardcover o.p. pa $18

Grades: 11 12 Adult   **960**
1. Africa—History
ISBN 0-679-40979-3; 0-679-73869-X (pa)
                   LC 97-36892

First published 1997 in the United Kingdom

This book discusses "the paleontology of the early African continent, covering a period of approximately three billion years. [Reader] then traces the history of human origins in Africa and proceeds to track the imprint of that beginning on human evolution, staying grounded in Africa as he marks the immigration of humans to other continents." Booklist

Reader "writes with sweeping historical perspective and an engaging familiarity with the continent and its people." Publ Wkly

Includes bibliographical references

Stewart, John, 1952-
African states and rulers. 3rd ed. McFarland & Co. 2006 423p $115 *

Grades: 9 10 11 12   **960**
1. Africa—History
ISBN 0-7864-2562-8; 978-0-7864-2562-4
                 LC 2006-5823

First published 1989

Arranged alphabetically by the country's official name, each entry gives the country's location, capital, other names, a brief history, and a chronological listing of its rulers and their official titles. Coverage includes contemporary nation-states and ancient tribal kingdoms.

This volume offers "the most in-depth treatment of Africa's changing political boundaries and heads of state." Booklist

Includes bibliographical references

962   Egypt and Sudan

Asante, Molefi K., 1942-
Culture and customs of Egypt; [by] Molefi Kete Asante. Greenwood Press 2002 168p il map (Culture and customs of Africa) $44.95

Grades: 9 10 11 12   **962**
1. Egypt—Social life and customs
ISBN 0-313-31740-2   LC 2002-21620

"The work is divided into seven . . . chapters. They include: land, people, and a historical overview; government, economy, education, and tourism; religion and worldview; architecture and art; social customs and lifestyles; the media and cinema; and literature, the performing arts, and music. These chapters address all relevant areas and provide the reader with a well-rounded picture of the culture and customs of Egypt." Recomm Ref Books for Small & Medium-sized Libr & Media Cent, 2003

Includes bibliographical references

963   Ethiopia and Eritrea

Mezlekia, Nega, 1958-
Notes from the Hyena's belly; an Ethiopian boyhood. Picador 2001 351p il map hardcover o.p. pa $14

Grades: 9 10 11 12   **963**
1. Ethiopia
ISBN 0-312-26988-9; 0-312-28914-6 (pa)
                   LC 00-50126

Mezlekia, Nega, 1958-—*Continued*
First published 2000 by Penguin
In this memoir, Mezlekia, "an Ethiopian who now
lives in Canada, . . . traces the years from his birth in
1958 through his flight in 1983 to the Netherlands and
on to Canada." N Y Times Book Rev
"Full of adventure, political struggle, and intrigue
[this] memoir works as a coming-of-age story as well as
a glimpse into a world of political corruption and change
that Westerners rarely get to know so intimately." Libr
J

966   West Africa and offshore islands

Conrad, David C.
Empires of medieval West Africa; Ghana, Mali,
and Songhay. Facts on File 2005 128p il map
(Great empires of the past) $35 *
Grades: 9 10 11 12   **966**
  1. Ghana Empire 2. Mali—History 3. Songhai Empire
  ISBN 0-8160-5562-9   LC 2004-28478
The author "explores the people, places, and ideas that
made up this trio of empires. Empires of Medieval West
Africa discusses the vital role salt and other natural re-
sources played in the development of the empires, the
rich and diverse cultures, and the influence of the grow-
ing Islamic Empire on everyday life." Publisher's note
Includes bibliographical references

966.4   Sierra Leone

Campbell, Greg
Blood diamonds; tracing the deadly path of the
world's most precious stones. Westview Press
2002 xxv, 251p maps hardcover o.p. pa $15.95
Grades: 11 12 Adult   **966.4**
  1. Diamonds 2. Sierra Leone
  ISBN 0-8133-3939-1; 0-8133-4220-1 (pa)
                                        LC 2002-4931
"Campbell explores the significance of the diamond
trade in Sierra Leone. . . . He recounts the horrors of
this war-torn nation. . . . The underlying motivation for
the violence and strife of Sierra Leone is centered in the
diamond trade, much of it illegal smuggling sanctioned
by the cartel DeBeers." Booklist
"This focused study of the catastrophic effect of blood
diamonds on Sierra Leone belongs in all libraries." Libr
J
Includes bibliographical references

966.62   Liberia

Reef, Catherine
This our dark country; the American settlers of
Liberia. Clarion Bks. 2002 136p il maps $17
Grades: 7 8 9 10   **966.62**
  1. American Colonization Society 2. African Ameri-
  cans—History 3. Slavery—United States
  ISBN 0-618-14785-3   LC 2002-3966

Contents: "These Free, Sunny Shores"; "Beyond the
Reach of Mixture"; Divine providence; Americans; Life
upriver; Progress; "Some Fertile Country"; "The Be-
clouded Sun"; Epilogue: Liberia, troubled land
Explores the history of the colony, later the independent nation of Liberia, which was established on the west
coast of Africa in 1822 as a haven for free African
Americans
"This photo-essay is a grim, disturbing history of Liberia. . . . Reef tells it in clear, plain style, always
showing the connections between the two homelands.
The handsome, very spacious design . . . makes the hard
facts accessible. . . . A must for history collections."
Booklist
Includes bibliographical references

966.9   Nigeria

Harmon, Dan
Nigeria; 1880 to the present: the struggle, the
tragedy, the promise; [by] Daniel Harmon. Chelsea
House 2000 144p il (Exploration of Africa, the
emerging nations) lib bdg $29.95
Grades: 9 10 11 12   **966.9**
  1. Nigeria
  ISBN 0-7910-5452-7   LC 99-58749
Photographs and text look at the past, development,
and present culture of Nigeria and its inhabitants
Includes bibliographical references

967   Central Africa and offshore islands

Davidson, Basil, 1914-
The African slave trade. rev and expanded ed.
Little, Brown 1980 304p il maps hardcover o.p. pa
$19.99 *
Grades: 11 12 Adult   **967**
  1. Central Africa—History 2. Slave trade
  ISBN 0-316-17439-4; 0-316-17438-6 (pa)
                                        LC 81-65588
"An Atlantic Monthly Press book"
First published 1961 with title: Black mother
An account of the slave trade and its impact on West
African society.
Includes bibliographical references

Oppong, Joseph R.
Africa South of the Sahara; series consulting
editor Charles F. Gritzner. Chelsea House
Publishers 2006 124p il map (Modern world
cultures) lib bdg $30
Grades: 6 7 8 9   **967**
  1. Sub-Saharan Africa
  ISBN 0-7910-8146-X
This describes the physical and historical geography,
population and settlement, cultures, politics, and economy of sub-Saharan Africa.
This "accessible [title is] generously illustrated with
colorful photos, maps, and clear charts, graphs, and other
statistical data." SLJ

967.5 Democratic Republic of the Congo, Rwanda, Burundi

Hochschild, Adam, 1942-
King Leopold's ghost; a story of greed, terror, and heroism in Colonial Africa. Houghton Mifflin 1998 366p il map hardcover o.p. pa $15
Grades: 11 12 Adult   **967.5**
1. Belgium—Colonies 2. Atrocities
ISBN 0-395-75924-2; 0-618-00190-5 (pa)
         LC 98-16813
The author "focuses on King Leopold's reign of terror in the Belgian Congo and the unswerving efforts by human rights activists (Sir Roger Casement, E.D. Morel, and others) and the Congo Reform Association to raise awareness of the enslavement, mutilation, and murder of millions of Congolese." Libr J
"Hochschild's impressively researched history records the roles of the famous and obscure, missionaries, journalists, opportunists, politicians, and royalty in this long-forgotten drama." Booklist
Includes bibliographical references

967.571 Rwanda

Gourevitch, Philip
We wish to inform you that tomorrow we will be killed with our families; stories from Rwanda. Farrar, Straus & Giroux 1998 355p hardcover o.p. pa $15
Grades: 11 12 Adult   **967.571**
1. Rwanda—Politics and government 2. Genocide
ISBN 0-374-28697-3; 0-312-24335-9 (pa)
         LC 98-22132
"In 1994, the world was informed of the inexplicable mass killings in Rwanda, in which over 800,000 were killed in 100 days. Gourevitch . . . spent over three years putting together an oral history of the mass killing that occurred in this small country." Libr J
This work is "readable and moving, Gourevitch is an impassioned and thoughtful observer. But this is not a work that gives much pleasure or comfort. Nor are its arguments fool-proof, its evidence complete, or its documentation thorough. . . . Still Gourevitch does struggle to come close to a great mystery of evil, and he makes us attend to great crimes." Commonweal

967.62 Kenya

Lekuton, Joseph
Facing the lion; growing up Maasai on the African savanna; by Joseph Lekuton with Herman Viola. National Geographic Soc. 2003 127p il map $15.95
Grades: 7 8 9 10 11 12   **967.62**
1. Masai (African people) 2. Kenya
ISBN 0-7922-5125-3   LC 2003-750
Contents: A lion hunt; The proud one; Cows; The pinching man; School; Herdsman; Initiation; Kabarak; Soccer; America; A warrior in two worlds

A member of the Masai people describes his life as he grew up in a northern Kenya village, travelled to America to attend college, and became an elementary school teacher in Virginia
"Lekuton's story touches a universal chord, and shows readers the beauty of another culture from the inside. Simple and direct enough for reluctant readers, and written in a conversational and occasionally wryly humorous style, this book will be enjoyed by a wide range of readers." SLJ

968 Southern Africa. Republic of South Africa

Beck, Roger
The history of South Africa; {by} Roger B. Beck. Greenwood Press 2000 xxx, 248p (Greenwood histories of the modern nations) $39.95 *
Grades: 11 12 Adult   **968**
1. South Africa—History
ISBN 0-313-30730-X   LC 99-58880
"Beginning with an overview of the modern nation, this narrative history traces South Africa from prehistory through the European invasions, the settlement by the Dutch, the imposition of British rule, the many internecine wars for control of the nation, the institution of apartheid, and, finally, freedom for all South Africans in 1994 and the Mandela years 1994-1999." Publisher's note
"The text is well written, easy to follow, and a good place to start for readers who have no prior knowledge of South African history." Am Ref Books Annu, 2001
Includes bibliographical references

Thompson, Leonard Monteath
A history of South Africa; [by] Leonard Thompson. 3rd ed. Yale Univ. Press 2001 xxiv, 358p il maps pa $17.95
Grades: 9 10 11 12   **968**
1. South Africa—History 2. South Africa—Race relations
ISBN 0-300-08776-4   LC 00-32101
First published 1990
This "exploration of South Africa's history—from the earliest known human settlement of the region to the present—focuses primarily on the experiences of its black inhabitants, rather than on those of its white minority." Publisher's note
Includes bibliographical references

968.06 Period as Republic, 1961-

Biko, Stephen, 1946-1977
I write what I like; selected writings; edited with a personal memoir by Aelred Stubbs; preface by Archbishop Desmond Tutu; introduction by Malusi and Thoko Mpumlwana; with a new foreword by Lewis R. Gordon. University of Chicago Press 2002 xxxiii, 216p pa $17
Grades: 9 10 11 12   968.06
1. South Africa—Race relations 2. South Africa—Politics and government
ISBN 0-226-04897-7   LC 2002-23951
First published 1978 in the United Kingdom
"This selection of writings by the South African black leader who died in custody . . . contains letters, addresses, conference papers and articles written for the newsletter of the South African Student's Organization." Publ Wkly
"Readers will find [Biko's] essential humaneness, intelligence, and lack of malice as impressive as his eloquence and compelling arguments." Libr J

Bradley, Catherine
The end of apartheid. Raintree Steck-Vaughn Pubs. 1996 79p il maps (Causes and consequences) lib bdg $28.54
Grades: 9 10 11 12   968.06
1. Apartheid 2. South Africa—Race relations
ISBN 0-8172-4055-1   LC 95-17669
Traces the origins of apartheid, the struggle against it, and the changes in South African society that brought about its end
Includes bibliographical references

Carter, Jason
Power lines; two years on South Africa's borders; introduction by Jimmy Carter. National Geographic Soc. 2002 xxiii, 278p il hardcover o.p. pa $14
Grades: 11 12 Adult   968.06
1. Peace Corps (U.S.) 2. South Africa—Description and travel
ISBN 0-7922-8012-1; 0-7922-4101-0 (pa)
LC 2002-22370
This is an account of life in the Peace Corps by the grandson of former President Jimmy Carter. "After graduating from college, Carter spent two years in the late 1990s volunteering in a former black homeland. . . . Assigned to the tiny, and poor, community of Lochiel, Carter takes the political and turns it into the personal as he writes candidly of his attempts to help create a new curriculum; he reflects on his efforts to raise teachers' self-esteem without trampling on their turf. Carter depicts life with humor and honesty and considers the limits of his stint, the way Western culture has become part of South Africans' lives and his guilt at enjoying its trappings as he travels around the country." Publ Wkly
"A great read for those who want more than vanishing-tribes exotica." Booklist

Finnegan, William
Crossing the line; a year in the land of apartheid. Persea Books 2006 434p map pa $20
Grades: 9 10 11 12   968.06
1. South Africa—Race relations 2. High schools—South Africa 3. Discrimination in education
ISBN 0-89255-325-1   LC 2006-47648
"A Karen and Michael Braziller book"
First published 1986 by Harper & Row
The author, an American school teacher, recalls his experiences in the segregated black schools of South Africa.

Mandela, Nelson
Nelson Mandela speaks; forging a democratic nonracial South Africa. Pathfinder Press 1993 296p il map hardcover o.p. pa $18.95 *
Grades: 11 12 Adult   968.06
1. African National Congress 2. South Africa—Politics and government 3. Apartheid
ISBN 0-87348-775-3 (lib bdg); 0-87348-774-5 (pa)
LC 93-85689
In this volume "the South African leader's significant speeches, letters, and interviews from the period since his February 1990 release from prison are brought together. . . . [The editor] provides a useful glossary and chronology of the 1990-93 period, and supplies a brief introduction to each entry." Booklist

Tutu, Desmond
The words of Desmond Tutu; selected by Naomi Tutu. Newmarket Press 1989 109p il hardcover o.p. pa $11.95
Grades: 11 12 Adult   968.06
1. South Africa—Race relations
ISBN 1-55704-038-9; 1-55704-282-9 (pa)
LC 88-34567
New edition in preparation
"This title contains quotations selected by Tutu's daughter Naomi, ranging in length from one sentence to one page. . . . The selections are separated into the topical categories of Apartheid, Faith and Responsibility, Nonviolence and Violence, Family, The Community—Black and White, and Toward a New South Africa." Voice Youth Advocates
Includes bibliographical references

968.91 Zimbabwe

Lessing, Doris May, 1919-
African laughter; four visits to Zimbabwe; [by] Doris Lessing. HarperCollins Pubs. 1992 442p hardcover o.p. pa $15
Grades: 11 12 Adult   968.91
1. Zimbabwe
ISBN 0-06-016854-4; 0-06-092433-0 (pa)
LC 92-52590
"After the wars fought by black nationalists for the liberation of Rhodesia ended in 1980 and the nation of Zimbabwe came into being, Lessing was able to return to the homeland that had officially exiled her 25 years

Lessing, Doris May, 1919-—*Continued*
earlier because of her opposition to the white government. The distinguished novelist . . . details four trips she made to Zimbabwe in 1982, 1988, 1989, and 1992 in a series of haunting vignettes dealing with facets of life there." Publ Wkly

970 North America

Purcell, L. Edward
Encyclopedia of battles in North America, 1517 to 1916; [by] L. Edward Purcell and Sarah J. Purcell. Facts on File 2000 383p maps (Facts on File library of American history) $66 *
Grades: 11 12 Adult   **970**
1. Battles 2. United States—Military history 3. Canada—Military history
ISBN 0-8160-3350-1   LC 99-38634
"Entries are in alphabetical order by battle name, from Adobe Walls to Yorktown, each one with bibliographic references. Many were from wars that are vaguely remembered today, if at all (e.g., the Pequot War of 1637 or the Russian-Indian War of 1804 in Alaska). There are cross references to alternate names, a comprehensive bibliography, a glossary, 50 maps, and indexes by war, year, and geographic area." Libr J
Includes bibliographical references

970.004 North American native peoples

American Indian tribes; edited by the editors of Salem Press; project editor, R. Kent Rasmussen. Salem Press 2000 2v (Magill's choice) set $99 *
Grades: 11 12 Adult   **970.004**
1. Native Americans
ISBN 0-89356-063-4   LC 00-44659
"Arranged by tribe, these volumes contain essays that originally appeared in Salem's three-volume *Ready Reference, American Indians* (1995). All of the bibliographies have been updated." Booklist
Includes bibliographical references

Bordewich, Fergus M.
Killing the white man's Indian; the reinvention of Native Americans at the end of the 20th century. Doubleday 1996 400p hardcover o.p. pa $15
Grades: 11 12 Adult   **970.004**
1. Native Americans
ISBN 0-385-42035-8; 0-385-42036-6 (pa)
                                     LC 95-23069
In separate chapters the author examines "historic Indian-white relations, modern Indian identity, the revival of tribal authority, Indians and environmentalism, conflicts between reinvigorated Indian property rights and archaeological research, new Indian claims to lands said to be sacred, Indian alcoholism, the reservation-based system of Indian colleges, and the promise and perils of growing economic and political cooperation with the world beyond the reservation." Booklist

Brown, Dee Alexander
Bury my heart at Wounded Knee; an Indian history of the American West; [by] Dee Brown. Thirtieth anniversary ed. Holt & Co. 2001 487p il $35; pa $16
Grades: 8 9 10 11 12 Adult   **970.004**
1. Native Americans—West (U.S.) 2. Native Americans—Wars 3. West (U.S.)—History
ISBN 0-8050-6634-9; 0-8050-6669-1 (pa)
                                     LC 00-40958
First published 1970
This is an account of the experience of the American Indian during the white man's expansion westward
Includes bibliographical references

Bruchac, Joseph, 1942-
Our stories remember; American Indian history, culture, & values through storytelling. Fulcrum 2003 192p map pa $16.95 *
Grades: 11 12 Adult   **970.004**
1. Native Americans—History 2. Storytelling
ISBN 1-555-91129-3   LC 2002-151236
Contents: The road of stories; Who are we?; Origins; Spirit: life and death; Trickster's turn; Contact: the coming of Europeans; Generations: parents, grandparents, children; All is living around us: animal, people, and plants; Epilogue: the drum is the heartbeat
"Synthesizes the stories of many different Indian nations, including Navajo, Abenaki, Cherokee, Cree, Sioux, and Tlingit in order to illustrate core values, which are pivotal to them all." Booklist
"This important volume includes a wealth of traditional stories and solid information." SLJ
Includes bibliographical references

Crow Dog, Leonard, 1942-
Crow Dog; four generations of Sioux medicine men; [by] Leonard Crow Dog and Richard Erdoes. HarperCollins Pubs. 1995 243p il hardcover o.p. pa $13
Grades: 11 12 Adult   **970.004**
1. American Indian Movement 2. Dakota Indians
ISBN 0-06-016861-7; 0-06-092682-1 (pa)
                                     LC 94-40695
Erdoes has recorded Leonard Crow Dog's oral narrative of the history of his family and his people, the Lakota. Mr. Crow Dog discusses "the generations of his family who have carried the name Crow Dog since the American government told them it would be their family name. . . . He tells of his involvement as the spiritual leader of the American Indian Movement and the occupation of Wounded Knee in the early 1970's." Booklist

Debo, Angie, 1890-1988
A history of the Indians of the United States. University of Okla. Press 1970 386p il maps (Civilization of the American Indian series) hardcover o.p. pa $24.95
Grades: 9 10 11 12   **970.004**

Debo, Angie, 1890-1988—*Continued*
1. Native Americans
ISBN 0-8061-0911-4; 0-8061-1888-1 (pa)
This historical survey of the Indians of North America, including the Eskimos and Aleuts of Alaska, discusses the first meetings with European explorers, their dispossession by colonial expansion, and their relations with the new American republic.
Includes bibliographical references

Deloria, Vine
Custer died for your sins; an Indian manifesto; by Vine Deloria, Jr. University of Oklahoma Press 1988 278p pa $19.95
Grades: 11 12 Adult   **970.004**
1. Native Americans
ISBN 0-8061-2129-7   LC 87-40561
First published 1969 by Macmillan
The author examines how anthropologists, missionaries, and government agencies have mistreated American Indians.

Encyclopedia of American Indian civil rights; edited by James S. Olson; associate editors, Mark Baxter {et al.}. Greenwood Press 1997 xxi, 417p il $68.50
Grades: 11 12 Adult   **970.004**
1. Native Americans—Government relations 2. Native Americans—Encyclopedias
ISBN 0-313-29338-4   LC 96-35352
This reference work "presents issues, individuals, court cases, and laws dealing with American Indian civil rights. There are more than six hundred alphabetical entries ranging from one paragraph to two pages in length. . . . This is a quality resource that will be welcomed by school and public libraries." Voice Youth Advocates
Includes bibliographical references

Encyclopedia of Native American wars and warfare; general editors, William B. Kessel, Robert Wooster. Facts on File 2005 398p il map $75; pa $21.95 *
Grades: 7 8 9 10   **970.004**
1. Native Americans—Wars—Encyclopedias
ISBN 0-8160-3337-4; 0-8160-6430-X (pa)
     LC 00-56200
"More than 600 entries provide access to information about the persons, tribes, treaties, battles, places, weaponry, and concepts related to armed conflicts between Native Americans and those of European descent, for the years between 1599 and 1890 and primarily the geographic locations now within the borders of the U.S." Booklist
"This encyclopedia offers readers a wide range of information about Native American history in North America after 1492." Choice
Includes bibliographical references

The **Encyclopedia** of North American Indians; general editor, D.L. Birchfield. Marshall Cavendish 1997 11v il maps set $657.07
Grades: 8 9 10 11 12 Adult   **970.004**
1. Native Americans—Encyclopedias
ISBN 0-7614-0227-6   LC 96-7700

A comprehensive reference work on the culture and history of Native Americans.
This "is a lavishly illustrated encyclopedia providing a multicultural perspective that will enhance the juvenile or general reference collections of any library." Libr J

Frazier, Ian
On the rez. Farrar, Straus & Giroux 2000 311p il $25; pa $14
Grades: 11 12 Adult   **970.004**
1. War Lance, Le 2. Oglala Indians 3. Pine Ridge Indian Reservation (S.D.)
ISBN 0-374-22638-5; 0-312-27859-4 (pa)
     LC 99-28353
Frazier discusses the history of the Oglala Sioux and the Indians that he met on the Pine Ridge Reservation in South Dakota, including his friend Le War Lance
"As Frazier serendipitously shuttles his narrative between Pine Ridge visits and snippets of Indian history, a fascinating picture emerges of a people struggling with the consequences of old wrongs and human orneriness." Time

From the heart; voices of the American Indian; edited and with narrative by Lee Miller. Knopf 1995 405p il hardcover o.p. pa $16 *
Grades: 11 12 Adult   **970.004**
1. Native Americans
ISBN 0-679-43549-2; 0-679-76891-2 (pa)
     LC 94-28492
An anthology of excerpts from speeches by Native Americans from the 16th to the 19th centuries.
"Arranged by region and chronology, these extraordinarily moving extracts are placed into appropriate historical context by Miller's descriptive narrative. In addition, pertinent quotations of non-Indian witnesses are also included. A haunting and eloquent anthology." Booklist
Includes bibliographical references

Gilbert, Joan
The Trail of Tears across Missouri. University of Mo. Press 1996 122p il map (Missouri heritage readers series) pa $9.95
Grades: 11 12 Adult   **970.004**
1. Cherokee Indians
ISBN 0-8262-1063-5   LC 96-10232
"Gilbert retells the tragic story of the removal of the Cherokees from their established homes in the southeastern United States to the Indian Territory that is now Oklahoma. . . . This title would be an excellent addition to both school and public libraries with an interest in Native American or Midwest cultural history." Libr J
Includes bibliographical references

Iverson, Peter
We are still here; American Indians in the twentieth century. Davidson, H. 1998 255p il (American history series) pa $14.95 *
Grades: 11 12 Adult   **970.004**
1. Native Americans
ISBN 0-88295-940-9   LC 97-38321

Iverson, Peter—*Continued*
The author "begins at Wounded Knee and tells the stories of Indian communities throughout the United States, including not only political leaders and activists, but also professionals, artists, soldiers and athletes." Publisher's note
Includes bibliographical references

Johansen, Bruce E. (Bruce Elliott), 1950-
The Native peoples of North America; a history. Praeger 2005 2v il set $99.95 *
Grades: 11 12 Adult   **970.004**
1. Native Americans—History
ISBN 0-275-98159-2   LC 2004-28732
This is a history of "cultures indigenous to North America from their earliest origins to the present. . . . Encompassing not only traditional historical records but also oral histories and biographical sketches, these two volumes will undoubtedly become an integral part of Native American history, an increasingly popular field." Booklist
Includes bibliographical references

Keenan, Jerry
Encyclopedia of American Indian wars, 1492-1890. Norton 1999 278p il pa $18.95 *
Grades: 9 10 11 12   **970.004**
1. Native Americans—Wars—Encyclopedias
ISBN 0-393-31915-6
First published 1997 by ABC-CLIO
"In over 450 separate entries (people, places, battles, terms); Keenan gives . . . coverage of most of the major elements in the 400-year struggle between the native peoples of the United States and the invading immigrants." Book Rep
Includes bibliographical references

Keoke, Emory Dean
Encyclopedia of American Indian contributions to the world; 15,000 years of inventions and innovations; {by} Emory Dean Keoke and Kay Marie Porterfield. Facts on File 2002 384p il $65 *
Grades: 11 12 Adult   **970.004**
1. Native Americans—Encyclopedias 2. Inventions
ISBN 0-8160-4052-4   LC 00-49034
This "volume describes more than 450 inventions and innovations that originated with indigenous peoples of North, Middle, and South America." Booklist
"This volume provides comprehensive coverage of the often-underreported contributions and achievements of the Indians of the western hemisphere." Book Rep
Includes bibliographical references

Lassieur, Allison
Before the storm; American Indians before the Europeans. Facts on File 1998 150p il maps (Library of American Indian history) $25
Grades: 7 8 9 10   **970.004**
1. Native Americans
ISBN 0-8160-3651-9   LC 97-50072

A narrative history about the various Indian people of North America and their way of life before contact with Europeans
"Archaeological evidence and the science of ethnographic and historical research are utilized throughout the book. Numerous side-bars enliven the text. . . . A well-researched account." SLJ
Includes bibliographical references

Nardo, Don, 1947-
The Native Americans. Lucent Bks. 2003 112p il maps (History of weapons and warfare) $27.45
Grades: 7 8 9 10   **970.004**
1. Military art and science 2. Native Americans—Wars
ISBN 1-59018-070-4   LC 2002-8589
Contents: Two very different concepts of warfare; Precontact offensive weapons; Weapons borrowed from the whites; Defensive weapons and tactics; Horses transform warfare on the plains; When Indians fought Indians; The struggle between Indians and whites; Faith as a weapon: the ghost dance
Discusses the weapons used by Native Americans and their different means of warfare.
Includes glossary and bibliographical references

Native American rights; Tamara L. Roleff, book editor. Greenhaven Press 1998 208p (Current controversies) lib bdg $31.20 *
Grades: 9 10 11 12   **970.004**
1. Native Americans—Government relations
ISBN 1-56510-685-7   LC 97-37078
This offers a variety of opinions concerning "Native culture, resources, sovereignty, and gaming. Each chapter begins with an introduction to one question, which is followed by three to six articles from a variety of sources. . . . Anyone looking for various viewpoints on these issues, or a subject to debate, need look no further." SLJ
Includes bibliographical references

Native universe; voices of Indian America; Gerald McMaster and Clifford E. Trafzer, editors. National Geographic Society 2004 320p il $40 *
Grades: 9 10 11 12   **970.004**
1. Native Americans—Social life and customs
ISBN 0-7922-5994-7   LC 2004-40221
"Published in conjunction with the fall 2004 opening of the Smithsonian's new National Museum of the American Indian, this . . . book is an overview of the diverse cultures of the American Indian. . . . The text is primarily essays, but also includes some poetry and even a scene from the screenplay, 'Smoke Signals.' The book is organized in sections that reflect the opening exhibits of the museum: Our Universes (spiritual beliefs and rituals); Our Peoples (key events in the history of Native America); and Our Lives (views of contemporary Native American life). . . . The strength of this book lies in the over 300 beautiful color illustrations, most of which are artifacts from the museum's vast collection. . . . Readers will gain much from simply browsing." Libr Media Connect
Includes bibliographical references

Philip, Neil
The great circle; a history of the First Nations; foreword by Dennis Hastings. Clarion Books 2006 153p il map $25
Grades: 7 8 9 10   **970.004**
     1. Native Americans
     ISBN 978-0-618-15941-3; 0-618-15941-X
                   LC 2005032743
"Philip takes on a huge challenge here: to present a unified narrative that explains the complex and confrontational relationships between Native Americans and white settlers. . . . He pulls it off, however, thanks to solid research, an engaging writing style, and a talent for making individual stories serve the whole. . . . Top marks, too, for the volume's photographs and historical renderings, which so intensely illustrate the pages." Booklist
Includes bibliographical references

Roberts, David, 1943-
In search of the old ones; exploring the Anasazi world of the Southwest. Simon & Schuster 1996 271p il map hardcover o.p. pa $14
Grades: 11 12 Adult   **970.004**
     1. Pueblo Indians 2. Native Americans—Antiquities
     ISBN 0-684-81078-6; 0-684-83212-7 (pa)
                   LC 95-46218
Roberts "chronicles the search for clues to the mystery of the Anasazi's abandonment of their extraordinary cliff dwellings some 700 years ago. Roberts blends accounts of his hiking adventures in the glorious canyon country of the Southwest with a chronicle of Anglos of the nineteenth century who shared his passion for studying the elusive Anasazi, especially the cowboy-archaeologist Richard Wetherell." Booklist
Includes bibliographical references

Sonneborn, Liz
Chronology of American Indian history. Updated ed. Facts on File 2007 472p il map (Facts on File library of American history) $71.50 *
Grades: 9 10 11 12   **970.004**
     1. Native Americans—History
     ISBN 0-8160-6770-8; 978-0-8160-6770-1
                   LC 2006-25396
First published 2001
This book "describes thousands of years of events that helped shape the lives and cultures of Native Americans—as well as American society as a whole—from their ancestors' arrival in North America to the present." Publisher's note
Includes bibliographical references

Vogel, Virgil J.
American Indian medicine. University of Okla. Press 1970 xx, 583p il (Civilization of the American Indian series) pa $29.95 hardcover o.p.
Grades: 11 12 Adult   **970.004**
     1. Native Americans—Medicine
     ISBN 0-8061-2293-5 (pa)
Covers "Indian theories of disease; early white doctors' and frontiersmen's observations in different parts of the country and among different tribes; Indians' influence on folk, fake, and patent medicine; Indian therapeutic methods in drug and drugless therapy, treatment of injuries, obstetrics, pediatrics, dentistry, diet, etc." Libr J
Includes bibliographical references

Voices from the Trail of Tears; edited by Vicki Rozema. Blair 2003 240p il maps (Real voices, real history series) pa $11.95 *
Grades: 9 10 11 12   **970.004**
     1. Cherokee Indians
     ISBN 0-89587-271-4   LC 2002-15299
Rozema "uses a variety of primary sources, including eyewitness accounts, to recount . . . {the Cherokees} sad fate, climaxed by a forced march to Oklahoma during which thousands died. Missionaries write outraged letters describing the mistreatment of Cherokees by white opportunists and government officials. Ordinary soldiers charged with rousting families from their homes describe the suffering of victims. This compilation is often stunning and heartbreaking in its impact." Booklist
Includes bibliographical references

Waldman, Carl
Atlas of the North American Indian; illustrations by Molly Braun. rev ed. Facts on File 2000 385p maps hardcover o.p. pa $21.95 *
Grades: 11 12 Adult   **970.004**
     1. Native Americans
     ISBN 0-8160-3974-7; 0-8160-3975-5 (pa)
                   LC 99-23678
First published 1985
"Details the migration of prehistoric tribes to North America from Asia. A unique section on 'Lifeways' provides information on all socioeconomic and religious aspects of Native American cultures, both pre- and post-contact with European Americans. Covers the Indian Wars, the Land Cessions, and contemporary Native American conditions." N Y Public Libr. Book of How & Where to Look It Up
Includes bibliographical references

Encyclopedia of Native American tribes. 3rd rev ed. Facts on File 2006 xxiv, 360p il map (Facts on File library of American history) $75; pa $21.95
Grades: 6 7 8 9 10 11 12 Adult   **970.004**
     1. Native Americans—Encyclopedias
     ISBN   0-8160-6273-0;   978-0-8160-6273-7; 0-8160-6274-9 (pa); 978-0-8160-6274-4 (pa)
                   LC 2006-12529
First published 1988
This book discusses "more than 200 American Indian tribes of North America, as well as prehistoric peoples and civilizations. . . . [The] text summarizes the historical record—locations, migrations, contacts with non-Indians, wars, and more—and includes present-day tribal affairs and issues. The book also covers traditional Indian lifeways, including diet, housing, transportation, tools, clothing, art, and rituals, as well as language families." Publisher's note
"This well-written and easily accessible encyclopedia of a good starting point for research on Native American tribes." Libr Media Connect
Includes bibliographical references

Wright, Ronald
Stolen continents; the Americas through Indian eyes since 1492. Houghton Mifflin 1992 424p il maps hardcover o.p. pa $17 *
Grades: 11 12 Adult   **970.004**
1. Native Americans 2. America—Exploration
ISBN 0-395-56500-6; 0-618-49240-2 (pa)
LC 91-36202
"A Peter Davison book"
The author "views the past 500 years from the native American perspective by drawing on long-neglected post-Columbian documents. Maintaining a five-track narrative, he follows the history of the distinct groups that survived the European invasion: the Aztecs of Mexico, the Maya of Guatemala and Yucatan, the Incas of Peru, and the Cherokees and Iroquois of North America. . . . Compelling, important, and well told." Booklist
Includes bibliographical references

970.01   North America--Early history to 1599

America in 1492; the world of the Indian peoples before the arrival of Columbus; edited and with an introduction by Alvin Josephy, Jr.; developed by Frederick E. Hoxie. Knopf 1992 477p il maps hardcover o.p. pa $20
Grades: 11 12 Adult   **970.01**
1. Native Americans—History 2. Native Americans—Antiquities 3. America—Exploration 4. America—Antiquities
ISBN 0-394-56438-3; 0-679-74337-5 (pa)
LC 90-26222
These essays depict "the diverse lives of the approximately 75 million people living in the Americas around the turn of the fifteenth century. Geography guides the first section. . . . Another section focuses on languages, spiritual beliefs and customs, art, and 'systems of knowledge.'" Booklist
Includes bibliographical references

Jones, Constance, 1961-
The European conquest of North America. Facts on File 1995 152p il maps (World history library) $25
Grades: 9 10 11 12   **970.01**
1. Native Americans 2. North America—History
ISBN 0-8160-3041-3   LC 94-12470
"This title covers the European conquest and settlement of North America, the resulting conflicts that arose between the colonizing nations and the indigenous peoples of the continent, and the effects of the conquest on those peoples. . . . There is an abundance of factual material, and the excellent chronology, index, and bibliography make this a useful source for student research." Voice Youth Advocates

Mann, Charles C.
1491; new revelations of the Americas before Columbus. Knopf 2005 465p il maps $30; pa $14.95
Grades: 11 12 Adult   **970.01**
1. Native Americans—History 2. America—Antiquities
ISBN 1-4000-4006-X; 1-4000-3205-9 (pa)
LC 2005-42178
U.S. title: Ancient Americans
The author "demonstrates that long before any European explorers set foot in the New World, Native American cultures were flourishing with a high degree of sophistication." Publ Wkly
"Mann navigates adroitly through the controversies. He approaches each in the best scientific tradition, carefully sifting the evidence, never jumping to hasty conclusions, giving everyone a fair hearing—the experts and the amateurs; the accounts of the Indians and their conquerors. And rarely is he less than enthralling." N Y Times Book Rev
Includes bibliographical references

971   Canada

Garrington, Sally, 1953-
Canada. Facts on File 2005 61p il map (Countries of the world) lib bdg $30 *
Grades: 7 8 9 10   **971**
1. Canada
ISBN 0-8160-6009-6   LC 2005040676
This describes Canada's "culture, history, geography, government, and economy. [It is] competently written and [contains] current information." SLJ

Riendeau, Roger E., 1950-
A brief history of Canada; [by] Roger Riendeau. 2nd ed. Facts on File 2007 444p il map $45 *
Grades: 11 12 Adult   **971**
1. Canada—History
ISBN 978-0-8160-6335-2   LC 2006-47130
First published 2000
This is a history of Canada "beginning with the exploration of the Northern American frontier and continuing through the rise and fall of the French and British empires to the foundations of Canadian nationhood and the present day." Publisher's note
Includes bibliographical references

971.9   Northern territories of Canada

Murphy, Claire Rudolf
Gold rush women; [by] Claire Rudolf Murphy & Jane G. Haigh. Alaska Northwest Bks. 1997 126p il maps pa $16.95
Grades: 9 10 11 12   **971.9**
1. Frontier and pioneer life—Klondike River valley (Yukon) 2. Women—History 3. Klondike River valley (Yukon)—Gold discoveries
ISBN 0-88240-484-9   LC 97-946

Murphy, Claire Rudolf—*Continued*

"During the late 1890s, one in 10 of the people who rushed to the Yukon looking for gold was a woman. Some came with husbands, some alone. Murphy and Haigh give accounts of these women and their contributions to Alaska and the Yukon territory during that period." Book Rep

"These stories of triumph, tragedy, hard work, and hard luck create a vibrant and multilayered picture of early Alaskan and of American society in the 1890s." SLJ

Includes bibliographical references

972　Middle America. Mexico

Foster, Lynn V.

A brief history of Mexico. Updated ed. Facts on File 2007 304p il map $45 *

Grades: 9 10 11 12 Adult　　　　　**972**

1. Mexico—History

ISBN 978-0-8160-7170-8; 0-8160-7170-5

　　　　　　　　　　　　　　LC 2006-52531

First published 1997

An overview of Mexican history covering pre-Columbian civilizations and contemporary indigenous cultures. Language, art, religion, politics and economics are discussed. A chronology and bibliography are included.

Includes bibliographical references

Guillermoprieto, Alma, 1949-

Looking for history; dispatches from Latin America. Pantheon Bks. 2001 303p il hardcover o.p. pa $13.95

Grades: 11 12 Adult　　　　　**972**

1. Mexico—Politics and government 2. Cuba—Politics and government 3. Colombia—Politics and government

ISBN 0-375-42094-0; 0-375-72582-2 (pa)

　　　　　　　　　　　　　　LC 00-62382

The author discusses conditions in Latin America, focusing particularly on Mexico, Colombia, and Cuba. "The essays . . . have been adapted from work which first appeared in the New Yorker and the New York Review of Books." Economist

"Among the stories, book reviews, and descriptions are perceptive and insightful observations of Latin American politics and society that help illuminate this important part of the world. This volume will be of interest to Latin American collections as well as current affairs libraries." Libr J

Kirkwood, Burton

The history of Mexico. Greenwood Press 2000 245p (Greenwood histories of the modern nations) $45

Grades: 11 12 Adult　　　　　**972**

1. Mexico—History

ISBN 0-313-30351-7　　　　　LC 99-33688

Also available in paperback from Palgrave Macmillan

A historical survey of Mexico and its people from the arrival of the first humans in the Western Hemisphere to the end of the 20th century. Topics range from Mexico's cultural past to current issues such as the war on drugs and the North American Free Trade Agreement.

Includes bibliographical references

The **Oxford** encyclopedia of Mesoamerican cultures; the civilizations of Mexico and Central America; David Carrasco, editor in chief. Oxford Univ. Press 2000 3v set $395

Grades: 11 12 Adult　　　　　**972**

1. Native Americans—Mexico—Encyclopedias

ISBN 0-19-510815-9　　　　　LC 00-32624

This encyclopedia includes parts of Mexico, Honduras, Nicaragua, and Costa Rica, as well as Guatemala, Belize, and El Salvador. Beginning with the Olmecs, coverage extends through the twentieth century. Essays discuss issues related to economic, social, religious, and political organization; practices and beliefs; and artistic expression, as well as the cultures, people, and sites of these regions

"This superb work should grace collections in art, archaeolgy, religious studies, anthropology, Native American studies, and Latin American history." Libr J

Includes bibliographical references

Smith, Michael Ernest, 1953-

The Aztecs; [by] Michael E. Smith. 2nd ed. Blackwell 2003 c2002 367p il maps (Peoples of America) hardcover o.p. pa $29.95

Grades: 11 12 Adult　　　　　**972**

1. Aztecs 2. Mexico—Antiquities

ISBN 0-631-23015-7; 0-631-23016-5 (pa)

　　　　　　　　　　　　　　LC 2001-6950

First published 1996

The author "summarizes the results of archaeological research conducted largely in the past 30 years into the everyday lives of ordinary people in the villages, hamlets, and farmsteads from many regions of central Mexico. His method permits a fresh view of such topics as agricultural methods, population size, market system, relations between city-states and the empire, and even human sacrifice. Smith carries his social account of these people through transformation under Spanish rule and their legacy in modern Mexico." Libr J [review of 1996 edition]

Includes bibliographical references

Townsend, Richard F.

The Aztecs. rev ed, 2nd ed. Thames & Hudson 2000 232p il maps (Ancient peoples and places) pa $18.95 *

Grades: 11 12 Adult　　　　　**972**

1. Aztecs

ISBN 0-500-28132-7　　　　　LC 99-70847

First published 1992

"In addition to analyzing the advancement and eventual dissolution of the extensive Aztec empire, the author also provides a fascinating record of the minutiae of daily life. . . . A compact introduction to the historical and sociological evolution of a prominent Meso-American civilization." Booklist {review of 1992 edition}

Includes bibliographical references

972.08 Mexico since 1867

Coerver, Don M., 1943-
Mexico: an encyclopedia of contemporary culture and history; [by] Don M. Coerver, Suzanne B. Pasztor, and Robert M. Buffington. ABC-CLIO 2004 xxiv, 621p il map $85 *
Grades: 9 10 11 12   **972.08**
1. Mexico—Civilization
ISBN 1-576-07132-4   LC 2004-14738
An "overview of 20th- and 21st-century Mexico, this volume explores the political, economic, social, and cultural history of the world's largest Spanish-speaking country." Publisher's note
"The book would probably be best for undergraduates taking a survey course on Mexico or Latin America or high-school students taking similar courses." Booklist
Includes bibliographical references

972.8 Central America

Foster, Lynn V.
A brief history of Central America. 2nd ed. Facts on File 2007 338p il map $45 *
Grades: 9 10 11 12   **972.8**
1. Central America—History
ISBN 978-0-8160-6671-1; 0-8160-6671-X
LC 2006-49760
First published 2000
This book "explores the history of the Central American isthmus from the pre-Columbian cultures to the contemporary nations that make up the region today: Belize, Costa Rica, El Salvador, Guatemala, Honduras, Nicaragua, and Panama." Publisher's note
Includes bibliographical references

972.9 West Indies and Bermuda

Rogozinski, Jan
A brief history of the Caribbean; from the Arawak and the Carib to the present. rev ed. Facts on File 1999 415p il maps $45 *
Grades: 9 10 11 12   **972.9**
ISBN 0-8160-3811-2   LC 98-51304
Available in paperback from Plume Bks.
First published 1991
New edition in preparation
This historical overview "covers Spanish rule, the northern European influence, the sugar empire, independence, and post-World War I development. Textual clarity, access to straightforward tables covering primarily demographic information, and various statistics will prove useful to the reader looking for a ready reference source." Libr J {review of 1991 edition}
Includes bibliographical references

972.91 Cuba

Castro's Cuba; Charles W. Carey Jr., book editor. Greenhaven Press 2004 205p il (History firsthand) $37.95; pa $23.70 *
Grades: 7 8 9 10   **972.91**
1. Castro, Fidel, 1926- 2. Cuba—Politics and government
ISBN 0-7377-1654-1; 0-7377-1655-X (pa)
LC 2003-47286
"Through the use of interviews, articles, and first-person narratives, this book focuses on the significance of the 1959 revolution and its aftermath. An extensive introduction explaining events precipitating the rise of Fidel Castro, the revolution, and the current situation in Cuba provides readers with a necessary overview to understand the succeeding chapters." SLJ
Includes bibliographical references

Encyclopedia of Cuba; people, history, culture; edited by Luis Martinez-Fernández {et al.}. Greenwood Press 2003 2v il maps set $174.95 *
Grades: 11 12 Adult   **972.91**
1. Cuba—Encyclopedias
ISBN 1-57356-334-X   LC 2002-70030
"An Oryx book"
"The editors intend this work to be a non-politicized look at Cuban people, politics, history, and culture. Chapters cover topics such as history, government, and popular culture. Within each chapter, entries are in alphabetical order. An excellent introduction to a colorful and important nation." Booklist
Includes bibliographical references

Harvey, David Alan, 1944-
Cuba; photographs by David Alan Harvey; essays by Elizabeth Newhouse. National Geographic Soc. 1999 215p il $50
Grades: 11 12 Adult   **972.91**
1. Cuba
ISBN 0-7922-7501-2   LC 99-32488
This collection of Harvey's photographs depicts "the effects of Cuba's totalitarian government and dire economy upon its remarkably resilient population. . . . These images are matched with staff writer Newhouse's historical overview, which discusses the country's rich architectural heritage, culture, and social conditions. Together these add up to a sympathetic understanding of what the island is like today." Libr J

Living through the Cuban Missile Crisis; edited by William S. McConnell. Greenhaven Press 2005 138p il map (Living through the Cold War) lib bdg $32.45
Grades: 9 10 11 12   **972.91**
1. Cuban Missile Crisis, 1962
ISBN 0-7377-2128-6 (lib bdg)   LC 2004-47476
"This volume examines the missile crisis from the perspective of U.S. citizens, includes articles that highlight the public response, and provides primary documents such as speeches and communiques to which the public had access through news media during the crisis period."

Living through the Cuban Missile Crisis—*Continued*
Publisher's note
Includes bibliographical references

Staten, Clifford L.
The history of Cuba. Greenwood Press 2003
162p map (Greenwood histories of the modern
nations) $45
Grades: 9 10 11 12   **972.91**
1. Cuba—History
ISBN 0-313-31690-2   LC 2002-35334
Also available in paperback from Palgrave Macmillan
The author presents an overview of Cuba's "history
from its early settlement by Taino Indians in 1250. Coverage includes its discovery by Christopher Columbus in
1492 and subsequent colonization by Spain; the wars of
independence and intervention by the United States in
the early twentieth century; the rise and fall of Fulgencio
Batista; and Fidel Castro's Marxist revolution in 1959
and its ties to the Soviet Union. More recent events discussed are the various economic reforms and the afteref-
fects of the end of the Cold War and the collapse of the
Soviet Union. The book concludes with an analytical
look at the current situation in Cuba, and offers educated
conjectures as to what the future might hold for this
troubled nation." Voice Youth Advocates
Includes bibliographical references

972.95   Puerto Rico

Fernandez, Ronald
Puerto Rico past and present; an encyclopedia;
[by] Ronald Fernandez, Serafín Méndez Méndez,
Gail Cueto. Greenwood Press 1998 xxxii, 375p il
$59.95
Grades: 11 12 Adult   **972.95**
1. Puerto Rico—Encyclopedias
ISBN 0-313-29822-X   LC 97-1689
"Along with biographical entries, included are colloquial and political terms and groups, court decisions,
buildings, and other items of Puerto Rican cultural and
historical developments. Each entry is approximately one
page." Voice Youth Advocates

973   United States

100 key documents in American democracy; edited
by Peter B. Levy; foreword by William E.
Leuchtenburg. Greenwood Press 1994 502p il
$59.95; pa $42.95 *
Grades: 11 12 Adult   **973**
1. United States—History—Sources
ISBN 0-313-28424-5; 0-275-96525-2 (pa)
                              LC 93-1137
"The work is arranged chronologically within sections,
such as 'The Early Republic' and 'The Progressive Era.'
Beginning with Powhatan's call for peace in his 1609
'Letter to John Smith' and concluding with Jesse Jack-
son's moving speech at the 1988 Democratic National
Convention. . . . Each piece is prefaced by a short chro-

nology that sets the historical context and a commentary
on the document that often refers to other writings in the
book. Shorter documents are reprinted in their entirety,
while longer ones have been edited." Booklist

American eras. Gale Res. 1997-1998 8v il set
$950
Grades: 11 12 Adult   **973**
1. United States—Civilization 2. United States—History
ISBN 0-7876-1477-7
Also available separately for $130
Contents: Early American civilizations and exploration
to 1600; The colonial era (1600-1754); The Revolutionary era (1754-1783); Development of a nation (1783-
1815); The reform era and eastern U.S. development
(1815-1850); Westward expansion (1801-1861); Civil
War and Reconstruction (1850-1877); Development of
the industrial U.S. (1877-1900)
This reference set "provides information on U.S. history, including social history, prior to the twentieth century. Each era-specific volume includes an introductory essay describing the time period to provide context and an
overview, 150 illustrations, an index of photographs, a
bibliography, a subject index and a list of contributors."
Publisher's note

The **American** presidency; edited by Alan
Brinkley and Davis Dyer. Houghton Mifflin Co
2004 572p il pa $19.95 *
Grades: 11 12 Adult   **973**
1. Presidents—United States 2. United States—Politics
and government
ISBN 0-618-38273-9   LC 2003-62513
An updated version of The reader's companion to the
American presidency (2000)
This work assesses "how presidents shape and define
culture and society and, at the same time, reflect them.
. . . [This] can serve as a beginning point for research
and should engage casual readers as well as students of
the American presidency." Choice
Includes bibliographical references

Americans at war; society, culture, and the
homefront; John P. Resch, Editor in Chief.
Macmillan Reference USA 2005 4v il set $395
Grades: 11 12 Adult   **973**
1. War and civilization 2. United States—Military history 3. United States—Civilization
ISBN 0-02-865806-X   LC 2004-17314
Contents: v. 1. 1500-1815 -- v. 2. 1816-1900 -- v. 3.
1901-1945 -- v. 4. 1946-present
This book "delivers well-written articles and would
make an excellent addition to high-school, academic, and
public libraries." Booklist
Includes bibliographical references

Anzovin, Steven, 1954-
Famous first facts about American politics; [by]
Steven Anzovin & Janet Podell. Wilson, H.W.
2001 756p $180 *
Grades: 11 12 Adult   **973**
1. United States—Politics and government 2. United
States—History
ISBN 0-8242-0971-0   LC 00-49960

Anzovin, Steven, 1954-—*Continued*
This offers over 5,000 entries of firsts in national, state, and local U.S. politics from the founding of the nation through the 2000 election and includes five indexes: subject, name, year, day, and place.
Includes bibliographical references

Basic documents in American history; [edited by] Richard B. Morris. Krieger 1980 c1965 193p pa $13.50
Grades: 9 10 11 12   **973**
1. United States—History—Sources
ISBN 0-89874-202-1   LC 80-12822
First published 1956. This is a reprint of the edition published 1965 by Van Nostrand
"A collection of documents, with brief analysis and evaluation for each selection, covering from 1620 to the 1960s." Wynar. Guide to Ref Books for Sch Media Cent. 3d edition

Creative Media Applications Inc.
Debatable issues in U.S. history. Greenwood Press 2004 5v il, maps (Middle school reference) set $200
Grades: 11 12 Adult   **973**
1. United States—History 2. United States—Politics and government 3. United States—Social conditions
ISBN 0-313-32910-9   LC 2003-56802
Contents: v. 1. From colonies to a country, 1635-1790 -- v. 2. Building the nation, 1791-1832 -- v. 3. A country divided, 1833-1868 -- v. 4. Entering the industrial age, 1869-1933 -- v. 5. A world power, 1934 to the present
"Covering the period from 1635 through the 2000 presidential election, this resource for junior high and high school students examines a variety of important issues that have sparked ongoing and emotional political and social debate in the United States. . . . The volumes are well organized, and the writing style is quite accessible." Voice Youth Advocates
Includes bibliographical references

Eyewitness to America; 500 years of America in the words of those who saw it happen; edited by David Colbert. Pantheon Bks. 1997 xxx, 599p hardcover o.p. pa $16.95 *
Grades: 11 12 Adult   **973**
1. United States—History—Sources
ISBN 0-679-44224-3; 0-679-76724-X (pa)
                                   LC 96-24150
This volume contains a "panorama of first-person accounts of moments in the country's story that stretch from an October 10, 1492, diary entry by one of Columbus's crewmen to a 1994 e-mail message from Bill Gates. The nearly 300 entries tend to be short, preceded by informative introductions. The result is a feeling for history that is both immediate and dramatic." Publ Wkly
Includes bibliographical references

Facts about the states; editors, Joseph Nathan Kane, Janet Podell, Steven Anzovin. 2nd ed. Wilson, H.W. 1994 c1993 624p il $115 *
Grades: 11 12 Adult   **973**
1. United States—Local history 2. State governments
ISBN 0-8242-0849-8   LC 93-30328

First published 1989
Provides geographic, demographic, economic, political, and cultural facts about the fifty states, Puerto Rico, and the District of Columbia. Part I presents state entries in alphabetical order. Part II provides comparative tables that rank states in categories such as population, geography, education, and finance.

Genovese, Michael A.
Encyclopedia of the American presidency; [by] Michael Genovese. Facts on File 2004 546p il (Facts on File library of American history) $85 *
Grades: 11 12 Adult   **973**
1. Presidents—United States—Encyclopedias
ISBN 0-8160-4699-9   LC 2003-49254
First published 2003 in the United Kingdom
Alphabetically arranged entries provide "information regarding elections, court cases, scandals, domestic and foreign policy issues, war and peace, political opponents and running mates, plus a number of other topics. . . . There are four appendixes: sections on the U.S. Constitution dealing with the presidency, an annotated chronology of presidential elections, a selected general bibliography, and a bibliography by president. This source promises to be a good first stop for students, journalists, history buffs, and general readers looking for information on the American executive branch." Booklist

Keegan, John, 1934-
Fields of battle; the wars for North America. Knopf 1996 c1995 348p il maps hardcover o.p. pa $15
Grades: 11 12 Adult   **973**
1. North America—Military history
ISBN 0-679-42413-X; 0-679-74664-1 (pa)
                                   LC 96-154385
First published 1995 in the United Kingdom with title: Warpaths: travels of a military historian in North America
The author "demonstrates how North America's geography has influenced its history: how its mountain chains and river systems have determined where people fought, and fought repeatedly. For example, the defenses that Cornwallis built at Yorktown to deter American forces were improved and reused by the Confederates almost a century later. Keegan's tour of the continent skips the Mexican War, and his book is atypically discursive. For Americans, the charm is the familiarity of its sites—Brooklyn, Pittsburgh, Laramie, and other home towns." New Yorker

Lubar, Steven D.
Legacies; collecting America's history at the Smithsonian; [by] Steven Lubar and Kathleen M. Kendrick. Smithsonian Institution Press 2001 256p il $39.95
Grades: 9 10 11 12   **973**
1. National Museum of American History (U.S.)
2. United States—Civilization
ISBN 1-56098-886-X   LC 2001-20399
An illustrated look at more than 200 representative objects from the Smithsonian's collection. "The eclectic

Lubar, Steven D.—*Continued*

collage of artifacts ranges from the curious (an 1860s phrenology model used to decipher personality and behavior) to the provocative (the uniform of a WWI woman contract-surgeon). Elegant acquisitions, such as first ladies' inaugural gowns, are preserved along with the mundane (the Veg-O-Matic) and popular culture (Archie and Edith Bunkers' chairs), as well as scientific and technological advances. In every case, stories are the key elements that transform each specimen into a legacy worth preserving." Publ Wkly

Includes bibliographical references

Opposing viewpoints in American history; William Dudley, volume editor; John C. Chalberg, consulting editor. Greenhaven Press 2007 2v v1 $59.95; v1 pa $39.95; v2 $59.95; v2 pa $39.95 *

Grades: 9 10 11 12   **973**

1. United States—History—Sources

ISBN 0-7377-3184-2 (v1); 978-0-7377-3184-2 (v1); 0-7377-3185-0 (v1 pa); 978-0-7377-3185-9 (v1 pa); 0737731869 (v2); 978-0-7377-3186-6 (v2); 0-7377-3187-7 (v2 pa); 978-0-7377-3187-3 (v2 pa)

LC 2006-24673

First published 1996

Contents: v. 1. From colonial times to Reconstruction — v. 2. From Reconstruction to the present

"Topics range chronologically from 'Origins of English Settlement' to 'National Security, Terrorism, and Iraq.' Essays, speeches, and letters by such notables as Elizabeth Cady Stanton, Malcolm X, and Bill Clinton provide historical context for the debates. Articles are clustered under prefaced general categories, such as 'The Gilded Age,' 'Antebellum America,' and 'New Challenges after the Cold War.'" SLJ

Includes bibliographical references

Our national archive; key documents, opinions, speeches, letters, and songs that shaped our nation; edited by Erik Bruun and Jay Crosby. Black Dog & Leventhal 1999 886p $29.98 *

Grades: 11 12 Adult   **973**

1. United States—History—Sources

ISBN 1-57912-067-9   LC 99-29451

An "anthology of 1000 chronologically arranged primary sources spanning 300 years of American history. . . . As the voices from history speak, one gains a vivid portrait of American life." SLJ

The **Reader's** companion to the American presidency; edited by Alan Brinkley and Davis Dyer. Houghton Mifflin 2000 566p il $40

Grades: 11 12 Adult   **973**

1. Presidents—United States 2. United States—Politics and government

ISBN 0-395-78889-7   LC 99-59638

"Essays written by professors and historians present an overview of each administration through factual details, anecdotes, and analysis. The amount of criticism in each article varies depending on the writer and the president. The text is academic but readable. . . . A detailed time line runs along the bottom of the pages and includes other important political and cultural events." SLJ

Includes bibliographical references

Savage, William W.

The cowboy hero; his image in American history & culture; by William W. Savage, Jr. University of Okla. Press 1979 179p il hardcover o.p. pa $19.95

Grades: 9 10 11 12   **973**

1. Cowhands

ISBN 0-8061-1587-4; 0-8061-1920-9 (pa)

LC 79-4730

The author's "research extends into all facets of Western history with emphasis on the popular glorification of the cowboy in books, movies, radio, and television. . . . Savage . . . appears to have a real affection for his subject." Libr J

Includes bibliographical references

United States. National Archives and Records Administration

Our documents; 100 milestone documents from the National Archives. Oxford University Press 2003 256p il $40; pa $24.95

Grades: 9 10 11 12   **973**

1. United States—History—Sources

ISBN 0-19-517206-X; 0-19-530959-6 (pa)

LC 2003-15080

A collection of one hundred documents that were important in the development of the United States from its founding to 1965, including the Declaration of Independence, Constitution, and lesser-known writings.

"Photographs and facsimile reproductions of documents are a highlight of the book—they let readers see the actual items. The appealing, clean layout is defined by clear blue and red headings and plenty of white space. A useful addition." SLJ

Includes bibliographical references

Virga, Vincent

Eyes of the nation; a visual history of the United States; by Vincent Virga and curators of the Library of Congress; historical commentary by Alan Brinkley. Knopf 1997 399p il $75

Grades: 9 10 11 12 Adult   **973**

ISBN 0-679-44330-4   LC 97-36603

Also available in paperback from Bunker Hill

This visual history "showcases more than 500 illustrations, manuscripts, engravings, prints, movie stills and other artifacts stretching back to the 15th century. The accompanying text by the historian Alan Brinkley rolls through the high and low points of the nation's history, but it is the captions that sparkle the brightest, adding context while offering surprising information." N Y Times Book Rev

War and American popular culture; a historical encyclopedia; edited by M. Paul Holsinger. Greenwood Press 1999 479p il $95

Grades: 11 12 Adult   **973**

1. Popular culture—United States 2. War and civilization 3. United States—Military history

ISBN 0-313-29908-0   LC 98-12141

Holsinger "has attempted to pull together in one volume 'many of the most significant representations in popular culture that deal with this nation's various wars.'

War and American popular culture—*Continued*
. . . The popular culture forms he examines include novels, short stories, poems, songs, plays, movies, radio and television, paintings, photographs, cartoons, toys, comic books, dime novels, slogans, and posters. The book is arranged chronologically, in chapters from 'Colonial Wars, 1565-1765' to 'The United States Military Since 1975.'" Booklist
Includes bibliographical references

Wetterau, Bruce
Congressional Quarterly's desk reference on the Presidency. CQ Press 2000 311p il (Desk reference series) $49.95 *
Grades: 11 12 Adult   **973**
1. Presidents—United States
ISBN 1-56802-589-0   LC 00-63024
Over 500 questions and answers on the organization, procedures, and history of the office and on the presidents and their wives. Topics covered include scandals, elections, the White House, and the executive branch
Includes bibliographical references

Wilkins, Roger W., 1932-
Jefferson's pillow; the founding fathers and the dilemma of Black patriotism; [by] Roger Wilkins. Beacon Press 2001 163p hardcover o.p. pa $14 *
Grades: 11 12 Adult   **973**
1. Mason, George, 1725-1792 2. Washington, George, 1732-1799 3. Jefferson, Thomas, 1743-1826 4. Madison, James, 1751-1836 5. United States—History 6. United States—Race relations
ISBN 0-8070-0956-3; 0-8070-0957-1 (pa)
                                  LC 2001-25117
"Wilkins returns to America's beginnings and the lives of the founding fathers to explore how . . . race and slavery still impede our progress. In . . . [an] analysis of the lives of George Washington, George Mason, James Madison, and . . . Thomas Jefferson, he explores how class, education, and personality allowed for the institution of slavery in a nation conceived under the premise that all men are created equal." Publisher's note
"This is an important look at the essential and ongoing contradictions at the heart of American ideals of liberty and patriotism." Booklist
Includes bibliographical references

Young, Dwight
Saving America's treasures; National Trust for Historic Preservation; photographs by Ira Block; text by Dwight Young; essays by Ian Frazier [et al.] National Geographic Soc. 2000 192p il $35
Grades: 11 12 Adult   **973**
1. Historic sites 2. United States—Description and travel 3. United States—Local history
ISBN 0-7922-7942-5   LC 00-56261
This guide includes "43 places, artifacts, and documents targeted by the National Trust for restoration and preservation. Each entry contains data on origin, present condition, and restoration and preservation plans. But it is the 150 photographs that make the book so absorbing. Featured places and items include the Manzanar Intern-

ment Camp in California, where 10,000 Japanese Americans were unjustly held during World War II; Harriet Tubman's home in Auburn, New York; Babe Ruth's scrapbooks in Cooperstown, New York; and the yacht *Coronet,* built in the 1800s for an oil tycoon, which is anchored off Newport, Rhode Island. This book is quite a treasure in and of itself." Booklist

973.03   United States--History-- Encyclopedias and dictionaries

Cornelison, Pam
The great American history fact-finder; the who, what, where, when, and why of American history; [by] Pam Cornelison and Ted Yanak. 2nd ed, updated and expanded. Houghton Mifflin 2004 608p il, maps pa $14.95
Grades: 11 12 Adult   **973.03**
1. United States—History—Dictionaries
ISBN 0-618-43941-2   LC 2004-47480
First published 1993 with authors' names in reverse order
This book provides "information about significant persons as well as political, legal, sporting, and cultural events in American history. Entries are alphabetically arranged, and related entries cross-referenced. . . . Besides an index, there are suggested readings and information on the states, presidents, vice presidents, population, Supreme Court, Articles of Confederation, Declaration of Independence, and US Constitution (with signers and nonsigners). This is a good quick reference." Choice

Dictionary of American history; Stanley I. Kutler, editor in chief. 3rd ed. Scribner 2003 10v il map set $1,050 *
Grades: 11 12 Adult   **973.03**
1. United States—History—Dictionaries
ISBN 0-684-80533-2   LC 2002-12433
First published 1940 in 5 volumes edited by James Truslow Adams
"This set provides 4,434 entries pertaining to American history. . . . Volumes 1-8 provide an alphabetic listing of key events, while volume 9 offers primary documents and archival maps and volume 10 offers a research guide and index to the set. Each article runs several paragraphs to several pages in length and each have a bibliography and *see also* references." Am Ref Books Annu, 2003
Includes bibliographical references

Encyclopedia of American cultural and intellectual history; edited by Mary Kupiec Cayton and Peter W. Williams. Scribner 2000 3v il set $400
Grades: 11 12 Adult   **973.03**
1. United States—Civilization—Encyclopedias 2. United States—Intellectual life—Encyclopedias
ISBN 0-684-80561-8   LC 2001-20005
Art movements, education and academia, the counterculture, the sciences, domestic life, social classes, Hollywood, and post-structuralism are among the topics covered. Each article includes illustrations, boxed biographies, or documentary excerpts

Encyclopedia of American historical documents; edited by Susan Rosenfeld. Facts on File 2004 3v (Facts on File library of American history) set $300 *

Grades: 11 12 Adult   **973.03**
1. United States—History—Sources
ISBN 0-8160-4995-5   LC 2003-51610

"Each section begins with an overview of the period and each document is introduced with commentary on when and why it was created and its significance, then and now. Entries include material 'with resonance for the 21st century' that represents turning points in U.S. history, and documents of a controversial nature. Students can read Supreme Court justices' opinions, presidential announcements and inaugural addresses, excerpts from noteworthy books that influenced American thought and action, and speeches of women and people of color. . . . Students and teachers will welcome this mammoth resource." SLJ

Includes bibliographical references

Encyclopedia of American history; Gary B. Nash, general editor. Facts on File 2003 11v il maps set $935

Grades: 11 12 Adult   **973.03**
1. United States—History—Encyclopedias
ISBN 0-8160-4371-X   LC 2001-51278

Contents: v1 Three worlds meet beginnings to 1607; v2 Colonization and settlement 1608 to 1760; v3 Revolution and new nation 1761 to 1812; v4 Expansion and reform 1813 to 1855; v5 Civil War and Reconstruction 1856 to 1869; v6 The development of the industrial United States 1870 to 1899; v7 The emergence of modern America 1900 to 1928; v8 The Great Depression and World War II 1929 to 1945; v9 Postwar United States 1946 to 1968; v10 Contemporary United States 1969 to the present; v11 Comprehensive index

"The volumes are organized chronologically, but the entries within each volume are alphabetical. Each book begins with a contents list, and there are copious see and cross-references. Essays of varying length cover events; 'major categories of the American experience' (education, urbanization, etc.); people, places, concepts, and more. At the end of each entry, one or more suggestions for further reading (generally adult titles) are offered. . . . This encyclopedia is a valuable resource for students of American history and can be used to support any classroom text, offering students ample opportunity for fuller exploration of topics of interest." SLJ

The **Encyclopedia** of American political history; edited by Paul Finkelman, Peter Wallenstein. CQ Press 2001 xxxii, 494p il map $140 *

Grades: 11 12 Adult   **973.03**
1. United States—Politics and government—Encyclopedias
ISBN 1-56802-511-4   LC 00-66812

This reference tool covers "significant events, people {and} concepts in U.S. political history. Organized alphabetically, the 225 entries vary in length from a few paragraphs to several pages. The book opens with a descriptive time line of political events and ends with an appendix of acronyms and abbreviations used in U.S. history." Libr J

Includes bibliographical references

Encyclopedia of American studies; edited by George T. Kurian [et al.] Grolier Educ. 2001 4v il set $399

Grades: 11 12 Adult   **973.03**
1. United States—Civilization—Encyclopedias
ISBN 0-7172-9222-3   LC 2001-23415

"Published under the sponsorship of the American Studies Association"

This work "brings together a range of topics related to the culture of the US, from political movements, arts, and religion to wars, landmark legal rulings, and technology. The preface explains the concept and discipline of 'American studies.' A table of contents groups by subject the 660 entries, nearly all written by academics. . . . Entries are clearly written with enough interesting detail to inspire high school or undergraduate students to conduct further research." Choice

Includes bibliographical references

Encyclopedia of the new American nation; the emergence of the United States, 1754-1829; Paul Finkelman, editor in chief. Thomson Gale 2005 3v il map set $395

Grades: 11 12 Adult   **973.03**
1. United States—History—1600-1775, Colonial period—Encyclopedias 2. United States—History—1775-1783, Revolution—Encyclopedias 3. United States—History—1783-1865—Encyclopedias
ISBN 0-684-31346-4   LC 2005-17783

The timeframe covered in this encyclopedia of major political events and figures "is roughly from 1754 (beginning of the Seven Years' War) to the inauguration of President Andrew Jackson (1829). Woven among this set of political markers and milestones are entries outlining the cultural development of the new nation, including entries on art, music, literature, dress and daily life." Publisher's note

The editor and contributors "have produced a wonderful reference source." Ref & User Services Quarterly

Includes bibliographical references

The **Greenwood** encyclopedia of American regional cultures; William Ferris, consulting editor. Greenwood Press 2004 8v il map set $699.95

Grades: 11 12 Adult   **973.03**
1. United States—Social life and customs—Encyclopedias 2. United States—Civilization—Encyclopedias
ISBN 0-313-33266-5

This "set explores the history and culture of U.S. regions from the Atlantic to the Pacific. The essay-long articles examine at length each region's art, ethnicity, fashion, film, folklore, food, literature, religion, sports, and more." Libr J

Includes bibliographical references

The **Oxford** companion to United States history; editor in chief, Paul S. Boyer; editors, Melvyn Dubofsky {et al.}. Oxford Univ. Press 2001 xliv, 940p il maps $75 *

Grades: 11 12 Adult   **973.03**
1. United States—History—Dictionaries
ISBN 0-19-508209-5   LC 00-55801

First published 1966 under the authorship of Thomas A. Johnson with title: The Oxford companion to American history

The Oxford companion to United States history—*Continued*

This reference work contains 1,400 alphabetically arranged signed entries. See and see also references are provided. Coverage starts with the colonial period and examines notable men and women and major events in U.S. history

Includes bibliographical references

The Reader's companion to American history; Eric Foner and John A. Garraty, editors; sponsored by the Society of American Historians. Houghton Mifflin 1991 xxii, 1226p $45 *

Grades: 11 12 Adult   **973.03**
1. United States—History—Encyclopedias
ISBN 0-395-51372-3   LC 91-19508
"The nearly 1000 entries, ranging from concise explanations to multipage essays, are all equally well written, crisp, and entertaining. Most entries are signed by the nearly 400 contributors, many of whom are acknowledged experts in their fields. . . . Brief bibliographies and thorough 'See also' references to related articles follow each entry." Libr J

Thompson, Peter, 1960-

Dictionary of American history: from 1763 to the present. Facts on File 2000 540p $71.50; pa $20.95 *

Grades: 11 12 Adult   **973.03**
1. United States—History—Dictionaries
ISBN 0-8160-4462-7; 0-8160-4463-5 (pa)
     LC 00-41079
Published in Great Britain with title: Dictionary of modern American history
Originally published in Great Britain under title: Cassell's dictionary of modern American history; Series statement from jacket
"The approximately 1,200 entries encompass political, diplomatic, military, economic, social, and cultural topics, as well as biographies, essential terms, battles, and key legislation. Most entries are two or three paragraphs in length, but some topics, like the Civil War and civil rights, are treated in several pages of interpretive essays. There are histories of all 50 states and synopses of important Supreme Court cases." Booklist
Includes bibliographical references

Worldmark encyclopedia of the states. Gale Res. 2v maps set $180 *

Grades: 9 10 11 12 Adult   **973.03**
1. United States—Encyclopedias
ISBN 0-7876-7338-2
First published 1981 by Harper & Row (7th edition 2006) Periodically revised
"Comprehensive examination of each state within the framework of 50 standard subject headings. Includes economic policy, energy and power, resources, education, the press, famous persons, etc." N Y Public Libr. Ref Books for Child Collect. 2d edition

973.2 United States--Colonial period, 1607-1775

Bogaert, Harmen Meyndertsz van den

Journey into Mohawk Country; as written by H.M. van den Bogaert, with artwork by George O'Connor and color by Hilary Sycamore. First Second 2006 144p il pa $17.95 *

Grades: 8 9 10 11 12   **973.2**
1. Graphic novels 2. United States—History—1600-1775, Colonial period—Graphic novels 3. New York (State)—History—1600-1775, Colonial period—Graphic novels
ISBN 1-59643-106-7
In 1634, young Dutch trader Harmen Meyndertsz van den Bogaert, several companions, and some native guides traveled deep into what is now New York State, trading tools and weapons and trying to establish new tribal friendships to bolster Dutch trade. van den Bogaert kept a journal throughout his journeys. O'Connor has kept the original text and conducted extensive research in order to make his illustrations as authentic as possible.

Colonial America; an encyclopedia of social, political, cultural, and economic history; edited by James Ciment. Sharpe Reference 2006 5v il map set $499

Grades: 11 12 Adult   **973.2**
1. United States—Civilization 2. United States—Social life and customs—1600-1775, Colonial period
ISBN 0-7656-8065-3; 978-0-7656-8065-5
     LC 2003-23235
"Seven opening essays provide an overview of major issues and the more than 450 signed, alphabetical entries that follow. The articles cover places, events, institutions, ideas, women, and minority peoples. . . . The final volume includes the text of 60 primary-source documents, each with an introduction that describes its contents and significance." SLJ
Includes bibliographical references

Copeland, David A., 1951-

Debating the issues in colonial newspapers; primary documents on events of the period. Greenwood Press 2000 397p il $59.95 *

Grades: 9 10 11 12   **973.2**
1. United States—History—1600-1775, Colonial period—Sources 2. Newspapers—United States
ISBN 0-313-30982-5   LC 99-89070
"Primary-source material on 31 events and issues from 1690 to 1776 including abolition, inoculation, women's rights, censorship, and separation from England. The principal source of communication for people during this period was the newspaper, and political and social concerns were debated there at length. . . . Following the colonialists' pro or con opinions, a number of questions are posed for students." SLJ
Includes bibliographical references

Events that changed America through the seventeenth century; edited by John E. Findling and Frank W. Thackeray. Greenwood Press 2000 193p (Greenwood Press "Events that changed America" series) $39.95

Grades: 11 12 Adult   **973.2**

1. United States—History—1600-1775, Colonial period 2. America—History

ISBN 0-313-29083-0   LC 00-20080

A look at ten of the most important events in what was to become the continental United States from the settlement of the earliest peoples to the close of the seventeenth century. Coronado's expedition, the founding of St. Augustine, and early European-Native American encounters are among the topics discussed

Includes bibliographical references

Gray, Edward G., 1964-

Colonial America: a history in documents. Oxford Univ. Press 2003 191p il maps (Pages from history) lib bdg $36.95 *

Grades: 7 8 9 10   **973.2**

1. United States—History—1600-1775, Colonial period

ISBN 0-19-513747-7   LC 2002-4285

Contents: England expands; New lands, new lives; Colonists confront first nations; Who built the colonies?; Ties that bind; A spiritual people; Gentle women and gentle men; A world of things

This title "presents excerpts from printed and pictorial primary sources that together form a compact portrait of the Colonial era in America from the late 15th century through 1763. . . . Each chapter begins with concise introductory remarks that create a clear context for the lists, letters, drawings, maps, portraits, ads, diagrams, news stories, diary entries, poems, and other documentation that follow. . . . A fine source for reports about this period." SLJ

Includes bibliographical references

Hawke, David Freeman

Everyday life in early America. Harper & Row 1988 195p il (Everyday life in America) pa $13 hardcover o.p. *

Grades: 11 12 Adult   **973.2**

1. United States—History—1600-1775, Colonial period 2. United States—Social life and customs

ISBN 0-06-091251-0 (pa)   LC 87-17667

The author "provides enlightening and colorful descriptions of early Colonial Americans and debunks many widely held assumptions about 17th century settlers." Publ Wkly

Includes bibliographical references

Hofstadter, Richard, 1916-1970

America at 1750; a social portrait. Knopf 1971 293p pa $11 hardcover o.p.

Grades: 11 12 Adult   **973.2**

1. United States—History—1600-1775, Colonial period 2. United States—Social conditions

ISBN 0-394-71795-3 (pa)

"Using primarily secondary accounts, Hofstadter examines the ethnic composition of the colonies in 1750; traces the development of white servitude, the slave trade, and the slave system; sketches briefly the middle-class framework of early America; and dissects the colonial religious paradigm and the impact of the Great Awakening." Choice

Includes bibliographical references

Purvis, Thomas L., 1949-

Colonial America to 1763. Facts on File 1999 381p il (Almanacs of American life) $95

Grades: 11 12 Adult   **973.2**

1. United States—History—1600-1775, Colonial period 2. United States—Social life and customs—1600-1775, Colonial period

ISBN 0-8160-2527-4   LC 98-29007

Series statement from jacket

This compendium is "divided into 19 chapters that cover such topics as 'Diet and Health,' 'Religion,' 'The Cities,' 'Science and Technology,' 'Crime and Violence,' and 'Popular Life and Recreation.' There are general details of Colonial life as well as obscure and difficult-to-find facts that students need and teachers always want. . . . Young adults will enjoy learning through all of the fascinating facts and curious bits of information, but the well-organized, complete, and accessible text will also provide an invaluable resource for research and term papers." SLJ

Includes bibliographical references

Saari, Peggy

Colonial America: primary sources; Julie Carnagie, editor. U.X.L 1999 297p il $67 *

Grades: 9 10 11 12   **973.2**

1. United States—History—1600-1775, Colonial period

ISBN 0-7876-3766-1   LC 99-34460

Presents the historical events and social issues of colonial America through twenty-four primary documents, including diary entries, poems, and personal narratives.

"Each chapter adds helpful material before and after the excerpt to explain its importance. Illustrations and sidebars are used in this volume also, and difficult words are defined." Booklist

Wolf, Stephanie Grauman

As various as their land; the everyday lives of eighteenth-century Americans. University of Arkansas Press 2000 304p il map pa $16.95 *

Grades: 9 10 11 12 Adult   **973.2**

1. United States—Social life and customs—1600-1775, Colonial period

ISBN 1-557-28599-3   LC 99-86042

First published 1993 by HarperCollins

The author examines the "diversity of experience that marked America's people in the 100 or so years preceding nationhood. Wolf's main concern is with immigrant cultures and their transfer to, and transformation of, the

Wolf, Stephanie Grauman—*Continued*
soil of New England, the Middle Atlantic region, and the American South." Libr J
"An excellent overview of the foundation of our society's successes and failures." Booklist
Includes bibliographical references

973.3   United States--Periods of Revolution and Confederation, 1775-1789

The **American** Revolution; Kirk D. Werner, book editor. Greenhaven Press 2000 224p (Turning points in world history) lib bdg $31.20
Grades: 9 10 11 12   973.3
1. United States—History—1775-1783, Revolution
ISBN 0-7377-0239-7   LC 99-38377
This volume "contains 16 essays by well-known historians that center on the background, politics, and effects of the [American Revolution]. . . . There is an extensive section of documents (Stamp Act resolutions, excerpts from first-person accounts, Articles of Confederation, etc.) An excellent resource for research." SLJ
Includes bibliographical references

The **American** Revolution; writings from the War of Independence. Library of Am. 2001 878p $40
*
Grades: 11 12 Adult   973.3
1. United States—History—1775-1783, Revolution
ISBN 1-88301-191-4   LC 00-45373
This collection includes "over 120 pieces by more than 70 Revolution-era writers from both sides of the War of Independence. The book begins with Paul Revere's personal account of his famous ride in April 1775 and ends with a description of George Washington's resignation from the command of the Continental Army in December 1783. . . . At the book's end one can find a long section that includes a chronology, biographical sketches of the authors, and other notes on the texts." Libr J
"This work will serve as a marvelous research tool for specialists, but general readers with an interest in American history will also find fascinating gems." Booklist
Includes bibliographical references

American Revolutionary War: a student encyclopedia; Gregory Fremont-Barnes, Richard Alan Ryerson, volume editors; James Arnold and Roberta Wiener, editors, documents volume; foreword by Jack P. Greene. ABC-CLIO 2007 5v il map set $485 *
Grades: 9 10 11 12   973.3
1. United States—History—1775-1783, Revolution—Encyclopedias
ISBN 978-1-85109-839-2; 1-85109-839-9
LC 2006-31100
"With over 800 entries and essays and a separate documents volume, . . . [this encyclopedia] covers every battle and campaign, every political debate and diplomatic encounter. It also introduces students to the broad spectrum of American culture at the time (day-to-day life, art, music) as well as the personal lives of all those

caught up in the war." Publisher's note
Includes bibliographical references

Aronson, Marc
The real revolution; the global story of American independence. Clarion Books 2005 238p il map lib bdg $21 *
Grades: 7 8 9 10   973.3
1. United States—History—1775-1783, Revolution
ISBN 0-618-18179-2   LC 2005-1088
In this "volume, Aronson investigates the origins of the American Revolution and discovers some startling global connections. The colonies' quest for independence is tied to such seemingly unrelated incidents as Robert Clive's triumph over the French in India in 1750 and John Wilkes's accusations against the king in his newspaper, The North Briton, in the 1760s. . . . This outstanding work is highly compelling reading and belongs in every library." SLJ
Includes bibliographical references

Barnes, Ian, 1946-
The historical atlas of the American Revolution; Charles Royster, consulting editor. Routledge 2000 223p il maps $50 *
Grades: 11 12 Adult   973.3
1. United States—Historical geography—Maps
ISBN 0-415-92243-7   LC 99-59920
"Although the emphasis is on the Revolution, the scope is much broader—from settlement to 1820. Chronologically arranged, each chapter opens with an overview, followed by readable double-page spreads on the time periods, specific battles, pertinent individuals or peoples, and other relevant issues. Maps are large enough to show troop movement. Legends are clear with dissimilar symbols. Portraits, illustrations, and other graphics are clearly identified. A concluding section provides brief biographical sketches. An excellent presentation of the era." SLJ
Includes bibliographical references

Bober, Natalie
Countdown to independence; a revolution of ideas in England and her American colonies: 1760-1776; by Natalie S. Bober. Atheneum Bks. for Young Readers 2000 xxv, 342p il $26.95 *
Grades: 9 10 11 12   973.3
1. United States—History—1775-1783, Revolution—Causes 2. United States—Politics and government—1775-1783, Revolution 3. Great Britain—History—1714-1837
ISBN 0-689-81329-5; 978-0-689-81329-0
LC 99-27086
Examines the people and events both in the American colonies and in Great Britain between 1760 and 1776 that led to the American Revolution.
This "is a compelling, yet scholarly resource that places readers at the center of the action, encouraging them to learn about the historic events and people, care about them, and, perhaps, learn more by investigating the extensive bibliography." Booklist
Includes bibliographical references

Draper, Theodore, 1912-2006

A struggle for power; the American Revolution. Times Bks. 1996 544p pa $13.56 hardcover o.p.

Grades: 11 12 Adult   **973.3**

1. United States—History—1775-1783, Revolution

ISBN 0-679-77642-7 (pa)   LC 95-11605

The author "maintains that the Revolution was really a power struggle spawned by the British system of chartering colonies, which placed fiscal control of public funds with the colonial assemblies." Libr J

This is an "elegantly written, masterful study. . . . Drawing freely on period pamphlets, letters, petitions, travelogues and assembly minutes, [the author] vividly evokes the populist discontent, intellectual gymnastics and mob violence that led to revolution." Publ Wkly

Includes bibliographical references

Fischer, David Hackett

Washington's crossing. Oxford University Press 2004 564p il maps (Pivotal moments in American history) $35; pa $16.95

Grades: 11 12 Adult   **973.3**

1. Washington, George, 1732-1799 2. United States—History—1775-1783, Revolution—Campaigns

ISBN 0-19-517034-2; 0-19-518159-X (pa)

      LC 2003-19858

Contents: Three armies in America -- A cataract of disaster -- The pivot point -- The crossing -- Risking it all -- The boldest stroke

The author describes how "Washington, his officers, and their men turn the early military defeats of Long Island and New York City into victory at Trenton and Princeton. The opening chapter is devoted to the painting *Washington Crossing the Delaware*. Then the author discusses the British, Hessian, and American military units that were involved in these campaigns and gives background on their officers. This is Fischer's strong suit: he tells stories and gives details that bring history alive. . . . In the hands of such a thorough researcher and talented writer, this is powerful stuff." SLJ

Includes bibliographical references

Freedman, Russell

Give me liberty! the story of the Declaration of Independence. Holiday House 2000 90p il $24.95; pa $12.95

Grades: 5 6 7 8 9   **973.3**

1. United States. Declaration of Independence 2. United States—Politics and government—1775-1783, Revolution

ISBN 0-8234-1448-5; 0-8234-1753-0 (pa)

      LC 99-57513

Describes the events leading up to the Declaration of Independence as well as the personalities and politics behind its framing

"Handsomely designed with a generous and thoughtful selection of period art, the book is dramatic and inspiring." Horn Book

Includes bibliographical references

Lefkowitz, Arthur S.

Bushnell's submarine; the best kept secret of the American Revolution. Scholastic Nonfiction 2006 136p il map $16.99

Grades: 7 8 9 10   **973.3**

1. Bushnell, David, 1742-1824 2. United States—History—1775-1783, Revolution 3. Submarines

ISBN 0-439-74352-4   LC 2005-42645

This "book relates the story of America's first submarine, the *Turtle*. Constructed by David Bushnell in time to see action during the American Revolution, the barrel-shaped submersible housed a single man, who sat blindly in the dark, wet contraption with no power source and dwindling fresh air while operating a variety of levers, pumps, and other devices. The climax of the account is a dramatic attempt to attach a mine to a British warship anchored near New York. Lefkowitz vividly conveys the ingenuity of the inventor, the courage of the Turtle's operator, and the pleasure of discovering lost bits of history." Booklist

Maier, Pauline, 1938-

American scripture; making the Declaration of Independence. Knopf 1997 xxi, 304p pa $14 hardcover o.p.

Grades: 11 12 Adult   **973.3**

1. United States. Declaration of Independence 2. United States—Politics and government—1775-1783, Revolution

ISBN 0-679-77908-6 (pa)   LC 97-2769

"In the spring of 1776, with a British invasion fleet on its way, the Second Continental Congress appointed a committee to compose a statement explaining America's decision to seek independence. Thomas Jefferson was the principal drafter of the statement, but Maier makes it clear that his task was to express the sentiments of the Congress, not his personal views, and she shows that when the congressmen edited his draft they improved it greatly (rather than 'mangling' it, as Jefferson ever after maintained). The Declaration of Independence is, she argues, a profoundly collective document, both in its origins and in our still-evolving interpretation of its self-evident truths." New Yorker

Morgan, Edmund Sears

The birth of the Republic, 1763-89. 3rd ed. University of Chicago Press 1992 206p (Chicago history of American civilization) hardcover o.p. pa $13

Grades: 11 12 Adult   **973.3**

1. United States—History—1775-1783, Revolution 2. United States—History—1783-1809

ISBN 0-226-53756-0; 0-226-53757-9 (pa)

      LC 92-8871

First published 1956

A brief study of the American revolutionary period from 1763 to 1789.

Includes bibliographical references

Purvis, Thomas L., 1949-
Revolutionary America, 1763-1800. Facts on File 1995 383p il maps (Almanacs of American life) $95 *
Grades: 11 12 Adult **973.3**
1. United States—History—1775-1783, Revolution 2. United States—Social life and customs
ISBN 0-8160-2528-2 LC 93-38382
"Arranged thematically, sections such as 'Climate,' 'Economy,' 'Population,' 'Health,' 'Religion,' 'Architecture,' and 'Education' provide statistical charts, graphs, and other data to show what life was like in the various parts of the country. . . . The text, covering perhaps a third of the book, explains and elaborates on the tabular information, pulling everything together in a relevant, interesting manner." SLJ
Includes bibliographical references

Raphael, Ray
A people's history of the American Revolution; how common people shaped the fight for independence. 1st Perennial ed. Perennial 2002 506p pa $13.95 *
Grades: 11 12 Adult **973.3**
1. United States—History—1775-1783, Revolution
ISBN 0-06-000440-1 LC 2002-16992
First published 2001 by New Press
This volume "collects the experiences of ordinary people during the American Revolution and sutures them into a story. And that story is that the rebellion and war inescapably influenced everyone—farmers, townspeople, women, Indians, free blacks and enslaved blacks, plutocrats and proletarians." Booklist
"Moving from broad overviews to stories of small groups or individuals, Raphael's study is impressive in both its sweep and its attention to the particular." Publ Wkly
Includes bibliographical references

Stokesbury, James L.
A short history of the American Revolution. Morrow 1991 304p maps hardcover o.p. pa $15.95
Grades: 11 12 Adult **973.3**
1. United States—History—1775-1783, Revolution
ISBN 0-688-08333-1; 0-688-12304-X (pa)
LC 90-29108
"Stokesbury's concise retelling of the war is spiced with his own insights and explanations. . . . This is shorter history at its best: informative, lively, and fun to read, yet thoughtful and erudite." Libr J
Includes bibliographical references

Wood, W. J. (William J.), 1917-
Battles of the Revolutionary War, 1775-1781; [by] W.J. Wood; with an introduction by John S.D. Eisenhower. Da Capo 2003 c1990 xxxii, 315p il map (Major battles and campaigns) pa $18.95
Grades: 9 10 11 12 **973.3**
1. United States—History—1775-1783, Revolution—Campaigns
ISBN 0-306-81329-7
First published 1990 by Algonquin Bks.

"Wood focuses on 10 major battles and campaigns of the American Revolution that have unique military qualities. Maps and new insights about the leadership of both armies make this a worthy addition to military history collections." Booklist
Includes bibliographical references

The **World** almanac of the American Revolution; edited by L. Edward Purcell and David F. Burg. World Almanac 1992 386p il hardcover o.p. pa $18.95 *
Grades: 11 12 Adult **973.3**
1. United States—History—1775-1783, Revolution
ISBN 0-88687-574-9; 0-88687-665-6 (pa)
LC 91-32057
A chronological examination of the events of the American Revolution and its aftermath, describing political and military actions. A separate section provides biographical information on important figures. Beginning with 1775, a one-page summary begins each year's events. Interspersed in the chronology are essays on special topics.
Includes bibliographical references

973.4 United States--Constitutional period, 1789-1809

Ellis, Joseph J.
Founding brothers; the revolutionary generation. Knopf 2000 288p $26.95; pa $14 *
Grades: 11 12 Adult **973.4**
1. United States—History—1783-1809 2. United States—Politics and government—1783-1809 3. Presidents—United States 4. United States—Biography
ISBN 0-375-40544-5; 0-375-70524-4 (pa)
LC 99-59304
This study looks at the intertwined lives of "Benjamin Franklin, Thomas Jefferson, John Adams, Alexander Hamilton, James Madison and Aaron Burr. . . . As Ellis sees it, the founding brethren not only 'created the American republic' but 'held it together throughout the volatile and vulnerable early years by sustaining their presence until national habits and customs took root.'" NY Times Book Rev
"Ellis' essays are angled, fascinating, and perfect for general-interest readers." Booklist
Includes bibliographical references

Heidler, David Stephen, 1955-
Daily life in the early American republic, 1790-1820; [by] David S. Heidler and Jeanne T. Heidler. Greenwood Press 2004 xxxi, 236p map (Greenwood Press "Daily life through history" series) $49.95 *
Grades: 9 10 11 12 **973.4**
1. United States—Social life and customs
ISBN 0-313-32391-7 LC 2004-11771
Contents: The time of their lives -- Historical narrative -- Cradle to grave: rituals of life, love, and death -- Life on the land -- A changing economy: artisans, factories, and money -- Leisure -- Faith and charity -- Beyond the mainstream -- The martial life

Heidler, David Stephen, 1955-—*Continued*
The authors "discuss the people who lived during this critical time, and uncover the essential and unexpected realities of ordinary life in the early American republic." Publisher's note
Includes bibliographical references

Purcell, Sarah J.
The early national period; [by] Sarah Purcell. Facts on File 2004 420p il map (Eyewitness history) $75 *
Grades: 11 12 Adult   973.4
1. United States—History—1783-1865
ISBN 0-8160-4769-3   LC 2003-14969
Contents: Post-revolutionary change: 1783-1786 -- Making a new Constitution: 1787-1788 -- A new nation: 1789-1792 -- Federalist order: 1793-1796 -- Federalist disorder: 1797-1800 -- Jeffersonian America: 1801-1803 -- Rising conflict: 1804-1807 -- Commercial crisis and the clamor for war: 1808-1811 -- The War of 1812: 1812-1815 -- The era of good feelings?: 1816-1819 -- Economic crisis, political stability: 1820-1823 -- Democracy: 1824-1828
"The introduction to each section summarizes major events and provides excerpts from primary resources including speeches, letters, newspaper accounts, diary entries, and advertisements." SLJ
"A serious history student will find this book invaluable." Libr Media Connect
Includes bibliographical references

Stefoff, Rebecca, 1951-
American voices from the new republic, 1783-1830. Benchmark Books 2004 c2005 xxiii, 116p (American voices from--) lib bdg $34.21
Grades: 6 7 8 9   973.4
1. United States—History—1783-1865
ISBN 0-7614-1695-1   LC 2004-11391
Contents: Birth of a nation; Forming a new government; Presidents and parties; International affairs; American affairs; African Americans and slavery; Arts and sciences; The age of new possibilities
Describes, through excerpts from diaries, speeches, newspaper articles, and other documents of the time, United States history from 1783 to 1830. Includes review questions.

973.5   United States--1809-1845

Encyclopedia of the War of 1812; David S. Heidler and Jeanne T. Heidler, editors. 1st Naval Institute Press pa. ed. Naval Institute Press 2004 c1997 xxxvii, 636p il map pa $37.50
Grades: 11 12 Adult   973.5
1. War of 1812—Encyclopedias
ISBN 1-591-14362-4   LC 2004-42695
First published 1997 by ABC-CLIO
This "encyclopedia contains more than 500 entries by some 70 authors, including leading authorities on the war such as Donald Hickey. Although all the military engagements are covered, this thorough and comprehensive book also treats such topics as African Americans, the

Federalist Party, and naval medicine. . . . This handsomely produced and easy-to-use book is fully indexed, with a special section of important documents." Libr J
Includes bibliographical references

Greenblatt, Miriam
War of 1812; John S. Bowman, general editor. Updated ed. Facts on File 2003 166p il maps (America at war) lib bdg $35 *
Grades: 7 8 9 10   973.5
1. War of 1812
ISBN 0-8160-4933-5   LC 2002-9555
First published 1994
Contents: "The darkest day"; "Free trade and sailors' rights"; Warriors and war hawks; The United States on the eve of war; "Go march to Canada"; The naval war; "O'er the land of the free"; The war in the South; Ghent, Hartford, and peace
An account of the events surrounding the War of 1812 between the newly established United States and Great Britain
This offers "high-quality writing . . . {a} wealth of information and good organization." SLJ
Includes glossary and bibliographical references

Heidler, David Stephen, 1955-
The War of 1812; [by] David S. Heidler and Jeanne T. Heidler. Greenwood Press 2002 xxiii, 217p il maps (Greenwood Press guides to historic events, 1500-1900) $44.95 *
Grades: 11 12 Adult   973.5
1. War of 1812
ISBN 0-313-31687-2   LC 2001-50102
This book discusses "the causes, battles, and personalities that surrounded the war. . . . The authors describe all of the factors that led to some of the more ignominious defeats and unexpected victories. . . . The book includes brief biographies of some of the major participants and some primary-source documents." SLJ
Includes glossary and bibliographical references

Howes, Kelly King
War of 1812; Julie L. Carnagie, editor. U.X.L 2002 xxvi, 318p $67
Grades: 7 8 9 10   973.5
1. War of 1812
ISBN 0-7876-5574-0   LC 2001-44240
Preliminary pagination continues after p.318
A chronological overview of the events of the War of 1812, accompanied by fifteen biographies of individuals associated with the war.
Includes glossary and bibliographical references

Marker, Sherry, 1941-
Plains Indian wars; John S. Bowman, general editor. Updated ed. Facts on File 2003 164p il maps (America at war) lib bdg $35 *
Grades: 7 8 9 10   973.5
1. Native Americans—Wars 2. Native Americans—Great Plains
ISBN 0-8160-4931-9   LC 2002-9556

Marker, Sherry, 1941---*Continued*
First published 1996
This is an account of the wars between Plains Indians and white settlers in the American West in the 19th century.
"Marker does an excellent job of detailing the cultural and social complexity of the many tribes of the Great Plains while offering both a political and social picture of the U.S. Army at this time. The work concludes with an excellent chapter on the history of the stereotypes of the Plains Indians." SLJ
Includes glossary and bibliographical references

Nardo, Don, 1947-
The War of 1812. Lucent Bks. 2000 128p il (World history series) $27.45
Grades: 9 10 11 12   **973.5**
1. War of 1812
ISBN 1-56006-581-8   LC 99-14587
Describes the War of 1812, including its prelude, battles and campaigns, conclusion, and aftermath
"A well-organized and well-documented presentation." SLJ
Includes bibliographical references

973.6   United States--1845-1861

Douglas, Stephen Arnold, 1813-1861
The Lincoln-Douglas debates of 1858; edited by Robert W. Johannsen. Oxford Univ. Press 1965 330p pa $23.95
Grades: 9 10 11 12   **973.6**
1. Lincoln-Douglas debates, 1858 2. United States—Politics and government—1815-1861
ISBN 0-19-500921-5
With introductions to give perspective, this "includes the seven debates of 1858 as well as Douglas's speech in Chicago that set the tone for the debates." Guide to Read in Am Hist
Includes bibliographical references

Mills, Bronwyn
U.S.-Mexican War; John S. Bowman, general editor. Updated ed. Facts on File 2003 143p il, maps (America at war) $35 *
Grades: 9 10 11 12   **973.6**
1. Mexican War, 1846-1848
ISBN 0-8160-4932-7   LC 2002-9557
First published 1992 with title: Mexican War
Contents: Crossing the boundary -- Blood on American soil! -- War along the Rio Grande -- California and the Southwest -- Mr. Polk's war -- Tampico and Vera Cruz -- Birds of peace and birds of prey -- To the Halls of Montezuma -- We take nothing by conquest, by God!
Chronicles the causes and events of the Mexican War, from Mexico's struggle for recognition as an independent country to the war's end in 1848
"The writing is strong, the illustrations are well chosen and often quite dramatic, and the organization is clear. . . . The story of the U.S.-Mexican War is told with novelistic aplomb, from the border skirmishes near the Rio Grande to Winfield Scott's invasion of Mexico City and the famous 'Halls of Montezuma.'" SLJ
Includes bibliographical references

973.7   United States--Administration of Abraham Lincoln, 1861-1865. Civil War

Armstrong, Jennifer, 1961-
Photo by Brady; a picture of the Civil War. Atheneum Books For Young Readers 2005 160p il $18.95
Grades: 6 7 8 9 10   **973.7**
1. Brady, Mathew B., ca. 1823-1896 2. United States—History—1861-1865, Civil War 3. Photography—History
ISBN 0-689-85785-3   LC 2004-8967
"Armstrong chronicles the Civil War from Lincoln's election to his death with both a storylike narrative of events and a photo-essay. . . . This book is also a look at early photographic techniques and offers a description of [Mathew] Brady's rare collection. . . . When readers remember that the pictures are more than 100 years old, they should recognize their exquisiteness, grandeur, and genius." SLJ
Includes bibliographical references

Barney, William L.
The Civil War and Reconstruction; a student companion. Oxford Univ. Press 2001 368p il maps (Oxford student companions to American history) $60
Grades: 7 8 9 10   **973.7**
1. Reconstruction (1865-1876) 2. United States—History—1861-1865, Civil War
ISBN 0-19-511559-7   LC 00-57444
This reference guide includes "articles on the military, political, social, economic, and cultural aspects of the war and its aftermath, as well as biographical sketches of major figures." SLJ
"The book is encyclopedic in format, with many useful access points, and bibliographic information is located both at the ends of the articles and in several appendixes that suggest books, historic sites and addresses, and Web sites." Voice Youth Advocates
Includes bibliographical references

Bolden, Tonya
Cause: Reconstruction America, 1863-1877. Knopf 2005 138p il $19.95; lib bdg $21.99 *
Grades: 7 8 9 10   **973.7**
1. Reconstruction (1865-1876) 2. United States—History—1865-1898
ISBN 0-375-82795-1; 0-375-92795-6 (lib bdg)
"This examination of America during Reconstruction covers Lincoln's Proclamation of Amnesty and Reconstruction, the Civil Rights Act of 1866, the troubles of freed slaves, the expansion of the nation and the plight of Native Americans, the 15th Amendment, and the women's suffrage movement. While this is well-documented nonfiction, Bolden writes in the voice of a storyteller. The excellent graphics include archival photos, political cartoons, and primary resources." SLJ

Browne, Ray Broadus

The Civil War and Reconstruction; [by] Ray B. Browne and Lawrence A. Kreiser, Jr. Greenwood Press 2003 215p il (American popular culture through history) $49.95 *

Grades: 9 10 11 12   973.7

1. United States—History—1861-1865, Civil War 2. Reconstruction (1865-1876) 3. Popular culture—United States

ISBN 0-313-31325-3   LC 2002-35206

"Browne and Kreiser begin with overview chapters on daily life for the general population, and then examine in detail 10 aspects of culture including advertising, clothing and fashion, food, leisure activities, travel and transportation, and several categories of performing and fine arts. The authors describe both the trends and important people that shaped popular culture and the impact of the war and its aftermath. For example, they relate how baseball became America's pastime when Civil War soldiers, who learned to play while in camps, carried the game home with them at the war's end. Each chapter is well documented. . . . This well-written and objective book deserves a place in all libraries." SLJ

Includes bibliographical references

The **Causes** of the Civil War; edited by Kenneth M. Stampp. 3rd rev ed. Simon & Schuster 1991 255p pa $14 *

Grades: 11 12 Adult   973.7

1. United States—History—1861-1865, Civil War—Causes 2. United States—History—1861-1865, Civil War—Sources

ISBN 0-671-75155-7   LC 91-36819

"A Touchstone book"

First published 1959 by Prentice-Hall

This book integrates the conclusions of various postwar historians with the thoughts of contemporary commentators like Jefferson Davis, Horace Greeley, and Lincoln. Political, cultural and economic aspects are emphasized

Includes bibliographical references

The **Civil** War; James Tackach, book editor. Greenhaven Press 2004 186p il (Turning points in world history) lib bdg $34.95

Grades: 7 8 9 10   973.7

1. United States—History—1861-1865, Civil War

ISBN 0-7377-1114-0   LC 2003-64297

"Comprised of 17 essays, this book is divided into four chapters: 'A Nation Divides: The Causes of the Civil War,' 'Early Battlefield Victories and the Prospect of European Intervention Fuel the South's Hope for Independence,' 'The North Gains the Advantage,' and 'A Changed Nation.' Many of the most respected Civil War historians . . . are excerpted. . . . Outstanding features of the book are discussion questions and the appendix of documents that are sure to inspire additional research and assist classroom teachers." SLJ

Includes bibliographical references

The **Civil** War chronicle; the only day-by-day portrait of America's tragic conflict as told by soldiers, journalists, politicians, farmers, nurses, slaves, and other eyewitnesses; general editor, J. Matthew Gallman; introduction by Eric Foner; edited by David Rubel and Russell Shorto. Crown 2000 544p il hardcover o.p. pa $14.99 *

Grades: 11 12 Adult   973.7

1. United States—History—1861-1865, Civil War—Sources

ISBN 0-8129-3114-9; 0-517-22181-0 (pa)
LC 00-55551

"An Agincourt Press book"

The editor has compiled "primary sources into a one-volume account of the war, showing the conflict through the eyes of witnesses in a day-by-day history that begins with reactions to Abraham Lincoln's 1860 election and ends with accounts of the Confederate defeat in May 1865. Various documents are reproduced, including letters from soldiers, private diaries, newspaper articles, government dispatches, and telegrams. Concentrating on campaigns and battles, this work is especially good in its inclusion of minor as well as major engagements." Libr J

Corrick, James A.

Life among the soldiers and cavalry. Lucent Bks. 2000 112p il maps (American war library, Civil War) $27.45 *

Grades: 9 10 11 12   973.7

1. Soldiers—United States 2. United States—History—1861-1865, Civil War

ISBN 1-56006-491-9   LC 99-28237

Discusses life among Civil War soldiers and cavalry, including joining up, uniforms and rifles, training and discipline on the march, battle, and returning home.

This "volume is fully documented, providing researchers with notes, a bibliography, a chronology, a glossary, and maps." Booklist

Includes bibliographical references

DeRamus, Betty

Forbidden fruit; love stories from the Underground Railroad. Atria Books 2005 269p il $25; pa $14

Grades: 11 12 Adult   973.7

1. Underground railroad 2. Slavery—United States 3. Love

ISBN 0-7434-8263-8; 978-0-7434-8263-9; 0-7434-8264-6 (pa); 978-0-7434-8264-6 (pa)
LC 2004-63414

"Debunking one of the myths used to justify separating families during slavery, de Ramus offers a collection of stories recording the love and devotion of slave couples, many of whom risked their lives to stay together." Booklist

This is an "uplifting and sometimes heartbreaking look at love during the U.S.'s slavery years." Publ Wkly

Includes bibliographical references

Detzer, David

Allegiance; Fort Sumter, Charleston, and the beginning of the Civil War. Harcourt 2001 367p $27; pa $15 *

Grades: 11 12 Adult   **973.7**

1. Fort Sumter (Charleston, S.C.) 2. United States—History—1861-1865, Civil War—Causes

ISBN 0-15-100641-5; 0-15-600741-X (pa)

LC 00-50570

The author "limns the daily lives of the men and women caught in the 1861 secession crisis in Charleston, SC, to show how personalities and circumstances determined the advent of the Civil War." Libr J

"The central figure in this drama is Maj. Robert Anderson, commander of the Union garrison in Charleston Harbor. . . . Detzer's writing style brings the reader into close contact with soldiers, civilians and politicians as they struggle to solve the fate of Anderson and his men." Publ Wkly

Includes bibliographical references

Dissonance; between Fort Sumter and Bull Run in the turbulent first days of the Civil War. Harcourt 2006 xxv, 371p $27; pa $15

Grades: 9 10 11 12   **973.7**

1. United States—History—1861-1865, Civil War

ISBN   978-0-15-101158-2;   0-15-101158-3; 978-0-15-603064-9 (pa); 0-15-603064-0 (pa)

LC 2005-20991

Third volume in the author's trilogy about the first 100 days of the Civil War, begun with Allegiance

The author "has written an engaging and comprehensive account of the early days of the Civil War that should have wide appeal." Publ Wkly

Includes bibliographical references

Donnybrook; the Battle of Bull Run, 1861. Harcourt 2004 490p il map $28; pa $16

Grades: 9 10 11 12   **973.7**

1. Bull Run, 1st Battle of, 1861 2. United States—History—1861-1865, Civil War

ISBN 0-15-100889-2; 0-15-603143-4 (pa)

LC 2004-5227

Second volume of the author's trilogy about the first 100 days of the Civil War, begun with Allegiance and followed by Dissonance

The author "provides a lucid narrative of the battle's course, judiciously assesses the causes and authors of the Union defeat, draws vivid thumbnail sketches of participants from generals to privates, and debunks the 'stone wall' legend and other enduring myths of the battle." Publ Wkly

Includes bibliographical references

Encyclopedia of the American Civil War; a political, social, and military history; David S. Heidler and Jeanne T. Heidler, editors; foreword by James W. McPherson; David J. Coles, associate editor; Gary W. Gallagher, James M. McPherson, Mark E. Neely, Jr., editorial board. ABC-CLIO 2000 5v il maps set $425

Grades: 11 12 Adult   **973.7**

1. United States—History—1861-1865, Civil War—Encyclopedias

ISBN 1-57607-066-2   LC 00-11195

Also available in a one-volume edition from Norton

"The editors have compiled a comprehensive source that provides a first-stop reference on broad areas or specific topics on the Civil War. The contemporary photographs and lithographs bring the human element into the encyclopedia, a type of reference known more for facts and figures than emotions. The primary-source-documents volume brings obscure resources together, which will further illumine the period for students."—"Outstanding Reference Sources." American Libraries, May 2001

Includes bibliographical references

Faust, Drew Gilpin

Mothers of invention; women of the slaveholding South in the American Civil War. University of N.C. Press 1996 326p il $37.50; pa $19.95 *

Grades: 11 12 Adult   **973.7**

1. United States—History—1861-1865, Civil War—Women 2. Women—Southern States

ISBN 0-8078-2255-8; 0-8078-5573-1 (pa)

LC 95-8896

Based on journals, letters and memoirs, this is an "analysis of the impact of secession, invasion and conquest on Southern white women. Antebellum images based on helplessness and dependence were challenged as women assumed an increasing range of social and economic responsibilities. . . . Faust's provocative analysis of a complex subject merits a place in all collections of U.S. history." Publ Wkly

Includes bibliographical references

Geary, Rick, 1946-

The murder of Abraham Lincoln; a chronicle of 62 days in the life of the American Republic, March 4-May 4, 1865; written and illustrated by Rick Geary. NBM ComicsLit 2005 unp il map (A treasury of Victorian murder) $15.95; pa $8.95 *

Grades: 7 8 9 10   **973.7**

1. Lincoln, Abraham, 1809-1865—Assassination 2. Booth, John Wilkes, 1838-1865 3. Graphic novels

ISBN   978-1-56163-425-5;   1-56163-425-5; 978-1-56163-426-2 (pa); 1-56163-426-3 (pa)

LC 2005-41468

This graphic novel "covers Lincoln's assassination, the events that led up to it, and the aftermath. Geary also makes a point of bringing up still-unanswered questions, like the whereabouts of the missing pages of John Wilkes Booth's journal. . . . Even teens who know nothing about the tragedy will find their heads chock-full of information when they're finished reading this book." SLJ

Includes bibliographical references

Hargrove, Hondon B., 1916-

Black Union soldiers in the Civil War. McFarland & Co. 1988 250p il hardcover o.p. pa $35 *

Grades: 11 12 Adult   973.7
1. United States. Army—History 2. United States—History—1861-1865, Civil War 3. African American soldiers
ISBN 0-89950-337-3; 0-7864-1697-1 (pa)
                              LC 88-42511
This volume "discusses the participation of Blacks in the Union Army during the Civil War. The chronologically arranged narrative covers Black soldiers in each battle. Special features include an extensive bibliography and nine appendixes that reprint documents and include rosters and statistics." Nichols. Guide to Ref Books for Sch Media Cent. 4th edition

Kirchberger, Joe H.

The Civil War and Reconstruction; an eyewitness history; [by] Joe Kirchberger. Facts on File 1991 389p il maps (Eyewitness history) $75 *

Grades: 7 8 9 10   973.7
1. United States—History—1861-1865, Civil War—Sources 2. Reconstruction (1865-1876)
ISBN 0-8160-2171-6   LC 90-40852
This work contains "quotations from eyewitnesses' memoirs, letters, diaries, newspapers, and official documents. Those quoted come from all walks of life. . . . Thirty-three documents are excerpted. Four appendixes contain valuable primary-source and reference materials. . . . Interspersed throughout are political cartoons, photographs, and paintings. . . . An excellent reference tool." SLJ
Includes bibliographical references

Leonard, Elizabeth D.

All the daring of the soldier; women of the Civil War armies. Penguin Books 2001 368p il pa $15

Grades: 11 12 Adult   973.7
1. Women soldiers 2. United States—History—1861-1865, Civil War—Women
ISBN 0-14-029858-4
First published 1999 by Norton
The author presents "stories of dozens of women who served in both the Union and Confederacy during the Civil War. Some were spies, but many more adopted men's names, dressed in men's clothes and lived and fought and died alongside mostly unsuspecting men." Publ Wkly
Includes bibliographical references

Lincoln, Abraham, 1809-1865

The portable Abraham Lincoln; edited and with an introduction by Andrew Delbanco. Viking 1992 xxxvii, 341p il pa $17 hardcover o.p. *

Grades: 11 12 Adult   973.7
1. United States—Politics and government—1815-1861 2. United States—Politics and government—1861-1865
ISBN 0-14-017031-6 (pa)   LC 91-37488

"The Viking portable library"
Material drawn from Speeches and writings, published by the Library of America (1989).
"This collection shows Lincoln at work in law, politics, and war. All the great Lincoln works are here, with the added bonus of several personal memos that show Lincoln's humor." Libr J
Includes bibliographical references

The **Lincoln** mailbag; America writes to the President, 1861-1865; edited by Harold Holzer. Southern Ill. Univ. Press 1998 xxxv, 236p il $32; pa $22.95

Grades: 9 10 11 12   973.7
1. Lincoln, Abraham, 1809-1865 2. United States—History—1861-1865, Civil War
ISBN 0-8093-2072-X; 0-8093-2685-X (pa)
                              LC 97-42164
This collection of letters to President Lincoln includes "death threats, requests for offices, requests for money, invitations to speak, unsolicited gifts, proposals for new weapons, and pesterings for favors from obscure relatives and impostors. . . . A revealing glimpse into how civil war and emancipation appeared from the White House, this browsable collection of epistles and replies enriches the body of Lincolniana." Booklist

Marrin, Albert, 1936-

Commander in Chief Abraham Lincoln and the Civil War. Dutton Children's Bks. 1997 246p il maps hardcover o.p. pa $14.99

Grades: 7 8 9 10   973.7
1. Lincoln, Abraham, 1809-1865 2. United States—History—1861-1865, Civil War
ISBN 0-525-45822-0; 0-525-47069-7 (pa)
                              LC 97-8518
The author places Lincoln in the context of his own personal background and the larger circumstances of the Civil War.
"The narrative is skillfully constructed and expressed in a strong, compelling style." SLJ
Includes bibliographical references

Marten, James, 1956-

Civil War America; voices from the home front. ABC-CLIO 2003 346p il $85 *

Grades: 11 12 Adult   973.7
1. United States—History—1861-1865, Civil War—Personal narratives
ISBN 1-576-07237-1   LC 2002-154377
"Marten offers a view of the war through the eyes of diverse noncombatants. Four parts of this five-part work each deal with Southerners, Northerners, children, and African Americans . . . Part five, 'Aftermaths,' includes descriptions of the postwar lives of veterans, orphans, and ex-slaves, and concludes with a chapter on the Civil War stories by Ambrose Bierce. Readers will find Marten's overarching theme of change—both immediate and long-range—revelatory and instructional." SLJ
Includes bibliographical references

McPherson, James M.

Abraham Lincoln and the second American Revolution. Oxford Univ. Press 1991 173p pa $16.95 hardcover o.p.

Grades: 11 12 Adult   **973.7**

1. Lincoln, Abraham, 1809-1865 2. United States—History—1861-1865, Civil War

ISBN 0-19-507606-0 (pa)   LC 90-6885

The author "examines Lincoln's role in the transformation wrought by the Civil War—the liberation of four million slaves, the overthrow of the social and political order of the South." Publ Wkly

Includes bibliographical references

Drawn with the sword; reflections on the American Civil War. Oxford Univ. Press 1996 258p $45; pa $18.95

Grades: 11 12 Adult   **973.7**

1. Lincoln, Abraham, 1809-1865 2. United States—History—1861-1865, Civil War

ISBN 0-19-509679-7; 0-19-511796-4 (pa)
                                    LC 95-38107

A collection of "essays on some of the most thought-provoking questions of the Civil War. All of the essays were published earlier but have been updated and revised for this compilation. The topics deal with such subjects as the origins of the Civil War, the slavery question in both North and South, why the North won the war and why the South lost, President Abraham Lincoln, and the change in historical writing." Libr J

"These pieces provide a lively reminder that the best scholarship is also often a pleasure to read." N Y Times Book Rev

For cause and comrades; why men fought in the Civil War. Oxford Univ. Press 1997 237p $25; pa $15.95

Grades: 11 12 Adult   **973.7**

1. Soldiers—United States 2. United States—History—1861-1865, Civil War

ISBN 0-19-509023-3; 0-19-512499-5 (pa)
                                    LC 96-24760

"Volumes have been written on the causes of the Civil War, but less has been written on what caused soldiers to risk their lives on the battlefield. McPherson . . . fills the gap. After studying thousands of letters and diaries, he discusses what really led soldiers to enlist, what kept them in the army, and what led them to the front lines." Libr J

Includes bibliographical references

Murphy, Jim, 1947-

The boys' war; Confederate and Union soldiers talk about the Civil War. Clarion Bks. 1990 110p il $18; pa $8.95

Grades: 5 6 7 8 9 10   **973.7**

1. United States—History—1861-1865, Civil War

ISBN 0-89919-893-7; 0-395-66412-8 (pa)
                                    LC 89-23959

This book includes diary entries, personal letters, and archival photographs to describe the experiences of boys, sixteen years old or younger, who fought in the Civil War.

"An excellent selection of more than 45 sepia-toned

contemporary photographs augment the text of this informative, moving work." SLJ

Includes bibliographical references

Nardo, Don, 1947-

The Civil War. Lucent Bks. 2003 109p il maps (History of weapons and warfare) $27.45

Grades: 7 8 9 10   **973.7**

1. Military art and science 2. United States—History—1861-1865, Civil War

ISBN 1-59018-068-2   LC 2002-11032

Contents: Muskets and rifles; Artillery guns and batteries; Infantry units and tactics; Cavalry units and tactics; Ships and naval warfare; Espionage and experimental weapons

Discusses the weapons of American Civil War soldiers and different means of warfare used during that conflict.

Includes glossary and bibliographical references

Netzley, Patricia D.

Civil War. Greenhaven Press 2004 336p il (Greenhaven encyclopedia of) lib bdg $74.95 *

Grades: 9 10 11 12   **973.7**

1. United States—History—1861-1865, Civil War—Encyclopedias

ISBN 0-7377-0438-1   LC 2003-11808

An alphabetical presentation of definitions and descriptions of terms, people, and events of the Civil War.

"Basic, accurate information about many aspects of the war. . . . The well-written, objective entries are cross-referenced. . . . Netzley's solid volume will be helpful to students needing introductory research material." SLJ

Includes bibliographical references

Sears, Stephen W.

Gettysburg. Houghton Mifflin 2003 623p il map $30; pa $17 *

Grades: 11 12 Adult   **973.7**

1. Gettysburg (Pa.), Battle of, 1863

ISBN 0-395-86761-4; 0-618-48538-4 (pa)
                                    LC 2002-191259

This is an "assessment of the battle of Gettysburg and the events leading up to it. . . . Sears examines several turning points during the battle's buildup and three-day duration. The resulting insights add to the excellent and dramatic narrative flow. . . . For all Civil War collections and academic libraries." Libr J

Includes bibliographical references

Seidman, Rachel Filene

The Civil war: a history in documents. Oxford Univ. Press 2001 206p il map (Pages from history) $36.95

Grades: 9 10 11 12   **973.7**

1. United States—History—1861-1865, Civil War—Sources

ISBN 0-19-511558-9   LC 00-37523

"Seidman's documents bookend the Civil War with the territorial expansion that preceded the conflict and with the Reconstruction that followed it. In this structure

Seidman, Rachel Filene—*Continued*
the documents, under the guidance of Seidman's linking
narrative, all make a powerful impression of immediacy
about ordinary people's experience of, and condemnation
or defense of, slavery." Booklist
Includes bibliographical references

Sullivan, George, 1933-
The Civil War at sea. 21st Cent. Bks.
(Brookfield) 2001 80p il lib bdg $27.90
Grades: 9 10 11 12   **973.7**
1. United States—History—1861-1865, Civil War—
Naval operations
ISBN 0-7613-1553-5   LC 00-41805
"Sullivan tells of the struggle between the Union and
Confederate forces at sea and in America's bays, rivers,
and harbors. He describes the two rival navies and their
most famous ships, most significant battles, and most
memorable commanders. He also looks at the lives of or-
dinary sailors." Booklist
"The illustrations and reproductions included here and
the lively text will appeal to every Civil War buff, and
will be an excellent source of information for reports."
SLJ
Includes bibliographical references

Swanson, Mark, 1951-
Atlas of the Civil War, month by month; major
battles and troop movements; maps by Mark
Swanson, with Jacqueline D. Langley. University
of Georgia Press 2004 141p il map $39.95
Grades: 11 12 Adult   **973.7**
1. United States—History—1861-1865, Civil War—
Maps
ISBN 0-8203-2658-5   LC 2004-12264
Contents: Introduction: origins of the Civil War -- The
rise of the Republican Party and the 1860 presidential
election -- The 1860 census and its implications for the
Civil War -- Month-by-month maps of the Civil War --
Appendix: the Civil War in the far West
This Civil War atlas depicts "multiple aspects of the
war's action in a month-by-month sequence from April
1861 to June 1865. . . . An absolute must for Civil War
studies." Univ Press Books for Public and Second Sch
Libr, 2006
Includes bibliographical references

Tobin, Jacqueline, 1950-
Hidden in plain view; the secret story of quilts
and the underground railroad; [by] Jacqueline L.
Tobin and Raymond G. Dobard. Doubleday 1999
208p il map hardcover o.p. pa $14
Grades: 11 12 Adult   **973.7**
1. Underground railroad 2. Ciphers 3. Quilts
ISBN 0-385-49137-9; 0-385-49767-9 (pa)
LC 98-49804
The authors present the "theory that slaves created
quilts coded with patterns to help one another flee to
freedom." N Y Times Book Rev
This is "a needed and valuable contribution to the lit-
erature of African American culture." Libr J
Includes bibliographical references

Walker, Sally M.
Secrets of a Civil War submarine; solving the
mysteries of the H.L. Hunley. Carolrhoda Books
2005 112p il lib bdg $17.95
Grades: 7 8 9 10   **973.7**
1. Hunley (Submarine) 2. United States—History—
1861-1865, Civil War—Naval operations
3. Shipwrecks 4. Underwater exploration
5. Submarines
ISBN 1-575-05830-8   LC 2004-19646
Contents: Prologue: a lost treasure; A seafaring stealth
weapon; Climb aboard; Disaster; Lieutenant Dixon's mission; A stunning discovery; The Hunley talks; Buried
treasures; In touch with the past; Forensic tales
This discusses "the Confederate submarine H. L.
Hunley. . . . Walker begins with the history of the
Hunley's design and construction as well as its place in
Civil War and naval history. She really hits her stride,
though, in explaining the complex techniques and loving
care used in raising the craft, recovering its contents, and
even reconstructing models of the crewmembers' bodies.
. . . Thoroughly researched, nicely designed, and well il-
lustrated with clear, color photos." Booklist
Includes glossary and bibliographical references

Woodworth, Steven E.
Atlas of the Civil War; by Steven Woodworth
and Kenneth J. Winkle; foreword by James M.
McPherson. Oxford University Press 2004 400p il
map $75 *
Grades: 11 12 Adult   **973.7**
1. United States—History—1861-1865, Civil War—
Maps
ISBN 0-19-522131-1   LC 2004-53112
"Each of five major chapters is devoted to a single
year from 1861 to 1865. In addition to every important
battle, there is coverage of nonmilitary topics, such as
population, the economy, transportation, elections, and
the home front. . . . The work ends with a list of major
battle sites, a chronology, a glossary, a short bibliography, and an index, which provides access to illustrations
and maps as well as names." Booklist
"Richly illustrated, this publication will be wanted by
all types of libraries. . . . The text entries are useful,
while the maps and illustrations are both informative and
eye-catching." Choice

Cultures in conflict: the American Civil War.
Greenwood Press 2000 xx, 220p (Greenwood
Press cultures in conflict series) $45 *
Grades: 11 12 Adult   **973.7**
1. United States—History—1861-1865, Civil War
ISBN 0-313-30651-6   LC 99-43165
"The history documents, including diary entries, letters, and photographs, provide a rich panorama of America's bloodiest conflict. Brief introductory paragraphs to
each document or set of documents remind readers about
the cultural differences that brought the country to the
point of war and continued to flourish throughout this
period and beyond." Voice Youth Advocates
Includes bibliographical references

973.8 United States--Reconstruction period, 1865-1901

Encyclopedia of the Gilded Age and Progressive Era; edited by John D. Buenker and Joseph Buenker. M.E. Sharpe 2005 3v il set $299
Grades: 11 12 Adult   **973.8**
  1. United States—History—1865-1898 2. United States—History—1898-1919
ISBN 0-7656-8051-3   LC 2003-24653
This set focuses "on a period between 1870 and 1920, when the United States emerged as an urban and industrial world power. Some 900 A-Z entries cover key individuals, events, and organizations of the times, and 17 essays discuss broad themes like the economy, politics, religion, and pop culture." Libr J
Includes bibliographical references

Foner, Eric
  Forever free; the story of emancipation and Reconstruction; illustrations edited and with commentary by Joshua Brown. Knopf 2005 xxx, 268p il $27.50; pa $15 *
Grades: 11 12 Adult   **973.8**
  1. Reconstruction (1865-1876) 2. Slavery—United States 3. United States—Politics and government—1865-1898
ISBN   0-375-40259-4;   978-0-375-40259-3; 0-375-70274-1 (pa); 978-0-375-70274-7 (pa)
     LC 2005-40706
"Forever Free project: Stephen B. Brier, Peter O. Almond, executive editors/producers; Christine Doudna, editor."
This "examination of the years of Emancipation and Reconstruction during and immediately following the Civil War emphasizes the era's political and cultural meaning for today's America." Publisher's note
This "is an invaluable and timely book about a subject central to U.S. history and still of obvious significance today—slavery, the Civil War, emancipation, Reconstruction, and both the immediate aftermath and longer-term consequences of those things." Rev Am Hist
Includes bibliographical references

The Gilded Age: a history in documents; [compiled by] Janette Thomas Greenwood. Oxford Univ. Press 2000 191p il map (Pages from history) $36.95; pa $19.95
Grades: 7 8 9 10   **973.8**
  1. United States—History—1865-1898
ISBN 0-19-510523-0; 0-19-516638-8 (pa)
     LC 99-98194
Uses a wide variety of documents to show how Americans dealt with an age of extremes from 1887 to 1900, including rapid industrialization, unemployment, unprecedented wealth, and immigration.
"There's plenty to absorb and much to capture the imagination. . . . Greenwood presents the history as a seamless tapestry sewn by the people who lived it." Booklist
Includes bibliographical references

Golay, Michael, 1951-
  Spanish-American War; John S. Bowman, general editor. Updated ed. Facts on File 2003 xxii, 154p il, maps (America at war) $35 *
Grades: 9 10 11 12   **973.8**
  1. Spanish-American War, 1898
ISBN 0-8160-4935-1   LC 2002-8764
First published 1995
A narrative account of the Spanish American War, covering the origins of dispute between the United States and Spain over Cuba, profiles of the key figures, and descriptions of major battles
This book "tells the story of this short conflict in Cuba, and the Philippines, with an eye for detail and a brisk style." SLJ
Includes bibliographical references

Grumet, Bridget Hall
  Reconstruction era: primary sources; Lawrence W. Baker, project editor. UXL 2004 xxv, 228p il (Reconstruction Era reference library) $60 *
Grades: 11 12 Adult   **973.8**
  1. Reconstruction (1865-1876)
ISBN 0-7876-9219-0   LC 2004-17309
This book "contains 19 complete or partial documents, such as the Fourteenth Amendment of the U.S. Constitution and Rutherford B. Hayes' inaugural address. Each document is accompanied by an introduction, keys to reading the document, a discussion of subsequent events related to the document, and other material." Booklist
Includes bibliographical references

Hansen, Joyce
  Bury me not in a land of slaves; African-Americans in the time of Reconstruction. Watts 2000 160p il lib bdg $23 *
Grades: 7 8 9 10   **973.8**
  1. African Americans—History 2. Reconstruction (1865-1876) 3. United States—Race relations
ISBN 0-531-11539-9 (lib bdg)   LC 99-30040
An account of African-American life in the period of Reconstruction following the Civil War, based on first-person narratives, contemporary documents, and other historical sources
"Readers of this balanced, well-written account will come away with a solid understanding of the period's events and how they contributed to the twentieth century's segregation and prejudice." Booklist
Includes bibliographical references

Reconstruction; opposing viewpoints in world history; Laura K. Egendorf, book editor. Greenhaven Press 2004 224p il map (Opposing viewpoints in world history) lib bdg $34.95; pa $23.70 *
Grades: 9 10 11 12   **973.8**
  1. Reconstruction (1865-1876)
ISBN 0-7377-1703-3 (lib bdg); 0-7377-1704-1 (pa)
     LC 2003-49016
"The book uses a pro/con format to present articles both from the time period, such as ones by Abraham Lincoln, Frederick Douglass, and W.E.B. Du Bois, and

Reconstruction—*Continued*

articles written retrospectively. . . . [This] should be available in every high school library and in every upper-level Social Studies and AP classroom." Libr Media Connect

Includes bibliographical references

Roosevelt, Theodore, 1858-1919

The Rough Riders; new introduction by Elting E. Morison. Da Capo Press 1990 298p il pa $16

Grades: 9 10 11 12   **973.8**

1. United States. Army. Volunteer Cavalry, 1st—History 2. Spanish-American War, 1898
ISBN 0-306-80405-0   LC 90-38860
Also available in paperback from Modern Library
A reprint of the title first published 1899 by Scribner
This is a history of the First United States Volunteer Cavalry, which fought in the Spanish-American War under the command of Theodore Roosevelt

Sandoz, Mari, 1896-1966

The Battle of the Little Bighorn. Lippincott 1966 191p maps (Great battles of history series) hardcover o.p. pa $12.95

Grades: 11 12 Adult   **973.8**

1. Custer, George Armstrong, 1839-1876 2. Little Bighorn, Battle of the, 1876
ISBN 0-397-00410-9; 0-8032-9100-0 (pa)
"An account of the United States Army expedition against the Sioux Nation with emphasis on the political motives and ambitions of General Custer." Publ Wkly
Includes bibliographical references

Schlereth, Thomas J.

Victorian America; transformations in everyday life, 1876-1915. HarperCollins Pubs. 1991 363p (Everyday life in America) pa $15 hardcover o.p.

Grades: 11 12 Adult   **973.8**

1. United States—Social life and customs
ISBN 0-06-092160-9 (pa)   LC 89-46555
The author surveys the objects, events, experiences, products and tastes that comprised what he terms America's Victorian culture (1876-1915) and shows how its values shaped modern life.
"What a wonderful book. . . . Schlereth is no wry compiler of trivia. His analysis of social context reveals truly profound, intangible transformations in how and where Americans spent their time during four pivotal decades." Booklist
Includes bibliographical references

Shifflett, Crandall A.

Victorian America, 1876 to 1913; {by} Crandall Shifflett. Facts on File 1996 408p il maps (Almanacs of American life) $95 *

Grades: 11 12 Adult   **973.8**

1. United States—Social life and customs
ISBN 0-8160-2531-2   LC 95-13553
This illustrated overview of 19th century America contains sections on: historical geography; native American life; government; popular culture; urban development; influential personalities; and arts and letters
Includes bibliographical references

Viola, Herman J., 1938-

It is a good day to die; Indian eyewitnesses tell the story of the Battle of the Little Bighorn; [by] Herman J. Viola with Jan Shelton Danis. University of Nebraska Press 2001 101p il map pa $12.95 *

Grades: 5 6 7 8 9 10   **973.8**

1. Custer, George Armstrong, 1839-1876 2. Little Bighorn, Battle of the, 1876 3. Dakota Indians—Wars 4. Cheyenne Indians
ISBN 0-8032-9626-6   LC 2001-34669
First published 1998 by Crown
A series of eyewitness accounts of the 1876 Battle of Little Bighorn and the defeat of General Custer as told by Native American participants in the war.
"This is a thought-provoking, accessible compilation that will give new insight to the study of American history." Bull Cent Child Books
Includes bibliographical references

Welch, James, 1940-2003

Killing Custer; the Battle of the Little Bighorn and the fate of the Plains Indians; by James Welch with Paul Stekler. Norton 1994 320p il pa $14.95 hardcover o.p. *

Grades: 11 12 Adult   **973.8**

1. Little Bighorn, Battle of the, 1876 2. Native Americans—Wars
ISBN 0-393-32939-9 (pa)   LC 94-5617
"Welch produced this history of the Indian wars of the northern plains as a by-product of his work scripting a television documentary on the Battle of the Little Bighorn. In addition to military history, it contains long sections describing the life of the Plains Indians, accounts of contemporary Indian radical groups, and Welch's reactions while visiting the various historic sites in the area." Libr J
Includes bibliographical references

973.9   United States--1901-

American decades. Gale Res. 1994-2000 10v set $995

Grades: 11 12 Adult   **973.9**

1. United States—Civilization 2. United States—History—20th century
ISBN 0-7876-5076-5
Also available American decades primary sources ten volume companion set $995 (ISBN 0-7876-6587-8)
"A Manly, Inc. book"
The set is divided as follows: 1900-1909 (ISBN 0-8103-5722-4); 1910-1919 (ISBN 0-8103-5723-2); 1920-1929 (ISBN 0-8103-5724-0); 1930-1939 (ISBN 0-8103-5725-9); 1940-1949 (ISBN 0-8103-5726-7); 1950-1959 (ISBN 0-8103-5727-5); 1960-1969 (ISBN 0-8103-8883-9); 1970-1979 (ISBN 0-8103-8882-0); 1980-1989 (ISBN 0-8103-8881-2); 1990-1999 (ISBN 0-7876-4030-1)
"A series of volumes covering the twentieth century by decades. . . . Fun to browse, each volume is divided into 13 sections covering topics such as the arts, government and politics, lifestyles and social trends, medicine and health, and sports. Each section opens with a chro-

American decades—*Continued*

nology and overview and closes with short biographies, deaths, and a bibliography of important books published in the decade. Sidebars highlight events and prominent individuals." Am Libr

American decades primary sources; Cynthia Rose, project editor. Gale 2004 10v il map set $1,055
Grades: 11 12 Adult   **973.9**
1. United States—Civilization 2. United States—History—20th century—Sources
ISBN 0-7876-6587-8   LC 2002-8155
Companion set to American decades published 1994-2000

Contents: [1] 1900-1909 -- [2] 1910-1919 -- [3] 1920-1929 -- [4] 1930-1939 -- [5] 1940-1949 -- [6] 1950-1959 -- [7] 1960-1969 -- [8] 1970-1979 -- [9] 1980-1989 -- [10] 1990-1999

"A treasure trove of more than 2,000 primary sources on U.S. history and culture, ranging from speeches and literary works to graphs and architectural drawings. Although many of the sources might be found on the Internet, they lack the organization and context provided here." Booklist

The **Century** that was; reflections on the last one hundred years; edited and with an introduction by James Cross Giblin. Atheneum Bks. for Young Readers 2000 166p il $19.95
Grades: 7 8 9 10   **973.9**
1. United States—History—20th century
ISBN 0-689-82281-2   LC 99-27011
A collection of essays by well-known authors for young people, reflecting on various aspects of life in twentieth-century America, including politics, the environment, sports, fashion, and civil rights

"The 11 essays show tremendous range in voice and scope. . . . What unites these perspectives are a sharp analysis of history, fine writing and, for the most part, an optimistic sense of progress to lead us into the next 100 years." Publ Wkly

Includes bibliographical references

Evans, Harold

The American century; by Harold Evans with Gail Buckland and Kevin Baker. Knopf 1998 xxiii, 710p il hardcover o.p. pa $35
Grades: 11 12 Adult   **973.9**
1. United States—History—20th century 2. United States—Politics and government—20th century
ISBN 0-679-41070-8; 0-375-70938-X (pa)
                                      LC 96-7449
This narrative history of the United States spans the years 1889-1989

This "compilation is a family album for all Americans to ponder; it smartly emphasizes the contributions of men and women other than presidents and top politicians, although these leaders are not slighted. The chapters are thematic, forthrightly exploring such overarching ideas as capitalism vs. communism, the contributions of immigrants, the struggle for civil rights, and the rise of conservatism at the century's close. Accompanying the text are 900 unforgettable (and many rarely seen) photographs." Libr J

Includes bibliographical references

Gordon, Lois G.

American chronicle; year by year through the twentieth century; {by} Lois Gordon and Alan Gordon; with an introduction by Roger Rosenblatt. Yale Univ. Press 1999 998p $49.95 *
Grades: 11 12 Adult   **973.9**
1. United States—Civilization
ISBN 0-300-07587-1   LC 99-24886
First published 1987 by Atheneum Pubs. with title: American chronicle; six decades in American life, 1920-1980; variant title: The Columbia chronicles of American life, 1910-1992

This volume presents in a year by year format the events, personalities, and elements of popular culture for each year of the period

Gould, Lewis L.

The modern American presidency; foreword by Richard Norton Smith. University Press of Kansas 2003 301p il $29.95; pa $15.95
Grades: 11 12 Adult   **973.9**
1. Presidents—United States
ISBN 0-7006-1252-1; 0-7006-1330-7 (pa)
                                      LC 2002-154108
Contents: The age of Cortelyou : William McKinley and Theodore Roosevelt -- The lawyer and the professor : William Howard Taft and Woodrow Wilson -- The modern presidency recedes : Warren G. Harding, Calvin Coolidge, and Herbert Hoover -- The modern presidency revives and grows : Franklin D. Roosevelt -- The presidency in the Cold War era : Harry S. Truman and Dwight D. Eisenhower -- The souring of the modern presidency : John F. Kennedy and Lyndon B. Johnson -- The rise of the continuous campaign : Richard Nixon -- The modern presidency under siege : Gerald Ford and Jimmy Carter -- The modern presidency in a Republican era : Ronald Reagan and George H.W. Bush -- Perils of the modern presidency : Bill Clinton

The author "does a solid job of reviewing the modern presidents, covering the high and low points of each administration, and giving a general audience a readable, engaging text." Libr J

Includes bibliographical references

The **Greenwood** guide to American popular culture; edited by M. Thomas Inge and Dennis Hall. Greenwood Press 2002 4v il set $399.95
Grades: 11 12 Adult   **973.9**
1. Popular culture—United States
ISBN 0-313-30878-0   LC 2002-71291
Based on the Handbook of American popular culture and Handbook of American popular literature

Contents: v1 Almanacs through do-it-yourself -- v2 Editorial cartoons through illustration -- v3 Jazz through propaganda -- v4 Pulps and dime novels through young adult fiction

This "offers overviews of various aspects of our culture. The 58 signed articles touch on topics from almanacs and amusement parks to pornography and propaganda, and from science fiction and self-help to television and young adult fiction. The selections cover trends from the 17th century to the present with a focus on the 20th century." SLJ

"Students searching for help in locating resources spe-

The Greenwood guide to American popular culture—*Continued*

cific to different aspects of popular culture will find these volumes an excellent starting point." Voice Youth Advocates

Includes bibliographical references

Lemann, Nicholas

The promised land; the great black migration and how it changed America. Knopf 1991 401p pa $16.95 hardcover o.p. *

Grades: 11 12 Adult   **973.9**

1. African Americans—Social conditions 2. Internal migration

ISBN 0-679-73347-7 (pa)   LC 90-52951

An "account of the migration of 6.5 million black people from rural South to urban North between 1910-1970." N Y Times Book Rev

The author "describes why the war on poverty did not succeed and why the civil rights movement yielded only partial victories in trying to win improvements. While Lemann's interviews establish the human drama of this process, his assessment of the consequences of this great movement both for African Americans and for the entire country raises substantial questions of justice and equality that cut to the heart of the social situation of the impoverished and oppressed today." Booklist

Includes bibliographical references

Roosevelt, Eleanor, 1884-1962

Courage in a dangerous world; the political writings of Eleanor Roosevelt; edited by Allida M. Black. Columbia Univ. Press 1999 362p il $34.50; pa $17.95

Grades: 11 12 Adult   **973.9**

1. United States—Politics and government—1933-1945 2. United States—Politics and government—1953-1961

ISBN 0-231-11180-0; 0-231-11181-9 (pa)

LC 98-33807

"This collection of columns, essays, speeches, and letters documents Eleanor Roosevelt's political transformation from self-effacing first lady to outspoken defender of democracy and human rights." Libr J

Includes bibliographical references

973.91   United States--1901-1953

Allen, Frederick Lewis, 1890-1954

Only yesterday; an informal history of the 1920's. Wiley 1997 285p (Wiley investment classics) $21.95 *

Grades: 11 12 Adult   **973.91**

1. United States—History—1919-1933 2. United States—Social conditions 3. United States—Economic conditions—1919-1933

ISBN 0-471-18952-9   LC 97-19930

Also available in paperback from HarperCollins Pubs.

A reissue of the title first published 1931 by Harper and Brothers

"An account of the years from the spring of 1919 to . . . {1931}. It is a kaleidoscopic picture of American politics, society, manners, morals, and economic conditions." Booklist

Includes bibliographical references

Burg, David F.

The Great Depression. Updated ed. Facts on File 2005 xx, 444p il (Eyewitness history) $75

Grades: 8 9 10 11 12   **973.91**

1. Great Depression, 1929-1939 2. United States—Economic conditions—1919-1933 3. United States—Economic conditions—1933-1945

ISBN 0-8160-5709-5; 978-0-8160-5709-2

LC 2004-29126

First published 1996

"The book is divided into seven chapters, each covering a specific timeframe beginning with causative events preceding the crisis (1919-1928) and ending with the emerging Second World War (1939-1941.) Each chapter opens with a narrative summary and analysis of the period, followed by a chronological listing of significant events and then by primary-source contemporary quotations from private citizens, politicians, radio broadcasts, and more." Voice Youth Advocates

Includes bibliographical references

Encyclopedia of the Great Depression; Robert McElvaine, editor in chief. Macmillan Reference USA 2004 2v set $265

Grades: 11 12 Adult   **973.91**

1. Great Depression, 1929-1939—Encyclopedias 2. New Deal, 1933-1939—Encyclopedias 3. United States—Economic conditions—1933-1945—Encyclopedias

ISBN 0-02-865686-5   LC 2003-10292

This "encyclopedia features entries on depression-era politics, government, business, economics, literature, the arts, society and culture. While its main focus is on the Great Depression within the United States, the global impact of the economic slow-down is also examined through articles on Canada, Mexico, Australia, Europe, Africa and Asia." Publisher's note

"This comprehensive, accessible set will serve as a useful supplement for research." SLJ

Includes bibliographical references

Gregory, Ross

Modern America, 1914 to 1945. Facts on File 1995 455p il maps (Almanacs of American life) $95

Grades: 11 12 Adult   **973.91**

1. United States—History—20th century 2. United States—Social life and customs

ISBN 0-8160-2532-0   LC 94-4168

The author "interweaves brief discussions with statistical tables to provide deeper perspectives of major themes in American history not found in annual almanacs. . . . Themes covered include population and immigration, transportation and communication, politics and government, religion, science, and the world wars." Libr J

Includes bibliographical references

Kennedy, David M., 1941-
Freedom from fear; the American people in depression and war, 1929-1945. Oxford Univ. Press 1999 936p il maps (Oxford history of the United States) $39.95; pa $22.50
Grades: 11 12 Adult   **973.91**
    1. United States—History—1919-1933 2. United States—History—1933-1945
    ISBN 0-19-503834-7; 0-19-514403-1 (pa)
                       LC 98-49580
Also available in a two-volume paperback edition
This narrative history of the United States spans the period from the Great Depression to the end of the Second World War
"Rarely does a work of historical synthesis combine such trenchant analysis and elegant writing. For its scope, its insight and its purring narrative engine, Kennedy's book will stand for years to come as the definitive account of the critical decades of the American century." Publ Wkly
Includes bibliographical references

McElvaine, Robert S., 1947-
The Depression and New Deal; a history in documents. Oxford Univ. Press 2000 192p il (Pages from history) lib bdg $36.95; pa $19.95 *
Grades: 7 8 9 10   **973.91**
    1. Great Depression, 1929-1939 2. United States—Economic conditions—1933-1945
    ISBN 0-19-510493-5 (lib bdg); 0-19-516636-1 (pa)
                       LC 99-36644
"A vast assortment of diary entries, newspaper articles, campaign memos and speeches, political cartoons, songs, poetry, art, advertisements, photographs, and personal letters provide students with a political, economic, and social picture of this nation during the Depression. . . . {This} provides a balanced, inclusive picture of the period through the senses of the people who lived it." SLJ
Includes bibliographical references

The **Roaring** twenties; Phillip Margulies, book editor. Greenhaven Press 2004 267p (Turning points in world history) $34.95
Grades: 7 8 9 10   **973.91**
    1. United States—Politics and government—1919-1933 2. United States—Social conditions 3. United States—Social life and customs
    ISBN 0-7377-1809-9   LC 2003-49370
"The twenties are seen today as a watershed, a time that saw the birth of mass consumer society as it exists today. This anthology examines the ingredients of that new society as well as individual turning points in the decade that brought us modern sales promotion, chain stores, radio, tabloid newspapers, jazz, mixed drinks, organized crime and the 1929 stock market crash." Publisher's note
Includes bibliographical references

Streissguth, Thomas, 1958-
The roaring twenties; [by] Tom Streissguth. Rev ed. Facts on File 2007 500p il map (Eyewitness history) $75
Grades: 9 10 11 12   **973.91**
    1. United States—History—1919-1933
    ISBN 0-8160-6423-7; 978-0-8160-6423-6
                       LC 2006-21723
First published 2001 as part of the Facts on File library of American history series
This book "provides hundreds of firsthand accounts of the period—from diary entries, letters, speeches, and newspaper accounts—that illustrate how historical events appeared to those who lived through them." Publisher's note
Includes bibliographical references

Terkel, Studs, 1912-
Hard times; an oral history of the great depression. Norton 2000 462p pa $14.95 *
Grades: 11 12 Adult   **973.91**
    1. Great Depression, 1929-1939 2. United States—Social conditions 3. United States—Economic conditions—1919-1933 4. United States—Economic conditions—1933-1945
    ISBN 1-56584-656-7   LC 2003-389318
A reissue of the title first published 1970 by Pantheon Bks.
"Persons of all ages, occupations, and classes scattered across the U.S. remember what they experienced or were told about the economic crisis of the 1930's. The result is a social document of immense interest." Booklist

U.S.A. Twenties. Grolier 2004 6v il set $419
    Grades: 11 12 Adult   **973.91**
    1. United States—History—1919-1933
    ISBN 0-7172-6013-5   LC 2004-40604
Contents: v. 1. Advertising industry-Cushing, Harvey Williams -- v. 2. Dance-Harding, Warren G. -- v. 3. Harlem renaissance-Lynd Report -- v. 4. Magazines-Politics, Local -- v. 5. Popular music-Sports -- v. 6. Sports, Professionalism and-Young Plan
"This set covers biographies and all aspects of life in the '20s from daily life to politics. . . . For American history or decade studies, this set is invaluable." Libr Media Connect
Includes bibliographical references

Watkins, T. H. (Tom H.), 1936-2000
The hungry years; a narrative history of the Great Depression in America. Holt & Co. 1999 587p il pa $17 hardcover o.p.
Grades: 11 12 Adult   **973.91**
    1. Great Depression, 1929-1939 2. United States—Economic conditions—1919-1933 3. United States—Economic conditions—1933-1945
    ISBN 0-8050-6506-7 (pa)   LC 99-10391
"A Marian Wood book"
"This book explores how everyday Americans across the country coped with economic disaster." Libr J
"The vignettes Watkins selects are gritty, visceral, and seamlessly sutured to the federal programs that rolled out in the course of the decade, making this a signal addition to the rich historiography of the Depression." Booklist
Includes bibliographical references

973.92   United States--1953-2001

Bok, Chip, 1952-
A recent history of the United States in political cartoons; a look Bok! University of Akron Press 2005 291p il (Series on law, politics, and society) $26.95; pa $16.95
Grades: 9 10 11 12   **973.92**
    1. United States—Politics and government—1974-1989—Cartoons and caricatures 2. United States—Politics and government—1989-—Cartoons and caricatures
ISBN 1-931968-11-X; 1-931968-12-8 (pa)
                                  LC 2005-41935
This is a collection of political cartoons satirizing the people and events of the late 20th and early 21st century.

Encyclopedia of contemporary American culture; edited by Gary W. McDonogh, Robert Gregg, and Cindy H. Wong. Routledge 2001 xxxiv, 839p $145 *
    Grades: 11 12 Adult   **973.92**
    1. Popular culture—United States 2. United States—Civilization
ISBN 0-415-16161-4   LC 00-55326
This presents a "synthesis of the United States after World War II. The text covers all aspects of culture, from business and politics to education, arts and sciences, society, and religion. The alphabetically arranged entries range from short definitions to longer overviews that span a couple pages and treat topics as varied as Haitian Americans, Camille Paglia, Disneyland, Prozac, and censorship. . . . This work provides a good starting point for information about the issues, events, people, and places that shape, define, or represent America today." Libr J
    Includes bibliographical references

Frum, David, 1960-
How we got here; the 70's: the decade that brought you modern life (for better or worse). Basic Bks. 2000 xxiv, 418p il pa $18.95 hardcover o.p.
Grades: 11 12 Adult   **973.92**
    1. United States—Civilization—1970-
ISBN 0-465-01496-5 (pa)
The author "aims 'to describe—and to judge' the transformation of American values during the '70s. Surveying politics, legal cases and opinion polls as well as popular culture, he links what he sees as America's loss of faith in government, the rise of 'sourness and cynicism' and the culture of licentiousness and divorce, among other social changes, to events in that decade." Publ Wkly
    Includes bibliographical references

Gregory, Ross
Cold War America, 1946 to 1990; Richard Balkin, general editor. Facts on File 2003 670p il map (Almanacs of American life) $105 *
    Grades: 11 12 Adult   **973.92**
    1. Cold war 2. United States—History—1945-3. United States—Social conditions
ISBN 0-8160-3868-6   LC 2001-51136
"This is a treasure trove of statistical information documenting the enormous changes in American life from 1945 to 1990. . . . Found herein are data on everything from the population by sex . . . region, and race, business formations and failures, bull and bear markets, and operations of the postal service to the federal debt, high school seniors and drugs, executions by gender and race, and recipients of National Book Awards and Pulitzer Prizes. . . . Enhancing the work's appeal are photographs throughout the text and an exhaustive index." Am Ref Books Annu, 2003
    Includes bibliographical references

Halberstam, David, 1934-2007
The fifties. Villard Bks. 1993 800p il pa $17.95 hardcover o.p.
Grades: 11 12 Adult   **973.92**
    1. United States—Social life and customs 2. United States—Politics and government—20th century 3. Popular culture—United States
ISBN 0-449-90933-6 (pa)   LC 92-56815
This is a social history of the United States during the 1950s
    The author's "sources are secondary and derivative, but his instinct for the revealing anecdote, his ear for the memorable quote, and his awesome powers of organization add up to a variegated overview that moves seamlessly between the serious shenanigans of Chief Justice Earl Warren and the frivolous ones of . . . Grace Metalious." Natl Rev
    Includes bibliographical references

Hurley, Jennifer A., 1973-
The 1960s. Greenhaven Press 2000 143p il maps (Opposing viewpoints digests) lib bdg $27.45; pa $17.45
Grades: 9 10 11 12   **973.92**
    1. United States—History—1961-1974 2. United States—Social conditions
ISBN 0-7377-0211-7 (lib bdg); 0-7377-0210-9 (pa)
                                      LC 99-38546
Presents opposing viewpoints on events of the 1960s including the Vietnam War, social rebellion, the civil rights movement, and the women's liberation movement
    Includes bibliographical references

Kort, Michael
The Columbia guide to the Cold War. Columbia Univ. Press 1998 366p (Columbia guides to American history and cultures) $60; pa $19.50
Grades: 11 12 Adult   **973.92**
    1. Cold war 2. United States—Foreign relations 3. United States—History—1945-
ISBN 0-231-10772-2; 0-231-10773-0 (pa)
                                      LC 98-7154

Kort, Michael—*Continued*

The author begins "with a narrative survey of the Cold War which explains some of the historiographical debates that have occupied historians for more than 50 years. Following this section is a mini-encyclopedia consisting of one- or two-page essays on a wide range of Cold War topics. The book concludes with a concise chronology and a comprehensive bibliography of books, films, novels, journal articles, and archival sources. Finally . . . Kort points out some of the relevant current websites and CD-ROM products." Libr J

Maga, Timothy P., 1952-

The 1960s. Facts on File 2003 xx, 396p il map (Eyewitness history) $75 *

Grades: 9 10 11 12   **973.92**

1. United States—History—1961-1974 2. United States—Civilization

ISBN 0-8160-4809-6   LC 2002-14119

Contents: To the "new frontier" : January 1960-December 1961; Lost in the Cold War : January 1962-September 1963; Lessons of the Cuban missile crisis : October 1962-December 1963; All the way with LBJ : 1964-1965; Beach Boys America : 1966-1967; The perils of power : 1968; How the "sixties" end : 1969-1970

This volume covers the 1960s "from the cold war days of the Cuban Missile Crisis to the assassinations of John F. Kennedy, Robert F. Kennedy, and Martin Luther King, Jr., to the Vietnam War; from the Beach Boys to the Beatles to the Rolling Stones; from Hippies and Yippies to race riots and Kent State. [These events are depicted] in the words of Americans who experienced the major events and issues of the decade." Publisher's note

Includes bibliographical references

McWilliams, John C., 1949-

The 1960s cultural revolution. Greenwood Press 2000 xxxvii, 187p (Greenwood Press guides to historic events of the twentieth century) $49.95 *

Grades: 11 12 Adult   **973.92**

1. United States—History—1961-1974

ISBN 0-313-29913-7   LC 99-58963

"The changes and challenges that manifested themselves in the 1960s did not begin and end in a neat 10-year package, so this book actually runs through to 1975 and the end of the Vietnam War. . . . The book has a lengthy chronology, a notable selection of primary documents, and an extensive annotated bibliography that includes videos and Web sites." SLJ

Includes bibliographical references

Postwar America; an encyclopedia of social, political, cultural, and economic history; James Ciment, editor. M.E. Sharpe 2006 4v il set $399

Grades: 11 12 Adult   **973.92**

1. United States—Civilization—Encyclopedias

ISBN 0-7656-8067-X; 978-0-7656-8067-9

LC 2004-13120

"A-Z entries address specific persons, groups, concepts, events, geographical locations, organizations, and cultural and technological phenomena. Sidebars highlight primary source materials, items of special interest, statis-

tical data, and other information; and Cultural Landmark entries chronologically detail the music, literature, arts, and cultural history of the era. Bibliographies covering literature from the postwar era and about the era are also included, as well as illustrations and specialized indexes." Publisher's note

Includes bibliographical references

Rather, Dan

The American dream; stories from the heart of our nation. Morrow 2001 xxii, 266p hardcover o.p. pa $12.95

Grades: 11 12 Adult   **973.92**

1. American national characteristics 2. United States—Social life and customs 3. United States—Social conditions

ISBN 0-688-17892-8; 0-06-093770-X (pa)

LC 2001-30031

In this book Rather tells stories of individual Americans and their dreams. He "groups his material into chapters that focus on elements of our national aspirations: liberty, enterprise, pursuit of happiness, family, fame, education, innovation, and 'giving back.' The Americans that Rather describes are a diverse group but, he urges, their stories are an inspirational reminder of the power of the nation's fundamental ideas to motivate a wide range of people." Booklist

Schwartz, Richard Alan, 1951-

The 1990s; [by] Richard A. Schwartz. Facts on File 2006 496p il (Eyewitness history) $75 *

Grades: 11 12 Adult   **973.92**

1. United States—History—1989- 2. United States—Politics and government—1989-

ISBN 0-8160-5696-X   LC 2004-28884

This book "provides hundreds of firsthand accounts of the 1990s—including diary entries, letters, speeches, and newspaper accounts—that illustrate how historical events appeared to those who lived through them. Each chapter provides an introductory essay and a chronology of events." Publisher's note

Includes bibliographical references

Sirimarco, Elizabeth, 1966-

American voices from The Cold War. Benchmark Books 2004 c2005 134p (American voices from--) lib bdg $23.95

Grades: 6 7 8 9 10   **973.92**

1. Cold war

ISBN 0-7614-1694-3   LC 2003-1933

Presents the history of the Cold War through excerpts from letters, newspaper articles, speeches, and songs dating from the period. Includes review questions.

This "excellent [resource stands] out . . . because [it deals] strictly with primary sources, [contains] topnotch illustrations, and [enables] students to grasp the concepts without being overwhelmed." SLJ

Sitkoff, Harvard
Postwar America; a student companion. Oxford Univ. Press 2000 292p il $45
Grades: 11 12 Adult   **973.92**
1. United States—History—1945-
ISBN 0-19-510300-9   LC 98-34183
"The articles in this volume cover events, people, documents, legal cases, and social and political movements and groups that have had an impact on our country since the end of World War II. The alphabetical entries range from one paragraph to four pages." SLJ
Includes bibliographical references

Sixties counterculture; Stuart A. Kallen, book editor. Greenhaven Press 2001 224p il (History firsthand) hardcover o.p. pa $19.95 *
Grades: 9 10 11 12   **973.92**
1. Counter culture 2. Radicalism 3. United States—History—1961-1974 4. United States—Social conditions
ISBN 0-7377-0407-1; 0-7377-0406-3 (pa)
     LC 00-29377
"Chapters touch on such topics as feminism, war protests, civil rights, free speech, the hippie culture, and the birth of yippies. The text comes from primary—source material—from figures such as Huey Newton, Carletta Fields, and Eldridge Cleaver—which was actually written during the '60s as well as as excerpts from books written well after that decade." SLJ
"The overview is interesting reading, and some of the excerpts are excellent. A few selections include language that may be objectionable, though a more sanitized approach would not accurately represent the era." Booklist
Includes bibliographical references

The **Sixties** in America; editor, Carl Singleton; project editor, Rowena Wildin. Salem Press 1999 3v il set $315
Grades: 11 12 Adult   **973.92**
1. United States—History—1961-1974—Encyclopedias 2. United States—Social life and customs
ISBN 0-89356-982-8   LC 98-49255
This set covers "the events, people, organizations, scientific advances, and popular culture of the sixties. The generally brief articles are alphabetically arranged and written chiefly by academic contributors. . . . Appendixes cover such topics as major legislation and important Supreme Court decisions and provide statistics and a time line of science and technology. An extensive, up-to-date bibliography and a mediagraphy listing electronic materials, videos, and Web sites conclude the set." SLJ

Woodger, Elin
The 1980s; [by] Elin Woodger and David F. Burg. Facts on File 2006 508p il map (Eyewitness history) $75
Grades: 9 10 11 12   **973.92**
1. United States—History—1974-1989 2. United States—Politics and government—1974-1989
ISBN 0-8160-5809-1; 978-0-8160-5809-1
     LC 2005-18732
This book provides a look at the 1980s, "illustrating how events appeared to those who lived through them. In addition to the firsthand accounts, each chapter pro-

vides an introductory essay and a chronology of events. The book also includes critical documents, as well as capsule biographies of key figures, a bibliography, an index, 92 black-and-white photographs and illustrations, and 13 maps and graphs." Publisher's note
Includes bibliographical references

973.921 United States-- Administration of Dwight D. Eisenhower, 1953-1961

Schwartz, Richard Alan, 1951-
The 1950s; {by} Richard A. Schwartz. Facts on File 2003 504p il maps (Eyewitness history) $75 *
Grades: 9 10 11 12   **973.921**
1. United States—Civilization 2. United States—History—1945-1953 3. United States—History—1953-1961
ISBN 0-8160-4597-6   LC 2002-1149
Contents: Introduction; Postwar prelude: 1945-1949; America becomes the world's policeman: 1950; The Cold War settles in: 1951; "I like Ike": 1952; New leadership in Washington and Moscow: 1953; Separate is not equal: 1954; Self-created annihilation becomes a possibility: 1955; Ike and Elvis, Budapest and the Suez: 1956; Sputnik and Little Rock: 1957; America enters outer space: 1958; America expands into the Pacific: 1959
The chapters in this volume "describe each year of the decade with a narrative account of the most significant social, cultural, and political developments; a chronology of events; and eyewitness testimonies drawn from newspapers, memoirs of private and public figures, literature, and other sources." Publisher's note
Includes bibliographical references

973.922 United States-- Administration of John F. Kennedy, 1961-1963

Benson, Michael
The encyclopedia of the JFK assassination. Facts on File 2002 348p il map (Facts on File library of American history) $75; pa $21.95
Grades: 11 12 Adult   **973.922**
1. Kennedy, John F. (John Fitzgerald), 1917-1963—Assassination
ISBN 0-8160-4476-7; 0-8160-4477-5 (pa)
     LC 2001-53212
"This volume provides a listing of people, places, and events related (however slightly) to November 22 to 24, 1963. Following an introduction that describes the events and summarizes conspiracy theories are hundreds of entries. . . . These range from a paragraph to identify people and groups . . . to 4 or 5 pages. . . . This volume is readable and intriguing." Booklist

Hampton, Wilborn
Kennedy assassinated! the world mourns: a
reporter's story. Candlewick Press 1997 96p il
$17.99; pa $8.99
Grades: 5 6 7 8 9   **973.922**
    1. Kennedy, John F. (John Fitzgerald), 1917-1963—
Assassination 2. Journalism
    ISBN 1-56402-811-9; 0-7636-1564-1 (pa)
                LC 96-25801
This is the author's "account of November 22, 1963,
when, as a cub reporter for UPI in Dallas, he was drafted
to cover JFK's assassination. His personal response to
the tragedy is fluidly juxtaposed with the nuts and bolts
of scooping the story in this insider's view of one of the
most pivotal events of our nation's recent history." Publ
Wkly
Includes bibliographical references

973.923 United States--
Administration of Lyndon B.
Johnson, 1963-1969

Pendergast, Tom, 1964-
The sixties in America. Almanac; [by] Tom
Pendergast and Sara Pendergast. U.X.L. 2005
xxxviii, 229p il (U-X-L the sixties in America
reference library) $63
Grades: 11 12 Adult   **973.923**
    1. United States—History—1961-1974
    ISBN 0-7876-9246-8   LC 2004-16601
This book provides "essays on social and political developments: the antiwar movement, civil rights, feminism
and the sexual revolution, and sweeping cultural changes
in popular entertainment, sports, and the arts." Booklist
Includes bibliographical references

Sixties in America. Primary sources; [by] Tom
Pendergast and Sara Pendergast. U.X.L 2005
xxxviii, 240p il (U-X-L the sixties in America
reference library) $60 *
Grades: 9 10 11 12   **973.923**
    1. United States—History—1961-1974
    ISBN 0-7876-9248-4   LC 2004-16602
This "volume contains primary documents including
including George Wallace's inaugural speech, an excerpt
from 'The Ballot or The Bullet' by Malcolm X, and
NOW's 'Bill of Rights for Women in 1968.' Chapters
are followed by Where to Learn More and an index.
Each except is accompanied by a glossary that defines
terms, people, and ideas." Libr Media Connect
Includes bibliographical references

Schomp, Virginia, 1953-
American voices from the Vietnam era.
Benchmark Books 2004 c2005 xxiii, 134p
(American voices from--) lib bdg $34.21 *
Grades: 6 7 8 9   **973.923**
    1. Vietnam War, 1961-1975 2. United States—Histo-
ry—1961-1974
    ISBN 0-7614-1693-5   LC 2003-1475

Contents: A television war; The unseen enemy; The
war at home: "doves" for peace; The war at home:
"hawks" for war; American youth and the counterculture;
The battle for civil rights; The women's liberation movement; The credibility gap; Coming home
Describes, through excerpts from diaries, speeches,
newspaper articles, and other documents of the time, the
Vietnam War and related events that occurred in the
United States during the 1960's, including the women's
movement, the struggle for civil rights, and the generation gap. Includes review questions.
Includes glossary and bibliographical references

973.924 United States--
Administration of Richard Nixon,
1969-1974

Bernstein, Carl
All the president's men; {by} Carl Bernstein,
Bob Woodward. Simon & Schuster 1999 349p il
hardcover o.p. pa $14
Grades: 11 12 Adult   **973.924**
    1. Washington post 2. Watergate Affair, 1972-1974
    ISBN 0-684-86355-3; 0-671-89441-2 (pa)
                LC 98-54773
A reissue of the title first published 1974
The two Washington Post reporters whose investigative journalism first revealed the Watergate scandal tell
the way it happened from the first suspicions, through
the trail of false leads, lies, secrecy, and high-level pressure, to the final moments when they were able to put
the pieces of the puzzle together and write the series that
won the Post a Pulitzer Prize

Caputo, Philip
13 seconds; a look back at the Kent State
shootings. Chamberlain Bros. 2005 198p $21.95 *
Grades: 11 12 Adult   **973.924**
    1. Kent State University 2. Vietnam War, 1961-
1975—Protest movements
    ISBN 1-59609-080-4   LC 2005-41328
    Includes DVD
The author reconstructs "the events of May 4, 1970,
when National Guard troops in Ohio opened fire on Kent
State University students during an antiwar rally, killing
four and wounding nine." Publ Wkly
"The book is packaged with a DVD containing the
2001 documentary Kent State: The Day the War Came
Home. Together, the images and Caputo's words serve as
a powerful antidote to the romanticization of an era."
Booklist

Genovese, Michael A.
The Watergate crisis. Greenwood Press 1999
xxix, 197p il (Greenwood Press guides to historic
events of the twentieth century) $46.95
Grades: 11 12 Adult   **973.924**
    1. Nixon, Richard M. (Richard Milhous), 1913-1994
2. Watergate Affair, 1972-1974
    ISBN 0-313-29878-5   LC 99-17858

Genovese, Michael A.—*Continued*
This book "provides a historical overview of the Watergate crisis, an account of the development of Nixon's political personality, a discussion of whether the president can ever act outside legal limits, a presentation of historical precedent for presidential corruption, an analysis of Nixon's relationships with the news media, and a conclusion about the Watergate legacy." SLJ

Includes glossary and bibliographical references

Olson, Keith W., 1931-
Watergate; the presidential scandal that shook America. University Press of Kansas 2003 220p il $35; pa $15.95
Grades: 11 12 Adult   **973.924**
1. Watergate Affair, 1972-1974
ISBN 0-7006-1250-5; 0-7006-1251-3 (pa)
                                     LC 2002-38058
The author describes "the White House-approved break-in at Democratic National Committee headquarters in Washington's Watergate complex and its aftermath—most importantly, the dramatic proceedings of the Senate Watergate Committee. . . . {This} book provides an excellent, compact narrative of a crucial moment in the history of the American presidency." Publ Wkly

Includes bibliographical references

Woodward, Bob, 1943-
The final days; {by} Bob Woodward, Carl Bernstein. Simon & Schuster 1976 476p il pa $16 hardcover o.p.
Grades: 11 12 Adult   **973.924**
1. Nixon, Richard M. (Richard Milhous), 1913-1994 2. Watergate Affair, 1972-1974 3. United States—Politics and government—1961-1974
ISBN 0-7432-7406-7 (pa)
The title refers to the final days of the Nixon Presidency. The authors have "constructed a two-part narrative, the first half covering the period from April 30, 1973—the day John Dean was fired as White House counsel—until late July 1974, and the second half covering the last two weeks in detail." N Y Times Book Rev

973.929 United States-- Administration of Bill Clinton, 1993- 2001

Aaseng, Nathan, 1953-
The impeachment of Bill Clinton. Lucent Bks. 2000 112p il (Famous trials) lib bdg $27.45
Grades: 9 10 11 12   **973.929**
1. Clinton, Bill, 1946-—Impeachment 2. United States—Politics and government—1989-
ISBN 1-56006-651-2   LC 99-39568
Examines the impeachment of Bill Clinton, discussing the history of impeachment, his actions, the struggle in the House, the Senate trial, and the conclusion of the proceedings
"The text is clearly written and accurate." SLJ

Includes bibliographical references

Cohen, Daniel, 1936-
The impeachment of William Jefferson Clinton. 21st Cent. Bks. (Brookfield) 2000 112p il lib bdg $23.90 *
Grades: 7 8 9 10   **973.929**
1. Clinton, Bill, 1946-—Impeachment 2. United States—Politics and government—1989-
ISBN 0-7613-1711-2   LC 99-56179
Examines the events leading to the impeachment of President Bill Clinton, including the Whitewater investigation, the media coverage, the grand jury proceedings, impeachment by the Senate, and the legacy of this scandal
"The chronology of events is smoothly presented, and issues of national importance which became part of the public debate . . . are clearly explained." Bull Cent Child Books

Includes bibliographical references

William J. Clinton; Todd Howard, book editor. Greenhaven Press 2001 212p il (Presidents and their decisions) lib bdg $31.20
Grades: 9 10 11 12   **973.929**
1. Clinton, Bill, 1946- 2. United States—Politics and government—1989-
ISBN 0-7377-0498-5 (lib bdg)   LC 00-57843
"After a 40-page biographical sketch that covers Clinton's political career and the recurring questions about his personal conduct, essays provide opposing positions on gays in the military, health-care reform, and his administration's foreign policy. The final chapter focuses on the impeachment. . . . The contributors include policy experts and commentators from across the political spectrum. Although there is little general background, the issues are clear." SLJ

Includes bibliographical references

973.931 United States-- Administration of George W. Bush, 2001-

America under attack: primary sources; Tamara Roleff, book editor. Lucent Bks. 2002 96p il map (Lucent terrorism library) $27.45
Grades: 7 8 9 10   **973.931**
1. September 11 terrorist attacks, 2001 2. Terrorism
ISBN 1-59018-216-2   LC 2002-1816
Contents: On the scene; America's response; Response from abroad; Who is to blame?; War on terrorism
Looks at the September 11, 2001 terrorist attack on the World Trade Center and Pentagon, U.S. response, world reaction, and the war on terrorism
"Roleff's useful compendium offers thematically arranged perspectives from witnesses in New York and Washington, DC, U.S. and world leaders, the blamed and the accusers, and war proponents and opponents. . . . This will be a sought-after research tool." SLJ

Includes bibliographical references

America's battle against terrorism; Andrea C. Nakaya, book editor. Greenhaven Press 2005 208p (Current controversies) lib bdg $34.95; pa $23.70 *

Grades: 9 10 11 12　　　　　**973.931**
1. War on terrorism 2. Terrorism
ISBN 0-7377-2783-7 (lib bdg); 0-7377-2784-5 (pa)
　　　　　　　　　　　　LC 2004-54122
"This volume explores the effectiveness of the tactics the United States uses against terrorists, the effect battling terrorism has on civil liberties in America, the impact of the war in Iraq, and whether the United States is prepared for another terrorist attack." Publisher's note
Includes bibliographical references

Bernstein, Richard
Out of the blue; the story of September 11, 2001, from Jihad to Ground Zero; {by} Richard Bernstein and the staff of the New York Times. Times Bks. 2002 287p il hardcover o.p. pa $15 *
Grades: 11 12 Adult　　　　　**973.931**
1. September 11 terrorist attacks, 2001 2. Terrorism
ISBN 0-8050-7240-3; 0-8050-7410-4 (pa)
　　　　　　　　　　　　LC 2002-20396
This account of the September 11, 2001 terrorist attacks focuses "on the personal—the victims, the perpetrators and heroes whose lives became tangled in catastrophe. . . . It uses these stories as a jumping-off point for a comprehensive look at the terror attacks—the reactions of New Yorkers, the nation and the world; the criticism of U.S. government agencies; the lingering effects of the tragedy. While some of this information has been published elsewhere, it has not been gathered so comprehensively—nor has it been written so well." Publ Wkly

The **Day** our world changed; children's art of 9/11; [edited by] Robin F. Goodman & Andrea Henderson Fahnestock; introduction by Rudolph W. Giuliani; forewords by Harold S. Koplewicz & Robert R. MacDonald; essays by Debbie Almontaser [et al.] Abrams 2002 128p il $19.95
Grades: 11 12 Adult　　　　　**973.931**
1. September 11 terrorist attacks, 2001 2. Children's art 3. Child psychology
ISBN 0-8109-3544-9　　　　LC 2002-104747
This is a collection of art works created by New York children and teenagers in response to the terrorist attacks of September 11, 2001, with commentary by psychologists and others
"Reproduced in expressive full color, the works are remarkable and also very graphic. . . . The artists, from five to 18 years old, created complex works that capture many aspects of grief." Libr J

Does the world hate the United States? Andrea C. Nakaya, book editor. Greenhaven Press 2005 139p (At issue) lib bdg $27.45; pa $18.70 *
Grades: 9 10 11 12　　　　　**973.931**
1. United States—Foreign opinion 2. United States—Foreign relations
ISBN 0-7377-2368-8 (lib bdg); 0-7377-2369-6 (pa)
　　　　　　　　　　　　LC 2004-47440

The authors in this anthology "offer various perspectives on the extent of anti-Americanism around the world. They also examine the causes of both love and hatred toward the United States, and the implications of these views for Americans." Introduction
Includes bibliographical references

Friedman, Thomas L.
Longitudes and attitudes; exploring the world after September 11. Farrar, Straus & Giroux 2002 383p $23
Grades: 11 12 Adult　　　　　**973.931**
1. September 11 terrorist attacks, 2001 2. Terrorism 3. United States—Politics and government—1989- 4. United States—Foreign relations
ISBN 0-374-19066-6　　　　LC 2002-74321
Also available in paperback from Anchor Bks.
This is a collection "of Friedman's *New York Times* columns from September 2001 through June 2002, with a lengthy postscript describing Friedman's travels and interviews throughout this period." Booklist
"Unapologetically pro-American, Friedman's deliberation on what changed on September 11 outside of the U.S. ultimately centers on the strength of American society and our place in the world." Publ Wkly
Includes bibliographical references

Hampton, Wilborn
September 11, 2001; attack on New York City. Candlewick Press 2003 145p il $17.99
Grades: 6 7 8 9　　　　　**973.931**
1. September 11 terrorist attacks, 2001 2. Terrorism
ISBN 0-7636-1949-3　　　　LC 2002-41204
Describes the September 11 attacks in the United States and presents several personal stories of tragedy told by New Yorkers who lived through the collapse of the World Trade Center.
"Hampton re-creates the terrible events of that day clearly. . . . There are many . . . books about 9/11 written for young people, but this is one of the best." Booklist
Includes bibliographical references

How should the United States treat prisoners in the war on terror? Lauri S. Friedman, book editor. Greenhaven Press 2005 110p (At issue) lib bdg $28.70; pa $19.95 *
Grades: 9 10 11 12　　　　　**973.931**
1. War on terrorism 2. Prisoners of war
ISBN 0-7377-3113-3 (lib bdg); 0-7377-3114-1 (pa)
　　　　　　　　　　　　LC 2004-53501
This book "explores the variety of perspectives regarding how the United States should deal with the prisoners in the war on terror." Publisher's note
Includes bibliographical references

Jacobson, Sidney
The 9/11 report; a graphic adaptation; by Sid Jacobson and Ernie Colón; [with a foreword by Thomas H. Kean and Lee H. Hamilton] Hill and Wang 2006 133p il $30; pa $16.95 *
Grades: 11 12 Adult　　　　　**973.931**

Jacobson, Sidney—*Continued*
1. September 11 terrorist attacks, 2001—Graphic novels 2. Graphic novels
ISBN   0-8090-5738-7;   978-0-8090-5738-2;
0-8090-5739-5 (pa); 978-0-8090-5739-9 (pa)
On cover: Based on the final report of the National Commission on Terrorist Attacks upon the United States
"The book aims to make . . . [The 9/11 Commission Report] more accessible to all readers and draw in young adults. . . . This graphic adaptation is an important and necessary part of any collection." Libr J

A **Just** response; the Nation on terrorism, democracy, and September 11, 2001; edited by Katrina van den Heuvel. Thunder's Mouth Press 2002 349p pa $14.95 *
Grades: 11 12 Adult   **973.931**
1. Nation (Periodical) 2. September 11 terrorist attacks, 2001 3. Terrorism
ISBN 1-56025-400-9
"Included in this . . . collection of essays, articles, and editorials published in the *Nation* since September 11 are contributions that address issues pertaining to First Amendment rights, civil liberties, social justice, disarmament, international law, and world opinion within the context of the current war on terrorism." Booklist
"Although the Nation's targets range from Defense Secretary Donald Rumsfeld to Bayer, the manufacturer of Cipro, the harshest criticism is reserved for the mainstream media. . . . Those who found the early coverage of America's 'War on Terror' to be monotonous will appreciate the Nation's radical point of view." Publ Wkly

National Commission on Terrorist Attacks Upon the United States
The 9/11 Commission report; final report of the National Commission on Terrorist Attacks Upon the United States. Norton 2004 567p il $19.95; pa $10
Grades: 11 12 Adult   **973.931**
1. Al Qaeda (Organization) 2. September 11 terrorist attacks, 2001 3. Terrorism 4. War on terrorism
5. National security—United States
ISBN 0-393-06041-1; 0-393-32671-3 (pa)
                                       LC 2004-57564
Also available in paperback from St. Martin's Press
"Authorized edition"
This work aims to describe how the terrorist attacks of September 11, 2001 occurred and to provide recommendations for the prevention of future attacks.
This book "reads like a Shakespearean drama. . . . This multi-author document produces an absolutely compelling narrative intelligence, one with clarity, a sense of shared mission and an overriding desire to *do* something about the situation." Publ Wkly
Includes bibliographical references

Spiegelman, Art
In the shadow of no towers. Pantheon Books 2004 various paging il $19.95
Grades: 11 12 Adult   **973.931**
1. September 11 terrorist attacks, 2001—Graphic novels 2. Graphic novels
ISBN 0-375-42307-9   LC 2004-43870

This is a "memoir of the attacks on the World Trade Center, which Spiegelman witnessed from close range, a rant on their effects on the world at large and within the author, and a monograph on the Sunday newspaper comic strips of the early 20th century." N Y Times Book Rev
The author "provides a hair-raising and wry account of his family's frantic efforts to locate one another on September 11 as well as a morbidly funny survey of his trademark sense of existential doom. . . . This is a powerful and quirky work of visual storytelling by a master comics artist." Publ Wkly

Terrorism; Lauri S. Friedman, book editor. Greenhaven Press 2005 128p il (Introducing issues with opposing viewpoints) lib bdg $32.45
Grades: 9 10 11 12   **973.931**
1. Terrorism 2. War on terrorism
ISBN 0-7377-3225-3   LC 2005-40416
This "collection of viewpoints investigates the scope of terrorism, its root causes and various ideas on how to prevent it." Publisher's note
Includes bibliographical references

The **war** on terrorism: opposing viewpoints; Karen F. Balkin, book editor. Greenhaven Press 2005 206p il lib bdg $33.70; pa $22.45
Grades: 9 10 11 12   **973.931**
1. War on terrorism 2. Terrorism
ISBN 0-7377-2336-X (lib bdg); 0-7377-2337-8 (pa)
                                       LC 2004-47442
"Opposing viewpoints series"
This book features 28 essays on topics such as Is the War on Terrorism Justified? and Is the Domestic War on Terrorism a Threat to Civil Liberties? Contributors include Dr. Leonard Peikoff, George W. Bush, Tom Ridge, and Colin Powell
Includes bibliographical references

974.7 New York

At ground zero; the young reporters who were there tell their stories; edited by Chris Bull and Sam Erman. Thunder's Mouth Press 2002 404p pa $15.95 *
Grades: 11 12 Adult   **974.7**
1. September 11 terrorist attacks, 2001 2. Terrorism
ISBN 1-56025-427-0   LC 2002-75210
The essays "describe the chaos and destruction . . . {and} the atmosphere and people of New York during the surprise attack and the sadness and grief that followed. An excellent collection from a talented group of up-and-coming journalists who strugged off inexperience, doubts, and fears to bring . . . the facts." Booklist

DeAngelis, Gina
The Triangle Shirtwaist Company fire of 1911; [by] Gina De Angelis. Chelsea House 2000 120p il (Great disasters, reforms and ramifications) $21.95
Grades: 9 10 11 12   **974.7**
1. Triangle Shirtwaist Company, Inc. 2. Factories
3. Clothing industry
ISBN 0-7910-5267-2   LC 99-86848

DeAngelis, Gina—*Continued*

Examines, using eyewitness accounts, the tragedy that killed 146 workers in a New York City garment factory

"DeAngelis's text conveys the urgency of the tragedy, and period photographs bring an immediacy to the event. This book should be of interest to students studying the labor movement, immigrant life, and early twentieth-century city life." Voice Youth Advocates

Includes bibliographical references

Dwyer, Jim, 1957-

102 minutes; the untold story of the fight to survive inside the Twin Towers; [by] Jim Dwyer and Kevin Flynn. Times Books 2005 322p il $26; pa $15 *

Grades: 11 12 Adult   **974.7**

1. World Trade Center terrorist attack, 2001
2. September 11 terrorist attacks, 2001

ISBN 0-8050-7682-4; 0-8050-8032-5 (pa)

LC 2004-55321

The authors "take us into the 102 minutes of hell experienced by those in the World Trade Center between the time the first jet crashed into the north tower and the last standing tower toppled. While other accounts have focused on the members of NYFD and NYPD who responded to the catastrophe, this book tells the stories of scores of civilians." Libr J

Dwyer and Flynn have "given us a fitting tribute to the people caught up in one of the great dramas of our time. And for people still haunted by the events of that day, reading '102 Minutes' provides a cathartic release." N Y Times Book Rev

Hopkinson, Deborah

Shutting out the sky; life in the tenements of New York, 1880-1924. Orchard Bks. 2003 134p il $17.95

Grades: 5 6 7 8 9 10   **974.7**

1. Poor 2. Immigrants—United States 3. Lower East Side (New York, N.Y.)

ISBN 0-439-37590-8   LC 2002-44781

Contents: Coming to the golden land; Tenements: shutting out the sky; Settling in: greenhorns and boarders; Everyone worked on; On the streets: pushcarts, pickles and play; A new language, a new life; Looking to the future: will it ever be different?

Photographs and text document the experiences of five individuals who came to live in the Lower East Side of New York City as children or young adults from Belarus, Italy, Lithuania, and Romania at the turn of the twentieth century.

"The text is supported by numerous tinted archival photos of living and working conditions. Although this book will appeal to students looking for material for projects, the writing lends immediacy and vivid images make it simply a fascinating read." SLJ

Includes bibliographical references

Lieurance, Suzanne

The Triangle Shirtwaist fire and sweatshop reform in American history. Enslow Pubs. 2003 128p il (In American history) $20.95

Grades: 7 8 9 10   **974.7**

1. Triangle Shirtwaist Company, Inc. 2. Clothing industry 3. Factories

ISBN 0-7660-1839-3   LC 2002-8761

Contents: Fire in the factory; A general strike is declared; A city mourns; Investigations and a trial; Steps to improve working conditions

Explores the people and events connected with the 1911 fire in a New York City sewing factory that killed 146 people and led to reforms in legislation regarding workplace safety.

This is written "in a clear, moving yet meticulously documented style. . . . Period photographs and judicious use of personal stories add a human face to the tragedy." Libr Media Connect

Includes bibliographical references

Von Drehle, Dave

Triangle: the fire that changed America. Atlantic Monthly Press 2003 340p il $25; pa $14

Grades: 11 12 Adult   **974.7**

1. Triangle Shirtwaist Company, Inc. 2. Fires 3. New York (N.Y.) 4. Clothing industry 5. Factories

ISBN 0-87113-874-3; 0-8021-4151-X (pa)

LC 2003-41835

"The tragic conflagration at the Triangle Shirtwaist Factory in March 1911 resulted in the deaths of 123 women (most of them young immigrants), caused widespread public outrage, and set in motion a wave of reform. Drehle's vivid retelling of this horrifying event begins with the strike that immediately preceded it and then examines the terrible fire, the unsuccessful prosecution of the factory owners, and the fight to prevent similar tragedies in the future." Libr J

"Von Drehle's engrossing account, which emphasizes the humanity of the victims and the theme of social justice, brings on of the pivotal and most shocking episodes of American labor history to life." Publ Wkly

Includes bibliographical references

975.3 District of Columbia (Washington)

The **White** House; an historic guide; White House Historical Association. 22nd ed. White House Historical Association 2003 159p il pa $7 *

Grades: 9 10 11 12   **975.3**

1. White House (Washington, D.C.)

ISBN 0-912308-91-5   LC 2004-366305

Contact publisher for purchase information

First published 1962. Periodically revised

This book traces the changing appearance of the White House through many administrations. It describes life in the White House under different presidents as well as its great furniture, paintings, collections of china, vermeil, and the furnishings of the official rooms

975.6   North Carolina

Miller, Lee
Roanoke; solving the mystery of the Lost Colony. Arcade Pub. 2001 362p il maps $25.95
Grades: 11 12 Adult   **975.6**
1. Roanoke Island (N.C.)—History
ISBN 1-55970-584-1   LC 2001-22446
Also available in paperback from Penguin
First published 2000 in the United Kingdom
The author "blames the colony's disappearance on treachery and murder she traces to the court of Elizabeth I. Conspiracy theorists should find much to savor in this convoluted story, which includes palace intrigues, cultural misunderstandings, and gray-eyed Native Americans. . . . This is an interesting, well-told tale." Libr J
Includes bibliographical references

975.8   Georgia

Foxfire 40th anniversary book; faith, family, and the land; edited by Angie Cheek, Lacy Hunter Nix, and Foxfire students. Anchor Books 2006 xxxix, 512p il pa $17.95 *
Grades: 11 12 Adult   **975.8**
1. Country life—Georgia 2. Appalachian region—Social life and customs 3. Handicraft
ISBN 0-307-27551-5; 978-0-307-27551-6
LC 2006-45311
"Drawing on the magazine's published talks by local high school students with elderly rural inhabitants, the books have explored the crafts, cooking, music, gardening and stories that have been passed down through the generations. The focus in this anniversary volume is on devotion to religion, family and the land. Collecting pieces from 40 years' worth of the magazine, the book inevitably covers topics covered in previous Foxfire collections, including snake handling, childhood toys and recipes. But the spoken words remain captivating, eloquent if plainspoken." Publ Wkly

976.1   Alabama

McWhorter, Diane
Carry me home; Birmingham, Alabama: the climactic battle of the civil rights revolution. Simon & Schuster 2001 701p il $35; pa $17
Grades: 11 12 Adult   **976.1**
1. African Americans—Civil rights 2. Birmingham (Ala.)—Race relations
ISBN 0-684-80747-5; 0-7432-1772-1 (pa)
LC 00-53827
McWhorter presents an account of the struggle for civil rights in Birmingham, Ala., both from a personal and societal perspective
"A daughter of Birmingham's privileged elite, McWhorter weaves a personal narrative through this startling account of the history, events, and major players on both sides of the civil rights battle in that city." Booklist
Includes bibliographical references

976.3   Louisiana

Dyson, Michael Eric, 1958-
Come hell or high water; Hurricane Katrina and the color of disaster. Basic Civitas 2006 258p $23
Grades: 11 12 Adult   **976.3**
1. Hurricane Katrina, 2005 2. Disaster relief 3. African Americans—Social conditions
ISBN 0-465-01761-4; 978-0-465-01761-4
LC 2007-310210
This book on Hurrican Katrina "not only chronicles what happened when, it also argues that the nation's failure to offer timely aid to Katrina's victims indicates deeper problems in race and class relations. . . . [The author's] contention that Katrina exposed a dominant culture pervaded not only by 'active malice' toward poor blacks but also by a long history of 'passive indifference' to their problems is both powerful and unsettling." Publ Wkly
Includes bibliographical references

Van Heerden, Ivor Ll., 1950-
The storm; what went wrong and why during Hurricane Katrina; [by] Ivor van Heerden and Mike Bryan. Viking 2006 308p il map $25.95
Grades: 11 12 Adult   **976.3**
1. Hurricane Katrina, 2005 2. Disaster relief
ISBN 0-670-03781-8   LC 2006-44727
This book focuses on public mismanagement relating to Hurricane Katrina.
"This serious, scientific explanation of what exactly happened in the hours—and years—leading up to Hurricane Katrina's devestation of New Orleans brings a fresh perspective to a tragedy that has generated remarkably similar news accounts over the past eight months." Publ Wkly
Includes bibliographical references

976.4   Texas

Roberts, Randy, 1951-
A line in the sand; the Alamo in blood and memory; {by} Randy Roberts, James S. Olson. Free Press 2001 356p il map hardcover o.p. pa $14
Grades: 11 12 Adult   **976.4**
1. Alamo (San Antonio, Tex.) 2. Texas—History
ISBN 0-684-83544-4; 0-743-21233-9 (pa)
LC 00-48421
The Alamo "was attacked by the Mexican Army under Santa Anna in 1836; its defenders, American and Tejano rebels, were quickly overwhelmed. In death, though, they became American folk heroes, symbols of frontier bravery and the unquenchable thirst for liberty. Roberts and Olson do a commendable job of re-creating the murky circumstances of the battle itself, but the real strength of this enjoyable, innovative book lies in its final movement, when the authors turn their attention to cultural criticism." New Yorker
Includes bibliographical references

977.3   Illinois

Murphy, Jim, 1947-
The great fire. Scholastic 1995 144p il maps $16.95
Grades: 5 6 7 8 9 10   **977.3**
1. Fires—Chicago (Ill.)
ISBN 0-590-47267-4   LC 94-9963
Newbery honor book, 1996
"Firsthand descriptions by persons who lived through the 1871 Chicago fire are woven into a gripping account of this famous disaster. Murphy also examines the origins of the fire, the errors of judgment that delayed the effective response, the organizational problems of the city's firefighters, and the postfire efforts to rebuild the city. Newspaper lithographs and a few historical photographs convey the magnitude of human suffering and confusion." Horn Book Guide
Includes bibliographical references

978   Western United States

Ambrose, Stephen E.
Lewis & Clark; voyage of discovery; {photographs by} Sam Abell. National Geographic Soc. 2002 255p il maps $35
Grades: 11 12 Adult   **978**
1. Lewis and Clark Expedition (1804-1806) 2. West (U.S.)—Exploration 3. West (U.S.)—Description and travel
ISBN 0-7922-6473-8   LC 2002-727771
First published 1998
Bicentennial edition
"Ambrose, drawing on his hikes and canoe trips to all the monuments between St. Louis and Fort Clatsop associated with the explorers, melds his memories and own journal entries with a . . . Lewis and Clark narrative spiced by entries from their journals." Booklist
"In addition to the superb writing, the book has stunning, full-color photographs of the places that Lewis and Clark so vividly described. . . . This combination of easy-to-read writing, high-quality photographs, and period artwork makes this book appealing to a wide range of readers." SLJ
Includes bibliographical references

The **American** frontier; James D. Torr, book editor. Greenhaven Press 2002 240p il (Turning points in world history) lib bdg $34.95; pa $23.70
Grades: 7 8 9 10   **978**
1. Frontier and pioneer life—West (U.S.) 2. United States—Territorial expansion 3. West (U.S.)—History
ISBN 0-7377-0786-0 (lib bdg); 0-7377-0785-2 (pa)
LC 2001-33514
This is a collection of essays about the American frontier, with an introduction and summaries
Includes bibliographical references

Duncan, Dayton
Lewis & Clark; the journey of the Corps of Discovery; based on a documentary film by Ken Burns, written by Dayton Duncan; with a preface by Ken Burns and conributions by Stephen E. Ambrose, Erica Funkhouser, William Least Heat-Moon. Knopf 1997 248p il maps $45; pa $25
*
Grades: 11 12 Adult   **978**
1. Lewis and Clark Expedition (1804-1806) 2. West (U.S.)—Exploration
ISBN 0-679-45450-0; 0-375-70652-6 (pa)
LC 97-73823
This is a companion volume to PBS television film 'Lewis and Clark: The journey of the Corps of Discovery,' by Ken Burns
An "attractive book with a well-written text and an excellent presentation of historic paintings, photographs, maps, and original quotations from various of Lewis and Clark's journals." Sci Books Films

Katz, William Loren
Black women of the Old West. Atheneum Bks. for Young Readers 1995 84p il $19.95
Grades: 5 6 7 8 9   **978**
1. African American women 2. Frontier and pioneer life—West (U.S.) 3. West (U.S.)—History
ISBN 0-689-31944-4   LC 95-9969
This work contains "vignettes and photographs of dozens of women, some famous, others unknown outside their own family circles, who lived across the West in the 19th and early 20th centuries." N Y Times Book Rev
"Katz succeeds in establishing that women of color were an important, if unsung, presence on the westward-shifting frontier." Bull Cent Child Books

Lawlor, Laurie
Window on the West; the frontier photography of William Henry Jackson. Holiday House 1999 132p il $18.95
Grades: 7 8 9 10   **978**
1. Jackson, William Henry, 1843-1942 2. West (U.S.)—History
ISBN 0-8234-1380-2   LC 98-56083
Presents the photographs taken by William Henry Jackson from 1869 to 1893, discussing his life and how his work captured and introduced the American West to the public
"Jackson's images are balanced by Lawlor's eloquent text, which folds in details about everything from the wonder of Yellowstone's geysers to the debasement of the Native Americans. . . . A memorable, bittersweet valentine to the Old West." Booklist
Includes glossary and bibliographical references

Lewis, Meriwether, 1774-1809
The essential Lewis and Clark; Landon Y. Jones, editor. Ecco Press 2000 xx, 203p hardcover o.p. pa $13.95 *
Grades: 11 12 Adult   **978**
   1. Lewis and Clark Expedition (1804-1806) 2. West (U.S.)—Exploration
   ISBN 0-06-019600-9; 0-06-001159-9 (pa)
                     LC 99-86335
Excerpts from the 1904-05 version of: Original journals of the Lewis and Clark expedition, 1804-1806; edited by Reuben Gold Thwaites
In this volume the editor presents excerpts from the journals of Lewis and Clark "that focus on the seminal junctures of the journey, including their reactions to the breathtaking physical majesty of the West, their initial encounters with various Native American tribes, and their fascinating accounts of the physical and moral courage of their fellow travelers." Booklist

Luchetti, Cathy, 1945-
Children of the West; family life on the frontier. Norton 2001 253p il $39.95 *
Grades: 11 12 Adult   **978**
   1. Children—West (U.S.) 2. Frontier and pioneer life—West (U.S.) 3. West (U.S.)—Social life and customs
   ISBN 0-393-04913-2   LC 00-53287
"In the nineteenth and early twentieth centuries, the children who resided in the sparsely populated plains and prairies of the western U.S. were subject to a unique variety of hardships and joys. . . . Utilizing more than 100 vintage photographs and excerpts from letters, diaries, and journals, Luchetti examines aspects of childbearing, child rearing, childhood, and adolescence on the American frontier." Booklist
Includes bibliographical references

MacGregor, Greg, 1941-
Lewis and Clark revisited; a photographer's trail; Iris Tillman Hill, editor. Center for Documentary Studies in association with the University of Washington Press 2003 199p il map $50; pa $29.95
Grades: 9 10 11 12   **978**
   1. Lewis and Clark Expedition (1804-1806) 2. West (U.S.)—Description and travel
   ISBN 0-295-98342-6; 0-295-98343-4 (pa)
                    LC 2003-53110
"A Lyndhurst book published by the Center for Documentary Studies in association with the University of Washington Press"
This is a photo "album of nearly 100 black-and-white images, which set forth places along . . . {Lewis and Clark's} 1804-06 route as they appear today. Although generally not a pretty sight, with dams, power plants, and grain elevators having supplanted waterfalls, campfires, and wildlife, there yet remain refuges of original scenery whose beauty so transported Lewis and which MacGregor ably arrests in an ethereal timelessness." Booklist

Peavy, Linda Sellers, 1943-
Frontier children; {by} Linda Peavy & Ursula Smith; foreword by Elliott West. University of Okla. Press 1999 164p il $24.95 *
Grades: 11 12 Adult   **978**
   1. Children—West (U.S.) 2. Frontier and pioneer life—West (U.S.) 3. West (U.S.)—History
   ISBN 0-8061-3161-6   LC 99-18932
The authors aim "to reconstruct stories of children on the frontier from later-life memories and from oral history transcripts. . . . Excellent use is made of photographic evidence, which is quite extensive." Booklist
Includes bibliographical references

Pendergast, Tom, 1964-
Westward expansion: almanac; {by} Tom Pendergast and Sara Pendergast; Christine Slovey, editor. U.X.L 2000 xlvi, 254p il $60 *
Grades: 9 10 11 12   **978**
   1. Frontier and pioneer life—West (U.S.) 2. West (U.S.)—History
   ISBN 0-7876-4862-0   LC 00-36375
This almanac "documents the chronological events that created a romantic national mythology around the pioneers who blazed trails through the wilderness." Publisher's note
Includes bibliographical references

Westward expansion: primary sources; {by} Tom Pendergast and Sara Pendergast; Christine Slovey, editor. U.X.L 2001 xxix, 260p $60 *
Grades: 7 8 9 10   **978**
   1. United States—Territorial expansion 2. West (U.S.)—History
   ISBN 0-7876-4864-7   LC 00-107861
This volume provides "full text or excerpts from diaries, books, letters and many other documents." Publisher's note
Includes bibliographical references

Quay, Sara E.
Westward expansion. Greenwood Press 2002 xx, 301p il (American popular culture through history) $49.95
Grades: 11 12 Adult   **978**
   1. Frontier and pioneer life—West (U.S.) 2. West (U.S.)—History 3. Popular culture—United States
   ISBN 0-313-31235-4   LC 2001-54546
"This volume covers U.S. frontier culture from the Gold Rush to the close of the 19th century and discusses how myths and images of the Wild West have influenced 20th- and 21st-century popular culture." SLJ
"This excellent title belongs on the reference shelves, and all staff members who assist with student research should be aware of and familiar with it." Voice Youth Advocates
Includes bibliographical references

Schlissel, Lillian

Women's diaries of the westward journey; [collected by] Lillian Schlissel; foreword by Mary Clearman Blew. Schocken Books 2004 278p il pa $14.95 *

Grades: 9 10 11 12   **978**

1. Overland journeys to the Pacific 2. Frontier and pioneer life—West (U.S.) 3. West (U.S.)—Description and travel 4. Women—Social conditions

ISBN 0-8052-1176-4   LC 2004-556208

First published 1982

This account of the experiences, attitudes and perceptions of some hundred women who migrated West is based on their reminiscences, diaries, and letters. The book concerns their daily lives as they travelled the Overland Trail from the midwest to California or Oregon between 1840 and 1870.

Includes bibliographical references

Tunis, Edwin, 1897-1973

Frontier living; written and illustrated by Edwin Tunis. Lyons Press 2000 165p il, maps pa $18.95 *

Grades: 5 6 7 8 9 10   **978**

1. Frontier and pioneer life—West (U.S.) 2. West (U.S.)—History

ISBN 1-585-74137-X   LC 00-710694

Companion volume to Colonial living (1976)

First published 1961 by World Publishing Company

On cover: An illustrated guide to pioneer life in America, including log cabins, furniture, tools, clothing, and more

This volume "portrays the manners and customs of the frontiersman and his family from the beginning of the westward movement through the 19th century in . . . text and more than 200 drawings." Wis Libr Bull

Westward expansion; James D. Torr, book editor. Greenhaven Press 2003 208p map (Interpreting primary documents) $33.70; pa $22.45 *

Grades: 7 8 9 10   **978**

1. Frontier and pioneer life—West (U.S.) 2. West (U.S.)—History

ISBN 0-7377-1134-5; 0-7377-1133-7 (pa)

      LC 2002-499

Contents: The lure of the west; Conquest of native America; Manifest Destiny; The Western railroads

Uses primary source materials, including letters and magazine articles of the time, to examine the exploration and conquest of the American West by explorers and settlers of European descent.

"Students will welcome the summary provided at the beginning of each document and the questions for consideration. A good choice for those who are eager to understand arguments and attitudes that shaped the history of the West." SLJ

Includes bibliographical references

978.03   Western United States-- Encyclopedias and dictionaries

Encyclopedia of the Great Plains; David J. Wishart, editor. University of Nebraska Press 2004 919p il map $75

Grades: 11 12 Adult   **978.03**

1. Great Plains—Encyclopedias

ISBN 0-8032-4787-7   LC 2003-21037

The author "presents 1,316 signed entries, written by some 1000 scholars and divided according to 27 topics that range from the Paleo-Indians to the 2000 census. The contents of each topic are outlined with an introductory essay, followed by specific articles arranged alphabetically within the topic. Historical figures are listed under their common names rather than their formal names." Libr J

"Here is a unique reference book that cuts a broad swath through parts of the U.S. and Canada, the region known as the heartland. The book's topical arrangement perfectly suits the cross-boundary approach." Booklist

The **New** encyclopedia of the American West; edited by Howard R. Lamar. Yale Univ. Press 1998 1324p il maps $60 *

Grades: 11 12 Adult   **978.03**

1. Frontier and pioneer life—West (U.S.)—Encyclopedias

ISBN 0-300-07088-8   LC 98-6231

First published 1977 by Crowell with title: The Reader's encyclopedia of the American West

This reference work covers "the history, geography, culture, literature, art, and natural history of both the real and the imaginary West. . . . {Coverage spans} prehistory to the present, and . . . {includes} events in the history of the trans-Mississippi West . . . {as well as} the frontier or 'western' stage of all 50 American states. Entries range from important events in the expansion of the U.S. . . . to the first European and American discoverers, among them Coronado, LaSalle, and Lewis and Clark." Publisher's note

Includes bibliographical references

978.1   Kansas

Stratton, Joanna L.

Pioneer women; voices from the Kansas frontier; introduction by Arthur M. Schlesinger, Jr. Simon & Schuster 1981 319p il $15 hardcover o.p.

Grades: 11 12 Adult   **978.1**

1. Women—Kansas 2. Frontier and pioneer life—Kansas 3. Kansas—History

ISBN 0-671-44748-3 (pa)   LC 80-15960

"A unique book based on the memoirs of nearly 800 pioneer women who lived in Kansas between 1854 and 1890. . . . The book presents personal and detailed accounts of life inside homes, the schools, and the social organizations of early Kansas." Choice

Includes bibliographical references

978.7   Wyoming

Meyer, Judith L., 1956-
The spirit of Yellowstone; the cultural evolution of a national park; photographs by Vance Howard. Roberts Rinehart 2003 145p il pa $19.95
Grades: 11 12 Adult   **978.7**
1. Yellowstone National Park 2. Human influence on nature
ISBN 1-570-98395-X   LC 2002-156320
A reissue of the title first published 1996 by Rowman & Littlefield
Contents: Revolutionary ideas and evolutionary processes; The discovery accounts; Following in the footsteps; The art of the Yellowstone; Experiencing Yellowstone; The idea of the ideal
The author "pays tribute to the park and all its glories, covering the park's history, its prime landmarks, and its prominence in art. The photographs are truly striking and not the typical landscape fare. Howard plays with light and texture to capture images that will amaze even those already familiar with the park's unprecedented beauty." Libr J

978.9   New Mexico

Bryan, Howard
Robbers, rogues, and ruffians; true tales of the Wild West in New Mexico; foreword by Tony Hillerman. Clear Light Pubs. 1991 318p il $22.95; pa $14.95
Grades: 11 12 Adult   **978.9**
1. Frontier and pioneer life—West (U.S.) 2. Thieves
ISBN 0-940666-04-9; 0-940666-23-5 (pa)
                     LC 91-72481
The author "concentrates on some of the lesser-known desperadoes whose colorful stories have rarely been told. The stories center in and around the New Mexico Territory, where the reader meets such interesting characters as Joel Fowler, 'the human exterminator'; Charles Kennedy, proprietor of the Inn of Death; and Bronco Sue, a real 'black widow'; and many others." Booklist

When we were young in the West; true stories of childhood; edited with an introduction and conclusion by Richard Melzer. Sunstone Press 2003 345p il map pa $19.95 *
Grades: 11 12 Adult   **978.9**
1. Children—West (U.S.)
ISBN 0-86534-338-1   LC 2003-42572
Presents biographical sketches of New Mexican children from different cultures, races, and classes who represent the strength and diversity of this state's heritage
"A unique and vastly informative book. . . . The richness of detail tells us as much about the past as it does about childhood." Booklist
Includes bibliographical references

979.1   Arizona

Pyne, Stephen J., 1949-
How the Canyon became Grand; a short history. Viking 1998 199p il maps pa $15 hardcover o.p.
Grades: 11 12 Adult   **979.1**
1. Grand Canyon (Ariz.)
ISBN 0-14-028056-1 (pa)   LC 98-20094
"To understand the canyon as a place and as a perspective, Pyne traces its history from the time of the Spanish conquistadors and later explorers like John Wesley Powell and Clarence Dutton to its status today as a natural wonder attracting more than five million visitors annually. He also explains how our attitude toward the canyon has changed." Libr J
Includes bibliographical references

980   South America. Latin America

Gritzner, Charles F.
Latin America. Chelsea House Publishers 2006 120p il map (Modern world cultures) lib bdg $30
Grades: 7 8 9 10   **980**
1. Latin America
ISBN 0-7910-8142-7; 978-0-7910-8142-6
                     LC 2005-32686
Contents: Introducing our Latin American neighbors — Diverse natural landscapes — Native cultures — European heritage — Population and settlement — Cultural geography — Political geography — Economic geography — Latin America looks ahead
This book "explores the diverse cultural, economic, political, and natural landscapes of this unique region." Publisher's note
Includes bibliographical references

982   Argentina

Parrado, Nando, 1949-
Miracle in the Andes; 72 days on the mountain and my long trek home; [by] Nando Parrado with Vince Rause. Crown Publishers 2006 291p il map $25 *
Grades: 11 12 Adult   **982**
1. Survival after airplane accidents, shipwrecks, etc. 2. Andes
ISBN 1-4000-9767-3; 978-1-4000-9767-8
                     LC 2005-21629
"In October 1972, a plane carrying an Uruguayan rugby team crashed in the Andes. Not immediately rescued, the survivors turned to cannibalism to survive and after 72 days were saved. Rugby team member Parrado has written a beautiful story of friendship, tragedy and perseverance." Publ Wkly

985   Peru

Bingham, Hiram, 1875-1956
Lost city of the Incas; the story of Machu
Picchu and its builders; with an introduction by
Hugh Thomson; photographs by Hugh Thomson.
Sterling 2002 274p il $35; pa $12.95 *
Grades: 11 12 Adult   **985**
1. Machu Picchu (Peru) 2. Peru—Antiquities 3. Incas
ISBN 0-2976-0759-6; 1-84212-585-0 (pa)
                                    LC 2002-483039
A reissue of the title first published 1948 by Duell
"In 1911 Bingham, an American explorer, found the
Inca city of Machu Picchu, which had been lost for 300
years. In this volume he tells of its origin, how it came
to be lost and how it was finally discovered." Libr J
Includes bibliographical references

Hemming, John, 1935-
The conquest of the Incas. Harcourt Brace
Jovanovich 1970 641p il maps pa $25 hardcover
o.p.
Grades: 11 12 Adult   **985**
1. Incas
ISBN 0-15-602826-3 (pa)
"This {study} focuses on relations of Spaniards and
Incas during the Spanish conquest of Peru launched by
Pizarro and partners. Spaniards and Incas speak frequent-
ly in their own words as preserved in Spanish docu-
ments. . . . Inca ways and achievements, the empire's
tragic vulnerability because of rivalrous leaders and civil
war, and conquest aftermath are made sharply manifest."
Booklist
Includes bibliographical references

Malpass, Michael
Daily life in the Inca empire; {by} Michael A.
Malpass. Greenwood Press 1996 xxix, 164p il
(Greenwood Press daily life through history series)
$49.95 *
Grades: 11 12 Adult   **985**
1. Incas
ISBN 0-313-29390-2   LC 95-44699
This book is "about the Inca social structure, religion,
family interaction, agriculture and labor, and the role
conquered people played in their society. Research for
this book is based on Spanish records, letters from clergy
working with the Incas, information passed on by Incas
to the Spaniards, and archaeological research done in
South America." Book Rep
Includes glossary and bibliographical references

Moseley, Michael Edward
The Incas and their ancestors; the archaeology
of Peru; {by} Michael E. Moseley. Thames &
Hudson 1992 272p il maps pa $31.95 hardcover
o.p.
Grades: 11 12 Adult   **985**
1. Incas 2. Peru—Antiquities
ISBN 0-500-28277-3 (pa)   LC 91-65309

This account of Andean prehistory and archaeology
takes us from the first settlement of 10,000 years ago to
the Spanish conquest
"Clearly presented, with a generous ration of maps
and illustrations, {the volume} is thoughtful and welcome." Times Lit Suppl

Somervill, Barbara A., 1948-
Empire of the Inca. Facts on File 2005 c2004
128p il map (Great empires of the past) $35 *
Grades: 9 10 11 12   **985**
1. Incas
ISBN 0-8160-5560-2   LC 2004-3952
Contents: The beginning of the empire -- The empire
at its greatest -- The final years of Inca rule -- Inca society -- Living among the Incas -- Inca art, science, and
culture
"This offers a fine starting point for students researching Incan civilization." Booklist
Includes bibliographical references

996   Polynesia and Micronesia

Alexander, Caroline, 1956-
The Bounty: the true story of the mutiny on the
Bounty. Viking 2003 491p il $27.95
Grades: 11 12 Adult   **996**
1. Bligh, William, 1754-1817 2. Christian, Fletcher,
1764-1793 3. Bounty (Ship) 4. Oceania
ISBN 0-670-03133-X   LC 2003-50158
Alexander reexamines the story of the 1789 mutiny on
the Bounty during a voyage in the South Pacific. She explores "the Royal Navy's efforts to bring the mutineers
who did not escape to Pitcairn [Island with Fletcher
Christian] to justice, a proceeding complicated by the political, legal and social influence exerted to defend Christian's reputation in absentia and that of one of his well-
born colleagues in mutiny. This was Peter Heywood." N
Y Times Book Rev
"A rollicking sea adventure told with enormous confidence and style." Booklist
Includes bibliographical references

Souhami, Diana
Selkirk's Island; the true and strange adventures
of the real Robinson Crusoe. Harcourt 2002 c2001
246p $24; pa $13
Grades: 11 12 Adult   **996**
1. Selkirk, Alexander, 1676-1721 2. Defoe, Daniel,
1661?-1731. Robinson Crusoe 3. Survival after airplane accidents, shipwrecks, etc. 4. Islands of the Pacific
ISBN 0-15-100526-5; 0-15-602717-8 (pa)
                                       LC 01-24979
First published 2001 in the United Kingdom
"Daniel Defoe based his 1719 novel *Robinson Crusoe*
on the trials and tribulations of Scottish seaman Alexander Selkirk. Souhami . . . draws on journals, maritime
histories and ship and parish records to detail his . . .
[story]. Complete with detailed comparisons between Defoe's novel and Selkirk's life, Souhami's account is a
well-researched investigation of a forgotten anti-hero."
Publ Wkly
Includes bibliographical references

998   Arctic islands and Antarctica

Alexander, Caroline, 1956-
The Endurance; Shackleton's legendary Antarctic expedition. Knopf 1998 211p il $29.95
Grades: 11 12 Adult   **998**
   1. Shackleton, Sir Ernest Henry, 1874-1922 2. Endurance (Ship) 3. Imperial Trans-Antarctic Expedition (1914-1917) 4. Antarctica—Exploration
   ISBN 0-375-40403-1
Published in association with the American Museum of Natural History
In 1914, Sir Ernest Shackleton "sailed to Antarctica with 27 men in hopes of being the first human to transverse the continent. But his ship, the *Endurance,* was trapped, then crushed, by ice in the Weddell Sea, propelling the party into a nightmare of cold and near starvation. Alexander, relying extensively on journals by crew members, some never published, as well as on myriad other sources, delivers a spellbinding story of human courage. . . . What makes this book especially exciting, however, are the 170 previously unpublished photos by the expedition's photographer, Frank Hurley." Publ Wkly

Antarctica: an encyclopedia from Abbott Ice Shelf to zooplankton; edited by Mary Trewby. Firefly Bks. 2002 208p il maps $35 *
Grades: 11 12 Adult   **998**
   1. Antarctica—Encyclopedias
   ISBN 1-55297-590-8   LC 2002-514992
This "guide to Antarctica features a true encyclopedia layout, with over 1000 concise, alphabetically arranged entries and 250 photographs that cover natural history, climate, geology, tourism, and more. . . . The entries in this book are easily accessible and particularly useful for quick reference." Libr J

Bryant, John H.
Dangerous crossings; the first modern polar expedition, 1925; [by] John H. Bryant and Harold N. Cones. Naval Inst. Press 2000 206p il maps $28.95
Grades: 9 10 11 12   **998**
   1. MacMillan, Donald, 1874-1970 2. McDonald, Eugene F., 1890-1958 3. Byrd, Richard Evelyn, 1888-1957 4. Arctic regions—Exploration
   ISBN 1-55750-187-4   LC 00-26344
This book recounts the expedition mounted by Donald B. MacMillan, a colleague of Robert Peary's, Eugene F. McDonald, founder of the Zenith Corporation; and Richard E. Byrd, a young naval aviator
"Perfect Storm-like moments, a lack of supplies, some conflict with Danish officials in Greenland, nascent corporate development and the extraordinary bravery of the personnel involved make this an unusually rich exploration narrative." Publ Wkly
Includes bibliographical references

Gurney, Alan
The race to the white continent; voyages to the Antarctic. Norton 2000 320p il maps hardcover o.p. pa $15.95
Grades: 11 12 Adult   **998**
   1. Antarctica—Exploration
   ISBN 0-393-05004-1; 0-393-32321-8 (pa)
                          LC 00-38673
This is an account "of the expeditions that paved the way for the race to the South Pole. All took place in the late 1830s and early 1840s. . . . One was French, another English, and the third was American. Their leaders were, respectively, Jules Sébastien César Dumont d'Urville, James Clark Ross and Charles Wilkes. They were all naval officers, sent out by their governments." Publ Wkly
Includes bibliographical references

Solomon, Susan, 1956-
The coldest March. Yale Univ. Press 2001 xxii, 383p il maps $29.95; pa $16.95
Grades: 11 12 Adult   **998**
   1. Scott, Robert Falcon, 1868-1912 2. British Antarctic ("Terra Nova") Expedition (1910-1913) 3. Antarctica—Exploration 4. South Pole
   ISBN 0-300-08967-8; 0-300-09921-5 (pa)
                          LC 00-54996
"In November 1911, Capt. Robert Falcon Scott and his British team set out to be the first to reach the South Pole. Battling the brutal weather of Antarctica, they reached the pole in January 1912 only to discover that a Norwegian team had beat them there by nearly a month. On their return from the Pole, Scott and four of his companions died in harsh conditions. Ever since, history has not known whether to label them heroes or bunglers. Solomon . . . analyzes all the factors present during Scott's expedition in an attempt to explain that his failure was due not to incompetence but to a combination of unpredictable weather, erroneous choices and bad luck." Libr J
Includes bibliographical references

Fic   FICTION

A number of subject headings have been added to the books in this section to aid in curriculum work. It is not necessarily recommended that these subjects be used in the library catalog.

Abdel-Fattah, Randa
Does my head look big in this? [by] Randa Abdel-Fattah. 1st ed. Orchard Books 2007 360p $16.99 *
Grades: 7 8 9 10 11 12   **Fic**
   1. Muslims—Fiction 2. Clothing and dress—Fiction 3. School stories 4. Australia—Fiction
   ISBN 978-0-439-91947-0; 0-439-91947-9
                       LC 2006029117
Year Eleven at an exclusive prep school in the suburbs of Melbourne, Australia, would be tough enough, but it is further complicated for Amal when she decides to wear the hijab, the Muslim head scarf, full-time as a badge of her faith – without losing her identity or sense

Abdel-Fattah, Randa—*Continued*
of style.

"While the novel deals with a number of serious issues, it is extremely funny and entertaining." SLJ

Abrahams, Peter, 1947-
Down the rabbit hole; an Echo Falls mystery. Laura Geringer Books 2005 375p $15.99; lib bdg $16.89; pa $6.99
Grades: 7 8 9 10   **Fic**
1. Mystery fiction
ISBN 0-06-073701-8; 0-06-073702-6 (lib bdg); 0-06-073703-4 (pa)   LC 2004-14778
Also available audiobook edition

"Ingrid Levin-Hill . . . has just been cast as the lead in Alice in Wonderland when she finds herself in a different role - murder detective. The corpse is that of 'Cracked-Up Katie,' whom Ingrid encountered when she attempted to get from her orthodontist to soccer practice." Publ Wkly

Ingrid "and the other main characters are all solidly drawn. . . . Deft use of literary allusions and ironic humor add further touches of class to a topnotch mystery." SLJ

Another title about Ingrid Levin-Hill is:
Behind the curtain (2006)

Abu-Jaber, Diana
Crescent. Norton 2003 349p hardcover o.p. pa $13.95 *
Grades: 11 12 Adult   **Fic**
1. Arab American women—Fiction
ISBN 0-393-05747-X; 0-393-32554-7 (pa)
LC 2002-152907

"Sirine's now-deceased missionary parents were Iraqi and American; she's been raised since she was nine by her beloved Iraqi uncle. Her world is his house, the café where she is chef, and the air of Los Angeles. She's nearly 40, and inside her pale skin and green eyes she feels the rhythms of her uncle's Arabic stories and the scent of Eastern spices. Hanif ('Han'), a professor of Arabic literature at the local university comes to the café for the tastes of home, and he and Sirine fall into an affair of wild, sweet tenderness. . . . Abu-Jaber's language is miraculous, whether describing the texture of Han's skin or Sirine's way with an onion. It is not possible to stop reading." Booklist

Acampora, Paul
Defining Dulcie. Dial Books 2006 168p $16.99
Grades: 7 8 9 10   **Fic**
1. Bereavement—Fiction 2. Runaway teenagers—Fiction
ISBN 0-8037-3046-2; 978-0-8037-3046-5
LC 2005-16186

When sixteen-year-old Dulcie's father dies, her mother makes a decision to move them to California, where Dulcie makes an equally radical decision to steal her dad's old truck and head back home.

"Strong and quirky characters who see life as an inextricable mix of sadness and humor, sorrow and hope, are the hallmark of this memorable first novel." SLJ

Achebe, Chinua, 1930-
Things fall apart; with an introduction by Kwame Anthony Appiah. Knopf 1995 xxi, 181p $15 *
Grades: 11 12 Adult   **Fic**
1. Igbo (African people)—Fiction 2. Nigeria—Fiction
ISBN 0-679-44623-0   LC 94-13429
Also available from McGraw-Hill College
"Everyman's library"

A reissue of the title first published 1958 in the United Kingdom and 1959 in the United States by McDowell, Obolensky

"The novel chronicles the life of Okonkwo, the leader of an Igbo (Ibo) community, from the events leading up to his banishment from the community for accidentally killing a clansman, through the seven years of his exile, to his return. The novel addresses the problem of the intrusion in the 1890s of white missionaries and colonial government into tribal Igbo society. It describes the simultaneous disintegration of its protaganist Okonkwo and of his village. The novel was praised for its intelligent and realistic treatment of tribal beliefs and of psychological disintegration coincident with social unraveling." Merriam-Webster's Ency of Lit

Adams, Douglas, 1952-2001
The hitchhiker's guide to the galaxy. 25th anniversary illustrated collector's ed. Harmony Books 2004 271p il $35 *
Grades: 7 8 9 10 11 12 Adult   **Fic**
1. Science fiction
ISBN 1-4000-5293-9   LC 2004-558987
Also available in paperback from Ballantine Bks.
First published 1980

"Based on a BBC radio series, . . . this is the episodic story of Arthur Dent, a contemporary Englishman who discovers first that his unpretentious house is about to be demolished to make way for a bypass, and second that a good friend is actually an alien galactic hitchhiker who announces that Earth itself will soon be demolished to make way for an intergalactic speedway. A suitably bewildered Dent soon finds himself hitching . . . rides throughout space, aided by a . . . reference book, The Hitchhiker's Guide to the Galaxy, a compendium of 'facts,' philosophies, and wild advice." Libr J

Other titles featuring Arthur Dent are:
Life, the universe and everything (1982)
Mostly harmless (1992)
The restaurant at the end of the universe (1981)
So long, and thanks for all the f ish (1984)

Adams, Richard, 1920-
Watership Down. Scribner classics ed. Scribner 1996 c1972 429p $30; pa $15
Grades: 6 7 8 9   **Fic**
1. Rabbits—Fiction 2. Allegories
ISBN 0-684-83605-X; 0-7432-7770-8 (pa)
First published 1972 in the United Kingdom; first United States edition 1974 by Macmillan

"Faced with the annihilation of its warren, a small group of male rabbits sets out across the English downs in search of a new home. Internal struggles for power surface in this intricately woven, realistically told adult

Adams, Richard, 1920-—_Continued_
adventure when the protagonists must coordinate tactics
in order to defeat an enemy rabbit fortress. It is clear that
the author has done research on rabbit behavior, for this
tale is truly authentic." Shapiro Fic for Youth. 3d edition

Adichie, Chimamanda Ngozi, 1977-
Purple hibiscus. Algonquin Bks. 2003 320p
$23.95 *
Grades: 11 12 Adult   **Fic**
1. Family life—Fiction 2. Nigeria—Fiction
ISBN 1-565-12387-5   LC 2003-51894
Also available in paperback from Anchor Bks.
"Fifteen-year-old Kambili lives comfortably with her
parents and older brother, Jaja, in Enugu, Nigeria. Respected and generous with his money, her fanatically religious father is nevertheless cruel when his wife and
children do not live up to his lofty expectations. When
Kambili and Jaja visit their widowed aunt Ifeoma in the
impoverished countryside, they endure many privations
but finally enjoy the pleasures of a warm and loving
family." Libr J
"Quiet, chilling, and heart wrenching, this debut novel
is both a superb portrait of an unfamiliar culture and an
unflinching depiction of the universal turmoil of adolescence." Voice Youth Advocates

Adlington, L. J., 1970-
The diary of Pelly D. Greenwillow Books 2005
282p $15; lib bdg $16.89
Grades: 7 8 9 10   **Fic**
1. Science fiction
ISBN 0-06-076615-8; 0-06-076616-6 (lib bdg)
                              LC 2004-52258
When Toni V, a construction worker on a futuristic
colony, finds the diary of a teenage girl whose life has
been turned upside-down by holocaust-like events, he begins to question his own beliefs.
"Adlington has crafted an original and disturbing
dystopian fantasy told in a smart and sympathetic teen
voice." Booklist

Adoff, Jaime
Names will never hurt me. Dutton Children's
Books 2004 186p $16.99
Grades: 9 10 11 12   **Fic**
1. School stories 2. School violence—Fiction
ISBN 0-525-47175-8   LC 2003-49271
Several high school students relate their feelings about
school, themselves, and events as they unfold on the
fateful one-year anniversary of the killing of a fellow
student
"This is high school at its most painful, seen through
the eyes of the kids living it—the jocks, the misfits, the
freaks, the truly miserable. . . . Adoff creates palpable
tension as he explores each character's state of mind
through the physical and emotional pain of being ignored, rejected, or terrorized. . . . This is a powerful,
complex, skillfully written novel that even the most reluctant reader will find accessible." Booklist

Agee, James, 1909-1955
A death in the family. Vintage Books 1998
310p il pa $13.95
Grades: 9 10 11 12   **Fic**
1. Family life—Fiction 2. Death—Fiction
3. Tennessee—Fiction
ISBN 0-375-70123-0   LC 99-164384
First published 1957 by McDowell, Obolensky
"Six-year-old Rufus Follet, his younger sister Catherine, his mother, and various relatives all react differently
to the unexpected announcement that Rufus's father has
been fatally injured in an automobile accident. The poignancy of sorrow, the strength of personal beliefs, and
the comforting love and support of a family are all elements of this compassionate novel." Shapiro. Fic for
Youth. 3d edition

Aidinoff, Elsie V.
The garden. Harper Tempest 2004 403p $16.99;
lib bdg $17.89
Grades: 9 10 11 12   **Fic**
1. Eve (Biblical figure)—Fiction 2. Adam (Biblical
figure)—Fiction
ISBN 0-06-055605-6; 0-06-055606-4 (lib bdg)
                              LC 2003-15841
Retells the tale of the Garden of Eden fron Eve's
point of view, as Serpent teaches her everthing from her
own name to why she should eat the forbidden fruit, and
then leaves her with Adam and the knowledge that her
choice has made mankind free
"There's no doubt this book will upset some people,
both in its depiction of God and because of its sexual
scenes, which, though not salacious, are intense and uncompromising. . . . Some readers, however, will find the
book liberating—a meditation on the role of humanity in
the world and on the compromises people make when
they choose freedom instead of obedience." Booklist

Alder, Elizabeth
The king's shadow. Bantam Doubleday Dell
Books for Young Readers 1997 259p pa $6.50
Grades: 9 10 11 12   **Fic**
1. Harold, King of England, 1022?-1066—Fiction
2. Orphans—Fiction 3. Great Britain—History—0-
1066—Fiction
ISBN 0-440-22011-4
A reissue of the title first published 1995 by Farrar,
Straus & Giroux
After he is orphaned and has his tongue cut out in a
clash with the bullying sons of a Welsh noble, Evyn is
sold as a slave and serves many masters, from the gra-
cious Lady Swan Neck to the valiant Harold Godwinson,
England's last Saxon king
"Readers will get their history almost without noticing
it, but will come to understand the complex society and
world within which these individuals functioned easily.
Evyn is easy to identify with as both a victim and an
outcast." Voice Youth Advocates

Alegría, Malín
Estrella's quinceañera. Simon & Schuster Books
for Young Readers 2006 260p $14.95
Grades: 7 8 9 10   **Fic**

Alegría, Malín—*Continued*
1. Mexican Americans—Fiction 2. Quinceañera (Social custom)—Fiction
ISBN 0-689-87809-5
Estrella's mother and aunt are planning a gaudy, traditional quinceañera for her, even though it is the last thing she wants.
"Alegria writes about Mexican American culture, first love, family, and of moving between worlds with poignant, sharp-sighted humor and authentic dialogue." Booklist

Ali, Thalassa
A singular hostage. Bantam Bks. 2002 352p il pa $13.95
Grades: 9 10 11 12   **Fic**
1. India—Fiction
ISBN 0-553-38176-8   LC 2001-56591
"Sent to relatives in India in 1838 to find a husband among the eligible suitors in the British officer corps . . . [Mariana] is allowed a Muslim *munshi*, or teacher. An eager, apt pupil of Hindustani language and culture, [she] becomes a translator for the straitlaced sisters of the Governor-General of India and travels with his entourage to Punjab. . . . When a charismatic boy held hostage by the ailing Maharaja, who believes the child has curative powers, disappears, his rescuers are led to Mariana, who agrees to hide him. The rest of her adventure . . . centers on Saboor, her determination to return him to his father, and the lengths to which she will go to protect this child. . . . By contrasting the British view of Indian culture and its people with the view of Punjabis themselves, rich and poor, this mesmerizing tale helps readers better understand a vitally important area of the world." SLJ

Allende, Isabel
Daughter of fortune; a novel; translated from the Spanish by Margaret Sayers Peden. HarperCollins Pubs. 1999 399p hardcover o.p. pa $7.99
Grades: 11 12 Adult   **Fic**
1. Adventure fiction 2. California—Gold discoveries—Fiction
ISBN 0-06-019491-X; 0-380-82101-X (pa)
                                        LC 99-26021
Original Spanish edition, 1999
A "historical novel flavored by four cultures—English, Chilean, Chinese and American—and set during the 1849 California Gold Rush. The . . . tale begins in Valparaiso, Chile, with young Eliza Sommers, who was left as a baby on the doorstep of wealthy British importers Miss Rose Sommers and her prim brother, Jeremy. Now a 16 year-old, and newly pregnant, Eliza decides to follow her lover, fiery clerk Joaquin Andieta, when he leaves for California to make his fortune in the gold rush. Enlisting the unlikely aid of Tao Chi'en, a Chinese shipboard cook, she stows away on a ship bound for San Francisco." Publ Wkly
"This novel has pretensions, but they are overridden by Allende's riproaring girl's adventure story. . . . Throughout it all, Allende projects a woman's point of view with confidence, control and an expansive definition of romance as a fact of life." Time

Eva Luna; translated by Margaret Sayers Peden. Knopf 1988 271p hardcover o.p. pa $14 *
Grades: 11 12 Adult   **Fic**
1. Latin America—Fiction
ISBN 0-394-57273-4; 0-553-38382-5 (pa)
                                        LC 88-45272
Original Spanish edition, 1987
This novel "gives us successive episodes in Eva's life, from illegitimate birth and orphanhood through drifting adolescence to relative stability and success, but also recounts in parallel the biography of Rolf Carle, from his wartime childhood in Austria to his emigration to Latin America, subsequent fame as a controversial documentary film-maker, and finally his encounter and love affair with Eva herself. A third narrative strand deals with the fortunes of Huberto Naranjo . . . guerrilla fighter and [Eva's] transient lover." Times Lit Suppl
This "wonderful novel, crammed with the strange and fantastical, the sensuous and the erotic, also speaks powerfully in the cause of freedom." Publ Wkly

Zorro; a novel; translated from the Spanish by Margaret Sayers Peden. HarperCollins Publishers 2005 390p maps $25.95; pa $14.95
Grades: 11 12 Adult   **Fic**
1. California—Fiction 2. Adventure fiction
ISBN 0-06-077897-0; 0-06-077900-4 (pa)
                                        LC 2005-46389
This "novel reimagines the legend of Zorro." N Y Times Book Rev
"Allende's lively retelling of the Zorro legend reads as effortlessly as the hero himself might slice his trademark 'Z' on the wall with a flash of his sword." Publ Wkly

Allison, Dorothy, 1949-
Bastard out of Carolina. Dutton 1992 309p hardcover o.p. pa $16
Grades: 11 12 Adult   **Fic**
1. Child abuse—Fiction 2. South Carolina—Fiction
ISBN 0-525-93425-1; 0-452-28705-7 (pa)
                                        LC 91-34607
"Set in the rural South, this tale centers around the Boatwright family, a proud and closeknit clan known for their drinking, fighting, and womanizing. Nicknamed Bone by her Uncle Earle, Ruth Anne is the bastard child of Anney Boatwright, who has fought tirelessly to legitimize her child. When she marries Glen, a man from a good family, it appears that her prayers have been answered. However, Anney suffers a miscarriage and Glen begins drifting. He develops a contentious relationship with Bone and then begins taking sexual liberties with her. . . . Unaware of her husband's abusive behavior, Anney stands by her man. Eventually, a violent encounter wrests Bone away from her stepfather." Libr J

Almond, David, 1951-
Clay. Delacorte Press 2006 247p $15.95; lib bdg $17.99 *
Grades: 7 8 9 10   **Fic**
1. Supernatural—Fiction 2. Horror fiction
ISBN 0-385-73171-X; 0-385-90208-5 (lib bdg)
                                        LC 2005-22681

Almond, David, 1951-—_Continued_

The developing relationship between teenager Davie and a mysterious new boy in town morphs into something darker and more sinister when Davie learns firsthand of the boy's supernatural powers.

"Rooted in the ordinariness of a community and in one boy's chance to play God, this story will grab readers with its gripping action and its important ideas." Booklist

Kit's wilderness. Delacorte Press 1999 229p $15.95; pa $5.99 *

Grades: 5 6 7 8 9   **Fic**

1. Coal mines and mining—Fiction 2. Ghost stories 3. Great Britain—Fiction

ISBN 0-385-32665-3; 0-440-41605-1 (pa)

LC 99-34332

Thirteen-year-old Kit goes to live with his grandfather in the decaying coal mining town of Stoneygate, England, and finds both the old man and the town haunted by ghosts of the past

The author "explores the power of friendship and family, the importance of memory, and the role of magic in our lives. This is a highly satisfying literary experience." SLJ

Skellig. Delacorte Press 1999 c1998 182p $16.95; pa $6.50

Grades: 5 6 7 8 9 10   **Fic**

1. Fantasy fiction

ISBN 0-385-32653-X; 0-440-41602-7 (pa)

LC 98-23121

First published 1998 in the United Kingdom

Unhappy about his baby sister's illness and the chaos of moving into a dilapidated old house, Michael retreats to the garage and finds a mysterious stranger who is something like a bird and something like an angel.

"The plot is beautifully paced and the characters are drawn with a graceful, careful hand. . . . A lovingly done, thought-provoking novel." SLJ

Alvarez, Julia, 1950-

Finding miracles; Julia Alvarez. Knopf 2004 264p $15.95; lib bdg $17.99

Grades: 9 10 11 12   **Fic**

1. Adoption—Fiction 2. School stories

ISBN 0-375-82760-9; 0-375-92760-3 (lib bdg)

LC 2003-25127

Fifteen-year-old Milly Kaufman is an average American teenager until Pablo, a new student at her school, inspires her to search for her birth family in his native country

"Complex multicultural characters and skillful depiction of Latino culture raises this well-written, readable novel, which is a school story, a family story, and a love story, to far above average." Voice Youth Advocates

How the García girls lost their accents. Algonquin Bks. 1991 290p $18.95 *

Grades: 11 12 Adult   **Fic**

1. Dominican Americans—Fiction

ISBN 0-945575-57-2   LC 90-48575

Also available in paperback from Plume Bks.

This novel "tells the story (in reverse chronological order) of four sisters and their family, as they become Americanized after fleeing the Dominican Republic in the 1960s. A family of privilege in the police state they leave, the Garcias experience understandable readjustment problems in the United States, particularly old world patriarch Papi. The sisters fare better but grow up conscious, like all immigrants, of living in two worlds." Libr J

"This is an account of parallel odysseys, as each of the four daughters adapts in her own way, and a large part of Alvarez's accomplishment is the complexity with which these vivid characters are rendered." Publ Wkly

Anaya, Rudolfo A.

Bless me, Ultima. Warner Bks. 1994 c1972 277p il pa $6.99 *

Grades: 9 10 11 12   **Fic**

1. Mexican Americans—Fiction

ISBN 0-446-51783-6   LC 93-30477

A reissue of the title first published 1972

A novel set in southeastern New Mexico in the 1940s. Antonio, a seven-year-old Chicano boy, learns about life, nature and death through his relationship with Ultima, an aging healer

Anderson, Laurie Halse, 1961-

Prom; Laurie Halse Anderson. Viking 2005 215p $16.99; pa $8.99

Grades: 9 10 11 12   **Fic**

1. School stories 2. Pennsylvania—Fiction

ISBN 0-670-05974-9; 0-14-240570-1 (pa)

LC 2004-14974

Eighteen-year-old Ash wants nothing to do with senior prom, but when disaster strikes and her desperate friend, Nat, needs her help to get it back on track, Ash's involvement transforms her life

"Whether or not readers have been infected by prom fever themselves, they will be enraptured and amused by Ashley's attitude-altering, life-changing commitment to a cause." Publ Wkly

Speak. Farrar, Straus & Giroux 1999 197p $16 *

Grades: 7 8 9 10   **Fic**

1. Rape—Fiction 2. School stories

ISBN 0-374-37152-0   LC 98-31933

Also available in paperback from Puffin Bks.

"Having broken up an end-of-summer party by calling the police, high school freshman Melinda Sordino begins the school year as a social outcast. She's the only person who knows the real reason behind her call: she was raped at the party by Andy Evans, a popular senior at her school." Booklist

The novel is "keenly aware of the corrosive details of outsiderhood and the gap between home and daily life at high school; kids whose exclusion may have less concrete cause than Melinda's will nonetheless find the picture recognizable. This is a gripping account of personal wounding and recovery." Bull Cent Child Books

Anderson, Laurie Halse, 1961——*Continued*
Twisted. Viking 2007 250p $16.99
Grades: 9 10 11 12   **Fic**
1. Family life—Fiction 2. School stories 3. Ohio—Fiction
ISBN 978-0-670-06101-3   LC 2006-31297
After finally getting noticed by someone other than school bullies and his ever-angry father, seventeen-year-old Tyler enjoys his tough new reputation and the attentions of a popular girl, but when life starts to go bad again, he must choose between transforming himself or giving in to his destructive thoughts.
"This is a gripping exploration of what it takes to grow up, really grow up, against the wishes of people and circumstances conspiring to keep you the victim they need you to be." Bull Cent Child Books

Anderson, M. T., 1968-
Feed. Candlewick Press 2002 237p $16.99; pa $7.99 *
Grades: 9 10 11 12   **Fic**
1. Science fiction 2. Satire
ISBN 0-7636-1726-1; 0-7636-2259-1 (pa)
                                            LC 2002-23738
In a future where most people have computer implants in their heads to control their environment, a boy meets an unusual girl who is in serious trouble
"An ingenious satire of corporate America and our present-day value system." Horn Book Guide

The Pox party; taken from accounts by [Octavius Nothing's] own hand and other sundry sources; collected by Mr. M.T. Anderson of Boston. Candlewick Press 2006 351p (The astonishing life of Octavian Nothing, traitor to the nation) $17.99 *
Grades: 9 10 11 12   **Fic**
1. Slavery—Fiction 2. African Americans—Fiction 3. United States—History—1775-1783, Revolution—Fiction
ISBN 0-7636-2402-0; 978-0-7636-2402-6
                                            LC 2006-43170
This is the first of projected two volumes in The astonishing life of Octavian Nothing, traitor to the nation series. Various diaries, letters, and other manuscripts chronicle the experiences of Octavian, a young African American, from birth to age sixteen, as he is brought up as part of a science experiment in the years leading up to and during the Revolutionary War.
"Teens looking for a challenge will find plenty to sink into here. The questions raised about race and freedom are well developed and leave a different perspective on the Revolutionary War than most novels." Voice Youth Advocates

Anthony, Piers
On a pale horse. Ballantine Bks. 1983 249p (Incarnations of immortality, bk1) hardcover o.p. pa $7.99
Grades: 9 10 11 12   **Fic**
1. Fantasy fiction
ISBN 0-345-30924-3; 0-345-33858-8 (pa)
                                            LC 83-6043
"A Del Rey book"

In this first volume of the Incarnations of immortality series "a young man named Zane tries to commit suicide and winds up killing Death instead, whereupon he has to take on the job himself. Zane subsequently learns the responsibilities of his position and deals with an array of logical complexities." Booklist
Other titles in the series are:
And eternity (1990)
Bearing an hourglass (1984)
Being a green mother (1987)
For love of evil (1988)
Wielding a red sword (1986)
With a tangled skein (1985)

Asimov, Isaac, 1920-1992
Fantastic voyage. Bantam Bks. 1988 186p pa $7.99 *
Grades: 9 10 11 12   **Fic**
1. Science fiction
ISBN 0-553-27572-0
First published 1966 by Houghton Mifflin
"Based on the screenplay by Harry Kleiner, from the original story by Otto Klement and Jay Lewis Bixby"
"Five people are sent on a rescue mission in a submarine, but this is no ordinary submarine moving through an ordinary sea. The people and the submarine are miniaturized. They are moving through a man's blood vessels to reach and break up a blood clot in his brain. The miniaturization will not last—they have only 60 minutes to do the job and leave the man's body, before they return to ordinary size." Publ Wkly

Foundation. Bantam Books 2004 244p $24; pa $7.99 *
Grades: 9 10 11 12   **Fic**
1. Science fiction
ISBN 0-553-80371-9; 0-553-29335-7 (pa)
                                            LC 2003-69137
A reissue of the title first published 1951 by Gnome Press
The first volume in the author's Foundation series narrating the fall of a great galactic empire and the efforts of the Foundations to combat the barbarism that follows
Other titles in the series are:
Forward the Foundation (1993)
Foundation and earth (1986)
Foundation and empire (1952)
Foundation's edge (1982)
Prelude to Foundation (1988)
Second Foundation (1986)

Atwood, Margaret, 1939-
The Handmaid's tale; with an introduction by Valerie Martin. Everyman's Library 2006 xxxiii, 350p $24 *
Grades: 11 12 Adult   **Fic**
1. Allegories
ISBN 0-307-26460-2   LC 2006-42618
Also available in paperback from Anchor Bks.
First published 1986 by Houghton Mifflin
"The time is the near future, the place is the Republic of Gilead—formerly known as the United States. A coup d'etat by religious fundamentalists has left the President

Atwood, Margaret, 1939——*Continued*
and Congress dead, The Constitution suspended, and the
borders sealed. . . . Atwood's storyteller, a 33-year-old
woman known only as Offred, serves as a handmaid to
one of the ruling Commanders of the Faithful, Fred, from
whom she takes her name. . . . Her sole function . . .
is to carry out a . . . version of Old Testament lore and
bear a child for the aging Commander, with the collusion
of his barren wife." Christ Sci Monit
   "A gripping suspense tale, The Handmaid's Tale is an
allegory of what results from a politics based on misogy-
ny, racism, and anti-Semitism." Ms

Auch, Mary Jane
   Ashes of roses. Holt & Co. 2002 250p $16.95
Grades: 7 8 9 10 11 12 Adult   **Fic**
   1. Triangle Shirtwaist Company, Inc. —Fiction
   2. Immigrants—Fiction 3. Irish Americans—Fiction
   4. New York (N.Y.)—Fiction
   ISBN 0-8050-6686-1   LC 2001-51896
Also available in paperback from Laurel Leaf Bks.
   Sixteen-year-old Margaret Rose Nolan, newly arrived
from Ireland, finds work at New York City's Triangle
Shirtwaist Factory shortly before the 1911 fire in which
146 employees died
   "Fast-paced, populated by distinctive characters, and
anchored in Auch's convincing sense of time and place,
this title is a good choice for readers who like historical
fiction." SLJ

Auseon, Andrew, 1976-
   Funny little monkey. Harcourt 2005 298p $17;
pa $6.95
Grades: 7 8 9 10   **Fic**
   1. Brothers—Fiction 2. Twins—Fiction 3. Size—Fiction 4. School stories
   ISBN 0-15-205334-4; 0-15-205413-8 (pa)
                                           LC 2004-19017
   Arty, an abnormally short fourteen-year-old boy, enlists the help of a group of students, known at school as
the "pathetic losers," to take revenge against his abusive,
tall fraternal twin brother.
   "The author taps into the painful experience of high
school, leavened with healthy doses of hyperbole, hope
and wry humor—which Auseon seems to understand just
may be the best tools for teenage survival." Publ Wkly

Austen, Jane, 1775-1817
   Persuasion. Alfred A. Knopf 1992 xxxvii, 260p
$18
Grades: 11 12 Adult   **Fic**
   1. Great Britain—Fiction
   ISBN 0-679-40986-6   LC 91-53181
Also available from other publishers
"Everyman's library"
First published 1818
   "The heroine, Anne Elliott, and her lover, Captain
Wentworth, had been engaged eight years before the sto-
ry opens but Anne had broken the engagement in defer-
ence to family and friends. Upon his return he finds her
'wretchedly altered,' but after numerous obstacles have
been overcome, the lovers are happily united." Gerwig.
Handb for Readers and Writers

   Pride and prejudice; introduction by Anna
Quindlen. Modern Library 1995 281p $14.95 *
Grades: 11 12 Adult   **Fic**
   1. Great Britain—Fiction
   ISBN 0-679-60168-6   LC 95-6310
Also available Thorndike Press large print edition and
from other publishers
First published 1813
   "Concerned mainly with the conflict between the prej-
udice of a young lady and the well-founded though mis-
interpreted pride of the aristocratic hero. The heroine's
father and mother cope in very different ways with the
problem of marrying off five daughters." Good Read
   "The characters are drawn with humor, delicacy, and
the intimate knowledge of men and women that Miss
Austen always shows." Keller. Reader's Dig of Books

   Sense and sensibility; with an introduction by
Peter Conrad. Knopf 1992 xxxix, 367p $16
Grades: 11 12 Adult   **Fic**
   1. Great Britain—Fiction
   ISBN 0-679-40987-4   LC 91-53182
Also available from other publishers
"Everyman's library"
First published 1811
   A story "in which two sisters, Elinor and Marianne
Dashwood represent 'sense' and 'sensibility' respectively.
Each is deserted by the young man from whom she has
been led to expect an offer of matrimony. Elinor bears
her deep disappointment with dignity and restraint while
Marianne violently expresses her grief." Reader's Ency.
4th edition

Bagdasarian, Adam
   Forgotten fire. DK Pub. 2000 273p $19.99
Grades: 7 8 9 10   **Fic**
   1. Armenian massacres, 1915-1923—Fiction
   2. Turkey—Fiction
   ISBN 0-7894-2627-7   LC 99-46465
Also available in paperback from Laurel Leaf
   "Based on a true story, this . . . historical novel tells
about the Turkish genocide of the Armenians. Vahan
Kenderian, age 12 when his home is torn apart, sees
many of his family and friends butchered before his
eyes." Booklist
   "Bagdasarian has created a story that is a tribute to
the human ability to endure. Because of the sexual and
physical violence, this book is recommended for mature
readers." Book Rep

Baldwin, James, 1924-1987
   Go tell it on the mountain. Knopf 1953 303p
$15.95; pa $6.99
Grades: 7 8 9 10   **Fic**
   1. African Americans—Fiction 2. Harlem (New York,
N.Y.)—Fiction
   ISBN 0-679-60154-6; 0-440-33007-6 (pa)
Also available in paperback from Laurel-Leaf Bks.
   This novel is an "autobiographical story of a Harlem
child's relationship with his father against the back-
ground of his being saved in the pentecostal church." Be-
net's Reader's Ency of Am Lit

Baldwin, James, 1924-1987—*Continued*

If Beale Street could talk. Dial Press (NY) 1974
197p hardcover o.p. pa $12.95
Grades: 11 12 Adult   Fic
1. African Americans—Fiction 2. New York (N.Y.)—
Fiction
ISBN 0-803-74169-3; 0-307-27593-0 (pa)

"Tish, aged 19, and Fonny, 22 years old, are in love
and pledged to marry, a decision hastened by Tish's unexpected pregnancy. Fonny is falsely accused of raping
a Puerto Rican woman and is sent to prison. The families
of the desperate couple search frantically for evidence
that will prove his innocence in order to reunite the lovers and provide a safe haven for the expected child.
There is some explicit sex but it is not treated in a sensational manner, nor is the use of street language gratuitous." Shapiro. Fic for Youth. 3d edition

Ballard, J. G., 1930-

Empire of the Sun; a novel. Simon & Schuster
1984 279p hardcover o.p. pa $13
Grades: 9 10 11 12 Adult   Fic
1. World War, 1939-1945—Fiction 2. Shanghai (China)—Fiction
ISBN 0-671-53051-8; 0-7432-6523-8 (pa)
LC 84-10630

"The day after Pearl Harbor, Shanghai is captured by
the Japanese, and 11-year-old Jim is separated from his
parents and spends some months living on his own. Then
he is captured and interned in a Japanese prison camp
with other civilians. The story of the next four years is
one of struggling to stay alive by any means possible."
Libr J

"This novel is much more than the gritty story of a
child's miraculous survival in the grimly familiar setting
of World War II's concentration camps. There is no nos-
talgia for a good war here, no sentimentality for the human spirit at extremes. Mr. Ballard is more ambitious
than romance usually allows. He aims to render a vision
of the apocalypse, and succeeds so well that it can hurt
to dwell upon his images." N Y Times Book Rev

Followed by The kindness of women (1991)

Banks, Russell, 1940-

Rule of the bone; a novel. HarperCollins Pubs.
1995 390p hardcover o.p. pa $13.95
Grades: 11 12 Adult   Fic
1. Adolescence—Fiction 2. Runaway teenagers—Fiction 3. Drug abuse—Fiction
ISBN 0-06-017275-4; 0-06-092724-0 (pa)
LC 95-11701

The protagonist of this novel, fourteen-year-old Bone,
"has a disturbed stepfather, a long-suffering mother, and
a long-gone father. The first half of the book chronicles
his willing but innocent drift into criminality. His life
takes a turn for the better when he moves into an abandoned school bus with a Jamaican mystic. He travels to
Jamaica with 'I-man,' and there he finds his self-centered
druggie father, turns 15, is sexually initiated, and loses
I-man in a violent drug deal." SLJ

"Intoxicating and unsparing, 'Rule of the Bone' is a
romance for a world fast running out of room for childhood." N Y Times Book Rev

Barker, Clive

Abarat. Joanna Cotler Bks. 2002 388, xxvp il
$24.99; pa $6.99
Grades: 7 8 9 10   Fic
1. Fantasy fiction
ISBN 0-06-028092-1; 0-06-059637-6 (pa)
LC 2002-1299

Candy Quackenbush of Chickentown, Minnesota,
"finds herself transported to the Abarat, a magical realm
composed of 25 islands, each representing one hour of
the day, with the mysterious Twenty-Fifth designated for
Time Outside of Time." SLJ

"The first of a planned four-book series, Barker imbues the traditional conventions of fantasy with a whimsical Wonderland quality, providing a host of bizarre
characters, a fabulous landscape, and a coherent underlying mythology." Booklist

Another title in this series is:
Days of magic, nights of war (2004)

Barr, Nevada

Track of the cat. Putnam 1993 238p hardcover
o.p. pa $7.99
Grades: 11 12 Adult   Fic
1. Mystery fiction
ISBN 0-399-13824-2; 0-425-19083-8 (pa)
LC 92-29694

In this first novel of the Anna Pigeon series, "Anna
Pigeon has fled New York City after the accidental death
of her husband, and she now works as a law enforcement
ranger at Guadaloupe Mountains National Park. There
she finds the remains of fellow ranger Sheila Drury, who
apparently was clawed to death by a mountain lion. Although an autopsy confirms this judgment, Anna becomes convinced that the claw marks have been faked.
Her superiors discourage her from probing further, but
another supposedly accidental death goads her into investigating Sheila's activities before her death—her campaign to open up the park to the public and her relationships with a young divorcee and with a powerful rancher
opposed to Park Service policies. . . . A park ranger herself, Barr develops a complex, credible and capable heroine who believes in truth and justice while remaining
conscious of the ambiguities of human existence." Publ
Wkly

Barry, Max

Jennifer Government; a novel. Doubleday 2003
321p hardcover o.p. pa $13.95
Grades: 11 12 Adult   Fic
1. Capitalism—Fiction 2. Science fiction
ISBN 0-385-50759-3; 1-4000-3092-7 (pa)
LC 2002-19436

"Free enterprise runs amok in Barry's satirical near-
future nightmare: the American government has been
privatized and now runs most of the world, including
'the Australian territories of the U.S.A.,' where the book
is set. American corporations sponsor everything from
schools to their employee's identities, and literally go to
war with one another. By taking a drink at the wrong
water cooler, Hack Nike, a merchandising officer at the
athletic shoe company whose name he bears, is coerced
into a nefarious marketing plot to raise demand for
Nike's new $2,500 sneakers by shooting teenagers." Publ

Barry, Max—*Continued*
Wkly
"Though pensive readers may extract political commentary from it, Barry's latest novel has more value as entertainment. A refreshingly creative and unique read." Booklist

Bates, Judy Fong, 1949-
Midnight at the Dragon Café. Counterpoint 2005 317p pa $14.95
Grades: 11 12 Adult   Fic
1. Chinese—Fiction 2. Family life—Fiction 3. Canada—Fiction
ISBN 1-58243-189-2; 978-1-58243-189-5
                     LC 2006-279843
First published 2004 in Canada
"Su-Jen Chou, the only daughter of parents who flee Communist China in the 1950s to become proprietors of a Chinese restaurant in an isolated Ontario town, watches as her family unravels." Publ Wkly
"The mounting suspense of family secrets makes this . . . novel a breathless read, even as the simple, beautiful words make you want to stop and read the sentences over and over again." Booklist

Bauer, Cat
Harley, like a person. Winslow Press 2000 248p hardcover o.p. pa $5.95
Grades: 9 10 11 12   Fic
1. Family life—Fiction 2. Adoption—Fiction
ISBN 1-89081-748-1; 1-58837-005-4 (pa)
                     LC 99-46814
Also available in paperback from Knopf Books for Young Readers
Fourteen-year-old Harley, an artistic teenager living with her alcoholic father and angry mother, suspects that she is adopted and begins a search for her biological parents.
"Bauer has created a vivid portrait of a teenage girl whose life is fraught with well-meaning deception; young-adult readers will sympathize with Harley's struggle." Bull Cent Child Books
Followed by Harley's ninth (2007)

Bauer, Joan
Hope was here. Putnam 2000 186p $16.99; pa $7.99
Grades: 7 8 9 10   Fic
1. Aunts—Fiction 2. Restaurants—Fiction 3. Wisconsin—Fiction
ISBN 0-399-23142-0; 0-14-240424-1 (pa)
                     LC 00-38232
A Newbery Medal honor book, 2001
When sixteen-year-old Hope and the aunt who has raised her move from Brooklyn to Mulhoney, Wisconsin, to work as waitress and cook in the Welcome Stairways diner, they become involved with the diner owner's political campaign to oust the town's corrupt mayor.
"Bauer manages to fill her heartfelt novel with gentle humor, quirky but appealing characters, and an engaging plot." Book Rep

Rules of the road. Putnam 1998 201p $16.99; pa $7.99 *
Grades: 7 8 9 10   Fic
1. Old age—Fiction
ISBN 0-399-23140-4; 0-14-240425-X (pa)
                     LC 97-32198
Sixteen-year-old Jenna gets a job driving the elderly owner of a chain of successful shoe stores from Chicago to Texas to confront the son who is trying to force her to retire, and along the way Jenna hones her talents as a saleswoman and finds the strength to face her alcoholic father.
"The author creates some fabulous and sometimes flamboyant characters, witty dialogue, and memorable scenes." SLJ
Followed by Best foot forward (2005)

Beagle, Peter S.
The last unicorn. Viking 1968 218p hardcover o.p. pa $14.95
Grades: 11 12 Adult   Fic
1. Unicorns—Fiction 2. Allegories
ISBN 0-670-41908-7; 0-451-45052-3 (pa)
"A beautiful and previously happy unicorn learns she may be the last unicorn left on earth. Wanting not to believe it, she sets off in quest of her fellows. In the course of her journey, she meets a carnival magician of little ability, has encounters with a Robin Hood-like band, a king presiding over a hate-filled and miserable land, with the aid of the mysterious Red Bull, and a glamorous, if previously ineffectual prince." Publ Wkly
"Beagle is a true magician with words, a master of prose and a deft practitioner in verse. He has been compared, not unreasonably, with Lewis Carroll and J. R. R. Tolkien, but he stands squarely and triumphantly on his own feet." Saturday Rev

Beard, Philip, 1963-
Dear Zoe; a novel. Viking 2005 196p $21.95; pa $13
Grades: 9 10 11 12   Fic
1. Letters—Fiction 2. Death—Fiction 3. Sisters—Fiction 4. Bereavement—Fiction
ISBN 0-670-03401-0; 0-452-28740-5 (pa)
                     LC 2004-57173
Also available Thorndike Press large print edition
"On the morning planes hit the World Trade Center towers, Tess DeNunzio's three-year-old sister, Zoe, ran into the street and was killed by a car. Fifteen-year-old Tess, who was supposed to be watching Zoe, was consumed by guilt. This novel is written in the form of a letter from Tess to Zoe, chronicling the year after Zoe's death. . . . Beard captures the raw emotion of a 15-year-old girl with impressive dexterity, following Tess through the many stages of grief." Booklist

Bechard, Margaret, 1953-
Hanging on to Max. Roaring Brook Press 2002 142p $15.95
Grades: 7 8 9 10   Fic
1. Teenage fathers—Fiction 2. Infants—Fiction
ISBN 0-7613-1579-9   LC 2001-48335
Also available in paperback from Simon & Schuster

Bechard, Margaret, 1953——*Continued*
When his girlfriend decides to give their baby away, seventeen-year-old Sam is determined to keep him and raise him alone.
"An easy read filled with practical wisdom, this book is highly recommended as an important edition for any adolescent classroom collection." ALAN

Bell, Hilari, 1958-
A matter of profit. HarperCollins Pubs. 2001 281p lib bdg $17.89; pa $6.99
Grades: 7 8 9 10   **Fic**
1. Science fiction 2. Mystery fiction
ISBN 0-06-029514-7 (lib bdg); 0-06-447300-7 (pa)
LC 00-50555
Sick of the horrors of conquering beings on other planets, Ahvren will end his service as a soldier and save his sister from an unhappy marriage if he can discover who is behind a rumored plot to assassinate the Emperor.
"This is well-written, thought-provoking, and exciting science fiction." SLJ

Bellow, Saul, 1915-2005
The adventures of Augie March. Penguin 2006 586p (Penguin Classics) pa $16
Grades: 9 10 11 12   **Fic**
1. Jews—Fiction
ISBN 0-14-303957-1
A reissue of the title first published 1953
"It is a picaresque story of a poor Jewish youth from Chicago, his progress, sometimes highly comic, through the world of the 20th century, and his attempts to make sense of it." Merriam-Webster's Ency of Lit

Benchley, Peter, 1940-2006
Jaws. Random House 2005 311p $15.95
Grades: 9 10 11 12   **Fic**
1. Sharks—Fiction 2. Adventure fiction
ISBN 1-4000-6456-2   LC 2005-46451
First published 1974
With a new introd. by the author
This is a "story about what happens when a great white shark terrorizes a small Long Island town. . . . A woman swimmer is devoured by the shark, and Police Chief Martin Brody insists on closing the beaches. But he's overruled by the town fathers who remind him that the community is dependent on summer visitors for economic survival. Two deaths later, the news can no longer be suppressed and Brody, an oceanographer and a fisherman go after the monster in an exciting chase." Publ Wkly

Benduhn, Tea
Gravel queen. Simon & Schuster Bks. for Young Readers 2003 152p $15.95
Grades: 9 10 11 12   **Fic**
1. Homosexuality—Fiction
ISBN 0-689-84994-X   LC 2002-3083
All Aurin wants to do the summer before her senior year in high school is hang out with her friends Kenney and Fred, but when she falls in love with Neila, every-

thing changes.
This "is a sensitive and realistic portrayal of the changing relationship that characterize adolescence. . . . Benduhn's characters, both gay and straight, are well developed." Voice Youth Advocates

Berg, Elizabeth, 1948-
Joy school. Random House 1997 208p hardcover o.p. pa $12.95
Grades: 11 12 Adult   **Fic**
1. Adolescence—Fiction 2. Missouri—Fiction
ISBN 0-679-44943-4; 0-345-42309-2 (pa)
LC 96-35245
For Katie, first introduced in the author's Durable Goods (1993), "being 13 is hard: she's still a child, but she thinks she's a woman—maybe. It's harder still because her mother is dead and her army colonel dad has moved her to a new town. At first, Katie makes no friends. Then she meets Jimmy and falls in love. She is sure that Jimmy returns her love and that they will have a life together. (So what if he's married and has a child?) Katie's first friends are Cynthia, a lonely girl with a too-perfect mother and an old, very Italian grandmother and Taylor, a model who introduces her to boys, stealing, and sex." Libr J
The "grim backdrop for . . . [this] novel is considerably lightened by Katie's clear-eyed view of events as she describes the trials of adolescence in an era of beehive hairdos and mandatory home economics classes." N Y Times Book Rev

Berman, Judith
Bear daughter. Ace Books 2005 422p pa $16
Grades: 9 10 11 12   **Fic**
1. Bears—Fiction 2. Fantasy fiction
ISBN 0-441-01322-8   LC 2005-41199
"One morning, young Cloud awakens in the form of a human girl, shedding the bear shape she inherited from her true father. Determined to learn to live in her new body, Cloud struggles to fit into the life of Sandspit Town, but her mother's human husband, King Rumble, despises her and seeks her downfall." Libr J
"Do not be fooled by this book's seemingly middle school cover; its dark tale will better suit horror collections, as slogging through its endless charnel-house descriptions is not for the squeamish. . . . Recommend this one to lovers of intelligent horror." Voice Youth Advocates

Berry, Liz
The China garden. HarperCollins Pubs. 1999 285p pa $6.99 hardcover o.p.
Grades: 9 10 11 12   **Fic**
1. Extrasensory perception—Fiction
ISBN 0-345-42309-2
First published 1994 in the United Kingdom; first United States edition 1996 by Farrar, Straus & Giroux
"Clare Meredith, 17 and waiting to hear the results of her school exams, goes with her widowed mother to Ravensmere, an ancient English estate, where she's oddly attracted to a handsome biker. Clare makes friends and enemies; sees visions; learns of past Ravensmere women and of her previously unknown connection to the area;

Berry, Liz—*Continued*
and rethinks her plans for the future." SLJ
"A lushly romantic tale that unfolds in layers and is firmly grounded in mythology and New Age mysticism." Booklist

Black, Holly, 1971-
Valiant: a modern faerie tale. Simon & Schuster 2005 314p hardcover o.p. pa $7.99
Grades: 9 10 11 12   **Fic**
1. Fantasy fiction 2. Fairies—Fiction 3. Runaway teenagers—Fiction 4. New York (N.Y.)—Fiction
ISBN 0-689-86822-7; 0-689-86823-5 (pa)
        LC 2005-298934
"When 17-year-old Valerie catches her boyfriend and her mother fooling around, she runs away to New York City. There she falls in with a small group of teens who live in the subway tunnels. But there is something more to their stories than that of normal street kids. When Valerie begins to notice odd things about the deliveries they make, and when she meets Ravus, a troll, she understands that there is an entire world that she has never known existed—the world of Faerie. . . . This dark fantasy includes drug use and strong language, but beneath its darkness readers find well-rendered characters, a gripping plot, and pure magic." SLJ

Blackman, Malorie, 1962-
Naughts & Crosses. Simon & Schuster 2005 386p $15.95; pa $7.99 *
Grades: 7 8 9 10   **Fic**
1. Prejudices—Fiction
ISBN 1-4169-0016-0; 1-4169-0017-9 (pa)
        LC 2004-16564
First published 2001 in the United Kingdom with title: Noughts & crosses
In a world where the pale-skinned Naughts are discriminated against by the politically and socially powerful dark-skinned Crosses, teenagers Callum—a Naught—and Sephy—a Cross—test whether their love is strong enough to survive their society's racism.
"Gripping and deeply layered, this book will make readers question everything: race relations, government, friendship." Booklist

Block, Francesca Lia
Dangerous angels; the Weetzie Bat books. HarperCollins Pubs. 1998 478p pa $12
Grades: 9 10 11 12   **Fic**
1. Los Angeles (Calif.)—Fiction
ISBN 0-06-440697-0   LC 97-40933
"Joanna Cotler books"
This is an omnibus edition of five Weetzie Bat books
Contents: Weetzie Bat; Witch baby; Cherokee Bat and the Goat Guys; Missing Angel Juan; Baby Be-Bop

Weetzie Bat. Harper & Row 1989 88p hardcover o.p. pa $7.99 *
Grades: 9 10 11 12   **Fic**
1. Friendship—Fiction
ISBN 0-06-020534-2; 0-06-073625-9 (pa)
        LC 88-6214
"A Charlotte Zolotow book"

Follows the wild adventures of Weetzie Bat and her Los Angeles punk friends, Dirk, Duck-Man, and Secret-Agent-Lover-Man
"A brief, off-beat tale that has great charm, poignancy, and touches of fantasy. . . . This creates the ambiance of Hollywood with no cynicism, from the viewpoint of denizens who treasure its unique qualities." SLJ
Other titles about Weetzie Bat and her friends are:
Witch baby (1991)
Cherokee Bat and the Goat Guys (1992)
Missing Angel Juan (1993)
Necklace of kisses (2005)

Bondoux, Anne-Laure
The killer's tears; translated from the French by Y. Maudet. Delacorte Press 2006 162p map $15.95; lib bdg $17.99
Grades: 8 9 10 11 12   **Fic**
1. Father-son relationship—Fiction 2. Thieves—Fiction 3. Chile—Fiction
ISBN   0-385-73293-7;   978-0-385-73293-2; 0-385-90314-6 (lib bdg); 978-0-385-90314-1 (lib bdg)
        LC 2005-8845
Original French edition, 2003
A young boy, Paolo, and the man who murdered his parents, Angel, gradually become like father and son as they live and work together on the remote Chilean farm where Paolo was born.
"This novel is filled with challenging ideas and potent language that will pull readers in new directions." Booklist

Booth, Coe
Tyrell. PUSH 2006 310p $16.99 *
Grades: 9 10 11 12   **Fic**
1. Homeless persons—Fiction 2. Poor—Fiction 3. African Americans—Fiction 4. Bronx (New York, N.Y.)—Fiction
ISBN 0-439-83879-7; 978-0-439-83879-5
        LC 2005-37330
Fifteen-year-old Tyrell, who is living in a Bronx homeless shelter with his spaced-out mother and his younger brother, tries to avoid temptation so he does not end up in jail like his father.
"The immediate first-person narrative is pitch perfect: fast, funny, and anguished (there's also lots of use of the n-word, though the term is employed in the colloquial sense, not as an insult). Unlike many books reflecting the contemporary street scene, this one is more than just a pat situation with a glib resolution; it's filled with surprising twists and turns that continue to the end." Booklist

Bosse, Malcolm J., 1934-2002
The examination. Farrar, Straus & Giroux 1994 296p $17; pa $7.50
Grades: 7 8 9 10   **Fic**
1. Brothers—Fiction 2. China—Fiction
ISBN 0-374-32234-1; 0-374-42223-0 (pa)
        LC 93-50955
Fifteen-year-old Hong and his older brother Chen face famine, flood, pirates, and jealous rivals on their journey

Bosse, Malcolm J., 1934-2002—*Continued*
through fifteenth century China as Chen pursues his calling as a scholar and Hong becomes involved with a secret society known as the White Lotus

"Bosse has constructed a compelling, picaresque novel which blends adventure and history into a seamless fabric." Horn Book

Boulle, Pierre, 1912-1994
The bridge over the River Kwai; translated by Xan Fielding. Amereon Limited 1988 224p $26.95
Grades: 11 12 Adult   **Fic**
1. Great Britain. Army—Officers—Fiction 2. World War, 1939-1945—Fiction 3. Thailand—Fiction
ISBN 0-8919-0571-5
Original French edition, 1952; first United States edition published 1954 by Vanguard Press

"In 1942 the Japanese military under the command of Col. Saito orders its British prisoners of war to construct a bridge over the 400-foot-wide River Kwai in the Siamese jungle. Complications arise when prisoner Col. Nicholson insists that officers not be treated like regular lower-class soldiers. Medical officer Clipton is much more humane, and this difference brings the two fellow prisoners into frequent conflict. When the bridge is finally completed, a British demolition team prepares to destroy it." Shapiro Fic for Youth. 3d edition

Planet of the apes; translated by Xan Feilding. Ballantine 2001 c1991 268p pa $6.99
Grades: 11 12 Adult   **Fic**
1. Science fiction
ISBN 0-345-44798-0
"A Del Rey book"
First published 1963 by Vanguard Press; published in the United Kingdom with title: Monkey planet

"Ulysse Merou writes of his experiences on an unusual planet where the roles of humans and apes are reversed. Gorillas wear clothing and run businesses, while humans are caged in zoos and are the subjects of scientific experiments. In the year 2500 a vacationing couple cruising through space spot a bottle-encased message, retrieve it, and soon become absorbed in Merou's tale." Shapiro. Fic for Youth. 3d edition

"In this Swiftian fable Boulle gives full play to his not inconsiderable gift for irony and satire." Libr J

Boylan, Jennifer Finney, 1958-
Getting in; a novel; {by} James Finney Boylan. Warner Bks. 1998 342p pa $14 *
Grades: 9 10 11 12   **Fic**
1. New England—Fiction
ISBN 0-446-67417-6   LC 97-51216
"Three adults and four high-school seniors undertake a journey of self-discovery when they set off in a Winnebago on a tour of eastern colleges. As they travel their route, beginning with Yale and ending with Wesleyan, they learn volumes about themselves, one another, and their complex connections. . . . Boylan cleverly manipulates the lives of this strangely assorted group, giving readers not only a good deal to laugh at but a good deal to think about as well." Booklist

Bradbury, Ray, 1920-
Fahrenheit 451. Simon & Schuster 2003 190p $23 *
Grades: 9 10 11 12 Adult   **Fic**
1. Science fiction
ISBN 0-7432-4722-1   LC 2003-66160
Also available in paperback from Ballantine Bks.
First published 1953 in paperback by Ballantine Bks.
On cover: With a new introduction by the author
Dystopian novel about a bookburner official in a future fascist state.

Something wicked this way comes. Avon Bks. 1999 293p $15.95; pa $7.99
Grades: 7 8 9 10   **Fic**
1. Horror fiction 2. Fantasy fiction
ISBN 0-380-97727-3; 0-380-72940-7 (pa)
A reissue of the title first published 1962 by Simon and Schuster

"We read here of the loss of innocence, the recognition of evil, the bond between generations, and the purely fantastic. These forces enter Green Town, Illinois, on the wheels of Cooger and Dark's Pandemonium Shadow Show. Will Halloway and Jim Nightshade, two 13-year-olds, explore the sinister carnival for excitement, which becomes desperation as the forces of the dark threaten to engulf them. Bradbury's gentle humanism and lyric style serve this fantasy well." Shapiro. Fic for Youth. 3d edition

Bradford, Richard, 1932-2002
Red sky at morning. Perennial Classics 1999 246p pa $13
Grades: 11 12 Adult   **Fic**
1. New Mexico—Fiction
ISBN 0-06-093190-6   LC 99-12690
First published 1968 by Lippincott
"Joshua Arnold and his mother move to their summer home in Corazon Sagrado, New Mexico, when the father joins the Navy during World War II. Josh copes with the Mexican and Anglo customs and is concerned with his mother's drinking. When his father dies in the war, he takes responsibility for his mother, his own life, and his father's business." Shapiro. Fic for Youth. 3d edition

Bradley, Marion Zimmer
The mists of Avalon. Ballantine Pub. Group 2000 876p $30; pa $16.95 *
Grades: 9 10 11 12   **Fic**
1. Arthur, King—Fiction 2. Fantasy fiction 3. Great Britain—History—0-1066—Fiction
ISBN 0-345-44118-4; 0-345-35049-9 (pa)
     LC 00-712415
"A Del Rey book"
A reissue of the title first published 1982 by Knopf
This "retelling of the Arthurian legend is dominated by the character of Morgan le Fay (here called Morgaine), the powerful sorceress who symbolizes the historical clash between Christianity and the early pagan religions of the British Isles." Publ Wkly

Bradshaw, Gillian, 1956-
The sand-reckoner. Forge 2000 351p hardcover
o.p. pa $14.95
Grades: 11 12 Adult   **Fic**
1. Archimedes, ca. 287-212 B.C.—Fiction 2. Greece—
Fiction
ISBN 0-312-87340-9; 0-312-87581-9 (pa)
                                          LC 99-89827
"A Tom Doherty Associates book"
"When the young Archimedes is called back to Syra-
cuse after three years in Alexandria, where he studied his
beloved mathematics at Ptolemy's museum, he discovers
that his father is gravely ill and the city itself is under
attack by the Roman army. . . . Two subplots are woven
into the novel's main thread: the growing love between
Archimedes and King Hieron's sister, and the difficult
situation that Marcus, Archimedes' Roman slave, finds
himself in as he discovers that his brother is one of the
Roman soldiers captured by the Syracusan army."
Booklist

Brashares, Ann, 1967-
The sisterhood of the traveling pants. Delacorte
Press 2001 294p $14.95; pa $8.95
Grades: 9 10 11 12   **Fic**
1. Friendship—Fiction
ISBN 0-385-72933-2; 0-385-73058-6 (pa)
                                          LC 2002-282046
"Four lifelong high-school friends and a magical pair
of jeans take summer journeys to discover love, disap-
pointment, and self-realization." Booklist
"The author shares her subjects' shrewdness at evalu-
ating social nuances and their ease with sarcastic slang.
. . . She is equally adept at describing anger toward an
absent parent, the difficulty of losing a beloved pet and
the awkwardness of newfound sexual desire." N Y Times
Book Rev
Other titles about the Sisterhood are:
Forever in blue (2007)
Girls in pants (2005)
The second summer of the sisterhood (2003)

Bray, Libba
A great and terrible beauty. Delacorte Press
2004 403p $16.95; lib bdg $18.99 *
Grades: 9 10 11 12   **Fic**
1. Great Britain—Fiction 2. Mystery fiction
ISBN 0-385-73028-4; 0-385-90161-5 (lib bdg)
                                          LC 2003-9472
Also available Thorndike press large print edition
After the suspicious death of her mother in 1895, sixteen-year-old Gemma returns to England, after many
years in India, to attend a finishing school where she becomes aware of her magical powers and ability to see
into the spirit world.
"The reader will race to the end to discover the mysterious and realistic challenges of an exciting teenage
gothic mystery." Lib Media Connect
Followed by Rebel angels (2005)

Brin, David, 1950-
The postman. Bantam Bks. 1985 294p hardcover
o.p. pa $7.99 *
Grades: 11 12 Adult   **Fic**
1. Science fiction 2. Nuclear warfare—Fiction
ISBN 0-553-05107-5; 0-553-27874-06 (pa)
                                          LC 85-47647
This novel opens with the "familiar portrait of an
America brought to the edge of extinction by nuclear
war. An itinerant storyteller, Gordon Krantz, finds an old
postman's uniform and bag and starts traveling across
country, taking people's letters to loved ones and telling
tales of a country on the road to recovery. Eventually he
becomes a major force for that recovery, as the hope he
gives the people rallies them." Booklist
"A well-crafted, realistic and often violent novel with
diverse elements woven together in expert style." Best
Sellers

Sundiver. Bantam 1985 pa $7.99
Grades: 11 12 Adult   **Fic**
1. Science fiction
ISBN 0-553-26982-8
A reissue of the title first published 1980
First novel in the Uplift series depicting a galactic civilization responsible for uplifting all forms of life. "No
species has ever reached for the stars without the guidance of a patron—except perhaps mankind. Did some
mysterious race begin the uplift of humanity aeons ago?
Circling the sun, under the caverns of Mercury, Expedition Sundiver prepares for the most momentous voyage
in history—a journey into the boiling inferno of the sun."
Publisher's note

Brontë, Charlotte, 1816-1855
Jane Eyre; Charlotte Brontë with an introduction
by Lucy Hughes-Hallet. Knopf 1991 xxxviii, 284p
$20 *
Grades: 11 12 Adult   **Fic**
1. Great Britain—Fiction
ISBN 0-679-40582-8   LC 91-52968
Also available from other publishers and Thorndike
Press large print edition
"Everyman's library"
First published 1847
"In both heroine and hero the author introduced types
new to English fiction. Jane Eyre is a shy, intense little
orphan, never for a moment, neither in her unhappy
school days nor her subsequent career as a governess,
displaying those qualities of superficial beauty and charm
that had marked the conventional heroine. Jane's lover,
Edward Rochester, to whose ward she is governess, is a
strange, violent man, bereft of conventional courtesy, a
law unto himself. Rochester's moodiness derives from
the fact that he is married to an insane wife, whose existence, long kept secret, is revealed on the very day of his
projected marriage to Jane. Years afterward the lovers
are reunited." Reader's Ency. 4th edition

Brontë, Emily, 1818-1848
Wuthering Heights; with an introduction by
Katherine Frank. Knopf 1991 xxxiii, 385p $22 *
Grades: 11 12 Adult   **Fic**
1. Great Britain—Fiction
ISBN 0-679-40543-7   LC 91-52969

Brontë, Emily, 1818-1848—*Continued*
Also available from other publishers
"Everyman's library"
First published 1847
Forced by a storm to spend the night at the home of the somber and unsociable Heathcliff, Mr. Lockwood has an encounter with the spirit of Catherine Linton. He gradually learns that Catherine's father, Mr. Earnshaw, had taken in Heathcliff as a young orphan. Heathcliff and Catherine began to fall in love, but after Mr. Earnshaw's death Catherine's brother treated Heathcliff in a degrading manner and Catherine married rich Edgar Linton. Heathcliff gradually worked his revenge against those who injured him
Includes bibliographical references

Brooks, Kevin, 1959-
Candy. Chicken House/Scholastic 2005 359p $16.95
Grades: 9 10 11 12   Fic
1. Drug abuse—Fiction 2. London (England)—Fiction
ISBN 0-439-68327-0
"In London for a doctor's appointment, Joe meets a captivating girl named Candy at the train station, but his rhapsody is cut short when a man who's clearly Candy's pimp breaks up the interlude by threatening Joe. She remains irresistible to Joe, who finds ways to see her again . . . and who develops a growing determination to save her from her dangerous life of drugs and prostitution, even if it endangers himself and his family." Bull Cent Child Books
"Brooks's plotting is masterful, and the action twists and builds to a frenzied and violent climax." SLJ

Kissing the rain. Scholastic 2004 320p $16.95
Grades: 9 10 11 12   Fic
1. Great Britain—Fiction
ISBN 0-439-57742-X   LC 2003-57395
"After fat, bullied British teen Moo witnesses a murder, he finds himself the center of a conflict between two unsavory factions that threaten his working-class father and himself. In a casual narrative that spikes with increasing panic, Moo tells his own story, stopping short of answering the pivotal question at book's end." Booklist

Lucas. Chicken House/Scholastic 2003 423p hardcover o.p. pa $6.99 *
Grades: 7 8 9 10   Fic
1. Prejudices—Fiction 2. Great Britain—Fiction
ISBN 0-439-45698-3; 0-439-53063-6 (pa)
LC 2002-29189
On an isolated English island, fifteen-year-old Caitlin McCann makes the painful journey from adolescence to adulthood through her experiences with a mysterious boy, whose presence has an unsettling effect on the island's inhabitants
"This beautifully written allegorical tale . . . stays with readers long after it ends. . . . All of the characters are sharply defined. Lucas, with his mixture of real and unearthly qualities, is unique and unforgettable. This is a powerful book to be savored by all who appreciate fine writing and a gripping read." SLJ

Martyn Pig; a novel. Scholastic 2002 230p hardcover o.p. pa $6.99
Grades: 7 8 9 10   Fic
1. Death—Fiction 2. Alcoholism—Fiction
ISBN 0-439-29595-5; 0-439-50752-9 (pa)
LC 2001-49414
"The Chicken House"
Faced with the possibility of living with a dreadful aunt, fifteen-year-old Martyn Pig decides not to tell authorities when his alcoholic father dies accidentally, instead asking a friend for her help in disposing of the body.
Readers "will be fascinated with the gripping plot twists and turns, and fully engaged by Martyn's distinctive voice. . . . The bleakness is tempered by some tongue-in-cheek and zany humor." SLJ

The road of the dead. Chicken House 2006 339p $16.99
Grades: 9 10 11 12   Fic
1. Homicide—Fiction 2. Brothers—Fiction
3. Gypsies—Fiction 4. Great Britain—Fiction
ISBN 0-439-78623-1; 978-0-439-78623-2
LC 2005-14793
First published 2004 in the United Kingdom
Two brothers, sons of an incarcerated gypsy, leave London traveling to an isolated and desolate village, in search of the brutal killer of their sister.
"The sustained violence of the final events will be familiar to fans of films by Tarantino or, for those with historic tastes, Peckinpah, and the moral ambiguity of the ending ('Did any of it matter?') will appeal to lovers of noir, making this a useful title for readers seeking the literary equivalent of edgy cinema." Bull Cent Child Books

Brooks, Martha, 1944-
True confessions of a heartless girl. Farrar, Straus & Giroux 2003 181p $16
Grades: 7 8 9 10   Fic
1. Canada—Fiction 2. City and town life—Fiction
ISBN 0-374-37806-1   LC 2002-72461
"Melanie Kroupa books"
A confused seventeen-year-old girl, a single mother and her young son, two elderly women, and a sad and lonely man, with their own individual tragedies to bear, come together in a small Manitoba town and find a way to a better future
"The writing is plain, with a flatness about it that mirrors the Canadian prairie where the story is set. The style also suits the novel's bleak mood; even the most horrific events seem somehow expected. The characterizations are bare-to-the-bones as well, but the people are so expertly revealed that their pain is palpable." Booklist

Brooks, Terry, 1944-
Armageddon's children. Del Rey 2006 371p $26.95
Grades: 11 12 Adult   Fic
1. Good and evil—Fiction 2. Fantasy fiction
ISBN 0-345-48408-8; 978-0-345-48408-6
LC 2006-40423
In this first volume in an untitled pre-Shannara series the "author envisions a chilling near-future U.S., where

Brooks, Terry, 1944——*Continued*

civilization has collapsed from environmental degradation, plagues, global warfare and supernatural threats. The last surviving members of the Knights of the Word, Logan Tom and Angel Perez, seek to keep the 'balance of the world's magic in check' as they battle the Void—embodied by demons, their leader Findo Cask and their vicious human mutant counterparts known as 'once-men.'" Publ Wkly

"Characterizations are dynamic and multidimensional, the descriptions of the land as well as the ruined cities and small towns are compelling, the action and battles are mesmerizing, and, as is Brooks' wont, the ending is a cliffhanger that leaves readers salivating for the sequel." Booklist

The sword of Shannara; illustrated by the Brothers Hildebrandt. Ballantine Bks. 1991 726p il hardcover o.p. pa $7.99 *

Grades: 11 12 Adult **Fic**
1. Fantasy fiction
ISBN 0-394-441333-4; 0-345-31425-5 (pa)
LC 90-43727
"A Del Rey book"

A reissue of the title first published 1977 by Random House

"Humans, trolls, dwarfs, elves, gnomes, sorcerers both good and evil, and battalions of knights and knaves populate this sweeping adult epic-fantasy. At the urging of a mysterious sorcerer, an adopted orphan named Shea reluctantly takes up the quest for the Sword of Shannara, a legendary elvin blade that alone can defeat the forces of evil engulfing the world." Booklist

This is an "engrossing saga of hardship and adventure with well-maintained action that will keep readers captive right up to a nicely-wrought finish." SLJ

Other titles in this epic-fantasy are:
The druids of Shannara (1991)
The Elf queen of Shannara (1992)
The Elfstones of Shannara (1982)
First king of Shannara (1996)
The scions of Shannara (1990)
The talismans of Shannara (1993)
The wishsong of Shannara (1985)

Bruchac, Joseph, 1942-
Code talker; a novel about the Navajo Marines of World War Two. Dial 2005 240p $16.99 *

Grades: 6 7 8 9 **Fic**
1. Navajo Indians—Fiction 2. World War, 1939-1945—Fiction
ISBN 0-8037-2921-9

After being taught in a boarding school run by whites that Navajo is a useless language, Ned Begay and other Navajo men are recruited by the Marines to become Code Talkers, sending messages during World War II in their native tongue.

"Bruchac's gentle prose presents a clear historical picture of young men in wartime. . . . Nonsensational and accurate, Bruchac's tale is quietly inspiring." SLJ

Includes bibliographical references

Geronimo. Scholastic Press 2006 360p $16.99

Grades: 7 8 9 10 **Fic**
1. Geronimo, Apache Chief, 1829-1909—Fiction
2. Apache Indians—Fiction
ISBN 0-439-35360-2 LC 2005-50007

"Starting in 1886 with Geronimo's final surrender, this novel is told from the perspective of his adopted grandson Little Foot, and follows the Chiricahua Apaches from their home in Arizona to Florida. . . . The fictional Little Foot affords Bruchac the perfect point of view to observe and interpret Geronimo's life, explaining where the history books got it wrong, and offering insights that won't be found there." SLJ

Buck, Pearl S. (Pearl Sydenstricker), 1892-1973
The good earth. Washington Square Press 2004 357p (Contemporary classics) pa $14 *

Grades: 11 12 Adult **Fic**
1. China—Fiction
ISBN 0-7432-7293-5
Also available from other publishers
First published 1931 by Day

This novel set in prerevolutionary China "describes the rise of Wang Lung, a Chinese peasant, from poverty to the position of a rich landowner, helped by his patient wife, O-lan. Their vigor, fortitude, persistence, and enduring love of the soil are emphasized throughout. Generally regarded as Pearl Buck's masterpiece, the book won universal acclaim for its sympathetically authentic picture of Chinese life." (Reader's Ency. 4th edition)
Reader's Ency. 4th edition

Buckhanon, Kalisha, 1977-
Upstate. St. Martin's Press 2005 247p hardcover o.p. pa $11.95

Grades: 9 10 11 12 **Fic**
1. Letters—Fiction 2. African Americans—Fiction
3. Prisoners—Fiction 4. Homicide—Fiction
5. Harlem (New York, N.Y.)—Fiction
ISBN 0-312-33268-8; 0-312-33269-6 (pa)
LC 2004-56651
Also available large print edition $30 (ISBN: 0-312-71222-7)

"Set in the 1990s, this . . . [novel] features Harlem teenagers Antonio, who has been convicted of involuntary manslaughter for killing his father, and his bright and ambitious girlfriend, Natasha. With Antonio in jail, the two maintain their intense relationship through the written correspondence that makes up the text." Libr J

"This is a moving, uplifting story of love and hope in the face of adversity." Publ Wkly

Budhos, Marina Tamar
Ask me no questions; [by] Marina Budhos. Atheneum Books for Young Readers 2006 162p $16.95 *

Grades: 7 8 9 10 **Fic**
1. School stories 2. Asian Americans—Fiction
3. Family life—Fiction 4. New York (N.Y.)—Fiction
ISBN 1-4169-0351-8 LC 2005-1831
"Ginee Seo Books"

Budhos, Marina Tamar—*Continued*

Fourteen-year-old Nadira, her sister, and their parents leave Bangladesh for New York City, but the expiration of their visas and the events of September 11, 2001, bring frustration, sorrow, and terror for the whole family.

"Nadira and Aisha's strategies for surviving and succeeding in high school offer sharp insight into the narrow margins between belonging and not belonging." Horn Book Guide

Bujold, Lois McMaster

The curse of Chalion; {by} Lois M. Bujold. HarperCollins Pubs. 2001 442p hardcover o.p. pa $13.95

Grades: 11 12 Adult   Fic
 1. Fantasy fiction
 ISBN 0-380-97901-2; 0-06-113424-4 (pa)
                                                  LC 00-46586

"Betrayed by an unknown enemy into slavery, former soldier and courtier Lupe dy Cazaril escapes his bondage and returns to the royal household he once served. Entrusted with the teaching of the sister to the heir to the throne of Chalion, Cazaril finds himself drawn into a tangled web of politics and dark magic as he battles a curse that threatens the lives and souls of a family he has come to love. . . . Compelling characters and richly detailed world building make this a strong addition to fantasy collections." Libr J

Burgess, Anthony, 1917-1993

A clockwork orange. [New American ed.] Norton 1988 192p hardcover o.p. pa $13.95 *

Grades: 10 11 12 Adult   Fic
 1. Juvenile delinquency—Fiction 2. Violence—Fiction
 3. Science fiction
 ISBN 0-393-02439-3; 0-393-31283-6 (pa)
                                                  LC 86-23843

First published 1962 in the United Kingdom

"A compelling and often comic vision of the way violence comes to dominate the mind. The novel is set in a future London and is told in curious but readable Russified argot by a juvenile deliquent whose brainwashing by the authorities has destroyed not only his murderous aggression but also his deeper-seated sense of humanity as typified by his compulsive love for the music of Beethoven. It is an ironic novel in the tradition of Zamiatin's and Orwell's anti-Utopias." Sci Fic Ency

Burgess, Melvin, 1954-

Smack. Holt & Co. 1997 327p $16.95

Grades: 9 10 11 12   Fic
 1. Runaway teenagers—Fiction 2. Drug abuse—Fiction 3. Great Britain—Fiction
 ISBN 0-8050-5801-X   LC 97-40629

Also available in paperback from Avon Bks.

First published 1996 in the United Kingdom with title: Junk

After running away from their troubled homes, two English teenagers move in with a group of squatters in the port city of Bristol and try to find ways to support their growing addiction to heroin

"Although the omnipresent British slang (most but not all of which is explained in a glossary) may put off some readers, lots of YAs will be drawn to this book because of the subject. Those who are will quickly find themselves absorbed in an honest, unpatronizing, unvarnished account of teen life on the skids." Booklist

Burns, Olive Ann

Cold Sassy tree. Ticknor & Fields 1984 391p $28

Grades: 11 12 Adult   Fic
 1. Georgia—Fiction
 ISBN 0-89919-309-9   LC 84-8570

Also available in paperback from Dial Press

"Young Will Tweedy lives in a small Georgia town called Cold Sassy in the early 1900s. He is hard working (when pushed) because he has chores to do at home and work to do at his Grandpa Blakeslee's store. That still leaves him time to plan practical jokes with his pals and to overhear family dramas. The biggest drama begins when Grandpa, only three weeks after the death of his wife whom he had dearly loved, marries Miss Love Simpson—young enough to be his daughter. Miss Love has to face not only the town gossip, but also rejection from Will's Mother and Grandpa's other daughter. The story has humor, excitement, and realistic family confrontations." Shapiro. Fic for Youth. 3d edition

Followed by Leaving Cold Sassy: the unfinished sequel (1992)

Butler, Octavia E., 1947-2006

Fledgling; a novel. Seven Stories 2005 317p $24.95

Grades: 11 12 Adult   Fic
 1. Vampires—Fiction 2. Science fiction
 ISBN 1-58322-690-7   LC 2005-5664

Also available in paperback from Warner Books

"Awaking blind, in pain, confused, and alone, Shori Matthews manages to survive amnesia and what should be crippling injuries and starts looking for answers—who hurt her, who she is, and where she comes from. She quickly learns that she is not a young human girl but a genetically altered vampire. Her black skin allows her to survive sunlight and remain alert during the day, but she faces grave danger from those threatened by her strength and heritage. Accompanied by several human hosts who feed and love her, Shori tries to protect her new family and friends from an increasingly hostile threat." Libr J

"In the feisty Shori, Butler has created a new vampire paradigm—one that's more prone to sci-fi social commentary than gothic romance—and given a tired genre a much-needed shot in the arm." Publ Wkly

Parable of the sower. Warner Books 2000 345p pa $13.99 *

Grades: 11 12 Adult   Fic
 1. California—Fiction 2. Adventure fiction
 ISBN 0-446-67550-4   LC 99-46567

First published 1993 by Four Walls Eight Windows

"Written in diary form, Parable chronicles the sometimes grim adventures of Lauren Olamina, an adolescent girl living in a barricaded village in Southern California amid the rampant socioeconomic decay of the early twenty-first century. After her neighborhood is overrun by a cult of drug-demented pyromaniacs, Lauren takes to

Butler, Octavia E., 1947-2006—*Continued*
the road and bands together with other refugees of violent attacks." Booklist

The author "infuses this tale with an allegorical quality that is part meditation, part warning. Simple, direct, and deeply felt, this should reach both mainstream and sf audiences." Libr J

Followed by Parable of the talents (1998)

Caletti, Deb
Honey, Baby, Sweetheart. Simon & Schuster Books for Young Readers 2004 308p $15.95
Grades: 9 10 11 12   **Fic**
1. Mother-daughter relationship—Fiction
ISBN 0-689-86765-4   LC 2003-18331
In the summer of her junior year, sixteen-year-old Ruby McQueen and her mother, both nursing broken hearts, set out on a journey to reunite an elderly woman with her long-lost love and in the process learn many things about "the real ties that bind" people to one another

"Young adults will see themselves in Ruby and, like her, have some laughs along the road to wisdom. A story full of heart, fun, and energy." SLJ

The nature of Jade. Simon & Schuster Books for Young Readers 2007 288p $16.99
Grades: 8 9 10 11 12   **Fic**
1. Zoos—Fiction 2. Elephants—Fiction 3. Family life—Fiction 4. Anxiety—Fiction 5. Seattle (Wash.)—Fiction
ISBN 978-1-4169-1005-3; 1-4169-1005-0
LC 2006-04632
Seattle high school senior Jade's life is defined by her anxiety disorder and dysfunctional family, until she spies a mysterious boy with a baby who seems to share her fascination with the elephants at a nearby zoo.

"Smooth, perceptive writing adds polish to an already compelling story that's sure to draw teens contemplating their own leaps into independence." Bull Cent Child Books

Wild roses. Simon & Schuster 2005 296p $15.95
Grades: 9 10 11 12   **Fic**
1. Mental illness—Fiction 2. Stepfathers—Fiction 3. Violinists—Fiction 4. Washington (State)—Fiction
ISBN 0-689-86766-2   LC 2004-23230
In Washington State, seventeen-year-old Cassie learns about the good and bad sides of both love and genius while living with her mother and brilliant, yet disturbed, violinist stepfather and falling in love with a gifted young musician.

"Readers struggling with their own turmoil will find Cassie a kindred spirit, while others may begin to appreciate the comparative calm of their lives." Bull Cent Child Books

Camus, Albert, 1913-1960
The plague; translated from the French by Stuart Gilbert. Knopf 1948 278p hardcover o.p. pa $12.95
Grades: 11 12 Adult   **Fic**

1. Plague—Fiction
ISBN 0-394-44061-7; 0-679-72021-9 (pa)
Original French edition, 1947
"Using an epidemic of bubonic plague in an Algerian city as a symbol for the absurdity of man's condition, Albert Camus has in this novel articulated his firm belief in mankind's heroism in struggling against the ultimate futility of life. The plague makes everyone in the city intensely aware both of mortality and of the fact that cooperation is the only logical consolation anyone will find in the face of certain death. Though each character, from doctor to priest, represents some aspect of mankind's attempts to deal with the absurd, none is a cardboard figure. The reader cares what happens to the men depicted here. One takes pleasure in the moments of deep human connection that leave us with the conviction that men are, on the whole, admirable." Shapiro. Fic for Youth. 3d edition

The stranger; translated from the French by Matthew Ward; with an introduction by Peter Dunwoodie. Knopf 1993 xxxv, 117p $15; pa $9 *
Grades: 9 10 11 12   **Fic**
1. Homicide—Fiction
ISBN 0-679-42026-6; 0-679-72020-0 (pa)
LC 92-54290
Original French edition, 1942; published in the United Kingdom with title: The outsider

This novel "reveals the 'Absurd' as the condition of man, who feels himself a stranger in his world. Meursault refuses to 'play the game,' by telling the conventional social white lies demanded of him or by believing in human love or religious faith. The unemotional style of his narrative lays naked his motives—or his absence of motive—for his lack of grief over his mother's death, his affair with Marie, his killing an Arab in the hot Algerian sun. Having rejected by honest self-analysis all interpretations which could explain or justify his existence, he nevertheless discovers, while in prison awaiting execution, a passion for the simple fact of life itself." Reader's Ency. 4th edition

Canales, Viola, 1957-
The tequila worm. Wendy Lamb Books 2005 199p $15.95; lib bdg $17.99
Grades: 6 7 8 9   **Fic**
1. Mexican Americans—Fiction 2. Texas—Fiction
ISBN 0-385-74674-1; 0-385-90905-5 (lib bdg)
LC 2004-24533
Sofia grows up in the close-knit community of the barrio in McAllen, Texas, then finds that her experiences as a scholarship student at an Episcopal boarding school in Austin only strengthen her ties to family and her "comadres."

"The explanations of cultural traditions . . . are always rooted in immediate, authentic family emotions, and in Canales' exuberant storytelling, which . . . finds both humor and absurdity in sharply observed, painful situations." Booklist

Card, Orson Scott
Ender's game. TOR Bks. 1991 c1985 xxi, 226p $24.95; pa $6.99
Grades: 7 8 9 10 11 12 Adult   **Fic**

Card, Orson Scott—*Continued*
1. Science fiction
ISBN 0-312-93208-1; 0-812-55070-6 (pa)
"A Tom Doherty Associates book"
A reissue of the title first published 1985
"Chosen as a six-year-old for his potential military genius, Ender Wiggin spends his childhood in outer space at the Battle School of the Belt. Severed from his family, isolated from his peers, and rigorously tested and trained, Ender pours all his talent into the war games that will one day repel the coming alien invasion." Libr J
"The key, of course, is Ender Wiggin himself. Mr. Card never makes the mistake of patronizing or sentimentalizing his hero. Alternately likable and insufferable, he is a convincing little Napoleon in short pants." N Y Times Book Rev
Other titles in the author's distant future series about Ender Wiggin are:
Speaker for the dead (1986)
Xenocide (1991)
Children of the mind (1996)
Ender's shadow (1999)
Shadow of the Hegemon (2001)
Shadow puppets (2002)
Shadow of the giant (2005)

Seventh son 1987 241p (Tales of Alvin Maker) pa $6.99
Grades: 11 12 Adult **Fic**
1. Fantasy fiction
ISBN 0-312-93019-4; 0-812-53305-4 (pa)
LC 86-51490
"A TOR book"
This first novel of the Tales of Alvin Maker series is a "fantasy set in early nineteenth century of an alternate-world America. Settlers beyond the Appalachians have brought with them powerful folk magic—charms, hexes, petitions—to ease the hard work and danger of everyday life. Into this world is born Alvin Miller, a seventh son carrying powerful magic. Unfortunately, Somebody or Something is determined that Alvin won't grow up." Booklist
"This beguiling book recalls Robert Penn Warren in its robust but reflective blend of folktale, history, parable and personal testimony, pioneer narrative." Publ Wkly
Followed by Red prophet

Carey, Janet Lee
Dragon's Keep. Harcourt 2007 302p $17 *
Grades: 7 8 9 10 **Fic**
1. Princesses—Fiction 2. Dragons—Fiction 3. Mother-daughter relationship—Fiction 4. Great Britain—History—1066-1154, Norman period—Fiction 5. Fantasy fiction
ISBN 978-0-15-205926-2; 0-15-205926-1
LC 2006-24669
In 1145 A.D., as foretold by Merlin, fourteen-year-old Rosalind, who will be the twenty-first Pendragon Queen of Wilde Island, has much to accomplish to fulfill her destiny, while hiding from her people the dragon's claw she was born with that reflects only one of her mother's dark secrets.
This is told "in stunning, lyrical prose. . . . Carey smoothly blends many traditional fantasy tropes here, but her telling is fresh as well as thoroughly compelling." Booklist

Cary, Kate
Bloodline; a novel. Razor Bill 2005 324p $16.99
Grades: 7 8 9 10 **Fic**
1. Vampires—Fiction 2. World War, 1914-1918—Fiction 3. Horror fiction
ISBN 1-59514-012-3
In this story told primarily through journal entries, a British soldier in World War I makes the horrifying discovery that his regiment commander is descended from Count Dracula.
"This story is an interesting blend of mystery, horror, and romance, and readers who love vampire novels will find it a refreshing twist to the classic story." SLJ
Followed by Bloodline: reckoning (2007)

Castellucci, Cecil, 1969-
Boy proof. Candlewick Press 2005 203p $15.99
Grades: 7 8 9 10 **Fic**
1. Motion pictures—Fiction 2. Los Angeles (Calif.)—Fiction
ISBN 0-7636-2333-4 LC 2004-50256
Feeling alienated from everyone around her, Los Angeles high school senior and cinephile Victoria Denton hides behind the identity of a favorite movie character until an interesting new boy arrives at school and helps her realize that there is more to life than just the movies.
This "novel's clipped, funny, first-person, present-tense narrative will grab teens . . . with its romance and the screwball special effects, and with the story of an outsider's struggle both to belong and to be true to herself." Booklist

The queen of cool. Candlewick Press 2006 166p $15.99 *
Grades: 9 10 11 12 **Fic**
1. School stories 2. Zoos—Fiction
ISBN 0-7636-2720-8 LC 2005-50174
Bored with her life, popular high school junior Libby signs up for an internship at the zoo and discovers that the "science nerds" she meets there may have a few things to teach her about friendship and life.
The author "offers a refreshingly nuanced and credible look at what lies behind the facade of cool." Bull Cent Child Books

Cather, Willa, 1873-1947
Death comes for the archbishop. Knopf 1992 xxvii, 297p $17; pa $11.95 *
Grades: 11 12 Adult **Fic**
1. New Mexico—Fiction 2. Catholic Church—Missions—Fiction
ISBN 0-679-41319-7; 0-679-72889-9 (pa)
Also available from other publishers
"Everyman's library"
First published 1927
"Bishop Jean Latour and his vicar Father Joseph Vaillant together create pioneer missions and organize the new diocese of New Mexico. . . . The two combine to triumph over the apathy of the Hopi and Navajo Indians, the opposition of corrupt Spanish priests, and adverse climatic and topographic conditions. They are assisted by Kit Carson and by such devoted Indians as the guide Ja-

Cather, Willa, 1873-1947—*Continued*
cinto. When Vaillant goes as a missionary bishop to Colorado, they are finally separated, but Latour dies soon after his friend, universally revered and respected, to lie in state in the great Santa Fe cathedral that he himself created." Oxford Companion to Am Lit. 6th edition

My Antonia; with an introduction by Lucy Hughes-Hallett. Knopf 1996 xxxiii, 272p $20

Grades: 11 12 Adult   **Fic**
1. Frontier and pioneer life—Fiction 2. Nebraska—Fiction 3. Czech Americans—Fiction
ISBN 0-679-44727-X   LC 96-223945
Also available in paperback from Houghton Mifflin "Everyman's library"
First published 1918 by Houghton Mifflin
"Told by Jim Burden, a New York lawyer recalling his boyhood in Nebraska, the story concerns Antonia Shimerda, who came with her family from Bohemia to settle on the prairies of Nebraska. The difficulties related to pioneering and the integration of immigrants into a new culture are clearly portrayed." Shapiro. Fic for Youth. 3d edition

O pioneers! edited with an introduction and notes by Marilee Lindemann. Oxford University Press 1999 xxxi, 179p (Oxford world's classics) pa $9.95 *

Grades: 11 12 Adult   **Fic**
1. Swedish Americans—Fiction 2. Frontier and pioneer life—Fiction
ISBN 0-19-283216-6   LC 98-35944
Also available in paperback from Vintage and in hardcover from Buccaneer Bks.
First published 1913 by Houghton Mifflin
"The heroic battle for survival of simple pioneer folk in the Nebraska country of the 1880's. John Bergson, a Swedish farmer, struggles desperately with the soil but dies unsatisfied. His daughter Alexandra resolves to vindicate his faith, and her strong character carries her weak older brothers and her mother along to a new zest for life. Years of privation, are rewarded on the farm. But when Alexandra falls in love with Carl Linstrum, and her family objects because he is poor, he leaves to seek a different career. After Alexandra's younger brother Emil is killed by the jealous husband of the French girl Marie Shabata, however, Carl gives up his plans to go to the Klondike, returns to marry Alexandra and take up the life of the farm." Haydn. Thesaurus of Book Dig

Cervantes Saavedra, Miguel de, 1547-1616
Don Quixote de la Mancha; [by] Miguel de Cervantes; translated, with a critical text based on the first editions of 1605 and 1615, and with variant readings, variorum notes, and an introduction by Samuel Putnam. Modern Library 1998 xl, 1239p $25.95

Grades: 11 12 Adult   **Fic**
1. Spain—Fiction
ISBN 0-679-60286-0   LC 97-47415
Also available from other publishers
Original Spanish edition, published in two parts, 1605 and 1615

"Originally conceived as a comic satire against the chivalric romances then in literary vogue, the novel describes realistically what befalls an elderly knight who, his head bemused by reading romances, sets out on his old horse Rosinante, with his pragmatic squire Sancho Panza, to seek adventure. In the process, he also finds love in the person of the pleasant Dulcinea. Contemporaries evidently did not take the book as seriously as later generations have done, but by the end of the 17th century it was deemed highly significant, especially abroad. It came to be seen as a mock epic in prose, and the 'grave and serious air' of the author's irony was much admired. In the history of the modern novel the role of *Don Quixote* is recognized as seminal." Merriam-Webster's Ency of Lit

Chambers, Aidan, 1934-
Postcards from no man's land. Dutton Children's Bks. 2002 312p $19.99

Grades: 11 12   **Fic**
1. World War, 1939-1945—Fiction 2. Netherlands—Fiction
ISBN 0-525-46863-3   LC 2002-16562
First published 1999 in the United Kingdom
"In Holland in 1944, Dutch teenager Geertrui fell passionately in love with a wounded young British soldier, and she hid him from the enemy. That soldier's grandson, Jacob, a British teenager, is now in Amsterdam to visit the grave of the grandfather he never knew, and he falls in love with a beautiful young woman, even as he's attracted to an openly gay young man." Booklist
"This novel is beautifully written, emotionally touching, and intellectually challenging." Voice Youth Advocates

Chbosky, Steve
The perks of being a wallflower; {by} Stephen Chbosky. Pocket Bks. 1999 213p pa $12 *

Grades: 9 10 11 12   **Fic**
ISBN 0-671-02734-4   LC 99-236288
This novel in letter form is narrated by Charlie, a high school freshman. "His favorite aunt passed away, and his best friend just committed suicide. The girl he loves wants him as a friend; a girl he does not love wants him as a lover. His 18-year-old sister is pregnant. The LSD he took is not sitting well. And he has a math quiz looming." Time
"Charlie, his friends, and family are palpably real. . . . This report on his life will engage teen readers for years to come." SLJ

Chevalier, Tracy, 1962-
Girl with a pearl earring. Dutton 2000 240p $21.95

Grades: 11 12 Adult   **Fic**
1. Vermeer, Johannes, 1632-1675—Fiction 2. Netherlands—Fiction
ISBN 0-525-94527-X   LC 99-32493
Also available in paperback from Plume Bks.
Chevalier examines the world of artist Johannes Vermeer and the city of Delft in the 17th century through the eyes of Griet, an illiterate 17-year-old. In this novel the fictional character of Griet, a servant in the Vermeer

Chevalier, Tracy, 1962-—*Continued*

household, acts as the model for the artist's portrait Girl With a Pearl Earring

The author "has done very well in creating the feel of a society with sharp divisions of status and creed. . . . Griet is a memorable character—reserved, wary, observant, and, although she does not know it, afflicted with a serious and ultimately dangerous crush on her employer. The situation makes a fine story, which is exceptionally well told." Atl Mon

Chotjewitz, David, 1964-

Daniel half human; and the good Nazi; translated by Doris Orgel. Atheneum Books for Young Readers 2004 298p $17.95 *

Grades: 7 8 9 10   Fic

1. Jews—Fiction 2. Germany—Fiction 3. National socialism—Fiction

ISBN 0-689-85747-0   LC 2003-25554

"A Richard Jackson Book"

In 1933, best friends Daniel and Armin admire Hitler, but as anti-Semitism buoys Hitler to power, Daniel learns he is half Jewish, threatening the friendship even as life in their beloved Hamburg, Germany, is becoming nightmarish. Also details Daniel and Armin's reunion in 1945 in interspersed chapters.

"Orgel's translation reads smoothly and movingly. An outstanding addition to the large body of World War II/Holocaust fiction." SLJ

Christie, Agatha, 1890-1976

The A.B.C. murders; a Hercule Poirot mystery. Distributed by Workman Pub. Co. 2006 252p $12 *

Grades: 11 12 Adult   Fic

1. Mystery fiction

ISBN 1-57912-624-3; 978-1-57912-624-7

LC 2006-45734

First published 1936 by Dodd, Mead & Company

Series statement from jacket

This novel is "about a serial killer who announces his apparently unmotivated killings in advance to Poirot; the only clue is a railway guide left at the scene of each crime. In the opinion of many critics, this is one of Dame Agatha's greatest detective novels." Ency of Mystery & Detection

And then there were none. St. Martin's Griffin 2004 264p pa $12.95 *

Grades: 11 12 Adult   Fic

1. Mystery fiction

ISBN 0-312-33087-1   LC 2004-41165

Also available in hardcover from Buccaneer Books

First published 1939 in the United Kingdom with title: Ten little niggers; first United States edition, 1940, by Dodd, Mead. Variant title: Ten little Indians

"A tour de force on the following trapeze: invitations go out to a group of people, all of whom have been responsible for the death of someone by negligence of intent. The island on which the party is gathered is owned by the would-be avenger of all those deaths. The events and the tension produced by the gradual polishing off of the undetected culprits are beautifully done. One improbability, well hidden, makes the whole thing plausible." Barzun. Cat of Crime. Rev and enl edition

Cisneros, Sandra

The house on Mango Street. Knopf 1994 134p $24 *

Grades: 7 8 9 10   Fic

1. Chicago (Ill.)—Fiction 2. Mexican Americans—Fiction

ISBN 0-679-43335-X   LC 93-43564

"Originally published by Arte Público Press in 1984." Verso of title page

Composed of a series of interconnected vignettes, this "is the story of Esperanza Cordero, a young girl growing up in the Hispanic quarter of Chicago. For Esperanza, Mango Street is a desolate landscape of concrete and run-down tenements, where she discovers the hard realities of life—the fetters of class and gender, the specter of racial enmity, the mysteries of sexuality, and more." Publisher's note

This is "a composite of evocative snapshots that manages to passionately recreate the milieu of the poor quarters of Chicago." Commonweal

Clancy, Tom, 1947-

The hunt for Red October. Naval Inst. Press 1984 387p $27.95

Grades: 11 12 Adult   Fic

1. Spies—Fiction

ISBN 0-87021-285-0   LC 84-16569

Also available in paperback from Berkley Bks.

"Based on a true incident—the attempted defection of a Soviet destroyer in 1975—the plot concerns the defection of the 'Red October', a Soviet submarine carrying 26 Seahawk missiles able to destroy 200 cities. Russia's fleet is ordered to find and destroy the sub; the U.S. Navy wants to find it and get it to an American port. An 18-day, 4,000-mile hunt across the Atlantic ensues." Booklist

Clark, Mary Higgins

Where are the children? [S & S classic ed] Simon & Schuster 1999 268p $25; pa $7.99

Grades: 9 10 11 12   Fic

1. Kidnapping—Fiction 2. Mystery fiction

ISBN 0-684-86356-1; 0-671-74118-7 (pa)

LC 98-55511

A reissue of the title first published 1975

This tale is "set against a background of Cape Cod in the dead of winter. Nancy Eldredge's past hides a terrible secret. She was once tried and almost convicted of the murder of her two young children from a first marriage. . . . She is now happily married again with another little boy and girl. When these children vanish from their front yard in a snowstorm, Nancy's past is raked up and the local police are certain she has killed again." Publ Wkly

Clarke, Arthur C., 1917-

2001: a space odyssey. New Am. Lib. 1968 221p pa $7.99 hardcover o.p. *

Grades: 7 8 9 10 11 12 Adult   Fic

1. Science fiction

ISBN 0-451-45799-4 (pa)

"Based on a screenplay by Stanley Kubrick and Arthur C. Clarke." Title page

Clarke, Arthur C., 1917-—*Continued*

Astronauts of the spaceship Discovery, aided by their computer, HAL, blast off in search of proof that extraterrestrial beings had a part in the development of intelligent life forms on Earth millions of years ago.

"By standing the universe on its head, the author makes us see the ordinary universe in a different light. . . . [This novel becomes] a complex allegory about the history of the world." New Yorker

Clement-Davies, David, 1961-

The sight. Dutton Bks. 2002 465p hardcover o.p. pa $7.99

Grades: 7 8 9 10 11 12 Adult   Fic

1. Wolves—Fiction 2. Fantasy fiction
ISBN 0-525-46723-8; 0-14-250047-X (pa)
LC 2002-16572

In Transylvania during the Middle Ages, a pack of wolves sets out on a perilous journey to prevent their enemy from calling upon a legendary evil one that will give her the power to control all animals

"The narrative is rich, complex, and most importantly, credible, but it requires a thoughtful and perceptive reader." Voice Youth Advocates

Clinton, Cathryn

A stone in my hand. Candlewick Press 2002 191p $15.99; pa $5.99 *

Grades: 9 10 11 12   Fic

1. Family life—Fiction
ISBN 0-7636-1388-6; 0-7636-2561-2 (pa)
LC 2001-58423

Eleven-year-old Malaak and her family are touched by the violence in Gaza between Jews and Palestinians when first her father disappears and then her older brother is drawn to the Islamic Jihad

"With a sharp eye for nuances of culture and the political situation in the Middle East, Clinton has created a rich, colorful cast of characters and created an emotionally charged novel." SLJ

Cohn, Rachel

Gingerbread. Simon & Schuster Bks. for Young Readers 2002 172p $15.95

Grades: 9 10 11 12   Fic

1. Parent-child relationship—Fiction
ISBN 0-689-84337-2   LC 00-52225

After being expelled from a fancy boarding school, Cyd Charisse's problems with her mother escalate after Cyd falls in love with a sensitive surfer and is subsequently sent from San Francisco to New York City to spend time with her biological father.

"Cohn works wonders with snappy dialogue, up-to-the-minute language, and funny repartee. Her contemporary voice is tempered with humor and deals with problems across two generations. Funny and irreverent reading with teen appeal that's right on target." SLJ

Other titles featuring Cyd Charisse are:
Shrimp (2005)
Cupcake (2007)

Nick & Norah's infinite playlist; [by] Rachel Cohn & David Levithan. Knopf 2006 183p $16.95; lib bdg $18.99 *

Grades: 9 10 11 12   Fic

1. Rock musicians—Fiction 2. New York (N.Y.)—Fiction
ISBN 978-0-375-83531-5;   0-375-83531-8;
978-0-375-93531-2 (lib bdg); 0-375-93531-2 (lib bdg)
LC 2005-12413

High school student Nick O'Leary, member of a rock band, meets college-bound Norah Silverberg and asks her to be his girlfriend for five minutes in order to avoid his ex-sweetheart.

"The would-be lovers are funny, do stupid things, doubt themselves, and teens will adore them. F-bombs are dropped throughout the book, but it works. These characters are not 'gosh' or 'shucks' people." Voice Youth Advocates

Cole, Stephen, 1971-

Thieves like us. Bloomsbury 2006 349p $16.95

Grades: 8 9 10 11 12   Fic

1. Adventure fiction
ISBN 978-1-58234-653-3; 1-58234-653-4
LC 2005030616

A mysterious benefactor hand-picks a group of teen geniuses to follow a set of clues leading to the secrets of everlasting life, secrets which they must steal and for which they risk being killed.

"This novel relies on fast action, cool gadgets, and clever problem solving." Booklist

Followed by Thieves till we die (2007)

Coleman, Evelyn, 1948-

Born in sin. Atheneum Bks. for Young Readers 2001 234p $16

Grades: 9 10 11 12   Fic

1. African Americans—Fiction 2. Swimming—Fiction
ISBN 0-689-83833-6   LC 00-25947

"A Richard Jackson book"

"Keisha, an inner-city high school freshman, wants to attend Avery College and then medical school. Instead, she finds herself in a summer camp for underprivileged kids. She not only learns to swim but is so good at it that an Olympic scout comes to watch her and wants her on the team." Book Rep

"In gritty vernacular, Keisha Wright narrates a testimonial depicting the racial stereotypes and socioeconomic hardships that many urban African-American teens struggle to overcome." SLJ

Connor, Leslie

Dead on town line; illustrations by Gina Triplett. Dial Books 2005 131p il $15.99

Grades: 7 8 9 10   Fic

1. Ghost stories 2. Homicide—Fiction
ISBN 0-8037-3021-7   LC 2004-15312

"Cassie's body lies hidden in a crevice, where she tries to figure out what happens next. She meets the ghost of Birdie, another murdered girl who was hidden in the same crevice years earlier. . . . Each verse/chapter adds a piece to the puzzle of Cassie's death until her body is found and the crime is solved. . . . This is an absorbing and moving story." SLJ

Conrad, Joseph, 1857-1924

Heart of darkness; with an introduction by Verlyn Klinkenborg. Knopf 1993 110p $15 *

Grades: 11 12 Adult   **Fic**
1. Africa—Fiction
ISBN 0-679-42801-1   LC 93-1855
"Everyman's library"
Originally published 1902 in the United Kingdom in the collection Youth, and two other stories
"Marlow tells his friends of an experience in the (then) Belgian Congo, where he once ran a river steamer for a trading company. Fascinated by reports about the powerful white trader Kurtz, Marlow went into the jungle in search of him, expecting to find in his character a clue to the evil around him. He found Kurtz living a depraved and abominable life, based on his exploitation of the natives. Without the pressures of society, and with the opportunity to wield absolute power, Kurtz succumbs to atavism." Reader's Ency. 4th edition

Lord Jim; a tale. Knopf 1992 xxxiii, 437p $19 *

Grades: 11 12 Adult   **Fic**
1. Islands of the Pacific—Fiction
ISBN 0-679-40544-5   LC 91-53223
"Everyman's library"
First published 1899; first Everyman's library edition 1935
A Borzoi Bk.
"The title character is a man haunted by guilt over an act of cowardice. He becomes an agent at an isolated East Indian trading post. There his feelings of inadequacy and responsibility are played out to their logical and inevitable end." Merriam-Webster's Ency of Lit

Conroy, Pat

The lords of discipline. Bantam Books 2002 c1980 561p pa $15

Grades: 11 12 Adult   **Fic**
1. Military education—Fiction 2. South Carolina—Fiction
ISBN 0-553-38156-3
A reissue of the title first published 1980 by Houghton Mifflin
The story is set in the late sixties at the time of the Vietnam War. The narrator, "Will McLean, recounts his four years at 'Carolina Military Institute.' . . . We follow the fates of four roommates and their reactions to the Institute. Will has been given the responsibility of helping the Institute's first black cadet make it through the first year. In doing that Will runs into a mysterious secret society." Libr J
The novel "is engrossing and well written. Pat Conroy . . . writes dialogue that reeks of witty Hollywood repartee, but his descriptions and characterizations are both sensitive and entertaining. He carefully draws Will as the young man who disdains military formalities and defends plebes." Saturday Rev

The prince of tides. Houghton Mifflin 1986 567p $35 *

Grades: 11 12 Adult   **Fic**
1. South Carolina—Fiction 2. New York (N.Y.)—Fiction
ISBN 0-395-35300-9   LC 86-10689

Also available in paperback from Bantam Bks.
"Savannah Wingo, a successful feminist poet who has suffered from hallucinations and suicidal tendencies since childhood, has never been able to reconcile her life in New York with her early South Carolina tidewater heritage. Her suicide attempt brings her twin brother, Tom, to New York, where he spends the next few months, at the request of Savannah's psychiatrist . . . helping to reconstruct and analyze her early life." Libr J

Constable, Kate

The singer of all songs. Arthur A. Levine Books 2004 c2002 297p $16.95

Grades: 7 8 9 10   **Fic**
1. Fantasy fiction 2. Magic—Fiction
ISBN 0-439-55478-0   LC 2003-9034
First published 2002 in Australia
Sequel: The waterless sea
Calwyn, a young priestess of ice magic, or chantment, joins with other chanters who have different magical skills to fight a sorcerer who wants to claim all powers for his own
"An impressive debut by an author who clearly has much to contribute to the fantasy genre." Booklist
Other available titles in this series are:
The waterless sea (2005)
The tenth power (2006)

Cook, K. L.

The girl from Charnelle; a novel. William Morrow 2006 371p $24.95; pa $14.95

Grades: 11 12 Adult   **Fic**
1. Family life—Fiction 2. Texas—Fiction
ISBN 0-06-082965-6; 978-0-06-082965-0; 0-06-082966-4 (pa); 978-0-06-082966-7 (pa)
     LC 2005-50234
"Laura Tate, barely 16 and in charge of the household after her mother runs away, is drawn into an affair with her father's married coworker and poker buddy." SLJ
This novel "considers more than a young girl's erotic and emotional awakening; it's the story of an entire generation growing up too quickly." Libr J

Cook, Karin, 1969-

What girls learn; a novel. Pantheon Bks. 1997 304p hardcover o.p. pa $13.95

Grades: 11 12 Adult   **Fic**
1. Mother-daughter relationship—Fiction
ISBN 0-679-44828-4; 0-679-76944-7 (pa)
     LC 96-30315
This novel "tells the story of two young sisters, Tilden and Elizabeth, and their relationship with their mother, Frances. Having spent their childhood as a close, happy threesome moving from house to house in Atlanta, the girls' lives are forever changed when Frances meets and falls in love with Nick, who moves the entire family to the North. Just when the girls have begun to make inroads at their new school, Frances discovers a lump in her breast." Booklist
"Cook has a deft touch in capturing the domestic dialogue of family life, the alternating innocence and wiseass cynicism of preteens, and the ache of a mother who tried to do the best for her girls." SLJ

Cook, Lorna J.

Departures. St. Martin's Press 2004 242p hardcover o.p. pa $12.95

Grades: 9 10 11 12 Fic

1. Siblings—Fiction

ISBN 0-312-32128-7; 0-312-32129-5 (pa)

LC 2003-58183

"Like all the members in their unsettled family, teen siblings Suzen and Evan dream of escaping their small midwestern town. Cook's understated, pitch-perfect prose captures fundamental high-school restlessness and a family's subtle, shifting fragility." Booklist

Cooney, Caroline B.

Code orange. Delacorte 2005 200p $15.95

Grades: 7 8 9 10 Fic

1. Smallpox—Fiction 2. School stories 3. New York (N.Y.)—Fiction

ISBN 0-385-90277-8 LC 2004-26422

While conducting research for a school paper on smallpox, Mitty finds an envelope containing 100-year-old smallpox scabs and fears that he has infected himself and all of New York City.

"Readers won't soon forget either the profoundly disturbing premise of this page-turner or its likable, ultimately heroic slacker protagonist." Booklist

Cooper, James Fenimore, 1789-1851

The Leatherstocking tales. Library of Am. 1985 2v ea $40

Grades: 11 12 Adult Fic

1. United States—History—1755-1763, French and Indian War—Fiction 2. Native Americans—Fiction 3. Frontier and pioneer life—Fiction 4. Adventure fiction

ISBN 0-940450-20-8 (v1); 0-940450-21-6 (v2)

LC 84-25060

Contents: v1 The pioneers; or, The sources of the Susquehanna, a descriptive tale; The last of the Mohicans; a narrative of 1757; The prairie; a tale; v2 The Pathfinder; or, The inland sea; The Deerslayer; or, The first warpath

These novels "are linked together by the career of Natty Bumppo, or Hawkeye, Cooper's inimitable backwoodsman, a romantic embodiment of the virtues of both races, and of Chingachgook, his Indian counterpart, equally idealized. . . . There is little historical background; but the vivid descriptions of wood, lake, and prairie, and of the daily life of Indian and huntsman, gives the finest imaginable picture extant of natural scenes and human conditions that have long passed away." Baker. Guide to the Best Fic

Cormier, Robert

After the first death. Dell Publishing 1991 c1979 233p pa $6.50 *

Grades: 7 8 9 10 Fic

1. Terrorism—Fiction

ISBN 0-440-20835-1

First published 1979 by Pantheon Bks.

"A busload of children is hijacked by a band of terrorists whose demands include the exposure of a military brainwashing project. The narrative line moves from the teenage terrorist Milo to Kate the bus driver and the involvement of Ben, whose father is the head of the military operation, in this confrontation. The conclusion has a shocking twist." Shapiro. Fic for Youth. 2d edition

The chocolate war; a novel. Pantheon Bks. 1974 253p $19.95 *

Grades: 7 8 9 10 Fic

1. School stories

ISBN 0-394-82805-4

Also available in paperback from Random House Children's Bks.

"In the Trinity School for Boys the environment is completely dominated by an underground gang, the Vigils. During a chocolate candy sale Brother Leon, the acting headmaster of the school, defers to the Vigils, who reign with terror in the school. Jerry Renault is first a pawn for the Vigils' evil deeds and finally their victim." Shapiro. Fic for Youth. 3d edition

Followed by Beyond the chocolate war (1985)

I am the cheese; a novel. Pantheon Bks. 1977 233p hardcover o.p. pa $6.50 *

Grades: 7 8 9 10 11 12 Adult Fic

1. Intelligence service—Fiction

ISBN 0-394-83462-3; 0-440-94060-5 (pa)

LC 76-55948

"Adam Farmer's mind has blanked out; his past is revealed in bits and pieces—partly by Adam himself, partly through a transcription of Adam's interviews with a government psychiatrist. Adam's father, a newspaper reporter, gave evidence at the trial of a criminal organization which had infiltrated the government itself. He and his family, marked for death, came under the protection of the super-secret Department of Re-Identification, which changed the family's name and kept them under constant surveillance. Now an adolescent, Adam is finally let in on his parents' terrible secret." SLJ

"The suspense builds relentlessly to an ending that, although shocking, is entirely plausible." Booklist

Cornish, D. M., 1972-

Foundling. Putnam's Sons 2006 434p il (Monster blood tattoo) $18.99

Grades: 8 9 10 11 12 Fic

1. Fantasy fiction

ISBN 0-399-24638-X

Having grown up in a home for foundlings and possessing a girl's name, Rossamünd sets out to report to his new job as a lamplighter and has several adventures along the way as he meets people and monsters who are more complicated than he previously thought.

"This first book in a trilogy presents a fantasy world remarkably well developed. Included in the book are maps, a 102-page glossary, appendixes, and the author's own illustrations of the characters. The descriptions are vivid and fascinating." Voice Youth Advocates

Corrigan, Eireann, 1977-

Splintering. Scholastic 2004 184p $16.95

Grades: 9 10 11 12 Fic

1. Violence—Fiction 2. Family life—Fiction

ISBN 0-439-53597-2 LC 2003-20056

Corrigan, Eireann, 1977-—*Continued*

Relates, in a series of poems from different perspectives, the events and after-effects of an intruder's violent attack on a family

"The poems offer insight into sibling relationships, rivalries and misunderstandings, as the brother and sister each rage against the other, struggle at cross-purposes and find ways to reach each other across the parentally imposed silences and secrets. The author does not demonize the parents, however, and in some of the most thought-provoking verses the children muse about evidence of love they had never noticed before. Although this novel captures several kinds of splintering, its climax imparts hope of a solid healing." Publ Wkly

Coy, John

Crackback. Scholastic 2005 201p $16.99 *
Grades: 7 8 9 10   Fic
1. School stories 2. Football—Fiction 3. Drug abuse—Fiction 4. Father-son relationship—Fiction
ISBN 0-439-69733-6   LC 2004-30972
Miles barely recalls when football was fun after being sidelined by a new coach, constantly criticized by his father, and pressured by his best friend to take performance-enhancing drugs.

The author "writes a moving, nuanced portrait of a teen struggling with adults who demand, but don't always deserve, respect." Booklist

Crane, Stephen, 1871-1900

The red badge of courage; an episode of the American Civil War; [by] Stephen Crane, with an introduction by Shelby Foote. Modern Library 1993 li, 246p $17.95 *
Grades: 7 8 9 10   Fic
1. Chancellorsville (Va.), Battle of, 1863—Fiction
ISBN 0-679-60296-8
Also available Thorndike Press large print edition and from other publishers
First published 1895
"A young Union soldier, Henry Fleming, tells of his feelings when he is under fire for the first time during the battle of Chancellorsville. He is overcome by fear and runs from the field. Later he returns to lead a charge that re-establishes his own reputation as well as that of his company. One of the great novels of the Civil War." Cincinnati Public Libr

Craven, Margaret

I heard the owl call my name. Doubleday 1973 166p hardcover o.p. pa $6.99
Grades: 7 8 9 10   Fic
1. Native Americans—Fiction 2. Clergy—Fiction 3. Death—Fiction
ISBN 0-385-02586-6; 0-440-34369-0 (pa)
Not knowing that he has a fatal illness, a young Anglican priest is assigned to serve a parish of Kwakiutl Indians in the seacoast wilds of British Columbia. Among these vanishing Indians, Mark Brian learns enough of the meaning of life not to fear death

The author's "writing glows with delicate, fleeting images and a sense of peace. Her characters' hearts are bared by a few words—or by the fact that nothing is said at all." Christ Sci Monit

Crichton, Michael, 1942-

The Andromeda strain. Avon Books 2003 c1969 331p pa $7.99
Grades: 11 12 Adult   Fic
1. Science fiction
ISBN 0-06-054181-4
First published 1969 by Knopf
"In these days of interplanetary exploration, this tale of the world's first space-age biological emergency may seem uncomfortably believable. When a contaminated space capsule drops to earth in a small Nevada town and all the town's residents suddenly die, four American scientists gather at an underground laboratory of Project Wildfire to search frantically for an antidote to the threat of a worldwide epidemic." Shapiro. Fic for Youth. 3d edition

Jurassic Park; a novel. Knopf 1990 399p $28.95; pa $7.99 *
Grades: 7 8 9 10   Fic
1. Science fiction 2. Dinosaurs—Fiction 3. Genetic engineering—Fiction
ISBN 0-394-58816-9; 0-345-37077-5 (pa)
                                           LC 90-52960
This novel "tells of a modern-day scientist bringing to life a horde of prehistoric animals." N Y Times Book Rev

"Crichton is a master at blending technology with fiction. . . . Suspense, excitement, and good adventure pervade this book." SLJ

Followed by The lost world (1995)

Crist-Evans, Craig

Amaryllis. Candlewick Press 2003 184p $15.99 *
Grades: 7 8 9 10   Fic
1. Brothers—Fiction 2. Father-son relationship—Fiction 3. Vietnamese Conflict, 1961-1975—Fiction 4. Florida—Fiction
ISBN 0-7636-1863-2   LC 2002-34997
Jimmy and his older brother Frank share a love of surfing and their problems with a drunken father, until Frank turns eighteen and goes to Vietnam

"Crist-Evans has written an interesting, although somber, account of a troubled family in emotional turmoil. Both teens are believable and likable characters with whom many young adults will identify. . . . This is a crisply written and a worthwhile addition to fiction collections." SLJ

Crowe, Chris

Mississippi trial, 1955. Penguin Putnam 2002 231p $17.99; pa $5.99
Grades: 7 8 9 10   Fic
1. Till, Emmett—Fiction 2. Grandfathers—Fiction
ISBN 0-8037-2745-3; 0-14-250192-1 (pa)
                                           LC 2001-40221
"Phyllis Fogelman books"
In Mississippi in 1955, a sixteen-year-old finds himself at odds with his grandfather over issues surrounding the kidnapping and murder of a fourteen-year-old African American from Chicago named Emmett Till

"By combining real events with their impact upon a

Crowe, Chris—*Continued*
single fictional character, Crowe makes the issues in this novel hard-hitting and personal. The characters are complex." Voice Youth Advocates

Crutcher, Chris, 1946-
Ironman; a novel. Greenwillow Bks. 1995 181p $16.99; pa $6.99
Grades: 9 10 11 12 **Fic**
1. Father-son relationship—Fiction 2. School stories 3. Triathlon—Fiction
ISBN 0-688-13503-X; 0-06-059840-9 (pa)
LC 94-1657
While training for a triathlon, seventeen-year-old Bo attends Mr. Nak's anger management group at school which leads him to examine his relationship with his father.
"Through Crutcher's masterful character development, readers will believe in Bo, empathize with the other members of the anger-management group, absorb the wisdom of Mr. Nak and despise, yet at times pity, the boy's father. This is not a light read, as many serious issues surface, though the author's trademark dark humor (and colorful use of street language) is abundant." SLJ

Running loose. Greenwillow Bks. 1983 190p $18.99; pa $6.99 *
Grades: 7 8 9 10 **Fic**
1. School stories
ISBN 0-688-02002-X; 0-06-009491-5 (pa)
LC 82-20935
"Louie Banks tells what happened to him in his senior year in a small town Idaho high school. Besides falling in love with Becky and losing her in a senseless accident, Louie takes a stand against the coach when he sets the team up to injure a black player on an opposing team, and learns that you can't be honorable with dishonorable men." Voice Youth Advocates
"This is a story of honor and principles, messages that are achieved without preaching. An unusually fine first novel." Bull Cent Child Books

Staying fat for Sarah Byrnes. Greenwillow Bks. 1993 216p $17.99; pa $6.99 *
Grades: 7 8 9 10 **Fic**
1. Obesity—Fiction 2. Child abuse—Fiction 3. Friendship—Fiction 4. Swimming—Fiction
ISBN 0-688-11552-7; 0-06-009489-3 (pa)
LC 91-40097
"An obese boy and a disfigured girl suffer the emotional scars of years of mockery at the hands of their peers. They share a hard-boiled view of the world until events in their senior year hurl them in very different directions. A story about a friendship with staying power, written with pathos and pointed humor." SLJ

Stotan! HarperTempest 2003 c1986 261p pa $6.99
Grades: 7 8 9 10 **Fic**
1. Swimming—Fiction
ISBN 0-06-009492-3 LC 85-12712
"A Greenwillow book"
First published 1986

A high school coach invites members of his swimming team to a memorable week of rigorous training that tests their moral fiber as well as their physical stamina.
"A subplot involving the boys' fight against local Neo-Nazi activists provides some immediate action, while the various characters' conflicts tighten the middle and ending. The pace lags through the story's introduction; nevertheless, this is a searching sports novel, with a tone varying from macho-tough to sensitive." Bull Cent Child Books

Danticat, Edwidge, 1969-
The farming of bones; a novel. Soho Press 1998 312p $23
Grades: 11 12 Adult **Fic**
1. Dominican-Haitian Conflict, 1937—Fiction 2. Plantation life—Fiction
ISBN 1-56947-126-6 LC 98-3655
Also available in paperback from Penguin
"The book is based on a historical incident in 1937, when Dominican dictator Trujillo ordered the massacre of 15,000 to 20,000 Haitian emigrants living in his country. The Farming of Bones recounts the story through the eyes of Amabelle Désir, a young Haitian woman who is working in the Dominican Republic as the servant to a patrician family." Time
"It's a testament to Danticat's skill that Amabelle's musical, sorrowing voice never falters, even during her stark descriptions of the bloodbath." New Yorker

Darrow, Sharon
The painters of Lexieville. Candlewick Press 2003 182p $16.99
Grades: 9 10 11 12 **Fic**
1. Poverty—Fiction 2. Country life—Fiction 3. Arkansas—Fiction
ISBN 0-7636-1437-8 LC 2002-41142
Seventeen-year-old Pert Lexie does not think things could get much worse in her small, impoverished community, but when her uncle's advances go too far, everthing—including her determination to leave as soon as possible—suddenly changes
"A harrowing, suspenseful, grudgingly hopeful book that will haunt the reader long after its conclusion." Booklist

Davidson, Dana, 1967-
Jason & Kyra. Jump at the Sun/Hyperion 2004 330p $16.99; pa $5.99
Grades: 9 10 11 12 **Fic**
1. African Americans—Fiction 2. School stories 3. Detroit (Mich.)—Fiction
ISBN 0-7868-1851-4; 0-7868-3653-9 (pa)
LC 2003-61277
Handsome and popular Jason tries to come to terms with his irascible, often absent father and his growing attraction to the quiet, studious Kyra
"Readers with an appetite for love stories are likely to follow Jason and Kyra's pas de deux from its beginning straight through to its satisfying end." Publ Wkly

Played. Hyperion/Jump at the Sun 2005 234p $16.99; pa $8.99
Grades: 9 10 11 12 **Fic**

Davidson, Dana, 1967-—*Continued*
1. School stories
ISBN 0-7868-3690-3; 0-7868-3691-1 (pa)
"When one of Ian's boys dares him to get plain-faced Kylie Winship to sleep with him in just three weeks, he thinks it'll be a breeze. Tall and fine, with honey-colored skin and eyes, Ian is used to getting what he wants from girls. And if he succeeds in playing Kylie, he'll be down with the most popular crew in his high school. But this girl who everyone considers a nobody is turning out to be more surprising than he ever could have imagined." Publisher's note
"Direct and affecting, this will pull at readers' heartstrings while also serving as fair warning for teenage girls everywhere." Booklist

Davis, Amanda
Wonder when you'll miss me. William Morrow 2003 259p $24.95; pa $12.95
Grades: 11 12 Adult   Fic
1. Runaway teenagers—Fiction 2. Rape—Fiction 3. Circus—Fiction
ISBN 0-688-16781-0; 0-06-053426-5 (pa)
LC 2002-24118
"After she is sexually assaulted under the school bleachers, 16-year-old Faith runs away from home, accompanied by the Fat Girl, a taunting, imaginary former self. At the circus, Faith finds a safe haven and a healing environment." Booklist
"Davis's writing is at its finest when the protagonist is struggling through the constant trials with her distant mother, her ineffectual teachers, and her one true friend's suicide. . . . The author succeeds in making this character unique, with flaws that teens will relate to. Readers will root for Faith, and the heartwarming conclusion will leave them satisfied." SLJ
Includes bibliographical references

De la Cruz, Melissa, 1971-
Blue bloods. Hyperion 2006 302p $15.99 *
Grades: 9 10 11 12   Fic
1. Vampires—Fiction 2. New York (N.Y.)—Fiction
ISBN 978-0-7868-3892-9; 0-7868-3892-2
LC 2005-44786
Select teenagers from some of New York City's wealthiest and most socially prominent families learn a startling secret about their bloodlines.
"History, mythology, and the contemporary New York prep-school and club scene blend seamlessly in this sexy and sophisticated riff on vampire lore that never collapses into camp." Bull Cent Child Books

Fresh off the boat. HarperCollins Publishers 2005 243p $15; lib bdg $16.89
Grades: 7 8 9 10   Fic
1. Filipino Americans—Fiction 2. Immigrants—Fiction 3. School stories
ISBN 0-06-054540-2; 0-06-054541-0 (lib bdg)
LC 2004-15513
When her family emigrates from the Philippines to San Francisco, California, fourteen-year-old Vicenza Arambullo struggles to fit in at her exclusive, all-girl private school.
"This well-written, heartfelt novel is a worthy addition to most YA collections, but especially where there are strong immigrant populations." SLJ

De la Peña, Matt
Ball don't lie. Delacorte Press 2005 280p $16.95; lib bdg $18.99; pa $7.99
Grades: 9 10 11 12   Fic
1. Basketball—Fiction 2. Obsessive-compulsive disorder—Fiction 3. Foster home care—Fiction 4. Race relations—Fiction 5. Los Angeles (Calif.)—Fiction
ISBN 0-385-73232-5; 0-385-90258-1 (lib bdg); 0-385-73425-7 (pa)   LC 2004-18057
Seventeen-year-old Sticky lives for basketball and plays at school and at the Lincoln Rec Center in Los Angeles but he is unaware of the many dangers—including his own past—that threaten his dream of playing professionally.
"The prose moves with the rhythm of a bouncing basketball and those who don't mind mixing their sports stories with some true grit may find themselves hypnotized by Sticky's grim saga." Publ Wkly

De Lint, Charles, 1951-
The blue girl; Charles de Lint. Viking 2004 368p $17.99; pa $7.99
Grades: 7 8 9 10   Fic
1. Fairies—Fiction 2. Ghost stories 3. School stories
ISBN 0-670-05924-2; 0-14-240545-0 (pa)
LC 2004-19051
New at her high school, Imogene enlists the help of her introverted friend Maxine and the ghost of a boy who haunts the school after receiving warnings through her dreams that soul-eaters are threatening her life
"The book combines the turmoil of high school intertwined with rich, detailed imagery drawn from traditional folklore and complex characters with realistic relationships. . . . This book is not just another ghost story, but a novel infused with the true sense of wonder and magic that is De Lint at his best. It is strongly recommended." Voice Youth Advocates

Defoe, Daniel, 1661?-1731
Robinson Crusoe; edited with an introduction by Thomas Keymer and notes by Thomas Keymer and James Kelly. Oxford University Press 2007 368p (Oxford world's classics) pa $7.95
Grades: 11 12 Adult   Fic
1. Survival after airplane accidents, shipwrecks, etc.—Fiction
ISBN 0-19-283342-1; 978-0-19-283342-6
LC 2006-26022
Also available from other publishers
First published 1719
"A minutely circumstantial account of the hero's shipwreck and escape to an uninhabited island, and the methodical industry whereby he makes himself a comfortable home. The story is founded on the actual experiences of Alexander Selkirk, who spent four years on the island of Juan Fernandez in the early 18th century." Lenrow. Reader's Guide to Prose Fic

Desai, Anita, 1937-
Clear light of day. Houghton Mifflin 2000 182p
pa $13

Grades: 11 12 Adult   **Fic**
1. India—Fiction 2. Family life—Fiction
ISBN 0-618-07451-1   LC 00-61326
"A Mariner book"
First published 1980 by Harper & Row
"The novel begins with the triennial visit of the younger sister Tara and her diplomat husband to the old family home, a decaying suburban mansion on the banks of
the Jumma outside Old Delhi. Here Bim the older sister,
lives with the youngest brother, Baba. Baba is autistic, a
childlike, speechless whisp of a man who spends his
days playing 'I'm Dreaming of a White Christmas' and
'Donkey Seranade' on an ancient windup gramophone.
The oldest brother, Raja, has moved away. The book divides itself equally between the present of Tara's visit
and the sisters' memories of the past. . . . The visit is
a strain—a series of under-the-surface estrangements and
rapprochements, with sisterly love ebbing and flowing.

Desai Hidier, Tanuja
Born confused. Scholastic Press 2002 413p
$16.95; pa $7.99 *

Grades: 7 8 9 10   **Fic**
1. East Indians—United States—Fiction
2. Friendship—Fiction
ISBN 0-439-35762-4; 0-439-51011-2 (pa)
                                          LC 2002-4515
Seventeen-year-old Dimple, whose family is from India, discovers that she is not Indian enough for the Indians and not American enough for the Americans, as she
sees her hypnotically beautiful, manipulative best friend
taking possession of both her heritage and the boy she
likes
"This involving story . . . will reward its readers. The
family background and richness in cultural information
add a new level to the familiar girl-meets-boy story."
SLJ

Dessen, Sarah, 1970-
Dreamland; a novel. Viking 2000 250p $15.99;
pa $7.99

Grades: 7 8 9 10   **Fic**
1. Violence—Fiction
ISBN 0-670-89122-3; 0-14-240175-7 (pa)
                                          LC 99-44102

After her older sister runs away, sixteen-year-old
Caitlin decides that she needs to make a major change
in her own life and begins an abusive relationship with
a boy who is mysterious, brilliant, and dangerous
"Dessen writes with utter realism as she describes
Caitlin's descent, first into drugs, then into sex, and finally into a relationship that turns violent. . . . It's not
only the plot that's vivid; the characters are also intensely real." Booklist

Just listen; a novel. Viking 2006 371p $17.99
Grades: 9 10 11 12   **Fic**
1. School stories 2. Friendship—Fiction 3. Family
life—Fiction
ISBN 0-670-06105-0; 978-0-670-06105-1
                                          LC 2006-472

Isolated from friends who believe the worst because
she has not been truthful with them, sixteen-year-old
Annabel finds an ally in classmate Owen, whose honesty
and passion for music help her to face and share what
really happened at the end-of-the-year party that changed
her life.
The author "weaves a sometimes funny, mostly emotional, and very satisfying story." Voice Youth Advocates

Deuker, Carl, 1950-
Painting the black. Avon Books 1999 248p pa
$5.99

Grades: 9 10 11 12   **Fic**
1. Baseball—Fiction 2. School stories
ISBN 0-380-73104-5
"An Avon Flare book"
First published 1997 by Houghton Mifflin
"After a disastrous fall from a tree, senior Ryan Ward
wrote off baseball. But he is swept back into the game
when cocky, charismatic Josh Daniels—a star quarterback with the perfect spiral pass as well as a pitcher with
a mean slider—moves into the neighborhood. . . . The
well-written sports scenes—baseball and football—will
draw reluctant readers, but it is Ryan's moral courage
that will linger when the reading is done." Booklist

Runner. Houghton Mifflin 2005 216p $16; pa
$7.99

Grades: 7 8 9 10   **Fic**
1. Smuggling—Fiction 2. Alcoholism—Fiction
3. Terrorism—Fiction
ISBN 0-618-54298-1; 0-618-73505-4 (pa)
                                          LC 2004-15781

Living with his alcoholic father on a broken-down
sailboat on Puget Sound has been hard on seventeen-
year-old Chance Taylor, but when his love of running
leads to a high-paying job, he quickly learns that the
money is not worth the risk
"Writing in a fast-paced, action-packed, but at the
same time reflective style, Deuker . . . uses running as
a hook to entice readers into a perceptive coming-of-age
novel." SLJ

Devoto, Pat Cunningham
The summer we got saved. Warner Books 2005
411p map $23.95; pa $14.95

Grades: 9 10 11 12   **Fic**
1. Civil rights demonstrations—Fiction 2. Race relations—Fiction 3. Alabama—Fiction
ISBN 0-446-57696-4; 0-446-69715-X (pa)
                                          LC 2004-10408
"In 1960s Alabama, young Tab and her sister are introduced to nonviolent protests and the lies told by both
white and black. Realistic, flawed characters, poignant
humor, and provocative questions about social injustice
combine in this compelling historical novel." Booklist

Diamant, Anita, 1951-

The red tent. St. Martin's Press 1997 321p
$24.95; pa $16.95

Grades: 11 12 Adult **Fic**
1. Dinah (Biblical figure)—Fiction 2. Bible. O.T. Genesis—Fiction
ISBN 0-312-16978-7; 0-312-35376-6 (pa)
LC 97-16825
Also available in paperback from Picador
This biblical tale "re-creates the life of Dinah, daughter of Leah and Jacob, from her birth and happy childhood in Mesopotamia through her years in Canaan and death in Egypt." Libr J
"Diamant's fiction debut links the passions of the early Israelites to the ongoing traditions of modern Jews, while the red tent of her title (where women retreat for menstruation, childbirth and illness) becomes a resonant symbol of womanly strength, love and wisdom. Despite a few unprofitable digressions, Diamant succeeds admirably in depicting the lives of women in the age that engendered our civilization and our most enduring values." Publ Wkly

Dick, Philip K.

The minority report. Pantheon Bks. 2002 103p
$12.95

Grades: 11 12 Adult **Fic**
1. Science fiction
ISBN 0-375-42187-4 LC 2002-72313
Originally published posthumously as a short story
"Police Commissioner John Anderton finds himself at the mercy of his own crime-prevention system when the prescient precogs he's hired to stop crime before it starts peg him as a soon-to-be murderer." Publ Wkly

Dickens, Charles, 1812-1870

David Copperfield; with the original illustrations by "Phiz"; introduced by Michael Slater. Knopf 1991 xlii, 891p il $25

Grades: 11 12 Adult **Fic**
1. Great Britain—Fiction
ISBN 0-679-40571-2 LC 91-52995
Also available from other publishers
"Everyman's library"
First published 1850
This novel "incorporates material from the autobiography Dickens had recently begun but soon abandoned and is written in the first person, a new technique for him. Although Copperfield differs from his creator in many ways, Dickens uses many early personal experiences that had meant much to him—his own period of work in a factory while his father was jailed, his schooling and reading, his passion for Maria Beadnell (a woman much like Dora Spenlow), and (more cursorily) his emergence from parliamentary reporting into successful novel writing." Merriam-Webster's Ency of Lit

Great expectations; illustrated by F.W. Pailthrope with an introduction by Michael Slater. Knopf 1992 xxxiv, 469p il $21 *

Grades: 11 12 Adult **Fic**
1. Great Britain—Fiction
ISBN 0-679-40579-8 LC 91-53219
Also available from other publishers

"Everyman's library"
First published 1861
"The first-person narrative relates the coming-of-age of Pip (Philip Pirrip). Reared in the marshes of Kent by his disagreeable sister and her sweet-natured husband, the blacksmith Joe Gargery, the young Pip one day helps a convict to escape. Later he is sent to live with Miss Havisham, a woman driven half-mad years earlier by her lover's departure on their wedding day. . . . When an anonymous benefactor makes it possible for Pip to go to London for an education, he credits Miss Havisham. . . . Pips benefactor turns out to have been Abel Magwitch, the convict he once aided, who dies awaiting trial after Pip is unable to help him a second time. Joe rescues Pip from despair and nurses him back to health." Merriam-Webster's Ency of Lit

Oliver Twist; with twenty-four illustrations by George Cruikshank; introduced by Michael Slater. Knopf 1992 xlvi, 427p il $20

Grades: 7 8 9 10 **Fic**
1. Great Britain—Fiction
ISBN 0-679-41724-9 LC 92-52899
Also available North Books large print edition and from other publishers
"Everyman's library"
First published 1837-1838
"A boy from an English workhouse falls into the hands of rogues who train him to be a pickpocket. The story of his struggles to escape from an environment of crime is one of hardship, danger and the severe obstacles overcome." Natl Counc of Teachers of Engl

A tale of two cities; with an introduction by Simon Schama and sixteen illustrations by Phiz. Knopf 1993 xxviii, 413p il $20 *

Grades: 11 12 Adult **Fic**
1. France—History—1789-1799, Revolution—Fiction
ISBN 0-679-42073-8 LC 92-73542
Also available HarperLargePrint large print edition and from other publishers
"Everyman's library"
First published 1859
"Although Dickens borrowed from Thomas Carlyle's history, *The French Revolution*, for his sprawling tale of London and revolutionary Paris, the novel offers more drama than accuracy. The scenes of large-scale mob violence are especially vivid, if superficial in historical understanding. The complex plot involves Sydney Carton's sacrifice of his own life on behalf of his friends Charles Darnay and Lucie Manette. While political events drive the story, Dickens takes a decidedly antipolitical tone, lambasting both aristocratic tyranny and revolutionary excess." Merriam-Webster's Ency of Lit

Dickinson, Peter, 1927-

Eva. Delacorte Press 1989 219p hardcover o.p.
pa $6.50 *

Grades: 7 8 9 10 **Fic**
1. Chimpanzees—Fiction 2. Science fiction
ISBN 0-385-29702-5; 0-440-20766-5 (pa)
LC 88-29435
"Eva wakes up from a deep coma that was the result of a terrible car accident and finds herself drastically al-

Dickinson, Peter, 1927--—*Continued*

tered. The accident leaves her so badly injured that her parents consent to a radical experiment to transplant her brain and memory into the body of a research chimpanzee. With the aid of a computer for communication, Eva slowly adjusts to her new existence while scientists monitor her progress, feelings, and insight into the animal world." Voice Youth Advocates

"Raising ethical and moral questions, Dickinson creates a vision both profound and chilling." SLJ

The ropemaker. Delacorte Press 2001 375p $15.95

Grades: 7 8 9 10   **Fic**
    1. Magic—Fiction 2. Fantasy fiction
    ISBN 0-385-72921-9   LC 2001-17422
When the magic that protects their Valley starts to fail, Tilja and her companions journey into the evil Empire to find the ancient magician Faheel, who originally cast those spells

"The suspense does not let up until the very last pages. While on one level this tale is a fantasy, it is also a wonderful coming-of-age story." SLJ

Disher, Garry, 1949-

The divine wind; a love story. Levine Bks. 2002 153p hardcover o.p. pa $5.99

Grades: 9 10 11 12   **Fic**
    1. World War, 1939-1945—Fiction 2. Australia—Fiction
    ISBN 0-439-36915-0; 0-439-36916-9 (pa)
                                     LC 2001-38645
On the eve of World War II, Hart, an Australian boy and Mitsy, a Japanese-Australian girl, fall in love but are driven apart

"It will take mature readers to understand the complex relationship between the characters. Although readers might stumble over some of the Aussie phrases and unfamiliar culture, they will finish the story with a better understanding of the depths of love." Voice Youth Advocates

Doctorow, E. L., 1931-

Ragtime. Modern Library 1997 320p $18.95

Grades: 11 12 Adult   **Fic**
    1. New York (State)—Fiction
    ISBN 0-679-60297-6   LC 97-42251
Also available from Plume and Random House Trade Paperbacks

This is a reissue of the title first published 1975 by Random House

"The lives of an upper-middle-class family in New Rochelle; a black ragtime musician who loses his love, his child, and his life because of bigotry; and a poor immigrant Jewish family are interwoven in this early-twentieth-century story. There are cameo appearances by well-known figures of that period: Houdini, anarchist Emma Goldman, actress Evelyn Nesbit, Henry Ford, and J.P. Morgan, whose magnificent library plays an important part in the story. The book mingles fact and fiction in portraying the era of ragtime." Shapiro. Fic for Youth. 3d edition

Doig, Ivan

The whistling season. Harcourt 2006 345p $25

Grades: 11 12 Adult   **Fic**
    1. Siblings—Fiction 2. Household employees—Fiction 3. Teachers—Fiction 4. Montana—Fiction 5. Western stories
    ISBN 978-0-15-101237-4; 0-15-101237-7
                                     LC 2005-25457
"Set in the early 1900s, this novel is a nostalgic, bittersweet story about a widower, his three sons, and the year these boys spend in a one-room country schoolhouse. The novel begins with the father, Oliver, hiring a widowed housekeeper named Rose from Minneapolis (her advertisement reads 'Can't Cook but Doesn't Bite'). She arrives with her unconventional brother, Morrie, in tow. Morrie is something of a scholar, and he soon finds himself pressed into service as a replacement teacher. During the course of the novel, these intriguing and unpredictable characters come together in surprising and uplifting ways. This is an affectionate, heartwarming tale that also celebrates a vanished way of life and laments its passing." Libr J

Donnelly, Jennifer

A northern light. Harcourt 2003 389p $17; pa $8.95

Grades: 9 10 11 12   **Fic**
    1. Farm life—Fiction
    ISBN 0-15-216705-6; 0-15-205310-7 (pa)
                                     LC 2002-5098
In 1906, sixteen-year-old Mattie, determined to attend college and be a writer against the wishes of her father and fiance, takes a job at a summer inn where she discovers the truth about the death of a guest. Based on a true story.

"Donnelly's characters ring true to life, and the meticulously described setting forms a vivid backdrop to this finely crafted story. An outstanding choice for historical-fiction fans." SLJ

Dorfman, Ariel

Burning city; [by] Ariel and Joaquín Dorfman. Random House 2005 c2003 259p $15.95; lib bdg $17.95; pa $7.95

Grades: 9 10 11 12   **Fic**
    1. Cycling—Fiction 2. New York (N.Y.)—Fiction
    ISBN 0-375-83203-3; 0-375-93203-8 (lib bdg); 0-375-83204-1 (pa)   LC 2004-9282
First published 2003 in the United Kingdom with title: The burning city

Sixteen-year-old Heller Highland, who is living with his grandparents while his parents are away, burns rubber across Manhattan delivering bad news by bicycle, and as a summer heat wave melts the city, he is struck by first love.

"Taut writing matches the fast, sweaty pace of Heller's extreme cycling through a sizzling New York summer. . . . Deft, playful dialogue furthers Heller's existential and romantic quests." Horn Book Guide

Dorris, Michael
A yellow raft in blue water. Holt & Co. 1987
343p hardcover o.p. pa $14 *
Grades: 11 12 Adult   **Fic**
  1. Mother-daughter relationship—Fiction 2. Native
Americans—Fiction 3. Family life—Fiction
4. Women—Fiction
ISBN 0-8050-0045-3; 0-312-42185-0 (pa)
                 LC 86-26947
"The bitter rifts and inevitable bonds between generations are highlighted as a teenaged daughter, mother, and
grand matriarch of an American Indian family tell their
life stories. Humorous and poignant, with unique characters." SLJ

Dostoyevsky, Fyodor, 1821-1881
Crime and punishment; translated from the
Russian by Constance Garnett; with an
introduction by Ernest J. Simmons. Modern
Library 1994 xxiv, 629p $19.95 *
Grades: 11 12 Adult   **Fic**
  1. Homicide—Fiction 2. Russia—Fiction
ISBN 0-679-60100-7
Also available from other publishers
Written 1866
"The novel is a psychological analysis of the poor student Raskolnikov, whose theory that humanitarian ends
justify evil means leads him to murder a St. Petersburg
pawnbroker. The act produces nightmarish guilt in
Raskolnikov. The narrative's feverish, compelling tone
follows the twists and turns of Raskolnikov's emotions
and elaborates his struggle with his conscience and his
mounting sense of horror as he wanders the city's hot,
crowded streets. In prison, Raskolnikov comes to the realization that happiness cannot be achieved by a reasoned
plan of existence but must be earned by suffering."
Merriam-Webster's Ency of Lit

Dowd, Siobhan
A swift pure cry. David Fickling Books 2007
309p $16.99; lib bdg $19.99
Grades: 9 10 11 12   **Fic**
  1. Family life—Fiction 2. Fathers—Fiction
3. Pregnancy—Fiction 4. Ireland—Fiction
ISBN   978-0-385-75108-7;   0-385-75108-7;
978-0-385-75109-4 (lib bdg); 0-385-75109-5 (lib bdg)
                 LC 2006-14562
Coolbar, Ireland, is a village of secrets and Shell,
caretaker to her younger brother and sister after the death
of their mother and with the absence of their father, is
not about to reveal hers until suspicion falls on the
wrong person.
"This book, with its serious tone and inclusion of social issues, will have appeal for American readers desir-
ing weightier material, and teachers might find it useful
in the classroom." Voice Youth Advocates

Doyle, Sir Arthur Conan, 1859-1930
The hound of the Baskervilles; introduction by
Laurie R. King; notes by James Danly. Modern
Library 2002 xx, 181p pa $7.95 *
Grades: 11 12 Adult   **Fic**
  1. Mystery fiction 2. Great Britain—Fiction
ISBN 0-8129-6606-6   LC 2002-29505

Also available from other publishers
First published 1902
This is the "case of the eerie howling on the moor and
strange deaths at Baskerville. Sir Charles Baskerville is
murdered, and Holmes and Watson move in to solve the
crime." Haydn. Thesaurus of Book Dig
"By a miracle of judgment, the supernatural is handled
with great effect and no letdown. The plot and subplots
are thoroughly integrated and the false clues put in and
removed with a master hand. The criminal is superb, Dr.
Mortimer memorable, and the secondary figures each
contribute to the total effect of brilliancy and grandeur
combined. One wishes one could be reading it for the
first time." Barzun. Cat of Crime. Rev and enl edition

Draper, Sharon M., 1950-
The Battle of Jericho. Atheneum Books for
Young Readers 2003 297p $16.95
Grades: 7 8 9 10   **Fic**
  1. Clubs—Fiction 2. School stories 3. Cousins—Fic-
tion 4. Death—Fiction
ISBN 0-689-84232-5   LC 2002-8612
"The Warriors of Distinction has been the school's
most exclusive club for 50 years, so when 16-year-old
Jericho is asked to pledge, he's excited—and intimidated.
. . . When the ceremony turns cruel—with the one girl
pledge being singled out for abuse—Jericho begins to
have second thoughts. Then the affair turns deadly."
Booklist
"This title is a compelling read that drives home im-
portant lessons about making choices." SLJ

Copper sun; [by] Sharon Draper. Atheneum
Books for Young Readers 2006 302p $16.95
Grades: 8 9 10 11 12   **Fic**
  1. Slavery—Fiction 2. African Americans—Fiction
ISBN 0-689-82181-6   LC 2005-05540
Two fifteen-year-old girls—one a slave and the other
an indentured servant—escape their Carolina plantation
and try to make their way to Fort Moses, Florida, a
Spanish colony that gives sanctuary to slaves.
"This action-packed, multifaceted, character-rich story
describes the shocking realities of the slave trade and
plantation life while portraying the perseverance, re-
sourcefulness, and triumph of the human spirit." Booklist

Tears of a tiger. Atheneum Pubs. 1994 162p
$16.95; pa $5.99
Grades: 7 8 9 10   **Fic**
  1. Death—Fiction 2. African Americans—Fiction
3. Suicide—Fiction
ISBN 0-689-31878-2; 0-689-80698-1 (pa)
                 LC 94-10278
The death of African American high school basketball
star Rob Washington in a drunk driving accident leads to
the suicide of his friend Andy, who was driving the car
"The story emerges through newspaper articles, journal entries, homework assignments, letters, and conversations that give the book immediacy; the teenage conversational idiom is contemporary and well written. Andy's
perceptions of the racism directed toward young black
males . . . will be recognized by African American
YAs." Booklist

Dumas, Alexandre, 1802-1870
The three musketeers; translated by Jacques Le Clercq. Modern Library 1999 xxi, 598p $24.95
Grades: 7 8 9 10   **Fic**
1. France—History—1589-1789, Bourbons—Fiction
ISBN 0-679-60332-8
Also available from other publishers
Original French edition, 1844
"D'Artagnan arrives in Paris one day in 1625 and manages to be involved in three duels with three musketeers . . . Athos, Porthos and Aramis. They become d'Artagnan's best friends. The account of their adventures from 1625 on develops against the rich historical background of the reign of Louis XIII and the early part of that of Louis XIV, the main plot being furnished by the antagonism between Cardinal de Richelieu and Queen Anne d'Autriche." Haydn. Thesaurus of Book Dig

Duncan, Lois, 1934-
Killing Mr. Griffin. Dell 1990 223p pa $6.50 *
Grades: 7 8 9 10   **Fic**
1. School stories 2. Kidnapping—Fiction
ISBN 0-440-94515-1
First published 1978 by Little, Brown
"Mr. Griffin, the stern highschool English teacher, is loathed by those who should appreciate his determination to educate them. Mark, a student, uses his cool glamour and cleverness to mesmerize classmates Jeff, David, Betsy and Sue, persuading them to kidnap Mr. Griffin, with the idea of scaring the teacher into handing out high grades for inferior work. They leave the man trussed and gagged in a remote spot, where he dies. Sue wants to go to the police with a confession, but Mark masterminds a frantic coverup." Publ Wkly
The author's "skillful plotting builds layers of tension that draws readers into the eye of the conflict. The ending is nicely handled in a manner which provides relief without removing any of the chilling implications." SLJ

Dunkle, Clare B.
By these ten bones. Henry Holt 2005 229p $16.95
Grades: 7 8 9 10   **Fic**
1. Werewolves—Fiction 2. Horror fiction 3. Scotland—Fiction
ISBN 0-8050-7496-1   LC 2004-52359
After a mysterious young wood carver with a horrifying secret arrives in her small Scottish town, Maddie gains his trust – and his heart – and seeks a way to save both him and her townspeople from an ancient evil.
"Readers with a taste for fantasy rooted in folklore and history, and a stomach for grisly horror, will happily roam the mist-shrouded Highlands of Dunkle's latest creation." Booklist

Durham, David Anthony, 1969-
Gabriel's story. Doubleday 2001 291p hardcover o.p. pa $13.95
Grades: 11 12 Adult   **Fic**
1. African Americans—Fiction 2. Kansas—Fiction 3. Frontier and pioneer life—Fiction
ISBN 0-385-49814-4; 0-385-72033-5 (pa)
LC 00-25291

In this "novel, set in the eighteen-seventies, Gabriel, a fifteen-year-old black boy from Baltimore, resents his new life on the Kansas plains when his widowed mother marries a homesteader. But then he falls in with a charismatic cowpunch and horse thief, and as they travel west to New Mexico a series of violent episodes brings Gabriel to swift maturity. The moral gravity of Durham's narrative is offset by his attentiveness to the primacy of nature in the Western landscape." New Yorker

Eddings, David
Belgarath the sorcerer; by David Eddings and Leigh Eddings 1995 644p hardcover o.p. pa $7.99
Grades: 11 12 Adult   **Fic**
1. Fantasy fiction
ISBN 0-345-37324-3; 0-345-40395-09 (pa)
"A Del Rey book"
The authors "return to the world of their multivolume sagas, *The Belgariad* and *The Malloreon*. This prequel to the earlier books, presented as Belgarath's memoirs, offers an absorbing story line and some memorable characters as, once again, the authors touch all the right fantasy bases, with warring gods, political intrigues, supernatural creatures and appealingly human magicians involved in a titanic war over the course of seven millennia." Publ Wkly

Ehrenberg, Pamela, 1972-
Ethan, suspended; written by Pamela Ehrenberg. Eerdmans Books for Young Readers 2007 266p $16
Grades: 7 8 9 10   **Fic**
1. Grandparents—Fiction 2. Race relations—Fiction 3. Jews—Fiction 4. Washington (D.C.)—Fiction
ISBN 978-0-8028-5324-0   LC 2006032697
After a school suspension and his parents' separation, Ethan is sent to live with his grandparents in Washington, D.C., which is worlds apart from his home in a Philadelphia suburb.
"Ehrenberg focuses on themes of race and class without sounding preachy. . . . Best of all are the portraits of [Ethan's] scrappy Jewish grandparents." Booklist

Ehrenhaft, Daniel
Drawing a blank, or, How I tried to solve a mystery, end a feud, and land the girl of my dreams; illustrations by Trevor Ristow. 1st ed. HarperCollins Publishers 2006 326p il $15.99; lib bdg $16.89
Grades: 7 8 9 10   **Fic**
1. Cartoons and comics—Fiction 2. Kidnapping—Fiction 3. Scotland—Fiction
ISBN 0-06-075252-1; 978-0-06-075252-1; 0-06-075253-X (lib bdg); 978-0-06-075253-8 (lib bdg)
LC 2005-20997
Carlton Dunne IV, an outcast boarding school student with a secret identity as a graphic novelist, teams up with a beautiful Scottish girl who yearns to be an American police officer, to resolve an ancient feud and rescue Carlton's kidnapped father.
"The short chapters, abundant one-liners and Carlton's engaging, self-deprecating narration make this a fun, light read." Publ Wkly

Ellison, Ralph

Invisible man; preface by Charles Johnson. Modern Lib. 1994 xxxiv, 572p $19.95; pa $12 *
Grades: 11 12 Adult   **Fic**

1. African Americans—Fiction

ISBN 0-679-60139-2; 0-679-73276-4 (pa)

LC 94-176953

A reissue of the title first published 1952 by Random House

"Acclaimed as a powerful representation of the lives of blacks during the Depression, this novel describes the experiences of one young black man during that period. Dismissed from a Negro college in the South for showing one of the founders how Negroes live there, he is used later as a symbol of repression by a Communist group in New York City. After a Harlem race riot, he is aware that he must contend with both whites and blacks, and that loss of social identity makes him invisible among his fellow beings." Shapiro. Fic for Youth. 3d edition

Emecheta, Buchi

The bride price. Braziller 1976 168p hardcover o.p. pa $14.95

Grades: 11 12 Adult   **Fic**

1. Women—Nigeria—Fiction 2. Igbo (African people)—Fiction 3. Culture conflict—Fiction

ISBN 0-8076-0818-1; 0-8076-0951-X (pa)

"When Aku-nna (translated 'father's wealth'), a delicately beautiful, educated teenager, loses her beloved father, the inexorable tribal protocol mandates that she, with her mother and younger brother, leave the urban life of Lagos, and become part of the extended family of her uncle, a rising rural chieftan. The conflicts engendered by her emerging womanhood, her star-crossed marriage to Chike, the university-bound, village schoolmaster and her gentle efforts to reconcile the countless, unchanging traditions of her ancestors with the ways of her country in the late fifties, are the matter of this . . . novel." Publ Wkly

Engdahl, Sylvia Louise, 1933-

Enchantress from the stars; foreword by Lois Lowry. Firebird 2003 288p pa $6.99

Grades: 7 8 9 10 11 12   **Fic**

1. Science fiction

ISBN 0-14-250037-2

A reissue of the title first published 1970 by Atheneum Pubs.

When young Elana unexpectedly joins the team leaving the spaceship to study the planet Andrecia, she becomes an integral part of an adventure involving three very different civilizations, each one centered on the third planet from the star in its own solar system

"Emphasis is on the intricate pattern of events rather than on characterization, and readers will find fascinating symbolism-and philosophical parallels to what they may have observed or thought. The book is completely absorbing and should have a wider appeal than much science fiction." Horn Book

Another title about Elana is:

The far side of evil (2003)

Enger, Leif

Peace like a river. Atlantic Monthly Press 2001 313p $24; pa $13.95

Grades: 11 12 Adult   **Fic**

1. Minnesota—Fiction

ISBN 0-87113-795-X; 0-8021-3925-6 (pa)

LC 2001-18873

Reuben, the narrator, "was an adolescent in Minnesota in the 1960s, when his brother, Davy, shot and killed two young men who were harassing the family. Reuben's father—in Reuben's estimation fully capable of performing miracles even though the outside world believes he is lost in the clouds—packs Reuben and his sister up and follows the trail Davy has left in his flight from the law." Booklist

Erdrich, Louise

The last report on the miracles at Little No Horse; a novel. HarperCollins Pubs. 2001 361p hardcover o.p. pa $13.95

Grades: 9 10 11 12   **Fic**

1. Catholic Church—Clergy—Fiction 2. Native Americans—Fiction 3. North Dakota—Fiction

ISBN 0-06-018727-1; 0-06-093122-1 (pa)

LC 00-47198

This novel features characters who have appeared previously in Erdrich's work: Father Damien Modeste and Agnes DeWitt. "Now these two merge into one person. . . . From 1912 to 1996, Agnes, disguised as Damien and thus a sham as both man and priest, tries to bring Roman Catholicism to the Ojibwas of Little No Horse Reservation on a loney patch of North Dakota." Time

"Even the small incidents in this novel are moments of tremendous power, stripped of sentimentality or pretension. Erdrich has developed a style that can sound as serious as death or ring with the haunting simplicity of ancient legend." Christ Sci Monit

Esquivel, Laura

Like water for chocolate; translated by Carol Christensen and Thomas Christensen. Doubleday 1992 245p $26; pa $13.95

Grades: 11 12 Adult   **Fic**

1. Women—Fiction 2. Cooking—Fiction 3. Mexico—Fiction

ISBN 0-385-42016-1; 0-385-42017-X (pa)

LC 91-47188

Original Spanish edition published 1989 in Mexico

Set in turn-of-the-century Mexico, this novel relates the story of Tita, "the youngest of three daughters. Practically raised in the kitchen, she is expected to spend her life waiting on Mama Elena and never to marry. Her habitual torment increases when her beloved Pedro becomes engaged to one of her sisters. Tita and he are thrown into tantalizing proximity and manage to communicate their affection through the dishes she prepares for him and his rapturous appreciation. Eventually, Tita's culinary wizardry unleashes uncontrollable forces, with surprising results." Booklist

"A poignant, funny story of love, life, and food which proves that all three are entwined and interdependent." Libr J

Farmer, Nancy, 1941-
The house of the scorpion. Atheneum Bks. for
Young Readers 2002 380p $17.95; pa $7.99 *
Grades: 7 8 9 10   **Fic**
  1. Cloning—Fiction 2. Science fiction
  ISBN 0-689-85222-3; 0-689-85223-1 (pa)
                                        LC 2001-56594
Also available Thorndike Press large print edition
"This is a powerful, ultimately hopeful, story that
builds on today's sociopolitical, ethical, and scientific is-
sues and prognosticates a compelling picture of what the
future could bring." Booklist

Faulkner, William, 1897-1962
Light in August; the corrected text. Modern
Library 2002 512p $21.95 *
Grades: 11 12 Adult   **Fic**
  1. Southern States—Fiction
  ISBN 0-679-64248-X   LC 2001-57933
Also available in paperback from McGraw-Hill
First published 1932 by Harrison Smith & Robert
Haas, Inc.
The novel "reiterates the author's concern with a society that classifies men according to race, creed, and origin. Joe Christmas, the central character and victim, appears to be white but is really part black; he has an affair
with Joanna Burden, a spinster whom the townsfold of
Jefferson regard with suspicion because of her New England background. Joe eventually kills her and sets fire
to her house; he is captured, castrated, and killed by the
outraged townspeople, to whom his victim has become a
symbol of the innocent white woman attacked and killed
by a black man. Other important characters are Lena
Grove, who comes to Jefferson far advanced in pregnancy, expecting to find the lover who has deserted her, and
Gail Hightower, the minister who ignores his wife and
loses his church because of his fanatic devotion to the
past." Reader's Ency. 4th edition

The reivers; a reminiscence. Vintage Books
1992 305p pa $12.95 *
Grades: 11 12 Adult   **Fic**
  1. Tennessee—Fiction
  ISBN 0-679-74192-5   LC 92-50095
First published 1932 by Harrison Smith & Robert
Haas, Inc.
"Told to his grandson as 'A Reminiscence,' Lucius
Priest's monologue recalls his adventures in 1905 as an
11-year-old, when he, the gigantic but childish part-
Indian Boon Hogganbeck, and a black family servant,
Ned William McCaslin, become reivers (stealthy plunder-
ers) of the automobile of his grandfather, the senior
banker of Jefferson, Miss." Oxford Companion to Am
Lit. 5th edition

Ferguson, Alane, 1957-
The Christopher killer; a forensic mystery.
Viking/Sleuth 2006 274p $15.99
Grades: 9 10 11 12   **Fic**
  1. Forensic sciences—Fiction 2. Father-daughter rela-
  tionship—Fiction 3. Homicide—Fiction 4. Mystery
  fiction
  ISBN 0-670-06008-9   LC 2005-15806

On the payroll as an assistant to her coroner father,
seventeen-year-old Cameryn Mahoney uses her knowledge of forensic medicine to catch the killer of a friend
while putting herself in terrible danger.
"This is worlds away from the Nancy Drew college
series in terms of gore, but CSI fans won't blink twice."
Booklist
Followed by Angel of death (2006)

Ferris, Jean, 1939-
Eight seconds. Harcourt 2000 186p $17 *
Grades: 7 8 9 10   **Fic**
  1. Homosexuality—Fiction 2. Prejudices—Fiction
  3. Rodeos—Fiction
  ISBN 0-15-202367-4   LC 99-48796
Also available in paperback from Puffin Bks.
Eighteen-year-old John must confront his own sexuality when he goes to rodeo school and finds himself
strangely attracted to Kit, an older boy who is smart,
tough, complicated, gorgeous, and gay
"Ferris burrows her story firmly, and very authentically, in the heart of her characters. Through John's
thoughts, Kit's dialogue, and a wealth of raging emotions
that pack dramatic punch, she compassionately shares the
challenges of gay teens." Booklist

Of sound mind. Farrar, Straus & Giroux 2001
215p $16; pa $6.95
Grades: 7 8 9 10   **Fic**
  1. Deaf—Fiction 2. Friendship—Fiction
  ISBN 0-374-35580-0; 0-374-45584-8 (pa)
                                        LC 00-68123
Also available Thorndike Press large print edition
Tired of interpreting for his deaf family and resentful
of their reliance on him, high school senior Theo finds
support and understanding from Ivy, a new student who
also has a deaf parent
"Both a thought-provoking study of just when being
deaf matters and when it does not, and an unusually rich
coming-of-age story that explores universal issues of
family responsibility, emotional maturation, love, and
loss." Booklist

Fforde, Jasper
The Eyre affair; a novel. Viking 2002 374p
hardcover o.p. pa $14
Grades: 11 12 Adult   **Fic**
  1. Fantasy fiction
  ISBN 0-670-03064-3; 0-14-200180-5 (pa)
                                        LC 2001-43775
First published 2001 in the United Kingdom
"It's 1985 in England, at least on the calendar; the
Crimean War is in its hundred-and-thirty-first year; time
travel is nothing new; Japanese tourists slip in and out
of Victorian novels; and the literary branch of the special
police, led gamely by the beguiling Thursday Next, are
pursuing Acheron Hades, who has stolen the manuscript
of 'Martin Chuzzlewit' and set his sights on kidnapping
the character Jane Eyre, a theft that could have disastrous
consequences for Brontë lovers who like their story
straight. This rambunctious caper could be taken as a
warning about what might happen if society considered
literature really important—like, say, energy futures or
accounting." New Yorker
Other titles featuring Thursday Next are:

Fforde, Jasper—*Continued*
Thursday Next in Lost in a good book (2003)
Thursday Next in Something rotten (2004)
Thursday Next in The well of lost plots (2004)

Fiedler, Lisa
Romeo's ex; Rosaline's story. Henry Holt 2006
246p $16.95
Grades: 9 10 11 12   **Fic**
1. Shakespeare, William, 1564-1616—Fiction
ISBN 978-0-8050-7500-7; 0-8050-7500-3
LC 2005-35692
In a story based on the Shakespeare play, sixteen-year-old Roseline, who is studying to be a healer, becomes romantically entangled with the Montague family even as her beloved young cousin, Juliet Capulet, defies the family feud to secretly marry Romeo.
"This novel manages to be both witty and multilayered, leaving readers with plenty to ponder." Publ Wkly

Fischer, Jackie
An egg on three sticks; [by] Jackie Moyer Fischer. Thomas Dunne Books 2004 309p pa $12.95
Grades: 9 10 11 12   **Fic**
1. Mother-daughter relationship—Fiction 2. Mental illness—Fiction 3. San Francisco (Calif.)—Fiction
ISBN 0-312-31775-1   LC 2003-9126
In the San Francisco Bay Area in the early 1970s, twelve-year-old Abby watches her mother fall apart and must take on the burden of holding her family together
"With acutely observed detail, Fischer describes a young adult's pull between the universal struggles of adolescence and the surreal anguish of losing a parent to disease." Booklist

Fitzgerald, F. Scott (Francis Scott), 1896-1940
The great Gatsby; preface by Matthew J. Bruccoli. Scribner Classics 1996 170p $25 *
Grades: 11 12 Adult   **Fic**
1. Wealth—Fiction 2. Long Island (N.Y.)—Fiction
ISBN 0-684-83042-6   LC 96-16596
First published 1925
"The mysterious Jay Gatsby lives in a luxurious mansion on the Long Island shore. . . . Nick Carraway, the narrator, lives next door to Gatsby, and Nick's cousin Daisy and her crude but wealthy husband Tom Buchanan live directly across the harbor. Gatsby reveals to Nick that he and Daisy had a brief affair before the war and her marriage to Tom. . . . He persuades Nick to bring him and Daisy together again but ultimately he is unable to win her away from Tom. Daisy, driving Gatsby's car, runs over and kills Tom's mistress Myrtle, unaware of her identity. Myrtle's husband traces the car and shoots Gatsby, who has remained silent in order to protect Daisy. Gatsby's friends and business associates have all deserted him, and only Gatsby's father, and one former guest attend the funeral." Reader's Ency. 4th edition
"The power of the novel derives from its sharp and antagonistic portrayal of wealthy society in New York City and Long Island. . . . The 'Jazz Age,' Fitzgerald's

constant subject, is exposed here in terms of its false glamor and cultural barrenness." Benet's Reader's Ency of Am Lit

Tender is the night. Scribner 1996 320p $25; pa $14
Grades: 9 10 11 12   **Fic**
ISBN 0-684-83050-7; 0-684-80154-X (pa)
LC 96-15215
First published 1934
The story of Dick Diver, a young psychiatrist whose career was thwarted and his genius numbed through his marriage to the exquisite and wealthy Nicole Warren. On the outside their life was all glitter and glamour, but beneath the smooth, beautiful surface lay the corroding falseness of their social values and the tragedy of her disturbed mind
"Despite the book's many terrifying scenes, the warm tenderness of its writing lifts it into the realm of genuine tragedy." Reader's Ency. 4th edition

Flake, Sharon G.
Bang! Jump at the Sun/Hyperion Books for Children 2005 298p $16.99
Grades: 8 9 10 11 12   **Fic**
1. Violence—Fiction 2. Family life—Fiction 3. African Americans—Fiction
ISBN 0-7868-1844-1   LC 2005-47434
A teenage boy must face the harsh realities of inner city life, a disintegrating family, and destructive temptations as he struggles to find his identity as a young man.
"This disturbing, thought-provoking novel will leave readers with plenty of food for thought and should fuel lively discussions." SLJ

Fleischman, Paul
Seek. Front St./Cricket Bks. 2001 167p $16.95
Grades: 7 8 9 10   **Fic**
1. Fathers—Fiction 2. Radio—Fiction
ISBN 0-8126-4900-1   LC 2001-28869
"A Marcato book"
"Using a script format, Rob relates his experiences growing up listening to local and distant radio stations, searching for the disk jockey father who abandoned him before birth." Horn Book Guide
"Fleischman has orchestrated a symphony that is both joyful and poignant with this book designed for reader's theatre." Voice Youth Advocates

Fletcher, Susan, 1951-
Alphabet of dreams. Atheneum Books for Young Readers 2006 294p map $16.95
Grades: 6 7 8 9   **Fic**
1. Jesus Christ—Nativity—Fiction 2. Iran—Fiction 3. Dreams—Fiction 4. Zoroastrianism—Fiction
ISBN 0-689-85042-5
"Ginee Seo Books"
Fourteen-year-old Mitra, of royal Persian lineage, and her five-year-old brother Babak, whose dreams foretell the future, flee for their lives in the company of the magus Melchoir and two other Zoroastrian priests, traveling through Persia as they follow star signs leading to a

Fletcher, Susan, 1951-—*Continued*

newly-born king in Bethlehem. Includes historical notes

"The characters are vivid and whole, the plot compelling, and the setting vast." Voice Youth Advocates

Flinn, Alex

Breathing underwater. HarperCollins Pubs. 2001 263p $15.95; lib bdg $15.89 *

Grades: 9 10 11 12   **Fic**

1. Domestic violence—Fiction

ISBN 0-06-029198-2; 0-06-029199-0 (lib bdg)

LC 00-44933

Sent to counseling for hitting his girlfriend, Caitlin, and ordered to keep a journal, sixteen-year-old Nick recounts his relationship with Caitlin, examines his controlling behavior and anger, and describes living with his abusive father.

"This book attempts to understand the root of domestic violence. Flinn has created sympathetic characters who are struggling with their insecurities. While it is difficult at first to be sympathetic towards Nick, it becomes easier as he examines his life and relationships. This is a good book to use in discussion with teens who have anger issues." Book Rep

Followed by Diva (2006)

Nothing to lose. HarperCollins 2004 277p $15.99; lib bdg $16.99

Grades: 9 10 11 12   **Fic**

1. Runaway teenagers—Fiction 2. Florida—Fiction

ISBN 0-06-051750-6; 0-06-051751-4 (lib bdg)

A year after running away with a traveling carnival to escape his unbearable home life, sixteen-year-old Michael returns to Miami, Florida, to find that his mother is going on trial for the murder of his abusive stepfather

This "is a fast-paced, readable mystery that is rooted in the psychology of battered-sponse syndrome and its impact on an entire family. An inside look at carnival life and Michael's growing love for another carny named Kirstie add gritty texture and a layer of emotional richness to the already intriguing plot." Booklist

Foer, Jonathan Safran, 1977-

Extremely loud & incredibly close. Houghton Mifflin 2005 326p il $24.95; pa $13.95

Grades: 11 12 Adult   **Fic**

1. September 11 terrorist attacks, 2001—Fiction 2. Father-son relationship—Fiction 3. New York (N.Y.)—Fiction

ISBN 0-618-32970-6; 0-618-71165-1 (pa)

LC 2004-65131

"Oskar Schell is an inventor, Francophile, tambourine player, Shakespearean actor, jeweler, pacifist. He is nine years old. And he is on an urgent, secret search through the five boroughs of New York to find the lock that fits a mysterious key belonging to his father, who died in the attacks on the World Trade Center." Publisher's note

The author's "depiction of Oskar's reaction to phone messages left by his father as he awaited rescue in the burning World Trade Center, his description of Oskar's grandfather's love affair . . . and his experiences during the bombing of Dresden—these passages underscore Mr. Foer's ability to evoke, with enormous compassion and psychological acuity, his characters' emotional experiences, and to show how these private moments intersect with the great public events of history." N Y Times (Late N Y Ed)

Forester, C. S. (Cecil Scott), 1899-1966

Beat to quarters. Little, Brown 1985 324p pa $13.95

Grades: 9 10 11 12   **Fic**

1. Sea stories 2. Adventure fiction 3. Naval battles—Fiction

ISBN 0-316-28932-9   LC 85-11609

First published 1937

First of a "series of novels set in the Napoleonic Wars, outlining the career of an introspective naval officer, not always fortunate and seldom truly happy, who hates cruelty and loves the Navy, and who rises in rank to Admiral and eventually becomes Lord Hornblower." Oxford Companion to 20th-century Lit in Engl

Other available titles in this series are:

Flying colours (1986)

Ship of the line (1985)

Forster, E. M. (Edward Morgan), 1879-1970

A passage to India; with an introduction by P.N. Furbank. Knopf 1991 xxxix, 293p $18

Grades: 11 12 Adult   **Fic**

1. British—India—Fiction 2. India—Fiction

ISBN 0-679-40549-6

Also available from other publishers

"Everyman's library"

First published 1924

"Politics and mysticism are potent forces in India just after World War I. Ronald Heaslop, magistrate of Chandrapore, has asked his mother, Mrs. Moore, to visit him along with his fiancée, Adela Quested. To add to their knowledge of the real India, Dr. Aziz, a young Moslem doctor, offers to take them to the Marabar Caves outside the city. The visit is a shattering experience. Mrs. Moore is struck by the thought that all her ideas about life are no more than the hollow echo she hears in the cave. Adela, entering another cave alone, emerges in a panic and accuses Dr. Aziz of having attacked her in the gloom of the cave. The trial that results from her accusation divides the groups in the city so acutely that a reconciliation appears impossible." Shapiro. Fic for Youth. 3d edition

Frank, E. R.

America; a novel. Atheneum Pubs. 2002 242p $18 *

Grades: 9 10 11 12   **Fic**

1. Racially mixed people—Fiction 2. Foster home care—Fiction

ISBN 0-689-84729-7   LC 2001-22984

"A Richard Jackson book"

Teenage America, a not-black, not-white, not-anything boy who has spent many years in institutions for disturbed, antisocial behavior, tries to piece his life together

The author "exposes with compassion, clarity, and deeply unsetting detail the profound shame and horror of abuse as well as the erratic nature of a medical system that tries to reclaim the victims. . . . A piercing, unforgettable novel." Booklist

Frank, E. R.—*Continued*

Life is funny; a novel. DK Ink 2000 263p $19.99

Grades: 7 8 9 10 **Fic**

1. Brooklyn (New York, N.Y.)—Fiction

ISBN 0-7894-2634-X LC 99-23452

Also available in paperback from Puffin Bks.

"A Richard Jackson book"

The lives of eleven young people of different races, economic backgrounds, and family situations living in Brooklyn, New York, become intertwined over a seven year period

"The voices ring true, and the talk is painful, vulgar, rough, sexy, funny, fearful, furious, gentle." Booklist

Frank, Hillary

Better than running at night. Houghton Mifflin 2002 263p $17; pa $10

Grades: 9 10 11 12 **Fic**

1. School stories

ISBN 0-618-10439-9; 0-618-25073-5 (pa)

LC 2002-218

"Ellie's a freshman at art college, and her new life is bringing her all the changes she could have desired. She's in an intense and strange introductory class, which is causing her to rethink her artistic priorities; more significantly, she's in her first serious and sexual relationship." Bull Cent Child Books

"With honesty, wit, and a wild first-person narrative, this first novel breaks boundaries in YA fiction." Booklist

Fredericks, Mariah

Crunch time. Atheneum Bks. for Young Readers 2006 317p $15.95

Grades: 8 9 10 11 12 **Fic**

1. Friendship—Fiction 2. School stories

ISBN 0-689-86938-X LC 2004-20008

"A Richard Jackson book"

Four students, who have formed a study group to prepare for the SAT exam, sustain each other through the emotional highs and lows of their junior year in high school.

"Fredericks writes about high school academics and social rules with sharp insight and spot-on humor." Booklist

Freymann-Weyr, Garret, 1965-

My heartbeat. Houghton Mifflin 2002 154p $15

Grades: 7 8 9 10 **Fic**

1. Siblings—Fiction 2. Homosexuality—Fiction

ISBN 0-618-14181-2 LC 2001-47059

Also available in paperback from Puffin Bks.

As she tries to understand the closeness between her older brother and his best friend, fourteen-year-old Ellen finds her relationship with each of them changing

"This beautiful novel tells a frank, upbeat story of teen bisexual love in all its uncertainty, pain, and joy. . . . The fast, clipped dialogue will sweep teens into the story, as will Ellen's immediate first-person, present-tense narrative." Booklist

Stay with me. Houghton Mifflin 2006 308p $16

Grades: 9 10 11 12 **Fic**

1. Sisters—Fiction 2. Suicide—Fiction 3. New York (N.Y.)—Fiction

ISBN 0-618-60571-1; 978-0-618-60571-2

LC 2005-10754

When her sister kills herself, sixteen-year-old Leila goes looking for a reason and, instead, discovers great love, her family's true history, and what her own place in it is.

"This novel pushes the markers of YA fiction onward and upward." Booklist

Friend, Natasha, 1972-

Lush. Scholastic Press 2006 178p $16.99

Grades: 7 8 9 10 **Fic**

1. Alcoholism—Fiction 2. Fathers—Fiction

ISBN 0-439-85346-X LC 2005-031333

Unable to cope with her father's alcoholism, thirteen-year-old Sam corresponds with an older student, sharing her family problems and asking for advice.

"Friend adeptly takes a teen problem and turns it into a believable, sensitive, character-driven story, with realistic dialogue." Booklist

Frost, Helen, 1949-

The braid. Farrar, Straus and Giroux 2006 95p $16 *

Grades: 7 8 9 10 **Fic**

1. Scotland—Fiction 2. Canada—Fiction 3. Sisters—Fiction 4. Immigrants—Fiction

ISBN 0-374-30962-0 LC 2005-40148

"Frances Foster books"

Two Scottish sisters, living on the western island of Barra in the 1850s, relate, in alternate voices and linked narrative poems, their experiences after their family is forcible evicted and separated with one sister accompanying their parents and younger siblings to Cape Breton, Canada, and the other staying behind with other family on the small island of Mingulay.

"The book will inspire both students and teachers to go back and study how the taut poetic lines manage to contain the powerful feelings." Booklist

Keesha's house. Frances Foster Bks./Farrar, Straus & Giroux 2003 116p $16

Grades: 7 8 9 10 **Fic**

ISBN 0-374-34064-1 LC 2002-22698

Seven teens facing such problems as pregnancy, closeted homosexuality, and abuse each describe in poetic forms what caused them to leave home and where they found home again

"Spare, eloquent, and elegantly concise. . . . Public, private, or correctional educators and librarians should put this must-read on their shelves." Voice Youth Advocates

Fuqua, Jonathon Scott

The reappearance of Sam Webber. Bancroft Press 1999 c1998 237p $24

Grades: 11 12 Adult **Fic**

1. Maryland—Fiction

ISBN 1-890862-02-9 LC 98-74800

Fuqua, Jonathon Scott—*Continued*

Also available in paperback from Candlewick Press

This "novel follows the life of a contemporary 11-year-old white boy named Sam Webber whose father, suffering from depression, abandons Sam and his mother. They are forced to move into a small apartment in the rundown Baltimore neighborhood of Charles Village. At school, Sam is bullied because of his small size and isolated because of his good grades. Eventually, he befriends a black janitor named Greely, who teaches Sam to face his fears." Libr J

Fuqua "has a sensitive understanding of the shaky emotional terrain of preadolescence, and he displays a good ear for dialogue and an intimate feel for Baltimore's rowhouses, creaky buses and broad sidewalks." Publ Wkly

Furey, Leo

The long run; a novel. Trumpeter 2006 376p $22.95

Grades: 11 12 Adult   **Fic**

1. Boys—Fiction 2. Orphanages—Fiction

ISBN 978-1-59030-411-2; 1-59030-411-X

LC 2006-14924

First published 2004 in Canada

This "tale takes place in a Newfoundland orphanage in the early 1960s. While the school is grim and the corporal punishment the students receive is brutal, the boys band together to create the families they all lack. The book is filled with vivid characters." Publ Wkly

Fusco, Kimberly Newton

Tending to Grace. Knopf 2004 167p $14.95; lib bdg $16.99

Grades: 7 8 9 10   **Fic**

1. Speech disorders—Fiction 2. Mothers—Fiction 3. Aunts—Fiction

ISBN 0-375-82862-1; 0-375-92862-6 (lib bdg)

LC 2003-60406

When Cornelia's mother runs off with a boyfriend, leaving her with an eccentric aunt, Cornelia must finally confront the truth about herself and her mother.

"This quiet, beautiful first novel makes the search for home a searing drama." Booklist

Gaiman, Neil, 1960-

American gods; a novel. Morrow 2001 465p $26

Grades: 11 12 Adult   **Fic**

1. Science fiction

ISBN 0-380-97365-0   LC 2001-30407

"A noirish sci-fi road trip novel in which the melting pot of the United States extends not merely to mortals but to a motley assortment of disgruntled gods and deities. Early in 'American Gods' we are introduced to Shadow, a man who has been released from prison only to learn that his wife has died in a car crash. With nothing to return home to, Shadow accepts a job protecting Mr. Wednesday, an omniscient one-eyed grifter. . . . Soon the ex-convict finds himself in an alternate universe, where he is haunted by prophetic nightmares and visited by his dead wife." N Y Times Book Rev

Anansi boys. William Morrow 2005 336p il $26.95; pa $7.99 *

Grades: 11 12 Adult   **Fic**

1. Fantasy fiction

ISBN 978-0-06-051518-8; 0-06-051518-X; 978-0-06-051519-5 (pa); 0-06-051519-8 (pa)

LC 2005-47176

Also available Thorndike Press large print edition

"Fat Charlie's life is about to be spiced up—his estranged father dies in a karaoke bar, and the handsome brother he never knew he had shows up on his doorstep with a gleam in his eye. Next thing he knows, Fat Charlie is being investigated by the police, his fiancée's falling in love with the wrong brother, and he finds out that his father was the god Anansi, Trickster and Spider, and that the beast gods of folklore are plotting their own revenge upon his family bloodline. A fun book with a little of everything—horror, mystery, magic, comedy, song, romance, ghosts, scary birds, ancient grudges, and trademark British wit." Libr J

Stardust. Avon Bks. 1999 238p hardcover o.p. pa $13.95

Grades: 9 10 11 12   **Fic**

1. Fantasy fiction

ISBN 0-380-97728-1; 0-06-114202-6 (pa)

LC 98-8773

Also available Thorndike Press large print edition

"Young Tristran Thorn has grown up in the isolated village of Wall, on the edge of the realm of Faerie. When Tristran and the lovely Victoria see a falling star during the special market fair, Victoria impulsively offers him his heart's desire if he will retrieve the star for her. Tristran crosses the border into Faerie and encounters witches, unicorns, and other strange creatures." Libr J

"Grounding his narrative in mythic tradition, Gaiman employs exquisitely rich language, natural wisdom, good humor and a dash of darkness to conjure up a fairy tale in the grand tradition." Publ Wkly

Gaines, Ernest J., 1933-

The autobiography of Miss Jane Pittman. Dial Press (NY) 1971 245p pa $6.99 hardcover o.p.

Grades: 7 8 9 10   **Fic**

1. African Americans—Fiction 2. Louisiana—Fiction

ISBN 0-553-26357-9 (pa)   LC 77-144380

"In the epic of Miss Jane Pittman, a 110-year-old exslave, the action begins at the time she is a small child watching both Union and Confederate troops come into the plantation on which she lives. It closes with the demonstrations of the sixties and the freedom walk she decides to make. This is a log of trials, heartaches, joys, love—but mostly of endurance." Shapiro. Fic for Youth. 3d edition

A gathering of old men. Knopf 1983 213p hardcover o.p. pa $11.95

Grades: 11 12 Adult   **Fic**

1. Race relations—Fiction 2. African Americans—Fiction 3. Homicide—Fiction 4. Louisiana—Fiction

ISBN 0-394-51468-8; 0-679-73890-8 (pa)

LC 82-49000

"The story opens with the murder of Beau Boutan, a Cajun farmer, on the Louisiana plantation of Candy Mar-

Gaines, Ernest J., 1933-—*Continued*

shall, a headstrong white owner. She claims to have done the shooting because she wished to protect one of her black workers, Mathu, who has been like a guardian to her following the death of her parents. In the plan to stand between Mapes, the local sheriff, and Mathu, Candy has set into motion an idea that has brought together a group of old black men with shotguns (unloaded), all claiming to have done the shooting. The threat of the South's way of punishing blacks by lynching hangs over the story like a pall. It meets opposition from Beau's young brother who has been friends with a black fellow-student and team-mate at his university." Shapiro. Fic for Youth. 3d edition

A lesson before dying. Knopf 1997 c1993 256p $26; pa $12.95 *

Grades: 9 10 11 12   Fic
   1. African Americans—Fiction 2. Mentally handicapped—Fiction 3. Prisoners—Fiction 4. Louisiana—Fiction
   ISBN 0-679-45561-2; 0-375-70270-9 (pa)
                                           LC 92-20335

First published 1993

"The story of two African American men struggling to attain manhood in a prejudiced society, the tale is set in Bayonne, La. . . in the late 1940s. It concerns Jefferson, a mentally slow, barely literate young man, who, though an innocent bystander to a shootout between a white store owner and two black robbers is convicted of murder, and the sophisticated, educated man who comes to his aid. When Jefferson's own attorney claims that executing him would be tantamount to killing a hog, his incensed godmother, Miss Emma, turns to teacher Grant Wiggins, pleading with him to gain access to the jailed youth and help him to face his death by electrocution with dignity." Publ Wkly

"YAs who seek thought-provoking reading will enjoy this glimpse of life in the rural South just before the civil rights movement." SLJ

García Márquez, Gabriel, 1928-

Love in the time of cholera; translated from the Spanish by Edith Grossman. Knopf 1988 348p $30 *

Grades: 11 12 Adult   Fic
   1. Latin America—Fiction
   ISBN 0-394-56161-9   LC 87-40484
Also available in paperback from Penguin Bks.

Original Spanish edition published 1985 in Colombia

"While delivering a message to her father, Florentino Ariza spots the barely pubescent Fermina Daza and immediately falls in love. What follows is the story of a passion that extends over 50 years, as Fermina is courted solely by letter, decisively rejects her suitor when he first speaks, and then joins the urbane Dr. Juvenal Urbino, much above her station, in a marriage initially loveless but ultimately remarkable in its strength. Florentino remains faithful in his fashion; paralleling the tale of the marriage is that of his numerous liaisons, all ultimately without the depth of love he again declares at Urbino's death." Libr J

"The poetry of the author's style, the humor in his voice, the joyous detail with which the plot is upholstered—all are reasons to live in this lush, luxurious novel for as long as you desire." Booklist

One hundred years of solitude; translated from the Spanish by Gregory Rabassa. Knopf 1995 416p $27.95 *

Grades: 11 12 Adult   Fic
   1. Colombia—Fiction
   ISBN 0-679-44465-3   LC 95-234911
Also available in hardcover and paperback from HarperCollins Pubs.

Original Spanish edition published 1967 in Argentina

This novel "relates the founding of Macondo by Jose Arcadio Buendia, the adventures of six generations of his descendants, and, ultimately, the town's destruction. It also presents a vast synthesis of social, economic, and political evils plaguing much of Latin America. Even more important from a literary point of view is its aesthetic representation of a world in microcosm, that is, a complete history, from Eden to Apocalypse, of a world in which miracles such as people riding on flying carpets and a dead man returning to life tend to erase the thin line between objective and subjective realities." Ency of World Lit in the 20th Century

Gardner, John, 1933-1982

Grendel; illustrated by Emil Antonucci. Knopf 1971 174p il hardcover o.p. pa $11.95

Grades: 11 12 Adult   Fic
   1. Monsters—Fiction
   ISBN 0-394-47143-1; 0-679-72311-0 (pa)

"To the heroes of 'Beowulf,' the monster Grendel, devourer of men, represented chaos and death and pagan darkness. This is Grendel's side of the story. . . . Grendel perceives that what the primeval dragon has told him is true: he is the brute existent by which men learn to define themselves. 'Grendel' may be read for what it says about the human condition, for its implicit comments on men's art, wars, fears, and hopes." Publ Wkly

"The world, Mr. Gardner seems to be suggesting in his violent, inspiring, awesome, terrifying narrative, has to defeat its Grendels, yet somehow, he hints, both ecologically and in deeper ways, that world is a poorer place when men and their monsters cannot coexist." Christ Sci Monit

Geras, Adèle

Troy. Harcourt 2001 340p $17; pa $6.95 *

Grades: 7 8 9 10   Fic
   1. Trojan War—Fiction
   ISBN 0-15-216492-8; 0-15-204570-8 (pa)
                                           LC 00-57262

Homer's "tales of Paris and Helen, Achilles and Hector, and Odysseus and the Trojan horse are recast in the form of a modern novel, using the heroes' fates as background and focus for the real subjects: the women of Troy." Horn Book Guide

"Mythology buffs will savor the author's ability to embellish stories of old without diminishing their original flavor, while the uninitiated will find this a captivating introduction to a pivotal event in classic Greek literature." Publ Wkly

Gibbons, Kaye, 1960-
Ellen Foster; a novel. Algonquin Bks. 1987
146p $16.95 *
Grades: 11 12 Adult   **Fic**
1. Southern States—Fiction 2. Foster home care—Fiction
ISBN 1-56512-205-4   LC 86-22136
Also available in paperback from Vintage Bks.

A "novel narrated by an adolescent girl, Ellen, who relates the day-to-day experiences she endured as a child in a troubled family. Ellen's mother died young, her father was abusive, her other relatives were equally bad; it wasn't until she was taken into a foster home that she found the sort of peace and freedom to be innocent that most normal childhoods afford." Booklist

"What might have been grim, melodramatic material in the hands of a less talented author is instead filled with lively humor, . . . compassion and intimacy. This short novel focuses on Ellen's strengths rather than her victimization, presenting a memorable heroine who rescues herself." N Y Times Book Rev

Followed by The life all around me by Ellen Foster (2006)

Giles, Gail
Playing in traffic. Roaring Brook Press 2004
176p $16.95
Grades: 9 10 11 12   **Fic**
1. Homicide—Fiction 2. School stories
ISBN 1-59643-005-2   LC 2003-17829
Also available in paperback from Simon & Schuster
"A Deborah Brodie book"

Shy and unremarkable, seventeen-year-old Matt Lathrop is surprised and flattered to find himself singled out for the sexual attentions of the alluring Skye Colbly, until he discovers the evil purpose behind her actions

"The book is fast paced and written in short chapters that will keep a reluctant reader going. The language is realistic for this MTV generation and sex plays a big part in the story. Although the book is suggested for ages 12 years and up, I recommend that you consider it for grades 10 through 12." Libr Media Connect

Shattering Glass. Roaring Brook Press 2002
152p $15.95; lib bdg $22.90
Grades: 7 8 9 10   **Fic**
1. School stories 2. Violence—Fiction
ISBN 0-7613-1581-0; 0-7613-2601-4 (lib bdg)
                                      LC 2001-41713
Also available in paperback from Simon & Schuster

When Rob, the charismatic leader of the senior class, turns Simon Glass, the school nerd, into Prince Charming, his actions lead to unexpected violence

"Tricky, surprising, and disquieting, this tension-filled story is a psychological thriller as well as a book about finding oneself and taking responsibility." Booklist

What happened to Cass McBride? a novel.
Little, Brown and Company 2006 211p $16.99; pa
$7.99 *
Grades: 11 12   **Fic**
1. Suicide—Fiction 2. Kidnapping—Fiction 3. Family life—Fiction
ISBN   978-0-316-16638-6;   0-316-16638-3;
978-0-316-16639-3 (pa); 0-316-16639-1 (pa)
                                      LC 2005-37298

After his younger brother commits suicide, Kyle Kirby decides to exact revenge on the person he holds responsible.

"Often brutal, this outstanding psychological thriller is recommended for older teens." Voice Youth Advocates

Glass, Linzi
The year the gypsies came. H. Holt 2006 260p
$16.95
Grades: 9 10 11 12   **Fic**
1. Family life—Fiction 2. South Africa—Fiction
ISBN 0-8050-7999-8; 978-0-8050-7999-9
                                      LC 2005-50314
In Johannesburg, South Africa, in the late 1960s, twelve-year-old Emily, who longs for affection from her quarreling parents, finds comfort in the stories of a Zulu servant and in her friendship with a young houseguest who has an equally troubled family.

"Suggest this one to readers who are always looking for a sad book." SLJ

Going, K. L.
Fat kid rules the world. Putnam 2003 187p
$17.99; pa $6.99 *
Grades: 7 8 9 10   **Fic**
1.   Obesity—Fiction   2.   Musicians—Fiction
3. Friendship—Fiction
ISBN 0-399-23990-1; 0-14-240208-7 (pa)
                                      LC 2002-67956
Seventeen-year-old Troy, depressed, suicidal, and weighing nearly 300 pounds, gets a new perspective on life when a homeless teenager who is a genius on guitar wants Troy to be the drummer in his rock band

"Going has put together an amazing assortment of characters. . . . This is an impressive debut that offers hope for all kids." Booklist

Saint Iggy. Harcourt 2006 260p $17
Grades: 9 10 11 12   **Fic**
1. Drug abuse—Fiction 2. Family life—Fiction
3. Poor—Fiction
ISBN 0-15-205795-1; 978-0-15-205795-4
                                      LC 2005-34857
Iggy Corso, who lives in city public housing, is caught physically and spiritually between good and bad when he is kicked out of high school, goes searching for his missing mother, and causes his friend to get involved with the same dangerous drug dealer who deals to his parents.

"Teens will connect with Iggy's powerful sense that although he notices everything, he is not truly seen and accepted himself." Booklist

Goldberg, Myla
Bee season; a novel. Doubleday 2000 275p
hardcover o.p. pa $13.95
Grades: 11 12 Adult   **Fic**
1. Family life—Fiction 2. Jews—United States—Fiction
ISBN 0-385-49879-9; 0-385-49880-2 (pa)
                                      LC 99-47933

Goldberg, Myla—*Continued*

This novel concerns an eleven-year-old girl, Eliza Naumann, who wins the National Spelling Bee. "Eliza's supernatural gift for spelling thrills her father, Saul, a self-styled Jewish scholar who now believes he can train his daughter to literally talk to God. Unfortunately, that means shunting aside Eliza's older brother, Aaron, who joins a religious cult, and her scarily remote mother, Miriam, who begins breaking into houses in search of missing pieces of herself." Newsweek

"Some of the events that unfold . . . seem a little contrived. But Goldberg engenders considerable suspense around both Eliza's string of spelling successes and the fates of the other Naumanns." Time

Golden, Arthur

Memoirs of a geisha; a novel. Knopf 1997 434p il $26.95; pa $7.99

Grades: 11 12 Adult   **Fic**
    1. Japan—Fiction 2. Geishas—Fiction
    ISBN 0-375-40011-7; 1-4000-9689-8 (pa)
                       LC 97-74747

"How nine-year-old Chiyo, sold with her sister into slavery by their father after their mother's death, becomes Sayuri, the beautiful geisha accomplished in the art of entertaining men, is the focus of this . . . novel. Narrating her life story from her elegant suite in the Waldorf Astoria, Sayuri tells of her traumatic arrival at the *Nitta okiya* (a geisha house), where she endures harsh treatment from Granny and Mother, the greedy owners, and from Hatsumomo, the sadistically cruel head geisha. But Sayuri's chance meeting with the Chairman, who shows her kindness, makes her determined to become a geisha. Under the tutelage of the renowned Mameha, she becomes a leading geisha of the 1930s and 1940s." Libr J

"Rarely has a world so closed and foreign been evoked with such natural assurance, from the aesthetics of the Kyoto geisha's 'art'—to the fetishized sexuality of Gion in the thirties and forties, at once delicate and crude, repressed and flagrant." New Yorker

Golding, William, 1911-1993

Lord of the flies; introduction by E. M. Forster; with a biographical and critical note by E. L. Epstein; illustrated by Ben Gibson. 50th anniversary ed. Berkley 2003 315p $23.95; pa $13 *

Grades: 9 10 11 12   **Fic**
    1. Allegories 2. Boys—Fiction
    ISBN 0-399-52920-9; 0-399-50148-7 (pa)
                       LC 2003-54825
"A Perigee book"

First published 1954 in the United Kingdom; first United States edition, 1955, by Coward-McCann

"Stranded on an island, a group of English schoolboys leave innocence behind in a struggle for survival. A political structure modeled after English government is set up and a hierarchy develops, but forces of anarchy and aggression surface. The boys' existence begins to degenerate into a savage one. They are rescued from their microcosmic society to return to an adult, stylized milieu filled with the same psychological tensions and moral voids. Adventure and allegory are brilliantly combined in this novel." Shapiro. Fic for Youth. 3d edition

Goodman, Allegra

Intuition; a novel. Dial Press 2006 344p $25; pa $13 *

Grades: 11 12 Adult   **Fic**
    1. Research—Fiction 2. Cancer—Fiction
    ISBN 0-385-33612-8; 0-385-33610-1 (pa)
                       LC 2005-51940

"The prestigious Philpott Institute in Cambridge, MA, is a virtually closed community dominated by a charismatic leader, oncologist Sandy Glass. Dr. Glass's enthusiasm galvanizes his ambitious scientists to work round the clock when experimental results yield a possible cancer cure, until one young researcher publicizes her suspicions of fraud." Libr J

The author "draws tender but unflinching portraits of the characters' personal lives for a truly humanist novel from the supposedly antiseptic halls of science." Publ Wkly

Gordimer, Nadine, 1923-

My son's story. Penguin Books 1991 277p pa $9.95

Grades: 9 10 11 12   **Fic**
    1. South Africa—Fiction
    ISBN 0-14-015975-4   LC 91-17273
    First published 1990 by Farrar, Straus & Giroux

"Sonny is a teacher of mixed race. He and his wife are . . . sympathetic to the plight of the 'real blacks,' yet ambitious that they may someday be accepted by the whites. Sonny's political education begins when he's fired for helping black children demonstrate in their township. Jailed for promoting boycotts and participating in illegal gatherings, Sonny meets and falls in love with a blond, blue-eyed woman who works for a human-rights organization. Sonny's adolescent son, Will, tells the story of his father's political and erotic development, the resentments and betrayals that ensue." Newsweek

This is a "thoughtful, poised, quietly poignant novel that not only recognizes the value and cost of political commitment, but also takes account of recent developments in South Africa and Eastern Europe in a way that Gordimer's previous work did not." Christ Sci Monit

Graham, Rosemary

Thou shalt not dump the skater dude and other commandments I have broken. Viking 2005 281p $16.99

Grades: 9 10 11 12   **Fic**
    1. School stories
    ISBN 0-670-06017-8; 978-0-670-06017-7
                       LC 2005-3928

Having endured the vicious rumors spread by her professional-skateboarder ex-boyfriend, high school sophomore Kelsey Wilcox tries to salvage her reputation while attempting to earn a place on her high school newspaper.

"Many young women will enjoy this light-handed, anti-romance and will cheer for Kelsey as she stands up for herself and learns that her worth and enjoyment of life are not tied to a boyfriend . . . Kelsey's romantic interludes are PG-13 and perfectly appropriate for middle-school as well as high school readers." Booklist

Gratz, Alan, 1972-
Samurai shortstop. Dial Books 2006 280p
$17.99 *
Grades: 7 8 9 10   **Fic**
1. Father-son relationship—Fiction 2. Baseball—Fiction 3. School stories 4. Tokyo (Japan)—Fiction
ISBN 0-8037-3075-6; 978-0-8037-3075-5
LC 2005-22081
While obtaining a Western education at a prestigious Japanese boarding school in 1890, sixteen-year-old Toyo also receives traditional samurai training which has profound effects on both his baseball game and his relationship with his father. This book features some scenes of graphic violence.
"This is an intense read about a fascinating time and place in world history." Publ Wkly

Graves, Robert, 1895-1985
I, Claudius; from the autobiography of Tiberius Claudius, born B.C. 10, murdered and deified A.D. 54. Modern Lib. 1983 c1934 432p hardcover o.p. pa $14.95 *
Grades: 11 12 Adult   **Fic**
1. Claudius, Emperor of Rome, 10 B.C.-54—Fiction 2. Augustus, Emperor of Rome, 63 B.C.-14 A.D.—Fiction 3. Rome—History—Fiction
ISBN 0-394-60811-9; 0-679-72477-X (pa)
First published 1934 by Harrison Smith and Robert Haas
"Claudius is lame and a stammerer who seems unlikely to carry on the family tradition of power in ancient Rome. Immersing himself in scholarly pursuits, Claudius observes and lives through the plots hatched by his grandmother, Livia, political conspiracies, murders, and corruption, and he survives a number of emperors. He becomes emperor at last and is a just and well-liked ruler, in contrast to those who preceded him." Shapiro. Fic for Youth. 3d edition

Gray, Dianne E.
Together apart. Houghton Mifflin 2002 193p
$16
Grades: 7 8 9 10   **Fic**
1. Sex role—Fiction 2. Blizzards—Fiction
ISBN 0-618-18721-9   LC 2002-408
In 1888 in Prairie Hill, Nebraska, a few months after barely surviving a deadly blizzard that has killed two of her brothers, fourteen-year-old Hannah goes to work at the home of a wealthy widow with progressive social ideas, where she finds Isaac, who is also trying to make a new life for himself. Told from alternating points of view of Hannah and Isaac
"The blossoming love story will keep readers involved, and Gray's memorable characters reveal the late 19th-century society's attitudes toward women's rights and class consciousness." Publ Wkly

Green, John, 1977-
An abundance of Katherines. Dutton Books 2006 227p $16.99 *
Grades: 9 10 11 12   **Fic**
1. Mathematics—Fiction
ISBN 0-525-47688-1; 978-0-525-47688-7
LC 2006-4191

Having been recently dumped for the nineteenth time by a girl named Katherine, recent high school graduate and former child prodigy Colin sets off on a road trip with his best friend to try to find some new direction in life while also trying to create a mathematical formula to explain his relationships.
This "is an enjoyable, thoughtful novel that will attract readers interested in romance, math, or just good storytelling." Voice Youth Advocates

Looking for Alaska. Dutton Books 2005 221p
$15.99; pa $7.99 *
Grades: 9 10 11 12   **Fic**
1. Death—Fiction 2. School stories 3. Birmingham (Ala.)—Fiction
ISBN 0-525-47506-0; 0-14-240251-6 (pa)
LC 2004-10827
Sixteen-year-old Miles' first year at Culver Creek Preparatory School in Alabama includes good friends and great pranks, but is defined by the search for answers about life and death after a fatal car crash
"The language and sexual situations are aptly and realistically drawn, but sophisticated in nature. Miles's narration is alive with sweet, self-deprecating humor, and his obvious struggle to tell the story truthfully adds to his believability." SLJ

Greenberg, Joanne, 1932-
I never promised you a rose garden; [by] Joanne Greenberg (Hannah Green); with a new afterword by the author. New American Library 2004 282p pa $13.95
Grades: 7 8 9 10 11 12 Adult   **Fic**
1. Mentally ill—Fiction 2. Antisemitism—Fiction
ISBN 0-451-21120-0   LC 2003-61424
First published 1964 by Holt & Co.
Sixteen-year-old Deborah "is sick of rebelling against the lies she hears, the hatred she feels, and, at a summer camp, the anti-Semitism she suffers. She is schizophrenic: she has invented for herself a mythical kingdom into which she retreats and only when her parents reluctantly commit her to an asylum does she begin with difficulty to face reality." Publ Wkly
"The hospital world and Deborah's fantasy world are strikingly portrayed, as is the girl's violent struggle between sickness and health, a struggle given added poignancy by youth, wit, and courage." Libr J

Greene, Graham, 1904-1991
The heart of the matter; introduction by James Wood. Deluxe ed. Penguin Books 2004 255p (Penguin classics) pa $15
Grades: 9 10 11 12   **Fic**
1. West Africa—Fiction
ISBN 0-14243799-9   LC 2004-275122
Also available Thorndike Press large print edition
First published 1948
"Set in West Africa, it is a suspense story ingeniously made to hinge on religious faith. . . . The hero is Scobie, an English Roman Catholic who has vowed to make his devout wife happy though he no longer loves her. He borrows money from a local criminal to send her out of harm's way to South Africa; then he falls in love

Greene, Graham, 1904-1991—*Continued*
with a young woman from a group of castaways whose
ship has been torpedoed. The return of his wife, the development of an adulterous affair, and blackmail drive
Scobie deeper into deception and lies. Forced to betray
someone, he betrays his god and himself, and finally
commits suicide." Reader's Ency. 4th edition

The power and the glory; introduction by John
Updike. Viking 1990 295p hardcover o.p. pa $14
*
Grades: 11 12 Adult   **Fic**
    1. Clergy—Fiction 2. Mexico—Fiction
    ISBN 0-670-83536-6; 0-14-243730-1 (pa)
                           LC 90-50052
Also available in hardcover from Amereon
First published 1940 with title: The labyrinthine ways
Set in Mexico, this novel "describes the desperate last
wanderings of a whisky priest as outlaw in his own state,
who, despite a sense of his own worthlessness (he drinks,
and has fathered a bastard daughter), is determined to
continue to function as priest until captured. . . . Like
many of Greene's works, it combines a conspicuous
Christian theme and symbolism with the elements of a
thriller." Oxford Companion to Engl Lit

Greif, Jean-Jacques, 1944-
The fighter. Bloomsbury Children's Books 2006
211p $16.95 *
Grades: 9 10 11 12   **Fic**
    1. Holocaust, 1933-1945—Fiction 2. Jews—Fiction
    ISBN 978-1-58234-891-9; 1-58234-891-X
                           LC 2006-01291
Moshe Wisniak, a poor Polish Jew, uses his physical
strength and cleverness, plus luck, to help him survive
the horrors he is subjected to in the concentration camps
of World War II. Based on the life of Moshé Garbarz.
"Tough, realistic reading with some raw language."
SLJ

Grey, Zane, 1872-1939
Riders of the purple sage. Five Star 2005 368p
$25.95
Grades: 11 12 Adult   **Fic**
    1. Western stories 2. Utah—Fiction 3. Mormons—Fic-
tion 4. Adventure fiction
    ISBN 1-59414-130-4   LC 2004-60017
Also available Thorndike Press large print edition and
from other publishers
First published 1912 by Harper
"Well handled melodramatic story of hair-breadth es-
capes from Mormon vengeance in southwestern Utah in
1871." Booklist

Griffin, Adele
Amandine. Hyperion Bks. for Children 2001
220p $15.99; pa $6.99 *
Grades: 7 8 9 10   **Fic**
    1. School stories 2. Friendship—Fiction
    ISBN 0-7868-0618-4; 0-7868-1441-1 (pa)
                           LC 00-54010

Her first week at a new high school, shy, plain Delia
befriends Amandine, not anticipating the dangerous turns
their friendship would take
"Griffin offers this cautionary message to readers in a
riveting, richly layered, and emotionally honest story."
Voice Youth Advocates

My almost epic summer. G. P. Putnam's Sons
2006 170p $15.99; pa $6.99
Grades: 7 8 9 10   **Fic**
    1. Babysitters—Fiction 2. Summer—Fiction
    ISBN 0-399-23784-4; 0-14-240860-3 (pa)
                           LC 2005013491
Stuck babysitting during the summer while her friends
take glamorous vacations, fourteen-year-old Irene learns
some lessons about life after meeting a beautiful, yet
troubled, girl.
"Griffin has created vivid scenes, believable dilemmas,
and satisfyingly human characters in this novel of self-
discovery." SLJ

Where I want to be. G.P. Putnam's Sons 2005
150p $15.99
Grades: 7 8 9 10   **Fic**
    1. Sisters—Fiction 2. Mental illness—Fiction
    3. Death—Fiction 4. Rhode Island—Fiction
    ISBN 0-399-23783-6   LC 2004-1887
Two teenaged sisters, separated by death but still connected, work through their feelings of loss over the
closeness they shared as children that was later destroyed
by one's mental illness, and finally make peace with
each other
"Thoughtful, unique, and ultimately life-affirming, this
is a fascinating take on the literary device of a main
character speaking after death." SLJ

Grimes, Nikki
Bronx masquerade. Dial Bks. 2002 167p $16.99;
pa $5.99 *
Grades: 7 8 9 10   **Fic**
    1. School stories 2. African Americans—Fiction
    3. Bronx (New York, N.Y.)—Fiction
    ISBN 0-8037-2569-8; 0-14-250189-1 (pa)
                           LC 00-31701
While studying the Harlem Renaissance, students at a
Bronx high school read aloud poems they've written, revealing their innermost thoughts and fears to their formerly clueless classmates
"Funny and painful, awkward and abstract, the poems
talk about race, abuse, parental love, neglect, death, and
body image. . . . Readers will enjoy the lively, smart
voices that talk bravely about real issues and secret fears.
A fantastic choice for readers' theater." Booklist

Dark sons. Jump at the Sun 2005 216p $15.99
Grades: 6 7 8 9   **Fic**
    1. Father-son relationship—Fiction 2. Stepfamilies—
Fiction
    ISBN 0-7868-1888-3   LC 2004-54208
Alternating poems compare and contrast the conflicted
feelings of Ishmael, son of the Biblical patriarch Abraham, and Sam, a teenager in New York City, as they try
to come to terms with being abandoned by their fathers
and with the love they feel for their younger stepbroth-

Grimes, Nikki—*Continued*
ers.

"The simple words eloquently reveal what it's like to miss someone. . . . but even more moving is the struggle to forgive and the affection each boy feels for the baby that displaces him. The elemental connections and the hope. . . will speak to a wide audience." Booklist

Grindle, Lucretia

The nightspinners; a novel. Random House 2003 288p $23.95; pa $11.95

Grades: 11 12 Adult   Fic
1. Sisters—Fiction 2. Twins—Fiction 3. Mystery fiction 4. Philadelphia (Pa.)—Fiction 5. Georgia—Fiction
ISBN 0-375-50776-0; 0-375-75984-0 (pa)
                                          LC 2002-69703
"As very young children, Susannah deBreem and her twin sister, Marina, discovered the ability to speak to each other without physically talking, calling it 'nightspinning.' Now a successful restaurant designer, Susannah thinks herself grown beyond such childish hobbies, especially since her sister was murdered over 18 months before the beginning of the story. But now Marina seems to be reaching out to her from the grave—perhaps even trying to kill her." Libr J

"Grindle takes her time crafting a thrilling and psychological tale that doesn't rely on forced plot twists for suspense." Booklist

Grisham, John

The client. Doubleday 1993 422p $29.95; pa $7.99

Grades: 11 12 Adult   Fic
1. Boys—Fiction 2. Mafia—Fiction 3. Lawyers—Fiction
ISBN 0-385-42471-X; 0-440-21352-5 (pa)
                                          LC 92-39079
"While sneaking into the woods to smoke forbidden cigarettes, preteen brothers Mark and Ricky find a lawyer committing suicide in his car. Mark tries to save the man but is instead grabbed by him and told the location of the body of a murdered U.S. senator—a murder for which the lawyer's Mafia-connected client is accused. Witnessing the successful suicide sends Ricky into shock and Mark into a web of lies, half-truths, and finally into refusal to tell the confided secret to the police. Mark accidentally but fortuitously hires a lawyer, Reggie Love, who steers him through a maze of FBI agents, legal proceedings, judges, ambitious lawyers, and hit men. . . . This thriller is unique in its theme and in its suspense mixed with humor. A sure 'all-night' read." SLJ

The firm. Doubleday 1991 421p $30

Grades: 11 12 Adult   Fic
1. Lawyers—Fiction 2. Mafia—Fiction 3. Memphis (Tenn.)—Fiction
ISBN 0-385-41634-2   LC 90-3945
"Fresh out of Harvard Law School, Mitchell McDeere is recruited by an elite Memphis law firm. . . . {His colleagues} put in 19-hour days for their front-office clients, while beavering behind the scenes on money-laundering operations for the Mafia. . . . Mitch, in fear for his life, agrees to work undercover for the F.B.I." N Y Times Book Rev

"The aphorism 'between a rock and a hard place' aptly describes the dilemma of a young attorney pressed by the FBI to reveal crime-related secrets of his firm, while also hounded by his employers to simply take his huge salary and zip his lip. No aphorism, though, can convey the suspense, wit, and polished writing of this laser-sharp candidate for the best recent updating of the David and Goliath story." Libr J

Gruber, Michael

The witch's boy. HarperTempest 2005 377p $16.99; lib bdg $17.89; pa $7.99 *

Grades: 7 8 9 10   Fic
1. Witches—Fiction 2. Fairy tales
ISBN 0-06-076164-4; 0-06-076165-2 (lib bdg); 0-06-076167-9 (pa)   LC 2004-20845
Also available Thorndike Press large print edition
"Gruber cleverly weaves elements from familiar fairy tales into a saga that moves across forest, earth, and sea." Booklist

Guène, Faïza

Kiffe kiffe tomorrow; [translated from the French by Sarah Adams] Harcourt 2006 179p pa $13

Grades: 11 12 Adult   Fic
1. Muslim women—Fiction 2. Poor—Fiction 3. Paris (France)—Fiction
ISBN 0-15-603048-9; 978-0-15-603048-9
                                          LC 2005-30456
"A Harvest original"
Original French edition, 2004
"Doria, 15, a child of Muslim immigrants, describes her daily struggle in Paris' rough housing projects in a contemporary narrative that's touching, furious, and very funny." Booklist

Guterson, David

Snow falling on cedars. Harcourt Brace & Co. 1994 345p $25 *

Grades: 11 12 Adult   Fic
1. Japanese Americans—Fiction 2. Trials—Fiction 3. Journalists—Fiction 4. Washington (State)—Fiction
ISBN 0-15-100100-6   LC 94-7535
Also available in paperback from Vintage Bks.
"Japanese American Kabuo Miyomoto is arrested in 1954 for the murder of a fellow fisherman, Carl Heine. Miyomoto's trial, which provides a focal point to the novel, stirs memories of past relationships and events in the minds and hearts of the San Piedro Islanders. Through these memories, Guterson illuminates the grief of loss, the sting of prejudice triggered by World War II, and the imperatives of conscience. With mesmerizing clarity he conveys the voices of Kabuo's wife, Hatsue, and Ishmael Chambers, Hatsue's first love who, having suffered the loss of her love and the ravages of war, ages into a cynical journalist now covering Kabuo's trial." Libr J

Haddix, Margaret Peterson, 1964-

Leaving Fishers. Simon & Schuster Bks. for Young Readers 1997 211p hardcover o.p. pa $5.99 *

Grades: 7 8 9 10   Fic
1. Cults—Fiction
ISBN 0-689-81125-X; 0-689-86793-X (pa)
LC 96-47857

After joining her new friends in the religious group called Fishers of Men, Dorry finds herself immersed in a cult from which she must struggle to extricate herself

"The novel does a credible job of showing the effect of a cult on a vulnerable person, without disavowing strong religious beliefs." Child Book Rev Serv

Haddon, Mark

The curious incident of the dog in the night-time. Today Show Book Club ed. Doubleday 2003 226p il $24.95 *

Grades: 9 10 11 12   Fic
1. Autism—Fiction 2. Parent-child relationship—Fiction 3. Great Britain—Fiction
ISBN 0-385-51210-4

Despite his overwhelming fear of interacting with people, Christopher, a mathematically-gifted, autistic fifteen-year-old boy, decides to investigate the murder of a neighbor's dog and uncovers secret information about his mother

"Unable to feel emotions himself, his story evokes emotions in readers—heartache and frustration for his well-meaning but clueless parents and deep empathy for the wonderfully honest, funny, and lovable protagonist. Readers will never view the behavior of an autistic person again without more compassion and understanding." SLJ

Halaby, Laila

West of the Jordan; a novel. Beacon Press 2003 220p (Bluestreak) pa $13

Grades: 9 10 11 12   Fic
1. Cousins—Fiction 2. Arab Americans—Fiction 3. Muslim women—Fiction
ISBN 0-8070-8359-3   LC 2002-154924

"In alternating chapters, four female cousins—Mawal, in the West Bank village of Nawara; Hala, in Arizona; and Khadija and Soraya, in California—tell their stories. Their experiences range from the orthodoxy that imbues Mawal's life to the freedoms that her American relatives find both exhilarating and frightening. The author focuses on the difficulties facing Arab women wherever they live, but especially when trying to navigate the crosscurrents of parental and traditional mores while seeking acceptance and success in a foreign country." SLJ

"Halaby's choice to alternate the narratives of the four young women offers real characterizations to latch onto, and her prose, often lyrical—particularly when the speakers relate other peoples' stories—deepens the complications of history and heritage. Contemplative and lush, this coming-of-age tale resonates with the challenges of cross-cultural life." Publ Wkly

Halam, Ann

Dr. Franklin's island. Wendy Lamb Bks. 2002 245p hardcover o.p. pa $6.50 *

Grades: 9 10 11 12   Fic
1. Survival after airplane accidents, shipwrecks, etc.—Fiction 2. Genetic engineering—Fiction 3. Science fiction
ISBN 0-385-73008-X; 0-440-23781-5 (pa)
LC 2001-50691

First published 2001 in the United Kingdom

When their plane crashes over the Pacific Ocean, three science students are left stranded on a tropical island and then imprisoned by a doctor who is performing horrifying experiments on humans involving the transfer of animal genes

"This exciting and well-developed book . . . will appeal to fans of horror and adventure. . . . However, the book is not for the squeamish. The description of the dead bodies found in the aftermath of the plane explosion and the physical changes the girls experience during their experiments is gruesomely detailed." SLJ

Siberia; a novel. Wendy Lamb Books 2005 262p hardcover o.p. pa $5.99

Grades: 7 8 9 10   Fic
1. Endangered species—Fiction 2. Wilderness survival—Fiction 3. Science fiction
ISBN 0-385-74659-4; 0-553-49414-7 (pa)

After spending two years at a prison school, thirteen-year-old Sloe sets off on a trek across frozen wastelands, tending to the secret "seeds" of wild animals her mother left in her care, trying to reach a new life for all of them.

"Halam intertwines issues of ecology, climate change, and nature conservancy with more personal themes of loneliness, identity, and trust. . . . The bitterly cold setting, the hunger, and fear are almost palpable." SLJ

Haldeman, Joe W., 1943-

The forever war; [by] Joe Haldeman. Eos 2003 277p pa $14.95 *

Grades: 9 10 11 12   Fic
1. Science fiction
ISBN 0-06-051086-2   LC 2003-48518

"The author's preferred ed. of the groundbreaking SF classic."—Cover

"Earth is battling the aliens from a planet in the constellation Taurus but in Haldeman's chronicle of the career of William Mandella from private to reluctant major, the war becomes an engrossing, poignant epic. Mandella was among the unlucky first recruits for a war that has been fought for 1,000 years." Booklist

"A naturalistic description of a war that lasts more than a thousand years, although the main characters age only a few years because of the relativistic effects of faster-than-light space travel. The situation of the soldiers fighting in this kind of war is complicated, however, by their alienation from their own societies by the time-dilation effect, and their growing disillusionment with the war." New Ency of Sci Fic

Haley, Alex, 1921-1992

Mama Flora's family. Delta 1999 462p pa $23

Grades: 9 10 11 12   Fic

Haley, Alex, 1921-1992—*Continued*
1. African Americans—Fiction
ISBN 0-440-61409-0
First published 1998 by Scribner
In this multigenerational family saga, the "lives of Mama Flora and her family provide a whirlwind survey of the 20th-century black experience. As a young woman in a small Tennessee town, Flora bears a son and sees his father killed at the hands of white racists. She realizes that education is the only way out of poverty. Soon, her daughter becomes a social worker while her son dabbles in communism and enlists to fight in World War II. As Flora lays dying, she can look back on her family and their accomplishments with pride." Libr J

Halpin, Brendan
Donorboy; a novel. Villard 2004 209p pa $12.95
Grades: 9 10 11 12   **Fic**
1. Father-daughter relationship—Fiction 2. Orphans—Fiction
ISBN 1-400-06277-2   LC 2004-43090
"14-year-old Rosalind's lesbian moms have been killed in a motor accident, and she is placed in the custody of Sean, 35, her sperm-donor dad. He knew her mothers, saw her, and loved her at birth, but she hasn't known him until now, when suddenly they are a family. . . . Told in a mix of personal narratives, including Rosalind and Sean's desperate e-mails to friends and to each other, her grief journal, instant messages, and taped disciplinary hearings with the school bureaucrats, the novel presents contemporary voices that are funny, tender, defiant, and immediate." Booklist

Hambly, Barbara
A free man of color. Bantam Bks. 1997 311p hardcover o.p. pa $5.99
Grades: 11 12 Adult   **Fic**
1. Race relations—Fiction 2. Homicide—Fiction 3. Creoles—Fiction
ISBN 0-553-10258-3; 0-553-57526-0 (pa)
                                       LC 96-44942
A romantic suspense novel set in 19th century New Orleans. "Benjamin January, a free Creole with dark brown skin, has returned to this society after living in Paris for more than a decade. He is trained as a surgeon, but in Louisiana, he makes his living playing the piano. Soon he is the main suspect in the death of a wealthy man's young mistress, found murdered at a ball. January spends the rest of the book gathering evidence in his defense." Libr J
"A few suspenseful moments not-withstanding, this isn't an action-packed or suspenseful whodunit. Rather, it's a richly detailed, telling portrait of an intricately structured racial hierarchy." Booklist

Hamill, Pete
Snow in August; a novel. Little, Brown 1997 327p hardcover o.p. pa $14
Grades: 11 12 Adult   **Fic**
1. Jews—Fiction 2. Prejudices—Fiction 3. Irish Americans—Fiction 4. Brooklyn (New York, N.Y.)—Fiction
ISBN 0-316-34094-4; 0-446-67525-3 (pa)
                                       LC 96-36043

"In Brooklyn in 1947, Michael Devlin, an 11-year-old Irish kid who spends his days reading *Captain Marvel* and anticipating the arrival of Jackie Robinson, makes the acquaintance of a recently emigrated Orthodox rabbi. In exchange for lessons in English and baseball, Rabbi Hirsch teaches him Yiddish and tells him of Jewish life in old Prague and of the mysteries of the Kabbalah. Anti-Semitism soon rears its head in the form of a gang of young Irish toughs out to rule the neighborhood." Libr J
"Mr. Hamill is not a subtle writer, but his gift for sensual description and his tabloid muscularity . . . fit this page turner of a fable." N Y Times Book Rev

Hardy, Thomas, 1840-1928
The return of the native. Knopf 1992 xxxix, 497p map $22
Grades: 11 12 Adult   **Fic**
1. Great Britain—Fiction
ISBN 0-679-41730-3   LC 92-52901
Also available from other publishers
"Everyman's library"
First published 1878
"The novel is set on Egdon Heath, a barren moor in the fictional Wessex in southwestern England. The native of the title is Clym Yeobright, who has returned to the area to become a schoolmaster after a successful but, in his opinion, a shallow career as a jeweler in Paris. He and his cousin Thomasin exemplify the traditional way of life, while Thomasin's husband, Damon Wildeve, and Clym's wife, Eustacia Vye, long for the excitement of city life. Disappointed that Clym is content to remain on the heath, Eustacia, willful and passionate, rekindles her affair with the reckless Damon. After a series of coincidences Eustacia comes to believe that she is responsible for the death of Clym's mother. Convinced that fate has doomed her to cause others pain, Eustacia flees and is drowned (by accident or intent). Damon drowns trying to save her." Merriam-Webster's Ency of Lit

Tess of the D'Urbervilles; with an introduction by Patricia Ingham. Knopf 1991 xlviii, 472p map $22
Grades: 11 12 Adult   **Fic**
1. Great Britain—Fiction
ISBN 0-679-40586-0   LC 91-52998
Also available from other publishers
"Everyman's library"
First published in complete form 1891
"The tragic history of a woman betrayed. . . . Tess the author contends, is sinned against, but not a sinner; her tragedy is the work of tyrannical circumstances and of the evil deeds of others in the past and the present, and more particularly of two men's baseness, the seducer, and the well-meaning intellectual who married her. . . . The pastoral surroundings, the varying aspects of field, river, sky, serve to deepen the pathos of each stage in the heroine's calamities, or to add beauty and dignity to her tragic personality." Baker. Guide to the Best Fic

Harris, Robert, 1957-
Pompeii; a novel. Random House 2003 278p
map hardcover o.p. pa $13.95
Grades: 11 12 Adult   **Fic**
1. Rome—History—Fiction 2. Volcanoes—Fiction
3. Adventure fiction
ISBN 0-679-42889-5; 0-8129-7461-1 (pa)
                              LC 2003-58446
"An upstanding Roman engineer rushes to repair an
aqueduct in the shadow of Mount Vesuvius, which, in
A.D. 79, is getting ready to blow its top. . . . Lively
writing, convincing but economical period details and
plenty of intrigue keep the pace quick." Publ Wkly

Hartinger, Brent, 1964-
Geography Club. HarperTempest 2003 226p
$15.99; lib bdg $16.89
Grades: 9 10 11 12   **Fic**
1. Homosexuality—Fiction 2. Clubs—Fiction
3. School stories
ISBN 0-06-001221-8; 0-06-001222-6 (lib bdg)
                              LC 2001-51736
A group of gay and lesbian teenagers finds mutual
support when they form the "Geography Club" at their
high school.
"Hartinger grasps the melodrama and teen angst of
high school well. . . . Frank language and the intimation
of sexual activity might put off some readers." Voice
Youth Advocates
Other titles in this series are:
The Order of the Poison Oak (2005)
Split screen (2007)

Hartnett, Sonya, 1968-
Surrender. Candlewick Press 2006 248p $16.99
*
Grades: 9 10 11 12   **Fic**
1. Family life—Fiction 2. Brothers—Fiction 3. Dogs—
Fiction
ISBN 0-7636-2768-2   LC 2005-54259
As he is dying, a twenty-year-old man known as Gabriel recounts his troubled childhood and his strange relationship with a dangerous counterpart named Finnigan.
"From the gripping cover showing a raging inferno to
the blood-chilling revelation of the final chapter, this
page-turner is a blistering yet dense psychological thriller." Voice Youth Advocates

Thursday's child. Candlewick Press 2002 261p
$15.99; pa $7.99
Grades: 7 8 9 10   **Fic**
1. Poverty—Fiction 2. Family life—Fiction 3. Farm
life—Fiction 4. Australia—Fiction
ISBN 0-7636-1620-6; 0-7636-2203-6 (pa)
                              LC 2001-25223
Harper Flute recounts her Australian farm family's
poverty during the Depression, her father's cowardice,
and her younger brother Tin's obsession for digging tunnels and living underground
"This coming-of-age story with allegorical overtones
will burrow into young people's deepest hopes and fears,
shining light in the darkest inner rooms." Booklist

Haruf, Kent, 1943-
Plainsong. Knopf 1999 301p $27.50
Grades: 11 12 Adult   **Fic**
1. Teachers—Fiction 2. Family life—Fiction
3. Colorado—Fiction
ISBN 0-375-40618-2   LC 99-15606
"Set in the plains of Colorado, east of Denver, the
novel comprises several story lines that flow into one.
Tom Guthrie, a high school history teacher, is having
problems with his wife and with an unruly student at
school—problems that affect his young sons, Ike and
Bob, as well. Meanwhile, the pregnant Victoria
Roubideaux has been abandoned by her family. With the
assistance of another teacher, Maggie Jones, she finds
refuge with the McPheron brothers—who seem to know
more about cows than people." Libr J
"From simple strands of language and cuttings of talk,
from the look of the high Colorado plains east of Denver
almost to the place where Nebraska and Kansas meet,
Haruf has made a novel so foursquare, so delicate and
lovely, that it has the power to exalt the reader." N Y
Times Book Rev
Another available title about the residents of Holt, Colorado is:
Eventide (2004)

Hautman, Pete, 1952-
Godless. Simon & Schuster Books for Young
Readers 2004 208p $15.95; pa $7.99 *
Grades: 7 8 9 10   **Fic**
1. Religion—Fiction
ISBN 0-689-86278-4; 1-4169-0816-1 (pa)
                              LC 2003-10468
When sixteen-year-old Jason Bock and his friends
create their own religion to worship the town's water
tower, what started out as a joke begins to take on a
power of its own
"The witty text and provocative subject will make this
a supremely enjoyable discussion-starter as well as pleasurable read." Bull Cent Child Books

Invisible. Simon & Schuster Books for Young
Readers 2005 149p $15.95; pa $7.99 *
Grades: 7 8 9 10   **Fic**
1. Mental illness—Fiction 2. Friendship—Fiction
ISBN 0-689-86800-6; 0-689-86903-7 (pa)
                              LC 2004-2484
Doug and Andy are unlikely best friends—one a loner
obsessed by his model trains, the other a popular student
involved in football and theater—who grew up together
and share a bond that nothing can sever
"With its excellent plot development and unforgettable, heartbreaking protagonist, this is a compelling novel
of mental illness." SLJ

Haworth-Attard, Barbara, 1953-
Theories of relativity. Henry Holt 2005 231p
$16.95 *
Grades: 9 10 11 12   **Fic**
1. Homeless persons—Fiction
ISBN 0-8050-7790-1; 978-0-8050-7790-2
First published 2003 in Canada

Haworth-Attard, Barbara, 1953---_Continued_

"Dylan Wallace, 16, lives on the streets of an unnamed Canadian city. His cruel, useless mother threw him out to make ready for her fourth man, whom she hopes to marry. The teen's only refuges are a youth center, a 24-hour doughnut shop, and the library. He keeps a biography of Einstein with him and tries to make sense of theories of time travel and black holes in the context of his own lack of 'relatives.'" SLJ

"The novel is sure to be a hit with teens everywhere. Order multiple copies. You will need them." Voice Youth Advocates

Hawthorne, Nathaniel, 1804-1864

The scarlet letter; with an introduction by Alfred Kazin. Knopf 1992 xxvii, 273p $18 *

Grades: 11 12 Adult   Fic
1. Puritans—Fiction 2. New England—Fiction
ISBN 0-679-41731-1   LC 92-52902

Also available Thorndike Press large print edition and from other editions

"Everyman's library"

"Set in 17th-century Salem, the novel is built around three scaffold scenes, which occur at the beginning, the middle, and the end. The story opens with the public condemnation of Hester Prynne, and the exhortation that she confess the name of the father of Pearl, her illegitimate child. Hester's husband, an old and scholarly physician, just arrived from England, assumes the name of Roger Chillingworth in order to seek out Hester's lover and revenge himself upon him. He attaches himself as physician to a respected and seemingly holy minister, Arthur Dimmesdale, suspecting that he is the father of the child. _The Scarlet Letter_ traces the effect of the actual and symbolic sin on all the characters." Benet's Reader's Ency of Am Lit

Hearn, Julie, 1958-

The minister's daughter. Atheneum Books for Young Readers 2005 263p $16.95; pa $7.99

Grades: 7 8 9 10   Fic
1. Witchcraft—Fiction 2. Supernatural—Fiction
3. Great Britain—History—1642-1660, Civil War and Commonwealth—Fiction 4. Salem (Mass.)—Fiction
ISBN 0-689-87690-4; 0-689-87691-2 (pa)
                                          LC 2004-18324

Published in United Kingdom with title: The Merrybegot

In 1645 in England, the daughters of the town minister successfully accuse a local healer and her granddaughter of witchcraft to conceal an out-of-wedlock pregnancy, but years later during the 1692 Salem trials their lie has unexpected repercussions.

"With its thought-provoking perceptions about human nature, magic and persecution, this tale will surely cast a spell over readers." Publ Wkly

Hearn, Lian

Across the nightingale floor. Riverhead Bks. 2002 287p (Tales of the Otori, bk 1) $24.95

Grades: 11 12 Adult   Fic
1. Japan—Fiction
ISBN 1-57322-225-9   LC 2002-22339

The first volume of a projected trilogy

"In an imaginary country reminiscent of feudal Japan, Takeo is adopted by Lord Shigeru after his village is wiped out, and he learns that the lord may have acted out of more than compassion as he himself is heir to powerful, mysterious abilities. A riveting start to an imaginative trilogy." Booklist

Other available titles in this series are:
Grass for his pillow (2003)
Brilliance of the moon (2004)

Heinlein, Robert A. (Robert Anson), 1907-1988

The moon is a harsh mistress. Orb 1997 382p il pa $14.95 *

Grades: 11 12 Adult   Fic
1. Science fiction
ISBN 0-312-86355-1
"A Tom Doherty Associates Book"
First published 1966 by Putnam

"Colonists of the Moon declare independence from Earth, and contrive to win the ensuing battle with the aid of a sentient computer. Action-adventure with some exploration of new possibilities in social organization and fierce assertion of the motto 'There Ain't No Such Thing as a Free Lunch.'" Anatomy of Wonder 4

The puppet masters. Doubleday 1951 219p

Grades: 11 12 Adult   Fic
1. Science fiction
ISBN 0-451-07339-8
"Heinlein's paranoia-laden tale of sluglike creatures, arrived in saucer-shaped craft to enslave humans by the particularly gruesome procedure of growing into each person's nervous system from a position on the upper back of the victim—making his or her profile humpbacked." Anatomy of Wonder. 3d edition

Stranger in a strange land. Putnam 1961 408p pa $16.95 hardcover o.p.

Grades: 11 12 Adult   Fic
1. Science fiction
ISBN 0-441-78838-6 (pa)
"The hero is a human born of space travelers from earth and raised by Martians. He is brought to the totalitarian post-World War III world that is in many ways depicted as a satire of the U.S. in the 1960s, marked by repressiveness in sexual morality and religion. The plot, which tells how the heroic stranger creates a Utopian society in which people preserve their individuality but share a brotherhood of community, made Heinlein and his novel cult objects for young people dedicated to a counterculture." Oxford Companion to Am Lit. 5th edition

Heller, Joseph

Catch-22; with an introduction by Malcolm Bradbury. Knopf 1995 xxxix, 568p $20 *

Grades: 11 12 Adult   Fic
1. World War, 1939-1945—Fiction
ISBN 0-679-43722-3   LC 94-13984

Also available in paperback from Simon & Schuster
"Everyman's library"

A reissue of the title first published 1961 by Simon & Schuster

Heller, Joseph—*Continued*

"A comic, satirical, surreal, and apocalyptic novel . . . which describes the ordeals and exploits of a group of American airmen based on a small Mediterranean island during the Italian campaign of the Second World War, and in particular the reactions of Captain Yossarian, the protagonist." Oxford Companion to Engl Lit. 5th edition

"By way of some of the funniest dialogue ever, Heller takes shots at the hypocrisy, meanness, and stupidities of our society." Shapiro. Fic for Youth. 3d edition

Followed by Closing time (1994)

Hemingway, Amanda

The Greenstone grail. Del Rey/Ballentine Books 2005 360p $16.95; pa $12.95

Grades: 11 12 Adult   **Fic**
1. Fantasy fiction
ISBN   0-345-46078-2;   978-0-345-46078-3; 0-345-46079-0 (pa); 978-0-345-46079-0 (pa)
           LC 2004-49396

First published 2004 in the United Kingdom

"Nathan Ward is just your typical 11-year-old of supernatural parentage, until he stumbles on a hidden altar that gives him visions of a green stone cup filled with blood. Soon he begins dreaming of Eos, a world that needs the grail for a spell to ward off a terrible plague. As the dreams become astral excursions, the grail surfaces in Nathan's world, but then is stolen and sent to Eos, at the wrong time and into the wrong hands. . . . The book glows with a blend of ancient magic and wide-eyed wonder that should captivate audiences on both sides of the Atlantic, especially readers weary of more conventional Arthurian epics." Publ Wkly

Other titles in the Sangreal Trilogy are:
The sword of straw (2005)

Hemingway, Ernest, 1899-1961

A farewell to arms. Scribner Classics 1997 297p $27.50

Grades: 11 12 Adult   **Fic**
1. World War, 1914-1918—Fiction
ISBN 0-684-83788-9   LC 96-53356
A reissue of the title first published 1929

This novel "deals with a love-affair conducted against the background of the war in Italy. Its excellence lies in the delicacy with which it conveys a sense of the impermanence of the best human feelings; the unobstrusive force of its symbolism of mountain and plain; above all the vast scope of its vision of war—the retreat from Caporetto is one of the great war-sequences of literature." Penguin Companion to Am Lit

For whom the bell tolls. Scribner 1996 495p $27.50; pa $14

Grades: 9 10 11 12   **Fic**
1. Spain—History—1936-1939, Civil War—Fiction
ISBN 0-684-83048-5; 0-684-80335-6 (pa)
           LC 96-7706

A reissue of the title first published 1940

"This war tale covers tension-ridden days in the life of Robert Jordan, an American in the Loyalist ranks during the Spanish Civil War. Having accomplished his mission to blow up a bridge with the aid of guerilla bands, he is injured when his horse falls and crushes his leg. As

enemy troops approach, he is left alone to meet their attack. Jordan's love for Maria, a young girl whom the Fascists had subjected to every possible indignity, adds another dimension to a story of courage, dedication—and treachery." Shapiro. Fic for Youth. 3d edition

The old man and the sea; illustrations by C.F. Tunnicliffe and Raymond Sheppard. Scribner Classics 1996 93p il $20 *

Grades: 11 12 Adult   **Fic**
1. Fishing—Fiction
ISBN 0-684-83049-3   LC 96-11419
A reissue of the title first published 1952

"The old fisherman Santiago had only one friend in the village, the boy Manolin. Everyone else thought he was unlucky because he had caught no fish in a long time. At noon on the 85th day of fishing, he hooked a large fish. He fought with the huge swordfish for three days and nights before he could harpoon it, but the battle came to nought when sharks destroyed the fish before Santiago could get back to the village." Shapiro. Fic for Youth. 3d edition

The sun also rises. Scribner Classics 1996 222p $26; pa $15

Grades: 9 10 11 12   **Fic**
ISBN 0-684-83051-5; 0-7432-9733-4 (pa)
           LC 96-11420

A reissue of the title first published 1926

This novel "deals with the lost generation of Americans who had fought in France during World War I and then had expatriated themselves from the America of Calvin Coolidge. The story is told by Jake Barnes, rendered impotent by a war wound. Lady Brett Ashley, a typical representative of the 'lost generation,' is divorcing her husband and diverts herself by her friendship, which sometimes seems like love, for Barnes. These two go to Spain with a group that includes Michael Campbell, whom Brett plans to marry; Bill Gorton, a friend of Jake; a Greek nobleman; and Robert Cohn, an American-Jewish writer." Reader's Ency. 4th edition

Hemphill, Helen, 1955-

Long gone daddy. Front Street 2006 176p $16.95

Grades: 8 9 10 11 12   **Fic**
1. Father-son relationship—Fiction 2. Grandfathers—Fiction 3. Christian life—Fiction 4. Las Vegas (Nev.)—Fiction
ISBN 1-932425-38-1   LC 2005-25105
Young Harlan Q. Stank gets a taste of life in the fast lane when he accompanies his preacher father on a road trip to Las Vegas to bury his grandfather and to fulfill the terms of the old man's will.

"Many teens will see their own questions about faith, worship, and independence in Harlan's heart-twisting feelings." Booklist

Herbert, Frank, 1920-1986

Dune. Ace Bks. 1999 c1965 517p il $27.95 *

Grades: 11 12 Adult   **Fic**
1. Science fiction
ISBN 0-441-00590-X
First published 1965 by Chilton

Herbert, Frank, 1920-1986—*Continued*

"Herbert combines several classic elements: a Machiavellian world of political intrigue worthy of fourteenth-century Italy, a huge cast of characters, and a detailed picture of a culture. Duke Leto Atreides and his family are coerced into exchanging their rich lands for a barren planet, Dune, which produces a unique drug. Duke's son, Paul, becomes the leader of a group that leads the Fremen of Dune against the enemy. This is a science fiction story with sociological and ecological import." Shapiro. Fic for Youth. 3d edition

Other titles about Dune are:
Chapterhouse: Dune (1985)
Children of Dune (1976)
Dune messiah (1969)
God Emperor of Dune (1981)
Heretics of Dune (1984)

Herrera, Juan Felipe, 1948-

Cinnamon girl; letters found inside a cereal box. Joanna Cotler Books 2005 164p $15.99; lib bdg $16.89

Grades: 7 8 9 10   **Fic**
1. September 11 terrorist attacks, 2001—Fiction 2. Puerto Ricans—Fiction 3. Uncles—Fiction 4. New York (N.Y.)—Fiction
ISBN 0-06-057984-6; 0-06-057985-4 (lib bdg)
LC 2004-26185
Yolanda, a Puerto Rican girl, tries to come to terms with her painful past as she waits to see if her uncle recovers from injuries he suffered when the towers collapsed on September 11, 2001

"Herrera depicts the immigration experience with intensity and drama, and even readers who aren't Latino will understand Yolanda's feelings." Booklist

Herrick, Steven, 1958-

By the river. Front Street 2006 238p $16.95

Grades: 8 9 10 11 12   **Fic**
1. Brothers—Fiction 2. Death—Fiction 3. Single parent family—Fiction 4. Australia—Fiction
ISBN 1-932425-72-1   LC 2005-23967
First published 2004 in the United Kingdom
A fourteen-year-old describes, through prose poems, his life in a small Australian town in 1962, where, since their mother's death, he and his brother have been mainly on their own to learn about life, death, and love.

"The poems are simple but potent in their simplicity, blending together in a compelling, evocative story of a gentle, intelligent boy growing up and learning to deal with a sometimes-ugly little world that he . . . will eventually escape." Voice Youth Advocates

Hersey, John, 1914-1993

The wall. Knopf 1950 632p pa $17.95 hardcover o.p.

Grades: 11 12 Adult   **Fic**
1. World War, 1939-1945—Fiction 2. Jews—Fiction 3. Warsaw (Poland)—Fiction
ISBN 0-394-75696-7 (pa)
"This novel is presented as a journal kept by a diarist during World War II. It tells of life in the Warsaw Ghetto, depicting Jewish interdependence in a struggle for

survival. The writer's observations enrich our understanding of Jewish culture. Although the diarist dies of pneumonia in 1944, his escape from the enclosure within which the Germans confined the Jews is a testament to hope and courage." Shapiro. Fic for Youth. 3d edition

Hesse, Hermann, 1877-1962

Siddhartha; translated by Hilda Rosner. New Directions 1951 153p $16.95; pa $6.95 *

Grades: 11 12 Adult   **Fic**
1. Buddhism—Fiction 2. India—Fiction
ISBN 0-8112-0292-5; 0-8112-0068-X (pa)
Also available in paperback from Bantam Bks.
Original German edition, 1923
"The young Indian Siddhartha endures many experiences in his search for the ultimate answer to the question, what is humankind's role on earth? He is also looking for the solution to loneliness and discontent, and he seeks that solution in the way of a wanderer, the company of a courtesan, and the high position of a successful businessman. His final relationship is with a humble but wise ferryman. This is an allegory that examines love, wealth, and freedom while the protagonist struggles toward self-knowledge." Shapiro. Fic for Youth. 3d edition

Steppenwolf; translated from the German by Basil Creighton. Holt & Co. 1929 309p pa $14 hardcover o.p. *

Grades: 11 12 Adult   **Fic**
ISBN 0-312-27867-5 (pa)
Available in hardcover from Amereon
Original German edition, 1927
"The hero, Harry Haller . . . is torn between his own frustrated artistic idealism and the inhuman nature of modern reality, which, in his eyes, is characterized entirely by philistinism and technology. It is his inability to be a part of the world and the resulting loneliness and desolation of his existence that cause him to think of himself as a 'Steppenwolf' (wolf of the Steppes). The novel, which is rich in surrealistic imagery throughout, ends in what is called the magic theater, a kind of allegorical sideshow. Here, Haller learns that in order to relate successfully to humanity and reality without sacrificing his ideals, he must overcome his own social and sexual inhibitions." Reader's Ency. 4th edition

Hinton, S. E.

The outsiders. Viking 1967 188p $16.99; pa $6.99 *

Grades: 7 8 9 10   **Fic**
1. Juvenile delinquency—Fiction
ISBN 0-670-53257-6; 0-14-038572-X (pa)
Also available in paperback from Puffin Books
"From the perspective of Ponyboy Curtis, the author relates the story of the Greasers, who are from the lower class, and their conflict with the Socs, who are their middle-class opposite number. For the Greasers, the gang comprises their street family, all the family that some of them have. In the collision between the two social factions, two buddies die, one as a hood, the other, a hero." Shapiro. Fic for Youth. 3d edition

"This remarkable novel by a seventeen-year-old girl gives a moving, credible view of the outsiders from the

Hinton, S. E.—*Continued*

inside—their loyalty to each other, their sensitivity under tough crusts, their understanding of self and society." Horn Book

Hobbs, Valerie, 1941-

Letting go of Bobby James, or, How I found myself of steam. Farrar Straus Giroux/Frances Foster Books 2004 135p $16

Grades: 8 9 10 11 12   **Fic**
    1. Wife abuse—Fiction 2. Florida—Fiction
    ISBN 0-374-34384-5; 978-0-374-34384-2
                                LC 2003-56377

After being left by her husband at a gas station in Florida, sixteen-year-old Sally Jo Walker, also known as Jody, makes some difficult decisions and a better life for herself.

"Readers will admire Jody's spunk and determination as she defeats one obstacle after another, grows increasingly independent and gains 'self of steam' along the way." Publ Wkly

Sonny's war. Farrar, Straus & Giroux 2002 215p $16

Grades: 7 8 9 10   **Fic**
    1. Vietnam War, 1961-1975—Fiction
    ISBN 0-374-37136-9   LC 2002-23891

"Frances Foster books"

In the late 1960s, fourteen-year-old Cory's life is greatly changed by the sudden death of her father and her brother's tour of duty in Vietnam

"Hobbs writes like a dream . . . but the Cory she conjures up for us is as real as real, completely believable in all her teenage vulnerability and sharp-eyed observation." Horn Book Guide

Hobbs, Will

Bearstone. Atheneum Pubs. 1989 154p pa $4.99 hardcover o.p.

Grades: 7 8 9 10   **Fic**
    1. Ute Indians—Fiction
    ISBN 0-689-87071-X (pa)   LC 89-6641

"Rebellious at being forced to abandon his family and his Ute Indian heritage to attend high school, Cloyd is sent to spend a summer with a lonely old rancher in Colorado. Upon arriving, Cloyd accidentally finds a turquoise bear totem in an Anasazi grave site, which serves as a touchstone between his cultural roots and his feelings. As time goes by, he also develops a mutual respect and friendship for the old man." ALAN

"The growth and maturity that Cloyd acquires as the summer progresses is juxtaposed poetically against the majestic Colorado landscape. Hobbs has creatively blended myth and reality as Cloyd forges a new identity for himself." Voice Youth Advocates

Followed by Beardance (1993)

Leaving Protection. HarperCollins 2004 178p il map $15.99; pa $5.99

Grades: 7 8 9 10   **Fic**
    1. Fishing—Fiction 2. Buried treasure—Fiction
    3. Alaska—Fiction
    ISBN 0-688-17475-2; 0-380-73312-9 (pa)
                                LC 2003-15545

Sixteen-year-old Robbie Daniels, happy to get a job aboard a troller fishing for king salmon off southeastern Alaska, finds himself in danger when he discovers that his mysterious captain is searching for long-buried Russian plaques that lay claim to Alaska and the Northwest

This "nautical thriller brims with detail about the fishing life and weaves in historical facts as well. . . . Robbie's doubts build to a climactic finale involving a dramatic and fateful storm at sea, grippingly rendered. Fans of maritime tales will relish the atmosphere and the bursts of action." Publ Wkly

The maze. Morrow Junior Bks. 1998 198p $15.99; pa $5.99 *

Grades: 7 8 9 10   **Fic**
    1. Runaway teenagers—Fiction 2. Condors—Fiction
    ISBN 0-688-15092-6; 0-380-72913-X (pa)
                                LC 98-10791

Rick, a fourteen-year-old foster child, escapes from a juvenile detention facility near Las Vegas and travels to Canyonlands National Park in Utah where he meets a bird biologist working on a project to reintroduce condors to the wild

"Hobbs spins an engrossing yarn, blending adventure with a strong theme, advocating the need for developing personal values." Horn Book Guide

Hoffman, Alice, 1952-

Blue diary. Putnam 2001 303p hardcover o.p. pa $14

Grades: 11 12 Adult   **Fic**
    1. Homicide—Fiction 2. Massachusetts—Fiction
    3. Family life—Fiction
    ISBN 0-399-14802-7; 0-425-18494-3 (pa)
                                LC 2001-19517

Ethan Ford is "suddenly arrested on suspicion of the rape and murder of teenager Rachel Morris 15 years earlier in Maryland. Ethan confesses to the crime, but says that he is now 'a different man,' who has redeemed himself through exemplary behavior. What this revelation means to his beautiful wife of 13 years, Jorie {and} his 12-year-old son, Collie . . . allows the novel to investigate the themes of devotion, betrayal, guilt and forgiveness in trenchantly effective ways." Publ Wkly

The foretelling. Little, Brown 2005 167p $16.99; pa $7.99

Grades: 7 8 9 10   **Fic**
    1. Amazons—Fiction 2. Sex role—Fiction
    ISBN 0-316-01018-9; 0-316-15409-1 (pa)
                                LC 2004-25102

Also available Thorndike Press large print edition

Growing up the daughter of an Amazon queen who shuns her, Rain rebels against the ways of her tribe through her sisterlike relationship with Io and her feelings for a boy from a tribe of wanderers.

The "first-person narration is accessible while evoking a sense of otherworldliness. . . . The story unfolds at a measured pace with little dialogue, but the language makes it compulsively readable." SLJ

Hoffman, Alice, 1952-—*Continued*

Incantation. Little, Brown 2006 166p $16.99 *
Grades: 7 8 9 10   **Fic**
  1. Prejudices—Fiction 2. Jews—Persecutions—Fiction
  3. Inquisition—Fiction 4. Spain—Fiction
  ISBN 978-0-316-01019-1; 0-316-01019-7
                                          LC 2005-37301
During the Spanish Inquisition, sixteen-year-old
Estrella, brought up a Catholic, discovers her family's
true Jewish identity, and when their secret is betrayed by
Estrella's best friend, the consequences are tragic. Includes some scenes of graphic violence.
  "Hoffman's lyrical prose and astute characterization
blend to create a riveting, horrific tale that unites despair
with elements of hope." SLJ

The probable future. Doubleday 2003 322p
hardcover o.p. pa $13.95
Grades: 11 12 Adult   **Fic**
  1. Women—Fiction 2. Mother-daughter relationship—
Fiction 3. New England—Fiction
  ISBN 0-385-50760-7; 0-345-45591-8 (pa)
                                          LC 2003-40960
Also available large print edition $26.95 (ISBN 0-375-
43216-7)
  "In a New England family in which generations of
women have magical powers, young Stella foresees a
murder, a crime that her father is then accused of committing." SLJ
  "Filled with vivid (if sometimes sketchy) characters
and cinematic descriptions of New England landscapes,
this book will be a hit wherever Hoffman is in demand."
Libr J

Hoffman, Mary, 1945-
The falconer's knot; a story of friars, flirtation
and foul play. Bloomsbury Children's Books 2007
297p $16.95
Grades: 7 8 9 10   **Fic**
  1. Religious life—Fiction 2. Renaissance—Fiction
  3. Italy—History—0-1559—Fiction
  ISBN 978-1-59990-056-8; 1-59990-056-4
                                          LC 2006-16365
Silvano and Chiara, teens sent to live in a friary and
a nunnery in Renaissance Italy, are drawn to one another
and dream of a future together, but when murders are
committed in the friary, they must discover who is behind the crimes before they can realize their love.
  "Hoffman creates utterly engaging characters and vivid settings, and she skillfully turns up the suspense,
wrapping her varied plot threads into a satisfying whole."
Booklist

Stravaganza: city of masks. Bloomsbury
Children's Bks. 2002 344p $17.95; pa $7.95
Grades: 7 8 9 10   • **Fic**
  1. Space and time—Fiction
  ISBN 1-58234-791-3; 1-58234-917-7 (pa)
                                          LC 2001-56464
While sick in bed with cancer, Lucien begins making
journeys to a place in a parallel world that resembles
Venice, Italy, and he becomes caught up in the political
intrigues surrounding the Duchessa who rules the city.
  "Utterly fascinating, this rich, rip-roaring adventure—

the first in a series—will no doubt whet readers' appe-
tites for Italian history and culture as well as the next in-
stallment." Booklist
  Other available titles in this series are:
Stravaganza: city of flowers (2005)
Stravaganza: city of stars (2003)

Holub, Josef, 1926-
An innocent soldier; translated by Michael
Hofmann. Arthur A. Levine Books 2005 231p
$16.99; pa $6.99
Grades: 8 9 10 11 12   **Fic**
  1. France—History—1799-1815—Fiction 2. Russia—
Fiction 3. War stories
  ISBN 0-439-62771-0; 0-439-62772-9 (pa)
A sixteen-year-old farmhand is tricked into fighting in
the Napoleonic Wars by the farmer for whom he works,
who secretly substitutes him for the farmer's own son.
  "This is a well-wrought psychological tale. . . . [It]
has a lot to offer to those seeking to build a deep historical fiction collection." SLJ

Hooker, Richard
MASH. Morrow 1968 219p pa $13 hardcover
o.p. *
Grades: 11 12 Adult   **Fic**
  1. Physicians—Fiction 2. Soldiers—Fiction 3. Korean
War, 1950-1953—Fiction
  ISBN 0-688-14955-3 (pa)   LC 68-29610
  "Captains Hawkeye Pierce, Duke Forrest, and 'Trap-
per' John McIntyre, all M.D.'s, are stationed in Korea
with the 4077th MASH (Mobile Army Surgical Hospital). The reader is soon involved in many operations and
medical jargon. It is, however, the off-duty activities of
these three that engages one's attention and laughter. Full
of martinis, or bored, or tired, or all three, the men soon
start raising hell. . . . Hilarious, occasionally very serious, full of warm, appealing eccentric characters, one
could enjoy a very pleasant evening with this sMASHing
novel." Libr J

Hopkins, Ellen, 1955-
Burned. Margaret K. McElderry Books 2006
532p $16.95 *
Grades: 9 10 11 12   **Fic**
  1. Family life—Fiction 2. Mormons—Fiction 3. Sex
role—Fiction 4. Child abuse—Fiction
  ISBN 1-4169-0354-2; 978-1-4169-0354-3
                                          LC 2005-32461
Seventeen-year-old Pattyn, the eldest daughter in a
large Mormon family, is sent to her aunt's Nevada ranch
for the summer, where she temporarily escapes her alcoholic, abusive father and finds love and acceptance, only
to lose everything when she returns home.
  "The free verses, many in the form of concrete poems,
create a compressed and intense reading experience with
no extraneous dialogue or description. . . . This book
will appeal to teens favoring realistic fiction and dramatic interpersonal stories." Voice Youth Advocates

Hopkinson, Nalo, 1960-
Brown girl in the ring. Warner Bks. 1998 250p
pa $13.95
Grades: 9 10 11 12   **Fic**
1. Science fiction 2. Canada—Fiction
ISBN 0-446-67433-8   LC 97-39151
"Toronto's economy has collapsed, and those who
couldn't flee with big business must farm in parks, hunt
pigeons and squirrels for meat, and avoid the Posse, the
gang that controls the streets. Ti-Jeanne Baines lives with
her grandmother, learning to make herbal medicines and
raising her child, conceived in an affair with {Tony}, a
former medical intern. . . . {Ti-Jeanne} asks her voo-
doo-practicing grandmother to help Tony escape {the
city} before the Posse kills him for defecting." Booklist
"Readers should be forewarned that this book includes
moments of stomach-turning horror, rendered in appall-
ingly clear language. But the pleasure of watching Ti-
Jeanne grow in knowledge and power seems recompense
enough." N Y Times Book Rev

Horniman, Joanne, 1951-
Mahalia. Knopf 2003 184p lib bdg $17.99
Grades: 9 10 11 12   **Fic**
1. Teenage fathers—Fiction
ISBN 0-375-92325-X   LC 2002-66149
First published 2001 in the United Kingdom
When his girlfriend leaves him and their five-month-
old baby, seventeen-year-old Matt struggles to make a
life for himself and Mahalia, the daughter he adores.
This novel "explores a real and relatively ignored issue—the problems and emotions of a teenage father.
Matt and Mahalia are winning, engaging, and genuine, as
are all of the characters in his novel. . . . A poignant
and memorable love story of a young father and his
daughter." SLJ

Hosseini, Khaled
The kite runner. Riverhead Bks. 2003 324p
$24.95; pa $14 *
Grades: 11 12 Adult   **Fic**
1. Taliban (Afghanistan)—Fiction 2. Friendship—Fiction 3. Social classes—Fiction 4. Afghanistan—Fiction
ISBN 1-57322-245-3; 1-59448-000-1 (pa)
                                            LC 2003-43106
"Amir, the son of a well-to-do Kabul merchant, is the
first-person narrator, who marries, moves to California
and becomes a successful novelist. But he remains haunted by a childhood incident in which he betrayed the trust
of his best friend, a Hazara boy named Hassan, who receives a brutal beating from some local bullies. After establishing himself in America, Amir learns that the
Taliban have murdered Hassan and his wife, raising
questions about the fate of his son, Sohrab. Spurred on
by childhood guilt, Amir makes the difficult journey to
Kabul, only to learn the boy has been enslaved by a former childhood bully who has become a prominent
Taliban official." Publ Wkly
"Khaled Hosseini gives us a vivid and engaging story
that reminds us how long his people have been struggling to triumph over the forces of violence." N Y Times
Book Rev

A thousand splendid suns. Riverhead Books
2007 372p $25.95
Grades: 11 12 Adult   **Fic**
1. Family life—Fiction 2. Afghanistan—Fiction
ISBN 978-1-59448-950-1; 1-59448-950-5
                                            LC 2007-8679
"Born a generation apart and with very different ideas
about love and family, Mariam and Laila are two women
brought jarringly together by war, by loss and by fate.
As they endure the ever escalating dangers around
them—in their home as well as in the streets of Kabul—
they . . . form a bond that makes them both sisters and
mother-daughter to each other." Publisher's note
"The texture of these characters' journey around the
craters of their country is no doubt well known to readers of international news. Rendered as fiction . . ., however, it devastates in a new way." Minneapolis Star Tri-
bune

Houston, James D.
Snow Mountain passage; a novel. Knopf 2001
317p $24
Grades: 11 12 Adult   **Fic**
1. Donner party—Fiction 2. California—Fiction
ISBN 0-375-41103-8   LC 00-62009
Also available in paperback from Harcourt
This is a novel about the Donner Party, a group of
California pioneers who became trapped in the mountains
during winter snowstorms in 1846 and resorted to cannibalism to survive.
"Houston has given himself an opportunity to explore
complex motives and characters, and his writerly skills
are a match for the task. . . . He has a sure sense of
place. . . . And most important, he has a clear-eyed
view of humanity's heart of darkness." Atl Mon

Houston, Julian, 1944-
New boy. Houghton Mifflin Co. 2005 282p $16
Grades: 8 9 10 11 12   **Fic**
1. Prejudices—Fiction 2. African Americans—Fiction
3. School stories
ISBN 0-618-43253-1   LC 2004-27207
"As the first black student in an elite Connecticut
boarding school in the late 1950s, Rob Garrett, 16,
knows he is making history. . . . When his friends in the
South plan a sit-in against segregation, he knows he must
be part of it. . . . The honest first-person narrative
makes stirring drama. . . . This brings up much for discussion about then and now." Booklist

Howe, Norma
The adventures of Blue Avenger. Holt & Co.
1999 230p $15.95
Grades: 7 8 9 10   **Fic**
1. Heroes and heroines—Fiction
ISBN 0-8050-6062-6   LC 98-29788
Also available in paperback from HarperCollins
On his sixteenth birthday, still trying to cope with the
unexpected death of his father, David Schumacher de-
cides--or does he--to change his name to Blue Avenger,
hoping to find a way to make a difference in his Oakland neighborhood and in the world.
"This is at once ingeniously plotted and howlingly
funny." Bull Cent Child Books

Howe, Norma—*Continued*
Other available titles about Blue Avenger are:
Blue Avenger and the theory of everything (2002)
Blue Avenger cracks the code (2000)

Hughes, Dean, 1943-
Search and destroy. Atheneum Books for Young Readers 2006 216p $16.95
Grades: 7 8 9 10   Fic
1. Vietnam War, 1961-1975—Fiction
ISBN 0-689-87023-X   LC 2005-11255
"Ginee Seo Books"
Recent high school graduate Rick Ward, undecided about his future and eager to escape his unhappy home life, joins the army and experiences the horrors of the war in Vietnam.
"This is a compelling, insightful story about the emotional, physical, and psychological scars that wars leave upon soldiers." Booklist

Hughes, Pat, 1933-
Open ice. Wendy Lamb Books 2005 271p $15.95; lib bdg $17.89
Grades: 8 9 10 11 12   Fic
1. Hockey—Fiction 2. Brain—Wounds and injuries—Fiction 3. School stories
ISBN 0-385-74675-X; 0-385-90906-3 (lib bdg)
             LC 2004-23113
Hockey has been Nick Taglio's life since he was five years old, so when a massive concussion benches him—possibly for good—everything seems to fall apart, including his schoolwork, his family relationships, his friendships, and his love life.
"Hughes's attention to detail in terms of both head injuries and the sport adds lots of pith and interest to this story, and her accurate portrayal of middle-class teen life (which includes sex, obscenities, and pot smoking) should keep reluctant readers turning pages." Booklist

Hugo, Victor, 1802-1885
Les misérables; translated from the French by Charles E. Wilbour; with an introduction by Peter Washington. Knopf 1997 xxxvii, 1432p $27
Grades: 11 12 Adult   Fic
1. Paris (France)—Fiction
ISBN 0-375-40317-5   LC 98-156450
Also available from other publishers
"Everyman's library"
Original French edition, 1862
"Set in the Parisian underworld and plotted like a detective story, the work follows Jean Valjean, a victim of society who has been imprisoned for 19 years for stealing a loaf of bread. A hardened criminal upon his release, he eventually reforms, becoming a successful industrialist and mayor of a northern town. Despite this he is haunted by an impulsive, regretted former crime and is pursued relentlessly by the police inspector Javert. Valjean eventually gives himself up for the sake of his adopted daughter, Cosette, and her husband, Marius. *Les Misérables* is a vast panorama of Parisian society and its underworld, and it contains many famous episodes and passages." Merriam-Webster's Ency of Lit

Hurston, Zora Neale, 1891-1960
Novels and stories. Library of Am. 1995 1041p $35 *
Grades: 11 12 Adult   Fic
1. African Americans—Fiction 2. Short stories
ISBN 0-940450-83-6   LC 94-25757
Companion volume to Folklore, memoirs, and other writings
This collection contains Hurston's four novels: Jonah's gourd vine, Their eyes were watching God, Moses, man of the mountain, and Seraph on the Suwanee. Also included are nine short stories
"Libraries without a complete set of Hurston's fiction will find this volume a necessary and easy purchase to fill that unfortunate gap." Booklist

Their eyes were watching God; with a foreword by Edwidge Danticat. HarperCollins Pubs. 2000 xxii, 231p $22; pa $15.95
Grades: 9 10 11 12   Fic
1. African Americans—Fiction 2. Florida—Fiction
ISBN 0-06-019949-0; 0-06-112006-0 (pa)
             LC 00-58186
First published 1937 by Lippincott
This novel "treats social problems from a racial and feminist perspective. Janie Crawford, raised by her grandmother in rural poverty, flees her old and dictatorial husband with Joe Starks, an ambitious man who becomes the mayor of Florida's first town run by African Americans. When Joe dies, Janie falls in love with the younger Teacake and follows him to the truck farming area of the Florida swamps. In the floods following a hurricane, he is bitten by a rabid dog and, crazed, attacks Janie. She shoots him, is charged with murder, and finally exonerated. When she returns to the town she and Joe built, she tells her story to a friend." HarperCollins Reader's Ency of Am Lit

Huser, Glen, 1943-
Stitches. Groundwood Books 2003 198p hardcover o.p. pa $6.95
Grades: 7 8 9 10   Fic
1. Bullies—Fiction 2. Puppets and puppet plays—Fiction 3. Sex role—Fiction 4. Canada—Fiction
ISBN 0-88899-553-9; 0-88899-578-4 (pa)
             LC 2003-363167
This story of two outsiders who become friends is set in rural Alberta. The protagonists "are Chantelle, who has a limp and a scarred face, and Travis, a boy completely unselfconscious about his love for puppets and sewing. Both kids have ragtaggle families. . . . Chantelle and Travis joined forces back in fifth grade, when she rescued him from the boys who called him 'girlie'; junior high brings new challenges as the teasing gets uglier and, eventually, violent." Horn Book
"Teachers will use this book in their classrooms, but it will appeal to leisure readers as well." Voice Youth Advocates

Huxley, Aldous, 1894-1963
Brave new world. Harper & Row 1946 xx, 311p pa $13.95 hardcover o.p.
Grades: 7 8 9 10   Fic

Huxley, Aldous, 1894-1963—*Continued*
1. Utopias—Fiction 2. Technology and civilization—
Fiction
ISBN 0-06-085052-3 (pa)
Also available in hardcover from Buccaneer Bks.
First published 1932 by Doubleday, Doran & Company

"The ironic title, which Huxley has taken from Shakespeare's 'The Tempest,' describes a world in which science has taken control over morality and humaneness. In this utopia humans emerge from test tubes, families are obsolete, and even pleasure is regulated. When a so-called savage who believes in spirituality is found and is imported to the community, he cannot accomodate himself to this world and ends his life." Shapiro. Fic for Youth. 3d edition

Hyde, Catherine Ryan
Becoming Chloe. Random House 2006 215p
$15.95; lib bdg $17.99
Grades: 9 10 11 12   **Fic**
1. Homeless persons—Fiction 2. Voyages and travels—Fiction
ISBN 0-375-83258-0; 0-375-93258-5 (lib bdg)
LC 2005-18949
"The young characters in . . . [this novel] are searching for signs of hope amid grim realities, which begin, here, with a gang rape on the first page. Seventeen-year-old Jordan tries to rescue 18-year-old Chloe from her attackers, and the two homeless teens form a fierce, siblinglike bond as they help each other survive the streets—a struggle that sometimes drives Jordan to prostitution. Both have deep scars: gay Jordan nearly died from his father's abuse; childlike Chloe can't speak directly about her past horrors, even to Jordan. At last, they strike out on a healing, cross-country trip in search of 'beauty . . . maybe even some decent, kind people.'"
Booklist
"This thought-provoking story of the power of hope . . . blends the realities of street life with the wonder of cross-country exploration." Voice Youth Advocates

Irving, John, 1942-
The Hotel New Hampshire. Ballantine Books 2001 401p pa $14.95
Grades: 11 12 Adult   **Fic**
1. Family life—Fiction 2. Hotels and motels—Fiction
ISBN 0-345-41795-X   LC 97-93266
First published 1981 by Dutton
This is "a family chronicle—a tale of generations of parents coping with children and siblings coping with each other. The chief parents are Win and Mary Berry of Dairy, New Hampshire, a couple brought together after high school at a seaside resort where, on summer jobs, they catch a glimpse of a joyous vocation (innkeeping). The Berry union produces five spirited and amusing children. . . . The story covers a quarter-century, beginning round about 1940, and the principal action takes place in three hotels, each called . . . The Hotel New Hampshire. (The hotels are situated in New Hampshire, Austria, and Maine.)" Atlantic
The author "keeps us moving, sacrificing rhetoric to pace, as in the most primitive narrative forms, the fable and the fairy tale. In fiction like this, meaning lies near the surface of the story and in the voice of the storyteller." New Repub

The world according to Garp. Modern Library 1998 688p $21.95 *
Grades: 11 12 Adult   **Fic**
1. Mother-son relationship—Fiction 2. Family life—Fiction
ISBN 0-679-60306-9   LC 97-39458
First published 1978 by Dutton
"Jenny Fields is the black sheep daughter of an aristocratic New England family; she becomes, almost by accident, a feminist leader ahead of her time. Her son, T. S. Garp (named for a father he never saw), has high ambitions for his artistic career, but he has an even higher, obsessive devotion to his wife and children. Surrounding Garp and Jenny are a wide assortment of people: schoolteachers and whores, wrestlers and radicals, editors and assassins, transsexuals and rapists, and husbands and wives." Publisher's note
This "is a long family novel, spanning four generations and two continents, crammed with incidents, characters, feelings and craft. The components of black comedy and melodrama, pathos and tragedy, mesh effortlessly in a tale that can also be read as a commentary on art and the imagination." Time

Ishiguro, Kazuo, 1954-
Never let me go. Knopf 2005 288p $24 *
Grades: 11 12 Adult   **Fic**
1. Science fiction 2. Bioethics—Fiction 3. School stories
ISBN 1-4000-4339-5   LC 2004-48966
This novel is "set in late 1990s England, in a parallel universe in which humans are cloned and raised expressly to 'donate' their healthy organs and thus eradicate disease from the normal population." Publ Wkly
"Highly recommended for literary merit and as an exceptional platform for the discussion of a controversial topic." SLJ

Jackson, Jeremy, 1956-
Life at these speeds. Thomas Dunne Bks. 2002 342p $24.95; pa $14 *
Grades: 11 12 Adult   **Fic**
1. Missouri—Fiction 2. School stories
ISBN 0-312-28808-5; 0-312-31366-7 (pa)
LC 2002-510283
"When the school van veers off a bridge and plunges into the river below, everyone on the track team is killed except star Kevin Schuler, who rode home with his parents that evening. Repressing almost all memory of that season, Kevin begins high school in a different district, where he remains isolated from other students and teammates. . . . The unforgettable and complex main character makes this novel well worth reading." Booklist

Jackson, Shirley, 1919-1965
The haunting of Hill House. Viking 1959 246p
pa $14 hardcover o.p. *
Grades: 11 12 Adult   **Fic**
1. Ghost stories 2. Horror fiction
ISBN 0-14-303998-9 (pa)
Also available in hardcover from Amereon

Jackson, Shirley, 1919-1965—*Continued*

"Dr. John Montague, an anthropologist, is interested in the analysis of supernatural manifestations. He rents Hill House, which is reported to be haunted, and plans to spend the summer there with research assistants. Eleanor Vance, one of the researchers, is at first repelled by the house but soon adjusts. Other people come and signs of psychic activity are rampant, many of them centered on Eleanor. When Dr. Montague insists that she leave to insure her safety, the house does not release her." Shapiro. Fic for Youth. 3d edition

We have always lived in a castle. Viking 1962 214p pa $14 hardcover o.p.

Grades: 11 12 Adult   **Fic**

1. Horror fiction

ISBN 0-14-303997-0 (pa)

Also available in hardcover from Amereon

"Since the time that Constance Blackwood was tried and acquitted of the murder of four members of her family, she has lived with her sister Mary Catherine and her Uncle Julian in the family mansion. Mary Catherine takes care of family chores and Uncle Julian is busy with the writing of a detailed account of the six-year-old murders. Cousin Charles's arrival on the scene disrupts the quiet peace of the family, and Mary Catherine's efforts to get rid of him unloose a chain of events that bring everything down in ruins." Shapiro. Fic for Youth. 3d edition

Jaffe, Michele, 1970-

Bad kitty. HarperCollins Publishers 2006 268p il $16.99; lib bdg $17.89

Grades: 9 10 11 12   **Fic**

1. Mystery fiction 2. Las Vegas (Nev.)—Fiction

ISBN   0-06-078108-4;   978-0-06-078108-8; 0-06-078109-2 (lib bdg); 978-0-06-078109-5 (lib bdg)

LC 2005-5733

While vacationing with her family in Las Vegas, seventeen-year-old Jasmine stumbles upon a murder mystery that she attempts to solve with the help of her friends, recently arrived from California.

"Readers will likely find themselves quickly clawing their way through this fun novel." Publ Wkly

James, Henry, 1843-1916

The portrait of a lady. Knopf 1991 xxv, 626p $20

Grades: 9 10 11 12   **Fic**

1. Europe—Fiction

ISBN 0-679-40562-3   LC 91-52999

Also available in paperback from Penguin Books

"Everyman's library"

First published 1881 by Houghton

"This is one of the best James's early works, in which he presents various types of American character transplanted into a European environment. The story centres in Isabel Archer, the 'Lady,' an attractive American girl. Around her we have the placid old American banker, Mr. Touchett; his hard repellent wife; his ugly, invalid, witty, charming son Ralph, whom England has thoroughly assimilated; and the outspoken, brilliant, indomitably American journalist Henrietta Stackpole. Isabel refuses the offer of marriage of a typical English peer, the excellent Lord Warburton, and of a bulldog-like New Englander, Casper Goodwood, to fall a victim, under the influence of the slightly sinister Madame Merle (another cosmopolitan American), to a worthless and spiteful dilettante, Gilbert Osmond, who marries her for her fortune and ruins her life; but to whom she remains loyal in spite of her realization of his vileness." Oxford Companion to Engl Lit. 6th edition

The turn of the screw; edited by Allan Lloyd Smith. J.M. Dent 1993 xxxii, 139p pa $8.95 *

Grades: 11 12 Adult   **Fic**

1. Horror fiction

ISBN 0-460-87299-0   LC 94-125860

Also available from other publishers

First published 1898

This novella "is told from the viewpoint of the leading character, a governess in love with her employer, who goes to an isolated English estate to take charge of Miles and Flora, two attractive and precocious children. She gradually realizes that her young charges are under the evil influence of two ghosts, Peter Quint, the ex-steward, and Miss Jessel, their former governess. At the climax of the story, she enters into open conflict with the children, as a result of which Flora is alienated and Miles dies of fright." Reader's Ency. 4th edition

Jansen, Hanna

Over a thousand hills I walk with you; translated from the German by Elizabeth D. Crawford. Carolrhoda Books 2006 342p $16.95 *

Grades: 7 8 9 10   **Fic**

1. Rwanda—Fiction

ISBN 1-57505-927-4 (lib bdg); 978-1-57505-927-3

LC 2005-21123

Original German edition, 2002

"Eight-year-old Jeanne was the only one of her family to survive the 1994 Rwanda genocide. Then a German family adopted her, and her adoptive mother now tells Jeanne's story in a compelling fictionalized biography that stays true to the traumatized child's bewildered viewpoint." Booklist

Jeapes, Ben

The new world order. Fickling 2005 435p $15.95; lib bdg $17.99

Grades: 7 8 9 10   **Fic**

1. Charles I, King of Great Britain, 1600-1649—Fiction 2. Cromwell, Oliver, 1599-1658—Fiction 3. Space and time—Fiction

ISBN 0-385-75013-7; 0-385-75015-3 (lib bdg)

LC 2004-3402

Having ended England's Civil War between the Roundheads and the Royalists in 1645, the Overlord of the Holekhor, a race from another world, and his half-English son question the decision to colonize the island and convert their beloved English to a faith characterised by witches and myriad gods

"The riveting story has enough twists and turns, battles and bloodshed to intrigue even hardcore sf fans, but readers will also get a painless lesson in English history." Booklist

Jen, Gish

Typical American. Plume 1992 296p (Plume contemporary fiction) pa $13.95 *

Grades: 9 10 11 12   **Fic**

1. Chinese Americans—Fiction

ISBN 0-452-26774-9   LC 91-33814

First published 1991 by Houghton Mifflin

"Yefing Chang becomes Ralph Chang in America and begins a hard struggle to achieve the American dream-a career, a family and a home of his own. In poverty, he succeeds finally to win a doctoral degree, a college position, a happy marriage to Helen, two delightful daughters and a close reunion with his older sister, Theresa. The dream becomes a nightmare when he meets Grover Ding whose corrupt influence over Ralph and Helen begins to unravel all that the Changs have managed to achieve. This is an honest novel that does not promise happy endings and recognizes the human weaknesses that can destroy a family's stability." Shapiro. Fic for Youth. 3d edition

Followed by Mona in the promised land (1996)

Jenkins, A. M. (Amanda McRaney)

Beating heart; a ghost story. HarperCollins Publishers 2006 244p $15.99; lib bdg $16.89

Grades: 8 9 10 11 12   **Fic**

1. Ghost stories 2. Divorce—Fiction 3. Moving—Fiction

ISBN 0-06-054607-7; 0-06-054608-5 (lib bdg)

LC 2005-05071

Following his parents' divorce, seventeen-year-old Evan moves with his mother and sister into an old house where the spirit of a teenager who died there awakens and mistakes him for her long-departed lover.

"Both accessible and substantive, this book will be an easy sell to teens." Booklist

Damage; by Amanda Jenkins. HarperCollins Pubs. 2001 186p lib bdg $15.89; pa $7.99 *

Grades: 9 10 11 12   **Fic**

1. Depression (Psychology)—Fiction 2. Football—Fiction

ISBN 0-06-029100-1 (lib bdg); 0-06-447255-8 (pa)

LC 00-54038

Also available Thorndike Press large print edition

"Popular, handsome, a talented athlete, Austin Reid seems to have it all. In reality, however, he's deeply depressed, and not even his beloved football or sex with the prettiest girl help. There are no simple solutions in this unflinching, powerful novel." Booklist

Out of order. HarperCollins Pubs. 2003 247p $15.99; lib bdg $16.89; pa $6.99

Grades: 7 8 9 10   **Fic**

1. School stories

ISBN 0-06-623968-0; 0-06-623969-9 (lib bdg); 0-06-447374-0 (pa)   LC 2002-15621

Sophomore Colt Trammel loves baseball and his girlfriend Grace, but he hates the rest of high school and maintains a tough facade to hide his feelings of inferiority

"The best part of this novel is the portrait of Colt. Every part rings true, from his rough language and obsession with sex to his need to act cool at all costs. It's also

a very funny portrait, without ever lapsing into stereotypes or becoming too broad. Readers looking for a dead-on look at high school will enjoy this novel." SLJ

Jinks, Catherine, 1963-

Evil genius; [by] Catherine Jinks. 1st ed. Harcourt 2007 486p $17

Grades: 7 8 9 10   **Fic**

1. Genius—Fiction 2. Crime—Fiction 3. Good and evil—Fiction 4. School stories 5. Australia—Fiction

ISBN 978-0-15-205988-0; 0-15-205988-1

LC 2006014476

First published 2005 in Australia

Child prodigy Cadel Piggot, an antisocial computer hacker, discovers his true identity when he enrolls as a first-year student at an advanced crime academy.

"Cadel's turnabout is convincingly hampered by his difficulty recognizing appropriate outlets for rage, and Jinks' whiplash-inducing suspense writing will gratify fans of Anthony Horowitz's high-tech spy scenarios." Booklist

Johnson, Angela, 1961-

The first part last. Simon & Schuster Bks. for Young Readers 2003 131p $15.95; pa $5.99

Grades: 7 8 9 10   **Fic**

1. Teenage fathers—Fiction 2. Infants—Fiction 3. African Americans—Fiction

ISBN 0-689-84922-2; 0-689-84923-0 (pa)

LC 2002-36512

Also available Thorndike Press large print edition

Prequel to Heaven (1998)

Bobby's carefree teenage life changes forever when he becomes a father and must care for his adored baby daughter.

"Brief, poetic, and absolutely riveting." SLJ

Johnson, Harriet McBryde

Accidents of nature. Holt 2006 229p $16.95 *

Grades: 9 10 11 12   **Fic**

1. Handicapped—Fiction 2. Camps—Fiction 3. Cerebral palsy—Fiction

ISBN 0-8050-7634-4; 978-0-8050-7634-9

LC 2005-24598

Also available Thorndike Press large print edition

Having always prided herself on blending in with "normal" people despite her cerebral palsy, seventeen-year-old Jean begins to question her role in the world while attending a summer camp for children with disabilities.

"This book is smart and honest, funny and eye-opening. A must-read." SLJ

Johnson, Kathleen Jeffrie

A fast and brutal wing. Roaring Brook Press 2004 191p $16.95

Grades: 9 10 11 12   **Fic**

1. Siblings—Fiction 2. Family life—Fiction 3. Mental illness—Fiction 4. Colorado—Fiction

ISBN 1-59643-013-3   LC 2004-13656

Johnson, Kathleen Jeffrie—*Continued*

A series of journal entries, emails, stories, and newspaper articles reveals the strange events that led to the disappearance of a reclusive author on Halloween night and the involvement of a teenager and his friends—a brother and sister some say can transform into animals and back again

Johnson, Lindsay Lee

Worlds apart. Front Street 2005 166p il $16.95 *

Grades: 7 8 9 10 **Fic**

1. Moving—Fiction 2. Psychiatric hospitals—Fiction

ISBN 1-932425-28-4 LC 2005-12052

A thirteen-year-old daughter of a surgeon finds herself wrenched away from a comfortable lifestyle to a home on the grounds of a mental hospital, where her father has accepted a five year contract.

"This story brings bias and prejudice to the forefront in a discussable and readable narrative." SLJ

Johnson, Maureen, 1973-

13 little blue envelopes. HarperCollins Publishers 2005 317p $15.99; lib bdg $16.89; pa $8.99 *

Grades: 8 9 10 11 12 **Fic**

1. Voyages and travels—Fiction 2. Aunts—Fiction 3. Europe—Fiction

ISBN 0-06-054141-5; 0-06-054142-3 (lib bdg); 0-06-054143-1 (pa) LC 2005-02658

When seventeen-year-old Ginny receives a packet of mysterious envelopes from her favorite aunt, she leaves New Jersey to criss-cross Europe on a sort of scavenger hunt that transforms her life.

"Equal parts poignant, funny and inspiring, this tale is sure to spark wanderlust." Publ Wkly

Devilish. Razorbill/Penguin Putnam 2006 263p $16.99

Grades: 8 9 10 11 12 **Fic**

1. Devil—Fiction 2. Supernatural—Fiction 3. Friendship—Fiction 4. School stories

ISBN 1-59514-060-3 LC 2006-10230

Jane Jarvis, a senior at a Catholic girl's school in Providence, Rhode Island, tries to save her best friend by making a pact with a demon—in the form of a cupcake-eating, very friendly teenage girl.

"Decorated in fine detail and well served by a terrific supporting cast, this page-turner will have high appeal and get great word-of-mouth." Booklist

Jolin, Paula

In the name of God. Roaring Brook Press 2007 208p $16.95

Grades: 9 10 11 12 **Fic**

1. Muslims—Fiction 2. Family life—Fiction 3. Islamic fundamentalism—Fiction 4. Syria—Fiction

ISBN 978-1-59643-211-6; 1-59643-211-X LC 2006-23834

Determined to follow the laws set down in the Qur'an, seventeen-year-old Nadia becomes involved in a violent revolutionary movement aimed at supporting Muslim rule in Syria and opposing the Western politics and materialism that increasingly affect her family.

"The well-written prose and short chapters give stories in the news a face and a character. Readers of this book will not be able to read or watch the news in the same way." Voice Youth Advocates

Jones, Diana Wynne

Cart and cwidder. Greenwillow Books 2001 c1995 214p $16.95

Grades: 9 10 11 12 **Fic**

1. Fantasy fiction

ISBN 0-06-623745-9

Also available in paperback from Oxford University Press

A reissue of the title first published 1975 in the United Kingdom; first United States edition, 1977 by Atheneum

"Accompanying their gregarious father, Clennen the Singer, on panhorns and cwidders (a lute-like instrument) and traversing the earldoms of Dalemark in their gaily decorated cart make up the only life 11-year-old Moril and his brother and sister have ever known. . . . When his father is suddenly killed, Moril becomes heir to the large, ancient cwidder supposedly owned once by an old bard and having mystical powers. . . . Jones strikes a note of timelessness and universality in her forest setting and her theme of the struggle against oppressive forces, developing her characters in depth." Booklist

Followed by Drowned Ammet (1995)

Jones, Patrick

Nailed. Walker & Co. 2006 216p $16.95

Grades: 9 10 11 12 **Fic**

1. School stories 2. Father-son relationship—Fiction

ISBN 0-8027-8077-6; 978-0-8027-8077-5 LC 2005-27447

An outcast in a school full of jocks, sixteen-year-old Bret struggles to keep his individuality through his interest in drama and music, while trying to reconnect with his father.

"A tough, revealing book worthy of discussion." Booklist

Joyce, James, 1882-1941

A portrait of the artist as a young man; with an introduction by Richard Brown. Knopf 1991 xli, 318p $18 *

Grades: 11 12 Adult **Fic**

1. Ireland—Fiction

ISBN 0-679-40575-5 LC 91-52979

Also available from other publishers

"Everyman's library"

First appeared serially, 1914-1915 in the United Kingdom; first United States edition published 1916 by Huebsch

This autobiographical novel "portrays the childhood, school days, adolescence, and early manhood of Stephen Dedalus, later one of the leading characters in Ulysses. Stephen's growing self-awareness as an artist forces him to reject the whole narrow world in which he has been brought up, including family ties, nationalism, and the Catholic religion. The novel ends when, having decided

Joyce, James, 1882-1941—*Continued*
to become a writer, he is about to leave Dublin for Paris. Rather than following a clear narrative progression, the book revolves around experiences that are crucial to Stephen's development as an artist; at the end of each chapter Stephen makes some assertion of identity. Through his use of the stream-of-consciousness technique, Joyce reveals the actual materials of his hero's world, the components of his thought processes." Reader's Ency. 4th edition

Kafka, Franz, 1883-1924
The trial; translated from the German by Willa and Edwin Muir; revised, with additional notes, by E. M. Butler. Knopf 1992 299p $19 *
Grades: 11 12 Adult   **Fic**
ISBN 0-679-40994-7
Also available in paperback from Schocken Bks.
"Everyman's library"
Original edition 1924; first Everyman's Library edition, 1922
"Joseph K., a respected bank assessor, is arrested and spends his remaining years fighting charges about which he has no knowledge. The helplessness of an insignificant individual within a mysterious bureaucracy where answers are never accessible is described in this provocative and disturbing book." Shapiro. Fic for Youth. 3d edition

Kaplow, Robert
Me and Orson Welles; a novel. MacAdam/Cage Pub. 2003 269p $18.50
Grades: 11 12 Adult   **Fic**
1. Welles, Orson, 1915-1985—Fiction 2. Actors—Fiction 3. New York (N.Y.)—Fiction
ISBN 1-931561-49-4   LC 2003-14982
Also available in paperback from Penguin Books
"Richard, 17, spends a hectic week in New York in 1938, where he gets a small part in *Julius Caesar* at the new Mercury Theatre and meets Orson Welles." SLJ
This is "a delightful escape into a pre-war coming-of-age, and coming-of-stage, story—perfect for a quick and totally entertaining read." Booklist

Kaslik, Ibolya, 1973-
Skinny; [by] Ibi Kaslik. Walker & Company 2006 244p $16.95
Grades: 11 12   **Fic**
1. Anorexia nervosa—Fiction 2. Sisters—Fiction 3. Father-daughter relationship—Fiction
ISBN 978-0-8027-9608-0; 0-8027-9608-7
                                      LC 2006-42140
First published 2004 in Canada
After the death of their father, two sisters struggle with various issues, including their family history, personal relationships, and an extreme eating disorder
"It's refreshing that Gigi's anorexia and briefly described lesbian romance are treated as only parts of a larger story, and the girls' grief following their father's death and the pressures they face growing up with immigrant parents add depth to the novel. . . . This is an ambitious, often moving offering, and older readers will

likely connect with the raw emotions and intelligent insights into a family's secrets, pain, and enduring love." Booklist

Kass, Pnina
Real time; by Pnina Moed Kass. Clarion Books 2004 186p $15; pa $7.99
Grades: 7 8 9 10   **Fic**
1. Israel—Fiction 2. Germans—Israel—Fiction 3. Terrorism—Fiction
ISBN 0-618-44203-0; 0-618-69174-X (pa)
                                      LC 2004-8481
Sixteen-year-old Tomas Wanninger persuades his mother to let him leave Germany to volunteer at a kibbutz in Israel, where he experiences a violent political attack and finds answers about his own past
This "volume is an exhausting but illuminating read that will provide much-needed insight into life in modern Israel. . . . The characters are deeply developed and painfully sympathetic." SLJ

Kearney, Meg
The secret of me. Persea Books 2005 136p $17.95
Grades: 7 8 9 10   **Fic**
1. Adoption—Fiction
ISBN 0-89255-322-7   LC 2005-15578
"A Karen and Michael Braziller book"
"This novel in verse follows 14-year-old Lizzie through a year in which, despite her loving family, a circle of good friends, and a potential first boyfriend, she is plagued with a personal secret. She desperately wants to find out the story behind her adoption and her own identity." SLJ
"On rare occasions one reads a book that is just plain touching, pulling the reader in and allowing one to feel what the character feels. Here is such a book." Voice Youth Advocates

Keneally, Thomas, 1935-
Schindler's list. Simon & Schuster 1982 400p $25; pa $14 *
Grades: 11 12 Adult   **Fic**
1. Schindler, Oskar, 1908-1974—Fiction 2. Holocaust, 1933-1945—Fiction 3. World War, 1939-1945—Fiction 4. Jews—Fiction
ISBN 0-671-51688-4; 0-671-88031-4 (pa)
                                      LC 82-10489
"An actual occurrence during the Nazi regime in Germany forms the basis for this story. Oskar Schindler, a Catholic German industrialist, chose to act differently from those Germans who closed their eyes to what was happening to the Jews. By spending enormous sums on bribes to the SS and on food and drugs for the Jewish prisoners whom he housed in his own camp-factory in Cracow, he succeeded in sheltering thousands of Jews, finally transferring them to a safe place in Czechoslovakia. Fifty Schindler survivors from seven nations helped the author with information." Shapiro. Fic for Youth. 3d edition

Kennedy, William, 1928-
Ironweed. Viking 1983 227p pa $14 hardcover
o.p.
Grades: 11 12 Adult   **Fic**
1. Great Depression, 1929-1939—Fiction 2. New York
(State)—Fiction
ISBN 0-14-007020-0 (pa)   LC 82-40370
Also available in paperback from Scribner
With this "tale of skid-row life in the Depression,
Kennedy adds another chapter to his 'Albany cycle'—a
group of novels set in the Albany, New York, underworld from the 1920s onward. Following 'Legs' and
'Billy Phelan's Greatest Game,' 'Ironweed' tells the story
of Francis Phelan, a 58-year-old bum with muscatel on
his breath and hallucinations on his mind. Chief among
the latter is a vision of his infant son, who died after
falling out of Francis' arms. It is the desire to reconcile
himself to the memory of his dead son that brings Francis home to Albany, ultimately opening the door to a
possible reconciliation with his family." Booklist

Kerouac, Jack, 1922-1969
On the road. Viking 1997 307p $24.95; pa $16
Grades: 11 12 Adult   **Fic**
1. Voyages and travels—Fiction 2. Friendship—Fiction
ISBN 0-670-87478-7; 0-14-303638-6 (pa)
           LC 97-12899
First published 1957
"Sal Paradise (a self-portrait of Kerouac), a struggling
author in his mid-twenties, tells of his meeting Dean
Moriarty (based on Neal Cassady), a fast-living teenager
just out of a New Mexico reform school, whose soul is
'wrapped up in a fast car, a coast to reach, and a woman
at the end of the road.' During the next five years they
travel coast to coast, either with each other or to each
other. Five trips are described." Oxford Companion to
Am Lit. 6th dition

Kerr, M. E., 1927-
Deliver us from Evie. HarperCollins Pubs. 1994
177p pa $6.99 *
Grades: 9 10 11 12   **Fic**
1. Lesbians—Fiction 2. Siblings—Fiction
ISBN 0-06-024475-5; 0-06-447128-4 (pa)
           LC 94-1296
Parr Burrman and his family face some difficult times
when word spreads through their rural Missouri town
that his older sister is a lesbian, and she leaves the family farm to live with the daughter of the town's banker
"The strong, multi-dimensional, well-plotted story addresses current issues with sensitivity, thoughtfulness,
and a touch of humor." Horn Book

Night kites. Harper & Row 1986 216p
hardcover o.p. pa $5.99 *
Grades: 7 8 9 10   **Fic**
1. Homosexuality—Fiction 2. Brothers—Fiction
3. AIDS (Disease)—Fiction
ISBN 0-06-023253-6; 0-06-447035-0
           LC 85-45386
"A Charlotte Zolotow book"

"Seventeen-year-old Erick suddenly learns that his
older brother, Pete, whom he admires and tries to emu-
late, is gay and sick with AIDS. He also struggles with
his feelings for his best friend's girl, Nicki, a non-
conformist with a 'fast' reputation. Pete and Nicki are
the 'night kites' of the title—they dare to be different."
BAYA Book Rev
"Pete and his methods of coping with his disease and
its effects on himself, his friends, his family, and ultimately, his community, are sensitively and non-
sentimentally drawn, and seem to be portrayed accurately. This is sure to be a popular title, and will be a natural for booktalks." Voice Youth Advocates

Slap your sides; a novel. HarperCollins Pubs.
2001 198p lib bdg $16.89; pa $5.99
Grades: 7 8 9 10   **Fic**
1. World War, 1939-1945—Fiction 2. Brothers—Fiction 3. Conscientious objectors—Fiction 4. Society of
Friends—Fiction
ISBN 0-06-029482-5 (lib bdg); 0-06-447274-4 (pa)
           LC 00-54037
Life in their Pennsylvania hometown changes for
Jubal Shoemaker and his family when his older brother
witnesses to his Quaker beliefs by becoming a conscientious objector during World War II
"The ideas are gripping, not only because Kerr is fair
to all sides but also because the characters are complicated." Booklist

Your eyes in stars; a novel. HarperCollins
Publishers 2006 229p $15.99; lib bdg $16.89
Grades: 9 10 11 12   **Fic**
1. Family life—Fiction 2. World War, 1939-1945—
Fiction 3. New York (State)—Fiction
ISBN   0-06-075682-9;   978-0-06-075682-6;
0-06-075683-7 (lib bdg); 978-0-06-075683-3 (lib bdg)
           LC 2005-8781
In their small New York town, two teenaged girls become friends while helping each other make sense of
their families, neighbors, and selves as they approach
adulthood in the years preceding World War II.
The author "explores issues of anti-Semitism, classism
and capital punishment through the eyes of ordinary people, and demonstrates that taking a stand on the small
things can mean the difference between justice and apathy." Publ Wkly

Kesey, Ken
One flew over the cuckoo's nest; a novel.
Viking 1962 311p hardcover o.p. pa $7.99 *
Grades: 11 12 Adult   **Fic**
1. Mentally ill—Fiction
ISBN 0-670-03058-9; 0-451-16396-6 (pa)
"Life in a mental institution is predictable and suffocating under the iron rule of Nurse Ratched, who toler-
ates no disruption of routine on her all-male ward. Half-
Indian Chief Bromden, almost invisible on the ward because he is thought to be deaf and dumb, describes the
arrival of rowdy Randle Patrick McMurphy. McMurphy
takes on the nurse as an adversary in his attempt to organize his fellow inmates and breathe some self-esteem and
joy into their lives. The battle is vicious on the part of
the nurse, who is relentless in her efforts to break
McMurphy, but a spark of human will brings an element

Kesey, Ken—*Continued*

of hope to counter the despotic institutional power." Shapiro. Fic for Youth. 3d edition

Keyes, Daniel, 1927-

Flowers for Algernon. Harcourt Brace & Co. 1995 c1966 286p $17 *

Grades: 9 10 11 12   **Fic**

1. Mentally handicapped—Fiction 2. Science fiction

ISBN 0-15-100163-4   LC 95-148312

Also available in paperback from Skylark Bks.

"A Harcourt Brace modern classic"

First published 1966

"Charlie Gordon, aged 32, is mentally retarded and enrolls in a class to 'become smart.' He keeps a journal of his progress after an experimental operation that increases his I.Q. Although Charlie becomes brilliant, he is unhappy because he cannot shed his former personality and is tormented by his memories. In the end he begins to lose the mental powers he has gained." Shapiro. Fic for Youth. 3d edition

Kidd, Sue Monk

The secret life of bees. Viking 2002 301p $24.95; pa $14 *

Grades: 11 12 Adult   **Fic**

1. African Americans—Fiction 2. Race relations—Fiction 3. South Carolina—Fiction

ISBN 0-670-89460-5; 0-14-200174-0 (pa)

LC 2001-26310

This is the "tale of a 14-year-old white girl named Lily Owen who is raised by the elderly African American Rosaleen after the accidental death of Lily's mother. Following a racial brawl in 1960s Tiburon, S.C, Lily and Rosaleen find shelter in a distant town with three black bee-keeping sisters." Libr J

"Lily is a wonderfully petulant and self-absorbed adolescent, and Kidd deftly portrays her sense of injustice as it expands to accommodate broader social evils." N Y Times Book Rev

Kincaid, Jamaica

Annie John. Farrar, Straus & Giroux 1985 148p hardcover o.p. pa $12 *

Grades: 11 12 Adult   **Fic**

1. Antigua and Barbuda—Fiction 2. Mother-daughter relationship—Fiction

ISBN 0-374-10521-9; 0-374-52510-2 (pa)

"Episodes from the young life of Annie John, aged 10 to 17, as she grows up on the Caribbean island of Antigua. This is a magical coming-of-age tale, ripe with the special ambience of its tropical setting and sustained by Annie's far from naive awareness of the world around her. Death, illness, and poverty intrude on the narrator's perceptive sensibility from time to time, but even these experiences instruct her and expand her understanding of life and its shifting reality. . . . A poetic and intensely moving work." Booklist

King, Laurie R.

The beekeeper's apprentice, or, On the segregation of the queen. Bantam Books 2002 xxi, 341p pa $12

Grades: 9 10 11 12   **Fic**

1. Doyle, Sir Arthur Conan, 1859-1930—Parodies, imitations, etc. 2. Mystery fiction 3. Great Britain—Fiction

ISBN 0-553-38152-0   LC 2001-43926

First published 1994 by St. Martin's Press

"In the early years of WWI, 15-year-old American Mary Russell encounters Holmes, retired in Sussex Downs where Conan Doyle left him raising bees. Mary, an orphan rebelling against her guardian aunt's strictures, impresses the sleuth with her intelligence and acumen. Holmes initiates her into the mysteries of detection, allowing her to participate in a few cases when she comes home from her studies at Oxford. The collaboration is ignited by the kidnapping in Wales of Jessica Simpson, daughter of an American senator." Publ Wkly

"A wonderfully original and entertaining story that is funny, heartwarming, and full of intrigue. . . . Holmes fans, history buffs, lovers of humor and adventure, and mystery devotees will all find King's book absorbing from beginning to end." Booklist

King, Stephen, 1947-

Carrie. Doubleday 1974 199p $32.50 *

Grades: 11 12 Adult   **Fic**

1. Extrasensory perception—Fiction 2. Horror fiction 3. Maine—Fiction

ISBN 0-385-08695-4

Also available in paperback from Pocket Bks.

"Carrie is 16, lonely, the butt of all her Maine classmates' tricks and jokes, an object of scorn even to her own mother, who is fanatically religious and believes anything remotely sexual is from the devil. Then one girl becomes ashamed of the cruelty being vented on Carrie and plans an act of kindness that will give her the first happiness in her young life. The only trouble is the act backfires horribly and Carrie is worse off than ever before. It is at this point, at the senior prom, that Carrie begins to put into effect her awesome telekinetic powers, powers with which she has only toyed before." Publ Wkly

"A terrifying treat for both horror and parapsychology fans." SLJ

Firestarter. Viking 1980 428p hardcover o.p. pa $7.99

Grades: 11 12 Adult   **Fic**

1. Psychokinesis—Fiction 2. Horror fiction

ISBN 0-670-31541-9; 0-451-16780-5 (pa)

LC 80-14793

"Two college students sign up as paid guinea pigs for a secret and unknowingly dangerous government experiment in telekinesis. . . . When the subjects marry and have a baby, however, their child develops not only telekinesis but pyrokinesis as well; in short, the tot can not only push things with her mind, but set them ablaze as well. The government's plan to use the girl as a human weapon set [the author's] plot into action, and an extended chase ensues with expected havoc wreaked in vivid detail." Booklist

"This is your advanced post-Watergate cynical Ameri-

King, Stephen, 1947-—*Continued*

can thriller with some eerie parapsychological twists, and it's been done so distinctively well that we'd better talk about genius rather than genre." Quill Quire

Kingsolver, Barbara

The bean trees; a novel. 10th anniversary ed. HarperFlamingo 1997 261p $19.95; pa $7.99 *

Grades: 11 12 Adult   **Fic**

1. Arizona—Fiction

ISBN 0-06-017579-6; 0-06-109731-4 (pa)

LC 97-2691

A reissue of the title first published 1988

In this novel, "Taylor Greer, a poor, young woman, flees her Kentucky home and heads west. . . . While passing through Oklahoma, she becomes responsible for a two-year-old Cherokee girl. The two continue on the road. When they roll off the highway in Tucson, Taylor and the child, whom she has named Turtle, . . . meet Mattie, a widow who runs Jesus Is Lord Used Tires and is active in the sanctuary movement on the side." Ms

This book "gives readers something that's increasingly hard to find today—a character to believe in and laugh with and admire." Christ Sci Monit

Followed by Pigs in heaven (1993)

The poisonwood Bible; a novel. HarperFlamingo 1998 546p $26; pa $15

Grades: 11 12 Adult   **Fic**

1. Congo (Republic)—Fiction 2. Christian missionaries—Fiction

ISBN 0-06-017540-0; 0-06-093053-5 (pa)

LC 98-19901

"In 1959, evangelical preacher Nathan Price moves his wife and four daughters from Georgia to a village in the Belgian Congo, later Zaire. Their dysfunction and cultural arrogance proves disastrous as the family is nearly destroyed by war, Nathan's tyranny, and Africa itself. Told in the voices of the mother and daughters, the novel spans 30 years as the women seek to understand each other and the continent that tore them apart." Libr J

"Buttressing her suspenseful chronicle with authentic background detail, Kingsolver's narrative is at once a compelling family saga and an astute look at Western imperialism in Africa." Publ Wkly

Kinsella, W. P.

Shoeless Joe. Houghton Mifflin 1982 265p hardcover o.p. pa $13.95 *

Grades: 9 10 11 12   **Fic**

1. Baseball—Fiction 2. Fantasy fiction

ISBN 0-395-32047-X; 0-395-95773-7 (pa)

LC 81-19196

In this fantasy, Iowan farmer Ray Kinsella "hears a voice say 'If you build it, he will come,' and knows that 'it' refers to a baseball park and 'he' to Shoeless Joe Jackson. . . . Ray builds his magic stadium and while watching Shoeless Joe and others play ball, hears the voice again, this time saying, 'Ease his pain.' The mission clearly means kidnapping J. D. Salinger and taking him to Fenway Park for a Red Sox game. Ray succeeds and Salinger . . . joins Ray on a further quest. Their odyssey culminates back at home plate in Iowa." Quill Quire

Klass, David, 1960-

California Blue. Scholastic 1994 200p hardcover o.p. pa $5.99

Grades: 7 8 9 10   **Fic**

1. Butterflies—Fiction 2. Environmental protection—Fiction

ISBN 0-590-46688-7; 0-590-46689-5

LC 93-13705

When seventeen-year-old John Rodgers discovers a new sub-species of butterfly which may necessitate closing the mill where his dying father works, they find themselves on opposite sides of the environmental conflict.

"The absorbing first-person narration rings true, projecting the credible voice of a teenager just beginning to break free from his emotional ties at home, family and friends. The fears, excitement, anger and energy of this awkward psychological time are movingly captured here." Publ Wkly

Dark angel. Farrar, Straus & Giroux 2005 311p $17

Grades: 7 8 9 10   **Fic**

1. Brothers—Fiction

ISBN 0-374-39950-6   LC 2004-53340

"Frances Foster books"

When his older brother is released from prison, seventeen-year-old Jeff's family secret is revealed, causing upheaval in his home, school and love life.

"The plot builds ferociously in tandem with Jeff's suffocating conflict and burgeoning courage. . . . Recommend this fast-paced, thoughtful story to older reluctant readers, especially boys." SLJ

Home of the Braves. Farrar, Straus & Giroux 2002 312p $18

Grades: 7 8 9 10   **Fic**

1. Soccer—Fiction 2. School stories

ISBN 0-374-39963-8   LC 2002-19391

Also available in paperback from HarperCollins

"Frances Foster books"

Eighteen-year-old Joe, captain of the soccer team, is dismayed when a hotshot player shows up from Brazil and threatens to take over both the team and the girl whom Joe hopes to date.

"A gritty, realistic story of a robust insider with his feet planted solidly on the ground. . . . More than a sports story, [this] is a first-rate coming-of-age novel." Voice Youth Advocates

You don't know me; a novel. Foster Bks. 2001 262p $17 *

Grades: 7 8 9 10   **Fic**

1. School stories 2. Child abuse—Fiction

ISBN 0-374-38706-0   LC 00-22709

Also available in paperback from HarperCollins

Fourteen-year-old John creates alternative realities in his mind as he tries to deal with his mother's abusive boyfriend, his crush on a beautiful, but shallow classmate and other problems at school

"Klass is effective with John's deliberately distanced voice, his constant dancing with and away from reality, . . . and his brittle and even dorky defenses, and the rising tension is suspenseful." Bull Cent Child Books

Klause, Annette Curtis

Blood and chocolate. Delacorte Press 1997 264p
pa $6.50 *

Grades: 7 8 9 10   **Fic**

1. Werewolves—Fiction 2. Horror fiction
ISBN 0-385-32305-0; 0-440-22668-6 (pa)
LC 96-35247

Having fallen for a human boy, a beautiful teenage
werewolf must battle both her packmates and the fear of
the townspeople to decide where she belongs and with
whom

"Klause's imagery is magnetic, and her language
fierce, rich, and beautiful. . . . Passion and philosophy
dovetail superbly in this powerful, unforgettable novel
for mature teens." Booklist

The silver kiss. Delacorte Press 1990 198p
hardcover o.p. pa $5.99 *

Grades: 9 10 11 12   **Fic**

1. Vampires—Fiction 2. Death—Fiction
ISBN 0-385-30160-X; 0-440-21346-0 (pa)
LC 89-48880

"One evening, when 17-year-old Zoë is sitting in the
park contemplating her mother's imminent death due to
cancer, her father's lack of support, and her best friend's
move, she meets Simon. Simon is startlingly handsome
and strangely compelling. As their friendship grows over
time, Simon reveals to Zoë his true identity: he is a vampire, trying to kill his younger vampire brother." SLJ

"There's inherent romantic appeal in the vampire legend, and Klause weaves all the gory details into a poignant love story that becomes both sensuous and suspenseful." Booklist

Klein, Lisa M., 1958-

Ophelia. Bloomsbury Children's Books 2006
328p $16.95

Grades: 9 10 11 12   **Fic**

1. Shakespeare, William, 1564-1616—Fiction
ISBN 978-1-58234-801-8; 1-58234-801-4
LC 2005-32601

In a story based on Shakespeare's Hamlet, Ophelia
tells of her life in the court at Elsinore, her love for
Prince Hamlet, and her escape from the violence in Denmark.

"Teens need not be familiar with Shakespeare's original to enjoy this fresh take—with the added romance and
a strong heroine at its center." Publ Wkly

Knowles, John, 1926-2001

A separate peace. Scribner Classics 1996 204p
$20; pa $11 *

Grades: 11 12 Adult   **Fic**

1. Friendship—Fiction 2. School stories
ISBN 0-684-83366-2; 0-7432-5397-3 (pa)
LC 96-25844

A reissue of the title published 1960 by Macmillan

"Gene Forrester looks back on his school days, spent
in a New England town just before World War II. He
both admires and envies his close friend and roommate,
Finny, who is a natural athlete, in contrast to Gene's special competence as a scholar. When Finny suffers a crippling accident, Gene must face his own involvement in
it." Shapiro. Fic for Youth. 3d edition

Knox, Elizabeth, 1959-

Dreamhunter; book one of the Dreamhunter
duet. Farrar, Straus & Giroux 2006 365p $19 *

Grades: 7 8 9 10   **Fic**

1. Fantasy fiction 2. Dreams—Fiction
ISBN 0-374-31853-0   LC 2005-46366
"Frances Foster books"

First published 2005 in the United Kingdom

In a world where select people can enter "The Place"
and find dreams of every kind to share with others for
a fee, a fifteen-year-old girl is training to be a
dreamhunter when her father disappears, leaving her to
carry on his mysterious mission.

This first of a projected two-book series is "a highly
original exploration of the idea of a collective unconscious, mixed with imagery from the raising of Lazarus
and with the brave, dark qualities of the psyche of an adolescent female." Horn Book Guide

Followed by Dreamquake (2007)

Koertge, Ronald

Margaux with an X; [by] Ron Koertge.
Candlewick Press 2004 165p $15.99; pa $6.99 *

Grades: 7 8 9 10   **Fic**

1. Domestic violence—Fiction
ISBN 0-7636-2401-2; 0-7636-2679-1 (pa)
LC 2003-65279

Margaux, known as a "tough chick" at her Los Angeles high school, makes a connection with Danny, who,
like her, struggles with the emotional impact of family
violence and abuse.

This book "excels in character development. It is an
intriguing story that constantly provokes readers' curiosity. . . . [The author's] language at times is advanced, an
accurate reflection of his characters' intellectual capacity." SLJ

Stoner & Spaz; [by] Ron Koertge. Candlewick
Press 2002 169p $15.99; pa $6.99 *

Grades: 7 8 9 10   **Fic**

1. Cerebral palsy—Fiction 2. School stories
ISBN 0-7636-1608-7; 0-7636-2150-1 (pa)
LC 2001-43050

A troubled youth with cerebral palsy struggles toward
self-acceptance with the help of a drug-addicted young
woman

"Funny, touching, and surprising, it is a hopeful yet
realistic view of things as they are and as they could be."
Booklist

Strays; [by] Ron Koertge. Candlewick Press
2007 167p $16.99

Grades: 7 8 9 10 11 12   **Fic**

1. Foster home care—Fiction 2. Orphans—Fiction
ISBN 978-0-7636-2705-8; 0-7636-2705-4
LC 2007-24096

After his parents are killed in a car accident, high
school senior Sam wonders whether he will ever feel
again or if he will remain numbed by grief.

"Though Koertge never soft pedals the horrors faced
by some foster children, this thoughtful novel about the
lost and abandoned is a hopeful one." Booklist

Koja, Kathe

The blue mirror. Farrar, Straus and Giroux 2004
119p $16

Grades: 9 10 11 12   **Fic**
1. Alcoholism—Fiction 2. Mother-daughter relationship—Fiction
ISBN 0-374-30849-7   LC 2003-48510
Also available in paperback from Puffin Books
"Frances Foster books"
Seventeen-year-old loner Maggy Klass, who frequently
seeks refuge from her alcoholic mother's apartment by
sitting and drawing in a local cafe, becomes involved in
a destructive relationship with a charismatic homeless
youth named Cole

Buddha Boy. Farrar, Straus & Giroux 2003
117p $16 *

Grades: 7 8 9 10   **Fic**
1. Artists—Fiction 2. Buddhism—Fiction 3. School
stories
ISBN 0-374-30998-1   LC 2002-25067
"Frances Foster books"
"When Jinsen arrives at Edward Rucher High School
coatless in winter, sporting a bald head, begging for
money in the school cafeteria, and talking about karma,
he is immediately dubbed 'Buddha Boy' by the resident
bullies. Justin, the narrator . . . is forced to work on a
school project with Jinsen and discovers the newcomer's
incredible artistic talent. . . . Mesmerized by Jinsen's art
and philosophy, Justin befriends him and learns about
Jinsen's hostile past." Voice Youth Advocates
"A compelling introduction to Buddhism and a credible portrait of how true friendship brings out the best in
people." Publ Wkly

Koontz, Dean R., 1945-

Watchers. Putnam 1987 352p hardcover o.p. pa
$7.99 *

Grades: 11 12 Adult   **Fic**
1. Horror fiction
ISBN 0-399-13263-5; 0-425-18880-9 (pa)
         LC 86-22687
"When the Russians sabotage a genetic research project in California, two mutated creatures escape from the
lab. One is a golden retriever with high enough intelligence to think and communicate with humans; the other
is the Outsider, a vicious monster created from a baboon
and bred to kill. Both the man who befriends and adopts
the dog and his new bride find themselves stalked by
government agents anxious to find the dog, a particularly
repulsive Mafia hit man intent on stealing him, and the
Outsider, with whom the dog is linked telepathically."
Libr J

Korman, Gordon, 1963-

Born to rock. Hyperion Books for Children
2006 261p $15.99

Grades: 7 8 9 10   **Fic**
1. Father-son relationship—Fiction 2. Rock music—
Fiction
ISBN 0-7868-0920-5   LC 2005-52652
High school senior Leo Caraway, a conservative Re-
publican, learns that his biological father is a punk rock

legend.
"Rock fans will appreciate the short riffs at chapter
breaks and the intriguing music-centric premise." Publ
Wkly

Jake, reinvented. Hyperion 2003 213p $15.99;
pa $5.99 *

Grades: 7 8 9 10   **Fic**
1. School stories
ISBN 0-7868-1957-X; 0-7868-5697-1 (pa)
         LC 2003-47804
Rick becomes friends with the popular new boy, Jake
Garrett, football player and host of superlative parties,
and in the process discovers the true nature of his
schoolmates and uncovers the mystery of Jake's past.
"Korman's reworking of The Great Gatsby places the
action in a modern framework, which makes it more recognizable for today's readers and may lead them to the
classic. Teens will find deeper issues to consider about
popularity, being true to one's self, and taking responsibility for one's actions as they relate to the setting and
characters." SLJ

Son of the mob. Hyperion Bks. for Children
2002 262p $15.99; pa $5.99 *

Grades: 7 8 9 10   **Fic**
1. Mafia—Fiction
ISBN 0-7868-0769-5; 0-7868-1593-0 (pa)
         LC 2002-68672
Seventeen-year-old Vince's life is constantly complicated by the fact that he is the son of a powerful Mafia
boss, a relationship that threatens to destroy his romance
with the daughter of an FBI agent
"The fast-paced, tightly focused story addresses the
problems of being an honest kid in a family of outlaws—and loving them anyway. Korman doesn't ignore
the seamier side of mob life, but even when the subject
matter gets violent . . . he keeps things light by relating
his tale in the first-person voice of a humorously sarcastic yet law-abiding wise guy." Horn Book
Another title about Vince is:
Son of the mob: Hollywood hustle (2004)

Kosinski, Jerzy N., 1933-1991

The painted bird; with an introduction by the
author. 2nd ed. Grove Press 1995 xxvi, 234p pa
$12

Grades: 11 12 Adult   **Fic**
1. Poland—Fiction 2. World War, 1939-1945—Fiction
3. Refugees—Fiction 4. Boys—Fiction
ISBN 0-8021-3422-X   LC 95-19520
First published 1965 by Houghton Mifflin
"In Eastern Europe during World War II a ten-year-
old boy is separated from his parents and struggles to
survive in primitive villages where he is viewed as an
unwanted outsider. Dark-haired and dark-eyed, he is unlike the Polish villagers among whom he tries to find
refuge. He is the gypsy, the 'painted bird,' and savage
abuse is heaped upon him time after time. He has, nevertheless, the will to transcend the sadism and superstition
of these ignorant people." Shapiro. Fic for Youth. 3d edition

Kositsky, Lynne, 1947-
Claire by moonlight. Tundra Books 2005 271p pa $9.95
Grades: 7 8 9 10   **Fic**
1. Nova Scotia—Fiction 2. Acadians—Fiction
ISBN 0-88776-659-5
"Claire Richard has already survived the death of her parents, deportation from her beloved Acadian village, and a violent storm at sea. British and French forces are at large in 1755, but she is determined to return to Acadia with her remaining sister and brother. She also seeks her true love, Sam, a reluctant British soldier. . . . Plenty of action and the determination of the strong female heroine move the story swiftly along." Booklist

Kostick, Conor
Epic. Viking 2007 364p $17.99 *
Grades: 7 8 9 10   **Fic**
1. Fantasy fiction 2. Video games—Fiction
ISBN 0-670-06179-4; 978-0-06179-2
LC 2006-19958
On New Earth, a world based on a video role-playing game, fourteen-year-old Erik pursuades his friends to aid him in some unusual gambits in order to save his father from exile and safeguard the futures of each of their families.
"There is intrigue and mystery throughout this captivating page-turner. Veins of moral and ethical social situations and decisions provide some great opportunities for discussion. Well written and engaging." SLJ

Krovatin, Christopher, 1985-
Heavy metal and you. Scholastic 2005 186p $16.95; pa $7.99
Grades: 9 10 11 12   **Fic**
1. School stories 2. Rock music—Fiction 3. New York (N.Y.)—Fiction
ISBN 0-439-73648-X; 0-439-74399-0 (pa)
LC 2004-23645
High schooler Sam begins losing himself when he falls for a preppy girl who wants him to give up getting wasted with his best friends and even his passion for heavy metal music in order to become a better person.
"From the terrific cover and portrait of selfish love to the clever CD player icons indicating narrative switches . . . this is an authentic portrayal of an obsession with music. Teens don't have to like heavy metal to appreciate this novel, which is guaranteed to attract readers looking for a book to reach their death-metal souls." Booklist

Lackey, Mercedes
Joust. DAW Bks. 2003 373p il $24.95; pa $7.99 *
Grades: 11 12 Adult   **Fic**
1. Dragons—Fiction 2. Fantasy fiction
ISBN 0-7564-0122-4; 0-7564-0153-4 (pa)
LC 2003-544990
Vetch, an Altan serf, must learn the secret of the Tian jousters and their dragons in order to save his people
"This uplifting tale, which contains a valuable lesson or two on the virtues of hard work, is a must-read for dragon lovers in particular and for fantasy fans in general." Publ Wkly

The outstretched shadow; {by} Mercedes Lackey and James Mallory. Tor 2003 604p (Obsidian trilogy, bk 1) $27.95
Grades: 9 10 11 12   **Fic**
1. Fantasy fiction
ISBN 0-7653-0219-5   LC 2003-55955
"A Tom Doherty Associates book"
"As the son of the Arch-Mage of the Council of Mages, Kellen lives an ordered life, structured by the principles of High Magick—until he discovers a set of forbidden books on Wild Magic and becomes anathema to his people. Banished in disgrace from his home, Kellen enters a wild world populated by elves and other magical creatures only to find that this world is threatened by the rise of demons deep within the Obsidian Mountain." Libr J
"Lackey and Mallory create a wide variety of multidimensional characters, especially Kellen who grows to manhood in realistic starts and stops, recognizing and accepting both his heritage and the consequences of his actions." Voice Youth Advocates

The serpent's shadow. DAW Bks. 2001 343p $24.95; pa $7.99
Grades: 11 12 Adult   **Fic**
1. Fantasy fiction
ISBN 0-88677-915-4; 0-7564-0061-9 (pa)
LC 2002-265143
"To an alternative Victorian London Dr. Maya Witherspoon, {daughter} of a Brahmin lady and an English physician, comes to practice. Besides standard Western medicine, Maya knows the magic of India, where she grew up. Maya's aunt Shivani has also come to England, but as a devotee of Kali, she hates her sister's marriage and is determined to wreak havoc on the English. Maya must seek the aid of British magical masters before the powers of Kali devastate London." Booklist

Lahiri, Jhumpa
The namesake. Houghton Mifflin 2003 291p $24; pa $14 *
Grades: 11 12 Adult   **Fic**
1. East Indians—United States—Fiction 2. Culture conflict—Fiction 3. Massachusetts—Fiction
ISBN 0-395-92721-8; 0-618-48522-8 (pa)
LC 2003-41718
"A novel about assimilation and generational differences. Gogol is so named because his father believes that sitting up in a sleeping car reading Nikolai Gogol's 'The Overcoat' saved him when the train he was on derailed and most passengers perished. After his arranged marriage, the man and his wife leave India for America, where he eventually becomes a professor. They adopt American ways, yet all of their friends are Bengalis. But for young Gogol and his sister, Boston is home, and trips to Calcutta to visit relatives are voyages to a foreign land." SLJ
"Its incorrigible mildness and its ungilded lilies aside, Lahiri's novel is unfailingly lovely in its treatment of Gogol's relationship with his father. This is the classic American parent-child bond." N Y Times Book Rev

L'Amour, Louis, 1908-1988

The daybreakers. Bantam 1984 224p pa $4.99

Grades: 9 10 11 12   **Fic**

1. Western stories

ISBN 0-553-27674-3

First published 1960

First book in series that explores the settling of the American West by focusing on the exploits of several generations of the Sackett family

Other titles in the series are:

Galloway (1974)

Jubal Sackett (1985)

Lando (1962)

The lonely men (1976)

Lonely on the mountain (1980)

Mojave crossing (1964)

Mustang man (1976)

Ride the dark trail (1972)

Ride the river (1983)

Sackett (1961)

The Sackett brand (1971)

Sackett's land (1975)

The sky-liners (1972)

To the far blue mountains (1976)

Treasure mountain (1979)

The warrior's path (1980)

Lansens, Lori

The girls; a novel. Little, Brown 2006 c2005 345p $23.95; pa $13.99 *

Grades: 11 12 Adult   **Fic**

1. Twins—Fiction 2. Sisters—Fiction

ISBN 978-0-316-06903-8; 0-316-06903-5; 978-0-316-06634-1 (pa); 0-316-06634-6 (pa)

LC 2005-24510

First published 2005 in Canada

"Since their birth, Rose and Ruby Darlen have been known simply as 'the girls.' They make friends, fall in love, have jobs, love their parents, and follow their dreams. But the Darlens are special. Now nearing their 30th birthday, they are history's oldest craniopagus twins, joined at the head by a spot the size of a bread plate." Publisher's note

"Through their alternating narratives, Lansens captures a contradictory longing for independence and togetherness that transcends the book's enormous conceit." Publ Wkly

Larbalestier, Justine, 1967-

Magic or madness. Razorbill 2005 288p $16.99; pa $7.99

Grades: 8 9 10 11 12   **Fic**

1. Magic—Fiction 2. Space and time—Fiction 3. Grandmothers—Fiction 4. New York (N.Y.)—Fiction 5. Australia—Fiction

ISBN 1-59514-022-0; 1-59514-124-3 (pa)

LC 2004-18263

From the Sydney, Australia home of a grandmother she believes is a witch, fifteen-year-old Reason Cansino is magically transported to New York City, where she discovers that friends and foes can be hard to distinguish

"Readers looking for layered, understated fantasy will follow the looping paths of Larbalestier's fine writing . . . with gratitude and awe." Booklist

Other titles about Reason Cansino are:

Magic lessons (2006)

Magic's child (2007)

LaRochelle, David, 1960-

Absolutely, positively not. Arthur A. Levine Books 2005 219p $16.95 *

Grades: 7 8 9 10   **Fic**

1. Homosexuality—Fiction 2. School stories

ISBN 0-439-59109-0   LC 2004-23558

Chronicles a teenage boy's humorous attempts to fit in at his Minnesota high school by becoming a macho, girl-loving, "Playboy" pinup-displaying heterosexual.

"The wry, first-person narrative is wonderful as it moves from personal angst to outright farce. . . . The characters are drawn with surprising depth." Booklist

Larson, Kirby, 1954-

Hattie Big Sky. Delacorte Press 2006 289p $15.95; lib bdg $17.99 *

Grades: 6 7 8 9 10   **Fic**

1. Frontier and pioneer life—Fiction 2. Orphans—Fiction 3. World War, 1914-1918—Fiction 4. Montana—Fiction

ISBN 0-385-73313-5; 0-385-90332-4 (lib bdg)

LC 2005-35039

A Newbery Medal honor book, 2007

After inheriting her uncle's homesteading claim in Montana, sixteen-year-old orphan Hattie Brooks travels from Iowa in 1917 to make a home for herself and encounters some unexpected problems related to the war being fought in Europe.

This is "a richly textured novel full of memorable characters." Booklist

Lavender, William, 1921-

Aftershocks. Harcourt 2006 344p $17

Grades: 8 9 10 11 12   **Fic**

1. Sex role—Fiction 2. Father-daughter relationship—Fiction 3. Chinese Americans—Fiction 4. Earthquakes—Fiction 5. San Francisco (Calif.)—Fiction

ISBN 0-15-205882-6   LC 2005-19695

In San Francisco from 1903 to 1908, teenager Jessie Wainwright determines to reach her goal of becoming a doctor while also trying to care for the illegitimate child of a liaison between her father and their Chinese maid.

This "is readable historical fiction about an engrossing event in U.S. history." Voice Youth Advocates

Lawhead, Steve, 1950-

Patrick, son of Ireland; a novel; {by} Stephen R. Lawhead. Morrow 2003 434p hardcover o.p. pa $7.99

Grades: 11 12 Adult   **Fic**

1. Patrick, Saint, 373?-463?—Fiction 2. Christian saints—Fiction 3. Ireland—Fiction

ISBN 0-06-001281-1; 0-06-001282-X (pa)

LC 2002-31535

This novel "portrays the famous saint's youth, beginning with his privileged, reckless young manhood in Wales. Patrick is captured by pirates and spends seven

Lawhead, Steve, 1950-—_Continued_
painful years as a slave to an Irish chieftain. At last he
escapes, in some ways betraying the woman he loves,
and makes his way to Gaul. He becomes a soldier, rises
in the ranks, and marries a Roman noblewoman."
Booklist

"Lawhead attempts to reclaim the lost years of the
legendary Saint Patrick's life, from his escape from slavery to his life in the dwindling Holy Roman Empire and
his eventual return to Ireland. . . . Filled with rich realism and believable characters, this first-person narrative
will engage readers interested in the legend of Saint Patrick as well as those simply attracted to novels that investigate medieval culture." Voice Youth Advocates

Lawlor, Laurie
The two loves of Will Shakespeare. Holiday
House 2006 278p $16.95
Grades: 9 10 11 12   **Fic**
 1. Shakespeare, William, 1564-1616—Fiction
2. Great Britain—History—1485-1603, Tudors—Fiction
ISBN 0-8234-1901-0; 978-0-8234-1901-2
                                     LC 2005-52537
After falling in love, eighteen-year-old Will Shakespeare, a bored apprentice in his father's glove business
and often in trouble for various misdeeds, vows to live
an upstanding life and pursue his passion for writing.

"Quoting lines from Shakespeare's sonnets and highlighting the dismal treatment of women in that brutally
repressive society, the author creates both a vivid setting
and a feckless protagonist, equally credible as an adolescent and as a product of his times." Booklist

Lawrence, D. H. (David Herbert), 1885-1930
Sons and lovers. Knopf 1991 xxvii, 403p $17
Grades: 11 12 Adult   **Fic**
 1. Mother-son relationship—Fiction 2. Great Britain—
Fiction
ISBN 0-679-40572-0   LC 91-53002
Also available in paperback from Modern Lib.
"Everyman's library"
First published 1913

"Paul Morel, adored youngest son of a middle-class
mother who feels that her coal-miner husband was unworthy of her, has difficulty in breaking away from her.
Mrs. Morel has given her son all her warmth and love
for so long a time that Paul finds it impossible to establish a relationship with another women. Miriam is supportive and understanding of his artistic nature but appeals mainly to his higher nature; Clara Dawes becomes
his mistress but she is married and will not divorce her
husband. After the death of his mother, Paul arranges a
reconciliation between Clara and her husband and, after
months of grieving for his mother, at last finds the
strength to strike out on his own." Shapiro. Fic For
Youth. 3d edition

Lawrence, Iain, 1955-
B for Buster. Delacorte Press 2004 321p $15.95;
lib bdg $17.95; pa $5.99
Grades: 7 8 9 10   **Fic**
 1. World War, 1939-1945—Fiction 2. Air pilots—Fiction
ISBN 0-385-73086-1; 0-385-90108-9 (lib bdg);
0-440-23810-2 (pa)   LC 2003-17345
In the spring of 1943, sixteen-year-old Kak, desperate
to escape his abusive parents, lies about his age to enlist
in the Canadian Air Force and soon finds himself based
in England as part of a crew flying bombing raids over
Germany

"Lawrence writes a gripping, affecting story about the
thrill of flying, the terrifying realities of war, and the ag-
ony of reconciling personal fears and ideals with duty
and bravery." Booklist

The lightkeeper's daughter. Delacorte Press
2002 246p $16.95; lib bdg $18.99; pa $7.95
Grades: 7 8 9 10   **Fic**
 1. Teenage mothers—Fiction 2. Islands—Fiction
ISBN 0-385-72925-1; 0-385-90062-7 (lib bdg);
0-385-73127-2 (pa)   LC 2002-578
When, after a four-year absence, seventeen-year-old
Squid returns to her childhood home on a remote lighthouse island off British Columbia with her young daughter in tow, she and her parents try to come to terms with
each other and the painful events of the past, especially
the death of her older brother

This "is not an easy or comfortable read but for sophisticated teens, this lyrical novel is an experience not
to be forgotten." SLJ

Lawrence, Michael
A crack in the line; Withern Rise, volume I; by
Michael Lawrence. 1st ed. Greenwillow Books
2004 c2003 323p $15.99; lib bdg $16.89; pa $7.99
Grades: 7 8 9 10   **Fic**
 1. Space and time—Fiction 2. Great Britain—Fiction
ISBN 0-06-072477-3; 0-06-072478-1 (lib bdg);
0-06-072479-X (pa)   LC 2003-56860
Sixteen-year-old Alaric discovers how to travel to an
alternate reality, where his mother is alive and his place
in the family is held by a girl named Naia

"The first in a trilogy, this complex story of choices,
fate, and acceptance is demanding. . . . [It] is sure to
spark passionate discussion." Booklist
 Other titles in this series are :
Small eternities (2005)
The Underwood See (2007)

Lawson, Mary, 1910-1941
Crow Lake. Dial Press (NY) 2002 291p
hardcover o.p. pa $14
Grades: 11 12 Adult   **Fic**
 1. Orphans—Fiction 2. Poverty—Fiction 3. Canada—
Fiction
ISBN 0-385-33611-X; 0-385-33763-9 (pa)
                                          LC 2001-53779
In this novel "four children living in northern Ontario
struggle to stay together after their parents die in an auto
accident. . . . Kate Morrison narrates the tale in flash-

Lawson, Mary, 1910-1941—*Continued*

back mode, starting with the fatal car accident that leaves seven-year-old Kate; her toddler sister, Bo; 19-year-old Luke; and 17-year-old Matt to fend for themselves." Publ Wkly

"Lawson achieves a breathless anticipatory quality in her surprisingly adept first novel, in which a child tells the story, but tells it very well indeed." Booklist

Le Carré, John, 1931-

The spy who came in from the cold. Walker & Company 2005 223p $19

Grades: 9 10 11 12   **Fic**
1. Spies—Fiction
ISBN 0-8027-1454-4
Also available in paperback from Scribner
First published 1963 in the United kingdom; first United States edition published 1964 by Coward-McCann
"The story of Alec Leamas, 50-year-old professional {secret agent} who has grown stale in espionage, who longs to 'come in from the cold' and how he undertakes one last assignment before that hoped-for retirement. Over the years Leamas has grown unsure where his workday carapace ends and his real self begins. . . . Recalled from Berlin after the death of his last East German contact at the Wall, Leamas lets himself be seduced into a pretended defection—thereby providing the East Germans with data from which they can deduce that the head of their own spy apparatus is a double agent." N Y Times Book Rev

Le Guin, Ursula K., 1929-

Gifts. Harcourt 2004 274p $17; pa $7.95

Grades: 7 8 9 10   **Fic**
1. Fantasy fiction
ISBN 0-15-205123-6; 0-15-205124-4 (pa)
                                          LC 2003-21449
When a young man in the Uplands blinds himself rather than use his gift of "unmaking"—a violent talent shared by members of his family—he upsets the precarious balance of power among rival, feuding families, each of which has a strange and deadly talent of its own.

"Although intriguing as a coming-of-age allegory, Orrec's story is also rich in . . . earthy magic and intelligent plot twists." Booklist
Followed by Voices (2006)

The lathe of heaven. Perennial Classics 2003 175p pa $12.95

Grades: 11 12 Adult   **Fic**
1. Science fiction 2. Dreams—Fiction
ISBN 0-06-051274-1   LC 2003-46573
First published 1971 by Scribner
"A psychiatrist sets out to use a patient whose dreams can alter reality to create utopia, but in usurping this power he is gradually delivered into madness." Anatomy of Wonder 4

"The author has done some profound research in psychology, cerebro-physiology and biochemistry. . . . In addition, her perceptions of such matters as geopolitics, race, socialized medicine and the patient/shrink relationship are razor-sharp and more than a little cutting." Natl Rev

The left hand of darkness. Ace Books 2000 304p pa $13.95 *

Grades: 9 10 11 12   **Fic**
1. Science fiction 2. Extrasensory perception—Fiction
ISBN 0-441-00731-7
A reissue of the title first published 1969 by Walker & Company

"This is a tale of political intrigue and danger on the world of Gethen, the Winter planet. Genly Ai, high official of the Eukemen—the commonwealth of worlds—is on Gethen to convince the royalty to join the Federation. He soon becomes a pawn in Gethen's power struggles, set against the elaborate mores of the Gethenians, a unisex hermaphroditic people whose intricate sexual physiology plays a key role in the conflict. Allied with Estraven, fallen lord, Genly is forced to cross the savage and impassable Gobrin Ice." Shapiro. Fic for Youth. 3d edition

Leavitt, Martine, 1953-

Keturah and Lord Death. Front Street 2006 216p $16.95 *

Grades: 8 9 10 11 12   **Fic**
1. Death—Fiction
ISBN 978-1-932425-29-1; 1-932425-29-2
                                          LC 2006-00799
When Lord Death comes to claim sixteen-year-old Keturah while she is lost in the King's Forest, she charms him with her story and is granted a twenty-four hour reprieve in which to seek her one true love

"The romance is intense, the writing is startling, and the story is spellbinding." Booklist

Lee, Harper, 1926-

To kill a mockingbird. 40th anniversary ed. HarperCollins Pubs. 1999 323p $19.95 *

Grades: 9 10 11 12   **Fic**
1. Race relations—Fiction 2. Alabama—Fiction
ISBN 0-06-019499-5
Also available large print edition $20 (ISBN 0-06-093327-5) and in paperback from Warner Bks.
A reissue of the title first published 1960 by Lippincott

"Scout, as Jean Louise is called, is a precocious child. She relates her impressions of the time when her lawyer father, Atticus Finch, is defending a black man accused of raping a white woman in a small Alabama town during the 1930's. Atticus's courageous act brings the violence and injustice that exists in their world sharply into focus as it intrudes into the lighthearted life that Scout and her brother Jem have enjoyed until that time." Shapiro. Fic for Youth. 3d edition

Leitch, Will

Catch. Razorbill 2005 288p pa $7.99

Grades: 9 10 11 12   **Fic**
1. Illinois—Fiction
ISBN 1-59514-069-7   LC 2005-08146
Teenager Tim Temples must decide if he wants to leave his comfortable life in a small town and go to college.

"This substantive title will entice both male and female YA readers with its thoughtful, authentic, and romantic young man's voice." Booklist

L'Engle, Madeleine, 1918-

A wrinkle in time. Farrar, Straus & Giroux 1962
211p $17

Grades: 5 6 7 8 9 10   **Fic**
    1. Fantasy fiction
    ISBN 0-374-38613-7
    Awarded the Newbery Medal, 1963
"A brother and sister, together with a friend, go in search of their scientist father who was lost while engaged in secret work for the government on the tesseract problem. A tesseract is a wrinkle in time. The father is a prisoner on a forbidding planet, and after awesome and terrifying experiences, he is rescued, and the little group returns safely to Earth and home." Child Books Too Good to Miss
"It makes unusual demands on the imagination and consequently gives great rewards." Horn Book
Followed by A wind in the door (1973)

Leroux, Gaston, 1868-1927

The phantom of the opera; introduction by Anne Perry. Modern Library 2002 xxiii, 286p (The Modern Library Classics) pa $8.95

Grades: 9 10 11 12   **Fic**
    1. Paris (France)—Fiction
    ISBN 0-375-76113-6   LC 2002-67075
    Also available Thorndike Press large print edition
    First published 1911 by The Bobbs-Merrill Company
This love story/thriller relates the tale of the mysterious masked terror who inhabits the cellars of the Paris Opera House

Les Becquets, Diane

Love, Cajun style. Bloomsbury 2005 296p $16.95; pa $7.95

Grades: 9 10 11 12   **Fic**
    1. Louisiana—Fiction
    ISBN 1-58234-674-7; 1-59990-030-0 (pa)
                   LC 2005-11948
Teenage Lucy learns about life and love with the help of her friends and saucy Tante Pearl over the course of one hot Louisiana summer before her senior year of high school.
"This is romantic, real, and lots of fun." Booklist

Lessing, Doris May, 1919-

The sweetest dream; [by] Doris Lessing. HarperCollins Pubs. 2002 478p hardcover o.p. pa $13.95

Grades: 11 12 Adult   **Fic**
    1. Feminism—Fiction 2. London (England)—Fiction
    ISBN 0-06-621334-7; 0-06-093755-6 (pa)
                  LC 2002-279950
The epicenter of this novel "is a grand old house in London, the holdfast of the seemingly impervious widow Julia. It's the early 1960s and when her selfish and feckless communist son, Johnny, callously abandons his wife, Frances, and their two young sons, Julia persuades her resilient daughter-in-law to move in with her. Soon Frances, a self-possessed yet endlessly empathic and accommodating earth mother, is presiding over a contentious commune of moody teenage 'waifs and strays.'" Booklist

"Lessing's understanding of relationships—both personal and political—has always been keen; now . . . it is unparalleled. This novel is warm and heartfelt, old-fashioned and ambitious in its historical sweep." New Statesman (1913)

Lester, Julius

Day of tears; a novel in dialogue. Hyperion 2005 177p $15.99; pa $7.99 *

Grades: 7 8 9 10   **Fic**
    1. Slavery—Fiction 2. African Americans—Fiction
    ISBN 0-7868-0490-4; 1-42310-409-0 (pa)
    Coretta Scott King award for text, 2006
"Jump at the sun"
Emma has taken care of the Butler children since Sarah and Frances's mother, Fanny, left. Emma wants to raise the girls to have good hearts, as a rift over slavery has ripped the Butler household apart. Now, to pay off debts, Pierce Butler wants to cash in his slave "assets", possibly including Emma.
"The horror of the auction and its aftermath is unforgettable. . . . The racism is virulent (there's widespread use of the n-word). The personal voices make this a stirring text for group discussion." Booklist

Time's memory. Farrar, Straus & Giroux 2006 230p $17

Grades: 8 9 10 11 12   **Fic**
    1. Slavery—Fiction 2. African Americans—Fiction
    ISBN 0-374-37178-4; 978-0-374-37178-4
                  LC 2005-47716
    Also available Thorndike Press large print edition
Ekundayo, a Dogon spirit brought to America from Africa, inhabits the body of a young African American slave on a Virginia plantation, where he experiences loss, sorrow, and reconciliation in the months preceding the Civil War.
"More than a picture of slavery through the eyes of those enslaved or their captors, Lester's narrative evokes spiritual images of Mali's Dogon people." SLJ

Levine, Gail Carson, 1947-

Fairest. HarperCollins 2006 326p $16.99; lib bdg $17.89

Grades: 6 7 8 9   **Fic**
    1. Fairy tales 2. Singing—Fiction
    ISBN 978-0-06-073408-4; 0-06-073408-6; 978-0-06-073409-1 (lib bdg); 0-06-073409-4 (lib bdg)
                  LC 2006-00337
    Also available Thorndike Press large print edition
In a land where beauty and singing are valued above all else, Aza eventually comes to reconcile her unconventional appearance and her magical voice, and learns to accept herself for who she truly is.
"The plot is fast-paced, and Aza's growth and maturity are well crafted and believable." SLJ

Levithan, David, 1972-

Are we there yet? Knopf 2005 215p $15.95; lib bdg $17.99; pa $8.99

Grades: 11 12   **Fic**

1. Brothers—Fiction 2. Travel—Fiction 3. Italy—Fiction

ISBN 0-375-82846-X; 0-375-92846-4 (lib bdg); 0-375-83956-9 (pa)   LC 2004-61546

Tricked by their parents into taking a trip to Italy together, two brothers—one in high school and the other recently graduated from college—reflect on the directions of their own lives and on the distance that has grown between them.

The author's "insights into traveling lyrically describe many travelers' experiences of discovery and adventure. Suggestive romance and marijuana use as well as contextual references of art and religion place this title for more mature teen readers." Libr Media Connect

Marly's ghost; a remix of Charles Dickens' A Christmas Carol; with illustrations by Brian Selznick. Dial Books 2006 167p il $14.99

Grades: 7 8 9 10   **Fic**

1. Valentine's Day—Fiction 2. Ghost stories

ISBN 0-8037-3063-2   LC 2005-16183

The spirit of Ben's girlfriend Marly returns with three other ghosts to haunt him with a painful journey though Valentine's Days past, present, and future.

"The magical realism is powerful throughout. . . . A solid story to mark the holiday." Booklist

Lewis, C. S. (Clive Staples), 1898-1963

Out of the silent planet. Scribner Classics 1996 158p $22; pa $13

Grades: 11 12 Adult   **Fic**

1. Mars (Planet)—Fiction 2. Science fiction

ISBN 0-684-83364-6; 0-7432-3490-1 (pa)
                                   LC 96-30110

A reissue of the title first published 1938 in the United Kingdom; first United States edition published 1943 by Macmillan

First volume of trilogy about the adventures of Dr. Ransom

"The trilogy can be read on two levels: first for its exciting plot and second as a theological allegory, although Lewis denied this interpretation. The stories are about temptation. They concern the classic battle between good, as represented by Ransom, the philologist, and evil, as represented by Weston, the physicist. The battle is played out on the planets of Malacondra (Mars), Perelandra (Venus), and Earth." Shapiro. Fic for Youth. 3d edition

Followed by Perelandra (1943) and That hideous strength (1945)

Lewis, Sinclair, 1885-1951

Main Street. Harcourt 2003 486p (An HBJ modern classic) $34 *

Grades: 11 12 Adult   **Fic**

1. Minnesota—Fiction

ISBN 0-15-155547-8

Also available in paperback from New American Library

A reissue of the title first published 1920

"Carol Milford, a girl of quick intelligence but no particular talent, after graduation from college meets and marries Will Kennicott, a sober, kindly, unimaginative physician of Gopher Prairie, Minn., who tells her that the town needs her abilities. She finds the village to be a smug, intolerant, unimaginatively standardized place, where the people will not accept her efforts to create more sightly homes, organize a dramatic association, and otherwise improve the village life." Oxford Companion to Am Lit. 6th edition

Main Street & Babbitt. Library of Am. 1992 898p $40

Grades: 11 12 Adult   **Fic**

1. Minnesota—Fiction

ISBN 0-940450-61-5   LC 91-58224

In addition to Main Street, this book also features Babbitt (1922), a satire on American middle-class conventions. Set in the Midwest, it focuses on the life of George Babbitt, a prosperous and self-satisfied real estate man.

Lipsyte, Robert

The contender. Harper & Row 1967 182p pa $5.99 hardcover o.p. *

Grades: 7 8 9 10   **Fic**

1. Boxing—Fiction 2. Harlem (New York, N.Y.)—Fiction 3. African Americans—Fiction

ISBN 0-06-447039-3

"After a street fight in which he is the chief target, Alfred wanders into a gym in his neighborhood. He decides not only to improve his physical condition but also to become a boxer. Because of this interest Alfred's life is completely changed. He assumes a more positive outlook on his immediate future, even within the confines of a black ghetto." Shapiro. Fic for Youth. 3d edition

Followed by The brave (1991) and The chief (1993)

One fat summer. Harper & Row 1977 152p hardcover o.p. pa $5.99

Grades: 7 8 9 10   **Fic**

1. Weight loss—Fiction 2. Obesity—Fiction

ISBN 0-06-023895-X; 0-06-447073-3 (pa)
                                   LC 76-49746

"Bobby Marks is 14 and fat. How fat, he doesn't know because he jumps off the scale when it hits 200 pounds. In one action-packed summer Bobby learns that altered physical appearance can bolster self-esteem. He's not sure he likes his friend Joanie's new nose and new ego, but he's certainly pleased with his own svelte new image. The slimming is a result of his summer job; tending the grounds of the town miser." West Coast Rev Books

"This is far superior to most of the summer-of-change stories; any change that takes place is logical and the protagonist learns by action and reaction to be both self-reliant and compassionate." Bull Cent Child Books

Followed by Summer rules (1981) and The summerboy (1982)

Lipsyte, Robert—*Continued*

Raiders night. HarperTempest 2006 232p
$15.99; lib bdg $16.89

Grades: 9 10 11 12   **Fic**

1. Football—Fiction 2. Drug abuse—Fiction 3. Rape—Fiction

ISBN   978-0-06-059946-1;   0-06-059946-4;
978-0-06-059947-8 (lib bdg); 0-06-059947-2 (lib bdg)
LC 2005-17865

Matt Rydeck, co-captain of his high school football
team, endures a traumatic season as he witnesses the
rape of a rookie player by teammates and grapples with
his own use of performance-enhancing drugs.

This is "is a riveting and chilling look inside contemporary high school football." Publ Wkly

Lockhart, E.

The boyfriend list; (15 guys, 11 shrink
appointments, 4 ceramic frogs, and me, Ruby
Oliver). Delacorte Press 2005 240p $15.95; lib bdg
$17.99; pa $8.95

Grades: 9 10 11 12   **Fic**

1. School stories 2. Dating (Social customs)—Fiction
3. Washington (State)—Fiction

ISBN 0-385-73206-6; 0-385-90238-7 (lib bdg);
0-385-73207-4 (pa)   LC 2004-6691

A Seattle fifteen-year-old explains some of the reasons
for her recent panic attacks, including breaking up with
her boyfriend, losing all her girlfriends, tensions between
her performance-artist mother and her father, and more.

"Readers will find many of Ruby's experiences familiar, and they'll appreciate the story as a lively, often entertaining read." Booklist

Followed by The boy book (2006)

London, Jack, 1876-1916

The call of the wild; pictures by Wendell Minor.
Atheneum Books for Young Readers 1999 112p il
$24

Grades: 5 6 7 8 9 10   **Fic**

1. Dogs—Fiction 2. Alaska—Fiction

ISBN 0-689-81836-X   LC 97-45019

Also available from other publishers
First published 1903 by Macmillan

"Buck, half-St. Bernard, half-Scottish sheepdog, is
stolen from his comfortable home in California and
pressed into service as a sledge dog in the Klondike. At
first he is abused by both man and dog, but he learns to
fight ruthlessly. He becomes lead dog on a sledge team,
after bettering Spitz, the vicious old leader, in a brutal
fight to the death. In John Thornton, he finally finds a
master whom he can respect and love. When Thornton
is killed by Indians, Buck breaks away to the wilds and
becomes the leader of a wolf pack, returning each year
to the site of Thornton's death." Reader's Ency. 4th edition

White Fang; pictures by Ed Young. Atheneum
Books for Young Readers 2000 260p il hardcover
o.p. pa $5.99

Grades: 5 6 7 8 9 10   **Fic**

1. Dogs—Fiction 2. Alaska—Fiction

ISBN 0-689-82431-9; 1-416-91414-5 (pa)
LC 98-19241

Also available from other publishers
First published 1906

White Fang "is about a dog, a cross-breed, sold to
Beauty Smith. This owner tortures the dog to increase
his ferocity and value as a fighter. A new owner
Weedom Scott, brings the dog to California, and, by kind
treatment, domesticates him. White Fang later sacrifices
his life to save Scott." Haydn. Thesaurus of Book Dig

Lowell, Pamela

Returnable girl; [by] Pamela Lowell. Marshall
Cavendish 2006 229p $16.99

Grades: 8 9 10 11   **Fic**

1. Foster home care—Fiction 2. Mothers—Fiction
3. Friendship—Fiction

ISBN 978-0-7614-5317-8; 0-7614-5317-2
LC 2006006398

Friendship with an outcast classmate and memories of
her mother's desertion interfere with the relationship thirteen-year-old Ronnie tries to establish with her new foster mother.

"With its clear, direct language and an appealing heroine, the book is likely to draw a wide range of teen readers." Voice Youth Advocates

Lowry, Lois

The giver. Houghton Mifflin 1993 180p $16

Grades: 6 7 8 9   **Fic**

1. Science fiction

ISBN 0-395-64566-2   LC 92-15034

Also available Thorndike Press large print edition and
in paperback from Laurel Leaf

Awarded the Newbery Medal, 1994

Given his lifetime assignment at the Ceremony of
Twelve, Jonas becomes the receiver of memories shared
by only one other in his community and discovers the
terrible truth about the society in which he lives.

"A riveting, chilling story that inspires a new appreciation for diversity, love, and even pain. Truly memorable." SLJ

Lubar, David, 1954-

Sleeping freshmen never lie. Dutton Books 2005
279p $16.99; pa $6.99

Grades: 7 8 9 10   **Fic**

1. Authorship—Fiction 2. School stories

ISBN 0-525-47311-4; 0-14-240780-1 (pa)
LC 2004-23067

While navigating his first year of high school and
awaiting the birth of his new baby brother, Scott loses
old friends and gains some unlikely new ones as he
hones his skills as a writer

"The plot is framed by Scott's journal of advice for
the unborn baby. The novel's absurd, comical mood is
evident in its entries. . . . The author brings the protagonist to three-dimensional life by combining these introspective musings with active, hilarious narration." SLJ

Lyga, Barry

The astonishing adventures of Fanboy & Goth Girl. Houghton Mifflin 2006 311p $16.95 *

Grades: 7 8 9 10 11 12   **Fic**

1. Cartoons and comics—Fiction 2. School stories 3. Friendship—Fiction

ISBN 0-618-72392-7   LC 2005-33259

A fifteen-year-old "geek" who keeps a list of the high school jocks and others who torment him, and pours his energy into creating a great graphic novel, encounters Kyra, Goth Girl, who helps change his outlook on almost everything, including himself.

"This engaging first novel has good characterization with genuine voices. . . . The book is compulsively readable." Voice Youth Advocates

Lynch, Chris

Freewill. HarperCollins Pubs. 2001 148p $15.95; lib bdg $15.89; pa $6.99

Grades: 9 10 11 12   **Fic**

1. Suicide—Fiction

ISBN 0-06-028176-6; 0-06-028177-4 (lib bdg); 0-06-447202-7 (pa)   LC 00-32050

Teenage Will, trying to recover from the tragic death of his father and stepmother believes himself to be somehow responsible for the rash of teen suicides occurring in his town

"It won't take long for readers to realize that Lynch's book is written in second person. It may take them a bit longer to grasp that the speaker, 17-year-old Will, is actually talking to himself. Lynch ably carries off this complicated construct, giving the story the immediacy of experience but also the restricted perspective of a disturbed young man." Booklist

Iceman. HarperCollins Pubs. 1994 181p hardcover o.p. pa $5.99 *

Grades: 7 8 9 10   **Fic**

1. Hockey—Fiction 2. Parent-child relationship—Fiction

ISBN 0-06-023340-0; 0-06-447114-4 (pa)

           LC 93-7776

"Fourteen-year-old Eric is an ice hockey player who has a well-earned reputation for playing a rough game and being physically violent on the ice. He is encouraged by his father, a second-rate public relations man, who lives vicariously through the team's winning. Whereas, his mother, a former nun, has made saving his soul a priority." Child Book Rev Serv

"Much better than the usual sports novel, this is an unsettling, complicated portrayal of growing up in a dysfunctional family. Lynch is a wizard with game color, and he challenges the violence of the game throughout the story." Booklist

Inexcusable. Atheneum Books for Young Readers 2005 165p $16.95; pa $6.99 *

Grades: 8 9 10 11 12   **Fic**

1. Rape—Fiction 2. Football—Fiction 3. School stories

ISBN 0-689-84789-0; 1-416-93972-5 (pa)

           LC 2004-30874

"Ginee Seo books"

High school senior and football player Keir sets out to enjoy himself on graduation night, but when he attempts to comfort a friend whose date has left her stranded, things go terribly wrong

"This finely crafted and thought-provoking page-turner carefully conveys that it is simply inexcusable to whitewash wrongs, and that those responsible should (and hopefully will) pay the price." SLJ

Slot machine. HarperCollins Pubs. 1995 241p hardcover o.p. pa $5.99 *

Grades: 7 8 9 10   **Fic**

1. Camps—Fiction 2. Sports—Fiction 3. Friendship—Fiction

ISBN 0-06-023584-5; 0-06-447140-3 (pa)

           LC 94-48235

When overweight thirteen-year-old Elvin Bishop is sent to camp at St. Paul's Seminary Retreat Center, he and his two best friends are forced to try out various sports in order to find out where they belong

"The religious setting is used to heighten the irony. There is some beer drinking. Pornography is discussed and in one scene described in an inoffensive way. Likewise, there is a scene or two of adolescent male exhibitionism, again not graphically described, and finally it is implied that Frank undergoes hazing of a homosexual nature." Book Rep

Other titles about Elvin Bishop are:

Extreme Elvin (1999)

Me, dead Dad & Alcatraz (2005)

Lynch, Scott, 1978-

The lies of Locke Lamora. Bantam 2006 499p map $23 *

Grades: 11 12 Adult   **Fic**

1. Swindlers and swindling—Fiction 2. Thieves—Fiction 3. Fantasy fiction

ISBN 0-553-80467-7; 978-0-553-80467-6

           LC 2006-42653

"A Bantam spectra book"

"Abandoned as an infant, the boy known as Locke Lamora grows up to become one of his city's most famous (or infamous) con artists, yet his good nature has made him a folk hero. Leading his own band of men, Locke falls into the center of a conspiracy that threatens those he holds dear." Libr J

"Fans of lavishly appointed fantasy will be in seventh heaven here, but it will be nearly as popular with readers of literary crime fiction. This is a true genre bender, at home on almost any kind of fiction shelf." Booklist

MacCullough, Carolyn

Stealing Henry. Roaring Brook Press 2005 196p $16.95

Grades: 9 10 11 12   **Fic**

1. Runaway teenagers—Fiction 2. Siblings—Fiction 3. Mother-daughter relationship—Fiction 4. Child abuse—Fiction

ISBN 1-596-43045-1   LC 2004-17550

"A Deborah Brodie book"

The experiences of high-schooler Savannah, following her decision to take her eight-year-old half brother from his abusive father and their oblivious mother, are inter-

MacCullough, Carolyn—_Continued_

spersed with the earlier story of her mother, Alice, as she meets Savannah's father and unexpectedly becomes pregnant.

"Young adult readers will find this [book] fascinating and appealing." Libr Media Connect

Mackall, Dandi Daley, 1949-

Eva underground. Harcourt 2006 239p $17 *

Grades: 9 10 11 12   **Fic**

1. Poland—Fiction 2. Father-daughter relationship—Fiction 3. Communism—Fiction

ISBN 0-15-205462-6; 978-0-15-205462-5

LC 2005-04195

In 1978, a high school senior is forced by her widowed father to move from their comfortable Chicago suburb to help with an underground education movement in communist Poland.

"Poland behind the Iron Curtain is rarely found in modern young adult literature, and Mackall has done a superb job in captivating high reader interest in this unique setting." Libr Media Connect

Mackler, Carolyn

The earth, my butt, and other big, round things. Candlewick Press 2003 246p $15.99; pa $8.99 *

Grades: 7 8 9 10   **Fic**

1. Family life—Fiction 2. Obesity—Fiction 3. School stories 4. New York (N.Y.)—Fiction

ISBN 0-7636-1958-2; 0-7636-2091-2 (pa)

LC 2002-73921

Feeling like she does not fit in with the other members of her family, who are all thin, brilliant, and goodlooking, fifteen-year-old Virginia tries to deal with her self-image, her first physical relationship, and her disillusionment with some of the people closest to her

"The e-mails {Virginia} exchanges . . . and the lists she makes (e.g., 'The Fat Girl Code of Conduct') add both realism and insight to her character. The heroine's transformation into someone who finds her own style and speaks her own mind is believable—and worthy of applause." Publ Wkly

Vegan virgin Valentine. Candlewick Press 2004 228p $16.99; pa $8.99

Grades: 9 10 11 12   **Fic**

1. Aunts—Fiction 2. School stories

ISBN 0-7636-2155-2; 0-7636-2613-9 (pa)

LC 2004-45774

Mara's niece, who is only one-year-younger, moves in bringing conflict between the two teenagers because of their opposite personalities

"Racily narrated by likeable Mara, this fast-paced coming-of-age story is charged with sarcasm, angst, honesty, and hope. Many teen girls will recognize parts of themselves within its pages." Voice Youth Advocates

Mahy, Margaret

Alchemy. Margaret K. McElderry Bks. 2003 207p $16.95; pa $7.99

Grades: 7 8 9 10   **Fic**

1. Alchemy—Fiction

ISBN 0-689-85053-0; 0-689-85054-9 (pa)

LC 2002-5973

Seventeen-year-old Roland discovers that an unpopular girl in his school is studying alchemy and finds that their destiny is linked with that of a power-hungry magician

"Mahy, whose thrillers are both complex and literary, once again provides a multilayered story that can be appreciated on several levels." Booklist

Malamud, Bernard, 1914-1986

The assistant; a novel. Farrar, Straus & Giroux 1957 246p pa $13 hardcover o.p.

Grades: 11 12 Adult   **Fic**

1. Jews—New York (N.Y.)—Fiction 2. Brooklyn (New York, N.Y.)—Fiction

ISBN 0-374-50484-9 (pa)

This novel is "set in the prison of a failing grocery store, where Morris Bober, its elderly, long-suffering Jewish owner, teaches his assistant, Frankie Alpine, what it means to be a Jew, and what it means to be a man. After decades in which Jewish protagonists struggled to assimilate to the non-Jewish world around them, _The Assistant_ is a tale about reverse assimilation, one in which Frankie takes over the store on Morris's death and undergoes a painful conversion to Judaism." Benet's Reader's Ency of Am Lit

The fixer. Farrar, Straus & Giroux 1966 355p pa $14 hardcover o.p. *

Grades: 11 12 Adult   **Fic**

1. Jews—Fiction   2. Jews—Russia—Fiction 3. Russia—Fiction

ISBN 0-374-52938-8 (pa)

"Yakov Bok, a handyman, is arrested and charged with the killing of a Christian boy. Innocent of the crime, he is only guilty of being a Jew in Czarist Russia. In jail he is mentally and physically tortured as a scapegoat for a crime he insists he did not commit. Although his suffering and degradation are unrelenting, Bok emerges a hero as he maintains his innocence. Malamud has fashioned a powerful story of injustice and endurance based on a true incident." Shapiro. Fic for Youth. 3d edition

Malloy, Brian

The year of ice. St. Martin's Press 2002 262p hardcover o.p. pa $12.95 *

Grades: 11 12 Adult   **Fic**

1. Homosexuality—Fiction 2. Father-son relationship—Fiction 3. Minnesota—Fiction

ISBN 0-312-28948-0; 0-312-31369-1 (pa)

LC 2002-510282

"A gay high school senior struggles to cope with his father's irresponsibility in Malloy's poignant, quietly effective debut, set in Minneapolis in the late '70s. From the outside looking in, protagonist Kevin Doyle seems like a normal, party-happy 17-year-old, but the combination of a troubled family life and his secret crush on one of his best friends definitely sets him apart from the pack." Publ Wkly

Manning, Sarra

Guitar girl. Dutton Children's Books 2004 217p $15.99; pa $6.99

Grades: 9 10 11 12   **Fic**

1. Musicians—Fiction 2. Great Britain—Fiction

ISBN 0-525-47234-7; 0-14-240318-0 (pa)

                LC 2004-299584

First published 2003 in the United Kingdom

"Yearning to be like her idol, rock star Ruby X, and desperate to be noticed, Molly decides to form a band with her two best school friends, Jane and Tara. 'The Hormones,' as Jane dubs them, then add cocky Dean, a guitarist, and T, his silent drummer friend . . . and pick up a manager who catapults them into the fast lane of British rock. Molly's pleased to have the chance to be a real rocker girl, but the experience is, overall, less pleasurable than frustrating. . . . The more she learns about where she stands, personally and legally, the more she realizes she's been completely out of her depth." Bull Cent Child Books

"Wryly funny, often sincere, and sometimes pressed into banshee-like behavior, Molly is endearing in her attempts to reach maturity, sort out what's important, and decide what needs to be left behind." SLJ

Marchetta, Melina, 1965-

Saving Francesca. 1st American ed. Knopf 2004 243p $15.95; lib bdg $17.99

Grades: 9 10 11 12   **Fic**

1. Mental illness—Fiction 2. Mother-daughter relationship—Fiction 3. School stories 4. Australia—Fiction

ISBN 0-375-82982-2; 0-375-92982-7 (lib bdg)

                LC 2004-3926

Sixteen-year-old Francesca could use her outspoken mother's help with the problems of being one of a handful of girls at a parochial school that has just turned co-ed, but her mother has suddenly become severely depressed

This book "has great characterizations, witty dialogue, a terrific relationship between Francesca and her younger brother, and a sweet romance. Teens will relate to this tender novel and will take to heart its solid messages and realistic treatment of a very real problem." SLJ

Marillier, Juliet

Daughter of the forest. TOR Bks. 2000 400p (Sevenwaters trilogy) $25.95; pa $14.95

Grades: 11 12 Adult   **Fic**

1. Fantasy fiction

ISBN 0-312-84879-X; 0-312-87530-4 (pa)

                LC 00-25216

"A Tom Doherty Associates book"

"As the only daughter and youngest child of Lord Colum of Sevenwaters, Sorcha grows up protected and pampered by her six older brothers. When a sorceress's evil magic ensorcels Colum's sons, transforming them into swans, only Sorcha's efforts can break the curse. . . . The author's keen understanding of Celtic paganism and early Irish Christianity adds texture to a rich and vibrant novel that belongs in most fantasy collections." Libr J

Other titles in the Sevenwaters trilogy are:

Child of the prophecy (2002)

Son of the shadows (2001)

Marino, Peter

Dough Boy. Holiday House 2005 221p $16.95
*

Grades: 7 8 9 10   **Fic**

1. Obesity—Fiction 2. Family life—Fiction 3. Bullies—Fiction 4. School stories

ISBN 0-8234-1873-1   LC 2004-40593

Overweight, fifteen-year-old Tristan, who lives happily with his divorced mother and her boyfriend Frank, suddenly finds that he must deal with intensified criticism about his weight and other aspects of his life when Frank's popular but troubled, nutrition-obsessed daughter moves in.

"Readers will easily feel the boy's anger and will applaud his resilience and resolve to remain true to himself." Publ Wkly

Markandaya, Kamala, 1924-2004

Nectar in a sieve; with a new introduction by Indira Ganesan. Signet Classic 2002 190p pa $6.95

Grades: 9 10 11 12   **Fic**

1. India—Fiction

ISBN 0-451-52823-9   LC 2001-49544

First published 1954 in the United Kingdom; first United States edition published 1955 by Day

"This realistic novel of peasant life in a southern Indian village portrays the struggle that Nathan and Rukmani must make to survive. Their first child is a daughter, Irawaddy, and there follow five other children, all sons, after an interval of seven years. Hardships are innumerable and insurmountable, whether they are disasters of nature such as drought, or such manmade catastrophes as the coming of a tannery to their village and a subsequent labor conflict. After many crises, Nathan and Rukmani come to the city to seek help from one of their sons, but he has disappeared. Nathan, finally destroyed by privation, dies, believing to the end that his life with Rukmani has been a happy one." Shapiro. Fic for Youth. 3d edition

Marks, Graham

Missing in Tokyo. Bloomsbury Children's Books 2006 253p $16.95

Grades: 9 10 11 12   **Fic**

1. Missing persons—Fiction 2. Siblings—Fiction 3. Tokyo (Japan)—Fiction

ISBN 1-58234-907-X; 978-1-58234-907-7

                LC 2005-57036

When his older sister is reported missing, teenager Adam travels from England to Tokyo, Japan, to look for her.

"The plot twists and turns in this fast-paced, intriguing novel that will keep readers guessing." SLJ

Marley, Louise, 1952-

Singer in the snow. Viking 2005 304p $16.99; pa $7.99

Grades: 7 8 9 10   **Fic**

1. Fantasy fiction

ISBN 0-670-05965-X; 0-14-240748-8 (pa)

                LC 2005-5575

Marley, Louise, 1952-—*Continued*

"This follow-up to the Singers of Nevya trilogy (1995-1997) features two young Singers with the psi-Gift who journey from their beloved Conservatory to the remote House of Tarus near the Frozen Sea. Mreen, a mute young woman of exceptional power, is Tarus' new Cantrix: one who uses music and magic to summon the light and heat necessary to survive the planet's deadly cold. Emle, whose musical talent is sublime but who for reasons unknown cannot summon a thing, acts as Mreen's interpreter. While Mreen adjusts to her new life, Emle explores the flaws of her gift and connects with a psychologically burdened stable boy. . . . This is satisfying fare for fantasy lovers and an easy entry point for teens new to the genre." Booklist

Marsden, John, 1950-

Tomorrow, when the war began. Houghton Mifflin 1995 286p $16

Grades: 7 8 9 10   **Fic**

1. War stories 2. Australia—Fiction

ISBN 0-395-70673-4   LC 94-29299

Also available in paperback from Dell

First published 1993 in Australia

"Australian teenager Ellie and six of her friends return from a winter break camping trip to find their homes burned or deserted, their families imprisoned, and their country occupied by a foreign military force in league with a band of disaffected Australians. As their shock wears off, the seven decide they must stick together if they are to survive." SLJ

"The novel is a riveting adventure through which Marsden explores the capacity for evil and the necessity of working together to oppose it." Horn Book

Other available titles in this series are:

Burning for revenge (2000)

Darkness, be my friend (1999)

The dead of night (1997)

A killing frost (1998)

The night is for hunting (2001)

The other side of dawn (2002)

Marshall, Catherine, 1914-1983

Christy. Avon Books 2006 576p pa $6.99

Grades: 9 10 11 12   **Fic**

1. Teachers—Fiction 2. Appalachian region—Fiction

ISBN 0-380-00141-1

A reissue of the title first published 1967 by McGraw-Hill

"A spirited young woman leaves the security of her home to become a teacher in Cutter Gap, Kentucky. It is 1912 and the needs of the Appalachian people are great. Christy learns much from the poverty and superstition of the mountain folk. Marshall's Christian faith and ideals are intertwined in the plot, which includes a love story." Shapiro. Fic for Youth. 3d edition

Martinez, Victor, 1954-

Parrot in the oven; a novel. Cotler Bks. 1996 216p $19.99; lib bdg $16.89; pa $5.99 *

Grades: 7 8 9 10   **Fic**

1. Mexican Americans—Fiction 2. Family life—Fiction

ISBN 0-06-026704-6; 0-06-026706-2 (lib bdg); 0-06-447186-1 (pa)   LC 96-2119

"Joanna Cotler books"

Manny relates his coming of age experiences as a member of a poor Mexican American family in which the alcoholic father only adds to everyone's struggle

The author "maintains the authenticity of his setting and characterizations through a razor-sharp combination of tense dialogue, coursing narrative and startlingly elegant imagery." Publ Wkly

Mason, Bobbie Ann

In country; a novel. Harper & Row 1985 247p hardcover o.p. pa $13.95 *

Grades: 11 12 Adult   **Fic**

1. Veterans—Fiction 2. Vietnam War, 1961-1975—Fiction 3. Kentucky—Fiction

ISBN 0-06-015469-1; 0-06-083517-0 (pa)

LC 85-42579

"Sam, 17, is obsessed with the Vietnam War and the effect it has had on her life—losing a father she never knew and now living with Uncle Emmett, who seems to be suffering from the effects of Agent Orange. In her own forthright way, she tries to sort out why and how Vietnam has altered the lives of the vets of Hopewell, Kentucky. . . . A harshly realistic, well-written look at the Vietnam War as well as the story of a young woman maturing." SLJ

Maugham, W. Somerset (William Somerset), 1874-1965

Of human bondage; introduction by Gore Vidal. Modern Library 1999 xxxix, 611p pa $11.95 *

Grades: 11 12 Adult   **Fic**

ISBN 0-375-75315-X   LC 98-46169

Also available from other publishers

First published 1915

This novel's "hero is Philip Carey, a sensitive, talented, club-footed orphan who is brought up by an unsympathetic aunt and uncle. It is a study of his struggle for independence, his intellectual development, and his attempt to become an artist. Philip gets entangled and obsessed by his love affair with Mildred, a waitress. After years of struggle as a medical student, he marries a nice woman, gives up his aspirations, and becomes a country doctor. The first part of the novel is partly autobiographical, and the book is regarded as Maugham's best work." Reader's Ency. 4th edition

Maynard, Joyce, 1953-

The cloud chamber. Atheneum Books for Young Readers 2005 274p $16.95; pa $7.99

Grades: 7 8 9 10   **Fic**

1. Depression (Psychology)—Fiction 2. Suicide—Fiction 3. School stories 4. Montana—Fiction

ISBN 0-689-87152-X; 1-416-92699-2 (pa)

LC 2004-18607

"An Anne Schwartz book"

In 1966, when his father's attempted suicide causes the ostracism of the family in their small Montana community, fourteen-year-old Nate copes with his sadness and anger by trying to win the school science fair.

"The plot moves quickly and engagingly through Nate's trials and small triumphs." SLJ

Mazer, Harry, 1925-
The last mission. Dell 1981 c1979 188p pa
$5.99
Grades: 7 8 9 10   **Fic**
1. World War, 1939-1945—Fiction 2. Prisoners of
war—Fiction 3. Jews—Fiction
ISBN 0-440-94797-9
First published 1979 by Delacorte Press
In 1944 a 15-year-old Jewish boy tells his family he
will travel in the West but instead, enlists in the United
States Air Corps and is subsequently taken prisoner by
the Germans.
"Told in a rapid journalistic style, occasionally peppered with barrack-room vulgarities, the story is a vivid
and moving account of a boy's experience during World
War II as well as a skillful, convincing portrayal of his
misgivings as a Jew on enemy soil and of his ability to
size up—in mature human fashion—the misery around
him." Horn Book

McBay, Bruce, 1946-
Waiting for Sarah; {by} Bruce McBay & James
Heneghan. Orca Book Publishers 2003 170p pa
$7.95
Grades: 9 10 11 12   **Fic**
1. Orphans—Fiction 2. Physically handicapped—Fic-
tion 3. Canada—Fiction
ISBN 1-55143-270-6   LC 2002-117768
After Mike loses his family and is severely injured in
a car accident, he withdraws until he meets mysterious
Sarah, a girl who is not who she seems
"This is a well-developed novel that shatters the teen
perceptions of invincibility, as well as dealing with loss,
handicaps, and positive ways to break through grief." Lib
Media Connect

McCaffrey, Anne
Dragonflight; volume 1 of "The Dragonriders of
Pern". Ballantine Bks. 1978 337p il (Dragonriders
of Pern) hardcover o.p. pa $12.95
Grades: 11 12 Adult   **Fic**
1. Dragons—Fiction 2. Fantasy fiction
ISBN 0-345-27749-X; 0-345-48426-6 (pa)
                                    LC 78-16707
"A Del Rey book"
First published 1968 in paperback. Based on two
award winning stories entitled: Weyr search and
Dragonrider
The planet Pern, originally colonized from Earth but
long out of contact with it, has been periodically threatened by the deadly silver Threads which fall from the
wandering Red Star. To combat them a life borne on the
planet was developed into winged, fire-breathing dragons.
Humans with a high degree of empathy and telepathic
power are needed to train and preserve these creatures.
As the story begins, Pern has fallen into decay, the threat
of the Red Star has been forgotten, the Dragonriders and
dragons are reduced in number and in disrepute, and the
evil Lord Fax has begun conquering neighboring holds
Fantasy titles set on Pern are:
All the Weyrs of Pern (1991)
The chronicles of Pern: first fall (1993)
Dragon's fire (2006)
Dragon's kin (2003)

Dragondrums (1979)
Dragonquest (1971)
Dragonsdawn (1988)
Dragonseye (1997)
D ragonsinger (1977)
Dragonsong (1976)
The masterharper of Pern (1998)
Morets: Dragonlady of Pern (1983)
Nerilka's story (1986)
The Renegades of Pern (1989)
The skies of Pern (2001)
White dragon (1978)

McCarthy, Cormac, 1933-
All the pretty horses. Knopf 1992 301p $27.50;
pa $14.95
Grades: 11 12 Adult   **Fic**
1. Mexico—Fiction 2. Cowhands—Fiction
ISBN 0-394-57474-5; 0-679-74439-8 (pa)
                                    LC 91-58560
First volume in the author's Border trilogy
In the spring of 1950, after the death of his grandfather, sixteen-year-old John Grady Cole "is evicted from
the Texas ranch where he grew up. He and another boy
Lacey Rawlins, head for Mexico on horseback, riding
south until they finally turn up at a vast ranch in mountainous Coahuila, the Hacienda de la Purisima, where
they sign on as vaqueros. . . . John Grady's unusual talent for breaking, training and understanding horses becomes crucial to the *hacendado* Don Hector's ambitious
breeding program. For John Grady, La Purisima is a paradise, complete with its Eve, Don Hector's daughter,
Alejandra." N Y Times Book Rev
"Though some readers may grow impatient with the
wild prairie rhythms of McCarthy's language, others will
find his voice completely transporting." Publ Wkly
Other titles in the Border trilogy are:
The crossing (1994)
Cities of the Plain (1998)

The road. Knopf 2006 241p $24 *
Grades: 11 12 Adult   **Fic**
1. Father-son relationship—Fiction 2. Voyages and
travels—Fiction 3. Survival after airplane accidents,
shipwrecks, etc.—Fiction
ISBN 978-0-307-26543-2; 0-307-26543-9
                                    LC 2006-23629
"A nuclear holocaust has reduced everything to ash,
mummifying all but a few unlucky souls, who must kill
or be killed (and eaten). The main characters are a father
and his son, who was born a few nights after the bombs
fell. 'We're still the good guys,' the man repeatedly assures the boy as they scavenge their way south for the
winter, trying to avoid 'bad guy' survival techniques.
. . . The horrors here—an infant 'headless and gutted
and blackening on the spit'—are extreme, and, deprived
of historical context, . . . [the author's] brutality can
seem willful. But McCarthy's prose retains its ability to
seduce . . . and there are nods to the gentler aspects of
the human spirit." New Yorker

McCarthy, Susan Carol

True fires. Bantam Books 2004 306p pa $13

Grades: 9 10 11 12 **Fic**

1. Race relations—Fiction 2. Segregation in education—Fiction 3. Florida—Fiction

ISBN 0-553-80170-8; 0-553-38104-0 (pa)

LC 2003-70885

"Recently widowed, Franklin Dare moves his family to Florida to start a new life in the lush citrus groves. But his young children catch the eye of a corrupt sheriff, K.A. DeLuth, who proclaims Daniel's hair too 'kinked' and Rebecca's nose too wide and bans them from Lake Esther Elementary (according to Florida law, any child deemed one-eighth black or more cannot attend an all-white school). Only unimpeachable evidence that Franklin has no black blood—in fact, he is part Croatan Indian—will result in the children's readmittance. . . . The ending may present more questions than answers, but it doesn't take away from McCarthy's flawless dialogue, warm characters and compassionate wit, all of which service a moving story about the powers of love and justice." Publ Wkly

McCaughrean, Geraldine, 1951-

The white darkness. HarperTempest 2007 c2005 384p $16.99; lib bdg $17.89

Grades: 8 9 10 11 12 **Fic**

1. Antarctica—Fiction 2. Wilderness survival—Fiction

ISBN 978-0-06-089035-3; 0-06-089035-5; 978-0-06-089036-0 (lib bdg); 0-06-089036-3 (lib bdg)

LC 2006-02503

First published 2005 in the United Kingdom

Taken to Antarctica by the man she thinks of as her uncle for what she believes to be a vacation, Symone—a troubled fourteen year old—discovers that he is dangerously obsessed with seeking Symme's Hole, an opening that supposedly leads into the center of a hollow Earth.

"McCaughrean's lyrical language actively engages the senses, plunging readers into a captivating landscape that challenges the boundaries of reality." Booklist

McCormick, Patricia

Cut. Front St. 2000 168p $16.95 *

Grades: 7 8 9 10 **Fic**

1. Self-mutilation—Fiction 2. Psychiatric hospitals—Fiction

ISBN 1-88691-061-8 LC 00-34840

Also available in paperback from Scholastic Bks.

While confined to a mental hospital, thirteen-year-old Callie slowly comes to understand some of the reasons behind her self-mutilation, and gradually starts to get better

"Realistic, sensitive, and heartfelt." Voice Youth Advocates

Sold. Hyperion 2006 263p $15.99 *

Grades: 9 10 11 12 **Fic**

1. Slavery—Fiction 2. Prostitution—Fiction 3. Nepal—Fiction

ISBN 0-7868-5171-6; 978-0-7868-5171-3

LC 2006-49594

Thirteen-year-old Lakshmi leaves her poor mountain home in Nepal thinking that she is to work in the city as a maid only to find that she has been sold into the sex slave trade in India and that there is no hope of escape.

"In beautiful clear prose and free verse that remains true to the child's viewpoint, first-person, present-tense vignettes fill in Lakshmi's story. The brutality and cruelty are ever present ('I have been beaten here, / locked away, / violated a hundred times / and a hundred times more'), but not sensationalized. . . . An unforgettable account of sexual slavery as it exists now." Booklist

McCullers, Carson, 1917-1967

The heart is a lonely hunter. Modern Lib. 1993 430p $14.95 *

Grades: 9 10 11 12 **Fic**

1. Deaf—Fiction 2. Southern States—Fiction

ISBN 0-679-42474-1 LC 92-51062

A reissue of the title first published 1940 by Houghton Mifflin

"After his friend is committed to a hospital for the insane, John Singer, a deaf mute, finds himself alone. He becomes the pivotal figure in a strange circle of four other lonely individuals: Biff Brannon, the owner of a cafe; Mick Kelly, a young girl; Jake Blount, a radical; and Benedict Copeland, the town's black doctor. Although Singer provides companionship for others, he remains outside the warmth of close relationships." Shapiro. Fic for Youth. 3d edition

The member of the wedding. Houghton Mifflin 1946 195p hardcover o.p. pa $7.95 *

Grades: 9 10 11 12 Adult **Fic**

1. Georgia—Fiction

ISBN 0-395-07981-0; 0-618-49239-9 (pa)

Also available in hardcover from Chelsea House

"Twelve-year-old Frankie is experiencing a boring summer until news arrives that her older brother will soon be returning to Georgia from his Alaska home in order to marry. Plotting to accompany the newlyweds on their honeymoon occupies much of Frankie's waking hours, while at the same time she is coping with the pressures of puberty and its effects on her body and mind. Particularly revealing are her conversations with her six-year-old cousin and the nurturing black family cook, Bernice." Shapiro. Fic for Youth. 3d edition

McDevitt, Jack

Moonfall. HarperCollins Pubs. 1998 464p hardcover o.p. pa $7.99

Grades: 9 10 11 12 **Fic**

1. Science fiction 2. Space colonies—Fiction 3. Comets—Fiction

ISBN 0-06-105036-9; 0-06-105112-8 (pa)

LC 98-147774

"The discovery of an interstellar comet on a collision course with the moon spells catastrophic destruction not only for Moonbase—Earth's first lunar colony—but for the planet itself. . . . McDevitt chronicles the countdown from sighting to impact to aftermath in taut vignettes that display the best and worst of humanity's reaction to impending doom. Compulsively readable." Libr J

McDonald, Janet, 1953-2007

Brother hood. Farrar, Straus and Giroux 2004 165p $16 *

Grades: 7 8 9 10   **Fic**

1. Gifted children—Fiction 2. African Americans—Fiction 3. School stories 4. Harlem (New York, N.Y.)—Fiction

ISBN 0-374-30995-7   LC 2003-60670

Also available Thorndike Press large print edition

"Frances Foster Books"

Sixteen-year-old Nate, an academically gifted student who attends an exclusive private boarding school, straddles two cultures as he returns home for occasional visits to see his family and "gangsta crew" in Harlem, New York.

"It's the anger, sadness, and laugh-out-loud honesty about the contemporary scene that will hold readers. . . . This is a stirring celebration of Harlem, its roots, diversity, and change." Booklist

Chill wind. Farrar, Straus & Giroux 2002 134p hardcover o.p. pa $6.95

Grades: 7 8 9 10   **Fic**

1. Teenage mothers—Fiction 2. African Americans—Fiction 3. Public welfare—Fiction 4. New York (N.Y.)—Fiction

ISBN 0-374-39958-1; 0-374-41183-2 (pa)

                                    LC 2001-54785

Also available Thorndike Press large print edition

"Frances Foster books"

Afraid that she will have nowhere to go when her welfare checks are stopped, nineteen-year-old high school dropout Aisha tries to figure out how she can support herself and her two young children in New York City

"McDonald writes with such honesty, wit, and insight that you want to quote from every page and read the story aloud to share the laughter and anguish, fury and tenderness." Booklist

Spellbound. Frances Foster Bks. 2001 138p $16

Grades: 7 8 9 10   **Fic**

1. Teenage mothers—Fiction 2. African Americans—Fiction

ISBN 0-374-37140-7   LC 00-29381

Also available Thorndike Press large print edition and in paperback from Puffin Bks.

Raven, a teenage mother and high school dropout living in a housing project, decides, with the help and sometime interference of her best friend Aisha, to study for a spelling bee which could lead to a college preparatory program and four-year scholarship

"The dialogue is lively and smart; the characters ring true." Booklist

Twists and turns. Frances Foster Bks./Farrar, Straus & Giroux 2003 135p $16; pa $6.95

Grades: 7 8 9 10   **Fic**

1. African Americans—Fiction 2. Public housing—Fiction 3. Sisters—Fiction 4. Brooklyn (New York, N.Y.)—Fiction

ISBN 0-374-39955-7; 0-374-40006-7 (pa)

                                    LC 2002-35313

Also available Thorndike Press large print edition

With the help of a couple of successful friends, eighteen- and nineteen-year-old Teesha and Keeba try to cap-italize on their talents by opening a hair salon in the run-down Brooklyn housing project where they live

"The poetry and wit are in the daily details. . . . The story is inspiring—not because of a slick resolution or a heavy message, but because McDonald shows how hard things are, even as she tells a story of teens who find the strength in themselves and in those around them to rebuild and carry on." Booklist

McGhee, Alison, 1960-

All rivers flow to the sea. Candlewick Press 2005 168p $15.99

Grades: 8 9 10 11 12   **Fic**

1. Sisters—Fiction 2. Traffic accidents—Fiction 3. Bereavement—Fiction 4. Adirondack Mountains (N.Y.)—Fiction

ISBN 0-7636-2591-4   LC 2004-54609

After a car accident in the Adirondacks leaves her older sister Ivy brain-dead, seventeen-year-old Rose struggles with her grief and guilt as she slowly learns to let her sister go.

"This somber, philosophical look at loss and the reestablishment of identity is sensitive and perceptive, and includes passages of beautiful writing. Supporting characters are complex and lovingly rendered." Booklist

McKenzie, Nancy

Grail prince; {by} Nancy Affleck McKenzie. Del Rey 2003 510p pa $14.95

Grades: 9 10 11 12   **Fic**

1. Great Britain—History—0-1066—Fiction

ISBN 0-345-45648-3   LC 2002-94133

In this sequel to Queen of Camelot, "the story focuses on Sir Galahad, son of Lancelot and Guinevere's cousin, Elaine. Legend says that when the Holy Grail and the spear of King Macsen, along with the sword Excalibur, are in the hands of the king, Britain will be forever invincible. Galahad's quest to find these relics, undertaken at Arthur's command, is for him a journey into manhood as well as one of expiation." Libr J

"Brimming with romance, myth, and magic, this intriguing retelling of an ever-appealing fable will appease fans eager for new twists and turns in the lives and times of King Arthur and the knights of the Round Table." Booklist

McKinley, Robin

Beauty; a retelling of the story of Beauty & the beast. Harper & Row 1978 247p $15.99; pa $5.99 *

Grades: 7 8 9 10   **Fic**

1. Fairy tales

ISBN 0-06-024149-7; 0-06-440477-3 (pa)

                                    LC 77-25636

"McKinley's version of this folktale is embellished with rich descriptions and settings and detailed characterizations. The author has not modernized the story but varied the traditional version to attract modern readers. The values of love, honor, and beauty are placed in a magical setting that will please the reader of fantasy." Shapiro. Fic for Youth. 3d edition

McKinley, Robin—*Continued*
The blue sword. Greenwillow Bks. 1982 272p
$16.99
Grades: 7 8 9 10   **Fic**
1. Fantasy fiction
ISBN 0-688-00938-7   LC 82-2895
Also available in paperback from Ace Bks.

Harry, bored with her sheltered life in the remote orange-growing colony of Daria, discovers magic in herself when she is kidnapped by a native king with mysterious powers.

"This is a zesty, romantic, heroic fantasy with an appealing stalwart heroine, a finely realixed mythical kingdom, and a grounding in reality." Booklist

McMurtry, Larry
Lonesome dove; a novel. Simon & Schuster
1985 843p hardcover o.p. pa $17
Grades: 9 10 11 12 Adult   **Fic**
1. West (U.S.)—Fiction 2. Frontier and pioneer life—Fiction
ISBN 0-671-50420-7; 0-684-85752-9 (pa)
                  LC 85-2192
"Two former Texas Rangers have been running a ramshackle stock operation near the Mexican border with a lot of work and not much success. When they hear rumors of freewheeling opportunities in the newly opened territory, they decide to break camp, pull up stakes, and head north. Their dusty trek is filled with troubles, violence, and unfulfilled yearning." Booklist

"'Lonesome Dove' shows, early on, just about every symptom of American Epic except pretentiousness. McMurtry has laconic Texas talk and leathery, slim-hipped machismo down pat, and he's able to refresh heroic clichés with exact observations about cowboy prudery, ignorance and fear of losing face." Newsweek
Other titles in the Lonesome dove trilogy are:
Streets of Laredo (1993)
Dead man's walk (1995)

McNamee, Graham
Acceleration. Wendy Lamb Bks. 2003 210p
$15.95; lib bdg $17.99; pa $6.50 *
Grades: 9 10 11 12   **Fic**
1. Homicide—Fiction 2. Mystery fiction 3. Canada—Fiction
ISBN 0-385-73119-1; 0-385-90144-5 (lib bdg);
0-440-23836-6 (pa)   LC 2003-3708
Stuck working in the Lost and Found of the Toronto Transit Authority for the summer, seventeen-year-old Duncan finds the diary of a serial killer and sets out to stop him
"Never overexploits the sensational potential of the subject and builds suspense layer upon layer, while injecting some surprising comedy relief." Booklist

McNeal, Laura
Crushed; [by] Laura & Tom McNeal. Knopf
2006 308p $15.95; lib bdg $17.99
Grades: 9 10 11 12   **Fic**
1. Family life—Fiction 2. School stories
ISBN 0-375-83105-3; 0-375-93105-8 (lib bdg)
              LC 2005-04320

Seventeen-year-old Audrey's life is turned upside down when she falls in love with a mysterious newcomer and a vicious gossip sheet exposes the secrets of both students and teachers at her school.

The authors "capture the emotions and struggles of teens accurately, and readers will relate to the pressures that the characters experience both at school and at home." Voice Youth Advocates

Zipped; {by} Laura and Tom McNeal. Knopf
2003 283p $15.95; lib bdg $17.99; pa $7.99 *
Grades: 9 10 11 12   **Fic**
1. Stepfamilies—Fiction
ISBN 0-375-81491-4; 0-375-91491-9 (lib bdg);
0-375-83098-7 (pa)   LC 2002-2781
At the end of their sophomore year in high school, the lives of four teenagers are woven together as they start a tough new job, face family problems, deal with changing friendships, and find love
"There's a realism here that takes the narrative beyond the problem novel and into one of relationships, their difficult demands in the face of human complexity and frailty, and their nonetheless often satisfying rewards. The book never loses sight of the kids at the heart of this, however, which keeps this accessible to the teens it's about." Bull Cent Child Books

Melling, O. R.
The Hunter's Moon. Amulet Books 2005 284p
(Chronicles of Faerie) $16.95; pa $7.95
Grades: 7 8 9 10   **Fic**
1. Magic—Fiction 2. Ireland—Fiction
ISBN 0-8109-5857-0; 0-8109-9214-0 (pa)
            LC 2004-22216
First published 1992 in Ireland
Two teenage cousins, one Irish, the other from the United States, set out to find a magic doorway to the Faraway Country, where humans must bow to the little people.
"This novel is a compelling blend of Irish mythology and geography. Characters that breathe and connect with readers, and a picturesque landscape that shifts between the present and the past, bring readers into the experience." SLJ
Another available title in this series is:
The Summer King (2006)

Melville, Herman, 1819-1891
Billy Budd, sailor; supplementary material written by Kathleen Helal. Pocket Books 2006 xxi, 166p pa $4.99   **Fic**
1. Sea stories
ISBN 978-1-416-52372-7; 1-416-52372-3
           LC 2006-299200
Written in 1891 but in a still "unfinished" manuscript stage when Melville died. First publication 1924 in the United Kingdom, as part of the Standard edition of Melville's complete works
"Narrates the hatred of petty officer Claggart by Billy, handsome Spanish sailor. Billy strikes and kills Claggart, and is condemned by Captain Vere even though the latter senses Billy's spiritual innocence." Haydn. Thesaurus of Book Dig
Includes bibliographical references

Melville, Herman, 1819-1891—*Continued*

Moby-Dick; or, The whale; illustrated by Rockwell Kent. Modern Library 1992 xxxv, 822p il $21 *

Grades: 11 12 Adult   **Fic**
1. Whaling—Fiction 2. Sea stories
ISBN 0-679-60010-8   LC 92-50222
Also available from other publishers
First published 1851

"Moby Dick is a ferocious white whale, who was known to whalers as Mocha Dick. He is pursued in a fury of revenge by Captain Ahab, whose leg he has bitten off; and under Melville's handling the chase takes on a significance beyond mere externals. Moby Dick becomes a symbol of the terrific forces of the natural universe, and Captain Ahab is doomed to disaster, even though Moby Dick is killed at last." Univ Handbook for Readers and Writers

"'Moby-Dick' had some initial critical appreciation, particularly in Britain, but only since the 1920s has it been recognized as a masterpiece, an epic tragedy of tremendous dramatic power and narrative drive." Oxford Companion to Engl Lit. 5th edition

Meyer, L. A., 1942-

Bloody Jack; being an account of the curious adventures of Mary "Jacky" Faber, ship's boy. Harcourt 2002 278p $17; pa $6.95

Grades: 7 8 9 10   **Fic**
1. Orphans—Fiction 2. Seafaring life—Fiction 3. Pirates—Fiction 4. Sex role—Fiction
ISBN 0-15-216731-5; 0-15-205085-X (pa)
    LC 2002-759

Reduced to begging and thievery in the streets of 18th-century London, a thirteen-year-old orphan disguises herself as a boy and connives her way onto a British warship set for high sea adventure in search of pirates

"From shooting a pirate in battle to foiling a shipmate's sexual attack to surviving when stranded alone on a Caribbean island, the action in Jacky's tale will entertain readers with a taste for adventure." Booklist

Other titles in this series are:
Curse of the blue tatoo (2004)
In the belly of The Bloodhound (2006)
Under the Jolly Roger (2005)

Meyer, Stephenie, 1973-

Twilight. Little, Brown and Co. 2005 498p $17.99; pa $8.99 *

Grades: 8 9 10 11 12   **Fic**
1. Vampires—Fiction 2. School stories 3. Washington (State)—Fiction
ISBN 0-316-16017-2; 0-316-01584-9 (pa)
    LC 2004-24730

"Megan Tingley books"

When seventeen-year-old Bella leaves Phoenix to live with her father in Forks, Washington, she meets an exquisitely handsome boy at school for whom she feels an overwhelming attraction and who she comes to realize is not wholly human.

"Realistic, subtle, succinct, and easy to follow, . . . [this book] will have readers dying to sink their teeth into it." SLJ

Other titles in this series are:

New moon (2006)
Eclipse (2007)

Miller, Mary Beth

Aimee; a novel. Dutton Bks. 2002 276p hardcover o.p. pa $6.99

Grades: 7 8 9 10   **Fic**
1. Suicide—Fiction 2. Friendship—Fiction
ISBN 0-525-46894-3; 0-14-240025-4 (pa)
    LC 2002-283987

It seems that everyone believes that Zoe helped her best friend, Aimee, commit suicide. Zoe is paralyzed by loneliness, guilt, and anger at everyone's suppression of the truth

"Despite the topic, there's no gratuitous violence, and the realistic yet not overly graphic suicide scene doesn't romanticize Aimee's action. The portrayal of therapy is especially good, and Miller's wholly believable, often irritating characters will alienate some readers but feel like a mirror for others." Booklist

On the head of a pin. Dutton Books 2006 250p $16.99 *

Grades: 9 10 11 12   **Fic**
1. Violence—Fiction
ISBN 0-525-47736-5   LC 2005-16768

While drinking alcohol and playing with a loaded gun at a party, a teenage boy accidentally shoots and kills another student and then tries to conceal her death.

This is an "edgy novel that skillfully weaves together numerous strands to create a horrifying yet thought-provoking and disturbingly real scenario." Booklist

Miller, Walter M., 1923-1996

A canticle for Leibowitz; a novel; by Walter M. Miller, Jr. Lippincott 1960 c1959 320p pa $13.95 hardcover o.p. *

Grades: 9 10 11 12 Adult   **Fic**
1. Science fiction
ISBN 0-06-089299-4

"Here is science fiction of the highest literary excellence and thematic intelligence. A monastery founded by the scientist Leibowitz is discovered decades after an atomic war. In the first part of the book a young novice in the monastery is the protagonist; in the second part we see scholars in a new period of enlightenment; and in the final section we observe man's proclivity for repeating mistakes and the apparent inevitability of history's repeating itself." Shapiro. Fic for Youth. 3d edition

Min, Katherine

Secondhand world; a novel. Knopf 2006 269p $23 *

Grades: 11 12 Adult   **Fic**
1. Korean Americans—Fiction 2. Parent-child relationship—Fiction 3. Family life—Fiction
ISBN 0-307-26344-4; 978-0-307-26344-5
    LC 2006-41038

The book "opens by introducing readers to 18-year-old Isadora Myung Hee Sohn, known as Isa to her mother and friends and Myung Hee to her father. Isa tells the absorbing story of a young woman's struggle to over-

Min, Katherine—_Continued_
come the obstacles of growing up Korean American in Albany, NY, during the 1970s. True to that stereotypically liberated period, Isa gets involved with sex, drugs, and rock'n'roll. . . . Touching and bittersweet, this novel is filled with universal themes presented through Isa's eyes and should resonate with teen readers of both today and yesterday." Libr J

Minchin, Adele
The beat goes on. Simon & Schuster Books for Young Readers 2004 212p $15.95 *
Grades: 9 10 11 12   Fic
1. AIDS (Disease)—Fiction 2. Cousins—Fiction 3. Great Britain—Fiction
ISBN 0-689-86611-9
First published 2001 in the United Kingdom
"Fifteen-year-old Leyla must keep her cousin's secret: Emma is HIV positive, and only her mother and Leyla know. The secret becomes a burden, especially when Leyla must lie to her parents in order to work with Emma's support group on their special project—to teach other HIV-positive teens how to play the drums. In spite of its heavy Briticisms and a didactic tone, this is one of the better YA books about HIV. The facts of transmission and symptoms are clearly presented, as are Emma's struggles to lead a normal, healthy life. Leyla's very proper mother's holier-than-thou response and the grief Emma and her mother feel are authentic and painful. Leyla's sadness and initial unease at being physically near her cousin are also palpably genuine. Minchin educates young readers while telling a gripping story that will keep personal tragedy aficionados turning the pages to the hopeful yet realistic conclusion." Booklist

Mitchell, David
Black swan green; a novel. Random House 2006 294p $23.95; pa $13.95 *
Grades: 11 12 Adult   Fic
1. Speech disorders—Fiction 2. Family life—Fiction 3. Great Britain—Fiction
ISBN 1-400-06379-5; 978-1-4000-6379-6; 0-8129-7401-8 (pa); 978-0-8129-7401-0 (pa)
LC 2005-52914
Also available Thorndike Press large print edition
This is a "portrait of a thirteen-year-old boy, growing up in Worcestershire in 1982, who is afflicted with a stammer, unhappy parents, and a snide older sister." New Yorker
"The author does not pull any punches when it comes to the casual cruelty that adolescent boys can inflict on one another, but it is this very brutality that underscores the sweetness of which they are also capable. With its British slang and complex twists and turns, this title is not a selection for reluctant readers, but teens who enjoy multifaceted coming-of-age stories will be richly rewarded." SLJ

Mochizuki, Ken
Beacon Hill boys. Scholastic Press 2002 201p $16.95; pa $5.99
Grades: 7 8 9 10   Fic
1. Japanese Americans—Fiction 2. Washington (State)—Fiction
ISBN 0-439-26749-8; 0-439-24906-6 (pa)
LC 2002-2343
In 1972 in Seattle, a teenager in a Japanese American family struggles for his own identity, along with a group of three friends who share his anger and confusion
"The author nicely balances universal experiences of male adolescence . . . with scenes that bring readers right into the complicated era, and his important, thought-provoking story asks tough questions about racial and cultural identity, prejudice, and family." Booklist

Moloney, James, 1954-
Black taxi. HarperCollins Publishers 2005 264p $15.99; lib bdg $16.89
Grades: 9 10 11 12   Fic
1. Mystery fiction 2. Crime—Fiction 3. Automobiles—Fiction 4. Great Britain—Fiction
ISBN 0-06-055937-3; 0-06-055938-1 (lib bdg)
LC 2003-27848
When Rosie agrees to take care of her grandfather's Mercedes while he is in jail, she gets more than she bargained for, including being thrust into the middle of a jewel heist mystery and being attracted to a dangerous boy.
"Love and larceny are center stage in this British import, which is best suited to older readers even though it has no explicit language or dicey situations. Only the main characters are developed, but the story is entertaining enough to appeal to fans of lightweight mystery who also relish a hint of romance." Booklist

Moranville, Sharelle Byars
A higher geometry. Henry Holt 2006 212p $16.95
Grades: 8 9 10 11   Fic
1. Sex role—Fiction 2. Mathematics—Fiction 3. School stories
ISBN 978-0-8050-7470-3; 0-8050-7470-8
LC 2005-21699
While grieving the death of her grandmother in 1959, teenager Anna is torn between her aspirations to study math in college and her family's expectations that she will marry and become a homemaker after high school.
"Readers will easily connect with the romance that's both thrilling and nurturing and with Anna's steady resolve to follow her passion for numbers and challenge a world of expectations." Booklist

Morgan, Nicola, 1961-
Fleshmarket. Delacorte Press 2004 208p hardcover o.p. lib bdg $17.99
Grades: 7 8 9 10   Fic
1. Knox, Robert, 1793-1862—Fiction 2. Medicine—Fiction 3. Physicians—Fiction 4. Poverty—Fiction 5. Scotland—Fiction
ISBN 0-385-73154-X; 0-385-90192-5 (lib bdg)
LC 2003-11441

Morgan, Nicola, 1961-—_Continued_

In nineteenth-century Scotland, following the death of his mother during surgery, Robbie decides to take revenge on the surgeon who performed the operation, Dr. Robert Knox, and in the process, makes a gruesome discovery about the lengths the medical profession will go to advance its knowledge of anatomy.

"The protagonist's need for revenge is palpable, and Morgan's story is fast paced and absorbing. Readers who are fascinated by forensics and anatomy will find this a gripping story." SLJ

Morgenroth, Kate

Echo. Simon & Schuster 2007 144p $15.99

Grades: 7 8 9 10   **Fic**

1. Death—Fiction 2. Post-traumatic stress disorder—Fiction

ISBN 1-4169-1438-2; 978-1-4169-1438-9

LC 2005-32984

After Justin witnesses his brother's accidental shooting death, he must live with the repercussions, as the same horrific day seems to happen over and over.

Jude. Simon & Schuster Books for Young Readers 2004 277p $16.95; pa $5.99

Grades: 7 8 9 10   **Fic**

1. Crime—Fiction 2. Mother-son relationship—Fiction

ISBN 0-689-86479-5; 1-416-91267-3 (pa)

LC 2003-20475

Still reeling from his drug-dealing father's murder, moving in with the wealthy mother he never knew, and transferring to a private school, fifteen-year-old Jude is tricked into pleading guilty to a crime he did not commit

"The plot is tight, deliberately paced, and full of delicious twists. . . . The story is quick and action packed enough to engage reluctant readers, especially older boys." SLJ

Moriarty, Jaclyn

The year of secret assignments. Arthur A. Levine Books 2004 340p $16.95; pa $7.99

Grades: 7 8 9 10   **Fic**

1. Friendship—Fiction 2. School stories 3. Australia—Fiction

ISBN 0-439-49881-3; 0-439-49882-1 (pa)

LC 2003-14278

Three female students from Ashbury High write to three male students from rival Brookfield High as part of a pen pal program, leading to romance, humiliation, revenge plots, and war between the schools

"There are a few coarse moments—a reference to a blow job and some caustic outbursts. . . . This is an unusual novel with an exhilarating pace, irrepressible characters, and a screwball humor that will easily attract teens." Booklist

Moriarty, Laura

The center of everything. Hyperion 2003 291p $22.95; pa $14

Grades: 9 10 11 12   **Fic**

1. Mother-daughter relationship—Fiction 2. Single parent family—Fiction 3. Kansas—Fiction

ISBN 1-401-30031-6; 0-7868-8845-8 (pa)

LC 2002-32898

Also available Thorndike Press large print edition

"Any map clearly shows that Kansas is the center of everything. Ten-year-old Evelyn Bucknow notices it on every map that she sees and truly believes that is where she belongs—in the center. Unfortunately, Evelyn is forced to parent her mother, a flighty, unrealistically romantic woman who is having an affair with her married boss. . . . Fortunately, Evelyn takes the events of her life and her mother's life and learns her lessons, with a few glitches along the way. Young people will find Evelyn appealing and real despite the book's setting in the age of Ronald Reagan and big hair, and they will respond positively to her determination." VOYA

Morpurgo, Michael

Private Peaceful. Scholastic Press 2004 c2003 202p $16.95; pa $5.99 *

Grades: 7 8 9 10   **Fic**

1. World War, 1914-1918—Fiction 2. Great Britain—Fiction

ISBN 0-439-63648-5; 0-439-63653-1 (pa)

LC 2003-65347

First published 2003 in the United Kingdom

When Thomas Peaceful's older brother is forced to join the British Army, Thomas decides to sign up as well, although he is only fourteen years old, to prove himself to his country, his family, his childhood love, Molly, and himself

"In this World War I story, the terse and beautiful narrative of a young English soldier is as compelling about the world left behind as about the horrific daily details of trench warfare. . . . Suspense builds right to the end, which is shocking, honest, and unforgettable." Booklist

Morrison, Toni, 1931-

Beloved; a novel. Knopf 1987 275p $29.95; pa $13.95 *

Grades: 9 10 11 12 Adult   **Fic**

1. African Americans—Fiction 2. Mother-daughter relationship—Fiction 3. Slavery—Fiction

ISBN 0-394-53597-9; 1-4000-3341-6 (pa)

Also available large print edition $19.95 (ISBN 0-375-70414-0)

This novel, "set in the third quarter of the 19th century, focuses on the life of the runaway slave woman Sethe and her struggle with the unspeakable pain of her past. Like Morrison's earlier novels, _Beloved_ is marked by rich and lyrical language, narratives shot through with exotic and magical elements, and a fragmented structure that requires readers to participate in the telling." Benet's Reader's Ency of Am Lit

The bluest eye; with a new afterword by the author. Knopf 2005 c1993 215p $19.95 *

Grades: 11 12 Adult   **Fic**

1. African Americans—Fiction 2. Ohio—Fiction

ISBN 0-375-41155-0   LC 93-43124

Also available in paperback from Plume

A reissue of the title first published 1970 by Holt, Rinehart & Winston

"This tragic study of a black adolescent girl's struggle to achieve white ideals of beauty and her consequent de-

Morrison, Toni, 1931-—*Continued*

scent into madness was acclaimed as an eloquent indictment of some of the more subtle forms of racism in American society. Pecola Breedlove longs to have 'the bluest eye' and thus to be acceptable to her family, schoolmates, and neighbors, all of whom have convinced her that she is ugly." Merriam-Webster's Ency of Lit

Sula. Knopf 1974 c1973 174p $26
Grades: 11 12 Adult   **Fic**
   1. African Americans—Fiction 2. Ohio—Fiction 3. Friendship—Fiction 4. Poverty—Fiction
ISBN 0-394-48044-9

This "is the story of two black women friends and of their community of Medallion, Ohio. The community has been stunted and turned inward by the racism of the larger society. The rage and disordered lives of the townspeople are seen as a reaction to their stifled hopes. The novel follows the lives of Sula and Nel from childhood to maturity to death." Merriam-Webster's Ency of Lit

Mosley, Walter

Fortunate son. Little, Brown and Co. 2006 313p $23.95
Grades: 11 12 Adult   **Fic**
   1. Brothers—Fiction 2. Race relations—Fiction
ISBN 978-0-316-11471-4; 0-316-11471-5
                            LC 2005-24477

"Tommy was born out of wedlock with a hole in his heart; he's also lame and black. Eric, on the other hand, glows with health; he is so beautiful that people want to touch him—and he's white. For a few years, the boys live together after Tommy's mother and Eric's widowed doctor father fall in love after meeting in the hospital ward. Then Tommy's mother dies, and Tommy is wrested from the only family he's known. Eric grows up leading a life that appears blessed, but with Tommy gone, he's lost all that is important to him. Tommy, meanwhile, ends up on the street but feels lucky simply to be alive. . . . The writing is crisp and the plotting impeccable." Libr J

Mowll, Joshua

Operation Red Jericho; [illustrated by Benjamin Mowll, Julek Heller, Niroot Puttapipat] Candlewick Press 2005 271p il map (The Guild of Specialists) $15.99
Grades: 9 10 11 12   **Fic**
   1. Adventure fiction 2. Siblings—Fiction 3. Uncles—Fiction
ISBN 0-7636-2634-1   LC 2005-45382

The posthumous papers of Rebecca MacKenzie document her adventures, along with her brother Doug, in 1920s China as the teenaged siblings are sent to live aboard their uncle's ship where they become involved in the dangerous activities of a mysterious secret society called the Honourable Guild of Specialists.

"Some readers may pore over the details in this novel; others will simply appreciate the comic adventure." SLJ
   Includes bibliographical references
Followed by Operation typhoon shore (2006)

Murdock, Catherine Gilbert

Dairy Queen; a novel. Houghton Mifflin 2006 275p $16 *
Grades: 7 8 9 10   **Fic**
   1. Football—Fiction 2. Farm life—Fiction
ISBN 0-618-68307-0   LC 2005-19077

After spending her summer running the family farm and training the quarterback for her school's rival football team, sixteen-year-old D.J. decides to go out for the sport herself, not anticipating the reactions of those around her.

"D. J.'s voice is funny, frank, and intelligent, and her story is not easily pigeonholed." Voice Youth Advocates
Followed by The off season (2007)

Myers, Walter Dean, 1937-

Autobiography of my dead brother; art by Christopher Myers. HarperTempest/Amistad 2005 212p il $15.99; lib bdg $16.89; pa $6.99 *
Grades: 7 8 9 10   **Fic**
   1. Violence—Fiction 2. African Americans—Fiction 3. Friendship—Fiction 4. Harlem (New York, N.Y.)—Fiction
ISBN 0-06-058291-X; 0-06-058292-8 (lib bdg); 0-06-058293-6 (pa)   LC 2004-27878

Jesse pours his heart and soul into his sketchbook to make sense of life in his troubled Harlem neighborhood and the loss of a close friend.

"This novel is like photorealism; it paints a vivid and genuine portrait of life that will have a palpable effect on its readers." SLJ

Fallen angels. Scholastic 1988 309p hardcover o.p. pa $5.99 *
Grades: 9 10 11 12   **Fic**
   1. Vietnam War, 1961-1975—Fiction 2. African American soldiers—Fiction
ISBN 0-590-40942-5; 0-590-40943-3 (pa)
                            LC 87-23236

"Black, seventeen, perceptive and sensitive, Richie (the narrator) has enlisted and been sent to Vietnam; in telling the story of his year of active service, Richie is candid about the horror of killing and the fear of being killed, the fear and bravery and confusion and tragedy of the war." Bull Cent Child Books

"Except for occasional outbursts, the narration is remarkably direct and understated; and the dialogue, with morbid humor sometimes adding comic relief, is steeped in natural vulgarity, without which verisimilitude would be unthinkable. In fact, the foul talk, which serves as the story's linguistic setting, is not nearly as obscene as are the events." Horn Book

Monster; illustrations by Christopher Myers. HarperCollins Pubs. 1999 281p il $14.95; lib bdg $14.89
Grades: 7 8 9 10   **Fic**
   1. Trials—Fiction 2. African Americans—Fiction
ISBN 0-06-028077-8; 0-06-028078-6 (lib bdg)
                            LC 98-40958

Coretta Scott King honor book text, 2000

While on trial as an accomplice to a murder, sixteen-year-old Steve Harmon records his experiences in prison and in the courtroom in the form of a film script as he

Myers, Walter Dean, 1937——_Continued_
tries to come to terms with the course his life has taken.

"Balancing courtroom drama and a sordid jailhouse setting with flashbacks to the crime, Myers adeptly allows each character to speak for him or herself, leaving readers to judge for themselves the truthfulness of the defendants, witnesses, lawyers, and, most compellingly, Steve himself." Horn Book Guide

Slam! Scholastic Press 1996 266p hardcover o.p. pa $5.99
Grades: 7 8 9 10   **Fic**
1. Basketball—Fiction 2. African Americans—Fiction 3. School stories
ISBN 0-590-48667-5; 0-590-48668-3 (pa)
           LC 95-46647
Coretta Scott King Award for text, 1997
Seventeen-year-old "Slam" Harris is counting on his noteworthy basketball talents to get him out of the inner city and give him a chance to succeed in life, but his coach sees things differently

Myers "descriptions of Slam on the court . . . use crisp details, not flowery language, to achieve their muscular poetry, and Myers is equally vivid in relating the torment Slam feels as he stares at a page of indecipherable algebra formulas. . . . [This is an] admirably realistic coming-of-age novel." Booklist

Street love. Amistad/Harper Tempest 2006 134p $15.99; lib bdg $16.89
Grades: 8 9 10 11 12   **Fic**
1. African Americans—Fiction 2. Harlem (New York, N.Y.)—Fiction
ISBN   978-0-06-028079-6;   0-06-028079-4; 978-0-06-028080-2 (lib bdg); 0-06-028080-8 (lib bdg)
           LC 2006-02457
This story told in free verse is set against a background of street gangs and poverty in Harlem in which seventeen-year-old African American Damien takes a bold step to ensure that he and his new love will not be separated.

"The realistic drama on the street and at home tells a gripping story." Booklist

Na, An, 1972-
A step from heaven. Front St. 2000 156p $15.95 *

Grades: 7 8 9 10   **Fic**
1. Korean Americans—Fiction 2. Family life—Fiction
ISBN 1-88691-058-8   LC 00-41083
Also available Thorndike Press large print edition and in paperback from Speak
A young Korean girl and her family find it difficult to learn English and adjust to life in America
"This isn't a quick read, especially at the beginning when the child is trying to decipher American words and customs, but the coming-of-age drama will grab teens and make them think of their own conflicts between home and outside. As in the best writing, the particulars make the story universal." Booklist

Wait for me. Putnam 2006 169p $15.99 *
Grades: 8 9 10 11 12   **Fic**
1. Mother-daughter relationship—Fiction 2. Korean Americans—Fiction 3. Sisters—Fiction 4. Deaf—Fiction
ISBN 0-399-24275-9   LC 2005-30931
As her senior year in high school approaches, Mina yearns to find her own path in life but working at the family business, taking care of her little sister, and dealing with her mother's impossible expectations are as stifling as the southern California heat, until she falls in love with a man who offers a way out.

"This is a well-crafted tale, sensitively told. . . . The mother-daughter conflict will resonate with teens of any culture who have wrestled parents for the right to choose their own paths." Bull Cent Child Books

Napoli, Donna Jo, 1948-
Beast. Atheneum Bks. for Young Readers 2000 260p $17; pa $8
Grades: 7 8 9 10   **Fic**
1. Fairy tales 2. Iran—Fiction
ISBN 0-689-83589-2; 0-689-87005-1 (pa)
           LC 99-89923
"In this take on 'Beauty and the Beast,' Napoli focuses on Beast before French beauty Belle enters his life. The first-person story begins in Persia, where proud prince Orasmyn, who loves roses, makes an unfortunate decision that sets in motion a curse: he becomes a lion who can only be restored by the love of a woman." Booklist
"The reader is immersed in the imagery and spirituality of ancient Persia. . . . Although Napoli uses Farsi (Persian) and Arabic words in the text (there is a glossary), this only adds to the texture and richness of her remarkable piece of writing." Book Rep

Bound. Atheneum Books for Young Readers 2004 186p $16.95; pa $5.99
Grades: 9 10 11 12   **Fic**
1. China—Fiction 2. Sex role—Fiction
ISBN 0-689-86175-3; 0-689-86178-8 (pa)
           LC 2004-365
Also available Thorndike Press large print edition
In a novel based on Chinese Cinderella tales, fourteen-year-old stepchild Xing-Xing endures a life of neglect and servitude, as her stepmother cruelly mutilates her own child's feet so that she alone might marry well
The author "fleshes out and enriches the story with well-rounded characters and with accurate information about a specific time and place in Chinese history; the result is a dramatic and masterful retelling." SLJ

The magic circle. Dutton Children's Bks. 1993 118p hardcover o.p. pa $4.99 *
Grades: 9 10 11 12   **Fic**
1. Fairy tales 2. Witchcraft—Fiction
ISBN 0-525-45127-7; 0-14-037439-6 (pa)
           LC 92-27008
After learning sorcery to become a healer, a good-hearted woman is turned into a witch by evil spirits and she fights their power until her encounter with Hansel and Gretel years later
"The strength of Napoli's writing and the clarity of

Napoli, Donna Jo, 1948-—*Continued*
her vision make this story fresh and absorbing. A brilliantly conceived and beautifully executed novel that is
sure to be appreciated by thoughtful readers." SLJ

Naslund, Sena Jeter
Four spirits; a novel. Morrow 2003 524p
hardcover o.p. pa $14.95 *
Grades: 9 10 11 12   **Fic**
1. Race relations—Fiction 2. Birmingham (Ala.)—Fiction
ISBN 0-06-621238-3; 0-06-093669-X (pa)
LC 2003-51170
"Stella, a white Birmingham, AL, college student in
the early 1960s, faces the problems of birth control,
women's 'liberation,' peaceful protest, and civil and
handicapped rights. . . . After the bombing of a Birmingham church that kills four black children, Stella and
her friend Cat begin to teach night classes at the black
high school, helping dropouts earn their GEDs. They
overcome the resentment and suspicion of the black
teachers and students only to be confronted by the Ku
Klux Klan. A major tragedy at a peaceful sit-in pushes
Stella firmly into the activist camp, where she finds her
soul mate." Libr J
"The book's last act, involving the murder of four
protesters at a sit-in, is violent and shocking and leads to
one of the few sermons in contemporary literature that I
can recall as vital and moving. . . . Naslund brings a
measure of dignity and moral complexity to her portrayal
of a city that came to be known as 'Bombingham.'" N
Y Times Book Rev

Naylor, Gloria
The men of Brewster Place. Hyperion 1998
173p
Grades: 11 12 Adult   **Fic**
1. African Americans—Fiction 2. Social problems—
Fiction
ISBN 0-7868-6421-4   LC 97-45987
"Ben, a neighborhood janitor (and chorus) resurrected
from the previous Brewster Place novel, narrates seven
tales of neighborhood men and the women who love
them. Their travails feature the familiar ills of the inner
city, yet Naylor lends these archetypal situations complexity and depth: Basil yearns to be the kind of father
he never had but chooses a path that leads to heartbreak;
Eugene's restlessness in his marriage and friendship with
a transsexual force him to face a difficult fact about himself; Reverend Moreland T. Woods rehearses his political
aspirations with maneuvers on his church's board; and
C.C. Baker, involved in local drug trafficking, keeps a
startling truth from the police." Publ Wkly

Nelson, Blake, 1960-
Paranoid Park. Viking 2006 180p $15.99
Grades: 7 8 9 10   **Fic**
1. Guilt—Fiction 2. Skateboarding—Fiction
3. Homicide—Fiction
ISBN 0-670-06118-2   LC 2006-00277
A sixteen-year-old Portland, Oregon skateboarder,
whose parents are going through a difficult divorce, is
engulfed by guilt and confusion when he accidentally

kills a security guard at a train yard.
"Readers will have a visceral reaction to this story,
but on a literary level, they'll also appreciate Nelson's
clever plotting and spot-on characterizations." Booklist

Rock star, superstar; by Blake Nelson. Viking
2004 229p $16.99; pa $6.99
Grades: 9 10 11 12   **Fic**
1. Musicians—Fiction 2. Rock music—Fiction
ISBN 0-670-05933-1; 0-14-240574-4 (pa)
LC 2003-27556
When Pete, a talented bass player, moves from playing in the school jazz band to playing in a popular rock
group, he finds the experience exhilarating even as his
new fame jeopardizes his relationship with girlfriend
Margaret
"A brilliant, tender, funny, and utterly believable novel about music and relationships. . . . Pete is one of the
best male protagonists in recent YA fiction and the other
characters are equally strong." SLJ

Newbery, Linda, 1952-
Sisterland. David Fickling Books 2004 369p
$15.95; lib bdg $17.99
Grades: 9 10 11 12   **Fic**
1. Grandmothers—Fiction 2. Alzheimer's disease—
Fiction 3. Holocaust, 1933-1945—Fiction 4. Great
Britain—Fiction
ISBN 0-385-75026-9; 0-385-75035-8 (lib bdg)
LC 2003-56547
Also available in paperback from Laurel Leaf
First published 2003 in the United Kingdom
When Hilly's grandmother becomes ill with
Alzheimer's disease, her family is turned upside down by
revelations from her life during World War II
"The time and character switches are initially confus-
ing, but the mystery drives the plot, bringing the political
history close to home without slick parallels between the
Holocaust horror and prejudice now." Booklist

Nicholson, William
Seeker; the first book of the Noble Warriors.
Harcourt 2006 413p $17; pa $7.95
Grades: 7 8 9 10   **Fic**
1. Fantasy fiction
ISBN   978-0-15-205768-8;   0-15-205768-4;
978-0-15-205866-1 (pa); 0-15-205866-4 (pa)
LC 2005-17171
"Seeker, Morning Star, and Wildman are three teens
who hope to join the Nomana, a society of noble warriors and worshippers of the All and Only (the god who
makes all things). . . . Conjuring up a plan to prove
their worth, this motley trio plays a key role in foiling
the murderous plans of the royalty in a nearby town."
Bull Cent Child Books
"The classic coming-of-age tale is combined with a
rich setting of cold villains, strange powers, and disturbing warriors." Voice Youth Advocates
Followed by Jango (2007)

Nilsson, Per, 1954-

Heart's delight; translated by Tara Chace. Front St. 2003 155p $16.95

Grades: 9 10 11 12   **Fic**

1. Sweden—Fiction

ISBN 1-88691-092-8   LC 2003-51167

Also available in paperback from Simon Pulse

"A 16-year-old boy suffers the agonies and ecstasies of first love. . . . The unnamed narrator ponders memorabilia from his relationship with Ann-Katrin—a bus pass, unused condoms, old movie tickets, a plant she gave him—and relives their courtship." SLJ

"Like its emotionally fragile main character, this affecting, uniquely constructed Swedish novel about first love—and first heartbreak—puts up a pretense of detachment." Horn Book Guide

You & you & you; translated by Tara Chace. Front Street 2005 301p $16.95 *

Grades: 9 10 11 12   **Fic**

1. Friendship—Fiction 2. Sweden—Fiction

ISBN 1-932425-19-5   LC 2004-30660

Original Swedish edition, 1998

Young Anon, who marches to the beat of a different drummer in galoshes to protect himself from radiation, touches the lives of all around him, resulting in disillusionment, loss, love, and more than a few surprises.

"Swedish magical realism comes alive in this mature, sometimes graphically sexual and violent, ultimately breathtaking and inspiring tale. . . . Many of the older YA readers to whom this book is directed will likely come away with a feeling of being somehow transformed or at least being given much to ponder." SLJ

Niven, Larry

The Mote in God's Eye; by Larry Niven & Jerry Pournelle 1974 537p pa $7.99 hardcover o.p.

Grades: 11 12 Adult   **Fic**

1. Science fiction

ISBN 0-671-74192-6

"Superior space opera in which Earth's interstellar navy contacts and does battle with an enormously hostile alien race. The scenes of space warfare are well handled, and the alien Moties are fascinating." Anatomy of Wonder 4

Another title about the war between humans and the Moties is:

The gripping hand (1993)

Ringworld. Ballantine Bks. 1970 342p pa $7.99 *

Grades: 11 12 Adult   **Fic**

1. Science fiction

ISBN 0-345-33392-6

"The Ringworld, a world shaped like a wheel so huge that it surrounds a sun, is almost too fantastic to conceive of. With a radius of 90 million miles and a length of 600 million miles, the Ringworld's mystery is compounded by the discovery that it is artificial. What phenomenal intelligence can be behind such a creation? Four unlikely explorers, two humans and two aliens, set out for the Ringworld, bound by mutual distrust and unsure of each other's motives." Shapiro. Fic for Youth. 3d edition

Other available titles in this series are:

The Ringworld engineers (1980)

The Ringworld throne (1996)

Ringworld's children (2004)

Nix, Garth, 1963-

Sabriel. HarperCollins Pubs. 1996 c1995 292p $17.99; pa $7.99 *

Grades: 7 8 9 10   **Fic**

1. Fantasy fiction

ISBN 0-06-027322-4; 0-06-447183-7 (pa)

        LC 96-1295

First published 1995 in Australia

Sabriel, daughter of the necromancer Abhorsen, must journey into the mysterious and magical Old Kingdom to rescue her father from the Land of the Dead

"The final battle is gripping, and the bloody cost of combat is forcefully presented. The story is remarkable for the level of originality of the fantastic elements . . . and for the subtle presentation, which leaves readers to explore for themselves the complex structure and significance of the magic elements." Horn Book

Other titles in this series are:

Abhorsen (2003)

Across the wall (2005)

Lirael, daughter of the Clayr (2001)

Nordhoff, Charles, 1887-1947

Mutiny on the Bounty; by Charles Nordhoff and James Norman Hall. Little, Brown 1932 396p hardcover o.p. pa $13.95

Grades: 11 12 Adult   **Fic**

1. Bligh, William, 1754-1817—Fiction 2. Bounty (Ship)—Fiction 3. Sea stories 4. Islands of the Pacific—Fiction

ISBN 0-316-61157-3; 0-316-61168-9 (pa)

Also available from Amereon

This narrative is "based on the famous mutiny that members of the crew of the 'Bounty', a British war vessel, carried out in 1787 against their cruel commander, Captain William Bligh. The authors kept the actual historical characters and background, using as narrator an elderly man, Captain Roger Byam, who had been a midshipman on the 'Bounty.' The story tells how the mate of the ship, Fletcher Christian, and a number of the crew rebel and set Captain Bligh adrift in an open boat with the loyal members of the crew." Reader's Ency. 4th edition

Other titles in the Bounty trilogy are:

Men against the sea (1934)

Pitcairn's Island (1934)

Oates, Joyce Carol, 1938-

Big Mouth & Ugly Girl. HarperCollins Pubs. 2002 265p $16.99; lib bdg $17.89; pa $7.99 *

Grades: 7 8 9 10   **Fic**

1. School stories 2. Friendship—Fiction

ISBN 0-06-623756-4; 0-06-623758-0 (lib bdg); 0-06-447347-3 (pa)   LC 2001-24601

"Readers will be propelled through these pages by an intense curiosity to learn how events will play out. Oates has written a fast-moving, timely, compelling story." SLJ

Oates, Joyce Carol, 1938-—*Continued*

Freaky green eyes. Harper Tempest 2003 341p lib bdg $17.89; pa $6.99

Grades: 7 8 9 10   **Fic**

1. Domestic violence—Fiction

ISBN 0-06-623757-2 (lib bdg); 0-06-447348-1 (pa)

LC 2002-32868

Fifteen-year-old Frankie relates the events of the year leading up to her mother's mysterious disappearance and her own struggle to discover and accept the truth about her parents' relationship.

"Oates pulls readers into a fast-paced, first-person thriller. . . . an absorbing page-turner." Booklist

O'Brien, Tim, 1946-

Going after Cacciato; a novel 1978 338p o.p. pa $14.95

Grades: 11 12 Adult   **Fic**

1. Vietnam War, 1961-1975—Fiction 2. Soldiers—Fiction 3. Dreams—Fiction

ISBN 0-440-02948-1; 0-7679-0442-7 (pa)

LC 77-11723

"Paul Berlin's squad is sent to retrieve Cacciato, a young deserter from the Vietnam War. Fantasy colors the progress of the squad as a dream of peace and the possibility of forsaking war follow them through many adventures. The horror and destruction of war is vividly conveyed and the language is rough, as would be expected. Cacciato becomes a kind of symbol for resisting bureaucratic militarism and an enviable model for Berlin himself." Shapiro. Fic for Youth. 3d edition

Odom, Mel, 1950-

The rover. TOR Bks. 2001 400p hardcover o.p. pa $6.99

Grades: 11 12 Adult   **Fic**

1. Fantasy fiction

ISBN 0-312-87882-6; 0-7653-4194-8 (pa)

LC 2001-27474

"A Tom Doherty Associates book"

"Although not particularly successful because he has never been promoted from his position as a Level Three Librarian at the Vault of All Known Knowledge, Edgewick 'Wick' Lamplighter loves his vocation even if it means that all of his adventures merely are borrowed from books. This situation completely changes for Wick when Grandmagister Frollo sends him on an errand to deliver a package to the Customs House at the docks of Blood-Soaked Sea." Voice Youth Advocates

"Pushing the conventions of fantasy to the max, Odom serves up a rip-roaring, pell-mell, often laugh-out-loud romp." Booklist

Other titles about Edgewick Lamplighter are:

The destruction of the books (2004)

Lord of the libraries (2005)

Olsen, Sylvia, 1955-

White girl. Sono Nis Press 2004 235p pa $8.95 *

Grades: 7 8 9 10   **Fic**

1. Native Americans—Fiction 2. Prejudices—Fiction

ISBN 1-5503-9147-X

"Until she was fourteen, Josie was pretty ordinary. Then her Mom meets Martin, 'a real ponytail Indian,' and before long, Josie finds herself living on a reserve outside town, with a new stepfather, a new stepbrother, and a new name 'Blondie.'" Publisher's note

"The talk is contemporary and relaxed, and the characters will hold readers as much as the novel's extraordinary sense of place." Booklist

Orenstein, Denise Gosliner, 1950-

Unseen companion. Katherine Tegen Bks. 2003 357p lib bdg $16.89; pa $7.99 *

Grades: 7 8 9 10   **Fic**

1. Inuit—Fiction 2. Alaska—Fiction

ISBN 0-06-052057-4 (lib bdg); 0-06-052058-2 (pa)

LC 2002-152944

"In distinctive voices, the four narrators tell their own involving stories. . . . A sensitive observer and a compelling storyteller, Orenstein offers a novel that is both touching and harsh." Booklist

Orwell, George, 1903-1950

Animal farm; with an introduction by Julian Symons. Knopf 1993 xl, 113p $16 *

Grades: 7 8 9 10   **Fic**

1. Animals—Fiction 2. Totalitarianism—Fiction

ISBN 0-679-42039-8   LC 92-54299

Also available from other publishers

"Everyman's library"

First published 1945 in the United Kingdom; first United States edition 1946

"The animals on Farmer Jones's farm revolt in a move led by the pigs, and drive out the humans. The pigs become the leaders, in spite of the fact that their government was meant to be 'classless.' The other animals soon find that they are suffering varying degrees of slavery. A totalitarian state slowly evolves in which 'all animals are equal but some animals are more equal than others.' This is a biting satire aimed at communism." Shapiro. Fic for Youth. 3d edition

Nineteen eighty-four; with an introduction by Julian Symonds. Knopf 1992 xlii, 325p $19 *

Grades: 11 12 Adult   **Fic**

1. Totalitarianism—Fiction

ISBN 0-679-41739-7   LC 92-52906

Also available in paperback from Plume

First published 1949 by Harcourt, Brace

"A dictatorship called Big Brother rules the people in a collectivist society where Winston Smith works in the Ministry of Truth. The Thought Police persuade the people that ignorance is strength and war is peace. Winston becomes involved in a forbidden love affair and joins the underground to resist this mind control." Shapiro. Fic for Youth. 3d edition

Osa, Nancy

Cuba 15. Delacorte Press 2003 277p $15.95; lib
bdg $17.99; pa $7.95

Grades: 7 8 9 10 **Fic**

1. Cuban Americans—Fiction

ISBN 0-385-73021-7; 0-385-90086-4 (lib bdg);
0-385-73233-3 (pa) LC 2002-13389

Violet Paz, who is half Cuban American, half Polish
American, reluctantly prepares for her upcoming
"quince," a Spanish nickname for the celebration of an
Hispanic girl's fifteenth birthday

"Violet's hilarious, cool first-person narrative veers
between slapstick and tenderness, denial and truth."
Booklist

Otsuka, Julie, 1962-

When the emperor was divine; a novel. Knopf
2002 141p hardcover o.p. pa $10.95 *

Grades: 11 12 Adult **Fic**

1. Japanese Americans—Evacuation and relocation,
1942-1945—Fiction 2. California—Fiction

ISBN 0-375-41429-0; 0-385-72181-1 (pa)
LC 2002-20814

Also available large print edition $20 (ISBN 0-375-
43278-7)

This novel traces the "fortunes of a Japanese-
American family from the spring of 1942—when President Roosevelt's evacuation order came through—to the
spring of 1946. In four brief chapters, we follow a mother, daughter and son from their comfortable home in
Berkeley through their five months in a temporary 'assembly center' (a converted stable at a racetrack south of
San Francisco) to an internment camp in Topaz, Utah,
where they spend three years." N Y Times Book Rev

Otsuka "demonstrates a breathtaking restraint and delicacy throughout this supple and devastating first novel."
Booklist

Packer, Ann

The dive from Clausen's pier; a novel. Knopf
2002 369p hardcover o.p. pa $14

Grades: 11 12 Adult **Fic**

1. Accidents—Fiction 2. Wisconsin—Fiction 3. New
York (N.Y.)—Fiction

ISBN 0-375-41282-4; 0-375-72713-2 (pa)
LC 2001-42522

"A reckless attempt to impress Carrie, Mike's dive off
Clausen's Pier rendered him paralyzed. Now Carrie finds
herself torn between the loyalty she's expected to feel toward Mike and her need to transform herself. She takes
a dive of her own—into adulthood—when she escapes to
New York." Booklist

Palwick, Susan

The necessary beggar. Tor 2005 316p $24.95;
pa $6.99

Grades: 9 10 11 12 **Fic**

1. Fantasy fiction 2. Refugees—Fiction

ISBN 0-765-31097-X; 978-0-765-31097-2;
0-765-34951-5 (pa); 978-0-765-34951-4 (pa)
LC 2005-41919

"A Tom Doherty Associates book"

"In the Glorious City of Lémabantunk, a young man
is found guilty of murder, and his punishment is exile—
along with his whole family—to another world from
which they can never return. Their new home is Earth,
where they are considered refugees who must begin their
lives anew. . . . [The author] has crafted a unique story
of a family's love and the power of forgiveness to transcend the boundary between life and death." Libr J

Paolini, Christopher

Eragon. Knopf 2003 509p (Inheritance) $18.95;
lib bdg $20.99; pa $6.99 *

Grades: 7 8 9 10 **Fic**

1. Dragons—Fiction 2. Fantasy fiction

ISBN 0-375-82668-8; 0-375-92668-2 (lib bdg);
0-440-23848-X (pa) LC 2003-47481

First published 2002 in different form by Paolini International

In Aagaesia, a fifteen-year-old boy of unknown lineage called Eragon finds a mysterious stone that weaves
his life into an intricate tapestry of destiny, magic, and
power, peopled with dragons, elves, and monsters

"This unusual, powerful tale . . . is the first book in
the planned Inheritance trilogy. . . . The telling remains
constantly fresh and fluid, and [the author] has done a
fine job of creating an appealing and convincing relationship between the youth and the dragon." Booklist

Another title in this series is:
Eldest (2005)

Parkhurst, Carolyn, 1971-

Lost and found. Little, Brown and Co. 2006
292p $23.95

Grades: 11 12 Adult **Fic**

1. Television programs—Fiction 2. Contests—Fiction
3. Mother-daughter relationship—Fiction
4. Homosexuality—Fiction 5. Adventure fiction

ISBN 978-0-316-15638-7; 0-316-15638-8
LC 2005-029741

Also available Thorndike Press large print edition

This "novel focuses on several characters competing
on an Amazing Race-like reality show called Lost and
Found, where teams of two travel from destination to
destination following enigmatic clues and collecting various items in hopes of winning the game. Laura wants to
connect with her sullen teenage daughter, Cassie, after a
traumatic experience highlighted the distance between
them. Justin and Abby believe they have cast off their
homosexual urges in favor of a traditional Christian marriage, but the game offers unexpected tests for their resolution. Carl and Jeff are two middle-aged, recently divorced brothers looking for adventure. Juliet and Dallas
are former child stars seeking to recapture fame and willing to do just about anything to achieve that end."
Booklist

"Older teens may find that this book presses just the
right buttons." SLJ

Parks, Gordon, 1912-2006

The learning tree. Ballantine Books 1989 c1963
240p pa $6.99

Grades: 9 10 11 12 **Fic**

1. African Americans—Fiction 2. Kansas—Fiction

ISBN 0-449-21504-0

"A Fawcett Crest book"

Parks, Gordon, 1912-2006—*Continued*
First published 1963 by Harper & Row
"At 12 years of age Newt is awakening to the world around him in his small town of Cherokee Flats, Kansas, in the 1920s. There is the impact of a first sexual experience and a first love, and because he is a Negro, special responsibility of behavior when one individual may represent an entire group in the eyes of the community." Shapiro. Fic for Youth. 3d edition

Pate, Alexs D., 1950-
West of Rehoboth; a novel. Morrow 2001 241p hardcover o.p. pa $12.95
Grades: 11 12 Adult   Fic
1. African Americans—Fiction 2. Delaware—Fiction
ISBN 0-380-97679-X; 0-380-80042-X (pa)
LC 2001-279030
Also available Thorndike Press large print edition
Twelve-year-old Edward Massey, "his mother, and his sister escape the violence in their 1960s Philadelphia neighborhood by spending the summer at Aunt Edna's house in all-black West Rehoboth. Behind Edna's house, a man called Rufus lives in a shack, spending his time drinking or disappearing for days. Edward thought Rufus was his uncle, but Rufus isn't ever allowed in the house, and Edna and his mother forbid any trips to the shack. Sneaking visits with Rufus, Edward finally unravels the mystery—though not without placing himself in grave danger." Booklist

Paterson, Katherine
Lyddie. Lodestar Bks. 1991 182p $17.99; pa $6.99 *
Grades: 5 6 7 8 9   Fic
1. United States—History—1815-1861—Fiction 2. Massachusetts—Fiction 3. Factories—Fiction
ISBN 0-525-67338-5; 0-14-034981-2 (pa)
LC 90-42944
Impoverished Vermont farm girl Lyddie Worthen is determined to gain her independence by becoming a factory worker in Lowell, Massachusetts, in the 1840s
"Not only does the book contain a riveting plot, engaging characters, and a splendid setting, but the language—graceful, evocative, and rhythmic—incorporates the rural speech patterns of Lyddie's folk, the simple Quaker expressions of the farm neighbors, and the lilt of fellow mill girl Bridget's Irish brogue. . . . A superb story of grit, determination, and personal growth." Horn Book

Paton, Alan
Cry, the beloved country. Scribner Classics 2003 316p $28; pa $15
Grades: 7 8 9 10 11 12 Adult   Fic
1. Race relations—Fiction 2. South Africa—Fiction
ISBN 0-7432-6195-X; 0-7432-6217-4 (pa)
First published 1948
"Reverend Kumalo, a black South African preacher, is called to Johannesburg to rescue his sister. There he learns that his son Absalom has been accused of murdering a young white attorney whose interests and sympathies had been with the natives. Despite this, the attorney's father comes to the aid of the minister to help the natives in their struggle to survive a drought." Shapiro. Fic for Youth. 3d edition

Paton Walsh, Jill, 1937-
A parcel of patterns. Farrar, Straus & Giroux 1983 136p hardcover o.p. pa $5.95
Grades: 7 8 9 10   Fic
1. Plague—Fiction 2. Great Britain—Fiction
ISBN 0-374-35750-1; 0-374-45743-3
LC 83-48143
Mall Percival tells how the plague came to her Derbyshire village of Eyam in the year 1665, how the villagers determined to isolate themselves to prevent further spread of the disease, and how three-fourths of them died before the end of the following year.
"Historical in broad outline, the narrative blends superb characterizations, skillful plotting, and convincing speech for a hauntingly memorable story that offers a richly textured picture of the period." Child Book Rev Serv

Paulsen, Gary
Soldier's heart; a novel of the Civil War. Delacorte Press 1998 106p $15.95; pa $5.99 *
Grades: 7 8 9 10   Fic
1. United States—History—1861-1865, Civil War—Fiction 2. Post-traumatic stress disorder—Fiction
ISBN 0-385-32498-7; 0-440-22838-7 (pa)
LC 98-10038
"Being the story of the enlistment and due service of the boy Charley Goddard in the First Minnesota Volunteers." Title page
"This compelling and realistic depiction of war is based on a true story. . . . Paulsen's writing is crisp and fast-paced, and this soldier's story will haunt readers long after they finish reading the novel." Book Rep

Pausewang, Gudrun, 1928-
Traitor; translated from the German by Rachel Ward. Carolrhoda Books 2006 220p $16.95
Grades: 7 8 9 10   Fic
1. World War, 1939-1945—Fiction 2. Germany—Fiction 3. Prisoners of war—Fiction
ISBN 0-8225-6195-6   LC 2005033379
During the closing months of World War II, a fifteen-year-old German girl must decide whether or not to help an escaped Russian prisoner of war, despite the serious consequences if she does so.
"Pausewang presents an exciting and thought-provoking novel." SLJ

Pearson, Mary
A room on Lorelei Street; [by] Mary E. Pearson. Henry Holt 2005 266p $16.95
Grades: 9 10 11 12   Fic
1. Alcoholism—Fiction 2. Family life—Fiction 3. Texas—Fiction
ISBN 0-8050-7667-0   LC 2004-54015
To escape a miserable existence taking care of her alcoholic mother, seventeen-year-old Zoe rents a room from an eccentric woman, but her earnings as a waitress after school are minimal and she must go to extremes to cover expenses.
"Readers drawn to rescue dramas may particularly appreciate this story of a girl who's trying against odds to rescue herself." Bull Cent Child Books

Peck, Richard, 1934-

The river between us. Dial Bks. 2003 164p
$16.99; pa $6.99

Grades: 7 8 9 10   Fic
1. United States—History—1861-1865, Civil War—
Fiction 2. Racially mixed people—Fiction 3. Race relations—Fiction
ISBN 0-8037-2735-6; 0-14-240310-5 (pa)
                             LC 2002-34815
During the early days of the Civil War, the Pruitt family takes in two mysterious young ladies who have fled
New Orleans to come north to Illinois
"The harsh realities of war are brutally related in a
complex, always surprising plot that resonates on mutiple
levels." Horn Book Guide

Peet, Mal

Keeper. Candlewick Press 2005 c2003 225p
$15.99

Grades: 8 9 10 11 12   Fic
1. Soccer—Fiction 2. Brazil—Fiction
ISBN 0-7636-2749-6   LC 2005-50786
First published 2003 in the United Kingdom
In an interview with a young journalist, World Cup
hero, El Gato, describes his youth in the Brazilian rain
forest and the events, experiences, and people that helped
make him a great goalkeeper and renowned soccer star.
"This is a well-written, fast-paced sports story that addresses far more than just the sport itself." SLJ

Tamar. Candlewick Press 2007 424p $17.99
Grades: 8 9 10 11 12   Fic
1. Grandfathers—Fiction 2. World War, 1939-1945—
Fiction 3. Netherlands—Fiction
ISBN 978-0-7636-3488-9; 0-7636-3488-3
                           LC 2006-51837
In 1995, 15-year-old Tamar inherits a box containing
a series of coded messages from his late grandfather. The
messages show Tamar the life that his grandfather lived
during World War II the life of an Allied undercover op-
erative in Nazi-occupied Holland.
"Peet's plot is tightly constructed, and striking, descriptive language, full of metaphor, grounds the story."
Booklist

Pennebaker, Ruth

Don't think twice. Holt & Co. 1996 262p
hardcover o.p. pa $7.95

Grades: 7 8 9 10   Fic
1. Pregnancy—Fiction 2. Unmarried mothers—Fiction
3. Adoption—Fiction
ISBN 0-8050-4407-8; 0-8050-6729-9 (pa)
                           LC 95-20499
Seventeen years old and pregnant, Anne lives with
other unwed mothers in a group home in rural Texas
where she learns to be herself before giving her child up
for adoption
"There is brutal honesty, tempered with sparkling adolescent wit throughout. . . . Some adults might react
with anxiety to the sometimes frank language, to Anne's
negative attitude towards religion, and to a minor segment in which one of the girls explains that she was mo-
lested by a clergyman. It would really be a shame, however, if those factors kept this moving book out of the
hands of teen readers." Voice Youth Advocates

Perkins, Mitali, 1963-

Monsoon summer. Delacorte Press 2004 257p
$15.95; pa $6.50

Grades: 7 8 9 10   Fic
1. India—Fiction 2. East Indians—United States—Fiction
ISBN 0-385-73123-X; 0-440-23840-4 (pa)
                           LC 2003-15168
Secretly in love with her best friend and business partner Steve, fifteen-year-old Jazz must spend the summer
away from him when her family goes to India during
that country's rainy season to help set up a clinic.
This "novel, written in Jazz's smart, funny, self-
deprecating voice, vividly evokes the smells, sights, and
sounds of India in the monsoon season." Booklist

Pesci, David

Amistad; the thunder of freedom. Marlowe &
Co. 1997 292p hardcover o.p. pa $12.95 *

Grades: 11 12 Adult   Fic
1. Adams, John Quincy, 1767-1848—Fiction
2. Amistad (Schooner)—Fiction 3. Slavery—Fiction
4. Trials—Fiction
ISBN 1-56924-748-X; 1-56924-703-X (pa)
                           LC 96-54050
"In August 1839, Singbe-Pleh, a Mende tribesman, led
his fellow African captives aboard the Spanish ship
Amistad in successful revolt. The Africans took over the
ship but could not sail it back to Africa. They were captured and put on trial in Connecticut. . . . The case was
politically charged, with pro-slavery President Van Buren's administration wanting to give the Africans to
Spain, abolitionists rallying for their freedom, and former
President John Quincy Adams eventually defending them
before the Supreme Court. Pesci deftly blends the facts
of this fascinating historical episode with story." SLJ

Peters, Julie Anne, 1952-

Luna; a novel. Little, Brown 2003 248p $16.95;
pa $7.99 *

Grades: 9 10 11 12   Fic
1. Transsexualism—Fiction 2. Siblings—Fiction
ISBN 0-316-73369-5; 0-316-01127-4 (pa)
                           LC 2003-58913
"Megan Tingley books"
Fifteen-year-old Regan's life, which has always re-
volved around keeping her older brother Liam's
transsexuality a secret, changes when Liam decides to
start the process of "transitioning" by first telling his
family and friends that he is a girl who was born in a
boy's body
"The author gradually reveals the issues facing a
transgender teen, educating readers without feeling too
instructional (Luna and Regan discuss lingo, hormones
and even sex change operations). Flashbacks throughout
help round out the story, explaining Liam/Luna's
longtime struggle with a dual existence, and funny, sar-
castic-but-strong Regan narrates with an authentic voice
that will draw readers into this new territory." Publ Wkly

Philbrick, W. R. (W. Rodman)
The last book in the universe; by Rodman Philbrick. Blue Sky Press (NY) 2001 223p $16.95; pa $5.99
Grades: 9 10 11 12   **Fic**
  1. Science fiction 2. Epilepsy—Fiction
  ISBN 0-439-08758-9; 0-439-08759-7 (pa)
                           LC 99-59878
Expanded from a short story in Tomorrowland edited by Michael Cart, published 1999 by Scholastic Press
After an earthquake has destroyed much of the planet, an epileptic teenager nicknamed Spaz begins the heroic fight to bring human intelligence back to the Earth of a distant future
"Enthralling, thought-provoking, and unsettling." Voice Youth Advocates

Picoult, Jodi, 1966-
My sister's keeper; a novel. Atria 2004 423p $25; pa $15 *
Grades: 11 12 Adult   **Fic**
  1. Sisters—Fiction 2. Mother-daughter relationship—Fiction 3. Bioethics—Fiction
  ISBN 0-7434-5452-9; 0-7434-5453-7 (pa)
               LC 2004-300043
"Thirteen-year-old Anna knows that she was conceived to provide life support for her critically ill sister. After enduring multiple surgeries, she sues her parents for the rights to her own body." Booklist
"Picoult's timely and compelling novel will appeal to anyone who has thought about the morality of medical decision making and any parent who must balance the needs of different children." Libr J

Pierce, Tamora, 1954-
Terrier. Random House 2006 581p il map (Beka Cooper) $18.95; lib bdg $20.99
Grades: 7 8 9 10   **Fic**
  1. Police—Fiction 2. Fantasy fiction 3. Magic—Fiction
  ISBN 978-0-375-81468-6; 0-375-81468-X; 978-0-375-91468-3 (lib bdg); 0-375-91468-4 (lib bdg)
              LC 2006-14834
When sixteen-year-old Beka becomes "Puppy" to a pair of "Dogs," as the Provost's Guards are called, she uses her police training, natural abilities and a touch of magic to help them solve the case of a murdered baby in Tortall's Lower City.
"Pierce deftly handles the novel's journal structure, and her clear homage to the police-procedural genre applies a welcome twist to the girl-legend-in-the-making story line." Booklist

The will of the empress. Scholastic Press 2005 550p $17.99; pa $8.99
Grades: 9 10 11 12   **Fic**
  1. Fantasy fiction
  ISBN 0-439-44171-4; 0-439-44172-2 (pa)
             LC 2005-02874
On visit to Namorn to visit her vast landholdings and her devious cousin, Empress Berenene, eighteen-year-old Sandry must rely on her childhood friends and fellow mages, Daja, Tris, and Briar, despite the distance that has grown between them
"This novel begins two years after the Circle of Magic and The Circle Opens series. . . . Readers will enjoy being reacquainted with these older but still very well-developed characters." SLJ

Placide, Jaira
Fresh girl. Wendy Lamb Bks. 2002 216p $15.95
Grades: 7 8 9 10   **Fic**
  1. Haitian Americans—Fiction 2. Haiti—Fiction 3. Brooklyn (New York, N.Y.)—Fiction
  ISBN 0-385-32753-6   LC 2001-32427
After having been sent, at a very young age, from New York to live with her grandmother in Haiti, fourteen-year-old Mardi returns to join her parents and try to shape a new life in Brooklyn
"The heart of the story is Mardi's relationship with her uncle, who helps her confront, first, her anger toward him and finally the horror of her rape when the soldiers came. The violence isn't sensationalized, and readers will appreciate that by the end, Mardi is beginning to feel at home." Booklist

Plath, Sylvia
The bell jar; foreword by Frances McCullough; biographical note by Lois Ames; drawings by Sylvia Plath. 25th anniversary ed. HarperCollins Publishers 1996 296p il $20; pa $16.95 *
                               Fic
  1. Mental illness—Fiction
  ISBN 0-06-017490-0; 0-06-114851-2 (pa)
             LC 96-211742
First published 1963 in the United Kingdom; first United States edition published 1971
"Esther Greenwood, having spent what should have been a glorious summer as guest editor for a young woman's magazine, came home from New York, had a nervous breakdown, and tried to commit suicide. Through months of therapy, Esther kept her rationality, if not her sanity. In telling the story of Esther Plath thinly disguised her own experience with attempted suicide and time spent in an institution." Shapiro. Fic for Youth. 3d edition

Porter, Connie Rose
Imani all mine; [by] Connie Porter. Houghton Mifflin 1999 212p hardcover o.p. pa $12
Grades: 11 12 Adult   **Fic**
  1. African Americans—Fiction 2. Unmarried mothers—Fiction 3. Rape—Fiction
  ISBN 0-395-83808-8; 0-618-05678-5 (pa)
             LC 98-37722
"Tasha is 15, an honors student struggling to live up to her mother's dreams of college and life beyond their poor black neighborhood. She is also a rape victim and a single mother, determined that she alone will give her baby, Imani, a good future in the midst of poverty, drugs, gangs, and ignorance. Even the baby's name is a sign of Tasha's hope—Imani means 'faith.' When gang violence assaults her family, Tasha's innocence is shattered, and she must summon every ounce of strength within her to survive." Libr J
The narrative, "told in Tasha's voice, is the story of great promise shining through monstrous obstacles." N Y Times Book Rev

Portman, Frank

King Dork. Delacorte Press 2006 344p il
$16.95; lib bdg $18.99

Grades: 10 11 12 Fic

1. Salinger, J. D. (Jerome David), 1919-—Fiction
2. Fathers—Fiction 3. School stories

ISBN   0-385-73291-0;   978-0-385-73291-8;
0-385-90312-X (lib bdg); 978-0-385-90312-7 (lib bdg)
LC 2005-12556

High school loser Tom Henderson discovers that "The
Catcher in the Rye" may hold the clues to the many
mysteries in his life.

"Mature situations, casual sexual experiences, and allusions to Salinger suggest an older teen audience, who
will also best appreciate the appended bandography and
the very funny glossary." Booklist

Potok, Chaim, 1929-2002

The chosen; a novel; with a foreword by the
author. 25th anniversary ed. Knopf 1992 c1967
295p hardcover o.p. pa $13.95 *

Grades: 11 12 Adult Fic

1. Jews—New York (N.Y.)—Fiction

ISBN 0-679-40222-5; 0-449-91154-3 (pa)
LC 91-58551

Available in hardcover from Holt, Rinehart and Winston

A reissue of the title first published 1967 by Simon &
Schuster

"Living only five blocks apart in the Williamsburg
section of Brooklyn, New York, Danny and Reuven meet
as opponents in a softball game. Out of this encounter
evolves a strong bond of friendship between a brilliant
Hasidic Jew and a scholar who is Orthodox in his religious thinking. During the course of their relationship
Reuven becomes the means by which Danny's father, a
rabbi, can communicate with his son, who has been
reared under a code of silence." Shapiro. Fic for Youth.
2d edition

Another title about Danny and Reuven is:
The promise (1969)

Powell, Randy

Three clams and an oyster. Farrar, Straus &
Giroux 2002 216p $16; pa $6.95 *

Grades: 7 8 9 10 Fic

1. Friendship—Fiction 2. Football—Fiction

ISBN 0-374-37526-7; 0-374-40007-5 (pa)
LC 2001-54833

During their humorous search to find a fourth player
for their flag football team, three high school juniors are
forced to examine their long friendship, their individual
flaws, and their inability to try new experiences

"Sometimes philosophical, sometimes comical, but always touching, Randy Powell writes an unusually moving story of adolescent male friends." Book Rep

Power, Susan, 1961-

The grass dancer. Putnam 1994 300p hardcover
o.p. pa $7.99 *

Grades: 11 12 Adult Fic

1. Dakota Indians—Fiction

ISBN 0-399-13911-7; 0-425-14962-5 (pa)
LC 93-47199

"Set on a North Dakota reservation, 'The Grass Dancer' tells the story of Harley Wind Soldier, a young Sioux
trying to understand his place among people whose intertwined lives and shared heritage move backward in time
in the narrative from the 1980's to the middle of the last
century." N Y Times Book Rev

This "is a passionate portrayal of universal human
emotions and a vivid account of Native American history
and culture." SLJ

Pratchett, Terry

The amazing Maurice and his educated rodents.
HarperCollins Pubs. 2001 241p $16.95; lib bdg
$17.89; pa $6.99

Grades: 7 8 9 10 Fic

1. Fantasy fiction 2. Rats—Fiction 3. Cats—Fiction

ISBN 0-06-001233-1; 0-06-001234-X (lib bdg);
0-06-001235-8 (pa) LC 2001-42411

A talking cat, intelligent rats, and a strange boy coop-
erate in a Pied Piper scam until they try to con the
wrong town and are confronted by a deadly evil rat king

"In this laugh-out-loud fantasy, his first 'Discworld'
novel for younger readers, Pratchett rethinks a classic
story and comes up with a winner." SLJ

Price, Charlie

Dead connection. Roaring Brook Press 2006
225p $16.95 *

Grades: 8 9 10 11 12 Fic

1. Ghost stories 2. Homicide—Fiction

ISBN 1-59643-114-8; 978-1-59643-114-0
LC 2005-17138

"A Deborah Brodie book"

A loner who communes with the dead in the town
cemetery hears the voice of a murdered cheerleader and
tries to convince the adults that he knows what happened
to her

"Readers will like the edginess and be intrigued by
the extrasensory elements as well as the darker turns the
mystery takes. This is something different." Booklist

Provoost, Anne, 1964-

In the shadow of the ark; translated by John
Nieuwenhuizen. Arthur A. Levine Books 2004
368p $17.95

Grades: 9 10 11 12 Fic

1. Noah's ark—Fiction

ISBN 0-439-44234-6 LC 2003-9622

Also available in paperback from Berkley

Original Dutch edition, 2001

This is a "story of the biblical Flood, recounted by Re
Jana, whose family leaves the marshes to find the ark.
The passion Re Jana finds with Ham, son of the Builder,
leads to a place on the ark, but this 'safe haven,' with
the stink and sounds of the animals, starvation, and repeated (if not lustful) rapes by Ham's brothers, tests her
in every way, even as she carries new life into the New
World. Exquisitely detailed and intelligently written, this
is a YA novel only in the broadest sense; no one would
blink if it appeared on an adult list." Booklist

Pullman, Philip, 1946-

The golden compass; his dark materials book I; [appendix illustrations by Ian Beck] Deluxe 10th anniversary ed. Alfred A. Knopf 2006 399p il $22.95; lib bdg $24.99 *

Grades: 7 8 9 10 11 12   **Fic**
1. Fantasy fiction
ISBN   978-0-375-83830-9;   0-375-83830-9; 978-0-375-93830-6 (lib bdg); 0-375-93830-3 (lib bdg)
LC 2005-32556

First published 1995 in the United Kingdom with title: Northern lights

Includes "Some papers from the Library at Jordan College" and other materials that complement the original text

This first title in a fantasy trilogy "introduces the characters and sets up the basic conflict, namely, a race to unlock the mystery of a newly discovered type of charged particles simply called 'dust' that may be a bridge to an alternate universe. The action follows 11-year-old protagonist Lyra Belacqua from her home at Oxford University to the frozen wastes of the North on a quest to save dozens of kidnapped children from the evil 'Gobblers,' who are using them as part of a sinister experiment involving dust." Libr J [review of 1996 edition]

Other titles in the His dark materials series are:
The amber spyglass (2000)
The subtle knife (1997)

The ruby in the smoke. Knopf 1987 c1985 230p hardcover o.p. pa $6.50 *

Grades: 7 8 9 10   **Fic**
1. Mystery fiction 2. Orphans—Fiction 3. London (England)—Fiction
ISBN 0-394-88826-x; 0-394-89589-4 (pa)
LC 86-20983

First published 1985 in the United Kingdom

This story "begins in 1872 on a 'cold, fretful' October afternoon in London. Sally Lockhart is the 16-year-old heroine who asks some innocent questions about her father's death that lead her into a world of stolen rubies and the opium trade." N Y Times Book Rev

"Pullman uses a cliff-hanger at the end of each chapter to keep readers enthralled in this fast-paced, intricate, and suspenseful novel. Sally's complex characterization as a resourceful, yet occasionally unsure, young woman, makes her both likable and memorable." Voice Youth Advocates

Other titles in the Sally Lockhart series are:
The shadow in the North (1988)
The tiger in the well (1990)

Rabb, Margo

Cures for heartbreak. Delacorte Press 2007 238p $15.99; lib bdg $18.99

Grades: 9 10 11 12   **Fic**
1. Parent-child relationship—Fiction 2. Death—Fiction 3. New York (N.Y.)—Fiction
ISBN   978-0-385-73402-8;   0-385-73402-6; 978-0-385-90414-8 (lib bdg); 0-385-90414-2 (lib bdg)
LC 2006-7333

As she navigates adolescence, ninth-grader Mia must deal with her mother's recent death and her father's illness while she searches for friendship and love in the world around her.

"Black humor, pitch-perfect detail, and compelling characters make this a terrific read, despite the pain that permeates every superbly written page." SLJ

Randle, Kristen D., 1952-

Breaking rank. Morrow Junior Bks. 1999 201p $15.95 *

Grades: 7 8 9 10   **Fic**
1. Gangs—Fiction 2. School stories
ISBN 0-688-16243-6   LC 98-27867

Seventeen-year-old Casey has some of her preconceived notions challenged when she begins to tutor Baby, a member of a ganglike non-conformist society called the Clan

"The alternating points of view and Randle's taut, poetic prose provide remarkable character depth and complexity. . . . Gritty, smart, and realistic, the novel perceptively explores issues of religion, sex and sexual abstinence, peer pressure, and integrity with grace and compassion." Booklist

Rapp, Adam

Under the wolf, under the dog. Candlewick Press 2004 310p $16.99 *

Grades: 9 10 11 12   **Fic**
1. Suicide—Fiction 2. Family life—Fiction 3. Illinois—Fiction
ISBN 0-7636-1818-7   LC 2004-50255

"Steve currently resides in a facility for troubled youth, but most are here for drug abuse or suicidal tendencies, and he doesn't really fit in either category. What's led him here, as he describes in his journal, is a series of life depredations that have sent him reeling into irrationality: his mother's long, horrible, and unsuccessful bout with cancer, his father's concomitant catatonic depression, his brother's drug-induced haze and subsequent suicide, and his own unintentional self-woundings along the way, from a lacerated leg to an injury that eventually results in blindness in one eye." Bull Cent Child Books

Rawles, Nancy, 1958-

My Jim; a novel. Crown Publishers 2005 174p hardcover o.p. pa $12.95

Grades: 9 10 11 12   **Fic**
1. Slavery—Fiction 2. African Americans—Fiction
ISBN 1-400-05400-1; 1-400-05401-X (pa)
LC 2004-11606

In this "retelling of the story of escaped slave Jim from Mark Twain's The Adventures of Huckleberry Finn, Rawles shifts the focus to Jim's wife, Sadie, whose unspeakable losses set the tone for Jim's flight." Publ Wkly

"Students reading Huckleberry Finn are a prime audience for this accessible and revealing new story, but teens who enjoy family romance or contemporary African American fiction will be rewarded and bring insight to the older text when later meeting it." Voice Youth Advocates

Razzell, Mary, 1930-

Snow apples. Groundwood Books 2006 209p
$15.95; pa $6.95

Grades: 9 10 11 12   **Fic**

1.   Mother-daughter   relationship—Fiction
2. Pregnancy—Fiction 3. British Columbia—Fiction

ISBN   0-88899-741-8;   978-0-88899-741-8;
0-88899-728-0 (pa); 978-0-88899-728-9 (pa)

First published 1984 in Canada

"In isolated, rural British Columbia, as World War II
is ending, Sheila Brary turns 16 and yearns for a life different from the sad existence of her mother. Struggling
to raise four sons and a daughter mostly on her own, the
woman has turned hard and cold, always angry at her
bright and emotional daughter who reminds her too much
of her unfaithful, undependable husband. . . . The teen
wins one struggle with her mother and manages to finish
high school, while she loses another with her own awakening sexuality and finds herself desperate and pregnant.
When she runs off to Vancouver, her distant father helps
her to abort the pregnancy and then abandons her one
last time. Sheila survives a terrifying miscarriage on her
own, returns to her family long enough to see what her
mother has sacrificed, and starts a new life with promise
and support. This is a quiet, introspective novel that
takes a while to build its power, and it has some stunningly dramatic scenes." SLJ

Reasoner, James

Manassas. Cumberland House 1999 336p $22.95

Grades: 9 10 11 12   **Fic**

1. United States—History—1861-1865, Civil War—
Fiction

ISBN 1-58182-008-9   LC 98-52494

This novel focuses on "the Brannon clan of Culpepper
County, Virginia. . . . Fiercely devoted to the Confederacy and to each other, the six Brannon siblings anxiously
await news of secession as a deadly feud erupts between
Will Brannon, sheriff of Culpepper County, and the law-
less Fogarty gang. When Will shoots and kills Joe
Fogarty, he is forced to leave the family farm in order
to ensure the safety of his mother, his sister, and his
brothers. Enlisting in the Army of Northern Virginia,
Will prepares for the Battle of Manassas, where he must
face both the Union army and the surviving Fogarty
brothers. Fraught with tension, drama, and tantalizing
hints of future romance, this vividly rendered family saga
will hook fans of meaty historical fiction." Booklist

Other titles in the Civil War battle series are:

Shiloh (1999)
Chancellorsville (2000)
Vicksburg (2001)
Gettysburg (2001)
Chickamauga (2002)
Shenandoah (2002)
Savannah (2003)
Appomattox (2003)

Rees, Celia, 1949-

Pirates! the true and remarkable adventures of
Minerva Sharpe and Nancy Kington, female
pirates. Bloomsbury 2003 379p $16.95; pa $8.95

Grades: 9 10 11 12   **Fic**

1. Pirates—Fiction 2. Adventure fiction 3. Sea stories
4. Jamaica—Fiction

ISBN 1-582-34816-2; 1-582-34665-8 (pa)

                 LC 2003-51861

Also available Thorndike Press large print edition

In 1722, after arriving with her brother at the family's
Jamaican plantation where she is to be married off, sixteen-year-old Nancy Kington escapes with her slave
friend, Minerva Sharpe, and together they become pirates
traveling the world in search of treasure.

"There's action aplenty . . . with storms and sea battles and a devilish suitor hot on the heels of an innocent
(except for the odd murder here and there) heroine. Add
popcorn and a supersized soda, and you've got a rousing
Saturday matinee." Bull Cent Child Books

Reeve, Philip, 1966-

Mortal engines; a novel. Eos 2003 c2001 310p
(Hungry city chronicles) $16.99; lib bdg $17.89

Grades: 7 8 9 10   **Fic**

1. Science fiction

ISBN 0-06-008207-0; 0-06-008208-9 (lib bdg)

                 LC 2002-38801

First published 2001 in the United Kingdom

In the distant future, when cities move about and con-
sume smaller towns, a fifteen-year-old apprentice is
pushed out of London by the man he most admires and
must seek answers in the perilous Out-Country, aided by
one girl and the memory of another.

"A page-turner, this adventure in a city-eat-city world
will have readers eagerly suspending disbelief to follow
the twists and turns of the imaginative plot." Booklist

Other titles in this series are:

Predator's gold (2004)
Infernal devices (2006)
A darkling plain (2007)

Reinhardt, Dana

A brief chapter in my impossible life. Wendy
Lamb Books 2006 228p $15.95; lib bdg $17.99

Grades: 9 10 11 12   **Fic**

1. Adoption—Fiction 2. Jews—Fiction 3. Family
life—Fiction 4. Massachusetts—Fiction

ISBN 0-385-74698-9; 0-385-90940-3 (lib bdg)

                 LC 2005-3972

Sixteen-year-old atheist Simone Turner-Bloom's life
changes in unexpected ways when her parents convince
her to make contact with her biological mother, an agnostic from a Jewish family who is losing her battle with
cancer.

"Besides offering insight into the customs of Hasidic
Jews, this intimate story celebrates family love and promotes tolerance of diverse beliefs. Readers will quickly
become absorbed in Simone's quest to understand her
heritage and herself." Publ Wkly

Remarque, Erich Maria, 1898-1970

All quiet on the western front; translated from the German by A. W. Wheen. Little, Brown 1929 291p $24.95 *

Grades: 11 12 Adult   Fic
  1. World War, 1914-1918—Fiction
  ISBN 0-316-73992-8
Also available in paperback from Fawcett Bks.

"Four German youths are pulled abruptly from school to serve at the front as soldiers in World War I. Only Paul survives, and he contemplates the needless violation of the human body by weapons of war. No longer innocent or lighthearted, he is repelled by the slaughter of soldiers and questions the usefulness of war as a means of adjudication. Although the young men in this novel are German, the message is universal in its delineation of the feelings of the common soldier." Shapiro. Fic for Youth. 3d edition

Followed by The road back

Renault, Mary, 1905-1983

Fire from heaven. 2nd Vintage Books ed. Vintage Books 2002 375p map pa $14.95

Grades: 11 12 Adult   Fic
  1. Alexander, the Great, 356-323 B.C.—Fiction 2. Philip II, King of Macedonia, 382-336 B.C.—Fiction 3. Greece—Fiction
  ISBN 0-375-72682-9   LC 2002-282848
First published 1969 by Pantheon Bks.

"This is the story of Alexander the Great from his earliest childhood until the death of his father, Philip of Macedonia. . . . We meet everyone who ever influenced the young Alexander—Aristotle, his teacher; Hephaiston, his friend and lover; Olympias, his strange priestess mother; and scores of others. This was a time of ritual feasts and bacchanalian orgies, of unbashed sexual freedom, of bloody wars and insidious plottings, of pageantry and splendor, myths and mysteries." Publ Wkly
  Other books in this fictional series about the life of Alexander the Great are:
The Persian boy (1972)
Funeral games (1981)

The king must die. Pantheon Bks. 1958 338p pa $14 hardcover o.p. *

Grades: 11 12 Adult   Fic
  1. Theseus (Greek Mythology)—Fiction 2. Classical mythology—Fiction 3. Greece—Fiction
  ISBN 0-394-75104-3
"Retold by its hero, the legend of Theseus becomes a logical sequence of adventures that befell a slight, wiry, quick-witted youth impelled to prove his manhood in a semibarbaric society that put a premium on size and brawn. Although, at seventeen, he was already a king and a seasoned warrior, Theseus obeyed his patron god's prompting and voluntarily joined a company of young people conscripted for the bull-dances in Crete, became a renowned bull-leaper, and took advantage of an earthquake to overthrow the Cretan kingdom." Booklist

Followed by The bull from the sea (1962)

Rennison, Louise, 1951-

Angus, thongs and full-frontal snogging; confessions of Georgia Nicolson. HarperCollins Pubs. 2000 c1999 247p $15.95; lib bdg $17.89; pa $6.95 *

Grades: 7 8 9 10   Fic
  1. Great Britain—Fiction
  ISBN 0-06-028814-0; 0-06-028871-X (lib bdg); 0-06-447227-2 (pa)   LC 99-40591
First published 1999 in the United Kingdom
Presents the humorous journal of a year in the life of Georgia, a fourteen-year-old British girl who tries to reduce the size of her nose, stop her mad cat from terrorizing the neighborhood animals, and win the love of handsome hunk Robbie

"Georgia is a wonderful character whose misadventures are not only hysterically funny but universally recognizable." Booklist
  Other titles about Georgia are:
Away laughing on a fast camel (2004)
Dancing in my nuddy-pants (2003)
Knocked out by my nunga-nungas (2002)
Love is a many trousered thing (2007)
On the bright side, I'm now the girlfriend of a sex god (2001)
Startled by his furry shorts (2006)
Then he ate my boy entrancers (2005)

Ritter, John H., 1951-

Under the baseball moon. Philomel Books 2006 283p $16.99

Grades: 7 8 9 10   Fic
  1. Softball—Fiction 2. Musicians—Fiction 3. California—Fiction
  ISBN 0-399-23623-6   LC 2005-27183
Andy and Glory, two fifteen-year-olds from Ocean Beach, California, pursue their respective dreams of becoming a famous musician and a professional softball player.

"Andy's poetic first-person narrative superbly catches the weird uniqueness of Ocean Beach and briskly moves the . . . story to a satisfying conclusion." SLJ

Robinson, Kim Stanley

Forty signs of rain. Bantam Books 2004 358p hardcover o.p. pa $7.99

Grades: 9 10 11 12   Fic
  1. Science fiction 2. Washington (D.C.)—Fiction
  ISBN 0-553-80311-5; 0-553-58580-0 (pa)
            LC 2003-63683
"The specter of global warming looms over the personal and professional lives of several scientists at the National Science Foundation and the delegation of Buddhist refugees from a drowned nation, who open an embassy next door." SLJ

The author's "portrayal of how actual scientists would deal with this disaster-in-the-making is utterly convincing. Robinson clearly cares deeply about our planet's future, and he makes the reader care as well." Publ Wkly
  Other titles in this series are:
Fifty degrees below (2005)
Sixty days and counting (2007)

Robinson, Kim Stanley—*Continued*

Red Mars. Bantam Books 1993 519p il hardcover o.p. pa $7.99

Grades: 11 12 Adult   **Fic**
1. Mars (Planet)—Fiction 2. Science fiction
ISBN 0-553-09204-9; 0-553-56073-5 (pa)
LC 92-21607

This novel, the first of a trilogy "concerns the first permanent settlement on Mars, a multinational band of 100 hardy experts, and their mission—to begin making Mars habitable for humans by releasing underground water and oxygen into the atmosphere. Unfortunately, they are divided over whether this is a desirable step in human evolution or an ecological crime." Booklist

"A novel fully inhabited both by detailed technical processes and by people whose careers those processes are; it is also a novel with a complex sense of political reality. . . . This is one of the finest works of American SF because it is one of the few that aspire to the dignity of the genuinely tragic." Times Lit Suppl

Other titles in the Mars trilogy are:
Green Mars (1994)
Blue Mars (1996)

Rosoff, Meg

How I live now. Wendy Lamb Books 2004 194p $16.95; lib bdg $18.99; pa $7.99 *

Grades: 7 8 9 10   **Fic**
1. War stories 2. Cousins—Fiction 3. Great Britain—Fiction
ISBN 0-385-74677-6; 0-385-90908-X (lib bdg); 0-553-37605-5 (pa)   LC 2004-6443

To get away from her pregnant stepmother in New York City, fifteen-year-old Daisy goes to England to stay with her aunt and cousins, with whom she instantly bonds, but soon war breaks out and rips apart the family while devastating the land

"Teens may feel that they have experienced a war themselves as they vicariously witness Daisy's worst nightmares. Like the heroine, readers will emerge from the rubble much shaken, a little wiser and with perhaps a greater sense of humanity." Publ Wkly

Roth, Philip

The plot against America. Houghton Mifflin 2004 391p $26

Grades: 11 12 Adult   **Fic**
1. Lindbergh, Charles, 1902-1974—Fiction 2. Jews—Fiction 3. New Jersey—Fiction 4. Antisemitism—Fiction
ISBN 0-618-50928-3   LC 2004-47490
Also available in paperback from Vintage

In this alternative history novel, "Charles Lindbergh is elected president in 1940 on a pro-Nazi platform, and a Jewish family in Newark suffers the consequences." N Y Times Book Rev

This book "engages readers in many ways. It prompts them to consider the nature of history, present times, and possible futures, and can lead to good discussions among thoughtful readers and teachers." SLJ

Rowling, J. K.

Harry Potter and the Sorcerer's Stone; illustrations by Mary Grandpré. Arthur A. Levine Bks. 1998 c1997 309p il $22.99; pa $8.99 *

Grades: 4 5 6 7 8 9 10   **Fic**
1. Fantasy fiction 2. Witches—Fiction
ISBN 0-590-35340-3; 0-590-35342-X (pa)
LC 97-39059

First published 1997 in the United Kingdom with title: Harry Potter and the Philosopher's Stone

Rescued from the outrageous neglect of his aunt and uncle, a young boy with a great destiny proves his worth while attending Hogwarts School for Witchcraft and Wizardry.

This "is a brilliantly imagined and beautifully written fantasy." Booklist

Other titles about Harry Potter are:
Harry Potter and the Chamber of Secrets (1999)
Harry Potter and prisoner of Azkaban (1999)
Harry Potter and Goblet of Fire (2000)
Harry Potter and the Order of the Phoenix (2003)
Harry Potter and the Half-Blood Prince (2005)
Harry Potter and the Deathly Hallows (2007)

Roy, Arundhati

The god of small things. HarperPerennial 1998 321p pa $14.95

Grades: 11 12 Adult   **Fic**
1. Family life—Fiction
ISBN 0-06-097749-3   LC 97-32562
First published 1997 by Random House

A novel "set in the tiny river town of Ayemenem in Kerala, India. The story revolves around a pair of twins, brother and sister, whose mother has left her violent husband to live with her blind mother and kind, if ineffectual, brother, Chacko. Chacko's ex-wife, an Englishwoman, has returned to Ayemenem after a long absence, bringing along her and Chacko's lovely young daughter. Their arrival not only unsettles the already tenuous balance of the divisive household, it also coincides with political unrest." Booklist

"If the symbolism is a trifle overdone, the lush local color and the incisive characterizations give the narrative power and drama." Publ Wkly

Rushdie, Salman

Haroun and the sea of stories. Granta Books in association with Viking 1990 219p pa $14 hardcover o.p.

Grades: 9 10 11 12 Adult   **Fic**
1. Allegories
ISBN 0-14-015737-9 (pa)   LC 90-45496

"This delightful fantasy is filled with adventures, amusing characters with names like Iff and Butt, and villains to fight against and defeat. Rushdie's puns and rhymes will be enjoyed by young and old—the catchy tunes by the younger readers and the political allegory by the adults. Rashid is a professional story-teller whose son, Haroun, delights in hearing them. When Rashid's source of stories seems to have disappeared Haroun faces many dangerous opponents to help his father regain his Gift of Gab." Shapiro. Fic for Youth. 3d edition

Russon, Penni

Undine. Greenwillow Books 2006 c2004 326p $15.99; lib bdg $16.89

Grades: 8 9 10 11 12   **Fic**
1. Magic—Fiction 2. Father-daughter relationship—Fiction 3. Australia—Fiction
ISBN 0-06-079389-9; 0-06-079390-2 (lib bdg)
     LC 2004-59757

First published 2004 in Australia

Sixteen-year-old Undine, hearing her presumably deceased father calling to her and feeling a strange force growing inside her, travels to the sea to discover the depths of her magical powers.

"The strength of Russon's writing and the intensity of the story itself will draw readers to Undine, but they will also find some familiar themes, such as unrequited love." SLJ

Followed by Breathe (2007)

Saenz, Benjamin Alire

Sammy and Juliana in Hollywood; by Benjamin Alire Saenz. Cinco Puntos Press 2004 294p $18.95 *

Grades: 9 10 11 12   **Fic**
1. Mexican Americans—Fiction 2. Violence—Fiction 3. New Mexico—Fiction
ISBN 0-938317-81-4   LC 2004-2414

Also available in paperback from Rayo

As a Chicano boy living in the unglamorous town of Hollywood, New Mexico, and a member of the graduating class of 1969, Sammy Santos faces the challenges of "gringo" racism, unpopular dress codes, the Vietnam War, barrio violence, and poverty

Saint-Exupéry, Antoine de, 1900-1944

The little prince; written and illustrated by Antoine de Saint-Exupery; translated from the French by Richard Howard. Harcourt 2000 83p il $18; pa $12

Grades: 11 12 Adult   **Fic**
1. Allegories
ISBN 0-15-202398-4; 0-15-601219-7 (pa)
     LC 99-50439

A new translation of the title first published 1943 by Reynal & Hitchcock

"This many-dimensional fable of an airplane pilot who has crashed in the desert is for readers of all ages. The pilot comes upon the little prince soon after the crash. The prince tells of his adventures on different planets and on Earth as he attempts to learn about the universe in order to live peacefully on his own small planet. A spiritual quality enhances the seemingly simple observations of the little prince." Shapiro. Fic for Youth. 3d edition

Salinger, J. D. (Jerome David), 1919-

The catcher in the rye. Little, Brown 1951 277p $24.95; pa $5.99 *

Grades: 11 12 Adult   **Fic**
1. New York (N.Y.)—Fiction
ISBN 0-316-76953-3; 0-316-76948-7 (pa)

"The story of adolescent Holden Caulfield who runs away from boarding-school in Pennsylvania to New York where he preserves his innocence despite various attempts to lose it. The colloquial, lively, first-person narration, with its attacks on the 'phoniness' of the adult world and its clinging to family sentiment in the form of Holden's affection for his sister Phoebe, made the novel accessible to and popular with a wide readership, particularly with the young." Oxford Companion to Engl Lit. 5th edition

Franny & Zooey. Little, Brown 1961 201p $24.95; pa $5.99

Grades: 11 12 Adult   **Fic**
1. Family life—Fiction 2. New York (N.Y.)—Fiction
ISBN 0-316-76954-1; 0-316-76949-5 (pa)

"At 20, Franny Glass is experiencing desperate dissatisfaction with her life and seems to be looking for help via a religious awakening. Her brother Zooey tries to help her out of this depression. He recalls the influence on their growth and development of their appearance as young radio performers on a network program called 'It's a Wise Child.' An older brother, Buddy, is also an important component of the interrelationships in the Glass family." Shapiro. Fic for Youth. 3d edition

Raise high the roof beam, carpenters, and Seymour: an introduction. Little, Brown 1963 248p $24.95

Grades: 11 12 Adult   **Fic**
1. Family life—Fiction 2. New York (N.Y.)—Fiction
ISBN 0-316-76957-6

This volume "reprints stories from *The New Yorker* (1955, 1959), in which Buddy Glass tells, first, of his return to New York during the war to attend his brother Seymour's wedding and of Seymour's jilting of the bride and then of their later elopement; and, second, after Seymour's suicide, of Buddy's own brooding, to the point of breakdown, upon Seymour's virtues, human and literary." Oxford Companion to Am Lit. 6th edition

Salisbury, Graham, 1944-

Eyes of the emperor. Wendy Lamb Books 2005 228p $15.95; lib bdg $17.99; pa $6.50 *

Grades: 7 8 9 10   **Fic**
1. World War, 1939-1945—Fiction 2. Japanese Americans—Fiction
ISBN 0-385-72971-5; 0-385-90874-1 (lib bdg); 0-440-22956-8 (pa)   LC 2004-15142

Following orders from the United States Army, several young Japanese American men train K-9 units to hunt Asians during World War II.

"Based on the experiences of 26 Hawaiian-Americans of Japanese ancestry, this novel tells an uncomfortable story. Yet it tells of belief in honor, respect, and love of country." Libr Media Connect

Jungle dogs. Delacorte Press 1998 183p pa $4.99 *

Grades: 9 10 11 12   **Fic**
1. Wild dogs—Fiction 2. Brothers—Fiction 3. Hawaii—Fiction
ISBN 0-385-32187-2; 0-440-41573-X (pa)
     LC 98-5561

While worrying about the wild dogs that supposedly lurk in the jungle along his paper route, Hawaiian sixth

Salisbury, Graham, 1944-—*Continued*
grader Boy Regis also seeks to stop his older brother Damon from fighting all his battles for him.
"The novel boasts a compelling narrative voice, a sympathetic protagonist, and throws in enough drama to bring the story to a satisfying end." ALAN

Under the blood-red sun. Delacorte Press 1994 246p pa $5.99 *
Grades: 9 10 11 12   **Fic**
1. Pearl Harbor (Oahu, Hawaii), Attack on, 1941—Fiction 2. World War, 1939-1945—Fiction 3. Japanese Americans—Fiction 4. Hawaii—Fiction
ISBN 0-385-32099-X; 0-440-41139-4 (pa)
                                        LC 94-444
Tomikazu Nakaji's biggest concerns are baseball, homework, and a local bully, until life with his Japanese family in Hawaii changes drastically after the bombing of Pearl Harbor in December 1941
"Character development of major figures is good, the setting is warmly realized, and the pace of the story moves gently though inexorably forward." SLJ

Sanchez, Alex, 1957-
Rainbow boys. Simon & Schuster 2001 233p $17
Grades: 10 11 12   **Fic**
1. Homosexuality—Fiction 2. School stories
ISBN 0-689-84100-0   LC 2001-20952
Three high school seniors, a jock with a girlfriend and an alcoholic father, a closeted gay, and a flamboyant gay rights advocate, struggle with family issues, gay bashers, first sex, and conflicting feelings about each other.
"Some of the language and sexual situations may be too mature for some readers, but overall there's enough conflict, humor and tenderness to make this story believable—and touching." Publ Wkly
Other titles featuring Nelson, Kyle, and Jason are:
Rainbow High (2004)
Rainbow road (2005)

Saroyan, William, 1908-1981
The human comedy. Rev by the author. Dell 1971 192p pa $7.50
Grades: 7 8 9 10 11 12 Adult   **Fic**
1. California—Fiction 2. Family life—Fiction
ISBN 0-440-33933-2
First published 1944 by Harcourt, Brace and Company
"Homer, the narrator, identifies himself in this novel as a night messenger for the Postal Telegraph office. He creates a view of family life in the 1940s in a small town in California. His mother, Ma Macauley, presides over the family and takes care of four children after her husband dies. Besides Homer, there is Marcus, the oldest, who is in the army; Bess; and Ulysses, the youngest, who describes the world from his perspective as a solemn four-year-old." Shapiro. Fic for Youth. 3d edition

Savage, Deborah
Kotuku. Houghton Mifflin 2002 291p $16 *
Grades: 9 10 11 12   **Fic**
ISBN 0-618-04756-5   LC 2001-39027

Still having difficulty facing the death of her best friend, Wim must deal with a difficult great-aunt and Maori visitors from New Zealand who uncover a dark family secret
"The multilayered, multifaceted story is peopled with complex characters, reaching across time, oceans, and continents. The superbly interwoven story strands yield amazing results in an enthralling novel with something for everyone." Voice Youth Advocates

Sayed, Kashua, 1975-
Let it be morning; translated from Hebrew by Miriam Shlesinger. Black Cat 2006 271p pa $13
Grades: 11 12 Adult   **Fic**
1. Journalists—Fiction 2. Israel-Arab conflicts—Fiction
ISBN 0-8021-7021-8; 978-0-8021-7021-7
                                        LC 2005-46768
Original Hebrew edition, 2004
"A young Arab-Israeli journalist moves from Tel Aviv back to his childhood village with his wife and baby daughter just in time to be caught up in a series of harrowing, dramatic events. In response to Israel's military presence in the village, neighbors and relatives find themselves fighting one another in order to survive. . . . The short chapters and fast pace, combined with the memories of youth that his return home elicits, make for an easy fit for older teens with an interest in other cultures or current events." SLJ

Sayres, Meghan Nuttall
Anahita's woven riddle. Amulet Books 2006 352p $16.95
Grades: 9 10 11 12   **Fic**
1. Marriage—Fiction 2. Sex role—Fiction 3. Weaving—Fiction 4. Muslim women—Fiction 5. Iran—Fiction
ISBN 978-0-8109-5481-6; 0-8109-5481-8
                                        LC 2006-19893
In Iran, more than 100 years ago, a young girl with three suitors gets permission from her father and a holy man to weave into her wedding rug a riddle to be solved by her future husband, which will ensure that he has wit to match hers.
"The exploration of another culture in an earlier time with a side of almost fairy-tale romance results in a satisfying read." Voice Youth Advocates

Scott, Amanda
Dreaming the eagle; {by} Manda Scott. Delacorte Press 2003 465p hardcover o.p. pa $14
Grades: 11 12 Adult   **Fic**
1. Boadicea, Queen, d. 62—Fiction 2. Great Britain—History—0-1066—Fiction
ISBN 0-385-33670-5; 0-385-33773-6 (pa)
                                        LC 2002-31462
This first part of a projected "trilogy about the life of Boudica, the warrior queen of Britannia who fought the Romans in the first century A.D. . . . runs from A.D. 32 to 43 and covers Boudica's youth (when she was known as Breaca), during which she kills her first opponent in battle and begins a life of leadership and bloodshed." Publ Wkly

Scott, Amanda—*Continued*

"Definitely not a tired old retelling of a legend, this novel is beautifully written and lovingly told, filled with drama and passion. Scott takes great care to draw secondary characters and evoke the feel of first-century Britain." Libr J

Sebold, Alice

The lovely bones. Little, Brown 2002 328p $21.95; pa $13.95 *

Grades: 11 12 Adult   **Fic**

1. Homicide—Fiction 2. Family life—Fiction

ISBN 0-316-66634-3; 0-316-16881-5 (pa)

LC 2001-50622

Also available Thorndike Press large print edition

Sebold's "heroine, 14-year-old Suzy Salmon, is murdered in the first chapter, on her way home from school. Suzy narrates the story from heaven, viewing the devastating effects of her murder on her family." Booklist

"As pleasant as Susie's heaven is, there's no God there, and certainly no Jesus. This is spirituality for an age that's ecumenical to a fault. But emotionally, it's faultless. Sebold never slips as she follows this family. The risks she walks are enough to give you vertigo." Christ Sci Monit

Sedgwick, Marcus

The foreshadowing. Wendy Lamb Books 2006 293p $16.95; lib bdg $18.99 *

Grades: 8 9 10 11   **Fic**

1. World War, 1914-1918—Fiction 2. Extrasensory perception—Fiction

ISBN   0-385-74646-6;   978-0-385-74646-5; 0-385-90881-4 (lib bdg); 978-0-385-90881-8 (lib bdg)

LC 2006-5135

Having always been able to know when someone is going to die, Alexandra poses as a nurse to go to France during World War I to locate her brother and to try to save him from the fate she has foreseen for him.

The author "skillfully connects young peoples' struggles for power and self-determination with the deepest questions about fate, free will, and the meaning of patriotism." Booklist

Seigel, Andrea, 1979-

Like the red panda; Andrea Seigel. 1st ed. Harcourt 2004 280p (A Harvest book) pa $13

Grades: 9 10 11 12   **Fic**

1. School stories 2. Suicide—Fiction 3. Orphans—Fiction 4. California—Fiction

ISBN 0-15-603024-1   LC 2003-17164

"A Harvest book"

"After the overdose deaths of her coke-addicted parents and six years in a chilly foster family, Princeton-bound high-school senior Stella Parrish has decided to commit suicide. Shortly before her graduation, morbid apathy sets in 'like pulling on sunglasses, but internally,' and the rest of the novel . . . is Stella's explanation of her decision." Booklist

"Seigel's novel is a keen portrait of young American angst and all its ironic posturing. The result veers between an earnest critique of the Columbine era and *Heathers*-like parody, which leaves its conclusion half tragedy, half punch line." Publ Wkly

Selvadurai, Shyam, 1965-

Swimming in the monsoon sea. Tundra Books 2005 274p $18.95 *

Grades: 9 10 11 12   **Fic**

1. Cousins—Fiction 2. Homosexuality—Fiction 3. Family life—Fiction 4. Sri Lanka—Fiction

ISBN 0-88776-735-4

"In Sri Lanka in 1980, 14-year-old Amrith is forced to confront his feelings about his birth family when Niresh, a cousin from Canada, visits. He falls in love with the boy, jealously refusing to share him with his adoptive sisters, in spite of their obvious interest. . . . The author's affection for the country of his childhood is evident in this sympathetic and insightful look at first love." SLJ

Senna, Danzy

Caucasia. Riverhead Bks. 1998 353p hardcover o.p. pa $14 *

Grades: 11 12 Adult   **Fic**

1. Interracial marriage—Fiction

ISBN 1-57322-091-4; 1-57322-716-1 (pa)

LC 97-28911

Birdie, the narrator of this novel, is "a biracial girl who must struggle for acceptance from blacks and whites alike. Birdie and Cole are the daughters of a white mother and an African American father whose marriage is disintegrating. When their activist mother must flee from the police, the girls are split between their parents: Cole goes with her father because she looks black, Birdie with her mother because she could pass for white. Living in a small town and forced to keep her family, her past, and her race a secret, Birdie spies upon racism in all its forms, from the overt comments of the town locals to the hypocrisy of the wealthy liberals." Libr J

Birdie's "struggles to fit in anywhere, to pass as anything, are vivid. . . . She tells this coming-of-age tale with impressive beauty and power." Newsweek

Setterfield, Diane

The thirteenth tale; a novel. 1st Atria Books hardcover ed. Atria Books 2006 406p $26

Grades: 11 12 Adult   **Fic**

1. Authors—Fiction 2. Ghost stories

ISBN 978-0-7432-9802-5; 0-7432-9802-0

LC 2006-42906

"Margaret Lea, a London bookseller's daughter, has written an obscure biography that suggests deep understanding of siblings. She is contacted by renowned aging author Vida Winter, who finally wishes to tell her own, long-hidden, life story. Margaret travels to Yorkshire, where she interviews the dying writer, walks the remains of her estate at Angelfield and tries to verify the old woman's tale of a governess, a ghost and more than one abandoned baby." Publ Wkly

"A wholly original work told in the vein of all the best gothic classics. Lovers of books about book lovers will be enthralled." Booklist

Shaara, Michael, 1929-1988

The killer angels; a novel of the Civil War. Modern Library 2004 xx, 337p map $22.95

Grades: 9 10 11 12   **Fic**

1. Gettysburg (Pa.), Battle of, 1863—Fiction

ISBN 0-679-64324-9   LC 2004-46877

Also available in paperback from Ballantine Bks.

A reissue of the title first published 1974 by David McKay

This is a fictionalized account of four days in July, 1863 at the Battle of Gettysburg. The point of view of the Southern forces is represented by Generals Robert E. Lee and James Longstreet, while Colonel Joshua Chamberlain and General John Buford are the focus for the North

"Shaara's version of private reflections and conversations are based on his reading of documents and letters. Although some of his judgments are not necessarily substantiated by historians, he demonstrates a knowledge of both the battle and the area. The writing is vivid and fast moving." Libr J

Sheldon, Dyan

Confessions of a teenage drama queen. Candlewick Press 1999 272p hardcover o.p. pa $7.99

Grades: 7 8 9 10   **Fic**

1. School stories

ISBN 0-7636-0822-X; 0-7636-2827-1 (pa)

LC 98-53914

In her first year at a suburban New Jersey high school, Mary Elizabeth Cep, who now calls herself "Lola," sets her sights on the lead in the annual drama production, and finds herself in conflict with the most popular girl in school.

"An exuberant and hilarious celebration of the ups and downs of high school life. . . . The story is off-beat, outrageous, and utterly charming." SLJ

Shelley, Mary Wollstonecraft, 1797-1851

Frankenstein; or, The modern Prometheus; with an introduction by Wendy Lesser. Knopf 1992 xxxiii, 231p $15 *

Grades: 7 8 9 10   **Fic**

ISBN 0-679-40999-8   LC 91-53195

Also available from other publishers

"Everyman's library"

First published 1818

"The tale relates the exploits of Frankenstein, an idealistic Genevan student of natural philosophy, who discovers at the university of Ingolstadt the secret of imparting life to inanimate matter. Collecting bones from charnel-houses, he constructs the semblance of a human being and gives it life. The creature, endowed with supernatural strength and size and terrible in appearance, inspires loathing in whoever sees it." Oxford Companion to Engl Lit. 5th edition

Shepard, Jim

Project X; a novel. Alfred A. Knopf 2004 163p hardcover o.p. pa $12 *

Grades: 9 10 11 12   **Fic**

1. School stories 2. School violence—Fiction

ISBN 1-4000-4071-X; 1-4000-3348-9 (pa)

LC 2003-47575

"Flake and Edwin are often bullied; at other times, they have the horrible feeling of being completely invisible to their classmates. Flake is even more alienated than Edwin and hatches a revenge plan involving guns that they call 'project x.' Disaster looms. . . . The vivid dialogue is sprinkled with profanity and is movingly expressive. This heartbreaking and wrenching novel will leave teens with plenty of questions and, hopefully, some answers." SLJ

Sherrill, Martha

The Ruins of California. Penguin Press 2006 318p $24.95

Grades: 11 12 Adult   **Fic**

1. Family life—Fiction 2. Divorce—Fiction 3. California—Fiction

ISBN 1-59420-080-7; 978-1-59420-080-9

LC 2005-49343

"Set in California in the 1970s, this beautifully written novel tells the story of a girl, trapped in a theatrical family, who manages to transform herself from an observer into the star of her own life." Booklist

Sheth, Kashmira

Koyal dark, mango sweet. Hyperion 2006 250p $15.99

Grades: 8 9 10 11 12   **Fic**

1. Family life—Fiction 2. India—Fiction

ISBN 0-7868-3857-4; 978-0-7868-3857-8

LC 2005-50338

Growing up with her family in Mumbai, India, sixteen-year-old Jeeta disagrees with much of her mother's traditional advice about how to live her life and tries to be more modern and independent.

"Eloquent and insightful, this book invites introspection and may lead to lively discussions about the pros and cons of honoring and breaking tradition." Publ Wkly

Shinn, Sharon, 1957-

Mystic and rider. Berkley Books 2005 440p il map $23.95; pa $7.99

Grades: 9 10 11 12   **Fic**

1. Cults—Fiction 2. Fantasy fiction

ISBN 0-441-01246-9; 0-441-01303-1 (pa)

LC 2004-59639

"In the land of Gillengaria, ill feeling toward magic and those who use it rises to a dangerous level. The king dispatches the Mystic woman Senneth on a journey to see firsthand how dire the situation is. Accompanying her are Shapeshifters and Riders—unlikely allies who will enter a land under the sway of a fanatical cult that would purge Gillengaria of all magic users." Publisher's note

"Never tripping over the plot twists and complications, Shinn gives us an easy, absorbing, high-quality read sans gratuitous bloodshed and violence." Booklist

Shinn, Sharon, 1957——*Continued*

The Safe-Keeper's secret. Viking 2004 222p
$16.99; pa $6.99

Grades: 7 8 9 10   **Fic**
  1. Fantasy fiction
  ISBN 0-670-05910-2; 0-14-240357-1 (pa)
                                       LC 2003-23538
Fiona is Safe-Keeper in the small village of
Tambleham, where neighbors and strangers alike come
one by one, in secret, to tell her things they dare not
share with anyone else.
  "Teens will connect with Shinn's vividly drawn fanta-
sy world as well as her provocative questions about
truth, justice, and individual destiny." Booklist
  A companion volume to:
The truth-teller's tale (2005)

Shulman, Polly
Enthusiasm. G. P. Putnam's Sons 2006 198p
$15.99

Grades: 7 8 9 10   **Fic**
  1. School stories
  ISBN 0-399-24389-5   LC 2005-13490
Julie and Ashleigh, high school sophomores and Jane
Austen fans, seem to fall for the same Mr. Darcy-like
boy and struggle to hide their true feelings from one another while rehearsing for a school musical.
  "While familiarity with Austen's world through her
books or, more likely, the movie renditions will deepen
readers' appreciation for Shulman's impressive . . . novel, it is by no means a prerequisite to enjoying this involving and often amusing narrative of friendship, courtship, and (of course) true love." Booklist

Shusterman, Neal
Downsiders. Simon & Schuster Bks. for Young
Readers 1999 246p hardcover o.p. pa $4.99

Grades: 9 10 11 12   **Fic**
  1. Subways—Fiction 2. New York (N.Y.)—Fiction
  ISBN 0-689-80375-3; 0-689-83969-3 (pa)
                                       LC 98-38555
When fourteen-year-old Lindsay meets Talon and dis-
covers the Downsiders world which had evolved from
the subway built in New York in 1867 by Alfred Ely
Beach, she and her new friend experience the clash of
their two cultures.
  "Shusterman has invented an alternate world in the
Downside that is both original and humorous." Voice
Youth Advocates

Everlost. Simon & Schuster Books for Young
Readers 2006 313p $16.95 *

Grades: 8 9 10 11 12   **Fic**
  1. Traffic accidents—Fiction 2. Death—Fiction
  3. Future life—Fiction
  ISBN 978-0-689-87237-2; 0-689-87237-2
                                       LC 2005-32244
When Nick and Allie are killed in a car crash, they
end up in Everlost, or limbo for lost souls, where although Nick is satisfied, Allie will stop at nothing—even
skinjacking—to break free.
  "Shusterman has reimagined what happens after death

and questions power and the meaning of charity. While
all this is going on, he has also managed to write a rip-
roaring adventure complete with monsters, blimps, and
high-diving horses." SLJ

Shute, Nevil, 1899-1960
On the beach. Ballantine Books 1983 278p pa
$6.99

Grades: 9 10 11 12 Adult   **Fic**
  1. Nuclear warfare—Fiction
  ISBN 0-345-31148-5
Also available in hardcover from Buccaneer Books
First published 1957 by Morrow
  "A nuclear war annihilates the world's Northern Hemisphere, and as atomic wastes are spreading southward,
residents of Australia try to come to grips with their
mortality. In spite of the inevitability of death, these people face their end with courage and live from day to day.
They even plant trees they may never see mature." Shapiro. Fic for Youth. 3d edition

Silbert, Leslie
The intelligencer. Atria Bks. 2004 335p
hardcover o.p. pa $14

Grades: 9 10 11 12   **Fic**
  1. Marlowe, Christopher, 1564-1593—Fiction
  2. Great Britain—History—1485-1603, Tudors—Fiction 3. Mystery fiction
  ISBN 0-7434-3292-4; 0-7434-3293-2 (pa)
                                       LC 2004-298225
This mystery "alternates between the present and the
England of Elizabeth I and Christopher Marlowe. In addition to being a skilled and popular playwright, Marlowe was a spy, or *intelligencer*, for both Cecil and
Essex, rivals for the favor of the Queen. Kate Morgan,
a present-day Renaissance scholar working as a PI for a
former agent still working clandestinely for the government, takes on a case involving a bound collection of
coded reports of intelligencers gathered by an employee
of Cecil, Essex, and others. The trail of the manuscript
and its codes intersects with modern investigations involving murders, a crooked but charming art dealer, a
charming but devious entrepreneur, a captured spy, Iranian prisons, Kate's father, a U.S. senator, and the current
CIA director. There are a lot of strands, but the pace is
quick and the action fascinating." SLJ

Simmons, Dan
Ilium. Eos 2003 576p $25.95

Grades: 11 12 Adult   **Fic**
  1. Homer—Parodies, imitations, etc. 2. Mars (Planet)—Fiction 3. Science fiction
  ISBN 0-380-97893-8   LC 2002-44791
  "Restored to life by the 'gods,' a race of beings who
dwell on the heights of Olympos, 20th-century scholar
Thomas Hockenberry travels back in time to observe the
events of the Trojan War, as chronicled in Homer's epic
poem. There, one of the gods recruits him in a secret
war against her brother and sister deities. Set in a far future in which the population of true humans is kept
strictly regulated by extraplanetary forces and machine
intelligences study Proust and Shakespeare as they perform their duties throughout the universe." Libr J

Simmons, Dan—*Continued*

"For answers to the mysteries laid out in 'Ilium'—from the true identity of the Olympian gods to the fate of robots and humans and of the 'little green men' on Mars for whom communication means death—you will have to wait for the promised sequel. For now, matching wits with Simmons and his lively creations should be reward enough." N Y Times Book Rev

Followed by Olympos (2005)

Simmons, Michael

Finding Lubchenko. Razorbill 2005 280p $16.99; pa $8.99

Grades: 8 9 10 11 12   Fic

1. Father-son relationship—Fiction 2. Homicide—Fiction 3. Terrorism—Fiction 4. Paris (France)—Fiction
ISBN   1-59514-021-2;   978-1-59514-021-0; 1-59514-075-1 (pa); 978-1-59514-075-3 (pa)
LC 2004-26075

"A Junior Library Guild selection"

When his father is framed for murder and bioterrorism, highschool junior Evan, using clues from a stolen laptop, travels from Seattle to Paris with two friends to find the real culprit.

This " is diversionary reading at its best, strong on plot and voice and humor, and completely satisfying in the moment." Horn Book

Followed by The rise of Lubchenko (2006)

Vandal. Roaring Brook Press 2006 173p $16.95

Grades: 7 8 9 10   Fic

1. Brothers—Fiction 2. Bands (Music)—Fiction
ISBN 978-1-59643-070-9; 1-59643-070-2
LC 2005-28741

The love-hate relationship between high school musician Will and his older brother Jason is fueled by the abuse Will suffers at Jason's hands but a devastating accident changes the everything for the boys and their family.

This is "a deftly structured, refreshingly unsentimental, and witty analysis of the resilient, complicated bonds that connect siblings." Booklist

Sinclair, April

Coffee will make you black. Avon Books 1994 239p pa $13.95

Grades: 9 10 11 12   Fic

1. African Americans—Fiction
ISBN 0-380-72459-6
First published 1994 by Hyperion

This novel's protagonist "is Jean ('Stevie') Stevenson, a spunky 11-year-old when the story begins; a highschool student when it concludes. The setting is Chicago, circa 1965-70. . . . Raised by a strict, if well-meaning, mother and an affectionate, if vague, father, Stevie soon finds herself caught up in one of the many riddles of youth: to be cool or be square. . . . Meanwhile, she is listening to Dr. Martin Luther King and Malcolm X and liberating herself from the confines of her upbringing and her fear of being 'different.'" Booklist

"Sinclair gives a realistic portrayal of personal awakening during a politically tumultuous time." Publ Wkly

Sinclair, Upton, 1878-1968

The jungle; introduction by Jane Jacobs. Modern Library 2002 xx, 382p pa $9.95 *

Grades: 11 12 Adult   Fic

1. Chicago (Ill.)—Fiction 2. Social problems—Fiction
ISBN 0-375-75950-6   LC 2001-44823
Also available from other publishers
First published 1906 by Doubleday, Page

"Jurgis Rudkus, an immigrant from Lithuania, arrives in Chicago with his father, his fiancée, and her family. He is determined to make a life for his bride in the new country. The deplorable conditions in the stockyards and the harrowing experiences of impoverished workers are vividly described by the author." Shapiro. Fic for Youth. 3d edition

Sitomer, Alan Lawrence

Hip-hop high school. Jump at the Sun/Hyperion Books For Children 2006 368p $16.99; pa $8.99

Grades: 7 8 9 10   Fic

1. School stories 2. African Americans—Fiction
ISBN 0-7868-5515-0; 1-4231-0644-X (pa)
LC 2005-43331

Follows an African-American teenager through four years at her inner-city high school.

The author "strikes a fair balance between serious issues and more lighthearted fare, writing in a smart, conversational voice loaded with wit, rhythm, and energy." Booklist

Followed by Homeboyz (2007)

The Hoopster. Jump at the Sun/Hyperion Books for Children 2005 218p $16.99 *

Grades: 7 8 9 10   Fic

1. Basketball—Fiction 2. Race relations—Fiction 3. African Americans—Fiction 4. Authorship—Fiction
ISBN 0-7868-5483-9

First published 2002 by Milk Mug Pub.

Andre Anderson, called "The Hoopster" for his basketball skills, is brutally attacked by racists in response to an article he writes for a national magazine.

"The dialogue-filled sparring is fresh and accurately portrays the dynamics among urban teens and their families." SLJ

Sittenfeld, Curtis

Prep; a novel. Random House 2005 406p $21.95; pa $13.95 *

Grades: 11 12 Adult   Fic

1. School stories 2. Massachusetts—Fiction
ISBN 1-400-06231-4; 0-812-97235-X
LC 2004-46858

During the late 1980s, a fourteen-year-old leaves her middle-class Indiana family to enroll in an elite New England boarding school, becoming a shrewd observer of the rituals and mores of upper-class Easterners

"This readable coming-of-age tale . . . [is] suitable for YA collections if mildly sexually explicit scenes are not objectionable." Libr J

Slade, Arthur G., 1967-

Megiddo's shadow. Wendy Lamb Books 2006 290p $15.95

Grades: 7 8 9 10   **Fic**

1. World War, 1914-1918—Fiction 2. Brothers—Fiction

ISBN 0-385-74701-2; 978-0-385-90945-7

LC 2006011494

After the death of his beloved older brother Hector in World War I, sixteen-year-old Edward leaves the family farm in Canada to enlist in Hector's batallion, where he attempts to come to terms with what has happened.

"An engrossing and thought-provoking story." SLJ

Sleator, William

House of stairs. Dutton 1974 166p hardcover o.p. pa $5.99 *

Grades: 7 8 9 10   **Fic**

1. Science fiction

ISBN 0-525-32335-X; 0-14-034580-9 (pa)

Available in hardcover from P. Smith

"Five 15-year-old orphans with widely ranging personality characteristics are involuntarily placed in a house of endless stairs and subjected to psychological experiments on conditioned human responses." Booklist

"The setting is bleak, dramatic and convincing; the interaction and development of the five young people as characters trapped in an abrasive situation are compelling. A very effective and provocative suspense story that can be read for plot alone or doubly enjoyed for the mystery and the message." Bull Cent Child Books

Sloan, Brian

A tale of two summers. Simon & Schuster Books for Young Readers 2006 241p $15.95 *

Grades: 9 10 11 12   **Fic**

1. Friendship—Fiction 2. Homosexuality—Fiction 3. Theater—Fiction

ISBN 978-0-689-87439-0; 0-689-87439-1

LC 2005-20697

Even though Hal is gay and Chuck is straight, the two fifteen-year-olds are best friends and set up a blog where Hal records his budding romance with a young Frenchman and Chuck falls for a summer theater camp diva.

"This book is for readers mature enough to handle some very direct, realistic, and often-humorous entries about heterosexuality, homosexuality, masturbation, and alcohol and marijuana use. This title would be ideal for discussion within Gay/Straight Alliance groups." Voice Youth Advocates

Sloan, Kay

The patron saint of red Chevies. Permanent Press 2004 221p $21.95

Grades: 9 10 11 12   **Fic**

1. Homicide—Fiction 2. Sisters—Fiction 3. Race relations—Fiction 4. Mississippi—Fiction

ISBN 1-57962-104-X   LC 2003-65550

"Mississippi, 1964: Bernice Starling, a blues singer of some repute, is stabbed to death. Her two young daughters decide they want to find the killer, but it's a tricky job, and there are plenty of suspects: a local bigot, their mother's lover, a random passerby, even their own father. . . . In the end, it doesn't matter whodunit, because this isn't really a mystery novel at all. It's a family drama, the coming-of-age story of two young girls who lose their mother and decide to do something about it. Fresh, enticing, often elegantly written." Booklist

Smelcer, John E., 1963-

The trap; [by] John Smelcer. Henry Holt and Co. 2006 170p $15.95 *

Grades: 6 7 8 9   **Fic**

1. Survival after airplane accidents, shipwrecks, etc.—Fiction 2. Grandfathers—Fiction 3. Native Americans—Fiction 4. Alaska—Fiction

ISBN 978-0-8050-7939-5; 0-8050-7939-4

LC 2005035740

In alternating chapters, seventeen-year-old Johnny Least-Weasel worries about his missing grandfather, and the grandfather, Albert Least-Weasel, struggles to survive, caught in his own steel trap in the Alaskan winter.

"In this story, Smelcer . . . seems to straddle the line flawlessly between an ancient legend and contemporary fiction. . . . His characters act with quiet dignity. . . . The suspense is played on an everyday level, which is why it works." Voice Youth Advocates

Smith, Cynthia Leitich

Tantalize. Candlewick Press 2007 310p $16.99

Grades: 9 10 11 12   **Fic**

1. Supernatural—Fiction 2. Vampires—Fiction 3. Werewolves—Fiction 4. Restaurants—Fiction 5. Texas—Fiction

ISBN 0-7636-2791-7; 978-0-7636-2791-1

LC 2005-58124

When multiple murders in Austin, Texas, threaten the grand reopening of her family's vampire-themed restaurant, seventeen-year-old, orphaned Quincie worries that her best friend-turned-love interest, Kieren, a werewolf-in-training, may be the prime suspect.

"Horror fans will be hooked by Kieren's quiet, hirsute hunkiness, and Texans by the premise that nearly everybody in their capitol is a shapeshifter." Publ Wkly

Smith, Diane

Letters from Yellowstone. Viking 1999 226p il map hardcover o.p. pa $12.95

Grades: 11 12 Adult   **Fic**

1. Yellowstone National Park—Fiction

ISBN 0-670-88631-9; 0-14-029181-4 (pa)

LC 99-12904

"Professor Merriam thinks Cornell University student A. E. Bartram will be a wonderful addition to his Yellowstone National Park field expedition—until he finds out Bartram is a strong nineteenth-century woman who is willing to trade comfort for adventure. A thoroughly enjoyable epistolary novel that mixes history, romance, and science." Booklist

Smith, Kirsten, 1970-
The geography of girlhood. Little, Brown 2006
184p $16.99; pa $7.99
Grades: 8 9 10 11 12   **Fic**
1. Family life—Fiction 2. School stories
ISBN 0-316-16021-0; 0-316-01735-3 (pa)
LC 2005-938431
Novel in poetry about a girl navigating the unknown,
the difficult limbo between youth and adulthood. A novel
written in verse follows Penny Morrow in her transition
from middle school to high school as her father remar-
ries, she acquires a new stepbrother, and she experiences
her first dance, first kiss, and other hazards of growing
up.
"There is some matter-of-fact mention of sexual situations and underage drinking. However, it is the clarity,
the keen understanding, and the apt metaphors that make
Penny's voice so memorable." SLJ

Solzhenitsyn, Aleksandr, 1918-
One day in the life of Ivan Denisovich;
translated from the Russian by H. T. Willets; with
an introduction by John Bayley. Knopf 1995 xxvii,
159p $15
Grades: 11 12 Adult   **Fic**
1. Prisoners—Fiction 2. Soviet Union—Fiction
ISBN 0-679-44464-5
Also available in paperback from Farrar, Straus &
Giroux
"Everyman's library"
Original Russian edition, 1962; this is a reissue of the
translation published 1991 by Farrar, Straus & Giroux
"Drawing on his own experiences, the author writes of
one day, from reveille to lights-out, in the prison existence of Ivan Denisovich Shukhov. Innocent of any
crime, he has been convicted of treason and sentenced to
ten years in one of Stalin's notorious slave-labor compounds. The protagonist is a simple man trying to survive the brutality of a totalitarian system." Shapiro. Fic
for Youth. 3d edition

Sones, Sonya
One of those hideous books where the mother
dies. Simon & Schuster Books for Young Readers
2004 268p $15.95; pa $6.99
Grades: 7 8 9 10   **Fic**
1.   Father-daughter   relationship—Fiction
2. Bereavement—Fiction 3. Actors—Fiction
ISBN 0-689-85820-5; 1-416-90788-2 (pa)
LC 2003-9355
Fifteen-year-old Ruby Milliken leaves her best friend,
her boyfriend, her aunt, and her mother's grave in Boston and reluctantly flies to Los Angeles to live with her
father, a famous movie star who divorced her mother before Ruby was born
"Ruby's affable personality is evident in her humorous
quips and clever wordplays. Her depth of character is revealed through her honest admissions, poignant revelations, and sensitive insights. . . . Ruby's story is gripping, enjoyable, and memorable." SLJ

Sonnenblick, Jordan
Notes from the midnight driver. Scholastic Press
2006 265p $16.99
Grades: 8 9 10 11 12   **Fic**
1.   Friendship—Fiction   2.   Old   age—Fiction
3. Musicians—Fiction
ISBN 0-439-75779-7   LC 2005-27972
After being assigned to perform community service at
a nursing home, sixteen-year-old Alex befriends a can-
tankerous old man who has some lessons to impart about
jazz guitar playing, love, and forgiveness.
The author "deftly infiltrates the teenage mind to produce a first-person narrative riddled with enough hapless
confusion, mulish equivocation, and beleaguered deadpan
humor to have readers nodding with recognition, sighing
with sympathy, and gasping with laughter—often on the
same page." Horn Book

Sorrells, Walter
Fake ID; Hunted: book one. Sleuth/Dutton 2005
313p $12.99
Grades: 7 8 9 10   **Fic**
1. Mystery fiction
ISBN 0-525-47514-1   LC 2004-21578
After a lifetime of moving and assuming new identities, sixteen-year-old Chass begins to piece together the
disturbing past that haunts her and her mother and which
involves a mysterious tape, a deceased popular singer,
and the secrets of several people in a small Alabama
town.
"Sorrells masterfully sustains suspense throughout,
spiking the drama with some truly frightening scenes that
make this a terrific read." Booklist
Another title about Chastity is:
Club Dread, Hunted: book two (2006)

Soto, Gary
The afterlife. Harcourt 2003 161p $16; pa $6.95
*
Grades: 7 8 9 10   **Fic**
1. Mexican Americans—Fiction 2. Ghost stories
ISBN 0-15-204774-3; 0-15-205220-8 (pa)
LC 2003-44995
A senior at East Fresno High School lives on as a
ghost after his brutal murder in the restroom of a club
where he had gone to dance.
"In many ways, this is as much a story about a hard-
scrabble place as it is about a boy who is murdered.
Both pulse with life and will stay in memory." Booklist

Buried onions. Harcourt Brace & Co. 1997 149p
$17; pa $6.95 *
Grades: 9 10 11 12   **Fic**
1. Violence—Fiction 2. Mexican Americans—Fiction
ISBN 0-15-201333-4; 0-15-206265-3 (pa)
LC 96-53112
When nineteen-year-old Eddie drops out of college, he
struggles to find a place for himself as a Mexican American living in a violence-infested neighborhood of Fresno, California.
"Soto has created a beautiful, touching, and truthful
story. . . . The lyrical language and Spanish phrases add
to the immediacy of setting and to the sensitivity the author brings to his character's life." Voice Youth Advocates

Southgate, Martha

The fall of Rome; a novel. Scribner 2002 223p hardcover o.p. pa $13 *

Grades: 11 12 Adult **Fic**

1. African Americans—Fiction 2. Teachers—Fiction 3. School stories

ISBN 0-684-86500-9; 0-7432-2721-2 (pa)

LC 2001-34225

A "novel about a token black teacher at an élite New England boarding school. Jerome Washington is a classics scholar who, armed with a Harvard education and an accent purged of his Georgia-sharecropper roots, has spent his life trying to defeat racism through sheer decorum. But his hermetic existence is threatened by the arrival of a black student from a Brooklyn ghetto and a white female teacher who fancies herself a champion of the underprivileged." New Yorker

The author "delves deeply into the social and emotional elements that unite and divide us. Issues of race, identity, and integrity are intensely explored through a tragic human triangle." Booklist

Spiegler, Louise

The amethyst road. Clarion Books 2005 328p $16

Grades: 9 10 11 12 **Fic**

1. Family life—Fiction 2. Prejudices—Fiction

ISBN 0-618-48572-4; 978-0-618-48572-7

LC 2005-4014

Having fled the city of Oestia after attacking an official, sixteen-year-old Serena—an outcast as well as a mixed-race child of a Gorgio father and Yulang mother—seeks to reunite her family and regain her honor.

"This novel of self-discovery is an intriguing blend of gritty urban fantasy and magical realism." Voice Youth Advocates

Spillebeen, Geert, 1956-

Kipling's choice; written by Geert Spillebeen; translated by Terese Edelstein. Houghton Mifflin Co 2005 147p $16; pa $7.99

Grades: 7 8 9 10 **Fic**

1. Kipling, John, 1897-1915—Fiction 2. World War, 1914-1918—Fiction 3. France—Fiction

ISBN 0-618-43124-1; 0-618-80035-2 (pa)

LC 2004-20856

In 1915, mortally wounded in Loos, France, eighteen-year-old John Kipling, son of writer Rudyard Kipling, remembers his boyhood and the events leading to what is to be his first and last World War I battle.

"This well-written novel combines facts with speculation about John Kipling's short life and gruesome death. A riveting account of World War I." SLJ

Springer, Nancy

I am Mordred; a tale from Camelot. Philomel Bks. 1998 184p hardcover o.p. pa $6.99 *

Grades: 7 8 9 10 **Fic**

1. Arthur, King—Fiction 2. Mordred (Legendary character)—Fiction 3. Great Britain—History—0-1066—Fiction

ISBN 0-399-23143-9; 0-698-11841-3 (pa)

LC 97-39740

"Mordred, the bad seed, the son of King Arthur and his sister, spends his youth learning who he is and then trying to deal with the prophecy made by Merlin that he will kill his father." SLJ

"Springer humanizes Arthurian archvillain Mordred in a thoroughly captivating and poignant tale." Booklist

I am Morgan le Fay; a tale from Camelot. Philomel Bks. 2001 227p hardcover o.p. pa $5.99

Grades: 7 8 9 10 **Fic**

1. Arthur, King—Fiction 2. Morgan le Fay (Legendary character)—Fiction 3. Great Britain—History—0-1066—Fiction

ISBN 0-399-23451-9; 0-698-11974-6 (pa)

LC 99-52847

In a war-torn England where her half-brother Arthur will eventually become king, the young Morgan le Fay comes to realize that she has magic powers and links to the faerie world

"Introspective, yet threaded with intrigue and adventure, this compelling study of the legendary villainess explores the ways that love, hate, jealousy, and the desire for power shape one young woman's fate and affect the destiny of others." Horn Book

Stahler, David, Jr.

Doppelganger; [by] David Stahler, Jr. HarperCollins Publishers 2006 258p $16.99; lib bdg $17.89 *

Grades: 8 9 10 11 12 **Fic**

1. Family life—Fiction 2. Child abuse—Fiction 3. Supernatural—Fiction 4. Horror fiction

ISBN 978-0-06-087232-8; 0-06-087232-2; 978-0-06-087233-5 (lib bdg); 0-06-087233-0 (lib bdg)

LC 2005-28484

When a sixteen-year-old member of a race of shape-shifting killers called doppelgangers assumes the life of a troubled teen, he becomes unexpectedly embroiled in human life—and it is nothing like what he has seen on television.

"This brooding story of literally stepping into someone else's shoes combines romance, horror, and angst to create a distinctive story of redemption. The abusive relationships in Chris's family are portrayed with realism and sensitivity." Voice Youth Advocates

Staples, Suzanne Fisher

Shabanu; daughter of the wind. Knopf 1989 240p hardcover o.p. pa $6.50 *

Grades: 9 10 11 12 **Fic**

1. Sex role—Fiction 2. Pakistan—Fiction

ISBN 0-394-84815-2; 0-440-23856-0 (pa)

LC 89-2714

When eleven-year-old Shabanu, the daughter of a nomad in the Cholistan Desert of present-day Pakistan, is pledged in marriage to an older man whose money will bring prestige to the family, she must either accept the decision, as is the custom, or risk the consequences of defying her father's wishes

"Interspersing native words throughout adds realism, but may trip up readers, who must be patient enough to find meaning through context. This use of language is, however, an important element in helping Staples paint an evocative picture of life in the desert that includes references to the hard facts of reality." Booklist

Staples, Suzanne Fisher—*Continued*
Followed by Haveli

Shiva's fire. Farrar, Straus & Giroux 1999 275p
$17
Grades: 7 8 9 10   Fic
1. Dance—Fiction 2. India—Fiction
ISBN 0-374-36824-4   LC 99-10626
Also available Thorndike Press large print edition and
in paperback from HarperCollins Pubs.
"A Frances Foster book"
In India, a talented dancer sacrifices friends and family for her art
"This novel draws the reader into the exotic setting
and spiritual world of sacred Hindu classical dance. The
glossary with pronunciation guide helps readers understand Indian terminology. . . . Readers will relate to
Parvati's dislike of being different and to her relief upon
finding her place as a master dancer, a place where her
unique abilities are honored, not feared." Voice Youth
Advocates

Stein, Tammar
Light years; a novel. Knopf, Distributed by
Random House 2005 263p $15.95; lib bdg $17.99
Grades: 7 8 9 10   Fic
1. Israel-Arab conflicts—Fiction 2. Bereavement—Fiction
ISBN 0-375-83023-5; 0-375-93023-X (lib bdg)
                                          LC 2004-7776
Maya Laor leaves her home in Israel to study astronomy at the University of Virginia after the tragic death of
her boyfriend in a suicide bombing.
"This well-paced first novel, a moving study of grief
and recovery, is also a love story that should appeal particularly to students interested in other ways of seeing
the world." SLJ
Includes bibliographical references

Steinbeck, John, 1902-1968
The grapes of wrath; introduction and notes by
Robert DeMott. Penguin Books 2006 lviii, 464p
(Penguin classics) pa $15
Grades: 11 12 Adult   Fic
1. Migrant agricultural laborers—Fiction
ISBN 0-14-303943-1   LC 2005-58182
First published 1939
"Awarded the Pulitzer Prize in 1940, this moving and
highly successful proletarian novel tells of the hardships
of the Joad family. 'Okie' farmers forced out of their
home in the Oklahoma dustbowl region by economic
desperation, they drive to California in search of work as
migrant fruitpickers. The grandparents die on the way;
on their arrival the others are harassed by the police and
participate in strike violence, during which Tom, the
Joad son, kills a man. At the conclusion of the novel,
throughout which descriptive and philosophical passages
alternate with narrative portions, the family is defeated
but still resolute." Reader's Ency. 4th edition

Of mice and men. Viking 1986 107p hardcover
o.p. pa $12 *
Grades: 11 12 Adult   Fic
1. Migrant labor—Fiction 2. Ranch life—Fiction
ISBN 0-670-52071-3; 0-14-200067-1 (pa)
                                          LC 86-1300
First published 1937 by Covici-Friede
"Two uneducated laborers dream of a time when they
can share the ownership of a rabbit farm in Califonia.
George is a plotter and a schemer, while Lennie is a
mentally deficient hulk of a man who has no concept of
his physical strength. As a team they are not particularly
successful, but their friendship is enduring." Shapiro. Fic
for Youth. 3d edition

The pearl; with drawings by José Clemente
Orozco. Viking 1947 122p il hardcover o.p. pa
$12 *
Grades: 7 8 9 10   Fic
1. Mexico—Fiction 2. Poverty—Fiction
ISBN 0-670-54575-9; 0-14-200069-8 (pa)
"Kino, a poor pearl-fisher, lives a happy albeit spartan
life with his wife and their child. When he finds a magnificent pearl, the Pearl of the World, he is besieged by
dishonest pearl merchants and envious neighbors. Even a
greedy doctor ties his professional treatment of their
baby when it is bitten by a scorpion to the possible acquisition of the pearl. After a series of disasters, Kino
throws the pearl away since it has brought him only unhappiness." Shapiro. Fic for Youth. 3d edition

Steinhöfel, Andreas
The center of the world; translated from the
German by Alisa Jaffa. Delacorte Press 2005 467p
$16.95; lib bdg $18.99; pa $7.99
Grades: 9 10 11 12   Fic
1. Homosexuality—Fiction 2. Family life—Fiction
3. Germany—Fiction
ISBN 0-385-72943-X; 0-385-90266-2 (lib bdg);
0-440-22932-4 (pa)   LC 2001-52987
As he works through his often difficult relationships
with his single mother, distant twin sister, his first boyfriend, and an odd assortment of friends, a teenage boy
learns about the wounds and healing brought by love
"This long novel . . . is not a quick read. But Jaffa's
translation is clear and immediate, and the funny, aching
first-person narrative will keep many teens enthralled
with the story about secrets and betrayal." Booklist

Stemple, Adam
Singer of souls. Tor 2005 237p $22.95; pa $6.99
Grades: 9 10 11 12   Fic
1. Fantasy fiction 2. Fairies—Fiction 3. Musicians—
Fiction 4. Drug abuse—Fiction
ISBN   0-7653-1170-4;   978-0-7653-1170-2;
0-7653-5027-0 (pa); 978-0-7653-5027-5 (pa)
                                          LC 2004-63758
"A Tom Doherty Associates book"
"Deciding to break free from his drug addiction,
Douglas McLaren decides to leave Minneapolis and visit
his Grandma McLaren in Edinburgh. Supporting himself
as a street-corner busker, he seems to be on his way to
reforming himself until he meets a young woman named

Stemple, Adam—*Continued*

Aine who gives him a white powder that opens his eyes. Suddenly, Douglas can see all the faeries in Edinburgh; furthermore, he becomes caught up in their wars and finds himself fighting for his life and sanity. . . . [The author] tells a strong, well-crafted tale of magic and mayhem built around one young man's discovery of a new world existing alongside the world of everyday." Libr J

Stevenson, Robert Louis, 1850-1894

The strange case of Dr. Jekyll and Mr. Hyde; with an introduction by Joyce Carol Oates. Vintage Books 1991 97p pa $8.95

Grades: 11 12 Adult   **Fic**
1. Horror fiction 2. Allegories
ISBN 0-679-73476-7   LC 90-50600
Also available from other publishers
First published 1886. Variant title: Dr. Jekyll and Mr. Hyde

"The disturbing tale of the dual personality of Dr. Jekyll, a physician. A generous and philanthropic man, he is preoccupied with the problems of good and evil and with the possibility of separating them into two distinct personalities. He develops a drug that transforms him into the demonic Mr. Hyde, in whose person he exhausts all the latent evil in his nature. He also creates an antidote that will restore him to his respectable existence as Dr. Jekyll. Gradually, however, the unmitigated evil of his darker self predominates, until finally he performs an atrocious murder. . . . The novel is of great psychological perception and strongly concerned with ethical problems." Reader's Ency. 4th edition

Stewart, Mary, 1916-

Mary Stewart's Merlin trilogy. Morrow 1980 919p maps $29.95 *

Grades: 11 12 Adult   **Fic**
1. Arthur, King—Fiction 2. Merlin (Legendary character)—Fiction 3. Great Britain—History—0-1066—Fiction
ISBN 0-688-00347-8   LC 80-21019
An omnibus edition of: The crystal cave, The hollow hills and The last enchantment, first published 1970, 1973 and 1979 respectively

The first novel in this trilogy based on Arthurian legends concerns the difficult childhood and youth of the magician Merlin who grows up as a bastard at the court of the King of Wales where he is believed to be the offspring of the King's daughter and the devil. He gains much knowledge from a learned wizard and escapes to "Less Britain" where he becomes involved in efforts to unite all of Britain. The second novel tells of Merlin's involvement with the childhood of Arthur and Arthur's search for the magical sword, Caliburn. The last novel deals with Merlin's death and Arthur's turbulent reign.

The author's "skill in creating colorful characters, suspense, and a brooding atmosphere serves her well in portraying England's Dark Ages, where witches, sorcerers, and tragic kings moved heroically through an enchanted land. Though Arthur's rise to power is the subject, the true star and narrator of the tale is Merlin the magician." Husband. Sequels

Includes bibliographical references

Stine, Catherine

Refugees. Delacorte 2005 277p $15.95; lib bdg $17.99; pa $5.99

Grades: 9 10 11 12   **Fic**
1. Refugees—Fiction 2. Runaway teenagers—Fiction 3. September 11 terrorist attacks, 2001—Fiction 4. New York (N.Y.)—Fiction 5. Afghanistan—Fiction
ISBN 0-385-73179-5; 0-385-90216-6 (lib bdg); 0-440-23876-5 (pa)   LC 2004-10128
Following the September 11, 2001, terrorist attacks, Dawn, a sixteen-year-old runaway from San Francisco, connects by phone and email with Johar, a gentle, fifteen-year-old Afghani who assists Dawn's foster mother, a doctor, at a Red Cross refugee camp in Peshawar

The author "tells an ambitious, haunting story that asks urgent questions about current conflicts, the human lives behind the headlines, and the healing that must follow." Booklist

Stoker, Bram, 1847-1912

Dracula; edited with an introduction and notes by Maurice Hindle; preface by Christopher Frayling. Penguin Books 2003 xlvii, 454p pa $11 *

Grades: 11 12 Adult   **Fic**
1. Horror fiction 2. Vampires—Fiction
ISBN 0-14-143984-X   LC 2003-269578
Also available Thorndike Press large print edition and in hardcover and paperback from other publishers
First published 1897

"Count Dracula, an 'undead' villain from Transylvania, uses his supernatural powers to lure and prey upon innocent victims from whom he gains the blood on which he lives. The novel is written chiefly in the form of journals kept by the principal characters—Jonathan Harker, who contacts the vampire in his Transylvanian castle; Harker's fiancée (later his wife), Mina, adored by the Count; the well-meaning Dr. Seward; and Lucy Westerna, a victim who herself becomes a vampire. The doctor and friends destroy Dracula in the end, but only after they drive a stake through Lucy's heart to save her soul." Merriam-Webster's Ency of Lit

Stone, Tanya Lee

A bad boy can be good for a girl. Wendy Lamb Books 2006 228p $14.95; lib bdg $16.99; pa $7.99 *

Grades: 9 10 11 12   **Fic**
1. School stories
ISBN 0-385-74702-0; 978-0-385-74702-8; 0-385-90946-2 (lib bdg); 978-0-385-90946-4 (lib bdg); 0-553-49509-7 (pa); 978-0-553-49509-6 (pa)
         LC 2006-272453
Josie, Nicolette, and Aviva all get mixed up with a senior boy who can talk them into doing almost anything he wants. In a blur of high school hormones and personal doubt, each girl struggles with how much to give up and what ultimately to keep for herself.

"The language is realistic and frank, and, while not graphic, it is filled with descriptions of the teens and their sexuality. This is not a book that will sit quietly on any shelf; it will be passed from girl to girl to girl." SLJ

Stowe, Harriet Beecher, 1811-1896
Uncle Tom's cabin; with an introduction by
Alfred Kazin. Knopf 1995 xxix, 494p $20
Grades: 11 12 Adult **Fic**
1. African Americans—Fiction 2. Slavery—Fiction
ISBN 0-679-44365-7
Also available in paperback from Bantam Classics
"Everyman's library"
"The book relates the trials, suffering, and human dig-
nity of Uncle Tom, an old slave. Cruelly treated by a
Yankee plantation owner, Simon Legree, Tom dies as the
result of a beating. Uncle Tom is devoted to Little Eva,
the daughter of his white owner, Augustine St. Clare.
Other important characters are the mulatto girl Eliza; the
impish black child Topsy; Miss Ophelia St. Clare, a New
England spinster; and Marks, the slave catcher. The setting is Kentucky and Louisiana." Reader's Ency. 4th edition

Strasser, Todd, 1950-
Give a boy a gun. Simon & Schuster Bks. for
Young Readers 2000 146p hardcover o.p. pa $5.99
*
Grades: 9 10 11 12 **Fic**
1. Violence—Fiction 2. School stories
ISBN 0-689-81112-8; 0-689-84893-5 (pa)
This documentary novel "charts the growing disaffec-
tion of Gary and Brendan, two teenage friends who
dream of taking revenge on the people (primarily members of the school's football team) who have tormented
them. Told in a variety of voices, which are presented as
excerpts from interview's with family, friends, teachers,
and others." Booklist
"Statistics, quotes, and facts related to actual incidents
of school violence appear in dark print at the bottom of
the pages. An appendix includes a chronology of school
shootings in the United States, the author's own treatise
on gun control, and places to get more information." SLJ

Stratton, Allan
Chanda's secrets. Annick Press 2004 193p
$19.95; pa $8.95 *
Grades: 7 8 9 10 **Fic**
1. AIDS (Disease)—Fiction 2. Africa—Fiction
ISBN 1-55037-835-X; 1-55037-834-1 (pa)
In this story "Chanda, a 16-year-old . . . girl living in
the small city of Bonang in Africa, must confront the un-
dercurrents of shame and stigma associated with
HIV/AIDS." Publisher's note
"The details of sub-Saharan African life are convincing and smoothly woven into this moving story of poverty and courage, but the real insight for readers will be
the appalling treatment of the AIDS victims. Strong language and frank description are appropriate to the subject
matter." SLJ

Stroud, Jonathan, 1970-
The Amulet of Samarkand. Hyperion Bks. for
Children 2003 462p (Bartimaeus trilogy) $17.95;
pa $7.99
Grades: 7 8 9 10 **Fic**
1. Fantasy fiction
ISBN 0-7868-1859-X; 0-7868-5255-0 (pa)
LC 2003-49904

Nathaniel, a magician's apprentice, summons up the
djinni Bartimaeus and instructs him to steal the Amulet
of Samarkand from the powerful magician Simon Lovelace.
"There is plenty of action, mystery, and humor to
keep readers turning the pages. This title, the first in a
trilogy, is a must for fantasy fans." SLJ
Other titles in this series are:
The golem's eye (2004)
Ptolemy's gate (2006)

Styron, William, 1925-2006
The confessions of Nat Turner. Modern Lib.
1994 xliv, 428p hardcover o.p. pa $14
Grades: 11 12 Adult **Fic**
1. Turner, Nat, 1800?-1831—Fiction 2. Slavery—Fic-
tion
ISBN 0-679-60101-5; 0-679-73663-8 (pa)
LC 94-9393
A reissue of the title first published 1967 by Random
House
This "account of an actual person and event is based
on the brief contemporary pamphlet of the same title
presented to a trial court as evidence and published in
Virginia a year after the revolt of fellow slaves led by
Turner in 1831. Imagining much of Turner's youth and
early manhood before the rebellion that he headed at the
age of 31, Styron in frequently rhetorical and pseudo-
Biblical style has Turner recall his religious faith and his
power of preaching to other slaves." Oxford Companion
to Am Lit. 5th edition

Sophie's choice. Modern Lib. 1998 599p $22;
pa $14
Grades: 11 12 Adult **Fic**
1. Authors—Fiction 2. Brooklyn (New York, N.Y.)—
Fiction
ISBN 0-679-60289-5; 0-679-73637-9 (pa)
LC 97-36895
A reissue of the title first published 1979
"Sophie Zawistowska is a Polish Catholic who has
somehow survived Auschwitz and resettled in America
after the war. Here, in a Jewish boarding house in
Flatbush, she meets two men—Nathan Landau, a brilliant
but dangerously unstable Jew who becomes her lover;
and Stingo, a young Southern writer (and autobiographical simulacrum of Styron himself). The novel traces
Stingo's intense involvement with the lovers—their eu-
phoric highs as well as their cataclysmic descents into
psychopathy—and his growing fascination with the horror of Sophie's past." Libr J
"It was a daring act for Styron, whose sensibilities are
wholly Southern, to venture into the territory of the
American Jew, to say nothing of his plunge into European history. The book is powerfully moving." Burgess. 99
Novels

Sutcliff, Rosemary, 1920-1992
The Shining Company. Farrar, Straus & Giroux
1990 295p hardcover o.p. pa $7.95
Grades: 9 10 11 12 **Fic**
1. Great Britain—History—0-1066—Fiction
ISBN 0-374-36807-4; 0-374-46616-5 (pa)
LC 89-46142

Sutcliff, Rosemary, 1920-1992—*Continued*

This novel is "based on 'The Gododdin,' the earliest surviving poem set in Northern Britain. Set in A.D. 600, the story is told by Prosper who, with his bodyservant Conn, joins Prince Gorthyn as a shieldbearer when the prince enlists in a company formed by King Mynyddog of the Gododdin in an effort to unite the British kingdoms against the ever-present Saxon threat. The bulk of the story concerns the forging of men from disparate parts of Britain into a fighting unit, combined in a common cause. The rousing climax comes with their first mission when, sent deep into Saxon territory, they are abandoned by Mynyddog." SLJ

"The realistic telling of the tale makes Sutcliff's story interesting. She creates a setting so genuine that readers will find themselves transposed into another time and place. Her language, reinforced by the Germanic influence of Old English, adds not only authenticity to the story but also a sense of poetry. This book will be cherished by the lover of history, the lover of literature, and the lover of adventure." Voice Youth Advocates

Swift, Jonathan, 1667-1745

Gulliver's travels; with an introduction by Pat Rogers. Knopf 1991 xlv, 318p map $20

Grades: 7 8 9 10   **Fic**
1. Fantasy fiction
ISBN 0-679-40545-3   LC 91-53011
Also available from other publishers
"Everyman's library"
First published 1726

"In the account of his four wonder-countries Swift satirizes contemporary manners and morals, art and politics—in fact the whole social scheme—from four different points of view. The huge Brobdingnagians reduce man to his natural insignificance, the little people of Lilliput parody Europe and its petty broils, in Laputa philosophers are ridiculed, and finally all Swift's hatred and contempt find their satisfaction in degrading humanity to a bestial condition." Baker. Guide to the Best Fic

Tal, Eve, 1947-

Double crossing. Cinco Puntos Press 2005 261p $16.95

Grades: 7 8 9 10   **Fic**
1. Immigrants—Fiction 2. Jews—Fiction
ISBN 0-938317-94-6   LC 2005-8188
In 1905, as life becomes increasingly difficult for Jews in Ukraine, eleven-year-old Raizel and her father flee to America in hopes of earning money to bring the rest of the family there, but her father's health and Orthodox faith become barriers.

"Tal's fictionalized account of her grandfather's journey to America is fast paced, full of suspense, and highly readable." SLJ

Tan, Amy

The Joy Luck Club. Putnam 1989 288p $24.95 *

Grades: 11 12 Adult   **Fic**
1. Chinese Americans—Fiction 2. Mother-daughter relationship—Fiction
ISBN 0-399-13420-4   LC 88-26492

"Four aging Chinese women who knew life in China before 1949 and now live in San Francisco meet regularly to play mah-jongg and share thoughts about their American-born children. In alternating sections we learn about the cultural differences between the elderly 'aunties' and the younger generation. When one of the older women dies, her daughter is pressed to take her place in the Joy Luck Club. Her feeling of being out of place gradually gives way to an understanding of the need to retain cultural continuity and an appreciation for the strength and endurance of the older women." Shapiro. Fic for Youth. 3d edition

Tanner, Mike, 1960-

Resurrection blues. Annick Press 2005 246p $19.95; pa $9.95 *

Grades: 9 10 11 12   **Fic**
1. Rock music—Fiction 2. Musicians—Fiction
ISBN 1-55037-897-X; 1-55037-896-1 (pa)

"In the middle of his senior year, 18-year-old Flynn Robinson drops out of high school to join a traveling bar band and chase his dream of being a professional musician like his uncle Ray. . . Flynn describes his six months on the road with the Sawyers band: the thrill of performing; his unease with his bandmates' adventures with drugs and sex; and ambivalence about his future, particularly his relationship with his high-school girlfriend. . . . Many readers, particularly teens who share his lyrically described musical passion, will easily connect with his questions, restlessness, and driving need for independence and expression." Booklist

Taylor, G. P.

Tersias the oracle. G.P. Putnam's Sons 2006 c2005 262p $17.99; pa $8.99

Grades: 8 9 10 11 12   **Fic**
1. Occultism—Fiction 2. London (England)—Fiction 3. Prophets—Fiction
ISBN 0-399-24258-9; 0-14-240846-8 (pa)
    LC 2005-14347
First published 2005 in the United Kingdom
Jonah, a young thief, and his friends and Tersias, a twelve-year-old boy who channels prophesies, become embroiled in the machinations of a magician, a politician, and a false prophet, as well as in the magic of a strange alabaster box.

"The story's gritty setting, moody tone, and brisk action will appeal to many." Booklist

Taylor, Kim

Bowery girl. Viking 2006 225p $16.99 *

Grades: 9 10 11 12   **Fic**
1. Thieves—Fiction 2. Poverty—Fiction 3. New York (N.Y.)—Fiction
ISBN 0-670-05966-8; 978-0-670-05966-9
    LC 2005-27892
In New York's tenements in 1883, two orphaned teenage girls realize that their dream of saving enough money to move to Brooklyn across the newly-built bridge may be achieved if they learn new trades at a nearby settlement house, rather than continuing their lives of prostitution and stealing.

"This novel is not just fine historical fiction; it is also

Taylor, Kim—_Continued_

splendid writing with mega teen appeal, as close a 'must-have' for any collection as this reviewer can imagine."
Voice Youth Advocates

Taylor, Mildred D.

Roll of thunder, hear my cry. 25th anniversary ed. Phyllis Fogelman Books 2001 276p $17.99; pa $7.99

Grades: 4 5 6 7 8 9   **Fic**
1. African Americans—Fiction 2. Mississippi—Fiction
ISBN 0-8037-2647-3; 0-14-240112-9 (pa)
                           LC 00-39378
Also available in paperback from Puffin Bks.
Awarded the Newbery medal, 1977
First published 1976 by Dial Press
"The time is 1933. The place is Spokane, Mississippi where the Logans, the only black family who own their own land, wage a courageous struggle to remain independent, displeasing a white plantation owner bent on taking their land. But this suspenseful tale is also about the story's young narrator, Cassie, and her three brothers who decide to wage their own personal battles to maintain the self-dignity and pride with which they were raised. . . . Ms. Taylor's richly textured novel shows a strong, proud black family . . . resisting rather than succumbing to oppression." Child Book Rev Serv
Other titles about the Logan family are:
Let the circle be unbroken (1981)
The road to Memphis (1990)
The land (2000)

Temple, Frances, 1945-1995

The Beduins' gazelle. HarperTrophy 1998 150p pa $5.99

Grades: 9 10 11 12   **Fic**
1. Bedouins—Fiction 2. Deserts—Fiction 3. Middle East—Fiction
ISBN 0-06-440669-5
First published 1996 by Orchard Books
"In 1302, Atiyah and Halima, cousins betrothed at birth, are separated when Atiyah travels from the desert to Fez to study. . . . While in Fez, Atiyah meets and befriends Etienne, a French pilgrim who is studying Arabic, whom readers met in 'The Ramsay Scallop'. . . . When word travels to Atiyah that Halima is lost, he and Etienne return to the desert to find her. But Halima is rescued by another tribe whose sheikh wants her as his newest wife." Voice Youth Advocates
"Told in short, rapid chapters, Temple's briskly paced story is fueled by a cast of complex, emotionally resonant characters." Publ Wkly

Thal, Lilli

Mimus; translated by John Brownjohn. Annick Press 2005 394p $19.95; pa $9.95 *

Grades: 7 8 9 10   **Fic**
1. Fools and jesters—Fiction 2. Fantasy fiction
ISBN 1-55037-925-9; 1-55037-924-0 (pa)
"Two mighty kingdoms are engaged in endless, merciless war, but change appears imminent. King Philip is meeting his archenemy, King Theodo, to sign a peace treaty. But King Philip and his men are tricked and consigned to the squalid dungeons of King Theodo's castle. Soon, his son, 12-year-old Prince Florin, is lured to the castle, where the same horror awaits him. On a whim, King Theodo decides to make the captive crown prince his second Fool, trained by Mimus, an enigmatic, occasionally spiteful, and unpredictable court jester." Publisher's note
"This outstanding translation from the German brings an author with rich, complex, and very clever storytelling skills to American teens. . . . This is a sophisticated and engrossing historical tale by a writer who brings exceptional attention to detail, character development, and theme." Booklist

Tharp, Tim, 1957-

Knights of the hill country. Alfred A. Knopf 2006 233p $16.95; lib bdg $18.99

Grades: 8 9 10 11 12   **Fic**
1. Football—Fiction 2. School stories 3. Oklahoma—Fiction
ISBN   978-0-375-83653-4;   0-375-83653-5; 978-0-375-93653-1 (lib bdg); 0-375-93653-X (lib bdg)
                         LC 2005-33279
In his senior year, high school star linebacker Hampton Greene finally begins to think for himself and discovers that he might be interested in more than just football.
"Taut scenes on the football field and the dilemmas about choosing what feels right over what's expected are all made memorable by Hamp's unforgettable, colloquial voice." Booklist

Thesman, Jean

Singer. Viking 2005 308p $17.99; pa $7.99

Grades: 7 8 9 10   **Fic**
1. Fantasy fiction
ISBN 0-670-05937-4; 0-14-240650-3 (pa)
                         LC 2004-14905
Also available Thorndike Press large print edition
Imprisoned by her wicked and power-hungry mother, Lady Rhiannon, Gwenore escapes to a women's healing community, later changing her name and becoming nursemaid and protector to the children of the magical king of Lir, who is now married to Rhiannon
The violent world of this "compulsively readable and satisfying medieval fantasy . . . seems a brutish place indeed. . . . Yet it's a breathtakingly magical world as well." Publ Wkly

Thompson, Kate

The new policeman. Greenwillow Books 2007 442p $16.99; lib bdg $17.89 *

Grades: 7 8 9 10   **Fic**
1. Space and time—Fiction 2. Fairies—Fiction 3. Music—Fiction 4. Ireland—Fiction 5. Fantasy fiction
ISBN   978-0-06-117427-8;   0-06-117427-0; 978-0-06-117428-5 (lib bdg); 0-06-117428-9 (lib bdg)
                         LC 2006-8246
First published 2005 in the United Kingdom
Irish teenager JJ Liddy discovers that time is leaking from his world into Tir na nOg, the land of the fairies,

Thompson, Kate—*Continued*
and when he attempts to stop the leak he finds out a lot
about his family history, the music that he loves, and a
crime his great-grandfather may or may not have committed.
"Mesmerizing and captivating, this book is guaranteed
to charm fantasy fans." Voice Youth Advocates

Tiernan, Cate, 1961-
A chalice of wind. Book 1: Balefire Series.
Penguin/Razorbill 2005 250p pa $5.99 *
Grades: 8 9 10 11 12   **Fic**
1. Witchcraft—Fiction 2. Twins—Fiction 3. Sisters—
Fiction 4. New Orleans (La.)—Fiction
ISBN 1-59514-045-X
Separated since birth, seventeen-year-old twins Thais
and Clio unexpectedly meet in New Orleans where they
seem to be pursued by a coven of witches who want to
harness the twins' magickal powers for its own ends.
"The suspenseful story moves quickly along, and a
love triangle between the twins and a mysterious young
man adds some depth. The action builds toward a tanta-
lizing twist." Booklist
Other titles in the Balefire series are:
A circle of ashes (2005)
A feather of stone (2005)
A necklace of water (2006)

Tiffany, Grace, 1958-
Ariel. Laura Geringer Books 2005 232p $16.99;
lib bdg $17.89
Grades: 7 8 9 10   **Fic**
1. Shakespeare, William, 1564-1616. The Tempest—
Fiction 2. Survival after airplane accidents, ship-
wrecks, etc.—Fiction 3. Magic—Fiction
ISBN 0-06-075327-7; 0-06-075327-6 (lib bdg)
"Tiffany takes the characters from Shakespeare's The
Tempest and provides background as to how they get to
the point where readers find them in the play." SLJ
"This lush, lyrical, and elegantly expressive work is a
strong mix of solid narrative storytelling, sensitive characterization, and fantasy." Booklist

Tingle, Rebecca
The edge on the sword. Putnam 2001 277p
$18.99; pa $6.99
Grades: 9 10 11 12   **Fic**
1. Great Britain—History—0-1066—Fiction
ISBN 0-399-23580-9; 0-14-250058-5 (pa)
                                             LC 00-55353
In ninth-century Britain, fifteen-year-old Aethelflaed,
daughter of King Alfred of West Saxony, finds she must
assume new responsibilities much sooner than expected
when she is betrothed to Ethelred of Mercia in order to
strengthen a strategic alliance against the Danes
This "story is filled with exciting action, interesting
characters, and convincing historical details of the late
ninth century that bring to life this distant and violent
time in Britain." SLJ
Another title about Aethelflaed and her family is:
Far traveler (2005)

**Tolkien, J. R. R. (John Ronald Reuel), 1892-
1973**
The hobbit, or, There and back again. Houghton
Mifflin 2001 330p il $18; pa $10
Grades: 4 5 6 7 8 9 10   **Fic**
1. Fantasy fiction
ISBN 0-618-16221-6; 0-618-26030-7 (pa)
                                             LC 2001276594
Also available from Houghton Mifflin in an edition
with illustrations by Michael Hague for $29.95 (ISBN
0395362903)
A reissue of the title first published 1938
"Text of this edition is based on that first published
in Great Britain by Collins Modern Classics in 1998 . . .
corrections have been made to that setting"—T.p. verso
"This fantasy features the adventures of hobbit Bilbo
Baggins, who joins a band of dwarves led by Gandalf
the Wizard. Together they seek to recover the stolen
treasure that is hidden in Lonely Mountain and guarded
by Smaug the Dragon. This book precedes the Lord of
the Rings trilogy." Shapiro. Fic for Youth. 3d edition
Followed by The lord of the rings, a trilogy intended
for older readers

The lord of the rings. 50th Anniversary ed.
Houghton Mifflin 2004 xxv, 1157p il map slip
case $100
Grades: 7 8 9 10   **Fic**
1. Fantasy fiction
ISBN 0-618-51765-0   LC 2004-275215
Also available as separate volumes in hardcover and
paperback editions
First published 1954 in the United Kingdom
Contents: The fellowship of the ring; The two towers;
The return of the king
"This is a tale of imaginary gnomelike creatures who
battle against evil. Led by Frodo, the hobbits embark on
a journey to prevent a magic ring from falling into the
grasp of the powers of darkness. The forces of good succeed in their fight against the Dark Lord of evil, and
Frodo and Sam bring the Ring to Mount Doom, where
it is destroyed." Shapiro. Fic for Youth. 3d edition

Tolstoy, Leo, graf, 1828-1910
Anna Karenina; translated from the Russian by
Louise and Aylmer Maude; with an introduction
by John Bayley. Knopf 1992 xlix, 963p $24
Grades: 9 10 11 12   **Fic**
1. Russia—Fiction
ISBN 0-679-41000-7   LC 91-53196
Also available in paperback from various publishers
"Everyman's Library"
Written in 1873-1876
This novel is "the story of a tragic, adulterous love.
Anna meets and falls in love with Aleksei Vronski, a
handsome young officer. She abandons her child and
husband in order to be with Vronski. When she thinks
Vronski has tired of her, she kills herself by leaping under a train. . . . A subplot concerns the contrasting happy marriage of Konstantin Levin and his young wife Kitty. Levin's search for meaning in his life and his love for
a natural, simple existence on his estate are reflections of
Tolstoy's own moods and thoughts of the time." Reader's Ency. 4th edition

Triana, Gaby

Cubanita. HarperCollins Pub. 2005 195p lib bdg $16.89; pa $7.99 *

Grades: 9 10 11 12   **Fic**

1. Cuban Americans—Fiction 2. Mother-daughter relationship—Fiction 3. Miami (Fla.)—Fiction

ISBN 0-06-056021-5 (lib bdg); 0-06-056022-3 (pa)

LC 2004-18462

Seventeen-year-old Isabel, eager to leave Miami to attend the University of Michigan and escape her overprotective Cuban mother, learns some truths about her family's past and makes important decisions about the type of person she wants to be.

"Isabel's story is an entertaining read that will be gobbled up by cubanitas and non-cubanitas alike." SLJ

Trice, Dawn Turner, 1956-

Only twice I've wished for heaven; a novel. Crown 1997 304p hardcover o.p. pa $12.95

Grades: 11 12 Adult   **Fic**

1. African Americans—Fiction 2. Chicago (Ill.)—Fiction

ISBN 0-517-70428-5; 0-385-49123-9 (pa)

LC 97-22164

"In 1975, the Saville family has won the chance to move into Lakeland, a planned community on Chicago's lakefront. Formed as a social experiment, Lakeland is home to many of the city's elite black professionals, but for 11-year-old Tempest, the residents, with their expensive clothes and prissy manners, have 'no color' at all. Slipping outside the walled community through a hole in the fence, she is drawn to the raucous environs of Thirty-fifth Street, particularly Miss Jonetta's liquor store." Booklist

"Trice creates vibrant characters via the counterpointed voices of Temmie and Jonetta. As each interprets events within the range of her knowledge and expectations, Trice obliquely provides insight into the crucial social issues that help shape the lives of African Americans." Publ Wkly

Trottier, Maxine

Three songs for courage. Tundra Books 2006 324p $16.95

Grades: 9 10 11 12   **Fic**

1. Bullies—Fiction 2. Homicide—Fiction 3. Brothers—Fiction 4. Canada—Fiction

ISBN 978-0-88776-745-6; 0-88776-745-1

LC 2005-927011

"Sixteen-year-old Gordon is looking forward to the summer—he has his best buddies; a new girlfriend, Mary; and his baby, a 1950 Pontiac named the Chief. The only sour note is Lancer Caldwell and his gang, whose violence follows Gordon wherever he goes. When Gordon finds his brother dead from a fall down the stairs, he thinks it's an accident like everyone else—until he finds evidence that Lancer was in his home that night." Booklist

"From native wisdom to flatulence humor and from sexual assault to pigs in dresses, Trottier handles the serious with poignancy and lighter moments with flair. . . . This coming-of-age novel is rich, readable, and substantive." Voice Youth Advocates

Trumbo, Dalton, 1905-1976

Johnny got his gun. Stuart, L. 1970 c1959 309p hardcover o.p. pa $15.95 *

Grades: 11 12 Adult   **Fic**

1. World War, 1914-1918—Fiction 2. Physically handicapped—Fiction

ISBN 0-818-40110-9; 0-8065-2847-8 (pa)

A reissue of the title first published 1939 by Lippincott

"Far more than an antiwar polemic, this compassionate description of the effects of war on one soldier is a poignant tribute to the human instinct to survive. Badly mutilated, blind, and deaf, Johnny fights to communicate with an uncomprehending medical world debating his fate." Shapiro. Fic for Youth. 3d edition

Tullson, Diane, 1958-

Red Sea. Orca Book Publishers 2005 169p pa $7.95

Grades: 7 8 9 10   **Fic**

1. Adventure fiction 2. Survival after airplane accidents, shipwrecks, etc.—Fiction

ISBN 1-55143-331-1

"Libby, 14, is on a yearlong sailing adventure with her mother and stepfather, Duncan. Stuck in Djibouti awaiting favorable seas, she makes her discontent known to everyone, at every turn. She deliberately dilly-dallies on the day of departure, which causes her boat to miss traveling with the flotilla as planned. Sailing through dangerous waters, Libby's family is alone when pirates attack. Duncan is killed, and her mother is badly wounded. The teen is left to her own devices to survive, nurse her mother, and find the right course to safety. An exciting and suspenseful survival tale." SLJ

Turner, Ann Warren, 1945-

Hard hit; [by] Ann Turner. Scholastic Press 2006 167p $16.99

Grades: 7 8 9 10   **Fic**

1. Father-son relationship—Fiction 2. Baseball—Fiction 3. Cancer—Fiction 4. Death—Fiction

ISBN 0-439-29680-3   LC 2005-49906

Also available Thorndike Press large print edition

A rising high school baseball star faces his most difficult challenge when his father is diagnosed with pancreatic cancer.

This is a "novel in verse that speaks volumes long after the book is closed." Voice Youth Advocates

Turner, Megan Whalen, 1965-

The thief. Greenwillow Bks. 1996 219p $16.99 *

Grades: 7 8 9 10   **Fic**

1. Adventure fiction 2. Thieves—Fiction

ISBN 0-688-14627-9   LC 95-41040

Also available in paperback from Puffin Bks.

A Newbery Medal honor book, 1997

"Gen languishes in prison for boasting of his skill as a thief. The magus—the king's powerful advisor—needing a clever thief to find an ancient ring that gives the owner the right to rule a neighboring country, bails Gen out. Their journey toward the treasure is marked by dan-

Turner, Megan Whalen, 1965-—*Continued*
ger and political intrigue, and features a motley cast, tales of old gods, and the revelation of Gen's true identity." Publisher's note

"A tantalizing, suspenseful, exceptionally clever novel. . . . The author's characterization of Gen is simply superb." Horn Book

Other titles in this series are:
The King of Attolia (2006)
The Queen of Attolia (2000)

Twain, Mark, 1835-1910
The adventures of Huckleberry Finn. Modern Library 1993 xx, 433p $16.95 *

Grades: 5 6 7 8 9 10 11 12 Adult **Fic**
1. Mississippi River—Fiction 2. Missouri—Fiction
ISBN 0-679-42470-9 LC 92-51065

Also available from other publishers
First published 1885. This is a companion volume to: The adventures of Tom Sawyer

This novel "begins with Huck's escape from his drunken, brutal father to the river, where he meets up with Jim, a runaway slave. The story of their journey downstream, with occasional forays into the society along the banks, is an American classic that captures the smells, rhythms, and sounds, the variety of dialects and the human activity of life on the great river. It is also a penetrating social commentary that reveals corruption, moral decay, and intellectual impoverishment through Huck and Jim's encounters with traveling actors and con men, lynch mobs, thieves, and Southern gentility." Reader's Ency. 4th edition

The adventures of Tom Sawyer; [illustrated by True W. Williams]; foreword and notes by John C. Gerber; text established by Paul Baender. University of California Press 2002 c1982 274p il pa $14.95

Grades: 5 6 7 8 9 10 11 12 Adult **Fic**
1. Mississippi River—Fiction 2. Missouri—Fiction
ISBN 0-520-23575-4

Also available from other publishers
First published 1876. This is a companion volume to: The adventures of Huckleberry Finn

"Tom, a shrewd and adventurous boy, is at home in the respectable world of his Aunt Polly, as well as in the self-reliant, parentless world of Huck Finn. The two friends, out in the cemetery under a full moon, attempt to cure warts with a dead cat. They accidentally witness a murder, of which Muff Potter is later wrongly accused. Knowing that the true murderer is Injun Joe, the boys are helpless with fear; they decide to run away to Jackson's Island. After a few pleasant days of smoking and swearing, they realize that the townspeople believe them dead. Returning in time to hear their funeral eulogies, they become town heroes. At the trial of Muff Potter, Tom, unable to let an innocent person be condemned, reveals his knowledge. Injun Joe flees. Later Tom and his sweetheart, Becky Thatcher, get lost in the cave in which the murderer is hiding. They escape, and Tom and Huck return to find the treasure Joe has buried." Reader's Ency. 4th edition

Tyler, Anne, 1941-
Dinner at the Homesick Restaurant. Knopf 1982 303p hardcover o.p. pa $14.95

Grades: 11 12 Adult **Fic**
1. Family life—Fiction 2. Maryland—Fiction
ISBN 0-394-52381-4; 0-449-91159-4 (pa)
LC 81-13694

"Pearl Tull, an angry woman who vacillates between excesses of maternal energy and spurts of terrifying rage, has been deserted by her husband and has brought up her three children alone. Cody, the eldest, is handsome, wild, and in a lifelong battle of jealousy with his young brother, the sweet-tempered and patient Ezra. Their sister Jenny tries, through three marriages, to find a stability which was never present in Pearl's home. Ezra also tries to achieve a permanence through his homey Homesick Restaurant in Baltimore, but he is cruelly tricked by his brother and is unable to establish any unity in the family." Shapiro. Fic for Youth. 3d edition

Uchida, Yoshiko, 1921-1992
Picture bride; a novel. University of Washington pa. ed. University of Washington Press 1997 216p pa $14.95

Grades: 11 12 Adult **Fic**
1. Japanese American women—Fiction 2. California—Fiction
ISBN 0-295-97616-0 LC 97-3

First published 1987 by Northland Press
"Carrying a photograph of the man she is to marry but has yet to meet, young Hana Omiya arrives in San Francisco, California, in 1917, one of several hundred Japanese 'picture brides' whose arranged marriages brought them to America in the early 1900s. Her story is intertwined with others: her husband, Taro Takeda, an Oakland shopkeeper; Kiku and her husband Henry, who reject demeaning city work to become farmers; Dr. Kaneda, a respected community leader who is destroyed by the adopted land he loves. All are caught up in the cruel turmoil of World War II, when West Coast Japanese Americans are uprooted from their homes and imprisoned in desert detention camps." Publisher's note

Updale, Eleanor
Montmorency; thief, liar, gentleman? Orchard Books 2004 c2003 232p $16.95

Grades: 6 7 8 9 10 **Fic**
1. London (England)—Fiction 2. Great Britain—History—19th century—Fiction 3. Thieves—Fiction
ISBN 0-439-58035-8 LC 2003-56345

Also available Thorndike Press large print edition
First published 2003 in the United Kingdom
In Victorian London, after his life is saved by a young physician, a thief utilizes the knowledge he gains in prison and from the scientific lectures he attends as the physician's case study exhibit to create a new, highly successful, double life for himself.

"Updale adroitly works the tradition of devilish schemes and narrow escapes, and the plot moves as nimbly as the master thief himself." Bull Cent Child Books

Other titles about Montmorency are:
Montmorency and the assassins (2006)
Montmorency on the rocks: doctor, aristocrat, murderer? (2005)
Montmorency's revenge (2007)

Uris, Leon, 1924-2003
Exodus. Doubleday 1958 626p il hardcover o.p. pa $7.99
Grades: 11 12 Adult   Fic
1. Zionism—Fiction
ISBN 0-385-05082-8; 0-553-25847-8 (pa)
"Following World War II the British forbade immigration of the Jews to Israel. European Jewish underground groups, aided by Palestinian agent Ari Ben Canaan, made every effort to aid these unfortunate victims of Nazi persecution. The novel provides insight into the heritage of the Jews and understanding of the danger involved in helping them reach a safe haven. It also includes the warm love story of Ari and a gentile nurse, Kitty Fremont, who cared very much for the welfare of the Jewish children caught in this nightmare." Shapiro. Fic for Youth. 3d edition

Vande Velde, Vivian, 1951-
The book of Mordred; [illustrations by Justin Gerard] Houghton Mifflin 2005 342p $18; pa $8.99
Grades: 8 9 10 11 12   Fic
1. Arthur, King—Fiction 2. Mordred (Legendary character)—Fiction 3. Knights and knighthood—Fiction 4. Great Britain—History—0-1066—Fiction
ISBN 0-618-50754-X; 0-618-80916-3 (pa)
                                        LC 2004-28223
As the peaceful King Arthur reigns, the five-year-old daughter of Lady Alayna, newly widowed of the village-wizard Toland, is abducted by knights who leave their barn burning and their only servant dead.
"All of the characters are well developed and have a strong presence throughout. . . . [This] provides an intriguing counterpoint to anyone who is interested in Arthurian legend." SLJ

Vargas Llosa, Mario, 1936-
The Feast of the Goat; translated from the Spanish by Edith Grossman. Farrar, Straus & Giroux 2001 404p $25; pa $14
Grades: 11 12 Adult   Fic
1. Trujillo Molina, Rafael Leónidas, 1891-1961—Fiction 2. Dictators—Fiction
ISBN 0-374-15476-7; 0-312-42027-7 (pa)
                                        LC 2001-33480
Original Spanish edition, 2000
"This fictional portrait of ruthless Dominican Republic dictator Rafael Trujillo focuses on the end of the old 'goat's' life. . . . Vargas Llosa relates Trujillo's story from the perspective of Urania Cabral, a successful New York lawyer who has spent a lifetime in exile but returns to her homeland when the tyrant is finally murdered. Urania hopes to rid herself of the demons that have possessed her since 1961, when as a teenager she was battered and humiliated by the impotent and vindictive old dictator." Libr J

Vaught, Susan
Stormwitch. Bloomsbury Children's Books 2005 208p $16.95
Grades: 7 8 9 10   Fic
1. Voodooism—Fiction 2. Haitian Americans—Fiction 3. Hurricanes—Fiction 4. Mississippi—Fiction
ISBN 1-58234-952-5   LC 2004-54681
In Pass Christian, Mississippi in 1969, sixteen-year-old Ruba, trained by her Haitian grandmother in both voodoo and Amazonian warrior tactics, uses her skills to fight against racism and the African witch Zashar, now coming ashore in the form of Hurricane Camille.
"This story offers a smooth blend of historical fact, suspense, and magic." SLJ

Trigger. Bloomsbury Children's Books 2006 292p $16.95 *
Grades: 9 10 11 12   Fic
1. Brain—Wounds and injuries—Fiction 2. Suicide—Fiction
ISBN 978-1-58234-920-6; 1-58234-920-7
                                        LC 2005-32249
Teenager Jersey Hatch must work through his extensive brain damage to figure out why he decided to shoot himself.
"Though teen suicide is a oft-chosen theme in young adult realism, Jersey's fresh voice, combined with the mystery elements fueled by his damaged memory, make this addition to the subgenre a compelling one." Bull Cent Child Books

Verdelle, A. J., 1960-
The good negress. Algonquin Bks. 1995 298p $19.95
Grades: 11 12 Adult   Fic
1. African Americans—Fiction 2. Detroit (Mich.)—Fiction
ISBN 1-56512-085-X   LC 94-40889
Also available in paperback from HarperCollins Pubs.
Set in Virginia and Detroit during the 1950s and 1960s, this novel "is the coming-of-age story of Denise Palms, who leaves her grandmother's rural home to return to her family in Detroit. Denise's family expects her to concentrate on housework and childcare, but her teacher pushes her to spend time on afterschool lessons in diction and grammar in order to 'better' herself." Libr J
"Verdelle's truly fine debut novel belongs in the ranks of other classics in African American folk vernacular." Choice

Verne, Jules, 1828-1905
Twenty thousand leagues under the sea; translated with an introduction and notes by William Butcher. Oxford University Press 1998 xlviii, 445p pa $10.95
Grades: 5 6 7 8 9 10 11 12 Adult   Fic
1. Submarines—Fiction 2. Sea stories 3. Science fiction
ISBN 0-19-282839-8   LC 97-29726
Also available from other publishers
Original French edition, 1870

Verne, Jules, 1828-1905—*Continued*
"The voyage of the Nautilus permitted Verne to describe the wonders of an undersea world almost totally unknown to the general public of the period. Indebted to literary tradition for his Atlantis, he made his major innovation in having the submarine completely powered by electricity, although the interest in electrical forces goes back to Poe and Shelley. So far as the enigmatic ending is concerned, his readers had to wait for the three-part The Mysterious Island (1874-1875) to learn that Nemo had been the Indian warrior-prince Dakkar, who had been involved in the Sepoy Mutiny of 1857." Anatomy of Wonder 4

Vijayaraghavan, Vineeta, 1972-
Motherland; a novel. Soho Press 2001 231p hardcover o.p. pa $12
Grades: 11 12 Adult   **Fic**
1. Culture conflict—Fiction 2. India—Fiction
ISBN 1-56947-217-3; 1-56947-283-1 (pa)
         LC 00-41011
"An American teenager spends the summer with her relatives in southern India and gains new insight into her past, her family and her heritage." Publ Wkly
"Readers will readily identify with Maya's American cultural instincts and impulses while gaining an appreciation and respect for her Indian heritage and values." SLJ

Vizzini, Ned, 1981-
It's kind of a funny story. Miramax Books/Hyperion Books For Children 2006 444p $16.95; pa $8.99 *
Grades: 9 10 11 12   **Fic**
1. Depression (Psychology)—Fiction 2. Psychiatric hospitals—Fiction 3. New York (N.Y.)—Fiction
ISBN 0-7868-5196-1; 0-7868-5797-X (pa)
         LC 2005-52670
A humorous account of a New York City teenager's battle with depression and his time spent in a psychiatric hospital.
"What's terrific about the book is Craig's voice—intimate, real, funny, ironic, and one kids will come closer to hear." Booklist

Volponi, Paul
Black and white. Viking 2005 185p $15.99; pa $6.99 *
Grades: 7 8 9 10   **Fic**
1. African Americans—Fiction 2. Race relations—Fiction 3. Basketball—Fiction
ISBN 0-670-06006-2; 0-14-240692-9 (pa)
         LC 2004-24543
Two star high school basketball players, one black and one white, experience the justice system differently after committing a crime together and getting caught.
"These complex characters share a mutual respect and struggle with issues of loyalty, honesty, and courage. Social conflicts, basketball fervor, and tough personal choices make this title a gripping story." SLJ

Rooftop. Viking 2006 199p $15.99; pa $6.99 *
Grades: 9 10 11 12   **Fic**
1. Death—Fiction 2. Race relations—Fiction 3. African Americans—Fiction 4. New York (N.Y.)—Fiction
ISBN 0-670-06069-0; 0-14-240844-1 (pa)
         LC 2005-22811
Still reeling from seeing police shoot his unarmed cousin to death on the roof of a New York City housing project, seventeen-year-old Clay is dragged into the whirlwind of political manipulation that follows.
"This thoughtfully crafted, deceptively simple story knits together a high-interest plot, a readable narrative crackling with street slang, and complex personal and societal issues that will engage teen readers." Booklist

Voltaire, 1694-1778
Candide; translated by Peter Constantine. Modern Library 2005 119p hardcover o.p. pa $8.95
Grades: 11 12 Adult   **Fic**
ISBN 0-679-64313-3; 0-812-97201-5 (pa)
         LC 2004-55244
Also available from other publishers
Original French edition, 1759
"In this philosophical fantasy, naive Candide sees and suffers such misfortune that he ultimately rejects the philosophy of his tutor Doctor Pangloss, who claims that 'all is for the best in this best of all possible worlds.' Candide and his companions—Pangloss, his beloved Cunegonde, and his servant Cacambo—display an instinct for survival that provides them hope in an otherwise somber setting. When they all retire together to a simple life on a small farm, they discover that the secret of happiness is 'to cultivate one's garden,' a practical philosophy that excludes excessive idealism and nebulous metaphysics." Merriam-Webster's Ency of Lit

Vonnegut, Kurt, 1922-2007
Cat's cradle. Dial Press trade paperback ed. Dial Press 2006 c1963 287p pa $14
Grades: 11 12 Adult   **Fic**
1. Science fiction
ISBN 0-385-33348-X; 978-0-385-33348-1
         LC 2005-285166
First published 1963 by Holt, Rinehart and Winston
"In this mordant satire on religion, research, government, and human nature, a freelance writer becomes the catalyst in a chain of events that unearths the secret of ice-nine. This is an element potentially more lethal than that produced by nuclear fission. The search leads to a mythical island, San Lorenzo, where the writer also discovers the leader of a new religion, Bokonon." Shapiro. Fic for Youth. 3d edition

Slaughterhouse-five; or, The children's crusade: a duty-dance with death. 25th anniversary ed. Delacorte Press 1994 205p il $22.50; pa $6.99 *
Grades: 11 12 Adult   **Fic**
1. World War, 1939-1945—Fiction 2. Science fiction
ISBN 0-385-31208-3; 0-440-18029-5 (pa)
         LC 94-171120
A reissue of the title first published 1969

Vonnegut, Kurt, 1922-2007—*Continued*

This novel "mixes a fictionalized account of the author's experience of the fire bombing of Dresden with a compensatory fantasy of the planet Tralfamadore, the science-fiction element is progressively dominated by the overall concerns of satire, black humor, and absurdism." Reader's Ency. 3d edition

"A masterpiece, in which Vonnegut penetrated to the heart of the issues developed in his earlier absurdist fabulations. A key work of modern SF." Anatomy of Wonder 4

Vrettos, Adrienne Maria

Skin. Margaret K. McElderry Books 2006 227p $16.95 *

Grades: 7 8 9 10   **Fic**

1. Siblings—Fiction 2. Anorexia nervosa—Fiction

ISBN 1-4169-0655-X   LC 2005001119

When his parents decide to separate, eighth-grader Donnie watches with horror as the physical condition of his sixteen-year old sister, Karen, deteriorates due to an eating disorder.

"The overwhelming alienation Donnie endures will speak to many teens, while his honest perspective will be welcomed by boys." Booklist

Walker, Alice, 1944-

The color purple. 10th anniversary ed. Harcourt Brace Jovanovich 1992 290p il $24; pa $14 *

Grades: 11 12 Adult   **Fic**

1. African Americans—Fiction 2. Sisters—Fiction 3. Southern States—Fiction

ISBN 0-15-119154-9; 0-15-602835-2 (pa)

LC 91-47202

A reissue of the title first published 1982

"A feminist novel about an abused and uneducated black woman's struggle for empowerment, the novel was praised for the depth of its female characters and for its eloquent use of black English vernacular." Merriam-Webster's Ency of Lit

Wallace, Rich, 1957-

Wrestling Sturbridge. Knopf 1996 135p hardcover o.p. pa $4.99 *

Grades: 7 8 9 10   **Fic**

1. Wrestling—Fiction 2. Friendship—Fiction

ISBN 0-679-87803-3; 0-679-88555-2 (pa)

LC 95-20468

"Narrator Ben, a high school senior, doesn't want to be like his father and so many others in Sturbridge, Pa., who after graduating get a job at the cinder block plant. Seemingly his only alternative is to become a state wrestling champion and thus win an athletic scholarship. But his way is firmly blocked by his buddy Al, who reigns supreme in their weight class." Publ Wkly

"The wresting scenes are thrilling. . . . Like Ben, whose voice is so strong and clear here, Wallace weighs his words carefully, making every one count in this excellent, understated first novel." Booklist

Watson, Larry

Montana 1948; a novel. Washington Square Press 1995 175p pa $12.95 *

Grades: 11 12 Adult   **Fic**

1. Family life—Fiction 2. Montana—Fiction

ISBN 0-671-50703-6

First published 1993 by Milkweed Eds.

David Hayden, the narrator "is on the brink of young manhood when he learns that his uncle, a doctor and a hero of World War II in the Pacific, has been sexually molesting local Indian women. The citizens of Bentrock, Mont., tolerate Uncle Frank's predilection until Marie Little Soldier, David's parents' housekeeper, dies while under his care. Frank's conduct poses a moral problem for Wes Hayden, David's father, who is also the town sheriff; despite pressure from the boy's grandfather, Wes arrests Frank as a suspect in Marie's death." N Y Times Book Rev

"The moral issues, and the consequences of following one's conscience, are made painfully evident here. Watson is to be congratulated for the honesty of his writing and the purity of his prose." Libr J

Weaver, Will

Full service. Farrar, Straus & Giroux 2005 231p $17

Grades: 7 8 9 10   **Fic**

1. Service stations—Fiction 2. Farm life—Fiction 3. Minnesota—Fiction

ISBN 0-374-32485-9   LC 2004-57671

In the summer of 1965, teenager Paul Sutton, a northern Minnesota farm boy, takes a job at a gas station in town, where his strict religious upbringing is challenged by new people and experiences.

"Weaver is a wonderful stylist and his beautifully chosen words put such a shine on his deeply felt story that most teens will be able to find their own faces reflected in its pages." Booklist

Memory boy; a novel. HarperCollins Pubs. 2001 152p $15.95; pa $6.50

Grades: 9 10 11 12   **Fic**

1. Wilderness survival—Fiction 2. Family life—Fiction

ISBN 0-06-028811-6; 0-06-440854-X (pa)

LC 00-32049

"The year is 2008, two years after a massive volcano has wreaked havoc in the United States. The air is polluted with ash, crops keep failing, fuel is scarce and looting is rampant. Sixteen-year-old Miles knows that the only way for his family to survive is to head to their cabin in the Minnesota wilderness. Relying on knowledge passed down to him from an elderly friend, Mr. Kurz, Miles constructs a man-powered vehicle out of bicycles and sailboat parts to transport himself, his parents and younger sister." Publ Wkly

"Vivid characterizations, nonstop action, and an entirely plausible plot combine for a thrilling story." Booklist

Striking out. HarperCollins Pubs. 1993 272p hardcover o.p. pa $6.99

Grades: 9 10 11 12   **Fic**

1. Baseball—Fiction

ISBN 0-06-023346-X; 0-06-447113-6 (pa)

LC 93-565

Weaver, Will—*Continued*

Since the death of his older brother, thirteen-year-old Billy Baggs has had a distant relationship with his father, but life on their farm in northern Minnesota begins to change when he starts to play baseball

"This has the classic trimmings of an American bildungsroman, with subtle incorporation of the young hero's initiation into adult complexities that include sex, work, honor—and dishonor." Bull Cent Child Books

Other titles about Billy Baggs are:

Farm team (1995)

Hard ball (1998)

Weis, Margaret, 1948-

Mistress of dragons. TOR Bks. 2003 381p $25.95; pa $7.99

Grades: 11 12 Adult   Fic
   1. Dragons—Fiction 2. Fantasy fiction
   ISBN 0-7653-0468-6; 0-7653-4390-8 (pa)
                      LC 2003-42618

"A Tom Doherty Associates book"

When the Amazonian order of priestesses, who have kept dragons from interfering with humans, is violated by men, a wild and magical conflict ensues, revealing a secret lineage and dark truth about the Parliament of Dragons.

"Full of intrigue, magic, and violence, this first book of Dragonvarld—a projected trilogy chronicling the battle to preserve the uneasy relationship between dragons and humans—launches the project powerfully. Weis has brilliantly conceived a world viable for both dragons and humans." Booklist

Other titles in the Dragonvarld series are:

The dragon's son (2004)

Master of the dragons (2005)

Well of darkness; [by] Margaret Weis and Tracy Hickman. HarperCollins Pubs. 2000 450p hardcover o.p. pa $7.99

Grades: 11 12 Adult   Fic
   1. Fantasy fiction
   ISBN 0-06-105180-2; 0-06-102057-5 (pa)
                      LC 00-41710

First title in the authors' Sovereign stone trilogy

"Chosen to serve as the whipping boy of the young Prince Dagnarus, Gareth becomes his master's friend and confidant as they grow to manhood and become embroiled in the affairs of the land. Tempted by dark powers, Gareth seeks to assist the prince in his search for love and glory, unaware of the greater paths each must follow to fulfill his destiny." Libr J

The authors "raise a fairly standard plot far above mediocrity with ingenious world-building touches. . . . Moreover, they render Gareth and Dagnarus' friendship convincingly; the characters' motives are plausible and fully developed, and both retain human appeal." Booklist

Another title in the Sovereign Stone trilogy is:

Guardians of the lost (2001)

Weisberg, Joseph

10th grade; a novel. Random House 2002 259p hardcover o.p. pa $13.95

Grades: 11 12 Adult   Fic
   1. School stories
   ISBN 0-375-50584-9; 0-8129-6662-7 (pa)
                      LC 2001-41916

This "novel is the journal of Jeremy Reskin, a tenth-grader with atrocious grammar who does not believe in the utility of commas and will stretch sentences across many lines because his writing teacher has told him to express himself. . . . The book is in fact quite charming and proves surprisingly readable. . . . Weisberg admirably captures the inarticulate voice of a suburban tenth-grader." Booklist

Wells, H. G. (Herbert George), 1866-1946

The invisible man. Penguin 2005 xxiv, 161p pa $6

Grades: 11 12 Adult   Fic
   1. Science fiction
   ISBN 0-14-143998-X

Also available from other publishers

First published 1897

"The story concerns the life and death of a scientist named Griffin who has gone mad. Having learned how to make himself invisible, Griffin begins to use his invisibility for nefarious purposes, including murder. When he is finally killed, his body becomes visible again." Merriam-Webster's Ency of Lit

The time machine. Penguin 2005 xxviii, 104p pa $9

Grades: 11 12 Adult   Fic
   1. Science fiction
   ISBN 0-14-143997-1

Also available Thorndike Press large print edition and from other publishers

First published 1895

"Wells advanced his social and political ideas in this narrative of a nameless Time Traveller who is hurtled into the year 802,701 by his elaborate ivory, crystal, and brass contraption. The world he finds is peopled by two races: the decadent Eloi, fluttery and useless, are dependent for food, clothing, and shelter on the simian subterranean Morlocks, who prey on them. The two races—whose names are borrowed from the Biblical Eli and Moloch—symbolize Wells's vision of the eventual result of unchecked capitalism: a neurasthenic upper class that would eventually be devoured by a proletariat driven to the depths." Merriam-Webster's Ency of Lit

The war of the worlds; illustrated by Edward Gorey. New York Review Books [2005] c1960 251p il $16.95 *

Grades: 7 8 9 10   Fic
   1. Science fiction
   ISBN 1-59017-158-6   LC 2005-3693

Also available from other publishers

First published 1898

"The inhabitants of Mars, a loathsome though highly organized race, invade England, and by their command of superior weapons subdue and prey on the people." Baker. Guide to the Best Fic

Wells, H. G. (Herbert George), 1866-1946—
Continued

In this novel the author "introduced the 'Alien' being into the role which became a cliché—a monstrous invader of Earth, a competitor in a cosmic struggle for existence. Though the Martians were a ruthless and terrible enemy, HGW was careful to point out that Man had driven many animal species to extinction, and that human invaders of Tasmania had behaved no less callously in exterminating their cousins." Sci Fic Ency

Wells, Rosemary, 1943-

Red moon at Sharpsburg. Viking 2007 236p $16.99

Grades: 6 7 8 9 10   **Fic**
1. United States—History—1861-1865, Civil War—Fiction
ISBN 0-670-03638-2; 978-0-670-03638-7

As the Civil War breaks out, India, a young Southern girl, summons her sharp intelligence and the courage she didn't know she had to survive the war that threatens to destroy her family, her Virginia home and the only life she has ever known.

"This powerful novel is unflinching in its depiction of war and the devastation it causes, yet shows the resilience and hope that can follow such a tragedy. India is a memorable, thoroughly believable character." SLJ

Werlin, Nancy, 1961-

Double helix. Dial Books 2004 252p $16.99; pa $6.99 *

Grades: 7 8 9 10   **Fic**
1. Genetic engineering—Fiction 2. Bioethics—Fiction
3. Science fiction
ISBN 0-8037-2606-6; 0-14-240327-X (pa)
LC 2003-12269

Eighteen-year-old Eli discovers a shocking secret about his life and his family while working for a Nobel Prizewinning scientist whose specialty is genetic engineering.

"Werlin clearly and dramatically raises fundamental bioethical issues for teens to ponder. She also creates a riveting story with sharply etched characters and complex relationships that will stick with readers long after the book is closed." SLJ

The killer's cousin. Delacorte Press 1998 229p hardcover o.p. pa $5.99

Grades: 7 8 9 10   **Fic**
1. Homicide—Fiction 2. Cousins—Fiction
ISBN 0-385-32560-6; 0-440-22751-8 (pa)
LC 98-12950

After being acquitted of murder, seventeen-year-old David goes to stay with relatives in Cambridge, Massachusetts, where he finds himself forced to face his past as he learns more about his strange young cousin Lily

"Teens will find this tautly plotted thriller, rich in complex, finely drawn characters, an absolute page-turner." Booklist

The rules of survival. Dial Books 2006 259p $16.99 *

Grades: 8 9 10 11 12   **Fic**
1. Child abuse—Fiction 2. Siblings—Fiction
ISBN 0-8037-3001-2   LC 2006-1675

Seventeen-year-old Matthew recounts his attempts, starting at a young age, to free himself and his sisters from the grip of their emotionally and physically abusive mother.

The author "tackles the topic of child abuse with grace and insight. . . . Teens will empathize with these siblings and the secrets they keep in this psychological horror story." SLJ

West, Dorothy, 1907-1998

The wedding. Doubleday 1995 240p hardcover o.p. pa $12.95

Grades: 11 12 Adult   **Fic**
1. African Americans—Fiction 2. Race relations—Fiction 3. Martha's Vineyard (Mass.)—Fiction
ISBN 0-385-47143-2; 0-385-47144-0 (pa)
LC 94-27285

This novel is "set on Martha's Vineyard during the 1950s and focuses on the black bourgeois community known as the Oval. Dr. Clark Coles and his wife, Corrine, highly respected Ovalites, are preparing for the wedding of their youngest daughter, Shelby, who, much to their consternation, is marrying a white jazz musician. Lute McNeil, a compulsive womanizer who has recently made a fortune in the furniture business, is determined to stop Shelby's wedding; he is confident that he can convince Shelby to marry him, which would bring him the social acceptance he has always craved." Booklist

"Through the ancestral histories of the Coles family, West . . . subtly reveals the ways in which color can burden and codify behavior. The author makes her points with a delicate hand, maneuvering with confidence and ease through a sometimes incendiary subject." Publ Wkly

West, Jessamyn, 1902-1984

The friendly persuasion. Harcourt 1945 214p hardcover o.p. pa $13

Grades: 11 12 Adult   **Fic**
1. Society of Friends—Fiction 2. Indiana—Fiction
ISBN 0-15-133605-9; 0-15-602909-X (pa)
Also available in hardcover from Amereon

"The Birdwell family of Indiana led a quiet life until the Civil War came into their lives. They were Quakers and tried to live according to the teachings of William Penn. Jess Birdwell, a nurseryman, loved a fast horse as well as his trees and the people he knew. Eliza, his wife, was a Quaker minister and a gentle, albeit strict, soul. When the war reached Indiana, Josh, the oldest son, was torn between his Quaker upbringing and his belief in the rightness of the Union cause; Mattie was at that difficult age between childhood and womanhood; and Little Jess, the youngest, ran into trouble with Eliza's geese. This is a wonderful family chronicle, with the laughter, tears, and tenderness that can be found in many families." Shapiro. Fic for Youth. 3d edition

Westerfeld, Scott

Peeps. Razorbill 2005 312p $16.99; pa $8.99 *

Grades: 9 10 11 12   **Fic**
1. Vampires—Fiction
ISBN 1-59514-031-X; 1-59514-083-2 (pa)
LC 2005-8151

Westerfeld, Scott—*Continued*

Cal Thompson is a carrier of a parasite that causes vampirism, and must hunt down all of the girlfriends he has unknowingly infected.

"This innovative and original vampire story, full of engaging characters and just enough horror without any gore, will appeal to a wide audience." SLJ

Followed by The last days (2006)

So yesterday; a novel. Razorbill 2004 225p $16.99; pa $7.99

Grades: 7 8 9 10 **Fic**

1. Missing persons—Fiction 2. Mystery fiction 3. New York (N.Y.)—Fiction

ISBN 1-59514-000-X; 1-59514-032-8 (pa)

LC 2004-2302

Hunter Braque, a New York City teenager who is paid by corporations to spot what is "cool," combines his analytical skills with girlfriend Jen's creative talents to find a missing person and thwart a conspiracy directed at the heart of consumer culture

"This hip, fascinating thriller aggressively questions consumer culture. . . . Teens will inhale this wholly entertaining, thought-provoking look at a system fueled by their purchasing power. " Booklist

Uglies. Simon Pulse 2005 425p pa $6.99 *

Grades: 7 8 9 10 **Fic**

1. Science fiction

ISBN 0-689-86538-4

Also available Thorndike Press large print edition

"Fifteen-year-old Tally's eerily harmonious, postapocalyptic society gives extreme makeovers to teens on their sixteenth birthdays. . . . When a top-secret agency threatens to leave Tally ugly forever unless she spies on runaway teens, she agrees to infiltrate the Smoke, a shadowy colony of refugees from the 'tyranny of physical perfection.' " Booklist

"Ethical concerns will provide a good source of discussion. . . . Characterization . . . is strong, and . . . the novel is highly readable with a convincing plot." SLJ

Other titles in this series are:

Pretties (2005)

Specials (2006)

Wharton, Edith, 1862-1937

Ethan Frome. Scribner 1911 195p pa $13 hardcover o.p.

Grades: 11 12 Adult **Fic**

ISBN 0-684-82591-0

Also available Thorndike Press large print edition and in hardcover from Buccaneer Bks.

This is "an ironic tragedy of love, frustration, jealousy, and sacrifice. The scene is a New England village, where Ethan barely makes a living out of a stony farm and is at odds with his wife Zeena (short for Zenobia), a whining hypochondriac. Mattie, a cousin of Zeena's comes to live with them, and love develops between her and Ethan. They try to end their impossible lives by steering a bobsled into a tree; instead ending up crippled and tied for the rest of their unhappy time on earth to Zeena and the barren farm. Zeena, however, is transformed into a devoted nurse and Mattie becomes the nagging invalid." Benet's Reader's Ency of Am Lit

Whelan, Gloria

Homeless bird. HarperCollins Pubs. 2000 216p $15.95; lib bdg $16.89; pa $5.99

Grades: 6 7 8 9 **Fic**

1. Women—India—Fiction 2. India—Fiction

ISBN 0-06-028454-4; 0-06-028452-8 (lib bdg); 0-06-440819-1 (pa) LC 99-33241

When thirteen-year-old Koly enters into an ill-fated arranged marriage, she must either suffer a destiny dictated by India's tradition or find the courage to oppose it

"This beautifully told, inspiring story takes readers on a fascinating journey through modern India and the universal intricacies of a young woman's heart." Booklist

Whitcomb, Laura, 1958-

A certain slant of light. Graphia 2005 282p $8.99

Grades: 9 10 11 12 **Fic**

1. Ghost stories 2. Future life—Fiction

ISBN 0-618-58532-X (pa) LC 2004-27208

After benignly haunting a series of people for 130 years, Helen meets a teenage boy who can see her and together they unlock the mysteries of their pasts.

The author "creatively pulls together a dramatic and compelling plot that cleverly grants rebellious teen romance a timeless grandeur." Bull Cent Child Books

White, Andrea

Surviving Antarctica; reality TV 2083. HarperCollins Publishers 2005 327p $15.99; lib bdg $16.89; pa $6.99

Grades: 7 8 9 10 **Fic**

1. Antarctica—Fiction 2. Science fiction

ISBN 0-06-055454-1; 0-06-055455-X (lib bdg); 0-06-055456-8 (pa) LC 2004-6249

In the year 2083, five fourteen-year-olds who were deprived by chance of the opportunity to continue their educations reenact Scott's 1910-1913 expedition to the South Pole as contestants on a reality television show, secretly aided by a Department of Entertainment employee

"A real page-turner, this novel will give readers pause as they ponder the ethics of teens risking their lives in adult-contrived situations for the entertainment of the masses." Booklist

White, Edmund, 1940-

A boy's own story; introduction by Allan Gurganus; afterword by the author. [Twentieth anniversary ed.] Modern Library 2002 xxxiii, 227p $18.95; pa $12.95 *

Grades: 11 12 Adult **Fic**

1. Homosexuality—Fiction 2. Adolescence—Fiction

ISBN 0-679-64254-4; 0-375-70740-9 (pa)

LC 2002020504

First published 1982 by Dutton

In this first volume of an autobiographical trilogy, a nameless narrator reminisces about his homosexual childhood and his conflicting emotions in coming of age during the 1950s. At fifteen years of age, the boy hopes that "he is just passing through a homosexual 'stage.' At prep school he goes to a . . . psychiatrist who pops pills and

White, Edmund, 1940——*Continued*

talks of his own problems—and with no help from this man he begins slowly to see the real dimensions of his own life." Newsweek

This first-person novel is "written with the flourish of a master stylist. . . . It is an endearing portrait of a child's longing to be charming, popular, powerful, and loved, and of his struggles with adults . . . told with sensitivity and elegance." Harpers

Other titles in this trilogy are:

The beautiful room is empty (1988)

The farewell symphony (1997)

White, T. H. (Terence Hanbury), 1906-1964

The once and future king. Putnam 1958 677p $25.95 *

Grades: 11 12 Adult   **Fic**

1. Arthur, King—Fiction 2. Great Britain—History—0-1066—Fiction

ISBN 0-399-10597-2   LC 58-10760

Also available in paperback from Ace Bks.

An omnibus edition of four novels; The sword in the stone (1939), The witch in the wood (1939, now called The Queen of Air and Darkness) and The ill-made knight (1940). A number of alterations have been made in the earlier books. Previously unpublished, The candle in the wind "deals with the plotting of Mordred and his kinsmen of the house of Orkney, and their undying enmity to King Arthur." Times Lit Suppl

"White's contemporary retelling of Malory's Le Morte d'Arthur is both romantic and exciting." Shapiro. Fic for Youth. 3d edition

Whitney, Kim Ablon

The perfect distance. Knopf 2005 256p $15.95; lib bdg $17.99; pa $5.99

Grades: 9 10 11 12   **Fic**

1. Horsemanship—Fiction 2. Mexican Americans—Fiction

ISBN 0-375-83243-2; 0-375-93243-7 (lib bdg); 0-553-49467-8 (pa)   LC 2005-40726

While competing in the three junior national equitation championships, seventeen-year-old Francie Martinez learns to believe in herself and makes some decisions about the type of person she wants to be

The author "inhabits Francie's character wholly and convincingly and gets the universals of serious competition just right—any athlete will recognize the imperious, unfeeling coach; the snotty front-runner; and the unparalleled thrill of hitting the zone." Booklist

See you down the road. Alfred A. Knopf 2004 188p $15.95; lib bdg $17.99; pa $5.99

Grades: 9 10 11 12   **Fic**

1. Irish travellers (Nomadic people)—Fiction 2. Irish Americans—Fiction 3. Family life—Fiction

ISBN 0-375-82467-7; 0-375-92467-1 (lib bdg); 0-440-23809-9 (pa)   LC 2003-47570

Sixteen-year-old Bridget, member of an Irish Traveller community in the United States, questions the traditions of her family's nomadic and criminal way of life and begins to wonder if she wants to continue living it

This is a "wonderful . . . novel that examines some important questions in society." VOYA

Wild, Margaret, 1948-

One night. Knopf 2004 236p $15.95; lib bdg $17.99; pa $5.99

Grades: 9 10 11 12   **Fic**

1. Pregnancy—Fiction 2. Teenage mothers—Fiction 3. Australia—Fiction

ISBN 0-375-82920-2; 0-375-92920-7 (lib bdg); 0-553-49434-1 (pa)   LC 2003-60619

In this novel written in free verse and narrated by alternating characters, a teenaged girl decides to have her baby and care for it on her own after a "one night stand" results in pregnancy

"Teen readers will love this story and will appreciate its hopeful ending." SLJ

Wilde, Oscar, 1854-1900

The picture of Dorian Gray. Modern Library 1992 254p $16.95 *

Grades: 11 12 Adult   **Fic**

ISBN 0-679-60001-9   LC 92-11593

Also available from other publishers

First published 1891 in the United Kingdom; first United States edition published 1895 by G. Munro's Sons

"An archetypal tale of a young man who purchases eternal youth at the expense of his soul, the novel was a romantic exposition of Wilde's Aestheticism. Dorian Gray is a wealthy Englishman who gradually sinks into a life of dissipation and crime. Despite his unhealthy behavior, his physical appearance remains youthful and unmarked by dissolution. Instead, a portrait of himself catalogues every evil deed by turning his once handsome features into a hideous mask." Merriam-Webster's Ency of Lit

Williams, Lori Aurelia

When Kambia Elaine flew in from Neptune. Simon & Schuster 2000 246p pa $10 *

Grades: 7 8 9 10   **Fic**

1. African Americans—Fiction 2. Houston (Tex.)—Fiction

ISBN 0-689-82468-8; 0-689-84593-6 (pa)

LC 99-65154

Also available Thorndike Press large print edition

"Williams weaves two tales in the first-person narrative of twelve-year-old Shayla: the story of Shayla's older sister and her sexual awakening; and the story of Kambia, Shayla's soon-to-be best friend, whose fantastic stories of transformation hide her real-life abuse." Horn Book Guide

"This is a strong and disturbing novel, told in beautiful language. Teens will find it engrossing." SLJ

Williams-Garcia, Rita

Every time a rainbow dies. HarperCollins Pubs. 2001 166p hardcover o.p. pa $6.99

Grades: 9 10 11 12   **Fic**

1. Rape—Fiction

ISBN 0-06-029202-4; 0-06-447303-1 (pa)

LC 00-38900

"As the novel opens, sixteen-year-old Jamaican-born Thulani's only friends are the pigeons he tends on the

Williams-Garcia, Rita—*Continued*

roof of the Brooklyn brownstone he shares with his brother and sister-in-law. From the roof, he witnesses a rape. After he intercedes on the victim's behalf, he becomes obsessed with her." Horn Book

"The rape and, later, a lovemaking scene between Ysa and Thulani, are explicitly drawn, yet the manner in which Williams-Garcia contrasts the violence of one and the gentleness of the other underscores the myriad ways in which their relationship heals old wounds. With its layered yet understated language, including snippets of Jamaican and Haitian 'patois' and complex yet truthful characterizations, this novel will hold the rapt attention of sophisticated readers." Publ Wkly

Like sisters on the homefront. Lodestar Bks. 1995 165p hardcover o.p. pa $5.99 *

Grades: 7 8 9 10   **Fic**
1. African Americans—Fiction 2. Family life—Fiction 3. Teenage mothers—Fiction
ISBN 0-525-67465-9; 0-14-038561-4 (pa)

LC 95-3690

"It's bad enough that 14-year-old Gayle has one baby, but when she becomes pregnant again by another boy, Mama's had enough. She takes Gayle for an abortion and then ships her and her baby south to stay with religious relatives. . . . With the help of her dying great-grandmother, who leaves Gayle the family's African-American oral tradition, she begins to mature and understand her place in the family and her future." Child Book Rev Serv

"Beautifully written, the text captures the cadence and rhythm of New York street talk and the dilemma of being poor, black, and uneducated. This is a gritty, realistic, well-told story." SLJ

Willis, Connie

To say nothing of the dog; or, How we found the bishop's bird stump at last. Bantam Bks. 1998 434p hardcover o.p. pa $7.99

Grades: 11 12 Adult   **Fic**
1. Science fiction
ISBN 0-553-09995-7; 0-553-57538-4 (pa)

LC 97-16002

"Rich dowager Lady Schrapnell has invaded Oxford University's time travel research project in 2057, promising to endow it if they help her rebuild Coventry Cathedral, destroyed by a Nazi air raid in 1940. . . . Time traveler Ned Henry is suffering from advanced time lag and has been sent, he thinks, for rest and relaxation to 1888, where he connects with time traveler Verity Kindle and discovers that he is actually there to correct an incongruity created when Verity inadvertently brought something forward from the past." Booklist

"No one mixes scientific mumbo jumbo and comedy of manners with more panache than Willis." N Y Times Book Rev

Wilson, Diane L.

Firehorse. Margaret K. McElderry Books 2006 325p $16.95

Grades: 7 8 9 10   **Fic**
1. Veterinary medicine—Fiction 2. Sex role—Fiction 3. Horses—Fiction 4. Arson—Fiction 5. Family life—Fiction 6. Boston (Mass.)—Fiction
ISBN 1-4169-1551-6; 978-1-4169-1551-5

LC 2005-30785

Spirited fifteen-year-old horse lover Rachel Selby determines to become a veterinarian, despite the opposition of her rigid father, her proper mother, and the norms of Boston in 1872, while that city faces a serial arsonist and an epidemic spreading through its firehorse population.

"Wilson paces the story well, with tension building. . . . The novel's finest achievement, though, is the convincing depiction of family dynamics in an era when men ruled the household and and women, who had few opportunities, folded their dreams and put them away with the linens they embroidered." Booklist

Winspear, Jacqueline, 1955-

Maisie Dobbs; a novel. Soho Press 2003 294p $24 *

Grades: 11 12 Adult   **Fic**
1. World War, 1914-1918—Fiction 2. Mystery fiction 3. Great Britain—Fiction
ISBN 1-56947-330-7   LC 2002-44656

In this novel "set in WWI-era England, humble housemaid Maisie Dobbs climbs . . . up Britain's social ladder, becoming in turn a university student, a wartime nurse and ultimately a private investigator. . . . Her first sleuthing case, which begins as a simple marital infidelity investigation, leads to a trail of war-wounded soldiers lured to a remote convalescent home in Kent from which no one seems to emerge alive." Publ Wkly

"For a clever and resourceful young woman who has just set herself up in business as a private investigator, Maisie seems a bit too sober and much too sad. Romantic readers sensing a story-within-a-story won't be disappointed. But first, they must prepare to be astonished at the sensitivity and wisdom with which Maisie resolves her first professional assignment." N Y Times Book Rev

Other titles about Maisie Dobbs are:
Birds of a feather (2004)
Pardonable lies (2005)

Wittlinger, Ellen, 1948-

Blind faith. Simon & Schuster Books for Young Readers 2006 280p $15.95

Grades: 7 8 9 10   **Fic**
1. Death—Fiction 2. Spiritualism—Fiction 3. Mother-daughter relationship—Fiction 4. Depression (Psychology)—Fiction 5. Religion—Fiction
ISBN 978-1-4169-0273-7; 1-4169-0273-2

LC 2005-08281

While coping with her grandmother's sudden death and her mother's resulting depression and fascination with a spiritualist church, whose ministers claim to communicate with the dead, fifteen-year-old Liz finds herself falling for a new neighbor whose mother is dying of cancer.

"Wittlinger brings readers right into a teen's roiling

Wittlinger, Ellen, 1948-—*Continued*
emotional life with sensitive, skillful descriptions."
Booklist

Hard love. Simon & Schuster Bks. for Young
Readers 1999 224p hardcover o.p. pa $8.99
Grades: 7 8 9 10   **Fic**
1. Authorship—Fiction 2. Lesbians—Fiction
ISBN 0-689-82134-4; 0-689-84154-X (pa)
                                    LC 98-6668
"John, cynical yet vulnerable, thinks he's immune to
emotion until he meets bright, brittle Marisol, the author
of his favorite zine. He falls in love, but Marisol, a lesbian, just wants to be friends. A love story of a different
sort—funny, poignant, and thoughtful." Booklist

Sandpiper. Simon & Schuster Books for Young
Readers 2005 227p $16.95; pa $6.99 *
Grades: 9 10 11 12   **Fic**
1. Dating (Social customs)—Fiction
ISBN 0-689-86802-2; 1-4169-3651-3 (pa)
                                  LC 2004-7576
When The Walker, a mysterious boy who walks constantly, intervenes in an argument between Sandpiper and
a boy she used to see, their lives become entwined in
ways that change them both.
"While heavy on message and mature in subject matter, the novel is notable for the bold look it takes at relationships and at the myth that oral sex is not really sex."
SLJ

Wolff, Tobias, 1945-
Old school; a novel. Knopf 2003 195p $22; pa
$12
Grades: 9 10 11 12   **Fic**
1. Authors—Fiction 2. School stories 3. New England—Fiction
ISBN 0-375-40146-6; 0-375-70149-4 (pa)
                                 LC 2003-52930
"The unnamed narrator of this coming-of-age story set
in 1960 is a scholarship student at a prestigious New England prep school that has a tradition of inviting literary
stars to the campus. Prior to the visit, the seniors are requested to write a piece to be 'judged' by the guest. The
winner is given a private meeting with the literary lumi-
nary and the story is published in the school paper. . . .
In his fervent desire to be chosen, the narrator 'borrows'
an idea and reveals a secret about his heritage that he
has carefully hidden. He wins, but the results of his story's publication are disastrous and his life is forever
changed. The events and ideas in this thoughtful and
thought-provoking novel remain with readers after the
story is over and could provide meat for discussion." SLJ

Wolff, Virginia Euwer
Make lemonade. Holt & Co. 1993 200p $17.95
*
Grades: 9 10 11 12   **Fic**
1. Teenage mothers—Fiction 2. Babysitters—Fiction
3. Poverty—Fiction
ISBN 0-8050-2228-7   LC 92-41182
Also available Thorndike Press large print edition and
in paperback from Scholastic

"Fourteen-year-old LaVaughn accepts the job of
babysitting Jolly's two small children but quickly realizes
that the young woman, a seventeen-year-old single mother, needs as much help and nurturing as her two neglected children. The four become something akin to a temporary family, and through their relationship each makes
progress toward a better life. Sixty-six brief chapters,
with words arranged on the page like poetry, perfectly
echo the patterns of teenage speech." Horn Book Guide
 Another title about LaVaughn is:
True believer (2001)

Wooding, Chris, 1977-
The haunting of Alaizabel Cray. Orchard Bks.
2004 292p $16.95; pa $7.99
Grades: 7 8 9 10   **Fic**
1. Horror fiction 2. Supernatural—Fiction 3. London
(England)—Fiction
ISBN 0-439-54656-7; 0-439-59851-6 (pa)
                                 LC 2003-69108
Also available Thorndike Press large print edition
First published 2001 in the United Kingdom
In a world similar to Victorian London, Thaniel, a
seventeen-year-old hunter of deadly, demonic creatures
called the wych-kin, takes in a lost, possessed girl, and
becomes embroiled in a plot to unleash evil on the world
"Eerie and exhilarating. . . . [The author] fuses to-
gether his best storytelling skills . . . to create a fabu-
lously horrific and ultimately timeless underworld." SLJ

Poison. Orchard Bks. 2005 c2003 273p $16.99;
pa $7.99
Grades: 7 8 9 10   **Fic**
1. Fantasy fiction 2. Storytelling—Fiction 3. Fairies—
Fiction
ISBN 0-439-75570-0; 0-439-75571-9 (pa)
                                 LC 2005-02174
Also available Thorndike Press large print edition
First published 2003 in the United Kingdom
When Poison leaves her home in the marshes of Gull
to retrieve the infant sister who was snatched by the
fairies, she and a group of unusual friends survive encounters with the inhabitants of various Realms, and Poison herself confronts a surprising destiny.
"Poison's story should please crowds of horror fans
who like their books fast-paced, darkly atmospheric, and
melodramatic." SLJ

The storm thief. Orchard Books 2006 310p
$16.99
Grades: 6 7 8 9   **Fic**
1. Science fiction
ISBN 0-439-86513-1   LC 2005-35993
With the help of a golem, two teenaged thieves try to
survive on the city island of Orokos, where unpredictable
probability storms continually change both the landscape
and the inhabitants.
The author "delivers memorable characters, such as
Vago, whose plight—Who am I and where do I belong
in the world?—will be understood by many teens. Wooding also creates a unique world for his characters to explore, and the setting serves as an excellent backdrop for
the author to develop his theme of order versus chaos
and the need for balance between the two." Voice Youth
Advocates

Woodrell, Daniel

Winter's bone; a novel. Little, Brown and Co. 2006 193p $22.99

Grades: 11 12 Adult **Fic**

1. Criminals—Fiction 2. Father-daughter relationship—Fiction 3. Mountain life—Fiction 4. Ozark Mountains—Fiction

ISBN 0-316-05755-X; 978-0-316-05755-4

LC 2005-17349

"In the poverty-stricken hills of the Ozarks, Rees Dolly, 17, struggles daily to care for her two brothers and an ill mother. When she learns that her absent father, a meth addict, has put up the family home as bond, she embarks on a dangerous search to find him and bring him home for an upcoming court date." SLJ

"This lyrical and haunting story exposes the dark underside of its scenic setting. . . . But the book is not for the young or the faint-of-heart; Ree is not a saint, and this gritty story requires maturity to appreciate." Voice Youth Advocates

Woodson, Jacqueline

If you come softly. Putnam 1998 181p $15.99; pa $5.99

Grades: 7 8 9 10 **Fic**

1. African Americans—Fiction 2. Race relations—Fiction 3. New York (N.Y.)—Fiction

ISBN 0-399-23112-9; 0-698-11862-6 (pa)

LC 97-32212

After meeting at their private school in New York, fifteen-year-old Jeremiah, who is black and whose parents are separated, and Ellie, who is white and whose mother has twice abandoned her, fall in love and then try to cope with people's reactions

"The gentle and melancholy tone of this book makes it ideal for thoughtful readers and fans of romance." Voice Youth Advocates

Another title about Jeremiah is:

Behind you (2004)

Miracle's boys. Putnam 2000 133p $15.99; pa $5.99

Grades: 9 10 11 12 **Fic**

1. Brothers—Fiction 2. Orphans—Fiction 3. African Americans—Fiction 4. New York (N.Y.)—Fiction

ISBN 0-399-23113-7; 0-698-11916-9 (pa)

LC 99-40050

Coretta Scott King award for text, 2001

Twelve-year-old Lafayette's close relationship with his older brother Charlie changes after Charlie is released from a detention home and blames Lafayette for the death of their mother

"The fast-paced narrative is physically immediate, and the dialogue is alive with anger and heartbreak." Booklist

Woolf, Virginia, 1882-1941

To the lighthouse; with an introduction by Julia Briggs. Knopf 1992 xxix, 242p $17

Grades: 9 10 11 12 **Fic**

1. Great Britain—Fiction

ISBN 0-679-40537-2

LC 92-52912

Arranged in three parts, the first "called 'The window,' describes a day during Mr. and Mrs. Ramsay's house party at their country home by the sea. Mr. Ramsay is a distinguished scholar . . . whose mind works rationally, heroically and rather icily. . . . The Ramsays have arranged to take a boat out to the lighthouse, the next morning, and their little son James is bitterly disappointed when a change in weather makes it impossible. The second section, called 'Time passes' describes the seasons and the house, unused and decaying, in the years after Mrs. Ramsay's death. In the third section, the 'Lighthouse,' Mr. Ramsay and his friends are back at the house. He takes the postponed trip to the lighthouse with his now sixteen-year-old son, who is at last able to communicate silently with him and forgive him for being different from his mother." Reader's Ency. 4th edition

Wouk, Herman, 1915-

The winds of war; a novel. Little, Brown 1971 885p pa $16.99 hardcover o.p.

Grades: 11 12 Adult **Fic**

1. World War, 1939-1945—Fiction

ISBN 0-316-95266-8

"On the broadest of tapestries, Wouk weaves the effect of the preparation and the actual outbreak of World War II upon the family of Commander 'Pug' Henry. The affairs of the Henry family became intertwined with those of others, in such varying scenes as Washington, Berlin, Rome, London, and Moscow. . . . Despite the novel's breadth, the development of Henry's character as the middle-class military leader America needed in the 1940's is surprisingly credible." Choice

Another title featuring the Henry family is:

War and remembrance (1978)

Wright, Richard, 1908-1960

Native son; with an introduction: "How 'Bigger' was born," by the author. Harper & Row 1969 c1940 xxxiv, 392p pa $14.95 hardcover o.p. *

Grades: 11 12 Adult **Fic**

1. African Americans—Fiction 2. Race relations—Fiction 3. Chicago (Ill.)—Fiction

ISBN 0-06-083756-X (pa)

Also available in hardcover from Buccaneer Bks.

A reissue of the title first published 1940

"Bigger Thomas is black. He is driven by anger, hate, and frustration, which are born out of the poverty that has dominated his life. When he gets a job with the Daltons, a white family, he is confused by their behavior and misinterprets their patronizing friendship. Tragedy follows when he accidentally kills Mary Dalton." Shapiro. Fic for Youth. 3d edition

Wyatt, Melissa, 1963-

Raising the griffin. Wendy Lamb Books 2004 279p lib bdg $18.99; pa $6.50

Grades: 9 10 11 12 **Fic**

1. Europe—Fiction

ISBN 0-385-90115-1 (lib bdg); 0-440-23821-8 (pa)

LC 2003-7925

When the people of Rovenia vote to restore their monarchy, sixteen-year-old Alex Varenhoff must suddenly leave his native England to become prince of a land he knows only from his grandfather's stories

Wyatt, Melissa, 1963-—*Continued*

"There are no easy answers in this powerfully affecting novel that avoids cliché and the expected fairy-tale ending. The characters, while not always likable, are real and complex, even the secondary ones. This is a compulsively readable book that lingers in the mind long after the final page." SLJ

Wyeth, Sharon Dennis

Orphea Proud. Delacorte Press 2004 189p $15.95; pa $5.99

Grades: 9 10 11 12   **Fic**

1. Lesbians—Fiction 2. Family life—Fiction 3. Poetry—Fiction 4. New York (N.Y.)—Fiction

ISBN 0-385-32497-9; 0-440-27706-2 (pa)

LC 2003-22727

While reciting her poetry at a club in Queens, New York, seventeen-year-old Orphea recounts her childhood in Pennsylvania, leaving after her parents and the girl she loves die, and learning about her family and herself while living with her great-aunts on a Virginia mountaintop

"Aspiring poets or teens questioning their sexuality will be especially moved by Orphea's struggle to verbalize her overwhelming experience." Booklist

Wynne-Jones, Tim

A thief in the house of memory. Farrar, Straus & Giroux 2004 210p $17

Grades: 7 8 9 10   **Fic**

1. Memory—Fiction 2. Mothers—Fiction 3. Canada—Fiction

ISBN 0-374-37478-3   LC 2004-53263

Also available Thorndike Press large print edition

"Melanie Kroupa books"

The death of an apparent stranger in the Steeple family's old home triggers troubling questions for sixteen-year-old Declan as he tries to make sense of his fragmented dreams, random memories, and unexplained coincidences, hoping to learn the truth about the mother who suddenly left when he was ten

"This rich and rewarding novel will appeal most to thoughtful readers who appreciate a sad and bittersweet read." SLJ

Yolen, Jane

Briar Rose. Doherty Assocs. 1992 190p (Fairy tale series) hardcover o.p. pa $6.99 *

Grades: 11 12 Adult   **Fic**

1. Fantasy fiction

ISBN 0-312-85135-9; 0-7653-4230-8 (pa)

LC 92-25456

"A TOR book"

"Yolen takes the story of Briar Rose (commonly known as Sleeping Beauty) and links it to the Holocaust. . . . Rebecca Berlin, a young woman who has grown up hearing her grandmother Gemma tell an unusual and frightening version of the Sleeping Beauty legend, realizes when Gemma dies that the fairy tale offers one of the very few clues she has to her grandmother's past. . . . By interpolating Gemma's vivid and imaginative story into the larger narrative, Yolen has created an engrossing novel." Publ Wkly

Zarr, Sara

Story of a girl; a novel. Little, Brown 2006 192p $16.99 *

Grades: 10 11 12   **Fic**

1. Family life—Fiction 2. California—Fiction

ISBN 978-0-316-01453-3; 0-316-01453-2

LC 2005-28467

In the three years since her father caught her in the back seat of a car with an older boy, sixteen-year-old Deanna's life at home and school has been a nightmare, but while dreaming of escaping with her brother and his family, she discovers the power of forgiveness.

"This highly recommended novel will find a niche with older, more mature readers because of frank references to sex and some x-rated language." Voice Youth Advocates

Zevin, Gabrielle, 1977-

Elsewhere. Farrar, Straus & Giroux 2005 275p $16; pa $6.95

Grades: 7 8 9 10   **Fic**

1. Future life—Fiction 2. Death—Fiction

ISBN 0-374-32091-8; 0-312-36746-5 (pa)

LC 2004-56279

Also available Thorndike Press large print edition

After fifteen-year-old Liz Hall is hit by a taxi and killed, she finds herself in a place that is both like and unlike Earth, where she must adjust to her new status and figure out how to "live."

"Zevin's third-person narrative calmly, but surely guides readers through the bumpy landscape of strongly delineated characters dealing with the most difficult issue that faces all of us. A quiet book that provides much to think about and discuss." SLJ

Zusak, Markus, 1975-

The book thief. Knopf 2006 552p il $16.95; lib bdg $18.99 *

Grades: 8 9 10 11 12   **Fic**

1. World War, 1939-1945—Fiction 2. Holocaust, 1933-1945—Fiction 3. Books and reading—Fiction 4. Death—Fiction

ISBN 0-375-83100-2; 0-375-93100-7 (lib bdg)

LC 2005-08942

Also available Thorndike Press large print edition

Trying to make sense of the horrors of World War II, Death relates the story of Liesel—a young German girl whose book-stealing and storytelling talents help sustain her family and the Jewish man they are hiding, as well as their neighbors.

"This hefty volume is an achievement—a challenging book in both length and subject, and best suited to sophisticated older readers." Publ Wkly

Getting the girl. Levine Bks. 2003 261p $16.95; pa $6.99

Grades: 7 8 9 10   **Fic**

1. Brothers—Fiction 2. Australia—Fiction

ISBN 0-439-38949-6; 0-439-38950-X (pa)

LC 2002-11411

First published 2001 in Australia with title: When dogs cry

Sequel to Fighting Ruben Wolfe (2001)

Zusak, Markus, 1975-—Continued

Tired of being the underdog, Cameron Wolfe hungers to become something worthwhile and finally finds a girl with whom he can share his words and feelings—his popular brother Rube's ex-girlfriend

"The interaction of the characters is a real strength of this novel. It is a story of family dynamics and coming of age, interspersed with the protagonist's poignant poems and observations." SLJ

I am the messenger. Knopf 2005 357p $16.95; lib bdg $18.99; pa $8.95 *

Grades: 9 10 11 12   **Fic**
  1. Mystery fiction
  ISBN 0-375-83099-5; 0-375-93099-X (lib bdg);
  0-375-83667-5 (pa)   LC 2003-27388

After capturing a bank robber, nineteen-year-old cab driver Ed Kennedy begins receiving mysterious messages that direct him to addresses where people need help, and he begins getting over his lifelong feeling of worthlessness

"Zusak's characters, styling, and conversations are believably unpretentious, well conceived, and appropriately raw. Together, these key elements fuse into an enigmatically dark, almost film-noir atmosphere where unknowingly lost Ed Kennedy stumbles onto a mystery—or series of mysteries—that could very well make or break his life." SLJ

S C STORY COLLECTIONS

Books in this class include collections of short stories by one author and collections by more than one author. Folk tales are entered in class 398.2

Adaptations: from short story to big screen; 35 great stories that have inspired great films; edited by Stephanie Harrison. Three Rivers Press 2005 619p il pa $15.95 *

Grades: 11 12 Adult   **S C**
  1. Short stories 2. Film adaptations
  ISBN 1-4000-5314-5   LC 2005-3441

"From science fiction to social satire, this . . . collection of 35 tales embraces literary greats like Chekhov and Cheever and memorable writings long out of print. . . . Harrison devotes a chapter to every imaginable genre, prefacing each with quotes and anecdotes from writers, directors, and actors associated with the creative endeavors selected." Booklist

Alexie, Sherman, 1966-

Ten little Indians; stories. Grove Press 2003 243p hardcover o.p. pa $13 *

Grades: 11 12 Adult   **S C**
  1. Native Americans—Fiction 2. Short stories
  ISBN 0-8021-1744-9; 0-8021-4117-X (pa)
       LC 2003-44832

"These short stories feature Spokane Indians from many urban walks of life. Alexie's characters include a student, a lawyer, a basketball player, and a feminist mother; their stories might be angry, tragic, humorous, or ironic—but they are all believable, and irresistibly engaging." SLJ

Alfred Hitchcock's mystery magazine presents fifty years of crime and suspense; edited by Linda Landrigan. Pegasus 2006 560p pa $16.95

Grades: 11 12 Adult   **S C**
  1. Mystery fiction 2. Short stories
  ISBN 1-933648-03-1

"To commemorate its 50th anniversary, Alfred Hitchcock's Mystery Magazine staff-with input from its readers-selected 34 stories and arranged them chronologically here, starting with Jim Thompson's 'The Frightening Frammis' from February 1957 and ending with 'Voodoo' by Rhys Bowen from December 2004. . . . These are uniformly satisfying stories that have stood the test of time." Libr J

Am I blue? coming out from the silence; edited by Marion Dane Bauer. HarperCollins Pubs. 1994 273p hardcover o.p. lib bdg $14.89 *

Grades: 9 10 11 12   **S C**
  1. Homosexuality—Fiction 2. Short stories
  ISBN 0-06-024253-1; 0-06-024254-X (lib bdg)
       LC 93-29574

This "collection includes stories by Bruce Coville, Lois Lowry, Jane Yolen, Nancy Garden, and others. While all the pieces center on themes of coming to terms with homosexuality, they also are stories of love, coming of age, adventure, and self-discovery. A powerful commentary about our social and emotional responses to homosexuality and our human need for love and acceptance." Horn Book Guide

American eyes; new Asian-American short stories for young adults; introduction by Cynthia Kadohata. Fawcett Juniper 1996 c1994 138p pa $6.99 *

Grades: 7 8 9 10   **S C**
  1. Asian Americans—Fiction 2. Short stories
  ISBN 0-449-70448-3

"A Fawcett Juniper book"

First published 1994 by Holt & Co.

These ten stories reflect the conflict Asian Americans face in balancing an ancient heritage and an unknown future.

American short story masterpieces; edited by Raymond Carver and Tom Jenks. Delacorte Press 1987 435p pa $7.50 hardcover o.p. *

Grades: 11 12 Adult   **S C**
  1. Short stories
  ISBN 0-440-20423-2   LC 86-19964

"Thirty-six stories are presented here. . . . These are all stories written in a realistic vein, with strong narrative drive. They 'moved and exhilarated' the compilers, and readers will have equally positive reactions. Bernard Malamud, Ann Beattie, John Updike, Grace Paley, Flannery O'Connor, and James Baldwin are just a few of the superior practitioners of the form found here." Booklist

Asimov, Isaac, 1920-1992

The complete stories. Doubleday 1990-1992 2v v1 pa $19.95; v2 o.p.

Grades: 11 12 Adult   **S C**
  1. Science fiction 2. Short stories
  ISBN 0-385-41627-X; (v1 pa)   LC 90-3136

Asimov, Isaac, 1920-1992—*Continued*
"A Foundation book"
This set contains all of Asimov's science fiction stories including the "collections 'Earth Is Room Enough' and 'Nine Tomorrows' from the 1950s as well as . . . 'Nightfall and Other Stories.'" SLJ

I, robot. Bantam hardcover ed. Bantam Books 2004 224p (Robot series) $24; pa $7.99 *
Grades: 7 8 9 10 11 12 Adult   S C
1. Science fiction 2. Robots—Fiction 3. Short stories
ISBN 0-553-80370-0; 0-553-29438-5 (pa)
                                        LC 2003-69139
First published 1950 by Gnome Press
"These loosely connected stories cover the career of Dr. Susan Calvin and United States Robots, the industry that she heads, from the time of the public's early distrust of these robots to its later dependency on them. This collection is an important introduction to a theme often found in science fiction: the encroachment of technology on our lives." Shapiro. Fic for Youth. 3d edition

Beagle, Peter S.
The line between. Tachyon Publications 2006 231p pa $14.95
Grades: 11 12 Adult   S C
1. Short stories 2. Fantasy fiction
ISBN 978-1-892391-36-0; 1-892391-36-8
Contents: Gordon, the self-made cat; Two hearts; The fable of the moth; The fable of the tyrannosaurus rex; The fable of the ostrich; The fable of the octopus; El Regalo; Quarry; Salt wine; Mr. Sigerson; A dance for Emilia
"This story collection from fantasy legend Beagle offers a sublime mix of reprints and original works. . . . This book is a fitting tribute to a beloved author." Publ Wkly

Bear, Greg, 1951-
The collected stories of Greg Bear. TOR Bks. 2002 653p hardcover o.p. pa $17.95
Grades: 11 12 Adult   S C
1. Science fiction 2. Short stories
ISBN 0-7653-0160-1; 0-7653-0161-X (pa)
                                        LC 2002-20466
"A Tom Doherty Associates book"
Contents: Blood music [novelette]; Sisters; A Martian Ricorso; Schrodinger's plague; Heads; The wind from a burning woman; The venging; Perihesperon; Scattershot; Plague of conscience; The white horse child; Dead run; Petra; Webster; Through road, no whither; Tangents; The visitation; Richie by the sea; Sleepside story; Judgment engine; The fall of the house of Escher; The way of all ghosts; MDIO ecosystes increase knowledge of DNA languages (2215 C.E.); Hardfought

The **Best** American mystery stories of the century; Tony Hillerman, editor; Otto Penzler, series editor; with an introduction by Tony Hillerman. Houghton Mifflin 2000 813p $28; pa $17.95
Grades: 11 12 Adult   S C

1. Mystery fiction 2. Short stories
ISBN 0-618-01267-2; 0-618-01271-0 (pa)
"Dating from 1904 to the present, these stories provide a rough chronology of 20th-century crime fiction. . . . All the great writers of the genre are here—Raymond Chandler, Ellery Queen, Sue Grafton, etc.—but so are writers not normally associated with crime fiction, e.g., Flannery O'Connor, John Steinbeck, and Harlan Ellison." Libr J
"This anthology is a cornerstone volume for any mystery library." Publ Wkly

Best of the best: 20 years of the Year's best science fiction; [edited by] Gardner Dozois. St. Martin's Griffin 2005 672p hardcover o.p. pa $19.95
Grades: 9 10 11 12   S C
1. Science fiction 2. Short stories
ISBN 0-312-33655-1; 0-312-33656-X (pa)
                                        LC 2004-51411
Dozois "collects 36 tales by some of the most notable authors currently active in the genre, among them Gene Wolfe, William Gibson, Connie Willis, Joe Haldeman and Tony Daniel. Robert Silverberg provides a foreword." Publ Wkly

Block, Francesca Lia
Girl goddess #9: nine stories. HarperCollins Pubs. 1996 181p hardcover o.p. pa $4.95
Grades: 9 10 11 12   S C
1. Short stories
ISBN 0-06-027211-2; 0-06-447187-X (pa)
                                        LC 95-52050
"Joanna Cotler books"
"In each of these nine selections, mostly female protagonists with unusual names such as Peachy Pie, Tuck, Tweetie, La, Pixie, and Pony experience the highs and lows of adolescence." SLJ
"Block requires a certain suspension of disbelief as the world she writes about is often a fantastical one, the settings surreal in their atmospherics, but her characters fight against spiritual annihilation by groping toward creative expression with a purity of purpose and inherent emotionality that is remarkably moving." Bull Cent Child Books

The rose and the beast; fairy tales retold. HarperCollins Pubs. 2000 229p hardcover o.p. pa $6.99
Grades: 7 8 9 10   S C
1. Fairy tales 2. Short stories
ISBN 0-06-028129-4; 0-06-440745-4 (pa)
                                        LC 00-22444
"Joanna Cotler books"
Nine classic fairy tales set in modern, magical landscapes and retold with a twist.
The author's "beautiful words turn modern-day Los Angeles into a fantastical world of fairies, angels, and charms. The context is very modern, with issues of drug addiction, rape, and suicide smoothly woven into the stories, which are infused with a palpable if not explicit eroticism." Booklist

Boyle, T. Coraghessan
The Human Fly and other stories; [by] T.C. Boyle. Viking 2005 179p $17.99; pa $9.99
Grades: 9 10 11 12   S C
   1. Short stories
   ISBN 0-670-06054-2; 0-14-240363-6 (pa)
               LC 2005047436
"In this collection of previously published and new stories, Boyle delivers compelling tales of humor, compassion, and intrigue." SLJ

Bradbury, Ray, 1920-
Bradbury stories; 100 of his most celebrated tales. Morrow 2003 893p $29.95; pa $17.95
Grades: 11 12 Adult   S C
   1. Science fiction 2. Short stories
   ISBN 0-06-054242-X; 0-06-054488-0 (pa)
               LC 2003-42189
"This massive retrospective of self-selected Bradbury stories offers a compendium of his eccentrics, misfits, losers, and small-town dreamers, who typically inhabit an uncanny setting or confront a strange, unsettling situation." Libr J

The illustrated man. Avon Books 1997 275p $15.95
Grades: 9 10 11 12 Adult   S C
   1. Science fiction 2. Short stories
   ISBN 0-380-97384-7   LC 97-93228
Also available in paperback from Spectra
First published 1951 by Doubleday; short stories originally published between 1948 and 1951
   Contents: Prologue: The illustrated man — The veldt Kaleidoscope — The other foot — The highway — The man — The long rain — The rocket man — The last night of the world — The exiles — No particular night or morning — The fox and the forest — The visitor — The concrete mixer — Marionettes, Inc. — The city — Zero hour — The rocket — The illustrated man
   In this work "the stories are given a linking framework; they are all seen as magical tattoos becoming living stories, springing from the body of the protagonist." Sci Fic Ency

The Martian chronicles. Avon Books 1997 268p $15.95 *
Grades: 7 8 9 10   S C
   1. Science fiction 2. Short stories
   ISBN 0-380-97383-9   LC 96-95071
Also available from other publishers
First published 1950 by Doubleday
This book's "closely interwoven short stories, linked by recurrent images and themes, tell of the repeated attempts by humans to colonize Mars, of the way they bring their old prejudices with them, and of the repeated, ambiguous meetings with the shape-changing Martians." Sci Fic Ency

Capote, Truman, 1924-1984
Breakfast at Tiffany's: a short novel and three stories. Modern Lib. 1994 161p $14.95; pa $11
Grades: 9 10 11 12   S C
   1. Short stories
   ISBN 0-679-60085-X; 0-679-74565-3 (pa)
               LC 93-43633
First published 1958 by Random House
The novella which gives the book its title is the tale of a Manhattan playgirl, Holly Golightly. Completing the volume are three short stories: House of flowers, A diamond guitar, and A Christmas memory

Card, Orson Scott
First meetings in the Enderverse. Tor Teen 2003 208p il $17.95; pa $6.99
Grades: 9 10 11 12   S C
   1. Science fiction 2. Short stories
   ISBN 0-7653-0873-8; 0-7653-4798-9 (pa)
               LC 2003-55951
"A Tom Doherty Associates book"
"Andrew 'Ender' Wiggins, a brilliant leader and tactician and destined to save Earth by destroying an entire alien civilization at the age of 12, was first introduced in Card's 'Ender's Game'. . . . That novella, plus three other stories (including one never before published) make up this . . . collection of tales, all dealing with first meetings that played significant roles in the life of Ender Wiggins. . . . All four stories use the future setting as a framework to explore various issues of religion, government control, population limits, education, and moral responsibility. Character, setting, plot—Card does them all right, and makes it look effortless. . . . For newcomers to Ender's universe and longtime fans, this book will hit the spot and whet the appetite for more." SLJ

Carter, Alden R.
Love, football, and other contact sports. Holiday House 2006 261p $16.95 *
Grades: 8 9 10 11 12   S C
   1. Football—Fiction 2. School stories 3. Short stories
   ISBN 978-0-8234-1975-3; 0-8234-1975-4
               LC 2005-46094
This "collection of short stories, which revolves around Argyle West High School's football team, features an ensemble cast of students during their sophomore, junior, and senior years. . . . Written with sensitivity and conviction, the realistic stories are leavened with occasional, often ironic humor." Booklist

A **Century** of great Western stories; edited by John Jakes. Forge 2000 525p $27.95; pa $18.95
Grades: 11 12 Adult   S C
   1. Western stories 2. Short stories
   ISBN 0-312-86986-X; 0-312-86985-1 (pa)
               LC 99-462096
"A Tom Doherty Associates book"
This anthology of 30 short stories includes pieces by such writers as Owen Wister, Zane Grey, Max Brand, Bill Pronzini, Elmer Kelton and Marcia Muller
"Romance, murder, action, mystery and suspense are mixed with hefty doses of moral dilemma, guilt and redemption in these carefully plotted tales. . . . Many of

A Century of great Western stories—*Continued*
the stories are appearing here for the first time since they were published in the pulps of the '30s, '40s and '50s, but their appeal is as fresh as ever." Publ Wkly

Includes bibliographical references

Chairman Mao would not be amused; fiction from today's China; edited by Howard Goldblatt. Grove Press 1995 321p pa $14 hardcover o.p.

Grades: 11 12 Adult   S C
1. China—Fiction 2. Short stories
ISBN 0-8021-3449-1   LC 95-1931
"The 20 authors represented here range from Wang Meng, the former minister of culture, to Su Tong, whose Raise the Red Lantern has been immortalized on screen." Libr J
"Translated ably enough to keep up with the colloquial tone, most tales are told with straightforward familiarity, drawing readers into small communities and personal histories that are anything but heroic." Publ Wkly

Cheever, John, 1912-1982
The stories of John Cheever. Knopf 1978 693p hardcover o.p. pa $17.95

Grades: 11 12 Adult   S C
1. Short stories
ISBN 0-394-50087-3; 0-375-72442-7 (pa)
LC 78-160
A "bringing together of 61 Cheever stories in a single binding. . . . Most of these pieces were initially published in 'The New Yorker.'" Choice
"Readers will delight in the delineation of Cheever's mythical landscapes. . . . Resonant with feeling and meaning, this is a collection to treasure." Publ Wkly

Chekhov, Anton Pavlovich, 1860-1904
The Russian master and other stories; [by] Anton Chekhov; translated with an introduction and notes by Ronald Hingley. Oxford Univ. Press 1999 233p (World's classics) pa $7.95

Grades: 9 10 11 12   S C
1. Russia—Fiction 2. Short stories
ISBN 0-19-283687-0   LC 00-268365
A collection of eleven short stories written between 1892 and 1899

Includes bibliographical references

Chopin, Kate, 1851-1904
The awakening and selected stories; edited with an introduction by Sandra M. Gilbert. Penguin Books 2003 286p (Penguin Classics) pa $8

Grades: 9 10 11 12   S C
1. Short stories
ISBN 0-14-243732-8   LC 2003-265744
In addition to the novel The awakening (1899) this volume also includes selected stories from Bayou folk (1894) and A night in Acadie (1897).

Christie, Agatha, 1890-1976
Miss Marple: the complete short stories. Putnam 1985 346p hardcover o.p. pa $12.95 *

Grades: 11 12 Adult   S C
1. Mystery fiction 2. Short stories
ISBN 0-396-08747-7; 0-425-09486-3 (pa)
LC 85-10220
This volume contains "all 20 short stories that Christie centered on the elderly sleuth. . . . The bulk of the stories are gathered from *The Tuesday Club* murders, chronicling the meetings of a group formed by Miss Marple and a handful of her friends." Publ Wkly

Cisneros, Sandra
Woman Hollering Creek and other stories. Random House 1991 165p pa $11.95 hardcover o.p. *

Grades: 11 12 Adult   S C
1. Mexican Americans—Fiction 2. Short stories
ISBN 0-679-73856-8   LC 90-52930
"Unforgettable characters march through a satisfying collection of tales about Mexican-Americans who know the score and cling to the anchor of their culture." N Y Times Book Rev

Clarke, Arthur C., 1917-
The collected stories of Arthur C. Clarke. TOR Bks. 2001 c2000 966p $29.95; pa $19.95 *

Grades: 11 12 Adult   S C
1. Short stories 2. Science fiction
ISBN 0-312-87821-4; 0-312-87860-5 (pa)
"A TOR book"
First published 2000 in the United Kingdom
"Although most of these stories date from between 1946 and 1970, seven earlier tales, rescued from what would now be called fanzines, extend coverage back to 1937, and a few snippets stretch it toward the present. At least two dozen stories bear titles that are household words among sf readers. . . . The stories demonstrate Clarke's dazzling and unique combination of command of the language, scientific and other kinds of erudition, and inimitable wit." Booklist

Coming of age in America; a multicultural anthology; edited by Mary Frosch; foreword by Gary Soto. New Press (NY) 1994 274p hardcover o.p. pa $14.95 *

Grades: 11 12 Adult   S C
1. Short stories
ISBN 1-56584-146-8; 1-56584-147-6 (pa)
LC 93-46921
This collection consists of sixteen short stories and excerpts from five novels, written by noted authors from a variety of ethnic backgrounds. Among the authors represented are Dorothy Allison, Cynthia Kadohata, Julia Alvarez, Frank Chin, Tobias Wolff, and Chaim Potok.

Cosmos latinos; an anthology of science fiction from Latin America and Spain; translated, edited, & with an introduction & notes by Andrea L. Bell & Yolanda Molina-Gavilán. Wesleyan Univ. Press 2003 352p (Wesleyan early classics of science fiction series) hardcover o.p. pa $24.95

Grades: 11 12 Adult S C

1. Science fiction 2. Short stories

ISBN 0-8195-6633-0; 0-8195-6634-9 (pa)

LC 2003-41182

Translated from the Spanish

This "is a survey of Spanish and Portuguese sf from both sides of the Atlantic, most of it never before translated into English. Coverage begins in the nineteenth century and continues through the early years of the genre's definition to include many more recent than older stories. . . . Many stories exploit familiar sf territory—the technologically advanced future, time travel and its repercussions, and so on—but obscurer corners are visited, too, as in an alternate Crucifixion occurring on a far-distant world just being explored by humans, and a re-casting of the conquistadors as spacefarers. A welcome expansion of the sf terrain for Anglophones." Booklist

Includes bibliographical references

Dahl, Roald

Skin and other stories. Viking 2000 212p $15.99; pa $8.99

Grades: 7 8 9 10 S C

1. Short stories

ISBN 0-670-89184-3; 0-14-131034-0 (pa)

LC 99-58600

A collection of 13 of the author's short stories written for adults. "Full of irony and unexpected twists, they smack of the master's touch—every word carefully chosen, characters fully fleshed out in only a few pages, the sense of place immediate." Booklist

Danticat, Edwidge, 1969-

Krik? Krak! Vintage Books 1996 224p (Vintage contemporaries) pa $12.95 *

Grades: 11 12 Adult S C

1. Haitian Americans—Fiction 2. Haiti—Fiction 3. Short stories

ISBN 0-679-76657-X LC 95-43449

First published 1995 by Soho Press

The author "touches upon life both in Haiti and in New York's Haitian community, though we spend most of our time in Port-au-Prince and the country town of Ville Rose. The best of these stories humanize, particularize, give poignancy to the lives of people we may have come to think of as faceless emblems of misery, poverty and brutality." N Y Times Book Rev

Destination unexpected: short stories; collected by Donald R. Gallo. Candlewick Press 2003 240p hardcover o.p. pa $8.99 *

Grades: 7 8 9 10 S C

1. Short stories

ISBN 0-7636-1764-4; 0-7636-3119-1 (pa)

LC 2002-71599

Contents: Something old, something new, by J. Sweeney; Brutal interlude, by R. Koertge; Bread on the water, by D. Lubar; My people, by M. P. Haddix; Bad blood, by W. Weaver; Keep smiling, by A. Flinn; August lights, by K. W. Holt; Mosquito, by G. Salisbury; The kiss in the carry-on bag, by R. Peck; Tourist trapped, by E. Wittlinger

This collection "features teen protagonists experiencing a transforming experience while on some kind of journey. . . . . Whether humorous or serious, the stories are consistently well written and engaging." Booklist

Don't cramp my style; stories about that time of the month; edited by Lisa Rowe Fraustino. Simon & Schuster for Young Readers 2004 295p $15.95

Grades: 7 8 9 10 S C

1. Menstruation—Fiction 2. Short stories

ISBN 0-689-85882-5

A collection of eleven stories concerning menstruation, by such authors as Pat Brisson, Alice McGill, David Lubar, and Joan Elizabeth Goodman.

"This highly recommended collection . . . encompasses an impressive variety of times, cultures, attitudes, and moods. . . . The writing . . . is consistently excellent." Voice Youth Advocates

Doyle, Sir Arthur Conan, 1859-1930

The complete Sherlock Holmes; with a preface by Christopher Morley. Doubleday 1960 c1930 1122p $27.95 *

Grades: 7 8 9 10 S C

1. Mystery fiction 2. Short stories

ISBN 0-385-00689-6

Also available in a two-volume paperback edition from Bantam Bks.

First published 1930

This book contains the following four Sherlock Holmes novels: A study in scarlet (1887); The sign of the four (1890); The hound of the Baskervilles (1902); The valley of fear (1915). It also contains fifty-eight Sherlock Holmes stories which were originally published in the following separate volumes: Adventures of Sherlock Holmes (1892); Memoirs of Sherlock Holmes (1894); The return of Sherlock Holmes (1905); His last bow (1917); The case book of Sherlock Holmes (1927).

Dreams and visions; fourteen flights of fantasy; edited by M. Jerry Weiss and Helen S. Weiss. Starscape 2006 251p $19.95; pa $5.99

Grades: 11 12 Adult S C

1. Fantasy fiction 2. Short stories

ISBN 0-765-31249-2; 978-0-765-31249-5; 0-765-35107-2 (pa); 978-0-765-35107-4 (pa)

LC 2005-16724

"A Tom Doherty Associates book"

A collection of fourteen science fiction and fantasy short stories by young adult fiction authors.

This "is a strong collection that surprises and delights with every turn of the page." Voice Youth Advocates

Every man for himself; ten short stories about being a guy; edited by Nancy E. Mercado. Dial Books 2005 154p il $16.99; pa $6.99 *
Grades: 7 8 9 10　　　　　　　　　　　S C
1. Short stories 2. Boys—Fiction
ISBN 0-8037-2896-4; 0-14-240813-1 (pa)
　　　　　　　　　　　　　　LC 2004-24069
"This collection provides a refreshing look at the values, decisions, and friendships that ultimately shape a boy into a man. The stories themselves are diverse, ranging from humorous to serious." SLJ

Face relations; 11 stories about seeing beyond color. Simon & Schuster Books for Young Readers 2004 224p $17.95
Grades: 7 8 9 10　　　　　　　　　　　S C
1. Race relations—Fiction 2. Short stories
ISBN 0-689-85637-7
Contents: Phat acceptance by Jess Mowry; Skins by Joseph Bruchac; Snow by Sherri Winston; The heartbeat of the soul of the world by René Saldaña, Jr.; Hum by Naomi Shihab Nye; Epiphany by Ellen Wittlinger; Black and white by Kyoko Mori; Hearing flower by M.E. Kerr; Gold by Marina Budhos; Mr. Ruben by Rita Williams-Garcia; Negress by Marilyn Singer
"Contributed by familiar writers for young people, including Ellen Wittlinger, M. E. Kerr, Rita Williams-Garcia, Naomi Shihab Nye, and Jess Mowry, the stories ask challenging questions about what role race plays in family life, at school, in friendships, and in love. . . . This is a provocative collection." Booklist

The **Faery** Reel; tales from the Twilight Realm; edited by Ellen Datlow & Terri Windling; introduction by Terri Windling; decorations by Charles Vess. Viking 2004 528p il $19.99; pa $9.99
Grades: 9 10 11 12　　　　　　　　　　S C
1. Fairies—Fiction 2. Short stories
ISBN 0-670-05914-5; 0-14-240406-3 (pa)
　　　　　　　　　　　　　　LC 2003-23537
Contents: The boys of Goose Hill \ by Charles de Lint -- Catnyp \ by Delia Sherman -- Elvenbrood \ by Tanith Lee -- Your garnet eyes \ by Katherine Vaz -- Tengu Mountain \ by Gregory Frost -- The faery handbag \ by Kelly Link -- The price of glamour \ by Steve Berman -- The night market \ by Holly Black -- Never never \ by Bruce Glassco -- Screaming for faeries \ by Ellen Steiber -- Immersed in matter \ by Nina Kiriki Hoffman -- Undine \ by Patricia A. McKillip -- The oakthing \ by Gregory Maguire -- Foxwife \ by Hiromi Goto -- The dream eaters \ by A.M. Dellamonica -- The Faery Reel \ by Neil Gaiman -- The shooter at the Heartrock waterhole \ by Bill Congreve -- The annals of Eelin-Ok \ by Jeffrey Ford -- De la tierra \ by Emma Bull -- How to find faery \ by Nan Fry
"A rewarding choice for those who like the traditional with a twist." Booklist

Faulkner, William, 1897-1962
Collected stories of William Faulkner. Random House 1950 900p pa $19.95 hardcover o.p.
Grades: 11 12 Adult　　　　　　　　　S C

1. Short stories
ISBN 0-679-76403-8 (pa)
"Forty-two short stories, including all from These Thirteen (1931), all but two from Doctor Martino and other stories (1934) and seventeen published in magazines, 1932-1948. . . . Many of the stories deal with characters and incidents related to those in his novels set in the mythical Yoknapatawpha County, Mississippi." Libr J

Selected short stories of William Faulkner. Modern Lib. 1993 310p $15.95 *
Grades: 9 10 11 12　　　　　　　　　　S C
1. Short stories
ISBN 0-679-42478-4　　　　　　　LC 92-51072
A reissue of the 1961 edition
A variety of the author's output, diverse in method and subject matter, ranging in original publication dates from 1930 to 1955

Feeling very strange; the Slipstream anthology; James Patrick Kelly & John Kessel, editors. Tachyon Publications 2006 288p pa $14.95
Grades: 11 12 Adult　　　　　　　　　S C
1. Science fiction 2. Fantasy fiction 3. Short stories
ISBN 978-1-892391-35-X; 1-892391-35-X
Contents: Al, by C. Emshwiller; The little magic shop, by B. Sterling; The healer, by A. Bender; The specialist's hat, by K. Link; Light and the sufferer, by J. Lethem; Sea Oak, by G. Saunders; Exhibit H: torn pages discovered in the vest pocket of an unidentified tourist, by J. VanderMeer; Hell is the absence of God, by T. Chiang; Lieserl, by K. J. Fowler; Bright morning, by J. Ford; Biographical notes to "A discourse on the nature of causality, with air-plane," by Benjamin Rosenbaum, by B. Rosenbaum; The god of dark laughter, by M. Chabon; The rose in twelve petals, by T. Goss; The lions are asleep this night, by H. Waldrop; You have never been here, by M. Rickert
"Is slipstream just science fiction and fantasy that doesn't know that it's science fiction or fantasy? Or is it more than that? Decide for yourself by slipping into short stories that are superb, whatever you choose to call them." SciFi.com

Firebirds rising; an anthology of original science fiction and fantasy; edited by Sharyn November. Firebird 2006 530p $19.99
Grades: 7 8 9 10　　　　　　　　　　　S C
1. Science fiction 2. Fantasy fiction 3. Short stories
ISBN 0-14-240549-3; 978-0-14-240549-9
This is a collection of sixteen stories by such authors as Tamora Pierce, Charles de Lint, Alan Dean Foster, Kelly Link, Patricia A. McKillip, and Diana Wynne Jones.
"This anthology is a wonderful choice for any young adult collection." Voice Youth Advocates

First crossing; stories about teen immigrants; edited by Donald R. Gallo. Candlewick Press 2004 224p $16.99; pa $8.99
Grades: 7 8 9 10　　　　　　　　　　　S C
1. Immigrants—Fiction 2. Short stories
ISBN 0-7636-2249-4; 0-7636-3291-0 (pa)
　　　　　　　　　　　　　　LC 2003-65255

First crossing—*Continued*

Contents: First crossing \ Pam Muñoz Ryan — Second culture kids \ Dian Curtis Regan — My favorite chaperone \ Jean Davies Okimoto — They don't mean it! \ Lensey Namioka — Pulling up stakes \ David Lubar — Lines of scrimmage \ Elsa Marston — The Swede \ Alden R. Carter — The Rose of Sharon \ Marie G. Lee — Make Maddie mad \ Rita Williams-Garcia — The green armchair \ Minfong Ho

Ten short stories about teen immigrants by such authors as Pam Muñoz Ryan, Lensey Namioka, and David Lubar.

"Covering a wide range of cultural and economical backgrounds, these stories by 11 well-known authors touch on a variety of teen experiences, with enough attitude and heartfelt angst to speak to young adults anywhere." SLJ

Fitzgerald, F. Scott (Francis Scott), 1896-1940

The short stories of F. Scott Fitzgerald; a new collection; edited and with a preface by Matthew J. Bruccoli. Scribner 1989 775p $37.50; pa $18 *
Grades: 11 12 Adult   S C
1. Short stories
ISBN 0-684-19160-1; 0-684-80445-X (pa)
LC 89-6351

"The 43 stories in this collection include both the famous ones and several that are less well known." Booklist

Flake, Sharon G.

Who am I without him? short stories about girls and the boys in their lives. Jump at the Sun/Hyperion Books for Children 2004 168p $15.99; pa $7.99 *
Grades: 7 8 9 10   S C
1. African Americans—Fiction 2. Short stories
ISBN 0-7868-0693-1; 1-4231-0383-1 (pa)

Ten short stories about African American teenage girls and their relationships with boys.

"Addressing issues and situations that many girls face in today's often complex society, this book is provocative and thought-provoking." SLJ

Gaiman, Neil, 1960-

Fragile things; short fictions and wonders. William Morrow 2006 xxxi, 360p $26.95 *
Grades: 11 12 Adult   S C
1. Short stories 2. Fantasy fiction 3. Horror fiction
ISBN 978-0-06-051522-5; 0-06-051522-8
LC 2006-48135

Also available large print edition $26.95 (ISBN: 0-06-124493-7; ISBN-13: 978-0-06-124493-3)

This "collection contains approximately twenty previously published pieces of short fiction—stories, verse, and an American Gods novella—plus one new piece written especially for this volume." Publisher's note

"The stories are by turns horrifying and fanciful, often blending the two with a little sex, violence, and humor. . . . Gaiman skips along the edge of many adolescent fascinations—life, death, the living dead, and the occult—and teens with a taste for the weird will enjoy this book." SLJ

Gotham Writers' Workshop fiction gallery;

exceptional short stories selected by New York's acclaimed creative writing school; edited by Thom Didato and Alexander Steele. 1st U.S. ed. Bloomsbury, Distributed to the trade by Holtzbrinck Publishers 2004 356p pa $14.95
Grades: 9 10 11 12   S C
1. Short stories
ISBN 1-582-34462-0   LC 2004-5432

Partial contents: Introduction -- Starting out. A trifle from life \ Anton Chekhov -- First confession \ Frank O'Connor -- Brownies \ ZZ Packer -- What the river told us to do \ Peter Markus -- Going for the Orange Julius \ Myla Goldberg -- Longings. Labors of the heart \ Claire Davis -- Crazy life \ Lou Mathews -- Sometimes you talk about Idaho \ Pam Houston -- After the plague \ T.C. Boyle -- Those we know. Here we are \ Dorothy Parker -- Whoever was using this bed \ Raymond Carver -- For a long time this was Griselda's story \ Anthony Doerr -- Home sweet home \ Hannah Tinti -- The job. Orientation \ Daniel Orozco -- Walking into the wind \ John O'Farrell -- Night women \ Edwidge Danticat -- The palace thief \ Ethan Canin -- Strangeness. The book of sand \ Jorge Luis Borges -- The next building I plan to bomb \ Charles Baxter -- The secrets of bats \ Jess Row -- The third and final continent \ Jhumpa Lahiri -- Sunset. The swimmer \ John Cheever

"Each story is captivating; some are shocking. The selections are great examples of how writers use words to craft great literature." SLJ

Includes bibliographical references

Gothic!; ten original dark tales; edited by Deborah

Noyes. Candlewick Press 2004 241p $15.99; pa $7.99 *
Grades: 7 8 9 10   S C
1. Horror fiction 2. Short stories
ISBN 0-7636-2243-5; 0-7636-2737-2 (pa)
LC 2004-45188

Contents: Lungewater by Joan Aiken; Morgan Roehmar's boys by Vivian Vande Velde; Watch and wake by M.T. Anderson; Forbidden brides of the faceless slaves in the nameless house of the night of dread desire by Neil Gaiman; The dead and the moonstruck by Caitlin R. Kiernan; Have no fear, Crumpot is here! by Barry Yourgrau; Stone tower by Janni Lee Simner; The prank by Gregory Maguire; Writing on the wall by Celia Rees; Endings by Garth Nix

This "collection features short stories by noted young adult authors such as M. T. Anderson, Caitlín R. Kiernan, Garth Nix, Celia Rees, Janni Lee Simner, and Barry Yourgrau. . . . These varied tales take place in the distant past and in the high-tech present. Some are humorous while others have surprising twists or are reminiscent of classic fairy tales full of malevolent characters, but all share a love of the surreal or supernatural. . . . A sophisticated, thought-provoking, and gripping read." SLJ

Growing up ethnic in America; contemporary

fiction about learning to be American; edited by Maria Mazziotti Gillan and Jennifer Gillan. Penguin Bks. 1999 374p pa $16.95 *
Grades: 9 10 11 12   S C
1. Short stories
ISBN 0-14-028063-4   LC 99-25762

Growing up ethnic in America—*Continued*

Includes index

This anthology of 35 stories illustrates the various ways young people of distinct ethnic communities come to terms with their identities, negotiating the differences between their cultures and American society. Among the writers included are Amy Tan, Toni Morrison, Gary Soto, Sherman Alexie, Veronica Chambers, and E. L. Doctorow

"This kind of collection, with its literary quality and multiple perspectives, is the best answer to those who expect only messages with multiculturalism and who sneer 'P.C.' at the mention of diversity." Booklist

Halkin, Hillel, 1939-

Tevye the dairyman and The railroad stories; [by] Sholom Aleichem; translated from the Yiddish and with an introduction by Hillel Halkin. Schocken Bks. 1987 xli, 309p pa $15 hardcover o.p.

Grades: 11 12 Adult   S C

1. Jews—Fiction 2. Short stories

ISBN 0-8052-1069-5 (pa)   LC 86-24835

"Library of Yiddish classics"

"In the first eight stories of this collection, Tevye, the Russian Jew so familiar from *Fiddler on the Roof*, bemoans his fate. In these as well as the following 21 tales, the author displays his splendid storytelling skills." Booklist

The Hard SF renaissance; edited by David G. Hartwell and Kathryn Cramer. TOR Bks. 2002 960p hardcover o.p. pa $23.95

Grades: 11 12 Adult   S C

1. Science fiction 2. Short stories

ISBN 0-312-87635-1; 0-312-87636-X (pa)

"A Tom Doherty Associates book"

"The 41 stories in this annotated anthology . . . [showcase] short fiction by veteran sf authors like Kim Stanley Robinson, Joe Haldeman, Bruce Sterling, Nancy Kress, Ben Bova and Arthur C. Clarke. . . . For libraries wanting a definitive collection of hard sf written since 1990, this is a priority purchase." Libr J

Hawthorne, Nathaniel, 1804-1864

Tales and sketches, including Twice-told tales, Mosses from an old manse, and The snow-image; A wonder book for girls and boys; Tanglewood tales for girls and boys, being a second Wonder book. Library of Am. 1982 1493p $39.50

Grades: 11 12 Adult   S C

1. Short stories

ISBN 0-940450-03-8   LC 81-20760

The stories in this collection have appeared in the five books: Twice-told tales (1837); Mosses from an old manse (1846); The snow-image (1852); A wonder book for girls and boys (1851); Tanglewood tales for girls and boys, being a second wonder book (1853)

This volume contains all of Hawthorne's tales and sketches, which are arranged in order of their periodical publication

The Heinemann book of contemporary African short stories; edited by Chinua Achebe and C. L. Innes. Heinemann Educ. Bks. 1992 200p (African writers series) pa $11.95 *

Grades: 9 10 11 12   S C

1. Africa—Fiction 2. Short stories

ISBN 0-435-90566-X   LC 93-106811

Spine title: Contemporary African writers

The twenty stories in this collection "are divided by region: five stories from Southern Africa; two from Central Africa; five from East Africa; two from Northern Africa; and six from West Africa. Region is important for, in many cases, the issues of the area are reflected in the selections. . . . The writing is mature, and the themes and moods are many, ranging from mystical to magical to supernatural to realistic. This anthology is a worthwhile addition to any library collection serving YAs." SLJ

Hemingway, Ernest, 1899-1961

The complete short stories of Ernest Hemingway; the Finca Vigía edition. Scribner 1987 650p pa $20 hardcover o.p. *

Grades: 11 12 Adult   S C

1. Short stories

ISBN 0-684-84332-3   LC 87-12888

"To the 49 standard *Short stories of Ernest Hemingway*, this edition adds 14 from other books or magazines and seven never published before. . . . For all the repetition of previous collections and possible incompleteness despite the title, this volume is pure Hemingway in his most consistently satisfying format and, as such, belongs in most libraries." Booklist

Henry, O., 1862-1910

The best short stories of O. Henry; selected and with an introduction by Bennett A. Cerf, and Van H. Cartmell. Modern Lib. 1994 c1945 340p $22.95 *

Grades: 11 12 Adult   S C

1. Short stories

ISBN 0-679-60122-8

First Modern Library edition published 1945

O. Henry "is best known for his observations on the diverse lives of everyday New Yorkers, 'the four million ' neglected by other writers. He had a fine gift of humor and was adept at the ingenious depiction of ironic circumstances, in plots frequently dependent upon coincidence." Oxford Companion to Am Lit. 6th edition

Hesse, Hermann, 1877-1962

The fairy tales of Hermann Hesse; translated and with an introduction by Jack Zipes; woodcut illustrations by David Frampton. Bantam Bks. 1995 xxxi, 266p il pa $14.95 hardcover o.p.

Grades: 11 12 Adult   S C

1. Fairy tales 2. Short stories

ISBN 0-553-37776-0 (pa)   LC 94-49166

"Quirky and evocative, Hesse's fairy tales stand alone, but also amplify the ideas and utopian longings of such counterculture avatars as *Siddhartha* and *Steppenwolf*." Publ Wkly

Hughes, Langston, 1902-1967

Short stories of Langston Hughes; edited by Akiba Sullivan Harper; with an introduction by Arnold Rampersad. Hill & Wang 1996 299p pa $16 hardcover o.p. *

Grades: 11 12 Adult   **S C**
 1. African Americans—Fiction 2. Short stories
 ISBN 0-8090-1603-6   LC 95-19554
 "Dating from 1919 to 1963, these pieces vary in theme, covering life at sea, the trials and tribulations of a young pianist and her elderly white patron, a visiting writer's experience in Cuba, a young girl's winning an art scholarship but losing it when it's learned she is black, and an ambitious black preacher trying to gain fame by being nailed to a cross. If you crave good reading don't pass up this gem." Libr J

Hurston, Zora Neale, 1891-1960

The complete stories; introduction by Henry Louis Gates, Jr. and Sieglinde Lemke. HarperCollins Pubs. 1995 xxiii, 305p pa $14 hardcover o.p. *

Grades: 11 12 Adult   **S C**
 1. African Americans—Fiction 2. Short stories
 ISBN 0-06-092171-4 (pa)   LC 91-50438
 This collection of Hurston's short fiction contains nineteen stories originally published between 1921 and 1951, arranged in the order in which they were published, and seven previously unpublished stories.
 Includes bibliographical references

Irving, Washington, 1783-1859

Bracebridge Hall; Tales of a traveller; The Alhambra. Library of Am. 1991 1104p $35

Grades: 11 12 Adult   **S C**
 ISBN 0-940450-59-3   LC 90-62267
 This volume contains three collections of stories and sketches: Bracebridge Hall (1822); Tales of a traveller (1824); and The Alhambra (1832)

Jackson, Shirley, 1919-1965

The lottery; or, The adventures of James Harris. Farrar, Straus & Giroux 1949 306p pa $14 hardcover o.p. *

Grades: 11 12 Adult   **S C**
 1. Short stories
 ISBN 0-374-52953-1
 The stories "in this collection seem to fall into three groups. There are the slight sketches, like genre paintings, dealing with episodes which are trivial in terms of plot but which by means of [the author's] precise, sensitive, and sharply focused style become luminous with meaning. . . . The second group comprises her social-problem sketches. . . . Her final group deals with fantasy, ranging from humorous whimsy to horrifying shock." Saturday Rev Lit

Join in; multiethnic short stories by outstanding writers for young adults; edited by Donald R. Gallo. Delacorte Press 1993 256p pa $5.99 hardcover o.p.

Grades: 9 10 11 12   **S C**
 1. Short stories
 ISBN 0-440-21957-4 (pa)   LC 92-43169
 "The 17 stories cross the boundaries of race and culture and probe the universal themes of belonging, acceptance, family, and friendship." Booklist
 "Uneven in quality, this will nevertheless offer grounds for discussion among young adults, who will appreciate the accessibility and brevity of the stories." Bull Cent Child Books

Joyce, James, 1882-1941

Dubliners. Knopf 1991 lxvii, 7-287p $19 *

Grades: 11 12 Adult   **S C**
 1. Ireland—Fiction 2. Short stories
 ISBN 0-679-40574-7   LC 91-53001
 First published 1914 in the United Kingdom; first United States edition published 1916 by Huebsch
 Contents: The sisters; An encounter; Araby; Eveline; After the race; Two gallants; The boarding house; A little cloud; Counterparts; Clay; A painful case; Ivy day in the committee room; A mother; Grace; The dead
 "This collection of 15 stories provides an introduction to the style and motifs found in Joyce's writing. The stories stand alone as individual scenes of Dublin society and are intertwined by the use of autobiography and symbolism." Shapiro. Fic for Youth. 3d edition

Kafka, Franz, 1883-1924

The metamorphosis and other stories; translated by Joachim Neugroschel. Scribner 1993 xxiii, 227p pa $13 hardcover o.p. *

Grades: 11 12 Adult   **S C**
 1. Short stories
 ISBN 0-684-80070-5   LC 92-43912
 Also available in paperback from Penguin Bks.
 This is a collection of thirty stories, some of which are quite short. The stories are arranged in order of their original publication dates.

King, Stephen, 1947-

Everything's eventual: 14 dark tales. Scribner 2002 459p $28

Grades: 11 12 Adult   **S C**
 1. Horror fiction 2. Short stories
 ISBN 0-7432-3515-0   LC 2002-17738
 "Fourteen stories, most of them gems, featuring an array of literary approaches, plus an opinionated intro from King about the '(Almost) Lost Art' of the short story." Publ Wkly

Four past midnight. Viking 1990 763p pa $7.99 hardcover o.p.

Grades: 11 12 Adult   **S C**
 1. Horror fiction 2. Short stories
 ISBN 0-451-17038-5 (pa)   LC 90-50046

King, Stephen, 1947-—*Continued*

This volume contains four novellas: The Langoliers; Secret window, secret garden; The library policeman; The sun dog.

This book "is hard to put down, truly chilling, and sure to be enjoyed by YA horror afficionados everywhere." SLJ

Night shift. Doubleday 1978 xxii, 336p $35
Grades: 11 12 Adult   S C
1. Short stories 2. Horror fiction
ISBN 0-385-12991-2   LC 77-75146
Also available in paperback from Signet Bks.

The stories "all begin in our normal world, where everything is safe and warm. But in almost every instance, something slips, and we find ourselves in the nightmare world of the not-quite real. . . . Such stories require a willing suspension of disbelief, of course, but they also require an author who is an expert manipulator. . . . King is an expert." Best Sellers

Skeleton crew. Putnam 1985 512p pa $7.99 hardcover o.p. *
Grades: 11 12 Adult   S C
1. Horror fiction 2. Short stories
ISBN 0-451-16861-5 (pa)   LC 84-15947
This "collection of King's shorter work is a hefty sampler from all stages of his career, and demonstrates the range of his abilities. . . . There are several stories here that must rank among King's best." Publ Wkly

Kinsella, W. P.

Shoeless Joe Jackson comes to Iowa: stories. Southern Methodist Univ. Press 1993 141p il $19.95; pa $8.89
Grades: 11 12 Adult   S C
1. Baseball—Fiction 2. Short stories
ISBN 0-87074-355-4; 0-87074-356-2 (pa)
LC 93-3935
First published 1980 in Canada
"The title story contains the germ of Kinsella's novel Shoeless Joe; not as deep and rich as the longer work, it remains pure and perfect in itself. Among the other gems: 'Fiona the First,' a portrait of a man doomed to spend eternity picking up girls at airports, 'First Names and Empty Pockets,' in which a doll-mender saves the broken Janis Joplin; and 'The Grecian Urn,' a tale of people traveling in time by becoming part of works of art. Few writers can match Kinsella's ability to establish tone, character, and a complete reality in just a few paragraphs, then sweep the reader into his imagined world." Libr J

Kipling, Rudyard, 1865-1936

Collected stories; selected and introduced by Robert Gottlieb. Knopf 1994 xxxvii, 911p $25
Grades: 11 12 Adult   S C
1. Short stories
ISBN 0-679-43592-1   LC 94-5854
"Everyman's library"
"There is an enormous range of subject matter, genre, styles, and tones in Kipling's prose work. . . . [He] is undoubtedly one of the great short-story writers in En-

glish and the subtlety of his early narrative technique has led some to claim him as a proto-Modernist." Oxford Companion to 20th Cent Lit in Engl

Includes bibliographical references

Lanagan, Margo, 1960-

Black juice. Eos 2005 201p $15.99; lib bdg $16.89; pa $5.99
Grades: 7 8 9 10   S C
1. Short stories
ISBN 0-06-074390-5; 0-06-074391-3 (lib bdg); 0-06-074392-1 (pa)   LC 2004-8715
Contents: Singing my sister down; My lord's man; Red nose day; Sweet Pippit; House of the many; Wooden bride; Earthly uses; Perpetual light; Yowlinin; Rite of spring

Provides glimpses of the dark side of civilization and the beauty of the human spirit through ten short stories that explore significant moments in people's lives, events leading to them, and their consequences.

"This book will satisfy readers hungry for intelligent, literary fantasies that effectively twist facets of our everyday world into something alien." SLJ

White time. Eos 2006 216p $15.99; lib bdg $16.89
Grades: 8 9 10 11 12   S C
1. Short stories
ISBN 978-0-06-074393-2; 0-06-074393-X; 978-0-06-074394-9 (lib bdg); 0-06-074394-8 (lib bdg)
LC 2005019755
Presents ten short stories, both dark and hopeful, that journey into the past, the future, and altered versions of the present.

"Each story underscores Lanagan's talent for inspiring curiosity, disturbing sensibilities, and provoking thought." Booklist

Le Guin, Ursula K., 1929-

Tales from Earthsea. Ace Books 2002 314p pa $13.95
Grades: 11 12 Adult   S C
1. Fantasy fiction 2. Short stories
ISBN 0-441-00932-8   LC 2001-56673
First published 2001 by Harcourt
Five fantasy tales set on the archipelago of Earthsea with an essay on the people, languages, history and magic of the place.

"Inhabited by people no better or worse than ourselves, Earthsea is dominated by the practice of magic as precise as any science and as unpredictable in its social consequences. Since it is based entirely on language, Earthsea's magic serves as a metaphor for the writer's own sorcery. Yet despite Le Guin's strong bias toward the didactic there is no hint of by-the-numbers allegory here." N Y Times Book Rev

Legends: short novels by the masters of modern fantasy; edited by Robert Silverberg. TOR Bks. 1998 715p il hardcover o.p. pa $17.95
Grades: 11 12 Adult   S C
1. Fantasy fiction 2. Short stories
ISBN 0-312-86787-5; 0-7653-0035-4 (pa)
LC 98-23593

Legends: short novels by the masters of modern fantasy—*Continued*

Seven of the short novels included in this collection also issued in paperback with designations Legends v2 and Legends v3

"A Tom Doherty Associates book"

Contents: The little sisters of Eluria, by S. King; The sea and little fishes, by T. Pratchett; Debt of bones, by T. Goodkind; Grinning man, by O. S. Card; The seventh shrine, by R. Silverberg; Dragonfly, by U. K. Le Guin; The burning man, by T. Williams; The hedge knight, by George R. R. Martin; Runner of Pern, by A. McCaffrey; The woodboy, by R. E. Feist; New spring, by R. Jordan

"What is so noteworthy about this collection is the fact that all the selections are first rate and are well integrated into their universes." Booklist

The **Literary** ghost; great contemporary ghost stories; edited and with an introduction by Larry Dark. Atlantic Monthly Press 1991 369p pa $13 hardcover o.p. *

Grades: 11 12 Adult S C

1. Ghost stories 2. Short stories

ISBN 0-87113-483-7 (pa) LC 91-15052

The ghost story "is alive and more than well, as proved by this anthology of 28 examples. . . . From the U.S., Britain, Canada, South Africa, and India, the authors showcased here who have taken their fiction in the direction of the supernatural are, specifically, such modern luminaries as Joyce Carol Oates, Nadine Gordimer, Graham Greene, and Isaac Singer. . . . The variety of approaches . . . represented here promises wide appeal." Booklist

The **Locus** awards; thirty years of the best in science fiction and fantasy; edited by Charles N. Brown and Jonathan Strahan. Eos 2004 512p pa $15.95 *

Grades: 9 10 11 12 S C

1. Science fiction 2. Fantasy fiction 3. Short stories

ISBN 0-06-059426-8 LC 2004-42054

Contents: The 1970s: The death of Doctor Island / Gene Wolfe -- The day before the revolution / Ursula K. Le Guin -- Jeffty is five / Harlan Ellison -- The persistence of vision / John Varley -- The 1980s: The way of cross and dragon / George R.R. Martin -- Souls / Joanna Russ Bloodchild / Octavia E. Butler -- The only neat thing to do / James Tiptree Jr. -- Rachel in love / Pat Murphy -- The scalehunter's beautiful daughter / Lucius Shepard -- The 1990s: Bears discover fire / Terry Bisson -- Buffalo / John Kessel -- Even the queen / Connie Willis -- Gone / John Crowley -- Maneki Neko / Bruce Sterling -- The 2000s: Border guards / Greg Egan -- Hell is the absence of God / Ted Chiang -- October in the chair / Neil Gaiman -- Previous winners

"Whether readers are catching up on legendary science fiction and fantasy, becoming reacquainted with old favorites, or grazing the field in hopes of discovering new ones, this anthology delivers some of the finest science fiction and fantasy ever written." SLJ

Make me over; 11 stories of transformation; edited by Marilyn Singer. Dutton Children's Books 2005 199p $17.99

Grades: 7 8 9 10 S C

1. Short stories

ISBN 0-525-47480-3 LC 2005-02109

These stories "delve into our culture's fascination with beauty and present different views about all kinds of makeovers. . . . Authors include Joseph Bruchac, Marina Budhos, Evelyn Coleman, Peni R. Griffin, Margaret Peterson Haddix, Norma Howe, Jess Mowry, René Saldaña, Jr., Marilyn Singer, Joyce Sweeney, and Terry Trueman." Publisher's note

"Sweet and spicy, tough and raw, these well-written stories will make a lasting impression on readers." Booklist

Malamud, Bernard, 1914-1986

The complete stories; introduction by Robert Giroux. Farrar, Straus & Giroux 1997 634p hardcover o.p. pa $18 *

Grades: 11 12 Adult S C

1. Short stories

ISBN 0-374-12639-9; 0-374-52575-7 (pa) LC 97-12394

"Whether, stark, comic or fanciful, Malamud's stories give us immigrant Jews and their descendants pondering moral questions and experiencing moments of magical intervention while enduring life's ridiculous situations. Yet the stories transcend their ethnic settings and achieve a universal resonance." Publ Wkly

Marston, Elsa

Figs and fate; stories about growing up in the Arab world today. Braziller 2005 135p hardcover o.p. pa $15.95 *

Grades: 9 10 11 12 S C

1. Arab countries—Fiction 2. Middle East—Fiction 3. Short stories

ISBN 0-8076-1551-X; 0-8076-1554-4 (pa) LC 2004-25818

Contents: In line; Hand of Fatima; Faces; The plan; Santa Claus in Bagdad

A collection of five stories portraying Arab life in Egypt, Lebanon, Syria, a Palestinian refugee camp in Lebanon, and Iraq today.

"Readers will recognize the universals of coming-of-age, even as they are drawn into the rich diversity and the desperation of daily life." Booklist

Masters of fantasy; edited by Bill Fawcett & Brian Thomsen. Baen Publishing Enterprises, Distributed by Simon & Schuster 2004 376p $25; pa $7.99 *

Grades: 9 10 11 12 S C

1. Fantasy fiction 2. Short stories

ISBN 0-7434-8822-9; 1-4165-0927-5 (pa) LC 2004-5565

"A Baen Books original"

Contents: Out of the deep: a Valdemar story / Mercedes Lackey -- Earthborne: a Witchworld story / Andre Norton -- Mything in dreamland: a Myth adventures in

Masters of fantasy—*Continued*

dreamland story / Robert Asprin & Jody Lynn Nye -- Race for the sky: a Bifrost story / Mickey Zucker Reichert -- Shadamehr and the old wive's tale: a Shadamehr story / Margaret Weis and Don Perrin -- Serenade: a Spellsinger story / Alan Dean Foster -- Child of prophecy: a War of light and shadow story / Janny Wurts -- The afterlife of St. Vidicon of Cathode: a Warlock story / Christopher Stasheff -- The elf house: an Isles story / David Drake -- Gifts: a World of Paksenarrian story / Elizabeth Moon -- The amorous broom: a John Justin Mallory story / Mike Resnick -- Web of deception: a Bahzell story / David Weber

"This volume presents . . . stories set in several series of proven and lasting popularity, by some of the best writers in the genre. . . . Though anthologies can be difficult for libraries to merchandise, this one could be very useful." SLJ

Maugham, W. Somerset (William Somerset), 1874-1965

Collected short stories. Penguin Bks. 1992-1993
4v v1 & v3 pa $13.95; v2 pa $15; v4 pa $14.95
Grades: 9 10 11 12   S C
1. Short stories
ISBN 0-14-018589-5 (v1); 0-14-018590-9 (v2); 0-14-018591-7 (v3); 0-14-018592-5 (v4)
First published 1963 in the United Kingdom
"Two qualities of Maugham as a writer brought him mastery of the short story: an economical and exact means of fixing the sense of place, often exotic places; and an equally economical skill in realizing the crisis of a story." Penguin Companion to Engl Lit

McKillip, Patricia A., 1948-

Harrowing the dragon. Ace Books 2005 310p hardcover o.p. pa $14
Grades: 9 10 11 12   S C
1. Fantasy fiction 2. Short stories
ISBN 0-441-01360-0; 0-441-01443-7 (pa)
LC 2005-51311
"This collection of 13 stories by one of fantasy's most elegant and luminescent writers brings together 25 years of short fiction into one lyrical volume." Libr J

McKinley, Robin

Water: tales of elemental spirits; [by] Robin McKinley, Peter Dickinson. Putnam 2002 266p $18.99; pa $6.99
Grades: 7 8 9 10   S C
1. Fantasy fiction 2. Mermaids and mermen—Fiction
3. Short stories
ISBN 0-399-23796-8; 0-14-240244-3 (pa)
LC 2001-41642
"These six stories, three by McKinley and three by her husband, Dickinson, feature the elemental spirits that inhabit Earth's waters." Voice Youth Advocates
"The masterfully written stories all feature distinct, richly detailed casts and settings . . . and focus as strongly on action as on character. There's plenty here to excite, enthrall, and move even the pickiest readers." SLJ

Michener, James A., 1907-1997

Tales of the South Pacific. Ballantine Books 1984 384p pa $7.99
Grades: 11 12 Adult   S C
1. World War, 1939-1945—Fiction 2. Short stories
ISBN 0-449-20652-1
First published 1947 by Macmillan
These 19 tales describe "the strain and the boredom, the careful planning and heroic action, the color and beauty of the islands, and all that made up life during the critical days of the war in the Pacific." Wis Libr Bull

Moccasin thunder; American Indians stories for today; edited by Lori Marie Carlson. HarperCollins 2005 156p $15.99; lib bdg $16.89 *

Grades: 7 8 9 10   S C
1. Native Americans—Fiction 2. Short stories
ISBN 0-06-623957-5; 0-06-623959-1 (lib bdg)
LC 2004-22186
Presents ten short stories about contemporary Native American teens by members of tribes of the United States and Canada, including Louise Erdrich and Joseph Bruchac
"This distinguished anthology offers powerful, beautifully written stories that are thoughtful and important for teens to hear." SLJ

Myers, Walter Dean, 1937-

145th Street; short stories. Delacorte Press 2000 151p $15.95; lib bdg $18.99; pa $5.50 *
Grades: 7 8 9 10   S C
1. Harlem (New York, N.Y.)—Fiction 2. African Americans—Fiction 3. Short stories
ISBN 0-385-32137-6; 0-385-90538-6 (lib bdg); 0-440-22916-2 (pa)   LC 99-36097
"These ten powerful stories create a vivid mosaic of life in the Harlem neighborhood of 145th Street. Memorable characters range from outgoing Big Joe, who decides to stage his own funeral party in *Big Joe's funeral*, to book-loving *Monkeyman*, who outsmarts the Tigros gang. . . . Beautifully told, Myers's stories offer an enticing collection for teens." Voice Youth Advocates

Necessary noise: stories about our families as they really are; edited by Michael Cart; illustrations by Charlotte Noruzi. Joanna Cotler Bks. 2003 239p $15.99; pa $8.99

Grades: 7 8 9 10   S C
1. Family life—Fiction 2. Short stories
ISBN 0-06-027499-9; 0-06-051437-X (pa)
LC 2002-151058
"Ten original stories provide ten distinct perspectives on the quagmire that is 'family.' The result is a collection with considerable range and depth. . . . The style of the writers varies as much as their subjects: Joyce Carol Thomas offers a 'Mom-Son Conversation' about the frightening onset of schizophrenia; Sonya Sones's prose poems portray a light-and-dark relationship with an abusive sibling in 'Dr. Jekyll and Sister Hyde'. . . . Lois Lowry gives us a terrific finale with a clever and truthful story that reads like a one-act play." Horn Book Guide

New skies: an anthology of today's science fiction; edited by Patrick Nielsen Hayden. Tor 2003 288p $19.95; pa $6.99

Grades: 7 8 9 10   S C

1. Science fiction 2. Short stories

ISBN 0-7653-0016-8; 0-7653-4004-6 (pa)

LC 2003-55952

"A Tom Doherty Associates book"

This collection "gathers 17 stories starring aliens and dimensions beyond the 3D world. In 'They're Made Out of Meat' by Terry Bisson, a pair of aliens are stunned to discover an intelligent species made not of machinery or gasses, but of flesh. A boy and his dog exchange bodies with a pair of tentacled aliens in 'Brian and the Aliens' by Will Shetterly. And in the award-winning 'Tangents' by Greg Bear, a scientist and a kid make contact with the fourth dimension." Publ Wkly

This "is the finest collection of SF short stories published specifically for young adult readers in recent memory. . . . This anthology is a must-purchase for all YA collections." Voice Youth Advocates

Night terrors; stories of shadow and substance; edited by Lois Duncan. Simon & Schuster Bks. for Young Readers 1996 175p pa $5.99 hardcover o.p.

Grades: 7 8 9 10   S C

1. Horror fiction 2. Short stories

ISBN 0-689-80724-4 (pa)   LC 95-44901

Contents: The monkey's wedding, by J. Aiken; Satan's shadow, by A. Ferguson; The chosen, by M. Harrah; The bogey man, by A. C. Klause; Bearing Paul, by C. Lynch; The beautiful thing, by H. Mazer; The house on Buffalo Street, by N. F. Mazer; The dark beast of death, by J. L. Nixon; Girl at the window, by R. Peck; The grind of an axe, by T. Taylor; Moon kill, by P. Windsor

"The stories deal with madness, witchcraft, homicide and incest. While the book should be popular with students, the subject matter may be too mature for some middle-schoolers." Voice Youth Advocates

Nightshade: 20th century ghost stories; edited by Robert Phillips. Carroll & Graf Pubs. 1999 470p hardcover o.p. pa $14

Grades: 11 12 Adult   S C

1. Ghost stories 2. Short stories

ISBN 0-7867-0614-7; 0-7867-0808-5 (pa)

This is a collection "of 27 paranormal tales. . . . Classics by Henry James, Rudyard Kipling, and Edith Wharton are included, as are stories like Elizabeth Bowen's 'The happy autumn fields,' all considered to be among the authors' best writings. . . . [Also included are] noted world writers such as Isak Dinesen, Franz Kafka, and Gabriel Garcia Marquez, and the contemporary voices of Christopher Tilghman and Max Eberts." Libr J

The **Norton** book of American short stories.

Norton 1988 779p $29.95 *

Grades: 11 12 Adult   S C

1. Short stories

ISBN 0-393-02619-1   LC 88-14181

"The 70 stories Prescott chose for inclusion in this comprehensive anthology show to great effect the ster-

ling quality of American short stories, from the dawn-days of Poe and Hawthorne to the . . . minimalism of Raymond Carver. A collection full of treasures." Booklist

The **Norton** book of science fiction; North American science fiction, 1960-1990; edited by Ursula K. Le Guin and Brian Attebery; Karen Joy Fowler, consultant. Norton 1993 869p pa $38.13 hardcover o.p. *

Grades: 11 12 Adult   S C

1. Science fiction 2. Short stories

ISBN 0-393-97241-0 (pa)   LC 93-16130

Damon Knight, Robert Silverberg, Connie Willis and Harlan Ellison are among the authors represented in this anthology of more than 60 stories.

A "compilation of intelligent and entertaining sf that belongs in virtually every fiction collection." Booklist

Not the only one; lesbian and gay fiction for teens; edited by Jane Summer. Alyson Publs. 2004 302p pa $13.95

Grades: 9 10 11 12   S C

1. Homosexuality—Fiction 2. Short stories

ISBN 1-55583-834-0

First published 1995

Some stories appeared previously in collection edited in 1995 by Tony Grima

"This collection of twenty . . . pieces, featuring lesbi-an/gay/bisexual/transgender (LGBT) characters in each story, are for all teens. . . . The stories are gems to be savored, with settings ranging from nineteenth-century New York City through today's Africa and on to contemporary American suburbs." Voice Youth Advocates

Oates, Joyce Carol, 1938-

Small avalanches and other stories. HarperCollins Pubs. 2003 390p $16.99; pa $7.99

Grades: 7 8 9 10   S C

1. Short stories

ISBN 0-06-001217-X; 0-06-001219-6 (pa)

LC 2002-23311

These "tales are about vulnerable, wild, rebellious, scared young women, several of whom fall victim to older, predatory males who know how to lure them with the thrill of danger and make them betray the best in themselves. . . . Oates makes poetry with ordinary words that take readers right into the restless psyches of young women terrified of their own violence. Far from role models, these characters wrestle with the fearful fantasies they dare not even articulate." Booklist

O'Brien, Tim, 1946-

The things they carried; a work of fiction. Broadway Books 1998 273p pa $14.95 *

Grades: 11 12 Adult   S C

1. Vietnam War, 1961-1975—Fiction 2. Short stories

ISBN 0-7679-0289-0   LC 98-49677

First published 1990 by Houghton Mifflin

This is a collection of stories about American soldiers in Vietnam. . . . All of the stories "deal with a single platoon, one of whose members is a character named Tim O'Brien." N Y Times Book Rev

O'Brien, Tim, 1946-—*Continued*

"This book may be selfconscious . . . but through its determination to treat these men with dignity and decency it proves immensely affecting." Newsweek

O'Connor, Flannery

Collected works. Library of Am. 1988 1281p $35 *

Grades: 11 12 Adult   **S C**
1. Short stories
ISBN 0-940450-37-2   LC 87-37829

Contents: Wise blood; A good man is hard to find; The violent bear it away; Everything that rises must converge; Stories and occasional prose; Letters

The complete stories. Farrar, Straus & Giroux 1971 555p pa $17 hardcover o.p.

Grades: 11 12 Adult   **S C**
1. Short stories
ISBN 0-374-51536-0

This collection is "arranged in chronological order from the story she wrote for her master's thesis at the University of Iowa to 'Judgement Day.' . . . The stories here include the original openings and other chapters of her two novels 'Wise Blood' and 'The Violent Bear It Away.'" N Y Times Book Rev

Once upon a cuento; edited by Lyn Miller-Lachman. Curbstone Press 2003 243p pa $15.95

Grades: 9 10 11 12   **S C**
1. Hispanic Americans—Fiction 2. Short stories
ISBN 1-88068-499-3   LC 2003-14667

Contents: Heritage, holidays, and contemporary culture: My ciguapa; A Nuyorican Christmas in el Bronx; Adventures in Mexican wrestling; Searching for Peter Z; Family life: Leaving before the snow; A special gift; Initiation; Good trouble for Lucy; The snake; Friends and other relationships: Sara and Panchito; Armpits, hair and other marks of beauty; Learning buddies; Indian summer sun; Dealing with differences: Leti's shoe escandalo; Dancing Miranda; That October; Grease

"Fourteen Latino authors have contributed to this collection of 17 short stories " SLJ

"Writing quality is consistently high throughout. . . . This book . . . succeeds admirably in proving, through literature, that there is no single 'Latino experience.'" Voice Youth Advocates

Ortiz Cofer, Judith, 1952-

An island like you; stories of the barrio. Puffin Books 1996 165p pa $6.99

Grades: 7 8 9 10 11 12   **S C**
1. Puerto Ricans—Fiction 2. New Jersey—Fiction 3. Short stories
ISBN 0-14-038068-X   LC 96-23203

A collection of twelve stories about young people in Paterson New Jersey caught between their Puerto Rican heritage and their American surroundings.

"The combination of interweaving of characters, intensity of emotion, and deft control of language make this a rewarding collection." Bull Cent Child Books

The **Oxford** book of English short stories; edited by A.S. Byatt. Oxford Univ. Press 1998 xxx, 439p hardcover o.p. pa $19.95

Grades: 11 12 Adult   **S C**
1. Short stories
ISBN 0-19-214238-0; 0-19-280376-X (pa)
                       LC 97-44998

In this anthology Byatt "includes necessary masters—Rudyard Kipling, Saki, D. H. Lawrence, and V. S. Pritchett, to name a few. But . . . she draws into the fold the work of several extremely talented writers of which few readers on this side of the Atlantic will have heard. Falling into this category are such writers as Malachi Whitaker, H. E. Bates, Sylvia Townsend Warner, and Charlotte Mew." Booklist

The **Oxford** book of gothic tales; edited by Chris Baldick. Oxford Univ. Press 1992 xxiii, 533p pa $19.95 hardcover o.p.

Grades: 11 12 Adult   **S C**
1. Horror fiction 2. Short stories 3. Gothic romances
ISBN 0-19-286219-7 (pa)   LC 91-27290

This chronologically arranged anthology contains thirty-seven stories dating from the 18th to 20th century. Among the authors are Hawthorne, Poe, Stevenson, Hardy, Faulkner, Welty, Borges, Angela Carter and Isabel Allende.

The **Oxford** book of Irish short stories; edited by William Trevor. Oxford Univ. Press 1989 567p $40; pa $17.95

Grades: 11 12 Adult   **S C**
1. Ireland—Fiction 2. Short stories
ISBN 0-19-214180-5; 0-19-280193-7 (pa)
                       LC 88-28147

"The great Irish writers—from Oliver Goldsmith and Oscar Wilde to James Joyce and Edna O'Brien—are represented in a collection for older advanced readers." Booklist

The **Oxford** book of short stories; chosen by V.S. Pritchett. Oxford Univ. Press 1981 547p $35; pa $16.95 *

Grades: 11 12 Adult   **S C**
1. Short stories
ISBN 0-19-214116-3; 0-19-282113-X (pa)
                       LC 81-156872

In addition to one of his own short stories, Pritchett has selected 40 others, written in English during the 19th and 20th centuries. Most of the authors are English, Irish or American and include Somerset Maugham, D. H. Lawrence, Faulkner, Twain, and Eudora Welty

Packer, ZZ, 1973-

Drinking coffee elsewhere. Riverhead Bks. 2003 238p hardcover o.p. pa $14

Grades: 11 12 Adult   **S C**
1. African Americans—Fiction 2. Short stories
ISBN 1-57322-234-8; 1-57322-378-6 (pa)
                       LC 2002-73971

"The predominantly African American characters in Packer's first collection of short fiction struggle to maintain their sense of self while they confront unexpected life events." Booklist

Past imperfect; edited by Martin H. Greenberg and Larry Segriff. DAW Bks. 2001 pa $6.99

Grades: 9 10 11 12   **S C**

1. Science fiction 2. Short stories

ISBN 0-7564-0012-0   LC 2002-560856

The authors of these "stories on the classic sf trope of time travel let it lead them as it may through genres including mystery, romance, space opera, and quiet reflection at home. The book's selections are excellent, which isn't surprising given the likes of Nina Kiriki Hoffman, Jody Lynn Nye, and James P. Hogan as contributors and the fact that lesser-knowns proffer fine stories, too. Altogether, they take us to both the future and the past. . . . A well-balanced and entertaining anthology." Booklist

Peck, Richard, 1934-

Past perfect, present tense: new and collected stories. Dial Bks. 2004 177p $16.99; pa $6.99

Grades: 9 10 11 12   **S C**

1. Short stories

ISBN 0-8037-2998-7; 0-14-240537-X (pa)

     LC 2003-10904

A collection of short stories, including two previously unpublished ones, that deal with the way things could be.

"The stories perfectly highlight Peck's range and expertise at characterization. Almost every one is a superb read-aloud. . . . This superior collection is a must for every library." SLJ

Poe, Edgar Allan, 1809-1849

Edgar Allan Poe's tales of mystery and madness; illustrated by Gris Grimley. Atheneum Books for Young Readers 2004 135p il $17.95 *

Grades: 9 10 11 12   **S C**

1. Horror fiction 2. Short stories

ISBN 0-689-84837-4   LC 2003-10565

Contents: The black cat; The masque of the Red Death; Hop Frog; The fall of the house of Usher

"With high-production values and gothic sensibilities thoroughly reflected in both text and art, this is an essential purchase for libraries. Adults can use it to lead young people to some great literature; readers will pluck it off the shelves themselves for creepy, entertaining fun." Booklist

Porter, Katherine Anne, 1890-1980

The collected stories of Katherine Anne Porter. Harcourt Brace & World 1965 495p pa $16 hardcover o.p.

Grades: 11 12 Adult   **S C**

1. Short stories

ISBN 0-15-618876-7

Contains three collections of short stories: Flowering Judas, and other stories (1935); The leaning tower, and other stories (1944); Pale horse, pale rider (1939); and four additional short stories: Virgin Violeta; The martyr; The fig tree; and Holiday.

"These are perfect examples of the short story and are representative not only of the best American writing but of the best in the world." SLJ

Pale horse, pale rider: three short novels. Harcourt Brace Jovanovich 1990 c1939 208p $17 *

Grades: 11 12 Adult   **S C**

1. Short stories

ISBN 0-15-170755-3   LC 89-26886

First published 1939

"These three short novels include the title story, which concerns a young newspaperwoman in love with a soldier who dies in the 1918 influenza epidemic; 'Noon Wine,' the narrative of a shooting in the glare of a Texas midday; and 'Old Mortality,' a three-stage account of a Southern family that tries to believe its own myths about itself." Good Read

The **restless** dead; ten original stories of the supernatural; edited by Deborah Noyes. Candlewick Press 2007 253p $16.99

Grades: 8 9 10 11 12   **S C**

1. Supernatural—Fiction 2. Horror fiction 3. Short stories

ISBN 0-7636-2906-5; 978-0-7636-2906-9

     LC 2007-22114

This is a "collection of terrifying stories from some of the most well-known authors writing for teens, including M. T. Anderson, Holly Black, Libby Bray, and Annette Curtis Klause. From vampires to vindictive ghosts, this diverse anthology has it all, and then some." Booklist

Rice, David, 1964-

Crazy loco; stories about growing up Chicano in southern Texas. Dial Bks. for Young Readers 2001 135p hardcover o.p. pa $6.99

Grades: 9 10 11 12   **S C**

1. Mexican Americans—Fiction 2. Texas—Fiction 3. Short stories

ISBN 0-8037-2598-1; 0-14-250056-9 (pa)

     LC 00-59042

A collection of nine stories about Mexican American kids growing up in the Rio Grande Valley of southern Texas.

"Two great strengths of these stories are the pitch-perfect sense for the speech and thought patterns of teens and the vivid depiction of the daily lives of Mexican-Americans in Texas's Rio Grande Valley." SLJ

Roth, Philip

Goodbye, Columbus, and five short stories. Modern Lib. 1995 298p hardcover o.p. pa $14 *

Grades: 11 12 Adult   **S C**

1. Jews—United States—Fiction 2. Short stories

ISBN 0-679-60159-7; 0-679-74826-1 (pa)

     LC 94-44528

A reissue of the title first published 1959 by Houghton Mifflin

"The title story in this collection is about a young Radcliffe girl and a Rutgers boy who learn that there is more to love than exuberance and passion. All of the stories dramatize the dilemma of modern American Jews, torn between two worlds." Publ Wkly

Salinger, J. D. (Jerome David), 1919-
Nine stories. Little, Brown 1953 302p $24.95;
pa $5.99 *
Grades: 11 12 Adult   **S C**
1. Short stories
ISBN 0-316-76956-8; 0-316-76950-9 (pa)
This collection "introduced various members of the
Glass family who would dominate the remainder of Salinger's work. Critical response divided itself between
high praise and cult worship. Most of the stories deal
with precocious, troubled children, whose religious
yearnings—often tilting toward the East—are in vivid
contrast to the materialistic and spiritually empty world
of their parents. The result was a perfect literary formula
for the 1950s." Benet's Reader's Ency of Am Lit

Salisbury, Graham, 1944-
Island boyz: short stories. Wendy Lamb Bks.
2002 260p hardcover o.p. pa $5.99
Grades: 7 8 9 10   **S C**
1. Hawaii—Fiction 2. Short stories
ISBN 0-385-72970-7; 0-440-22955-3 (pa)
                                LC 2001-32425
"Eleven short stories chronicle pivotal episodes in the
lives of teenage boys growing up in the Hawaiian islands. . . . Themes are timeless in their appeal—guys
testing their mettle against hurricanes and bullies and the
irresponsible dares of their best friends, against fear of
sharks and fear of failure and fear of war—and plotting
is exceptionally well crafted to maximize suspense and to
meticulously develop a teen narrator's frame of mind and
state of conscience." Bull Cent Child Books

Shattered: stories of children and war; edited by
    Jennifer Armstrong. Knopf 2002 166p hardcover
    o.p. pa $6.50 *
Grades: 7 8 9 10   **S C**
1. War stories 2. Short stories
ISBN 0-375-81112-5; 0-440-23765-3 (pa)
                                LC 2001-18609
"This anthology of short stories (and one memoir),
mostly by well-known writers for YAs, shows how war's
violence affects individual young people in countries
across the world." Booklist
"These selections will make teens cry, will make them
angry, but most of all they will make them think." SLJ

Singer, Isaac Bashevis, 1904-1991
The collected stories of Isaac Bashevis Singer.
Farrar, Straus & Giroux 1982 610p hardcover o.p.
pa $20 *
Grades: 11 12 Adult   **S C**
1. Short stories 2. Jews—Fiction
ISBN 0-374-12631-3; 0-374-51788-6 (pa)
This is a selection of forty-seven stories chosen by the
author from eight prior collections

Sixteen: short stories by outstanding writers for
    young adults; edited by Donald R. Gallo.
    Delacorte Press 1984 179p hardcover o.p. pa
    $5.99 *
Grades: 7 8 9 10   **S C**
1. Short stories
ISBN 0-440-97757-6; 0-385-29346-1 (pa)
                                LC 84-3250
"This is a collection of sixteen short stories for young
adults especially commissioned from such authors as
Joan Aiken, M. E. Kerr, Richard Peck, and Norma and
Harry Mazer. Divided into five sections ('Friendships',
'Turmoils', 'Lovers', 'Decisions', and 'Families'), some
of the stories are fantasies, some are realistic, others are
funny, scary, or poignant, but all are choice examples of
their genre." Child Book Rev Serv

Sixteen: stories about that sweet and bitter
    birthday; edited by Megan McCafferty. Three
    Rivers Press 2004 318p pa $10.95
Grades: 9 10 11 12   **S C**
1. Short stories
ISBN 1-400-05270-X   LC 2003-27919
Contents: Infinity / Sarah Dessen -- Relent/Persist /
Zoe Trope -- The future lives of Emily Milty / Julianna
Baggott -- Rutford becomes a man / Ned Vizzini -- The
grief diet / Emma Forrest -- Mona Lisa, Jesus, Chad, and
me / Carolyn Mackler -- The alumni interview / David
Levithan -- Cat got your tongue? / Sonya Sones -- The
day I turned chickenhearted / Steve Almond -- Venetian
fan / Cat Bauer -- Kissing lessons / Joseph Weisberg --
Nebraska 99 / Jacqueline Woodson -- The perfect kiss /
Sarah Mlynowski -- Cowgirls & Indie boys / Tanuja
Desai Hidier -- The mud and fever dialogues / M.T. Anderson -- Fifteen going on... / Megan McCafferty
"Diverse as the teens the stories represent, this collection features Native Americans, teen mothers, queer boys
and questioning girls, ancient Greeks, students abroad,
and a teen author. . . . Adults wanting to relive their
youth will get as much mileage out of the combined joy
and misery of the protagonists as teens seeking assurance
they are not alone at this bittersweet crossroads of life."
Voice Youth Advocates

Sleator, William
Oddballs; stories. Dutton Children's Bks. 1993
134p hardcover o.p. pa $5.99
Grades: 6 7 8 9 10   **S C**
1. Short stories
ISBN 0-525-45057-2; 0-14-037438-8 (pa)
                                LC 92-27666
A collection of stories based on experiences from the
author's youth and peopled with an unusual assortment
of family and friends.
"Fresh, funny, and slightly gross, the quasi-
autobiographical glimpses will grab the reader's attention." Horn Book Guide

Somehow tenderness survives; stories of Southern
    Africa; selected by Hazel Rochman. Harper &
    Row 1988 147p hardcover o.p. pa $5.99
Grades: 7 8 9 10   **S C**
1. Short stories 2. South Africa—Race relations—Fiction
ISBN 0-06-025022-4; 0-06-447063-6 (pa)
                                LC 88-916

Somehow tenderness survives—*Continued*

A collection of eight short stories and two "autobiographical accounts which vividly evoke what it means to come of age in South Africa under apartheid. The contributors, including Doris Lessing and Nadine Gordimer, as well as lesser-known writers, are of various races and their stories cover a time span of 35 years. . . . This title should be in every YA collection. A glossary and notes on contributors are included." Voice Youth Advocates

Spider Woman's granddaughters; traditional tales and contemporary writing by Native American women; edited and with an introduction by Paula Gunn Allen. Fawcett Columbine 1990 c1989 279p pa $15

Grades: 11 12 Adult   **S C**

1. Native Americans—Fiction 2. Short stories

ISBN 0-449-90508-X

First published 1989 by Beacon Press

This is a collection of twenty-four stories by Native American women authors arranged in three thematic sections, 'The Warriors,' 'The Casualties,' and 'The Resistance.' The contributors include Marmon Silko, E. Pauline Johnson, Vickie L. Sears, Anna Lee Walters, Soge Track, LeAnne Howe and Louise Erdrich.

"Each of the stories in this collection, whether traditional or modern, expresses the urgency of survival—of not vanishing either individually or politically. And the quality of the stories is stunning." Women's Rev Books

Includes bibliographical references

Such a pretty face; short stories; edited by Ann Angel. Amulet Books 2007 267p $18.95

Grades: 9 10 11 12   **S C**

1. Short stories

ISBN 978-0-8109-1607-4; 0-8109-1607-X

LC 2006-23612

For this short story collection, the editor has "chosen stories reflecting the many definitions and ramifications of physical beauty. . . . This powerful, thought-provoking anthology will certainly find a place in public libraries. High school librarians are strongly urged to consider it for purchase, despite a few instances of profane language and several sexual references." Voice Youth Advocates

Tolkien, J. R. R. (John Ronald Reuel), 1892-1973

The Silmarillion; edited by Christopher Tolkien. 2nd ed. Houghton Mifflin 2001 xxiv, 365p il $28; pa $14

Grades: 9 10 11 12   **S C**

1. Fantasy fiction 2. Short stories

ISBN 0-618-13504-9; 0-618-12698-8 (pa)

LC 2001-16971

First published 1977

"J.R.R. Tolkien Quenta Silmarillion (The history of the Silmarils) together with Ainudalë (The music of the Ainur) and Valaquenta (Account of the Valar) To which is appended Akallabêth (The downfall of Númenor) and of the Rings of Power and the Third age." Facing title page

"Tolkien began writing these introductory legends in 1917 and, sporadically throughout his life, continued adding to them; his son Christopher has edited and compiled the various versions into a single cohesive work. Two brief tales, which outline the origin of the world and describe the gods who create and rule, precede the title story about the Silmarils—three brilliant, jewel-like creatures who are desired and fought over, setting up a clash between good and evil." Booklist

Tolstoy, Leo, graf, 1828-1910

Great short works of Leo Tolstoy; with an introduction by John Bayley; in the translations by Louise and Aylmer Maude. Harper & Row 1967 685p pa $15.95 hardcover o.p.

Grades: 9 10 11 12   **S C**

1. Russia—Fiction 2. Short stories

ISBN 0-06-058697-4 (pa)

"A Perennial classic"

Contents: Family happiness; The Cossacks; The death of Ivan Ilych; The devil; The Kreutzer Sonata; Master and man; Father Sergius; Hadji Murád; Alyosha the Pot

Twain, Mark, 1835-1910

The complete short stories of Mark Twain; now collected for the first time; edited with an introduction by Charles Neider. Doubleday 1957 xxiv, 676p pa $15.95 hardcover o.p. *

Grades: 11 12 Adult   **S C**

1. Short stories

ISBN 0-06-058697-4 (pa)

Also available in hardcover from Buccaneer Bks.

"The sixty pieces which are here hospitably called short stories illustrate both the weaknesses and the strengths of Mark Twain as a writer of fiction." N Y Times Book Rev

Twice told; original stories inspired by original art; drawings by Scott Hunt. Dutton 2006 259p il $19.99 *

Grades: 7 8 9 10   **S C**

1. Short stories

ISBN 0-525-46818-8; 978-0-525-46818-9

LC 2005-18694

Presents nine drawings by a single illustrator, each of which has been translated into a story by two different authors writing about what they imagine is going on in the picture.

"The collection showcases authors' distinct voices and effectively samples a variety of styles." Horn Book Guide

Ultimate sports; short stories by outstanding writers for young adults; edited by Donald R. Gallo. Delacorte Press 1995 333p hardcover o.p. pa $6.50 *

Grades: 7 8 9 10   **S C**

1. Sports—Fiction 2. Short stories

ISBN 0-440-22707-0; 0-385-32152-X (pa)

LC 94-49610

This anthology includes stories by: Chris Crutcher; Will Weaver; Norma Fox Mazer; Robert Lipsyte; Thomas J. Dygard and Chris Lynch.

"There is a terrific mix of the serious and the light-hearted, female and male characters, and traditional and nontraditional games. A winning collection." SLJ

Updike, John

Pigeon feathers, and other stories. Knopf 1962
278p $29.95; pa $14 *

Grades: 11 12 Adult   **S C**

1. Short stories

ISBN 0-394-44056-0; 0-449-91225-6 (pa)

These stories "are filled with gentle humor and irony.
Youth, marriage, and family life provide most of the
themes." Cincinnati Public Libr

Vande Velde, Vivian, 1951-

Being dead; stories. Harcourt 2001 203p
hardcover o.p. pa $6.95

Grades: 7 8 9 10   **S C**

1. Supernatural—Fiction 2. Horror fiction 3. Short stories

ISBN 0-15-216320-4; 0-15-204912-6 (pa)

LC 00-12996

This is a collection of seven "creepy tales featuring
ghosts, cemeteries, suicides, murders, and other death-
related themes." SLJ

"Often humorous and sometimes evoking sympathy,
this anthology will be enjoyed by lovers of mild horror
as well as by those who like clever short stories." Voice
Youth Advocates

Vonnegut, Kurt, 1922-2007

Bagombo snuff box: uncollected short fiction.
Putnam 1999 295p hardcover o.p. pa $13.95

Grades: 11 12 Adult   **S C**

1. Short stories

ISBN 0-399-14505-2; 0-425-17446-8 (pa)

LC 99-13665

"The 23 stories in this collection were published in
magazines . . . during the Fifties and are collected here
for the first time. The topics covered include space travel
('Thanasphere'), which describes the first manned orbit
of Earth; finding the American dream ('The package'),
about a new home full of the latest accessories; and an
attempt to impress an old girlfriend (the title story). . . .
Although many of the stories are topically dated, the
ironic insights and illumination of character are timeless,
and no one does it better than Vonnegut." Libr J

Wallace, Rich, 1957-

Losing is not an option: stories. Knopf 2003
127p $15.95; pa $5.99

Grades: 7 8 9 10   **S C**

1. Short stories

ISBN 0-375-81351-9; 0-440-23844-7 (pa)

LC 2002-34036

Nine episodes in the life of a young man, from sneaking into his tenth football game in a row with his best
friend in sixth grade to running his last high school race,
the Pennsylvania state championships.

"Readers will nod with recognition as they follow this
jock/poet/regular guy from the cusp of adolescence to the
edge of adulthood." Horn Book Guide

Welty, Eudora, 1909-2001

The collected stories of Eudora Welty. Harcourt
Brace Jovanovich 1980 622p hardcover o.p. pa
$16 *

Grades: 11 12 Adult   **S C**

1. Short stories

ISBN 0-15-118994-3; 0-15-618921-6 (pa)

LC 80-7947

This volume contains four previously published collections: A curtain of green, and other stories; The wide
net, and other stories; The golden apples and The bride
of the Innisfallen, and other stories. Also included in this
volume are two uncollected pieces: Where is the voice
coming from? and The demonstrators.

What a song can do; 12 riffs on the power of
music; edited by Jennifer Armstrong. Knopf
2004 200p $15.95; pa $5.99

Grades: 7 8 9 10   **S C**

1. Music—Fiction 2. Short stories

ISBN 0-375-82499-5; 0-440-23816-1 (pa)

LC 2003-24306

Twelve stories describe the power of music in young
people's lives, from forming a community of individuals
in a high school band to helping a young man connect
to his Indian heritage through ancient songs.

These stories "show the power of both words and music to express the turbulent emotions of growing up."
Booklist

Who do you think you are? stories of friends and
enemies; selected by Hazel Rochman and
Darlene Z. McCampbell. Little, Brown 1993
170p pa $9.99 hardcover o.p.

Grades: 7 8 9 10   **S C**

1. Friendship—Fiction 2. Short stories

ISBN 0-316-75320-3 (pa)   LC 93-314

"Joy Street books"

"Louise Erdrich, John Updike, Ray Bradbury, Joyce
Carol Oates, Sandra Cisneros, Tim O'Brien, Richard
Peck, and Maya Angelou are among the 15 writers repre-
sented in this anthology of stories [two prose excerpts
and a poem] about friendship and loss of friendship."
Booklist

"Meticulously chosen and arranged, these works
crystalize moments of vulnerability, sorrow and understanding; together, they serve as an excellent introduction
to modern American writing." Publ Wkly

Wolfe, Thomas, 1900-1938

The complete short stories of Thomas Wolfe;
edited by Francis E. Skipp; foreword by James
Dickey. Scribner 1987 xxix, 621p pa $27.50
hardcover o.p.

Grades: 11 12 Adult   **S C**

1. Short stories

ISBN 0-02-040891-9 (pa)   LC 86-13782

"All 58 of Wolfe's short stories . . . have been edited
by Skipp in a way that represents what Wolfe himself
may have wanted his audience to read." Booklist

Working days: stories about teenagers and work; edited by Anne Mazer. Persea Bks. 1997 207p pa $9.95 hardcover o.p.

Grades: 9 10 11 12   **S C**

1. Work—Fiction 2. Short stories

ISBN 0-89255-224-7 (pa)   LC 96-50243

Fifteen stories relate the experiences of teenagers working for many different reasons in a variety of jobs. Lois Metzger, Victor Martinez, Norman Wong and Thylias Moss are among the contributors.

"This multicultural collection would fit any high school curriculum. Senior high school students and adults will identify with many of these protagonists while being challenged at the same time." ALAN

Wright, Richard, 1908-1960

Uncle Tom's children; five long stories. Harper & Row 1938 xxx, 384p pa $13.95 hardcover o.p.

Grades: 11 12 Adult   **S C**

1. African Americans—Fiction 2. Short stories

ISBN 0-06-058714-8 (pa)

The stories in this collection deal with conflicts between whites and blacks in the South.

The **Year's** best science fiction and fantasy for teens: first annual collection; edited by Jane Yolen and Patrick Nielsen Hayden. TOR 2005 288p $17.95; pa $12.95

Grades: 9 10 11 12   **S C**

1. Science fiction 2. Fantasy fiction 3. Short stories

ISBN 0-765-31383-9; 978-0-7653-1383-6; 0-765-31384-7 (pa); 978-0-7653-1384-3 (pa)

LC 2005-299191

"A Tom Doherty Associates book"

A collection of science and fantasy fiction from some of today's most popular writers, including Garth Nix, David Gerrold, and Delia Sherman.

"Faery handbags, culture-clash-befuddled Bronze Age warriors, powerful babies hatched of golden eggs and hapless babies replaced with malevolent changelings, New York Between (replete with a charming and often sleepy living library catalog), and traveling levitated cities all make appearances in this strong, accessible collection." Booklist

Young warriors; stories of strength; edited by Tamora Pierce and Josepha Sherman. Random House 2005 312p $17.95; lib bdg $19.99; pa $8.95

Grades: 7 8 9 10   **S C**

1. Fantasy fiction 2. Short stories

ISBN 0-375-82962-8; 978-0-375-82962-8; 0-375-92962-2 (lib bdg); 978-0-375-92962-5 (lib bdg); 0-375-82963-6 (pa); 978-0-375-82963-5 (pa)

LC 2004-16432

Fifteen original short stories by various authors relate the exploits of teenage warriors who defeat their enemies with cunning and skill as they strive to fulfill their destinies.

"This timely and appealing anthology will surely help swell the ranks of teenage fantasy readers." SLJ

LIST OF RECOMMENDED PERIODICALS

The following list of recommended periodicals for a High School Library is divided into two parts: Part I, Professional, which lists titles for librarians and teachers, and Part II, Young Adult, which lists titles for students.

PART I

PROFESSIONAL

The **ALAN** Review. National Council of Teachers of English, Assembly on Literature for Adolescents $20 per year (individuals), $30 per year (institutions) (Professional)
ISSN 0882-2840

http://scholar.lib.vt.edu/ejournals/ALAN/alan-review.html

3 times a year.

This publication "is unique in being devoted entirely to adolescent literature. Each issue contains 'Clip and File' reviews of approximately twenty new hardbacks or paperbacks and includes [several] feature articles, news announcements, and occasional in-depth reviews of professional books." Donelson. Literature for Today's Young Adults

Art Education. National Art Education Association $50 per year (Professional)
ISSN 0004-3125

http://www.naea-reston.org

Bimonthly.

"Articles on current directions, problems, and exemplary approaches in visual art education at all instructional levels. Articles may focus on the art curriculum, teaching strategies, innovative programs, or a special area of the curriculum such as studio, art criticism, or art history. Each issue of Art Education includes four full-color reproductions of works of art, with commentary and lesson plan suggestions for use at both elementary and secondary levels." NAEA website

Arts and Activities; the nation's leading arts education magazine. Publishers Development Corp. $30 per year (Professional)
ISSN 0004-3931

http://www.artsandactivities.com/

Monthly September through June.

"A magazine dedicated to providing an exchange of professional experiences, opinions, and new ideas for art educators. Contributors share strategies for art instruction, approaches to art history, techniques for engaging students in evaluating art, and programs and lessons to expand students' appreciation of art. Articles have covered a broad range of topics such as art appreciation, ceramics, computer art, drawing and painting, mixed media, papier-mache, collage, and three-dimensional design for grades K-12. A regular feature is a pullout clip-and-save art print. For the practitioner, the magazine publishes an annual buyers' guide and a listing of summer art programs." Katz. Mag for Libr. 13th edition

AudioFile; the magazine for people who love audiobooks. AudioFile Publs. $19.95 per year (individuals), $29.95 per year (institutions) (Professional)
ISSN 1063-0244

http://www.audiofilemagazine.com/

6 times a year.

Price of subscription includes *AudioFile* issues and the *Audiobook Reference Guide*.

"AudioFile reviews unabridged and abridged audiobooks, original audio programs, commentary and dramatizations in the spoken-word format. Our focus is the audio presentation, not the critique of the written material." Publisher's note

Booklist. American Library Association $89.95 per year (Professional)
ISSN 0006-7385

http://www.booklistonline.com/

Bimonthly (22/yr.).

"Intended chiefly as a guide for librarians in public and school libraries, each issue covers titles in five major areas: forthcoming titles, adult books, books for youth, audiovisual media, and reference books. . . . Because of its selectivity, its early reviews, and its broad coverage of popular non-print media, Booklist is essential reading for public, school, and many academic libraries." Katz. Mag for Libr. 10th edition

The **Education** Digest; essential readings condensed for quick review. Prakken Publications, Inc. $48 per year (Professional)
ISSN 0013-127X

http://www.eddigest.com/

Monthly (nine issues a year, September through May).

"This publication provides a condensation of current articles on the themes chosen for the individual ED issues, allowing educators, students, and other interested readers an opportunity to quickly update their knowledge of particular education topics. In addition, there are regular columns such as the free-ranging discussions in 'The Teachers' Lounge,' capsules of education news in Washington and elsewhere, book reviews and lists, and web resources. This is a handy, pocket-sized resource that is useful for school and public libraries." Katz. Mag for Libr. 13th edition

Educational Leadership. Association for Supervision and Curriculum Development $36 per year (Professional)
ISSN 0013-1784

http://www.ascd.org/portal/site/ascd/

Bimonthly September through May.

This magazine discusses "teaching and learning, new ideas and practices relevant to practicing educators, and the latest trends and issues affecting prekindergarten through higher education." ASCD website

Edutopia: The World of Learning. The George Lucas Educational Foundation Free to qualified personnel, otherwise $29.95 per year (Professional)
ISSN 1552-9029

http://www.edutopia.org

Bimonthly.

Published by the George Lucas Foundation and evolved from their website that features multimedia streaming video to support many of the journal articles, Edutopia focuses on the newest research, theories, and practices in K-12 education and relates it to schools around the world that are already implementing them. Best New Publication 2005 Maggie Awards.

English Journal. National Council of Teachers of English $25 per year (price for members) (Professional)
ISSN 0013-8274

http://www.ncte.org/pubs/journals/ej

Bimonthly September through July.

"A journal of ideas for English language arts teachers in junior and senior high schools and middle schools. EJ presents information on the teaching of writing and reading, literature, and language. Each issue examines the relationship of theory and research to classroom practice and reviews current materials of interest to English teachers, including books and electronic media." NCTE website

Journal of Physical Education, Recreation and Dance. American Alliance for Health, Physical Education, Recreation and Dance $165 per year (institutions), $73 (non-members), free to members (Professional)
ISSN 0730-3084

http://www.aahperd.org/aahperd/
template.cfm?template=johperd%5Fmain.html

Monthly (except July).

Variant title: JOPERD

The Journal of Physical Education, Recreation & Dance is the professional magazine for the American Alliance of Health, Physical, Recreation, and Dance. It addresses a variety of HPERD issues including articles on teaching strategies, fitness, legal issues, assessment, dancing, teacher education, adapted physical education, leisure for older adults, the use of technology, and ethics and gender equity in sports and physical education.

Kliatt; reviews of selected current paperbacks, hardcover fiction, audiobooks, and educational software. Kliatt $39 per year (Professional)
ISSN 1065-8602

http://hometown.aol.com/kliatt/

Bimonthly.

This magazine "publishes reviews of paperback books, hardcover fiction for adolescents, audiobooks, and educational software recommended for libraries and classrooms serving young adults." Publisher's note
"A recommended selection tool for junior high, high school, and YA librarians." Katz. Mag for Libr

Knowledge Quest. American Library Association $40 per year (Professional)
ISSN 1094-9046

http://www.ala.org/ala/aasl/aaslpubsandjournals/
kqweb/kqweb.htm

Bimonthly September through May.

This publication, along with its companion website KQonline, "is devoted to offering substantive information to assist building-level library media specialists, supervisors, library educators, and other decision makers concerned with the development of school library media programs and services. Articles address the integration of theory and practice in school librarianship and new developments in education, learning theory, and relevant disciplines." ALA website

Learning and Leading with Technology. International Society for Technology in Education Subscription included with membership (Professional)
ISSN 1082-5754

http://www.iste.org/ll/

Monthly (except June, July, August), bimonthly December/January.

Member subscription of the International Society for Technology in Education, introduces classroom applications of newer technology, integration strategies, and leadership strategies for implementing instructional technology into schools.

Library Media Connection; magazine for secondary school library media and technology specialists. Linworth Publishing, Inc. $69 per year (Professional)
ISSN 1542-4715

http://www.linworth.com/lmc/

7 times a year.

The magazine provides articles and advice for managing school libraries, along with reviews of books, multimedia, and videos written by school librarians. Each review contains grade level recommendations.

Mathematics Teacher. National Council of Teachers of Mathematics $76 per year (individual members); $99 per year (institutional members) (Professional)
ISSN 0025-5769

http://my.nctm.org/eresources/
journal_home.asp?journal_id=2

9 times a year (Sep.-May).

"Mathematics Teacher (MT) offers activities, lesson ideas, teaching strategies, and problems through in-depth articles, departments, and features. Great resources for secondary teachers, preservice teachers, and teacher educators. Article downloads are free to individual members who subscribe." Publisher's note

Media & Methods; educational products, technologies & programs for schools & universities. American Society of Educators $35 per year (Professional)
ISSN 0025-6897

http://www.media-methods.com

5 times a year.

"Each issue has feature articles and departments. Articles are easy to read and provide hands-on experiences to meet the practical needs of media specialists and school librarians. Because media and school library services have become increasingly computer dependent, it is not surprising that many articles deal with computer-related technologies. Readers will also find valuable information on selection and evaluation of various media products, including laptops, digital cameras, DVD players, multimedia projectors, multimedia TV, and visual presenters." Katz. Mag for Libr

MultiMedia & Internet@Schools; the media and technology specialist's guide to electronic tools and resources for K-12. Information Today, Inc. $42.95 per year (Professional)
ISSN 1546-4636

http://www.mmischools.com/

6 times a year.

This magazine for library media specialists and technology coordinators reviews and evaluates new software and hardware, offers purchasing recommendations and technical advice, and profiles high-tech products.

Phi Delta Kappan. Phi Delta Kappa International, Inc. $58 per year (members), $65 per year (institutions) (Professional)
ISSN 0031-7217

http://www.pdkintl.org/kappan/kappan.htm

Monthly (except July and August).

"The professional print journal for education, addresses policy issues for educators at all levels. Advocating research-based school reform, the Kappan provides a forum for debate on controversial subjects." PDKINTL website

Preventing School Failure. Heldref Publications $57 per year (individuals), $134 per year (institutions) (Professional)
ISSN 1045-988X

http://www.heldref.org

Quarterly.

"Helps educators and other professionals seeking to promote the success of students who have learning and behavioral problems. It offers examples of programs and practices that help children and youth in schools, clinics, correctional institutions, and other settings." Heldref website

SB&F; Science Books and Films: your guide to science resources for all ages. American Association for the Advancement of Science $45 per year (Professional)
ISSN 1533-5046

http://SBFonline.com

Bimonthly.

"Published by the American Association for the Advancement of Science (AAAS), SB&F is the only critical review journal devoted exclusively to print and nonprint materials in all of the sciences and for all age groups. Every year, SB&F evaluates nearly 1,000 books, videos and DVDs, and software packages for general audiences, professionals, teachers, and students from kindergarten through college." AAAS website

School Library Journal; the magazine of children, young adults & school librarians. Reed Business Information $129.99 per year (Professional)
ISSN 0362-8930

http://www.schoollibraryjournal.com/

Monthly.

In addition to the feature articles this journal includes "a calendar of events, news from the field, notes on people, columns . . . as well as many reviews of professional reading, books for children and young adults, audiovisuals, and computer software. . . . This is an essential professional journal for school and public librarians." Katz. Mag for Libr. 10th edition

School Library Media Research. American Library Association Free (Professional)
ISSN 1523-4320

http://www.ala.org/aasl/SLMR

5 times a year.

This is a web-based only publication

"An official journal of the American Association of School Librarians. It is the successor to School Library Media Quarterly Online. The purpose of School Library Media Research is to promote and publish high quality original research concerning the management, implementation, and evaluation of school library media programs. The journal will also emphasize research on instructional theory, teaching methods, and critical issues relevant to school library media." Publisher's note

Science. American Association for the Advancement of Science $142 for professional members and K-12 teachers (with 6 print issues of Science Books & Films plus online access); $99 for K-12 teachers with online only access to Science Books & Films; $75 for students (Professional)
ISSN 0036-8075

http://sciencemag.org

Weekly.

Articles on subjects like global warming, genetics, and the possibility of water on Mars. Published by the American Association for the Advancement of Science, with assistance of Stanford University's HighWire Press.

Social Education; the official journal of the National Council for the Social Studies. National Council for the Social Studies $55 per year (members), $75 per year (institutions) (Professional)
ISSN 0037-7724

http://www.socialstudies.org

Monthly in September, October, March, April. Bimonthly November/December, January/February, May/June.

This journal, which includes the supplement *Middle Level Learning* featuring lesson ideas focused on the middle grades (3 times yearly) "contains a balance of theoretical content and practical ideas for classroom use. Our award-winning resources include techniques for using teaching materials in the classroom, information on the latest instructional technology, reviews of educational media, research on significant topics related to social studies, and lesson plans that can be applied to various disciplines." NCSS website

Teacher Librarian; the journal for school library professionals. Scarecrow Press, Inc. $54 per year (Professional)
ISSN 1481-1782

http://www.teacherlibrarian.com/

5 times a year.

"This monthly publication provides useful information and resources for library staff who serve children and young adults. Feature articles cover a broad spectrum of topics, including management, advocacy, technology, leadership, information literacy, and collaboration. Reviews evaluate new books, e-zines, computer software, Internet resources, and electronic databases. Past issues have discussed gender discrimination in the school library, data use, strategic planning, and metacognition. Especially recommended for school librarians and library media specialists." Katz. Mag for Libr. 13th edition

Teacher Magazine. Editorial Projects in Education $17.94 per year (Professional)
ISSN 1046-6193

http://www.teachermagazine.org

Bimonthly (except for July and single-month October issue).

A sister publication of Education Week, Teacher Magazine is focused upon current news and stories of interest to classroom teachers.

Teaching Tolerance Magazine. Teaching Tolerance No charge to educators (Professional)
ISSN 1066-2847

http://www.teachingtolerance.org

Twice a year.

"Founded in 1991 by the Southern Poverty Law Center, Teaching Tolerance provides educators with free educational materials that promote respect for differences and appreciation of diversity in the classroom and beyond. Published twice a year, our magazine profiles educators, schools and programs promoting diversity and equity in inspirational and replicable ways." Teaching Tolerance website

Technology and Learning; the leading magazine of electronic education. NewBay Media Free to qualified personnel (Professional)
ISSN 1053-6728

http://www.techlearning.com/

Monthly.

"The Resource for Education Technology Leaders" targets teachers as well as technology coordinators and administrators with ideas for and the theory behind the educational use of technology resources in the classroom.

University press books selected for public and secondary school libraries. Association of Am. Univ. Presses Free (Professional)
ISSN 1055-4173

http://aaupnet.org/librarybooks/

Annual. First published 1967 as University Press books for secondary school libraries, merged with University Press books for public libraries in 1991

"Books published by cooperating university presses are reviewed for selection for this source by committees of the Public Library Association and the American Association of School Librarians. Selected books are arranged by Dewey Class or Divisions. Each title is given an indicator labeling it as outstanding, for a general audience, for special interest, or for regional general or special interest. The AASL committee also indicates if items are appropriate for junior high or high school collections. This is a useful source as many of these materials are not reviewed in the standard school review sources." Safford. Guide to Ref Materials for Sch Libr Media Cent. 5th edition

PART II

YOUNG ADULT

Astronomy. Kalmbach Publishing Co. $42.95 per year (11 12 Adult)
ISSN 0091-6358

http://www.astronomy.com/asy/default.aspx

Monthly.

"Explore the universe in your own backyard with the most popular amateur astronomy magazine. Every issue includes a monthly star and planet chart, tips on telescope observing, breathtaking photography, product reviews and up-to-the-minute space news." DealTime

Atlantic Monthly. Atlantic Monthly Co. $24.50 per year (11 12 Adult)
ISSN 1072-7825

http://www.theatlantic.com/

10 times a year.

"Originally a monthly publication, the magazine, subscribed to by 480,000 readers, now publishes ten times a year and features articles in the fields of political science and foreign affairs, as well as book reviews." Wikipedia

Audubon. National Audubon Society $20 per year (11 12 Adult)
ISSN 0097-7136

http://magazine.audubon.org/index.html

Bimonthly.

"Reports on the state of the earth. It offers views on environmental problems and proposes solutions regarding ecology, conservation, wildlife, policy, recreation, and technology." MagazineCity.com

Authors & artists for young adults. Gale Res. $130 per issue (7 8 9 10 11 12)
ISSN 1040-5682

http://www.gale.com/

Bimonthly. First published 1988

Editors vary

"Each volume contains 20-25 entries offering personal, behind-the-scenes information, . . . sidelights, portraits, movie stills, bibliographies, cumulative index and much more. Its international scope ranges from contemporary to classic, fantasy to nonfiction." Publisher's note

Biography index; a cumulative index to biographical material in books and magazines. Wilson, H.W. Annual subscription $340 (11 12 Adult)
ISSN 0006-3053

http://www.hwwilson.com/

Quarterly, November, February, May, and August, with bound annual and permanent two-year cumulations. First issued September 1946

"Indexes biographical articles published in . . . periodicals, current books of individual and collected biography, obituaries, letters, diaries, memoirs, and incidental biographical material in otherwise nonbiographical books. Includes an index by professions and occupations. Annual and three-year cumulations." Ref Sources for Small & Medium-sized Libr. 6th edition

Business Week. McGraw-Hill Companies, Inc. $64 per year (11 12 Adult)
ISSN 0007-7135

http://www.businessweek.com/

Weekly.

"Business Week features in-depth perspectives on the financial markets, industries, trends, technology, and people guiding the global economy." MagazineCity.com

Car and Driver. Hachette Filipacchi Media U.S., Inc. $12 per year (11 12 Adult)
ISSN 0008-6002

http://www.caranddriver.com/

Car and Driver—*Continued*

Monthly.

"An American automotive enthusiast magazine. Its total circulation is 1.36 million. It is owned by Hachette Filipacchi Magazines. Originally headquartered in New York City, the magazine has been based in Ann Arbor, Michigan since the late 1970s." Wikipedia

Civil War Times; a magazine for persons interested in the American Civil War, its people, and its era. Weider History Group $27.95 per year (11 12 Adult)
ISSN 1546-9980

http://www.historynet.com/magazines/ civil_war_times

Bi-monthly.

"Civil War Times Illustrated Magazine delivers the complete story of America's greatest internal conflict with all its actions, emotion, drama and modern significance. In Civil War Times, leading historians and authors take readers on a journey into the experience of the real people who lived the history from the greatest commanders and politicians to the rank and file soldiers and their families at home. Beautifully illustrated with period artwork and photography, Civil War Times Illustrated provides readers with a window into America's most dramatic days." MagazineCity.com

The Concord Review. Concord Review $40 per year (9 10 11 12)
ISSN 0895-0539

http://www.tcr.org/tcr/index.htm

Quarterly.

The goal of this magazine is "to recognize and to publish exemplary history essays by high school students in the English-speaking world." Publisher's note

Congress and the Nation; a review of government and politics. Congressional Quarterly $293 per volume (11 12 Adult)
ISSN 1047-1324

http://www.cqpress.com/

Every 4 years.

"Overview and detailed coverage of presidential, legislative, and political events in every major subject area." N Y Public Libr Book of How & Where to Look It Up

Consumer Reports. Consumers Union of the United States, Inc. $26 per year (11 12 Adult)
ISSN 0010-7174

http://www.consumerreports.org

Monthly (except s-m. Dec.).

"Consumer Reports® and ConsumerReports.org® are published by Consumers Union, an expert, independent nonprofit organization whose mission is to work for a fair, just, and safe marketplace for all consumers and to empower consumers to protect themselves. To achieve this mission, we test, inform, and protect. To maintain our independence and impartiality, CU accepts no outside advertising, no free test samples, and has no agenda other than the interests of consumers. CU supports itself through the sale of our information products and services, individual contributions, and a few noncommercial grants. Consumers Union is governed by a board of 18 directors, who are elected by CU members and meet three times a year. CU's President, James Guest, oversees a staff of more than 450." Publisher's note

Contemporary literary criticism. Gale Res. $225 subscription per volume (11 12 Adult)
ISSN 0091-3421   LC 76-38938

http://www.gale.com/

Irregular. Started publication in 1973

"Excerpts from criticism of the works of today's novelists, poets, playwrights, short story writers, scriptwriters, and other creative writers." Title page

"This multivolume, ongoing series offers significant passages from contemporary criticism on authors who are now living or who have died since December 31, 1959. . . . Brief author sketches are followed by critical excerpts, presented in chronological order. The number of authors covered in each volume has varied over the years." Ref Sources for Small & Medium-sized Libr. 6th edition

Contemporary musicians; profiles of the people in music. Gale Res. $125 per volume (9 10 11 12)
ISSN 1044-2197

http://www.gale.com/

Irregular. First published 1989. Editors vary

Each volume provides "information on 80 to 100 musical artists from all the genres that form the broad spectrum of contemporary music . . . as well as selected classical artists who have achieved 'crossover' success with the general public." Introduction

Discover: the world of science. Disney Publishing Worldwide Inc. $29.95 per year (11 12 Adult)
ISSN 0274-7529

http://discovermagazine.com/

Monthly.

"An award-winning, general interest magazine devoted to the world of science and technology. It explores all areas of science from archeology to ecology, technology to medicine, and astronomy to physics. Reports the latest breakthroughs on such subjects as the origin of life, the evolution of the universe, the inner workings of the human brain, and the mass extinction of the dinosaurs." Publisher's note

History behind the headlines; the origins of conflicts worldwide; Meghan Appel O'Meara, editor. Gale Group $110 per volume (9 10 11 12)
ISSN 1531-7307

http://www.gale.com/

Irregular. Released biannually 2001-2003. Started publication 2001

This series covers "current political, environmental, territorial, social, and economic struggles. Each alphabetically arranged, 7- to 18-page entry begins with a synopsis of the clash and a brief chronology. Each essay provides historical background and, in greater detail, an outline of the main aspects of each dispute. The possibility of a resolution is also discussed. . . . The writing is succinct, accurate, and impartial. . . . This title will be useful for research into current events." SLJ

Hostelling North America; the official guide to hostels in Canada and the United States of America. American Youth Hostels $3 per year (11 12 Adult)
ISSN 1540-8116

Annual. First published 1934. Title varies

An annual directory of the youth hostels in the United States and Canada, published by American Youth Hostels and Canadian Hostelling Association.

Math Horizons. Mathematical Association of America $29 per year (members); $38 per year (non-members) (11 12 Adult)
ISSN 1072-4117

http://www.maa.org/mathhorizons/

This is "is a glossy, popular magazine intended 'to introduce [undergraduate] students to the world of mathematics outside the classroom.' . . . Of all the journals covering mathematics, this is probably the most accessible to a general adult audience." Katz. Mag for Libr

Muslim Girl. Muslim Girl Magazine $19.99 per year (7 8 9 10 11 12)
ISSN 1934-5127

http://www.muslimgirlmagazine.com/

Bi-monthly.

"A magazine for and about young Muslim women, Muslim Girl, with its tastefully progressive outlook on fashion, education, health, culture, sports, and politics, is a welcome addition to the newsstands." Libr J

National Geographic. National Geographic Society $19 per year (11 12 Adult)
ISSN 0027-9358

http://www.nationalgeographic.com

Monthly.

"A magazine with an editorial focus that spans the globe, probing the farthest reaches of the universe. With a subscription to National Geographic also includes a membership in the National Geographic Society." MagazineCity.com

National Wildlife; dedicated to the conservation of our nation's natural resources. National Wildlife Federation $20 per year (11 12 Adult)
ISSN 0028-0402

http://www.nwf.org

Bi-monthly.

"National Wildlife Magazine is specifically designed to inspire individuals and organizations to conserve and protect wildlife and the environment. Issues include lengthy features on various animal species, including interesting facts, research news, and conservation status. National Wildlife also keeps readers updated on government environmental regulations and efforts of the National Wildlife Federation, and its chapters' and affiliates' efforts to protect nature in the United States." MagazineCity.com

Newsweek. Newsweek, Inc. $20 per year (11 12 Adult)
ISSN 0028-9604

http://www.newsweek.com

Weekly.

A weekly news magazine that covers all current events, national and international news, political and social leaders, business, movies, books and more.

Newtype U S A; the moving pictures magazine. Newtype USA, Inc. $89.95 per year (9 10 11 12)
ISSN 1541-4817

http://www.newtype-usa.com

Monthly.

This magazine is a source for information on anime and manga, the American version of a magzine published in Japan. Also features reviews of toys, games, and music. Each issue is packaged with a sampler DVD.

Novels for students. Gale Group $100 per volume (9 10 11 12)
ISSN 1094-3552

http://www.gale.com

Irregular. Started publication 1997

"Presenting analysis, context and criticism on commonly studied novels." Title page

The entries for each title include an author biography, plot summary, character profiles and a discussion of themes and style. Critical material placing the work within its historical context is included.

PC World. I D G Communications Inc. $19.97 per year (11 12 Adult)
ISSN 0737-8939

http://www.pcworld.com/

Monthly.

PC publication for PC buyers and users. Every issue provides PC product rankings, reviews, multimedia and Internet coverage how-tos, and tips.

Plays; the drama magazine for young people. Plays Magazine $39 per year (5 6 7 8 9 10 11 12)
ISSN 0032-1540

http://www.playsmag.com

Monthly October through May, except January/February combined.

"Each issue contains between 9 and 12 short plays, with subjects ranging from historic to holidays, to skits and comedies, to a dramatized classic (e.g., Puccini's Gianni Schicchi). The plays are arranged by general grade level (Junior and Senior High, Middle and Lower Grade), and each contains production notes that include casting and staging suggestions. . . . This magazine should be included in the library of any school with a drama program or club. It should also be included in public libraries' children's collections." Katz. Mag for Libr.

Popular Mechanics. Hearst Corporation $12 per year (11 12 Adult)
ISSN 0032-4558

http://popularmechanics.com

Monthly.

"Popular Mechanics regularly covers advancements in science, technology, electronics, photography, transportation, defense, telecommunications, home improvement and other areas of special interest to readers." MagazineCity.com

Readers' guide to periodical literature. Wilson, H.W. $385 per year (11 12 Adult)
ISSN 0034-0464

http://www.hwwilson.com/

Monthly. Permanent bound annual cumulations. First published 1900

A cumulative author and subject index to over 300 periodicals. Coverage includes computers, business, health, fashion, politics, education, science, sports, arts and literature with criticism of individual dramatic works, videodiscs and videotapes, operas, ballets, musicals, movies, phonograph records, dance, and television and radio programs. A free pamphlet: How to use the Reader's guide to periodical literature, is available for download in PDF format from publisher's website or upon request.

"This is a modern index of the best type." Sheehy. Guide to Ref Books. 10th edition

Representative American speeches. Wilson, H.W. $50 per issue (11 12 Adult)
ISSN 0197-6923

Annual. First published 1937-1938

Editors vary

A compilation containing a selection of speeches of the year made by eminent men and women on major trends and events. Each speech is prefaced by a note about the speaker and the occasion. The appendix in each volume contains biographical notes.

Rolling Stone. Rolling Stone LLC $12.97 per year (11 12 Adult)
ISSN 0035-791X

http://www.rollingstone.com/

Bi-weekly.

"For almost 40 years, Rolling Stone has been a primary source for the latest news about American popular culture, music, celebrities, and politics. High-quality journalism, as well as authoritative recording, book, and film reviews add to its value." Katz. Mag for Libr

The **Scholarship** book. Prentice-Hall $30 per year (9 10 11 12)
ISSN 1528-9079

http://www.prenhall.com

Annual.

This is a "listing of private-sector awards offered by a wide range of corporations, unions, trust funds, religious and fraternal organizations, associations, and private philanthropists. . . . [It covers] tips for determining which awards you qualify for, helps you write . . . essays, applications, and cover letters, alerts you to scams and rip-offs, and provides . . . lists of recommended websites and publications." Publisher's note

Scholastic Art. Scholastic, Inc. Price is based on the total number of subscriptions (7 8 9 10 11 12)
ISSN 1060-832X

http://teacher.scholastic.com/products/classmags/art.htm

6 times a year.

Each issue is centered on an art related theme and explains the historical and cultural contexts in which works or styles of fine art were created. It also includes an "Art Workshop" to teach students how to replicate theme-related techniques.

Scientific American. Scientific American, Inc. $24.97 per year (11 12 Adult)
ISSN 0036-8733

http://www.sciam.com

Monthly.

"Scientific American reviews the vital role science discovery has in medicine, energy, technology, the environment and business." MagazineCity.com

Sex, Etc.: a national newsletter by teens for teens. Network for Family Life Education (Rutgers) $10 per year (9 10 11 12)

http://www.sexetc.org/

3 times per year (September, January and April).

"This 'telling like it is' national sex-education newsletter, edited by teenagers for other teens, does not mince words or sugarcoat the topic. Topics cover a range as you might expect, but the language is blunt and explicit. . . . In its eight pages, it manages to stimulate, educate and address succinctly and accurately the concerns of American youth today. . . . A highly recommended addition to your collection." Katz. Mag for Libr.

Shojo Beat; manga from the heart. VIZ Media, Llc $29.95 per year (7 8 9 10 11 12)

http://www.shojobeat.com

Monthly.

This magazine showcases Japanese manga aimed at a female audience. Also contains interviews with shojo manga creators and information on video and card games, toys, and anime.

Shonen Jump. Viz Communications, Inc. $29.95 per year (7 8 9 10 11 12)
ISSN 1545-7818

http://www.shonenjump.com

Monthly.

"Shonen Jump is a hefty magazine (typically over 250 pages per issue, frequently more) that serializes sixteen Manga titles: Dragon Ball, Dragon Ball Z, Yu-Gi-Oh!, Naruto, Sand Land, One Piece, Yuyu Hakusho, Shaman King, Knights of the Zodiac, Rurouni Kenshin, Hikaru No Go, Ultimate Muscle, The Prince of Tennis, Bleach, Whistle!, and Beet the Vandel Buster. Each chapter is preceded by a summary of the story from the previous issue and typically includes a brief character guide. The visual elements of Manga make this a highly appealing media, and anything that attracts and keeps kids reading—and begging for more—has to be appreciated by parents who just wish video games would disappear from the planet." Katz. Mag for Libr

Short stories for students. Gale Group $100 per volume (9 10 11 12)
ISSN 1092-7735

http://www.gale.com

Irregular. Started publication 1997

"Presenting analysis, context and criticism on commonly studied short stories." Title page

"Each volume contains entries for 20 stories arranged alphabetically by title. . . . Each entry includes a brief biographical sketch of the writer; a plot summary; descriptions of characters; a discussion of the major themes and style (use of irony, symbolism, points of view, etc.); an introduction to the historical and cultural period during which the story was written; a critical overview; and an essay written for this resource along with excerpts from the work of other critics." SLJ

Short story index. Wilson, H.W. $210 per year (11 12 Adult)
ISSN 0360-9774   LC 75-649762

http://www.hwwilson.com/

Annual (with 5 yr. cumulations).

Also available Short story index: collections indexed 1900-1978 $235 (ISBN 0-8242-0643-6)

This index offers a single-alphabet listing of stories by author, title and subject. The List of collections indexed provides full bibliographic information. Includes a Directory of periodicals.

"These indexes provide valuable access to short stories in collections published since 1900." Ref Sources for Small & Medium-sized Libr. 6th edition

Sky & Telescope; the essential magazine of astronomy. Sky Publishing Corp. $42.95 per year (11 12 Adult)
ISSN 0037-6604

http://www.SkyandTelescope.com

Monthly.

"World's leading source of accurate and up-to-date information about astronomy and space science since 1941." MagazineCity.com

Smithsonian. Smithsonian Magazine $19 per year (11 12 Adult)
ISSN 0037-7333

http://www.smithsonianmagazine.com/

Monthly.

"Published by the Smithsonian Institution, the Smithsonian Magazine is published by the Smithsonian Institution and is an entertaining and informative resource on Americana, natural history, science, ecology, contemporary society and the arts. Also included in each issue of Smithsonian Magazine are spectacular photo essays and in-depth articles highlighting current Smithsonian exhibits." MagazineCity.com

Teen Ink; written by teens. Young Authors Foundation $25 per year (6 7 8 9 10 11 12)
ISSN 1545-1283

http://www.teenink.com

Monthly.

Each issue of this national magazine written and illustrated by teenagers features fiction, nonfiction, interviews, poetry, photography, and art.

Teen Voices. Women Express $20 per year (6 7 8 9 10 11 12)
ISSN 1074-7494

http://www.teenvoices.com

Twice a year.

This magazine written and illustrated by teenage girls addresses such issues as body image, racism, rape, and drug abuse.

Time. Time, Inc $29.95 per year (11 12 Adult)
ISSN 0040-781X

http://www.time.com/time/

Weekly.

Insightful analysis of today's important events, revealing what they mean to you and your family. Articles on politics, scientific breakthroughs, the arts, business, and society.

Transworld Skateboarding. Time4 Media, Inc. $17.97 per year (9 10 11 12)
ISSN 0748-7401

http://www.skateboarding.com/skate/

Monthly.

"This glossy magazine for the avid skateboarder contains almost 300 pages and is filled with photographs of daring rides, stunts, and flips. . . . Regular columns include letters to the editor; short news reports of people, contests, events, and products; trick tips; profiles of young skaters; travel stories; and interviews with leading skaters." Katz. Mag for Libr

The **ultimate** audition book for teens; 111 one-minute monologues. Smith & Kraus $11.95 per year (7 8 9 10 11 12)

http://www.smithkraus.com/

Annual.

A series of collections of 111 original monologues, all about one minute long, to be used by male and female teenage actors in auditions.

"Some suggestive sexual situations described here will not be acceptable in some classrooms. Drama teachers may, however, welcome some of this material for beginning acting students." Book Rep [review of volume one]

US News & World Report. U S News & World Report Inc. $29.97 per year (11 12 Adult)
ISSN 0041-5537

http://www.usnews.com

Weekly.

"A weekly magazine that covers national and world affairs, business trends as well as entertaining editorials and features about lifestyle and health." MagazineCity.com

Wired. Conde Nast Publications Inc. $12 per year (11 12 Adult)
ISSN 1059-1028

http://www.wired.com/wired

Monthly.

"Wired lays out the possibilities, hopes and opportunities of the digital frontier and the techno changes affecting work, business and our culture." MagazineCity.com

LIST OF RECOMMENDED ELECTRONIC RESOURCES

Access Science. McGraw-Hill $795/yr. for up to 500 users; $995/yr. for 501-2,000 users; $1,795/yr. for 2,001 or more users (9 10 11 12)

http://www.accessscience.com/

By subscription only. Tel. 888-307-5984

This database "provides high school students with a wealth of notable materials taken from the McGraw-Hill print collection. It includes full-text search capabilities of the ninth edition of the McGraw-Hill Encyclopedia of Science and Technology; new trends and developments in science and technology from the McGraw-Hill Yearbooks of Science and Technology; access to 110,000 definitions from the McGraw-Hill Dictionary of Scientific and Technical Terms; biographies of scientists; latebreaking science and technology news; bibliographies containing more than 28,000 literature citations; links to evaluated related Web sites; learning resources and study guides; additional illustrations, animations, and image galleries; and a question-and-answer section." SLJ

The African American Experience. Greenwood Publishing Group $450/yr for up to 500 users; $650/yr. for 500-1000 users; $900 for 1001-2000 users (9 10 11 12)

http://www.greenwood.com/mosaic/aae/productInfo.aspx

By subscription only. Tel 800-225-5800

"Greenwood's African American Experience is the first in its database family called American Mosaic (future products will cover Latino Americans, Native Americans, and Asian Americans). As an online library of information rather than an online encyclopedia of resources, the African American Experience offers more than 35,000 articles from over 300 print volumes including reference titles, narrative books and monographs, biographies, and early texts dating back to the 1800's. With a wealth of searchable slave narratives, over 1800+ images, 200+ vetted web links, and 4,500 primary documents—all within a single resource—this database provides a unique opportunity for students to easily investigate and explore the rich history and heritage of African American culture. Topics covered include history, art, folklore, biography, music, literature, pop culture, slavery, sports, politics, business, civil rights, education, science and technology, and more. . . . Alongside the depth of information provided within the database, African American Experience also contains over 88 lesson plans compiled by education and subject experts. These lessons integrate primary documents, introductory essays, and other background materials into easy-to-use and thought-provoking classroom activities for high school students." SLJ

Africans in America. Public Broadcasting Service and WGBH, Boston Free (9 10 11 12)

http://www.pbs.org/wgbh/aia/

"Africans in America is an online companion to the PBS television series, but also functions as a self-contained source of information and primary source documents relating to the topic of slavery in the United States. The main content is divided into four sections spanning the years from 1450 to 1865: The Terrible Transformation (1450-1750), Revolution (1750-1805), Brotherly Love (1791-1831), and Judgment Day (1831-1865). Each of these sections is subdivided into a Narrative, a Resource Bank, and a Teacher's Guide. . . . Africans in America strikes a sound balance between providing factual details and personal stories that bring life to the historical record. Teachers should be aware that authentic documents and accounts dealing with slavery inevitably portray violence and injustice, and may be upsetting to some students." Evalutech

Alt HealthWatch. EBSCO Publishing Contact producer for pricing (8 9 10 11 12 Adult)

http://www.epnet.com

By subscription only. Tel. 800-653-2726

Alt HealthWatch is a reference resource Internet tool that focuses on complementary, holistic, and integrated approaches to health care and wellness. It includes articles from over 180 international, peer-reviewed and professional journals, magazines, reports, proceedings, and association and consumer newsletters (most from 1990 to the present), pamphlets, booklets, special reports, original research, and book excerpts. The database indexes each article by more than 225 subject categories, 16 article types, and 11 publication types. It provides coverage across the spectrum of subject areas covered by the term, "Alternative Medicine."

Altavista's Babel Fish. Overture Services, Inc. Free (9 10 11 12 Adult)

http://www.babelfish.altavista.com

"This site from Altavista will translate individual words, short paragraphs (up to 150 words), or whole Web pages between various languages. . . . While the results are by no means perfect, the site may be useful in providing a general idea of the subject matter of short passages or a Web page." Ref & User Services Quarterly

American family immigration history center. The statue of liberty—Ellis island foundation, Inc. Free (7 8 9 10 11 12)

http://www.ellisisland.org

Explore your family history by accessing the records of all immigrants to pass through Ellis Island and the Port of New York from 1892 to 1924. A simple name search on the home page is the starting point. You can also search ship's manifests, create and maintain a family scrapbook and create printouts.

American Government. ABC-CLIO $499/yr. (6 7 8 9 10)

http://www.abc-clio.com/products/overview.aspx?productid=109714

By subscription only. Tel. 800-368-6868

Comprehensive resource on all aspects of American Government that includes topic overviews, essays, court cases, biographies, speeches, and historical documents. Students can explore pre-designed topics such as Congressional Powers, the Presidency, Civil Rights, and Po-

American Government—*Continued*

litical Parties or search by key word. Advanced searches can be limited by topic and categories (movements, organizations, statistics, quotes, etc.). The Home page provides changing news articles and feature stories linked to related articles in the database. Instructors can customize the site by adding announcements, syllabi, calendar of assignments, tests, etc. Teachers also have access to professional articles and links to additional resources. Includes the *Merriam Webster Dictionary*.

"Well designed, with good content and strategically placed links. Students will enjoy digging deep into this source." Libr J

American History. ABC-CLIO $599/yr. (6 7 8 9 10)

http://www.abc-clio.com/products/
overview.aspx?productid=109716

By subscription only. Tel. 800-368-6868

Provides coverage and resources on American history from 1350 to the present. The Home page includes feature stories and current events with links to related articles. Information can be searched by key word or phrase as well as through advanced searches by category, including documents, quotes, timelines, and type of multimedia. Instructors can customize the site by adding announcements, syllabi, calendar of assignments, tests, etc. Teachers also have access to professional articles and links to additional resources. Includes the *Merriam Webster Dictionary*.

"An easily navigable, appealing and comprehensive resource that would be extremely useful for the study of United States history." Evalutech

American Rhetoric. Michael E. Eidenmuller Free (9 10 11 12 Adult)

http://www.americanrhetoric.com

This website, which contains banner advertising, "combines the Online Speech Bank and The Top 100 Speeches into one easy-to-use, searchable reference database for all ages. According to the Web site, the online speech bank is an index to and growing database of more than five thousand full-text, audio, and video (streaming) versions of public speeches, sermons, legal proceedings, lectures, debates, interviews, and other recorded media events. . . . The top one hundred speeches in the Web site are an index to and partial database of full-text transcriptions of the one hundred most significant American political speeches of the twentieth century." Ref & User Services Quarterly

American verse project. University of Michigan Free (7 8 9 10 11 12)

http://www.hti.umich.edu/a/amverse/

A collaboration between the University of Michigan Humanities Text Initiative and the University of Michigan Press to assemble an electronic archive of volumes of American poetry prior to 1920. Search types include basic, proximity, Boolean, and citations. A word index and browse features are also included. There are over 125 volumes available by authors such as Whittier, Teasdale and Poe. Some of the volumes available, including those by a number of African-American and women poets, are the only existing editions of the author's work.

AmericanPresident.org. Miller Center of Public Affairs—University of Virginia Free (9 10 11 12 Adult)

http://www.millercenter.virginia.edu/academic/
americanpresident/

"The site consists of two sections. The Presidency in History section presents biographies and timelines for each president, first lady, cabinet member, and staff along with a list of key events and an image gallery for each president. The Presidency in Action section includes an organizational chart of administrative units and office holders, along with essays and bibliographies on key areas of presidential responsibility such as economic and domestic policy, national security, and legislative affairs." Ref & User Services Quarterly

Ancient History: Egyptians. British Broadcasting Corporation Free (9 10 11 12)

http://www.bbc.co.uk/history/ancient/egyptians

This website "covers a broad spectrum of topics relating to Egyptian civilization in ancient times. Major sections are devoted to mummification, gods and beliefs, sacred animals, Tutankhamun, the twelve great dynasties, the culture, health and medicine, and hieroglyphics. Each of these sections is comprised of a series of photographs with explication, and a bibliography of related print resources. The fascinating facts and explanation on this site are supplemented by several interactive, Flash-based games such as Death in Sakkara, an Indiana Jones-style archeological adventure." Evalutech

Answers.com. Guru-Net Corporation Free (11 12 Adult)

http://www.answers.com

"Answers.com is a search engine that searches and cross-indexes online research tools. Its 100-plus resources include The Columbia Electronic Encyclopedia, Merriam-Webster's Dictionary, Who2, and Wikipedia." Ref & User Services Quarterly

Asia source. Asia Society Free (11 12 Adult)

http://www.asiasource.org/

Provides a variety of information pertaining to Asia including: food, business, events, news, holidays, maps, and statistics. Specific resource sections provide information on holidays, chronologies, country comparisons, embassies, bibliographies, biographies, timelines, and languages. A searchable glossary of terms, dictionary and ask an expert features are included.

Atlapedia online. Latimer Clarke Corporation Pty Ltd Free (9 10 11 12)

http://www.atlapedia.com/index.html

Full color physical and political maps from countries around the world, plus facts and statistics on geography, climate, people, religion, language, history, and economy. Indexed by country.

Background Notes. United States Department of State Free (9 10 11 12 Adult)

http://www.state.gov/r/pa/ei/bgn/

"Prepared by the regional bureaus of the United States Department of State, Background Notes are factual publications about the land, people, history, government, political conditions, economy, and foreign relations of independent states, some dependencies, and areas of special sovereignty." Ref & User Services Quarterly

Bartleby.com. Alibris Free (7 8 9 10 11 12 Adult)

http://www.bartleby.com/

Access to full text of books on the web including reference, verse, fiction and nonfiction. Sections are indexed by author, subject and title and feature a browse function

Bartleby.com—*Continued*
for each section. Reference texts include: Columbia Encyclopedia, American Heritage Dictionary, Roget's II: The new Thesaurus, American Heritage Book of English Usage, Columbia World of Quotations, Simpson's Contemporary Quotations, Bartlett's Familiar Quotations, King James Bible, Oxford Shakespeare, Gray's Anatomy, Strunk's Elements of Style, World Factbook and Columbia Gazetteer. Includes banner advertising.

BBC News. BBC News Free (11 12 Adult)
http://news.bbc.co.uk
"BBC News is the largest news broadcaster in the world, with more than two thousand journalists in forty-eight bureaus around the globe. Visitors to this site will find extensive, in-depth coverage of the world's news that strives to be 'impartial, fair, and accurate,' offering an alternative perspective to that of American-based news media. Sections of the site focus on world regions, business, health, science and nature, technology, and entertainment. Articles are well illustrated, and often supplemented by links to audio and video coverage." Ref & User Services Quarterly

Ben's guide to U.S. Government. U.S. Government Printing Office Free (K 1 2 3 4 5 6 7 8 9 10)
http://bensguide.gpo.gov/
Quick facts and information about the U.S. Government designed for students, divided by grade levels. Topics include: Our nation, historical documents, branches of Government, how laws are made, National versus State Government, election process, and citizenship. Students can put together, state by state, and interactive puzzle of the nation or access Print games including word searches and crossword puzzles.

Bibliomania. Biblomania.com Ltd. Free (7 8 9 10 11 12)
http://www.bibliomania.com
Free access to thousands of e-books, poems, articles, short stories and plays on the Internet. Study guides are written by Oxford and Cambridge University graduates and include summaries, discussions and commentaries on the texts. The reference section includes biographies, classic nonfiction and religious texts. Each section can be quickly accessed by using the search features on the left side of the screen by section type and author. A book store function is also featured.

Big6: Information Skills for Student Achievement. Linworth $49/yr. for personal subscriptions; $69/yr. for personal teacher subscription; $495/yr. for grades K-5; $995/yr. for grades 6-12; $695/yr. for a district license (Professional)
http://www.big6.com/
By subscription only. Tel. 888-342-2446
"The program provides several modules, or tools, that students can use throughout their research: Big6 Planner, TurboCite, TurboReport, TurboWrite, TurboLinks, and TurboRater. Each student (in the Enterprise edition) has a Locker that allows him or her to keep electronic note cards, lists of possible research sources, bibliographic information, and assignments. Projects are created individually and each one contains all of the resources and information in one filemaking it less likely that students will lose their resources. A Big6™ Planner creates a road map of the assignment so students are able to determine

how the project is progressing. A citation program called TurboCite allows for easy tracking of resources and citation notes. By plugging in the resource information, TurboCite provides an accurate citation of any source used. A variety of tools are also available including a dictionary; a comprehensive list of stages in the Big6™ process; an instant messaging tool, TurboTalk, that allows collaboration with teachers or peers from within the software program; a list of Big6-related Web sites; the Planner that uses questions, answers, and video clips to guide students through the problem-solving process; TurboReport, a collection of report templates that enable teachers and librarians to generate customized reports; TurboWrite, a fully functioning word processor for printing reports, labels, captions, graphics, and more; and TurboRater, a tool for generating tests and evaluations using a variety of question types that can be completed by the student online and saved, printed, or e-mailed to the teacher." SLJ

Biography of America. WGBH Interactive for Annenberg Media Free (9 10 11 12)
http://www.learner.org/biographyofamerica/
This website "covers the history of our country in twenty-six sessions, beginning with pre-European events and ending in 1999. The Web site is based on a series of videos that are available for purchase, or viewable for free as streaming videos (in Windows Media format). Each of the sections is organized in the same fashion. A timeline of events is provided, with links to text coverage of most of the events listed. A map provides a visual context for key concepts, and a complete transcript of the video is provided. A collection of relevant Web resources is included, and a bibliography of print resources is available in another location on the site." Evalutech

Biography Reference Bank. H. W. Wilson Contact producer for pricing (7 8 9 10 11 12 Adult)
http://www.hwwilson.com
By subscription only. Tel. 800-367-6770
This database features substantial full-text biographies of over 500,000 people, current and historical. Biographies are linked to related indexing, abstracts, full-text articles, and page images from the full range of Wilson databases to keep information up to date. There are also over 36,000 pictures of people profiled. Uniform name authority control facilitates searching.

BLS Career Information. U.S. Bureau of Labor Statistics Free (5 6 7 8 9 10 11 12)
http://www.bls.gov/k12/
Provides vocational guidance for young people interested in the arts, mathematics, science, physical activities, the outdoors, social science, or reading.

C.E.R.F. (Curriculum and Education Resource Finder). Media Flex Contact producer for pricing (Professional)
http://www.cerfinfo.com/
By subscription only. Tel. 877-331-1022
A directory of weekly updated Web sites that have been pre-screened and selected for use in the instructional setting. Users can search for sites by key word (with Boolean operators), by topic lists, or by grade level range (including professional). Information about each site includes the title, hyperlinked URL, relevant subject areas, correlations to McREL standards, and cross references to related topics. Sites can also be saved to a bibliography with an option to e-mail results.

C.E.R.F. (Curriculum and Education Resource Finder)—*Continued*

"A big plus for C.E.R.F. is the extensive use of links from outside the United States, giving a more global perspective to inquiry." Book Report

calisphere. The University of California Free (9 10 11 12)

http://www.calisphere.universityofcalifornia.edu/

"Although calisphere focuses on the history of California, its relevance extends handily into the broader study of North American civilization. Topics of high interest to a general audience include the Japanese-American Internment, the Great Depression, the Gold Rush, and World War II. The collection of photographs and documents on calisphere includes over 150,000 items and comprises an excellent resource for public domain primary source materials." Evalutech

Cambridge Dictionaries online. Cambridge University Press Free (7 8 9 10 11 12 Adult)

http://dictionary.cambridge.org/

A simple to use search functions allows access to Cambridge dictionaries. Enter a word in the box, click search, and users can immediately access dictionary information. Also included are activities and worksheets, information for language researchers and a top forty word list.

The CIA world factbook. Central Intelligence Agency Free (7 8 9 10 11 12 Adult)

http://www.odci.gov/cia/publications/factbook/index.html

Quick reference to information for all countries including: geography (including maps), people, government, economy, military, communication, travel, and transnational issues. All countries can be accessed from the browse list on the left side of the home page. Appendixes include: abbreviations, international organizations and groups, international environmental agreements, cross-reference list of country data codes, cross-reference list of hydrographic data codes, and cross-reference list of geographic names. Also included is a comprehensive collection of reference maps and a definitions and abbreviations section.

Connected University. Classroom Connect Contact producer for pricing (Professional)

http://www.cu.classroom.com

By subscription only. Tel. 800-638-1639

Connected University offers educators 24-hour a day access to instructor-led courses, self-paced courses, technology "how to" tips, and software tutorials. Courses are available on a broad range of topics from teaching reading standards to how to build a Web page. Graduate credits and continuing education units can be obtained from partner universities. Thousands of pre-screened, educator-friendly web sites are provided in the CU Library.

Constitution Finder. University of Richmond Free (9 10 11 12 Adult)

http://confinder.richmond.edu/index.php

This "Web site features a well-placed pull-down index to more than two hundred countries ranging from Afghanistan to Zimbabwe. Constitutions are offered in original languages and English (and sometimes Spanish) translations." Ref & User Services Quarterly

ConsumerSearch. ConsumerSearch, Inc. Free (9 10 11 12 Adult)

http://www.consumersearch.com

"ConsumerSearch aims to be the starting place for consumers researching top-rated products in thirteen catagories including Photo and Video, Health and Fitness, Computers, Automotive, and Sports and Leisure." Ref & User Service Quarterly

Crash Course in Copyright. University of Texas System, Georgia K. Harper Free (Professional)

http://www.utsystem.edu/ogc/intellectualproperty/cprtindx.htm

"This very comprehensive site covers copyright and fair use as well as the broader area of intellectual property for creators and users. Content includes the background of fair use, using multimedia, digital content in libraries, copyright management, licensing resources, online presentations, a copyright tutorial, and links to additional information elsewhere." Ref & User Services Quarterly

Curriculum Resource Center. Facts on File $650/yr for up to 500 users; $860/yr. for 500-1000 users (Professional)

http://www.factsonfile.com

By subscription only. Tel. 800-322-8755

Database of copyright-free, reproducible, black-and-white and color maps, historical maps, graphs, charts, timelines, illustrations, and other hand-out materials with visual content and text. Subjects dealt with include religion, geography, health and fitness, general science, mathematics, U.S and world history, and government. The materials in this database display in Adobe Acrobat (link to free download provided).

Digital History. University of Houston Free (9 10 11 12)

http://www.digitalhistory.uh.edu

"This is an extensive and well-organized site featuring 'high quality historical resources for teachers and students for free and without advertising.'" Ref & User Services Quarterly

DigitalCurriculum.com. AIMS Multimedia Contact producer for pricing (Professional)

http://www.digitalcurriculum.com/

By subscription only. Tel. 800-367-2467

DigitalCurriculum.com "is a curriculum video-on-demand teaching and learning system that fully integrates full-length educational videos, key concept video clips, still images, Encyclopaedia Britannica content, teacher guides, lesson plans, and interactive online assessments and assignments into a . . . learning tool for teachers, students, and administrators with complete record-keeping and an internal messaging service. DigitalCurriculum offers multimedia components for every K-12 subject, state and national framework correlations, multiple bit-rate encoding for school and home use, and simple incorporation of local content." Publisher's note

Distinguished women of past and present. Distinguishedwomen.com Free (7 8 9 10 11 12)

http://www.distinguishedwomen.com/

Search for biographical information by subject or name of women writers, educators, scientists, heads of state, politicians, civil rights crusaders, artists, and enter-

Distinguished women of past and present—*Continued*

tainers. This site features bibliography information links to Amazon.com.

Documenting the American South Free (9 10 11 12 Adult)

http://docsouth.unc.edu

This website "is a large-scale, digital publishing initiative that features primary resources in history for the study of the history, literature, and culture of the American South. It is an indispensable resource for study of the Civil War and the antebellum South, African-American history, and Southern literature." Ref & User Services Quarterly

Earth Trends: The Environmental Information Portal. The World Resources Institute Free (9 10 11 12)

http://earthtrends.wri.org/

This website "is a collection of online databases that provide access to massive amounts of data relating to the environment, geography, and economics of countries around the world. The databases are compiled by the World Resources Institute, in collaboration with the United Nations, the World Bank, and the Federal Government's USAID program. The ten topics covered include Coastal and Marine Ecosystems, Climate and Atmosphere, Agriculture and Food, and Energy and Resources. The type of information provided within each topic includes data tables, country profiles, maps, and feature articles. For casual users EarthTrends permits three data requests per week without registration. More extensive use requires registration, which is a free process with minimal personal information required (name, email address and general location)." Evalutech

eLibrary Science. ProQuest $1,495/yr. (9 10 11 12)

http://www.proquestk12.com/productinfo/elibrary_science.shtml

By subscription only. Tel. 800-521-0600 x3344

"Through a recent partnership with reference publisher Salem Press, eLibrary Science provides more than 20 of Salem's reference titles, such as Animal Life and Plant Life from the Magill's Encyclopedia of Science program, science-related titles from the Great Events in History series, the Encyclopedia of Genetics, and over 400 other science publications. Students, teachers, and librarians will find updated science news links, information about famous scientists, a 'Today in Science History' feature, hundreds of educator-approved Web sites from Homework Central, dozens of model BookCarts of durable links, and other features. To support both the regular and AP science courses." SLJ

eNature.com. Audubon Society Free (4 5 6 7 8 9 10)

http://www.enature.com

Audubon field guides online and searchable, with descriptions and color photographs of over 4,800 North American plants and animals. If given a zip code, the site will provide descriptions and pictures of birds native to that region.

Encarta. Microsoft Corporation Free (5 6 7 8 9 10 11 12 Adult)

http://encarta.msn.com/

Online access to the Encarta encyclopedia by entering a question or a keyword. Sections include: reference, homework, college prep, grad school, e-learning, parents, genealogy, and products. Quick reference tools include encyclopedia, dictionary and atlas. Content includes text, graphic, audio and video files. Quicktime three is needed for playing video files.

Encyclopedia Americana. Grolier Educational Contact producer for pricing; minimum of two databases (7 8 9 10 11 12)

http://www.go.grolier.com

By subscription only. Tel. 888-326-6546

General encyclopedia comprised of 45,000 articles and more than 25 million words contributed by over 6,500 specialists in their respective disciplines covering all academic fields and curriculum topics. The new online addition is organized around four editorial "modules": Americana encyclopedia database, Americana Journal, Profiles, and Editor's Picks and is American with Disabilities Act (ADA)/Section 508 compliant. Many of the articles link to the Online Computer Library Center's (OCLC) WorldCat bibliographic database which contains merged catalogs of libraries from around the world providing up to 25 bibliographic citations per entry which can be filtered by zip or postal code to locate libraries holding the work.

"EA remains a good choice for any highschool, college, or public library collection. Libraries that can afford the online version, updated quarterly, will get the benefit of hundreds of new and revised articles each year that do not appear in the print set, as well as other online features." Booklist

Encyclopedia Britannica. Encyclopedia Britannica, Inc. $69.95/yr. (7 8 9 10 11 12 Adult)

http://www.britannica.com

By subscription only. Tel. 800-323-1229

This site offers Britannica's well-researched, clearly written articles packaged with a search engine, videos and pictures, a Web site directory, periodical articles, and the Merriam-Webster dictionary and thesaurus. Search results provide topic headings, encyclopedia articles, Web site listings, and an opportunity to search the periodical database. A browse section gives one access to the topic headings in alphabetical order, although without the cross-references found in print versions. There is also a set of subject classifications bringing together articles on related subjects. A student edition is also available. Includes banner advertising.

eTAP. eTAP, Inc. Contact producer for pricing (Professional)

http://www.etap.org

By subscription only. Tel. 949-497-2200

Short for "electronic teaching assistance program," this resource provides a K-12 curriculum in the subjects of mathematics, English, history and science. It provides educators with lesson plans, instructions for assignments, links to web sites on key topics, practice exercises that can be used as worksheet assignments for students, tests modeled after standardized exams, and a problem section that can be printed out and used for student assessment.

Eternal Egypt. Egyptian Center for Documentation of Cultural and Natural Heritage Free (9 10 11 12)

http://www.eternalegypt.org/

Eternal Egypt—*Continued*

"Exploring more than 'five thousand years of Egyptian civilization,' this multimedia presentation offers cultural highlights, maps, timelines, and libraries and museums of information." Ref & User Services Quarterly

Ethnic NewsWatch. Proquest Contact producer for pricing (7 8 9 10 11 12 Adult)

http://www.proquest.com/products_pq/descriptions/ethnic_newswatch.shtml

By subscription only. Tel. 1-800-521-0600

Ethnic NewsWatch, a reference resource tool, includes a full-text collection from 250 newspapers, magazines and other publications from the ethnic, minority and native press in America. It includes coverage of issues in Ireland, Israel and the Middle East, Mexico, Bosnia, Armenia, China, Nigeria, and Ukraine among other countries. The resource covers current topics and other social, political and educational subjects, especially African-American and Hispanic topics. The database includes full-text articles in English and in Spanish, and roughly 7500 new articles are added each month.

Ethnologue. SIL International Free (7 8 9 10 11 12)

http://www.ethnologue.com/web.asp

Information about over 6,900 languages and 41,000 alternative dialects from around the world. Users can search for world language information by using the interactive world map to drill down to particular countries or search by language name, codes or families. Specific information for each language includes population, region, alternate names, classification and comments.

Explore the Constitution. National Constitution Center Free (9 10 11 12)

http://www.constitutioncenter.org/explore/TheU.S.Constitution/

"The National Constitution Center has created an online resource that explores various aspects of the Constitution and other documents significant in U.S. history. The mainstay of Explore the Constitution is the Interactive Constitution. Students may search this resource by keyword, or use the pop-up menus that allow browsing sections of the document by topic or important Supreme Court cases. Annotations are provided from Linda Monk's book The Words We Live By. The Web site builds on this base by providing printable versions of the Constitution in Acrobat format, a Spanish language version, and the text of other important documents such as the Magna Carta, The Mayflower Compact, and the Articles of Confederation." Evalutech

Exploring Data. Education Queensland Free (9 10 11 12)

http://exploringdata.cqu.edu.au/

"For many students who wish to embark into the world of statistics, the whole process can be a bit daunting. Fortunately, the Exploring Data website makes such a proposition a bit easier for both students and teachers. The site is easy to navigate, and the homepage contains an index of topics and materials ranging from linear regression to sampling. Each of these sections includes activities, worksheets, and datasets that can be used in a variety of ways. More advanced students will appreciate the fact that the site also contains material that goes beyond some of the basic concepts within the field, and educators will also want to recommend this site to students who might need a bit of a refresher on certain key areas." 2007 Internet Scout Project

Federal Resources for Educational Excellence. U.S. Department of Education Free (5 6 7 8 9 10 11 12)

http://www.free.ed.gov/

Lists hundreds of educational Web sites supported by U.S. government agencies. Subjects include arts, history, health and physical education, language arts, mathematics, science, and world studies.

The **Federal** Web Locator. Villanova Center for Information law and policy Free (7 8 9 10 11 12 Adult)

http://www.lib.auburn.edu/madd/docs/fedloc.html

A comprehensive guide to federal government information, with links to major government agencies, departments and offices.

Foreign Relations of the United States. University of Wisconsin System Board of Regents Free (9 10 11 12)

http://digicoll.library.wisc.edu/FRUS/

"With the very official title of 'Foreign Relations of the United States' (FRUS), this important United States government series serves as the official documentary historical record of major foreign policy decisions. Produced by the State Department's Office of the Historian, many of these printed volumes have been digitized and placed online here as part of the University of Wisconsin Digital Collections project. Working with collaborators at the University of Illinois at Chicago, this archive includes those volumes published from 1861 to the year 1960. It is easy to search through the volumes, and visitors may also want to just browse through different volumes at their leisure. Users should also be mindful that the organization of FRUS, while generally chronological, does not always correspond to the dates of documentary history. Fortunately, each volume has a subject and author index available for consultation. Students of political science, United States history, and international relations will find this website indispensable." 2007 Internet Scout Project

The **Gateway** to 21st Century Skills. U. S. Department of Education Free (Professional)

http://www.thegateway.org

Direct access to collections of educational resources found on various federal, state, university, nonprofit, and commercial Internet sites including lesson plans, activities, and projects. Lists and search functions are organized by subject, type, level, keyword, mediator, beneficiary, and pricecode.

Get a Clue: language arts software. FableVision Contact producer for price (Professional)

http://www.getaclue.com

By subscription only. Tel. 888-240-3734

Get a Clue is a vocabulary development program based on word etymology. Students use the inductive reasoning skills of application, analysis, and synthesis to work through a word's derivation and 5 "Clues." Students develop understanding of word meaning by examining multimedia feedback and explanation at each step. The program provides online progress tracking, review features, and customized printable quizzes. Designed for use with grades 5 and up.

Girls Health. The National Women's Health Information Center, Washington, D C. Free (4 5 6 7 8 9 10)

http://www.girlshealth.gov/

Girls Health—*Continued*

"Designed for girls ages 10 to 16, GirlsHealth, covers a wide range of health topics—but doesn't focus on sexuality as other health sites do. There are particularly useful sections, including 'Bullying' and 'Drugs, Alcohol & Smoking.' (Check out the 'Guess what's in a cigarette?' quiz.) Sections entitled 'For Parents & Caregivers' and 'For Educators' are also worthy of review." SLJ

The **Greeks:** Crucible of Civilization. The Public Broadcasting System Free (9 10 11 12)

http://www.pbs.org/empires/thegreeks/

This website "offers a broad range of multimedia resources covering the Golden Age of Greece. Interactive panoramas include simulated impressions of the Acropolis and the Parthenon as they may have existed at the time of Pericles. An interactive map provides an overview of ancient Athens, and a streaming video depicts the extraordinary beauty of the Parthenon and the works of art within. Life in ancient Athens is also covered in detail, with extensive information on social customs, political life, and military history. Another interactive feature allows the visitor to role play in order to learn about the varying lifestyles of Greeks from different backgrounds and circumstances. The major figures in the development of Greek democracy are presented in illustrated profiles that include Cleisthenes, Themistocles, Pericles, Aspasia, and Socrates. Areas of special interest about the Greeks are covered in articles on topics such as the theater, the Olympics, and women's role in society. One valuable feature of The Greeks is an overview that establishes the relative place of the Golden Age in the context of world history." Evalutech

Grolier Multimedia Encyclopedia Online. Grolier Educational Contact producer for pricing; minimum of two databases (5 6 7 8 9 10)

http://www.go.grolier.com

By subscription only. Tel. 888-326-6546

General encyclopedia covering all subjects with multimedia and current events. Information can be located by browsing categories such U.S. history, language and literature, life sciences, and technology or by key word searches. Advanced searches can be limited to article titles or full text with the use of Boolean operators. Articles include hyperlinked cross references, related Web links, and bibliographies. There are also links to related magazine articles provided by EBSCO. The Brain Jam feature changes frequently and explores a topic in more depth, enhanced with Web links, activities, and teacher resources.

"A wonderfully easy-to-use title that provides good overviews to large topics, good definitions and brief biographies, and highly useful cross-referencing. . . . Highly recommended for public and school libraries." Libr J

Healthfinder. Office of Disease Prevention and Health Promotion/ U.S. Department of Health and Human Services Free (7 8 9 10 11 12 Adult)

http://www.healthfinder.gov

This government site serves as an all-purpose source of free medical and health information for the general public. It features a Health Library, browsable by topic and with links to special resources; a section on information about doctors, dentists, hospitals, health insurance, Medicare, etc.; and a directory of selected health information Web sites from government agencies, clearinghouses, nonprofit organizations, and universities. There is also a Spanish version and a version for kids.

Historic Jamestowne. The Association for the Preservation of Virginia Antiquities Free (9 10 11 12)

http://historicjamestowne.org/

This website "is particularly effective when used in conjunction with its sister Web site, Jamestown Rediscovery (http://www.apva.org/jr.html).Lesson plans are provided that span the elementary through high school curriculum from English language arts and social studies through science and math. Representative topics include critical thinking, map skills, interpreting tree rings, archeology, economics, and Native Americans. Background material on the site is plentiful. A PowerPoint presentation, 'Archeology 101,' can be useful as an introductory activity. A glossary, a list of related Web links, and a bibliography round out a strong offering of curriculum materials. Historic Jamestowne also includes sections appropriate for student use. The History and Dig sections provide information on the early settlement of the Colony and on the archeological techniques used to uncover the past. The latter section features articles on significant artifacts recovered from the historic site, and includes numerous photographs. Two interactive modules allow students to experience the techniques and thought patterns employed by professional archeologists when interpreting artifacts and historical sites." Evalutech

HistorySolutions.com. History Solutions, Inc. Contact producer for pricing (Professional)

http://www.historysolutions.com

By subscription only. Tel. 973-701-6770

This history Internet workbook contains 16 units of U.S. History. Each unit contains six lessons. In Historical Simulation students act as advisors to historical figures, weigh options, consider consequences, and try to make the "historically accurate" decision. Students create notes in the interactive Cognitive Organizer. The Primary Source Analysis Guide has students interpret documents. In the Prediction Center students attempt to predict how certain events will affect the United States. The Quiz at the end of each unit checks mastery of the content-based simulations. Students work in the Writer's Workshop where they are guided through the process of writing an expository essay based on the content in the historical simulation, and evaluate their essay. The program provides opportunities for students to learn historical content, critical thinking skills, historical perspective, conceptual thinking, and expository writing.

Homeroom.com. The Princeton Review Contact producer for pricing (Professional)

http://k12.princetonreview.com/homeroom_index.asp

By subscription only. Tel. 800-REVIEW-2

Homeroom.com is a web based assessment and diagnostic tool containing over 130,000 math, reading, and language arts questions and over 10,000 instructional resources aligned to all state standards, major classroom textbooks, and specific state and national tests. There are an average of 10 instructional resources per tested skill. The program can be used to assess, analyze, and remediate strengths and weaknesses of student skills. It allows teachers to generate practice assessments that are correlated to state or city standards and the textbook used in the classroom. It directs teachers and students to targeted educational resources, customized to each tested skill, based on individual and group performance.

Homework Center. Multnomah Public Library Free (4 5 6 7 8 9 10 11 12)

http://www.multcolib.org/homework/index.html

Homework Center—*Continued*

This browsable selection of internet resources is organized by topics most commonly requested for homework assignments. Sites are selected and annotated by librarians and an online question feature allows immediate access to a librarian of the Mulnomah Public Library.

Hotmath.com. Hotmath.com $29 for 60 days; $49/yr. (7 8 9 10 11 12)

http://www.hotmath.com

By subscription only. Tel. 510-524-5525

This website provides tutorial solutions to homework problems in selected state-approved mathematics textbooks. Solutions include hints, Socratic questions, graphs, figures, and steps leading up to and including the final answer.

How Products Are Made. Thomson Gale Free (9 10 11 12)

http://www.madehow.com

"The seven-volume print set, How Products Are Made, published by Thomson Gale from 1994 through 2002, now has an electronic coutnerpart. . . . Each entry includes understated advertising links related to the product, a background, perhaps a history, diagrams, the raw materials needed, the manufacturing process, quality control, the future of the product, and a short bibliography titled 'Where To Learn More.'" Ref & User Services Quarterly

Iemily. iEmily, Inc Free (7 8 9 10 11 12)

http://www.iemily.com

"This unique site, from iEmily, Inc., in Cambridge, MA, includes information on herbs, natural remedies and beauty tips, and yoga. 'My Story' offers up essays written by girls about grief, living with a disability, self-image, and self-injury. 'Healthy Eating' contains recipes that will appeal to young people. Parents may want to review sections on sexuality and alternative lifestyles before sharing with their kids. Don't miss: A printable list of health hotline telephone numbers." SLJ

INFOMINE. Regents of the University of California Free (11 12 Adult)

http://infomine.ucr.edu/

Provides access to a collection of resources like databases, electronic journals, electronic books, bulletin boards, mailing lists, online library card catalogs, articles, directories of researchers, and other types of information built by librarians at 30 contributing universities.

Infoplease.com. Family Education Network, Inc. Free (7 8 9 10 11 12 Adult)

http://www.infoplease.com/

A collection of almanacs as well as a searchable dictionary, encyclopedia, and atlas. Contains banner advertising.

InfoTrac Student Edition. Gale Group Contact producer for pricing (9 10 11 12)

http://www.galegroup.com

By subscription only. Tel. 800-877-4253

Designed for the secondary school student, this resource offers full-text content from fourteen different reference books, including Asimov's Chronology of Science & Discovery; Merriam-Webster's Biographical Dictionary; Encyclopedia of American Facts and Dates; The Columbia Encyclopedia; and World Almanac Book of Facts.

Infrared Astronomy. Infrared Processing and Analysis Center, California Institute of Technology Free (9 10 11 12)

http://coolcosmos.ipac.caltech.edu/
cosmic_classroom/ir_tutorial/

"Despite the claims of certain science fiction novels and films, humans cannot see in infrared. As many people know, the primary source of infrared radiation is heat, and the study of infrared astronomy allows scientists to detect radiation emitted from objects throughout the universe. This delightful website (created by NASA and the Infrared Processing and Analysis Center at the California Institute of Technology) provides a wide range of material on this fascinating area of scientific study. Visitors can lean about the discovery of infrared, learn about the technology that is used in such endeavors, and of course, look over dozens of infrared images and video clips. Educators will be glad to learn that there are a number of activities offered here for use in the classroom, including one that will help students learn how to build a photocell detector." 2007 Internet Scout Project

The Internet Public library. Regents of the University of Michigan Free (7 8 9 10 11 12 Adult)

http://www.ipl.org/

This virtual library provides easy access to reference resources, books, magazines, and other web sites on the Internet. It is organized around basic content areas by subject. There is also a section especially for teens.

The Internet Scout Report. Internet Scout Project Free (7 8 9 10 11 12 Adult)

http://scout.wisc.edu/Reports/ScoutReport/Current/

Published each Friday online and by email, the report provides information about valuable resources on the Internet. Resources are selected, researched and annotated by a team of professional librarians and subject matter experts.

Introduction to Genetics. GlaxoSmithKline Free (9 10 11 12)

http://genetics.gsk.com/overview.htm

"Keeping the world of base pairs straight can be a challenge, but fortunately this well-developed introduction to the world of genetics will be a boon to students and those members of the public who are craving a refresher on this exciting area of science. Created by GlaxoSmithKline, the site includes a number of interactive animations that illustrate the workings of DNA and genes. Along with these animations, visitors can read over brief introductory pieces on mutations and genetic disorders. The site also has a brief multiple choice quiz that users can take after they make their way through the different sections here." 2007 Internet Scout Project

JetStream: An Online School for Weather. The National Weather Service Southern Region Free (9 10 11 12)

http://www.srh.noaa.gov/srh/jetstream/

This website "covers the fundamentals of weather and severe weather in an online experience that is easy to follow. The major areas addressed are Weather on the Web (forecasting), the Atmosphere, The Ocean, Global Weather, Synoptic Meteorology, Thunderstorms, Lightning, Tropical Weather, Remote Sensing, and the National Weather Service. Each major topic is covered with clear explanations, illustrations, and charts, as well as with lesson plans and handouts." Evalutech

Kepler's Three Laws of Planetary Motion. David P. Stern Free (Professional)

http://www.phy6.org/stargaze/Kep3laws.htm

"Four hundred years ago, the German astronomer Johannes Kepler described his concept of the laws of planetary motion in his work, 'Astronomia nova'. These important laws remain important concepts for students of physics, and those who work with such students will find much of interest on this particular site. Created by David P. Stern (a retired physicist at the Goddard Space Flight Center), the site consists of an overview of Kepler's laws, with examples, applications, problems and related history. The material is based on a talk that Stern gave in Maryland, and visitors will find that this resource is both accessible and very thorough." 2007 Internet Scout Project

Lands and Peoples Online. Grolier Educational Contact producer for pricing; minimum of two databases (4 5 6 7 8 9 10)

http://www.go.grolier.com

By subscription only. Tel. 888-326-6546

An international geography reference based on the print version. Articles have hyperlinked outlines and cross references and include photos, maps, flags, facts and figures, and Internet links. A Culture Cross feature enables users to compare two countries, continents, or states/provinces from the perspective of land, people, economy, history, or facts and figures. Also included are highlights of current events around the world, an atlas, an almanac, and games and quizzes for students.

"The ease of navigation and the multiple access points make it easy for beginning researchers to find what they need. The ability to create specific searches and locate precise elements of information make Lands and Peoples online attractive for more sophisticated assignments as well." Booklist

Legends of Tuskegee. National Park Service Museum Management Program Free (9 10 11 12)

http://www.cr.nps.gov/museum/exhibits/tuskegee/

"The important heritage of the Tuskegee Institute is presented in this Web site from the National Park Service. The site's subject matter centers on the achievements of Booker T. Washington, George Washington Carver, and the Tuskegee Airmen. Content is drawn from the collections of three National Park historic sites and museums, as well as from several other Federal agencies." Evalutech

Librarians' Internet Index. Library of California Free (7 8 9 10 11 12 Adult)

http://lii.org/

This is a searchable collection of over 20,000 Internet resources selected by librarians at the Library of California for their usefulness to users of public libraries. A browsing function is included.

The **Library** of Congress. Library of Congress Free (7 8 9 10 11 12 Adult)

http://www.loc.gov/

Provides access to Library of Congress digital collections of text, audio, and graphics. Collections include: American Memory from the Library of Congress (http://memory.loc.gov/); Global Gateway: World Culture and Resources (http://international.loc.gov/intldl/intldlhome.html); America's Library (http://www.americaslibrary.gov/cgi-bin/page.cgi) for kids and family; THOMAS (http://thomas.loc.gov/) legislative information; Exhibitions (http://www.loc.gov/exhibits/) Online galleries. Other services include: search functions, including catalogues and A-Z index, web casting and Ask a Librarian feature.

MagillOnLiterature Plus. EBSCO Publishing Contact producer for pricing (9 10 11 12)

http://www.epnet.com

By subscription only. Tel. 800-653-2726

"This database is composed of approximately 35,000 critical analyses of individual works of literature, 6,500 biographical records, more than 1,000 images, and a glossary of 1,310 literary terms. MagillOnLiterature Plus contains editorially reviewed critical essays, brief plot summaries, extended character profiles, and . . . setting discussions covering works by more than 8,500 long and short fiction writers, poets, dramatists, essayists, and philosophers. The biographical essays reflect extended coverage of the 2,500 most studied authors and include . . . lists of each author's principal works and current secondary bibliographies. In addition, 395 . . . genre-driven overview essays provide details about important literary genres, time periods, and national literatures." EBSCO website

Mark Twain's Mississippi River. Northern Illinois University Libraries Free (9 10 11 12)

http://dig.lib.niu.edu/twain/index.html

"In a very real way, Samuel Clemens cut his teeth on the Mississippi River as an apprentice steamboat captain in the late 1850s. Years later he would draw on these experiences for a number of the works he would write under the name, 'Mark Twain'. This multimedia website created at Northern Illinois University explores his time in and around Big Muddy through a number of interactive maps, historic images, and audio content. By clicking on the 'Twain's Life and Works' section, visitors can read a number of essays written by Gregg Camfield of the University of the Pacific on such topics as the economic importance of the river during Twain's life, as well as other pieces on related topics. Moving along, visitors can perform detailed searches across the entire database and also listen to songs from the period, such as 'Steamboat Bill'." 2007 Internet Scout Project

The **Martin** Luther King, Jr. Research and Education Institute. Stanford University Free (Professional)

http://www.stanford.edu/group/King/index.htm

"Stanford University has been the home of the Martin Luther King, Jr. Papers Project for over twenty years, and they also have the Martin Luther King, Jr. Research and Education Institute. On their website, visitors can learn about their work, which includes sponsoring conferences, providing research fellowships, and developing the Liberation curriculum for educators interested in nonviolent movements. The Liberation Curriculum section is actually a fine place to start exploring the site, as it contains lesson plans and other online resources (such as transcripts of King's speeches) that will assist teachers in crafting valuable classroom experiences. Visitors will also want to make sure and visit the King Papers Project section of the site as well. Here they can find transcripts of some of King's most important works and a number of audio recordings of his sermons and speeches." 2007 Internet Scout Project

MAS Ultra—School Edition. EBSCO Publishing Contact producer for pricing (9 10 11 12)

http://www.epnet.com

MAS Ultra—School Edition—*Continued*

By subscription only. Tel. 800-653-2726

This "database, designed specifically for high school libraries, contains full text for nearly 500 popular, high school magazines including America's Civil War, American Heritage, American History, Archaeology, Astronomy, Bioscience, Careers & Colleges, Civil War Times, Congressional Digest, Discover, Economist, History Today, Nation, National Review, New Republic, New Scientist, Popular Science, Science News, Scientific American, Smithsonian, World War II, etc. All full text articles are assigned a reading level indicator (Lexiles). Full text is also available for 84,774 biographies and 100,554 primary source documents. Additionally, MAS Ultra—School Edition contains more than 350 reference books (including the Columbia Encyclopedia, the CIA World Fact Book and World Almanac & Book of Facts), an Image Collection of 276,132 photos, maps & flags, color PDFs and expanded full text backfiles (back to 1975) for key magazines." EBSCO website

Medical Dictionary. MedicineNet.com Free (11 12 Adult)

http://www.medterms.com/script/main/hp.asp

"For nurses and other health care professionals who seek to distinguish the habitus from the humerus, this online medical dictionary provided by MedicineNet will be a place to bookmark for repeat visits. The dictionary contains well-written explanations for over 16,000 medical terms, and users can go ahead and browse around, or enter keywords or phrases into the search engine that resides on the page. The site also features a 'Word of the Day', and visitors can also look through recent news items that address different health issues and also look over the latest entries to the dictionary. The site is rounded out by a list of the 'Top 10 Medterms', which is also a good way to start exploring the materials here." 2007 Internet Scout Project

Medline Plus. National Library of Medicine/ National Institutes of Health Free (7 8 9 10 11 12 Adult)

http://www.nlm.nih.gov/medlineplus

This site is devoted to medical and health information for the public and for health professionals. It features information on conditions, diseases and wellness topics, and a medical encyclopedia; drug information; several medical dictionaries; access to directories with locations and credentials of doctors, dentists, and hospitals; and access to medical organizations, consumer health libraries, international sites, and medical publications.

Merriam-Webster online. Merriam-Webster Inc. Free (7 8 9 10 11 12 Adult)

http://www.m-w.com/home.htm

Site provides quick access to Merriam-Webster's Collegiate Dictionary, Collegiate Thesaurus, Spanish-English Dictionary, and Medical Dictionary by entering a word in a box on the home page and selecting the product you want to search. Other features include: Word of the Day, word games, and word for the wise. You can also add a free dictionary button to your browser, add a free dictionary search box on your web site or receive the word of the day by e-mail.

The Middle East in Early Prints and Photographs. New York Public Library Free (9 10 11 12)

http://digitalgallery.nypl.org/nypldigital/explore/dgexplore.cfm?col_id=179

"The New York Public Library has plenty of material on the Middle East, and in fact, they have created this very fine digital collection which brings together early prints and photographs of the region. With over 8800 items online, the collection contains engravings, lithographs, and salt prints, along with a number of complete photograph albums and archival compilations. Visitors can perform a general search of these materials, and they may also wish to read the background essay offered here as well. Clicking on the 'Collection Contents' section will bring up a list of the works that make up the digital collection, which include Francis Frith's 1862 work, 'Upper Egypt and Ethiopia' and an ordnance survey executed by Colonel Sir Henry James in 1865." 2007 Internet Scout Project

Monticello Explorer. The Thomas Jefferson Foundation Free (9 10 11 12)

http://explorer.monticello.org/

This website "offers a virtual visit to the grounds and buildings of the Monticello plantation. In 1809, when Jefferson retired to Monticello, the plantation comprised 5000 acres and was served by over 200 workers. Monticello Explorer is a multimedia window into Jefferson's world at that time. The centerpiece of the Web site is an interactive map with a selection tool that permits the visitor to choose an area of the estate and zoom in for a closer look." Evalutech

A More Perfect Union: Japanese Americans & the U.S. Constitution. Smithsonian National Museum of American History Free (9 10 11 12)

http://americanhistory.si.edu/perfectunion/experience/

This website "gives a balanced and comprehensive portrayal of the internment of Japanese Americans during World War II. The site may be viewed in a Flash-based interactive format or in a more typical page-oriented layout. Through transcripts of oral interviews and narrative writing, A More Perfect Union transforms the abstract concept of unjust policy into the concrete reality of the harrowing impact on individuals." Evalutech

Napoleonic Period Collection. University of Washington Libraries Free (9 10 11 12 Adult)

http://content.lib.washington.edu/napoleonweb/index.html

"Napoleon Bonaparte never visited the part of North America that would later become Washington State, but he probably would have been intrigued by this online collection created by the good folks at the University of Washington Libraries Digital Collection project. This latest collection brings together 83 satirical drawings from the Napoleonic period, and there are a number of real gems amidst this visually arresting collection. As might be expected they all offer a variety of political commentary on various events during this period. The site includes information about the Napoleonic Era, complete with a nice timeline, and a comparison between the French and English drawings is included in this trove of visual ephemera. Finally, the site also contains a brief piece on the publishing scene of the late 18th and early 19th centuries, along with a very nice bibliography of additional resources." 2007 Internet Scout Project

NASA Explores. NASA Free (4 5 6 7 8 9 10 11 12)

http://www.nasaexplores.com/

This site contains articles discussing recent scientific research at NASA. Each article is available at reading

NASA Explores—*Continued*
levels appropriate for elementary school students, middle school students, and high school students and comes replete with teacher lesson plans and student worksheets.

National Library of Virtual Manipulatives for Interactive Mathematics. Utah State University with funding from the National Science Foundation Free (Professional)

http://nlvm.usu.edu/en/nav/vlibrary.html

This "Web site hosts a comprehensive collection of online, interactive mathematics activities (Java applets) that comprise a major curriculum resource for teachers and students of mathematics. A matrix provides access to the resources, categorizing them by grade level and by the general topics of Number & Operations, Algebra, Geometry, Measurement, and Data Analysis and Probability." Evalutech

National Museum of the American Indian Free (9 10 11 12)

http://www.nmai.si.edu/

This site offers a virtual tour of the museum's New York annex, in which images can be enlarged and rotated in three dimensions.

NationMaster.com. NationMaster.com; Luke Metcalfe, Manager/Developer Free (11 12 Adult)

http://www.nationmaster.com/

This website "is a vast compilation of data from such sources as the CIA World Factbook, United Nations, World Health Organization, World Bank, World Resources Institute, UNESCO, UNICEF and OECD." NationMaster website

NativeTech: Native American Technology and Art. Tara Prindle Free (9 10 11 12 Adult)

http://www.nativetech.org/

This website "is devoted to the arts, crafts, and technology of the eastern woodland Native Americans. The major topics addressed include beadwork, birds and feathers, pottery, clothing, metal work, plants and trees, porcupine quills, stonework and tools, and weaving. Each topic features multiple articles incorporating drawings and photographs into a textual explanation of the history and techniques involved. NativeTech also includes stories and poems by Native Americans, and an extensive array of recipes organized by region and main ingredients, and a collection of interactive Java-based games with Native American motifs, and information on Native American toys and games. The Virtual Woodland Tour provides a glimpse of the Native lifestyle in the 16th century. This Web site does not specifically target the K-12 audience, and the inclusion of some commercialism and news directed at an adult audience indicates that it should be used with teacher supervision." Evalutech

NetLibrary. OCLC Contact producer for pricing (5 6 7 8 9 10 11 12 Adult)

http://www.netlibrary.com

By subscription only. Tel. 1-800-898-6252

This database "offers an easy-to-use information retrieval system for accessing the full text of reference, scholarly, and professional books, as well as others. NetLibrary's ebooks are full-text electronic versions of published books that library patrons can search, borrow, read, and return over the Internet. Ebooks are available to users at terminals in the library or from their personal computers via the Internet. NetLibrary's ebook collection for schools (available through Baker & Taylor) is called TitleSelect. It contains approximately 122,700 titles with both professional and recreational titles. In addition to informational material, the program provides fiction for students as young as second grade. The American Heritage Dictionary of the English Language is embedded in all NetLibrary ebooks " SLJ

The **New** Book of Popular Science Online. Grolier Educational Starts at $398/yr.; minimum of two databases (5 6 7 8 9 10)

http://www.go.grolier.com

By subscription only. Tel. 888-326-6546

"Since 1924, the New Book of Popular Science has been one of the leading science reference sources for students; the online version provides some of the same features that users have come to expect from the print edition, but with 21st-century style. With over 400 articles, 600 photographs, and 660 illustrations, the New Book of Popular Science Online continues to provide accessible information on science, medicine, and technology for students in grades four through 12. One unique feature is that the database is available in two versions: one graphical, the other text-only. Students may switch instantly from one version to the other by clicking on the 'toggle' link. Schools can use the database with adaptive technology that requires text-only formats. For visually impaired students, the database is also ADA compliant." SLJ

The **New** York Times on the web Learning Network. The New York Times Company Free (7 8 9 10 11 12)

http://www.nytimes.com/learning/index.html

Users can search and access front page and news stories from the New York Times for current and past years. Sections for students, teachers and parents provide lesson plans, puzzles, quizzes and information.

North American mammals. The Smithsonian National Museum of Natural History Free (3 4 5 6 7 8 9 10 11 12)

http://www.mnh.si.edu/mna/

"The content of two major reference books, The Smithsonian Book of North American Mammals (Don E. Wilson and Sue Ruff) and Mammals of North America (Roland W. Kays and Don E. Wilson), are incorporated into this interactive Web site. . . . Each of the over 400 profiles on the site includes scientific information such as average weight and length, a drawing of the animal, a map with its distribution range, and an explanation of the animal's habits, alternative names, and other characteristics. Some profiles include Quicktime panoramas that can be manipulated by the viewer, and several have sound clips such as a coyote's howl. . . . An interactive map search allows users to select an area of North America and identify the mammals in that range. . . . Students will find North American Mammals to be a delight for browsing as well as a valuable tool for research." Evalutech

NoveList. EBSCO Publishing $750 for public library; $350 High School; $250 Middle and Elementary/yr. (9 10 11 12)

http://www.epnet.com

By subscription only. Tel. 800-653-2726

An online readers' advisory service designed to assist users in locating new fiction books based on books they

NoveList—_Continued_

have read or topics in which they are interested. Books can be located by title, genre, setting, time period, character name, theme, author, or by describing a book's plot. The database includes subject and key word access to more than 147,000 fiction titles. 36,000 subject headings for fiction are based on the Hennepin County Public Library's cataloging system. Included are over 500 theme-oriented books lists and over 350 award lists. There are also 100,000 full-text book reviews and descriptions from Library Journal, Publishers Weekly, Booklist, and School Library Journal, as well as links to author Home pages and other fiction-related Web sites.

"NoveList is a reader's paradise and a reference librarian's dream. . . . Public, academic, special-librarian's everywhere—just do yourselves a favor, and subscribe." Libr J

Nutrition.gov. National Agricultural Library, Food and Nutrition Information Center Free (9 10 11 12 Adult)

http://www.nutrition.gov

"Nutrition.gov provides access to nutritional information from numerous government databases. . . . The site answers numerous nutrition-related questions, provides helpful hints on planning nutrition meals, food recalls, and food safety. People trying to lose weight can find suggestions for weight control through exercise and proper nutrition." Ref & User Services Quarterly

OFFSTATS: Official Statistics on the Web. Rainer Wolcke, University of Auckland Library Free (11 12 Adult)

http://www.library.auckland.ac.nz/subjects/stats/offstats/

This is "a metasite that pulls together links to official statistics from countries, government agencies and intergovernmental organizations. . . . Statistics can be found by country, region, or topic." Ref & User Service Quarterly

Online Exhibits. Field Museum Free (3 4 5 6 7 8 9 10)

http://www.fmnh.org/exhibits/online_exhib.htm

Collection of exhibits shows such things as photographs of a 19th-century hunt for two lions who had eaten 128 workers building a Ugandan railway bridge, an animated, insect's-eye view of life underground, and images from the Field Museum's anthropology collections.

Online Reader. EBSCO Publishing Contact producer for pricing (4 5 6 7 8 9 10 11 12)

http://www.epnet.com/thisTopic.php?marketID=9&topicID=202

By subscription only. Tel. 800-653-2726

This database "is an interdisciplinary database of expository reading content designed to build students' reading comprehension skills across content areas. Its direct-assign format allows teachers to choose from high interest, nonfiction magazine articles and assign them to students according to individual reading needs. Lexile™ readability indicators are available for each article to facilitate selection. Each Online Reader article has a reading comprehension test that is automatically graded and question types are similar to those found on standardized tests. Online grade book and progress report features track student performance and achievement. Thematic teacher guides provide activities correlated to standards and explore expository writing and expression." EBSCO

website

"An outstanding, valuable resource. Teachers can use it to improve student comprehension of informational material, provide background information, improve student test-taking skills, and much more. The program can be an important tool to help students prepare for state-administered tests nationwide." MultiMedia Schools

Oxford Digital Reference Shelf. Oxford University Press $295/yr. for core collection subscription; $395/yr for premium collection subscription (11 12 Adult)

http://www.oup.com/online/digitalreference/

By subscription only. Tel. 800-624-0153

This database "provides not just access but ownership through a one-time-only purchase. In the Digital Reference Shelf, 17 scholarly reference titles are sold separately and include choices such as The Oxford Encyclopedia of American Literature, The Oxford Encyclopedia of Latinos and Latinas in the United States, The Encyclopedia of Evolution, and more. Each title is searchable as a stand-alone resource or can be cross-searched through the optional Oxford Reference Online Premium subscription." SLJ

Oxford Reference Online. Oxford University Press $395 per title (11 12 Adult)

http://www.oxfordreference.com/pub/views/home.html

By subscription only. Tel. 800-334-4249 x6484

This database "is a comprehensive resource that contains over 130 reference titles from science, medicine, social sciences, business, and the humanities. Among the titles in the core collection are the Oxford Companion to American Literature, the Oxford Companion to American Theatre, the Oxford Companion to English Literature, The Dictionary of Biology, and more. A complete list of the subjects with URLs, the titles with ISBNs and URLs, as well as a set of MARC records are available Two premium collection additions can be added: the Literature Collection, which includes 14 of the best Oxford Companion literature titles, and the Western Civilization collection, with six reference titles ranging from the Byzantium period to the Renaissance. Oxford Reference Online is updated at least three times a year with new titles, new editions, and additional features. " SLJ

Papal Encyclicals Online. Papal Encyclicals Online Free (11 12 Adult)

http://www.papalencyclicals.net

This website "provides papal encyclicals and other Catholic Church documents from 1226 to the present. It is currently the most complete website for these materials." Ref & User Services Quarterly

Peterson's Planner. Thomson Peterson Free (9 10 11 12 Adult)

http://www.petersons.com

This website "is a searchable guide for choosing schools, from K-12 to college and from graduate schools to continuing-education programs, even summer camps. Admission-test preparation and financial-aid planning are important elements available for both students and parents, along with information on study-abroad programs and help for international students." Ref & User Services Quarterly

Physlets. Wolfgang Christian (Davidson University) Free (Professional)

http://qbx6.ltu.edu/s_schneider/physlets/main/index.shtml

"Understanding how various concepts and processes in physics can be an exasperating experience for students beginning to study the field, so finding sites like this one can be quite a delight. These Java-based applets were developed at Davidson University by Wolfgang Christian, and they are a real delight. First-time visitors may wish to read through the introduction on using these physlets, and then move on to look through the different sections on the site. In total, there are over 100 physlets here, and they include those that illustrate (or animate) such processes as linear momentum, elastic linear collisions, and the movement of sound waves." 2007 Internet Scout Project

The PLANTS Database. U. S. Department of Agriculture Free (7 8 9 10 11 12 Adult)

http://plants.usda.gov/

A database of plant information by common name, scientific name and symbol. Also included are special topics such as: alternative crops, cultural significance, distribution update, and fact sheets. Tools include a crop nutrient tool, ecological site information system and plant materials.

Poe Museum. The Museum of Edgar Allan Poe Free (9 10 11 12)

http://www.poemuseum.org/

"The Museum of Edgar Allan Poe in Richmond, Virginia hosts this Web site providing basic information about the life and works of Edgar Allan Poe. The biographical information includes a timeline and family tree, along with a discussion of Poe's connection to Richmond. A selection of online readings includes five short stories and 'The Raven.' There is also an online quiz for students, and a collection of links to other Poe sites. An Educator Information Packet is available at a cost of $4 plus shipping and handling. Poe Museum is well suited for students looking for basic information about the author." Evalutech

POTUS: Presidents of the United States. Internet Public Library and School of Information University of Michigan Free (9 10 11 12)

http://www.ipl.org/div/potus/

"The POTUS site is part of the Internet Public Library and is a quick biography source for all the U.S. presidents. Individual links to the different presidents provide basic biographical information, election results, cabinet-member biographies, and notable events that occurred in each administration." Ref & User Services Quarterly

ProQuest AP Science. ProQuest $2,575/yr. (10 11 12)

http://www.proquestk12.com/productinfo/pq_ap_science.shtml

By subscription only. Tel. 800-521-0600 x3344

"If you're looking for higher-level science materials that provide the content and full-text resources for advanced placement students, ProQuest AP Science should meet those needs. With citations, abstracts, full-text articles, and full-page images, AP Science provides journal coverage from 1971 to the present. It contains more than 500 magazines and scholarly journals to support advanced placement and college-prep level science studies. Disciplines include earth, life, physical, medical, and ap-plied sciences. Coverage is nearly 100 percent full-text from professional and scholarly journals not generally found in high school collections. A deep backfile allows students to search for information relating to AP or college science coursework without going to a university library. In addition to the full-text and full-image content, students can create durable links for presentations." SLJ

ProQuest Historical Newspapers. ProQuest Contact publisher for pricing (7 8 9 10 11 12)

http://www.proquestk12.com/

By subscription only. Tel. 1-800-521-0600 x3344

ProQuest Historical Newspapers is a full-text, full-content, and graphics archive of the New York Times from the present back to the first issue in 1851. The database is indexed by subject and searchable by keyword. It is intended to support student research activities that require primary sources. It provides models for students of book reviews, letters, speeches, news writing, and editorials.

Readers' Guide Full Text, Mega Edition. H. W. Wilson Contact producer for pricing (7 8 9 10 11 12 Adult)

http://www.hwwilson.com/

By subscription only. Tel. 800-367-6770

This online version of the Readers' Guide to Periodical Literature features indexing and abstracting of nearly 400 popular magazines and journals (including *The New York Times*) going back to 1983, with full text for around 200 of those back to 1994. The full text is in both HTML files and PDF page images to capture graphics and pictures. The topics covered include art and antiques, business, computers, dance, drama, education, entertainment, fashion, food, health, history, literature, music, news and current events, photography, politics, sports, and travel, among others. Also available as a full-text-only database at a lower price.

RefDesk.com. RefDesk.com Free (7 8 9 10 11 12 Adult)

http://www.refdesk.com/

A searchable reference source for facts on the Internet. This index provides quick access to information using its search and browse features. Also provides free subscription service to "dailies" such as the Site of the Day and the Thought of the Day.

Riverdeep.net. Riverdeep, Inc. Contact producer for pricing (Professional)

http://www.riverdeep.net

By subscription only. Tel. 888-242-6747

A curriculum resource with a variety of programs, activities, and reference tools including Destination Math, Destination Success (for professional development), DK Anatomy, the Edmark Functional Word series, the Imagination Express series, Mighty Math, Oregon Trail, Reader Rabbit, Skill Detective (for elementary and middle grades) and Skill Navigator (for high school grades), and Where In The World Is Carmen Sandiego? A Living Library section offers searchable reference materials such as the *World Book International*, Time.com for Kids, *Bartlett's Quotations*, almanacs, dictionaries, etc.

Science Buddies. Kenneth Lafferty Hess Family Charitable Foundation Free (9 10 11 12)

http://www.sciencebuddies.org/

Science Buddies—*Continued*

"Science Buddies is a nonprofit organization that focuses on promoting student-produced science projects and on providing assistance to students working on them. The basics of science projects are covered in sections that explain the scientific method and strategies for selecting an appropriate topic. Extra resources include a PDF document about keeping a logbook, a tip section for engineering and programming projects, and information about the judging process and evaluation standards. An interactive topic selection wizard will assist the student in selecting and narrowing a science project concept. An online bulletin board system (Ask the Expert) provides assistance during the development of the project. There is also a collection of downloadable resources for teachers to use, with promotional brochures targeting specific states." Evalutech

Science Café. University of California, San Francisco Free (9 10 11 12)

http://www.ucsf.edu/sciencecafe/index.html

"More and more, research institutes and specialized centers of learning are turning to the world of podcasts, vodcasts, and other such multimedia devices to reach out to people from Peoria to Patagonia. The University of California, San Francisco recently opened up their own virtual science café, and this website represents an attempt to provide lively and interesting conversations about the 'story of science.' As a statement on their website remarks, 'From stem cells and what sells to great ideas, yeasty trends and budding controversies, we will be developing a menu for your mind.' They have delivered on this intriguing promise quite well, as visitors to the site will quickly discover. With close to a dozen talks online so far, visitors can learn about the mysteries of aging from researcher Cynthia Kenyon and how the world of basic science research differs in the United States as compared with Germany. One can imagine that this program could be used as a nice complement in science education courses for both high school and college." 2007 Internet Scout Project

Science Online. Facts on File $530/yr. (6 7 8 9 10 11 12)

http://www.factsonfile.com

By subscription only. Tel. 800-322-8755

"Science Online, just one of many specialized databases offered by Facts On File, represents a comprehensive, authoritative overview of science for students in grades six through 12. With diagrams, experiments, essays, biographies, and definitions organized by topic and subject area, as well as by the National Science Education Standards, Science Online provides users access to a wide range of specialized resources. Specifically, Science Online offers approximately 2,500 biographies of scientists throughout history; over 6,000 essays on current issues in science and technology; more than 3,300 diagrams; over 600 science experiments indexed by grade level and subject categories; a science timeline organized by historical period or topic; and over 29,000 definitions." SLJ

Science Reference Center. EBSCO $995/yr. (7 8 9 10 11 12)

http://www.ebscohost.com/
thisTopic.php?marketID=7&topicID=612

By subscription only. Tel. 800-653-2726

"The database contains more than 640 full text titles including science encyclopedias, reference books, and periodicals, as well as biographies, images, and PDF files of original journal articles. With content consisting primarily of scientist biographies, full-text reference titles, and science magazines from around the world, Science Reference Center enters the science database market with some of the most interesting resources. Subjects include biology, chemistry, earth and space science, environmental science, health and medicine, life science, physics, technology, and wildlife. Lexile reading levels are specified for all information. Publishers include Crabtree Publishing, Facts On File, Great Neck Publishing, Houghton Mifflin, Lerner Publishing Group, Mason Crest Publishers, Oxford University Press, Scholastic, Weekly Reader, and more." SLJ

Science Resource Center. Thomson Gale $2,500/yr. (9 10 11 12)

http://www.gale.com/SciRC/

By subscription only. Tel. 800-877-4253

"Thomson Gale's Science Resource Center offers students and teachers thousands of topic overviews, experiments, biographies, pictures, and illustrations, along with the latest scientific developments from over 270 full-text magazines and academic journals with PDF formats available, as well as links to selected science Web sites. The database also offers over 14,800 multimedia formats including pictures, illustrations, audio clips, and video clips. Science Resource Center covers curriculum-related science topics and offers teachers an easy-to-use tool to identify content directly correlated to state and national standards. In addition, the database reflects curriculum trends and focuses on key concepts taught in school classrooms such as earth science, science history, life science, physical science, science and technology, space, and much more. With about 58 reference titles, the Science Resource Center provides a healthy dose of digitized print content, including many Gale sources such as the Encyclopedia of Medicine, third edition; Science of Everyday Things; and World of Microbiology and Immunology. Also, the list of scholarly journals is comparable to the holdings of many small colleges." SLJ

SciLinks. National Science Teacher's Association Free (7 8 9 10 11 12)

http://www.scilinks.org/

This site is the product of a partnership between textbook publishers and the National Science Teachers Association. SciLinks provides access to web sites to expand student's understanding of concepts, science news to add context to learning, activities to expand learning opportunities, and experts to answers questions. A coding system in the margins of the textbooks is used to direct students to the correct teacher selected information on the SciLinks web site. Participating publishers include Harcourt, Holt, Rinehart, and Winston, Kendall/Hunt Publishing Company and WGBH.

Seaturtle.org Free (9 10 11 12)

http://www.seaturtle.org/

"Sea turtles are fascinating creatures, and they have a lovely online home here at the Seaturtle website. It is an ambitious site that contains everything from the latest scientific research on seaturtles to a blend of materials designed for the more casual visitor as well. From the homepage, visitors can read the Marine Turtle Newsletter, view recent news headlines about these animals, and also view updated announcements about job opportunities in the field of marine animal research and advocacy. The 'Tracking' section is a true gem, as visitors can look at an interactive map that shows the location of tagged sea turtles and also learn more about the status of sea turtles who are in marine hospitals. Additionally, the 'Multime-

Seaturtle.org—*Continued*
dia' area contains some fine podcasts that deal with sea turtle conservation efforts and rehabilitation." 2007 Internet Scout Project

SkyscraperPage. SkyscraperPage.com Free (9 10 11 12 Adult)

http://skyscraperpage.com/

"Beautiful architectural drawings of thousands of tall buildings around the globe, contributed by members of the SkyscraperPage Illustrators Association, can be found on this site. Users can browse by city, country, or continent, or can use the sophisticated search form." Ref & User Services Quarterly

Smithsonian Expeditions. Smithsonian Institution Free (5 6 7 8 9 10 11 12)

http://www.mnh.si.edu/anthro/laexped

Tells the story of the North and Latin American naturalists who collaborated on anthropological, botanical, and zoological expeditions to South America in the 19th and early 20th centuries.

SOS Math. Math Medics, L.L.C. Free (4 5 6 7 8 9 10 11 12)

http://www.sosmath.com/index.html

Provides tutorials and practice exams on elementary to college-level mathematics. Also available in a CD-ROM version for $19.95.

Star Journey. National Geographic Free (4 5 6 7 8 9 10)

http://www.nationalgeographic.com/features/97/stars

This site provides a star chart with embedded links to thirty-nine Hubble space telescope photographs of the corresponding heavenly bodies. Also includes articles on the Hubble space telescope and on constellations.

State Geography. ABC-CLIO $499/yr. (4 5 6 7 8 9 10 11 12)

http://www.abc-clio.com/products/overview.aspx?productid=109715

By subscription only. Tel. 800-368-6868

Covers the people, places, events, trends, statistics, news, attractions, politics, culture, environment, government, and history of all 50 states in the U.S. The site also includes biographies and primary source documents. Searchable by key word and advanced search options that allow filtering by categories. Teachers can customize the site by setting up classes and posting information such as announcements, syllabi, discussion questions, handouts, and tests. The Home page has frequently updated news articles and feature stories that are linked to related articles in the database. Includes the *Merriam Webster Dictionary*.

"The site's entries are authoritative and well linked. This online reference would be a boon to busy teachers who want to use the Internet in the instruction of geography. Highly recommended." Book Report

Student Research Center. EBSCO Publishing Contact producer for pricing (9 10 11 12)

http://www.epnet.com/thisTopic.php?marketID=5&topicID=13

By subscription only. Tel. 800-653-2726

A subscription product designed to search across 18 EBSCO databases appropriate for secondary school students' research needs.

Students.gov. U.S. Department of Education Free (9 10 11 12)

http://www.students.gov/

Provides students access to information and services of the U.S. Government for planning their education and career development. The site was developed with the cooperation of federal agencies, students, and the higher education community.

SunSite. Regents of the University of California Free (9 10 11 12 Adult)

http://sunsite.berkeley.edu/

Provides links to digital library catalogs and indexes and collections of text and images on information on the Internet utilizing a Boolean search function.

TeachingBooks. Nick Glass $325/yr. for one school (Professional)

http://www.teachingbooks.net/

"TeachingBooks . . . allows educators, students, librarians, and parents not only to learn more about more than 6,500 titles for pre-school through high school but also to become enveloped and inspired by the 'behind the scenes' activities, thoughts, and ideas used by authors and illustrators to develop their works." SLJ

testGEAR. Bridges Contact producer for pricing (5 6 7 8 9 10 11 12)

http://www.testu.com/frameset.asp

By subscription only. Tel. 800-281-1168

This is a test preparation program that provides interactive instruction in English-Language Arts, mathmatics, social studies and science topics tested on the exit-level examination. It supplies lessons on test-taking strategies, and offers practice tests in a variety of formats.

Thoreau Reader: The Works of Henry D. Thoreau, 1817-1862. Richard Lenat, Iowa State University, and the Thoreau Society Free (9 10 11 12)

http://thoreau.eserver.org/

"Richard Lenat has assembled an impressive collection of resources for The Thoreau Reader and organized them in a manner consistent with Thoreau's tenet, 'Simplify, simplify.' The texts of Walden, The Maine Woods, and Cape Cod are presented in their entirety, along with the essays Civil Disobedience, Life Without Principle, Slavery in Massachusetts, and Walking. The texts are annotated with hyperlinked footnotes that explain some of the more esoteric references, and a search page for the 1903 version of Webster's Unabridged Dictionary (from the University of Chicago's ARTfl Project Web site) is included to provide assistance with archaic words. The Thoreau Reader also includes reproductions of early photographs and items such as Thoreau's 1846 survey map of Walden Pond. Numerous teaching resources, lesson ideas, and miscellaneous documents add to the site's usefulness in the classroom, and the fact that the texts are searchable enhances their usefulness for those doing research and writing papers. Lenat's tips for reading online texts are particularly helpful in ensuring that students fully appreciate their visits to The Thoreau Reader." Evalutech

Timelines of Art History. Metropolitan Museum of Art Free (9 10 11 12 Adult)

http://www.metmuseum.org/toah/splash.htm

Timelines of Art History—*Continued*

This website "is a chronological, geographical, and thematic exploration of the history of art from around the world, as illustrated especially by the Metropolitan Museum of Art's collection." Timeline of Art History website

Treehouses on the Tree of Life. Tree of Life Project Free (5 6 7 8 9 10)

http://tolweb.org/tree/home.pages/treehouses.html

The Tree of Life is a web project developed by biologists around the world that is composed of more than 2,000 web pages and provides information about phylogeny and biodiversity. Treehouses is the section of the Tree of Life aimed at K-16 learners and teachers. The site features "treehouses" or sections including investigations (science reports and experiments with photos, diagrams, and videos), stories, games, and teacher resources.

U.S. Capitol Virtual Tour. United States Senate Free (9 10 11 12)

http://www.senate.gov/vtour/

"The U.S. Senate Virtual Tour uses Java technology to create an interactive experience that reveals the majesty and history of the U.S. Capitol building in Washington, D.C. The viewer can control a panoramic view of selected rooms in the building using the mouse to rotate the panorama and the keyboard to zoom in and out on various features." Evalutech

U.S. Census Bureau. U.S. Census Bureau Free (9 10 11 12 Adult)

http://www.census.gov

Complete U.S. data listed in a variety of ways (such as by region, county, city, etc.). Also includes downloadable software tools to use in accessing data tables. The American FactFinder feature provides popular tables and maps for the nation, states, counties, cities, towns, and Indian reservations. A simple search is available for the complete site.

U.S. Naval Observatory Astronomical Applications: Data Services. United States Naval Observatory Astronomical Applications Department Free (9 10 11 12 Adult)

http://aa.usno.navy.mil/data/

"This comprehensive and practical Web resource provides a myriad of information on all types of astronomical phenomena. Data covered includes moon phases, sun and moon positions, eclipses, date of Easter, the Earth's seasons, and Julian calendar date conversion, as well as information on sunrise, sunset, moonrise, moonset, and twilight times." Ref & User Services Quarterly

Ultra Online Package for High Schools. EBSCO Contact producer for pricing (9 10 11 12)

http://www.epnet.com/
thisTopic.php?marketID=7&topicID=155

By subscription only. Tel. 800-623-2726

Ultra Online Package for High schools includes ERIC, Health Source: Consumer Edition, MAS Ultra—School Edition, Newspaper Source, Professional Development Collection, and TOPICsearch. ERIC is the Education Resource Information Center, which covers education resources and literature. Health Source: Consumer Edition provides access to over 130 full-text consumer health magazines as well as pamphlets and health reference books. Newspaper Source provides access to 28 complete full-text national newspapers as well as selected full-text

for over 260 regional newspapers and news transcripts from television and radio. Professional Development Collection includes full-text for 520 high-quality education journals and 722 indexed and abstracted education and library science journals. The TOPICsearch database explores social, political,a nd economic issues, scientific discoveries and other popular current event topics.

unitedstreaming. Discovery Education Starting at $1,495/yr. for K-8 schools and $1,995/yr. for high schools (Professional)

http://www.unitedstreaming.com

By subscription only. Tel. 800-323-9084

Unitedstreaming.com is an online library of over 50,000 video clips aligned to state standards for grades K-12. The library is searchable by keyword, subject area, grade level, and curriculum strand. Video clips are supported by materials for teachers and students, and can be streamed or downloaded as PDF files, printed, and distributed.

Urban Legends Reference Pages. Barbara and David P. Mikkelson Free (11 12 Adult)

http://www.snopes.com

This website contains banner advertising. "This searchable archive and repository offers insight to urban legends, 'common fallacies, misinformation, old wives' tales, strange news stories, rumors, celebrity gossip, and similar items.'" Ref & User Services Quarterly

USA.gov. Office of Citizen Services and Communications, U.S. General Services Administration Free (7 8 9 10 11 12 Adult)

http://www.usa.gov/

The official U.S. Government gateway for citizens, business and government employees. Provides one-click access to federal, state, local, tribal, and international government information.

The USGenWeb Project. The USGenWeb Project Free (7 8 9 10 11 12 Adult)

http://usgenweb.org/

Provides links to all state and county web sites for genealogical research with resources for postings of unknown county queries, family reunion bulletin boards, state histories, and maps showing the changing county boundaries. Special projects include the collection of African American historical records, the reuniting of families with lost photos and tombstone transcription.

Weather Scope: An Investigative Study of Weather and Climate. Center for Innovation in Engineering and Science Education at Stevens Institute of Technology Free (6 7 8 9 10 11 12)

http://www.k12science.org/curriculum/
weatherproj2/en/

"Weather Scope immerses students in a hands-on, data-driven approach to the study of weather and climate. Based on National science and math standards, the program begins by having students construct their own weather instruments, including a thermometer, wind vane, anemometer, rain gauge, and barometer. Using these devices and inexpensive commercial equipment, the participants then engage in a project involving the use of their locally-gathered information and real-time data collected from the Internet to study weather basics, change, and forecasting." Evalutech

Webopedia. INT Media Group, Inc. Free (7 8 9 10 11 12 Adult)

http://www.webopedia.com/

An online dictionary and search engine for computer and Internet technology information. Features include: term of the day, top 15 terms and information, job listings, and quick reference section for information on everything technological. Contains banner advertising.

Wikipedia. Nupedia.com Free (11 12 Adult)

http://en.wikipedia.org/

"Wikipedia is a free, Web-based encyclopedia edited by its readers. Each of its more than 1 million articles may be edited, corrected, or updated by anyone in the world." Ref & User Services Quarterly

Wise: Web-based inquiry science environment. Wise, UC Berkeley Free (Professional)

http://wise.berkeley.edu/

This web-based science learning environment supported by the National Science Foundation helps students learn about and respond to scientific controversies through designing, debating and critiquing solutions. Topics include hybrid cars, static electricity, and global warming.

The **Wordsmyth** Educational Dictionary-Thesaurus (WEDT). Wordsmyth Collaboratory Free (7 8 9 10 11 12)

http://www.wordsmyth.net/

Users can search this online American English dictionary (with an integrated thesaurus of over 50,000 headwords) and hyperlinked synonyms by entering a word on the homepage. Choose from three levels of search: exact, broad, and spelled-like. Entry includes syllabication, part of speech, pronunciation, definitions, browse words alphabetically around entry, and see other entries that contain entry. Also included are discussion area, word of the week, wordlink and thinktank (key discussions on popular topics) features. Includes Glossary Maker, Crossword Puzzle Helper, Quiz Builder, and Anagram Solver.

World Atlas. Facts on File Contact producer for pricing (6 7 8 9 10 11 12)

http://www.factsonfile.com/

By subscription only. Tel. 800-322-8755

An interactive database of maps and information related to geographic regions and countries of the world, as well as states and Canadian provinces. The site provides full-color political, elevation, and outline maps of each geographic area as well as multiple maps depicting information ranging from political and economic data to energy and natural resources. "Fact Files" have information on countries such as vital statistics, government, history, and chronologies. Links to related Web sites are included.

"Allows for easy access to current information in lieu of hard copy versions that become outdated quickly. This is a worthwhile purchase for classroom and media center use for research." Evalutech

World Book Online. World Book Publishing Contact producer for pricing (4 5 6 7 8 9 10 11 12)

http://www.worldbookonline.com

By subscription only. Tel. 800-975-3250

General reference encyclopedia with all articles from the print version of World Book Encyclopedia along with multimedia elements and updated articles and information (750 new articles, 550 new Back in Time articles, 60 special reports, and 4500 revised articles were added in a single year). This online reference also has links to full text articles in over 250 magazines and newspapers as well as links to more than 10,000 editor approved Web sites. Back in Time articles, taken from World Book Yearbooks dating to 1922, provide coverage of people and events from the perspective of the times. Includes a fully integrated dictionary.

"This flexible, easy-to-use, online resource is an excellent tool for student research. By integrating historical background and current information, it makes history more relevant to events of the day. Highly recommended." Book Report

The **World** Flag Database. The World Flag Database and Graham Bartram Free (7 8 9 10 11 12)

http://www.flags.net/

A comprehensive database of information and graphics of flags around the world. Listed by country, information is given for capital city and main city as well as specific flag information and graphics for national flag, civil ensign, naval ensign, and government ensign. Searchable using the quick buttons on the left side of the home page.

World Geography. ABC-CLIO Contact producer for pricing (5 6 7 8 9 10 11 12)

http://www.abc-clio.com/products/overview.aspx?productid=109713

By subscription only. Tel. 800-368-6868

Provides information for a catalog of countries and regions. Each country page provides an overview of the nation, historical and governmental information, facts and figures, important events, biographies, primary source documents, lists of organizations, and maps. Articles are cross-referenced through hyperlinks. In addition to key word searches, there are advanced search options to limit by categories of information. Teachers can customize the site by adding discussion questions, handouts, tests, etc. The site also features daily news articles and feature stories with links to related articles. Includes the *Merriam-Webster Collegiate Dictionary* and *Merriam-Webster's Collegiate Thesaurus*.

"An excellent reference tool . . . that also can be used as a daily organizational resource for students logging on to find their assignments for the day." Evalutech

World History Collection. EBSCO Contact producer for pricing (9 10 11 12)

http://www.epnet.com/thisTopic.php?marketID=7&topicID=150

By subscription only. Tel. 800-653-2726

This database "offers a global look at history with content from Africa, Asia, North and South America, Europe and the Middle East. World History Collection contains cover-to-cover full text for 150 titles, including many peer-reviewed journals. Full text dates as far back as 1964. These hand-selected information sources cover a . . . range of historical topics including anthropology, art, culture, economics, government, heritage, military, politics, regional issues, and more. In addition to the full text, indexing and abstracts are provided for all journals in the collection." EBSCO website

The **Writers** Almanac. Minnesota Public Radio Free (7 8 9 10 11 12 Adult)

http://almanac.mpr.org/

The Writers Almanac—*Continued*

Provides archival access to audio and text files from past programs of The Writers Almanac, a daily program of poetry and history hosted by Garrison Keillor, on National Public Radio stations. Information includes author background and text of reading selections as well as program schedule.

yourDictionary.com. yourDictionary.com Free (7 8 9 10 11 12 Adult)

http://www.yourdictionary.com

Provides a portal for language and language-related products and services on the web including 2500 dictionaries with more than 300 languages. All dictionaries on the site are searchable via a Google powered search engine and include language, specialty, translation, synonym, acronym, rhyming and more. There is a translation feature and gameroom. Specialty areas include access to endangered languages and research.

AUTHOR, TITLE, SUBJECT, AND ANALYTICAL INDEX

This index to the books in the Classified Collection includes author, title, subject, and analytical entries; added entries for publishers' series, for joint authors, and for editors of works entered under title; and name and subject cross references; all arranged in one alphabet. The number or symbol in bold face type at the end of each entry refers to the Dewey Decimal Classification or to the Fiction or Story Collection Section where the book will be found. Works classed in 92 will be found under the heading for the person written about. For further information about this index and for examples of entries, see Directions for Use of the Collection.

1/3, 1/3, 1/3. Brautigan, R.
   In American short story masterpieces   **S C**
2BR02B. Vonnegut, K.
   In Vonnegut, K. Bagombo snuff box: uncollected short fiction p259-67   **S C**
2Pac *See* Shakur, Tupac
3-D displays for libraries, schools and media centers. Evans, E. G.   **027.62**
4 plays. Inge, W.   **812**
#8. Ritchie, J.
   In Alfred Hitchcock's mystery magazine presents fifty years of crime and suspense   **S C**
The **9/11** report. Jacobson, S.   **973.931**
The **9/11** Commission report. National Commission on Terrorist Attacks Upon the United States   **973.931**
10 things employers want you to learn in college. Coplin, W. D.   **378**
10^{16} to 1. Kelly, J. P.
   In Best of the best: 20 years of the Year's best science fiction   **S C**
10th grade. Weisberg, J.   **Fic**
The **13** clocks. Thurber, J.
   In Thurber, J. Writings and drawings   **818**
13 little blue envelopes. Johnson, M.   **Fic**
13 seconds. Caputo, P.   **973.924**
15 short plays. McNally, T.   **812**
19 varieties of gazelle. Nye, N. S.   **811**
20th-century perspectives [series]
   Allan, T. The causes of World War I   **940.3**
21st century science [series]
   Major systems of the body   **612**
   The Structure of the body   **611**
24 favorite one-act plays   **808.82**
27 wagons full of cotton. Williams, T.
   In 24 favorite one-act plays p94-116   **808.82**
50% chance of lightning. Salat, C.
   In Am I blue?; coming out from the silence p227-43   **S C**

56-0. Boyle, T. C.
   In Boyle, T. C. The Human Fly and other stories   **S C**
100 decisive battles. Davis, P. K.   **904**
100 essential modern poems   **821.008**
100 great monologues from the neo-classical theatre   **808.82**
100 great monologues from the Renaissance theatre   **822.008**
100 great poems of the twentieth century   **821.008**
The **100** greatest baseball players of the 20th century ranked. McGuire, M.   **796.357**
100 key documents in American democracy   **973**
100 more popular young adult authors. Drew, B. A.   **810.9**
The **100** most popular young adult authors. Drew, B. A.   **810.9**
100 myths about the Middle East. Halliday, F.   **956**
100 ready-to-use pathfinders for the Web. Wilson, A. P.   **001.4**
100 research topic guides for students. Borne, B. W.   **025.5**
100 world-class thin books. See Bodart, J. R. The world's best thin books   **028.1**
100 years of the World Series. Enders, E.   **796.357**
The **101** best graphic novels. Weiner, S.   **016.7**
101 questions about blood and circulation, with answers straight from the heart. Brynie, F. H.   **612.1**
101 questions about reproduction. Brynie, F. H.   **612.6**
101 questions about sex and sexuality—. Brynie, F. H.   **613.9**
101 questions about sleep and dreams that kept you awake nights . . . until now. Brynie, F. H.   **612.8**
101 questions about your immune system you felt defenseless to answer . . . until now. Brynie, F. H.   **616.07**

885

101+ teen programs that work. Honnold, R.
027.62

102 minutes. Dwyer, J.   974.7

109 East Palace. Conant, J.   623.4

112 acting games. Levy, G.   792

145th Street. Myers, W. D.   S C

150 years of popular musical theatre. Lamb, A.
792.6

180 more   811.008

222 monologues, 2 minutes & under from literature. See The Ultimate audition book
808.82

500 great books by women. Bauermeister, E.
016.3054

500 great books for teens. Silvey, A.   028.5

501 recipes for a low-carb life. Gillespie, G. R.
613.2

911: the book of help   810.8

The 1000s   940.1

1001 ideas for science projects. Brisk, M. A.
507.8

1001 legal words you need to know. Feinman, J.
M.   340

1066: the year of the conquest. Howarth, D. A.
942.02

1089 and all that. Acheson, D. J.   510

The 1100s   909

The 1200s   909

The 1300s   909

1408. King, S.
In King, S. Everything's eventual: 14 dark
tales   S C

1491. Mann, C. C.   970.01

1800-1820: the nineteenth century   909.81

1820-1840: the nineteenth century   909.81

1840-1860: the nineteenth century   909.81

1860-1880: the nineteenth century   909.81

1880-1900: the nineteenth century   909.81

1900-1920: the twentieth century   909.82

1920-1940: the twentieth century   909.82

1940-1960: the twentieth century   909.82

The 1950s. Schwartz, R. A.   973.921

1960-1980: the twentieth century   909.82

The 1960s. Hurley, J. A.   973.92

The 1960s. Maga, T. P.   973.92

The 1960s cultural revolution. McWilliams, J. C.
973.92

1980-2000: the twentieth century   909.82

The 1980s. Woodger, E.   973.92

The 1990s. Schwartz, R. A.   973.92

2001: a space odyssey. Clarke, A. C.   Fic

2004-05: the naming of names. Bradbury, R.
In Bradbury, R. Bradbury stories; 100 of his
most celebrated tales   S C

2064, or thereabouts. Bunch, D. R.
In The Norton book of science fiction; North
American science fiction, 1960-1990
p93-97   S C

5,000 miles to freedom. Fradin, J. B.   326

The $30,000 bequest. Twain, M.
In Twain, M. The complete short stories of
Mark Twain; now collected for the first
time   S C

The £1,000,000 bank-note. Twain, M.
In Twain, M. The complete short stories of
Mark Twain; now collected for the first
time   S C

A

A & P. Updike, J.
In Updike, J. Pigeon feathers, and other stories p187-96   S C

A to Z of African Americans [series]
Aaseng, N. African-American athletes
920.003
Bader, P. African-American writers   920.003
Reef, C. African Americans in the military
920.003

A to Z of earth scientists. Gates, A. E.
920.003

A to Z of mathematicians. McElroy, T.
920.003

A to Z of women in science and math. Yount, L.
920.003

A to Z of women in world history. Kuhlman, E.
A.   920.003

The A.B.C. murders. Christie, A.   Fic

A-bomb victims *See* Atomic bomb victims

A.I.D.S. (Disease) *See* AIDS (Disease)

A. Philip Randolph and the African American labor movement. Miller, C. C.   92

AACR *See* Anglo-American cataloguing rules

Aamidor, Abraham
(ed) Real sports reporting. See Real sports reporting   070.4

Aaron, Hank, 1934-
About
Stanton, T. Hank Aaron and the home run that
changed America   92

Aaron, Henry *See* Aaron, Hank, 1934-

Aaseng, Nathan, 1953-
African-American athletes   920.003
Athletes   920
Black inventors   920
The impeachment of Bill Clinton   973.929
Navajo code talkers   940.54

Abarat. Barker, C.   Fic

Abbotson, Susan C. W., 1961-
Critical companion to Arthur Miller   812.009
Student companion to Arthur Miller   812.009

Abbott, Berenice, 1898-1991
About
Sullivan, G. Berenice Abbott, photographer
92

Abbreviations
Dictionaries
The Barnhart abbreviations dictionary   421.03

ABC-CLIO's history of science series
Lawson, R. M. Science in the ancient world
509

The **Actor's** book of movie monologues **791.43**

The **Actor's** book of scenes from new plays **808.82**

Actresses *See* Actors

Acts of faith. McBain, L.
In Young warriors; stories of strength **S C**

Aczel, Amir D.
The riddle of the compass **912**

Ad astra. Faulkner, W.
In Faulkner, W. Collected stories of William Faulkner p407-29 **S C**

Adair, Robert Kemp
The physics of baseball **796.357**

Adam (Biblical figure)
Fiction
Aidinoff, E. V. The garden **Fic**

Adam and Eve. Kazakov, Y. P.
In The portable twentieth-century Russian reader **891.7**

Adamec, Christine A., 1949-
(jt. auth) Minocha, A. The encyclopedia of the digestive system and digestive disorders **616.3**

Adams, Amy
The muscular system **612.7**

Adams, Ansel, 1902-1984
About
Gherman, B. Ansel Adams **92**

Adams, Douglas, 1952-2001
The hitchhiker's guide to the galaxy **Fic**
See/See also pages in the following book(s):
Reid, S. E. Presenting young adult science fiction **813.009**

Adams, Harriet Stratemeyer *See* Keene, Carolyn

Adams, J. Q.
(jt. auth) Welsch, J. R. Multicultural films **791.43**

Adams, John
(jt. auth) Dixon, D. The future is wild **576.8**

Adams, John, 1735-1826
See/See also pages in the following book(s):
Ellis, J. J. Founding brothers **973.4**

Adams, John Quincy, 1767-1848
See/See also pages in the following book(s):
Kennedy, J. F. Profiles in courage **920**
Fiction
Pesci, D. Amistad **Fic**

Adams, Richard, 1920-
Watership Down **Fic**

Adams, Samuel, 1722-1803
About
Irvin, B. Samuel Adams **92**

Adamson, Lynda G.
Literature connections to American history, 7-12 **016.973**
Literature connections to world history, 7-12 **016.9**
Notable women in world history **920.003**
(jt. auth) Dickinson, A. T. American historical fiction **016.8**

Adaptation (Biology)
Gross, M. Life on the edge **578.4**

Adaptations, Film *See* Film adaptations

Adaptations: from short story to big screen **S C**

ADD *See* Attention deficit disorder

Addams, Jane, 1860-1935
About
Fradin, J. B. Jane Addams **92**

Addiction: opposing viewpoints **362.29**

Addiction to alcohol *See* Alcoholism

Addiction to work *See* Workaholism

Addicts, Drug *See* Drug addicts

Addresses *See* Speeches

Addy, Esi Sutherland- *See* Sutherland-Addy, Esi

Adelman, Bob
(jt. auth) Johnson, C. R. King: the photobiography of Martin Luther King, Jr. **92**

Adelson-Goldstein, Jayme
(jt. auth) Shapiro, N. The Oxford picture dictionary, English-Korean **495.7**

Adichie, Chimamanda Ngozi, 1977-
Purple hibiscus **Fic**

Adirondack Mountains (N.Y.)
Fiction
McGhee, A. All rivers flow to the sea **Fic**

Adkins, Lesley
Dictionary of Roman religion **292**
Handbook to life in ancient Greece **938**
Handbook to life in ancient Rome **937**

Adkins, Roy
(jt. auth) Adkins, L. Dictionary of Roman religion **292**
(jt. auth) Adkins, L. Handbook to life in ancient Greece **938**
(jt. auth) Adkins, L. Handbook to life in ancient Rome **937**

Adler, C. S. (Carole S.), 1932-
Michael's little sister
In Am I blue?; coming out from the silence p147-62 **S C**

Adler, Carole S. *See* Adler, C. S. (Carole S.), 1932-

Adler, David A., 1947-
We remember the Holocaust **940.53**

Adler, Kraig
(ed) Firefly encyclopedia of reptiles and amphibians. See Firefly encyclopedia of reptiles and amphibians **597.9**

Adler, Mortimer J., 1902-2001
Aristotle for everybody **185**
How to think about the great ideas **080**
Six great ideas **111**
(ed) Great treasury of Western thought. See Great treasury of Western thought **080**

Adler, Robert E., 1946-
Medical firsts **610.9**
Science firsts: from the creation of science to the science of creation **509**

Adler, Stephen J.
(ed) Women's letters. See Women's letters
305.4

Adlington, L. J., 1970-
The diary of Pelly D   **Fic**

Administering the school library media center.
Morris, B. J.   **027.8**

Administration of criminal justice
See also Corrections
Alternatives to prisons   **364**
Banks, C. Punishment in America   **364.6**
Berger, L. The grand jury   **345**
Encyclopedia of crime and punishment
    364.03
Famous American crimes and trials   **364**
Hanes, R. C. Crime and punishment in America,
Almanac   **364**
Hanes, R. C. Crime and punishment in America,
Biographies   **920**
Hanes, S. M. Crime and punishment in America, Primary sources   **364**
Should juveniles be tried as adults?   **345**

Administration of justice
Jacobs, T. A. They broke the law, you be the judge   **345**

Admirals
Brager, B. L. John Paul Jones   **92**
Czisnik, M. Horatio Nelson   **92**

Admissions applications *See* College applications

Adoff, Arnold, 1935-
(ed) I am the darker brother. See I am the darker brother   **811.008**

Adoff, Jaime
The god of St. James and Vine
In Twice told; original stories inspired by original art   **S C**
Names will never hurt me   **Fic**

Adolescence
Feig, P. Kick me   **305.23**
Jukes, M. It's a girl thing   **305.23**
See/See also pages in the following book(s):
Espeland, P. The gifted kids' survival guide p47-64   **155.5**
Fiction
Banks, R. Rule of the bone   **Fic**
Berg, E. Joy school   **Fic**
White, E. A boy's own story   **Fic**

Adolescent fathers *See* Teenage fathers

Adolescent mothers *See* Teenage mothers

Adolescent pregnancy *See* Teenage pregnancy

Adolescent psychology
Fitzgerald, H. The grieving teen   **155.9**

Adolescents *See* Teenagers

Adolf Hitler [biographical essays]   **92**

Adolf Hitler and Nazi Germany. Rice, E.   **92**

Adolph, José B., 1933-
The falsifier
In Cosmos latinos; an anthology of science fiction from Latin America and Spain
    S C

Adoptees
Miró, A. Daughter of the Ganges   **92**

Adoption
See also Adoptees
Adoption   **362.7**
Adoption: opposing viewpoints   **362.7**
Lanchon, A. All about adoption   **649**
Tucker, N. Love in the driest season   **362.7**
Fiction
Alvarez, J. Finding miracles   **Fic**
Bauer, C. Harley, like a person   **Fic**
Kearney, M. The secret of me   **Fic**
Pennebaker, R. Don't think twice   **Fic**
Reinhardt, D. A brief chapter in my impossible life   **Fic**

Adoption, Interracial *See* Interracial adoption

Adoption   **362.7**

Adoption: opposing viewpoints   **362.7**

Adorno, Juan Nepomuceno, 1807-1880
The distant future
In Cosmos latinos; an anthology of science fiction from Latin America and Spain
    S C

Adult adoptees *See* Adoptees

Advanced backpacking. Berger, K.   **796.51**

Adventure and adventurers
Stark, P. Last breath   **616**
Fiction
See Adventure fiction

Adventure divas (Television program)
Morris, H. Adventure divas   **791.45**

Adventure fiction
See also Science fiction; Sea stories
Allende, I. Daughter of fortune   **Fic**
Allende, I. Zorro   **Fic**
Benchley, P. Jaws   **Fic**
Butler, O. E. Parable of the sower   **Fic**
Cole, S. Thieves like us   **Fic**
Cooper, J. F. The Leatherstocking tales   **Fic**
Forester, C. S. Beat to quarters   **Fic**
Grey, Z. Riders of the purple sage   **Fic**
Harris, R. Pompeii   **Fic**
Mowll, J. Operation Red Jericho   **Fic**
Parkhurst, C. Lost and found   **Fic**
Poe, E. A. Narrative of A. Gordon Pym
In Poe, E. A. The collected tales and poems of Edgar Allan Poe   **818**
Rees, C. Pirates!   **Fic**
Tullson, D. Red Sea   **Fic**
Turner, M. W. The thief   **Fic**
Bibliography
Gannon, M. B. Blood, bedlam, bullets, and badguys   **016.8**

Adventure graphic novels
Daly, P. Athena Voltaire   **741.5**
Kibuishi, K. Daisy Kutter   **741.5**
Kubo, T. Bleach, Vol. 1   **741.5**
Miyuki, T. Musashi #9, Vol. 1   **741.5**
Sakai, S. Usagi Yojimbo, book one   **741.5**

Adventure heroes. Rovin, J.   **700**

The **adventure** of Black Peter. Doyle, Sir A. C.
In Doyle, Sir A. C. The complete Sherlock Holmes   **S C**

The **adventure** of Charles Augustus Milverton.
Doyle, Sir A. C.
In Doyle, Sir A. C. The complete Sherlock
Holmes   **S C**

The **adventure** of Shoscombe Old Place. Doyle,
Sir A. C.
In Doyle, Sir A. C. The complete Sherlock
Holmes   **S C**

The **adventure** of the Abbey Grange. Doyle, Sir
A. C.
In Doyle, Sir A. C. The complete Sherlock
Holmes   **S C**

The **adventure** of the Beryl Coronet. Doyle, Sir
A. C.
In Doyle, Sir A. C. The complete Sherlock
Holmes   **S C**

The **adventure** of the blanched soldier. Doyle, Sir
A. C.
In Doyle, Sir A. C. The complete Sherlock
Holmes   **S C**

The **adventure** of the Blue Carbuncle. Doyle, Sir
A. C.
In Doyle, Sir A. C. The complete Sherlock
Holmes   **S C**

The **adventure** of the Bruce-Partington plans.
Doyle, Sir A. C.
In Doyle, Sir A. C. The complete Sherlock
Holmes   **S C**

The **adventure** of the cardboard box. Doyle, Sir
A. C.
In Doyle, Sir A. C. The complete Sherlock
Holmes   **S C**

The **adventure** of the copper beeches. Doyle, Sir
A. C.
In Doyle, Sir A. C. The complete Sherlock
Holmes   **S C**

The **adventure** of the creeping man. Doyle, Sir A.
C.
In Doyle, Sir A. C. The complete Sherlock
Holmes   **S C**

The **adventure** of the dancing men. Doyle, Sir A.
C.
In Doyle, Sir A. C. The complete Sherlock
Holmes   **S C**

The **adventure** of the devil's foot. Doyle, Sir A.
C.
In Doyle, Sir A. C. The complete Sherlock
Holmes   **S C**

The **adventure** of the dying detective. Doyle, Sir
A. C.
In Doyle, Sir A. C. The complete Sherlock
Holmes   **S C**

The **adventure** of the empty house. Doyle, Sir A.
C.
In Doyle, Sir A. C. The complete Sherlock
Holmes   **S C**

The **adventure** of the engineer's thumb. Doyle,
Sir A. C.
In Doyle, Sir A. C. The complete Sherlock
Holmes   **S C**

The **adventure** of the golden pince-nez. Doyle, Sir
A. C.
In Doyle, Sir A. C. The complete Sherlock
Holmes   **S C**

The **adventure** of the illustrious client. Doyle, Sir
A. C.
In Doyle, Sir A. C. The complete Sherlock
Holmes   **S C**

The **adventure** of the lion's mane. Doyle, Sir A.
C.
In Doyle, Sir A. C. The complete Sherlock
Holmes   **S C**

The **adventure** of the Mazarin stone. Doyle, Sir
A. C.
In Doyle, Sir A. C. The complete Sherlock
Holmes   **S C**

The **adventure** of the missing three-quarter.
Doyle, Sir A. C.
In Doyle, Sir A. C. The complete Sherlock
Holmes   **S C**

The **adventure** of the noble bachelor. Doyle, Sir
A. C.
In Doyle, Sir A. C. The complete Sherlock
Holmes   **S C**

The **adventure** of the Norwood builder. Doyle, Sir
A. C.
In Doyle, Sir A. C. The complete Sherlock
Holmes   **S C**

The **adventure** of the President's half disme.
Queen, E.
In The Best American mystery stories of the
century p344-62   **S C**

The **adventure** of the priory school. Doyle, Sir A.
C.
In Doyle, Sir A. C. The complete Sherlock
Holmes   **S C**

The **adventure** of the red circle. Doyle, Sir A. C.
In Doyle, Sir A. C. The complete Sherlock
Holmes   **S C**

The **adventure** of the retired colourman. Doyle,
Sir A. C.
In Doyle, Sir A. C. The complete Sherlock
Holmes   **S C**

The **adventure** of the second stain. Doyle, Sir A.
C.
In Doyle, Sir A. C. The complete Sherlock
Holmes   **S C**

The **adventure** of the six Napoleons. Doyle, Sir
A. C.
In Doyle, Sir A. C. The complete Sherlock
Holmes   **S C**

The **adventure** of the solitary cyclist. Doyle, Sir
A. C.
In Doyle, Sir A. C. The complete Sherlock
Holmes   **S C**

The **adventure** of the speckled band. Doyle, Sir
A. C.
In Doyle, Sir A. C. The complete Sherlock
Holmes   **S C**

The **adventure** of the Sussex vampire. Doyle, Sir
A. C.
In Doyle, Sir A. C. The complete Sherlock
Holmes   **S C**

The **adventure** of the three gables. Doyle, Sir A.
C.
In Doyle, Sir A. C. The complete Sherlock
Holmes   **S C**

African Americans in literature—*Continued*
African-American voices in young adult litera-
ture **810.9**
African Americans in the military. Reef, C.
920.003
The **African** and Middle Eastern world, 600-1500.
Pouwels, R. L. **956**
African art
Kasfir, S. L. Contemporary African art **709**
African civilization *See* Africa—Civilization
African diaspora
Encyclopedias
Africana: the encyclopedia of the African and
African American experience **909**
African folktales **398.2**
African laughter. Lessing, D. M. **968.91**
African literature
Collections
Women writing Africa: the eastern region
896
Women writing Africa: the southern region
896
Women writing Africa: West Africa and the
Sahel **896**
African literature and its times **809**
African morning. Hughes, L.
In Hughes, L. Short stories of Langston
Hughes **S C**
African National Congress
Mandela, N. Nelson Mandela speaks **968.06**
African poetry
Collections
The Penguin book of modern African poetry
896
The **African** prayer book **242**
African religion. Lugira, A. M. **299.6**
The **African** slave trade. Davidson, B. **967**
African states and rulers. Stewart, J. **960**
An **African** story. Dahl, R.
In Dahl, R. Skin and other stories **S C**
An **African** story. Hemingway, E.
In Hemingway, E. The complete short stories
of Ernest Hemingway; the Finca Vigía
edition p545-54 **S C**
African voices of the Atlantic slave trade. Bailey,
A. C. **326**
African writers series
The Heinemann book of contemporary African
short stories **S C**
Africana: the encyclopedia of the African and Af-
rican American experience **909**
After Jackie. Fussman, C. **92**
After the days of Dead-Eye 'Dee. Cadigan, P.
In The Norton book of science fiction; North
American science fiction, 1960-1990
p605-15 **S C**
After the fall. Miller, A.
In Miller, A. The portable Arthur Miller
812
After the first death. Cormier, R. **Fic**

After the plague. Boyle, T. C.
In Gotham Writers' Workshop fiction gallery:
exceptional short stories selected by New
York's acclaimed creative writing school
S C
After the race. Joyce, J.
In Joyce, J. Dubliners **S C**
After the storm. Hemingway, E.
In Hemingway, E. The complete short stories
of Ernest Hemingway; the Finca Vigía
edition p283-87 **S C**
After you, my dear Alphonse. Jackson, S.
In Jackson, S. The lottery; or, The adventures
of James Harris **S C**
The **afterlife.** Soto, G. **Fic**
The **afterlife** of St. Vidicon of Cathode: a Warlock
story. Stasheff, C.
In Masters of fantasy **S C**
Aftermath. Burrill, M. P.
In Black theatre USA; plays by African
Americans, 1847 to today **812.008**
Afternoon in linen. Jackson, S.
In Jackson, S. The lottery; or, The adventures
of James Harris **S C**
An **afternoon** in the woods. O'Connor, F.
In O'Connor, F. Collected works p763-72
S C
Afternoon of an author. Fitzgerald, F. S.
In Fitzgerald, F. S. The short stories of F.
Scott Fitzgerald; a new collection p734-
38 **S C**
Aftershocks. Lavender, W. **Fic**
Agamemnon. Aeschylus
In Four Greek plays **882.008**
In Seven famous Greek plays **882.008**
Agard, John, 1949-
Half-caste and other poems **821**
Age *See* Old age
Age of bronze [series]
Shanower, E. A thousand ships **939**
The **age** of chivalry. Bulfinch, T.
In Bulfinch, T. Bulfinch's mythology
398.2
The **age** of fable. Bulfinch, T.
In Bulfinch, T. Bulfinch's mythology
398.2
The **age** of genius. Bradley, M. J. **920**
The **age** of reason. Paine, T.
In Paine, T. Collected writings p663-830
320
The **Age** of Revolution **909.7**
The **age** of Shakespeare. Kermode, F. **792.09**
Aged *See* Elderly
Agee, James, 1909-1955
A death in the family **Fic**
Aggressiveness (Psychology)
Evans, P. Teen torment **158**
Lorenz, K. On aggression **152.4**
Aging
Aging in America **362.6**
Panno, J. Aging **612.6**
Aging in America **362.6**

Akbar, Said Hyder
Come back to Afghanistan **958.1**

Akhnilo. Salter, J.
In American short story masterpieces **S C**

Akutagawa, Ryunosuke, 1892-1927
In a grove
In Adaptations: from short story to big screen; 35 great stories that have inspired great films **S C**

Al. Emshwiller, C.
In Feeling very strange; the Slipstream anthology **S C**

Al-Khalili, Jim, 1962-
Black holes, wormholes & time machines **530.1**

Al Qaeda (Organization)
National Commission on Terrorist Attacks Upon the United States. The 9/11 Commission report **973.931**

Al-Windawi, Thura
Thura's diary **956.7**

ALA fundamental series
Giesecke, J. Fundamentals of library supervision **023**

ALA readers' advisory series
Booth, H. Serving teens through readers' advisory **028.5**
Saricks, J. G. The readers' advisory guide to genre fiction **025.5**
Spratford, B. S. The horror readers' advisory **025.5**

Alabama
Fiction
Devoto, P. C. The summer we got saved **Fic**
Lee, H. To kill a mockingbird **Fic**

Alabiso, Vincent
(ed) Flash!: the Associated Press covers the world. See Flash!: the Associated Press covers the world **070.4**

Alamo (San Antonio, Tex.)
Roberts, R. A line in the sand **976.4**

Alaska
Description and travel
Krakauer, J. Into the wild [biography of Christopher McCandless] **92**
Fiction
Hobbs, W. Leaving Protection **Fic**
London, J. The call of the wild **Fic**
London, J. White Fang **Fic**
Orenstein, D. G. Unseen companion **Fic**
Smelcer, J. E. The trap **Fic**

Alba, Alicia Gaspar de *See* Gaspar de Alba, Alicia, 1958-

Albala, Ken, 1964-
Food in early modern Europe **641.3**
(jt. auth) Cox, C. Opening up North America, 1497-1800 **917**

Albee, Edward, 1928-
Who's afraid of Virginia Woolf? **812**

Albert Einstein and the frontiers of physics. Bernstein, J. **92**

Albert Nobbs. Moore, G.
In The Oxford book of Irish short stories p109-51 **S C**

Albrecht, Gary L.
(ed) Encyclopedia of disability. See Encyclopedia of disability **362.4**

An **album** of memories. Brokaw, T. **940.54**

Albyn, Carole Lisa, 1955-
The multicultural cookbook for students **641.5**

Alcestis. Euripides
In Four Greek plays **882.008**
In Seven famous Greek plays **882.008**

Alchemy
Fiction
Mahy, M. Alchemy **Fic**

Alcindor, Lew *See* Abdul-Jabbar, Kareem, 1947-

Alcohol **362.292**

Alcohol: an opposing viewpoints guide **362.292**

Alcohol and teenagers *See* Teenagers—Alcohol use

Alcohol and your liver. Booley, T. A. **616.86**

Alcohol and youth *See* Youth—Alcohol use

Alcoholic beverages
See also Drinking of alcoholic beverages

Alcoholics Anonymous
Rosengren, J. Big book unplugged **362.292**

Alcoholism
See also Drinking of alcoholic beverages
Addiction: opposing viewpoints **362.29**
Alcohol **362.292**
Alcohol: an opposing viewpoints guide **362.292**
Booley, T. A. Alcohol and your liver **616.86**
Gottfried, T. The facts about alcohol **362.292**
Rosengren, J. Big book unplugged **362.292**
The Truth about alcohol **362.292**
Fiction
Brooks, K. Martyn Pig **Fic**
Deuker, C. Runner **Fic**
Friend, N. Lush **Fic**
Koja, K. The blue mirror **Fic**
Pearson, M. A room on Lorelei Street **Fic**

Alcorn, Stephen, 1958-
(il) Gottfried, T. Children of the slaughter **940.53**
(il) Gottfried, T. Deniers of the Holocaust **940.53**
(il) Gottfried, T. Heroes of the Holocaust **940.53**

Alcott, Louisa May, 1832-1888
The selected letters of Louisa May Alcott **92**

Aldenderfer, Mark S.
(ed) Great events from history, The ancient world, prehistory-476 C.E. See Great events from history, The ancient world, prehistory-476 C.E. **930**

Alder, Elizabeth
The king's shadow **Fic**

Aliki
William Shakespeare & the Globe   **822.3**

Alistair, James *See* Goligorsky, Eduardo, 1931-

Alive. Read, P. P.   **910.4**

All about adoption. Lanchon, A.   **649**

All about techniques in acrylics   **751.4**

All American [biography of Jim Thorpe] Crawford, B.   **92**

All-American Girls Professional Baseball League
Encyclopedia of women and baseball
796.357

All creatures great and small. Herriot, J.   **92**

All Gold Canyon. London, J.
In A Century of great Western stories
S C
In London, J. The portable Jack London p100-17   **818**

The **all-in-one** college guide. Nemko, M.
378.1

All on a summer's night. Bradbury, R.
In Bradbury, R. Bradbury stories; 100 of his most celebrated tales   **S C**

All over but the shoutin'. Bragg, R.   **92**

All quiet on the western front. Remarque, E. M.
Fic

All rivers flow to the sea. McGhee, A.   **Fic**

All terrain bicycles *See* Mountain bikes

All terrain cycling *See* Mountain biking

All that you love will be carried away. King, S.
In King, S. Everything's eventual: 14 dark tales   **S C**

All the daring of the soldier. Leonard, E. D.
973.7

All the dead pilots. Faulkner, W.
In Faulkner, W. Collected stories of William Faulkner p511-31   **S C**

All the president's men. Bernstein, C.   **973.924**

All the pretty horses. McCarthy, C.   **Fic**

All the time in the world. Clarke, A. C.
In Clarke, A. C. The collected stories of Arthur C. Clarke   **S C**

All the troubles of the world. Asimov, I.
In Asimov, I. The complete stories p263-76
S C

All the way to Berlin. Megellas, J.   **940.54**

All the words on stage. Scheeder, L.   **822.3**

All things Shakespeare. Olsen, K.   **822.3**

Allaby, Michael, 1933-
A chronology of weather   **363.34**
Droughts   **551.57**
Encyclopedia of weather and climate   **551**
Makers of science   **920.003**

Allan, Tony, 1946-
The causes of World War I   **940.3**
Life, myth, and art in Ancient Rome   **937**

Allegiance. Detzer, D.   **973.7**

Allegories
Adams, R. Watership Down   **Fic**
Atwood, M. The Handmaid's tale   **Fic**
Beagle, P. S. The last unicorn   **Fic**

Golding, W. Lord of the flies   **Fic**
Rushdie, S. Haroun and the sea of stories
Fic
Saint-Exupéry, A. d. The little prince   **Fic**
Stevenson, R. L. The strange case of Dr. Jekyll and Mr. Hyde   **Fic**

Allegra, Donna, 1953-
God lies in the details
In Not the only one; lesbian and gay fiction for teens   **S C**

Allegro. Wallace, R.
In Dreams and visions; fourteen flights of fantasy   **S C**

Allen, Frederick Lewis, 1890-1954
Only yesterday   **973.91**

Allen, John L., 1965-
The rise of Benedict XVI   **282**

Allen, John O.
(jt. auth) Jewett, C. E. Slavery in the South
326

Allen, Paula Gunn
A deep purple
In Spider Woman's granddaughters; traditional tales and contemporary writing by Native American women   **S C**
Raven's road [excerpt]
In Growing up gay; an anthology for young people p105-09   **808.8**
About
Coltelli, L. Winged words: American Indian writers speak   **897**
(ed) Spider Woman's granddaughters. See Spider Woman's granddaughters   **S C**

Allen, Stewart Lee
In the devil's garden   **641**

Allen, Thomas B., 1929-
The shark almanac   **597**

Allen, William Rodney
(ed) Vonnegut, K. Conversations with Kurt Vonnegut   **92**

Allen, Zita
Black women leaders of the civil rights movement   **323.1**

Allenbaugh, Kay
(comp) Chocolate for a teen's heart. See Chocolate for a teen's heart   **152.4**

Allende, Isabel
Daughter of fortune   **Fic**
Eva Luna   **Fic**
If you touched my heart
In The Oxford book of gothic tales p519-26
S C
Paula   **92**
Zorro   **Fic**

Allende family
About
Allende, I. Paula   **92**

Allergies, Food *See* Food allergy

Allergy
See also Food allergy
Brynie, F. H. 101 questions about your immune system you felt defenseless to answer . . . until now   **616.07**

Alvarez, Julia, 1950-—Continued
How the García girls lost their accents
Fic
[excerpt]
In Coming of age in America; a multicultural
anthology p226-38 **S C**
Snow
In Latina: women's voices from the border-
lands p127-28 **810.8**
The woman I kept to myself **811**

Alvarez, Walter, 1940-
T. rex and the Crater of Doom **551.7**

Alyosha the Pot. Tolstoy, L., graf
In The portable twentieth-century Russian
reader **891.7**
In Tolstoy, L., graf. Great short works of Leo
Tolstoy p669-77 **S C**

Alzheimer's disease
Landau, E. Alzheimer's disease **616.8**
Fiction
Newbery, L. Sisterland **Fic**

Alzheimer's disease. Landau, E. **616.8**

Am I blue? **S C**

Am I blue? [story] Coville, B.
In Am I blue?; coming out from the silence
p1-16 **S C**

Amandine. Griffin, A. **Fic**

Amar, Akhil Reed
America's constitution **342**

Amaryllis. Crist-Evans, C. **Fic**

The **Amateur** astronomer **520**

Amato, Joseph Anthony
(jt. auth) Rorer, A. Dust **551.51**

The **amazing** Maurice and his educated rodents.
Pratchett, T. **Fic**

The **amazing** two-headed boy. Wallace, R.
In Wallace, R. Losing is not an option: stories
S C

Amazons
Fiction
Hoffman, A. The foretelling **Fic**

The **ambitious** guest. Hawthorne, N.
In Hawthorne, N. Tales and sketches, including Twice-told tales, Mosses from an old
manse, and The snow-image; A wonder
book for girls and boys; Tanglewood
tales for girls and boys, being a second
Wonder book p299-307 **S C**

Ambitious sophomore. Vonnegut, K.
In Vonnegut, K. Bagombo snuff box: uncollected short fiction p123-34 **S C**

Ambling into history: the unlikely odyssey of
George W. Bush. Bruni, F. **92**

Ambrose, Alison *See* Cole, Alison

Ambrose, Stephen E.
Lewis & Clark **978**

Ambrus, Victor G., 1935-
(il) McCarty, N. The Iliad **883**

Ambush. O'Brien, T.
In O'Brien, T. The things they carried; a
work of fiction **S C**
In Who do you think you are?; stories of
friends and enemies p152-55 **S C**

Amelia Earhart's daughters. Haynsworth, L.
629.13

The **amen** corner. Baldwin, J.
In Black theatre USA; plays by African
Americans, 1847 to today **812.008**

America
See also Latin America; North America
Antiquities
America in 1492 **970.01**
Mann, C. C. 1491 **970.01**
Exploration
America in 1492 **970.01**
Cox, C. Opening up North America, 1497-1800
917
Goetzmann, W. H. The atlas of North American
exploration **911**
Smith, T. Discovery of the Americas, 1492-1800
909
Wright, R. Stolen continents **970.004**
History
Events that changed America through the seven-
teenth century **973.2**

America. Card, O. S.
In The Norton book of science fiction; North
American science fiction, 1960-1990
p665-88 **S C**

America. Frank, E. R. **Fic**

America at 1750. Hofstadter, R. **973.2**

America at war [series]
Bosco, P. I. World War I **940.3**
Carlisle, R. P. Iraq war **956.7**
Golay, M. Spanish-American War **973.8**
Greenblatt, M. War of 1812 **973.5**
Isserman, M. Korean war **951.9**
Isserman, M. Vietnam War **959.704**
Marker, S. Plains Indian wars **973.5**
Mills, B. U.S.-Mexican War **973.6**

America in 1492 **970.01**

America in Vietnam **959.704**

America under attack: primary sources
973.931

American Airlines Flight 11 hijacking, 2001 *See*
World Trade Center terrorist attack, 2001

American art
The American art book **709.73**
Bearden, R. A history of African-American art-
ists **709.73**
Harlem Renaissance **709.73**
Heart to heart **811.008**
Roark, E. L. Artists of colonial America
709.73

The **American** art book **709.73**

American artists *See* Artists—United States

American arts *See* Arts—United States

American Association of School Librarians
Information power **027.8**

American authors
Anecdotes
See Authors, American—Anecdotes
American authors, 1600-1900 **920.003**

The **American** Bar Association guide to workplace
law **344**

Ancient civilization
> *See also* Classical civilization

Aveni, A. F. Stairways to the stars   **520**
Classical Greece and Rome   **938**
Hakim, J. The story of science: Aristotle leads the way   **509**
Kaufman, C. K. Cooking in ancient civilizations   **641.3**
The Oxford history of the biblical world   **220.9**

Encyclopedias
Encyclopedia of the ancient world   **930**

Ancient Egypt   **932**
Ancient Egyptian literature   **892**
Ancient Egyptians. Baker, R. F.   **932**
Ancient geography
Obregón, M. Beyond the edge of the sea   **930**

Ancient Greece   **938.003**
Ancient Greek literature   **880.9**
Ancient Greeks. Baker, R. F.   **938**
Ancient history
> *See also* Classical dictionaries

Craig, S. Sports and games of the ancients   **796**
Great events from history, The ancient world, prehistory-476 C.E.   **930**
Great lives from history, The ancient world, pre-history-476 C.E   **920.003**
Starr, C. G. A history of the ancient world   **930**

Ancient inventions. James, P.   **609**
An **ancient** manuscript. Kafka, F.
> *In* Kafka, F. The metamorphosis and other stories p197-200   **S C**

Ancient philosophy
See/See also pages in the following book(s):
Ancient Greek literature   **880.9**

Ancient Romans. Baker, R. F.   **937**
And justice for all   **940.53**
And the angels sing. Wilhelm, K.
> *In* The Norton book of science fiction; North American science fiction, 1960-1990 p797-813   **S C**

And the band played on. Shilts, R.   **362.1**
And the rock cried out. Bradbury, R.
> *In* Bradbury, R. Bradbury stories; 100 of his most celebrated tales   **S C**

And the sailor, home from the sea. Bradbury, R.
> *In* Bradbury, R. Bradbury stories; 100 of his most celebrated tales   **S C**

And the soul shall dance. Yamauchi, W.
> *In* American dragons: twenty-five Asian American voices p144-54   **810.8**

And then there were none. Christie, A.   **Fic**
And they all sang. Terkel, S.   **780.9**
Andersen, Richard, 1946-
   Arthur Miller   **92**
   Toni Morrison   **92**
Anderson, Anna, d. 1984
See/See also pages in the following book(s):
Massie, R. K. The Romanovs   **947.08**

Anderson, Frederick Irving, 1877-1947
   Blind man's buff
> *In* The Best American mystery stories of the century p58-72   **S C**

Anderson, Garland, 1886-1939
   Appearances
> *In* Black theatre USA; plays by African Americans, 1847 to today   **812.008**

Anderson, Ho Che, 1969-
   King: a comic book biography   **92**
Anderson, James Maxwell, 1933-
   Daily life during the French Revolution   **944.04**

Anderson, Laurie Halse, 1961-
   Prom   **Fic**
   Speak   **Fic**
   Twisted   **Fic**
Anderson, M. T., 1968-
   Angel's food
> *In* Twice told; original stories inspired by original art   **S C**

   Feed   **Fic**
   The gray boy's work
> *In* The restless dead; ten original stories of the supernatural   **S C**

   The mud and fever dialogues
> *In* Sixteen: stories about that sweet and bitter birthday   **S C**

   The Pox party   **Fic**
   Watch and wake
> *In* Gothic!; ten original dark tales   **S C**

Anderson, Marian, 1897-1993
About
Keiler, A. Marian Anderson   **92**
Anderson, Poul, 1926-2001
   Genesis
> *In* The Hard SF renaissance   **S C**

   Kyrie
> *In* The Norton book of science fiction; North American science fiction, 1960-1990 p201-10   **S C**

Anderson, Sheila B.
   Extreme teens   **027.62**
   (ed) Serving older teens. See Serving older teens   **027.62**
Anderson, Sherwood, 1876-1941
   Death in the woods
> *In* The Norton book of American short stories p220-30   **S C**

   I want to know why
> *In* The Oxford book of short stories p238-46   **S C**

Anderson, Terry H., 1946-
   The movement and the sixties   **303.4**
Andes
Parrado, N. Miracle in the Andes   **982**
Read, P. P. Alive   **910.4**
Andrea, Alfred J., 1941-
   Encyclopedia of the crusades   **909.07**
Andreas Vesalius the anatomist. Borel, P.
> *In* The Oxford book of gothic tales p70-81   **S C**

Andre's mother. McNally, T.
  In McNally, T. 15 short plays p347-52
    812

Andrews, John F.
  (ed) Shakespeare's world and work. See Shakespeare's world and work   **822.3**

Andrews, Robert, 1957-
  The Columbia dictionary of quotations
    808.88
  Famous lines   **808.88**

The **Andromeda** strain. Crichton, M.   **Fic**

Anecdotes
  See also Wit and humor

Anesthetics
  See/See also pages in the following book(s):
  Friedman, M. Medicine's 10 greatest discoveries
    610.9

Ang, Tom
  KISS guide to digital photography   **775**

Angel, Ann, 1952-
  Such a pretty face
    In Such a pretty face; short stories   **S C**
  (ed) Such a pretty face. See Such a pretty face
    S C

Angel, Heather, 1941-
  Pandas   **599.78**

Angel. Chekhov, A. P.
  In Chekhov, A. P. The Russian master and other stories p172-82   **S C**

Angel, all innocence. Weldon, F.
  In The Literary ghost; great contemporary ghost stories p230-46   **S C**

Angel-baby. Salisbury, G.
  In Salisbury, G. Island boyz: short stories p196-219   **S C**

Angel Levine. Malamud, B.
  In Malamud, B. The complete stories   **S C**

The **angel** of the bridge. Cheever, J.
  In Cheever, J. The stories of John Cheever p490-97   **S C**

The **Angel** of the Odd. Poe, E. A.
  In Poe, E. A. The collected tales and poems of Edgar Allan Poe p376-83   **818**

An **angel** on the porch. Wolfe, T.
  In Wolfe, T. The complete short stories of Thomas Wolfe p3-9   **S C**

Angela's ashes. McCourt, F.   **92**

Angela's eyes. Myers, W. D.
  In Myers, W. D. 145th Street; short stories
    S C

Angell, Judie, 1937-
  Turmoil in a blue and beige bedroom
    In Sixteen: short stories by outstanding writers for young adults p72-82   **S C**

Angell, Roger
  Game time: a baseball companion   **796.357**

Angelo, Bonnie
  First families   **920**

Angelo, Joseph A.
  Encyclopedia of space and astronomy   **520.3**
  The Facts on File dictionary of space technology   **629.4**
  Space technology   **629.4**

Spacecraft for astronomy   **522**

Angelou, Maya
  The complete collected poems of Maya Angelou
    811
  I know why the caged bird sings
    92
  [excerpt]
    In Who do you think you are?; stories of friends and enemies p156-63   **S C**
  Wouldn't take nothing for my journey now
    814

About
  Maya Angelou [critical essays]   **818**
  Maya Angelou's I know why the caged bird sings   **818**

Angels

Dictionaries
  Guiley, R. E. The encyclopedia of angels
    200

Angel's food. Anderson, M. T.
  In Twice told; original stories inspired by original art   **S C**

Angels in America. Kushner, T.   **812**

Anglo-American cataloguing rules
  Fritz, D. A. Cataloging with AACR2 and MARC21   **025.3**
  Gorman, M. The concise AACR2   **025.3**

Anglo-American invasion of Iraq, 2003 *See* Iraq War, 2003

Anglo-Saxon literature *See* English literature—Old English period

Angst! teen verses from the edge!   **811.008**

Anguiano religious articles rosaries statues medals incense candles talismans perfumes oils herbs. Cisneros, S.
  In Cisneros, S. Woman Hollering Creek and other stories   **S C**

Angus, thongs and full-frontal snogging. Rennison, L.   **Fic**

Anichkov, N. N. (Nikolai Nikolaevich), 1885-1964

About
  Friedman, M. Medicine's 10 greatest discoveries
    610.9

Anichkov, Nikolai Nikolaevich *See* Anichkov, N. N. (Nikolai Nikolaevich), 1885-1964

Animal abuse *See* Animal welfare

Animal attacks
  Capuzzo, M. Close to shore   **597**

Animal behavior
  See also Animal defenses
  Crump, M. L. Headless males make great lovers
    591.5
  Encyclopedia of animal behavior   **591.5**
  Grandin, T. Animals in translation   **591.5**
  McDougall, L. The complete tracker   **591.5**

Animal cloning. Panno, J.   **660.6**

Animal communication
  Agosta, W. C. Thieves, deceivers, and killers
    577
  Friend, T. Animal talk   **591.59**

Animal defenses
  Eisner, T. Secret weapons   **595.7**

Anzovin, Steven, 1954——*Continued*
(jt. auth) Kane, J. N. Famous first facts
031.02

AP *See* Associated Press

Apache Indians
Sweeney, E. R. Cochise, Chiricahua Apache chief **92**
Fiction
Bruchac, J. Geronimo **Fic**

Apartheid
Bradley, C. The end of apartheid **968.06**
Houze, D. Twilight people **92**
Mandela, N. Nelson Mandela speaks **968.06**

Ape. Keels, J. J.
In Such a pretty face; short stories **S C**

An **ape** about the house. Clarke, A. C.
In Clarke, A. C. The collected stories of Arthur C. Clarke **S C**

Apel, Melanie Ann
Cystic fibrosis **616.2**

Apes
See also Chimpanzees; Gorillas; Orangutan
World atlas of great apes and their conservation **599.8**

Apfelbaum, Nina
(jt. auth) Rosen, P. Bearing witness **016.94053**

Apiculture *See* Beekeeping; Bees

The **Apollo** of Bellac. Giraudoux, J.
In 24 favorite one-act plays p308-32 **808.82**

Apollo Project *See* Project Apollo

An **apology**. Malamud, B.
In Malamud, B. The complete stories **S C**

An **apology** to the moon furies. Vega, E.
In Growing up Latino; memoirs and stories p47-72 **810.8**

The **apostate**. London, J.
In London, J. The portable Jack London p118-35 **818**

Appalachian Mountain region *See* Appalachian region

Appalachian region
Reece, E. Lost mountain **622**
Fiction
Marshall, C. Christy **Fic**
Social life and customs
Foxfire 40th anniversary book **975.8**

Appearance and reality. Maugham, W. S.
In Maugham, W. S. Collected short stories **S C**

Appearances. Anderson, G.
In Black theatre USA; plays by African Americans, 1847 to today **812.008**

Appelt, Kathi, 1954-
Poems from homeroom **811**

Appetite disorders *See* Eating disorders

Appiah, Anthony
(ed) Africana: the encyclopedia of the African and African American experience. See Africana: the encyclopedia of the African and African American experience **909**

(ed) Gloria Naylor: critical perspectives past and present. See Gloria Naylor: critical perspectives past and present **813.009**
(ed) Langston Hughes. See Langston Hughes [critical essays] **818**
(ed) Richard Wright. See Richard Wright [critical essays] **813.009**

Appiah, Kwame Anthony *See* Appiah, Anthony

Appignanesi, Richard
Manga Shakespeare: Romeo and Juliet **822.3**

Apple, Hope
(jt. auth) Jacob, M. To be continued **016.8**

Apple, Max
Bridging
In The Norton book of American short stories p692-700 **S C**

The **apple** orchard. Anaya, R. A.
In Growing up Latino; memoirs and stories p292-304 **810.8**

Applications for college *See* College applications

Applications for positions
Bolles, R. N. What color is your parachute? for teens **331.7**
Potter, R. Résumés that get jobs **650.14**

Appointment with death. Christie, A.
In Christie, A. The mousetrap and other plays **822**

Apprentices
Paquette, P. H. Apprenticeship **331.2**

Apprenticeship. Paquette, P. H. **331.2**

The **approximate** cost of loving Caroline. Green, J.
In Twice told; original stories inspired by original art **S C**

April 2005: Usher II. Bradbury, R.
In Bradbury, R. Bradbury stories; 100 of his most celebrated tales **S C**

April 2026: the long years. Bradbury, R.
In Bradbury, R. Bradbury stories; 100 of his most celebrated tales **S C**

April, late April. Wolfe, T.
In Wolfe, T. The complete short stories of Thomas Wolfe p323-31 **S C**

April twilights, and other poems. Cather, W.
In Cather, W. Stories, poems, and other writings **818**

Aquanauts *See* Underwater exploration

Aquariums
See also Marine aquariums
Maître-Allain, T. Aquariums **639.34**
Encyclopedias
Dawes, J. Complete encyclopedia of the freshwater aquarium **639.34**

Aquatic animals *See* Marine animals

Aquinas, Saint Thomas *See* Thomas, Aquinas, Saint, 1225?-1274

Aquinas, Thomas *See* Thomas, Aquinas, Saint, 1225?-1274

Arab American voices. Hall, L. **305.8**

Arab American women
Fiction
Abu-Jaber, D. Crescent **Fic**

Aristotle, 384-322 B.C.—*Continued*
Metaphysics
In Aristotle. The basic works of Aristotle
p689-926 **888**
Nicomachean ethics
In Aristotle. The basic works of Aristotle
p927-1112 **888**
On generation and corruption
In Aristotle. The basic works of Aristotle
p470-531 **888**
On the soul
In Aristotle. The basic works of Aristotle
p535-603 **888**
Organon
In Aristotle. The basic works of Aristotle p1-
212 **888**
Parva naturalia
In Aristotle. The basic works of Aristotle
p607-30 **888**
Physica
In Aristotle. The basic works of Aristotle
p213-394 **888**
Poetics
In Aristotle. The basic works of Aristotle
p1455-87 **888**
Politics
In Aristotle. The basic works of Aristotle
p1127-1316 **888**
About
Adler, M. J. Aristotle for everybody **185**
See/See also pages in the following book(s):
Durant, W. J. The story of philosophy **109**
Russell, B. A history of Western philosophy
109
Aristotle for everybody. Adler, M. J. **185**
Arizona
Fiction
Kingsolver, B. The bean trees **Fic**
Arkansas
Fiction
Darrow, S. The painters of Lexieville **Fic**
Race relations
Fradin, J. B. The power of one [biography of
Daisy Bates] **92**
Armageddon's children. Brooks, T. **Fic**
Armaments industries *See* Defense industry
Armaments race. Clarke, A. C.
In Clarke, A. C. The collected stories of Ar-
thur C. Clarke **S C**
Der Arme Dolmetscher. Vonnegut, K.
In Vonnegut, K. Bagombo snuff box: uncol-
lected short fiction p183-87 **S C**
Armenian massacres, 1915-1923
See/See also pages in the following book(s):
Naimark, N. M. Fires of hatred **364.1**
Fiction
Bagdasarian, A. Forgotten fire **Fic**
Armies
See also Great Britain. Army
Armistice. Malamud, B.
In Malamud, B. The complete stories **S C**
Arms and armor *See* Weapons
Arms control
Schram, M. Avoiding armageddon **327.1**

Arms sales *See* Defense industry
The **arms** trade. Gifford, C. **382**
Armstrong, Jennifer, 1961-
Photo by Brady **973.7**
The song of stones river
In What a song can do; 12 riffs on the power
of music **S C**
Witness
In Shattered: stories of children and war
p133-38 **S C**
(ed) Shattered: stories of children and war. See
Shattered: stories of children and war **S C**
(ed) What a song can do. See What a song can
do **S C**
Armstrong, Karen
The battle for God **200**
Buddha **92**
Islam **297**
Jerusalem **956.94**
Muhammad **92**
The spiral staircase **92**
Armstrong, Lance
It's not about the bike **92**
Army life *See* Soldiers
Army Nurse Corps *See* United States. Army
Nurse Corps
Arnason, Eleanor
The warlord of Saturn's moons
In The Norton book of science fiction; North
American science fiction, 1960-1990
p305-12 **S C**
Arnett, Ross H., Jr.
Simon and Schuster's guide to insects **595.7**
Arnold Pentland. Wolfe, T.
In Wolfe, T. The complete short stories of
Thomas Wolfe p222-28 **S C**
Aronson, Elliot
Nobody left to hate **371.7**
Aronson, Marc
Art attack **700**
Exploding the myths **028.5**
John Winthrop, Oliver Cromwell, and the Land
of Promise [dual biography of John Winthrop
and Oliver Cromwell] **92**
The real revolution **973.3**
Sir Walter Ralegh and the quest for El Dorado
92
Witch-hunt: mysteries of the Salem witch trials
133.4
(ed) 911: the book of help. See 911: the book
of help **810.8**
Arouet, François Marie *See* Voltaire, 1694-1778
Arreola, Juan José, 1918-2001
Baby H.P.
In Cosmos latinos; an anthology of science
fiction from Latin America and Spain
S C
Arrian, ca. 96-ca. 180
Alexander the Great **92**
Arrianus, Flavius *See* Arrian, ca. 96-ca. 180
The **ARRL** handbook for radio communications
2007 **621.3841**

Arson
Fiction
Wilson, D. L. Firehorse **Fic**
Art

See also Artistic anatomy; Children's art; Symbolism in art
Kampen O'Riley, M. Art beyond the west
709
15th and 16th centuries
Cole, A. Renaissance **709.02**
Graham-Dixon, A. Renaissance **709.02**
19th century
See also Impressionism (Art)
20th century
Heart to heart **811.008**
Kasfir, S. L. Contemporary African art **709**
Dictionaries
Carr-Gomm, S. Dictionary of symbols in Western art **704.9**
Hall, J. Dictionary of subject and symbols in art **704.9**
Langmuir, E. Yale dictionary of art and artists
703
The Oxford companion to western art **703**
The Oxford dictionary of art **703**
Encyclopedias
Facts on File encyclopedia of art **703**
Landi, A. Schirmer encyclopedia of art **703**
Graphic novels
Castellucci, C. The Plain Janes **741.5**
History
Cole, B. Art of the Western world **709**
Gardner, H. Gardner's art through the ages
709
Gombrich, E. H. The story of art **709**
Hartt, F. Art: a history of painting, sculpture, architecture **709**
Hollingsworth, M. Art in world history **709**
Janson, H. W. Janson's history of art **709**
Little, S. . . . isms: understanding art **709**
History—Maps
Atlas of world art **709**
Internet resources
Eyerdam, P. J. Using Internet primary sources to teach critical thinking skills in visual arts
700
Philosophy
See/See also pages in the following book(s):
Hamilton, E. The Greek way **880.9**
Study and teaching
Eyerdam, P. J. Using Internet primary sources to teach critical thinking skills in visual arts
700
Technique
Smith, R. The artist's handbook **702.8**
Art, Abstract *See* Abstract art
Art, African *See* African art
Art, African American *See* African American art
Art, American *See* American art
Art, Chinese *See* Chinese art
Art, Christian *See* Christian art
Art, Egyptian *See* Egyptian art
Art, Graphic *See* Graphic arts

Art, Hispanic American *See* Hispanic American art
Art, Indian *See* Native American art
Art, Islamic *See* Islamic art
Art, Latin American *See* Latin American art
Art, Medieval *See* Medieval art
Art, Modern *See* Modern art
Art, Prehistoric *See* Prehistoric art
Art, Renaissance *See* Art—15th and 16th centuries
Art, Roman *See* Roman art
Art: a history of painting, sculpture, architecture. Hartt, F. **709**
The **art** and craft of poetry. Bugeja, M. J.
808.1
Art appreciation
Beckett, W. Sister Wendy's 1000 masterpieces
759
How to read a painting **753**
Yenawine, P. Key art terms for beginners
701
Art attack. Aronson, M. **700**
Art beyond the west. Kampen O'Riley, M.
709
Art deco
Arwas, V. Art deco **709.04**
Art from the ashes **940.53**
Art in world history. Hollingsworth, M. **709**
Art Institute of Chicago
Treasures from the Art Institute of Chicago
708
The **art** of calligraphy. Harris, D. **745.6**
The **art** of fiction. Gardner, J. **808.3**
The **art** of loving. Fromm, E. **152.4**
Art of mentoring [series]
Brustein, R. Letters to a young actor **792**
Campolo, A. Letters to a young evangelical
248.4
Freedman, S. G. Letters to a young journalist
070.4
Gitlin, T. Letters to a young activist **322.4**
Stewart, I. Letters to a young mathematician
510
The **art** of spelling. Vos Savant, M. M. **421**
The **art** of the author interview. Johnson, S. A.
808
The **art** of the comic book. Harvey, R. C.
741.5
Art of the Middle Ages. Snyder, J. **709.02**
Art of the Western world. Cole, B. **709**
Art thefts
Dolnick, E. The rescue artist **364.1**
Artemis, the honest well digger. Cheever, J.
In Cheever, J. The stories of John Cheever p650-71 **S C**
Arthur, King
About
Ashe, G. The discovery of King Arthur **92**
Malory, Sir T. Le morte Darthur, or, The hoole book of Kyng Arthur and of his noble knyghtes of the Rounde Table **398.2**

Aslan, Reza
No god but God **297**

ASPCA complete cat care manual. Edney, A. T.
B. **636.8**

ASPCA complete dog training manual. See Fogle,
B. New complete dog training manual
636.7

Aspey, Lynette
Sleeping dragons
In The Year's best science fiction and fantasy
for teens: first annual collection **S C**

Asphodel. Welty, E.
In Welty, E. The collected stories of Eudora
Welty p200-08 **S C**

Asprin, Robert
Mything in dreamland: a Myth adventures in
dreamland story
In Masters of fantasy **S C**

Assassination vacation. Vowell, S. **920**

The **assault** on the record. Hoffius, S.
In Ultimate sports; short stories by outstand-
ing writers for young adults p161-78
S C

The **assignation**. Poe, E. A.
In Poe, E. A. The collected tales and poems
of Edgar Allan Poe p293-302 **818**

The **assistant**. Malamud, B. **Fic**

Assisted suicide *See* Euthanasia

Assisted suicide **179.7**

Associated Press
Flash!: the Associated Press covers the world
070.4

**Association for Educational Communications
and Technology**
American Association of School Librarians. Information power **027.8**

**Association for the Study of American Indian
Literatures (U.S.)**
Returning the gift. See Returning the gift
897

Associations
See also Clubs

Astaire, Fred
See/See also pages in the following book(s):
Ford, C. T. Legends of American dance and
choreography **920**

Asteroids
Erickson, J. Asteroids, comets, and meteorites
551.3
Norton, O. R. Rocks from space **523.5**

Asteroids, comets, and meteorites. Erickson, J.
551.3

Asthma
Asthma information for teens **616.2**
Fanta, C. H. The Harvard Medical School guide
to taking control of asthma **616.2**
Paquette, P. H. Asthma **616.2**

Asthma information for teens **616.2**

Aston, Margaret
(ed) The panorama of the Renaissance. See The
panorama of the Renaissance **940.2**

The **astonishing** adventures of Fanboy & Goth
Girl. Lyga, B. **Fic**

The **astonishing life of Octavian Nothing, traitor
to the nation** [series]
Anderson, M. T. The Pox party **Fic**

The **astral** body of a U.S. mail truck. Herlihy, J.
L.
In Nightshade: 20th century ghost stories
p229-39 **S C**

The **Astrologer's** prediction; or, The maniac's fate
In The Oxford book of gothic tales p63-69
S C

Astrology
Woolfolk, J. M. The only astrology book you'll
ever need **133.5**
Encyclopedias
Lewis, J. R. The astrology book **133.5**

The **astrology** book. Lewis, J. R. **133.5**

The **astrology** encyclopedia. See Lewis, J. R. The
astrology book **133.5**

Astronautics
See also Space flight
Angelo, J. A. Space technology **629.4**
Benjamin, M. Rocket dreams **303.4**
Burrows, W. E. This new ocean **629.4**
National Geographic encyclopedia of space
629.4
Zimmerman, R. The chronological encyclopedia
of discoveries in space **629.4**
Dictionaries
Angelo, J. A. The Facts on File dictionary of
space technology **629.4**
International cooperation
Launius, R. D. Frontiers of space exploration
629.45
United States
Kranz, E. F. Failure is not an option **629.45**
Reynolds, D. W. Kennedy Space Center
629.47
Space exploration **333.9**
Walsh, P. J. Echoes among the stars **629.4**
Wolfe, T. The right stuff **629.45**

Astronauts
See also Women astronauts
Wolfe, T. The right stuff **629.45**

The **astronomer**. Updike, J.
In Updike, J. Pigeon feathers, and other stories p179-86 **S C**

Astronomers
See also Women astronomers
Ferris, T. Seeing in the dark **520**
Litwin, L. B. Benjamin Banneker **92**
Voelkel, J. R. Johannes Kepler and the new as-
tronomy **92**

Astronomical almanac for the year 2008 **528**

Astronomical enigmas. Kidger, M. R. **520**

Astronomical instruments
Angelo, J. A. Spacecraft for astronomy **522**
Stephenson, B. The universe unveiled **522**

Astronomical observatories
Angelo, J. A. Spacecraft for astronomy **522**

Astronomy
See also Radio astronomy; Stars
The Amateur astronomer **520**
Barnes-Svarney, P. Through the telescope
522

Augustus, Emperor of Rome, 63 B.C.-14 A.D.
Fiction
Graves, R. I, Claudius　　　　　　　**Fic**

Augustus. Hesse, H.
　In Hesse, H. and Zipes, J. D. The fairy tales
　　of Hermann Hesse　　　　　　**S C**

Aumakua. Salisbury, G.
　In Salisbury, G. Island boyz: short stories
　　p95-117　　　　　　　　　**S C**

Aunt Millicent. Steele, M.
　In Read all about it!; great read-aloud stories,
　　poems, and newspaper pieces for
　　preteens and teens p12-28　　**808.8**

Aunt Parnetta's electric blisters. Glancy, D.
　In The Norton book of science fiction; North
　　American science fiction, 1960-1990
　　p814-18　　　　　　　　　**S C**

Aunts
Fiction
Bauer, J. Hope was here　　　　　**Fic**
Fusco, K. N. Tending to Grace　　　**Fic**
Johnson, M. 13 little blue envelopes　**Fic**
Mackler, C. Vegan virgin Valentine　**Fic**

Auroras
See/See also pages in the following book(s):
Jago, L. The northern lights [biography of
　Kristian Birkeland]　　　　　　**92**

Auschwitz (Poland: Concentration camp)
Graphic novels
Croci, P. Auschwitz　　　　　　**940.53**

Auseon, Andrew, 1976-
Funny little monkey　　　　　　**Fic**

Austen, Jane, 1775-1817
Persuasion　　　　　　　　　**Fic**
Pride and prejudice　　　　　　**Fic**
Sense and sensibility　　　　　　**Fic**
About
Critical essays on Jane Austen　　**823.009**
Jane Austen [critical essays]　　　**823.009**
Olsen, K. All things Austen　　　**823.009**
Poplawski, P. A Jane Austen encyclopedia
　　　　　　　　　　　　823.009
Shields, C. Jane Austen　　　　　**92**

Auster, Paul, 1947-
Auggie Wren's Christmas story
　In Adaptations: from short story to big
　　screen; 35 great stories that have inspired
　　great films　　　　　　　**S C**
(ed) I thought my father was God and other true
　tales from the National Story Project. See I
　thought my father was God and other true
　tales from the National Story Project
　　　　　　　　　　　　810.8

Australia
Fiction
Abdel-Fattah, R. Does my head look big in this?
　　　　　　　　　　　　Fic
Disher, G. The divine wind　　　　**Fic**
Hartnett, S. Thursday's child　　　**Fic**
Herrick, S. By the river　　　　　**Fic**
Jinks, C. Evil genius　　　　　　**Fic**
Larbalestier, J. Magic or madness　**Fic**
Marchetta, M. Saving Francesca　　**Fic**
Marsden, J. Tomorrow, when the war began
　　　　　　　　　　　　Fic

Moriarty, J. The year of secret assignments
　　　　　　　　　　　　Fic
Russon, P. Undine　　　　　　　**Fic**
Wild, M. One night　　　　　　　**Fic**
Zusak, M. Getting the girl　　　　**Fic**
Natural history
　See Natural history—Australia

Authoritarianism *See* Totalitarianism
Authors
　See also Literature—Bio-bibliography;
　Women authors
Burt, D. S. The literary 100　　　**809**
Gillespie, J. T. The Newbery/Printz companion
　　　　　　　　　　　　028.5
Read all about it!　　　　　　　**808.8**
Dictionaries
Encyclopedia of world writers　　**920.003**
Popular contemporary writers　　**920.003**
Science fiction, fantasy, and horror writers
　　　　　　　　　　　　920.003
World authors, 1950-1970　　　**920.003**
World authors, 1970-1975　　　**920.003**
World authors, 1975-1980　　　**920.003**
World authors, 1980-1985　　　**920.003**
World authors, 1985-1990　　　**920.003**
World authors, 1990-1995　　　**920.003**
World authors, 1995-2000　　　**920.003**
World authors, 2000-2005　　　**920.003**
Fiction
Setterfield, D. The thirteenth tale　**Fic**
Wolff, T. Old school　　　　　　**Fic**
Homes and haunts
　See Literary landmarks

Authors, African American *See* African American authors

Authors, American
Alcott, L. M. The selected letters of Louisa May
　Alcott　　　　　　　　　**92**
Andersen, R. Arthur Miller　　　**92**
Andersen, R. Toni Morrison　　　**92**
Asimov, I. It's been a good life　　**92**
Baldwin, J. Conversations with James Baldwin
　　　　　　　　　　　　92
Boon, K. A. F. Scott Fitzgerald　**92**
Bruchac, J. Bowman's store　　　**92**
Caravantes, P. Writing is my business　**92**
Conroy, P. My losing season　　　**92**
Crutcher, C. King of the mild frontier: an ill-
　advised autobiography　　　　**92**
Dear author　　　　　　　　**028.5**
Fitzgerald, F. S. A life in letters　**92**
Gaines, E. J. Conversations with Ernest Gaines
　　　　　　　　　　　　92
Gantos, J. Hole in my life　　　　**92**
Haskins, J. Toni Morrison: telling a tale untold
　　　　　　　　　　　　92
King, S. On writing　　　　　　**92**
Meltzer, M. Edgar Allan Poe　　**92**
Meltzer, M. Milton Meltzer　　　**92**
Morrison, T. Conversations with Toni Morrison
　　　　　　　　　　　　92
Myers, W. D. Bad boy　　　　　**92**
Open your eyes　　　　　　　**910.4**
Paulsen, G. The beet fields　　　**92**
Paulsen, G. Eastern sun, winter moon　**92**

The **autobiography** of Alice B. Toklas. Stein, G.
  In Stein, G. Selected writings p1-237   **818**
The **autobiography** of Malcolm X. Malcolm X
    92
The **autobiography** of Miss Jane Pittman. Gaines, E. J.   **Fic**
Autobiography of my dead brother. Myers, W. D.
    Fic
The **autobiography** of Thomas Jefferson. Jefferson, T.
  In Jefferson, T. Writings   **818**
Autobiography, Poor Richard, and later writings. Franklin, B.   **818**
Automata *See* Robots
Automated information networks *See* Information networks
The **automatic** exemption. Sholem Aleichem
  In Halkin, H. and Sholem Aleichem. Tevye the dairyman and The railroad stories
    S C
Automobile accidents *See* Traffic accidents
Automobile drivers
  Gravelle, K. The driving book   **629.28**
Automobile racing
  Menzer, J. The wildest ride   **796.72**
  O'Malley, J. J. Daytona 24 Hours   **796.72**
  Thunder and glory   **796.72**
Automobile service stations *See* Service stations
Automobiles
    See also Electric automobiles
  Edmonston, L.-P. Car smarts   **629.222**
    Design and construction
  Vose, K. E. Inside Monster garage   **629.28**
    Fiction
  Moloney, J. Black taxi   **Fic**
    Maintenance and repair
  Chilton's auto repair manual   **629.28**
  Christensen, L. Clueless about cars   **629.28**
  Florence, M. The everything car care book
    629.28
Autopsy room four. King, S.
  In King, S. Everything's eventual: 14 dark tales   **S C**
Avakian, Monique
  Atlas of Asian-American history   **305.8**
Avalanches
  Fredston, J. A. Snowstruck   **551.3**
The **Avalon** Ballroom. Hood, A.
  In Working days: stories about teenagers and work   **S C**
Aveni, Anthony F.
  Empires of time   **529**
  Stairways to the stars   **520**
Averett, Edward, 1951-
  Pig lessons
  In Every man for himself; ten short stories about being a guy   **S C**
Avi, 1937-
    About
  Bloom, S. P. Presenting Avi   **813.009**
Avian influenza
  Siegel, M. Bird flu   **614.5**

Aviation *See* Aeronautics
Aviation century [series]
  Dick, R. The golden age   **629.13**
  Dick, R. War & peace in the air   **629.13**
Aviators *See* Air pilots
Avila, Inés Hernández- *See* Hernández-Avila, Inés
Avisson young adult series
  Zach, K. K. Hidden from history   **920**
Avoiding armageddon. Schram, M.   **327.1**
The **awakening.** Chopin, K.
  In Chopin, K. The awakening and selected stories   **S C**
The **awakening.** Clarke, A. C.
  In Clarke, A. C. The collected stories of Arthur C. Clarke   **S C**
The **awakening** and selected stories. Chopin, K.
    S C
An **axe** for men. Edghill, R.
  In Young warriors; stories of strength   **S C**
Axelrod, Alan, 1952-
  The encyclopedia of the American armed forces
    355
  (jt. auth) Phillips, C. Encyclopedia of wars
    355
Aya. Abouet, M.   **741.5**
Ayer, Eleanor H.
  In the ghettos   **940.53**
  Parallel journeys   **940.53**
Aykroyd, Clarissa
  Savage satire [biography of Jonathan Swift]
    92
Aymar, Brandt
  (ed) Men in sports. See Men in sports   **796**
The **Ayn** Rand reader. Rand, A.   **191**
Ayto, John
  (ed) Brewer's dictionary of modern phrase & fable. See Brewer's dictionary of modern phrase & fable   **803**
  (ed) Brewer's dictionary of phrase & fable. See Brewer's dictionary of phrase & fable
    803
Azaceta, Paul
  (il) Sable, M. Grounded, Vol. 1: Powerless
    741.5
Aztecs
  Smith, M. E. The Aztecs   **972**
  Townsend, R. F. The Aztecs   **972**
  See/See also pages in the following book(s):
  Ceram, C. W. Gods, graves, and scholars
    930.1
  Wright, R. Stolen continents   **970.004**
Azuma, Kiyohiko, 1968-
  Azumanga Daioh, Vol. 1   **741.5**
Azumanga Daioh, Vol. 1. Azuma, K.   **741.5**

B

B., David, 1959-
  Epileptic   **616.8**
B for Buster. Lawrence, I.   **Fic**

Baba Yaga and the sorcerer's son. McKillip, P. A.
  In McKillip, P. A. Harrowing the dragon
  S C

Babbitt. Lewis, S.
  In Lewis, S. Main Street & Babbitt **Fic**

Babe: the life and legend of Babe Didrikson Zaharias. Cayleff, S. E. **92**

Babel´, I. (Isaac), 1894-1940
  How it was done in Odessa
  In The portable twentieth-century Russian reader **891.7**
  My first fee
  In The portable twentieth-century Russian reader **891.7**
  My first goose
  In The portable twentieth-century Russian reader **891.7**

Babel´, Isaac *See* Babel´, I. (Isaac), 1894-1940

Babel, Tower of
  See/See also pages in the following book(s):
  Ceram, C. W. Gods, graves, and scholars
  930.1

Babies *See* Infants

Baby Be-Bop. Block, F. L.
  In Block, F. L. Dangerous angels; the Weetzie Bat books **Fic**

Baby care *See* Infants—Care

Baby H.P. Arreola, J. J.
  In Cosmos latinos; an anthology of science fiction from Latin America and Spain
  S C

The **baby** in the icebox. Cain, J. M.
  In The Best American mystery stories of the century p178-192 **S C**
  In The Norton book of American short stories p297-311 **S C**

Babylon revisited. Fitzgerald, F. S.
  In Adaptations: from short story to big screen; 35 great stories that have inspired great films **S C**
  In Fitzgerald, F. S. The short stories of F. Scott Fitzgerald; a new collection p616-33 **S C**

The **babysitter**. Coover, R.
  In The Norton book of American short stories p595-618 **S C**

Babysitters
  Fiction
  Griffin, A. My almost epic summer **Fic**
  Wolff, V. E. Make lemonade **Fic**

Babysitting
  Dayee, F. S. Babysitting **649**

Bach, Johann Sebastian, 1685-1750
  See/See also pages in the following book(s):
  Grout, D. J. A history of western music
  780.9

Bachel, Beverly K., 1957-
  What do you really want? **153.8**

Bachleda, F. Lynne, 1951-
  Dangerous wildlife in California & Nevada
  591.6
  Dangerous wildlife in the mid-Atlantic **591.6**
  Dangerous wildlife in the Southeast **591.6**

Bachman, Richard *See* King, Stephen, 1947-

Bacho, Peter
  A matter of faith
  In American eyes; new Asian-American short stories for young adults **S C**

The **back** of beyond. Maugham, W. S.
  In Maugham, W. S. Collected short stories
  S C

Backgrounds to American literature [series]
  Phillips, J. Romanticism and transcendentalism: 1800-1860 **810.9**

Backgrounds to English literature **820.9**

Backpacking
  Berger, K. Advanced backpacking **796.51**
  Hart, J. Walking softly in the wilderness
  796.51

A **backward** glance. Wharton, E.
  In Wharton, E. Novellas and other writings
  818

Bacon, Francis, 1561-1626
  See/See also pages in the following book(s):
  Durant, W. J. The story of philosophy **109**

Bacon, Tony
  The ultimate guitar book **787.87**

Bacteria
  Bakalar, N. Where the germs are **616**
  Shnayerson, M. The killers within **616**

Bacterial infections
  Freeman-Cook, L. Staphylococcus aureus infections **616.9**

Bacteriology
  See also Germ theory of disease
  See/See also pages in the following book(s):
  Friedman, M. Medicine's 10 greatest discoveries
  610.9

Bad blood. Weaver, W.
  In Destination unexpected: short stories
  S C

Bad boy. Myers, W. D. **92**

A **bad** boy can be good for a girl. Stone, T. L.
  Fic

Bad day for baseball. Salisbury, G.
  In Shattered: stories of children and war p23-39 **S C**

Bad girls. Oates, J. C.
  In Oates, J. C. Small avalanches and other stories **S C**

Bad habits. McNally, T.
  In McNally, T. 15 short plays p195-268
  812

Bad hair day. Myracle, L.
  In Such a pretty face; short stories **S C**

Bad Heart Buffalo, Amos, ca. 1869-1913
  The life and death of Crazy Horse **92**

Bad influence. Ortiz Cofer, J.
  In Leaving home: stories p63-90 **808.8**
  In Ortiz Cofer, J. An island like you; stories of the barrio **S C**

Bad kitty. Jaffe, M. **Fic**

Bad things. Bray, L.
  In The restless dead; ten original stories of the supernatural **S C**

Baddeley, Alan D., 1934-
  Your memory **153.1**

The **baddest** dog in Harlem. Myers, W. D.
In Myers, W. D. 145th Street; short stories
S C

Bader, Jenny Lyn
None of the above
In Under 30; plays for a new generation
812.008

Bader, Philip
African-American writers **920.003**

Badge of valor. Ashabranner, B. K. **363.2**

Badger, David
(jt. auth) Netherton, J. Lizards **597.9**

Badminton (Game)
Boga, S. Badminton **796.34**

Baechler, Lea
(ed) Modern American women writers. See
Modern American women writers **810.9**

Baek, Hongyong, 1912-2002
About
Lee, H. Still life with rice [biography of
Hongyong Baek] **92**

A **bag** of oranges. Athanas, S.
In Coming of age in America; a multicultural
anthology p216-25 **S C**

Bagdasarian, Adam
Forgotten fire **Fic**

Baggott, Julianna
The future lives of Emily Milty
In Sixteen: stories about that sweet and bitter
birthday **S C**

Bagombo snuff box. Vonnegut, K.
In Vonnegut, K. Bagombo snuff box: uncollected short fiction p135-46 **S C**

Bagombo snuff box: uncollected short fiction.
Vonnegut, K. **S C**

Bahai Faith
Hartz, P. Baha'i Faith **297**

Baha'i Faith. Hartz, P. **297**

Bahaism *See* Bahai Faith

Bahn, Paul G.
The Cambridge illustrated history of prehistoric
art **709.01**

Baigrie, Brian S. (Brian Scott)
(ed) History of modern science and mathematics. See History of modern science and mathematics **509**
(ed) The Renaissance and the scientific revolution. See The Renaissance and the scientific
revolution **920.003**

Bailey, Anne C.
African voices of the Atlantic slave trade
326

Bailey, Frankie Y.
(ed) Famous American crimes and trials. See
Famous American crimes and trials **364**

Bailey, Jill
(ed) The Facts on File dictionary of botany. See
The Facts on File dictionary of botany
580

Bailey, John
The lost German slave girl [biography of Salomé Muller] **92**

Bailey, Kristen
(ed) How should prisons treat inmates? See
How should prisons treat inmates? **365**
(ed) Sex education. See Sex education **613.9**

Bailey, Lee Worth
(ed) Introduction to the world's major religions.
See Introduction to the world's major religions **200**

Bailey, R. A.
(jt. auth) Rittner, D. Encyclopedia of chemistry
540.3

Bailey, Robin W.
Doing time
In Past imperfect **S C**

Bailey, Wayne, 1955-
The complete marching band resource manual
784.8

Baines, Anthony
The Oxford companion to musical instruments
784.19

Bair, Barbara
Though justice sleeps
In The Young Oxford history of African
Americans **305.8**

Baird, Robin W.
Killer whales of the world **599.5**

Bakalar, Nick
Where the germs are **616**

Baker, Alan
The knight **940.1**

Baker, Beth A., 1964-
(ed) Holidays and anniversaries of the world.
See Holidays and anniversaries of the world
394.26

Baker, Charles F., III
(jt. auth) Baker, R. F. Ancient Egyptians
932
(jt. auth) Baker, R. F. Ancient Greeks **938**
(jt. auth) Baker, R. F. Ancient Romans **937**

Baker, Kevin, 1958-
(jt. auth) Evans, H. The American century
973.9

Baker, Kyle
Nat Turner Encore Edition Vol. 1 **92**

Baker, Lawrence W.
(jt. auth) Bruno, L. C. Math and mathematicians
920
(ed) Grumet, B. H. Reconstruction era: primary
sources **973.8**
(jt. auth) Hillstrom, K. American Civil War: biographies **920**
(ed) Matuz, R. Reconstruction era: biographies
920
(jt. auth) Newton, D. E. Chemical elements
546
(ed) Outman, J. L. U.S. immigration and migration. Biographies **920**
(ed) U.S. immigration and migration, Prim
sources. See U.S. immigration and mi
Primary sources

Baker, Nancy L., 1950-
A research guide for under

The **balloon-hoax**. Poe, E. A.
In Poe, E. A. The collected tales and poems of Edgar Allan Poe p71-81 **818**

Balmer, Randall Herbert
Religion in twentieth century America **200.9**

Balo. Toomer, J.
In Black theatre USA; plays by African Americans, 1847 to today **812.008**

Baltimore Orioles (Baseball team)
See/See also pages in the following book(s):
Ripken, C., Jr. The only way I know **92**

Bambara, Toni Cade
Gorilla, my love
In The Norton book of American short stories p675-80 **S C**
Raymond's run
In Who do you think you are?; stories of friends and enemies p47-57 **S C**

Bamford, Janet
Street wise **332.6**

Banal story. Hemingway, E.
In Hemingway, E. The complete short stories of Ernest Hemingway; the Finca Vigía edition p274-75 **S C**

Banana bottom [excerpt] McKay, C.
In The Portable Harlem Renaissance reader p395-408 **810.8**

Banana Sunday. Nibot, R. **741.5**

Bancroft, Tom
Creating characters with personality **741.6**

Bands (Music)
Bailey, W. The complete marching band resource manual **784.8**
Fiction
Simmons, M. Vandal **Fic**

Banerjee, Dillon
So you want to join the Peace Corps **361.6**

Bang!. Flake, S. G. **Fic**

Bang! you're dead!. Bradbury, R.
In Bradbury, R. Bradbury stories; 100 of his most celebrated tales **S C**

Bangs, Richard
Mystery of the Nile **916**

Banish, Roslyn, 1942-
Focus on living **362.1**

Banjo [excerpt] McKay, C.
In The Portable Harlem Renaissance reader p389-94 **810.8**

Banjos
Ellis, R. M. With a banjo on my knee **787.8**

Bankier, William, 1928-
Making a killing with Mama Cass
In Alfred Hitchcock's mystery magazine presents fifty years of crime and suspense **S C**

Banks, Arthur S.
(ed) Political handbook of the world 2007. See Political handbook of the world 2007 **324.025**

Banks, Cyndi
Punishment in America **364.6**

Banks, Robert B.
Slicing pizzas, racing turtles, and further adventures in applied mathematics **793.74**

Banks, Russell, 1940-
Rule of the bone **Fic**

Bankston, Carl L., III, 1952-
(ed) Immigration in U.S. history. See Immigration in U.S. history **304.8**

Banned books *See* Books—Censorship

Banned plays. Sova, D. B. **792.09**

Banneker, Benjamin, 1731-1806
About
Litwin, L. B. Benjamin Banneker **92**

Banner, Lois W.
Elizabeth Cady Stanton **92**

Banshee. Bradbury, R.
In Bradbury, R. Bradbury stories; 100 of his most celebrated tales **S C**

Bar mitzvah
Oppenheimer, M. Thirteen and a day **296.4**

Baraka, Imamu Amiri, 1934-
Dutchman
In Black theatre USA; plays by African Americans, 1847 to today **812.008**

Barakat, Ibtisam
Piano obsession
In What a song can do; 12 riffs on the power of music **S C**
The second day
In Shattered: stories of children and war p5-13 **S C**
Tasting the sky **92**

Barancik, Sue, 1944-
Guide to collective biographies for children and young adults **016.9**

Baranovich Station. Sholem Aleichem
In Halkin, H. and Sholem Aleichem. Tevye the dairyman and The railroad stories **S C**

Barbara of the House of Grebe. Hardy, T.
In The Oxford book of gothic tales p218-44 **S C**

Barbary States *See* North Africa

Barbauld, Anna Letitia Aikin, 1743-1825
Sir Bertrand
In The Oxford book of gothic tales p3-6 **S C**

Barber, Peter, 1948-
(ed) The Map book. See The Map book **526**

The **barber**. O'Connor, F.
In O'Connor, F. Collected works p714-24 **S C**
In O'Connor, F. The complete stories p15-25 **S C**

Barbie-Q. Cisneros, S.
In Cisneros, S. Woman Hollering Creek and other stories **S C**

Barbosa Monteiro, Jerônimo *See* Monteiro, Jerônimo, 1908-1970

Barbour, Scott, 1963-
(ed) Alcohol. See Alcohol **362.292**
(ed) Gangs. See Gangs **364.1**

Barbour, Scott, 1963- —*Continued*
(ed) Genetic engineering. See Genetic engineering   **174.2**
(ed) How can school violence be prevented? See How can school violence be prevented?   **371.7**

Barbour, William, 1963-
See also Barbour, Scott, 1963-

Barceló, Elia, 1957-
First time
In Cosmos latinos; an anthology of science fiction from Latin America and Spain   **S C**

Bardin, Matt
Zen in the art of the SAT   **378.1**

Barefoot heart. Hart, E. T.   **92**

Barefoot in the park. Simon, N.
In Simon, N. The collected plays of Neil Simon   **812**

The **barefoot** serpent. Morse, S.   **741.5**

Barefootin'. Blackwell, U.   **92**

Barghusen, Joan D., 1935-
Cults   **209**

Barkan, Elazar
The guilt of nations   **341.6**

Barker, Clive
Abarat   **Fic**

Barker, Lucius Jefferson, 1928-
(ed) Civil liberties and the constitution. See Civil liberties and the constitution   **342**

Barks, Coleman
See/See also pages in the following book(s):
Fooling with words   **808.1**

Barlow, Philip L.
(jt. auth) Gaustad, E. S. New historical atlas of religion in America   **200.9**

Barn burning. Faulkner, W.
In Faulkner, W. Collected stories of William Faulkner p3-25   **S C**
In Faulkner, W. Selected short stories of William Faulkner   **S C**

Barnavi, Eli
(ed) A Historical atlas of the Jewish people. See A Historical atlas of the Jewish people   **909**

Barnes, Ian, 1946-
The historical atlas of the American Revolution   **973.3**

Barnes, Jessica
(ed) GirlSource. See GirlSource   **305.23**

Barnes, Gregory Fremont- *See* Fremont-Barnes, Gregory

Barnes-Svarney, Patricia
Through the telescope   **522**

Barney, William L.
The Civil War and Reconstruction   **973.7**

Barnhart, Robert K.
(ed) The Barnhart abbreviations dictionary. See The Barnhart abbreviations dictionary   **421.03**

The **Barnhart** abbreviations dictionary   **421.03**

Barnicoat, John, 1924-
Posters: a concise history   **741.6**

Barnouw, David
(ed) Frank, A. The diary of Anne Frank: the critical edition   **92**

Barnstone, Aliki
(ed) A Book of women poets from antiquity to now. See A Book of women poets from antiquity to now   **808.81**

Barnstone, Willis, 1927-
(ed) A Book of women poets from antiquity to now. See A Book of women poets from antiquity to now   **808.81**
(ed) The Gnostic Bible. See The Gnostic Bible   **299**

Barone, Michael
The almanac of American politics, 2006   **328.73**

Barough, Nina
Walking for fitness   **613.7**

Barr, Catherine
(jt. auth) Gillespie, J. T. Best books for high school readers   **011.6**
(jt. auth) Thomas, R. L. Popular series fiction for middle school and teen readers   **016.8**

Barr, Nevada
Track of the cat   **Fic**

Barrett, Carole A.
(ed) American Indian biographies. See American Indian biographies   **920.003**

Barrett, Joanne R., 1960-
Teaching and learning about computers   **004**

Barrett, Tracy, 1955-
(jt. auth) Kleeman, T. F. The ancient Chinese world   **931**

Barron, Neil, 1934-
What do I read next? 2007. See What do I read next? 2007   **016.8**
(ed) Anatomy of wonder. See Anatomy of wonder   **016.8**
(ed) Fantasy and horror. See Fantasy and horror   **016.8**

Barron, Pamela Petrick, 1946-
(jt. auth) Doll, C. A. Managing and analyzing your collection   **025.2**

Barron's ACT assessment   **378.1**

Barron's How to prepare for the ACT assessment. See Barron's ACT assessment   **378.1**

Barron's How to prepare for the American College Testing Program (ACT). See Barron's ACT assessment   **378.1**

Barron's profiles of American colleges 2007   **378.73**

Barrow, Lloyd H.
Science fair projects investigating earthworms   **592**

Barry, Lynda
One hundred demons   **741.5**

Barry, Max
Jennifer Government   **Fic**

Barth, Kelly
(ed) The rise and fall of the Taliban. See The rise and fall of the Taliban   **958.1**

Barth, Kelly—*Continued*
(ed) The Tiananmen Square massacre. See The
Tiananmen Square massacre   **951.05**

Barthelmas, Della Gray, 1920-
The signers of the Declaration of Independence
920.003

Barthelme, Donald
The death of Edward Lear
In The Literary ghost; great contemporary
ghost stories p111-14   **S C**
Robert Kennedy saved from drowning
In The Norton book of American short stories
p587-95   **S C**

Bartimaeus trilogy [series]
Stroud, J. The Amulet of Samarkand   **Fic**

Bartlett, John, 1820-1905
Bartlett's familiar quotations   **808.88**

Bartlett's familiar quotations. Bartlett, J.
808.88

Bartlett's Roget's thesaurus   **423**

Bartoletti, Susan Campbell, 1958-
Black potatoes   **941.5**
Hitler Youth   **943.086**

Barton, Clara, 1821-1912
About
Oates, S. B. A woman of valor: Clara Barton
and the Civil War   **92**

Baryshnikov, Mikhail, 1948-
See/See also pages in the following book(s):
Ford, C. T. Legends of American dance and
choreography   **920**

Bas mitzvah *See* Bat mitzvah

Baseball
See also Negro leagues; Softball; World se-
ries (Baseball)
Adair, R. K. The physics of baseball
796.357
Angell, R. Game time: a baseball companion
796.357
Asinof, E. Eight men out   **796.357**
Baseball: a literary anthology   **810.8**
Baseball, the perfect game   **796.357**
Biographical dictionary of American sports,
Baseball   **796.357**
Encyclopedia of women and baseball
796.357
Enders, E. 100 years of the World Series
796.357
Hogan, L. D. Shades of glory   **796.357**
Kahn, R. Beyond the boys of summer
796.357
Kelley, B. P. Voices from the Negro leagues
796.357
McGuire, M. The 100 greatest baseball players
of the 20th century ranked   **796.357**
Owens, T. Collecting baseball memorabilia
790.1
Ripken, C., Jr. Play baseball the Ripken way
796.357
Sokolove, M. Y. The ticket out: Darryl Straw-
berry and the boys of Crenshaw   **796.357**
Total baseball   **796.357**
Vecsey, G. Baseball: a history of America's fa-
vorite game   **796.357**

Wendel, T. The new face of baseball
796.357
Wilson, N. Voices from the pastime   **796.357**
Biography
Fussman, C. After Jackie   **92**
Jeter, D. The life you imagine   **92**
Maraniss, D. Clemente   **92**
Morris, J. The oldest rookie   **92**
New York Times Company. Sultans of swat
920
Ripken, C., Jr. The only way I know   **92**
Robinson, J. I never had it made   **92**
Stanton, T. Hank Aaron and the home run that
changed America   **92**
Wells, D. Perfect I'm not   **92**
Encyclopedias
Light, J. F. The cultural encyclopedia of base-
ball   **796.357**
Fiction
Deuker, C. Painting the black   **Fic**
Gratz, A. Samurai shortstop   **Fic**
Kinsella, W. P. Shoeless Joe   **Fic**
Turner, A. W. Hard hit   **Fic**
Weaver, W. Striking out   **Fic**
Graphic novels
Sturm, J. James Sturm's America   **741.5**
Pictorial works
Baseball's best shots   **796.357**
Statistics
Neft, D. S. The sports encyclopedia: baseball
2007   **796.357**

Baseball: a literary anthology   **810.8**

The **baseball** glove. Martinez, V.
In Working days: stories about teenagers and
work   **S C**

Baseball in Iraq (being the true story of the ghost
of Gunnery Sergeant T.J. McVeigh). Ritter, J.
H.
In Dreams and visions; fourteen flights of
fantasy   **S C**

Baseball, the perfect game   **796.357**

Baseball's best shots   **796.357**

The **basement** room. Greene, G.
In Adaptations: from short story to big
screen; 35 great stories that have inspired
great films   **S C**

Basic book repair methods. Schechter, A. A.
025.7

Basic documents in American history   **973**

A **basic** guide to ice hockey   **796.962**

Basic Japanese-English dictionary   **495.6**

Basic life skills *See* Life skills

Basic nutrition. Smolin, L. A.   **613.2**

Basic rights *See* Civil rights; Human rights

Basic weight training for men and women. Fahey,
T. D.   **613.7**

The **basic** works of Aristotle. Aristotle   **888**

The **basic** writings of C. G. Jung. De Laszlo, V.
S.   **150.19**

The **basic** writings of Sigmund Freud. Freud, S.
150.19

The **basics** of biology. Stone, C. L.   **570**

The **basics** of chemistry. Myers, R.   **540**

Bauer, Joan—*Continued*
Hardware
In Necessary noise: stories about our families as they really are p1-20 **S C**
Hope was here **Fic**
Rules of the road **Fic**

Bauer, Marion Dane, 1938-
Dancing backwards
In Am I blue?; coming out from the silence p261-72 **S C**
(ed) Am I blue? See Am I blue? **S C**

Bauermeister, Erica
500 great books by women **016.3054**

Baugh, Bryan
(jt. auth) Miller, S. Scared!: how to draw fantastic horror comic characters **741.5**

Baughman, Judith
(ed) Fitzgerald, F. S. A life in letters **92**

Baum, Lawrence
The Supreme Court **347**

Baumbach, Donna
Less is more **025.2**

Baumfree, Isabella *See* Truth, Sojourner, d. 1883

Bawden-Davis, Julie
Flower gardening **635.9**

Baxandall, Rosalyn Fraad, 1939-
(ed) America's working women. See America's working women **331.4**

Baxter, Charles
The next building I plan to bomb
In Gotham Writers' Workshop fiction gallery; exceptional short stories selected by New York's acclaimed creative writing school **S C**

Baxter, Stephen
Gossamer
In The Hard SF renaissance **S C**
On the orion line
In The Hard SF renaissance **S C**
People came from earth
In Best of the best: 20 years of the Year's best science fiction **S C**

Bayless, Lanie
(jt. auth) Bayless, R. Rick & Lanie's excellent kitchen adventures **641.5**

Bayless, Rick
Rick & Lanie's excellent kitchen adventures **641.5**

Bazooka Joe and the Chaos Kid. Howe, N.
In Make me over; 11 stories of transformation **S C**

Be afraid, be very afraid **398.2**

Be aggressive. Weisman, A.
In Under 30; plays for a new generation **812.008**

Beach, Rex, 1877-1949
The weight of obligation
In A Century of great Western stories **S C**

Beacham's encyclopedia of popular fiction **809.3**

Beachworld. King, S.
In King, S. Skeleton crew **S C**

Beacon Hill boys. Mochizuki, K. **Fic**

Beads
Discover beading **745.58**

Beadwork
Discover beading **745.58**
Taylor, C. Creative bead jewelry **745.58**

Beagle, Peter S.
The last unicorn **Fic**
The line between **S C**
Contents: Gordon, the self-made cat; Two hearts; The fable of the moth; The fable of the tyrannosaurus rex; The fable of the ostrich; The fable of the octopus; El Regalo; Quarry; Salt wine; Mr. Sigerson; A dance for Emilia

Beah, Ishmael, 1980-
A long way gone **92**

The **bean** trees. Kingsolver, B. **Fic**

Beane, Douglas Carter
As bees in honey drown
In Under 30; plays for a new generation **812.008**

Bear, Greg, 1951-
Blood music
In Best of the best: 20 years of the Year's best science fiction **S C**
The collected stories of Greg Bear **S C**
Schrödinger's plague
In The Norton book of science fiction; North American science fiction, 1960-1990 p477-84 **S C**
Tangents
In New skies: an anthology of today's science fiction **S C**

The **bear**. Chekhov, A. P.
In Chekhov, A. P. The plays of Anton Chekhov p19-33 **891.7**

Bear daughter. Berman, J. **Fic**

A **bear** hunt. Faulkner, W.
In Faulkner, W. Collected stories of William Faulkner p63-79 **S C**

Beard, Jocelyn
(ed) 100 great monologues from the neo-classical theatre. See 100 great monologues from the neo-classical theatre **808.82**
(ed) 100 great monologues from the Renaissance theatre. See 100 great monologues from the Renaissance theatre **822.008**
(ed) The Best men's stage monologues of 2006. See The Best men's stage monologues of 2006 **808.82**
(ed) The Best women's stage monologues of 2006. See The Best women's stage monologues of 2006 **808.82**
(ed) Scenes from classic plays, 468 B.C. to 1970 A.D. See Scenes from classic plays, 468 B.C. to 1970 A.D. **808.82**
(ed) The Ultimate audition book. See The Ultimate audition book **808.82**

Beard, Philip, 1963-
Dear Zoe **Fic**

Bearden, Romare, 1914-1988
A history of African-American artists **709.73**

Bierce, Ambrose, 1842-1914?—*Continued*
The coup de grâce
In The Oxford book of short stories p78-83
S C
A vine on a house
In The Oxford book of gothic tales p299-301
S C

Bierhorst, John, 1936-
(ed) Latin American folktales. See Latin American folktales **398.2**

Big bang cosmology *See* Big bang theory

Big bang theory
Kaku, M. Parallel worlds **523.1**
The **big** book of blues. Santelli, R. **781.643**
The **big** book of library grant money, 2006 **025.1**
Big book unplugged. Rosengren, J. **362.292**
Big boy leaves home. Wright, R.
In Wright, R. Uncle Tom's children; five long stories **S C**
Big Chicago. Carter, A. R.
In Carter, A. R. Love, football, and other contact sports **S C**
Big game hunt. Clarke, A. C.
In Clarke, A. C. The collected stories of Arthur C. Clarke **S C**

Big game hunting *See* Hunting

Big Joe's funeral. Myers, W. D.
In Myers, W. D. 145th Street; short stories **S C**
Big meeting. Hughes, L.
In Hughes, L. Short stories of Langston Hughes **S C**
Big Mouth & Ugly Girl. Oates, J. C. **Fic**
The **big** night out. Beker, J. **646.7**
The **big** one. Page, J. **551.2**
Big rage. Lanagan, M.
In Lanagan, M. White time **S C**
The **big** splat; or, How our moon came to be. Mackenzie, D. **523.3**
Big two-hearted river: part I. Hemingway, E.
In Hemingway, E. The complete short stories of Ernest Hemingway; the Finca Vigía edition p163-69 **S C**
Big two-hearted river: part II. Hemingway, E.
In Hemingway, E. The complete short stories of Ernest Hemingway; the Finca Vigía edition p173-80 **S C**
Big wheels: a tale of the laundry game (Milkman #2). King, S.
In King, S. Skeleton crew **S C**
Big white fog. Ward, T.
In Black theatre USA; plays by African Americans, 1847 to today **812.008**

Bigsby, C. W. E.
(ed) Miller, A. The portable Arthur Miller **812**

Bikes, Mountain *See* Mountain bikes

Biko, Stephen, 1946-1977
I write what I like **968.06**

Bilingual books
English-Chinese
Liu Siyu. A thousand peaks **895.1**
English-Spanish
Cool salsa **811.008**
Red hot salsa **811.008**
The Tree is older than you are **860.8**

Bilingual education
Bilingual education **370.117**
Bilingual education **370.117**

The **bill**. Malamud, B.
In Malamud, B. The complete stories **S C**

Bill of rights (U.S.) *See* United States. Constitution. 1st-10th amendments

The **Bill** of Rights **342**
The **Bill** of Rights. Patrick, J. J. **342**

Bill of Rights [series]
Freedom from cruel and unusual punishment **345**
Freedom of religion **342**
Freedom of speech **342**
The right to a trial by jury **345**

The **billiard** ball. Asimov, I.
In Asimov, I. The complete stories p362-76 **S C**

Billings, Charlene W., 1941-
Supercomputers **004**

Billitteri, Thomas J.
Alternative medicine **615.5**

Billy Budd, sailor. Melville, H. **Fic**

Biloxi blues. Simon, N.
In Simon, N. The collected plays of Neil Simon **812**

Bily, Cynthia A.
(ed) Global warming: opposing viewpoints. See Global warming: opposing viewpoints **363.7**

Bingham, Hiram, 1875-1956
Lost city of the Incas **985**

Bingo!. Riggio, A.
In Such a pretty face; short stories **S C**

Biochemistry
Research
Watson, J. D. The double helix **572.8**

Bioengineered foods *See* Food—Biotechnology

Bioethics
Biomedical ethics: opposing viewpoints **174.2**
See/See also pages in the following book(s):
Ethics: opposing viewpoints **170**
Fiction
Ishiguro, K. Never let me go **Fic**
Picoult, J. My sister's keeper **Fic**
Werlin, N. Double helix **Fic**

Bioethics and medical issues in literature. Stripling, M. Y. **809**

Biogeography
World atlas of great apes and their conservation **599.8**

Biograph. Martone, M.
In The Norton book of American short stories p749-63 **S C**

Bishop, Elizabeth, 1911-1979
The complete poems, 1927-1979 **811**

Bishop, Michael, 1945-
The Bob Dylan Tambourine Software & Satori Support Services Consortium, Ltd.
In The Norton book of science fiction; North American science fiction, 1960-1990 p616-27 **S C**

Bishop, Morris, 1893-1973
The Middle Ages **940.1**

The **bishop**. Chekhov, A. P.
In The portable twentieth-century Russian reader **891.7**

Bismarck, Otto, Fürst von, 1815-1898
See/See also pages in the following book(s):
Fulbrook, M. A concise history of Germany **943**

Bissinger, Buzz *See* Bissinger, H. G.

Bissinger, H. G.
Friday night lights **796.332**

Bisson, Terry
Bears discover fire
In Best of the best: 20 years of the Year's best science fiction **S C**
In The Locus awards; thirty years of the best in science fiction and fantasy **S C**
They're made out of meat
In New skies: an anthology of today's science fiction **S C**

Bitter cane. Lim, G.
In The Oxford book of women's writing in the United States p407-40 **810.8**

Bitter grounds. Gaiman, N.
In Gaiman, N. Fragile things; short fictions and wonders **S C**

Bitton-Jackson, Livia
I have lived a thousand years **940.53**

Bjornlund, Britta
The Cold War ends: 1980 to the present **909.82**

Blachford, Stacey
(ed) Drugs and controlled substances. See Drugs and controlled substances **362.29**

Black, Allida M., 1952-
(ed) Roosevelt, E. Courage in a dangerous world **973.9**

Black, Eric
Bosnia **949.7**

Black, Holly, 1971-
Heartless
In Young warriors; stories of strength **S C**
The night market
In The Faery Reel; tales from the Twilight Realm **S C**
The poison eaters
In The restless dead; ten original stories of the supernatural **S C**
Valiant: a modern faerie tale **Fic**

Black, Jeremy
The Cambridge illustrated atlas of warfare: Renaissance to revolution, 1492-1792 **355**
(ed) World history atlas. See World history atlas **911**

Black, Laura
The stem cell debate **174.2**

Black Americans *See* African Americans
The **Black** Americans **305.8**

Black and white. Mori, K.
In Face relations; 11 stories about seeing beyond color **S C**

Black and white. Volponi, P. **Fic**

Black art (Magic) *See* Witchcraft

Black ass at the cross roads. Hemingway, E.
In Hemingway, E. The complete short stories of Ernest Hemingway; the Finca Vigía edition p579-89 **S C**

Black authors
See also African American authors

Black belt tae kwon do. Park, Y. H. **796.8**

Black boy. Wright, R. **92**
also in Wright, R. Works **818**

The **Black** Bull of Norroway
In Hearne, B. G. Beauties and beasts p92-96 **398.2**

The **black** cat. Poe, E. A.
In Poe, E. A. The collected tales and poems of Edgar Allan Poe p223-30 **818**
In Poe, E. A. Edgar Allan Poe's tales of mystery and madness **S C**

Black cat bone. Lewis, J. P. **811**

Black death *See* Plague
The **black** death. Byrne, J. P. **614.5**

Black death. Hurston, Z. N.
In Hurston, Z. N. The complete stories p202-08 **S C**

Black diaspora *See* African diaspora
The **black** doctor. Aldridge, I.
In Black theatre USA; plays by African Americans, 1847 to today **812.008**

Black drama (American) *See* American drama—African American authors

Black Elk, 1863-1950
Black Elk speaks **92**

Black firsts: 4,000 ground-breaking and pioneering historical events **305.8**

Black folktales. Lester, J. **398.2**

Black heritage sites. Curtis, N. C. **917.3**

Black holes and baby universes and other essays. Hawking, S. W. **523.1**

Black holes, wormholes & time machines. Al-Khalili, J. **530.1**

Black ice. Cary, L. **92**

Black Indians. Katz, W. L. **305.8**

Black inventors. Aaseng, N. **920**

Black is my favorite color. Malamud, B.
In Malamud, B. The complete stories **S C**

Black Jack. Kipling, R.
In Kipling, R. The portable Kipling **828**

Black juice. Lanagan, M. **S C**

Black leaders of the nineteenth century **920**

Black like me. Griffin, J. H. **305.8**

Black literature (American) *See* American literature—African American authors

Blazek, Ronald David, 1936-
(jt. auth) Muccigrosso, R. Term paper resource guide to twentieth-century United States history **016.973**

Bleach, Vol. 1. Kubo, T. **741.5**

Bledsoe, Lucy Jane
Teamwork
In Growing up gay; an anthology for young people p240-43 **808.8**

Bless me, father, for I have sinned. Bradbury, R.
In Bradbury, R. Bradbury stories; 100 of his most celebrated tales **S C**

Bless me, Ultima. Anaya, R. A. **Fic**

Blessed among all women. Ellsberg, R. **920**

Blessed assurance. Hughes, L.
In Hughes, L. Short stories of Langston Hughes **S C**

The **blessed** man of Boston, my grandmother's thimble, and Fanning Island. Updike, J.
In Updike, J. Pigeon feathers, and other stories p227-45 **S C**

Blessings. Surface, M. H.
In Surface, M. H. Most valuable player and four other all-star plays for middle and high school audiences **812**

Bligh, William, 1754-1817
About
Alexander, C. The Bounty: the true story of the mutiny on the Bounty **996**
Fiction
Nordhoff, C. Mutiny on the Bounty **Fic**

Blight, David W.
(ed) Passages to freedom. See Passages to freedom **326**

Blind
Keller, H. Helen Keller: selected writings **92**
Keller, H. The story of my life **92**
Roberts, J. A sense of the world [biography of James Holman] **92**

Blind alley. Asimov, I.
In Asimov, I. The complete stories p45-64 **S C**

Blind faith. Wittlinger, E. **Fic**

Blind man's buff. Anderson, F. I.
In The Best American mystery stories of the century p58-72 **S C**

Blink: the power of thinking without thinking. Gladwell, M. **153.4**

Blish, James, 1921-1975
How beautiful with banners
In The Norton book of science fiction; North American science fiction, 1960-1990 p133-41 **S C**

Blizzards
Fiction
Gray, D. E. Together apart **Fic**

Blk love song #1. Kalamu ya Salaam
In Black theatre USA; plays by African Americans, 1847 to today **812.008**

Block, Francesca Lia
Blood roses
In Firebirds rising; an anthology of original science fiction and fantasy **S C**

Dangerous angels **Fic**
Contents: Weetzie Bat; Witch baby; Cherokee Bat and the Goat Guys; Missing Angel Juan; Baby Be-Bop
Girl goddess #9: nine stories **S C**
Contents: Tweetie Sweet Pea; Blue; Dragons in Manhattan; Girl goddess #9; Rave; The canyon; Pixie and Pony; Winnie and Cubby; Orpheus
The rose and the beast **S C**
Weetzie Bat **Fic**
Winnie and Tommy
In Am I blue?; coming out from the silence p29-44 **S C**

Block, Ira
(jt. auth) Young, D. Saving America's treasures **973**

Block, Lawrence, 1938-
By the dawn's early light
In The Best American mystery stories of the century p597-14 **S C**
A candle for the bag lady
In Alfred Hitchcock's mystery magazine presents fifty years of crime and suspense **S C**

Block party—145th Street style. Myers, W. D.
In Myers, W. D. 145th Street; short stories **S C**

Blocked. Bauer, J.
In Dreams and visions; fourteen flights of fantasy **S C**

Blog!: how the newest media revolution is changing politics, business, and culture. Kline, D. **006.7**

Blomquist, Jean M.
(jt. auth) Bolles, R. N. What color is your parachute? for teens **331.7**

Blonde. Min, K.
In American eyes; new Asian-American short stories for young adults **S C**

Blood
Brynie, F. H. 101 questions about blood and circulation, with answers straight from the heart **612.1**
Circulation
See also Cardiovascular system
See/See also pages in the following book(s):
Friedman, M. Medicine's 10 greatest discoveries **610.9**

Blood and chocolate. Klause, A. C. **Fic**

Blood, bedlam, bullets, and badguys. Gannon, M. B. **016.8**

Blood diamonds. Campbell, G. **966.4**

Blood disease. McGrath, P.
In The Oxford book of gothic tales p502-18 **S C**

Blood evidence. Lee, H. C. **614**

Blood lines. McClelland, J.
In International plays for young audiences; contemporary works from leading playwrights p97-129 **808.82**

Blood music. Bear, G.
In Bear, G. The collected stories of Greg Bear **S C**
In Best of the best: 20 years of the Year's best science fiction **S C**

Blood roses. Block, F. L.
In Firebirds rising; an anthology of original
science fiction and fantasy **S C**

Blood sister. Yolen, J.
In Am I blue?; coming out from the silence
p191-212 **S C**

Blood song. Drooker, E. **741.5**

Blood trail. Rusch, K. K.
In Past imperfect **S C**

Blood Wolf. Stirling, S. M.
In The Year's best science fiction and fantasy
for teens: first annual collection **S C**

Bloodchild. Butler, O. E.
In The Locus awards; thirty years of the best
in science fiction and fantasy **S C**

Bloodline. Cary, K. **Fic**

Bloods: an oral history of the Vietnam War by
black veterans **959.704**

The **bloodstained** pavement. Christie, A.
In Christie, A. Miss Marple: the complete
short stories **S C**

Bloody Blanche. Schwob, M.
In The Oxford book of gothic tales p245-48
S C

The **bloody** countess. Pizarnik, A.
In The Oxford book of gothic tales p466-77
S C

Bloody Jack. Meyer, L. A. **Fic**

Bloom, Harold, 1930-
Dramatists and dramas **809.2**
The epic **809**
Essayists and prophets **100**
Hamlet: poem unlimited **822.3**
Novelists and novels **809.3**
Poets and poems **809.1**
Shakespeare: the invention of the human
822.3
Short story writers and short stories **809.3**
(ed) Aeschylus. See Aeschylus [critical essays]
882
(ed) African-American poets: Phillis Wheatley
through Melvin B. Tolson. See African-
American poets: Phillis Wheatley through
Melvin B. Tolson **811.009**
(ed) African-American poets: Robert Hayden
through Rita Dove. See African-American poets: Robert Hayden through Rita Dove
811.009
(ed) Alice Walker. See Alice Walker [critical
essays] **813.009**
(ed) American religious poems. See American
religious poems **811.008**
(ed) The American renaissance. See The American renaissance **810.9**
(ed) Arthur Miller's Death of a salesman. See
Arthur Miller's Death of a salesman [critical
essays] **812.009**
(ed) August Wilson. See August Wilson [critical
essays] **812.009**
(ed) Ben Jonson. See Ben Jonson [critical es-
says] **822.009**
(ed) The Best poems of the English language.
See The Best poems of the English language
821.008

(ed) Elizabeth Barrett Browning. See Elizabeth
Barrett Browning [critical essays] **821.009**
(ed) Ernest Hemingway. See Ernest Hemingway
[critical essays] **813.009**
(ed) Eudora Welty. See Eudora Welty [critical
essays] **813.009**
(ed) Eugene O'Neill. See Eugene O'Neill [criti-
cal essays] **812.009**
(ed) Franz Kafka's The metamorphosis. See
Franz Kafka's The metamorphosis [study
guide] **833.009**
(ed) Gwendolyn Brooks. See Gwendolyn Brooks
[critical essays] **811.009**
(ed) The Harlem Renaissance. See The Harlem
Renaissance [critical essays] **810.9**
(ed) Harper Lee's To kill a mockingbird. See
Harper Lee's To kill a mockingbird [study
guide] **813.009**
(ed) Hermann Hesse. See Hermann Hesse [criti-
cal essays] **838**
(ed) Homer. See Homer **883**
(ed) J.D. Salinger's The catcher in the rye. See
J.D. Salinger's The catcher in the rye [study
guide] **813.009**
(ed) Jane Austen. See Jane Austen [critical es-
says] **823.009**
(ed) Jean-Paul Sartre. See Jean-Paul Sartre [crit-
ical essays] **848**
(ed) Langston Hughes. See Langston Hughes
[critical essays] **818**
(ed) Leo Tolstoy: comprehensive research and
study guide. See Leo Tolstoy: comprehensive
research and study guide **891.7**
(ed) Literature of the Holocaust. See Literature
of the Holocaust **809**
(ed) Lord of the Flies. See Lord of the Flies
[critical essays] **823.009**
(ed) Mark Twain's The adventures of Huckleberry Finn. See Mark Twain's The adventures
of Huckleberry Finn **813.009**
(ed) Mary Shelley's Frankenstein. See Mary
Shelley's Frankenstein [study guide]
823.009
(ed) Maya Angelou. See Maya Angelou [critical
essays] **818**
(ed) Maya Angelou's I know why the caged
bird sings. See Maya Angelou's I know why
the caged bird sings **818**
(ed) Molière. See Molière [critical essays]
842
(ed) Poets of World War I: Rupert Brooke &
Siegfried Sassoon. See Poets of World War I:
Rupert Brooke & Siegfried Sassoon
821.009
(ed) Poets of World War I: Wilfred Owen &
Isaac Rosenberg. See Poets of World War I:
Wilfred Owen & Isaac Rosenberg **821.009**
(ed) Romantic poetry and prose. See Romantic
poetry and prose **820.8**
(ed) Shakespeare's histories. See Shakespeare's
histories **822.3**
(ed) Sophocles' Oedipus rex. See Sophocles'
Oedipus rex [critical essays] **882**
(ed) Sylvia Plath. See Sylvia Plath [critical es-
says] **811.009**
(ed) Thomas Hardy. See Thomas Hardy [critical
essays] **823.009**

Bohr, Niels Henrik David, 1885-1962
About
Ottaviani, J. Suspended in language   **92**
See/See also pages in the following book(s):
Cropper, W. H. Great physicists   **920**
Henderson, H. Nuclear physics   **539.7**

"**Boil** some water—lots of it". Fitzgerald, F. S.
In Fitzgerald, F. S. The short stories of F.
Scott Fitzgerald; a new collection p751-56   **S C**

Bojaxhiu, Agnes Gonxha *See* Teresa, Mother, 1910-1997

Bok, Chip, 1952-
A recent history of the United States in political cartoons   **973.92**

Boland, Robert, 1925-
Musicals!   **792.6**

Bolden, Tonya
Cause: Reconstruction America, 1863-1877   **973.7**
Maritcha [biography of Maritcha Rémond Lyons]   **92**
Wake up our souls   **704**

Boleyn, Anne *See* Anne Boleyn, Queen, consort of Henry VIII, King of England, 1507-1536

Bolles, Richard Nelson
What color is your parachute? for teens   **331.7**

The **Bolshevik** revolution and Russian Civil War. Wade, R. A.   **947.084**

Bolshevism *See* Communism

Bolt, Bruce A., 1930-2005
Earthquakes   **551.2**

Bolt, Marvin, 1963-
(jt. auth) Stephenson, B. The universe unveiled   **522**

Bolt, Robert
A man for all seasons   **822**

Bombers (Terrorists)
See also Suicide bombers

Bon-bon. Poe, E. A.
In Poe, E. A. The collected tales and poems of Edgar Allan Poe p522-34   **818**

Bonaparte, Napoleon *See* Napoleon I, Emperor of the French, 1769-1821

Bond, James (Fictitious character)
Parker, B. R. Death rays, jet packs, stunts, & supercars   **600**

Bonde, Robert K.
(jt. auth) Reep, R. L. The Florida manatee   **599.5**

Bondoux, Anne-Laure
The killer's tears   **Fic**

Bone [excerpt] Ng, F. M.
In American eyes; new Asian-American short stories for young adults   **S C**

Bone detective [biography of Diane France] Hopping, L. J.   **92**

The **bone** of contention. Hurston, Z. N.
In Hurston, Z. N. The complete stories p209-20   **S C**
In Hurston, Z. N. Novels and stories p968-78   **Fic**

Bone sharps, cowboys, and thunder lizards. Ottaviani, J.   **560**

Bones
Kelly, E. B. The skeletal system   **612.7**

Bones. Strasser, T.
In Ultimate sports; short stories by outstanding writers for young adults p238-50   **S C**

The **bones** of the earth. Le Guin, U. K.
In Le Guin, U. K. Tales from Earthsea   **S C**

Bonham, Frank
Burn him out
In A Century of great Western stories   **S C**

Bonham-Boveé, Jonita Ruth, d. 1994
See/See also pages in the following book(s):
Mendoza, P. M. Extraordinary people in extraordinary times   **920**

Bonner, Marita, 1899-1971
The purple flower
In Black theatre USA; plays by African Americans, 1847 to today   **812.008**

Bonner, Nigel *See* Bonner, W. Nigel (William Nigel)

Bonner, W. Nigel (William Nigel)
Whales of the world   **599.5**

Bonner, William Nigel *See* Bonner, W. Nigel (William Nigel)

Bonnin, Gertrude Simmons *See* Zitkala-Ša, 1876-1938

Bontemps, Arna Wendell, 1902-1973
Black thunder [excerpt]
In The Portable Harlem Renaissance reader p674-79   **810.8**
God sends Sunday [excerpt]
In The Portable Harlem Renaissance reader p667-74   **810.8**

The **boogeyman.** King, S.
In King, S. Night shift   **S C**

The **book-bag.** Maugham, W. S.
In Maugham, W. S. Collected short stories   **S C**

Book industry
See also Publishers and publishing

A **book** of autographs. Hawthorne, N.
In Hawthorne, N. Tales and sketches, including Twice-told tales, Mosses from an old manse, and The snow-image; A wonder book for girls and boys; Tanglewood tales for girls and boys, being a second Wonder book p959-74   **S C**

Book of changes *See* I ching

Book of Harlem. Hurston, Z. N.
In Hurston, Z. N. The complete stories p221-26   **S C**
In Hurston, Z. N. Novels and stories p979-84   **Fic**

The **book** of inventions. Harrison, I.   **609**

A **Book** of love poetry   **808.81**

A **Book** of luminious things   **808.81**

The **Book** of monologues for aspiring actors
808.82

The **book** of Mordred. Vande Velde, V. **Fic**

The **book** of sand. Borges, J. L.
In Gotham Writers' Workshop fiction gallery; exceptional short stories selected by New York's acclaimed creative writing school **S C**

The **book** of scenes for aspiring actors. Cassady, M. **808.82**

The **book** of survival. Greenbank, A. H. **613.6**

The **Book** of the states, 2006 **352.13**

A **Book** of women poets from antiquity to now
808.81

Book report biography [series]
Cockcroft, J. D. Latino visions **704**

Book selection
Lyga, A. A. W. Graphic novels in your media center **025.2**
Miller, S. Developing and promoting graphic novel collections **025.2**

Book talks
Bromann, J. Booktalking that works **028.5**
Bromann, J. More booktalking that works
028.5
Gillespie, J. T. Classic teenplots **011.6**

The **book** thief. Zusak, M. **Fic**

Bookbanning in America. Noble, W. **098**

Books
See/See also pages in the following book(s):
Davis, W. S. A day in old Rome **937**
Censorship
Noble, W. Bookbanning in America **098**
Classification
See Classified catalogs
Conservation and restoration
Schechter, A. A. Basic book repair methods
025.7

Books, Filmed *See* Film adaptations

Books and reading
De Vos, G. Storytelling for young adults
372.6
Donelson, K. L. Literature for today's young adults **028.5**
Edwards, M. A. The fair garden and the swarm of beasts **027.62**
Fadiman, C. The new lifetime reading plan
028
Herald, D. T. Genreflecting **016.8**
Jones, P. Connecting young adults and libraries
027.62
Lyga, A. A. W. Graphic novels in your media center **025.2**
Miller, S. Developing and promoting graphic novel collections **025.2**
Peck, R. Invitations to the world **808.06**
Planet on the table **809.1**
Prose, F. Reading like a writer **808**
Best books
See Best books
Fiction
Zusak, M. The book thief **Fic**

Books for children *See* Children's literature

Books for the teen age, 2007. New York Public Library **011.6**

Books for you **011.6**

Booktalking *See* Book talks

Booktalking that works. Bromann, J. **028.5**

Booley, Theresa Anne
Alcohol and your liver **616.86**

Boom Town. Wolfe, T.
In Wolfe, T. The complete short stories of Thomas Wolfe p120-41 **S C**

Boon, Kevin A.
F. Scott Fitzgerald **92**

Boorstin, Daniel J., 1914-2004
The creators **909**
The discoverers **909**
The seekers **909**

Booth, Coe
Tyrell **Fic**

Booth, Heather, 1978-
Serving teens through readers' advisory
028.5

Booth, John Wilkes, 1838-1865
About
Geary, R. The murder of Abraham Lincoln
973.7

Border guards. Egan, G.
In The Locus awards; thirty years of the best in science fiction and fantasy **S C**

Borderlines. Kraus, C. **92**

Bordewich, Fergus M.
Killing the white man's Indian **970.004**

Bordman, Gerald Martin
American musical theatre **792.6**
The Oxford companion to American theatre
792.03

Borel, Pétrus, 1809-1859
Andreas Vesalius the anatomist
In The Oxford book of gothic tales p70-81
S C

Borgenicht, David
(jt. auth) Piven, J. The worst-case scenario survival handbook **613.6**

Borges, Jorge Luis, 1899-1986
The book of sand
In Gotham Writers' Workshop fiction gallery; exceptional short stories selected by New York's acclaimed creative writing school
S C
The Gospel according to Mark
In The Oxford book of gothic tales p478-82
S C
Selected poems **861**

Born beautiful. Fornay, A. **646.7**

Born confused. Desai Hidier, T. **Fic**

Born in sin. Coleman, E. **Fic**

Born on the Fourth of July. Kovic, R.
959.704

Born to rock. Korman, G. **Fic**

Borne, Barbara Wood, 1945-
100 research topic guides for students **025.5**

Borowitz, Sidney, 1918-
Farewell fossil fuels **333.79**

Borrero, Mauricio, 1959-
Russia: a reference guide from the Renaissance to the present   **947**

Bortman, Marci
(ed) Environmental encyclopedia. See Environmental encyclopedia   **363.7**

Bortolotti, Dan
Hope in hell   **610**

Bortz, Alfred B., 1944-
Beyond Jupiter [biography of Heidi Hammel]   **92**

Borus, Audrey
A student's guide to Emily Dickinson   **811.009**

Bosch, Hieronymus, d. 1516
About
Campbell, W. J. The essential Hieronymus Bosch   **759.9492**

Bosco, Antoinette
(jt. auth) Bosco, P. I. World War I   **940.3**

Bosco, Peter I.
World War I   **940.3**

The **Boscombe** Valley mystery. Doyle, Sir A. C.
In Doyle, Sir A. C. The complete Sherlock Holmes   **S C**

Boslough, John
Stephen Hawking's universe   **523.1**

Bosnia and Hercegovina
Black, E. Bosnia   **949.7**
See/See also pages in the following book(s):
Naimark, N. M. Fires of hatred   **364.1**

Boss, Laura, 1938-
Myrna and me
In Growing up ethnic in America; contemporary fiction about learning to be American   **S C**

Bosse, Malcolm J., 1934-2002
The examination   **Fic**

Boston (Mass.)
Fiction
Wilson, D. L. Firehorse   **Fic**

Boston Red Sox (Baseball team)
Halberstam, D. Summer of '49   **796.357**

Botanists
Lowman, M. Life in the treetops   **92**

Botany
See also Plants
Plant   **580**
Plant sciences   **580**
Encyclopedias
Magill's encyclopedia of science   **580**

Botany, Medical *See* Medical botany

Botticelli. McNally, T.
In McNally, T. 15 short plays p51-60   **812**

Botulism
Emmeluth, D. Botulism   **614.5**

Boucquey, Thierry
(ed) Encyclopedia of world writers. See Encyclopedia of world writers   **920.003**

Boudicca *See* Boadicea, Queen, d. 62

Boulle, Pierre, 1912-1994
The bridge over the River Kwai   **Fic**

Planet of the apes   **Fic**

Bound. Napoli, D. J.   **Fic**

Bound for the North Star. Fradin, D. B.   **326**

Bounty (Ship)
Alexander, C. The Bounty: the true story of the mutiny on the Bounty   **996**
Fiction
Nordhoff, C. Mutiny on the Bounty   **Fic**

Bourdain, Anthony
Typhoid Mary   **92**

Bourgeois, Louise
About
Greenberg, J. Runaway girl: the artist Louise Bourgeois   **92**

Bourjaily, Vance, 1922-
The Amish farmer
In American short story masterpieces   **S C**

Bourke-White, Margaret, 1904-1971
About
Rubin, S. G. Margaret Bourke-White   **92**
See/See also pages in the following book(s):
Colman, P. Where the action was   **070.4**

Boustani, Rafic
(jt. auth) Fargues, P. The atlas of the Arab world   **909**

Bova, Ben, 1932-
Mount Olympus
In The Hard SF renaissance   **S C**

Boveé, Jonita Ruth Bonham- *See* Bonham-Boveé, Jonita Ruth, d. 1994

Bow and arrow
See also Archery

Bowden, John, 1935-
(ed) Encyclopedia of Christianity. See Encyclopedia of Christianity   **230.003**

Bowen, Catherine Drinker, 1897-1973
Miracle at Philadelphia   **342**

Bowen, Elizabeth, 1899-1973
The demon lover
In The Oxford book of short stories p346-52   **S C**
The happy autumn fields
In Nightshade: 20th century ghost stories p47-64   **S C**
Her table spread
In The Oxford book of Irish short stories p311-18   **S C**

Bowen, Mark
Thin ice   **551.51**

Bowen, Nancy
Ralph Nader   **92**

Bowen, Rhys, 1941-
Voodoo
In Alfred Hitchcock's mystery magazine presents fifty years of crime and suspense   **S C**

Bower, B. M., 1871-1940
The lamb of the Flying U
In A Century of great Western stories   **S C**

Bowery girl. Taylor, K.   **Fic**

Bowker, John, 1935-
World religions   **200**

Boys, Teenage See Teenagers

Boys and literacy. Knowles, E.   **028.5**

The **boys'** crusade. Fussell, P.   **940.54**

A **boy's** own story. White, E.   **Fic**

Boys to men. Goldstein, M. A.   **613**

The **boys'** war. Murphy, J.   **973.7**

Boz See Dickens, Charles, 1812-1870

Bracebridge Hall. Irving, W.
> In Irving, W. Bracebridge Hall; Tales of a traveller; The Alhambra p1-377   **S C**

Bracebridge Hall; Tales of a traveller; The Alhambra. Irving, W.   **S C**

Brackett, Virginia, 1950-
> Restless genius [biography of Virginia Woolf]   **92**
>
> (ed) The Facts on File companion to the British novel. See The Facts on File companion to the British novel   **823.009**

Bradburn, Frances Bryant
> Output measures for school library media programs   **027.8**

Bradbury, Ray, 1920-
> 2004-05: the naming of names
> > In Bradbury, R. Bradbury stories; 100 of his most celebrated tales   **S C**
>
> Bradbury speaks   **814**
> Bradbury stories   **S C**

Contents: The whole town's sleeping; The rocket; Season of disbelief; And the rock cried out; The drummer boy of Shiloh; The beggar on O'Connell Bridge; The flying machine; Heavyset; The first night of Lent; Lafayette, farewell; Remember Sascha?; Junior; That woman on the lawn; February 1999: Ylla; Banshee; One for his lordship, and one for the road!; The Laurel and Hardy love affair; Unterderseaboat doktor; Another fine mess; The dwarf; A wild night in Galway; The wind; No news, or what killed the dog?; A little journey; Any friend of Nicholas Nickleby's is a friend of mine; The garbage collector; The visitor; The man; Henry the ninth; The messiah; Bang! you're dead!; Darling Adolf; The beautiful shave; Colonel Stonesteel's genuine homemade truly Egyptian mummy; I see you never; The exiles; At midnight, in the month of June; The witch door; The watchers; 200405: the naming of names; Hopscotch; The illustrated man; The dead man; June 2001: and the moon be still as bright; The burning man; G.B.S.—Mark V; A blade of grass; The sound of summer running; And the sailor, home from the sea; The lonely ones; The Finnegan; On the Orient, North; The smiling people; The fruit at the bottom of the bowl; Bug; Downwind from Gettysburg; Time in thy flight; Changeling; The dragon; Let's play "poison"; The cold wind and the warm; The meadow; The Kilimanjaro device; The man in the Rorschach shirt; Blees me, father, for I have sinned; The pedestrian; Trapdoor; The swan; The sea shell; Once more, Legato; 2003: way in the middle of the air; The wonderful death of Dudley Stone; By the numbers!; April 2005: Usher II; The square pegs; The trolley; The smile; The miracles of Jamie; A far-away guitar; The cistern; The machineries of joy; Bright phoenix; The wish; The lifework of Juan Diaz; Time intervening/interim; Almost the end of the world; The great collision of Monday last; The poems; April 2026: the long years; Icarus Montgolfier Wright; Death and the maiden; Zero hour; The Toynbee convector; Forever and the earth; The handler; Getting through Sunday somehow; The Pumpernickel; Last rites; The watchful poker chip of H. Matisse; All on a summer's night

> Fahrenheit 451   **Fic**
> Good grief
> > In Who do you think you are?; stories of friends and enemies p3-13   **S C**
>
> The illustrated man   **S C**

Contents: Prologue: The illustrated man — The veldt — Kaleidoscope — The other foot — The highway — The man — The long rain — The rocket man — The last night of the world — The exiles — No particular night or morning — The fox and the forest — The visitor — The concrete mixer — Marionettes, Inc. — The city — Zero hour — The rocket — The illustrated man

The Martian chronicles   **S C**
The ravine
> In Read all about it!; great read-aloud stories, poems, and newspaper pieces for preteens and teens p252-71   **808.8**

Something wicked this way comes   **Fic**

Bradbury speaks. Bradbury, R.   **814**

Bradbury stories. Bradbury, R.   **S C**

Bradford, Richard, 1932-2002
> Red sky at morning   **Fic**

Bradley, Catherine
> The end of apartheid   **968.06**

Bradley, James
> Flags of our fathers   **940.54**

Bradley, Marion Zimmer
> Elbow room
> > In The Norton book of science fiction; North American science fiction, 1960-1990 p412-26   **S C**
>
> The mists of Avalon   **Fic**

Bradley, Michael J., 1956-
> The age of genius   **920**
> The birth of mathematics   **920**
> The foundations of mathematics   **920**
> Mathematics frontiers   **920**
> Modern mathematics   **920**

Bradshaw, Gillian, 1956-
> The sand-reckoner   **Fic**

Brady, Mathew B., ca. 1823-1896
> ### About
> Armstrong, J. Photo by Brady   **973.7**

Brady, Patricia, 1943-
> Martha Washington   **92**

Brager, Bruce L., 1949-
> John Paul Jones   **92**

Bragg, Rick
> All over but the shoutin'   **92**

Brahms, William B.
> Notable last facts   **031.02**

Brahms, Bill See Brahms, William B.

The **braid**. Frost, H.   **Fic**

Brain
> Fleischman, J. Phineas Gage: a gruesome but true story about brain science   **362.1**
> Hains, B. C. Pain   **616**
> Hudmon, A. Learning and memory   **612.8**
> Morgan, M. The midbrain   **612.8**
> Rose, S. P. R. The future of the brain   **153**
> Sagan, C. The dragons of Eden   **153**
> ### Diseases
> See also Encephalitis
> ### Encyclopedias
> Turkington, C. The encyclopedia of the brain and brain disorders   **612.8**
> ### Wounds and injuries—Fiction
> Hughes, P. Open ice   **Fic**
> Vaught, S. Trigger   **Fic**

Brain damaged children
> Esherick, J. The journey toward recovery   **618.92**

The **brain** encyclopedia. See Turkington, C. The encyclopedia of the brain and brain disorders   **612.8**

Breazeal, Cynthia
About
Brown, J. Robo world [biography of Cyntia Breazeal] **92**

Brecht, Bertolt, 1898-1956
Galileo **832**

Breed, Clara E., 1906-1994
About
Oppenheim, J. Dear Miss Breed **940.53**

Breedlove, Sarah *See* Walker, C. J., Madame, 1867-1919

"**Breeds** there a man . . . ?". Asimov, I.
In Asimov, I. The complete stories p408-37 **S C**

Breiter, Matthias
Bears: [a year in the life] **599.78**

Brennan, Herbie
The necromancers
In The restless dead; ten original stories of the supernatural **S C**

Brennan, J. H.
The magical I ching **299.5**

Brenner, Barbara, 1925-
(ed) Voices: poetry and art from around the world. See Voices: poetry and art from around the world **808.81**

Brenner, Samuel
(ed) The death penalty. See The death penalty [Issues on trial series] **345**
(ed) Living through the Vietnam War. See Living through the Vietnam War **959.704**

Brent, Linda *See* Jacobs, Harriet A., 1813-1897

Breuilly, Elizabeth
Religions of the world **201**

Brewer, Gene
Alejandro
In Twice told; original stories inspired by original art **S C**

Brewer's dictionary of modern phrase & fable **803**

Brewer's dictionary of phrase & fable **803**

Brewster, W. Herbert, d. 1987
See/See also pages in the following book(s):
We'll understand it better by and by **782.25**

Brian and the aliens. Shetterly, W.
In New skies: an anthology of today's science fiction **S C**

Briar Rose. Yolen, J. **Fic**

Brickell, Christopher
(ed) The American Horticultural Society A-Z encyclopedia of garden plants. See The American Horticultural Society A-Z encyclopedia of garden plants **635.9**
(ed) American Horticultural Society encyclopedia of plants and flowers. See American Horticultural Society encyclopedia of plants and flowers **635.9**

The **bridal** party. Fitzgerald, F. S.
In Fitzgerald, F. S. The short stories of F. Scott Fitzgerald; a new collection p561-76 **S C**
In The Norton book of American short stories p326-41 **S C**

The **bride** of the Innisfallen. Welty, E.
In Welty, E. The collected stories of Eudora Welty p495-518 **S C**

The **bride** of the Innisfallen, and other stories. Welty, E.
In Welty, E. The collected stories of Eudora Welty p463-600 **S C**

Bride price. Crew, L.
In Join in; multiethnic short stories by outstanding writers for young adults p111-26 **S C**

The **bride** price. Emecheta, B. **Fic**

The **bridge** over the River Kwai. Boulle, P. **Fic**

Bridges
Brown, D. J. Bridges: three thousand years of defying nature **624.2**
See/See also pages in the following book(s):
Macaulay, D. Building big **720**

Bridging. Apple, M.
In The Norton book of American short stories p692-700 **S C**

A **brief** chapter in my impossible life. Reinhardt, D. **Fic**

A **brief** history of Canada. Riendeau, R. E. **971**

A **brief** history of Central America. Foster, L. V. **972.8**

A **brief** history of Israel. Reich, B. **956.94**

A **brief** history of Mexico. Foster, L. V. **972**

A **brief** history of the Caribbean. Rogozinski, J. **972.9**

The **briefcase**. Carter, A. R.
In Carter, A. R. Love, football, and other contact sports **S C**

A **briefer** history of time. Hawking, S. W. **523.1**

Brier, Bob
The murder of Tutankhamen **932**

The **brigadier** and the golf widow. Cheever, J.
In Cheever, J. The stories of John Cheever p498-511 **S C**

Bright and morning star. Wright, R.
In Wright, R. Uncle Tom's children; five long stories **S C**

Bright morning. Ford, J.
In Feeling very strange; the Slipstream anthology **S C**

Bright phoenix. Bradbury, R.
In Bradbury, R. Bradbury stories; 100 of his most celebrated tales **S C**

Brighton Beach memoirs. Simon, N. **812**
also in Simon, N. The collected plays of Neil Simon **812**

Brigstocke, Hugh
(ed) The Oxford companion to western art. See The Oxford companion to western art **703**

Brill, A. A. (Abraham Arden), 1874-1948
(ed) Freud, S. The basic writings of Sigmund Freud **150.19**

Brill, Abraham Arden *See* Brill, A. A. (Abraham Arden), 1874-1948

Bromann, Jennifer
Booktalking that works   **028.5**
More booktalking that works   **028.5**

Bronchial asthma *See* Asthma

Brontë, Charlotte, 1816-1855
Jane Eyre   **Fic**

Brontë, Emily, 1818-1848
Brontë: poems   **821**
Wuthering Heights   **Fic**

Bronx (New York, N.Y.)
Fiction
Booth, C. Tyrell   **Fic**
Grimes, N. Bronx masquerade   **Fic**

Bronx masquerade. Grimes, N.   **Fic**

The **brooch**. Faulkner, W.
In Faulkner, W. Collected stories of William
    Faulkner p647-65   **S C**

Brooke, Rupert, 1887-1915
About
Poets of World War I: Rupert Brooke & Sieg-
    fried Sassoon   **821.009**

Brooklyn (New York, N.Y.)
Fiction
Frank, E. R. Life is funny   **Fic**
Hamill, P. Snow in August   **Fic**
Malamud, B. The assistant   **Fic**
McDonald, J. Twists and turns   **Fic**
Placide, J. Fresh girl   **Fic**

Brooklyn dreams. DeMatteis, J. M.   **741.5**

Brooks, Brad
(jt. auth) Pilcher, T. The essential guide to
    world comics   **741.5**

Brooks, Cleanth, 1906-1994
(ed) Understanding poetry. See Understanding
    poetry   **821.008**

Brooks, Gwendolyn
In Montgomery, and other poems   **811**
Selected poems   **811**
About
Gwendolyn Brooks [critical essays]   **811.009**
Hill, C. M. Gwendolyn Brooks   **92**
Rhynes, M. E. Gwendolyn Brooks   **92**

Brooks, Kevin, 1959-
Candy   **Fic**
Kissing the rain   **Fic**
Lucas   **Fic**
Martyn Pig   **Fic**
The road of the dead   **Fic**

Brooks, Martha, 1944-
A boy and his dog
In Who do you think you are?; stories of
    friends and enemies p58-63   **S C**
True confessions of a heartless girl   **Fic**

Brooks, Philip *See* Wilkinson, Philip, 1955-

Brooks, Rodney Allen
Flesh and machines   **629.8**

Brooks, Terry, 1944-
Armageddon's children   **Fic**
The sword of Shannara   **Fic**
See/See also pages in the following book(s):
MacRae, C. D. Presenting young adult fantasy
    fiction   **813.009**

Brother hood. McDonald, J.   **Fic**

Brother Imás. Hinojosa, R.
In Growing up Latino; memoirs and stories
    p250-58   **810.8**

Brother Square-Toes. Kipling, R.
In Kipling, R. The portable Kipling   **828**

Brothers
Fiction
Auseon, A. Funny little monkey   **Fic**
Bosse, M. J. The examination   **Fic**
Brooks, K. The road of the dead   **Fic**
Crist-Evans, C. Amaryllis   **Fic**
Hartnett, S. Surrender   **Fic**
Herrick, S. By the river   **Fic**
Kerr, M. E. Night kites   **Fic**
Kerr, M. E. Slap your sides   **Fic**
Klass, D. Dark angel   **Fic**
Levithan, D. Are we there yet?   **Fic**
Mosley, W. Fortunate son   **Fic**
Salisbury, G. Jungle dogs   **Fic**
Simmons, M. Vandal   **Fic**
Slade, A. G. Megiddo's shadow   **Fic**
Trottier, M. Three songs for courage   **Fic**
Woodson, J. Miracle's boys   **Fic**
Zusak, M. Getting the girl   **Fic**

Brothers and sisters *See* Siblings; Twins

The **brothers** Shu. Su Tong
In Chairman Mao would not be amused; fic-
    tion from today's China   **S C**

Brower, Kenneth, 1944-
Yosemite   **917.9**

Brown, Angela
Mrs. Houdini's wife
In Not the only one; lesbian and gay fiction
    for teens   **S C**

Brown, Bobbi
Bobbi Brown teenage beauty   **646.7**

Brown, Bradford B., 1929-
While you're here, Doc   **92**

Brown, Charles N.
(ed) The Locus awards. See The Locus awards
    S C

Brown, Clara, 1800-1885
See/See also pages in the following book(s):
Stefoff, R. Women pioneers   **920**

Brown, Clarence, 1929-
(ed) The portable twentieth-century Russian
    reader. See The portable twentieth-century
    Russian reader   **891.7**

Brown, Claude, 1937-2002
Manchild in the promised land   **92**

Brown, Daniel, 1951-
Under a flaming sky   **634.9**

Brown, David E.
Inventing modern America   **609**

Brown, David J., 1946-
Bridges: three thousand years of defying nature
    624.2

Brown, Dee Alexander
Bury my heart at Wounded Knee   **970.004**

Brown, Jean E., 1945-
Teaching young adult literature   **809**

Bunin, Ivan Alekseevich, 1870-1953
Light breathing
In The portable twentieth-century Russian
reader **891.7**
Bunny boy. Flinn, A.
In Twice told; original stories inspired by
original art **S C**
Bunson, Margaret R.
Encyclopedia of ancient Egypt **932**
Bunson, Matthew
Encyclopedia of the Roman Empire **937**
Buonarotti, Michelangelo *See* Michelangelo Buo-
narroti, 1475-1564
Buonarroti, Michel Angelo *See* Michelangelo
Buonarroti, 1475-1564
Burchfield, R. W. (Robert W.)
(jt. auth) Fowler, H. W. Fowler's modern En-
glish usage **428**
Burchfield, Robert W. *See* Burchfield, R. W.
(Robert W.)
Burden, Ernest E., 1934-
Illustrated dictionary of architecture **720.3**
Burdick, Alan
Out of Eden **577**
Burfoot, Amby
(ed) Complete book of running. See Complete
book of running **796.42**
Burg, David F.
Almanac of World War I **940.3**
The Great Depression **973.91**
(jt. auth) Woodger, E. The 1980s **973.92**
(ed) The World almanac of the American Revo-
lution. See The World almanac of the Ameri-
can Revolution **973.3**
Burgan, Michael
Empire of the Mongols **951**
Burger, Joanna
Birds: a visual guide **598**
Burger, William C., 1932-
Flowers: how they changed the world
582.13
Burgess, Anthony, 1917-1993
A clockwork orange **Fic**
Burgess, Melvin, 1954-
Smack **Fic**
Burgin, Robert
(ed) Nonfiction reader's advisory. See Nonfic-
tion reader's advisory **025.5**
Burgos-Debray, Elisabeth
(ed) Menchú, R. I, Rigoberta Menchú **92**
Burial
Colman, P. Corpses, coffins, and crypts **393**
The **burial** of Letty Strayhorn. Kelton, E.
In A Century of great Western stories
S C
The **buried** mirror. Fuentes, C. **946**
Buried onions. Soto, G. **Fic**
Buried treasure
Fiction
Hobbs, W. Leaving Protection **Fic**

Burke, Ed, 1949-
The complete book of long-distance cycling
613.7
Burke, Jan
The muse
In Alfred Hitchcock's mystery magazine pres-
ents fifty years of crime and suspense
S C
Burke, Larry
(jt. auth) Ripken, C., Jr. Play baseball the
Ripken way **796.357**
Burkett, Richard
(jt. auth) Nelson, G. C. Ceramics: a potter's
handbook **738.1**
Burkhead, Cynthia
Student companion to John Steinbeck
813.009
Burkholder, J. Peter (James Peter)
(jt. auth) Grout, D. J. A history of western mu-
sic **780.9**
Burl, Aubrey
The stone circles of Britain, Ireland and Brittany
936.1
Burlend, Rebecca, 1793-1872
See/See also pages in the following book(s):
Stefoff, R. Women pioneers **920**
Burn him out. Bonham, F.
In A Century of great Western stories
S C
The **burn** journals. Runyon, B. **92**
Burned out. Sholem Aleichem
In Halkin, H. and Sholem Aleichem. Tevye
the dairyman and The railroad stories
S C
Burner, David, 1937-
John F. Kennedy and a new generation **92**
Burnham, Robert
Great comets **523.6**
Burnham, Terry
Mean genes **155.2**
The **burning**. Welty, E.
In Welty, E. The collected stories of Eudora
Welty p482-94 **S C**
A **burning** brand. Twain, M.
In Twain, M. The complete short stories of
Mark Twain; now collected for the first
time **S C**
Burning city. Dorfman, A. **Fic**
The **burning** man. Bradbury, R.
In Bradbury, R. Bradbury stories; 100 of his
most celebrated tales **S C**
The **burning** man. Williams, T.
In Legends: short novels by the masters of
modern fantasy p397-450 **S C**
Burns, Allan
Thematic guide to American poetry **811.009**
Burns, Eric
Infamous scribblers **071**
Burns, James MacGregor
(ed) Encyclopedia of leadership. See Encyclope-
dia of leadership **658.4**

Businesspeople
  Business leader profiles for students   **920.003**
  Carey, C. W. American inventors, entrepreneurs, and business visionaries   **920**

Buso Renkin, Vol. 1. Watsuki, N.   **741.5**

Bussey, Jennifer A.
  (ed) 1820-1840: the nineteenth century. See 1820-1840: the nineteenth century   **909.81**
  (ed) 1940-1960: the twentieth century. See 1940-1960: the twentieth century   **909.82**
  (ed) 1960-1980: the twentieth century. See 1960-1980: the twentieth century   **909.82**

Bussing-Burks, Marie, 1958-
  Influential economists   **920**

But what if I don't want to go to college? Unger, H. G.   **331.7**

Butler, Alban, 1711-1773
  Butler's Lives of the saints   **920.003**

Butler, Colin
  The practical Shakespeare   **822.3**

Butler, Daniel Allen
  Unsinkable: the full story of the RMS Titanic   **910.4**

Butler, Octavia E., 1947-2006
  Bloodchild
    In The Locus awards; thirty years of the best in science fiction and fantasy   **S C**
  Fledgling   **Fic**
  Parable of the sower   **Fic**
  Speech sounds
    In The Norton book of science fiction; North American science fiction, 1960-1990 p513-24   **S C**
  See/See also pages in the following book(s):
  Reid, S. E. Presenting young adult science fiction   **813.009**

Butler, Rebecca P.
  Copyright for teachers and librarians   **346.04**

Butler, William S.
  Secret messages   **652**

Butler's Lives of the saints. Butler, A.   **920.003**

Butterflies
  Brock, J. P. Kaufman field guide to butterflies of North America   **595.7**
  Pyle, R. M. The Audubon Society field guide to North American butterflies   **595.7**
  Sbordoni, V. Butterflies of the world   **595.7**
    Fiction
  Klass, D. California Blue   **Fic**

Butterflies. Haddix, M. P.
  In Make me over; 11 stories of transformation   **S C**

Butterflies of North America. See Brock, J. P. Kaufman field guide to butterflies of North America   **595.7**

Butterflies of the world. Sbordoni, V.   **595.7**

Butterfly, The *See* Whistler, James McNeill, 1834-1903

The **butterfly** and the tank. Hemingway, E.
  In Hemingway, E. The complete short stories of Ernest Hemingway; the Finca Vigía edition p429-36   **S C**

Butterfly boy. González, R.   **92**

The **Butterfly's** way   **810.9**

Butts, Edward, 1951-
  She dared   **920**

Butts, Lauren
  Okay, so now you're a vegetarian   **641.5**

Bütz, Richard
  How to carve wood   **731.4**

Buxton, Ted
  Soccer skills for young players   **796.334**

Buying *See* Consumer education

By far the worst pupil at Long Point School. Peck, R.
  In Peck, R. Past perfect, present tense: new and collected stories   **S C**

By order of the president. Robinson, G.   **940.53**

By the dawn's early light. Block, L.
  In The Best American mystery stories of the century p597-14   **S C**

By the numbers!. Bradbury, R.
  In Bradbury, R. Bradbury stories; 100 of his most celebrated tales   **S C**

By the river. Herrick, S.   **Fic**

By these ten bones. Dunkle, C. B.   **Fic**

Byatt, A. S. (Antonia Susan), 1936-
  The next room
    In The Literary ghost; great contemporary ghost stories p257-81   **S C**
  (ed) The Oxford book of English short stories. See The Oxford book of English short stories   **S C**

Byers, Andrew R.
  (ed) The Canadian atlas. See The Canadian atlas   **912**

Bynoe, Yvonne
  Encyclopedia of rap and hip-hop culture   **782.42**

Bynum, W. F. (William F.), 1943-
  (ed) Oxford dictionary of scientific quotations. See Oxford dictionary of scientific quotations   **500**

Byrd, Richard Evelyn, 1888-1957
    About
  Bryant, J. H. Dangerous crossings   **998**

Byrd, Susannah Mississippi, 1971-
  Bienvenidos! = Welcome!   **027.6**

The **Byrds**. Coney, M.
  In The Norton book of science fiction; North American science fiction, 1960-1990 p501-12   **S C**

Byrne, Deborah J.
  MARC manual   **025.3**

Byrne, Joseph Patrick
  The black death   **614.5**

Byron, George Gordon Byron, 6th Baron, 1788-1824
  Byron   **821**
    About
  Graham, P. W. Lord Byron   **821.009**

The **bystander**. Berriault, G.
  In American short story masterpieces   **S C**

C

C-chute. Asimov, I.
    In Asimov, I. The complete stories p438-67
                S C

A **cabin** on the coast. Wolfe, G.
    In Best of the best: 20 years of the Year's
        best science fiction   **S C**

Cabinet officers
    See also Prime ministers

Cable, George Washington, 1844-1925
    Belles Demoiselles plantation
    In The Norton book of American short stories
        p97-110   **S C**
    Jean-ah Poquelin
    In The Oxford book of gothic tales p165-82
                S C

Cactus
    Hewitt, T. The complete book of cacti & succulents   **635.9**

Cadavers *See* Dead

Cadigan, Pat
    After the days of Dead-Eye 'Dee
    In The Norton book of science fiction; North
        American science fiction, 1960-1990
        p605-15   **S C**
    Roadside rescue
    In Best of the best: 20 years of the Year's
        best science fiction   **S C**

Cadnum, Michael
    Daphne
    In The Green Man: tales from the mythic forest p44-49   **808.8**

Caesar, Julius, 100-44 B.C.
    The Gallic War   **878**
    See/See also pages in the following book(s):
    Hamilton, E. The Roman way   **870.9**

Cafferty, Stephen
    (ed) Firefly Encyclopedia of trees. See Firefly
        Encyclopedia of trees   **582.16**

Cages. Gurnah, A.
    In The Heinemann book of contemporary African short stories p87-93   **S C**

Cahill, Thomas, 1940-
    The gifts of the Jews   **909**
    Sailing the wine-dark sea   **909**

Cahill, Tom *See* Cahill, Thomas, 1940-

Cahn, Victor L.
    The plays of Shakespeare   **822.3**

Cail, Carol
    Sinkhole
    In Alfred Hitchcock's mystery magazine presents fifty years of crime and suspense
                S C

Cain, James M. (James Mallahan), 1892-1977
    The baby in the icebox
    In The Best American mystery stories of the
        century p178-192   **S C**
    In The Norton book of American short stories
        p297-311   **S C**

Cain, William E., 1952-
    (ed) A Historical guide to Henry David Thoreau. See A Historical guide to Henry David
    Thoreau   **818**

Cain rose up. King, S.
    In King, S. Skeleton crew   **S C**

Cairo Museum *See* Egyptian Museum
The **Cairo** Museum. See Egyptian treasures from
    the Egyptian Museum in Cairo   **709.32**

Cajal, Santiago Ramón y *See* Ramón y Cajal,
    Santiago, 1852-1934

Calculus
    Berlinski, D. A tour of the calculus   **515**
    Maor, E. The Facts on File calculus handbook
                515

Caldecott, Julian Oliver
    (ed) World atlas of great apes and their conservation. See World atlas of great apes and
    their conservation   **599.8**

Caldwell, Ben, 1937-
    Prayer meeting; or, The first militant preacher
    In Black theatre USA; plays by African
        Americans, 1847 to today   **812.008**

Caldwell, Erskine, 1903-1987
    Kneel to the rising sun
    In The Norton book of American short stories
        p374-94   **S C**

Calendars
    Chase's calendar of events 2006   **394.26**
    Religious holidays and calendars   **203**
    Richards, E. G. Mapping time   **529**
    The Wilson calendar of world history   **902**

Caletti, Deb
    Honey, Baby, Sweetheart   **Fic**
    The nature of Jade   **Fic**
    Wild roses   **Fic**

Calhoun, Charles W. (Charles William), 1948-
    Benjamin Harrison   **92**

Calhoun, Craig J., 1952-
    (ed) Dictionary of the social sciences. See Dictionary of the social sciences   **300.3**

Calhoun, John C. (John Caldwell), 1782-1850
    See/See also pages in the following book(s):
    McPherson, J. M. Drawn with the sword
                973.7

Calhoun, Yael
    (ed) Climate change. See Climate change
                363.7
    (ed) Conservation. See Conservation   **333.72**
    (ed) Environmental policy. See Environmental
    policy   **363.7**
    (ed) Water pollution. See Water pollution
                363.7
    (ed) Wildlife protection. See Wildlife protection
                333.95

Calia, Charles Laird
    The stargazing year   **523.8**

California
    Fiction
    Allende, I. Zorro   **Fic**
    Butler, O. E. Parable of the sower   **Fic**
    Houston, J. D. Snow Mountain passage   **Fic**
    Otsuka, J. When the emperor was divine
                Fic

Capote, Truman, 1924-1984—*Continued*
The Thanksgiving visitor
In Capote, T. A Christmas memory, One
Christmas, & The Thanksgiving visitor
p55-107 **818**

Caprara, Giovanni
(ed) The solar system. See The solar system
523.2

Capricorn. Oates, J. C.
In Oates, J. C. Small avalanches and other
stories **S C**

Captain Jack *See* Kintpuash, Modoc Chief,
1837?-1873

The **captured** shadow. Fitzgerald, F. S.
In Fitzgerald, F. S. The short stories of F.
Scott Fitzgerald; a new collection p412-
30 **S C**

Caputo, Philip
13 seconds **973.924**
Ghosts of Tsavo **599.75**
A rumor of war **959.704**

Caputo, Robert
National Geographic photography field guide
778.9

Capuzzo, Mike
Close to shore **597**

Car design *See* Automobiles—Design and construction

Car smarts. Edmonston, L.-P. **629.222**

Caras, Roger A.
(jt. auth) Foster, S. A field guide to venomous
animals and poisonous plants **578.6**

Caravantes, Peggy, 1935-
Best of times: the story of Charles Dickens
92
Deep woods [biography of Robert Frost] **92**
Writing is my business **92**

Carbon dioxide greenhouse effect *See* Greenhouse effect

Carcassonne. Faulkner, W.
In Faulkner, W. Collected stories of William
Faulkner p895-900 **S C**

Card, Orson Scott
America
In The Norton book of science fiction; North
American science fiction, 1960-1990
p665-88 **S C**
Ender's game **Fic**
First meetings in the Enderverse **S C**
Contents: The Polish boy — Teacher's pest — Ender's game
— Investment counselor
Grinning man
In Legends: short novels by the masters of
modern fantasy p215-53 **S C**
The Polish boy
In Card, O. S. First meetings in the
Enderverse **S C**
Salvage
In New skies: an anthology of today's science
fiction **S C**
Seventh son **Fic**

About
Tyson, E. S. Orson Scott Card **813.009**

See/See also pages in the following book(s):
Reid, S. E. Presenting young adult science fiction **813.009**

Card tricks
Hugard, J. Encyclopedia of card tricks **795.4**

Cardiovascular system
See also Blood—Circulation; Heart
Brynie, F. H. 101 questions about blood and cir-
culation, with answers straight from the heart
612.1
Mertz, L. A. The circulatory system **616.1**

Cards of grief. Yolen, J.
In New skies: an anthology of today's science
fiction **S C**

Care-free plants **635.9**

Care of children *See* Child care

Care of the dying *See* Terminal care

Career development series
Scheeder, L. All the words on stage **822.3**

Career guidance *See* Vocational guidance

Career ideas for teens [series]
Reeves, D. L. Career ideas for teens in architecture and construction **624**
Reeves, D. L. Career ideas for teens in education and training **331.7**
Reeves, D. L. Career ideas for teens in health
science **610.69**

Career ideas for teens in architecture and construction. Reeves, D. L. **624**

Career ideas for teens in education and training.
Reeves, D. L. **331.7**

Career ideas for teens in health science. Reeves,
D. L. **610.69**

A **career** in sexual chemistry. Stableford, B. M.
In The Hard SF renaissance **S C**

Careers *See* Occupations

Carey, Charles W.
American inventors, entrepreneurs, and business
visionaries **920**
(ed) Castro's Cuba. See Castro's Cuba
972.91
(ed) The Kennedy assassination. See The Kennedy assassination **364.1**

Carey, Ernestine Gilbreth
(jt. auth) Gilbreth, F. B. Cheaper by the dozen
92

Carey, Gary
A multicultural dictionary of literary terms
803

Carey, Janet Lee
Dragon's Keep **Fic**

Caribbean region
Antiquities
Macaulay, D. Ship **387.2**

Caricatures *See* Cartoons and caricatures

Caricaturists *See* Cartoonists

Carle, Jill
(jt. auth) Carle, M. Teens cook **641.5**

Carle, Judi
(jt. auth) Carle, M. Teens cook **641.5**

Carle, Megan
Teens cook **641.5**

Carleton, William, 1794-1869
The death of a devotee
In The Oxford book of Irish short stories p52-72 **S C**

Carlin, John, 1955-
(ed) Masters of American comics. See Masters of American comics **741.5**

Carlisle, Rodney P.
Iraq war **956.7**
Scientific American inventions and discoveries **609**
World War I **940.3**

Carlsen, Henrik Kurt, 1915-1989
About
Delaney, F. Simple courage **910.4**

Carlsen, Kurt *See* Carlsen, Henrik Kurt, 1915-1989

Carlson, Dale Bick, 1935-
In and out of your mind **500**

Carlson, Laurie M., 1952-
A fever in Salem **133.4**

Carlson, Lori M.
(ed) American eyes. See American eyes **S C**
(ed) Cool salsa. See Cool salsa **811.008**
(ed) Moccasin thunder. See Moccasin thunder **S C**
(ed) Red hot salsa. See Red hot salsa **811.008**

Carlson, Shawn
(ed) The Amateur astronomer. See The Amateur astronomer **520**

Carlson, W. Bernard
(ed) Technology in world history. See Technology in world history **909**

Carlton Fredericks and my mother. Gillan, M.
In Growing up ethnic in America; contemporary fiction about learning to be American **S C**

Carman, L. Kay
(ed) Reaching out to religious youth. See Reaching out to religious youth **027.62**

Carmichael, Chris
The ultimate ride **796.6**

Carnagie, Julie
Renaissance & Reformation: almanac. See Renaissance & Reformation: almanac **940.2**
Renaissance & Reformation: primary sources. See Renaissance & Reformation: primary sources **940.2**
(ed) Howes, K. K. War of 1812 **973.5**

Carnegie Library of Pittsburgh. Science and Technology Dept.
The Handy science answer book. See The Handy science answer book **500**

Carneiro, André, 1922-
Brain transplant
In Cosmos latinos; an anthology of science fiction from Latin America and Spain **S C**

Carnes, Mark C. (Mark Christopher), 1950-
(ed) American national biography. See American national biography **920.003**
(ed) Invisible giants. See Invisible giants **920**

Caroline's wedding. Danticat, E.
In Danticat, E. Krik? Krak! **S C**

Caroselli, Joanne
(il) Hearne, B. G. Beauties and beasts **398.2**

Carpenter, Robert 1973-, 1973-
(jt. auth) Hinkson, J. Lacrosse for dummies **796.34**

Carpetbag rule *See* Reconstruction (1865-1876)

Carpets *See* Weaving

Carr, Gerald A., 1936-
Fundamentals of track and field **796.42**

Carr-Gomm, Sarah
Dictionary of symbols in Western art **704.9**

Carrasco, David
(ed) The Oxford encyclopedia of Mesoamerican cultures. See The Oxford encyclopedia of Mesoamerican cultures **972**

Carrie. King, S. **Fic**

Carrington, Leonora, 1917-
My flannel knickers
In The Oxford book of English short stories p369-71 **S C**

Carroll, David L., 1942-
(jt. auth) Zugibe, F. T. Dissecting death **614**

Carroll, Jamuna
(ed) Civil liberties and war. See Civil liberties and war **342**
(ed) Do children have rights? See Do children have rights? **323.3**
(ed) Marijuana: opposing viewpoints. See Marijuana: opposing viewpoints **362.29**
(ed) Students' rights: opposing viewpoints. See Students' rights: opposing viewpoints **344**
(ed) Television: opposing viewpoints. See Television: opposing viewpoints **302.23**

Carroll, Rebecca
(ed) Sugar in the raw. See Sugar in the raw **305.23**

Carroll, Sean B.
The making of the fittest **572.8**

Carroll, Kristi L. Thomason- *See* Thomason-Carroll, Kristi L.

Carry me home. McWhorter, D. **976.1**

Cars (Automobiles) *See* Automobiles

Carson, Clayborne, 1944-
(ed) The Eyes on the prize civil rights reader. See The Eyes on the prize civil rights reader **323.1**

Carson, Rachel, 1907-1964
The edge of the sea **577.7**
Silent spring **363.7**
About
Levine, E. Rachel Carson **92**

Carson-DeWitt, Rosalyn
(ed) Drugs, alcohol, and tobacco. See Drugs, alcohol, and tobacco **362.29**
(ed) Encyclopedia of drugs, alcohol & addictive behavior. See Encyclopedia of drugs, alcohol & addictive behavior **362.29**

Carson McCullers [critical essays] **813.009**

Cart, Michael
The heart has its reasons **813.009**

Cart, Michael—*Continued*

Sailing away

In Necessary noise: stories about our families as they really are p145-69   **S C**

(ed) 911: the book of help. See 911: the book of help   **810.8**

(ed) Necessary noise: stories about our families as they really are. See Necessary noise: stories about our families as they really are   **S C**

Cart and cwidder. Jones, D. W.   **Fic**

Carter, Alden R.

Love, football, and other contact sports   **S C**

Contents: A girl's guide to football players; A football player's guide to love; Kickoff (or never trust a girl who steals your ice cream sandwich); Trashback; Pig brains; Buck's head; Satyagraha; Elvis; The Ogre of Mensa; The gully; Kicker wanted; The briefcase; Jersey Day; Big Chicago; The ghost of Mum-Mum; The Doughnut boots his reputation; A good game.

No Win Phuong

In Join in; multiethnic short stories by outstanding writers for young adults p62-84   **S C**

The Swede

In First crossing; stories about teen immigrants p137-56   **S C**

Carter, Angela, 1940-1992

The kiss

In The Oxford book of English short stories p400-02   **S C**

The lady of the house of love

In The Oxford book of gothic tales p483-97   **S C**

Carter, James Earl See Carter, Jimmy, 1924-

Carter, Jason

Power lines   **968.06**

Carter, Jimmy, 1924-

An hour before daylight   **92**

Carter, Julie

Cat

In Growing up gay; an anthology for young people p138-44   **808.8**

Carter, Robert, 1728-1804

About

Levy, A. The first emancipator [biography of Robert Carter]   **92**

Carter, Stephen L.

God's name in vain   **322**

Carter, Susan B.

(ed) Historical statistics of the United States. See Historical statistics of the United States   **317.3**

Carter family

About

Carter, J. An hour before daylight   **92**

Cartmell, Van Henry

(ed) 24 favorite one-act plays. See 24 favorite one-act plays   **808.82**

(jt. auth) Cerf, B. The best short stories of O. Henry   **S C**

Cartography See Maps

The **cartoon** history of the modern world [part 1] Gonick, L.   **909.08**

Cartooning for the beginner. Hart, C.   **741.5**

Cartoonists

Jones, G. Men of tomorrow   **741.5**

Lehman, T. Manga: masters of the art   **741.5**

Masters of American comics   **741.5**

Dictionaries

Pendergast, T. U-X-L graphic novelists   **920.003**

Cartoons, Animated See Animated films

Cartoons and caricatures

See also Comic books, strips, etc.

Bancroft, T. Creating characters with personality   **741.6**

Chiarello, M. The DC Comics guide to coloring and lettering comics   **741.5**

Hart, C. Cartooning for the beginner   **741.5**

Hart, C. Drawing cutting edge anatomy   **741.5**

McCloud, S. Reinventing comics   **741.5**

Miller, S. Scared!: how to draw fantastic horror comic characters   **741.5**

Cartoons and comics

The Superhero book   **741.5**

Fiction

Ehrenhaft, D. Drawing a blank, or, How I tried to solve a mystery, end a feud, and land the girl of my dreams   **Fic**

Lyga, B. The astonishing adventures of Fanboy & Goth Girl   **Fic**

Carus, Marianne

(ed) 911: the book of help. See 911: the book of help   **810.8**

Caruso, Sandra

The young actor's book of improvisation   **808.82**

Carvajal, Carol Styles

(ed) The Oxford Spanish dictionary. See The Oxford Spanish dictionary   **463**

Carver, George Washington, 1864?-1943

About

Nelson, M. Carver, a life in poems   **811**

Carver, Raymond

Fever

In American short story masterpieces   **S C**

Jerry and Molly and Sam

In Adaptations: from short story to big screen; 35 great stories that have inspired great films   **S C**

What we talk about when we talk about love

In The Norton book of American short stories p651-61   **S C**

Whoever was using this bed

In Gotham Writers' Workshop fiction gallery; exceptional short stories selected by New York's acclaimed creative writing school   **S C**

(ed) American short story masterpieces. See American short story masterpieces   **S C**

Carver, a life in poems. Nelson, M.   **811**

Carving, Wood See Wood carving

Cary, Joyce, 1888-1957

Bush River

In The Oxford book of Irish short stories p277-86   **S C**

Cary, Kate
Bloodline **Fic**

Cary, Lorene
Black ice **92**

Casa, Ricard de la See Casa Pérez, Ricard de la, 1954-

Casa i Pérez, Ricard de la See Casa Pérez, Ricard de la, 1954-

Casa Pérez, Ricard de la, 1954-
The day we went through the transition
In Cosmos latinos; an anthology of science fiction from Latin America and Spain
S C

The **case** book of Sherlock Holmes. Doyle, Sir A. C.
In Doyle, Sir A. C. The complete Sherlock Holmes **S C**

A **case** of identity. Doyle, Sir A. C.
In Doyle, Sir A. C. The complete Sherlock Holmes **S C**

The **case** of the caretaker. Christie, A.
In Christie, A. Miss Marple: the complete short stories **S C**

The **case** of the perfect maid. Christie, A.
In Christie, A. Miss Marple: the complete short stories **S C**

The **casebook** of forensic detection. Evans, C.
614

Cash, Johnny
About
Neimark, A. E. Johnny Cash **92**

Cash and credit information for teens: tips for a successful financial life **332.024**

The **cask** of Amontillado. Poe, E. A.
In Poe, E. A. The collected tales and poems of Edgar Allan Poe p274-79 **818**

Cassady, Marsh, 1936-
The book of scenes for aspiring actors
808.82
(ed) The Book of monologues for aspiring actors. See The Book of monologues for aspiring actors **808.82**
(ed) Great scenes from minority playwrights. See Great scenes from minority playwrights
812.008

Cassatt, Mary, 1844-1926
About
Gouveia, G. The essential Mary Cassatt
759.13

Cassell, Dana K.
Encyclopedia of obesity and eating disorders
616.85

The **Cassell** dictionary of English idioms **427**

Cassell dictionary of humorous quotations. See Cassell's humorous quotations **808.88**

Cassell's chronology of world history. Williams, H. **902**

Cassell's dictionary of first names. See Room, A. Dictionary of first names **929.4**

Cassell's dictionary of slang. Green, J. **427**

Cassell's humorous quotations **808.88**

Cassell's Latin dictionary **473**

Cassell's Spanish dictionary. See Cassell's Spanish-English, English-Spanish dictionary
463

Cassell's Spanish-English, English-Spanish dictionary **463**

Cassette tape recordings, Video See Videotapes

Cassirer, Nadine Gordimer See Gordimer, Nadine, 1923-

Casson, Lionel, 1914-
Everyday life in ancient Egypt **932**

Castaway. Clarke, A. C.
In Clarke, A. C. The collected stories of Arthur C. Clarke **S C**

Castellucci, Cecil, 1969-
Boy proof **Fic**
The Plain Janes **741.5**
The queen of cool **Fic**

Castillo-Speed, Lillian, 1949-
(ed) Latina: women's voices from the borderlands. See Latina: women's voices from the borderlands **810.8**

Castle waiting. Medley, L. **741.5**

Castles
Gies, J. Life in a medieval castle **940.2**
Macaulay, D. Castle **728.8**

Castro, Fidel, 1926-
About
Castro's Cuba **972.91**
Coltman, Sir L. The real Fidel Castro **92**

Castro, Pablo
Exerion
In Cosmos latinos; an anthology of science fiction from Latin America and Spain
S C

Castro Hermosilla, Pablo See Castro, Pablo

Castro's Cuba **972.91**

A **casual** affair. Maugham, W. S.
In Maugham, W. S. Collected short stories
S C

Cat. Carter, J.
In Growing up gay; an anthology for young people p138-44 **808.8**

Cat got your tongue? Sones, S.
In Sixteen: stories about that sweet and bitter birthday **S C**

Cat in the rain. Hemingway, E.
In Hemingway, E. The complete short stories of Ernest Hemingway; the Finca Vigía edition p129-31 **S C**

The **cat** that walked by himself. Kipling, R.
In Kipling, R. The portable Kipling **828**

Cataloging
Byrne, D. J. MARC manual **025.3**
Fritz, D. A. Cataloging with AACR2 and MARC21 **025.3**
Gorman, M. The concise AACR2 **025.3**
Intner, S. S. Standard cataloging for school and public libraries **025.3**

Cataloging with AACR2 and MARC21. Fritz, D. A. **025.3**

Cataloging with AACR2R and USMARC. See Fritz, D. A. Cataloging with AACR2 and MARC21 **025.3**

Catalogs *See* Audiovisual materials—Catalogs; School libraries—Catalogs

Catastrophes (Geology)
Alvarez, W. T. rex and the Crater of Doom **551.7**
Frankel, C. The end of the dinosaurs **551.3**
Powell, J. L. Night comes to the Cretaceous **576.8**

Catastrophic extinction of species *See* Mass extinction of species

The **catbird** seat. Thurber, J.
In The Best American mystery stories of the century p279-87 **S C**

Catch-22. Heller, J. **Fic**

Catch that rabbit. Asimov, I.
In Asimov, I. I, robot **S C**

Catch the fire!!! **811.008**

Catch the moon. Ortiz Cofer, J.
In Ortiz Cofer, J. An island like you; stories of the barrio **S C**

The **catcher** in the rye. Salinger, J. D. **Fic**

Catharine Howard, Queen, consort of Henry VIII, King of England, d. 1542
See/See also pages in the following book(s):
Starkey, D. Six wives: the queens of Henry VIII **920**

Catharine Parr, Queen, consort of Henry VIII, King of England, 1512-1548
See/See also pages in the following book(s):
Starkey, D. Six wives: the queens of Henry VIII **920**

Cathcart, Brian
The fly in the cathedral **539.7**

Cather, Willa, 1873-1947
Alexander's bridge
In Cather, W. Stories, poems, and other writings **818**
April twilights, and other poems
In Cather, W. Stories, poems, and other writings **818**
Death comes for the archbishop **Fic**
My Antonia **Fic**
My mortal enemy
In Cather, W. Stories, poems, and other writings **818**
Not under forty
In Cather, W. Stories, poems, and other writings **818**
O pioneers! **Fic**
Obscure destinies
In Cather, W. Stories, poems, and other writings **818**
The old beauty, and others
In Cather, W. Stories, poems, and other writings **818**
Old Mrs. Harris
In The Oxford book of women's writing in the United States p229-72 **810.8**
Paul's case
In The Best American mystery stories of the century p8-25 **S C**

In The Norton book of American short stories p203-20 **S C**
Stories, poems, and other writings **818**
Youth and the bright Medusa
In Cather, W. Stories, poems, and other writings **818**

Catherine II, the Great, Empress of Russia, 1729-1796
About
Whitelaw, N. Catherine the Great and the Enlightenment in Russia **92**

Catherine
See/See also pages in the following book(s):
Starkey, D. Six wives: the queens of Henry VIII **920**

Catherine Howard *See* Catharine Howard, Queen, consort of Henry VIII, King of England, d. 1542

Catherine Parr *See* Catharine Parr, Queen, consort of Henry VIII, King of England, 1512-1548

Catherine the Great and the Enlightenment in Russia. Whitelaw, N. **92**

Cathey, Henry Marcellus, 1928-
(ed) The American Horticultural Society A-Z encyclopedia of garden plants. See The American Horticultural Society A-Z encyclopedia of garden plants **635.9**

Cathleen ni Houlihan. Yeats, W. B.
In 24 favorite one-act plays p391-402 **808.82**

Catholic Church
See also Inquisition
The Catholic Church: opposing viewpoints **282**
New Catholic encyclopedia: jubilee volume, the Wojtyla years **282**
See/See also pages in the following book(s):
Russell, B. A history of Western philosophy **109**
Clergy—Fiction
Erdrich, L. The last report on the miracles at Little No Horse **Fic**
Encyclopedias
Flinn, F. K. Encyclopedia of Catholicism **282**
New Catholic encyclopedia **282**
Missions—Fiction
Cather, W. Death comes for the archbishop **Fic**

The **Catholic** Church: opposing viewpoints **282**

Catholic encyclopedia. See New Catholic encyclopedia **282**

CATNYP. Sherman, D.
In The Faery Reel; tales from the Twilight Realm **S C**
In The Year's best science fiction and fantasy for teens: first annual collection **S C**

Cats
Christensen, W. The Humane Society of the United States complete guide to cat care **636.8**
Davis, C. Essential cat **636.8**

Chekhov, Anton Pavlovich, 1860-1904—*Continued*

The bishop
In The portable twentieth-century Russian reader **891.7**

The cherry orchard
In Chekhov, A. P. The plays of Anton Chekhov p331-87 **891.7**

The dangers of tobacco
In Chekhov, A. P. The plays of Anton Chekhov p323-29 **891.7**

The festivities
In Chekhov, A. P. The plays of Anton Chekhov p191-205 **891.7**

Ivanov
In Chekhov, A. P. The plays of Anton Chekhov p51-108 **891.7**

The lady with the dog
In The Portable nineteenth-century Russian reader p534-49 **891.7**

The lady with the pet dog
In Adaptations: from short story to big screen; 35 great stories that have inspired great films **S C**

A marriage proposal
In 24 favorite one-act plays p403-16 **808.82**

The plays of Anton Chekhov **891.7**

The proposal
In Chekhov, A. P. The plays of Anton Chekhov p35-49 **891.7**

A reluctant tragic hero
In Chekhov, A. P. The plays of Anton Chekhov p165-73 **891.7**

The Russian master and other stories **S C**
Contents: His wife; A lady with a dog; The duel; A hard case; Gooseberries; Concerning love; Peasants; Angel; The Russian master; Terror; The Order of St. Anne

The seagull
In Chekhov, A. P. The plays of Anton Chekhov p109-64 **891.7**

Swan song
In Chekhov, A. P. The plays of Anton Chekhov p9-17 **891.7**

Three sisters
In Chekhov, A. P. The plays of Anton Chekhov p257-322 **891.7**

A trifle from life
In Gotham Writers' Workshop fiction gallery; exceptional short stories selected by New York's acclaimed creative writing school **S C**

Uncle Vanya
In Chekhov, A. P. The plays of Anton Chekhov p207-55 **891.7**
In The Portable nineteenth-century Russian reader p549-607 **891.7**

The wedding
In Chekhov, A. P. The plays of Anton Chekhov p175-89 **891.7**

About
Malcolm, J. Reading Chekhov **891.7**

Chemical elements
Knapp, B. J. Elements **546**
Krebs, R. E. The history and use of our earth's chemical elements **546**
Miller, R. The elements **546**
Newton, D. E. Chemical elements **546**
Stwertka, A. A guide to the elements **546**

Chemical engineering
See also Biotechnology
A **chemical** history tour. Greenberg, A. **540.9**

Chemical pollution *See* Pollution

Chemical warfare
Biological and chemical weapons **358**
Gay, K. Silent death **358**
Russell, E. War and nature **577.2**
Weapons of mass destruction **358**
See/See also pages in the following book(s):
Schram, M. Avoiding armageddon **327.1**
Weapons of mass destruction: opposing viewpoints **358**

Chemistry
See also Biochemistry
Cobb, C. The joy of chemistry **540**
The Facts on File chemistry handbook **540**
Le Couteur, P. Napoleon's buttons **540**
Myers, R. The basics of chemistry **540**
Dictionaries
The Facts on File dictionary of chemistry **540.3**
Encyclopedias
Chemistry: foundations and applications **540.3**
Rittner, D. Encyclopedia of chemistry **540.3**
History
Greenberg, A. A chemical history tour **540.9**
Study and teaching
Cracking the SAT: chemistry subject test, 2007-2008 edition **540**
Tables
CRC handbook of chemistry and physics **540**
Lange's handbook of chemistry **540**

Chemistry, Physical and theoretical *See* Physical chemistry

Chemistry: foundations and applications **540.3**

Chemists
McClafferty, C. K. Something out of nothing [biography of Marie Curie] **92**
Pasachoff, N. E. Linus Pauling **92**
Yannuzzi, D. A. New elements [biography of Marie Curie] **92**

Chen, Mary F.
Knuckles
In American eyes; new Asian-American short stories for young adults **S C**

Chen Cun
Footsteps on the roof
In Chairman Mao would not be amused; fiction from today's China **S C**

Chen Jan, 1962-
Sunshine between the lips
In Chairman Mao would not be amused; fiction from today's China **S C**

Chen Ran *See* Chen Jan, 1962-

Cheney, Annie
Body brokers **617.9**

Chermak, Steven M.
(ed) Famous American crimes and trials. See Famous American crimes and trials **364**

A **chip** of glass ruby. Gordimer, N.
In Somehow tenderness survives; stories of
Southern Africa p105-18 **S C**

Chippings with a chisel. Hawthorne, N.
In Hawthorne, N. Tales and sketches, including Twice-told tales, Mosses from an old
manse, and The snow-image; A wonder
book for girls and boys; Tanglewood
tales for girls and boys, being a second
Wonder book p616-25 **S C**

Chittister, Joan
The tent of Abraham **222**

Chiu, Christina
Rain
In Not the only one; lesbian and gay fiction
for teens **S C**

Chivalry
See also Medieval civilization
Bulfinch, T. Bulfinch's mythology **398.2**

Chocolate
Almond, S. Candyfreak: a journey through the
chocolate underbelly of America **338.4**
Rosenblum, M. Chocolate: a bittersweet saga of
dark and light **641.3**

Chocolate almond torte. Sleator, W.
In Twice told; original stories inspired by
original art **S C**

Chocolate for a teen's heart **152.4**

The **chocolate** war. Cormier, R. **Fic**

Choice (Psychology)
See also Decision making

Choice of college *See* College choice

A **choice** of profession. Malamud, B.
In Malamud, B. The complete stories **S C**

Choice of school *See* School choice

Choiniere, Joseph
What's that bird? **598**

Cholera
Coleman, W. H. Cholera **616.9**
Johnson, S. The ghost map **614.5**

Cholesterol
See/See also pages in the following book(s):
Friedman, M. Medicine's 10 greatest discoveries
610.9

Chollet, Laurence B.
The essential Frank O. Gehry **720.973**

Chopin, Kate, 1851-1904
The awakening and selected stories **S C**
Contents: The awakening —Emancipation: a life fable — At
the 'Cadian ball — Désirée's baby — La belle Zoraïde — At
Chênière Caminada — The story of an hour — Lilacs —
Athénaïse — A pair of silk stockings — Nég Créol — Elizabeth
Stock's one story — The storm: a sequel to "The 'Cadian ball."
A pair of silk stockings
In The Oxford book of women's writing in
the United States p63-67 **810.8**
The story of an hour
In Gotham Writers' Workshop fiction gallery;
exceptional short stories selected by New
York's acclaimed creative writing school
S C
In The Norton book of American short stories
p123-25 **S C**

About
Skaggs, P. Kate Chopin **813.009**

Chopra, Deepak
Fire in the heart **204**

Choreographers
Ford, C. T. Legends of American dance and
choreography **920**
Freedman, R. Martha Graham, a dancer's life
92
Gottlieb, R. A. George Balanchine: the ballet
maker **92**

The **chosen**. Harrah, M.
In Night terrors; stories of shadow and substance **S C**

The **chosen**. Potok, C. **Fic**

Chotjewitz, David, 1964-
Daniel half human **Fic**

Chow, Cheryl, 1952-
(jt. auth) Chow, J. H. The encyclopedia of hepatitis and other liver diseases **616.3**

Chow, James H., 1948-
The encyclopedia of hepatitis and other liver
diseases **616.3**

Christ *See* Jesus Christ

Christen, Carol
(jt. auth) Bolles, R. N. What color is your parachute? for teens **331.7**

Christensen, Karen
(ed) Berkshire encyclopedia of world sport. See
Berkshire encyclopedia of world sport
796.03
(ed) International encyclopedia of women and
sports. See International encyclopedia of
women and sports **796.03**

Christensen, Lisa
Clueless about cars **629.28**

Christensen, Wendy
The Humane Society of the United States complete guide to cat care **636.8**

Christian, Fletcher, 1764-1793
About
Alexander, C. The Bounty: the true story of the
mutiny on the Bounty **996**

Christian art
Snyder, J. Art of the Middle Ages **709.02**

Christian fiction
Bibliography
Walker, B. J. The librarian's guide to developing Christian fiction collections for young
adults **025.2**

Christian fundamentalism
See/See also pages in the following book(s):
Armstrong, K. The battle for God **200**

Christian life
Campolo, A. Letters to a young evangelical
248.4
Lewis, C. S. The Screwtape letters **248**
Fiction
Hemphill, H. Long gone daddy **Fic**
Quotations
The Quotable saint **230**

Cooking—*Continued*

Kaufman, C. K. Cooking in ancient civilizations **641.3**

Lieberman, D. Young and hungry **641.5**

McFeely, M. D. Can she bake a cherry pie? **641.5**

The new American Heart Association cookbook **641.5**

The new American plate cookbook **641.5**

Rolland, J. L. The food encyclopedia **641.03**

Rombauer, I. v. S. Joy of cooking **641.5**

Stern, S. Cooking up a storm **641.5**

Webb, L. S. Holidays of the world cookbook for students **641.5**

Zanger, M. H. The American history cookbook **641.5**

See/See also pages in the following book(s):

Shanley, E. L. Fueling the teen machine p139-53 **613.2**

Fiction

Esquivel, L. Like water for chocolate **Fic**

Natural foods

See also Natural foods

Cooking in ancient civilizations. Kaufman, C. K. **641.3**

Cooking up a storm. Stern, S. **641.5**

Cool careers without college [series]

Hayhurst, C. Cool careers without college for animal lovers **636**

Cool careers without college for animal lovers. Hayhurst, C. **636**

Cool colleges for the hyper-intelligent, self-directed, late blooming, and just plain different. Asher, D. **378.73**

Cool salsa **811.008**

Cool stuff and how it works **600**

Cool women, hot jobs . . . and how you can go for it, too!. Schwager, T. **650.14**

Cooney, Caroline B.

Code orange **Fic**

Cooper, Bob, 1963-

(jt. auth) Greiner, T. Analyzing library collection use with Excel **025.2**

Cooper, Dan

Enrico Fermi and the revolutions in modern physics **92**

Cooper, Gail, 1950-

New virtual field trips **025.5**

Cooper, Garry

(jt. auth) Cooper, G. New virtual field trips **025.5**

Cooper, Ilene, 1948-

Jack: the early years of John F. Kennedy **92**

Cooper, James Fenimore, 1789-1851

The Leatherstocking tales **Fic**

Coover, Colleen

(il) Nibot, R. Banana Sunday **741.5**

Coover, Robert

The babysitter

In The Norton book of American short stories p595-618 **S C**

The **cop** and the anthem. Henry, O.

In Henry, O. The best short stories of O. Henry **S C**

Cope, E. D. (Edward Drinker), 1840-1897

About

Ottaviani, J. Bone sharps, cowboys, and thunder lizards **560**

Cope, Edward Drinker *See* Cope, E. D. (Edward Drinker), 1840-1897

Copeland, David A., 1951-

Debating the issues in colonial newspapers **973.2**

Coplin, William D.

10 things employers want you to learn in college **378**

Coppard, A. E. (Alfred Edgar), 1878-1957

The field of mustard

In The Oxford book of short stories p247-54 **S C**

Some talk of Alexander

In The Oxford book of English short stories p180-87 **S C**

Coppard, Alfred Edgar *See* Coppard, A. E. (Alfred Edgar), 1878-1957

Coppens, Linda Miles, 1944-

What American women did, 1789-1920 **305.4**

Copper sun. Draper, S. M. **Fic**

Coppinger, Lorna

(jt. auth) Coppinger, R. Dogs **636.7**

Coppinger, Raymond

Dogs **636.7**

Coppola, Francis Ford, 1939-

See/See also pages in the following book(s):

Koopmans, A. Filmmakers **920**

Copyright

See also Fair use (Copyright)

Butler, R. P. Copyright for teachers and librarians **346.04**

Complete copyright **346.04**

Crews, K. D. Copyright law for librarians and educators **346.04**

Gordon, S. M. Downloading copyrighted stuff from the Internet **346.04**

Hoffmann, G. M. Copyright in cyberspace 2 **346.04**

Simpson, C. M. Copyright catechism **346.04**

Simpson, C. M. Copyright for schools **346.04**

Music

Internet piracy **346.04**

Copyright catechism. Simpson, C. M. **346.04**

Copyright essentials for librarians and educators. See Crews, K. D. Copyright law for librarians and educators **346.04**

Copyright for school libraries. See Simpson, C. M. Copyright for schools **346.04**

Copyright for schools. Simpson, C. M. **346.04**

Copyright for teachers and librarians. Butler, R. P. **346.04**

Copyright in cyberspace 2. Hoffmann, G. M. **346.04**

The **coup** de grâce. Bierce, A.
  In The Oxford book of short stories p78-83
  S C

The **couple** next door. Millar, M.
  In The Best American mystery stories of the century p443-57 **S C**

Courage
  Kennedy, J. F. Profiles in courage **920**
  McCain, J. S. Why courage matters **179**
  Profiles in courage for our time **920**

Courage in a dangerous world. Roosevelt, E.
  973.9

The **Courage** to be yourself **305.23**

Coursen, Herbert R.
  Macbeth **822.3**

The **courting** of Dinah Shadd. Kipling, R.
  In Kipling, R. The portable Kipling **828**

Courts
  See also Juvenile courts
  United States
  U.S. court cases **347**

Courts and courtiers
  See also Fools and jesters; Princesses; Queens

A **courtship**. Faulkner, W.
  In Faulkner, W. Collected stories of William Faulkner p361-80 **S C**

Cousins
  Fiction
  Draper, S. M. The Battle of Jericho **Fic**
  Halaby, L. West of the Jordan **Fic**
  Minchin, A. The beat goes on **Fic**
  Rosoff, M. How I live now **Fic**
  Selvadurai, S. Swimming in the monsoon sea
  Fic
  Werlin, N. The killer's cousin **Fic**

Cousins. Dean, P.
  In Firebirds rising; an anthology of original science fiction and fantasy **S C**

Cousins. Fugard, A. **92**

Couto, Mia, 1955-
  The birds of God
  In The Heinemann book of contemporary African short stories p67-71 **S C**

Couturier, Lisa, 1962-
  The hopes of snakes **591.7**

Cover, Arthur Byron
  Macbeth **822.3**

Coverlets *See* Quilts

Coville, Bruce
  Am I blue? [story]
  In Am I blue?; coming out from the silence p1-16 **S C**
  Saying no to Nick
  In Twice told; original stories inspired by original art **S C**

Covington, Melody Mauldin
  (jt. auth) Downing, D. Dictionary of computer and Internet terms **004**

Covington, Michael A., 1957-
  (jt. auth) Downing, D. Dictionary of computer and Internet terms **004**

Coward, Noel
  Hands across the sea
  In 24 favorite one-act plays p151-69
  808.82

The **cowboy** hero. Savage, W. W. **973**

Cowgirls & Indie boys. Desai Hidier, T.
  In Sixteen: stories about that sweet and bitter birthday **S C**

Cowhands
  Savage, W. W. The cowboy hero **973**
  Fiction
  McCarthy, C. All the pretty horses **Fic**

Cowles, Frederick I., 1900-1948
  The vampire of Kaldenstein
  In The Oxford book of gothic tales p407-23
  S C

Cowles, Virginia, 1915-1983
  See/See also pages in the following book(s):
  Colman, P. Where the action was **070.4**

Cowley, Malcolm, 1898-1989
  (ed) Emerson, R. W. The portable Emerson
  818

Cowtown. Moore, A.
  In Under 30; plays for a new generation
  812.008

Cox, Barry, 1931-
  (jt. auth) Whitfield, P. J. Biomes and habitats
  577.8

Cox, Caroline, 1954-
  Opening up North America, 1497-1800 **917**

Cox, Daniel J., 1960-
  (jt. auth) Grambo, R. L. Wolf: legend, enemy, icon **599.77**

Cox, Lynne
  Swimming to Antarctica **92**

Coy, John
  Crackback **Fic**

Coye, Dale F.
  Pronouncing Shakespeare's words **822.3**

CQ's American government A to Z series
  Congress A to Z **328.73**
  Jost, K. The Supreme Court A to Z **347**
  Moore, J. L. Elections A to Z **324.6**
  The Presidency A to Z **352.23**

CQ's politics in America **328.73**

CQ's state fact finder 2007 **317.3**

A **crack** in the line. Lawrence, M. **Fic**

Crackback. Coy, J. **Fic**

The **cracked** looking-glass. Porter, K. A.
  In Porter, K. A. The collected stories of Katherine Anne Porter **S C**

Cracking the PSAT/NMSQT, 2008 edition
  378.1

Cracking the SAT, 2008 edition **378.1**

Cracking the SAT: biology E/M subject test, 2007-2008 edition **570**

Cracking the SAT: chemistry subject test, 2007-2008 edition **540**

Cracking the SAT: French subject test, 2007-2008 edition **440**

Cracking the SAT: literature subject test, 2007-2008 edition **800**

Criminals—*Continued*
Dictionaries
MacNee, M. J. Outlaws, mobsters & crooks
920.003
Fiction
Woodrell, D. Winter's bone **Fic**
Identification
See also Fingerprints
Rehabilitation programs
See Corrections

Crips (Gang)
Simpson, C. Inside the Crips **92**

Crisfield, Deborah
(jt. auth) Monteleone, J. J. The Louisville Slugger complete book of women's fast-pitch softball **796.357**

Crisis management
See also Conflict management

Crist-Evans, Craig
Amaryllis **Fic**

Cristiano, Lynda M.
(jt. auth) Fanta, C. H. The Harvard Medical School guide to taking control of asthma
616.2

The **critic** as artist. Wilde, O.
In Wilde, O. The portable Oscar Wilde p51-136 **828**

Critical companion to Arthur Miller. Abbotson, S. C. W. **812.009**

Critical companion to Charles Dickens. Davis, P. B. **823.009**

Critical companion to Chaucer. Rossignol, R. **821.009**

Critical companion to Emily Dickinson. Leiter, S. **811.009**

Critical companion to Ernest Hemingway. Oliver, C. M. **813.009**

Critical companion to F. Scott Fitzgerald. Tate, M. J. **813.009**

Critical companion to Herman Melville. Rollyson, C. **813.009**

Critical companion to James Joyce. Fargnoli, A. N. **823.009**

Critical companion to John Steinbeck. Schultz, J. D. **813.009**

Critical companion to Jonathan Swift. DeGategno, P. J. **828**

Critical companion to Mark Twain. Rasmussen, R. K. **818**

Critical companion to Nathaniel Hawthorne. Wright, S. B. **813.009**

Critical companion to Robert Frost. Fagan, D. **811.009**

Critical companion to Tennessee Williams. Heintzelman, G. **812.009**

Critical companion to Walt Whitman. Oliver, C. M. **811.009**

Critical companion to William Shakespeare. Boyce, C. **822.3**

Critical companions to popular contemporary writers [series]
Russell, S. A. Revisiting Stephen King
813.009
Russell, S. A. Stephen King: a critical companion **813.009**

Critical essays on British literature [series]
Critical essays on Jane Austen **823.009**

Critical essays on Jane Austen **823.009**

Critical issue series
Daniels, R. Prisoners without trial **940.53**

Critical mass. Clarke, A. C.
In Clarke, A. C. The collected stories of Arthur C. Clarke **S C**

Critical perspectives on the past [series]
Lerner, G. Fireweed **92**

Critical survey of drama **809.2**

Critical survey of short fiction **809.3**

Croce, Benedetto, 1866-1952
See/See also pages in the following book(s):
Durant, W. J. The story of philosophy **109**

The **crochet** answer book. Eckman, E. **746.43**

Crocheting
Eckman, E. The crochet answer book
746.43

Croci, Pascal
Auschwitz **940.53**

Crocodiles
See also Alligators
Behler, J. L. Alligators & crocodiles **597.98**

Croddy, Eric, 1966-
(ed) Weapons of mass destruction. See Weapons of mass destruction **358**

Crofton, Ian
(ed) Brewer's dictionary of modern phrase & fable. See Brewer's dictionary of modern phrase & fable **803**

Croke, Vicki
The lady and the panda **599.78**

Cromartie High School, Vol. 1. Nonaka, E.
741.5

Cromwell, Oliver, 1599-1658
About
Aronson, M. John Winthrop, Oliver Cromwell, and the Land of Promise [dual biography of John Winthrop and Oliver Cromwell] **92**
Fiction
Jeapes, B. The new world order **Fic**

The **crooked** man. Doyle, Sir A. C.
In Doyle, Sir A. C. The complete Sherlock Holmes **S C**

Crookenden, Isaac
The vindictive monk; or, The fatal ring
In The Oxford book of gothic tales p51-59
S C

Crooker, Constance Emerson
Gun control and gun rights **363.33**

Croom, Emily Anne
(jt. auth) Smith, F. C. A genealogist's guide to discovering your African-American ancestors
929

The **crop**. O'Connor, F.
  In O'Connor, F. Collected works p732-40
  S C
  In O'Connor, F. The complete stories p33-41
  S C

Cropper, William H.
  Great physicists **920**

Crops *See* Farm produce

Crosby, Jay
  (ed) Our national archive. See Our national archive **973**

Crosby, Molly Caldwell
  The American plague **614.5**

Cross, Gary S.
  (ed) Encyclopedia of recreation and leisure in America. See Encyclopedia of recreation and leisure in America **790**

Cross-country skiing. Cazeneuve, B. **796.93**

Cross-country snow. Hemingway, E.
  In Hemingway, E. The complete short stories of Ernest Hemingway; the Finca Vigía edition p143-47 **S C**

Cross cultural conflict *See* Culture conflict

Cross-X. Miller, J. **808.53**

Crossing into America **810.8**

Crossing lines. Powell, J.
  In Not the only one; lesbian and gay fiction for teens **S C**

Crossing the danger water **810.8**

Crossing the line. Finnegan, W. **968.06**

Crossing the water. Plath, S. **811**

Crossword puzzles
Dictionaries
  Pulliam, T. The New York times crossword puzzle dictionary **793.73**

Crouch, Tom D.
  The Wright brothers and the invention of the aerial age **92**

Crow. Hogan, L.
  In Moccasin thunder; American Indians stories for today **S C**

Crow Dog, Leonard, 1942-
  Crow Dog **970.004**

Crow Dog, Mary *See* Brave Bird, Mary

The **crow** in the woods. Updike, J.
  In Updike, J. Pigeon feathers, and other stories p221-26 **S C**

Crow Lake. Lawson, M. **Fic**

Crowe, Chris
  Getting away with murder: the true story of the Emmett Till case **364.1**
  Mississippi trial, 1955 **Fic**

Crowley, John, 1942-
  Gone
  In The Locus awards; thirty years of the best in science fiction and fantasy **S C**
  Snow
  In Best of the best: 20 years of the Year's best science fiction **S C**
  In The Norton book of science fiction; North American science fiction, 1960-1990 p591-604 **S C**

A **crown** of feathers. Singer, I. B.
  In The Literary ghost; great contemporary ghost stories p342-65 **S C**

Crowther, Nicky
  The ultimate mountain bike book **796.6**

Crowther, Peter
  Things I didn't know my father knew
  In Past imperfect **S C**

The **crucible**. Miller, A. **812**
  also in Miller, A. The portable Arthur Miller **812**

The **cruel** sky. Clarke, A. C.
  In Clarke, A. C. The collected stories of Arthur C. Clarke **S C**

Cruel world. Nicholas, L. H. **940.53**

Cruelty to animals *See* Animal welfare

The **cruise** of The Jolly Roger. Vonnegut, K.
  In Vonnegut, K. Bagombo snuff box: uncollected short fiction p99-108 **S C**

Cruising through research. Volkman, J. D.
  025.5

'Cruiter. Matheus, J. F.
  In Black theatre USA; plays by African Americans, 1847 to today **812.008**

Crumley, James, 1939-
  Hot springs
  In The Best American mystery stories of the century p678-93 **S C**

Crump, Martha L.
  Headless males make great lovers **591.5**

Crunch time. Fredericks, M. **Fic**

Crusade. Clarke, A. C.
  In Clarke, A. C. The collected stories of Arthur C. Clarke **S C**

Crusades
  Jones, J. S. The Crusades, Biographies
  920.003
  Jones, J. S. The Crusades, Primary sources
  909.07
  O'Neal, M. The Crusades, Almanac **909.07**
  The Oxford illustrated history of the Crusades
  909.07
Encyclopedias
  Andrea, A. J. Encyclopedia of the crusades
  909.07
  The Crusades **909.07**

The **Crusades** **909.07**

The Crusades reference library [series]
  Jones, J. S. The Crusades, Biographies
  920.003
  Jones, J. S. The Crusades, Primary sources
  909.07
  O'Neal, M. The Crusades, Almanac **909.07**

Crushed. McNeal, L. **Fic**

Crutcher, Chris, 1946-
  Ironman **Fic**
  King of the mild frontier: an ill-advised autobiography **92**
  Running loose **Fic**
  Staying fat for Sarah Byrnes **Fic**
  Stotan! **Fic**

The **daemon** lover. Jackson, S.
   In Jackson, S. The lottery; or, The adventures
     of James Harris   **S C**

Dahl, Roald
   Skin and other stories   **S C**
   Contents: Skin; Lamb to the slaughter; The sound machine; An
African story; Galloping Foxley; The wish; The surgeon; Dip in
the pool; The champion of the world; Beware of the dog; My
lady love, my dove
     About
   Gelletly, L. Gift of imagination [biography of
     Roald Dahl]   **92**

Dailey, Donna
   London   **820.9**

Daily life during the French Revolution. Anderson,
   J. M.   **944.04**

Daily life in Chaucer's England. Singman, J. L.
     942.03

Daily life in Elizabethan England. Singman, J. L.
     942.05

Daily life in medieval Europe. Singman, J. L.
     940.1

Daily life in Renaissance Italy. Cohen, E. S.
     945

Daily life in the early American republic, 1790-
   1820. Heidler, D. S.   **973.4**

Daily life in the Inca empire. Malpass, M.
     985

Daily life in the Soviet Union. Eaton, K. B.
     947.084

Daily life in Victorian England. Mitchell, S.
     941.081

Daintith, John
   (ed) The Facts on File dictionary of astronomy.
   See The Facts on File dictionary of astronomy   **520.3**
   (ed) The Facts on File dictionary of chemistry.
   See The Facts on File dictionary of chemistry
     540.3
   (ed) The Facts on File dictionary of computer
   science. See The Facts on File dictionary of
   computer science   **004**
   (ed) The Facts on File dictionary of mathematics. See The Facts on File dictionary of mathematics   **510.3**
   (ed) The Facts on File dictionary of physics. See
   The Facts on File dictionary of physics
     530

Dairy Queen. Murdock, C. G.   **Fic**

Daisy Kutter. Kibuishi, K.   **741.5**

Dakota Indians
   See also Oglala Indians
   Brave Bird, M. Lakota woman   **92**
   Crow Dog, L. Crow Dog   **970.004**
   McMurtry, L. Crazy Horse   **92**
   See/See also pages in the following book(s):
   Freedman, R. Indian chiefs   **920**
     Fiction
   Power, S. The grass dancer   **Fic**
     Wars
   Viola, H. J. It is a good day to die   **973.8**

Dalai Lama II, 1476-1542
     About
   Mullin, G. H. The second Dalai Lama   **92**

Dalai Lama XIV, 1935-
   Ethics for the new millennium   **294.3**
   Freedom in exile   **92**

Dalby, Andrew
   Dictionary of languages   **410**

Dalí, Salvador, 1904-1989
     About
   Goff, R. The essential Salvador Dali   **759.6**
   Ross, M. E. Salvador Dali and the surrealists
     92

Dalkey, Kara, 1953-
   Hives
   In Firebirds rising; an anthology of original
     science fiction and fantasy   **S C**

Dalle, Eric
   Facts about China. See Facts about China
     951

Dallek, Robert
   Let every nation know [biography of John F.
   Kennedy]   **92**

Dalston, Teresa R., 1965-
   (jt. auth) Hallam, A. Managing budgets and finances   **025.1**

D'Aluisio, Faith, 1957-
   (jt. auth) Menzel, P. Hungry planet   **641.3**

Daly, Kathleen N.
   Greek and Roman mythology A to Z   **292**
   Norse mythology A to Z   **293**

Daly, Paul
   Athena Voltaire   **741.5**

Dalzell, Tom, 1951-
   (ed) The new Partridge dictionary of slang and
   unconventional English. See The new Partridge dictionary of slang and unconventional
   English   **427**

Damage. Jenkins, A. M.   **Fic**

Dame, Enid
   Drowning kittens
   In Growing up ethnic in America; contempo-
     rary fiction about learning to be Ameri-
     can   **S C**

Damned lies and statistics. Best, J.   **303.3**

Dams
   See/See also pages in the following book(s):
   Macaulay, D. Building big   **720**

Dana's eyes. Juratovac, N.
   In American dragons: twenty-five Asian
     American voices p75-95   **810.8**

Dance, Daryl Cumber
   (ed) Honey, hush! See Honey, hush!
     817.008

Dance
   See also Ballet; Modern dance
   Reynolds, N. No fixed points   **792.8**
     Dictionaries
   Craine, D. The Oxford dictionary of dance
     792.8
     Fiction
   Staples, S. F. Shiva's fire   **Fic**

A **dance** for Emilia. Beagle, P. S.
   In Beagle, P. S. The line between   **S C**

Dancer. Sears, V.
   In Leaving home: stories p19-25   **808.8**

Dancer in the dark. Gerrold, D.
In The Year's best science fiction and fantasy for teens: first annual collection **S C**

Dancers
Fishman, K. D. Attitude!: eight young dancers come of age at the Ailey School **792.8**
Ford, C. T. Legends of American dance and choreography **920**
Freedman, R. Martha Graham, a dancer's life **92**

Dancing *See* Dance

Dancing backwards. Bauer, M. D.
In Am I blue?; coming out from the silence p261-72 **S C**

Dancing solo. Surface, M. H.
In Surface, M. H. Most valuable player and four other all-star plays for middle and high school audiences **812**

Dancing with Marjorie's ghost. Vande Velde, V.
In Vande Velde, V. Being dead; stories **S C**

Dando, Marc
(jt. auth) Compagno, L. J. V. Sharks of the world **597**

Dangerous angels. Block, F. L. **Fic**

Dangerous animals
See also Animal attacks; Poisonous animals
Bachleda, F. L. Dangerous wildlife in California & Nevada **591.6**
Bachleda, F. L. Dangerous wildlife in the mid-Atlantic **591.6**
Bachleda, F. L. Dangerous wildlife in the Southeast **591.6**

Dangerous crossings. Bryant, J. H. **998**

Dangerous water: a biography of the boy who became Mark Twain. Powers, R. **92**

Dangerous weather [series]
Allaby, M. A chronology of weather **363.34**
Allaby, M. Droughts **551.57**

Dangerous wildlife in California & Nevada. Bachleda, F. L. **591.6**

Dangerous wildlife in the mid-Atlantic. Bachleda, F. L. **591.6**

Dangerous wildlife in the Southeast. Bachleda, F. L. **591.6**

The **dangers** of tobacco. Chekhov, A. P.
In Chekhov, A. P. The plays of Anton Chekhov p323-29 **891.7**

Daniel, Tony
A dry, quiet war
In Best of the best: 20 years of the Year's best science fiction **S C**

Daniel half human. Chotjewitz, D. **Fic**

Daniels, Jim
(ed) Letters to America. See Letters to America **811.008**

Daniels, Les, 1943-
Marvel **741.5**

Daniels, Roger
Coming to America **325.73**
Prisoners without trial **940.53**

Daniels, Ted, 1939-
(ed) A Doomsday reader. See A Doomsday reader **301**

Danis, Jan S.
(jt. auth) Viola, H. J. It is a good day to die **973.8**

Danish authors *See* Authors, Danish

Danson, Edwin, 1948-
Weighing the world **526**

Dante Alighieri, 1265-1321
The Divine comedy
In Dante Alighieri. The portable Dante **851**
The new life [La vita nuova]
In Dante Alighieri. The portable Dante **851**
In Emerson, R. W. Collected poems & translations **811**
The portable Dante **851**
Purgatorio **851**
Emerson, R. W. Collected poems & translations **811**

See/See also pages in the following book(s):
Highet, G. The classical tradition **809**
The new life; criticism
In Emerson, R. W. Collected poems & translations **811**

Danticat, Edwidge, 1969-
The farming of bones **Fic**
Krik? Krak! **S C**
Contents: Between the pool and the gardenias; Caroline's wedding; Children of the sea; The missing peace; New York day women; Night women; Nineteen thirty-seven; Seeing things simply; A wall of fire rising
Night women
In Gotham Writers' Workshop fiction gallery; exceptional short stories selected by New York's acclaimed creative writing school **S C**
(ed) The Butterfly's way. See The Butterfly's way **810.9**

Danziger, Danny
(jt. auth) Lacey, R. The year 1000 **942.01**

Daphne. Cadnum, M.
In The Green Man: tales from the mythic forest p44-49 **808.8**

Darion, Joe, 1917-2001
Man of La Mancha **812**

Dark, Larry
(ed) The Literary ghost. See The Literary ghost **S C**

Dark Ages *See* Middle Ages

Dark angel. Klass, D. **Fic**

The **dark** at the top of the stairs. Inge, W.
In Inge, W. 4 plays p221-304 **812**

The **dark** beast of death. Nixon, J. L.
In Night terrors; stories of shadow and substance **S C**

Dark cosmos. Hooper, D. **523.1**

Dark dreams [biography of Stephen King] Whitelaw, N. **92**

Dark in the forest, strange as time. Wolfe, T.
In Wolfe, T. The complete short stories of Thomas Wolfe p167-76 **S C**

The **dark** messiah. Wolfe, T.
In Wolfe, T. The complete short stories of Thomas Wolfe p459-64   **S C**

The **dark** princess [excerpt] Du Bois, W. E. B.
In The Portable Harlem Renaissance reader p511-35   **810.8**

The **dark** snow. DuBois, B.
In The Best American mystery stories of the century p694-712   **S C**

Dark sons. Grimes, N.   **Fic**

Darkrose and Diamond. Le Guin, U. K.
In Le Guin, U. K. Tales from Earthsea   **S C**

Darling, David J.
The universal book of astronomy from the Andromeda Galaxy to the zone of avoidance   **520.3**
The universal book of mathematics   **510.3**

Darling Adolf. Bradbury, R.
In Bradbury, R. Bradbury stories; 100 of his most celebrated tales   **S C**

Darrow, Sharon
The painters of Lexieville   **Fic**

Darwin, Charles, 1809-1882
The portable Darwin   **576.8**
About
Eldredge, N. Darwin: discovering the tree of life   **92**
Quammen, D. The reluctant Mr. Darwin   **92**
See/See also pages in the following book(s):
Horvitz, L. A. Eureka!: scientific breakthroughs that changed the world   **509**
Tudge, C. The time before history   **599.93**
(jt. auth) Ridley, M. The Darwin reader   **576.8**

Darwinism *See* Evolution

Darwin's ghost. Jones, S.   **576.8**

Dasch, E. Julius (Ernest Julius), 1932-
(ed) Water: science and issues. See Water: science and issues   **553.7**

Dasch, Ernest Julius *See* Dasch, E. Julius (Ernest Julius), 1932-

Dasch, Pat
(ed) Space sciences. See Space sciences   **500.5**

Dashefsky, H. Steven
Zoology: high school science fair experiments   **590.7**

Data processing
See also Artificial intelligence; Computer science
Barrett, J. R. Teaching and learning about computers   **004**
Ceruzzi, P. E. A history of modern computing   **004**
Katz, J. Geeks   **338.7**
Dictionaries
Pfaffenberger, B. Webster's New World computer dictionary   **004**

Data storage and retrieval systems *See* Information systems

Dating (Social customs)
Dating   **646.7**

Turner, J. S. Dating and sexuality in America   **306.7**
Drama
Soto, G. Novio boy   **812**
Fiction
Lockhart, E. The boyfriend list   **Fic**
Wittlinger, E. Sandpiper   **Fic**

Dating   **646.7**

Dating and sexuality in America. Turner, J. S.   **306.7**

Datlow, Ellen
(ed) The Faery Reel. See The Faery Reel   **S C**
(ed) The Green Man: tales from the mythic forest. See The Green Man: tales from the mythic forest   **808.8**

Daubert, Stephen
Threads from the web of life   **508**

Dauenhauer, Nora
Egg boat
In Working days: stories about teenagers and work   **S C**

Daughter of fortune. Allende, I.   **Fic**

Daughter of invention. Alvarez, J.
In Growing up Latino; memoirs and stories p3-15   **810.8**

Daughter of the forest. Marillier, J.   **Fic**

Daughter of the Ganges. Miró, A.   **92**

A **daughter** of the sea. Wartski, M. C.
In Join in; multiethnic short stories by outstanding writers for young adults p86-96   **S C**

Daughters and fathers *See* Father-daughter relationship

Daughters and mothers *See* Mother-daughter relationship

Davenport, Basil, 1905-1966
(ed) The Portable Roman reader. See The Portable Roman reader   **870.8**

David, A. Rosalie (Ann Rosalie)
Handbook to life in ancient Egypt   **932**

David Copperfield. Dickens, C.   **Fic**

David H. Levy's guide to observing and discovering comets. Levy, D. H.   **523.6**

David Swan. Hawthorne, N.
In Hawthorne, N. Tales and sketches, including Twice-told tales, Mosses from an old manse, and The snow-image; A wonder book for girls and boys; Tanglewood tales for girls and boys, being a second Wonder book p429-34   **S C**

Davidorf, Jonathan M., 1965-
(jt. auth) Kornmehl, E. W. LASIK: a guide to laser vision correction   **617.7**

Davidson, Alan, 1924-2003
The Oxford companion to food   **641.03**

Davidson, Avram, 1923-1993
The cost of Kent Castwell
In Alfred Hitchcock's mystery magazine presents fifty years of crime and suspense   **S C**

The **dead** and the moonstruck. Kiernan, C. R.
   In Gothic!; ten original dark tales   **S C**

Dead connection. Price, C.   **Fic**

Dead end. Anaya, R. A.
   In Join in; multiethnic short stories by out-
     standing writers for young adults p101-
     09   **S C**

Dead High yearbook   **741.5**

Dead languages. Hensher, P.
   In The Oxford book of English short stories
     p435-39   **S C**

The **dead** man. Bradbury, R.
   In Bradbury, R. Bradbury stories; 100 of his
     most celebrated tales   **S C**

Dead on town line. Connor, L.   **Fic**

The **dead** past. Asimov, I.
   In Asimov, I. The complete stories p3-40
     S C

Dead run. Bear, G.
   In Bear, G. The collected stories of Greg
     Bear   **S C**

The **Dead** Sea scrolls Bible. Bible. O.T.   **221**

Dead women's things. Chwedyk, K.
   In Nightshade: 20th century ghost stories p74-
     76   **S C**

Deadly diseases and epidemics [series]
   Bloom, O. Encephalitis   **616.8**
   Brands, D. A. Salmonella   **615.9**
   Coleman, W. H. Cholera   **616.9**
   Cramer, S. D. Prostate cancer   **616.99**
   Decker, J. M. Anthrax   **616.9**
   Decker, J. M. Mononucleosis   **616.9**
   Emmeluth, D. Botulism   **614.5**
   Emmeluth, D. Influenza   **616.2**
   Ferreiro, C. Lung cancer   **616.99**
   Finer, K. R. Tuberculosis   **616.2**
   Freeman-Cook, L. Staphylococcus aureus infec-
     tions   **616.9**
   Guilfoile, P. Antibiotic-resistant bacteria
     616.9
   Hecht, A. Polio   **616.8**
   Kienzle, T. E. Rabies   **616.9**
   Sehgal, A. Leprosy   **614.5**
   Serradell, J. SARS   **616.2**
   Shmaefsky, B. Syphilis   **616.95**
   Smith, T. C. Ebola   **616.9**
   Spencer, J. V. Cervical cancer   **616.99**
   Spencer, J. V. Herpes   **616.95**

Deadly invaders. Grady, D.   **614.4**

Deaf
   Coffey, W. R. Winning sounds like this
     796.323
   Keller, H. Helen Keller: selected writings   **92**
   Keller, H. The story of my life   **92**
   Vasishta, M. Deaf in Delhi   **92**
         Drama
   Medoff, M. H. Children of a lesser god   **812**
         Fiction
   Ferris, J. Of sound mind   **Fic**
   McCullers, C. The heart is a lonely hunter
     Fic
   Na, A. Wait for me   **Fic**

Means of communication
   See also Sign language
   Cohen, L. H. Train go sorry   **371.9**

Deaf in Delhi. Vasishta, M.   **92**

Deaf lives [series]
   Vasishta, M. Deaf in Delhi   **92**

Deafness
   Mayo Clinic on hearing   **617.8**

Dean, Pamela
   Cousins
   In Firebirds rising; an anthology of original
     science fiction and fantasy   **S C**

Dean, Ruth, 1947-
   (jt. auth) Thomson, M. Women of the Renais-
     sance   **940.2**

DeAngelis, Gina
   The Triangle Shirtwaist Company fire of 1911
     974.7

Dear, I. C. B. *See* Dear, Ian, 1935-

Dear, Ian, 1935-
   (ed) The Oxford companion to World War II.
     See The Oxford companion to World War II
     940.53

Dear Alexandros. Updike, J.
   In Updike, J. Pigeon feathers, and other sto-
     ries p102-08   **S C**

Dear America: letters home from Vietnam
   959.704

Dear author   **028.5**

Dear Miss Breed. Oppenheim, J.   **940.53**

Dear Zoe. Beard, P.   **Fic**

Dearing, Joel
   Volleyball fundamentals   **796.325**

Dearly beloved. Fitzgerald, F. S.
   In Fitzgerald, F. S. The short stories of F.
     Scott Fitzgerald; a new collection p773-
     75   **S C**

Deas, Nilo MarXia Fabra y *See* Fabra, Nilo Ma-
   ría, 1843-1903

Death
   See also Longevity; Terminal care
   Death and dying: opposing viewpoints   **179.7**
   Gootman, M. E. When a friend dies   **155.9**
   Hughes, L. B. You are not alone   **155.9**
   Kübler-Ross, E. On death and dying   **155.9**
   Lynch, T. Bodies in motion and at rest   **113**
   Stark, P. Last breath   **616**
   See/See also pages in the following book(s):
   Colman, P. Corpses, coffins, and crypts   **393**
         Encyclopedias
   Macmillan encyclopedia of death and dying
     306.9
         Fiction
   Agee, J. A death in the family   **Fic**
   Beard, P. Dear Zoe   **Fic**
   Brooks, K. Martyn Pig   **Fic**
   Craven, M. I heard the owl call my name
     Fic
   Draper, S. M. The Battle of Jericho   **Fic**
   Draper, S. M. Tears of a tiger   **Fic**
   Green, J. Looking for Alaska   **Fic**
   Griffin, A. Where I want to be   **Fic**
   Herrick, S. By the river   **Fic**

Debating the issues in colonial newspapers. Copeland, D. A. **973.2**

Debo, Angie, 1890-1988
A history of the Indians of the United States **970.004**

Debray, Elisabeth Burgos- *See* Burgos-Debray, Elisabeth

Debt of bones. Goodkind, T.
In Legends: short novels by the masters of modern fantasy p139-214 **S C**

Decade of the wolf. Smith, D. W. **599.77**

Decision making
Gladwell, M. Blink: the power of thinking without thinking **153.4**

Decker, Janet M.
Anthrax **616.9**
Mononucleosis **616.9**

Declaration of Independence *See* United States. Declaration of Independence

The **decline** and fall of the Roman Empire. Ermatinger, J. W. **937**

DeCurtis, Anthony
(ed) The Rolling Stone illustrated history of rock & roll. See The Rolling Stone illustrated history of rock & roll **781.66**

Dedication. Lanagan, M.
In Lanagan, M. White time **S C**

Dee, Catherine, 1964-
(ed) The Girls' book of wisdom. See The Girls' book of wisdom **808.88**

The **deep.** Asimov, I.
In Asimov, I. The complete stories p112-28 **S C**

Deep ocean. Rice, T. **551.46**

A **deep** purple. Allen, P. G.
In Spider Woman's granddaughters; traditional tales and contemporary writing by Native American women **S C**

The **deep** range. Clarke, A. C.
In Clarke, A. C. The collected stories of Arthur C. Clarke **S C**

Deep woods [biography of Robert Frost] Caravantes, P. **92**

Deering, Kathryn R.
(ed) Cash and credit information for teens: tips for a successful financial life. See Cash and credit information for teens: tips for a successful financial life **332.024**
(ed) Savings and investment information for teens. See Savings and investment information for teens **332.024**

The **Deerslayer.** Cooper, J. F.
In Cooper, J. F. The Leatherstocking tales p483-1030 **Fic**

The **defeat** of the city. Henry, O.
In Henry, O. The best short stories of O. Henry **S C**

The **defender.** Lipsyte, R.
In Ultimate sports; short stories by outstanding writers for young adults p180-92 **S C**

Defender of the faith. Roth, P.
In Roth, P. Goodbye, Columbus, and five short stories **S C**

The **defenestration** of Ermintrude Inch. Clarke, A. C.
In Clarke, A. C. The collected stories of Arthur C. Clarke **S C**

Defense, Civil *See* Civil defense

Defense industry
Gifford, C. The arms trade **382**

Defense mechanisms (Zoology) *See* Animal defenses

Defense policy *See* Military policy

Defining Dulcie. Acampora, P. **Fic**

Defining moments [series]
Hill, J. Prohibition **363.4**
Telgen, D. Brown v. Board of Education **344**

Defoe, Daniel, 1661?-1731
Robinson Crusoe **Fic**
Robinson Crusoe; criticism
In Souhami, D. Selkirk's Island **996**

DeGategno, Paul J.
Critical companion to Jonathan Swift **828**

Deities *See* Gods and goddesses

DeJean, Joan E.
The essence of style **391**

Del Testa, David W.
(ed) Global history. See Global history **909**

Delacampagne, Ariane, 1959-
Here be dragons **700**

Delacampagne, Christian, 1949-
(jt. auth) Delacampagne, A. Here be dragons **700**

Delahunty, Andrew
(ed) The Oxford dictionary of allusions. See The Oxford dictionary of allusions **422**

Delaney, Frank, 1942-
Simple courage **910.4**

Delany, Annie Elizabeth *See* Delany, Bessie

Delany, Bessie
(jt. auth) Delany, S. Having our say **92**

Delany, Sadie
Having our say **92**

Delany, Samuel R.
High weir
In The Norton book of science fiction; North American science fiction, 1960-1990 p183-200 **S C**

Delany, Sarah Louise *See* Delany, Sadie

Delany family
About
Delany, S. Having our say **92**

Delaware
Fiction
Pate, A. D. West of Rehoboth **Fic**

Delbanco, Andrew, 1952-
(ed) Lincoln, A. The portable Abraham Lincoln **973.7**

Dice, brassknuckles & guitar. Fitzgerald, F. S.
In Fitzgerald, F. S. The short stories of F. Scott Fitzgerald; a new collection p237-58   **S C**

Dick, Philip K.
The alien mind
In New skies: an anthology of today's science fiction   **S C**
Frozen journey
In The Norton book of science fiction; North American science fiction, 1960-1990 p386-401   **S C**
The minority report   **Fic**
also in Adaptations: from short story to big screen; 35 great stories that have inspired great films   **S C**

Dick, Ron, 1931-
The golden age   **629.13**
War & peace in the air   **629.13**

Dickens, Charles, 1812-1870
David Copperfield   **Fic**
Great expectations   **Fic**
The haunted house
In The Oxford book of English short stories p18-43   **S C**
Oliver Twist   **Fic**
A tale of two cities   **Fic**
About
Caravantes, P. Best of times: the story of Charles Dickens   **92**
Davis, P. B. Critical companion to Charles Dickens   **823.009**
Smiley, J. Charles Dickens   **92**

Dickey, James
The whole motion   **811**

Dickinson, A. T.
American historical fiction   **016.8**

Dickinson, Emily, 1830-1886
The complete poems of Emily Dickinson   **811**
Final harvest   **811**
The selected poems of Emily Dickinson   **811**
About
Borus, A. A student's guide to Emily Dickinson   **811.009**
Leiter, S. Critical companion to Emily Dickinson   **811.009**
Longsworth, P. The world of Emily Dickinson   **92**
Meltzer, M. Emily Dickinson   **92**
(jt. auth) Shurr, W. New poems of Emily Dickinson   **811**

Dickinson, Peter, 1927-
Eva   **Fic**
Kraken
In McKinley, R. and Dickinson, P. Water: tales of elemental spirits p170-207   **S C**
Mermaid song
In McKinley, R. and Dickinson, P. Water: tales of elemental spirits p1-29   **S C**
The ropemaker   **Fic**

Sea serpent
In McKinley, R. and Dickinson, P. Water: tales of elemental spirits p78-118   **S C**
(jt. auth) McKinley, R. Water: tales of elemental spirits   **S C**

Dickinson, Terence
The universe and beyond   **520**
(ed) NightWatch: a practical guide to viewing the universe. See NightWatch: a practical guide to viewing the universe   **520**

Dickson, Paul
Slang!   **427**

Dictators
Adolf Hitler [biographical essays]   **92**
Cunningham, K. Joseph Stalin and the Soviet Union   **92**
Hitler and his henchmen   **92**
Rice, E. Adolf Hitler and Nazi Germany   **92**
Scandiffio, L. Evil masters   **920**
Fiction
Vargas Llosa, M. The Feast of the Goat   **Fic**

Dictionaries *See* Encyclopedias and dictionaries

Dictionaries, Biographical *See* Biography—Dictionaries

Dictionaries, Classical *See* Classical dictionaries

Dictionaries, Multilingual *See* Polyglot dictionaries

Dictionaries, Picture *See* Picture dictionaries

Dictionary for school library media specialists. McCain, M. M.   **020**

Dictionary of American family names   **929.4**

Dictionary of American history   **973.03**

Dictionary of American history: from 1763 to the present. Thompson, P.   **973.03**

A **Dictionary** of American proverbs   **398.9**

Dictionary of architecture & construction   **720.3**

A **Dictionary** of astronomy   **520.3**

Dictionary of computer and Internet terms. Downing, D.   **004**

A **dictionary** of creation myths. Leeming, D. A.   **201.03**

The **dictionary** of cultural literacy. See Hirsch, E. D. The new dictionary of cultural literacy   **031**

A **dictionary** of earth sciences. See The Facts on File dictionary of earth science   **550.3**

Dictionary of first names. Room, A.   **929.4**

A **dictionary** of folklore. Pickering, D.   **398.2**

Dictionary of Hispanic biography   **920.003**

Dictionary of languages. Dalby, A.   **410**

A **dictionary** of literary and thematic terms. Quinn, E.   **803**

Dictionary of Mexican literature   **860.3**

Dictionary of modern American history. See Thompson, P. Dictionary of American history: from 1763 to the present   **973.03**

A **dictionary** of modern American usage. See Garner, B. A. Garner's modern American usage   **423**

Dinesen, Isak, 1885-1962
The monkey
In The Oxford book of gothic tales p344-85
S C

The supper at Elsinore
In Nightshade: 20th century ghost stories
p100-49 **S C**
About
Leslie, R. Isak Dinesen **92**

Dining
Tannahill, R. Food in history **641.3**
Dinner at the Homesick Restaurant. Tyler, A.
Fic

Dinner in Audoghast. Sterling, B.
In Best of the best: 20 years of the Year's
best science fiction **S C**

Dinner with Father. Jacobs, B. A.
In Growing up ethnic in America; contemporary fiction about learning to be American **S C**

Dinosaur encyclopedia. Lambert, D. **567.9**
Dinosaur in a haystack. Gould, S. J. **508**

Dinosaurs
Alvarez, W. T. rex and the Crater of Doom
551.7
Haines, T. The complete guide to prehistoric life
560
Parker, S. Dinosaurus **567.9**
Powell, J. L. Night comes to the Cretaceous
576.8
Encyclopedias
Lambert, D. Dinosaur encyclopedia **567.9**
Fiction
Crichton, M. Jurassic Park **Fic**
Dinosaurus. Parker, S. **567.9**

Dinwiddie, R. (Robert)
Universe. See Universe **523.1**

Dinwiddie, Robert *See* Dinwiddie, R. (Robert)

Dion, Nathalie, 1964-
(il) Beker, J. The big night out **646.7**

Diorio, Mary Ann L.
A student's guide to Herman Melville
813.009

Dip in the pool. Dahl, R.
In Dahl, R. Skin and other stories **S C**

Direction (Motion pictures) *See* Motion pictures—Production and direction

Direction (Theater) *See* Theater—Production and
direction

Directory of distance learning opportunities, K-12
371.3

Directory of financial aids for women 2007-2009.
Schlachter, G. A. **378.3**

Dirty hands. Sartre, J. P.
In Sartre, J. P. No exit, and three other plays
842

Disabled *See* Handicapped

Disabled students *See* Handicapped students

Disadvantaged children *See* Socially handicapped
children

The **disappearance** of Lady Frances Carfax.
Doyle, Sir A. C.
In Doyle, Sir A. C. The complete Sherlock
Holmes **S C**

Disarmament *See* Arms control

Disaster planning. Halsted, D. D. **025.8**

Disaster relief
Dyson, M. E. Come hell or high water
976.3
Halsted, D. D. Disaster planning **025.8**
Hurricane Katrina **363.34**
Katrina: state of emergency **363.34**
Van Heerden, I. L. The storm **976.3**

Disasters
See also Accidents; Natural disasters
Davis, L. A. Man-made catastrophes **904**
Garner, J. We interrupt this broadcast **070.1**
Gunn, A. M. Unnatural disasters **304.2**
Moore, R. A time to die **910**

Discipline *See* Punishment

Discipline of children *See* Child rearing

Discover beading **745.58**

The **discoverers**. Boorstin, D. J. **909**

Discoveries (in geography) *See* Exploration

The **discoveries**. Lightman, A. P. **509**

Discovering the world through debate **808.53**

Discovering world cultures [series]
The Middle East **956**

Discovery! [series]
Fleisher, P. Parasites **578.6**
Goldsmith, C. Invisible invaders **614.4**
Seiple, S. Mutants, clones, and killer corn
660.6

Discovery and exploration [series]
Cox, C. Opening up North America, 1497-1800
917
Isserman, M. Exploring North America, 1800-
1900 **917**
Smith, T. Discovery of the Americas, 1492-1800
909
Vail, M. Exploring the Pacific **919**
White, P. Exploration in the world of the Mid-
dle Ages, 500-1500 **910.4**

Discovery Channel reptiles & amphibians
597.9

The **discovery** of King Arthur. Ashe, G. **92**

Discovery of the Americas, 1492-1800. Smith, T.
909

Discrimination
See also Hate crimes; Race discrimination;
Sex discrimination
See/See also pages in the following book(s):
Affirmative action [Greenwood Press] **331.1**

Discrimination in education
See also Segregation in education
Affirmative action [Greenhaven Press] **331.1**
Finnegan, W. Crossing the line **968.06**

Discrimination in employment
See also Affirmative action programs

Disease germs *See* Bacteria; Germ theory of disease

DNA

Carroll, S. B. The making of the fittest **572.8**

Polcovar, J. Rosalind Franklin and the structure of life **92**

Watson, J. D. DNA: the secret of life **576.5**

Watson, J. D. The double helix **572.8**

See/See also pages in the following book(s):

Friedman, M. Medicine's 10 greatest discoveries **610.9**

DNA fingerprinting

Fridell, R. DNA fingerprinting **614**

Lee, H. C. Blood evidence **614**

Tocci, S. High-tech IDs **614**

Do children have rights? **323.3**

Do infectious diseases pose a serious threat? **614.4**

Do it right!. Jones, P. **027.62**

Do not go gentle. Alexie, S.

In Alexie, S. Ten little Indians; stories **S C**

Do nuclear weapons pose a serious threat? **355.8**

Do with me what you will. Oates, J. C.

In The Best American mystery stories of the century p556-67 **S C**

Do you know where I am? Alexie, S.

In Alexie, S. Ten little Indians; stories **S C**

Do you want my opinion? Kerr, M. E.

In Sixteen: short stories by outstanding writers for young adults p93-100 **S C**

Dobard, Raymond

(jt. auth) Tobin, J. Hidden in plain view **973.7**

Dobkin, David S.

(jt. auth) Ehrlich, P. R. The birder's handbook **598**

Dobson, Michael

(ed) The Oxford companion to Shakespeare. See The Oxford companion to Shakespeare **822.3**

The **doctor** and the doctor's wife. Hemingway, E.

In Hemingway, E. The complete short stories of Ernest Hemingway; the Finca Vigía edition p73-76 **S C**

The **doctor** in spite of himself. Molière

In Molière. The misanthrope and other plays **842**

Doctorow, E. L., 1931-

Ragtime **Fic**

Willi

In American short story masterpieces **S C**

The writer in the family

In Growing up ethnic in America; contemporary fiction about learning to be American **S C**

Doctors *See* Physicians

The **doctor's** wife. Updike, J.

In Updike, J. Pigeon feathers, and other stories p197-210 **S C**

Doctors Without Borders (Organization) *See* Médecins Sans Frontières (Organization)

Documentary photography

Through the lens **779**

Dodge, Hazel

(jt. auth) Connolly, P. The ancient city **937**

Dodson, Owen, 1914-1983

The confession stone

In Black theatre USA; plays by African Americans, 1847 to today **812.008**

Doerr, Anthony, 1973-

For a long time this was Griselda's story

In Gotham Writers' Workshop fiction gallery; exceptional short stories selected by New York's acclaimed creative writing school **S C**

Does my head look big in this? Abdel-Fattah, R. **Fic**

Does the world hate the United States? **973.931**

Dog racing

See also Iditarod Trail Sled Dog Race, Alaska; Sled dog racing

Dog Star. Clarke, A. C.

In Clarke, A. C. The collected stories of Arthur C. Clarke **S C**

A **dog** year. Katz, J. **636.7**

Doggett, Sandra L.

(jt. auth) Montgomery, P. K. Beyond the book **025.04**

Dogs

American Kennel Club. The complete dog book **636.7**

Budiansky, S. The truth about dogs **636.7**

Coppinger, R. Dogs **636.7**

Davis, C. Essential dog **636.7**

Dibra, B. Dogspeak **636.7**

Geeson, E. Ultimate dog grooming **636.7**

Katz, J. A dog year **636.7**

Katz, J. A good dog **636.7**

The Original dog bible **636.7**

Sidman, J. The world according to dog **810.8**

Encyclopedias

Fogle, B. The new encyclopedia of the dog **636.7**

Fiction

Hartnett, S. Surrender **Fic**

London, J. The call of the wild **Fic**

London, J. White Fang **Fic**

Psychology

Thomas, E. M. The hidden life of dogs **636.7**

Training

Fogle, B. New complete dog training manual **636.7**

Dogs, Wild *See* Wild dogs

A **dog's** tale. Twain, M.

In Twain, M. The complete short stories of Mark Twain; now collected for the first time **S C**

Dogspeak. Dibra, B. **636.7**

The **doi** store monkey. Salisbury, G.

In Salisbury, G. Island boyz: short stories p165-95 **S C**

Dornstein, Ken
The boy who fell out of the sky [biography of David Scott Dornstein]   **92**

Dorothea Lange—a visual life   **92**

Dorothy and my grandmother and the sailors. Jackson, S.
In Jackson, S. The lottery; or, The adventures of James Harris   **S C**

Dorris, Michael
A yellow raft in blue water   **Fic**
About
Coltelli, L. Winged words: American Indian writers speak   **897**

Dorsey, Candas Jane
(Learning about) machine sex
In The Norton book of science fiction; North American science fiction, 1960-1990 p746-61   **S C**

Dorsey, Thomas A., 1899-1993
See/See also pages in the following book(s):
We'll understand it better by and by   **782.25**

D'Orso, Michael
Eagle blue   **796.323**
(jt. auth) Lewis, J. Walking with the wind   **92**

Dostoevskiĭ, Fedor Mikhaĭlovich *See* Dostoyevsky, Fyodor, 1821-1881

Dostoyevsky, Fyodor, 1821-1881
Crime and punishment   **Fic**
The Grand Inquisitor
In The Portable nineteenth-century Russian reader p413-33   **891.7**

Doty, Mark
See/See also pages in the following book(s):
Fooling with words   **808.1**

A **double-barreled** detective story. Twain, M.
In Twain, M. The complete short stories of Mark Twain; now collected for the first time   **S C**

Double crossing. Tal, E.   **Fic**

The **double** helix. Watson, J. D.   **572.8**

Double helix. Werlin, N.   **Fic**

A **double** life [excerpt] Pavlova, K.
In The Portable nineteenth-century Russian reader p282-91   **891.7**

Double victory. Takaki, R. T.   **940.53**

Doubt *See* Belief and doubt

Dough Boy. Marino, P.   **Fic**

The **Dough** prince
In Hearne, B. G. Beauties and beasts p151-53   **398.2**

The **Doughnut** boots his reputation. Carter, A. R.
In Carter, A. R. Love, football, and other contact sports   **S C**

Douglas, Aaron, 1898-1979
See/See also pages in the following book(s):
Harlem Renaissance   **709.73**

Douglas, H. Ford, 1831-1865
See/See also pages in the following book(s):
Katz, W. L. Black pioneers   **920**

Douglas, Paul
Tennis   **796.342**

Douglas, Stephen Arnold, 1813-1861
The Lincoln-Douglas debates of 1858   **973.6**

Douglas-Klotz, Neil
(jt. auth) Chittister, J. The tent of Abraham   **222**

Douglass, Frederick, 1817?-1895
Autobiographies   **92**
Frederick Douglass: selected speeches and writings   **326**
Life and times of Frederick Douglass
In Douglass, F. Autobiographies   **92**
My bondage and my freedom
In Douglass, F. Autobiographies   **92**
Narrative of the life of Frederick Douglass, an American slave
In Douglass, F. Autobiographies   **92**
See/See also pages in the following book(s):
Abdul-Jabbar, K. Black profiles in courage   **920**
Garrison, M. Slaves who dared   **920**
Slave narratives [Library of Am.]   **326**

Dove, Rita
American smooth   **811**
Mother love   **811**
On the bus with Rosa Parks   **811**
Selected poems   **811**

Dover, Jeffrey S.
(jt. auth) Turkington, C. The encyclopedia of skin and skin disorders   **616.5**

Dover, Kenneth James
(ed) Ancient Greek literature. See Ancient Greek literature   **880.9**

Dow, James R.
(jt. auth) Mercatante, A. S. The Facts on File encyclopedia of world mythology and legend   **201.03**

Dow, Kirstin, 1963-
The atlas of climate change   **551.6**

Dow, Sheila M.
(ed) Business leader profiles for students. See Business leader profiles for students   **920.003**

Dowd, Siobhan
A swift pure cry   **Fic**

Dowhan, Adrienne
(jt. auth) Kaufman, D. Essays that will get you into college   **378**

Dowhan, Chris
(jt. auth) Kaufman, D. Essays that will get you into college   **378**

Dowling, Elizabeth M.
(ed) Encyclopedia of religious and spiritual development. See Encyclopedia of religious and spiritual development   **200.3**

Down, Oliphant
The maker of dreams
In 24 favorite one-act plays p256-71   **808.82**

Down at the dinghy. Salinger, J. D.
In Salinger, J. D. Nine stories p111-30   **S C**

Down by the riverside. Wright, R.
In Wright, R. Uncle Tom's children; five long stories   **S C**

Down syndrome
Libal, A. My name is not Slow   **362.3**
Down the rabbit hole. Abrahams, P.   **Fic**
Downer, Deborah A., 1954-
(ed) Classic American ghost stories. See Classic American ghost stories   **133.1**
Downfall. Frank, R. B.   **940.54**
Downie, N. A., 1956-
Vacuum bazookas, electric rainbow jelly, and 27 other Saturday science projects   **507.8**
Downing, Douglas
Dictionary of computer and Internet terms   **004**
Downing, Thomas E.
(jt. auth) Dow, K. The atlas of climate change   **551.6**
Downloading copyrighted stuff from the Internet. Gordon, S. M.   **346.04**
Downs, Todd
The bicycling guide to complete bicycle maintenance & repair   **629.28**
Downsiders. Shusterman, N.   **Fic**
The **downward** path to wisdom. Porter, K. A.
In Porter, K. A. The collected stories of Katherine Anne Porter   **S C**
Downwind from Gettysburg. Bradbury, R.
In Bradbury, R. Bradbury stories; 100 of his most celebrated tales   **S C**
Doyle, Sir Arthur Conan, 1859-1930
Adventures of Sherlock Holmes
In Doyle, Sir A. C. The complete Sherlock Holmes   **S C**
The case book of Sherlock Holmes
In Doyle, Sir A. C. The complete Sherlock Holmes   **S C**
The complete Sherlock Holmes   **S C**
The collections included and their contents are as follows: Adventures of Sherlock Holmes: A scandal in Bohemia; The Redheaded League; A case of identity; The Boscombe Valley mystery; The five orange pips; The man with the twisted lip; The adventure of the Blue Carbuncle; The adventure of the speckled band; The adventure of the engineer's thumb; The adventure of the noble bachelor; The adventure of the Beryl Coronet; The adventure of the copper beeches
Memoirs of Sherlock Holmes: Silver Blaze; They yellow face; The stock-broker's clerk; The "Gloria Scott"; The Musgrave ritual; The Reigate puzzle; The crooked man; The resident patient; The Greek interpreter; The naval treaty; The final problem
The return of Sherlock Holmes: The adventure of the empty house; The adventure of the Norwood builder; The adventure of the dancing men; The adventure of the solitary cyclist; The adventure of the priory school; The adventure of Black Peter; The adventure of Charles Augustus Milverton; The adventure of the six Napoleons; The adventure of the three students; The adventure of the golden pince-nez; The adventure of the missing three-quarter; The adventure of the Abbey Grange; The adventure of the second stain
His last bow: The adventure of Wisteria Lodge; The adventure of the cardboard box; The adventure of the red circle; The adventure of the Bruce-Partington plans; The adventure of the dying detective; The disappearance of Lady Frances Carfax; The adventure of the Devil's foot; His last bow
The case book of Sherlock Holmes: The adventure of the illustrious client; The adventure of the blanched soldier; The adventure of the Mazarin stone; The adventure of the Three Gables; The adventure of the Sussex vampire; The adventure of the three Garridebs; The problem of Thor Bridge; The adventure of the creeping man; The adventure of the lion's mane; The adventure of the veiled lodger; The adventure of Shoscombe Old Place; The adventure of the retired colourman

His last bow
In Doyle, Sir A. C. The complete Sherlock Holmes   **S C**
The hound of the Baskervilles   **Fic**
also in Doyle, Sir A. C. The complete Sherlock Holmes   **S C**
Memoirs of Sherlock Holmes
In Doyle, Sir A. C. The complete Sherlock Holmes   **S C**
The return of Sherlock Holmes
In Doyle, Sir A. C. The complete Sherlock Holmes   **S C**
The sign of the four
In Doyle, Sir A. C. The complete Sherlock Holmes   **S C**
A study in scarlet
In Doyle, Sir A. C. The complete Sherlock Holmes   **S C**
The valley of fear
In Doyle, Sir A. C. The complete Sherlock Holmes   **S C**
Parodies, imitations, etc.
King, L. R. The beekeeper's apprentice, or, On the segregation of the queen   **Fic**
Doyle, Conan *See* Doyle, Sir Arthur Conan, 1859-1930
Doyle, Debra
Uncle Joshua and the Grogglemen
In New skies: an anthology of today's science fiction   **S C**
Doyle, Kelly
(ed) 1860-1880: the nineteenth century. See 1860-1880: the nineteenth century   **909.81**
(ed) Is gun ownership a right? See Is gun ownership a right?   **344**
Doyle, William, 1942-
The Oxford history of the French Revolution   **944.04**
Dozois, Gardner R.
(ed) Best of the best: 20 years of the Year's best science fiction. See Best of the best: 20 years of the Year's best science fiction   **S C**
Dr. Bullivant. Hawthorne, N.
In Hawthorne, N. Tales and sketches, including Twice-told tales, Mosses from an old manse, and The snow-image; A wonder book for girls and boys; Tanglewood tales for girls and boys, being a second Wonder book p34-41   **S C**
Dr. Franklin's island. Halam, A.   **Fic**
Dr. Heidegger's experiment. Hawthorne, N.
In Gotham Writers' Workshop fiction gallery; exceptional short stories selected by New York's acclaimed creative writing school   **S C**
In Hawthorne, N. Tales and sketches, including Twice-told tales, Mosses from an old manse, and The snow-image; A wonder book for girls and boys; Tanglewood tales for girls and boys, being a second Wonder book p470-79   **S C**
Dr. Jekyll and Mr. Hyde. See Stevenson, R. L. The strange case of Dr. Jekyll and Mr. Hyde   **Fic**

Dr. Jekyll and Sister Hyde. Sones, S.
In Necessary noise: stories about our families as they really are p173-216 **S C**

Dr. Knoegle's end. Hesse, H.
In Hesse, H. and Zipes, J. D. The fairy tales of Hermann Hesse **S C**

Dr. Martino. Faulkner, W.
In Faulkner, W. Collected stories of William Faulkner p565-85 **S C**

Dr. Melissa Palmer's guide to hepatitis & liver disease. Palmer, M. **616.3**

Drabble, Margaret, 1939-
(ed) The Oxford companion to English literature. See The Oxford companion to English literature **820.3**

Dracula *See* Vlad III, Prince of Wallachia, 1430 or 31-1476 or 7

Dracula. Stoker, B. **Fic**

Dracula [biography of Vlad II] Florescu, R. R. N. **92**

Draft resisters
See also Conscientious objectors

The **dragon.** Bradbury, R.
In Bradbury, R. Bradbury stories; 100 of his most celebrated tales **S C**

Dragonflight. McCaffrey, A. **Fic**

Dragonfly. Le Guin, U. K.
In Le Guin, U. K. Tales from Earthsea **S C**
In Legends: short novels by the masters of modern fantasy p333-95 **S C**

Dragons
See/See also pages in the following book(s):
Nigg, J. Wonder beasts **398**
Fiction
Carey, J. L. Dragon's Keep **Fic**
Lackey, M. Joust **Fic**
McCaffrey, A. Dragonflight **Fic**
Paolini, C. Eragon **Fic**
Weis, M. Mistress of dragons **Fic**

Dragons in Manhattan. Block, F. L.
In Block, F. L. Girl goddess #9: nine stories **S C**

Dragon's Keep. Carey, J. L. **Fic**

The **dragons** of Eden. Sagan, C. **153**

The **dragon's** teeth. Hawthorne, N.
In Hawthorne, N. Tales and sketches, including Twice-told tales, Mosses from an old manse, and The snow-image; A wonder book for girls and boys; Tanglewood tales for girls and boys, being a second Wonder book p1356-81 **S C**

Dragonwagon, Crescent
Passionate vegetarian **641.5**

Drake, David, 1945-
The elf house: an Isles story
In Masters of fantasy **S C**

Drama
See also American drama; Comedy; English drama; Motion picture plays; One act plays; Tragedy
See/See also pages in the following book(s):
Highet, G. The classical tradition **809**

Bio-bibliography
Partnow, E. The female dramatist **809.2**
Collections
24 favorite one-act plays **808.82**
The Actor's book of scenes from new plays **808.82**
Cassady, M. The book of scenes for aspiring actors **808.82**
International plays for young audiences **808.82**
Latrobe, K. H. Readers theatre for young adults **808.5**
Multicultural scenes for young actors **808.82**
The Scenebook for actors **808.82**
Scenes from classic plays, 468 B.C. to 1970 A.D. **808.82**
Stevens, C. Sensational scenes for teens **808.82**
Dictionaries
Critical survey of drama **809.2**
Griffiths, T. R. The Ivan R. Dee guide to plays and playwrights **809.2**
Patterson, M. The Oxford dictionary of plays **809.2**
History and criticism
Bloom, H. Dramatists and dramas **809.2**
Brockett, O. G. History of the theatre **792.09**
Sova, D. B. Banned plays **792.09**
Indexes
Play index **808.82**
Technique
Straczynski, J. M. The complete book of scriptwriting **808.2**
Women authors
Partnow, E. The female dramatist **809.2**

Drama in education
Latrobe, K. H. Readers theatre for young adults **808.5**

Dramatists
Fugard, A. Cousins **92**
Hansberry, L. To be young, gifted, and Black **92**

Dramatists and dramas. Bloom, H. **809.2**

Draper, Sharon M., 1950-
The Battle of Jericho **Fic**
Copper sun **Fic**
Tears of a tiger **Fic**

Draper, Theodore, 1912-2006
A struggle for power **973.3**

Draw 3-D. DuBosque, D. **742**

Draw your own Manga. Nagatomo, H. **741.5**

Drawing
See also Artistic anatomy; Colored pencil drawing; Figure drawing
Chiarello, M. The DC Comics guide to coloring and lettering comics **741.5**
Complete guide to drawing & painting **741.2**
DuBosque, D. Draw 3-D **742**
Graves, D. R. Drawing portraits **743**
Hart, C. How to draw animation **741.5**
Miller, S. Scared!: how to draw fantastic horror comic characters **741.5**
Nagatomo, H. Draw your own Manga **741.5**

Droughts

Allaby, M. Droughts **551.57**

Drowne's wooden image. Hawthorne, N.

In Hawthorne, N. Tales and sketches, including Twice-told tales, Mosses from an old manse, and The snow-image; A wonder book for girls and boys; Tanglewood tales for girls and boys, being a second Wonder book p932-44 **S C**

Drowning. Bush, M. B.

In Growing up ethnic in America; contemporary fiction about learning to be American **S C**

Drowning kittens. Dame, E.

In Growing up ethnic in America; contemporary fiction about learning to be American **S C**

Drucker, Malka, 1945-

The widest heart

In Not the only one; lesbian and gay fiction for teens **S C**

Drucker, Olga Levy, 1927-

Kindertransport **940.53**

Druckman, Nancy

American flags **929.9**

Drug abuse

See also Hallucinogens; Solvent abuse

Addiction: opposing viewpoints **362.29**

Club drugs **362.29**

Drug abuse: opposing viewpoints **362.29**

Drugs and controlled substances **362.29**

Hyde, M. O. Drugs 101 **362.29**

LeVert, S. The facts about cocaine **362.29**

LeVert, S. The facts about LSD and other hallucinogens **362.29**

The war on drugs: opposing viewpoints **363.4**

See/See also pages in the following book(s):

Jukes, M. It's a girl thing **305.23**

Fiction

Banks, R. Rule of the bone **Fic**

Brooks, K. Candy **Fic**

Burgess, M. Smack **Fic**

Coy, J. Crackback **Fic**

Going, K. L. Saint Iggy **Fic**

Lipsyte, R. Raiders night **Fic**

Stemple, A. Singer of souls **Fic**

Testing

See Drug testing

Drug abuse counseling

See also Drug addicts—Rehabilitation

Drug abuse: opposing viewpoints **362.29**

Drug addicts

Rehabilitation

Frey, J. A million little pieces **92**

Drug plants *See* Medical botany

Drug testing

Kowalski, K. M. The Earls case and the student drug testing debate **344**

Drug therapy

See also Pharmacology

Drug trade, Illicit *See* Drug traffic

Drug traffic

See/See also pages in the following book(s):

The war on drugs: opposing viewpoints **363.4**

Drugs

See also Designer drugs; Hallucinogens; Materia medica; Pharmacology; Steroids

Drugs and controlled substances **362.29**

Facklam, M. Modern medicines **615**

Guilfoile, P. Antibiotic-resistant bacteria **616.9**

Hyde, M. O. Drugs 101 **362.29**

Kowalski, K. M. Attack of the superbugs **616.9**

The Merck index **615**

Adulteration and analysis

See Pharmacology

Law and legislation

Ruschmann, P. Legalizing marijuana **345**

See/See also pages in the following book(s):

The war on drugs: opposing viewpoints **363.4**

Drugs, Designer *See* Designer drugs

Drugs [series]

Gottfried, T. The facts about alcohol **362.292**

Gottfried, T. The facts about marijuana **362.29**

LeVert, S. The facts about cocaine **362.29**

LeVert, S. The facts about ecstasy **362.29**

LeVert, S. The facts about LSD and other hallucinogens **362.29**

LeVert, S. The facts about steroids **362.29**

Menhard, F. R. The facts about inhalants **362.29**

Drugs 101. Hyde, M. O. **362.29**

Drugs, alcohol, and tobacco **362.29**

Drugs and controlled substances **362.29**

Drugs and crime

See also Drug traffic

Drugs and sports *See* Athletes—Drug use

Drugs and sports **362.29**

Drugs: the straight facts [series]

Mehling, R. Hallucinogens **615**

Druids and Druidism

Green, M. J. The world of the Druids **299**

Drum Kiss. Power, S.

In Moccasin thunder; American Indians stories for today **S C**

The **drummer** boy of Shiloh. Bradbury, R.

In Bradbury, R. Bradbury stories; 100 of his most celebrated tales **S C**

Drunk driving

Alcohol **362.292**

Drunk driving **363.1**

Drunk driving **363.1**

Drury, John, 1950-

The poetry dictionary **808.1**

A **dry,** quiet war. Daniel, T.

In Best of the best: 20 years of the Year's best science fiction **S C**

Economic entomology *See* Insect pests

Economic policy
> *See also* Sanctions (International law)

Economic sanctions *See* Sanctions (International law)

Economic zoology
> *See also* Insect pests

Economics
> *See also* Consumption (Economics)
> Heilbroner, R. L. The worldly philosophers
> **330.1**

The **Economist** desk companion **530.8**

Economists
> Bussing-Burks, M. Influential economists
> **920**
> Heilbroner, R. L. The worldly philosophers
> **330.1**

Ecstasy (Drug)
> Club drugs **362.29**
> LeVert, S. The facts about ecstasy **362.29**

Eddings, David
> Belgarath the sorcerer **Fic**

Eddings, Leigh, d. 2007
> (jt. auth) Eddings, D. Belgarath the sorcerer
> **Fic**

Edelman, Bernard
> (ed) Dear America: letters home from Vietnam. See Dear America: letters home from Vietnam **959.704**

Edelman, Rob
> (ed) Freedom of the press. See Freedom of the press **342**

Edelson, Edward, 1932-
> Francis Crick and James Watson and the building blocks of life **92**

Edey, Maitland Armstrong, 1910-1992
> (jt. auth) Johanson, D. C. Lucy: the beginnings of humankind **599.93**

Edgar, Blake
> (jt. auth) Johanson, D. C. From Lucy to language **599.93**

Edgar Allan Poe. Meltzer, M. **92**

Edgar Allan Poe, A-Z. Sova, D. B. **818**

Edgar Allan Poe's tales of mystery and madness. Poe, E. A. **S C**

The **edge** of the sea. Carson, R. **577.7**

The **edge** on the sword. Tingle, R. **Fic**

Edgeworth, Maria, 1767-1849
> The Limerick gloves
> *In* The Oxford book of Irish short stories p27-51 **S C**

Edghill, India
> Devil wind
> *In* Young warriors; stories of strength **S C**

Edghill, Rosemary
> An axe for men
> *In* Young warriors; stories of strength **S C**

Edible plants
> *See/See also pages in the following book(s):*
> The Cambridge world history of food **641.3**

Edison, Thomas A. (Thomas Alva), 1847-1931
> **About**
> Essig, M. R. Edison & the electric chair
> **364.66**
> Jonnes, J. Empires of light **621.3**
> Tagliaferro, L. Thomas Edison **92**

Edison & the electric chair. Essig, M. R.
> **364.66**

Edlow, Jonathan A., 1952-
> Bull's-eye: unraveling the medical mystery of Lyme disease **616.9**

Edmonds, Randolph, 1900-1983
> Old man Pete
> *In* Black theatre USA; plays by African Americans, 1847 to today **812.008**

Edmonds, Sheppard Randolph *See* Edmonds, Randolph, 1900-1983

Edmonston, Louis-Philippe
> Car smarts **629.222**

Edney, A. T. B.
> ASPCA complete cat care manual **636.8**

Edney, Andrew *See* Edney, A. T. B.

An **educated** American woman. Cheever, J.
> *In* Cheever, J. The stories of John Cheever p521-35 **S C**

Education
> *See also* Colleges and universities; Internet in education; Military education; Teaching
> Reeves, D. L. Career ideas for teens in education and training **331.7**
> *See/See also pages in the following book(s):*
> The information revolution **303.4**
> **Curricula**
> *See also* Colleges and universities—Curricula
> Managing curriculum and assessment **375**
> *See/See also pages in the following book(s):*
> Goleman, D. Emotional intelligence **152.4**
> **Government policy**
> Hester, J. P. Public school safety **371.7**
> **Rome**
> *See/See also pages in the following book(s):*
> Davis, W. S. A day in old Rome **937**
> **United States**—Encyclopedias
> Unger, H. G. Encyclopedia of American education **370**

Education, Bilingual *See* Bilingual education

Education, Discrimination in *See* Discrimination in education

Education, Higher *See* Higher education

Education, Intercultural *See* Multicultural education

Education, Segregation in *See* Segregation in education

Education and church *See* Church and education

Education and state *See* Education—Government policy

Education: opposing viewpoints **371**

Educational achievement *See* Academic achievement

Educational counseling
> *See also* Vocational guidance

Elsewhere. Zevin, G.   **Fic**

Elster, Jean Alicia, 1953-
(ed) The Death penalty. See The Death penalty
[History of issues series]   **364.66**

Elul. Sholem Aleichem
In Halkin, H. and Sholem Aleichem. Tevye
the dairyman and The railroad stories   **S C**

Elvenbrood. Lee, T.
In The Faery Reel; tales from the Twilight
Realm   **S C**

Elvis. Carter, A. R.
In Carter, A. R. Love, football, and other contact sports   **S C**

Emadi, Hafizullah
Culture and customs of Afghanistan   **958.1**

Emancipation: a life fable. Chopin, K.
In Chopin, K. The awakening and selected
stories   **S C**

Emancipation Proclamation (1863)
See/See also pages in the following book(s):
McPherson, J. M. Drawn with the sword
973.7

Emanuel, Kerry A., 1955-
Divine wind   **551.55**

Emblems *See* Signs and symbols

Embryology
See also Fetus
Nilsson, L. A child is born   **612.6**

Emecheta, Buchi
The bride price   **Fic**

Emergency. Johnson, D.
In Adaptations: from short story to big
screen; 35 great stories that have inspired
great films   **S C**

Emergency relief *See* Disaster relief

Emergency survival *See* Survival skills

Emerging legacy. Durgin, D.
In Young warriors; stories of strength   **S C**

Emerson, Ralph Waldo, 1803-1882
Collected poems & translations   **811**
English traits
In Emerson, R. W. The portable Emerson
p395-518   **818**
Essays: first and second series
In Emerson, R. W. The portable Emerson
p111-290   **818**
Nature
In Emerson, R. W. The portable Emerson p7-
50   **818**
The portable Emerson   **818**

Emigrants *See* Immigrants

Emigration *See* Immigration and emigration

Emily Post's Etiquette. Post, P.   **395**

Emily Post's teen etiquette. Post, E. L.   **395**

Eminent lives [series]
Armstrong, K. Muhammad   **92**
Gottlieb, R. A. George Balanchine: the ballet
maker   **92**
Johnson, P. George Washington: the Founding
Father   **92**
Morris, E. Beethoven: the universal composer
92

Ridley, M. Francis Crick   **92**

Emmeluth, Donald
Botulism   **614.5**
Influenza   **616.2**

Emotional bankruptcy. Fitzgerald, F. S.
In Fitzgerald, F. S. The short stories of F.
Scott Fitzgerald; a new collection p546-
60   **S C**

Emotional intelligence. Goleman, D.   **152.4**

Emotional stress *See* Stress (Psychology)

Emotionally disturbed children
See/See also pages in the following book(s):
Goleman, D. Emotional intelligence   **152.4**

Emotions
See also Anxiety
Canfield, J. Chicken soup for the teenage soul
[I-III]   **158**
Chicken soup for the teenage soul's the real
deal   **158**
Goleman, D. Emotional intelligence   **152.4**
Goleman, D. Social intelligence   **158**

The **empire**. Hesse, H.
In Hesse, H. and Zipes, J. D. The fairy tales
of Hermann Hesse   **S C**

Empire. Laxer, J.   **327.73**

Empire in the east: the story of Genghis Khan.
Rice, E.   **92**

Empire of Alexander the Great. Skelton, D.
930

Empire of ancient Greece. Williams, J. K.
938

Empire of the Inca. Somervill, B. A.   **985**

Empire of the Mongols. Burgan, M.   **951**

Empire of the Sun. Ballard, J. G.   **Fic**

Empire State Building (New York, N.Y.)
Macaulay, D. Unbuilding   **690**

Empires of light. Jonnes, J.   **621.3**

Empires of medieval West Africa. Conrad, D. C.
966

Empires of time. Aveni, A. F.   **529**

Employees
See also Personnel management
Training
See also Apprentices

Employer-employee relations *See* Industrial relations

Employment applications *See* Applications for
positions

Employment guidance *See* Vocational guidance

Employment management *See* Personnel management

Employment of women *See* Women—Employment

The **empty** ocean. Ellis, R.   **577.7**

Emshwiller, Carol
Al
In Feeling very strange; the Slipstream anthol-
ogy   **S C**
Overlooking
In The Green Man: tales from the mythic for-
est p223-36   **808.8**

Emshwiller, Carol—*Continued*
Quill
In Firebirds rising; an anthology of original
science fiction and fantasy **S C**
The start of the end of the world
In The Norton book of science fiction; North
American science fiction, 1960-1990
p466-76 **S C**

Encephalitis
Bloom, O. Encephalitis **616.8**

The **Enchanted** prince
In Hearne, B. G. Beauties and beasts p109-14
398.2

The **enchanted** profile. Henry, O.
In Henry, O. The best short stories of O.
Henry **S C**

The **Enchanted** Tsarevitch
In Hearne, B. G. Beauties and beasts p14-17
398.2

Enchantress from the stars. Engdahl, S. L.
Fic

Encinosa, Michel *See* Encinosa Fú, Michel

Encinosa Fú, Michel
Like the roses had to die
In Cosmos latinos; an anthology of science
fiction from Latin America and Spain
S C

An **encounter**. Joyce, J.
In Joyce, J. Dubliners **S C**

Encounter in the dawn. Clarke, A. C.
In Clarke, A. C. The collected stories of Arthur C. Clarke **S C**

Encountering enchantment. Fichtelberg, S.
016.8

Encyclopaedia Britannica almanac, 2006
031.02

The **Encyclopedia** Americana **031**

Encyclopedia Latina **305.8**

The **encyclopedia** of addictive drugs. Miller, R. L.
615

Encyclopedia of African-American culture and
history **305.8**

Encyclopedia of African American history, 1619-
1895 **305.8**

Encyclopedia of African American society
305.8

Encyclopedia of African history **960**

Encyclopedia of African history and culture
960

Encyclopedia of air. Newton, D. E. **551**

Encyclopedia of American cultural and intellectual
history **973.03**

Encyclopedia of American education. Unger, H.
G. **370**

Encyclopedia of American foreign policy. Hastedt,
G. P. **327.73**

Encyclopedia of American historical documents
973.03

Encyclopedia of American history **973.03**

Encyclopedia of American Indian civil rights
970.004

Encyclopedia of American Indian costume.
Paterek, J. **391**

Encyclopedia of American law **349**

Encyclopedia of American literature **810.3**

Encyclopedia of American literature. See The Oxford encyclopedia of American literature
810.3

Encyclopedia of American military history
355

Encyclopedia of American poetry, the twentieth
century **811.009**

The **Encyclopedia** of American political history
973.03

Encyclopedia of American religion and politics.
Djupe, P. A. **322**

The **encyclopedia** of American religious history.
Queen, E. L. **200.9**

Encyclopedia of American social movements
303.4

Encyclopedia of American studies **973.03**

The **encyclopedia** of American television, broadcast programming Post World War II to 2000.
Lackmann, R. W. **791.45**

Encyclopedia of American war literature **810.9**

Encyclopedia of ancient Asian civilizations.
Higham, C. **950**

Encyclopedia of ancient Egypt. Bunson, M. R.
932

The **encyclopedia** of angels. Guiley, R. E. **200**

Encyclopedia of animal behavior **591.5**

The **encyclopedia** of animals **590.3**

The **encyclopedia** of animated cartoon series. See
Lenburg, J. The encyclopedia of animated
cartoons **791.43**

The **encyclopedia** of animated cartoons. Lenburg,
J. **791.43**

Encyclopedia of aquarium & pond fish. Alderton,
D. **639.34**

The **encyclopedia** of aquatic life. See The new encyclopedia of aquatic life **591.9**

The **encyclopedia** of autism spectrum disorders.
Turkington, C. **616.85**

Encyclopedia of battles in North America, 1517 to
1916. Purcell, L. E. **970**

Encyclopedia of biology. Rittner, D. **570.3**

The **encyclopedia** of birds. See Firefly encyclopedia of birds **598**

Encyclopedia of British writers, 16th-18th centuries **820.9**

Encyclopedia of card tricks. Hugard, J. **795.4**

Encyclopedia of careers and vocational guidance
331.7

Encyclopedia of Catholicism. Flinn, F. K. **282**

The **encyclopedia** of censorship. Green, J.
363.31

Encyclopedia of chemistry. Rittner, D. **540.3**

Encyclopedia of women [series]
  Yount, L. A to Z of women in science and math
  920.003

Encyclopedia of women and baseball **796.357**

Encyclopedia of women and sport in America
  796.03

Encyclopedia of women and world religion
  200

Encyclopedia of women in American history
  305.4

Encyclopedia of women in the Middle Ages.
  Lawler, J. **305.4**

Encyclopedia of women's autobiography
  920.003

Encyclopedia of women's history in America.
  Cullen-DuPont, K. **305.4**

Encyclopedia of women's travel and exploration.
  Netzley, P. D. **910.4**

The **Encyclopedia** of wood **674**

Encyclopedia of world biography **920.003**

Encyclopedia of world history **903**

Encyclopedia of world poverty **362.5**

The **encyclopedia** of world religions **200.3**

Encyclopedia of world religions [series]
  Flinn, F. K. Encyclopedia of Catholicism
  282

Encyclopedia of world scientists. Oakes, E. H.
  920.003

Encyclopedia of world terrorism **303.6**

Encyclopedia of world writers **920.003**

Encyclopedia of world writers: 19th and 20th centuries. See Encyclopedia of world writers
  920.003

Encyclopedia of youth and war. Sherrow, V.
  305.23

Encyclopedias and dictionaries
  See also Picture dictionaries; Polyglot dictionaries names of languages with the subdivision *Dictionaries* and subjects with the subdivision *Dictionaries* or *Encyclopedias*
  Brahms, W. B. Notable last facts **031.02**
  The Encyclopedia Americana **031**
  Famous first facts, international edition
  031.02
  Kane, J. N. Famous first facts **031.02**
  Merriam-Webster's collegiate encyclopedia
  031
  The New Encyclopaedia Britannica **031**
  The New York Public Library desk reference
  031.02
  The New York times guide to essential knowledge **031.02**
  Webster's new explorer desk encyclopedia
  031
  The World Book encyclopedia **031**

The **End** of ancient Rome **937**

The **end** of apartheid. Bradley, C. **968.06**

The **end** of something. Hemingway, E.
  In Hemingway, E. The complete short stories of Ernest Hemingway; the Finca Vigía edition p79-82 **S C**

The **end** of the dinosaurs. Frankel, C. **551.3**

The **end** of the flight. Maugham, W. S.
  In Maugham, W. S. Collected short stories
  S C

Endangered oceans: opposing viewpoints
  333.95

Endangered species
  See also Wildlife conservation
  Ellis, R. The empty ocean **577.7**
  Endangered species: opposing viewpoints
  578.68
  Hoose, P. M. The race to save the Lord God Bird **598**
  Matthiessen, P. The birds of heaven **598**
  O'Brien, S. J. Tears of the cheetah **591.3**
  Smith, D. W. Decade of the wolf **599.77**
    Fiction
  Halam, A. Siberia **Fic**

Endangered species: opposing viewpoints
  578.68

Enders, Eric
  100 years of the World Series **796.357**

Ender's game. Card, O. S. **Fic**

Endicott and the Red Cross. Hawthorne, N.
  In Hawthorne, N. Tales and sketches, including Twice-told tales, Mosses from an old manse, and The snow-image; A wonder book for girls and boys; Tanglewood tales for girls and boys, being a second Wonder book p542-48 **S C**

Endings. Nix, G.
  In Gothic!; ten original dark tales **S C**
  In The Year's best science fiction and fantasy for teens: first annual collection **S C**

Endocrine glands
  Watson, S. The endocrine system **612.4**

The **endocrine** system. Watson, S. **612.4**

Endowments
    Directories
  The big book of library grant money, 2006
  025.1

Endurance, Physical *See* Physical fitness

Endurance (Ship)
  Alexander, C. The Endurance **998**

The **enduring** chill. O'Connor, F.
  In O'Connor, F. Collected works p547-72
  S C
  In O'Connor, F. The complete stories p357-82
  S C

Enedina's story. Hernández-Avila, I.
  In Latina: women's voices from the borderlands p229-39 **810.8**

Enelow, Wendy S.
  Best resumes for people without a four-year degree **650.14**

Enemies. O'Brien, T.
  In O'Brien, T. The things they carried; a work of fiction **S C**

An **enemy** of the people. Ibsen, H.
  In Ibsen, H. and Johnston, B. Ibsen: four major plays **839.8**

Energy *See* Force and energy

Energy alternatives: opposing viewpoints
  333.79

Everything that rises must converge [story] O'Connor, F.
In O'Connor, F. The complete stories p405-20 **S C**

Everything we had **959.704**

Everything you need to know about food additives. Hayhurst, C. **664**

Everything you need to know about organic foods. Dunn-Georgiou, E. **641.3**

Everything's eventual. King, S.
In King, S. Everything's eventual: 14 dark tales **S C**

Everything's eventual: 14 dark tales. King, S. **S C**

Evidence. Asimov, I.
In Asimov, I. The complete stories p65-84 **S C**
In Asimov, I. I, robot **S C**

Evil *See* Good and evil

Evil genius. Jinks, C. **Fic**

Evil masters. Scandiffio, L. **920**

The **evitable** conflict. Asimov, I.
In Asimov, I. I, robot **S C**

Evolution
Arthur, W. Creatures of accident **591.3**
Carroll, S. B. The making of the fittest **572.8**
Creationism versus evolution **576.8**
Darwin, C. The Darwin reader **576.8**
Darwin, C. The portable Darwin **576.8**
Dixon, D. The future is wild **576.8**
Evolution [Exploring science and medical discoveries series] **576.8**
Evolution [Don Nardo, ed.] **576.8**
Gibbons, A. The first human **599.93**
Gould, S. J. I have landed **578**
Gould, S. J. The richness of life **508**
Jolly, A. Lucy's legacy **599.93**
Jones, S. Darwin's ghost **576.8**
Larson, E. J. Evolution: the remarkable history of a scientific theory **576.8**
Leakey, R. E. The sixth extinction **304.2**
Parker, A. In the blink of an eye **576.8**
Pennock, R. T. Tower of Babel **576.8**
Scott, E. C. Evolution vs. creationism **576.8**
Sloan, C. The human story **599.93**
Tattersall, I. Extinct humans **599.93**
Tudge, C. The time before history **599.93**
Wade, N. Before the dawn **599.93**
Wells, S. The journey of man **599.93**
Whitfield, P. J. Evolution **576.8**
Young, C. C. Evolution and creationism **576.8**
Zimmer, C. Evolution **576.8**
Dictionaries
Mai, L. L. The Cambridge Dictionary of human biology and evolution **612**
Encyclopedias
Encyclopedia of evolution **576.8**
Rice, S. A. Encyclopedia of evolution **576.8**
Study and teaching
Hanson, F. O. The Scopes monkey trial **345**
Larson, E. J. The Scopes trial **345**
Larson, E. J. Summer for the gods **345**

Evolution [Don Nardo, ed.] **576.8**

Evolution [Exploring science and medical discoveries series] **576.8**

Evolution and creationism. Young, C. C. **576.8**

Evolution: the remarkable history of a scientific theory. Larson, E. J. **576.8**

Evolution vs. creationism. Scott, E. C. **576.8**

Ewen, David, 1907-1985
(ed) Musicians since 1900. See Musicians since 1900 **920.003**

Ex, Kris
(jt. auth) Scott, D. How to draw hip-hop **741.2**

Ex-service men *See* Veterans

The **examination.** Bosse, M. J. **Fic**

Examinations
See/See also pages in the following book(s):
Espeland, P. The gifted kids' survival guide p47-64 **155.5**

Examining issues through political cartoons [series]
Civil liberties and war **323**

Excavations (Archeology)
Kurson, R. Shadow divers **940.54**

Excel (Computer program)
Greiner, T. Analyzing library collection use with Excel **025.2**

Excellence in library services to young adults **027.62**

Exceptional children
See also Brain damaged children

Exchange rate. Clement, H.
In The Hard SF renaissance **S C**

Executions *See* Capital punishment

Executive ability
See also Leadership

Executive departments
United States
See also Presidents—United States—Staff

Exercise
See also Physical fitness; Tai chi; Weight lifting

Exercises, Reducing *See* Weight loss

Exerion. Castro, P.
In Cosmos latinos; an anthology of science fiction from Latin America and Spain **S C**

Exhibit H: torn pages discovered in the vest pocket of an unidentified tourist. VanderMeer, J.
In Feeling very strange; the Slipstream anthology **S C**

Exhibitions
See also Fairs
Rydell, R. W. Fair America **394**

Exile to Hell. Asimov, I.
In Asimov, I. The complete stories p377-80 **S C**

Exiles *See* Refugees

The **exiles**. Bradbury, R.
In Bradbury, R. Bradbury stories; 100 of his
most celebrated tales **S C**
In Bradbury, R. The illustrated man **S C**

Exodus, Book of *See* Bible. O.T. Exodus

Exodus. Uris, L. **Fic**

An **exorcism**. Malamud, B.
In Malamud, B. The complete stories **S C**

Expanding universe *See* Universe

Experience of the McWilliamses with membranous croup. Twain, M.
In Twain, M. The complete short stories of
Mark Twain; now collected for the first
time **S C**

Experimentation on animals *See* Animal experimentation

The **experts'** guide to 100 things everyone should
know how to do **640**

Exploding the myths. Aronson, M. **028.5**

Exploration
Boorstin, D. J. The discoverers **909**
De Porti, A. Explorers **910**
Farrington, K. Historical atlas of expeditions
911
Fleming, F. Off the map **910**
Paine, L. P. Ships of discovery and exploration
910.4
Vail, M. Exploring the Pacific **919**
Waldman, C. Encyclopedia of exploration
910.3
White, P. Exploration in the world of the Middle Ages, 500-1500 **910.4**

Exploration in the world of the Middle Ages,
500-1500. White, P. **910.4**

Exploration of Africa, the emerging nations [series]
Harmon, D. Nigeria **966.9**

Explorers
Aronson, M. Sir Walter Ralegh and the quest
for El Dorado **92**
Cox, C. Opening up North America, 1497-1800
917
De Porti, A. Explorers **910**
Farrington, K. Historical atlas of expeditions
911
Fleming, F. Off the map **910**
Goetzmann, W. H. The atlas of North American
exploration **911**
Isserman, M. Exploring North America, 1800-
1900 **917**
Obregón, M. Beyond the edge of the sea
930
Smith, T. Discovery of the Americas, 1492-1800
909
Vail, M. Exploring the Pacific **919**
Waldman, C. Encyclopedia of exploration
910.3

Explorers house. Poole, R. M. **910**

Exploring ecosystems [series]
Martin, P. A. F. Woods and forests **577.3**

Exploring North America, 1800-1900. Isserman,
M. **917**

Exploring science and medical discoveries [series]
Cloning **176**
Evolution **576.8**
Gene therapy **615.8**

Exploring social issues through literature [series]
Johnson, C. D. Labor and workplace issues in
literature **810.9**
Stripling, M. Y. Bioethics and medical issues in
literature **809**
Wilson, C. E. Race and racism in literature
810.9

Exploring tech careers **331.7**
Exploring the Pacific. Vail, M. **919**
Exploring the world of the Druids. See Green, M.
J. The world of the Druids **299**

Exposing a city slicker. Kafka, F.
In Kafka, F. The metamorphosis and other
stories p26-28 **S C**

Expositions *See* Exhibitions

Exposures. Benford, G.
In The Norton book of science fiction; North
American science fiction, 1960-1990
p445-56 **S C**

Extenuating circumstances. Oates, J. C.
In The Oxford book of women's writing in
the United States p148-53 **810.8**

Extermination of pests *See* Pest control

Extinct animals
See also Mass extinction of species
Marven, N. Chased by sea monsters **560**

Extinct humans. Tattersall, I. **599.93**

Extinction of species, Mass *See* Mass extinction
of species

Extract from Captain Stormfield's visit to heaven.
Twain, M.
In Twain, M. The complete short stories of
Mark Twain; now collected for the first
time **S C**

Extraordinary essays. Orr, T. **808.4**
Extraordinary oral presentations. Ryan, M.
808.5
Extraordinary people in extraordinary times.
Mendoza, P. M. **920**
Extraordinary women of the Medieval and Renaissance world **920.003**

Extrasensory perception
Fiction
Berry, L. The China garden **Fic**
King, S. Carrie **Fic**
Le Guin, U. K. The left hand of darkness
Fic
Sedgwick, M. The foreshadowing **Fic**

Extraterrestrial bases
See also Space colonies

Extraterrestrial life **576.8**

Extreme sports [series]
Masoff, J. Snowboard! **796.93**
Extreme teens. Anderson, S. B. **027.62**
Extreme weather. Burt, C. C. **551.5**

Facts on File science library—*Continued*
Bell, S. The Facts on File dictionary of forensic science **363.2**
Erickson, J. An introduction to fossils and minerals **560**
Erickson, J. Plate tectonics: unraveling the mysteries of the earth **551.1**
Erickson, J. Rock formations and unusual geologic structures **550**
The Facts on File biology handbook **570**
The Facts on File chemistry handbook **540**
The Facts on File dictionary of astronomy **520.3**
The Facts on File dictionary of biology **570.3**
The Facts on File dictionary of chemistry **540.3**
The Facts on File dictionary of computer science **004**
The Facts on File dictionary of mathematics **510.3**
The Facts on File dictionary of physics **530**
The Facts on File dictionary of weather and climate **551.5**
The Facts on File Earth science handbook **550**
The Facts on File physics handbook **530**
Gates, A. E. Encyclopedia of earthquakes and volcanoes **551.2**
Gorini, C. A. The Facts on File geometry handbook **516**
Kusky, T. M. Encyclopedia of earth science **550.3**
Oakes, E. H. Encyclopedia of world scientists **920.003**
Rice, S. A. Encyclopedia of evolution **576.8**
Rittner, D. Encyclopedia of chemistry **540.3**
Tanton, J. S. Encyclopedia of mathematics **510.3**
Wyman, B. C. The Facts on File dictionary of environmental science **363.7**

Facts on File writer's library [series]
The Facts on File dictionary of classical and biblical allusions **809**

Fadiman, Clifton, 1904-1999
The new lifetime reading plan **028**
(ed) World poetry. See World poetry **808.81**

The **faery** handbag. Link, K.
In The Faery Reel; tales from the Twilight Realm **S C**
In The Year's best science fiction and fantasy for teens: first annual collection **S C**

The **Faery** Reel **S C**

Fagan, Brian M., 1936-
The Little Ice Age **551.6**
The long summer: how climate changed civilization **551.6**
(ed) The Oxford companion to archaeology. See The Oxford companion to archaeology **930.1**
(ed) The Seventy great inventions of the ancient world. See The Seventy great inventions of the ancient world **609**

Fagan, Deirdre
Critical companion to Robert Frost **811.009**

Fagan, Eleanora *See* Holiday, Billie, 1915-1959

Fagles, Robert
(tr) Homer. The Iliad **883**
(tr) Homer. The Odyssey **883**
(tr) Virgil. The Aeneid **873**

Fahey, Thomas D., 1947-
Basic weight training for men and women **613.7**

Fahrenheit 451. Bradbury, R. **Fic**

Failure is not an option. Kranz, E. F. **629.45**

Fair America. Rydell, R. W. **394**

The **fair** garden and the swarm of beasts. Edwards, M. A. **027.62**

Fair use (Copyright)
Butler, R. P. Copyright for teachers and librarians **346.04**
Simpson, C. M. Copyright catechism **346.04**
Simpson, C. M. Copyright for schools **346.04**

Fairbank, John King, 1907-1991
The great Chinese revolution: 1800-1985 **951**

Fairbanks, Stephanie S., 1950-
Spotlight **812**

Fairchild, B. H. (Bertram H.), 1942-
Early occult memory systems of the Lower Midwest **811**

Fairest. Levine, G. C. **Fic**

Fairies
Fiction
Black, H. Valiant: a modern faerie tale **Fic**
De Lint, C. The blue girl **Fic**
The Faery Reel **S C**
Stemple, A. Singer of souls **Fic**
Thompson, K. The new policeman **Fic**
Wooding, C. Poison **Fic**

Fairs
See also Exhibitions
Rydell, R. W. Fair America **394**

The **Fairy** serpent
In Hearne, B. G. Beauties and beasts p29-31 **398.2**

The **fairy** tale about the wicker chair. Hesse, H.
In Hesse, H. and Zipes, J. D. The fairy tales of Hermann Hesse **S C**

Fairy tales
See also Fantasy fiction
Best-loved folktales of the world **398.2**
Block, F. L. The rose and the beast **S C**
Favorite folktales from around the world **398.2**
Gruber, M. The witch's boy **Fic**
Hearne, B. G. Beauties and beasts **398.2**
Hesse, H. The fairy tales of Hermann Hesse **S C**
Levine, G. C. Fairest **Fic**
McKinley, R. Beauty **Fic**
Medley, L. Castle waiting **741.5**
Meeting the other crowd **398.2**
Napoli, D. J. Beast **Fic**
Napoli, D. J. The magic circle **Fic**
The **fairy** tales of Hermann Hesse. Hesse, H. **S C**

Faith
Gaskins, P. I believe in—   **200**
Faith & doubt   **808.81**
The **faithful** bull. Hemingway, E.
In Hemingway, E. The complete short stories
of Ernest Hemingway; the Finca Vigía
edition p485-86   **S C**
Faithful Ruslan [excerpt] Vladimov, G. N.
In The portable twentieth-century Russian
reader   **891.7**
The **faithless** wife. O'Faoláin, S.
In The Oxford book of Irish short stories
p319-37   **S C**
Faizabad harvest, 1980. Staples, S. F.
In Shattered: stories of children and war
p108-21   **S C**
Fake ID. Sorrells, W.   **Fic**
Fakes & forgeries. Innes, B.   **364.1**
Falcetti, Cara
(jt. auth) Blanchard, M. L. Poets for young
adults   **920.003**
The **falconer's** knot. Hoffman, M.   **Fic**
Falcons
Tennant, A. On the wing   **598**
Faldum. Hesse, H.
In Hesse, H. and Zipes, J. D. The fairy tales
of Hermann Hesse   **S C**
The **fall** of Edward Barnard. Maugham, W. S.
In Maugham, W. S. Collected short stories
                                         S C
The **fall** of Rome. Southgate, M.   **Fic**
The **fall** of the house of Escher. Bear, G.
In Bear, G. The collected stories of Greg
Bear   **S C**
The **fall** of the House of Usher. Poe, E. A.
In The Oxford book of gothic tales p85-101
                                         S C
In The Oxford book of short stories p43-60
                                         S C
In Poe, E. A. The collected tales and poems
of Edgar Allan Poe p231-45   **818**
In Poe, E. A. Edgar Allan Poe's tales of mys-
tery and madness   **S C**
Falla, P. S. (Paul Stephen), 1913-
(ed) Oxford Russian dictionary. See Oxford
Russian dictionary   **491.7**
Fallen angels. Myers, W. D.   **Fic**
Falling off the Empire State Building. Mazer, H.
In Ultimate sports; short stories by outstand-
ing writers for young adults p302-13
                                         S C
Fallis, Greg
Lord of obstacles
In Alfred Hitchcock's mystery magazine pres-
ents fifty years of crime and suspense
                                         S C
Fallon, Robert Thomas
A theatergoer's guide to Shakespeare   **822.3**
Falola, Toyin, 1953-
Key events in African history   **960**
False dawn. Wharton, E.
In Wharton, E. Novellas and other writings
                                         818

The **falsifier**. Adolph, J. B.
In Cosmos latinos; an anthology of science
fiction from Latin America and Spain
                                         S C
Fame and the poet. Wolfe, T.
In Wolfe, T. The complete short stories of
Thomas Wolfe p290-95   **S C**
Familiar flowers of North America: eastern re-
gion. Spellenberg, R.   **582.13**
Familiar flowers of North America: western re-
gion. Spellenberg, R.   **582.13**
Familiar trees of North America: eastern region
                                         582.16
Familiar trees of North America: western region
                                         582.16
Family
See also types of family members
United States
The Truth about family life   **306.8**
Family. Olsen, L.
In The Literary ghost; great contemporary
ghost stories p206-15   **S C**
Family farms
Pyle, G. Raising less corn, more hell   **338.1**
Family finance *See* Personal finance
Family happiness. Tolstoy, L., graf
In Tolstoy, L., graf. Great short works of Leo
Tolstoy p1-81   **S C**
Family histories *See* Genealogy
A **family** illness: a mom-son conversation. Thom-
as, J. C.
In Necessary noise: stories about our families
as they really are p97-128   **S C**
Family life
Kafka, F. The metamorphosis
In Kafka, F. The metamorphosis and other
stories p117-92   **Fic**
Fiction
Adichie, C. N. Purple hibiscus   **Fic**
Agee, J. A death in the family   **Fic**
Anderson, L. H. Twisted   **Fic**
Bates, J. F. Midnight at the Dragon Café
                                         Fic
Bauer, C. Harley, like a person   **Fic**
Budhos, M. T. Ask me no questions   **Fic**
Caletti, D. The nature of Jade   **Fic**
Clinton, C. A stone in my hand   **Fic**
Cook, K. L. The girl from Charnelle   **Fic**
Corrigan, E. Splintering   **Fic**
Desai, A. Clear light of day   **Fic**
Dessen, S. Just listen   **Fic**
Dorris, M. A yellow raft in blue water   **Fic**
Dowd, S. A swift pure cry   **Fic**
Flake, S. G. Bang!   **Fic**
Giles, G. What happened to Cass McBride?
                                         Fic
Glass, L. The year the gypsies came   **Fic**
Going, K. L. Saint Iggy   **Fic**
Goldberg, M. Bee season   **Fic**
Hartnett, S. Surrender   **Fic**
Hartnett, S. Thursday's child   **Fic**
Haruf, K. Plainsong   **Fic**
Hoffman, A. Blue diary   **Fic**
Hopkins, E. Burned   **Fic**

Family life—Fiction—*Continued*

Hosseini, K. A thousand splendid suns   **Fic**
Irving, J. The Hotel New Hampshire   **Fic**
Irving, J. The world according to Garp   **Fic**
Johnson, K. J. A fast and brutal wing   **Fic**
Jolin, P. In the name of God   **Fic**
Kerr, M. E. Your eyes in stars   **Fic**
Mackler, C. The earth, my butt, and other big, round things   **Fic**
Marino, P. Dough Boy   **Fic**
Martinez, V. Parrot in the oven   **Fic**
McNeal, L. Crushed   **Fic**
Min, K. Secondhand world   **Fic**
Mitchell, D. Black swan green   **Fic**
Na, A. A step from heaven   **Fic**
Necessary noise: stories about our families as they really are   **S C**
Pearson, M. A room on Lorelei Street   **Fic**
Rapp, A. Under the wolf, under the dog   **Fic**
Reinhardt, D. A brief chapter in my impossible life   **Fic**
Roy, A. The god of small things   **Fic**
Salinger, J. D. Franny & Zooey   **Fic**
Salinger, J. D. Raise high the roof beam, carpenters, and Seymour: an introduction   **Fic**
Saroyan, W. The human comedy   **Fic**
Sebold, A. The lovely bones   **Fic**
Selvadurai, S. Swimming in the monsoon sea   **Fic**
Sherrill, M. The Ruins of California   **Fic**
Sheth, K. Koyal dark, mango sweet   **Fic**
Smith, K. The geography of girlhood   **Fic**
Spiegler, L. The amethyst road   **Fic**
Stahler, D., Jr. Doppelganger   **Fic**
Steinhöfel, A. The center of the world   **Fic**
Tyler, A. Dinner at the Homesick Restaurant   **Fic**
Watson, L. Montana 1948   **Fic**
Weaver, W. Memory boy   **Fic**
Whitney, K. A. See you down the road   **Fic**
Williams-Garcia, R. Like sisters on the homefront   **Fic**
Wilson, D. L. Firehorse   **Fic**
Wyeth, S. D. Orphea Proud   **Fic**
Zarr, S. Story of a girl   **Fic**
See/See also pages in the following book(s):
Sleator, W. Oddballs   **S C**

Graphic novels

Lat. Kampung boy   **741.5**
Thompson, C. Blankets   **92**

Family planning *See* Birth control

Family reunion. Eliot, T. S.
In Eliot, T. S. The complete poems and plays, 1909-1950 p223-94   **818**

Family size

See also Birth control

Family violence *See* Domestic violence

Famines

Bartoletti, S. C. Black potatoes   **941.5**

Famous American crimes and trials   **364**

Famous first facts. Kane, J. N.   **031.02**

Famous first facts about American politics. Anzovin, S.   **973**

Famous first facts about sports. Franck, I. M.   **796**

Famous first facts, international edition   **031.02**

Famous lines. Andrews, R.   **808.88**

Famous people *See* Celebrities

Famous trials [series]
Aaseng, N. The impeachment of Bill Clinton   **973.929**

The **fanatic**. O'Flaherty, L.
In The Oxford book of Irish short stories p300-10   **S C**

Fancy dress *See* Costume

Fancy's show box. Hawthorne, N.
In Hawthorne, N. Tales and sketches, including Twice-told tales, Mosses from an old manse, and The snow-image; A wonder book for girls and boys; Tanglewood tales for girls and boys, being a second Wonder book p450-55   **S C**

Fanta, Christopher H.
The Harvard Medical School guide to taking control of asthma   **616.2**

Fantastic fiction *See* Fantasy fiction

Fantastic voyage. Asimov, I.   **Fic**

Fantasy and horror   **016.8**

Fantasy fiction

See also Fairy tales; Science fiction. A spell for chameleon   **Fic**
Almond, D. Skellig   **Fic**
Anthony, P. On a pale horse   **Fic**
Barker, C. Abarat   **Fic**
Beagle, P. S. The line between   **S C**
Berman, J. Bear daughter   **Fic**
Black, H. Valiant: a modern faerie tale   **Fic**
Bradbury, R. Something wicked this way comes   **Fic**
Bradley, M. Z. The mists of Avalon   **Fic**
Brooks, T. Armageddon's children   **Fic**
Brooks, T. The sword of Shannara   **Fic**
Bujold, L. M. The curse of Chalion   **Fic**
Card, O. S. Seventh son   **Fic**
Carey, J. L. Dragon's Keep   **Fic**
Clement-Davies, D. The sight   **Fic**
Constable, K. The singer of all songs   **Fic**
Cornish, D. M. Foundling   **Fic**
Dickinson, P. The ropemaker   **Fic**
Dreams and visions   **S C**
Eddings, D. Belgarath the sorcerer   **Fic**
Feeling very strange   **S C**
Fforde, J. The Eyre affair   **Fic**
Firebirds rising   **S C**
Gaiman, N. Anansi boys   **Fic**
Gaiman, N. Fragile things   **S C**
Gaiman, N. Stardust   **Fic**
Hemingway, A. The Greenstone grail   **Fic**
Jones, D. W. Cart and cwidder   **Fic**
Kinsella, W. P. Shoeless Joe   **Fic**
Knox, E. Dreamhunter   **Fic**
Kostick, C. Epic   **Fic**
Lackey, M. Joust   **Fic**
Lackey, M. The outstretched shadow   **Fic**
Lackey, M. The serpent's shadow   **Fic**
Le Guin, U. K. Gifts   **Fic**
Le Guin, U. K. Tales from Earthsea   **S C**
Legends: short novels by the masters of modern fantasy   **S C**

Faulkner, William, 1897-1962—*Continued*
Dry September
In The Oxford book of short stories p330-40
S C
An error in chemistry
In The Best American mystery stories of the
century p318-34 S C
Light in August Fic
The reivers Fic
A rose for Emily
In The Oxford book of gothic tales p322-30
S C
Selected short stories of William Faulkner
S C
Contents: Barn burning; Two soldiers; A rose for Emily; Dry
September; That evening sun; Red leaves; Lo!; Turnabout; Hon-
or; There was a queen; Mountain victory; Beyond; Race at morn-
ing
Tomorrow
In Adaptations: from short story to big
screen; 35 great stories that have inspired
great films S C
Wash
In The Norton book of American short stories
p342-52 S C
About
Fargnoli, A. N. William Faulkner A to Z
813.009

Faurie, Bernadette
The horse riding & care handbook 636.1

Faurot, Jeannette L.
(ed) Asian-Pacific folktales and legends. See
Asian-Pacific folktales and legends 398.2

Fauset, Jessie Redmon, 1882-1961
Plum bun [excerpt]
In The Portable Harlem Renaissance reader
p348-50 810.8
There is confusion [excerpt]
In The Portable Harlem Renaissance reader
p340-48 810.8

Faust, Drew Gilpin
Mothers of invention 973.7

Favorite folktales from around the world
398.2

Fawcett, Bill
(ed) Masters of fantasy. See Masters of fantasy
S C

Fayer, Steve, 1935-
(jt. auth) Hampton, H. Voices of freedom
323.1

FBI *See* United States. Federal Bureau of Investigation
FBI careers. Ackerman, T. H. 363.2

Feagin, Joe R.
White men on race 305.8

Fear
See also Anxiety; Phobias
Wynbrandt, J. The encyclopedia of genetic dis-
orders and birth defects 616
Fear. Davies, R.
In Read all about it!; great read-aloud stories,
poems, and newspaper pieces for
preteens and teens p223-29 808.8

Fear. Pronzini, B.
In A Century of great Western stories
S C
Fear. Trueman, T.
In Every man for himself; ten short stories
about being a guy S C
The **Feast** of the Goat. Vargas Llosa, M. Fic
Feather tigers. Wolfe, G.
In The Norton book of science fiction; North
American science fiction, 1960-1990
p280-86 S C
Feathertop. Hawthorne, N.
In Hawthorne, N. Tales and sketches, includ-
ing Twice-told tales, Mosses from an old
manse, and The snow-image; A wonder
book for girls and boys; Tanglewood
tales for girls and boys, being a second
Wonder book p1103-23 S C
February 1999: Ylla. Bradbury, R.
In Bradbury, R. Bradbury stories; 100 of his
most celebrated tales S C
Federal Bureau of Investigation (U.S.) *See* Unit-
ed States. Federal Bureau of Investigation
Federal courts *See* Courts—United States
Fee, fie, foe, et cetera. Maguire, G.
In The Green Man: tales from the mythic for-
est p238-59 808.8
Feed. Anderson, M. T. Fic
Feeders and eaters. Gaiman, N.
In Gaiman, N. Fragile things; short fictions
and wonders S C
The **feeling** of power. Asimov, I.
In Asimov, I. The complete stories p208-16
S C
Feeling very strange S C
Contents: Al, by C. Emshwiller; The little magic shop, by B.
Sterling; The healer, by A. Bender; The specialist's hat, by K.
Link; Light and the sufferer, by J. Lethem; Sea Oak, by G.
Saunders; Exhibit H: torn pages discovered in the vest pocket of
an unidentified tourist, by J. VanderMeer; Hell is the absence of
God, by T. Chiang; Lieserl, by K. J. Fowler; Bright morning, by
J. Ford; Biographical notes to "A discourse on the nature of cau-
sality, with airplane," by Benjamin Rosenbaum, by B.
Rosenbaum; The god of dark laughter, by M. Chabon; The rose
in twelve petals, by T. Goss; The lions are asleep this night, by
H. Waldrop; You have never been here, by M. Rickert
Feelings, Tom, 1933-2003
The middle passage 759.13
(il) Lester, J. To be a slave 326
Feig, Paul
Kick me 305.23
Feik, LuAnne
(jt. auth) Jay, A. Stars in your eyes—feet on the
ground 792
Feinberg, Barbara Silberdick, 1938-
The Articles of Confederation 342
Feingold, Russ
See/See also pages in the following book(s):
Profiles in courage for our time 920
Feinman, Jay M.
1001 legal words you need to know 340
Law 101 340
Feinsilber, Mike
(jt. auth) Webber, E. Merriam-Webster's dictio-
nary of allusions 803

The **field**. Hong, Y.
   In Chairman Mao would not be amused; fiction from today's China   **S C**

Field athletics *See* Track athletics

A **field** guide to freshwater fishes: North America north of Mexico. Page, L. M.   **597**

The **field** guide to geology. Lambert, D.   **551**

Field guide to grasshoppers, crickets, and katydids of the United States. Capinera, J. L.   **595.7**

A **field** guide to mushrooms, North America. McKnight, K. H.   **579.6**

A **field** guide to reptiles & amphibians. Conant, R.   **597.9**

A **field** guide to rocks and minerals. Pough, F. H.   **549**

A **field** guide to the birds. See Peterson, R. T. A field guide to the birds of eastern and central North America   **598**

A **field** guide to the birds of eastern and central North America. Peterson, R. T.   **598**

Field guide to the birds of North America. See National Geographic field guide to the birds of North America   **598**

Field guide to the sharks of the world. See Compagno, L. J. V. Sharks of the world   **597**

A **field** guide to venomous animals and poisonous plants. Foster, S.   **578.6**

A **field** guide to western birds. Peterson, R. T.   **598**

Field guide to wildflowers, eastern region. See Thieret, J. W. National Audubon Society field guide to North American wildflowers: eastern region   **582.13**

Field hockey
   Swissler, B. Winning field hockey for girls   **796.355**

Field notes from a catastrophe. Kolbert, E.   **363.7**

The **field** of mustard. Coppard, A. E.
   In The Oxford book of short stories p247-54   **S C**

Field trip. O'Brien, T.
   In O'Brien, T. The things they carried; a work of fiction   **S C**

Field trips
   Cooper, G. New virtual field trips   **025.5**

Fields of battle. Keegan, J.   **973**

Fies, Brian
   Mom's cancer   **616.99**

Fifteen going on . . . McCafferty, M.
   In Sixteen: stories about that sweet and bitter birthday   **S C**

Fifteen painted cards from a vampire tarot. Gaiman, N.
   In Gaiman, N. Fragile things; short fictions and wonders   **S C**

Fifteen short plays. See McNally, T. 15 short plays   **812**

Fifteenth century *See* World history—15th century

The **fifties**. Halberstam, D.   **973.92**

Fifty grand. Hemingway, E.
   In Hemingway, E. The complete short stories of Ernest Hemingway; the Finca Vigía edition p231-49   **S C**

Fifty signs of mental illness. Hicks, J. W.   **616.89**

The **fight** for peace. Gottfried, T.   **303.6**

The **fighter**. Greif, J.-J.   **Fic**

Fighter. Myers, W. D.
   In Myers, W. D. 145th Street; short stories   **S C**

Figs and fate. Marston, E.   **S C**

Figure drawing
   Hart, C. Drawing cutting edge anatomy   **741.5**
   Hart, C. Human anatomy made amazingly easy   **743**

Filipino Americans
   Fiction
   De la Cruz, M. Fresh off the boat   **Fic**

Filipovic, Zlata
   (ed) Stolen voices. See Stolen voices   **920**

Filloux, Catherine
   Photographs from S-21
   In Under 30; plays for a new generation   **812.008**

Film adaptations
   Adaptations: from short story to big screen   **S C**

Film: an international history of the medium. See Sklar, R. A world history of film   **791.43**

Film direction *See* Motion pictures—Production and direction

Film production *See* Motion pictures—Production and direction

Filmmakers. Koopmans, A.   **920**

Filmmaking *See* Motion pictures—Production and direction

Films *See* Motion pictures

The **final** days. Woodward, B.   **973.924**

Final harvest. Dickinson, E.   **811**

The **final** problem. Doyle, Sir A. C.
   In Doyle, Sir A. C. The complete Sherlock Holmes   **S C**

Final rites. Allyn, D.
   In Alfred Hitchcock's mystery magazine presents fifty years of crime and suspense   **S C**

Financial aid, Student *See* Student aid

Financial aid for the disabled and their families, 2006-2008. Schlachter, G. A.   **378.3**

Financial planning, Personal *See* Personal finance

Financiers *See* Capitalists and financiers

Financing Finnegan. Fitzgerald, F. S.
   In Fitzgerald, F. S. The short stories of F. Scott Fitzgerald; a new collection p739-46   **S C**

Finckenstein, Maria von *See* Von Finckenstein, Maria

Find me a dream. Vonnegut, K.
   In Vonnegut, K. Bagombo snuff box: uncollected short fiction p233-41   **S C**

The **finder**. Le Guin, U. K.
   In Le Guin, U. K. Tales from Earthsea
                        S C

Finding Lubchenko. Simmons, M.   **Fic**

Finding miracles. Alvarez, J.   **Fic**

Findling, John E.
   (ed) Events that changed America through the seventeenth century. See Events that changed America through the seventeenth century   **973.2**
   (ed) Events that changed Great Britain, from 1066 to 1714. See Events that changed Great Britain, from 1066 to 1714   **941**
   (ed) Events that changed Great Britain since 1689. See Events that changed Great Britain since 1689   **941**
   (ed) Events that changed the world in the eighteenth century. See Events that changed the world in the eighteenth century   **909.7**
   (ed) Events that changed the world in the nineteenth century. See Events that changed the world in the nineteenth century   **909.81**
   (ed) Events that changed the world in the seventeenth century. See Events that changed the world in the seventeenth century   **909**
   (ed) Events that changed the world in the twentieth century. See Events that changed the world in the twentieth century   **909.82**
   (ed) Events that changed the world through the sixteenth century. See Events that changed the world through the sixteenth century   **909**
   (jt. auth) Rydell, R. W. Fair America   **394**

Fine, Susan
   (jt. auth) Bardin, M. Zen in the art of the SAT   **378.1**

Fine accommodations. Hughes, L.
   In Hughes, L. Short stories of Langston Hughes   **S C**

Fine arts *See* Arts

A **fine** old firm. Jackson, S.
   In Jackson, S. The lottery; or, The adventures of James Harris   **S C**

Finer, Kim R., 1956-
   Tuberculosis   **616.2**

Fingerprints
   Tocci, S. High-tech IDs   **614**

Finkelman, Paul, 1949-
   Landmark decisions of the United States Supreme Court   **347**
   (ed) Encyclopedia of African American history, 1619-1895. See Encyclopedia of African American history, 1619-1895   **305.8**
   (ed) The Encyclopedia of American political history. See The Encyclopedia of American political history   **973.03**
   (ed) Encyclopedia of the Harlem Renaissance. See Encyclopedia of the Harlem Renaissance   **700**
   (ed) Encyclopedia of the new American nation. See Encyclopedia of the new American nation   **973.03**

Finkelstein, Norman H., 1941-
   Forged in freedom   **305.8**

Finlay, Victoria
   Color: a natural history of the palette   **535.6**

Finnegan, William
   Crossing the line   **968.06**

The **Finnegan**. Bradbury, R.
   In Bradbury, R. Bradbury stories; 100 of his most celebrated tales   **S C**

Finneran, Richard J.
   (ed) Yeats, W. B. The poems   **821**
   (ed) Yeats, W. B. The Yeats reader   **828**

Fiona the first. Kinsella, W. P.
   In Kinsella, W. P. Shoeless Joe Jackson comes to Iowa: stories   **S C**

Firbank, Ronald, 1886-1926
   A tragedy in green
   In The Oxford book of English short stories p233-42   **S C**

Fire and cloud. Wright, R.
   In Wright, R. Uncle Tom's children; five long stories   **S C**

The **fire** and the cloud. Hurston, Z. N.
   In Hurston, Z. N. The complete stories p117-21   **S C**
   In Hurston, Z. N. Novels and stories p997-1000   **Fic**

Fire fighters
                     Biography
   Unger, Z. Working fire   **92**

Fire fighters   **628.9**

Fire fighting
   Fire fighters   **628.9**

Fire from heaven. Renault, M.   **Fic**

The **fire** in the flint [excerpt] White, W. F.
   In The Portable Harlem Renaissance reader p351-62   **810.8**

Fire in the heart. Chopra, D.   **204**

Fire in the lake. FitzGerald, F.   **959.704**

Fire in the turtle house. Davidson, O. G.   **597.92**

Fire under the snow. See Palden Gyatso. The autobiography of a Tibetan monk   **92**

Fire-worship. Hawthorne, N.
   In Hawthorne, N. Tales and sketches, including Twice-told tales, Mosses from an old manse, and The snow-image; A wonder book for girls and boys; Tanglewood tales for girls and boys, being a second Wonder book p841-48   **S C**

Firearms
   Atkin, S. B. Gunstories   **363.33**
                Law and legislation
   See Gun control

Firearms industry
   See also Defense industry
   Gifford, C. The arms trade   **382**

Firebirds rising   **S C**

Firefly astronomy dictionary   **520.3**

Firefly atlas of North America   **912**

Firefly atlas of the universe   **523**

The **Firefly** encyclopedia of astronomy   **520.3**

Fischer, David Hackett
Washington's crossing   973.3
Fischer, Jackie
An egg on three sticks   Fic
Fischetti, Mark
(jt. auth) Berners-Lee, T. Weaving the Web
    025.04
Fish, Robert L., 1912-
The wager
   In The Best American mystery stories of the
     century p547-55   S C
Fish culture
    See also Aquariums
Fisher, James Maxwell McConnell, 1912-1970
    About
Weidensaul, S. Return to wild America   578
Fisher, Jerilyn
(ed) Women in literature. See Women in litera-
ture   809
**Fisher, M. F. K. (Mary Frances Kennedy),
1908-1992**
The lost, strayed, stolen
   In The Literary ghost; great contemporary
     ghost stories p5-30   S C
Fisher, Ronald M., 1938-
National Geographic historical atlas of the Unit-
ed States   911
Fisher, Rudolph, 1897-1934
The walls of Jericho [excerpt]
   In The Portable Harlem Renaissance reader
     p537-47   810.8
The **fisherman** from Chihuahua. Connell, E. S.
   In American short story masterpieces   S C
Fishes
    See also Aquariums; Eels; Rays (Fishes);
    Salmon
Rogers, G. Focus on freshwater aquarium fish
    639.34
    Encyclopedias
Alderton, D. Encyclopedia of aquarium & pond
   fish   639.34
Dawes, J. Complete encyclopedia of the fresh-
   water aquarium   639.34
    North America
Gilbert, C. R. National Audubon Society field
   guide to fishes, North America   597
Page, L. M. A field guide to freshwater fishes:
   North America north of Mexico   597
Fishing
    See also Fly casting
Mason, B. Sports illustrated fly fishing
    799.1
Merwin, J. Fly fishing   799.1
Paulsen, G. Father water, Mother woods
    799
    Fiction
Hemingway, E. The old man and the sea
    Fic
Hobbs, W. Leaving Protection   Fic
Fishing. Hoffman, J.
   In Under 30; plays for a new generation
    812.008

Fishman, Katharine Davis
Attitude!: eight young dancers come of age at
   the Ailey School   792.8
Fiske, Edward B.
The Fiske guide to colleges 2008   378.73
The Fiske guide to getting into the right college
    378
The **Fiske** guide to colleges 2008. Fiske, E. B.
    378.73
The **Fiske** guide to getting into the right college.
   Fiske, E. B.   378
Fitoussi, Michèle
(jt. auth) Oufkir, M. Stolen lives   92
Fitts, Dudley, 1903-1968
(ed) Four Greek plays. See Four Greek plays
    882.008
FitzGerald, Edward, 1809-1883
(tr) Omar Khayyam. Rubáiyát of Omar Khay-
yám   891
Fitzgerald, F. Scott (Francis Scott), 1896-1940
Babylon revisited
   In Adaptations: from short story to big
     screen; 35 great stories that have inspired
     great films   S C
The bridal party
   In The Norton book of American short stories
     p326-41   S C
The great Gatsby   Fic
A life in letters   92
The short stories of F. Scott Fitzgerald   S C
Contents: Head and shoulders; Bernice bobs her hair; The ice
palace; The offshore pirate; May Day; The jelly-bean; The curi-
ous case of Benjamin Button; The diamond as big as the Ritz;
Winter dreams; Dice, brassknuckles & guitar; Absolution; Rags
Martin-Jones and the Pr-nce of W-les; "The sensible thing"; Love
in the night; The rich boy; Jacob's ladder; A short trip home;
The bowl; The captured shadow; Basil and Cleopatra; The last of
the belles; Majesty; At your age; The swimmers; Two wrongs;
First blood; Emotional bankruptcy; The bridal party; One trip
abroad; The hotel child; Babylon revisited; A new leaf; A freeze-
out; Six of one—; What a handsome pair!; Crazy Sunday; More
than just a house; Afternoon of an author; Financing Finnegan;
The lost decade; "Boil some water—lots of it"; Last kiss; Dearly
beloved
Tender is the night   Fic
    About
Boon, K. A. F. Scott Fitzgerald   92
Gale, R. L. An F. Scott Fitzgerald encyclopedia
    813.009
Tate, M. J. Critical companion to F. Scott Fitz-
gerald   813.009
FitzGerald, Frances, 1940-
Fire in the lake   959.704
Fitzgerald, Francis Scott *See* Fitzgerald, F. Scott
   (Francis Scott), 1896-1940
Fitzgerald, Helen
The grieving teen   155.9
Fitzgerald, John J.
(jt. auth) Young, M. B. The Vietnam War: a
   history in documents   959.704
Fitzgerald, Penelope
At Hiruharama
   In The Oxford book of English short stories
     p362-68   S C
Fitzgerald, Robert, 1910-1985
(tr) Homer. The Odyssey   883

The **five** boons of life. Twain, M.
In Twain, M. The complete short stories of Mark Twain; now collected for the first time **S C**

Five equations that changed the world. Guillen, M. **530.1**

The **five-forty-eight**. Cheever, J.
In Cheever, J. The stories of John Cheever p236-47 **S C**

Five helpful hints. Peck, R.
In Peck, R. Past perfect, present tense: new and collected stories **S C**

Five hundred great books by women. *See* Bauermeister, E. 500 great books by women **016.3054**

Five hundred great books for teens. *See* Silvey, A. 500 great books for teens **028.5**

Five hundred one recipes for a low-carb life. *See* Gillespie, G. R. 501 recipes for a low-carb life **613.2**

The **five** orange pips. Doyle, Sir A. C.
In Doyle, Sir A. C. The complete Sherlock Holmes **S C**

Five plays. Hughes, L. **812**

Five thousand miles to freedom. *See* Fradin, J. B. 5,000 miles to freedom **326**

Five-twenty. White, P.
In The Oxford book of short stories p443-65 **S C**

Fixed ideas *See* Obsessive-compulsive disorder

Fixed ideas: America since 9.11. Didion, J. **320.5**

The **fixer**. Malamud, B. **Fic**

Flag: an American biography. Leepson, M. **929.9**

Flags
United States
Druckman, N. American flags **929.9**
Leepson, M. Flag: an American biography **929.9**
Schneider, R. H. Stars & stripes forever **929.9**
Shearer, B. F. State names, seals, flags, and symbols **929.9**

Flags of our fathers. Bradley, J. **940.54**

Flake, Sharon G.
Bang! **Fic**
Who am I without him? **S C**
Contents: So I ain't no good girl; The ugly one; Wanted: a thug; I know a stupid boy when I see one; Mookie in love; Don't be disrespecting me; I like white boys; Jacob's rules; Hunting for boys; A letter to my daughter

Flanagan, Robert, 1941-
Teller's ticket
In The Norton book of American short stories p681-92 **S C**

Flannery, Tim F. (Tim Fridjof), 1956-
The weather makers **363.7**

Flash!: the Associated Press covers the world **070.4**

The **flattering** word. Kelly, G.
In 24 favorite one-act plays p272-300 **808.82**

Fledgling. Butler, O. E. **Fic**

Fleischman, John
Phineas Gage: a gruesome but true story about brain science **362.1**

Fleischman, Paul
Seek **Fic**
Zap **812**

Fleischner, Jennifer
Mrs. Lincoln and Mrs. Keckley **92**

Fleisher, Paul
Parasites **578.6**

Fleming, Alexander, 1881-1955
About
Friedman, M. Medicine's 10 greatest discoveries **610.9**
See/See also pages in the following book(s):
Horvitz, L. A. Eureka!: scientific breakthroughs that changed the world **509**

Fleming, Fergus, 1959-
Off the map **910**

Fleming, John, 1919-2001
(ed) The Penguin dictionary of architecture and landscape architecture. *See* The Penguin dictionary of architecture and landscape architecture **720.3**

Fleming, Louis B.
(jt. auth) Yamazaki, J. N. Children of the atomic bomb **92**

Fleming, Robert
The African American writer's handbook **808**

Flesh and machines. Brooks, R. A. **629.8**

Fleshmarket. Morgan, N. **Fic**

Fletcher, Lucille, 1912-2000
Sorry, wrong number
In 24 favorite one-act plays p117-32 **808.82**

Fletcher, Nick
(jt. auth) Rogers, G. Focus on freshwater aquarium fish **639.34**

Fletcher, Susan, 1951-
Alphabet of dreams **Fic**

Flies. Asimov, I.
In Asimov, I. The complete stories p515-20 **S C**

The **flies**. Sartre, J. P.
In Sartre, J. P. No exit, and three other plays **842**

Flight. Updike, J.
In Updike, J. Pigeon feathers, and other stories p49-73 **S C**

Flight: 100 years of aviation. Grant, R. G. **629.13**

Flight patterns. Alexie, S.
In Alexie, S. Ten little Indians; stories **S C**

Flight v2 **741.5**
Flight v3 **741.5**

Flinn, Alex
Breathing underwater **Fic**
Bunny boy
In Twice told; original stories inspired by original art **S C**

Flinn, Alex—*Continued*
Keep smiling
In Destination unexpected: short stories
S C

Nothing to lose **Fic**

Flinn, Alexandra *See* Flinn, Alex

Flinn, Frank K.
Encyclopedia of Catholicism **282**

The **Flints** of memory lane. Gaiman, N.
In Gaiman, N. Fragile things; short fictions
and wonders **S C**

Floater. Wittlinger, E.
In Twice told; original stories inspired by
original art **S C**

The **floating** world [excerpt] Kadohata, C.
In Coming of age in America; a multicultural
anthology p122-35 **S C**

Flora, Joseph M.
(ed) The Companion to southern literature. *See*
The Companion to southern literature
810.3

Florence, Mike
The everything car care book **629.28**

A **Florentine** tragedy. Wilde, O.
In 24 favorite one-act plays p434-43
808.82

Flores, Angel, 1900-1992
Spanish American authors **920.003**

Florescu, Radu R. N.
Dracula [biography of Vlad II] **92**

Florey, Howard, Baron Florey, 1898-1968
About
Friedman, M. Medicine's 10 greatest discoveries
610.9

Florida
Fiction
Crist-Evans, C. Amaryllis **Fic**
Flinn, A. Nothing to lose **Fic**
Hobbs, V. Letting go of Bobby James, or, How
I found myself of steam **Fic**
Hurston, Z. N. Their eyes were watching God
Fic
McCarthy, S. C. True fires **Fic**

The **Florida** manatee. Reep, R. L. **599.5**

Florio, James J.
See/See also pages in the following book(s):
Profiles in courage for our time **920**

Flotsam and Jetsam. Maugham, W. S.
In Maugham, W. S. Collected short stories
S C

Flower garden. Jackson, S.
In Jackson, S. The lottery; or, The adventures
of James Harris **S C**

Flower gardening
Bawden-Davis, J. Flower gardening **635.9**

Flowering Judas. Porter, K. A.
In The Oxford book of short stories p310-21
S C
In Porter, K. A. The collected stories of Kath-
erine Anne Porter **S C**

Flowering Judas, and other stories. Porter, K. A.
In Porter, K. A. The collected stories of Katherine Anne Porter **S C**

Flowers
See also Wild flowers
Burger, W. C. Flowers: how they changed the
world **582.13**

Flowers for Algernon. Keyes, D. **Fic**

Flowers for Marjorie. Welty, E.
In Welty, E. The collected stories of Eudora
Welty p98-106 **S C**

Floyd, Samuel A.
The power of black music **780.89**

Flu *See* Influenza

Fluffy the gangbuster. Peck, R.
In Peck, R. Past perfect, present tense: new
and collected stories **S C**

Flute dream. Hesse, H.
In Hesse, H. and Zipes, J. D. The fairy tales
of Hermann Hesse **S C**

The **fly.** Langelaan, G.
In Adaptations: from short story to big
screen; 35 great stories that have inspired
great films **S C**

Fly casting
Mason, B. Sports illustrated fly fishing
799.1
Merwin, J. Fly fishing **799.1**

Fly fishing. Merwin, J. **799.1**

The **fly** in the cathedral. Cathcart, B. **539.7**

Flying Enterprise (Ship)
Delaney, F. Simple courage **910.4**

The **flying** machine. Bradbury, R.
In Bradbury, R. Bradbury stories; 100 of his
most celebrated tales **S C**

Flying Officer X *See* Bates, H. E. (Herbert Ernest), 1905-1974

Flying saucer rock and roll. Waldrop, H.
In Best of the best: 20 years of the Year's
best science fiction **S C**

Flying saucers *See* Unidentified flying objects

Flynn, Kevin, 1956-
(jt. auth) Dwyer, J. 102 minutes **974.7**

Flynn, Michael
Built upon the sands of time
In The Hard SF renaissance **S C**

Flynn, Raymond
John Paul II **92**

Focus on freshwater aquarium fish. Rogers, G.
639.34

Focus on living. Banish, R. **362.1**

Fo'Dolla'. Michener, J. A.
In Michener, J. A. Tales of the South Pacific
S C

Fodor, Margie Druss
Megan's law **362.7**

Foe, Daniel *See* Defoe, Daniel, 1661?-1731

Foer, Jonathan Safran, 1977-
Extremely loud & incredibly close **Fic**

Foerstel, Herbert N.
From Watergate to Monicagate **070.4**

The **fog** man. Boyle, T. C.
In Boyle, T. C. The Human Fly and other
stories **S C**

Ford, Jeffrey, 1955——*Continued*
Bright morning
In Feeling very strange; the Slipstream anthology   **S C**
The green word
In The Green Man: tales from the mythic forest p353-82   **808.8**
Ford, Michael Thomas
Sara
In Not the only one; lesbian and gay fiction for teens   **S C**
Ford, R. A.
Homemade lightning   **621.31**
Ford, Richard, 1944-
Rock Springs
In American short story masterpieces   **S C**
Forecast Earth [biography of Inez Fung] Skelton, R.   **92**
Forecasting
    See also Weather forecasting
Dixon, D. The future is wild   **576.8**
The next fifty years   **501**
Foreign oil dependence   **333.8**
Foreign population *See* Immigrants
Foreign relations *See* International relations
Foreign study
    Directories
Balaban, M. Study away   **378**
Study abroad, 2007   **378**
The **foreigner,** sister of the foreign woman. Djebar, A.
In The Heinemann book of contemporary African short stories p121-28   **S C**
Foreigners *See* Immigrants
Foreman, Laura, d. 2001
Alexander the Conqueror   **92**
Foreman, Michael, 1938-
(il) Garfield, L. Shakespeare stories {I}-II   **822.3**
Forensic anthropology
Bass, W. M. Death's acre   **614**
Hopping, L. J. Bone detective [biography of Diane France]   **92**
Pringle, H. A. The mummy congress   **393**
See/See also pages in the following book(s):
Massie, R. K. The Romanovs   **947.08**
The **forensic** casebook. Genge, N.   **363.2**
Forensic medicine *See* Medical jurisprudence
Forensic pharmacology. Zedeck, B. E.   **614**
Forensic sciences
Evans, C. The casebook of forensic detection   **614**
Fridell, R. DNA fingerprinting   **614**
Friedlander, M. P. When objects talk   **363.2**
Genge, N. The forensic casebook   **363.2**
Lee, H. C. Blood evidence   **614**
Owen, D. Hidden evidence   **363.2**
Platt, R. Crime scene   **363.2**
Wagner, E. J. The science of Sherlock Holmes   **363.2**
Wecht, C. H. Tales from the morgue   **614**
Yount, L. Forensic science   **363.2**
Zedeck, B. E. Forensic pharmacology   **614**

Zugibe, F. T. Dissecting death   **614**
See/See also pages in the following book(s):
Newton, M. The encyclopedia of high-tech crime and crime-fighting   **364.1**
    Dictionaries
Bell, S. The Facts on File dictionary of forensic science   **363.2**
    Encyclopedias
Bell, S. Encyclopedia of forensic science   **363.2**
    Fiction
Ferguson, A. The Christopher killer   **Fic**
Forensics. Greco, S.
In Not the only one; lesbian and gay fiction for teens   **S C**
The **forest** dweller. Hesse, H.
In Hesse, H. and Zipes, J. D. The fairy tales of Hermann Hesse   **S C**
Forest ecology
Martin, P. A. F. Woods and forests   **577.3**
Forest fires
Brown, D. Under a flaming sky   **634.9**
Forest reserves
    See also National parks and reserves
Forester, C. S. (Cecil Scott), 1899-1966
Beat to quarters   **Fic**
Forester, Cecil Scott *See* Forester, C. S. (Cecil Scott), 1899-1966
Forestiero, Saverio
(jt. auth) Sbordoni, V. Butterflies of the world   **595.7**
Forests and forestry
    See also Trees
The **foretelling.** Hoffman, A.   **Fic**
Forever and the earth. Bradbury, R.
In Bradbury, R. Bradbury stories; 100 of his most celebrated tales   **S C**
Forever free. Foner, E.   **973.8**
The **forever** war. Haldeman, J. W.   **Fic**
Forged in freedom. Finkelstein, N. H.   **305.8**
Forgery
Innes, B. Fakes & forgeries   **364.1**
The **forgotten** enemy. Clarke, A. C.
In Clarke, A. C. The collected stories of Arthur C. Clarke   **S C**
Forgotten fire. Bagdasarian, A.   **Fic**
Former Soviet republics
    See also Eastern Europe—History—1989-; Soviet Union
Fornay, Alfred
Born beautiful   **646.7**
Forrest, Emma
The grief diet
In Sixteen: stories about that sweet and bitter birthday   **S C**
Forster, E. M. (Edward Morgan), 1879-1970
A passage to India   **Fic**
Forsyth, Adrian
Mammals of North America   **599**
Forsyth, Elizabeth Held
(jt. auth) Hyde, M. O. Depression   **616.85**

The **four** Dutchmen. Maugham, W. S.
  In Maugham, W. S. Collected short stories
    S C
Four Greek plays **882.008**
The **four** lost men. Wolfe, T.
  In Wolfe, T. The complete short stories of
    Thomas Wolfe p106-19 **S C**
Four past midnight. King, S. **S C**
Four plays. Ionesco, E. **842**
Four plays. See Inge, W. 4 plays **812**
Four quartets. Eliot, T. S.
  In Eliot, T. S. The complete poems and plays,
    1909-1950 p117-45 **818**
Four saints in three acts. Stein, G.
  In Stein, G. Selected writings p577-612
    818
Four spirits. Naslund, S. J. **Fic**
The **four** suspects. Christie, A.
  In Christie, A. Miss Marple: the complete
    short stories **S C**
Four wings and a prayer. Halpern, S. M.
    595.7
Fourteenth century See World history—14th century
The **fourth** alarm. Cheever, J.
  In Cheever, J. The stories of John Cheever
    p645-49 **S C**
Fourth dimension
  Gott, J. R. Time travel in Einstein's universe
    530.1
Fourth of July. Brancato, R. F.
  In Sixteen: short stories by outstanding writers for young adults p102-12 **S C**
Fourth World See Developing countries
Fowler, H. W., 1858-1933.
  Fowler's modern English usage **428**
Fowler, Karen Joy
  The lake was full of artificial things
    In The Norton book of science fiction; North American science fiction, 1960-1990 p580-90 **S C**
  Lieserl
    In Feeling very strange; the Slipstream anthology **S C**
Fowler, Sarah L.
  (jt. auth) Compagno, L. J. V. Sharks of the world **597**
Fowler's modern English usage. Fowler, H. W.
    428
The **fox** and the forest. Bradbury, R.
  In Bradbury, R. The illustrated man **S C**
Fox hunt. Faulkner, W.
  In Faulkner, W. Collected stories of William Faulkner p587-607 **S C**
Fox hunt. Namioka, L.
  In Join in; multiethnic short stories by outstanding writers for young adults p13-21 **S C**
Foxfire 40th anniversary book **975.8**
Foxwife. Goto, H.
  In The Faery Reel; tales from the Twilight Realm **S C**

Fradin, Dennis B.
  Bound for the North Star **326**
  (jt. auth) Fradin, J. B. 5,000 miles to freedom **326**
  (jt. auth) Fradin, J. B. Jane Addams **92**
  (jt. auth) Fradin, J. B. The power of one [biography of Daisy Bates] **92**
Fradin, Judith Bloom
  5,000 miles to freedom **326**
  Jane Addams **92**
  The power of one [biography of Daisy Bates]
    92
Fragile things. Gaiman, N. **S C**
Fragments from the journal of a solitary man. Hawthorne, N.
  In Hawthorne, N. Tales and sketches, including Twice-told tales, Mosses from an old manse, and The snow-image; A wonder book for girls and boys; Tanglewood tales for girls and boys, being a second Wonder book p487-500 **S C**
Frampton, David
  (jt. auth) Giblin, J. When plague strikes
    614.4
France, Diane L.
  About
  Hopping, L. J. Bone detective [biography of Diane France] **92**
France, Peter, 1935-
  (ed) The New Oxford companion to literature in French. See The New Oxford companion to literature in French **840.3**
France
  Civilization
  Haine, W. S. Culture and customs of France
    944
  Fiction
  Spillebeen, G. Kipling's choice **Fic**
  History—0-1328
  Kelly, A. R. Eleanor of Aquitaine and the four kings **92**
  Sapet, K. Eleanor of Aquitaine **92**
  History—1328-1589, House of Valois
  Pernoud, R. Joan of Arc: her story **92**
  History—1589-1789, Bourbons
  Lever, E. Marie Antoinette **92**
  History—1589-1789, Bourbons—Fiction
  Dumas, A. The three musketeers **Fic**
  History—1789-1799, Revolution
  Anderson, J. M. Daily life during the French Revolution **944.04**
  Doyle, W. The Oxford history of the French Revolution **944.04**
  History—1789-1799, Revolution—Encyclopedias
  The encyclopedia of the French revolutionary and Napoleonic Wars **944.04**
  History—1789-1799, Revolution—Fiction
  Dickens, C. A tale of two cities **Fic**
  History—1799-1815
  Streissguth, T. The Napoleonic wars **940.2**
  History—1799-1815—Encyclopedias
  The encyclopedia of the French revolutionary and Napoleonic Wars **944.04**
  History—1799-1815—Fiction
  Holub, J. An innocent soldier **Fic**

A **fratricide**. Kafka, F.
  In Kafka, F. The metamorphosis and other
    stories p207-09   **S C**

Fraud
  Innes, B. Fakes & forgeries   **364.1**

Fraud, Computer *See* Computer crimes

Fraustino, Lisa Rowe, 1961-
  Sleeping Beauty
    In Don't cramp my style; stories about that
      time of the month p131-44   **S C**
  Things happen
    In Shattered: stories of children and war p87-
      107   **S C**
  (ed) Don't cramp my style. See Don't cramp my
    style   **S C**

Frazer, Sir James George, 1854-1941
  The new golden bough   **201**

Frazier, Ian
  On the rez   **970.004**

Frazier, Nishani
  (ed) Freedom on my mind. See Freedom on my
    mind   **305.8**

Freaky green eyes. Oates, J. C.   **Fic**

Frederick Douglass [critical essays]   **92**

Fredericks, Mariah
  Crunch time   **Fic**

Fredston, Jill A.
  Snowstruck   **551.3**

A **free** man of color. Hambly, B.   **Fic**

Free speech   **342**

Freedman, David Noel, 1922-
  (ed) Eerdmans dictionary of the Bible. See
    Eerdmans dictionary of the Bible   **220.3**

Freedman, Russell
  Babe Didrikson Zaharias   **92**
  Eleanor Roosevelt   **92**
  Franklin Delano Roosevelt   **92**
  Give me liberty!   **973.3**
  Indian chiefs   **920**
  Lincoln: a photobiography   **92**
  Martha Graham, a dancer's life   **92**
  The Wright brothers: how they invented the air-
    plane   **92**
  (jt. auth) Bad Heart Buffalo, A. The life and
    death of Crazy Horse   **92**

Freedman, Samuel G.
  Letters to a young journalist   **070.4**

Freedom
  Adler, M. J. Six great ideas   **111**
  Fromm, E. Escape from freedom   **323.44**

Freedom, Academic *See* Academic freedom

Freedom. Larsen, N.
  In The Oxford book of women's writing in
    the United States p95-99   **810.8**

The **freedom** fighters of Parkview. Sleator, W.
  In Sleator, W. Oddballs; stories p27-42
                                                   S C

Freedom from cruel and unusual punishment
                                                   345

Freedom from fear. Kennedy, D. M.   **973.91**

Freedom in exile. Dalai Lama   **92**

Freedom marches for civil rights *See* Civil rights
  demonstrations

Freedom of choice movement *See* Pro-choice
  movement

Freedom of information
    See also Censorship

Freedom of religion
  Freedom of religion   **342**
  Head, T. Freedom of religion   **342**
  See/See also pages in the following book(s):
  Haynes, C. C. First freedoms   **342**
  Religion in America: opposing viewpoints
                                                   200.9
Freedom of religion   **342**

Freedom of speech
  Free speech   **342**
  Freedom of speech   **342**
  Friedman, I. C. Freedom of speech and the press
                                                   342
  Icenoggle, J. Schenck v. United States and the
    freedom of speech debate   **342**
  Peck, R. S. Libraries, the First Amendment, and
    cyberspace   **025.04**
  See/See also pages in the following book(s):
  Censorship: opposing viewpoints   **363.31**
  Civil liberties   **342**
  Civil liberties: opposing viewpoints   **323**
  Haynes, C. C. First freedoms   **342**
Freedom of speech   **342**

Freedom of speech and the press. Friedman, I. C.
                                                   342

Freedom of the press
  Freedom of the press   **342**
  Friedman, I. C. Freedom of speech and the press
                                                   342
  Phillips, T. A. Hazelwood v. Kuhlmeier and the
    school newspaper censorship debate   **342**
  See/See also pages in the following book(s):
  Haynes, C. C. First freedoms   **342**
Freedom of the press   **342**

Freedom of worship *See* Freedom of religion

Freedom on my mind   **305.8**

Freedom: the story of my second life. Oufkir, M.
                                                   92

The **Freedom** Writers diary   **305.23**

Freedom's daughters. Olson, L.   **323.1**

Freeman, Mary Eleanor Wilkins, 1852-1930
  Luella Miller
    In The Norton book of American short stories
      p125-36   **S C**
  The revolt of "Mother"
    In The Oxford book of women's writing in
      the United States p27-40   **810.8**

Freeman, Michael, 1945-
  The complete guide to digital photography
                                                   775

Freeman-Cook, Kevin D.
  (jt. auth) Freeman-Cook, L. Staphylococcus
    aureus infections   **616.9**

Freeman-Cook, Lisa
  Staphylococcus aureus infections   **616.9**

Freese, Barbara
  Coal: a human history   **553.2**

Friedman, Lauri S.—*Continued*
(ed) Smoking. *See* Smoking   **362.29**
(ed) Terrorism. *See* Terrorism [Lauri S. Friedman]   **973.931**
(ed) What motivates suicide bombers? *See* What motivates suicide bombers?   **303.6**

Friedman, Meyer, 1910-2001
Medicine's 10 greatest discoveries   **610.9**

Friedman, Thomas L.
Longitudes and attitudes   **973.931**

Friel, Brian
The diviner
   In The Oxford book of Irish short stories p471-81   **S C**

Friend, Natasha, 1972-
Lush   **Fic**

Friend, Tim
Animal talk   **591.59**

A **friend** in need. Maugham, W. S.
   In Maugham, W. S. Collected short stories   **S C**

The **Friend** who got away   **158**

Friendly Brook. Kipling, R.
   In Kipling, R. The portable Kipling   **828**

The **friendly** persuasion. West, J.   **Fic**

Friends, Society of *See* Society of Friends

Friends. O'Brien, T.
   In O'Brien, T. The things they carried; a work of fiction   **S C**

The **friends** of the friends. James, H.
   In Nightshade: 20th century ghost stories p254-81   **S C**

Friendship
The Friend who got away   **158**
Winick, J. Pedro and me   **362.1**
     Fiction
Block, F. L. Weetzie Bat   **Fic**
Brashares, A. The sisterhood of the traveling pants   **Fic**
Crutcher, C. Staying fat for Sarah Byrnes   **Fic**
Desai Hidier, T. Born confused   **Fic**
Dessen, S. Just listen   **Fic**
Ferris, J. Of sound mind   **Fic**
Fredericks, M. Crunch time   **Fic**
Going, K. L. Fat kid rules the world   **Fic**
Griffin, A. Amandine   **Fic**
Hautman, P. Invisible   **Fic**
Hosseini, K. The kite runner   **Fic**
Johnson, M. Devilish   **Fic**
Kerouac, J. On the road   **Fic**
Knowles, J. A separate peace   **Fic**
Lowell, P. Returnable girl   **Fic**
Lyga, B. The astonishing adventures of Fanboy & Goth Girl   **Fic**
Lynch, C. Slot machine   **Fic**
Miller, M. B. Aimee   **Fic**
Moriarty, J. The year of secret assignments   **Fic**
Morrison, T. Sula   **Fic**
Myers, W. D. Autobiography of my dead brother   **Fic**
Nilsson, P. You & you & you   **Fic**
Oates, J. C. Big Mouth & Ugly Girl   **Fic**

Powell, R. Three clams and an oyster   **Fic**
Sloan, B. A tale of two summers   **Fic**
Sonnenblick, J. Notes from the midnight driver   **Fic**
Wallace, R. Wrestling Sturbridge   **Fic**
Who do you think you are?   **S C**
See/See also pages in the following book(s):
Sleator, W. Oddballs   **S C**
     Graphic novels
Abouet, M. Aya   **741.5**
Castellucci, C. The Plain Janes   **741.5**
Friedman, A. Breaking up   **741.5**

Friesner, Esther M.
Thunderbolt
   In Young warriors; stories of strength   **S C**

The **frightening** Frammis. Thompson, J.
   In Alfred Hitchcock's mystery magazine presents fifty years of crime and suspense   **S C**

Frisco. Michener, J. A.
   In Michener, J. A. Tales of the South Pacific   **S C**

Fritter hollow chronicles. Wang Xiangfu
   In Chairman Mao would not be amused; fiction from today's China   **S C**

Fritz, Deborah A. (Deborah Angela), 1955-
Cataloging with AACR2 and MARC21   **025.3**

Froehner, Melissa Alberti, 1963-
(jt. auth) Palmer, P. Teen esteem   **155.5**

Frogs
   See also Toads
Beltz, E. Frogs: inside their remarkable world   **597.8**

The **frogs.** Aristophanes
   In Seven famous Greek plays   **882.008**

Frolund, Tina
Genrefied classics   **016.8**

From a raw deal to a new deal? Trotter, J. W.
   In The Young Oxford history of African Americans   **305.8**

From both sides now   **811.008**
From conception to birth. Tsiaras, A.   **618.3**
From Hinton to Hamlet. Herz, S. K.   **809**
From Lucy to language. Johanson, D. C.   **599.93**
From school to a career. Jell, J. R.   **378**
From slavery to freedom. Franklin, J. H.   **305.8**
From the cabby's seat. Henry, O.
   In Henry, O. The best short stories of O. Henry   **S C**
From the country of eight islands   **895.6**
From the heart   **970.004**
From totems to hip-hop   **811.008**
From Watergate to Monicagate. Foerstel, H. N.   **070.4**

Frome, Keith W., 1960-
(ed) The Columbia book of Civil War poetry. *See* The Columbia book of Civil War poetry   **811.008**

Fuller, Charles
A soldier's play
In Black theatre USA; plays by African
Americans, 1847 to today **812.008**

Fuller, John, 1937-
My story
In The Oxford book of English short stories
p398-99 **S C**
Telephone
In The Oxford book of English short stories
p396-97 **S C**

Fuller, Meta Vaux Warrick, 1877-1968
See/See also pages in the following book(s):
Harlem Renaissance **709.73**

The **fun** they had. Asimov, I.
In Asimov, I. The complete stories p120-22
S C

Fund raising
Gerding, S. K. Grants for libraries **025.1**

Fundamental acting. Kuritz, P. **792**

Fundamental life skills *See* Life skills

Fundamentalism *See* Christian fundamentalism;
Islamic fundamentalism

Fundamentalism and education *See* Church and
education; Religion in the public schools

Fundamentalism and evolution *See* Creationism

Fundamentalist movements *See* Religious fundamentalism

Fundamentalists and extremists. Long, D. **306**

Fundamentals of library supervision. Giesecke, J.
023

Fundamentals of track and field. Carr, G. A.
796.42

Funds, Scholarship *See* Scholarships

Funeral rites and ceremonies
Colman, P. Corpses, coffins, and crypts **393**

Fung, Inez, 1949-
About
Skelton, R. Forecast Earth [biography of Inez
Fung] **92**

Fungi
See also Mushrooms
See/See also pages in the following book(s):
Reader's Digest North American wildlife, trees
and nonflowering plants **582.16**

Funnies *See* Comic books, strips, etc.

Funny in Farsi. Dumas, F. **92**

Funny little monkey. Auseon, A. **Fic**

Funnyhouse of a Negro. Kennedy, A.
In Black theatre USA; plays by African
Americans, 1847 to today **812.008**

Fuqua, Jonathon Scott
The reappearance of Sam Webber **Fic**

Furey, Joan A.
(ed) Visions of war, dreams of peace. See Visions of war, dreams of peace **811.008**

Furey, Leo
The long run **Fic**

Furia, Philip, 1943-
The poets of Tin Pan Alley **782.42**

Furlough—1944. Mazer, H.
In Sixteen: short stories by outstanding writers for young adults p83-92 **S C**

The **furnished** room. Henry, O.
In Henry, O. The best short stories of O.
Henry **S C**

Fury. Bethancourt, T. E.
In Ultimate sports; short stories by outstand-
ing writers for young adults p21-49
S C

Fusco, Kimberly Newton
Tending to Grace **Fic**

Fussell, Paul, 1924-
The boys' crusade **940.54**

Fussman, Cal
After Jackie **92**

Futrelle, Jacques, 1875-1912
The problem of cell 13
In The Best American mystery stories of the
century p26-57 **S C**

Future. Britto García, L.
In Cosmos latinos; an anthology of science
fiction from Latin America and Spain
S C

The **future** is in eggs. Ionesco, E.
In Ionesco, E. Rhinoceros, and other plays
842

The **future** is wild. Dixon, D. **576.8**

Future life
Is there life after death? **133.9**
Roach, M. Spook **133.9**
See/See also pages in the following book(s):
Death and dying: opposing viewpoints **179.7**
Fiction
Shusterman, N. Everlost **Fic**
Whitcomb, L. A certain slant of light **Fic**
Zevin, G. Elsewhere **Fic**

The **future** lives of Emily Milty. Baggott, J.
In Sixteen: stories about that sweet and bitter
birthday **S C**

The **future** of the brain. Rose, S. P. R. **153**

Future shock *See* Culture conflict

Future tense. Lipsyte, R.
In Sixteen: short stories by outstanding writers for young adults p60-70 **S C**

Futurology *See* Forecasting

G

G.B.S.—Mark V. Bradbury, R.
In Bradbury, R. Bradbury stories; 100 of his
most celebrated tales **S C**

G.I. nightingales. Tomblin, B. **940.54**

G.I.'s *See* Soldiers—United States

Gabriel's story. Durham, D. A. **Fic**

Gaddis, John Lewis
The Cold War **909.82**

Gage, Carolyn
Harriet Tubman visits a therapist
In Under 30; plays for a new generation
812.008

Gelfant, Blanche H., 1922-
(ed) The Columbia companion to the twentieth-century American short story. See The Columbia companion to the twentieth-century American short story   **813.009**

Gell-Mann, Murray, 1929-
See/See also pages in the following book(s):
Cropper, W. H. Great physicists   **920**
Henderson, H. Nuclear physics   **539.7**

Gelletly, LeeAnne
Gift of imagination [biography of Roald Dahl]   **92**

Gellhorn, Martha
See/See also pages in the following book(s):
Colman, P. Where the action was   **070.4**

Gems
   See also Precious stones
Oldershaw, C. Firefly guide to gems   **553.8**

Gemstones of the world. Schumann, W.   **553.8**

Gender identity See Sex role

Gene hunter [biography of Nancy Wexler] Glimm, A.   **92**

Gene mapping
   See also Genomes
See/See also pages in the following book(s):
Biomedical ethics: opposing viewpoints   **174.2**

Gene splicing See Genetic engineering

Gene therapy
Gene therapy [Roman Espejo, book editor]   **615.8**
Gene therapy [Clay Farris Naff, book editor]   **615.8**
Panno, J. Gene therapy   **615.8**
Gene therapy [Clay Farris Naff, book editor]   **615.8**
Gene therapy [Roman Espejo, book editor]   **615.8**

Gene wars. McAuley, P. J.
   In The Hard SF renaissance   **S C**

A **genealogist's** guide to discovering your African-American ancestors. Smith, F. C.   **929**

Genealogy
Shepherdson, N. Ancestor hunt   **929**
Smith, F. C. A genealogist's guide to discovering your African-American ancestors   **929**

The **genealogy** of Greek mythology. Beauman, S.   **292**

Generals
Blount, R. Robert E. Lee   **92**
Robertson, J. I., Jr. Robert E. Lee   **92**
Robertson, J. I., Jr. Standing like a stone wall: the life of General Thomas J. Jackson   **92**

Generative organs See Reproductive system

Generators, Electric See Electric generators

Genesis, Book of See Bible. O.T. Genesis

Genesis. Anderson, P.
   In The Hard SF renaissance   **S C**

Genetic engineering
   See also Biotechnology; Cloning
The Ethics of genetic engineering   **174.2**
Genetic engineering   **174.2**

Genetic engineering: opposing viewpoints   **174.2**
Shannon, T. A. Genetic engineering   **660.6**
Yount, L. Biotechnology and genetic engineering   **660.6**
Yount, L. Modern genetics   **576.5**
See/See also pages in the following book(s):
Animal experimentation: opposing viewpoints   **179**
Biomedical ethics: opposing viewpoints   **174.2**
Global resources: opposing viewpoints   **333.71**
Hyde, M. O. Medicine's brave new world   **610**
Fiction
Crichton, M. Jurassic Park   **Fic**
Halam, A. Dr. Franklin's island   **Fic**
Werlin, N. Double helix   **Fic**

Genetic engineering   **174.2**

Genetic engineering: opposing viewpoints   **174.2**

Genetic fingerprints See DNA fingerprinting

Genetically engineered food. Cummins, R.   **363.1**

Genetically engineered foods   **363.1**

Genetics
   See also Gene mapping; Genomes; Medical genetics
Ackerman, J. Chance in the house of fate   **599.93**
Burnham, T. Mean genes   **155.2**
Edelson, E. Francis Crick and James Watson and the building blocks of life   **92**
O'Brien, S. J. Tears of the cheetah   **591.3**
Ridley, M. Francis Crick   **92**
Ridley, M. Genome   **599.93**
Ridley, M. Nature via nurture   **155.7**
Sagan, C. The dragons of Eden   **153**
Watson, J. D. DNA: the secret of life   **576.5**
Wells, S. The journey of man   **599.93**
Yount, L. Modern genetics   **576.5**
Encyclopedias
Encyclopedia of genetics   **576.5**
Genetics   **576.5**
Law and legislation
See/See also pages in the following book(s):
Biomedical ethics: opposing viewpoints   **174.2**

Genetics   **576.5**

Genetics and environment See Nature and nurture

Genge, Ngaire
The forensic casebook   **363.2**

Genghis Khan, 1162-1227
About
Lane, G. Genghis Khan and Mongol rule   **950**
Rice, E. Empire in the east: the story of Genghis Khan   **92**

Genitalia See Reproductive system

Genius
Streznewski, M. K. Gifted grownups   **153.9**

Genius—*Continued*
Fiction
Jinks, C. Evil genius   **Fic**
Genocide
Cocker, M. Rivers of blood, rivers of gold
     909
Gourevitch, P. We wish to inform you that tomorrow we will be killed with our families
     967.571
Naimark, N. M. Fires of hatred   **364.1**
Springer, J. Genocide   **304.6**
Encyclopedias
Encyclopedia of genocide and crimes against humanity   **304.6**
Genome mapping *See* Gene mapping
Genomes
Ridley, M. Genome   **599.93**
Genovese, Michael A.
Encyclopedia of the American presidency
     973
The Watergate crisis   **973.924**
Genrefied classics. Frolund, T.   **016.8**
Genreflecting. Herald, D. T.   **016.8**
Genreflecting advisory series
Fichtelberg, S. Encountering enchantment
     016.8
Frolund, T. Genrefied classics   **016.8**
Gannon, M. B. Blood, bedlam, bullets, and badguys   **016.8**
Herald, D. T. Genreflecting   **016.8**
Herald, D. T. Strictly science fiction   **016.8**
Johnson, S. L. Historical fiction   **016.8**
Pawuk, M. G. Graphic novels   **016.7**
The **gentle** boy. Hawthorne, N.
In Hawthorne, N. Tales and sketches, including Twice-told tales, Mosses from an old manse, and The snow-image; A wonder book for girls and boys; Tanglewood tales for girls and boys, being a second Wonder book p108-38   **S C**
The **gentle** vultures. Asimov, I.
In Asimov, I. The complete stories p250-62
     S C
Gentlemen of the press. See Wolfe, T. The newspaper
Gentry, April
(jt. auth) Rollyson, C. Critical companion to Herman Melville   **813.009**
Gentry, Curt, 1931-
(jt. auth) Bugliosi, V. Helter skelter   **364.1**
A **genuine** alectryomancer. Willeford, C. R.
In Alfred Hitchcock's mystery magazine presents fifty years of crime and suspense
     S C
Geoffrey, of Monmouth, Bishop of St. Asaph, 1100?-1154
See/See also pages in the following book(s):
Ashe, G. The discovery of King Arthur   **92**
Historia Britonum; criticism
In Ashe, G. The discovery of King Arthur
     92

Geographic names
United States
Shearer, B. F. State names, seals, flags, and symbols   **929.9**
Geographical distribution of animals and plants
See Biogeography
Geographical distribution of people *See* Human geography
Geography
See also Maps; Voyages and travels
The DK geography of the world   **910**
Worldmark chronology of the nations   **910**
Dictionaries
Firefly geography dictionary   **910.3**
Merriam-Webster's geographical dictionary
     910.3
Encyclopedias
Worldmark encyclopedia of the nations
     910.3
Geography, Ancient *See* Ancient geography
Geography Club. Hartinger, B.   **Fic**
Geography of extreme environments [series]
Gritzner, C. F. Deserts   **577.5**
Gritzner, C. F. Polar regions   **577.5**
The **geography** of girlhood. Smith, K.   **Fic**
Geological hazards. Kusky, T. M.   **363.34**
Geology
See also Catastrophes (Geology); Submarine geology
Erickson, J. An introduction to fossils and minerals   **560**
Erickson, J. Rock formations and unusual geologic structures   **550**
Kusky, T. M. Geological hazards   **363.34**
Lambert, D. The field guide to geology   **551**
Geology, Stratigraphic *See* Stratigraphic geology
Geometry
Gorini, C. A. The Facts on File geometry handbook   **516**
Livio, M. The golden ratio   **516.2**
Mlodinow, L. Euclid's window   **516**
Tabak, J. Geometry: the language of space and form   **516**
The **geometry** of love. Cheever, J.
In Cheever, J. The stories of John Cheever p594-602   **S C**
George, Henry, 1839-1897
See/See also pages in the following book(s):
Heilbroner, R. L. The worldly philosophers
     330.1
George, Sam
(ed) The Perfect day. See The Perfect day
     797.3
George-Warren, Holly
(ed) The Rolling Stone illustrated history of rock & roll. See The Rolling Stone illustrated history of rock & roll   **781.66**
George Washington and the founding of a nation. Marrin, A.   **92**
Georgia
Fiction
Burns, O. A. Cold Sassy tree   **Fic**
Grindle, L. The nightspinners   **Fic**

Georgia—Fiction—*Continued*
McCullers, C. The member of the wedding
    Fic
Georgiou, Elisha Dunn- *See* Dunn-Georgiou, Elisha
The **geranium**. O'Connor, F.
  In O'Connor, F. Collected works p701-13
    S C
  In O'Connor, F. The complete stories p3-14
    S C
Geranium house. Curry, P. S.
  In A Century of great Western stories
    S C
Geras, Adèle
Ruby
  In Twice told; original stories inspired by
    original art   **S C**
Troy   **Fic**
Gerdes, Louise
(ed) Addiction: opposing viewpoints. See Addiction: opposing viewpoints   **362.29**
(ed) Cloning. See Cloning [Introducing issues with opposing viewpoints series]   **176**
(ed) Drunk driving. See Drunk driving
    363.1
(ed) Endangered oceans: opposing viewpoints. See Endangered oceans: opposing viewpoints
    333.95
(ed) Espionage and intelligence gathering. See Espionage and intelligence gathering
    327.12
(ed) Gangs: opposing viewpoints. See Gangs: opposing viewpoints   **364.1**
(ed) Genetic engineering: opposing viewpoints. See Genetic engineering: opposing viewpoints
    174.2
(ed) Globalization: opposing viewpoints. See Globalization: opposing viewpoints   **303.4**
(ed) Immigration. See Immigration   **325.73**
(ed) Media violence: opposing viewpoints. See Media violence: opposing viewpoints
    303.6
(ed) The Patriot Act: opposing viewpoints. See The Patriot Act: opposing viewpoints   **345**
(ed) Police brutality. See Police brutality
    363.2
(ed) Pollution: opposing viewpoints. See Pollution: opposing viewpoints   **363.7**
(ed) Rogue nations: opposing viewpoints. See Rogue nations: opposing viewpoints   **355**
(ed) War: opposing viewpoints. See War: opposing viewpoints   **355**
Gerding, Stephanie K.
Grants for libraries   **025.1**
Gerges, Fawaz A.
Journey of the Jihadist   **322.4**
Germ theory of disease
Bakalar, N. Where the germs are   **616**
Germ warfare *See* Biological warfare
German Democratic Republic *See* Germany (East)
German Harry. Maugham, W. S.
  In Maugham, W. S. Collected short stories
    S C

German language
    Dictionaries
Random House Webster's German-English, English-German dictionary   **433**
German literature
    Bio-bibliography
Garland, H. B. The Oxford companion to German literature   **830.3**
    History and criticism
The Cambridge history of German literature
    830.9
The **German** refugee. Malamud, B.
  In Malamud, B. The complete stories   **S C**
Germans
    Israel—Fiction
Kass, P. Real time   **Fic**
Germany
    Civilization
Bernstein, E. Culture and customs of Germany
    943.087
    Fiction
Chotjewitz, D. Daniel half human   **Fic**
Pausewang, G. Traitor   **Fic**
Steinhöfel, A. The center of the world   **Fic**
    History
Fulbrook, M. A concise history of Germany
    943
    History—1933-1945
Ayer, E. H. Parallel journeys   **940.53**
Bartoletti, S. C. Hitler Youth   **943.086**
Feldman, G. Understanding the Holocaust
    940.53
Goldhagen, D. Hitler's willing executioners
    940.53
Hay, J. A history of the Third Reich
    943.086
    History—1945-1990
Schmemann, S. When the wall came down
    943
    Politics and government—1933-1945
Adolf Hitler [biographical essays]   **92**
Dvorson, A. The Hitler Youth   **943.086**
Feldman, G. Understanding the Holocaust
    940.53
Hitler and his henchmen   **92**
Keeley, J. Life in the Hitler Youth   **943.086**
Rice, E. Adolf Hitler and Nazi Germany   **92**
Germany (East)
    Politics and government
Schmemann, S. When the wall came down
    943
Germs *See* Bacteria
The **Gernsback** continuum. Gibson, W.
  In The Norton book of science fiction; North American science fiction, 1960-1990 p457-65   **S C**
Geronimo, Apache Chief, 1829-1909
See/See also pages in the following book(s):
Brown, D. A. Bury my heart at Wounded Knee
    970.004
    Fiction
Bruchac, J. Geronimo   **Fic**
Gerontology
  See also Aging; Old age

Gerrard, Jon
(jt. auth) Park, Y. H. Black belt tae kwon do
796.8

Gerrold, David, 1944-
Dancer in the dark
In The Year's best science fiction and fantasy
for teens: first annual collection **S C**

Gershman, Gary P.
Death penalty on trial **345**

Gerstenberg, Alice, 1885-1972
Overtones
In The Oxford book of women's writing in
the United States p381-92 **810.8**

Get a seeing-eyed dog. Hemingway, E.
In Hemingway, E. The complete short stories
of Ernest Hemingway; the Finca Vigía
edition p487-91 **S C**

Getting away with murder: the true story of the
Emmett Till case. Crowe, C. **364.1**

Getting graphic!. Gorman, M. **741.5**

Getting in. Boylan, J. F. **Fic**

Getting ready for college. Berent, P. **378**

Getting the girl. Zusak, M. **Fic**

Getting through Sunday somehow. Bradbury, R.
In Bradbury, R. Bradbury stories; 100 of his
most celebrated tales **S C**

Gettysburg (Pa.), Battle of, 1863
Sears, S. W. Gettysburg **973.7**
Fiction
Shaara, M. The killer angels **Fic**

Ghafur, Saleemah Abdul- *See* Abdul-Ghafur,
Saleemah

Ghana Empire
Conrad, D. C. Empires of medieval West Africa
966

Gherman, Beverly, 1934-
Ansel Adams **92**
The **ghost**. Sexton, A.
In The Literary ghost; great contemporary
ghost stories p225-29 **S C**
The **ghost**. Vande Velde, V.
In Vande Velde, V. Being dead; stories
S C

Ghost and flesh, water and dirt. Goyen, W.
In The Literary ghost; great contemporary
ghost stories p304-13 **S C**

Ghost hunt, Vol. 1. Inada, S. **741.5**

The **ghost** map. Johnson, S. **614.5**

The **ghost** of Mum-Mum. Carter, A. R.
In Carter, A. R. Love, football, and other contact sports **S C**

The **ghost** soldiers. O'Brien, T.
In The Literary ghost; great contemporary
ghost stories p185-205 **S C**
In O'Brien, T. The things they carried; a
work of fiction **S C**

Ghost stories
Almond, D. Kit's wilderness **Fic**
Connor, L. Dead on town line **Fic**
De Lint, C. The blue girl **Fic**
Jackson, S. The haunting of Hill House **Fic**
Jenkins, A. M. Beating heart **Fic**
Levithan, D. Marly's ghost **Fic**

The Literary ghost **S C**
Nightshade: 20th century ghost stories **S C**
Price, C. Dead connection **Fic**
Setterfield, D. The thirteenth tale **Fic**
Soto, G. The afterlife **Fic**
Whitcomb, L. A certain slant of light **Fic**

A **ghost** story. Twain, M.
In Twain, M. The complete short stories of
Mark Twain; now collected for the first
time **S C**

The **ghost** who vanished by degrees. Davies, R.
In The Literary ghost; great contemporary
ghost stories p54-63 **S C**

Ghostly populations. Matthews, J.
In The Literary ghost; great contemporary
ghost stories p171-84 **S C**

Ghosts
Classic American ghost stories **133.1**
Encyclopedias
Guiley, R. E. The encyclopedia of ghosts and
spirits **133.1**

Ghosts. Ibsen, H.
In Ibsen, H. and Johnston, B. Ibsen: four major plays **839.8**

The **ghosts** of August. García Márquez, G.
In Nightshade: 20th century ghost stories
p344-46 **S C**

Ghosts of Tsavo. Caputo, P. **599.75**

Ghosts on the lake. Aichinger, I.
In Nightshade: 20th century ghost stories p1-6
S C

Giant panda
Angel, H. Pandas **599.78**
Croke, V. The lady and the panda **599.78**

Gibaldi, Joseph, 1942-
MLA handbook for writers of research papers
808

Gibbons, Ann
The first human **599.93**

Gibbons, Kaye, 1960-
Ellen Foster **Fic**

Gibian, George
(ed) The Portable nineteenth-century Russian
reader. See The Portable nineteenth-century
Russian reader **891.7**

Giblin, James, 1933-
Charles A. Lindbergh **92**
Three Mondays in July
In Am I blue?; coming out from the silence
p105-24 **S C**
When plague strikes **614.4**
(ed) The Century that was. See The Century that
was **973.9**

Gibran, Kahlil, 1883-1931
The Prophet **811**

Gibson, Craig, 1954-
(ed) Student engagement and information literacy. See Student engagement and information
literacy **028.7**

Gibson, Graeme, 1934-
(comp) The Bedside book of birds. See The
Bedside book of birds **598**

Gillan, Maria
Carlton Fredericks and my mother
In Growing up ethnic in America; contemporary fiction about learning to be American   **S C**
(ed) Growing up ethnic in America. See Growing up ethnic in America   **S C**
(ed) Unsettling America. See Unsettling America   **811.008**
Gilles de la Tourette's syndrome *See* Tourette syndrome
Gillespie, Gregg R., 1934-
501 recipes for a low-carb life   **613.2**
Gillespie, John Thomas, 1928-
Best books for high school readers   **011.6**
Classic teenplots   **011.6**
The Newbery/Printz companion   **028.5**
Gillespie, Kellie M., 1960-
Teen volunteer services in libraries   **021.2**
Gillespie, Michael Patrick
(jt. auth) Fargnoli, A. N. Critical companion to James Joyce   **823.009**
Gillette, J. Michael
Theatrical design and production   **792**
Gillispie, Charles Coulston
(ed) Dictionary of scientific biography. See Dictionary of scientific biography   **920.003**
Gilman, Charlotte Perkins, 1860-1935
The yellow wallpaper
In The Norton book of American short stories p137-50   **S C**
In The Oxford book of gothic tales p249-63   **S C**
In The Oxford book of women's writing in the United States p41-55   **810.8**
Gilman, Laura Anne
Serpent's rock
In Young warriors; stories of strength   **S C**
Gimmicks three. Asimov, I.
In Asimov, I. The complete stories p57-61   **S C**
Gimpel the fool. Singer, I. B.
In The Norton book of American short stories p394-406   **S C**
Gingerbread. Cohn, R.   **Fic**
The **gingerbread** lady. Simon, N.
In Simon, N. The collected plays of Neil Simon   **812**
Ginsberg, Allen, 1926-1997
Collected poems, 1947-1997   **811**
Cosmopolitan greetings: poems, 1986-1992   **811**
In Ginsberg, A. Collected poems, 1947-1997   **811**
Death & fame: poems 1993-1997
In Ginsberg, A. Collected poems, 1947-1997   **811**
White shroud: poems 1980-1985
In Ginsberg, A. Collected poems, 1947-1997   **811**
Gioia, Dana
(ed) Twentieth-century American poetry. See Twentieth-century American poetry   **811.008**

Gioia, Ted
The history of jazz   **781.65**
Gioseffi, Daniela, 1941-
(ed) Women on war. See Women on war   **303.6**
Giovanni, Nikki
Blues   **811**
Quilting the black-eyed pea   **811**
The selected poems of Nikki Giovanni (1968-1995)   **811**
(ed) Grand mothers: poems, reminiscences, and short stories about the keepers of our traditions. See Grand mothers: poems, reminiscences, and short stories about the keepers of our traditions   **810.8**
(ed) Shimmy shimmy shimmy like my sister Kate. See Shimmy shimmy shimmy like my sister Kate   **811.008**
Giovanni's room [excerpt] Baldwin, J.
In Growing up gay; an anthology for young people p85-89   **808.8**
Gipsies *See* Gypsies
Giraudoux, Jean, 1882-1944
The Apollo of Bellac
In 24 favorite one-act plays p308-32   **808.82**
Girl at the window. Peck, R.
In Night terrors; stories of shadow and substance   **S C**
In Peck, R. Past perfect, present tense: new and collected stories   **S C**
The **girl** from Charnelle. Cook, K. L.   **Fic**
Girl goddess #9. Block, F. L.
In Block, F. L. Girl goddess #9: nine stories   **S C**
Girl goddess #9: nine stories. Block, F. L.   **S C**
The **girl** of my dreams. Malamud, B.
In Malamud, B. The complete stories   **S C**
Girl sleuth. Rehak, M.   **813.009**
Girl stories. Weinstein, L.   **741.5**
Girl with a pearl earring. Chevalier, T.   **Fic**
Girlbomb. Erlbaum, J.   **92**
Girls
See also Young women
Chocolate for a teen's heart   **152.4**
Jukes, M. It's a girl thing   **305.23**
Things I have to tell you   **810.8**
Yell-oh girls!   **305.23**
Health and hygiene
Nichter, M. Fat talk   **613.2**
Girls, Teenage *See* Teenagers
The **girls**. Lansens, L.   **Fic**
The **Girls'** book of wisdom   **808.88**
A **girl's** guide to football players. Carter, A. R.
In Carter, A. R. Love, football, and other contact sports   **S C**
The **girls** of summer. Longman, J.   **796.334**
GirlSource   **305.23**
GIs *See* Soldiers—United States
Gitlin, Todd
Letters to a young activist   **322.4**

Giulia Lazzari. Maugham, W. S.
  In Maugham, W. S. Collected short stories
                    S C

Give a boy a gun. Strasser, T.   **Fic**
Give me liberty!. Freedman, R.   **973.3**
The **giver.** Lowry, L.   **Fic**

Gjertsen, Derek
  (jt. auth) Allaby, M. Makers of science
                920.003

Glaciers
  Gordon, J. E. Glaciers   **551.3**

Gladwell, Malcolm
  Blink: the power of thinking without thinking
                153.4

Glancey, Jonathan
  Architecture   **720.9**

Glancy, Diane
  Aunt Parnetta's electric blisters
    In The Norton book of science fiction; North
      American science fiction, 1960-1990
      p814-18   **S C**
  Portrait of the lone survivor
    In Growing up ethnic in America; contempo-
      rary fiction about learning to be Ameri-
      can   **S C**

Glancy, Ruth F., 1948-
  Thematic guide to British poetry   **821.009**

Glasgow, Ellen
  Jordan's end
    In The Oxford book of gothic tales p302-15
                  S C
  The shadowy third
    In Nightshade: 20th century ghost stories
      p166-90   **S C**

Glaspell, Susan, 1876-1948
  A jury of her peers
    In The Best American mystery stories of the
      century p85-104   **S C**
  ·Trifles
    In 24 favorite one-act plays p333-46
                 808.82
    In The Oxford book of women's writing in
      the United States p393-406   **810.8**

Glass, Linzi
  The year the gypsies came   **Fic**

Glass blower of Venice. Malamud, B.
  In Malamud, B. The complete stories **S C**
The **glass** castle. Walls, J.   **92**
The **glass** menagerie. Williams, T.   **812**

Glassco, Bruce
  Never never
    In The Faery Reel; tales from the Twilight
      Realm   **S C**

Glavan, James
  (jt. auth) Corson, R. Stage makeup   **792**

Glazer, Evan, 1971-
  Real-life math   **510**
  Using Internet primary sources to teach critical
    thinking skills in mathematics   **510**

GLBTQ (Gay, Lesbian, Bisexual, Transgender,
  Questioning). Huegel, K.   **306.76**

Gleaves, David H.
  (jt. auth) Cassell, D. K. Encyclopedia of obesity
    and eating disorders   **616.85**

Gleick, James
  Faster   **529**

Glenn, Calvin
  In my own space
    In Growing up gay; an anthology for young
      people p235-39   **808.8**

Glenn, Mel, 1943-
  Ryan and Angel in the green room, a heavenly
    fantasy; or, the ultimate in high-stakes testing
    In Dreams and visions; fourteen flights of
      fantasy   **S C**

Glimm, Adele
  Gene hunter [biography of Nancy Wexler]
                  92

Glimmerings on blue glass. Schwarz, M.-J.
  In Cosmos latinos; an anthology of science
    fiction from Latin America and Spain
                 S C

Glisson, Susan M., 1967-
  (jt. auth) Haynes, C. C. First freedoms **342**
Global AIDS crisis. Marlink, R. G.   **614.5**
Global history   **909**
Global resources: opposing viewpoints **333.71**
Global studies [series]
  Hanks, R. R. Central Asia   **958**
Global terrorism. Henderson, H.   **303.6**
Global warming *See* Greenhouse effect
Global warming   **363.7**
Global warming: opposing viewpoints   **363.7**
Globalization
  Globalization: opposing viewpoints   **303.4**
Globalization   **327.1**
Globalization: opposing viewpoints   **303.4**
Globe Theatre (London, England)
  See also Shakespeare's Globe (London, En-
    gland)
  Aliki. William Shakespeare & the Globe
                822.3

Gloria Naylor: critical perspectives past and pres-
  ent   **813.009**
The **'Gloria** Scott'. Doyle, Sir A. C.
  In Doyle, Sir A. C. The complete Sherlock
    Holmes   **S C**

Glory (Motion picture)
  See/See also pages in the following book(s):
  McPherson, J. M. Drawn with the sword
               973.7

Glory in the flower. Inge, W.
  In 24 favorite one-act plays p133-50
               808.82

Gloss, Molly
  Interlocking pieces
    In The Norton book of science fiction; North
      American science fiction, 1960-1990
      p571-76   **S C**
  Lambing season
    In Best of the best: 20 years of the Year's
      best science fiction   **S C**

Glossaries *See* Encyclopedias and dictionaries

A **glossary** of literary terms. Abrams, M. H.
803

Glover, Linda K.
(ed) National Geographic encyclopedia of space. See National Geographic encyclopedia of space **629.4**

Glynn, Ian, 1928-
The life and death of smallpox **616.9**

Glynn, Jenifer
(jt. auth) Glynn, I. The life and death of smallpox **616.9**

The **Gnostic** Bible **299**

Gnosticism
The Gnostic Bible **299**

Go ask Ogre. Siana, J. **92**

Go back for murder. Christie, A.
In Christie, A. The mousetrap and other plays **822**

Go climb a tree if you don't like it. Sholem Aleichem
In Halkin, H. and Sholem Aleichem. Tevye the dairyman and The railroad stories
S C

Go tell it on the mountain. Baldwin, J. **Fic**

God
See/See also pages in the following book(s):
Sagan, C. Broca's brain **500**

The **God** effect. Clegg, B. **530.1**

God lies in the details. Allegra, D.
In Not the only one; lesbian and gay fiction for teens **S C**

The **god** of dark laughter. Chabon, M.
In Feeling very strange; the Slipstream anthology **S C**

The **god** of small things. Roy, A. **Fic**

The **god** of St. James and Vine. Adoff, J.
In Twice told; original stories inspired by original art **S C**

God rest you merry, gentlemen. Hemingway, E.
In Hemingway, E. The complete short stories of Ernest Hemingway; the Finca Vigía edition p298-301 **S C**

God sends Sunday [excerpt] Bontemps, A. W.
In The Portable Harlem Renaissance reader p667-74 **810.8**

Goddesses *See* Gods and goddesses

Godless. Hautman, P. **Fic**

Godmother. Mathis, S. B.
In Join in; multiethnic short stories by outstanding writers for young adults p173-99 **S C**

Gods and goddesses
See also Religions names of individual gods and goddesses
Patel, S. The little book of Hindu deities **704.9**
See/See also pages in the following book(s):
Hamilton, E. Mythology **292**

God's favorite. Simon, N.
In Simon, N. The collected plays of Neil Simon **812**

God's fool: the life and times of Francis of Assisi. Green, J. **92**

Gods, graves, and scholars. Ceram, C. W.
930.1

God's name in vain. Carter, S. L. **322**

God's wrath. Malamud, B.
In Malamud, B. The complete stories **S C**

Godwin, Gail, 1937-
Dream children
In American short story masterpieces **S C**

Goethals, George R.
(ed) Encyclopedia of leadership. See Encyclopedia of leadership **658.4**

Goetzmann, William H.
The atlas of North American exploration
911

Goff, Robert
The essential Salvador Dali **759.6**

Gogh, Vincent van, 1853-1890
About
Bernard, B. Van Gogh **759.9492**
Greenberg, J. Vincent Van Gogh **92**
Schaffner, I. The essential Vincent van Gogh
759.9492

Gogol´, Nikolaĭ Vasil´evich, 1809-1852
The overcoat
In The Portable nineteenth-century Russian reader p202-32 **891.7**

Goin' a buffalo. Bullins, E.
In Black theatre USA; plays by African Americans, 1847 to today **812.008**

Going, K. L.
Fat kid rules the world **Fic**
Saint Iggy **Fic**

Going after Cacciato. O'Brien, T. **Fic**

Going for the Orange Julius. Goldberg, M.
In Gotham Writers' Workshop fiction gallery; exceptional short stories selected by New York's acclaimed creative writing school
S C

Going home. Trevor, W.
In The Oxford book of short stories p520-38
S C

Going live. Seib, P. M. **070.1**

Going to Naples. Welty, E.
In Welty, E. The collected stories of Eudora Welty p567-600 **S C**

Going to school. McNickle, D.
In Coming of age in America; a multicultural anthology p154-65 **S C**

Golay, Michael, 1951-
Spanish-American War **973.8**
(jt. auth) Fargnoli, A. N. William Faulkner A to Z **813.009**

Gold, Alison Leslie
(jt. auth) Gies, M. Anne Frank remembered
940.53

Gold, Susan Dudley, 1949-
Korematsu v. United States **323.1**

Gold. Budhos, M. T.
In Face relations; 11 stories about seeing beyond color **S C**

Golub, Leon
Nearest star **523.7**

Golway, Terry, 1955-
(jt. auth) Dallek, R. Let every nation know [biography of John F. Kennedy] **92**

Gombrich, E. H. (Ernst Hans), 1909-2001
The story of art **709**

Gombrich, Ernst Hans *See* Gombrich, E. H. (Ernst Hans), 1909-2001

Gomez, Magdalena, 1954-
The daydreamer
In Working days: stories about teenagers and work **S C**

Goncharov, Ivan Aleksandrovich, 1812-1891
Oblomov's dream
In The Portable nineteenth-century Russian reader p295-333 **891.7**

Gone. Crowley, J.
In The Locus awards; thirty years of the best in science fiction and fantasy **S C**

Gone a-whaling. Murphy, J. **639.2**

Gone girl. Macdonald, R.
In The Best American mystery stories of the century p375-404 **S C**

Gonick, Larry
The cartoon history of the modern world [part 1] **909.08**

Gonzales, Doreen
The Manhattan Project and the atomic bomb in American history **623.4**

González, Federico Schaffler *See* Schaffler González, Federico, 1959-

Gonzalez, Genaro, 1949-
Un hijo del sol
In Growing up Latino; memoirs and stories p38-46 **810.8**

Gonzalez, Gloria
Viva New Jersey
In Join in; multiethnic short stories by outstanding writers for young adults p51-60 **S C**

Gonzalez, Henry B., 1916-2000
See/See also pages in the following book(s):
Profiles in courage for our time **920**

Gonzalez, Juan
Harvest of empire **305.8**

González, Kathleen Ann
That was living
In Latina: women's voices from the borderlands p97-106 **810.8**

González, Rigoberto, 1970-
Butterfly boy **92**

Gonzalez, Gabriela *See* Triana, Gaby

Gooch, Anthony
(ed) Cassell's Spanish-English, English-Spanish dictionary. See Cassell's Spanish-English, English-Spanish dictionary **463**

Good and evil
Adler, M. J. Six great ideas **111**
Fiction
Brooks, T. Armageddon's children **Fic**
Jinks, C. Evil genius **Fic**

Good boys deserve favors. Gaiman, N.
In Gaiman, N. Fragile things; short fictions and wonders **S C**

Good-by, Jack. London, J.
In London, J. The portable Jack London p178-86 **818**

Good country people. O'Connor, F.
In O'Connor, F. Collected works p263-84 **S C**
In O'Connor, F. The complete stories p271-91 **S C**

The **good** doctor. Simon, N.
In Simon, N. The collected plays of Neil Simon **812**

A **good** dog. Katz, J. **636.7**

The **good** earth. Buck, P. S. **Fic**

Good form. O'Brien, T.
In O'Brien, T. The things they carried; a work of fiction **S C**

A **good** game. Carter, A. R.
In Carter, A. R. Love, football, and other contact sports **S C**

The **good** good pig. Montgomery, S. **636.4**

Good grief. Bradbury, R.
In Who do you think you are?; stories of friends and enemies p3-13 **S C**

Good grooming *See* Personal grooming

The **good** lion. Hemingway, E.
In Hemingway, E. The complete short stories of Ernest Hemingway; the Finca Vigía edition p482-84 **S C**

Good man, bad man. Weidman, J.
In The Best American mystery stories of the century p508-22 **S C**

A **good** man is hard to find. O'Connor, F.
In American short story masterpieces **S C**
In O'Connor, F. Collected works p137-53 **S C**
In O'Connor, F. The complete stories p117-33 **S C**

A **good** man is hard to find, and other stories. O'Connor, F.
In O'Connor, F. Collected works p133-327 **S C**

A **good** man's miracles. Hawthorne, N.
In Hawthorne, N. Tales and sketches, including Twice-told tales, Mosses from an old manse, and The snow-image; A wonder book for girls and boys; Tanglewood tales for girls and boys, being a second Wonder book p868-72 **S C**

Good morning, America. Sandburg, C.
In Sandburg, C. The complete poems of Carl Sandburg p315-435 **811**

The **good** negress. Verdelle, A. J. **Fic**

Good news from the Vatican. Silverberg, R.
In The Norton book of science fiction; North American science fiction, 1960-1990 p242-49 **S C**

Good night! Good night!. Westlake, D. E.
In Alfred Hitchcock's mystery magazine presents fifty years of crime and suspense **S C**

Gorini, Catherine A.
The Facts on File geometry handbook   **516**

Gorky, Maksim, 1868-1936
Recollections of Leo Tolstoy
In The portable twentieth-century Russian
reader   **891.7**
Twenty-six men and one girl
In The Portable nineteenth-century Russian
reader p618-29   **891.7**

Gorky, Maxim *See* Gorky, Maksim, 1868-1936

Gorman, Edward
Wolf moon
In A Century of great Western stories
S C

Gorman, Michael, 1941-
The concise AACR2   **025.3**

Gorman, Michele
Getting graphic!   **741.5**
(jt. auth) Jones, P. Connecting young adults and
libraries   **027.62**

Gorman, Robert F.
Great debates at the United Nations   **341.23**

Gormley, Michael Sean, 1960-
(jt. auth) McGuire, M. The 100 greatest baseball
players of the 20th century ranked
796.357

Gorodischer, Angélica
The violet's embryos
In Cosmos latinos; an anthology of science
fiction from Latin America and Spain
S C

Gorog, Judith, 1938-
Those three wishes
In Read all about it!; great read-aloud stories,
poems, and newspaper pieces for
preteens and teens p475-78   **808.8**

The **gospel** according to Krenzwinkle. Klass, D.
In Ultimate sports; short stories by outstand-
ing writers for young adults p274-98
S C

The **Gospel** according to Mark. Borges, J. L.
In The Oxford book of gothic tales p478-82
S C

Gospel music
We'll understand it better by and by   **782.25**

Goss, Theodora
The rose in twelve petals
In Feeling very strange; the Slipstream anthol-
ogy   **S C**
The wings of Meister Wilhelm
In The Year's best science fiction and fantasy
for teens: first annual collection   **S C**

Gossamer. Baxter, S.
In The Hard SF renaissance   **S C**

Got a letter from Jimmy. Jackson, S.
In Jackson, S. The lottery; or, The adventures
of James Harris   **S C**

Gotama Siddhatta *See* Gautama Buddha

Gotham Writers' Workshop fiction gallery
S C

Gothic!   **S C**

Gothic revival literature
Snodgrass, M. E. Encyclopedia of Gothic literature   **809**

Gothic romances
The Oxford book of gothic tales   **S C**

Gothic sports, Vol. 1. Hage, A.   **741.5**

Gotlieb, Phyllis, 1926-
Tauf Aleph
In The Norton book of science fiction; North
American science fiction, 1960-1990
p427-44   **S C**

Goto, Hiromi
Foxwife
In The Faery Reel; tales from the Twilight
Realm   **S C**

Gott, J. Richard, 1947-
Time travel in Einstein's universe   **530.1**

Gottesman, Greg
College survival   **378**

Gottesman, Jane
Game face. See Game face   **796**

Gottfried, Ted, 1928-
Children of the slaughter   **940.53**
Deniers of the Holocaust   **940.53**
Displaced persons   **940.53**
The facts about alcohol   **362.292**
The facts about marijuana   **362.29**
The fight for peace   **303.6**
Heroes of the Holocaust   **940.53**
Homeland security versus constitutional rights
363.32
The road to Communism   **947**

Gottlieb, Lori
Stick figure   **92**

Gottlieb, Robert Adams, 1931-
George Balanchine: the ballet maker   **92**

Gould, Lewis L.
The modern American presidency   **973.9**

Gould, Stephen Jay, 1941-2002
Dinosaur in a haystack   **508**
I have landed   **578**
The richness of life   **508**

Gould, Steven, 1955-
Peaches for Mad Molly
In New skies: an anthology of today's science
fiction   **S C**

Gould, William, 1947-
(ed) The Facts on File dictionary of astronomy.
See The Facts on File dictionary of astronomy   **520.3**

Gourdine, Traci L.
(ed) Night is gone, day is still coming. See
Night is gone, day is still coming   **808.8**

Gourevitch, Philip
We wish to inform you that tomorrow we will
be killed with our families   **967.571**

Gourley, Robbin
(jt. auth) Dragonwagon, C. Passionate vegetarian
641.5

Gouveia, Georgette
The essential Mary Cassatt   **759.13**

Gove, Philip Babcock, 1902-1972
(ed) Webster's third new international dictionary of the English language, unabridged. See Webster's third new international dictionary of the English language, unabridged **423**

Government See Political science

Government by magic spell. Herzi, S. H.-D.
In The Heinemann book of contemporary African short stories p94-99 **S C**

Government housing See Public housing

Government information
Directories
Hernon, P. U.S. government on the Web **025.04**
The United States government Internet manual 2007 **025.04**

Governments of the world **320.3**

Gowing, Sir Lawrence, 1918-1991
(ed) Biographical encyclopedia of artists. See Biographical encyclopedia of artists **920.003**
(ed) Facts on File encyclopedia of art. See Facts on File encyclopedia of art **703**

Goyen, William
Ghost and flesh, water and dirt
In The Literary ghost; great contemporary ghost stories p304-13 **S C**
A shape of light
In Nightshade: 20th century ghost stories p191-216 **S C**

Grace. Joyce, J.
In Joyce, J. Dubliners **S C**
In The Oxford book of short stories p255-74 **S C**

Grace. Sears, V.
In Spider Woman's granddaughters; traditional tales and contemporary writing by Native American women **S C**

A **gracious** rain. Tilghman, C.
In Nightshade: 20th century ghost stories p388-04 **S C**

Grady, Denise
Deadly invaders **614.4**
The New York Times guide to alternative health. See The New York Times guide to alternative health **615.5**

Grady, Sean M., 1965-
Biohazards **614.5**
(jt. auth) Billings, C. W. Supercomputers **004**
(jt. auth) Facklam, M. Modern medicines **615**

Graff Hysell, Shannon
(ed) American reference books annual 2007 edition. See American reference books annual 2007 edition **011**
(ed) Recommended reference books for small and medium-sized libraries and media centers. See Recommended reference books for small and medium-sized libraries and media centers **011**

Graffiti
Ganz, N. Graffiti world **751**

Graffiti world. Ganz, N. **751**

Grafton, Sue
The Parker shotgun
In The Best American mystery stories of the century p649-64 **S C**

Graham, Billy, 1918-
See/See also pages in the following book(s):
Aikman, D. Great souls **920**

Graham, Martha
About
Freedman, R. Martha Graham, a dancer's life **92**
See/See also pages in the following book(s):
Ford, C. T. Legends of American dance and choreography **920**

Graham, Peter W., 1951-
Lord Byron **821.009**
(ed) Darwin, C. The portable Darwin **576.8**

Graham, Rosemary
Thou shalt not dump the skater dude and other commandments I have broken **Fic**

Graham, Tom See Lewis, Sinclair, 1885-1951

Graham, William Franklin See Graham, Billy, 1918-

Graham-Dixon, Andrew
Renaissance **709.02**

Grail
Fiction
Pyle, H. The story of the Grail and the passing of Arthur **398.2**
The **grail** bird. Gallagher, T. **598**
Grail prince. McKenzie, N. **Fic**

Grambo, Rebecca L., 1963-
Wolf: legend, enemy, icon **599.77**

Gramma. King, S.
In King, S. Skeleton crew **S C**

Grammar
See also English language—Grammar

Grand Canyon (Ariz.)
Pyne, S. J. How the Canyon became Grand **979.1**

Grand Central Park. Sherman, D.
In The Green Man: tales from the mythic forest p21-42 **808.8**

The **Grand** Inquisitor. Dostoyevsky, F.
In The Portable nineteenth-century Russian reader p413-33 **891.7**

Grand mothers: poems, reminiscences, and short stories about the keepers of our traditions **810.8**

Grand slam. Chávez, D.
In Latina: women's voices from the borderlands p135-40 **810.8**

Grand Theft Galaxy, Vol. 1. Hale, T. R. **741.5**

Grand vampire. See Sfar, J. Vampire loves **741.5**

Grandfathers
Fiction
Crowe, C. Mississippi trial, 1955 **Fic**
Hemphill, H. Long gone daddy **Fic**
Peet, M. Tamar **Fic**
Smelcer, J. E. The trap **Fic**

Grandin, Temple
Animals in translation **591.5**

Grandmothers
Grand mothers: poems, reminiscences, and short stories about the keepers of our traditions **810.8**

Fiction
Larbalestier, J. Magic or madness **Fic**
Newbery, L. Sisterland **Fic**

Grandparents

Fiction
Ehrenberg, P. Ethan, suspended **Fic**
Grandpa's "Chicaudies". Gardaphé, F. L.
In Growing up ethnic in America; contemporary fiction about learning to be American **S C**

Grandpré, Mary, 1954-
(il) Rowling, J. K. Harry Potter and the Sorcerer's Stone **Fic**

Granfield, Linda
I remember Korea **951.9**

Granja Carneiro, André *See* Carneiro, André, 1922-

Grant, Edward, 1926-
Science and religion, 400 B.C. to A.D. 1550 **261.5**

Grant, Gordon
Canoeing **797.1**

Grant, Mark
Roman cookery **641.5**

Grant, Michael, 1914-2004
Greek and Latin authors, 800 B.C.-A.D. 1000 **920.003**

Grant, R. G. (Reg G.)
Flight: 100 years of aviation **629.13**

Grant, Reg G. *See* Grant, R. G. (Reg G.)

Grant, Tina
(ed) Ethics: opposing viewpoints. See Ethics: opposing viewpoints **170**

Grant, Ulysses S. (Ulysses Simpson), 1822-1885
About
Rice, E. Ulysses S. Grant: defender of the Union **92**
See/See also pages in the following book(s):
Marrin, A. Commander in Chief Abraham Lincoln and the Civil War **973.7**
McPherson, J. M. Drawn with the sword **973.7**

Grants for libraries. Gerding, S. K. **025.1**

Grants-in-aid
Gerding, S. K. Grants for libraries **025.1**

Grapes, Bryan J.
(ed) 1980-2000: the twentieth century. See 1980-2000: the twentieth century **909.82**
(ed) Sexually transmitted diseases. See Sexually transmitted diseases [Current controversies] **616.95**

The **grapes** of wrath. Steinbeck, J. **Fic**
also in Steinbeck, J. The grapes of wrath and other writings, 1936-1941 **818**

The **grapes** of wrath and other writings, 1936-1941. Steinbeck, J. **818**

Graphic arts
Bancroft, T. Creating characters with personality **741.6**

Graphic Classics Volume Eleven: O. Henry **741.5**

Graphic fiction *See* Graphic novels

Graphic novels
See also Adventure graphic novels; Autobiographical graphic novels; Biographical graphic novels; Fantasy graphic novels; Horror graphic novels; Humorous graphic novels; Manga; Mystery graphic novels; Romance graphic novels; Science fiction graphic novels; Superhero graphic novels; Supernatural graphic novels
Abouet, M. Aya **741.5**
Anderson, H. C. King: a comic book biography **92**
Appignanesi, R. Manga Shakespeare: Romeo and Juliet **822.3**
Asamiya, K. Batman: child of dreams **741.5**
Azuma, K. Azumanga Daioh, Vol. 1 **741.5**
B., David. Epileptic **616.8**
Baker, K. Nat Turner Encore Edition Vol. 1 **92**
Barry, L. One hundred demons **741.5**
Batman in the eighties **741.5**
Batman in the forties **741.5**
Beatty, S. Batgirl: year one **741.5**
Bogaert, H. M. v. d. Journey into Mohawk Country **973.2**
Busiek, K. Superman: secret identity **741.5**
Castellucci, C. The Plain Janes **741.5**
Cover, A. B. Macbeth **822.3**
Croci, P. Auschwitz **940.53**
Daly, P. Athena Voltaire **741.5**
Dead High yearbook **741.5**
Delisle, G. Pyongyang: a journey in North Korea **951.93**
DeMatteis, J. M. Brooklyn dreams **741.5**
Drooker, E. Blood song **741.5**
Eldred, T. Grease monkey **741.5**
Fies, B. Mom's cancer **616.99**
Flight v2 **741.5**
Flight v3 **741.5**
Friedman, A. Breaking up **741.5**
Fujii, M. Gals! Vol. 1 **741.5**
Gaiman, N. Marvel 1602 **741.5**
Gallagher, F. Megatokyo v2 **741.5**
Geary, R. The murder of Abraham Lincoln **973.7**
Goldsmith, F. Graphic novels now **025.2**
Gonick, L. The cartoon history of the modern world [part 1] **909.08**
Graphic Classics Volume Eleven: O. Henry **741.5**
Hale, T. R. Grand Theft Galaxy, Vol. 1 **741.5**
Helfer, A. Malcolm X **92**
Hickman, T. Common Grounds: Baker's dozen **741.5**
Hinds, G. Beowulf **741.5**
Hornschemeier, P. Mother, come home **741.5**
Ikuta, T. Project X Challengers: Seven Eleven **658.8**

Graves, Douglas R.
Drawing portraits   **743**

Graves, Mark A., 1963-
(ed) Encyclopedia of American war literature.
See Encyclopedia of American war literature
    810.9

Graves, Robert, 1895-1985
The Greek myths   **292**
I, Claudius   **Fic**

Gravett, Paul
Graphic novels   **741.5**

Graveyard shift. King, S.
In King, S. Night shift   **S C**

Graveyards of the Pacific. Ballard, R. D.
    940.54

Gravitation
See/See also pages in the following book(s):
Feynman, R. P. Six easy pieces   **530**

Gray, Dianne E.
Together apart   **Fic**

Gray, Edward G., 1964-
Colonial America: a history in documents
    973.2

Gray, Farrah
Reallionaire   **332.024**

Gray, Jeffrey, 1944-
(ed) The Greenwood encyclopedia of American
poets and poetry. See The Greenwood encyclopedia of American poets and poetry
    811.009

The **gray** boy's work. Anderson, M. T.
In The restless dead; ten original stories of
the supernatural   **S C**

The **gray** champion. Hawthorne, N.
In Hawthorne, N. Tales and sketches, including Twice-told tales, Mosses from an old
manse, and The snow-image; A wonder
book for girls and boys; Tanglewood
tales for girls and boys, being a second
Wonder book p236-43   **S C**

Gray matter. King, S.
In King, S. Night shift   **S C**

Gray matter [series]
Hains, B. C. Pain   **616**
Hudmon, A. Learning and memory   **612.8**
Morgan, M. The midbrain   **612.8**
Rosen, M. Meditation and hypnosis   **154.7**

Gray noise. Rojo, P.
In Cosmos latinos; an anthology of science
fiction from Latin America and Spain
    S C

Graydon, Shari
In your face   **391**

Gray's anatomy   **611**

Grayson, Gabriel
Talking with your hands, listening with your
eyes   **419**

Grealy, Lucy, 1963-2002
About
Patchett, A. Truth & beauty [biography of Lucy
Grealy]   **92**

Grease monkey. Eldred, T.   **741.5**

Greasy Lake. Boyle, T. C.
In Boyle, T. C. The Human Fly and other
stories   **S C**

The **great** age of Greek literature. See Hamilton,
E. The Greek way   **880.9**

The **great** American history fact-finder.
Cornelison, P.   **973.03**

A **great** and terrible beauty. Bray, L.   **Fic**

Great-aunts *See* Aunts

Great Barrier Reef (Australia)
Love, R. Reefscape   **508**

Great books of the Western world
Adler, M. J. How to think about the great ideas
    080

Great Britain
Antiquities
Burl, A. The stone circles of Britain, Ireland and
Brittany   **936.1**
Armed forces
See also Great Britain. Army
Civilization
Backgrounds to English literature   **820.9**
Mitchell, S. Daily life in Victorian England
    941.081
See/See also pages in the following book(s):
Emerson, R. W. The portable Emerson   **818**
Colonies
James, L. The rise and fall of the British Empire
    909
Colonies—America
See/See also pages in the following book(s):
Tuchman, B. W. The march of folly   **909.08**
Description and travel
Raymo, C. Walking zero   **526**
Fiction
Almond, D. Kit's wilderness   **Fic**
Austen, J. Persuasion   **Fic**
Austen, J. Pride and prejudice   **Fic**
Austen, J. Sense and sensibility   **Fic**
Bray, L. A great and terrible beauty   **Fic**
Brontë, C. Jane Eyre   **Fic**
Brontë, E. Wuthering Heights   **Fic**
Brooks, K. Kissing the rain   **Fic**
Brooks, K. Lucas   **Fic**
Brooks, K. The road of the dead   **Fic**
Burgess, M. Smack   **Fic**
Dickens, C. David Copperfield   **Fic**
Dickens, C. Great expectations   **Fic**
Dickens, C. Oliver Twist   **Fic**
Doyle, Sir A. C. The hound of the Baskervilles
    Fic
Haddon, M. The curious incident of the dog in
the night-time   **Fic**
Hardy, T. The return of the native   **Fic**
Hardy, T. Tess of the D'Urbervilles   **Fic**
King, L. R. The beekeeper's apprentice, or, On
the segregation of the queen   **Fic**
Lawrence, D. H. Sons and lovers   **Fic**
Lawrence, M. A crack in the line   **Fic**
Manning, S. Guitar girl   **Fic**
Minchin, A. The beat goes on   **Fic**
Mitchell, D. Black swan green   **Fic**
Moloney, J. Black taxi   **Fic**
Morpurgo, M. Private Peaceful   **Fic**
Newbery, L. Sisterland   **Fic**

Great Depression, 1929-1939—*Continued*
McElvaine, R. S. The Depression and New Deal
    973.91
Terkel, S. Hard times   **973.91**
Watkins, T. H. The hungry years   **973.91**
See/See also pages in the following book(s):
Lifetimes: the Great War to the stock market
    crash: American history through biography
    and primary documents   **920**
Encyclopedias
Encyclopedia of the Great Depression
    973.91
Fiction
Kennedy, W. Ironweed   **Fic**
Great disasters, reforms and ramifications [series]
DeAngelis, G. The Triangle Shirtwaist Company
    fire of 1911   **974.7**
Great discoveries [series]
Quammen, D. The reluctant Mr. Darwin   **92**
Great empires of the past [series]
Burgan, M. Empire of the Mongols   **951**
Conrad, D. C. Empires of medieval West Africa
    966
Skelton, D. Empire of Alexander the Great
    930
Somervill, B. A. Empire of the Inca   **985**
Williams, J. K. Empire of ancient Greece
    938
Great events   **909.82**
Great events from history, The 17th century,
    1601-1700   **909**
Great events from history, The 18th century,
    1701-1800   **909.7**
Great events from history, The 19th century,
    1801-1900   **909.81**
Great events from history, The ancient world, pre-
    history-476 C.E.   **930**
Great events from history, The Middle Ages, 477-
    1453   **909.07**
Great events from history, The Renaissance &
    early modern era, 1454-1600   **909**
Great expectations. Dickens, C.   **Fic**
Great feuds in history. Evans, C.   **909**
Great feuds in medicine. Hellman, H.   **610.9**
The **great** fire. Murphy, J.   **977.3**
The **great** Gatsby. Fitzgerald, F. S.   **Fic**
The **great** goodbye. Wilson, R. C.
    In New skies: an anthology of today's science
    fiction   **S C**
Great Hispanic heritage [series]
Hasday, J. L. Ellen Ochoa   **92**
McNeese, T. Pablo Picasso   **92**
Sterngass, J. José Martí   **92**
Great horned owl *See* Owls
Great ideas in physics. Lightman, A. P.   **530**
Great lives from history, The 17th century, 1601-
    1700   **920.003**
Great lives from history, The 18th century, 1701-
    1800   **920.003**
Great lives from history, The 19th century, 1801-
    1900   **920.003**

Great lives from history, The ancient world, pre-
    history-476 C.E   **920.003**
Great lives from history, the Middle Ages, 477-
    1453   **920.003**
Great lives from history, the Renaissance & early
    modern era, 1454-1600   **920.003**
Great medical discoveries   **610.9**
Great monologues for young actors   **812.008**
The **great** mortality. Kelly, J.   **614.5**
Great news from the mainland. Hemingway, E.
    In Hemingway, E. The complete short stories
    of Ernest Hemingway; the Finca Vigía
    edition p602-04   **S C**
Great physicists. Cropper, W. H.   **920**
Great Plains
Encyclopedias
Encyclopedia of the Great Plains   **978.03**
Great projects. Tobin, J.   **620**
Great scenes from minority playwrights
    812.008
Great short works of Leo Tolstoy. Tolstoy, L.,
    graf   **S C**
Great souls. Aikman, D.   **920**
Great speeches in history series
The Arab-Israeli conflict   **956.04**
Civil rights   **323.1**
The **great** stone face. Hawthorne, N.
    In Hawthorne, N. Tales and sketches, includ-
    ing Twice-told tales, Mosses from an old
    manse, and The snow-image; A wonder
    book for girls and boys; Tanglewood
    tales for girls and boys, being a second
    Wonder book p1068-86   **S C**
Great thinkers of the Western world   **190**
Great treasury of Western thought   **080**
Great trials of the 20th century [series]
Sorensen, L. The Scottsboro Boys Trial   **345**
Great Wall of China
Slavicek, L. C. The Great Wall of China
    951
Great wall of Mars. Reynolds, A.
    In The Hard SF renaissance   **S C**
Great world trials   **347**
Great writers in 90 minutes [series]
Strathern, P. Hemingway in 90 minutes   **92**
Strathern, P. Poe in 90 minutes   **92**
The **greatest** asset. Asimov, I.
    In Asimov, I. The complete stories p403-08
    S C
The **greatest** stories never told. Beyer, R.   **904**
The **Grecian** Urn. Kinsella, W. P.
    In Kinsella, W. P. Shoeless Joe Jackson
    comes to Iowa: stories   **S C**
Greco, Stephen
Forensics
    In Not the only one; lesbian and gay fiction
    for teens   **S C**
Greece
Biography
Baker, R. F. Ancient Greeks   **938**

Greece—*Continued*
Civilization
Adkins, L. Handbook to life in ancient Greece
    938
Baker, R. F. Ancient Greeks   **938**
Cahill, T. Sailing the wine-dark sea   **909**
Classical Greek civilization, 800-323 B.C.E
    938
Connolly, P. The ancient city   **937**
Hamilton, E. The Greek way   **880.9**
Williams, J. K. Empire of ancient Greece
    938
See/See also pages in the following book(s):
Russell, B. A history of Western philosophy
    109
Fiction
Bradshaw, G. The sand-reckoner   **Fic**
Renault, M. Fire from heaven   **Fic**
Renault, M. The king must die   **Fic**
History
Arrian. Alexander the Great   **92**
Foreman, L. Alexander the Conqueror   **92**
Skelton, D. Empire of Alexander the Great
    930
History—0-323
Williams, J. K. Empire of ancient Greece
    938
History—431-404 B.C., Peloponnesian War
Tritle, L. A. The Peloponnesian War   **938**
History—Encyclopedias
Ancient Greece   **938.003**
Sacks, D. Encyclopedia of the ancient Greek
  world   **938.003**
Religion
See/See also pages in the following book(s):
Hamilton, E. The Greek way   **880.9**
Greek and Latin authors, 800 B.C.-A.D. 1000.
  Grant, M.   **920.003**
Greek and Roman medicine. Dawson, I. **610.9**
Greek and Roman mythology A to Z. Daly, K. N.
    292

Greek drama
Collections
Four Greek plays   **882.008**
The **Greek** interpreter. Doyle, Sir A. C.
  In Doyle, Sir A. C. The complete Sherlock
  Holmes   **S C**
Greek literature
  See also Classical literature
The **Greek** myths. Graves, R.   **292**
Greek tragedy in new translations [series]
Sophocles. Antigone   **882**
Sophocles. Oedipus the King   **882**
The **Greek** way. Hamilton, E.   **880.9**
Green, Carolyn Eve, 1966-
  (ed) Meeting the other crowd. See Meeting the
  other crowd   **398.2**
Green, Hannah *See* Greenberg, Joanne, 1932-
Green, Jacob D., b. 1813
See/See also pages in the following book(s):
Slave narratives [Library of Am.]   **326**
Green, John, 1977-
An abundance of Katherines   **Fic**

The approximate cost of loving Caroline
  In Twice told; original stories inspired by
  original art   **S C**
Looking for Alaska   **Fic**
Green, Jonathon
Cassell's dictionary of slang   **427**
The encyclopedia of censorship   **363.31**
Green, Julien, 1900-1998
God's fool: the life and times of Francis of As-
  sisi   **92**
Green, Miranda J. (Miranda Jane)
The world of the Druids   **299**
Green, William Scott
  (ed) The HarperCollins dictionary of religion.
  See The HarperCollins dictionary of religion
    200.3
The **green** armchair. Ho, M.
  In First crossing; stories about teen immi-
  grants p201-24   **S C**
Green earth mother. Bei, A.
  In Chairman Mao would not be amused; fic-
  tion from today's China   **S C**
Green inheritance. Huxley, A. J.   **580**
The **Green** Man: tales from the mythic forest
    808.8
Green patches. Asimov, I.
  In Asimov, I. The complete stories p363-75
    S C
Green tea. Le Fanu, J. S.
  In The Oxford book of Irish short stories p78-
  108   **S C**
The **green** word. Ford, J.
  In The Green Man: tales from the mythic for-
  est p353-82   **808.8**
Greenbank, Anthony Hunt, 1933-
The book of survival   **613.6**
Greenberg, Arthur
A chemical history tour   **540.9**
Greenberg, Ellen
The House and Senate explained   **328.73**
Greenberg, Jan, 1942-
Andy Warhol   **92**
Runaway girl: the artist Louise Bourgeois
    92
Vincent Van Gogh   **92**
(ed) Heart to heart. See Heart to heart
    811.008
Greenberg, Joanne, 1932-
I never promised you a rose garden   **Fic**
Greenberg, Keith Elliot, 1959-
Pro wrestling   **796.8**
Greenberg, Martin Harry
  (ed) Past imperfect. See Past imperfect **S C**
Greenblatt, Miriam
War of 1812   **973.5**
Greenblatt, Stephen J. (Stephen Jay)
The Norton Shakespeare   **822.3**
Greene, Bette, 1934-
An ordinary woman
  In Sixteen: short stories by outstanding writ-
  ers for young adults p125-32   **S C**
Greene, Gloria Kaufer, 1950-
The new Jewish holiday cookbook   **641.5**

Griboedov, Aleksandr Sergeevich *See* Griboyedov, Aleksandr Sergeyevich, 1795-1829

Griboyedov, Aleksandr Sergeyevich, 1795-1829
The trouble with reason
In The Portable nineteenth-century Russian reader p35-128   **891.7**

Grice, Gordon, 1944-
The red hourglass   **591.5**

The **grief** diet. Forrest, E.
In Sixteen: stories about that sweet and bitter birthday   **S C**

The **grieving** teen. Fitzgerald, H.   **155.9**

Griffin, Adele
Amandine   **Fic**
My almost epic summer   **Fic**
Where I want to be   **Fic**

Griffin, Geoff
(ed) Are athletes good role models? See Are athletes good role models?   **306.4**
(ed) How can the poor be helped? See How can the poor be helped?   **362.5**

Griffin, Gerald, 1803-1840
The Brown Man
In The Oxford book of Irish short stories p73-77   **S C**

Griffin, John Howard, 1920-1980
Black like me   **305.8**

Griffin, Lynne
The Truth about family life. See The Truth about family life   **306.8**

Griffin, Peni R.
Vision quest
In Make me over; 11 stories of transformation   **S C**

Griffin, Robert, 1951-
(ed) The Folklore of world holidays. See The Folklore of world holidays   **394.26**

Griffin's egg. Swanwick, M.
In The Hard SF renaissance   **S C**

Griffith, Tom
(tr) Plato. The republic   **888**

Griffiths, Rodney
(il) Gamble, C. Leopards   **599.75**

Griffiths, Trevor R., 1949-
The Ivan R. Dee guide to plays and playwrights   **809.2**

Grimes, Nikki
Bronx masquerade   **Fic**
Dark sons   **Fic**
The throwaway: a suite
In Necessary noise: stories about our families as they really are p71-78   **S C**

Grimké, Angelina Emily, 1805-1879
Rachel
In Black theatre USA; plays by African Americans, 1847 to today   **812.008**

Grimké, Angelina Weld, 1880-1958
The closing door [excerpt]
In The Portable Harlem Renaissance reader p486-500   **810.8**

Grimly, Gris
(il) Poe, E. A. Edgar Allan Poe's tales of mystery and madness   **S C**

The **grind** of an axe. Taylor, T.
In Night terrors; stories of shadow and substance   **S C**

Grindle, Lucretia
The nightspinners   **Fic**

Grinning man. Card, O. S.
In Legends: short novels by the masters of modern fantasy p215-53   **S C**

Grisham, John
The client   **Fic**
The firm   **Fic**

Griswold del Castillo, Richard
César Chávez   **92**

Gritzner, Charles F.
Deserts   **577.5**
Latin America   **980**
Polar regions   **577.5**

The **grizzly** almanac. Busch, R.   **599.78**

Grizzly bear
Busch, R. The grizzly almanac   **599.78**
Turbak, G. Grizzly bears   **599.78**

Grobman, Alex
(jt. auth) Shermer, M. Denying history   **940.53**

Grob's basic electronics. Schultz, M. E.   **621.381**

The **grocery** store. Malamud, B.
In Malamud, B. The complete stories   **S C**

Gronniosaw, James Albert Ukawsaw
See/See also pages in the following book(s):
Slave narratives [Library of Am.]   **326**

Grooming, Personal *See* Personal grooming

Gross, John J.
(ed) The New Oxford book of literary anecdotes. See The New Oxford book of literary anecdotes   **828**

Gross, Melissa
(jt. auth) Dresang, E. T. Dynamic youth services through outcome-based planning and evaluation   **025.1**

Gross, Michael, 1963-
Life on the edge   **578.4**

Grossman, David
Death as way of life   **956.94**

Grossman, Edith
(jt. auth) Vargas Llosa, M. The Feast of the Goat   **Fic**

Grossman, Elizabeth, 1957-
High tech trash   **363.7**

Grossman, James R.
A chance to make good
In The Young Oxford history of African Americans   **305.8**

Grossman, Mark
World military leaders   **920.003**

Grosvenor, Mary B.
(jt. auth) Smolin, L. A. Basic nutrition   **613.2**
(jt. auth) Smolin, L. A. Nutrition and weight management   **613.2**

Guys write for Guys Read   **810.8**
Gwendolyn Brooks [critical essays]   **811.009**
Gymnastics
    Ryan, J. Little girls in pretty boxes   **796.44**
Gynecology *See* Women—Health and hygiene
Gypsies
    Lewy, G. The Nazi persecution of the gypsies
        940.53

                Fiction
    Brooks, K. The road of the dead   **Fic**
The **gypsy's** violin. Giles, G.
    In What a song can do; 12 riffs on the power
        of music   **S C**

H

Haaga, John, 1953-
    (ed) The American people. *See* The American
    people   **304.6**
Haas, Jessie
    Hoofprints: horse poems   **811**
Haas, Peter J. (Peter Jerome)
    (ed) Human rights and the world's major reli-
    gions. *See* Human rights and the world's ma-
    jor religions   **201**
Haase, Ynez D.
    (jt. auth) Beck, W. A. Historical atlas of the
    American West   **911**
Habitat (Ecology)
        See also types of ecology, e.g. Desert ecol-
    ogy; Marine ecology
    Fothergill, A. Planet Earth   **508**
Habitat for Humanity. Lubar, D.
    In Twice told; original stories inspired by
        original art   **S C**
Hacienda. Porter, K. A.
    In Porter, K. A. The collected stories of Kath-
    erine Anne Porter   **S C**
Hackett, Albert, 1900-1995
    (jt. auth) Goodrich, F. The diary of Anne Frank
        812
Haddix, Margaret Peterson, 1964-
    Butterflies
    In Make me over; 11 stories of transformation
        S C
    Essie and Clem
    In Twice told; original stories inspired by
        original art   **S C**
    Leaving Fishers   **Fic**
    My people
    In Destination unexpected: short stories
        S C
Haddon, Mark
    The curious incident of the dog in the night-
    time   **Fic**
Hadji Murád. Tolstoy, L., graf
    In Tolstoy, L., graf. Great short works of Leo
    Tolstoy p547-668   **S C**
Haerens, Margaret
    (ed) Illegal immigration: opposing viewpoints.
    See Illegal immigration: opposing viewpoints
        325.73

    (ed) Sexually transmitted diseases: opposing
    viewpoints. *See* Sexually transmitted diseases:
    opposing viewpoints   **616.95**
Haesly, Richard, 1969-
    (ed) Women's suffrage. *See* Women's suffrage
        324.6
Hafner, Katie
    Where wizards stay up late   **004**
Hage, Anika
    Gothic sports, Vol. 1   **741.5**
Hager, Alan
    (ed) Encyclopedia of British writers, 16th-18th
    centuries. *See* Encyclopedia of British writers,
    16th-18th centuries   **820.9**
Hager, Thomas
    The demon under the microscope   **615**
Hahn, David
                About
    Silverstein, K. The radioactive boy scout [biog-
    raphy of David Hahn]   **92**
Haigh, Jane G.
    (jt. auth) Murphy, C. R. Gold rush women
        971.9
Haiku
    Higginson, W. J. The haiku handbook   **808.1**
    One man's moon   **895.6**
Haiku. Wright, R.   **811**
The **haiku** handbook. Higginson, W. J.   **808.1**
Haine, W. Scott
    Culture and customs of France   **944**
Haines, Tim
    The complete guide to prehistoric life   **560**
Hains, Bryan C.
    Pain   **616**
Hair. Faulkner, W.
    In Faulkner, W. Collected stories of William
    Faulkner p131-48   **S C**
Haircut. Lardner, R.
    In The Best American mystery stories of the
    century p133-43   **S C**
The **hairless** Mexican. Maugham, W. S.
    In Maugham, W. S. Collected short stories
        S C
Haiti
    Galembo, P. Vodou   **299.6**
                Fiction
    Danticat, E. Krik? Krak!   **S C**
    Placide, J. Fresh girl   **Fic**
Haitian Americans
                Fiction
    Danticat, E. Krik? Krak!   **S C**
    Placide, J. Fresh girl   **Fic**
    Vaught, S. Stormwitch   **Fic**
Haitian-Dominican Conflict, 1937 *See* Domini-
    can-Haitian Conflict, 1937
Hakakian, Roya
    Journey from the land of no   **92**
Hakim, Joy
    The story of science: Aristotle leads the way
        509
    The story of science: Newton at the center
        509

Hallucinogenic drugs *See* Hallucinogens

Hallucinogenic plants *See* Hallucinogens

Hallucinogens

    See also Ecstasy (Drug)

  Hallucinogens   **615**

  LeVert, S. The facts about LSD and other hallu-
    cinogens   **362.29**

  Mehling, R. Hallucinogens   **615**

Hallucinogens   **615**

Hallwas, John E.

  (jt. auth) Masters, E. L. Spoon River anthology
    811

Halo. Schroeder, K.

  In The Hard SF renaissance   **S C**

Halpern, Sue M.

  Four wings and a prayer   **595.7**

Halpin, Brendan

  Donorboy   **Fic**

Halpin, Mikki

  It's your world—if you don't like it, change it
    361.2

Halsted, Deborah D.

  Disaster planning   **025.8**

Hamas

  Rosaler, M. Hamas: Palestinian terrorists
    956.94

Hamberger, Lars

  (jt. auth) Nilsson, L. A child is born   **612.6**

Hambly, Barbara

  A free man of color   **Fic**

  See/See also pages in the following book(s):

  MacRae, C. D. Presenting young adult fantasy
    fiction   **813.009**

Hamill, Pete

  Piecework   **814**

  Snow in August   **Fic**

Hamilton, Alexander, 1757-1804

  See/See also pages in the following book(s):

  Ellis, J. J. Founding brothers   **973.4**

Hamilton, Alice

  See/See also pages in the following book(s):

  Zach, K. K. Hidden from history   **920**

Hamilton, Clive *See* Lewis, C. S. (Clive Staples),
  1898-1963

Hamilton, Donald, 1916-

  The guns of William Longley

  In A Century of great Western stories
    S C

Hamilton, Edith, 1867-1963

  The Greek way   **880.9**

  Mythology   **292**

  The Roman way   **870.9**

Hamilton, Neil A., 1949-

  Presidents: a biographical dictionary   **920.003**

  Rebels and renegades   **322.4**

  (ed) Lifetimes: the Great War to the stock mar-
    ket crash: American history through biogra-
    phy and primary documents. See Lifetimes:
    the Great War to the stock market crash:
    American history through biography and pri-
    mary documents   **920**

Hamilton, Roger, 1945-

  (jt. auth) Bishop, A. C. Guide to minerals, rocks
    & fossils   **552**

Hamilton, W. R. *See* Hamilton, Roger, 1945-

Hamlet: poem unlimited. Bloom, H.   **822.3**

The **Hamlyn** guide to minerals, rocks, and fossils.
  See Bishop, A. C. Guide to minerals, rocks &
  fossils   **552**

Hammel, Heidi B.

About

  Bortz, A. B. Beyond Jupiter [biography of Heidi
    Hammel]   **92**

Hammer from above. Stout, J. A.   **956.7**

The **hammer** of God. Clarke, A. C.

  In Clarke, A. C. The collected stories of Ar-
    thur C. Clarke   **S C**

  In The Hard SF renaissance   **S C**

Hammett, Dashiell, 1894-1961

  The gutting of Couffignal

  In The Best American mystery stories of the
    century p105-32   **S C**

Hammond, Bruce

  (jt. auth) Fiske, E. B. The Fiske guide to getting
    into the right college   **378**

Hammond atlas of United States history   **911**

Hammond world atlas   **912**

Hampton, Henry

  Voices of freedom   **323.1**

Hampton, Wilborn

  Kennedy assassinated!   **973.922**

  September 11, 2001   **973.931**

Hancock, Paul L.

  (ed) The Oxford companion to the earth. See
    The Oxford companion to the earth   **550.3**

Hancocks, David

  A different nature   **590.73**

Hand of Fatima: a story from Lebanon. Marston,
  E.

  In Marston, E. Figs and fate; stories about
    growing up in the Arab world today
    S C

Handal, Kathleen A.

  (ed) The American Red Cross first aid and safe-
    ty handbook. See The American Red Cross
    first aid and safety handbook   **616.02**

Handbook of chemistry and physics. See CRC
  handbook of chemistry and physics   **540**

Handbook of denominations in the United States.
  Mead, F. S.   **280**

The **handbook** of knots. Pawson, D.   **623.88**

Handbook of Russian literature   **891.7**

The **handbook** of the Middle East. Kort, M.
    956

The **handbook** of the new Eastern Europe. Kort,
  M.   **943**

Handbook to life in ancient Egypt. David, A. R.
    932

Handbook to life in ancient Greece. Adkins, L.
    938

Handbook to life in ancient Rome. Adkins, L.
    937

Handbook to life in Renaissance Europe. Sider, S.
940.2

A **handbook** to literature. Harmon, W.   803

Handel, George Frideric, 1685-1759
See/See also pages in the following book(s):
Grout, D. J. A history of western music
780.9

Handicapped
  See also Mentally handicapped; Physically handicapped
McHugh, M. Special siblings   362.4
Encyclopedias
Encyclopedia of disability   362.4
Fiction
Johnson, H. M. Accidents of nature   **Fic**

Handicapped children
  See also Brain damaged children; Socially handicapped children

Handicapped students
A Guide to high school success for students with disabilities   371.9

Handicraft
Arendt, M. Altered art for the first time
745.5
Foxfire 40th anniversary book   975.8
Taylor, T. Altered art   745.5

The **handler**. Bradbury, R.
  In Bradbury, R. Bradbury stories; 100 of his most celebrated tales   **S C**

The **handler**. Knight, D. F.
  In The Norton book of science fiction; North American science fiction, 1960-1990 p45-48   **S C**

Handley, Graham
(comp) Shakespeare, W. Poems   821

The **Handmaid's** tale. Atwood, M.   **Fic**

Hands. London, J.
  In Am I blue?; coming out from the silence p215-23   **S C**

Hands across the sea. Coward, N.
  In 24 favorite one-act plays p151-69
808.82

Handwriting
  See also Calligraphy

The **Handy** science answer book   500

Hanes, Richard Clay, 1946-
Crime and punishment in America, Almanac
364
Crime and punishment in America, Biographies
920

Hanes, Sharon M.
Crime and punishment in America, Primary sources   364
(jt. auth) Hanes, R. C. Crime and punishment in America, Almanac   364

Haney, Eric L.
Inside Delta Force   356

Haney-López, Ian
Racism on trial   305.8

Hanging on to Max. Bechard, M.   **Fic**

Hank Aaron and the home run that changed America. Stanton, T.   92

Hanks, Patrick
A concise dictionary of first names   929.4
(ed) Dictionary of American family names. See Dictionary of American family names
929.4

Hanks, Reuel R.
Central Asia   958

Hannah, Barry
Water liars
  In American short story masterpieces   **S C**

Hanrahan, Clare
(ed) America's prisons: opposing viewpoints. See America's prisons: opposing viewpoints
365

Hansberry, Lorraine, 1930-1965
A raisin in the sun   812
  also in Black theatre USA; plays by African Americans, 1847 to today   812.008
To be young, gifted, and Black   92

Hansen, Brad
The dictionary of multimedia   006.6

Hansen, Joyce
Bury me not in a land of slaves   973.8

Hansen, Mark Victor
(jt. auth) Canfield, J. Chicken soup for the teenage soul [I-III]   158
(comp) Chicken soup for the teenage soul's the real deal. See Chicken soup for the teenage soul's the real deal   158

Hanson, Freya Ottem, 1949-
The Scopes monkey trial   345

Hanson, Nicholas P., 1978-
(jt. auth) Nevraumont, E. J. The ultimate improv book   792.7

The **happiest** man in all Kodny. Sholem Aleichem
  In Halkin, H. and Sholem Aleichem. Tevye the dairyman and The railroad stories
     S C

The **happy** autumn fields. Bowen, E.
  In Nightshade: 20th century ghost stories p47-64   **S C**

Happy birthday. Prener, N.
  In Not the only one; lesbian and gay fiction for teens   **S C**

The **happy** couple. Maugham, W. S.
  In Maugham, W. S. Collected short stories
     S C

The **happy** journey. Wilder, T.
  In 24 favorite one-act plays p194-209
808.82

The **happy** man. Maugham, W. S.
  In Maugham, W. S. Collected short stories
     S C

Haralson, Carol
(ed) The Arts of the North American Indian. See The Arts of the North American Indian
704

Haralson, Eric L.
(ed) Encyclopedia of American poetry, the twentieth century. See Encyclopedia of American poetry, the twentieth century   811.009

Harassment, Sexual *See* Sexual harassment

The **harrowing** of the dragon of Hoarsbreath. McKillip, P. A.
In McKillip, P. A. Harrowing the dragon
S C

Harrowing the dragon. McKillip, P. A. **S C**

Harry Potter and the Philosopher's Stone. See Rowling, J. K. Harry Potter and the Sorcerer's Stone **Fic**

Harry Potter and the Sorcerer's Stone. Rowling, J. K. **Fic**

Hart, Christopher
Cartooning for the beginner **741.5**
Drawing cutting edge anatomy **741.5**
How to draw animation **741.5**
Human anatomy made amazingly easy **743**

Hart, Elva Trevino
Barefoot heart **92**

Hart, Gary, 1936-
James Monroe **92**

Hart, James David, 1911-1990
The Oxford companion to American literature **810.3**

Hart, John, 1948-
Walking softly in the wilderness **796.51**

Hart, Mickey
Songcatchers **780.9**

Harte, Bret, 1836-1902
The Iliad of Sandy Bar
In The Oxford book of short stories p67-77 **S C**
The outcasts of Poker Flat
In The Norton book of American short stories p65-74 **S C**
Selina Sedilia
In The Oxford book of gothic tales p158-64 **S C**

Harter, Penny
(jt. auth) Higginson, W. J. The haiku handbook **808.1**

Hartinger, Brent, 1964-
Geography Club **Fic**
Swords that talk
In Young warriors; stories of strength **S C**
Throwing rocks at cats
In Not the only one; lesbian and gay fiction for teens **S C**

Hartley, L. P. (Leslie Poles), 1895-1972
W.S.
In Nightshade: 20th century ghost stories p217-28 **S C**

Hartley, Leslie Poles *See* Hartley, L. P. (Leslie Poles), 1895-1972

The **Hartleys.** Cheever, J.
In Cheever, J. The stories of John Cheever p58-64 **S C**

Hartman, Gary R.
Landmark Supreme Court cases **347**

Hartmann, William K.
A traveler's guide to Mars **523.4**

Hartnett, Sonya, 1968-
Surrender **Fic**
Thursday's child **Fic**

Hartt, Frederick, 1914-1991
Art: a history of painting, sculpture, architecture **709**
Michelangelo **759.5**

Hartwell, David G.
(ed) The Hard SF renaissance. See The Hard SF renaissance **S C**

Hartz, Paula
Baha'i Faith **297**
Native American religions **299.7**
Shinto **299.5**
Taoism **299.5**

Haruf, Kent, 1943-
Plainsong **Fic**

The **Harvard** concise dictionary of music and musicians **780.3**

The **Harvard** guide to African-American history **305.8**

The **Harvard** Medical School family health guide **610**

The **Harvard** Medical School guide to taking control of asthma. Fanta, C. H. **616.2**

Harvard University Press reference library [series]
The Harvard guide to African-American history **305.8**

The **harvest** gypsies. Steinbeck, J.
In Steinbeck, J. The grapes of wrath and other writings, 1936-1941 **818**

Harvest of empire. Gonzalez, J. **305.8**

Harvey, David Alan, 1944-
Cuba **972.91**

Harvey, Henry Paul *See* Harvey, Sir Paul, 1869-1948

Harvey, Joy
(ed) The Biographical dictionary of women in science. See The Biographical dictionary of women in science **920.003**

Harvey, Sir Paul, 1869-1948
The Oxford companion to classical literature. See The Oxford companion to classical literature **880.3**

Harvey, Robert C.
The art of the comic book **741.5**

Harvey, William, 1578-1657
About
Friedman, M. Medicine's 10 greatest discoveries **610.9**

See/See also pages in the following book(s):
Hellman, H. Great feuds in medicine **610.9**

Harvey Pekar's American splendor. Pekar, H. **92**

Hasan, Asma Gull
American Muslims **297**

Hasan, Heather
Archimedes: the father of mathematics **92**

Hasday, Judy L., 1957-
Ellen Ochoa **92**

Haskins, James, 1941-2005
Toni Morrison: telling a tale untold **92**

Hassell, Sandra Hughes- *See* Hughes-Hassell, Sandra

Hassrick, Peter H.
Charles M. Russell 92

Hastedt, Glenn P., 1950-
Encyclopedia of American foreign policy
327.73

Hastings, Max
The Korean War 951.9
Overlord: D-Day and the battle for Normandy
940.54

Hastings, Penny
Sports for her 796

Hastings (East Sussex, England), Battle of, 1066
Howarth, D. A. 1066: the year of the conquest
942.02

Hat of clouds. Salisbury, G.
In Salisbury, G. Island boyz: short stories
p220-60 S C

Hatch, James Vernon, 1928-
(ed) Black theatre USA. See Black theatre USA
812.008

Hatch, Robert
The hero project 920

Hatch, William
(jt. auth) Hatch, R. The hero project 920

Hatching the Phoenix. Pohl, F.
In The Hard SF renaissance S C

Hate. Clarke, A. C.
In Clarke, A. C. The collected stories of Arthur C. Clarke S C

Hate crimes
Altschiller, D. Hate crimes 364.1
Hate groups: opposing viewpoints 364.1
See/See also pages in the following book(s):
Racial discrimination 342

Hate groups: opposing viewpoints 364.1

Hatfield, Charles, 1965-
Alternative comics 741.5

Hatha yoga *See* Yoga

Hats
Scott, G. Headwraps 391

Hattie Big Sky. Larson, K. Fic

Haugen, David, 1969-
Legalized gambling 363.4
(ed) Adoption. See Adoption 362.7
(ed) China: opposing viewpoints. See China: opposing viewpoints 951
(ed) Domestic violence: opposing viewpoints. See Domestic violence: opposing viewpoints 362.82
(ed) Poverty. See Poverty 362.5
(ed) Terrorism. See Terrorism [David Haugen and Matthew J. Box, eds.] 303.6
(ed) The Third World: opposing viewpoints. See The Third World: opposing viewpoints 909

Haunted. Oates, J. C.
In Oates, J. C. Small avalanches and other stories S C

The **haunted** house. Dickens, C.
In The Oxford book of English short stories p18-43 S C

The **haunted** mind. Hawthorne, N.
In Hawthorne, N. Tales and sketches, including Twice-told tales, Mosses from an old manse, and The snow-image; A wonder book for girls and boys; Tanglewood tales for girls and boys, being a second Wonder book p200-04 S C

The **haunted** quack. Hawthorne, N.
In Hawthorne, N. Tales and sketches, including Twice-told tales, Mosses from an old manse, and The snow-image; A wonder book for girls and boys; Tanglewood tales for girls and boys, being a second Wonder book p49-60 S C

The **haunting** of Alaizabel Cray. Wooding, C.
Fic

The **haunting** of Hill House. Jackson, S. Fic

Hautman, Pete, 1952-
Godless Fic
Invisible Fic

Have a nice day—no problem!: a dictionary of cliches. See Ammer, C. The Facts on File dictionary of clichés 423

Have no fear, Crumpot is here!. Yourgrau, B.
In Gothic!; ten original dark tales S C

Have not have. Ryman, G.
In Best of the best: 20 years of the Year's best science fiction S C

Havemann, Ernst
A farm at Raraba
In Somehow tenderness survives; stories of Southern Africa p119-34 S C

Haver, Kenan E.
(jt. auth) Fanta, C. H. The Harvard Medical School guide to taking control of asthma
616.2

Having our say. Delany, S. 92

Hawaii
Description and travel
Twain, M. Roughing it 818
Fiction
Salisbury, G. Island boyz: short stories S C
Salisbury, G. Jungle dogs Fic
Salisbury, G. Under the blood-red sun Fic
Graphic novels
Morse, S. The barefoot serpent 741.5

Hawass, Zahi A.
Tutankhamun and the golden age of the pharaohs 932

Hawes, Louise, 1943-
Sideshow
In Such a pretty face; short stories S C

Hawk, Tony, 1968-
Hawk 92

Hawke, David Freeman
Everyday life in early America 973.2

Hawking, Stephen W., 1942-
Black holes and baby universes and other essays
523.1
A briefer history of time 523.1
The nature of space and time 530.1
The universe in a nutshell 530.1

Hayden, Patrick Nielsen *See* Nielsen Hayden, Patrick

Haydn, Joseph, 1732-1809
See/See also pages in the following book(s):
Grout, D. J. A history of western music
780.9

Hayhurst, Chris
Cool careers without college for animal lovers
636
Euclid: the great geometer **92**
Everything you need to know about food additives
664

Haynes, Charles C.
First freedoms **342**

Haynsworth, Leslie
Amelia Earhart's daughters **629.13**

Hayslip, Le Ly
When heaven and earth changed places **92**

Hazelwood School District v. Kuhlmeier
Phillips, T. A. Hazelwood v. Kuhlmeier and the school newspaper censorship debate **342**

Hazelwood v. Kuhlmeier and the school newspaper censorship debate. Phillips, T. A. **342**

Hazen, Edith P.
(ed) The Columbia Granger's dictionary of poetry quotations. See The Columbia Granger's dictionary of poetry quotations **808.88**

The **hazing**. Asimov, I.
In Asimov, I. The complete stories p16-29
S C

He. Porter, K. A.
In Porter, K. A. The collected stories of Katherine Anne Porter **S C**

Head, Dominic
(ed) The Cambridge guide to literature in English. See The Cambridge guide to literature in English **820.9**

Head, Tom
Freedom of religion **342**

Head and shoulders. Fitzgerald, F. S.
In Fitzgerald, F. S. The short stories of F. Scott Fitzgerald; a new collection p3-24
S C

The **head** of the district. Kipling, R.
In Kipling, R. The portable Kipling **828**

Headless males make great lovers. Crump, M. L.
591.5

Headline court cases [series]
Hanson, F. O. The Scopes monkey trial **345**
Monroe, J. The Sacco and Vanzetti controversial murder trial
345

Headlines in history [series]
The 1000s **940.1**
The 1100s **909**
The 1200s **909**
The 1300s **909**

Heads. Bear, G.
In Bear, G. The collected stories of Greg Bear **S C**

Heads of state
See also Dictators; Kings and rulers; Presidents; Prime ministers

Opfell, O. S. Women prime ministers and presidents **920**

Headwraps. Scott, G. **391**

The **healer**. Bender, A.
In Feeling very strange; the Slipstream anthology **S C**

Healing drugs: the history of pharmacology. See Facklam, M. Modern medicines **615**

Health
See also Physical fitness
The Harvard Medical School family health guide **610**

Environmental aspects
See Environmental health

Health, Public *See* Public health

Health foods *See* Natural foods

Health reference series
Lung disorders sourcebook **616.2**
Vegetarian sourcebook **613.2**

Health self-care
American Medical Association family medical guide **616.02**

Heaney, Seamus
Electric light **821**
Opened ground **821**
(tr) Beowulf. Beowulf **829**

Heaphy, Leslie A., 1964-
(ed) Encyclopedia of women and baseball. See Encyclopedia of women and baseball
796.357

Hear me out: true stories of Teens Educating and Confronting Homophobia **306.76**

Hearing
Mayo Clinic on hearing **617.8**

Hearing flower. Kerr, M. E.
In Face relations; 11 stories about seeing beyond color **S C**

Hearing impaired
See also Deaf

Hearn, Julie, 1958-
The minister's daughter **Fic**

Hearn, Lian
Across the nightingale floor **Fic**

Hearne, Betsy Gould, 1942-
Beauties and beasts **398.2**

Heart
See also Blood—Circulation
Brynie, F. H. 101 questions about blood and circulation, with answers straight from the heart
612.1

Heart full of grace **808.88**

The **heart** has its reasons. Cart, M. **813.009**

The **heart** is a lonely hunter. McCullers, C.
Fic

Heart of a champion. Boyle, T. C.
In Boyle, T. C. The Human Fly and other stories **S C**

The **heart** of another. Sedgwick, M.
In The restless dead; ten original stories of the supernatural **S C**

Heart of darkness. Conrad, J. **Fic**

Helprin, Mark—*Continued*
In The Norton book of American short stories
p722-32 **S C**

Helter skelter. Bugliosi, V. **364.1**

Hemings, Sally, 1773-1835
See/See also pages in the following book(s):
Lanier, S. Jefferson's children **920**

Hemings family
See/See also pages in the following book(s):
Lanier, S. Jefferson's children **920**

Hemingway, Amanda
The Greenstone grail **Fic**

Hemingway, Ernest, 1899-1961
The complete short stories of Ernest Hemingway
S C

Contents: The short happy life of Francis Macomber; The capital of the world; The snows of Kilimanjaro; Old man at the bridge; Up in Michigan; On the quai at Smyrna; Indian camp; The doctor and the doctor's wife; The end of something; The three-day blow; The battler; A very short story; Soldier's home; The revolutionist; Mr. and Mrs. Elliot; Cat in the rain; Out of season; Cross-country snow; My old man; Big two-hearted river: part I; Big two-hearted river: part II; The undefeated; In another country; Hills like white elephants; The killers; Che ti dice la patria?; Fifty grand; A simple enquiry; Ten Indians; A canary for one; An Alpine idyll; A pursuit race; Today is Friday; Banal story; Now I lay me; After the storm; A clean, well-lighted place; The light of the world; God rest you merry, gentlemen; The sea change; A way you'll never be; The mother of a queen; One reader writes; Homage to Switzerland; A day's wait; A natural history of the dead; Wine of Wyoming; The gambler, the nun, and the radio; Fathers and sons; One trip across; The tradesman's return; The denunciation; The butterfly and the tank; Night before battle; Under the ridge; Nobody ever dies; The good lion; The faithful bull; Get a seeing-eyed dog; A man of the world; Summer people; The last good country; An African story; A train trip; The porter; Black ass at the cross roads; Landscape with figures; I guess everything reminds you of something; Great news from the mainland

A farewell to arms **Fic**
For whom the bell tolls **Fic**
Hills like white elephants
In The Norton book of American short stories
p352-57 **S C**
In The Oxford book of short stories p341-45
S C
The killers
In Adaptations: from short story to big screen; 35 great stories that have inspired great films **S C**
The old man and the sea **Fic**
The sun also rises **Fic**
About
Ernest Hemingway [critical essays] **813.009**
A Historical guide to Ernest Hemingway
813.009
Oliver, C. M. Critical companion to Ernest Hemingway **813.009**
Pingelton, T. J. A student's guide to Ernest Hemingway **813.009**
Strathern, P. Hemingway in 90 minutes **92**

Hemingway in 90 minutes. Strathern, P. **92**

Hemmendinger, David
(ed) Encyclopedia of computer science. See Encyclopedia of computer science **004**

Hemming, John, 1935-
The conquest of the Incas **985**

Hemphill, Helen, 1955-
Long gone daddy **Fic**

Hemphill, Stephanie
Your own, Sylvia **811**

Henderson, Andrea
(ed) The Day our world changed. See The Day our world changed **973.931**

Henderson, C. J.
The encyclopedia of science fiction movies
791.43

Henderson, Harry, 1914-
(jt. auth) Bearden, R. A history of African-American artists **709.73**

Henderson, Harry, 1951-
Artificial intelligence **006.3**
Campaign and election reform **324.6**
Capital punishment **364.66**
Communications and broadcasting **384**
Encyclopedia of computer science and technology **004**
Global terrorism **303.6**
Gun control **363.33**
Internet predators **364.1**
Mathematics: powerful patterns in nature and society **510**
Modern robotics **629.8**
Nuclear physics **539.7**
Power of the news media **070.1**
Terrorist challenge to America **363.32**

Henderson, Helene, 1963-
(ed) Holidays, festivals, and celebrations of the world dictionary. See Holidays, festivals, and celebrations of the world dictionary
394.26
(ed) Twentieth-century literary movements dictionary. See Twentieth-century literary movements dictionary **809**

Henderson, Roxanne
(jt. auth) Lewis, K. B. Sign language made simple **419**

Henderson, Zenna, 1917-1989
As simple as that
In The Norton book of science fiction; North American science fiction, 1960-1990 p231-41 **S C**

Hendrick, George
The Creole mutiny **326**

Hendrick, Willene, 1928-
(jt. auth) Hendrick, G. The Creole mutiny
326

Hendrickson, Robert, 1933-
The Facts on File dictionary of American regionalisms **427**
The Facts on File encyclopedia of word and phrase origins **422.03**

Hendrickson, Susan
See/See also pages in the following book(s):
Malone, J. W. It doesn't take a rocket scientist **920**

Heneghan, James, 1930-
(jt. auth) McBay, B. Waiting for Sarah **Fic**

Henke, James
(ed) The Rolling Stone illustrated history of rock & roll. See The Rolling Stone illustrated history of rock & roll **781.66**

Hennessey, Maureen Hart
Norman Rockwell **759.13**

Henningfeld, Diane Andrews
(ed) The death penalty: opposing viewpoints.
See The death penalty: opposing viewpoints
364.66

Henry, Laurie
The fiction dictionary **808.3**

Henry, O., 1862-1910
Mammon and the archer
In The Norton book of American short stories
p151-56 **S C**
A retrieved reformation
In The Best American mystery stories of the
century p1-7 **S C**
Telemachus, friend
In The Oxford book of short stories p167-73
S C
About
Caravantes, P. Writing is my business **92**
Adaptations
Graphic Classics Volume Eleven: O. Henry
741.5
(jt. auth) Cerf, B. The best short stories of O.
Henry **S C**

Henry IV, part I. See Shakespeare, W. The first
part of King Henry the Fourth **822.3**

Henry the ninth. Bradbury, R.
In Bradbury, R. Bradbury stories; 100 of his
most celebrated tales **S C**

Hensher, Philip
Dead languages
In The Oxford book of English short stories
p435-39 **S C**

Henson, Josiah, 1789-1883
See/See also pages in the following book(s):
Garrison, M. Slaves who dared **920**

Hensrud, Donald D.
(ed) Mayo Clinic on healthy weight. See Mayo
Clinic on healthy weight **613.2**

Hepatitis See Liver—Diseases

Her blue body everything we know. Walker, A.
811

Her other son. Rice, D.
In Rice, D. Crazy loco; stories about growing
up Chicano in southern Texas p14-28
S C

Her sister's wedding. Stelboum, J. P.
In Not the only one; lesbian and gay fiction
for teens **S C**

Her table spread. Bowen, E.
In The Oxford book of Irish short stories
p311-18 **S C**

Heracles (Legendary character) See Hercules
(Legendary character)

Herald, Diana Tixier
Genreflecting **016.8**
Strictly science fiction **016.8**
Teen genreflecting **016.8**

Herb gardening
Smith, M. Your backyard herb garden **635**
The **herb** of death. Christie, A.
In Christie, A. Miss Marple: the complete
short stories **S C**

Herbal medicine See Medical botany

Herbert, Frank, 1920-1986
Dune **Fic**

Herbert, Patricia
The life of the Buddha **92**

Herbert George Morley Roberts Wells, Esq.
Clarke, A. C.
In Clarke, A. C. The collected stories of Ar-
thur C. Clarke **S C**

Herbert West—Reanimator: six shots by moonlight. Lovecraft, H. P.
In Adaptations: from short story to big
screen; 35 great stories that have inspired
great films **S C**

Herbs
Smith, M. Your backyard herb garden **635**

Hercegovina See Bosnia and Hercegovina

Hercules (Legendary character)
See/See also pages in the following book(s):
Hamilton, E. Mythology **292**

Here be dragons. Delacampagne, A. **700**

Here be dragons. Koerner, D. **576.8**

Here in Harlem. Myers, W. D. **811**

Here there be tygers. King, S.
In King, S. Skeleton crew **S C**

Here we are. Parker, D.
In 24 favorite one-act plays p210-18
808.82
In Gotham Writers' Workshop fiction gallery;
exceptional short stories selected by New
York's acclaimed creative writing school
S C

Heredity
See also Gene mapping
Ackerman, J. Chance in the house of fate
599.93

Heredity and environment See Nature and nurture

Hérelle, Félix d', 1873-1949
See/See also pages in the following book(s):
Malone, J. W. It doesn't take a rocket scientist
920

Herlihy, James Leo, 1927-1993
The astral body of a U.S. mail truck
In Nightshade: 20th century ghost stories
p229-39 **S C**

Herman Melville A to Z. See Rollyson, C. Critical companion to Herman Melville
813.009

Hermann, Spring
A student's guide to Tennessee Williams
812.009

Hermann Hesse [critical essays] **838**

Hermetic art and philosophy See Alchemy

Hermosilla, Pablo Castro See Castro, Pablo

Hermsen, Sarah
(ed) Benson, S. U.S. immigration and migration
almanac **304.8**
(ed) Hanes, R. C. Crime and punishment in
America, Almanac **364**
(ed) Hanes, R. C. Crime and punishment in
America, Biographies **920**

The **hidden** life of dogs. Thomas, E. M.
636.7

Hidden warriors. Mahy, M.
In Young warriors; stories of strength   **S C**

Hide-and-seek. Clarke, A. C.
In Clarke, A. C. The collected stories of Arthur C. Clarke   **S C**

Hidier, Tanuja Desai *See* Desai Hidier, Tanuja

The **hiding** of Black Bill. Henry, O.
In Henry, O. The best short stories of O. Henry   **S C**

Hieroglyphics
See also Picture writing; Rosetta stone inscription
See/See also pages in the following book(s):
Ceram, C. W. Gods, graves, and scholars
930.1

Higginbotham, Evelyn Brooks, 1945-
(ed) African American lives. See African American lives   **920.003**
(ed) The Harvard guide to African-American history. See The Harvard guide to African-American history   **305.8**

Higgins, Aidan
The bird I fancied
In The Oxford book of Irish short stories p445-54   **S C**

Higgins, Kathleen Marie
(jt. auth) Solomon, R. C. A short history of philosophy   **109**

Higgins, Marguerite, 1920-1966
See/See also pages in the following book(s):
Colman, P. Where the action was   **070.4**

Higginson, William J., 1938-
The haiku handbook   **808.1**

High, Linda Oatman, 1958-
The uterus fairy
In Don't cramp my style; stories about that time of the month p265-83   **S C**

High definition   **004**

High John de Conquer. Hurston, Z. N.
In Hurston, Z. N. The complete stories p139-48   **S C**

High school. Sholem Aleichem
In Halkin, H. and Sholem Aleichem. Tevye the dairyman and The railroad stories   **S C**

High school libraries
See also Young adults' libraries
Doggett, S. L. Beyond the book   **025.04**
Leslie, R. Igniting the spark   **027.8**

High school senior's guide to merit and other no-need funding. Schlachter, G. A.   **378.3**

High school students
Bluestein, J. High school's not forever   **373.1**
Robbins, A. The overachievers   **305.23**
Graphic novels
Azuma, K. Azumanga Daioh, Vol. 1   **741.5**
Castellucci, C. The Plain Janes   **741.5**
Dead High yearbook   **741.5**
DeMatteis, J. M. Brooklyn dreams   **741.5**
Friedman, A. Breaking up   **741.5**
Hage, A. Gothic sports, Vol. 1   **741.5**

Nibot, R. Banana Sunday   **741.5**
Nonaka, E. Cromartie High School, Vol. 1   **741.5**
Sable, M. Grounded, Vol. 1: Powerless   **741.5**
Suenobu, K. Life, Vol. 1   **741.5**
Wight, E. My dead girlfriend, Vol. 1   **741.5**

High schools
South Africa
Finnegan, W. Crossing the line   **968.06**

High school's not forever. Bluestein, J.   **373.1**

High tech *See* Technology

High-tech IDs. Tocci, S.   **614**

High tech trash. Grossman, E.   **363.7**

High tide. Lynas, M.   **363.7**

High weir. Delany, S. R.
In The Norton book of science fiction; North American science fiction, 1960-1990 p183-200   **S C**

Higham, Charles
Encyclopedia of ancient Asian civilizations
950

The **highboy**. Lurie, A.
In Nightshade: 20th century ghost stories p328-43   **S C**

Higher education
See also Colleges and universities
Rosen, L., Ph. D. College is not for everyone
378.1

A **higher** geometry. Moranville, S. B.   **Fic**

Highet, Gilbert, 1906-1978
The classical tradition   **809**

Highsmith, Patricia, 1921-1995
The terrapin
In The Best American mystery stories of the century p466-78   **S C**

The **highway**. Bradbury, R.
In Bradbury, R. The illustrated man   **S C**

Un **hijo** del sol. Gonzalez, G.
In Growing up Latino; memoirs and stories p38-46   **810.8**

Hijuelos, Oscar
The Mambo Kings play songs of love [excerpt]
In Growing up Latino; memoirs and stories p16-21   **810.8**

Hiking
See also Walking

Hildebrandt, Greg, 1939-
(jt. auth) Brooks, T. The sword of Shannara
Fic

Hildebrandt, Tim, 1939-
(jt. auth) Brooks, T. The sword of Shannara
Fic

Hildy, Franklin J. (Franklin Joseph), 1953-
(jt. auth) Brockett, O. G. History of the theatre
792.09

Hill, Abram, 1910-1986
On strivers row
In Black theatre USA; plays by African Americans, 1847 to today   **812.008**

Hill, Christine M.
Gwendolyn Brooks   **92**

Hobson, J. Allan
Dreaming **154.6**

Hobson, John Atkinson, 1858-1940
See/See also pages in the following book(s):
Heilbroner, R. L. The worldly philosophers
330.1

Hoch, Edward D., 1930-
The long way down
In Alfred Hitchcock's mystery magazine presents fifty years of crime and suspense
S C

Hochschild, Adam, 1942-
King Leopold's ghost **967.5**

Hockenberry, John
Moving violations **92**

Hockensmith, Steve
Erie's last day
In Alfred Hitchcock's mystery magazine presents fifty years of crime and suspense
S C

Hockey
A basic guide to ice hockey **796.962**
McKinley, M. Hockey: a people's history
796.962

Fiction
Hughes, P. Open ice **Fic**
Lynch, C. Iceman **Fic**

Hodges, Flavia
(jt. auth) Hanks, P. A concise dictionary of first names **929.4**

Hodges, Larry, 1960-
Table tennis **796.34**

Hodgins, Eric, 1899-1971
Mr. Blandings builds his castle
In Adaptations: from short story to big screen; 35 great stories that have inspired great films **S C**

Hodl. Sholem Aleichem
In Halkin, H. and Sholem Aleichem. Tevye the dairyman and The railroad stories
S C

Hoehner, Jane
Outlaws, mobsters & crooks **920.003**

Hoff, Brent H.
Mapping epidemics **614**

Hoffer, Peter Charles
The Salem witchcraft trials **345**
(jt. auth) Hull, N. E. H. Roe v. Wade **344**

Hoffius, Stephen
The assault on the record
In Ultimate sports; short stories by outstanding writers for young adults p161-78
S C

Hoffman, Alice, 1952-
Blue diary **Fic**
The foretelling **Fic**
Incantation **Fic**
The probable future **Fic**

Hoffman, Jeff
Fishing
In Under 30; plays for a new generation
812.008

Hoffman, Mary, 1945-
The falconer's knot **Fic**

Stravaganza: city of masks **Fic**

Hoffman, Nina Kiriki
Grounded
In The Green Man: tales from the mythic forest p191-220 **808.8**
Immersed in matter
In The Faery Reel; tales from the Twilight Realm **S C**
Mint condition
In Past imperfect **S C**
Unwrapping
In Firebirds rising; an anthology of original science fiction and fantasy **S C**

Hoffman, Roy, 1953-
Ice cream man
In Working days: stories about teenagers and work **S C**

Hoffmann, Gretchen McCord
Copyright in cyberspace 2 **346.04**

Hofstadter, Richard, 1916-1970
America at 1750 **973.2**

Hogan, Desmond
The Airedale
In The Oxford book of Irish short stories p553-63 **S C**

Hogan, James P.
Convolution
In Past imperfect **S C**
Madam Butterfly
In The Hard SF renaissance **S C**

Hogan, Lawrence D., 1944-
Shades of glory **796.357**

Hogan, Linda
Crow
In Moccasin thunder; American Indians stories for today **S C**
Making do
In Spider Woman's granddaughters; traditional tales and contemporary writing by Native American women **S C**
About
Coltelli, L. Winged words: American Indian writers speak **897**

Hogan, Walter
Humor in young adult literature **813.009**

Hold them in your heart. Mondowney, J. G.
027.62

Holding, James, 1907-
Recipe for murder
In Alfred Hitchcock's mystery magazine presents fifty years of crime and suspense
S C

Holding. Lowry, L.
In Am I blue?; coming out from the silence p175-87 **S C**

Hole in my life. Gantos, J. **92**

The **hole** in the universe. Cole, K. C. **530**

Holiday, Billie, 1915-1959
Lady sings the blues **92**

Holiday. Porter, K. A.
In Porter, K. A. The collected stories of Katherine Anne Porter **S C**

Holiday on the moon. Clarke, A. C.
    In Clarke, A. C. The collected stories of Arthur C. Clarke   **S C**
Holiday symbols. See Thompson, S. E. Holiday symbols and customs   **394.26**
Holiday symbols and customs. Thompson, S. E.   **394.26**
Holidays
    See also Christmas; New Year; Religious holidays; Thanksgiving Day; Valentine's Day
    The American book of days   **394.26**
    Chase's calendar of events 2006   **394.26**
    Christianson, S. G. The international book of days   **394.26**
    Encyclopedia of holidays and celebrations   **394.26**
    The Folklore of world holidays   **394.26**
    Holidays and anniversaries of the world   **394.26**
    Holidays, festivals, and celebrations of the world dictionary   **394.26**
    Rajtar, S. United States holidays and observances   **394.26**
    Thompson, S. E. Holiday symbols and customs   **394.26**
    Webb, L. S. Holidays of the world cookbook for students   **641.5**
Holidays, Jewish *See* Jewish holidays
Holidays and anniversaries of the world   **394.26**
Holidays, festivals, and celebrations of the world dictionary   **394.26**
Holidays of the world cookbook for students. Webb, L. S.   **641.5**
Holkeboer, Katherine Strand
    Patterns for theatrical costumes   **646.4**
Holland, Peter, 1951-
    (ed) Shakespeare, W. Much ado about nothing   **822.3**
    (ed) Shakespeare, W. Romeo and Juliet   **822.3**
    (ed) Shakespeare, W. The tempest   **822.3**
Holland *See* Netherlands
Hollander, John
    (ed) American poetry: the nineteenth century. See American poetry: the nineteenth century   **811.008**
    (ed) Animal poems. See Animal poems   **808.81**
    (ed) The Literature of Renaissance England. See The Literature of Renaissance England   **820.8**
Hollen, Kathryn H.
    The reproductive system   **618**
Holler if you hear me: searching for Tupac Shakur. Dyson, M. E.   **92**
Holley, Marietta, 1836-1926
    A male Magdalene [excerpt]
    In The Oxford book of women's writing in the United States p56-62   **810.8**
Holliday, Laurel, 1946-
    (comp) Children in the Holocaust and World War II. See Children in the Holocaust and World War II   **940.53**

    (ed) Children of Israel, children of Palestine. See Children of Israel, children of Palestine   **956.94**
Hollingsworth, Mary
    Art in world history   **709**
The **hollow**. Christie, A.
    In Christie, A. The mousetrap and other plays   **822**
The **hollow** hills. Stewart, M.
    In Stewart, M. Mary Stewart's Merlin trilogy   **Fic**
The **hollow** men. Wolfe, T.
    In Wolfe, T. The complete short stories of Thomas Wolfe p485-91   **S C**
The **hollow** of the three hills. Hawthorne, N.
    In Hawthorne, N. Tales and sketches, including Twice-told tales, Mosses from an old manse, and The snow-image; A wonder book for girls and boys; Tanglewood tales for girls and boys, being a second Wonder book p7-11   **S C**
The **hollyhock** sowers. Wolfe, T.
    In Wolfe, T. The complete short stories of Thomas Wolfe p465-68   **S C**
Hollywood 101 [series]
    Stevens, C. Sensational scenes for teens   **808.82**
Hollywood and the pits. Lee, C.
    In American dragons: twenty-five Asian American voices p34-47   **810.8**
Holman, C. Hugh (Clarence Hugh), 1914-
    (jt. auth) Harmon, W. A handbook to literature   **803**
Holman, Clarence Hugh *See* Holman, C. Hugh (Clarence Hugh), 1914-
Holman, James, 1786-1857
About
    Roberts, J. A sense of the world [biography of James Holman]   **92**
Holmes, George, 1927-
    (ed) The Oxford history of Italy. See The Oxford history of Italy   **945**
    (ed) The Oxford history of medieval Europe. See The Oxford history of medieval Europe   **940.1**
Holmes, Hannah, 1963-
    The secret life of dust   **551.51**
Holmes, Sherlock (Fictitious character)
    Wagner, E. J. The science of Sherlock Holmes   **363.2**
Holocaust, 1933-1945
    See also Holocaust survivors; World War, 1939-1945—Jews
    Ayer, E. H. Parallel journeys   **940.53**
    Bartoletti, S. C. Hitler Youth   **943.086**
    Berenbaum, M. The world must know   **940.53**
    Chesnoff, R. Z. Pack of thieves   **940.53**
    Dawidowicz, L. S. The war against the Jews, 1933-1945   **940.53**
    Epstein, H. Children of the Holocaust   **940.53**
    Feldman, G. Understanding the Holocaust   **940.53**

Horses—*Continued*
Encyclopedias
Edwards, E. H. The new encyclopedia of the horse **636.1**
Fiction
Wilson, D. L. Firehorse **Fic**
Poetry
Haas, J. Hoofprints: horse poems **811**

A **horse's** tale. Twain, M.
In Twain, M. The complete short stories of Mark Twain; now collected for the first time **S C**

Horst, Heather A.
Jamaican Americans **305.8**

Horton, Edward
(jt. auth) Stewart, R. Mysteries of history **902**

Horton, James Oliver
Slavery and the making of America **326**

Horton, Lois E.
(jt. auth) Horton, J. O. Slavery and the making of America **326**

Horvitz, Leslie Alan
Eureka!: scientific breakthroughs that changed the world **509**

Horwood, Jane
(ed) The Oxford Spanish dictionary. See The Oxford Spanish dictionary **463**

Horwood, Roger
The woodworker's handbook **684**

Hospital, Carolina, 1957-
Catskill snows
In Working days: stories about teenagers and work **S C**

Hospitals
See also Psychiatric hospitals

Hosseini, Khaled
The kite runner **Fic**
A thousand splendid suns **Fic**

Hostess. Asimov, I.
In Asimov, I. The complete stories p376-407 **S C**

Hostetler, John A., 1918-
Amish society **289.7**
(ed) Amish roots. See Amish roots **289.7**

Hot springs. Crumley, J.
In The Best American mystery stories of the century p678-93 **S C**

The **hot** zone. Preston, R. **614.5**

The **hotel.** Maja-Pearce, A.
In The Heinemann book of contemporary African short stories p146-48 **S C**

The **hotel** child. Fitzgerald, F. S.
In Fitzgerald, F. S. The short stories of F. Scott Fitzgerald; a new collection p598-615 **S C**

The **Hotel** New Hampshire. Irving, J. **Fic**

Hotels and motels
Fiction
Irving, J. The Hotel New Hampshire **Fic**

Houle, Michelle E.
(ed) Terrorism. See Terrorism [Michelle E. Houle, ed.] **303.6**

The **hound** of the Baskervilles. Doyle, Sir A. C. **Fic**
also in Doyle, Sir A. C. The complete Sherlock Holmes **S C**

An **hour** before daylight. Carter, J. **92**

An **hour** with Abuelo. Ortiz Cofer, J.
In Ortiz Cofer, J. An island like you; stories of the barrio **S C**

Housden, Roger
(ed) Risking everything. See Risking everything **808.81**

House, Callie, 1861-1928
About
Berry, M. F. My face is black is true [biography of Callie House] **92**

The **House** and Senate explained. Greenberg, E. **328.73**

The **house** and the locket. Wooding, C.
In The restless dead; ten original stories of the supernatural **S C**

House of flowers. Capote, T.
In Capote, T. Breakfast at Tiffany's: a short novel and three stories **S C**

House of Representatives (U.S.) *See* United States. Congress. House

House of Romanov
About
Massie, R. K. The Romanovs **947.08**

House of stairs. Sleator, W. **Fic**

The **house** of the far and lost. Wolfe, T.
In Wolfe, T. The complete short stories of Thomas Wolfe p147-66 **S C**

House of the many. Lanagan, M.
In Lanagan, M. Black juice **S C**

The **house** of the scorpion. Farmer, N. **Fic**

The **house** on Buffalo Street. Mazer, N. F.
In Night terrors; stories of shadow and substance **S C**

The **house** on Mango Street. Cisneros, S. **Fic**

The **house** on the planet. Lee, T.
In Firebirds rising; an anthology of original science fiction and fantasy **S C**

House painting
Lord, G. It's faux easy by Gary Lord **698**

The **house** the Blakeneys built. Davidson, A.
In The Norton book of science fiction; North American science fiction, 1960-1990 p115-24 **S C**

The **House:** the history of the House of Representatives. Remini, R. V. **328.73**

The **housebreaker** of Shady Hill. Cheever, J.
In Cheever, J. The stories of John Cheever p253-69 **S C**

The **housegirl.** Chigbo, O.
In The Heinemann book of contemporary African short stories p149-64 **S C**

Household employees
Fiction
Doig, I. The whistling season **Fic**

Household moving *See* Moving

Household pests
See also Insect pests

Hughes, Langston, 1902-1967—*Continued*

Something in common; Mysterious Madame Shaghai; Never room with a couple; Powder-white faces; Pushcart man; Rouge high; Patron of the arts; Thank you, m'am'; Sorrow for a midget; Blessed assurance; Early autumn; Fine accommodations; The gun; His last affair; No place to make love; Rock, church; Mary Winosky; Those who have no turkey; Seventy-five dollars; The childhood of Jimmy

Simply heavenly

    In Hughes, L. Five plays p113-81   **812**

Slave on the block

    In The Norton book of American short stories p367-74   **S C**

Soul gone home

    In Hughes, L. Five plays p37-42   **812**

Tambourines to glory

    In Hughes, L. Five plays p183-258   **812**

Thank you, m'am

    In Read all about it!; great read-aloud stories, poems, and newspaper pieces for preteens and teens p82-89   **808.8**

About

Langston Hughes [critical essays]   **818**

Leach, L. F. Langston Hughes   **92**

Hughes, Lynne Barribeau

You are not alone   **155.9**

Hughes, Pat, 1933-

Open ice   **Fic**

Hughes, Ted, 1930-1998

Selected poems, 1957-1994   **821**

(tr) Ovid. Tales from Ovid   **873**

(ed) Shakespeare, W. The essential Shakespeare   **822.3**

Hughes-Hassell, Sandra

Collection management for youth   **025.2**

(ed) Curriculum connections through the library. See Curriculum connections through the library   **027.8**

Hugo, Victor, 1802-1885

Les misérables   **Fic**

Huling, Nancy, 1950-

(jt. auth) Baker, N. L. A research guide for undergraduate students   **800**

Hull, Gary

(ed) Rand, A. The Ayn Rand reader   **191**

Hull, N. E. H., 1949-

Roe v. Wade   **344**

Hull House (Chicago, Ill.)

Fradin, J. B. Jane Addams   **92**

Hum. Nye, N. S.

    In Face relations; 11 stories about seeing beyond color   **S C**

HUM-ISHU-MA *See* Mourning Dove, 1888-1936

Human anatomy

    See also Human body

Abrahams, P. H. McMinn's color atlas of human anatomy   **611**

Gray's anatomy   **611**

Leonardo, da Vinci. Leonardo on the human body   **611**

Major systems of the body   **612**

McMillan, B. Human body   **612**

The Structure of the body   **611**

Walker, R. Encyclopedia of the human body   **612**

See/See also pages in the following book(s):

Friedman, M. Medicine's 10 greatest discoveries   **610.9**

Atlases

Photographic atlas of the body   **611**

Human anatomy made amazingly easy. Hart, C.   **743**

Human behavior

    See also Behaviorism

Waal, F. d. Our inner ape   **156**

Human body

Margulies, S. The fascinating body   **612**

Human body. McMillan, B.   **612**

Human body systems [series]

Adams, A. The muscular system   **612.7**

Hollen, K. H. The reproductive system   **618**

Kelly, E. B. The skeletal system   **612.7**

McDowell, J. The lymphatic system   **612.4**

McDowell, J. The nervous system and sense organs   **612.8**

Mertz, L. A. The circulatory system   **616.1**

Petechuk, D. The respiratory system   **612.2**

Watson, S. The endocrine system   **612.4**

Watson, S. The urinary system   **616.6**

Windelspecht, M. The digestive system   **612.3**

Human cargo. Moorehead, C.   **305.9**

The **human** comedy. Saroyan, W.   **Fic**

Human diseases and conditions   **616**

Human ecology

The Atlas of US and Canadian environmental history   **304.2**

The Environment: opposing viewpoints   **363.7**

Hillstrom, K. North America   **363.7**

Magoc, C. J. Environmental issues in American history   **333.7**

Mongillo, J. F. Teen guides to environmental science   **333.72**

Walters, M. J. Six modern plagues and how we are causing them   **614.4**

The **human** element. Maugham, W. S.

    In Maugham, W. S. Collected short stories   **S C**

Human engineering

Parks, D. Nature's machines [biography of Mimi Koehl]   **92**

Human experimentation in medicine

Roach, M. Stiff   **611**

Uschan, M. V. Forty years of medical racism   **174.2**

Human figure in art *See* Artistic anatomy

The **Human** Fly. Boyle, T. C.

    In Boyle, T. C. The Human Fly and other stories   **S C**

The **Human** Fly and other stories. Boyle, T. C.   **S C**

Human geography

How geography affects the United States   **304.2**

Human influence on nature

Are the world's coral reefs threatened?   **333.95**

Hunting for boys. Flake, S. G.
   In Flake, S. G. Who am I without him?; short stories about girls and the boys in their lives p135-56   **S C**

Hunting the deceitful turkey. Twain, M.
   In Twain, M. The complete short stories of Mark Twain; now collected for the first time   **S C**

Huntington's chorea
   Glimm, A. Gene hunter [biography of Nancy Wexler]   **92**

Huntress. Pierce, T.
   In Firebirds rising; an anthology of original science fiction and fantasy   **S C**

Hurley, Jennifer A., 1973-
   The 1960s   **973.92**
   (ed) Dating. See Dating   **646.7**
   (ed) Eating disorders: opposing viewpoints. See Eating disorders: opposing viewpoints   **616.85**

Hurley, Jessica
   (jt. auth) Hill, J. One makes the difference   **333.72**

Hurmence, Belinda, 1921-
   (ed) My folks don't want me to talk about slavery. See My folks don't want me to talk about slavery   **920**

Hurricane. Hurston, Z. N.
   In Hurston, Z. N. The complete stories p149-61   **S C**

The **hurricane**. Salisbury, G.
   In Salisbury, G. Island boyz: short stories p68-94   **S C**

Hurricane almanac 2007. Norcross, B.   **551.55**

Hurricane Katrina, 2005
   Dyson, M. E. Come hell or high water   **976.3**
   Hurricane Katrina   **363.34**
   Katrina: state of emergency   **363.34**
   Van Heerden, I. L. The storm   **976.3**

Hurricane Katrina   **363.34**

Hurricanes
   Emanuel, K. A. Divine wind   **551.55**
   Norcross, B. Hurricane almanac 2007   **551.55**

Fiction
   Vaught, S. Stormwitch   **Fic**

Hurst of Hurstcote. Nesbit, E.
   In The Oxford book of gothic tales p286-96   **S C**

Hurston, Zora Neale, 1891-1960
   The complete stories   **S C**
   Contents: John Redding goes to sea; Drenched in light; Spunk; Magnolia Flower; Muttsy; 'Possum or pig?; The Eatonville anthology; Sweat; The gilded six-bits; Mother Catherine; Uncle Monday; The fire and the cloud; Cock Robin Beale Street; Story in Harlem slang; High John de Conquer; Hurricane; The conscience of the court; Escape from Pharaoh; The tablets of the law; Black death; The bone of contention; Book of Harlem; Harlem slanguage; Now you cookin' with gas; The seventh veil; The woman in Gaul
   Drenched in light
      In The Portable Harlem Renaissance reader p695-702   **810.8**
   Dust tracks on a road   **92**
      also in Hurston, Z. N. Folklore, memoirs, and other writings   **818**

The Eatonville anthology
   In The Norton book of American short stories p357-67   **S C**
The first one
   In Black theatre USA; plays by African Americans, 1847 to today   **812.008**
Folklore, memoirs, and other writings   **818**
Jonah's gourd vine
   In Hurston, Z. N. Novels and stories p1-171   **Fic**
[excerpt]
   In The Portable Harlem Renaissance reader p719-28   **810.8**
Moses, man of the mountain
   In Hurston, Z. N. Novels and stories p335-595   **Fic**
Mules and men
   In Hurston, Z. N. Folklore, memoirs, and other writings   **818**
Novels and stories   **Fic**
   Contents: Short stories included are: John Redding goes to sea; Drenched in light; Spunk; Sweat; The bones of contention; Book of Harlem; The gilded six-bits; The fire and the cloud; Story in Harlem slang
Seraph on the Suwanee
   In Hurston, Z. N. Novels and stories p597-920   **Fic**
Sweat
   In The Oxford book of women's writing in the United States p101-10   **810.8**
Tell my horse
   In Hurston, Z. N. Folklore, memoirs, and other writings   **818**
Their eyes were watching God   **Fic**
   also in Hurston, Z. N. Novels and stories p173-333   **Fic**

About
   Lyons, M. E. Sorrow's kitchen [biography of Zora Neale Hurston]   **92**

Hurvitz, Mitchell M.
   (jt. auth) Karesh, S. E. Encyclopedia of Judaism   **296.03**

Husain, Saddam *See* Hussein, Ṣaddām

Husain, Sarah
   (ed) Voices of resistance. See Voices of resistance   **305.4**

Ḥusayn, Ṣaddām *See* Hussein, Ṣaddām

Huser, Glen, 1943-
   Stitches   **Fic**

Hussein, Ṣaddām
About
   Salbi, Z. Between two worlds   **92**

Hussey, Mark, 1956-
   Virginia Woolf A-Z   **828**

Hutchings, R. T.
   (jt. auth) Abrahams, P. H. McMinn's color atlas of human anatomy   **611**

Hutchinson, S., 1959-
   Oceans: a visual guide   **551.46**

Hutchinson, Stephen *See* Hutchinson, S., 1959-

Hutson, James H.
   (ed) The Founders on religion. See The Founders on religion   **200**

Huxley, Aldous, 1894-1963
   Brave new world   **Fic**

I want to live!. Jones, T.
   In Gotham Writers' Workshop fiction gallery; exceptional short stories selected by New York's acclaimed creative writing school **S C**

I write what I like. Biko, S.   **968.06**

Ian, Janis, 1951-
   Eli and the dybbuk
   In Young warriors; stories of strength   **S C**

Ibn al-Haytham. Steffens, B.   **92**

Ibo (African people) *See* Igbo (African people)

Ibsen, Henrik, 1828-1906
   A doll's house
   In Ibsen, H. and Johnston, B. Ibsen: four major plays   **839.8**
   An enemy of the people
   In Ibsen, H. and Johnston, B. Ibsen: four major plays   **839.8**
   Ghosts
   In Ibsen, H. and Johnston, B. Ibsen: four major plays   **839.8**
   Hedda Gabler
   In Ibsen, H. and Johnston, B. Ibsen: four major plays   **839.8**
   Ibsen: four major plays   **839.8**

Icarus Montgolfier Wright. Bradbury, R.
   In Bradbury, R. Bradbury stories; 100 of his most celebrated tales   **S C**

Icarus's mother. Shepard, S.
   In Under 30; plays for a new generation   **812.008**

Ice. Bruchac, J.
   In Moccasin thunder; American Indians stories for today   **S C**

Ice cream man. Hoffman, R.
   In Working days: stories about teenagers and work   **S C**

Ice hockey *See* Hockey

The ice palace. Fitzgerald, F. S.
   In Fitzgerald, F. S. The short stories of F. Scott Fitzgerald; a new collection p48-69   **S C**

Ice skating
   Jackson, J. On edge   **92**
   Ryan, J. Little girls in pretty boxes   **796.44**

Iceman. Lynch, C.   **Fic**

The iceman cometh. O'Neill, E.   **812**

Icenoggle, Jodi, 1967-
   Schenck v. United States and the freedom of speech debate   **342**

Iconography *See* Christian art; Religious art

An ideal craftsman. De la Mare, W.
   In The Oxford book of short stories p202-18   **S C**

An ideal husband. Wilde, O.
   In Wilde, O. The importance of being earnest and other plays   **822**

Ideal states *See* Utopias

Identification
   See also DNA fingerprinting; Forensic anthropology

Idioms *See* English language—Idioms

Idiots first. Malamud, B.
   In Malamud, B. The complete stories   **S C**
   In The Norton book of American short stories p460-64   **S C**

Iditarod Trail Sled Dog Race, Alaska
   Paulsen, G. Winterdance   **798.8**

The Idol House of Astarte. Christie, A.
   In Christie, A. Miss Marple: the complete short stories   **S C**

If Beale Street could talk. Baldwin, J.   **Fic**

'If I forget thee, oh Earth . . .'. Clarke, A. C.
   In Clarke, A. C. The collected stories of Arthur C. Clarke   **S C**

If the war continues. Hesse, H.
   In Hesse, H. and Zipes, J. D. The fairy tales of Hermann Hesse   **S C**

If you can't be lucky . . . Deuker, C.
   In Ultimate sports; short stories by outstanding writers for young adults p72-91   **S C**

If you come softly. Woodson, J.   **Fic**

If you touched my heart. Allende, I.
   In The Oxford book of gothic tales p519-26   **S C**

Igbo (African people)
Fiction
   Achebe, C. Things fall apart   **Fic**
   Emecheta, B. The bride price   **Fic**

Igniting the spark. Leslie, R.   **027.8**

Ikuta, Tadashi
   Project X Challengers: Seven Eleven   **658.8**

Ile forest. Le Guin, U. K.
   In American short story masterpieces   **S C**

The Iliad. Homer   **883**

The Iliad. McCarty, N.   **883**

The Iliad of Sandy Bar. Harte, B.
   In The Oxford book of short stories p67-77   **S C**

Ilium. Simmons, D.   **Fic**

I'll give you my word. Jones, D. W.
   In Firebirds rising; an anthology of original science fiction and fantasy   **S C**

The ill-made knight. White, T. H.
   In White, T. H. The once and future king   **Fic**

I'll see you when this war is over. Kerr, M. E.
   In Shattered: stories of children and war p40-51   **S C**

Illegal aliens
   Illegal immigration: opposing viewpoints   **325.73**
   Nazario, S. Enrique's journey   **305.23**
   What rights should illegal immigrants have?   **342**

Illegal immigration: opposing viewpoints   **325.73**

Illinois
Fiction
   Leitch, W. Catch   **Fic**
   Rapp, A. Under the wolf, under the dog   **Fic**

Illinois history of sports [series]
Guttmann, A. The Olympics, a history of the modern games **796.48**

Illiteracy *See* Literacy

Illness *See* Diseases

Illusions *See* Hallucinations and illusions

Illustrated dictionary of architecture. Burden, E. E. **720.3**

Illustrated dictionary of religions. Wilkinson, P. **200.3**

Illustrated great decisions of the Supreme Court. Mauro, T. **347**

The **Illustrated** guide to world religions **200**

An **illustrated** history of the First World War. Keegan, J. **940.3**

The **illustrated** man. Bradbury, R. **S C**

The **illustrated** man [story] Bradbury, R.
In Bradbury, R. Bradbury stories; 100 of his most celebrated tales **S C**
In Bradbury, R. The illustrated man **S C**

Illustrations, Humorous *See* Cartoons and caricatures

I'm in Marsport without Hilda. Asimov, I.
In Asimov, I. The complete stories p239-49 **S C**

The **imaginary** invalid. Molière
In Molière. The misanthrope and other plays **842**

Imalhayene, Fatma-Zohra *See* Djebar, Assia, 1936-

Imani all mine. Porter, C. R. **Fic**

Immell, Myra
(ed) Ethnic violence. See Ethnic violence **305.8**
(ed) World War II. See World War II [Turning points in world history series] **940.53**

Immersed in matter. Hoffman, N. K.
In The Faery Reel; tales from the Twilight Realm **S C**

Immersion. Benford, G.
In The Hard SF renaissance **S C**

Immigrants
Crossing into America **810.8**
Nguyen, T. We are all suspects now **323.1**
Fiction
Auch, M. J. Ashes of roses **Fic**
De la Cruz, M. Fresh off the boat **Fic**
First crossing **S C**
Frost, H. The braid **Fic**
Tal, E. Double crossing **Fic**
United States
Hopkinson, D. Shutting out the sky **974.7**
Horst, H. A. Jamaican Americans **305.8**
Rangaswamy, P. Indian Americans **305.8**

Immigrants in literature
New immigrant literatures in the United States **810.9**

Immigration **325.73**

Immigration and emigration
See also Canada—Immigration and emigration; Children of immigrants; Immigrants; Refugees names of countries with the subdivision *Immigration and emigration*; and names of nationality groups
Pagden, A. Peoples and empires **909**

Immigration in U.S. history **304.8**

The **Immortal** Bard. Asimov, I.
In Asimov, I. The complete stories p135-37 **S C**

Immortality
See also Future life

Immroth, Barbara Froling
(ed) Library services to youth of Hispanic heritage. See Library services to youth of Hispanic heritage **027.6**

Immune system
Brynie, F. H. 101 questions about your immune system you felt defenseless to answer . . . until now **616.07**

Immunization *See* Vaccination

Immunological system *See* Immune system

The **imp** of the perverse. Poe, E. A.
In Poe, E. A. The collected tales and poems of Edgar Allan Poe p280-84 **818**

The **impeachment** of Bill Clinton. Aaseng, N. **973.929**

The **impeachment** of William Jefferson Clinton. Cohen, D. **973.929**

Imperial Trans-Antarctic Expedition (1914-1917)
Alexander, C. The Endurance **998**

Imperialism
Cocker, M. Rivers of blood, rivers of gold **909**
Heilbroner, R. L. The worldly philosophers **330.1**
Laxer, J. Empire **327.73**
Smith, B. Imperialism **909**

The **importance** of being Earnest. Wilde, O.
In The Oxford anthology of English literature **820.8**
In Wilde, O. The importance of being earnest and other plays **822**
In Wilde, O. The portable Oscar Wilde p430-507 **828**

The **importance** of being earnest and other plays. Wilde, O. **822**

Impressionism (Art)
Waldron, A. Claude Monet **92**
Welton, J. Impressionism **759.05**

Improving the neighbourhood. Clarke, A. C.
In Clarke, A. C. The collected stories of Arthur C. Clarke **S C**

Impulse control disorders
Williams, J. Pyromania, kleptomania, and other impulse control disorders. **616.85**

In a far country. London, J.
In London, J. The portable Jack London p11-25 **818**

Incas—*Continued*

Malpass, M. Daily life in the Inca empire
985

Moseley, M. E. The Incas and their ancestors
985

Somervill, B. A. Empire of the Inca   **985**
See/See also pages in the following book(s):
Aveni, A. F. Stairways to the stars   **520**
Wright, R. Stolen continents   **970.004**

The **Incas** and their ancestors. Moseley, M. E.
985

Incentive (Psychology) *See* Motivation (Psychology)

Incest
Strong at the heart   **362.7**

Incredibly disgusting drugs [series]
Booley, T. A. Alcohol and your liver
616.86

Index of majors and graduate degrees. See College Entrance Examination Board. The College Board book of majors   **378.73**

Index to the Wilson authors series   **920.003**

India
Fiction
Ali, T. A singular hostage   **Fic**
Desai, A. Clear light of day   **Fic**
Forster, E. M. A passage to India   **Fic**
Hesse, H. Siddhartha   **Fic**
Markandaya, K. Nectar in a sieve   **Fic**
Perkins, M. Monsoon summer   **Fic**
Sheth, K. Koyal dark, mango sweet   **Fic**
Staples, S. F. Shiva's fire   **Fic**
Vijayaraghavan, V. Motherland   **Fic**
Whelan, G. Homeless bird   **Fic**
History
See Mogul Empire
History—1526-1765
McLeod, J. The history of India   **954**
Politics and government
Gandhi, M. Gandhi on non-violence   **322.4**
Martin, C. Mohandas Gandhi   **92**

Indian Americans. Rangaswamy, P.   **305.8**

Indian camp. Hemingway, E.
In Hemingway, E. The complete short stories of Ernest Hemingway; the Finca Vigía edition p67-70   **S C**

Indian chiefs. Freedman, R.   **920**

Indian literature (American) *See* American literature—Native American authors

Indian literature (North American Indian) *See* Native American literature

Indiana
Fiction
West, J. The friendly persuasion   **Fic**

Indianapolis (Cruiser)
Nelson, P. Left for dead   **940.54**
Stanton, D. In harm's way   **940.54**

Indians (of India) *See* East Indians

Indians of North America *See* Native Americans

Indigenous peoples *See* Ethnology

Individual rights and the police   **345**

Indoctrination, Forced *See* Brainwashing

Industrial arts
See also Technology

Industrial plants *See* Factories

Industrial relations
See/See also pages in the following book(s):
Goleman, D. Emotional intelligence   **152.4**

Industrial research
See also Technological innovations

Industrial revolution
Benson, S. Development of the industrial U.S.: Almanac   **330.973**
Benson, S. Development of the industrial U.S.: Biographies   **920**
Benson, S. Development of the industrial U.S.: Primary sources   **330.973**
The Industrial revolution: opposing viewpoints
330.973
Outman, J. L. Industrial Revolution: almanac
330.9
Outman, J. L. Industrial Revolution: biographies
920
Outman, J. L. Industrial Revolution: primary sources   **330.9**

Industrial Revolution: biographies. Outman, J. L.
920

The **Industrial** revolution: opposing viewpoints
330.973

Industrial revolution reference library [series]
Outman, J. L. Industrial Revolution: almanac
330.9
Outman, J. L. Industrial Revolution: biographies
920
Outman, J. L. Industrial Revolution: primary sources   **330.9**

Industries
See also Defense industry
Japan
See also Retail trade—Japan
United States
Benson, S. Development of the industrial U.S.: Almanac   **330.973**
Benson, S. Development of the industrial U.S.: Biographies   **920**
Benson, S. Development of the industrial U.S.: Primary sources   **330.973**

Inequality *See* Equality

Inexcusable. Lynch, C.   **Fic**

Infamous scribblers. Burns, E.   **071**

Infantile paralysis *See* Poliomyelitis

Infants
Care
See also Babysitting
Stoppard, M. Complete baby & child care
649
Fiction
Bechard, M. Hanging on to Max   **Fic**
Johnson, A. The first part last   **Fic**

Infants of the spring [excerpt] Thurman, W.
In The Portable Harlem Renaissance reader p649-53   **810.8**

Infection and infectious diseases *See* Communicable diseases

Jamaica

Fiction

Rees, C. Pirates! **Fic**

Jamaican Americans. Horst, H. A. **305.8**

Jameel and the House of Djinn. Staples, S. F.

In Dreams and visions; fourteen flights of
fantasy **S C**

James, Delores C. S., 1961-
(ed) Nutrition and well-being A to Z. See Nutrition and well-being A to Z **613.2**

James, Edward T.
(ed) Notable American women, 1607-1950. See
Notable American women, 1607-1950
920.003

James, Henry, 1843-1916
The friends of the friends
In Nightshade: 20th century ghost stories
p254-81 **S C**
The middle years
In The Norton book of American short stories
p80-96 **S C**
Paste
In The Oxford book of short stories p84-98
S C
The portrait of a lady **Fic**
The turn of the screw **Fic**

James, J. Alison, 1962-
The audition
In What a song can do; 12 riffs on the power
of music **S C**

James, Jasper
(jt. auth) Marven, N. Chased by sea monsters
560

James, Lawrence
The rise and fall of the British Empire **909**

James, M. R. (Montague Rhodes), 1862-1936
Two doctors
In The Oxford book of English short stories
p97-104 **S C**

James, Montague Rhodes *See* James, M. R.
(Montague Rhodes), 1862-1936

James, Peter
Ancient inventions **609**

James, William, 1842-1910
See/See also pages in the following book(s):
Durant, W. J. The story of philosophy **109**

James Bond (Fictitious character) *See* Bond,
James (Fictitious character)

James Herriot's cat stories. Herriot, J. **636.8**

James Joyce A to Z. See Fargnoli, A. N. Critical
companion to James Joyce **823.009**

James Sturm's America. Sturm, J. **741.5**

Jamestown (Va.)
History
See/See also pages in the following book(s):
Woodward, G. S. Pocahontas **92**

Janaczewska, Noëlle
Madagascar, Lily
In International plays for young audiences;
contemporary works from leading playwrights p257-96 **808.82**

Jane. Maugham, W. S.
In Maugham, W. S. Collected short stories
S C

Jane Austen [critical essays] **823.009**

A **Jane** Austen encyclopedia. Poplawski, P.
823.009

Jane Eyre. Brontë, C. **Fic**

**Jane Seymour, Queen, consort of Henry VIII,
King of England, 1509?-1537**
See/See also pages in the following book(s):
Starkey, D. Six wives: the queens of Henry VIII
920

Janeczko, Paul B., 1945-
(comp) I feel a little jumpy around you. See I
feel a little jumpy around you **808.81**
(comp) Poetry from A to Z. See Poetry from A
to Z **808.1**
(comp) A Poke in the I. See A Poke in the I
811.008
(comp) Seeing the blue between. See Seeing the
blue between **808.1**
(comp) Wherever home begins. See Wherever
home begins **811.008**

Janos, Leo
(jt. auth) Yeager, C. Yeager **92**

Jansen, Barbara A.
(jt. auth) McGhee, M. W. The principal's guide
to a powerful library media program
025.1

Jansen, Hanna
Over a thousand hills I walk with you **Fic**

Janson, H. W. (Horst Woldemar), 1913-1982
Janson's history of art **709**

Janson, Horst Woldemar *See* Janson, H. W.
(Horst Woldemar), 1913-1982

Janson's history of art. Janson, H. W. **709**

Japan
The Cambridge encyclopedia of Japan **952**
Civilization
Dunn, C. J. Everyday life in traditional Japan
952
Kamachi, N. Culture and customs of Japan
952
Schomp, V. Japan in the days of the samurai
952
Fiction
Golden, A. Memoirs of a geisha **Fic**
Hearn, L. Across the nightingale floor **Fic**
Food industry
See Food industry—Japan
Graphic novels
Gallagher, F. Megatokyo v2 **741.5**
History
Buruma, I. Inventing Japan, 1853-1964
952.03
Roberson, J. R. Japan meets the world **952**
History—1868-1945
Frank, R. B. Downfall **940.54**
Religion
Hartz, P. Shinto **299.5**
Social life and customs
Dunn, C. J. Everyday life in traditional Japan
952

Japan 1945. O'Donnell, J. **779**

Jeanne d'Arc, Saint *See* Joan, of Arc, Saint, 1412-1431

Jeans (Clothing)
Sullivan, J. Jeans: a cultural history of an American icon **687**

Jeapes, Ben
The new world order **Fic**

Jefferson, Jon
(jt. auth) Bass, W. M. Death's acre **614**

Jefferson, Thomas, 1743-1826
The autobiography of Thomas Jefferson
In Jefferson, T. Writings **818**
Notes on the State of Virginia
In Jefferson, T. Writings **818**
A summary view of the rights of British America
In Jefferson, T. Writings **818**
Writings **818**
About
Wilkins, R. W. Jefferson's pillow **973**
See/See also pages in the following book(s):
Ellis, J. J. Founding brothers **973.4**
Lanier, S. Jefferson's children **920**
Malone, J. W. It doesn't take a rocket scientist **920**

Jefferson family
See/See also pages in the following book(s):
Lanier, S. Jefferson's children **920**

Jefferson's children. Lanier, S. **920**

Jefferson's pillow. Wilkins, R. W. **973**

Jeff's best joke. Lindskold, J. M.
In Past imperfect **S C**

Jeffty is five. Ellison, H.
In The Locus awards; thirty years of the best in science fiction and fantasy **S C**

Jell, John R.
From school to a career **378**

The **jelly-bean**. Fitzgerald, F. S.
In Fitzgerald, F. S. The short stories of F. Scott Fitzgerald; a new collection p142-58 **S C**

Jen, Gish
In the American society
In The Oxford book of women's writing in the United States p176-89 **810.8**
Typical American **Fic**
What means switch
In Coming of age in America; a multicultural anthology p175-94 **S C**
In Growing up ethnic in America; contemporary fiction about learning to be American **S C**
In Who do you think you are?; stories of friends and enemies p96-118 **S C**

Jenkins, A. M. (Amanda McRaney)
Beating heart **Fic**
Damage **Fic**
Out of order **Fic**

Jenkins, Amanda McRaney *See* Jenkins, A. M. (Amanda McRaney)

Jenkins, Christine, 1949-
(jt. auth) Cart, M. The heart has its reasons **813.009**

Jenkins, George
(jt. auth) Davis, S. The pact: three young men make a promise and fulfill a dream **920**

Jenkins, Robert L., 1945-
(ed) The Malcolm X encyclopedia. See The Malcolm X encyclopedia **92**

Jenkins, Roy, Baron, 1920-2003
Franklin Delano Roosevelt **92**

Jenkins, Sally
(jt. auth) Armstrong, L. It's not about the bike **92**

Jenks, Tom
(ed) American short story masterpieces. See American short story masterpieces **S C**

Jenner, Edward, 1749-1823
About
Friedman, M. Medicine's 10 greatest discoveries **610.9**

Jennifer Government. Barry, M. **Fic**

Jennings, Kevin, 1963-
Mama's boy, preacher's son **92**

Jensen, Richard J.
(jt. auth) Smith, J. D. World War II on the Web **025.04**

Jerome, Judson
The poet's handbook **808.1**

Jerry and Molly and Sam. Carver, R.
In Adaptations: from short story to big screen; 35 great stories that have inspired great films **S C**

Jersey Day. Carter, A. R.
In Carter, A. R. Love, football, and other contact sports **S C**

The **Jerusalem** Bible. See Bible. The new Jerusalem Bible **220.5**

Jerusalem's Lot. King, S.
In King, S. Night shift **S C**

The **jest** of Hahalaba. Dunsany, E. J. M. D. P., Baron
In 24 favorite one-act plays p367-76 **808.82**

Jesters *See* Fools and jesters

Jestice, Phyllis G.
(ed) Holy people of the world. See Holy people of the world **920.003**

Jesus Christ
Nativity—Fiction
Fletcher, S. Alphabet of dreams **Fic**

Jesus land. Scheeres, J. **92**

Jeter, Derek, 1974-
The life you imagine **92**

The **Jewbird**. Malamud, B.
In Malamud, B. The complete stories **S C**

Jewelry
Codina, C. The complete book of jewelry making **739.27**
Discover beading **745.58**
Taylor, C. Creative bead jewelry **745.58**

Jewels *See* Gems; Precious stones

The **jewels** of the Cabots. Cheever, J.
In Cheever, J. The stories of John Cheever p681-93 **S C**

Just before the war with the Eskimos. Salinger, J. D.
In Salinger, J. D. Nine stories p57-82
S C

Just dessert. Ponce, M. H.
In Latina: women's voices from the border-lands p185-98
810.8

Just like a woman. Newman, L.
In Not the only one; lesbian and gay fiction for teens
S C

Just once. Dygard, T. J.
In Ultimate sports; short stories by outstanding writers for young adults p196-205
S C

Just one more time. Cheever, J.
In Cheever, J. The stories of John Cheever p248-52
S C

A **Just** response
973.931

Just tell me who it was. Cheever, J.
In Cheever, J. The stories of John Cheever p370-85
S C

Justice
Adler, M. J. Six great ideas
111

Justice, Administration of *See* Administration of justice

A **justice**. Faulkner, W.
In Faulkner, W. Collected stories of William Faulkner p343-60
S C

Justice is blind. Wolfe, T.
In Wolfe, T. The complete short stories of Thomas Wolfe p589-95
S C

Juvenile courts
Cohen, L. The Gault case and young people's rights
345
Jacobs, T. A. They broke the law, you be the judge
345

Juvenile crime: opposing viewpoints
364.36

Juvenile delinquency
See also Gangs; Juvenile delinquents
Hubner, J. Last chance in Texas
365
Juvenile crime: opposing viewpoints
364.36
Salzman, M. True notebooks
808
Fiction
Burgess, A. A clockwork orange
Fic
Hinton, S. E. The outsiders
Fic

Juvenile delinquents
Should juveniles be tried as adults?
345

K

Kadohata, Cynthia
The floating world [excerpt]
In Coming of age in America; a multicultural anthology p122-35
S C
Jack's girl
In The Literary ghost; great contemporary ghost stories p247-56
S C
Singing apples
In American eyes; new Asian-American short stories for young adults
S C

Kaffir boy [excerpt] Mathabane, M.
In Somehow tenderness survives; stories of Southern Africa p87-103
S C

Kafka, Franz, 1883-1924
Blumfeld, an elderly bachelor
In Nightshade: 20th century ghost stories p282-304
S C
The metamorphosis
In Kafka, F. The metamorphosis and other stories p117-92
Fic
The metamorphosis; adaptation. See Kuper, P.
The metamorphosis
741.5
The metamorphosis and other stories
S C
The longer stories included are: Conversation with the worshiper; Conversation with the drunk; Children on the highway; Exposing a city slicker; The businessman; Unhappiness; The judgment; The stoker; The metamorphosis; An ancient manuscript; Jackals and Arabs; A fratricide; A dream; A report for an Academy
The trial
Fic
About
Franz Kafka's The metamorphosis [study guide]
833.009

Kagan, Andrew
Marc Chagall
92

Kagan, Neil, 1949-
(ed) National Geographic concise history of the world. See National Geographic concise history of the world
902

Kahn, Roger, 1927-
Beyond the boys of summer
796.357

Kakalios, James
The physics of superheroes
530

Kaku, Michio
Parallel worlds
523.1

Kalamu ya Salaam, 1947-
Blk love song #1
In Black theatre USA; plays by African Americans, 1847 to today
812.008

Kaleidoscope. Bradbury, R.
In Bradbury, R. The illustrated man
S C

Kaler, James B.
The hundred greatest stars
523.8

Kallen, Stuart A., 1955-
Primary sources [American war library, The Cold War]
909.82
Witches
133.4
(ed) The Age of Revolution. See The Age of Revolution
909.7
(ed) Are privacy rights being violated? See Are privacy rights being violated?
342
(ed) Biological and chemical weapons. See Biological and chemical weapons
358
(ed) Food safety. See Food safety
363.1
(ed) How should America's wilderness be managed? See How should America's wilderness be managed?
333.7
(ed) Media bias. See Media bias
302.23
(ed) Sixties counterculture. See Sixties counterculture
973.92
(ed) What are the most serious threats to national security? See What are the most serious threats to national security?
355
(ed) What energy sources should be pursued? See What energy sources should be pursued?
333.79

Kamachi, Noriko
Culture and customs of Japan
952

Kelly, Evelyn B.
The skeletal system **612.7**

Kelly, George, 1887-1974
The flattering word
In 24 favorite one-act plays p272-300
808.82

Kelly, James Patrick
10^{16} to 1
In Best of the best: 20 years of the Year's best science fiction **S C**
Rat
In The Norton book of science fiction; North American science fiction, 1960-1990 p654-64 **S C**
Think like a dinosaur
In The Hard SF renaissance **S C**
(ed) Feeling very strange. See Feeling very strange **S C**

Kelly, John, 1945-
The great mortality **614.5**

Kelly-Gangi, Carol
Miranda v. Arizona and the rights of the accused **345**

Kelso, Megan, 1968-
The squirrel mother **741.5**

Kelton, Elmer, 1926-
The burial of Letty Strayhorn
In A Century of great Western stories **S C**

Kemelgor, Carol, 1944-
(jt. auth) Etzkowitz, H. Athena unbound **500**

Kemelman, Harry
The nine mile walk
In The Best American mystery stories of the century p335-43 **S C**

Kemp Owyne
In Hearne, B. G. Beauties and beasts p143-44 **398.2**

Kendrick, Kathleen M.
(jt. auth) Lubar, S. D. Legacies **973**

Keneally, Thomas, 1935-
Abraham Lincoln **92**
Schindler's list **Fic**

Kennebec Indians *See* Abnaki Indians

Kennedy, Adrienne
Funnyhouse of a Negro
In Black theatre USA; plays by African Americans, 1847 to today **812.008**

Kennedy, Caroline
(ed) A Patriot's handbook. See A Patriot's handbook **810.8**
(ed) Profiles in courage for our time. See Profiles in courage for our time **920**

Kennedy, David M., 1941-
Freedom from fear **973.91**

Kennedy, J. Gerald
(ed) A Historical guide to Edgar Allan Poe. See A Historical guide to Edgar Allan Poe **818**

Kennedy, John F. (John Fitzgerald), 1917-1963
Profiles in courage **920**
About
Burner, D. John F. Kennedy and a new generation **92**

Cooper, I. Jack: the early years of John F. Kennedy **92**
Dallek, R. Let every nation know [biography of John F. Kennedy] **92**
Kenney, C. John F. Kennedy **92**
Assassination
Benson, M. The encyclopedia of the JFK assassination **973.922**
Hampton, W. Kennedy assassinated! **973.922**
The Kennedy assassination **364.1**
President Kennedy has been shot **364.1**

Kennedy, Randall
Nigger **305.8**

Kennedy, Richard S., 1920-
E.E. Cummings revisited **811.009**

Kennedy, William, 1928-
Ironweed **Fic**

Kennedy assassinated!. Hampton, W. **973.922**
The **Kennedy** assassination **364.1**

Kennedy Cuomo, Kerry
Speak truth to power **920**

Kennedy Space Center *See* John F. Kennedy Space Center

Kennedy Space Center. Reynolds, D. W. **629.47**

Kenney, Charles
John F. Kennedy **92**

Kent-Drury, Roxanne M.
Using Internet primary sources to teach critical thinking skills in world literature **800**

Kent State University
Caputo, P. 13 seconds **973.924**

Kentucky
Fiction
Mason, B. A. In country **Fic**

Kenya
Lekuton, J. Facing the lion **967.62**

Keoke, Emory Dean
Encyclopedia of American Indian contributions to the world **970.004**

Kepler, Johannes, 1571-1630
About
Voelkel, J. R. Johannes Kepler and the new astronomy **92**

Keppler, Johannes *See* Kepler, Johannes, 1571-1630

Kermode, Frank, 1919-
The age of Shakespeare **792.09**
(ed) Modern British literature. See Modern British literature **820.8**
(ed) Modern British literature; ed. by F. Kermode and J. Hollander. See Modern British literature; ed. by F. Kermode and J. Hollander **820.8**

Kern, Robert W., 1934-
The regions of Spain **946**

Kernfeld, Barry, 1950-
(ed) The New Grove dictionary of jazz. See The New Grove dictionary of jazz **781.65**

Kerns, Roshni Rustomji- *See* Rustomji-Kerns, Roshni, 1938-

Kerouac, Jack, 1922-1969
On the road **Fic**

Kerouac, Jack, 1922-1969—_Continued_
Pomes all sizes   **811**
The portable Jack Kerouac   **818**

Kerouac, Jean _See_ Kerouac, Jack, 1922-1969

Kerouac, Jeanlouis _See_ Kerouac, Jack, 1922-1969

Kerr, M. E., 1927-
Deliver us from Evie   **Fic**
Do you want my opinion?
   _In_ Sixteen: short stories by outstanding writers for young adults p93-100   **S C**
Hearing flower
   _In_ Face relations; 11 stories about seeing beyond color   **S C**
I'll see you when this war is over
   _In_ Shattered: stories of children and war p40-51   **S C**
Night kites   **Fic**
   [excerpt]
   _In_ Growing up gay; an anthology for young people p190-95   **808.8**
Slap your sides   **Fic**
We might as well all be strangers
   _In_ Am I blue?; coming out from the silence p19-26   **S C**
Your eyes in stars   **Fic**

Kerrod, Robin, 1938-
Hubble   **522**
The star guide   **523.8**

Kersting, M. Patricia, 1947-
(jt. auth) Mai, L. L. The Cambridge Dictionary of human biology and evolution   **612**

Kesey, Ken
One flew over the cuckoo's nest   **Fic**

Kessel, John
Buffalo
   _In_ The Locus awards; thirty years of the best in science fiction and fantasy   **S C**
Invaders
   _In_ The Norton book of science fiction; North American science fiction, 1960-1990 p830-50   **S C**
The pure product
   _In_ Best of the best: 20 years of the Year's best science fiction   **S C**
(ed) Feeling very strange. See Feeling very strange   **S C**

Kessel, William B.
(ed) Encyclopedia of Native American wars and warfare. See Encyclopedia of Native American wars and warfare   **970.004**

Kesselman, Wendy Ann
(jt. auth) Goodrich, F. The diary of Anne Frank   **812**

Kessler, James H.
Distinguished African American scientists of the 20th century. See Distinguished African American scientists of the 20th century   **920**

Kett, Joseph F.
(jt. auth) Hirsch, E. D. The new dictionary of cultural literacy   **031**

Kettlewell, Caroline
Electric dreams   **629.22**

Kettmann, Steve
(jt. auth) Angell, R. Game time: a baseball companion   **796.357**

Keturah and Lord Death. Leavitt, M.   **Fic**

Kevles, Bettyann
Almost heaven   **629.45**

The **key**. Asimov, I.
   _In_ Asimov, I. The complete stories p337-61   **S C**

The **key**. Welty, E.
   _In_ Welty, E. The collected stories of Eudora Welty p29-37   **S C**

Key art terms for beginners. Yenawine, P.   **701**

Key events in African history. Falola, T.   **960**

Key item. Asimov, I.
   _In_ Asimov, I. The complete stories p381-83   **S C**

Keyes, Daniel, 1927-
Flowers for Algernon   **Fic**

Keynes, John Maynard, 1883-1946
See/See also pages in the following book(s):
Bussing-Burks, M. Influential economists   **920**
Heilbroner, R. L. The worldly philosophers   **330.1**

Khalili, Nasser D., 1945-
Islamic art and culture   **709.1**

Khan, Lin Shi
Scottsboro, Alabama   **345**

Khlebnikov, Velimir, 1885-1922
Nikolai
   _In_ The portable twentieth-century Russian reader   **891.7**

Khlebnikov, Viktor Vladimirovich _See_ Khlebnikov, Velimir, 1885-1922

Khomeini, Ruhollah
About
Moin, B. Khomeini   **92**

Kibuishi, Kazu
Daisy Kutter   **741.5**
(ed) Flight v2. See Flight v2   **741.5**
(ed) Flight v3. See Flight v3   **741.5**

Kick me. Feig, P.   **305.23**

Kicker wanted. Carter, A. R.
   _In_ Carter, A. R. Love, football, and other contact sports   **S C**

Kickoff (or never trust a girl who steals your ice-cream sandwich). Carter, A. R.
   _In_ Carter, A. R. Love, football, and other contact sports   **S C**

Kid stuff. Asimov, I.
   _In_ Asimov, I. The complete stories p62-72   **S C**

Kidd, J. S. (Jerry S.)
Air pollution   **363.7**
Potent natural medicines   **615**

Kidd, Jerry S. _See_ Kidd, J. S. (Jerry S.)

Kidd, Renee A.
(jt. auth) Kidd, J. S. Air pollution   **363.7**
(jt. auth) Kidd, J. S. Potent natural medicines   **615**

King, Ross, 1962-
Brunelleschi's dome   **726**

King, Stephen, 1947-
Carrie   **Fic**
Everything's eventual: 14 dark tales   **S C**
Contents: Autopsy room four; The man in the black suit; All that you love will be carried away; The death of Jack Hamilton; In the deathroom; The Little Sisters of Eluria; Everything's eventual; L.T.'s theory of pets; The road virus heads north; Lunch at the Gotham Café; That feeling, you can only say what it is in French; 1408; Riding the Bullet; Luckey quarter
Firestarter   **Fic**
Four past midnight   **S C**
Contents: The Langoliers; Secret window, secret garden; The library policeman; The sun dog
The Langoliers
In King, S. Four past midnight p1-246   **S C**
The library policeman
In King, S. Four past midnight p401-604   **S C**
The little sisters of Eluria
In Legends: short novels by the masters of modern fantasy p17-88   **S C**
Night shift   **S C**
Contents: Jerusalem's Lot; Graveyard shift; Night surf; I am the doorway; The mangler; The boogeyman; Gray matter; Battleground; Trucks; Sometimes they come back; Strawberry spring; The ledge; The lawnmower man; Quitters, Inc.; I know what you need; Children of the corn; The last rung of the ladder; The man who loved flowers; One for the road; The woman in the room
On writing   **92**
Quitters, Inc.
In The Best American mystery stories of the century p568-86   **S C**
Secret window, secret garden
In King, S. Four past midnight p247-399   **S C**
Skeleton crew   **S C**
Contents: The mist; Here there be tygers; The monkey; Cain rose up; Mrs. Todd's shortcut; The jaunt; The wedding gig; Paranoid: A chant; The raft; Word processor of the gods; The man who would not shake hands; Beachworld; The reaper's image; Nona; For Owen; Survivor type; Uncle Otto's truck; Morning deliveries (Milkman #1); Big wheels: a tale of the laundry game (Milkman #2); Gramma; The ballad of the flexible bullet; The reach
The sun dog
In King, S. Four past midnight p605-763   **S C**

About
Russell, S. A. Revisiting Stephen King   **813.009**
Russell, S. A. Stephen King: a critical companion   **813.009**
Whitelaw, N. Dark dreams [biography of Stephen King]   **92**

King, Wilma, 1942-
Stolen childhood   **326**

King: a comic book biography. Anderson, H. C.   **92**

King Dork. Portman, F.   **Fic**

King Lear. Shakespeare, W.   **822.3**

King Leopold's ghost. Hochschild, A.   **967.5**

The **king** must die. Renault, M.   **Fic**

King of the buckskin breed. Savage, L., Jr.
In A Century of great Western stories   **S C**

King of the mild frontier: an ill-advised autobiography. Crutcher, C.   **92**

King of the world: Muhammad Ali and the rise of an American hero. Remnick, D.   **92**

King Pest. Poe, E. A.
In Poe, E. A. The collected tales and poems of Edgar Allan Poe p720-29   **818**

King: the photobiography of Martin Luther King, Jr. Johnson, C. R.   **92**

The **kingdom** of infinite number. Bunch, B. H.   **513**

Kings and rulers
See also Dictators; Queens
Arrian. Alexander the Great   **92**
Florescu, R. R. N. Dracula [biography of Vlad II]   **92**
Foreman, L. Alexander the Conqueror   **92**
Wilson, D. A. Charlemagne   **92**
Dictionaries
World monarchies and dynasties   **903**

The **King's** ankus. Kipling, R.
In Kipling, R. The portable Kipling   **828**

The **king's** shadow. Alder, E.   **Fic**

Kingsley, Anna, d. 1870
About
Schafer, D. L. Anna Madgigine Jai Kingsley   **92**

Kingsolver, Barbara
The bean trees   **Fic**
The poisonwood Bible   **Fic**
Small wonder   **814**

Kingston, Maxine Hong
A sea worry
In American dragons: twenty-five Asian American voices p112-17   **810.8**

Kinney, Anne Behnke
(jt. auth) Hardy, G. The establishment of the Han empire and imperial China   **931**

Kinsella, Thomas, 1928-
(ed) The New Oxford book of Irish verse. *See* The New Oxford book of Irish verse   **821.008**

Kinsella, W. P.
Shoeless Joe   **Fic**
Shoeless Joe Jackson comes to Iowa
In Adaptations: from short story to big screen; 35 great stories that have inspired great films   **S C**
Shoeless Joe Jackson comes to Iowa: stories   **S C**
Contents: Fiona the first; A quite incredible dance; Shoeless Joe Jackson comes to Iowa; Waiting for the call; Sister Ann of the Cornfields; The Grecian Urn; Mankiewitz won't be bowling Tuesday nights anymore; A picture of the virgin; The blacksmith shop caper; First names and empty pockets

Kintpuash, Modoc Chief, 1837?-1873
See/See also pages in the following book(s):
Brown, D. A. Bury my heart at Wounded Knee   **970.004**

Kiowa Indians
See/See also pages in the following book(s):
Freedman, R. Indian chiefs   **920**

Kipfer, Barbara Ann
(ed) Roget's 21st century thesaurus in dictionary form. See Roget's 21st century thesaurus in dictionary form   **423**

Kiple, Kenneth F., 1939-
(ed) The Cambridge world history of food. See The Cambridge world history of food
  641.3

Kipling, John, 1897-1915
Fiction
Spillebeen, G. Kipling's choice   **Fic**

Kipling, Rudyard, 1865-1936
Collected stories   **S C**
Contents: In the house of Suddhoo; Beyond the pale; A bank fraud; Pig; On Greenhow Hill; "Love-o'-women"; The drums of the fore and aft; Dray wara yow dee; "The City of Dreadful Night"; Without benefit of clergy; The head of the district; Jews in Shushan; The man who would be king; "The finest story in the world"; The mark of the beast; The strange ride of Morrowbie Jukes; The disturber of traffic; Mrs. Hauksbee sits out {play}; A wayside comedy; Baa baa, black sheep; The bridge-builders; The maltese cat; "In ambush"; A sahibs' war; "Wireless"; Mrs. Bathurst; "Swept and garnished"; Mary Postgate; "Dymchurch flit"; With the night mail; The house surgeon; The wish house; The Janeites; The bull that thought; A madonna of the trenches; The eye of Allah; The gardener; Dayspring mishandled; The church that was at Antioch; The manner of men
Complete verse   **821**
The portable Kipling   **828**
Includes the following stories: The strange ride of Morrowbie Jukes; The man who would be king; Without benefit of clergy; Lispeth; The head of the district; The miracle of Purun Bhagat; The story of Muhammad Din; Jews in Shushan; The courting of Dinah Shadd; On Greenhow Hill; Black Jack; Toomai of the Elephants; The King's ankus; How the Rhinoceros got his skin; The cat that walked by himself; The village that voted the Earth was flat; Brugglesmith; Brother Square-Toes; 'A priest in spite of himself'; The church that was at Antioch; The Eye of Allah; As easy as A.B.C.; Mrs. Bathurst; Friendly Brook; The wish house; Mary Postgate; The gardener; Dayspring mishandled
The record of Badalia Herodsfoot
  In The Oxford book of short stories p147-66   **S C**
Rikki-tikki-tavi
  In Read all about it!; great read-aloud stories, poems, and newspaper pieces for preteens and teens p155-74   **808.8**
"They"
  In Nightshade: 20th century ghost stories p305-27   **S C**
  In The Year's best science fiction and fantasy for teens: first annual collection   **S C**
'Wireless'
  In The Oxford book of English short stories p110-26   **S C**

Kipling's choice. Spillebeen, G.   **Fic**

Kirberger, Kimberly, 1953-
(jt. auth) Canfield, J. Chicken soup for the teenage soul [I-III]   **158**

Kirby, John T.
(ed) Classical Greek civilization, 800-323 B.C.E. See Classical Greek civilization, 800-323 B.C.E   **938**

Kirby, Megan, 1965-
(ed) The Michaels book of paper crafts. See The Michaels book of paper crafts   **745.54**

Kirchberger, Joe H.
The Civil War and Reconstruction   **973.7**

Kirinyaga. Resnick, M.
  In Best of the best: 20 years of the Year's best science fiction   **S C**
  In The Norton book of science fiction; North American science fiction, 1960-1990 p716-32   **S C**

Kirk, Connie Ann, 1951-
J.K. Rowling: a biography   **92**
A student's guide to Robert Frost   **811.009**

Kirkman, Robert
Invincible: ultimate collection, Vol. 1   **741.5**

Kirkpatrick, Helen, 1909-
See/See also pages in the following book(s):
Colman, P. Where the action was   **070.4**

Kirkwood, Burton
The history of Mexico   **972**

Kirsch, Jonathan
Moses   **222**

Kishimoto, Masashi, 1974-
Naruto. vol. 1, The tests of the Ninja   **741.5**

The kiss. Carter, A.
  In The Oxford book of English short stories p400-02   **S C**

KISS guide to digital photography. Ang, T.
  775

The kiss in the carry-on bag. Peck, R.
  In Destination unexpected: short stories   **S C**
  In Peck, R. Past perfect, present tense: new and collected stories   **S C**

Kissing dead boys. Klause, A. C.
  In The restless dead; ten original stories of the supernatural   **S C**

Kissing lessons. Weisberg, J.
  In Sixteen: stories about that sweet and bitter birthday   **S C**

Kissing the rain. Brooks, K.   **Fic**

The kite. Maugham, W. S.
  In Maugham, W. S. Collected short stories   **S C**

The kite runner. Hosseini, K.   **Fic**

Kit's wilderness. Almond, D.   **Fic**

Kittleson, Mark J., 1952-
(ed) The Truth about alcohol. See The Truth about alcohol   **362.292**
(ed) The truth about divorce. See The truth about divorce   **306.89**
(ed) The Truth about eating disorders. See The Truth about eating disorders   **616.85**
(ed) The Truth about family life. See The Truth about family life   **306.8**
(ed) The Truth about fear and depression. See The Truth about fear and depression
  616.85

Kittredge, William
(ed) The Portable Western reader. See The Portable Western reader   **810.8**

Kitty and Mack: a love story. Myers, W. D.
  In Myers, W. D. 145th Street; short stories   **S C**

Kiyosaki, Robert T., 1947-
Rich dad, poor dad for teens   **332.024**

Labor policy
See also Vocational education

Labor relations *See* Industrial relations

Labor unions
Miller, C. C. A. Philip Randolph and the African American labor movement **92**

Laboratory animal experimentation *See* Animal experimentation

Labors of the heart. Davis, C.
In Gotham Writers' Workshop fiction gallery; exceptional short stories selected by New York's acclaimed creative writing school **S C**

The **labyrinthine** ways. See Greene, G. The power and the glory **Fic**

Lace, William W.
The Vatican **945**

Lacey, Robert
The year 1000 **942.01**

Lachmann, Lyn Miller- *See* Miller-Lachmann, Lyn, 1956-

Lackey, Mercedes
Joust **Fic**
Out of the deep: a Valdemar story
In Masters of fantasy **S C**
The outstretched shadow **Fic**
The serpent's shadow **Fic**

Lackmann, Ronald W.
The encyclopedia of American television, broadcast programming Post World War II to 2000 **791.45**

Lacrosse
Hinkson, J. Lacrosse for dummies **796.34**
Swissler, B. Winning lacrosse for girls **796.34**
Urick, D. Sports illustrated lacrosse **796.34**
Lacrosse for dummies. Hinkson, J. **796.34**

Lacy, Ed, 1911-1968
The "method" sheriff
In Alfred Hitchcock's mystery magazine presents fifty years of crime and suspense **S C**

Ladd, Andrew
(jt. auth) Phillips, J. Romanticism and transcendentalism: 1800-1860 **810.9**

Ladies in spring. Welty, E.
In Welty, E. The collected stories of Eudora Welty p519-30 **S C**

Ladies' voices. Stein, G.
In Stein, G. Selected writings p555-56 **818**

The **lady** and the panda. Croke, V. **599.78**

Lady Eltringham; or, The castle of Ratcliffe Cross. Wadham, J.
In The Oxford book of gothic tales p82-84 **S C**

The **lady** of the house of love. Carter, A.
In The Oxford book of gothic tales p483-97 **S C**

The **lady** of the lake. Malamud, B.
In Malamud, B. The complete stories **S C**

Lady of the skulls. McKillip, P. A.
In McKillip, P. A. Harrowing the dragon **S C**

Lady sings the blues. Holiday, B. **92**

The **lady** vanishes. Sheffield, C.
In The Hard SF renaissance **S C**

Lady Windermere's fan. Wilde, O.
In Wilde, O. The importance of being earnest and other plays **822**

A **lady** with the dog. Chekhov, A. P.
In Chekhov, A. P. The Russian master and other stories p7-21 **S C**
In The Portable nineteenth-century Russian reader p534-49 **891.7**

The **lady** with the pet dog. Chekhov, A. P.
In Adaptations: from short story to big screen; 35 great stories that have inspired great films **S C**

Læssøe, Thomas
Mushrooms **579.6**

Lafayette, farewell. Bradbury, R.
In Bradbury, R. Bradbury stories; 100 of his most celebrated tales **S C**

Lafferty, R. A., 1914-2002
Nine hundred grandmothers
In The Norton book of science fiction; North American science fiction, 1960-1990 p142-50 **S C**

The **lagoon.** Conrad, J.
In Conrad, J. The portable Conrad **828**

Lagowski, J. J.
(ed) Chemistry: foundations and applications. See Chemistry: foundations and applications **540.3**

LaGuardia, Cheryl M.
(ed) Magazines for libraries. See Magazines for libraries **011**

LaGumina, Salvatore John, 1928-
(ed) The Italian American experience. See The Italian American experience **305.8**

Lahiri, Jhumpa
The namesake **Fic**
The third and final continent
In Gotham Writers' Workshop fiction gallery; exceptional short stories selected by New York's acclaimed creative writing school **S C**

The **Laidly** worm of Spindleston Heughs
In Hearne, B. G. Beauties and beasts p139-42 **398.2**

Laing, Kojo, 1946-
Vacancy for the post of Jesus Christ
In The Heinemann book of contemporary African short stories p185-96 **S C**

Laird, Charlton, 1901-
Webster's New World Roget's A-Z thesaurus **423**

Laird's promptory. See Laird, C. Webster's New World Roget's A-Z thesaurus **423**

The **lake** was full of artificial things. Fowler, K. J.
In The Norton book of science fiction; North American science fiction, 1960-1990 p580-90 **S C**

Lakota woman. Brave Bird, M.   **92**

Lalor, Brian, 1941-
(ed) The Encyclopedia of Ireland. See The Encyclopedia of Ireland   **941.5**

Lamar, Howard Roberts
(ed) The New encyclopedia of the American West. See The New encyclopedia of the American West   **978.03**

Lamar, Lucius Quintus Cincinnatus, 1825-1893
See/See also pages in the following book(s):
Kennedy, J. F. Profiles in courage   **920**

Lamb, Andrew
150 years of popular musical theatre   **792.6**

The **lamb** of the Flying U. Bower, B. M.
In A Century of great Western stories
   S C

Lamb to the slaughter. Dahl, R.
In Dahl, R. Skin and other stories   **S C**

Lambert, David, 1932-
Dinosaur encyclopedia   **567.9**
The field guide to geology   **551**

Lambing season. Gloss, M.
In Best of the best: 20 years of the Year's best science fiction   **S C**

The **lame** shall enter first. O'Connor, F.
In O'Connor, F. Collected works p595-632
   S C
In O'Connor, F. The complete stories p445-82
   S C

Lamkin, Kurtis
See/See also pages in the following book(s):
Fooling with words   **808.1**

Lammers, Wayne P., 1951-
Japanese the manga way   **495.6**

L'Amour, Louis, 1908-1988
The daybreakers   **Fic**
The gift of Cochise
In A Century of great Western stories
   S C

Lanagan, Margo, 1960-
Black juice   **S C**
Contents: Singing my sister down; My lord's man; Red nose day; Sweet Pippit; House of the many; Wooden bride; Earthly uses; Perpetual light; Yowlinin; Rite of spring
White time   **S C**
Contents: White time; Dedication; Tell and kiss; The queen's notice; Big rage; The night lily; The boy who didn't yearn; Midsummer mission; Welcome blue; Wealth

Lancelot (Legendary character)
Pyle, H. The story of Sir Launcelot and his companions   **398.2**

Lanchon, Anne
All about adoption   **649**

Land reform
See also Agriculture—Government policy

Land surveying *See* Surveying

Landau, Elaine
Alzheimer's disease   **616.8**

Landforms
See also Coasts

Landi, Ann
Schirmer encyclopedia of art   **703**

The **landing** on Kuralei. Michener, J. A.
In Michener, J. A. Tales of the South Pacific
   S C

Landis, Geoffrey A.
A walk in the sun
In The Hard SF renaissance   **S C**
In New skies: an anthology of today's science fiction   **S C**

Landlord of the crystal fountain. Whitaker, M.
In The Oxford book of English short stories p264-69   **S C**

Landmark decisions of the United States Supreme Court. Finkelman, P.   **347**

Landmark law cases & American society [series]
Hoffer, P. C. The Salem witchcraft trials
   345
Hull, N. E. H. Roe v. Wade   **344**

Landmark Supreme Court cases. Hartman, G. R.
   347

Landmark Supreme Court cases. Lively, D. E.
   342

Landmark Supreme Court cases [series]
DeVillers, D. Marbury v. Madison   **347**
Sherrow, V. Cherokee Nation v. Georgia
   346
Sherrow, V. Gideon v. Wainwright   **345**

Landmarks, Literary *See* Literary landmarks

Landor's cottage. Poe, E. A.
In Poe, E. A. The collected tales and poems of Edgar Allan Poe p616-25   **818**

Landrigan, Linda
(ed) Alfred Hitchcock's mystery magazine presents fifty years of crime and suspense. See Alfred Hitchcock's mystery magazine presents fifty years of crime and suspense   **S C**

Landsberg, Brian K.
(ed) Major acts of Congress. See Major acts of Congress   **348**

Landscape architecture
Step-by-step yard & garden basics   **635**

Landscape gardening
Care-free plants   **635.9**

Landscape with figures. Hemingway, E.
In Hemingway, E. The complete short stories of Ernest Hemingway; the Finca Vigía edition p590-96   **S C**

Lane, Eric
Sweet hunk o' trash
In Under 30; plays for a new generation
   812.008
(ed) The Actor's book of scenes from new plays. See The Actor's book of scenes from new plays   **808.82**
(ed) Under 30. See Under 30   **812.008**

Lane, George, 1952-
Genghis Khan and Mongol rule   **950**

Lang, Kenneth R.
The Cambridge encyclopedia of the sun
   523.7

Lange, Dianne
(ed) Informed decisions. See Informed decisions
   616.99

The **last** refuge. Goligorsky, E.
> *In* Cosmos latinos; an anthology of science fiction from Latin America and Spain
> **S C**

The **last** report on the miracles at Little No Horse. Erdrich, L.　　**Fic**

Last rites. Bradbury, R.
> *In* Bradbury, R. Bradbury stories; 100 of his most celebrated tales　　**S C**

The **last** rung of the ladder. King, S.
> *In* King, S. Night shift　　**S C**

The **last** snow of the Virgin Mary. Van Camp, R.
> *In* Moccasin thunder; American Indians stories for today　　**S C**

The **last** trump. Asimov, I.
> *In* Asimov, I. The complete stories p106-19
> **S C**

The **last** unicorn. Beagle, P. S.　　**Fic**

The **last** Yankee. Miller, A.
> *In* Miller, A. The portable Arthur Miller
> **812**

Lat
> Kampung boy　　**741.5**

A **late** encounter with the enemy. O'Connor, F.
> *In* O'Connor, F. Collected works p252-62
> **S C**
> *In* O'Connor, F. The complete stories p134-44
> **S C**
> *In* The Oxford book of women's writing in the United States p126-34　　**810.8**

Latham, Alison
> (ed) The Oxford companion to music. See The Oxford companion to music　　**780.3**

The **lathe** of heaven. Le Guin, U. K.　　**Fic**

Latimer, Lewis Howard, 1848-1928
> *See/See also pages in the following book(s):*
> Aaseng, N. Black inventors　　**920**
> Abdul-Jabbar, K. Black profiles in courage
> **920**

Latin America
> Gritzner, C. F. Latin America　　**980**
> **Civilization**
> Fuentes, C. The buried mirror　　**946**
> **Fiction**
> Allende, I. Eva Luna　　**Fic**
> García Márquez, G. Love in the time of cholera
> **Fic**
> **Folklore**
> *See* Folklore—Latin America

Latin American art
> Makosz, R. Latino arts and their influence on the United States　　**700**
> Scott, J. F. Latin American art　　**709.8**

Latin American art. Scott, J. F.　　**709.8**

Latin American fiction
> **History and criticism**
> Williams, R. L. The modern Latin American novel　　**863.009**

Latin American folktales　　**398.2**

Latin American literature
> *See also* Mexican literature

Bio-bibliography
> Concise encyclopedia of Latin American literature　　**860.3**
> Flores, A. Spanish American authors
> **920.003**
> **Encyclopedias**
> Concise encyclopedia of Latin American literature　　**860.3**
> **History and criticism**
> Moss, J. Latin American literature and its times
> **860.9**

Latin American literature and its times. Moss, J.
> **860.9**

Latin American music *See* Music—Latin America

The **Latin** beat. Morales, E.　　**781.64**

Latin language
> **Dictionaries**
> Cassell's Latin dictionary　　**473**

Latin literature
> *See also* Classical literature
> **Collections**
> Atchity, K. J. The classical Roman reader
> **870.8**
> The Portable Roman reader　　**870.8**
> **History and criticism**
> Hamilton, E. The Roman way　　**870.9**

Latin poetry
> The Roman poets　　**871.008**

Latina: women's voices from the borderlands
> **810.8**

Latino arts and their influence on the United States. Makosz, R.　　**700**

Latino biography library [series]
> Cruz, B. César Chávez　　**92**

Latino periodicals　　**011.6**

The **Latino** student's guide to college success
> **378**

Latino visions. Cockcroft, J. D.　　**704**

Latinos (U.S.) *See* Hispanic Americans

Latrobe, Kathy Howard
> Readers theatre for young adults　　**808.5**

Latter-day Saints *See* Church of Jesus Christ of Latter-day Saints

Lauer, Josh
> (ed) Contemporary novelists. See Contemporary novelists　　**920.003**
> (ed) Science and its times. See Science and its times　　**509**

The **laughing** man. Salinger, J. D.
> *In* Salinger, J. D. Nine stories p83-110
> **S C**

Laughlin, Mildred, 1922-1994
> (jt. auth) Latrobe, K. H. Readers theatre for young adults　　**808.5**

Laughter
> Provine, R. R. Laughter　　**152.4**

Laughter on the 23rd floor. Simon, N.
> *In* Simon, N. The collected plays of Neil Simon　　**812**

Laughton, Charles, 1899-1962
> (jt. auth) Brecht, B. Galileo　　**832**

Le Guin, Ursula K., 1929-
Coming of age in Karhide
  In Best of the best: 20 years of the Year's
    best science fiction   **S C**
The day before the revolution
  In The Locus awards; thirty years of the best
    in science fiction and fantasy   **S C**
Dragonfly
  In Legends: short novels by the masters of
    modern fantasy p333-95   **S C**
Gifts   **Fic**
Ile forest
  In American short story masterpieces   **S C**
The lathe of heaven   **Fic**
The left hand of darkness   **Fic**
May's lion
  In The Oxford book of women's writing in
    the United States p190-96   **810.8**
The new Atlantis
  In The Norton book of science fiction; North
    American science fiction, 1960-1990
    p317-36   **S C**
The ones who walk away from Omelas
  In The Norton book of American short stories
    p566-71   **S C**
Sixty odd   **811**
Tales from Earthsea   **S C**
  Contents: The finder — Darkrose and Diamond — The bones
of the earth — On the high marsh — Dragonfly — A description
of Earthsea
(ed) The Norton book of science fiction. See
  The Norton book of science fiction   **S C**

Le Vert, Suzanne *See* LeVert, Suzanne

Leach, Laurie F.
Langston Hughes   **92**

The **leader**. Ionesco, E.
  In Ionesco, E. Rhinoceros, and other plays
     842

Leadership
        Encyclopedias
Encyclopedia of leadership   **658.4**

Leadership and the school librarian   **025.1**

The **leaf-sweeper**. Spark, M.
  In Nightshade: 20th century ghost stories
    p422-27   **S C**

Leah's stories. Sleator, W.
  In Sleator, W. Oddballs; stories p83-101
     S C

Leahy, Christopher W.
The birdwatcher's companion to North American birdlife   **598**

Leakey, Richard E., 1944-
The origin of humankind   **599.93**
Origins reconsidered   **599.93**
The sixth extinction   **304.2**

Leal, Alvaro Menendez *See* Menen Desleal,
  Alvaro

The **leaning** tower. Porter, K. A.
  In Porter, K. A. The collected stories of Kath-
    erine Anne Porter   **S C**

The **leaning** tower, and other stories. Porter, K. A.
  In Porter, K. A. The collected stories of Kath-
    erine Anne Porter   **S C**

The **learned** women. Molière
  In Molière. The misanthrope and other plays
     842

Learning, Art of *See* Study skills

Learning, Psychology of *See* Psychology of learning

(Learning about) machine sex. Dorsey, C. J.
  In The Norton book of science fiction; North
    American science fiction, 1960-1990
    p746-61   **S C**

Learning and libraries in an information age
     027.62

Learning and memory. Hudmon, A.   **612.8**

Learning and scholarship
  See also Education
  See/See also pages in the following book(s):
  Emerson, R. W. The portable Emerson   **818**

Learning disabilities
  See also Attention deficit disorder
  Abeel, S. My thirteenth winter   **92**
  Colleges with programs for students with learn-
    ing disabilities or attention deficit disorders
     378.73
  Paquette, P. H. Learning disabilities   **371.9**

Learning resource centers *See* Instructional materials centers

Learning right from wrong in the digital age.
  Johnson, D.   **004.6**

The **learning** tree. Parks, G.   **Fic**

The **Leatherstocking** saga. See Cooper, J. F. The
  Leatherstocking tales   **Fic**

The **Leatherstocking** tales. Cooper, J. F.   **Fic**

Leaves of grass. Whitman, W.   **811**
  also in Whitman, W. Complete poetry and
    collected prose   **818**

Leaving. Vassanji, M. G.
  In The Heinemann book of contemporary Af-
    rican short stories p114-20   **S C**

Leaving Fishers. Haddix, M. P.   **Fic**

Leaving home: stories   **808.8**
  Includes the following stories: The first day, by E. P. Jones;
Dancer, by V. Sears; A gift of laughter, by A. Sherman; Rules
of the game, by A. Tan; The circuit, by F. Jiménez; Bad influence, by J. Ortiz Cofer; Dawn, by T. Wynne-Jones; Trip in a
summer dress, by A. Sanford; On the rainy river, by T. O'Brien;
The setting sun and the rolling world, by C. Mungoshi; Zelzah:
a tale from long ago, by N. F. Mazer; "Recitatif", by T. Morrison

Leaving Nairobi. McBain, E.
  In Alfred Hitchcock's mystery magazine pres-
    ents fifty years of crime and suspense
     S C

Leaving Protection. Hobbs, W.   **Fic**

Leavitt, David, 1961-
The lost language of cranes [excerpt]
  In Growing up gay; an anthology for young
    people p110-16   **808.8**

Leavitt, Henrietta Swan, 1868-1921
  See/See also pages in the following book(s):
  Malone, J. W. It doesn't take a rocket scientist
     920

Leavitt, Martine, 1953-
Keturah and Lord Death   **Fic**

Legends of the Province-House. Hawthorne, N.
In Hawthorne, N. Tales and sketches, including Twice-told tales, Mosses from an old manse, and The snow-image; A wonder book for girls and boys; Tanglewood tales for girls and boys, being a second Wonder book p626-77 **S C**

Legends: short novels by the masters of modern fantasy **S C**

LeGuin, Ursula *See* Le Guin, Ursula K., 1929-

Lehane, Dennis
Running out of dog
In The Best American mystery stories of the century p770-99 **S C**

Lehman, David, 1948-
(ed) The Oxford book of American poetry. See The Oxford book of American poetry **811.008**

Lehman, Jeffrey, 1969-
(ed) Gale encyclopedia of multicultural America. See Gale encyclopedia of multicultural America **305.8**
(ed) West's encyclopedia of American law. See West's encyclopedia of American law **349**

Lehman, Timothy
Manga: masters of the art **741.5**

Lehmann, Rosamond, 1901-1990
A dream of winter
In The Oxford book of English short stories p286-94 **S C**

Leiber, Fritz, 1910-1992
The winter flies
In The Norton book of science fiction; North American science fiction, 1960-1990 p171-82 **S C**

Leibnitz, Gottfried Wilhelm von *See* Leibniz, Gottfried Wilhelm, Freiherr von, 1646-1716

Leibniz, Gottfried Wilhelm, Freiherr von, 1646-1716
See/See also pages in the following book(s):
Russell, B. A history of Western philosophy **109**

Leigh, Mitch, 1928-
(jt. auth) Darion, J. Man of La Mancha **812**

Leighton, Robert B., 1919-1997
(jt. auth) Feynman, R. P. Six easy pieces **530**

Leininger, Phillip, 1928-
(ed) HarperCollins Reader's encyclopedia of American literature. See HarperCollins Reader's encyclopedia of American literature **810.3**
(jt. auth) Hart, J. D. The Oxford companion to American literature **810.3**

Leitch, Will
Catch **Fic**

Leiter, Sharon
Critical companion to Emily Dickinson **811.009**

Lekh-Lekho. Sholem Aleichem
In Halkin, H. and Sholem Aleichem. Tevye the dairyman and The railroad stories **S C**

Lekuton, Joseph
Facing the lion **967.62**

Lemann, Nicholas
The promised land **973.9**

LeMaster, J. R., 1934-
(ed) The Mark Twain encyclopedia. See The Mark Twain encyclopedia **818**

Lemay, J. A. Leo (Joseph A. Leo), 1935-
(ed) Franklin, B. Autobiography, Poor Richard, and later writings **818**

Lemay, Joseph A. Leo *See* Lemay, J. A. Leo (Joseph A. Leo), 1935-

Lenburg, Jeff
The encyclopedia of animated cartoons **791.43**

Lend-lease. Shalamov, V. T.
In The portable twentieth-century Russian reader **891.7**

Lend me your ears **808.85**

Lenderman, Lois
(il) Costello, E. Random House American sign language dictionary **419**

Lending of library materials *See* Library circulation

L'Engle, Madeleine, 1918-
A wrinkle in time **Fic**

Lenihan, Edmund
(ed) Meeting the other crowd. See Meeting the other crowd **398.2**

Lennon, John, 1940-1980
About
Partridge, E. John Lennon **92**

Lenny. Asimov, I.
In Asimov, I. The complete stories p272-83 **S C**

Leo Tolstoy: comprehensive research and study guide **891.7**

Leonard, Elizabeth D.
All the daring of the soldier **973.7**

Leonard, Elmore, 1925-
About
Devlin, J. E. Elmore Leonard **813.009**

Leonard, Thomas M., 1937-
(ed) Encyclopedia of the developing world. See Encyclopedia of the developing world **909**

Leonard Maltin's movie guide 2007. Maltin, L. **791.43**

Leonardo, da Vinci, 1452-1519
Leonardo on the human body **611**
About
Marani, P. C. Leonardo da Vinci—the complete paintings **759.5**
Wasserman, J. Leonardo **759.5**

Leonardo Da Vinci on the human body. See Leonardo, da Vinci. Leonardo on the human body **611**

Leonardo on the human body. Leonardo, da Vinci **611**

Leone, Bruno, 1939-
(ed) Cloning. See Cloning **176**

Leone, Daniel A., 1969-
(ed) Space exploration. See Space exploration **333.9**

A **letter** from the Clearys. Willis, C.
 In New skies: an anthology of today's science
  fiction **S C**
A **letter** to my daughter. Flake, S. G.
 In Flake, S. G. Who am I without him?; short
  stories about girls and the boys in their
  lives p157-68 **S C**
Letter writing
 See also Business letters
Letters
 See also American letters
 First daughters: letters between U.S. presidents
  and their daughters **920**
     Fiction
 Beard, P. Dear Zoe **Fic**
 Buckhanon, K. Upstate **Fic**
Letters from the Samantha. Helprin, M.
 In American short story masterpieces **S C**
 In The Norton book of American short stories
  p722-32 **S C**
Letters from Yellowstone. Smith, D. **Fic**
Letters of the century **816**
Letters to a young activist. Gitlin, T. **322.4**
Letters to a young actor. Brustein, R. **792**
Letters to a young artist. Smith, A. D. **700**
Letters to a young brother. Harper, H. **170**
Letters to a young evangelical. Campolo, A.
     248.4
Letters to a young journalist. Freedman, S. G.
     070.4
Letters to America **811.008**
Letting go of Bobby James, or, How I found my-
 self of steam. Hobbs, V. **Fic**
LeVay, Simon
 (jt. auth) Koerner, D. Here be dragons
     576.8
Levenson, J. C. (Jacob Claver), 1922-
 (ed) Crane, S. Prose and poetry **818**
Leventhal, Alice Walker *See* Walker, Alice,
 1944-
Leventhal, Josh, 1971-
 (ed) Baseball, the perfect game. See Baseball,
  the perfect game **796.357**
Lever, Evelyne
 Marie Antoinette **92**
Leverage your library program to help raise test
 scores. Church, A. P. **027.8**
LeVert, Suzanne
 The facts about cocaine **362.29**
 The facts about ecstasy **362.29**
 The facts about LSD and other hallucinogens
     362.29
 The facts about steroids **362.29**
Levertov, Denise, 1923-1997
 Sands of the well **811**
 This great unknowing **811**
Levin, Carole, 1948-
 Extraordinary women of the Medieval and Re-
  naissance world. See Extraordinary women of
  the Medieval and Renaissance world
     920.003

Levin, Judith, 1956-
 Hugo Chávez **92**
Levine, Ellen, 1939-
 Rachel Carson **92**
Levine, Gail Carson, 1947-
 Fairest **Fic**
Levinson, David, 1947-
 (ed) Berkshire encyclopedia of world sport. See
  Berkshire encyclopedia of world sport
     796.03
 (ed) Encyclopedia of crime and punishment. See
  Encyclopedia of crime and punishment
     364.03
 (ed) Encyclopedia of homelessness. See Ency-
  clopedia of homelessness **362.5**
 (ed) The Wilson chronology of the world's reli-
  gions. See The Wilson chronology of the
  world's religions **200**
Levinson, Paul
 The mendelian lamp case
  In The Hard SF renaissance **S C**
Levitation. Ozick, C.
 In The Norton book of American short stories
  p554-66 **S C**
Levithan, David, 1972-
 The alumni interview
  In Sixteen: stories about that sweet and bitter
   birthday **S C**
 Are we there yet? **Fic**
 Marly's ghost **Fic**
 Princes
  In Every man for himself; ten short stories
   about being a guy **S C**
 What a song can do
  In What a song can do; 12 riffs on the power
   of music **S C**
 (jt. auth) Cohn, R. Nick & Norah's infinite
  playlist **Fic**
 (ed) The Full spectrum. See The Full spectrum
     306.76
 (ed) Where we are, what we see. See Where we
  are, what we see **810.8**
Levitt, Eric J., 1970-
 (jt. auth) Seamon, M. P. Digital cameras in the
  classroom **775**
Levitt, Susan
 Teen feng shui **133.3**
Levy, Andrew, 1962-
 The first emancipator [biography of Robert Car-
  ter] **92**
Levy, Ariel, 1974-
 Female chauvinist pigs **305.4**
Levy, David H., 1948-
 David H. Levy's guide to observing and discov-
  ering comets **523.6**
 See/See also pages in the following book(s):
 Malone, J. W. It doesn't take a rocket scientist
     920
Levy, Debbie
 Medical ethics **174.2**
Levy, Gavin
 112 acting games **792**

Libraries—*Continued*

Administration

Curzon, S. C. Managing change   **025.1**

Dresang, E. T. Dynamic youth services through outcome-based planning and evaluation   **025.1**

Giesecke, J. Fundamentals of library supervision   **023**

Leadership and the school librarian   **025.1**

MacDonell, C. Essential documents for school libraries   **025.1**

Matthews, J. R. Strategic planning and management for library managers   **025.1**

Automation

Cuddy, C. Using PDAs in libraries   **004**

Censorship

Intellectual freedom manual   **323.44**

Kravitz, N. E. Censorship and the school library media center   **025.2**

Peck, R. S. Libraries, the First Amendment, and cyberspace   **025.04**

Symons, A. K. Protecting the right to read   **025.2**

Collection development

Baumbach, D. Less is more   **025.2**

Crawford, P. C. Graphic novels 101   **741.5**

Doll, C. A. Managing and analyzing your collection   **025.2**

Greiner, T. Analyzing library collection use with Excel   **025.2**

Hughes-Hassell, S. Collection management for youth   **025.2**

Exhibitions

Evans, E. G. 3-D displays for libraries, schools and media centers   **027.62**

Skaggs, G. Off the wall!   **027.8**

Law and legislation

Torrans, L. A. Law for K-12 libraries and librarians   **344**

Public relations

Valenza, J. K. Power tools recharged   **027.8**

Wolfe, L. A. Library public relations, promotions, and communications   **021.7**

Special collections

Goldsmith, F. Graphic novels now   **025.2**

Reaching out to religious youth   **027.62**

Walker, B. J. The librarian's guide to developing Christian fiction collections for young adults   **025.2**

United States

The whole library handbook 4   **027**

Libraries, School *See* School libraries

Libraries, Young adults' *See* Young adults' libraries

Libraries and community

Farkas, M. Social software in libraries   **025.5**

Lukenbill, W. B. Community resources in the school library media center   **025.2**

Schuckett, S. Political advocacy for school librarians   **027.8**

Libraries and Hispanic Americans

Byrd, S. M. Bienvenidos! = Welcome!   **027.6**

Library services to youth of Hispanic heritage   **027.6**

Libraries and students

Student engagement and information literacy   **028.7**

Thinking outside the book   **027.62**

Libraries, the First Amendment, and cyberspace. Peck, R. S.   **025.04**

Libraries Unlimited professional guides for young adult librarians [series]

Anderson, S. B. Extreme teens   **027.62**

Farmer, L. S. J. Digital inclusion, teens, and your library   **027.62**

Koelling, H. Classic connections   **027.62**

Kunzel, B. L. The teen-centered book club   **027.62**

Lerch, M. T. Serving homeschooled teens and their parents   **027.6**

Ott, V. A. Teen programs with punch   **027.62**

Reaching out to religious youth   **027.62**

Serving older teens   **027.62**

Thinking outside the book   **027.62**

Libraries Unlimited professional guides in school librarianship [series]

Eyerdam, P. J. Using Internet primary sources to teach critical thinking skills in visual arts   **700**

Johnson, C. Using Internet primary sources to teach critical thinking skills in the sciences   **500**

Kent-Drury, R. M. Using Internet primary sources to teach critical thinking skills in world literature   **800**

Kravitz, N. E. Censorship and the school library media center   **025.2**

Shiveley, J. M. Using Internet primary sources to teach critical thinking skills in government, economics, and contemporary world issues   **900**

Taylor, J. Information literacy and the school library media center   **028.7**

Library and information problem-solving skills series

Doggett, S. L. Beyond the book   **025.04**

Library and information science text series

Woolls, E. B. The school library media manager   **027.8**

Library circulation

Greiner, T. Analyzing library collection use with Excel   **025.2**

Library classification

Intner, S. S. Standard cataloging for school and public libraries   **025.3**

Library exhibits *See* Libraries—Exhibitions

Library finance

The big book of library grant money, 2006   **025.1**

Hallam, A. Managing budgets and finances   **025.1**

Library in a book [series]

Ferro, J. Prisons   **365**

Haugen, D. Legalized gambling   **363.4**

Henderson, H. Campaign and election reform   **324.6**

Henderson, H. Capital punishment   **364.66**

Henderson, H. Global terrorism   **303.6**

Life in the iron-mills. Davis, R. H.
In The Oxford book of women's writing in
the United States p198-228   **810.8**

Life in the sea [series]
Walker, P. The coral reef   **577.7**

Life in the treetops. Lowman, M.   **92**

Life in the undergrowth. Attenborough, D.   **592**

Life is better than death. Malamud, B.
In Malamud, B. The complete stories   **S C**

Life is funny. Frank, E. R.   **Fic**

Life line. SAnzaldúa, G.
In Growing up gay; an anthology for young
people p90-92   **808.8**

Life lists for teens. Espeland, P.   **646.7**

Life, myth, and art in Ancient Rome. Allan, T.
937

Life of an American soldier. Yancey, D.
959.704

The **life** of anybody. Sheckley, R.
In The Norton book of science fiction; North
American science fiction, 1960-1990
p569-70   **S C**

The **life** of birds. Attenborough, D.   **598**

The **life** of mammals. Attenborough, D.   **599**

The **life** of Pope John Paul . . . in comics!.
Mainardi, A.   **92**

The **life** of the Buddha. Herbert, P.   **92**

Life on earth   **333.95**

Life on other planets
Extraterrestrial life   **576.8**
Koerner, D. Here be dragons   **576.8**

Life on the edge. Gross, M.   **578.4**

Life on the Mississippi. Twain, M.   **818**

Life sciences
Life sciences before the twentieth century
920.003
Life sciences in the twentieth century
920.003

Life sciences before the twentieth century
920.003

Life sciences in the twentieth century   **920.003**

Life skills
Espeland, P. Life lists for teens   **646.7**
The experts' guide to 100 things everyone
should know how to do   **640**
Morgenstern, J. Organizing from the inside out
for teens   **646.7**
The New York Times practical guide to practi-
cally everything   **646.7**
Taylor, S. On my own   **646.7**
Willdorf, N. City chic   **646.7**
Williams, T. Stay strong   **305.23**

Life under the Taliban. Stewart, G.   **958.1**

Life, Vol. 1. Suenobu, K.   **741.5**

Life: World War 2   **940.53**

The **life** you imagine. Jeter, D.   **92**

The **life** you save may be your own. O'Connor, F.
In O'Connor, F. Collected works p172-83
S C
In O'Connor, F. The complete stories p145-56
S C

Lifeguard. Updike, J.
In The Oxford book of short stories p539-44
S C
In Updike, J. Pigeon feathers, and other sto-
ries p211-20   **S C**

Lifesaving
See also First aid

Lifetimes: the Great War to the stock market
crash: American history through biography
and primary documents   **920**

The **lifework** of Juan Diaz. Bradbury, R.
In Bradbury, R. Bradbury stories; 100 of his
most celebrated tales   **S C**

Ligeia. Poe, E. A.
In Poe, E. A. The collected tales and poems
of Edgar Allan Poe p654-66   **818**

Light, Alan
The skills to pay the bills   **920**
(ed) The Vibe history of hip hop. See The Vibe
history of hip hop   **782.42**

Light, Douglas B.
Cells, tissues, and skin   **611**

Light, Jonathan Fraser, 1957-
The cultural encyclopedia of baseball
796.357

Light, Richard J.
Making the most of college   **378.1**

Light and the sufferer. Lethem, J.
In Feeling very strange; the Slipstream anthology   **S C**

Light breathing. Bunin, I. A.
In The portable twentieth-century Russian
reader   **891.7**

Light-gathering poems   **808.81**

Light in August. Faulkner, W.   **Fic**

Light of darkness. Clarke, A. C.
In Clarke, A. C. The collected stories of Arthur C. Clarke   **S C**

The **light** of the world. Hemingway, E.
In Hemingway, E. The complete short stories
of Ernest Hemingway; the Finca Vigía
edition p292-97   **S C**

Light verse. Asimov, I.
In Asimov, I. The complete stories p437-40
S C

Light years. Stein, T.   **Fic**

Lighting the way. Schiff, K. G.   **920**

The **lightkeeper's** daughter. Lawrence, I.   **Fic**

Lightman, Alan P., 1948-
The discoveries   **509**
Great ideas in physics   **530**

Lihamba, Amandina
(ed) Women writing Africa: the eastern region.
See Women writing Africa: the eastern region
896

Like mother used to make. Jackson, S.
In Jackson, S. The lottery; or, The adventures
of James Harris   **S C**

Like sisters on the homefront. Williams-Garcia, R.
Fic

Like the red panda. Seigel, A.   **Fic**

The **lion** and the lark. McKillip, P. A.
In McKillip, P. A. Harrowing the dragon
S C

The **lion** at morning. Wolfe, T.
In Wolfe, T. The complete short stories of
Thomas Wolfe p499-513 **S C**

The **lion** of Comarre. Clarke, A. C.
In Clarke, A. C. The collected stories of Arthur C. Clarke **S C**

Lioness. Service, P. F.
In Young warriors; stories of strength **S C**

Lionheart. Martin, J. **910.4**

Lionizing. Poe, E. A.
In Poe, E. A. The collected tales and poems
of Edgar Allan Poe p743-47 **818**

Lions
Caputo, P. Ghosts of Tsavo **599.75**

The **lions** are asleep this night. Waldrop, H.
In Feeling very strange; the Slipstream anthology **S C**

The **lion's** pride: Theodore Roosevelt and his family in peace and war. Renehan, E. J. **92**

The **lion's** skin. Maugham, W. S.
In Maugham, W. S. Collected short stories **S C**

Lipstick jihad. Moaveni, A. **92**

Lipsyte, Robert
The contender **Fic**
The defender
In Ultimate sports; short stories by outstanding writers for young adults p180-92 **S C**
Future tense
In Sixteen: short stories by outstanding writers for young adults p60-70 **S C**
One fat summer **Fic**
Raiders night **Fic**

Liquor makes you smart. Loos, A.
In The Norton book of American short stories p311-18 **S C**

Liquor problem *See* Drinking of alcoholic beverages

Lispeth. Kipling, R.
In Kipling, R. The portable Kipling **828**

List of subject headings for small libraries. See
Sears list of subject headings **025.4**

Literacy
Braun, L. W. Teens, technology, and literacy;
or, Why bad grammar isn't always bad **373.1**

Literacy, Information *See* Information literacy

The **literary** 100. Burt, D. S. **809**

Literary conversations series
Baldwin, J. Conversations with James Baldwin **92**
Gaines, E. J. Conversations with Ernest Gaines **92**
Morrison, T. Conversations with Toni Morrison **92**
Steinbeck, J. Conversations with John Steinbeck **92**
Vonnegut, K. Conversations with Kurt Vonnegut **92**

The **Literary** ghost **S C**

Literary landmarks
Dailey, D. London **820.9**
Foster, B. Rome **809**
Tomedi, J. Dublin **820.9**

The **literary** life of Laban Goldman. Malamud, B.
In Malamud, B. The complete stories **S C**

The **literary** life of Thingum Bob, Esq. Poe, E. A.
In Poe, E. A. The collected tales and poems
of Edgar Allan Poe p322-37 **818**

Literary movements for students **809**

Literary prizes
See also Newbery Medal

Literature
See also African Americans in literature;
Characters and characteristics in literature;
Children's literature; Classical literature; Developing countries in literature; Ethics in literature; Feminism in literature; Gothic revival
literature; Homosexuality in literature; London
(England) in literature; Medicine in literature;
Mythology in literature; Native American literature; Race in literature; Renaissance literature; Spies in literature; Symbolism in literature; Teenagers' writings; War in literature;
West (U.S.) in literature; Women in literature;
Work in literature; Young adult literature
names of national literatures, e.g. *English literature*

Bio-bibliography
European authors, 1000-1900 **920.003**
Magill's survey of American literature **810.9**
Popular contemporary writers **920.003**
World authors, 1950-1970 **920.003**
World authors, 1970-1975 **920.003**
World authors, 1975-1980 **920.003**
World authors, 1980-1985 **920.003**
World authors, 1985-1990 **920.003**
World authors, 1990-1995 **920.003**
World authors, 1995-2000 **920.003**
World authors, 2000-2005 **920.003**
World writers in English **820.9**
Writers of the American Renaissance **920.003**

Collections
Growing up gay **808.8**
Journalistas **808.8**
Nothing makes you free **808.8**
Read all about it! **808.8**

Dictionaries
Abrams, M. H. A glossary of literary terms **803**
Baldick, C. The concise Oxford dictionary of
literary terms **803**
Benét's reader's encyclopedia **803**
Brewer's dictionary of modern phrase & fable **803**
Brewer's dictionary of phrase & fable **803**
Carey, G. A multicultural dictionary of literary
terms **803**
The Facts on File dictionary of classical and
biblical allusions **809**
Harmon, W. A handbook to literature **803**
Oxford dictionary of phrase and fable **803**

Lush. Friend, N.   **Fic**

Lüsted, Greg
(jt. auth) Lüsted, M. A. A nuclear power plant
       621.48

Lüsted, Marcia Amidon, 1962-
A nuclear power plant   **621.48**

Luttikhuizen, Henry, 1964-
(jt. auth) Snyder, J. Art of the Middle Ages
       709.02

Luxbacher, Joe
Soccer: steps to success   **796.334**

Lyddie. Paterson, K.   **Fic**

Lyga, Allyson A. W.
Graphic novels in your media center   **025.2**

Lyga, Barry
The astonishing adventures of Fanboy & Goth
Girl   **Fic**
(jt. auth) Lyga, A. A. W. Graphic novels in
your media center   **025.2**

Lyme disease
Edlow, J. A. Bull's-eye: unraveling the medical
mystery of Lyme disease   **616.9**

Lymphatic system
McDowell, J. The lymphatic system   **612.4**

Lynas, Mark, 1973-
High tide   **363.7**

Lynch, Chris
Bearing, Paul
In Night terrors; stories of shadow and sub-
stance   **S C**
Freewill   **Fic**
The hobbyist
In Ultimate sports; short stories by outstand-
ing writers for young adults p315-33
       S C
Iceman   **Fic**
Inexcusable   **Fic**
Red rover, red rover
In Such a pretty face; short stories   **S C**
Slot machine   **Fic**

Lynch, Patricia Ann
Native American mythology A to Z   **398.2**

Lynch, Scott, 1978-
The lies of Locke Lamora   **Fic**

Lynch, Thomas, 1948-
Bodies in motion and at rest   **113**

Lynching
Crowe, C. Getting away with murder: the true
story of the Emmett Till case   **364.1**
Poetry
Nelson, M. A wreath for Emmett Till   **811**

Lynn, Elizabeth Cook- *See* Cook-Lynn, Elizabeth

Lynton, Norbert
(jt. auth) Langmuir, E. Yale dictionary of art
and artists   **703**

Lyon, Matthew
(jt. auth) Hafner, K. Where wizards stay up late
       004

Lyons, Maritcha Rémond, 1848-1929
About
Bolden, T. Maritcha [biography of Maritcha
Rémond Lyons]   **92**

Lyons, Mary E.
Sorrow's kitchen [biography of Zora Neale
Hurston]   **92**

Lyricists
Furia, P. The poets of Tin Pan Alley
       782.42

Lysergic acid diethylamide *See* LSD (Drug)

Lysistrata. Aristophanes   **882**

M

Ma Rainey's black bottom. Wilson, A.   **812**

Mabbott, Thomas Ollive, 1898-1968
(jt. auth) Poe, E. A. Complete poems   **811**

Mabel. Maugham, W. S.
In Maugham, W. S. Collected short stories
       S C

Mabinogion
See/See also pages in the following book(s):
Bulfinch, T. Bulfinch's mythology   **398.2**

Mabunda, L. Mpho
(ed) The African American almanac. See The
African American almanac   **305.8**
(ed) Dictionary of Hispanic biography. See Dictionary of Hispanic biography   **920.003**

Mabuza, Lindiwe
Wake . . .
In The Heinemann book of contemporary Af-
rican short stories p33-56   **S C**

MacArthur, Brian
(ed) The Penguin book of twentieth-century
speeches. See The Penguin book of twentieth-
century speeches   **808.85**

Macaulay, David, 1946-
Building big   **720**
Castle   **728.8**
City: a story of Roman planning and construc-
tion   **711**
Mill   **690**
Mosque   **726**
Motel of the mysteries   **817**
The new way things work   **600**
Pyramid   **726**
Ship   **387.2**
Unbuilding   **690**
Underground   **624**

Macbeth. Coursen, H. R.   **822.3**

Macbeth. Cover, A. B.   **822.3**

Macbeth. Shakespeare, W.   **822.3**

MacCambridge, Michael, 1963-
America's game   **796.332**

MacCullough, Carolyn
Stealing Henry   **Fic**

Macdonald, Anne L., 1920-
Feminine ingenuity   **609**

Macdonald, David W.
(ed) The encyclopedia of mammals. See The encyclopedia of mammals   **599**

MacDonald, John D. (John Dann), 1916-1986
The homesick Buick
In The Best American mystery stories of the
century p363-74   **S C**

MacDonald, Randall M., 1961-
Successful keyword searching **025.04**

Macdonald, Ross, 1915-1983
Gone girl
In The Best American mystery stories of the
century p375-404 **S C**

MacDonald, Susan Priest, 1958-
(jt. auth) MacDonald, R. M. Successful keyword
searching **025.04**

MacDonell, Colleen
Essential documents for school libraries

025.1

Macey, J. David, Jr.
(ed) The Greenwood encyclopedia of African
American literature. See The Greenwood encyclopedia of African American literature
810.9

MacGregor, Greg, 1941-
Lewis and Clark revisited **978**

Machiavelli, Niccolò, 1469-1527
The prince **320**

Machine design
See also Human engineering
Gurstelle, W. Adventures from the technology
underground **621.8**

Machine quilting *See* Quilting

Machine readable catalog system *See* MARC
formats

The **machine** that won the war. Asimov, I.
In Asimov, I. The complete stories p593-97
S C

The **machineries** of joy. Bradbury, R.
In Bradbury, R. Bradbury stories; 100 of his
most celebrated tales **S C**

Machinery
See also Mills
Macaulay, D. The new way things work
600
See/See also pages in the following book(s):
Sagan, C. Broca's brain **500**
Design and construction
See Machine design

Machu Picchu (Peru)
Bingham, H. Lost city of the Incas **985**

Mackall, Dandi Daley, 1949-
Eva underground **Fic**

MacKellar, Pamela H.
(jt. auth) Gerding, S. K. Grants for libraries
025.1

Mackenzie, Dana
The big splat; or, How our moon came to be
523.3

MacKethan, Lucinda Hardwick
(ed) The Companion to southern literature. See
The Companion to southern literature
810.3

Mackintosh. Maugham, W. S.
In Maugham, W. S. Collected short stories
S C

Mackler, Carolyn
The earth, my butt, and other big, round things
Fic

Mona Lisa, Jesus, Chad, and me
In Sixteen: stories about that sweet and bitter
birthday **S C**
Vegan virgin Valentine **Fic**

Mackrell, Judith
(jt. auth) Craine, D. The Oxford dictionary of
dance **792.8**

MacLaverty, Bernard
Life drawing
In The Oxford book of Irish short stories
p541-51 **S C**

MacLean, Katherine, 1925-
Night-rise
In The Norton book of science fiction; North
American science fiction, 1960-1990
p376-85 **S C**

MacLeish, Archibald, 1892-1982
Collected poems, 1917-1982 **811**

MacLeod, Ian
Breathmoss
In Best of the best: 20 years of the Year's
best science fiction **S C**

MacMahon, Bryan, 1909-1998
The ring
In The Oxford book of Irish short stories
p388-91 **S C**

MacMillan, Donald, 1874-1970
About
Bryant, J. H. Dangerous crossings **998**

Macmillan encyclopedia of death and dying
306.9

Macmillan living universe series
Whitfield, P. J. Biomes and habitats **577.8**

Macmillan science library [series]
Animal sciences **590.3**

MacNee, Marie J.
(jt. auth) Hoehner, J. Outlaws, mobsters &
crooks **920.003**
(ed) Science fiction, fantasy, and horror writers.
See Science fiction, fantasy, and horror writers **920.003**

MacNeil, Robert, 1931-
(jt. auth) McCrum, R. The story of English
420

MacPherson, Malcolm C., 1943-
Roberts ridge **958.1**

MacRae, Cathi Dunn
Presenting young adult fantasy fiction
813.009

Macy, Anne Sullivan *See* Sullivan, Anne, 1866-
1936

Mad about physics. Jargodzki, C. **530**

Madagascar, Lily. Janaczewska, N.
In International plays for young audiences;
contemporary works from leading playwrights p257-96 **808.82**

Madam Butterfly. Hogan, J. P.
In The Hard SF renaissance **S C**

Madame de Troyes. Wharton, E.
In Wharton, E. Novellas and other writings
818

Madison, Deborah
Vegetarian cooking for everyone **641.5**

Maguire, Gregory—*Continued*
The oakthing
In The Faery Reel; tales from the Twilight
Realm **S C**
The prank
In Gothic!; ten original dark tales **S C**

Mahabharata
The Mahābhārata **891**

Mahabharata. Bhagavadgita
Bhagavad Gita **891**

Mahalia. Horniman, J. **Fic**

Mahjoub, Jamal, 1960-
Road block
In The Heinemann book of contemporary African short stories p129-33 **S C**

Mahomet *See* Muḥammad, d. 632

Mahony, Phillip, 1955-
(ed) From both sides now. *See* From both sides now **811.008**

Mahy, Margaret
Alchemy **Fic**
Hidden warriors
In Young warriors; stories of strength **S C**

Mai, Larry L.
The Cambridge Dictionary of human biology and evolution **612**

The **maid's** shoes. Malamud, B.
In Malamud, B. The complete stories **S C**

Maier, Pauline, 1938-
American scripture **973.3**

Main-street. Hawthorne, N.
In Hawthorne, N. Tales and sketches, including Twice-told tales, Mosses from an old manse, and The snow-image; A wonder book for girls and boys; Tanglewood tales for girls and boys, being a second Wonder book p1023-50 **S C**

Main Street. Lewis, S. **Fic**
also in Lewis, S. Main Street & Babbitt **Fic**

Main Street & Babbitt. Lewis, S. **Fic**

Mainardi, Alessandro
The life of Pope John Paul . . . in comics! **92**

Maine
Fiction
King, S. Carrie **Fic**

Mair, Victor H., 1943-
(ed) The Shorter Columbia anthology of traditional Chinese literature. *See* The Shorter Columbia anthology of traditional Chinese literature **895.1**

Maisie Dobbs. Winspear, J. **Fic**

Maison, Jérôme
(il) Jacquet, L. March of the penguins **598**

Maître-Allain, Thierry
Aquariums **639.34**

Maja-Pearce, Adewale
The hotel
In The Heinemann book of contemporary African short stories p146-48 **S C**

Majesty. Fitzgerald, F. S.
In Fitzgerald, F. S. The short stories of F. Scott Fitzgerald; a new collection p464-80 **S C**

The **majesty** of the law. O'Connor, F.
In The Oxford book of Irish short stories p354-62 **S C**

Major, John S., 1942-
(jt. auth) Fadiman, C. The new lifetime reading plan **028**
(ed) World poetry. *See* World poetry **808.81**

Major, Kevin, 1949-
Three people and two seats
In Sixteen: short stories by outstanding writers for young adults p113-24 **S C**

Major acts of Congress **348**

Major battles and campaigns [series]
Wood, W. J. Battles of the Revolutionary War, 1775-1781 **973.3**

Major issues in American history [series]
Magoc, C. J. Environmental issues in American history **333.7**
Strom, S. H. Women's rights **305.4**

Major systems of the body **612**

The **major** works. Keats, J. **821**

Majority rules. Shusterman, N.
In Dreams and visions; fourteen flights of fantasy **S C**

Majure, Janet, 1954-
Breast cancer **616.99**

Make lemonade. Wolff, V. E. **Fic**

Make Maddie mad. Williams-Garcia, R.
In First crossing; stories about teen immigrants p180-200 **S C**

Make me over **S C**

The **maker** of dreams. Down, O.
In 24 favorite one-act plays p256-71 **808.82**

Makers of America [series]
Scott, R. A. Chief Joseph and the Nez Percés **92**

Makers of modern science [series]
Spangenburg, R. Wernher von Braun **92**

Makers of science. Allaby, M. **920.003**

Makes me wanna holler. McCall, N. **92**

Makeup, Theatrical *See* Theatrical makeup

Making a killing with Mama Cass. Bankier, W.
In Alfred Hitchcock's mystery magazine presents fifty years of crime and suspense **S C**

Making comics. McCloud, S. **741.5**

Making do. Hogan, L.
In Spider Woman's granddaughters; traditional tales and contemporary writing by Native American women **S C**

Making it all the way into the future on Gaxton Falls of the red planet. Malzberg, B. N.
In The Norton book of science fiction; North American science fiction, 1960-1990 p313-16 **S C**

A **marriage** of convenience. Maugham, W. S.
  In Maugham, W. S. Collected short stories
                              S C

A **marriage** proposal. Chekhov, A. P.
  In 24 favorite one-act plays p403-16
                              808.82

Marrin, Albert, 1936-
  Commander in Chief Abraham Lincoln and the
    Civil War   **973.7**
  George Washington and the founding of a na-
    tion   **92**
  Old Hickory [biography of Andrew Jackson]
                              92

Marrow. Reed, R.
  In The Hard SF renaissance   **S C**

The **marry** month of May. Henry, O.
  In Henry, O. The best short stories of O.
    Henry   **S C**

Mars (Planet)
  Hartmann, W. K. A traveler's guide to Mars
                            523.4

           Fiction
  Lewis, C. S. Out of the silent planet   **Fic**
  Robinson, K. S. Red Mars   **Fic**
  Simmons, D. Ilium   **Fic**

Marsalis, Wynton
  Jazz A-B-Z   **781.65**
  Marsalis on music   **780**

Marsalis on music. Marsalis, W.   **780**

Marsden, John, 1950-
  Tomorrow, when the war began   **Fic**

Marsden, Peter, 1945-
  The Taliban   **958.1**

Marsden, William, 1754-1836
  (tr) Polo, M. The travels of Marco Polo **915**

Marsh, Don, 1957-
  Calligraphy   **745.6**

Marsh, Othniel Charles, 1831-1899
           About
  Ottaviani, J. Bone sharps, cowboys, and thunder
    lizards   **560**

Marshall, Catherine, 1914-1983
  Christy   **Fic**

Marshall, David
  Wild about flying!   **629.13**

Marshall, Peter H., 1946-
  Nature's web   **113**

Marshall, Sarah Catherine Wood *See* Marshall,
  Catherine, 1914-1983

Marshall, Stephen A.
  Insects: their natural history and diversity
                          595.7

Marshall, Thurgood, 1908-1993
  Thurgood Marshall   **92**
           About
  Williams, J. Thurgood Marshall   **92**

Marston, Daniel, 1970-
  (ed) The Pacific war companion. See The Pacif-
    ic war companion   **940.54**

Marston, Elsa
  Figs and fate   **S C**
  <small>Contents: In line; Hand of Fatima; Faces; The plan; Santa
Claus in Bagdad</small>

Lines of scrimmage
  In First crossing; stories about teen immi-
    grants p110-36   **S C**
Rima's song
  In Join in; multiethnic short stories by out-
    standing writers for young adults p153-
    71   **S C**

Marszalek, John F., 1939-
  (ed) The Greenwood encyclopedia of African
    American civil rights. See The Greenwood
    encyclopedia of African American civil rights
                          305.8

Marta del Angel. Feyder, L.
  In Latina: women's voices from the border-
    lands p172-78   **810.8**

Marten, James, 1956-
  Civil War America   **973.7**

Martha Graham, a dancer's life. Freedman, R.
                          92

Martha's Vineyard (Mass.)
           Fiction
  West, D. The wedding   **Fic**

Martí, José, 1853-1895
           About
  Sterngass, J. José Martí   **92**
  See/See also pages in the following book(s):
  Mendoza, P. M. Extraordinary people in extraor-
    dinary times   **920**

Martial arts
    See also Tae kwon do; Tai chi
  Lee, B. Bruce Lee   **92**
  Miller, D. The Tao of Bruce Lee   **92**
  Salzman, M. Iron & silk   **915.1**

Martial arts series
  Pedro, J. Judo techniques & tactics **796.8**

The **Martian** chronicles. Bradbury, R.   **S C**

A **Martian** Ricorso. Bear, G.
  In Bear, G. The collected stories of Greg
    Bear   **S C**

The **Martian** way. Asimov, I.
  In Asimov, I. The complete stories p129-65
                          S C

Martin, Christopher, 1923-
  Mohandas Gandhi   **92**

Martin, George R. R.
  The hedge knight
  In Legends: short novels by the masters of
    modern fantasy p451-533   **S C**
  The way of cross and dragon
  In The Locus awards; thirty years of the best
    in science fiction and fantasy   **S C**

Martin, James
  My life with the saints   **920**

Martin, Jesse
  Lionheart   **910.4**

Martin, Judith, 1938-
  Miss Manners' guide to excruciatingly correct
    behavior   **395**

Martin, Linda Wagner- *See* Wagner-Martin, Linda

Martin, Patricia A. Fink, 1955-
  Woods and forests   **577.3**

Martin, Patricia Preciado
The ruins
In Growing up Latino; memoirs and stories p73-84 **810.8**

Martin, Roberta, 1907-1969
See/See also pages in the following book(s):
We'll understand it better by and by **782.25**

Martin, Waldo E., 1951-
(ed) Civil rights in the United States. See Civil rights in the United States **323.1**

Martinez, Demetria
MotherTongue [excerpt]
In Latina: women's voices from the borderlands p274-79 **810.8**

Martínez, Rubén
The new Americans **305.9**

Martinez, Victor, 1954-
The baseball glove
In Working days: stories about teenagers and work **S C**
Parrot in the oven **Fic**

Martínez-Fernández, Luis, 1960-
(ed) Encyclopedia of Cuba. See Encyclopedia of Cuba **972.91**

Martone, Michael
Biograph
In The Norton book of American short stories p749-63 **S C**

Marty, Martin E., 1928-
(jt. auth) Breuilly, E. Religions of the world **201**

Martyn Pig. Brooks, K. **Fic**
The **martyr**. Porter, K. A.
In Porter, K. A. The collected stories of Katherine Anne Porter **S C**

Marusek, David
The wedding album
In Best of the best: 20 years of the Year's best science fiction **S C**

Marvel, Laura
(ed) Salem witch trials. See Salem witch trials **133.4**

Marvel. Daniels, L. **741.5**
Marvel 1602. Gaiman, N. **741.5**

Marvel comics (New York, N.Y.)
Daniels, L. Marvel **741.5**

Marven, Nigel
Chased by sea monsters **560**

Marx, Karl, 1818-1883
See/See also pages in the following book(s):
Heilbroner, R. L. The worldly philosophers **330.1**

Marx, Tracy
To walk with kings
In Working days: stories about teenagers and work **S C**

Marxism
See also Communism; Socialism

Mary Magdalene, Saint
About
Ehrman, B. D. Peter, Paul, and Mary Magdalene **225.9**

Mary Postgate. Kipling, R.
In Kipling, R. The portable Kipling **828**

Mary Shelley, her life, her fiction, her monsters. Mellor, A. K. **823.009**

Mary Shelley's Frankenstein [study guide] **823.009**

Mary Stewart's Merlin trilogy. Stewart, M. **Fic**

Mary Winosky. Hughes, L.
In Hughes, L. Short stories of Langston Hughes **S C**

Maryland
Fiction
Fuqua, J. S. The reappearance of Sam Webber **Fic**
Tyler, A. Dinner at the Homesick Restaurant **Fic**

Marzilli, Alan, 1970-
Fetal rights **342**

Masai (African people)
Lekuton, J. Facing the lion **967.62**

MASH. Hooker, R. **Fic**
The **mask** of Nostradamus. Randi, J. **92**

The masks of God [series]
Campbell, J. Creative mythology **201**
Campbell, J. Occidental mythology **201**
Campbell, J. Oriental mythology **201**
Campbell, J. Primitive mythology **201**

Maslon, Laurence, 1959-
(jt. auth) Kantor, M. Broadway: the American musical **792.6**

Masoff, Joy, 1951-
Snowboard! **796.93**

Mason, Bill, 1929-
Sports illustrated fly fishing **799.1**

Mason, Bobbie Ann
Elvis Presley **92**
In country **Fic**
Shiloh
In American short story masterpieces **S C**

Mason, David, 1954-
(ed) Twentieth-century American poetry. See Twentieth-century American poetry **811.008**

Mason, George, 1725-1792
About
Wilkins, R. W. Jefferson's pillow **973**

The **masque** of the Red Death. Poe, E. A.
In Poe, E. A. The collected tales and poems of Edgar Allan Poe p269-73 **818**
In Poe, E. A. Edgar Allan Poe's tales of mystery and madness **S C**

Mass communication *See* Communication; Telecommunication

Mass extinction of species
Frankel, C. The end of the dinosaurs **551.3**
Leakey, R. E. The sixth extinction **304.2**
Powell, J. L. Night comes to the Cretaceous **576.8**

Mass media
See also Native Americans in mass media
Censorship [Contemporary issues companion] **363.31**

Maugham, W. Somerset (William Somerset), 1874-1965—*Continued*
An official position
In The Oxford book of short stories p219-37
S C

Maugham, William Somerset *See* Maugham, W. Somerset (William Somerset), 1874-1965

Mauki. London, J.
In London, J. The portable Jack London p187-99 **818**

Maule, Jeremy
(ed) The Oxford book of classical verse in translation. *See* The Oxford book of classical verse in translation **881.008**

Maunder, Andrew
The Facts on File companion to the British short story **823.009**

Maurer-Mathison, Diane V., 1944-
Paper art **745.54**

Mauro, Tony
Illustrated great decisions of the Supreme Court **347**

Maus, Derek C.
(ed) Living through the red scare. *See* Living through the red scare **320**
(ed) Living under the threat of nuclear war. *See* Living under the threat of nuclear war **355**

Maus. Spiegelman, A. **940.53**
Mauve. Garfield, S. **667**
Maxims *See* Proverbs

May, Charles E. (Charles Edward), 1941-
(ed) Critical survey of short fiction. *See* Critical survey of short fiction **809.3**
(ed) Short story writers. *See* Short story writers **809.3**

May, Mel Anthony
(ed) Encyclopedia of women and baseball. *See* Encyclopedia of women and baseball **796.357**

May, Nathaniel
(ed) Shark: stories of life and death from the world's most dangerous waters. *See* Shark: stories of life and death from the world's most dangerous waters **597**

May day. Fitzgerald, F. S.
In Fitzgerald, F. S. The short stories of F. Scott Fitzgerald; a new collection p97-141 **S C**

May I have your autograph? Sharmat, M. W.
In Sixteen: short stories by outstanding writers for young adults p15-21 **S C**

The **may-pole** of Merry Mount. Hawthorne, N.
In Hawthorne, N. Tales and sketches, including Twice-told tales, Mosses from an old manse, and The snow-image; A wonder book for girls and boys; Tanglewood tales for girls and boys, being a second Wonder book p360-70 **S C**

Maya Angelou [critical essays] **818**
Maya Angelou's I know why the caged bird sings **818**

Mayas
See/See also pages in the following book(s):
Aveni, A. F. Stairways to the stars **520**
Ceram, C. W. Gods, graves, and scholars **930.1**
Wright, R. Stolen continents **970.004**

Mayer, Robert H.
(ed) The Civil Rights Act of 1964. *See* The Civil Rights Act of 1964 **342**

Mayhew. Maugham, W. S.
In Maugham, W. S. Collected short stories **S C**

Maynard, Joyce, 1953-
The cloud chamber **Fic**

Mayo Clinic on healthy weight **613.2**
Mayo Clinic on hearing **617.8**
Mayo Clinic on managing diabetes **616.4**

Mayor, F. M. (Flora Macdonald), 1872-1932
Miss de Mannering of Asham
In The Oxford book of gothic tales p386-406 **S C**

Mayor, Flora Macdonald *See* Mayor, F. M. (Flora Macdonald), 1872-1932

Mays, Dorothy A.
Women in early America **305.4**

May's lion. Le Guin, U. K.
In The Oxford book of women's writing in the United States p190-96 **810.8**

The **maze**. Hobbs, W. **Fic**

Mazer, Anne, 1953-
The pill factory
In Working days: stories about teenagers and work **S C**
(ed) Working days: stories about teenagers and work. *See* Working days: stories about teenagers and work **S C**

Mazer, Harry, 1925-
The beautiful thing
In Night terrors; stories of shadow and substance **S C**
Falling off the Empire State Building
In Ultimate sports; short stories by outstanding writers for young adults p302-13 **S C**
Furlough—1944
In Sixteen: short stories by outstanding writers for young adults p83-92 **S C**
The last mission **Fic**

Mazer, Norma Fox, 1931-
Cutthroat
In Ultimate sports; short stories by outstanding writers for young adults p148-59 **S C**
The house on Buffalo Street
In Night terrors; stories of shadow and substance **S C**
How to survive a name
In Such a pretty face; short stories **S C**
I, hungry Hannah Cassandra Glen . . .
In Sixteen: short stories by outstanding writers for young adults p2-14 **S C**
Zelzah: a tale from long ago
In Leaving home: stories p179-99 **808.8**

McLean, Will
(jt. auth) Singman, J. L. Daily life in Chaucer's England   **942.03**

McLeod, John, 1963-
The history of India   **954**

McLuhan, Marshall, 1911-1980
Understanding media   **302.23**

McMahon, Pat See Hoch, Edward D., 1930-

McMaster, Gerald R.
(ed) Native universe. See Native universe   **970.004**

McMillan, Beverly
Human body   **612**

McMillan, Naomi See Grimes, Nikki

McMillian, John Campbell
(ed) Freedom on my mind. See Freedom on my mind   **305.8**
(ed) The Radical reader. See The Radical reader   **303.4**

McMinn, R. M. H. (Robert Matthew Hay)
(jt. auth) Abrahams, P. H. McMinn's color atlas of human anatomy   **611**

McMinn, Robert Matthew Hay See McMinn, R. M. H. (Robert Matthew Hay)

McMinn's color atlas of human anatomy. Abrahams, P. H.   **611**

McMullin, Jordan
(ed) Marijuana. See Marijuana   **615**

McMurtry, Larry
Crazy Horse   **92**
Lonesome dove   **Fic**

McNab, Claire
Fooling around
In Not the only one; lesbian and gay fiction for teens   **S C**

McNally, Raymond T., 1931-2002
(jt. auth) Florescu, R. R. N. Dracula [biography of Vlad II]   **92**

McNally, Terrence, 1939-
15 short plays   **812**
Contents: Bringing it all back; Noon; Botticelli; Next; ¡Cuba si!; Sweet Eros; Witness; Whiskey; Bad habits; The Ritz; Prelude & Liebestod; Andre's mother; The wibbly, wobbly, wiggly dance that Cleopatterer did; Street talk; Hidden agendas

McNamee, Graham
Acceleration   **Fic**

McNeal, Laura
Crushed   **Fic**
Zipped   **Fic**

McNeal, Tom
(jt. auth) McNeal, L. Crushed   **Fic**
(jt. auth) McNeal, L. Zipped   **Fic**

McNeese, Tim
Pablo Picasso   **92**

McNeil, Beth
(jt. auth) Giesecke, J. Fundamentals of library supervision   **023**

McNeill, Robert
About
Pekar, H. Harvey Pekar's American splendor   **92**

McNeill, William Hardy, 1917-
(ed) Berkshire encyclopedia of world history. See Berkshire encyclopedia of world history   **903**

McNickle, D'Arcy, 1904-1977
Going to school
In Coming of age in America; a multicultural anthology p154-65   **S C**

McPhee, Andrew T.
Sleep and dreams   **616.8**

McPherson, James Alan, 1943-
The story of a scar
In American short story masterpieces   **S C**

McPherson, James M.
Abraham Lincoln and the second American Revolution   **973.7**
Drawn with the sword   **973.7**
For cause and comrades   **973.7**
(ed) To the best of my ability. See To the best of my ability   **920**

McPherson, Stephanie Sammartino
The Bakke case and the affirmative action debate   **344**

McVay, Charles Butler, III
About
Nelson, P. Left for dead   **940.54**

McVeigh, Mark, 1964-
(ed) Dead High yearbook. See Dead High yearbook   **741.5**

McWhorter, Diane
Carry me home   **976.1**

McWilliams, John C., 1949-
The 1960s cultural revolution   **973.92**

The **McWilliamses** and the burglar alarm. Twain, M.
In Twain, M. The complete short stories of Mark Twain; now collected for the first time   **S C**

MDIO ecosystems increase knowledge of DNA languages (2215 C.E.). Bear, G.
In Bear, G. The collected stories of Greg Bear   **S C**

MDMA (Drug)
See also Ecstasy (Drug)

Me and Orson Welles. Kaplow, R.   **Fic**

Mead, Frank Spencer, 1898-1982
Handbook of denominations in the United States   **280**

Mead, Margaret, 1901-1978
About
Mark, J. T. Margaret Mead   **92**

The **meadow**. Bradbury, R.
In Bradbury, R. Bradbury stories; 100 of his most celebrated tales   **S C**

Meagher, Timothy J.
The Columbia guide to Irish American history   **305.8**

Meal planning See Menus; Nutrition

Mean genes. Burnham, T.   **155.2**

The **meaning** of it all. Feynman, R. P.   **500**

The **meaning** of the glorious Koran. Koran   **297.1**

Medieval and early modern world [series]
Pouwels, R. L. The African and Middle Eastern world, 600-1500   **956**

Medieval architecture
Snyder, J. Art of the Middle Ages   **709.02**

Medieval art
Snyder, J. Art of the Middle Ages   **709.02**
See/See also pages in the following book(s):
Bishop, M. The Middle Ages   **940.1**
Medieval art. See Snyder, J. Art of the Middle Ages   **709.02**

Medieval civilization
The 1000s   **940.1**
The 1100s   **909**
The 1200s   **909**
The 1300s   **909**
Bishop, M. The Middle Ages   **940.1**
The Early Middle Ages   **909.07**
Gies, F. Life in a medieval village   **940.1**
Great events from history, The Middle Ages, 477-1453   **909.07**
Knight, J. Middle ages: almanac   **909.07**
Knight, J. Middle ages: biographies   **920**
Medieval world   **909.07**
Singman, J. L. Daily life in medieval Europe   **940.1**
Snodgrass, M. E. Who's who in the Middle Ages   **920.003**

Medieval English literature
In The Oxford anthology of English literature   **820.8**

Medieval literature
Encyclopedias
Ruud, J. Encyclopedia of medieval literature   **809**

A **medieval** romance. Twain, M.
In Twain, M. The complete short stories of Mark Twain; now collected for the first time   **S C**

Medieval world   **909.07**

Medieval writers and their work. Burrow, J. A.   **820.9**

Medina, Loreta M.
(ed) Bilingual education. See Bilingual education   **370.117**
(ed) Euthanasia. See Euthanasia   **179.7**

Meditation
Rosen, M. Meditation and hypnosis   **154.7**

Meditation and hypnosis. Rosen, M.   **154.7**

Medley, Linda
Castle waiting   **741.5**

Medoff, Mark Howard
Children of a lesser god   **812**

Meeks, Kenneth, 1963-
Driving while black   **363.2**

Meet the Beatles. Stark, S. D.   **920**

Meeting the other crowd   **398.2**

A **meeting** with Medusa. Clarke, A. C.
In Clarke, A. C. The collected stories of Arthur C. Clarke   **S C**

Megan's law. Fodor, M. D.   **362.7**

Megatokyo v2. Gallagher, F.   **741.5**

Megellas, James
All the way to Berlin   **940.54**

Megiddo's shadow. Slade, A. G.   **Fic**

Mehling, Randi
Hallucinogens   **615**

Mehus-Roe, Kristin
(ed) The Original dog bible. See The Original dog bible   **636.7**

Meier, August, 1923-2003
(ed) Black leaders of the nineteenth century. See Black leaders of the nineteenth century   **920**

Meitner, Lise, 1878-1968
See/See also pages in the following book(s):
Henderson, H. Nuclear physics   **539.7**

Melling, O. R.
The Hunter's Moon   **Fic**

Mellonta Tauta. Poe, E. A.
In Poe, E. A. The collected tales and poems of Edgar Allan Poe p384-94   **818**

Mellor, Anne Kostelanetz
Mary Shelley, her life, her fiction, her monsters   **823.009**

Melton, J. Gordon
(ed) Flinn, F. K. Encyclopedia of Catholicism   **282**

Meltzer, Milton, 1915-
Edgar Allan Poe   **92**
Emily Dickinson   **92**
Milton Meltzer   **92**
Never to forget: the Jews of the Holocaust   **940.53**
Walt Whitman   **92**
(ed) The Black Americans. See The Black Americans   **305.8**

Melville, Herman, 1819-1891
Billy Budd, sailor   **Fic**
Moby-Dick; or, The whale   **Fic**
About
Diorio, M. A. L. A student's guide to Herman Melville   **813.009**
Rollyson, C. Critical companion to Herman Melville   **813.009**

Melzer, Richard
(ed) When we were young in the West. See When we were young in the West   **978.9**

The **member** of the wedding. McCullers, C.   **812**

The **member** of the wedding. McCullers, C.   **Fic**

Memento mori. Nolan, J.
In Adaptations: from short story to big screen; 35 great stories that have inspired great films   **S C**

Memoir of a visionary: Antonia Pantoja. Pantoja, A.   **92**

Memoirs *See* Autobiography

Memoirs of a geisha. Golden, A.   **Fic**

Memoirs of Sherlock Holmes. Doyle, Sir A. C.
In Doyle, Sir A. C. The complete Sherlock Holmes   **S C**

Memory
Baddeley, A. D. Your memory   **153.1**

The **metamorphosis**. Kafka, F.
In Kafka, F. The metamorphosis and other
stories p117-92 **Fic**
The **metamorphosis**. Kuper, P. **741.5**
The **metamorphosis** and other stories. Kafka, F.
S C
Metaphors dictionary **423**
Metaphysics. Aristotle
In Aristotle. The basic works of Aristotle
p689-926 **888**
Meteorites
Erickson, J. Asteroids, comets, and meteorites
551.3
Norton, O. R. The Cambridge encyclopedia of
meteorites **523.5**
Norton, O. R. Rocks from space **523.5**
Meteorology
See also Climate; Droughts; Weather;
Weather forecasting
Buckley, B. Weather: a visual guide **551.5**
Newton, D. E. Encyclopedia of air **551**
Reynolds, R. Cambridge guide to the weather
551.5
Dictionaries
Allaby, M. Encyclopedia of weather and climate
551
The Facts on File dictionary of weather and cli-
mate **551.5**
Meth (Drug) *See* Methamphetamine
Methamphetamine
Amphetamines **615**
The **"method"** sheriff. Lacy, E.
In Alfred Hitchcock's mystery magazine pres-
ents fifty years of crime and suspense
S C
Metzengerstein. Poe, E. A.
In Poe, E. A. The collected tales and poems
of Edgar Allan Poe p672-78 **818**
Metzger, Bruce Manning
(ed) The Oxford companion to the Bible. See
The Oxford companion to the Bible **220.3**
(ed) The Oxford guide to people & places of the
Bible. See The Oxford guide to people &
places of the Bible **220.9**
Metzger, Lois
Seashell Motel
In Working days: stories about teenagers and
work **S C**
Snap, crackle, pop
In Shattered: stories of children and war p71-
86 **S C**
Metzger, Tom
See/See also pages in the following book(s):
Langer, E. A hundred little Hitlers **305.8**
Mew, Charlotte Mary, 1869-1928
A white night
In The Oxford book of English short stories
p139-54 **S C**
The **Mexican**. London, J.
In London, J. The portable Jack London
p291-313 **818**
Mexican Americans
Cruz, B. César Chávez **92**
González, R. Butterfly boy **92**

Griswold del Castillo, R. César Chávez **92**
Haney-López, I. Racism on trial **305.8**
Hart, E. T. Barefoot heart **92**
The Mexicans **305.8**
Rodriguez, R. Hunger of memory **92**
Biography
O'Connell, D. People person [biography of Mar-
ta Tienda] **92**
Drama
Soto, G. Novio boy **812**
Fiction
Alegría, M. Estrella's quinceañera **Fic**
Anaya, R. A. Bless me, Ultima **Fic**
Canales, V. The tequila worm **Fic**
Cisneros, S. The house on Mango Street **Fic**
Cisneros, S. Woman Hollering Creek and other
stories **S C**
Martinez, V. Parrot in the oven **Fic**
Rice, D. Crazy loco **S C**
Saenz, B. A. Sammy and Juliana in Hollywood
Fic
Soto, G. The afterlife **Fic**
Soto, G. Buried onions **Fic**
Whitney, K. A. The perfect distance **Fic**
Poetry
Mora, P. My own true name **811**
Mexican literature
Collections
The Tree is older than you are **860.8**
Mexican movies. Cisneros, S.
In Cisneros, S. Woman Hollering Creek and
other stories **S C**
Mexican War, 1846-1848
Mills, B. U.S.-Mexican War **973.6**
Mexican War. See Mills, B. U.S.-Mexican War
973.6
Mexicans
United States
See also Mexican Americans
The **Mexicans** **305.8**
Mexico
Antiquities
Smith, M. E. The Aztecs **972**
Civilization
Coerver, D. M. Mexico: an encyclopedia of con-
temporary culture and history **972.08**
Fiction
Esquivel, L. Like water for chocolate **Fic**
Greene, G. The power and the glory **Fic**
McCarthy, C. All the pretty horses **Fic**
Steinbeck, J. The pearl **Fic**
History
Foster, L. V. A brief history of Mexico **972**
Kirkwood, B. The history of Mexico **972**
Politics and government
Guillermoprieto, A. Looking for history **972**
Meyer, Judith L., 1956-
The spirit of Yellowstone **978.7**
Meyer, L. A., 1942-
Bloody Jack **Fic**
Meyer, Marvin W., 1948-
(ed) The Gnostic Bible. See The Gnostic Bible
299

Minkin, Mary Jane
The Yale guide to women's reproductive health
618.1

Minnesota
Brown, D. Under a flaming sky **634.9**
Paulsen, G. Woodsong **796.5**
Fiction
Enger, L. Peace like a river **Fic**
Lewis, S. Main Street **Fic**
also in Lewis, S. Main Street & Babbitt
Fic
Lewis, S. Main Street & Babbitt **Fic**
Malloy, B. The year of ice **Fic**
Weaver, W. Full service **Fic**

Minocha, Anil, 1957-
The encyclopedia of the digestive system and
digestive disorders **616.3**

Minor leagues. Ott, G.
In International plays for young audiences;
contemporary works from leading playwrights p353-89 **808.82**

Minorities
See also Discrimination; Ethnic relations
Barkan, E. The guilt of nations **341.6**
Daniels, R. Coming to America **325.73**
Encyclopedias
Gale encyclopedia of multicultural America
305.8
The Greenwood encyclopedia of multiethnic
American literature **810.9**

Minorities in literature
Great scenes from minority playwrights
812.008
New immigrant literatures in the United States
810.9

Minorities in motion pictures
Welsch, J. R. Multicultural films **791.43**

The **minority** report. Dick, P. K. **Fic**
also in Adaptations: from short story to big
screen; 35 great stories that have inspired
great films **S C**

The **Minotaur**. Hawthorne, N.
In Hawthorne, N. Tales and sketches, including Twice-told tales, Mosses from an old
manse, and The snow-image; A wonder
book for girls and boys; Tanglewood
tales for girls and boys, being a second
Wonder book p1313-37 **S C**

Mint condition. Hoffman, N. K.
In Past imperfect **S C**

The **miracle**. Mutia, B.
In The Heinemann book of contemporary African short stories p165-78 **S C**

Miracle at Philadelphia. Bowen, C. D. **342**

Miracle in the Andes. Parrado, N. **982**

The **miracle** of Hoshana Rabbah. Sholem
Aleichem
In Halkin, H. and Sholem Aleichem. Tevye
the dairyman and The railroad stories
S C

The **miracle** of Purun Bhagat. Kipling, R.
In Kipling, R. The portable Kipling **828**

The **miracle** worker. Gibson, W. **812**

Miracle's boys. Woodson, J. **Fic**

The **miracles** of Jamie. Bradbury, R.
In Bradbury, R. Bradbury stories; 100 of his
most celebrated tales **S C**

The **miraculous** fever tree. Rocco, F. **616.9**

The **miraculous** pitcher. Hawthorne, N.
In Hawthorne, N. Tales and sketches, including Twice-told tales, Mosses from an old
manse, and The snow-image; A wonder
book for girls and boys; Tanglewood
tales for girls and boys, being a second
Wonder book p1259-75 **S C**

Mirage. Maugham, W. S.
In Maugham, W. S. Collected short stories
S C

Miraldi, Robert
(ed) Kahn, R. Beyond the boys of summer
796.357

Miranda, Ernesto
About
Kelly-Gangi, C. Miranda v. Arizona and the
rights of the accused **345**
Ruschmann, P. Miranda rights **345**
Sonneborn, L. Miranda v. Arizona **345**

Miranda rights. Ruschmann, P. **345**

Miranda v. Arizona. Sonneborn, L. **345**

Miranda v. Arizona and the rights of the accused.
Kelly-Gangi, C. **345**

Miró, Asha, 1967-
Daughter of the Ganges **92**

Mirror image. Asimov, I.
In Asimov, I. The complete stories p409-21
S C

The **misanthrope**. Molière
In Molière. The misanthrope and other plays
842

The **misanthrope** and other plays. Molière
842

A **miscalculation**. Schaffler González, F.
In Cosmos latinos; an anthology of science
fiction from Latin America and Spain
S C

Miscellaneous facts *See* Curiosities and wonders

A **miscellany** of characters that will not appear.
Cheever, J.
In Cheever, J. The stories of John Cheever
p467-72 **S C**

The **mischievous** machinations of Scapin. Molière
In Molière. The misanthrope and other plays
842

The **miseducation** of women. Tooley, J.
371.82

The **miser**. Molière
In Molière. The misanthrope and other plays
842

Les **misérables**. Hugo, V. **Fic**

The **misfits**. Miller, A.
In American short story masterpieces **S C**

Mishler, Clifford
(jt. auth) Krause, C. L. Standard catalog of
world coins **737.4**

Misiroglu, Gina Renée
(ed) The Superhero book. See The Superhero
book **741.5**

Miss Butterfly. Mori, T.
In American dragons: twenty-five Asian
American voices p26-33 **810.8**

Miss Clairol. Viramontes, H. M.
In Latina: women's voices from the borderlands p120-25 **810.8**
In The Oxford book of women's writing in
the United States p154-58 **810.8**

Miss de Mannering of Asham. Mayor, F. M.
In The Oxford book of gothic tales p386-406
S C

Miss King. Maugham, W. S.
In Maugham, W. S. Collected short stories
S C

Miss Manners' guide to excruciatingly correct behavior. Martin, J. **395**

Miss Marple tells a story. Christie, A.
In Christie, A. Miss Marple: the complete
short stories **S C**

Miss Marple: the complete short stories. Christie,
A. **S C**

Missing Angel Juan. Block, F. L.
In Block, F. L. Dangerous angels; the
Weetzie Bat books **Fic**

Missing in Tokyo. Marks, G. **Fic**

The **missing** peace. Danticat, E.
In Danticat, E. Krik? Krak! **S C**

Missing persons
See also Runaway teenagers
Fiction
Marks, G. Missing in Tokyo **Fic**
Westerfeld, S. So yesterday **Fic**

Missionaries, Christian See Christian missionaries

Missionaries of Charity
Spink, K. Mother Teresa **92**

Missions
India
Spink, K. Mother Teresa **92**

Mississippi
Fiction
Sloan, K. The patron saint of red Chevies
Fic
Taylor, M. D. Roll of thunder, hear my cry
Fic
Vaught, S. Stormwitch **Fic**
Poetry
Lewis, J. P. Black cat bone **811**
Nelson, M. A wreath for Emmett Till **811**
Race relations
Crowe, C. Getting away with murder: the true
story of the Emmett Till case **364.1**

Mississippi River
Fiction
Twain, M. The adventures of Huckleberry Finn
Fic
Twain, M. The adventures of Tom Sawyer
Fic

Mississippi River valley
Twain, M. Life on the Mississippi **818**
Mississippi trial, 1955. Crowe, C. **Fic**

Mississippi valley See Mississippi River valley

Missouri
Fiction
Berg, E. Joy school **Fic**
Jackson, J. Life at these speeds **Fic**
Twain, M. The adventures of Huckleberry Finn
Fic
Twain, M. The adventures of Tom Sawyer
Fic

Missouri Boy. Myrick, L. **92**

Missouri heritage readers series
Gilbert, J. The Trail of Tears across Missouri
970.004

The **mist**. King, S.
In King, S. Skeleton crew **S C**

Mister and Mistress Elliot. See Hemingway, E.
Mr. and Mrs. Elliot

Mister Malone. See Wolfe, T. Mr. Malone

Mistral. Faulkner, W.
In Faulkner, W. Collected stories of William
Faulkner p843-76 **S C**

Mistress of dragons. Weis, M. **Fic**

The **mists** of Avalon. Bradley, M. Z. **Fic**

Mitcham, Carl
(ed) Encyclopedia of science, technology, and
ethics. See Encyclopedia of science, technology, and ethics **503**

Mitchell, David
Black swan green **Fic**

Mitchell, John G.
National Geographic, the wildlife photographs
779

Mitchell, Sally, 1937-
Daily life in Victorian England **941.081**

Mitchell, Stephen, 1943-
(tr) Gilgamesh. Gilgamesh **892**
(tr) Mahabharata. Bhagavadgita. Bhagavad Gita
891

The **Mitchell** Beazley world atlas of birds. See
The world atlas of birds **598**

Mixed marriage See Interracial marriage

Mixed race people See Racially mixed people

Miyuki, Takahashi
Musashi #9, Vol. 1 **741.5**

MLA handbook for writers of research papers.
Gibaldi, J. **808**

Mlodinow, Leonard
Euclid's window **516**
(jt. auth) Hawking, S. W. A briefer history of
time **523.1**

Mlynowski, Sarah, 1977-
The perfect kiss
In Sixteen: stories about that sweet and bitter
birthday **S C**

Mnemonics. Vonnegut, K.
In Vonnegut, K. Bagombo snuff box: uncollected short fiction p29-32 **S C**

Mo, Yen See Mo Yan, 1956-

Mo Yan, 1956-
The cure
In Chairman Mao would not be amused; fic-
tion from today's China **S C**

Molière, 1622-1673
The doctor in spite of himself
In Molière. The misanthrope and other plays
842
The imaginary invalid
In Molière. The misanthrope and other plays
842
The learned women
In Molière. The misanthrope and other plays
842
The misanthrope
In Molière. The misanthrope and other plays
842
The misanthrope and other plays **842**
The mischievous machinations of Scapin
In Molière. The misanthrope and other plays
842
The miser
In Molière. The misanthrope and other plays
842
The would-be gentleman
In Molière. The misanthrope and other plays
842

About
Molière [critical essays] **842**
Molière [critical essays] **842**
Molin, Paulette Fairbanks
American Indian themes in young adult litera-
ture **810.9**
(jt. auth) Hirschfelder, A. B. The encyclopedia
of Native American religions **299.7**
Molina, Rafael Leónidas Trujillo *See* Trujillo
Molina, Rafael Leónidas, 1891-1961
Molina-Gavilán, Yolanda, 1963-
(ed) Cosmos latinos. See Cosmos latinos
S C
Mollel, Tololwa M. (Tololwa Marti)
A night out
In The Heinemann book of contemporary Af-
rican short stories p100-03 **S C**
Moloney, James, 1954-
Black taxi **Fic**
Molotch, Harvey Luskin
Where stuff comes from **620**
Momaday, N. Scott
About
Coltelli, L. Winged words: American Indian
writers speak **897**
The **moment** of decision. Ellin, S.
In The Best American mystery stories of the
century p405-25 **S C**
Mom's cancer. Fies, B. **616.99**
Mona Lisa, Jesus, Chad, and me. Mackler, C.
In Sixteen: stories about that sweet and bitter
birthday **S C**
Monarch butterflies
Halpern, S. M. Four wings and a prayer
595.7
Schappert, P. The last Monarch butterfly
595.7
The **monarch** of the glen. Gaiman, N.
In Gaiman, N. Fragile things; short fictions
and wonders **S C**
Monarchs *See* Kings and rulers

Monarchy
See also Queens
Mondowney, JoAnn G.
Hold them in your heart **027.62**
Monet, Claude, 1840-1926
About
Morris, C. The essential Claude Monet
759.4
Waldron, A. Claude Monet **92**
Money
See also Paper money
Mongillo, John F.
Encyclopedia of environmental science **363.7**
Teen guides to environmental science **333.72**
Mongillo, Peter A.
(jt. auth) Mongillo, J. F. Teen guides to environ-
mental science **333.72**
Mongolia
Kings and rulers
Rice, E. Empire in the east: the story of Gen-
ghis Khan **92**
Mongolians *See* Mongols
Mongols
Burgan, M. Empire of the Mongols **951**
Lane, G. Genghis Khan and Mongol rule
950
The **monkey**. Dinesen, I.
In The Oxford book of gothic tales p344-85
S C
The **monkey**. King, S.
In King, S. Skeleton crew **S C**
The **monkey** garden. Cisneros, S.
In Growing up Latino; memoirs and stories
p288-91 **810.8**
Monkey planet. See Boulle, P. Planet of the apes
Fic
Monkey son-in-law
In Hearne, B. G. Beauties and beasts p32-34
398.2
Monkeyman. Myers, W. D.
In Myers, W. D. 145th Street; short stories
S C
Monkeys
Graphic novels
Nibot, R. Banana Sunday **741.5**
The **monkey's** finger. Asimov, I.
In Asimov, I. The complete stories p166-74
S C
The **monkey's** wedding. Aiken, J.
In Night terrors; stories of shadow and sub-
stance **S C**
Mono (Disease) *See* Mononucleosis
Monologue audition series
100 great monologues from the neo-classical
theatre **808.82**
Monologue audition series [series]
The Ultimate audition book **808.82**
Monologues
100 great monologues from the neo-classical
theatre **808.82**
100 great monologues from the Renaissance the-
atre **822.008**

Morgenstern, Julie
Organizing from the inside out for teens
646.7

Morgenstern-Colón, Jessi
(jt. auth) Morgenstern, J. Organizing from the inside out for teens **646.7**

Mori, Kyoko, 1957-
Black and white
In Face relations; 11 stories about seeing beyond color **S C**

Mori, Toshio, 1910-1980
Miss Butterfly
In American dragons: twenty-five Asian American voices p26-33 **810.8**

Moriarty, Jaclyn
The year of secret assignments **Fic**

Moriarty, Laura
The center of everything **Fic**

Morkes, Andrew
(ed) They teach that in college!? See They teach that in college!? **378.73**

Mormon Church *See* Church of Jesus Christ of Latter-day Saints

Mormons
Remini, R. V. Joseph Smith **92**
Fiction
Grey, Z. Riders of the purple sage **Fic**
Hopkins, E. Burned **Fic**

Mormons in America. Bushman, C. L. **289.3**

Morning deliveries (Milkman #1). King, S.
In King, S. Skeleton crew **S C**

Mornings like this. Dillard, A. **811**

Morpurgo, Michael
Private Peaceful **Fic**

Morris, Betty J.
Administering the school library media center
027.8

Morris, Catherine
The essential Claude Monet **759.4**

Morris, Edmund
Beethoven: the universal composer **92**

Morris, Holly, 1965-
Adventure divas **791.45**

Morris, Jim
The oldest rookie **92**

Morris, JoAnne Prichard
(jt. auth) Blackwell, U. Barefootin' **92**

Morris, Kenneth
See/See also pages in the following book(s):
We'll understand it better by and by **782.25**

Morris, Richard Brandon, 1904-1989
(ed) Basic documents in American history. See Basic documents in American history **973**

Morrison, Arthur, 1863-1945
Behind the shade
In The Oxford book of English short stories p105-09 **S C**

Morrison, Gordon
(jt. auth) Leahy, C. W. The birdwatcher's companion to North American birdlife **598**

Morrison, M. A. (Martha A.), 1948-
Judaism **296**

Morrison, Martha A. *See* Morrison, M. A. (Martha A.), 1948-

Morrison, Theodore, 1901-1988
(ed) Chaucer, G. The portable Chaucer **821**

Morrison, Toni, 1931-
Beloved **Fic**
The bluest eye **Fic**
[excerpt]
In Growing up ethnic in America; contemporary fiction about learning to be American **S C**
Conversations with Toni Morrison **92**
"Recitatif"
In Leaving home: stories p201-27 **808.8**
In The Oxford book of women's writing in the United States p159-75 **810.8**
Sula **Fic**
About
Andersen, R. Toni Morrison **92**
Crayton, L. A. A student's guide to Toni Morrison **813.009**
The Toni Morrison encyclopedia **813.009**

Morrow, Charlene, 1948-
(ed) Notable women in mathematics. See Notable women in mathematics **920.003**

Morse, Scott
The barefoot serpent **741.5**

Mortal engines. Reeve, P. **Fic**

Le **morte** Darthur, or, The hoole book of Kyng Arthur and of his noble knyghtes of the Rounde Table. Malory, Sir T. **398.2**

Mortimer, Sean
(jt. auth) Hawk, T. Hawk **92**

Mortimer Gray's History of death. Stableford, B. M.
In Best of the best: 20 years of the Year's best science fiction **S C**

Morton Arboretum (Lisle, Ill.)
Plotnik, A. The urban tree book **582.16**

Mosby, Rebekah Presson
(ed) Poetry speaks. See Poetry speaks
808.81

Moseley, Michael Edward
The Incas and their ancestors **985**

Moser, Diane, 1944-
(jt. auth) Spangenburg, R. The history of science **509**
(jt. auth) Spangenburg, R. Wernher von Braun **92**

Moser, Kit *See* Moser, Diane, 1944-

Moses (Biblical figure)
About
Kirsch, J. Moses **222**

Moses, William
She won't bite
In Not the only one; lesbian and gay fiction for teens **S C**

Moses, man of the mountain. Hurston, Z. N.
In Hurston, Z. N. Novels and stories p335-595 **Fic**

Mosier, John, 1944-
The myth of the Great War **940.4**

Moslem countries *See* Islamic countries

Mr. and Mrs. Elliot. Hemingway, E.
In Hemingway, E. The complete short stories
of Ernest Hemingway; the Finca Vigía
edition p123-25   **S C**

Mr. Blandings builds his castle. Hodgins, E.
In Adaptations: from short story to big
screen; 35 great stories that have inspired
great films   **S C**

Mr. Harrington's washing. Maugham, W. S.
In Maugham, W. S. Collected short stories
    S C

Mr. Higginbotham's catastrophe. Hawthorne, N.
In Hawthorne, N. Tales and sketches, including Twice-told tales, Mosses from an old
manse, and The snow-image; A wonder
book for girls and boys; Tanglewood
tales for girls and boys, being a second
Wonder book p188-99   **S C**

Mr. Know-all. Maugham, W. S.
In Maugham, W. S. Collected short stories
    S C

Mr. Malone. Wolfe, T.
In Wolfe, T. The complete short stories of
Thomas Wolfe p300-07   **S C**

Mr. Mendelsohn. Mohr, N.
In Growing up Latino; memoirs and stories
p131-46   **810.8**

Mr. Ruben. Williams-Garcia, R.
In Face relations; 11 stories about seeing beyond color   **S C**

Mr. Sigerson. Beagle, P. S.
In Beagle, P. S. The line between   **S C**

Mrs. Acland's ghosts. Trevor, W.
In Nightshade: 20th century ghost stories
p405-21   **S C**

Mrs. Bathurst. Kipling, R.
In Kipling, R. The portable Kipling   **828**

Mrs. Bullfrog. Hawthorne, N.
In Hawthorne, N. Tales and sketches, including Twice-told tales, Mosses from an old
manse, and The snow-image; A wonder
book for girls and boys; Tanglewood
tales for girls and boys, being a second
Wonder book p406-13   **S C**

Mrs. Fortescue. Lessing, D. M.
In The Oxford book of short stories p487-500
    S C

Mrs. Houdini's wife. Brown, A.
In Not the only one; lesbian and gay fiction
for teens   **S C**

Mrs. Hutchinson. Hawthorne, N.
In Hawthorne, N. Tales and sketches, including Twice-told tales, Mosses from an old
manse, and The snow-image; A wonder
book for girls and boys; Tanglewood
tales for girls and boys, being a second
Wonder book p18-24   **S C**

Mrs. Lincoln and Mrs. Keckley. Fleischner, J.
    92

Mrs. McWilliams and the lightning. Twain, M.
In Twain, M. The complete short stories of
Mark Twain; now collected for the first
time   **S C**

Mrs. Noonan. Salisbury, G.
In Salisbury, G. Island boyz: short stories
p20-48   **S C**

Mrs. Todd's shortcut. King, S.
In King, S. Skeleton crew   **S C**

Ms. found in a bottle. Poe, E. A.
In Poe, E. A. The collected tales and poems
of Edgar Allan Poe p118-26   **818**

Muccigrosso, Robert
Term paper resource guide to twentieth-century
United States history   **016.973**

Much ado about nothing. Shakespeare, W.
    822.3

The **mud** and fever dialogues. Anderson, M. T.
In Sixteen: stories about that sweet and bitter
birthday   **S C**

Muḥammad, d. 632
About
Armstrong, K. Muhammad   **92**

Muhammedanism *See* Islam

Muhammedans *See* Muslims

Muir, John, 1838-1914
About
Ehrlich, G. John Muir   **92**
Wilkins, T. John Muir   **92**

Muir, John Kenneth, 1969-
The encyclopedia of superheroes on film and
television   **791.43**

Mulatto. Hughes, L.
In Black theatre USA; plays by African
Americans, 1847 to today   **812.008**
In Hughes, L. Five plays p1-35   **812**

Muldoon, Paul
See/See also pages in the following book(s):
Fooling with words   **808.1**

Mule in the yard. Faulkner, W.
In Faulkner, W. Collected stories of William
Faulkner p249-64   **S C**

Mules and men. Hurston, Z. N.
In Hurston, Z. N. Folklore, memoirs, and other writings   **818**

Mulholland, Garry
This is uncool: the 500 greatest singles since
punk and disco   **781.66**

Mulkerns, Val, 1925-
Loser
In The Oxford book of Irish short stories
p437-44   **S C**

Mullane, Deirdre
(ed) Crossing the danger water. See Crossing
the danger water   **810.8**

Muller, Marcia
Sweet cactus wine
In A Century of great Western stories
    S C

Muller, Salomé, b. ca. 1809
About
Bailey, J. The lost German slave girl [biography
of Salomé Muller]   **92**

Mullin, Glenn H.
The second Dalai Lama   **92**

The **multicultural** cookbook for students. Albyn,
C. L.   **641.5**

My so-called digital life. Pletka, B. **779**

My son the murderer. Malamud, B.
In Malamud, B. The complete stories **S C**

My son, the physicist. Asimov, I.
In Asimov, I. The complete stories p598-601 **S C**

My son's story. Gordimer, N. **Fic**

My story. Fuller, J.
In The Oxford book of English short stories p398-99 **S C**

My sweet sixteenth. Wilkinson, B. S.
In Join in; multiethnic short stories by outstanding writers for young adults p128-40 **S C**

My thirteenth winter. Abeel, S. **92**

My tocaya. Cisneros, S.
In Cisneros, S. Woman Hollering Creek and other stories **S C**

My visit to Niagara. Hawthorne, N.
In Hawthorne, N. Tales and sketches, including Twice-told tales, Mosses from an old manse, and The snow-image; A wonder book for girls and boys; Tanglewood tales for girls and boys, being a second Wonder book p244-50 **S C**

My vocation. Lavin, M.
In The Oxford book of short stories p432-42 **S C**

My watch. Twain, M.
In Twain, M. The complete short stories of Mark Twain; now collected for the first time **S C**

Mycology *See* Fungi

Myer, Valerie Grosvenor
(ed) The Continuum encyclopedia of British literature. See The Continuum encyclopedia of British literature **820.3**

Myers, Allen C., 1945-
(ed) Eerdmans dictionary of the Bible. See Eerdmans dictionary of the Bible **220.3**

Myers, Christopher
(il) Cummings, E. E. Love **811**
(jt. auth) Myers, W. D. Autobiography of my dead brother **Fic**
(il) Myers, W. D. Harlem **811**

Myers, Edward, 1950-
When will I stop hurting? **155.9**

Myers, Jack Elliott, 1941-
Dictionary of poetic terms **808.1**

Myers, Richard, 1951-
The basics of chemistry **540**

Myers, Walter Dean, 1937-
145th Street **S C**
Contents: Big Joe's funeral; The baddest dog in Harlem; Fighter; Angela's eyes; The streak; Monkeyman; Kitty and Mack: a love story; A Chirstmas story; A story in three parts; Block party—145th Street style
Autobiography of my dead brother **Fic**
Bad boy **92**
Fallen angels **Fic**
Harlem **811**
Here in Harlem **811**
Monster **Fic**
One more river to cross **779**

The prom prize
In Every man for himself; ten short stories about being a guy **S C**
Slam! **Fic**
Street love **Fic**
Visit
In Necessary noise: stories about our families as they really are p81-93 **S C**

Myerson, Joel
(ed) Alcott, L. M. The selected letters of Louisa May Alcott **92**
(ed) A Historical guide to Ralph Waldo Emerson. See A Historical guide to Ralph Waldo Emerson **814**

Myracle, Lauren, 1969-
Bad hair day
In Such a pretty face; short stories **S C**

Myrick, Leland
Missouri Boy **92**

Myrna and me. Boss, L.
In Growing up ethnic in America; contemporary fiction about learning to be American **S C**

MySpace (Web site)
Magid, L. J. MySpace unraveled **004.6**

MySpace unraveled. Magid, L. J. **004.6**

Mysteries of history. Stewart, R. **902**

Mysterious creatures. Eberhart, G. M. **001.9**

Mysterious Madame Shanghai. Hughes, L.
In Hughes, L. Short stories of Langston Hughes **S C**

The **mysterious** stranger. Twain, M.
In Twain, M. The complete short stories of Mark Twain; now collected for the first time **S C**

Mystery and detective stories *See* Mystery fiction

Mystery and suspense writers **809.3**

Mystery fiction
Abrahams, P. Down the rabbit hole **Fic**
Alfred Hitchcock's mystery magazine presents fifty years of crime and suspense **S C**
Barr, N. Track of the cat **Fic**
Bell, H. A matter of profit **Fic**
The Best American mystery stories of the century **S C**
Bray, L. A great and terrible beauty **Fic**
Christie, A. The A.B.C. murders **Fic**
Christie, A. And then there were none **Fic**
Christie, A. Miss Marple: the complete short stories **S C**
Clark, M. H. Where are the children? **Fic**
Doyle, Sir A. C. The complete Sherlock Holmes **S C**
Doyle, Sir A. C. The hound of the Baskervilles **Fic**
Ferguson, A. The Christopher killer **Fic**
Grindle, L. The nightspinners **Fic**
Jaffe, M. Bad kitty **Fic**
King, L. R. The beekeeper's apprentice, or, On the segregation of the queen **Fic**
McNamee, G. Acceleration **Fic**
Moloney, J. Black taxi **Fic**
Pullman, P. The ruby in the smoke **Fic**
Silbert, L. The intelligencer **Fic**

Near East *See* Middle East

Nearest star. Golub, L.   **523.7**

Nebraska

Fiction

Cather, W. My Antonia   **Fic**

Nebraska 99. Woodson, J.

     In Sixteen: stories about that sweet and bitter birthday   **S C**

Nebraska Crane. Wolfe, T.

     In Wolfe, T. The complete short stories of Thomas Wolfe p469-77   **S C**

Nebulae, Extragalactic *See* Galaxies

The **necessary** beggar. Palwick, S.   **Fic**

Necessary noise. Donoghue, E.

     In Necessary noise: stories about our families as they really are p51-67   **S C**

Necessary noise: stories about our families as they really are   **S C**

     Contents: Hardware, by J. Bauer; Siskiyou Sloan and the eye of the giraffe, by N. Howe; Necessary noise, by E. Donoghue; The throwaway: a suite, by N. Grimes; Visit, by W. D. Myers; A family illness: a mom-son conversation, by J. C. Thomas; A woman's touch, by R. Williams-Garcia; Sailing away, by M. Cart; Dr. Jekyll and Sister Hyde, by S. Sones; Snowbound, by L. Lowry

Neches, Neil

     (ed) Poetry in motion. See Poetry in motion   **808.81**

The **necromancers**. Brennan, H.

     In The restless dead; ten original stories of the supernatural   **S C**

Nectar in a sieve. Markandaya, K.   **Fic**

Need to know library [series]

     Dunn-Georgiou, E. Everything you need to know about organic foods   **641.3**

     Hayhurst, C. Everything you need to know about food additives   **664**

Neeley, Bill

     The last Comanche chief: the life and times of Quanah Parker   **92**

Neft, David S.

     The sports encyclopedia: baseball 2007   **796.357**

Nég Créol. Chopin, K.

     In Chopin, K. The awakening and selected stories   **S C**

Negotiation

     See also Conflict management

Negress. Singer, M.

     In Face relations; 11 stories about seeing beyond color   **S C**

The **Negro** almanac. See The African American almanac   **305.8**

Negro leagues

     Hogan, L. D. Shades of glory   **796.357**

Nehlen, Don, 1936-

     (ed) Complete guide to special teams. See Complete guide to special teams   **796.332**

The **neighborhood**. Gordon, M.

     In Coming of age in America; a multicultural anthology p7-16   **S C**

Neihardt, John Gneisenau, 1881-1973

     (jt. auth) Black Elk. Black Elk speaks   **92**

Neil MacAdam. Maugham, W. S.

     In Maugham, W. S. Collected short stories   **S C**

Neimark, Anne E., 1935-

     Johnny Cash   **92**

Nelson, Alice Moore Dunbar- *See* Dunbar-Nelson, Alice Moore, 1875-1935

Nelson, Blake, 1960-

     Paranoid Park   **Fic**

     Rock star, superstar   **Fic**

Nelson, Emmanuel S. (Emmanuel Sampath), 1954-

     (ed) Contemporary African American novelists. See Contemporary African American novelists   **920.003**

     (ed) The Greenwood encyclopedia of multiethnic American literature. See The Greenwood encyclopedia of multiethnic American literature   **810.9**

Nelson, Glenn C.

     Ceramics: a potter's handbook   **738.1**

Nelson, Horatio Nelson, Viscount, 1758-1805

About

     Czisnik, M. Horatio Nelson   **92**

Nelson, Marilyn, 1946-

     Carver, a life in poems   **811**

     Fortune's bones   **811**

     A wreath for Emmett Till   **811**

Nelson, Michael, 1949-

     (ed) Guide to the presidency. See Guide to the presidency   **352.23**

     (ed) The Presidency A to Z. See The Presidency A to Z   **352.23**

Nelson, Pete

     Left for dead   **940.54**

Nelson, W. Dale

     Interpreters with Lewis and Clark: the story of Sacagawea and Toussaint Charbonneau   **92**

Nelson Mandela and apartheid in world history. Gaines, A.   **92**

Nelson Mandela speaks. Mandela, N.   **968.06**

Nemesis. Clarke, A. C.

     In Clarke, A. C. The collected stories of Arthur C. Clarke   **S C**

Nemiroff, Robert, d. 1991

     (jt. auth) Hansberry, L. To be young, gifted, and Black   **92**

Nemko, Marty, 1945-

     The all-in-one college guide   **378.1**

Neo-fascism *See* Fascism

Neo-Nazis

     See/See also pages in the following book(s):

     Laqueur, W. Fascism   **320.5**

Nepal

Fiction

     McCormick, P. Sold   **Fic**

Neruda, Pablo, 1904-1973

     The poetry of Pablo Neruda   **861**

     Selected odes of Pablo Neruda   **861**

     Twenty love poems and a song of despair   **861**

Nerve endings. Rapport, R.   **612.8**

New Catholic encyclopedia: jubilee volume, the Wojtyla years **282**

New complete do-it-yourself manual. See Complete do-it-yourself manual **643**

New complete dog training manual. Fogle, B. **636.7**

New complete sailing manual. Sleight, S. **797.1**

The new comprehensive American rhyming dictionary. Young, S. **423**

New Deal, 1933-1939
Encyclopedias
Encyclopedia of the Great Depression **973.91**

The new dictionary of cultural literacy. Hirsch, E. D. **031**

New dictionary of the history of ideas **903**

New directions for library service to young adults **027.62**

New elements [biography of Marie Curie] Yannuzzi, D. A. **92**

The New Encyclopaedia Britannica **031**

The new encyclopedia of aquatic life **591.9**

The new encyclopedia of golf. Campbell, M. **796.352**

The New encyclopedia of Judaism [New York University Press] **296.03**

The new encyclopedia of Judaism. See The student's encyclopedia of Judaism **296.03**

The New encyclopedia of the American West **978.03**

The new encyclopedia of the cat. Fogle, B. **636.8**

The new encyclopedia of the dog. Fogle, B. **636.7**

The new encyclopedia of the horse. Edwards, E. H. **636.1**

New England
Fiction
Boylan, J. F. Getting in **Fic**
Hawthorne, N. The scarlet letter **Fic**
Hoffman, A. The probable future **Fic**
Wolff, T. Old school **Fic**

New England
History
Demos, J. Entertaining Satan **133.4**

A New English-Chinese dictionary **495.1**

The new face of baseball. Wendel, T. **796.357**

The new Fowler's modern English usage. See Fowler, H. W. Fowler's modern English usage **428**

The new golden bough. Frazer, Sir J. G. **201**

The New Grove dictionary of jazz **781.65**

New historical atlas of religion in America. Gaustad, E. S. **200.9**

The new how things work. Langone, J. **600**

New immigrant literatures in the United States **810.9**

The new immigrants [series]
Horst, H. A. Jamaican Americans **305.8**
Rangaswamy, P. Indian Americans **305.8**

New Jersey
Fiction
Ortiz Cofer, J. An island like you **S C**
Roth, P. The plot against America **Fic**

The new Jerusalem Bible. Bible **220.5**

The new Jewish holiday cookbook. Greene, G. K. **641.5**

A new leaf. Fitzgerald, F. S.
In Fitzgerald, F. S. The short stories of F. Scott Fitzgerald; a new collection p634-47 **S C**

The new life [La vita nuova] Dante Alighieri
In Dante Alighieri. The portable Dante **851**

In Emerson, R. W. Collected poems & translations **811**

The new lifetime reading plan. Fadiman, C. **028**

New Mexico
Fiction
Bradford, R. Red sky at morning **Fic**
Cather, W. Death comes for the archbishop **Fic**
Saenz, B. A. Sammy and Juliana in Hollywood **Fic**

The new negro. Pinckney, D.
In Growing up ethnic in America; contemporary fiction about learning to be American **S C**

New neighbor. Powell, T.
In Alfred Hitchcock's mystery magazine presents fifty years of crime and suspense **S C**

The New new journalism **071**

New Orleans (La.)
Fiction
Tiernan, C. A chalice of wind Book 1 **Fic**

The New Oxford American dictionary **423**

The New Oxford book of Irish verse **821.008**

The New Oxford book of literary anecdotes **828**

The New Oxford book of Victorian verse **821.008**

The New Oxford companion to literature in French **840.3**

The new Partridge dictionary of slang and unconventional English **427**

The new Penguin dictionary of science **503**

New poems of Emily Dickinson. Dickinson, E. **811**

The new policeman. Thompson, K. **Fic**

The New quotable woman. See The Quotable woman **808.88**

New skies: an anthology of today's science fiction **S C**

Contents: They're made out of meat / Terry Bisson -- A walk in the sun / Geoffrey A. Landis -- Peaches for Mad Molly / Steven Gould -- Serpents' teeth / Spider Robinson -- Uncle Joshua and the Grooglemen / Debra Doyle and James D. Macdonald -- A letter from the Clearys / Connie Willis -- Brian and the aliens / Will Shetterly -- Different kinds of darkness / David Langford -- Will you be an astronaut? / Greg van Eekhout -- Cards of grief

New skies: an anthology of today's science fiction—*Continued*
/ Jane Yolen -- Tangents / Greg Bear -- The alien mind / Philip K. Dick -- Out of all them bright stars / Nancy Kress -- The Lincoln train / Maureen F. McHugh -- Arthur Sternbach brings the curveball to Mars / Kim Stanley Robinson -- Salvage / Orson Scott Card -- The great goodbye / Robert Charles Wilson

New spring. Jordan, R.
    In Legends: short novels by the masters of modern fantasy p631-715   **S C**
The **New** Times selective guide to colleges. See Fiske, E. B. The Fiske guide to colleges 2008   **378.73**

New town. Siy, A.
    In What a song can do; 12 riffs on the power of music   **S C**

New virtual field trips. Cooper, G.   **025.5**
The **new** way things work. Macaulay, D.   **600**
The **new** world order. Jeapes, B.   **Fic**

New Year
    Gulevich, T. Encyclopedia of Christmas and New Year's celebrations   **394.26**

New Year's Day. Wharton, E.
    In Wharton, E. Novellas and other writings   **818**

New York (N.Y.)
    See also Lower East Side (New York, N.Y.)
    Von Drehle, D. Triangle: the fire that changed America   **974.7**

Fiction

Auch, M. J. Ashes of roses   **Fic**
Baldwin, J. If Beale Street could talk   **Fic**
Black, H. Valiant: a modern faerie tale   **Fic**
Budhos, M. T. Ask me no questions   **Fic**
Cohn, R. Nick & Norah's infinite playlist   **Fic**
Conroy, P. The prince of tides   **Fic**
Cooney, C. B. Code orange   **Fic**
De la Cruz, M. Blue bloods   **Fic**
Dorfman, A. Burning city   **Fic**
Foer, J. S. Extremely loud & incredibly close   **Fic**
Freymann-Weyr, G. Stay with me   **Fic**
Herrera, J. F. Cinnamon girl   **Fic**
Kaplow, R. Me and Orson Welles   **Fic**
Krovatin, C. Heavy metal and you   **Fic**
Larbalestier, J. Magic or madness   **Fic**
Mackler, C. The earth, my butt, and other big, round things   **Fic**
McDonald, J. Chill wind   **Fic**
Packer, A. The dive from Clausen's pier   **Fic**
Rabb, M. Cures for heartbreak   **Fic**
Salinger, J. D. The catcher in the rye   **Fic**
Salinger, J. D. Franny & Zooey   **Fic**
Salinger, J. D. Raise high the roof beam, carpenters, and Seymour: an introduction   **Fic**
Shusterman, N. Downsiders   **Fic**
Stine, C. Refugees   **Fic**
Taylor, K. Bowery girl   **Fic**
Vizzini, N. It's kind of a funny story   **Fic**
Volponi, P. Rooftop   **Fic**
Westerfeld, S. So yesterday   **Fic**
Woodson, J. If you come softly   **Fic**
Woodson, J. Miracle's boys   **Fic**

Wyeth, S. D. Orphea Proud   **Fic**

Race relations
    Bolden, T. Maritcha [biography of Maritcha Rémond Lyons]   **92**

New York (State)

Fiction

Doctorow, E. L. Ragtime   **Fic**
Kennedy, W. Ironweed   **Fic**
Kerr, M. E. Your eyes in stars   **Fic**

History—1600-1775, Colonial period—Graphic novels
    Bogaert, H. M. v. d. Journey into Mohawk Country   **973.2**

New York day women. Danticat, E.
    In Danticat, E. Krik? Krak!   **S C**

New York in June. Sloan, B.
    In Not the only one; lesbian and gay fiction for teens   **S C**

New York Public Library
    Books for the teen age, 2007   **011.6**
The **New** York Public Library African American desk reference   **305.8**
The **New** York Public Library business desk reference   **651**
The **New** York Public Library desk reference   **031.02**

New York Stock Exchange, Inc.
    Blumenthal, K. Six days in October   **332.6**
The **New** York Times almanac, 2007   **031.02**

New York Times Company
    Sultans of swat   **920**
The **New** York times crossword puzzle dictionary. Pulliam, T.   **793.73**
The **New** York Times essential library: Jazz. See Ratliff, B. Jazz: a critic's guide to the 100 most important recordings   **781.65**
The **New** York Times guide to alternative health   **615.5**
The **New** York times guide to essential knowledge   **031.02**
The **New** York Times practical guide to practically everything   **646.7**
The **New** York Times second book of science questions and answers. Ray, C. C.   **500**

New York Vietnam Veterans Memorial Commission
    Dear America: letters home from Vietnam. See Dear America: letters home from Vietnam   **959.704**

New York Yankees (Baseball team)
    Halberstam, D. Summer of '49   **796.357**
    McGough, M. Bat boy   **92**
    New York Times Company. Sultans of swat   **920**

See/See also pages in the following book(s):
    Jeter, D. The life you imagine   **92**

Newbery, Linda, 1952-
    Sisterland   **Fic**
The **Newbery/Printz** companion. Gillespie, J. T.   **028.5**

Newbery Medal
    Gillespie, J. T. The Newbery/Printz companion   **028.5**

Nikolai. Khlebnikov, V.
   In The portable twentieth-century Russian
     reader   **891.7**
Nile River
   Bangs, R. Mystery of the Nile   **916**
Nilsen, Alleen Pace
   (jt. auth) Donelson, K. L. Literature for today's
     young adults   **028.5**
Nilsson, Lennart, 1922-
   A child is born   **612.6**
Nilsson, Per, 1954-
   Heart's delight   **Fic**
   You & you & you   **Fic**
The **nine/eleven** report. See Jacobson, S. The 9/11
   report   **973.931**
The **nine** billion names of God. Clarke, A. C.
   In Clarke, A. C. The collected stories of Ar-
     thur C. Clarke   **S C**
Nine eleven: the book of help. See 911: the book
   of help   **810.8**
Nine hundred grandmothers. Lafferty, R. A.
   In The Norton book of science fiction; North
     American science fiction, 1960-1990
     p142-50   **S C**
The **nine** mile walk. Kemelman, H.
   In The Best American mystery stories of the
     century p335-43   **S C**
Nine stories. Salinger, J. D.   **S C**
The **nineteen-eighties**. See Woodger, E. The
   1980s   **973.92**
Nineteen eighty-four. Orwell, G.   **Fic**
Nineteen-eighty - Two thousand: the twentieth
   century. See 1980-2000: the twentieth century
     909.82
The **nineteen** fifties. See Schwartz, R. A. The
   1950s   **973.921**
Nineteen-forty - Nineteen-sixty: the twentieth cen-
   tury. See 1940-1960: the twentieth century
     909.82
Nineteen hundred - Nineteen-forty: the twentieth
   century. See 1900-1920: the twentieth century
     909.82
The **nineteen-nineties**. See Schwartz, R. A. The
   1990s   **973.92**
Nineteen-sixty - Nineteen-eighty: the twentieth
   century. See 1960-1980: the twentieth century
     909.82
Nineteen thirty-seven. Danticat, E.
   In Danticat, E. Krik? Krak!   **S C**
Nineteen-twenty - Nineteen-forty: the twentieth
   century. See 1920-1940: the twentieth century
     909.82
Nineteen varieties of gazelle. See Nye, N. S. 19
   varieties of gazelle   **811**
Nineteenth-century American women writers
     810.9
Nishi, Dennis, 1967-
   (ed) The Korean War. See The Korean War
     951.9
Nist, Sherrie L. (Sherrie Lee), 1946-
   College rules!   **378**
Niven, Larry
   The Mote in God's Eye   **Fic**
   Ringworld   **Fic**

Nix, Garth, 1963-
   Endings
   In Gothic!; ten original dark tales   **S C**
   In The Year's best science fiction and fantasy
     for teens: first annual collection   **S C**
   Sabriel   **Fic**
Nix, Lacy Hunter, 1979-
   (ed) Foxfire 40th anniversary book. See Foxfire
     40th anniversary book   **975.8**
Nixon, Joan Lowery, 1927-2003
   The dark beast of death
   In Night terrors; stories of shadow and sub-
     stance   **S C**
Nixon, Richard M. (Richard Milhous), 1913-
   1994
            About
   Genovese, M. A. The Watergate crisis
     973.924
   Woodward, B. The final days   **973.924**
No cure for it. Wolfe, T.
   In Wolfe, T. The complete short stories of
     Thomas Wolfe p533-36   **S C**
No door. Wolfe, T.
   In Wolfe, T. The complete short stories of
     Thomas Wolfe p67-105   **S C**
No easy answers [biography of Bayard Rustin]
   Miller, C. C.   **92**
No exit. Sartre, J. P.
   In Sartre, J. P. No exit, and three other plays
     842
No exit, and three other plays. Sartre, J. P.
     842
No fixed points. Reynolds, N.   **792.8**
No god but God. Aslan, R.   **297**
No more birds will die today. Acampora, P.
   In Every man for himself; ten short stories
     about being a guy   **S C**
No more rivers. Wolfe, T.
   In Wolfe, T. The complete short stories of
     Thomas Wolfe p596-611   **S C**
No morning after. Clarke, A. C.
   In Clarke, A. C. The collected stories of Ar-
     thur C. Clarke   **S C**
No news, or what killed the dog? Bradbury, R.
   In Bradbury, R. Bradbury stories; 100 of his
     most celebrated tales   **S C**
No one loved gorillas more [biography of Dian
   Fossey] De la Bédoyère, C.   **92**
No particular night or morning. Bradbury, R.
   In Bradbury, R. The illustrated man   **S C**
No place for you, my love. Welty, E.
   In Welty, E. The collected stories of Eudora
     Welty p465-81   **S C**
No place to make love. Hughes, L.
   In Hughes, L. Short stories of Langston
     Hughes   **S C**
Nō plays
   The Classic Noh theatre of Japan   **895.6**
No pretty pictures. Lobel, A.   **92**
The **no-talent** kid. Vonnegut, K.
   In Vonnegut, K. Bagombo snuff box: uncol-
     lected short fiction p63-73   **S C**

No visible power. Noyes, D.
  In The restless dead; ten original stories of the supernatural   **S C**

No Win Phuong. Carter, A. R.
  In Join in; multiethnic short stories by outstanding writers for young adults p62-84   **S C**

Noah's ark
Fiction
  Provoost, A. In the shadow of the ark   **Fic**

Nobel Prize-winning scientists [series]
  Pasachoff, N. E. Linus Pauling   **92**

Nobel Prizes
  Feldman, B. The Nobel Prize   **001.4**

Noble, William, 1932-
  Bookbanning in America   **098**

Noble Warriors [series]
  Nicholson, W. Seeker   **Fic**

Nobody ever dies. Hemingway, E.
  In Hemingway, E. The complete short stories of Ernest Hemingway; the Finca Vigía edition p470-81   **S C**

Nobody left to hate. Aronson, E.   **371.7**

Nocerino, Kathryn
  Americanism
  In Growing up ethnic in America; contemporary fiction about learning to be American   **S C**

Nofi, Albert A.
  (jt. auth) Dunnigan, J. F. The Pacific War encyclopedia   **940.54**

Nolan, Han, 1956-
  Maroon
  In Don't cramp my style; stories about that time of the month p182-208   **S C**

Nolan, Jonathan
  Memento mori
  In Adaptations: from short story to big screen; 35 great stories that have inspired great films   **S C**

Nolan, Michael, 1955-
  (ed) American humor. See American humor   **817.009**

Noll, Richard, 1959-
  The encyclopedia of schizophrenia and other psychotic disorders   **616.89**

Non-proliferation of nuclear weapons See Arms control

Non-violence in peace and war; excerpts. See Gandhi, M. Gandhi on non-violence   **322.4**

Nona. King, S.
  In King, S. Skeleton crew   **S C**

Nonaka, Eiji
  Cromartie High School, Vol. 1   **741.5**

Nonbook materials See Audiovisual materials

Nonconformity See Dissent

None of the above. Bader, J. L.
  In Under 30; plays for a new generation   **812.008**

None so blind. Haldeman, J. W.
  In Best of the best: 20 years of the Year's best science fiction   **S C**

Nonfiction reader's advisory   **025.5**

Nonsense verses
  Silverstein, S. Where the sidewalk ends   **811**

Nonverbal communication
  See also Deaf—Means of communication
  Fast, J. Body language   **153.6**

Noon. McNally, T.
  In McNally, T. 15 short plays p23-50   **812**

Noon wine. Porter, K. A.
  In Porter, K. A. The collected stories of Katherine Anne Porter   **S C**
  In Porter, K. A. Pale horse, pale rider: three short novels   **S C**

Norcross, Bryan
  Hurricane almanac 2007   **551.55**

Nordhoff, Charles, 1887-1947
  Mutiny on the Bounty   **Fic**

Nordley, G. David
  Into the miranda rift
  In The Hard SF renaissance   **S C**

Normandy (France), Attack on, 1944
  Hastings, M. Overlord: D-Day and the battle for Normandy   **940.54**

Norrie, Christine
  (il) Friedman, A. Breaking up   **741.5**

Norris, George William, 1861-1944
  See/See also pages in the following book(s):
  Kennedy, J. F. Profiles in courage   **920**

Norse mythology
  Hamilton, E. Mythology   **292**
Dictionaries
  Daly, K. N. Norse mythology A to Z   **293**

Norse mythology A to Z. Daly, K. N.   **293**

Norsemen See Vikings

North, Andrew See Norton, Andre, 1912-2005

North Africa
Encyclopedias
  Encyclopedia of the modern Middle East & North Africa   **956**

North America
Gazetteers
  The Columbia gazetteer of North America   **917**
History
  Jones, C. The European conquest of North America   **970.01**
Military history
  Keegan, J. Fields of battle   **973**
Natural history
  See Natural history—North America

North America. Hillstrom, K.   **363.7**

North American Indians See Native Americans

North American wildlife, trees and nonflowering plants. See Reader's Digest North American wildlife, trees and nonflowering plants   **582.16**

North Atlantic Treaty Organization
  Daalder, I. H. Winning ugly   **949.7**

North Carolina
Race relations
  Tillage, L. Leon's story   **92**

North Dakota
Fiction
Erdrich, L. The last report on the miracles at
Little No Horse **Fic**
North Korea *See* Korea (North)
North Korea **951.93**
North Pole
See also Arctic regions
Northern Ireland
Cottrell, R. C. Northern Ireland and England
941.6
A **northern** light. Donnelly, J. **Fic**
Northern lights *See* Auroras
The **northern** lights [biography of Kristian
Birkeland] Jago, L. **92**
Northern lights. See Pullman, P. The golden com-
pass **Fic**
Northmen *See* Vikings
Norton, Alice Mary *See* Norton, Andre, 1912-
2005
Norton, Andre, 1912-2005
Earthborne: a Witchworld story
In Masters of fantasy **S C**
Norton, O. Richard
The Cambridge encyclopedia of meteorites
523.5
Rocks from space **523.5**
The **Norton** anthology of African American litera-
ture **810.8**
The **Norton** anthology of literature by women
820.8
The **Norton** anthology of modern and contempo-
rary poetry **821.008**
The **Norton** anthology of modern poetry. See The
Norton anthology of modern and contempo-
rary poetry **821.008**
The **Norton** book of American short stories
S C
The **Norton** book of classical literature **880.8**
The **Norton** book of light verse **821.008**
The **Norton** book of science fiction **S C**
The **Norton** Shakespeare. Shakespeare, W.
822.3
Norway, Nevil Shute *See* Shute, Nevil, 1899-1960
Nostbakken, Faith, 1964-
Understanding Macbeth **822.3**
Nostradamus, 1503-1566
About
Randi, J. The mask of Nostradamus **92**
Not a laughing matter. Hunter, E.
In Alfred Hitchcock's mystery magazine pres-
ents fifty years of crime and suspense
S C
Not final!. Asimov, I.
In Asimov, I. The complete stories p1-15
S C
Not for ourselves alone: the story of Elizabeth
Cady Stanton and Susan B. Anthony. Ward,
G. C. **92**
Not much to it. Saldaña, R.
In Make me over; 11 stories of transformation
S C

Not out of Africa. Lefkowitz, M. R. **960**
Not the only one **S C**
Not under forty. Cather, W.
In Cather, W. Stories, poems, and other writ-
ings **818**
Not without laughter [excerpt] Hughes, L.
In The Portable Harlem Renaissance reader
p592-99 **810.8**
Not your usual founding father. Franklin, B.
92
Notable American women **920.003**
Notable American women, 1607-1950 **920.003**
Notable Asian Americans **920.003**
Notable last facts. Brahms, W. B. **031.02**
Notable Latino writers **920.003**
Notable poets **920.003**
Notable scientists [series]
Gates, A. E. A to Z of earth scientists
920.003
McElroy, T. A to Z of mathematicians
920.003
Yount, L. A to Z of biologists **920.003**
Notable women in mathematics **920.003**
Notable women in the life sciences **920.003**
Notable women in world history. Adamson, L. G.
920.003
A **note** on experts: Dexter Vespasian Joyner.
Wolfe, T.
In Wolfe, T. The complete short stories of
Thomas Wolfe p438-46 **S C**
Notes. O'Brien, T.
In O'Brien, T. The things they carried; a
work of fiction **S C**
Notes from a lady at a dinner party. Malamud, B.
In Malamud, B. The complete stories **S C**
Notes from the Hyena's belly. Mezlekia, N.
963
Notes from the midnight driver. Sonnenblick, J.
Fic
Notes on the State of Virginia. Jefferson, T.
In Jefferson, T. Writings **818**
Nothing makes you free **808.8**
The **nothing** that is. Kaplan, R. **511**
Nothing to lose. Flinn, A. **Fic**
The **notorious** jumping frog of Calaveras County.
Twain, M.
In Twain, M. The complete short stories of
Mark Twain; now collected for the first
time **S C**
Noughts & Crosses. See Blackman, M. Naughts &
Crosses **Fic**
Nouveau petit Larousse illustré. See Le petit La-
rousse illustré **443**
Nova Scotia
Fiction
Kositsky, L. Claire by moonlight **Fic**
Novak, Joseph *See* Kosinski, Jerzy N., 1933-1991
Novak, Philip
(jt. auth) Smith, H. Buddhism: a concise intro-
duction **294.3**

Nye, Jody Lynn, 1957-
Theory of relativity
In Past imperfect   **S C**

Nye, Naomi Shihab, 1952-
19 varieties of gazelle   **811**
Hum
In Face relations; 11 stories about seeing beyond color   **S C**
Red velvet dress
In Growing up ethnic in America; contemporary fiction about learning to be American   **S C**
You & yours: poems   **811**
(comp) I feel a little jumpy around you. See I feel a little jumpy around you   **808.81**
(ed) Is this forever, or what? See Is this forever, or what?   **811.008**
(comp) The Space between our footsteps. See The Space between our footsteps   **808.81**
(comp) This same sky. See This same sky   **808.81**
(comp) The Tree is older than you are. See The Tree is older than you are   **860.8**

NYSE *See* New York Stock Exchange, Inc.

O

O, Se-Yong, 1955-
Buja's diary   **741.5**

The **O-Bon** cat. Parker, I. J.
In Alfred Hitchcock's mystery magazine presents fifty years of crime and suspense   **S C**

Ó Cadhain, Máirtín
The hare-lip
In The Oxford book of Irish short stories p375-81   **S C**

Ó Conaire, Pádraic, 1883-1928
My little black ass
In The Oxford book of Irish short stories p267-70   **S C**

O city of broken dreams. Cheever, J.
In Cheever, J. The stories of John Cheever p42-57   **S C**

O Yes. Olsen, T.
In The Oxford book of women's writing in the United States p111-25   **810.8**

O youth and beauty!. Cheever, J.
In Cheever, J. The stories of John Cheever p210-18   **S C**

Oakes, Elizabeth H., 1951-
The encyclopedia of sports medicine   **617.1**
Encyclopedia of world scientists   **920.003**

The **oakthing**. Maguire, G.
In The Faery Reel; tales from the Twilight Realm   **S C**

Oates, Joyce Carol, 1938-
Big Mouth & Ugly Girl   **Fic**
Do with me what you will
In The Best American mystery stories of the century p556-67   **S C**
The doll
In Nightshade: 20th century ghost stories p347-69   **S C**
Extenuating circumstances
In The Oxford book of women's writing in the United States p148-53   **810.8**
Freaky green eyes   **Fic**
How I contemplated the world from the Detroit House of Correction and began my life over again
In The Norton book of American short stories p662-75   **S C**
The others
In The Literary ghost; great contemporary ghost stories p64-68   **S C**
Secret observations on the goat-girl
In The Oxford book of gothic tales p498-501   **S C**
Small avalanches and other stories   **S C**
Contents: Where are you going, where have you been?; The sky blue bell; Small avalanches; Haunted; Bad girls; How I contemplated the world; "Shot"; Why don't you come live with me: it's time; Life after high school; Capricorn; The visit; The model
Where are you going, where have you been?
In Adaptations: from short story to big screen; 35 great stories that have inspired great films   **S C**
In American short story masterpieces   **S C**
In Who do you think you are?; stories of friends and enemies p14-35   **S C**
(ed) The Best American essays of the century. See The Best American essays of the century   **814**

Oates, Stephen B., 1936-
A woman of valor: Clara Barton and the Civil War   **92**

Oates, Whitney Jennings, 1904-1973
(ed) Seven famous Greek plays. See Seven famous Greek plays   **882.008**

Oba, Ryan
Home now
In American eyes; new Asian-American short stories for young adults   **S C**

Obejas, Achy, 1956-
Polaroids
In Latina: women's voices from the borderlands p162-70   **810.8**

Obesity
Ingram, S. Want fries with that?   **613.2**
Kuffel, F. Passing for thin   **92**
Nichter, M. Fat talk   **613.2**
Obesity: opposing viewpoints   **613.2**
Control
See Weight loss
Encyclopedias
Cassell, D. K. Encyclopedia of obesity and eating disorders   **616.85**
Fiction
Crutcher, C. Staying fat for Sarah Byrnes   **Fic**
Going, K. L. Fat kid rules the world   **Fic**
Lipsyte, R. One fat summer   **Fic**
Mackler, C. The earth, my butt, and other big, round things   **Fic**
Marino, P. Dough Boy   **Fic**

Obesity: opposing viewpoints   **613.2**

Obituary. Asimov, I.
In Asimov, I. The complete stories p306-19   **S C**

Object lesson. Queen, E.
In Read all about it!; great read-aloud stories, poems, and newspaper pieces for preteens and teens p53-66 **808.8**

Oblomov's dream. Goncharov, I. A.
In The Portable nineteenth-century Russian reader p295-333 **891.7**

The **oblong** box. Poe, E. A.
In Poe, E. A. The collected tales and poems of Edgar Allan Poe p711-19 **818**

Obregón, Mauricio
Beyond the edge of the sea **930**

O'Brien, Edna
Irish revel
In The Oxford book of Irish short stories p495-514 **S C**

O'Brien, Eileen, 1972-
(jt. auth) Feagin, J. R. White men on race **305.8**

O'Brien, Joanne, 1959-
(jt. auth) Breuilly, E. Religions of the world **201**

O'Brien, Patrick Karl
(ed) Atlas of world history. See Atlas of world history **911**

O'Brien, Stephen J.
Tears of the cheetah **591.3**

O'Brien, Tim, 1946-
Ambush
In Who do you think you are?; stories of friends and enemies p152-55 **S C**
The ghost soldiers
In The Literary ghost; great contemporary ghost stories p185-205 **S C**
Going after Cacciato **Fic**
The man I killed
In Who do you think you are?; stories of friends and enemies p146-51 **S C**
On the rainy river
In Leaving home: stories p133-56 **808.8**
The things they carried **S C**

Obscenity (Law)
See also Pornography

Obscure destinies. Cather, W.
In Cather, W. Stories, poems, and other writings **818**

Observatories, Astronomical *See* Astronomical observatories

Obsession (Psychology) *See* Obsessive-compulsive disorder

Obsessive-compulsive disorder
Hyman, B. M. Obsessive-compulsive disorder **616.85**
Traig, J. Devil in the details **92**
Fiction
De la Peña, M. Ball don't lie **Fic**

Obsessive-compulsive neuroses *See* Obsessive-compulsive disorder

Obstfeld, Loretta
(ed) The Renaissance. See The Renaissance [Greenhaven Press] **940.2**

Obstfeld, Raymond, 1952-
(ed) The Renaissance. See The Renaissance [Greenhaven Press] **940.2**

An **occasion** of sin. Montague, J.
In The Oxford book of Irish short stories p482-94 **S C**

Occidental mythology. Campbell, J. **201**

Occomy, Marita Odette Bonner *See* Bonner, Marita, 1899-1971

Occult sciences *See* Occultism

Occultism
See also Alchemy; Astrology; Divination; Fortune telling; Prophecies; Satanism
Eberhart, G. M. Mysterious creatures **001.9**
Fiction
Taylor, G. P. Tersias the oracle **Fic**

Occupational guidance *See* Vocational guidance

Occupational outlook handbook 2006-2007. United States. Bureau of Labor Statistics **331.7**

Occupational training
Paquette, P. H. Apprenticeship **331.2**
Unger, H. G. But what if I don't want to go to college? **331.7**

Occupations
Encyclopedia of careers and vocational guidance **331.7**
Exploring tech careers **331.7**
O*NET dictionary of occupational titles
Reber, D. In their shoes **331.4**
Schwager, T. Cool women, hot jobs . . . and how you can go for it, too! **650.14**
United States. Bureau of Labor Statistics. Occupational outlook handbook 2006-2007 **331.7**

Ocean
See also Pacific Ocean; Seashore
Davidson, O. G. Fire in the turtle house **597.92**
Rice, T. Deep ocean **551.46**
Stow, D. A. V. Oceans: an illustrated reference **551.46**

The **ocean**. Cheever, J.
In Cheever, J. The stories of John Cheever p567-83 **S C**

Ocean currents
See also El Niño Current

Ocean sciences *See* Marine sciences

Oceania
Alexander, C. The Bounty: the true story of the mutiny on the Bounty **996**

Oceanography
Crane, K. Sea legs **92**
Hutchinson, S. Oceans: a visual guide **551.46**
Rice, T. Deep ocean **551.46**
Stow, D. A. V. Oceans: an illustrated reference **551.46**
Encyclopedias
Ellis, R. Encyclopedia of the sea **551.46**

Oceans: a visual guide. Hutchinson, S. **551.46**

Oceans: an illustrated reference. Stow, D. A. V. **551.46**

Ochiltree, Dianne, 1953-
The women's house
In Don't cramp my style; stories about that
time of the month p68-100 **S C**

Ochoa, Annette Piña
(ed) Night is gone, day is still coming. See
Night is gone, day is still coming **808.8**

Ochoa, Ellen, 1958-
About
Hasday, J. L. Ellen Ochoa **92**

Ochoa, George
The Wilson chronology of ideas **909**
The Wilson chronology of science and technolo-
gy **502**
The Wilson chronology of the arts **700**

O'Clair, Robert, 1923-1989
(ed) The Norton anthology of modern and contemporary poetry. See The Norton anthology
of modern and contemporary poetry
821.008

O'Connell, Diane
People person [biography of Marta Tienda]
92
Strong force [biography of Shirley Ann Jackson]
92

O'Connell, Jennifer
(ed) Everything I needed to know about being
a girl I learned from Judy Blume. See Everything I needed to know about being a girl I
learned from Judy Blume **814**

O'Connell, Jenny *See* O'Connell, Jennifer

O'Conner, Patricia T.
Woe is I **428**

O'Connor, Ann
(ed) Congress A to Z. See Congress A to Z
328.73

O'Connor, Flannery
Collected works **S C**
The comforts of home
In The Best American mystery stories of the
century p489-507 **S C**
The complete stories **S C**
Contents: The geranium; The barber; Wildcat; The crop; The
turkey; The train; The peeler; The heart of the park; A stroke of
good fortune; Enoch and the gorilla; A good man is hard to find;
A late encounter with the enemy; The life you save may be your
own; The river; A circle in the fire; The displaced person; A
Temple of the Holy Ghost; The artificial nigger; Good country
people; You can't be any poorer than dead; Greenleaf; A view
of the woods; The enduring chill; The comforts of home; Every-
thing that rises must converge; The Partridge festival; The lame
shall enter first; Why do the heathen rage?; Revelation; Parker's
back; Judgement Day
Everything that rises must converge
In O'Connor, F. Collected works p481-695
S C
A good man is hard to find
In American short story masterpieces **S C**
A good man is hard to find, and other stories
In O'Connor, F. Collected works p133-327
S C
A late encounter with the enemy
In The Oxford book of women's writing in
the United States p126-34 **810.8**
Parker's back
In The Oxford book of short stories p501-19
S C

Revelation
In The Norton book of American short stories
p536-54 **S C**
The violent bear it away
In O'Connor, F. Collected works p329-479
S C
Wise blood
In O'Connor, F. Collected works p1-131
S C

O'Connor, Frank, 1903-1966
First confession
In Gotham Writers' Workshop fiction gallery;
exceptional short stories selected by New
York's acclaimed creative writing school
S C
Guests of the nation
In The Oxford book of Irish short stories
p342-53 **S C**
In The Oxford book of short stories p371-81
S C
The majesty of the law
In The Oxford book of Irish short stories
p354-62 **S C**

O'Connor, George
(il) Bogaert, H. M. v. d. Journey into Mohawk
Country **973.2**

O'Connor, Ian
The jump [biography of Sebastian Telfair]
92

O'Connor, Mary Flannery *See* O'Connor,
Flannery

O'Connor, Rebecca
(ed) Is there life after death? See Is there life after death? **133.9**

Octavian *See* Augustus, Emperor of Rome, 63
B.C.-14 A.D.

October chill. Vande Velde, V.
In Vande Velde, V. Being dead; stories
S C

October in the chair. Gaiman, N.
In Gaiman, N. Fragile things; short fictions
and wonders **S C**
In The Locus awards; thirty years of the best
in science fiction and fantasy **S C**

The odd couple. Simon, N.
In Simon, N. The collected plays of Neil Simon **812**

Odd couple (female version). Simon, N.
In Simon, N. The collected plays of Neil Simon **812**

Oddballs. Sleator, W. **S C**
In Sleator, W. Oddballs; stories p129-34
S C

Oddities *See* Curiosities and wonders

Odekon, Mehmet
(ed) Encyclopedia of world poverty. See Encyclopedia of world poverty **362.5**

Odes, Rebecca
The looks book **646.7**

Odlum, Jacqueline Cochran *See* Cochran, Jacqueline, 1910?-1980

Odom, Mel, 1950-
The rover **Fic**

O'Hara, John, 1905-1970
Over the river and through the wood
In The Norton book of American short stories
p406-412 **S C**

O'Hara, Mary, 1885-1980
My friend Flicka
In Adaptations: from short story to big screen; 35 great stories that have inspired great films **S C**

Ohio
Fiction
Anderson, L. H. Twisted **Fic**
Morrison, T. The bluest eye **Fic**
Morrison, T. Sula **Fic**

Oil painting *See* Painting

Ojeda, Auriana, 1977-
(ed) Civil liberties: opposing viewpoints. See Civil liberties: opposing viewpoints **323**
(ed) Homosexuality: opposing viewpoints. See Homosexuality: opposing viewpoints **306.76**
(ed) Male/female roles: opposing viewpoints. See Male/female roles: opposing viewpoints **305.3**
(ed) Slavery today. See Slavery today **326**

Okay, so now you're a vegetarian. Butts, L. **641.5**

O'Keeffe, Georgia, 1887-1986
About
Eldredge, C. C. Georgia O'Keeffe **759.13**

O'Kelly, Helen Watanabe- *See* Watanabe-O'Kelly, Helen

O'Kelly, Seumas, 1881-1918
The weaver's grave
In The Oxford book of Irish short stories p182-227 **S C**

Okey, Shannon
Knitgrrl **746.43**
Knitgrrl 2 **746.43**

Okimoto, Jean Davies, 1942-
My favorite chaperone
In First crossing; stories about teen immigrants p44-79 **S C**
Next month . . . Hollywood!
In Join in; multiethnic short stories by outstanding writers for young adults p35-46 **S C**

Okinawa. Leckie, R. **940.54**

Oklahoma
Fiction
Tharp, T. Knights of the hill country **Fic**

Oklahoma western biographies [series]
Griswold del Castillo, R. César Chávez **92**
Wilkins, T. John Muir **92**

Okri, Ben
Converging city
In The Heinemann book of contemporary African short stories p134-45 **S C**

Oktoberfest. Wolfe, T.
In Wolfe, T. The complete short stories of Thomas Wolfe p308-15 **S C**

Olalla. Stevenson, R. L.
In The Oxford book of gothic tales p183-217 **S C**

Old age
See also Aging; Longevity
Fiction
Bauer, J. Rules of the road **Fic**
Sonnenblick, J. Notes from the midnight driver **Fic**

The **old** apple-dealer. Hawthorne, N.
In Hawthorne, N. Tales and sketches, including Twice-told tales, Mosses from an old manse, and The snow-image; A wonder book for girls and boys; Tanglewood tales for girls and boys, being a second Wonder book p714-20 **S C**

The **old** beauty, and others. Cather, W.
In Cather, W. Stories, poems, and other writings **818**

Old Catawba. Wolfe, T.
In Wolfe, T. The complete short stories of Thomas Wolfe p214-21 **S C**

The **old** chief Mshlanga. Lessing, D. M.
In Somehow tenderness survives; stories of Southern Africa p19-35 **S C**

Old English literature *See* English literature—Old English period

Old-fashioned. Asimov, I.
In Asimov, I. The complete stories p530-37 **S C**

Old Hickory [biography of Andrew Jackson] Marrin, A. **92**

The **old** maid. Wharton, E.
In Wharton, E. Novellas and other writings **818**

The **old** man and the sea. Hemingway, E. **Fic**

Old man at the bridge. Hemingway, E.
In Hemingway, E. The complete short stories of Ernest Hemingway; the Finca Vigía edition p57-58 **S C**

Old Man Coyote, the young man and two otter sisters
In Hearne, B. G. Beauties and beasts p154-56 **398.2**

Old man of the temple. Narayan, R. K.
In The Literary ghost; great contemporary ghost stories p330-35 **S C**

Old man Pete. Edmonds, R.
In Black theatre USA; plays by African Americans, 1847 to today **812.008**

Old Man Rivers. Wolfe, T.
In Wolfe, T. The complete short stories of Thomas Wolfe p563-88 **S C**

Old mortality. Porter, K. A.
In Porter, K. A. The collected stories of Katherine Anne Porter **S C**
In Porter, K. A. Pale horse, pale rider: three short novels **S C**

Old Mr. Marblehall. Welty, E.
In Welty, E. The collected stories of Eudora Welty p91-97 **S C**

Old Mrs. Harris. Cather, W.
In The Oxford book of women's writing in the United States p229-72 **810.8**

On leprechauns. Wolfe, T.
 In Wolfe, T. The complete short stories of Thomas Wolfe p537-41 **S C**

On my own. Taylor, S. **646.7**

On strivers row. Hill, A.
 In Black theatre USA; plays by African Americans, 1847 to today **812.008**

On the beach. Shute, N. **Fic**

On the bus with Rosa Parks. Dove, R. **811**

On the edge. Pospisil, C.
 In Under 30; plays for a new generation **812.008**

On the edge of the cliff. Pritchett, V. S.
 In The Oxford book of English short stories p270-85 **S C**

On the head of a pin. Miller, M. B. **Fic**

On the high marsh. Le Guin, U. K.
 In Le Guin, U. K. Tales from Earthsea **S C**

On the market day. Mativo, K.
 In The Heinemann book of contemporary African short stories p104-13 **S C**

On the Orient, North. Bradbury, R.
 In Bradbury, R. Bradbury stories; 100 of his most celebrated tales **S C**

On the orion line. Baxter, S.
 In The Hard SF renaissance **S C**

On the planet Mars. Fabra, N. M.
 In Cosmos latinos; an anthology of science fiction from Latin America and Spain **S C**

On the quai at Smyrna. Hemingway, E.
 In Hemingway, E. The complete short stories of Ernest Hemingway; the Finca Vigía edition p63-64 **S C**

On the rainy river. O'Brien, T.
 In Leaving home: stories p133-56 **808.8**
 In O'Brien, T. The things they carried; a work of fiction **S C**

On the rez. Frazier, I. **970.004**

On the road. Hughes, L.
 In Hughes, L. Short stories of Langston Hughes **S C**

On the road. Kerouac, J. **Fic**

On the road to Texas: Pete Fonseca. Rivera, T.
 In Growing up Latino; memoirs and stories p147-54 **810.8**

On the shoulders of giants. See Spangenburg, R. The history of science **509**

On the soul. Aristotle
 In Aristotle. The basic works of Aristotle p535-603 **888**

On the way home. Hughes, L.
 In Hughes, L. Short stories of Langston Hughes **S C**

On the wing. Tennant, A. **598**

On trial [series]
 Gershman, G. P. Death penalty on trial **345**

On writing. King, S. **92**

The **once** and future king. White, T. H. **Fic**

Once more, Legato. Bradbury, R.
 In Bradbury, R. Bradbury stories; 100 of his most celebrated tales **S C**

Once upon a cuento **S C**

Once upon a number. Paulos, J. A. **519.5**

One act plays
 24 favorite one-act plays **808.82**
 Dabrowski, K. Twenty 10-minute plays for teens **812**
 Garner, J. Stagings **812**
 See/See also pages in the following book(s):
 Under 30 **812.008**

One Christmas. Capote, T.
 In Capote, T. A Christmas memory, One Christmas, & The Thanksgiving visitor p31-53 **818**

One day in the life of Ivan Denisovich. Solzhenitsyn, A. **Fic**

One fat summer. Lipsyte, R. **Fic**

One flew over the cuckoo's nest. Kesey, K. **Fic**

One for his lordship, and one for the road!. Bradbury, R.
 In Bradbury, R. Bradbury stories; 100 of his most celebrated tales **S C**

One for the road. King, S.
 In King, S. Night shift **S C**

One Friday morning. Hughes, L.
 In Hughes, L. Short stories of Langston Hughes **S C**

One holy night. Cisneros, S.
 In Cisneros, S. Woman Hollering Creek and other stories **S C**

One hundred and one questions about blood and circulation, with answers straight from the heart. See Brynie, F. H. 101 questions about blood and circulation, with answers straight from the heart **612.1**

One hundred and one questions about reproduction. See Brynie, F. H. 101 questions about reproduction **612.6**

One hundred and one questions about sex and sexuality. See Brynie, F. H. 101 questions about sex and sexuality— **613.9**

One hundred decisive battles. See Davis, P. K. 100 decisive battles **904**

One hundred demons. Barry, L. **741.5**

One hundred eighty more. See 180 more **811.008**

One hundred essential modern poems. See 100 essential modern poems **821.008**

One hundred fifty years of popular musical theatre. See Lamb, A. 150 years of popular musical theatre **792.6**

One hundred great monologues from the neoclassical theatre **808.82**

One hundred great monologues from the Renaissance theatre. See 100 great monologues from the Renaissance theatre **822.008**

One hundred key documents in American democracy. See 100 key documents in American democracy **973**

Orphans

Fiction

Alder, E. The king's shadow	Fic
Halpin, B. Donorboy	Fic
Koertge, R. Strays	Fic
Larson, K. Hattie Big Sky	Fic
Lawson, M. Crow Lake	Fic
McBay, B. Waiting for Sarah	Fic
Meyer, L. A. Bloody Jack	Fic
Pullman, P. The ruby in the smoke	Fic
Seigel, A. Like the red panda	Fic
Woodson, J. Miracle's boys	Fic

Orphea Proud. Wyeth, S. D.   Fic

Orpheus. Block, F. L.
    In Block, F. L. Girl goddess #9: nine stories
                            S C

Orr, Mary
The wisdom of Eve
    In Adaptations: from short story to big
    screen; 35 great stories that have inspired
    great films   **S C**

Orr, Tamra
Extraordinary essays	808.4
Violence in our schools	371.7

Ortiz, Simon J., 1941-
To change in a good way
    In Growing up ethnic in America; contempo-
    rary fiction about learning to be Ameri-
    can   **S C**

About

Coltelli, L. Winged words: American Indian
    writers speak   **897**

Ortiz Cofer, Judith, 1952-
American history
    In Growing up ethnic in America; contempo-
    rary fiction about learning to be Ameri-
    can   **S C**
    In Who do you think you are?; stories of
    friends and enemies p36-46   **S C**
Bad influence
    In Leaving home: stories p63-90   **808.8**
An island like you   **S C**
    Contents: Day in the barrio — Bad influence — Arturo's flight
    — Beauty lessons — Catch the moon — An hour with Abuelo
    — The one who watches — Matoa's mirror — Don Jose of La
    Mancha — Abuela invents the zero — A job for Valentin —
    Home to El Building — White balloons

Orwell, George, 1903-1950
Animal farm	Fic
Nineteen eighty-four	Fic

About

Brunsdale, M. Student companion to George Or-
    well   **828**
Means, A. L. A student's guide to George Or-
    well   **828**

Oryx multicultural folktale series
Hearne, B. G. Beauties and beasts   **398.2**

Osa, Nancy
Cuba 15   Fic

O'Shea, Mark
Venomous snakes of the world   **597.96**

Oshinsky, David M., 1944-
Polio   **614.5**

Ostler, Rosemarie
Dewdroppers, waldos, and slackers   **428**

Ostrom, Hans A.
    (ed) The Greenwood encyclopedia of African
    American literature. See The Greenwood en-
    cyclopedia of African American literature
                           810.9

Otaño, Magdalena Moujan *See* Moujan Otaño,
    Magdalena

Otfinoski, Steven, 1949-
Afghanistan	958.1
Ukraine	947.7

Othello. Shakespeare, W.   **822.3**
Othello. See Shakespeare, W. The tragedy of
    Othello, the Moor of Venice   **822.3**

The **other** foot. Bradbury, R.
    In Bradbury, R. The illustrated man   **S C**
Other people. Gaiman, N.
    In Gaiman, N. Fragile things; short fictions
    and wonders   **S C**
Other people's words. Francis, B.   **808**
The **other** side of the sky. Clarke, A. C.
    In Clarke, A. C. The collected stories of Ar-
    thur C. Clarke   **S C**
The **other** tiger. Clarke, A. C.
    In Clarke, A. C. The collected stories of Ar-
    thur C. Clarke   **S C**
The **other** two. Wharton, E.
    In The Oxford book of women's writing in
    the United States p68-82   **810.8**
The **other** victims. Friedman, I. R.   **940.53**
The **others**. Oates, J. C.
    In The Literary ghost; great contemporary
    ghost stories p64-68   **S C**

O'Toole, Christopher
    (ed) The Firefly encyclopedia of insects and spi-
    ders. See The Firefly encyclopedia of insects
    and spiders   **595.7**

Otsuka, Julie, 1962-
When the emperor was divine   Fic

Ott, Gustavo
Minor leagues
    In International plays for young audiences;
    contemporary works from leading play-
    wrights p353-89   **808.82**

Ott, Valerie A.
Teen programs with punch   **027.62**

Ottaviani, Jim
Bone sharps, cowboys, and thunder lizards
                           560
Dignifying science: stories about women scien-
    tists   **920**
Suspended in language   **92**

Ottley, Ryan
    (il) Kirkman, R. Invincible: ultimate collection,
    Vol. 1   **741.5**

Ottmann, Klaus, 1954-
The essential Michelangelo   **759.5**

Oubrerie, Clément
    (il) Abouet, M. Aya   **741.5**

Oufkir, Malika
Freedom: the story of my second life	92
Stolen lives	92

Our affair with El Niño. Philander, S. G.
                          551.6

P.'s correspondence. Hawthorne, N.
In Hawthorne, N. Tales and sketches, including Twice-told tales, Mosses from an old manse, and The snow-image; A wonder book for girls and boys; Tanglewood tales for girls and boys, being a second Wonder book p1006-22   **S C**

Pachino, Jamie
Race
In International plays for young audiences; contemporary works from leading playwrights p297-315   **808.82**

Pacific Area *See* Pacific region

Pacific Islands *See* Islands of the Pacific

Pacific Ocean
Heyerdahl, T. Kon-Tiki   **910.4**
Vail, M. Exploring the Pacific   **919**

Pacific region
History
The Wilson chronology of Asia and the Pacific   **950**

The **Pacific** war companion   **940.54**

The **Pacific** War encyclopedia. Dunnigan, J. F.   **940.54**

Pacifism
See also Conscientious objectors
Gottfried, T. The fight for peace   **303.6**

The **pacifist.** Clarke, A. C.
In Clarke, A. C. The collected stories of Arthur C. Clarke   **S C**

Pack of thieves. Chesnoff, R. Z.   **940.53**

The **package.** Vonnegut, K.
In Vonnegut, K. Bagombo snuff box: uncollected short fiction p45-61   **S C**

Packard, William
The poet's dictionary   **808.1**

Packed dirt, churchgoing, a dying cat, a traded car. Updike, J.
In Updike, J. Pigeon feathers, and other stories p246-79   **S C**

Packer, Alex J., 1951-
The how rude! handbook of family manners for teens   **395**
The how rude! handbook of school manners for teens   **395**

Packer, Ann
The dive from Clausen's pier   **Fic**

Packer, ZZ, 1973-
The ant of the self
In Packer, Z. Drinking coffee elsewhere   **S C**
Brownies
In Gotham Writers' Workshop fiction gallery; exceptional short stories selected by New York's acclaimed creative writing school   **S C**
In Packer, Z. Drinking coffee elsewhere   **S C**
Doris is coming
In Packer, Z. Drinking coffee elsewhere   **S C**
Drinking coffee elsewhere   **S C**

Contents: Brownies; Every tongue shall confess; Our Lady of Peace; The ant of the self; Drinking coffee elsewhere; Speaking in tongues; Geese; Doris is coming [story]
In Packer, Z. Drinking coffee elsewhere   **S C**
Every tongue shall confess
In Packer, Z. Drinking coffee elsewhere   **S C**
Geese
In Packer, Z. Drinking coffee elsewhere   **S C**
Our Lady of Peace
In Packer, Z. Drinking coffee elsewhere   **S C**
Speaking in tongues
In Packer, Z. Drinking coffee elsewhere   **S C**

Paddock, Lisa
Facts about the Supreme Court of the United States   **347**
(jt. auth) Rollyson, C. Critical companion to Herman Melville   **813.009**

Paddock, Lisa Olson
Encyclopedia of American literature. See Encyclopedia of American literature   **810.3**

Padgett, Ron
(ed) World poets. See World poets   **920.003**

Pagano, Joan
Strength training for women   **613.7**

Pagden, Anthony
Peoples and empires   **909**

Page, Jake
The big one   **551.2**

Page, Lawrence M.
A field guide to freshwater fishes: North America north of Mexico   **597**

Page, Lisa Frazier
(jt. auth) Davis, S. The pact: three young men make a promise and fulfill a dream   **920**

Page, Willie F., 1929-
(ed) Encyclopedia of African history and culture. See Encyclopedia of African history and culture   **960**

Pagel, Mark D.
(ed) Encyclopedia of evolution. See Encyclopedia of evolution   **576.8**

Pages from a journal found in a shoebox left in a Greyhound bus somewhere between Tulsa, Oklahoma, and Louisville, Kentucky. Gaiman, N.
In Gaiman, N. Fragile things; short fictions and wonders   **S C**

Pages from history [series]
Coetzee, F. World War I: a history in documents   **940.3**
The Gilded Age: a history in documents   **973.8**
Gray, E. G. Colonial America: a history in documents   **973.2**
McElvaine, R. S. The Depression and New Deal   **973.91**
Patrick, J. J. The Bill of Rights   **342**
Schoppa, R. K. Twentieth century China   **951.05**

Parr, Katherine *See* Catharine Parr, Queen, consort of Henry VIII, King of England, 1512-1548

Parrado, Nando, 1949-
Miracle in the Andes   982

The Parricide punished
In The Oxford book of gothic tales p27-30
    S C

Parrot in the oven. Martinez, V.   Fic

Parsons, Ellen *See* Dragonwagon, Crescent

Parties
Beker, J. The big night out   646.7

Partnow, Elaine, 1941-
The female dramatist   809.2
(comp) The Quotable woman. See The Quotable woman   808.88

Partridge, Elizabeth
John Lennon   92
Restless spirit: the life and work of Dorothea Lange   92
This land was made for you and me: the life and songs of Woody Guthrie   92
(ed) Dorothea Lange—a visual life. See Dorothea Lange—a visual life   92

The Partridge festival. O'Connor, F.
In O'Connor, F. Collected works p773-96
    S C
In O'Connor, F. The complete stories p421-44
    S C

Parva naturalia. Aristotle
In Aristotle. The basic works of Aristotle p607-30   888

Pas, Julian F.
(ed) The Wisdom of the Tao. See The Wisdom of the Tao   299.5

Pasachoff, Jay M.
(jt. auth) Golub, L. Nearest star   523.7

Pasachoff, Naomi E., 1947-
Linus Pauling   92

Pascal, Janet B.
Jacob Riis   92

Paschen, Elise
(ed) Poetry in motion. See Poetry in motion
    808.81
(ed) Poetry speaks. See Poetry speaks
    808.81

A passage to India. Forster, E. M.   Fic

Passages from a relinquished work. Hawthorne, N.
In Hawthorne, N. Tales and sketches, including Twice-told tales, Mosses from an old manse, and The snow-image; A wonder book for girls and boys; Tanglewood tales for girls and boys, being a second Wonder book p174-87   S C

Passages to freedom   326

Passero, Barbara
(ed) Energy alternatives: opposing viewpoints. See Energy alternatives: opposing viewpoints
    333.79

Passing [excerpt] Larsen, N.
In The Portable Harlem Renaissance reader p460-85   810.8

Passing for thin. Kuffel, F.   92

The passing of Black Eagle. Henry, O.
In Henry, O. The best short stories of O. Henry   S C

Passion. Michener, J. A.
In Michener, J. A. Tales of the South Pacific
    S C

Passionate vegetarian. Dragonwagon, C.   641.5

Passive resistance
Gandhi, M. Gandhi on non-violence   322.4
Martin, C. Mohandas Gandhi   92

The past and the punishments. Yu Hua
In Chairman Mao would not be amused; fiction from today's China   S C

Past imperfect   S C

Past perfect, present tense: new and collected stories. Peck, R.   S C

Paste. James, H.
In The Oxford book of short stories p84-98
    S C

Pasternak, Boris Leonidovich, 1890-1960
Varykino
In The portable twentieth-century Russian reader   891.7

Pasteur, Louis, 1822-1895
About
Ackerman, J. Louis Pasteur and the founding of microbiology   92
See/See also pages in the following book(s):
Hellman, H. Great feuds in medicine   610.9

Pastorale. Boyle, P.
In The Oxford book of Irish short stories p363-74   S C

Pasztor, Suzanne B., 1964-
(jt. auth) Coerver, D. M. Mexico: an encyclopedia of contemporary culture and history
    972.08

Patchett, Ann
Truth & beauty [biography of Lucy Grealy]
    92

Patchwork quilts *See* Quilts

Pate, Alexs D., 1950-
West of Rehoboth   Fic

Pâté de foie gras. Asimov, I.
In Asimov, I. The complete stories p231-43
    S C

Patel, Sanjay
The little book of Hindu deities   704.9

Patent pending. Clarke, A. C.
In Clarke, A. C. The collected stories of Arthur C. Clarke   S C

Patently female. Vare, E. A.   920

Paterek, Josephine
Encyclopedia of American Indian costume
    391

Paterson, Katherine
Lyddie   Fic

The Pathfinder. Cooper, J. F.
In Cooper, J. F. The Leatherstocking tales p1-482   Fic

Pathologies of power. Farmer, P.   305

The patient's guide to medical tests. Segen, J. C.
    616.07

Pearce, Philippa, 1920-2006
Who's afraid?
In Read all about it!; great read-aloud stories, poems, and newspaper pieces for preteens and teens p230-35 **808.8**

The **pearl**. Steinbeck, J. **Fic**

Pearl Harbor (Oahu, Hawaii), Attack on, 1941
The Attack on Pearl Harbor **940.54**
Lord, W. Day of infamy **940.54**
Fiction
Salisbury, G. Under the blood-red sun **Fic**
Pictorial works
Goldstein, D. M. The way it was **940.54**

Pearlman, Ann
(jt. auth) Simpson, C. Inside the Crips **92**

Pearson, Mary
A room on Lorelei Street **Fic**

Peasantry
See/See also pages in the following book(s):
Bishop, M. The Middle Ages **940.1**

Peasants. Chekhov, A. P.
In Chekhov, A. P. The Russian master and other stories p144-71 **S C**

Peavy, Linda Sellers, 1943-
Frontier children **978**
Pioneer women **305.4**

Peck, Richard, 1934-
Girl at the window
In Night terrors; stories of shadow and substance **S C**
How to write a short story
In Peck, R. Past perfect, present tense: new and collected stories **S C**
Invitations to the world **808.06**
The kiss in the carry-on bag
In Destination unexpected: short stories **S C**
Past perfect, present tense: new and collected stories **S C**
Contents: Priscilla and the wimps; The electric summer; Shotgun Cheatham's last night above ground; The special powers of Blossom Culp; By far the worst pupil at Long Point School; Girl at the window; The most important night of Melanie's life; Waiting for Sebastian; Shadows; Fluffy the gangbuster; I go along; The kiss in the carry-on bag; The three-century woman; How to write a short story; Five helpful hints
Priscilla and the wimps
In Sixteen: short stories by outstanding writers for young adults p42-46 **S C**
In Who do you think you are?; stories of friends and enemies p92-95 **S C**
The river between us **Fic**

Peck, Robert S.
Libraries, the First Amendment, and cyberspace **025.04**

Pedagogy *See* Teaching

Peden, Margaret Sayers
(tr) Allende, I. Paula **92**

Pederson, Jay P.
(ed) African American breakthroughs. See African American breakthroughs **305.8**
(ed) Twentieth-century literary movements dictionary. See Twentieth-century literary movements dictionary **809**

The **pedestrian**. Bradbury, R.
In Bradbury, R. Bradbury stories; 100 of his most celebrated tales **S C**

The **pedlar's** revenge. O'Flaherty, L.
In The Oxford book of Irish short stories p287-99 **S C**

Pedrick, Cherry
(jt. auth) Hyman, B. M. Obsessive-compulsive disorder **616.85**

Pedro, Jimmy, 1970-
Judo techniques & tactics **796.8**

Pedro and me. Winick, J. **362.1**

The **peeler**. O'Connor, F.
In O'Connor, F. The complete stories p63-80 **S C**

Peeps. Westerfeld, S. **Fic**

Peet, Mal
Keeper **Fic**
Tamar **Fic**

Peikoff, Leonard
(ed) Rand, A. The Ayn Rand reader **191**

Pekar, Harvey
Harvey Pekar's American splendor **92**

Pellant, Chris
Rocks and minerals **549**

Pelle, Kimberly D.
(jt. auth) Rydell, R. W. Fair America **394**

Pelliccia, Hayden
(ed) Plato. The selected dialogues of Plato **184**

The **Peloponnesian** War. Tritle, L. A. **938**

Pendergast, Sara
(jt. auth) Pendergast, T. Constitutional amendments: from freedom of speech to flag burning **342**
(jt. auth) Pendergast, T. The sixties in America. Almanac **973.923**
(jt. auth) Pendergast, T. The sixties in America. Biographies **920**
(jt. auth) Pendergast, T. Sixties in America. Primary sources **973.923**
(jt. auth) Pendergast, T. U-X-L graphic novelists **920.003**
(jt. auth) Pendergast, T. Westward expansion: almanac **978**
(jt. auth) Pendergast, T. Westward expansion: primary sources **978**
(jt. auth) Pendergast, T. World War I almanac **940.3**

Pendergast, Tom, 1964-
Constitutional amendments: from freedom of speech to flag burning **342**
The sixties in America. Almanac **973.923**
The sixties in America. Biographies **920**
Sixties in America. Primary sources **973.923**
U-X-L graphic novelists **920.003**
Westward expansion: almanac **978**
Westward expansion: biographies **920**
Westward expansion: primary sources **978**
World War I almanac **940.3**

The **pendulum**. Henry, O.
In Henry, O. The best short stories of O. Henry **S C**

A **pool** in the desert. McKinley, R.
   In McKinley, R. and Dickinson, P. Water:
   tales of elemental spirits p208-66
                        S C

Poole, Adrian
  (ed) The Oxford book of classical verse in
  translation. See The Oxford book of classical
  verse in translation   **881.008**

Poole, Joyce, 1956-
  Elephants   **599.67**

Poole, Robert M.
  Explorers house   **910**

Poor
  Hopkinson, D. Shutting out the sky   **974.7**
Encyclopedias
  Encyclopedia of world poverty   **362.5**
Fiction
  Booth, C. Tyrell   **Fic**
  Going, K. L. Saint Iggy   **Fic**
  Guène, F. Kiffe kiffe tomorrow   **Fic**
Medical care
  Farmer, P. Pathologies of power   **305**
United States
  Poverty   **362.5**

Poor little rich town. Vonnegut, K.
   In Vonnegut, K. Bagombo snuff box: uncollected short fiction p75-87   **S C**

Pop art
  Greenberg, J. Andy Warhol   **92**
  Livingstone, M. Pop art: a continuing history
                        709.04

Popes
  See/See also pages in the following book(s):
  Tuchman, B. W. The march of folly   **909.08**

Poplawski, Paul
  A Jane Austen encyclopedia   **823.009**

Popular contemporary writers   **920.003**

Popular culture
  Johnson, S. Everything bad is good for you
                        306
United States
  Browne, R. B. The Civil War and Reconstruc-
  tion   **973.7**
  Encyclopedia of contemporary American culture
                        973.92
  The Greenwood guide to American popular cul-
  ture   **973.9**
  Halberstam, D. The fifties   **973.92**
  Harvey, R. C. The art of the comic book
                        741.5
  Popular culture: opposing viewpoints **302.23**
  Professional sports   **796**
  Quay, S. E. Westward expansion   **978**
  War and American popular culture   **973**

Popular culture: opposing viewpoints **302.23**

Popular music
    See also Blues music; Gospel music; Rap
  music; Rock music
  Furia, P. The poets of Tin Pan Alley
                        782.42
Dictionaries
  Baker's biographical dictionary of popular musicians since 1990   **920.003**

Writing and publishing
  Songwriter's market 2007   **782.42**

Popular psychology. Cordón, L. A.   **150.3**

Popular series fiction for middle school and teen
  readers. Thomas, R. L.   **016.8**

Population
  Population: opposing viewpoints   **304.6**

Population: opposing viewpoints   **304.6**

Porcellino, Michael R.
  (jt. auth) Barnes-Svarney, P. Through the telescope   **522**

Pornography
  Pornography: opposing viewpoints   **363.4**
  See/See also pages in the following book(s):
  Mass media: opposing viewpoints   **302.23**

Pornography: opposing viewpoints   **363.4**

The **portable** Abraham Lincoln. Lincoln, A.
                        973.7

The **portable** Arthur Miller. Miller, A. **812**

The **portable** Blake. Blake, W.   **828**

The **portable** Chaucer. Chaucer, G.   **821**

The **portable** Conrad. Conrad, J.   **828**

The **portable** Dante. Dante Alighieri   **851**

The **portable** Darwin. Darwin, C.   **576.8**

The **portable** Emerson. Emerson, R. W. **818**

The **Portable** Greek reader   **880.8**

The **Portable** Harlem Renaissance reader
                        810.8

The **portable** Hawthorne. Hawthorne, N. **818**

The **portable** Jack Kerouac. Kerouac, J. **818**

The **portable** Jack London. London, J. **818**

The **portable** Kipling. Kipling, R.   **828**

The **portable** Milton. Milton, J.   **828**

The **portable** Nietzsche. Nietzsche, F. W. **193**

The **Portable** nineteenth-century Russian reader
                        891.7

The **portable** Oscar Wilde. Wilde, O. **828**

The **Portable** Roman reader   **870.8**

The **Portable** sixties reader   **810.8**

The **portable** twentieth-century Russian reader
                        891.7

The **portable** Voltaire. Voltaire   **848**

The **Portable** Western reader   **810.8**

Porter, Connie Rose
  Imani all mine   **Fic**

Porter, David L., 1941-
  (ed) Biographical dictionary of American sports,
  Baseball. See Biographical dictionary of
  American sports, Baseball   **796.357**

Porter, Duncan M.
  (ed) Darwin, C. The portable Darwin **576.8**

Porter, Katherine Anne, 1890-1980
  The collected stories of Katherine Anne Porter
                        S C
  Flowering Judas
   In The Oxford book of short stories p310-21
                        S C
  Flowering Judas, and other stories
   In Porter, K. A. The collected stories of Kath-
   erine Anne Porter   **S C**

Puerto Rico
Encyclopedias
Fernandez, R. Puerto Rico past and present
972.95

Puerto Rico past and present. Fernandez, R.
972.95

Pulitzer Prizes
Written into history **071**

Pulliam, June Michele
(jt. auth) Fonseca, A. J. Hooked on horror
016.8

Pulliam, Tom
The New York times crossword puzzle dictionary **793.73**

Pulling up stakes. Lubar, D.
In First crossing; stories about teen immigrants p95-109 **S C**

Pullman, Philip, 1946-
The golden compass **Fic**
The ruby in the smoke **Fic**
About
Speaker-Yuan, M. Philip Pullman **92**

The **pumpernickel**. Bradbury, R.
In Bradbury, R. Bradbury stories; 100 of his most celebrated tales **S C**

Pumping iron *See* Weight lifting

Punctuation
Truss, L. Eats, shoots & leaves **428**

Punishment
Banks, C. Punishment in America **364.6**
Freedom from cruel and unusual punishment
345

The **puppet** masters. Heinlein, R. A. **Fic**

Puppetry. Blumenthal, E. **791.5**

Puppets and puppet plays
Blumenthal, E. Puppetry **791.5**
Fiction
Huser, G. Stitches **Fic**

Purcell, L. Edward
Encyclopedia of battles in North America, 1517 to 1916 **970**
(jt. auth) Burg, D. F. Almanac of World War I
940.3
(ed) Vice presidents. See Vice presidents
920.003
(ed) The World almanac of the American Revolution. See The World almanac of the American Revolution **973.3**

Purcell, Sarah J.
The early national period **973.4**
(jt. auth) Purcell, L. E. Encyclopedia of battles in North America, 1517 to 1916 **970**

Purdy, James, 1923-
Dawn
In Growing up gay; an anthology for young people p175-78 **808.8**

The **pure** product. Kessel, J.
In Best of the best: 20 years of the Year's best science fiction **S C**

Purgatorio. Dante Alighieri **851**

Puritans
Aronson, M. John Winthrop, Oliver Cromwell, and the Land of Promise [dual biography of John Winthrop and Oliver Cromwell] **92**
Gaustad, E. S. Roger Williams **92**
Fiction
Hawthorne, N. The scarlet letter **Fic**

The **purloined** letter. Poe, E. A.
In Poe, E. A. The collected tales and poems of Edgar Allan Poe p208-22 **818**

The **purple** flower. Bonner, M.
In Black theatre USA; plays by African Americans, 1847 to today **812.008**

The **purple** hat. Welty, E.
In Welty, E. The collected stories of Eudora Welty p222-27 **S C**

Purple hibiscus. Adichie, C. N. **Fic**

A **pursuit** race. Hemingway, E.
In Hemingway, E. The complete short stories of Ernest Hemingway; the Finca Vigía edition p267-70 **S C**

Purvis, Thomas L., 1949-
Colonial America to 1763 **973.2**
Revolutionary America, 1763-1800 **973.3**

Pusan nights. Limón, M.
In Alfred Hitchcock's mystery magazine presents fifty years of crime and suspense
S C

Pushcart man. Hughes, L.
In Hughes, L. Short stories of Langston Hughes **S C**

Puzzles
See also Crossword puzzles

Pygmalion . . . and My fair lady. Shaw, B.
822

The **Pygmies**. Hawthorne, N.
In Hawthorne, N. Tales and sketches, including Twice-told tales, Mosses from an old manse, and The snow-image; A wonder book for girls and boys; Tanglewood tales for girls and boys, being a second Wonder book p1338-55 **S C**

Pyle, David
What every artist needs to know about paints & colors **752**

Pyle, George, 1956-
Raising less corn, more hell **338.1**

Pyle, Howard, 1853-1911
The story of King Arthur and his knights
398.2
The story of Sir Launcelot and his companions
398.2
The story of the champions of the Round Table
398.2
The story of the Grail and the passing of Arthur
398.2

Pyle, Robert Michael
The Audubon Society field guide to North American butterflies **595.7**

Pyle, Rod
Destination moon **629.45**

Pyne, Stephen J., 1949-
How the Canyon became Grand **979.1**

Rampersad, Arnold—*Continued*
(ed) The Oxford anthology of African-American poetry. See The Oxford anthology of African-American poetry **811.008**

Ranch life
Fiction
Steinbeck, J. Of mice and men **Fic**

Rand, Ayn, 1905-1982
The Ayn Rand reader **191**

Rand McNally Goode's world atlas. See Goode, J. P. Goode's world atlas **912**

Rand McNally road atlas. See The road atlas '07: U.S., Canada, Mexico **912**

Randall, Dudley, 1914-2000
(ed) Black poets. See Black poets **811.008**

Randel, Don Michael
(ed) The Harvard concise dictionary of music and musicians. See The Harvard concise dictionary of music and musicians **780.3**

Randi, James
The mask of Nostradamus **92**

Randle, Kristen D., 1952-
Breaking rank **Fic**

Randolph, Asa Philip, 1889-1979
About
Miller, C. C. A. Philip Randolph and the African American labor movement **92**

Random House American sign language dictionary. Costello, E. **419**

The **Random** House international encyclopedia of golf. See Campbell, M. The new encyclopedia of golf **796.352**

Random House Roget's college thesaurus. See Random House Webster's college thesaurus **423**

Random House thesaurus. See Random House Webster's college thesaurus **423**

Random House Webster's college dictionary **423**

Random House Webster's college thesaurus **423**

Random House Webster's easy English dictionary **423**

Random House Webster's French-English, English-French dictionary **443**

Random House Webster's German-English, English-German dictionary **433**

Random House Webster's intermediate English dictionary **423**

Random House Webster's quotationary **808.88**
Random House Webster's school & office dictionary. See The essential high school dictionary **423**

Random House Webster's unabridged dictionary **423**

Rangaswamy, Padma, 1945-
Indian Americans **305.8**

Rankin, Jeannette, 1880-1973
See/See also pages in the following book(s):
Mendoza, P. M. Extraordinary people in extraordinary times **920**

Ransom. Buck, P. S.
In The Best American mystery stories of the century p212-34 **S C**

The **ransom** of Red Chief. Henry, O.
In Henry, O. The best short stories of O. Henry **S C**

Rap music
Chang, J. Can't stop, won't stop **781.64**
Dyson, M. E. Holler if you hear me: searching for Tupac Shakur **92**
Light, A. The skills to pay the bills **920**
Lommel, C. The history of rap music **782.42**
The Vibe history of hip hop **782.42**
White, A. Rebel for the hell of it [biography of Tupac Shakur] **92**
Encyclopedias
Bynoe, Y. Encyclopedia of rap and hip-hop culture **782.42**

Rape
Sexual violence: opposing viewpoints **364.1**
Strong at the heart **362.7**
Fiction
Anderson, L. H. Speak **Fic**
Davis, A. Wonder when you'll miss me **Fic**
Lipsyte, R. Raiders night **Fic**
Lynch, C. Inexcusable **Fic**
Porter, C. R. Imani all mine **Fic**
Williams-Garcia, R. Every time a rainbow dies **Fic**

Raphael, Lev
Abominations
In Growing up gay; an anthology for young people p249-52 **808.8**

Raphael, Ray
A people's history of the American Revolution **973.3**

Rapoport, Ron
(jt. auth) Einhorn, E. How march became madness **796.323**

Rapp, Adam
Under the wolf, under the dog **Fic**

Rappaccini's daughter. Hawthorne, N.
In Hawthorne, N. Tales and sketches, including Twice-told tales, Mosses from an old manse, and The snow-image; A wonder book for girls and boys; Tanglewood tales for girls and boys, being a second Wonder book p975-1005 **S C**
In The Oxford book of gothic tales p133-57 **S C**

Rapport, Richard
Nerve endings **612.8**

Rara avis. Boyle, T. C.
In Boyle, T. C. The Human Fly and other stories **S C**

Rare animals
See also Endangered species; Extinct animals

Rare plants
See also Endangered species

Raschka, Christopher
(il) A Poke in the I. See A Poke in the I **811.008**

Reagon, Bernice Johnson, 1942-
(ed) We'll understand it better by and by. See We'll understand it better by and by **782.25**

The **real** Fidel Castro. Coltman, Sir L. **92**

A **real** life blond Cherokee and his equally annoyed soul mate. Smith, C. L.
In Moccasin thunder; American Indians stories for today **S C**

Real-life math. Glazer, E. **510**

The **real** revolution. Aronson, M. **973.3**

Real sports reporting **070.4**

The **real** thing. Goodman, A.
In Firebirds rising; an anthology of original science fiction and fantasy **S C**

Real time. Kass, P. **Fic**

Real voices, real history series
Voices from the Trail of Tears **970.004**

Real world (Television program)
Winick, J. Pedro and me **362.1**

The **real** world. Utley, S.
In Best of the best: 20 years of the Year's best science fiction **S C**

Reality check. Brin, D.
In The Hard SF renaissance **S C**

Reallionaire. Gray, F. **332.024**

The **reaper's** image. King, S.
In King, S. Skeleton crew **S C**

The **reappearance** of Sam Webber. Fuqua, J. S. **Fic**

Rear window. Woolrich, C.
In The Best American mystery stories of the century p288-317 **S C**

Rear window [originally titled "It had to be murder"]. Woolrich, C.
In Adaptations: from short story to big screen; 35 great stories that have inspired great films **S C**

Reason. Asimov, I.
In Asimov, I. I, robot **S C**

Reasoner, James
Manassas **Fic**

Reasons to be cheerful. Egan, G.
In The Hard SF renaissance **S C**

Rebecca. Werlin, N.
In Twice told; original stories inspired by original art **S C**

Rebel for the hell of it [biography of Tupac Shakur] White, A. **92**

Rebels and renegades. Hamilton, N. A. **322.4**

Reber, Arthur S.
The Penguin dictionary of psychology **150**

Reber, Deborah
In their shoes **331.4**
(comp) Chicken soup for the teenage soul's real deal. See Chicken soup for the teenage soul's the real deal **158**

Reber, Emily S., 1969-
(jt. auth) Reber, A. S. The Penguin dictionary of psychology **150**

Reber, Grote, 1911-2002
See/See also pages in the following book(s):
Malone, J. W. It doesn't take a rocket scientist **920**

Rebolledo, Tey Diana, 1937-
(ed) Infinite divisions: an anthology of Chicana literature. See Infinite divisions: an anthology of Chicana literature **810.8**

A **recent** history of the United States in political cartoons. Bok, C. **973.92**

Recipe for murder. Holding, J.
In Alfred Hitchcock's mystery magazine presents fifty years of crime and suspense **S C**

Recipes *See* Cooking

"Recitatif". Morrison, T.
In Leaving home: stories p201-27 **808.8**
In The Oxford book of women's writing in the United States p159-75 **810.8**

Recitations *See* Monologues

Recollections of Leo Tolstoy. Gorky, M.
In The portable twentieth-century Russian reader **891.7**

Recollections of my life as a woman [excerpt] Di Prima, D.
In Growing up ethnic in America; contemporary fiction about learning to be American **S C**

Recommended reference books for small and medium-sized libraries and media centers **011**

Reconstruction (1865-1876)
See also Ku Klux Klan
Barney, W. L. The Civil War and Reconstruction **973.7**
Bolden, T. Cause: Reconstruction America, 1863-1877 **973.7**
Browne, R. B. The Civil War and Reconstruction **973.7**
Foner, E. Forever free **973.8**
Grumet, B. H. Reconstruction era: primary sources **973.8**
Hansen, J. Bury me not in a land of slaves **973.8**
Kirchberger, J. H. The Civil War and Reconstruction **973.7**
Matuz, R. Reconstruction era: biographies **920**
Reconstruction **973.8**

Reconstruction **973.8**

Reconstruction Era reference library [series]
Grumet, B. H. Reconstruction era: primary sources **973.8**
Matuz, R. Reconstruction era: biographies **920**

The **record** of Badalia Herodsfoot. Kipling, R.
In The Oxford book of short stories p147-66 **S C**

Recording angel. McDonald, I.
In Best of the best: 20 years of the Year's best science fiction **S C**

Recreation
See also Amusements

Reilly, Edwin D.
Milestones in computer science and information technology **004**
(ed) Encyclopedia of computer science. See Encyclopedia of computer science **004**

Reilly, Philip, 1947-
Is it in your genes? **599.93**

Reinhardt, Dana
A brief chapter in my impossible life **Fic**

Reinventing comics. McCloud, S. **741.5**

Reiss, Johanna
The upstairs room **92**

Reitci, John George See Ritchie, Jack, 1922-1983

The **reivers**. Faulkner, W. **Fic**

Relations among ethnic groups See Ethnic relations

Relativity (Physics)
Strathern, P. Einstein and relativity **92**
See/See also pages in the following book(s):
Lightman, A. P. Great ideas in physics **530**

Relent/persist. Trope, Z.
In Sixteen: stories about that sweet and bitter birthday **S C**

A **relic** of the Pliocene. London, J.
In London, J. The portable Jack London p32-41 **818**

Relics of General Chassé: a tale of Antwerp. Trollope, A.
In The Oxford book of English short stories p44-62 **S C**

Religion
See also Religious fundamentalism; Theology
Bowker, J. World religions **200**
Feynman, R. P. The meaning of it all **500**
See/See also pages in the following book(s):
Bishop, M. The Middle Ages **940.1**
Emerson, R. W. The portable Emerson **818**
Sagan, C. Broca's brain **500**
Bibliography
Reaching out to religious youth **027.62**
Fiction
Hautman, P. Godless **Fic**
Wittlinger, E. Blind faith **Fic**
History—Chronology
The Wilson chronology of the world's religions **200**

Religion and modern culture [series]
McIntosh, K. When religion & politics mix **201**

Religion and politics
See also Islam and politics
Carter, S. L. God's name in vain **322**
Djupe, P. A. Encyclopedia of American religion and politics **322**
Long, D. Fundamentalists and extremists **306**
McIntosh, K. When religion & politics mix **201**
The Middle East: opposing viewpoints **956**

Religion and science
Creationism versus evolution **576.8**
Grant, E. Science and religion, 400 B.C. to A.D. 1550 **261.5**

Olson, R. Science and religion, 1450-1900 **261.5**
Pennock, R. T. Tower of Babel **576.8**
Roach, M. Spook **133.9**

Religion and state See Church and state

Religion and war See War—Religious aspects

Religion in America: opposing viewpoints **200.9**

Religion in American life [series]
Balmer, R. H. Religion in twentieth century America **200.9**
Bushman, C. L. Mormons in America **289.3**
Mann, G. S. Buddhists, Hindus, and Sikhs in America **294**

Religion in the public schools
Dudley, M. E. Engel v. Vitale (1962) **344**
See/See also pages in the following book(s):
Education: opposing viewpoints **371**

Religion in twentieth century America. Balmer, R. H. **200.9**

Religions
See also Gods and goddesses; Occultism; Sects
Bowker, J. World religions **200**
Breuilly, E. Religions of the world **201**
The Cambridge illustrated history of religions **200.9**
Frazer, Sir J. G. The new golden bough **201**
Human rights and the world's major religions **201**
The Illustrated guide to world religions **200**
Introduction to the world's major religions **200**
Encyclopedias
Encyclopedia of religious rites, rituals, and festivals **203**
The encyclopedia of world religions **200.3**

Religions of the world. Breuilly, E. **201**

Religious art
See also Christian art
Campbell, J. The power of myth **201**

Religious belief See Faith

Religious biography
Ellsberg, R. Blessed among all women **920**
Goldman, E. Believers **920**
Holy people of the world **920.003**

Religious ceremonies See Rites and ceremonies

Religious cults See Cults

Religious freedom See Freedom of religion

Religious fundamentalism
See also Islamic fundamentalism
Armstrong, K. The battle for God **200**
Long, D. Fundamentalists and extremists **306**

Religious holidays
See also Jewish holidays
Religious holidays and calendars **203**

Religious holidays and calendars **203**

Religious life
Fiction
Hoffman, M. The falconer's knot **Fic**

Respiratory system
  Petechuk, D. The respiratory system   **612.2**
Restaurants
  Fast food   **363.1**
  Spurlock, M. Don't eat this book   **614.5**
Fiction

  Bauer, J. Hope was here   **Fic**
  Smith, C. L. Tantalize   **Fic**
The **restless** dead   **S C**
Restless genius [biography of Virginia Woolf]
  Brackett, V.   **92**
Restless spirit: the life and work of Dorothea
  Lange. Partridge, E.   **92**
The **Restoration** and the eighteenth century
  In The Oxford anthology of English literature
   820.8

Résumés (Employment)
  Enelow, W. S. Best resumes for people without
   a four-year degree   **650.14**
  Fry, R. W. Your first resume   **650.14**
  Hinds, M. J. The Ferguson guide to resumes and
   job hunting skills   **650.14**
  Potter, R. Résumés that get jobs   **650.14**
  Thomason-Carroll, K. L. Young adult's guide to
   business communications   **651.7**
  Troutman, K. K. Creating your high school re-
   sume   **650.14**
Résumés that get jobs. Potter, R.   **650.14**
The **resurrection**. Mowry, J.
  In Make me over; 11 stories of transformation
   S C
Resurrection blues. Tanner, M.   **Fic**
Retail trade
Japan—Graphic novels

  Ikuta, T. Project X Challengers: Seven Eleven
   658.8
Retreat from Earth. Clarke, A. C.
  In Clarke, A. C. The collected stories of Ar-
   thur C. Clarke   **S C**
A **retrieved** reformation. Henry, O.
  In The Best American mystery stories of the
   century p1-7   **S C**
  In Henry, O. The best short stories of O.
   Henry   **S C**
Retter, Yolanda, 1947-
  (ed) Gay and lesbian rights in the United States.
   See Gay and lesbian rights in the United
   States   **306.76**
Return. Wolfe, T.
  In Wolfe, T. The complete short stories of
   Thomas Wolfe p296-99   **S C**
The **return** of Chorb. Nabokov, V. V.
  In The portable twentieth-century Russian
   reader   **891.7**
The **return** of Sherlock Holmes. Doyle, Sir A. C.
  In Doyle, Sir A. C. The complete Sherlock
   Holmes   **S C**
The **return** of Simple. Hughes, L.   **818**
The **return** of the native. Hardy, T.   **Fic**
The **return** of the prodigal. Wolfe, T.
  In Wolfe, T. The complete short stories of
   Thomas Wolfe p542-62   **S C**
Return to Titanic. Ballard, R. D.   **910.4**

Return to wild America. Weidensaul, S.   **578**
Returnable girl. Lowell, P.   **Fic**
Returning the gift   **897**
Reunion. Cheever, J.
  In Cheever, J. The stories of John Cheever
   p518-20   **S C**
Reunion. Clarke, A. C.
  In Clarke, A. C. The collected stories of Ar-
   thur C. Clarke   **S C**
Revelation. O'Connor, F.
  In The Norton book of American short stories
   p536-54   **S C**
  In O'Connor, F. Collected works p633-54
   S C
  In O'Connor, F. The complete stories p488-
   509   **S C**
Revenant as typewriter. Lively, P.
  In The Literary ghost; great contemporary
   ghost stories p156-70   **S C**
Revenge and forgiveness   **808.81**
Revenge of the lawn. Brautigan, R.
  In The Norton book of American short stories
   p622-26   **S C**
The **reverent** wooing of Archibald. Wodehouse, P.
  G.
  In The Oxford book of English short stories
   p188-203   **S C**
Reverie. Clarke, A. C.
  In Clarke, A. C. The collected stories of Ar-
   thur C. Clarke   **S C**
Revisiting Stephen King. Russell, S. A.
   813.009
Revivals
Graphic novels

  Sturm, J. James Sturm's America   **741.5**
Music

  See Gospel music
The **revolt** of "Mother". Freeman, M. E. W.
  In The Oxford book of women's writing in
   the United States p27-40   **810.8**
Revolution, Industrial *See* Industrial revolution
Revolution from within. Steinem, G.   **155.2**
Revolutionary America, 1763-1800. Purvis, T. L.
   973.3
Revolutionary citizens. Littlefield, D. C.
  In The Young Oxford history of African
   Americans   **305.8**
Revolutionary studies series
  U.S. labor in the twentieth century   **331**
The **revolutionist**. Hemingway, E.
  In Hemingway, E. The complete short stories
   of Ernest Hemingway; the Finca Vigía
   edition p119-20   **S C**
Rewald, John, 1912-1994
  Cézanne   **92**
Rexroth, Kenneth, 1905-1982
  (ed) One hundred poems from the Chinese. See
   One hundred poems from the Chinese
   895.1
  (ed) One hundred poems from the Japanese. See
   One hundred poems from the Japanese
   895.6

Rottman, S. L., 1970-
Red sky
In Dreams and visions; fourteen flights of fantasy **S C**

Rouge high. Hughes, L.
In Hughes, L. Short stories of Langston Hughes **S C**

The **Rough** Riders. Roosevelt, T. **973.8**

Roughing it. Twain, M. **818**

The **round** dozen. Maugham, W. S.
In Maugham, W. S. Collected short stories **S C**

Rousseau, Jean-Jacques, 1712-1778
The social contract
In Social contract; essays by Locke, Hume, and Rousseau p167-307 **320.1**
About
Conroy, P. V. Jean-Jacques Rousseau **848**
See/See also pages in the following book(s):
Russell, B. A history of Western philosophy **109**

The **Routledge** atlas of the Holocaust. Gilbert, M. **940.53**

Routledge encyclopedias of religion and society [series]
Encyclopedia of religious rites, rituals, and festivals **203**

The **rover**. Odom, M. **Fic**

Rovin, Jeff
Adventure heroes **700**

Row, Jess, 1974-
The secrets of bats
In Gotham Writers' Workshop fiction gallery; exceptional short stories selected by New York's acclaimed creative writing school **S C**

Rowling, J. K.
Harry Potter and the Sorcerer's Stone **Fic**
About
Kirk, C. A. J.K. Rowling: a biography **92**

Roy, Arundhati
The god of small things **Fic**

Roy, Christian, 1963-
Traditional festivals **394.26**

The **Royal** Horticultural Society gardeners' encyclopedia of plants and flowers. See American Horticultural Society encyclopedia of plants and flowers **635.9**

Royalty *See* Kings and rulers; Princesses; Queens

Royster, Charles
(jt. auth) Barnes, I. The historical atlas of the American Revolution **973.3**

Royte, Elizabeth
Garbage land **363.7**

Rozan, S. J.
Body English
In Alfred Hitchcock's mystery magazine presents fifty years of crime and suspense **S C**

Rozema, Vicki, 1954-
(ed) Voices from the Trail of Tears. See Voices from the Trail of Tears **970.004**

Rozett, Robert
(ed) Encyclopedia of the Holocaust. See Encyclopedia of the Holocaust [Facts on File] **940.53**

Ruanda *See* Rwanda

Rubáiyát of Omar Khayyám. Omar Khayyam **891**

The **rubbish** dump. Chimombo, S.
In The Heinemann book of contemporary African short stories p72-80 **S C**

Rubenstein, Jeff
Crash course for the new SAT **378.1**
Cracking the PSAT/NMSQT, 2008 edition. See Cracking the PSAT/NMSQT, 2008 edition **378.1**

Rubin, Gretchen Craft
Forty ways to look at Winston Churchill **92**

Rubin, Robert Alden, 1958-
(ed) Poetry out loud. See Poetry out loud **821.008**

Rubin, Susan Goldman, 1939-
Margaret Bourke-White **92**

Ruby, Aaron, 1967-
(jt. auth) Chaplin, H. Smartbomb **338.4**

Ruby. Geras, A.
In Twice told; original stories inspired by original art **S C**

The **ruby** in the smoke. Pullman, P. **Fic**

Rubyfruit jungle [excerpt] Brown, R. M.
In Growing up gay; an anthology for young people p253-59 **808.8**

Rudd, Kelly, 1954-
(jt. auth) Hanes, R. C. Crime and punishment in America, Biographies **920**

Ruden, Sarah
(tr) Aristophanes. Lysistrata **882**

Rudof, Joanne Weiner
(ed) Witness. See Witness **940.53**

Rugg, Jim
(il) Castellucci, C. The Plain Janes **741.5**

Ruins *See* Excavations (Archeology)

The **ruins**. Martin, P. P.
In Growing up Latino; memoirs and stories p73-84 **810.8**

The **Ruins** of California. Sherrill, M. **Fic**

The **Ruins** of the Abbey of Fitz-Martin
In The Oxford book of gothic tales p31-50 **S C**

The **rule** book. See Rules of the game **796.03**

Rule of the bone. Banks, R. **Fic**

Rulers *See* Heads of state; Kings and rulers; Queens

Rulers and their times [series]
Mann, K. Isabel, Ferdinand and fifteenth-century Spain **946**

Rules of order *See* Parliamentary practice

The **rules** of survival. Werlin, N. **Fic**

Rules of the game **796.03**

Rules of the game. Tan, A.
In Growing up ethnic in America; contemporary fiction about learning to be American **S C**

Rules of the game—*Continued*
  In Leaving home: stories p35-52   **808.8**
Rules of the road. Bauer, J.   **Fic**
A **rumor** of war. Caputo, P.   **959.704**
Rumors. Simon, N.
  In Simon, N. The collected plays of Neil Simon   **812**
Runaround. Asimov, I.
  In Asimov, I. I, robot   **S C**
The **runaway**. Callaghan, M.
  In The Oxford book of short stories p382-90   **S C**
Runaway girl: the artist Louise Bourgeois. Greenberg, J.   **92**
Runaway teenagers
  Erlbaum, J. Girlbomb   **92**
Fiction
  Acampora, P. Defining Dulcie   **Fic**
  Banks, R. Rule of the bone   **Fic**
  Black, H. Valiant: a modern faerie tale   **Fic**
  Burgess, M. Smack   **Fic**
  Davis, A. Wonder when you'll miss me   **Fic**
  Flinn, A. Nothing to lose   **Fic**
  Hobbs, W. The maze   **Fic**
  MacCullough, C. Stealing Henry   **Fic**
  Stine, C. Refugees   **Fic**
Graphic novels
  Talbot, B. The tale of one bad rat   **741.5**
Runaways. Vonnegut, K.
  In Vonnegut, K. Bagombo snuff box: uncollected short fiction p243-57   **S C**
Runner. Deuker, C.   **Fic**
Runner of Pern. McCaffrey, A.
  In Legends: short novels by the masters of modern fantasy p535-93   **S C**
Runner's world complete book of running. See Complete book of running   **796.42**
Runner's world complete book of women's running. Scott, D.   **796.42**
Running
  Scott, D. Runner's world complete book of women's running   **796.42**
Running. Howard, E.
  In Am I blue?; coming out from the silence p85-101   **S C**
Running loose. Crutcher, C.   **Fic**
Running out of dog. Lehane, D.
  In The Best American mystery stories of the century p770-99   **S C**
Runyon, Alfred Damon *See* Runyon, Damon, 1884-1946
Runyon, Brent
  The burn journals   **92**
Runyon, Damon, 1884-1946
  Sense of humor
  In The Best American mystery stories of the century p204-211   **S C**
Rural life *See* Country life; Farm life
Rurouni Kenshin. Watsuki, N.   **741.5**
Rusch, Kristine Kathryn
  Blood trail
  In Past imperfect   **S C**

Ruschmann, Paul
  Legalizing marijuana   **345**
  Miranda rights   **345**
Rush, Barbara
  The Jewish year   **296.4**
Rushdie, Salman
  Haroun and the sea of stories   **Fic**
Russ, Joanna, 1937-
  A few things I know about Whileaway
  In The Norton book of science fiction; North American science fiction, 1960-1990 p337-49   **S C**
  Souls
  In The Locus awards; thirty years of the best in science fiction and fantasy   **S C**
Russell, Bertrand, 1872-1970
  A history of Western philosophy   **109**
  See/See also pages in the following book(s):
  Durant, W. J. The story of philosophy   **109**
Russell, Bruce J.
  (jt. auth) Rainis, K. G. A guide to microlife   **579**
Russell, Carrie
  (ed) Complete copyright. See Complete copyright   **346.04**
Russell, Charles M. (Charles Marion), 1864-1926
About
  Hassrick, P. H. Charles M. Russell   **92**
Russell, Colin Archibald
  Michael Faraday   **92**
Russell, Edmund, 1957-
  War and nature   **577.2**
Russell, Emily
  (jt. auth) Kuper, P. The jungle   **741.5**
Russell, Ray
  Sardonicus
  In The Oxford book of gothic tales p435-65   **S C**
Russell, Roy, 1954-
  (ed) The Oxford Spanish dictionary. See The Oxford Spanish dictionary   **463**
Russell, Sharon A.
  Revisiting Stephen King   **813.009**
  Stephen King: a critical companion   **813.009**
Russell Baker's book of American humor   **817.008**
Russia
  See also Russia (Federation); Soviet Union
Civilization
  Schultze, S. Culture and customs of Russia   **947**
Fiction
  Chekhov, A. P. The Russian master and other stories   **S C**
  Dostoyevsky, F. Crime and punishment   **Fic**
  Holub, J. An innocent soldier   **Fic**
  Malamud, B. The fixer   **Fic**
  Tolstoy, L., graf. Anna Karenina   **Fic**
  Tolstoy, L., graf. Great short works of Leo Tolstoy   **S C**
History
  Kurth, P. Tsar: the lost world of Nicholas and Alexandra   **947.08**

Salter, Mark
(jt. auth) McCain, J. S. Why courage matters
179

Saltykov, Mikhail Evgrafovich, 1826-1889
The story of how one Russian peasant fed two generals
In The Portable nineteenth-century Russian reader p609-15 **891.7**

Saltykov-Shchedrin, Mikhail *See* Saltykov, Mikhail Evgrafovich, 1826-1889

Salvador. Shepard, L.
In Best of the best: 20 years of the Year's best science fiction **S C**

Salvador Dali and the surrealists. Ross, M. E.
92

Salvador late or early. Cisneros, S.
In Cisneros, S. Woman Hollering Creek and other stories **S C**

Salvadori, Mario George, 1907-1997
(jt. auth) Levy, M. Why the earth quakes
551.2

Salvage. Card, O. S.
In New skies: an anthology of today's science fiction **S C**

Salvatore. Maugham, W. S.
In Maugham, W. S. Collected short stories
S C

Salzman, Mark
Iron & silk **915.1**
True notebooks **808**

Same-sex marriage
Gay and lesbian families **306.8**
Gay marriage **306.8**

Samjatin, Jewgenij *See* Zamiâtin, Evgeniĭ Ivanovich, 1884-1937

Sammy and Juliana in Hollywood. Saenz, B. A.
Fic

Samson Agonistes. Milton, J.
In Milton, J. The portable Milton **828**
In The Oxford anthology of English literature
820.8

Samuel, Wolfgang W. E.
The war of our childhood **940.53**

Samuel. London, J.
In London, J. The portable Jack London p214-31 **818**

Samurai shortstop. Gratz, A. **Fic**

San Francisco (Calif.)
Fiction
Fischer, J. An egg on three sticks **Fic**
Lavender, W. Aftershocks **Fic**

Sanatorium. Maugham, W. S.
In Maugham, W. S. Collected short stories
S C

Sanchez, Alex, 1957-
Rainbow boys **Fic**

Sanctions (International law)
See/See also pages in the following book(s):
U.S. policy toward rogue nations **327.73**

Sanctuaries, Wildlife *See* Wildlife refuges

Sanctuary. Christie, A.
In Christie, A. Miss Marple: the complete short stories **S C**

Sanctuary movement
See also Refugees

Sand Creek, Battle of, 1864
See/See also pages in the following book(s):
Mendoza, P. M. Extraordinary people in extraordinary times **920**

The **sand-reckoner.** Bradshaw, G. **Fic**

Sandberg, R. N.
Convivencia
In International plays for young audiences; contemporary works from leading playwrights p131-72 **808.82**

Sandburg, Carl, 1878-1967
Chicago poems
In Sandburg, C. The complete poems of Carl Sandburg p3-76 **811**
The complete poems of Carl Sandburg **811**
Cornhuskers
In Sandburg, C. The complete poems of Carl Sandburg p79-147 **811**
Good morning, America
In Sandburg, C. The complete poems of Carl Sandburg p315-435 **811**
Honey and salt
In Sandburg, C. The complete poems of Carl Sandburg p706-71 **811**
The people, yes
In Sandburg, C. The complete poems of Carl Sandburg p439-617 **811**
Poems for the people **811**
Selected poems **811**
Slabs of the sunburnt West
In Sandburg, C. The complete poems of Carl Sandburg p271-314 **811**
Smoke and steel
In Sandburg, C. The complete poems of Carl Sandburg p149-268 **811**

Sanders, William
The undiscovered
In Best of the best: 20 years of the Year's best science fiction **S C**

Sandler, Martin W.
Photography: an illustrated history **770.9**

Sandoz, Mari, 1896-1966
The Battle of the Little Bighorn **973.8**

Sandpiper. Wittlinger, E. **Fic**

Sands, Matthew L. (Matthew Linzee)
(jt. auth) Feynman, R. P. Six easy pieces
530

Sands of the well. Levertov, D. **811**

Sanello, Frank
Reel v. real **791.43**

Sanford, Annette
Trip in a summer dress
In Leaving home: stories p119-31 **808.8**

Sanger, Margaret, 1879-1966
About
Reed, M. Margaret Sanger: her life in her words
92

Sankaran, Neeraja
Microbes and people: an A-Z of microorganisms in our lives **579**

Saturn rising. Clarke, A. C.
   In Clarke, A. C. The collected stories of Arthur C. Clarke   **S C**

Satyagraha. Carter, A. R.
   In Carter, A. R. Love, football, and other contact sports   **S C**

Saunders, George
   Sea Oak
   In Feeling very strange; the Slipstream anthology   **S C**

Savage, Candace, 1949-
   Prairie   **508**

Savage, David G., 1950-
   Guide to the U.S. Supreme Court   **347**
   The Supreme Court and individual rights   **342**

Savage, Deborah
   Kotuku   **Fic**

Savage, Les, Jr.
   King of the buckskin breed
   In A Century of great Western stories   **S C**

Savage, Steele
   (il) Hamilton, E. Mythology   **292**

Savage, Stephen, 1965-
   (jt. auth) Martin, P. A. F. Woods and forests   **577.3**

Savage, Steve, 1965- *See* Savage, Stephen, 1965-

Savage, William W.
   The cowboy hero   **973**

Savage satire [biography of Jonathan Swift] Aykroyd, C.   **92**

Savant, Marilyn Mach Vos *See* Vos Savant, Marilyn Mach

Saving America's treasures. Young, D.   **973**

Saving and investment
   Bamford, J. Street wise   **332.6**
   Savings and investment information for teens   **332.024**

Saving Francesca. Marchetta, M.   **Fic**

Savings and investment information for teens   **332.024**

Sawa, Maureen
   (jt. auth) Edmonston, L.-P. Car smarts   **629.222**

Sawyer, P. H., 1928-
   (ed) The Oxford illustrated history of the Vikings. See The Oxford illustrated history of the Vikings   **948**

Sawyer, Robert J., 1960-
   The shoulders of giants
   In The Hard SF renaissance   **S C**

Sax, Benjamin C., 1950-
   (ed) Western civilization. See Western civilization   **909**

Sayed, Kashua, 1975-
   Let it be morning   **Fic**

Saying no to Nick. Coville, B.
   In Twice told; original stories inspired by original art   **S C**

Sayler, Mary Harwell
   The encyclopedia of the muscle and skeletal systems and disorders   **616.7**

Sayres, Meghan Nuttall
   Anahita's woven riddle   **Fic**

Sbordoni, Valerio
   Butterflies of the world   **595.7**

The **scalehunter's** beautiful daughter. Shepard, L.
   In The Locus awards; thirty years of the best in science fiction and fantasy   **S C**

A **scandal** in Bohemia. Doyle, Sir A. C.
   In Doyle, Sir A. C. The complete Sherlock Holmes   **S C**

Scandiffio, Laura
   Evil masters   **920**

Scandinavians
   See also Vikings

Scarecrow studies in young adult literature [series]
   Aronson, M. Exploding the myths   **028.5**
   Cart, M. The heart has its reasons   **813.009**
   Hogan, W. Humor in young adult literature   **813.009**
   Molin, P. F. American Indian themes in young adult literature   **810.9**
   Reed, A. J. S. Norma Fox Mazer   **813.009**
   Tyson, E. S. Orson Scott Card   **813.009**

Scared!: how to draw fantastic horror comic characters. Miller, S.   **741.5**

The **scarlet** letter. Hawthorne, N.   **Fic**
   also in Hawthorne, N. The portable Hawthorne   **818**

The **scarlet** moving van. Cheever, J.
   In Cheever, J. The stories of John Cheever p359-69   **S C**

Scarlett, W. George
   (ed) Encyclopedia of religious and spiritual development. See Encyclopedia of religious and spiritual development   **200.3**

Scattershot. Bear, G.
   In Bear, G. The collected stories of Greg Bear   **S C**

Scaturro, Pasquale
   (jt. auth) Bangs, R. Mystery of the Nile   **916**

Scenarios *See* Motion picture plays

The **Scenebook** for actors   **808.82**

Scenes from classic plays, 468 B.C. to 1970 A.D.   **808.82**

Schaap, Phil, 1951-
   (jt. auth) Marsalis, W. Jazz A-B-Z   **781.65**

Schacter, Daniel L.
   The seven sins of memory   **153.1**

Schaefer, Emmett Robert, 1947-
   (jt. auth) Thompson, C. White men challenging racism   **323**

Schaefer, Jack Warner, 1907-1991
   Sergeant Houck
   In A Century of great Western stories   **S C**

Schafer, Daniel L.
   Anna Madgigine Jai Kingsley   **92**

Schram, Martin
Avoiding armageddon   **327.1**

Schrock, Kathleen
(ed) The Technology connection. See The Technology connection   **027.8**

Schrödinger's plague. Bear, G.
In Bear, G. The collected stories of Greg Bear   **S C**
In The Norton book of science fiction; North American science fiction, 1960-1990 p477-84   **S C**

Schroeder, Karl, 1962-
Halo
In The Hard SF renaissance   **S C**

Schuckett, Sandy
Political advocacy for school librarians
    027.8

Schuerger, Michele, 1961-
(jt. auth) Schwager, T. Cool women, hot jobs . . . and how you can go for it, too!
    650.14

Schulberg, Budd
Your Arkansas traveler
In Adaptations: from short story to big screen; 35 great stories that have inspired great films   **S C**

Schulman, Grace
(jt. auth) Moore, M. The poems of Marianne Moore   **811**

Schultz, David A., 1958-
The encyclopedia of the Supreme Court   **347**
(ed) Encyclopedia of American law. See Encyclopedia of American law   **349**

Schultz, Jeffrey D., 1966-
Critical companion to John Steinbeck
    813.009

Schultz, Margaret A.
Teens with single parents   **306.8**

Schultz, Mitchel E.
Grob's basic electronics   **621.381**

Schultze, Sydney
Culture and customs of Russia   **947**

Schumann, Walter
Gemstones of the world   **553.8**

Schur, Joan Brodsky
(ed) The Arabs. See The Arabs   **305.8**

Schutz, Samantha, 1978-
I don't want to be crazy   **92**

Schuyler, George Samuel, 1895-1977
Black no more
In The Portable Harlem Renaissance reader p655-66   **810.8**

Schwager, Tina, 1964-
Cool women, hot jobs . . . and how you can go for it, too!   **650.14**

Schwartz, Adam
Where is it written?
In Coming of age in America; a multicultural anthology p82-99   **S C**

Schwartz, Ellen, 1949-
I love yoga   **613.7**

Schwartz, Jeffrey H.
(jt. auth) Tattersall, I. Extinct humans
    599.93

Schwartz, Lynne Sharon
Killing the bees
In Growing up ethnic in America; contemporary fiction about learning to be American   **S C**

Schwartz, Maxime, 1940-
How the cows turned mad   **616.8**

Schwartz, Richard Alan, 1951-
The 1950s   **973.921**
The 1990s   **973.92**
Encyclopedia of the Persian Gulf War   **956.7**

Schwartz, Tina P., 1969-
Organ transplants   **617.9**

Schwarz, Mauricio-José
Glimmerings on blue glass
In Cosmos latinos; an anthology of science fiction from Latin America and Spain   **S C**

Schwarzschild radius. Willis, C.
In The Norton book of science fiction; North American science fiction, 1960-1990 p689-704   **S C**

Schwedt, Rachel E., 1944-
Young adult poetry   **809.1**

Schweid, Richard
Consider the eel   **597**

Schwob, Marcel, 1867-1905
Bloody Blanche
In The Oxford book of gothic tales p245-48   **S C**

Science
See also Computer science
Bryson, B. A short history of nearly everything   **500**
Carlson, D. B. In and out of your mind   **500**
Feynman, R. P. The meaning of it all   **500**
Great thinkers of the Western world   **190**
The Handy science answer book   **500**
The next fifty years   **501**
Oxford dictionary of scientific quotations
    500
Ray, C. C. The New York Times second book of science questions and answers   **500**
Sagan, C. Broca's brain   **500**
Sagan, C. The demon-haunted world   **001.9**
Scientific American's ask the experts   **500**
Shermer, M. Why people believe weird things
    001.9
Tabak, J. Mathematics and the laws of nature
    510
Wiggins, A. W. The five biggest unsolved problems in science   **500**
Dictionaries
The American Heritage science dictionary
    503
The American Heritage student science dictionary   **503**
The new Penguin dictionary of science   **503**
Encyclopedias
Gale encyclopedia of science   **503**
McGraw-Hill concise encyclopedia of science & technology   **503**

Scott, Damion
How to draw hip-hop **741.2**

Scott, Danna
Boxing: the complete guide to training and fitness **796.8**

Scott, Eugenie Carol, 1945-
Evolution vs. creationism **576.8**

Scott, Georgia
Headwraps **391**

Scott, Hunter
About
Nelson, P. Left for dead **940.54**

Scott, Jeffry
Unbearable temptations
In Alfred Hitchcock's mystery magazine presents fifty years of crime and suspense **S C**

Scott, John F., 1936-
Latin American art **709.8**

Scott, Sir Peter Markham, Sir, 1909-1989
(ed) The world atlas of birds. See The world atlas of birds **598**

Scott, Ralph D.
(jt. auth) Capinera, J. L. Field guide to grasshoppers, crickets, and katydids of the United States **595.7**

Scott, Robert Alan
Chief Joseph and the Nez Percés **92**

Scott, Robert Falcon, 1868-1912
About
Solomon, S. The coldest March **998**

Scott, Sir Walter, 1771-1832
The two drovers
In The Oxford book of short stories p1-26 **S C**

Scott-Kilvert, Ian
(ed) British writers. See British writers **920.003**

Scottsboro, Alabama. Khan, L. S. **345**

The **Scottsboro** Boys Trial. Sorensen, L. **345**

Scottsboro case
Khan, L. S. Scottsboro, Alabama **345**

Scrap-books *See* Scrapbooks

Scrapbooks
Sowell, S. Paper cutting techniques for scrapbooks & cards **745.54**
See/See also pages in the following book(s):
The Michaels book of paper crafts **745.54**

Screaming for faeries. Steiber, E.
In The Faery Reel; tales from the Twilight Realm **S C**

Screen plays *See* Motion picture plays

The **Screwtape** letters. Lewis, C. S. **248**

Scribner American civilization series
Encyclopedia of recreation and leisure in America **790**

The **Scribner** encyclopedia of American lives **920.003**

Scribner science reference series
Life sciences before the twentieth century **920.003**
Life sciences in the twentieth century **920.003**

The Renaissance and the scientific revolution **920.003**

Scribner turning points library [series]
Tobacco in history and culture **394.1**

The **Scrowrers.** Doyle, Sir A. C.
In Doyle, Sir A. C. The complete Sherlock Holmes **S C**

The **sea** and little fishes. Pratchett, T.
In Legends: short novels by the masters of modern fantasy p91-138 **S C**

Sea animals *See* Marine animals

The **sea** change. Hemingway, E.
In Hemingway, E. The complete short stories of Ernest Hemingway; the Finca Vigía edition p302-05 **S C**

Sea changes. Duder, T.
In Ultimate sports; short stories by outstanding writers for young adults p252-72 **S C**

The **sea-king's** son. McKinley, R.
In McKinley, R. and Dickinson, P. Water: tales of elemental spirits p30-77 **S C**

Sea legs. Crane, K. **92**

Sea life *See* Seafaring life

Sea lions *See* Seals (Animals)

Sea monsters
Marven, N. Chased by sea monsters **560**

Sea Oak. Saunders, G.
In Feeling very strange; the Slipstream anthology **S C**

Sea serpent. Dickinson, P.
In McKinley, R. and Dickinson, P. Water: tales of elemental spirits p78-118 **S C**

The **sea** shell. Bradbury, R.
In Bradbury, R. Bradbury stories; 100 of his most celebrated tales **S C**

Sea stories
Forester, C. S. Beat to quarters **Fic**
Melville, H. Billy Budd, sailor **Fic**
Melville, H. Moby-Dick; or, The whale **Fic**
Nordhoff, C. Mutiny on the Bounty **Fic**
Poe, E. A. Narrative of A. Gordon Pym
In Poe, E. A. The collected tales and poems of Edgar Allan Poe **818**
Rees, C. Pirates! **Fic**
Verne, J. Twenty thousand leagues under the sea **Fic**

Sea turtles
Davidson, O. G. Fire in the turtle house **597.92**
Ripple, J. Sea turtles **597.92**
Spotila, J. R. Sea turtles **597.92**

A **sea** worry. Kingston, M. H.
In American dragons: twenty-five Asian American voices p112-17 **810.8**

Seabiscuit (Race horse)
Hillenbrand, L. Seabiscuit **798.4**

Seafaring life
Fiction
Meyer, L. A. Bloody Jack **Fic**

Self-realization

See also Success

Self-reliance

See also Survival skills

Self-respect *See* Self-esteem

Selina Sedilia. Harte, B.

In The Oxford book of gothic tales p158-64
S C

Selkirk, Alexander, 1676-1721

About

Souhami, D. Selkirk's Island   **996**

Selkirk's Island. Souhami, D.   **996**

Selvadurai, Shyam, 1965-

Swimming in the monsoon sea   **Fic**

Selznick, Brian

(jt. auth) Levithan, D. Marly's ghost   **Fic**

Semantics

Hayakawa, S. I. Language in thought and action
412

Seminary boy. Cornwell, J.   **92**

Semiotics

See also Semantics

Semmelweis, Ignác Fülöp, 1818-1865

See/See also pages in the following book(s):
Hellman, H. Great feuds in medicine   **610.9**

Seneca, Lucius Annaeus, the Younger, 4 B.C.-65 A.D.

Medea

In The Portable Roman reader p487-527
870.8

Senior citizens *See* Elderly

Senna, Danzy

Caucasia   **Fic**

Sensational scenes for teens. Stevens, C.
808.82

Sense and sensibility. Austen, J.   **Fic**

Sense of humor. Runyon, D.

In The Best American mystery stories of the
century p204-211   **S C**

A **sense** of shelter. Updike, J.

In Updike, J. Pigeon feathers, and other stories p83-101   **S C**

A **sense** of the world [biography of James Holman] Roberts, J.   **92**

Senses and sensation

See also Pain

McDowell, J. The nervous system and sense organs   **612.8**

The **sentinel**. Clarke, A. C.

In Adaptations: from short story to big screen; 35 great stories that have inspired great films   **S C**

In Clarke, A. C. The collected stories of Arthur C. Clarke   **S C**

A **separate** peace. Knowles, J.   **Fic**

September 11, 2001. Hampton, W.   **973.931**

September 11 terrorist attacks, 2001

See also World Trade Center terrorist attack, 2001

911: the book of help   **810.8**

America under attack: primary sources
973.931

At ground zero   **974.7**

Bernstein, R. Out of the blue   **973.931**

The Day our world changed   **973.931**

Didion, J. Fixed ideas: America since 9.11
320.5

Dwyer, J. 102 minutes   **974.7**

Friedman, T. L. Longitudes and attitudes
973.931

Hampton, W. September 11, 2001   **973.931**

A Just response   **973.931**

National Commission on Terrorist Attacks Upon the United States. The 9/11 Commission report   **973.931**

Nguyen, T. We are all suspects now   **323.1**

See/See also pages in the following book(s):
Does the world hate the United States?
973.931

Fiction

Foer, J. S. Extremely loud & incredibly close
Fic

Herrera, J. F. Cinnamon girl   **Fic**

Stine, C. Refugees   **Fic**

Graphic novels

Jacobson, S. The 9/11 report   **973.931**

Spiegelman, A. In the shadow of no towers
973.931

Serafin, Steven

(ed) The Continuum encyclopedia of British literature. See The Continuum encyclopedia of British literature   **820.3**

Seraph on the Suwanee. Hurston, Z. N.

In Hurston, Z. N. Novels and stories p597-920   **Fic**

Seraw, Mulugeta

About

Langer, E. A hundred little Hitlers   **305.8**

Serbs

Judah, T. The Serbs   **949.6**

Serenade: a Spellsinger story. Foster, A. D.

In Masters of fantasy   **S C**

Sergeant Chip. Denton, B.

In The Year's best science fiction and fantasy for teens: first annual collection   **S C**

Sergeant Houck. Schaefer, J. W.

In A Century of great Western stories
S C

Serial publications

See also Newspapers

Series on law, politics, and society

Bok, C. A recent history of the United States in political cartoons   **973.92**

Sermons

American sermons   **252**

King, M. L., Jr. Strength to love   **252**

The **Serpent** and the grape-grower's daughter

In Hearne, B. G. Beauties and beasts p56-59
398.2

Serpent's rock. Gilman, L. A.

In Young warriors; stories of strength   **S C**

The **serpent's** shadow. Lackey, M.   **Fic**

Serpents' teeth. Robinson, S.
    In New skies: an anthology of today's science
      fiction   **S C**

Serradell, Joaquima
    SARS   **616.2**

Servants *See* Household employees

Service, Pamela F.
    Lioness
    In Young warriors; stories of strength   **S C**
    See/See also pages in the following book(s):
    Reid, S. E. Presenting young adult science fic-
      tion   **813.009**

Service stations
            Fiction
    Weaver, W. Full service   **Fic**

Serving homeschooled teens and their parents.
    Lerch, M. T.   **027.6**

Serving older teens   **027.62**

Serving teens through readers' advisory. Booth, H.
            028.5

Servitude *See* Slavery

Setaro, John F.
    (jt. auth) Hyde, M. O. Drugs 101   **362.29**
    (jt. auth) Hyde, M. O. Medicine's brave new
      world   **610**
    (jt. auth) Hyde, M. O. Smoking 101   **616.86**

Setterfield, Diane
    The thirteenth tale   **Fic**

The **setting** sun and the rolling world. Mungoshi,
    C.
    In Leaving home: stories p157-64   **808.8**

Setzer, Paul M.
    (il) Costello, E. Random House American sign
      language dictionary   **419**

Seven famous Greek plays   **882.008**

The **seven** sins of memory. Schacter, D. L.
            153.1

Seven types of ambiguity. Jackson, S.
    In Jackson, S. The lottery; or, The adventures
      of James Harris   **S C**

The **seven** vagabonds. Hawthorne, N.
    In Hawthorne, N. Tales and sketches, includ-
      ing Twice-told tales, Mosses from an old
      manse, and The snow-image; A wonder
      book for girls and boys; Tanglewood
      tales for girls and boys, being a second
      Wonder book p139-55   **S C**

Seventeen syllables. Yamamoto, H.
    In The Oxford book of women's writing in
      the United States p83-94   **810.8**

Seventeenth century *See* World history—17th
    century

The **seventh** shrine. Silverberg, R.
    In Legends: short novels by the masters of
      modern fantasy p255-332   **S C**

Seventh son. Card, O. S.   **Fic**

The **seventh** veil. Hurston, Z. N.
    In Hurston, Z. N. The complete stories p242-
      60   **S C**

The **seventy** architectural wonders of our world.
    See The Seventy wonders of the modern
    world   **720.9**

Seventy-five dollars. Hughes, L.
    In Hughes, L. Short stories of Langston
      Hughes   **S C**

The **Seventy** great inventions of the ancient world
            609

The **Seventy** wonders of the modern world
            720.9

Sevenwaters trilogy [series]
    Marillier, J. Daughter of the forest   **Fic**

Severe acute respiratory syndrome *See* SARS
    (Disease)

Sewerage
    See/See also pages in the following book(s):
    Macaulay, D. Underground   **624**

Sewing
    The complete book of sewing   **646.2**
    The complete photo guide to sewing   **646.2**
    Holkeboer, K. S. Patterns for theatrical costumes
            646.4

Sex *See* Sexual behavior

Sex (Biology)
    See also Reproductive system

Sex bias *See* Sexism

Sex change *See* Transsexualism

Sex crimes
    See also Child sexual abuse
    Fodor, M. D. Megan's law   **362.7**
    Sexual violence: opposing viewpoints   **364.1**

Sex discrimination
    See/See also pages in the following book(s):
    Sports and athletes: opposing viewpoints
            796

Sex education
    Bell, R. Changing bodies, changing lives
            613.9
    Brynie, F. H. 101 questions about reproduction
            612.6
    Brynie, F. H. 101 questions about sex and sexu-
      ality—   **613.9**
    Jukes, M. It's a girl thing   **305.23**
    Pardes, B. Doing it right   **613.9**
    Sex education   **613.9**
    Sexual health information for teens   **613.9**
    Teenage pregnancy and parenting   **306.8**
    Teenage sexuality: opposing viewpoints
            613.9
    See/See also pages in the following book(s):
    Teen sex   **306.7**

Sex education   **613.9**

Sex: opposing viewpoints   **306.7**

Sex organs *See* Reproductive system

Sex role
    The Full spectrum   **306.76**
    Male/female roles: opposing viewpoints
            305.3
    Wolf, N. The beauty myth   **305.4**
            Fiction
    Gray, D. E. Together apart   **Fic**
    Hoffman, A. The foretelling   **Fic**
    Hopkins, E. Burned   **Fic**
    Huser, G. Stitches   **Fic**
    Lavender, W. Aftershocks   **Fic**
    Meyer, L. A. Bloody Jack   **Fic**

Silverstein, Ken

The radioactive boy scout [biography of David Hahn] **92**

Silverstein, Shel

Where the sidewalk ends **811**

Silverstein, Virginia B.

(jt. auth) Silverstein, A. Cancer **616.99**

(jt. auth) Silverstein, A. Parkinson's disease **616.8**

(jt. auth) Silverstein, A. Polio **616.8**

Silvey, Anita

500 great books for teens **028.5**

Simak, Clifford D., 1904-1988

Over the river and through the woods

In The Norton book of science fiction; North American science fiction, 1960-1990 p125-32 **S C**

Simmons, Dan

Ilium **Fic**

Simmons, Michael

Finding Lubchenko **Fic**

Vandal **Fic**

Simner, Janni Lee

Stone tower

In Gothic!; ten original dark tales **S C**

Simon, Beth

About

Simon, R. Riding the bus with my sister **92**

Simon, Lizzie

Detour **92**

Simon, Neil

Barefoot in the park

In Simon, N. The collected plays of Neil Simon **812**

Biloxi blues

In Simon, N. The collected plays of Neil Simon **812**

Brighton Beach memoirs **812**

also in Simon, N. The collected plays of Neil Simon **812**

Broadway bound

In Simon, N. The collected plays of Neil Simon **812**

California suite

In Simon, N. The collected plays of Neil Simon **812**

Chapter two

In Simon, N. The collected plays of Neil Simon **812**

The collected plays of Neil Simon **812**

Come blow your horn

In Simon, N. The collected plays of Neil Simon **812**

Fools

In Simon, N. The collected plays of Neil Simon **812**

The gingerbread lady

In Simon, N. The collected plays of Neil Simon **812**

God's favorite

In Simon, N. The collected plays of Neil Simon **812**

The good doctor

In Simon, N. The collected plays of Neil Simon **812**

I ought to be in pictures

In Simon, N. The collected plays of Neil Simon **812**

Jake's women

In Simon, N. The collected plays of Neil Simon **812**

Last of the red hot lovers

In Simon, N. The collected plays of Neil Simon **812**

Laughter on the 23rd floor

In Simon, N. The collected plays of Neil Simon **812**

Little me

In Simon, N. The collected plays of Neil Simon **812**

London suite

In Simon, N. The collected plays of Neil Simon **812**

Lost in Yonkers **812**

also in Simon, N. The collected plays of Neil Simon **812**

The odd couple

In Simon, N. The collected plays of Neil Simon **812**

Odd couple (female version)

In Simon, N. The collected plays of Neil Simon **812**

Plaza suite

In Simon, N. The collected plays of Neil Simon **812**

The prisoner of Second Avenue

In Simon, N. The collected plays of Neil Simon **812**

Promises, promises

In Simon, N. The collected plays of Neil Simon **812**

Rumors

In Simon, N. The collected plays of Neil Simon **812**

The star-spangled girl

In Simon, N. The collected plays of Neil Simon **812**

The Sunshine Boys

In Simon, N. The collected plays of Neil Simon **812**

Sweet Charity

In Simon, N. The collected plays of Neil Simon **812**

They're playing our song

In Simon, N. The collected plays of Neil Simon **812**

Simon, Rachel, 1959-

Riding the bus with my sister **92**

Simon and Schuster's guide to insects. Arnett, R. H., Jr. **595.7**

Simonis, Doris A.

(ed) Scientists, mathematicians, and inventors. See Scientists, mathematicians, and inventors **920.003**

Simple courage. Delaney, F. **910.4**

A **simple** enquiry. Hemingway, E.

In Hemingway, E. The complete short stories of Ernest Hemingway; the Finca Vigía edition p250-52 **S C**

Simply heavenly. Hughes, L.
   In Hughes, L. Five plays p113-81   **812**

Simply super paper. Foose, S. L.   **745.54**

Simpson, Carol Mann, 1949-
   Copyright catechism   **346.04**
   Copyright for schools   **346.04**
   Internet for schools   **004.6**

Simpson, Colton
   Inside the Crips   **92**

Simpson, D. P.
   Cassell's Latin dictionary. See Cassell's Latin
   dictionary   **473**

Simpson, Martha Seif, 1954-
   Reading programs for young adults   **027.62**

Simpson, William Kelly
   (ed) The Literature of ancient Egypt. See The
   Literature of ancient Egypt   **890**

Sinclair, April
   Coffee will make you black   **Fic**

Sinclair, Bertha Muzzy *See* Bower, B. M., 1871-
1940

Sinclair, Upton, 1878-1968
   The jungle   **Fic**
   The jungle; adaptation. See Kuper, P. The jun-
   gle   **741.5**

Singer, Bennett L.
   (ed) Growing up gay. See Growing up gay
       808.8

Singer, Beverly R.
   (ed) Rising voices. See Rising voices   **810.8**

Singer, Isaac Bashevis, 1904-1991
   The collected stories of Isaac Bashevis Singer
       S C

   Contents: Gimpel the fool; The gentleman from Cracow; Joy;
The little shoemakers; The unseen; The Spinoza of Market Street;
The destruction of Kreshev; Taibele and her demon; Alone; Yentl
the yeshiva boy; Zeidlus the Pope; The last demon; Short Friday;
The séance; The slaughterer; The dead fiddler; Henne Fire; The
letter writer; A friend of Kafka; The cafeteria; The joke; Powers;
Something is there; A crown of feathers; A day in Coney Island;
The cabalist of East Broadway; A quotation from Klopstock; A
dance and a hop; Grandfather and grandson; Old love; The admirer; The yearning heifer; A tale of two sisters; Three encounters; Passions; Brother Beetle; The betrayer of Israel; The psychic
journey; The manuscript; The power of darkness; The bus; A
night in the poorhouse; Escape from civilization; Vanvild Kava;
The reencounter; Neighbors; Moon and madness

   A crown of feathers
      In The Literary ghost; great contemporary
      ghost stories p342-65   **S C**
   Gimpel the fool
      In The Norton book of American short stories
      p394-406   **S C**

Singer, Marilyn, 1948-
   Bedhead red, peekaboo pink
      In Make me over; 11 stories of transformation
         S C
   Negress
      In Face relations; 11 stories about seeing be-
      yond color   **S C**
   Shattered
      In Shattered: stories of children and war p14-
      22   **S C**
   Word of the day
      In Twice told; original stories inspired by
      original art   **S C**
   (ed) Face relations. See Face relations   **S C**

   (ed) Make me over. See Make me over   **S C**

Singer, Ronald
   (ed) Encyclopedia of paleontology. See Encyclopedia of paleontology   **560**

Singer. Thesman, J.   **Fic**

Singer in the snow. Marley, L.   **Fic**

The **singer** of all songs. Constable, K.   **Fic**

Singer of souls. Stemple, A.   **Fic**

Singers
    See also African American singers
   Partridge, E. This land was made for you and
    me: the life and songs of Woody Guthrie
       92
   Talamon, B. Bob Marley   **92**

Singh, Patwant, 1925-
   The Sikhs   **954**

Singh, Simon
   The code book   **652**

Singing
           Fiction
   Levine, G. C. Fairest   **Fic**

Singing apples. Kadohata, C.
   In American eyes; new Asian-American short
    stories for young adults   **S C**

The **singing** bell. Asimov, I.
   In Asimov, I. The complete stories p175-88
       S C

Singing my sister down. Lanagan, M.
   In Lanagan, M. Black juice   **S C**

The **Singing,** soaring lark
   In Hearne, B. G. Beauties and beasts p60-65
       398.2

Singing to Cuba [excerpt] Engle, M.
   In Latina: women's voices from the border-
    lands p222-27   **810.8**

Single parent family
    See also Children of divorced parents; Un-
    married mothers
   Schultz, M. A. Teens with single parents
       306.8
           Fiction
   Herrick, S. By the river   **Fic**
   Moriarty, L. The center of everything   **Fic**

Singleton, Carl
   (ed) The Sixties in America. See The Sixties in
   America   **973.92**

Singman, Jeffrey L.
   Daily life in Chaucer's England   **942.03**
   Daily life in Elizabethan England   **942.05**
   Daily life in medieval Europe   **940.1**

A **singular** hostage. Ali, T.   **Fic**

Siniavskiĭ, Andrei *See* Sinyavsky, Andrei, 1925-
1997

Sinkhole. Cail, C.
   In Alfred Hitchcock's mystery magazine pres-
    ents fifty years of crime and suspense
       S C

Sinkler, Adrian
   Iraq   **956.7**
   Pakistan   **954.91**

Sinners. O'Faoláin, S.
In The Oxford book of short stories p362-70
    S C

Sinte-galeshka *See* Spotted Tail, Brulé Sioux Chief, 1823-1881

Sinyavsky, Andrei, 1925-1997
Pkhentz
In The portable twentieth-century Russian reader   **891.7**

Siouan Indians
    See also Dakota Indians; Oglala Indians

Sioux Indians *See* Dakota Indians

Sir Bertrand. Barbauld, A. L. A.
In The Oxford book of gothic tales p3-6
    S C

Sir Gawain and the Green Knight. Gawain and the Grene Knight (Middle English poem)   **821**
also in The Oxford anthology of English literature   **820.8**

Sir Gawain and the loathly lady
In Hearne, B. G. Beauties and beasts p131-38
    398.2

Sir Rabbit. Welty, E.
In Welty, E. The collected stories of Eudora Welty p331-41   **S C**

Sir Walter Ralegh and the quest for El Dorado. Aronson, M.   **92**

Sir William Pepperell. Hawthorne, N.
In Hawthorne, N. Tales and sketches, including Twice-told tales, Mosses from an old manse, and The snow-image; A wonder book for girls and boys; Tanglewood tales for girls and boys, being a second Wonder book p166-73   **S C**

Sir William Phips. Hawthorne, N.
In Hawthorne, N. Tales and sketches, including Twice-told tales, Mosses from an old manse, and The snow-image; A wonder book for girls and boys; Tanglewood tales for girls and boys, being a second Wonder book p12-17   **S C**

Sirimarco, Elizabeth, 1966-
American voices from The Cold War   **973.92**

'SiseneG'. Clarke, A. C.
In Clarke, A. C. The collected stories of Arthur C. Clarke   **S C**

Siskiyou Sloan and the eye of the giraffe. Howe, N.
In Necessary noise: stories about our families as they really are p23-48   **S C**

Sister Ann of the Cornfields. Kinsella, W. P.
In Kinsella, W. P. Shoeless Joe Jackson comes to Iowa: stories   **S C**

Sister in the Band of Brothers. Skiba, K. M.
    956.7

Sister to sister   **810.8**

Sister Wendy's 1000 masterpieces. Beckett, W.
    759

The **sister** years. Hawthorne, N.
In Hawthorne, N. Tales and sketches, including Twice-told tales, Mosses from an old manse, and The snow-image; A wonder book for girls and boys; Tanglewood tales for girls and boys, being a second Wonder book p678-84   **S C**

The **sisterhood** of the traveling pants. Brashares, A.   **Fic**

Sisterland. Newbery, L.   **Fic**

Sisters
Fiction
Beard, P. Dear Zoe   **Fic**
Freymann-Weyr, G. Stay with me   **Fic**
Frost, H. The braid   **Fic**
Griffin, A. Where I want to be   **Fic**
Grindle, L. The nightspinners   **Fic**
Kaslik, I. Skinny   **Fic**
Lansens, L. The girls   **Fic**
McDonald, J. Twists and turns   **Fic**
McGhee, A. All rivers flow to the sea   **Fic**
Na, A. Wait for me   **Fic**
Picoult, J. My sister's keeper   **Fic**
Sloan, K. The patron saint of red Chevies   **Fic**
Tiernan, C. A chalice of wind Book 1   **Fic**
Walker, A. The color purple   **Fic**
Graphic novels
Nowak, N. Unholy kinship   **741.5**

Sisters. Bear, G.
In Bear, G. The collected stories of Greg Bear   **S C**

The **sisters**. Joyce, J.
In Joyce, J. Dubliners   **S C**

Sisters and brothers *See* Siblings

Sitkoff, Harvard
Postwar America   **973.92**

Sitomer, Alan Lawrence
Hip-hop high school   **Fic**
The Hoopster   **Fic**

Sittenfeld, Curtis
Prep   **Fic**

Sitting Bull, Dakota Chief, 1831-1890
See/See also pages in the following book(s):
Freedman, R. Indian chiefs   **920**

Sivananda Yoga Vedanta Center (London, England)
Yoga, mind & body. See Yoga, mind & body
    294.5

Six American poets   **811.008**

Six days in October. Blumenthal, K.   **332.6**

Six easy pieces. Feynman, R. P.   **530**

Six great ideas. Adler, M. J.   **111**

Six modern plagues and how we are causing them. Walters, M. J.   **614.4**

Six of one—. Fitzgerald, F. S.
In Fitzgerald, F. S. The short stories of F. Scott Fitzgerald; a new collection p667-79   **S C**

Six questions of Socrates. Phillips, C.   **179**

Six wives: the queens of Henry VIII. Starkey, D.
    920

Sixteen: short stories by outstanding writers for young adults **S C**

Sixteen: stories about that sweet and bitter birthday **S C**

Sixteenth century *See* World history—16th century

The **sixth** extinction. Leakey, R. E. **304.2**

Sixties counterculture **973.92**

The **Sixties** in America **973.92**

The **sixties** in America. Almanac. Pendergast, T. **973.923**

The **sixties** in America. Biographies. Pendergast, T. **920**

Sixties in America. Primary sources. Pendergast, T. **973.923**

Sixty odd. Le Guin, U. K. **811**

Siy, Alexandra
New town
In What a song can do; 12 riffs on the power of music **S C**

Size
Fiction
Auseon, A. Funny little monkey **Fic**

Size and shape *See* Size

Sizer, Paul
Moped army, Vol. 1 **741.5**

Sizzling summer reading programs for young adults. Kan, K. **027.62**

Skaggs, Gayle, 1952-
Off the wall! **027.8**

Skaggs, Peggy
Kate Chopin **813.009**

Skancke, Jennifer
(ed) Alternatives to prisons. See Alternatives to prisons **364**

Skateboarding
Jay, J. Skateboarding basics **796.22**
Fiction
Nelson, B. Paranoid Park **Fic**

Skateboarding basics. Jay, J. **796.22**

Skating *See* Ice skating

The **skeletal** system. Kelly, E. B. **612.7**

Skeleton
Kelly, E. B. The skeletal system **612.7**

Skeleton crew. King, S. **S C**

Skellig. Almond, D. **Fic**

Skelton, Debra
Empire of Alexander the Great **930**

Skelton, Renee
Forecast Earth [biography of Inez Fung] **92**

Skepticism
See also Belief and doubt

Sketches from memory. Hawthorne, N.
In Hawthorne, N. Tales and sketches, including Twice-told tales, Mosses from an old manse, and The snow-image; A wonder book for girls and boys; Tanglewood tales for girls and boys, being a second Wonder book p338-51 **S C**

Skiba, Katherine M.
Sister in the Band of Brothers **956.7**

Skiing
Cazeneuve, B. Cross-country skiing **796.93**

Skills, Life *See* Life skills

The **skills** to pay the bills. Light, A. **920**

Skin
Light, D. B. Cells, tissues, and skin **611**
Care
Brown, B. Bobbi Brown teenage beauty **646.7**
Encyclopedias
Turkington, C. The encyclopedia of skin and skin disorders **616.5**

Skin. Dahl, R.
In Dahl, R. Skin and other stories **S C**

Skin. Vrettos, A. M. **Fic**

Skin and bones. Duffield, N.
In International plays for young audiences; contemporary works from leading playwrights p45-69 **808.82**

Skin and other stories. Dahl, R. **S C**

The **skin** between us. Ragusa, K. **92**

Skin deep. See Turkington, C. The encyclopedia of skin and skin disorders **616.5**

The **skin** of our teeth. Wilder, T.
In Wilder, T. Three plays: Our town, The skin of our teeth, The matchmaker; with a preface **812**

Skinheads *See* White supremacy movements

Skinner, B. F. (Burrhus Frederic), 1904-1990
About behaviorism **150.19**

Skinner, Brian J., 1928-
(ed) The Oxford companion to the earth. See The Oxford companion to the earth **550.3**

Skinner, Burrhus Frederic *See* Skinner, B. F. (Burrhus Frederic), 1904-1990

Skinny. Kaslik, I. **Fic**

Skins. Bruchac, J.
In Face relations; 11 stories about seeing beyond color **S C**

Skipp, Francis E.
The complete short stories of Thomas Wolfe **S C**
Contents: An angel on the porch; The train and the city; Death the proud brother; No door; The four lost men; Boom town; The sun and the rain; The house of the far and lost; Dark in the forest, strange as time; For professional appearance; The names of the nation; One of the girls in our party; Circus at dawn; His father's earth; Old Catawba; Arnold Pentland; The face of the war; Gulliver, the story of a tall man; In the park; Only the dead know Brooklyn; Polyphemus; The far and the near; The bums at sunset; The bell remembered; Fame and the poet; Return; Mr. Malone; Oktoberfest; 'E: a recollection; April, late April; The child by tiger; Katamoto; The lost boy; Chickamauga; The company; A prologue to America; Portrait of a literary critic; The birthday; A note on experts: Dexter Vespasian Joyner; Three o'clock; The winter of our discontent; The dark Messiah; The hollyhock sowers; Nebraska Crane; So this is man; The promise of America; The hollow men; The anatomy of loneliness; The lion at morning; The plumed knight; The newspaper; No cure for it; On leprechauns; The return of the prodigal; Old Man Rivers; Justice is blind; No more rivers; The Spanish letter

Skis and skiing *See* Skiing

Sklar, Robert
A world history of film **791.43**

Snow. Alvarez, J.
In Latina: women's voices from the borderlands p127-28 **810.8**

Snow. Crowley, J.
In Best of the best: 20 years of the Year's
best science fiction **S C**
In The Norton book of science fiction; North
American science fiction, 1960-1990
p591-604 **S C**

Snow. Winston, S.
In Face relations; 11 stories about seeing beyond color **S C**

Snow apples. Razzell, M. **Fic**

Snow falling on cedars. Guterson, D. **Fic**

Snow-flakes. Hawthorne, N.
In Hawthorne, N. Tales and sketches, including Twice-told tales, Mosses from an old
manse, and The snow-image; A wonder
book for girls and boys; Tanglewood
tales for girls and boys, being a second
Wonder book p593-97 **S C**

The **snow-image**. Hawthorne, N.
In Hawthorne, N. Tales and sketches, including Twice-told tales, Mosses from an old
manse, and The snow-image; A wonder
book for girls and boys; Tanglewood
tales for girls and boys, being a second
Wonder book p1087-1102 **S C**

Snow in August. Hamill, P. **Fic**

Snow Mountain passage. Houston, J. D. **Fic**

The **snow** queen. McKillip, P. A.
In McKillip, P. A. Harrowing the dragon
S C

Snowboard!. Masoff, J. **796.93**

Snowboarding
Kleh, C. Snowboarding skills **796.93**
Masoff, J. Snowboard! **796.93**

Snowboarding skills. Kleh, C. **796.93**

Snowbound. Lowry, L.
In Necessary noise: stories about our families
as they really are p219-38 **S C**

The **snows** of Kilimanjaro. Hemingway, E.
In Hemingway, E. The complete short stories
of Ernest Hemingway; the Finca Vigía
edition p39-56 **S C**

Snowstruck. Fredston, J. A. **551.3**

Snyder, Carrie L.
(ed) Euthanasia: opposing viewpoints. See Euthanasia: opposing viewpoints **179.7**

Snyder, James
Art of the Middle Ages **709.02**

Snyder, Midori, 1954-
Charlie's away
In The Green Man: tales from the mythic for-
est p137-65 **808.8**

So I ain't no good girl. Flake, S. G.
In Flake, S. G. Who am I without him?; short
stories about girls and the boys in their
lives p1-9 **S C**

So this is man. Wolfe, T.
In Wolfe, T. The complete short stories of
Thomas Wolfe p478-81 **S C**

So yesterday. Westerfeld, S. **Fic**

So you want to join the Peace Corps. Banerjee, D.
361.6

So you want to write. Piercy, M. **808.3**

Soanes, Catherine
(ed) Concise Oxford English dictionary. See
Concise Oxford English dictionary **423**

Sobel, Dava
Longitude **526**
The Planets **523.2**

Sobey, Ed
How to build your own prize-winning robot
629.8

Soccer
Buxton, T. Soccer skills for young players
796.334
Longman, J. The girls of summer **796.334**
Luongo, A. M. Soccer drills **796.334**
Luxbacher, J. Soccer: steps to success
796.334
Fiction
Klass, D. Home of the Braves **Fic**
Peet, M. Keeper **Fic**
Graphic novels
Hage, A. Gothic sports, Vol. 1 **741.5**

Soccer drills. Luongo, A. M. **796.334**

Soccer skills for young players. Buxton, T.
796.334

Social action
Halpin, M. It's your world—if you don't like it,
change it **361.2**

Social anthropology *See* Ethnology

Social behavior *See* Human behavior

Social change
Diamond, J. M. Collapse: how societies choose
to fail or succeed **304.2**
Diamond, J. M. Guns, germs, and steel
303.4
Fischer, C. S. Century of difference **306**
Wade, N. Before the dawn **599.93**

Social classes
See also Working class
Fiction
Hosseini, K. The kite runner **Fic**

Social conflict
See also Conflict management

Social contract **320.1**

The **social** contract. Rousseau, J.-J.
In Social contract; essays by Locke, Hume,
and Rousseau p167-307 **320.1**

Social customs *See* Manners and customs

Social democracy *See* Socialism

Social drinking *See* Drinking of alcoholic beverages

Social equality *See* Equality

Social ethics
See also Bioethics
Callahan, D. The cheating culture **174**

Social intelligence. Goleman, D. **158**

Social issues firsthand [series]
Adoption **362.7**
Poverty **362.5**
Terrorism **303.6**

Solvent abuse
Menhard, F. R. The facts about inhalants
362.29

Solzhenitsyn, Aleksandr, 1918-
Matryona's home
In The portable twentieth-century Russian reader **891.7**
One day in the life of Ivan Denisovich **Fic**
See/See also pages in the following book(s):
Aikman, D. Great souls **920**

Some learned fables for good old boys and girls. Twain, M.
In Twain, M. The complete short stories of Mark Twain; now collected for the first time **S C**

Some people call me Maurice. Sweeney, J.
In Make me over; 11 stories of transformation **S C**

Some talk of Alexander. Coppard, A. E.
In The Oxford book of English short stories p180-87 **S C**

Some words with a Mummy. Poe, E. A.
In Poe, E. A. The collected tales and poems of Edgar Allan Poe p535-48 **818**

Somebody's boyfriend. Winter, L.
In Not the only one; lesbian and gay fiction for teens **S C**

Someday. Asimov, I.
In Asimov, I. The complete stories p138-45 **S C**

Somehow tenderness survives **S C**

Somers, Jane *See* Lessing, Doris May, 1919-

Somerset Fry, Peter *See* Somerset Fry, Plantagenet, 1931-

Somerset Fry, Plantagenet, 1931-
The Dorling Kindersley history of the world **909**

Somervill, Barbara A., 1948-
Empire of the Inca **985**
Michelangelo **92**

Somerville, Edith Anna Œnone, 1858-1949
Philippa's fox-hunt
In The Oxford book of Irish short stories p157-71 **S C**

Something in common. Hughes, L.
In Hughes, L. Short stories of Langston Hughes **S C**

Something old, something new. Sweeney, J.
In Destination unexpected: short stories **S C**

Something out of nothing [biography of Marie Curie] McClafferty, C. K. **92**

Something permanent. Rylant, C. **811**

Something wicked this way comes. Bradbury, R. **Fic**

Sometimes they come back. King, S.
In King, S. Night shift **S C**

Sometimes you talk about Idaho. Houston, P.
In Gotham Writers' Workshop fiction gallery; exceptional short stories selected by New York's acclaimed creative writing school **S C**

Somewhere in my mind there is a painting box. De Lint, C.
In The Green Man: tales from the mythic forest p51-83 **808.8**

Sommer, Elyse
(ed) Metaphors dictionary. See Metaphors dictionary **423**

Son of the mob. Korman, G. **Fic**

Sonata for harp and bicycle. Aiken, J.
In Nightshade: 20th century ghost stories p7-16 **S C**

Sones, Sonya
Cat got your tongue?
In Sixteen: stories about that sweet and bitter birthday **S C**
Dr. Jekyll and Sister Hyde
In Necessary noise: stories about our families as they really are p173-216 **S C**
One of those hideous books where the mother dies **Fic**

The **song** of one or the journey of Ti Marie. Hippolyte, K.
In International plays for young audiences; contemporary works from leading playwrights p173-226 **808.82**

The **song** of Roland. Chanson de Roland **841**

The **song** of stones river. Armstrong, J.
In What a song can do; 12 riffs on the power of music **S C**

Songbird journeys. Chu, M. **598**

Songcatchers. Hart, M. **780.9**

Songhai Empire
Conrad, D. C. Empires of medieval West Africa **966**

Songs
See also National songs; Popular music

Songs, American *See* American songs

Songs from this Earth on turtle's back **811.008**

The **songs** of distant Earth. Clarke, A. C.
In Clarke, A. C. The collected stories of Arthur C. Clarke **S C**

Songs of innocence and experience. Blake, W.
In Blake, W. The portable Blake **828**

Songwriters *See* Composers; Lyricists

Songwriter's market 2007 **782.42**

Sonneborn, Liz
Chronology of American Indian history **970.004**
Miranda v. Arizona **345**

Sonnenblick, Jordan
Notes from the midnight driver **Fic**

The **sonnets.** Shakespeare, W. **821**

Sonnets from the Portuguese. Browning, E. B. **821**

Sonny's blues. Baldwin, J.
In American short story masterpieces **S C**

Sonny's war. Hobbs, V. **Fic**

Sons and fathers *See* Father-son relationship

Sons and lovers. Lawrence, D. H. **Fic**

South Carolina—Fiction—*Continued*

Conroy, P. The prince of tides **Fic**

Kidd, S. M. The secret life of bees **Fic**

South Korea *See* Korea (South)

The **South** Pacific. Michener, J. A.

In Michener, J. A. Tales of the South Pacific
S C

South Pacific Region *See* Oceania

South Pole

See also Antarctica

Solomon, S. The coldest March **998**

South Sea Islands *See* Oceania

South Seas *See* Oceania

South Vista Education Center (Richfield, Minn.)

Daycare and diplomas **306.8**

Southeast Asia

Phillips, D. A. Southeast Asia **959**

Southeast Asia **959**

Graphic novels

Neufeld, J. A few perfect hours and other stories from Southeast Asia and Central Europe
910

Southeast Asia **959**

Southern, Eileen

The music of black Americans **780.89**

Southern Africa

Women writing Africa: the southern region
896

Southern Rhodesia *See* Zimbabwe

Southern States

Economic conditions

See/See also pages in the following book(s):

The Causes of the Civil War **973.7**

Fiction

Faulkner, W. Light in August **Fic**

Gibbons, K. Ellen Foster **Fic**

McCullers, C. The heart is a lonely hunter
Fic

Walker, A. The color purple **Fic**

Folklore

See Folklore—Southern States

Intellectual life

The Companion to southern literature **810.3**

Race relations

Remembering Jim Crow **305.8**

Southgate, Martha

The fall of Rome **Fic**

Southwest Pacific Region *See* Oceania

Souvenir. Vonnegut, K.

In Vonnegut, K. Bagombo snuff box: uncollected short fiction p89-98 **S C**

Sova, Dawn B.

Banned plays **792.09**

Edgar Allan Poe, A-Z **818**

Sovereigns *See* Kings and rulers; Queens

Soviet Union

See also Russia; Russia (Federation)

Fiction

Solzhenitsyn, A. One day in the life of Ivan Denisovich **Fic**

Foreign relations—United States

Kallen, S. A. Primary sources [American war library, The Cold War] **909.82**

Rice, E. The Cold War **327.47**

Speakman, J. The Cold War **940.55**

Winkler, A. M. The Cold War **909.82**

History

Cunningham, K. Joseph Stalin and the Soviet Union **92**

Eaton, K. B. Daily life in the Soviet Union
947.084

Langley, A. The collapse of the Soviet Union
947.085

Riasanovsky, N. V. A history of Russia **947**

The Rise and fall of the Soviet Union
947.084

History—1917-1921, Revolution

Gottfried, T. The road to Communism **947**

Wade, R. A. The Bolshevik revolution and Russian Civil War **947.084**

Sowell, Sharyn

Paper cutting techniques for scrapbooks & cards
745.54

Space, Outer *See* Outer space

Space. Chaikin, A. **629.4**

Space and time

See also Fourth dimension

Al-Khalili, J. Black holes, wormholes & time machines **530.1**

Bodanis, D. $E=mc^2$ **530.1**

Gott, J. R. Time travel in Einstein's universe
530.1

Hawking, S. W. The nature of space and time
530.1

Fiction

Hoffman, M. Stravaganza: city of masks **Fic**

Jeapes, B. The new world order **Fic**

Larbalestier, J. Magic or madness **Fic**

Lawrence, M. A crack in the line **Fic**

Thompson, K. The new policeman **Fic**

The **Space** between our footsteps **808.81**

Space colonies

Fiction

McDevitt, J. Moonfall **Fic**

Space exploration **333.9**

Space flight

Kranz, E. F. Failure is not an option **629.45**

Space flight to the moon

Pyle, R. Destination moon **629.45**

Space probes

Angelo, J. A. Spacecraft for astronomy **522**

Space sciences

Angelo, J. A. Space technology **629.4**

Cavelos, J. The science of Star Wars **791.43**

Space sciences **500.5**

Encyclopedias

Angelo, J. A. Encyclopedia of space and astronomy **520.3**

Space sciences **500.5**

Space technology. Angelo, J. A. **629.4**

Space Telescope *See* Hubble Space Telescope

Spacecraft for astronomy. Angelo, J. A. **522**

Speech disorders—Fiction—*Continued*
Mitchell, D. Black swan green   **Fic**

The **speech** of Polly Baker. Franklin, B.
In The Norton book of American short stories
p23-25   **S C**

Speech sounds. Butler, O. E.
In The Norton book of science fiction; North
American science fiction, 1960-1990
p513-24   **S C**

Speeches
The Arab-Israeli conflict   **956.04**
Civil rights   **323.1**
Lend me your ears   **808.85**
The Penguin book of twentieth-century speeches
    808.85
UXL Asian American voices   **815.008**

Speeches, addresses, etc., American *See* American speeches

Speed, Lillian Castillo- *See* Castillo-Speed, Lillian, 1949-

Speed (Drug) *See* Methamphetamine

Speight, James G.
(ed) Lange's handbook of chemistry. See
Lange's handbook of chemistry   **540**

Speleology *See* Caves

A **spell** for chameleon.   **Fic**

Spell my name with an S. Asimov, I.
In Asimov, I. The complete stories p277-89
    S C

A **spell** of kona weather. Watanabe, S.
In Coming of age in America; a multicultural
anthology p166-74   **S C**

Spellbound. McDonald, J.   **Fic**

Spellbound: from ancient gods to modern Merlins.
Alexander, D.   **133.4**

Spellenberg, Richard
Familiar flowers of North America: eastern region   **582.13**
Familiar flowers of North America: western region   **582.13**
National Audubon Society field guide to North
American wildflowers, western region
    582.13

Spells *See* Magic

Spence, Eulalie, 1894-1981
Undertow
In Black theatre USA; plays by African
Americans, 1847 to today   **812.008**

Spencer, Elizabeth
Owl
In Nightshade: 20th century ghost stories
p384-87   **S C**

Spencer, Herbert, 1820-1903
See/See also pages in the following book(s):
Durant, W. J. The story of philosophy   **109**

Spencer, Juliet V.
Cervical cancer   **616.99**
Herpes   **616.95**

Spengemann, William C.
(ed) Hawthorne, N. The portable Hawthorne
    818

The **Sphinx**. Poe, E. A.
In Poe, E. A. The collected tales and poems
of Edgar Allan Poe p471-74   **818**

The **Sphinx** without a secret. Wilde, O.
In The Oxford book of Irish short stories
p152-56   **S C**

Spider Woman's granddaughters   **S C**

Spiders
Eisner, T. Secret weapons   **595.7**
The Firefly encyclopedia of insects and spiders
    595.7

Spiders in the hairdo. Holt, D.   **398.2**

Spiegelman, Art
In the shadow of no towers   **973.931**
Maus   **940.53**

Spiegelman, Vladek
About
Spiegelman, A. Maus   **940.53**

Spiegler, Louise
The amethyst road   **Fic**

Spies
Owen, D. Spies: the undercover world of secrets, gadgets and lies   **327.12**
Fiction
Clancy, T. The hunt for Red October   **Fic**
Le Carré, J. The spy who came in from the cold
    Fic
Graphic novels
Miyuki, T. Musashi #9, Vol. 1   **741.5**

Spies in literature
Mystery and suspense writers   **809.3**

Spillebeen, Geert, 1956-
Kipling's choice   **Fic**

Spin. O'Brien, T.
In O'Brien, T. The things they carried; a
work of fiction   **S C**

Spink, Kathryn
Mother Teresa   **92**

Spinoza, Benedictus de, 1632-1677
See/See also pages in the following book(s):
Durant, W. J. The story of philosophy   **109**
Russell, B. A history of Western philosophy
    109

The **spiral** staircase. Armstrong, K.   **92**

Spirit capture   **779**

The **spirit** of Yellowstone. Meyer, J. L.   **978.7**

Spirit seizures. Pritchard, M.
In The Literary ghost; great contemporary
ghost stories p144-55   **S C**

Spiritism *See* Spiritualism

Spirits *See* Angels; Ghosts

Spiritual life
Campbell, J. The power of myth   **201**
Chopra, D. Fire in the heart   **204**

Spiritualism
Fiction
Wittlinger, E. Blind faith   **Fic**

A **spiritualist**. Rhys, J.
In Nightshade: 20th century ghost stories
p380-83   **S C**

Stoff, Laurie
(ed) The Rise and fall of the Soviet Union. See
The Rise and fall of the Soviet Union
947.084

Stoics
See/See also pages in the following book(s):
Russell, B. A history of Western philosophy
109

Stoker, Bram, 1847-1912
Dracula **Fic**

The **stoker**. Kafka, F.
In Kafka, F. The metamorphosis and other
stories p75-116 **S C**

Stokes, Gale
The walls came tumbling down **947**

Stokesbury, James L.
A short history of the American Revolution
973.3
A short history of the Korean War **951.9**
A short history of World War I **940.3**

Stolen childhood. King, W. **326**

Stolen continents. Wright, R. **970.004**

Stolen lives. Oufkir, M. **92**

Stolen voices **920**

The **stolen** White Elephant. Twain, M.
In Twain, M. The complete short stories of
Mark Twain; now collected for the first
time **S C**

Stolley, Richard B.
(ed) Life: World War 2. See Life: World War
2 **940.53**

Stone, Biz
Who let the blogs out? **006.7**

Stone, Carol Leth
The basics of biology **570**

Stone, Tanya Lee
A bad boy can be good for a girl **Fic**
(ed) Scientists: their lives and works. See Scientists: their lives and works **920.003**

The **stone** circles of Britain, Ireland and Brittany.
Burl, A. **936.1**

The **stone** circles of the British Isles. See Burl, A.
The stone circles of Britain, Ireland and Brittany **936.1**

A **stone** in my hand. Clinton, C. **Fic**

Stone tower. Simner, J. L.
In Gothic!; ten original dark tales **S C**

Stonehenge (England)
See/See also pages in the following book(s):
Aveni, A. F. Stairways to the stars **520**

Stoner & Spaz. Koertge, R. **Fic**

Stoneware See Pottery

Stoplight. Yoon, S. C.-N.
In American dragons: twenty-five Asian
American voices p14-25 **810.8**

Stoppard, Miriam
Complete baby & child care **649**

Stoppard, Tom
Rosencrantz and Guildenstern are dead **822**

Stores See Retail trade

Stories don't have endings. Gallagher, M.
In Spider Woman's granddaughters; traditional tales and contemporary writing by Native American women **S C**

The **stories** of John Cheever. Cheever, J. **S C**

Stories, poems, and other writings. Cather, W.
818

Stories without words
Drooker, E. Blood song **741.5**
Kuper, P. Sticks and stones **741.5**

The **storm**. Van Heerden, I. L. **976.3**

The **storm:** a sequel to "The 'Cadian ball". Chopin, K.
In Chopin, K. The awakening and selected
stories **S C**

The **storm** thief. Wooding, C. **Fic**

Storms
See also Hurricanes
Junger, S. The perfect storm **910.4**

Stormwitch. Vaught, S. **Fic**

Story in Harlem slang. Hurston, Z. N.
In Hurston, Z. N. The complete stories p127-
38 **S C**
In Hurston, Z. N. Novels and stories p1001-
10 **Fic**

A **story** in three parts. Myers, W. D.
In Myers, W. D. 145th Street; short stories
S C

Story of a girl. Zarr, S. **Fic**

The **story** of a scar. McPherson, J. A.
In American short story masterpieces **S C**

The **story** of an hour. Chopin, K.
In Chopin, K. The awakening and selected
stories **S C**
In Gotham Writers' Workshop fiction gallery;
exceptional short stories selected by New
York's acclaimed creative writing school
S C
In The Norton book of American short stories
p123-25 **S C**

The **story** of architecture. See Glancey, J. Architecture **720.9**

The **story** of art. Gombrich, E. H. **709**

A **story** of Don Juan. Pritchett, V. S.
In The Literary ghost; great contemporary
ghost stories p69-73 **S C**

The **story** of English. McCrum, R. **420**

The **Story** of Five Heads
In Hearne, B. G. Beauties and beasts p115-19
398.2

The **story** of Green-blanket Feet. Mourning Dove
In Spider Woman's granddaughters; traditional tales and contemporary writing by Native American women **S C**

The **story** of how one Russian peasant fed two
generals. Saltykov, M. E.
In The Portable nineteenth-century Russian
reader p609-15 **891.7**

The **story** of King Arthur and his knights. Pyle, H.
398.2

The **story** of Muhammad Din. Kipling, R.
In Kipling, R. The portable Kipling **828**

The **story** of my life. Keller, H. **92**

The **story** of philosophy. Durant, W. J. **109**

The **story** of philosophy. Magee, B. **190**

Story of science [series]
Hakim, J. The story of science: Aristotle leads the way **509**
Hakim, J. The story of science: Newton at the center **509**

The **story** of science: Aristotle leads the way. Hakim, J. **509**

The **story** of science: Newton at the center. Hakim, J. **509**

The **story** of the bad little boy. Twain, M.
In Twain, M. The complete short stories of Mark Twain; now collected for the first time **S C**

The **story** of the champions of the Round Table. Pyle, H. **398.2**

The **story** of the good little boy. Twain, M.
In Twain, M. The complete short stories of Mark Twain; now collected for the first time **S C**

The **story** of the Old Ram. Twain, M.
In Twain, M. The complete short stories of Mark Twain; now collected for the first time **S C**

Story of your life. Chiang, T.
In Best of the best: 20 years of the Year's best science fiction **S C**

A **story** without an end. Twain, M.
In Twain, M. The complete short stories of Mark Twain; now collected for the first time **S C**

Storytelling
Bruchac, J. Our stories remember **970.004**
De Vos, G. Storytelling for young adults **372.6**

Fiction
Wooding, C. Poison **Fic**

Storytelling for young adults. De Vos, G. **372.6**

Stotan!. Crutcher, C. **Fic**

Stout, Jay A., 1959-
Hammer from above **956.7**

Stow, Dorrik A. V.
Oceans: an illustrated reference **551.46**

Stowe, Harriet Beecher, 1811-1896
The Oxford Harriet Beecher Stowe reader **818**
Uncle Tom's cabin **Fic**
also in Stowe, H. B. The Oxford Harriet Beecher Stowe reader p78-405 **818**
See/See also pages in the following book(s):
McPherson, J. M. Drawn with the sword **973.7**
Uncle Tom's cabin; criticism
In McPherson, J. M. Drawn with the sword **973.7**

Stowe, Harriet Elizabeth *See* Stowe, Harriet Beecher, 1811-1896

Strachan, Hew
The First World War **940.3**

Straczynski, J. Michael, 1954-
The complete book of scriptwriting **808.2**

Strada, Jennifer L., 1970-
Eating disorders **616.85**

Stradling, R. A.
(jt. auth) Vincent, M. Cultural atlas of Spain and Portugal **946**

Strahan, Jonathan
(ed) The Locus awards. See The Locus awards **S C**

Straight flush. Maugham, W. S.
In Maugham, W. S. Collected short stories **S C**

Strain (Psychology) *See* Stress (Psychology)

Strand, Mark, 1934-
Chicken, shadow, moon and more **811**
(ed) 100 great poems of the twentieth century. See 100 great poems of the twentieth century **821.008**

The **strange** case of Dr. Jekyll and Mr. Hyde. Stevenson, R. L. **Fic**

Strange jest. Christie, A.
In Christie, A. Miss Marple: the complete short stories **S C**

Strange little girls. Gaiman, N.
In Gaiman, N. Fragile things; short fictions and wonders **S C**

Strange new land. Wood, P. H.
In The Young Oxford history of African Americans **305.8**

Strange news from another planet. Hesse, H.
In Hesse, H. and Zipes, J. D. The fairy tales of Hermann Hesse **S C**

Strange powers. Thompson, C.
In Every man for himself; ten short stories about being a guy **S C**

The **strange** ride of Morrowbie Jukes. Kipling, R.
In Kipling, R. The portable Kipling **828**

Strange wine. Ellison, H.
In The Norton book of science fiction; North American science fiction, 1960-1990 p350-56 **S C**

The **stranger**. Camus, A. **Fic**

The **stranger**. McKillip, P. A.
In McKillip, P. A. Harrowing the dragon **S C**

Stranger in a strange land. Heinlein, R. A. **Fic**

Stranger in paradise. Asimov, I.
In Asimov, I. The complete stories p441-62 **S C**

Strangers from a different shore. Takaki, R. T. **305.8**

Strasser, Todd, 1950-
Bones
In Ultimate sports; short stories by outstanding writers for young adults p238-50 **S C**
Give a boy a gun **Fic**

Strategic planning and management for library managers. Matthews, J. R. **025.1**

Stross, Charles
Lobsters
In Best of the best: 20 years of the Year's best science fiction **S C**

Stroud, Jonathan, 1970-
The Amulet of Samarkand **Fic**

Struck by lightning. Rosenthal, J. **519.2**

The **Structure** of the body **611**

A **struggle** for power. Draper, T. **973.3**

The **Struggle** to be strong **305.23**

Strunk, William, 1869-1946
The elements of style **808**

Stubblefield, R. Jay
(jt. auth) DeGategno, P. J. Critical companion to Jonathan Swift **828**

Stubbs, Aelred
(jt. auth) Biko, S. I write what I like **968.06**

Stubbs, Harry Clement *See* Clement, Hal, 1922-2003

Student aid
See also Scholarships; Student loan funds
Schlachter, G. A. College student's guide to merit and other no-need funding 2007-2009 **378.3**
Schlachter, G. A. High school senior's guide to merit and other no-need funding **378.3**

Student cheating *See* Cheating (Education)

Student companion to Arthur Miller. Abbotson, S. C. W. **812.009**

Student companion to Edgar Allan Poe. Magistrale, T. **818**

Student companion to George Orwell. Brunsdale, M. **828**

Student companion to John Steinbeck. Burkhead, C. **813.009**

Student companion to Stephen Crane. Sorrentino, P. **813.009**

Student companions to classic writers [series]
Abbotson, S. C. W. Student companion to Arthur Miller **812.009**
Brunsdale, M. Student companion to George Orwell **828**
Burkhead, C. Student companion to John Steinbeck **813.009**
Magistrale, T. Student companion to Edgar Allan Poe **818**
Sorrentino, P. Student companion to Stephen Crane **813.009**

Student dishonesty *See* Cheating (Education)

Student engagement and information literacy **028.7**

Student guide to research in the digital age. Stebbins, L. F. **025.5**

Student loan funds
College Board guide to getting financial aid, 2007 **378.3**
College money handbook 2007 **378.3**

Student Nonviolent Coordinating Committee
Lewis, J. Walking with the wind **92**

Student of ostriches. Pierce, T.
In Young warriors; stories of strength **S C**

Student success and library media programs. Farmer, L. S. J. **027.8**

Students
See also College students; High school students
Civil rights
Students' rights **344**
Students' rights: opposing viewpoints **344**
Law and legislation
Kowalski, K. M. The Earls case and the student drug testing debate **344**
Phillips, T. A. Hazelwood v. Kuhlmeier and the school newspaper censorship debate **342**
Students' rights **344**
Political activity
See/See also pages in the following book(s):
Hurley, J. A. The 1960s **973.92**

Students, Handicapped *See* Handicapped students

Students and libraries *See* Libraries and students

The **student's** encyclopedia of Judaism **296.03**

A **student's** guide to Arthur Miller. Dunkleberger, A. **812.009**

A **student's** guide to Emily Dickinson. Borus, A. **811.009**

A **student's** guide to Ernest Hemingway. Pingelton, T. J. **813.009**

A **student's** guide to George Orwell. Means, A. L. **828**

A **student's** guide to Herman Melville. Diorio, M. A. L. **813.009**

A **student's** guide to Jack London. Buckwalter, S. **813.009**

A **student's** guide to John Steinbeck. Newman, G. **813.009**

A **student's** guide to Robert Frost. Kirk, C. A. **811.009**

A **student's** guide to Tennessee Williams. Hermann, S. **812.009**

A **student's** guide to Toni Morrison. Crayton, L. A. **813.009**

Students helping students [series]
Navigating your freshman year **378**

Students' rights **344**

Students' rights: opposing viewpoints **344**

Studies in environment and history [series]
Russell, E. War and nature **577.2**

Studies in popular culture [series]
Harvey, R. C. The art of the comic book **741.5**

Study, Method of *See* Study skills

Study abroad, 2007 **378**

Study away. Balaban, M. **378**

A **study** in emerald. Gaiman, N.
In Gaiman, N. Fragile things; short fictions and wonders **S C**

A **study** in scarlet. Doyle, Sir A. C.
In Doyle, Sir A. C. The complete Sherlock Holmes **S C**

Study skills
Nist, S. L. College rules! **378**

Textile industry
History
Macaulay, D. Mill **690**

Thackeray, Frank W.
(ed) Events that changed America through the seventeenth century. See Events that changed America through the seventeenth century **973.2**
(ed) Events that changed Great Britain, from 1066 to 1714. See Events that changed Great Britain, from 1066 to 1714 **941**
(ed) Events that changed Great Britain since 1689. See Events that changed Great Britain since 1689 **941**
(ed) Events that changed the world in the eighteenth century. See Events that changed the world in the eighteenth century **909.7**
(ed) Events that changed the world in the nineteenth century. See Events that changed the world in the nineteenth century **909.81**
(ed) Events that changed the world in the seventeenth century. See Events that changed the world in the seventeenth century **909**
(ed) Events that changed the world in the twentieth century. See Events that changed the world in the twentieth century **909.82**
(ed) Events that changed the world through the sixteenth century. See Events that changed the world through the sixteenth century **909**

Thailand
Fiction
Boulle, P. The bridge over the River Kwai **Fic**

Thal, Lilli
Mimus **Fic**

Thanasphere. Vonnegut, K.
In Vonnegut, K. Bagombo snuff box: uncollected short fiction p13-27 **S C**

Thank you, m'am. Hughes, L.
In Hughes, L. Short stories of Langston Hughes **S C**
In Read all about it!; great read-aloud stories, poems, and newspaper pieces for preteens and teens p82-89 **808.8**

Thanksgiving. Wallace, R.
In Wallace, R. Losing is not an option: stories **S C**

Thanksgiving Day
Fiction
Capote, T. The Thanksgiving visitor
In Capote, T. A Christmas memory, One Christmas, & The Thanksgiving visitor p55-107 **818**

Thanksgiving in a monsoonless land. Rustomji-Kerns, R.
In Growing up ethnic in America; contemporary fiction about learning to be American **S C**

The **Thanksgiving** visitor. Capote, T.
In Capote, T. A Christmas memory, One Christmas, & The Thanksgiving visitor p55-107 **818**

Tharp, Tim, 1957-
Knights of the hill country **Fic**

Tharp, Twyla
See/See also pages in the following book(s):
Ford, C. T. Legends of American dance and choreography **920**

That evening sun. Faulkner, W.
In Faulkner, W. Collected stories of William Faulkner p289-309 **S C**
In Faulkner, W. Selected short stories of William Faulkner **S C**

That feeling, you can only say what it is in French. King, S.
In King, S. Everything's eventual: 14 dark tales **S C**

That thou art mindful of him. Asimov, I.
In Asimov, I. The complete stories p463-82 **S C**

That tree. Porter, K. A.
In Porter, K. A. The collected stories of Katherine Anne Porter **S C**

That was living. González, K. A.
In Latina: women's voices from the borderlands p97-106 **810.8**

That will be fine. Faulkner, W.
In Faulkner, W. Collected stories of William Faulkner p265-88 **S C**

That woman on the lawn. Bradbury, R.
In Bradbury, R. Bradbury stories; 100 of his most celebrated tales **S C**

Theater
See also Acting; Musicals
Dictionaries
Griffiths, T. R. The Ivan R. Dee guide to plays and playwrights **809.2**
Fiction
Sloan, B. A tale of two summers **Fic**
History
Brockett, O. G. History of the theatre **792.09**
The Oxford illustrated history of theatre **792.09**
Production and direction
See also Motion pictures—Production and direction
Lee, R. L. Everything about theatre! **792**
Varley, J. Places, please! **792**
Japan
See also Nō plays
United States—Dictionaries
Bordman, G. M. The Oxford companion to American theatre **792.03**
Cambridge guide to American theatre **792.03**

A **theatergoer's** guide to Shakespeare. Fallon, R. T. **822.3**

Theaters
Stage setting and scenery
Gillette, J. M. Theatrical design and production **792**

The **theatre** guide. See Griffiths, T. R. The Ivan R. Dee guide to plays and playwrights **809.2**

Theatrical costume *See* Costume

Theatrical design and production. Gillette, J. M. **792**

Theatrical makeup
Corson, R. Stage makeup **792**

Theft. Porter, K. A.
In The Norton book of American short stories p292-97 **S C**
In Porter, K. A. The collected stories of Katherine Anne Porter **S C**

Their eyes were watching God. Hurston, Z. N. **Fic**
also in Hurston, Z. N. Novels and stories p173-333 **Fic**

Thematic guide to American poetry. Burns, A. **811.009**

Thematic guide to British poetry. Glancy, R. F. **821.009**

Theodosia. Mandelstam, O.
In The portable twentieth-century Russian reader **891.7**

Theology
See also Faith
Great thinkers of the Western world **190**

Theoretical chemistry *See* Physical chemistry

Theories of relativity. Haworth-Attard, B. **Fic**

Theory of relativity. Nye, J. L.
In Past imperfect **S C**

Therapeutics
See also Gene therapy

Therapy, Gene *See* Gene therapy

There is confusion [excerpt] Fauset, J. R.
In The Portable Harlem Renaissance reader p340-48 **810.8**

There was a man, there was a woman. Cisneros, S.
In Cisneros, S. Woman Hollering Creek and other stories **S C**

There was a queen. Faulkner, W.
In Faulkner, W. Collected stories of William Faulkner p727-44 **S C**
In Faulkner, W. Selected short stories of William Faulkner **S C**

There's no reason to get romantic. Slater, A. T.
In American dragons: twenty-five Asian American voices p185-99 **810.8**

Thermodynamics
See/See also pages in the following book(s):
Lightman, A. P. Great ideas in physics **530**
Shachtman, T. Absolute zero and the conquest of cold **536**

These are my rivers. Ferlinghetti, L. **811**

Theseus (Greek mythology)
See/See also pages in the following book(s):
Hamilton, E. Mythology **292**
Fiction
Renault, M. The king must die **Fic**

Thesman, Jean
Singer **Fic**

"They". Kipling, R.
In Nightshade: 20th century ghost stories p305-27 **S C**
In The Year's best science fiction and fantasy for teens: first annual collection **S C**

They broke the law, you be the judge. Jacobs, T. A. **345**

They don't mean it!. Namioka, L.
In First crossing; stories about teen immigrants p80-94 **S C**

They made America. Evans, H. **920**

They marched into sunlight. Maraniss, D. **959.704**

They teach that in college!? **378.73**

They that sit in darkness. Burrill, M. P.
In Black theatre USA; plays by African Americans, 1847 to today **812.008**

They're made out of meat. Bisson, T.
In New skies: an anthology of today's science fiction **S C**

They're playing our song. Simon, N.
In Simon, N. The collected plays of Neil Simon **812**

The **thief**. Turner, M. W. **Fic**

A **thief** in the house of memory. Wynne-Jones, T. **Fic**

Thieret, John W., 1926-2005
National Audubon Society field guide to North American wildflowers: eastern region **582.13**

Thieves
Bryan, H. Robbers, rogues, and ruffians **978.9**
Fiction
Bondoux, A.-L. The killer's tears **Fic**
Lynch, S. The lies of Locke Lamora **Fic**
Taylor, K. Bowery girl **Fic**
Turner, M. W. The thief **Fic**
Updale, E. Montmorency **Fic**

Thieves, deceivers, and killers. Agosta, W. C. **577**

Thieves like us. Cole, S. **Fic**

Thieves of Baghdad. Bogdanos, M. **956.7**

A **thin** cosmic rain. Friedlander, M. W. **539.7**

Thin ice. Bowen, M. **551.51**

Things fall apart. Achebe, C. **Fic**

Things happen. Fraustino, L. R.
In Shattered: stories of children and war p87-107 **S C**

Things I didn't know my father knew. Crowther, P.
In Past imperfect **S C**

Things I have to tell you **810.8**

The **things** they carried. O'Brien, T.
In O'Brien, T. The things they carried; a work of fiction **S C**

The **things** they carried. O'Brien, T. **S C**

Think: a compelling introduction to philosophy. Blackburn, S. **100**

Think like a dinosaur. Kelly, J. P.
In The Hard SF renaissance **S C**

Thinking *See* Thought and thinking

Thinking outside the book **027.62**

The **third** and final continent. Lahiri, J.
  In Gotham Writers' Workshop fiction gallery; exceptional short stories selected by New York's acclaimed creative writing school **S C**

Third class. Sholem Aleichem
  In Halkin, H. and Sholem Aleichem. Tevye the dairyman and The railroad stories **S C**

A **third** kind of funny. Ellis, S.
  In What a song can do; 12 riffs on the power of music **S C**

The **third** voice. Ferguson, W.
  In The Literary ghost; great contemporary ghost stories p125-26 **S C**

Third World *See* Developing countries

The **Third** World: opposing viewpoints **909**

Thirteen and a day. Oppenheimer, M. **296.4**

The **thirteen** hundreds. See The 1300s **909**

Thirteen seconds. See Caputo, P. 13 seconds **973.924**

Thirteenth century *See* World history—13th century

The **thirteenth** tale. Setterfield, D. **Fic**

This boy's life [excerpt] Wolff, T.
  In Coming of age in America; a multicultural anthology p197-211 **S C**
  In Who do you think you are?; stories of friends and enemies p83-91 **S C**

This boy's life: a memoir. Wolff, T. **92**

This far by faith. Williams, J. **200**

This great unknowing. Levertov, D. **811**

This is our youth. Lonergan, K.
  In Under 30; plays for a new generation **812.008**

This is uncool: the 500 greatest singles since punk and disco. Mulholland, G. **781.66**

This is what it means to say Phoenix, Arizona. Alexie, S.
  In Adaptations: from short story to big screen; 35 great stories that have inspired great films **S C**
  In Growing up ethnic in America; contemporary fiction about learning to be American **S C**

This land was made for you and me: the life and songs of Woody Guthrie. Partridge, E. **92**

This new ocean. Burrows, W. E. **629.4**

This our dark country. Reef, C. **966.62**

This same sky **808.81**

This son of mine. Vonnegut, K.
  In Vonnegut, K. Bagombo snuff box: uncollected short fiction p201-15 **S C**

Thom, Kara Douglass
  (ed) Becoming an ironman. See Becoming an ironman **796**

Thomas, Aquinas, Saint, 1225?-1274
About
  Strathern, P. Thomas Aquinas in 90 minutes **92**
  See/See also pages in the following book(s):
  Russell, B. A history of Western philosophy **109**

Thomas, Carol G., 1938-
  The Trojan War **939**

Thomas, Dylan, 1914-1953
  A child's Christmas in Wales [illustrated by Chris Raschka] **828**
  The poems of Dylan Thomas **821**
  Selected poems, 1934-1952 **821**
  Under milk wood **822**

Thomas, Elizabeth Marshall, 1931-
  The hidden life of dogs **636.7**

Thomas, Hugh, 1931-
  The slave trade **326**

Thomas, Joyce Carol
  A family illness: a mom-son conversation
  In Necessary noise: stories about our families as they really are p97-128 **S C**

Thomas, Rebecca L.
  Popular series fiction for middle school and teen readers **016.8**

Thomas Aquinas in 90 minutes. Strathern, P. **92**

Thomas Green Fessenden. Hawthorne, N.
  In Hawthorne, N. Tales and sketches, including Twice-told tales, Mosses from an old manse, and The snow-image; A wonder book for girls and boys; Tanglewood tales for girls and boys, being a second Wonder book p571-84 **S C**

Thomas Hardy [critical essays] **823.009**

Thomason-Carroll, Kristi L.
  Young adult's guide to business communications **651.7**

Thompson, Bruce E. R., 1952-
  The Greenhaven encyclopedia of capital punishment **364.66**

Thompson, Cliff
  World musicians. See World musicians **920.003**
  (ed) World authors, 1990-1995. See World authors, 1990-1995 **920.003**
  (ed) World authors, 1995-2000. See World authors, 1995-2000 **920.003**

Thompson, Colleen A.
  (jt. auth) Shanley, E. L. Fueling the teen machine **613.2**

Thompson, Cooper, 1950-
  White men challenging racism **323**

Thompson, Craig, 1975-
  Blankets **92**
  Strange powers
  In Every man for himself; ten short stories about being a guy **S C**

Thompson, Della
  (ed) Oxford Russian dictionary. See Oxford Russian dictionary **491.7**

Thompson, Ida
  The Audubon Society field guide to North American fossils **560**

Thompson, Jim
  The frightening Frammis
  In Alfred Hitchcock's mystery magazine presents fifty years of crime and suspense **S C**

Thompson, Kate
The new policeman   **Fic**

Thompson, Leonard Monteath
A history of South Africa   **968**

Thompson, Peter, 1960-
Dictionary of American history: from 1763 to the present   **973.03**

Thompson, Sue Ellen, 1948-
Holiday symbols and customs   **394.26**

Thompson, Thomas, 1913-
Gun job
In A Century of great Western stories   **S C**

Thoms, Annie
(ed) With their eyes. See With their eyes   **812**

Thomsen, Brian
(ed) Masters of fantasy. See Masters of fantasy   **S C**

Thomson, Melissa
Women of the Renaissance   **940.2**

Thorburn, John E., Jr.
The Facts on File companion to classical drama   **880**

Thoreau, Henry David, 1817-1862
Collected essays and poems   **818**
Walden, or, Life in the woods   **818**
About
Emerson, R. W. The portable Emerson   **818**
A Historical guide to Henry David Thoreau   **818**

Thorn, John, 1947-
(ed) Total baseball. See Total baseball   **796.357**

Thorpe, James Francis *See* Thorpe, Jim, 1888-1953

Thorpe, Jim, 1888-1953
About
Crawford, B. All American [biography of Jim Thorpe]   **92**
See/See also pages in the following book(s):
Aaseng, N. Athletes   **920**

Thorpe, Nick
(jt. auth) James, P. Ancient inventions   **609**

Those three wishes. Gorog, J.
In Read all about it!; great read-aloud stories, poems, and newspaper pieces for preteens and teens p475-78   **808.8**

Those who fraternize. Michener, J. A.
In Michener, J. A. Tales of the South Pacific   **S C**

Those who have no turkey. Hughes, L.
In Hughes, L. Short stories of Langston Hughes   **S C**

"Thou art the man". Poe, E. A.
In Poe, E. A. The collected tales and poems of Edgar Allan Poe p490-501   **818**

Thou shalt not dump the skater dude and other commandments I have broken. Graham, R.   **Fic**

Though justice sleeps. Bair, B.
In The Young Oxford history of African Americans   **305.8**

Thought and thinking
Hayakawa, S. I. Language in thought and action   **412**

Thought control *See* Brainwashing

The thousand-and-second tale of Scheherazade. Poe, E. A.
In Poe, E. A. The collected tales and poems of Edgar Allan Poe p104-17   **818**

A thousand peaks. Liu Siyu   **895.1**

A thousand ships. Shanower, E.   **939**

A thousand splendid suns. Hosseini, K.   **Fic**

Thrall, William Flint, b. 1880
(jt. auth) Harmon, W. A handbook to literature   **803**

Thrawn Janet. Stevenson, R. L.
In The Oxford book of short stories p99-108   **S C**

Threads from the web of life. Daubert, S.   **508**

Threatened species *See* Endangered species

Three centuries of American poetry, 1623-1923   **811.008**

The three-century woman. Peck, R.
In Peck, R. Past perfect, present tense: new and collected stories   **S C**

Three clams and an oyster. Powell, R.   **Fic**

Three contributions to the theory of sex. Freud, S.
In Freud, S. The basic writings of Sigmund Freud   **150.19**

The Three daughters of King O'Hara
In Hearne, B. G. Beauties and beasts p84-91   **398.2**

The three-day blow. Hemingway, E.
In Hemingway, E. The complete short stories of Ernest Hemingway; the Finca Vigía edition p85-93   **S C**

Three-Dot-Po. Paretsky, S.
In The Best American mystery stories of the century p635-48   **S C**

The three fat women of Antibes. Maugham, W. S.
In Maugham, W. S. Collected short stories   **S C**

The three golden apples. Hawthorne, N.
In Hawthorne, N. Tales and sketches, including Twice-told tales, Mosses from an old manse, and The snow-image; A wonder book for girls and boys; Tanglewood tales for girls and boys, being a second Wonder book p1236-53   **S C**

The three linden trees. Hesse, H.
In Hesse, H. and Zipes, J. D. The fairy tales of Hermann Hesse   **S C**

Three Mondays in July. Giblin, J.
In Am I blue?; coming out from the silence p105-24   **S C**

The three musketeers. Dumas, A.   **Fic**

Three o'clock. Wolfe, T.
In Wolfe, T. The complete short stories of Thomas Wolfe p447-50   **S C**

Three people and two seats. Major, K.
In Sixteen: short stories by outstanding writers for young adults p113-24   **S C**

To say nothing of the dog; or, How we found the bishop's bird stump at last. Willis, C. **Fic**

To the best of my ability **920**

To the flag. Ellis, R. **323.6**

To the lighthouse. Woolf, V. **Fic**

To the man on trail. London, J.
In London, J. The portable Jack London p3-10 **818**

To the reader. Sholem Aleichem
In Halkin, H. and Sholem Aleichem. Tevye the dairyman and The railroad stories **S C**

To-to *See* Li Shizheng, 1951-

To walk with kings. Marx, T.
In Working days: stories about teenagers and work **S C**

Toad. McKillip, P. A.
In McKillip, P. A. Harrowing the dragon **S C**

Toads
Beltz, E. Frogs: inside their remarkable world **597.8**

Tobacco
Hyde, M. O. Smoking 101 **616.86**
Encyclopedias
Tobacco in history and culture **394.1**

Tobacco and smoking: opposing viewpoints **362.29**

Tobacco habit
Addiction: opposing viewpoints **362.29**
Smoking **362.29**
Tobacco and smoking: opposing viewpoints **362.29**

Tobacco in history and culture **394.1**

Tobacco industry
Tobacco and smoking: opposing viewpoints **362.29**

Tobin, Jacqueline, 1950-
Hidden in plain view **973.7**

Tobin, James, 1956-
Great projects **620**
To conquer the air **629.13**
Reporting America at war. See Reporting America at war **070.4**

Tocci, Salvatore
High-tech IDs **614**

Today is Friday. Hemingway, E.
In Hemingway, E. The complete short stories of Ernest Hemingway; the Finca Vigía edition p271-73 **S C**

Today's children. Sholem Aleichem
In Halkin, H. and Sholem Aleichem. Tevye the dairyman and The railroad stories **S C**

Todd, Mark
Whatcha mean, what's a zine? **070.5**

Together apart. Gray, D. E. **Fic**

The **toilet**. Mhlophe, G.
In Somehow tenderness survives; stories of Southern Africa p77-86 **S C**

Tokyo (Japan)
Fiction
Gratz, A. Samurai shortstop **Fic**
Marks, G. Missing in Tokyo **Fic**

Told in the drooling ward. London, J.
In London, J. The portable Jack London p282-90 **818**

Tolkien, J. R. R. (John Ronald Reuel), 1892-1973
The hobbit, or, There and back again **Fic**
The lord of the rings **Fic**
The Silmarillion **S C**
Contents: Ainulindale; Valaquenta; Quenta Silmarillion: Of the beginning of days; Quenta Silmarillion: Of Autë and Yavanna; Quenta Silmarillion: Of the coming of the elves and the captivity of Melkor; Quenta Silmarillion: Of Thingol and Melian; Quenta Silmarillion: Of Eldamar and the princes of the Eldalië; Quenta Silmarillion: Of Fëanor and the unchaining of Melkor; Quenta Silmarillion: Of the Silmarils and the unrest of the Noldor; Quenta Silmarillion: Of the darkening of Valinor; Quenta Silmarillion: Of the flight of the Noldor; Quenta Silmarillion: Of the Sindar; Quenta Silmarillion: Of the sun and moon and the hiding of Valinor; Quenta Silmarillion: Of men; Quenta Silmarillion: Of the return of the Noldor; Quenta Silmarillion: Of Beleriand and its realms; Quenta Silmarillion: Of the Noldor in Beleriand; Quenta Silmarillion: Of Maeglin; Quenta Silmarillion: Of the coming of men into the West; Quenta Silmarillion: Of the ruin of Beleriand and the fall of Fingollin; Quenta Silmarillion: Of Beren and Lúthien; Quenta Silmarillion: Of the fifth battle: Niraeth Arnoediad; Quenta Silmarillion: Of Turin Turambar; Quenta Silmarillion: Of the ruin of Doriath; Quenta Silmarillion: Of Tuor and the fall of Gondolin; Quenta Silmarillion: Of the voyage of Eärendil and the war of wrath; Akallabeth; Of the Rings of Power and the Third Age
About
Fonstad, K. W. The atlas of Middle-earth **823.009**
Shippey, T. A. J.R.R. Tolkien **828**

Tolkien, John Ronald Reuel *See* Tolkien, J. R. R. (John Ronald Reuel), 1892-1973

The **toll-gatherer's** day. Hawthorne, N.
In Hawthorne, N. Tales and sketches, including Twice-told tales, Mosses from an old manse, and The snow-image; A wonder book for girls and boys; Tanglewood tales for girls and boys, being a second Wonder book p508-13 **S C**

Tolstoy, Leo, graf, 1828-1910
Alyosha the Pot
In The portable twentieth-century Russian reader **891.7**
Anna Karenina **Fic**
The death of Ivan Ilych
In The Portable nineteenth-century Russian reader p440-89 **891.7**
Great short works of Leo Tolstoy **S C**
Contents: Family happiness; The Cossacks; The death of Ivan Ilych; The devil; The Kreutzer Sonata; Master and man; Father Sergius; Hadji Murád; Alyosha the Pot
Master and man
In The Portable nineteenth-century Russian reader p489-529 **891.7**
About
Leo Tolstoy: comprehensive research and study guide **891.7**

Toltecs
See also Aztecs

Tom, Karen
(ed) Angst! teen verses from the edge! See Angst! teen verses from the edge!
811.008

Tom, Linda C.
(il) Costello, E. Random House American sign language dictionary **419**

Tom Quartz. Twain, M.
In Twain, M. The complete short stories of Mark Twain; now collected for the first time **S C**

Tomblin, Barbara
G.I. nightingales **940.54**

Tomedi, John, 1978-
Dublin **820.9**
(jt. auth) Dailey, D. London **820.9**

Tommasini, Anthony, 1948-
Opera: a critic's guide to the 100 most important recordings **782**

Tomorrow. Faulkner, W.
In Adaptations: from short story to big screen; 35 great stories that have inspired great films **S C**

Tomorrow, when the war began. Marsden, J.
Fic

Tompkins, Cynthia, 1958-
(ed) Teen life in Latin America and the Caribbean. See Teen life in Latin America and the Caribbean **305.23**

Tompson, Richard S.
Great Britain: a reference guide from the Renaissance to the present **941**

Tom's husband. Jewett, S. O.
In The Oxford book of women's writing in the United States p10-20 **810.8**

The Toni Morrison encyclopedia **813.009**

Tony's wife. Dunbar-Nelson, A. M.
In The Oxford book of women's writing in the United States p21-26 **810.8**

Too many crooks. Westlake, D. E.
In The Best American mystery stories of the century p665-77 **S C**

Tooley, James
The miseducation of women **371.82**

Toomai of the Elephants. Kipling, R.
In Kipling, R. The portable Kipling **828**

Toomer, Jean, 1894-1967
Balo
In Black theatre USA; plays by African Americans, 1847 to today **812.008**
Becky
In The Norton book of American short stories p324-26 **S C**
Cane [excerpt]
In The Portable Harlem Renaissance reader p318-32 **810.8**

Toomey, David M.
(jt. auth) Haynsworth, L. Amelia Earhart's daughters **629.13**

The tooth. Jackson, S.
In Jackson, S. The lottery; or, The adventures of James Harris **S C**

The top 10 of everything 2008. Ash, R.
031.02

The Top 500 poems **821.008**

Top hand. Short, L.
In A Century of great Western stories **S C**

Topeka (Kan.). Board of Education
Telgen, D. Brown v. Board of Education **344**

The Torah: the five books of Moses. Bible. O.T. Pentateuch **222**

Torch song. Cheever, J.
In Cheever, J. The stories of John Cheever p89-102 **S C**

Tories, American *See* American Loyalists

Torn between two cultures. Aseel, M. Q. **92**

Torr, James D., 1974-
(ed) Abortion: opposing viewpoints. See Abortion: opposing viewpoints **363.46**
(ed) The American frontier. See The American frontier **978**
(ed) Crime and criminals: opposing viewpoints. See Crime and criminals: opposing viewpoints **364**
(ed) The Internet: opposing viewpoints. See The Internet: opposing viewpoints **303.4**
(ed) Internet piracy. See Internet piracy **346.04**
(ed) Professional sports. See Professional sports **796**
(ed) Race relations: opposing viewpoints. See Race relations: opposing viewpoints **305.8**
(ed) Slavery. See Slavery **326**
(ed) Sports and athletes: opposing viewpoints. See Sports and athletes: opposing viewpoints **796**
(ed) U.S. policy toward rogue nations. See U.S. policy toward rogue nations **327.73**
(ed) Weapons of mass destruction: opposing viewpoints. See Weapons of mass destruction: opposing viewpoints **358**
(ed) Westward expansion. See Westward expansion [Interpreting primary documents] **978**

Torrans, Lee Ann, 1952-
Law for K-12 libraries and librarians **344**

Tortoises *See* Turtles

Tortoises and turtles. Ferri, V. **597.92**

Total baseball **796.357**

The total cat. Wilbourn, C. **636.8**

Totalitarianism
See also Dictators
Fromm, E. Escape from freedom **323.44**
Huxley, A. Brave new world revisited **303.3**
Fiction
Orwell, G. Animal farm **Fic**
Orwell, G. Nineteen eighty-four **Fic**

Totem and taboo. Freud, S.
In Freud, S. The basic writings of Sigmund Freud **150.19**

A touch through time. Massie-Ferch, K. M.
In Past imperfect **S C**

Tough acts to follow. Ullom, S. **812**

Trevor, William, 1928-—*Continued*
(ed) The Oxford book of Irish short stories. See
The Oxford book of Irish short stories
S C

Trewby, Mary
(ed) Antarctica: an encyclopedia from Abbott
Ice Shelf to zooplankton. See Antarctica: an
encyclopedia from Abbott Ice Shelf to zoo-
plankton **998**
The **trial**. Kafka, F. **Fic**
A **trial**. Twain, M.
In Twain, M. The complete short stories of
Mark Twain; now collected for the first
time **S C**
Trial by combat. Jackson, S.
In Jackson, S. The lottery; or, The adventures
of James Harris **S C**
Trials
Aronson, M. Witch-hunt: mysteries of the Salem
witch trials **133.4**
Burns, W. E. Witch hunts in Europe and Ameri-
ca **133.4**
Great world trials **347**
Hoffer, P. C. The Salem witchcraft trials
345
Larson, E. J. Summer for the gods **345**
Salem witch trials **133.4**
Sorensen, L. The Scottsboro Boys Trial **345**
Weiner, M. S. Black trials **342**
Fiction
Guterson, D. Snow falling on cedars **Fic**
Myers, W. D. Monster **Fic**
Pesci, D. Amistad **Fic**
Trials (Espionage)
Philipson, I. J. Ethel Rosenberg **92**
Trials (Homicide)
Crowe, C. Getting away with murder: the true
story of the Emmett Till case **364.1**
Monroe, J. The Sacco and Vanzetti controversial
murder trial **345**
Trials (Murder) *See* Trials (Homicide)
The **trials** of Simon Erickson. Twain, M.
In Twain, M. The complete short stories of
Mark Twain; now collected for the first
time **S C**
Triana, Gaby
Cubanita **Fic**
The **triangle**. Stephens, J.
In The Oxford book of Irish short stories
p271-76 **S C**
Triangle Shirtwaist Company, Inc.
DeAngelis, G. The Triangle Shirtwaist Company
fire of 1911 **974.7**
Lieurance, S. The Triangle Shirtwaist fire and
sweatshop reform in American history
974.7
Von Drehle, D. Triangle: the fire that changed
America **974.7**
Fiction
Auch, M. J. Ashes of roses **Fic**
The **Triangle** Shirtwaist Company fire of 1911.
DeAngelis, G. **974.7**
The **Triangle** Shirtwaist fire and sweatshop reform
in American history. Lieurance, S. **974.7**

Triangle: the fire that changed America. Von
Drehle, D. **974.7**
Triathlon
Becoming an ironman **796**
Fiction
Crutcher, C. Ironman **Fic**
Trice, Dawn Turner, 1956-
Only twice I've wished for heaven **Fic**
Tricks
See also Card tricks
The **tridget** of Greva. Lardner, R.
In 24 favorite one-act plays p301-07
808.82
A **trifle** from life. Chekhov, A. P.
In Gotham Writers' Workshop fiction gallery;
exceptional short stories selected by New
York's acclaimed creative writing school
S C
Trifles. Glaspell, S.
In 24 favorite one-act plays p333-46
808.82
In The Oxford book of women's writing in
the United States p393-406 **810.8**
Trigger. Vaught, S. **Fic**
Trilling, Lionel, 1905-1975
(ed) Victorian prose and poetry. See Victorian
prose and poetry **820.8**
The **trimmed** lamp. Henry, O.
In Henry, O. The best short stories of O.
Henry **S C**
Trinity. Kress, N.
In Best of the best: 20 years of the Year's
best science fiction **S C**
Trip in a summer dress. Sanford, A.
In Leaving home: stories p119-31 **808.8**
Tritle, Lawrence A., 1946-
The Peloponnesian War **938**
The **triumph** of numbers. Cohen, I. B. **519.5**
Trivia *See* Curiosities and wonders
Troilus and Cressida. Chaucer, G.
In Chaucer, G. The portable Chaucer **821**
Trojan War
Homer. The Iliad **883**
McCarty, N. The Iliad **883**
Thomas, C. G. The Trojan War **939**
See/See also pages in the following book(s):
Hamilton, E. Mythology **292**
Tuchman, B. W. The march of folly **909.08**
Fiction
Geras, A. Troy **Fic**
Graphic novels
Shanower, E. A thousand ships **939**
The **troll**. White, T. H.
In The Oxford book of English short stories
p345-54 **S C**
A **troll** and two roses. McKillip, P. A.
In McKillip, P. A. Harrowing the dragon
S C
The **trolley**. Bradbury, R.
In Bradbury, R. Bradbury stories; 100 of his
most celebrated tales **S C**

Uchida, Yoshiko, 1921-1992
Picture bride **Fic**

UFOs *See* Unidentified flying objects

Uglies. Westerfeld, S. **Fic**

The **ugly** duckling. Milne, A. A.
In 24 favorite one-act plays p347-66
808.82

The **ugly** little boy. Asimov, I.
In Asimov, I. The complete stories p301-33
S C

The **ugly** one. Flake, S. G.
In Flake, S. G. Who am I without him?; short
stories about girls and the boys in their
lives p10-18 **S C**

Uh huh!: the story of Ray Charles. Duggleby, J.
92

Uhle, Mary E.
(jt. auth) Shields, N. E. Where credit is due
808

Ujifusa, Grant
(jt. auth) Barone, M. The almanac of American
politics, 2006 **328.73**

Ukraine
Otfinoski, S. Ukraine **947.7**

Ullom, Shirley, 1938-
Tough acts to follow **812**

The **Ultimate** audition book **808.82**

Ultimate dog grooming. Geeson, E. **636.7**

Ultimate golf techniques. Campbell, M.
796.352

The **ultimate** guitar book. Bacon, T. **787.87**

The **ultimate** Harley-Davidson book. Wilson, H.
629.227

The **ultimate** improv book. Nevraumont, E. J.
792.7

The **ultimate** melody. Clarke, A. C.
In Clarke, A. C. The collected stories of Arthur C. Clarke **S C**

The **ultimate** mountain bike book. Crowther, N.
796.6

The **ultimate** ride. Carmichael, C. **796.6**

Ultimate robot. Malone, R. **629.8**

Ultimate sports **S C**

Ultimate visual dictionary. See Visual dictionary
423

UN *See* United Nations

Unamuno, Miguel de, 1864-1936
Mechanopolis
In Cosmos latinos; an anthology of science
fiction from Latin America and Spain
S C

Unbearable temptations. Scott, J.
In Alfred Hitchcock's mystery magazine pres-
ents fifty years of crime and suspense
S C

The **unbeatable.** Willems, M.
In Every man for himself; ten short stories
about being a guy **S C**

Unbegaun, B. O., 1898-1973.
(ed) Oxford Russian dictionary. See Oxford
Russian dictionary **491.7**

Unborn child *See* Fetus

Unbuilding. Macaulay, D. **690**

Uncle Joshua and the Grogglemen. Doyle, D.
In New skies: an anthology of today's science
fiction **S C**

Uncle Monday. Hurston, Z. N.
In Hurston, Z. N. The complete stories p106-
16 **S C**

Uncle Otto's truck. King, S.
In King, S. Skeleton crew **S C**

Uncle Shelby *See* Silverstein, Shel

Uncle Tom's cabin. Stowe, H. B. **Fic**
also in Stowe, H. B. The Oxford Harriet Beecher Stowe reader p78-405 **818**

Uncle Tom's children. Wright, R. **S C**
also in Wright, R. Works **Fic**

Uncle Tungsten. Sacks, O. W. **92**

Uncle Vanya. Chekhov, A. P.
In Chekhov, A. P. The plays of Anton Chekhov p207-55 **891.7**
In The Portable nineteenth-century Russian
reader p549-607 **891.7**

Uncle Wiggily in Connecticut. Salinger, J. D.
In Salinger, J. D. Nine stories p27-56
S C

Uncle Willy. Faulkner, W.
In Faulkner, W. Collected stories of William
Faulkner p225-47 **S C**

Uncles
Fiction
Herrera, J. F. Cinnamon girl **Fic**
Mowll, J. Operation Red Jericho **Fic**

Uncommon women and others. Wasserstein, W.
In Wasserstein, W. The Heidi chronicles and
other plays **812**

The **unconquered.** Maugham, W. S.
In Maugham, W. S. Collected short stories
S C

The **undefeated.** Hemingway, E.
In Hemingway, E. The complete short stories
of Ernest Hemingway; the Finca Vigía
edition p183-205 **S C**

Under 30 **812.008**

Under a flaming sky. Brown, D. **634.9**

Under milk wood. Thomas, D. **822**

Under the baseball moon. Ritter, J. H. **Fic**

Under the blood-red sun. Salisbury, G. **Fic**

Under the knife. Wells, H. G.
In The Oxford book of English short stories
p127-38 **S C**

Under the ridge. Hemingway, E.
In Hemingway, E. The complete short stories
of Ernest Hemingway; the Finca Vigía
edition p460-69 **S C**

Under the wolf, under the dog. Rapp, A. **Fic**

Under thirty. See Under 30 **812.008**

Underdeveloped areas *See* Developing countries

Undergraduates *See* College students

Underground. Macaulay, D. **624**

Underground railroad
DeRamus, B. Forbidden fruit **973.7**
Fradin, D. B. Bound for the North Star **326**

Vargas Llosa, Mario, 1936-
The Feast of the Goat   **Fic**

Variations on a theme. Koertge, R.
In What a song can do; 12 riffs on the power of music   **S C**

Various temptations. Sansom, W.
In The Oxford book of short stories p417-31   **S C**

Varley, John, 1947-
Lollipop and the tar baby
In The Norton book of science fiction; North American science fiction, 1960-1990 p257-76   **S C**
The persistence of vision
In The Locus awards; thirty years of the best in science fiction and fantasy   **S C**

Varley, Joy
Places, please!   **792**

Varley, Lynn
(jt. auth) Miller, F. Batman: the Dark Knight strikes again   **741.5**

Varykino. Pasternak, B. L.
In The portable twentieth-century Russian reader   **891.7**

Vasishta, Madan, 1941-
Deaf in Delhi   **92**

Vassanji, M. G. (Moyez G.), 1950-
Leaving
In The Heinemann book of contemporary African short stories p114-20   **S C**

Vassanji, Moyez G. *See* Vassanji, M. G. (Moyez G.), 1950-

Vatican City
Lace, W. W. The Vatican   **945**

Vaught, Susan
Stormwitch   **Fic**
Trigger   **Fic**

Vaz, Katherine
A world painted by birds
In The Green Man: tales from the mythic forest p168-88   **808.8**
Your garnet eyes
In The Faery Reel; tales from the Twilight Realm   **S C**

VCRs *See* Video recording

VD *See* Sexually transmitted diseases

Veague, Heather Barnett
Personality disorders   **616.85**

Veblen, Thorstein, 1857-1929
See/See also pages in the following book(s):
Heilbroner, R. L. The worldly philosophers   **330.1**

Vecchione, Glen
Blue ribbon science fair projects   **507.8**

Vecchione, Patrice
(ed) The Body eclectic. See The Body eclectic   **808.81**
(ed) Faith & doubt. See Faith & doubt   **808.81**
(ed) Revenge and forgiveness. See Revenge and forgiveness   **808.81**

Vecsey, George
Baseball: a history of America's favorite game   **796.357**

Vega, Ed
An apology to the moon furies
In Growing up Latino; memoirs and stories p47-72   **810.8**

Vegan planet. Robertson, R.   **641.5**

Vegan virgin Valentine. Mackler, C.   **Fic**

Vegetarian cooking
Butts, L. Okay, so now you're a vegetarian   **641.5**
Dragonwagon, C. Passionate vegetarian   **641.5**
Madison, D. Vegetarian cooking for everyone   **641.5**
Robertson, R. Vegan planet   **641.5**

Vegetarian cooking for everyone. Madison, D.   **641.5**

Vegetarian sourcebook   **613.2**

Vegetarianism
Vegetarian sourcebook   **613.2**
See/See also pages in the following book(s):
Shanley, E. L. Fueling the teen machine p139-53   **613.2**

Veiga, Marisella
Fresh fruit
In Latina: women's voices from the borderlands p180-83   **810.8**

The veldt. Bradbury, R.
In Bradbury, R. The illustrated man   **S C**

Velez, Ivan, Jr.
(ed) Dead High yearbook. See Dead High yearbook   **741.5**

Velikovsky, Immanuel, 1895-1979
See/See also pages in the following book(s):
Sagan, C. Broca's brain   **500**

Venereal diseases *See* Sexually transmitted diseases

Venetian fan. Bauer, C.
In Sixteen: stories about that sweet and bitter birthday   **S C**

Venezuela
Levin, J. Hugo Chávez   **92**

The venging. Bear, G.
In Bear, G. The collected stories of Greg Bear   **S C**

Venn, John, 1834-1923
About
Edwards, A. W. F. Cogwheels of the mind   **511.3**

Venomous animals and poisonous plants. See Foster, S. A field guide to venomous animals and poisonous plants   **578.6**

Venomous snakes of the world. O'Shea, M.   **597.96**

Venture to the moon. Clarke, A. C.
In Clarke, A. C. The collected stories of Arthur C. Clarke   **S C**

Venzon, Anne Cipriano, 1951-
(ed) The United States in the First World War. See The United States in the First World War   **940.3**

Violence

See also Domestic violence; School violence

The Central Intelligence Agency	**327.12**
Ethnic violence	**305.8**
Guns and violence [Current controversies]	**363.33**
Media violence: opposing viewpoints	**303.6**
Sexual violence: opposing viewpoints	**364.1**
Violence against women	**362.83**

See/See also pages in the following book(s):

Mass media: opposing viewpoints	**302.23**

Encyclopedias

Encyclopedia of murder and violent crime	**364.1**

Fiction

Burgess, A. A clockwork orange	**Fic**
Corrigan, E. Splintering	**Fic**
Dessen, S. Dreamland	**Fic**
Flake, S. G. Bang!	**Fic**
Giles, G. Shattering Glass	**Fic**
Miller, M. B. On the head of a pin	**Fic**
Myers, W. D. Autobiography of my dead brother	**Fic**
Saenz, B. A. Sammy and Juliana in Hollywood	**Fic**
Soto, G. Buried onions	**Fic**
Strasser, T. Give a boy a gun	**Fic**

Violence against women **362.83**

Violence in our schools. Orr, T. **371.7**

The **violent** bear it away. O'Connor, F.
In O'Connor, F. Collected works p329-479 **S C**

The **violet's** embryos. Gorodischer, A.
In Cosmos latinos; an anthology of science fiction from Latin America and Spain **S C**

Violinists

Fiction

Caletti, D. Wild roses	**Fic**

Viramontes, Helena Maria, 1954-
Miss Clairol
In Latina: women's voices from the borderlands p120-25 **810.8**
In The Oxford book of women's writing in the United States p154-58 **810.8**
The moths
In Growing up ethnic in America; contemporary fiction about learning to be American **S C**
In Growing up Latino; memoirs and stories p32-37 **810.8**

Virga, Vincent
Eyes of the nation **973**

Virgil
The Aeneid **873**
See/See also pages in the following book(s):
Hamilton, E. The Roman way **870.9**

Virgin Violeta. Porter, K. A.
In Porter, K. A. The collected stories of Katherine Anne Porter **S C**

Virginia

Natural history
See Natural history—Virginia

Virginia Woolf A-Z. Hussey, M. **828**
The **Virginia** Woolf reader. Woolf, V. **828**
Virtual field trips. See Cooper, G. New virtual field trips **025.5**
Virtue. Maugham, W. S.
In Maugham, W. S. Collected short stories **S C**

A **virtuoso's** collection. Hawthorne, N.
In Hawthorne, N. Tales and sketches, including Twice-told tales, Mosses from an old manse, and The snow-image; A wonder book for girls and boys; Tanglewood tales for girls and boys, being a second Wonder book p697-713 **S C**

Viruses

See also Ebola virus; Epstein-Barr virus; Herpesvirus diseases

Crawford, D. H. The invisible enemy **616**
The **vision** of the fountain. Hawthorne, N.
In Hawthorne, N. Tales and sketches, including Twice-told tales, Mosses from an old manse, and The snow-image; A wonder book for girls and boys; Tanglewood tales for girls and boys, being a second Wonder book p324-29 **S C**

A **vision** of the world. Cheever, J.
In Cheever, J. The stories of John Cheever p512-17 **S C**

Vision quest. Griffin, P. R.
In Make me over; 11 stories of transformation **S C**

Visions of the cosmos. Petersen, C. C. **520**
Visions of war, dreams of peace **811.008**
Visit. Myers, W. D.
In Necessary noise: stories about our families as they really are p81-93 **S C**

The **visit**. Oates, J. C.
In Oates, J. C. Small avalanches and other stories **S C**

A **visit** of charity. Welty, E.
In The Oxford book of short stories p411-16 **S C**
In Welty, E. The collected stories of Eudora Welty p113-18 **S C**

A **visit** to the clerk of the weather. Hawthorne, N.
In Hawthorne, N. Tales and sketches, including Twice-told tales, Mosses from an old manse, and The snow-image; A wonder book for girls and boys; Tanglewood tales for girls and boys, being a second Wonder book p390-94 **S C**

The **visit** to the museum. Nabokov, V. V.
In The portable twentieth-century Russian reader **891.7**

The **visitation**. Bear, G.
In Bear, G. The collected stories of Greg Bear **S C**

The **visitor**. Bradbury, R.
In Bradbury, R. Bradbury stories; 100 of his most celebrated tales **S C**

The visitor—*Continued*
In Bradbury, R. The illustrated man   **S C**
Visual dictionary   **423**
A **visual** dictionary of architecture. Ching, F.
   720.3
The **visual** display of quantitative information.
Tufte, E. R.   **001.4**
Vitale, William J.
About
Dudley, M. E. Engel v. Vitale (1962)   **344**
Vitamins
See also Dietary supplements
The Encyclopedia of vitamins, minerals, and
supplements   **613.2**
Viva New Jersey. Gonzalez, G.
In Join in; multiethnic short stories by out-
standing writers for young adults p51-60
   S C
Vivar, Rodrigo Díaz de *See* Cid, ca. 1043-1099
Vizenor, Gerald Robert, 1934-
About
Coltelli, L. Winged words: American Indian
writers speak   **897**
Vizzini, Ned, 1981-
It's kind of a funny story   **Fic**
Rutford becomes a man
In Sixteen: stories about that sweet and bitter
birthday   **S C**
**Vlad III, Prince of Wallachia, 1430 or 31-1476
or 7**
About
Florescu, R. R. N. Dracula [biography of Vlad
II]   **92**
Vladimov, Georgiĭ Nikolaevich, 1931-2003
Faithful Ruslan [excerpt]
In The portable twentieth-century Russian
reader   **891.7**
Vocal music
See/See also pages in the following book(s):
Grout, D. J. A history of western music
   780.9
Vocational education
Coplin, W. D. 10 things employers want you to
learn in college   **378**
Jell, J. R. From school to a career   **378**
Paquette, P. H. Apprenticeship   **331.2**
Unger, H. G. But what if I don't want to go to
college?   **331.7**
Vocational guidance
Ackerman, T. H. FBI careers   **363.2**
Bolles, R. N. What color is your parachute? for
teens   **331.7**
Brustein, R. Letters to a young actor   **792**
Coplin, W. D. 10 things employers want you to
learn in college   **378**
Encyclopedia of careers and vocational guidance
   331.7
Freedman, S. G. Letters to a young journalist
   070.4
Gordon, R. S. Best career and education Web
sites   **025.04**
Hayhurst, C. Cool careers without college for
animal lovers   **636**
Jell, J. R. From school to a career   **378**

Reber, D. In their shoes   **331.4**
Reeves, D. L. Career ideas for teens in architecture and construction   **624**
Reeves, D. L. Career ideas for teens in educa-
tion and training   **331.7**
Reeves, D. L. Career ideas for teens in health
science   **610.69**
Rosen, L., Ph. D. College is not for everyone
   378.1
Schwager, T. Cool women, hot jobs . . . and
how you can go for it, too!   **650.14**
Unger, H. G. But what if I don't want to go to
college?   **331.7**
United States. Bureau of Labor Statistics. Occu-
pational outlook handbook 2006-2007
   331.7
Vocational training *See* Occupational training
Vocations *See* Occupations
Vodou. Galembo, P.   **299.6**
Voelkel, James R., 1962-
Johannes Kepler and the new astronomy   **92**
Vogel, Virgil J.
American Indian medicine   **970.004**
A **voice** of her own. Schiwy, M. A.   **808**
The **voice** of the turtle. Maugham, W. S.
In Maugham, W. S. Collected short stories
   S C
Voices from the Negro leagues. Kelley, B. P.
   796.357
Voices from the pastime. Wilson, N.   **796.357**
Voices from the Trail of Tears   **970.004**
Voices of freedom. Hampton, H.   **323.1**
Voices of resistance   **305.4**
Voices of the Holocaust   **940.53**
Voices of war   **355**
Voices: poetry and art from around the world
   808.81
Voĭnovich, Vladimir, 1932-
A circle of friends
In The portable twentieth-century Russian
reader   **891.7**
Volcanoes
Clarkson, P. Volcanoes   **551.2**
Levy, M. Why the earth quakes   **551.2**
Encyclopedias
Gates, A. E. Encyclopedia of earthquakes and
volcanoes   **551.2**
Fiction
Harris, R. Pompeii   **Fic**
Volkman, John D.
Cruising through research   **025.5**
Volleyball
Dearing, J. Volleyball fundamentals   **796.325**
Volpe, Lane E., 1976-
(ed) Battered women. See Battered women
   362.82
Volponi, Paul
Black and white   **Fic**
Rooftop   **Fic**
Voltaire, 1694-1778
Candide   **Fic**
Micromegas
In Voltaire. The portable Voltaire   **848**

Wadham, J.
Lady Eltringham; or, The castle of Ratcliffe Cross
In The Oxford book of gothic tales p82-84 **S C**

The **wager**. Fish, R. L.
In The Best American mystery stories of the century p547-55 **S C**

Wages
Minimum wage
See Minimum wage

Wagner, E. J.
The science of Sherlock Holmes **363.2**

Wagner, Linda Welshimer *See* Wagner-Martin, Linda

Wagner, Viqi
(ed) Do infectious diseases pose a serious threat? See Do infectious diseases pose a serious threat? **614.4**

Wagner-Martin, Linda
(ed) A Historical guide to Ernest Hemingway. See A Historical guide to Ernest Hemingway **813.009**
(ed) The Oxford book of women's writing in the United States. See The Oxford book of women's writing in the United States **810.8**

Wainwright, Louie L.
About
Sherrow, V. Gideon v. Wainwright **345**

Wait for me. Na, A. **Fic**

Waiting for Godot. Beckett, S. **842**

Waiting for Sarah. McBay, B. **Fic**

Waiting for Sebastian. Peck, R.
In Peck, R. Past perfect, present tense: new and collected stories **S C**

Waiting for the call. Kinsella, W. P.
In Kinsella, W. P. Shoeless Joe Jackson comes to Iowa: stories **S C**

Waiting for the war. Salisbury, G.
In Salisbury, G. Island boyz: short stories p142-64 **S C**

Wake . . . Mabuza, L.
In The Heinemann book of contemporary African short stories p33-56 **S C**

Wake up our souls. Bolden, T. **704**

Wakefield. Hawthorne, N.
In Hawthorne, N. Tales and sketches, including Twice-told tales, Mosses from an old manse, and The snow-image; A wonder book for girls and boys; Tanglewood tales for girls and boys, being a second Wonder book p290-98 **S C**

The **Wakefield** Second Shepherd's play
In The Oxford anthology of English literature **820.8**

Wakeman, John, 1928-
(ed) World authors, 1950-1970. See World authors, 1950-1970 **920.003**
(ed) World authors, 1970-1975. See World authors, 1970-1975 **920.003**

Waking up American **305.4**

Walcott, Derek
Collected poems, 1948-1984 **811**
Omeros **811**

Wald, Elijah
Escaping the delta [biography of Robert Johnson] **92**

Waldbauer, Gilbert
Insights from insects **632**
Millions of monarchs, bunches of beetles **595.7**
A walk around the pond **595.7**
What good are bugs? **595.7**

Walden, Sarah
Whistler and his mother: an unexpected relationship **709**

Walden, or, Life in the woods. Thoreau, H. D. **818**

Waldman, Carl
Atlas of the North American Indian **970.004**
Encyclopedia of exploration **910.3**
Encyclopedia of Native American tribes **970.004**

Waldman, Michael, 1960-
(comp) My fellow Americans. See My fellow Americans **352.23**

Waldron, Ann
Claude Monet **92**

Waldrop, Howard
Flying saucer rock and roll
In Best of the best: 20 years of the Year's best science fiction **S C**
The lions are asleep this night
In Feeling very strange; the Slipstream anthology **S C**
". . . the world, as we know't"
In The Norton book of science fiction; North American science fiction, 1960-1990 p485-500 **S C**

A **walk** around the pond. Waldbauer, G. **595.7**

A **walk** in the dark. Clarke, A. C.
In Clarke, A. C. The collected stories of Arthur C. Clarke **S C**

A **walk** in the sun. Landis, G. A.
In The Hard SF renaissance **S C**
In New skies: an anthology of today's science fiction **S C**

Walk on the wild side **811.008**

Walker, Aidan
(ed) The Encyclopedia of wood. See The Encyclopedia of wood **674**

Walker, Alice, 1944-
Anything we love can be saved **818**
The color purple **Fic**
Communist
In The Norton book of American short stories p700-14 **S C**
Everyday use
In The Norton book of American short stories p714-22 **S C**
Her blue body everything we know **811**
About
Alice Walker [critical essays] **813.009**

Weather forecasting
Reynolds, R. Cambridge guide to the weather
551.5
The **weather** makers. Flannery, T. F.   **363.7**
Weaver, Afaa M., 1951-
Honey boy
In Growing up ethnic in America; contemporary fiction about learning to be American   **S C**
Weaver, Michael S. *See* Weaver, Afaa M., 1951-
Weaver, Stewart Angas
(jt. auth) Lasch, C. Plain style   **808**
Weaver, Will
Bad blood
In Destination unexpected: short stories
S C
Full service   **Fic**
Memory boy   **Fic**
Stealing for girls
In Ultimate sports; short stories by outstanding writers for young adults p93-116
S C
Striking out   **Fic**
Weaverdom. Sallah, T. M.
In The Heinemann book of contemporary African short stories p179-84   **S C**
The **weaver's** grave. O'Kelly, S.
In The Oxford book of Irish short stories p182-227   **S C**
Weaving
Fiction
Sayres, M. N. Anahita's woven riddle   **Fic**
Weaving the Web. Berners-Lee, T.   **025.04**
Web-based instruction. Smith, S. S.   **005.7**
Web of deception: a Bahzell story. Weber, D.
In Masters of fantasy   **S C**
Web sites
See also MySpace (Web site)
College exploration on the internet   **378.73**
Gordon, R. S. Best career and education Web sites   **025.04**
Hernon, P. U.S. government on the Web
025.04
Smith, J. D. World War II on the Web
025.04
Smith, S. S. Web-based instruction   **005.7**
The United States government Internet manual 2007   **025.04**
See/See also pages in the following book(s):
Braun, L. W. Teens.library   **027.62**
Webb, Lois Sinaiko, 1922-
Holidays of the world cookbook for students
641.5
(jt. auth) Albyn, C. L. The multicultural cookbook for students   **641.5**
Webb, Robyn
(jt. auth) Warshaw, H. S. The diabetes food & nutrition bible   **616.4**
Webber, Elizabeth, 1946-
Merriam-Webster's dictionary of allusions
803
Weber, David, 1952-
Web of deception: a Bahzell story
In Masters of fantasy   **S C**

Weber, R. David, 1941-
(jt. auth) Schlachter, G. A. College student's guide to merit and other no-need funding 2007-2009   **378.3**
(jt. auth) Schlachter, G. A. Financial aid for the disabled and their families, 2006-2008
378.3
(jt. auth) Schlachter, G. A. High school senior's guide to merit and other no-need funding
378.3
Weblogs
Kline, D. Blog!: how the newest media revolution is changing politics, business, and culture
006.7
Stone, B. Who let the blogs out?   **006.7**
See/See also pages in the following book(s):
Farkas, M. Social software in libraries   **025.5**
Webster, Daniel, 1782-1852
See/See also pages in the following book(s):
Kennedy, J. F. Profiles in courage   **920**
Webster, Raymond B.
African American firsts in science and technology   **509**
Webster. Bear, G.
In Bear, G. The collected stories of Greg Bear   **S C**
Webster's collegiate thesaurus. See Merriam-Webster's collegiate thesaurus   **423**
Webster's dictionary of English usage. See Merriam-Webster's dictionary of English usage   **428**
Webster's geographical dictionary. See Merriam-Webster's geographical dictionary   **910.3**
Webster's II new college dictionary   **423**
Webster's new explorer desk encyclopedia
031
Webster's new explorer medical dictionary
610.3
Webster's New World computer dictionary. Pfaffenberger, B.   **004**
Webster's New World dictionary of computer terms. See Pfaffenberger, B. Webster's New World computer dictionary   **004**
Webster's New World Roget's A-Z thesaurus. Laird, C.   **423**
Webster's New World thesaurus. See Laird, C. Webster's New World Roget's A-Z thesaurus
423
Webster's third new international dictionary of the English language, unabridged   **423**
Wecht, Cyril H., 1931-
Tales from the morgue   **614**
The **wedding**. Chekhov, A. P.
In Chekhov, A. P. The plays of Anton Chekhov p175-89   **891.7**
The **wedding**. West, D.   **Fic**
The **wedding**. Williams, J.
In American short story masterpieces   **S C**
The **wedding** album. Marusek, D.
In Best of the best: 20 years of the Year's best science fiction   **S C**
Wedding day. Bennett, G.
In The Portable Harlem Renaissance reader p363-69   **810.8**

Weitzman, Lenore J.
(ed) Women in the Holocaust. See Women in the Holocaust **940.53**

Weizmann, Chaim, 1874-1952
About
Greenfeld, H. A promise fulfilled **956.94**

Welch, David, 1950-
(jt. auth) Cull, N. J. Propaganda and mass persuasion **303.3**

Welch, James, 1940-2003
Killing Custer **973.8**
About
Coltelli, L. Winged words: American Indian writers speak **897**

Welch, Janet, 1953-
(jt. auth) Lerch, M. T. Serving homeschooled teens and their parents **027.6**

Welch, Robert, 1947-
(ed) The Oxford companion to Irish literature. See The Oxford companion to Irish literature **820.9**

Welcome. Sebestyen, O.
In Sixteen: short stories by outstanding writers for young adults p47-59 **S C**

Welcome blue. Lanagan, M.
In Lanagan, M. White time **S C**

Weldon, Fay
Angel, all innocence
In The Literary ghost; great contemporary ghost stories p230-46 **S C**

Well of darkness. Weis, M. **Fic**

The **well** of loneliness [excerpt] Hall, R.
In Growing up gay; an anthology for young people p34-35 **808.8**

We'll understand it better by and by **782.25**

Welles, Orson, 1915-1985
Fiction
Kaplow, R. Me and Orson Welles **Fic**

Wells, David
Perfect I'm not **92**

Wells, H. G. (Herbert George), 1866-1946
The invisible man **Fic**
The time machine **Fic**
Under the knife
In The Oxford book of English short stories p127-38 **S C**
The war of the worlds **Fic**

Wells, Herbert George *See* Wells, H. G. (Herbert George), 1866-1946

Wells, Ken R.
(ed) Teenage sexuality: opposing viewpoints. See Teenage sexuality: opposing viewpoints **613.9**

Wells, Rosemary, 1943-
Red moon at Sharpsburg **Fic**

Wells, Spencer, 1969-
The journey of man **599.93**

Wells, Stanley W., 1930-
(ed) Shakespeare, W. The complete works **822.3**

Welsch, Janice R.
Multicultural films **791.43**

Weltner, Charles L., 1927-1992
See/See also pages in the following book(s):
Profiles in courage for our time **920**

Welton, Jude, 1955-
Impressionism **759.05**

Welty, Eudora, 1909-2001
The bride of the Innisfallen, and other stories
In Welty, E. The collected stories of Eudora Welty p463-600 **S C**
Clytie
In The Oxford book of gothic tales p424-34 **S C**
The collected stories of Eudora Welty **S C**
Contents: Lily Daw and the three ladies; A piece of news; Petrified man; The key; Keela, the outcast Indian maiden; Why I live at the P.O.; The whistle; The hitch-hikers; A memory; Clytie; Old Mr. Marblehall; Flowers for Marjorie; A curtain of green; A visit of charity; Death of a traveling salesman; Powerhouse; A worn path; First love; The wide net; A still moment; Asphodel; The winds; The purple hat; Livvie; At the landing; Shower of gold; June recital; Sir Rabbit; Moon Lake; The whole world knows; Music from Spain; The wanderers; No place for you, my love; The burning; The bride of the Innisfallen; Ladies in spring; Circe; Kin; Going to Naples; Where is the voice coming from?; The demonstrators
A curtain of green
In Welty, E. The collected stories of Eudora Welty p107-112 **S C**
A curtain of green, and other stories
In Welty, E. The collected stories of Eudora Welty p1-149 **S C**
The golden apples
In Welty, E. The collected stories of Eudora Welty
One writer's beginnings **92**
A visit of charity
In The Oxford book of short stories p411-16 **S C**
Why I live at the P.O.
In The Norton book of American short stories p420-31 **S C**
The wide net, and other stories
In Welty, E. The collected stories of Eudora Welty p151-258 **S C**
A worn path
In The Oxford book of women's writing in the United States p135-42 **810.8**
About
Eudora Welty [critical essays] **813.009**

Wendel, Tim
The new face of baseball **796.357**

Wenger, J. Michael
(jt. auth) Goldstein, D. M. The way it was **940.54**

Werblowsky, R. J. Zwi (Raphael Jehudah Zwi), 1924-
(ed) The Oxford dictionary of the Jewish religion. See The Oxford dictionary of the Jewish religion **296.03**

Werblowsky, Raphael Jehudah Zwi *See* Werblowsky, R. J. Zwi (Raphael Jehudah Zwi), 1924-

Werewolves
Encyclopedias
Guiley, R. E. The encyclopedia of vampires, werewolves, and other monsters **133.4**
Fiction
Dunkle, C. B. By these ten bones **Fic**

Westfahl, Gary—*Continued*
(ed) Science fiction quotations. See Science fiction quotations **808.88**

Westinghouse, George, 1846-1914
About
Jonnes, J. Empires of light **621.3**

Westlake, Donald E.
Good night! Good night!
In Alfred Hitchcock's mystery magazine presents fifty years of crime and suspense **S C**
Too many crooks
In The Best American mystery stories of the century p665-77 **S C**

Westmacott, Mary, 1890-1976
See also Christie, Agatha, 1890-1976

West's encyclopedia of American law **349**

Westward expansion. Quay, S. E. **978**
[Interpreting primary documents] **978**

Westward expansion: biographies. Pendergast, T. **920**

Westward expansion: primary sources. Pendergast, T. **978**

Westward movement *See* West (U.S.)—History

Wetlands
Guide to wetlands **578.7**
Knapp, B. America's wetland **333.91**

Wetterau, Bruce
Congressional Quarterly's desk reference on the Presidency **973**

Wexler, Alan
(jt. auth) Waldman, C. Encyclopedia of exploration **910.3**

Wexler, Nancy S.
About
Glimm, A. Gene hunter [biography of Nancy Wexler] **92**

Whacky. Clarke, A. C.
In Clarke, A. C. The collected stories of Arthur C. Clarke **S C**

Whales
Baird, R. W. Killer whales of the world **599.5**
Bonner, W. N. Whales of the world **599.5**
Clapham, P. Whales of the world **599.5**

Whales of the world. Bonner, W. N. **599.5**

Whales of the world. Clapham, P. **599.5**

Whaling
Clapham, P. Whales of the world **599.5**
Fiction
Melville, H. Moby-Dick; or, The whale **Fic**
History
Murphy, J. Gone a-whaling **639.2**

The **wharf** rats. Walrond, E.
In The Portable Harlem Renaissance reader p549-58 **810.8**

Wharton, Edith, 1862-1937
A backward glance
In Wharton, E. Novellas and other writings **818**
Ethan Frome **Fic**

also in Wharton, E. Novellas and other writings **818**

False dawn
In Wharton, E. Novellas and other writings **818**

Madame de Troyes
In Wharton, E. Novellas and other writings **818**

The mother's recompense
In Wharton, E. Novellas and other writings **818**

New Year's Day
In Wharton, E. Novellas and other writings **818**

Novellas and other writings **818**

The old maid
In Wharton, E. Novellas and other writings **818**

Old New York
In Wharton, E. Novellas and other writings **818**

The other two
In The Oxford book of women's writing in the United States p68-82 **810.8**

Pomegranate seed
In Nightshade: 20th century ghost stories p428-60 **S C**
In The Norton book of American short stories p156-82 **S C**

The spark
In Wharton, E. Novellas and other writings **818**

Summer
In Wharton, E. Novellas and other writings **818**

What a handsome pair!. Fitzgerald, F. S.
In Fitzgerald, F. S. The short stories of F. Scott Fitzgerald; a new collection p680-97 **S C**

What a song can do **S C**

What a song can do. Levithan, D.
In What a song can do; 12 riffs on the power of music **S C**

What American women did, 1789-1920. Coppens, L. M. **305.4**

What are my rights? Jacobs, T. A. **346**

What are the most serious threats to national security? **355**

What are the odds? Orkin, M. **519.2**

What are you? **305.8**

What color is your parachute? for teens. Bolles, R. N. **331.7**

What do I read next? 2007 **016.8**

What do you really want? Bachel, B. K. **153.8**

What energy sources should be pursued? **333.79**

What ever happened to Frank Snake Church? Alexie, S.
In Alexie, S. Ten little Indians; stories **S C**

What every artist needs to know about paints & colors. Pyle, D. **752**

What girls learn. Cook, K. **Fic**

Where is it written? Schwartz, A.
In Coming of age in America; a multicultural anthology p82-99 **S C**

Where is the voice coming from? Welty, E.
In Welty, E. The collected stories of Eudora Welty p603-07 **S C**

Where stuff comes from. Molotch, H. L. **620**

Where the action was. Colman, P. **070.4**

Where the germs are. Bakalar, N. **616**

Where the sidewalk ends. Silverstein, S. **811**

Where we are, what we see **810.8**

Where wizards stay up late. Hafner, K. **004**

Wherever home begins **811.008**

Wheye, Darryl
(jt. auth) Ehrlich, P. R. The birder's handbook **598**

While you're here, Doc. Brown, B. B. **92**

The **whimper** of whipped dogs. Ellison, H.
In The Best American mystery stories of the century p530-46 **S C**

The **whirligig** of life. Henry, O.
In Henry, O. The best short stories of O. Henry **S C**

Whiskey. McNally, T.
In McNally, T. 15 short plays p139-97 **812**

A **whisper** in the veins. Wolverton, T.
In Growing up gay; an anthology for young people p196-207 **808.8**

The **whistle**. Welty, E.
In Welty, E. The collected stories of Eudora Welty p57-61 **S C**

Whistler, James McNeill, 1834-1903
About
Walden, S. Whistler and his mother: an unexpected relationship **709**

Whistler and his mother: an unexpected relationship. Walden, S. **709**

The **whistling** season. Doig, I. **Fic**

Whitaker, John O., Jr.
National Audubon Society field guide to North American mammals **599**

Whitaker, Malachi, 1895-1975
Landlord of the crystal fountain
In The Oxford book of English short stories p264-69 **S C**

Whitaker, Richard, 1947-
(jt. auth) Buckley, B. Weather: a visual guide **551.5**

Whitcomb, Laura, 1958-
A certain slant of light **Fic**

White, Andrea
Surviving Antarctica **Fic**

White, Armond
Rebel for the hell of it [biography of Tupac Shakur] **92**

White, Deborah Gray
Let my people go
In The Young Oxford history of African Americans **305.8**

White, E. B. (Elwyn Brooks), 1899-1985
(jt. auth) Strunk, W. The elements of style **808**

White, Edmund, 1940-
A boy's own story **Fic**

White, Evelyn C., 1954-
(ed) The Black women's health book. See The Black women's health book **613**

White, Graham J.
(jt. auth) White, S. The sounds of slavery **326**

White, Laura Mooneyham
(ed) Critical essays on Jane Austen. See Critical essays on Jane Austen **823.009**

White, Margaret Bourke- *See* Bourke-White, Margaret, 1904-1971

White, Pamela
Exploration in the world of the Middle Ages, 500-1500 **910.4**

White, Patricia Holden
(jt. auth) Fogle, B. New complete dog training manual **636.7**

White, Patrick, 1912-1990
Five-twenty
In The Oxford book of short stories p443-65 **S C**

White, Ryan
Ryan White: my own story **92**

White, Shane
The sounds of slavery **326**

White, T. H. (Terence Hanbury), 1906-1964
The candle in the wind
In White, T. H. The once and future king **Fic**
The ill-made knight
In White, T. H. The once and future king **Fic**
The once and future king **Fic**
The Queen of Air and Darkness
In White, T. H. The once and future king **Fic**
The sword in the stone
In White, T. H. The once and future king **Fic**
The troll
In The Oxford book of English short stories p345-54 **S C**
The witch in the wood
In White, T. H. The once and future king **Fic**

White, Terence de Vere, 1912-1994
Desert island
In The Oxford book of Irish short stories p401-11 **S C**

White, Terence Hanbury *See* White, T. H. (Terence Hanbury), 1906-1964

White, Walter Francis, 1893-1955
The fire in the flint [excerpt]
In The Portable Harlem Renaissance reader p351-62 **810.8**

White Aryan Resistance
See/See also pages in the following book(s):
Langer, E. A hundred little Hitlers **305.8**

Who's who in the Middle Ages. Snodgrass, M. E.
920.003

Why courage matters. McCain, J. S. **179**

Why do buses come in threes? Eastaway, R.
510

Why do clocks run clockwise? and other imponderables. Feldman, D. **031.02**

Why do the heathen rage? O'Connor, F.
In O'Connor, F. Collected works p797-800
S C
In O'Connor, F. The complete stories p483-87
S C

Why don't you come live with me: it's time.
Oates, J. C.
In Oates, J. C. Small avalanches and other
stories **S C**

Why I live at the P.O. Welty, E.
In The Norton book of American short stories
p420-31 **S C**
In Welty, E. The collected stories of Eudora
Welty p46-56 **S C**

Why people believe weird things. Shermer, M.
001.9

Why the earth quakes. Levy, M. **551.2**

Why the little Frenchman wears his hand in a
sling. Poe, E. A.
In Poe, E. A. The collected tales and poems
of Edgar Allan Poe p517-21 **818**

Why we are at war. United States. Food Adminis-
tration
In Black theatre USA; plays by African
Americans, 1847 to today **812.008**

Why we buy. Underhill, P. **658.8**

Why we can't wait. King, M. L., Jr. **323.1**

Why, you reckon? Hughes, L.
In Hughes, L. Short stories of Langston
Hughes **S C**

The wibbly, wobbly, wiggly dance that
Cleopatterer did. McNally, T.
In McNally, T. 15 short plays p353-62
812

Wicomb, Zoë, 1948-
When the train comes
In Somehow tenderness survives; stories of
Southern Africa p61-76 **S C**

Wide awake: a Buddhist guide for teens. Winston,
D. **294.3**

The wide net. Welty, E.
In Welty, E. The collected stories of Eudora
Welty p169-88 **S C**

The wide net, and other stories. Welty, E.
In Welty, E. The collected stories of Eudora
Welty p151-258 **S C**

The widest heart. Drucker, M.
In Not the only one; lesbian and gay fiction
for teens **S C**

Widmer, Edward L.
Martin Van Buren **92**

A widow's quilt. Warner, S. T.
In The Oxford book of English short stories
p243-49 **S C**

Wieder, Laurance, 1946-
(ed) Chapters into verse. See Chapters into verse
821.008

Wiegand, Wayne A., 1946-
(ed) Herald, D. T. Genreflecting **016.8**

Wiesel, Elie, 1928-
Night **92**
See/See also pages in the following book(s):
Aikman, D. Great souls **920**

Wiesel, Eliezer *See* Wiesel, Elie, 1928-

Wife abuse
See also Abused women
Fiction
Hobbs, V. Letting go of Bobby James, or, How
I found myself of steam **Fic**

Wife-wooing. Updike, J.
In Updike, J. Pigeon feathers, and other stories p109-15 **S C**

A wig. Malamud, B.
In Malamud, B. The complete stories **S C**

Wiget, Andrew
(ed) Dictionary of Native American literature.
See Dictionary of Native American literature
897

Wiggins, Arthur W.
The five biggest unsolved problems in science
500

Wiggins, Marianne
Herself in love
In The Norton book of American short stories
p732-41 **S C**

Wight, Eric, 1974-
My dead girlfriend, Vol. 1 **741.5**

Wight, James Alfred *See* Herriot, James

Wigoder, Geoffrey, 1922-1999
(ed) The New encyclopedia of Judaism. See The
New encyclopedia of Judaism [New York
University Press] **296.03**
(ed) The Oxford dictionary of the Jewish religion. See The Oxford dictionary of the Jewish
religion **296.03**
(ed) The student's encyclopedia of Judaism. See
The student's encyclopedia of Judaism
296.03

Wilbourn, Carole, 1940-
The total cat **636.8**

Wilbur, Richard, 1921-
(ed) Poe, E. A. Poems and poetics **811**

Wild, Margaret, 1948-
One night **Fic**

Wild about flying!. Marshall, D. **629.13**

Wild cats
See also Cats; Leopards; Lions
Alderton, D. Wild cats of the world **599.75**

Wild cats of the world. Alderton, D. **599.75**

Wild dogs
Fiction
Salisbury, G. Jungle dogs **Fic**

Wild flowers
Spellenberg, R. Familiar flowers of North America: eastern region **582.13**
Spellenberg, R. Familiar flowers of North America: western region **582.13**

Wilson, Patricia J. (Patricia Jane)
(jt. auth) Leslie, R. Igniting the spark   **027.8**
Wilson, Patricia Potter *See* Wilson, Patricia J.
(Patricia Jane)
Wilson, Robert Charles, 1953-
The great goodbye
In New skies: an anthology of today's science
fiction   **S C**
Wilson, Sondra K.
(ed) Johnson, J. W. Complete poems   **811**
Wilson, Tracey Scott
Small world
In Under 30; plays for a new generation
812.008
Wilson, Woodrow, 1856-1924
About
Lukes, B. L. Woodrow Wilson and the Progres-
sive Era   **92**
The **Wilson** calendar of world history   **902**
The **Wilson** chronology of Asia and the Pacific
950
The **Wilson** chronology of ideas. Ochoa, G.
909
The **Wilson** chronology of science and technology.
Ochoa, G.   **502**
The **Wilson** chronology of the arts. Ochoa, G.
700
The **Wilson** chronology of the world's religions
200
The **Wilson** chronology of women's achievements.
Franck, I. M.   **305.4**
Winbush, Raymond A.
(ed) Should America pay? See Should America
pay?   **305.8**
The **wind**. Bradbury, R.
In Bradbury, R. Bradbury stories; 100 of his
most celebrated tales   **S C**
The **wind** from a burning woman. Bear, G.
In Bear, G. The collected stories of Greg
Bear   **S C**
The **wind** from the sun. Clarke, A. C.
In Clarke, A. C. The collected stories of Ar-
thur C. Clarke   **S C**
Windawi, Thura al- *See* Al-Windawi, Thura
Windelspecht, Michael, 1963-
The digestive system   **612.3**
Groundbreaking scientific experiments, inven-
tions, and discoveries of the 19th century
509
(jt. auth) McDowell, J. The lymphatic system
612.4
Windling, Terri, 1958-
(ed) The Faery Reel. See The Faery Reel
S C
(ed) The Green Man: tales from the mythic for-
est. See The Green Man: tales from the myth-
ic forest   **808.8**
Window on the West. Lawlor, L.   **978**
The **winds**. Welty, E.
In Welty, E. The collected stories of Eudora
Welty p209-21   **S C**
The **winds** of war. Wouk, H.   **Fic**

Windsor, Patricia, 1938-
Moon kill
In Night terrors; stories of shadow and sub-
stance   **S C**
Wine for the mess at Segi. Michener, J. A.
In Michener, J. A. Tales of the South Pacific
S C
Wine in the wilderness. Childress, A.
In Black theatre USA; plays by African
Americans, 1847 to today   **812.008**
Wine of Wyoming. Hemingway, E.
In Hemingway, E. The complete short stories
of Ernest Hemingway; the Finca Vigía
edition p342-54   **S C**
Wine on the desert. Brand, M.
In A Century of great Western stories
S C
Winfield, Julia *See* Armstrong, Jennifer, 1961-
Wingard-Nelson, Rebecca
Algebra I and algebra II   **512**
Winged words: American Indian writers speak.
Coltelli, L.   **897**
The **wings** of Meister Wilhelm. Goss, T.
In The Year's best science fiction and fantasy
for teens: first annual collection   **S C**
Winick, Judd, 1970-
Pedro and me   **362.1**
Winkle, Kenneth J.
(jt. auth) Woodworth, S. E. Atlas of the Civil
War   **973.7**
Winkler, Allan M., 1945-
The Cold War   **909.82**
Winkler, Anthony C.
Writing the research paper   **808**
Winks, Robin W., 1930-2003
(ed) Mystery and suspense writers. See Mystery
and suspense writers   **809.3**
Winnie and Cubby. Block, F. L.
In Block, F. L. Girl goddess #9: nine stories
S C
Winnie and Tommy. Block, F. L.
In Am I blue?; coming out from the silence
p29-44   **S C**
Winning bowling. Anthony, E.   **794.6**
Winning field hockey for girls. Swissler, B.
796.355
Winning lacrosse for girls. Swissler, B.
796.34
Winning sounds like this. Coffey, W. R.
796.323
Winning track and field for girls. Housewright, E.
796.42
Winning ugly. Daalder, I. H.   **949.7**
Winspear, Jacqueline, 1955-
Maisie Dobbs   **Fic**
Winston, Diana
Wide awake: a Buddhist guide for teens
294.3
Winston, Sherri
Snow
In Face relations; 11 stories about seeing be-
yond color   **S C**

Witch hunts in Europe and America. Burns, W. E.
133.4

The **witch** in the wood. White, T. H.
In White, T. H. The once and future king
Fic

The **witch** in the wood. See White, T. H. The
Queen of Air and Darkness

Witchcraft
See also Magic
Aronson, M. Witch-hunt: mysteries of the Salem
witch trials **133.4**
Carlson, L. M. A fever in Salem **133.4**
Demos, J. Entertaining Satan **133.4**
Kallen, S. A. Witches **133.4**
Salem witch trials **133.4**
Drama
Miller, A. The crucible **812**
Encyclopedias
Burns, W. E. Witch hunts in Europe and America **133.4**
The Greenhaven encyclopedia of witchcraft
133.4
Guiley, R. E. The encyclopedia of witches and
witchcraft **133.4**
Fiction
Hearn, J. The minister's daughter **Fic**
Napoli, D. J. The magic circle **Fic**
Tiernan, C. A chalice of wind Book 1 **Fic**

Witches
Fiction
Gruber, M. The witch's boy **Fic**
Rowling, J. K. Harry Potter and the Sorcerer's
Stone **Fic**
Witches. Kallen, S. A. **133.4**
The **witches** of Junket. McKillip, P. A.
In McKillip, P. A. Harrowing the dragon
S C
The **witch's** boy. Gruber, M. **Fic**
With a banjo on my knee. Ellis, R. M. **787.8**
With their eyes **812**
Withern Rise [series]
Lawrence, M. A crack in the line **Fic**
Without benefit of clergy. Kipling, R.
In Kipling, R. The portable Kipling **828**
Witness **940.53**
Witness. Armstrong, J.
In Shattered: stories of children and war
p133-38 **S C**
Witness. McNally, T.
In McNally, T. 15 short plays p113-38
812
Witness for the prosecution. Christie, A.
In Christie, A. The mousetrap and other plays
822
Witnesses of war. Stargardt, N. **940.53**
Witten, Edward
See/See also pages in the following book(s):
Mlodinow, L. Euclid's window **516**
Wittlinger, Ellen, 1948-
Blind faith **Fic**
Cheekbones
In Such a pretty face; short stories **S C**

Epiphany
In Face relations; 11 stories about seeing be-
yond color **S C**
Floater
In Twice told; original stories inspired by
original art **S C**
Hard love **Fic**
Sandpiper **Fic**
Tourist trapped
In Destination unexpected: short stories
S C
The **wives** of the dead. Hawthorne, N.
In Hawthorne, N. Tales and sketches, includ-
ing Twice-told tales, Mosses from an old
manse, and The snow-image; A wonder
book for girls and boys; Tanglewood
tales for girls and boys, being a second
Wonder book p61-67 **S C**
The **wizards** of Perfil. Link, K.
In Firebirds rising; an anthology of original
science fiction and fantasy **S C**
**Wodehouse, P. G. (Pelham Grenville), 1881-
1975**
The reverent wooing of Archibald
In The Oxford book of English short stories
p188-203 **S C**
Wodehouse, Pelham Grenville See Wodehouse,
P. G. (Pelham Grenville), 1881-1975
Woe is I. O'Conner, P. T. **428**
Wojtyła, Karol See John Paul II, Pope, 1920-2005
Wolbrink, Shelley
(ed) Great lives from history, the Middle Ages,
477-1453. See Great lives from history, the
Middle Ages, 477-1453 **920.003**
Wolf, Naomi
The beauty myth **305.4**
Wolf, Stephanie Grauman
As various as their land **973.2**
Wolf: legend, enemy, icon. Grambo, R. L.
599.77
Wolf moon. Gorman, E.
In A Century of great Western stories
S C
Wolfe, David W.
Tales from the underground **578**
Wolfe, Gene, 1931-
A cabin on the coast
In Best of the best: 20 years of the Year's
best science fiction **S C**
The death of Doctor Island
In The Locus awards; thirty years of the best
in science fiction and fantasy **S C**
Feather tigers
In The Norton book of science fiction; North
American science fiction, 1960-1990
p280-86 **S C**
Wolfe, George C.
The colored museum
In Black theatre USA; plays by African
Americans, 1847 to today **812.008**
Wolfe, Lisa Ann
Library public relations, promotions, and com-
munications **021.7**

Wolfe, Thomas, 1900-1938
(jt. auth) Skipp, F. E. The complete short stories
of Thomas Wolfe **S C**

Wolfe, Tom
The right stuff **629.45**

Wolff, Tobias, 1945-
The liar
In American short story masterpieces **S C**
Old school **Fic**
This boy's life [excerpt]
In Coming of age in America; a multicultural
anthology p197-211 **S C**
In Who do you think you are?; stories of
friends and enemies p83-91 **S C**
This boy's life: a memoir **92**

Wolff, Virginia Euwer
Brownian motion
In Ultimate sports; short stories by outstand-
ing writers for young adults p207-36
S C
Make lemonade **Fic**

Wolfie. Phillips, R. S.
In Nightshade: 20th century ghost stories
p370-79 **S C**

Wolfinger, Anne, 1953-
(jt. auth) Gordon, R. S. Best career and education Web sites **025.04**

Wolin, Sybil
(ed) The Struggle to be strong. *See* The Struggle
to be strong **305.23**

Wolinsky, Art
Internet power research using the Big6 approach
025.04

Wolverton, Terry
A whisper in the veins
In Growing up gay; an anthology for young
people p196-207 **808.8**

Wolves
Grambo, R. L. Wolf: legend, enemy, icon
599.77
Smith, D. W. Decade of the wolf **599.77**
Steinhart, P. The company of wolves **599.77**
Fiction
Clement-Davies, D. The sight **Fic**

The **woman** at the store. Mansfield, K.
In The Oxford book of short stories p300-09
S C

The **woman** at the Washington Zoo. Jarrell, R.
In Jarrell, R. The complete poems **811**

Woman Hollering Creek. Cisneros, S.
In Cisneros, S. Woman Hollering Creek and
other stories **S C**

Woman Hollering Creek and other stories. Cisneros, S. **S C**

The **woman** I kept to myself. Alvarez, J. **811**

The **woman** in Gaul. Hurston, Z. N.
In Hurston, Z. N. The complete stories p261-
83 **S C**

The **woman** in the room. King, S.
In King, S. Night shift **S C**

A **woman** of fifty. Maugham, W. S.
In Maugham, W. S. Collected short stories
S C

A **woman** of valor: Clara Barton and the Civil
War. Oates, S. B. **92**

The **woman** who fell from the sky. Harjo, J.
811

A **woman** without a country. Cheever, J.
In Cheever, J. The stories of John Cheever
p423-28 **S C**

A **woman's** touch. Williams-Garcia, R.
In Necessary noise: stories about our families
as they really are p131-42 **S C**

Woman's work [biography of Betty Friedan]
Bohannon, L. F. **92**

Women
See also Abused women; Young women
and women of particular racial or ethnic
groups, e.g. *African American women;* and
women in various occupations and professions
Wolf, N. The beauty myth **305.4**
Bibliography
Bauermeister, E. 500 great books by women
016.3054
Biography
Butts, E. She dared **920**
Ellsberg, R. Blessed among all women **920**
Extraordinary women of the Medieval and Re-
naissance world **920.003**
Opfell, O. S. Women prime ministers and presi-
dents **920**
Biography—Dictionaries
Adamson, L. G. Notable women in world histo-
ry **920.003**
Kuhlman, E. A. A to Z of women in world his-
tory **920.003**
Biography—Encyclopedias
Encyclopedia of women's autobiography
920.003

Civil rights
See Women's rights
Education
Peril, L. College girls **305.4**
Schlachter, G. A. Directory of financial aids for
women 2007-2009 **378.3**
Tooley, J. The miseducation of women
371.82
Employment
Reber, D. In their shoes **331.4**
Schwager, T. Cool women, hot jobs . . . and
how you can go for it, too! **650.14**
Fiction
Dorris, M. A yellow raft in blue water **Fic**
Esquivel, L. Like water for chocolate **Fic**
Hoffman, A. The probable future **Fic**
Health and hygiene
Minkin, M. J. The Yale guide to women's re-
productive health **618.1**
Our bodies, ourselves **613**
Pagano, J. Strength training for women
613.7
See/See also pages in the following book(s):
Jukes, M. It's a girl thing **305.23**
History
Extraordinary women of the Medieval and Re-
naissance world **920.003**
Franck, I. M. The Wilson chronology of wom-
en's achievements **305.4**

Woodford, Chris, 1943-
Cool stuff and how it works. See Cool stuff and how it works **600**

Woodger, Elin
The 1980s **973.92**

Wooding, Chris, 1977-
The haunting of Alaizabel Cray **Fic**
The house and the locket
In The restless dead; ten original stories of the supernatural **S C**
Poison **Fic**
The storm thief **Fic**

Woodpeckers
Gallagher, T. The grail bird **598**
Hoose, P. M. The race to save the Lord God Bird **598**

Woodrell, Daniel
Winter's bone **Fic**

Woodring, Carl, 1919-
(ed) The Columbia anthology of British poetry. See The Columbia anthology of British poetry **821.008**

Woodrow Wilson and the Progressive Era. Lukes, B. L. **92**

Woodruff, John, 1915-
(ed) Firefly astronomy dictionary. See Firefly astronomy dictionary **520.3**

Woods, Granville, 1856-1910
See/See also pages in the following book(s):
Aaseng, N. Black inventors **920**

Woods and forests. Martin, P. A. F. **577.3**

Woodson, Jacqueline
If you come softly **Fic**
Miracle's boys **Fic**
My crazy, beautiful world
In Such a pretty face; short stories **S C**
Nebraska 99
In Sixteen: stories about that sweet and bitter birthday **S C**
Slipping away
In Am I blue?; coming out from the silence p47-59 **S C**

Woodson, Sarah Jane
See/See also pages in the following book(s):
Katz, W. L. Black pioneers **920**

Woodsong. Paulsen, G. **796.5**

Woodward, Bob, 1943-
The final days **973.924**
(jt. auth) Bernstein, C. All the president's men **973.924**

Woodward, Grace Steele, b. 1899
Pocahontas **92**

Woodward, John, 1958-
War **303.6**
(ed) The ethics of human cloning. See The ethics of human cloning **176**
(ed) Israel: opposing viewpoints. See Israel: opposing viewpoints **956.94**
(ed) Popular culture: opposing viewpoints. See Popular culture: opposing viewpoints **302.23**
(ed) The right to die. See The right to die **179.7**
(ed) Teen suicide. See Teen suicide **362.28**

Woodwork
Horwood, R. The woodworker's handbook **684**
Taunton's complete illustrated guide to woodworking **684**

The **woodworker's** handbook. Horwood, R. **684**

Woodworth, Steven E.
Atlas of the Civil War **973.7**
Cultures in conflict: the American Civil War **973.7**

Woolf, Greg
(ed) Cambridge illustrated history of the Roman world. See Cambridge illustrated history of the Roman world **937**

Woolf, Virginia, 1882-1941
A room of one's own **305.4**
Solid objects
In The Oxford book of English short stories p204-09 **S C**
To the lighthouse **Fic**
The Virginia Woolf reader **828**
About
Brackett, V. Restless genius [biography of Virginia Woolf] **92**
Hussey, M. Virginia Woolf A-Z **828**
Mills, C. Virginia Woolf **92**

Woolfolk, Joanna Martine
The only astrology book you'll ever need **133.5**

Woolley, Alan Robert
(jt. auth) Bishop, A. C. Guide to minerals, rocks & fossils **552**

Woolls, E. Blanche
The school library media manager **027.8**
(ed) The Whole school library handbook. See The Whole school library handbook **027.8**

Woolrich, Cornell, 1903-1968
Rear window
In The Best American mystery stories of the century p288-317 **S C**
Rear window [originally titled "It had to be murder"]
In Adaptations: from short story to big screen; 35 great stories that have inspired great films **S C**

Wooster, Robert, 1956-
(ed) Encyclopedia of Native American wars and warfare. See Encyclopedia of Native American wars and warfare **970.004**

Word games
See also Crossword puzzles

Word of mouth **811.008**

Word of the day. Singer, M.
In Twice told; original stories inspired by original art **S C**

Word parts dictionary. Sheehan, M. **423**

Word processor of the gods. King, S.
In King, S. Skeleton crew **S C**

The **words** of Desmond Tutu. Tutu, D. **968.06**

Wordsworth, William, 1770-1850
Poems **821**
About
William Wordsworth [critical essays] **821**

Writings, 1932-1946. Stein, G.   **818**
Writings and drawings. Thurber, J.   **818**
Writings of teenagers *See* Teenagers' writings
Written into history   **071**
The **wrong** grave. Link, K.
  In The restless dead; ten original stories of
    the supernatural   **S C**
The **wrong** lunch line. Mohr, N.
  In Coming of age in America; a multicultural
    anthology p52-57   **S C**
The **Wrysons.** Cheever, J.
  In Cheever, J. The stories of John Cheever
    p319-24   **S C**
Wu, William F., 1951-
  Black powder
  In American dragons: twenty-five Asian
    American voices p211-34   **810.8**
Wukasch, Don C.
  (jt. auth) Myers, J. E. Dictionary of poetic terms
    808.1
Wurts, Janny
  Child of prophecy: a War of light and shadow
    story
  In Masters of fantasy   **S C**
Wurts, Jay
  (jt. auth) Hayslip, L. L. When heaven and earth
    changed places   **92**
Wuthering Heights. Brontë, E.   **Fic**
WWII: the people's story   **940.53**
Wyatt, Melissa, 1963-
  Raising the griffin   **Fic**
Wyeth, Andrew, 1917-
  Andrew Wyeth, autobiography   **92**
Wyeth, Sharon Dennis
  An interview with the actress Celeste; or, the
    dreamer and the dreamed
  In Dreams and visions; fourteen flights of
    fantasy   **S C**
  Orphea Proud   **Fic**
Wyman, Bruce C.
  The Facts on File dictionary of environmental
    science   **363.7**
Wynbrandt, James
  The encyclopedia of genetic disorders and birth
    defects   **616**
Wyndham, Jeremy
  (jt. auth) Eastaway, R. Why do buses come in
    threes?   **510**
Wynn, Charles M.
  (jt. auth) Wiggins, A. W. The five biggest un-
    solved problems in science   **500**
Wynne-Jones, Tim
  Bella in five acts
  In Such a pretty face; short stories   **S C**
  Dawn
  In Leaving home: stories p91-114   **808.8**
  A thief in the house of memory   **Fic**
Wyse, Liz
  (jt. auth) Lambert, D. Dinosaur encyclopedia
    567.9

X

X-ing a paragrab. Poe, E. A.
  In Poe, E. A. The collected tales and poems
    of Edgar Allan Poe p361-66   **818**
X-rays
  See/See also pages in the following book(s):
  Friedman, M. Medicine's 10 greatest discoveries
    610.9
Xenophon, ca. 431-ca. 352 B.C.
  See/See also pages in the following book(s):
  Hamilton, E. The Greek way   **880.9**

Y

Yabu, Julie
  A lesson from the heart
  In American dragons: twenty-five Asian
    American voices p161-65   **810.8**
Yachts and yachting
  See also Sailing
Yagoda, Ben
  Will Rogers   **92**
Yahk fahn, Auntie. Lum, D. H. Y.
  In American dragons: twenty-five Asian
    American voices p5-13   **810.8**
Yai. Hirunpidok, V.
  In American dragons: twenty-five Asian
    American voices p168-84   **810.8**
The **Yale** book of quotations   **808.88**
Yale dictionary of art and artists. Langmuir, E.
  703
The **Yale** guide to women's reproductive health.
  Minkin, M. J.   **618.1**
Yale Nota bene [series]
  Bloom, J. Islam: a thousand years of faith and
    power   **297**
Yale University Press health & wellness [series]
  Hicks, J. W. Fifty signs of mental illness
    616.89
Yamamoto, Hisaye
  Seventeen syllables
  In The Oxford book of women's writing in
    the United States p83-94   **810.8**
Yamanaka, Lois-Ann, 1961-
  Wild meat and the bully burgers [excerpt]
  In American eyes; new Asian-American short
    stories for young adults   **S C**
Yamauchi, Wakako
  And the soul shall dance
  In American dragons: twenty-five Asian
    American voices p144-54   **810.8**
Yamazaki, James N., 1916-
  Children of the atomic bomb   **92**
Yanak, Ted
  (jt. auth) Cornelison, P. The great American his-
    tory fact-finder   **973.03**
Yancey, Diane
  The internment of the Japanese   **940.53**
  Life of an American soldier   **959.704**
  STDs   **616.95**

Young adults
Books and reading
See Teenagers—Books and reading

Young adult's guide to business communications. Thomason-Carroll, K. L.   **651.7**

Young adults' libraries
See also High school libraries

Anderson, S. B. Extreme teens   **027.62**

Booth, H. Serving teens through readers' advisory   **028.5**

Braun, L. W. Technically involved   **027.62**

Braun, L. W. Teens.library   **027.62**

Bromann, J. Booktalking that works   **028.5**

Bromann, J. More booktalking that works   **028.5**

Edwards, K. Teen library events   **027.62**

Edwards, M. A. The fair garden and the swarm of beasts   **027.62**

Excellence in library services to young adults   **027.62**

Farmer, L. S. J. Digital inclusion, teens, and your library   **027.62**

Harris, F. J. I found it on the Internet   **025.04**

Honnold, R. 101+ teen programs that work   **027.62**

Honnold, R. More teen programs that work   **027.62**

Honnold, R. The teen reader's advisor   **028.5**

Jones, P. Connecting young adults and libraries   **027.62**

Jones, P. Do it right!   **027.62**

Kan, K. Sizzling summer reading programs for young adults   **027.62**

Kunzel, B. L. The teen-centered book club   **027.62**

Lerch, M. T. Serving homeschooled teens and their parents   **027.6**

Library services to youth of Hispanic heritage   **027.6**

Mondowney, J. G. Hold them in your heart   **027.62**

New directions for library service to young adults   **027.62**

Ott, V. A. Teen programs with punch   **027.62**

Reynolds, T. K. Teen reading connections   **028.5**

Serving older teens   **027.62**

Simpson, M. S. Reading programs for young adults   **027.62**

Thinking outside the book   **027.62**

Tuccillo, D. Library teen advisory groups   **027.62**

Young and hungry. Lieberman, D.   **641.5**

The **young** glory of him. Hughes, L.
In Hughes, L. Short stories of Langston Hughes   **S C**

Young Goodman Brown. Hawthorne, N.
In Hawthorne, N. Tales and sketches, including Twice-told tales, Mosses from an old manse, and The snow-image; A wonder book for girls and boys; Tanglewood tales for girls and boys, being a second Wonder book p276-89   **S C**

In The Norton book of American short stories p35-46   **S C**

Young musicians in world history. Earls, I.   **920**

Young Owl, Marcus
(jt. auth) Mai, L. L. The Cambridge Dictionary of human biology and evolution   **612**

The **young** Oxford companion to the Congress of the United States. See Ritchie, D. A. The Congress of the United States   **328.73**

The **young** Oxford companion to the presidency of the United States. See Pious, R. M. The presidency of the United States   **352.23**

The **young** Oxford companion to the Supreme Court of the United States. See Patrick, J. J. The Supreme Court of the United States   **347**

The **Young** Oxford history of African Americans   **305.8**

Young people's libraries See Young adults' libraries

Young warriors   **S C**

Young women
GirlSource   **305.23**

Willdorf, N. City chic   **646.7**

Youngerman, Barry
The Truth about alcohol. See The Truth about alcohol   **362.292**

The truth about divorce. See The truth about divorce   **306.89**

The **youngest** one. Springer, N.
In Dreams and visions; fourteen flights of fantasy   **S C**

Yount, Lisa
A to Z of biologists   **920.003**

A to Z of women in science and math   **920.003**

Animal rights   **179**

Biotechnology and genetic engineering   **660.6**

Energy supply   **333.79**

Forensic science   **363.2**

Modern astronomy   **520**

Modern genetics   **576.5**

Modern marine science   **551.4**

Right to die and euthanasia   **179.7**

(ed) Cloning. See Cloning [Contemporary issues companion]   **176**

(ed) Euthanasia. See Euthanasia   **179.7**

Younts, Shane Ann
(jt. auth) Scheeder, L. All the words on stage   **822.3**

Your Arkansas traveler. Schulberg, B.
In Adaptations: from short story to big screen; 35 great stories that have inspired great films   **S C**

Your backyard herb garden. Smith, M.   **635**

Your body, how it works [series]
Light, D. B. Cells, tissues, and skin   **611**

Your eyes in stars. Kerr, M. E.   **Fic**

Your first resume. Fry, R. W.   **650.14**

Your garnet eyes. Vaz, K.
In The Faery Reel; tales from the Twilight Realm   **S C**